PETERSON'S
COLLEGE
MONEY
HANDBOOK
1998

FIFTEENTH EDITION

Peterson's
Princeton, New Jersey

About Peterson's

Peterson's is the country's largest educational information/communications company, providing the academic, consumer, and professional communities with books, software, and on-line services in support of lifelong education access and career choice. Well-known references include Peterson's annual guides to private schools, summer programs, colleges and universities, graduate and professional programs, financial aid, international study, adult learning, and career guidance. Peterson's Web site at petersons.com is the only comprehensive—and most heavily traveled—education resource on the Internet. The site carries all of Peterson's fully searchable major databases and includes financial aid sources, test-prep help, job postings, direct inquiry and application features, and specially created Virtual Campuses for every accredited academic institution and summer program in the U.S. and Canada that offers in-depth narratives, announcements, and multimedia features.

Peterson's Career Focus Books: helping people make successful job choices, maximize career potential, and stay competitive in today's workplace

Visit Peterson's Education Center on the Internet (World Wide Web) at http://www.petersons.com

Previously published as *Peterson's College Money Handbook* © 1983, 1984, 1985, 1986, 1987, 1988, 1989, 1990, 1991, 1996 and as *Paying Less for College* © 1992, 1993, 1994, 1995

ISSN 1089-831X

ISBN 1-56079-832-7

Printed in the United States of America

10 9 8 7 6 5 4 3 2 1

CONTENTS

The Financial Aid System

College Financial Aid Information

SECTION 8: COLLEGE FINANCIAL AID PROFILES

SECTION 9: COLLEGE FINANCIAL AID INDEXES

SECTION 1

In most families, parents assume the major responsibility for paying college expenses even though the child is the primary beneficiary of the education. Therefore, this book is geared for parents, although we hope that students also will read it and participate in family discussions on how their education will be financed.

How to Use This Book

This book is both a quick resource and an in-depth reference that puts at your fingertips valuable information about college costs and financial aid opportunities. It contains:

- Easy-to-use charts, tables and lists
- An overview of federal financial aid and the programs available
- A guide to help you through the maze of applying for financial aid
- A state-by-state description of each state-administered financial aid program
- Financial aid profiles of more than 1,700 individual colleges

The challenge of paying for college requires forethought, organization, and resourcefulness. However, there are many ways to manage college costs and many channels through which you can receive help. If typical financial aid packages are taken into consideration, the actual cost of four years of college is likely to be less than what most families spend on a new car, and, unlike a car, the value a college education will increase as time goes on. We wish you success in your quest and hope that *Peterson's College Money Handbook* will prove to be helpful both

in your child's college selection and in helping you finance the cost of his or her education.

Contents

A Guide to Financing Your Child's College Education

More and more families must count on financial aid. In this generation, financial aid is a basic and essential component in paying the costs of college. Most students and their families should plan on tapping the river of governmental and institutional financial aid subsidies that will supplement, and occasionally supersede, their personal saving and borrowing plans. If you do not consider how these sources may help you to pay for college costs, you are likely making a real mistake.

However, the financial aid system and its process can seem overwhelming, confusing, and complex, especially the first time you go through it. In "A Guide to Financing Your Child's College Education," Don Betterton, Director of Undergraduate Financial Aid at Princeton University, provides a clear, concise picture of what families need to know. A noted author, Betterton's twenty-five years of experience enable him to pinpoint the trouble areas and questions that most concern parents and students. Reading his article will give you the background and understanding necessary to make the best use of this book.

Common Questions Answered

Here are answers to the questions most often asked of financial aid administrators.

Federal Financial Aid

This section provides a description of the federal programs that serve as the foundation of financial assistance. Included are descriptions of the two federal grant programs, the Federal Work-Study program, and the two families of loans, each of which has loan programs for both students and parents.

State-Sponsored College Savings Programs

By the end of 1997, twenty-four states will be actively operating a prepaid tuition program, college savings plan trust program, or savings bond purchase program with special features for college savers. This number is rapidly increasing as more states consider and adopt programs to encourage families to save for college. This section discusses the advantages and disadvantages of these programs and provides details for the existing ones.

State Scholarship and Grant Programs

This section lists more than 300 specific grants and loans state by state. Eligibility requirements, award amounts, and contacts for further information are given for all programs.

Freshman-Year Out-of-Pocket Costs: Looking Beyond the Sticker Price

The amount of aid available at colleges can vary widely. The first question you are no doubt asking yourself is what is the likely amount of aid one might expect from a particular college? The table en-

Where Our Information Comes From

The college data were collected in the winter and spring of 1997 through Peterson's Annual Survey of Undergraduate Institutions and the associated Freshman Financial Aid Survey. We sent detailed questionnaires to more than 3,500 institutions of higher education that are accredited in the U.S. and U.S. territories and offer full four- or five-year baccalaureate degrees via full-time, on-campus programs of study. Officials at the colleges—usually the financial aid or admission officers but sometimes the registrars or institutional research staff—completed and returned the forms. We entered the information we received into our database, verifying anything that seemed unusual. Because of the comprehensive editorial review that takes place in our offices, we have every reason to believe that the data presented in this book are accurate. However, students should always confirm costs and other facts with a specific school at the time of application, since colleges can and do change policies and fees whenever necessary.

The state aid data presented in *Peterson's College Money Handbook 1998* were submitted by state officials (usually the director of the state scholarship commission) to Peterson's in the spring of 1997. Because regulations for any government-sponsored program may be changed at any time, readers should request written descriptive materials from the office administering a program in which they are interested.

titled "Freshman-Year Out-of-Pocket Costs: Looking Beyond the Sticker Price" provides some quick answers to this.

College Financial Aid Profiles

After the federal government, colleges provide the largest amount of financial aid to students. Colleges also control a great deal of federal and state money channeled to students. This section shows you the pattern and extent of each college's current awards.

Detailed profiles present facts and statistics on more than 1,700 undergraduate institutions of higher education. The profiles, which appear in alphabetical order by school name, contain data supplied by each college and university for full-time students enrolled as of the fall of 1996 (unless otherwise noted). Each profile provides specific information on expenses; basic facts about the school; a summary of the school's undergraduate financial aid resources; detailed data on need-based and non-need awards for freshmen and what is required to apply for each; a list of money-saving options to consider; and the name, title, and telephone number of the person to contact for further information.

College Financial Aid Indexes

Six indexes in the back of the book provide valuable information from the college profiles for easy reference. Prospective students with special abilities, interests, characteristics, or circumstances will find these indexes helpful. A listing of colleges that offer money-saving options and tuition payment plans is also included

Non-Need Scholarships

Lists colleges that offer scholarships not based on need to freshmen with specific academic strengths, talents in the creative or performing arts, special achievements or activities, and students in a wide variety of particular circumstances. Some of these circumstances are students with parents in specific professions; residents of particular geographic areas; spouses, children, and siblings of other students; and handicapped students.

Athletic Grants

Lists colleges that award athletic scholarships in each of thirty-two sports.

Cooperative Education

Lists colleges that offer cooperative education programs (a formal arrangement with an off-campus employer that allows students to combine study and work in order to earn money, often while gaining degree-related experience).

ROTC Programs

Lists colleges that offer Reserve Officers' Training Corps programs in one or more of the armed services.

Tuition Waivers

Lists colleges that offer full or partial tuition waivers for minority students, children of alumni, adult students, or senior citizens.

Payment Alternatives

Lists colleges that offer tuition payment alternatives (deferred payment plans, guaranteed tuition plans, installment payment plans, and tuition prepayment plans).

SECTION 2

A Guide to Financing Your Child's College Education

by Don Betterton, Director of Undergraduate Financial Aid, Princeton University

iven the lifelong benefit of a college degree (college graduates are projected to earn in a lifetime $600,000 more than those with only a high school diploma), higher education is a very worthwhile investment. However, it is also an expensive one made even harder to manage by cost increases that have outpaced both inflation and gains in family income. This reality of higher education economics means that parental concern about how to pay a child's college costs is a dilemma that shows no sign of getting easier.

Because of the high cost involved (even the most inexpensive four-year education at a public institution costs about $10,000 a year), good information about college budgets and strategies for reducing the "sticker price"

is essential. You have made a good start by taking the time to read *Peterson's College Money Handbook*. In the chapters that follow, you will find valuable information about the four main sources of aid—federal, state, college, and private. Before you learn about the various programs, however, it will be helpful if you have an overview of how the college financial aid system operates and what long-range financing strategies are available.

Financial Aid

Financial aid refers to money that is awarded to a student, usually in a "package" that consists of a scholarship (also called grant or gift aid), student loan, and campus job.

College Costs

The starting point for organizing a plan to pay for your child's college education is making a good estimate of the yearly cost. You can use the college cost worksheet on page 4 to do so. And *Peterson's College Money Handbook* makes this first step easy for you by listing the costs for 1997–98.

To estimate your college costs for next year (1998–99), refer to the tuition and fees and room and board figures shown in Section 8, Financial Aid Profiles, and inflate the numbers by 5 percent. If your child will commute from your home, use $2000 instead of the college's room and board charges, $900 for transportation, $750 for books, and $1300 for personal expenses. Finally, estimate the cost of two round trips if your home is more than a few hundred miles from the college. Add the items to calculate the total budget. You should now have a reasonably good estimate of college costs for 1998–99. (To determine the costs for later years, adding 5 percent per year will probably give you a fairly accurate estimate.)

Do You Qualify for Need-Based Aid?

The next step is to evaluate whether or not your child is likely to qualify for financial aid based on need. This step is critical, since more than 90 percent of the yearly total of $50 billion in student aid is awarded only after a determination is made that the family lacks sufficient financial resources to pay the full cost of college on its own. To judge your chance of receiving need-based aid, it is neces-

College Cost Worksheet

	College 1	College 2	College 3	Commuter College
Tuition and Fees	___	___	___	___
Room and Board	___	___	___	$2000
Books	$ 750	$ 750	$ 750	$ 750
Personal Expenses	$1300	$1300	$1300	$1300
Travel	___	___	___	$ 900
Total Budget	═══	═══	═══	═══

sary to estimate an expected Family Contribution (EFC) according to a government formula known as the Federal Methodology. You can do so by referring to the Family Contribution Table on page 6.

Applying for Need-Based Aid

Because the federal government provides about 75 percent of all aid awarded, the application and need evaluation process is controlled by Congress and the U.S. Department of Education. The application used is the Free Application for Federal Student Aid (FAFSA), and the method used for need determination is known as the Federal Methodology (FM). In addition, nearly every state that offers student assistance uses the federal government's system to award its own aid. You apply for a state scholarship (see Section 6) by checking a box on the FAFSA. Furthermore, many colleges, besides arranging for the pay-

ment of federal and state aid, use the FAFSA to award their own funds to needy students. (NOTE: In addition to the FAFSA, many colleges also ask the family to complete the Financial Aid PROFILE application. See the box titled *What is the Financial Aid PROFILE?* on page 7.)

The FAFSA is your "passport" to receiving your share of the billions of dollars awarded annually in need-based aid. If the college cost worksheet shows that your child might qualify for aid, ask him or her to pick up a FAFSA from the high school guidance office after mid-November, 1997. The form will ask for 1997 financial data and it should be filed after January 1, 1998, in time to meet the earliest college or state scholarship deadline. Within two to four weeks after you submit the form, you will receive a summary of the FAFSA information, which is called the Student Aid Report. The SAR will give you an estimated family contribution and also allow you to make corrections to the data you submitted.

Students can apply for 1997–98 federal student aid over the Internet using the interactive FAFSA on the Web. The 1998–99 FAFSA and an interactive renewal application will be available in December 1997. FAFSA on the Web can be accessed at http://www.fafsa.ed.gov/ with Netscape Navigator 3.0 or higher. It can be used with any computer, including Macintosh and UNIX.

Many colleges provide the option to apply for early-decision admission. If you apply for this before January 1, which is prior to when FAFSA can be is used, follow the college's instructions. Many colleges use either PROFILE or their own application form for early admission candidates.

How Aid Matches Need

	COLLEGE X	COLLEGE Y
Total Cost	$10,000	$24,000
– Family Contribution	– 5,500	– 5,500
= Financial Need	$ 4,500	$18,500
Financial Need	$ 4,500	$18,500
– Grant Aid Awarded	– 675	–14,100
– Federal Work-Study	– 1,400	– 1,300
– Student Loan Awarded	– 3,000	– 2,625
= Unmet Need	0	0

Awarding Aid

About the same time you receive the SAR, the colleges your child lists will receive the FAFSA information so they can calculate a financial aid award in a package that typically includes aid from at least one of the major sources—federal, state, college, or private. In addition, the award will probably consist of a combination of scholarship or grant, loan, and campus job. These last two pieces—loan and job—are called self-help aid because they require effort on the part of the student (that is, it must be either earned through work or paid back later). Scholarships or grants are outright gifts that have no such obligation.

It is important that you understand each part of the package so that you can determine your true costs. You'll want to know, for example: How much is gift aid? What are the interest rate and repayment terms of the student loan? How many hours per week does the campus job require? There should be an enclosure with the award letter that answers these kinds of questions. If not, make a list of your questions and call or visit the financial aid office.

Once you understand the terms of each item in the award letter, you should turn your attention to the "bottom line"—how much you and your child will have to pay for each college to which he or she was admitted. In addition to understanding the aid award, this means having a good estimate of the college budget so you can accurately calculate how much you and your family will have to contribute (often an aid package does not cover the entire need). Colleges follow different practices in how fully they explain these elements in their award notifications. Many colleges provide full information—types and amounts of aid, yearly costs, and the expected family contribution divided

---

Worksheet

Comparing Financial Aid Awards and Family Contribution

	College 1	College 2	College 3
Total Budget	_____	_____	_____
Aid Awarded	_____	_____	_____
Grant/Scholarship	_____	_____	_____
Loan	_____	_____	_____
Job	_____	_____	_____
Total Aid	_____	_____	_____
Family Contribution	_____	_____	_____
Student Contribution	_____	_____	_____
Parent Contribution	_____	_____	_____

---

between the parent and student share. If these important items are missing or incomplete, you can easily do the work on your own. (See the Comparing Awards and Family Contribution worksheet on this page.) For example, if only the college's direct charges for tuition, room, and board are shown on the award letter, make your own estimate of indirect costs like books, personal expenses, and travel using the figures provided earlier. Then subtract the total aid awarded from the yearly budget to get the expected Family Contribution. A portion of that amount may be your child's student contribution (35 percent of your child's savings and 50 percent of earnings over $2500) and the remainder is the parental share. If you can afford this amount out of your current income and assets at your child's first-choice college, the financial aid system has worked well for you and your child's college attendance plans can go forward.

But if you think your parental contribution is too high, you should contact the college's financial aid office and ask whether additional aid is available. Many colleges, private high-cost colleges in particular, have a service perspective—they are willing to work with families to help make education at their colleges affordable. Most colleges also allow applicants to appeal their financial aid awards, the budget used for the student, or any of the elements used to determine the family contribution, especially if there are extenuating circumstances or if the information has changed since the application was submitted. Some colleges may also reconsider an award based on a "competitive appeal," the submission of a more favorable award letter from another college.

If your appeal is unsuccessful, and there is still a gap between the expected parental contribution and what you feel you can pay from income and savings,

Family Contribution Table

Consult the following family contribution table using estimated 1997 income and likely asset holdings as of December 31, 1997. First, locate the approximate parental contribution in the table. If more than one family member will be in college at least half-time during 1998–99, divide the parental contribution by the number in college. If your child has savings, add 35 percent of that amount.

If your child earned in excess of $2500 in 1997, include 50 percent of the amount over $2500 in the income figure. To see whether or not you might qualify for need-based aid, subtract the family contribution from each college's budget. If the family contribution is only a few thousand dollars over the budget, it is still worthwhile to apply for aid since this procedure is only intended to give

you a preliminary estimate of college costs and your family contribution.

If you may be eligible for aid at one or more of the colleges, pay close attention to the section Applying for Need-Based Aid on page 4. If, on the other hand, the possibility of showing need seems unlikely, you should concentrate on the sections describing merit aid and financial planning.

Approximate Expected Family Contribution for 1998–99

ASSETS▼	FAMILY SIZE	$ 20,000	30,000	40,000	50,000	60,000	70,000	80,000	90,000	100,000
$ 20,000										
	3	$ 800	2,700	4,400	6,800	9,500	12,600	15,600	18,500	21,400
	4	0	2,000	2,600	4,700	8,200	11,400	14,300	17,200	20,200
	5	0	900	1,900	3,700	7,000	10,200	13,100	16,000	19,000
	6	0	0	1,200	2,800	5,800	8,800	11,800	14,700	17,600
$ 30,000										
	3	$ 800	2,700	3,400	5,800	9,500	12,600	15,600	18,500	21,400
	4	0	2,000	2,600	4,700	8,200	11,400	14,300	17,200	20,200
	5	0	900	1,900	3,700	7,000	10,200	13,100	16,000	19,000
	6	0	0	1,200	2,800	5,800	8,800	11,800	14,700	17,600
$ 40,000										
	3	$ 800	2,700	3,400	5,800	9,500	12,600	15,600	18,500	21,400
	4	0	2,000	2,600	4,700	8,200	11,400	14,300	17,200	20,200
	5	0	900	1,900	3,700	7,000	10,200	13,100	16,000	19,000
	6	0	0	1,200	2,800	5,800	8,800	11,800	14,700	17,600
$ 50,000										
	3	$ 1,000	2,900	4,300	7,300	10,100	13,600	16,100	19,100	22,000
	4	400	2,300	3,500	6,200	8,800	11,900	14,900	17,800	20,700
	5	0	1,700	2,800	5,000	7,600	10,700	13,700	16,600	19,500
	6	0	200	2,100	4,000	6,300	9,400	12,300	15,300	18,200
$ 60,000										
	3	$ 1,300	3,200	4,100	7,900	10,600	14,100	16,700	19,600	22,700
	4	700	2,500	3,200	6,700	9,400	12,900	15,400	18,300	21,400
	5	300	1,900	2,500	5,500	8,200	11,700	14,200	17,200	20,200
	6	0	1,200	1,700	4,500	6,800	10,400	12,900	15,800	18,800
$ 80,000										
	3	$ 1,800	3,800	5,800	9,000	11,800	14,900	17,800	20,700	23,700
	4	900	3,000	4,700	7,700	10,500	13,600	16,500	19,400	22,400
	5	400	2,400	3,900	6,400	9,300	12,400	15,400	18,200	21,200
	6	0	1,700	3,100	5,200	7,900	11,100	14,000	16,800	19,900
$100,000										
	3	$ 2,800	4,000	6,900	10,200	12,900	16,000	19,000	21,800	24,800
	4	1,500	3,200	5,700	8,900	11,600	14,800	17,700	20,500	23,500
	5	900	2,500	4,700	7,500	10,400	13,600	16,500	19,300	22,300
	6	400	1,800	3,800	6,100	9,100	12,200	15,100	18,000	21,000
$120,000										
	3	$ 3,900	4,900	8,000	11,300	14,000	17,100	21,000	23,200	25,800
	4	2,600	4,000	6,500	10,100	12,700	15,900	18,800	21,700	24,600
	5	1,900	3,200	5,400	8,800	11,500	14,700	17,600	20,500	23,400
	6	1,200	2,500	4,300	7,200	10,200	13,300	16,300	19,200	22,400
$140,000										
	3	$ 4,600	5,900	9,200	12,400	15,400	18,200	21,200	23,800	28,200
	4	3,200	4,800	7,800	11,100	13,900	17,000	19,900	21,900	26,900
	5	2,500	3,900	6,400	9,800	12,700	15,800	18,800	21,700	25,700
	6	1,700	3,200	5,200	8,300	11,300	14,500	17,400	20,300	23,300

(Income before taxes shown across the top; Assets and Family Size shown down the left.)

you are left with two choices. One option is to have your child attend a college where paying your share of the bill will not be a problem. (This assumes that an affordable option was included on the original list of colleges, a wise admission application strategy.) The second is to look into an alternate method of financing. At this stage, parental loans and tuition payment plans are the available financing options. A parental loan can bring the yearly cost down to a manageable level by spreading payments over a number of years. This is the type of financing families use when purchasing a home or automobile. A tuition payment plan is essentially a short-term loan and allows you to pay the costs over 10–12 months. It is an option for families who have the resources available but need help with managing their cash-flow. See the section on financing for more information.

Aid Not Based on Need

Whether or not your child might qualify for a need-based award, it is always worthwhile to look into merit, or non-need, scholarships from sources such as foundations, agencies, religious groups, and service organizations. For a family that isn't eligible for need-based aid, merit scholarships are the only form of gift aid available. If your child later qualifies for a need-based award, a merit scholarship can be quite helpful in providing additional resources when the aid does not fully cover the costs. Even if the college meets 100 percent of need, a merit scholarship can benefit the student by reducing the self-help (loan and job) portion of an award.

In searching for outside merit-based scholarships, keep in mind that there are relatively few awards (compared to those that are need-based) and most of them are highly competitive. Looking for a merit scholarship is like betting on a long shot in a horse race—the chances of winning are slim but the payoff can be large. Use the following checklist when investigating merit scholarships.

■ Take advantage of any scholarships

The financial aid award letter tells you the amount of discount to subtract from the college's "sticker price." You don't know how much college will cost until you've completed this step.

---

for which your child is automatically eligible based on employer benefits, military service, associational or church membership, other affiliations, or student or parent attributes (ethnic background, nationality, etc.). Company or union tuition remissions are the most common examples of these awards.

■ Look for other awards for which your child might be eligible based on the characteristics and affiliations indicated above, but where there is a selection process and an application is required. Computerized searches are available on the Internet. Scholarship directories, such as *Peterson's Scholarships, Grants & Prizes*, which details some 2,200 scholarship programs, are useful resources and can be found in bookstores, high school guidance offices, or public libraries.

■ Read Section 6 to see if your state has a merit scholarship program.

■ Look into national scholarship competitions. High school guidance counselors usually know about these scholarships. Examples of these awards are the National Merit Scholarship, Coca-Cola Scholarship, Aid Association for Lutherans, Westinghouse Science Talent Search, and the U.S. Senate Youth Program. *Winning Money for College* (Peterson's, 2nd ed., 1997) provides detailed profiles of fifty of the most lucrative and prestigious competitions open to high school students.

■ ROTC (Reserve Officers' Training Corps) scholarships are offered by the Army, Navy, Air Force and Marine Corps. A full ROTC scholarship can cover virtually all tuition, fees and textbook costs. Acceptance of an ROTC scholarship entails a commitment to take a military science course and to serve for a specific number of years as an officer in the sponsoring branch of the service. ROTC is not available at every college. Competition is heavy, and preference may be given to students in certain fields of study, such as nursing, engineering, science, or business. Application procedures vary by service. Contact

What is the Financial Aid PROFILE?

There are many complexities in the financial aid process: separate application procedures for merit and need-based aid; understanding the difference between grants, loans, and work-study; and determining whether funds are from federal, state, college, or private sources.

To add to the confusion, the aid application process itself can involve more than the Free Application for Federal Student Aid (FAFSA) and Federal Methodology (FM). Among the approximately 2,000 four-year colleges, about 600 are private institutions with over $2 billion of their own scholarships. Many of these colleges feel that the federal aid system (FAFSA and FM) does not collect or evaluate information thoroughly enough to be used to award their institutional funds. These colleges have made an arrangement with the College Scholarship Service, a branch of the College Board, to establish a separate application system to meet their needs.

The application is called the Financial Aid PROFILE, and the means of need determination is known as the Institutional Methodology (IM). If your student applies for financial aid at one of the approximately 400 colleges that use PROFILE, the admission material will state that PROFILE is required in addition to the FAFSA. You should read the information carefully and file PROFILE to meet the earliest deadline among the colleges involved. Before you can receive the PROFILE form, however, you must register, providing enough basic information so the PROFILE package can be designed specifically for you. Also, while the FAFSA is free, there is a charge for PROFILE.

In addition to the requirement by certain colleges that you submit both the FAFSA and PROFILE (when used, PROFILE is always in addition to the FAFSA; it does not replace it), you should also realize that each system has its own method for analyzing family ability to pay for college. The main differences between the Institutional Methodology as calculated using PROFILE and the Federal Methodology based on the FAFSA are as follows:

- PROFILE includes equity in the family home as an asset; the FAFSA doesn't.

- PROFILE expects a minimum student contribution, usually in the form of summer earnings. The FAFSA has no such minimum.

- PROFILE considers only the number of children in college, not parents; if a parent attends college, these expenses are treated on an individual basis. The FAFSA divides the parent contribution by all family members in college, including both children and parents.

- PROFILE allows for much more professional judgment than the FAFSA. Medical expenses, private secondary school costs, and a variety of special circumstances are considered under PROFILE subject to the discretion of the aid counselor on campus.

To summarize: PROFILE's Institutional Methodology (IM) tends to be both more complete in its data collection and more rigorous in its analysis than the FAFSA's Federal Methodology (FM). On average, this means that IM will usually come up with a higher expected parental contribution than FM. However, for an individual family, the results will vary depending on how the aid counselor treats special circumstances.

Creditworthiness

If you will be borrowing to pay for your child's college education, making sure you qualify for a loan is critical. For the most part, that means your credit record must be free of default or delinquency. You can check your credit history with one or more of the following three major credit bureaus and clean up any adverse information that appears. The numbers below will provide specific information on what you need to provide in order to obtain a report. You will need to send a signed written request and a fee (usually $8 or less) that varies depending upon the state in which you reside. Usually you will be asked to provide your full name, phone number, Social Security number, birth date, and addresses for the last five years.

Equifax Information Service Center P.O. Box 740241 Atlanta, GA 30374-0241 (800) 685-1111	Trans Union Corporation P.O. Box 390 Springfield, PA 19064-0390 (610) 690-4909	Experian National Consumer Assistance Center P.O. Box 949 Allen, TX 75013-0949 (888) 397-3742

an armed services recruiter or high school guidance counselor for further information.

■ Investigate community scholarships. The high school guidance counselor usually has a list of these awards, and announcements are published in the town newspaper. Most common are awards given by service organizations like the American Legion, Rotary International, and the local women's club.

If your child is strong academically (for example, a National Merit Commended Scholar or better) or is very talented in fields such as athletics or performing/creative arts, you may want to consider colleges that offer their own merit awards to gifted students they wish to enroll. Refer to the Non-Need Scholarships for Undergraduates Index for lists of colleges that award non-need scholarships.

In addition to merit scholarships, there are loan and job opportunities for students who do not qualify for need-based aid. The federal loan program is called the unsubsidized Federal Stafford or Direct loan. See Section 4: Federal Financial Aid for more information. Some of the organizations that sponsor scholarships—for example, the Air Force Aid Society, also provide loans.

Work opportunities during the academic year are another type of assistance that is not restricted to aid recipients. Many colleges, after assigning jobs to students on aid, will open campus positions to all students looking for work. In addition, there are usually off-campus employment opportunities available to everyone.

Financing Your Child's College Education

In this section, "financing" means arranging for the use of resources to pay balances due to the college over and above payments from the primary sources of aid—scholarships, student loans, and jobs. Financing strategies are important because the high cost of a college education today often requires a family, whether they receive aid or not, to think about stretching the payment for college beyond the four-year period of enrollment. For high-cost colleges, it is not unreasonable to think about a 10-4-10 plan: ten years of saving; four years of paying college bills out of current income, savings, and borrowing; and ten years to repay a parental loan.

Savings

Although saving for college is always a good idea, many families are unclear about its advantages. Families do not save for two reasons. First, after expenses have been covered, many families do not have much money to set aside. An affordable but regular savings plan through a payroll deduction is usually the answer to the problem of spending your entire paycheck every month.

The second reason that saving for college is not a high priority is the belief that the financial aid system penalizes a family by lowering aid eligibility. The Federal Methodology of need determination is very kind to savers. In fact, savings are ignored completely for families that earn less than $50,000. Savings in the form of home equity are excluded from the calculation. And even when savings are counted, a maximum of 5.6 percent of the total is expected each year. In other words, if a family has $40,000 in savings after an asset protection allowance is considered, the contribution is no greater than $2240, an amount very close to the yearly interest that is accumulated. Therefore, it is possible

NOTE:

A point of clarification about whether to put college savings in the parents' or student's name: If you are certain that you will not be a candidate for need-based aid, there may be a tax advantage to accumulating money in the student's name. However, when it comes to maximizing aid eligibility, it is important to understand that student assets are assessed at a 35 percent rate and parental assets at about 5 percent. Therefore, if your college savings are in your child's name, it is probably wise to move these funds a full year before your child's senior year in high school.

for a family to meet its savings contribution without depleting the face value of its investments.

A sensible savings plan is important because of the financial advantage of saving compared to borrowing. The amount of money students borrow for college is now greater than the amount they receive in grants and scholarships. With loans becoming so widespread, savings should be carefully considered as an alternative to borrowing. Your incentive for saving is that a dollar saved is a dollar not borrowed.

Borrowing

Once you've calculated your "bottom-line" parental contribution and determined that the amount is not affordable out of your current income and assets, the most likely alternative is borrowing. First determine if your child is eligible for a larger Subsidized Federal Stafford or Direct Loan. Because no interest is due while a student attends college, these are the most favorable loans. If this is not possible, look into the Unsubsidized Stafford or Direct Loan, which does not require a needs test but where the interest is due each year. The freshman year limit (either Subsidized or Unsubsidized) is $2625.

After you have taken out the maximum amount of student loans, the next step is to look into parental loans. The federal government's parent loan program is called the PLUS loan and is the standard against which other loans are judged. A local bank that participates in the PLUS program can give you a schedule of monthly repayments per $1000 borrowed. Use this repayment figure to compare other parental loans available through commercial lenders (including home equity loans), state programs, or colleges

themselves. Choose the one that offers the best terms after all up-front costs, tax advantages, and the amount of monthly payments are considered.

Make Financial Aid Work for You

This overview is intended to provide you with a road map to help you think about financing strategies and navigate through the complexities of the financial aid process. Much of the information you will need to help you determine your plan to pay for your child's education can be found within the pages of this publication. First use the parental contribution tables in conjunction with the college cost worksheet to estimate need eligibility. If there is any chance you could qualify for aid, complete the FAFSA (and PROFILE if required). At the same time look into merit scholarships. Once your child is accepted by colleges that award aid, use the Comparing Awards and Family Contribution worksheet to figure out your parental obligation. If you can't afford the payment, present your arguments to the college's financial aid office before checking out the terms of PLUS and parental loan options. And finally, if there are younger children at home, think about starting a college savings fund to get a head start on future costs.

If you are like millions of families that benefit from financial aid, it is likely that your child's college plans can go forward without undue worry about the costs involved. The key is to understand the financial aid system and to follow the best path for your family. The result of good information and good planning should be that you will receive your fair share of the billions of dollars available each year and that the cost of college will not prevent your child from attending.

SECTION 3

Common Questions
Answered

Q *Are a student's chances of being admitted to a college reduced if the student applies for financial aid?*

A Generally not. Most colleges have a policy of "need-blind" admissions, which means that a student's financial need is not taken into account in the admission decision. However, there are a few colleges that do consider ability to pay before deciding whether or not to admit a student. There are a few more that look at ability to pay of those whom they placed on a waiting list to get in or those students who applied late. Some colleges will mention this in their literature, others may not. In making decisions about the college application and financing process, however, families should apply for financial aid if the student needs the aid to attend college.

Q *Are parents penalized for saving money for college?*

A No. As a matter of fact, families that have made a concerted effort to save money for college are in a much better position. For example, a student from a family that has saved money may not have to borrow as much in student loans, which are part of most financial aid packages. Also, when the expected parent contribution is calculated for federal aid, only about 5 percent of the parents' assets are assessed, and none of the home equity is included. That means that a parent who saved $40,000 (after an asset protection allowance has been considered) for college expenses will have about $2400 counted as part of the parental contribution. When students have assets in their name, 35 percent of those assets count toward the calculated family contribution. The reason for the difference is that the student will be the direct beneficiary of the college education.

Q *How does the financial aid system work in cases of divorce or separation? How are stepparents treated?*

A In cases of divorce or separation, the financial aid application(s) should be completed by the parent with whom the student lived for the longest period of time in the last twelve months. If the custodial parent has remarried, the stepparent is considered a family member and must complete the application along with the natural parent. If your family has any special circumstances, you can discuss these directly with the financial aid office. (Note: Colleges that award their own aid may ask the non-custodial natural parent to contribute.)

Q *When are students considered independent of parental support in applying for financial aid?*

A The student must be 24 years of age in order to be considered independent. The only exceptions are if the student is married, is a graduate or professional student, has legal dependents other than a spouse, is an orphan or ward of the court, or is a veteran of the armed forces.

Q *What can a family do if a job loss occurs?*

A Financial aid eligibility is based on the previous year's income. So the family's 1997 income would be reported to determine eligibility for the 1998–99 academic year. In that way, the family's income can be verified with an income tax return. But the previous year's income may not accurately reflect the current financial situation, particularly if a parent lost a job or retired. In these instances, the projected income for the coming year can be used instead. Families should discuss the situation directly with the financial aid office and be prepared to provide appropriate documentation.

Q *When my daughter first went to college, we applied for financial aid and were denied because our family contribution was too high. Now, my son is a high school senior and we will soon have two in college. Will we get the same results?*

A The results will definitely be different. You still may not qualify based on need. But both your son and daughter should apply. As we described earlier, need-based financial aid is based on your calculated "family contribution." When you have two in college, this amount is divided in half for each child.

Q *I've heard about the "middle-income squeeze" in regard to financial aid. What is it?*

A The so-called "middle-income squeeze" is the idea that low-income families qualify for aid, high-income families already have adequate resources to pay for education, and those in the middle are caught in between, not eligible for aid but without the ability to pay full college costs. There is no provision in the Federal Methodology that treats middle-income students differently than others (such as an income cutoff for eligibility). The expected family contribution rises proportionately as income and assets increase. If a middle-income family does not qualify for aid, it is because the need analysis formula yields a contribution that exceeds college costs. But keep in mind that if a $60,000-income family does not qualify for aid at a public university with a $10,000 budget, the same family will likely be eligible for aid at a private college with a cost of $20,000 or more. Also, there

are now loan programs available to parents and students that are not based on need. Middle-income families should realize, however, that many of the grant programs funded by federal and state governments are directed at lower-income families. It is therefore likely that a larger share of an aid package for a middle-income student will consist of loans rather than grants.

Q *Given our financial condition, my daughter will be receiving financial aid. We will help out as much as we can and, in fact, will be borrowing ourselves. But I am concerned that she will have to take on a lot of loans in order to go to the college of her choice. Does she have any options?*

A Absolutely. If offered a loan, she can decline all or part of it. One option is for her to ask in the financial aid office to have some of the loan changed to Federal Work-Study. If this is not possible, she can find her own part-time job. Often there is an employment office on campus that can help her locate a job. If she finds work, she should tell the financial aid office so that they don't continue to process her loan application.

Q *Is it possible to change your financial aid package?*

A Yes. Most colleges have an appeals process. Requests to change need-based loans to Federal Work-Study are often approved if funds are available. Requests to alter a student's budget or to change an element used in the need-analysis formula may also be granted if the expense is nondiscretionary and can be documented.

At most colleges, requests for more grant are rarely approved unless they are based on a change in the information reported. Applicants should speak with the financial aid office if they have concerns about their package. Some colleges may even respond to a competitive appeal, that is, a request to match another college's offer.

Q *My son was awarded a Federal Stafford Loan as part of his financial aid package. His award letter also indicated that we could take out a PLUS loan and could borrow from a private source to meet our expected contribution. How do we go about choosing our lender? Do we go to our local bank?*

A Choosing a lender should not be taken lightly. Chances are you will have a long relationship with your lender. Your family may even have several loans with that same lender, including both student and parent loans. If the college is not one of the schools participating in the Direct Lending program, often they will send a list of participating lenders with your son's award letter. In addition to most banks and savings and loans, there are private organizations such as Academic Management Service, Inc., The Education Resources Institute, and The College Board that offer both subsidized and unsubsidized Federal Stafford Loans as well as private loans. You are free to choose any lender that participates in the Federal Stafford Loan program. But you might want to check with the financial aid office first since they may have made special arrangements with a bank to expedite loan processing.

Q *The cost of attending college seems to be going up so much faster than the Consumer Price Index. Why is that and how can I plan for my child's four years?*

A The cost of higher education cannot be compared to the Consumer Price Index. Neither the CPI nor even the Higher Education Price Index takes into account some of the fastest-changing costs. For example, the dollars that universities spend on need-based grants and scholarships have soared to match the rise in tuition, food, housing, and books. Secondly, most universities have increased enrollment of students from less affluent families, further increasing the need for institutional financial aid. Third, colleges are expected to be on the cutting edge of technology, not only in research but also in the classroom and in the library. Lastly, during the high inflation years of the 1970s, most colleges deferred needed maintenance and repairs that can no longer be put off. In general you can expect that college costs will rise about 2 to 3 percent faster than inflation. A financial institution (like Merrill Lynch) can provide projections and savings alternatives.

Q *I will be receiving a scholarship from my local high school. How will this scholarship be treated in my financial aid award?*

A Federal student aid regulations specify that all forms of aid must be included within the definition of need and need-based aid recipients cannot receive more than the cost of education. This means that additional aid such as outside scholarships must be combined with any need-based aid you will receive.

It may not be kept separate and used to reduce your family's contribution. If the college has not filled 100 percent of your need, they will usually earmark outside scholarships to close the gap. Once your total need has been met, however, the college must reduce other aid and replace it with the outside award. Most colleges will allow you to use at least part of an outside scholarship to replace self-help aid (loans and Federal Work-Study) rather than grant aid.

Q *I know we're supposed to apply for financial aid as soon as possible after January 1. What if I don't have my W-2's yet and my tax return isn't done?*

A Although you can't apply for federal financial aid until after January 1 of each year, you don't have to have your application in until the school's deadline. The first deadlines are in early February, and many are much later. Chances are you'll have your W-2's by then but won't have a completed tax return yet. If that is the case, complete the financial aid application using your best estimates. Then, when you receive the Student Aid Report (SAR), you can make any needed corrections.

Q *Is there enough aid available to make it worthwhile for me to consider colleges that are more expensive than I can afford?*

A Definitely. More than $50 billion in aid is awarded to undergraduates every year. With more than half of all enrolled students qualifying for some type of assistance, this comes to over $5000 per student. You

should view financial aid as a large, national system of tuition discounts, some given according to a student's ability and talent, others based on what a student's family can afford to pay. If you qualify for need-based financial aid, you will essentially pay only your calculated family contribution, regardless of the cost of the college. You will not pay the "sticker price" (the yearly budget listed in the college catalog) but a lower rate that is reduced by the amount of aid you receive. No college should be ruled out until after financial aid is considered. In addition, when deciding which college to attend, consider that the short-term cost of a college education is only one criterion. If a school meets your educational needs and you are convinced it can launch you on an exciting career, a significant up-front investment may turn out to be a bargain over the long run.

Q *If I don't qualify for need-based aid, what options are available?*

A If you are not eligible for need-based aid, you should try to put together your own aid package to help reduce your parents' share. There are basically three sources to look into. First is the search for merit scholarships that you start during the initial stages of the aid application process. Second is employment, both during the summer and the academic year. The student employment office on campus should be able to help you find a job during the school year. Third is borrowing. Even if you don't qualify for the need-based loan programs, the Unsubsidized Federal Stafford or Direct Loan programs are available to all students. The terms and conditions are the same as the subsidized loan programs except that interest accrues while you are in college.

COMMON QUESTIONS ANSWERED

After you have contributed what you can through scholarships, working, and borrowing, your parents are left with their share of the college bill. Many colleges have monthly payment plans that allow families to spread their payment over the academic year. If these monthly payments turn out to be more than your parents can afford, they can take out a parent loan. By borrowing from the college itself, from a commercial agency or lender, or through the Federal PLUS Loan, parents can extend their college payments over a ten-year period or longer. Borrowing reduces the monthly obligation to its lowest level, but the total amount paid will be the highest due to principal and interest payments.

SECTION 4

Federal Financial Aid Programs

here are a number of sources of financial aid available to students: the federal government, state governments, private lenders, foundations and private agencies, and the institutions themselves. In addition, as discussed earlier, there are three different forms of aid: grants, earnings, and loans.

The federal government is the single largest source of financial aid for students, accounting for about 74 percent of the $50 billion available annually. At the present time there are two federal grant programs—the Federal Pell Grant and the Federal Supplemental Educational Opportunity Grant (FSEOG); three loan programs—the Federal Perkins Loan, the Federal Direct Loan and the Federal Stafford Loan; and a work program that helps colleges provide jobs for students, the Federal Work-Study (FWS).

The two grants, Federal Work-Study, Federal Perkins Loan, and two other loan programs, the Subsidized Federal Direct Loan and the Subsidized Federal Stafford Loan, are awarded to students with demonstrated financial need. Interest on the loans is paid by the government during the time the student is in school. For the Federal Unsubsidized Direct Loan and Federal Unsubsidized Stafford Loan, the interest begins to accrue as soon as the money is received. There is also a parental loan (PLUS) available under the Direct or Stafford programs.

Federal Pell Grant

The Federal Pell Grant is the largest grant program; over 5 million students receive awards annually. This grant is intended to be the base, or starting point, of assistance for lower-income families. Eligibility for a Federal Pell Grant depends on the Expected Family Contribution (EFC). The amount your child receives will depend on your EFC, the cost of education at the college or university your child will attend, and whether your child attends full-time or part-time. The highest award depends on how much the program is funded. The maximum for 1997–98 was $2700.

To give you some idea of the distribution of Federal Pell Grant dollars in 1996–97, the table below may be helpful. The amounts shown are based on a family size of five, with one in college, no emergency expenses, no contribution from student income or assets, and college costs of at least $2500 per year.

Table Used to Estimate Federal Pell Grants for 1997–98

Family Assets

Adjusted Gross Income	$50,000	$55,000	$60,000	$65,000	$70,000	$75,000	$80,000	$85,000
$ 5000	$2700	$2700	$2700	$2700	$2700	$2700	$2700	$2700
$10,000	2700	2700	2700	2700	2700	2700	2700	2700
$15,000	2700	2700	2700	2700	2700	2700	2700	2600
$20,000	2500	2400	2300	2200	2100	1900	1800	1700
$25,000	1700	1600	1500	1300	1200	1000	900	800
$30,000	800	700	700	400	400	0	0	0
$35,000	400	400	400	400	0	0	0	0

Federal Supplemental Educational Opportunity Grant (FSEOG)

As its name implies, the Federal Supplemental Educational Opportunity Grant (FSEOG) provides additional need-based federal grant money to supplement the Federal Pell Grant. Each participating college is given funds ·to award to especially needy students. The maximum award is $4000 per year, but the amount your child receives will depend on the college's policy, the availability of FSEOG funds, the total cost of education, and the amount of other aid awarded.

Federal Work-Study (FWS)

This program provides jobs for students who need financial aid for their educational expenses. The salary is paid by funds from the federal government and the college (or the employer). Your child works on an hourly basis in jobs on- or off-campus and must be paid at least the federal minimum wage. Your child may earn only up to the amount awarded, which depends on the calculated financial need and the total amount of money available to the college.

Federal Perkins Loan

This loan is a low-interest (5 percent) loan for students with exceptional financial need (students with the lowest Expected Family Contribution). Federal Perkins Loans are made through the college's financial aid office. That is, the college is the lender. Students may borrow a maximum of $3000 per year for up to five years of undergraduate study. They may take up to ten

Federal Financial Aid Programs

Name of Program	Type of Program	Maximum Award Per Year
Federal Pell Grant	Need-based grant	$2700
Federal Supplemental Educational Opportunity Grant (FSEOG)	Need-based grant	$4000
Federal Work-Study	Need-based part-time job	no maximum
Federal Perkins Loan	Need-based loan	$3000
Federal Stafford Loan/ Federal Direct Loan (Subsidized)	Need-based student loan	$2625 (first year)
Federal Stafford Loan/ Federal Direct Loan (Unsubsidized)	Non-need-based student loan	$2625 (first year, dependent student)
Federal PLUS Loan	Non-need-based parent loan	Up to the cost of education

Note: The Direct and Stafford Loans have higher maximums after the freshman year.

years to repay the loan, beginning nine months after they graduate, leave school, or drop below half-time status. No interest accrues while they are in school and, under certain conditions (e.g., they teach in low-income areas, work in law enforcement, are full-time nurses or medical technicians, serve as Peace Corps or VISTA volunteers, etc.), some or all of the loan can be canceled or payments deferred.

Federal Stafford Loan

A Federal Stafford Loan may be borrowed from a participating commercial lender such as a bank, credit union, or savings and loan association. The interest rate varies annually (up to a maximum of 8.25 percent), and the rate for 1996–97 is 7.66 percent. If your child qualifies for a need-based,

subsidized Federal Stafford Loan, the interest is paid by the federal government while your child is enrolled in school. There is also an unsubsidized Federal Stafford Loan not based on need for which your child is eligible regardless of your family income.

The maximum amount dependent students may borrow in any one year is $2625 for freshmen, $3500 for sophomores, and $5500 for juniors and seniors, with a maximum of $23,000 for the total undergraduate program. The maximum amount independent students can borrow is $6625 for freshmen (no more than $2625 in subsidized Stafford Loans), $7500 for sophomores (no more than $3500 in subsidized Stafford Loans), and $10,500 for juniors and seniors (no more than $5500 in subsidized Stafford Loans). Borrowers must pay a 4 percent fee, which is deducted from the loan proceeds.

To apply for a Federal Stafford Loan, your child must first complete a FAFSA to determine eligibility for a subsidized loan, then a separate loan application that is submitted to a lender. The financial aid office can help in selecting a lender, or you can contact your state department of higher education to find a participating lender. The lender will send a promissory note that your child must sign agreeing to repay the loan. The proceeds of the loan, less the origination fee, will be sent to your child's school to be either credited to the student account or paid to your child directly.

If your child qualifies for a subsidized Federal Stafford Loan, your child does not have to pay interest while in school. For an unsubsidized Federal Stafford Loan, your child will be responsible for paying the interest from the time the loan is established. However, some lenders will permit borrowers to delay making payments and will add the interest to the loan. Once the repayment period starts, borrowers of both subsidized and unsubsidized Federal Stafford Loans will have to pay a combination of interest and principal monthly for up to a ten-year period.

Federal PLUS Loan

The Federal PLUS loan is a loan for parents of dependent students designed to help families with cash-flow problems. There is no needs test to qualify, and the loans are made by participating lenders. The loan has a variable interest rate that cannot exceed 9 percent (the rate from July 1997 to June 1998 is 8.72 percent). There is no specific yearly limit; you can borrow up to the cost of your child's education less other financial aid received. Repayment begins sixty days after the money is advanced. A 4 percent fee is subtracted from the proceeds. Parent borrowers must generally have a good credit record to qualify for Federal PLUS Loans.

The PLUS loan will be processed under either the Direct or Stafford system, depending on the type of loan program for which the college has contracted.

Federal Direct Student Loans

The Federal Direct Student Loan is a relatively new program that is basically the same as the Federal Stafford. The difference is that the U.S. Department of Education is the lender rather than a bank. Not all colleges participate in this program, and if your child's college does not, he or she can still apply for a Federal Stafford Loan.

Many of the terms of the new Federal Direct Student Loan are similar to those of the Federal Stafford Loan. In particular, the interest rate, loan maximums, deferments, and cancellation benefits are the same. However, under the terms of the Federal Direct Student Loan, students have a choice of repayment plans. They may choose either a fixed monthly payment for ten years; a different fixed monthly payment for twelve to thirty years at a rate that varies with the loan balance; or a variable monthly payment for up to twenty-five years that is based on a percentage of income. Students cannot receive both a Federal Direct Student Loan and a Federal Stafford Loan for the same period of time, but may receive both in different enrollment periods.

National and Community Service Plan

The National and Community Service Plan is a program for a limited number of students. Participants work in a public or private nonprofit agency providing service to the community in one of four priority areas: education, human services, the environment, and public safety. In exchange, they earn a stipend of between $7400 and $14,800 a year for living expenses and up to $4725 for up to two years to apply toward college expenses. Students can work either before, during, or after they go to college and can use the funds to pay either current educational expenses or repay federal student loans. We suggest speaking to the college financial aid office for more details about this program and any other new initiatives available to students.

State-Sponsored College Savings Programs

Types of Programs

As college tuition costs continue to inflate at a rate double that of general inflation, state governments in increasing numbers are enacting new programs to help families save for college education. Although specific details vary considerably from one state to the next, there are two basic categories of these programs:

Prepaid or guaranteed tuition. In exchange for early tuition purchase, accomplished either through a one-time lump-sum purchase or monthly installments, this program locks in a tuition rate at the plan's participating colleges or universities.

Savings plan trusts. These programs allow participants to save money in a college savings account on behalf of a prospective student. These special accounts guarantee a minimum 4 percent return and exempt the interest from state, but not federal, taxes. The accrued savings may be spent at any college.

In addition to the two specialized types of programs, a third category, savings bond purchase programs that provide special features for college savers, is offered by six states: Arkansas, California, Illinois, Nevada, New Hampshire, and Oregon. These plans sell, often at discount, general obligation, zero-coupon, or municipal bonds to program participants who are saving for a child's education. Interest is compounded over the life of the bonds. The proceeds may be used to pay any costs related to college attendance. A number of states have evolved from a college-focused savings bond programs into prepaid tuition or savings plan trust programs, and four of the above six states (California, Illinois, Nevada, and New Hampshire) are actively considering offering a prepaid tuition program or college savings trust.

A fourth category, modeled on an IRA is under study in a number of states. Under this proposal, a special account, set up for the prospective student and funded either by a one-time purchase or installment payments, would be invested by a third party. States would allow an income adjustment for the plan earnings to help protect them from state income taxes.

Growth of the Plans

Although New Jersey's discontinued Garden State Savings Bonds program instituted in 1959 was historically the first state college savings promotion plan, all the currently active plans were instituted in the last decade. The Michigan Education Trust (MET), begun in 1986, was the first of these, and it has become a prototype for other states' prepaid tuition plans. Between 1987 and 1990 Alabama, Florida, and Ohio also introduced prepaid tuition plans. The first college savings plan trust was Kentucky's Educational Savings Trust Plan, established in 1988.

The Michigan Education Trust was enacted with the expectation that participants would be entitled to both federal and state tax exemptions. However, the Internal Revenue Service refused exemption on the grounds that helping to pay for college was not an essential function of state government and so not entitled to tax-exempt status. This situation was resolved in 1996 when Congress redefined the tax treatment of state college savings programs. This at last made it attractive and practical for state governments to establish prepaid tuition programs and college savings trusts. Interest by state governments in these plans has been growing rapidly since then.

As of mid-1997, twelve states actively operate prepaid tuition or savings plan trust programs Before the end of 1997, this number will expand to eighteen. In addition, six states have savings bond purchase programs with special provisions for college savers. Some form of college savings program is under active consideration in twenty-one states.

Advantages

These programs appeal to many families for a number of reasons:

Regimented saving. Funds cannot be withdrawn early without serious penalty. Many families find the disincentive to casually withdraw funds and the encouragement to save on a regular program to be major benefits of the plans.

Portability. Money accrued in savings plan trusts or savings bonds may be spent at any college. Most prepaid tuition programs allow a degree of portability to out-of-state or private institutions. The usual stipulation is that the benefits paid out will be equal to the tuition rates of the colleges participating in the state plan in which the contributor invested.

Transferability. If a student transfers to another school, benefits transfer as well. In the event that the beneficiary receives a scholarship, the saved funds can be accessed immediately as a refund to be used for other college costs, the use can be deferred, or the savings can be transferred to other family members. Transfer of savings is allowed in cases of death, disability, or decision not to attend college. If funds are not transferred or needed for college costs, a refund with interest is given.

Minimal risk. Many of the programs actually are risk-free, backed by the full faith and credit of the state government.

Most financial counselors advise that college savings, especially as the time approaches when they will be used, should be in lower-risk investments of the kind that make up the state plans.

Affordability. In most state plans, a low monthly payment is made from the child's fifth birthday through to high school graduation. Many plans allow a great variety of low-contribution savings options. The Pennsylvania Tuition Account Program, for example, allows payments as low as $3.25 per unit price (a unit is a portion of a credit) for a community college. Kentucky's monthly payment is as low as $25, and Ohio's, $15.

Tax exemption. All plans, except Alabama's and Michigan's, are exempt from state taxes. The federal tax obligation is based on the child's rate and is deferred until the savings are tapped.

Locked-in prices. Prepaid tuition plans, in addition to the above advantages shared with other forms of savings plans, guarantee that tuition in the next decade will be locked in at today's rates.

Negative Aspects

There are some potentially negative aspects to these plans:

Relatively low interest rates. These plans are low risk and are not subject to the unpredictability and volatility of the stock market. The plans are indexed to keep pace with tuition rates, typically between 6 percent and 8 percent per year. This conservative investment policy also means that the potential returns are less than they could be with riskier investments. A family that has the time, knowledge, discipline, and desire to invest the funds on their own probably would do better.

Negative impact on federal student aid eligibility. Funds paid by state plans are figured at 100 percent in reducing the amount of federal aid to a student. So, if a student is likely to benefit from federal need-based grants, he or she would lose money by previously paying into a state program. On the other hand, reliance on federal grants to pay a major part of college expenses could be unwise. The federal grant aid contribution as been steadily declining for twenty years and shows no sign of turning around. Also, most families tend to experience an increase in wealth as time goes by. So, families usually can expect to see their eligibility for federal need-based aid diminish as a child approaches college age.

Prepaid tuition plans have some unique disadvantages:

Limitation on choice of college. The prepaid plans are designed for students who intend to enroll at a state college or university. This, according to General Accounting Office figures, is about 72 percent of all freshmen. For the other 15 to 28 percent who will enroll either at a private college or an out-of-state public institution, most prepaid plans will cover costs equivalent to the average at the state's public colleges. However, a primary benefit of the plans, the locking in of tuition rates, is nullified. Some savings plans provide a lower rate of return if the student goes to college out of the state.

Plan fees. Prepaid tuition plans charge fees, ranging from $25 to $75, when the family enrolls and frequently assess charges for late payments, early withdrawals, and other actions beyond the routine.

Limits on kinds of costs covered. Coverage of most plans is limited to tuition and fees. Only Florida and Mississippi cover room expenses and only Mississippi, room and board.

Future of State Plans

Parents are worried about their ability to pay for college in the face of rising tuitions and cutbacks in federal financial aid help. Faced with this concern from citizens and alert to long-range economic benefits to a state that possesses a large college-educated work force, there is a trend among state governments to introduce plans to support college attendance. The clarification of the state savings plans' tax status has encouraged many states to consider these programs. By the end of the decade it is quite possible that more than half of the states will have a college savings program in place.

PREPAID TUITION PLANS

(* means that the plan is scheduled to start in the latter half of 1997)

ALABAMA

Plan Name: Prepaid Affordable College Tuition (PACT) **Year started: 1990 Participating colleges:** 16 Four-Year; 22 Two-Year, 9 Technical Alabama public colleges **Private/out-of-state colleges:** paid at Alabama average rate **Purchaser buys** contract **Restrictions:** Beneficiary and parents must be state residents **Refunds and transferability:** Refunds minus interest with $150 cancellation fee. Transferable to immediate family. **Fees:** $75 enrollment. Also: late payment, early withdrawal, beneficiary substitution, transfer, private or out-of-state attendance, maintenance fees. **Contact for Information:** 800-ALA-PACT

ALASKA

Plan Name: University of Alaska Advanced College Tuition (ACT) Payment Plan **Year started:** 1991 **Participating colleges:** 3 Four-Year, 1 Two-Year Alaska public colleges **Private/out-of-state colleges:** up to 15 credits per semester paid at Alaska average rate **Purchaser buys** credits or units **Restrictions:** Beneficiary or purchaser must be

state resident **Refunds and transferability:** Refunds for reason; transferable on approval. **Fees:** $40 enrollment. Also: withdrawal, beneficiary substitution fees.

Contact for Information: 800-478-0003 (Alaska, only); other: 907-474-7711.

COLORADO

Plan Name: Colorado Student Obligation Bond Authority **Year started:** 1997* **Participating colleges:** 9 Four-Year, 12 Two-Year Colorado public colleges **Private/out-of-state colleges:** Savings refunded with reduced interest **Purchaser buys** contract **Refunds and transferability:** Refund with reduced interest.

Contact for Information: 1-800-448-2424

FLORIDA

Plan Name: Florida Prepaid College Program **Year started:** 1988 **Participating colleges:** 10 Four-Year, 28 Two-Year Florida public colleges **Purchaser buys** contract **Restrictions:** Beneficiary must be state resident **Refunds and transferability:** Refunds for reason; transferable to siblings **Fees:** $42 enrollment fee. Also: late payment, beneficiary substitution, transfer, out-of-state attendance, fees.

Contact for Information: 800-552-GRAD

MASSACHUSETTS

Plan Name: U-Plan - The Massachusetts College Savings Plan **Year started:** 1995 **Participating colleges:** 14 Four-Year Public, 25 Two-Year Public, 46 Private Massachusetts colleges **Private/out-of-state colleges:** Savings are refundable **Purchaser buys** general obligation bonds

redeemable for a percentage of tuition and fees **Restrictions:** No residency restrictions **Refunds and transferability:** Refundable with compounded interest indexed to Consumer Price Index; Transferable to family **Fees:** $25 enrollment. Also: early withdrawal, beneficiary substitution, transfer fees.

Contact for Information: 800-449-MEFA

MICHIGAN

Plan Name: Michigan Education Trust (MET) **Year started:** 1988 **Participating colleges:** Any Michigan public college **Private/out-of-state colleges:** Full tuition not covered **Purchaser buys contract Restrictions:** Beneficiary must be state resident **Refunds and transferability:** Refund for reason; transferable to immediate family **Fees:** $25 enrollment fee. Also: late payment, beneficiary termination fees.

Contact for Information: 800-MET-4KID

MISSISSIPPI

Plan Name: Mississippi Prepaid Affordable College Tuition Program (MPACT) **Year started:** 1997 **Participating colleges:** 8 Four-Year Public, 15 Two-Year Public, 9 Private Mississippi colleges **Private/out-of-state colleges:** Paid at Mississippi average rate **Purchaser buys** contract **Restrictions:** Beneficiary or purchaser must be state resident **Refunds and transferability:** Conditional refunds; conditional transferability **Fees:** $60 enrollment fee. Also: late payment, out-of-state attendance fees. **Contact for Information:** 888-308-1997

OHIO

Plan Name: Ohio Tuition Trust Authority **Year started:** 1989
Participating colleges: 13 Four-Year, 23 Two Year Ohio public colleges
Private/out-of-state colleges: Paid at Ohio average rate. **Purchaser buys** Credits or units **Restrictions:** Beneficiary must be state resident
Refunds and transferability: Refund with reduced interest; refunds with interest for reason; transferable to immediate family **Fees:** $50 enrollment fee. Also: beneficiary substitution fees.
Contact for Information: 800-AFFORD-IT

PENNSYLVANIA

Plan Name: Pennsylvania Tuition Account Program **Year started:** 1993
Participating colleges: 18 Four-Year, 15 Two-Year Pennsylvania public colleges **Private/out-of-state colleges:** Paid at Pennsylvania average rate **Purchaser buys** credits or units **Restrictions:** Beneficiary or purchaser must be state resident
Refunds and transferability: Refunds for reason; transferable to immediate family. **Fees:** $65 enrollment fee. Also: early withdrawal, beneficiary substitution, transfer fees.
Contact for Information: 800-440-4000

TENNESSEE

Plan Name: Tennessee Baccalaureate Education System Trust (BEST) **Year started:** 1997* **Participating colleges:** Any Tennessee public college **Private/out-of-state colleges:** Tuition, fees at any accredited college payable at Tennessee average rate **Purchaser buys** credits or units **Restrictions:** Beneficiary must be state resident **Refunds and transferability:** Transferable to siblings.
Contact for Information: 888-486-BEST

TEXAS

Plan Name: Texas TOMORROW Fund **Year started:** 1996 **Participating colleges:** 35 Four-Year Public, 50 Two-Year Public, 1 Technical Public, 38 Private Texas colleges **Private/out-of-state colleges:** Some private Texas colleges are in the plan. Others are paid at the average Texas rate **Purchaser buys contract Restrictions:** Beneficiary or purchaser must be state resident **Refunds and transferability:** Refunds for reason; transferable to siblings or half-siblings **Fees:** $50 enrollment fee. Also: late payment, early withdrawal, beneficiary substitution, transfer, maintenance fees.
Contact for Information: 800-445-4723

VIRGINIA

Plan Name: Virginia Prepaid Education Program (VPEP) **Year started:** 1996 **Participating colleges:** 15 Four-Year Public, 24 Two-Year Public, 28 private Virginia colleges **Private/out-of-state colleges:** Some private Virginia colleges are in the plan. Others are paid at variable amounts **Purchaser buys** contract **Restrictions:** Beneficiary or purchaser must be state resident **Refunds and transferability:** Refunds for reason; transferable to younger sibling **Fees:** $85 enrollment fee. Also: late payment, out-of-state attendance, maintenance fees.
Contact for Information: 888-567-0540

WISCONSIN

Plan Name: EdVest Wisconsin (Wisconsin Education Investment Program) **Year started:** 1997*
Participating colleges: May be used at any accredited college **Private/out-of-state colleges:** Payment based on University of Wisconsin rate **Purchaser buys** credits or units **Restrictions:** Beneficiary or purchaser must be state resident **Refunds and transferability:** Refunds available, may be paid over four years; transferable to siblings **Fees:** $50 enrollment fee.
Contact for Information: 888-EDVESTWI

SAVINGS PLAN TRUSTS

COLORADO

Plan Name: Colorado Student Obligation Authority **Year started:** 1997* **Notes:** Details to be announced.
Contact for Information: 800-448-2424

INDIANA

Plan Name: Indiana Education Savings Authority **Year started:** 1996 **Notes:** Consists of two programs: the Save Indiana Program and the Family College Savings Program. The Save Indiana Program has student participants who save a predetermined amount over a required number of years to become eligible for a grant award toward tuition. This grant is the same for all eligible students but can vary from year to year. The Family College Savings Program is a savings plan trust for parents and other family participants.
Contact for Information: 317-232-6386

KENTUCKY

Plan Name: Kentucky Educational Savings Plan **Year started:** 1990

Notes: Accepts $25 contributions. Guarantees a 4 percent return.

Contact for Information: 800-338-0318

LOUISIANA

Plan Name: Louisiana Student Tuition Assistance & Revenue Trust Program (START) **Year started:** 1997 **Notes:** As an enhancement, need-based grants to qualifying participants are indexed according to the amounts saved.

Contact for Information: 800-259-5626, ext. 1012

UTAH

Plan Name: Utah Educational Savings Plan Trust **Year started:** 1996 **Notes:** Funds may be established on behalf of any child under age 17, regardless of relationship.

Contact for Information: 800-418-2551

SECTION 6

State Scholarship and Grant Programs

Each state government has established one or more state-administered financial aid programs for qualified students. In many instances, these state programs are restricted to legal residents of the state. However, they often are available to out-of-state students who will be or are attending colleges or universities within the state. In addition to residential status, other qualifications frequently exist.

Gift aid and forgivable loan programs open to undergraduate students for all states and the District of Columbia are described below. They are arranged in alphabetical order, first by state name, then by program name. The annotation for each program provides information about the program, eligibility, and the contact addresses for applications or further information. Unless otherwise stated. this information refers to awards for 1997–98. Information is provided by the state sponsoring agency in response to Peterson's Annual Survey of Peterson's Non-institutional Aid, which is conducted between November 1996 and January 1997. Information is accurate when Peterson's receives it. However, it is always advisable to check with the sponsor to ascertain that the information remains correct.

Students or parents should write to the address given for each program to request that award details for 1998–99 be sent to them as soon as these are available. Usually descriptive information brochures and application forms for state scholarship programs also are available from the financial aid offices of public colleges or universities within the specific state. High school guidance offices often have information and relevant forms for awards for which high school seniors may be eligible. Increasingly, state government agencies are putting state scholarship information on state government agency Web sites. However, in many states the higher education agency is separate from the state's general education office, which is often responsible for elementary and secondary education. Also, the financial aid page of state-administered college or university sites frequently has a list of state-sponsored scholarships and financial aid programs. College and university Web sites easily can be accessed through Peterson's Education Center (http://www.petersons.com).

Names of scholarship programs frequently are used inconsistently or become abbreviated in use. Many programs have variant names by which they are known. The program's sponsor has approved the title of the program that Peterson's uses. However, this name sometimes differs from the program's official name or from the most commonly used name.

States may also offer internship or work-study programs, graduate fellowships and grants, or low-interest loans in addition to the grant aid and forgivable loans programs listed below. If you are interested in learning more about these other kinds of programs, the state education office that supplies information or applications for the undergraduate scholarship programs should be able to provide information about other kinds of higher education financial aid programs that may be sponsored by the state.

ALABAMA

Alabama GI Dependents' Scholarship Program. This program provides full scholarships to students who are dependents of Alabama disabled, Prisoners of War, or Missing in Action veterans. Applicants must be children or stepchildren and under age 26 (in certain situations, an age 30 deadline may apply). There is no age restriction for eligible spouses or widows.

Obtain the application form and further information from Alabama GI Dependents Scholarship, Department of Veterans Affairs, P.O. Box 1509, Montgomery, Alabama 36102-1509.

Alabama National Guard Educational Assistance Program. These scholarships aid Alabama residents who are members of the Alabama National Guard and are enrolled in a degree-seeking program at an accredited Alabama college or university. The maximum award is $1000 per academic year and awards are renewable. Forms must be signed by a representative of the Alabama Military Department and the college's financial aid officer.

Obtain an application form from any unit of the Alabama National Guard.

Alabama Student Grant Program. This program provides aid to Alabama residents for undergraduate study at certain independent colleges in Alabama. These renewable awards range up to a maximum of $1200.

Application forms are available from the financial aid office at participating Alabama colleges. The deadlines for applying are September 15, January 15, and February 15.

Junior and Community College Athletic Scholarships. This renewable award, based on demonstrated athletic ability, is for Alabama residents enrolled full-time at public junior and community colleges in Alabama.

Contact the financial aid officer at any public Alabama junior or community college.

Junior and Community College Performing Arts Scholarships. These one-time awards at Alabama public junior and community colleges

are for full-time students with talent in the performing arts. Awards are based on demonstrated ability. Applicants must be Alabama residents.

Contact the financial aid officer at any Alabama junior or community college.

Nursing Scholarship Program. This program provides renewable scholarships to Alabama residents enrolled in approved nursing programs at colleges in Alabama. Recipients must agree to practice nursing in Alabama for at least one year.

Application forms are available from the financial aid office at Alabama colleges offering nursing programs.

Police Officers and Fire Fighters Survivors Education Assistance Program. This program provides tuition, fees, books, and supplies to dependents of full-time police officers and fire fighters who were killed in the line of duty. Recipients must be Alabama residents and must attend an Alabama college or university. Awards are renewable annually.

Application forms are available from the Grants and Scholarships Department, Alabama Commission on Higher Education, P.O. Box 302000, Montgomery, Alabama 36130.

Senior Adult Scholarship Program-Alabama. These renewable full tuition grants are available to Alabama residents over sixty years old for use at any two-year public institution in Alabama.

Application forms are available from the Grants and Scholarships Department, Alabama Commission on Higher Education, P.O. Box 302000, Montgomery, Alabama 36130.

Student Assistance Program. This is a need-based program for Alabama residents pursuing an undergraduate education at a public or private college or university in Alabama. These one-time awards range from $300 to $2500.

Application forms are available at the financial aid office of any Alabama college.

Two-Year College Academic Scholarship Program. This award is for Alabama residents enrolled at two-year postsecondary institutions in Alabama and is based on demonstrated academic merit. Recipients must have a minimum 2.5 GPA. Awards may be renewed if students maintain academic excellence.

Contact the financial aid office at any Alabama junior or community college.

ALASKA

Alaska Student Loan Program. This loan program provides renewable loans to Alaska residents for full-time or part-time study in career, undergraduate, or graduate programs. Loans may be used for tuition, fees, room, board, books, and supplies. Students must attend an approved college or university in a program leading to a certificate, degree, or diploma. Awards range up to $6500. Interest rate varies. Repayment begins no later than twelve months from the time the recipient terminates full-time-student status, and it is spread over a ten-year period.

Applications are available from the Student Financial Aid Division, Alaska Commission on Postsecondary Education, 3030 Vintage Boulevard, Juneau, Alaska 99801-7109.

Family Education Loan Program.
This program was created to provide low-interest (5 percent) renewable loans to families to assist in paying the costs of postsecondary education. Loans are made to a family member on behalf of a student, and the maximum amount is $6500. The borrower must be an Alaska resident. Loans may only be used for attendance at an approved institution.

For further information, contact the Alaska Commission on Postsecondary Education, 3030 Vintage Boulevard, Juneau, Alaska 99801-7109.

Robert C. Thomas Memorial Scholarship Loan Fund. This program provides loans to students who wish to pursue a degree program leading to a career in education, public administration, or other closely related fields at an accredited college or university. Funds of up to $1000 a year are available for full-time undergraduate or graduate study. Upon degree completion, the recipient receives forgiveness of 20 percent of the total loan indebtedness for each year of full-time employment in education or public administration in Alaska.

For further information and applications, contact the Department of Education, 801 West 10th Street, Suite 200, Juneau, Alaska 99801-1894. Applications are due by March 1.

State Educational Incentive Grant Program. This program aids residents of Alaska enrolled full-time or eligible for admission at an approved college or university. Recipients must show substantial financial need and maintain satisfactory academic performance. Awards range up to $1500 per academic year.

To apply, complete and file the State Educational Incentive Grant Program application form, available from the Alaska Commission on Postsecondary Education, 3030 Vintage Boulevard, Juneau, Alaska 99801-7109. The application deadline is May 31.

Teacher Scholarship Loan Program. This program was established to encourage Alaska high school graduates to pursue teaching careers in rural elementary and secondary schools in the state. Applicants must be nominated by a rural school district. Students may borrow up to $7500 per year for in-state or out-of-state study. If the borrower is employed as a teacher in a rural elementary or secondary school in Alaska after graduation, he or she may be eligible for up to 100 percent forgiveness of the loan.

Teacher Scholarship Loan application forms are sent by the Commission to nominated recipients for completion and submission by July 1. For more information and to apply, students should contact their local high school guidance office.

ARIZONA

Arizona State Student Incentive Grant. This program offers renewable loans to Arizona residents attending accredited institutions within the state. Recipients must be enrolled at least half-time. Awards range from $100 to $2500 per year.

To apply, contact the financial aid office of the postsecondary institution you plan to attend for application procedures. The deadline for applying is June 1.

ARKANSAS

Arkansas Minority Teacher Scholars Program. This program is designed to provide forgivable renewable loans to a maximum amount of $5000 per academic year to college juniors who are African-American and are enrolled full-time in a teacher certification program. Applicant must be an Arkansas resident with a minimum 2.5 grade point average. Recipients must teach in Arkansas for three to five years to receive forgiveness of the loan.

Applications are available from the Arkansas Department of Higher Education, Financial Aid Division, 114 East Capitol, Little Rock, AR 72201-3818. The application deadline is June 1.

Arkansas Student Assistance Grant Program. This program aids graduating Arkansas high school seniors who have at least a 2.5 grade point average, score at least 19 on American College Test, and have financial need. Awards range up to $1500 and are renewable up to three additional years.

Inquire for details from the Financial Aid Coordinator, Arkansas Department of Higher Education, 114 East Capitol, Little Rock, Arkansas 72201-3818.

Emergency Secondary Education Loan Program. This program has been established to aid students majoring in secondary teacher education programs in mathematics, science, special education, or foreign language. Applicants must be Arkansas residents enrolled full-time in an approved Arkansas institution. Recipients must teach in an Arkansas secondary school for at least five years. Students may receive a renewable scholarship of up to $2500 per academic year. I1,1For further information, contact the Emergency Secondary Education Loan Program, Arkansas Department of Higher Education, 114 East Capitol, Little Rock, Arkansas 72201-3818. The application deadline is April 1.

Freshman/Sophomore Minority Grant Program. This program is designed for college freshmen and sophomores at an Arkansas institution who are African-American and pursuing a career in teaching. Renewable stipends of up to $1000 per academic year can be awarded. Applicants must be Arkansas residents.

Interested students should contact the Arkansas Department of Higher Education, Financial Aid Division, 114 East Capitol, Little Rock, Arkansas 72201-3818.

Governor's Scholars. This program aids outstanding Arkansas high school seniors. Applicants must be Arkansas residents and must have earned a grade point average of at least 3.6 or have scored at least 27 on the ACT. Recipients receive grant awards of $4000 per year for four years of full-time undergraduate study.

Applications are available from the Arkansas Department of Higher Education, Financial Aid Division, 114 East Capitol, Little Rock, AR 72201-3818. The application deadline is March 1.

Law Enforcement Officers' Dependents Scholarship. This renewable award is a waiver of tuition, fees, and room charges at two-year or four-year Arkansas institutions for dependents under twenty-four years old of Arkansas law-enforcement officers killed or permanently disabled in the line of duty. Applicants must submit proof of casualty.

For details, contact the Arkansas Department of Higher Education, Financial Aid Division, 114 East Capitol, Little Rock, AR 72201-3818.

Missing in Action/Killed in Action Dependent's Scholarship. A renewable waiver of tuition, fees, room and board at Arkansas state-supported institutions is available to Arkansas residents whose parent or spouse was Missing in Action, Killed in Action or was a Prisoner of War. Applicants must submit proof.

For details, contact the Arkansas Department of Higher Education, Financial Aid Division, 114 East Capitol, Little Rock, AR 72201-3818. Deadlines are August 1, December 1, May 1, or July 1.

CALIFORNIA

Assumption Program of Loans for Education (APLE). This program aids up to 500 college and university students who are planning to become teachers. To be eligible, students must be California residents who are planning to teach in a state public school and maintain a minimum 2.5 GPA. Students must commit themselves to three consecutive years of teaching. Once APLE participants have obtained their California teaching credentials and qualifying positions in the state's K-12 public school system, they are entitled to up to $8000 in loan assumption benefits. Participants must maintain satisfactory academic progress and continue to satisfy all program requirements.

Obtain an application form after March 1 from any California college or university financial aid office. Other application requirements include transcripts, test scores, an essay, references, and an interview. The deadline for applying is June 30.

Cal Grant A. This program provides over 17,000 awards to students attending approved colleges or universities within the state. Recipients must be California residents and are selected on the basis of financial need and academic ability. Awards range from $1584 to $5250. The application deadline is March 2. Applicants for a Cal Grant A are also required to submit a verified grade point average to the commission by the deadline date of March 2. Application forms are available from high school guidance offices and college financial aid offices.

Cal Grant B. The Cal Grant B program is intended to help up to 12,250 high school seniors from disadvantaged/low-income families who would not be able to get a postsecondary education without aid. For college freshmen, the Cal Grant B award is usually limited to nontuition costs, such as living expenses, books and supplies, and transportation, although exceptions may be made for unusually needy or disadvantaged applicants. When renewed during the sophomore, junior, or senior year, a Cal Grant B may also include tuition/fee costs. Awards range from $1410 to $6660. Applicants must attend a California institution. Other specific requirements apply. Application forms are available from high school guidance offices and college financial aid offices. The deadline for applying is March 2.

Cal Grant C. This program provides renewable awards to vocationally oriented students. It will not meet the needs of the academically oriented student seeking to broaden his or her general educational background. Cal Grant C may not be used to pursue a four-year degree program, graduate study, course prerequisites, or general education.

Cal Grant C is ideally suited for students whose interests and talents center on school workshops, labs, and work experience functions and for those who can profit most by the short-term, highly specialized vocational training currently offered in community colleges, accredited proprietary schools, and hospital schools. Training under the Cal Grant C program must lead to a recognized occupational goal, i.e., a diploma, an associate degree, license qualification, or a certificate, that indicates at least an entry-level skill. Course length must be between four and twenty-four months, and attendance may be full- or part-time. Over 1,500 Cal Grant C awards are offered to help defray tuition and fees up to $2360 per year.

Applications must be received by March 2. Applications are available from the California Student Aid Commission, Cal Grant C, P.O. Box 510845, Sacramento, California 94245-0845.

COLORADO

Colorado Student Grant. This need-based program assists over 17,000 Colorado residents attending eligible public, private, or vocational institutions within the state. Awards are renewable for undergraduates.

The program is administered by eligible schools. Contact the financial aid office at the institution you plan to attend for complete information and details about application

procedures and deadlines, as well as about the institution's renewal policy.

Colorado Student Incentive Grant. This grant helps Colorado residents with substantial financial need meet the tuition costs of an eligible public, private, or vocational institution within the state. The maximum grant is $5000 per academic year.

This program is administered by the colleges. Contact the financial aid office at the institution you plan to attend for complete information and details about application procedures and deadlines, as well as about the institution's renewal policy.

Colorado Work-Study Program. This is an employment program designed to allow Colorado resident undergraduate students to earn funds to help pay the cost of attending eligible institutions in the state. Funds are awarded to students who have demonstrated financial need and to others without regard to financial need. Awards range up to $1451 and over 7,000 awards are available. For additional information, contact the Colorado Commission on Higher Education, 1300 Broadway, Second Floor, Denver, Colorado 80203.

Law Enforcement/POW-MIA Dependents Tuition Assistance Program. This program pays tuition costs only at eligible institutions within the state for Colorado residents who are dependents of law enforcement officers, fire personnel, or national guard members killed or disabled in the line of duty and of prisoners of war or service personnel listed as missing in action. Dependents of disabled personnel must have demonstrated financial need. Application deadlines vary. Applications are available from the Colorado Commission on Higher

Education, Second Floor, 1300 Broadway, Denver, Colorado 80203.

CONNECTICUT

Aid for Public College Students Grant Program. This renewable award helps students at Connecticut public colleges and universities. Students must be state residents and must be enrolled on at least a half-time basis. Eligibility is based on financial need and satisfactory academic progress.

To apply, contact the Financial Aid Office, Connecticut Department of Higher Education, 61 Woodland Street, Hartford CT 06105.

Connecticut Independent College Student Grant Program. This program helps Connecticut residents attending an independent college or university in Connecticut on at least a half-time basis. Renewable awards are based on financial need. The maximum annual award is $7000.

To apply, contact the Financial Aid Office, Connecticut Department of Higher Education, 61 Woodland Street, Hartford CT 06105

Connecticut Tuition Waiver for Senior Citizens. Renewable tuition waivers for undergraduate study only are available to Connecticut senior citizens at accredited two-year or four-year institutions in Connecticut. Applicants must show financial need and prove senior citizen status.

To apply, contact the Financial Aid Office, Connecticut Department of Higher Education, 61 Woodland Street, Hartford, CT 06105-2391.

Connecticut Tuition Waiver for Veterans. Renewable tuition waivers for are available to Connecticut veterans at accredited two-year or four-year institutions in Connecticut. Military separation papers are required.

To apply, contact the Financial Aid Office, Connecticut Department of Higher Education, 61 Woodland Street, Hartford, CT 06105.

Scholastic Achievement Grant Program. This program aids Connecticut residents attending a college or university in Connecticut or in a state with reciprocity (Massachusetts, Rhode Island, Vermont, New Hampshire, Maine, Pennsylvania, Delaware, or Washington, DC). To be eligible, students must rank in the top twenty percent of their high school class or score 1200 or better on the Scholastic Assessment Test (SAT I) and demonstrate financial need. Awards range from $300 to $2000.

Application forms are available from the Financial Aid Office, Department of Higher Education, 61 Woodland Street, Hartford, Connecticut 06105-2391. The application deadline is February 15.

Tuition Aid for Needy Students Program. This is a need-based program that assists Connecticut residents who are enrolled at Connecticut state-supported colleges and universities. Award amounts are variable.

To apply, request an application form from the Connecticut Department of Higher Education, 61 Woodland Street, Hartford, CT 06105. Deadlines vary by college.

DELAWARE

Educational Benefits for Children of Deceased Military and State Police. This program aids three Delaware residents under the age of 25 who are children of military service personnel or state police

officers killed in the line of duty. The deceased parent must have been a resident of Delaware. Students must attend a state-supported college or university in Delaware; a private college in Delaware, if the desired program is not available in Delaware public colleges or universities; or a private or public college or university outside the state, if the desired program is unavailable at Delaware public or private colleges or universities. Awards are renewable upon reapplication through the FAFSA.

To obtain an application form, contact the Delaware Higher Education Commission, Fourth Floor, 820 North French Street, Wilmington, Delaware 19801.

Scholarship Incentive Program. This is a need-based program that assists state residents in meeting college costs. Grants may be used at Delaware colleges and, under certain conditions, at out-of-state colleges as well. Awards are made for full-time study at Delaware colleges and universities and at out-of-state schools if the student's chosen major is not offered in Delaware. The amount of each grant varies depending on student resources, academic merit, tuition, and other financial assistance for which a student may be eligible. Maximum grants of $1000 are awarded. Awards are renewable upon reapplication, provided that the student has continued need and makes satisfactory academic progress.

To apply, complete and file the Free Application for Federal Student Aid and authorize the Department of Education to release application data to the state agency. Only applicants whose state of legal residence is Delaware will be considered. The deadline for receipt of the application

form by the processor is April 15 each year. For information, contact Nancy Holm, Associate Director, Delaware Higher Education Commission, 820 North French Street, Wilmington, Delaware 19801.

DISTRICT OF COLUMBIA

State Student Incentive Grant. This renewable award is offered only to residents of the District of Columbia who have financial need. Applicants must also apply for the Federal Pell Grant and must attend college on at least a half-time basis. Awards range from $400 to $1000. Application forms must be received by June 27. For more information, contact the Office of Postsecondary Education, Suite 401, 2100 Martin Luther King Jr. Avenue, SE, Washington, DC 20020.

FLORIDA

Florida Postsecondary Student Assistance Grant. Theses renewable grants of $200 to $1500 are available to Florida residents who are United States citizens attending as full-time students at degree-granting private Florida colleges or universities. Recipients must have financial need but not qualify for the Florida Private Student Assistance Grant.

Contact the Office of Student Financial Assistance, Florida Department of Education, 1344 Florida Education Center, Tallahassee FL 32399.

Florida Private Student Assistance Grant. This program provides grants to full-time undergraduate students who are Florida residents and United States citizens..Recipients must attend an eligible independent nonprofit college or university in Florida. Awards range from $200 to $1500 per academic year and are renewable for up to nine semesters, fourteen quarters, or until receipt of a bachelor's degree. Substantial financial need must be demonstrated, and the Free Application for Federal Student Aid (FAFSA) must be completed and filed.

Contact the Office of Student Financial Assistance, Florida Department of Education, 1344 Florida Education Center, Tallahassee, Florida 32399.

Florida Teacher Scholarship and Forgivable Loan Program. This program is comprised of a renewable two-year scholarship for freshmen or sophomores with a minimum 3.0 grade point average and a two-year loan program for juniors or seniors with a minimum 2.5 grade point average. The amount of the scholarship is $1500 per year for a maximum of two years. The amount of the undergraduate loan may not exceed $4000 per year for a maximum of two years. Recipients must be Florida residents enrolled in an approved teacher education program in Florida.

For further information, contact the Office of Student Financial Assistance, Florida Department of Education, 1344 Florida Education Center, Tallahassee, Florida 32399.

Florida Undergraduate Scholars' Fund and Challenger Astronauts Memorial Scholarship. This program provides renewable scholarships ranging up to $4000 for the academically top-ranked high school seniors from each Florida county. Eligible students must have a minimum 3.5 grade point average and have a minimum 1270 SAT score or minimum 28 ACT score. Awards are renewable annually.

Obtain an application form the Office of Student Financial Assistance, Florida Department of Education, 1344 Florida Education Center, Tallahassee, Florida 32399. Applications must be postmarked by April 1 of the student's last year in high school.

Jose Marti Scholarship Challenge Grant Fund. This need-based scholarship grant is available to Hispanic American students who were born in, or whose parent was born in an Hispanic country. Applicants must have been resident in Florida for at least one year. Recipients must be enrolled as full-time students at an eligible Florida institution and have earned a minimum grade point average of 3.0. The renewable scholarship is $2000 per academic year.

Contact the Office of Student Financial Assistance, Florida Department of Education, 1344 Florida Education Center, Tallahassee, Florida 32399. The application deadline is May 15.

Mary McLeod Bethune Scholarship. This need-based scholarship awards $3000 per academic year to Florida high school seniors with a grade point average of 3.0 for undergraduate study at Florida Agricultural and Mechanical University, Bethune-Cookman College, Edward Waters College, or Florida Memorial College. Recipients must reapply to renew this award.

For information contact the Office of Student Financial Assistance, Florida Department of Education, 1344 Florida Education Center, Tallahassee, Florida 32399. The grant's application deadline is April 30.

Nicaraguan and Haitian Scholarship Program. This program provides a one-time award of between $4000 and $5000 to one Nicaraguan student and one Haitian student Recipients must have a minimum cumulative high school grade point average of 3.0 and attend a Florida State University System institution. The applicant must live in Florida and be a United States citizen or permanent resident, but have been either born in Nicaragua or Haiti or been a Nicaraguan or Haitian citizen

More information is available from the Office of Student Assistance, Florida Department of Education, 1344 Florida Education Center, Tallahassee, Florida 32399. The deadline for applying is July 1.

Occupational Therapist and Physical Therapist Scholarship Loan Program. This program provides renewable financial assistance to Florida residents enrolled full-time in occupational or physical therapy or therapy assistant programs at an eligible Florida institution. The loan may be repaid in cash or by working for a minimum of three years as a therapist in Florida public schools. repay loan. The annual amount of the award is the cost of education up to a maximum of $4000.

Complete information about eligibility requirements and applications are available from Dr. Cynthia Burton, BSSEE, Florida Department of Education, 601 Florida Education Center, Tallahassee, Florida 32399. Applications, including all required documentation, must be postmarked by April 15.

Rosewood Family Scholarship. This scholarship fund provides renewable financial assistance for a maximum of 25 eligible African American, Hispanic, Asian, Pacific Islander, American Indian, or Alaskan native students to attend Florida public postsecondary institution on a full-time basis. Students who are direct descendants of African-American Rosewood families affected by the incidents of January 1923 receive preference for awards. The annual award is $4000.

Complete eligibility requirements and applications are available from the Office of Student Financial Assistance, Florida Department of Education, 1344 Florida Education Center, Tallahassee, Florida 32399-0400. Applications must be postmarked by April 1.

Scholarships for Children of Deceased or Disabled Veterans or Children of Servicemen Classified as POW or MIA. This program provides full tuition and fees for two semesters of undergraduate study to Florida residents between sixteen and twenty-two years old who are children of deceased or disabled service members and are enrolled full-time at a Florida public postsecondary institution. The scholarship is renewable for a maximum of eight semesters.

Obtain the application form from the Office of Student Financial Assistance, Florida Department of Education, 1344 Florida Education Center, Tallahassee, Florida 32399. The application deadline is April 1.

Seminole and Miccosukee Indian Scholarships Program. These scholarships aid Florida Seminole and Miccosukee Indians attending an approved Florida college or university either full-time or part-time. Eligibility is based on financial need. The amount of the scholarship and renewal is determined by the respective tribe.

The deadline for applying is Sept. 1.

Information is available from the Office of Student Financial Assistance, Florida Department of Education, 1344 Florida Education Center, Tallahassee, Florida 32399

Vocational Gold Seal Endorsement Scholarship Program. This scholarship program provides scholarships to Florida public high school seniors whose diploma has the Vocational Gold Seal Endorsement. Awards are a maximum of $2000 toward expenses at Florida postsecondary institutions. Applicants must enroll for a minimum of twelve credit hours per term. Renewal is possible.

Applications are available at public high school guidance offices or from the Office of Student Financial Assistance, Florida Department of Education, 1344 Florida Education Center, Tallahassee, Florida 32399. Applications must be postmarked by April 1.

GEORGIA

Georgia Tuition Equalization Grant (GTEG). This grant helps students pursuing undergraduate study at an accredited two-year or four-year Georgia institution. Students must be residents of Georgia. Grants are $1000 per academic year. Recipients may receive an additional $1500 from the HOPE program.

To apply, complete the Georgia Student Grant Application. Contact the Grants Director, Georgia Student Finance Commission, 2082 East Exchange Place, Suite 100, Tucker GA 30084. Deadlines vary by school.

Governor's Scholarship. The Governor's Scholarship Program assists with a one-time award of up to $1,575 Georgia high school gradu-

ates of exceptional merit. To be eligible to receive a Governor's Scholarship, a recipient must be a Georgia Scholar, STAR student, valedictorian, or salutatorian enrolled or accepted for enrollment as a full-time freshman student at an eligible two-year or four-year college or university located in Georgia.

For more information, students should contact the Grants Director, Georgia Student Finance Commission, 2082 East Exchange Place, Suite 100, Tucker GA 30084.

HOPE-Helping Outstanding Pupils Educationally. The HOPE Grant program aids undergraduates at accredited two-year or four-year Georgia institutions who are Georgia residents. Tuition and fees that are not covered by federal aid may be covered by the grant. The award is renewable if student maintains a minimum 3.0 grade point average grades and reapplies.

For more information, students should contact the Grants Director, Georgia Student Finance Commission, 2082 East Exchange Place, Suite 100, Tucker GA 30084.

Law Enforcement Personnel Dependents Grant. This one-time award of $2,000 aids children of Georgia law enforcement officers, fire fighters, and prison guards who have been killed or permanently disabled in the line of duty. Students must be residents of Georgia and must attend an accredited Georgia postsecondary school within the state. The scholarship is $2000 per academic year.

To apply, complete the Law Enforcement Personnel Dependents application. For more information, applicants should contact the Grants Director, Georgia Student Finance

Commission, 2082 East Exchange Place, Suite 100, Tucker GA 30084.

Student Incentive Grant. This grant helps students meet costs at postsecondary schools in Georgia. Students must have substantial financial need and be Georgia residents. Awards range from $300 to $5000 per academic year but are not available during summer terms. Applicants must complete the Free Application for Federal Student Aid (FAFSA).

Contact the Grants Director, Georgia Student Finance Commission, 2082 East Exchange Place, Suite 100, Tucker GA 30084.

HAWAII

Hawaii Student Incentive Grants (HSIG). These grants aid undergraduates with financial need attending eligible public or private colleges or universities within the state on a full-time basis. Recipients must be eligible for a Federal Pell Grant and must be legal residents of Hawaii. The award is for the amount of tuition or $2000, whichever is less.

To apply, complete and file the Hawaii Financial Aid Form (FAF) with the College Scholarship Service (CSS). The deadline for applying is March 1. The FAF is available from high school guidance offices and college financial aid offices.

Tuition Waivers. This program aids both resident and nonresident students attending campuses of the University of Hawaii. Eligible students must have financial need or be enrolled in certain programs (as designated by their college). This one-time award is for the amount of tuition. Aid is not restricted to students currently in high school.

Contact the financial aid office at the University of Hawaii campus you plan to attend to obtain application information. The deadline for applying is March 1.

IDAHO

Education Incentive Loan Forgiveness. This waiver was established to assist and encourage students to enroll in Idaho postsecondary institutions for training as teachers or nurses and pursue teaching or nursing careers within the state. Recipients must have graduated from a secondary school in Idaho within two years of receiving the waiver, must rank within the top 15 percent of their high school graduating class or have earned a cumulative grade point average of 3.0 or higher, and must enroll full-time at an Idaho college or university in a program of study leading to an Idaho teaching certificate or the licensure examination approved by the Board of Nursing to become a registered nurse. After completing their program of study, recipients must teach in an Idaho school or pursue a nursing career in the state for a minimum of two years.

For further information, contact the financial aid office at your college or university.

Idaho Minority and "At Risk" Student Scholarship. This renewable award was established by the state legislature in 1991 to help students who are disabled or are members of a minority group and have financial need. The award amount is $2700. To be eligible, applicants must be Idaho residents and Idaho high school graduates. In addition, recipients must be or plan to be enrolled full-time as undergraduates in one of eight eligible postsecondary institu-

tions in the state. For more information, contact your high school counselor or the financial aid office of the college or university you plan to attend.

Deadlines vary by institution.

Idaho State Student Incentive Grant. This one-time grant aids students attending a public or private college or university within the state of Idaho, regardless of their state of residence. Eligible students must demonstrate financial need. Theology and divinity majors are not eligible for consideration for this state-funded award. Awards range up to $5000 per academic year for full-time students.

To apply, contact the financial aid office at the college you plan to attend for its application forms and information about deadlines.

Paul L. Fowler Memorial Scholarship Program. Under this program, students who have demonstrated outstanding ability and willingness to work in the field of higher education are eligible to apply for scholarships of $2830 per year. Recipients must be residents of Idaho who plan to enroll as full-time students in an academic program at an institution of higher learning. These one-time scholarships are awarded on the basis of class rank and ACT scores.

The application deadline is January 31 of each year for awards beginning the following school year. For further information and an application form, contact your high school guidance office or the Scholarship Assistant, State Board of Education, Room 307 Len B. Jordan Building, P.O. Box 83720, Boise, Idaho 83720-0037.

State of Idaho Scholarship Program. This renewable scholarship aids academically outstanding seniors who are graduating from an Idaho high school and will be attending an approved college or university within the state full-time. Eligibility is based on class rank and scores on the American College Testing examination. Recipients receive $2650 per academic year for a maximum of four years. Vocational students may also apply. Twenty-five percent of the initial scholarships are awarded each year to vocational students.

The application deadline is January 31 of each year for awards beginning the following school year. For further information, contact the Caryl Smith, State Board of Education, P.O. Box 83720, Boise, Idaho 83720-0037.

ILLINOIS

Correctional Officer's Grant. This award will cover tuition and fees, up to $3800, for eight semesters or twelve quarters of the spouse, natural, adopted, or custodial child, who were dependents of Illinois Department of Correction employees who were killed or ninety percent disabled in the line of duty. The injury or the death must have occurred after January 1, 1960. Recipients must attend a nonprofit college or university within the state on at least a half-time basis.

For application information, contact the Illinois Student Assistance Commission, 1755 Lake Cook Road, Deerfield, IL 60015-5209.

Illinois Department of Children and Family Services Scholarships. Twenty-four renewable awards are available each year to Illinois residents who are wards of the state. The program provides a tuition

waiver and $250 per month at an Illinois state four-year college or university.

Contact Patricia James-Davis, PSA, Illinois Department of Children and Family Services, 406 East Monroe Street, #50, Springfield IL 62701-1498.

Illinois Educational Opportunities for Children of Veterans. These renewable awards are provided annually to Illinois residents who are children between the ages of ten and eighteen of a veteran who died or became totally disabled as a result of service during World War II, the Korean War, or Vietnam War.

Contact Eva Palmer, Illinois Department of Veterans Affairs, P.O. Box 19432, Springfield IL 62794-9432.

Illinois Korean, Vietnam, and Persian Gulf Conflict Bonus. This one-time award is available to veterans who received a service medal for service during the Korean, Vietnam, or Persian Gulf conflict. Recipient must have been an Illinois resident for one year prior to service. Disabled survivors are entitled to $1000 if their disability is service-related.

Inquiries should be directed to Kathy Davis, Illinois Department of Veterans Affairs, P.O. Box 19432, Springfield IL 62794-9432.

Illinois MIA/POW Scholarships. These one-time awards for veterans or children of veterans who were Missing in Action or Prisoners of War must be used at a trade/technical school in Illinois. Applicants must be United States citizens with minimum 3.0 grade point average. High school students are not eligible.

Contact Tracy Mahan, Illinois Department of Veterans Affairs, P.O. Box 19432, Springfield IL 62794-9432.

Illinois National Guard Grant. This program aids currently enlisted members up to the rank of captain who have served at least one year in the Illinois National Guard. The award covers tuition and some mandatory fees for up to eight semesters or twelve quarters of credit for full-time or part-time study at an Illinois college.

Obtain the application form from the Illinois Student Assistance Commission, 1755 Lake Cook Road, Deerfield, IL, 60015-5209.

Illinois Survivor Compensation. A $1000 bonus is payable to surviving dependents of military service people killed by terrorist acts or hostile activities during performance of their duties in periods not recognized as wartime. Residency of one year in Illinois prior to service is required.

Contact Kathy Davis, Illinois Department of Veterans Affairs, P.O. Box 19432, Springfield IL 62794-9432.

Illinois Veteran Grant (IVG). This renewable award pays tuition and certain fees for undergraduate or graduate study at all state-supported Illinois colleges, universities, and community colleges for Illinois veterans. Recipients may use their grant assistance for a maximum of 120 eligibility points. Students applying for this grant must complete an application form and provide discharge information.

Application forms and additional information are available from the Manager, Scholarships and Grants, Illinois Student Assistance Commission, 1755 Lake Cook Road, Deerfield, Illinois 60015-5209.

Merit Recognition Scholarship (MRS). This program provides a one-time $1000 scholarship to Illinois students who rank in the top five percent of their high school class at the end of the seventh semester. The MRS may be used to meet undergraduate tuition, fees, or other expenses at approved Illinois institutions.

Eligible seniors from all approved Illinois high schools are automatically considered for the MRS. The high schools certify to the Illinois Student Assistance Commission (ISAC) the names of students who are eligible applicants. ISAC notifies potential MRS recipients in accordance with annual funding levels. Eligible students are then sent applications that must be completed, in part, by their chosen college or university. Receipt by ISAC of this properly completed application constitutes a request for payment. Funds are remitted to institutions on behalf of the qualified students. This program is dependent upon funding from the General Assembly each year. Inquiries should be directed to the Manager, Scholarships and Grants, Illinois Student Assistance Commission, 1755 Lake Cook Road, Deerfield, Illinois 60015-5209.

Minority Teachers of Illinois Scholarship. This one-time, merit-based scholarship provides up to $5000 per year to assist minority students who plan to become teachers at the elementary or secondary level. Recipients must be undergraduates at the sophomore level or above at an approved Illinois public or private college or university and must sign a teaching commitment to teach one year for each year assistance is received.

To apply, contact the college's financial aid administrator or Minority Affairs Office or the Manager, Scholarships and Grants, Illinois Student Assistance Commission, 1755 Lake Cook Road, Deerfield, Illinois 60015-5209. The deadline for applying is August 1.

Monetary Award Program (MAP). This grant program aids students with financial need attending a public or private college in Illinois on at least a half-time basis. Eligible students must be residents of Illinois. Awards range from $400 to $4000 per year and are renewable for up to five years.

To apply, complete and file the Free Application for Federal Student Aid (FAFSA) need analysis form. Be sure to read carefully the question giving the U.S. Department of Education permission to send information from the FAFSA to the Illinois Students Assistance Commission. The application forms are available from high school guidance offices or college financial aid offices. For more information, contact the Monetary Award Program, Illinois Student Assistance Commission, 1755 Lake Cook Road, Deerfield, Illinois 60015-5209. The deadlines for applying are May 31 and September 30.

Police Officer/Fire Officer Survivor Grant. This grant pays tuition and mandatory fees, up to $3800, for ten semesters or fifteen quarters of credit, for the dependent spouse and children under the age of twenty-five of Illinois police or fire personnel killed in the line of duty. Eligible students must be enrolled at least a half-time basis at any approved Illinois college or university.

For more information, contact the Manager, Scholarships and Grants, Illinois Student Assistance Commission, 1755 Lake Cook Road, Deerfield, Illinois 60015-5209. Check school for deadline.

Student-to-Student Grant (STS). In this renewable awards program, voluntary student contributions, donated by other students, are matched by the Illinois Student Assistance Commission (ISAC) and are paid to participating institutions. These funds are then made available to needy students through procedures established by each college's financial aid office. Eligible students must be Illinois residents enrolled at a participating Illinois two-or four-year college or university.

For more information, contact the Manager, Scholarships and Grants, Illinois Student Assistance Commission, 1755 Lake Cook Road, Deerfield, Illinois 60015-5209.

INDIANA

Hoosier Scholar Award. Up to eight-hundred one-time scholarships are given to Indiana's top prospective college freshmen who are in top twenty percent of their graduating class and are determined by their high school to be the most academically qualified of any in their class. Students must attend an approved Indiana college or university. Winners receive a nonrenewable $500 scholarship.

For additional information, contact the Grant Division, Indiana State Student Assistance Commission, 150 West Market Street, Suite 500, Indianapolis, Indiana 46204-2811. The deadline for applying is March 1.

Indiana Free Tuition-Children of POW/MIAs in Vietnam. This renewable award is for residents of Indiana who are children of veterans declared Missing in Action or Prisoners of War after January 1, 1960. The award provides tuition at Indiana institutions for undergraduate study.

For additional information, contact the Indiana Department of Veterans Affairs, 302 West Washington Street, Room E-120, Indianapolis, Indiana 46204-2738.

Indiana Freedom of Choice Grants. These renewable grants provide additional funds for Indiana residents who receive the Indiana Higher Education Award and plan to attend an eligible private institution in Indiana. Awards range from $200 to $2850.

No separate application is necessary. Every recipient of an Indiana Higher Education Award automatically will be considered for a Freedom of Choice Grant. For additional information, contact the Grant Division, State Student Assistance Commission, 150 West Market Street, Suite 500, Indianapolis, Indiana 46204-2811.

Indiana Higher Education Award. This renewable award aids Indiana residents attend full-time approved Indiana colleges or universities. Eligibility is based on financial need. Awards range from $200 to $2700.

To apply, complete the Free Application for Federal Student Aid (FAFSA). For additional information, contact the Grant Division, State Student Assistance Commission, 150 West Market Street, Suite 500, Indianapolis, Indiana 46204-2811. The application deadline is March 1.

Indiana Nursing Scholarship Fund. This renewable program aids Indiana residents who are pursuing nursing degrees at eligible Indiana institutions. The awards are up to $5000. Applicants must have a minimum 2.5 grade point average and show financial need. Recipients must agree to work as a nurse in Indiana for at least two years.

Applications are available from eligible colleges. For applications or additional information, contact the Special Programs Director, State Student Assistance Commission, 150 West Market Street, Suite 500, Indianapolis, Indiana 46204-2811.

Indiana Remission of Fees for Children of Deceased or Disabled Veterans or Purple Heart Recipients. This renewable benefit pays partial tuition at Indiana state supported institutions for Indiana residents who are the children of veterans who received the Purple Heart Medal, are rated with a service-connected disability, or died from a service-related disease or injury. Applicants must submit proof of the decoration.

Further inquiries should be directed to the Indiana Department of Veterans Affairs, 302 West Washington Street, Room E-120, Indianapolis, Indiana 46204-2738.

Minority Teacher and Special Education Services Scholarship Program. This award is for African-American or Hispanic students seeking teacher certification in special education or physical/occupational therapy. The awards are for $1000 per year and are renewable for up to four years. Upon certification, recipients are required to teach in Indiana. Recipients must be Indiana residents and have a minimum 2.0 GPA.

Applications are available from the Program Director, State Student Assistance Commission, 150 West Market Street, Suite 500, Indianapolis, Indiana 46204.

Special Education Services and Occupational or Physical Therapy Scholarship. This program provides assistance to Indiana residents who are pursuing degrees in special education, or occupational/physical therapy in Indiana. The scholarship is $1000, renewable up to four years. Applicants must have a minimum 2.5 grade point average and teach or practice full-time for three years in Indiana following certification.

Applications are available from eligible colleges. For additional information, contact the Special Programs Director, State Student Assistance Commission, 150 West Market Street, Suite 500, Indianapolis, Indiana 46204-2811.

Twenty-first Century Scholars Award. This need-based renewable award of $1000 to $3000 is for Indiana residents for use at two-year or four-year postsecondary institutions in Indiana.

Write for details and deadlines to Philip A. Seabrook, Director, Office of 21st Century Scholars, 150 West Market Street, Suite 500, Indianapolis, Indiana 46204.

IOWA

Iowa Grants (for Undergraduate Study). Up to $1000 may be available to Iowa residents enrolled at least half-time in an undergraduate program in an eligible Iowa institution. This award is renewable based on continuing eligibility.

Contact the Iowa College Student Aid Commission, 200 Tenth Street, Fourth Floor, Des Moines, IA 50309-3609.

Iowa Tuition Grant Program. This program aids Iowa residents attending an eligible independent college, business school, or nursing school in Iowa. Eligibility is based on financial need. The maximum grant is $3150 for each year of full-time undergraduate study.

To apply, forms are available from high school guidance offices and college financial aid offices. For more information, contact the Grants Administrator, Iowa College Student Aid Commission, 200 Tenth Street, Fourth Floor, Des Moines, IA 50309-3609. Complete and file a needs analysis form by April 20.

Iowa Vocational-Technical Tuition Program. This program aids Iowa residents attending an Iowa public college for a vocational-technical career education or career option program. Eligibility is based on financial need. Recipients must be enrolled full-time in a program of at least twelve months' duration. The maximum grant is $600 for a full year, for a maximum of two years. Recipients must reapply each year.

Forms are available from high school guidance offices, college financial aid offices, and the Iowa College Student Aid Commission, 200 Tenth Street, Fourth Floor, Des Moines, Iowa 50309-3609. Apply by April 20.

State of Iowa Scholarship Program (Freshman Year Only). This one-time scholarship aids Iowa residents who graduate in top 15 percent of their high school classes and receive a high American College Test Program (ACT) score. Applicants must take ACT by October of their senior year. The award of $410 is only for freshman year attendance at an Iowa college or university.

Contact the Iowa College Student Aid Commission, 200 Tenth Street, Fourth Floor, Des Moines, IA 50309-3609. Deadline is December 1.

KANSAS

Kansas Educational Benefits for Children of MIA, POW, & Deceased Veterans of the Vietnam War. This full tuition scholarship at Kansas colleges is awarded to children of veterans who were missing in action, prisoner of war, or killed in action in the Vietnam War. Applicants must show proof of their parent's status. Kansas residence is required.

For more information, write to the Scholarship Administrator, Kansas Commission on Veterans Affairs, Jayhawk Tower, #701, 700 Southwest Jackson, Topeka, Kansas 66603.

Kansas Minority Scholarship Program. This renewable scholarship, ranging up to $1500, is available to minority members with demonstrated scholastic ability and financial need who are attending Kansas postsecondary schools. Recipients may receive the scholarship for a maximum of four years (eight semesters), provided that they continue to meet all eligibility criteria. Applicants must be Kansas residents All applicants must submit the Free Application for Federal Student Aid (FAFSA) and the Kansas Student Aid Application. There is a $10 application fee.

For more information, write to the Kansas Board of Regents, Security Benefit Building, Suite 1410, 700 Southwest Harrison, Topeka, Kansas 66603. The priority deadline is April 1.

Kansas Nursing Scholarship Program. This program provides scholarship assistance of $2500 to $3500 per year to Kansas residents who are enrolled in programs leading to licensure as a licensed practical nurse or registered nurse. A portion of each nursing scholarship will be funded by the state of Kansas, and a portion will be funded by a sponsoring medical care provider. Applicants are required to secure sponsorship prior to submitting the scholarship application. Recipients are required to practice one year for each year of scholarship assistance received. Applicants must submit the Free Application for Federal Student Aid (FAFSA), the Kansas Student Aid Application, and a sponsor agreement. There is a $10 application fee.

For more information, write to the Kansas Board of Regents, Security Benefit Building, Suite 1410, 700 Southwest Harrison, Topeka, Kansas 66603. The application deadline is May 1.

Kansas State Scholarship Program. This renewable award of $200 to $1000 aids Kansas residents who attend approved Kansas postsecondary schools. Eligibility is based on academic achievement and financial need. Applicants must take the ACT and file the Free Application for Federal Student Aid (FAFSA) and the Kansas Student Aid Application. There is a $10 application fee.

For more information, write to the Kansas Board of Regents, Security Benefit Building, Suite 1410, 700 Southwest Harrison, Topeka, Kansas 66603. For priority funding consideration the deadline is April 1

Kansas Teacher Scholarship Program. This program awards $5000 annually for up to five years to students who are pursuing teaching careers. Recipients must teach in a "hard to fill" discipline in Kansas for one year for each scholarship received.

For more information, write to the Kansas Board of Regents, Security Benefit Building, Suite 1410, 700 Southwest Harrison, Topeka, Kansas 66603. The application deadline is April 1.

Kansas Tuition Grant Program. This need-based renewable award aids Kansas residents who are attending independent colleges or universities in Kansas. To apply, complete and file the Free Application for Federal Student Aid (FAFSA) and the Kansas State Student Aid application.

For more information, students should contact their high school guidance office or the financial aid office at the college of their choice. For priority funding consideration, the processing deadline is April 1.

Regents Supplemental Grant. These renewable grants of up to $900 each are available for Kansas residents who enroll in full-time undergraduate study at Kansas Regents institutions.

For more information contact your college financial aid office or the Kansas Board of Regents, 700 Southwest Harrison, Suite 410, Topeka, Kansas 66603. For priority funding consideration, the processing deadline is April 1.

Vocational Education Scholarship Program. This program provides several scholarships for Kansas residents who are enrolled in a vocational education program at an eligible Kansas institution and who have graduated from a Kansas-accredited high school, The award of up to $500 is based on ability and aptitude. Awards are renewable annually.

Request an application form from the Kansas Board of Regents, Security Benefit Building, Suite 1410, 700 Southwest Harrison, Topeka, Kansas 66603. Application deadlines vary by school.

KENTUCKY

Benefits for Veterans and their Dependents. A tuition waiver for undergraduate study at a Kentucky state college is available to Kentucky residents who are dependents of veterans who were killed or totally disabled in the service. Recipient must be under twenty-five years of age.

Contact Larry W. Garrett, Coordinator, Kentucky department of Veterans Affairs, 545 South Third Street, Louisville KY 40202-9095.

College Access Program (CAP) Grant. The program provides to financially needy undergraduates payments of $42 per semester hour enrolled for a minimum of six hours per semester. To qualify for a CAP Grant, an applicant must be a U.S. citizen and a Kentucky resident. He or she must be attending an eligible Kentucky college and not have previously earned a college degree. Applicants seeking degrees in religion are not eligible. Applicants must file the Free Application for Federal Student Aid (FAFSA).

For more information about the program, contact the Kentucky Higher Education Assistance Authority, 1050 U.S. 127 South, Frankfort KY 40601-4323.

Environmental Protection Scholarships. These renewable awards for college juniors, seniors, and graduate students will pay tuition, fees, and room and board at a Kentucky State University. A minimum 2.5 grade point average is required. Recipients must agree to work full-time for the Kentucky Natural Resources and Environmental Protection Cabinet upon graduation.

For more information about the program, contact the Scholarship Program Coordinator, Kentucky Water Resources Research Institute, 233 Mining/Minerals Building, Lexington KY 40506.

Kentucky Department of Education Minority Educator Scholarship Program. Scholarships of $3000 are available to sophomores, juniors, or seniors enrolled in teaching programs, who are Kentucky residents and members of a minority. Recipients must teach in the state of Kentucky for one year per award or pay back amount in full. Merit is considered in making the award.

Contact the Minority Scholarship Program, Kentucky Department of Education, Capitol Plaza Tower, 1st Floor, Frankfort KY 40601-9095.

Kentucky Tuition Grant (KTG). 6000 to 6500 grants of up to $1500 based on financial need available to Kentucky residents who are full-time undergraduates at an independent non-profit college in Kentucky. Recipients must not be enrolled in a religion program.

For more information about the program, contact the Kentucky Higher Education Assistance Authority, 1050 U.S. 127 South, Frankfort KY 40601-4323.

Nursing Incentive Scholarship Program. Renewable award of $2,000 of $2000 offered to Kentucky residents who have been accepted into a nursing program. Recipients must work as a nurse in Kentucky one year for each year funded. Preference is given to financial need, LPNs pursuing RN education, and RNs pursuing graduate nursing education.

Write or call for details. Contact Darlene Chilton, Kentucky Board of Nursing, 312 Whittington Parkway, Suite 300, Louisville, KY 40222-5172.

Teacher Scholarship Program. The purpose of the program is to encourage academically talented students to become certified teachers in the commonwealth and to assist teachers to become recertified in a critical-shortage area. The award may go up to $5000. Recipients are required to provide teaching service for each semester or summer scholarship received; those who teach in a critical-shortage area have two semesters canceled for each semester of teaching service. To be eligible, the applicant must be a Kentucky resident and pursue a teaching degree at a Kentucky institution.

To apply, obtain an application form from your high school guidance office or a financial aid office at any Kentucky college.

LOUISIANA

Louisiana Honors Scholarship Program. This program provides renewable awards for Louisiana high school graduates to attend Louisiana institutions. Recipients must be in the top five percent of the state's high school graduates. The award amount is tuition at a Louisiana college or university. Applicants must be United States citizens with a minimum 3.5 grade point average.

For further information, contact Community Supervisor, Louisiana Office of Student Financial Assistance, P.O. Box 91202, Baton Rouge, Louisiana 70821-9202.

Louisiana State Student Incentive Grant (SSIG). This grant helps full-time students who are Louisiana residents to meet educational expenses at Louisiana institutions. Eligibility is based on both financial need and academic requirements (minimum 2.0 GPA). A Free Application For Student Aid (FAFSA) must be filed. Annual awards range from $200 to $2000.

Contact the financial aid office of the school you plan to attend for additional information and eligibility requirements. The deadline for applying is March 15.

Louisiana Tuition Assistance Plan. This renewable program offered to high school seniors provides tuition support for Louisiana residents who are pursuing an undergraduate degree or trade/technical degree at a Louisiana public college and university. Awards range from $640 to $2666 annually. Applicants must have United States citizenship.

For further information, contact the Community Supervisor, Louisiana Office of Student Financial Assistance, P.O. Box 91202, Baton Rouge, Louisiana 70821-9202. The deadline for applying is March 15.

Rockefeller State Wildlife Scholarship. The program offers renewable scholarships to Louisiana residents who are full-time students majoring in wildlife, forestry, or marine sciences at Louisiana public colleges or universities. The award is $500 per semester or $1000 per year for up to five years of undergraduate study and two years of graduate study.

Applicants must have taken the ACT and must have a high school grade point average of at least 2.5.

For further information, contact the Office of Student Financial Assistance, Scholarship Section, P.O. Box 91202, Baton Rouge, Louisiana 70821. The deadline for applying is March 15.

State Aid for Veterans' Dependents. This program provides educational assistance for dependents and spouses of veterans who in the line of duty died or who were 100 percent disabled. Recipients must be Louisiana residents enrolled full-time in state-supported Louisiana colleges, universities, or trade schools. The award is a waiver of tuition and fees for a maximum of four years.

For further information, contact the Department of Veterans' Affairs, P.O. Box 94095, Capitol Station, Baton Rouge, Louisiana 70804. Application deadlines vary by school.

T. H. Harris State Academic Scholarship. This program offers renewable scholarships based on academic achievement for up to five years to Louisiana residents who graduate from a Louisiana high school and attend a Louisiana public college or university. Minimum requirements are a 2.5 high school grade point average and submission of ACT scores. The award is $400 per year.

For further information, contact the Office of Student Financial Assistance, P.O. Box 91202, Baton Rouge, Louisiana 70821. The deadline for applying is March 15.

MAINE

Maine Student Incentive Scholarship Program. These scholarships aid residents of Maine who attend full-time an eligible public or private institution in Maine, New Hampshire, Vermont, Massachusetts, Rhode Island, Connecticut, Pennsylvania, Delaware, Maryland, Washington, D.C., or Alaska. Eligibility is based on financial need. To apply, complete the Free Application for Federal Student Aid (FAFSA). Awards range from $500 to $1000. Recipients must reapply annually.

Contact Rochelle Bridgham, Program Assistant, Financial Authority of Maine, 119 State House Station, Augusta ME 04333-0119. The application deadline is May 1.

Veterans Dependents Educational Benefits. This one-time award for use at Maine institutions is for the dependents under 22 years old or spouses of veterans, who were prisoners of war or missing in action, or permanently disabled as a result of service. The veteran must have been Maine resident at his or her service entry or during the five years preceding application. Applicants must be high school graduates and submit a birth certificate.

Contact the State of Maine Division of Veterans Services, 117 State House Station, Augusta ME 04333-0117.

MARYLAND

Child Care Provider Program. This program aids full- or part-time students enrolled in a child development program at an eligible Maryland institution. These awards range from $500 to $2000 per year and may be held for up to four years with reapplication. Recipients must serve as professional day care providers in Maryland for one year per award. The deadline for applying is June 30. For details and application forms, contact the Maryland Higher

Education Commission, State Scholarship Administration, 16 Francis Street, Annapolis, Maryland 21401-1781.

Delegate Scholarships. These scholarships help Maryland residents attending Maryland degree granting institutions, certain career schools, or nursing diploma schools. Recipients may attend out-of-state institutions if their major is not available at a Maryland institution. For application information and procedures, students should contact the delegate in their legislative district.

Distinguished Scholar Award. This award aids academically and artistically outstanding Maryland students planning to enroll full-time in degree-granting institutions within the state. Recipients receive $3000 per year, renewable for three additional years provided that they maintain an average of at least 3.0 on a 4.0 scale in a full-time program.

Each year, 350 new scholars are selected in three categories. Applicants should write for details. A minimum 3.7 GPA is required. Students in the arts must be nominated by their high schools in the spring of their junior year and must audition.

To be considered for these awards, all interested candidates should contact the Maryland Higher Education Commission, State Scholarship Administration, 16 Francis Street, Annapolis, Maryland 21401-1781.

Distinguished Scholar Teacher Education Awards. This award is available to recipients of the Distinguished Scholar Award who agree to enroll full-time in an undergraduate program leading to a Maryland teaching certificate. Recipients of this award receive

$3000 annually in addition to the value of the Distinguished Scholar Award. Following graduation, recipients are required to teach for one year in a Maryland public school for each year of award use. Distinguished Scholar Award recipients who wish to apply for this additional award should contact the Maryland Higher Education Commission, State Scholarship Administration, 16 Francis Street, Annapolis, Maryland 21401-1781.

Educational Assistance Grant Program. This program aids Maryland residents enrolled full-time at an approved college or university or hospital nursing school program within the state. Eligible students must demonstrate financial need. Awards range from $200 to $3000 per academic year for a maximum of four years. Recipients must reapply to renew the award.

To apply, complete the Free Application for Federal Student Aid (FAFSA) and file it after January 1 but prior to the March 1 deadline. Contact the Maryland Higher Education Commission, State Scholarship Administration, 16 Francis Street, Annapolis, Maryland 21401-1781 for an application form.

Edward T. Conroy Memorial Scholarship Program. This program aids dependents of deceased or 100 percent disabled veterans, Vietnam MIA/POWs, deceased state personnel, or deceased or disabled public safety personnel who were residents of Maryland at the time of death. Recipients of this award must attend a Maryland institution. Awards range up to $3800.

Contact the Maryland Higher Education Commission, State

Scholarship Administration, 16 Francis Street, Annapolis, Maryland 21401-1781 for an application form. The deadline is July 15.

Guaranteed Access Grant Program. This need-based program guarantees that low-income Maryland residents under age 22 have access to postsecondary education in Maryland. Award amounts range up to $8000. Recipients must enroll in college on a full-time basis within one year of graduating high school, must have graduated with a minimum 2.5 GPA, must qualify for the Federal Free Lunch Program, and must file the FAFSA.

For application information and procedures, contact the Maryland Higher Education Commission, State Scholarship Administration, 16 Francis Street, Annapolis, Maryland 21401-1781.

Maryland State Nursing Scholarship and Living Expenses Award. This award applies to Maryland undergraduate and graduate students studying on a full- or part-time basis. The student must be enrolled in a degree granting institution or nursing diploma program in a Maryland school and have a minimum grade point average of 3.0 on a 4.0 scale. The awards range to a maximum of $4800. Recipients must agree to serve as a full-time nurse in a Maryland area of shortage for one year for each year of scholarship award.

Application forms are available in March, and the application deadline is mid-June. For additional information, contact the Maryland Higher Education Commission, State Scholarship Administration, 16 Francis Street, Annapolis, Maryland 21401-1781.

Part-Time Grant Program. This need-based program is for Maryland residents studying part-time (6-11 credit hours) in an undergraduate-degree-granting program at a Maryland institution. Grants range between $200 and $1000. To apply for, complete the Free Application for Federal Student Aid (FAFSA) by March 1. Contact the financial aid office at the Maryland college or university of your choice for further information.

Physical and Occupational Therapists and Assistants Scholarship Program. This program aids Maryland students training as physical or occupational therapists, or as assistants, in Maryland postsecondary institutions. Awards are for up to $2000 and require recipients to provide one year of service for each year of the award to handicapped school children or at a hospital in Maryland.

Applications may be obtained from the Maryland Higher Education Commission, State Scholarship Administration, 16 Francis Street, Annapolis, Maryland 21401-1781 and must be filed by July 1.

Professional Scholarship Program. This program provides need-based financial assistance to full-time Maryland students attending a Maryland school of medicine, dentistry, law, pharmacy, or undergraduate nursing. Scholarships range from $200 to $1000, renewable for up to four years. To apply, complete the Free Application for Federal Student Aid (FAFSA) and file it after January 1 but prior to the March 1 deadline. Also complete a separate application form available from the Maryland Higher Education Commission, State Scholarship

Administration, 16 Francis Street, Annapolis, Maryland 21401-1781.

Tuition Reimbursement for Firefighters and Rescue Squad Members. This program aids Maryland firefighters and ambulance and rescue squad members pursuing a program of study in fire service or emergency medical technology at either a two-year or four-year school.. Students may be full-time or part-time and must maintain their affiliation with the fire department or rescue squad throughout their academic career. Reimbursement of tuition is made after successful completion of each year of study.

Contact the Maryland Higher Education Commission, State Scholarship Administration, 16 Francis Street, Annapolis, Maryland 21401-1781. The application deadline is July 1.

Senatorial Scholarships. These scholarships aid full- or part-time students attending approved proprietary schools, colleges, or universities within the state. Eligible students must be Maryland residents with financial need. Recipients may attend out-of-state institutions if their academic major is not available at a Maryland institution. Awards range from $200 to $2000 per academic year for up to four years.

To apply for, complete the Free Application for Federal Student Aid (FAFSA) and file it after January 1 but prior to the March 1 deadline. For more information, contact the Maryland Higher Education Commission, State Scholarship Administration, 16 Francis Street, Annapolis, Maryland 21401-1781.

Sharon Christa McAuliffe Teacher Education—Critical Shortage Grant Program. This program aids

Maryland residents with a superior academic record who agree to prepare for and enter the teaching profession in a certification field that has been designated as a critical-shortage area. Recipients are required to be in their junior or senior year of undergraduate school or graduate students in a Maryland teacher education program and must teach after graduation in a Maryland public school for up to one year for each year of award use. Applicants must submit a college transcript showing a cumulative grade point average of at least 3.0 on a 4.0 scale. The maximum value of an annual award is $9200. The deadline for applying is December 31.

For more information, contact the Maryland Higher Education Commission, State Scholarship Administration, 16 Francis Street, Annapolis, Maryland 21401-1781.

Tolbert Grant Program. This grant aids Maryland residents attending Maryland-approved private career schools on a full-time basis. Applicants are nominated by the individual schools. Awards are based on financial need and are renewable for a second year. Recipients receive from $200 to $1500 per academic year and are nominated by individual schools.

To apply, complete the Free Application for Federal Student Aid (FAFSA). Applications are processed continuously. Contact the financial aid office at any Maryland private career school for information on applying.

MASSACHUSETTS

Christian A. Herter Memorial Scholarship. This renewable award provides up to fifty percent of undergraduate costs for Mas-

sachusetts residents who are in the tenth and eleventh grades and can exhibit severe personal or family-related difficulties, medical problems, or a personal obstacle that has been overcome.

Contact Cynthia Miles Gray, Massachusetts Office of Student Financial Assistance, 330 Stuart Street, Boston, Massachusetts 02116

Gilbert Grant. Need-based scholarships for at least one year of between $200 and $2500 are available to Massachusetts residents attending full-time at an independent, regionally accredited Massachusetts school. To qualify, file the Free Application for Federal Student Aid (FAFSA). immediately after January 1.

Contact the college financial aid office or Scholarship Director, Massachusetts Office of Student Financial Assistance, 330 Stuart Street, Boston, Massachusetts 02116 for complete details.

Massachusetts Grant. Renewable need-based scholarships of between $200 and $2500 are available to Massachusetts residents attending undergraduate postsecondary institutions in Maine, Vermont, Rhode Island, Connecticut, Pennsylvania, New Jersey, Maryland, and Washington, DC. High school seniors may apply.

Write for information to Scholarship Director, Massachusetts Office of Student Financial Assistance, 330 Stuart Street, Boston, Massachusetts 02116 for complete details.

Public Service Scholarship. Grants of $1026 to $2220 are available for Massachusetts residents who are children of deceased veterans who are Prisoners of War or Missing in Action, or whose death was service related, or children or spouses of

deceased members of fire, police, or corrections departments. The awards are applicable to attending Massachusetts institutions.

Contact Jill McTague, Senior Counselor, Massachusetts Office of Student Financial Assistance, 330 Stuart Street, Boston, Massachusetts 02116 for complete details.

Tuition Waiver (General). A tuition waiver at Massachusetts institutions of higher education are available for full-time students who are permanent Massachusetts residents. The waivers are need based, and the applicant must file the Free Application For Student Aid (FAFSA) soon after January 1.

Contact the Scholarship Director, Massachusetts Office of Student Financial Assistance, 330 Stuart Street, Boston, Massachusetts 02116 for complete details.

Tuition Waiver Program (Military Service). Renewable tuition exemption for up to four years is available to active Massachusetts members of the Air Force, Army, Navy, Marines, or Coast Guard. For use at a Massachusetts college or university. Deadlines vary. Contact veterans coordinator at college.

Contact the Scholarship Director, Massachusetts Office of Student Financial Assistance, 330 Stuart Street, Boston, Massachusetts 02116 for complete details.

MICHIGAN

Michigan Adult Part-Time Grant. This grant provides assistance of up to $600 to financially needy, independent students. Eligible students must be Michigan residents enrolled part-time at approved public or private degree-granting colleges in

Michigan. Eligibility is limited to two years. The Free Application for Federal Student Aid (FAFSA) must be filed.

Further inquiries should be addressed to the Office of Scholarships and Grants, Michigan Higher Education Assistance Authority, P.O. Box 30466, Lansing MI 48909-7966.

Michigan Competitive Scholarship. This awards are limited to the college's tuition up to $1200. Michigan residents attending a Michigan college or university are eligible dependent on financial need and their academic ability, as determined by scores on the ACT Assessment. If the ACT is taken after October of the senior year in high school, the student is considered a late applicant. The scholarship is renewable if recipients maintain a C average and meet the college's academic progress requirements. Applicants must file the Free Application For Student Aid (FAFSA).

Further inquiries should be addressed to the Office of Scholarships and Grants, Michigan Higher Education Assistance Authority, P.O. Box 30462, Lansing MI 48909-7962. Deadlines are February 21 for high school seniors or March 21 for college students.

Michigan Educational Opportunity Grant. This need-based, one-time award of up to $1000 is available to Michigan residents who are enrolled at least half-time at a public Michigan college. Applicants must file the Free Application For Student Aid (FAFSA).

For further information, contact the desired college's financial aid office or the Office of Scholarships and Grants, Michigan Higher Educa-

tion Assistance Authority, P.O. Box 30466, Lansing MI 48909-7966.

Michigan Tuition Grants. These need-based grants aid students attending an approved Michigan private, nonprofit, degree-granting college or university. Students must be Michigan residents enrolled on at least a half-time basis. Awards are renewable for undergraduate and graduate study. Applicants must file the Free Application For Student Aid (FAFSA).

For further program information, students should contact their high school counselor, college financial aid officer, or the Office of Scholarships and Grants, Michigan Higher Education Assistance Authority, P.O. Box 30462, Lansing MI 48909-7962.

Tuition Incentive Program (TIP). This program encourages high school completion by helping to pay college tuition and mandatory fees for students who are receiving or have received Medicaid through the Family Independence Agency. The TIP Scholarship provides two years tuition towards an associate degree at a Michigan college or university. Applicants must apply before graduation from high school or receiving a GED.

For an informational brochure, including an application, and for more information, contact the Tuition Incentive Program, Family Independence Agency, P.O. Box 30037, Lansing, MI 48909.

MINNESOTA

Educational Assistance for Veterans. This one-time $350 stipend may be given to veterans who have used up all other federal funds yet have time remaining on their delimiting period. The applicant must be a

Minnesota resident attending a Minnesota college or university.

Send all inquiries to the Minnesota Department of Veterans Affairs, Veterans Service Building, 20 West 12th Street, Second Floor, St. Paul, Minnesota 55155.

Minnesota Educational Assistance for War Orphans. This program provides tuition benefits of $350 per year for children of veterans who died in service. Children of deceased veterans may qualify for free tuition at state university, college, or vocational/technical schools, but not at University of Minnesota.

To apply, contact the Minnesota Department of Veterans Affairs, Veterans Service Building, 20 West 12th Street, Second Floor, St. Paul, Minnesota 55155.

Minnesota Nursing Grants for Persons of Color. These scholarships of $2000 to $4000 can aid minority Minnesota residents who are nursing students enrolled in a four-year or advanced nursing program in Minnesota.

For details, contact the Minnesota Higher Education Services Office, Suite 400, Capitol Square Building, 550 Cedar Street, St. Paul MN 55101.

Minnesota Reciprocal Agreement. This program waives all or part of the non-resident tuition surcharges for Minnesota residents attending a public college or university in Wisconsin, Iowa, South Dakota, North Dakota, Michigan, Nebraska, Missouri, or Kansas.

Application forms are available from participating colleges and university admissions offices or from high school counselors. The application deadline is the last day of each academic term. To be considered for benefits for a full academic year, apply by the last day of scheduled classes for the fall term.

Minnesota Safety Officers' Survivor Program. This program provides tuition and fee benefits to dependent children and surviving spouses of Minnesota public safety officers killed or permanently or totally disabled in the line of duty. Awards are renewable and can be used at Minnesota two-year and four-year colleges participating in the State Grant Program. Applicants must submit proof of death or disability.

Write for details to Brenda Larter, Program Assistant, Minnesota Higher Education Services Office, Suite 400, Capitol Square Building, 550 Cedar Street, St. Paul, Minnesota 55101.

Minnesota State Grant Program. This program aids Minnesota residents who are attending an approved Minnesota institution. To be eligible, students must demonstrate financial need. Awards amounts range from $300 to $5932 and are based on deducting the Pell Grant and Expected Family Contribution from half the cost of attendance.

For more information, contact the Minnesota Higher Education Services Office, Suite 400, Capitol Square Building, 550 Cedar Street, St. Paul, Minnesota 55101. The application deadline is June 30.

Minnesota State Veterans' Dependents Assistance Program. This program provides tuition assistance at Minnesota two-year and four year institutions to students who are dependents of veterans classified after August 1, 1958, as Prisoner of War (POW) or Missing in Action (MIA).

Information is available from college financial aid offices or the Min-

nesota Higher Education Services Office, Suite 400, Capitol Square Building, 550 Cedar Street, St. Paul, Minnesota 55101.

Non-AFDC Child Care Grant Program. This renewable need-based grant for child care is available to Minnesota residents who are enrolled at a Minnesota two-year or four-year college and who are not receiving Aid to Families with Dependent Children. The award calculated from a maximum award chart based on income cannot exceed actual child care costs.

Information is available from college financial aid offices. For more information, contact the Minnesota Higher Education Services Office, Suite 400, Capitol Square Building, 550 Cedar Street, St. Paul, Minnesota 55101.

MISSISSIPPI

Career Ladder Nursing Scholarship Loan Program. A registered nurse who is a current resident in Mississippi may request a nursing scholarship grant. The recipient must be admitted on a full-time basis to an accredited Bachelor of Science program in Nursing and agree to practice nursing in Mississippi upon completion of the college program for the same length of time for which the scholarship was received or repay the amount as a loan. Scholarships range from $1500 to $2000 per year.

For more information, contact Board of Trustees of State Institutions of Higher Learning, 3825 Ridgewood Road, Jackson, Mississippi 39211-6453. The application deadline is June 15.

Law Enforcement Officer and Firemen Scholarship Program. This program provides college scholar-

ships for the dependents of law enforcement officers and fire fighters who were killed or disabled in the performance of their official duties. Recipients must be Mississippi residents. The award is a full tuition waiver renewable annually at any state-supported college or university in Mississippi.

For more information, contact Board of Trustees of State Institutions of Higher Learning, 3825 Ridgewood Road, Jackson, Mississippi 39211-6453.

Mississippi Health Care Professions Loan/Scholarship Program. This renewable award provides a full tuition waiver renewable annually at any state-supported college or university in Mississippi for junior and senior undergraduates in an allied health program in critical demand.

For more information, contact Board of Trustees of State Institutions of Higher Learning, 3825 Ridgewood Road, Jackson, Mississippi 39211-6453.

Nursing Education BSN (Bachelor of Science in Nursing) Program. This is a renewable aid program for Mississippi residents studying in order to earn BSN degree in an approved nursing program within the state of Mississippi. Include transcript, financial aid form, and references with application.

For more information, Board of Trustees of State Institutions of Higher Learning, 3825 Ridgewood Road, Jackson, Mississippi 39211-6453. The application deadline is June 15.

Southeast Asia POW/MIA Scholarship Program. This program provides college scholarships for the biological children of veterans currently or formerly listed as Prisoners of War or Missing in Action in Southeast Asia or as a result of military action against the naval vessel *Pueblo*. Eligible students are entitled to an eight-semester tuition waiver. Recipients must be Mississippi residents.

For more information, contact Board of Trustees of State Institutions of Higher Learning, 3825 Ridgewood Road, Jackson, Mississippi 39211-6453

State Student Incentive Grant (SSIG). Students who are Mississippi residents enrolled in a full-time program of study at a Mississippi college or university and who demonstrate financial need are eligible for this renewable award. The amount of the award ranges from $100 to $1500 per academic year.

For further information, contact a college financial aid office or Board of Trustees of State Institutions of Higher Learning, 3825 Ridgewood Road, Jackson, Mississippi 39211-6453. Deadline varies with each institution.

William F. Winter Teacher Scholar Loan Program. This program provides scholarships to students enrolled in a full-time program leading to a Class A certification. Scholarships range from $1000 to $3000 per year. The recipient must maintain a 2.5 grade point average. In return for the scholarship award, the recipient agrees to work as teacher in the for one year for each year of the loan.

For more information, contact Board of Trustees of State Institutions of Higher Learning, 3825 Ridgewood Road, Jackson, Mississippi 39211-6453. The application deadline is June 15.

MISSOURI

Missouri Higher Education Academic Scholarship Program.

This program provides between 6000 and 6400 scholarships of $2,000 per academic year to top ranking Missouri high school seniors to attend a participating Missouri postsecondary institution full-time. To be eligible, a student must be a high school senior, a citizen or permanent resident of the United States, and a Missouri resident with a composite score on the American College Testing (ACT) exam or the Scholastic Assessment Test (SAT I) in the top 3 percent of all Missouri students taking those tests. To be eligible for scholarship renewal, the student attend full-time at a participating Missouri postsecondary institution and maintain satisfactory academic progress according to standards determined by the institution.

Applications are available from Missouri high schools, college financial aid offices, or the Missouri Coordinating Board for Higher Education, 3515 Amazonas Drive, Jefferson City MO 65109. Applications must be received by July 31.

Missouri Minority Teacher Education Scholarship. This renewable merit-based award for use for up to four years at a Missouri institution is for minority residents of Missouri. Recipients must be enrolled in an approved mathematics or science education program and commit to teach math or science in Missouri for five years following graduation.

Further inquiries should be directed to the Missouri Minority Teaching Scholarship, Missouri Department of Elementary and Secondary Education, P.O. Box 480, Jefferson City MO 65102-0480.

Missouri Student Grant Program. These state grants provide financial assistance to Missouri residents attending an approved Missouri public or private college or university on a full-time basis. Recipients must demonstrate financial need. The amount of the award ranges from $100 to $1500. Recipients may reapply until the he or she has obtained a baccalaureate degree or for a maximum of ten semesters.

Application forms may be obtained from high school guidance offices, college financial aid offices, or the Missouri Coordinating Board for Higher Education, 3515 Amazonas Drive, Jefferson City MO 65109. The application period is from January 1 to April 1.

Missouri Teacher Education Scholarship (General). This nonrenewable merit-based award of $2000 is for Missouri high school seniors, resident college freshmen, or sophomores in an approved teacher training program at Missouri four-year institution. Recipients must rank in the top fifteen percent of either their high school class or of scores on the American College Test or Scholastic Assessment Test.

Further inquiries should be directed to the Missouri Teacher Education Scholarships, Missouri Department of Elementary and Secondary Education, P.O. Box 480, Jefferson City MO 65102-0480.

MONTANA

State Student Incentive Grant. This grant helps Montana residents attending an approved college or university within the state. Eligible students must be enrolled full-time and have substantial financial need.

To apply, complete the Financial Aid Form (FAF) and Supplement, and submit them to the College Scholarship Service (CSS). Also, complete the Montana Student Information Form and forward it directly to the college you plan to attend. Both forms are available from high school guidance offices or college financial aid offices. The application deadline is after January 1 but prior to April 1.

NEBRASKA

Nebraska National Guard Tuition Credit. This renewable benefit pays one-half of a Nebraska National Guard enlistee's tuition until he or she has received a baccalaureate degree.

Further inquiries should be directed to the State Tuition Office, Nebraska Military Department, 1300 Military Road, Lincoln NE 68508-1090.

Nebraska Scholarship Assistance Program. Assistance is available to Pell Grant recipients who are Nebraska residents attending a participating Nebraska postsecondary institution. Awards are determined by each participating institution.

Further inquiries should be directed to the Scholarship Coordinator, Postsecondary Education Commission, P.O. Box 95005, Lincoln NE 68509-9500.

Nebraska State Scholarship Award Program. Pell Grant recipients who are not Nebraska residents but who attend a participating postsecondary institution in Nebraska may be eligible for these scholarships. Awards are determined by each participating institution.

Further inquiries should be directed to the Scholarship Coordinator, Postsecondary Education Commission, P.O. Box 95005, Lincoln NE 68509-9500.

Nebraska Tuition Credit for Active Reservists. Renewable credit of fifty percent of tuition charges is available for active Nebraska reservists with at least two years remaining on their enlistment. The reservist must have agreed to serve a minimum of three years and be enrolled in a degree program at a state-supported Nebraska institution.

Further inquiries should be directed to Keith E. Fickenscher, Nebraska Department of Veterans Affairs, P.O. Box 95083, Lincoln NE 68509.

Nebraska Tuition Waiver for Veterans' Dependents. Nebraska residents are eligible for a renewable tuition waiver at a Nebraska institution if they are children under 26, spouses, widows, or widowers of veterans were totally disabled or who died as the result of a service-connected casualty. The veteran must have been disabled, died, or been classified as Missing in Action or Prisoner of War after August 4, 1964.

Further inquiries should be directed to Keith E. Fickenscher, Nebraska Department of Veterans Affairs, P.O. Box 95083, Lincoln NE 68509.

Postsecondary Education Award Program. Pell Grant recipients attending a participating Nebraska private, nonprofit postsecondary institution may be eligible for these awards. Nebraska residency is required. The awards are determined by each participating institution.

Further inquiries should be directed to the Scholarship Coordinator, Postsecondary Education Commission, P.O. Box 95005, Lincoln NE 68509-9500.

NEVADA

Nevada Student Incentive Grant Program. This program aids Nevada residents attending an approved college or university within the state. Recipients must have financial need and must be enrolled at least half-time. Awards range from $200 to $5000 per academic year and are renewable, provided the student has continued financial need.

Contact the financial aid office of the college you plan to attend for application forms and deadlines, since the program is administered individually by the colleges and universities in Nevada.

NEW HAMPSHIRE

New Hampshire Incentive Program (NHIP). This program aids New Hampshire residents attending a regionally accredited college or university in New Hampshire, Massachusetts, Maine, Vermont, Rhode Island, or Connecticut. Recipients must be full-time students with financial need. To apply, complete the Free Application for Federal Student Aid (FAFSA). Grants range from $450 to $1000 per academic year.

Direct inquiries to the New Hampshire Postsecondary Education Commission, Two Industrial Park Drive, Concord, NH 03301-8512. The application deadline is May 1.

New Hampshire Nursing Education Grant. These grants aid New Hampshire residents attending state-approved nursing schools. Recipients must agree to practice nursing in New Hampshire for one year following licensing by the state. Awards are based on need.

To apply, obtain an application from the financial aid office of the nursing school or from Lynn Duke, New Hampshire Postsecondary Education Commission, Two Industrial Park Drive, Concord, New Hampshire 03301-8512. The application deadlines are June 1 for the summer/fall term and December 15 for the spring term.

Scholarships for Orphans of Veterans. These scholarships help New Hampshire residents under age 26 who are the children of veterans who died as a result of service in the Southeast Asian Conflict. Benefits include possible full tuition payment, plus an award of up to $1000 per year for the duration of the undergraduate degree program. Awards are renewable.

Contact Julia Pingree, New Hampshire Postsecondary Education Commission, Two Industrial Park Drive, Concord, New Hampshire 03301-8512.

NEW JERSEY

Educational Opportunity Fund (EOF) Grants. These grants are designed for students from educationally disadvantaged backgrounds who have exceptional financial need. Students must be matriculated and attending an accredited New Jersey college or university on a full-time basis. Garden State Scholars are not eligible for this award. Grants range from $400 to $2100 per year. Grants may be renewed subject to continued student eligibility.

Application forms are available at high school guidance offices and college financial aid offices.

Edward J. Bloustein Distinguished Scholars Program. This program is for students who have demonstrated the highest level of academic achievement, as demonstrated by

their high school record (3.5 GPA) and their SAT scores. Students are selected for consideration by their high school, and final determination of awards is made by the New Jersey Department of Higher Education. From those selected for consideration, awards of $1000 per year will be offered to high school seniors who intend to enroll at a New Jersey college or university as full-time undergraduate students. Recipients must be residents of New Jersey. The award is renewable for four years, based upon satisfactory academic progress, continued undergraduate enrollment in a New Jersey college or university, and continued program funding.

Interested students should contact their guidance counselor.

Garden State Scholarship (GSS). This program is for students who have demonstrated high academic achievement based upon their high school record (3.5 GPA) and their SAT scores. Recipients must be New Jersey residents enrolled as full-time undergraduate students in a New Jersey college or university. Candidates are selected for consideration by their high schools Students awarded a GSS receive $500 per year. The GSS is renewable based upon satisfactory academic progress, continued undergraduate enrollment in a New Jersey college or university, and continued program funding.

Students should file the New Jersey Financial Aid Form (NJFAF) with the College Scholarship Service (CSS) after January 1 in order to be considered for additional financial aid. Interested students should contact their guidance counselor for more information.

POW/MIA Program. This program provides assistance to dependent children of military service personnel who were officially declared Prisoner of War (POW) or Person Missing in Action (MIA). The POW or MIA must have been a resident of New Jersey at the time he or she entered the services of the United States Armed Forces or must have an official residence in New Jersey. Grants provide tuition for undergraduate students attending any public or independent institution in New Jersey.

Application forms may be obtained by contacting Barbara J. Gilsenan, New Jersey Department of Military & Veterans Affairs, Eggert Crossing Road, CN 340, Trenton, New Jersey 08625-0340.

Public Tuition Benefit Program (PTBP). This benefit program aids dependents of emergency service personnel, civil defense and disaster control workers, and other law enforcement officials killed in the line of duty. The award recipients must be residents of New Jersey who are attending a New Jersey public or independent institution of higher education as undergraduate students. Grants pay the actual cost of tuition charges incurred at any New Jersey public college or university. The program will pay recipients who attend New Jersey independent institutions up to the highest tuition charged at a New Jersey public institution.

Application forms may be obtained by calling the New Jersey Financial Aid Hotline (800-792-8670) from any location in New Jersey, Monday through Friday, 9 a.m. to 5 p.m. The application deadlines are October 1 if aid is desired for both the fall and spring terms and March 1 if aid is desired for the spring term only.

Tuition Aid Grant (TAG).

This grant program is open to residents of New Jersey who are or intend to be full-time undergraduates at a New Jersey college. Grants range from $760 to $5570 and are renewable for up to four years of undergraduate study, provided that an application is filed each year, eligibility continues, and the student is making satisfactory academic progress.

All applicants must file the FAFSA form. Application forms are available at high school guidance offices and deadlines vary.

Veterans Tuition Credit Program.

U.S. veterans who were or are eligible for federal veterans' assistance and served in the armed forces of the United States between December 31, 1960, and May 7, 1975, may apply. Applicants must have been New Jersey residents at the time of induction or discharge or for at least one year prior to the time of application, excluding the time of active duty. Eligible veterans may receive a maximum award of $400 a year for full-time attendance or $200 a year for half-time attendance.

Applications can be obtained by contacting Barbara J. Gilsenan, New jersey Department of Military & Veterans Affairs, Eggert Crossing Road, CN340, Trenton, New Jersey 08625-0340. Applications must be filed before October 1 (for fall and spring terms) and March 1 (for spring term only).

NEW MEXICO

New Mexico Allied Health Student Loan Program.

This is need-based program offers renewable loans for study in a variety of allied health fields including nursing, physical therapy, health medicine, dental hygiene, and others. It is intended to increase the number of health professionals in medically underserved areas in New Mexico. Students must declare their intention to practice in a medically underserved area in New Mexico in order to receive loan forgiveness.

Students may borrow a maximum of $12,000 per year for four years. Loans may be forgiven through service, or they may be repaid.

For more information, contact the financial aid officer of the New Mexico postsecondary institution of your choice. Deadlines vary by school.

Children of Deceased Veterans Scholarship Program.

This program offers nonrenewable awards to New Mexico residents who are children of veterans retired from active duty, killed or disabled as a result of service, POWs, or MIAs. Applicants must be between the ages of 16 and 26. Scholarships may be used only at New Mexico schools for undergraduate study. Eleven awards are currently offered.

For further information, contact Alan Martinez, New Mexico Veterans' Service Commission, P.O. Box 2324, Santa Fe, New Mexico 87503.

NEW YORK

Educational Opportunity Program (EOP).

These renewable awards aid New York State residents who plan to pursue postsecondary education in New York State. Recipients must demonstrate financial need.

Write for more information to Scholarship Coordinator, New York State Higher Education Services Corporation, 99 Washington Avenue, Albany, New York 12255.

New York Aid for Part-Time Study (APTS).

This tuition assistance program aids New York state residents who are enrolled part-time at New York accredited institutions. Renewable scholarship is based on need and the amount of money available at the institution. Award amounts vary up to $2000.

To apply, contact the Scholarship Coordinator, New York State Higher Education Services Corporation, 99 Washington Avenue, Albany, New York 12255.

Primary Care Services Corps Scholarship Program.

This competitive scholarship program awards up to $15,000 per year to students enrolled in full-time or part-time programs of study for midwives, nurse practitioners, or physicians' assistants. Scholarship recipients must agree to work in an underserved area for eighteen months per full-time award or for nine months per part-time award. Recipients must be New York residents.

Scholarship applications can be obtained from the New York State Primary Care Service Corps, Room 1602, Corning Tower, Empire State Plaza, Albany, New York 12237-0053. The deadline for applying is April 1.

Regents Award for Children of Deceased or Disabled Veterans.

This program aids students who are New York residents and are children of veterans who died while serving in the armed forces, incurred a service-related disability, were classified as Prisoner of War (POW), or are classified as Missing in Action (MIA). The amount of this renewable award is

$450 per academic year for four years of full-time undergraduate study at a college in New York.

Obtain more information and the special application form from the Scholarship Coordinator, New York State Higher Education Services Corporation, 99 Washington Avenue, Albany, New York 12255. The deadline for applying is May 1.

Regents Award for Children of Deceased Police Officers, Fire Fighters, or Corrections Officers. This program aids students who are New York residents and are children of police officers, fire fighters, or corrections officers who served in New York State and were killed in the line of duty. Awards are $450 per academic year and are normally renewable for four years of full-time undergraduate study at a college in New York State.

Obtain a special application form from the Scholarship Coordinator, New York State Higher Education Services Corporation, 99 Washington Avenue, Albany, New York 12255. The deadline for applying is May 1.

New York Supplemental Tuition Assistance Program (STAP). This program of renewable awards aids New York residents who are undergraduates at New York institutions and are in need of remedial study during a summer term. Awards range from $25 to $975, based on financial need.

For more information, contact the Scholarship Coordinator, New York State Higher Education Services Corporation, 99 Washington Avenue, Albany, New York 12255. Students must apply by May 1.

New York Tuition Assistance Program. This program aids residents of New York enrolled full-time in New York postsecondary institutions. Recipients must show financial need and must be U.S. citizens. Recipients must not be in default on other state education assistance programs. Undergraduate awards range from $75 to $3900 per year for up to four years of study.

For more information, contact the Scholarship Coordinator, New York State Higher Education Services Corporation, 99 Washington Avenue, Albany, New York 12255. The deadline for applying is May 1.

Vietnam Veterans Tuition Awards (VVTA). This program aids New York residents who served in the U.S. armed forces in Vietnam, and are attending a New York institution. Renewable awards range from $500 up to $1000 per academic year.

An application can be obtained from the New York State Higher Education Services Corporation, 99 Washington Avenue, Albany, New York 12255. The deadline for applying is May 1.

NORTH CAROLINA

Incentive Scholarship and Grant Program for Native American Indians. This program aids North Carolina residents enrolled full-time as undergraduates in program at one of the one of the sixteen universities of the University of North Carolina System.who are members of a recognized Native American Indian tribe. Awards are based on academic achievement and financial need. Awards may be renewable dependent on academic progress.

To apply, contact the Scholarship and Grant Officer, University of North Carolina, P.O. Box 2688, Chapel Hill NC 27515-2688.

North Carolina Community College Scholarship Program. This renewable award aids North Carolina residents enrolled in a North Carolina community college. 756 scholarships of $557 each are available. Each college selects recipients from applicants meeting criteria based on financial need. Awards may be renewed each year.

Contact the Director of Financial Aid at any North Carolina community college. Deadline varies with each community college.

North Carolina Freshmen Scholars Program. This is a one-time award for high school seniors who are North Carolina residents planning to attend a participating North Carolina university. Covers tuition, fees, and books for freshman year. Each school has specific eligibility requirements.

To apply, write for details to the Grant Administrator, University of North Carolina General Administration, P.O. Box 2688, Chapel Hill NC 27515-2688.

North Carolina Legislative Tuition Grant Program. This renewable award aids residents of North Carolina attending an approved private college or university within the state. Recipients must be enrolled full-time in an undergraduate program of study not designed primarily for career preparation in a religious vocation. The maximum annual award has been $1300. Financial need is not a requirement of this program.

Contact the financial aid office or registrar of the North Carolina private college you plan to attend for application forms and deadlines.

North Carolina National Guard Tuition Assistance Program (TAP). This program aids members of the

North Carolina Air and Army National Guard who will remain in the service for two years following the end of tuition assistance is provided. Recipients must enroll in a college or university in North Carolina. The award amount is up to $1000 per year for tuition assistance, subject to annual renewal.

For an application form and information contact Education Services, North Carolina National Guard, 4105 Reedy Creek Road, Raleigh, North Carolina 27607-6467.

North Carolina State Assistance Authority Minority Presence Grant. The aim of this program is to increase the presence of minority students at four-year state institutions in North Carolina. The recipient must be a United States citizen, a North Carolina resident, demonstrate financial need, and be a member of a racial group that is in the minority at the attending institution. The amount of the award depends upon the financial need of the recipient and the availability of funds.

To apply, write for further details to Scholarship and Grant Services, North Carolina State Education Assistance Authority, P.O. Box 2688, Chapel Hill, North Carolina 27615-2688.

North Carolina Student Incentive Grant. This renewable award is for North Carolina residents who are enrolled full-time at a North Carolina postsecondary institution. Applicants must demonstrate substantial financial need by completing the Free Application For Student Aid (FAFSA). Recipients must be United States citizens and maintain satisfactory academic progress.

To apply, contact the financial aid office of any North Carolina college.

North Carolina Student Loan Program for Health, Science, and Mathematics. This renewable award is for residents of North Carolina studying health related fields, or science or math education. Recipients are selected on the basis of merit, financial need, and promise of service as a health professional or educator in an underserved area of North Carolina. Loans range from $3000 to $8500 a year. Loans must be supported by a promissory note with notarized signatures from the recipient and two cosigners.

Applications must be received by April 1. For more information, contact the North Carolina Student Loan Program, North Carolina State Education Assistance Authority, P.O. Box 20549, Raleigh, North Carolina 27619-0549.

North Carolina Rehabilitation Assistance for the Visually Handicapped. This renewable award aids North Carolina residents who are blind or visually impaired and require vocational rehabilitation in order to secure employment. Scholarships covers tuition and other assistance. The amount of the scholarship is based on need. Documentation of a visual impairment is required.

To apply, contact James D. Roberts, Division of Services for the Blind, 309 Ashe Avenue, Raleigh, North Carolina 27606.

North Carolina Teaching Fellows Program. This merit-based, state-funded program awards $5000 per year to up to 400 North Carolina high school graduates to enter teacher-training programs at one of fourteen approved schools in North Carolina. A Teaching Fellow must agree to teach in a North Carolina

public or government school for four years or repay award.

Teaching Fellow applications are available from the North Carolina Teaching Fellows Commission, Koger Center, Cumberland Building, 3739 National Drive, Suite 210, Raleigh, North Carolina 27612.

North Carolina Veterans Scholarships. This award is available to children of veterans who are deceased, disabled, or listed as Prisoner of War (POW) or Missing in Action (MIA). The veteran must have been a legal resident of North Carolina at the time of entry into the service. Full scholarships provide for four academic years of tuition, room and board allowances, and mandatory fees at North Carolina institution. These renewable scholarships range from $1500 to $4500.

For further information, contact the North Carolina Division of Veterans Affairs, 325 North Salisbury Street, Raleigh, North Carolina 27603.

State Contractual Scholarship Fund. This scholarship fund aids North Carolina residents already attending an approved private college or university within the state. Eligible students must have financial need and not enrolled in a program leading to a religious vocation. The amount of this renewable award varies according to financial need and available funds.

Contact the financial aid office of any private North Carolina college or university office for deadline and information.

NORTH DAKOTA

North Dakota Indian Scholarship Program. Thus program grants from $600 to $2000 to Native American

North Dakota residents to help pay for a college education at a North Dakota institution. Priority is given to full-time undergraduates with a cumulative grade point average of 3.5 or higher. Financial need is a factor in setting the amount of the grant. Certification of tribal enrollment is required.

For further information, contact the North Dakota Indian Scholarship Program, North Dakota University System, State Capitol, 10th Floor, 600 East Boulevard, Bismarck, North Dakota 58505-0230. The application deadline is July 15.

North Dakota Scholars Program.

This program provides scholarships equal to the cost of tuition at the North Dakota public colleges for North Dakota high school seniors who score at or above the 95th percentile on the ACT Assessment and who rank in the top 20 percent of their high school graduating class. Applicants must take the ACT test in the fall.

For further information, contact the Student Financial Assistance Program, North Dakota University System, State Capitol, 10th Floor, 600 East Boulevard, Bismarck, North Dakota 58505-0230

North Dakota State Department of Transportation Educational Grant.

This renewable award of $1000 based on financial need and academic progress is for sophomores, juniors, and seniors studying civil engineering study at a North Dakota institution. The grant may be used for tuition, fees, books and other educational expenditures. Experience may be given consideration in awarding the grant.

Further inquires should be directed to Ms Marlene Larson, Human

Resources, North Dakota State Department of Transportation, 608 East Boulevard Avenue, Bismarck ND 58505-0700.

North Dakota Student Financial Assistance Grants.

This need-based program aids North Dakota residents attending an approved North Dakota college or university. Recipients must enroll in a course of study of at least nine months in length. The award is renewable for up to four years. The grant amount is determined annually. The current maximum is $600. The Free Application for Federal Student Aid (FAFSA) must be filed.

For further information, contact the Student Financial Assistance Program, North Dakota University System, State Capitol, 10th Floor, 600 East Boulevard, Bismarck, North Dakota 58505-0230. The application deadline is April 15.

OHIO

Ohio Academic Scholarship Program.

This program aids academically outstanding Ohio residents planning to attend an approved Ohio college. Applicants must be high school seniors who intend to enroll as full-time undergraduates. The award is $2000 per year for up to four years, provided that recipients make satisfactory academic progress.

Contact your high school guidance office or the Administrator, Ohio Student Aid Commission, P.O. Box 182452, Columbus OH 43218-2452 to apply. The application deadline is February 23.

Ohio Instructional Grant.

This grant aids low-income and middle-income Ohio residents attending an approved public, proprietary, or private college of nursing in Ohio or

Pennsylvania. Recipients must be enrolled full-time and must have financial need. The average award is $630, but range up to $3750.

To apply, obtain an application form from a high school guidance office, college financial aid office, or the Administrator, Ohio Student Aid Commission, P.O. Box 182452, Columbus OH 43218-2452. The application deadline for full-year awards is October 1.

Ohio Missing in Action and Prisoners of War Orphans Scholarship.

This program of renewable full tuition awards aid the children of Vietnam war service personnel who have been classified as Missing in Action (MIA) or Prisoner of War (POW). Recipients must be Ohio residents between the ages of sixteen and twenty-one years old and enrolled full-time at an Ohio college or university.

For information about how to apply, contact a high school guidance office, college financial aid office, or the Administrator, Ohio Student Aid Commission, P.O. Box 182452, Columbus OH 43218-2452.

Ohio Safety Officers College Memorial Fund.

These renewable scholarships are available to children under 26 years of age of Ohio peace officers and fire fighters killed in the line of duty. Applicants must be Ohio residents and enrolled full-time in an Ohio college or university.

Inquiries should be addressed to the Administrator, Ohio Student Aid Commission, P.O. Box 182452, Columbus OH 43218-2452.

Ohio Student Choice Grant Program.

This program aids Ohio residents enrolled full-time in a bachelor's degree program at an eligible private, nonprofit college or university in Ohio. Awards range up to $678 and are renewable.

The eligible institutions determine which students are eligible and submit those students' names to the Ohio Student Aid Commission. For more information, students should contact their college's financial aid office.

Ohio War Orphans Scholarship. This award at eligible Ohio colleges is available to residents of Ohio who are children of deceased or severely disabled veterans of war. Applicants must be between 16 and 21 years of age and have a minimum 2.0 grade point average. If living, the veteran must be sixty percent or greater service-related disabled, or one-hundred percent non-service connected disabled, and receiving veterans benefits. Award amounts vary and are to be used to pay tuition and fees. Awards are automatically . renewable for up to four years.

For the application form and additional information, contact a college financial office or Sue Minturn, Program Administrator, Ohio Student Aid Commission, P.O. Box 182452, Columbus OH 43218-2452. The application deadline is July 1.

Part-Time Student Instructional Grant. These renewable grants for part-time undergraduates who are Ohio residents who have financial need. Recipients must attend an Ohio institution.

Inquiries should be addressed to the Administrator, Ohio Student Aid Commission, P.O. Box 182452, Columbus OH 43218-2452. The deadline is October 1st for full year awards.

OKLAHOMA

Academic Scholars Program. This program encourage students of high academic ability to attend institutions of higher education in Oklahoma. Oklahoma residence is not required. The program provides funding for tuition and other fees, room and board, and required course materials for up to five years of study at approved state colleges and universities. The recipient must have graduated from high school after July 1, 1988, and received an ACT score at or above the 99.5 percentile. Annual awards range from $3100 to $5000.

For more information, contact the Academic Scholars Program, Oklahoma State Regents for Higher Education, 500 Education Building, Oklahoma City, Oklahoma 73105.

Future Teacher Scholarship Program. This program is open to outstanding high school graduates who agree to teach in shortage areas identified by the State Department of Education. Applicants must rank in the top fifteen percent of their high school graduating class and must score at or above the 85th percentile on the ACT or other similar test. Awards range up to $1500 per year for full-time students. Recipients must reapply to renew.

Students are nominated by their college or university. For further information , contact the Future Teachers Scholarship Program, Oklahoma State Regents for Higher Education, 500 Education Building, Oklahoma City, Oklahoma 73105. The application deadline is July 1.

Oklahoma Tuition Aid Grant. This program aids Oklahoma residents who have demonstrated financial need may take advantage of this program to attend Oklahoma

postsecondary educational institutions or vocational or technical schools. Eligible students must carry at least 6 credit hours per semester in a program leading to a degree or certificate. Awards up to $1000 are granted. Students may receive grants for a maximum of ten semesters of full-time study. Students must file the Free Application for Federal Student Aid (FAFSA) form.

Applications are available from high school guidance offices, college financial aid offices, or the Tuition Aid Grant Program, Oklahoma State Regents for Higher Education, P.O. Box 3020, Oklahoma City, Oklahoma 73101-3020. Application deadline is April 30.

William P. Willis Scholarship Program. This program provides renewable annual awards to Oklahoma residents with incomes of less than $20,000 who are enrolled as full-time undergraduates at a member institution of the Oklahoma State System of Higher Education. Awards range from $1700 to $2600.

Applicants must be nominated by their institution. For more information, contact the William P. Willis Scholarship Program, Oklahoma State Regents for Higher Education, 500 Education Building, Oklahoma City, Oklahoma 73105-9925. The application deadline is May 20.

OREGON

Barber and Hairdresser Grant Program. This grant aids Oregon residents attending an eligible school of barbering, hair design, cosmetology, or manicure located in and licensed by the state of Oregon. Recipients must be enrolled full-time in programs of at least nine months in length. Eligibility is based on financial need. Recipients are limited to fifteen months of eligibility.

The maximum award amount is $1500. To apply, complete and submit any federally approved need analysis form. Students should apply by December 31. Awards are granted until funds are spent. Applications are available from high school guidance and college financial aid offices. For further information, contact the school you plan to attend.

Children of Disabled/Deceased Peace Officers Grant. This program aids children and stepchildren of Oregon peace officers killed or severely and permanently disabled in the line of duty. The award covers the cost of tuition and required fees at an Oregon community college or at one of the colleges or universities of the Oregon State System of Higher Education. Awardees must demonstrate financial need at least equal to the sum of tuition and required fees at the institution attended. Grants are available for up to four years of undergraduate education, provided the student continues to demonstrate the requisite need.

To apply, complete and submit any federally approved need analysis form. In addition, you must file a separate application form. For more information, contact the Oregon State Scholarship Commission, 1500 Valley River Drive, Suite 100, Eugene, Oregon 97401 (telephone 503-687-7395 or 800-452-8807, toll-free in Oregon).

Need Grant. This grant aids Oregon residents attending an approved two- or four-year nonprofit college or university or any eligible hospital school within Oregon. Recipients must be enrolled full-time in programs other than theology, divinity, or religious education. Eligibility is based on financial need. The amount of the award depends on the level of need and the cost of education. Awards are renewable for up to four years, provided there is continued need and satisfactory academic progress.

To apply, complete and submit any federally approved need analysis form. Students should apply as soon after January 1 as possible, since awards are granted until funds are spent. Applications are available from high school guidance and college financial aid offices. For further information, contact the Oregon State Scholarship Commission, 1500 Valley River Drive, Suite 100, Eugene, Oregon 97401 (telephone 503-687-7395 or 800-452-8807, toll-free in Oregon).

PENNSYLVANIA

Paul Douglas Teacher Scholarship Program. The Pennsylvania Higher Education Assistance Agency administers this federal teacher scholarship program in Pennsylvania. Applicants must be in the top 10 percent of their high school or college class, have the support of school officials, and be majoring in education. Awards are $5000 per year but are reduced by the amount of other grants so that a student may not make a profit through financial aid. Nevertheless, many students have virtually the entire cost of their education paid by the scholarship. Recipients must teach two years in exchange for each year of scholarship assistance or repay the award as if it were a loan. However, those who teach in shortage areas as defined by the U.S. Department of Education need teach only one year for each year of aid.

To apply, contact your guidance counselor or the financial aid office or head of the education department at the school or college you are attending or plan to attend.

Pennsylvania State Grant. This grant aids residents of Pennsylvania attending an approved postsecondary institution in most states. Recipients must be enrolled full-time in a program of at least two years' duration. The award is based on financial need and may be received for a maximum of eight semesters, provided that the student demonstrates continued need and satisfactory academic progress. Awards are limited to 80 percent of tuition and fees, not to exceed $600 for recipients attending out-of-state institutions or $2632 for those attending Pennsylvania institutions.

To apply, complete and submit the Free Application for Federal Student Aid (FAFSA). The application form may be obtained from high school guidance offices and college financial aid offices. The application deadline is May 1.

Prisoner of War/Missing in Action Dependents Grant. This program aids dependents of Pennsylvania military service personnel who are classified as Prisoners of War or Missing in Action. Recipients will receive up to $1200 for study at in-state institutions and up to $800 for study at out-of-state institutions. The student's parent must have been a Pennsylvania resident, although the student does not have to be. Applications for this renewable award are accepted anytime during the academic year, but those sent earliest are more likely to receive funding.

Write to the Pennsylvania Higher Education Assistance Agency, Grant Division, 1200 North Seventh Street, Harrisburg, Pennsylvania 17102, for application forms and information.

Veterans Grant. This grant aids residents of Pennsylvania who are qualified veterans attending an approved postsecondary institution on a full-time basis. Eligibility is based on educational costs and the resources of the student, without regard to the financial information or status of the veteran's parents or guardian. Awards are limited to 80 percent of tuition and fees, not to exceed $2632 for recipients attending in-state institutions or $800 for those attending out-of-state institutions.

To apply, complete and file the Pennsylvania Higher Education Assistance Agency (PHEAA) State Grant Application. The application form may be obtained from high school guidance offices, from college financial aid offices, and from the PHEAA Grant Division, 1200 North Seventh Street, Harrisburg, Pennsylvania 17102. The application deadline is May 1 for renewal applicants. First-time students may file anytime. As long as funds permit, students will be considered for full-year aid if their application is received before February 1 of the academic year and for final-term aid if received before April 1 of the academic year. For information about federal student loans available to students from Pennsylvania, contact the Pennsylvania Higher Education Assistance Agency, Loan Division, 660 Boas Street, Harrisburg, Pennsylvania 17102 (telephone 800-692-7392).

RHODE ISLAND

Rhode Island Higher Education Grant Program. These grants aid Rhode Island residents attending an approved college or university in the United States, Canada, or Mexico. Eligibility is based on financial need.

Awards range from $250 to $700 and are renewable for up to four years, provided the student remains in good academic standing.

For further information contact the Rhode Island Higher Education Assistance Authority, Grant Division, 560 Jefferson Boulevard, Warwick, Rhode Island 02886. The application deadline is March 1.

SOUTH CAROLINA

Free Tuition for Children of Deceased or Disabled South Carolina Firemen, Law Officers, Civil Air Patrol, or Rescue Squad Members. These renewable awards aid the children of deceased or disabled fire fighters, law officers, Civil Air Patrol, or rescue squad members. Recipients must attend a public postsecondary institution in South Carolina and be a South Carolina resident.

To apply, contact the South Carolina Commission on Higher Education, 1333 Main Street, Suite 200, Columbia, South Carolina 29201.

Free Tuition for Children of Deceased or Disabled Wartime South Carolina Veterans. These renewable awards are for South Carolina residents who are dependents of deceased or totally disabled wartime veterans. Recipients must be between the ages of eighteen and twenty-six and attend a South Carolina college, university, or trade school.

To apply, contact the South Carolina Division of Veterans Affairs, Edgar Brown Building, 1205 Pendleton Street, Room 226, Columbia, South Carolina 29201.

Palmetto Fellows Scholarship. These automatically renewable awards of up to $5000 aid South

Carolina high school seniors attend four-year South Carolina colleges and universities.

Application form is available from Dr. Karen Woodfaulk, South Carolina Commission on Higher Education, 1333 Main Street, Suite 200, Columbia, South Carolina 29201. The application, with a transcript, test scores, and essay must be submitted by October 1.

South Carolina State Student Incentive Grant. These renewable awards of up to $2000 are for full-time study at a participating South Carolina institution. Awards are based on substantial financial need. South Carolina residence is not required.

Contact the South Carolina Commission on Higher Education, 1333 Main Street, Suite 200, Columbia, South Carolina 29201. Deadlines vary by institution.

South Carolina Teacher Loan and South Carolina Governor's Teaching Scholarship Loan. These one-time awards of $2500 to $5000 are for South Carolina residents attending four-year postsecondary institutions in South Carolina. Recipients must teach in the South Carolina public school system in a critical-need area after graduation. 20% of the loan is forgiven for each year of service.

To learn of additional requirements, write to Ann Gregory, South Carolina Student Loan Corporation, P.O. Box 21487, Columbia, South Carolina 29221. The application deadline is May 15.

South Carolina Tuition Grants Program. These grants aid residents of South Carolina attending one of twenty approved South Carolina colleges within the state. Eligibility is based on academic merit and financial need. Freshman applicants should be in the upper three quarters of their high school class or have a combined Scholastic Assessment Test (SAT I) score of at least 900. Upper-class students must complete a minimum of 24 semester hours per year. The awards, which range up to $3420 per academic year for up to four years, must be reapplied for each year.

To apply, contact the South Carolina Tuition Grants Commission, 1310 Lady Street, Suite 811, P.O. Box 12159, Columbia, South Carolina 29211-2159. The deadline for applying is June 30.

Tuition Waiver for Senior Citizens. These renewable awards are available to South Carolina residents who are 60 and over and are attending South Carolina public colleges. The award is equal to the tuition at the public college attended.

To apply, contact the South Carolina Commission on Higher Education, 1333 Main Street, Suite 200, Columbia, South Carolina 29201. Application deadlines vary by institution.

Vocational Rehabilitation Benefits. Based on financial need, South Carolina residents who have physical or mental handicaps that limit vocational opportunities may be eligible for these renewable awards of up to $2000. Additional funds are available to cover special services.

To apply, contact the South Carolina Commission on Higher Education, 1333 Main Street, Suite 200, Columbia, South Carolina 29201. Application deadlines vary by institution.

War Orphans Benefits. South Carolina residents under 23 years of age who are children of deceased or disabled veterans of the United States

Armed Forces are eligible for these renewable scholarships.

To apply, contact the Veterans Administration Office, 1205 Pendleton Street, Columbia, South Carolina 29201.

SOUTH DAKOTA

Aid to National Guardsmen. This program aids South Dakota residents who are active members of the South Dakota Army or Air National Guard and are attending a state-supported South Dakota university or postsecondary vocational school. Recipients are granted a reduction of one half the tuition for up to four years.

To apply, contact the Aid Director, Department of Military and Veterans Affairs, 44 East Capitol Avenue, Pierre SD 57501-3185.

South Dakota Board of Regents Annis I. Fowler/Kaden Scholarship. This scholarship of $1000 is available to South Dakota high school seniors to pursue a career in elementary education at a South Dakota public university. Applicants must have a minimum 3.0 grade point average.

Award inquiries should be directed to the Senior Administrator, South Dakota Board of Regents, 207 East Capitol Avenue, Pierre SD 57501-3159. Application deadline is February 18.

South Dakota Board of Regents Bjugstad Scholarship. This scholarship of $500 is available to South Dakota or North Dakota high school seniors who are Native American. Applicants must demonstrate academic achievement, character, leadership abilities, and submit proof of tribal enrollment.

Award inquiries should be directed to the Senior Administrator, South Dakota Board of Regents, 207 East Capitol Avenue, Pierre SD 57501-3159. Application deadline is February 18.

South Dakota Board of Regents Haines Memorial Scholarship. This scholarship of $1750 is available to sophomores, juniors, or seniors who are majoring in education at a South Dakota public university and have a 2.5 or better grade point average. Applicants should submit resumes with their applications.

Award inquiries should be directed to the Senior Administrator, South Dakota Board of Regents, 207 East Capitol Avenue, Pierre SD 57501-3159. Application deadline is February 18.

South Dakota Board of Regents Marlin R. Scarborough Memorial Scholarship. This merit-based scholarship of $1500 is available to a college junior who has completed three semesters at a South Dakota public university. Applicants must have graduated from a South Dakota high school and be nominated by their university.

Award inquiries should be directed to the Senior Administrator, South Dakota Board of Regents, 207 East Capitol Avenue, Pierre SD 57501-3159. Application deadline is February 18.

South Dakota State Student Incentive Grant. This program aids residents of South Dakota attending an eligible South Dakota institution on at least a half-time basis. Eligibility is based on financial need. Awards are renewable until attainment of the bachelor's degree. Awards range from $100 to $600.

Obtain the application forms from a high school guidance counselor, college financial aid officer, or the Scholarship Chairman, South Dakota Department of Education, 700 Governors Drive, Pierre SD 57501-2291. Deadlines vary by school.

South Dakota Tuition Equalization Grant Program. This program aids residents of South Dakota attending on a full-time basis an approved private college or university in South Dakota. Awards of up to $300 are based on financial need. Awards are renewable annually.

Application forms may be obtained from college financial aid offices, or the Scholarship Chairman, South Dakota Department of Education, 700 Governors Drive, Pierre SD 57501-2291. Deadlines vary by school.

TENNESSEE

Minority Teaching Fellows Program. This program is a forgivable loan program designed to encourage Tennessee residents from minority groups to pursue a teaching career. Awardees can receive a $5000 loan each year for up to four years. One year of the award will be forgiven for every year spent teaching. Otherwise, the award will be repaid as a loan. Applicants must be in the top quarter of their high school class and must submit a statement of intent, test scores, and transcripts with the application. The deadline is May 15 each year that funding is available.

Further information and application forms are available from Michael C. Roberts, Tennessee Student Assistance Corporation, 404 James Robertson Parkway, Suite 1950, Nashville TN 37343.

Ned McWherter Scholars Program. This program is intended to encourage Tennessee residents with high academic ability to attend Tennessee colleges. The award pays up to $6000 per year for up to four years for attendance at a college in Tennessee. Only high school seniors may apply. Students are eligible for the award if they have a cumulative grade point average of 3.5 or higher and have scored in the top five percent on the ACT or SAT.

Applications are available from the Tennessee Student Assistance Corporation, Suite 1950, Parkway Towers, 404 James Robertson Parkway, Nashville, Tennessee 37243. Deadline for applications is February 15.

Tennessee Student Assistance Award Program. This program aids Tennessee residents who attend an approved college or university in Tennessee. Awards range up to $2682 per year. Eligibility is based on financial need. It is necessary to file the Free Application for Federal Student Aid (FAFSA).

Application forms are available from high school guidance offices and college financial aid offices in Tennessee. The application deadline is May 1.

Tennessee Teaching Scholars Program. This program provides forgivable loans for college juniors, seniors, and post-bachelor students with a minimum GPA of 2.75 who have enrolled in an education program in Tennessee. Students must commit to teach in a Tennessee public school for one year for each year of the award. Loans range from $1000 to $3000.

Application forms are available from the Tennessee Student

Assistance Corporation (TSAC), Suite 1950, Parkway Towers, 404 James Robertson Parkway, Nashville, Tennessee 37243.

TEXAS

Scholarship Programs for Nursing Students. The Texas Higher Education Coordinating Board provides numerous scholarships for programs leading to LVN, ADN, and BSN degrees for students meeting various criteria, including Texas residents from rural counties, students at colleges in non-metropolitan counties, members of minority groups, and unlicensed nurses or LVNs advanced degrees leading to licensure or advanced nursing degrees.

Application forms and further information may be obtained from the Texas Higher Education Coordinating Board, PO Box 12788, Capitol Station, Austin TX 78711-2788.

State Scholarship Program for Ethnic Recruitment. This program aids minority students whose ethnic group constitutes less than 40 percent of the enrollment at the institution in which the recipient enrolls. Freshmen and first-time transfer students enrolling in a four-year public college or university in Texas are eligible on the basis of financial need and grade point average. The awards range up to $2000.

An application form may be obtained from the Grants Director, Texas Higher Education Coordinating Board, Tuition Exemption, P.O. Box 12788, Capitol Station, Austin, TX 78711-2788.

State Student Incentive Grant (SSIG). This grant aids residents and nonresidents attending public colleges or universities in Texas. Students must be enrolled at least half-time and show financial need. Students receiving a Tuition Equalization Grant may also qualify for up to $1250 in State Student Incentive Grant funds.

To apply, contact the Texas Higher Education Coordinating Board, Tuition Exemption, P.O. Box 12788, Capitol Station, Austin, TX 78711-2788.

State Tuition Exemption Program: Veterans and Dependents. This program of tuition and fee exemption at public colleges and universities in Texas aids veterans who have been honorably discharged and the dependents of veterans who have been honorably discharged or killed in the line of duty. The veteran must have been a resident of Texas at the time of his or her entry into the service. The award recipient must have exhausted his or her federal education benefits.

Contact the Grants Director, Texas Higher Education Coordinating Board, Tuition Exemption, P.O. Box 12788, Capitol Station, Austin, TX 78711-2788.

Students from Other Nations of the American Hemisphere. This provides exemption from tuition for certain students residing in Texas who are citizens of another country of the Americas. The student must attend public college in Texas. Each recipient must be scholastically qualified.

To apply, obtain an application form and additional information from the Texas Higher Education Coordinating Board, Tuition Exemption, P.O. Box 12788, Capitol Station, Austin, TX 78711-2788.

Texas Outstanding Rural Scholar Forgiveness Loan. This is a forgivable loan for use at Texas institutions

for Texas residents who will pursue a health-related career in rural Texas. Applicants need a sponsoring rural community to nominate and apply for student. Graduates must work one year for the sponsoring community for each award received. This is award is renewable based on merit. Deadlines are the third Fridays in September, January, and May.

Contact the ORS Program Administrator, Center for Rural Health Initiatives, PO Box 1708, Austin TX 78767-1708.

Texas Public Educational Grant. This renewable grant aids students currently enrolled in a public college or university in Texas. Eligibility is based on need; the amount of each award is determined by the financial aid office of each institution. Texas residence is not necessary. Deadlines vary.

Application forms may be obtained from the Texas Higher Education Coordinating Board, Tuition Exemption, P.O. Box 12788, Capitol Station, Austin, TX 78711-2788.

Texas State Tuition Exemption Program: Highest-Ranking High School Graduate. This award aids the highest-ranking graduate of each accredited high school within the state. Eligible recipients must attend a public college or university within Texas. The award exempts the student from certain tuition charges for the first two semesters following graduation from high school.

Contact Grants Director, Texas Higher Education Coordinating Board, Tuition Exemption, P.O. Box 12788, Capitol Station, Austin, TX 78711-2788. Deadlines vary.

Tuition and Fee Exemption for Blind or Deaf Students. This program aids certain blind or deaf

students by exempting them from payment of tuition and fees at public colleges and universities. To be eligible, a student must be a Texas resident and present certification of deafness or blindness. The program is renewable.

Contact the Grants Director, Texas Higher Education Coordinating Board, Tuition Exemption, P.O. Box 12788, Capitol Station, Austin, TX 78711-2788. Deadlines vary from college to college.

Tuition and Fee Exemption for Children of Disabled Firemen and Peace Officers. This program aids children of deceased or disabled firemen, peace officers, custodial employees of the Department of Corrections, or game wardens whose death or disability occurred in the line of duty. Recipients must attend a college in Texas. Candidates must apply before their 21st birthday.

Contact the Grant Program Director, Texas Higher Education Coordinating Board, Tuition Exemption, P.O. Box 12788, Capitol Station, Austin, TX 78711 2788 for application information and further details.

Tuition and Fee Exemption for Children of Prisoners of War or Persons Missing in Action. This renewable tuition and fee exemption aids Texas residents who are the children of either prisoners of war (POW) or veterans missing in action (MIA). Recipients must attend a public college or university within Texas. Students must apply before their 21st birthday.

Contact the Grants Director, Texas Higher Education Coordinating Board, Tuition Exemption, P.O. Box 12788, Capitol Station, Austin, TX 78711-2788.

Tuition and Fee Exemption for Firemen Enrolled in Fire Science

Courses. This exemption from tuition and laboratory fees assists fire fighters enrolled in fire science courses as part of a fire science curriculum at publicly supported colleges and universities. Texas residency is not required. This is a one-time award.

Application forms and further information may be obtained from Texas Higher Education Coordinating Board, Tuition Exemption, P.O. Box 12788, Capitol Station, Austin, TX 78711-2788

Tuition Equalization Grant (TEG). This program aids Texas residents attending independent colleges or universities within the state. Recipients must be enrolled at least half-time, must show financial need, and must not be enrolled in a religious degree program or receiving an athletic scholarship. The amount of this renewable award varies according to need up to a maximum of $2640.

To apply, Grants Director, Texas Higher Education Coordinating Board, Tuition Exemption, P.O. Box 12788, Capitol Station, Austin, TX 78711-2788. Deadlines vary by institution.

UTAH

Educationally Disadvantaged Program. This program aids educationally disadvantaged residents of Utah attending a public institution within the state. Students must demonstrate financial need and must be making satisfactory progress in their studies. Awards are renewable, provided that the student maintains good academic standing.

Contact the financial aid office of the college you plan to attend for information about applying.

State Student Incentive Grant. This program aids residents of Utah with substantial financial need. Awards are renewable and range up to $2500 per academic year.

This program is administered independently by the colleges in the state. Contact the college you plan to attend for application forms and deadlines.

Tuition Waiver. This program aids residents of Utah attending eligible institutions within the state. Awards range from partial to full tuition waivers, depending on a student's financial need and on the institution's policies. A limited number of waivers are also available to nonresidents. Awards are renewable, provided that the student maintains good academic standing.

Contact the financial aid office of the college you plan to attend for information about applying. Deadlines vary by institution.

Utah Career Teaching Scholarships. This program makes available two types of awards to Utah residents in teacher education programs within the state. Recipients must agree to teach in Utah after the completion of certification or to repay the amount of the award. The basic award covers the cost of tuition and fees per academic year. The second type of award is a $3000 stipend plus the cost of tuition and fees. Awards are renewable and up to 365 scholarships are offered annually.

This program is administered independently by the colleges in the state. The deadline for applying is March 30. Contact the financial aid office at the college or university you plan to attend to obtain an application form.

VERMONT

Vermont Incentive Grants. These renewable grants aid undergraduates who are Vermont residents and U.S. citizens with financial need. The maximum grant per academic year for students is $5200.

Contact the Vermont Student Assistance Corporation, Champlain Mill, P.O. Box 2000, Winooski, Vermont 05404-2000. The deadline for applying is March 31.

Vermont Non-Degree Student Grant Program. These renewable grants aid Vermont residents enrolled in nondegree programs at colleges, vocational centers, and in high school adult courses. Applicants must demonstrate financial need. A student can receive funds for a maximum of two enrollment periods per year.

To apply, request an application from the Vermont Student Assistance Corporation, Champlain Mill, P.O. Box 2000, Winooski, Vermont 05404-2000.

Vermont Part-Time Student Grants. These grants aid undergraduates enrolled at any approved postsecondary institution in program who are taking fewer than twelve credits per semester. Recipients must be Vermont residents with financial need.

To apply, obtain the Financial Aid Packet for Vermont Students from your high school guidance office or college financial aid office. The application, as well as additional information, may be obtained by writing to the Vermont Student Assistance Corporation, Champlain Mill, P.O. Box 2000, Winooski, Vermont 05404-2601.

VIRGINIA

Granville P. Meade Scholarship.
The will of the late Granville P. Meade provided an endowment, the income from which is to be used in awarding scholarships on a competitive basis to qualified Virginia residents who are Virginians by birth and plan to attend a Virginia college or university. No new applicants will be accepted until 1997. Those students currently enrolled in the program will continue to receive funding.

For further information, contact the Office of Student Financial Aid, Virginia Council of Higher Education for Virginia, James Monroe Building, Tenth Floor, 101 North Fourteenth Street, Richmond, Virginia 23219.

Lee-Jackson Foundation Scholarship. The Lee Jackson Foundation of Charlottesville perpetuates the memory of the exemplary character and soldierly virtues of Generals Robert E. Lee and Thomas J. "Stonewall" Jackson by awarding one-time college scholarships of $1000 each for outstanding essays that demonstrate an appreciation of these virtues. Any student who is classified as a senior or junior in a Virginia public or private high school may apply. Consideration will be given to the applicant's good standing in his or her school.

Applications for this scholarship can be obtained from high school principals in late September. Persons interested may file their application and essay with the division superintendent in the county or city of their residence by February 3.

National Science Scholars Program.
This program awards scholarships to high school seniors who have demonstrated outstanding academic achievement in the physical, life, or computer sciences or mathematics or engineering during their secondary school education. The amount of the award is based on appropriations. Scholarships may be renewed for an additional four years if the student maintains full-time status in one of the areas named above and meets the postsecondary institution's definition of satisfactory academic progress.

Applications for this scholarship can be obtained from high school principals in mid-September. Applications must be sent to the State Council of Higher Education for Virginia, James Monroe Building, 101 North Fourteenth Street, Richmond, Virginia 23219 by October 15.

Undergraduate Student Financial Assistance Program. This is a need-based grant designed to assist minority Virginia students in attending state-supported colleges and universities on at least a half-time basis. Recipients must be domiciliary residents of Virginia. The minimum grant is $200 for any one term of undergraduate study and is renewable. Deadlines vary by school.

For more information, contact the financial aid office at the school you plan to attend.

Virginia College Scholarship Assistance Program (CSAP). The CSAP provides renewable grants of between $400 and $2000 to undergraduates with financial need who are enrolled for at least 6 credit hours at an approved public or private college or university within the state. Recipients must be domiciliary residents of Virginia. They may not be enrolled in a program of religious training or theological education.

To apply, contact the financial aid office at the Virginia college or university you plan to attend. Deadlines vary by institution.

Virginia Transfer Grant Program (VTGP). The VTGP provides aid for minority Virginia residents enrolled at a four-year college or university in Virginia. Recipients must be domiciliary residents of Virginia, must meet minimum merit criteria, and must qualify for entry as first-time transfer students. The grant is for up to full tuition and mandatory fees.

To apply, contact the financial aid office at the college or university you wish to attend. Deadlines vary by institution.

Virginia Tuition Assistance Grant Program (TAGP). The TAGP aids undergraduate, graduate, and first-professional-degree students attending an approved private college or university within the state, regardless of financial need. Recipients must be domiciliary residents of Virginia and must be enrolled full-time. This award may not be used for religious study.

Application forms are available from financial aid offices at participating private colleges and universities in Virginia. Deadlines for applying vary by institution.

WASHINGTON

Educational Opportunity Grant.
This program provides renewable awards to financially needy students who have completed an associate degree or its equivalent to help them to complete their four-year degree at an eligible institution that has enrollment capacity. Recipients must demonstrate sufficient financial need, must reside in one of twelve coun-

ties, and be unable to relocate. Some 200 awards are currently available at $2500 each. The deadline for applying is June 1. For more information, contact Barbara Theiss, Program Manager, Higher Education Coordinating Board, 917 Lakeridge Way, P.O. Box 43430, Olympia, Washington 98504-3430.

Health Professional Loan Repayment and Scholarship Program.
The purpose of this program is to encourage eligible health-care professionals to serve in shortage areas by providing financial support in the form of conditional scholarships to attend school or loan repayment if the participant renders health-care service in medically underserved areas or professional shortage areas within Washington State for no less than three years. Scholarship recipients receive payment from the program for the purpose of paying educational costs incurred while enrolled in a program of health professional training leading to licensure in Washington State. Recipients who do not provide service in a health professional shortage area in Washington State are required to repay the award plus penalty and interest. Awards may be renewed for up to five years for eligible participants. Applications are available in mid-January. The deadline for applying is April 1.

To obtain an application form, contact Kathy McVay, Program Manager, Higher Education Coordinating Board, 917 Lakeridge Way, P.O. Box 43430, Olympia, Washington 98504-3430.

State of Washington Need Grant Program. This program aids residents of Washington attending institutions within the state.

Recipients must have financial need and may be enrolled full-time or part-time. Students with dependents can receive a dependent-care allowance. Students pursuing a degree in theology are not eligible.

The maximum award is for ten semesters or fifteen quarters. Some 42,000 individual awards are currently available.

For further information, contact Terri May, Program Manager, Higher Education Coordinating Board, 917 Lakeridge Way, P.O. Box 43430, Olympia, Washington 98504-3430.

State Work Study. This program provides on- and off-campus employment opportunities to part-time and full-time students. Awards are based on financial need demonstrated through the FAFSA form. The program's purpose is to assist students in finding employment related to their academic pursuits or career goals. Preference is given to Washington residents and applicants must be over 18. For more information, students should contact the financial aid office at the college or university they plan to attend.

Washington Scholars. This program provides renewable scholarships to three high school seniors from each of the state's legislative districts. Applicants must be nominated by their high school principals and be in the top 1 percent of their graduating class.

Recipients must maintain a minimum 3.3 grade point average. For more information, contact Ann McLendon, Program Administrator, Higher Education Coordinating Board, 917 Lakeridge Way, P.O. Box 43430, Olympia, Washington 98504-3430.

WEST VIRGINIA

Tuition and Fee Waiver Program.
This program aids students attending public colleges or universities within West Virginia. The renewable award is granted to those with financial need and outstanding academic backgrounds. The award covers tuition, registration, higher education resources fees, and the faculty improvement fee. State residence is not required.

Contact the financial aid office of the college you plan to attend for information. Deadlines vary by institution.

Underwood-Smith Teacher Scholarship Program. This is a state-funded student aid program designed to enable and encourage outstanding high school graduates to pursue teaching careers at the preschool, elementary, or secondary level. Undergraduate and graduate scholarships range up to $5000 per academic year and are awarded on the basis of academic qualifications and interest in teaching.

To qualify for this program, a student must be a West Virginia resident and must have graduated or be about to graduate in the top 10 percent of his or her high school class, score in the top 10 percent statewide on the ACT, or have a cumulative grade point average of 3.25 after the successful completion of two years of course work at an approved institution. The applicant must also be enrolled or accepted for enrollment at a West Virginia institution of higher education as a full-time student in a course of study leading to certification as a teacher at the preschool, elementary, or secondary level. Recipients must agree to teach at the public preschool, elementary, or secondary level in West Virginia for two years for each year of scholarship assistance received. The deadline for applying is April 1. For additional information, contact the Underwood-Smith Teacher Scholarship Program, Central Office of the State College and University Systems, P.O. Box 4007, Charleston, West Virginia 25364-4007.

West Virginia Higher Education Grant Program. This program aids residents of West Virginia attending an approved two-year or four-year institution in West Virginia or Pennsylvania. Recipients must be enrolled full-time, show financial need, and have an acceptable level of academic performance. Awards range from $350 to $2136 per academic year.

To apply, complete and file the Free Application for Federal Student Aid (FAFSA). The application deadline is March 1 for priority consideration. For more information, contact the West Virginia Higher Education Grant Program, P.O. Box 4007, Charleston, West Virginia 25364-4007.

WISCONSIN

Minority Retention Grant. This $2500 scholarship provides financial assistance to Wisconsin residents who are African-American, Native American, Hispanic, or former citizens of Laos, Vietnam, or Cambodia. Recipients must enroll in a Wisconsin four-year college or a vocational school.

Contact the financial aid office of any university, college or technical college in Wisconsin for further information.

Minority Teacher Loan Program. Under this program, forgivable loans are made available to Wisconsin residents from minority groups who are juniors or seniors majoring in education at a Wisconsin colleges and university. Recipients may borrow up to $2500 per academic year. Loans are forgiven at a rate of twenty-five percent of the amount borrowed for each year of employment as a teacher in an eligible Wisconsin school district. Repayment of unforgiven loans is required.

Interested students should contact the financial aid office of the Wisconsin college where they are enrolled.

Talent Incentive Program. This program of awards of $600-$1,800 assists residents of Wisconsin who have substantial financial need and are attending a public or private institution in Wisconsin. Recipients must meet specific income criteria and be deemed economically disadvantaged. Awards are renewable for up to ten semesters if the student remains in good academic standing.

Additional information is available from the Program Office, Wisconsin Educational Opportunity, Suite 204, 101 West Pleasant Street, Milwaukee WI 53212.

Visual and Hearing Impaired Program. These grants are available to residents of Wisconsin who are legally deaf or blind. If the handicap prevents the student from attending a Wisconsin college, the grant may be used at an out-of-state college that specializes in teaching the blind or deaf. Awards range up to $1800 per academic year and are based on financial need.

For more information, contact the Wisconsin Higher Educational Aid Board, P.O. Box 7885, Madison WI 53707-7885.

Wisconsin Academic Excellence Scholarship. The school board of each public secondary school district and the governing body of each private high school will nominate the graduating senior who has the highest grade point average from each Wisconsin high school. Scholars choosing to attend an institution within the University of Wisconsin System, a participating private nonprofit college or university in Wisconsin, or a Wisconsin Vocational, Technical, and Adult Education District school are exempt from all tuition and related fees for up to four years if the recipient continues to be enrolled full-time and maintains a 3.0 grade point average. The total value of the scholarship at other non-profit Wisconsin institutions is up to $2250 depending upon the institution attended and the funds available.

For more information, students should contact their high school guidance office or the Wisconsin Higher Education Aid Board, P.O. Box 7885, Madison WI 53707-7885.

Wisconsin Department of Veterans Affairs Retraining Grants. Renewable awards of up to $3000 are available to veterans, unmarried spouses of deceased veterans, or dependents of deceased veterans. Recipients must be residents of Wisconsin and attend an institution in Wisconsin. Veterans who receive the grant must be recently unemployed and show financial need.

Award inquiries should be addressed to Retraining Grants,

Wisconsin Department of Veterans Affairs, P.O. Box 7843, Madison WI 53707-7843.

Wisconsin Higher Education Grants (WHEG). These grants aid residents of Wisconsin attending the University of Wisconsin or public vocational, technical, or adult education institutions in Wisconsin. Recipients must be enrolled at least half-time and must demonstrate financial need. The maximum award is $1800 per academic year and is renewable for up to five years.

The application form is available from high school guidance offices, and Wisconsin college financial aid offices.

Wisconsin National Guard Tuition Grant. A renewable award of half the tuition at a qualifying school, but not to exceed half of the maximum undergraduate tuition charged by University of Wisconsin-Madison, is available to active members of the Wisconsin National Guard.

Additional information is available from Linda McDermott, Wisconsin National Guard, P.O. Box 14587, Madison WI 53714-0587.

Wisconsin Native American Student Grant. This program assists residents of Wisconsin who are at least one-quarter Native American. Recipients must attend an approved Wisconsin college or university. The maximum award is $1100 per academic year, renewable for up to five years of full-time study.

Application forms are available from high school guidance offices and Wisconsin college financial aid offices.

Wisconsin Tuition Grant Program. This program aids Wisconsin residents attending an eligible

nonprofit college or university in Wisconsin that charges more than the University of Wisconsin-Madison. Recipients must be enrolled at least half-time and demonstrate financial need. The maximum award is $2172 per academic year. Awards are renewable if the student remains in good academic standing.

Application forms are available from high school guidance offices and Wisconsin college financial aid offices.

Wisconsin Veterans Part-time Study Reimbursement Grant. This grant of up to $1100 is open only to Wisconsin veterans and dependents of deceased Wisconsin veterans.

Contact Reimbursement Grant, Wisconsin Department of Veterans Affairs, 30 West Mifflin Street, Madison WI 53707-7843 for more details.

WYOMING

County Commissioners' Scholarships. These one-time scholarships aid Wyoming high school graduates attending a public college or university within the state. Scholarships are generally for the entire amount of tuition and fees, are awarded on the basis of academic achievement, and are for undergraduate study only. Recipients must maintain a minimum 2.5 GPA.

Contact the Board of County Commissioners in your county of residence for application information.

President's Honor Scholarships. These scholarships aid Wyoming high school seniors who have demonstrated high scholastic achievement and qualities of leadership and who will be attending a public college or university within the state. Scholarships are for the entire

amount of tuition and fees. Recipients must maintain a minimum 2.5 GPA.

The deadline for applying is October 1. For information, students should contact their high school guidance office.

State Student Incentive Grant. This grant aids Wyoming residents attending participating colleges or universities within the state. Eligibility is based on financial need. Recipients are selected by the financial aid officers of their colleges. Grants range up to $2000 per academic year for a maximum of four years.

Contact the financial aid office at the college you plan to attend for application forms. The deadline for applying is March 1.

Superior Student in Education Loan Fund. This scholarship is available to Wyoming high school graduates who have demonstrated a high level of academic achievement and plan to pursue a teaching career in Wyoming public schools. Awards are for the amount of tuition and fees at a Wyoming institution. Recipients must maintain a minimum 3.0 GPA.

Applications are available from the College of Education at the University of Wyoming.

Vietnam Veterans Award. Wyoming veterans in active service with the U.S. armed forces between August 5, 1964, and May 7, 1975, who received a Vietnam service medal between those dates may be eligible for free tuition at the University of Wyoming or at any of the state's community colleges.

For more information, contact the financial aid office at the University of Wyoming or any state community college.

Freshman-Year

Out-of-Pocket Costs:

Looking Beyond the

Sticker Price

"It's important to remember that an investment in higher education is an investment for a lifetime. A wise choice will return far more than just the dollar value of the initial investment."

Michael Steidel
Director of Admissions
Carnegie Mellon University

The sticker-price cost of a private college education falls in the range of $12,000 to $28,000 annually for tuition, room and board. On average, public college education is about half this. However, your actual cost depends upon your financial aid award. No matter what your family's income level or your academic record, you likely are eligible for some form of financial aid. That's why it's important to look beyond the "sticker price" of attending the college of your choice and apply for financial aid before ruling out a college based on cost.

Your Expected Family Contribution is determined by a formulation of need based on a your family's income and assets. However, whether you demonstrate 100 percent financial need or hardly any, you can look to the Financial Aid Office of the college that has accepted you to work with you to create a financial aid package that addresses your unique situation and makes your college education an investment that you can afford.

Whether it's in the form of scholarships, awards, grants, loans or student employment, most colleges endeavor to provide financial assistance to admitted freshmen that will enable these selected students to enroll at their institution. The

Financial Aid Offices in any college will guide you to the financial aid options available from a variety of sources—state and federal government programs, friends of the College, alumni, and the College itself. The actual amount of a financial aid package is determined not only from the evaluation of your personal financial situation, but also is influenced by the unique financial resources, policies, and practices of each institution. Financial aid packages vary significantly from school to school.

To help shed some light on the typical patterns of financial aid by colleges, we have prepared the following table. This table can help you to better understand financial aid practices in general, form realistic expectations about the amounts of aid that might be provided by specific colleges or universities, and prepare for meaningful discussions with the financial aid officers at colleges you are considering. The data appearing in the table have been supplied by the schools themselves and are also shown in the individual college profiles.

Published costs are based on the total of full-time tuition and mandatory fees for the 1997–98 academic year (or estimated 1997–98) or for the 1996–97 academic year if 1997–98 figures were not available. More information about these costs, as well as the costs of room and board and the year for which they are current, can be found in the individual college profiles. For institutions that have two or more tuition rates for different categories of students or types of programs, the lowest rate is used in figuring the cost. If the published cost figure reported in the table includes room and board, that total is marked with an asterisk (*).

The colleges are listed alphabetically by name. An "NR" in any individual column indicates that the applicable data element was "Not Reported."

The table is divided into five columns of information for each college:

A. *Published tuition and fees:* not including room and board, unless indicated by an asterisk (*).

B. *Room and board:* the costs of room and board. If a school has room and board costs that vary according the type of accommodation and meal plan, either the lowest figures are represented, or the figures are for the most common room arrangement and a full meal plan. If a school has only housing arrangements, a dagger appears to the right of the number. An *"NA"* will appear in this column if no college-owned or operated housing facilities are offered at all.

C. *Percent of freshmen who applied for aid:* calculated from the total number of new, full-time freshmen enrolled in fall 1996.

D. *Average aid package for freshmen:* the average dollar amount from all sources, including *gift aid* (scholarships and grants) and *self-help* (jobs and loans), awarded to aided freshmen. Note that this aid package may exceed tuition and fees if the average aid package included coverage of room and board expenses.

E. *Average cost after aid:* average aid package subtracted from published costs (tuition, fees, room and board) to produce what the average family will have to pay.

Because personal situations vary widely, it is very important to note that an individual's aid package can be quite different from the averages. Moreover, the data shown for each school can fluctuate widely from year to year, depending on the number of applicants, the amount of need to be met, and the financial resources and policies of the college. Our intent in presenting this table is to provide you with useful facts and figures that can serve as general guidelines in your pursuit of financial aid. We caution you to use the data only as a jumping-off point for further investigation and analysis, not as a means to rank or select colleges.

After you have narrowed down the colleges in which you are interested based on academic and personal criteria, we recommend that you carefully study this table. From it, you can develop a list of questions for financial aid officers at the colleges you are seriously considering attending. Here are just a few questions you might want to ask:

- What specifically are the types and sources of the aid provided to freshmen at this school?

- What factors does this college consider in determining whether a financial aid applicant is qualified for its need-based aid programs?

- How does the college determine the combination of types of aid that make up an individual's package?

- How are non-need awards treated: as a part of the aid package or as a part of the parental/family contribution?

- Does this school "guarantee" financial aid and, if so, how is its policy implemented? Guaranteed aid means that by policy, 100 percent of need is met for all students judged to have need. Implementation determines *how* need is met and varies widely from school to school. For example, grade point average may determine the proportioning of scholarship, loan, and work-study aid. Rules for freshmen may be different from those for upperclass students.

- To what degree is the admission process "need-blind"? Need-blindness means that admission decisions are made without regard to the student's need for financial aid.

- What are the norms and practices for upperclass students? Our table presents information on *freshman* financial aid only; however, the financial aid office should be able and willing to provide you with comparable figures for upperclass students. A college might offer a wonderful package for the freshman year, then leave you mostly on your own to fund the remaining three years. Or the school may provide a higher proportion of scholarship money for freshmen, then rebalance its aid packages to contain more self-help aid (loans and work-study) in upperclass years. There is an assumption that, all other factors being equal, students who have settled into the pattern of college time management can handle more work-study hours than freshmen. Grade point average, tuition increases, changes in parental financial circumstances, and other factors may also affect the redistribution.

Freshman-Year Out-of-Pocket Costs: Looking Beyond the Sticker Price

This chart presents average costs. Actual costs may vary.

	Published tuition and fees	Room and board	Percent of freshmen who applied for aid	Average aid package for freshmen	Average cost after aid
Abilene Christian University, Abilene, TX	$9080	$2340	90%	$7737	$3683
Academy of Art College, San Francisco, CA	$12,435	$5000†	48%	$3300	$14,135
Adams State College, Alamosa, CO	$1958	$4640	94%	$5622	$976
Adelphi University, Garden City, NY	$14,000	$6520	85%	$12,950	$7570
Adrian College, Adrian, MI	$12,350	$3670	94%	$12,051	$3969
The Advertising Arts College, San Diego, CA	$8650	NA	NR	NR	NR
Agnes Scott College, Decatur, GA	$14,460	$6020	87%	$13,392	$7088
Alabama Agricultural and Mechanical University, Normal, AL	$2076	$2930	90%	$4233	$773
Alabama State University, Montgomery, AL	$2090	$3112	90%	NR	NR
Alaska Bible College, Glennallen, AK	$3790	$3570	83%	$2441	$4919
Alaska Pacific University, Anchorage, AK	$8480	$4150	NR	$7332	$5298
Albany College of Pharmacy of Union University, Albany, NY	$10,213	$4800	NR	NR	NR
Albany State University, Albany, GA	$1860	$3180	85%	$5743	$0
Albertson College of Idaho, Caldwell, ID	$15,365	$3300	NR	$11,982	$6683
Albertus Magnus College, New Haven, CT	$16,180	$5956	83%	$8199	$13,937
Albion College, Albion, MI	$16,160	$4890	82%	$13,979	$7071
Albright College, Reading, PA	$17,395	$5180	90%	$14,722	$7853
Alcorn State University, Lorman, MS	$2389	$2229	NR	$1852	$2766
Alderson-Broaddus College, Philippi, WV	$12,215	$4165	NR	$6082	$10,298
Alfred University, Alfred, NY	$18,972	$6042	95%	$18,600	$6414
Alice Lloyd College, Pippa Passes, KY	$360	$2680	100%	$7623	$0
Allegheny College, Meadville, PA	$18,720	$4670	92%	$16,363	$7027
Allegheny University of the Health Sciences, Philadelphia, PA	$4060	$4800†	82%	$3961	$4899
Allen College of Nursing, Waterloo, IA	$4041	NA	NR	NR	NR
Allentown College of St. Francis de Sales, Center Valley, PA	$11,120	$5260	90%	$8925	$7455
Allen University, Columbia, SC	$4750	$4210	NR	NR	NR
Alma College, Alma, MI	$13,823	$4905	78%	$12,385	$6343
Alvernia College, Reading, PA	$10,650	$4600	80%	$13,310	$1940
Alverno College, Milwaukee, WI	$9338	$3890	84%	$5158	$8070
American Baptist College of American Baptist Theological Seminary, Nashville, TN	$2530	$752†	100%	NR	NR
The American College, Los Angeles, CA	$10,725	$6375†	NR	$6625	$10,475
The American College, Atlanta, GA	$9855	$3900†	36%	$9462	$4293
American Conservatory of Music, Chicago, IL	$8575	NA	0%	$0	$8575
American Indian College of the Assemblies of God, Inc., Phoenix, AZ	$3280	$3150	NR	NR	NR
American International College, Springfield, MA	$10,926	$5310	89%	$9420	$6816
American University, Washington, DC	$17,744	$4366	64%	$16,065	$6045
American University of Puerto Rico, Bayamón, PR	$3070	NA	97%	NR	NR
Amherst College, Amherst, MA	$22,007	$5820	56%	$20,527	$7300
Anderson College, Anderson, SC	$9475	$4145	NR	$2728	$10,892
Anderson University, Anderson, IN	$12,040	$3980	90%	$13,223	$2797
Andrews University, Berrien Springs, MI	$11,577	$3510	NR	NR	NR

*NA = not applicable; NR = not reported; * = includes room and board; † = room only.*

Freshman-Year Out-of-Pocket Costs: Looking Beyond the Sticker Price

This chart presents average costs. Actual costs may vary.

	Published tuition and fees	Room and board	Percent of freshmen who applied for aid	Average aid package for freshmen	Average cost after aid
Angelo State University, San Angelo, TX	$2006	$3808	NR	$3850	$1964
Anna Maria College, Paxton, MA	$11,780	$5128	NR	$13,833	$3075
Antioch College, Yellow Springs, OH	$17,832	$3796	NR	NR	NR
Appalachian Bible College, Bradley, WV	$5510	$3010	NR	NR	NR
Appalachian State University, Boone, NC	$1664	$2840	61%	$5455	$0
Aquinas College, Grand Rapids, MI	$12,574	$4198	91%	$12,367	$4405
Arizona Bible College, Phoenix, AZ	$5886	$1728†	94%	$4735	$2879
Arizona State University, Tempe, AZ	$2009	$4287	NR	$6591	$0
Arkansas State University, Jonesboro, AR	$1970	$2620	83%	$2300	$2290
Arkansas Tech University, Russellville, AR	$2007	$2732	NR	$3760	$979
Arlington Baptist College, Arlington, TX	$2490	$1500†	100%	$1032	$2958
Armstrong Atlantic State University, Savannah, GA	$1836	$3921	NR	$2500	$3257
Art Academy of Cincinnati, Cincinnati, OH	$10,925	NA	83%	NR	NR
Art Center College of Design, Pasadena, CA	$16,200	NA	NR	$7483	$8717
Art Institute of Boston, Boston, MA	$11,170	$7100	78%	$7461	$10,809
Art Institute of Southern California, Laguna Beach, CA	$10,500	NA	72%	$5486	$5014
Asbury College, Wilmore, KY	$11,225	$3150	NR	$8396	$5979
Ashland University, Ashland, OH	$12,900	$5001	97%	$10,987	$6914
Assumption College, Worcester, MA	$13,845	$5410	NR	NR	NR
Atlanta Christian College, East Point, GA	$6002	$3170	NR	NR	NR
Atlanta College of Art, Atlanta, GA	$11,900	$3750†	NR	$8249	$7401
Atlantic Union College, South Lancaster, MA	$12,000	$3900	92%	NR	NR
Auburn University, Auburn, AL	$2355	$1650†	51%	$5903	$0
Auburn University at Montgomery, Montgomery, AL	$2130	$1770†	NR	NR	NR
Audrey Cohen College, New York, NY	$8690	NA	97%	NR	NR
Augsburg College, Minneapolis, MN	$13,286	$4794	90%	$13,625	$4455
Augustana College, Rock Island, IL	$14,700	$4449	90%	$12,751	$6398
Augustana College, Sioux Falls, SD	$12,488	$3701	78%	$12,537	$3652
Augusta State University, Augusta, GA	$1800	NA	NR	$4226	$0
Austin College, Sherman, TX	$12,800	$4976	67%	$12,766	$5010
Austin Peay State University, Clarksville, TN	$2108	$2870	NR	$6200	$0
Averett College, Danville, VA	$11,850	$4150	NR	NR	NR
Azusa Pacific University, Azusa, CA	$13,596	$4200	74%	$11,336	$6460
Babson College, Wellesley, MA	$18,835	$5150	50%	$15,660	$8325
Baker University, Baldwin City, KS	$10,003	$4400	NR	NR	NR
Baldwin-Wallace College, Berea, OH	$12,765	$4740	NR	$10,485	$7020
Ball State University, Muncie, IN	$3188	$3952	NR	$4511	$2629
Baltimore Hebrew University, Baltimore, MD	$3620	NA	NR	NR	NR
Baptist Bible College, Springfield, MO	$2430	$3090	NR	NR	NR
Baptist Bible College of Pennsylvania, Clarks Summit, PA	$7530	$4312	NR	NR	NR
Baptist Missionary Association Theological Seminary, Jacksonville, TX	$1710	$1980†	NR	NR	NR

*NA = not applicable; NR = not reported; * = includes room and board; † = room only.*

Freshman-Year Out-of-Pocket Costs: Looking Beyond the Sticker Price

This chart presents average costs. Actual costs may vary.

	Published tuition and fees	Room and board	Percent of freshmen who applied for aid	Average aid package for freshmen	Average cost after aid
Barat College, Lake Forest, IL	$12,570	$4966	NR	NR	NR
Barber-Scotia College, Concord, NC	$5214	$3220	97%	$4233	$4201
Barclay College, Haviland, KS	$5000	$2900	96%	$4944	$2956
Bard College, Annandale-on-Hudson, NY	$21,384	$6645	65%	$19,137	$8892
Barnard College, New York, NY	$20,324	$8374	66%	$19,682	$9016
Barry University, Miami Shores, FL	$13,050	$5680	79%	$15,253	$3477
Bartlesville Wesleyan College, Bartlesville, OK	$8100	$3700	NR	NR	NR
Barton College, Wilson, NC	$8984	$4066	91%	NR	NR
Baruch College of the City University of New York, New York, NY	$3320	NA	90%	$4491	$0
Bassist College, Portland, OR	$8990	$2775†	59%	$8000	$3765
Bates College, Lewiston, ME	$27,415*	NA	56%	$18,021	$9394
Bayamón Central University, Bayamón, PR	$3230	NA	NR	NR	NR
Baylor University, Waco, TX	$9428	$4433	73%	$7578	$6283
Bay Path College, Longmeadow, MA	$11,240	$6350	NR	NR	NR
Beaver College, Glenside, PA	$15,840	$6520	NR	$14,890	$7470
Becker College–Leicester Campus, Leicester, MA	$10,130	$4890	NR	NR	NR
Becker College–Worcester Campus, Worcester, MA	$10,130	$4890	95%	$5950	$9070
Belhaven College, Jackson, MS	$9370	$3380	92%	$7654	$5096
Bellarmine College, Louisville, KY	$10,320	$3480	82%	$7932	$5868
Bellevue University, Bellevue, NE	$3650	NA	76%	NR	NR
Bellin College of Nursing, Green Bay, WI	$8191	NA	NR	$0	$8191
Belmont Abbey College, Belmont, NC	$10,408	$5346	84%	$5613	$10,141
Belmont University, Nashville, TN	$10,300	$3890	NR	$5553	$8637
Beloit College, Beloit, WI	$18,230	$3980	92%	$14,776	$7434
Bemidji State University, Bemidji, MN	$2925	$3300	NR	$5398	$827
Benedict College, Columbia, SC	$6820	$3620	NR	NR	NR
Benedictine College, Atchison, KS	$10,650	$4386	98%	$10,459	$4577
Benedictine University, Lisle, IL	$11,790	$4470	85%	$9632	$6628
Bennett College, Greensboro, NC	$7615	$3375	88%	$7500	$3490
Bennington College, Bennington, VT	$25,800*	NA	80%	$20,400	$5400
Bentley College, Waltham, MA	$15,745	$6480	77%	$13,020	$9205
Berea College, Berea, KY	$195	$3168	100%	$17,023	$0
Berklee College of Music, Boston, MA	$14,340	$7650	47%	$12,489	$9501
Berry College, Mount Berry, GA	$9678	$4380	100%	$12,200	$1858
Bethany College, Lindsborg, KS	$9980	$2690	94%	$10,188	$2482
Bethany College, Bethany, WV	$17,349	$5716	NR	NR	NR
Bethel College, Mishawaka, IN	$10,350	$3300	89%	$6504	$7146
Bethel College, North Newton, KS	$9900	$4030	88%	$7385	$6545
Bethel College, St. Paul, MN	$13,200	$4690	88%	$12,048	$5842
Bethel College, McKenzie, TN	$7240	$3660	NR	NR	NR
Beth-El College of Nursing and Health Sciences, Colorado Springs, CO	$5833	NA	40%	$5540	$293

*NA = not applicable; NR = not reported; * = includes room and board; † = room only.*

Freshman-Year Out-of-Pocket Costs: Looking Beyond the Sticker Price

This chart presents average costs. Actual costs may vary.

	Published tuition and fees	Room and board	Percent of freshmen who applied for aid	Average aid package for freshmen	Average cost after aid
Bethune-Cookman College, Daytona Beach, FL	$6780	$3874	95%	$9060	$1594
Beulah Heights Bible College, Atlanta, GA	$3280	$1300†	NR	NR	NR
Biola University, La Mirada, CA	$14,286	$4468	81%	$8317	$10,437
Birmingham-Southern College, Birmingham, AL	$13,310	$4290	72%	$10,741	$6859
Blackburn College, Carlinville, IL	$7510	$2990	98%	$7500	$3000
Black Hills State University, Spearfish, SD	$2662	$2537	83%	$2006	$3193
Bloomfield College, Bloomfield, NJ	$9250	$4650	NR	$9500	$4400
Bloomsburg University of Pennsylvania, Bloomsburg, PA	$4162	$3090	84%	$6717	$535
Bluefield College, Bluefield, VA	$9100	$4610	NR	NR	NR
Bluefield State College, Bluefield, WV	$2044	NA	NR	NR	NR
Blue Mountain College, Blue Mountain, MS	$4640	$2350	83%	$2342	$4648
Bluffton College, Bluffton, OH	$11,250	$4641	NR	$7680	$8211
Boise Bible College, Boise, ID	$4090	$3424	84%	$2103	$5411
Boise State University, Boise, ID	$2104	$3200	NR	NR	NR
Boricua College, New York, NY	$6400	NA	NR	$2863	$3537
Boston Architectural Center, Boston, MA	$5010	NA	57%	NR	NR
Boston College, Chestnut Hill, MA	$19,298	$7530	46%	$15,000	$11,828
Boston Conservatory, Boston, MA	$14,780	$6675	98%	$13,917	$7538
Boston University, Boston, MA	$22,278	$7570	71%	$17,529	$12,319
Bowdoin College, Brunswick, ME	$21,750	$6010	56%	$18,634	$9126
Bowie State University, Bowie, MD	$3102	$4410	NR	NR	NR
Bowling Green State University, Bowling Green, OH	$4190	$3914	93%	$5351	$2753
Bradford College, Bradford, MA	$15,770	$6590	69%	$16,278	$6082
Bradley University, Peoria, IL	$12,090	$4800	85%	$8100	$8790
Brandeis University, Waltham, MA	$21,917	$6910	NR	$17,566	$11,261
Brenau University, Gainesville, GA	$10,350	$6330	84%	$11,550	$5130
Brescia College, Owensboro, KY	$8400	$3456	98%	$7960	$3896
Brewton-Parker College, Mt. Vernon, GA	$5520	$2565	NR	NR	NR
Briar Cliff College, Sioux City, IA	$11,880	$4180	100%	$9119	$6941
Bridgewater College, Bridgewater, VA	$13,270	$5630	89%	$11,372	$7528
Bridgewater State College, Bridgewater, MA	$3803	$4550	80%	$4095	$4258
Brigham Young University, Provo, UT	$2630	$3805	85%	$3391	$3044
Brigham Young University–Hawaii Campus, Laie, Oahu, HI	$2665	$4900	NR	NR	NR
Brooklyn College of the City University of New York, Brooklyn, NY	$3387	NA	NR	NR	NR
Brooks Institute of Photography, Santa Barbara, CA	$14,910	NA	NR	NR	NR
Brown University, Providence, RI	$22,120	$6538	54%	$17,923	$10,735
Bryan College, Dayton, TN	$10,000	$3950	99%	$9910	$4040
Bryant and Stratton College, Cleveland, OH	$6745	$2500†	96%	$2300	$6945
Bryant College, Smithfield, RI	$13,900	$6700	NR	$11,992	$8608
Bryn Athyn College of the New Church, Bryn Athyn, PA	$4686	$3915	46%	$3170	$5431
Bryn Mawr College, Bryn Mawr, PA	$20,645	$7370	71%	$18,610	$9405

NA = not applicable; NR = not reported; * = includes room and board; † = room only.

Freshman-Year Out-of-Pocket Costs: Looking Beyond the Sticker Price

This chart presents average costs. Actual costs may vary.

	Published tuition and fees	Room and board	Percent of freshmen who applied for aid	Average aid package for freshmen	Average cost after aid
Bucknell University, Lewisburg, PA	$20,360	$5060	63%	$15,523	$9897
Buena Vista University, Storm Lake, IA	$14,458	$4125	99%	$15,467	$3116
Burlington College, Burlington, VT	$7208	NA	100%	$6800	$408
Butler University, Indianapolis, IN	$14,900	$5020	79%	$11,642	$8278
Cabrini College, Radnor, PA	$13,200	$6900	91%	$11,774	$8326
Caldwell College, Caldwell, NJ	$10,050	$5100	82%	$9502	$5648
California Baptist College, Riverside, CA	$8236	$4594	91%	$5150	$7680
California College of Arts and Crafts, San Francisco, CA	$15,052	$5300	46%	NR	NR
California Institute of Technology, Pasadena, CA	$18,216	$5478	71%	$18,385	$5309
California Institute of the Arts, Valencia, CA	$17,315	$5200	NR	NR	NR
California Lutheran University, Thousand Oaks, CA	$14,250	$5440	89%	$14,402	$5288
California Maritime Academy, Vallejo, CA	$3762	$5020	79%	$11,007	$0
California Polytechnic State University, San Luis Obispo, San Luis Obispo, CA	$2075	$4927	67%	$4164	$2838
California State Polytechnic University, Pomona, Pomona, CA	$1896	$5094	61%	$4974	$2016
California State University, Bakersfield, Bakersfield, CA	$1957	$4125	76%	$4892	$1190
California State University, Chico, Chico, CA	$2046	$4981	NR	NR	NR
California State University, Dominguez Hills, Carson, CA	$1821	$2946†	NR	$5300	$0
California State University, Fresno, Fresno, CA	$1822	$4498	77%	$5571	$749
California State University, Fullerton, Fullerton, CA	$1927	$3476†	NR	$4126	$1277
California State University, Hayward, Hayward, CA	$1800	$3009†	NR	NR	NR
California State University, Long Beach, Long Beach, CA	$1826	$5300	81%	$4000	$3126
California State University, Los Angeles, Los Angeles, CA	$1742	NA	88%	$4883	$0
California State University, Northridge, Northridge, CA	$1970	$4956	NR	$5600	$1326
California State University, Sacramento, Sacramento, CA	$2000	$4744	73%	$4645	$2099
California State University, San Bernardino, San Bernardino, CA	$2034	$4108	NR	NR	NR
California State University, San Marcos, San Marcos, CA	$1720	$2475†	NR	$4252	$0
California State University, Stanislaus, Turlock, CA	$1915	$5500	68%	$2343	$5072
California University of Pennsylvania, California, PA	$4304	$3992	86%	$5124	$3172
Calumet College of Saint Joseph, Whiting, IN	$5610	NA	68%	$3000	$2610
Calvary Bible College and Theological Seminary, Kansas City, MO	$3964	$2950	NR	$5018	$1896
Calvin College, Grand Rapids, MI	$11,680	$4160	81%	$9280	$6560
Cameron University, Lawton, OK	$1760	$2711	62%	$2200	$2271
Campbell University, Buies Creek, NC	$9513	$3550	89%	NR	NR
Canisius College, Buffalo, NY	$12,926	$5825	90%	$11,704	$7047
Capital University, Columbus, OH	$14,200	$4000	97%	$15,076	$3124
Capitol College, Laurel, MD	$9252	$2952†	88%	$10,100	$2104
Cardinal Stritch University, Milwaukee, WI	$9010	$3880	NR	NR	NR
Caribbean University, Bayamón, PR	$2800	NA	NR	NR	NR
Carleton College, Northfield, MN	$21,120	$4290	68%	$16,020	$9390
Carlow College, Pittsburgh, PA	$11,064	$4692	97%	$6196	$9560
Carnegie Mellon University, Pittsburgh, PA	$19,500	$6080	74%	$15,868	$9712

*NA = not applicable; NR = not reported; * = includes room and board; † = room only.*

Freshman-Year Out-of-Pocket Costs: Looking Beyond the Sticker Price

This chart presents average costs. Actual costs may vary.

	Published tuition and fees	Room and board	Percent of freshmen who applied for aid	Average aid package for freshmen	Average cost after aid
Carroll College, Helena, MT	$10,574	$4190	82%	$9779	$4985
Carroll College, Waukesha, WI	$13,890	$4160	NR	NR	NR
Carson-Newman College, Jefferson City, TN	$9990	$3670	94%	$6865	$6795
Carthage College, Kenosha, WI	$14,600	$4195	96%	$12,316	$6479
Cascade College, Portland, OR	$7500	$3300	NR	NR	NR
Case Western Reserve University, Cleveland, OH	$17,940	$5050	NR	$17,429	$5561
Castleton State College, Castleton, VT	$4330	$4936	81%	$7835	$1431
Catawba College, Salisbury, NC	$10,726	$4250	99%	$11,618	$3358
The Catholic University of America, Washington, DC	$16,152	$7594	81%	$15,485	$8261
Cazenovia College, Cazenovia, NY	$11,648	$5468	94%	$11,000	$6116
Cedar Crest College, Allentown, PA	$15,210	$5525	96%	$13,542	$7193
Cedarville College, Cedarville, OH	$8586	$4716	82%	$4527	$8775
Centenary College, Hackettstown, NJ	$12,598	$5600	NR	$12,355	$5843
Centenary College of Louisiana, Shreveport, LA	$10,720	$3800	98%	$9431	$5089
Center for Creative Studies—College of Art and Design, Detroit, MI	$13,276	$2600†	NR	$5974	$9902
Central Baptist College, Conway, AR	$4376	$2856	NR	$7850	$0
Central Bible College, Springfield, MO	$4750	$3200	100%	$4625	$3325
Central Christian College of the Bible, Moberly, MO	$4076	$2470	98%	NR	NR
Central College, Pella, IA	$12,304	$3808	94%	$12,545	$3567
Central Connecticut State University, New Britain, CT	$3542	$5182	41%	NR	NR
Central Methodist College, Fayette, MO	$10,220	$3960	95%	$9000	$5180
Central Michigan University, Mount Pleasant, MI	$3443	$4176	73%	$5777	$1842
Central Missouri State University, Warrensburg, MO	$2520	$3858	72%	$6000	$378
Central State University, Wilberforce, OH	$3318	$4470	95%	$8293	$0
Central Washington University, Ellensburg, WA	$2505	$4400	NR	$5705	$1200
Central Yeshiva Tomchei Tmimim-Lubavitch, Brooklyn, NY	$4800	$2300	NR	NR	NR
Centre College, Danville, KY	$14,000	$4600	78%	$12,870	$5730
Chadron State College, Chadron, NE	$1938	$2926	NR	NR	NR
Chaminade University of Honolulu, Honolulu, HI	$10,850	$5200	92%	$13,747	$2303
Chapman University, Orange, CA	$18,520	$6454	91%	$16,909	$8065
Charles R. Drew University of Medicine and Science, Los Angeles, CA	$6850	NA	100%	$3220	$3630
Charleston Southern University, Charleston, SC	$8724	$3360	NR	$8485	$3599
Chatham College, Pittsburgh, PA	$15,340	$5716	93%	$14,132	$6924
Chestnut Hill College, Philadelphia, PA	$13,148	$5772	96%	$10,560	$8360
Cheyney University of Pennsylvania, Cheyney, PA	$3923	$4351	93%	$7800	$474
Chicago State University, Chicago, IL	$2818	$4990	NR	NR	NR
Chowan College, Murfreesboro, NC	$9650	$3780	75%	$9037	$4393
Christendom College, Front Royal, VA	$10,545	$3700	NR	$7610	$6635
Christian Brothers University, Memphis, TN	$11,030	$3530	NR	$8860	$5700
Christian Heritage College, El Cajon, CA	$9600	$4395	NR	NR	NR
Christopher Newport University, Newport News, VA	$3366	$4650	NR	$5314	$2702

NA = not applicable; NR = not reported; * = includes room and board; † = room only.

Freshman-Year Out-of-Pocket Costs: Looking Beyond the Sticker Price

This chart presents average costs. Actual costs may vary.

	Published tuition and fees	Room and board	Percent of freshmen who applied for aid	Average aid package for freshmen	Average cost after aid
Cincinnati Bible College and Seminary, Cincinnati, OH	$5944	$3550	81%	$6812	$2682
Cincinnati College of Mortuary Science, Cincinnati, OH	$9075	NA	0%	$0	$9075
Circleville Bible College, Circleville, OH	$4414	$3820	97%	$6990	$1244
The Citadel, The Military College of South Carolina, Charleston, SC	$4070	$3679	NR	$6221	$1528
City College of the City University of New York, New York, NY	$3309	NA	89%	$4300	$0
Claflin College, Orangeburg, SC	$5166	$2810	96%	$6882	$1094
Claremont McKenna College, Claremont, CA	$18,460	$6510	72%	$15,100	$9870
Clarion University of Pennsylvania, Clarion, PA	$4238	$3140	NR	$3135	$4243
Clark Atlanta University, Atlanta, GA	$8830	$5170	NR	NR	NR
Clarke College, Dubuque, IA	$11,966	$4480	92%	$9945	$6501
Clarkson College, Omaha, NE	$8268	$1850†	89%	$4350	$5768
Clarkson University, Potsdam, NY	$17,843	$6064	82%	$17,350	$6557
Clark University, Worcester, MA	$20,040	$4250	77%	$14,642	$9648
Clayton College & State University, Morrow, GA	$1842	NA	99%	NR	NR
Clear Creek Baptist Bible College, Pineville, KY	$2370	$2480	100%	$1198	$3652
Clearwater Christian College, Clearwater, FL	$7300	$3500	NR	NR	NR
Cleary College, Ypsilanti, MI	$7290	NA	NR	NR	NR
Clemson University, Clemson, SC	$3112	$3136	60%	$5712	$536
Cleveland College of Jewish Studies, Beachwood, OH	$4950	NA	NR	NR	NR
Cleveland Institute of Art, Cleveland, OH	$12,676	$4650	96%	NR	NR
Cleveland Institute of Music, Cleveland, OH	$16,178	$5065	89%	NR	NR
Cleveland State University, Cleveland, OH	$3510	$4350	NR	NR	NR
Clinch Valley College of the University of Virginia, Wise, VA	$3258	$3960	NR	$4297	$2921
Coastal Carolina University, Conway, SC	$2930	$4265	NR	NR	NR
Coe College, Cedar Rapids, IA	$15,535	$4455	NR	$13,195	$6795
Cogswell Polytechnical College, Sunnyvale, CA	$7360	NA	NR	NR	NR
Coker College, Hartsville, SC	$13,400	$4551	NR	NR	NR
Colby College, Waterville, ME	$22,190	$5710	62%	$17,500	$10,400
Colby-Sawyer College, New London, NH	$16,310	$6240	90%	$13,571	$8979
Colegio Universitario del Este, Carolina, PR	$3512	NA	96%	$1740	$1772
Coleman College, La Mesa, CA	$5000	NA	90%	$4380	$620
Colgate University, Hamilton, NY	$22,770	$6110	49%	$19,539	$9341
College Misericordia, Dallas, PA	$12,880	$6050	97%	$5815	$13,115
College of Aeronautics, Flushing, NY	$8240	$3365†	88%	$9120	$2485
College of Charleston, Charleston, SC	$3190	$3340	NR	NR	NR
College of Insurance, New York, NY	$13,090	$7650	100%	$17,034	$3706
College of Mount St. Joseph, Cincinnati, OH	$11,350	$4950	91%	$12,500	$3800
College of Mount Saint Vincent, Riverdale, NY	$13,000	$6240	92%	NR	NR
The College of New Jersey, Trenton, NJ	$4446	$5544	85%	NR	NR
College of New Rochelle, New Rochelle, NY	$11,100	$5700	NR	$12,870	$3930
College of Notre Dame, Belmont, CA	$14,400	$6200	76%	$18,237	$2363

*NA = not applicable; NR = not reported; * = includes room and board; † = room only.*

Freshman-Year Out-of-Pocket Costs: Looking Beyond the Sticker Price

This chart presents average costs. Actual costs may vary.

	Published tuition and fees	Room and board	Percent of freshmen who applied for aid	Average aid package for freshmen	Average cost after aid
College of Notre Dame of Maryland, Baltimore, MD	$13,365	$6130	76%	$13,990	$5505
College of Our Lady of the Elms, Chicopee, MA	$12,950	$5000	81%	$6585	$11,365
College of Saint Benedict, Saint Joseph, MN	$13,996	$4541	92%	$12,350	$6187
College of St. Catherine, St. Paul, MN	$13,702	$4582	88%	$13,246	$5038
College of Saint Elizabeth, Morristown, NJ	$12,220	$5600	NR	$12,499	$5321
College of St. Francis, Joliet, IL	$11,950	$4740	96%	$11,245	$5445
College of St. Joseph, Rutland, VT	$10,100	$5800	NR	NR	NR
College of Saint Mary, Omaha, NE	$11,814	$4290	99%	NR	NR
College of St. Scholastica, Duluth, MN	$13,131	$3807	NR	$10,721	$6217
College of Santa Fe, Santa Fe, NM	$12,754	$4566	78%	$11,277	$6043
College of Staten Island of the City University of New York, Staten Island, NY	$3316	NA	NR	NR	NR
College of the Atlantic, Bar Harbor, ME	$17,066	$4905	NR	$15,495	$6476
College of the Holy Cross, Worcester, MA	$20,070	$6750	72%	$14,067	$12,753
College of the Ozarks, Point Lookout, MO	$150	$2200	100%	NR	NR
College of the Southwest, Hobbs, NM	$4430	$3504	100%	NR	NR
College of Visual Arts, St. Paul, MN	$8970	NA	NR	$5500	$3470
The College of West Virginia, Beckley, WV	$3360	$1980†	54%	NR	NR
College of William and Mary, Williamsburg, VA	$4906	$4470	60%	$4180	$5196
The College of Wooster, Wooster, OH	$19,300	$5100	88%	$16,579	$7821
Colorado Christian University, Lakewood, CO	$8855	$3930	NR	$7646	$5139
The Colorado College, Colorado Springs, CO	$19,026	$4824	NR	NR	NR
Colorado School of Mines, Golden, CO	$5069	$4730	NR	$5200	$4599
Colorado State University, Fort Collins, CO	$2855	$4152	66%	$5620	$1387
Colorado Technical University, Colorado Springs, CO	$6468	NA	NR	NR	NR
Columbia College, Chicago, IL	$8190	$4523†	NR	NR	NR
Columbia College, Columbia, MO	$8974	$4024	85%	$10,617	$2381
Columbia College, New York, NY	$21,446	$7160	61%	$17,897	$10,709
Columbia College, Columbia, SC	$11,595	$4160	NR	$12,236	$3519
Columbia College–Hollywood, Hollywood, CA	$6705	NA	46%	$6625	$80
Columbia College of Nursing, Milwaukee, WI	$14,610	$4280	NR	NR	NR
Columbia International University, Columbia, SC	$7451	$3970	81%	NR	NR
Columbia Union College, Takoma Park, MD	$11,790	$4140	NR	NR	NR
Columbia University, School of Engineering and Applied Science, New York, NY	$21,446	$7160	66%	$19,076	$9530
Columbus College of Art and Design, Columbus, OH	$11,880	$5800	NR	NR	NR
Columbus State University, Columbus, GA	$2106	$3825	90%	$3218	$2713
Community Hospital of Roanoke Valley–College of Health Sciences, Roanoke, VA	$4500	$1300†	NR	NR	NR
Conception Seminary College, Conception, MO	$7042	$3274	100%	$9730	$586
Concord College, Athens, WV	$2218	$3464	89%	$4832	$850
Concordia College, Selma, AL	$4600	$2600	NR	$3286	$3914
Concordia College, Ann Arbor, MI	$11,450	$4650	98%	NR	NR
Concordia College, Moorhead, MN	$12,145	$3525	85%	$9825	$5845

*NA = not applicable; NR = not reported; * = includes room and board; † = room only.*

70

Freshman-Year Out-of-Pocket Costs: Looking Beyond the Sticker Price

This chart presents average costs. Actual costs may vary.

	Published tuition and fees	Room and board	Percent of freshmen who applied for aid	Average aid package for freshmen	Average cost after aid
Concordia College, St. Paul, MN	$11,355	$4200	91%	$10,952	$4603
Concordia College, Seward, NE	$10,650	$3640	95%	$9179	$5111
Concordia College, Bronxville, NY	$11,400	$5310	98%	$10,515	$6195
Concordia University, Irvine, CA	$13,800	$5180	80%	$7500	$11,480
Concordia University, River Forest, IL	$11,571	$4852	84%	$9000	$7423
Concordia University, Portland, OR	$11,030	$3530	95%	$8700	$5860
Concordia University at Austin, Austin, TX	$9400	$4750	NR	$8195	$5955
Concordia University Wisconsin, Mequon, WI	$10,760	$3700	NR	NR	NR
Connecticut College, New London, CT	$27,375*	NA	NR	$19,872	$7503
Converse College, Spartanburg, SC	$14,445	$4080	NR	$13,137	$5388
The Corcoran School of Art, Washington, DC	$12,200	$4360†	100%	NR	NR
Cornell College, Mount Vernon, IA	$17,220	$4670	92%	$14,409	$7481
Cornell University, Ithaca, NY	$20,974	$7035	74%	$167,000	$0
Cornerstone College, Grand Rapids, MI	$9450	$4418	80%	$9086	$4782
Cornish College of the Arts, Seattle, WA	$10,990	NA	91%	NR	NR
Covenant College, Lookout Mountain, GA	$11,780	$3800	NR	$10,206	$5374
Creighton University, Omaha, NE	$12,210	$4726	75%	$10,261	$6675
Crichton College, Memphis, TN	$6360	$1650†	NR	$2624	$5386
The Criswell College, Dallas, TX	$3064	NA	NR	NR	NR
Crown College, St. Bonifacius, MN	$9335	$4020	95%	$7500	$5855
Culver-Stockton College, Canton, MO	$8800	$4000	90%	$9821	$2979
Cumberland College, Williamsburg, KY	$8430	$3776	89%	$8899	$3307
Cumberland University, Lebanon, TN	$8190	$3400	NR	$5630	$5960
Curry College, Milton, MA	$15,255	$6230	NR	$10,627	$10,858
The Curtis Institute of Music, Philadelphia, PA	$675	NA	NR	NR	NR
Daemen College, Amherst, NY	$10,330	$5200	69%	$8335	$7195
Dakota State University, Madison, SD	$2658	$2676	87%	$5206	$128
Dakota Wesleyan University, Mitchell, SD	$8825	$3240	100%	$9458	$2607
Dallas Baptist University, Dallas, TX	$7440	$3250	64%	$8655	$2035
Dallas Christian College, Dallas, TX	$3840	$2640	NR	NR	NR
Dana College, Blair, NE	$10,950	$3780	NR	$4725	$10,005
Daniel Webster College, Nashua, NH	$13,845	$5406	88%	$13,257	$5994
Dartmouth College, Hanover, NH	$21,951	$6282	65%	$19,958	$8275
Davenport College of Business, Grand Rapids, MI	$8188	$2025†	NR	NR	NR
Davenport College of Business, Kalamazoo Campus, Kalamazoo, MI	$8010	NA	NR	NR	NR
Davenport College of Business, Lansing Campus, Lansing, MI	$8182	NA	NR	NR	NR
David Lipscomb University, Nashville, TN	$7907	$3650	69%	NR	NR
David N. Myers College, Cleveland, OH	$7500	NA	100%	$3000	$4500
Davidson College, Davidson, NC	$20,118	$5636	54%	$15,600	$10,154
Davis & Elkins College, Elkins, WV	$10,780	$4890	NR	$10,496	$5174
Deaconess College of Nursing, St. Louis, MO	$7170	$3010	86%	$3670	$6510

NA = not applicable; NR = not reported; * = includes room and board; † = room only.

Freshman-Year Out-of-Pocket Costs: Looking Beyond the Sticker Price

This chart presents average costs. Actual costs may vary.

	Published tuition and fees	Room and board	Percent of freshmen who applied for aid	Average aid package for freshmen	Average cost after aid
The Defiance College, Defiance, OH	$13,475	$3950	88%	$11,568	$5857
Delaware State University, Dover, DE	$2636	$4704	88%	$7006	$334
Delaware Valley College, Doylestown, PA	$13,708	$5490	NR	$12,391	$6807
Delta State University, Cleveland, MS	$2334	$2400	NR	$4000	$734
Denison University, Granville, OH	$19,470	$5160	60%	$19,430	$5200
DePaul University, Chicago, IL	$12,780	$5210	88%	$10,700	$7290
DePauw University, Greencastle, IN	$16,180	$5400	NR	$15,898	$5682
Design Institute of San Diego, San Diego, CA	$9000	NA	NR	$8500	$500
Detroit College of Business, Dearborn, MI	$8526	NA	85%	$6148	$2378
Detroit College of Business–Flint, Flint, MI	$6321	NA	99%	$5819	$502
Detroit College of Business, Warren Campus, Warren, MI	$8526	NA	92%	$5659	$2867
DeVry Institute of Technology, Phoenix, AZ	$6968	NA	95%	NR	NR
DeVry Institute of Technology, Long Beach, CA	$6968	NA	95%	NR	NR
DeVry Institute of Technology, Pomona, CA	$6968	NA	95%	NR	NR
DeVry Institute of Technology, Decatur, GA	$6968	NA	NR	NR	NR
DeVry Institute of Technology, Addison, IL	$6968	NA	95%	NR	NR
DeVry Institute of Technology, Chicago, IL	$6968	NA	95%	NR	NR
DeVry Institute of Technology, Kansas City, MO	$6968	NA	95%	NR	NR
DeVry Institute of Technology, Columbus, OH	$6968	NA	95%	NR	NR
DeVry Institute of Technology, Irving, TX	$6968	NA	95%	NR	NR
Dickinson College, Carlisle, PA	$20,750	$5660	70%	$18,210	$8200
Dickinson State University, Dickinson, ND	$1970	$2328	NR	NR	NR
Dillard University, New Orleans, LA	$7500	$3950	90%	$9630	$1820
Doane College, Crete, NE	$10,950	$3290	93%	$9447	$4793
Dominican College of Blauvelt, Orangeburg, NY	$10,015	$6000	NR	$2824	$13,191
Dominican College of San Rafael, San Rafael, CA	$14,670	$6370	87%	$14,512	$6528
Dominican University, River Forest, IL	$12,950	$4880	93%	$11,669	$6161
Dordt College, Sioux Center, IA	$10,900	$2900	90%	$10,727	$3073
Dowling College, Oakdale, NY	$11,670	$3350†	88%	$6000	$9020
Drake University, Des Moines, IA	$14,380	$4870	77%	$13,920	$5330
Drew University, Madison, NJ	$20,402	$5972	75%	$15,878	$10,496
Drexel University, Philadelphia, PA	$14,472	$6909	NR	NR	NR
Drury College, Springfield, MO	$10,060	$3856	85%	$8421	$5495
Duke University, Durham, NC	$21,124	$6605	59%	$18,252	$9477
Duquesne University, Pittsburgh, PA	$13,396	$5803	99%	$11,907	$7292
D'Youville College, Buffalo, NY	$9700	$4600	91%	$9025	$5275
Earlham College, Richmond, IN	$17,898	$4412	NR	$12,000	$10,310
East Carolina University, Greenville, NC	$1752	$3480	80%	NR	NR
East Central University, Ada, OK	$1724	$1832	NR	NR	NR
East Coast Bible College, Charlotte, NC	$4863	$2740	78%	$4599	$3004
Eastern College, St. Davids, PA	$12,700	$5440	92%	$13,200	$4940

*NA = not applicable; NR = not reported; * = includes room and board; † = room only.*

Freshman-Year Out-of-Pocket Costs: Looking Beyond the Sticker Price

This chart presents average costs. Actual costs may vary.

	Published tuition and fees	Room and board	Percent of freshmen who applied for aid	Average aid package for freshmen	Average cost after aid
Eastern Connecticut State University, Willimantic, CT	$3594	$5048	75%	$5800	$2842
Eastern Illinois University, Charleston, IL	$2916	$3362	99%	$4551	$1727
Eastern Kentucky University, Richmond, KY	$1970	$2706	NR	NR	NR
Eastern Mennonite University, Harrisonburg, VA	$12,120	$4500	NR	$14,907	$1713
Eastern Michigan University, Ypsilanti, MI	$3293	$4400	80%	$5308	$2385
Eastern Nazarene College, Quincy, MA	$11,440	$3975	97%	$14,656	$759
Eastern New Mexico University, Portales, NM	$1654	$2810	NR	$4740	$0
Eastern Oregon University, La Grande, OR	$3011	$3966	NR	$6847	$130
Eastern Washington University, Cheney, WA	$2445	$4294	NR	$7500	$0
East Stroudsburg University of Pennsylvania, East Stroudsburg, PA	$4196	$3626	NR	NR	NR
East Tennessee State University, Johnson City, TN	$1928	$2430	NR	$5156	$0
East Texas Baptist University, Marshall, TX	$6440	$2790	NR	NR	NR
East-West University, Chicago, IL	$6960	NA	NR	$3709	$3251
Eckerd College, St. Petersburg, FL	$16,625	$4460	75%	$14,306	$6779
Edgewood College, Madison, WI	$10,280	$4380	87%	$9600	$5060
Edinboro University of Pennsylvania, Edinboro, PA	$4068	$3616	90%	$5295	$2389
Edward Waters College, Jacksonville, FL	$4800	$5200	NR	NR	NR
Electronic Data Processing College of Puerto Rico, San Juan, PR	$3231	NA	NR	$2264	$967
Elizabeth City State University, Elizabeth City, NC	$1688	$3248	98%	$3800	$1136
Elizabethtown College, Elizabethtown, PA	$15,890	$4700	90%	$13,171	$7419
Elmhurst College, Elmhurst, IL	$11,066	$4660	92%	$11,908	$3818
Elmira College, Elmira, NY	$17,950	$4730	90%	$15,497	$7183
Elon College, Elon College, NC	$10,667	$4170	NR	$6400	$8437
Embry-Riddle Aeronautical University, Prescott, AZ	$8740	$4080	66%	$9011	$3809
Embry-Riddle Aeronautical University, Daytona Beach, FL	$8740	$3640	72%	NR	NR
Emerson College, Boston, MA	$17,826	$8250	71%	$13,092	$12,984
Emmanuel College, Franklin Springs, GA	$5560	$3300	NR	NR	NR
Emmanuel College, Boston, MA	$14,550	$6785	NR	$12,800	$8535
Emmaus Bible College, Dubuque, IA	$2170	$4510	NR	$3700	$2980
Emory & Henry College, Emory, VA	$11,572	$4800	92%	$10,580	$5792
Emory University, Atlanta, GA	$20,110	$4786	61%	$17,524	$7372
Emporia State University, Emporia, KS	$1834	$3320	NR	NR	NR
Endicott College, Beverly, MA	$12,725	$6625	73%	$8813	$10,537
Erskine College, Due West, SC	$13,087	$4490	NR	$13,583	$3994
Escuela de Artes Plasticas de Puerto Rico, San Juan, PR	$1728	NA	59%	$1156	$572
Eugene Bible College, Eugene, OR	$4977	$3048	95%	$1276	$6749
Eugene Lang College, New School for Social Research, New York, NY	$16,920	$8860	NR	$16,500	$9280
Eureka College, Eureka, IL	$13,216	$4142	NR	$11,512	$5846
Evangel College, Springfield, MO	$8065	$3440	NR	$6005	$5500
The Evergreen State College, Olympia, WA	$2544	$4470	NR	$5923	$1091
Fairfield University, Fairfield, CT	$17,360	$6800	69%	$9363	$14,797

*NA = not applicable; NR = not reported; * = includes room and board; † = room only.*

Freshman-Year Out-of-Pocket Costs: Looking Beyond the Sticker Price

This chart presents average costs. Actual costs may vary.

	Published tuition and fees	Room and board	Percent of freshmen who applied for aid	Average aid package for freshmen	Average cost after aid
Fairleigh Dickinson University, Teaneck–Hackensack and Florham–Madison campuses, Teaneck, NJ/Madison, NJ	$14,712	$6040	89%	$14,501	$6251
Fairmont State College, Fairmont, WV	$1918	$3358	NR	$3005	$2271
Faith Baptist Bible College and Theological Seminary, Ankeny, IA	$6220	$3276	89%	NR	NR
Fashion Institute of Technology, New York, NY	$2610	$5340	75%	$5167	$2783
Faulkner University, Montgomery, AL	$6860	$3500	NR	$3600	$6760
Fayetteville State University, Fayetteville, NC	$1616	$3250	97%	$3775	$1091
Felician College, Lodi, NJ	$9382	NA	48%	NR	NR
Ferris State University, Big Rapids, MI	$3665	$4631	93%	$5860	$2436
Ferrum College, Ferrum, VA	$10,200	$4700	88%	$11,692	$3208
Fisk University, Nashville, TN	$7328	$4062	84%	NR	NR
Fitchburg State College, Fitchburg, MA	$3246	$4110	90%	$4913	$2443
Five Towns College, Dix Hills, NY	$8800	$4390	72%	NR	NR
Flagler College, St. Augustine, FL	$5760	$3580	83%	$5500	$3840
Florida Agricultural and Mechanical University, Tallahassee, FL	$1982	$3074	NR	NR	NR
Florida Atlantic University, Boca Raton, FL	$1900	$4365	91%	$3246	$3019
Florida Baptist Theological College, Graceville, FL	$2934	$1500†	NR	$1402	$3032
Florida Bible College, Miramar, FL	$4928	$2200†	NR	$750	$6378
Florida Christian College, Kissimmee, FL	$5174	$1240†	NR	$1421	$4993
Florida Institute of Technology, Melbourne, FL	$15,100	$4392	80%	NR	NR
Florida International University, Miami, FL	$1875	$2400†	98%	$2841	$1434
Florida Memorial College, Miami, FL	$5850	$3236	NR	NR	NR
Florida Metropolitan University–Orlando College, North, Orlando, FL	$4140	NA	NR	$4500	$0
Florida Metropolitan University–Tampa College, Pinellas, Clearwater, FL	$4464	NA	NR	NR	NR
Florida Metropolitan University–Tampa College, Lakeland, Lakeland, FL	$5220	NA	NR	$4500	$720
Florida Metropolitan University–Tampa College, Tampa, FL	$5220	NA	NR	NR	NR
Florida Southern College, Lakeland, FL	$9970	$5300	NR	$12,700	$2570
Florida State University, Tallahassee, FL	$1882	$4472	NR	$8045	$0
Fontbonne College, St. Louis, MO	$10,150	$4400	80%	NR	NR
Fordham University, New York, NY	$16,000	$7125	94%	$13,764	$9361
Fort Hays State University, Hays, KS	$1929	$3398	81%	$2177	$3150
Fort Lewis College, Durango, CO	$2050	$3740	NR	$4259	$1531
Fort Valley State University, Fort Valley, GA	$2040	$2925	86%	$6970	$0
Framingham State College, Framingham, MA	$3228	$3855	71%	$4801	$2282
Franciscan University of Steubenville, Steubenville, OH	$10,870	$4700	NR	NR	NR
Francis Marion University, Florence, SC	$3100	$3138	NR	NR	NR
Franklin and Marshall College, Lancaster, PA	$26,400*	NA	68%	$15,509	$10,891
Franklin College of Indiana, Franklin, IN	$12,360	$4080	98%	$11,884	$4556
Franklin Pierce College, Rindge, NH	$15,010	$4930	NR	$12,600	$7340
Franklin University, Columbus, OH	$5066	NA	63%	NR	NR
Freed-Hardeman University, Henderson, TN	$7120	$3620	86%	$8500	$2240

*NA = not applicable; NR = not reported; * = includes room and board; † = room only.*

Freshman-Year Out-of-Pocket Costs: Looking Beyond the Sticker Price

This chart presents average costs. Actual costs may vary.

	Published tuition and fees	Room and board	Percent of freshmen who applied for aid	Average aid package for freshmen	Average cost after aid
Free Will Baptist Bible College, Nashville, TN	$4830	$3749	NR	$2717	$5862
Fresno Pacific University, Fresno, CA	$11,936	$4100	96%	$10,750	$5286
Friends University, Wichita, KS	$9975	$3200	NR	NR	NR
Frostburg State University, Frostburg, MD	$3544	$4786	88%	$2625	$5705
Furman University, Greenville, SC	$15,514	$4304	NR	$10,500	$9318
Gallaudet University, Washington, DC	$6182	$6708	75%	$10,044	$2846
Gannon University, Erie, PA	$11,694	$4710	90%	$9542	$6862
Gardner-Webb University, Boiling Springs, NC	$8990	$4470	89%	$13,000	$460
Geneva College, Beaver Falls, PA	$10,864	$4600	96%	$8200	$7264
George Fox University, Newberg, OR	$14,520	$4640	NR	$14,872	$4288
George Mason University, Fairfax, VA	$4248	$5100	65%	$5216	$4132
Georgetown College, Georgetown, KY	$9740	$4050	84%	$10,912	$2878
Georgetown University, Washington, DC	$20,388	$7763	54%	$16,817	$11,334
The George Washington University, Washington, DC	$19,980	$6240	69%	$15,417	$10,803
Georgia Baptist College of Nursing, Atlanta, GA	$7200	$1134†	NR	NR	NR
Georgia College and State University, Milledgeville, GA	$1923	$3345	NR	NR	NR
Georgia Institute of Technology, Atlanta, GA	$2685	$4560	92%	$6035	$1210
Georgian Court College, Lakewood, NJ	$11,116	$4750	NR	$8953	$6913
Georgia Southern University, Statesboro, GA	$2055	$3675	NR	$4285	$1445
Georgia Southwestern State University, Americus, GA	$2025	$3033	84%	$7667	$0
Georgia State University, Atlanta, GA	$2385	$3790†	NR	NR	NR
Gettysburg College, Gettysburg, PA	$21,616	$4760	60%	$17,750	$8626
Glenville State College, Glenville, WV	$1860	$3348	NR	$4350	$858
GMI Engineering & Management Institute, Flint, MI	$13,696	$3730	NR	NR	NR
Goddard College, Plainfield, VT	$15,650	$5084	NR	NR	NR
God's Bible School and College, Cincinnati, OH	$3850	$2550	NR	NR	NR
Golden Gate University, San Francisco, CA	$8414	NA	44%	NR	NR
Goldey-Beacom College, Wilmington, DE	$7200	$3290†	85%	$3900	$6590
Gonzaga University, Spokane, WA	$15,350	$5020	78%	$11,115	$9255
Gordon College, Wenham, MA	$14,690	$4760	85%	$13,677	$5773
Goshen College, Goshen, IN	$10,900	$3880	100%	$10,284	$4496
Goucher College, Baltimore, MD	$17,760	$6570	75%	$16,681	$7649
Grace Bible College, Grand Rapids, MI	$5800	$3600	95%	$5079	$4321
Grace College, Winona Lake, IN	$9506	$4146	100%	$9136	$4516
Graceland College, Lamoni, IA	$10,340	$3310	93%	$10,804	$2846
Grace University, Omaha, NE	$7484	$3230	93%	NR	NR
Grambling State University, Grambling, LA	$2088	$2636	NR	$5159	$0
Grand Canyon University, Phoenix, AZ	$8946	$2750	86%	$5083	$6613
Grand Valley State University, Allendale, MI	$3226	$4380	83%	$5607	$1999
Grand View College, Des Moines, IA	$11,410	$3775	87%	NR	NR
Great Lakes Christian College, Lansing, MI	$4658	$3200	NR	NR	NR

*NA = not applicable; NR = not reported; * = includes room and board; † = room only.*

Freshman-Year Out-of-Pocket Costs: Looking Beyond the Sticker Price
This chart presents average costs. Actual costs may vary.

	Published tuition and fees	Room and board	Percent of freshmen who applied for aid	Average aid package for freshmen	Average cost after aid
Green Mountain College, Poultney, VT	$15,140	$3320	75%	$11,143	$7317
Greensboro College, Greensboro, NC	$9550	$4040	89%	$8670	$4920
Greenville College, Greenville, IL	$11,770	$4750	88%	$12,425	$4095
Grinnell College, Grinnell, IA	$17,134	$4926	91%	$14,652	$7408
Grove City College, Grove City, PA	$6478	$3652	NR	$5117	$5013
Guilford College, Greensboro, NC	$14,450	$5270	81%	$14,162	$5558
Gustavus Adolphus College, St. Peter, MN	$15,530	$3900	86%	$12,400	$7030
Gwynedd-Mercy College, Gwynedd Valley, PA	$11,794	$5800	96%	$11,706	$5888
Hamilton College, Clinton, NY	$22,700	$5650	63%	$18,500	$9850
Hamilton Technical College, Davenport, IA	$5250	NA	NR	NR	NR
Hamline University, St. Paul, MN	$14,344	$4536	98%	$14,768	$4112
Hampden-Sydney College, Hampden-Sydney, VA	$14,506	$5344	70%	$12,631	$7219
Hampshire College, Amherst, MA	$22,900	$5990	NR	$18,400	$10,490
Hannibal-LaGrange College, Hannibal, MO	$7140	$2610	100%	NR	NR
Hanover College, Hanover, IN	$9585	$3915	94%	$4704	$8796
Harding University, Searcy, AR	$6825	$3797	95%	$8141	$2481
Hardin-Simmons University, Abilene, TX	$7530	$3240	96%	$8252	$2518
Harid Conservatory, Boca Raton, FL	$0	NA	NR	NR	NR
Harrington Institute of Interior Design, Chicago, IL	$9949	NA	57%	$3412	$6537
Hartwick College, Oneonta, NY	$20,805	$5570	70%	$16,825	$9550
Harvard University, Cambridge, MA	$21,901	$6995	64%	$19,713	$9183
Harvey Mudd College, Claremont, CA	$19,426	$7197	79%	NR	NR
Hastings College, Hastings, NE	$10,724	$3594	100%	$8694	$5624
Haverford College, Haverford, PA	$20,890	$6810	55%	$20,092	$7608
Hawaii Pacific University, Honolulu, HI	$7100	$7310	37%	$10,988	$3422
Hebrew College, Brookline, MA	$8940	NA	NR	NR	NR
Hebrew Theological College, Skokie, IL	$6500	$5510	NR	NR	NR
Heidelberg College, Tiffin, OH	$15,594	$4985	NR	$15,000	$5579
Hellenic College, Brookline, MA	$7700	$5600	NR	NR	NR
Henderson State University, Arkadelphia, AR	$2034	$2720	79%	NR	NR
Hendrix College, Conway, AR	$10,028	$3640	NR	NR	NR
Henry Cogswell College, Everett, WA	$9360	NA	NR	$0	$9360
Heritage Bible College, Dunn, NC	$2850	$2035	79%	NR	NR
Heritage College, Toppenish, WA	$6470	NA	97%	NR	NR
High Point University, High Point, NC	$10,420	$5060	65%	$9125	$6355
Hilbert College, Hamburg, NY	$8930	$4450	NR	NR	NR
Hillsdale College, Hillsdale, MI	$12,320	$5180	80%	$9840	$7660
Hiram College, Hiram, OH	$15,890	$4936	NR	$13,984	$6842
Hobart and William Smith Colleges, Geneva, NY	$21,381	$6315	78%	$17,138	$10,558
Hobe Sound Bible College, Hobe Sound, FL	$4400	$2600	88%	$7000	$0
Hofstra University, Hempstead, NY	$12,766	$4600†	78%	$6939	$10,427

NA = not applicable; NR = not reported; * = includes room and board; † = room only.

Freshman-Year Out-of-Pocket Costs: Looking Beyond the Sticker Price

This chart presents average costs. Actual costs may vary.

	Published tuition and fees	Room and board	Percent of freshmen who applied for aid	Average aid package for freshmen	Average cost after aid
Hollins College, Roanoke, VA	$14,810	$5975	76%	$14,488	$6297
Holy Apostles College and Seminary, Cromwell, CT	$5030	$6400	50%	$0	$11,430
Holy Family College, Philadelphia, PA	$10,120	NA	97%	NR	NR
Holy Names College, Oakland, CA	$13,870	$5790	100%	NR	NR
Hood College, Frederick, MD	$16,418	$6592	91%	$14,460	$8550
Hope College, Holland, MI	$14,310	$4516	NR	$11,954	$6872
Hope International University, Fullerton, CA	$9265	$3619	97%	$6191	$6693
Houghton College, Houghton, NY	$12,060	$3998	NR	NR	NR
Houston Baptist University, Houston, TX	$8755	$2630	88%	$7315	$4070
Howard Payne University, Brownwood, TX	$6450	$3450	NR	NR	NR
Howard University, Washington, DC	$8985	$4162	NR	NR	NR
Humboldt State University, Arcata, CA	$1956	$5710	67%	$5398	$2268
Humphreys College, Stockton, CA	$5880	$4660	94%	NR	NR
Hunter College of the City University of New York, New York, NY	$3318	$1400†	NR	NR	NR
Huntingdon College, Montgomery, AL	$10,600	$4650	72%	$9338	$5912
Huntington College, Huntington, IN	$11,520	$4340	97%	$8000	$7860
Huron University, Huron, SD	$7878	$3470	NR	NR	NR
Husson College, Bangor, ME	$8500	$4490	85%	$8560	$4430
Huston-Tillotson College, Austin, TX	$5940	$4051	NR	NR	NR
Idaho State University, Pocatello, ID	$1726	$3398	NR	$8868	$0
Illinois College, Jacksonville, IL	$9150	$4150	87%	$9444	$3856
The Illinois Institute of Art, Chicago, IL	$9984	NA	NR	NR	NR
Illinois Institute of Technology, Chicago, IL	$16,460	$4620	87%	$15,807	$5273
Illinois State University, Normal, IL	$3720	$3765	74%	$5666	$1819
Illinois Wesleyan University, Bloomington, IL	$17,490	$4590	NR	$13,964	$8116
Immaculata College, Immaculata, PA	$11,580	$5855	NR	$13,998	$3437
Indiana Institute of Technology, Fort Wayne, IN	$10,030	$4130	NR	NR	NR
Indiana State University, Terre Haute, IN	$3072	$3995	30%	$1741	$5326
Indiana University Bloomington, Bloomington, IN	$3751	$4220	62%	$5136	$2835
Indiana University East, Richmond, IN	$2728	NA	78%	$3778	$0
Indiana University Kokomo, Kokomo, IN	$2652	NA	50%	$3032	$0
Indiana University Northwest, Gary, IN	$2768	NA	60%	$3866	$0
Indiana University of Pennsylvania, Indiana, PA	$4064	$3332	90%	$5142	$2254
Indiana University–Purdue University Fort Wayne, Fort Wayne, IN	$3007	NA	NR	NR	NR
Indiana University–Purdue University Indianapolis, Indianapolis, IN	$3565	$3000	61%	$3840	$2725
Indiana University South Bend, South Bend, IN	$2838	NA	59%	$2810	$28
Indiana University Southeast, New Albany, IN	$2718	NA	68%	$2731	$0
Indiana Wesleyan University, Marion, IN	$10,722	$4158	NR	NR	NR
Inter American University of Puerto Rico, Aguadilla Campus, Aguadilla, PR	$2500	NA	100%	NR	NR
Inter American University of Puerto Rico, Arecibo Campus, Arecibo, PR	$2500	$3266	NR	NR	NR
Inter American University of Puerto Rico, Barranquitas Campus, Barranquitas, PR	$2390	NA	100%	NR	NR

*NA = not applicable; NR = not reported; * = includes room and board; † = room only.*

Freshman-Year Out-of-Pocket Costs: Looking Beyond the Sticker Price

This chart presents average costs. Actual costs may vary.

	Published tuition and fees	Room and board	Percent of freshmen who applied for aid	Average aid package for freshmen	Average cost after aid
Inter American University of Puerto Rico, Fajardo Campus, Fajardo, PR	$2500	NA	NR	NR	NR
Inter American University of Puerto Rico, Guayama Campus, Guayama, PR	$2500	NA	NR	NR	NR
Inter American University of Puerto Rico, Metropolitan Campus, Hato Rey, PR	$2500	NA	NR	NR	NR
Inter American University of Puerto Rico, Ponce Campus, Mercedita, PR	$2500	NA	NR	NR	NR
Inter American University of Puerto Rico, San Germán Campus, San Germán, PR	$2500	$2200	NR	NR	NR
International Academy of Merchandising & Design, Inc., Tampa, FL	$8910	NA	NR	NR	NR
International Academy of Merchandising & Design, Ltd., Chicago, IL	$9270	NA	91%	NR	NR
International Baptist College, Tempe, AZ	$3540	$2600	NR	NR	NR
International Bible College, Florence, AL	$4934	$2900	NR	$3446	$4388
International College, Naples, FL	$6735	NA	NR	NR	NR
Iona College, New Rochelle, NY	$12,520	$7520	86%	$13,085	$6955
Iowa State University of Science and Technology, Ames, IA	$2666	$3508	79%	$6400	$0
Iowa Wesleyan College, Mount Pleasant, IA	$11,300	$3840	100%	$12,100	$3040
Ithaca College, Ithaca, NY	$16,130	$6990	80%	$13,143	$9977
Jackson State University, Jackson, MS	$2380	$3138	86%	$5113	$405
Jacksonville State University, Jacksonville, AL	$1940	$2870	74%	NR	NR
Jacksonville University, Jacksonville, FL	$13,900	$4900	94%	$12,315	$6485
James Madison University, Harrisonburg, VA	$4104	$4666	NR	NR	NR
Jamestown College, Jamestown, ND	$8770	$3080	82%	NR	NR
Jarvis Christian College, Hawkins, TX	$6694	$3750	NR	NR	NR
Jersey City State College, Jersey City, NJ	$3528	$5000	82%	$4953	$3575
Jewish Hospital College of Nursing and Allied Health, St. Louis, MO	$8680	$1856†	NR	NR	NR
Jewish Theological Seminary of America, New York, NY	$7490	$4150†	NR	NR	NR
John Brown University, Siloam Springs, AR	$9120	$4390	68%	$8240	$5270
John Carroll University, University Heights, OH	$13,883	$5662	85%	$12,684	$6861
John F. Kennedy University, Orinda, CA	$9435	NA	NR	$0	$9435
John Jay College of Criminal Justice, the City University of New York, New York, NY	$3059	NA	NR	NR	NR
Johns Hopkins University, Baltimore, MD	$21,675	$7400	69%	$17,662	$11,413
Johnson & Wales University, North Miami, FL	$11,952	$3180†	76%	$10,090	$5042
Johnson & Wales University, Providence, RI	$11,952	$5337	NR	$8868	$8421
Johnson & Wales University, Charleston, SC	$10,836	$3414†	80%	$7341	$6909
Johnson Bible College, Knoxville, TN	$5000	$3270	96%	$1190	$7080
Johnson C. Smith University, Charlotte, NC	$7473	$3253	69%	$5600	$5126
Johnson State College, Johnson, VT	$4340	$4936	81%	$4322	$4954
John Wesley College, High Point, NC	$4654	$1600†	95%	$5402	$852
Jones College, Jacksonville, FL	$4350	NA	72%	$2500	$1850
Judson College, Marion, AL	$6400	$3950	100%	$8201	$2149
Judson College, Elgin, IL	$11,350	$4780	NR	$13,547	$2583
The Juilliard School, New York, NY	$14,200	$6500	NR	NR	NR
Juniata College, Huntingdon, PA	$17,260	$4820	95%	$15,252	$6828
Kalamazoo College, Kalamazoo, MI	$17,284	$5421	81%	$14,513	$8192

*NA = not applicable; NR = not reported; * = includes room and board; † = room only.*

Freshman-Year Out-of-Pocket Costs: Looking Beyond the Sticker Price

This chart presents average costs. Actual costs may vary.

	Published tuition and fees	Room and board	Percent of freshmen who applied for aid	Average aid package for freshmen	Average cost after aid
Kansas City Art Institute, Kansas City, MO	$16,320	$4695	90%	$10,196	$10,819
Kansas Newman College, Wichita, KS	$8500	$3770	100%	$6500	$5770
Kansas State University, Manhattan, KS	$2373	$3490	NR	$7100	$0
Kansas Wesleyan University, Salina, KS	$9800	$3500	97%	$11,164	$2136
Kean College of New Jersey, Union, NJ	$3367	$4970	NR	$3200	$5137
Keene State College, Keene, NH	$3794	$4508	81%	$5947	$2355
Kehilath Yakov Rabbinical Seminary, Brooklyn, NY	$4000	$2000	87%	NR	NR
Kendall College, Evanston, IL	$10,128	$5091	NR	$8728	$6491
Kendall College of Art and Design, Grand Rapids, MI	$10,550	NA	NR	$8437	$2113
Kennesaw State University, Kennesaw, GA	$1824	NA	82%	NR	NR
Kent State University, Kent, OH	$4288	$4030	NR	NR	NR
Kentucky Christian College, Grayson, KY	$5984	$3764	96%	$5450	$4298
Kentucky Mountain Bible College, Vancleve, KY	$3050	$2770	NR	$4136	$1684
Kentucky State University, Frankfort, KY	$1950	$3088	NR	NR	NR
Kentucky Wesleyan College, Owensboro, KY	$9100	$4400	96%	$12,590	$910
Kenyon College, Gambier, OH	$22,010	$3820	55%	$17,962	$7868
Keuka College, Keuka Park, NY	$10,790	$5040	NR	$10,853	$4977
King College, Bristol, TN	$10,550	$3444	88%	$10,017	$3977
King's College, Wilkes-Barre, PA	$12,980	$5780	96%	$9930	$8830
Knox College, Galesburg, IL	$18,393	$4896	92%	$16,663	$6626
Knoxville College, Knoxville, TN	$5792	$3450	NR	NR	NR
Kol Yaakov Torah Center, Monsey, NY	$3300	$2900	NR	NR	NR
Kutztown University of Pennsylvania, Kutztown, PA	$4098	$3258	80%	$4189	$3167
Laboratory Institute of Merchandising, New York, NY	$11,450	NA	86%	$8500	$2950
Lafayette College, Easton, PA	$20,383	$6335	65%	$15,491	$11,227
LaGrange College, LaGrange, GA	$9114	$3990	88%	$8992	$4112
Lake Erie College, Painesville, OH	$12,950	$4905	96%	$12,740	$5115
Lake Forest College, Lake Forest, IL	$19,560	$4550	89%	$18,064	$6046
Lakeland College, Sheboygan, WI	$11,230	$4380	NR	NR	NR
Lamar University, Beaumont, TX	$1796	$3280	NR	$2454	$2622
Lambuth University, Jackson, TN	$6194	$3950	97%	$6028	$4116
Lancaster Bible College, Lancaster, PA	$8120	$3850	80%	$6754	$5216
Lander University, Greenwood, SC	$3600	$3000	NR	NR	NR
Lane College, Jackson, TN	$5400	$3400	NR	$9169	$0
Langston University, Langston, OK	$1482	$2580	NR	NR	NR
La Roche College, Pittsburgh, PA	$9912	$5198	92%	$10,700	$4410
La Salle University, Philadelphia, PA	$13,940	$5950	93%	$12,855	$7035
Lasell College, Newton, MA	$13,275	$6425	83%	$10,770	$8930
La Sierra University, Riverside, CA	$13,545	$3990	NR	$14,000	$3535
Lawrence Technological University, Southfield, MI	$6944	$1980†	82%	$4418	$4506
Lawrence University, Appleton, WI	$18,864	$4455	81%	$17,053	$6266

*NA = not applicable; NR = not reported; * = includes room and board; † = room only.*

Freshman-Year Out-of-Pocket Costs: Looking Beyond the Sticker Price

This chart presents average costs. Actual costs may vary.

	Published tuition and fees	Room and board	Percent of freshmen who applied for aid	Average aid package for freshmen	Average cost after aid
Lebanon Valley College, Annville, PA	$15,360	$4940	NR	$12,760	$7540
Lees-McRae College, Banner Elk, NC	$9670	$3530	NR	$9171	$4029
Lee University, Cleveland, TN	$5372	$3540	71%	$6020	$2892
Lehigh University, Bethlehem, PA	$20,500	$6020	62%	$17,267	$9253
Lehman College of the City University of New York, Bronx, NY	$3320	NA	97%	$4500	$0
Le Moyne College, Syracuse, NY	$12,620	$5390	95%	$13,895	$4115
LeMoyne-Owen College, Memphis, TN	$6000	$3916	95%	$6840	$3076
Lenoir-Rhyne College, Hickory, NC	$11,416	$4074	92%	$8905	$6585
Lesley College, Cambridge, MA	$13,850	$6440	85%	$15,156	$5134
LeTourneau University, Longview, TX	$10,220	$4630	93%	$9042	$5808
Lewis & Clark College, Portland, OR	$17,740	$5780	80%	$14,519	$9001
Lewis-Clark State College, Lewiston, ID	$1626	$3130	63%	$5047	$0
Lewis University, Romeoville, IL	$12,416	$5200	NR	NR	NR
Lexington Baptist College, Lexington, KY	$2480	NA	NR	$792	$1688
LIFE Bible College, San Dimas, CA	$4785	$2800	NR	$400	$7185
Limestone College, Gaffney, SC	$8200	$3700	97%	$7739	$4161
Lincoln Christian College, Lincoln, IL	$5140	$3320	NR	$3786	$4674
Lincoln Memorial University, Harrogate, TN	$7350	$3300	90%	$6760	$3890
Lincoln University, Jefferson City, MO	$2046	$2788	50%	$6695	$0
Lincoln University, Lincoln University, PA	$4180	$4060	88%	$10,000	$0
Lindenwood College, St. Charles, MO	$9900	$5000	NR	NR	NR
Lindsey Wilson College, Columbia, KY	$8280	$4230	84%	$9054	$3456
Linfield College, McMinnville, OR	$15,096	$4642	93%	$12,786	$6952
Livingstone College, Salisbury, NC	$6090	$3450	87%	NR	NR
Lock Haven University of Pennsylvania, Lock Haven, PA	$3988	$3784	84%	NR	NR
Long Island University, Brooklyn Campus, Brooklyn, NY	$13,596	$5090	89%	$8590	$10,096
Long Island University, C.W. Post Campus, Brookville, NY	$13,690	$5950	95%	$10,728	$8912
Long Island University, Southampton College, Southampton, NY	$13,760	$6550	NR	$11,342	$8968
Longwood College, Farmville, VA	$4370	$4222	71%	$5666	$2926
Loras College, Dubuque, IA	$12,660	$4545	90%	$9394	$7811
Louise Salinger Academy of Fashion, San Francisco, CA	$12,540	NA	NR	NR	NR
Louisiana College, Pineville, LA	$6459	$2994	NR	$4700	$4753
Louisiana State University and Agricultural and Mechanical College, Baton Rouge, LA	$2687	$3570	45%	$4821	$1436
Louisiana State University in Shreveport, Shreveport, LA	$2210	NA	NR	NR	NR
Louisiana Tech University, Ruston, LA	$2352	$2595	58%	$2239	$2708
Lourdes College, Sylvania, OH	$7700	NA	NR	$6584	$1116
Loyola College, Baltimore, MD	$15,710	$6280	73%	$10,460	$11,530
Loyola Marymount University, Los Angeles, CA	$16,495	$6736	86%	$16,688	$6543
Loyola University Chicago, Chicago, IL	$14,820	$6210	NR	NR	NR
Loyola University New Orleans, New Orleans, LA	$13,266	$5830	NR	$11,676	$7420
Lubbock Christian University, Lubbock, TX	$8136	$3590	NR	NR	NR

*NA = not applicable; NR = not reported; * = includes room and board; † = room only.*

Freshman-Year Out-of-Pocket Costs: Looking Beyond the Sticker Price

This chart presents average costs. Actual costs may vary.

	Published tuition and fees	Room and board	Percent of freshmen who applied for aid	Average aid package for freshmen	Average cost after aid
Lutheran Bible Institute of Seattle, Issaquah, WA	$5310	$4345	NR	$5500	$4155
Luther College, Decorah, IA	$14,900	$3650	83%	$10,770	$7780
Luther Rice Bible College and Seminary, Lithonia, GA	$2512	NA	NR	$0	$2512
Lycoming College, Williamsport, PA	$16,160	$4600	95%	$15,017	$5743
Lyme Academy of Fine Arts, Old Lyme, CT	$8690	NA	43%	$1990	$6700
Lynchburg College, Lynchburg, VA	$14,820	$4400	NR	$14,535	$4685
Lyndon State College, Lyndonville, VT	$4340	$4936	90%	$9795	$0
Lynn University, Boca Raton, FL	$16,700	$6250	NR	$17,886	$5064
Lyon College, Batesville, AR	$9470	$4238	79%	$10,003	$3705
Macalester College, St. Paul, MN	$18,758	$5430	NR	NR	NR
Machzikei Hadath Rabbinical College, Brooklyn, NY	$5200	$1800	NR	NR	NR
MacMurray College, Jacksonville, IL	$10,940	$4000	96%	$11,038	$3902
Madonna University, Livonia, MI	$5820	$4168	NR	$6058	$3930
Magnolia Bible College, Kosciusko, MS	$4000	$930	67%	NR	NR
Maharishi University of Management, Fairfield, IA	$13,976	$4800	67%	$18,225	$551
Maine College of Art, Portland, ME	$13,905	$6060	84%	$8682	$11,283
Maine Maritime Academy, Castine, ME	$5580	$4895	76%	$5925	$4550
Malone College, Canton, OH	$10,765	$4100	NR	$10,164	$4701
Manchester College, North Manchester, IN	$12,710	$4500	96%	$10,527	$6683
Manhattan Christian College, Manhattan, KS	$5300	$2730	95%	$4520	$3510
Manhattan College, Riverdale, NY	$13,930	$7150	NR	$14,995	$6085
Manhattan School of Music, New York, NY	$16,330	$4160†	73%	$12,586	$7904
Manhattanville College, Purchase, NY	$16,640	$7680	69%	$17,632	$6688
Mankato State University, Mankato, MN	$2896	$2965	NR	NR	NR
Mannes College of Music, New School for Social Research, New York, NY	$14,805	$6500†	NR	NR	NR
Mansfield University of Pennsylvania, Mansfield, PA	$4234	$3612	NR	$7460	$386
Maranatha Baptist Bible College, Watertown, WI	$5670	$3250	96%	$3368	$5552
Marian College, Indianapolis, IN	$11,692	$4032	NR	NR	NR
Marian College of Fond du Lac, Fond du Lac, WI	$11,370	$4188	91%	$8040	$7518
Marietta College, Marietta, OH	$15,490	$4410	98%	$14,100	$5800
Marist College, Poughkeepsie, NY	$12,390	$6600	97%	$8930	$10,060
Marlboro College, Marlboro, VT	$19,882	$6445	90%	$17,000	$9327
Marquette University, Milwaukee, WI	$14,934	$5130	79%	$15,363	$4701
Marshall University, Huntington, WV	$2116	$4240	71%	$5240	$1116
Mars Hill College, Mars Hill, NC	$8900	$3800	NR	$10,000	$2700
Martin Luther College, New Ulm, MN	$4465	$2205	NR	$4706	$1964
Martin Methodist College, Pulaski, TN	$6350	$2950	85%	$5492	$3808
Martin University, Indianapolis, IN	$6960	NA	NR	NR	NR
Mary Baldwin College, Staunton, VA	$13,360	$7000	NR	$10,723	$9637
Marycrest International University, Davenport, IA	$10,951	$3904	NR	$6330	$8525
Marygrove College, Detroit, MI	$9056	$4160	100%	$13,000	$216

*NA = not applicable; NR = not reported; * = includes room and board; † = room only.*

Freshman-Year Out-of-Pocket Costs: Looking Beyond the Sticker Price

This chart presents average costs. Actual costs may vary.

	Published tuition and fees	Room and board	Percent of freshmen who applied for aid	Average aid package for freshmen	Average cost after aid
Maryland Institute, College of Art, Baltimore, MD	$16,100	$5490	82%	$11,500	$10,090
Marymount College, Tarrytown, NY	$13,815	$7200	NR	$10,922	$10,093
Marymount Manhattan College, New York, NY	$11,900	$5600	NR	$9952	$7548
Marymount University, Arlington, VA	$12,770	$5810	85%	$12,819	$5761
Maryville College, Maryville, TN	$13,255	$4500	100%	$14,500	$3255
Maryville University of Saint Louis, St. Louis, MO	$10,340	$4900	90%	$9122	$6118
Mary Washington College, Fredericksburg, VA	$3318	$5024	75%	$4263	$4079
Marywood University, Scranton, PA	$13,185	$5200	NR	$10,305	$8080
Massachusetts College of Art, Boston, MA	$4034	$5588	73%	$3730	$5892
Massachusetts College of Pharmacy and Allied Health Sciences, Boston, MA	$13,400	$7250	NR	$10,622	$10,028
Massachusetts Institute of Technology, Cambridge, MA	$22,000	$6350	76%	$19,968	$8382
Massachusetts Maritime Academy, Buzzards Bay, MA	$3093	$3900	83%	$6183	$810
The Master's College and Seminary, Santa Clarita, CA	$11,050	$5400	100%	$6413	$10,037
Mayo School of Health-Related Sciences, Rochester, MN	$1000	NA	NR	$0	$1000
Mayville State University, Mayville, ND	$1920	$2382	75%	$6500	$0
McKendree College, Lebanon, IL	$8400	$4200	93%	$4605	$7995
McMurry University, Abilene, TX	$7950	$3500	95%	$7520	$3930
McNeese State University, Lake Charles, LA	$1997	$2620	84%	$3318	$1299
McPherson College, McPherson, KS	$9970	$3730	NR	NR	NR
Medaille College, Buffalo, NY	$9950	$4400	86%	$9553	$4797
Medgar Evers College of the City University of New York, Brooklyn, NY	$3240	NA	NR	NR	NR
Medical College of Georgia, Augusta, GA	$2364	$1305†	NR	$0	$3669
Memphis College of Art, Memphis, TN	$10,300	$4275	NR	$6120	$8455
Menlo College, Atherton, CA	$16,180	$6500	NR	NR	NR
Mercer University, Macon, GA	$13,896	$4215	96%	$13,956	$4155
Mercyhurst College, Erie, PA	$11,619	$4464	90%	$5261	$10,822
Meredith College, Raleigh, NC	$8490	$3750	91%	$7946	$4294
Merrimack College, North Andover, MA	$13,980	$6900	NR	$14,314	$6566
Mesa State College, Grand Junction, CO	$1933	$4100	75%	$5667	$366
Messenger College, Joplin, MO	$2880	NA	NR	NR	NR
Messiah College, Grantham, PA	$11,888	$5400	84%	$8642	$8646
Methodist College, Fayetteville, NC	$11,250	$4400	90%	$5200	$10,450
Metropolitan State College of Denver, Denver, CO	$1960	NA	NR	NR	NR
Metropolitan State University, St. Paul, MN	$2570	NA	54%	NR	NR
Miami University, Oxford, OH	$5172	$4440	59%	$6197	$3415
Michigan Christian College, Rochester Hills, MI	$6120	$3700	NR	$5690	$4130
Michigan State University, East Lansing, MI	$4655	$3972	NR	$8940	$0
Michigan Technological University, Houghton, MI	$3948	$4284	100%	$5586	$2646
Mid-America Bible College, Oklahoma City, OK	$4684	$3098	NR	NR	NR
MidAmerica Nazarene University, Olathe, KS	$9256	$4496	NR	NR	NR
Mid-Continent Baptist Bible College, Mayfield, KY	$3260	$2532	74%	$1290	$4502

*NA = not applicable; NR = not reported; * = includes room and board; † = room only.*

Freshman-Year Out-of-Pocket Costs: Looking Beyond the Sticker Price

This chart presents average costs. Actual costs may vary.

	Published tuition and fees	Room and board	Percent of freshmen who applied for aid	Average aid package for freshmen	Average cost after aid
Middlebury College, Middlebury, VT	$28,020*	NA	54%	$21,183	$6837
Middle Tennessee State University, Murfreesboro, TN	$2014	$2558	55%	$4070	$502
Midland Lutheran College, Fremont, NE	$12,250	$3200	96%	$11,019	$4431
Midway College, Midway, KY	$8160	$4250	NR	$3112	$9298
Midwestern State University, Wichita Falls, TX	$1888	$3366	45%	$1546	$3708
Miles College, Birmingham, AL	$4450	$2750	NR	$6800	$400
Millersville University of Pennsylvania, Millersville, PA	$4268	$4300	85%	NR	NR
Milligan College, Milligan College, TN	$9500	$3440	86%	$6152	$6788
Millikin University, Decatur, IL	$14,079	$5070	NR	$12,498	$6651
Millsaps College, Jackson, MS	$13,088	$4902	89%	$13,411	$4579
Mills College, Oakland, CA	$15,755	$5740	NR	NR	NR
Milwaukee Institute of Art and Design, Milwaukee, WI	$14,100	$6000	NR	$8122	$11,978
Milwaukee School of Engineering, Milwaukee, WI	$13,305	$3615	93%	$11,166	$5754
Minneapolis College of Art and Design, Minneapolis, MN	$14,782	$2000†	NR	$8568	$8214
Minnesota Bible College, Rochester, MN	$5239	$1440†	94%	$6022	$657
Minot State University, Minot, ND	$2224	$2049	NR	NR	NR
Mississippi College, Clinton, MS	$7650	$3550	NR	$6574	$4626
Mississippi State University, Mississippi State, MS	$2591	$3215	NR	$4625	$1181
Mississippi University for Women, Columbus, MS	$2749	$2557	100%	$5013	$293
Mississippi Valley State University, Itta Bena, MS	$2278	$2384	NR	$4200	$462
Missouri Baptist College, St. Louis, MO	$8450	$4000	89%	$6491	$5959
Missouri Southern State College, Joplin, MO	$2330	$3200	NR	$4113	$1417
Missouri Technical School, St. Louis, MO	$7396	NA	NR	$7500	$0
Missouri Valley College, Marshall, MO	$10,300	$5000	98%	$11,925	$3375
Missouri Western State College, St. Joseph, MO	$2414	$2726	NR	$4600	$540
Molloy College, Rockville Centre, NY	$9994	NA	NR	$9575	$419
Monmouth College, Monmouth, IL	$14,630	$4350	98%	NR	NR
Monmouth University, West Long Branch, NJ	$13,800	$5808	93%	$8816	$10,792
Montana State University–Billings, Billings, MT	$2388	$3000	NR	$2384	$3004
Montana State University–Bozeman, Bozeman, MT	$2504	$4034	NR	$6000	$538
Montana State University–Northern, Havre, MT	$2350	$3600	86%	$2500	$3450
Montana Tech of The University of Montana, Butte, MT	$2373	$3560	NR	$3500	$2433
Montclair State University, Upper Montclair, NJ	$3254	$5334	76%	$6335	$2253
Montreat College, Montreat, NC	$10,042	$3940	96%	$9324	$4658
Montserrat College of Art, Beverly, MA	$11,675	$3200†	NR	$5814	$9061
Moody Bible Institute, Chicago, IL	$830	$4300	NR	$0	$5130
Moore College of Art and Design, Philadelphia, PA	$14,422	$5604	NR	NR	NR
Moorhead State University, Moorhead, MN	$2881	$3078	95%	$4195	$1764
Moravian College, Bethlehem, PA	$16,621	$5225	87%	NR	NR
Morehead State University, Morehead, KY	$2090	$2950	NR	$4369	$671
Morehouse College, Atlanta, GA	$9254	$5976	93%	$8000	$7230

*NA = not applicable; NR = not reported; * = includes room and board; † = room only.*

Freshman-Year Out-of-Pocket Costs: Looking Beyond the Sticker Price

This chart presents average costs. Actual costs may vary.

	Published tuition and fees	Room and board	Percent of freshmen who applied for aid	Average aid package for freshmen	Average cost after aid
Morgan State University, Baltimore, MD	$3412	$5090	NR	NR	NR
Morningside College, Sioux City, IA	$11,612	$4528	96%	$12,702	$3438
Morris College, Sumter, SC	$5105	$2691	NR	$4000	$3796
Mount Aloysius College, Cresson, PA	$8780	$3920	95%	$5032	$7668
Mount Angel Seminary, Saint Benedict, OR	$8400	$4500	NR	$10,000	$2900
Mount Carmel College of Nursing, Columbus, OH	$6026	$2312†	NR	NR	NR
Mount Holyoke College, South Hadley, MA	$21,390	$6250	86%	$20,975	$6665
Mount Marty College, Yankton, SD	$8734	$3470	NR	$8073	$4131
Mount Mary College, Milwaukee, WI	$10,230	$3490	87%	$9195	$4525
Mount Mercy College, Cedar Rapids, IA	$11,860	$3945	100%	$13,500	$2305
Mount Olive College, Mount Olive, NC	$8490	$3325	NR	$7166	$4649
Mount St. Clare College, Clinton, IA	$11,640	$4020	NR	NR	NR
Mount Saint Mary College, Newburgh, NY	$9480	$5000	84%	$7157	$7323
Mount St. Mary's College, Los Angeles, CA	$14,965	$6000	NR	NR	NR
Mount Saint Mary's College and Seminary, Emmitsburg, MD	$14,885	$6250	75%	$11,530	$9605
Mount Senario College, Ladysmith, WI	$8980	$3250	NR	NR	NR
Mount Union College, Alliance, OH	$13,880	$3760	81%	$11,200	$6440
Mount Vernon College, Washington, DC	$15,430	$7340	88%	$11,175	$11,595
Mount Vernon Nazarene College, Mount Vernon, OH	$9977	$3843	99%	$8764	$5056
Muhlenberg College, Allentown, PA	$18,100	$4870	79%	$11,277	$11,693
Multnomah Bible College and Biblical Seminary, Portland, OR	$7100	$2990	NR	NR	NR
Murray State University, Murray, KY	$2120	$3410	NR	$4516	$1014
Musicians Institute, Hollywood, CA	$12,000	NA	25%	NR	NR
Muskingum College, New Concord, OH	$10,785	$4500	83%	$10,675	$4610
NAES College, Chicago, IL	$4340	NA	100%	$2886	$1454
National American University, Denver, CO	$7920	NA	NR	NR	NR
National College, Colorado Springs, CO	$7995	NA	NR	NR	NR
National College, Kansas City, MO	$8003	NA	NR	NR	NR
National College, Albuquerque, NM	$8210	NA	NR	NR	NR
National College, Rapid City, SD	$8475	$3360	NR	NR	NR
National College–St. Paul Campus, St. Paul, MN	$8160	NA	NR	NR	NR
National College–Sioux Falls Branch, Sioux Falls, SD	$7680	NA	NR	NR	NR
The National Hispanic University, San Jose, CA	$3875	NA	58%	$1338	$2537
National-Louis University, Evanston, IL	$11,250	$4740	NR	$7306	$8684
National University, La Jolla, CA	$6660	NA	NR	$4000	$2660
Nazarene Bible College, Colorado Springs, CO	$5055	NA	98%	NR	NR
Nazarene Indian Bible College, Albuquerque, NM	$4170	$900†	100%	$3784	$1286
Nazareth College of Rochester, Rochester, NY	$12,130	$5324	91%	$10,799	$6655
Nebraska Christian College, Norfolk, NE	$4330	$2660	100%	$4938	$2052
Nebraska Methodist College of Nursing and Allied Health, Omaha, NE	$8320	$2000	NR	$4029	$6291
Nebraska Wesleyan University, Lincoln, NE	$10,714	$3520	83%	$8265	$5969

*NA = not applicable; NR = not reported; * = includes room and board; † = room only.*

Freshman-Year Out-of-Pocket Costs: Looking Beyond the Sticker Price

This chart presents average costs. Actual costs may vary.

	Published tuition and fees	Room and board	Percent of freshmen who applied for aid	Average aid package for freshmen	Average cost after aid
Neumann College, Aston, PA	$12,870	NA	92%	$10,096	$2774
Newberry College, Newberry, SC	$12,326	$3218	86%	$9690	$5854
New College of California, San Francisco, CA	$8326	NA	NR	NR	NR
New College of the University of South Florida, Sarasota, FL	$2167	$4017	NR	NR	NR
New England College, Henniker, NH	$14,974	$5732	80%	$13,477	$7229
New England Conservatory of Music, Boston, MA	$17,300	$8000	NR	$11,380	$13,920
New Hampshire College, Manchester, NH	$12,980	$5756	NR	$8500	$10,236
New Jersey Institute of Technology, Newark, NJ	$5466	$5210	88%	$10,075	$601
New Mexico Highlands University, Las Vegas, NM	$1608	$2410	NR	NR	NR
New Mexico Institute of Mining and Technology, Socorro, NM	$1998	$3426	100%	$6553	$0
New Mexico State University, Las Cruces, NM	$2196	$3288	NR	NR	NR
New Orleans Baptist Theological Seminary, New Orleans, LA	$1800	$1125†	NR	NR	NR
Newschool of Architecture, San Diego, CA	$10,080	$6000	83%	$10,295	$5785
New York Institute of Technology, Old Westbury, NY	$11,060	$6060	NR	NR	NR
New York School of Interior Design, New York, NY	$12,800	NA	NR	$7500	$5300
New York University, New York, NY	$20,756	$7882	NR	$13,497	$15,141
Niagara University, Niagara Falls, NY	$12,256	$5388	95%	$11,926	$5718
Nicholls State University, Thibodaux, LA	$2017	$2700	NR	NR	NR
Nichols College, Dudley, MA	$11,295	$6200	78%	$13,068	$4427
Norfolk State University, Norfolk, VA	$2865	$4096	85%	$6064	$897
North Adams State College, North Adams, MA	$3485	$4502	87%	$5350	$2637
North Carolina Agricultural and Technical State University, Greensboro, NC	$1561	$3410	85%	$4437	$534
North Carolina Central University, Durham, NC	$2510	$3270	NR	NR	NR
North Carolina School of the Arts, Winston-Salem, NC	$2229	$3798	NR	$6244	$0
North Carolina State University, Raleigh, NC	$2200	$3350	NR	$6180	$0
North Carolina Wesleyan College, Rocky Mount, NC	$7430	$4830	92%	$3048	$9212
North Central Bible College, Minneapolis, MN	$7030	$3550	NR	NR	NR
North Central College, Naperville, IL	$13,194	$4854	85%	$12,244	$5804
North Dakota State University, Fargo, ND	$2410	$2968	73%	$4432	$946
Northeastern Illinois University, Chicago, IL	$2657	NA	65%	NR	NR
Northeastern State University, Tahlequah, OK	$1650	$2520	NR	$2619	$1551
Northeastern University, Boston, MA	$13,497	$7905	79%	$10,451	$10,951
Northeast Louisiana University, Monroe, LA	$1926	$2160	NR	$3616	$470
Northern Arizona University, Flagstaff, AZ	$2080	$3390	NR	$5747	$0
Northern Illinois University, De Kalb, IL	$3378	$3600	96%	$8500	$0
Northern Kentucky University, Highland Heights, KY	$2020	$3164	44%	$5645	$0
Northern Michigan University, Marquette, MI	$2939	$4141	NR	$5957	$1123
Northern State University, Aberdeen, SD	$2490	$2672	87%	$5861	$0
North Georgia College & State University, Dahlonega, GA	$1956	$3057	NR	NR	NR
North Greenville College, Tigerville, SC	$6900	$4080	NR	$7676	$3304
Northland College, Ashland, WI	$12,365	$4215	NR	$10,385	$6195

NA = not applicable; NR = not reported; * = includes room and board; † = room only.

Freshman-Year Out-of-Pocket Costs: Looking Beyond the Sticker Price

This chart presents average costs. Actual costs may vary.

	Published tuition and fees	Room and board	Percent of freshmen who applied for aid	Average aid package for freshmen	Average cost after aid
North Park University, Chicago, IL	$13,990	$4820	91%	$12,347	$6463
Northwest Christian College, Eugene, OR	$10,310	$4310	NR	NR	NR
Northwest College of Art, Poulsbo, WA	$7600	NA	63%	$4137	$3463
Northwest College of the Assemblies of God, Kirkland, WA	$8940	$4310	84%	$6060	$7190
Northwestern College, Orange City, IA	$10,850	$3250	92%	$11,627	$2473
Northwestern College, St. Paul, MN	$12,750	$4020	NR	$11,195	$5575
Northwestern Oklahoma State University, Alva, OK	$1650	$1932	NR	$2300	$1282
Northwestern State University of Louisiana, Natchitoches, LA	$2254	$2216	73%	$3565	$905
Northwestern University, Evanston, IL	$18,144	$6054	67%	$15,355	$8843
Northwest Missouri State University, Maryville, MO	$2535	$3780	74%	$4820	$1495
Northwood University, Midland, MI	$10,530	$4734	NR	$11,372	$3892
Northwood University, Florida Campus, West Palm Beach, FL	$10,874	$6013	55%	$9805	$7082
Northwood University, Texas Campus, Cedar Hill, TX	$10,530	$4709	NR	$10,487	$4752
Norwich University, Northfield, VT	$14,634	$5536	NR	NR	NR
Notre Dame College, Manchester, NH	$11,840	$5295	94%	$8200	$8935
Notre Dame College of Ohio, South Euclid, OH	$11,130	$4095	NR	$7476	$7749
Nova Southeastern University, Fort Lauderdale, FL	$9820	$5380	NR	$8125	$7075
Nyack College, Nyack, NY	$10,260	$4420	NR	$11,063	$3617
Oak Hills Bible College, Bemidji, MN	$7680	$2475	86%	$6429	$3726
Oakland City University, Oakland City, IN	$7966	$3146	NR	$5500	$5612
Oakland University, Rochester, MI	$3702	$4250	78%	$4184	$3768
Oakwood College, Huntsville, AL	$7628	$4500	71%	$8078	$4050
Oberlin College, Oberlin, OH	$21,576	$6174	NR	$18,564	$9186
Occidental College, Los Angeles, CA	$19,210	$5660	78%	$20,726	$4144
Oglethorpe University, Atlanta, GA	$15,170	$4790	97%	$14,498	$5462
Ohio Dominican College, Columbus, OH	$8910	$4570	91%	$8536	$4944
Ohio Northern University, Ada, OH	$17,970	$4500	91%	$17,062	$5408
The Ohio State University, Columbus, OH	$3468	$4907	NR	$6950	$1425
Ohio University, Athens, OH	$4080	$4473	84%	$7000	$1553
Ohio University–Chillicothe, Chillicothe, OH	$3021	NA	NR	NR	NR
Ohio University–Eastern, St. Clairsville, OH	$3021	NA	NR	NR	NR
Ohio University–Lancaster, Lancaster, OH	$3021	NA	NR	NR	NR
Ohio University–Zanesville, Zanesville, OH	$3051	NA	NR	NR	NR
Ohio Wesleyan University, Delaware, OH	$18,228	$5994	66%	$18,277	$5945
Oklahoma Baptist University, Shawnee, OK	$7656	$3180	85%	$4890	$5946
Oklahoma Christian University of Science and Arts, Oklahoma City, OK	$7478	$3840	80%	$6885	$4433
Oklahoma City University, Oklahoma City, OK	$8135	$3990	NR	NR	NR
Oklahoma Panhandle State University, Goodwell, OK	$1653	$2070	NR	NR	NR
Oklahoma State University, Stillwater, OK	$1708	$4160	73%	$7861	$0
Old Dominion University, Norfolk, VA	$4116	$4770	75%	$8100	$786
Olivet College, Olivet, MI	$12,660	$4038	98%	$12,733	$3965

NA = not applicable; NR = not reported; * = includes room and board; † = room only.

Freshman-Year Out-of-Pocket Costs:
Looking Beyond the Sticker Price
This chart presents average costs. Actual costs may vary.

	Published tuition and fees	Room and board	Percent of freshmen who applied for aid	Average aid package for freshmen	Average cost after aid
Olivet Nazarene University, Kankakee, IL	$10,166	$4460	NR	$10,669	$3957
O'More College of Design, Franklin, TN	$7500	NA	NR	NR	NR
Oral Roberts University, Tulsa, OK	$9934	$4724	NR	$13,388	$1270
Oregon College of Art and Craft, Portland, OR	$9918	NA	NR	$0	$9918
Oregon Institute of Technology, Klamath Falls, OR	$3144	$3910	NR	NR	NR
Oregon State University, Corvallis, OR	$3447	$4587	NR	NR	NR
Otis College of Art and Design, Los Angeles, CA	$15,350	NA	59%	NR	NR
Ottawa University, Ottawa, KS	$8990	$3920	94%	$12,600	$310
Otterbein College, Westerville, OH	$14,997	$4750	90%	$13,603	$6144
Ouachita Baptist University, Arkadelphia, AR	$7650	$2970	95%	$7600	$3020
Our Lady of Holy Cross College, New Orleans, LA	$5112	NA	NR	$4300	$812
Our Lady of the Lake University of San Antonio, San Antonio, TX	$9794	$3300	100%	$11,010	$2084
Ozark Christian College, Joplin, MO	$4025	$3220	NR	NR	NR
Pace University, New York, NY	$13,030	$5340	94%	$9742	$8628
Pacific Lutheran University, Tacoma, WA	$15,136	$4814	87%	$13,071	$6879
Pacific Northwest College of Art, Portland, OR	$10,362	NA	NR	NR	NR
Pacific University, Forest Grove, OR	$15,654	$4067	88%	$13,601	$6120
Paier College of Art, Inc., Hamden, CT	$10,595	NA	71%	$5200	$5395
Paine College, Augusta, GA	$6640	$3020	NR	$9200	$460
Palm Beach Atlantic College, West Palm Beach, FL	$9300	$4310	82%	$9000	$4610
Palmer College of Chiropractic, Davenport, IA	$13,905	NA	NR	NR	NR
Park College, Parkville, MO	$4200	$4220	NR	NR	NR
Parsons School of Design, New School for Social Research, New York, NY	$18,540	$8555	NR	$10,500	$16,595
Patten College, Oakland, CA	$6672	$2300†	NR	NR	NR
Paul Quinn College, Dallas, TX	$4685	$3450	NR	NR	NR
Peabody Conservatory of Music of The Johns Hopkins University, Baltimore, MD	$16,520	$6940	67%	$11,400	$12,060
Pennsylvania State University Abington College, Abington, PA	$5452	NA	NR	NR	NR
Pennsylvania State University Altoona College, Altoona, PA	$5452	$4170	NR	NR	NR
Pennsylvania State University at Erie, The Behrend College, Erie, PA	$5624	$4170	NR	NR	NR
Pennsylvania State University Berks–Lehigh Valley College, Reading, PA	$5452	$4170	NR	NR	NR
Pennsylvania State University Harrisburg Campus of the Capital College, Middletown, PA	$5624	$4170	NR	NR	NR
Pennsylvania State University Schuylkill Campus of the Capital College, Schuylkill Haven, PA	$5452	$4170	NR	NR	NR
Pennsylvania State University University Park Campus, State College, PA	$5624	$4170	NR	NR	NR
Pepperdine University, Malibu, CA	$20,210	$6860	71%	$18,352	$8718
Peru State College, Peru, NE	$1936	$2966	99%	$3900	$1002
Pfeiffer University, Misenheimer, NC	$9260	$4000	90%	NR	NR
Philadelphia College of Bible, Langhorne, PA	$9120	$4820	NR	$7907	$6033
Philadelphia College of Pharmacy and Science, Philadelphia, PA	$12,330	$5090	76%	$8500	$8920
Philadelphia College of Textiles and Science, Philadelphia, PA	$12,716	$5874	NR	$12,516	$6074
Philander Smith College, Little Rock, AR	$3288	$2746	NR	NR	NR

*NA = not applicable; NR = not reported; * = includes room and board; † = room only.*

Freshman-Year Out-of-Pocket Costs: Looking Beyond the Sticker Price

This chart presents average costs. Actual costs may vary.

	Published tuition and fees	Room and board	Percent of freshmen who applied for aid	Average aid package for freshmen	Average cost after aid
Phillips University, Enid, OK	$7105	$3904	80%	NR	NR
Piedmont Bible College, Winston-Salem, NC	$5250	$3090	73%	$6095	$2245
Piedmont College, Demorest, GA	$7200	$3930	100%	$6553	$4577
Pikeville College, Pikeville, KY	$6500	$3050	99%	$10,195	$0
Pine Manor College, Chestnut Hill, MA	$10,700	$6900	66%	$14,900	$2700
Pittsburg State University, Pittsburg, KS	$1876	$3188	77%	$3356	$1708
Pitzer College, Claremont, CA	$21,086	$6094	53%	$20,040	$7140
Plymouth State College of the University System of New Hampshire, Plymouth, NH	$3926	$4000	73%	$8374	$0
Point Loma Nazarene College, San Diego, CA	$11,824	$4730	85%	$4820	$11,734
Point Park College, Pittsburgh, PA	$10,637	$5072	NR	$10,500	$5209
Polytechnic University, Brooklyn Campus, Brooklyn, NY	$18,350	$4240	95%	$9449	$13,141
Polytechnic University, Farmingdale Campus, Farmingdale, NY	$18,350	$4400	92%	$9905	$12,845
Polytechnic University of Puerto Rico, Hato Rey, PR	$4140	NA	74%	NR	NR
Pomona College, Claremont, CA	$19,710	$7860	67%	$20,500	$7070
Pontifical Catholic University of Puerto Rico, Ponce, PR	$3514	$2660	NR	$2000	$4174
Pontifical College Josephinum, Columbus, OH	$5896	$4044	75%	$2402	$7538
Portland State University, Portland, OR	$3180	$4500	NR	$6612	$1068
Practical Bible College, Bible School Park, NY	$5000	$3350	97%	$6746	$1604
Prairie View A&M University, Prairie View, TX	$1900	$3620	NR	$4500	$1020
Pratt Institute, Brooklyn, NY	$17,151	$7153	NR	$12,120	$12,184
Presbyterian College, Clinton, SC	$14,121	$4034	91%	$14,052	$4103
Presentation College, Aberdeen, SD	$7090	$3046	NR	NR	NR
Princeton University, Princeton, NJ	$22,920	$6515	53%	$18,690	$10,745
Principia College, Elsah, IL	$14,112	$5586	NR	NR	NR
Providence College, Providence, RI	$15,980	$6670	77%	$13,850	$8800
Puget Sound Christian College, Edmonds, WA	$6075	$3870	91%	$5425	$4520
Purchase College, State University of New York, Purchase, NY	$3865	$5096	71%	$8150	$811
Purdue University, West Lafayette, IN	$3208	$4520	NR	NR	NR
Purdue University Calumet, Hammond, IN	$2971	NA	98%	NR	NR
Purdue University North Central, Westville, IN	$2610	NA	81%	$3127	$0
Queens College, Charlotte, NC	$12,980	$5600	NR	$11,467	$7113
Queens College of the City University of New York, Flushing, NY	$3387	NA	NR	NR	NR
Quincy University, Quincy, IL	$11,450	$4380	99%	$11,000	$4830
Quinnipiac College, Hamden, CT	$14,120	$6770	82%	$8436	$12,454
Rabbinical Academy Mesivta Rabbi Chaim Berlin, Brooklyn, NY	$4750	$2900	NR	NR	NR
Rabbinical Seminary of America, Forest Hills, NY	$4000	$2800	NR	NR	NR
Radford University, Radford, VA	$4344	$4416	61%	$4855	$3905
Ramapo College of New Jersey, Mahwah, NJ	$3752	$5678	64%	$5003	$4427
Randolph-Macon College, Ashland, VA	$15,630	$3895	NR	$13,430	$6095
Randolph-Macon Woman's College, Lynchburg, VA	$15,740	$6520	86%	$15,349	$6911
Reed College, Portland, OR	$21,490	$6000	59%	$18,175	$9315

*NA = not applicable; NR = not reported; * = includes room and board; † = room only.*

Freshman-Year Out-of-Pocket Costs: Looking Beyond the Sticker Price

This chart presents average costs. Actual costs may vary.

	Published tuition and fees	Room and board	Percent of freshmen who applied for aid	Average aid package for freshmen	Average cost after aid
Reformed Bible College, Grand Rapids, MI	$6736	$3350	94%	$6484	$3602
Regis College, Weston, MA	$14,500	$6600	73%	$15,014	$6086
Regis University, Denver, CO	$14,170	$5980	NR	$12,584	$7566
Reinhardt College, Waleska, GA	$5592	$4253	NR	$5300	$4545
Rensselaer Polytechnic Institute, Troy, NY	$19,652	$6377	NR	$15,567	$10,462
Research College of Nursing–Rockhurst College, Kansas City, MO	$11,300	$4260	NR	NR	NR
Rhode Island College, Providence, RI	$2999	$5367	80%	$5776	$2590
Rhode Island School of Design, Providence, RI	$18,630	$6618	54%	$13,500	$11,748
Rhodes College, Memphis, TN	$16,550	$5110	54%	$13,576	$8084
Rice University, Houston, TX	$13,200	$6000	67%	$14,573	$4627
The Richard Stockton College of New Jersey, Pomona, NJ	$3472	$4487	84%	$4867	$3092
Rider University, Lawrenceville, NJ	$14,690	$6030	83%	$14,630	$6090
Ringling School of Art and Design, Sarasota, FL	$12,900	$6650	81%	$7109	$12,441
Ripon College, Ripon, WI	$17,000	$4400	NR	$17,073	$4327
Rivier College, Nashua, NH	$12,500	$5380	NR	$8225	$9655
Roanoke Bible College, Elizabeth City, NC	$4340	$2930	100%	$1325	$5945
Roanoke College, Salem, VA	$14,750	$4850	85%	$14,593	$5007
Robert Morris College, Chicago, IL	$9750	NA	96%	$9977	$0
Robert Morris College, Moon Township, PA	$7740	$4744	85%	$4350	$8134
Roberts Wesleyan College, Rochester, NY	$11,640	$4056	92%	$12,604	$3092
Rochester Institute of Technology, Rochester, NY	$15,651	$6135	81%	$14,428	$7358
Rockford College, Rockford, IL	$14,100	$4500	85%	$15,016	$3584
Rockhurst College, Kansas City, MO	$11,790	$4760	NR	NR	NR
Rocky Mountain College, Billings, MT	$10,099	$3822	NR	$7131	$6790
Rocky Mountain College of Art & Design, Denver, CO	$6840	NA	NR	NR	NR
Roger Williams University, Bristol, RI	$15,100	$6860	77%	$15,091	$6869
Rollins College, Winter Park, FL	$19,075	$5885	45%	$18,644	$6316
Rose-Hulman Institute of Technology, Terre Haute, IN	$16,968	$4956	92%	$12,170	$9754
Rosemont College, Rosemont, PA	$13,340	$6500	74%	$10,661	$9179
Rowan University, Glassboro, NJ	$3751	$4768	NR	$3743	$4776
Russell Sage College, Troy, NY	$13,670	$5560	95%	$7664	$11,566
Rust College, Holly Springs, MS	$5025	$2275	90%	$6726	$574
Rutgers, The State University of New Jersey, Camden College of Arts and Sciences, Camden, NJ	$4948	$5134	85%	$7378	$2704
Rutgers, The State University of New Jersey, College of Engineering, Piscataway, NJ	$5524	$5134	77%	$7653	$3005
Rutgers, The State University of New Jersey, College of Nursing, Newark, NJ	$4880	$5134	80%	$8698	$1316
Rutgers, The State University of New Jersey, College of Pharmacy, Piscataway, NJ	$5524	$5134	75%	$8230	$2428
Rutgers, The State University of New Jersey, Cook College, New Brunswick, NJ	$5528	$5134	76%	$7677	$2985
Rutgers, The State University of New Jersey, Douglass College, New Brunswick, NJ	$5080	$5134	74%	$7716	$2498
Rutgers, The State University of New Jersey, Livingston College, New Brunswick, NJ	$5130	$5134	77%	$7523	$2741
Rutgers, The State University of New Jersey, Mason Gross School of the Arts, New Brunswick, NJ	$5080	$5134	71%	$7750	$2464

*NA = not applicable; NR = not reported; * = includes room and board; † = room only.*

Freshman-Year Out-of-Pocket Costs:
Looking Beyond the Sticker Price
This chart presents average costs. Actual costs may vary.

	Published tuition and fees	Room and board	Percent of freshmen who applied for aid	Average aid package for freshmen	Average cost after aid
Rutgers, The State University of New Jersey, Newark College of Arts and Sciences, Newark, NJ	$4902	$5134	76%	$6637	$3399
Rutgers, The State University of New Jersey, Rutgers College, New Brunswick, NJ	$5126	$5134	73%	$7501	$2759
Sacred Heart Major Seminary, Detroit, MI	$4855	$4220	67%	NR	NR
Sacred Heart University, Fairfield, CT	$12,712	$6380	94%	$8761	$10,331
Saginaw Valley State University, University Center, MI	$3349	$4140	100%	$7302	$187
St. Ambrose University, Davenport, IA	$12,300	$4400	95%	$7000	$9700
St. Andrews Presbyterian College, Laurinburg, NC	$12,182	$5315	80%	$5300	$12,197
Saint Anselm College, Manchester, NH	$14,950	$5710	88%	$12,684	$7976
Saint Augustine's College, Raleigh, NC	$6560	$4000	NR	NR	NR
St. Bonaventure University, St. Bonaventure, NY	$12,439	$5074	91%	$10,944	$6569
St. Charles Borromeo Seminary, Overbrook, Wynnewood, PA	$6700	$4250	29%	NR	NR
St. Cloud State University, St. Cloud, MN	$2904	$3027	48%	$3771	$2160
St. Edward's University, Austin, TX	$10,400	$4116	73%	$9049	$5467
Saint Francis College, Fort Wayne, IN	$10,220	$4070	95%	$9125	$5165
St. Francis College, Brooklyn Heights, NY	$7700	NA	93%	$7963	$0
Saint Francis College, Loretto, PA	$13,238	$5650	NR	$11,700	$7188
St. John Fisher College, Rochester, NY	$12,150	$5580	NR	$10,370	$7360
St. John's College, Annapolis, MD	$20,040	$5950	67%	$17,203	$8787
St. John's College, Santa Fe, NM	$18,720	$6055	72%	$15,662	$9113
St. John's Seminary College, Camarillo, CA	$7080	$3023	92%	$10,634	$0
Saint John's Seminary College of Liberal Arts, Brighton, MA	$5200	$2600	71%	$7120	$680
Saint John's University, Collegeville, MN	$13,996	$4392	88%	$13,290	$5098
St. John's University, Jamaica, NY	$11,380	NA	80%	$8220	$3160
St. John Vianney College Seminary, Miami, FL	$7000	$4000	11%	$2470	$8530
Saint Joseph College, West Hartford, CT	$13,800	$5300	91%	NR	NR
Saint Joseph's College, Rensselaer, IN	$12,590	$4640	97%	$10,879	$6351
Saint Joseph's College, Standish, ME	$11,285	$5380	93%	$12,526	$4139
St. Joseph's College, New York, Brooklyn, NY	$8326	NA	89%	$7800	$526
St. Joseph's College, Suffolk Campus, Patchogue, NY	$8356	NA	80%	$6500	$1856
Saint Joseph Seminary College, Saint Benedict, LA	$5780	$4550	33%	$12,723	$0
Saint Joseph's University, Philadelphia, PA	$14,700	$6450	81%	$9790	$11,360
St. Lawrence University, Canton, NY	$20,560	$6110	59%	$19,599	$7071
Saint Leo College, Saint Leo, FL	$10,496	$5060	95%	$11,360	$4196
St. Louis Christian College, Florissant, MO	$4380	$3070	48%	$5626	$1824
St. Louis College of Pharmacy, St. Louis, MO	$11,120	$4850	84%	$2847	$13,123
Saint Louis University, St. Louis, MO	$14,010	$5150	93%	$12,717	$6443
Saint Martin's College, Lacey, WA	$13,120	$4590	NR	$10,292	$7418
Saint Mary College, Leavenworth, KS	$9750	$4200	NR	$7786	$6164
Saint Mary-of-the-Woods College, Saint Mary-of-the-Woods, IN	$12,360	$4570	NR	NR	NR
Saint Mary's College, Notre Dame, IN	$14,933	$4970	75%	$11,441	$8462

NA = not applicable; NR = not reported; * = includes room and board; † = room only.

Freshman-Year Out-of-Pocket Costs:
Looking Beyond the Sticker Price
This chart presents average costs. Actual costs may vary.

	Published tuition and fees	Room and board	Percent of freshmen who applied for aid	Average aid package for freshmen	Average cost after aid
Saint Mary's College, Orchard Lake, MI	$6330	$4100	100%	$6227	$4203
Saint Mary's College of California, Moraga, CA	$15,098	$6909	70%	$12,435	$9572
St. Mary's College of Maryland, St. Mary's City, MD	$6575	$5480	78%	$6047	$6008
Saint Mary's University of Minnesota, Winona, MN	$11,615	$3900	84%	$10,317	$5198
St. Mary's University of San Antonio, San Antonio, TX	$10,608	$4308	96%	$10,926	$3990
Saint Meinrad College, Saint Meinrad, IN	$7025	$4550	92%	$9027	$2548
Saint Michael's College, Colchester, VT	$14,785	$6375	81%	$11,483	$9677
St. Norbert College, De Pere, WI	$14,434	$5120	NR	$13,343	$6211
St. Olaf College, Northfield, MN	$15,780	$3850	77%	$13,538	$6092
Saint Paul's College, Lawrenceville, VA	$6760	$4040	NR	NR	NR
Saint Peter's College, Jersey City, NJ	$14,214	$5530	88%	$11,500	$8244
St. Thomas Aquinas College, Sparkill, NY	$10,400	$6500	NR	NR	NR
St. Thomas University, Miami, FL	$11,220	$4000	NR	$7281	$7939
Saint Vincent College, Latrobe, PA	$12,400	$4410	94%	$10,633	$6177
Saint Xavier University, Chicago, IL	$12,080	$4985	86%	$10,919	$6146
Salem College, Winston-Salem, NC	$11,835	$6970	NR	NR	NR
Salem-Teikyo University, Salem, WV	$12,121	$3952	80%	$12,000	$4073
Salisbury State University, Salisbury, MD	$3842	$5060	60%	$5528	$3374
Salve Regina University, Newport, RI	$15,190	$6900	81%	$13,625	$8465
Samford University, Birmingham, AL	$9070	$3930	65%	$8203	$4797
Sam Houston State University, Huntsville, TX	$1730	$3160	29%	$3707	$1183
Samuel Merritt College, Oakland, CA	$13,930	$3330†	100%	$11,000	$6260
San Diego State University, San Diego, CA	$1902	$6192	68%	$6627	$1467
San Francisco Art Institute, San Francisco, CA	$16,416	NA	NR	$17,507	$0
San Francisco Conservatory of Music, San Francisco, CA	$15,050	NA	62%	$6300	$8750
San Francisco State University, San Francisco, CA	$1982	$5600	NR	$6883	$699
San Jose Christian College, San Jose, CA	$7014	$3564	NR	NR	NR
San Jose State University, San Jose, CA	$2004	$4875	NR	$3680	$3199
Santa Clara University, Santa Clara, CA	$15,624	$6780	73%	$14,330	$8074
Sarah Lawrence College, Bronxville, NY	$21,976	$6902	67%	$17,520	$11,358
Savannah College of Art and Design, Savannah, GA	$12,600	$5700	67%	$3750	$14,550
Savannah State University, Savannah, GA	$2556	$2970	NR	NR	NR
School of the Art Institute of Chicago, Chicago, IL	$16,320	$4980†	77%	$15,074	$6226
School of the Museum of Fine Arts, Boston, MA	$15,125	NA	NR	$8299	$6826
School of Visual Arts, New York, NY	$13,890	$5800†	NR	$8200	$11,490
Scripps College, Claremont, CA	$18,800	$7650	64%	$18,495	$7955
Seattle Pacific University, Seattle, WA	$13,680	$5244	81%	NR	NR
Seattle University, Seattle, WA	$14,265	$5283	NR	$15,689	$3859
Seton Hall University, South Orange, NJ	$13,670	$7084	81%	$13,312	$7442
Seton Hill College, Greensburg, PA	$12,640	$4730	98%	$10,772	$6598
Shasta Bible College, Redding, CA	$3430	$1107†	NR	NR	NR

*NA = not applicable; NR = not reported; * = includes room and board; † = room only.*

Freshman-Year Out-of-Pocket Costs: Looking Beyond the Sticker Price

This chart presents average costs. Actual costs may vary.

	Published tuition and fees	Room and board	Percent of freshmen who applied for aid	Average aid package for freshmen	Average cost after aid
Shawnee State University, Portsmouth, OH	$2976	$3945	NR	NR	NR
Shaw University, Raleigh, NC	$5746	$3824	83%	$10,500	$0
Sheldon Jackson College, Sitka, AK	$9300	$4800	94%	$11,201	$2899
Shenandoah University, Winchester, VA	$13,700	$4200	NR	NR	NR
Shepherd College, Shepherdstown, WV	$2160	$3970	74%	$4712	$1418
Shimer College, Waukegan, IL	$13,800	$1725†	NR	NR	NR
Shippensburg University of Pennsylvania, Shippensburg, PA	$4230	$3700	NR	$5002	$2928
Shorter College, Rome, GA	$8260	$4250	NR	$8062	$4448
Siena College, Loudonville, NY	$12,710	$5635	86%	$9357	$8988
Siena Heights College, Adrian, MI	$10,700	$4330	92%	NR	NR
Sierra Nevada College, Incline Village, NV	$9450	$5200	100%	$8125	$6525
Silver Lake College, Manitowoc, WI	$9400	$4054	NR	NR	NR
Simmons College, Boston, MA	$18,040	$7228	80%	$17,838	$7430
Simon's Rock College of Bard, Great Barrington, MA	$20,795	$5860	NR	$13,000	$13,655
Simpson College, Redding, CA	$8474	$3800	90%	$7793	$4481
Simpson College, Indianola, IA	$12,650	$4145	100%	$13,428	$3367
Sinte Gleska University, Rosebud, SD	$1980	NA	NR	NR	NR
Skidmore College, Saratoga Springs, NY	$20,895	$6110	52%	$17,266	$9739
Slippery Rock University of Pennsylvania, Slippery Rock, PA	$4119	$3552	NR	$4438	$3233
Smith College, Northampton, MA	$20,538	$6920	67%	$19,045	$8413
Sojourner-Douglass College, Baltimore, MD	$5225	NA	75%	$3000	$2225
Sonoma State University, Rohnert Park, CA	$2130	$5328	61%	$4786	$2672
South College, Savannah, GA	$5710	NA	NR	NR	NR
South Dakota School of Mines and Technology, Rapid City, SD	$3430	$2864	NR	NR	NR
South Dakota State University, Brookings, SD	$2784	$2344	81%	$4452	$676
Southeastern Baptist College, Laurel, MS	$2220	$1800	NR	$720	$3300
Southeastern Bible College, Birmingham, AL	$5040	$2940	54%	$4000	$3980
Southeastern College of the Assemblies of God, Lakeland, FL	$4804	$3046	NR	$5821	$2029
Southeastern Louisiana University, Hammond, LA	$2050	$2320	NR	NR	NR
Southeastern Oklahoma State University, Durant, OK	$1709	$2619	NR	NR	NR
Southeastern University, Washington, DC	$5700	NA	73%	NR	NR
Southeast Missouri State University, Cape Girardeau, MO	$3100	$4000	80%	$3968	$3132
Southern Adventist University, Collegedale, TN	$9156	$3782	54%	$7368	$5570
Southern Arkansas University–Magnolia, Magnolia, AR	$1800	$2500	NR	$2597	$1703
Southern California College, Costa Mesa, CA	$11,848	$4860	NR	NR	NR
Southern California Institute of Architecture, Los Angeles, CA	$13,990	NA	NR	NR	NR
Southern Christian University, Montgomery, AL	$6576	NA	NR	$0	$6576
Southern Connecticut State University, New Haven, CT	$3444	$5308	NR	$4450	$4302
Southern Illinois University at Carbondale, Carbondale, IL	$3260	$3472	90%	NR	NR
Southern Illinois University at Edwardsville, Edwardsville, IL	$2469	$3960	90%	NR	NR
Southern Methodist University, Dallas, TX	$15,990	$5338	55%	$7641	$13,687

NA = not applicable; NR = not reported; * = includes room and board; † = room only.

Freshman-Year Out-of-Pocket Costs: Looking Beyond the Sticker Price

This chart presents average costs. Actual costs may vary.

	Published tuition and fees	Room and board	Percent of freshmen who applied for aid	Average aid package for freshmen	Average cost after aid
Southern Nazarene University, Bethany, OK	$8222	$3968	NR	NR	NR
Southern Oregon University, Ashland, OR	$3147	$4200	100%	NR	NR
Southern Polytechnic State University, Marietta, GA	$1851	$3930	57%	$3516	$2265
Southern University and Agricultural and Mechanical College, Baton Rouge, LA	$2028	$3022	NR	NR	NR
Southern Utah University, Cedar City, UT	$1800	$2070	NR	NR	NR
Southern Vermont College, Bennington, VT	$11,300	$4934	77%	$10,268	$5966
Southern Wesleyan University, Central, SC	$10,180	$3540	84%	$7119	$6601
Southwest Baptist University, Bolivar, MO	$7872	$2623	NR	NR	NR
Southwestern Adventist University, Keene, TX	$8092	$3926	NR	$6659	$5359
Southwestern Assemblies of God University, Waxahachie, TX	$4402	$3390	NR	$4455	$3337
Southwestern Christian College, Terrell, TX	$5150	$2862	78%	$2961	$5051
Southwestern College, Phoenix, AZ	$6300	$2650	NR	$4767	$4183
Southwestern College, Winfield, KS	$9260	$3840	NR	$9890	$3210
Southwestern College of Christian Ministries, Bethany, OK	$4324	$2700	NR	NR	NR
Southwestern Oklahoma State University, Weatherford, OK	$1584	$2096	68%	$2266	$1414
Southwestern University, Georgetown, TX	$13,400	$5025	63%	$12,540	$5885
Southwest Missouri State University, Springfield, MO	$3060	$3472	NR	$5246	$1286
Southwest State University, Marshall, MN	$2980	$2900	NR	$5288	$592
Southwest Texas State University, San Marcos, TX	$2156	$3787	54%	$5612	$331
Spalding University, Louisville, KY	$9696	$2680	100%	$9206	$3170
Spelman College, Atlanta, GA	$9500	$6130	NR	$10,000	$5630
Spring Arbor College, Spring Arbor, MI	$10,686	$4190	95%	$7492	$7384
Springfield College, Springfield, MA	$12,700	$5800	NR	$8923	$9577
Spring Hill College, Mobile, AL	$13,140	$4960	NR	$9746	$8354
Stanford University, Stanford, CA	$20,618	$7340	55%	$19,600	$8358
State University of New York at Binghamton, Binghamton, NY	$4045	$4814	40%	NR	NR
State University of New York at Buffalo, Buffalo, NY	$4190	$5455	70%	$6139	$3506
State University of New York at New Paltz, New Paltz, NY	$3825	$5030	66%	$6500	$2355
State University of New York at Oswego, Oswego, NY	$3887	$5460	82%	$5412	$3935
State University of New York at Stony Brook, Stony Brook, NY	$3879	$5594	70%	$6865	$2608
State University of New York College at Brockport, Brockport, NY	$3915	$4780	87%	$6287	$2408
State University of New York College at Buffalo, Buffalo, NY	$3791	$4460	69%	$5496	$2755
State University of New York College at Cortland, Cortland, NY	$3842	$5020	75%	$7814	$1048
State University of New York College at Fredonia, Fredonia, NY	$4013	$4900	92%	$4938	$3975
State University of New York College at Geneseo, Geneseo, NY	$3984	$4540	81%	$5491	$3033
State University of New York College at Old Westbury, Old Westbury, NY	$3731	$5407	NR	NR	NR
State University of New York College at Oneonta, Oneonta, NY	$3758	$5590	78%	$6000	$3348
State University of New York College at Plattsburgh, Plattsburgh, NY	$3837	$4250	81%	$6030	$2057
State University of New York College at Potsdam, Potsdam, NY	$3739	$4900	87%	$6419	$2220
State University of New York College of Environmental Science and Forestry, Syracuse, NY	$3413	$6910	100%	$6500	$3823
State University of New York Health Science Center at Syracuse, Syracuse, NY	$3615	$3419†	NR	NR	NR

*NA = not applicable; NR = not reported; * = includes room and board; † = room only.*

Freshman-Year Out-of-Pocket Costs: Looking Beyond the Sticker Price

This chart presents average costs. Actual costs may vary.

	Published tuition and fees	Room and board	Percent of freshmen who applied for aid	Average aid package for freshmen	Average cost after aid
State University of New York Maritime College, Throgs Neck, NY	$3876	$5000	95%	$5200	$3676
Stephen F. Austin State University, Nacogdoches, TX	$1513	$3680	NR	$1916	$3277
Stephens College, Columbia, MO	$14,830	$5540	NR	NR	NR
Sterling College, Sterling, KS	$9696	$3784	98%	$10,700	$2780
Stetson University, DeLand, FL	$14,735	$5090	49%	$10,729	$9096
Stevens Institute of Technology, Hoboken, NJ	$18,570	$6490	91%	$19,277	$5783
Stillman College, Tuscaloosa, AL	$5200	$3100	NR	NR	NR
Stonehill College, Easton, MA	$14,856	$6996	83%	$13,822	$8030
Strayer College, Washington, DC	$7650	NA	40%	NR	NR
Sue Bennett College, London, KY	$7780	$3895	NR	NR	NR
Suffolk University, Boston, MA	$12,106	$8350	76%	$10,483	$9973
Sullivan College, Louisville, KY	$8904	$2700†	NR	NR	NR
Sul Ross State University, Alpine, TX	$1680	$3020	NR	$3773	$927
Susquehanna University, Selinsgrove, PA	$17,690	$5080	82%	$15,590	$7180
Swarthmore College, Swarthmore, PA	$21,054	$7176	72%	$21,535	$6695
Sweet Briar College, Sweet Briar, VA	$15,115	$6510	73%	$14,794	$6831
Syracuse University, Syracuse, NY	$17,142	$7440	76%	$14,500	$10,082
Tabor College, Hillsboro, KS	$10,560	$4000	100%	$8868	$5692
Talladega College, Talladega, AL	$6084	$2964	98%	$6338	$2710
Tarleton State University, Stephenville, TX	$1938	$2324	NR	NR	NR
Taylor University, Upland, IN	$12,774	$4220	NR	$10,321	$6673
Taylor University, Fort Wayne Campus, Fort Wayne, IN	$11,420	$4010	NR	NR	NR
Teikyo Post University, Waterbury, CT	$12,260	$5600	NR	$6356	$11,504
Temple University, Philadelphia, PA	$5848	$5712	89%	$8210	$3350
Tennessee State University, Nashville, TN	$1916	$2720	NR	$4580	$56
Tennessee Technological University, Cookeville, TN	$1920	$3720	NR	$2350	$3290
Tennessee Temple University, Chattanooga, TN	$6270	$4750	NR	$6895	$4125
Tennessee Wesleyan College, Athens, TN	$6600	$3870	NR	$7545	$2925
Texas A&M International University, Laredo, TX	$1947	NA	100%	NR	NR
Texas A&M University, College Station, TX	$2488	$2496	NR	$4798	$186
Texas A&M University at Galveston, Galveston, TX	$2120	$3653	NR	NR	NR
Texas A&M University–Commerce, Commerce, TX	$2288	$3678	NR	NR	NR
Texas A&M University–Corpus Christi, Corpus Christi, TX	$1986	$2817†	55%	$4631	$172
Texas A&M University–Kingsville, Kingsville, TX	$1772	$3484	NR	NR	NR
Texas Christian University, Fort Worth, TX	$10,510	$3800	47%	$11,103	$3207
Texas Lutheran University, Seguin, TX	$10,370	$3772	82%	$9233	$4909
Texas Southern University, Houston, TX	$2064	$4000	NR	$10,200	$0
Texas Tech University, Lubbock, TX	$2326	$4084	NR	NR	NR
Texas Wesleyan University, Fort Worth, TX	$7600	$3484	97%	$7483	$3601
Texas Woman's University, Denton, TX	$1929	$3170	NR	$5650	$0
Thiel College, Greenville, PA	$12,650	$5090	97%	$14,030	$3710

*NA = not applicable; NR = not reported; * = includes room and board; † = room only.*

Freshman-Year Out-of-Pocket Costs: Looking Beyond the Sticker Price

This chart presents average costs. Actual costs may vary.

	Published tuition and fees	Room and board	Percent of freshmen who applied for aid	Average aid package for freshmen	Average cost after aid
Thomas Aquinas College, Santa Paula, CA	$13,900	$5300	84%	$13,798	$5402
Thomas College, Thomasville, GA	$4875	NA	NR	$2253	$2622
Thomas College, Waterville, ME	$11,200	$6025	96%	$9804	$7421
Thomas More College, Crestview Hills, KY	$10,620	$3706	NR	NR	NR
Thomas More College of Liberal Arts, Merrimack, NH	$8200	$6000	63%	$8578	$5622
Tiffin University, Tiffin, OH	$9210	$4400	95%	$7481	$6129
Toccoa Falls College, Toccoa Falls, GA	$7419	$3708	NR	$2816	$8311
Tougaloo College, Tougaloo, MS	$6212	$2696	NR	NR	NR
Touro College, New York, NY	$9060	$4500†	NR	$8500	$5060
Towson University, Towson, MD	$4120	$4830	90%	$4212	$4738
Transylvania University, Lexington, KY	$12,640	$4810	NR	$5966	$11,484
Trevecca Nazarene University, Nashville, TN	$8644	$3890	NR	$11,500	$1034
Trinity Baptist College, Jacksonville, FL	$3698	$2800	NR	NR	NR
Trinity Bible College, Ellendale, ND	$5548	$3184	NR	NR	NR
Trinity Christian College, Palos Heights, IL	$11,700	$4460	NR	$9228	$6932
Trinity College, Hartford, CT	$21,410	$6120	62%	$18,411	$9119
Trinity College, Washington, DC	$12,490	$6580	NR	$12,915	$6155
Trinity College of Florida, New Port Richey, FL	$3470	$2400	NR	NR	NR
Trinity College of Vermont, Burlington, VT	$12,420	$6012	NR	$9174	$9258
Trinity International University, Deerfield, IL	$11,918	$4450	94%	$12,764	$3604
Trinity International University, South Florida Campus, Miami, FL	$7808	NA	NR	NR	NR
Trinity University, San Antonio, TX	$13,644	$5545	50%	$13,188	$6001
Tri-State University, Angola, IN	$11,100	$4644	NR	$7503	$8241
Troy State University, Troy, AL	$2175	$3000	NR	NR	NR
Troy State University Dothan, Dothan, AL	$2100	NA	NR	NR	NR
Troy State University Montgomery, Montgomery, AL	$2025	NA	NR	$2822	$0
Truman State University, Kirksville, MO	$3026	$3808	58%	NR	NR
Tufts University, Medford, MA	$21,957	$6540	48%	$17,768	$10,729
Tulane University, New Orleans, LA	$21,236	$6314	NR	$19,380	$8170
Tusculum College, Greeneville, TN	$11,150	$3700	NR	$7772	$7078
Tuskegee University, Tuskegee, AL	$8020	$4050	NR	$12,124	$0
Union College, Barbourville, KY	$8750	$3120	85%	$6167	$5703
Union College, Lincoln, NE	$9550	$3120	NR	$6267	$6403
Union College, Schenectady, NY	$20,995	$6329	68%	$18,340	$8984
The Union Institute, Cincinnati, OH	$7296	NA	75%	$3000	$4296
Union University, Jackson, TN	$8180	$3005	84%	$5800	$5385
United States International University, San Diego, CA	$11,745	$4800	80%	$10,500	$6045
Unity College, Unity, ME	$10,530	$5050	89%	$8858	$6722
Universidad Adventista de las Antillas, Mayagüez, PR	$3730	$2150	NR	$1786	$4094
Universidad del Turabo, Gurabo, PR	$2860	NA	NR	NR	NR
Universidad Metropolitana, Río Piedras, PR	$3512	NA	NR	NR	NR

*NA = not applicable; NR = not reported; * = includes room and board; † = room only.*

Freshman-Year Out-of-Pocket Costs: Looking Beyond the Sticker Price

This chart presents average costs. Actual costs may vary.

	Published tuition and fees	Room and board	Percent of freshmen who applied for aid	Average aid package for freshmen	Average cost after aid
University at Albany, State University of New York, Albany, NY	$4130	$5050	77%	$6005	$3175
The University of Akron, Akron, OH	$3486	$4120	NR	$5300	$2306
The University of Alabama at Birmingham, Birmingham, AL	$2700	$6384	36%	$3361	$5723
The University of Alabama in Huntsville, Huntsville, AL	$2698	$3645	NR	$3640	$2703
University of Alaska Anchorage, Anchorage, AK	$2263	$2800†	68%	$3054	$2009
University of Alaska Fairbanks, Fairbanks, AK	$2430	$3790	NR	$8000	$0
University of Alaska Southeast, Juneau, AK	$1714	$2900†	NR	NR	NR
University of Arizona, Tucson, AZ	$2009	$4410	69%	$5878	$541
University of Arkansas, Fayetteville, AR	$2410	$3780	NR	NR	NR
University of Arkansas at Little Rock, Little Rock, AR	$2879	$2410†	59%	$727	$4562
University of Arkansas at Monticello, Monticello, AR	$1906	$2400	NR	NR	NR
University of Arkansas at Pine Bluff, Pine Bluff, AR	$1890	$2900	NR	NR	NR
University of Biblical Studies and Seminary, Bethany, OK	$2325	NA	NR	NR	NR
University of Bridgeport, Bridgeport, CT	$13,144	$6810	77%	$16,771	$3183
University of California, Berkeley, Berkeley, CA	$3956	$6710	68%	$12,050	$0
University of California, Davis, Davis, CA	$4230	$5468	NR	NR	NR
University of California, Irvine, Irvine, CA	$4050	$5565	NR	$8364	$1251
University of California, Los Angeles, Los Angeles, CA	$4006	$6147	94%	$7568	$2585
University of California, Riverside, Riverside, CA	$4105	$5870	82%	$9475	$500
University of California, San Diego, La Jolla, CA	$4198	$6837	84%	$8266	$2769
University of California, Santa Barbara, Santa Barbara, CA	$4098	$6131	NR	NR	NR
University of California, Santa Cruz, Santa Cruz, CA	$4136	$6222	NR	$7919	$2439
University of Central Arkansas, Conway, AR	$2092	$2710	97%	$2900	$1902
University of Central Florida, Orlando, FL	$1925	$4240	96%	$4881	$1284
University of Central Oklahoma, Edmond, OK	$1716	$2431	91%	$4200	$0
The University of Charleston, Charleston, WV	$11,600	$4040	94%	$13,485	$2155
University of Chicago, Chicago, IL	$21,300	$7275	NR	NR	NR
University of Cincinnati, Cincinnati, OH	$4321	$5049	NR	NR	NR
University of Colorado at Boulder, Boulder, CO	$2840	$4370	NR	$8209	$0
University of Colorado at Colorado Springs, Colorado Springs, CO	$2493	$4700	NR	NR	NR
University of Colorado at Denver, Denver, CO	$2183	NA	NR	NR	NR
University of Connecticut, Storrs, CT	$5096	$5461	NR	$6199	$4358
University of Dallas, Irving, TX	$12,144	$4830	86%	$12,060	$4914
University of Dayton, Dayton, OH	$13,640	$4430	85%	$13,716	$4354
University of Delaware, Newark, DE	$4430	$4590	NR	$6250	$2770
University of Denver, Denver, CO	$21,622	$5538	87%	$13,318	$13,842
University of Detroit Mercy, Detroit, MI	$12,291	$4552	NR	NR	NR
University of Dubuque, Dubuque, IA	$12,370	$4340	98%	$14,046	$2664
University of Evansville, Evansville, IN	$13,270	$4080	85%	$10,587	$6763
The University of Findlay, Findlay, OH	$13,112	$5210	90%	$11,000	$7322
University of Florida, Gainesville, FL	$1793	$4500	57%	$7956	$0

*NA = not applicable; NR = not reported; * = includes room and board; † = room only.*

Freshman-Year Out-of-Pocket Costs: Looking Beyond the Sticker Price

This chart presents average costs. Actual costs may vary.

	Published tuition and fees	Room and board	Percent of freshmen who applied for aid	Average aid package for freshmen	Average cost after aid
University of Georgia, Athens, GA	$2694	$4045	97%	$4655	$2084
University of Great Falls, Great Falls, MT	$5180	$2010	93%	$2465	$4725
University of Guam, Mangilao, GU	$2068	$3242	NR	NR	NR
University of Hartford, West Hartford, CT	$16,415	$6545	66%	$15,001	$7959
University of Hawaii at Hilo, Hilo, HI	$1322	$3480	NR	$4065	$737
University of Hawaii at Manoa, Honolulu, HI	$2950	$4740	33%	$4365	$3325
University of Houston, Houston, TX	$1726	$4405	NR	$3623	$2508
University of Houston–Downtown, Houston, TX	$1977	NA	97%	NR	NR
University of Idaho, Moscow, ID	$1768	$3600	NR	$4200	$1168
University of Illinois at Chicago, Chicago, IL	$3776	$5188	NR	NR	NR
University of Illinois at Urbana–Champaign, Champaign, IL	$4186	$4560	NR	$7300	$1446
University of Indianapolis, Indianapolis, IN	$12,350	$4330	NR	$11,288	$5392
The University of Iowa, Iowa City, IA	$2646	$3688	67%	NR	NR
University of Kansas, Lawrence, KS	$2310	$3640	64%	$3771	$2179
University of Kentucky, Lexington, KY	$2736	$3198	NR	$6150	$0
University of La Verne, La Verne, CA	$14,710	$4330	91%	$13,339	$5701
University of Louisville, Louisville, KY	$2570	$3330	54%	$4464	$1436
University of Maine, Orono, ME	$4139	$4842	NR	NR	NR
University of Maine at Farmington, Farmington, ME	$3370	$4142	NR	NR	NR
University of Maine at Fort Kent, Fort Kent, ME	$3040	$3600	NR	$5331	$1309
University of Maine at Machias, Machias, ME	$2995	$3895	92%	$6545	$345
University of Maine at Presque Isle, Presque Isle, ME	$3060	$3704	86%	$4667	$2097
University of Mary, Bismarck, ND	$7740	$2990	NR	$8468	$2262
University of Mary Hardin-Baylor, Belton, TX	$6524	$3412	NR	NR	NR
University of Maryland Baltimore County, Baltimore, MD	$4136	$4746	75%	$7542	$1340
University of Maryland College Park, College Park, MD	$4169	$5442	NR	NR	NR
University of Maryland Eastern Shore, Princess Anne, MD	$3036	$4130	NR	NR	NR
University of Massachusetts Amherst, Amherst, MA	$5413	$4228	NR	$9423	$218
University of Massachusetts Boston, Boston, MA	$4348	NA	NR	NR	NR
University of Massachusetts Dartmouth, North Dartmouth, MA	$4151	$4718	NR	NR	NR
University of Massachusetts Lowell, Lowell, MA	$4422	$4165	NR	NR	NR
The University of Memphis, Memphis, TN	$2180	$1680†	NR	$4000	$0
University of Miami, Coral Gables, FL	$19,513	$7352	74%	$19,448	$7417
University of Michigan, Ann Arbor, MI	$5888	$5137	NR	NR	NR
University of Michigan–Dearborn, Dearborn, MI	$4040	NA	NR	NR	NR
University of Michigan–Flint, Flint, MI	$3434	NA	NR	$4400	$0
University of Minnesota, Crookston, Crookston, MN	$4251	$3492	76%	NR	NR
University of Minnesota, Duluth, Duluth, MN	$4187	$3774	80%	$5573	$2388
University of Minnesota, Morris, Morris, MN	$4554	$3594	78%	$6000	$2148
University of Minnesota, Twin Cities Campus, Minneapolis, MN	$4090	$4056	68%	$5503	$2643
University of Mississippi, Oxford, MS	$2631	$1660†	NR	NR	NR

NA = not applicable; NR = not reported; * = includes room and board; † = room only.

Freshman-Year Out-of-Pocket Costs: Looking Beyond the Sticker Price

This chart presents average costs. Actual costs may vary.

	Published tuition and fees	Room and board	Percent of freshmen who applied for aid	Average aid package for freshmen	Average cost after aid
University of Missouri–Columbia, Columbia, MO	$3868	$4172	62%	$6354	$1686
University of Missouri–Kansas City, Kansas City, MO	$3799	$3750	63%	$10,119	$0
University of Missouri–Rolla, Rolla, MO	$4213	$4026	NR	$5755	$2484
University of Missouri–St. Louis, St. Louis, MO	$3383	$4341	48%	$3829	$3895
University of Mobile, Mobile, AL	$6960	$3880	97%	$8500	$2340
The University of Montana–Missoula, Missoula, MT	$2484	$3962	NR	NR	NR
University of Montevallo, Montevallo, AL	$2850	$3504	NR	$2337	$4017
University of Nebraska at Kearney, Kearney, NE	$2145	$4100	83%	$2820	$3425
University of Nebraska at Omaha, Omaha, NE	$2328	NA	69%	NR	NR
University of Nebraska–Lincoln, Lincoln, NE	$2713	$3525	NR	$4460	$1778
University of Nevada, Las Vegas, Las Vegas, NV	$2045	$5300	NR	$2584	$4761
University of Nevada, Reno, Reno, NV	$2034	$4695	NR	NR	NR
University of New England, Biddeford, ME	$13,560	$5520	NR	$8774	$10,306
University of New Hampshire, Durham, NH	$5261	$4354	NR	NR	NR
University of New Hampshire at Manchester, Manchester, NH	$3566	NA	NR	$4061	$0
University of New Haven, West Haven, CT	$12,390	$5630	92%	$7840	$10,180
University of New Mexico, Albuquerque, NM	$2071	$3968	68%	$4394	$1645
University of North Alabama, Florence, AL	$1998	$3130	NR	$1351	$3777
University of North Carolina at Asheville, Asheville, NC	$1773	$3650	65%	$4963	$460
The University of North Carolina at Chapel Hill, Chapel Hill, NC	$2161	$4500	57%	$6730	$0
University of North Carolina at Charlotte, Charlotte, NC	$1718	$3120	68%	$4782	$56
University of North Carolina at Greensboro, Greensboro, NC	$1943	$3505	NR	$5398	$50
University of North Carolina at Pembroke, Pembroke, NC	$1467	$3320	93%	$3555	$1232
University of North Carolina at Wilmington, Wilmington, NC	$1748	$3900	63%	$1566	$4082
University of North Dakota, Grand Forks, ND	$2946	$2910	71%	$4800	$1056
University of Northern Colorado, Greeley, CO	$2378	$4270	NR	$7124	$0
University of Northern Iowa, Cedar Falls, IA	$2650	$3264	81%	$8768	$0
University of North Florida, Jacksonville, FL	$1884	$2830	NR	$4578	$136
University of North Texas, Denton, TX	$2044	$3767	NR	NR	NR
University of Notre Dame, Notre Dame, IN	$18,956	$4800	67%	$13,241	$10,515
University of Oklahoma, Norman, OK	$2126	$3904	56%	$4879	$1151
University of Oregon, Eugene, OR	$3540	$4342	NR	$6764	$1118
University of Pennsylvania, Philadelphia, PA	$21,130	$7500	56%	$19,885	$8745
University of Pittsburgh, Pittsburgh, PA	$5870	$4964	NR	NR	NR
University of Pittsburgh at Bradford, Bradford, PA	$5826	$4450	NR	NR	NR
University of Pittsburgh at Greensburg, Greensburg, PA	$5600	$3870	87%	$3612	$5858
University of Pittsburgh at Johnstown, Johnstown, PA	$5902	$4770	89%	$5546	$5126
University of Portland, Portland, OR	$14,400	$4380	84%	$14,314	$4466
University of Puerto Rico, Aguadilla Regional College, Aguadilla, PR	$1638	NA	NR	NR	NR
University of Puerto Rico, Cayey University College, Cayey, PR	$996	NA	90%	NR	NR
University of Puerto Rico, Humacao University College, Humacao, PR	$1090	NA	84%	NR	NR

*NA = not applicable; NR = not reported; * = includes room and board; † = room only.*

Freshman-Year Out-of-Pocket Costs: Looking Beyond the Sticker Price

This chart presents average costs. Actual costs may vary.

	Published tuition and fees	Room and board	Percent of freshmen who applied for aid	Average aid package for freshmen	Average cost after aid
University of Puerto Rico, Medical Sciences Campus, San Juan, PR	$1450	NA	NR	NR	NR
University of Puerto Rico, Río Piedras, Río Piedras, PR	$1262	$1000†	98%	NR	NR
University of Puget Sound, Tacoma, WA	$18,170	$4800	79%	$14,165	$8805
University of Redlands, Redlands, CA	$17,846	$6775	85%	$16,670	$7951
University of Rhode Island, Kingston, RI	$4460	$5824	NR	NR	NR
University of Richmond, University of Richmond, VA	$16,740	$3595	52%	$11,827	$8508
University of Rio Grande, Rio Grande, OH	$2100	$4263	85%	NR	NR
University of Rochester, Rochester, NY	$20,080	$6930	94%	$19,367	$7643
University of St. Thomas, St. Paul, MN	$14,660	$4769	79%	$12,767	$6662
University of St. Thomas, Houston, TX	$11,070	$4250	NR	NR	NR
University of San Diego, San Diego, CA	$15,780	$6970	NR	$13,095	$9655
University of San Francisco, San Francisco, CA	$15,020	$6553	73%	$15,155	$6418
University of Science and Arts of Oklahoma, Chickasha, OK	$1604	$2670	88%	$2507	$1767
University of Scranton, Scranton, PA	$14,096	$6600	91%	$10,850	$9846
University of Sioux Falls, Sioux Falls, SD	$10,750	$3450	90%	NR	NR
University of South Alabama, Mobile, AL	$2694	$2835	NR	$4060	$1469
University of South Carolina, Columbia, SC	$3362	$3692	34%	$6408	$646
University of South Carolina–Aiken, Aiken, SC	$2848	$2830	NR	NR	NR
University of South Carolina–Spartanburg, Spartanburg, SC	$2848	NA	NR	NR	NR
University of South Dakota, Vermillion, SD	$2884	$2647	NR	$4670	$861
University of Southern California, Los Angeles, CA	$19,516	$6712	NR	NR	NR
University of Southern Colorado, Pueblo, CO	$2092	$4180	NR	$5988	$284
University of Southern Indiana, Evansville, IN	$2510	$1812†	78%	$3575	$747
University of Southern Maine, Portland, ME	$3710	$4554	88%	$4988	$3276
University of Southern Mississippi, Hattiesburg, MS	$2518	$2505	NR	$3308	$1715
University of South Florida, Tampa, FL	$1961	$4598	53%	$4570	$1989
University of Southwestern Louisiana, Lafayette, LA	$1897	$2350	85%	$3634	$613
The University of Tampa, Tampa, FL	$14,132	$4410	81%	$12,100	$6442
University of Tennessee at Chattanooga, Chattanooga, TN	$2064	$1430†	71%	$6812	$0
The University of Tennessee at Martin, Martin, TN	$2014	$2990	70%	$4455	$549
University of Tennessee, Knoxville, Knoxville, TN	$2200	$3620	50%	$3939	$1881
The University of Texas at Arlington, Arlington, TX	$2221	$2900	70%	$4022	$1099
The University of Texas at Austin, Austin, TX	$2612	$4550	53%	$6200	$962
The University of Texas at Dallas, Richardson, TX	$2093	$5102	NR	NR	NR
The University of Texas at El Paso, El Paso, TX	$2056	$1850†	NR	$1832	$2074
The University of Texas at San Antonio, San Antonio, TX	$2194	$2833†	93%	$5443	$0
The University of Texas of the Permian Basin, Odessa, TX	$1920	$1350†	100%	$7123	$0
The University of Texas–Pan American, Edinburg, TX	$1593	$2050	NR	$1699	$1944
University of the Arts, Philadelphia, PA	$14,350	$3980†	NR	NR	NR
University of the District of Columbia, Washington, DC	$1850	NA	NR	NR	NR
University of the Ozarks, Clarksville, AR	$7140	$3400	77%	$9982	$558

*NA = not applicable; NR = not reported; * = includes room and board; † = room only.*

Freshman-Year Out-of-Pocket Costs: Looking Beyond the Sticker Price

This chart presents average costs. Actual costs may vary.

	Published tuition and fees	Room and board	Percent of freshmen who applied for aid	Average aid package for freshmen	Average cost after aid
University of the Pacific, Stockton, CA	$18,800	$5636	72%	$17,778	$6658
University of the Sacred Heart, Santurce, PR	$4035	$1400†	NR	NR	NR
University of the South, Sewanee, TN	$16,965	$4460	50%	NR	NR
University of the Virgin Islands, Charlotte Amalie, St. Thomas, VI	$2136	$4810	NR	NR	NR
University of Toledo, Toledo, OH	$3778	$4092	NR	$7268	$602
University of Tulsa, Tulsa, OK	$12,940	$4580	73%	$14,270	$3250
University of Utah, Salt Lake City, UT	$2514	$6633	56%	$3703	$5444
University of Vermont, Burlington, VT	$7211	$4706	NR	$13,043	$0
University of Virginia, Charlottesville, VA	$4648	$3962	55%	$8928	$0
University of Washington, Seattle, WA	$3250	$4455	NR	$6958	$747
The University of West Alabama, Livingston, AL	$2784	$2634	64%	$1367	$4051
University of West Florida, Pensacola, FL	$1819	$4134	NR	NR	NR
University of Wisconsin–Eau Claire, Eau Claire, WI	$2574	$2904	63%	$3755	$1723
University of Wisconsin–Green Bay, Green Bay, WI	$2545	$2550	67%	$4536	$559
University of Wisconsin–La Crosse, La Crosse, WI	$2635	$2800	NR	$3890	$1545
University of Wisconsin–Madison, Madison, WI	$3040	$4650	NR	$5277	$2413
University of Wisconsin–Milwaukee, Milwaukee, WI	$3104	$2912	74%	$5877	$139
University of Wisconsin–Oshkosh, Oshkosh, WI	$2419	$2511	68%	NR	NR
University of Wisconsin–Parkside, Kenosha, WI	$2523	$3166	NR	NR	NR
University of Wisconsin–Platteville, Platteville, WI	$2591	$2787	71%	$4104	$1274
University of Wisconsin–River Falls, River Falls, WI	$2565	$2908	NR	$5110	$363
University of Wisconsin–Stevens Point, Stevens Point, WI	$2522	$3106	NR	$4841	$787
University of Wisconsin–Stout, Menomonie, WI	$2619	$2922	NR	$2647	$2894
University of Wisconsin–Superior, Superior, WI	$2465	$3100	100%	$4324	$1241
University of Wisconsin–Whitewater, Whitewater, WI	$2586	$2702	NR	NR	NR
University of Wyoming, Laramie, WY	$2326	$4245	NR	NR	NR
Upper Iowa University, Fayette, IA	$9750	$3770	NR	NR	NR
Urbana University, Urbana, OH	$10,530	$4350	NR	NR	NR
Ursinus College, Collegeville, PA	$16,600	$5490	89%	$15,845	$6245
Ursuline College, Pepper Pike, OH	$10,710	$4330	100%	$9870	$5170
Utah State University, Logan, UT	$1971	$3639	NR	NR	NR
Utica College of Syracuse University, Utica, NY	$14,206	$5380	NR	$15,786	$3800
Valdosta State University, Valdosta, GA	$2043	$3300	NR	$4105	$1238
Valley City State University, Valley City, ND	$1893	$2770	79%	$5190	$0
Valley Forge Christian College, Phoenixville, PA	$6560	$3480	NR	$5061	$4979
Valparaiso University, Valparaiso, IN	$13,980	$3450	NR	$10,479	$6951
Vanderbilt University, Nashville, TN	$20,474	$7002	48%	$16,370	$11,106
VanderCook College of Music, Chicago, IL	$9650	$4795	93%	$6936	$7509
Vassar College, Poughkeepsie, NY	$21,150	$6310	64%	$18,734	$8726
Villa Julie College, Stevenson, MD	$8610	$3240†	94%	$6672	$5178
Villanova University, Villanova, PA	$17,790	$7470	68%	$12,788	$12,472

*NA = not applicable; NR = not reported; * = includes room and board; † = room only.*

Freshman-Year Out-of-Pocket Costs: Looking Beyond the Sticker Price

This chart presents average costs. Actual costs may vary.

	Published tuition and fees	Room and board	Percent of freshmen who applied for aid	Average aid package for freshmen	Average cost after aid
Virginia Commonwealth University, Richmond, VA	$4071	$4352	73%	$6024	$2399
Virginia Intermont College, Bristol, VA	$10,175	$4250	94%	$7200	$7225
Virginia Military Institute, Lexington, VA	$5355	$3435	51%	$7185	$1605
Virginia Polytechnic Institute and State University, Blacksburg, VA	$4131	$2910	NR	NR	NR
Virginia State University, Petersburg, VA	$3291	$4845	95%	$7940	$196
Virginia Union University, Richmond, VA	$9069	$3780	95%	$3771	$9078
Virginia Wesleyan College, Norfolk, VA	$12,700	$5550	86%	$9491	$8759
Viterbo College, La Crosse, WI	$11,150	$4050	NR	$10,542	$4658
Voorhees College, Denmark, SC	$4784	$2706	100%	$6323	$1167
Wabash College, Crawfordsville, IN	$14,825	$4620	84%	$15,117	$4328
Wadhams Hall Seminary-College, Ogdensburg, NY	$4700	$4200	56%	NR	NR
Wagner College, Staten Island, NY	$16,000	$6000	84%	$9777	$12,223
Wake Forest University, Winston-Salem, NC	$15,500	$5100	NR	$12,914	$7686
Walla Walla College, College Place, WA	$12,693	$3380	64%	$12,721	$3352
Walsh University, North Canton, OH	$10,200	$4760	NR	$5932	$9028
Warner Pacific College, Portland, OR	$9642	$3750	NR	NR	NR
Warner Southern College, Lake Wales, FL	$7780	$3816	100%	$7808	$3788
Warren Wilson College, Asheville, NC	$12,500	$4000	61%	$8900	$7600
Wartburg College, Waverly, IA	$13,000	$3970	NR	$12,401	$4569
Washburn University of Topeka, Topeka, KS	$2912	$3110	NR	NR	NR
Washington and Jefferson College, Washington, PA	$17,470	$4205	82%	$14,500	$7175
Washington and Lee University, Lexington, VA	$15,435	$5360	49%	$11,855	$8940
Washington Bible College, Lanham, MD	$5220	$3990	32%	$5376	$3834
Washington College, Chestertown, MD	$17,250	$5740	NR	$14,002	$8988
Washington State University, Pullman, WA	$3270	$4150	NR	$6342	$1078
Washington University, St. Louis, MO	$21,210	$6593	60%	$18,785	$9018
Waynesburg College, Waynesburg, PA	$10,040	$3870	NR	$9946	$3964
Wayne State College, Wayne, NE	$1938	$2870	81%	$4554	$254
Wayne State University, Detroit, MI	$3399	$3880†	NR	NR	NR
Webber College, Babson Park, FL	$7390	$3300	52%	$7811	$2879
Webb Institute, Glen Cove, NY	$0	$6050	NR	NR	NR
Weber State University, Ogden, UT	$1863	$3270	95%	$3850	$1283
Webster University, St. Louis, MO	$10,292	$4842	NR	$10,041	$5093
Wellesley College, Wellesley, MA	$20,554	$6416	NR	$16,029	$10,941
Wells College, Aurora, NY	$17,540	$5900	89%	$15,902	$7538
Wesleyan College, Macon, GA	$13,400	$5100	99%	$13,372	$5128
Wesleyan University, Middletown, CT	$21,910	$6030	57%	$19,027	$8913
Wesley College, Dover, DE	$11,665	$5019	96%	$6949	$9735
Wesley College, Florence, MS	$2120	$2400	85%	$4200	$320
West Chester University of Pennsylvania, West Chester, PA	$4032	$4312	NR	NR	NR
Western Baptist College, Salem, OR	$12,350	$4820	96%	$11,331	$5839

*NA = not applicable; NR = not reported; * = includes room and board; † = room only.*

Freshman-Year Out-of-Pocket Costs: Looking Beyond the Sticker Price

This chart presents average costs. Actual costs may vary.

	Published tuition and fees	Room and board	Percent of freshmen who applied for aid	Average aid package for freshmen	Average cost after aid
Western Carolina University, Cullowhee, NC	$1805	$2674	52%	$3285	$1194
Western Connecticut State University, Danbury, CT	$3626	$4718	NR	NR	NR
Western Illinois University, Macomb, IL	$2885	$3838	92%	$6334	$389
Western Kentucky University, Bowling Green, KY	$2030	$2666	78%	$4300	$396
Western Maryland College, Westminster, MD	$16,125	$5365	83%	$15,953	$5537
Western Michigan University, Kalamazoo, MI	$3332	$4257	70%	$6845	$744
Western Montana College of The University of Montana, Dillon, MT	$2162	$3524	84%	$5090	$596
Western New England College, Springfield, MA	$11,448	$6120	NR	$10,277	$7291
Western New Mexico University, Silver City, NM	$1711	$3014	86%	$1802	$2923
Western Oregon University, Monmouth, OR	$3096	$3839	NR	$6360	$575
Western State College of Colorado, Gunnison, CO	$2076	$4649	75%	$4980	$1745
Western Washington University, Bellingham, WA	$2613	$4478	NR	$4650	$2441
Westfield State College, Westfield, MA	$3162	$4146	NR	$6285	$1023
West Liberty State College, West Liberty, WV	$2020	$3100	48%	$5600	$0
Westmar University, Le Mars, IA	$10,276	$3750	98%	NR	NR
Westminster Choir College of Rider University, Princeton, NJ	$14,676	$6344	95%	$13,950	$7070
Westminster College, Fulton, MO	$11,940	$4330	94%	$12,024	$4246
Westminster College, New Wilmington, PA	$14,850	$4120	90%	$12,642	$6328
Westminster College of Salt Lake City, Salt Lake City, UT	$10,270	$4900	99%	$11,455	$3715
Westmont College, Santa Barbara, CA	$17,998	$6048	86%	$15,000	$9046
West Texas A&M University, Canyon, TX	$1854	$2846	42%	$5000	$0
West Virginia State College, Institute, WV	$2116	$3450	48%	NR	NR
West Virginia University, Morgantown, WV	$2262	$4584	82%	$7694	$0
West Virginia University Institute of Technology, Montgomery, WV	$2298	$3660	79%	$4301	$1657
West Virginia Wesleyan College, Buckhannon, WV	$15,175	$3975	NR	NR	NR
Wheaton College, Wheaton, IL	$13,100	$4550	NR	$10,540	$7110
Wheaton College, Norton, MA	$19,890	$6250	67%	$16,379	$9761
Wheeling Jesuit University, Wheeling, WV	$13,000	$4870	90%	$11,265	$6605
Wheelock College, Boston, MA	$15,520	$6000	93%	$12,300	$9220
Whitman College, Walla Walla, WA	$18,805	$5420	86%	$11,877	$12,348
Whittier College, Whittier, CA	$18,088	$6047	83%	$17,163	$6972
Whitworth College, Spokane, WA	$14,424	$5100	92%	$13,700	$5824
Wichita State University, Wichita, KS	$2489	$3639	NR	$4128	$2000
Widener University, Chester, PA	$13,560	$5910	NR	$12,737	$6733
Wilberforce University, Wilberforce, OH	$7820	$4100	NR	$9900	$2020
Wiley College, Marshall, TX	$4556	$3138	NR	NR	NR
Wilkes University, Wilkes-Barre, PA	$13,147	$5708	90%	$12,312	$6543
Willamette University, Salem, OR	$18,390	$5070	83%	$13,700	$9760
William Carey College, Hattiesburg, MS	$5760	$1550	NR	$5600	$1710
William Jewell College, Liberty, MO	$11,850	$3560	97%	$11,757	$3653
William Paterson University of New Jersey, Wayne, NJ	$3380	$4960	70%	$5732	$2608

*NA = not applicable; NR = not reported; * = includes room and board; † = room only.*

Freshman-Year Out-of-Pocket Costs: Looking Beyond the Sticker Price

This chart presents average costs. Actual costs may vary.

	Published tuition and fees	Room and board	Percent of freshmen who applied for aid	Average aid package for freshmen	Average cost after aid
William Penn College, Oskaloosa, IA	$11,490	$4110	NR	$12,194	$3406
Williams Baptist College, Walnut Ridge, AR	$4990	$2722	NR	$3500	$4212
Williams College, Williamstown, MA	$21,860	$6140	55%	$18,774	$9226
William Tyndale College, Farmington Hills, MI	$6000	$3600†	NR	NR	NR
William Woods University, Fulton, MO	$12,200	$5000	100%	$11,626	$5574
Wilmington College, New Castle, DE	$6130	NA	58%	NR	NR
Wilmington College, Wilmington, OH	$11,910	$4370	NR	NR	NR
Wilson College, Chambersburg, PA	$12,149	$5338	84%	$13,626	$3861
Wingate University, Wingate, NC	$11,690	$4100	78%	$9927	$5863
Winona State University, Winona, MN	$3116	$3200	90%	$3880	$2436
Winston-Salem State University, Winston-Salem, NC	$1484	$3265	67%	$2244	$2505
Winthrop University, Rock Hill, SC	$3818	$3662	82%	$6459	$1021
Wisconsin Lutheran College, Milwaukee, WI	$11,000	$4160	NR	NR	NR
Wittenberg University, Springfield, OH	$18,228	$4718	78%	$16,764	$6182
Wofford College, Spartanburg, SC	$14,675	$4185	69%	$12,392	$6468
Woodbury University, Burbank, CA	$14,145	$5685	77%	$10,596	$9234
Worcester Polytechnic Institute, Worcester, MA	$18,060	$5940	86%	$14,577	$9423
Worcester State College, Worcester, MA	$2683	$4120	81%	$3816	$2987
Wright State University, Dayton, OH	$3600	$4005	75%	NR	NR
Xavier University, Cincinnati, OH	$13,650	$5440	91%	NR	NR
Xavier University of Louisiana, New Orleans, LA	$8000	$3500	94%	$4267	$7233
Yale University, New Haven, CT	$22,200	$6680	61%	$21,900	$6980
Yeshiva Karlin Stolin, Brooklyn, NY	$4200	$2600	NR	NR	NR
Yeshiva Ohr Elchonon Chabad/West Coast Talmudical Seminary, Los Angeles, CA	$4600	$3300	100%	$5000	$2900
Yeshiva Toras Chaim Talmudical Seminary, Denver, CO	$4000	$4500	NR	NR	NR
Yeshiva University, New York, NY	$13,960	$6570	53%	NR	NR
York College, York, NE	$6565	$3300	87%	$4813	$5052
York College of Pennsylvania, York, PA	$5790	$4500	76%	$4347	$5943
York College of the City University of New York, Jamaica, NY	$3292	NA	NR	$3540	$0
Youngstown State University, Youngstown, OH	$3366	$4200	NR	NR	NR

*NA = not applicable; NR = not reported; * = includes room and board; † = room only.*

SECTION 8

College Financial Aid Profiles

After the federal government, colleges provide the largest amount of financial aid to students. In addition, they control a great deal of the money channeled to students from the federal government. The following section of this book shows you the pattern and extent of each college's current awards.

Here, there is a great deal of information about aid based on need as well as other types of aid. Whether or not you think that you will need financial aid, we encourage you to consider all the ways in which you can help yourself that can be found in the profiles that follow.

The profiles present detailed factual and statistical data for each school in a uniform format to make easy quick reference and comparisons. Items that could not be collected in time for publication are designated as *not reported*. Items for which the specific figures could not be gathered in time are given as *available*. The phrase *not offered* is used to designate items that a college has said it does not

offer. Colleges that supplied no usable data are listed by name and address only so that you do not overlook them in your search for colleges.

The following outline of the profile format explains what is covered in each section to help you understand the definition and significance of each item.

About the Institution

This paragraph gives the reader a brief introduction to a college. It contains the following elements:

Institutional control. Private institutions are designated as *independent* (nonprofit), *independent/religious* (sponsored by or affiliated with a religious group or having a non-denominational or interdenominational religious orientation), or *proprietary* (profit-making). Public institutions are designated by their primary source of support, such as *federal, state, commonwealth* (Puerto Rico), *territory* (U.S. territories), *county, district* (an administrative unit of public education, often having boundaries different from units of local government), *city, state* and *local* ("local" refers to

county, district, or city), or *state-related* (funded primarily by the state but administered autonomously).

You will notice that private colleges usually have larger financial aid programs, but that public colleges are usually less expensive, especially for in-state or local students.

Type of student body. The categories are *men* (100 percent of student body), *primarily men, women* (100 percent of student body), *primarily women*, and *coed*.

Degrees awarded. *A*– associate degree; *B*– bachelor's degree (baccalaureate); *M*– master's degree; *D*– doctoral degree (doctorate); *P*– first professional degree (in such fields as law and medicine). There are no colleges in this book that award the associate degree only. Many award the bachelor's as their highest degree. You will need to talk to your family and guidance counselor to decide whether you want to attend a college that concentrates on undergraduate education or an institution with professional schools and research activities.

Number of undergraduate majors. This shows the number of academic fields in which the institution offers associate and/or bachelor's degrees. The purpose of this is to give you a brief indication of the range of subjects available. For a full list of each college's majors, refer to Peterson's Guide to Four-Year Colleges.

Enrollment. These figures are based on the actual number of full-time and part-time students enrolled in degree programs as of fall 1996. In most instances, they are designated as total enrollment (for the specific college or university) and *freshmen*. If the institution is a university and its total enrollment figure includes graduate students, a separate figure for *undergraduates* may be provided. If the profiled institution is a subunit of a university, the figures may be designated *total university enrollment* for the entire university and *total unit enrollment* for the specific subunit. Following the undergraduate enrollment figure, the percentages of undergraduate students that are state residents are given in parentheses.

You may have some feeling for the college size that would suit you best. Be sure to look carefully at the relationship between total enrollment and undergraduate enrollment. However, be aware that although a university may have a relatively small number of undergraduates, it could be one of the many large universities that has successfully cultivated a small-college atmosphere for its undergraduate students.

Undergraduate Expenses

This section shows you at a glance the total basic cost of one year at each college.

Expenses are given for the 1997–98 academic year (actual or estimated), or for the 1996–97 academic year if more recent figures were not yet available at the time of data collection. Annual expenses may be expressed as a comprehensive fee (this includes full-time tuition, mandatory fees, and college room and board) or as separate figures for full-time tuition, mandatory fees, college room and board, or college room only. For public institutions where tuition differs according to residence, separate figures are given

for area and/or state residents and for out-of-state residents.

The tuition structure at some institutions is complex in that freshmen and sophomores may be charged a different rate from that for juniors and seniors, or a professional or vocational division may have a different fee structure than the liberal arts division of the same institution. In such cases, the lowest tuition appears in the profile, followed by the notation "minimum." Also, in instances where colleges report room and board costs which vary depending on the type of accommodation and meal plan, the figures given are either for the most common room arrangement and a full meal plan, or for the lowest figures, followed by the notation "minimum."

Remember, when thinking of costs, that you have to be sure to allow yourself spending money and transportation costs, as well as figuring on some $500 to $1000 for books and other course-related supplies.

Applications

This section will tell you what percentage of students at each college apply for financial aid and what the necessary forms and deadlines are.

Figures are given for the percentage of full-time undergraduates who enrolled in fall 1996 who applied for financial aid, the percentage of these students who were determined to have need according to Federal Methodology, and the percentage of these students who received aid from any source. Federal Methodology is the need analysis formula used by the U.S. Department of Education to determine the Expected Family Contribution (EFC), which, when subtracted from the cost of attendance at an institution, determines the financial need of a student.

The college's financial aid application deadline is noted as the *financial aid deadline* and is shown in one of three ways: as a specific date if it is an absolute deadline; noted as *(continuous)*, which means processing goes on up to a specific date or until all available aid has been awarded; or as *(priority)*, meaning that students are encouraged to apply before that date in order to have the best chance of obtaining aid.

The financial aid forms and supporting data that a student will have to submit in applying for financial aid are grouped into three categories: "required, acceptable (may be submitted in lieu of a required form), and required for some."

Be prepared to check early with the colleges you are interested in as to exactly which forms will be required from you. All colleges require the *Free Application for Federal Student Aid (FAFSA)* for students applying for federal aid. Other types of supporting data most commonly required are the following:

AFSSA-CSX. CSX Technology's Application for Federal and State Student Aid.

CSS Financial Aid PROFILE. The College Scholarship Service's supplementary financial aid form. To see if the college you are applying to requires this application, check the PROFILE registration forms that are available from high school guidance offices and college financial aid offices. This will provide you with a list of colleges and universities requiring this application for 1997–98.

FARE. Financial Aid Report of Eligibility.

Financial Aid Transcript. A record of aid previously received for college study, required of transfer applicants.

Institutional form. A college's own financial aid application form.

State form. A state aid application form, such as the Tuition Assistance Program form (TAP) for New York or the Pennsylvania Higher Education Assistance Agency (PHEAA) form.

The *admission application deadline* is noted either as an actual date or rolling, so that you will know whether the two parts of your application, financial aid and admissions, will be due together or separately. Rolling application means that applications are processed as they are received and students are accepted as long as there are openings. In general, it is a good idea to ask early for full information about aid so that you don't miss out on any part of an aid program. The application deadline for nonresidents is given if it differs from the date for state residents. Early decision and early action deadlines are also indicated if a college offers those options. If you plan to apply early, you will have to be sure to get all the right materials to also apply for early aid consideration.

Summary of Aid to Needy Students

This section presents a picture of the need-based aid situation at each college. All items refer to aid awarded to undergraduates enrolled full-time in the fall of 1996 who were judged to have need either by Federal Methodology or Institutional Methodology.

In this paragraph, the percentage of need met from both *gift aid* and *self-help* (if applicable) is listed, and the *average financial aid package* awarded to undergraduates is expressed as the average dollar amount received from all sources. The breakdown in percent-

ages (if provided) follows in parentheses and is defined as *gift aid* (scholarships and grants) and *self-help* (jobs and loans). The total amount of gift aid awarded to all needy undergraduates is shown, broken down into aid from college's own funds, other college-administered sources, and external sources.

Lastly, the number and average dollar amount of *Student jobs*: Federal Work-Study (FWS) jobs and other campus part-time jobs are represented. FWS is a federally funded program that enables students with demonstrated need to earn money by working on or off campus, usually in a nonprofit organization. FWS jobs are a special category of jobs that are open to students only through the financial aid office. Other kinds of part-time jobs are routinely available at most colleges and may vary widely.

You can form a rough idea of your chances of receiving aid at a specific college and some sense of whether it would be enough if you match this information to your own estimate of need and the cost of college. For example, if you think you would need $5000 to attend a particular college, yet that college aided fewer than half of their aid applicants and, further, met only half of their need, you could conclude that your chances of receiving all the aid you need are slim. You can also get an idea of a college's ability to help applicants directly from the proportion of self-help in the aid package (the lower it is, the less the burden on the student and her or his family) and from the proportion of scholarship money that comes from the college rather than from outside (student-located) sources.

Need-Based Scholarships and Grants

Scholarships and grants are gifts awarded to students that do not need to be repaid. Need-based scholarships and grants are awarded because of a student's or parents' inability or great difficulty in paying college costs. Award types listed here include Federal Pell Grants, Federal Supplemental Educational Opportunity Grants (FSEOG), ROTC Scholarships, and state, private, and institutional scholarships/grants. A student must demonstrate financial need to be eligible for Pell Grants, FSEOG, most state and institutional scholarships, and some private scholarships.

Loans

Loans are forms of aid that must be repaid. Loans listed here include Federal Perkins Loans, PLUS Loans, Subsidized and Unsubsidized Stafford Loans, Federal Nursing Student Loans, Primary Care Loans (PCL), and state, private, and institutional loans. Institutional loans are defined as short-term and low-interest long-term loans from college funds.

Non-Need Awards

This section covers college-administered scholarships awarded to undergraduates on the basis of merit or personal attributes without regard to need, although they may certainly be given to students who also happen to qualify for need-based aid.

The total number of non-need awards made in 1996 is given. This overall figure is then broken down into five categories: *academic interests/achievements, creative arts/performance, special achievement/activities, special characteristics*, and *athletic* awards. For each category in which a college has reported specific information about the awards it offers to undergraduates, the total number awarded and total dollar amount awarded for 1996–97 are given. Following the total amounts are types of scholarships offered within each category. If a college indicated that it awards scholarships in particular categories but was not able to report specific information, the word available appears following the category name. If a college indicated that it does not award any non-need scholarships at all, the phrase Not offered appears.

Other Money-Saving Options

This section shows you the availability of several types of special programs that many colleges offer in addition to the usual forms of direct aid.

Used in place of or in combination with the traditional sources of financial aid, these options can make a considerable contribution toward reducing college costs, and they do not require that you demonstrate need. These programs can be of particular help for students who don't quite qualify for aid but will still find going to college a strain on the budget.

Accelerated degree. If you are a very good student, you may earn a bachelor's degree in three academic years instead of the usual four at some colleges, thereby saving as much as a full year's expenses.

Co-op program (also known as "cooperative education"). Co-op programs provide a formal arrangement with off-campus employers that allows students to combine work and study, either at the same time or in alternating terms. Generally, these programs begin at the end of the sophomore year and add a year or a semester to the length of the degree

program. Co-op programs enable students to earn regular marketplace wages while gaining experience, often specifically related to the field they are studying or the career they are preparing for.

ROTC. Army, Naval, and Air Force ROTC programs offer such benefits as tuition, the cost of textbooks, and living allowances. In return, students must fulfill a service obligation after graduating from college. Because they can be a significant help in paying for college, these programs are increasing in popularity. In the profile, a program offered on campus is indicated without comment; a program offered by arrangement on another campus is indicated by the word cooperative.

Off-campus living. This indicates whether students are permitted to live off campus in noncollege housing; in some cases this is permitted only after a period of required on-campus residence. By living off campus and economizing on personal expenses, a student often can lower the living expenses portion of the total yearly cost of college.

Tuition prepayment plans: If a college has a prepayment plan, an entering student may lock in the current tuition rate for the entire term of enrollment by paying the full amount in advance rather than year by year. Colleges that offer such a plan may also help the student to arrange financing, which in the long run can cost less than the total of four years' worth under conditions of increasing tuition rates.

Guaranteed tuition plan. If a college has a guaranteed tuition plan, it promises that the tuition rate of an entering student will not increase for the entire term of enrollment, from entrance to graduation. This helps you to plan the

total cost of your education and saves you from the financial distress sometimes caused by tuition hikes.

Tuition waivers. Some colleges offer full or partial tuition waivers for minority students, children of alumni, adult students, senior citizens, or college employees or children of employees.

Contact

The name, title, address, telephone number, and fax number of the person to contact for further information (student financial aid contact, chief financial aid officer, or office of financial aid) are given at the end of the profile. You should feel free to write or call for any materials you need, or if you have questions.

How Schools Get into the Guide

Peterson's College Money Handbook 1998 covers accredited baccalaureate-degree-granting institutions in the United States and U.S. territories. Institutions have full accreditation or candidate-for-accreditation (preaccreditation) status granted by an institutional or specialized accrediting body recognized by the U.S. Department of Education or Council for Higher Education Accreditation. Recognized institutional accrediting bodies, which consider each institution as a whole, are the following: the six regional associations of schools and colleges (Middle States, New England, North Central, Northwest, Southern, and Western), each of which is responsible for a specified portion of the United States and its territories; the Accrediting Association of Bible Colleges (AABC); the Accrediting Council for Independent Colleges and Schools (ACICS); the Accrediting Commission of Career Schools/Colleges of Technology (ACCSCT); the Distance Education and Training Council (DETC); the American Academy for Liberal Education; the Council on Occupational Education; and the Transnational Association of Christian Schools (TRACS). Program registration by the New York State Board of Regents is considered to be the equivalent of institutional accreditation, since the Board requires that all programs offered by an institution meet its standards before recognition is granted. There are recognized specialized accrediting bodies in over forty different fields, each of which is authorized to accredit specific programs in its particular field. This can serve as the equivalent of institutional accreditation for specialized institutions that offer programs in one field only (schools of art, music, optometry, theology, etc.). For a full explanation of the accrediting process and complete information on recognized accrediting bodies, the reader should refer to *Peterson's Register of Higher Education.*

Research Procedures

The data contained in the college chart, profiles, and indexes were collected between fall 1996 and spring 1997 through Peterson's Annual Survey of Undergraduate Financial Aid and Peterson's Annual Survey of Undergraduate Institutions. Questionnaires were sent to the more than 1,700 colleges and universities that meet the criteria for inclusion outlined above. All data included in this edition have been submitted by officials (usually financial aid officers, registrars, or institutional research personnel) at the schools themselves. In addition, the great majority of institutions that submitted data were contacted directly by Peterson's editorial staff to verify unusual figures, resolve discrepancies, and obtain additional data. All usable information received in time for publication has been included. The omission of any particular item from an index or profile listing signifies that the item is either not applicable to that institution or that data were not available. Because of the comprehensive editorial review that takes place in our offices and because all material comes directly from college officials, we have every reason to believe that the information presented in this guide is accurate. However, students should check with a specific college or university at the time of application to verify such figures as tuition and fees, which may have changed since the publication of this volume.

ABILENE CHRISTIAN UNIVERSITY
Abilene, Texas

About the Institution Independent/religious, coed. Degrees awarded: A, B, M, D, P. Offers 92 undergraduate majors. Total enrollment: 4,397. Undergraduates: 3,754 (64% state residents). Freshmen: 896.

Undergraduate Expenses (1996–97) Comprehensive fee of $11,420 includes tuition ($8640), mandatory fees ($440), and college room and board ($2340 minimum). College room only: $1540 (minimum).

Applications Of all full-time undergraduates enrolled in fall 1996, 82% of those who applied for aid were judged to have need according to Federal Methodology, of whom 89% were aided. *Financial aid deadline (priority):* 3/1. *Financial aid forms:* FAFSA, institutional form required; CSS Financial Aid PROFILE, state form acceptable. *Admission application deadline:* rolling.

Summary of Aid to Needy Students *From gift & self-help combined:* Average need met: 70%. Average amount awarded: $7707 (49% gift aid, 51% self-help). *Gift aid:* Total: $8,093,202 (54% from college's own funds, 24% from other college-administered sources, 22% from external sources). 322 Federal Work-Study jobs (averaging $480); 605 part-time jobs.

Need-Based Scholarships & Grants Pell, FSEOG, state, private, college/university.

Loans Perkins, PLUS, Stafford, Unsubsidized Stafford, state, private, college/university long-term loans ($2000 average).

Non-Need Awards In 1996, a total of 3,012 non-need awards were made. *Academic Interests/Achievement Awards:* 2,267 ($5,397,753 total): general academic, agriculture, biological sciences, business, communication, education, English, foreign languages, home economics, mathematics, physical sciences, religion/biblical studies, social sciences. *Creative Arts/Performance Awards:* 93 ($126,890 total): art/fine arts, debating, journalism/publications, music, theater/drama. *Special Achievements/Activities Awards:* 88 ($85,200 total): cheerleading/drum major, leadership. *Special Characteristics Awards:* 346 ($1,019,713 total): children of faculty/staff, local/state students, out-of-state students, relatives of clergy, religious affiliation. *Athletic:* Total: 218 ($1,659,210); Men: 158 ($1,140,577); Women: 60 ($518,633).

Other Money-Saving Options Accelerated degree, co-op program, cooperative Army ROTC, off-campus living (after sophomore year). *Payment Plans:* tuition prepayment, installment. *Waivers:* full or partial for minority students and employees or children of employees.

Contact Office of Financial Aid, Abilene Christian University, ACU Station, Box 29007, Abilene, TX 79699-9007, 915-674-2000.

ACADEMY OF ART COLLEGE
San Francisco, California

About the Institution Proprietary, coed. Degrees awarded: B, M. Offers 18 undergraduate majors. Total enrollment: 4,568. Undergraduates: 3,953 (56% state residents). Freshmen: 1,260.

Undergraduate Expenses (1997–98) Tuition: $14,850. Mandatory fees: $60. College room only: $6000 (minimum).

Applications 47% of all full-time undergraduates enrolled in fall 1996 applied for aid; of these, 95% were judged to have need according to Federal Methodology, of whom 97% were aided. *Financial aid deadline (priority):* 5/1. *Financial aid forms:* FAFSA, institutional form required; state form acceptable. *Admission application deadline:* rolling.

Summary of Aid to Needy Students *From gift & self-help combined:* Average amount awarded: $4190 (30% gift aid, 70% self-help). *Gift aid:* Total: $1,300,000 (1% from college's own funds, 49% from other college-administered sources, 50% from external sources). 42 Federal Work-Study jobs; 73 part-time jobs.

Need-Based Scholarships & Grants Pell, state.

Loans PLUS, Stafford, Unsubsidized Stafford.

Non-Need Awards In 1996, a total of 6 non-need awards were made. *Creative Arts/Performance Awards:* 6 ($15,000 total): art/fine arts.

Other Money-Saving Options Off-campus living. *Payment Plan:* installment.

Contact Mr. Joe Vollaro, Vice-President–Financial Aid, Academy of Art College, 79 New Montgomery Street, San Francisco, CA 94105-3410, 415-274-8688, fax: 415-546-9737.

ACADEMY OF THE NEW CHURCH COLLEGE
Bryn Athyn, Pennsylvania

See Bryn Athyn College of the New Church

ADAMS STATE COLLEGE
Alamosa, Colorado

About the Institution State-supported, coed. Degrees awarded: A, B, M. Offers 56 undergraduate majors. Total enrollment: 2,444. Undergraduates: 2,176 (80% state residents). Freshmen: 566.

Undergraduate Expenses (1997–98 estimated) State resident tuition: $1496. Nonresident tuition: $5456. Mandatory fees: $462. College room and board: $4640. College room only: $2100.

Applications Of all full-time undergraduates enrolled in fall 1996, 100% of those judged to have need according to Federal Methodology were aided. *Financial aid deadline (priority):* 4/15. *Financial aid forms:* FAFSA required; CSS Financial Aid PROFILE acceptable. *Admission application deadline:* 8/1.

Summary of Aid to Needy Students *From gift & self-help combined:* Average need met: 63%. Average amount awarded: $6701 (36% gift aid, 64% self-help). *Gift aid:* Total: $4,107,623 (20% from college's own funds, 22% from other college-administered sources, 58% from external sources). 260 Federal Work-Study jobs (averaging $1250); 588 part-time jobs.

Need-Based Scholarships & Grants Pell, FSEOG, state, private, college/university.

Loans Perkins, PLUS, Stafford, Unsubsidized Stafford, college/university short-term loans ($200 average), college/university long-term loans.

Non-Need Awards In 1996, a total of 1,219 non-need awards were made. *Academic Interests/Achievement Awards:* 615 ($1,035,081 total): general academic, biological sciences, business, communication, computer science, education, English, foreign languages, health fields, humanities, mathematics, premedicine, social sciences. *Creative Arts/Performance Awards:* 58 ($30,350 total): art/fine arts, music, performing arts, theater/drama. *Special Achievements/Activities Awards:* 22 ($38,500 total): community service, leadership, memberships. *Special Characteristics Awards:* 308 ($683,985 total): out-of-state students. *Athletic:* Total: 216 ($367,575); Men: 144 ($223,344); Women: 72 ($144,231).

Other Money-Saving Options Accelerated degree, off-campus living (after sophomore year). *Payment Plan:* installment.

Contact Mr. Ted Laws, Director of Financial Aid, Adams State College, Alamosa, CO 81102, 719-587-7306, fax: 719-587-7522.

ADELPHI UNIVERSITY
Garden City, New York

About the Institution Independent, coed. Degrees awarded: B, M, D. Offers 36 undergraduate majors. Total enrollment: 5,969. Undergraduates: 2,787 (91% state residents). Freshmen: 337.

Undergraduate Expenses (1996–97) Comprehensive fee of $20,520 includes tuition ($13,830), mandatory fees ($170), and college room and board ($6520). College room only: $3620.

Applications 71% of all full-time undergraduates enrolled in fall 1996 applied for aid; of these,100% were judged to have need according to Federal Methodology, of whom 98% were aided. *Financial aid deadline (priority):* 2/15. *Financial aid forms:* FAFSA required; state form acceptable. Institutional form, CSS Business Supplement required for some. *Admission application deadline:* rolling.

Summary of Aid to Needy Students *From gift & self-help combined:* Average need met: 100%. Average amount awarded: $11,300 (56% gift aid, 44% self-help). *Gift aid:* Total: $10,283,511 (58% from college's own funds, 4% from other college-administered sources, 38% from external sources). 190 Federal Work-Study jobs (averaging $1500); 340 part-time jobs.

Need-Based Scholarships & Grants Pell, FSEOG, state, private, college/university.

Loans Perkins, PLUS, Stafford, Unsubsidized Stafford, Federal Nursing, private.

Non-Need Awards In 1996, a total of 661 non-need awards were made. *Academic Interests/Achievement Awards:* 512 ($2,550,353 total): general academic. *Creative Arts/Performance Awards:* 49 ($146,000 total): art/fine arts, dance, music, performing arts, theater/drama. *Special Characteristics Awards:* 12 ($24,000 total): children and siblings of alumni, ethnic background, international students. *Athletic:* Total: 88 ($819,900); Men: 48 ($489,100); Women: 40 ($330,800).

Other Money-Saving Options Cooperative Army ROTC, cooperative Air Force ROTC, off-campus living. *Payment Plans:* tuition prepayment, installment, deferred payment. *Waivers:* full or partial for employees or children of employees.

Contact Mr. Joseph Posillico, Assistant Director, Student Financial Services, Adelphi University, South Avenue, Garden City, NY 11530, 516-877-3365, fax: 516-877-3380.

ADRIAN COLLEGE
Adrian, Michigan

About the Institution Independent/religious, coed. Degrees awarded: A, B. Offers 48 undergraduate majors. Total enrollment: 1,049 (79% state residents). Freshmen: 298.

Undergraduate Expenses (1997–98) Comprehensive fee of $16,710 includes tuition ($12,730), mandatory fees ($100), and college room and board ($3880 minimum). College room only: $1880 (minimum).

Applications 90% of all full-time undergraduates enrolled in fall 1996 applied for aid; of these, 89% were judged to have need according to Federal Methodology, of whom 100% were aided. *Financial aid deadline (priority):* 3/15. *Financial aid forms:* FAFSA required. Institutional form required for some. *Admission application deadline:* 8/15.

Summary of Aid to Needy Students *From gift & self-help combined:* Average need met: 92%. Average amount awarded: $12,051 (61% gift aid, 39% self-help). *Gift aid:* Total: $5,745,420 (62% from college's own funds, 25% from other college-administered sources, 13% from external sources). 359 Federal Work-Study jobs (averaging $1500); 155 part-time jobs.

Need-Based Scholarships & Grants Pell, FSEOG, state, private, college/university.

Loans Perkins, PLUS, Stafford, Unsubsidized Stafford, state, private, college/university short-term loans ($30 average).

Non-Need Awards In 1996, a total of 459 non-need awards were made. *Academic Interests/Achievement Awards:* 359 ($1,312,783 total): general academic, business. *Creative Arts/Performance Awards:* 48 ($46,250 total): art/fine arts, music, theater/drama. *Special Achievements/Activities Awards:* 43 ($86,000 total): leadership. *Special Characteristics Awards:* 9 ($76,100 total): children of faculty/staff.

Other Money-Saving Options Off-campus living (after junior year). *Payment Plans:* installment, deferred payment. *Waivers:* full or partial for employees or children of employees.

Contact Mr. Chris Howard, Assistant Director of Student Financial Services, Adrian College, 110 South Madison Street, Adrian, MI 49221-2575, 800-877-2246.

THE ADVERTISING ARTS COLLEGE
San Diego, California

About the Institution Proprietary, coed. Degrees awarded: A, B. Offers 7 undergraduate majors. Total enrollment: 300 (77% state residents). Freshmen: 165.

Undergraduate Expenses (1997–98) Tuition: $8650.

Applications 73% of all full-time undergraduates enrolled in fall 1996 applied for aid; of these, 88% were judged to have need according to Federal Methodology, of whom 100% were aided. *Financial aid deadline:* continuous. *Financial aid forms:* FAFSA, institutional form required; CSS Financial Aid PROFILE acceptable. State form required for some. *Admission application deadline:* rolling.

Summary of Aid to Needy Students *From gift & self-help combined:* Average need met: 88%. Average amount awarded: $7427 (16% gift aid, 84% self-help). *Gift aid:* Total: $223,817 (2% from college's own funds, 44% from other college-administered sources, 54% from external sources). 3 Federal Work-Study jobs (averaging $2739); 5 part-time jobs.

Need-Based Scholarships & Grants Pell, FSEOG, state, private, college/university.

Loans PLUS, Stafford, Unsubsidized Stafford.

Non-Need Awards Not offered.

Other Money-Saving Options *Payment Plans:* tuition prepayment, installment.

Contact Ms. Sue Wheeler, Financial Aid Administrator, The Advertising Arts College, 10025 Mesa Rim Road, San Diego, CA 92121, 619-546-0602, fax: 619-546-0274.

AGNES SCOTT COLLEGE
Decatur, Georgia

About the Institution Independent/religious, women. Degrees awarded: B, M. Offers 26 undergraduate majors. Total enrollment: 715. Undergraduates: 694 (48% state residents). Freshmen: 232.

Undergraduate Expenses (1997–98) Comprehensive fee of $21,190 includes tuition ($14,825), mandatory fees ($135), and college room and board ($6230).

Applications 79% of all full-time undergraduates enrolled in fall 1996 applied for aid; of these, 86% were judged to have need according to Federal Methodology, of whom 100% were aided. *Financial aid deadline (priority):* 3/15. *Financial aid forms:* FAFSA required; CSS Financial Aid PROFILE acceptable. State form, institutional form required for some. *Regular admission application deadline:* 3/1. Early decision deadline: 11/15.

Summary of Aid to Needy Students *From gift & self-help combined:* Average need met: 95%. Average amount awarded: $16,053 (70% gift aid, 30% self-help). *Gift aid:* Total: $5,036,991 (75% from college's own funds, 2% from other college-administered sources, 23% from external sources). 249 Federal Work-Study jobs (averaging $1300); 60 part-time jobs.

Need-Based Scholarships & Grants Pell, FSEOG, state, private, college/university.

Loans PLUS, Stafford, Unsubsidized Stafford, college/university long-term loans ($1892 average).

Non-Need Awards *Academic Interests/Achievement Awards:* general academic, biological sciences, English, mathematics, physical sciences. *Creative Arts/Performance Awards:* music. *Special Achievements/Activities Awards:* general special achievements/activities, community service. *Special Characteristics Awards:* adult students, children of educators, children of faculty/staff, handicapped students.

Other Money-Saving Options Accelerated degree, cooperative Naval ROTC, cooperative Air Force ROTC. *Payment Plan:* installment. *Waivers:* full or partial for employees or children of employees.

Contact Financial Aid Office, Agnes Scott College, 141 East College Avenue, Decatur, GA 30030-3797, 404-638-6395.

ALABAMA AGRICULTURAL AND MECHANICAL UNIVERSITY
Normal, Alabama

About the Institution State-supported, coed. Degrees awarded: A, B, M, D. Offers 61 undergraduate majors. Total enrollment: 5,263. Undergraduates: 3,852 (66% state residents). Freshmen: 721.

Undergraduate Expenses (1997–98) State resident tuition: $1932. Nonresident tuition: $3864. Mandatory fees: $236. College room and board: $2678. College room only: $1164.

Applications Of all full-time undergraduates enrolled in fall 1996, 64% of those who applied for aid were judged to have need according to Federal Methodology, of whom 100% were aided. *Financial aid deadline (priority):* 4/1. *Financial aid forms:* FAFSA, institutional form required; CSS Financial Aid PROFILE acceptable. *Admission application deadline:* rolling.

Summary of Aid to Needy Students *From gift & self-help combined:* Average need met: 88%. Average amount awarded: $4955 (44% gift aid, 56% self-help). *Gift aid:* Total: $4,393,261 (26% from college's own funds, 4% from other college-administered sources, 70% from external sources). 121 Federal Work-Study jobs (averaging $1432); 155 part-time jobs.

Need-Based Scholarships & Grants Pell, FSEOG, state.

Loans Perkins, PLUS, Stafford, Unsubsidized Stafford, private.

Non-Need Awards *Academic Interests/Achievement Awards:* 469 ($1,117,256 total): general academic. *Creative Arts/Performance Awards:* 283 ($726,565 total): music. *Athletic:* Total: 94 ($293,899); Men: 70 ($221,926); Women: 24 ($71,973).

Other Money-Saving Options Accelerated degree, co-op program, Army ROTC, off-campus living (after freshman year). *Payment Plan:* deferred payment. *Waivers:* full or partial for employees or children of employees.

Contact Office of Financial Aid, Alabama Agricultural and Mechanical University, PO Box 907, Normal, AL 35762-0907, 205-851-5000.

ALABAMA STATE UNIVERSITY
Montgomery, Alabama

About the Institution State-supported, coed. Degrees awarded: A, B, M. Offers 47 undergraduate majors. Total enrollment: 5,554. Undergraduates: 4,778 (62% state residents). Freshmen: 1,075.

Undergraduate Expenses (1996–97) State resident tuition: $1800. Nonresident tuition: $3600. Mandatory fees: $290. College room and board: $3112.

Applications Of all full-time undergraduates enrolled in fall 1996, 100% of those judged to have need according to Federal Methodology were aided. *Financial aid deadline (priority):* 5/1. *Financial aid forms:* FAFSA required. *Admission application deadline:* 8/26.

Summary of Aid to Needy Students *From gift & self-help combined:* Average need met: 75%. *Gift aid:* Total: $6,705,955 (6% from college-administered sources, 94% from external sources). 825 Federal Work-Study jobs (averaging $1888); 137 part-time jobs.

Need-Based Scholarships & Grants Pell, FSEOG, state.

Loans Perkins, PLUS, Stafford, Unsubsidized Stafford, college/university short-term loans ($300 average).

Non-Need Awards In 1996, a total of 1,238 non-need awards were made. *Academic Interests/Achievement Awards:* 476 ($916,563 total): general academic, biological sciences, education, mathematics. *Creative Arts/Performance Awards:* 64 ($53,286 total): art/fine arts, music, performing arts. *Special Achievements/Activities Awards:* 42 ($30,301 total): general special achievements/activities, cheerleading/drum major, leadership. *Special Characteristics Awards:* 510 ($612,091 total): ethnic background, handicapped students, ROTC participants, veterans' children. *Athletic:* Total: 146 ($388,181); Men: 109 ($296,587); Women: 37 ($91,594).

Other Money-Saving Options Accelerated degree, co-op program, Air Force ROTC, cooperative Army ROTC, off-campus living.

Contact Mrs. Dorenda A. Adams, Director of Financial Aid, Alabama State University, PO Box 271, Montgomery, AL 36101-0271, 334-229-4323, fax: 334-299-4924.

ALASKA BIBLE COLLEGE
Glennallen, Alaska

About the Institution Independent/religious, coed. Degrees awarded: A, B. Offers 5 undergraduate majors. Total enrollment: 34 (47% state residents). Freshmen: 17.

Undergraduate Expenses (1997–98) Comprehensive fee of $7360 includes tuition ($3790) and college room and board ($3570).

Applications 68% of all full-time undergraduates enrolled in fall 1996 applied for aid; of these,100% were judged to have need according to Federal Methodology, of whom 100% were aided. *Financial aid deadline:* 8/5. *Financial aid forms:* institutional form required; FAFSA, CSS Financial Aid PROFILE, state form acceptable. *Admission application deadline:* 8/1.

Summary of Aid to Needy Students *From gift & self-help combined:* Average amount awarded: $2441 (64% gift aid, 36% self-help). *Gift aid:* Total: $34,102 (45% from college's own funds, 55% from external sources). 13 part-time jobs.

Need-Based Scholarships & Grants College/university.

Loans State.

Non-Need Awards *Academic Interests/Achievement Awards:* 6 ($600 total): general academic. *Creative Arts/Performance Awards:* 1 ($100 total): music. *Special Achievements/Activities Awards:* 2 ($350 total): religious involvement. *Special Characteristics Awards:* children of faculty/staff, local/state students, religious affiliation, spouses of current students.

Other Money-Saving Options Off-campus living (after sophomore year). *Payment Plan:* installment. *Waivers:* full or partial for employees or children of employees.

Contact Mr. Ken Pregizer, Business Manager, Alaska Bible College, Box 289, Glennallen, AK 99588-0289, 907-822-3201, fax: 907-822-5027.

ALASKA PACIFIC UNIVERSITY
Anchorage, Alaska

About the Institution Independent/religious, coed. Degrees awarded: A, B, M. Offers 10 undergraduate majors. Total enrollment: 450. Undergraduates: 261 (87% state residents). Freshmen: 29.

Undergraduate Expenses (1997–98) Comprehensive fee of $12,630 includes tuition ($8400), mandatory fees ($80), and college room and board ($4150 minimum). College room only: $1800.

Applications *Financial aid deadline (priority):* 3/15. *Financial aid forms:* FAFSA, institutional form required. State form required for some. *Regular admission application deadline:* 2/1. Early decision deadline: 1/1.

Summary of Aid to Needy Students *From gift & self-help combined:* Average need met: 74%. Average amount awarded: $7382 (55% gift aid, 45% self-help). *Gift aid:* Total: $835,503 (68% from college's own funds, 17% from other college-administered sources, 15% from external sources). 47 Federal Work-Study jobs (averaging $1152); 39 part-time jobs.

Need-Based Scholarships & Grants Pell, FSEOG, private, college/university.

Loans PLUS, Stafford, Unsubsidized Stafford, state, college/university short-term loans ($350 average).

Non-Need Awards In 1996, a total of 147 non-need awards were made. *Academic Interests/Achievement Awards:* 79 ($184,604 total): general academic. *Special Achievements/Activities Awards:* 46 ($95,221 total): general special achievements/activities, leadership. *Special Characteristics Awards:* 22 ($74,256 total): ethnic background, international students, local/state students, out-of-state students, religious affiliation.

Other Money-Saving Options Accelerated degree, off-campus living. *Payment Plan:* deferred payment. *Waivers:* full or partial for employees or children of employees and senior citizens.

Contact Mr. Roger Frierson, Assistant Director of Financial Aid, Alaska Pacific University, 4101 University Drive, Anchorage, AK 99508-4672, 907-564-8342, fax: 907-564-8317.

ALBANY COLLEGE OF PHARMACY OF UNION UNIVERSITY
Albany, New York

About the Institution Independent, coed. Degrees awarded: B, P. Offers 1 undergraduate major. Total enrollment: 722. Undergraduates: 696 (90% state residents). Freshmen: 124.

Undergraduate Expenses (1996–97) Comprehensive fee of $15,013 includes tuition ($10,000), mandatory fees ($213), and college room and board ($4800).

Applications 92% of all full-time undergraduates enrolled in fall 1996 applied for aid; of these,100% were judged to have need according to Federal Methodology, of whom 100% were aided. *Financial aid deadline (priority):* 2/1. *Financial aid forms:* FAFSA, state form, state income tax form required; CSS Financial Aid PROFILE acceptable. *Admission application deadline:* rolling.

Summary of Aid to Needy Students *From gift & self-help combined:* Average need met: 90%. Average amount awarded: $7847 (35% gift aid, 65% self-help). *Gift aid:* Total: $1,625,000 (35% from college's own funds, 49% from other college-administered sources, 16% from external sources). Federal Work-Study jobs; 30 part-time jobs.

Need-Based Scholarships & Grants Pell, FSEOG, state, private, college/university.

Loans Perkins, PLUS, Stafford, Unsubsidized Stafford, college/university short-term loans ($350 average), college/university long-term loans ($1200 average), health profession student loans.

Non-Need Awards *Academic Interests/Achievement Awards:* general academic. *Special Characteristics Awards:* children and siblings of alumni.

Other Money-Saving Options Off-campus living (after freshman year). *Payment Plan:* installment. *Waivers:* full or partial for employees or children of employees.

Contact Mr. Thomas J. Dalton, Director of Financial Aid, Albany College of Pharmacy of Union University, Albany, NY 12208-3425, 518-445-7256.

ALBANY STATE UNIVERSITY
Albany, Georgia

About the Institution State-supported, coed. Degrees awarded: A, B, M. Offers 28 undergraduate majors. Total enrollment: 3,150. Undergraduates: 2,801 (93% state residents). Freshmen: 515.

Undergraduate Expenses (1996–97) State resident tuition: $1440 (minimum). Nonresident tuition: $4320 (minimum). Mandatory fees: $420. College room and board: $3180. College room only: $1515.

Applications Of all full-time undergraduates enrolled in fall 1996, 84% of those who applied for aid were judged to have need according to Federal Methodology, of whom 94% were aided. *Financial aid deadline (priority):* 4/15. *Financial aid forms:* FAFSA required; CSS Financial Aid PROFILE acceptable. State form, institutional form required for some. *Admission application deadline:* 9/1.

Summary of Aid to Needy Students *From gift & self-help combined:* Average need met: 85%. Average amount awarded: $6425 (44% gift aid, 56% self-help). *Gift aid:* Total: $4,923,270 (2% from college's own funds, 16% from other college-administered sources, 82% from external sources). Federal Work-Study jobs; part-time jobs.

Need-Based Scholarships & Grants Pell, FSEOG, state, private.

Loans Perkins, PLUS, Stafford, Unsubsidized Stafford, state, private.

Non-Need Awards In 1996, a total of 292 non-need awards were made. *Academic Interests/Achievement Awards:* 66 ($157,293 total): general academic, biological sciences, health fields, social sciences. *Creative Arts/Performance Awards:* 92 ($19,000 total): music. *Athletic:* Total: 134 ($683,775); Men: 95 ($499,243); Women: 39 ($184,532).

Other Money-Saving Options Co-op program, Army ROTC, off-campus living. *Waivers:* full or partial for senior citizens.

Contact Ms. Kathleen J. Caldwell, Director of Admissions and Financial Aid, Albany State University, 504 College Drive, Albany, GA 31705-2717, 912-430-4650.

ALBERT A. LIST COLLEGE OF JEWISH STUDIES
New York, New York

See Jewish Theological Seminary of America

ALBERTSON COLLEGE OF IDAHO
Caldwell, Idaho

About the Institution Independent, coed. Degrees awarded: B. Offers 31 undergraduate majors. Total enrollment: 651 (73% state residents). Freshmen: 194.

Undergraduate Expenses (1997–98) Comprehensive fee of $18,665 includes tuition ($15,100), mandatory fees ($265), and college room and board ($3300). College room only: $1200.

Applications 90% of all full-time undergraduates enrolled in fall 1996 applied for aid; of these, 76% were judged to have need according to Federal Methodology, of whom 100% were aided. *Financial aid deadline (priority):* 2/15. *Financial aid forms:* FAFSA, institutional form required. *Admission application deadline:* 6/1.

Summary of Aid to Needy Students *From gift & self-help combined:* Average need met: 74%. Average amount awarded: $13,183 (63% gift aid, 37% self-help). *Gift aid:* Total: $4,619,959 (79% from college's own funds, 8% from other college-administered sources, 13% from external sources). 131 Federal Work-Study jobs (averaging $1148); 106 part-time jobs.

Need-Based Scholarships & Grants Pell, FSEOG, state, private, college/university.

Loans Perkins, PLUS, Stafford, Unsubsidized Stafford, Key Alternative Loans, Preston-Cappell Loans, Alaska Loans.

Non-Need Awards In 1996, a total of 1,385 non-need awards were made. *Academic Interests/Achievement Awards:* 1,022 ($1,801,455 total): general academic, biological sciences, business, education, humanities, mathematics, physical sciences, premedicine, religion/biblical studies. *Creative Arts/Performance Awards:* 82 ($184,694 total): art/fine arts, music, theater/drama. *Special Achievements/Activities Awards:* 0: Junior Miss, rodeo. *Special Characteristics Awards:* 128 ($428,046 total): children and siblings of alumni, children of faculty/staff, ethnic background, local/state students, members of minorities, religious affiliation. *Athletic:* Total: 153 ($654,868); Men: 91 ($430,303); Women: 62 ($224,565).

Other Money-Saving Options Accelerated degree, off-campus living (after freshman year). *Payment Plan:* installment. *Waivers:* full or partial for children of alumni, employees or children of employees, adult students, senior citizens.

Contact Mr. Ron E. Christianson, Director, Office of Student Financial Services, Albertson College of Idaho, 2112 Cleveland Boulevard, Box 39, Caldwell, ID 83605-4494, 208-459-5308, fax: 208-454-2077.

ALBERTUS MAGNUS COLLEGE
New Haven, Connecticut

About the Institution Independent/religious, coed. Degrees awarded: A, B, M. Offers 46 undergraduate majors. Total enrollment: 1,177. Undergraduates: 975 (70% state residents). Freshmen: 126.

Undergraduate Expenses (1997–98) Comprehensive fee of $24,860 includes tuition ($16,864), mandatory fees ($360), and college room and board ($7636).

Applications 83% of all full-time undergraduates enrolled in fall 1996 applied for aid; of these, 79% were judged to have need according to Federal Methodology, of whom 94% were aided. *Financial aid deadline (priority):* 2/15. *Financial aid forms:* FAFSA, institutional form required. Federal income tax form required for some. *Admission application deadline:* rolling.

Summary of Aid to Needy Students *From gift & self-help combined:* Average amount awarded: $5723 (61% gift aid, 39% self-help). *Gift aid:* Total: $837,952 (42% from college's own funds, 35% from other college-administered sources, 23% from external sources). Federal Work-Study jobs; part-time jobs.

Need-Based Scholarships & Grants Pell, FSEOG, state, private, college/university.

Loans Perkins, PLUS, Stafford, Unsubsidized Stafford.

Non-Need Awards In 1996, a total of 22 non-need awards were made. *Academic Interests/Achievement Awards:* 22 ($82,920 total): general academic.

Other Money-Saving Options Accelerated degree, off-campus living. *Payment Plan:* installment. *Waivers:* full or partial for employees or children of employees and senior citizens.

Contact Ms. Mercy Goodnow, Assistant Director, Albertus Magnus College, 700 Prospect Street, New Haven, CT 06511-1189, 203-773-8508, fax: 203-773-8972.

ALBION COLLEGE
Albion, Michigan

About the Institution Independent/religious, coed. Degrees awarded: B. Offers 37 undergraduate majors. Total enrollment: 1,527 (86% state residents). Freshmen: 434.

Undergraduate Expenses (1997–98) Comprehensive fee of $21,786 includes tuition ($16,640), mandatory fees ($166), and college room and board ($4980).

Applications Of all full-time undergraduates enrolled in fall 1996, 94% of those who applied for aid were judged to have need according to Federal Methodology, of whom 99% were aided. *Financial aid deadline (priority):* 2/21. *Financial aid forms:* FAFSA required. *Regular admission application deadline:* rolling. Early decision deadline: 12/1.

Summary of Aid to Needy Students *From gift & self-help combined:* Average need met: 93%. Average amount awarded: $14,639 (74% gift aid, 26% self-help). *Gift aid:* Total: $11,176,404 (72% from college's own funds, 20% from other college-administered sources, 8% from external sources). 514 Federal Work-Study jobs (averaging $1280); 385 part-time jobs.

Need-Based Scholarships & Grants Pell, FSEOG, state, private, college/university.

Loans Perkins, PLUS, Stafford, Unsubsidized Stafford, state.

Non-Need Awards In 1996, a total of 973 non-need awards were made. *Academic Interests/Achievement Awards:* 858 ($5,631,611 total): general academic, business. *Creative Arts/Performance Awards:* 115 ($87,875 total): art/fine arts, music, theater/drama.

Other Money-Saving Options *Payment Plan:* deferred payment. *Waivers:* full or partial for employees or children of employees.

Contact Mr. Skip Zabel, Associate Director of Financial Aid, Albion College, Albion, MI 49224-1831, 517-629-0440, fax: 517-629-0581.

ALBRIGHT COLLEGE
Reading, Pennsylvania

About the Institution Independent/religious, coed. Degrees awarded: B. Offers 39 undergraduate majors. Total enrollment: 1,193 (66% state residents). Freshmen: 354.

Undergraduate Expenses (1997–98) Comprehensive fee of $23,760 includes tuition ($17,710), mandatory fees ($600), and college room and board ($5450). College room only: $3050.

Applications 86% of all full-time undergraduates enrolled in fall 1996 applied for aid; of these, 84% were judged to have need according to Federal Methodology, of whom 100% were aided. *Financial aid deadline (priority):* 3/1. *Financial aid forms:* FAFSA, institutional form required; CSS Financial Aid PROFILE acceptable. State form required for some. *Admission application deadline:* 2/15.

Summary of Aid to Needy Students *From gift & self-help combined:* Average need met: 90%. Average amount awarded: $15,056 (69% gift aid, 31% self-help). *Gift aid:* Total: $8,330,092 (79% from college's own funds, 14% from other college-administered sources, 7% from external sources). 492 Federal Work-Study jobs (averaging $940); 25 part-time jobs.

Need-Based Scholarships & Grants Pell, FSEOG, state, private, college/university.

Loans Perkins, PLUS, Stafford, Unsubsidized Stafford, private.

Non-Need Awards In 1996, a total of 742 non-need awards were made. *Academic Interests/Achievement Awards:* 485 ($2,977,000 total): general academic. *Creative Arts/Performance Awards:* 42 ($42,750 total): music, theater/drama. *Special Characteristics Awards:* 215 ($1,131,387 total): children and siblings of alumni, children of faculty/staff, international students, local/state students, members of minorities, religious affiliation, siblings of current students.

Other Money-Saving Options Accelerated degree, off-campus living (after freshman year). *Payment Plan:* installment. *Waivers:* full or partial for employees or children of employees and senior citizens.

Contact Ms. Joyce M. Ballaban, Director of Financial Aid, Albright College, 13th and Bern Streets, Reading, PA 19612-5234, 610-921-7515, fax: 610-921-7294.

ALCORN STATE UNIVERSITY
Lorman, Mississippi

About the Institution State-supported, coed. Degrees awarded: A, B, M. Offers 43 undergraduate majors. Total enrollment: 3,073. Undergraduates: 2,722 (88% state residents). Freshmen: 631.

Undergraduate Expenses (1996–97) State resident tuition: $2389. Nonresident tuition: $4890. College room and board: $2229.

Applications 100% of all full-time undergraduates enrolled in fall 1996 applied for aid; of these,100% were judged to have need according to Federal Methodology, of whom 100% were aided. *Financial aid deadline (priority):* 4/15. *Financial aid forms:* FAFSA, CSS Financial Aid PROFILE, institutional form required. *Admission application deadline:* 8/15.

Summary of Aid to Needy Students *From gift & self-help combined:* Average need met: 97%. Average amount awarded: $2309 (58% gift aid, 42% self-help). *Gift aid:* Total: $3,874,986 (39% from college's own funds, 9% from other college-administered sources, 52% from external sources). 286 Federal Work-Study jobs (averaging $513); part-time jobs.

Need-Based Scholarships & Grants Pell, FSEOG, state, private, college/university.

Loans PLUS, Stafford, Unsubsidized Stafford.

Non-Need Awards In 1996, a total of 287 non-need awards were made. *Academic Interests/Achievement Awards:* 119 ($767,977 total): general academic. *Creative Arts/Performance Awards:* 33 ($58,822 total): music. *Athletic:* Total: 135 ($344,712); Men: 97 ($248,862); Women: 38 ($95,850).

Other Money-Saving Options Accelerated degree, co-op program, Army ROTC, off-campus living. *Waivers:* full or partial for children of alumni and employees or children of employees.

Contact Mrs. Juanita McKenzie-Russell, Director of Financial Aid, Alcorn State University, 1000 ASU Drive #28, Lorman, MS 39096-9402, 601-877-6190, fax: 601-877-6110.

ALDERSON-BROADDUS COLLEGE
Philippi, West Virginia

About the Institution Independent/religious, coed. Degrees awarded: A, B, M. Offers 44 undergraduate majors. Total enrollment: 740. Undergraduates: 692 (66% state residents). Freshmen: 117.

Undergraduate Expenses (1997–98) Comprehensive fee of $16,380 includes tuition ($12,115), mandatory fees ($100), and college room and board ($4165). College room only: $1980.

Applications Of all full-time undergraduates enrolled in fall 1996, 100% of those judged to have need according to Federal Methodology were aided. *Financial aid deadline (priority):* 7/31. *Financial aid forms:* FAFSA, institutional form required; CSS Financial Aid PROFILE acceptable. State form required for some. *Admission application deadline:* rolling.

Summary of Aid to Needy Students *From gift & self-help combined:* Average need met: 90%. Average amount awarded: $6520 (60% gift aid, 40% self-help). *Gift aid:* Total: $2,155,136 (58% from college's own funds, 15% from other college-administered sources, 27% from external sources). 168 Federal Work-Study jobs (averaging $1200); 183 part-time jobs.

Need-Based Scholarships & Grants Pell, FSEOG, state, private, college/university.

Loans Perkins, PLUS, Stafford, Unsubsidized Stafford, Federal Nursing, private.

Non-Need Awards In 1996, a total of 747 non-need awards were made. *Academic Interests/Achievement Awards:* 446 ($163,251 total): general academic, education, health fields, humanities, physical sciences, social sciences. *Creative Arts/Performance Awards:* 74 ($219,359

total): art/fine arts, creative writing, debating, music, performing arts, theater/drama. *Special Achievements/Activities Awards:* 127 ($92,227 total): general special achievements/activities, leadership. *Special Characteristics Awards:* 40 ($119,941 total): general special characteristics, children of faculty/staff, international students, relatives of clergy, religious affiliation. *Athletic:* Total: 60 ($340,867); Men: 34 ($182,504); Women: 26 ($158,363).

Other Money-Saving Options Cooperative Army ROTC. *Payment Plans:* installment, deferred payment. *Waivers:* full or partial for employees or children of employees.

Contact Ms. Mamie R. Argo, Director of Financial Aid, Alderson-Broaddus College, College Hill, Box 247, Philippi, WV 26416, 304-457-6250, fax: 304-457-6239.

ALFRED UNIVERSITY
Alfred, New York

About the Institution Independent, coed. Degrees awarded: B, M, D. Offers 68 undergraduate majors. Total enrollment: 2,397. Undergraduates: 2,011 (69% state residents). Freshmen: 497.

Undergraduate Expenses (1997–98) Comprehensive fee of $25,378 includes tuition ($18,498), mandatory fees ($474), and college room and board ($6406). College room only: $3334.

Applications 94% of all full-time undergraduates enrolled in fall 1996 applied for aid; of these, 98% were judged to have need according to Federal Methodology, of whom 100% were aided. *Financial aid deadline (priority):* 4/1. *Financial aid forms:* FAFSA, institutional form required; CSS Financial Aid PROFILE acceptable. State form, financial aid transcript (for transfers) required for some. *Regular admission application deadline:* 2/1. Early decision deadline: 12/1.

Summary of Aid to Needy Students *From gift & self-help combined:* Average amount awarded: $18,250 (73% gift aid, 27% self-help). *Gift aid:* Total: $15,180,000 (86% from college's own funds, 9% from other college-administered sources, 5% from external sources). 725 Federal Work-Study jobs (averaging $1100); 400 part-time jobs.

Need-Based Scholarships & Grants Pell, FSEOG, state, private, college/university.

Loans Perkins, PLUS, Stafford, Unsubsidized Stafford, private, college/university short-term loans ($75 average), college/university long-term loans ($1500 average).

Non-Need Awards In 1996, a total of 350 non-need awards were made. *Academic Interests/Achievement Awards:* 330 ($2,998,000 total): general academic, biological sciences, business, communication, computer science, education, engineering/technologies, English, foreign languages, humanities, international studies, mathematics, physical sciences, premedicine, social sciences. *Creative Arts/Performance Awards:* 17 ($42,000 total): general creative, art/fine arts, performing arts. *Special Achievements/Activities Awards:* 0: leadership, memberships. *Special Characteristics Awards:* 3 ($9400 total): international students, ROTC participants.

Other Money-Saving Options Accelerated degree, co-op program, cooperative Army ROTC, off-campus living (after sophomore year). *Payment Plans:* tuition prepayment, installment, deferred payment. *Waivers:* full or partial for employees or children of employees.

Contact Office of Financial Aid, Alfred University, Alumni Hall, Saxon Drive, Alfred, NY 14802-1205, 607-871-2111.

ALICE LLOYD COLLEGE
Pippa Passes, Kentucky

About the Institution Independent, coed. Degrees awarded: B. Offers 12 undergraduate majors. Total enrollment: 511 (93% state residents). Freshmen: 177.

Undergraduate Expenses (1996–97) State resident tuition: $0 (minimum). Nonresident tuition: $3800. Mandatory fees: $360 (minimum). College room and board: $2680. College room only: $1100.

Applications Of all full-time undergraduates enrolled in fall 1996, 100% of those judged to have need according to Federal Methodology were aided. *Financial aid deadline (priority):* 3/1. *Financial aid forms:* FAFSA required. State form required for some. *Admission application deadline:* 8/1.

Summary of Aid to Needy Students *From gift & self-help combined:* Average need met: 80%. Average amount awarded: $7985 (76% gift aid, 24% self-help). *Gift aid:* Total: $1,829,350 (50% from college's own funds, 7% from other college-administered sources, 43% from external sources). 360 Federal Work-Study jobs (averaging $1520).

Need-Based Scholarships & Grants Pell, FSEOG, state, private, college/university.

Loans Perkins, PLUS, Stafford, Unsubsidized Stafford, college/university short-term loans ($75 average), college/university long-term loans ($300 average).

Non-Need Awards In 1996, a total of 41 non-need awards were made. *Special Characteristics Awards:* 3 ($5240 total): members of minorities. *Athletic:* Total: 38 ($266,204); Men: 26 ($193,867); Women: 12 ($72,337).

Other Money-Saving Options *Payment Plan:* installment. *Waivers:* full or partial for employees or children of employees.

Contact Ms. Nancy M. Melton, Director of Financial Aid, Alice Lloyd College, 100 Purpose Road, Pippa Passes, KY 41844, 606-368-2101, fax: 606-368-2125.

ALLEGHENY COLLEGE
Meadville, Pennsylvania

About the Institution Independent/religious, coed. Degrees awarded: B. Offers 43 undergraduate majors. Total enrollment: 1,846 (60% state residents). Freshmen: 526.

Undergraduate Expenses (1997–98) Comprehensive fee of $24,080 includes tuition ($19,090), mandatory fees ($270), and college room and board ($4720). College room only: $2320.

Applications Of all full-time undergraduates enrolled in fall 1996, 94% of those who applied for aid were judged to have need according to Federal Methodology, of whom 100% were aided. *Financial aid deadline (priority):* 2/15. *Financial aid forms:* FAFSA, federal income tax form required. State form required for some. *Regular admission application deadline:* 2/15. Early decision deadline: 1/15.

Summary of Aid to Needy Students *From gift & self-help combined:* Average need met: 93%. Average amount awarded: $16,042 (69% gift aid, 31% self-help). *Gift aid:* Total: $16,390,056 (77% from college's own funds, 3% from other college-administered sources, 20% from external sources). 1,247 Federal Work-Study jobs (averaging $1400); 167 part-time jobs.

Need-Based Scholarships & Grants Pell, FSEOG, state, private, college/university, National Methodist Scholarships.

Loans Perkins, PLUS, Stafford, Unsubsidized Stafford, state, private, college/university long-term loans ($3000 average).

Non-Need Awards In 1996, a total of 1,076 non-need awards were made. *Academic Interests/Achievement Awards:* 1,033 ($5,556,620 total): general academic. *Creative Arts/Performance Awards:* general creative. *Special Achievements/Activities Awards:* general special achievements/activities. *Special Characteristics Awards:* 43 ($223,000 total): local/state students, members of minorities.

Other Money-Saving Options Accelerated degree, cooperative Army ROTC, off-campus living (after sophomore year). *Payment Plans:* tuition prepayment, installment. *Waivers:* full or partial for employees or children of employees.

Contact Office of Financial Aid, Allegheny College, Meadville, PA 16335, 814-332-3100.

ALLEGHENY UNIVERSITY OF THE HEALTH SCIENCES
Philadelphia, Pennsylvania

About the Institution Independent, coed. Degrees awarded: B, M, D, P. Offers 8 undergraduate majors. Total enrollment: 3,154. Undergraduates: 1,117 (55% state residents). Freshmen: 683.

Undergraduate Expenses (1996–97) Tuition: $4000 (minimum). Mandatory fees: $60. College room only: $4800.

Applications Of all full-time undergraduates enrolled in fall 1996, 96% of those who applied for aid were judged to have need according to Federal Methodology, of whom 98% were aided. *Financial aid deadline:* Applications processed continuously. *Financial aid forms:* FAFSA, state form, institutional form required. *Admission application deadline:* rolling.

Summary of Aid to Needy Students *From gift & self-help combined:* Average need met: 43%. Average amount awarded: $6694 (32% gift aid, 68% self-help). *Gift aid:* Total: $1,116,821 (3% from college's own funds, 68% from other college-administered sources, 29% from external sources). 230 Federal Work-Study jobs (averaging $1039).

Need-Based Scholarships & Grants Pell, FSEOG, state, private, college/university.

Loans Perkins, PLUS, Stafford, Unsubsidized Stafford, Federal Nursing, Primary Care, state, private, college/university long-term loans ($985 average).

Non-Need Awards Not offered.

Other Money-Saving Options Co-op program, off-campus living. *Payment Plan:* installment. *Waivers:* full or partial for employees or children of employees.

Contact University Student Financial Affairs, Allegheny University of the Health Sciences, Philadelphia, PA 19102-1192, 215-762-7739.

ALLEN COLLEGE OF NURSING
Waterloo, Iowa

About the Institution Independent, coed. Degrees awarded: B. Offers 1 undergraduate major. Total enrollment: 244 (97% state residents). Freshmen: 28.

Undergraduate Expenses (1996–97) Tuition: $3581 (minimum). Mandatory fees: $460 (minimum).

Applications 77% of all full-time undergraduates enrolled in fall 1996 applied for aid; of these, 95% were judged to have need according to Federal Methodology, of whom 96% were aided. *Financial aid deadline (priority):* 4/15. *Financial aid forms:* FAFSA, institutional form required.

Summary of Aid to Needy Students *Gift aid:* Total: $458,771 (8% from college's own funds, 65% from other college-administered sources, 27% from external sources). Federal Work-Study jobs; part-time jobs.

Need-Based Scholarships & Grants Pell, FSEOG, state, college/university.

Loans PLUS, Stafford, Unsubsidized Stafford, Federal Nursing.

Non-Need Awards Not offered.

Other Money-Saving Options Cooperative Army ROTC, off-campus living. *Payment Plan:* installment.

Contact Ms. Jen Fassman, Financial Aid Director, Allen College of Nursing, Waterloo, IA 50703, 319-235-3983.

ALLENTOWN COLLEGE OF ST. FRANCIS DE SALES
Center Valley, Pennsylvania

About the Institution Independent/religious, coed. Degrees awarded: B, M. Offers 31 undergraduate majors. Total enrollment: 2,158. Undergraduates: 1,716 (79% state residents). Freshmen: 283.

Undergraduate Expenses (1997–98) Comprehensive fee of $17,220 includes tuition ($11,600), mandatory fees ($150), and college room and board ($5470). College room only: $2874.

Applications 89% of all full-time undergraduates enrolled in fall 1996 applied for aid; of these, 88% were judged to have need according to Federal Methodology, of whom 89% were aided. *Financial aid deadline (priority):* 2/1. *Financial aid forms:* FAFSA, institutional form required. State form required for some. *Admission application deadline:* 8/1.

Summary of Aid to Needy Students *From gift & self-help combined:* Average need met: 70%. Average amount awarded: $10,113 (68% gift aid, 32% self-help). *Gift aid:* Total: $5,189,258 (58% from college's own funds, 34% from other college-administered sources, 8% from external sources). 442 Federal Work-Study jobs (averaging $1000); 132 part-time jobs.

Need-Based Scholarships & Grants Pell, FSEOG, state, private, college/university.

Loans Perkins, PLUS, Stafford, Unsubsidized Stafford, Federal Nursing, state, private.

Non-Need Awards In 1996, a total of 665 non-need awards were made. *Academic Interests/Achievement Awards:* 143 ($201,590 total): general academic, biological sciences, business, communication, computer science, education, English, foreign languages, health fields, humanities, mathematics, physical sciences, premedicine, religion/biblical studies, social sciences. *Creative Arts/Performance Awards:* 90 ($128,350 total): general creative, cinema/film/broadcasting, dance, debating, music, theater/drama. *Special Achievements/Activities Awards:* 243 ($919,130 total): general special achievements/activities, leadership, memberships, religious involvement. *Special Characteristics Awards:* 189 ($410,885 total): general special characteristics, adult students, children of educators, children of faculty/staff, international students, local/state students, members of minorities, relatives of clergy, religious affiliation, ROTC participants, siblings of current students.

Other Money-Saving Options Accelerated degree, cooperative Army ROTC, cooperative Air Force ROTC, off-campus living. *Payment Plans:* installment, deferred payment. *Waivers:* full or partial for employees or children of employees.

Contact Ms. Catherine A. McIntyre, Director of Financial Aid, Allentown College of St. Francis de Sales, 2755 Station Avenue, Center Valley, PA 18034-9568, 610-282-1100 Ext. 1287, fax: 610-282-2254.

ALLEN UNIVERSITY
Columbia, South Carolina

About the Institution Independent/religious, coed. Degrees awarded: B. Offers 14 undergraduate majors. Total enrollment: 281 (68% state residents). Freshmen: 98.

Undergraduate Expenses (1997–98) Comprehensive fee of $8960 includes tuition ($4650), mandatory fees ($100), and college room and board ($4210).

Applications *Financial aid deadline (priority):* 3/15. *Financial aid forms:* FAFSA, CSS Financial Aid PROFILE required. State form required for some. *Admission application deadline:* rolling.

Summary of Aid to Needy Students Federal Work-Study jobs; part-time jobs.

Non-Need Awards *Academic Interests/Achievement Awards:* general academic. *Creative Arts/Performance Awards:* music. *Athletic:* available.

Another Money-Saving Option Off-campus living.

Contact Office of Financial Aid, Allen University, 1530 Harden Street, Columbia, SC 29204-1085, 803-254-4165.

ALMA COLLEGE
Alma, Michigan

About the Institution Independent/religious, coed. Degrees awarded: B. Offers 62 undergraduate majors. Total enrollment: 1,363 (96% state residents). Freshmen: 377.

Undergraduate Expenses (1997–98 estimated) Comprehensive fee of $18,728 includes tuition ($13,690), mandatory fees ($133), and college room and board ($4905).

Applications Of all full-time undergraduates enrolled in fall 1996, 90% of those who applied for aid were judged to have need according to Federal Methodology, of whom 100% were aided. *Financial aid deadline (priority):* 2/15. *Financial aid forms:* FAFSA required; CSS Financial Aid PROFILE acceptable. *Regular admission application deadline:* rolling. Early decision deadline: 11/1.

Summary of Aid to Needy Students *From gift & self-help combined:* Average need met: 84%. Average amount awarded: $12,521 (71% gift aid, 29% self-help). *Gift aid:* Total: $9,518,025 (70% from college's own funds, 2% from other college-administered sources, 28% from external sources). 170 Federal Work-Study jobs (averaging $850); 420 part-time jobs.

Need-Based Scholarships & Grants Pell, FSEOG, state, private, college/university.

Loans Perkins, PLUS, Stafford, Unsubsidized Stafford, college/university short-term loans ($700 average), college/university long-term loans ($1000 average).

Non-Need Awards In 1996, a total of 1,647 non-need awards were made. *Academic Interests/Achievement Awards:* 1,319 ($5,375,891 total): general academic, humanities. *Creative Arts/Performance Awards:* 270 ($310,652 total): art/fine arts, dance, music, performing arts, theater/drama. *Special Characteristics Awards:* 58 ($376,733 total): children of faculty/staff, previous college experience.

Other Money-Saving Options Accelerated degree, cooperative Army ROTC. *Payment Plans:* tuition prepayment, installment. *Waivers:* full or partial for employees or children of employees.

Contact Office of Financial Aid, Alma College, 614 West Superior, Alma, MI 48801-1599, 517-463-7111.

ALVERNIA COLLEGE
Reading, Pennsylvania

About the Institution Independent/religious, coed. Degrees awarded: A, B. Offers 34 undergraduate majors. Total enrollment: 1,347 (93% state residents). Freshmen: 171.

Undergraduate Expenses (1997–98) Comprehensive fee of $16,320 includes tuition ($10,850), mandatory fees ($470), and college room and board ($5000). College room only: $2500.

Applications 79% of all full-time undergraduates enrolled in fall 1996 applied for aid; of these, 89% were judged to have need according to Federal Methodology, of whom 100% were aided. *Financial aid deadline:* Applications processed continuously. *Financial aid forms:* FAFSA required. *Admission application deadline:* rolling.

Summary of Aid to Needy Students *From gift & self-help combined:* Average need met: 65%. Average amount awarded: $12,310 (39% gift aid, 61% self-help). *Gift aid:* Total: $2,670,950 (41% from college's

own funds, 4% from other college-administered sources, 55% from external sources). 40 Federal Work-Study jobs (averaging $1000); 70 part-time jobs.

Need-Based Scholarships & Grants Pell, FSEOG, state, private, college/university.

Loans Perkins, PLUS, Stafford, Unsubsidized Stafford, Federal Nursing, state, private.

Non-Need Awards In 1996, a total of 116 non-need awards were made. *Academic Interests/Achievement Awards:* 110 ($407,800 total): general academic. *Special Characteristics Awards:* 6 ($40,000 total): children of faculty/staff, international students, members of minorities.

Other Money-Saving Options Accelerated degree, cooperative Army ROTC, off-campus living. *Payment Plan:* installment. *Waivers:* full or partial for employees or children of employees and senior citizens.

Contact Ms. Vali G. Heist, Director of Financial Aid, Alvernia College, 400 Saint Bernardine Street, Reading, PA 19607-1799, 610-796-8215, fax: 610-796-8336.

ALVERNO COLLEGE
Milwaukee, Wisconsin

About the Institution Independent/religious, women. Degrees awarded: A, B, M. Offers 25 undergraduate majors. Total enrollment: 2,191. Undergraduates: 2,161 (96% state residents). Freshmen: 235.

Undergraduate Expenses (1997–98) Comprehensive fee of $13,762 includes tuition ($9672 minimum), mandatory fees ($50), and college room and board ($4040).

Applications 83% of all full-time undergraduates enrolled in fall 1996 applied for aid; of these, 87% were judged to have need according to Federal Methodology, of whom 100% were aided. *Financial aid deadline (priority):* 4/1. *Financial aid forms:* FAFSA, institutional form required; CSS Financial Aid PROFILE acceptable. *Admission application deadline:* 8/1.

Summary of Aid to Needy Students *From gift & self-help combined:* Average need met: 75%. Average amount awarded: $5646 (41% gift aid, 59% self-help). *Gift aid:* Total: $3,609,045 (25% from college's own funds, 12% from other college-administered sources, 63% from external sources). 155 Federal Work-Study jobs (averaging $1246); 147 part-time jobs.

Need-Based Scholarships & Grants Pell, FSEOG, state, private, college/university.

Loans Perkins, PLUS, Stafford, Unsubsidized Stafford, private.

Non-Need Awards In 1996, a total of 308 non-need awards were made. *Academic Interests/Achievement Awards:* 277 ($498,841 total): general academic. *Creative Arts/Performance Awards:* 16 ($12,797 total): art/fine arts, music. *Special Characteristics Awards:* 15 ($5725 total): children and siblings of alumni, siblings of current students.

Other Money-Saving Options Co-op program, cooperative Air Force ROTC, off-campus living (after sophomore year). *Payment Plans:* installment, deferred payment. *Waivers:* full or partial for employees or children of employees.

Contact Mr. Robert P. Jacobson, Director of Financial Aid, Alverno College, 3401 South 39 Street, PO Box 343922, Milwaukee, WI 53234-3922, 414-382-6046, fax: 414-382-6354.

AMERICAN BAPTIST COLLEGE OF AMERICAN BAPTIST THEOLOGICAL SEMINARY
Nashville, Tennessee

About the Institution Independent/religious, coed. Degrees awarded: A, B. Offers 2 undergraduate majors. Total enrollment: 125 (25% state residents). Freshmen: 22.

Undergraduate Expenses (1997–98) Tuition: $2530. College room only: $752 (minimum).

Applications 100% of all full-time undergraduates enrolled in fall 1996 applied for aid; of these, 36% were judged to have need according to Federal Methodology, of whom 100% were aided. *Financial aid deadline (priority):* 6/1. *Financial aid forms:* FAFSA, institutional form required; CSS Financial Aid PROFILE acceptable. *Admission application deadline:* 7/1.

Summary of Aid to Needy Students *From gift & self-help combined:* Average need met: 75%. *Gift aid:* Total: $239,002 (73% from college-administered sources, 27% from external sources). Federal Work-Study jobs; 8 part-time jobs.

Need-Based Scholarships & Grants Pell, FSEOG, state.

Non-Need Awards In 1996, a total of 125 non-need awards were made. *Special Characteristics Awards:* 125 ($165,000 total): religious affiliation.

Other Money-Saving Options Accelerated degree, co-op program, off-campus living.

Contact Financial Aid Director, American Baptist College of American Baptist Theological Seminary, 1800 Baptist World Center Drive, Nashville, TN 37207, 615-228-7877.

THE AMERICAN COLLEGE
Los Angeles, California

About the Institution Proprietary, coed. Degrees awarded: A, B, M. Offers 11 undergraduate majors. Total enrollment: 450 (38% state residents). Freshmen: 385.

Undergraduate Expenses (1997–98) Tuition: $11,250. College room only: $4185.

Applications Of all full-time undergraduates enrolled in fall 1996, 100% of those who applied for aid were judged to have need according to Federal Methodology, of whom 91% were aided. *Financial aid deadline:* continuous. *Financial aid forms:* FAFSA, institutional form required; state form, Stafford Student Loan form acceptable. *Admission application deadline:* rolling.

Summary of Aid to Needy Students *From gift & self-help combined:* Average need met: 83%. Average amount awarded: $7500 (13% gift aid, 87% self-help). *Gift aid:* Total: $150,000. Federal Work-Study jobs.

Need-Based Scholarships & Grants Pell, FSEOG, state.

Loans PLUS, Stafford, Unsubsidized Stafford.

Non-Need Awards *Creative Arts/Performance Awards:* applied art and design. *Special Achievements/Activities Awards:* general special achievements/activities.

Other Money-Saving Options Accelerated degree, off-campus living. *Payment Plans:* installment, deferred payment. *Waivers:* full or partial for employees or children of employees.

Contact Mr. Joe Johnson, Financial Aid Counselor, The American College, Los Angeles, CA 90024-5603, 310-470-2000 Ext. 35.

THE AMERICAN COLLEGE
Atlanta, Georgia

About the Institution Proprietary, coed. Degrees awarded: A, B, M. Offers 11 undergraduate majors. Total enrollment: 960 (38% state residents). Freshmen: 350.

Undergraduate Expenses (1996–97) Tuition: $9120. Mandatory fees: $735. College room only: $3900.

Applications 40% of all full-time undergraduates enrolled in fall 1996 applied for aid; of these, 70% were judged to have need according to Federal Methodology, of whom 100% were aided. *Financial aid deadline:*

continuous. *Financial aid forms:* FAFSA, CSS Financial Aid PROFILE, institutional form required; state form acceptable. *Admission application deadline:* rolling.

Summary of Aid to Needy Students *From gift & self-help combined:* Average need met: 85%. Average amount awarded: $11,268 (11% gift aid, 89% self-help). *Gift aid:* Total: $262,000 (9% from college's own funds, 13% from other college-administered sources, 78% from external sources). Federal Work-Study jobs.

Need-Based Scholarships & Grants Pell, state.

Loans PLUS, Stafford, Unsubsidized Stafford, state, private.

Non-Need Awards Not offered.

Other Money-Saving Options Accelerated degree, off-campus living. *Waivers:* full or partial for employees or children of employees.

Contact Ms. Constance King, Vice-President/Director of Financial Aid, The American College, 3330 Peachtree Road, NE, Atlanta, GA 30326-1019, 404-231-9000, fax: 404-365-0736.

AMERICAN CONSERVATORY OF MUSIC
Chicago, Illinois

About the Institution Independent, coed. Degrees awarded: A, B, M, D. Offers 6 undergraduate majors. Total enrollment: 117. Undergraduates: 90 (45% state residents). Freshmen: 14.

Undergraduate Expenses (1997–98) Tuition: $8500 (minimum). Mandatory fees: $75 (minimum).

Applications *Financial aid forms:* institutional form required; FAFSA, CSS Financial Aid PROFILE, state form acceptable. *Admission application deadline:* rolling.

Non-Need Awards In 1996, a total of 2 non-need awards were made. *Creative Arts/Performance Awards:* 2 ($4527 total): music.

Other Money-Saving Options Accelerated degree. *Payment Plan:* installment.

Contact Office of Financial Aid, American Conservatory of Music, 36 South Wabash #800, Chicago, IL 60603-2901, 312-263-4161.

AMERICAN INDIAN COLLEGE OF THE ASSEMBLIES OF GOD, INC.
Phoenix, Arizona

About the Institution Independent/religious, coed. Degrees awarded: A, B. Offers 4 undergraduate majors. Total enrollment: 106 (57% state residents). Freshmen: 25.

Undergraduate Expenses (1997–98) Comprehensive fee of $6430 includes tuition ($2880), mandatory fees ($400), and college room and board ($3150).

Applications 96% of all full-time undergraduates enrolled in fall 1996 applied for aid; of these, 97% were judged to have need according to Federal Methodology, of whom 100% were aided. *Financial aid deadline (priority):* 4/01. *Financial aid forms:* FAFSA required; CSS Financial Aid PROFILE acceptable. *Admission application deadline:* 8/15.

Summary of Aid to Needy Students *From gift & self-help combined:* Average amount awarded: $6482 (64% gift aid, 36% self-help). *Gift aid:* Total: $363,213. Federal Work-Study jobs; part-time jobs.

Need-Based Scholarships & Grants Pell, FSEOG, college/university.

Loans PLUS, Stafford, Unsubsidized Stafford.

Non-Need Awards *Academic Interests/Achievement Awards:* general academic.

Contact Office of Student Financial Aid, American Indian College of the Assemblies of God, Inc., Phoenix, AZ 85021-2199, 800-933-3828.

AMERICAN INTERNATIONAL COLLEGE
Springfield, Massachusetts

About the Institution Independent, coed. Degrees awarded: A, B, M, D. Offers 45 undergraduate majors. Total enrollment: 1,986. Undergraduates: 1,420 (59% state residents). Freshmen: 261.

Undergraduate Expenses (1996–97) Comprehensive fee of $16,236 includes tuition ($10,400), mandatory fees ($526 minimum), and college room and board ($5310).

Applications 97% of all full-time undergraduates enrolled in fall 1996 applied for aid; of these, 80% were judged to have need according to Federal Methodology, of whom 100% were aided. *Financial aid deadline (priority):* 4/15. *Financial aid forms:* FAFSA, institutional form required. *Regular admission application deadline:* rolling. Early decision deadline: 11/15.

Summary of Aid to Needy Students *From gift & self-help combined:* Average need met: 80%. Average amount awarded: $8700 (51% gift aid, 49% self-help). *Gift aid:* Total: $4,043,987 (61% from college's own funds, 7% from other college-administered sources, 32% from external sources). 350 Federal Work-Study jobs (averaging $1600); 275 part-time jobs.

Need-Based Scholarships & Grants Pell, FSEOG, state, private, college/university.

Loans Perkins, PLUS, Stafford, Unsubsidized Stafford, Federal Nursing, state, private, college/university short-term loans ($1000 average).

Non-Need Awards In 1996, a total of 180 non-need awards were made. *Academic Interests/Achievement Awards:* 43 ($351,763 total): general academic. *Athletic:* Total: 137 ($1,246,339); Men: 80 ($735,111); Women: 57 ($511,228).

Other Money-Saving Options Accelerated degree, cooperative Army ROTC, cooperative Air Force ROTC, off-campus living (after sophomore year). *Payment Plans:* tuition prepayment, installment, deferred payment. *Waivers:* full or partial for employees or children of employees and senior citizens.

Contact Office of Financial Aid, American International College, Springfield, MA 01109-3189, 413-737-7000.

AMERICAN UNIVERSITY
Washington, District of Columbia

About the Institution Independent/religious, coed. Degrees awarded: A, B, M, D, P. Offers 77 undergraduate majors. Total enrollment: 11,285. Undergraduates: 5,042 (5% district residents). Freshmen: 1,176.

Undergraduate Expenses (1997–98) Comprehensive fee of $23,137 includes tuition ($18,300), mandatory fees ($255), and college room and board ($4582 minimum). College room only: $3382 (minimum).

Applications Of all full-time undergraduates enrolled in fall 1996, 88% of those who applied for aid were judged to have need according to Federal Methodology, of whom 98% were aided. *Financial aid deadline (priority):* 3/1. *Financial aid forms:* FAFSA, institutional form required. *Regular admission application deadline:* 2/1. Early decision deadline: 11/15.

Summary of Aid to Needy Students *From gift & self-help combined:* Average amount awarded: $18,814 (56% gift aid, 44% self-help). *Gift aid:* Total: $24,790,905 (91% from college's own funds, 3% from other college-administered sources, 6% from external sources). 1,724 Federal Work-Study jobs (averaging $1500); part-time jobs.

Need-Based Scholarships & Grants Pell, FSEOG, state, private, college/university.

Loans Perkins, PLUS, Stafford, Unsubsidized Stafford, private, college/university short-term loans ($100 average), college/university long-term loans ($1000 average).

Non-Need Awards In 1996, a total of 1,133 non-need awards were made. *Academic Interests/Achievement Awards:* 992 ($7,064,725 total): general academic, area/ethnic studies, biological sciences, business, communication, computer science, education, English, foreign languages, health fields, humanities, international studies, mathematics, social sciences. *Athletic:* Total: 141 ($1,647,320); Men: 73 ($932,002); Women: 68 ($715,318).

Other Money-Saving Options Co-op program, cooperative Army ROTC, cooperative Air Force ROTC, off-campus living. *Payment Plans:* tuition prepayment, installment, deferred payment. *Waivers:* full or partial for employees or children of employees and senior citizens.

Contact Office of Financial Aid, American University, 4400 Massachusetts Avenue, NW, Washington, DC 20016-8001, 202-885-6100.

AMERICAN UNIVERSITY OF PUERTO RICO
Bayamón, Puerto Rico

About the Institution Independent, coed. Degrees awarded: A, B. Offers 9 undergraduate majors. Total enrollment: 3,110 (99% commonwealth residents). Freshmen: 732.

Undergraduate Expenses (1996–97) Tuition: $3000. Mandatory fees: $70.

Applications 96% of all full-time undergraduates enrolled in fall 1996 applied for aid; of these,100% were judged to have need according to Federal Methodology, of whom 100% were aided. *Financial aid deadline:* 6/30. *Financial aid forms:* FAFSA required. *Admission application deadline:* 7/1.

Summary of Aid to Needy Students *From gift & self-help combined:* Average need met: 48%. Average amount awarded: $2695 (89% gift aid, 11% self-help). *Gift aid:* Total: $7,877,549 (14% from college's own funds, 8% from other college-administered sources, 78% from external sources). Federal Work-Study jobs; 22 part-time jobs.

Loans Stafford, Unsubsidized Stafford.

Non-Need Awards *Academic Interests/Achievement Awards:* available. *Special Achievements/Activities Awards:* available. *Special Characteristics Awards:* available. *Athletic:* available.

Other Money-Saving Options Co-op program, cooperative Army ROTC. *Payment Plan:* guaranteed tuition.

Contact Ms. Johanna Arroyo, Student Financial Aid Director, American University of Puerto Rico, PO Box 602037, Bayamón, PR 00960-2037, 787-798-2040 Ext. 233.

AMHERST COLLEGE
Amherst, Massachusetts

About the Institution Independent, coed. Degrees awarded: B. Offers 37 undergraduate majors. Total enrollment: 1,607 (14% state residents). Freshmen: 419.

Undergraduate Expenses (1997–98) Comprehensive fee of $29,107 includes tuition ($22,680), mandatory fees ($347), and college room and board ($6080). College room only: $3080.

Applications Of all full-time undergraduates enrolled in fall 1996, 87% of those who applied for aid were judged to have need according to Federal Methodology, of whom 100% were aided. *Financial aid deadline (priority):* 2/15. *Financial aid forms:* FAFSA, CSS Financial Aid PROFILE, institutional form required. State form required for some. *Regular admission application deadline:* 12/31. Early decision deadline: 11/15.

Summary of Aid to Needy Students *From gift & self-help combined:* Average need met: 100%. Average amount awarded: $20,428 (79% gift aid, 21% self-help). *Gift aid:* Total: $11,806,000 (90% from college's own funds, 3% from other college-administered sources, 7% from external sources). 603 Federal Work-Study jobs (averaging $1461); 86 part-time jobs.

Need-Based Scholarships & Grants Pell, FSEOG, state, private, college/university.

Loans Perkins, PLUS, Stafford, Unsubsidized Stafford, state, private, college/university short-term loans ($300 average), college/university long-term loans ($2523 average).

Non-Need Awards Not offered.

Other Money-Saving Options Off-campus living (after freshman year). *Payment Plans:* installment, deferred payment.

Contact Office of Financial Aid, Amherst College, 202 Converse Hall PO Box 5000, Amherst, MA 01002-5000, 413-542-2000.

ANDERSON COLLEGE
Anderson, South Carolina

About the Institution Independent/religious, coed. Degrees awarded: A, B. Offers 32 undergraduate majors. Total enrollment: 900 (75% state residents). Freshmen: 209.

Undergraduate Expenses (1997–98) Comprehensive fee of $13,620 includes tuition ($8680), mandatory fees ($795), and college room and board ($4145). College room only: $2086.

Applications Of all full-time undergraduates enrolled in fall 1996, 94% of those judged to have need according to Federal Methodology were aided. *Financial aid deadline (priority):* 6/30. *Financial aid forms:* FAFSA, CSS Financial Aid PROFILE, institutional form required. State form required for some. *Admission application deadline:* 7/15.

Summary of Aid to Needy Students *From gift & self-help combined:* Average amount awarded: $6123 (79% gift aid, 21% self-help). *Gift aid:* Total: $2,734,736 (45% from college's own funds, 35% from other college-administered sources, 20% from external sources). Federal Work-Study jobs; 7 part-time jobs.

Need-Based Scholarships & Grants Pell, FSEOG, state, college/university.

Loans Perkins, PLUS, Stafford, Unsubsidized Stafford, private, college/university long-term loans.

Non-Need Awards In 1996, a total of 1,012 non-need awards were made. *Academic Interests/Achievement Awards:* 148 ($187,530 total): general academic, biological sciences, business, communication, computer science, education, English, physical sciences, religion/biblical studies. *Creative Arts/Performance Awards:* 89 ($200,691 total): applied art and design, art/fine arts, journalism/publications, music, theater/drama. *Special Achievements/Activities Awards:* 48 ($48,400 total): leadership, religious involvement. *Special Characteristics Awards:* 512 ($468,314 total): general special characteristics, adult students, children and siblings of alumni, children of current students, children of faculty/staff, out-of-state students, parents of current students, relatives of clergy, religious affiliation, siblings of current students, spouses of current students, twins. *Athletic:* Total: 215 ($402,012); Men: 142 ($236,640); Women: 73 ($165,372).

Other Money-Saving Options Cooperative Army ROTC, cooperative Air Force ROTC, off-campus living (after sophomore year). *Payment Plan:* installment. *Waivers:* full or partial for employees or children of employees, adult students, senior citizens.

Contact Ms. Ann Clardy, Counselor, Anderson College, 316 Boulevard, Anderson, SC 29621-4035, 864-231-2070, fax: 864-231-2008.

ANDERSON UNIVERSITY
Anderson, Indiana

About the Institution Independent/religious, coed. Degrees awarded: A, B, M, D, P. Offers 53 undergraduate majors. Total enrollment: 2,136. Undergraduates: 1,949 (62% state residents). Freshmen: 421.

Undergraduate Expenses (1997–98) Comprehensive fee of $16,850 includes tuition ($12,500), mandatory fees ($200), and college room and board ($4150). College room only: $2310.

Applications 85% of all full-time undergraduates enrolled in fall 1996 applied for aid; of these, 90% were judged to have need according to Federal Methodology, of whom 98% were aided. *Financial aid deadline (priority):* 3/1. *Financial aid forms:* FAFSA required. *Admission application deadline:* 8/25.

Summary of Aid to Needy Students *From gift & self-help combined:* Average need met: 100%. Average amount awarded: $13,696 (52% gift aid, 48% self-help). *Gift aid:* Total: $8,212,164 (60% from college's own funds, 22% from other college-administered sources, 18% from external sources). 791 Federal Work-Study jobs (averaging $1910); 200 part-time jobs.

Need-Based Scholarships & Grants Pell, FSEOG, state, private, college/university.

Loans Perkins, PLUS, Stafford, Unsubsidized Stafford.

Non-Need Awards In 1996, a total of 1,732 non-need awards were made. *Academic Interests/Achievement Awards:* 1,145 ($3,414,092 total): general academic. *Creative Arts/Performance Awards:* 93 ($70,175 total): general creative, music. *Special Characteristics Awards:* 494 ($1,719,349 total): adult students, children of faculty/staff, international students, out-of-state students, relatives of clergy.

Other Money-Saving Options Accelerated degree, co-op program, off-campus living (after junior year). *Payment Plan:* installment. *Waivers:* full or partial for employees or children of employees and adult students.

Contact Office of Financial Aid, Anderson University, 1100 East Fifth Street, Anderson, IN 46012-3495, 765-649-9071.

ANDREWS UNIVERSITY
Berrien Springs, Michigan

About the Institution Independent/religious, coed. Degrees awarded: A, B, M, D, P. Offers 108 undergraduate majors. Total enrollment: 3,133. Undergraduates: 1,853 (36% state residents). Freshmen: 302.

Undergraduate Expenses (1997–98) Comprehensive fee of $15,087 includes tuition ($11,340), mandatory fees ($237), and college room and board ($3510 minimum). College room only: $2070.

Applications *Financial aid deadline (priority):* 3/31. *Financial aid forms:* institutional form required; CSS Financial Aid PROFILE acceptable. FAFSA, state form required for some. *Admission application deadline:* rolling.

Summary of Aid to Needy Students Federal Work-Study jobs; part-time jobs.

Loans College/university short-term loans.

Non-Need Awards *Academic Interests/Achievement Awards:* general academic. *Special Characteristics Awards:* available.

Other Money-Saving Options Accelerated degree. *Payment Plan:* installment. *Waivers:* full or partial for employees or children of employees and senior citizens.

Contact Office of Financial Aid, Andrews University, Berrien Springs, MI 49104, 616-471-7771.

ANGELO STATE UNIVERSITY
San Angelo, Texas

About the Institution State-supported, coed. Degrees awarded: A, B, M. Offers 37 undergraduate majors. Total enrollment: 6,200. Undergraduates: 5,800 (96% state residents). Freshmen: 1,200.

Undergraduate Expenses (1996–97) State resident tuition: $1024. Nonresident tuition: $7872. Mandatory fees: $982. College room and board: $3808 (minimum).

Applications *Financial aid deadline (priority):* 6/1. *Financial aid forms:* FAFSA, institutional form, required. *Admission application deadline:* 8/1.

Summary of Aid to Needy Students *From gift & self-help combined:* Average amount awarded: $4886 (50% gift aid, 50% self-help). *Gift aid:* Total: $7,292,700 (34% from college's own funds, 25% from other college-administered sources, 41% from external sources). 139 Federal Work-Study jobs; 384 part-time jobs.

Need-Based Scholarships & Grants Pell, FSEOG, state, private, college/university.

Loans Perkins, PLUS, Stafford, Unsubsidized Stafford, state, college/university short-term loans ($750 average), college/university long-term loans ($1577 average).

Non-Need Awards In 1996, a total of 850 non-need awards were made. *Academic Interests/Achievement Awards:* 532 ($425,310 total): general academic, agriculture, biological sciences, business, communication, computer science, education, English, international studies, military science, physical sciences, premedicine. *Creative Arts/Performance Awards:* 144 ($32,020 total): music, theater/drama. *Special Achievements/Activities Awards:* 40 ($8060 total): cheerleading/drum major. *Athletic:* Total: 134 ($237,430); Men: 84 ($128,799); Women: 50 ($108,631).

Other Money-Saving Options Accelerated degree, Air Force ROTC, off-campus living (after sophomore year). *Payment Plan:* installment.

Contact Mr. James B. Parker, Director of Financial Aid, Angelo State University, PO Box 11015, ASU Station, San Angelo, TX 76909, 915-942-2246, fax: 915-942-2082.

ANNA MARIA COLLEGE
Paxton, Massachusetts

About the Institution Independent/religious, coed. Degrees awarded: A, B, M. Offers 34 undergraduate majors. Total enrollment: 1,927. Undergraduates: 866 (90% state residents). Freshmen: 112.

Undergraduate Expenses (1997–98) Comprehensive fee of $17,676 includes tuition ($11,600), mandatory fees ($640), and college room and board ($5436).

Applications 83% of all full-time undergraduates enrolled in fall 1996 applied for aid; of these, 99% were judged to have need according to Federal Methodology, of whom 100% were aided. *Financial aid deadline (priority):* 3/1. *Financial aid forms:* FAFSA, CSS Financial Aid PROFILE, state form required. *Admission application deadline:* rolling.

Summary of Aid to Needy Students *From gift & self-help combined:* Average need met: 91%. *Gift aid:* Total: $2,189,397 (70% from college's own funds, 16% from other college-administered sources, 14% from external sources). 116 Federal Work-Study jobs (averaging $876); 15 part-time jobs.

Need-Based Scholarships & Grants Pell, FSEOG, state, private, college/university.

Loans Perkins, PLUS, Stafford, Unsubsidized Stafford, state, private, college/university long-term loans ($1970 average).

Non-Need Awards *Academic Interests/Achievement Awards:* general academic. *Creative Arts/Performance Awards:* 5 ($3500 total): music. *Special Achievements/Activities Awards:* cheerleading/drum major, leadership, religious involvement. *Special Characteristics Awards:* 82 ($356,534 total): general special characteristics, children and siblings of alumni, children of faculty/staff, ethnic background, members of minorities, siblings of current students.

Other Money-Saving Options Accelerated degree, cooperative Army ROTC, off-campus living. *Payment Plans:* tuition prepayment, installment. *Waivers:* full or partial for children of alumni, employees or children of employees, senior citizens.

Contact Ms. Laurie Peltier, Director of Financial Aid, Anna Maria College, Sunset Lane, Paxton, MA 01612, 508-849-3366, fax: 508-849-3362.

ANTIOCH COLLEGE
Yellow Springs, Ohio

About the Institution Independent, coed. Degrees awarded: B. Offers 56 undergraduate majors. Total enrollment: 640 (19% state residents). Freshmen: 143.

Undergraduate Expenses (1996–97) Comprehensive fee of $21,628 includes tuition ($16,322), mandatory fees ($1510), and college room and board ($3796). College room only: $1764.

Applications *Financial aid deadline (priority):* 3/1. *Financial aid forms:* FAFSA, institutional form, W-2 forms, federal income tax form, Divorced/Separated Parents' Statement (first year only) required; CSS Financial Aid PROFILE acceptable. State form required for some. *Regular admission application deadline:* 2/1. Early decision deadline: 11/15. Early action deadline: 11/15.

Summary of Aid to Needy Students Federal Work-Study jobs (averaging $1800).

Need-Based Scholarships & Grants Pell, FSEOG, state, college/university.

Loans Perkins, PLUS, Stafford, Unsubsidized Stafford.

Non-Need Awards *Academic Interests/Achievement Awards:* general academic, biological sciences, education, humanities, mathematics, physical sciences. *Special Achievements/Activities Awards:* community service.

Other Money-Saving Options Co-op program. *Payment Plan:* installment. *Waivers:* full or partial for employees or children of employees.

Contact Ms. Sandy Tarbox, Financial Aid Director, Antioch College, 795 Livermore Street, Yellow Springs, OH 45387-1697, 937-767-6367, fax: 937-767-6452.

APPALACHIAN BIBLE COLLEGE
Bradley, West Virginia

About the Institution Independent/religious, coed. Degrees awarded: A, B. Offers 2 undergraduate majors. Total enrollment: 291 (33% state residents). Freshmen: 80.

Undergraduate Expenses (1997–98) Comprehensive fee of $8520 includes tuition ($4650), mandatory fees ($860), and college room and board ($3010).

Applications *Financial aid deadline (priority):* 8/1. *Financial aid forms:* FAFSA required. *Admission application deadline:* rolling.

Summary of Aid to Needy Students Federal Work-Study jobs; 50 part-time jobs.

Need-Based Scholarships & Grants Pell, FSEOG, state, private, college/university.

Loans PLUS, Stafford, Unsubsidized Stafford.

Non-Need Awards *Academic Interests/Achievement Awards:* general academic.

Other Money-Saving Options *Payment Plan:* installment. *Waivers:* full or partial for employees or children of employees.

Contact Ms. Shirley Carfrey, Director of Financial Aid, Appalachian Bible College, Bradley, WV 25818, 304-877-6428.

APPALACHIAN STATE UNIVERSITY
Boone, North Carolina

About the Institution State-supported, coed. Degrees awarded: B, M, D. Offers 81 undergraduate majors. Total enrollment: 11,909. Undergraduates: 10,878 (89% state residents). Freshmen: 2,032.

Undergraduate Expenses (1996–97) State resident tuition: $874. Nonresident tuition: $8028. Mandatory fees: $790. College room and board: $2840. College room only: $1500.

Applications 44% of all full-time undergraduates enrolled in fall 1996 applied for aid; of these, 74% were judged to have need according to Federal Methodology, of whom 95% were aided. *Financial aid deadline (priority):* 3/15. *Financial aid forms:* CSS Financial Aid PROFILE required; institutional form acceptable. FAFSA required for some. *Admission application deadline:* 4/15.

Summary of Aid to Needy Students *From gift & self-help combined:* Average need met: 100%. Average amount awarded: $5623 (29% gift aid, 71% self-help). *Gift aid:* Total: $4,739,944 (16% from college's own funds, 37% from other college-administered sources, 47% from external sources). 436 Federal Work-Study jobs (averaging $1718); 2,404 part-time jobs.

Need-Based Scholarships & Grants Pell, FSEOG, state, private, college/university.

Loans Perkins, PLUS, Stafford, Unsubsidized Stafford, private, college/university short-term loans ($200 average).

Non-Need Awards In 1996, a total of 423 non-need awards were made. *Academic Interests/Achievement Awards:* 170 ($97,800 total): general academic. *Athletic:* Total: 253 ($1,160,888); Men: 184 ($878,795); Women: 69 ($282,093).

Other Money-Saving Options Accelerated degree, Army ROTC, off-campus living (after freshman year). *Waivers:* full or partial for employees or children of employees and senior citizens.

Contact Financial Aid Office, Appalachian State University, Hagaman Hall, Boone, NC 28608, 704-262-2190.

AQUINAS COLLEGE
Grand Rapids, Michigan

About the Institution Independent/religious, coed. Degrees awarded: A, B, M. Offers 62 undergraduate majors. Total enrollment: 2,385. Undergraduates: 1,825 (95% state residents). Freshmen: 283.

Undergraduate Expenses (1997–98) Comprehensive fee of $17,274 includes tuition ($12,910), mandatory fees ($40), and college room and board ($4324).

Applications 88% of all full-time undergraduates enrolled in fall 1996 applied for aid; of these, 91% were judged to have need according to Federal Methodology, of whom 99% were aided. *Financial aid deadline (priority):* 3/31. *Financial aid forms:* FAFSA required. *Admission application deadline:* rolling.

Summary of Aid to Needy Students *From gift & self-help combined:* Average need met: 91%. Average amount awarded: $10,787 (81% gift aid, 19% self-help). *Gift aid:* Total: $7,140,013 (68% from college's own funds, 26% from other college-administered sources, 6% from external sources). 183 Federal Work-Study jobs (averaging $759); 394 part-time jobs.

Need-Based Scholarships & Grants Pell, FSEOG, state, private, college/university.

Loans Perkins, PLUS, Stafford, Unsubsidized Stafford.

Non-Need Awards In 1996, a total of 319 non-need awards were made. *Academic Interests/Achievement Awards:* 29 ($233,010 total): general academic. *Special Achievements/Activities Awards:* 20 ($89,200 total): community service, leadership, memberships. *Special Characteristics Awards:* 8 ($14,000 total): children and siblings of alumni. *Athletic:* Total: 262 ($204,143); Men: 138 ($112,543); Women: 124 ($91,600).

Other Money-Saving Options Accelerated degree, co-op program, off-campus living (after sophomore year). *Payment Plans:* installment, deferred payment. *Waivers:* full or partial for children of alumni and employees or children of employees.

Contact Mr. David J. Steffee, Director of Financial Aid, Aquinas College, 1607 Robinson Road, SE, Grand Rapids, MI 49506-1799, 616-459-8281 Ext. 5127.

ARIZONA BIBLE COLLEGE
Phoenix, Arizona

About the Institution Independent/religious, coed. Degrees awarded: A, B. Offers 7 undergraduate majors. Total enrollment: 106 (68% state residents). Freshmen: 19.

Undergraduate Expenses (1996–97) Tuition: $5746. Mandatory fees: $140. College room only: $1728.

Applications 94% of all full-time undergraduates enrolled in fall 1996 applied for aid; of these, 93% were judged to have need according to Federal Methodology, of whom 96% were aided. *Financial aid deadline (priority):* 4/15. *Financial aid forms:* FAFSA required; CSS Financial Aid PROFILE acceptable. State form, institutional form required for some. *Admission application deadline:* 8/5.

Summary of Aid to Needy Students *From gift & self-help combined:* Average need met: 46%. Average amount awarded: $5107 (44% gift aid, 56% self-help). *Gift aid:* Total: $126,804 (27% from college's own funds, 9% from other college-administered sources, 64% from external sources). 7 Federal Work-Study jobs (averaging $1235); 9 part-time jobs.

Need-Based Scholarships & Grants Pell, FSEOG, state, college/university.

Loans PLUS, Stafford, Unsubsidized Stafford.

Non-Need Awards In 1996, a total of 24 non-need awards were made. *Academic Interests/Achievement Awards:* 13 ($15,000 total): general academic, education. *Creative Arts/Performance Awards:* 3 ($3000 total): music. *Special Achievements/Activities Awards:* 4 ($4000 total): religious involvement. *Special Characteristics Awards:* 4 ($4000 total): general special characteristics, children and siblings of alumni, children of faculty/staff, religious affiliation, siblings of current students.

Other Money-Saving Options Off-campus living (after freshman year). *Payment Plan:* installment. *Waivers:* full or partial for employees or children of employees.

Contact Office of Financial Aid, Arizona Bible College, 2045 West Northern Avenue, Phoenix, AZ 85015-1701, 602-242-6400.

ARIZONA STATE UNIVERSITY
Tempe, Arizona

About the Institution State-supported, coed. Degrees awarded: B, M, D, P. Offers 114 undergraduate majors. Total enrollment: 38,664. Undergraduates: 30,680 (72% state residents). Freshmen: 4,245.

Undergraduate Expenses (1996–97) State resident tuition: $1940. Nonresident tuition: $8308. Mandatory fees: $69. College room and board: $4287. College room only: $2587.

Applications Of all full-time undergraduates enrolled in fall 1996, 100% of those judged to have need according to Federal Methodology were aided. *Financial aid deadline (priority):* 3/1. *Financial aid forms:* FAFSA required. *Regular admission application deadline:* rolling. Early action deadline: 11/1.

Summary of Aid to Needy Students *From gift & self-help combined:* Average need met: 88%. Average amount awarded: $7543 (26% gift aid, 74% self-help). *Gift aid:* Total: $30,515,777. 663 Federal Work-Study jobs (averaging $2247); 4,116 part-time jobs.

Need-Based Scholarships & Grants Pell, FSEOG, state, private, college/university.

Loans Perkins, PLUS, Stafford, Unsubsidized Stafford, Federal Nursing, state, private, college/university short-term loans, college/university long-term loans.

Non-Need Awards *Academic Interests/Achievement Awards:* general academic. *Creative Arts/Performance Awards:* general creative. *Special*

Achievements/Activities Awards: general special achievements/activities. *Special Characteristics Awards:* general special characteristics. *Athletic:* available.

Other Money-Saving Options Accelerated degree, co-op program, Army ROTC, Air Force ROTC, off-campus living. *Waivers:* full or partial for employees or children of employees.

Contact Student Financial Assistance, Arizona State University, Tempe, AZ 85287, 602-965-3355, fax: 602-965-9484.

ARKANSAS BAPTIST COLLEGE
Little Rock, Arkansas

About the Institution Independent/religious, coed. Degrees awarded: A, B. Offers 8 undergraduate majors.

Applications *Financial aid deadline (priority):* 3/15. *Financial aid forms:* FAFSA required. *Admission application deadline:* rolling.

Summary of Aid to Needy Students *From gift & self-help combined:* Average need met: 70%. *Gift aid:* Total: $340,000. Federal Work-Study jobs; part-time jobs.

Need-Based Scholarships & Grants Pell, FSEOG, state, private.

Loans Stafford, Unsubsidized Stafford.

Non-Need Awards *Athletic:* available.

Other Money-Saving Options Accelerated degree, off-campus living.

Contact Ms. Evelyn Jones, Director of Financial Aid, Arkansas Baptist College, 1600 Bishop Street, Little Rock, AR 72202-6067, 501-374-7856.

ARKANSAS STATE UNIVERSITY
Jonesboro, Arkansas

About the Institution State-supported, coed. Degrees awarded: A, B, M, D. Offers 86 undergraduate majors. Total enrollment: 9,828. Undergraduates: 8,762 (86% state residents). Freshmen: 1,653.

Undergraduate Expenses (1997–98) State resident tuition: $2000. Nonresident tuition: $5090. Mandatory fees: $290. College room and board: $2620 (minimum).

Applications 70% of all full-time undergraduates enrolled in fall 1996 applied for aid; of these, 92% were judged to have need according to Federal Methodology, of whom 86% were aided. *Financial aid deadline (priority):* 4/1. *Financial aid forms:* FAFSA required; state form, institutional form acceptable. *Admission application deadline:* rolling.

Summary of Aid to Needy Students *From gift & self-help combined:* Average need met: 76%. Average amount awarded: $2700 (60% gift aid, 40% self-help). *Gift aid:* Total: $6,423,376 (36% from college's own funds, 28% from other college-administered sources, 36% from external sources). 290 Federal Work-Study jobs (averaging $1134); 845 part-time jobs.

Need-Based Scholarships & Grants Pell, FSEOG, state, private, college/university.

Loans Perkins, PLUS, Stafford, Unsubsidized Stafford, state, private, college/university long-term loans ($1600 average).

Non-Need Awards In 1996, a total of 1,569 non-need awards were made. *Academic Interests/Achievement Awards:* 966 ($1,399,513 total): general academic, agriculture, biological sciences, business, communication, computer science, education, engineering/technologies, English, foreign languages, health fields, mathematics, physical sciences, premedicine, social sciences. *Creative Arts/Performance Awards:* 218 ($263,159 total): art/fine arts, music, theater/drama. *Special Achievements/Activities Awards:* 29 ($12,439 total): general special achievements/activities. *Special Characteristics Awards:* 162 ($241,303 total): general special characteristics, adult students, children and siblings of alumni, children of union members/company employees, children with a deceased or disabled parent, ethnic background, handicapped students, local/state students, members of minorities, out-of-state students, ROTC participants. *Athletic:* Total: 194 ($1,014,288); Men: 142 ($745,132); Women: 52 ($269,156).

Other Money-Saving Options Accelerated degree, co-op program, Army ROTC, off-campus living (after sophomore year). *Payment Plan:* installment. *Waivers:* full or partial for children of alumni, employees or children of employees, senior citizens.

Contact Mr. Gerald Craig, Director of Financial Aid, Arkansas State University, PO Box 1620, State University, AR 72467, 501-972-2310, fax: 501-972-2794.

ARKANSAS TECH UNIVERSITY
Russellville, Arkansas

About the Institution State-supported, coed. Degrees awarded: A, B, M. Offers 54 undergraduate majors. Total enrollment: 4,490. Undergraduates: 4,166 (96% state residents). Freshmen: 704.

Undergraduate Expenses (1997–98) State resident tuition: $2016. Nonresident tuition: $4032. Mandatory fees: $110. College room and board: $2380 (minimum).

Applications Of all full-time undergraduates enrolled in fall 1996, 75% of those who applied for aid were judged to have need according to Federal Methodology, of whom 93% were aided. *Financial aid deadline (priority):* 4/15. *Financial aid forms:* FAFSA, institutional form required. *Admission application deadline:* 9/15.

Summary of Aid to Needy Students *From gift & self-help combined:* Average need met: 92%. Average amount awarded: $5363 (65% gift aid, 35% self-help). *Gift aid:* Total: $6,211,132 (7% from college's own funds, 27% from other college-administered sources, 66% from external sources). 77 Federal Work-Study jobs (averaging $2067); 161 part-time jobs.

Need-Based Scholarships & Grants Pell, FSEOG, state.

Loans Perkins, PLUS, Stafford, Unsubsidized Stafford.

Non-Need Awards In 1996, a total of 966 non-need awards were made. *Academic Interests/Achievement Awards:* 442 ($882,052 total): general academic, agriculture. *Creative Arts/Performance Awards:* 202 ($329,465 total): creative writing, journalism/publications, music. *Special Achievements/Activities Awards:* 28 ($39,428 total): general special achievements/activities, cheerleading/drum major. *Special Characteristics Awards:* 169 ($65,020 total): adult students, children of faculty/staff. *Athletic:* Total: 125 ($401,965); Men: 97 ($309,610); Women: 28 ($92,355).

Other Money-Saving Options Accelerated degree, cooperative Army ROTC, off-campus living (after sophomore year). *Payment Plan:* deferred payment. *Waivers:* full or partial for employees or children of employees and senior citizens.

Contact Ms. Sonya McAnally, Student Aid Officer, Arkansas Tech University, Bryan Hall, Russellville, AR 72801-2222, 501-968-0377, fax: 501-964-0857.

ARLINGTON BAPTIST COLLEGE
Arlington, Texas

About the Institution Independent/religious, coed. Degrees awarded: B. Offers 7 undergraduate majors. Total enrollment: 198 (78% state residents). Freshmen: 43.

Undergraduate Expenses (1996–97) Tuition: $2240. Mandatory fees: $250. College room only: $1500.

Applications 42% of all full-time undergraduates enrolled in fall 1996 applied for aid; of these, 94% were judged to have need according to Federal Methodology, of whom 100% were aided. *Financial aid deadline (priority):* 10/1. *Financial aid forms:* institutional form required; FAFSA acceptable. *Admission application deadline:* rolling.

Summary of Aid to Needy Students *From gift & self-help combined:* Average amount awarded: $2911 (50% gift aid, 50% self-help). *Gift aid:* Total: $97,631 (38% from college's own funds, 62% from external sources). 7 part-time jobs.

Need-Based Scholarships & Grants Pell.

Loans PLUS, Stafford, Unsubsidized Stafford.

Non-Need Awards Not offered.

Other Money-Saving Options Accelerated degree. *Payment Plans:* installment, deferred payment.

Contact Mr. David B. Clogston Jr., Business Manager, Arlington Baptist College, Arlington, TX 76012-3425, 817-461-8741, fax: 817-274-1138.

ARMSTRONG ATLANTIC STATE UNIVERSITY
Savannah, Georgia

About the Institution State-supported, coed. Degrees awarded: A, B, M. Offers 39 undergraduate majors. Total enrollment: 5,617. Undergraduates: 5,042 (93% state residents). Freshmen: 654.

Undergraduate Expenses (1997–98 estimated) State resident tuition: $1836. Nonresident tuition: $5715. College room and board: $3921.

Applications *Financial aid deadline (priority):* 4/15. *Financial aid forms:* FAFSA, institutional form required; state form acceptable. *Admission application deadline:* 8/15.

Summary of Aid to Needy Students *From gift & self-help combined:* Average need met: 80%. Average amount awarded: $3200 (45% gift aid, 55% self-help). *Gift aid:* Total: $5,474,399 (9% from college's own funds, 37% from other college-administered sources, 54% from external sources). 49 Federal Work-Study jobs (averaging $1712); 200 part-time jobs.

Need-Based Scholarships & Grants Pell, FSEOG, state, private, college/university.

Loans PLUS, Stafford, Unsubsidized Stafford, college/university short-term loans ($400 average).

Non-Need Awards In 1996, a total of 397 non-need awards were made. *Academic Interests/Achievement Awards:* 223 ($293,007 total): general academic, biological sciences, computer science, education, engineering/technologies, health fields, humanities, mathematics. *Creative Arts/Performance Awards:* 42 ($30,691 total): art/fine arts, music. *Special Characteristics Awards:* 52 ($201,708 total): out-of-state students. *Athletic:* Total: 80 ($311,773).

Other Money-Saving Options Accelerated degree, co-op program, Army ROTC, Naval ROTC, off-campus living. *Waivers:* full or partial for senior citizens.

Contact Financial Aid Office, Armstrong Atlantic State University, Savannah, GA 31419-1997, 912-921-5272.

ARNOLD & MARIE SCHWARTZ COLLEGE OF PHARMACY AND HEALTH SCIENCES
Brooklyn, New York

See Long Island University, Brooklyn Campus

ART ACADEMY OF CINCINNATI
Cincinnati, Ohio

About the Institution Independent, coed. Degrees awarded: A, B, M. Offers 8 undergraduate majors. Total enrollment: 168. Undergraduates: 158 (65% state residents). Freshmen: 42.

Undergraduate Expenses (1997–98) Tuition: $10,800. Mandatory fees: $125.

Applications Of all full-time undergraduates enrolled in fall 1996, 92% of those who applied for aid were judged to have need according to Federal Methodology, of whom 100% were aided. *Financial aid deadline:* continuous. *Financial aid forms:* FAFSA required. State form required for some. *Admission application deadline:* 8/15.

Summary of Aid to Needy Students *From gift & self-help combined:* Average amount awarded: $8404 (52% gift aid, 48% self-help). *Gift aid:* Total: $407,000 (37% from college's own funds, 11% from other college-administered sources, 52% from external sources). Federal Work-Study jobs; 20 part-time jobs.

Need-Based Scholarships & Grants Pell, FSEOG, state.

Loans PLUS, Stafford, Unsubsidized Stafford, college/university short-term loans ($1000 average), college/university long-term loans ($1000 average).

Non-Need Awards *Creative Arts/Performance Awards:* applied art and design , art/fine arts.

Other Money-Saving Options Cooperative Army ROTC, cooperative Naval ROTC, cooperative Air Force ROTC. *Payment Plan:* installment. *Waivers:* full or partial for employees or children of employees.

Contact Ms. Karen Geiger, Director of Financial Aid, Art Academy of Cincinnati, Cincinnati, OH 45202-1700, 513-721-5205.

ART CENTER COLLEGE OF DESIGN
Pasadena, California

About the Institution Independent, coed. Degrees awarded: B, M. Offers 10 undergraduate majors. Total enrollment: 1,477. Undergraduates: 1,402 (52% state residents). Freshmen: 200.

Undergraduate Expenses (1997–98) Tuition: $16,200.

Applications Of all full-time undergraduates enrolled in fall 1996, 96% of those who applied for aid were judged to have need according to Federal Methodology, of whom 98% were aided. *Financial aid deadline (priority):* 3/1. *Financial aid forms:* FAFSA, institutional form required. State form required for some. *Admission application deadline:* rolling.

Summary of Aid to Needy Students *From gift & self-help combined:* Average amount awarded: $11,014 (34% gift aid, 66% self-help). *Gift aid:* Total: $2,870,903 (42% from college's own funds, 35% from other college-administered sources, 23% from external sources). 168 Federal Work-Study jobs (averaging $1008); part-time jobs.

Need-Based Scholarships & Grants Pell, FSEOG, state, private.

Loans Perkins, PLUS, Stafford, Unsubsidized Stafford, college/university long-term loans ($1296 average).

Non-Need Awards Not offered.

Other Money-Saving Options Accelerated degree. *Payment Plan:* installment. *Waivers:* full or partial for employees or children of employees.

Contact Office of Financial Aid, Art Center College of Design, 1700 Lida Street, Pasadena, CA 91103-1999, 818-396-2200.

ART INSTITUTE OF BOSTON
Boston, Massachusetts

About the Institution Independent, coed. Degrees awarded: B. Offers 9 undergraduate majors. Total enrollment: 461 (56% state residents). Freshmen: 115.

Undergraduate Expenses (1997–98) Comprehensive fee of $18,670 includes tuition ($11,100), mandatory fees ($670 minimum), and college room and board ($6900 minimum).

Applications Of all full-time undergraduates enrolled in fall 1996, 91% of those who applied for aid were judged to have need according to Federal Methodology, of whom 100% were aided. *Financial aid deadline (priority):* 3/15. *Financial aid forms:* FAFSA, CSS Financial Aid PROFILE,

institutional form, financial aid transcript (for transfers), state income tax form required. State form required for some. *Admission application deadline:* rolling.

Summary of Aid to Needy Students *From gift & self-help combined:* Average amount awarded: $8458 (36% gift aid, 64% self-help). *Gift aid:* Total: $616,823 (55% from college's own funds, 22% from other college-administered sources, 23% from external sources). 42 Federal Work-Study jobs (averaging $1680); 18 part-time jobs.

Need-Based Scholarships & Grants Pell, FSEOG, state, private, college/university.

Loans PLUS, Stafford, Unsubsidized Stafford, state, private.

Non-Need Awards In 1996, a total of 66 non-need awards were made. *Academic Interests/Achievement Awards:* 1 ($1500 total): general academic. *Creative Arts/Performance Awards:* 62 ($180,925 total): applied art and design, art/fine arts. *Special Achievements/Activities Awards:* 1 ($600 total): memberships. *Special Characteristics Awards:* 2 ($3500 total): local/state students, members of minorities.

Other Money-Saving Options Off-campus living. *Payment Plan:* installment. *Waivers:* full or partial for employees or children of employees, adult students, senior citizens.

Contact Ms. Atoosa Malekani, Assistant Financial Aid Officer, Art Institute of Boston, 700 Beacon Street, Boston, MA 02215-2598, 617-262-1223 Ext. 318, fax: 617-437-1226.

THE ART INSTITUTE OF ILLINOIS
Chicago, Illinois

See Illinois Institute of Art

ART INSTITUTE OF SOUTHERN CALIFORNIA
Laguna Beach, California

About the Institution Independent, coed. Degrees awarded: B. Offers 4 undergraduate majors. Total enrollment: 181 (60% state residents). Freshmen: 38.

Undergraduate Expenses (1997–98) Tuition: $10,900.

Applications Of all full-time undergraduates enrolled in fall 1996, 96% of those who applied for aid were judged to have need according to Federal Methodology, of whom 100% were aided. *Financial aid deadline (priority):* 8/15. *Financial aid forms:* CSS Financial Aid PROFILE, institutional form required. FAFSA, state form required for some. *Admission application deadline:* rolling.

Summary of Aid to Needy Students *From gift & self-help combined:* Average amount awarded: $9500 (46% gift aid, 54% self-help). *Gift aid:* Total: $188,699 (27% from college's own funds, 32% from other college-administered sources, 41% from external sources). 10 Federal Work-Study jobs.

Need-Based Scholarships & Grants Pell, FSEOG, state, college/university.

Loans PLUS, Stafford, Unsubsidized Stafford.

Non-Need Awards *Academic Interests/Achievement Awards:* general academic. *Creative Arts/Performance Awards:* 53 ($50,500 total): applied art and design, art/fine arts.

Other Money-Saving Options *Payment Plans:* guaranteed tuition, installment.

Contact Ms. Tamara L. Broker, Director of Financial Aid, Art Institute of Southern California, 2222 Laguna Canyon Road, Laguna Beach, CA 92651-1136, 714-497-3309, fax: 714-497-4399.

ASBURY COLLEGE
Wilmore, Kentucky

About the Institution Independent/religious, coed. Degrees awarded: B. Offers 40 undergraduate majors. Total enrollment: 1,167 (22% state residents). Freshmen: 295.

Undergraduate Expenses (1997–98) Comprehensive fee of $14,375 includes tuition ($11,100), mandatory fees ($125), and college room and board ($3150).

Applications 76% of all full-time undergraduates enrolled in fall 1996 applied for aid; of these, 94% were judged to have need according to Federal Methodology, of whom 100% were aided. *Financial aid deadline (priority):* 3/1. *Financial aid forms:* FAFSA, institutional form required. State form required for some. *Admission application deadline:* rolling.

Summary of Aid to Needy Students *From gift & self-help combined:* Average need met: 83%. Average amount awarded: $8640 (48% gift aid, 52% self-help). *Gift aid:* Total: $3,167,094 (59% from college's own funds, 9% from other college-administered sources, 32% from external sources). 400 Federal Work-Study jobs (averaging $1006); 321 part-time jobs.

Need-Based Scholarships & Grants Pell, FSEOG, state, private, college/university.

Loans Perkins, PLUS, Stafford, Unsubsidized Stafford, private, college/university long-term loans ($907 average).

Non-Need Awards In 1996, a total of 355 non-need awards were made. *Academic Interests/Achievement Awards:* 276 ($807,207 total): general academic. *Creative Arts/Performance Awards:* 10 ($18,560 total): music. *Special Characteristics Awards:* 69 ($188,248 total): children and siblings of alumni, international students.

Other Money-Saving Options Cooperative Army ROTC. *Payment Plans:* installment, deferred payment. *Waivers:* full or partial for employees or children of employees and senior citizens.

Contact Mr. Douglas B. Cleary, Director of Financial Aid, Asbury College, 1 Macklem Drive, Wilmore, KY 40390-1198, 606-858-3511 Ext. 2195.

ASHLAND UNIVERSITY
Ashland, Ohio

About the Institution Independent/religious, coed. Degrees awarded: A, B, M. Offers 81 undergraduate majors. Total enrollment: 5,733. Undergraduates: 2,591 (91% state residents). Freshmen: 441.

Undergraduate Expenses (1997–98) Comprehensive fee of $18,717 includes tuition ($13,293), mandatory fees ($308), and college room and board ($5116). College room only: $2715.

Applications 97% of all full-time undergraduates enrolled in fall 1996 applied for aid; of these, 84% were judged to have need according to Federal Methodology, of whom 100% were aided. *Financial aid deadline (priority):* 3/1. *Financial aid forms:* FAFSA, institutional form required; CSS Financial Aid PROFILE acceptable. *Admission application deadline:* rolling.

Summary of Aid to Needy Students *From gift & self-help combined:* Average need met: 90%. Average amount awarded: $11,515 (69% gift aid, 31% self-help). *Gift aid:* Total: $11,137,000 (72% from college's own funds, 20% from other college-administered sources, 8% from external sources). 782 Federal Work-Study jobs (averaging $1130); 50 part-time jobs.

Need-Based Scholarships & Grants Pell, FSEOG, state, college/university.

Loans Perkins, PLUS, Stafford, Unsubsidized Stafford, private, college/university short-term loans ($200 average), college/university long-term loans ($1000 average).

Non-Need Awards In 1996, a total of 2,195 non-need awards were made. *Academic Interests/Achievement Awards:* 1,544 ($3,542,000 total): general academic. *Creative Arts/Performance Awards:* 142 ($195,000 total): art/fine arts, music, theater/drama. *Special Achievements/Activities Awards:* 27 ($15,000 total): leadership. *Special Characteristics Awards:* 226 ($925,000 total): children and siblings of alumni, children of faculty/staff, religious affiliation, siblings of current students. *Athletic:* Total: 256 ($1,471,000); Men: 169 ($945,000); Women: 87 ($526,000).

Other Money-Saving Options Accelerated degree, cooperative Air Force ROTC. *Payment Plan:* installment. *Waivers:* full or partial for employees or children of employees.

Contact Mr. Stephen C. Howell, Director of Financial Aid, Ashland University, 401 College Avenue, Room 312, Ashland, OH 44805-3702, 419-289-5002, fax: 419-289-5333.

ASSUMPTION COLLEGE
Worcester, Massachusetts

About the Institution Independent/religious, coed. Degrees awarded: B, M. Offers 38 undergraduate majors. Total enrollment: 2,596. Undergraduates: 1,649 (60% state residents). Freshmen: 452.

Undergraduate Expenses (1997–98) Comprehensive fee of $20,675 includes tuition ($14,700), mandatory fees ($145), and college room and board ($5830 minimum). College room only: $3430 (minimum).

Applications *Financial aid deadline (priority):* 3/1. *Financial aid forms:* FAFSA, CSS Financial Aid PROFILE, state form required. *Regular admission application deadline:* 3/1. Early decision deadline: 11/1.

Summary of Aid to Needy Students Federal Work-Study jobs; part-time jobs.

Non-Need Awards *Athletic:* available.

Other Money-Saving Options Cooperative Army ROTC, cooperative Naval ROTC, cooperative Air Force ROTC, off-campus living. *Payment Plan:* installment. *Waivers:* full or partial for minority students and employees or children of employees.

Contact Office of Financial Aid, Assumption College, 500 Salisbury Street, PO Box 15005, Worcester, MA 01615-0005, 508-767-7000.

ATLANTA CHRISTIAN COLLEGE
East Point, Georgia

About the Institution Independent/religious, coed. Degrees awarded: A, B. Offers 15 undergraduate majors. Total enrollment: 276 (89% state residents). Freshmen: 54.

Undergraduate Expenses (1997–98) Comprehensive fee of $9596 includes tuition ($6048), mandatory fees ($378), and college room and board ($3170).

Applications *Financial aid deadline (priority):* 7/1. *Financial aid forms:* FAFSA required. State form required for some. *Admission application deadline:* 8/1.

Summary of Aid to Needy Students *From gift & self-help combined:* Average amount awarded: $2375 (47% gift aid, 53% self-help). *Gift aid:* Total: $225,000. Federal Work-Study jobs; part-time jobs.

Loans PLUS, Stafford, Unsubsidized Stafford, state, private.

Non-Need Awards *Academic Interests/Achievement Awards:* general academic. *Creative Arts/Performance Awards:* music. *Special Achievements/Activities Awards:* memberships, religious involvement. *Special Characteristics Awards:* children of faculty/staff.

Other Money-Saving Options Off-campus living (after freshman year). *Payment Plan:* installment. *Waivers:* full or partial for employees or children of employees and senior citizens.

Contact Ms. Inez Morris, Director of Financial Aid, Atlanta Christian College, 2605 Ben Hill Road, East Point, GA 30344-1999, 404-761-8861.

ATLANTA COLLEGE OF ART
Atlanta, Georgia

About the Institution Independent, coed. Degrees awarded: B. Offers 13 undergraduate majors. Total enrollment: 396 (36% state residents). Freshmen: 69.

Undergraduate Expenses (1997–98 estimated) Tuition: $11,900. College room only: $3750.

Applications 63% of all full-time undergraduates enrolled in fall 1996 applied for aid; of these, 89% were judged to have need according to Federal Methodology, of whom 100% were aided. *Financial aid deadline (priority):* 3/15. *Financial aid forms:* FAFSA, institutional form, need-based aid application required. State form required for some. *Admission application deadline:* rolling.

Summary of Aid to Needy Students *From gift & self-help combined:* Average need met: 70%. Average amount awarded: $8552 (58% gift aid, 42% self-help). *Gift aid:* Total: $1,196,998 (55% from college's own funds, 10% from other college-administered sources, 35% from external sources). 51 Federal Work-Study jobs (averaging $1550); 33 part-time jobs.

Need-Based Scholarships & Grants Pell, FSEOG, state, private, college/university.

Loans PLUS, Stafford, Unsubsidized Stafford, private, college/university short-term loans ($500 average).

Non-Need Awards In 1996, a total of 122 non-need awards were made. *Academic Interests/Achievement Awards:* 44 ($32,500 total): general academic. *Creative Arts/Performance Awards:* 78 ($133,427 total): art/fine arts.

Other Money-Saving Options Co-op program, off-campus living. *Payment Plans:* installment, deferred payment. *Waivers:* full or partial for employees or children of employees.

Contact Ms. Teresa Tantillo, Director of Financial Aid, Atlanta College of Art, Atlanta, GA 30309-3582, 404-733-5111.

ATLANTIC UNION COLLEGE
South Lancaster, Massachusetts

About the Institution Independent/religious, coed. Degrees awarded: A, B, M. Offers 45 undergraduate majors. Total enrollment: 642. Undergraduates: 592 (52% state residents). Freshmen: 149.

Undergraduate Expenses (1997–98) Comprehensive fee of $15,900 includes tuition ($11,330), mandatory fees ($670), and college room and board ($3900). College room only: $2100.

Applications 95% of all full-time undergraduates enrolled in fall 1996 applied for aid; of these, 93% were judged to have need according to Federal Methodology, of whom 100% were aided. *Financial aid deadline (priority):* 3/1. *Financial aid forms:* FAFSA, institutional form required. *Admission application deadline:* 8/1.

Summary of Aid to Needy Students *From gift & self-help combined:* Average need met: 75%. Average amount awarded: $9309 (43% gift aid, 57% self-help). *Gift aid:* Total: $1,586,355 (50% from college's own funds, 21% from other college-administered sources, 29% from external sources). 100 Federal Work-Study jobs (averaging $1500); 250 part-time jobs.

Need-Based Scholarships & Grants Pell, FSEOG, state, private, college/university.

Loans Perkins, PLUS, Stafford, Unsubsidized Stafford, state, college/university short-term loans ($1200 average), college/university long-term loans, TERI Loans.

Non-Need Awards In 1996, a total of 80 non-need awards were made. *Academic Interests/Achievement Awards:* 38 ($86,295 total): general academic. *Creative Arts/Performance Awards:* 16 ($26,500 total): music. *Athletic:* Total: 26 ($44,200); Men: 10 ($14,000); Women: 16 ($30,200).

Other Money-Saving Options Co-op program. *Payment Plan:* installment. *Waivers:* full or partial for employees or children of employees and senior citizens.

Contact Ms. Linda L. Mularczyk, Director of Financial Aid, Atlantic Union College, PO Box 1000, South Lancaster, MA 01561-1000, 508-368-2284, fax: 508-368-2283.

AUBURN UNIVERSITY
Auburn, Alabama

About the Institution State-supported, coed. Degrees awarded: B, M, D, P. Offers 136 undergraduate majors. Total enrollment: 21,778. Undergraduates: 18,396 (65% state residents). Freshmen: 3,315.

Undergraduate Expenses (1997–98) State resident tuition: $2565 (minimum). Nonresident tuition: $7695 (minimum). College room only: $1575 (minimum).

Applications Of all full-time undergraduates enrolled in fall 1996, 81% of those who applied for aid were judged to have need according to Federal Methodology, of whom 46% were aided. *Financial aid deadline (priority):* 4/15. *Financial aid forms:* FAFSA, institutional form required. *Admission application deadline:* 9/1.

Summary of Aid to Needy Students *From gift & self-help combined:* Average amount awarded: $6489 (26% gift aid, 74% self-help). *Gift aid:* Total: $6,589,180 (25% from college's own funds, 11% from other college-administered sources, 64% from external sources). 508 Federal Work-Study jobs (averaging $1800); 4,570 part-time jobs.

Need-Based Scholarships & Grants Pell, FSEOG, state, private, college/university.

Loans Perkins, PLUS, Stafford, Unsubsidized Stafford, private, college/university short-term loans ($200 average), college/university long-term loans ($990 average).

Non-Need Awards *Academic Interests/Achievement Awards:* 1,310 ($2,143,772 total): general academic, agriculture, architecture, biological sciences, business, communication, computer science, education, engineering/technologies, English, foreign languages, health fields, humanities, international studies, mathematics, physical sciences, premedicine, social sciences. *Creative Arts/Performance Awards:* 67 ($17,868 total): music. *Special Achievements/Activities Awards:* 18 ($30,615 total): cheerleading/drum major, memberships. *Special Characteristics Awards:* 75 ($177,620 total): ethnic background, members of minorities. *Athletic:* available.

Other Money-Saving Options Accelerated degree, co-op program, Army ROTC, Naval ROTC, Air Force ROTC, off-campus living. *Waivers:* full or partial for employees or children of employees.

Contact Office of Financial Aid, Auburn University, 203 Martin Hall, Auburn University, AL 36849-5144, 334-844-4000.

AUBURN UNIVERSITY AT MONTGOMERY
Montgomery, Alabama

About the Institution State-supported, coed. Degrees awarded: B, M. Offers 24 undergraduate majors. Total enrollment: 5,645. Undergraduates: 4,771 (99% state residents). Freshmen: 844.

Undergraduate Expenses (1997–98) State resident tuition: $2289. Nonresident tuition: $6867. College room only: $1830.

Applications *Financial aid deadline (priority):* 3/15. *Financial aid forms:* FAFSA, institutional form required. *Admission application deadline:* 9/1.

Summary of Aid to Needy Students *From gift & self-help combined:* Average need met: 75%. Federal Work-Study jobs; part-time jobs.

Need-Based Scholarships & Grants Pell, FSEOG.

Loans Perkins, PLUS, Stafford, Unsubsidized Stafford.

Non-Need Awards *Academic Interests/Achievement Awards:* general academic. *Athletic:* available.

Other Money-Saving Options Accelerated degree, co-op program, Army ROTC, cooperative Air Force ROTC, off-campus living. *Payment Plan:* deferred payment.

Contact Office of Financial Aid, Auburn University at Montgomery, Montgomery, AL 36124-4023, 334-244-3571.

AUDREY COHEN COLLEGE
New York, New York

About the Institution Independent, coed. Degrees awarded: B, M. Offers 2 undergraduate majors. Total enrollment: 1,180. Undergraduates: 1,084 (92% state residents). Freshmen: 311.

Undergraduate Expenses (1996–97) Tuition: $8650 (minimum). Mandatory fees: $40.

Applications 96% of all full-time undergraduates enrolled in fall 1996 applied for aid; of these,100% were judged to have need according to Federal Methodology, of whom 67% were aided. *Financial aid deadline (priority):* 8/15. *Financial aid forms:* FAFSA, state form required; CSS Financial Aid PROFILE acceptable. *Admission application deadline:* 8/15.

Summary of Aid to Needy Students *From gift & self-help combined:* Average amount awarded: $2920 (76% gift aid, 24% self-help). *Gift aid:* Total: $1,312,415 (9% from college's own funds, 2% from other college-administered sources, 89% from external sources). Federal Work-Study jobs; 25 part-time jobs.

Need-Based Scholarships & Grants Pell, FSEOG.

Loans PLUS, Stafford, Unsubsidized Stafford.

Non-Need Awards In 1996, a total of 200 non-need awards were made. *Academic Interests/Achievement Awards:* 200 ($273,553 total): general academic.

Other Money-Saving Options Accelerated degree, co-op program. *Payment Plans:* guaranteed tuition, installment. *Waivers:* full or partial for employees or children of employees.

Contact Office of Financial Aid, Audrey Cohen College, 75 Varick Street, New York, NY 10013-1919, 212-343-1234 Ext. 5004, fax: 212-343-7399.

AUGSBURG COLLEGE
Minneapolis, Minnesota

About the Institution Independent/religious, coed. Degrees awarded: B, M. Offers 71 undergraduate majors. Total enrollment: 2,862. Undergraduates: 2,559 (83% state residents). Freshmen: 291.

Undergraduate Expenses (1997–98) Comprehensive fee of $18,982 includes tuition ($13,850), mandatory fees ($146), and college room and board ($4986).

Applications 87% of all full-time undergraduates enrolled in fall 1996 applied for aid; of these, 88% were judged to have need according to Federal Methodology, of whom 99% were aided. *Financial aid deadline (priority):* 4/15. *Financial aid forms:* FAFSA, institutional form required; CSS Financial Aid PROFILE, state form acceptable. *Regular admission application deadline:* 5/1. Early decision deadline: 12/15.

Summary of Aid to Needy Students *From gift & self-help combined:* Average need met: 82%. Average amount awarded: $13,966 (54% gift aid, 46% self-help). *Gift aid:* Total: $8,076,638 (52% from college's own funds, 35% from other college-administered sources, 13% from external sources). 331 Federal Work-Study jobs (averaging $999); part-time jobs.

Need-Based Scholarships & Grants Pell, FSEOG, state, private, college/university.

Loans Perkins, PLUS, Stafford, Unsubsidized Stafford, Federal Nursing, state, private, college/university long-term loans ($2154 average).

Non-Need Awards In 1996, a total of 658 non-need awards were made. *Academic Interests/Achievement Awards:* 523 ($2,210,946 total): general academic. *Creative Arts/Performance Awards:* 46 ($57,750 total): music, performing arts. *Special Achievements/Activities Awards:* 89 ($45,788 total): community service, leadership, religious involvement.

Other Money-Saving Options Accelerated degree, co-op program, cooperative Naval ROTC, cooperative Air Force ROTC, off-campus living. *Payment Plans:* installment, deferred payment. *Waivers:* full or partial for employees or children of employees and senior citizens.

Contact Mr. Hearld A. Johnson, Director of Student Financial Services, Augsburg College, 2211 Riverside Avenue, Minneapolis, MN 55454-1351, 612-330-1046, fax: 612-330-1649.

AUGUSTANA COLLEGE
Rock Island, Illinois

About the Institution Independent/religious, coed. Degrees awarded: B. Offers 70 undergraduate majors. Total enrollment: 2,214 (84% state residents). Freshmen: 576.

Undergraduate Expenses (1997–98) Comprehensive fee of $19,989 includes tuition ($15,195), mandatory fees ($105), and college room and board ($4689). College room only: $2391.

Applications 84% of all full-time undergraduates enrolled in fall 1996 applied for aid; of these, 90% were judged to have need according to Federal Methodology, of whom 99% were aided. *Financial aid deadline (priority):* 4/1. *Financial aid forms:* FAFSA, institutional form required; CSS Financial Aid PROFILE acceptable. State form required for some. *Admission application deadline:* 4/1.

Summary of Aid to Needy Students *From gift & self-help combined:* Average need met: 99%. Average amount awarded: $13,023 (68% gift aid, 32% self-help). *Gift aid:* Total: $14,457,353 (64% from college's own funds, 2% from other college-administered sources, 34% from external sources). 1,338 Federal Work-Study jobs (averaging $1074); 433 part-time jobs.

Need-Based Scholarships & Grants Pell, FSEOG, state, private, college/university.

Loans Perkins, PLUS, Stafford, Unsubsidized Stafford, Norwest Collegiate Loans.

Non-Need Awards In 1996, a total of 1,739 non-need awards were made. *Academic Interests/Achievement Awards:* 1,055 ($4,243,253 total): general academic, biological sciences. *Creative Arts/Performance Awards:* 263 ($425,421 total): art/fine arts, creative writing, debating, music, theater/drama. *Special Characteristics Awards:* 421 ($2,044,095 total): children and siblings of alumni, children of faculty/staff, international students, members of minorities, religious affiliation, siblings of current students.

Other Money-Saving Options Co-op program, off-campus living (after junior year). *Payment Plans:* tuition prepayment, installment. *Waivers:* full or partial for employees or children of employees.

Contact Office of Financial Aid, Augustana College, 639 38th Street, Rock Island, IL 61201-2296, 309-794-7000.

AUGUSTANA COLLEGE
Sioux Falls, South Dakota

About the Institution Independent/religious, coed. Degrees awarded: A, B, M. Offers 47 undergraduate majors. Total enrollment: 1,750. Undergraduates: 1,589 (45% state residents). Freshmen: 386.

Undergraduate Expenses (1997–98) Comprehensive fee of $17,015 includes tuition ($12,968), mandatory fees ($144), and college room and board ($3903 minimum). College room only: $1904 (minimum).

Applications Of all full-time undergraduates enrolled in fall 1996, 80% of those who applied for aid were judged to have need according to

Federal Methodology, of whom 97% were aided. *Financial aid deadline (priority):* 3/1. *Financial aid forms:* FAFSA required. State form, institutional form required for some. *Admission application deadline:* rolling.

Summary of Aid to Needy Students *From gift & self-help combined:* Average need met: 96%. Average amount awarded: $12,052 (56% gift aid, 44% self-help). *Gift aid:* Total: $6,461,837 (71% from college's own funds, 8% from other college-administered sources, 21% from external sources). 519 Federal Work-Study jobs (averaging $986); 115 part-time jobs.

Need-Based Scholarships & Grants Pell, FSEOG, state, private, college/university.

Loans Perkins, PLUS, Stafford, Unsubsidized Stafford, Federal Nursing, private, college/university long-term loans ($1835 average).

Non-Need Awards *Academic Interests/Achievement Awards:* ($3,376,423 total): general academic, biological sciences, business, communication, education, English, mathematics, physical sciences, religion/biblical studies, social sciences. *Creative Arts/Performance Awards:* 170 ($285,630 total): art/fine arts, debating, music, theater/drama. *Special Characteristics Awards:* ($1,720,997 total): children and siblings of alumni, international students, religious affiliation, siblings of current students, spouses of current students, veterans. *Athletic:* Total: 187 ($1,294,179); Men: 132 ($928,801); Women: 55 ($365,378).

Other Money-Saving Options Accelerated degree, co-op program, off-campus living (after sophomore year). *Payment Plans:* guaranteed tuition, installment. *Waivers:* full or partial for employees or children of employees, adult students, senior citizens.

Contact Ms. Brenda Murtha, Assistant Director of Financial Aid, Augustana College, 2001 South Summit Avenue, Sioux Falls, SD 57197, 605-336-5216.

AUGUSTA STATE UNIVERSITY
Augusta, Georgia

About the Institution State-supported, coed. Degrees awarded: A, B, M. Offers 32 undergraduate majors. Total enrollment: 5,561. Undergraduates: 4,733 (88% state residents). Freshmen: 843.

Undergraduate Expenses (1996–97) State resident tuition: $1584. Nonresident tuition: $5463. Mandatory fees: $216.

Applications Of all full-time undergraduates enrolled in fall 1996, 93% of those judged to have need according to Federal Methodology were aided. *Financial aid deadline (priority):* 4/15. *Financial aid forms:* FAFSA required. State form required for some. *Admission application deadline:* 8/15.

Summary of Aid to Needy Students *From gift & self-help combined:* Average need met: 62%. Average amount awarded: $2883 (39% gift aid, 61% self-help). *Gift aid:* Total: $2,953,216 (9% from college's own funds, 41% from other college-administered sources, 50% from external sources). 112 Federal Work-Study jobs (averaging $2529); 187 part-time jobs.

Need-Based Scholarships & Grants Pell, FSEOG, state, private, college/university.

Loans Perkins, PLUS, Stafford, Unsubsidized Stafford, state, private, college/university short-term loans ($200 average).

Non-Need Awards In 1996, a total of 202 non-need awards were made. *Academic Interests/Achievement Awards:* 47 ($59,304 total): general academic, business, education, English, health fields, mathematics, military science, physical sciences. *Creative Arts/Performance Awards:* 28 ($15,710 total): art/fine arts, music, theater/drama. *Special Achievements/Activities Awards:* 0: hobbies/interest. *Special Characteristics Awards:* 0: international students. *Athletic:* Total: 127 ($444,661); Men: 73 ($262,185); Women: 54 ($182,476).

Other Money-Saving Options Co-op program, Army ROTC. *Waivers:* full or partial for employees or children of employees and senior citizens.

Contact Ms. Roxanne Padgett, Assistant Director of Financial Aid, Augusta State University, 2500 Walton Way, Augusta, GA 30904-2200, 706-737-1431, fax: 706-737-1777.

AUSTIN COLLEGE
Sherman, Texas

About the Institution Independent/religious, coed. Degrees awarded: B, M. Offers 30 undergraduate majors. Total enrollment: 1,149. Undergraduates: 1,114 (92% state residents). Freshmen: 344.

Undergraduate Expenses (1996–97) Comprehensive fee of $17,776 includes tuition ($12,675), mandatory fees ($125), and college room and board ($4976). College room only: $2265.

Applications 74% of all full-time undergraduates enrolled in fall 1996 applied for aid; of these, 86% were judged to have need according to Federal Methodology, of whom 100% were aided. *Financial aid deadline (priority):* 4/1. *Financial aid forms:* FAFSA required. State form, institutional form required for some. *Regular admission application deadline:* rolling. Early decision deadline: 12/1. Early action deadline: 2/1.

Summary of Aid to Needy Students *From gift & self-help combined:* Average need met: 89%. Average amount awarded: $11,988 (67% gift aid, 33% self-help). *Gift aid:* Total: $5,667,894 (70% from college's own funds, 18% from other college-administered sources, 12% from external sources). 375 Federal Work-Study jobs (averaging $1300); 50 part-time jobs.

Need-Based Scholarships & Grants Pell, FSEOG, state, private, college/university.

Loans Perkins, PLUS, Stafford, Unsubsidized Stafford, state, private, college/university short-term loans ($100 average), college/university long-term loans ($1500 average).

Non-Need Awards In 1996, a total of 1,114 non-need awards were made. *Academic Interests/Achievement Awards:* 1,038 ($3,553,233 total): general academic, biological sciences, business, communication, education, engineering/technologies, English, foreign languages, health fields, humanities, international studies, physical sciences, premedicine, religion/biblical studies, social sciences. *Creative Arts/Performance Awards:* 12 ($29,000 total): art/fine arts, journalism/publications, music, theater/drama. *Special Achievements/Activities Awards:* 44 ($291,525 total): general special achievements/activities, leadership, religious involvement. *Special Characteristics Awards:* 20 ($167,205 total): children of faculty/staff, ethnic background, first-generation college students, handicapped students, international students, local/state students, relatives of clergy.

Other Money-Saving Options Accelerated degree, off-campus living (after junior year). *Payment Plan:* installment. *Waivers:* full or partial for employees or children of employees.

Contact Office of Financial Aid, Austin College, 900 North Grand, Suite 61562, Sherman, TX 75090-4440, 903-813-2000.

AUSTIN PEAY STATE UNIVERSITY
Clarksville, Tennessee

About the Institution State-supported, coed. Degrees awarded: A, B, M. Offers 94 undergraduate majors. Total enrollment: 8,187. Undergraduates: 7,556 (85% state residents). Freshmen: 1,012.

Undergraduate Expenses (1996–97) State resident tuition: $1714. Nonresident tuition: $6050. Mandatory fees: $394. College room and board: $2870. College room only: $1580.

Applications Of all full-time undergraduates enrolled in fall 1996, 69% of those who applied for aid were judged to have need according to

Federal Methodology, of whom 100% were aided. *Financial aid deadline (priority):* 4/1. *Financial aid forms:* FAFSA required. *Admission application deadline:* 7/27.

Summary of Aid to Needy Students *From gift & self-help combined:* Average need met: 80%. Average amount awarded: $7380 (44% gift aid, 56% self-help). *Gift aid:* Total: $7,617,570 (28% from college's own funds, 32% from other college-administered sources, 40% from external sources). 224 Federal Work-Study jobs (averaging $1467); 670 part-time jobs.

Need-Based Scholarships & Grants Pell, FSEOG, state.

Loans Perkins, PLUS, Stafford, Unsubsidized Stafford, college/university short-term loans ($50 average).

Non-Need Awards In 1996, a total of 1,171 non-need awards were made. *Academic Interests/Achievement Awards:* 331 ($889,680 total): general academic. *Creative Arts/Performance Awards:* 527 ($558,697 total): art/fine arts, debating, music. *Special Achievements/Activities Awards:* 80 ($115,500 total): leadership. *Athletic:* Total: 233 ($889,680).

Other Money-Saving Options Accelerated degree, co-op program, Army ROTC, off-campus living (after freshman year). *Waivers:* full or partial for employees or children of employees.

Contact Ms. Brenda D. Burney, Associate Director, Austin Peay State University, PO Box 4546, Clarksville, TN 37044-0001, 615-648-7907, fax: 615-648-6305.

AVERETT COLLEGE
Danville, Virginia

About the Institution Independent/religious, coed. Degrees awarded: A, B, M. Offers 80 undergraduate majors. Total enrollment: 2,540. Undergraduates: 1,661 (82% state residents). Freshmen: 164.

Undergraduate Expenses (1996–97) Comprehensive fee of $16,000 includes tuition ($11,450), mandatory fees ($400), and college room and board ($4150).

Applications *Financial aid deadline (priority):* 4/1. *Financial aid forms:* FAFSA required; CSS Financial Aid PROFILE acceptable. State form required for some. *Admission application deadline:* 8/15.

Summary of Aid to Needy Students *From gift & self-help combined:* Average need met: 88%. Average amount awarded: $7244 (40% gift aid, 60% self-help). *Gift aid:* Total: $3,294,073 (40% from college's own funds, 27% from other college-administered sources, 33% from external sources). 142 Federal Work-Study jobs (averaging $1200); 50 part-time jobs.

Need-Based Scholarships & Grants Pell, FSEOG, state, private, college/university.

Loans Perkins, PLUS, Stafford, Unsubsidized Stafford, private.

Non-Need Awards *Academic Interests/Achievement Awards:* ($477,238 total): general academic, health fields. *Special Achievements/Activities Awards:* ($36,875 total): leadership. *Special Characteristics Awards:* ($92,841 total): general special characteristics, local/state students, relatives of clergy, religious affiliation.

Other Money-Saving Options Accelerated degree, off-campus living (after junior year). *Payment Plan:* installment. *Waivers:* full or partial for employees or children of employees and senior citizens.

Contact Ms. Linda W. Shields, Director of Financial Aid, Averett College, Danville, VA 24541-3692, 804-791-5646, fax: 804-791-5647.

AZUSA PACIFIC UNIVERSITY
Azusa, California

About the Institution Independent/religious, coed. Degrees awarded: B, M, D. Offers 34 undergraduate majors. Total enrollment: 4,547. Undergraduates: 2,279 (86% state residents). Freshmen: 525.

Undergraduate Expenses (1996–97) Comprehensive fee of $17,796 includes tuition ($13,540), mandatory fees ($56), and college room and board ($4200). College room only: $1980.

Applications Of all full-time undergraduates enrolled in fall 1996, 93% of those who applied for aid were judged to have need according to Federal Methodology, of whom 100% were aided. *Financial aid deadline (priority):* 3/1. *Financial aid forms:* FAFSA, CSS Financial Aid PROFILE, institutional form required; state form acceptable. *Admission application deadline:* 7/15.

Summary of Aid to Needy Students *From gift & self-help combined:* Average need met: 87%. Average amount awarded: $15,090 (31% gift aid, 69% self-help). *Gift aid:* Total: $7,332,943 (57% from college's own funds, 4% from other college-administered sources, 39% from external sources). 147 Federal Work-Study jobs (averaging $1500); 272 part-time jobs.

Need-Based Scholarships & Grants Pell, FSEOG, state, private, college/university.

Loans Perkins, PLUS, Stafford, Unsubsidized Stafford, private.

Non-Need Awards In 1996, a total of 1,835 non-need awards were made. *Academic Interests/Achievement Awards:* 764 ($2,294,961 total): general academic, health fields, religion/biblical studies. *Creative Arts/Performance Awards:* 428 ($396,785 total): music, theater/drama. *Special Achievements/Activities Awards:* 10 ($3070 total): religious involvement. *Special Characteristics Awards:* 429 ($985,668 total): children of faculty/staff, ethnic background, international students, relatives of clergy, siblings of current students. *Athletic:* Total: 204 ($1,550,271); Men: 142 ($883,654); Women: 62 ($666,617).

Other Money-Saving Options Accelerated degree, co-op program, cooperative Army ROTC, off-campus living. *Payment Plan:* installment. *Waivers:* full or partial for employees or children of employees.

Contact Ms. Diane LeJeune, Director, Student Financial Services, Azusa Pacific University, 901 East Alosta Avenue, Azusa, CA 91702-7000, 818-812-3009, fax: 818-815-3815.

BABSON COLLEGE
Wellesley, Massachusetts

About the Institution Independent, coed. Degrees awarded: B, M. Offers 10 undergraduate majors. Total enrollment: 3,270. Undergraduates: 1,627 (38% state residents). Freshmen: 369.

Undergraduate Expenses (1997–98) Comprehensive fee of $26,675 includes tuition ($18,940), mandatory fees ($735), and college room and board ($7000).

Applications 47% of all full-time undergraduates enrolled in fall 1996 applied for aid; of these, 95% were judged to have need according to Federal Methodology, of whom 100% were aided. *Financial aid deadline:* 2/15. *Financial aid forms:* FAFSA, CSS Financial Aid PROFILE required. State form, Divorced/Separated Parents' Statement, Business/Farm Supplement required for some. *Regular admission application deadline:* 2/1. Early decision deadline: 11/15. Early action deadline: 11/15.

Summary of Aid to Needy Students *From gift & self-help combined:* Average need met: 85%. Average amount awarded: $15,930 (65% gift aid, 35% self-help). *Gift aid:* Total: $7,644,000 (88% from college's own funds, 5% from other college-administered sources, 7% from external sources). 800 Federal Work-Study jobs (averaging $1800); 350 part-time jobs.

Need-Based Scholarships & Grants Pell, FSEOG, state, private, college/university.

Loans Perkins, PLUS, Stafford, Unsubsidized Stafford, state, private, college/university short-term loans ($200 average), college/university long-term loans ($4000 average).

Non-Need Awards *Academic Interests/Achievement Awards:* general academic.

Other Money-Saving Options Accelerated degree, cooperative Army ROTC, off-campus living (after freshman year). *Payment Plan:* installment. *Waivers:* full or partial for employees or children of employees.

Contact Ms. Melissa Shaak, Director of Financial Aid, Babson College, Babson Park, MA 02157-0310, 617-239-4219, fax: 617-239-5510.

BAKER UNIVERSITY
Baldwin City, Kansas

About the Institution Independent/religious, coed. Degrees awarded: B, M. Offers 38 undergraduate majors. Total enrollment: 2,508. Undergraduates: 1,439 (64% state residents). Freshmen: 186.

Undergraduate Expenses (1997–98) Comprehensive fee of $15,500 includes tuition ($10,900) and college room and board ($4600).

Applications 97% of all full-time undergraduates enrolled in fall 1996 applied for aid; of these, 76% were judged to have need according to Federal Methodology, of whom 99% were aided. *Financial aid deadline (priority):* 3/1. *Financial aid forms:* FAFSA, institutional form required. State form required for some. *Admission application deadline:* rolling.

Summary of Aid to Needy Students *From gift & self-help combined:* Average need met: 75%. Average amount awarded: $9582 (62% gift aid, 38% self-help). *Gift aid:* Total: $3,507,097 (65% from college's own funds, 18% from other college-administered sources, 17% from external sources). 225 Federal Work-Study jobs (averaging $900); 180 part-time jobs.

Need-Based Scholarships & Grants Pell, FSEOG, state, private, college/university.

Loans Perkins, PLUS, Stafford, Unsubsidized Stafford, college/university long-term loans ($700 average).

Non-Need Awards *Academic Interests/Achievement Awards:* ($1,164,399 total): general academic, biological sciences, business, communication, computer science, education, English, humanities, international studies, mathematics, physical sciences, religion/biblical studies, social sciences. *Creative Arts/Performance Awards:* 172 ($106,115 total): art/fine arts, journalism/publications, music, theater/drama. *Special Achievements/Activities Awards:* 12 ($4750 total): cheerleading/drum major, religious involvement. *Special Characteristics Awards:* ($279,010 total): children of faculty/staff, international students, members of minorities, out-of-state students, relatives of clergy. *Athletic:* Total: 310 ($413,978); Men: 230 ($315,714); Women: 80 ($98,264).

Other Money-Saving Options Accelerated degree, cooperative Army ROTC, off-campus living (after junior year). *Payment Plan:* installment. *Waivers:* full or partial for employees or children of employees and senior citizens.

Contact Mrs. Jeanne Mott, Financial Aid Director, Baker University, PO Box 65, Baldwin City, KS 66006-0065, 913-594-6451 Ext. 595, fax: 913-594-8358.

BALDWIN-WALLACE COLLEGE
Berea, Ohio

About the Institution Independent/religious, coed. Degrees awarded: B, M. Offers 70 undergraduate majors. Total enrollment: 4,621. Undergraduates: 4,028 (93% state residents). Freshmen: 634.

Undergraduate Expenses (1997–98) Comprehensive fee of $18,156 includes tuition ($13,275) and college room and board ($4881). College room only: $2415.

Applications Of all full-time undergraduates enrolled in fall 1996, 95% of those who applied for aid were judged to have need according to Federal Methodology, of whom 100% were aided. *Financial aid deadline (priority):* 5/1. *Financial aid forms:* FAFSA, state form, institutional form required; CSS Financial Aid PROFILE acceptable. *Admission application deadline:* rolling.

Summary of Aid to Needy Students *From gift & self-help combined:* Average need met: 98%. Average amount awarded: $8952 (54% gift aid, 46% self-help). *Gift aid:* Total: $9,409,452 (54% from college's own funds, 5% from other college-administered sources, 41% from external sources). 1,618 Federal Work-Study jobs (averaging $1436).

Need-Based Scholarships & Grants Pell, FSEOG, state, private, college/university.

Loans Perkins, PLUS, Stafford, Unsubsidized Stafford, state, private, college/university long-term loans ($1800 average).

Non-Need Awards In 1996, a total of 2,119 non-need awards were made. *Academic Interests/Achievement Awards:* 1,342 ($3,511,946 total): general academic. *Creative Arts/Performance Awards:* 105 ($219,100 total): music. *Special Achievements/Activities Awards:* 633 ($1,223,995 total): leadership. *Special Characteristics Awards:* 39 ($221,469 total): members of minorities.

Other Money-Saving Options Accelerated degree, cooperative Army ROTC, cooperative Air Force ROTC, off-campus living (after freshman year). *Payment Plans:* installment, deferred payment. *Waivers:* full or partial for employees or children of employees.

Contact Dr. George L. Rolleston, Director of Financial Aid, Baldwin-Wallace College, Berea, OH 44017-2088, 216-826-2108.

BALL STATE UNIVERSITY
Muncie, Indiana

About the Institution State-supported, coed. Degrees awarded: A, B, M, D. Offers 128 undergraduate majors. Total enrollment: 18,594. Undergraduates: 16,558 (92% state residents). Freshmen: 3,711.

Undergraduate Expenses (1997–98) State resident tuition: $3316. Nonresident tuition: $8872. Mandatory fees: $98. College room and board: $4120.

Applications Of all full-time undergraduates enrolled in fall 1996, 78% of those who applied for aid were judged to have need according to Federal Methodology, of whom 99% were aided. *Financial aid deadline (priority):* 3/1. *Financial aid forms:* FAFSA required. *Admission application deadline:* rolling.

Summary of Aid to Needy Students *From gift & self-help combined:* Average need met: 80%. Average amount awarded: $5196 (42% gift aid, 58% self-help). *Gift aid:* Total: $17,137,995 (16% from college's own funds, 7% from other college-administered sources, 77% from external sources). 492 Federal Work-Study jobs (averaging $1200); 7,000 part-time jobs.

Need-Based Scholarships & Grants Pell, FSEOG, state, private, college/university.

Loans Perkins, PLUS, Stafford, Unsubsidized Stafford, private, college/university short-term loans ($700 average).

Non-Need Awards In 1996, a total of 3,025 non-need awards were made. *Academic Interests/Achievement Awards:* 2,232 ($3,724,337 total): general academic, architecture, biological sciences, business, communication, education, English, foreign languages, health fields, mathematics, social sciences. *Creative Arts/Performance Awards:* 225 ($161,986 total): general creative, art/fine arts, dance, journalism/publications, music, theater/drama. *Special Achievements/Activities Awards:* 37 ($82,820 total): leadership. *Special Characteristics Awards:* 235 ($346,418 total): children of faculty/staff. *Athletic:* Total: 296 ($2,039,123); Men: 184 ($1,295,682); Women: 112 ($743,441).

Other Money-Saving Options Accelerated degree, co-op program, Army ROTC, off-campus living (after freshman year). *Payment Plan:* installment. *Waivers:* full or partial for children of employees and senior citizens.

Contact Dr. Clarence L. Casazza, Director of Scholarships and Financial Aid, Ball State University, Ball State University Financial Aid Office, Muncie, IN 47306-1099, 317-285-8924, fax: 317-285-2173.

BALTIMORE HEBREW UNIVERSITY
Baltimore, Maryland

About the Institution Independent, coed. Degrees awarded: A, B, M, D. Offers 14 undergraduate majors. Total enrollment: 334. Undergraduates: 236 (96% state residents). Freshmen: 83.

Undergraduate Expenses (1996–97) Tuition: $3600. Mandatory fees: $20.

Applications 100% of all full-time undergraduates enrolled in fall 1996 applied for aid; of these,100% were judged to have need according to Federal Methodology, of whom 100% were aided. *Financial aid deadline:* continuous. *Financial aid forms:* FAFSA, institutional form required. *Admission application deadline:* rolling.

Need-Based Scholarships & Grants Pell, state, private, college/university.

Loans PLUS, Stafford, Unsubsidized Stafford.

Non-Need Awards Not offered.

Other Money-Saving Options Accelerated degree. *Payment Plan:* installment. *Waivers:* full or partial for employees or children of employees and senior citizens.

Contact Ms. Alexandra Kremenchugskaya, Financial Aid Counselor, Baltimore Hebrew University, 5800 Park Heights Avenue, Baltimore, MD 21215-3996, 410-578-6913.

BAPTIST BIBLE COLLEGE
Springfield, Missouri

About the Institution Independent/religious, coed. Degrees awarded: A, B, M. Offers 8 undergraduate majors. Total enrollment: 893. Undergraduates: 848 (5% state residents). Freshmen: 319.

Undergraduate Expenses (1997–98) Comprehensive fee of $5742 includes tuition ($2528 minimum) and college room and board ($3214).

Applications *Financial aid deadline:* continuous. *Financial aid forms:* FAFSA required. *Admission application deadline:* rolling.

Summary of Aid to Needy Students Part-time jobs.

Non-Need Awards available.

Another Money-Saving Option Cooperative Army ROTC.

Contact Office of Financial Aid, Baptist Bible College, Springfield, MO 65803-3498, 417-268-6060.

BAPTIST BIBLE COLLEGE OF PENNSYLVANIA
Clarks Summit, Pennsylvania

About the Institution Independent/religious, coed. Degrees awarded: A, B, M, D. Offers 14 undergraduate majors. Total enrollment: 820. Undergraduates: 540 (37% state residents). Freshmen: 192.

Undergraduate Expenses (1997–98 estimated) Comprehensive fee of $11,842 includes tuition ($6750), mandatory fees ($780), and college room and board ($4312). College room only: $1790.

Applications *Financial aid deadline (priority):* 5/1. *Financial aid forms:* FAFSA required; state form, institutional form acceptable. *Admission application deadline:* rolling.

Summary of Aid to Needy Students *Gift aid:* Total: $518,500 (4% from college's own funds, 44% from other college-administered sources, 52% from external sources). Part-time jobs.

Need-Based Scholarships & Grants Pell, state, college/university.

Loans PLUS, Stafford, Unsubsidized Stafford, private.

Non-Need Awards *Academic Interests/Achievement Awards:* general academic, education, religion/biblical studies. *Creative Arts/Performance Awards:* music. *Special Achievements/Activities Awards:* leadership,

religious involvement. *Special Characteristics Awards:* general special characteristics, children and siblings of alumni, married students, relatives of clergy.

Other Money-Saving Options Cooperative Army ROTC. *Payment Plan:* installment. *Waivers:* full or partial for employees or children of employees.

Contact Mr. Thomas Pollock, Director of Student Financial Services, Baptist Bible College of Pennsylvania, 538 Venard Road, Clarks Summit, PA 18411-1297, 717-587-1172 Ext. 205.

BAPTIST MISSIONARY ASSOCIATION THEOLOGICAL SEMINARY
Jacksonville, Texas

About the Institution Independent/religious, primarily men. Degrees awarded: A, B, M. Offers 1 undergraduate major. Total enrollment: 61. Undergraduates: 30 (73% state residents). Freshmen: 7.

Undergraduate Expenses (1997–98) Tuition: $1920. Mandatory fees: $60. College room only: $1980 (minimum).

Applications 83% of all full-time undergraduates enrolled in fall 1996 applied for aid; of these,100% were judged to have need according to Federal Methodology, of whom 100% were aided. *Financial aid deadline (priority):* 8/1. *Financial aid forms:* FAFSA, institutional form required. *Admission application deadline:* 7/17.

Summary of Aid to Needy Students *From gift & self-help combined:* Average need met: 25%. Average amount awarded: $2126 (53% gift aid, 47% self-help). *Gift aid:* Total: $5590 (100% from external sources). 2 part-time jobs.

Need-Based Scholarships & Grants Pell, private.

Loans Stafford, Unsubsidized Stafford.

Non-Need Awards Not offered.

Other Money-Saving Options Off-campus living. *Payment Plan:* installment. *Waivers:* full or partial for employees or children of employees.

Contact Dr. W. K. Benningfield, Dean/Registrar, Baptist Missionary Association Theological Seminary, 1530 East Pine Street, Jacksonville, TX 75766-5407, 903-586-2501, fax: 903-586-0378.

BARAT COLLEGE
Lake Forest, Illinois

About the Institution Independent/religious, coed. Degrees awarded: B. Offers 51 undergraduate majors. Total enrollment: 757 (43% state residents). Freshmen: 128.

Undergraduate Expenses (1997–98) Comprehensive fee of $17,536 includes tuition ($12,570) and college room and board ($4966).

Applications *Financial aid deadline (priority):* 4/15. *Financial aid forms:* FAFSA, institutional form required; CSS Financial Aid PROFILE acceptable. State form, state income tax form required for some. *Admission application deadline:* rolling.

Summary of Aid to Needy Students *From gift & self-help combined:* Average need met: 97%. Average amount awarded: $9223 (62% gift aid, 38% self-help). *Gift aid:* Total: $2,810,340 (57% from college's own funds, 34% from other college-administered sources, 9% from external sources). 193 Federal Work-Study jobs (averaging $2000); 32 part-time jobs.

Need-Based Scholarships & Grants Pell, FSEOG, state, private, college/university.

Loans Perkins, PLUS, Stafford, Unsubsidized Stafford, college/university long-term loans ($2250 average).

Non-Need Awards In 1996, a total of 191 non-need awards were made. *Academic Interests/Achievement Awards:* 125 ($228,500 total): general academic, biological sciences, physical sciences. *Creative Arts/*

Performance Awards: 46 ($54,000 total): art/fine arts, dance, theater/drama. *Athletic:* Total: 20 ($70,000); Men: 13 ($50,000); Women: 7 ($20,000).

Other Money-Saving Options Accelerated degree, off-campus living. *Payment Plan:* deferred payment. *Waivers:* full or partial for employees or children of employees.

Contact Ms. Sharon L. Stang, Director of Student Financial Planning, Barat College, 700 East Westleigh Road, Lake Forest, IL 60045-3297, 847-234-3000 Ext. 5675, fax: 847-234-1084.

BARBER-SCOTIA COLLEGE
Concord, North Carolina

About the Institution Independent/religious, coed. Degrees awarded: B. Offers 24 undergraduate majors. Total enrollment: 435 (53% state residents). Freshmen: 166.

Undergraduate Expenses (1997–98) Comprehensive fee of $8814 includes tuition ($5394), mandatory fees ($200), and college room and board ($3220). College room only: $1654.

Applications Of all full-time undergraduates enrolled in fall 1996, 70% of those who applied for aid were judged to have need according to Federal Methodology, of whom 100% were aided. *Financial aid deadline (priority):* 8/31. *Financial aid forms:* FAFSA, CSS Financial Aid PROFILE, institutional form required. *Admission application deadline:* rolling.

Summary of Aid to Needy Students *From gift & self-help combined:* Average need met: 89%. Average amount awarded: $4233 (62% gift aid, 38% self-help). *Gift aid:* Total: $772,422 (25% from college's own funds, 35% from other college-administered sources, 40% from external sources). 180 Federal Work-Study jobs (averaging $500); 5 part-time jobs.

Need-Based Scholarships & Grants Pell, FSEOG, state, private, college/university.

Loans PLUS, Stafford, Unsubsidized Stafford.

Non-Need Awards In 1996, a total of 69 non-need awards were made. *Academic Interests/Achievement Awards:* 14 ($18,779 total): general academic. *Creative Arts/Performance Awards:* 8 ($8797 total): music. *Athletic:* Total: 47 ($107,557); Men: 28 ($58,360); Women: 19 ($49,197).

Other Money-Saving Options Co-op program, cooperative Army ROTC. *Payment Plan:* installment. *Waivers:* full or partial for employees or children of employees.

Contact Ms. Tangar Young, Financial Aid Assistant/Counselor, Barber-Scotia College, 145 Cabarrus Avenue, Concord, NC 28025-5187, 704-789-2909, fax: 704-789-2911.

BARCLAY COLLEGE
Haviland, Kansas

About the Institution Independent/religious, coed. Degrees awarded: A, B. Offers 7 undergraduate majors. Total enrollment: 106 (52% state residents). Freshmen: 29.

Undergraduate Expenses (1997–98) Comprehensive fee of $7900 includes tuition ($4400), mandatory fees ($600), and college room and board ($2900). College room only: $900.

Applications 89% of all full-time undergraduates enrolled in fall 1996 applied for aid; of these, 100% were judged to have need according to Federal Methodology, of whom 90% were aided. *Financial aid deadline (priority):* 4/1. *Financial aid forms:* FAFSA required; CSS Financial Aid PROFILE acceptable. State form, institutional form required for some. *Admission application deadline:* 9/1.

Summary of Aid to Needy Students *From gift & self-help combined:* Average need met: 84%. Average amount awarded: $7609 (39% gift aid, 61% self-help). *Gift aid:* Total: $239,081 (35% from college's own

funds, 7% from other college-administered sources, 58% from external sources). 17 Federal Work-Study jobs (averaging $500); 50 part-time jobs.

Need-Based Scholarships & Grants Pell, FSEOG, state, private, college/university.

Loans PLUS, Stafford, Unsubsidized Stafford.

Non-Need Awards In 1996, a total of 92 non-need awards were made. *Academic Interests/Achievement Awards:* 34 ($39,175 total): general academic. *Special Achievements/Activities Awards:* 4 ($2000 total): general special achievements/activities, leadership. *Special Characteristics Awards:* 54 ($25,522 total): children and siblings of alumni, international students, religious affiliation.

Other Money-Saving Options Accelerated degree. *Waivers:* full or partial for employees or children of employees.

Contact Mr. John Unruh, Financial Aid Director, Barclay College, 607 North Kingman, PO Box 288, Haviland, KS 67059-0288, 800-862-0226, fax: 316-862-5403.

BARD COLLEGE
Annandale-on-Hudson, New York

About the Institution Independent, coed. Degrees awarded: B, M. Offers 68 undergraduate majors. Total enrollment: 1,244. Undergraduates: 1,076 (24% state residents). Freshmen: 326.

Undergraduate Expenses (1997–98) Comprehensive fee of $29,032 includes tuition ($21,700), mandatory fees ($520), and college room and board ($6812). College room only: $3416.

Applications Of all full-time undergraduates enrolled in fall 1996, 94% of those who applied for aid were judged to have need according to Federal Methodology, of whom 100% were aided. *Financial aid deadline (priority):* 3/15. *Financial aid forms:* FAFSA, CSS Financial Aid PROFILE required. *Regular admission application deadline:* 1/31. Early action deadline: 12/1.

Summary of Aid to Needy Students *From gift & self-help combined:* Average need met: 88%. Average amount awarded: $19,199 (79% gift aid, 21% self-help). *Gift aid:* Total: $11,393,425 (88% from college's own funds, 3% from other college-administered sources, 9% from external sources). 400 Federal Work-Study jobs (averaging $1500); 36 part-time jobs.

Need-Based Scholarships & Grants Pell, FSEOG, state, private, college/university.

Loans Perkins, PLUS, Stafford, Unsubsidized Stafford, college and university loans from institutional funds (only to international students).

Non-Need Awards In 1996, a total of 40 non-need awards were made. *Academic Interests/Achievement Awards:* 40 ($734,573 total): general academic, biological sciences, physical sciences.

Other Money-Saving Options Accelerated degree, off-campus living (after freshman year). *Payment Plan:* installment. *Waivers:* full or partial for employees or children of employees.

Contact Mr. Gerald E. Kelly, Director of Financial Aid, Bard College, Annandale Road, Annandale-on-Hudson, NY 12504, 914-758-7525, fax: 914-758-7336.

BARNARD COLLEGE
New York, New York

About the Institution Independent, women. Degrees awarded: B. Offers 52 undergraduate majors. Total university enrollment: 19,000. Undergraduates: 2,294 (39% state residents). Freshmen: 576.

Undergraduate Expenses (1996–97) Comprehensive fee of $28,698 includes tuition ($19,576), mandatory fees ($748), and college room and board ($8374). College room only: $5228.

Applications 63% of all full-time undergraduates enrolled in fall 1996 applied for aid; of these, 83% were judged to have need according to Federal Methodology, of whom 100% were aided. *Financial aid deadline:* 2/1. *Financial aid forms:* FAFSA, CSS Financial Aid PROFILE, institutional form, business supplement and noncustodial parents' statement required. State form required for some. *Regular admission application deadline:* 1/15. Early decision deadline: 12/15.

Summary of Aid to Needy Students *From gift & self-help combined:* Average need met: 100%. Average amount awarded: $20,147 (74% gift aid, 26% self-help). *Gift aid:* Total: $17,655,480 (82% from college's own funds, 3% from other college-administered sources, 15% from external sources). 300 Federal Work-Study jobs (averaging $1160); 577 part-time jobs.

Need-Based Scholarships & Grants Pell, FSEOG, state, private, college/university.

Loans Perkins, PLUS, Stafford, Unsubsidized Stafford, state, private, college/university short-term loans ($120 average), college/university long-term loans ($2500 average).

Non-Need Awards Not offered.

Other Money-Saving Options Accelerated degree, off-campus living. *Payment Plans:* tuition prepayment, installment, deferred payment. *Waivers:* full or partial for employees or children of employees.

Contact Ms. SuzanneClair Guard, Director of Financial Aid, Barnard College, 3009 Broadway, New York, NY 10027-6598, 212-854-2154, fax: 212-854-7491.

BARRY UNIVERSITY
Miami Shores, Florida

About the Institution Independent/religious, coed. Degrees awarded: B, M, D. Offers 52 undergraduate majors. Total enrollment: 7,016. Undergraduates: 4,773. Freshmen: 270.

Undergraduate Expenses (1997–98) Comprehensive fee of $19,460 includes tuition ($13,290), mandatory fees ($260), and college room and board ($5910).

Applications 76% of all full-time undergraduates enrolled in fall 1996 applied for aid; of these, 70% were judged to have need according to Federal Methodology, of whom 98% were aided. *Financial aid deadline (priority):* 2/15. *Financial aid forms:* FAFSA, state form, institutional form required. *Admission application deadline:* rolling.

Summary of Aid to Needy Students *From gift & self-help combined:* Average need met: 100%. Average amount awarded: $16,087 (70% gift aid, 30% self-help). *Gift aid:* Total: $9,040,563 (64% from college's own funds, 24% from other college-administered sources, 12% from external sources). 490 Federal Work-Study jobs (averaging $971); 590 part-time jobs.

Need-Based Scholarships & Grants Pell, FSEOG, state, private, college/university.

Loans Perkins, PLUS, Stafford, Unsubsidized Stafford, private, college/university long-term loans ($1523 average).

Non-Need Awards In 1996, a total of 999 non-need awards were made. *Academic Interests/Achievement Awards:* 300 ($1,726,536 total): general academic, biological sciences, business, education, health fields. *Creative Arts/Performance Awards:* 2 ($2500 total): applied art and design, art/fine arts, theater/drama. *Special Achievements/Activities Awards:* 315 ($1,346,246 total): general special achievements/activities, community service, leadership, memberships, religious involvement. *Special Characteristics Awards:* 304 ($1,525,150 total): general special characteristics, adult students, children and siblings of alumni, children of faculty/staff, handicapped students, international students, members of minorities, religious affiliation, siblings of current students. *Athletic:* Total: 78 ($460,871); Men: 35 ($196,823); Women: 43 ($264,048).

Other Money-Saving Options Accelerated degree, cooperative Air Force ROTC, off-campus living (after freshman year). *Payment Plan:* installment. *Waivers:* full or partial for employees or children of employees.

Contact Mr. Dart Humeston, Associate Director of Financial Aid, Barry University, 11300 Northeast Second Avenue, Miami Shores, FL 33161-6695, 305-899-3673, fax: 305-899-3104.

BARTLESVILLE WESLEYAN COLLEGE
Bartlesville, Oklahoma

About the Institution Independent/religious, coed. Degrees awarded: A, B. Offers 35 undergraduate majors. Total enrollment: 571 (58% state residents). Freshmen: 84.

Undergraduate Expenses (1997–98) Comprehensive fee of $11,800 includes tuition ($7800), mandatory fees ($300), and college room and board ($3700). College room only: $1800.

Applications 75% of all full-time undergraduates enrolled in fall 1996 applied for aid; of these, 94% were judged to have need according to Federal Methodology, of whom 100% were aided. *Financial aid deadline (priority):* 3/1. *Financial aid forms:* FAFSA, state form, institutional form required; CSS Financial Aid PROFILE acceptable. *Admission application deadline:* rolling.

Summary of Aid to Needy Students *From gift & self-help combined:* Average amount awarded: $14,194 (37% gift aid, 63% self-help). *Gift aid:* Total: $1,405,492 (58% from college's own funds, 6% from other college-administered sources, 36% from external sources). Federal Work-Study jobs; 30 part-time jobs.

Need-Based Scholarships & Grants Pell, FSEOG, state.

Loans Perkins, PLUS, Stafford, Unsubsidized Stafford.

Non-Need Awards In 1996, a total of 374 non-need awards were made. *Academic Interests/Achievement Awards:* 106 ($234,440 total): general academic. *Creative Arts/Performance Awards:* 8 ($5225 total): debating, music, performing arts, theater/drama. *Special Achievements/ Activities Awards:* 11 ($4966 total): religious involvement. *Special Characteristics Awards:* 179 ($250,390 total): children and siblings of alumni, children of faculty/staff, relatives of clergy, religious affiliation, siblings of current students. *Athletic:* Total: 70 ($114,600); Men: 37 ($58,700); Women: 33 ($55,900).

Other Money-Saving Options *Payment Plans:* installment, deferred payment. *Waivers:* full or partial for employees or children of employees and senior citizens.

Contact Ms. Carrie Thomas, Financial Aid Counselor, Bartlesville Wesleyan College, 2201 Silver Lake Road, Bartlesville, OK 74006-6299, 918-335-6282.

BARTON COLLEGE
Wilson, North Carolina

About the Institution Independent/religious, coed. Degrees awarded: B. Offers 50 undergraduate majors. Total enrollment: 1,295 (76% state residents). Freshmen: 249.

Undergraduate Expenses (1997–98) Comprehensive fee of $13,050 includes tuition ($8342), mandatory fees ($642), and college room and board ($4066). College room only: $2176.

Applications Of all full-time undergraduates enrolled in fall 1996, 95% of those judged to have need according to Federal Methodology were aided. *Financial aid deadline (priority):* 6/1. *Financial aid forms:* FAFSA, institutional form required; CSS Financial Aid PROFILE acceptable. State form required for some. *Admission application deadline:* rolling.

Summary of Aid to Needy Students *From gift & self-help combined:* Average need met: 83%. Average amount awarded: $7609 (33% gift aid, 67% self-help). *Gift aid:* Total: $1,460,934 (23% from college's

own funds, 40% from other college-administered sources, 37% from external sources). 433 Federal Work-Study jobs (averaging $978).

Need-Based Scholarships & Grants Pell, FSEOG, state, college/university.

Loans Perkins, PLUS, Stafford, Unsubsidized Stafford.

Non-Need Awards In 1996, a total of 1,996 non-need awards were made. *Academic Interests/Achievement Awards:* 385 ($483,945 total): general academic, biological sciences, business, communication, computer science, education, English, foreign languages, health fields, humanities, international studies, mathematics, physical sciences, religion/biblical studies, social sciences. *Creative Arts/Performance Awards:* 25 ($16,826 total): art/fine arts, music, theater/drama. *Special Achievements/Activities Awards:* 151 ($155,102 total): leadership, religious involvement. *Special Characteristics Awards:* 1,306 ($1,230,221 total): children of faculty/staff, children of union members/company employees, handicapped students, international students, local/state students, members of minorities, relatives of clergy, religious affiliation, veterans. *Athletic:* Total: 129 ($429,656); Men: 66 ($238,373); Women: 63 ($191,283).

Other Money-Saving Options Accelerated degree, off-campus living (after sophomore year). *Payment Plan:* installment. *Waivers:* full or partial for employees or children of employees and adult students.

Contact Mrs. Miriam Landing, Director of Financial Aid, Barton College, 5385 College Station, Wilson, NC 27893, 919-399-6316, fax: 919-237-1620.

BARUCH COLLEGE OF THE CITY UNIVERSITY OF NEW YORK
New York, New York

About the Institution State & locally supported, coed. Degrees awarded: B, M, D. Offers 40 undergraduate majors. Total enrollment: 15,223. Undergraduates: 12,854 (90% state residents). Freshmen: 1,449.

Undergraduate Expenses (1996–97) State resident tuition: $3200. Nonresident tuition: $6800. Mandatory fees: $120.

Applications 93% of all full-time undergraduates enrolled in fall 1996 applied for aid; of these, 93% were judged to have need according to Federal Methodology, of whom 89% were aided. *Financial aid deadline (priority):* 5/1. *Financial aid forms:* FAFSA, state form required. *Admission application deadline:* 6/15.

Summary of Aid to Needy Students *From gift & self-help combined:* Average need met: 65%. Average amount awarded: $5358 (81% gift aid, 19% self-help). *Gift aid:* Total: $26,875,286 (2% from college's own funds, 60% from other college-administered sources, 38% from external sources). 520 Federal Work-Study jobs; 610 part-time jobs.

Need-Based Scholarships & Grants Pell, FSEOG, state, college/university.

Loans Perkins, PLUS, Stafford, Unsubsidized Stafford.

Non-Need Awards *Academic Interests/Achievement Awards:* general academic.

Other Money-Saving Options *Waivers:* full or partial for employees or children of employees and senior citizens.

Contact Financial Aid Office, Baruch College of the City University of New York, 151 East 25th Street, Room 720, New York, NY 10010-5585, 212-802-2240.

BASSIST COLLEGE
Portland, Oregon

About the Institution Proprietary, coed. Degrees awarded: A, B. Offers 4 undergraduate majors. Total enrollment: 101 (64% state residents). Freshmen: 61.

Undergraduate Expenses (1996–97) Tuition: $8900. Mandatory fees: $90. College room only: $2775.

Applications 72% of all full-time undergraduates enrolled in fall 1996 applied for aid; of these, 90% were judged to have need according to Federal Methodology, of whom 100% were aided. *Financial aid deadline (priority):* 6/1. *Financial aid forms:* FAFSA, institutional form, financial aid transcript (for transfers) required. *Admission application deadline:* 9/1.

Summary of Aid to Needy Students *From gift & self-help combined:* Average need met: 75%. Average amount awarded: $7020 (9% gift aid, 91% self-help). *Gift aid:* Total: $35,668 (38% from college's own funds, 17% from other college-administered sources, 45% from external sources). 20 part-time jobs.

Need-Based Scholarships & Grants Pell, FSEOG, state, private.

Loans Perkins, PLUS, Stafford, Unsubsidized Stafford.

Non-Need Awards In 1996, a total of 23 non-need awards were made. *Academic Interests/Achievement Awards:* 23 ($13,697 total): general academic, English.

Other Money-Saving Options Accelerated degree, off-campus living. *Payment Plans:* guaranteed tuition, installment, deferred payment. *Waivers:* full or partial for employees or children of employees.

Contact Ms. Holly Havens, Director of Financial Aid, Bassist College, 2000 Southwest Fifth Avenue, Portland, OR 97201-4907, 503-228-6528 Ext. 102, fax: 503-228-4227.

BATES COLLEGE
Lewiston, Maine

About the Institution Independent, coed. Degrees awarded: B. Offers 31 undergraduate majors. Total enrollment: 1,672 (12% state residents). Freshmen: 534.

Undergraduate Expenses (1997–98) Comprehensive fee: $28,650.

Applications 56% of all full-time undergraduates enrolled in fall 1996 applied for aid; of these, 85% were judged to have need according to Federal Methodology, of whom 100% were aided. *Financial aid deadline:* 1/15. *Financial aid forms:* FAFSA, CSS Financial Aid PROFILE required. State form, Divorced/Separated Parents' Statement, Business/Farm Supplement required for some. *Regular admission application deadline:* 1/15. Early decision deadline: 1/1.

Summary of Aid to Needy Students *From gift & self-help combined:* Average need met: 100%. Average amount awarded: $16,959 (71% gift aid, 29% self-help). *Gift aid:* Total: $9,722,615 (92% from college's own funds, 5% from other college-administered sources, 3% from external sources). 736 Federal Work-Study jobs (averaging $1365); 200 part-time jobs.

Need-Based Scholarships & Grants Pell, FSEOG, state, private, college/university.

Loans Perkins, PLUS, Stafford, Unsubsidized Stafford, state, private, college/university long-term loans ($1411 average).

Non-Need Awards Not offered.

Other Money-Saving Options Accelerated degree, off-campus living (after freshman year). *Payment Plan:* installment.

Contact Office of Financial Aid, Bates College, Lindholm House, 23 Campus Avenue, Lewiston, ME 04240-6028, 207-786-6255.

BAYAMÓN CENTRAL UNIVERSITY
Bayamón, Puerto Rico

About the Institution Independent/religious, coed. Degrees awarded: A, B, M. Offers 24 undergraduate majors. Total enrollment: 3,144. Undergraduates: 2,864 (99% commonwealth residents). Freshmen: 581.

Undergraduate Expenses (1996–97) Tuition: $3130. Mandatory fees: $100.

Applications *Financial aid deadline (priority): 4/15. Financial aid forms:* FAFSA, CSS Financial Aid PROFILE, commonwealth form, institutional form required. *Admission application deadline: 4/15.*

Summary of Aid to Needy Students *From gift & self-help combined:* Average need met: 75%. *Gift aid:* Total: $3,178,170 (3% from college's own funds, 10% from other college-administered sources, 87% from external sources). 1,200 Federal Work-Study jobs (averaging $800).

Need-Based Scholarships & Grants Pell, FSEOG, state, college/university.

Loans Stafford, Unsubsidized Stafford.

Non-Need Awards *Athletic:* Total: ($83,648); Men: ($58,553); Women: ($25,095).

Other Money-Saving Options Accelerated degree, cooperative Army ROTC, cooperative Air Force ROTC.

Contact Mr. Henry Miranda Vázquez, Financial Aid Director, Bayamón Central University, PO Box 1725, Bayamón, PR 00960-1725, 787-786-3030 Ext. 2115, fax: 787-740-2200.

BAYAMÓN TECHNOLOGICAL UNIVERSITY COLLEGE
Bayamón, Puerto Rico

About the Institution Commonwealth-supported, coed. Degrees awarded: A, B. Offers 25 undergraduate majors.

Applications *Financial aid deadline (priority): 5/1. Financial aid forms:* FAFSA, institutional form, state income tax form required. *Admission application deadline: 12/15.*

Summary of Aid to Needy Students Federal Work-Study jobs.

Non-Need Awards *Academic Interests/Achievement Awards:* general academic. *Creative Arts/Performance Awards:* music, theater/drama. *Athletic:* available.

Other Money-Saving Options Co-op program, Army ROTC, cooperative Air Force ROTC.

Contact Office of Financial Aid, Bayamón Technological University College, Bayamón, PR 00959-1919, 787-786-2885.

BAYLOR UNIVERSITY
Waco, Texas

About the Institution Independent/religious, coed. Degrees awarded: B, M, D, P. Offers 113 undergraduate majors. Total enrollment: 12,391. Undergraduates: 10,500 (78% state residents). Freshmen: 2,476.

Undergraduate Expenses (1997–98) Comprehensive fee of $13,861 includes tuition ($8640), mandatory fees ($788), and college room and board ($4433). College room only: $1900.

Applications 73% of all full-time undergraduates enrolled in fall 1996 applied for aid; of these, 61% were judged to have need according to Federal Methodology, of whom 83% were aided. *Financial aid deadline (priority): 3/1. Financial aid forms:* FAFSA, institutional form required. *Admission application deadline:* rolling.

Summary of Aid to Needy Students *From gift & self-help combined:* Average need met: 71%. Average amount awarded: $9221 (46% gift aid, 54% self-help). *Gift aid:* Total: $15,928,721 (43% from college's own funds, 28% from other college-administered sources, 29% from external sources). 1,351 Federal Work-Study jobs; 653 part-time jobs.

Need-Based Scholarships & Grants Pell, FSEOG, state, private, college/university.

Loans Perkins, PLUS, Stafford, Unsubsidized Stafford, Federal Nursing, state, private, college/university long-term loans ($1100 average).

Non-Need Awards In 1996, a total of 2,133 non-need awards were made. *Academic Interests/Achievement Awards:* 1,287 ($3,150,272 total). *Creative Arts/Performance Awards:* 288 ($745,808 total): music, theater/drama. *Special Achievements/Activities Awards:* 23 ($65,400 total): community service, leadership, religious involvement. *Special Characteristics Awards:* 223 ($1,507,287 total): children of faculty/staff, ROTC participants. *Athletic:* Total: 312 ($3,077,117); Men: 202 ($2,020,703); Women: 110 ($1,056,414).

Other Money-Saving Options Accelerated degree, Air Force ROTC, off-campus living. *Payment Plan:* guaranteed tuition. *Waivers:* full or partial for employees or children of employees.

Contact Office of Financial Aid, Baylor University, PO Box 97028, Waco, TX 76798-7028, 817-755-1011.

BAY PATH COLLEGE
Longmeadow, Massachusetts

About the Institution Independent, women. Degrees awarded: A, B. Offers 19 undergraduate majors. Total enrollment: 608 (54% state residents). Freshmen: 109.

Undergraduate Expenses (1997–98) Comprehensive fee of $17,660 includes tuition ($11,800) and college room and board ($5860 minimum).

Applications 91% of all full-time undergraduates enrolled in fall 1996 applied for aid; of these, 95% were judged to have need according to Federal Methodology, of whom 98% were aided. *Financial aid deadline (priority): 3/15. Financial aid forms:* FAFSA, institutional form required; CSS Financial Aid PROFILE acceptable. State form required for some. *Regular admission application deadline:* rolling. Early decision deadline: 11/15.

Summary of Aid to Needy Students *From gift & self-help combined:* Average need met: 88%. Average amount awarded: $10,050 (58% gift aid, 42% self-help). *Gift aid:* Total: $2,208,387 (70% from college's own funds, 14% from other college-administered sources, 16% from external sources). 149 Federal Work-Study jobs (averaging $1222); 14 part-time jobs.

Need-Based Scholarships & Grants Pell, FSEOG, state, private, college/university.

Loans Perkins, PLUS, Stafford, Unsubsidized Stafford, state, private.

Non-Need Awards In 1996, a total of 311 non-need awards were made. *Academic Interests/Achievement Awards:* 171 ($585,825 total): general academic. *Creative Arts/Performance Awards:* 0: dance, performing arts, theater/drama. *Special Achievements/Activities Awards:* 38 ($34,000 total): general special achievements/activities. *Special Characteristics Awards:* 102 ($94,435 total): general special characteristics, adult students, children of faculty/staff, children of public servants, children with a deceased or disabled parent, international students, out-of-state students, siblings of current students, twins.

Other Money-Saving Options Cooperative Army ROTC, off-campus living (after sophomore year). *Payment Plans:* installment, deferred payment. *Waivers:* full or partial for employees or children of employees and senior citizens.

Contact Ms. Caroline Brown, Assistant Director of Financial Aid, Bay Path College, 588 Longmeadow Street, Longmeadow, MA 01106-2292, 413-567-0621 Ext. 261, fax: 413-567-0753.

BEAVER COLLEGE
Glenside, Pennsylvania

About the Institution Independent/religious, coed. Degrees awarded: B, M. Offers 49 undergraduate majors. Total enrollment: 2,567. Undergraduates: 1,637 (60% state residents). Freshmen: 274.

Undergraduate Expenses (1997–98) Comprehensive fee of $22,360 includes tuition ($15,560), mandatory fees ($280), and college room and board ($6520).

Applications Of all full-time undergraduates enrolled in fall 1996, 87% of those who applied for aid were judged to have need according to Federal Methodology, of whom 100% were aided. *Financial aid deadline (priority):* 3/1. *Financial aid forms:* FAFSA, institutional form required; CSS Financial Aid PROFILE acceptable. State form required for some. *Regular admission application deadline:* rolling. Early decision deadline: 11/1.

Summary of Aid to Needy Students *From gift & self-help combined:* Average need met: 95%. Average amount awarded: $14,813 (64% gift aid, 36% self-help). *Gift aid:* Total: $8,901,077 (67% from college's own funds, 17% from other college-administered sources, 16% from external sources). 698 Federal Work-Study jobs (averaging $1124); 66 part-time jobs.

Need-Based Scholarships & Grants Pell, state, private, college/ university.

Loans Perkins, PLUS, Stafford, Unsubsidized Stafford, college/university long-term loans ($1791 average).

Non-Need Awards In 1996, a total of 741 non-need awards were made. *Academic Interests/Achievement Awards:* 428 ($1,944,300 total): general academic, communication, English, mathematics. *Creative Arts/ Performance Awards:* 41 ($82,500 total): art/fine arts. *Special Achievements/Activities Awards:* 272 ($586,550 total): community service, leadership.

Other Money-Saving Options Accelerated degree, co-op program, cooperative Army ROTC, off-campus living. *Payment Plans:* installment, deferred payment. *Waivers:* full or partial for employees or children of employees.

Contact Ms. Elizabeth Rihl, Associate Director of Enrollment Management, Beaver College, 450 South Easton Road, Glenside, PA 19038-3295, 215-572-2956, fax: 215-572-4049.

BECKER COLLEGE–LEICESTER CAMPUS
Leicester, Massachusetts

About the Institution Independent, coed. Degrees awarded: A, B. Offers 31 undergraduate majors. Total enrollment: 378 (60% state residents). Freshmen: 187.

Undergraduate Expenses (1997–98) Comprehensive fee of $15,020 includes tuition ($9940), mandatory fees ($190), and college room and board ($4890).

Applications *Financial aid deadline (priority):* 4/1. *Financial aid forms:* FAFSA, institutional form required. *Admission application deadline:* rolling.

Summary of Aid to Needy Students *From gift & self-help combined:* Average need met: 67%. Average amount awarded: $7251 (45% gift aid, 55% self-help). *Gift aid:* Total: $2,519,312 (26% from college's own funds, 23% from other college-administered sources, 51% from external sources). 348 Federal Work-Study jobs (averaging $859); part-time jobs.

Need-Based Scholarships & Grants Pell, FSEOG, state, private, college/ university.

Loans Perkins, PLUS, Stafford, Unsubsidized Stafford, state, private.

Non-Need Awards *Academic Interests/Achievement Awards:* 8 ($12,500 total): general academic. *Special Achievements/Activities Awards:* general special achievements/activities, leadership. *Special Characteristics Awards:* 17 ($170,659 total): children of educators, children of faculty/ staff, siblings of current students, spouses of current students, twins. *Athletic:* Total: 93 ($71,550); Men: 51 ($39,300); Women: 42 ($32,250).

Other Money-Saving Options Co-op program, cooperative Army ROTC, cooperative Naval ROTC, cooperative Air Force ROTC, off-campus

living (after sophomore year). *Payment Plan:* installment. *Waivers:* full or partial for employees or children of employees and senior citizens.

Contact Ms. Pam Prizio, Financial Aid Counselor, Becker College–Leicester Campus, 3 Paxton Street, Leicester, MA 01524-1197, 508-791-9241, fax: 508-892-0330.

BECKER COLLEGE–WORCESTER CAMPUS
Worcester, Massachusetts

About the Institution Independent, coed. Degrees awarded: A, B. Offers 32 undergraduate majors. Total enrollment: 905 (78% state residents). Freshmen: 354.

Undergraduate Expenses (1997–98) Comprehensive fee of $15,020 includes tuition ($9940 minimum), mandatory fees ($190), and college room and board ($4890).

Applications 95% of all full-time undergraduates enrolled in fall 1996 applied for aid; of these, 92% were judged to have need according to Federal Methodology, of whom 100% were aided. *Financial aid deadline (priority):* 4/1. *Financial aid forms:* FAFSA, institutional form required. *Admission application deadline:* rolling.

Summary of Aid to Needy Students *From gift & self-help combined:* Average need met: 60%. Average amount awarded: $6015 (41% gift aid, 59% self-help). *Gift aid:* Total: $1,139,361. 264 Federal Work-Study jobs (averaging $604); part-time jobs.

Need-Based Scholarships & Grants Pell, FSEOG, state, private, college/ university.

Loans Perkins, PLUS, Stafford, Unsubsidized Stafford, state, private.

Non-Need Awards In 1996, a total of 131 non-need awards were made. *Academic Interests/Achievement Awards:* 8 ($12,500 total): general academic. *Special Achievements/Activities Awards:* 4 ($4500 total): leadership. *Special Characteristics Awards:* 17 ($170,659 total): children of current students, children of faculty/staff, parents of current students, siblings of current students, spouses of current students, twins. *Athletic:* Total: 102 ($88,000); Men: 41 ($44,000); Women: 61 ($44,000).

Other Money-Saving Options Co-op program, cooperative Army ROTC, cooperative Naval ROTC, cooperative Air Force ROTC, off-campus living (after sophomore year). *Payment Plan:* installment. *Waivers:* full or partial for employees or children of employees and senior citizens.

Contact Ms. Lisa Flynn, Director of Financial Aid, Becker College–Worcester Campus, 61 Sever Street, PO Box 15071, Worcester, MA 01615-0071, 508-791-9241 Ext. 242, fax: 508-890-1500.

BELHAVEN COLLEGE
Jackson, Mississippi

About the Institution Independent/religious, coed. Degrees awarded: B, M. Offers 21 undergraduate majors. Total enrollment: 1,256. Undergraduates: 1,208 (85% state residents). Freshmen: 85.

Undergraduate Expenses (1996–97) Comprehensive fee of $12,750 includes tuition ($8990), mandatory fees ($380), and college room and board ($3380).

Applications 91% of all full-time undergraduates enrolled in fall 1996 applied for aid; of these, 87% were judged to have need according to Federal Methodology, of whom 100% were aided. *Financial aid deadline (priority):* 4/1. *Financial aid forms:* FAFSA, institutional form required. State form required for some. *Admission application deadline:* rolling.

Summary of Aid to Needy Students *From gift & self-help combined:* Average need met: 88%. Average amount awarded: $10,645 (44% gift aid, 56% self-help). *Gift aid:* Total: $3,426,132 (70% from college's own funds, 13% from other college-administered sources, 17% from external sources). 95 Federal Work-Study jobs (averaging $1360).

Need-Based Scholarships & Grants Pell, FSEOG, state, private, college/university.

Loans Perkins, PLUS, Stafford, Unsubsidized Stafford, college/university long-term loans ($1000 average).

Non-Need Awards *Academic Interests/Achievement Awards:* 680 ($2,400,000 total): general academic, religion/biblical studies. *Creative Arts/Performance Awards:* art/fine arts, dance, music. *Special Achievements/Activities Awards:* Junior Miss, leadership. *Special Characteristics Awards:* children of faculty/staff, international students, relatives of clergy, religious affiliation, veterans. *Athletic:* Total: 125 ($630,269); Men: 78 ($429,990); Women: 47 ($200,279).

Other Money-Saving Options Accelerated degree, off-campus living (after freshman year). *Payment Plan:* installment. *Waivers:* full or partial for employees or children of employees and senior citizens.

Contact Ms. Linda Phillips, Director of Financial Aid, Belhaven College, 1500 Peachtree Street, Jackson, MS 39202-1789, 601-968-5933.

BELLARMINE COLLEGE
Louisville, Kentucky

About the Institution Independent/religious, coed. Degrees awarded: B, M. Offers 37 undergraduate majors. Total enrollment: 2,180. Undergraduates: 1,764 (79% state residents). Freshmen: 329.

Undergraduate Expenses (1996–97) Comprehensive fee of $13,800 includes tuition ($10,200), mandatory fees ($120), and college room and board ($3480). College room only: $2180.

Applications Of all full-time undergraduates enrolled in fall 1996, 88% of those who applied for aid were judged to have need according to Federal Methodology, of whom 88% were aided. *Financial aid deadline (priority):* 3/15. *Financial aid forms:* FAFSA required. *Admission application deadline:* 8/1.

Summary of Aid to Needy Students *From gift & self-help combined:* Average need met: 80%. Average amount awarded: $7541 (61% gift aid, 39% self-help). *Gift aid:* Total: $3,262,307 (60% from college's own funds, 28% from other college-administered sources, 12% from external sources). 198 Federal Work-Study jobs (averaging $2250); 8 part-time jobs.

Need-Based Scholarships & Grants Pell, FSEOG, state, private, college/university.

Loans Perkins, PLUS, Stafford, Unsubsidized Stafford, private, college/university long-term loans ($1000 average).

Non-Need Awards In 1996, a total of 1,219 non-need awards were made. *Academic Interests/Achievement Awards:* 801 ($1,341,424 total): general academic, biological sciences, business. *Creative Arts/Performance Awards:* 40 ($11,425 total): art/fine arts, music. *Special Achievements/Activities Awards:* 127 ($73,950 total): cheerleading/drum major, community service, leadership, religious involvement. *Special Characteristics Awards:* 67 ($100,672 total): adult students, children of faculty/staff, ethnic background, international students, local/state students, out-of-state students, previous college experience, ROTC participants. *Athletic:* Total: 184 ($302,155); Men: 80 ($142,570); Women: 104 ($159,585).

Other Money-Saving Options Accelerated degree, cooperative Army ROTC, cooperative Air Force ROTC, off-campus living (after sophomore year). *Payment Plans:* installment, deferred payment. *Waivers:* full or partial for employees or children of employees and senior citizens.

Contact Mr. David R. Wuinee, Director of Financial Aid, Bellarmine College, 2001 Newburg Road, Louisville, KY 40205-0671, 502-452-8131, fax: 502-452-8002.

BELLEVUE UNIVERSITY
Bellevue, Nebraska

About the Institution Independent, coed. Degrees awarded: B, M. Offers 21 undergraduate majors. Total enrollment: 2,600. Undergraduates: 2,205 (88% state residents). Freshmen: 183.

Undergraduate Expenses (1997–98) Tuition: $3600. Mandatory fees: $50.

Applications 75% of all full-time undergraduates enrolled in fall 1996 applied for aid; of these,100% were judged to have need according to Federal Methodology, of whom 100% were aided. *Financial aid deadline:* Applications processed continuously. *Financial aid forms:* FAFSA, institutional form required. *Admission application deadline:* rolling.

Summary of Aid to Needy Students *From gift & self-help combined:* Average need met: 95%. *Gift aid:* Total: $1,386,580 (31% from college's own funds, 11% from other college-administered sources, 58% from external sources). 13 Federal Work-Study jobs (averaging $3500); 10 part-time jobs.

Need-Based Scholarships & Grants Pell, FSEOG, state, college/university.

Loans PLUS, Stafford, Unsubsidized Stafford.

Non-Need Awards In 1996, a total of 332 non-need awards were made. *Academic Interests/Achievement Awards:* 85 ($76,300 total): general academic, business, humanities, mathematics, social sciences. *Creative Arts/Performance Awards:* 3 ($4000 total): art/fine arts. *Special Achievements/Activities Awards:* 18 ($8800 total): leadership. *Special Characteristics Awards:* 124 ($107,500 total): general special characteristics. *Athletic:* Total: 102 ($121,500); Men: 65 ($67,500); Women: 37 ($54,000).

Other Money-Saving Options Accelerated degree, cooperative Army ROTC, cooperative Air Force ROTC. *Payment Plans:* installment, deferred payment. *Waivers:* full or partial for employees or children of employees.

Contact Office of Financial Aid, Bellevue University, 1000 Galvin Road South, Bellevue, NE 68005-3098, 402-291-8100.

BELLIN COLLEGE OF NURSING
Green Bay, Wisconsin

About the Institution Independent, primarily women. Degrees awarded: B. Offers 1 undergraduate major. Total enrollment: 194 (90% state residents). Freshmen: 23.

Undergraduate Expenses (1996–97) Tuition: $8025. Mandatory fees: $166.

Applications 55% of all full-time undergraduates enrolled in fall 1996 applied for aid; of these, 83% were judged to have need according to Federal Methodology, of whom 100% were aided. *Financial aid deadline (priority):* 3/1. *Financial aid forms:* FAFSA required. CSS Financial Aid PROFILE required for some. *Admission application deadline:* rolling.

Summary of Aid to Needy Students *From gift & self-help combined:* Average need met: 86%. Average amount awarded: $8917 (51% gift aid, 49% self-help). *Gift aid:* Total: $379,666 (42% from college's own funds, 21% from other college-administered sources, 37% from external sources). 6 Federal Work-Study jobs (averaging $1167).

Need-Based Scholarships & Grants Pell, FSEOG, state, private, college/university.

Loans PLUS, Stafford, Unsubsidized Stafford, college/university short-term loans, college/university long-term loans.

Non-Need Awards In 1996, a total of 16 non-need awards were made. *Academic Interests/Achievement Awards:* 16 ($15,124 total): general academic.

Other Money-Saving Options Cooperative Army ROTC. *Payment Plan:* installment.

Contact Ms. Lena C. Terry, Director of Financial Aid, Bellin College of Nursing, 725 South Webster Avenue, PO Box 23400, Green Bay, WI 54305-3400, 414-433-5801, fax: 414-433-7416.

BELMONT ABBEY COLLEGE
Belmont, North Carolina

About the Institution Independent/religious, coed. Degrees awarded: B, M. Offers 24 undergraduate majors. Total enrollment: 959. Undergraduates: 835 (59% state residents). Freshmen: 215.

Undergraduate Expenses (1997–98) Comprehensive fee of $16,700 includes tuition ($10,516), mandatory fees ($518), and college room and board ($5666).

Applications 85% of all full-time undergraduates enrolled in fall 1996 applied for aid; of these, 76% were judged to have need according to Federal Methodology, of whom 100% were aided. *Financial aid deadline (priority):* 4/1. *Financial aid forms:* FAFSA required. State form required for some. *Admission application deadline:* 8/15.

Summary of Aid to Needy Students *From gift & self-help combined:* Average need met: 56%. Average amount awarded: $6892 (59% gift aid, 41% self-help). *Gift aid:* Total: $1,876,382 (62% from college's own funds, 20% from other college-administered sources, 18% from external sources). 229 Federal Work-Study jobs (averaging $1600); 20 part-time jobs.

Need-Based Scholarships & Grants Pell, FSEOG, state, private, college/university.

Loans Perkins, PLUS, Stafford, Unsubsidized Stafford.

Non-Need Awards In 1996, a total of 382 non-need awards were made. *Academic Interests/Achievement Awards:* 168 ($606,872 total): general academic. *Special Characteristics Awards:* 93 ($175,176 total): international students, religious affiliation. *Athletic:* Total: 121 ($348,114); Men: 63 ($183,252); Women: 58 ($164,862).

Other Money-Saving Options Accelerated degree, cooperative Army ROTC, cooperative Air Force ROTC. *Payment Plan:* installment. *Waivers:* full or partial for employees or children of employees and senior citizens.

Contact Ms. Julie Hodge, Associate Director of Financial Aid, Belmont Abbey College, 100 Belmont Mt. Holly Road, Belmont, NC 28012, 704-825-6718, fax: 704-825-6882.

BELMONT UNIVERSITY
Nashville, Tennessee

About the Institution Independent/religious, coed. Degrees awarded: B, M. Offers 74 undergraduate majors. Total enrollment: 2,926. Undergraduates: 2,553 (62% state residents). Freshmen: 425.

Undergraduate Expenses (1997–98) Comprehensive fee of $14,190 includes tuition ($10,050), mandatory fees ($250), and college room and board ($3890 minimum). College room only: $1990.

Applications Of all full-time undergraduates enrolled in fall 1996, 72% of those who applied for aid were judged to have need according to Federal Methodology, of whom 98% were aided. *Financial aid deadline (priority):* 3/1. *Financial aid forms:* FAFSA, institutional form required; CSS Financial Aid PROFILE acceptable. State form required for some. *Admission application deadline:* 8/1.

Summary of Aid to Needy Students *From gift & self-help combined:* Average need met: 80%. Average amount awarded: $5393 (34% gift aid, 66% self-help). *Gift aid:* Total: $2,151,240. 80 Federal Work-Study jobs (averaging $1727); 294 part-time jobs.

Need-Based Scholarships & Grants Pell, FSEOG, state, private, college/university.

Loans Perkins, PLUS, Stafford, Unsubsidized Stafford, private, college/university short-term loans, college/university long-term loans ($1140 average).

Non-Need Awards *Academic Interests/Achievement Awards:* general academic. *Creative Arts/Performance Awards:* music. *Special Achievements/Activities Awards:* available. *Special Characteristics Awards:* children of faculty/staff. *Athletic:* Total: 148 ($798,259); Men: 100 ($434,395); Women: 48 ($363,864).

Other Money-Saving Options Accelerated degree, co-op program, cooperative Army ROTC, off-campus living (after sophomore year). *Payment Plans:* installment, deferred payment. *Waivers:* full or partial for employees or children of employees and senior citizens.

Contact Ms. Paula Gill, Director of Financial Aid, Belmont University, 1900 Belmont Boulevard, Nashville, TN 37212-3757, 615-460-6403.

BELOIT COLLEGE
Beloit, Wisconsin

About the Institution Independent, coed. Degrees awarded: B. Offers 55 undergraduate majors. Total enrollment: 1,273. Undergraduates: 1,271 (21% state residents). Freshmen: 295.

Undergraduate Expenses (1997–98) Comprehensive fee of $23,190 includes tuition ($18,850), mandatory fees ($200), and college room and board ($4140). College room only: $2010.

Applications 86% of all full-time undergraduates enrolled in fall 1996 applied for aid; of these, 78% were judged to have need according to Federal Methodology, of whom 100% were aided. *Financial aid deadline (priority):* 2/15. *Financial aid forms:* FAFSA, institutional form required; CSS Financial Aid PROFILE, state form acceptable. *Regular admission application deadline:* rolling. Early decision deadline: 12/1.

Summary of Aid to Needy Students *From gift & self-help combined:* Average need met: 100%. Average amount awarded: $16,257 (64% gift aid, 36% self-help). *Gift aid:* Total: $7,895,417 (86% from college's own funds, 7% from other college-administered sources, 7% from external sources). 462 Federal Work-Study jobs (averaging $1350); 365 part-time jobs.

Need-Based Scholarships & Grants Pell, FSEOG, state, private, college/university.

Loans Perkins, PLUS, Stafford, Unsubsidized Stafford, state, private, college/university short-term loans ($100 average), college/university long-term loans ($2161 average).

Non-Need Awards *Academic Interests/Achievement Awards:* general academic. *Creative Arts/Performance Awards:* music. *Special Achievements/Activities Awards:* general special achievements/activities. *Special Characteristics Awards:* members of minorities, siblings of current students.

Other Money-Saving Options Off-campus living (after junior year). *Payment Plan:* installment. *Waivers:* full or partial for employees or children of employees.

Contact Mr. Tom Kreiser, Director of International Admissions and Freshman Financial Aid, Beloit College, 700 College Street, Beloit, WI 53511-5596, 800-356-0751.

BEMIDJI STATE UNIVERSITY
Bemidji, Minnesota

About the Institution State-supported, coed. Degrees awarded: A, B, M. Offers 72 undergraduate majors. Total enrollment: 4,019. Undergraduates: 3,905 (88% state residents). Freshmen: 576.

Undergraduate Expenses (1996–97) State resident tuition: $2520. Nonresident tuition: $5631. Mandatory fees: $405. College room and board: $3300.

Applications Of all full-time undergraduates enrolled in fall 1996, 74% of those who applied for aid were judged to have need according to Federal Methodology, of whom 82% were aided. *Financial aid deadline*

(priority): 5/15. *Financial aid forms:* FAFSA, institutional form required. Financial aid transcript (for transfers) required for some. *Admission application deadline:* 8/15.

Summary of Aid to Needy Students *From gift & self-help combined:* Average amount awarded: $6720 (43% gift aid, 57% self-help). *Gift aid:* Total: $5,618,071 (4% from college's own funds, 50% from other college-administered sources, 46% from external sources). 376 Federal Work-Study jobs (averaging $1410); 1,310 part-time jobs.

Need-Based Scholarships & Grants Pell, FSEOG, state, private.

Loans Alaska Loans, Canadian Student Loans, Norwest Loans.

Non-Need Awards *Academic Interests/Achievement Awards:* ($311,936 total): general academic. *Creative Arts/Performance Awards:* 9 ($3950 total): music, theater/drama. *Athletic:* Total: 116 ($100,444); Men: 57 ($52,600); Women: 59 ($47,844).

Other Money-Saving Options Accelerated degree, co-op program, off-campus living. *Waivers:* full or partial for employees or children of employees and senior citizens.

Contact Financial Aid Office, Bemidji State University, 1500 Birchmont Drive, NE, Bemidji, MN 56601-2699, 218-755-2034, fax: 218-755-4361.

BENEDICT COLLEGE
Columbia, South Carolina

About the Institution Independent/religious, coed. Degrees awarded: B. Offers 32 undergraduate majors. Total enrollment: 2,138 (83% state residents). Freshmen: 647.

Undergraduate Expenses (1996–97) Comprehensive fee of $10,440 includes tuition ($6304), mandatory fees ($516), and college room and board ($3620).

Applications 95% of all full-time undergraduates enrolled in fall 1996 applied for aid; of these,100% were judged to have need according to Federal Methodology, of whom 100% were aided. *Financial aid deadline (priority):* 3/15. *Financial aid forms:* FAFSA, institutional form required. State form required for some. *Regular admission application deadline:* rolling. Early decision deadline: 11/15.

Summary of Aid to Needy Students Federal Work-Study jobs.

Need-Based Scholarships & Grants Pell, FSEOG, state, private.

Loans Perkins, PLUS, Stafford, Unsubsidized Stafford, state, college/university short-term loans.

Non-Need Awards *Academic Interests/Achievement Awards:* general academic. *Creative Arts/Performance Awards:* general creative, music. *Athletic:* available.

Other Money-Saving Options Army ROTC, cooperative Air Force ROTC, off-campus living. *Waivers:* full or partial for employees or children of employees and senior citizens.

Contact Financial Aid Office, Benedict College, Columbia, SC 29204, 803-253-5105.

BENEDICTINE COLLEGE
Atchison, Kansas

About the Institution Independent/religious, coed. Degrees awarded: A, B, M. Offers 52 undergraduate majors. Total enrollment: 964. Undergraduates: 925 (44% state residents). Freshmen: 192.

Undergraduate Expenses (1996–97) Comprehensive fee of $15,036 includes tuition ($10,650) and college room and board ($4386). College room only: $1986.

Applications 96% of all full-time undergraduates enrolled in fall 1996 applied for aid; of these, 80% were judged to have need according to Federal Methodology, of whom 100% were aided. *Financial aid deadline (priority):* 3/1. *Financial aid forms:* institutional form, financial aid

transcript (for transfers) required; CSS Financial Aid PROFILE acceptable. FAFSA, state form required for some. *Admission application deadline:* 8/15.

Summary of Aid to Needy Students *From gift & self-help combined:* Average need met: 80%. Average amount awarded: $10,972 (64% gift aid, 36% self-help). *Gift aid:* Total: $3,951,262 (72% from college's own funds, 15% from other college-administered sources, 13% from external sources). 319 Federal Work-Study jobs (averaging $1022); 33 part-time jobs.

Need-Based Scholarships & Grants Pell, FSEOG, state.

Loans Perkins, PLUS, Stafford, Unsubsidized Stafford.

Non-Need Awards In 1996, a total of 1,236 non-need awards were made. *Academic Interests/Achievement Awards:* 521 ($1,878,545 total): general academic. *Creative Arts/Performance Awards:* 40 ($82,300 total): art/fine arts, journalism/publications, music, theater/drama. *Special Achievements/Activities Awards:* 16 ($23,800 total): general special achievements/activities, cheerleading/drum major. *Special Characteristics Awards:* 369 ($976,642 total): general special characteristics, children of educators, children of faculty/staff, ethnic background, local/state students, members of minorities, previous college experience, religious affiliation. *Athletic:* Total: 290 ($644,384); Men: 196 ($437,410); Women: 94 ($206,974).

Other Money-Saving Options Accelerated degree, co-op program, Army ROTC, off-campus living (after junior year). *Payment Plan:* installment. *Waivers:* full or partial for employees or children of employees and senior citizens.

Contact Mr. Gilbert R. Estrada, Director of Student Financial Aid, Benedictine College, 1020 North Second, Atchison, KS 66002-1499, 913-367-5340 Ext. 2484, fax: 913-367-3676.

BENEDICTINE UNIVERSITY
Lisle, Illinois

About the Institution Independent/religious, coed. Degrees awarded: B, M, D. Offers 45 undergraduate majors. Total enrollment: 2,579. Undergraduates: 1,596 (91% state residents). Freshmen: 234.

Undergraduate Expenses (1997–98) Comprehensive fee of $17,050 includes tuition ($11,990), mandatory fees ($340), and college room and board ($4720). College room only: $1980 (minimum).

Applications 76% of all full-time undergraduates enrolled in fall 1996 applied for aid; of these, 77% were judged to have need according to Federal Methodology, of whom 100% were aided. *Financial aid deadline (priority):* 4/15. *Financial aid forms:* institutional form required; CSS Financial Aid PROFILE acceptable. FAFSA, state form required for some. *Admission application deadline:* rolling.

Summary of Aid to Needy Students *From gift & self-help combined:* Average need met: 100%. Average amount awarded: $9632 (63% gift aid, 37% self-help). *Gift aid:* Total: $4,218,942 (36% from college's own funds, 53% from other college-administered sources, 11% from external sources). 280 Federal Work-Study jobs (averaging $909); 250 part-time jobs.

Need-Based Scholarships & Grants Pell, FSEOG, state, private, college/university.

Loans Perkins, PLUS, Stafford, Unsubsidized Stafford, private.

Non-Need Awards In 1996, a total of 686 non-need awards were made. *Academic Interests/Achievement Awards:* 570 ($1,837,116 total): general academic, humanities, physical sciences. *Creative Arts/Performance Awards:* 25 ($40,150 total): music. *Special Characteristics Awards:* 91 ($45,425 total): children and siblings of alumni, previous college experience.

Other Money-Saving Options Accelerated degree, cooperative Army ROTC, off-campus living. *Payment Plans:* installment, deferred payment. *Waivers:* full or partial for children of alumni and employees or children of employees.

Contact Ms. Jane L. Smith, Associate Dean of Enrollment Management, Benedictine University, 5700 College Road, Lisle, IL 60532-0900, 630-829-6300, fax: 630-829-6456.

BENNETT COLLEGE
Greensboro, North Carolina

About the Institution Independent/religious, women. Degrees awarded: B. Offers 25 undergraduate majors. Total enrollment: 550 (24% state residents). Freshmen: 111.

Undergraduate Expenses (1997–98) Comprehensive fee of $10,990 includes tuition ($6210), mandatory fees ($1405), and college room and board ($3375). College room only: $1603.

Applications 90% of all full-time undergraduates enrolled in fall 1996 applied for aid; of these, 90% were judged to have need according to Federal Methodology, of whom 98% were aided. *Financial aid deadline (priority):* 3/15. *Financial aid forms:* FAFSA, state form, institutional form required; CSS Financial Aid PROFILE acceptable. *Admission application deadline:* rolling.

Summary of Aid to Needy Students *From gift & self-help combined:* Average need met: 71%. Average amount awarded: $7000 (26% gift aid, 74% self-help). *Gift aid:* Total: $1,181,098 (18% from college's own funds, 20% from other college-administered sources, 62% from external sources). 176 Federal Work-Study jobs (averaging $967); 40 part-time jobs.

Need-Based Scholarships & Grants Pell, FSEOG, state, private, college/university.

Loans Perkins, PLUS, Stafford, Unsubsidized Stafford.

Non-Need Awards *Academic Interests/Achievement Awards:* general academic. *Special Characteristics Awards:* 11 ($28,000 total): children of faculty/staff, relatives of clergy, religious affiliation.

Other Money-Saving Options Co-op program, cooperative Army ROTC, cooperative Air Force ROTC, off-campus living (after sophomore year). *Payment Plan:* deferred payment. *Waivers:* full or partial for employees or children of employees.

Contact Office of Financial Aid, Bennett College, 900 East Washington Street, Greensboro, NC 27401-3239, 910-273-4431.

BENNINGTON COLLEGE
Bennington, Vermont

About the Institution Independent, coed. Degrees awarded: B, M. Offers 68 undergraduate majors. Total enrollment: 380. Undergraduates: 300 (6% state residents). Freshmen: 120.

Undergraduate Expenses (1997–98) Comprehensive fee: $26,400.

Applications 86% of all full-time undergraduates enrolled in fall 1996 applied for aid; of these, 96% were judged to have need according to Federal Methodology, of whom 100% were aided. *Financial aid deadline (priority):* 3/1. *Financial aid forms:* FAFSA, institutional form, parent and student tax returns, Divorced/Separated Parents' Statement required for some required. *Regular admission application deadline:* 2/1. Early decision deadline: 12/1.

Summary of Aid to Needy Students *From gift & self-help combined:* Average need met: 84%. Average amount awarded: $19,300 (74% gift aid, 26% self-help). *Gift aid:* Total: $3,450,500 (84% from college's own funds, 9% from other college-administered sources, 7% from external sources). 187 Federal Work-Study jobs (averaging $1155); 53 part-time jobs.

Need-Based Scholarships & Grants Pell, FSEOG, state, private, college/university.

Loans PLUS, Stafford, Unsubsidized Stafford, college/university long-term loans ($3250 average).

Non-Need Awards In 1996, a total of 55 non-need awards were made. *Academic Interests/Achievement Awards:* 31 ($179,000 total): general academic. *Special Characteristics Awards:* 24 ($133,000 total): general special characteristics.

Other Money-Saving Options *Payment Plan:* installment. *Waivers:* full or partial for employees or children of employees.

Contact Office of Financial Aid, Bennington College, Bennington, VT 05201-9993, 802-442-5401.

BENTLEY COLLEGE
Waltham, Massachusetts

About the Institution Independent, coed. Degrees awarded: B, M. Offers 15 undergraduate majors. Total enrollment: 6,169. Undergraduates: 4,162 (64% state residents). Freshmen: 754.

Undergraduate Expenses (1997–98) Comprehensive fee of $23,305 includes tuition ($16,400), mandatory fees ($95), and college room and board ($6810 minimum). College room only: $3560 (minimum).

Applications Of all full-time undergraduates enrolled in fall 1996, 92% of those who applied for aid were judged to have need according to Federal Methodology, of whom 97% were aided. *Financial aid deadline:* 2/1. *Financial aid forms:* FAFSA, CSS Financial Aid PROFILE required. *Regular admission application deadline:* 2/15. Early decision deadline: 12/1. Early action deadline: 12/1.

Summary of Aid to Needy Students *From gift & self-help combined:* Average need met: 77%. Average amount awarded: $14,170 (58% gift aid, 42% self-help). *Gift aid:* Total: $15,401,000 (85% from college's own funds, 8% from other college-administered sources, 7% from external sources). 1,187 Federal Work-Study jobs (averaging $1810); 275 part-time jobs.

Need-Based Scholarships & Grants Pell, FSEOG, private, college/university.

Loans Perkins, PLUS, Stafford, Unsubsidized Stafford, private, college/university short-term loans ($700 average).

Non-Need Awards In 1996, a total of 690 non-need awards were made. *Academic Interests/Achievement Awards:* 646 ($1,920,000 total): general academic. *Special Achievements/Activities Awards:* 24 ($120,000 total): community service. *Athletic:* Total: 20 ($493,869); Men: 10 ($247,038); Women: 10 ($246,831).

Other Money-Saving Options Accelerated degree, cooperative Army ROTC, cooperative Air Force ROTC, off-campus living. *Payment Plans:* tuition prepayment, installment. *Waivers:* full or partial for employees or children of employees.

Contact Office of Financial Aid, Bentley College, 175 Forest Street, Waltham, MA 02154-4705, 617-891-2000.

BEREA COLLEGE
Berea, Kentucky

About the Institution Independent, coed. Degrees awarded: B. Offers 43 undergraduate majors. Total enrollment: 1,524 (42% state residents). Freshmen: 395.

Undergraduate Expenses (1996–97) Comprehensive fee of $3363 includes tuition ($0), mandatory fees ($195), and college room and board ($3168).

Applications *Financial aid deadline:* continuous. *Financial aid forms:* FAFSA required; CSS Financial Aid PROFILE acceptable. Institutional form required for some. *Admission application deadline:* rolling.

Summary of Aid to Needy Students *From gift & self-help combined:* Average need met: 85%. Average amount awarded: $16,659 (92% gift aid, 8% self-help). *Gift aid:* Total: $22,719,800 (84% from college's own funds, 1% from other college-administered sources, 15% from external sources). 1,270 Federal Work-Study jobs (averaging $1089); 289 part-time jobs.

Need-Based Scholarships & Grants Pell, FSEOG, state, private, college/university.

Loans Perkins, PLUS, Stafford, Unsubsidized Stafford, college/university long-term loans ($398 average).

Non-Need Awards Not offered.

Another Money-Saving Option *Payment Plan:* deferred payment.

Contact Labor and Financial Aid Office, Berea College, Berea, KY 40404, 606-986-9341.

BERKLEE COLLEGE OF MUSIC
Boston, Massachusetts

About the Institution Independent, coed. Degrees awarded: B. Offers 9 undergraduate majors. Total enrollment: 2,809 (31% state residents). Freshmen: 832.

Undergraduate Expenses (1997–98) Comprehensive fee of $21,990 includes tuition ($14,150), mandatory fees ($190), and college room and board ($7650).

Applications Of all full-time undergraduates enrolled in fall 1996, 91% of those who applied for aid were judged to have need according to Federal Methodology, of whom 100% were aided. *Financial aid deadline (priority):* 3/31. *Financial aid forms:* FAFSA, state form, institutional form required for some. *Admission application deadline:* 3/1.

Summary of Aid to Needy Students *From gift & self-help combined:* Average need met: 72%. Average amount awarded: $13,440 (27% gift aid, 73% self-help). *Gift aid:* Total: $3,698,668 (61% from college's own funds, 12% from other college-administered sources, 27% from external sources). 149 Federal Work-Study jobs (averaging $2802); 79 part-time jobs.

Need-Based Scholarships & Grants Pell, FSEOG, state, private, college/university.

Loans Perkins, PLUS, Stafford, Unsubsidized Stafford, state, private.

Non-Need Awards In 1996, a total of 539 non-need awards were made. *Creative Arts/Performance Awards:* 539 ($1,713,526 total): music.

Other Money-Saving Options Accelerated degree, off-campus living (after sophomore year). *Payment Plan:* installment. *Waivers:* full or partial for employees or children of employees.

Contact Ms. Anna Kelly, Associate Director of Financial Aid, Berklee College of Music, 1140 Boylston Street, Boston, MA 02215-3693, 617-266-1400 Ext. 2273, fax: 617-424-1843.

BERRY COLLEGE
Mount Berry, Georgia

About the Institution Independent, coed. Degrees awarded: B, M. Offers 61 undergraduate majors. Total enrollment: 2,085. Undergraduates: 1,856 (81% state residents). Freshmen: 578.

Undergraduate Expenses (1997–98) Comprehensive fee of $14,746 includes tuition ($10,210) and college room and board ($4536). College room only: $2600.

Applications 99% of all full-time undergraduates enrolled in fall 1996 applied for aid; of these, 62% were judged to have need according to Federal Methodology, of whom 100% were aided. *Financial aid deadline (priority):* 4/1. *Financial aid forms:* FAFSA, institutional form required. State form, federal income tax form required for some. *Admission application deadline:* rolling.

Summary of Aid to Needy Students *From gift & self-help combined:* Average need met: 90%. Average amount awarded: $12,200 (73% gift aid, 27% self-help). *Gift aid:* Total: $9,971,719 (55% from college's own funds, 4% from other college-administered sources, 41% from external sources). 230 Federal Work-Study jobs (averaging $1700); 1,200 part-time jobs.

Need-Based Scholarships & Grants Pell, FSEOG, private, college/university.

Loans Perkins, PLUS, Stafford, Unsubsidized Stafford, college/university short-term loans ($250 average), college/university long-term loans.

Non-Need Awards In 1996, a total of 1,287 non-need awards were made. *Academic Interests/Achievement Awards:* 600 ($2,250,000 total): general academic, English, humanities, religion/biblical studies. *Creative Arts/Performance Awards:* 150 ($240,000 total): journalism/publications, music, theater/drama. *Special Achievements/Activities Awards:* 80 ($30,000 total): community service. *Special Characteristics Awards:* 300 ($495,000 total): adult students, children of faculty/staff, local/state students, members of minorities. *Athletic:* Total: 157 ($911,722); Men: 115 ($614,009); Women: 42 ($297,713).

Other Money-Saving Options Accelerated degree, co-op program, off-campus living (after sophomore year). *Payment Plan:* installment. *Waivers:* full or partial for employees or children of employees, adult students, senior citizens.

Contact Mr. William G. Fron, Director of Financial Aid, Berry College, 5007 Berry College, Mount Berry, GA 30149-0159, 706-236-2276, fax: 706-290-2160.

BETHANY COLLEGE
Lindsborg, Kansas

About the Institution Independent/religious, coed. Degrees awarded: B. Offers 43 undergraduate majors.

Undergraduate Expenses (1996–97) Comprehensive fee of $12,670 includes tuition ($9875), mandatory fees ($105), and college room and board ($2690 minimum). College room only: $1495 (minimum).

Applications 85% of all full-time undergraduates enrolled in fall 1996 applied for aid; of these, 94% were judged to have need according to Federal Methodology, of whom 100% were aided. *Financial aid deadline (priority):* 3/15. *Financial aid forms:* institutional form required; FAFSA, CSS Financial Aid PROFILE acceptable. State form required for some. *Admission application deadline:* rolling.

Summary of Aid to Needy Students *From gift & self-help combined:* Average need met: 72%. Average amount awarded: $9849 (50% gift aid, 50% self-help). *Gift aid:* Total: $2,488,339 (58% from college's own funds, 5% from other college-administered sources, 37% from external sources). 322 Federal Work-Study jobs (averaging $1000); 126 part-time jobs.

Need-Based Scholarships & Grants Pell, FSEOG, state, private, college/university.

Loans Perkins, PLUS, Stafford, Unsubsidized Stafford, private, college/university short-term loans ($200 average).

Non-Need Awards In 1996, a total of 925 non-need awards were made. *Academic Interests/Achievement Awards:* 430 ($1,007,726 total): general academic. *Creative Arts/Performance Awards:* 132 ($123,921 total): art/fine arts, music, theater/drama. *Special Achievements/Activities Awards:* 10 ($5000 total): cheerleading/drum major. *Special Characteristics Awards:* 15 ($21,645 total): international students, relatives of clergy. *Athletic:* Total: 338 ($418,500); Men: 225 ($278,950); Women: 113 ($139,550).

Other Money-Saving Options Accelerated degree, co-op program. *Payment Plan:* installment.

Contact Ms. Brenda L. Meagher, Interim Director of Financial Aid, Bethany College, 421 North First Street, Lindsborg, KS 67456-1897, 913-227-3311 Ext. 8114, fax: 913-227-2004.

BETHANY COLLEGE
Bethany, West Virginia

About the Institution Independent/religious, coed. Degrees awarded: B. Offers 44 undergraduate majors. Total enrollment: 761 (21% state residents). Freshmen: 242.

Undergraduate Expenses (1997–98) Comprehensive fee of $23,065 includes tuition ($17,022), mandatory fees ($327), and college room and board ($5716). College room only: $2238.

Applications *Financial aid deadline (priority):* 4/1. *Financial aid forms:* FAFSA, institutional form required. State form required for some. *Admission application deadline:* rolling.

Summary of Aid to Needy Students *Gift aid:* Total: $7,700,675 (86% from college's own funds, 9% from other college-administered sources, 5% from external sources). Federal Work-Study jobs; 38 part-time jobs.

Need-Based Scholarships & Grants Pell, FSEOG, state, private, college/university.

Loans Perkins, PLUS, Stafford.

Non-Need Awards In 1996, a total of 737 non-need awards were made. *Academic Interests/Achievement Awards:* 312 ($1,830,660 total): general academic. *Special Achievements/Activities Awards:* 224 ($454,558 total): leadership, religious involvement. *Special Characteristics Awards:* 201 ($818,025 total): children of faculty/staff, ethnic background, local/state students, relatives of clergy, religious affiliation.

Other Money-Saving Options Accelerated degree. *Payment Plan:* installment. *Waivers:* full or partial for employees or children of employees.

Contact Financial Aid Office, Bethany College, Bethany, WV 26032, 304-829-7141.

BETHEL COLLEGE
Mishawaka, Indiana

About the Institution Independent/religious, coed. Degrees awarded: A, B, M. Offers 57 undergraduate majors. Total enrollment: 1,467. Undergraduates: 1,409 (81% state residents). Freshmen: 212.

Undergraduate Expenses (1997–98) Comprehensive fee of $14,450 includes tuition ($11,100) and college room and board ($3350).

Applications 85% of all full-time undergraduates enrolled in fall 1996 applied for aid; of these, 89% were judged to have need according to Federal Methodology, of whom 99% were aided. *Financial aid deadline (priority):* 3/1. *Financial aid forms:* FAFSA, institutional form required; CSS Financial Aid PROFILE acceptable. *Admission application deadline:* 8/1.

Summary of Aid to Needy Students *From gift & self-help combined:* Average amount awarded: $6574 (61% gift aid, 39% self-help). *Gift aid:* Total: $2,021,300 (42% from college's own funds, 39% from other college-administered sources, 19% from external sources). 144 Federal Work-Study jobs (averaging $800); 80 part-time jobs.

Need-Based Scholarships & Grants Pell, FSEOG, state, private, college/university.

Loans Perkins, PLUS, Stafford, Unsubsidized Stafford, private, college/university long-term loans ($1286 average).

Non-Need Awards In 1996, a total of 993 non-need awards were made. *Academic Interests/Achievement Awards:* 328 ($840,667 total): general academic, biological sciences, business, communication, education, English, health fields, mathematics, physical sciences, religion/biblical studies, social sciences. *Creative Arts/Performance Awards:* 45 ($89,950 total): art/fine arts, theater/drama. *Special Achievements/Activities Awards:* 96 ($118,880 total): cheerleading/drum major, leadership. *Special Characteristics Awards:* 378 ($664,180 total): adult students, children of faculty/staff, international students, relatives of

clergy, religious affiliation, siblings of current students, spouses of current students. *Athletic:* Total: 146 ($435,908); Men: 80 ($216,797); Women: 66 ($219,111).

Other Money-Saving Options Accelerated degree, cooperative Naval ROTC, cooperative Air Force ROTC, off-campus living (after sophomore year). *Payment Plan:* installment. *Waivers:* full or partial for employees or children of employees and adult students.

Contact Mr. Guy A. Fisher, Director of Financial Aid, Bethel College, 1001 West McKinley Avenue, Mishawaka, IN 46545-5591, 219-257-3316.

BETHEL COLLEGE
North Newton, Kansas

About the Institution Independent/religious, coed. Degrees awarded: B. Offers 49 undergraduate majors. Total enrollment: 618 (68% state residents). Freshmen: 101.

Undergraduate Expenses (1997–98) Comprehensive fee of $14,490 includes tuition ($10,290) and college room and board ($4200 minimum).

Applications 87% of all full-time undergraduates enrolled in fall 1996 applied for aid; of these, 99% were judged to have need according to Federal Methodology, of whom 98% were aided. *Financial aid deadline (priority):* 3/1. *Financial aid forms:* FAFSA required. *Admission application deadline:* 8/15.

Summary of Aid to Needy Students *From gift & self-help combined:* Average need met: 87%. Average amount awarded: $11,747 (48% gift aid, 52% self-help). *Gift aid:* Total: $2,558,795 (55% from college's own funds, 19% from other college-administered sources, 26% from external sources). 218 Federal Work-Study jobs (averaging $1200); 140 part-time jobs.

Need-Based Scholarships & Grants Pell, FSEOG, state, college/university.

Loans Perkins, PLUS, Stafford, Unsubsidized Stafford.

Non-Need Awards In 1996, a total of 506 non-need awards were made. *Academic Interests/Achievement Awards:* 270 ($464,333 total): general academic. *Creative Arts/Performance Awards:* 87 ($98,875 total): art/fine arts, music, theater/drama. *Special Characteristics Awards:* 11 ($32,430 total): relatives of clergy. *Athletic:* Total: 138 ($192,916); Men: 95 ($137,250); Women: 43 ($55,666).

Other Money-Saving Options Accelerated degree. *Payment Plans:* installment, deferred payment. *Waivers:* full or partial for employees or children of employees.

Contact Office of Financial Aid, Bethel College, 300 East 27th Street, North Newton, KS 67117, 316-283-2500.

BETHEL COLLEGE
St. Paul, Minnesota

About the Institution Independent/religious, coed. Degrees awarded: A, B, M. Offers 54 undergraduate majors. Total enrollment: 2,584. Undergraduates: 2,368 (67% state residents). Freshmen: 544.

Undergraduate Expenses (1996–97) Comprehensive fee of $17,890 includes tuition ($13,180), mandatory fees ($20), and college room and board ($4690). College room only: $2640.

Applications 90% of all full-time undergraduates enrolled in fall 1996 applied for aid; of these, 80% were judged to have need according to Federal Methodology, of whom 99% were aided. *Financial aid deadline (priority):* 4/15. *Financial aid forms:* institutional form required. FAFSA required for some. *Admission application deadline:* rolling.

Summary of Aid to Needy Students *From gift & self-help combined:* Average need met: 85%. Average amount awarded: $11,460 (57% gift aid, 43% self-help). *Gift aid:* Total: $9,171,534 (54% from college's

own funds, 5% from other college-administered sources, 41% from external sources). 727 Federal Work-Study jobs (averaging $1688); 203 part-time jobs.

Need-Based Scholarships & Grants Pell, FSEOG, state, private, college/university.

Loans Perkins, PLUS, Stafford, Unsubsidized Stafford, state, private, college/university short-term loans ($500 average).

Non-Need Awards In 1996, a total of 1,846 non-need awards were made. *Academic Interests/Achievement Awards:* 775 ($1,119,864 total): general academic. *Creative Arts/Performance Awards:* 48 ($48,000 total): art/fine arts, debating, music, theater/drama. *Special Achievements/Activities Awards:* 10 ($10,000 total): community service, Junior Miss, leadership. *Special Characteristics Awards:* 1,013 ($603,350 total): ethnic background, international students, members of minorities, out-of-state students, relatives of clergy, religious affiliation, ROTC participants.

Other Money-Saving Options Cooperative Army ROTC, cooperative Naval ROTC, cooperative Air Force ROTC, off-campus living (after sophomore year). *Payment Plan:* installment. *Waivers:* full or partial for employees or children of employees and senior citizens.

Contact Mr. Daniel C. Nelson, Director of College Financial Planning, Bethel College, 3900 Bethel Drive, St. Paul, MN 55112-6999, 612-638-6241, fax: 612-638-6001.

BETHEL COLLEGE
McKenzie, Tennessee

About the Institution Independent/religious, coed. Degrees awarded: B, M. Offers 28 undergraduate majors. Total enrollment: 558. Undergraduates: 504 (70% state residents). Freshmen: 183.

Undergraduate Expenses (1997–98) Comprehensive fee of $10,900 includes tuition ($6990), mandatory fees ($250), and college room and board ($3660).

Applications *Financial aid deadline (priority):* 6/15. *Financial aid forms:* CSS Financial Aid PROFILE acceptable. FAFSA, institutional form required for some. *Admission application deadline:* 8/10.

Summary of Aid to Needy Students Federal Work-Study jobs.

Non-Need Awards *Academic Interests/Achievement Awards:* general academic, religion/biblical studies. *Creative Arts/Performance Awards:* music. *Special Characteristics Awards:* religious affiliation. *Athletic:* available.

Other Money-Saving Options Accelerated degree. *Payment Plan:* installment. *Waivers:* full or partial for employees or children of employees.

Contact Office of Financial Aid, Bethel College, McKenzie, TN 38201, 901-352-1000.

BETH-EL COLLEGE OF NURSING AND HEALTH SCIENCES
Colorado Springs, Colorado

About the Institution City-supported, primarily women. Degrees awarded: B, M. Offers 1 undergraduate major. Total enrollment: 439. Undergraduates: 335 (90% state residents).

Undergraduate Expenses (1996–97) Tuition: $5728. Mandatory fees: $105.

Applications Of all full-time undergraduates enrolled in fall 1996, 92% of those who applied for aid were judged to have need according to Federal Methodology, of whom 100% were aided. *Financial aid deadline (priority):* 6/1. *Financial aid forms:* FAFSA required. *Admission application deadline:* 2/15.

Summary of Aid to Needy Students *From gift & self-help combined:* Average need met: 55%. Average amount awarded: $5600 (22% gift

aid, 78% self-help). *Gift aid:* Total: $115,645 (10% from college-administered sources, 90% from external sources). 5 Federal Work-Study jobs (averaging $1500); 3 part-time jobs.

Need-Based Scholarships & Grants Pell, FSEOG.

Loans Perkins, PLUS, Stafford, Unsubsidized Stafford, college/university short-term loans ($75 average), college/university long-term loans ($1000 average).

Non-Need Awards Not offered.

Other Money-Saving Options Cooperative Army ROTC. *Payment Plans:* installment, deferred payment.

Contact Ms. Margaret S. Smith, Financial Aid Officer, Beth-El College of Nursing and Health Sciences, 2790 North Academy Boulevard, Suite 200, Colorado Springs, CO 80917-5399, 719-475-5170, fax: 719-475-5742.

BETH HAMEDRASH SHAAREI YOSHER INSTITUTE
Brooklyn, New York

About the Institution Independent/religious, men.

Applications *Financial aid deadline:* continuous. *Financial aid forms:* FAFSA required.

Summary of Aid to Needy Students Federal Work-Study jobs; part-time jobs.

Need-Based Scholarships & Grants Pell, FSEOG, private.

Non-Need Awards Not offered.

Contact Financial Aid Office, Beth HaMedrash Shaarei Yosher Institute, Brooklyn, NY 11204, 718-854-2290.

BETHUNE-COOKMAN COLLEGE
Daytona Beach, Florida

About the Institution Independent/religious, coed. Degrees awarded: B. Offers 30 undergraduate majors. Total enrollment: 2,335 (77% state residents). Freshmen: 601.

Undergraduate Expenses (1997–98) Comprehensive fee of $11,554 includes tuition ($7280) and college room and board ($4274). College room only: $2360.

Applications 96% of all full-time undergraduates enrolled in fall 1996 applied for aid; of these, 97% were judged to have need according to Federal Methodology, of whom 100% were aided. *Financial aid deadline (priority):* 3/1. *Financial aid forms:* FAFSA required. *Admission application deadline:* 7/30.

Summary of Aid to Needy Students *From gift & self-help combined:* Average need met: 87%. Average amount awarded: $9110 (46% gift aid, 54% self-help). *Gift aid:* Total: $8,849,897 (18% from college's own funds, 44% from other college-administered sources, 38% from external sources). 450 Federal Work-Study jobs (averaging $1100); 50 part-time jobs.

Need-Based Scholarships & Grants Pell, FSEOG, state, private, college/university.

Loans Perkins, PLUS, Stafford, Unsubsidized Stafford, private.

Non-Need Awards In 1996, a total of 735 non-need awards were made. *Academic Interests/Achievement Awards:* 230 ($629,000 total): general academic. *Creative Arts/Performance Awards:* 230 ($590,000 total): music. *Special Achievements/Activities Awards:* 10 ($5000 total): religious involvement. *Athletic:* Total: 265 ($1,741,500); Men: 178 ($1,237,000); Women: 87 ($504,500).

Other Money-Saving Options Accelerated degree, co-op program, Army ROTC, cooperative Air Force ROTC, off-campus living (after freshman year). *Waivers:* full or partial for employees or children of employees.

Contact Mr. Joseph Coleman, Director of Financial Aid, Bethune-Cookman College, 640 Mary McLeod Bethune Boulevard, Daytona Beach, FL 32114-3099, 904-255-1401 Ext. 307, fax: 904-255-9284.

BEULAH HEIGHTS BIBLE COLLEGE
Atlanta, Georgia

About the Institution Independent/religious, coed. Degrees awarded: A, B. Offers 2 undergraduate majors. Total enrollment: 374 (70% state residents). Freshmen: 101.

Undergraduate Expenses (1996–97) Tuition: $3200. Mandatory fees: $80. College room only: $1300.

Applications Of all full-time undergraduates enrolled in fall 1996, 100% of those who applied for aid were judged to have need according to Federal Methodology, of whom 100% were aided. *Financial aid deadline (priority):* 6/15. *Financial aid forms:* FAFSA, institutional form required. *Admission application deadline:* rolling.

Summary of Aid to Needy Students *From gift & self-help combined:* Average need met: 60%. Average amount awarded: $2952 (39% gift aid, 61% self-help). *Gift aid:* Total: $190,000. Federal Work-Study jobs.

Need-Based Scholarships & Grants Pell, FSEOG.

Loans Stafford, Unsubsidized Stafford.

Non-Need Awards Not offered.

Other Money-Saving Options Accelerated degree, co-op program, off-campus living. *Payment Plans:* installment, deferred payment.

Contact Ms. Patricia Banks, Financial Aid Director, Beulah Heights Bible College, Atlanta, GA 30316, 404-627-2681.

BIOLA UNIVERSITY
La Mirada, California

About the Institution Independent/religious, coed. Degrees awarded: B, M, D. Offers 70 undergraduate majors. Total enrollment: 3,039. Undergraduates: 1,926 (75% state residents). Freshmen: 407.

Undergraduate Expenses (1997–98) Comprehensive fee of $18,754 includes tuition ($14,286) and college room and board ($4468 minimum). College room only: $2546.

Applications Of all full-time undergraduates enrolled in fall 1996, 91% of those who applied for aid were judged to have need according to Federal Methodology, of whom 100% were aided. *Financial aid deadline (priority):* 3/2. *Financial aid forms:* FAFSA, institutional form required. State form required for some. *Admission application deadline:* 6/1.

Summary of Aid to Needy Students *From gift & self-help combined:* Average need met: 82%. Average amount awarded: $12,355 (64% gift aid, 36% self-help). *Gift aid:* Total: $10,860,362 (59% from college's own funds, 6% from other college-administered sources, 35% from external sources). 50 Federal Work-Study jobs (averaging $2378); 500 part-time jobs.

Need-Based Scholarships & Grants Pell, FSEOG, state, private, college/university.

Loans Perkins, PLUS, Stafford, Unsubsidized Stafford, Federal Nursing, private, college/university long-term loans ($1000 average).

Non-Need Awards In 1996, a total of 1,318 non-need awards were made. *Academic Interests/Achievement Awards:* 674 ($2,319,182 total): general academic, communication, health fields. *Creative Arts/Performance Awards:* 151 ($357,363 total): art/fine arts, debating, music, performing arts. *Special Characteristics Awards:* 402 ($1,206,068 total): adult students, children of faculty/staff, ethnic background, relatives of clergy. *Athletic:* Total: 91 ($482,598); Men: 53 ($342,693); Women: 38 ($139,905).

Other Money-Saving Options Accelerated degree, co-op program, cooperative Army ROTC, cooperative Naval ROTC, cooperative Air Force ROTC. *Payment Plan:* installment. *Waivers:* full or partial for employees or children of employees.

Contact Financial Aid Officer-Counselor on Call, Biola University, 13800 Biola Avenue, La Mirada, CA 90639-0001, 562-903-4742, fax: 562-906-4541.

BIRMINGHAM-SOUTHERN COLLEGE
Birmingham, Alabama

About the Institution Independent/religious, coed. Degrees awarded: B, M. Offers 43 undergraduate majors. Total enrollment: 1,492. Undergraduates: 1,266 (80% state residents). Freshmen: 273.

Undergraduate Expenses (1997–98) Comprehensive fee of $18,240 includes tuition ($13,750), mandatory fees ($210), and college room and board ($4280 minimum).

Applications 56% of all full-time undergraduates enrolled in fall 1996 applied for aid; of these, 76% were judged to have need according to Federal Methodology, of whom 100% were aided. *Financial aid deadline (priority):* 3/1. *Financial aid forms:* FAFSA, institutional form required; state form acceptable. Verification worksheet required for some. *Regular admission application deadline:* 5/1. Early action deadline: 12/1.

Summary of Aid to Needy Students *From gift & self-help combined:* Average need met: 85%. Average amount awarded: $12,108 (72% gift aid, 28% self-help). *Gift aid:* Total: $4,111,297 (74% from college's own funds, 11% from other college-administered sources, 15% from external sources). 185 Federal Work-Study jobs (averaging $1000); 40 part-time jobs.

Need-Based Scholarships & Grants Pell, FSEOG, state, private, college/university.

Loans Perkins, PLUS, Stafford, Unsubsidized Stafford, college/university long-term loans ($2500 average).

Non-Need Awards In 1996, a total of 997 non-need awards were made. *Academic Interests/Achievement Awards:* 696 ($3,215,173 total): general academic, business, computer science, education, health fields, premedicine. *Creative Arts/Performance Awards:* 43 ($163,000 total): art/fine arts, dance, music, performing arts, theater/drama. *Special Achievements/Activities Awards:* 3 ($7500 total): Junior Miss, memberships. *Special Characteristics Awards:* 152 ($656,862 total): children of faculty/staff, relatives of clergy, religious affiliation. *Athletic:* Total: 103 ($909,754); Men: 74 ($716,254); Women: 29 ($193,500).

Other Money-Saving Options Accelerated degree, cooperative Army ROTC, cooperative Air Force ROTC. *Payment Plan:* installment. *Waivers:* full or partial for children of alumni and employees or children of employees.

Contact Financial Aid Office, Birmingham-Southern College, Box 549016, Birmingham, AL 35254, 205-226-4688, fax: 205-226-3064.

BLACKBURN COLLEGE
Carlinville, Illinois

About the Institution Independent/religious, coed. Degrees awarded: B. Offers 28 undergraduate majors. Total enrollment: 576 (86% state residents). Freshmen: 162.

Undergraduate Expenses (1997–98) Comprehensive fee of $10,500 includes tuition ($7425), mandatory fees ($85), and college room and board ($2990).

Applications 96% of all full-time undergraduates enrolled in fall 1996 applied for aid; of these, 90% were judged to have need according to Federal Methodology, of whom 100% were aided. *Financial aid deadline (priority):* 4/1. *Financial aid forms:* FAFSA required. *Admission application deadline:* rolling.

Summary of Aid to Needy Students *From gift & self-help combined:* Average need met: 100%. Average amount awarded: $7385 (73% gift aid, 27% self-help). *Gift aid:* Total: $2,411,003 (41% from college's own funds, 44% from other college-administered sources, 15% from external sources). 30 part-time jobs.

Need-Based Scholarships & Grants Pell, FSEOG, state, college/university.

Loans Perkins, PLUS, Stafford, Unsubsidized Stafford, college/university long-term loans ($1200 average).

Non-Need Awards In 1996, a total of 143 non-need awards were made. *Academic Interests/Achievement Awards:* 143 ($377,236 total): general academic.

Other Money-Saving Options Accelerated degree, co-op program. *Payment Plan:* installment. *Waivers:* full or partial for employees or children of employees.

Contact Ms. Cheryl Gardner, Financial Aid Administrator, Blackburn College, 700 College Avenue, Carlinville, IL 62626-1498, 217-854-3231 Ext. 4227, fax: 217-854-3731.

BLACK HILLS STATE UNIVERSITY
Spearfish, South Dakota

About the Institution State-supported, coed. Degrees awarded: A, B, M. Offers 54 undergraduate majors. Total enrollment: 2,866. Undergraduates: 2,769 (71% state residents). Freshmen: 451.

Undergraduate Expenses (1997–98) State resident tuition: $1728. Nonresident tuition: $5496. Mandatory fees: $1150. College room and board: $2958. College room only: $1382.

Applications Of all full-time undergraduates enrolled in fall 1996, 85% of those who applied for aid were judged to have need according to Federal Methodology, of whom 95% were aided. *Financial aid deadline (priority):* 3/1. *Financial aid forms:* FAFSA required. State form required for some. *Admission application deadline:* rolling.

Summary of Aid to Needy Students *From gift & self-help combined:* Average need met: 80%. Average amount awarded: $2235 (30% gift aid, 70% self-help). *Gift aid:* Total: $1,063,078 (14% from college's own funds, 86% from external sources). 339 Federal Work-Study jobs (averaging $812); 395 part-time jobs.

Need-Based Scholarships & Grants Pell, FSEOG, state.

Loans Perkins, PLUS, Stafford, Unsubsidized Stafford, college/university short-term loans ($210 average).

Non-Need Awards *Academic Interests/Achievement Awards:* 303 ($184,758 total): general academic, biological sciences, communication, computer science, education, humanities, mathematics, military science, physical sciences, social sciences. *Creative Arts/Performance Awards:* music. *Special Characteristics Awards:* 5 ($1500 total): members of minorities. *Athletic:* Total: 103 ($83,900); Men: 79 ($63,950); Women: 24 ($19,950).

Other Money-Saving Options Co-op program, Army ROTC, off-campus living (after sophomore year). *Payment Plan:* installment. *Waivers:* full or partial for employees or children of employees and senior citizens.

Contact Mr. David W. Martin, Director of Financial Aid, Black Hills State University, University Station, Box 9509, Spearfish, SD 5779-9509, 605-642-6254.

BLOOMFIELD COLLEGE
Bloomfield, New Jersey

About the Institution Independent/religious, coed. Degrees awarded: B. Offers 36 undergraduate majors. Total enrollment: 2,054 (95% state residents). Freshmen: 238.

Undergraduate Expenses (1996–97) Comprehensive fee of $13,900 includes tuition ($9100), mandatory fees ($150), and college room and board ($4650).

Applications 90% of all full-time undergraduates enrolled in fall 1996 applied for aid; of these, 97% were judged to have need according to Federal Methodology, of whom 98% were aided. *Financial aid deadline (priority):* 6/1. *Financial aid forms:* FAFSA, institutional form required. *Admission application deadline:* rolling.

Summary of Aid to Needy Students *From gift & self-help combined:* Average need met: 85%. Average amount awarded: $8936 (80% gift aid, 20% self-help). *Gift aid:* Total: $8,440,238 (26% from college's own funds, 7% from other college-administered sources, 67% from external sources). 123 Federal Work-Study jobs (averaging $1310); 90 part-time jobs.

Need-Based Scholarships & Grants Pell, FSEOG, state, private, college/university.

Loans Perkins, PLUS, Stafford, Unsubsidized Stafford, state.

Non-Need Awards In 1996, a total of 191 non-need awards were made. *Academic Interests/Achievement Awards:* 76 ($163,830 total): general academic. *Special Characteristics Awards:* 28 ($18,903 total): children and siblings of alumni, children of current students, local/state students, relatives of clergy, siblings of current students. *Athletic:* Total: 87 ($413,751); Men: 48 ($230,260); Women: 39 ($183,491).

Other Money-Saving Options Accelerated degree, cooperative Army ROTC, off-campus living. *Payment Plans:* installment, deferred payment. *Waivers:* full or partial for children of alumni, employees or children of employees, adult students, senior citizens.

Contact Ms. Janet Mariano Merli, Associate Director of Financial Aid, Bloomfield College, Bloomfield, NJ 07003-9981, 973-748-9000, fax: 973-743-3998.

BLOOMSBURG UNIVERSITY OF PENNSYLVANIA
Bloomsburg, Pennsylvania

About the Institution State-supported, coed. Degrees awarded: A, B, M. Offers 48 undergraduate majors. Total enrollment: 7,438. Undergraduates: 6,392 (90% state residents). Freshmen: 1,566.

Undergraduate Expenses (1996–97) State resident tuition: $3368. Nonresident tuition: $8566. Mandatory fees: $794. College room and board: $3090.

Applications Of all full-time undergraduates enrolled in fall 1996, 80% of those who applied for aid were judged to have need according to Federal Methodology, of whom 90% were aided. *Financial aid deadline (priority):* 3/15. *Financial aid forms:* FAFSA, state form required. Institutional form required for some. *Admission application deadline:* rolling.

Summary of Aid to Needy Students *From gift & self-help combined:* Average need met: 73%. Average amount awarded: $6946 (33% gift aid, 67% self-help). *Gift aid:* Total: $8,281,876 (15% from college's own funds, 5% from other college-administered sources, 80% from external sources). 817 Federal Work-Study jobs (averaging $841); 1,055 part-time jobs.

Need-Based Scholarships & Grants Pell, FSEOG, state, private, college/university.

Loans Perkins, PLUS, Stafford, Unsubsidized Stafford, state, private, college/university short-term loans ($373 average).

Non-Need Awards In 1996, a total of 551 non-need awards were made. *Academic Interests/Achievement Awards:* 222 ($471,924 total): general academic, biological sciences, business, communication, computer science, education, English, foreign languages, health fields, humanities, international studies, mathematics, physical sciences, religion/biblical studies, social sciences. *Special Characteristics Awards:*

152 ($433,487 total): children of faculty/staff, international students. *Athletic:* Total: 177 ($306,516); Men: 44 ($65,355); Women: 133 ($241,161).

Other Money-Saving Options Co-op program, Army ROTC, cooperative Air Force ROTC, off-campus living (after freshman year). *Waivers:* full or partial for minority students and employees or children of employees.

Contact Office of Financial Aid, Bloomsburg University of Pennsylvania, Ben Franklin Building, Room 19, Bloomsburg, PA 17815-1905, 717-389-4000.

BLUEFIELD COLLEGE
Bluefield, Virginia

About the Institution Independent/religious, coed. Degrees awarded: A, B. Offers 39 undergraduate majors. Total enrollment: 758 (53% state residents). Freshmen: 144.

Undergraduate Expenses (1997–98) Comprehensive fee of $13,710 includes tuition ($8770), mandatory fees ($330), and college room and board ($4610). College room only: $1750.

Applications Of all full-time undergraduates enrolled in fall 1996, 99% of those judged to have need according to Federal Methodology were aided. *Financial aid deadline (priority):* 3/10. *Financial aid forms:* FAFSA, state form, institutional form required; CSS Financial Aid PROFILE acceptable. *Admission application deadline:* rolling.

Summary of Aid to Needy Students *From gift & self-help combined:* Average need met: 65%. Average amount awarded: $7314 (72% gift aid, 28% self-help). *Gift aid:* Total: $2,597,500 (62% from college's own funds, 26% from other college-administered sources, 12% from external sources). 30 Federal Work-Study jobs (averaging $700); 32 part-time jobs.

Need-Based Scholarships & Grants Pell, FSEOG, state, private, college/university.

Loans PLUS, Stafford, Unsubsidized Stafford, private.

Non-Need Awards In 1996, a total of 949 non-need awards were made. *Academic Interests/Achievement Awards:* 358 ($1,022,680 total): general academic. *Creative Arts/Performance Awards:* 15 ($16,600 total): art/fine arts. *Special Achievements/Activities Awards:* 22 ($10,650 total): religious involvement. *Special Characteristics Awards:* 461 ($668,319 total): local/state students, members of minorities, relatives of clergy. *Athletic:* Total: 93 ($262,060); Men: 59 ($175,260); Women: 34 ($86,800).

Other Money-Saving Options Off-campus living (after junior year). *Payment Plan:* installment. *Waivers:* full or partial for employees or children of employees, adult students, senior citizens.

Contact Ms. Eleanor Barnett, Director, Financial Aid, Bluefield College, 3000 College Drive, Bluefield, VA 24605-1799, 540-326-4243, fax: 540-326-4288.

BLUEFIELD STATE COLLEGE
Bluefield, West Virginia

About the Institution State-supported, coed. Degrees awarded: A, B. Offers 34 undergraduate majors. Total enrollment: 2,609 (92% state residents). Freshmen: 533.

Undergraduate Expenses (1997–98) State resident tuition: $2044. Nonresident tuition: $4968.

Applications *Financial aid deadline (priority):* 3/1. *Financial aid forms:* FAFSA, CSS Financial Aid PROFILE, institutional form required. *Admission application deadline:* rolling.

Summary of Aid to Needy Students *From gift & self-help combined:* Average need met: 36%. Average amount awarded: $2968 (58% gift aid, 42% self-help). *Gift aid:* Total: $2,053,992. Federal Work-Study jobs; 130 part-time jobs.

Need-Based Scholarships & Grants Pell, FSEOG, college/university.
Loans Perkins, PLUS, Stafford, Unsubsidized Stafford.
Non-Need Awards *Academic Interests/Achievement Awards:* general academic, engineering/technologies. *Special Achievements/Activities Awards:* general special achievements/activities. *Special Characteristics Awards:* general special characteristics. *Athletic:* available.
Another Money-Saving Option *Waivers:* full or partial for employees or children of employees.
Contact Mr. Tom Iles, Director of Financial Aid, Bluefield State College, Bluefield, WV 24701-2198, 304-327-4020.

BLUE MOUNTAIN COLLEGE
Blue Mountain, Mississippi

About the Institution Independent/religious, primarily women. Degrees awarded: B. Offers 27 undergraduate majors. Total enrollment: 420 (87% state residents).

Undergraduate Expenses (1997–98) Comprehensive fee of $6990 includes tuition ($4640) and college room and board ($2350). College room only: $750.

Applications 81% of all full-time undergraduates enrolled in fall 1996 applied for aid; of these, 74% were judged to have need according to Federal Methodology, of whom 100% were aided. *Financial aid deadline (priority):* 4/1. *Financial aid forms:* FAFSA, institutional form required for some. *Admission application deadline:* rolling.

Summary of Aid to Needy Students *From gift & self-help combined:* Average amount awarded: $1985. 30 Federal Work-Study jobs (averaging $1100); 40 part-time jobs.

Need-Based Scholarships & Grants Pell, FSEOG, state, college/university.

Loans Perkins, PLUS, Stafford, Unsubsidized Stafford.

Non-Need Awards *Academic Interests/Achievement Awards:* general academic. *Creative Arts/Performance Awards:* music. *Special Achievements/Activities Awards:* memberships, religious involvement. *Athletic:* available.

Other Money-Saving Options Accelerated degree. *Payment Plan:* installment. *Waivers:* full or partial for employees or children of employees.
Contact Office of Financial Aid, Blue Mountain College, PO Box 267, Blue Mountain, MS 38610-9509, 601-685-4771 Ext. 41, fax: 601-685-4776.

BLUFFTON COLLEGE
Bluffton, Ohio

About the Institution Independent/religious, coed. Degrees awarded: B, M. Offers 55 undergraduate majors. Total enrollment: 1,090. Undergraduates: 1,065 (94% state residents). Freshmen: 185.

Undergraduate Expenses (1997–98) Comprehensive fee of $16,707 includes tuition ($11,835) and college room and board ($4872). College room only: $1974.

Applications Of all full-time undergraduates enrolled in fall 1996, 92% of those who applied for aid were judged to have need according to Federal Methodology, of whom 100% were aided. *Financial aid deadline (priority):* 5/1. *Financial aid forms:* FAFSA, CSS Financial Aid PROFILE required. State form required for some. *Admission application deadline:* 5/31.

Summary of Aid to Needy Students *From gift & self-help combined:* Average need met: 100%. Average amount awarded: $9414 (59% gift aid, 41% self-help). *Gift aid:* Total: $4,131,037 (50% from college's own funds, 3% from other college-administered sources, 47% from external sources). 511 Federal Work-Study jobs (averaging $1188); 220 part-time jobs.

Need-Based Scholarships & Grants Pell, FSEOG, state, private, college/university.

Loans Perkins, PLUS, Stafford, Unsubsidized Stafford, state, private.

Non-Need Awards In 1996, a total of 602 non-need awards were made. *Academic Interests/Achievement Awards:* 318 ($1,422,995 total): general academic. *Creative Arts/Performance Awards:* 17 ($15,925 total): art/fine arts, music. *Special Achievements/Activities Awards:* 79 ($140,486 total): community service, leadership. *Special Characteristics Awards:* 188 ($465,749 total): children of faculty/staff, international students, members of minorities, relatives of clergy, religious affiliation.

Other Money-Saving Options Accelerated degree. *Payment Plan:* installment. *Waivers:* full or partial for employees or children of employees.

Contact Office of Financial Aid, Bluffton College, 280 West College Avenue, Bluffton, OH 45817-1196, 419-358-3266, fax: 419-358-3232.

BOISE BIBLE COLLEGE
Boise, Idaho

About the Institution Independent/religious, coed. Degrees awarded: A, B. Offers 7 undergraduate majors. Total enrollment: 113 (23% state residents). Freshmen: 26.

Undergraduate Expenses (1997–98) Comprehensive fee of $7764 includes tuition ($4340) and college room and board ($3424).

Applications 81% of all full-time undergraduates enrolled in fall 1996 applied for aid; of these, 93% were judged to have need according to Federal Methodology, of whom 100% were aided. *Financial aid deadline (priority):* 5/1. *Financial aid forms:* FAFSA, institutional form required. *Admission application deadline:* rolling.

Summary of Aid to Needy Students *From gift & self-help combined:* Average need met: 22%. Average amount awarded: $2703 (65% gift aid, 35% self-help). *Gift aid:* Total: $123,882 (31% from college's own funds, 7% from other college-administered sources, 62% from external sources). 4 Federal Work-Study jobs (averaging $1053); part-time jobs.

Need-Based Scholarships & Grants Pell, FSEOG, state, private.

Loans PLUS, Stafford, Unsubsidized Stafford, Key Alternative Loans.

Non-Need Awards In 1996, a total of 77 non-need awards were made. *Academic Interests/Achievement Awards:* 34 ($26,612 total): general academic, religion/biblical studies. *Creative Arts/Performance Awards:* 9 ($11,440 total): music. *Special Achievements/Activities Awards:* 21 ($9395 total): leadership, religious involvement. *Special Characteristics Awards:* 13 ($8990 total): adult students, children of faculty/staff, international students, relatives of clergy, spouses of current students.

Other Money-Saving Options *Payment Plan:* installment. *Waivers:* full or partial for employees or children of employees and senior citizens.

Contact Mrs. Joyce Anderson, Financial Aid Officer, Boise Bible College, 8695 Marigold Street, Boise, ID 83714-1220, 208-376-7731, fax: 208-376-7743.

BOISE STATE UNIVERSITY
Boise, Idaho

About the Institution State-supported, coed. Degrees awarded: A, B, M, D. Offers 93 undergraduate majors. Total enrollment: 15,137. Undergraduates: 13,154 (90% state residents). Freshmen: 1,960.

Undergraduate Expenses (1997–98) State resident tuition: $0. Nonresident tuition: $5880. Mandatory fees: $2294. College room and board: $3264.

Applications *Financial aid deadline (priority):* 3/1. *Financial aid forms:* FAFSA required. Institutional form required for some. *Admission application deadline:* 7/23.

Summary of Aid to Needy Students *From gift & self-help combined:* Average amount awarded: $4380 (23% gift aid, 77% self-help). *Gift aid:* Total: $8,057,830 (9% from college's own funds, 14% from other college-administered sources, 77% from external sources). 300 Federal Work-Study jobs (averaging $1100); 656 part-time jobs.

Need-Based Scholarships & Grants Pell, FSEOG, state, private, college/university.

Loans Perkins, PLUS, Stafford, Unsubsidized Stafford, Federal Nursing, private, college/university short-term loans ($250 average), college/university long-term loans ($1285 average).

Non-Need Awards In 1996, a total of 1,576 non-need awards were made. *Academic Interests/Achievement Awards:* 1,100 ($1,009,600 total): general academic, biological sciences, business, communication, computer science, education, engineering/technologies, English, foreign languages, health fields, mathematics, military science, premedicine, social sciences. *Creative Arts/Performance Awards:* 230 ($149,890 total): art/fine arts, journalism/publications, music, performing arts, theater/drama. *Special Achievements/Activities Awards:* 15 ($20,000 total): cheerleading/drum major, rodeo. *Special Characteristics Awards:* 28 ($231,000 total): ethnic background, first-generation college students, international students, out-of-state students. *Athletic:* Total: 203 ($1,454,287); Men: 129 ($950,599); Women: 74 ($503,688).

Other Money-Saving Options Army ROTC, off-campus living. *Payment Plan:* deferred payment. *Waivers:* full or partial for employees or children of employees and senior citizens.

Contact Financial Aid Office, Boise State University, 1910 University Drive, Boise, ID 83725-1315, 208-385-1664, fax: 208-385-1305.

BORICUA COLLEGE
New York, New York

About the Institution Independent, coed. Degrees awarded: A, B, M. Offers 7 undergraduate majors. Total enrollment: 1,052. Undergraduates: 1,037 (100% state residents). Freshmen: 157.

Undergraduate Expenses (1996–97) Tuition: $6400.

Applications *Financial aid deadline (priority):* 3/31. *Financial aid forms:* FAFSA, CSS Financial Aid PROFILE, state form, institutional form required. *Admission application deadline:* rolling.

Summary of Aid to Needy Students *From gift & self-help combined:* Average need met: 85%. Average amount awarded: $2912 (98% gift aid, 2% self-help). *Gift aid:* Total: $2,866,166 (1% from college's own funds, 59% from other college-administered sources, 40% from external sources). Federal Work-Study jobs.

Need-Based Scholarships & Grants Pell, FSEOG, state, private, college/university.

Loans College/university long-term loans ($250 average).

Non-Need Awards Not offered.

Other Money-Saving Options Accelerated degree. *Payment Plan:* deferred payment. *Waivers:* full or partial for employees or children of employees.

Contact Ms. Rosalia Cruz, Financial Aid Administrator, Boricua College, New York, NY 10032-1560, 212-694-1000 Ext. 226, fax: 212-694-1015.

BOSTON ARCHITECTURAL CENTER
Boston, Massachusetts

About the Institution Independent, coed. Degrees awarded: B. Offers 2 undergraduate majors. Total enrollment: 623 (80% state residents). Freshmen: 150.

Undergraduate Expenses (1997–98) Tuition: $5290. Mandatory fees: $20.

Applications Of all full-time undergraduates enrolled in fall 1996, 82% of those who applied for aid were judged to have need according to Federal Methodology, of whom 100% were aided. *Financial aid deadline (priority):* 6/1. *Financial aid forms:* FAFSA, institutional form required. *Admission application deadline:* rolling.

Summary of Aid to Needy Students *From gift & self-help combined:* Average need met: 40%. *Gift aid:* Total: $150,800 (36% from college's own funds, 17% from other college-administered sources, 47% from external sources).

Need-Based Scholarships & Grants Pell, state, private, college/university.

Loans PLUS, Stafford, Unsubsidized Stafford, private.

Non-Need Awards Not offered.

Other Money-Saving Options Co-op program. *Payment Plan:* deferred payment.

Contact Ms. Cheryl Zelanakas, Financial Aid Counselor, Boston Architectural Center, 320 Newbury Street, Boston, MA 02115-2795, 617-536-3170.

BOSTON COLLEGE
Chestnut Hill, Massachusetts

About the Institution Independent/religious, coed. Degrees awarded: B, M, D, P. Offers 57 undergraduate majors. Total enrollment: 14,830. Undergraduates: 8,958 (28% state residents). Freshmen: 2,474.

Undergraduate Expenses (1997–98) Comprehensive fee of $28,077 includes tuition ($19,770), mandatory fees ($537), and college room and board ($7770 minimum). College room only: $4340 (minimum).

Applications 65% of all full-time undergraduates enrolled in fall 1996 applied for aid; of these, 84% were judged to have need according to Federal Methodology, of whom 100% were aided. *Financial aid deadline (priority):* 2/1. *Financial aid forms:* FAFSA, CSS Financial Aid PROFILE, institutional form required. State form required for some. *Regular admission application deadline:* 1/10. Early action deadline: 11/1.

Summary of Aid to Needy Students *From gift & self-help combined:* Average need met: 92%. Average amount awarded: $12,350 (61% gift aid, 39% self-help). *Gift aid:* Total: $36,662,143 (79% from college's own funds, 6% from other college-administered sources, 15% from external sources). 1,470 Federal Work-Study jobs (averaging $1650); 1,150 part-time jobs.

Need-Based Scholarships & Grants Pell, FSEOG, state, private, college/university.

Loans Perkins, PLUS, Stafford, Unsubsidized Stafford, Federal Nursing, state, private.

Non-Need Awards *Academic Interests/Achievement Awards:* 10 ($94,100 total): general academic. *Special Characteristics Awards:* children of faculty/staff, ROTC participants. *Athletic:* available.

Other Money-Saving Options Accelerated degree, cooperative Army ROTC, cooperative Naval ROTC, cooperative Air Force ROTC, off-campus living. *Payment Plans:* tuition prepayment, installment. *Waivers:* full or partial for employees or children of employees.

Contact Mr. Bernie Pekala, Director of Financial Aid, Boston College, 116 Lyons, 140 Commonwealth Avenue, Chestnut Hill, MA 02167-9991, 617-552-3320.

BOSTON CONSERVATORY
Boston, Massachusetts

About the Institution Independent, coed. Degrees awarded: B, M. Offers 9 undergraduate majors. Total enrollment: 452. Undergraduates: 324 (23% state residents). Freshmen: 100.

Undergraduate Expenses (1997–98) Comprehensive fee of $23,075 includes tuition ($15,300), mandatory fees ($625), and college room and board ($7150).

Applications 92% of all full-time undergraduates enrolled in fall 1996 applied for aid; of these, 71% were judged to have need according to Federal Methodology, of whom 86% were aided. *Financial aid deadline (priority):* 3/1. *Financial aid forms:* FAFSA, institutional form required. *Regular admission application deadline:* rolling. Early action deadline: 11/15.

Summary of Aid to Needy Students *From gift & self-help combined:* Average need met: 82%. Average amount awarded: $13,891 (35% gift aid, 65% self-help). *Gift aid:* Total: $836,643 (69% from college's own funds, 13% from other college-administered sources, 18% from external sources). 63 Federal Work-Study jobs (averaging $840); 31 part-time jobs.

Need-Based Scholarships & Grants Pell, FSEOG, state, private, college/university.

Loans PLUS, Stafford, Unsubsidized Stafford, state, college/university long-term loans ($4000 average).

Non-Need Awards In 1996, a total of 102 non-need awards were made. *Creative Arts/Performance Awards:* 102: dance, music, theater/drama.

Another Money-Saving Option Off-campus living.

Contact Office of Financial Aid, Boston Conservatory, Boston, MA 02215, 617-536-6340.

BOSTON UNIVERSITY
Boston, Massachusetts

About the Institution Independent, coed. Degrees awarded: B, M, D, P. Offers 128 undergraduate majors. Total enrollment: 29,664. Undergraduates: 15,414 (25% state residents). Freshmen: 3,969.

Undergraduate Expenses (1997–98) Comprehensive fee of $29,848 includes tuition ($21,970), mandatory fees ($308), and college room and board ($7570). College room only: $4640.

Applications 63% of all full-time undergraduates enrolled in fall 1996 applied for aid; of these, 92% were judged to have need according to Federal Methodology, of whom 96% were aided. *Financial aid deadline (priority):* 2/15. *Financial aid forms:* FAFSA, CSS Financial Aid PROFILE required. State form, financial aid transcript (for mid-year transfers) required for some. *Regular admission application deadline:* 1/15. Early decision deadline: 11/1.

Summary of Aid to Needy Students *From gift & self-help combined:* Average need met: 89%. Average amount awarded: $17,542 (72% gift aid, 28% self-help). *Gift aid:* Total: $105,406,158 (90% from college's own funds, 2% from other college-administered sources, 8% from external sources). 3,031 Federal Work-Study jobs (averaging $2076); part-time jobs.

Need-Based Scholarships & Grants Pell, FSEOG, state, private, college/university.

Loans Perkins, PLUS, Stafford, Unsubsidized Stafford, Primary Care, state, private, college/university short-term loans, Health Professions Loans.

Non-Need Awards In 1996, a total of 3,182 non-need awards were made. *Academic Interests/Achievement Awards:* 1,798 ($17,271,000 total): general academic. *Creative Arts/Performance Awards:* 156 ($1,135,000 total): art/fine arts, music, theater/drama. *Special Characteristics Awards:* 965 ($7,144,000 total): children and siblings of alumni, local/state students, relatives of clergy, religious affiliation, ROTC participants. *Athletic:* Total: 263 ($5,440,000); Men: 154 ($3,465,000); Women: 109 ($1,975,000).

Other Money-Saving Options Co-op program, Army ROTC, Naval ROTC, Air Force ROTC, off-campus living (after freshman year). *Pay-*

ment Plans: tuition prepayment, installment. *Waivers:* full or partial for employees or children of employees and senior citizens.

Contact Mr. Ryan Williams, Director of Financial Assistance, Boston University, 881 Commonwealth Avenue, 5th Floor, Boston, MA 02215, 617-353-6782, fax: 617-353-8200.

BOWDOIN COLLEGE
Brunswick, Maine

About the Institution Independent, coed. Degrees awarded: B. Offers 37 undergraduate majors. Total enrollment: 1,581 (14% state residents). Freshmen: 443.

Undergraduate Expenses (1997–98) Comprehensive fee of $29,090 includes tuition ($22,460), mandatory fees ($445), and college room and board ($6185). College room only: $2790.

Applications Of all full-time undergraduates enrolled in fall 1996, 99% of those who applied for aid were judged to have need according to Federal Methodology, of whom 76% were aided. *Financial aid deadline (priority):* 3/1. *Financial aid forms:* FAFSA, CSS Financial Aid PROFILE, institutional form required. Divorced/Separated Parents' Statement, Business/Farm Supplement required for some. *Regular admission application deadline:* 1/1. Early decision deadline: 11/15.

Summary of Aid to Needy Students *From gift & self-help combined:* Average need met: 100%. Average amount awarded: $18,267 (75% gift aid, 25% self-help). *Gift aid:* Total: $9,556,435 (89% from college's own funds, 8% from other college-administered sources, 3% from external sources). 590 Federal Work-Study jobs (averaging $1972); 60 part-time jobs.

Need-Based Scholarships & Grants Pell, FSEOG, state, private, college/university.

Loans Perkins, PLUS, Stafford, Unsubsidized Stafford, state, private, college/university long-term loans ($2455 average).

Non-Need Awards Not offered.

Other Money-Saving Options Accelerated degree, off-campus living (after freshman year). *Payment Plan:* installment. *Waivers:* full or partial for employees or children of employees.

Contact Mr. Stephen Joyce, Associate Director of Student Aid, Bowdoin College, Brunswick, ME 04011-2546, 207-725-3273, fax: 207-725-3101.

BOWIE STATE UNIVERSITY
Bowie, Maryland

About the Institution State-supported, coed. Degrees awarded: B, M. Offers 42 undergraduate majors. Total enrollment: 5,067. Undergraduates: 3,110 (93% state residents). Freshmen: 325.

Undergraduate Expenses (1996–97) State resident tuition: $2380. Nonresident tuition: $6304. Mandatory fees: $722. College room and board: $4410. College room only: $2616.

Applications 77% of all full-time undergraduates enrolled in fall 1996 applied for aid; of these, 84% were judged to have need according to Federal Methodology, of whom 71% were aided. *Financial aid deadline (priority):* 4/1. *Financial aid forms:* FAFSA, institutional form required. State form required for some. *Admission application deadline:* 4/1.

Summary of Aid to Needy Students *From gift & self-help combined:* Average need met: 60%. Average amount awarded: $4053 (35% gift aid, 65% self-help). *Gift aid:* Total: $2,888,900 (21% from college's own funds, 30% from other college-administered sources, 49% from external sources). 200 Federal Work-Study jobs (averaging $1000); 225 part-time jobs.

Need-Based Scholarships & Grants Pell, FSEOG, state, private, college/university.

Loans Perkins, PLUS, Stafford, Unsubsidized Stafford.

Non-Need Awards *Academic Interests/Achievement Awards:* 221 ($266,063 total): general academic. *Creative Arts/Performance Awards:* 25 ($60,000 total): general creative, applied art and design, art/fine arts, music. *Special Characteristics Awards:* 10 ($125,000 total): out-of-state students. *Athletic:* available.

Other Money-Saving Options Accelerated degree, co-op program, Army ROTC, cooperative Air Force ROTC, off-campus living. *Payment Plan:* deferred payment. *Waivers:* full or partial for employees or children of employees and senior citizens.

Contact Ms. Mindy Schaffer, Interim Director of Financial Aid, Bowie State University, 14000 Jericho Park Road, Bowie, MD 20715, 301-464-6546, fax: 301-464-7234.

BOWLING GREEN STATE UNIVERSITY
Bowling Green, Ohio

About the Institution State-supported, coed. Degrees awarded: B, M, D. Offers 139 undergraduate majors. Total enrollment: 17,564. Undergraduates: 14,416 (91% state residents). Freshmen: 3,273.

Undergraduate Expenses (1996–97) State resident tuition: $4190. Nonresident tuition: $8930. College room and board: $3914. College room only: $2372.

Applications Of all full-time undergraduates enrolled in fall 1996, 91% of those who applied for aid were judged to have need according to Federal Methodology, of whom 100% were aided. *Financial aid deadline:* continuous. *Financial aid forms:* FAFSA required. *Admission application deadline:* rolling.

Summary of Aid to Needy Students *From gift & self-help combined:* Average need met: 90%. Average amount awarded: $5351 (23% gift aid, 77% self-help). *Gift aid:* Total: $9,907,800 (13% from college's own funds, 44% from other college-administered sources, 43% from external sources). Federal Work-Study jobs; 3,500 part-time jobs.

Need-Based Scholarships & Grants Pell, FSEOG, state, college/university.

Loans Perkins, PLUS, Stafford, Unsubsidized Stafford, Federal Nursing, state, private, college/university short-term loans ($617 average), college/university long-term loans.

Non-Need Awards *Academic Interests/Achievement Awards:* general academic. *Creative Arts/Performance Awards:* art/fine arts, cinema/film/broadcasting, debating, music, theater/drama. *Special Achievements/Activities Awards:* general special achievements/activities, leadership. *Special Characteristics Awards:* general special characteristics, members of minorities. *Athletic:* Total: 336 ($1,992,383).

Other Money-Saving Options Accelerated degree, co-op program, Army ROTC, Air Force ROTC, off-campus living (after sophomore year). *Payment Plan:* installment. *Waivers:* full or partial for employees or children of employees and senior citizens.

Contact Office of Financial Aid, Bowling Green State University, 231 Administration Building, Bowling Green, OH 43403, 419-372-2651, fax: 419-372-0404.

BRADFORD COLLEGE
Bradford, Massachusetts

About the Institution Independent, coed. Degrees awarded: B. Offers 46 undergraduate majors. Total enrollment: 568 (52% state residents). Freshmen: 195.

Undergraduate Expenses (1997–98) Comprehensive fee of $23,035 includes tuition ($15,850), mandatory fees ($465), and college room and board ($6720). College room only: $3770.

Applications Of all full-time undergraduates enrolled in fall 1996, 71% of those who applied for aid were judged to have need according to Federal Methodology, of whom 100% were aided. *Financial aid deadline*

(priority): 2/15. *Financial aid forms:* FAFSA, institutional form, nontaxable income verification required. State form required for some. *Admission application deadline:* rolling.

Summary of Aid to Needy Students *From gift & self-help combined:* Average need met: 95%. Average amount awarded: $17,489 (69% gift aid, 31% self-help). *Gift aid:* Total: $4,292,805 (80% from college's own funds, 3% from other college-administered sources, 17% from external sources). 294 Federal Work-Study jobs (averaging $955); 30 part-time jobs.

Need-Based Scholarships & Grants Pell, FSEOG, state, private, college/university.

Loans Perkins, PLUS, Stafford, Unsubsidized Stafford, state, private.

Non-Need Awards *Academic Interests/Achievement Awards:* 11 ($103,966 total): general academic. *Creative Arts/Performance Awards:* 1 ($4000 total): general creative. *Special Achievements/Activities Awards:* community service, leadership.

Other Money-Saving Options Accelerated degree, co-op program, off-campus living (after sophomore year). *Payment Plans:* installment, deferred payment. *Waivers:* full or partial for employees or children of employees.

Contact Ms. Elizabeth Keuffel, Assistant Director of Financial Aid, Bradford College, 320 South Main Street, Bradford, MA 01835, 508-372-7161, fax: 508-372-5240.

BRADLEY UNIVERSITY
Peoria, Illinois

About the Institution Independent, coed. Degrees awarded: B, M. Offers 80 undergraduate majors. Total enrollment: 5,900. Undergraduates: 4,949 (77% state residents). Freshmen: 951.

Undergraduate Expenses (1997–98) Comprehensive fee of $17,380 includes tuition ($12,610), mandatory fees ($80), and college room and board ($4690 minimum). College room only: $2840 (minimum).

Applications Of all full-time undergraduates enrolled in fall 1996, 70% of those who applied for aid were judged to have need according to Federal Methodology, of whom 100% were aided. *Financial aid deadline (priority):* 3/1. *Financial aid forms:* FAFSA required; CSS Financial Aid PROFILE acceptable. *Admission application deadline:* rolling.

Summary of Aid to Needy Students *From gift & self-help combined:* Average need met: 50%. Average amount awarded: $9872 (55% gift aid, 45% self-help). *Gift aid:* Total: $15,452,000 (41% from college's own funds, 5% from other college-administered sources, 54% from external sources). 583 Federal Work-Study jobs (averaging $1520).

Need-Based Scholarships & Grants Pell, FSEOG, state, private, college/university.

Loans Perkins, PLUS, Stafford, Unsubsidized Stafford, Federal Nursing, college/university long-term loans ($4388 average).

Non-Need Awards In 1996, a total of 2,011 non-need awards were made. *Academic Interests/Achievement Awards:* 1,521 ($5,240,000 total): general academic. *Creative Arts/Performance Awards:* 236 ($90,150 total): art/fine arts, debating, music, theater/drama. *Special Characteristics Awards:* 53 ($180,000 total): children and siblings of alumni, members of minorities. *Athletic:* Total: 201 ($1,393,166); Men: 101 ($672,690); Women: 100 ($720,476).

Other Money-Saving Options Accelerated degree, co-op program, Army ROTC, off-campus living (after sophomore year). *Payment Plans:* installment, deferred payment. *Waivers:* full or partial for employees or children of employees and senior citizens.

Contact Mr. David L. Pardieck, Director of Financial Assistance, Bradley University, 1501 West Bradley Avenue, 14 Swords Hall, Peoria, IL 61625-0002, 309-677-3089, fax: 309-677-2798.

BRANDEIS UNIVERSITY
Waltham, Massachusetts

About the Institution Independent, coed. Degrees awarded: B, M, D. Offers 51 undergraduate majors. Total enrollment: 4,219. Undergraduates: 3,020 (28% state residents). Freshmen: 770.

Undergraduate Expenses (1997–98) Comprehensive fee of $29,821 includes tuition ($22,360), mandatory fees ($491), and college room and board ($6970). College room only: $3890.

Applications Of all full-time undergraduates enrolled in fall 1996, 100% of those judged to have need according to Federal Methodology were aided. *Financial aid deadline (priority):* 2/15. *Financial aid forms:* FAFSA, CSS Financial Aid PROFILE, institutional form required. State form required for some. *Regular admission application deadline:* 2/1. Early decision deadline: 1/1.

Summary of Aid to Needy Students Federal Work-Study jobs; part-time jobs.

Need-Based Scholarships & Grants Pell, FSEOG, state, private, college/university.

Loans College/university long-term loans.

Non-Need Awards *Academic Interests/Achievement Awards:* general academic. *Special Achievements/Activities Awards:* community service. *Special Characteristics Awards:* local/state students.

Other Money-Saving Options Cooperative Army ROTC, cooperative Air Force ROTC, off-campus living. *Payment Plans:* tuition prepayment, installment. *Waivers:* full or partial for employees or children of employees.

Contact Office of Financial Aid, Brandeis University, 415 South Street Kutz Hall 121, Waltham, MA 02254-9110, 617-736-2000.

BRENAU UNIVERSITY
Gainesville, Georgia

About the Institution Independent, primarily women. Degrees awarded: B, M. Offers 45 undergraduate majors. Total enrollment: 2,225. Undergraduates: 1,423 (83% state residents). Freshmen: 262.

Undergraduate Expenses (1996–97) Comprehensive fee of $16,680 includes tuition ($10,350) and college room and board ($6330).

Applications 65% of all full-time undergraduates enrolled in fall 1996 applied for aid; of these, 87% were judged to have need according to Federal Methodology, of whom 100% were aided. *Financial aid deadline (priority):* 5/1. *Financial aid forms:* FAFSA required. State form, institutional form required for some. *Regular admission application deadline:* rolling. Early decision deadline: 11/14.

Summary of Aid to Needy Students *From gift & self-help combined:* Average need met: 88%. Average amount awarded: $10,230 (66% gift aid, 34% self-help). *Gift aid:* Total: $4,248,054 (42% from college's own funds, 5% from other college-administered sources, 53% from external sources). 83 Federal Work-Study jobs (averaging $1430); 10 part-time jobs.

Need-Based Scholarships & Grants Pell, FSEOG, private, college/university.

Loans Perkins, PLUS, Stafford, Unsubsidized Stafford, state.

Non-Need Awards In 1996, a total of 280 non-need awards were made. *Academic Interests/Achievement Awards:* 144 ($671,932 total): general academic, communication, humanities. *Creative Arts/Performance Awards:* 66 ($122,150 total): applied art and design, art/fine arts, dance, music, theater/drama. *Special Characteristics Awards:* 56 ($119,928 total): children of faculty/staff, international students, members of minorities. *Athletic:* Total: 14 ($68,050); Men: 0; Women: 14 ($68,050).

Other Money-Saving Options Accelerated degree. *Waivers:* full or partial for employees or children of employees.

Contact Office of Financial Aid, Brenau University, 1 Centennial Circle, Gainesville, GA 30501-3697, 770-534-6299.

BRESCIA COLLEGE
Owensboro, Kentucky

About the Institution Independent/religious, coed. Degrees awarded: A, B, M. Offers 42 undergraduate majors. Total enrollment: 753. Undergraduates: 716 (91% state residents). Freshmen: 83.

Undergraduate Expenses (1996–97) Comprehensive fee of $11,856 includes tuition ($8400) and college room and board ($3456).

Applications 96% of all full-time undergraduates enrolled in fall 1996 applied for aid; of these,100% were judged to have need according to Federal Methodology, of whom 100% were aided. *Financial aid deadline (priority):* 4/1. *Financial aid forms:* FAFSA required. *Admission application deadline:* rolling.

Summary of Aid to Needy Students *From gift & self-help combined:* Average need met: 100%. Average amount awarded: $7960 (56% gift aid, 44% self-help). *Gift aid:* Total: $1,800,000 (44% from college's own funds, 17% from other college-administered sources, 39% from external sources). 80 Federal Work-Study jobs (averaging $1020); 43 part-time jobs.

Need-Based Scholarships & Grants Pell, FSEOG, state, private, college/university.

Loans Perkins, PLUS, Stafford, Unsubsidized Stafford, college/university long-term loans ($1400 average).

Non-Need Awards In 1996, a total of 227 non-need awards were made. *Academic Interests/Achievement Awards:* 123 ($353,000 total): general academic. *Creative Arts/Performance Awards:* 10 ($14,500 total): art/fine arts, creative writing, music. *Special Characteristics Awards:* 30 ($52,500 total): general special characteristics, children and siblings of alumni, children of faculty/staff. *Athletic:* Total: 64 ($288,000); Men: 35 ($156,000); Women: 29 ($132,000).

Other Money-Saving Options Accelerated degree, co-op program, off-campus living (after freshman year). *Payment Plan:* deferred payment. *Waivers:* full or partial for children of alumni, employees or children of employees, senior citizens.

Contact Ms. Vivian Pearson, Director of Financial Aid, Brescia College, 717 Frederick Street, Owensboro, KY 42301-3023, 502-686-4290, fax: 502-686-4266.

BREWTON-PARKER COLLEGE
Mt. Vernon, Georgia

About the Institution Independent/religious, coed. Degrees awarded: A, B. Offers 45 undergraduate majors. Total enrollment: 1,582 (92% state residents). Freshmen: 239.

Undergraduate Expenses (1996–97) Comprehensive fee of $8085 includes tuition ($5265), mandatory fees ($255), and college room and board ($2565).

Applications Of all full-time undergraduates enrolled in fall 1996, 100% of those judged to have need according to Federal Methodology were aided. *Financial aid deadline (priority):* 7/1. *Financial aid forms:* FAFSA, institutional form required; CSS Financial Aid PROFILE acceptable. State form required for some. *Admission application deadline:* rolling.

Summary of Aid to Needy Students *From gift & self-help combined:* Average need met: 82%. *Gift aid:* Total: $10,029,000 (22% from college's own funds, 5% from other college-administered sources, 73% from external sources). Federal Work-Study jobs; part-time jobs.

Need-Based Scholarships & Grants Pell, FSEOG, state, private, college/university.

Loans Perkins, PLUS, Stafford, Unsubsidized Stafford.

Non-Need Awards *Academic Interests/Achievement Awards:* general academic, religion/biblical studies. *Creative Arts/Performance Awards:* music, theater/drama. *Special Achievements/Activities Awards:* leadership, religious involvement. *Special Characteristics Awards:* children of faculty/staff, members of minorities. *Athletic:* available.

Other Money-Saving Options Co-op program, off-campus living (after sophomore year). *Payment Plan:* installment. *Waivers:* full or partial for employees or children of employees.

Contact Ms. Cecelia Hightower, Director of Financial Aid, Brewton-Parker College, Mt. Vernon, GA 30445, 912-583-2241.

BRIAR CLIFF COLLEGE
Sioux City, Iowa

About the Institution Independent/religious, coed. Degrees awarded: A, B. Offers 41 undergraduate majors. Total enrollment: 1,116 (68% state residents). Freshmen: 185.

Undergraduate Expenses (1997–98) Comprehensive fee of $16,060 includes tuition ($11,730), mandatory fees ($150), and college room and board ($4180). College room only: $2065.

Applications 92% of all full-time undergraduates enrolled in fall 1996 applied for aid; of these, 95% were judged to have need according to Federal Methodology, of whom 100% were aided. *Financial aid deadline (priority):* 3/1. *Financial aid forms:* FAFSA required. State form required for some. *Admission application deadline:* rolling.

Summary of Aid to Needy Students *From gift & self-help combined:* Average need met: 95%. Average amount awarded: $7594 (62% gift aid, 38% self-help). *Gift aid:* Total: $5,274,849 (59% from college's own funds, 3% from other college-administered sources, 38% from external sources). 519 Federal Work-Study jobs (averaging $1500); 200 part-time jobs.

Need-Based Scholarships & Grants Pell, FSEOG, state, college/university.

Loans Perkins, PLUS, Stafford, Unsubsidized Stafford, college/university short-term loans ($200 average), college/university long-term loans ($2000 average).

Non-Need Awards In 1996, a total of 997 non-need awards were made. *Academic Interests/Achievement Awards:* 508 ($1,628,350 total): general academic, biological sciences, business, communication, computer science, education, English, foreign languages, health fields, humanities, mathematics, physical sciences, religion/biblical studies, social sciences. *Creative Arts/Performance Awards:* 63 ($121,956 total): art/fine arts, music, theater/drama. *Special Achievements/Activities Awards:* 178 ($118,329 total): leadership, religious involvement. *Special Characteristics Awards:* 28 ($110,116 total): international students, members of minorities. *Athletic:* Total: 220 ($522,504); Men: 107 ($266,528); Women: 113 ($255,976).

Other Money-Saving Options Accelerated degree, off-campus living (after junior year). *Payment Plan:* deferred payment. *Waivers:* full or partial for employees or children of employees, adult students, senior citizens.

Contact Financial Aid Office, Briar Cliff College, 3303 Rebecca Street, PO Box 2100, Sioux City, IA 51104-2100, 712-279-5440, fax: 712-279-5410.

BRIDGEWATER COLLEGE
Bridgewater, Virginia

About the Institution Independent/religious, coed. Degrees awarded: B. Offers 44 undergraduate majors. Total enrollment: 1,033 (71% state residents). Freshmen: 317.

Undergraduate Expenses (1997–98) Comprehensive fee of $18,900 includes tuition ($12,270), mandatory fees ($1000), and college room and board ($5630).

Applications 81% of all full-time undergraduates enrolled in fall 1996 applied for aid; of these, 92% were judged to have need according to Federal Methodology, of whom 100% were aided. *Financial aid deadline (priority):* 3/1. *Financial aid forms:* FAFSA required. State form required for some. *Admission application deadline:* rolling.

Summary of Aid to Needy Students *From gift & self-help combined:* Average need met: 83%. Average amount awarded: $11,391 (66% gift aid, 34% self-help). *Gift aid:* Total: $5,772,073 (72% from college's own funds, 3% from other college-administered sources, 25% from external sources). 314 Federal Work-Study jobs (averaging $978); 50 part-time jobs.

Need-Based Scholarships & Grants Pell, FSEOG, state, private, college/university.

Loans Perkins, PLUS, Stafford, Unsubsidized Stafford, college/university long-term loans.

Non-Need Awards In 1996, a total of 679 non-need awards were made. *Academic Interests/Achievement Awards:* 557 ($2,596,975 total): general academic. *Creative Arts/Performance Awards:* 17 ($17,000 total): music. *Special Characteristics Awards:* 105 ($247,000 total): religious affiliation.

Other Money-Saving Options Accelerated degree. *Payment Plan:* installment. *Waivers:* full or partial for employees or children of employees.

Contact Mr. J. Vern Fairchilds Jr., Director of Financial Aid, Bridgewater College, College Box 27, Bridgewater, VA 22812-1599, 540-828-5376, fax: 540-828-5497.

BRIDGEWATER STATE COLLEGE
Bridgewater, Massachusetts

About the Institution State-supported, coed. Degrees awarded: B, M. Offers 61 undergraduate majors. Total enrollment: 8,711. Undergraduates: 7,372 (96% state residents). Freshmen: 1,177.

Undergraduate Expenses (1997–98) State resident tuition: $1270. Nonresident tuition: $5950. Mandatory fees: $2102. College room and board: $4152 (minimum). College room only: $2360 (minimum).

Applications 80% of all full-time undergraduates enrolled in fall 1996 applied for aid; of these, 79% were judged to have need according to Federal Methodology, of whom 87% were aided. *Financial aid deadline (priority):* 3/1. *Financial aid forms:* FAFSA required. *Regular admission application deadline:* 3/1. Early action deadline: 11/15.

Summary of Aid to Needy Students *From gift & self-help combined:* Average need met: 69%. Average amount awarded: $4482 (34% gift aid, 66% self-help). *Gift aid:* Total: $4,755,303 (9% from college's own funds, 31% from other college-administered sources, 60% from external sources). 444 Federal Work-Study jobs (averaging $1721); 496 part-time jobs.

Need-Based Scholarships & Grants Pell, FSEOG, state, college/university.

Loans Perkins, PLUS, Stafford, Unsubsidized Stafford, private, college/university short-term loans ($50 average), college/university long-term loans ($1003 average).

Non-Need Awards In 1996, a total of 43 non-need awards were made. *Academic Interests/Achievement Awards:* 43 ($56,196 total): general academic.

Other Money-Saving Options Air Force ROTC, cooperative Army ROTC, off-campus living. *Payment Plan:* installment. *Waivers:* full or partial for employees or children of employees.

Contact Office of Financial Aid, Bridgewater State College, Tillinghast Hall, Bridgewater, MA 02325-0001, 508-697-1341.

BRIGHAM YOUNG UNIVERSITY
Provo, Utah

About the Institution Independent/religious, coed. Degrees awarded: B, M, D, P. Offers 173 undergraduate majors. Total enrollment: 30,563. Undergraduates: 27,706 (33% state residents). Freshmen: 4,277.

Undergraduate Expenses (1997–98) Comprehensive fee of $6435 includes tuition ($2630 minimum) and college room and board ($3805).

Applications 74% of all full-time undergraduates enrolled in fall 1996 applied for aid; of these, 53% were judged to have need according to Federal Methodology, of whom 88% were aided. *Financial aid deadline (priority):* 3/1. *Financial aid forms:* FAFSA, institutional form required. *Admission application deadline:* 2/15.

Summary of Aid to Needy Students *From gift & self-help combined:* Average need met: 52%. Average amount awarded: $4202 (47% gift aid, 53% self-help). *Gift aid:* Total: $16,392,475 (12% from college's own funds, 26% from other college-administered sources, 62% from external sources). 11,000 part-time jobs.

Need-Based Scholarships & Grants Pell, private, college/university.

Loans PLUS, Stafford, Unsubsidized Stafford, college/university short-term loans ($1285 average).

Non-Need Awards *Academic Interests/Achievement Awards:* 6,000 ($11,300,000 total): general academic. *Creative Arts/Performance Awards:* 160 ($200,000 total): applied art and design, art/fine arts, cinema/film/broadcasting, dance, journalism/publications, music, theater/drama. *Special Achievements/Activities Awards:* general special achievements/activities. *Special Characteristics Awards:* 164 ($484,020 total): ROTC participants. *Athletic:* Total: 311 ($913,659); Men: 231 ($793,659); Women: 80 ($120,000).

Other Money-Saving Options Accelerated degree, co-op program, Army ROTC, Air Force ROTC, off-campus living. *Waivers:* full or partial for employees or children of employees.

Contact Financial Aid Office, Brigham Young University, A-41 Abraham Smoot Building, Provo, UT 84602-1001, 801-378-4104, fax: 801-378-4264.

BRIGHAM YOUNG UNIVERSITY
HAWAII CAMPUS
Laie, Oahu, Hawaii

About the Institution Independent/religious, coed. Degrees awarded: A, B. Offers 37 undergraduate majors. Total enrollment: 2,287 (31% state residents). Freshmen: 541.

Undergraduate Expenses (1997–98) Comprehensive fee of $7565 includes tuition ($2665 minimum) and college room and board ($4900). College room only: $2200.

Applications *Financial aid deadline (priority):* 4/30. *Financial aid forms:* FAFSA, institutional form required for some. *Admission application deadline:* 3/31.

Summary of Aid to Needy Students 900 part-time jobs.

Need-Based Scholarships & Grants Pell, state, private, college/university.

Loans Stafford, Unsubsidized Stafford, college/university short-term loans ($1000 average).

Non-Need Awards *Academic Interests/Achievement Awards:* general academic, area/ethnic studies, biological sciences, business, communication, computer science, education, English, foreign languages, humanities, international studies, library science, mathematics, physical sciences, religion/biblical studies, social sciences. *Creative Arts/Performance Awards:* art/fine arts, creative writing, journalism/publications, music, theater/drama. *Special Achievements/Activities*

Awards: Junior Miss, leadership. *Special Characteristics Awards:* children of educators, children of faculty/staff, ethnic background, international students, religious affiliation. *Athletic:* available.

Other Money-Saving Options Accelerated degree, co-op program, cooperative Army ROTC, cooperative Air Force ROTC, off-campus living (after freshman year). *Waivers:* full or partial for employees or children of employees.

Contact Office of Financial Aid, Brigham Young University–Hawaii Campus, PO Box 1980, Laie, Oahu, HI 96762-1294, 808-293-3530.

BROOKLYN COLLEGE OF THE CITY UNIVERSITY OF NEW YORK
Brooklyn, New York

About the Institution State & locally supported, coed. Degrees awarded: B, M. Offers 63 undergraduate majors. Total enrollment: 13,267. Undergraduates: 10,504 (97% state residents). Freshmen: 1,311.

Undergraduate Expenses (1996–97) State resident tuition: $3200. Nonresident tuition: $6800. Mandatory fees: $187.

Applications *Financial aid deadline (priority):* 4/1. *Financial aid forms:* FAFSA required. State form required for some. *Admission application deadline:* 7/30.

Summary of Aid to Needy Students *From gift & self-help combined:* Average need met: 100%. Average amount awarded: $3763 (71% gift aid, 29% self-help). *Gift aid:* Total: $25,817,489 (1% from college's own funds, 37% from other college-administered sources, 62% from external sources). 1,500 Federal Work-Study jobs (averaging $800); 300 part-time jobs.

Need-Based Scholarships & Grants Pell, FSEOG, state, private, college/university.

Loans Perkins, PLUS, Stafford, Unsubsidized Stafford.

Non-Need Awards *Academic Interests/Achievement Awards:* general academic. *Creative Arts/Performance Awards:* general creative. *Special Achievements/Activities Awards:* general special achievements/activities. *Special Characteristics Awards:* general special characteristics.

Other Money-Saving Options *Waivers:* full or partial for employees or children of employees and senior citizens.

Contact Financial Aid Office, Brooklyn College of the City University of New York, 2900 Bedford Avenue, Brooklyn, NY 11210-2889, 718-951-5051.

BROOKS INSTITUTE OF PHOTOGRAPHY
Santa Barbara, California

About the Institution Proprietary, coed. Degrees awarded: B, M. Offers 2 undergraduate majors. Total enrollment: 351. Undergraduates: 324 (35% state residents). Freshmen: 115.

Undergraduate Expenses (1997–98 estimated) Tuition: $14,700. Mandatory fees: $210.

Applications *Financial aid deadline (priority):* 7/1. *Financial aid forms:* FAFSA, institutional form required. *Admission application deadline:* rolling.

Summary of Aid to Needy Students Federal Work-Study jobs; part-time jobs.

Loans College/university short-term loans.

Non-Need Awards Not offered.

Other Money-Saving Options Accelerated degree. *Payment Plans:* installment, deferred payment.

Contact Office of Financial Aid, Brooks Institute of Photography, 801 Alston Road, Santa Barbara, CA 93108-2399, 805-966-3888.

BROWN UNIVERSITY
Providence, Rhode Island

About the Institution Independent, coed. Degrees awarded: B, M, D, P. Offers 80 undergraduate majors. Total enrollment: 7,626. Undergraduates: 5,963 (3% state residents). Freshmen: 1,511.

Undergraduate Expenses (1997–98) Comprehensive fee of $29,900 includes tuition ($22,592), mandatory fees ($532), and college room and board ($6776). College room only: $4154.

Applications Of all full-time undergraduates enrolled in fall 1996, 89% of those who applied for aid were judged to have need according to Federal Methodology, of whom 100% were aided. *Financial aid deadline:* 1/22. *Financial aid forms:* FAFSA, CSS Financial Aid PROFILE, institutional form required. State form, Divorced/Separated Parents' Statement, Business/Farm Supplement required for some. *Regular admission application deadline:* 1/1. Early action deadline: 11/1.

Summary of Aid to Needy Students *From gift & self-help combined:* Average need met: 100%. Average amount awarded: $18,193 (64% gift aid, 36% self-help). *Gift aid:* Total: $27,145,502 (86% from college's own funds, 3% from other college-administered sources, 11% from external sources). 1,969 Federal Work-Study jobs (averaging $1768); 97 part-time jobs.

Need-Based Scholarships & Grants Pell, FSEOG, state, private, college/university.

Loans Perkins, PLUS, Stafford, Unsubsidized Stafford, state, private, college/university short-term loans ($200 average), college/university long-term loans ($6000 average).

Non-Need Awards Not offered.

Other Money-Saving Options Accelerated degree, cooperative Army ROTC. *Payment Plans:* tuition prepayment, installment, deferred payment. *Waivers:* full or partial for employees or children of employees.

Contact Mr. Paul Langhammer, Associate Director of Financial Aid, Brown University, 8 Fones Alley, Providence, RI 02912, 401-863-2721, fax: 401-863-7575.

BRYAN COLLEGE
Dayton, Tennessee

About the Institution Independent/religious, coed. Degrees awarded: A, B. Offers 28 undergraduate majors. Total enrollment: 455 (39% state residents). Freshmen: 124.

Undergraduate Expenses (1997–98 estimated) Comprehensive fee of $13,950 includes tuition ($9700), mandatory fees ($300), and college room and board ($3950). College room only: $1750.

Applications 97% of all full-time undergraduates enrolled in fall 1996 applied for aid; of these, 78% were judged to have need according to Federal Methodology, of whom 100% were aided. *Financial aid deadline (priority):* 5/1. *Financial aid forms:* FAFSA, institutional form required; CSS Financial Aid PROFILE acceptable. State form required for some. *Admission application deadline:* rolling.

Summary of Aid to Needy Students *From gift & self-help combined:* Average need met: 82%. Average amount awarded: $9950 (53% gift aid, 47% self-help). *Gift aid:* Total: $1,744,972 (67% from college's own funds, 14% from other college-administered sources, 19% from external sources). 199 Federal Work-Study jobs (averaging $900); 83 part-time jobs.

Need-Based Scholarships & Grants Pell, FSEOG, state, college/university.

Loans Perkins, PLUS, Stafford, Unsubsidized Stafford, college/university short-term loans ($500 average).

Non-Need Awards *Academic Interests/Achievement Awards:* 210 ($522,500 total): general academic. *Creative Arts/Performance Awards:* 28 ($20,800 total): music. *Special Achievements/Activities Awards:* 23

($6490 total): leadership. *Special Characteristics Awards:* 242 ($457,085 total): children and siblings of alumni, children of faculty/staff, local/state students, relatives of clergy, religious affiliation, spouses of current students. *Athletic:* available.

Other Money-Saving Options *Payment Plan:* installment. *Waivers:* full or partial for employees or children of employees.

Contact Office of Financial Aid, Bryan College, PO Box 7000, Dayton, TN 37321-7000, 423-775-2041.

BRYANT AND STRATTON COLLEGE
Cleveland, Ohio

About the Institution Proprietary, coed. Degrees awarded: A, B. Offers 6 undergraduate majors. Total enrollment: 339 (97% state residents). Freshmen: 117.

Undergraduate Expenses (1996–97) Tuition: $6720. Mandatory fees: $25. College room only: $2500.

Applications 94% of all full-time undergraduates enrolled in fall 1996 applied for aid; of these, 69% were judged to have need according to Federal Methodology, of whom 100% were aided. *Financial aid deadline (priority):* 10/1. *Financial aid forms:* FAFSA, institutional form required. *Admission application deadline:* rolling.

Summary of Aid to Needy Students *From gift & self-help combined:* Average need met: 96%. Average amount awarded: $2300 (41% gift aid, 59% self-help). *Gift aid:* Total: $285,831 (2% from college's own funds, 48% from other college-administered sources, 50% from external sources). 11 Federal Work-Study jobs (averaging $720); 3 part-time jobs.

Need-Based Scholarships & Grants Pell, FSEOG, state, private.

Loans Perkins, PLUS, Stafford, Unsubsidized Stafford.

Non-Need Awards In 1996, a total of 99 non-need awards were made. *Academic Interests/Achievement Awards:* 99 ($10,099 total): general academic.

Other Money-Saving Options Accelerated degree, off-campus living. *Payment Plan:* guaranteed tuition. *Waivers:* full or partial for employees or children of employees.

Contact Mr. Scott A. Heers, Financial Aid Director, Bryant and Stratton College, 1700 East 13th Street, #40, OH 44114-3203, 216-771-1700, fax: 216-771-7787.

BRYANT COLLEGE
Smithfield, Rhode Island

About the Institution Independent, coed. Degrees awarded: A, B, M. Offers 12 undergraduate majors. Total enrollment: 3,332. Undergraduates: 2,748 (28% state residents). Freshmen: 556.

Undergraduate Expenses (1997–98) Comprehensive fee of $21,500 includes tuition ($14,800) and college room and board ($6700). College room only: $3950.

Applications Of all full-time undergraduates enrolled in fall 1996, 100% of those judged to have need according to Federal Methodology were aided. *Financial aid deadline:* 2/15. *Financial aid forms:* FAFSA, state form required. CSS Financial Aid PROFILE, institutional form required for some. *Regular admission application deadline:* rolling. Early action deadline: 11/1.

Summary of Aid to Needy Students *From gift & self-help combined:* Average need met: 88%. Average amount awarded: $10,258 (57% gift aid, 43% self-help). *Gift aid:* Total: $10,043,068 (89% from college's own funds, 2% from other college-administered sources, 9% from external sources). Federal Work-Study jobs; 1,319 part-time jobs.

Need-Based Scholarships & Grants Pell, FSEOG, state, private, college/university.

Loans Perkins, PLUS, Stafford, Unsubsidized Stafford, private.

Non-Need Awards In 1996, a total of 917 non-need awards were made. *Academic Interests/Achievement Awards:* 630 ($2,803,825 total): general academic. *Special Achievements/Activities Awards:* 206 ($616,250 total): leadership. *Special Characteristics Awards:* 60 ($81,065 total): siblings of current students. *Athletic:* Total: 21 ($420,292); Men: 11 ($215,827); Women: 10 ($204,465).

Other Money-Saving Options Accelerated degree, Army ROTC, off-campus living. *Payment Plan:* installment. *Waivers:* full or partial for employees or children of employees and senior citizens.

Contact Mr. Dave Deblois, Director of Financial Aid, Bryant College, 1150 Douglas Pike, Smithfield, RI 02917-1284, 401-232-6020, fax: 401-232-6319.

BRYN ATHYN COLLEGE OF THE NEW CHURCH
Bryn Athyn, Pennsylvania

About the Institution Independent/religious, coed. Degrees awarded: A, B, P. Offers 10 undergraduate majors. Total enrollment: 145. Undergraduates: 129 (49% state residents). Freshmen: 57.

Undergraduate Expenses (1997–98) Comprehensive fee of $8991 includes tuition ($4179), mandatory fees ($741), and college room and board ($4071).

Applications 53% of all full-time undergraduates enrolled in fall 1996 applied for aid; of these, 86% were judged to have need according to Federal Methodology, of whom 100% were aided. *Financial aid deadline (priority):* 6/1. *Financial aid forms:* institutional form, federal income tax form required. *Admission application deadline:* rolling.

Summary of Aid to Needy Students *From gift & self-help combined:* Average need met: 53%. Average amount awarded: $3812. *Gift aid:* Total: $224,917 (98% from college's own funds, 2% from external sources). 70 part-time jobs.

Need-Based Scholarships & Grants Private, college/university.

Loans College/university short-term loans, college/university long-term loans ($1912 average).

Non-Need Awards In 1996, a total of 5 non-need awards were made. *Academic Interests/Achievement Awards:* 5 ($3000 total): general academic.

Other Money-Saving Options Accelerated degree, co-op program, off-campus living (after freshman year). *Payment Plan:* installment. *Waivers:* full or partial for employees or children of employees and senior citizens.

Contact Mr. Duane D. Hyatt, Business Manager, Bryn Athyn College of the New Church, PO Box 711, Bryn Athyn, PA 19009-0717, 215-938-2635, fax: 215-938-2616.

BRYN MAWR COLLEGE
Bryn Mawr, Pennsylvania

About the Institution Independent, women. Degrees awarded: B, M, D. Offers 54 undergraduate majors. Total enrollment: 1,886. Undergraduates: 1,205 (14% state residents). Freshmen: 360.

Undergraduate Expenses (1996–97) Comprehensive fee of $28,015 includes tuition ($20,210), mandatory fees ($435), and college room and board ($7370).

Applications Of all full-time undergraduates enrolled in fall 1996, 84% of those who applied for aid were judged to have need according to Federal Methodology, of whom 100% were aided. *Financial aid deadline:* 1/15. *Financial aid forms:* FAFSA, CSS Financial Aid PROFILE, institutional form required. State form required for some. *Regular admission application deadline:* 1/15. Early decision deadline: 11/15.

Summary of Aid to Needy Students *From gift & self-help combined:* Average need met: 100%. Average amount awarded: $18,600 (72%

gift aid, 28% self-help). *Gift aid:* Total: $8,913,000 (90% from college's own funds, 4% from other college-administered sources, 6% from external sources). 560 Federal Work-Study jobs (averaging $1400); 350 part-time jobs.

Loans College/university short-term loans ($100 average), college/university long-term loans ($700 average).

Non-Need Awards Not offered.

Other Money-Saving Options Accelerated degree, cooperative Air Force ROTC, off-campus living (after freshman year). *Payment Plans:* tuition prepayment, installment, deferred payment. *Waivers:* full or partial for employees or children of employees and senior citizens.

Contact Ms. Carolyn Dent, Associate Director of Admissions and Financial Aid, Bryn Mawr College, 101 North Merion Avenue, Bryn Mawr, PA 19010-2899, 610-526-5246, fax: 610-526-7926.

BUCKNELL UNIVERSITY
Lewisburg, Pennsylvania

About the Institution Independent, coed. Degrees awarded: B, M. Offers 57 undergraduate majors. Total enrollment: 3,573. Undergraduates: 3,347 (33% state residents). Freshmen: 894.

Undergraduate Expenses (1996–97) Comprehensive fee of $25,420 includes tuition ($20,230), mandatory fees ($130), and college room and board ($5060). College room only: $2710.

Applications Of all full-time undergraduates enrolled in fall 1996, 85% of those who applied for aid were judged to have need according to Federal Methodology, of whom 100% were aided. *Financial aid deadline (priority):* 1/1. *Financial aid forms:* FAFSA, CSS Financial Aid PROFILE, state form required. *Regular admission application deadline:* 1/1. Early decision deadline: 12/1.

Summary of Aid to Needy Students *From gift & self-help combined:* Average need met: 99%. Average amount awarded: $15,935 (78% gift aid, 22% self-help). *Gift aid:* Total: $18,106,000 (84% from college's own funds, 2% from other college-administered sources, 14% from external sources). 900 Federal Work-Study jobs (averaging $1500); 36 part-time jobs.

Need-Based Scholarships & Grants Pell, FSEOG, state, private, college/university.

Loans Perkins, PLUS, Stafford, Unsubsidized Stafford, private.

Non-Need Awards Not offered.

Other Money-Saving Options Accelerated degree, Army ROTC, off-campus living (after freshman year). *Payment Plans:* tuition prepayment, installment. *Waivers:* full or partial for employees or children of employees.

Contact Mr. Ronald T. Laszewski, Director of Financial Aid, Bucknell University, Lewisburg, PA 17837, 717-524-1331.

BUENA VISTA UNIVERSITY
Storm Lake, Iowa

About the Institution Independent/religious, coed. Degrees awarded: B, M. Offers 49 undergraduate majors. Total enrollment: 1,173. Undergraduates: 1,154 (84% state residents). Freshmen: 312.

Undergraduate Expenses (1997–98) Comprehensive fee of $19,223 includes tuition ($14,848) and college room and board ($4375).

Applications 95% of all full-time undergraduates enrolled in fall 1996 applied for aid; of these, 96% were judged to have need according to Federal Methodology, of whom 99% were aided. *Financial aid deadline (priority):* 4/21. *Financial aid forms:* FAFSA required; CSS Financial Aid PROFILE, institutional form acceptable. State form required for some. *Admission application deadline:* rolling.

Summary of Aid to Needy Students *From gift & self-help combined:* Average need met: 94%. Average amount awarded: $15,913 (68% gift

aid, 32% self-help). *Gift aid:* Total: $11,014,170 (60% from college's own funds, 11% from other college-administered sources, 29% from external sources). 639 Federal Work-Study jobs (averaging $794); 122 part-time jobs.

Need-Based Scholarships & Grants Pell, FSEOG, state, college/university.

Loans Perkins, PLUS, Stafford, Unsubsidized Stafford, college/university short-term loans ($50 average), college/university long-term loans ($1118 average).

Non-Need Awards In 1996, a total of 937 non-need awards were made. *Academic Interests/Achievement Awards:* 190 ($484,826 total): general academic, biological sciences, computer science, education, humanities, mathematics. *Creative Arts/Performance Awards:* 148 ($150,660 total): art/fine arts, music, theater/drama. *Special Achievements/Activities Awards:* 351 ($1,039,065 total): general special achievements/activities, leadership. *Special Characteristics Awards:* 248 ($586,533 total): international students, out-of-state students, religious affiliation, siblings of current students.

Other Money-Saving Options *Payment Plan:* installment. *Waivers:* full or partial for employees or children of employees.

Contact Office of Financial Aid, Buena Vista University, 610 West Fourth Street, Storm Lake, IA 50588, 712-749-2351.

BURLINGTON COLLEGE
Burlington, Vermont

About the Institution Independent, coed. Degrees awarded: A, B. Offers 10 undergraduate majors. Total enrollment: 198 (95% state residents). Freshmen: 15.

Undergraduate Expenses (1996–97) Tuition: $7013. Mandatory fees: $195 (minimum).

Applications 100% of all full-time undergraduates enrolled in fall 1996 applied for aid; of these, 92% were judged to have need according to Federal Methodology, of whom 100% were aided. *Financial aid deadline:* continuous. *Financial aid forms:* FAFSA, institutional form required; CSS Financial Aid PROFILE acceptable. State form required for some. *Admission application deadline:* rolling.

Summary of Aid to Needy Students *From gift & self-help combined:* Average need met: 75%. Average amount awarded: $7165 (43% gift aid, 57% self-help). *Gift aid:* Total: $157,037 (6% from college's own funds, 22% from other college-administered sources, 72% from external sources). 50 Federal Work-Study jobs (averaging $1600).

Need-Based Scholarships & Grants Pell, FSEOG, state, college/university.

Loans Perkins, PLUS, Stafford, Unsubsidized Stafford, college/university short-term loans ($50 average), college/university long-term loans ($540 average).

Non-Need Awards Not offered.

Other Money-Saving Options Accelerated degree, co-op program. *Payment Plan:* installment. *Waivers:* full or partial for employees or children of employees and senior citizens.

Contact Ms. Yvonne Whitaker, Assistant Director, VSAC Financial Aid Services, c/o Burlington College, PO Box 2000, Winooski, VT 05404, 802-654-3793, fax: 802-654-3765.

BUTLER UNIVERSITY
Indianapolis, Indiana

About the Institution Independent, coed. Degrees awarded: A, B, M. Offers 60 undergraduate majors. Total enrollment: 3,932. Undergraduates: 3,165 (66% state residents). Freshmen: 777.

Undergraduate Expenses (1997–98) Comprehensive fee of $20,870 includes tuition ($15,570 minimum) and college room and board ($5300). College room only: $2420.

Applications 76% of all full-time undergraduates enrolled in fall 1996 applied for aid; of these, 87% were judged to have need according to Federal Methodology, of whom 100% were aided. *Financial aid deadline:* Applications processed continuously. *Financial aid forms:* FAFSA, institutional form required; CSS Financial Aid PROFILE acceptable. *Regular admission application deadline:* 8/15. Early action deadline: 11/1.

Summary of Aid to Needy Students *From gift & self-help combined:* Average amount awarded: $11,765 (67% gift aid, 33% self-help). *Gift aid:* Total: $16,170,662 (80% from college's own funds, 16% from other college-administered sources, 4% from external sources). 141 Federal Work-Study jobs (averaging $1600); 325 part-time jobs.

Need-Based Scholarships & Grants Pell, FSEOG, state, private, college/university.

Loans Perkins, PLUS, Stafford, Unsubsidized Stafford.

Non-Need Awards In 1996, a total of 1,794 non-need awards were made. *Academic Interests/Achievement Awards:* 1,465 ($5,628,148 total): general academic, biological sciences, business, communication, computer science, education, English, foreign languages, humanities, international studies, mathematics, physical sciences, premedicine, religion/biblical studies, social sciences. *Creative Arts/Performance Awards:* 92 ($823,738 total): art/fine arts, dance, music, theater/drama. *Special Achievements/Activities Awards:* 38 ($136,853 total): leadership. *Athletic:* Total: 199 ($1,959,143); Men: 106 ($941,245); Women: 93 ($1,017,898).

Other Money-Saving Options Accelerated degree, cooperative Army ROTC, cooperative Air Force ROTC, off-campus living (after freshman year). *Payment Plans:* tuition prepayment, installment. *Waivers:* full or partial for employees or children of employees.

Contact Ms. Kristine Butz, Senior Assistant Director of Financial Aid, Butler University, 4600 Sunset Avenue, Indianapolis, IN 46208-3485, 317-940-8200, fax: 317-940-8150.

CABRINI COLLEGE
Radnor, Pennsylvania

About the Institution Independent/religious, coed. Degrees awarded: B, M. Offers 35 undergraduate majors. Total enrollment: 2,042. Undergraduates: 1,621 (77% state residents). Freshmen: 247.

Undergraduate Expenses (1997–98 estimated) Comprehensive fee of $20,100 includes tuition ($12,700), mandatory fees ($500), and college room and board ($6900).

Applications 83% of all full-time undergraduates enrolled in fall 1996 applied for aid; of these, 90% were judged to have need according to Federal Methodology, of whom 99% were aided. *Financial aid deadline (priority):* 4/1. *Financial aid forms:* FAFSA required; CSS Financial Aid PROFILE acceptable. State form, institutional form required for some. *Admission application deadline:* rolling.

Summary of Aid to Needy Students *From gift & self-help combined:* Average need met: 86%. Average amount awarded: $11,008 (57% gift aid, 43% self-help). *Gift aid:* Total: $4,718,150 (69% from college's own funds, 2% from other college-administered sources, 29% from external sources). 250 Federal Work-Study jobs (averaging $1000); 10 part-time jobs.

Need-Based Scholarships & Grants Pell, FSEOG, state, private, college/university.

Loans Perkins, PLUS, Stafford, Unsubsidized Stafford, private, college/university long-term loans ($1000 average).

Non-Need Awards In 1996, a total of 320 non-need awards were made. *Academic Interests/Achievement Awards:* 261 ($874,237 total):

general academic. *Special Characteristics Awards:* 59 ($61,400 total): children and siblings of alumni, children of faculty/staff, siblings of current students, twins.

Other Money-Saving Options Accelerated degree, co-op program, cooperative Army ROTC, off-campus living. *Payment Plan:* installment. *Waivers:* full or partial for children of alumni, employees or children of employees, senior citizens.

Contact Ms. Christine Melton, Financial Aid Counselor, Cabrini College, 610 King of Prussia Road, Radnor, PA 19087-3698, 610-902-8420, fax: 610-902-8426.

CAD INSTITUTE
Phoenix, Arizona

See University of Advancing Computer Technology

CALDWELL COLLEGE
Caldwell, New Jersey

About the Institution Independent/religious, coed. Degrees awarded: B, M. Offers 22 undergraduate majors. Total enrollment: 1,750. Undergraduates: 1,646 (93% state residents). Freshmen: 203.

Undergraduate Expenses (1997–98) Comprehensive fee of $16,200 includes tuition ($10,800) and college room and board ($5400).

Applications 72% of all full-time undergraduates enrolled in fall 1996 applied for aid; of these, 81% were judged to have need according to Federal Methodology, of whom 98% were aided. *Financial aid deadline (priority):* 4/15. *Financial aid forms:* FAFSA, institutional form required. *Admission application deadline:* rolling.

Summary of Aid to Needy Students *From gift & self-help combined:* Average need met: 74%. Average amount awarded: $11,604 (65% gift aid, 35% self-help). *Gift aid:* Total: $3,456,081 (37% from college's own funds, 49% from other college-administered sources, 14% from external sources). 213 Federal Work-Study jobs (averaging $950); 10 part-time jobs.

Need-Based Scholarships & Grants Pell, FSEOG, state, private, college/university.

Loans Perkins, PLUS, Stafford, Unsubsidized Stafford, state, private.

Non-Need Awards In 1996, a total of 273 non-need awards were made. *Academic Interests/Achievement Awards:* 110 ($549,908 total): general academic. *Creative Arts/Performance Awards:* 11 ($15,500 total): art/fine arts, music. *Special Achievements/Activities Awards:* 37 ($66,700 total): Junior Miss, leadership. *Special Characteristics Awards:* 64 ($93,931 total): children and siblings of alumni, children of faculty/staff, international students, out-of-state students, religious affiliation, siblings of current students. *Athletic:* Total: 51 ($119,415); Men: 31 ($68,450); Women: 20 ($50,965).

Other Money-Saving Options Accelerated degree, co-op program, cooperative Army ROTC, off-campus living. *Payment Plans:* installment, deferred payment. *Waivers:* full or partial for employees or children of employees and senior citizens.

Contact Ms. Lissa B. Anderson, Director of Financial Aid, Caldwell College, 9 Ryerson Avenue, Caldwell, NJ 07006-6195, 973-228-4424 Ext. 221, fax: 973-403-1784.

CALIFORNIA BAPTIST COLLEGE
Riverside, California

About the Institution Independent/religious, coed. Degrees awarded: B, M. Offers 38 undergraduate majors. Total enrollment: 2,687. Undergraduates: 1,403 (87% state residents). Freshmen: 238.

Undergraduate Expenses (1997–98 estimated) Comprehensive fee of $12,830 includes tuition ($7800), mandatory fees ($436), and college room and board ($4594). College room only: $2030.

Applications 94% of all full-time undergraduates enrolled in fall 1996 applied for aid; of these, 95% were judged to have need according to Federal Methodology, of whom 100% were aided. *Financial aid deadline (priority):* 4/1. *Financial aid forms:* FAFSA, institutional form required. State form required for some. *Admission application deadline:* rolling.

Summary of Aid to Needy Students *From gift & self-help combined:* Average need met: 63%. Average amount awarded: $7940 (52% gift aid, 48% self-help). *Gift aid:* Total: $4,294,615 (51% from college's own funds, 29% from other college-administered sources, 20% from external sources). 57 Federal Work-Study jobs (averaging $800); 74 part-time jobs.

Need-Based Scholarships & Grants Pell, FSEOG, state, private, college/university.

Loans Perkins, PLUS, Stafford, Unsubsidized Stafford, private.

Non-Need Awards In 1996, a total of 633 non-need awards were made. *Academic Interests/Achievement Awards:* 185 ($495,960 total): general academic, religion/biblical studies. *Creative Arts/Performance Awards:* 145 ($229,593 total): music, theater/drama. *Special Achievements/Activities Awards:* 11 ($16,500 total): cheerleading/drum major. *Special Characteristics Awards:* 76 ($186,357 total): children of faculty/staff, relatives of clergy. *Athletic:* Total: 216 ($839,600); Men: 120 ($449,200); Women: 96 ($390,400).

Other Money-Saving Options Accelerated degree, co-op program, cooperative Army ROTC, cooperative Air Force ROTC. *Payment Plans:* installment, deferred payment. *Waivers:* full or partial for employees or children of employees.

Contact Mr. Phillip Martinez, Director of Enrollment Services, California Baptist College, 8432 Magnolia Avenue, Riverside, CA 92504-3297, 909-343-4346, fax: 909-351-1808.

CALIFORNIA COLLEGE FOR HEALTH SCIENCES
National City, California

About the Institution Proprietary, coed. Degrees awarded: A, B, M. Offers 5 undergraduate majors. Total enrollment: 9,100. Undergraduates: 8,500.

Applications *Financial aid deadline (priority):* 9/12. *Financial aid forms:* FAFSA, institutional form, income verification required. *Admission application deadline:* rolling.

Summary of Aid to Needy Students *From gift & self-help combined:* Average need met: 65%. Average amount awarded: $5500 (34% gift aid, 66% self-help). *Gift aid:* Total: $70,630 (100% from external sources).

Need-Based Scholarships & Grants Pell.

Loans PLUS, Stafford, Unsubsidized Stafford, private.

Non-Need Awards Not offered.

Other Money-Saving Options Accelerated degree, co-op program. *Payment Plan:* installment. *Waivers:* full or partial for employees or children of employees.

Contact Ms. Gilda M. Maldonado, Financial Aid Director, California College for Health Sciences, 222 West 24th Street, National City, CA 91950-6605, 619-477-4800 Ext. 318, fax: 619-477-4360.

CALIFORNIA COLLEGE OF ARTS AND CRAFTS
San Francisco, California

About the Institution Independent, coed. Degrees awarded: B, M. Offers 19 undergraduate majors. Total enrollment: 1,056. Undergraduates: 979 (71% state residents). Freshmen: 71.

Undergraduate Expenses (1997–98 estimated) Comprehensive fee of $20,352 includes tuition ($14,952), mandatory fees ($100), and college room and board ($5300). College room only: $2150.

Applications Of all full-time undergraduates enrolled in fall 1996, 97% of those who applied for aid were judged to have need according to Federal Methodology, of whom 100% were aided. *Financial aid deadline (priority):* 3/2. *Financial aid forms:* FAFSA, state form, institutional form, financial aid transcript (for transfers) required. *Admission application deadline:* rolling.

Summary of Aid to Needy Students *From gift & self-help combined:* Average need met: 65%. Average amount awarded: $15,450 (45% gift aid, 55% self-help). *Gift aid:* Total: $4,465,000. Federal Work-Study jobs; 90 part-time jobs.

Need-Based Scholarships & Grants Pell, FSEOG, state, college/university.

Loans Perkins, PLUS, Stafford, Unsubsidized Stafford, private, college/university short-term loans ($200 average).

Non-Need Awards *Creative Arts/Performance Awards:* general creative, applied art and design, art/fine arts. *Special Characteristics Awards:* ethnic background.

Other Money-Saving Options Off-campus living. *Payment Plans:* installment, deferred payment. *Waivers:* full or partial for employees or children of employees.

Contact Ms. Anita Kermes, Director of Financial Aid, California College of Arts and Crafts, 450 Irwin Street, San Francisco, CA 94107, 415-703-9530.

CALIFORNIA INSTITUTE OF TECHNOLOGY
Pasadena, California

About the Institution Independent, coed. Degrees awarded: B, M, D. Offers 32 undergraduate majors. Total enrollment: 1,902. Undergraduates: 882 (30% state residents). Freshmen: 216.

Undergraduate Expenses (1997–98) Comprehensive fee of $24,511 includes tuition ($18,600), mandatory fees ($211), and college room and board ($5700).

Applications 76% of all full-time undergraduates enrolled in fall 1996 applied for aid; of these, 87% were judged to have need according to Federal Methodology, of whom 100% were aided. *Financial aid deadline (priority):* 1/15. *Financial aid forms:* FAFSA, CSS Financial Aid PROFILE required; institutional form acceptable. State form required for some. *Regular admission application deadline:* 1/1. Early action deadline: 11/1.

Summary of Aid to Needy Students *From gift & self-help combined:* Average need met: 100%. Average amount awarded: $18,992 (79% gift aid, 21% self-help). *Gift aid:* Total: $8,811,243 (86% from college's own funds, 3% from other college-administered sources, 11% from external sources). 426 Federal Work-Study jobs (averaging $1861); 100 part-time jobs.

Need-Based Scholarships & Grants Pell, FSEOG, state, private, college/university.

Loans Perkins, PLUS, Stafford, Unsubsidized Stafford, private, college/university short-term loans ($600 average), college/university long-term loans ($2225 average).

Non-Need Awards In 1996, a total of 71 non-need awards were made. *Academic Interests/Achievement Awards:* 71 ($737,500 total): general academic.

Other Money-Saving Options Cooperative Army ROTC, cooperative Air Force ROTC, off-campus living (after freshman year). *Payment Plans:* installment, deferred payment. *Waivers:* full or partial for employees or children of employees.

Contact Office of Financial Aid, California Institute of Technology, Financial Aid Office, 12-63, Pasadena, CA 91125-0001, 818-395-6811.

CALIFORNIA INSTITUTE OF THE ARTS
Valencia, California

About the Institution Independent, coed. Degrees awarded: B, M. Offers 15 undergraduate majors. Total enrollment: 1,125. Undergraduates: 730 (35% state residents). Freshmen: 116.

Undergraduate Expenses (1997–98) Comprehensive fee of $22,515 includes tuition ($17,250), mandatory fees ($65), and college room and board ($5200 minimum). College room only: $2600 (minimum).

Applications *Financial aid deadline (priority):* 3/1. *Financial aid forms:* FAFSA required. *Admission application deadline:* 2/1.

Summary of Aid to Needy Students *From gift & self-help combined:* Average need met: 86%. Federal Work-Study jobs; part-time jobs.

Need-Based Scholarships & Grants Pell, FSEOG, state, private.

Loans Perkins, Stafford, Unsubsidized Stafford, college/university long-term loans.

Non-Need Awards *Creative Arts/Performance Awards:* applied art and design, art/fine arts, cinema/film/broadcasting, dance, music.

Other Money-Saving Options Co-op program, off-campus living. *Waivers:* full or partial for employees or children of employees.

Contact Ms. Bobbi Heuer, Director of Financial Aid, California Institute of the Arts, 24700 McBean Parkway, Valencia, CA 91355-2340, 805-253-7869, fax: 805-287-3816.

CALIFORNIA LUTHERAN UNIVERSITY
Thousand Oaks, California

About the Institution Independent/religious, coed. Degrees awarded: B, M. Offers 48 undergraduate majors. Total enrollment: 2,457. Undergraduates: 1,511 (84% state residents). Freshmen: 230.

Undergraduate Expenses (1997–98) Comprehensive fee of $20,590 includes tuition ($14,780) and college room and board ($5810). College room only: $2840.

Applications 80% of all full-time undergraduates enrolled in fall 1996 applied for aid; of these, 80% were judged to have need according to Federal Methodology, of whom 100% were aided. *Financial aid deadline (priority):* 3/1. *Financial aid forms:* FAFSA required; CSS Financial Aid PROFILE acceptable. State form required for some. *Admission application deadline:* 6/1.

Summary of Aid to Needy Students *From gift & self-help combined:* Average need met: 80%. Average amount awarded: $12,179 (54% gift aid, 46% self-help). *Gift aid:* Total: $5,078,051 (64% from college's own funds, 5% from other college-administered sources, 31% from external sources). 295 Federal Work-Study jobs (averaging $1400); 254 part-time jobs.

Need-Based Scholarships & Grants Pell, FSEOG, state, private, college/university.

Loans Perkins, PLUS, Stafford, Unsubsidized Stafford, private, college/university short-term loans ($200 average), college/university long-term loans ($2265 average).

Non-Need Awards In 1996, a total of 819 non-need awards were made. *Academic Interests/Achievement Awards:* 319 ($1,922,900 total): general academic, biological sciences, business, communication, computer science, education, English, foreign languages, mathematics, physical sciences, religion/biblical studies, social sciences. *Creative Arts/Performance Awards:* 68 ($60,070 total): art/fine arts, creative writing, music, theater/drama. *Special Achievements/Activities Awards:* 129 ($58,200 total): leadership, religious involvement. *Special Characteristics Awards:* 303 ($782,311 total): adult students, children and siblings of alumni, children of faculty/staff, international students, relatives of clergy, religious affiliation.

Other Money-Saving Options Accelerated degree, co-op program, cooperative Army ROTC, cooperative Air Force ROTC, off-campus living (after junior year). *Payment Plan:* installment. *Waivers:* full or partial for employees or children of employees.

Contact Mrs. Betsy Kocher, Dictor of Student Financial Planning, California Lutheran University, 60 Olsen Road, Thousand Oaks, CA 91360-2787, 805-493-3115.

CALIFORNIA MARITIME ACADEMY
Vallejo, California

About the Institution State-supported, primarily men. Degrees awarded: B. Offers 6 undergraduate majors. Total enrollment: 400 (88% state residents).

Undergraduate Expenses (1996–97) State resident tuition: $0. Nonresident tuition: $7380. Mandatory fees: $3762. College room and board: $5020.

Applications 71% of all full-time undergraduates enrolled in fall 1996 applied for aid; of these, 83% were judged to have need according to Federal Methodology, of whom 99% were aided. *Financial aid deadline (priority):* 3/1. *Financial aid forms:* FAFSA acceptable. *Admission application deadline:* 7/1.

Summary of Aid to Needy Students *From gift & self-help combined:* Average need met: 80%. Average amount awarded: $13,472 (27% gift aid, 73% self-help). *Gift aid:* Total: $799,040 (5% from college's own funds, 57% from other college-administered sources, 38% from external sources). 45 Federal Work-Study jobs (averaging $1500); 80 part-time jobs.

Need-Based Scholarships & Grants Pell, FSEOG, state, private, college/university.

Loans Perkins, PLUS, Stafford, Unsubsidized Stafford.

Non-Need Awards *Special Characteristics Awards:* general special characteristics, members of minorities.

Another Money-Saving Option Cooperative Naval ROTC.

Contact Ms. Debbie Khoury, Student Personnel Technician, Financial Aid, California Maritime Academy, 200 Maritime Academy Drive, Vallejo, CA 94590-0644, 707-648-4227.

CALIFORNIA POLYTECHNIC STATE UNIVERSITY, SAN LUIS OBISPO
San Luis Obispo, California

About the Institution State-supported, coed. Degrees awarded: B, M. Offers 63 undergraduate majors. Total enrollment: 17,000. Undergraduates: 15,947 (96% state residents). Freshmen: 2,827.

Undergraduate Expenses (1996–97) State resident tuition: $0. Nonresident tuition: $7380. Mandatory fees: $2075. College room and board: $4927.

Applications 58% of all full-time undergraduates enrolled in fall 1996 applied for aid; of these, 78% were judged to have need according to Federal Methodology, of whom 97% were aided. *Financial aid deadline (priority):* 3/2. *Financial aid forms:* FAFSA required; CSS Financial Aid PROFILE acceptable. State form required for some. *Admission application deadline:* 11/30.

Summary of Aid to Needy Students *From gift & self-help combined:* Average amount awarded: $5961 (44% gift aid, 56% self-help). *Gift* *aid:* Total: $17,312,003 (6% from college's own funds, 50% from other college-administered sources, 44% from external sources). 381 Federal Work-Study jobs (averaging $1400); part-time jobs.

Need-Based Scholarships & Grants Pell, FSEOG, state, private, college/university.

Loans Perkins, PLUS, Stafford, Unsubsidized Stafford, college/university short-term loans ($300 average), college/university long-term loans ($2956 average).

Non-Need Awards *Academic Interests/Achievement Awards:* general academic, agriculture, architecture, biological sciences, business, communication, computer science, education, engineering/technologies, English, foreign languages, health fields, home economics, humanities, international studies, library science, mathematics, military science, physical sciences, social sciences. *Creative Arts/Performance Awards:* general creative, applied art and design, art/fine arts, cinema/film/broadcasting, creative writing, dance, debating, journalism/publications, music, performing arts, theater/drama. *Special Achievements/Activities Awards:* general special achievements/activities, community service, leadership, rodeo. *Special Characteristics Awards:* general special characteristics, ROTC participants. *Athletic:* Total: 608 ($979,865).

Other Money-Saving Options Co-op program, Army ROTC, off-campus living. *Payment Plan:* installment. *Waivers:* full or partial for employees or children of employees and senior citizens.

Contact Ms. Mary E. Spady, Associate Director of Financial Aid, California Polytechnic State University, San Luis Obispo, One Grand Avenue, San Luis Obispo, CA 93407, 805-756-5886, fax: 805-756-7243.

CALIFORNIA STATE POLYTECHNIC UNIVERSITY, POMONA
Pomona, California

About the Institution State-supported, coed. Degrees awarded: B, M. Offers 87 undergraduate majors. Total enrollment: 16,803. Undergraduates: 15,038 (90% state residents). Freshmen: 1,922.

Undergraduate Expenses (1996–97) State resident tuition: $0. Nonresident tuition: $7708. Mandatory fees: $1896. College room and board: $5094 (minimum).

Applications Of all full-time undergraduates enrolled in fall 1996, 90% of those who applied for aid were judged to have need according to Federal Methodology, of whom 94% were aided. *Financial aid deadline (priority):* 3/2. *Financial aid forms:* FAFSA required. State form required for some. *Admission application deadline:* rolling.

Summary of Aid to Needy Students *From gift & self-help combined:* Average need met: 74%. Average amount awarded: $5771 (47% gift aid, 53% self-help). *Gift aid:* Total: $16,265,178 (2% from college's own funds, 45% from other college-administered sources, 53% from external sources). 209 Federal Work-Study jobs (averaging $1992); part-time jobs.

Need-Based Scholarships & Grants Pell, FSEOG, state, private, college/university.

Loans Perkins, PLUS, Stafford, Unsubsidized Stafford, private, college/university short-term loans ($580 average), college/university long-term loans ($1000 average).

Non-Need Awards In 1996, a total of 349 non-need awards were made. *Academic Interests/Achievement Awards:* 165 ($130,426 total): general academic, agriculture, architecture, biological sciences, business, computer science, education, engineering/technologies, humanities, mathematics, physical sciences, social sciences. *Special Achievements/Activities Awards:* 20 ($34,032 total): hobbies/interest, leadership. *Special Characteristics Awards:* 36 ($28,350 total): children and siblings of alumni, children of current students, members of minorities. *Athletic:* Total: 128 ($274,481); Men: 72 ($140,783); Women: 56 ($133,698).

Other Money-Saving Options Accelerated degree, co-op program, Army ROTC, off-campus living. *Payment Plan:* installment. *Waivers:* full or partial for employees or children of employees and senior citizens.

Contact Office of Financial Aid, California State Polytechnic University, Pomona, 3801 West Temple Avenue, Pomona, CA 91768-2557, 909-869-7659.

CALIFORNIA STATE UNIVERSITY, BAKERSFIELD
Bakersfield, California

About the Institution State-supported, coed. Degrees awarded: B, M. Offers 45 undergraduate majors. Total enrollment: 5,435. Undergraduates: 4,189 (97% state residents). Freshmen: 432.

Undergraduate Expenses (1996–97) State resident tuition: $0. Nonresident tuition: $7380. Mandatory fees: $1957. College room and board: $4125.

Applications Of all full-time undergraduates enrolled in fall 1996, 91% of those who applied for aid were judged to have need according to Federal Methodology, of whom 94% were aided. *Financial aid deadline (priority):* 3/2. *Financial aid forms:* FAFSA required. *Admission application deadline:* 9/23.

Summary of Aid to Needy Students *From gift & self-help combined:* Average need met: 76%. Average amount awarded: $5529 (56% gift aid, 44% self-help). *Gift aid:* Total: $5,645,504 (6% from college's own funds, 44% from other college-administered sources, 50% from external sources). 74 Federal Work-Study jobs (averaging $1156); 350 part-time jobs.

Need-Based Scholarships & Grants Pell, FSEOG, state, private.

Loans Perkins, PLUS, Stafford, Unsubsidized Stafford, Federal Nursing, college/university short-term loans ($150 average), college/university long-term loans.

Non-Need Awards In 1996, a total of 412 non-need awards were made. *Academic Interests/Achievement Awards:* 172 ($157,021 total): general academic, biological sciences, business, communication, education, English, health fields, humanities, physical sciences, social sciences. *Creative Arts/Performance Awards:* 22 ($11,375 total): art/fine arts, creative writing, journalism/publications, music, performing arts, theater/drama. *Special Achievements/Activities Awards:* 0: general special achievements/activities. *Special Characteristics Awards:* 75 ($69,997 total): ethnic background, local/state students, members of minorities. *Athletic:* Total: 143 ($337,796); Men: 72 ($145,002); Women: 71 ($192,794).

Other Money-Saving Options Accelerated degree, co-op program, off-campus living. *Payment Plan:* installment. *Waivers:* full or partial for employees or children of employees and senior citizens.

Contact Mr. John Casdorph, Associate Director, Financial Aid, California State University, Bakersfield, 9001 Stockdale Highway, Bakersfield, CA 93311-1099, 805-664-3016, fax: 805-665-6800.

CALIFORNIA STATE UNIVERSITY, CHICO
Chico, California

About the Institution State-supported, coed. Degrees awarded: B, M. Offers 95 undergraduate majors. Total enrollment: 13,919. Undergraduates: 12,298 (98% state residents). Freshmen: 1,561.

Undergraduate Expenses (1996–97) State resident tuition: $0. Nonresident tuition: $7380. Mandatory fees: $2046. College room and board: $4981. College room only: $2952.

Applications *Financial aid deadline (priority):* 3/1. *Financial aid forms:* FAFSA required. *Admission application deadline:* rolling.

Summary of Aid to Needy Students *From gift & self-help combined:* Average amount awarded: $7714 (38% gift aid, 62% self-help). *Gift* *aid:* Total: $16,800,000 (2% from college's own funds, 51% from other college-administered sources, 47% from external sources). 575 Federal Work-Study jobs (averaging $1000); 833 part-time jobs.

Need-Based Scholarships & Grants Pell, FSEOG, state, private, college/university.

Loans Perkins, PLUS, Stafford, Unsubsidized Stafford, college/university short-term loans ($250 average).

Non-Need Awards *Academic Interests/Achievement Awards:* general academic, agriculture, area/ethnic studies, biological sciences, business, communication, computer science, education, engineering/technologies, English, foreign languages, health fields, humanities, international studies, mathematics, physical sciences, social sciences. *Creative Arts/Performance Awards:* general creative, applied art and design, art/fine arts, cinema/film/broadcasting, creative writing, dance, debating, journalism/publications, music, performing arts, theater/drama. *Special Achievements/Activities Awards:* general special achievements/activities, community service, hobbies/interest, leadership, memberships. *Special Characteristics Awards:* adult students, children of faculty/staff, ethnic background, first-generation college students, handicapped students, international students, local/state students, married students, members of minorities, out-of-state students.

Other Money-Saving Options Co-op program, off-campus living. *Payment Plan:* installment. *Waivers:* full or partial for employees or children of employees and senior citizens.

Contact Mr. Dan Reed, Financial Aid Adviser, California State University, Chico, 1st and Normal Streets, Chico, CA 95929-0722, 916-878-6451, fax: 916-898-6883.

CALIFORNIA STATE UNIVERSITY, DOMINGUEZ HILLS
Carson, California

About the Institution State-supported, coed. Degrees awarded: B, M. Offers 71 undergraduate majors. Total enrollment: 10,400. Undergraduates: 7,023 (88% state residents). Freshmen: 532.

Undergraduate Expenses (1996–97) State resident tuition: $0. Nonresident tuition: $7380. Mandatory fees: $1821. College room only: $2946.

Applications Of all full-time undergraduates enrolled in fall 1996, 100% of those who applied for aid were judged to have need according to Federal Methodology, of whom 100% were aided. *Financial aid deadline (priority):* 4/15. *Financial aid forms:* FAFSA, institutional form required; CSS Financial Aid PROFILE, state form acceptable. *Regular admission application deadline:* rolling. Early action deadline: 11/30.

Summary of Aid to Needy Students *From gift & self-help combined:* Average need met: 97%. Average amount awarded: $4800 (47% gift aid, 53% self-help). *Gift aid:* Total: $10,239,338 (1% from college's own funds, 37% from other college-administered sources, 62% from external sources). Federal Work-Study jobs; part-time jobs.

Need-Based Scholarships & Grants Pell, FSEOG, state, private, college/university.

Loans Perkins, PLUS, Stafford, Unsubsidized Stafford, college/university short-term loans ($100 average), college/university long-term loans ($914 average).

Non-Need Awards *Academic Interests/Achievement Awards:* general academic. *Special Characteristics Awards:* ethnic background, members of minorities. *Athletic:* Total: 100 ($116,462); Men: 44 ($56,295); Women: 56 ($60,167).

Other Money-Saving Options Co-op program, cooperative Army ROTC, cooperative Air Force ROTC, off-campus living. *Waivers:* full or partial for employees or children of employees.

Contact Mr. James Woods, Director of Financial Aid, California State University, Dominguez Hills, 1000 East Victoria Street, Carson, CA 90747-0001, 310-243-3691.

CALIFORNIA STATE UNIVERSITY, FRESNO
Fresno, California

About the Institution State-supported, coed. Degrees awarded: B, M, D. Offers 114 undergraduate majors. Total enrollment: 17,213. Undergraduates: 14,100 (91% state residents). Freshmen: 1,546.

Undergraduate Expenses (1996–97) State resident tuition: $0. Nonresident tuition: $7380. Mandatory fees: $1822. College room and board: $4498.

Applications 80% of all full-time undergraduates enrolled in fall 1996 applied for aid; of these, 89% were judged to have need according to Federal Methodology, of whom 96% were aided. *Financial aid deadline (priority):* 3/1. *Financial aid forms:* financial aid transcript (for transfers) required. FAFSA, CSS Financial Aid PROFILE, state form, institutional form required for some. *Admission application deadline:* 5/15.

Summary of Aid to Needy Students *From gift & self-help combined:* Average need met: 88%. Average amount awarded: $5646 (46% gift aid, 54% self-help). *Gift aid:* Total: $21,589,932 (2% from college's own funds, 31% from other college-administered sources, 67% from external sources). 231 Federal Work-Study jobs (averaging $2215); 1,070 part-time jobs.

Need-Based Scholarships & Grants Pell, FSEOG, state.

Loans Perkins, PLUS, Stafford, Unsubsidized Stafford, Federal Nursing, college/university short-term loans ($600 average).

Non-Need Awards In 1996, a total of 1,245 non-need awards were made. *Academic Interests/Achievement Awards:* 850 ($721,651 total): general academic, agriculture, architecture, area/ethnic studies, biological sciences, business, communication, computer science, education, engineering/technologies, English, health fields, home economics, humanities, mathematics, physical sciences, premedicine, social sciences. *Creative Arts/Performance Awards:* 19 ($5500 total): journalism/publications, music, theater/drama. *Special Characteristics Awards:* 15 ($4200 total): handicapped students, veterans, veterans' children. *Athletic:* Total: 361 ($2,037,098); Men: 227 ($1,316,727); Women: 134 ($720,371).

Other Money-Saving Options Accelerated degree, co-op program, Army ROTC, Air Force ROTC, off-campus living. *Waivers:* full or partial for employees or children of employees and senior citizens.

Contact Financial Aid Office, California State University, Fresno, 5150 North Maple Avenue, Mail Stop 64, Fresno, CA 93704-8026, 209-278-2182.

CALIFORNIA STATE UNIVERSITY, FULLERTON
Fullerton, California

About the Institution State-supported, coed. Degrees awarded: B, M. Offers 91 undergraduate majors. Total enrollment: 24,040. Undergraduates: 20,090 (80% state residents). Freshmen: 2,205.

Undergraduate Expenses (1996–97) State resident tuition: $0. Nonresident tuition: $7626. Mandatory fees: $1927. College room only: $3476.

Applications 53% of all full-time undergraduates enrolled in fall 1996 applied for aid; of these, 83% were judged to have need according to Federal Methodology, of whom 91% were aided. *Financial aid deadline (priority):* 3/1. *Financial aid forms:* FAFSA, state form required. *Admission application deadline:* rolling.

Summary of Aid to Needy Students *From gift & self-help combined:* Average need met: 64%. Average amount awarded: $5167 (41% gift aid, 59% self-help). *Gift aid:* Total: $11,597,768 (14% from college-administered sources, 86% from external sources). 350 Federal Work-Study jobs (averaging $1450); 1,052 part-time jobs.

Need-Based Scholarships & Grants Pell, FSEOG, state.

Loans Perkins, PLUS, Stafford, Unsubsidized Stafford, college/university short-term loans ($300 average).

Non-Need Awards In 1996, a total of 294 non-need awards were made. *Academic Interests/Achievement Awards:* 79 ($28,000 total): general academic, business, communication, engineering/technologies, humanities, mathematics, social sciences. *Creative Arts/Performance Awards:* 12 ($6000 total): art/fine arts, music. *Athletic:* Total: 203 ($782,000); Men: 173 ($640,000); Women: 30 ($142,000).

Other Money-Saving Options Accelerated degree, co-op program, Army ROTC, off-campus living. *Waivers:* full or partial for minority students and employees or children of employees.

Contact Ms. Deborah S. Gordon, Director of Financial Aid, California State University, Fullerton, 800 North State College Boulevard, Fullerton, CA 92831-3599, 714-278-3128, fax: 714-278-7090.

CALIFORNIA STATE UNIVERSITY, HAYWARD
Hayward, California

About the Institution State-supported, coed. Degrees awarded: B, M. Offers 81 undergraduate majors. Total enrollment: 12,734. Undergraduates: 9,853 (90% state residents). Freshmen: 704.

Undergraduate Expenses (1996–97) State resident tuition: $0. Nonresident tuition: $7380. Mandatory fees: $1800. College room only: $3009.

Applications *Financial aid deadline (priority):* 3/4. *Financial aid forms:* FAFSA required. State form required for some. *Admission application deadline:* 9/12.

Summary of Aid to Needy Students *Gift aid:* Total: $18,953,782 (71% from college-administered sources, 29% from external sources). 488 Federal Work-Study jobs (averaging $2125); part-time jobs.

Need-Based Scholarships & Grants Pell, FSEOG, state, private, college/university.

Loans Perkins, PLUS, Stafford, Unsubsidized Stafford, private, college/university short-term loans ($300 average).

Non-Need Awards *Academic Interests/Achievement Awards:* general academic. *Creative Arts/Performance Awards:* music.

Other Money-Saving Options Accelerated degree, co-op program, off-campus living. *Payment Plan:* installment. *Waivers:* full or partial for employees or children of employees and senior citizens.

Contact Office of Financial Aid, California State University, Hayward, 25800 Carlos Bee Boulevard, Hayward, CA 94542-3028, 510-885-3616, fax: 510-885-4627.

CALIFORNIA STATE UNIVERSITY, LONG BEACH
Long Beach, California

About the Institution State-supported, coed. Degrees awarded: B, M. Offers 118 undergraduate majors. Total enrollment: 27,431. Undergraduates: 22,052 (97% state residents). Freshmen: 2,477.

Undergraduate Expenses (1996–97) State resident tuition: $0. Nonresident tuition: $7380. Mandatory fees: $1826. College room and board: $5300.

Applications Of all full-time undergraduates enrolled in fall 1996, 75% of those who applied for aid were judged to have need according to Federal Methodology, of whom 94% were aided. *Financial aid deadline (priority):* 3/2. *Financial aid forms:* FAFSA required. *Admission application deadline:* 11/30.

Summary of Aid to Needy Students *From gift & self-help combined:* Average need met: 60%. Average amount awarded: $6606 (44% gift aid, 56% self-help). *Gift aid:* Total: $24,594,592 (35% from college-administered sources, 65% from external sources). 560 Federal Work-Study jobs (averaging $2000); part-time jobs.

Need-Based Scholarships & Grants Pell, FSEOG, state.

Loans Perkins, PLUS, Stafford, Unsubsidized Stafford, private, college/university short-term loans ($400 average).

Non-Need Awards In 1996, a total of 369 non-need awards were made. *Academic Interests/Achievement Awards:* 150 ($250,000 total): general academic. *Creative Arts/Performance Awards:* 60 ($80,000 total): applied art and design, cinema/film/broadcasting, dance, music, performing arts, theater/drama. *Athletic:* Total: 159 ($738,000).

Other Money-Saving Options Co-op program, Army ROTC, Air Force ROTC, off-campus living. *Payment Plan:* installment. *Waivers:* full or partial for employees or children of employees.

Contact Office of Financial Aid, California State University, Long Beach, 1250 Bellflower Boulevard, Long Beach, CA 90840-0119, 562-985-4641.

CALIFORNIA STATE UNIVERSITY, LOS ANGELES
Los Angeles, California

About the Institution State-supported, coed. Degrees awarded: B, M. Offers 103 undergraduate majors. Total enrollment: 18,849. Undergraduates: 13,995 (95% state residents). Freshmen: 1,381.

Undergraduate Expenses (1996–97) State resident tuition: $0. Nonresident tuition: $7626. Mandatory fees: $1742.

Applications Of all full-time undergraduates enrolled in fall 1996, 98% of those who applied for aid were judged to have need according to Federal Methodology, of whom 97% were aided. *Financial aid deadline (priority):* 3/1. *Financial aid forms:* FAFSA, CSS Financial Aid PROFILE, institutional form acceptable. State form required for some. *Admission application deadline:* 6/15.

Summary of Aid to Needy Students *From gift & self-help combined:* Average need met: 71%. Average amount awarded: $5271 (66% gift aid, 34% self-help). *Gift aid:* Total: $22,894,666 (38% from college-administered sources, 62% from external sources). 192 Federal Work-Study jobs (averaging $3152); part-time jobs.

Need-Based Scholarships & Grants Pell, FSEOG, state, private, college/university.

Loans Perkins, PLUS, Stafford, Unsubsidized Stafford, Federal Nursing.

Non-Need Awards In 1996, a total of 571 non-need awards were made. *Academic Interests/Achievement Awards:* general academic, health fields. *Creative Arts/Performance Awards:* general creative. *Special Achievements/Activities Awards:* general special achievements/activities. *Special Characteristics Awards:* general special characteristics, ethnic background, members of minorities. *Athletic:* Total: 226 ($325,647); Men: 125 ($155,152); Women: 101 ($170,495).

Other Money-Saving Options Accelerated degree, co-op program, cooperative Army ROTC, cooperative Air Force ROTC, off-campus living. *Waivers:* full or partial for employees or children of employees.

Contact Ms. Kim Miles, Senior Financial Aid Advisor, California State University, Los Angeles, 5151 State University Drive, Los Angeles, CA 90032-8530, 213-343-3349, fax: 213-343-3166.

CALIFORNIA STATE UNIVERSITY, NORTHRIDGE
Northridge, California

About the Institution State-supported, coed. Degrees awarded: B, M. Offers 136 undergraduate majors. Total enrollment: 25,020. Undergraduates: 20,024 (98% state residents). Freshmen: 2,138.

Undergraduate Expenses (1996–97) State resident tuition: $0. Nonresident tuition: $7626. Mandatory fees: $1970. College room and board: $4956 (minimum). College room only: $3326.

Applications Of all full-time undergraduates enrolled in fall 1996, 78% of those who applied for aid were judged to have need according to Federal Methodology, of whom 100% were aided. *Financial aid deadline (priority):* 3/2. *Financial aid forms:* FAFSA, state form required. Institutional form required for some. *Regular admission application deadline:* 11/30. Early action deadline: 8/30.

Summary of Aid to Needy Students *From gift & self-help combined:* Average need met: 74%. Average amount awarded: $6916 (42% gift aid, 58% self-help). *Gift aid:* Total: $27,100,000 (8% from college's own funds, 37% from other college-administered sources, 55% from external sources). 1,200 Federal Work-Study jobs (averaging $2000); 1,950 part-time jobs.

Need-Based Scholarships & Grants Pell, FSEOG, state, private, college/university.

Loans Perkins, PLUS, Stafford, Unsubsidized Stafford, college/university short-term loans ($300 average).

Non-Need Awards In 1996, a total of 440 non-need awards were made. *Academic Interests/Achievement Awards:* 100 ($100,000 total): general academic, business, computer science, education, engineering/technologies, social sciences. *Creative Arts/Performance Awards:* 40 ($40,000 total): journalism/publications, music. *Athletic:* Total: 300 ($1,181,000); Men: 178 ($654,000); Women: 122 ($527,000).

Other Money-Saving Options Accelerated degree, cooperative Army ROTC, cooperative Air Force ROTC, off-campus living. *Waivers:* full or partial for senior citizens.

Contact Financial Aid Office, California State University, Northridge, 18111 Nordhoff Street, Northridge, CA 91330-8307, 818-677-3000.

CALIFORNIA STATE UNIVERSITY, SACRAMENTO
Sacramento, California

About the Institution State-supported, coed. Degrees awarded: B, M. Offers 81 undergraduate majors. Total enrollment: 23,420. Undergraduates: 18,713 (97% state residents). Freshmen: 1,523.

Undergraduate Expenses (1996–97) State resident tuition: $0. Nonresident tuition: $7626. Mandatory fees: $2000. College room and board: $4744 (minimum).

Applications 62% of all full-time undergraduates enrolled in fall 1996 applied for aid; of these, 90% were judged to have need according to Federal Methodology, of whom 95% were aided. *Financial aid deadline (priority):* 3/2. *Financial aid forms:* FAFSA, state form, institutional form required. *Regular admission application deadline:* 5/1. Early action deadline: 2/1.

Summary of Aid to Needy Students *From gift & self-help combined:* Average amount awarded: $5433 (54% gift aid, 46% self-help). *Gift aid:* Total: $18,353,473 (1% from college's own funds, 35% from other college-administered sources, 64% from external sources). 238 Federal Work-Study jobs (averaging $1947); 1,300 part-time jobs.

Need-Based Scholarships & Grants Pell, FSEOG, state, private, college/university.

Loans Perkins, PLUS, Stafford, Unsubsidized Stafford, Federal Nursing, state, private, college/university short-term loans ($650 average).

Non-Need Awards *Academic Interests/Achievement Awards:* available. *Creative Arts/Performance Awards:* available. *Special Achievements/Activities Awards:* available. *Special Characteristics Awards:* available. *Athletic:* available.

Other Money-Saving Options Co-op program, cooperative Army ROTC, cooperative Naval ROTC, cooperative Air Force ROTC, off-campus living. *Payment Plan:* installment. *Waivers:* full or partial for employees or children of employees and senior citizens.

Contact Office of Financial Aid, California State University, Sacramento, 6000 J Street, Sacramento, CA 95819-6044, 916-278-6011.

CALIFORNIA STATE UNIVERSITY, SAN BERNARDINO
San Bernardino, California

About the Institution State-supported, coed. Degrees awarded: B, M. Offers 55 undergraduate majors. Total enrollment: 12,153. Undergraduates: 9,094 (96% state residents). Freshmen: 942.

Undergraduate Expenses (1996–97) State resident tuition: $0. Nonresident tuition: $7708. Mandatory fees: $2034. College room and board: $4108.

Applications *Financial aid deadline (priority):* 3/1. *Financial aid forms:* FAFSA, state form required; CSS Financial Aid PROFILE acceptable. *Admission application deadline:* rolling.

Summary of Aid to Needy Students Federal Work-Study jobs; part-time jobs.

Need-Based Scholarships & Grants Pell, FSEOG, state, college/university.

Loans Perkins, PLUS, Stafford, Unsubsidized Stafford, college/university short-term loans ($300 average).

Non-Need Awards In 1996, a total of 199 non-need awards were made. *Academic Interests/Achievement Awards:* 57 ($98,300 total): general academic, business, computer science, education, health fields, humanities, mathematics, military science. *Creative Arts/Performance Awards:* 18 ($14,950 total): general creative, music, performing arts. *Special Characteristics Awards:* 50 ($50,400 total): children with a deceased or disabled parent, ethnic background, first-generation college students, local/state students. *Athletic:* Total: 74 ($142,257); Men: 42 ($84,580); Women: 32 ($57,677).

Other Money-Saving Options Co-op program, Army ROTC, Air Force ROTC, off-campus living.

Contact Financial Aid Office, California State University, San Bernardino, 5500 University Parkway, San Bernardino, CA 92407-2397, 909-880-7800.

CALIFORNIA STATE UNIVERSITY, SAN MARCOS
San Marcos, California

About the Institution State-supported, coed. Degrees awarded: B, M. Offers 17 undergraduate majors. Total enrollment: 3,841. Undergraduates: 3,511 (99% state residents). Freshmen: 339.

Undergraduate Expenses (1996–97) State resident tuition: $0. Nonresident tuition: $7626. Mandatory fees: $1720. College room only: $2475 (minimum).

Applications *Financial aid deadline (priority):* 3/2. *Financial aid forms:* FAFSA required. State form required for some. *Admission application deadline:* rolling.

Summary of Aid to Needy Students *From gift & self-help combined:* Average need met: 36%. Average amount awarded: $4418 (48% gift aid, 52% self-help). *Gift aid:* Total: $5,081,000 (3% from college's own funds, 36% from other college-administered sources, 61% from external sources). 58 Federal Work-Study jobs (averaging $1655); part-time jobs.

Need-Based Scholarships & Grants Pell, FSEOG, state, private, college/university.

Loans Perkins, PLUS, Stafford, Unsubsidized Stafford, college/university short-term loans ($200 average), college/university long-term loans ($3000 average).

Non-Need Awards Not offered.

Other Money-Saving Options Cooperative Air Force ROTC. *Waivers:* full or partial for employees or children of employees and senior citizens.

Contact Mr. Paul Phillips, Director of Financial Aid, California State University, San Marcos, San Marcos, CA 92096, 619-750-4851, fax: 619-750-3047.

CALIFORNIA STATE UNIVERSITY, STANISLAUS
Turlock, California

About the Institution State-supported, coed. Degrees awarded: B, M. Offers 64 undergraduate majors. Total enrollment: 6,100. Undergraduates: 4,817 (99% state residents). Freshmen: 433.

Undergraduate Expenses (1996–97) State resident tuition: $0. Nonresident tuition: $7626. Mandatory fees: $1915. College room and board: $5500 (minimum).

Applications 86% of all full-time undergraduates enrolled in fall 1996 applied for aid; of these, 76% were judged to have need according to Federal Methodology, of whom 77% were aided. *Financial aid deadline (priority):* 3/1. *Financial aid forms:* FAFSA, state form required; CSS Financial Aid PROFILE acceptable. *Admission application deadline:* 7/31.

Summary of Aid to Needy Students *From gift & self-help combined:* Average need met: 72%. Average amount awarded: $5201 (39% gift aid, 61% self-help). *Gift aid:* Total: $934,557 (2% from college's own funds, 48% from other college-administered sources, 50% from external sources). 113 Federal Work-Study jobs (averaging $1671); part-time jobs.

Need-Based Scholarships & Grants Pell, FSEOG, state, private, college/university.

Loans Perkins, PLUS, Stafford, Unsubsidized Stafford, college/university short-term loans ($95 average).

Non-Need Awards In 1996, a total of 101 non-need awards were made. *Academic Interests/Achievement Awards:* 43 ($54,675 total): general academic, biological sciences, business, communication, computer science, education, English, mathematics, physical sciences, social sciences. *Creative Arts/Performance Awards:* 26 ($9150 total): art/fine arts, music. *Special Achievements/Activities Awards:* 16 ($9500 total): leadership. *Special Characteristics Awards:* 16 ($14,650 total): general special characteristics, children of faculty/staff, first-generation college students, local/state students, members of minorities.

Other Money-Saving Options Accelerated degree, co-op program, off-campus living. *Waivers:* full or partial for senior citizens.

Contact Ms. Joan R. Hillery, Director of Financial Aid, California State University, Stanislaus, 801 West Monte Vista Avenue, Turlock, CA 95382, 209-667-3336.

CALIFORNIA UNIVERSITY OF PENNSYLVANIA
California, Pennsylvania

About the Institution State-supported, coed. Degrees awarded: A, B, M. Offers 112 undergraduate majors. Total enrollment: 5,636. Undergraduates: 4,779 (94% state residents). Freshmen: 834.

Undergraduate Expenses (1996–97) State resident tuition: $3368. Nonresident tuition: $8566. Mandatory fees: $936. College room and board: $3992.

Applications Of all full-time undergraduates enrolled in fall 1996, 88% of those who applied for aid were judged to have need according to Federal Methodology, of whom 95% were aided. *Financial aid deadline (priority):* 4/1. *Financial aid forms:* FAFSA required. *Admission application deadline:* 7/30.

Summary of Aid to Needy Students *From gift & self-help combined:* Average need met: 79%. Average amount awarded: $5532 (46% gift aid, 54% self-help). *Gift aid:* Total: $7,687,758 (10% from college's

own funds, 45% from other college-administered sources, 45% from external sources). 350 Federal Work-Study jobs (averaging $1100); 950 part-time jobs.

Need-Based Scholarships & Grants Pell, FSEOG, state.

Loans College/university short-term loans ($200 average).

Non-Need Awards In 1996, a total of 283 non-need awards were made. *Academic Interests/Achievement Awards:* general academic. *Creative Arts/Performance Awards:* general creative. *Special Characteristics Awards:* members of minorities. *Athletic:* Total: 158 ($515,000); Men: 102 ($304,000); Women: 56 ($211,000).

Other Money-Saving Options Accelerated degree, co-op program, Army ROTC, off-campus living. *Payment Plan:* installment. *Waivers:* full or partial for employees or children of employees.

Contact Financial Aid Office, California University of Pennsylvania, 250 University Avenue, California, PA 15419-1394, 412-938-4415.

CALUMET COLLEGE OF SAINT JOSEPH
Whiting, Indiana

About the Institution Independent/religious, coed. Degrees awarded: A, B. Offers 28 undergraduate majors. Total enrollment: 1,018 (86% state residents).

Undergraduate Expenses (1997–98) Tuition: $6293.

Applications *Financial aid deadline (priority):* 10/8. *Financial aid forms:* FAFSA, CSS Financial Aid PROFILE, institutional form required. State form required for some. *Admission application deadline:* rolling.

Summary of Aid to Needy Students *From gift & self-help combined:* Average need met: 90%. Average amount awarded: $3000 (88% gift aid, 12% self-help). *Gift aid:* Total: $1,595,625 (25% from college's own funds, 34% from other college-administered sources, 41% from external sources). Federal Work-Study jobs.

Need-Based Scholarships & Grants Pell, FSEOG, state, private, college/university.

Loans Perkins, PLUS, Stafford, Unsubsidized Stafford, college/university long-term loans ($1500 average).

Non-Need Awards *Academic Interests/Achievement Awards:* 8 ($21,000 total): general academic. *Special Achievements/Activities Awards:* 1 ($1000 total): leadership. *Special Characteristics Awards:* ($384,000 total): adult students, children of faculty/staff, local/state students, previous college experience, religious affiliation.

Other Money-Saving Options Accelerated degree, co-op program. *Payment Plan:* installment. *Waivers:* full or partial for employees or children of employees and senior citizens.

Contact Ms. Barbara Jerzyk, Director of Financial Aid, Calumet College of Saint Joseph, 2400 New York Avenue, Whiting, IN 46394-2195, 219-473-4219.

CALVARY BIBLE COLLEGE AND THEOLOGICAL SEMINARY
Kansas City, Missouri

About the Institution Independent/religious, coed. Degrees awarded: A, B, M. Offers 15 undergraduate majors. Total enrollment: 317. Undergraduates: 267 (36% state residents). Freshmen: 43.

Undergraduate Expenses (1997–98) Comprehensive fee of $7520 includes tuition ($4200), mandatory fees ($370), and college room and board ($2950). College room only: $1200.

Applications Of all full-time undergraduates enrolled in fall 1996, 53% of those who applied for aid were judged to have need according to Federal Methodology, of whom 100% were aided. *Financial aid deadline:* Applications processed continuously. *Financial aid forms:* FAFSA, institutional form required; state form acceptable. *Admission application deadline:* rolling.

Summary of Aid to Needy Students *From gift & self-help combined:* Average need met: 85%. Average amount awarded: $6399 (49% gift aid, 51% self-help). *Gift aid:* Total: $232,609 (53% from college's own funds, 47% from external sources). 85 part-time jobs.

Need-Based Scholarships & Grants Pell, private, college/university.

Loans PLUS, Stafford, Unsubsidized Stafford.

Non-Need Awards In 1996, a total of 160 non-need awards were made. *Academic Interests/Achievement Awards:* 69 ($36,750 total): general academic, education, religion/biblical studies. *Special Achievements/ Activities Awards:* 24 ($10,545 total): general special achievements/ activities, religious involvement. *Special Characteristics Awards:* 67 ($75,202 total): children of current students, parents of current students, relatives of clergy, siblings of current students, spouses of current students.

Other Money-Saving Options Accelerated degree. *Payment Plans:* installment, deferred payment. *Waivers:* full or partial for children of alumni, employees or children of employees, senior citizens.

Contact Ms. Brenda L. Rigier, Financial Aid Assistant, Calvary Bible College and Theological Seminary, Kansas City, MO 64147-1341, 816-322-5152 Ext. 1313, fax: 816-331-4474.

CALVIN COLLEGE
Grand Rapids, Michigan

About the Institution Independent/religious, coed. Degrees awarded: B, M. Offers 81 undergraduate majors. Total enrollment: 4,051. Undergraduates: 3,993 (55% state residents). Freshmen: 962.

Undergraduate Expenses (1996–97) Comprehensive fee of $15,840 includes tuition ($11,655), mandatory fees ($25), and college room and board ($4160).

Applications Of all full-time undergraduates enrolled in fall 1996, 98% of those who applied for aid were judged to have need according to Federal Methodology, of whom 100% were aided. *Financial aid deadline (priority):* 2/15. *Financial aid forms:* FAFSA, institutional form required; CSS Financial Aid PROFILE acceptable. *Admission application deadline:* rolling.

Summary of Aid to Needy Students *From gift & self-help combined:* Average need met: 77%. Average amount awarded: $9380 (61% gift aid, 39% self-help). *Gift aid:* Total: $15,141,000 (67% from college's own funds, 24% from other college-administered sources, 9% from external sources). 800 Federal Work-Study jobs (averaging $960); 800 part-time jobs.

Need-Based Scholarships & Grants Pell, FSEOG, state, private, college/university.

Loans Perkins, PLUS, Stafford, Unsubsidized Stafford, state, private, college/university short-term loans, college/university long-term loans ($2580 average).

Non-Need Awards In 1996, a total of 4,445 non-need awards were made. *Academic Interests/Achievement Awards:* 1,707 ($3,490,000 total): general academic, biological sciences, business, communication, education, engineering/technologies, English, health fields, humanities, physical sciences, premedicine, religion/biblical studies, social sciences. *Creative Arts/Performance Awards:* 56 ($46,400 total): art/ fine arts, music, performing arts, theater/drama. *Special Achievements/ Activities Awards:* 82 ($58,000 total): community service, religious involvement. *Special Characteristics Awards:* 2,600 ($2,327,000 total): children of faculty/staff, ethnic background, handicapped students, international students, members of minorities, religious affiliation.

Other Money-Saving Options Co-op program, off-campus living (after sophomore year). *Payment Plans:* tuition prepayment, installment. *Waivers:* full or partial for employees or children of employees.

Contact Ms. Sharron Pridgeon, Financial Aid Counselor, Calvin College, 3201 Burton Street, SE, Grand Rapids, MI 49546-4388, 616-957-6134, fax: 616-957-8551.

CAMDEN COLLEGE OF ARTS AND SCIENCES
Camden, New Jersey

See Rutgers, The State University of New Jersey, Camden College of Arts and Sciences

CAMERON UNIVERSITY
Lawton, Oklahoma

About the Institution State-supported, coed. Degrees awarded: A, B, M. Offers 35 undergraduate majors. Total enrollment: 5,231. Undergraduates: 5,044 (98% state residents). Freshmen: 939.

Undergraduate Expenses (1996–97) State resident tuition: $1760 (minimum). Nonresident tuition: $4205 (minimum). College room and board: $2711 (minimum).

Applications 58% of all full-time undergraduates enrolled in fall 1996 applied for aid; of these, 81% were judged to have need according to Federal Methodology, of whom 92% were aided. *Financial aid deadline (priority):* 6/15. *Financial aid forms:* FAFSA required; CSS Financial Aid PROFILE acceptable. *Admission application deadline:* rolling.

Summary of Aid to Needy Students *From gift & self-help combined:* Average need met: 75%. Average amount awarded: $3294 (49% gift aid, 51% self-help). *Gift aid:* Total: $1,882,679 (19% from college-administered sources, 81% from external sources). 250 Federal Work-Study jobs (averaging $800); 200 part-time jobs.

Need-Based Scholarships & Grants Pell, FSEOG, state, private.

Loans PLUS, Stafford, Unsubsidized Stafford.

Non-Need Awards In 1996, a total of 348 non-need awards were made. *Academic Interests/Achievement Awards:* 91 ($103,403 total): general academic, business, communication, English, mathematics. *Creative Arts/Performance Awards:* 13 ($7600 total): art/fine arts, creative writing, debating, journalism/publications, music, theater/drama. *Special Achievements/Activities Awards:* 111 ($222,771 total): leadership. *Special Characteristics Awards:* 40 ($102,495 total): members of minorities, ROTC participants. *Athletic:* Total: 93 ($185,898); Men: 51 ($98,169); Women: 42 ($87,729).

Other Money-Saving Options Army ROTC, off-campus living.

Contact Mrs. Caryn Pacheco, Financial Aid Director, Cameron University, 2800 West Gore Boulevard, Lawton, OK 73505-6377, 405-581-2293, fax: 405-581-5514.

CAMPBELL UNIVERSITY
Buies Creek, North Carolina

About the Institution Independent/religious, coed. Degrees awarded: A, B, M, P. Offers 81 undergraduate majors. Total enrollment: 6,920. Undergraduates: 5,832 (62% state residents). Freshmen: 582.

Undergraduate Expenses (1996–97) Comprehensive fee of $13,063 includes tuition ($9350), mandatory fees ($163), and college room and board ($3550). College room only: $1600.

Applications 72% of all full-time undergraduates enrolled in fall 1996 applied for aid; of these, 73% were judged to have need according to Federal Methodology, of whom 100% were aided. *Financial aid deadline (priority):* 3/15. *Financial aid forms:* FAFSA required. State form required for some. *Admission application deadline:* rolling.

Summary of Aid to Needy Students *From gift & self-help combined:* Average need met: 87%. Average amount awarded: $12,762 (55% gift aid, 45% self-help). *Gift aid:* Total: $7,664,765 (41% from college's own funds, 43% from other college-administered sources, 16% from external sources). 585 Federal Work-Study jobs (averaging $480); 350 part-time jobs.

Need-Based Scholarships & Grants Pell, FSEOG, state, private, college/university.

Loans Perkins, PLUS, Stafford, Unsubsidized Stafford.

Non-Need Awards In 1996, a total of 1,289 non-need awards were made. *Academic Interests/Achievement Awards:* 825 ($2,795,449 total): general academic. *Creative Arts/Performance Awards:* 45 ($19,700 total): art/fine arts, creative writing, journalism/publications, music, theater/drama. *Special Achievements/Activities Awards:* 125 ($110,600 total): cheerleading/drum major, Junior Miss, religious involvement. *Special Characteristics Awards:* 120 ($285,464 total): children of faculty/staff, relatives of clergy. *Athletic:* Total: 174 ($1,138,652).

Other Money-Saving Options Accelerated degree, co-op program, Army ROTC. *Payment Plan:* installment. *Waivers:* full or partial for employees or children of employees.

Contact Office of Financial Aid, Campbell University, Buies Creek, NC 27506, 910-893-1313.

CANISIUS COLLEGE
Buffalo, New York

About the Institution Independent/religious, coed. Degrees awarded: A, B, M. Offers 47 undergraduate majors. Total enrollment: 4,746. Undergraduates: 3,275 (94% state residents). Freshmen: 692.

Undergraduate Expenses (1996–97) Comprehensive fee of $18,751 includes tuition ($12,600), mandatory fees ($326), and college room and board ($5825).

Applications Of all full-time undergraduates enrolled in fall 1996, 94% of those who applied for aid were judged to have need according to Federal Methodology, of whom 100% were aided. *Financial aid deadline (priority):* 1/31. *Financial aid forms:* FAFSA, state form, institutional form required. *Admission application deadline:* rolling.

Summary of Aid to Needy Students *Gift aid:* Total: $16,693,751 (69% from college's own funds, 22% from other college-administered sources, 9% from external sources). 779 Federal Work-Study jobs (averaging $1344); 116 part-time jobs.

Need-Based Scholarships & Grants Pell, FSEOG, state, private, college/university.

Loans Perkins, PLUS, Stafford, Unsubsidized Stafford, private, college/university short-term loans ($200 average), college/university long-term loans ($2262 average).

Non-Need Awards In 1996, a total of 391 non-need awards were made. *Academic Interests/Achievement Awards:* 70 ($831,693 total): general academic. *Special Achievements/Activities Awards:* 105 ($104,667 total): general special achievements/activities, community service, leadership. *Athletic:* Total: 216 ($1,078,020); Men: 112 ($522,627); Women: 104 ($555,393).

Other Money-Saving Options Army ROTC, off-campus living. *Payment Plans:* tuition prepayment, installment, deferred payment. *Waivers:* full or partial for employees or children of employees.

Contact Office of Financial Aid, Canisius College, 2001 Main Street, Buffalo, NY 14208-1098, 716-883-7000.

CAPITAL UNIVERSITY
Columbus, Ohio

About the Institution Independent/religious, coed. Degrees awarded: B, M, P. Offers 54 undergraduate majors. Total enrollment: 4,035. Undergraduates: 1,874 (90% state residents). Freshmen: 506.

Undergraduate Expenses (1997–98) Comprehensive fee of $18,960 includes tuition ($14,760) and college room and board ($4200).

Applications Of all full-time undergraduates enrolled in fall 1996, 93% of those who applied for aid were judged to have need according to Federal Methodology, of whom 100% were aided. *Financial aid deadline*

(priority): 3/01. *Financial aid forms:* FAFSA required. Institutional form required for some. *Admission application deadline:* rolling.

Summary of Aid to Needy Students *From gift & self-help combined:* Average need met: 90%. Average amount awarded: $14,905 (60% gift aid, 40% self-help). *Gift aid:* Total: $13,788,246. Federal Work-Study jobs (averaging $1200); part-time jobs.

Need-Based Scholarships & Grants Pell, FSEOG, state, college/university.

Loans Perkins, PLUS, Stafford, Unsubsidized Stafford, Federal Nursing, private, college/university short-term loans ($50 average), college/university long-term loans ($1000 average).

Non-Need Awards *Academic Interests/Achievement Awards:* ($9,135,997 total): general academic. *Creative Arts/Performance Awards:* ($972,190 total): music. *Special Achievements/Activities Awards:* ($9100 total): hobbies/interest, leadership. *Special Characteristics Awards:* ($1,470,474 total): children and siblings of alumni, children of faculty/staff, ethnic background, international students, members of minorities, relatives of clergy, religious affiliation, ROTC participants, siblings of current students.

Other Money-Saving Options Army ROTC, off-campus living (after junior year). *Payment Plan:* installment. *Waivers:* full or partial for employees or children of employees and senior citizens.

Contact Office of Financial Aid, Capital University, 2199 East Main Street, Columbus, OH 43209-2394, 614-236-6511.

CAPITOL COLLEGE
Laurel, Maryland

About the Institution Independent, coed. Degrees awarded: A, B, M. Offers 7 undergraduate majors. Total enrollment: 709. Undergraduates: 609 (78% state residents). Freshmen: 41.

Undergraduate Expenses (1996–97) Tuition: $9192. Mandatory fees: $60 (minimum). College room only: $2952 (minimum).

Applications 72% of all full-time undergraduates enrolled in fall 1996 applied for aid; of these, 90% were judged to have need according to Federal Methodology, of whom 100% were aided. *Financial aid deadline (priority):* 3/1. *Financial aid forms:* FAFSA, institutional form required; CSS Financial Aid PROFILE, state form acceptable. *Admission application deadline:* rolling.

Summary of Aid to Needy Students *From gift & self-help combined:* Average need met: 78%. Average amount awarded: $8341 (35% gift aid, 65% self-help). *Gift aid:* Total: $629,559 (29% from college's own funds, 48% from other college-administered sources, 23% from external sources). 23 Federal Work-Study jobs (averaging $2000); 15 part-time jobs.

Need-Based Scholarships & Grants Pell, FSEOG, state, private, college/university.

Loans Perkins, PLUS, Stafford, Unsubsidized Stafford, college/university short-term loans ($125 average).

Non-Need Awards In 1996, a total of 15 non-need awards were made. *Academic Interests/Achievement Awards:* 15 ($27,000 total): general academic.

Other Money-Saving Options Accelerated degree, co-op program, cooperative Army ROTC, cooperative Naval ROTC, cooperative Air Force ROTC, off-campus living. *Payment Plans:* installment, deferred payment. *Waivers:* full or partial for employees or children of employees.

Contact Ms. Sheila Sauls-White, Director, Financial Aid, Capitol College, 11301 Springfield Road, Laurel, MD 20708-9759, 301-369-2800, fax: 301-953-1442.

CARDINAL STRITCH UNIVERSITY
Milwaukee, Wisconsin

About the Institution Independent/religious, coed. Degrees awarded: A, B, M. Offers 42 undergraduate majors. Total enrollment: 5,526. Undergraduates: 3,161 (80% state residents). Freshmen: 169.

Undergraduate Expenses (1996–97) Comprehensive fee of $12,890 includes tuition ($8960), mandatory fees ($50), and college room and board ($3880 minimum). College room only: $1240.

Applications *Financial aid deadline (priority):* 8/1. *Financial aid forms:* institutional form required; FAFSA, CSS Financial Aid PROFILE acceptable. *Admission application deadline:* rolling.

Summary of Aid to Needy Students Federal Work-Study jobs; part-time jobs.

Need-Based Scholarships & Grants Pell, FSEOG.

Loans Perkins, PLUS, Stafford.

Non-Need Awards *Academic Interests/Achievement Awards:* general academic. *Creative Arts/Performance Awards:* art/fine arts. *Special Achievements/Activities Awards:* leadership.

Other Money-Saving Options Accelerated degree, off-campus living. *Payment Plan:* installment. *Waivers:* full or partial for employees or children of employees.

Contact Office of Financial Aid, Cardinal Stritch University, 6801 North Yates Road, Milwaukee, WI 53217-3985, 414-410-4000.

CARIBBEAN UNIVERSITY
Bayamón, Puerto Rico

About the Institution Independent, coed. Degrees awarded: A, B. Offers 26 undergraduate majors.

Applications *Financial aid deadline:* Applications processed continuously. *Financial aid forms:* FAFSA, institutional form required. *Admission application deadline:* rolling.

Summary of Aid to Needy Students Federal Work-Study jobs.

Need-Based Scholarships & Grants Pell, FSEOG, state.

Loans Stafford, Unsubsidized Stafford.

Non-Need Awards Not offered.

Other Money-Saving Options Accelerated degree, cooperative Army ROTC.

Contact Ms. Yolanda Cazull, Director of Financial Aid, Caribbean University, Bayamón, PR 00960-0493, 787-780-0070 Ext. 315.

CARLETON COLLEGE
Northfield, Minnesota

About the Institution Independent, coed. Degrees awarded: B. Offers 33 undergraduate majors. Total enrollment: 1,698 (22% state residents). Freshmen: 475.

Undergraduate Expenses (1996–97) Comprehensive fee of $25,410 includes tuition ($20,988), mandatory fees ($132), and college room and board ($4290).

Applications Of all full-time undergraduates enrolled in fall 1996, 72% of those who applied for aid were judged to have need according to Federal Methodology, of whom 100% were aided. *Financial aid deadline (priority):* 2/15. *Financial aid forms:* FAFSA, CSS Financial Aid PROFILE required. *Regular admission application deadline:* 1/15. Early decision deadline: 11/15.

Summary of Aid to Needy Students *From gift & self-help combined:* Average need met: 100%. Average amount awarded: $16,722 (69% gift aid, 31% self-help). *Gift aid:* Total: $12,251,767 (83% from col-

lege's own funds, 4% from other college-administered sources, 13% from external sources). 206 Federal Work-Study jobs (averaging $1966); 1,064 part-time jobs.

Need-Based Scholarships & Grants Pell, FSEOG, state, college/university.

Loans Perkins, PLUS, Stafford, Unsubsidized Stafford, state, private, college/university long-term loans ($2914 average).

Non-Need Awards In 1996, a total of 106 non-need awards were made. *Academic Interests/Achievement Awards:* 106 ($82,333 total): general academic.

Other Money-Saving Options Accelerated degree, off-campus living (after freshman year). *Payment Plans:* tuition prepayment, installment.

Contact Office of Financial Aid, Carleton College, One North College Street, Northfield, MN 55057-4001, 507-646-4000.

CARLOW COLLEGE
Pittsburgh, Pennsylvania

About the Institution Independent/religious, primarily women. Degrees awarded: B, M. Offers 28 undergraduate majors. Total enrollment: 2,339. Undergraduates: 2,085 (96% state residents). Freshmen: 170.

Undergraduate Expenses (1996–97) Comprehensive fee of $15,756 includes tuition ($10,730), mandatory fees ($334), and college room and board ($4692).

Applications 97% of all full-time undergraduates enrolled in fall 1996 applied for aid; of these, 95% were judged to have need according to Federal Methodology, of whom 100% were aided. *Financial aid deadline (priority):* 5/1. *Financial aid forms:* FAFSA, state form, institutional form, federal income tax form required. *Admission application deadline:* rolling.

Summary of Aid to Needy Students *From gift & self-help combined:* Average need met: 85%. Average amount awarded: $4776 (51% gift aid, 49% self-help). *Gift aid:* Total: $1,960,526 (34% from college's own funds, 7% from other college-administered sources, 59% from external sources). 291 Federal Work-Study jobs (averaging $324).

Need-Based Scholarships & Grants Pell, FSEOG, state, private, college/university.

Loans Perkins, PLUS, Stafford, Unsubsidized Stafford, Federal Nursing, private.

Non-Need Awards In 1996, a total of 207 non-need awards were made. *Academic Interests/Achievement Awards:* 119 ($192,491 total): general academic, biological sciences, business, communication, computer science, education, English, humanities, mathematics, social sciences. *Creative Arts/Performance Awards:* 2 ($3500 total): creative writing. *Special Achievements/Activities Awards:* 28 ($24,690 total): leadership, religious involvement. *Special Characteristics Awards:* 18 ($4500 total): children of current students, religious affiliation, siblings of current students, spouses of current students. *Athletic:* Total: 40 ($44,125); Men: 0; Women: 40 ($44,125).

Other Money-Saving Options Accelerated degree, cooperative Army ROTC, cooperative Naval ROTC, cooperative Air Force ROTC, off-campus living. *Payment Plans:* installment, deferred payment. *Waivers:* full or partial for employees or children of employees and adult students.

Contact Ms. Natalie L. Wilson, Director of Financial Aid, Carlow College, 3333 Fifth Avenue, Pittsburgh, PA 15213-3165, 412-578-6058, fax: 412-578-6668.

CARNEGIE MELLON UNIVERSITY
Pittsburgh, Pennsylvania

About the Institution Independent, coed. Degrees awarded: B, M, D. Offers 117 undergraduate majors. Total enrollment: 7,758. Undergraduates: 4,823 (25% state residents). Freshmen: 1,386.

Undergraduate Expenses (1996–97) Comprehensive fee of $25,580 includes tuition ($19,400), mandatory fees ($100), and college room and board ($6080). College room only: $3710.

Applications Of all full-time undergraduates enrolled in fall 1996, 89% of those who applied for aid were judged to have need according to Federal Methodology, of whom 95% were aided. *Financial aid deadline (priority):* 2/15. *Financial aid forms:* FAFSA, CSS Financial Aid PROFILE, institutional form required. State form required for some. *Regular admission application deadline:* 1/15. Early decision deadline: 12/1.

Summary of Aid to Needy Students *From gift & self-help combined:* Average need met: 100%. Average amount awarded: $15,054 (65% gift aid, 35% self-help). *Gift aid:* Total: $27,435,000 (81% from college's own funds, 11% from other college-administered sources, 8% from external sources). Federal Work-Study jobs; 1,250 part-time jobs.

Need-Based Scholarships & Grants Pell, FSEOG, state, private, college/university.

Loans Perkins, PLUS, Stafford, Unsubsidized Stafford.

Non-Need Awards *Academic Interests/Achievement Awards:* 1,499 ($6,318,000 total): general academic. *Creative Arts/Performance Awards:* music. *Special Characteristics Awards:* 70 ($1,300,000 total): ROTC participants.

Other Money-Saving Options Accelerated degree, co-op program, Army ROTC, Naval ROTC, Air Force ROTC, off-campus living (after freshman year). *Payment Plan:* installment. *Waivers:* full or partial for employees or children of employees.

Contact Enrollment Services, Carnegie Mellon University, 5000 Forbes Avenue, Pittsburgh, PA 15213-3891, 412-268-8186.

CARROLL COLLEGE
Helena, Montana

About the Institution Independent/religious, coed. Degrees awarded: A, B. Offers 48 undergraduate majors. Total enrollment: 1,352 (68% state residents). Freshmen: 281.

Undergraduate Expenses (1997–98) Comprehensive fee of $15,700 includes tuition ($11,316) and college room and board ($4384).

Applications 88% of all full-time undergraduates enrolled in fall 1996 applied for aid; of these, 72% were judged to have need according to Federal Methodology, of whom 100% were aided. *Financial aid deadline (priority):* 3/1. *Financial aid forms:* FAFSA required. State form required for some. *Admission application deadline:* 6/1.

Summary of Aid to Needy Students *From gift & self-help combined:* Average need met: 78%. Average amount awarded: $9291 (58% gift aid, 42% self-help). *Gift aid:* Total: $3,826,147 (75% from college's own funds, 4% from other college-administered sources, 21% from external sources). 178 Federal Work-Study jobs (averaging $1350); 138 part-time jobs.

Need-Based Scholarships & Grants Pell, FSEOG, state, college/university.

Loans Perkins, PLUS, Stafford, Unsubsidized Stafford, college/university short-term loans.

Non-Need Awards In 1996, a total of 703 non-need awards were made. *Academic Interests/Achievement Awards:* 422 ($1,328,450 total): general academic. *Creative Arts/Performance Awards:* 23 ($29,150 total): debating, theater/drama. *Special Achievements/Activities Awards:* 12 ($13,000 total): leadership. *Special Characteristics Awards:* 160 ($472,909 total): children and siblings of alumni, local/state students, siblings of current students. *Athletic:* Total: 86 ($667,409); Men: 59 ($436,510); Women: 27 ($230,899).

Other Money-Saving Options Accelerated degree, co-op program, off-campus living (after sophomore year). *Payment Plan:* installment. *Waivers:* full or partial for employees or children of employees and senior citizens.

Contact Financial Aid Office, Carroll College, 1601 North Benton Avenue, Helena, MT 59625-0002, 406-447-4300, fax: 406-447-4533.

CARROLL COLLEGE
Waukesha, Wisconsin

About the Institution Independent/religious, coed. Degrees awarded: B, M. Offers 54 undergraduate majors. Total enrollment: 2,464. Undergraduates: 2,414 (84% state residents). Freshmen: 461.

Undergraduate Expenses (1997–98) Comprehensive fee of $18,050 includes tuition ($13,670), mandatory fees ($220), and college room and board ($4160). College room only: $2260.

Applications 91% of all full-time undergraduates enrolled in fall 1996 applied for aid; of these, 85% were judged to have need according to Federal Methodology, of whom 100% were aided. *Financial aid deadline (priority):* 3/15. *Financial aid forms:* FAFSA required; CSS Financial Aid PROFILE acceptable. *Admission application deadline:* rolling.

Summary of Aid to Needy Students *From gift & self-help combined:* Average need met: 100%. Average amount awarded: $12,200 (66% gift aid, 34% self-help). *Gift aid:* Total: $10,010,499 (77% from college's own funds, 16% from other college-administered sources, 7% from external sources). Federal Work-Study jobs (averaging $900); 185 part-time jobs.

Need-Based Scholarships & Grants Pell, FSEOG, state, private, college/university.

Loans Perkins, PLUS, Stafford, Unsubsidized Stafford, college/university short-term loans ($200 average).

Non-Need Awards *Academic Interests/Achievement Awards:* general academic. *Creative Arts/Performance Awards:* music, theater/drama. *Special Characteristics Awards:* children and siblings of alumni.

Other Money-Saving Options Accelerated degree, off-campus living (after sophomore year). *Payment Plans:* installment, deferred payment. *Waivers:* full or partial for employees or children of employees.

Contact Office of Financial Aid, Carroll College, 100 North East Avenue, Waukesha, WI 53186-5593, 414-547-1211.

CARSON-NEWMAN COLLEGE
Jefferson City, Tennessee

About the Institution Independent/religious, coed. Degrees awarded: A, B, M. Offers 87 undergraduate majors. Total enrollment: 2,265. Undergraduates: 2,060 (60% state residents). Freshmen: 424.

Undergraduate Expenses (1997–98) Comprehensive fee of $13,660 includes tuition ($9500), mandatory fees ($490), and college room and board ($3670). College room only: $1470.

Applications 91% of all full-time undergraduates enrolled in fall 1996 applied for aid; of these, 97% were judged to have need according to Federal Methodology, of whom 99% were aided. *Financial aid deadline (priority):* 3/1. *Financial aid forms:* FAFSA, institutional form required; CSS Financial Aid PROFILE acceptable. *Admission application deadline:* 8/1.

Summary of Aid to Needy Students *From gift & self-help combined:* Average need met: 83%. Average amount awarded: $8683 (61% gift aid, 39% self-help). *Gift aid:* Total: $8,484,912 (66% from college's own funds, 17% from other college-administered sources, 17% from external sources). 171 Federal Work-Study jobs (averaging $850); 153 part-time jobs.

Need-Based Scholarships & Grants Pell, FSEOG, state, private, college/university.

Loans Perkins, PLUS, Stafford, Unsubsidized Stafford, college/university long-term loans ($2000 average).

Non-Need Awards In 1996, a total of 1,173 non-need awards were made. *Academic Interests/Achievement Awards:* 167 ($824,500 total):

general academic. *Creative Arts/Performance Awards:* 104 ($167,000 total): art/fine arts, debating, music. *Special Achievements/Activities Awards:* 459 ($760,500 total): leadership. *Special Characteristics Awards:* 135 ($128,350 total): children and siblings of alumni, siblings of current students. *Athletic:* Total: 308 ($915,114); Men: 202 ($649,020); Women: 106 ($266,094).

Other Money-Saving Options Accelerated degree, Army ROTC, cooperative Air Force ROTC, off-campus living (after junior year). *Payment Plan:* installment. *Waivers:* full or partial for employees or children of employees and senior citizens.

Contact Mr. Don Elia, Director of Financial Aid, Carson-Newman College, Russell Avenue, Jefferson City, TN 37760, 423-475-9061, fax: 423-471-3502.

CARTHAGE COLLEGE
Kenosha, Wisconsin

About the Institution Independent/religious, coed. Degrees awarded: B, M. Offers 48 undergraduate majors. Total enrollment: 2,164. Undergraduates: 2,109 (61% state residents). Freshmen: 401.

Undergraduate Expenses (1997–98) Comprehensive fee of $19,780 includes tuition ($15,365) and college room and board ($4415).

Applications 90% of all full-time undergraduates enrolled in fall 1996 applied for aid; of these, 88% were judged to have need according to Federal Methodology, of whom 100% were aided. *Financial aid deadline (priority):* 2/15. *Financial aid forms:* FAFSA required. *Regular admission application deadline:* rolling. Early action deadline: 7/1.

Summary of Aid to Needy Students *From gift & self-help combined:* Average need met: 82%. Average amount awarded: $12,791 (67% gift aid, 33% self-help). *Gift aid:* Total: $10,333,979 (79% from college's own funds, 11% from other college-administered sources, 10% from external sources). 265 Federal Work-Study jobs (averaging $1200); 415 part-time jobs.

Need-Based Scholarships & Grants Pell, FSEOG, state, private, college/university.

Loans Perkins, PLUS, Stafford, Unsubsidized Stafford, private, college/university long-term loans ($1000 average).

Non-Need Awards In 1996, a total of 2,345 non-need awards were made. *Academic Interests/Achievement Awards:* 1,098 ($3,521,659 total): general academic, biological sciences, health fields, mathematics, physical sciences, premedicine. *Creative Arts/Performance Awards:* 85 ($165,178 total): art/fine arts, music, theater/drama. *Special Achievements/Activities Awards:* 462 ($874,631 total): general special achievements/activities, leadership. *Special Characteristics Awards:* 700 ($398,211 total): children and siblings of alumni, children of public servants, local/state students, previous college experience, relatives of clergy, religious affiliation, siblings of current students.

Other Money-Saving Options Accelerated degree, cooperative Air Force ROTC. *Payment Plan:* installment. *Waivers:* full or partial for children of alumni and employees or children of employees.

Contact Ms. Kristi Blabaum, Assistant Director, Carthage College, 2001 Alford Park Drive, WI 53140-1994, 414-551-6001, fax: 414-551-5762.

CASCADE COLLEGE
Portland, Oregon

About the Institution Independent/religious, coed. Degrees awarded: B. Offers 5 undergraduate majors. Total enrollment: 255 (42% state residents). Freshmen: 92.

Undergraduate Expenses (1997–98) Comprehensive fee of $11,850 includes tuition ($7550) and college room and board ($4300).

Applications 95% of all full-time undergraduates enrolled in fall 1996 applied for aid; of these, 78% were judged to have need according to Federal Methodology, of whom 100% were aided. *Financial aid deadline*

(priority): 8/1. *Financial aid forms:* FAFSA required. *Regular admission application deadline:* rolling. Nonresident deadline: rolling.

Summary of Aid to Needy Students *From gift & self-help combined:* Average need met: 70%. Average amount awarded: $8504 (41% gift aid, 59% self-help). *Gift aid:* Total: $660,661 (66% from college's own funds, 12% from other college-administered sources, 22% from external sources). 75 part-time jobs.

Need-Based Scholarships & Grants Pell, college/university.

Loans PLUS, Stafford, Unsubsidized Stafford.

Non-Need Awards In 1996, a total of 589 non-need awards were made. *Academic Interests/Achievement Awards:* 451 ($640,355 total): general academic. *Creative Arts/Performance Awards:* 58 ($81,300 total): music, theater/drama. *Special Characteristics Awards:* 34 ($50,690 total): children of faculty/staff, siblings of current students. *Athletic:* Total: 46 ($164,110); Men: 33 ($117,858); Women: 13 ($46,252).

Other Money-Saving Options Accelerated degree, cooperative Army ROTC, cooperative Air Force ROTC. *Waivers:* full or partial for employees or children of employees.

Contact Ms. Kaelea Graul, Assistant Director of Financial Aid, Cascade College, 9101 East Burnside Street, Portland, OR 97216-1515, 503-257-1218.

CASE WESTERN RESERVE UNIVERSITY
Cleveland, Ohio

About the Institution Independent, coed. Degrees awarded: B, M, D, P. Offers 69 undergraduate majors. Total enrollment: 9,970. Undergraduates: 3,679 (59% state residents). Freshmen: 739.

Undergraduate Expenses (1997–98) Comprehensive fee of $22,990 includes tuition ($17,800), mandatory fees ($140), and college room and board ($5050). College room only: $3080.

Applications 74% of all full-time undergraduates enrolled in fall 1996 applied for aid; of these, 96% were judged to have need according to Federal Methodology, of whom 100% were aided. *Financial aid deadline (priority):* 2/1. *Financial aid forms:* FAFSA, CSS Financial Aid PROFILE required. State form, institutional form required for some. *Regular admission application deadline:* 2/1. Early decision deadline: 1/1.

Summary of Aid to Needy Students *From gift & self-help combined:* Average need met: 99%. Average amount awarded: $18,548 (63% gift aid, 37% self-help). *Gift aid:* Total: $25,928,973 (80% from college's own funds, 13% from other college-administered sources, 7% from external sources). 1,159 Federal Work-Study jobs (averaging $1567); 51 part-time jobs.

Need-Based Scholarships & Grants Pell, FSEOG, state, private, college/university.

Loans Perkins, PLUS, Stafford, Unsubsidized Stafford, Federal Nursing, state, private, college/university short-term loans ($480 average), college/university long-term loans ($2901 average).

Non-Need Awards In 1996, a total of 965 non-need awards were made. *Academic Interests/Achievement Awards:* 734 ($7,326,276 total): general academic. *Creative Arts/Performance Awards:* 20 ($118,200 total): art/fine arts, creative writing, dance, music, theater/drama. *Special Achievements/Activities Awards:* 78 ($210,750 total): leadership. *Special Characteristics Awards:* 133 ($2,045,702 total): children of faculty/staff, ROTC participants.

Other Money-Saving Options Accelerated degree, co-op program, cooperative Army ROTC, cooperative Air Force ROTC. *Payment Plans:* tuition prepayment, installment. *Waivers:* full or partial for employees or children of employees.

Contact Ms. Nancy Issa, Associate Director, Case Western Reserve University, 1090 Euclid Avenue, Cleveland, OH 44106-7049, 216-368-4530, fax: 216-368-5054.

CASTLETON STATE COLLEGE
Castleton, Vermont

About the Institution State-supported, coed. Degrees awarded: A, B, M. Offers 48 undergraduate majors. Total enrollment: 1,854. Undergraduates: 1,494 (62% state residents). Freshmen: 396.

Undergraduate Expenses (1996–97) State resident tuition: $3620. Nonresident tuition: $8380. Mandatory fees: $710. College room and board: $4936.

Applications Of all full-time undergraduates enrolled in fall 1996, 89% of those who applied for aid were judged to have need according to Federal Methodology, of whom 99% were aided. *Financial aid deadline (priority):* 3/15. *Financial aid forms:* FAFSA required. State form required for some. *Admission application deadline:* rolling.

Summary of Aid to Needy Students *From gift & self-help combined:* Average need met: 100%. Average amount awarded: $8103 (23% gift aid, 77% self-help). *Gift aid:* Total: $1,834,642 (5% from college's own funds, 23% from other college-administered sources, 72% from external sources). Federal Work-Study jobs; part-time jobs.

Loans College/university short-term loans.

Non-Need Awards *Academic Interests/Achievement Awards:* general academic, foreign languages. *Creative Arts/Performance Awards:* music.

Other Money-Saving Options Co-op program, off-campus living (after freshman year). *Payment Plan:* installment. *Waivers:* full or partial for employees or children of employees.

Contact Office of Financial Aid, Castleton State College, Castleton, VT 05735, 802-468-5611.

CATAWBA COLLEGE
Salisbury, North Carolina

About the Institution Independent/religious, coed. Degrees awarded: B, M. Offers 51 undergraduate majors. Total enrollment: 1,178. Undergraduates: 1,168 (57% state residents). Freshmen: 296.

Undergraduate Expenses (1997–98) Comprehensive fee of $15,852 includes tuition ($11,352) and college room and board ($4500).

Applications 98% of all full-time undergraduates enrolled in fall 1996 applied for aid; of these, 63% were judged to have need according to Federal Methodology, of whom 99% were aided. *Financial aid deadline (priority):* 3/1. *Financial aid forms:* FAFSA, institutional form required; CSS Financial Aid PROFILE acceptable. State form required for some. *Admission application deadline:* rolling.

Summary of Aid to Needy Students *From gift & self-help combined:* Average need met: 95%. Average amount awarded: $11,033 (81% gift aid, 19% self-help). *Gift aid:* Total: $6,137,512 (78% from college's own funds, 1% from other college-administered sources, 21% from external sources). 86 Federal Work-Study jobs (averaging $954); 318 part-time jobs.

Need-Based Scholarships & Grants Pell, FSEOG, state, college/university.

Loans Perkins, PLUS, Stafford, Unsubsidized Stafford, private, college/university long-term loans ($1800 average), TERI Loans, Advantage Loans, Nellie Mae Loans.

Non-Need Awards In 1996, a total of 1,681 non-need awards were made. *Academic Interests/Achievement Awards:* 1,317 ($3,319,344 total): general academic. *Creative Arts/Performance Awards:* 60 ($85,000 total): performing arts. *Special Achievements/Activities Awards:* 26 ($30,625 total): leadership. *Special Characteristics Awards:* 26 ($40,875 total): children of faculty/staff, relatives of clergy, religious affiliation, siblings of current students. *Athletic:* Total: 252 ($951,299); Men: 152 ($673,581); Women: 100 ($277,718).

Other Money-Saving Options Army ROTC, off-campus living (after sophomore year). *Payment Plan:* installment. *Waivers:* full or partial for employees or children of employees.

Contact Financial Assistance Office, Catawba College, Salisbury, NC 28144-2488, 704-637-4416.

THE CATHOLIC UNIVERSITY OF AMERICA
Washington, District of Columbia

About the Institution Independent/religious, coed. Degrees awarded: B, M, D, P. Offers 63 undergraduate majors. Total enrollment: 5,974. Undergraduates: 2,380 (8% district residents). Freshmen: 479.

Undergraduate Expenses (1997–98) Comprehensive fee of $24,916 includes tuition ($16,500 minimum), mandatory fees ($610), and college room and board ($7806). College room only: $4748.

Applications 73% of all full-time undergraduates enrolled in fall 1996 applied for aid; of these, 84% were judged to have need according to Federal Methodology, of whom 100% were aided. *Financial aid deadline:* continuous. *Financial aid forms:* FAFSA acceptable. Institutional form required for some. *Regular admission application deadline:* 2/15. Early action deadline: 11/15.

Summary of Aid to Needy Students *From gift & self-help combined:* Average need met: 90%. Average amount awarded: $15,482 (49% gift aid, 51% self-help). *Gift aid:* Total: $9,937,088 (81% from college's own funds, 10% from other college-administered sources, 9% from external sources). 642 Federal Work-Study jobs (averaging $1000); 47 part-time jobs.

Need-Based Scholarships & Grants Pell, FSEOG, state, private, college/university.

Loans Perkins, PLUS, Stafford, Unsubsidized Stafford, Federal Nursing, private.

Non-Need Awards In 1996, a total of 665 non-need awards were made. *Academic Interests/Achievement Awards:* 360 ($3,386,010 total): general academic. *Creative Arts/Performance Awards:* 101 ($316,650 total): music. *Special Achievements/Activities Awards:* 5 ($26,450 total): religious involvement. *Special Characteristics Awards:* 199 ($1,871,711 total): children of faculty/staff, religious affiliation.

Other Money-Saving Options Accelerated degree, cooperative Army ROTC, cooperative Naval ROTC, cooperative Air Force ROTC, off-campus living (after sophomore year). *Payment Plan:* deferred payment. *Waivers:* full or partial for employees or children of employees.

Contact Ms. Doris Torosian, Acting Director of Financial Aid, The Catholic University of America, Cardinal Station, Washington, DC 20064, 202-319-5307.

CAZENOVIA COLLEGE
Cazenovia, New York

About the Institution Independent, coed. Degrees awarded: A, B. Offers 21 undergraduate majors. Total enrollment: 727 (90% state residents). Freshmen: 177.

Undergraduate Expenses (1997–98 estimated) Comprehensive fee of $17,116 includes tuition ($11,232), mandatory fees ($416), and college room and board ($5468). College room only: $2734.

Applications Of all full-time undergraduates enrolled in fall 1996, 100% of those judged to have need according to Federal Methodology were aided. *Financial aid deadline (priority):* 3/15. *Financial aid forms:* FAFSA required; CSS Financial Aid PROFILE acceptable. State form required for some. *Admission application deadline:* rolling.

Summary of Aid to Needy Students *From gift & self-help combined:* Average need met: 34%. Average amount awarded: $11,180 (67% gift aid, 33% self-help). *Gift aid:* Total: $4,489,367 (51% from college's

own funds, 3% from other college-administered sources, 46% from external sources). 245 Federal Work-Study jobs (averaging $896); 25 part-time jobs.

Need-Based Scholarships & Grants Pell, FSEOG, state, college/university.

Loans PLUS, Stafford, Unsubsidized Stafford, college/university short-term loans ($50 average), college/university long-term loans ($5035 average).

Non-Need Awards In 1996, a total of 362 non-need awards were made. *Academic Interests/Achievement Awards:* 297 ($200,000 total): general academic. *Creative Arts/Performance Awards:* 65 ($100,000 total): applied art and design, art/fine arts.

Other Money-Saving Options Co-op program, cooperative Army ROTC, cooperative Air Force ROTC, off-campus living (after sophomore year). *Payment Plan:* installment. *Waivers:* full or partial for employees or children of employees.

Contact Ms. Christine L. Mandel, Director of Financial Aid, Cazenovia College, 13 Nickerson Street, Cazenovia, NY 13035, 315-655-8181, fax: 315-655-4860.

CEDAR CREST COLLEGE
Allentown, Pennsylvania

About the Institution Independent/religious, primarily women. Degrees awarded: A, B, M. Offers 69 undergraduate majors. Total enrollment: 1,699. Undergraduates: 1,683 (86% state residents). Freshmen: 239.

Undergraduate Expenses (1997–98) Comprehensive fee of $21,565 includes tuition ($15,820) and college room and board ($5745). College room only: $3100.

Applications 95% of all full-time undergraduates enrolled in fall 1996 applied for aid; of these, 91% were judged to have need according to Federal Methodology, of whom 100% were aided. *Financial aid deadline:* Applications processed continuously. *Financial aid forms:* FAFSA, state form, institutional form required; CSS Financial Aid PROFILE acceptable. *Admission application deadline:* rolling.

Summary of Aid to Needy Students *From gift & self-help combined:* Average need met: 92%. Average amount awarded: $14,603 (65% gift aid, 35% self-help). *Gift aid:* Total: $6,266,193 (75% from college's own funds, 2% from other college-administered sources, 23% from external sources). 75 Federal Work-Study jobs (averaging $1100); 275 part-time jobs.

Need-Based Scholarships & Grants Pell, FSEOG, state, private, college/university.

Loans Perkins, PLUS, Stafford, Unsubsidized Stafford, Federal Nursing, private, college/university long-term loans ($1500 average).

Non-Need Awards In 1996, a total of 325 non-need awards were made. *Academic Interests/Achievement Awards:* 202 ($836,109 total): general academic, biological sciences, education, health fields, premedicine. *Creative Arts/Performance Awards:* 15 ($22,500 total): art/fine arts, theater/drama. *Special Achievements/Activities Awards:* 27 ($55,750 total): general special achievements/activities, memberships. *Special Characteristics Awards:* 81 ($144,521 total): general special characteristics, previous college experience, relatives of clergy, religious affiliation.

Other Money-Saving Options Accelerated degree, cooperative Army ROTC. *Payment Plan:* installment. *Waivers:* full or partial for employees or children of employees.

Contact Ms. Judith A. Neyhart, Director of Financial Aid, Cedar Crest College, 100 College Drive, Allentown, PA 18104-6196, 610-437-4471.

CEDARVILLE COLLEGE
Cedarville, Ohio

About the Institution Independent/religious, coed. Degrees awarded: A, B. Offers 61 undergraduate majors. Total enrollment: 2,509 (34% state residents). Freshmen: 676.

Undergraduate Expenses (1997–98) Comprehensive fee of $14,028 includes tuition ($9168), mandatory fees ($144), and college room and board ($4716). College room only: $2532.

Applications Of all full-time undergraduates enrolled in fall 1996, 90% of those who applied for aid were judged to have need according to Federal Methodology, of whom 98% were aided. *Financial aid deadline (priority):* 3/1. *Financial aid forms:* FAFSA, institutional form required; CSS Financial Aid PROFILE acceptable. State form required for some. *Admission application deadline:* rolling.

Summary of Aid to Needy Students *From gift & self-help combined:* Average need met: 70%. Average amount awarded: $5470 (40% gift aid, 60% self-help). *Gift aid:* Total: $3,204,507 (39% from college's own funds, 42% from other college-administered sources, 19% from external sources). 120 Federal Work-Study jobs (averaging $1300); 750 part-time jobs.

Need-Based Scholarships & Grants Pell, FSEOG, state, private, college/university.

Loans Perkins, PLUS, Stafford, Unsubsidized Stafford, Federal Nursing, private, college/university short-term loans ($1500 average), college/university long-term loans ($1500 average).

Non-Need Awards In 1996, a total of 450 non-need awards were made. *Academic Interests/Achievement Awards:* 240 ($322,333 total): general academic. *Creative Arts/Performance Awards:* 20 ($16,050 total): debating, music. *Special Achievements/Activities Awards:* 75 ($76,084 total): leadership. *Special Characteristics Awards:* 25 ($127,425 total): general special characteristics, children of faculty/staff, religious affiliation, ROTC participants, veterans. *Athletic:* Total: 90 ($176,728); Men: 42 ($118,378); Women: 48 ($58,350).

Other Money-Saving Options Accelerated degree, cooperative Army ROTC, cooperative Air Force ROTC. *Payment Plan:* installment. *Waivers:* full or partial for employees or children of employees and senior citizens.

Contact Office of Financial Aid, Cedarville College, Box 601, Cedarville, OH 45314-0601, 937-766-2211.

CENTENARY COLLEGE
Hackettstown, New Jersey

About the Institution Independent/religious, coed. Degrees awarded: A, B, M. Offers 25 undergraduate majors. Total enrollment: 968. Undergraduates: 931 (85% state residents). Freshmen: 88.

Undergraduate Expenses (1997–98) Comprehensive fee of $19,060 includes tuition ($12,900), mandatory fees ($220), and college room and board ($5940).

Applications 77% of all full-time undergraduates enrolled in fall 1996 applied for aid; of these, 91% were judged to have need according to Federal Methodology, of whom 100% were aided. *Financial aid deadline (priority):* 5/1. *Financial aid forms:* FAFSA, institutional form required. Nontaxable income verification required for some. *Admission application deadline:* rolling.

Summary of Aid to Needy Students *From gift & self-help combined:* Average need met: 87%. Average amount awarded: $11,413 (65% gift aid, 35% self-help). *Gift aid:* Total: $2,554,141 (44% from college's own funds, 9% from other college-administered sources, 47% from external sources). 65 Federal Work-Study jobs (averaging $1000); 85 part-time jobs.

Need-Based Scholarships & Grants Pell, FSEOG, state, college/university.

Loans Perkins, PLUS, Stafford, Unsubsidized Stafford, state.

Non-Need Awards In 1996, a total of 205 non-need awards were made. *Academic Interests/Achievement Awards:* 181 ($745,670 total): general academic. *Special Achievements/Activities Awards:* 22 ($105,000 total): leadership. *Special Characteristics Awards:* 2 ($25,000 total): religious affiliation.

Other Money-Saving Options *Payment Plan:* installment. *Waivers:* full or partial for employees or children of employees and senior citizens.

Contact Mrs. Carol Strauss, Associate Director of Financial Aid, Centenary College, 400 Jefferson Street, Hackettstown, NJ 07840-2100, 908-852-1400 Ext. 2350, fax: 908-813-1984.

CENTENARY COLLEGE OF LOUISIANA
Shreveport, Louisiana

About the Institution Independent/religious, coed. Degrees awarded: B, M. Offers 66 undergraduate majors. Total enrollment: 971. Undergraduates: 744 (57% state residents). Freshmen: 181.

Undergraduate Expenses (1997–98) Comprehensive fee of $15,300 includes tuition ($11,050), mandatory fees ($350), and college room and board ($3900). College room only: $1650.

Applications 90% of all full-time undergraduates enrolled in fall 1996 applied for aid; of these, 63% were judged to have need according to Federal Methodology, of whom 99% were aided. *Financial aid deadline:* 3/1. *Financial aid forms:* FAFSA required; CSS Financial Aid PROFILE acceptable. State form, institutional form required for some. *Admission application deadline:* 3/1.

Summary of Aid to Needy Students *From gift & self-help combined:* Average need met: 85%. Average amount awarded: $9922 (71% gift aid, 29% self-help). *Gift aid:* Total: $2,894,121 (64% from college's own funds, 23% from other college-administered sources, 13% from external sources). 162 Federal Work-Study jobs (averaging $1350); 32 part-time jobs.

Need-Based Scholarships & Grants Pell, FSEOG, state, private, college/university.

Loans Perkins, PLUS, Stafford, Unsubsidized Stafford.

Non-Need Awards In 1996, a total of 1,340 non-need awards were made. *Academic Interests/Achievement Awards:* 546 ($1,748,995 total): general academic, biological sciences, business, education, engineering/technologies, English, foreign languages, humanities, mathematics, physical sciences, premedicine, religion/biblical studies, social sciences. *Creative Arts/Performance Awards:* 178 ($341,098 total): art/fine arts, dance, music, theater/drama. *Special Achievements/Activities Awards:* 96 ($101,285 total): leadership, religious involvement. *Special Characteristics Awards:* 380 ($512,580 total): general special characteristics, children of educators, children of faculty/staff, international students, local/state students, members of minorities, relatives of clergy, religious affiliation. *Athletic:* Total: 140 ($885,688); Men: 80 ($497,634); Women: 60 ($388,054).

Other Money-Saving Options Accelerated degree, cooperative Army ROTC. *Payment Plans:* tuition prepayment, installment, deferred payment. *Waivers:* full or partial for employees or children of employees.

Contact Ms. Mary Sue Rix, Director of Financial Aid, Centenary College of Louisiana, PO Box 41188, Shreveport, LA 71134-1188, 318-869-5137, fax: 318-869-5026.

CENTER FOR CREATIVE STUDIES—COLLEGE OF ART AND DESIGN
Detroit, Michigan

About the Institution Independent, coed. Degrees awarded: B. Offers 15 undergraduate majors. Total enrollment: 921 (83% state residents). Freshmen: 141.

Undergraduate Expenses (1996–97) Tuition: $13,110. Mandatory fees: $166. College room only: $2600 (minimum).

Applications Of all full-time undergraduates enrolled in fall 1996, 100% of those judged to have need according to Federal Methodology were aided. *Financial aid deadline (priority):* 2/15. *Financial aid forms:* FAFSA, institutional form required; CSS Financial Aid PROFILE acceptable. *Admission application deadline:* rolling.

Summary of Aid to Needy Students *From gift & self-help combined:* Average need met: 55%. Average amount awarded: $8803 (64% gift aid, 36% self-help). *Gift aid:* Total: $2,835,519 (48% from college's own funds, 10% from other college-administered sources, 42% from external sources). 96 Federal Work-Study jobs (averaging $1000); 84 part-time jobs.

Need-Based Scholarships & Grants Pell, FSEOG, state, private, college/university.

Loans PLUS, Stafford, Unsubsidized Stafford, college/university short-term loans ($200 average), alternative loans.

Non-Need Awards In 1996, a total of 385 non-need awards were made. *Creative Arts/Performance Awards:* 385 ($823,170 total): applied art and design, art/fine arts.

Other Money-Saving Options Off-campus living. *Payment Plans:* installment, deferred payment. *Waivers:* full or partial for employees or children of employees.

Contact Financial Aid Office, Center for Creative Studies—College of Art and Design, 201 East Kirby, Detroit, MI 48202-4034, 313-872-3118 Ext. 442, fax: 313-872-1521.

CENTRAL BAPTIST COLLEGE
Conway, Arkansas

About the Institution Independent/religious, coed. Degrees awarded: A, B. Offers 9 undergraduate majors. Total enrollment: 283 (73% state residents). Freshmen: 94.

Undergraduate Expenses (1996–97) Comprehensive fee of $7232 includes tuition ($4176), mandatory fees ($200), and college room and board ($2856). College room only: $976.

Applications *Financial aid deadline (priority):* 7/1. *Financial aid forms:* FAFSA required; state form acceptable. Institutional form required for some. *Admission application deadline:* 8/15.

Summary of Aid to Needy Students *From gift & self-help combined:* Average need met: 82%. Average amount awarded: $7850. Federal Work-Study jobs; part-time jobs.

Need-Based Scholarships & Grants Pell, FSEOG, state, college/university.

Loans PLUS, Stafford, Unsubsidized Stafford, private, college/university long-term loans ($1500 average).

Non-Need Awards *Academic Interests/Achievement Awards:* general academic. *Creative Arts/Performance Awards:* journalism/publications, music. *Special Achievements/Activities Awards:* religious involvement. *Special Characteristics Awards:* general special characteristics, adult students, relatives of clergy.

Other Money-Saving Options Cooperative Army ROTC. *Payment Plans:* installment, deferred payment. *Waivers:* full or partial for employees or children of employees.

Contact Ms. Christi Bell, Financial Aid Director, Central Baptist College, 1501 College Avenue, Conway, AR 72032-6470, 800-205-6872 Ext. 108, fax: 501-329-2941.

CENTRAL BIBLE COLLEGE
Springfield, Missouri

About the Institution Independent/religious, coed. Degrees awarded: A, B. Offers 7 undergraduate majors. Total enrollment: 976 (20% state residents). Freshmen: 241.

Undergraduate Expenses (1997–98) Comprehensive fee of $7950 includes tuition ($4440), mandatory fees ($310), and college room and board ($3200).

Applications 78% of all full-time undergraduates enrolled in fall 1996 applied for aid; of these, 92% were judged to have need according to Federal Methodology, of whom 96% were aided. *Financial aid deadline (priority):* 5/1. *Financial aid forms:* FAFSA required. *Admission application deadline:* rolling.

Summary of Aid to Needy Students *From gift & self-help combined:* Average need met: 55%. Average amount awarded: $5650 (32% gift aid, 68% self-help). *Gift aid:* Total: $1,133,081 (34% from college's own funds, 9% from other college-administered sources, 57% from external sources). 100 Federal Work-Study jobs (averaging $1300); 130 part-time jobs.

Need-Based Scholarships & Grants Pell, FSEOG.

Loans Perkins, PLUS, Stafford, Unsubsidized Stafford, private, college/university short-term loans ($250 average), college/university long-term loans ($1000 average).

Non-Need Awards In 1996, a total of 384 non-need awards were made. *Academic Interests/Achievement Awards:* 142 ($87,984 total): general academic. *Creative Arts/Performance Awards:* 54 ($54,804 total): art/fine arts, music, theater/drama. *Special Achievements/Activities Awards:* 36 ($28,988 total): community service, religious involvement. *Special Characteristics Awards:* 152 ($161,868 total): children of faculty/staff, ethnic background, relatives of clergy, religious affiliation, siblings of current students.

Other Money-Saving Options *Payment Plan:* installment. *Waivers:* full or partial for employees or children of employees and senior citizens.

Contact Mrs. Donna Shelton, Director of Financial Aid, Central Bible College, 3000 North Grant, Springfield, MO 65803-1096, 417-833-2551.

CENTRAL CHRISTIAN COLLEGE OF THE BIBLE
Moberly, Missouri

About the Institution Independent/religious, coed. Degrees awarded: A, B. Offers 8 undergraduate majors. Total enrollment: 135 (74% state residents). Freshmen: 55.

Undergraduate Expenses (1996–97) Comprehensive fee of $6546 includes tuition ($3450), mandatory fees ($626), and college room and board ($2470).

Applications *Financial aid deadline (priority):* 3/15. *Financial aid forms:* FAFSA, institutional form required; CSS Financial Aid PROFILE acceptable. *Admission application deadline:* rolling.

Summary of Aid to Needy Students *From gift & self-help combined:* Average need met: 75%. Average amount awarded: $3063 (76% gift aid, 24% self-help). *Gift aid:* Total: $277,536 (37% from college's own funds, 41% from other college-administered sources, 22% from external sources). 7 Federal Work-Study jobs (averaging $737); 30 part-time jobs.

Need-Based Scholarships & Grants Pell, state, college/university, vocational rehabilitation awards.

Loans PLUS, Stafford, Unsubsidized Stafford.

Non-Need Awards *Academic Interests/Achievement Awards:* general academic, communication, religion/biblical studies. *Creative Arts/*

Performance Awards: music, theater/drama. *Special Achievements/Activities Awards:* leadership, religious involvement. *Special Characteristics Awards:* adult students, children and siblings of alumni, children of faculty/staff, married students, relatives of clergy, spouses of current students.

Other Money-Saving Options *Payment Plan:* deferred payment. *Waivers:* full or partial for children of alumni and employees or children of employees.

Contact Mr. Russell E. Cobb, Director of Financial Aid, Central Christian College of the Bible, 911 Urbandale Drive East, Moberly, MO 65270-1997, 816-263-3900, fax: 816-263-3936.

CENTRAL COLLEGE
Pella, Iowa

About the Institution Independent/religious, coed. Degrees awarded: B. Offers 36 undergraduate majors. Total enrollment: 1,299 (75% state residents). Freshmen: 305.

Undergraduate Expenses (1996–97) Comprehensive fee of $16,112 includes tuition ($12,152), mandatory fees ($152), and college room and board ($3808). College room only: $1704.

Applications 89% of all full-time undergraduates enrolled in fall 1996 applied for aid; of these, 93% were judged to have need according to Federal Methodology, of whom 99% were aided. *Financial aid deadline (priority):* 4/1. *Financial aid forms:* institutional form required. FAFSA required for some. *Admission application deadline:* rolling.

Summary of Aid to Needy Students *From gift & self-help combined:* Average need met: 96%. Average amount awarded: $12,715 (66% gift aid, 34% self-help). *Gift aid:* Total: $8,069,354 (61% from college's own funds, 3% from other college-administered sources, 36% from external sources). 631 Federal Work-Study jobs (averaging $932); 463 part-time jobs.

Need-Based Scholarships & Grants Pell, FSEOG, state, private, college/university.

Loans Perkins, PLUS, Stafford, Unsubsidized Stafford, private, college/university short-term loans ($50 average), college/university long-term loans ($1700 average).

Non-Need Awards In 1996, a total of 1,537 non-need awards were made. *Academic Interests/Achievement Awards:* 1,117 ($3,548,246 total): general academic, biological sciences, business, communication, education, foreign languages, humanities, international studies, mathematics, physical sciences, religion/biblical studies. *Creative Arts/Performance Awards:* 109 ($187,850 total): art/fine arts, music, theater/drama. *Special Achievements/Activities Awards:* 16 ($50,300 total): religious involvement. *Special Characteristics Awards:* 295 ($925,045 total): children and siblings of alumni, children of faculty/staff, international students, local/state students, members of minorities, out-of-state students, relatives of clergy, religious affiliation, siblings of current students.

Other Money-Saving Options *Payment Plan:* installment. *Waivers:* full or partial for employees or children of employees.

Contact Ms. Jean Vander Wert, Director of Student Financial Planning, Central College, 812 University Street, Pella, IA 50219-1999, 515-628-5268, fax: 515-628-5316.

CENTRAL CONNECTICUT STATE UNIVERSITY
New Britain, Connecticut

About the Institution State-supported, coed. Degrees awarded: B, M. Offers 50 undergraduate majors. Total enrollment: 9,520. Undergraduates: 7,798 (95% state residents). Freshmen: 1,093.

Undergraduate Expenses (1997–98) State resident tuition: $2062. Nonresident tuition: $6674. Mandatory fees: $1552 (minimum). College room and board: $4850 (minimum). College room only: $2800 (minimum).

Applications Of all full-time undergraduates enrolled in fall 1996, 74% of those who applied for aid were judged to have need according to Federal Methodology, of whom 100% were aided. *Financial aid deadline (priority):* 4/22. *Financial aid forms:* FAFSA required. *Admission application deadline:* 5/1.

Summary of Aid to Needy Students *From gift & self-help combined:* Average need met: 80%. *Gift aid:* Total: $4,339,906 (40% from college's own funds, 18% from other college-administered sources, 42% from external sources). 400 Federal Work-Study jobs (averaging $800); 500 part-time jobs.

Need-Based Scholarships & Grants Pell, FSEOG, state, private, college/university.

Loans Perkins, PLUS, Stafford, Unsubsidized Stafford, private, college/university short-term loans ($500 average).

Non-Need Awards *Academic Interests/Achievement Awards:* general academic. *Special Characteristics Awards:* 84 ($67,350 total): members of minorities. *Athletic:* Total: 155 ($770,780); Men: 86 ($419,430); Women: 69 ($351,350).

Other Money-Saving Options Co-op program, cooperative Army ROTC, cooperative Air Force ROTC, off-campus living. *Payment Plans:* installment, deferred payment. *Waivers:* full or partial for employees or children of employees and senior citizens.

Contact Mrs. Jean Main, Counselor, Central Connecticut State University, 1615 Stanley Street, New Britain, CT 06050-4010, 860-832-2200, fax: 860-832-1105.

CENTRAL METHODIST COLLEGE
Fayette, Missouri

About the Institution Independent/religious, coed. Degrees awarded: A, B, M. Offers 43 undergraduate majors. Total enrollment: 1,152 (89% state residents). Freshmen: 212.

Undergraduate Expenses (1996–97) Comprehensive fee of $14,180 includes tuition ($9950), mandatory fees ($270), and college room and board ($3960). College room only: $1840.

Applications Of all full-time undergraduates enrolled in fall 1996, 68% of those who applied for aid were judged to have need according to Federal Methodology, of whom 98% were aided. *Financial aid deadline (priority):* 4/1. *Financial aid forms:* FAFSA required; CSS Financial Aid PROFILE acceptable. *Admission application deadline:* rolling.

Summary of Aid to Needy Students *From gift & self-help combined:* Average need met: 80%. Average amount awarded: $9000 (40% gift aid, 60% self-help). *Gift aid:* Total: $2,347,381 (38% from college's own funds, 6% from other college-administered sources, 56% from external sources). 125 Federal Work-Study jobs (averaging $800); 180 part-time jobs.

Need-Based Scholarships & Grants Pell, FSEOG, state, private, college/university.

Loans Perkins, PLUS, Stafford, Unsubsidized Stafford.

Non-Need Awards In 1996, a total of 1,893 non-need awards were made. *Academic Interests/Achievement Awards:* 521 ($966,262 total). *Creative Arts/Performance Awards:* 201 ($133,314 total): music, theater/drama. *Special Achievements/Activities Awards:* 282 ($250,226 total): cheerleading/drum major, leadership, religious involvement. *Special Characteristics Awards:* 342 ($471,268 total): general special characteristics, children of faculty/staff, international students, relatives of clergy, religious affiliation, siblings of current students, spouses of current students. *Athletic:* Total: 547 ($820,698); Men: 397 ($570,385); Women: 150 ($250,313).

Other Money-Saving Options Accelerated degree, cooperative Army ROTC. *Payment Plan:* installment. *Waivers:* full or partial for employees or children of employees and senior citizens.

Contact Mrs. Roberta Knipp, Director of Financial Aid, Central Methodist College, 411 Central Methodist Square, Fayette, MO 65248-1198, 816-248-3391.

CENTRAL MICHIGAN UNIVERSITY
Mount Pleasant, Michigan

About the Institution State-supported, coed. Degrees awarded: B, M, D. Offers 107 undergraduate majors. Total enrollment: 16,597. Undergraduates: 14,640 (97% state residents). Freshmen: 2,826.

Undergraduate Expenses (1996–97) State resident tuition: $2973. Nonresident tuition: $7721. Mandatory fees: $470. College room and board: $4176. College room only: $2004.

Applications 66% of all full-time undergraduates enrolled in fall 1996 applied for aid; of these, 78% were judged to have need according to Federal Methodology, of whom 97% were aided. *Financial aid deadline (priority):* 2/21. *Financial aid forms:* FAFSA required. *Admission application deadline:* rolling.

Summary of Aid to Needy Students *From gift & self-help combined:* Average need met: 84%. Average amount awarded: $5646 (32% gift aid, 68% self-help). *Gift aid:* Total: $12,292,835 (28% from college's own funds, 28% from other college-administered sources, 44% from external sources). 878 Federal Work-Study jobs (averaging $1411); 3,797 part-time jobs.

Need-Based Scholarships & Grants Pell, FSEOG, state, college/university.

Loans Perkins, PLUS, Stafford, Unsubsidized Stafford, state, private.

Non-Need Awards In 1996, a total of 5,128 non-need awards were made. *Academic Interests/Achievement Awards:* 2,136 ($2,508,058 total): general academic. *Creative Arts/Performance Awards:* 114 ($117,659 total): music, theater/drama. *Special Characteristics Awards:* 2,596 ($3,858,522 total): adult students, children of faculty/staff, international students, local/state students, members of minorities, ROTC participants, veterans, veterans' children. *Athletic:* Total: 282 ($1,581,477); Men: 178 ($980,895); Women: 104 ($600,582).

Other Money-Saving Options Accelerated degree, Army ROTC, off-campus living (after sophomore year). *Waivers:* full or partial for employees or children of employees.

Contact Office of Financial Aid, Central Michigan University, WA 205, Mount Pleasant, MI 48859, 517-774-4000.

CENTRAL MISSOURI STATE UNIVERSITY
Warrensburg, Missouri

About the Institution State-supported, coed. Degrees awarded: A, B, M. Offers 104 undergraduate majors. Total enrollment: 10,770. Undergraduates: 8,934 (92% state residents). Freshmen: 1,351.

Undergraduate Expenses (1997–98) State resident tuition: $2728. Nonresident tuition: $5456. College room and board: $4022 (minimum). College room only: $2692 (minimum).

Applications 69% of all full-time undergraduates enrolled in fall 1996 applied for aid; of these, 70% were judged to have need according to Federal Methodology, of whom 91% were aided. *Financial aid deadline (priority):* 3/1. *Financial aid forms:* FAFSA required. *Admission application deadline:* rolling.

Summary of Aid to Needy Students *From gift & self-help combined:* Average need met: 90%. Average amount awarded: $6700 (21% gift aid, 79% self-help). *Gift aid:* Total: $4,400,000 (9% from college-administered sources, 91% from external sources). 425 Federal Work-Study jobs (averaging $1400); 1,700 part-time jobs.

Need-Based Scholarships & Grants Pell, FSEOG, state, private, college/university.

Loans Perkins, PLUS, Stafford, Unsubsidized Stafford, college/university short-term loans ($250 average).

Non-Need Awards In 1996, a total of 1,923 non-need awards were made. *Academic Interests/Achievement Awards:* 930 ($185,901 total): general academic, agriculture, biological sciences, business, communication, computer science, education, English, foreign languages, health fields, home economics, humanities, library science, mathematics, military science, physical sciences, premedicine, social sciences. *Creative Arts/Performance Awards:* 460 ($92,675 total): art/fine arts, debating, music, theater/drama. *Special Achievements/Activities Awards:* 64 ($18,200 total): cheerleading/drum major, leadership. *Special Characteristics Awards:* 261 ($308,230 total): adult students, children and siblings of alumni, children of faculty/staff, out-of-state students. *Athletic:* Total: 208 ($669,560); Men: 134; Women: 74.

Other Money-Saving Options Accelerated degree, co-op program, Army ROTC, off-campus living (after freshman year). *Payment Plan:* installment. *Waivers:* full or partial for employees or children of employees.

Contact Mr. Phil Shreves, Director of Financial Aid, Central Missouri State University, Warrensburg, MO 64093, 816-543-4040, fax: 816-543-8080.

CENTRAL STATE UNIVERSITY
Wilberforce, Ohio

About the Institution State-supported, coed. Degrees awarded: B, M. Offers 72 undergraduate majors. Total enrollment: 1,976. Undergraduates: 1,954 (62% state residents). Freshmen: 357.

Undergraduate Expenses (1997–98) State resident tuition: $3318. Nonresident tuition: $7293. College room and board: $4695. College room only: $2415.

Applications Of all full-time undergraduates enrolled in fall 1996, 100% of those who applied for aid were judged to have need according to Federal Methodology, of whom 100% were aided. *Financial aid deadline (priority):* 3/31. *Financial aid forms:* FAFSA, CSS Financial Aid PROFILE, state form, institutional form required. *Admission application deadline:* 6/15.

Summary of Aid to Needy Students *From gift & self-help combined:* Average need met: 94%. Average amount awarded: $8244 (69% gift aid, 31% self-help). *Gift aid:* Total: $9,615,765 (18% from college's own funds, 58% from other college-administered sources, 24% from external sources). 543 Federal Work-Study jobs (averaging $1100); part-time jobs.

Need-Based Scholarships & Grants Pell, FSEOG, state, private, college/university.

Loans PLUS, Stafford, Unsubsidized Stafford, private.

Non-Need Awards In 1996, a total of 381 non-need awards were made. *Academic Interests/Achievement Awards:* 153 ($337,060 total): general academic, business, computer science, education, engineering/technologies, physical sciences. *Creative Arts/Performance Awards:* 92 ($143,834 total): music. *Special Achievements/Activities Awards:* 7 ($13,872 total): leadership. *Special Characteristics Awards:* 77 ($502,423 total): children of faculty/staff, international students, ROTC participants, veterans, veterans' children. *Athletic:* Total: 52 ($212,386); Men: 39 ($116,348); Women: 13 ($96,038).

Other Money-Saving Options Co-op program, Army ROTC, off-campus living (after freshman year).

Contact Ms. Edie Marshall, Financial Aid Counselor, Central State University, 21400 Brush Row Road, Wilberforce, OH 45384, 937-376-6574, fax: 937-376-6648.

CENTRAL WASHINGTON UNIVERSITY
Ellensburg, Washington

About the Institution State-supported, coed. Degrees awarded: B, M. Offers 102 undergraduate majors. Total enrollment: 8,569. Undergraduates: 7,772 (96% state residents). Freshmen: 1,115.

Undergraduate Expenses (1996–97) State resident tuition: $2430. Nonresident tuition: $8616. Mandatory fees: $75. College room and board: $4400.

Applications 58% of all full-time undergraduates enrolled in fall 1996 applied for aid; of these, 83% were judged to have need according to Federal Methodology, of whom 98% were aided. *Financial aid deadline (priority):* 3/1. *Financial aid forms:* FAFSA required. *Admission application deadline:* 3/1.

Summary of Aid to Needy Students *From gift & self-help combined:* Average need met: 82%. Average amount awarded: $6329 (36% gift aid, 64% self-help). *Gift aid:* Total: $7,355,204 (48% from college-administered sources, 52% from external sources). 298 Federal Work-Study jobs (averaging $2347); 2,000 part-time jobs.

Loans College/university short-term loans ($800 average), college/university long-term loans ($2000 average).

Non-Need Awards In 1996, a total of 82 non-need awards were made. *Academic Interests/Achievement Awards:* 29 ($71,220 total): general academic. *Creative Arts/Performance Awards:* 32 ($30,195 total): music. *Special Achievements/Activities Awards:* 2 ($5760 total): hobbies/interest, memberships. *Special Characteristics Awards:* 19 ($11,394 total): adult students.

Other Money-Saving Options Accelerated degree, co-op program, Army ROTC, Air Force ROTC, off-campus living (after freshman year). *Waivers:* full or partial for employees or children of employees and senior citizens.

Contact Office of Financial Aid, Central Washington University, 400 East 8th Avenue, Ellensburg, WA 98926-7495, 509-963-1111.

CENTRAL YESHIVA TOMCHEI TMIMIM-LUBAVITCH
Brooklyn, New York

About the Institution Independent/religious, men. Offers 1 undergraduate major. Total enrollment: 376.

Undergraduate Expenses (1996–97) Comprehensive fee of $7100 includes tuition ($4800) and college room and board ($2300).

Applications *Financial aid deadline:* continuous. *Financial aid forms:* FAFSA required.

Summary of Aid to Needy Students Federal Work-Study jobs.

Need-Based Scholarships & Grants Pell, FSEOG, private.

Loans Stafford, Unsubsidized Stafford.

Non-Need Awards Not offered.

Contact Rabbi Moshe M. Gluckowsky, Director of Financial Aid, Central Yeshiva Tomchei Tmimim-Lubavitch, 841-853 Ocean Parkway, Brooklyn, NY 11230, 718-859-2277.

CENTRE COLLEGE
Danville, Kentucky

About the Institution Independent, coed. Degrees awarded: B. Offers 31 undergraduate majors. Total enrollment: 968 (65% state residents). Freshmen: 285.

Undergraduate Expenses (1996–97) Comprehensive fee of $18,600 includes tuition ($13,000), mandatory fees ($1000), and college room and board ($4600). College room only: $2300.

Applications 68% of all full-time undergraduates enrolled in fall 1996 applied for aid; of these, 80% were judged to have need according to Federal Methodology, of whom 99% were aided. *Financial aid deadline:* Applications processed continuously. *Financial aid forms:* FAFSA, institutional form required. *Regular admission application deadline:* 3/1. Early decision deadline: 11/15. Early action deadline: 11/15.

Summary of Aid to Needy Students *From gift & self-help combined:* Average need met: 90%. Average amount awarded: $13,180 (72% gift aid, 28% self-help). *Gift aid:* Total: $4,950,999 (78% from college's own funds, 2% from other college-administered sources, 20% from external sources). 381 Federal Work-Study jobs (averaging $1200); 31 part-time jobs.

Need-Based Scholarships & Grants Pell, FSEOG, state, private, college/university.

Loans Perkins, PLUS, Stafford, Unsubsidized Stafford, college/university long-term loans ($2700 average).

Non-Need Awards In 1996, a total of 794 non-need awards were made. *Academic Interests/Achievement Awards:* 627 ($2,120,337 total): general academic. *Special Characteristics Awards:* 167 ($494,200 total): children and siblings of alumni, children of faculty/staff, local/state students, members of minorities, ROTC participants.

Other Money-Saving Options Cooperative Army ROTC, cooperative Air Force ROTC, off-campus living (after sophomore year). *Payment Plan:* installment. *Waivers:* full or partial for employees or children of employees.

Contact Ms. Elaine Larson, Director of Student Financial Planning, Centre College, 600 West Walnut Street, Danville, KY 40422-1394, 606-238-5365, fax: 606-238-5373.

CHADRON STATE COLLEGE
Chadron, Nebraska

About the Institution State-supported, coed. Degrees awarded: B, M. Offers 31 undergraduate majors. Total enrollment: 2,983. Undergraduates: 2,569 (78% state residents). Freshmen: 476.

Undergraduate Expenses (1996–97) State resident tuition: $1650. Nonresident tuition: $3300. Mandatory fees: $288. College room and board: $2926 (minimum). College room only: $1424 (minimum).

Applications 72% of all full-time undergraduates enrolled in fall 1996 applied for aid; of these, 90% were judged to have need according to Federal Methodology, of whom 100% were aided. *Financial aid deadline (priority):* 6/1. *Financial aid forms:* FAFSA, institutional form required; CSS Financial Aid PROFILE acceptable. *Admission application deadline:* rolling.

Summary of Aid to Needy Students *From gift & self-help combined:* Average need met: 90%. Average amount awarded: $3600 (46% gift aid, 54% self-help). *Gift aid:* Total: $856,971 (11% from college-administered sources, 89% from external sources). 330 Federal Work-Study jobs (averaging $500); part-time jobs.

Need-Based Scholarships & Grants Pell, FSEOG, state.

Loans Perkins, PLUS, Stafford, Unsubsidized Stafford.

Non-Need Awards In 1996, a total of 823 non-need awards were made. *Academic Interests/Achievement Awards:* 184 ($138,926 total): general academic, health fields. *Creative Arts/Performance Awards:* 34 ($19,044 total): art/fine arts. *Special Achievements/Activities Awards:* 19 ($5198 total): general special achievements/activities, rodeo. *Special Characteristics Awards:* 415 ($304,412 total): general special characteristics, children of faculty/staff, international students, local/state students, members of minorities, out-of-state students, veterans, veterans' children. *Athletic:* Total: 171 ($110,727); Men: 129 ($87,221); Women: 42 ($23,506).

Other Money-Saving Options Co-op program, off-campus living (after freshman year). *Payment Plan:* installment. *Waivers:* full or partial for employees or children of employees and senior citizens.

Contact Ms. Sherry Douglas, Director of Financial Aid, Chadron State College, 1000 Main Street, Chadron, NE 69337, 308-432-6230, fax: 308-432-6229.

CHAMINADE UNIVERSITY OF HONOLULU
Honolulu, Hawaii

About the Institution Independent/religious, coed. Degrees awarded: A, B, M. Offers 25 undergraduate majors. Total enrollment: 2,674. Undergraduates: 2,098 (55% state residents). Freshmen: 180.

Undergraduate Expenses (1997–98) Comprehensive fee of $16,050 includes tuition ($10,800), mandatory fees ($50), and college room and board ($5200 minimum). College room only: $1425.

Applications 73% of all full-time undergraduates enrolled in fall 1996 applied for aid; of these, 59% were judged to have need according to Federal Methodology, of whom 100% were aided. *Financial aid deadline (priority):* 3/29. *Financial aid forms:* FAFSA, institutional form, financial aid transcript (for transfers) required; CSS Financial Aid PROFILE acceptable. State form required for some. *Admission application deadline:* rolling.

Summary of Aid to Needy Students *From gift & self-help combined:* Average need met: 83%. Average amount awarded: $11,464 (72% gift aid, 28% self-help). *Gift aid:* Total: $2,810,927 (64% from college's own funds, 8% from other college-administered sources, 28% from external sources). 146 Federal Work-Study jobs (averaging $1793); part-time jobs.

Need-Based Scholarships & Grants Pell, FSEOG, state, private, college/university.

Loans Perkins, PLUS, Stafford, Unsubsidized Stafford, private, college/university long-term loans ($1757 average).

Non-Need Awards *Academic Interests/Achievement Awards:* 87 ($323,150 total): general academic. *Special Characteristics Awards:* children and siblings of alumni, children of faculty/staff, international students, local/state students, out-of-state students, religious affiliation, ROTC participants, siblings of current students, spouses of current students, veterans. *Athletic:* Total: 81 ($548,290); Men: 49 ($402,690); Women: 32 ($145,600).

Other Money-Saving Options Cooperative Army ROTC, cooperative Air Force ROTC, off-campus living. *Payment Plan:* deferred payment. *Waivers:* full or partial for employees or children of employees.

Contact Ms. Reyna Sugimoto, Assistant Director of Financial Aid, Chaminade University of Honolulu, Honolulu, HI 96816-1578, 808-735-4780.

CHAPMAN UNIVERSITY
Orange, California

About the Institution Independent/religious, coed. Degrees awarded: B, M, P. Offers 66 undergraduate majors. Total enrollment: 3,673. Undergraduates: 2,299 (90% state residents). Freshmen: 392.

Undergraduate Expenses (1997–98) Comprehensive fee of $25,556 includes tuition ($18,510), mandatory fees ($240), and college room and board ($6806 minimum).

Applications 92% of all full-time undergraduates enrolled in fall 1996 applied for aid; of these, 89% were. judged to have need according to Federal Methodology, of whom 95% were aided. *Financial aid deadline (priority):* 3/1. *Financial aid forms:* FAFSA required. State form required for some. *Regular admission application deadline:* 3/1. Early action deadline: 11/15.

Summary of Aid to Needy Students *From gift & self-help combined:* Average need met: 96%. Average amount awarded: $15,642 (72% gift aid, 28% self-help). *Gift aid:* Total: $19,752,636 (81% from college's

own funds, 11% from other college-administered sources, 8% from external sources). 559 Federal Work-Study jobs (averaging $2000); 636 part-time jobs.

Need-Based Scholarships & Grants Pell, FSEOG, state, college/university.

Loans Perkins, PLUS, Stafford, Unsubsidized Stafford, private, college/university short-term loans ($300 average), college/university long-term loans ($3200 average).

Non-Need Awards *Academic Interests/Achievement Awards:* 203 ($1,440,296 total): general academic, business, social sciences. *Creative Arts/Performance Awards:* 129 ($1,117,724 total): art/fine arts, cinema/film/broadcasting, creative writing, dance, journalism/publications, music, theater/drama. *Special Achievements/Activities Awards:* leadership, religious involvement. *Special Characteristics Awards:* children and siblings of alumni, children of faculty/staff, relatives of clergy, religious affiliation.

Other Money-Saving Options Accelerated degree, co-op program, cooperative Army ROTC, cooperative Air Force ROTC. *Payment Plans:* installment, deferred payment. *Waivers:* full or partial for children of alumni and employees or children of employees.

Contact Ms. Phyllis Coldiron, Director of Financial Aid, Chapman University, 333 North Glassell, Orange, CA 92866, 714-997-6741, fax: 714-997-6743.

CHARLES R. DREW UNIVERSITY OF MEDICINE AND SCIENCE
Los Angeles, California

About the Institution Independent, coed. Degrees awarded: A, B, D. Offers 6 undergraduate majors. Total enrollment: 320. Undergraduates: 218. Freshmen: 135.

Undergraduate Expenses (1997–98) Tuition: $6750. Mandatory fees: $100.

Applications 93% of all full-time undergraduates enrolled in fall 1996 applied for aid; of these,100% were judged to have need according to Federal Methodology, of whom 100% were aided. *Financial aid deadline (priority):* 5/30. *Financial aid forms:* FAFSA, institutional form required; state form acceptable. *Admission application deadline:* 2/28.

Summary of Aid to Needy Students *From gift & self-help combined:* Average need met: 63%. *Gift aid:* Total: $292,295 (19% from college's own funds, 18% from other college-administered sources, 63% from external sources). Federal Work-Study jobs (averaging $3000).

Need-Based Scholarships & Grants Pell, FSEOG, state, college/university.

Loans Perkins, PLUS, Stafford, Unsubsidized Stafford, private.

Non-Need Awards Not offered.

Contact Ms. Lida Castillo, Financial Aid Administrator, Charles R. Drew University of Medicine and Science, 1621 East 120th Street MP 21A, Los Angeles, CA 90059, 213-563-4824, fax: 213-569-0597.

CHARLESTON SOUTHERN UNIVERSITY
Charleston, South Carolina

About the Institution Independent/religious, coed. Degrees awarded: A, B, M. Offers 43 undergraduate majors. Total enrollment: 2,329. Undergraduates: 2,060 (85% state residents). Freshmen: 334.

Undergraduate Expenses (1997–98) Comprehensive fee of $12,810 includes tuition ($9248) and college room and board ($3562).

Applications *Financial aid deadline (priority):* 4/15. *Financial aid forms:* FAFSA, institutional form required. *Admission application deadline:* rolling.

Summary of Aid to Needy Students *From gift & self-help combined:* Average need met: 94%. Average amount awarded: $9378 (47% gift

aid, 53% self-help). *Gift aid:* Total: $7,070,505 (44% from college's own funds, 38% from other college-administered sources, 18% from external sources). 454 Federal Work-Study jobs (averaging $800); 110 part-time jobs.

Need-Based Scholarships & Grants Pell, FSEOG, state, private, college/university.

Loans Perkins, PLUS, Stafford, Unsubsidized Stafford, state, college/university short-term loans ($800 average).

Non-Need Awards In 1996, a total of 1,037 non-need awards were made. *Academic Interests/Achievement Awards:* 190 ($979,041 total): general academic. *Creative Arts/Performance Awards:* 67 ($160,126 total): art/fine arts, music, performing arts. *Special Achievements/Activities Awards:* 251 ($240,958 total): cheerleading/drum major, community service, Junior Miss, leadership, memberships, religious involvement. *Special Characteristics Awards:* 270 ($566,730 total): adult students, children of faculty/staff, out-of-state students, relatives of clergy, ROTC participants. *Athletic:* Total: 259 ($1,102,628); Men: 164 ($718,292); Women: 95 ($384,336).

Other Money-Saving Options Accelerated degree, Air Force ROTC.

Contact Ms. Elizabeth O. Rudy, Assistant Director of Financial Aid, Charleston Southern University, PO Box 118087, Charleston, SC 29423-8087, 803-863-7050, fax: 803-863-7070.

CHARTER OAK STATE COLLEGE
Newington, Connecticut

About the Institution State-supported, coed. Degrees awarded: A, B. Offers 4 undergraduate majors. Total enrollment: 1,252 (79% state residents).

Undergraduate Expenses (1997–98 estimated) Mandatory fees: $265 (minimum).

Applications *Financial aid deadline (priority):* 8/10. *Financial aid forms:* institutional form required.

Summary of Aid to Needy Students *Gift aid:* Total: $14,242 (100% from college's own funds).

Loans Private.

Non-Need Awards In 1996, a total of 19 non-need awards were made. *Academic Interests/Achievement Awards:* 19 ($4500 total): general academic.

Another Money-Saving Option Accelerated degree.

Contact Mr. Paul Morganti, Convener, Financial Aid Committee, Charter Oak State College, 66 Cedar Street, Newington, CT 06111-2646, 860-666-4595 Ext. 25, fax: 860-666-4852.

CHATHAM COLLEGE
Pittsburgh, Pennsylvania

About the Institution Independent, primarily women. Degrees awarded: B, M. Offers 33 undergraduate majors. Total enrollment: 801. Undergraduates: 483 (89% state residents). Freshmen: 103.

Undergraduate Expenses (1997–98) Comprehensive fee of $21,056 includes tuition ($15,184), mandatory fees ($156), and college room and board ($5716 minimum). College room only: $2858.

Applications 95% of all full-time undergraduates enrolled in fall 1996 applied for aid; of these, 87% were judged to have need according to Federal Methodology, of whom 100% were aided. *Financial aid deadline (priority):* 3/15. *Financial aid forms:* FAFSA, institutional form required. State form required for some. *Regular admission application deadline:* rolling. Early decision deadline: 11/30.

Summary of Aid to Needy Students *From gift & self-help combined:* Average need met: 92%. Average amount awarded: $13,654 (65% gift aid, 35% self-help). *Gift aid:* Total: $2,517,136 (70% from college's

own funds, 3% from other college-administered sources, 27% from external sources). 228 Federal Work-Study jobs (averaging $1725); 56 part-time jobs.

Need-Based Scholarships & Grants Pell, FSEOG, state, private, college/university.

Loans Perkins, PLUS, Stafford, Unsubsidized Stafford, private, college/university short-term loans.

Non-Need Awards In 1996, a total of 158 non-need awards were made. *Academic Interests/Achievement Awards:* 80 ($442,207 total): general academic, biological sciences, humanities, physical sciences, social sciences. *Creative Arts/Performance Awards:* 7 ($25,192 total): music, theater/drama. *Special Achievements/Activities Awards:* 30 ($75,000 total): community service, leadership. *Special Characteristics Awards:* 41 ($128,545 total): adult students, children and siblings of alumni, children of faculty/staff, international students.

Other Money-Saving Options Accelerated degree, cooperative Army ROTC, cooperative Naval ROTC, cooperative Air Force ROTC, off-campus living. *Payment Plan:* installment. *Waivers:* full or partial for employees or children of employees.

Contact Office of Admissions and Financial Aid, Chatham College, Woodland Road, Pittsburgh, PA 15232-2826, 800-837-1240, fax: 412-365-1609.

CHESTNUT HILL COLLEGE
Philadelphia, Pennsylvania

About the Institution Independent/religious, women. Degrees awarded: A, B, M. Offers 30 undergraduate majors. Total enrollment: 1,340. Undergraduates: 754 (73% state residents). Freshmen: 81.

Undergraduate Expenses (1996–97) Comprehensive fee of $18,920 includes tuition ($12,748), mandatory fees ($400), and college room and board ($5772).

Applications 86% of all full-time undergraduates enrolled in fall 1996 applied for aid; of these, 78% were judged to have need according to Federal Methodology, of whom 100% were aided. *Financial aid deadline (priority):* 3/15. *Financial aid forms:* state form, institutional form required; CSS Financial Aid PROFILE acceptable. FAFSA required for some. *Admission application deadline:* rolling.

Summary of Aid to Needy Students *From gift & self-help combined:* Average need met: 83%. Average amount awarded: $10,081 (99% gift aid, 1% self-help). *Gift aid:* Total: $2,741,864 (84% from college's own funds, 4% from other college-administered sources, 12% from external sources). Federal Work-Study jobs; 205 part-time jobs.

Need-Based Scholarships & Grants College/university.

Non-Need Awards *Academic Interests/Achievement Awards:* 0: general academic.

Other Money-Saving Options Accelerated degree, co-op program, cooperative Army ROTC, off-campus living. *Payment Plans:* installment, deferred payment. *Waivers:* full or partial for employees or children of employees and senior citizens.

Contact Mr. Michael Wisniewski, Director of Financial Aid, Chestnut Hill College, 9601 Germantown Avenue, Philadelphia, PA 19118-2695, 215-248-7101.

CHEYNEY UNIVERSITY OF PENNSYLVANIA
Cheyney, Pennsylvania

About the Institution State-supported, coed. Degrees awarded: B, M. Offers 32 undergraduate majors. Total enrollment: 1,360. Undergraduates: 1,076 (86% state residents). Freshmen: 237.

Undergraduate Expenses (1996–97) State resident tuition: $3368. Nonresident tuition: $8566. Mandatory fees: $555. College room and board: $4351. College room only: $2050.

Applications *Financial aid deadline (priority):* 3/1. *Financial aid forms:* FAFSA, state form required. *Admission application deadline:* rolling.

Summary of Aid to Needy Students *From gift & self-help combined:* Average need met: 98%. Average amount awarded: $6942 (42% gift aid, 58% self-help). *Gift aid:* Total: $3,419,324 (4% from college's own funds, 49% from other college-administered sources, 47% from external sources). 304 Federal Work-Study jobs (averaging $1000).

Need-Based Scholarships & Grants Pell, FSEOG, state, private, college/university.

Loans Perkins, PLUS, Stafford, Unsubsidized Stafford.

Non-Need Awards In 1996, a total of 65 non-need awards were made. *Academic Interests/Achievement Awards:* 37 ($36,000 total): general academic, biological sciences, computer science, education, mathematics. *Special Characteristics Awards:* 21 ($50,330 total): children of faculty/staff, ethnic background. *Athletic:* Total: 7 ($10,900); Men: 4 ($7600); Women: 3 ($3300).

Other Money-Saving Options Co-op program, Army ROTC, cooperative Air Force ROTC, off-campus living. *Payment Plan:* deferred payment. *Waivers:* full or partial for employees or children of employees.

Contact Mr. James Brown, Diector of Financial Aid, Cheyney University of Pennsylvania, Cheyney, PA 19319, 610-399-2331, fax: 610-399-2411.

CHICAGO STATE UNIVERSITY
Chicago, Illinois

About the Institution State-supported, coed. Degrees awarded: B, M. Offers 64 undergraduate majors. Total enrollment: 9,412. Undergraduates: 8,471 (98% state residents).

Undergraduate Expenses (1996–97) State resident tuition: $2420. Nonresident tuition: $7077. Mandatory fees: $398. College room and board: $4990.

Applications *Financial aid deadline (priority):* 5/1. *Financial aid forms:* institutional form required; FAFSA, CSS Financial Aid PROFILE acceptable. *Admission application deadline:* rolling.

Summary of Aid to Needy Students Federal Work-Study jobs; part-time jobs.

Loans College/university short-term loans.

Non-Need Awards *Academic Interests/Achievement Awards:* general academic, physical sciences. *Creative Arts/Performance Awards:* art/fine arts, journalism/publications, music. *Special Achievements/Activities Awards:* leadership. *Athletic:* available.

Other Money-Saving Options Accelerated degree, co-op program, Army ROTC, cooperative Naval ROTC, cooperative Air Force ROTC, off-campus living. *Payment Plan:* deferred payment. *Waivers:* full or partial for employees or children of employees and senior citizens.

Contact Office of Financial Aid, Chicago State University, Chicago, IL 60628, 773-995-2000.

CHOWAN COLLEGE
Murfreesboro, North Carolina

About the Institution Independent/religious, coed. Degrees awarded: B. Offers 32 undergraduate majors. Total enrollment: 746 (35% state residents). Freshmen: 259.

Undergraduate Expenses (1997–98) Comprehensive fee of $14,930 includes tuition ($10,710), mandatory fees ($50), and college room and board ($4170). College room only: $1700.

Applications 67% of all full-time undergraduates enrolled in fall 1996 applied for aid; of these, 89% were judged to have need according to Federal Methodology, of whom 100% were aided. *Financial aid deadline (priority):* 4/1. *Financial aid forms:* FAFSA required. *Admission application deadline:* rolling.

Summary of Aid to Needy Students *From gift & self-help combined:* Average need met: 82%. Average amount awarded: $9019 (43% gift aid, 57% self-help). *Gift aid:* Total: $1,674,981 (61% from college's own funds, 22% from other college-administered sources, 17% from external sources). 308 Federal Work-Study jobs (averaging $1123); 100 part-time jobs.

Need-Based Scholarships & Grants Pell, FSEOG, state, private, college/university.

Loans Perkins, PLUS, Stafford, Unsubsidized Stafford, college/university short-term loans ($50 average).

Non-Need Awards In 1996, a total of 639 non-need awards were made. *Academic Interests/Achievement Awards:* 627 ($1,674,990 total): general academic. *Special Characteristics Awards:* 12 ($65,340 total): children of faculty/staff, children of union members/company employees, relatives of clergy.

Other Money-Saving Options *Payment Plan:* installment. *Waivers:* full or partial for employees or children of employees and senior citizens.

Contact Mr. Clifton S. Collins, Director of Financial Aid, Chowan College, PO Box 1848, Murfreesboro, NC 27855, 919-398-1229, fax: 919-398-1190.

CHRISTENDOM COLLEGE
Front Royal, Virginia

About the Institution Independent/religious, coed. Degrees awarded: B, M. Offers 7 undergraduate majors. Total enrollment: 213 (28% state residents). Freshmen: 58.

Undergraduate Expenses (1997–98) Comprehensive fee of $14,245 includes tuition ($10,395), mandatory fees ($150), and college room and board ($3700).

Applications 55% of all full-time undergraduates enrolled in fall 1996 applied for aid; of these, 95% were judged to have need according to Federal Methodology, of whom 100% were aided. *Financial aid deadline (priority):* 4/1. *Financial aid forms:* institutional form required; FAFSA, CSS Financial Aid PROFILE acceptable. *Regular admission application deadline:* rolling. Early action deadline: 12/31.

Summary of Aid to Needy Students *From gift & self-help combined:* Average need met: 94%. Average amount awarded: $7275 (32% gift aid, 68% self-help). *Gift aid:* Total: $263,418 (100% from college's own funds). 114 part-time jobs.

Need-Based Scholarships & Grants College/university.

Loans College/university long-term loans ($2975 average).

Non-Need Awards In 1996, a total of 52 non-need awards were made. *Academic Interests/Achievement Awards:* 52 ($137,494 total): general academic.

Other Money-Saving Options Accelerated degree. *Payment Plan:* installment. *Waivers:* full or partial for employees or children of employees.

Contact Mrs. Alisa Polk, Financial Aid Officer, Christendom College, 134 Christendom Drive, Front Royal, VA 22630-5103, 540-636-2900, fax: 540-636-1655.

CHRISTIAN BROTHERS UNIVERSITY
Memphis, Tennessee

About the Institution Independent/religious, coed. Degrees awarded: B, M. Offers 28 undergraduate majors. Total enrollment: 1,785. Undergraduates: 1,564 (70% state residents). Freshmen: 330.

Undergraduate Expenses (1997–98) Comprehensive fee of $15,660 includes tuition ($11,600), mandatory fees ($330), and college room and board ($3730).

Applications 91% of all full-time undergraduates enrolled in fall 1996 applied for aid; of these, 71% were judged to have need according to Federal Methodology, of whom 100% were aided. *Financial aid deadline (priority):* 4/1. *Financial aid forms:* FAFSA required; CSS Financial Aid PROFILE acceptable. *Admission application deadline:* 7/1.

Summary of Aid to Needy Students *From gift & self-help combined:* Average need met: 65%. Average amount awarded: $8731 (65% gift aid, 35% self-help). *Gift aid:* Total: $4,498,543 (79% from college's own funds, 3% from other college-administered sources, 18% from external sources). 130 Federal Work-Study jobs (averaging $1000); 232 part-time jobs.

Need-Based Scholarships & Grants Pell, FSEOG, state, private, college/university.

Loans Perkins, PLUS, Stafford, Unsubsidized Stafford, college/university long-term loans ($1800 average).

Non-Need Awards *Academic Interests/Achievement Awards:* 972 ($2,916,149 total): general academic. *Creative Arts/Performance Awards:* general creative. *Special Achievements/Activities Awards:* general special achievements/activities. *Special Characteristics Awards:* general special characteristics. *Athletic:* Total: 134 ($461,774); Men: 76 ($255,620); Women: 58 ($206,154).

Other Money-Saving Options Accelerated degree, cooperative Army ROTC, cooperative Naval ROTC, cooperative Air Force ROTC, off-campus living (after freshman year). *Payment Plans:* installment, deferred payment. *Waivers:* full or partial for children of alumni and employees or children of employees.

Contact Mr. Jim Shannon, Student Financial Resources Director, Christian Brothers University, 650 East Parkway South, Memphis, TN 38104-5581, 901-321-3305.

CHRISTIAN HERITAGE COLLEGE
El Cajon, California

About the Institution Independent/religious, coed. Degrees awarded: B. Offers 29 undergraduate majors. Total enrollment: 555 (84% state residents). Freshmen: 74.

Undergraduate Expenses (1997–98) Comprehensive fee of $13,995 includes tuition ($9600) and college room and board ($4395).

Applications 90% of all full-time undergraduates enrolled in fall 1996 applied for aid; of these, 100% were judged to have need according to Federal Methodology, of whom 100% were aided. *Financial aid deadline (priority):* 3/2. *Financial aid forms:* FAFSA, CSS Financial Aid PROFILE, institutional form required. State form required for some. *Admission application deadline:* rolling.

Summary of Aid to Needy Students *From gift & self-help combined:* Average amount awarded: $10,033 (53% gift aid, 47% self-help). *Gift aid:* Total: $2,324,500 (55% from college's own funds, 30% from other college-administered sources, 15% from external sources). 45 Federal Work-Study jobs (averaging $1000); 50 part-time jobs.

Need-Based Scholarships & Grants Pell, FSEOG, state, private, college/university.

Loans Perkins, PLUS, Stafford, Unsubsidized Stafford.

Non-Need Awards In 1996, a total of 191 non-need awards were made. *Academic Interests/Achievement Awards:* 47 ($95,000 total): general academic. *Creative Arts/Performance Awards:* 15 ($60,000 total): music. *Special Characteristics Awards:* 80 ($109,450 total): children of faculty/staff, international students, out-of-state students, relatives of clergy. *Athletic:* Total: 49 ($225,000); Men: 28 ($135,000); Women: 21 ($90,000).

Other Money-Saving Options Cooperative Army ROTC, cooperative Air Force ROTC. *Payment Plan:* installment. *Waivers:* full or partial for employees or children of employees.

Contact Ms. Marcie Bonebright, Financial Aid Officer, Christian Heritage College, El Cajon, CA 92019-1157, 619-590-1786.

CHRISTOPHER NEWPORT UNIVERSITY
Newport News, Virginia

About the Institution State-supported, coed. Degrees awarded: B, M. Offers 72 undergraduate majors. Total enrollment: 4,558. Undergraduates: 4,406 (90% state residents). Freshmen: 543.

Undergraduate Expenses (1996–97) State resident tuition: $3326. Nonresident tuition: $7946. Mandatory fees: $40. College room and board: $4650.

Applications 60% of all full-time undergraduates enrolled in fall 1996 applied for aid; of these, 90% were judged to have need according to Federal Methodology, of whom 99% were aided. *Financial aid deadline (priority):* 4/1. *Financial aid forms:* FAFSA, institutional form required. *Admission application deadline:* 8/1.

Summary of Aid to Needy Students *From gift & self-help combined:* Average need met: 75%. Average amount awarded: $5314 (37% gift aid, 63% self-help). *Gift aid:* Total: $2,995,579 (53% from college-administered sources, 47% from external sources). 51 Federal Work-Study jobs (averaging $1478); 167 part-time jobs.

Need-Based Scholarships & Grants Pell, FSEOG, state, private, college/university.

Loans Perkins, PLUS, Stafford, Unsubsidized Stafford, state, college/university short-term loans ($25 average).

Non-Need Awards In 1996, a total of 44 non-need awards were made. *Academic Interests/Achievement Awards:* 38 ($44,160 total): general academic, education, military science. *Creative Arts/Performance Awards:* 6 ($4500 total): art/fine arts, music.

Other Money-Saving Options Accelerated degree, co-op program, Army ROTC, off-campus living (after freshman year). *Payment Plan:* installment. *Waivers:* full or partial for employees or children of employees and senior citizens.

Contact Office of Financial Aid, Christopher Newport University, 50 Shoe Lane, Newport News, VA 23606-2998, 757-594-7000.

CINCINNATI BIBLE COLLEGE AND SEMINARY
Cincinnati, Ohio

About the Institution Independent/religious, coed. Degrees awarded: A, B, M. Offers 13 undergraduate majors. Total enrollment: 848. Undergraduates: 600 (59% state residents). Freshmen: 216.

Undergraduate Expenses (1997–98) Comprehensive fee of $9494 includes tuition ($5775), mandatory fees ($169), and college room and board ($3550). College room only: $1750.

Applications 84% of all full-time undergraduates enrolled in fall 1996 applied for aid; of these, 97% were judged to have need according to Federal Methodology, of whom 100% were aided. *Financial aid deadline (priority):* 5/1. *Financial aid forms:* FAFSA, institutional form required; CSS Financial Aid PROFILE, state form acceptable. *Admission application deadline:* 8/10.

Summary of Aid to Needy Students *From gift & self-help combined:* Average need met: 90%. Average amount awarded: $6812 (34% gift aid, 66% self-help). *Gift aid:* Total: $926,200 (28% from college's own funds, 44% from other college-administered sources, 28% from external sources). 120 Federal Work-Study jobs (averaging $1000); part-time jobs.

Need-Based Scholarships & Grants Pell, FSEOG, state, college/university.

Loans PLUS, Stafford, Unsubsidized Stafford, private.

Non-Need Awards *Academic Interests/Achievement Awards:* general academic. *Creative Arts/Performance Awards:* music. *Special Characteristics Awards:* children and siblings of alumni, international students, relatives of clergy, spouses of current students.

Other Money-Saving Options Off-campus living (after junior year). *Payment Plan:* deferred payment. *Waivers:* full or partial for children of alumni, employees or children of employees, senior citizens.

Contact Ms. Carrie Stewart, Financial Aid Coordinator, Cincinnati Bible College and Seminary, 2700 Glenway Avenue, Cincinnati, OH 45204-1799, 513-244-8450, fax: 513-244-8140.

CINCINNATI COLLEGE OF MORTUARY SCIENCE
Cincinnati, Ohio

About the Institution Independent, coed. Degrees awarded: A, B. Offers 1 undergraduate major. Total enrollment: 145 (60% state residents). Freshmen: 76.

Undergraduate Expenses (1996–97) Tuition: $8325. Mandatory fees: $750.

Applications 50% of all full-time undergraduates enrolled in fall 1996 applied for aid; of these, 100% were judged to have need according to Federal Methodology, of whom 100% were aided. *Financial aid deadline:* continuous. *Financial aid forms:* financial aid transcript (for transfers) required; FAFSA, CSS Financial Aid PROFILE, state form, institutional form acceptable. *Admission application deadline:* rolling.

Summary of Aid to Needy Students *From gift & self-help combined:* Average amount awarded: $5471 (15% gift aid, 85% self-help). *Gift aid:* Total: $32,703 (9% from college's own funds, 91% from external sources).

Need-Based Scholarships & Grants Pell, state, private.

Loans Stafford, Unsubsidized Stafford.

Non-Need Awards Not offered.

Another Money-Saving Option *Waivers:* full or partial for employees or children of employees.

Contact Ms. Pat Leon, Financial Aid Officer, Cincinnati College of Mortuary Science, 645 West North Bend Road, Cincinnati, OH 45224-1428, 513-761-2020.

CIRCLEVILLE BIBLE COLLEGE
Circleville, Ohio

About the Institution Independent/religious, coed. Degrees awarded: A, B. Offers 10 undergraduate majors. Total enrollment: 203 (69% state residents). Freshmen: 65.

Undergraduate Expenses (1996–97) Comprehensive fee of $8234 includes tuition ($3864 minimum), mandatory fees ($550), and college room and board ($3820). College room only: $1692.

Applications 98% of all full-time undergraduates enrolled in fall 1996 applied for aid; of these, 100% were judged to have need according to Federal Methodology, of whom 100% were aided. *Financial aid deadline (priority):* 5/1. *Financial aid forms:* FAFSA, CSS Financial Aid PROFILE, institutional form required. *Admission application deadline:* rolling.

Summary of Aid to Needy Students *From gift & self-help combined:* Average need met: 80%. Average amount awarded: $7552 (37% gift aid, 63% self-help). *Gift aid:* Total: $458,465 (16% from college's own funds, 11% from other college-administered sources, 73% from external sources). 25 Federal Work-Study jobs (averaging $500); 20 part-time jobs.

Need-Based Scholarships & Grants Pell, FSEOG, state, private, college/university.

Loans Perkins, PLUS, Stafford, Unsubsidized Stafford, private, college/university short-term loans ($300 average).

Non-Need Awards In 1996, a total of 117 non-need awards were made. *Academic Interests/Achievement Awards:* 43 ($30,000 total): general academic, religion/biblical studies. *Creative Arts/Performance Awards:* 2 ($2250 total): music. *Special Characteristics Awards:* 72

($87,000 total): children of faculty/staff, international students, relatives of clergy, religious affiliation, veterans, veterans' children.

Other Money-Saving Options *Payment Plan:* installment. *Waivers:* full or partial for employees or children of employees and senior citizens.

Contact Office of Financial Aid, Circleville Bible College, 1476 Lancaster Pike, Circleville, OH 43113-9487, 614-474-8896.

THE CITADEL, THE MILITARY COLLEGE OF SOUTH CAROLINA
Charleston, South Carolina

About the Institution State-supported, coed. Degrees awarded: B, M. Offers 15 undergraduate majors. Total enrollment: 4,319. Undergraduates: 1,967 (50% state residents). Freshmen: 475.

Undergraduate Expenses (1996–97) State resident tuition: $3297. Nonresident tuition: $7536. Mandatory fees: $773. College room and board: $3679.

Applications 49% of all full-time undergraduates enrolled in fall 1996 applied for aid; of these, 78% were judged to have need according to Federal Methodology, of whom 97% were aided. *Financial aid deadline:* Applications processed continuously. *Financial aid forms:* FAFSA required. *Admission application deadline:* 7/1.

Summary of Aid to Needy Students *From gift & self-help combined:* Average need met: 86%. Average amount awarded: $6222 (59% gift aid, 41% self-help). *Gift aid:* Total: $2,525,700 (45% from college's own funds, 14% from other college-administered sources, 41% from external sources). 57 Federal Work-Study jobs (averaging $1000); 309 part-time jobs.

Need-Based Scholarships & Grants Pell, FSEOG, state, college/university.

Loans Perkins, PLUS, Stafford, Unsubsidized Stafford, college/university long-term loans ($1500 average).

Non-Need Awards In 1996, a total of 294 non-need awards were made. *Academic Interests/Achievement Awards:* 85 ($600,000 total): general academic, biological sciences, engineering/technologies, military science. *Creative Arts/Performance Awards:* 5 ($5000 total): journalism/publications, music. *Special Achievements/Activities Awards:* 3 ($3000 total): leadership, religious involvement. *Special Characteristics Awards:* 25 ($25,000 total): children and siblings of alumni, children with a deceased or disabled parent, local/state students, ROTC participants. *Athletic:* Total: 176 ($1,263,714); Men: 176 ($1,263,714); Women: 0.

Other Money-Saving Options Army ROTC, Naval ROTC, Air Force ROTC.

Contact Major Hank M. Fuller, Director of Financial Aid and Scholarships, The Citadel, The Military College of South Carolina, 171 Moultrie Street, Charleston, SC 29409, 803-953-5187.

CITY COLLEGE OF THE CITY UNIVERSITY OF NEW YORK
New York, New York

About the Institution State & locally supported, coed. Degrees awarded: B, M, D. Offers 62 undergraduate majors. Total enrollment: 12,494. Undergraduates: 9,616 (85% state residents). Freshmen: 824.

Undergraduate Expenses (1996–97) State resident tuition: $3200. Nonresident tuition: $6800. Mandatory fees: $109.

Applications Of all full-time undergraduates enrolled in fall 1996, 88% of those who applied for aid were judged to have need according to Federal Methodology, of whom 99% were aided. *Financial aid deadline (priority):* 5/23. *Financial aid forms:* FAFSA, institutional form required. *Admission application deadline:* rolling.

Summary of Aid to Needy Students *From gift & self-help combined:* Average need met: 66%. Average amount awarded: $4228 (71% gift aid, 29% self-help). *Gift aid:* Total: $15,527,000 (1% from college's own funds, 7% from other college-administered sources, 92% from external sources). 1,545 Federal Work-Study jobs (averaging $950); part-time jobs.

Need-Based Scholarships & Grants Pell, FSEOG, state, private, college/university.

Loans Perkins, PLUS, Stafford, Unsubsidized Stafford.

Non-Need Awards In 1996, a total of 78 non-need awards were made. *Academic Interests/Achievement Awards:* 78 ($140,000 total): general academic.

Other Money-Saving Options Co-op program, cooperative Army ROTC, cooperative Air Force ROTC. *Payment Plan:* deferred payment. *Waivers:* full or partial for senior citizens.

Contact Ms. Thelma Mason, Director of Financial Aid, City College of the City University of New York, 160 Convent Avenue, New York, NY 10031-6977, 212-650-5819, fax: 212-650-5829.

CLAFLIN COLLEGE
Orangeburg, South Carolina

About the Institution Independent/religious, coed. Degrees awarded: B. Offers 19 undergraduate majors. Total enrollment: 979 (85% state residents). Freshmen: 258.

Undergraduate Expenses (1997–98) Comprehensive fee of $8624 includes tuition ($5580) and college room and board ($3044). College room only: $1332.

Applications 97% of all full-time undergraduates enrolled in fall 1996 applied for aid; of these, 96% were judged to have need according to Federal Methodology, of whom 100% were aided. *Financial aid deadline (priority):* 4/15. *Financial aid forms:* FAFSA, state form, institutional form required. *Admission application deadline:* rolling.

Summary of Aid to Needy Students *From gift & self-help combined:* Average need met: 68%. Average amount awarded: $6882 (58% gift aid, 42% self-help). *Gift aid:* Total: $3,431,453 (16% from college's own funds, 12% from other college-administered sources, 72% from external sources). 250 Federal Work-Study jobs (averaging $1050).

Need-Based Scholarships & Grants Pell, FSEOG, state, private, college/university.

Loans Perkins, PLUS, Stafford, Unsubsidized Stafford, college/university long-term loans.

Non-Need Awards In 1996, a total of 212 non-need awards were made. *Academic Interests/Achievement Awards:* 92 ($364,564 total): general academic. *Creative Arts/Performance Awards:* 42 ($29,000 total): applied art and design, art/fine arts, music. *Special Achievements/Activities Awards:* 0: cheerleading/drum major. *Special Characteristics Awards:* 12 ($30,225 total): children of faculty/staff, relatives of clergy, religious affiliation. *Athletic:* Total: 66 ($109,548); Men: 28 ($49,339); Women: 38 ($60,209).

Other Money-Saving Options Army ROTC, off-campus living. *Waivers:* full or partial for employees or children of employees.

Contact Ms. Yvonne C. Clarkson, Director of Student Financial Aid, Claflin College, 700 College Avenue, Orangeburg, SC 29115, 803-535-5331, fax: 803-531-2860.

CLAREMONT MCKENNA COLLEGE
Claremont, California

About the Institution Independent, coed. Degrees awarded: B. Offers 51 undergraduate majors. Total enrollment: 954 (60% state residents). Freshmen: 246.

Undergraduate Expenses (1997–98) Comprehensive fee of $25,480 includes tuition ($18,860), mandatory fees ($160), and college room and board ($6460 minimum). College room only: $3190 (minimum).

Applications 96% of all full-time undergraduates enrolled in fall 1996 applied for aid; of these, 92% were judged to have need according to Federal Methodology, of whom 100% were aided. *Financial aid deadline (priority):* 2/1. *Financial aid forms:* FAFSA, CSS Financial Aid PROFILE required. State form required for some. *Regular admission application deadline:* 1/15. Early decision deadline: 11/15.

Summary of Aid to Needy Students *From gift & self-help combined:* Average need met: 100%. Average amount awarded: $14,803 (78% gift aid, 22% self-help). *Gift aid:* Total: $7,266,960 (76% from college's own funds, 14% from other college-administered sources, 10% from external sources). 459 Federal Work-Study jobs (averaging $1354); 165 part-time jobs.

Need-Based Scholarships & Grants Pell, FSEOG, state, private, college/university.

Loans Perkins, PLUS, Stafford, Unsubsidized Stafford, private, college/university short-term loans ($325 average), college/university long-term loans ($2917 average).

Non-Need Awards In 1996, a total of 105 non-need awards were made. *Academic Interests/Achievement Awards:* 105 ($296,000 total): general academic.

Other Money-Saving Options Accelerated degree, Army ROTC, cooperative Naval ROTC, cooperative Air Force ROTC, off-campus living (after freshman year). *Payment Plan:* installment. *Waivers:* full or partial for employees or children of employees.

Contact Ms. Georgette R. DeVeres, Director of Financial Aid/Associate Dean of Admission, Claremont McKenna College, 890 Columbia Avenue, Claremont, CA 91711, 909-621-8356.

CLARION UNIVERSITY OF PENNSYLVANIA
Clarion, Pennsylvania

About the Institution State-supported, coed. Degrees awarded: A, B, M. Offers 53 undergraduate majors. Total enrollment: 5,886. Undergraduates: 5,410 (97% state residents). Freshmen: 1,313.

Undergraduate Expenses (1996–97) State resident tuition: $3368. Nonresident tuition: $8566. Mandatory fees: $870. College room and board: $3140 (minimum). College room only: $1860 (minimum).

Applications 85% of all full-time undergraduates enrolled in fall 1996 applied for aid; of these, 89% were judged to have need according to Federal Methodology, of whom 94% were aided. *Financial aid deadline:* Applications processed continuously. *Financial aid forms:* FAFSA, state form required; institutional form acceptable. *Admission application deadline:* rolling.

Summary of Aid to Needy Students *From gift & self-help combined:* Average need met: 79%. Average amount awarded: $5807 (40% gift aid, 60% self-help). *Gift aid:* Total: $8,134,614 (6% from college's own funds, 10% from other college-administered sources, 84% from external sources). 255 Federal Work-Study jobs (averaging $1425); 715 part-time jobs.

Need-Based Scholarships & Grants Pell, FSEOG, state, private, Negro Emergency Education Drive.

Loans PLUS, Stafford, Unsubsidized Stafford, private, college/university short-term loans ($200 average).

Non-Need Awards *Academic Interests/Achievement Awards:* 844 ($1,672,872 total): general academic, biological sciences, business, communication, computer science, education, English, foreign languages, humanities, international studies, library science, mathematics, physical sciences, premedicine, social sciences. *Creative Arts/Performance Awards:* 20 ($10,000 total): art/fine arts, performing arts. *Special Characteristics Awards:* local/state students, members of minorities. *Athletic:* available.

Other Money-Saving Options Accelerated degree, co-op program, off-campus living. *Payment Plan:* installment. *Waivers:* full or partial for employees or children of employees.

Contact Ms. Mary Jo Phillips, Freshman Financial Aid Advisor, Clarion University of Pennsylvania, 104 Egbert Hall, Clarion, PA 16214-1232, 814-226-2315, fax: 814-226-2520.

CLARK ATLANTA UNIVERSITY
Atlanta, Georgia

About the Institution Independent/religious, coed. Degrees awarded: B, M, D. Offers 49 undergraduate majors. Total enrollment: 5,798. Undergraduates: 4,391 (56% state residents). Freshmen: 1,277.

Undergraduate Expenses (1997–98) Comprehensive fee of $14,948 includes tuition ($9148), mandatory fees ($200), and college room and board ($5600). College room only: $3300.

Applications *Financial aid deadline (priority):* 4/15. *Financial aid forms:* CSS Financial Aid PROFILE required; institutional form acceptable. FAFSA, state form required for some. *Admission application deadline:* 3/1.

Summary of Aid to Needy Students Federal Work-Study jobs.

Non-Need Awards *Academic Interests/Achievement Awards:* general academic. *Creative Arts/Performance Awards:* music. *Special Achievements/Activities Awards:* general special achievements/activities, leadership. *Special Characteristics Awards:* ROTC participants. *Athletic:* available.

Other Money-Saving Options Accelerated degree, co-op program, Army ROTC, Naval ROTC, off-campus living. *Payment Plan:* deferred payment. *Waivers:* full or partial for employees or children of employees.

Contact Office of Financial Aid, Clark Atlanta University, Atlanta, GA 30314, 404-880-8000.

CLARKE COLLEGE
Dubuque, Iowa

About the Institution Independent/religious, coed. Degrees awarded: A, B, M. Offers 61 undergraduate majors. Total enrollment: 1,082. Undergraduates: 1,066 (64% state residents). Freshmen: 195.

Undergraduate Expenses (1997–98) Comprehensive fee of $16,994 includes tuition ($12,199), mandatory fees ($240), and college room and board ($4555). College room only: $2246.

Applications 91% of all full-time undergraduates enrolled in fall 1996 applied for aid; of these, 97% were judged to have need according to Federal Methodology, of whom 100% were aided. *Financial aid deadline (priority):* 3/15. *Financial aid forms:* FAFSA required; CSS Financial Aid PROFILE acceptable. *Admission application deadline:* rolling.

Summary of Aid to Needy Students *From gift & self-help combined:* Average need met: 95%. Average amount awarded: $8889 (53% gift aid, 47% self-help). *Gift aid:* Total: $2,994,151 (56% from college's own funds, 32% from other college-administered sources, 12% from external sources). 186 Federal Work-Study jobs (averaging $1081); 69 part-time jobs.

Need-Based Scholarships & Grants Pell, FSEOG, state, private, college/university.

Loans Perkins, PLUS, Stafford, Unsubsidized Stafford, Federal Nursing, private, college/university short-term loans ($500 average), college/university long-term loans ($1275 average).

Non-Need Awards In 1996, a total of 355 non-need awards were made. *Academic Interests/Achievement Awards:* 218 ($597,464 total): general academic, computer science, education. *Creative Arts/Performance Awards:* 46 ($66,500 total): art/fine arts, music, theater/drama. *Special Achievements/Activities Awards:* 21 ($21,000 total): leadership. *Special Characteristics Awards:* 70 ($180,591 total): children and siblings of alumni, children of faculty/staff, local/state students, relatives of clergy, siblings of current students.

Other Money-Saving Options Co-op program, off-campus living (after junior year). *Payment Plans:* installment, deferred payment. *Waivers:* full or partial for children of alumni, employees or children of employees, adult students, senior citizens.

Contact Mr. Michael Pope, Director of Financial Aid, Clarke College, 1550 Clarke Drive, Dubuque, IA 52001-3198, 319-588-6327, fax: 319-588-6789.

CLARKSON COLLEGE
Omaha, Nebraska

About the Institution Independent/religious, coed. Degrees awarded: A, B, M. Offers 5 undergraduate majors. Total enrollment: 570. Undergraduates: 362 (85% state residents). Freshmen: 23.

Undergraduate Expenses (1997–98) Tuition: $8704. Mandatory fees: $544. College room only: $2040 (minimum).

Applications 95% of all full-time undergraduates enrolled in fall 1996 applied for aid; of these, 93% were judged to have need according to Federal Methodology, of whom 100% were aided. *Financial aid deadline (priority):* 4/1. *Financial aid forms:* FAFSA, institutional form required; CSS Financial Aid PROFILE acceptable. State form required for some. *Admission application deadline:* rolling.

Summary of Aid to Needy Students *From gift & self-help combined:* Average need met: 85%. Average amount awarded: $5385 (18% gift aid, 82% self-help). *Gift aid:* Total: $206,000 (45% from college's own funds, 12% from other college-administered sources, 43% from external sources). Federal Work-Study jobs (averaging $1900).

Need-Based Scholarships & Grants Pell, FSEOG, state, private, college/university.

Loans PLUS, Stafford, Unsubsidized Stafford, Federal Nursing, college/university short-term loans ($200 average).

Non-Need Awards In 1996, a total of 110 non-need awards were made. *Academic Interests/Achievement Awards:* 80 ($200,000 total): general academic, business, health fields. *Special Characteristics Awards:* 30 ($75,000 total): children and siblings of alumni, children of faculty/staff, ethnic background, international students, ROTC participants, veterans.

Other Money-Saving Options Accelerated degree, cooperative Army ROTC, off-campus living. *Payment Plans:* installment, deferred payment. *Waivers:* full or partial for minority students and employees or children of employees.

Contact Ms. Jennifer Wurth, Financial Aid Counselor, Clarkson College, 101 South 42nd Street, Omaha, NE 68131-2739, 402-552-3470, fax: 402-522-6165.

CLARKSON UNIVERSITY
Potsdam, New York

About the Institution Independent, coed. Degrees awarded: B, M, D. Offers 56 undergraduate majors. Total enrollment: 2,670. Undergraduates: 2,356 (69% state residents). Freshmen: 664.

Undergraduate Expenses (1997–98) Comprehensive fee of $25,103 includes tuition ($18,250), mandatory fees ($343), and college room and board ($6510). College room only: $3180.

Applications Of all full-time undergraduates enrolled in fall 1996, 94% of those who applied for aid were judged to have need according to Federal Methodology, of whom 100% were aided. *Financial aid deadline (priority):* 2/15. *Financial aid forms:* FAFSA required. CSS Financial Aid PROFILE, state form required for some. *Regular admission application deadline:* 3/15. Early decision deadline: 12/1.

Summary of Aid to Needy Students *From gift & self-help combined:* Average need met: 92%. Average amount awarded: $16,600 (61% gift aid, 39% self-help). *Gift aid:* Total: $19,301,361 (70% from college's

own funds, 20% from other college-administered sources, 10% from external sources). 300 Federal Work-Study jobs (averaging $800); 600 part-time jobs.

Need-Based Scholarships & Grants Pell, FSEOG, state, private, college/university.

Loans Perkins, PLUS, Stafford, Unsubsidized Stafford, private, college/university long-term loans ($3000 average), Quick Loan Funds.

Non-Need Awards In 1996, a total of 1,056 non-need awards were made. *Academic Interests/Achievement Awards:* 840 ($1,669,692 total): general academic, biological sciences, business, computer science, engineering/technologies, humanities, mathematics, military science, physical sciences. *Special Achievements/Activities Awards:* 81 ($538,000 total): leadership. *Special Characteristics Awards:* 114 ($1,147,084 total): general special characteristics, children of faculty/staff, international students, local/state students, members of minorities, ROTC participants. *Athletic:* Total: 21 ($437,490); Men: 21 ($437,490).

Other Money-Saving Options Accelerated degree, co-op program, Army ROTC, Air Force ROTC. *Payment Plan:* installment. *Waivers:* full or partial for employees or children of employees.

Contact Office of Financial Aid, Clarkson University, Lewis House, Potsdam, NY 13699-5615, 315-268-6400.

CLARK UNIVERSITY
Worcester, Massachusetts

About the Institution Independent, coed. Degrees awarded: B, M, D. Offers 55 undergraduate majors. Total enrollment: 2,732. Undergraduates: 1,869 (37% state residents). Freshmen: 534.

Undergraduate Expenses (1997–98) Comprehensive fee of $25,190 includes tuition ($20,500), mandatory fees ($440), and college room and board ($4250). College room only: $2250.

Applications Of all full-time undergraduates enrolled in fall 1996, 94% of those who applied for aid were judged to have need according to Federal Methodology, of whom 100% were aided. *Financial aid deadline (priority):* 2/1. *Financial aid forms:* FAFSA, financial aid transcript (for transfers) required. CSS Financial Aid PROFILE, institutional form required for some. *Regular admission application deadline:* 2/1. Early decision deadline: 12/1.

Summary of Aid to Needy Students *From gift & self-help combined:* Average need met: 94%. Average amount awarded: $15,132 (69% gift aid, 31% self-help). *Gift aid:* Total: $14,987,000 (87% from college's own funds, 6% from other college-administered sources, 7% from external sources). 908 Federal Work-Study jobs (averaging $1300); part-time jobs.

Need-Based Scholarships & Grants Pell, FSEOG, state, college/university.

Loans Perkins, PLUS, Stafford, Unsubsidized Stafford, state, private.

Non-Need Awards In 1996, a total of 303 non-need awards were made. *Academic Interests/Achievement Awards:* 303 ($1,306,000 total): general academic.

Other Money-Saving Options Accelerated degree, cooperative Army ROTC, cooperative Air Force ROTC, off-campus living (after sophomore year). *Payment Plans:* tuition prepayment, installment. *Waivers:* full or partial for employees or children of employees.

Contact Financial Aid Office, Clark University, 950 Main Street, Worcester, MA 01610-1477, 508-793-7478.

CLAYTON COLLEGE & STATE UNIVERSITY
Morrow, Georgia

About the Institution State-supported, coed. Degrees awarded: A, B. Offers 80 undergraduate majors. Total enrollment: 4,687 (97% state residents). Freshmen: 847.

Undergraduate Expenses (1996–97) State resident tuition: $1584. Nonresident tuition: $5463. Mandatory fees: $258.

Applications 75% of all full-time undergraduates enrolled in fall 1996 applied for aid; of these, 80% were judged to have need according to Federal Methodology, of whom 99% were aided. *Financial aid deadline (priority):* 6/1. *Financial aid forms:* FAFSA, institutional form required. *Admission application deadline:* 8/15.

Summary of Aid to Needy Students *Gift aid:* Total: $12,683,263 (1% from college's own funds, 69% from other college-administered sources, 30% from external sources). 12 Federal Work-Study jobs (averaging $1056).

Need-Based Scholarships & Grants Pell, FSEOG, state.

Loans Stafford, Unsubsidized Stafford, Federal Nursing, state, college/university short-term loans ($500 average).

Non-Need Awards *Academic Interests/Achievement Awards:* general academic. *Creative Arts/Performance Awards:* music. *Athletic:* Total: 56 ($38,686); Men: 32 ($22,581); Women: 24 ($16,105).

Other Money-Saving Options Co-op program, cooperative Army ROTC. *Waivers:* full or partial for senior citizens.

Contact Financial Aid Office, Clayton College & State University, PO Box 285, Morrow, GA 30273, 770-961-3511.

CLEAR CREEK BAPTIST BIBLE COLLEGE
Pineville, Kentucky

About the Institution Independent/religious, primarily men. Degrees awarded: A, B. Offers 2 undergraduate majors. Total enrollment: 150 (70% state residents). Freshmen: 48.

Undergraduate Expenses (1996–97) Comprehensive fee of $4850 includes tuition ($2170 minimum), mandatory fees ($200), and college room and board ($2480 minimum). College room only: $1060.

Applications 84% of all full-time undergraduates enrolled in fall 1996 applied for aid; of these, 91% were judged to have need according to Federal Methodology, of whom 100% were aided. *Financial aid deadline (priority):* 7/31. *Financial aid forms:* FAFSA, institutional form, federal income tax form required; CSS Financial Aid PROFILE acceptable. *Admission application deadline:* 7/15.

Summary of Aid to Needy Students *From gift & self-help combined:* Average need met: 41%. Average amount awarded: $1660. *Gift aid:* Total: $154,337 (30% from college's own funds, 20% from other college-administered sources, 50% from external sources). 70 part-time jobs.

Need-Based Scholarships & Grants Pell, private, college/university.

Non-Need Awards *Academic Interests/Achievement Awards:* area/ethnic studies, religion/biblical studies. *Creative Arts/Performance Awards:* 2 ($800 total): music. *Special Achievements/Activities Awards:* 3 ($450 total): religious involvement. *Special Characteristics Awards:* children of faculty/staff, ethnic background, handicapped students.

Other Money-Saving Options Off-campus living. *Payment Plan:* installment.

Contact Mr. Sam Risner, Director of Financial Aid, Clear Creek Baptist Bible College, 300 Clear Creek Road, Pineville, KY 40977-9754, 606-337-3196, fax: 606-337-2372.

CLEARWATER CHRISTIAN COLLEGE
Clearwater, Florida

About the Institution Independent/religious, coed. Degrees awarded: A, B. Offers 24 undergraduate majors. Total enrollment: 518 (62% state residents). Freshmen: 180.

Undergraduate Expenses (1997–98) Comprehensive fee of $10,800 includes tuition ($7000), mandatory fees ($300 minimum), and college room and board ($3500).

Applications *Financial aid deadline (priority):* 5/1. *Financial aid forms:* FAFSA required. *Admission application deadline:* 8/1.

Summary of Aid to Needy Students Federal Work-Study jobs; 35 part-time jobs.

Need-Based Scholarships & Grants Pell, FSEOG, state, college/university.

Loans Stafford, Unsubsidized Stafford, college/university short-term loans.

Non-Need Awards *Academic Interests/Achievement Awards:* general academic, business, education, mathematics, premedicine, religion/biblical studies. *Creative Arts/Performance Awards:* music. *Special Characteristics Awards:* children of educators, local/state students.

Other Money-Saving Options Cooperative Army ROTC, cooperative Air Force ROTC. *Payment Plan:* installment.

Contact Ms. Ruth Strum, Director of Financial Aid, Clearwater Christian College, Clearwater, FL 34619-4595, 813-726-1153 Ext. 220.

CLEARY COLLEGE
Ypsilanti, Michigan

About the Institution Independent, coed. Degrees awarded: A, B. Offers 9 undergraduate majors. Total enrollment: 782 (94% state residents). Freshmen: 29.

Undergraduate Expenses (1997–98) Tuition: $7200. Mandatory fees: $90.

Applications *Financial aid deadline (priority):* 7/1. *Financial aid forms:* FAFSA, institutional form required. *Admission application deadline:* rolling.

Summary of Aid to Needy Students *Gift aid:* Total: $492,502. Federal Work-Study jobs.

Need-Based Scholarships & Grants Pell, FSEOG, state, private, college/university.

Loans PLUS, Stafford, Unsubsidized Stafford, college/university short-term loans ($100 average).

Non-Need Awards *Academic Interests/Achievement Awards:* general academic. *Special Achievements/Activities Awards:* general special achievements/activities, community service. *Special Characteristics Awards:* children of faculty/staff.

Other Money-Saving Options Accelerated degree, co-op program, cooperative Air Force ROTC. *Payment Plans:* installment, deferred payment. *Waivers:* full or partial for employees or children of employees.

Contact Ms. Rose M. Smith, Director of Regulatory Compliance, Cleary College, 2170 Washtenaw Avenue, Ypsilanti, MI 48197-1788, 313-483-4400 Ext. 3315.

CLEMSON UNIVERSITY
Clemson, South Carolina

About the Institution State-supported, coed. Degrees awarded: B, M, D. Offers 81 undergraduate majors. Total enrollment: 16,537. Undergraduates: 12,717 (72% state residents). Freshmen: 2,546.

Undergraduate Expenses (1996–97) State resident tuition: $2922. Nonresident tuition: $8126. Mandatory fees: $190. College room and board: $3136 (minimum). College room only: $1560 (minimum).

Applications Of all full-time undergraduates enrolled in fall 1996, 68% of those who applied for aid were judged to have need according to Federal Methodology, of whom 90% were aided. *Financial aid deadline (priority):* 4/1. *Financial aid forms:* FAFSA required. *Admission application deadline:* 5/1.

Summary of Aid to Needy Students *From gift & self-help combined:* Average need met: 73%. Average amount awarded: $6349 (37% gift aid, 63% self-help). *Gift aid:* Total: $10,481,005 (30% from college's

own funds, 23% from other college-administered sources, 47% from external sources). 575 Federal Work-Study jobs (averaging $1375); 2,600 part-time jobs.

Need-Based Scholarships & Grants Pell, FSEOG, state, private, college/university.

Loans Perkins, PLUS, Stafford, Unsubsidized Stafford, private, college/university short-term loans ($200 average).

Non-Need Awards In 1996, a total of 2,867 non-need awards were made. *Academic Interests/Achievement Awards:* 2,465 ($2,887,801 total): general academic, agriculture, architecture, biological sciences, business, communication, computer science, education, engineering/technologies, English, foreign languages, health fields, humanities, international studies, mathematics, military science, physical sciences, premedicine, social sciences. *Special Characteristics Awards:* 8 ($8000 total): children of faculty/staff. *Athletic:* Total: 394 ($2,399,410); Men: 265 ($1,603,687); Women: 129 ($795,723).

Other Money-Saving Options Accelerated degree, co-op program, Army ROTC, Air Force ROTC, off-campus living (after freshman year). *Payment Plan:* deferred payment. *Waivers:* full or partial for senior citizens.

Contact Mr. Marvin G. Carmichael, Director of Financial Aid, Clemson University, G01 Sikes Hall, Clemson, SC 29634, 864-656-2280.

CLEVELAND COLLEGE OF JEWISH STUDIES
Beachwood, Ohio

About the Institution Independent, coed. Degrees awarded: B, M. Offers 10 undergraduate majors. Total enrollment: 75. Undergraduates: 22 (90% state residents). Freshmen: 4.

Undergraduate Expenses (1996–97) Tuition: $4950.

Applications *Financial aid deadline (priority):* 9/1. *Financial aid forms:* institutional form required. *Admission application deadline:* rolling.

Need-Based Scholarships & Grants College/university.

Non-Need Awards Not offered.

Other Money-Saving Options Co-op program. *Payment Plan:* installment. *Waivers:* full or partial for employees or children of employees and senior citizens.

Contact Ms. Linda Rosen, Registrar/Bursar, Cleveland College of Jewish Studies, 26500 Shaker Boulevard, Beachwood, OH 44122-7116, 216-464-4050, fax: 216-464-5827.

CLEVELAND INSTITUTE OF ART
Cleveland, Ohio

About the Institution Independent, coed. Degrees awarded: B. Offers 16 undergraduate majors. Total enrollment: 513 (70% state residents). Freshmen: 98.

Undergraduate Expenses (1997–98) Comprehensive fee of $18,364 includes tuition ($12,870), mandatory fees ($564), and college room and board ($4930). College room only: $2870.

Applications 94% of all full-time undergraduates enrolled in fall 1996 applied for aid; of these, 94% were judged to have need according to Federal Methodology, of whom 92% were aided. *Financial aid deadline (priority):* 3/15. *Financial aid forms:* FAFSA, institutional form required; CSS Financial Aid PROFILE acceptable. State form required for some. *Regular admission application deadline:* rolling. Early decision deadline: 11/15.

Summary of Aid to Needy Students *From gift & self-help combined:* Average need met: 98%. *Gift aid:* Total: $1,906,673 (59% from college's own funds, 5% from other college-administered sources, 36% from external sources). 200 Federal Work-Study jobs (averaging $1500).

Need-Based Scholarships & Grants Pell, FSEOG, state, private, college/university.

Loans Perkins, PLUS, Stafford, Unsubsidized Stafford, state, private, college/university short-term loans ($200 average).

Non-Need Awards *Creative Arts/Performance Awards:* art/fine arts.

Other Money-Saving Options Co-op program, off-campus living (after freshman year). *Payment Plan:* installment.

Contact Ms. Nancy Maldonado-Dillard, Director of Financial Aid, Cleveland Institute of Art, 11141 East Boulevard, Cleveland, OH 44106-1700, 216-421-7425, fax: 216-421-7438.

CLEVELAND INSTITUTE OF MUSIC
Cleveland, Ohio

About the Institution Independent, coed. Degrees awarded: B, M, D. Offers 7 undergraduate majors. Total enrollment: 354. Undergraduates: 226 (15% state residents). Freshmen: 47.

Undergraduate Expenses (1997–98) Comprehensive fee of $22,249 includes tuition ($16,365), mandatory fees ($664), and college room and board ($5220). College room only: $3250.

Applications 95% of all full-time undergraduates enrolled in fall 1996 applied for aid; of these,100% were judged to have need according to Federal Methodology, of whom 100% were aided. *Financial aid deadline (priority):* 3/1. *Financial aid forms:* FAFSA, institutional form required. CSS Financial Aid PROFILE, state form required for some. *Admission application deadline:* 12/15.

Summary of Aid to Needy Students *From gift & self-help combined:* Average need met: 95%. Average amount awarded: $11,694 (58% gift aid, 42% self-help). *Gift aid:* Total: $1,445,951 (89% from college's own funds, 8% from other college-administered sources, 3% from external sources). 100 Federal Work-Study jobs (averaging $1000); 60 part-time jobs.

Need-Based Scholarships & Grants Pell, FSEOG, state, private, college/university.

Loans Perkins, PLUS, Stafford, Unsubsidized Stafford, college/university long-term loans ($1000 average).

Non-Need Awards *Creative Arts/Performance Awards:* music.

Other Money-Saving Options Accelerated degree, off-campus living (after sophomore year). *Payment Plan:* installment. *Waivers:* full or partial for employees or children of employees.

Contact Ms. Carol E. Peffer, Director of Financial Aid, Cleveland Institute of Music, 11021 East Boulevard, Cleveland, OH 44106-1776, 216-791-5000 Ext. 262.

CLEVELAND STATE UNIVERSITY
Cleveland, Ohio

About the Institution State-supported, coed. Degrees awarded: B, M, D, P. Offers 64 undergraduate majors. Total enrollment: 15,522. Undergraduates: 10,728 (99% state residents). Freshmen: 1,120.

Undergraduate Expenses (1996–97) State resident tuition: $3442. Nonresident tuition: $6883. Mandatory fees: $68. College room and board: $4350.

Applications *Financial aid deadline (priority):* 4/15. *Financial aid forms:* FAFSA, state form, institutional form required. CSS Financial Aid PROFILE required for some. *Admission application deadline:* 8/1.

Summary of Aid to Needy Students Federal Work-Study jobs; part-time jobs.

Loans College/university short-term loans.

Non-Need Awards *Academic Interests/Achievement Awards:* general academic. *Creative Arts/Performance Awards:* art/fine arts, music, theater/drama. *Special Achievements/Activities Awards:* available. *Special Characteristics Awards:* available. *Athletic:* available.

Other Money-Saving Options Accelerated degree, co-op program, Army ROTC, cooperative Air Force ROTC, off-campus living. *Payment Plan:* installment. *Waivers:* full or partial for employees or children of employees and senior citizens.

Contact Office of Financial Aid, Cleveland State University, 2344 Euclid Avenue #201, Cleveland, OH 44115, 216-687-2000.

CLINCH VALLEY COLLEGE OF THE UNIVERSITY OF VIRGINIA
Wise, Virginia

About the Institution State-supported, coed. Degrees awarded: B. Offers 14 undergraduate majors. Total enrollment: 1,387 (95% state residents). Freshmen: 221.

Undergraduate Expenses (1997–98 estimated) State resident tuition: $3258. Nonresident tuition: $7782. College room and board: $3960. College room only: $2196.

Applications Of all full-time undergraduates enrolled in fall 1996, 91% of those who applied for aid were judged to have need according to Federal Methodology, of whom 100% were aided. *Financial aid deadline (priority):* 4/1. *Financial aid forms:* FAFSA required. *Admission application deadline:* 8/15.

Summary of Aid to Needy Students *From gift & self-help combined:* Average need met: 100%. Average amount awarded: $4297 (60% gift aid, 40% self-help). *Gift aid:* Total: $2,125,227 (4% from college's own funds, 52% from other college-administered sources, 44% from external sources). 189 Federal Work-Study jobs (averaging $994); 75 part-time jobs.

Need-Based Scholarships & Grants Pell, FSEOG, state, private, college/university.

Loans Perkins, PLUS, Stafford, Unsubsidized Stafford, college/university short-term loans ($300 average), college/university long-term loans ($1000 average).

Non-Need Awards *Academic Interests/Achievement Awards:* general academic, agriculture, biological sciences, business, computer science, education, English, health fields, humanities, mathematics, physical sciences, premedicine, social sciences. *Creative Arts/Performance Awards:* general creative, creative writing, journalism/publications, music, performing arts, theater/drama. *Special Characteristics Awards:* ethnic background, local/state students. *Athletic:* Total: 100 ($166,981); Men: 72 ($121,791); Women: 28 ($45,190).

Other Money-Saving Options Co-op program, off-campus living. *Waivers:* full or partial for senior citizens.

Contact Mr. Russell D. Necessary, Coordinator of Financial Aid Services, Clinch Valley College of the University of Virginia, One College Avenue, Wise, VA 24293, 540-328-0103, fax: 540-328-0251.

COASTAL CAROLINA UNIVERSITY
Conway, South Carolina

About the Institution State-supported, coed. Degrees awarded: B, M. Offers 29 undergraduate majors. Total enrollment: 4,477. Undergraduates: 4,304 (70% state residents). Freshmen: 833.

Undergraduate Expenses (1996–97) State resident tuition: $2930. Nonresident tuition: $7840. College room and board: $4265. College room only: $2810.

Applications Of all full-time undergraduates enrolled in fall 1996, 72% of those who applied for aid were judged to have need according to Federal Methodology, of whom 76% were aided. *Financial aid deadline (priority):* 4/1. *Financial aid forms:* FAFSA required. *Admission application deadline:* 8/15.

Summary of Aid to Needy Students *From gift & self-help combined:* Average need met: 74%. Average amount awarded: $7425. *Gift aid:*

Total: $2,700,000 (41% from college-administered sources, 56% from external sources). 110 Federal Work-Study jobs (averaging $2000); 152 part-time jobs.

Need-Based Scholarships & Grants Pell, FSEOG, state.

Loans Perkins, PLUS, Stafford, Unsubsidized Stafford.

Non-Need Awards In 1996, a total of 368 non-need awards were made. *Academic Interests/Achievement Awards:* 150 ($102,000 total): general academic. *Creative Arts/Performance Awards:* 14 ($10,500 total): art/fine arts, music, theater/drama. *Special Characteristics Awards:* 34 ($27,500 total): general special characteristics, members of minorities, veterans' children. *Athletic:* Total: 170 ($1,274,695); Men: 98 ($640,710); Women: 72 ($633,985).

Other Money-Saving Options Accelerated degree, off-campus living. *Payment Plans:* installment, deferred payment. *Waivers:* full or partial for employees or children of employees and senior citizens.

Contact Office of Financial Aid, Coastal Carolina University, PO Box 261954, Conway, SC 29528-6054, 803-349-2313, fax: 803-349-2347.

COE COLLEGE
Cedar Rapids, Iowa

About the Institution Independent/religious, coed. Degrees awarded: B, M. Offers 48 undergraduate majors. Total enrollment: 1,247. Undergraduates: 1,202 (62% state residents). Freshmen: 248.

Undergraduate Expenses (1996–97) Comprehensive fee of $19,990 includes tuition ($15,410), mandatory fees ($125), and college room and board ($4455). College room only: $1990.

Applications 97% of all full-time undergraduates enrolled in fall 1996 applied for aid; of these, 96% were judged to have need according to Federal Methodology, of whom 100% were aided. *Financial aid deadline (priority):* 3/1. *Financial aid forms:* FAFSA required; CSS Financial Aid PROFILE acceptable. State form, institutional form required for some. *Regular admission application deadline:* 3/1. Early decision deadline: 11/15. Early action deadline: 12/15.

Summary of Aid to Needy Students *From gift & self-help combined:* Average need met: 100%. Average amount awarded: $13,635 (69% gift aid, 31% self-help). *Gift aid:* Total: $9,070,010 (77% from college's own funds, 1% from other college-administered sources, 22% from external sources). 142 Federal Work-Study jobs (averaging $900); 200 part-time jobs.

Need-Based Scholarships & Grants Pell, FSEOG, state, private, college/university.

Loans Perkins, PLUS, Stafford, Unsubsidized Stafford, state, private, college/university long-term loans ($1500 average).

Non-Need Awards *Academic Interests/Achievement Awards:* 12 ($184,920 total): general academic, biological sciences, foreign languages, physical sciences, premedicine. *Creative Arts/Performance Awards:* 176 ($417,121 total): art/fine arts, creative writing, music, performing arts, theater/drama. *Special Characteristics Awards:* children and siblings of alumni, international students, religious affiliation.

Other Money-Saving Options Accelerated degree, cooperative Army ROTC, cooperative Air Force ROTC. *Payment Plans:* tuition prepayment, installment. *Waivers:* full or partial for employees or children of employees and adult students.

Contact Mr. Robert Baird, Director of Financial Aid and Associate Dean of Admissions, Coe College, 1220 1st Avenue, NE, Cedar Rapids, IA 52402-5070, 319-399-8540, fax: 319-399-8816.

COGSWELL COLLEGE NORTH
Kirkland, Washington

See Henry Cogswell College

COGSWELL POLYTECHNICAL COLLEGE
Sunnyvale, California

About the Institution Independent, coed. Degrees awarded: A, B. Offers 12 undergraduate majors. Total enrollment: 458 (80% state residents). Freshmen: 32.

Undergraduate Expenses (1996–97) Tuition: $7320. Mandatory fees: $40.

Applications Of all full-time undergraduates enrolled in fall 1996, 100% of those who applied for aid were judged to have need according to Federal Methodology, of whom 100% were aided. *Financial aid deadline:* continuous. *Financial aid forms:* FAFSA, state form, institutional form, financial aid transcript (for transfers) required; CSS Financial Aid PROFILE acceptable. *Admission application deadline:* rolling.

Summary of Aid to Needy Students Federal Work-Study jobs.

Need-Based Scholarships & Grants Pell, FSEOG, state, college/university.

Loans PLUS, Stafford, Unsubsidized Stafford.

Non-Need Awards *Academic Interests/Achievement Awards:* computer science , engineering/technologies.

Other Money-Saving Options Accelerated degree, cooperative Army ROTC, cooperative Air Force ROTC. *Payment Plan:* deferred payment. *Waivers:* full or partial for employees or children of employees.

Contact Office of Financial Aid, Cogswell Polytechnical College, 1175 Bordeaux Drive, Sunnyvale, CA 95112, 408-541-0100.

COKER COLLEGE
Hartsville, South Carolina

About the Institution Independent, coed. Degrees awarded: B. Offers 52 undergraduate majors. Total enrollment: 666 (80% state residents). Freshmen: 140.

Undergraduate Expenses (1997–98) Comprehensive fee of $17,951 includes tuition ($13,200), mandatory fees ($200), and college room and board ($4551). College room only: $1881.

Applications Of all full-time undergraduates enrolled in fall 1996, 100% of those judged to have need according to Federal Methodology were aided. *Financial aid deadline (priority):* 3/30. *Financial aid forms:* FAFSA required. *Admission application deadline:* rolling.

Summary of Aid to Needy Students *From gift & self-help combined:* Average amount awarded: $10,587 (54% gift aid, 46% self-help). *Gift aid:* Total: $3,458,647 (78% from college's own funds, 3% from other college-administered sources, 19% from external sources). 110 Federal Work-Study jobs (averaging $1000); 5 part-time jobs.

Need-Based Scholarships & Grants Pell, FSEOG, state, private, college/university.

Loans Perkins, PLUS, Stafford, Unsubsidized Stafford.

Non-Need Awards *Academic Interests/Achievement Awards:* general academic. *Creative Arts/Performance Awards:* art/fine arts, dance, music, theater/drama. *Special Characteristics Awards:* children and siblings of alumni. *Athletic:* Total: 110 ($352,814); Men: ($216,000); Women: ($136,814).

Other Money-Saving Options Accelerated degree, co-op program, off-campus living (after junior year). *Payment Plans:* guaranteed tuition, installment. *Waivers:* full or partial for employees or children of employees and adult students.

Contact Mr. Hal Lewis, Director of Financial Aid, Coker College, Hartsville, SC 29550, 803-383-8055.

COLBY COLLEGE
Waterville, Maine

About the Institution Independent, coed. Degrees awarded: B. Offers 36 undergraduate majors. Total enrollment: 1,764 (12% state residents). Freshmen: 471.

Undergraduate Expenses (1997–98) Comprehensive fee: $29,190.

Applications Of all full-time undergraduates enrolled in fall 1996, 85% of those who applied for aid were judged to have need according to Federal Methodology, of whom 100% were aided. *Financial aid deadline (priority):* 2/1. *Financial aid forms:* FAFSA, institutional form required. State form, federal income tax returns required for some. *Regular admission application deadline:* 1/15. Early decision deadline:

Summary of Aid to Needy Students *From gift & self-help combined:* Average need met: 100%. Average amount awarded: $16,000 (69% gift aid, 31% self-help). *Gift aid:* Total: $9,490,000 (88% from college's own funds, 6% from other college-administered sources, 6% from external sources). 527 Federal Work-Study jobs (averaging $1500); 20 part-time jobs.

Need-Based Scholarships & Grants Pell, FSEOG, state, private, college/university.

Loans Perkins, PLUS, Stafford, Unsubsidized Stafford, state, private, college/university short-term loans ($200 average), college/university long-term loans ($2000 average).

Non-Need Awards *Special Characteristics Awards:* children of faculty/staff , ROTC participants.

Other Money-Saving Options Cooperative Army ROTC, off-campus living (after junior year). *Payment Plan:* installment. *Waivers:* full or partial for employees or children of employees and senior citizens.

Contact Ms. Lucia Whittelsey, Director, Colby College, 4450 Mayflower Hill, Waterville, ME 04901, 800-723-4033, fax: 207-872-3474.

COLBY-SAWYER COLLEGE
New London, New Hampshire

About the Institution Independent, coed. Degrees awarded: A, B. Offers 16 undergraduate majors. Total enrollment: 755 (34% state residents). Freshmen: 227.

Undergraduate Expenses (1997–98) Comprehensive fee of $22,550 includes tuition ($16,310) and college room and board ($6240). College room only: $3430.

Applications 87% of all full-time undergraduates enrolled in fall 1996 applied for aid; of these, 89% were judged to have need according to Federal Methodology, of whom 91% were aided. *Financial aid deadline (priority):* 3/1. *Financial aid forms:* FAFSA, institutional form required. *Admission application deadline:* rolling.

Summary of Aid to Needy Students *From gift & self-help combined:* Average need met: 77%. Average amount awarded: $12,994 (72% gift aid, 28% self-help). *Gift aid:* Total: $4,808,914 (89% from college's own funds, 2% from other college-administered sources, 9% from external sources). 304 Federal Work-Study jobs (averaging $1121); 26 part-time jobs.

Need-Based Scholarships & Grants Pell, FSEOG, state, private, college/university.

Loans Perkins, PLUS, Stafford, Unsubsidized Stafford, private, college/university long-term loans ($2800 average).

Non-Need Awards In 1996, a total of 154 non-need awards were made. *Academic Interests/Achievement Awards:* 63 ($219,250 total): general academic. *Creative Arts/Performance Awards:* 33 ($108,170 total): general creative, art/fine arts, music. *Special Achievements/Activities Awards:* 39 ($195,000 total): community service, leadership. *Special Characteristics Awards:* 19 ($290,425 total): children of educators, children of faculty/staff.

Other Money-Saving Options Accelerated degree, cooperative Army ROTC, cooperative Air Force ROTC, off-campus living (after sophomore year). *Waivers:* full or partial for employees or children of employees.

Contact Office of Financial Aid, Colby-Sawyer College, 100 Main Street, New London, NH 03257-4648, 603-526-3000.

COLEGIO BIBLICO PENTECOSTAL
St. Just, Puerto Rico

About the Institution Independent/religious. Degrees awarded: B.

Applications 76% of all full-time undergraduates enrolled in fall 1996 applied for aid; of these, 92% were judged to have need according to Federal Methodology, of whom 100% were aided. *Financial aid deadline (priority):* 5/1. *Financial aid forms:* FAFSA required. Institutional form required for some.

Summary of Aid to Needy Students *From gift & self-help combined:* Average need met: 90%. Average amount awarded: $2417. *Gift aid:* Total: $145,000 (3% from college's own funds, 97% from external sources).

Need-Based Scholarships & Grants Pell, state.

Non-Need Awards Not offered.

Contact Mr. Eric Ayala, Director of Financial Aid, Colegio Biblico Pentecostal, St. Just, PR 00978-0901, 787-761-0640.

COLEGIO UNIVERSITARIO DEL ESTE
Carolina, Puerto Rico

About the Institution Independent, coed. Degrees awarded: A, B. Offers 12 undergraduate majors. Total enrollment: 4,405 (95% commonwealth residents). Freshmen: 2,040.

Undergraduate Expenses (1997–98) Tuition: $3392. Mandatory fees: $120.

Applications *Financial aid deadline (priority):* 7/30. *Financial aid forms:* FAFSA required. *Admission application deadline:* 3/15.

Summary of Aid to Needy Students *From gift & self-help combined:* Average need met: 45%. Average amount awarded: $2433 (94% gift aid, 6% self-help). *Gift aid:* Total: $8,096,242 (1% from college's own funds, 11% from other college-administered sources, 88% from external sources). 471 Federal Work-Study jobs.

Need-Based Scholarships & Grants Pell, FSEOG, state, private, college/university.

Loans Stafford, Unsubsidized Stafford.

Non-Need Awards *Athletic:* available.

Contact Mr. Clotilde Santiago, Director of Financial Aid, Colegio Universitario del Este, Apartado 2010, Carolina, PR 00928, 787-257-7373 Ext. 3300.

COLEMAN COLLEGE
La Mesa, California

About the Institution Independent, coed. Degrees awarded: A, B, M. Offers 5 undergraduate majors. Total enrollment: 930. Undergraduates: 915 (90% state residents). Freshmen: 302.

Undergraduate Expenses (1996–97) Tuition: $5000 (minimum).

Applications Of all full-time undergraduates enrolled in fall 1996, 95% of those judged to have need according to Federal Methodology were aided. *Financial aid deadline:* continuous. *Financial aid forms:* FAFSA, institutional form required; CSS Financial Aid PROFILE acceptable. State form required for some. *Admission application deadline:* rolling.

Summary of Aid to Needy Students *From gift & self-help combined:* Average need met: 60%. Average amount awarded: $4380 (25% gift aid, 75% self-help). *Gift aid:* Total: $828,800 (3% from college's own funds, 12% from other college-administered sources, 85% from external sources). 25 Federal Work-Study jobs (averaging $2000).

Need-Based Scholarships & Grants Pell, FSEOG, state, college/university.

Loans PLUS, Stafford, Unsubsidized Stafford, college/university long-term loans.

Non-Need Awards In 1996, a total of 8 non-need awards were made. *Academic Interests/Achievement Awards:* 7 ($28,000 total): general academic. *Special Characteristics Awards:* 1 ($800 total): children and siblings of alumni.

Other Money-Saving Options Accelerated degree. *Payment Plans:* guaranteed tuition, installment. *Waivers:* full or partial for employees or children of employees.

Contact Financial Aid Office, Coleman College, La Mesa, CA 91942-1532, 619-465-3990.

COLGATE UNIVERSITY
Hamilton, New York

About the Institution Independent, coed. Degrees awarded: B, M. Offers 50 undergraduate majors. Total enrollment: 2,859. Undergraduates: 2,849 (34% state residents). Freshmen: 721.

Undergraduate Expenses (1997–98 estimated) Comprehensive fee of $28,880 includes tuition ($22,605), mandatory fees ($165), and college room and board ($6110). College room only: $2950.

Applications Of all full-time undergraduates enrolled in fall 1996, 88% of those who applied for aid were judged to have need according to Federal Methodology, of whom 100% were aided. *Financial aid deadline (priority):* 2/1. *Financial aid forms:* FAFSA, CSS Financial Aid PROFILE, institutional form required. State form required for some. *Regular admission application deadline:* 1/15. Early decision deadline:

Summary of Aid to Needy Students *From gift & self-help combined:* Average need met: 97%. Average amount awarded: $18,515 (80% gift aid, 20% self-help). *Gift aid:* Total: $18,699,977 (90% from college's own funds, 2% from other college-administered sources, 8% from external sources). 918 Federal Work-Study jobs (averaging $1212); 865 part-time jobs.

Need-Based Scholarships & Grants Pell, FSEOG, state, college/university.

Loans Perkins, PLUS, Stafford, Unsubsidized Stafford, private.

Non-Need Awards Not offered.

Other Money-Saving Options *Payment Plans:* tuition prepayment, installment, deferred payment. *Waivers:* full or partial for employees or children of employees.

Contact Mrs. Marcelle Tyburski, Director of Financial Aid, Colgate University, 13 Oak Drive, Hamilton, NY 13346-1386, 315-824-7431.

COLLEGE FOR LIFELONG LEARNING OF THE UNIVERSITY SYSTEM OF NEW HAMPSHIRE
Concord, New Hampshire

See University System College for Lifelong Learning

COLLEGE MISERICORDIA
Dallas, Pennsylvania

About the Institution Independent/religious, coed. Degrees awarded: B, M. Offers 28 undergraduate majors. Total enrollment: 1,736. Undergraduates: 1,590 (80% state residents). Freshmen: 248.

Undergraduate Expenses (1997–98) Comprehensive fee of $19,760 includes tuition ($13,120), mandatory fees ($710), and college room and board ($5930). College room only: $3400.

Applications 96% of all full-time undergraduates enrolled in fall 1996 applied for aid; of these, 97% were judged to have need according to Federal Methodology, of whom 100% were aided. *Financial aid deadline (priority):* 3/1. *Financial aid forms:* FAFSA, institutional form required; CSS Financial Aid PROFILE acceptable. State form required for some. *Admission application deadline:* rolling.

Summary of Aid to Needy Students *From gift & self-help combined:* Average need met: 68%. Average amount awarded: $7315 (46% gift aid, 54% self-help). *Gift aid:* Total: $3,790,535 (39% from college's own funds, 6% from other college-administered sources, 55% from external sources). 144 Federal Work-Study jobs (averaging $1000); 160 part-time jobs.

Need-Based Scholarships & Grants Pell, FSEOG, state, private, college/university.

Loans Perkins, PLUS, Stafford, Unsubsidized Stafford, Federal Nursing, private.

Non-Need Awards In 1996, a total of 542 non-need awards were made. *Academic Interests/Achievement Awards:* 542 ($2,020,000 total): general academic, humanities.

Other Money-Saving Options Accelerated degree, co-op program, cooperative Army ROTC, cooperative Air Force ROTC, off-campus living. *Payment Plans:* installment; deferred payment. *Waivers:* full or partial for employees or children of employees.

Contact Ms. Jane F. Dessoye, Executive Director of Financial Aid and Admissions, College Misericordia, 301 Lake Street, Dallas, PA 18612-1098, 717-674-6313, fax: 717-675-2441.

COLLEGE OF AERONAUTICS
Flushing, New York

About the Institution Independent, primarily men. Degrees awarded: A, B. Offers 10 undergraduate majors. Total enrollment: 960 (94% state residents). Freshmen: 310.

Undergraduate Expenses (1996–97) Tuition: $7990. Mandatory fees: $250. College room only: $3365.

Applications Of all full-time undergraduates enrolled in fall 1996, 89% of those who applied for aid were judged to have need according to Federal Methodology, of whom 95% were aided. *Financial aid deadline (priority):* 3/1. *Financial aid forms:* FAFSA required; CSS Financial Aid PROFILE acceptable. State form required for some. *Admission application deadline:* rolling.

Summary of Aid to Needy Students *From gift & self-help combined:* Average need met: 79%. Average amount awarded: $10,870 (69% gift aid, 31% self-help). *Gift aid:* Total: $3,635,675 (17% from college's own funds, 3% from other college-administered sources, 80% from external sources). 45 Federal Work-Study jobs (averaging $1300); 234 part-time jobs.

Need-Based Scholarships & Grants Pell, FSEOG, state, private, college/university.

Loans Perkins, PLUS, Stafford, Unsubsidized Stafford, college/university short-term loans ($700 average).

Non-Need Awards *Academic Interests/Achievement Awards:* general academic.

Other Money-Saving Options Air Force ROTC, off-campus living. *Payment Plan:* installment.

Contact Office of Financial Aid, College of Aeronautics, La Guardia Airport, 8681 23rd Ave., Flushing, NY 11371, 718-429-6600.

COLLEGE OF ASSOCIATED ARTS
St. Paul, Minnesota

See College of Visual Arts

COLLEGE OF CHARLESTON
Charleston, South Carolina

About the Institution State-supported, coed. Degrees awarded: B. Offers 37 undergraduate majors. Total enrollment: 11,053. Undergraduates: 9,060 (70% state residents). Freshmen: 1,502.

Undergraduate Expenses (1996–97) State resident tuition: $3190. Nonresident tuition: $6380. College room and board: $3340 (minimum). College room only: $2350.

Applications 83% of all full-time undergraduates enrolled in fall 1996 applied for aid; of these, 76% were judged to have need according to Federal Methodology, of whom 96% were aided. *Financial aid deadline (priority):* 3/15. *Financial aid forms:* financial aid transcript (for transfers) required; FAFSA acceptable. *Admission application deadline:* 7/1.

Summary of Aid to Needy Students *From gift & self-help combined:* Average amount awarded: $7369 (37% gift aid, 63% self-help). *Gift aid:* Total: $10,922,006 (26% from college's own funds, 12% from other college-administered sources, 62% from external sources). 157 Federal Work-Study jobs (averaging $1000); 542 part-time jobs.

Need-Based Scholarships & Grants Pell, FSEOG, state, private, college/university.

Loans Perkins, PLUS, Stafford, Unsubsidized Stafford, private, college/university short-term loans ($250 average).

Non-Need Awards In 1996, a total of 908 non-need awards were made. *Academic Interests/Achievement Awards:* 501 ($1,587,057 total). *Creative Arts/Performance Awards:* 63 ($45,995 total): art/fine arts, music, performing arts, theater/drama. *Special Achievements/Activities Awards:* 23 ($31,380 total): community service, leadership, religious involvement. *Special Characteristics Awards:* 135 ($194,731 total): adult students, children and siblings of alumni, children of faculty/staff, children with a deceased or disabled parent, ethnic background, handicapped students, international students, local/state students, religious affiliation, spouses of deceased or disabled public servants. *Athletic:* Total: 186 ($674,372); Men: 99 ($339,647); Women: 87 ($334,725).

Other Money-Saving Options Accelerated degree, co-op program, cooperative Air Force ROTC, off-campus living. *Payment Plan:* installment. *Waivers:* full or partial for senior citizens.

Contact Mr. Robert N. Kersey, IV, Associate Director of Student Financial Aid, College of Charleston, 66 George Street, Charleston, SC 29424-0002, 803-953-5540, fax: 803-953-7192.

COLLEGE OF GREAT FALLS
Great Falls, Montana

See University of Great Falls

COLLEGE OF INSURANCE
New York, New York

About the Institution Independent, coed. Degrees awarded: A, B, M. Offers 3 undergraduate majors. Total enrollment: 2,379. Undergraduates: 2,204 (80% state residents). Freshmen: 61.

Undergraduate Expenses (1996–97) Comprehensive fee of $20,740 includes tuition ($12,730), mandatory fees ($360), and college room and board ($7650).

Applications 88% of all full-time undergraduates enrolled in fall 1996 applied for aid; of these, 94% were judged to have need according to

Federal Methodology, of whom 100% were aided. *Financial aid deadline (priority):* 6/1. *Financial aid forms:* FAFSA required. State form, institutional form required for some. *Regular admission application deadline:* 5/1. Early decision deadline: 12/1.

Summary of Aid to Needy Students *From gift & self-help combined:* Average need met: 88%. Average amount awarded: $14,508 (78% gift aid, 22% self-help). *Gift aid:* Total: $713,645 (48% from college's own funds, 12% from other college-administered sources, 40% from external sources). 7 Federal Work-Study jobs (averaging $2279); 13 part-time jobs.

Need-Based Scholarships & Grants Pell, FSEOG, state, private.

Loans Perkins, PLUS, Stafford, Unsubsidized Stafford, private, college/university short-term loans ($1600 average), college/university long-term loans ($2239 average).

Non-Need Awards *Academic Interests/Achievement Awards:* general academic. *Special Characteristics Awards:* children of faculty/staff.

Other Money-Saving Options Co-op program, off-campus living. *Payment Plan:* installment.

Contact Ms. Marjorie Melikian, Financial Aid Officer, College of Insurance, 101 Murray Street, New York, NY 10007-2165, 212-815-9222, fax: 212-964-3381.

COLLEGE OF MOUNT ST. JOSEPH
Cincinnati, Ohio

About the Institution Independent/religious, coed. Degrees awarded: A, B, M. Offers 40 undergraduate majors. Total enrollment: 2,205. Undergraduates: 2,083 (85% state residents). Freshmen: 227.

Undergraduate Expenses (1997–98) Comprehensive fee of $17,000 includes tuition ($11,900), mandatory fees ($50), and college room and board ($5050). College room only: $2600.

Applications Of all full-time undergraduates enrolled in fall 1996, 89% of those who applied for aid were judged to have need according to Federal Methodology, of whom 100% were aided. *Financial aid deadline (priority):* 3/1. *Financial aid forms:* FAFSA required. *Admission application deadline:* 8/15

Summary of Aid to Needy Students *From gift & self-help combined:* Average need met: 90%. Average amount awarded: $12,892 (50% gift aid, 50% self-help). *Gift aid:* Total: $6,177,729 (63% from college's own funds, 1% from other college-administered sources, 36% from external sources). 74 Federal Work-Study jobs (averaging $1250); 180 part-time jobs.

Need-Based Scholarships & Grants Pell, FSEOG, state, private, college/university.

Loans Perkins, PLUS, Stafford, Unsubsidized Stafford, Federal Nursing, state, private.

Non-Need Awards In 1996, a total of 552 non-need awards were made. *Academic Interests/Achievement Awards:* 465 ($1,477,263 total): general academic. *Creative Arts/Performance Awards:* 28 ($63,680 total): art/fine arts, music. *Special Achievements/Activities Awards:* 36 ($16,890 total): leadership. *Special Characteristics Awards:* 23 ($26,030 total): adult students, children and siblings of alumni.

Other Money-Saving Options Accelerated degree, co-op program, cooperative Army ROTC, cooperative Air Force ROTC, off-campus living (after sophomore year). *Payment Plan:* installment. *Waivers:* full or partial for employees or children of employees and senior citizens.

Contact Ms. Kathryn Kelly, Director of Financial Aid, College of Mount St. Joseph, 5701 Delhi Road, Cincinnati, OH 45233-1670, 513-244-4418, fax: 513-244-4201.

COLLEGE OF MOUNT SAINT VINCENT
Riverdale, New York

About the Institution Independent, coed. Degrees awarded: A, B, M. Offers 35 undergraduate majors. Total enrollment: 1,500. Undergraduates: 1,300 (93% state residents). Freshmen: 207.

Undergraduate Expenses (1997–98) Comprehensive fee of $20,010 includes tuition ($13,520), mandatory fees ($60), and college room and board ($6430).

Applications Of all full-time undergraduates enrolled in fall 1996, 94% of those who applied for aid were judged to have need according to Federal Methodology, of whom 100% were aided. *Financial aid deadline (priority):* 3/15. *Financial aid forms:* FAFSA required; CSS Financial Aid PROFILE, institutional form acceptable. State form required for some. *Regular admission application deadline:* rolling. Early decision deadline: 11/15.

Summary of Aid to Needy Students *From gift & self-help combined:* Average need met: 78%. Average amount awarded: $9052 (59% gift aid, 41% self-help). *Gift aid:* Total: $3,961,167 (37% from college's own funds, 5% from other college-administered sources, 58% from external sources). 248 Federal Work-Study jobs (averaging $700); 50 part-time jobs.

Need-Based Scholarships & Grants Pell, FSEOG, state, private, college/university.

Loans Perkins, PLUS, Stafford, Unsubsidized Stafford, Federal Nursing, private.

Non-Need Awards *Academic Interests/Achievement Awards:* 249 ($1,229,000 total): general academic. *Special Achievements/Activities Awards:* 44 ($181,500 total): leadership. *Special Characteristics Awards:* children and siblings of alumni, children of faculty/staff, siblings of current students.

Other Money-Saving Options Accelerated degree, cooperative Army ROTC, cooperative Air Force ROTC, off-campus living. *Payment Plan:* installment. *Waivers:* full or partial for employees or children of employees and senior citizens.

Contact Ms. Monica Simotas, Director of Financial Aid, College of Mount Saint Vincent, Riverdale, NY 10471-1093, 718-405-3289.

THE COLLEGE OF NEW JERSEY
Trenton, New Jersey

About the Institution State-supported, coed. Degrees awarded: B, M. Offers 45 undergraduate majors. Total enrollment: 6,704. Undergraduates: 5,744 (95% state residents). Freshmen: 1,014.

Undergraduate Expenses (1996–97) State resident tuition: $3465. Nonresident tuition: $6051. Mandatory fees: $981. College room and board: $5544 (minimum).

Applications *Financial aid deadline (priority):* 4/1. *Financial aid forms:* FAFSA, institutional form required; CSS Financial Aid PROFILE acceptable. *Regular admission application deadline:* 3/1. Early decision deadline: 11/15.

Summary of Aid to Needy Students 211 Federal Work-Study jobs (averaging $950); 1,272 part-time jobs.

Need-Based Scholarships & Grants Pell, FSEOG, state, college/university.

Loans Perkins, PLUS, Stafford, Unsubsidized Stafford, Federal Nursing, state, college/university short-term loans ($100 average).

Non-Need Awards In 1996, a total of 1,592 non-need awards were made. *Academic Interests/Achievement Awards:* 1,382 ($1,906,990 total): general academic, engineering/technologies. *Creative Arts/Performance Awards:* 17 ($21,000 total): music. *Special Characteristics Awards:* 193 ($458,966 total): members of minorities.

Other Money-Saving Options Cooperative Army ROTC, cooperative Air Force ROTC, off-campus living. *Payment Plans:* installment, deferred payment. *Waivers:* full or partial for senior citizens.

Contact Financial Aid Office, The College of New Jersey, Trenton, NJ 08650-4700, 609-771-2211.

COLLEGE OF NEW ROCHELLE
New Rochelle, New York

About the Institution Independent, primarily women. Degrees awarded: B, M. Offers 38 undergraduate majors. Total enrollment: 2,698. Undergraduates: 1,116 (90% state residents). Freshmen: 167.

Undergraduate Expenses (1997–98) Comprehensive fee of $16,800 includes tuition ($11,000), mandatory fees ($100), and college room and board ($5700).

Applications *Financial aid deadline (priority):* 9/1. *Financial aid forms:* FAFSA, state form, institutional form, federal income tax form, state income tax form required for some required; CSS Financial Aid PROFILE acceptable. *Admission application deadline:* rolling.

Summary of Aid to Needy Students *From gift & self-help combined:* Average need met: 100%. Average amount awarded: $12,870 (53% gift aid, 47% self-help). *Gift aid:* Total: $5,095,189 (54% from college's own funds, 27% from other college-administered sources, 19% from external sources). 473 Federal Work-Study jobs (averaging $1500); 46 part-time jobs.

Need-Based Scholarships & Grants Pell, FSEOG, state, private, college/university.

Loans Perkins, PLUS, Stafford, Unsubsidized Stafford, Federal Nursing.

Non-Need Awards In 1996, a total of 240 non-need awards were made. *Academic Interests/Achievement Awards:* 163 ($653,352 total): general academic, area/ethnic studies, biological sciences, business, communication, education, English, foreign languages, health fields, humanities, mathematics, physical sciences, religion/biblical studies, social sciences. *Creative Arts/Performance Awards:* 30 ($120,000 total): general creative, applied art and design, art/fine arts, cinema/film/broadcasting, creative writing, dance, debating, journalism/publications, music, performing arts, theater/drama. *Special Achievements/Activities Awards:* 30 ($120,000 total): general special achievements/activities, community service, hobbies/interest, Junior Miss, leadership, memberships. *Special Characteristics Awards:* 17 ($130,759 total): general special characteristics, children of current students, children of faculty/staff, out-of-state students, parents of current students, siblings of current students, spouses of current students.

Other Money-Saving Options Accelerated degree, co-op program, off-campus living. *Payment Plan:* tuition prepayment. *Waivers:* full or partial for employees or children of employees and senior citizens.

Contact Dr. Ronald Pollack, Director of Financial Aid, College of New Rochelle, 29 Castle Place, New Rochelle, NY 10805-2339, 914-654-5225, fax: 914-654-5554.

COLLEGE OF NOTRE DAME
Belmont, California

About the Institution Independent/religious, coed. Degrees awarded: B, M. Offers 41 undergraduate majors. Total enrollment: 1,743. Undergraduates: 973 (91% state residents). Freshmen: 134.

Undergraduate Expenses (1997–98) Comprehensive fee of $19,760 includes tuition ($14,976) and college room and board ($4784 minimum).

Applications 76% of all full-time undergraduates enrolled in fall 1996 applied for aid; of these, 96% were judged to have need according to Federal Methodology, of whom 100% were aided. *Financial aid deadline*

(priority): 3/2. *Financial aid forms:* FAFSA, institutional form required; CSS Financial Aid PROFILE acceptable. State form required for some. *Admission application deadline:* 6/1.

Summary of Aid to Needy Students *From gift & self-help combined:* Average need met: 80%. Average amount awarded: $17,458 (51% gift aid, 49% self-help). *Gift aid:* Total: $4,058,653 (69% from college's own funds, 16% from other college-administered sources, 15% from external sources). 200 Federal Work-Study jobs (averaging $1500); 10 part-time jobs.

Need-Based Scholarships & Grants Pell, FSEOG, state, private, college/university.

Loans Perkins, PLUS, Stafford, Unsubsidized Stafford, college/university short-term loans ($200 average).

Non-Need Awards *Academic Interests/Achievement Awards:* ($75,000 total): general academic. *Creative Arts/Performance Awards:* ($20,000 total): music. *Special Achievements/Activities Awards:* 30 ($75,000 total): general special achievements/activities.

Other Money-Saving Options Accelerated degree, co-op program, cooperative Army ROTC, cooperative Naval ROTC, cooperative Air Force ROTC, off-campus living. *Payment Plan:* installment. *Waivers:* full or partial for employees or children of employees.

Contact Office of Financial Aid, College of Notre Dame, 1500 Ralston Avenue, Belmont, CA 94404, 415-508-3509, fax: 415-637-0493.

COLLEGE OF NOTRE DAME OF MARYLAND
Baltimore, Maryland

About the Institution Independent/religious, women. Degrees awarded: B, M. Offers 48 undergraduate majors. Total enrollment: 3,237. Undergraduates: 2,519 (71% state residents). Freshmen: 161.

Undergraduate Expenses (1997–98) Comprehensive fee of $19,495 includes tuition ($13,125), mandatory fees ($240), and college room and board ($6130).

Applications 69% of all full-time undergraduates enrolled in fall 1996 applied for aid; of these, 91% were judged to have need according to Federal Methodology, of whom 100% were aided. *Financial aid deadline (priority):* 2/15. *Financial aid forms:* FAFSA, institutional form required. *Regular admission application deadline:* 2/15. Early action deadline: 11/15.

Summary of Aid to Needy Students *From gift & self-help combined:* Average need met: 100%. Average amount awarded: $11,573 (73% gift aid, 27% self-help). *Gift aid:* Total: $3,374,101 (71% from college's own funds, 2% from other college-administered sources, 27% from external sources). 297 Federal Work-Study jobs (averaging $700); part-time jobs.

Need-Based Scholarships & Grants Pell, FSEOG, state, private, college/university.

Loans Perkins, PLUS, Stafford, Unsubsidized Stafford, private, college/university long-term loans ($1938 average).

Non-Need Awards In 1996, a total of 350 non-need awards were made. *Academic Interests/Achievement Awards:* 268 ($1,442,480 total): general academic. *Creative Arts/Performance Awards:* 35 ($83,500 total): general creative, art/fine arts. *Special Achievements/Activities Awards:* 46 ($229,284 total): leadership, religious involvement. *Special Characteristics Awards:* 1 ($13,100 total): international students.

Other Money-Saving Options Accelerated degree, cooperative Army ROTC, off-campus living. *Payment Plan:* installment. *Waivers:* full or partial for employees or children of employees.

Contact Ms. Teresa Drzewiecki, Director of Financial Aid, College of Notre Dame of Maryland, 4701 North Charles Street, Baltimore, MD 21210-2476, 410-532-5749, fax: 410-532-6287.

COLLEGE OF OUR LADY OF THE ELMS
Chicopee, Massachusetts

About the Institution Independent/religious, women. Degrees awarded: B, M. Offers 45 undergraduate majors. Total enrollment: 1,133. Undergraduates: 961 (94% state residents). Freshmen: 114.

Undergraduate Expenses (1996–97) Comprehensive fee of $17,950 includes tuition ($12,450), mandatory fees ($500), and college room and board ($5000).

Applications Of all full-time undergraduates enrolled in fall 1996, 95% of those who applied for aid were judged to have need according to Federal Methodology, of whom 100% were aided. *Financial aid deadline (priority):* 2/15. *Financial aid forms:* FAFSA, institutional form required. CSS Financial Aid PROFILE, state form required for some. *Admission application deadline:* rolling.

Summary of Aid to Needy Students *From gift & self-help combined:* Average need met: 76%. Average amount awarded: $9205 (42% gift aid, 58% self-help). *Gift aid:* Total: $1,702,063 (43% from college's own funds, 31% from other college-administered sources, 26% from external sources). 130 Federal Work-Study jobs (averaging $1250); 3 part-time jobs.

Need-Based Scholarships & Grants Pell, FSEOG, state, private, college/university.

Loans Perkins, PLUS, Stafford, Unsubsidized Stafford, state.

Non-Need Awards In 1996, a total of 95 non-need awards were made. *Academic Interests/Achievement Awards:* 95 ($300,763 total).

Other Money-Saving Options Accelerated degree, cooperative Army ROTC, cooperative Air Force ROTC, off-campus living. *Payment Plans:* tuition prepayment, installment. *Waivers:* full or partial for employees or children of employees.

Contact Ms. Lisa Prolman, Financial Aid Counselor, College of Our Lady of the Elms, 291 Springfield Street, Chicopee, MA 01013-2839, 413-594-2761, fax: 413-594-2781.

COLLEGE OF SAINT BENEDICT
Saint Joseph, Minnesota

About the Institution Independent/religious, women. Degrees awarded: B. Offers 55 undergraduate majors. Total enrollment: 1,958 (83% state residents). Freshmen: 499.

Undergraduate Expenses (1996–97) Comprehensive fee of $18,537 includes tuition ($13,858), mandatory fees ($138), and college room and board ($4541). College room only: $2430.

Applications 89% of all full-time undergraduates enrolled in fall 1996 applied for aid; of these, 79% were judged to have need according to Federal Methodology, of whom 100% were aided. *Financial aid deadline (priority):* 8/15. *Financial aid forms:* FAFSA, institutional form required; CSS Financial Aid PROFILE acceptable. *Admission application deadline:* rolling.

Summary of Aid to Needy Students *From gift & self-help combined:* Average need met: 96%. Average amount awarded: $13,500 (59% gift aid, 41% self-help). *Gift aid:* Total: $10,545,153 (58% from college's own funds, 4% from other college-administered sources, 38% from external sources). 512 Federal Work-Study jobs (averaging $1575); 367 part-time jobs.

Need-Based Scholarships & Grants Pell, FSEOG, state, private, college/university.

Loans Perkins, PLUS, Stafford, Unsubsidized Stafford, state, private, MN SELF Loans.

Non-Need Awards In 1996, a total of 502 non-need awards were made. *Academic Interests/Achievement Awards:* 351 ($1,328,312 total): general academic. *Creative Arts/Performance Awards:* 66 ($36,400 total): art/fine arts, music, theater/drama. *Special Achievements/*

Activities Awards: 34 ($29,575 total): Junior Miss, memberships. *Special Characteristics Awards:* 51 ($142,203 total): ethnic background, international students, members of minorities.

Other Money-Saving Options Cooperative Army ROTC, off-campus living (after freshman year). *Payment Plans:* tuition prepayment, installment, deferred payment. *Waivers:* full or partial for employees or children of employees.

Contact Ms. Jane Haugen, Director of Financial Aid, College of Saint Benedict, 37 South College Avenue, Saint Joseph, MN 56374-2099, 320-363-5388, fax: 320-363-6099.

COLLEGE OF ST. CATHERINE
St. Paul, Minnesota

About the Institution Independent/religious, women. Degrees awarded: B, M. Offers 63 undergraduate majors. Total enrollment: 2,695. Undergraduates: 2,248 (85% state residents). Freshmen: 216.

Undergraduate Expenses (1996–97) Comprehensive fee of $18,284 includes tuition ($13,472), mandatory fees ($230), and college room and board ($4582). College room only: $2590.

Applications 86% of all full-time undergraduates enrolled in fall 1996 applied for aid; of these, 88% were judged to have need according to Federal Methodology, of whom 100% were aided. *Financial aid deadline (priority):* 4/1. *Financial aid forms:* FAFSA, institutional form required. *Admission application deadline:* 8/15.

Summary of Aid to Needy Students *From gift & self-help combined:* Average need met: 100%. Average amount awarded: $13,285 (54% gift aid, 46% self-help). *Gift aid:* Total: $7,388,241 (52% from college's own funds, 7% from other college-administered sources, 41% from external sources). 160 Federal Work-Study jobs (averaging $1412); 601 part-time jobs.

Need-Based Scholarships & Grants Pell, FSEOG, state, private, college/university.

Loans Perkins, PLUS, Stafford, Unsubsidized Stafford, Federal Nursing, state, private, college/university long-term loans ($4172 average).

Non-Need Awards In 1996, a total of 269 non-need awards were made. *Academic Interests/Achievement Awards:* 181 ($926,070 total): general academic. *Creative Arts/Performance Awards:* 23 ($26,270 total): music. *Special Achievements/Activities Awards:* 17 ($50,750 total): general special achievements/activities, community service, memberships. *Special Characteristics Awards:* 48 ($387,653 total): children and siblings of alumni, children of faculty/staff, international students, siblings of current students.

Other Money-Saving Options Accelerated degree, cooperative Air Force ROTC, off-campus living. *Payment Plan:* installment. *Waivers:* full or partial for employees or children of employees and senior citizens.

Contact Ms. Pam Johnson, Director of Financial Aid, College of St. Catherine, Mail #F-11, 2004 Randolph Avenue, St. Paul, MN 55105-1794, 612-690-6540, fax: 612-690-6024.

COLLEGE OF SAINT ELIZABETH
Morristown, New Jersey

About the Institution Independent/religious, primarily women. Degrees awarded: B, M. Offers 40 undergraduate majors. Total enrollment: 1,694. Undergraduates: 1,385 (94% state residents). Freshmen: 124.

Undergraduate Expenses (1997–98) Comprehensive fee of $19,010 includes tuition ($12,500), mandatory fees ($560), and college room and board ($5950).

Applications 90% of all full-time undergraduates enrolled in fall 1996 applied for aid; of these, 26% were judged to have need according to Federal Methodology, of whom 100% were aided. *Financial aid deadline*

(priority): 4/15. *Financial aid forms:* FAFSA required; institutional form acceptable. *Regular admission application deadline:* rolling. Early decision deadline: 11/15.

Summary of Aid to Needy Students *From gift & self-help combined:* Average need met: 94%. Average amount awarded: $12,244 (83% gift aid, 17% self-help). *Gift aid:* Total: $3,077,260. 14 Federal Work-Study jobs (averaging $1000); 214 part-time jobs.

Need-Based Scholarships & Grants Pell, FSEOG, state, private, college/university.

Loans Perkins, PLUS, Stafford, Unsubsidized Stafford, state.

Non-Need Awards *Academic Interests/Achievement Awards:* general academic. *Creative Arts/Performance Awards:* art/fine arts. *Special Achievements/Activities Awards:* Junior Miss. *Special Characteristics Awards:* children and siblings of alumni, handicapped students, international students.

Other Money-Saving Options Accelerated degree, off-campus living. *Payment Plan:* installment. *Waivers:* full or partial for employees or children of employees and senior citizens.

Contact Office of Financial Aid, College of Saint Elizabeth, 2 Convent Road, Morristown, NJ 07961, 973-290-4000.

COLLEGE OF ST. FRANCIS
Joliet, Illinois

About the Institution Independent/religious, coed. Degrees awarded: B, M. Offers 37 undergraduate majors. Total enrollment: 1,500. Undergraduates: 1,300 (97% state residents). Freshmen: 143.

Undergraduate Expenses (1997–98 estimated) Comprehensive fee of $16,690 includes tuition ($11,680), mandatory fees ($270), and college room and board ($4740).

Applications 85% of all full-time undergraduates enrolled in fall 1996 applied for aid; of these, 87% were judged to have need according to Federal Methodology, of whom 100% were aided. *Financial aid deadline (priority):* 5/1. *Financial aid forms:* FAFSA, institutional form required. *Admission application deadline:* 7/1.

Summary of Aid to Needy Students *From gift & self-help combined:* Average need met: 100%. Average amount awarded: $11,221 (64% gift aid, 36% self-help). *Gift aid:* Total: $4,170,236 (57% from college's own funds, 36% from other college-administered sources, 7% from external sources). 155 Federal Work-Study jobs (averaging $1638); 210 part-time jobs.

Need-Based Scholarships & Grants Pell, FSEOG, state, private, college/university.

Loans Perkins, PLUS, Stafford, Unsubsidized Stafford.

Non-Need Awards In 1996, a total of 809 non-need awards were made. *Academic Interests/Achievement Awards:* 414 ($1,236,947 total): general academic, biological sciences. *Creative Arts/Performance Awards:* 18 ($18,000 total): music. *Special Achievements/Activities Awards:* 12 ($14,400 total): cheerleading/drum major. *Special Characteristics Awards:* 133 ($144,740 total): children of educators, ethnic background, siblings of current students. *Athletic:* Total: 232 ($1,161,015); Men: 167 ($846,665); Women: 65 ($314,350).

Other Money-Saving Options Accelerated degree, co-op program, off-campus living. *Payment Plan:* installment. *Waivers:* full or partial for children of alumni and employees or children of employees.

Contact Office of Financial Aid, College of St. Francis, 500 North Wilcox, Joliet, IL 60435-6188, 815-740-3360.

COLLEGE OF ST. JOSEPH
Rutland, Vermont

About the Institution Independent/religious, coed. Degrees awarded: A, B, M. Offers 26 undergraduate majors. Total enrollment: 478. Undergraduates: 353 (66% state residents). Freshmen: 70.

Undergraduate Expenses (1997–98 estimated) Comprehensive fee of $15,900 includes tuition ($10,000), mandatory fees ($100), and college room and board ($5800).

Applications *Financial aid deadline (priority):* 3/1. *Financial aid forms:* FAFSA required; CSS Financial Aid PROFILE acceptable. *Admission application deadline:* rolling.

Summary of Aid to Needy Students *From gift & self-help combined:* Average need met: 87%. Average amount awarded: $9420 (42% gift aid, 58% self-help). *Gift aid:* Total: $669,000 (48% from college's own funds, 10% from other college-administered sources, 42% from external sources). 45 Federal Work-Study jobs (averaging $1000); 13 part-time jobs.

Need-Based Scholarships & Grants Pell, FSEOG, state, college/university.

Loans Perkins, PLUS, Stafford, Unsubsidized Stafford.

Non-Need Awards *Academic Interests/Achievement Awards:* 25 ($31,000 total): general academic. *Special Achievements/Activities Awards:* community service, leadership. *Special Characteristics Awards:* religious affiliation. *Athletic:* Total: 35 ($88,000); Men: 19 ($51,000); Women: 16 ($37,000).

Other Money-Saving Options Accelerated degree. *Payment Plan:* installment. *Waivers:* full or partial for employees or children of employees and senior citizens.

Contact Ms. Susan Sampson, Financial Aid Coordinator, College of St. Joseph, Rutland, VT 05701-3899, 802-773-5900.

COLLEGE OF SAINT MARY
Omaha, Nebraska

About the Institution Independent/religious, women. Degrees awarded: A, B. Offers 33 undergraduate majors. Total enrollment: 1,069 (84% state residents). Freshmen: 128.

Undergraduate Expenses (1997–98) Comprehensive fee of $16,104 includes tuition ($11,434), mandatory fees ($380), and college room and board ($4290 minimum).

Applications 94% of all full-time undergraduates enrolled in fall 1996 applied for aid; of these, 77% were judged to have need according to Federal Methodology, of whom 100% were aided. *Financial aid deadline (priority):* 3/1. *Financial aid forms:* FAFSA, institutional form required; CSS Financial Aid PROFILE, state form acceptable. *Admission application deadline:* rolling.

Summary of Aid to Needy Students *From gift & self-help combined:* Average amount awarded: $11,430 (64% gift aid, 36% self-help). *Gift aid:* Total: $2,763,681 (78% from college's own funds, 7% from other college-administered sources, 15% from external sources). 96 Federal Work-Study jobs (averaging $1100); 21 part-time jobs.

Need-Based Scholarships & Grants Pell, FSEOG, state, private, college/university.

Loans Perkins, PLUS, Stafford, Unsubsidized Stafford, Federal Nursing, private, college/university long-term loans ($1000 average).

Non-Need Awards In 1996, a total of 578 non-need awards were made. *Academic Interests/Achievement Awards:* 331 ($951,699 total): general academic. *Special Achievements/Activities Awards:* 126 ($127,100 total): leadership, religious involvement. *Special Characteristics Awards:* 56 ($122,250 total): out-of-state students, parents of current students, siblings of current students, spouses of current students. *Athletic:* Total: 65 ($319,689).

Other Money-Saving Options Cooperative Army ROTC, cooperative Air Force ROTC, off-campus living (after junior year). *Payment Plans:* installment, deferred payment. *Waivers:* full or partial for employees or children of employees and senior citizens.

Contact Office of Financial Aid, College of Saint Mary, 1901 South 72nd Street, Omaha, NE 68124-2377, 402-399-2400.

COLLEGE OF ST. SCHOLASTICA
Duluth, Minnesota

About the Institution Independent/religious, coed. Degrees awarded: B, M. Offers 45 undergraduate majors. Total enrollment: 2,101. Undergraduates: 1,474 (88% state residents). Freshmen: 292.

Undergraduate Expenses (1996–97) Comprehensive fee of $16,938 includes tuition ($13,056), mandatory fees ($75), and college room and board ($3807 minimum). College room only: $1860 (minimum).

Applications 86% of all full-time undergraduates enrolled in fall 1996 applied for aid; of these, 97% were judged to have need according to Federal Methodology, of whom 100% were aided. *Financial aid deadline (priority):* 3/15. *Financial aid forms:* state form required; CSS Financial Aid PROFILE acceptable. FAFSA, institutional form required for some. *Admission application deadline:* rolling.

Summary of Aid to Needy Students *From gift & self-help combined:* Average need met: 87%. Average amount awarded: $11,412 (49% gift aid, 51% self-help). *Gift aid:* Total: $6,112,097 (55% from college's own funds, 34% from other college-administered sources, 11% from external sources). 356 Federal Work-Study jobs (averaging $1350).

Need-Based Scholarships & Grants Pell, FSEOG, state, private, college/university.

Loans Perkins, PLUS, Stafford, Unsubsidized Stafford, Federal Nursing, state, private.

Non-Need Awards In 1996, a total of 426 non-need awards were made. *Academic Interests/Achievement Awards:* 318 ($462,422 total): general academic. *Creative Arts/Performance Awards:* 8 ($2175 total): music. *Special Characteristics Awards:* 100 ($738,003 total): children and siblings of alumni, children of faculty/staff, international students, ROTC participants.

Other Money-Saving Options Cooperative Army ROTC, cooperative Air Force ROTC, off-campus living. *Payment Plan:* installment. *Waivers:* full or partial for employees or children of employees and senior citizens.

Contact Office of Financial Aid, College of St. Scholastica, 1200 Kenwood Avenue, Duluth, MN 55811-4199, 218-723-6000.

COLLEGE OF SANTA FE
Santa Fe, New Mexico

About the Institution Independent, coed. Degrees awarded: A, B, M. Offers 46 undergraduate majors. Total enrollment: 1,469. Undergraduates: 1,290 (70% state residents). Freshmen: 165.

Undergraduate Expenses (1997–98) Comprehensive fee of $17,964 includes tuition ($13,000), mandatory fees ($240), and college room and board ($4724). College room only: $2308.

Applications 85% of all full-time undergraduates enrolled in fall 1996 applied for aid; of these, 86% were judged to have need according to Federal Methodology, of whom 100% were aided. *Financial aid deadline (priority):* 3/1. *Financial aid forms:* FAFSA, institutional form, federal verification worksheet and tax returns required; CSS Financial Aid PROFILE acceptable. *Regular admission application deadline:* rolling. Early decision deadline: 11/15.

Summary of Aid to Needy Students *From gift & self-help combined:* Average need met: 78%. Average amount awarded: $10,116 (44% gift aid, 56% self-help). *Gift aid:* Total: $1,996,542 (44% from college's

own funds, 36% from other college-administered sources, 20% from external sources). 141 Federal Work-Study jobs (averaging $2000); 65 part-time jobs.

Need-Based Scholarships & Grants Pell, FSEOG, state, private, college/university.

Loans Perkins, PLUS, Stafford, Unsubsidized Stafford, college/university long-term loans ($1000 average).

Non-Need Awards *Academic Interests/Achievement Awards:* general academic, business, education, humanities, physical sciences, social sciences. *Creative Arts/Performance Awards:* art/fine arts, cinema/film/broadcasting, creative writing, music, performing arts, theater/drama. *Special Characteristics Awards:* adult students, children of faculty/staff.

Other Money-Saving Options Co-op program, off-campus living (after freshman year). *Payment Plan:* installment. *Waivers:* full or partial for employees or children of employees and senior citizens.

Contact Office of Financial Aid, College of Santa Fe, 1600 Saint Michael's Drive, Santa Fe, NM 87505-7634, 505-473-6011.

COLLEGE OF STATEN ISLAND OF THE CITY UNIVERSITY OF NEW YORK
Staten Island, New York

About the Institution State & locally supported, coed. Degrees awarded: A, B, M. Offers 58 undergraduate majors. Total enrollment: 12,208. Undergraduates: 10,709 (95% state residents). Freshmen: 1,816.

Undergraduate Expenses (1996–97) State resident tuition: $3200. Nonresident tuition: $6800. Mandatory fees: $116.

Applications *Financial aid deadline (priority):* 5/29. *Financial aid forms:* FAFSA required. *Admission application deadline:* rolling.

Summary of Aid to Needy Students *From gift & self-help combined:* Average amount awarded: $2679 (67% gift aid, 33% self-help). *Gift aid:* Total: $10,041,000. Federal Work-Study jobs; part-time jobs.

Need-Based Scholarships & Grants Pell, FSEOG, state, private, college/university.

Loans Perkins, PLUS.

Non-Need Awards *Academic Interests/Achievement Awards:* general academic, biological sciences, education, engineering/technologies, health fields, humanities, physical sciences, social sciences. *Creative Arts/Performance Awards:* music, performing arts. *Special Achievements/Activities Awards:* community service, leadership. *Special Characteristics Awards:* general special characteristics, handicapped students.

Other Money-Saving Options *Payment Plan:* deferred payment. *Waivers:* full or partial for employees or children of employees and senior citizens.

Contact Office of Financial Aid, College of Staten Island of the City University of New York, Staten Island, NY 10314-6600, 718-982-2030.

COLLEGE OF THE ATLANTIC
Bar Harbor, Maine

About the Institution Independent, coed. Degrees awarded: B, M. Offers 38 undergraduate majors. Total enrollment: 254. Undergraduates: 251 (22% state residents). Freshmen: 90.

Undergraduate Expenses (1997–98) Comprehensive fee of $21,971 includes tuition ($16,895), mandatory fees ($171), and college room and board ($4905). College room only: $2985.

Applications *Financial aid deadline (priority):* 2/15. *Financial aid forms:* FAFSA, institutional form, financial aid transcript (for transfers) required. *Regular admission application deadline:* 3/1. Early decision deadline: 12/1.

Summary of Aid to Needy Students *From gift & self-help combined:* Average need met: 95%. Average amount awarded: $13,661 (66% gift

aid, 34% self-help). *Gift aid:* Total: $1,569,389 (85% from college's own funds, 2% from other college-administered sources, 13% from external sources). 147 Federal Work-Study jobs (averaging $1800); 6 part-time jobs.

Need-Based Scholarships & Grants Pell, FSEOG, state, college/university.

Loans Perkins, PLUS, Stafford, Unsubsidized Stafford, college/university short-term loans ($200 average), college/university long-term loans ($923 average).

Non-Need Awards In 1996, a total of 6 non-need awards were made. *Academic Interests/Achievement Awards:* 6 ($24,800 total): general academic.

Other Money-Saving Options Accelerated degree, co-op program, off-campus living. *Payment Plan:* installment. *Waivers:* full or partial for employees or children of employees and adult students.

Contact Mrs. Jean Boddy, Financial Aid Office Manager, College of the Atlantic, 105 Eden Street, Bar Harbor, ME 04609-1198, 207-288-5015, fax: 207-288-4126.

COLLEGE OF THE HOLY CROSS
Worcester, Massachusetts

About the Institution Independent/religious, coed. Degrees awarded: B. Offers 42 undergraduate majors. Total enrollment: 2,636 (38% state residents). Freshmen: 699.

Undergraduate Expenses (1997–98) Comprehensive fee of $27,980 includes tuition ($20,700), mandatory fees ($380), and college room and board ($6900).

Applications 63% of all full-time undergraduates enrolled in fall 1996 applied for aid; of these, 96% were judged to have need according to Federal Methodology, of whom 100% were aided. *Financial aid deadline (priority):* 2/1. *Financial aid forms:* FAFSA, CSS Financial Aid PROFILE required. Institutional form required for some. *Regular admission application deadline:* 1/15. Early decision deadline: 12/15.

Summary of Aid to Needy Students *From gift & self-help combined:* Average need met: 100%. Average amount awarded: $14,393 (67% gift aid, 33% self-help). *Gift aid:* Total: $15,638,190 (87% from college's own funds, 2% from other college-administered sources, 11% from external sources). 1,120 Federal Work-Study jobs (averaging $1401); 55 part-time jobs.

Need-Based Scholarships & Grants Pell, FSEOG, state, college/university.

Loans Perkins, PLUS, Stafford, Unsubsidized Stafford, private, college/university short-term loans ($100 average).

Non-Need Awards In 1996, a total of 40 non-need awards were made. *Academic Interests/Achievement Awards:* 8 ($157,500 total): humanities. *Creative Arts/Performance Awards:* 3 ($49,250 total): music. *Special Characteristics Awards:* 29 ($108,000 total): ROTC participants.

Other Money-Saving Options Accelerated degree, Naval ROTC, cooperative Army ROTC, cooperative Air Force ROTC, off-campus living. *Payment Plans:* tuition prepayment, installment. *Waivers:* full or partial for employees or children of employees.

Contact Dr. Francis H. Delaney Jr., Director of Financial Aid, College of the Holy Cross, One College Street, Worcester, MA 01610, 508-793-2265.

COLLEGE OF THE OZARKS
Point Lookout, Missouri

About the Institution Independent/religious, coed. Degrees awarded: B. Offers 71 undergraduate majors. Total enrollment: 1,525 (66% state residents). Freshmen: 314.

Undergraduate Expenses (1997–98) Comprehensive fee of $2350 includes tuition ($0), mandatory fees ($150), and college room and board ($2200).

Applications 100% of all full-time undergraduates enrolled in fall 1996 applied for aid; of these, 90% were judged to have need according to Federal Methodology, of whom 100% were aided. *Financial aid deadline:* Applications processed continuously. *Financial aid forms:* FAFSA, state form required. *Admission application deadline:* rolling.

Summary of Aid to Needy Students *From gift & self-help combined:* Average need met: 100%. *Gift aid:* Total: $11,844,540 (79% from college's own funds, 5% from other college-administered sources, 16% from external sources). 500 Federal Work-Study jobs (averaging $1026); 791 part-time jobs.

Need-Based Scholarships & Grants Pell, FSEOG, state, private, college/university.

Loans College/university short-term loans ($200 average), college/university long-term loans ($2200 average).

Non-Need Awards In 1996, a total of 177 non-need awards were made. *Academic Interests/Achievement Awards:* 129 ($1,316,060 total): general academic. *Special Characteristics Awards:* 0: ROTC participants. *Athletic:* Total: 48 ($105,600); Men: 24 ($52,800); Women: 24 ($52,800).

Other Money-Saving Options Accelerated degree, co-op program, Army ROTC.

Contact Mrs. Helen Youngblood, Director of Financial Aid, College of the Ozarks, Point Lookout, MO 65726, 417-334-6411 Ext. 4290, fax: 417-335-2618.

COLLEGE OF THE SOUTHWEST
Hobbs, New Mexico

About the Institution Independent, coed. Degrees awarded: B, M. Offers 22 undergraduate majors. Total enrollment: 538 (85% state residents). Freshmen: 32.

Undergraduate Expenses (1997–98 estimated) Comprehensive fee of $7934 includes tuition ($4290), mandatory fees ($140), and college room and board ($3504).

Applications 100% of all full-time undergraduates enrolled in fall 1996 applied for aid; of these, 90% were judged to have need according to Federal Methodology, of whom 100% were aided. *Financial aid deadline (priority):* 6/1. *Financial aid forms:* institutional form required; CSS Financial Aid PROFILE, state form acceptable. FAFSA required for some. *Admission application deadline:* rolling.

Summary of Aid to Needy Students *From gift & self-help combined:* Average need met: 79%. Average amount awarded: $8194 (52% gift aid, 48% self-help). *Gift aid:* Total: $1,309,917 (35% from college's own funds, 35% from other college-administered sources, 30% from external sources). 12 Federal Work-Study jobs (averaging $1380); 50 part-time jobs.

Need-Based Scholarships & Grants Pell, FSEOG, state, private, college/university.

Loans PLUS, Stafford, Unsubsidized Stafford, state, private.

Non-Need Awards In 1996, a total of 260 non-need awards were made. *Academic Interests/Achievement Awards:* 156 ($206,847 total). *Creative Arts/Performance Awards:* 3 ($1800 total): music, theater/drama. *Special Achievements/Activities Awards:* 43 ($57,666 total): general special achievements/activities. *Athletic:* Total: 58 ($146,990); Men: 31 ($71,890); Women: 27 ($75,100).

Other Money-Saving Options Accelerated degree, off-campus living. *Payment Plan:* deferred payment. *Waivers:* full or partial for employees or children of employees.

Contact Mr. David L. Arnold, Director of Financial Aid, College of the Southwest, 6610 Lovington Highway, Hobbs, NM 88240-9129, 505-392-6561 Ext. 337.

COLLEGE OF VISUAL ARTS
St. Paul, Minnesota

About the Institution Independent, coed. Degrees awarded: B. Offers 8 undergraduate majors. Total enrollment: 203 (90% state residents). Freshmen: 32.

Undergraduate Expenses (1997–98) Tuition: $9400.

Applications 86% of all full-time undergraduates enrolled in fall 1996 applied for aid; of these, 89% were judged to have need according to Federal Methodology, of whom 99% were aided. *Financial aid deadline:* Applications processed continuously. *Financial aid forms:* FAFSA, institutional form required. *Admission application deadline:* rolling.

Summary of Aid to Needy Students *From gift & self-help combined:* Average amount awarded: $6500 (44% gift aid, 56% self-help). *Gift aid:* Total: $532,632 (14% from college's own funds, 4% from other college-administered sources, 82% from external sources). 9 Federal Work-Study jobs (averaging $500); 10 part-time jobs.

Need-Based Scholarships & Grants Pell, FSEOG, state, college/university.

Loans PLUS, Stafford, Unsubsidized Stafford, state, private.

Non-Need Awards In 1996, a total of 8 non-need awards were made. *Creative Arts/Performance Awards:* 8 ($20,000 total).

Another Money-Saving Option *Waivers:* full or partial for employees or children of employees.

Contact Ms. Carolyn M. Chesebrough, Director of Financial Aid, College of Visual Arts, 344 Summit Avenue, St. Paul, MN 55102-2124, 612-224-3416, fax: 612-224-8854.

THE COLLEGE OF WEST VIRGINIA
Beckley, West Virginia

About the Institution Independent, coed. Degrees awarded: A, B. Offers 29 undergraduate majors. Total enrollment: 1,983 (98% state residents). Freshmen: 665.

Undergraduate Expenses (1996–97) Tuition: $2760. Mandatory fees: $600. College room only: $1980.

Applications Of all full-time undergraduates enrolled in fall 1996, 75% of those who applied for aid were judged to have need according to Federal Methodology, of whom 71% were aided. *Financial aid deadline (priority):* 5/1. *Financial aid forms:* FAFSA, institutional form required; state form acceptable. *Admission application deadline:* rolling.

Summary of Aid to Needy Students *From gift & self-help combined:* Average need met: 57%. Average amount awarded: $5733 (36% gift aid, 64% self-help). *Gift aid:* Total: $2,895,156 (2% from college's own funds, 29% from other college-administered sources, 69% from external sources). 35 Federal Work-Study jobs (averaging $1500); 29 part-time jobs.

Need-Based Scholarships & Grants Pell, FSEOG, state, private.

Loans PLUS, Stafford, Unsubsidized Stafford, private, college/university long-term loans ($25 average).

Non-Need Awards *Academic Interests/Achievement Awards:* general academic, business, computer science, health fields, humanities, social sciences. *Special Characteristics Awards:* children of faculty/staff. *Athletic:* available.

Other Money-Saving Options Accelerated degree, co-op program, off-campus living. *Payment Plan:* installment. *Waivers:* full or partial for employees or children of employees.

Contact Mr. Roger H. Widmer, Director of Financial Aid, The College of West Virginia, PO Box AG, Beckley, WV 25802-2830, 304-253-7351 Ext. 339.

COLLEGE OF WILLIAM AND MARY
Williamsburg, Virginia

About the Institution State-supported, coed. Degrees awarded: B, M, D, P. Offers 41 undergraduate majors. Total enrollment: 7,722. Undergraduates: 5,618 (66% state residents). Freshmen: 1,333.

Undergraduate Expenses (1997–98) State resident tuition: $2890. Nonresident tuition: $13,262. Mandatory fees: $2142. College room and board: $4586. College room only: $2606.

Applications 47% of all full-time undergraduates enrolled in fall 1996 applied for aid; of these, 65% were judged to have need according to Federal Methodology, of whom 100% were aided. *Financial aid deadline (priority):* 2/15. *Financial aid forms:* FAFSA required. *Regular admission application deadline:* 1/15. Early decision deadline: 11/1.

Summary of Aid to Needy Students *From gift & self-help combined:* Average need met: 85%. Average amount awarded: $4630 (64% gift aid, 36% self-help). *Gift aid:* Total: $5,008,000 (20% from college's own funds, 65% from other college-administered sources, 15% from external sources). 300 Federal Work-Study jobs (averaging $1200); part-time jobs.

Need-Based Scholarships & Grants Pell, FSEOG, state, private, college/university.

Loans College/university short-term loans ($200 average).

Non-Need Awards *Academic Interests/Achievement Awards:* general academic. *Athletic:* available.

Other Money-Saving Options Accelerated degree, Army ROTC, off-campus living (after freshman year). *Payment Plan:* installment. *Waivers:* full or partial for employees or children of employees and senior citizens.

Contact Financial Aid Office, College of William and Mary, PO Box 8795, Williamsburg, VA 23187-8795, 757-221-2420.

THE COLLEGE OF WOOSTER
Wooster, Ohio

About the Institution Independent/religious, coed. Degrees awarded: B. Offers 49 undergraduate majors. Total enrollment: 1,650 (48% state residents). Freshmen: 519.

Undergraduate Expenses (1997–98 estimated) Comprehensive fee of $24,400 includes tuition ($19,300) and college room and board ($5100). College room only: $2318.

Applications Of all full-time undergraduates enrolled in fall 1996, 84% of those who applied for aid were judged to have need according to Federal Methodology, of whom 99% were aided. *Financial aid deadline (priority):* 2/15. *Financial aid forms:* FAFSA required. CSS Financial Aid PROFILE, institutional form required for some. *Regular admission application deadline:* 2/15. Early decision deadline: 12/1.

Summary of Aid to Needy Students *From gift & self-help combined:* Average need met: 92%. Average amount awarded: $16,414 (79% gift aid, 21% self-help). *Gift aid:* Total: $14,225,841 (85% from college's own funds, 3% from other college-administered sources, 12% from external sources). 619 Federal Work-Study jobs (averaging $1117); 104 part-time jobs.

Need-Based Scholarships & Grants Pell, FSEOG, state, private, college/university.

Loans Perkins, PLUS, Stafford, Unsubsidized Stafford, private, college/university long-term loans ($2000 average).

Non-Need Awards In 1996, a total of 1,189 non-need awards were made. *Academic Interests/Achievement Awards:* 838 ($4,713,556 total): general academic, biological sciences, English, mathematics, physical sciences, social sciences. *Creative Arts/Performance Awards:* 42 ($171,000 total): dance, music, theater/drama. *Special Achievements/Activities Awards:* 104 ($471,049 total): community service, religious involvement. *Special Characteristics Awards:* 205 ($2,615,864 total): children of faculty/staff, handicapped students, international students, local/state students, members of minorities.

Other Money-Saving Options Off-campus living (after freshman year). *Payment Plan:* installment. *Waivers:* full or partial for minority students.

Contact Office of Financial Aid, The College of Wooster, Wooster, OH 44691, 330-263-2317.

COLORADO CHRISTIAN UNIVERSITY
Lakewood, Colorado

About the Institution Independent/religious, coed. Degrees awarded: A, B, M. Offers 24 undergraduate majors. Total enrollment: 3,006. Undergraduates: 2,641 (72% state residents). Freshmen: 210.

Undergraduate Expenses (1996–97) Comprehensive fee of $12,785 includes tuition ($8855) and college room and board ($3930). College room only: $2390.

Applications 79% of all full-time undergraduates enrolled in fall 1996 applied for aid; of these, 75% were judged to have need according to Federal Methodology, of whom 98% were aided. *Financial aid deadline (priority):* 3/15. *Financial aid forms:* FAFSA, institutional form required. *Admission application deadline:* 8/15.

Summary of Aid to Needy Students *From gift & self-help combined:* Average need met: 64%. Average amount awarded: $8554 (32% gift aid, 68% self-help). *Gift aid:* Total: $1,865,645 (64% from college's own funds, 7% from other college-administered sources, 29% from external sources). 50 Federal Work-Study jobs (averaging $2520); 58 part-time jobs.

Need-Based Scholarships & Grants Pell, FSEOG, college/university.

Loans Perkins, PLUS, Stafford, Unsubsidized Stafford.

Non-Need Awards In 1996, a total of 866 non-need awards were made. *Academic Interests/Achievement Awards:* 304 ($438,257 total): general academic, business, education, humanities, international studies. *Creative Arts/Performance Awards:* 97 ($81,526 total): art/fine arts, music, theater/drama. *Special Achievements/Activities Awards:* 162 ($91,850 total): leadership, religious involvement. *Special Characteristics Awards:* 185 ($247,975 total): children and siblings of alumni, children of faculty/staff, relatives of clergy, religious affiliation, siblings of current students, spouses of current students. *Athletic:* Total: 118 ($594,469); Men: 64 ($279,224); Women: 54 ($315,245).

Other Money-Saving Options Accelerated degree, co-op program, cooperative Army ROTC, cooperative Air Force ROTC, off-campus living (after freshman year). *Payment Plan:* installment. *Waivers:* full or partial for children of alumni and employees or children of employees.

Contact Mr. Kent McGowan, Director of Financial Aid, Colorado Christian University, 180 South Garrison Street, Lakewood, CO 80226-7499, 303-202-0100 Ext. 117, fax: 303-274-7560.

THE COLORADO COLLEGE
Colorado Springs, Colorado

About the Institution Independent, coed. Degrees awarded: B, M. Offers 42 undergraduate majors. Total enrollment: 2,099. Undergraduates: 2,052 (25% state residents). Freshmen: 593.

Undergraduate Expenses (1997–98) Comprehensive fee of $25,188 includes tuition ($19,980) and college room and board ($5208). College room only: $2682.

Applications *Financial aid deadline (priority):* 2/15. *Financial aid forms:* FAFSA, CSS Financial Aid PROFILE required. Institutional form required for some. *Regular admission application deadline:* 1/15. Early action deadline: 11/15.

Summary of Aid to Needy Students Federal Work-Study jobs; part-time jobs.

Loans College/university short-term loans, college/university long-term loans.

Non-Need Awards *Academic Interests/Achievement Awards:* general academic, physical sciences. *Special Characteristics Awards:* international students. *Athletic:* available.

Other Money-Saving Options Cooperative Army ROTC, off-campus living (after junior year). *Payment Plan:* installment. *Waivers:* full or partial for employees or children of employees.

Contact Office of Financial Aid, The Colorado College, 14 East Cache La Poudre, Colorado Springs, CO 80903-3294, 719-389-6000.

COLORADO SCHOOL OF MINES
Golden, Colorado

About the Institution State-supported, coed. Degrees awarded: B, M, D. Offers 19 undergraduate majors. Total enrollment: 3,203. Undergraduates: 2,353 (69% state residents). Freshmen: 557.

Undergraduate Expenses (1997–98 estimated) State resident tuition: $4494. Nonresident tuition: $13,980. Mandatory fees: $575. College room and board: $4730.

Applications 77% of all full-time undergraduates enrolled in fall 1996 applied for aid; of these, 94% were judged to have need according to Federal Methodology, of whom 100% were aided. *Financial aid deadline (priority):* 3/1. *Financial aid forms:* FAFSA, institutional form required. *Admission application deadline:* 6/1.

Summary of Aid to Needy Students *From gift & self-help combined:* Average need met: 100%. Average amount awarded: $6606 (46% gift aid, 54% self-help). *Gift aid:* Total: $5,050,000 (59% from college's own funds, 16% from other college-administered sources, 25% from external sources). 150 Federal Work-Study jobs (averaging $800); 350 part-time jobs.

Need-Based Scholarships & Grants Pell, FSEOG, state, private, college/university.

Loans Perkins, PLUS, Stafford, Unsubsidized Stafford, private, college/university short-term loans ($200 average), college/university long-term loans ($1800 average).

Non-Need Awards In 1996, a total of 1,290 non-need awards were made. *Academic Interests/Achievement Awards:* 700 ($2,000,000 total): general academic. *Creative Arts/Performance Awards:* 85 ($150,000 total): music. *Special Characteristics Awards:* 260 ($980,000 total): children and siblings of alumni, members of minorities, ROTC participants. *Athletic:* Total: 245 ($905,000); Men: 175 ($660,000); Women: 70 ($245,000).

Other Money-Saving Options Accelerated degree, co-op program, Army ROTC, cooperative Air Force ROTC, off-campus living. *Payment Plan:* installment.

Contact Mr. Roger A. Koester, Director of Financial Aid, Colorado School of Mines, 1500 Illinois Street, Golden, CO 80401-1887, 303-273-3207, fax: 303-273-3278.

COLORADO STATE UNIVERSITY
Fort Collins, Colorado

About the Institution State-supported, coed. Degrees awarded: B, M, D, P. Offers 108 undergraduate majors. Total enrollment: 21,970. Undergraduates: 18,451 (78% state residents). Freshmen: 2,733.

Undergraduate Expenses (1996–97) State resident tuition: $2224. Nonresident tuition: $9160. Mandatory fees: $631. College room and board: $4152 (minimum).

Applications Of all full-time undergraduates enrolled in fall 1996, 58% of those who applied for aid were judged to have need according to Federal Methodology, of whom 100% were aided. *Financial aid deadline*

(priority): 3/1. *Financial aid forms:* FAFSA required; CSS Financial Aid PROFILE acceptable. *Admission application deadline:* 7/1.

Summary of Aid to Needy Students *From gift & self-help combined:* Average amount awarded: $4953 (30% gift aid, 70% self-help). *Gift aid:* Total: $12,298,428 (13% from college's own funds, 33% from other college-administered sources, 54% from external sources). 597 Federal Work-Study jobs (averaging $1800); 4,800 part-time jobs.

Need-Based Scholarships & Grants Pell, FSEOG, state, private, college/university.

Loans Perkins, PLUS, Stafford, Unsubsidized Stafford, private, college/university short-term loans ($300 average).

Non-Need Awards In 1996, a total of 2,767 non-need awards were made. *Academic Interests/Achievement Awards:* 1,956 ($2,825,903 total): general academic. *Creative Arts/Performance Awards:* 266 ($191,500 total): art/fine arts, creative writing, dance, debating, music. *Special Characteristics Awards:* 171 ($739,725 total): first-generation college students. *Athletic:* Total: 374 ($2,182,769); Men: 198 ($1,408,072); Women: 176 ($774,697).

Other Money-Saving Options Accelerated degree, co-op program, Army ROTC, Air Force ROTC, off-campus living (after freshman year). *Payment Plan:* installment. *Waivers:* full or partial for employees or children of employees.

Contact Mr. Mark Francisco, Accountant, Colorado State University, Financial Aid Office, Room 103 Administration Annex, Fort Collins, CO 80523-0015, 970-491-1971, fax: 970-491-5010.

COLORADO TECHNICAL UNIVERSITY
Colorado Springs, Colorado

About the Institution Proprietary, coed. Degrees awarded: A, B, M, D. Offers 9 undergraduate majors. Total enrollment: 1,521. Undergraduates: 1,053 (97% state residents). Freshmen: 44.

Undergraduate Expenses (1996–97) Tuition: $6300. Mandatory fees: $168.

Applications Of all full-time undergraduates enrolled in fall 1996, 91% of those who applied for aid were judged to have need according to Federal Methodology, of whom 91% were aided. *Financial aid deadline (priority):* 10/1. *Financial aid forms:* FAFSA, state form, institutional form required. *Admission application deadline:* rolling.

Summary of Aid to Needy Students *From gift & self-help combined:* Average need met: 84%. Average amount awarded: $1130 (23% gift aid, 77% self-help). *Gift aid:* Total: $54,385 (4% from college's own funds, 42% from other college-administered sources, 54% from external sources). 26 Federal Work-Study jobs (averaging $3000); 10 part-time jobs.

Need-Based Scholarships & Grants Pell, FSEOG, state, college/university.

Loans Perkins, PLUS, Stafford, Unsubsidized Stafford.

Non-Need Awards In 1996, a total of 316 non-need awards were made. *Academic Interests/Achievement Awards:* 316 ($47,400 total): general academic.

Other Money-Saving Options Accelerated degree, co-op program, cooperative Army ROTC. *Payment Plan:* installment. *Waivers:* full or partial for employees or children of employees.

Contact Office of Financial Aid, Colorado Technical University, 4435 North Chestnut Street, Colorado Springs, CO 80907-3896, 719-598-0200.

COLUMBIA COLLEGE
Chicago, Illinois

About the Institution Independent, coed. Degrees awarded: B, M. Offers 33 undergraduate majors. Total enrollment: 8,066. Undergraduates: 7,510 (84% state residents). Freshmen: 1,136.

Undergraduate Expenses (1997–98) Tuition: $8498. Mandatory fees: $100. College room only: $4523.

Applications 61% of all full-time undergraduates enrolled in fall 1996 applied for aid. *Financial aid deadline:* continuous. *Financial aid forms:* FAFSA required; CSS Financial Aid PROFILE acceptable. *Admission application deadline:* rolling.

Summary of Aid to Needy Students *From gift & self-help combined:* Average amount awarded: $9900 (47% gift aid, 53% self-help). *Gift aid:* Total: $11,053,000 (5% from college's own funds, 64% from other college-administered sources, 31% from external sources). 92 Federal Work-Study jobs (averaging $2054); 496 part-time jobs.

Need-Based Scholarships & Grants Pell, FSEOG, state, private, college/university.

Loans PLUS, Stafford, Unsubsidized Stafford, private.

Non-Need Awards *Academic Interests/Achievement Awards:* ($360,700 total): general academic.

Other Money-Saving Options Off-campus living. *Payment Plan:* deferred payment. *Waivers:* full or partial for employees or children of employees.

Contact Mr. John Olino, Director of Financial Aid, Columbia College, Chicago, IL 60605-1997, 312-663-1600 Ext. 5144.

COLUMBIA COLLEGE
Columbia, Missouri

About the Institution Independent/religious, coed. Degrees awarded: A, B, M. Offers 51 undergraduate majors. Total enrollment: 855 (76% state residents). Freshmen: 255.

Undergraduate Expenses (1997–98) Comprehensive fee of $13,388 includes tuition ($9244) and college room and board ($4144). College room only: $2600.

Applications 84% of all full-time undergraduates enrolled in fall 1996 applied for aid; of these, 73% were judged to have need according to Federal Methodology, of whom 100% were aided. *Financial aid deadline (priority):* 4/1. *Financial aid forms:* FAFSA, institutional form required; CSS Financial Aid PROFILE acceptable. State form required for some. *Admission application deadline:* rolling.

Summary of Aid to Needy Students *From gift & self-help combined:* Average amount awarded: $11,099 (56% gift aid, 44% self-help). *Gift aid:* Total: $2,595,432 (64% from college's own funds, 6% from other college-administered sources, 30% from external sources). Federal Work-Study jobs; 28 part-time jobs.

Need-Based Scholarships & Grants Pell, FSEOG, state.

Loans Perkins, Stafford, Unsubsidized Stafford, college/university short-term loans ($50 average).

Non-Need Awards In 1996, a total of 297 non-need awards were made. *Academic Interests/Achievement Awards:* 151 ($522,535 total): general academic. *Creative Arts/Performance Awards:* 39 ($34,800 total): applied art and design, music. *Special Achievements/Activities Awards:* 17 ($17,000 total): Junior Miss, leadership, memberships. *Special Characteristics Awards:* 17 ($8500 total): children and siblings of alumni, religious affiliation, ROTC participants. *Athletic:* Total: 73 ($519,917); Men: 45 ($309,935); Women: 28 ($209,982).

Other Money-Saving Options Accelerated degree, cooperative Army ROTC, cooperative Naval ROTC, cooperative Air Force ROTC, off-campus living (after sophomore year). *Payment Plan:* deferred payment. *Waivers:* full or partial for children of alumni, employees or children of employees, senior citizens.

Contact Ms. Mary Lou Lang, Director of Financial Aid, Columbia College, 1001 Rogers, Columbia, MO 65216-0002, 573-875-7362.

COLUMBIA COLLEGE
New York, New York

About the Institution Independent, coed. Degrees awarded: B. Offers 54 undergraduate majors. Total university enrollment: 19,000. Undergraduates: 3,726 (19% state residents). Freshmen: 975.

Undergraduate Expenses (1996–97) Comprehensive fee of $28,606 includes tuition ($20,884), mandatory fees ($562), and college room and board ($7160 minimum).

Applications 55% of all full-time undergraduates enrolled in fall 1996 applied for aid; of these, 89% were judged to have need according to Federal Methodology, of whom 100% were aided. *Financial aid deadline:* 2/10. *Financial aid forms:* FAFSA, CSS Financial Aid PROFILE, institutional form required. State form required for some. *Regular admission application deadline:* 1/1. Early decision deadline: 11/1.

Summary of Aid to Needy Students *From gift & self-help combined:* Average need met: 100%. Average amount awarded: $18,573 (66% gift aid, 34% self-help). *Gift aid:* Total: $22,377,000 (83% from college's own funds, 3% from other college-administered sources, 14% from external sources). Federal Work-Study jobs; part-time jobs.

Need-Based Scholarships & Grants Pell, FSEOG, state, private, college/university.

Loans Perkins, PLUS, Stafford, Unsubsidized Stafford, private.

Non-Need Awards Not offered.

Other Money-Saving Options Off-campus living (after freshman year). *Payment Plans:* tuition prepayment, installment. *Waivers:* full or partial for employees or children of employees.

Contact Office of Financial Aid, Columbia College, 100 Hamilton Hall, New York, NY 10027, 212-854-1754.

COLUMBIA COLLEGE
Caguas, Puerto Rico

About the Institution Proprietary, coed. Degrees awarded: A, B. Offers 3 undergraduate majors.

Applications *Financial aid deadline:* continuous. *Financial aid forms:* FAFSA, institutional form required. *Admission application deadline:* rolling.

Summary of Aid to Needy Students Federal Work-Study jobs; part-time jobs.

Non-Need Awards *Academic Interests/Achievement Awards:* general academic.

Other Money-Saving Options Accelerated degree. *Payment Plan:* guaranteed tuition.

Contact Office of Financial Aid, Columbia College, Caguas, PR 00726, 787-258-1501.

COLUMBIA COLLEGE
Columbia, South Carolina

About the Institution Independent/religious, women. Degrees awarded: B, M. Offers 48 undergraduate majors. Total enrollment: 1,321. Undergraduates: 1,269 (93% state residents). Freshmen: 256.

Undergraduate Expenses (1996–97) Comprehensive fee of $15,755 includes tuition ($11,535), mandatory fees ($60), and college room and board ($4160).

Applications 93% of all full-time undergraduates enrolled in fall 1996 applied for aid; of these, 91% were judged to have need according to Federal Methodology, of whom 99% were aided. *Financial aid deadline (priority):* 4/1. *Financial aid forms:* FAFSA required; CSS Financial Aid PROFILE acceptable. *Admission application deadline:* rolling.

Summary of Aid to Needy Students *From gift & self-help combined:* Average need met: 81%. Average amount awarded: $12,188 (65% gift aid, 35% self-help). *Gift aid:* Total: $7,374,885 (45% from college's own funds, 2% from other college-administered sources, 53% from external sources). 339 Federal Work-Study jobs (averaging $811); 138 part-time jobs.

Need-Based Scholarships & Grants Pell, FSEOG, state, private, college/university.

Loans Perkins, PLUS, Stafford, Unsubsidized Stafford, state, private.

Non-Need Awards In 1996, a total of 778 non-need awards were made. *Academic Interests/Achievement Awards:* 476 ($1,428,850 total): general academic, biological sciences, business, communication, education, English, foreign languages, mathematics, religion/biblical studies. *Creative Arts/Performance Awards:* 135 ($154,150 total): applied art and design, art/fine arts, dance, music. *Special Achievements/Activities Awards:* 132 ($280,150 total): leadership. *Special Characteristics Awards:* 17 ($108,895 total): children of faculty/staff, relatives of clergy. *Athletic:* Total: 18 ($39,600).

Other Money-Saving Options Accelerated degree, cooperative Army ROTC, off-campus living. *Payment Plan:* installment. *Waivers:* full or partial for employees or children of employees.

Contact Office of Financial Aid, Columbia College, 1301 Columbia College Drive, Columbia, SC 29203-5998, 803-786-3012.

COLUMBIA COLLEGE–HOLLYWOOD
Hollywood, California

About the Institution Independent, coed. Degrees awarded: A, B. Offers 5 undergraduate majors. Total enrollment: 234 (50% state residents). Freshmen: 67.

Undergraduate Expenses (1997–98) Tuition: $6480. Mandatory fees: $225.

Applications 50% of all full-time undergraduates enrolled in fall 1996 applied for aid; of these, 100% were judged to have need according to Federal Methodology, of whom 100% were aided. *Financial aid deadline (priority):* 6/15. *Financial aid forms:* FAFSA, institutional form required; CSS Financial Aid PROFILE acceptable. State form required for some. *Regular admission application deadline:* rolling. Early action deadline: 1/15.

Summary of Aid to Needy Students *From gift & self-help combined:* Average need met: 100%. Average amount awarded: $7500. *Gift aid:* Total: $122,000 (29% from college-administered sources, 71% from external sources). 1 Federal Work-Study jobs (averaging $2430); 5 part-time jobs.

Need-Based Scholarships & Grants Pell, FSEOG, state, private.

Loans PLUS, Stafford, Unsubsidized Stafford.

Non-Need Awards Not offered.

Other Money-Saving Options Accelerated degree. *Payment Plan:* installment.

Contact Mrs. Natasha Kobrinsky, Student Affairs Director, Columbia College–Hollywood, 925 North La Brea Avenue, Hollywood, CA 90038-2392, 213-851-0550, fax: 213-851-6401.

COLUMBIA COLLEGE OF NURSING
Milwaukee, Wisconsin

About the Institution Independent, coed. Degrees awarded: B. Offers 1 undergraduate major. Total enrollment: 373 (97% state residents). Freshmen: 50.

Undergraduate Expenses (1997–98) Comprehensive fee of $18,890 includes tuition ($14,140), mandatory fees ($470), and college room and board ($4280). College room only: $2260.

Applications *Financial aid deadline (priority):* 3/1. *Financial aid forms:* CSS Financial Aid PROFILE, institutional form required. *Admission application deadline:* rolling.

Summary of Aid to Needy Students Federal Work-Study jobs; part-time jobs.

Non-Need Awards *Special Characteristics Awards:* children of faculty/staff, siblings of current students.

Other Money-Saving Options Off-campus living (after sophomore year). *Waivers:* full or partial for employees or children of employees.

Contact Office of Financial Aid, Columbia College of Nursing, 2121 East Newport Avenue, Milwaukee, WI 53211-2952, 414-961-3530.

COLUMBIA INTERNATIONAL UNIVERSITY
Columbia, South Carolina

About the Institution Independent/religious, coed. Degrees awarded: A, B, M. Offers 11 undergraduate majors. Total enrollment: 1,032. Undergraduates: 519 (47% state residents). Freshmen: 88.

Undergraduate Expenses (1997–98) Comprehensive fee of $12,001 includes tuition ($7740), mandatory fees ($151), and college room and board ($4110).

Applications 42% of all full-time undergraduates enrolled in fall 1996 applied for aid; of these, 94% were judged to have need according to Federal Methodology, of whom 100% were aided. *Financial aid deadline (priority):* 3/1. *Financial aid forms:* FAFSA required. *Admission application deadline:* rolling.

Summary of Aid to Needy Students *From gift & self-help combined:* Average need met: 61%. Average amount awarded: $9044 (33% gift aid, 67% self-help). *Gift aid:* Total: $538,000 (18% from college's own funds, 46% from other college-administered sources, 36% from external sources). Federal Work-Study jobs; 72 part-time jobs.

Need-Based Scholarships & Grants Pell, FSEOG, state, private, college/university.

Loans PLUS, Stafford, Unsubsidized Stafford, college/university short-term loans.

Non-Need Awards In 1996, a total of 63 non-need awards were made. *Academic Interests/Achievement Awards:* 10 ($61,000 total): general academic. *Creative Arts/Performance Awards:* 12 ($4500 total): music. *Special Characteristics Awards:* 41 ($57,861 total): children and siblings of alumni, international students, members of minorities.

Other Money-Saving Options Accelerated degree. *Payment Plan:* installment. *Waivers:* full or partial for employees or children of employees.

Contact Ms. Carrie Miller, Financial Aid Counselor, Columbia International University, Columbia, SC 29230-3122, 803-754-4100 Ext. 3036, fax: 803-691-0739.

COLUMBIA UNION COLLEGE
Takoma Park, Maryland

About the Institution Independent/religious, coed. Degrees awarded: A, B. Offers 29 undergraduate majors. Total enrollment: 1,163 (47% state residents). Freshmen: 162.

Undergraduate Expenses (1996–97) Comprehensive fee of $15,930 includes tuition ($11,500), mandatory fees ($290), and college room and board ($4140 minimum). College room only: $2250.

Applications *Financial aid deadline (priority):* 5/31. *Financial aid forms:* FAFSA, institutional form required; state form acceptable. CSS Financial Aid PROFILE required for some. *Regular admission application deadline:* 8/1. Early action deadline: 10/31.

Summary of Aid to Needy Students 40 Federal Work-Study jobs (averaging $1500); 339 part-time jobs.

Need-Based Scholarships & Grants Pell, FSEOG, state, private, college/university.

Loans Perkins, PLUS, Stafford, Unsubsidized Stafford.

Non-Need Awards *Academic Interests/Achievement Awards:* ($209,984 total): general academic. *Creative Arts/Performance Awards:* ($234,608 total): music. *Special Achievements/Activities Awards:* ($17,212 total): leadership, memberships, religious involvement. *Special Characteristics Awards:* local/state students. *Athletic:* Total: ($421,180).

Other Money-Saving Options Co-op program. *Payment Plans:* installment, deferred payment. *Waivers:* full or partial for employees or children of employees, adult students, senior citizens.

Contact Ms. Brenda Billingy, Director, Financial Aid, Columbia Union College, 7600 Flower Avenue, Takoma Park, MD 20912-7794, 301-891-4005, fax: 301-891-4131.

COLUMBIA UNIVERSITY, BARNARD COLLEGE
New York, New York

See Barnard College

COLUMBIA UNIVERSITY, COLUMBIA COLLEGE
New York, New York

See Columbia College (NY)

COLUMBIA UNIVERSITY, SCHOOL OF ENGINEERING AND APPLIED SCIENCE
New York, New York

About the Institution Independent, coed. Degrees awarded: B, M, D. Offers 17 undergraduate majors. Total university enrollment: 19,000. Undergraduates: 1,093. Freshmen: 289.

Undergraduate Expenses (1996–97) Comprehensive fee of $28,606 includes tuition ($20,884), mandatory fees ($562), and college room and board ($7160 minimum).

Applications 62% of all full-time undergraduates enrolled in fall 1996 applied for aid; of these, 94% were judged to have need according to Federal Methodology, of whom 100% were aided. *Financial aid deadline:* 2/10. *Financial aid forms:* FAFSA, CSS Financial Aid PROFILE, institutional form required. State form required for some. *Regular admission application deadline:* 1/1. Early decision deadline: 11/1.

Summary of Aid to Needy Students *From gift & self-help combined:* Average need met: 100%. Average amount awarded: $20,116 (68% gift aid, 32% self-help). *Gift aid:* Total: $8,791,972 (77% from college's own funds, 6% from other college-administered sources, 17% from external sources). Federal Work-Study jobs; part-time jobs.

Need-Based Scholarships & Grants Pell, FSEOG, state, private, college/university.

Loans Perkins, PLUS, Stafford, Unsubsidized Stafford, private.

Non-Need Awards Not offered.

Other Money-Saving Options Accelerated degree, off-campus living (after freshman year). *Payment Plans:* tuition prepayment, installment, deferred payment. *Waivers:* full or partial for minority students and employees or children of employees.

Contact Office of Financial Aid, Columbia University, School of Engineering and Applied Science, 100 Hamilton Hall, New York, NY 10027, 212-854-1754.

COLUMBUS COLLEGE OF ART AND DESIGN
Columbus, Ohio

About the Institution Independent, coed. Degrees awarded: B. Offers 13 undergraduate majors. Total enrollment: 1,494 (69% state residents). Freshmen: 239.

Undergraduate Expenses (1997–98) Comprehensive fee of $17,680 includes tuition ($11,880) and college room and board ($5800).

Applications Of all full-time undergraduates enrolled in fall 1996, 63% of those who applied for aid were judged to have need according to Federal Methodology, of whom 100% were aided. *Financial aid deadline (priority):* 4/15. *Financial aid forms:* FAFSA, CSS Financial Aid PROFILE, state form, institutional form required. *Admission application deadline:* rolling.

Summary of Aid to Needy Students *Gift aid:* Total: $9,147,215 (41% from college's own funds, 51% from other college-administered sources, 8% from external sources). 150 Federal Work-Study jobs (averaging $2300); 25 part-time jobs.

Need-Based Scholarships & Grants Pell, FSEOG, state, private, college/university.

Loans Perkins, PLUS, Stafford, Unsubsidized Stafford, state.

Non-Need Awards In 1996, a total of 1,654 non-need awards were made. *Creative Arts/Performance Awards:* 901 ($3,732,675 total): art/fine arts. *Special Characteristics Awards:* 753 ($3,114,016 total): local/state students.

Other Money-Saving Options Off-campus living (after freshman year). *Payment Plan:* installment. *Waivers:* full or partial for employees or children of employees and senior citizens.

Contact Ms. Anna Wall, Director of Financial Aid, Columbus College of Art and Design, 107 North Ninth Street, Columbus, OH 43215-1758, 614-224-9101, fax: 614-222-3218.

COLUMBUS STATE UNIVERSITY
Columbus, Georgia

About the Institution State-supported, coed. Degrees awarded: A, B, M. Offers 67 undergraduate majors. Total enrollment: 5,536. Undergraduates: 4,766 (81% state residents). Freshmen: 707.

Undergraduate Expenses (1996–97) State resident tuition: $1845. Nonresident tuition: $5724. Mandatory fees: $261. College room and board: $3825.

Applications 81% of all full-time undergraduates enrolled in fall 1996 applied for aid; of these, 68% were judged to have need according to Federal Methodology, of whom 100% were aided. *Financial aid deadline (priority):* 7/1. *Financial aid forms:* institutional form required; CSS Financial Aid PROFILE acceptable. FAFSA required for some. *Admission application deadline:* 8/30.

Summary of Aid to Needy Students *From gift & self-help combined:* Average need met: 60%. Average amount awarded: $4536 (60% gift aid, 40% self-help). *Gift aid:* Total: $4,407,950 (4% from college's own funds, 3% from other college-administered sources, 93% from external sources). Federal Work-Study jobs; 228 part-time jobs.

Need-Based Scholarships & Grants FSEOG, state, college/university.

Loans College/university short-term loans ($475 average), college/university long-term loans ($1050 average).

Non-Need Awards *Academic Interests/Achievement Awards:* general academic. *Creative Arts/Performance Awards:* 91 ($64,021 total): art/fine arts, music. *Athletic:* Total: 71 ($88,112); Men: 41 ($50,251); Women: 30 ($37,861).

Other Money-Saving Options Accelerated degree, co-op program, Army ROTC, off-campus living. *Waivers:* full or partial for employees or children of employees and senior citizens.

Contact Financial Aid Office, Columbus State University, 4225 University Avenue, Columbus, GA 31907-5645, 706-568-2036.

COMMUNITY HOSPITAL OF ROANOKE VALLEY–COLLEGE OF HEALTH SCIENCES
Roanoke, Virginia

About the Institution Independent, coed. Degrees awarded: A, B. Offers 11 undergraduate majors. Total enrollment: 561 (99% state residents). Freshmen: 6.

Undergraduate Expenses (1996–97) Tuition: $4500 (minimum). College room only: $1300.

Applications *Financial aid deadline (priority):* 4/1. *Financial aid forms:* FAFSA, institutional form required; state form acceptable. *Regular admission application deadline:* 7/31. Early decision deadline: 10/15.

Summary of Aid to Needy Students 9 Federal Work-Study jobs (averaging $1500); 7 part-time jobs.

Need-Based Scholarships & Grants Pell, FSEOG, state, private, college/university.

Loans PLUS, Stafford, Unsubsidized Stafford, college/university short-term loans ($200 average).

Non-Need Awards available.

Other Money-Saving Options Off-campus living. *Waivers:* full or partial for employees or children of employees.

Contact Office of Financial Aid, Community Hospital of Roanoke Valley–College of Health Sciences, Roanoke, VA 24031-3186, 540-985-8483.

CONCEPTION SEMINARY COLLEGE
Conception, Missouri

About the Institution Independent/religious, primarily men. Degrees awarded: B. Offers 3 undergraduate majors. Total enrollment: 64 (45% state residents). Freshmen: 11.

Undergraduate Expenses (1996–97) Comprehensive fee of $10,316 includes tuition ($6912), mandatory fees ($130), and college room and board ($3274).

Applications 89% of all full-time undergraduates enrolled in fall 1996 applied for aid; of these, 95% were judged to have need according to Federal Methodology, of whom 100% were aided. *Financial aid deadline (priority):* 07/15. *Financial aid forms:* FAFSA required for some. *Admission application deadline:* 7/31.

Summary of Aid to Needy Students *From gift & self-help combined:* Average need met: 72%. Average amount awarded: $8708 (69% gift aid, 31% self-help). *Gift aid:* Total: $301,790 (22% from college's own funds, 5% from other college-administered sources, 73% from external sources). 40 Federal Work-Study jobs (averaging $525); 24 part-time jobs.

Need-Based Scholarships & Grants Pell, FSEOG.

Loans PLUS, Stafford, Unsubsidized Stafford.

Non-Need Awards In 1996, a total of 44 non-need awards were made. *Academic Interests/Achievement Awards:* 14 ($19,100 total): general academic, religion/biblical studies. *Special Characteristics Awards:* 30 ($40,000 total): general special characteristics, religious affiliation.

Contact Br. Justin Hernandez, Director of Financial Aid, Conception Seminary College, Conception, MO 64433-0502, 816-944-2851.

CONCORD COLLEGE
Athens, West Virginia

About the Institution State-supported, coed. Degrees awarded: B. Offers 36 undergraduate majors. Total enrollment: 2,357 (88% state residents). Freshmen: 610.

Undergraduate Expenses (1997–98) State resident tuition: $2310. Nonresident tuition: $5000. College room and board: $3708. College room only: $1658.

Applications Of all full-time undergraduates enrolled in fall 1996, 93% of those judged to have need according to Federal Methodology were aided. *Financial aid deadline (priority):* 4/15. *Financial aid forms:* FAFSA, institutional form required. *Admission application deadline:* rolling.

Summary of Aid to Needy Students *From gift & self-help combined:* Average need met: 88%. Average amount awarded: $5363 (48% gift aid, 52% self-help). *Gift aid:* Total: $2,664,533 (9% from college's own funds, 16% from other college-administered sources, 75% from external sources). Federal Work-Study jobs; 469 part-time jobs.

Need-Based Scholarships & Grants Pell, FSEOG, state, private, college/university.

Loans Perkins, PLUS, Stafford, Unsubsidized Stafford, college/university short-term loans ($100 average), college/university long-term loans ($473 average).

Non-Need Awards *Academic Interests/Achievement Awards:* general academic. *Creative Arts/Performance Awards:* art/fine arts, music, theater/drama. *Special Achievements/Activities Awards:* community service. *Athletic:* available.

Other Money-Saving Options Accelerated degree. *Payment Plans:* installment, deferred payment.

Contact Financial Aid Office, Concord College, Athens, WV 24712-1000, 304-384-6075.

CONCORDIA COLLEGE
Selma, Alabama

About the Institution Independent/religious, coed. Degrees awarded: A, B. Offers 5 undergraduate majors. Total enrollment: 476 (90% state residents).

Undergraduate Expenses (1997–98) Comprehensive fee of $7200 includes tuition ($4600) and college room and board ($2600 minimum). College room only: $1200 (minimum).

Applications *Financial aid deadline (priority):* 8/15. *Financial aid forms:* FAFSA, institutional form required; CSS Financial Aid PROFILE acceptable. State form required for some. *Admission application deadline:* 9/2.

Summary of Aid to Needy Students *From gift & self-help combined:* Average need met: 76%. Average amount awarded: $3286 (93% gift aid, 7% self-help). *Gift aid:* Total: $670,000 (14% from college's own funds, 22% from other college-administered sources, 64% from external sources). 117 Federal Work-Study jobs (averaging $300).

Need-Based Scholarships & Grants Private.

Non-Need Awards *Academic Interests/Achievement Awards:* general academic, business, computer science, education, religion/biblical studies. *Athletic:* Total: 45 ($49,000); Men: 28 ($30,000); Women: 17 ($19,000).

Other Money-Saving Options Off-campus living. *Payment Plan:* installment. *Waivers:* full or partial for employees or children of employees.

Contact Financial Aid Office, Concordia College, 1804 Green Street, Selma, AL 36701, 334-874-7143.

CONCORDIA COLLEGE
Ann Arbor, Michigan

About the Institution Independent/religious, coed. Degrees awarded: A, B. Offers 30 undergraduate majors. Total enrollment: 601 (86% state residents). Freshmen: 81.

Undergraduate Expenses (1996–97) Comprehensive fee of $16,100 includes tuition ($11,210), mandatory fees ($240), and college room and board ($4650).

Applications *Financial aid deadline (priority):* 5/15. *Financial aid forms:* FAFSA, institutional form required. State form required for some. *Admission application deadline:* rolling.

Summary of Aid to Needy Students *From gift & self-help combined:* Average amount awarded: $8459 (57% gift aid, 43% self-help). *Gift aid:* Total: $2,381,488 (56% from college's own funds, 33% from other college-administered sources, 11% from external sources). 112 Federal Work-Study jobs (averaging $1572); 264 part-time jobs.

Need-Based Scholarships & Grants Pell, FSEOG, state, private, college/university.

Loans Perkins, PLUS, Stafford, Unsubsidized Stafford, state, private.

Non-Need Awards In 1996, a total of 451 non-need awards were made. *Academic Interests/Achievement Awards:* 118 ($266,928 total): general academic. *Creative Arts/Performance Awards:* 40 ($43,750 total): art/fine arts, music. *Special Achievements/Activities Awards:* 17 ($17,375 total): general special achievements/activities. *Special Characteristics Awards:* 200 ($178,628 total): children and siblings of alumni, relatives of clergy, religious affiliation. *Athletic:* Total: 76 ($178,050).

Other Money-Saving Options Cooperative Army ROTC, cooperative Air Force ROTC. *Payment Plan:* installment. *Waivers:* full or partial for employees or children of employees.

Contact Office of Financial Aid, Concordia College, Ann Arbor, MI 48105-2797, 313-995-7408.

CONCORDIA COLLEGE
Moorhead, Minnesota

About the Institution Independent/religious, coed. Degrees awarded: B. Offers 69 undergraduate majors. Total enrollment: 2,928 (61% state residents). Freshmen: 751.

Undergraduate Expenses (1997–98) Comprehensive fee of $15,670 includes tuition ($12,040), mandatory fees ($105), and college room and board ($3525). College room only: $1550.

Applications Of all full-time undergraduates enrolled in fall 1996, 89% of those who applied for aid were judged to have need according to Federal Methodology, of whom 98% were aided. *Financial aid deadline:* continuous. *Financial aid forms:* FAFSA, institutional form required. *Admission application deadline:* rolling.

Summary of Aid to Needy Students *From gift & self-help combined:* Average need met: 99%. Average amount awarded: $9831 (60% gift aid, 40% self-help). *Gift aid:* Total: $12,598,552 (59% from college's own funds, 6% from other college-administered sources, 35% from external sources). 804 Federal Work-Study jobs (averaging $1012); 629 part-time jobs.

Need-Based Scholarships & Grants Pell, FSEOG, state, private, college/university.

Loans Perkins, PLUS, Stafford, Unsubsidized Stafford, state, private, college/university short-term loans ($50 average), college/university long-term loans ($1470 average).

Non-Need Awards In 1996, a total of 374 non-need awards were made. *Academic Interests/Achievement Awards:* 243 ($1,099,575 total): general academic. *Creative Arts/Performance Awards:* 131 ($236,500 total): debating, music, theater/drama.

Other Money-Saving Options Co-op program, cooperative Army ROTC, cooperative Air Force ROTC, off-campus living (after sophomore year). *Payment Plan:* installment. *Waivers:* full or partial for employees or children of employees.

Contact Mr. Dale E. Thornton, Financial Aid Director, Concordia College, 901 South 8th Street, Moorhead, MN 56562, 218-299-3010, fax: 218-299-3947.

CONCORDIA COLLEGE
St. Paul, Minnesota

About the Institution Independent/religious, coed. Degrees awarded: A, B, M. Offers 44 undergraduate majors. Total enrollment: 1,259. Undergraduates: 1,255 (82% state residents). Freshmen: 164.

Undergraduate Expenses (1996–97) Comprehensive fee of $15,555 includes tuition ($11,355) and college room and board ($4200).

Applications 91% of all full-time undergraduates enrolled in fall 1996 applied for aid; of these, 95% were judged to have need according to Federal Methodology, of whom 100% were aided. *Financial aid deadline (priority):* 4/15. *Financial aid forms:* FAFSA, institutional form required. *Admission application deadline:* 8/15.

Summary of Aid to Needy Students *From gift & self-help combined:* Average need met: 86%. Average amount awarded: $10,579 (65% gift aid, 35% self-help). *Gift aid:* Total: $4,560,715 (58% from college's own funds, 6% from other college-administered sources, 36% from external sources). 304 Federal Work-Study jobs (averaging $1339); 137 part-time jobs.

Need-Based Scholarships & Grants Pell, FSEOG, state, private, college/university.

Loans Perkins, PLUS, Stafford, Unsubsidized Stafford, state.

Non-Need Awards In 1996, a total of 278 non-need awards were made. *Academic Interests/Achievement Awards:* 250 ($416,317 total): general academic, religion/biblical studies. *Creative Arts/Performance Awards:* 10 ($4250 total): music. *Special Characteristics Awards:* 18 ($99,736 total): children of faculty/staff.

Other Money-Saving Options Accelerated degree, cooperative Army ROTC, cooperative Naval ROTC, cooperative Air Force ROTC. *Payment Plan:* installment. *Waivers:* full or partial for employees or children of employees and senior citizens.

Contact Ms. Kay C. Rindal, Assistant Financial Aid Director, Concordia College, 275 North Syndicate Street, St. Paul, MN 55104-5494, 612-641-8835, fax: 612-659-0207.

CONCORDIA COLLEGE
Seward, Nebraska

About the Institution Independent/religious, coed. Degrees awarded: B, M. Offers 51 undergraduate majors. Total enrollment: 951. Undergraduates: 913 (35% state residents). Freshmen: 248.

Undergraduate Expenses (1997–98) Comprehensive fee of $14,290 includes tuition ($10,650) and college room and board ($3640).

Applications Of all full-time undergraduates enrolled in fall 1996, 100% of those judged to have need according to Federal Methodology were aided. *Financial aid deadline (priority):* 8/15. *Financial aid forms:* FAFSA, institutional form required; CSS Financial Aid PROFILE acceptable. *Admission application deadline:* rolling.

Summary of Aid to Needy Students *From gift & self-help combined:* Average need met: 81%. Average amount awarded: $10,418 (62% gift aid, 38% self-help). *Gift aid:* Total: $5,003,422 (53% from college's own funds, 15% from other college-administered sources, 32% from external sources). 298 Federal Work-Study jobs (averaging $687); 56 part-time jobs.

Need-Based Scholarships & Grants Pell, FSEOG, state, private, college/university.

Loans Perkins, PLUS, Stafford, Unsubsidized Stafford.

Non-Need Awards In 1996, a total of 2,024 non-need awards were made. *Academic Interests/Achievement Awards:* 1,018 ($1,131,105 total): general academic, biological sciences, business, communication, computer science, education, English, humanities, mathematics, religion/biblical studies, social sciences. *Creative Arts/Performance Awards:* 324 ($208,695 total): art/fine arts, music, theater/drama. *Special Characteristics Awards:* 375 ($268,074 total): children and siblings of alumni, children of faculty/staff, local/state students, religious affiliation. *Athletic:* Total: 307 ($404,215); Men: 187 ($254,670); Women: 120 ($149,545).

Other Money-Saving Options Army ROTC, Air Force ROTC, cooperative Naval ROTC. *Payment Plans:* installment, deferred payment. *Waivers:* full or partial for employees or children of employees.

Contact Mrs. Eveline Zwick, Director of Financial Aid, Concordia College, 800 North Columbia Avenue, Seward, NE 68434-1599, 402-643-7270, fax: 402-643-4073.

CONCORDIA COLLEGE
Bronxville, New York

About the Institution Independent/religious, coed. Degrees awarded: A, B. Offers 33 undergraduate majors. Total enrollment: 556 (82% state residents). Freshmen: 104.

Undergraduate Expenses (1997–98) Comprehensive fee of $17,540 includes tuition ($11,990) and college room and board ($5550).

Applications 75% of all full-time undergraduates enrolled in fall 1996 applied for aid; of these, 82% were judged to have need according to Federal Methodology, of whom 100% were aided. *Financial aid deadline (priority):* 4/1. *Financial aid forms:* FAFSA required; state form acceptable. *Admission application deadline:* 3/15.

Summary of Aid to Needy Students *From gift & self-help combined:* Average need met: 78%. Average amount awarded: $13,277 (63% gift aid, 37% self-help). *Gift aid:* Total: $2,448,214 (68% from college's own funds, 3% from other college-administered sources, 29% from external sources). 53 Federal Work-Study jobs (averaging $960); 124 part-time jobs.

Need-Based Scholarships & Grants Pell, FSEOG, state, private, college/university.

Loans PLUS, Stafford, Unsubsidized Stafford, private, college/university long-term loans ($1000 average).

Non-Need Awards In 1996, a total of 483 non-need awards were made. *Academic Interests/Achievement Awards:* 151 ($451,675 total): general academic, education, religion/biblical studies, social sciences. *Creative Arts/Performance Awards:* 32 ($71,550 total): music. *Special Characteristics Awards:* 199 ($197,150 total): children of faculty/staff, relatives of clergy, religious affiliation. *Athletic:* Total: 101 ($461,535); Men: 59 ($301,235); Women: 42 ($160,300).

Other Money-Saving Options Accelerated degree, off-campus living. *Payment Plan:* installment. *Waivers:* full or partial for employees or children of employees and senior citizens.

Contact Mr. Ken Fick, Director of Financial Aid, Concordia College, Bronxville, NY 10708-1998, 914-337-9300 Ext. 2146.

CONCORDIA UNIVERSITY
Irvine, California

About the Institution Independent/religious, coed. Degrees awarded: B, M. Offers 35 undergraduate majors. Total enrollment: 1,027. Undergraduates: 944 (79% state residents). Freshmen: 161.

Undergraduate Expenses (1997–98) Comprehensive fee of $18,980 includes tuition ($12,880), mandatory fees ($920), and college room and board ($5180). College room only: $3100.

Applications 82% of all full-time undergraduates enrolled in fall 1996 applied for aid; of these, 80% were judged to have need according to Federal Methodology, of whom 85% were aided. *Financial aid deadline (priority):* 3/15. *Financial aid forms:* FAFSA, state form, institutional form required. *Admission application deadline:* rolling.

Summary of Aid to Needy Students *From gift & self-help combined:* Average need met: 75%. Average amount awarded: $8471 (65% gift aid, 35% self-help). *Gift aid:* Total: $1,880,000 (48% from college's own funds, 28% from other college-administered sources, 24% from external sources). 35 Federal Work-Study jobs (averaging $1950); 150 part-time jobs.

Need-Based Scholarships & Grants Pell, FSEOG, state, college/university.

Loans PLUS, Stafford, Unsubsidized Stafford, private.

Non-Need Awards *Academic Interests/Achievement Awards:* general academic. *Creative Arts/Performance Awards:* music, theater/drama. *Special Achievements/Activities Awards:* general special achievements/activities, religious involvement. *Special Characteristics Awards:* children of faculty/staff, members of minorities, relatives of clergy, religious affiliation. *Athletic:* available.

Other Money-Saving Options Co-op program. *Waivers:* full or partial for employees or children of employees.

Contact Office of Financial Aid, Concordia University, Irvine, CA 92612-3299, 714-854-8002 Ext. 171, fax: 714-854-6709.

CONCORDIA UNIVERSITY
River Forest, Illinois

About the Institution Independent/religious, coed. Degrees awarded: B, M. Offers 49 undergraduate majors. Total enrollment: 2,107. Undergraduates: 1,343 (68% state residents). Freshmen: 214.

Undergraduate Expenses (1997–98) Comprehensive fee of $16,423 includes tuition ($11,488), mandatory fees ($83), and college room and board ($4852). College room only: $1684.

Applications Of all full-time undergraduates enrolled in fall 1996, 90% of those who applied for aid were judged to have need according to Federal Methodology, of whom 100% were aided. *Financial aid deadline:* Applications processed continuously. *Financial aid forms:* FAFSA, institutional form required. *Admission application deadline:* rolling.

Summary of Aid to Needy Students *From gift & self-help combined:* Average need met: 75%. Average amount awarded: $9900. *Gift aid:* Total: $6,303,000 (54% from college's own funds, 24% from other college-administered sources, 22% from external sources). 172 Federal Work-Study jobs (averaging $1316); part-time jobs.

Need-Based Scholarships & Grants Pell, FSEOG, state, private, college/university.

Loans Perkins, PLUS, Stafford, Unsubsidized Stafford.

Non-Need Awards *Academic Interests/Achievement Awards:* general academic. *Creative Arts/Performance Awards:* music. *Special Characteristics Awards:* general special characteristics, religious affiliation.

Other Money-Saving Options Accelerated degree, off-campus living (after sophomore year). *Waivers:* full or partial for employees or children of employees.

Contact Ms. Deborah A. Ness, Director of Financial Aid, Concordia University, 7400 Augusta, River Forest, IL 60305-1499, 708-209-3113.

CONCORDIA UNIVERSITY
Portland, Oregon

About the Institution Independent/religious, coed. Degrees awarded: A, B, M. Offers 25 undergraduate majors. Total enrollment: 1,020. Undergraduates: 971 (59% state residents). Freshmen: 94.

Undergraduate Expenses (1997–98 estimated) Comprehensive fee of $14,560 includes tuition ($11,030) and college room and board ($3530). College room only: $1830.

Applications Of all full-time undergraduates enrolled in fall 1996, 94% of those who applied for aid were judged to have need according to Federal Methodology, of whom 100% were aided. *Financial aid deadline (priority):* 8/1. *Financial aid forms:* FAFSA, institutional form required; CSS Financial Aid PROFILE acceptable. *Admission application deadline:* rolling.

Summary of Aid to Needy Students *From gift & self-help combined:* Average need met: 90%. Average amount awarded: $9400 (44% gift aid, 56% self-help). *Gift aid:* Total: $2,600,000 (74% from college's own funds, 6% from other college-administered sources, 20% from external sources). 45 Federal Work-Study jobs (averaging $1500); 180 part-time jobs.

Need-Based Scholarships & Grants Pell, FSEOG, state, private, college/university.

Loans Perkins, PLUS, Stafford, Unsubsidized Stafford.

Non-Need Awards In 1996, a total of 346 non-need awards were made. *Academic Interests/Achievement Awards:* 106 ($390,000 total): general academic. *Creative Arts/Performance Awards:* 3 ($3000 total): music. *Special Achievements/Activities Awards:* 83 ($260,000 total): religious involvement. *Special Characteristics Awards:* 24 ($21,000 total): relatives of clergy. *Athletic:* Total: 130 ($328,000); Men: 80 ($178,000); Women: 50 ($150,000).

Other Money-Saving Options Accelerated degree, off-campus living. *Payment Plan:* installment. *Waivers:* full or partial for employees or children of employees and senior citizens.

Contact Mr. James W. Cullen, Director of Financial Aid, Concordia University, 2811 Northeast Holman, Portland, OR 97211-6099, 503-280-8514, fax: 503-280-8531.

CONCORDIA UNIVERSITY AT AUSTIN
Austin, Texas

About the Institution Independent/religious, coed. Degrees awarded: A, B. Offers 19 undergraduate majors. Total enrollment: 723 (91% state residents). Freshmen: 119.

Undergraduate Expenses (1997–98) Comprehensive fee of $14,150 includes tuition ($8800), mandatory fees ($600), and college room and board ($4750).

Applications 68% of all full-time undergraduates enrolled in fall 1996 applied for aid; of these, 86% were judged to have need according to Federal Methodology, of whom 100% were aided. *Financial aid deadline (priority):* 4/15. *Financial aid forms:* FAFSA, institutional form required. *Admission application deadline:* 8/1.

Summary of Aid to Needy Students *From gift & self-help combined:* Average need met: 92%. Average amount awarded: $9175 (64% gift aid, 36% self-help). *Gift aid:* Total: $1,964,271 (57% from college's own funds, 26% from other college-administered sources, 17% from external sources). 81 Federal Work-Study jobs (averaging $1200); 29 part-time jobs.

Need-Based Scholarships & Grants Pell, FSEOG, state, college/university.

Loans PLUS, Stafford, Unsubsidized Stafford, state.

Non-Need Awards *Academic Interests/Achievement Awards:* ($120,650 total): general academic. *Creative Arts/Performance Awards:* 16 ($18,350 total): music. *Special Achievements/Activities Awards:* 104 ($136,050 total): leadership. *Special Characteristics Awards:* 8 ($9240 total): religious affiliation. *Athletic:* Total: 60 ($248,447); Men: 36 ($134,767); Women: 24 ($113,680).

Other Money-Saving Options Co-op program, cooperative Army ROTC, cooperative Naval ROTC, cooperative Air Force ROTC, off-campus living (after freshman year). *Payment Plan:* installment. *Waivers:* full or partial for employees or children of employees.

Contact Ms. Pat M. Jost, Director of Financial Assistance, Concordia University at Austin, 3400 Interstate 35 North, Austin, TX 78705-2799, 512-452-7661, fax: 512-459-8517.

CONCORDIA UNIVERSITY WISCONSIN
Mequon, Wisconsin

About the Institution Independent/religious, coed. Degrees awarded: B, M. Offers 52 undergraduate majors. Total enrollment: 3,659. Undergraduates: 1,269 (73% state residents). Freshmen: 263.

Undergraduate Expenses (1997–98) Comprehensive fee of $14,460 includes tuition ($10,700), mandatory fees ($60), and college room and board ($3700).

Applications *Financial aid deadline (priority):* 5/1. *Financial aid forms:* FAFSA, institutional form required. *Admission application deadline:* 8/15.

Summary of Aid to Needy Students *From gift & self-help combined:* Average need met: 90%. Average amount awarded: $7500. Federal Work-Study jobs; 205 part-time jobs.

Need-Based Scholarships & Grants Pell, FSEOG, state, private, college/university.

Loans PLUS, Stafford, Unsubsidized Stafford.

Non-Need Awards *Academic Interests/Achievement Awards:* general academic. *Creative Arts/Performance Awards:* music, performing arts. *Special Achievements/Activities Awards:* leadership, religious involvement. *Special Characteristics Awards:* religious affiliation.

Other Money-Saving Options Off-campus living. *Payment Plans:* installment, deferred payment. *Waivers:* full or partial for employees or children of employees.

Contact Mr. R. Edward Schroeder, Director of Financial Aid, Concordia University Wisconsin, 12800 North Lake Shore Drive, Mequon, WI 53097-2402, 414-243-4347.

CONNECTICUT COLLEGE
New London, Connecticut

About the Institution Independent, coed. Degrees awarded: B, M. Offers 41 undergraduate majors. Total enrollment: 1,918. Undergraduates: 1,702 (28% state residents). Freshmen: 450.

Undergraduate Expenses (1997–98) Comprehensive fee: $28,475.

Applications 60% of all full-time undergraduates enrolled in fall 1996 applied for aid; of these, 92% were judged to have need according to Federal Methodology, of whom 100% were aided. *Financial aid deadline (priority):* 2/1. *Financial aid forms:* FAFSA, CSS Financial Aid PROFILE required. *Regular admission application deadline:* 1/15. Early decision deadline: 11/15.

Summary of Aid to Needy Students *From gift & self-help combined:* Average need met: 100%. Average amount awarded: $17,788 (74% gift aid, 26% self-help). *Gift aid:* Total: $11,955,250 (90% from college's own funds, 7% from other college-administered sources, 3% from external sources). 737 Federal Work-Study jobs (averaging $1003); part-time jobs.

Need-Based Scholarships & Grants Pell, FSEOG, state, private, college/university.

Loans Perkins, PLUS, Stafford, Unsubsidized Stafford, college/university short-term loans ($100 average), college/university long-term loans ($1800 average).

Non-Need Awards Not offered.

Other Money-Saving Options Accelerated degree. *Payment Plan:* installment. *Waivers:* full or partial for employees or children of employees.

Contact Ms. Elaine Solinga, Director of Financial Aid, Connecticut College, 270 Mohegan Avenue, New London, CT 06320-4196, 860-439-2058, fax: 860-439-5357.

CONSERVATORY OF MUSIC OF PUERTO RICO
San Juan, Puerto Rico

About the Institution Commonwealth-supported, coed. Degrees awarded: B. Offers 6 undergraduate majors.

Applications 54% of all full-time undergraduates enrolled in fall 1996 applied for aid; of these, 95% were judged to have need according to Federal Methodology, of whom 100% were aided. *Financial aid deadline (priority):* 8/31. *Financial aid forms:* FAFSA, institutional form required. *Admission application deadline:* 4/15.

Summary of Aid to Needy Students *From gift & self-help combined:* Average need met: 27%. Average amount awarded: $3214 (64% gift aid, 36% self-help). *Gift aid:* Total: $292,393. 35 Federal Work-Study jobs (averaging $485).

Need-Based Scholarships & Grants Pell, FSEOG, state, private, college/university.

Loans Stafford, Unsubsidized Stafford.

Non-Need Awards Not offered.

Another Money-Saving Option Cooperative Army ROTC.

Contact Mr. Jorge Medina, Director of Financial Aid, Conservatory of Music of Puerto Rico, San Juan, PR 00918, 787-751-0160 Ext. 235.

CONVERSE COLLEGE
Spartanburg, South Carolina

About the Institution Independent, women. Degrees awarded: B, M. Offers 42 undergraduate majors. Total enrollment: 1,250. Undergraduates: 824 (58% state residents). Freshmen: 202.

Undergraduate Expenses (1997–98) Comprehensive fee of $18,525 includes tuition ($14,445) and college room and board ($4080).

Applications 76% of all full-time undergraduates enrolled in fall 1996 applied for aid; of these, 96% were judged to have need according to Federal Methodology, of whom 100% were aided. *Financial aid deadline:* continuous. *Financial aid forms:* FAFSA required. *Regular admission application deadline:* 8/1. Early action deadline: 6/25.

Summary of Aid to Needy Students *From gift & self-help combined:* Average need met: 95%. Average amount awarded: $12,004 (76% gift aid, 24% self-help). *Gift aid:* Total: $4,648,309 (65% from college's own funds, 2% from other college-administered sources, 33% from external sources). Federal Work-Study jobs; 39 part-time jobs.

Need-Based Scholarships & Grants Pell, FSEOG, state, private, college/university.

Loans Perkins, PLUS, Stafford, Unsubsidized Stafford, state, private.

Non-Need Awards In 1996, a total of 762 non-need awards were made. *Academic Interests/Achievement Awards:* 674 ($3,710,222 total): general academic. *Creative Arts/Performance Awards:* 88 ($432,500 total): music.

Other Money-Saving Options Accelerated degree, cooperative Army ROTC. *Payment Plan:* installment. *Waivers:* full or partial for employees or children of employees, adult students, senior citizens.

Contact Office of Financial Aid, Converse College, 580 East Main Street, Spartanburg, SC 29302-0006, 864-596-9000.

COOK COLLEGE
New Brunswick, New Jersey

See Rutgers, The State University of New Jersey, Cook College

COOPER UNION FOR THE ADVANCEMENT OF SCIENCE AND ART
New York, New York

About the Institution Independent, coed. Degrees awarded: B, M. Offers 8 undergraduate majors. Total enrollment: 927. Undergraduates: 872 (63% state residents). Freshmen: 178.

Applications *Financial aid deadline:* 4/15. *Financial aid forms:* FAFSA required. State form required for some.

Summary of Aid to Needy Students *From gift & self-help combined:* Average need met: 100%. 68 Federal Work-Study jobs (averaging $1000); 120 part-time jobs.

Need-Based Scholarships & Grants Pell, FSEOG, private, college/university.

Loans Perkins, PLUS, Stafford, Unsubsidized Stafford, college/university short-term loans ($500 average), college/university long-term loans ($2466 average).

Non-Need Awards Not offered.

Another Money-Saving Option Off-campus living.

Contact Office of Financial Aid, Cooper Union for the Advancement of Science and Art, 30 Cooper Square, New York, NY 10003-7120, 212-353-4100.

THE CORCORAN SCHOOL OF ART
Washington, District of Columbia

About the Institution Independent, coed. Degrees awarded: B. Offers 10 undergraduate majors. Total enrollment: 340 (15% district residents). Freshmen: 87.

Undergraduate Expenses (1997–98) Tuition: $12,800. College room only: $3865 (minimum).

Applications 66% of all full-time undergraduates enrolled in fall 1996 applied for aid; of these,100% were judged to have need according to Federal Methodology, of whom 100% were aided. *Financial aid deadline (priority):* 3/15. *Financial aid forms:* FAFSA, institutional form required. *Admission application deadline:* rolling.

Summary of Aid to Needy Students *From gift & self-help combined:* Average amount awarded: $7072 (42% gift aid, 58% self-help). *Gift aid:* Total: $658,821 (67% from college's own funds, 6% from other college-administered sources, 27% from external sources). 42 Federal Work-Study jobs (averaging $850); 22 part-time jobs.

Need-Based Scholarships & Grants Pell, FSEOG, state, college/university.

Loans Perkins, PLUS, Stafford, Unsubsidized Stafford.

Non-Need Awards In 1996, a total of 149 non-need awards were made. *Creative Arts/Performance Awards:* 149 ($231,761 total): art/fine arts.

Other Money-Saving Options Off-campus living. *Payment Plan:* installment. *Waivers:* full or partial for employees or children of employees.

Contact Ms. Wandra Miller, Director of Financial Aid, The Corcoran School of Art, 500 17th Street, NW, Washington, DC 20006-4804, 202-639-1816, fax: 202-639-1802.

CORNELL COLLEGE
Mount Vernon, Iowa

About the Institution Independent/religious, coed. Degrees awarded: B. Offers 50 undergraduate majors. Total enrollment: 1,105 (26% state residents). Freshmen: 320.

Undergraduate Expenses (1996–97) Comprehensive fee of $21,890 includes tuition ($17,080), mandatory fees ($140), and college room and board ($4670). College room only: $2140.

Applications 93% of all full-time undergraduates enrolled in fall 1996 applied for aid; of these, 93% were judged to have need according to Federal Methodology, of whom 100% were aided. *Financial aid deadline (priority):* 3/1. *Financial aid forms:* FAFSA, institutional form required. *Regular admission application deadline:* 3/1. Early decision deadline: 12/1.

Summary of Aid to Needy Students *From gift & self-help combined:* Average need met: 93%. Average amount awarded: $14,850 (72% gift aid, 28% self-help). *Gift aid:* Total: $10,131,297 (84% from college's own funds, 8% from other college-administered sources, 8% from external sources). 502 Federal Work-Study jobs (averaging $1000); 185 part-time jobs.

Need-Based Scholarships & Grants Pell, FSEOG, state, private, college/university.

Loans Perkins, PLUS, Stafford, Unsubsidized Stafford, college/university long-term loans.

Non-Need Awards *Academic Interests/Achievement Awards:* 335 ($1,991,155 total): general academic. *Creative Arts/Performance Awards:* 38 ($220,216 total): art/fine arts, music, theater/drama. *Special Achievements/Activities Awards:* 156 ($814,385 total): leadership. *Special Characteristics Awards:* children of faculty/staff.

Other Money-Saving Options Accelerated degree, off-campus living (after freshman year). *Payment Plan:* installment. *Waivers:* full or partial for employees or children of employees, adult students, senior citizens.

Contact Ms. Cindi P. Reints, Director of Financial Assistance, Cornell College, Wade House, 600 1st Street West, Mount Vernon, IA 52314-1098, 319-895-4216, fax: 319-895-4451.

CORNELL UNIVERSITY
Ithaca, New York

About the Institution Independent, coed. Degrees awarded: B, M, D, P. Offers 147 undergraduate majors. Total enrollment: 18,849. Undergraduates: 13,512 (43% state residents). Freshmen: 3,212.

Undergraduate Expenses (1996–97) Comprehensive fee of $28,009 includes tuition ($20,900), mandatory fees ($74), and college room and board ($7035). Tuition for state-supported programs: $8800 for state residents, $17,060 for nonresidents.

Applications Of all full-time undergraduates enrolled in fall 1996, 80% of those who applied for aid were judged to have need according to Federal Methodology, of whom 100% were aided. *Financial aid deadline (priority):* 2/15. *Financial aid forms:* FAFSA, CSS Financial Aid PROFILE, state form, institutional form required. *Regular admission application deadline:* 1/1. Early decision deadline: 11/1.

Summary of Aid to Needy Students *From gift & self-help combined:* Average need met: 100%. Average amount awarded: $15,910 (59% gift aid, 41% self-help). *Gift aid:* Total: $64,139,000 (77% from college's own funds, 7% from other college-administered sources, 16% from external sources). 5,395 Federal Work-Study jobs (averaging $1715); 4,315 part-time jobs.

Need-Based Scholarships & Grants Pell, FSEOG, state, private, college/university.

Loans Perkins, PLUS, Stafford, Unsubsidized Stafford, college/university short-term loans ($750 average), college/university long-term loans ($1670 average).

Non-Need Awards Not offered.

Other Money-Saving Options Co-op program, Army ROTC, Naval ROTC, Air Force ROTC, off-campus living. *Payment Plans:* tuition prepayment, installment. *Waivers:* full or partial for employees or children of employees.

Contact Mr. Thomas Keane, Director of Financial Aid, Cornell University, 203 Day Hall, Ithaca, NY 14853-0001, 607-255-5145, fax: 607-255-5022.

CORNERSTONE COLLEGE
Grand Rapids, Michigan

About the Institution Independent/religious, coed. Degrees awarded: A, B. Offers 38 undergraduate majors. Total enrollment: 1,082 (81% state residents). Freshmen: 300.

Undergraduate Expenses (1997–98) Comprehensive fee of $13,868 includes tuition ($8832), mandatory fees ($618), and college room and board ($4418). College room only: $2036.

Applications 86% of all full-time undergraduates enrolled in fall 1996 applied for aid; of these, 87% were judged to have need according to Federal Methodology, of whom 100% were aided. *Financial aid deadline (priority):* 3/1. *Financial aid forms:* FAFSA, institutional form required. *Admission application deadline:* rolling.

Summary of Aid to Needy Students *From gift & self-help combined:* Average need met: 83%. Average amount awarded: $9586 (43% gift aid, 57% self-help). *Gift aid:* Total: $2,650,000. Federal Work-Study jobs; 300 part-time jobs.

Need-Based Scholarships & Grants Pell, FSEOG, state, private, college/university.

Loans Perkins, PLUS, Stafford, Unsubsidized Stafford, state, private.

Non-Need Awards *Academic Interests/Achievement Awards:* available. *Creative Arts/Performance Awards:* music. *Special Achievements/Activities Awards:* leadership, religious involvement. *Special Characteristics Awards:* general special characteristics, children of faculty/staff, children of union members/company employees, spouses of current students. *Athletic:* Total: 174 ($302,000); Men: 99 ($189,000); Women: 75 ($113,000).

Other Money-Saving Options Cooperative Army ROTC, off-campus living (after junior year). *Payment Plan:* installment. *Waivers:* full or partial for employees or children of employees.

Contact Mr. Edward Kerestly, Director of Financial Aid, Cornerstone College, 1001 East Beltline Avenue, NE, Grand Rapids, MI 49505-5897, 616-222-1424, fax: 616-222-1400.

CORNISH COLLEGE OF THE ARTS
Seattle, Washington

About the Institution Independent, coed. Degrees awarded: B. Offers 11 undergraduate majors. Total enrollment: 640 (66% state residents).

Undergraduate Expenses (1996–97) Tuition: $10,990.

Applications Of all full-time undergraduates enrolled in fall 1996, 92% of those who applied for aid were judged to have need according to Federal Methodology, of whom 100% were aided. *Financial aid deadline (priority):* 2/15. *Financial aid forms:* FAFSA, institutional form required; CSS Financial Aid PROFILE acceptable. *Admission application deadline:* 8/15.

Summary of Aid to Needy Students *From gift & self-help combined:* Average need met: 84%. *Gift aid:* Total: $1,710,000 (44% from college's own funds, 24% from other college-administered sources, 32% from external sources). 250 Federal Work-Study jobs (averaging $3000).

Need-Based Scholarships & Grants Pell, FSEOG, state, private, college/university.

Loans Perkins, PLUS, Stafford, Unsubsidized Stafford, private, college/university short-term loans ($500 average).

Non-Need Awards In 1996, a total of 470 non-need awards were made. *Creative Arts/Performance Awards:* 450 ($700,000 total): art/fine arts, dance, music, theater/drama. *Special Characteristics Awards:* 20 ($50,000 total): members of minorities.

Other Money-Saving Options *Payment Plan:* installment. *Waivers:* full or partial for employees or children of employees.

Contact Office of Admissions and Financial Aid, Cornish College of the Arts, 710 East Roy Street, Seattle, WA 98102-4696, 206-726-5014, fax: 206-720-1011.

COVENANT COLLEGE
Lookout Mountain, Georgia

About the Institution Independent/religious, coed. Degrees awarded: A, B, M. Offers 18 undergraduate majors. Total enrollment: 763. Undergraduates: 711 (19% state residents). Freshmen: 205.

Undergraduate Expenses (1997–98) Comprehensive fee of $16,690 includes tuition ($12,550), mandatory fees ($330), and college room and board ($3810). College room only: $1690 (minimum).

Applications 72% of all full-time undergraduates enrolled in fall 1996 applied for aid; of these, 100% were judged to have need according to Federal Methodology, of whom 99% were aided. *Financial aid deadline (priority):* 3/31. *Financial aid forms:* FAFSA, institutional form required. Merit Scholarship form required for some. *Admission application deadline:* rolling.

Summary of Aid to Needy Students *From gift & self-help combined:* Average need met: 80%. Average amount awarded: $10,449 (57% gift aid, 43% self-help). *Gift aid:* Total: $2,715,407 (78% from college's own funds, 10% from other college-administered sources, 12% from external sources). 232 Federal Work-Study jobs (averaging $1320); part-time jobs.

Need-Based Scholarships & Grants Pell, FSEOG, private, college/university.

Loans Perkins, PLUS, Stafford, Unsubsidized Stafford, private.

Non-Need Awards In 1996, a total of 723 non-need awards were made. *Academic Interests/Achievement Awards:* 218 ($612,425 total): general academic. *Creative Arts/Performance Awards:* 59 ($48,655 total): music. *Special Characteristics Awards:* 360 ($744,230 total): children of faculty/staff, international students, members of minorities, religious affiliation. *Athletic:* Total: 86 ($269,310); Men: 44 ($144,360); Women: 42 ($124,950).

Other Money-Saving Options Accelerated degree, co-op program, cooperative Army ROTC, off-campus living (after junior year). *Waivers:* full or partial for employees or children of employees and senior citizens.

Contact Mrs. Carolyn Hays, Student Financial Planning Coordinator, Covenant College, Scenic Highway, Lookout Mountain, GA 30750, 706-820-1560, fax: 706-820-2165.

CREIGHTON UNIVERSITY
Omaha, Nebraska

About the Institution Independent/religious, coed. Degrees awarded: A, B, M, D, P. Offers 47 undergraduate majors. Total enrollment: 6,158. Undergraduates: 3,679 (46% state residents). Freshmen: 881.

Undergraduate Expenses (1997–98) Comprehensive fee of $17,696 includes tuition ($12,246), mandatory fees ($510), and college room and board ($4940). College room only: $2740.

Applications Of all full-time undergraduates enrolled in fall 1996, 86% of those who applied for aid were judged to have need according to Federal Methodology, of whom 100% were aided. *Financial aid deadline (priority):* 4/1. *Financial aid forms:* FAFSA, institutional form required; CSS Financial Aid PROFILE acceptable. *Admission application deadline:* rolling.

Summary of Aid to Needy Students *From gift & self-help combined:* Average amount awarded: $12,136 (37% gift aid, 63% self-help). *Gift aid:* Total: $4,810,316 (66% from college's own funds, 18% from other college-administered sources, 16% from external sources). 600 Federal Work-Study jobs (averaging $1400); 1,200 part-time jobs.

Need-Based Scholarships & Grants Pell, FSEOG, state, college/university.

Loans Perkins, PLUS, Stafford, Unsubsidized Stafford, Federal Nursing, Primary Care, private, college/university short-term loans ($200 average), college/university long-term loans ($2000 average).

Non-Need Awards In 1996, a total of 2,736 non-need awards were made. *Academic Interests/Achievement Awards:* 1,774 ($4,569,557 total): general academic. *Special Characteristics Awards:* 817 ($3,545,540 total): children of faculty/staff, local/state students, members of minorities, religious affiliation, ROTC participants, siblings of current students. *Athletic:* Total: 145 ($1,340,321); Men: 66 ($615,071); Women: 79 ($725,250).

Other Money-Saving Options Accelerated degree, Army ROTC, cooperative Air Force ROTC, off-campus living (after sophomore year). *Payment Plan:* installment. *Waivers:* full or partial for employees or children of employees and adult students.

Contact Ms. Paula Kohles, Assistant Director of Financial Aid, Creighton University, 2500 California Plaza, Omaha, NE 68178-0001, 402-280-2731.

CRICHTON COLLEGE
Memphis, Tennessee

About the Institution Independent, coed. Degrees awarded: B. Offers 10 undergraduate majors. Total enrollment: 560 (80% state residents). Freshmen: 56.

Undergraduate Expenses (1997–98) Tuition: $6360. College room only: $1650.

Applications *Financial aid deadline (priority):* 7/15. *Financial aid forms:* FAFSA, institutional form required; CSS Financial Aid PROFILE acceptable. *Admission application deadline:* 8/31.

Summary of Aid to Needy Students *From gift & self-help combined:* Average amount awarded: $2776 (36% gift aid, 64% self-help). *Gift aid:* Total: $433,498 (68% from college's own funds, 23% from other college-administered sources, 9% from external sources). 29 Federal Work-Study jobs (averaging $3800); 6 part-time jobs.

Need-Based Scholarships & Grants Pell, FSEOG, state, private, college/university.

Loans Perkins, Stafford, Unsubsidized Stafford, college/university short-term loans ($1100 average).

Non-Need Awards In 1996, a total of 276 non-need awards were made. *Academic Interests/Achievement Awards:* 123 ($90,203 total): general academic. *Creative Arts/Performance Awards:* 24 ($10,535 total): music, theater/drama. *Special Achievements/Activities Awards:* 97 ($47,015 total): community service, leadership, religious involvement. *Special Characteristics Awards:* 32 ($35,304 total): general special characteristics, children and siblings of alumni, members of minorities, relatives of clergy, religious affiliation.

Other Money-Saving Options Off-campus living. *Waivers:* full or partial for minority students, children of alumni, employees or children of employees, adult students, senior citizens.

Contact Ms. Lisa Becker, Financial Aid Counselor, Crichton College, PO Box 757830, Memphis, TN 38175-7830, 901-367-9800, fax: 901-367-3866.

THE CRISWELL COLLEGE
Dallas, Texas

About the Institution Independent/religious, coed. Degrees awarded: A, B, M, P. Offers 5 undergraduate majors. Total enrollment: 442. Undergraduates: 326 (58% state residents). Freshmen: 25.

Undergraduate Expenses (1996–97) Tuition: $2944. Mandatory fees: $120.

Applications *Financial aid deadline (priority):* 5/1. *Financial aid forms:* institutional form required. *Admission application deadline:* 8/15.

Summary of Aid to Needy Students *From gift & self-help combined:* Average need met: 70%. Average amount awarded: $1413 (82% gift aid, 18% self-help). *Gift aid:* Total: $320,000 (100% from college's own funds). 45 part-time jobs.

Need-Based Scholarships & Grants College/university.

Loans Private.

Non-Need Awards In 1996, a total of 141 non-need awards were made. *Academic Interests/Achievement Awards:* 21 ($11,000 total): general academic. *Special Achievements/Activities Awards:* 120 ($85,000 total): religious involvement.

Other Money-Saving Options *Payment Plan:* installment. *Waivers:* full or partial for employees or children of employees.

Contact Mr. Richard Grimm, Vice-President of Enrollment Services, The Criswell College, Dallas, TX 75246-1537, 800-899-0012.

CROWN COLLEGE
St. Bonifacius, Minnesota

About the Institution Independent/religious, coed. Degrees awarded: A, B, M. Offers 28 undergraduate majors. Total enrollment: 629. Undergraduates: 618 (58% state residents). Freshmen: 114.

Undergraduate Expenses (1997–98) Comprehensive fee of $13,355 includes tuition ($8640), mandatory fees ($695), and college room and board ($4020). College room only: $1996.

Applications *Financial aid deadline (priority):* 5/1. *Financial aid forms:* FAFSA, institutional form required; CSS Financial Aid PROFILE acceptable. *Admission application deadline:* rolling.

Summary of Aid to Needy Students *From gift & self-help combined:* Average amount awarded: $6968 (94% gift aid, 6% self-help). *Gift aid:* Total: $3,922,061 (19% from college's own funds, 51% from other college-administered sources, 30% from external sources). 65 Federal Work-Study jobs.

Need-Based Scholarships & Grants Pell, FSEOG, state, private, college/university.

Loans Perkins, PLUS, Stafford, Unsubsidized Stafford, state, private.

Non-Need Awards In 1996, a total of 40 non-need awards were made. *Academic Interests/Achievement Awards:* 20 ($40,000 total): general academic. *Special Achievements/Activities Awards:* 5 ($15,000 total): leadership. *Special Characteristics Awards:* 15 ($30,000 total): children of educators, children of faculty/staff, relatives of clergy.

Other Money-Saving Options *Payment Plan:* installment. *Waivers:* full or partial for employees or children of employees.

Contact Mrs. Janice Lanpher, Director of Financial Aid, Crown College, 6425 County Road 30, St. Bonifacius, MN 55375-9001, 612-446-4100, fax: 612-446-4149.

CULVER-STOCKTON COLLEGE
Canton, Missouri

About the Institution Independent/religious, coed. Degrees awarded: B. Offers 36 undergraduate majors. Total enrollment: 1,031 (54% state residents). Freshmen: 276.

Undergraduate Expenses (1996–97) Comprehensive fee of $12,800 includes tuition ($8800) and college room and board ($4000). College room only: $1800.

Applications 88% of all full-time undergraduates enrolled in fall 1996 applied for aid; of these, 64% were judged to have need according to Federal Methodology, of whom 100% were aided. *Financial aid deadline (priority):* 3/1. *Financial aid forms:* FAFSA required. *Admission application deadline:* rolling.

Summary of Aid to Needy Students *From gift & self-help combined:* Average need met: 100%. Average amount awarded: $10,310 (59% gift aid, 41% self-help). *Gift aid:* Total: $2,860,588 (73% from college's own funds, 13% from other college-administered sources, 14% from external sources). 76 Federal Work-Study jobs (averaging $836); 364 part-time jobs.

Need-Based Scholarships & Grants Pell, FSEOG, state, private, college/university.

Loans Perkins, PLUS, Stafford, Unsubsidized Stafford, college/university short-term loans ($100 average), college/university long-term loans ($1562 average).

Non-Need Awards In 1996, a total of 1,192 non-need awards were made. *Academic Interests/Achievement Awards:* 530 ($2,308,514 total): general academic. *Creative Arts/Performance Awards:* 207 ($265,528 total): art/fine arts, debating, music, theater/drama. *Special Characteristics Awards:* 264 ($392,165 total): children and siblings of alumni, local/state students, religious affiliation. *Athletic:* Total: 191 ($422,790); Men: 142 ($308,300); Women: 49 ($114,490).

Other Money-Saving Options Accelerated degree. *Payment Plan:* installment. *Waivers:* full or partial for children of alumni, employees or children of employees, adult students, senior citizens.

Contact Ms. Carla D. Boren, Director of Student Financial Planning, Culver-Stockton College, 1 College Hill, Canton, MO 63435-1299, 217-231-6306, fax: 217-231-6618.

CUMBERLAND COLLEGE
Williamsburg, Kentucky

About the Institution Independent/religious, coed. Degrees awarded: B, M. Offers 37 undergraduate majors. Total enrollment: 1,614. Undergraduates: 1,517 (54% state residents). Freshmen: 423.

Undergraduate Expenses (1997–98 estimated) Comprehensive fee of $12,206 includes tuition ($8398), mandatory fees ($32), and college room and board ($3776).

Applications Of all full-time undergraduates enrolled in fall 1996, 96% of those who applied for aid were judged to have need according to Federal Methodology, of whom 100% were aided. *Financial aid deadline (priority):* 3/15. *Financial aid forms:* FAFSA required. *Admission application deadline:* rolling.

Summary of Aid to Needy Students *From gift & self-help combined:* Average need met: 85%. Average amount awarded: $8659 (58% gift aid, 42% self-help). *Gift aid:* Total: $6,759,087 (66% from college's own funds, 17% from other college-administered sources, 17% from external sources). 448 Federal Work-Study jobs (averaging $1500); 200 part-time jobs.

Need-Based Scholarships & Grants Pell, FSEOG, state, private.

Loans Perkins, PLUS, Stafford, Unsubsidized Stafford, college/university short-term loans ($50 average), college/university long-term loans ($3000 average).

Non-Need Awards In 1996, a total of 1,263 non-need awards were made. *Academic Interests/Achievement Awards:* 792 ($1,696,198 total): general academic, biological sciences, business, communication, computer science, education, engineering/technologies, English, foreign languages, health fields, mathematics, military science, physical sciences, premedicine, religion/biblical studies, social sciences. *Creative Arts/Performance Awards:* 21 ($13,500 total): art/fine arts, music. *Special Achievements/Activities Awards:* 17 ($21,500 total): cheerleading/drum major. *Special Characteristics Awards:* 163 ($291,406 total): children and siblings of alumni, children of faculty/staff, relatives of clergy, siblings of current students. *Athletic:* Total: 270 ($879,364); Men: 177 ($551,171); Women: 93 ($328,193).

Other Money-Saving Options Accelerated degree, Army ROTC, off-campus living (after sophomore year). *Payment Plan:* installment. *Waivers:* full or partial for employees or children of employees.

Contact Mr. Jack Stanfill, Director, Student Financial Planning, Cumberland College, 6190 College Station Drive, Williamsburg, KY 40769-1372, 606-549-2200.

CUMBERLAND UNIVERSITY
Lebanon, Tennessee

About the Institution Independent, coed. Degrees awarded: A, B, M. Offers 19 undergraduate majors. Total enrollment: 1,062. Undergraduates: 922 (80% state residents). Freshmen: 140.

Undergraduate Expenses (1997–98) Comprehensive fee of $11,590 includes tuition ($7990), mandatory fees ($200), and college room and board ($3400).

Applications Of all full-time undergraduates enrolled in fall 1996, 70% of those who applied for aid were judged to have need according to Federal Methodology, of whom 100% were aided. *Financial aid deadline (priority):* 3/1. *Financial aid forms:* institutional form required; CSS Financial Aid PROFILE acceptable. FAFSA required for some. *Admission application deadline:* rolling.

Summary of Aid to Needy Students *From gift & self-help combined:* Average need met: 85%. Average amount awarded: $5250 (57% gift aid, 43% self-help). *Gift aid:* Total: $1,939,138 (77% from college's own funds, 10% from other college-administered sources, 13% from external sources). 38 Federal Work-Study jobs (averaging $800); 125 part-time jobs.

Need-Based Scholarships & Grants Pell, FSEOG, state, private, college/university.

Loans Perkins, PLUS, Stafford, Unsubsidized Stafford, private.

Non-Need Awards In 1996, a total of 664 non-need awards were made. *Academic Interests/Achievement Awards:* 318 ($794,231 total): general academic. *Creative Arts/Performance Awards:* 10 ($11,500 total): art/fine arts. *Special Achievements/Activities Awards:* 16 ($19,600 total): leadership. *Athletic:* Total: 320 ($766,617); Men: 225 ($534,165); Women: 95 ($232,452).

Other Money-Saving Options Co-op program, off-campus living. *Payment Plan:* installment. *Waivers:* full or partial for employees or children of employees and senior citizens.

Contact Ms. Jamie Stewart, Financial Aid Coordinator, Cumberland University, South Greenwood Street, Lebanon, TN 37087-3554, 615-444-2562 Ext. 244, fax: 615-444-2569.

CURRY COLLEGE
Milton, Massachusetts

About the Institution Independent, coed. Degrees awarded: B, M. Offers 27 undergraduate majors. Total enrollment: 1,909. Undergraduates: 1,867 (62% state residents). Freshmen: 294.

Undergraduate Expenses (1997–98) Comprehensive fee of $21,515 includes tuition ($15,250), mandatory fees ($450), and college room and board ($5815 minimum). College room only: $3215 (minimum).

Applications 69% of all full-time undergraduates enrolled in fall 1996 applied for aid; of these, 94% were judged to have need according to Federal Methodology, of whom 100% were aided. *Financial aid deadline (priority):* 3/15. *Financial aid forms:* FAFSA, institutional form required. *Regular admission application deadline:* 4/1. Early decision deadline: 12/1.

Summary of Aid to Needy Students *From gift & self-help combined:* Average need met: 72%. Average amount awarded: $11,576 (66% gift aid, 34% self-help). *Gift aid:* Total: $7,918,622 (49% from college's own funds, 46% from other college-administered sources, 5% from external sources). Federal Work-Study jobs; 45 part-time jobs.

Need-Based Scholarships & Grants Pell, FSEOG, state, private, college/university.

Loans Perkins, PLUS, Stafford, Unsubsidized Stafford, state, private, college/university long-term loans ($2500 average).

Non-Need Awards Not offered.

Other Money-Saving Options Accelerated degree, cooperative Army ROTC, off-campus living. *Payment Plan:* installment. *Waivers:* full or partial for children of alumni, employees or children of employees, senior citizens.

Contact Mr. Michael Mullaney, Director of Financial Aid, Curry College, 1071 Blue Hill Avenue, Milton, MA 02186-9984, 617-333-2325, fax: 617-333-6860.

THE CURTIS INSTITUTE OF MUSIC
Philadelphia, Pennsylvania

About the Institution Independent, coed. Degrees awarded: B, M. Offers 5 undergraduate majors. Total enrollment: 165. Undergraduates: 145 (55% state residents). Freshmen: 37.

Undergraduate Expenses (1996–97) Tuition: $0. Mandatory fees: $675.

Applications *Financial aid deadline:* 3/3. *Financial aid forms:* FAFSA, CSS Financial Aid PROFILE, state form, institutional form, Foreign Student Financial Aid Application required. *Admission application deadline:* 1/15.

Summary of Aid to Needy Students 38 part-time jobs.

Need-Based Scholarships & Grants Pell, state, college/university.

Loans PLUS, Stafford, Unsubsidized Stafford, college/university short-term loans ($250 average).

Non-Need Awards *Creative Arts/Performance Awards:* music.

Another Money-Saving Option Accelerated degree.

Contact Office of Financial Aid, The Curtis Institute of Music, Philadelphia, PA 19103-6107, 215-893-5252.

C.W. POST CAMPUS OF LONG ISLAND UNIVERSITY
Brookville, New York

See Long Island University, C.W. Post Campus

DAEMEN COLLEGE
Amherst, New York

About the Institution Independent, coed. Degrees awarded: B, M. Offers 26 undergraduate majors. Total enrollment: 1,815. Undergraduates: 1,792 (91% state residents). Freshmen: 377.

Undergraduate Expenses (1996–97) Comprehensive fee of $15,530 includes tuition ($9950), mandatory fees ($380), and college room and board ($5200).

Applications 96% of all full-time undergraduates enrolled in fall 1996 applied for aid; of these, 92% were judged to have need according to Federal Methodology, of whom 100% were aided. *Financial aid deadline (priority):* 3/15. *Financial aid forms:* FAFSA, state form, institutional form required. *Regular admission application deadline:* rolling. Early action deadline: 8/1.

Summary of Aid to Needy Students *From gift & self-help combined:* Average need met: 82%. Average amount awarded: $8397 (58% gift aid, 42% self-help). *Gift aid:* Total: $5,558,966 (55% from college's own funds, 5% from other college-administered sources, 40% from external sources). 350 Federal Work-Study jobs (averaging $1400); 60 part-time jobs.

Need-Based Scholarships & Grants Pell, FSEOG, state, private, college/university.

Loans Perkins, PLUS, Stafford, Unsubsidized Stafford, college/university long-term loans ($1500 average), alternative loans.

Non-Need Awards In 1996, a total of 544 non-need awards were made. *Academic Interests/Achievement Awards:* 499 ($797,529 total): general academic, education, health fields. *Special Characteristics Awards:* 21 ($26,239 total): general special characteristics, children and siblings of alumni, siblings of current students. *Athletic:* Total: 24 ($175,583); Men: 10 ($83,952); Women: 14 ($91,631).

Other Money-Saving Options Co-op program, cooperative Army ROTC, off-campus living. *Payment Plans:* installment, deferred payment. *Waivers:* full or partial for children of alumni, employees or children of employees, senior citizens.

Contact Office of Financial Aid, Daemen College, 4380 Main Street, Amherst, NY 14226-3592, 716-839-3600.

DAKOTA STATE UNIVERSITY
Madison, South Dakota

About the Institution State-supported, coed. Degrees awarded: A, B. Offers 32 undergraduate majors. Total enrollment: 1,231 (86% state residents). Freshmen: 203.

Undergraduate Expenses (1997–98) State resident tuition: $1728. Nonresident tuition: $5496. Mandatory fees: $1299. College room and board: $2694 (minimum). College room only: $1300 (minimum).

Applications Of all full-time undergraduates enrolled in fall 1996, 100% of those judged to have need according to Federal Methodology were aided. *Financial aid deadline (priority):* 3/1. *Financial aid forms:* FAFSA required. Institutional form required for some. *Admission application deadline:* rolling.

Summary of Aid to Needy Students *From gift & self-help combined:* Average need met: 81%. Average amount awarded: $2477 (27% gift aid, 73% self-help). *Gift aid:* Total: $545,861 (24% from college's own funds, 10% from other college-administered sources, 66% from external sources). Federal Work-Study jobs; 100 part-time jobs.

Need-Based Scholarships & Grants Pell, FSEOG, state, college/university.

Loans Perkins, PLUS, Stafford, Unsubsidized Stafford.

Non-Need Awards *Academic Interests/Achievement Awards:* general academic, communication, computer science. *Creative Arts/Performance Awards:* music. *Athletic:* available.

Other Money-Saving Options Co-op program, cooperative Air Force ROTC, off-campus living (after sophomore year). *Payment Plan:* deferred payment. *Waivers:* full or partial for employees or children of employees and senior citizens.

Contact Ms. Rose M. Jamison, Financial Aid Director, Dakota State University, 103 Heston Hall, Madison, SD 57042-1799, 605-256-5152.

DAKOTA WESLEYAN UNIVERSITY
Mitchell, South Dakota

About the Institution Independent/religious, coed. Degrees awarded: A, B, M. Offers 36 undergraduate majors. Total enrollment: 710 (84% state residents). Freshmen: 148.

Undergraduate Expenses (1997–98 estimated) Comprehensive fee of $12,065 includes tuition ($8825) and college room and board ($3240).

Applications 100% of all full-time undergraduates enrolled in fall 1996 applied for aid; of these, 73% were judged to have need according to Federal Methodology, of whom 100% were aided. *Financial aid deadline (priority):* 4/1. *Financial aid forms:* institutional form, Education Assistance Corporation's Application for Student Aid required; FAFSA, CSS Financial Aid PROFILE acceptable. State form required for some. *Admission application deadline:* 8/26.

Summary of Aid to Needy Students *From gift & self-help combined:* Average need met: 82%. Average amount awarded: $9458 (52% gift aid, 48% self-help). *Gift aid:* Total: $2,094,091 (56% from college's own funds, 7% from other college-administered sources, 37% from external sources). Federal Work-Study jobs; 65 part-time jobs.

Need-Based Scholarships & Grants Pell, FSEOG, state.

Loans Perkins, PLUS, Stafford, Unsubsidized Stafford, college/university short-term loans ($200 average), Methodist Loans (members of Methodist Church).

Non-Need Awards *Academic Interests/Achievement Awards:* business. *Creative Arts/Performance Awards:* art/fine arts, debating, music, theater/drama. *Special Achievements/Activities Awards:* leadership. *Special Characteristics Awards:* ethnic background, religious affiliation. *Athletic:* available.

Other Money-Saving Options Accelerated degree, co-op program. *Payment Plan:* installment. *Waivers:* full or partial for employees or children of employees.

Contact Ms. Alice Kaye, Assistant Director of Financial Aid, Dakota Wesleyan University, 1120 State Avenue, Mitchell, SD 57301-4398, 605-995-2659, fax: 605-995-2699.

DALLAS BAPTIST UNIVERSITY
Dallas, Texas

About the Institution Independent/religious, coed. Degrees awarded: A, B, M. Offers 44 undergraduate majors. Total enrollment: 3,283. Undergraduates: 2,661 (93% state residents). Freshmen: 190.

Undergraduate Expenses (1996–97) Comprehensive fee of $10,690 includes tuition ($7440) and college room and board ($3250 minimum). College room only: $1390.

Applications 79% of all full-time undergraduates enrolled in fall 1996 applied for aid; of these, 73% were judged to have need according to Federal Methodology, of whom 95% were aided. *Financial aid deadline (priority):* 5/1. *Financial aid forms:* FAFSA, CSS Financial Aid PROFILE, institutional form required; state form acceptable. *Admission application deadline:* rolling.

Summary of Aid to Needy Students *From gift & self-help combined:* Average need met: 98%. Average amount awarded: $9842 (46% gift aid, 54% self-help). *Gift aid:* Total: $2,379,926 (51% from college's own funds, 24% from other college-administered sources, 25% from external sources). 107 Federal Work-Study jobs (averaging $2407).

Need-Based Scholarships & Grants Pell, FSEOG, state, private, college/university.

Loans Perkins, PLUS, Stafford, Unsubsidized Stafford, private, college/university long-term loans ($1362 average).

Non-Need Awards In 1996, a total of 933 non-need awards were made. *Academic Interests/Achievement Awards:* 224 ($1,514,197 total): general academic. *Creative Arts/Performance Awards:* 72 ($240,236

total): music. *Special Achievements/Activities Awards:* 221 ($706,409 total): leadership, memberships. *Special Characteristics Awards:* 358 ($620,858 total): general special characteristics, children and siblings of alumni, children of faculty/staff. *Athletic:* Total: 58 ($244,622); Men: 33 ($165,972); Women: 25 ($78,650).

Other Money-Saving Options Cooperative Army ROTC, cooperative Air Force ROTC. *Payment Plan:* installment. *Waivers:* full or partial for employees or children of employees.

Contact Ms. Mari Notley, Assistant Director of Financial Aid, Dallas Baptist University, 3000 Mountain Creek Parkway, Dallas, TX 75211-9299, 214-333-5461, fax: 214-333-5586.

DALLAS CHRISTIAN COLLEGE
Dallas, Texas

About the Institution Independent/religious, coed. Degrees awarded: A, B. Offers 4 undergraduate majors. Total enrollment: 240 (86% state residents). Freshmen: 48.

Undergraduate Expenses (1996–97) Comprehensive fee of $6480 includes tuition ($3840) and college room and board ($2640).

Applications *Financial aid deadline (priority):* 7/1. *Financial aid forms:* FAFSA, institutional form required. *Admission application deadline:* rolling.

Summary of Aid to Needy Students Federal Work-Study jobs; part-time jobs.

Non-Need Awards *Academic Interests/Achievement Awards:* general academic. *Creative Arts/Performance Awards:* music. *Special Characteristics Awards:* religious affiliation.

Other Money-Saving Options *Payment Plan:* installment. *Waivers:* full or partial for employees or children of employees.

Contact Office of Financial Aid, Dallas Christian College, Dallas, TX 75234-7299, 972-241-3371.

DANA COLLEGE
Blair, Nebraska

About the Institution Independent/religious, coed. Degrees awarded: B. Offers 57 undergraduate majors. Total enrollment: 614 (55% state residents). Freshmen: 133.

Undergraduate Expenses (1997–98) Comprehensive fee of $15,190 includes tuition ($11,130), mandatory fees ($450), and college room and board ($3610). College room only: $1560.

Applications 90% of all full-time undergraduates enrolled in fall 1996 applied for aid; of these, 95% were judged to have need according to Federal Methodology, of whom 100% were aided. *Financial aid deadline (priority):* 4/1. *Financial aid forms:* FAFSA, institutional form required; CSS Financial Aid PROFILE, state form acceptable. *Admission application deadline:* 8/1.

Summary of Aid to Needy Students *From gift & self-help combined:* Average need met: 86%. Average amount awarded: $5191 (59% gift aid, 41% self-help). *Gift aid:* Total: $1,521,538 (69% from college's own funds, 14% from other college-administered sources, 17% from external sources). 203 Federal Work-Study jobs (averaging $600); 60 part-time jobs.

Need-Based Scholarships & Grants Pell, FSEOG, state, private, college/university.

Loans Perkins, PLUS, Stafford, Unsubsidized Stafford, private, college/university short-term loans ($500 average), college/university long-term loans ($1000 average).

Non-Need Awards In 1996, a total of 1,261 non-need awards were made. *Academic Interests/Achievement Awards:* 332 ($460,529 total): general academic. *Creative Arts/Performance Awards:* 128 ($110,680 total): applied art and design, art/fine arts, debating, music, theater/

drama. *Special Achievements/Activities Awards:* 222 ($147,774 total): general special achievements/activities. *Special Characteristics Awards:* 370 ($326,388 total): children and siblings of alumni, children of faculty/staff, ethnic background, international students, local/state students, members of minorities, out-of-state students, relatives of clergy, religious affiliation, siblings of current students, spouses of current students. *Athletic:* Total: 209 ($364,185); Men: 149 ($245,200); Women: 60 ($118,985).

Other Money-Saving Options Cooperative Army ROTC, cooperative Air Force ROTC, off-campus living (after junior year). *Payment Plan:* installment. *Waivers:* full or partial for minority students, children of alumni, employees or children of employees.

Contact Ms. Pam Shelton, Financial Aid Counselor, Dana College, Blair, NE 68008-1099, 402-426-7226, fax: 402-426-7386.

DANIEL WEBSTER COLLEGE
Nashua, New Hampshire

About the Institution Independent, coed. Degrees awarded: A, B. Offers 16 undergraduate majors. Total enrollment: 476 (17% state residents). Freshmen: 145.

Undergraduate Expenses (1996–97) Comprehensive fee of $19,251 includes tuition ($13,590), mandatory fees ($255), and college room and board ($5406 minimum). College room only: $2670 (minimum).

Applications 87% of all full-time undergraduates enrolled in fall 1996 applied for aid; of these, 97% were judged to have need according to Federal Methodology, of whom 100% were aided. *Financial aid deadline (priority):* 3/15. *Financial aid forms:* FAFSA, institutional form required. *Admission application deadline:* rolling.

Summary of Aid to Needy Students *From gift & self-help combined:* Average need met: 60%. Average amount awarded: $12,910 (50% gift aid, 50% self-help). *Gift aid:* Total: $2,378,534 (87% from college's own funds, 2% from other college-administered sources, 11% from external sources). 142 Federal Work-Study jobs (averaging $1824).

Need-Based Scholarships & Grants Pell, FSEOG, state, private, college/university.

Loans Perkins, PLUS, Stafford, Unsubsidized Stafford, private.

Non-Need Awards In 1996, a total of 197 non-need awards were made. *Academic Interests/Achievement Awards:* 197 ($683,737 total): general academic, business, computer science.

Other Money-Saving Options Co-op program, Air Force ROTC, cooperative Army ROTC, off-campus living. *Payment Plan:* installment. *Waivers:* full or partial for employees or children of employees and senior citizens.

Contact Ms. Kathie Taylor, Director of Financial Assistance, Daniel Webster College, 20 University Drive, Nashua, NH 03063-1300, 603-577-6590, fax: 603-577-6001.

DARKEI NOAM RABBINICAL COLLEGE
Brooklyn, New York

About the Institution Independent/religious, men. Offers 1 undergraduate major.

Applications 22% of all full-time undergraduates enrolled in fall 1996 applied for aid; of these, 70% were judged to have need according to Federal Methodology, of whom 100% were aided. *Financial aid deadline:* continuous. *Financial aid forms:* FAFSA required.

Summary of Aid to Needy Students *From gift & self-help combined:* Average need met: 50%. Average amount awarded: $9000. Federal Work-Study jobs.

Need-Based Scholarships & Grants Pell, FSEOG, college/university.

Loans Stafford, Unsubsidized Stafford.

Non-Need Awards In 1996, a total of 5 non-need awards were made. *Academic Interests/Achievement Awards:* 5 ($20,000 total): religion/biblical studies.

Another Money-Saving Option Off-campus living.

Contact Ms. Rivi Horowitz, Director of Financial Aid, Darkei Noam Rabbinical College, Brooklyn, NY 11219, 718-338-6464.

DARTMOUTH COLLEGE
Hanover, New Hampshire

About the Institution Independent, coed. Degrees awarded: B, M, D. Offers 46 undergraduate majors. Total enrollment: 5,300. Undergraduates: 4,285 (3% state residents). Freshmen: 1,095.

Undergraduate Expenses (1997–98) Comprehensive fee of $29,231 includes tuition ($22,896), mandatory fees ($116), and college room and board ($6219). College room only: $3714.

Applications Of all full-time undergraduates enrolled in fall 1996, 78% of those who applied for aid were judged to have need according to Federal Methodology, of whom 100% were aided. *Financial aid deadline:* 2/1. *Financial aid forms:* FAFSA, CSS Financial Aid PROFILE required. Institutional form required for some. *Regular admission application deadline:* 1/1. Early decision deadline: 11/01.

Summary of Aid to Needy Students *From gift & self-help combined:* Average need met: 100%. Average amount awarded: $19,619 (70% gift aid, 30% self-help). *Gift aid:* Total: $26,556,000 (86% from college's own funds, 5% from other college-administered sources, 9% from external sources). Federal Work-Study jobs; part-time jobs.

Need-Based Scholarships & Grants Pell, FSEOG, state, private, college/university.

Loans Perkins, PLUS, Stafford, Unsubsidized Stafford, private, college/university short-term loans, college/university long-term loans.

Non-Need Awards Not offered.

Other Money-Saving Options Accelerated degree, Army ROTC, off-campus living (after freshman year). *Payment Plans:* tuition prepayment, installment.

Contact Ms. Virginia S. Hazen, Director of Financial Aid, Dartmouth College, 6024 McNutt Hall, Hanover, NH 03755, 603-646-2451, fax: 603-646-1414.

DAVENPORT COLLEGE OF BUSINESS
Grand Rapids, Michigan

About the Institution Independent, coed. Degrees awarded: A, B. Offers 16 undergraduate majors. Total enrollment: 2,719 (98% state residents). Freshmen: 655.

Undergraduate Expenses (1996–97) Tuition: $8188. College room only: $2025.

Applications *Financial aid forms:* CSS Financial Aid PROFILE, state form, institutional form required; FAFSA acceptable. Nontaxable income verification required for some. *Admission application deadline:* rolling.

Summary of Aid to Needy Students Federal Work-Study jobs; part-time jobs.

Non-Need Awards *Academic Interests/Achievement Awards:* general academic.

Other Money-Saving Options Accelerated degree, co-op program, off-campus living.

Contact Office of Financial Aid, Davenport College of Business, 415 East Fulton, Grand Rapids, MI 49503, 616-451-3511.

DAVENPORT COLLEGE OF BUSINESS, KALAMAZOO CAMPUS
Kalamazoo, Michigan

About the Institution Independent, primarily women. Degrees awarded: A, B. Offers 15 undergraduate majors. Total enrollment: 1,200 (98% state residents). Freshmen: 400.

Undergraduate Expenses (1996–97) Tuition: $8010.

Applications *Financial aid deadline (priority):* 3/15. *Financial aid forms:* FAFSA, institutional form required. *Admission application deadline:* rolling.

Summary of Aid to Needy Students Federal Work-Study jobs.

Need-Based Scholarships & Grants Pell, FSEOG, state, private, college/university.

Loans Perkins, PLUS, Stafford, Unsubsidized Stafford.

Non-Need Awards *Academic Interests/Achievement Awards:* general academic.

Other Money-Saving Options *Payment Plans:* installment, deferred payment. *Waivers:* full or partial for employees or children of employees.

Contact Office of Financial Aid, Davenport College of Business, Kalamazoo Campus, 4123 West Main Street, Kalamazoo, MI 49006-2791, 616-382-2835.

DAVENPORT COLLEGE OF BUSINESS, LANSING CAMPUS
Lansing, Michigan

About the Institution Independent, coed. Degrees awarded: A, B. Offers 10 undergraduate majors. Total enrollment: 1,218 (100% state residents). Freshmen: 287.

Undergraduate Expenses (1996–97) Tuition: $8010. Mandatory fees: $172.

Applications *Financial aid deadline (priority):* 9/1. *Financial aid forms:* FAFSA, institutional form required. State form required for some. *Admission application deadline:* 9/15.

Summary of Aid to Needy Students *From gift & self-help combined:* Average need met: 70%. Average amount awarded: $7500. *Gift aid:* Total: $4,000,000. 20 Federal Work-Study jobs; part-time jobs.

Need-Based Scholarships & Grants Pell, FSEOG, state, private, college/university.

Loans Perkins, PLUS, Stafford, Unsubsidized Stafford, state.

Non-Need Awards Not offered.

Other Money-Saving Options Accelerated degree, co-op program, cooperative Army ROTC. *Payment Plan:* installment.

Contact Financial Aid Office, Davenport College of Business, Lansing Campus, Lansing, MI 48933-2197, 517-484-2600.

DAVID LIPSCOMB UNIVERSITY
Nashville, Tennessee

About the Institution Independent/religious, coed. Degrees awarded: B, M. Offers 60 undergraduate majors. Total enrollment: 2,543. Undergraduates: 2,457 (65% state residents). Freshmen: 544.

Undergraduate Expenses (1997–98) Comprehensive fee of $13,283 includes tuition ($9273), mandatory fees ($40), and college room and board ($3970). College room only: $1980.

Applications 78% of all full-time undergraduates enrolled in fall 1996 applied for aid; of these, 67% were judged to have need according to Federal Methodology, of whom 90% were aided. *Financial aid deadline (priority):* 2/28. *Financial aid forms:* FAFSA required; CSS Financial Aid PROFILE acceptable. State form required for some. *Regular admission application deadline:* rolling. Early action deadline: 11/15.

Summary of Aid to Needy Students *From gift & self-help combined:* Average need met: 95%. 90 Federal Work-Study jobs (averaging $1000); 240 part-time jobs.

Need-Based Scholarships & Grants Pell, FSEOG, state, private, college/university.

Loans Perkins, PLUS, Stafford, Unsubsidized Stafford, state, private.

Non-Need Awards In 1996, a total of 1,506 non-need awards were made. *Academic Interests/Achievement Awards:* 1,155 ($2,924,000 total): general academic. *Creative Arts/Performance Awards:* 91 ($94,523 total): art/fine arts, debating, journalism/publications, music, theater/drama. *Special Achievements/Activities Awards:* 39 ($25,750 total): cheerleading/drum major, leadership, religious involvement. *Special Characteristics Awards:* 81 ($161,000 total): children of faculty/staff, children with a deceased or disabled parent, relatives of clergy. *Athletic:* Total: 140 ($566,041); Men: 87 ($358,036); Women: 53 ($208,005).

Other Money-Saving Options Accelerated degree, cooperative Army ROTC, cooperative Air Force ROTC. *Payment Plan:* installment. *Waivers:* full or partial for minority students and employees or children of employees.

Contact Mr. R. Gerald Masterson, Assistant Vice President of Student Aid Services, David Lipscomb University, 3901 Granny White Pike, Nashville, TN 37204-3951, 615-269-1791, fax: 615-269-1804.

DAVID N. MYERS COLLEGE
Cleveland, Ohio

About the Institution Independent, coed. Degrees awarded: A, B. Offers 15 undergraduate majors. Total enrollment: 1,178 (100% state residents). Freshmen: 180.

Undergraduate Expenses (1996–97) Tuition: $7500.

Applications 96% of all full-time undergraduates enrolled in fall 1996 applied for aid; of these, 79% were judged to have need according to Federal Methodology, of whom 93% were aided. *Financial aid deadline (priority):* 4/30. *Financial aid forms:* FAFSA required. State form required for some. *Admission application deadline:* 9/1.

Summary of Aid to Needy Students *From gift & self-help combined:* Average need met: 80%. Average amount awarded: $3255 (73% gift aid, 27% self-help). *Gift aid:* Total: $1,329,277 (31% from college's own funds, 42% from other college-administered sources, 27% from external sources). 36 Federal Work-Study jobs (averaging $1342); 12 part-time jobs.

Need-Based Scholarships & Grants Pell, FSEOG, state, private, college/university.

Loans Perkins, PLUS, Stafford, Unsubsidized Stafford, college/university short-term loans.

Non-Need Awards In 1996, a total of 6 non-need awards were made. *Academic Interests/Achievement Awards:* 1 ($500 total): general academic, business. *Special Achievements/Activities Awards:* 4 ($4320 total): leadership. *Special Characteristics Awards:* 1 ($1512 total): children of faculty/staff, first-generation college students, public servants, veterans, veterans' children.

Other Money-Saving Options Accelerated degree, co-op program. *Payment Plans:* installment, deferred payment. *Waivers:* full or partial for employees or children of employees.

Contact Ms. Susan Alexander, Financial Aid Administrator, David N. Myers College, 112 Prospect Avenue, Cleveland, OH 44115-1096, 216-523-3816, fax: 216-696-6430.

DAVIDSON COLLEGE
Davidson, North Carolina

About the Institution Independent/religious, coed. Degrees awarded: B. Offers 22 undergraduate majors. Total enrollment: 1,613 (20% state residents). Freshmen: 442.

Undergraduate Expenses (1997–98) Comprehensive fee of $26,513 includes tuition ($19,883), mandatory fees ($712), and college room and board ($5918). College room only: $3129.

Applications 43% of all full-time undergraduates enrolled in fall 1996 applied for aid; of these, 88% were judged to have need according to Federal Methodology, of whom 99% were aided. *Financial aid deadline:* 2/15. *Financial aid forms:* FAFSA, CSS Financial Aid PROFILE required. State form required for some. *Regular admission application deadline:* 1/15. Early decision deadline: 11/10.

Summary of Aid to Needy Students *From gift & self-help combined:* Average need met: 95%. Average amount awarded: $15,300 (77% gift aid, 23% self-help). *Gift aid:* Total: $7,378,552 (84% from college's own funds, 7% from other college-administered sources, 9% from external sources). 179 Federal Work-Study jobs (averaging $1267); 450 part-time jobs.

Need-Based Scholarships & Grants Pell, FSEOG, state, private, college/university, need-linked special talent scholarships.

Loans Perkins, PLUS, Stafford, Unsubsidized Stafford, private.

Non-Need Awards In 1996, a total of 313 non-need awards were made. *Academic Interests/Achievement Awards:* 75 ($525,000 total): general academic, biological sciences, education, foreign languages, physical sciences. *Creative Arts/Performance Awards:* 40 ($150,000 total): art/fine arts, creative writing, music. *Special Achievements/Activities Awards:* 30 ($100,000 total): general special achievements/activities, leadership, religious involvement. *Special Characteristics Awards:* 60 ($200,000 total): children of faculty/staff, first-generation college students, relatives of clergy, ROTC participants. *Athletic:* Total: 108 ($840,000); Men: 48 ($430,724); Women: 60 ($409,276).

Other Money-Saving Options Army ROTC, cooperative Air Force ROTC. *Payment Plan:* installment. *Waivers:* full or partial for employees or children of employees.

Contact Office of Financial Aid, Davidson College, PO Box 1539, Davidson, NC 28036-1719, 704-892-2000.

DAVIS & ELKINS COLLEGE
Elkins, West Virginia

About the Institution Independent/religious, coed. Degrees awarded: A, B. Offers 55 undergraduate majors. Total enrollment: 732 (60% state residents). Freshmen: 154.

Undergraduate Expenses (1997–98) Comprehensive fee of $15,460 includes tuition ($10,580 minimum), mandatory fees ($200), and college room and board ($4680). College room only: $2000.

Applications 85% of all full-time undergraduates enrolled in fall 1996 applied for aid; of these, 92% were judged to have need according to Federal Methodology, of whom 100% were aided. *Financial aid deadline (priority):* 5/1. *Financial aid forms:* FAFSA, CSS Financial Aid PROFILE required. *Admission application deadline:* rolling.

Summary of Aid to Needy Students *From gift & self-help combined:* Average need met: 95%. Average amount awarded: $10,496 (64% gift aid, 36% self-help). *Gift aid:* Total: $3,440,470 (63% from college's own funds, 5% from other college-administered sources, 32% from external sources). 200 Federal Work-Study jobs (averaging $1200); 188 part-time jobs.

Need-Based Scholarships & Grants Pell, FSEOG, state, private, college/university.

Loans Perkins, PLUS, Stafford, Unsubsidized Stafford, private, college/university short-term loans ($500 average), college/university long-term loans ($1000 average).

Non-Need Awards In 1996, a total of 352 non-need awards were made. *Academic Interests/Achievement Awards:* 153 ($383,575 total): general academic, biological sciences, engineering/technologies, health fields, physical sciences, religion/biblical studies. *Creative Arts/Performance Awards:* 52 ($105,950 total): art/fine arts, music, performing arts, theater/drama. *Special Characteristics Awards:* 44 ($66,050 total): local/state students, religious affiliation. *Athletic:* Total: 103 ($395,450); Men: 51 ($227,495); Women: 52 ($167,955).

Other Money-Saving Options Accelerated degree, co-op program. *Payment Plan:* installment. *Waivers:* full or partial for employees or children of employees.

Contact Mr. John T. Elza, Director of Financial Aid, Davis & Elkins College, 100 Campus Drive, Elkins, WV 26241-3996, 304-637-1282, fax: 304-637-1413.

DEACONESS COLLEGE OF NURSING
St. Louis, Missouri

About the Institution Independent/religious, coed. Degrees awarded: A, B. Offers 1 undergraduate major. Total enrollment: 380 (80% state residents). Freshmen: 70.

Undergraduate Expenses (1996–97) Comprehensive fee of $10,180 includes tuition ($7170) and college room and board ($3010 minimum).

Applications 81% of all full-time undergraduates enrolled in fall 1996 applied for aid; of these, 77% were judged to have need according to Federal Methodology, of whom 100% were aided. *Financial aid deadline (priority):* 7/1. *Financial aid forms:* FAFSA, institutional form required; CSS Financial Aid PROFILE, state form acceptable. *Admission application deadline:* rolling.

Summary of Aid to Needy Students *From gift & self-help combined:* Average need met: 85%. Average amount awarded: $5952 (40% gift aid, 60% self-help). *Gift aid:* Total: $330,090 (50% from college's own funds, 16% from other college-administered sources, 34% from external sources). Federal Work-Study jobs; 10 part-time jobs.

Need-Based Scholarships & Grants Pell, FSEOG, state, college/university.

Loans PLUS, Stafford, Unsubsidized Stafford, college/university long-term loans ($2000 average).

Non-Need Awards In 1996, a total of 110 non-need awards were made. *Academic Interests/Achievement Awards:* 97 ($172,810 total): general academic, health fields. *Special Achievements/Activities Awards:* 4 ($6000 total): leadership. *Special Characteristics Awards:* 9 ($7000 total): religious affiliation.

Other Money-Saving Options Off-campus living. *Payment Plans:* installment, deferred payment.

Contact Ms. June Marlowe, Student Financial Planning Counselor, Deaconess College of Nursing, 6150 Oakland Avenue, St. Louis, MO 63139-3215, 314-768-5604, fax: 314-768-5673.

THE DEFIANCE COLLEGE
Defiance, Ohio

About the Institution Independent/religious, coed. Degrees awarded: A, B, M. Offers 45 undergraduate majors. Total enrollment: 826. Undergraduates: 789 (85% state residents). Freshmen: 152.

Undergraduate Expenses (1997–98) Comprehensive fee of $17,425 includes tuition ($13,400), mandatory fees ($75), and college room and board ($3950).

Applications 82% of all full-time undergraduates enrolled in fall 1996 applied for aid; of these, 100% were judged to have need according to

Federal Methodology, of whom 100% were aided. *Financial aid deadline (priority):* 3/1. *Financial aid forms:* FAFSA, institutional form required; CSS Financial Aid PROFILE acceptable. *Admission application deadline:* 8/15.

Summary of Aid to Needy Students *From gift & self-help combined:* Average need met: 94%. Average amount awarded: $11,306 (65% gift aid, 35% self-help). *Gift aid:* Total: $4,592,419 (42% from college's own funds, 51% from other college-administered sources, 7% from external sources). Federal Work-Study jobs (averaging $1360); 285 part-time jobs.

Need-Based Scholarships & Grants Pell, FSEOG, state, private, college/university.

Loans Perkins, PLUS, Stafford, Unsubsidized Stafford, private.

Non-Need Awards *Academic Interests/Achievement Awards:* general academic, biological sciences, business, communication, computer science, education, humanities, mathematics, physical sciences, premedicine, religion/biblical studies, social sciences. *Creative Arts/Performance Awards:* 6: debating, music, theater/drama. *Special Achievements/Activities Awards:* general special achievements/activities, community service, leadership, religious involvement. *Special Characteristics Awards:* general special characteristics, children and siblings of alumni, children of current students, children of faculty/staff, children with a deceased or disabled parent, ethnic background, first-generation college students, local/state students, members of minorities, out-of-state students, parents of current students, previous college experience, relatives of clergy, religious affiliation, siblings of current students, spouses of current students, twins.

Other Money-Saving Options Co-op program, off-campus living (after junior year). *Waivers:* full or partial for employees or children of employees and senior citizens.

Contact Ms. Amy Francis, Director of Financial Aid, The Defiance College, 701 North Clinton Street, Defiance, OH 43512-1610, 419-784-4010.

DELAWARE STATE UNIVERSITY
Dover, Delaware

About the Institution State-supported, coed. Degrees awarded: B, M. Offers 79 undergraduate majors. Total enrollment: 3,328. Undergraduates: 3,030 (59% state residents). Freshmen: 604.

Undergraduate Expenses (1996–97) State resident tuition: $2496. Nonresident tuition: $6096. Mandatory fees: $140. College room and board: $4704.

Applications 77% of all full-time undergraduates enrolled in fall 1996 applied for aid; of these, 90% were judged to have need according to Federal Methodology, of whom 97% were aided. *Financial aid deadline (priority):* 3/1. *Financial aid forms:* FAFSA required. *Admission application deadline:* 6/1.

Summary of Aid to Needy Students *From gift & self-help combined:* Average need met: 77%. Average amount awarded: $7216 (38% gift aid, 62% self-help). *Gift aid:* Total: $5,257,746 (15% from college's own funds, 45% from other college-administered sources, 40% from external sources). Federal Work-Study jobs; part-time jobs.

Need-Based Scholarships & Grants Pell, FSEOG, state, private, college/university.

Loans Perkins, PLUS, Stafford, Unsubsidized Stafford, college/university short-term loans.

Non-Need Awards *Academic Interests/Achievement Awards:* 133 ($217,000 total): general academic. *Creative Arts/Performance Awards:* 98 ($120,000 total): music. *Special Achievements/Activities Awards:* leadership. *Special Characteristics Awards:* out-of-state students. *Athletic:* Total: 118 ($369,017); Men: 58 ($186,423); Women: 60 ($182,594).

Other Money-Saving Options Accelerated degree, co-op program, Army ROTC, Air Force ROTC, off-campus living. *Payment Plans:* installment, deferred payment. *Waivers:* full or partial for senior citizens.

Contact Ms. Martha M. Hopkins, Associate Director of Financial Aid, Delaware State University, Dover, DE 19901-2277, 302-739-4908.

DELAWARE VALLEY COLLEGE
Doylestown, Pennsylvania

About the Institution Independent, coed. Degrees awarded: A, B. Offers 24 undergraduate majors. Total enrollment: 1,380 (74% state residents). Freshmen: 395.

Undergraduate Expenses (1997–98) Comprehensive fee of $20,584 includes tuition ($14,929) and college room and board ($5655). College room only: $2485.

Applications *Financial aid deadline (priority):* 5/1. *Financial aid forms:* FAFSA, institutional form required; CSS Financial Aid PROFILE acceptable. State form required for some. *Regular admission application deadline:* rolling. Early action deadline: 12/01.

Summary of Aid to Needy Students *From gift & self-help combined:* Average need met: 86%. Average amount awarded: $12,789 (60% gift aid, 40% self-help). *Gift aid:* Total: $7,797,150 (74% from college's own funds, 18% from other college-administered sources, 8% from external sources). 110 Federal Work-Study jobs (averaging $1500); 230 part-time jobs.

Need-Based Scholarships & Grants Pell, FSEOG, state, private, college/university.

Loans Perkins, PLUS, Stafford, Unsubsidized Stafford, private.

Non-Need Awards *Academic Interests/Achievement Awards:* general academic, agriculture, biological sciences, business, computer science, education, English, mathematics, premedicine, social sciences.

Other Money-Saving Options Co-op program, off-campus living. *Payment Plan:* installment. *Waivers:* full or partial for employees or children of employees.

Contact Mr. Robert Sauer, Director of Student Financial Aid, Delaware Valley College, 700 East Butler Avenue, Doylestown, PA 18901-2697, 215-489-2297, fax: 215-489-4959.

DELTA STATE UNIVERSITY
Cleveland, Mississippi

About the Institution State-supported, coed. Degrees awarded: B, M, D. Offers 39 undergraduate majors. Total enrollment: 3,860. Undergraduates: 3,305 (95% state residents). Freshmen: 450.

Undergraduate Expenses (1997–98) State resident tuition: $2294. Nonresident tuition: $4888. Mandatory fees: $40. College room and board: $2400.

Applications Of all full-time undergraduates enrolled in fall 1996, 77% of those who applied for aid were judged to have need according to Federal Methodology, of whom 100% were aided. *Financial aid deadline (priority):* 5/1. *Financial aid forms:* FAFSA, institutional form required; state form acceptable. *Admission application deadline:* rolling.

Summary of Aid to Needy Students *From gift & self-help combined:* Average need met: 90%. Average amount awarded: $4400 (51% gift aid, 49% self-help). *Gift aid:* Total: $4,982,166 (33% from college's own funds, 19% from other college-administered sources, 48% from external sources). 349 Federal Work-Study jobs (averaging $1200); 1,512 part-time jobs.

Need-Based Scholarships & Grants FSEOG, state, private, college/university.

Loans Perkins, PLUS, Stafford, Unsubsidized Stafford, private, college/university long-term loans ($1000 average).

Non-Need Awards In 1996, a total of 2,139 non-need awards were made. *Academic Interests/Achievement Awards:* 1,083 ($1,267,724 total): general academic. *Creative Arts/Performance Awards:* 235 ($322,900 total): art/fine arts, music. *Special Achievements/Activities Awards:* 391 ($110,550 total): general special achievements/activities, leadership. *Special Characteristics Awards:* 129 ($157,791 total): children and siblings of alumni, children of faculty/staff, out-of-state students. *Athletic:* Total: 301 ($542,212).

Other Money-Saving Options Accelerated degree, Army ROTC, Air Force ROTC, off-campus living. *Payment Plan:* installment. *Waivers:* full or partial for children of alumni, employees or children of employees, senior citizens.

Contact Ms. Ann Margaret Mullins, Director of Financial Aid, Delta State University, Cleveland, MS 38733-0001, 601-846-4670.

DENISON UNIVERSITY
Granville, Ohio

About the Institution Independent, coed. Degrees awarded: B. Offers 39 undergraduate majors. Total enrollment: 2,017 (39% state residents). Freshmen: 644.

Undergraduate Expenses (1997–98) Comprehensive fee of $25,620 includes tuition ($19,310), mandatory fees ($940), and college room and board ($5370). College room only: $2960.

Applications 53% of all full-time undergraduates enrolled in fall 1996 applied for aid; of these, 89% were judged to have need according to Federal Methodology, of whom 96% were aided. *Financial aid deadline (priority):* 3/1. *Financial aid forms:* FAFSA, institutional form required. *Regular admission application deadline:* 2/1. Early decision deadline: 1/1.

Summary of Aid to Needy Students *From gift & self-help combined:* Average need met: 74%. Average amount awarded: $18,016 (76% gift aid, 24% self-help). *Gift aid:* Total: $12,388,947 (84% from college's own funds, 8% from other college-administered sources, 8% from external sources). 660 Federal Work-Study jobs (averaging $1720); 453 part-time jobs.

Need-Based Scholarships & Grants Pell, FSEOG, state, private, college/university.

Loans Perkins, PLUS, Stafford, Unsubsidized Stafford, private, college/university long-term loans ($2283 average).

Non-Need Awards *Academic Interests/Achievement Awards:* general academic, biological sciences, humanities, physical sciences. *Creative Arts/Performance Awards:* music. *Special Achievements/Activities Awards:* leadership. *Special Characteristics Awards:* available.

Other Money-Saving Options *Payment Plan:* installment. *Waivers:* full or partial for employees or children of employees.

Contact Office of Financial Aid, Denison University, PO Box M, Granville, OH 43023, 614-587-0810.

DENVER INSTITUTE OF TECHNOLOGY
Denver, Colorado

About the Institution Proprietary, coed. Degrees awarded: A, B. Offers 13 undergraduate majors. Total enrollment: 950 (75% state residents). Freshmen: 240.

Applications *Financial aid deadline:* continuous. *Financial aid forms:* FAFSA, institutional form required; CSS Financial Aid PROFILE acceptable. State form required for some. *Admission application deadline:* rolling.

Summary of Aid to Needy Students Federal Work-Study jobs; part-time jobs.

Non-Need Awards available.

Other Money-Saving Options Accelerated degree. *Payment Plans:* guaranteed tuition, installment, deferred payment. *Waivers:* full or partial for employees or children of employees.

Contact Office of Financial Aid, Denver Institute of Technology, Denver, CO 80221-3653, 303-650-5050.

DENVER TECHNICAL COLLEGE
Denver, Colorado

About the Institution Proprietary, coed. Degrees awarded: A, B, M. Offers 17 undergraduate majors. Total enrollment: 1,500 (85% state residents). Freshmen: 280.

Applications Of all full-time undergraduates enrolled in fall 1996, 100% of those who applied for aid were judged to have need according to Federal Methodology, of whom 100% were aided. *Financial aid deadline:* continuous. *Financial aid forms:* FAFSA, institutional form required. *Admission application deadline:* rolling.

Summary of Aid to Needy Students *From gift & self-help combined:* Average need met: 100%. Average amount awarded: $9851 (17% gift aid, 83% self-help). *Gift aid:* Total: $1,893,844 (23% from college-administered sources, 77% from external sources). Federal Work-Study jobs; 24 part-time jobs.

Need-Based Scholarships & Grants Pell, FSEOG, state, private.

Loans PLUS, Stafford, Unsubsidized Stafford, college/university short-term loans.

Non-Need Awards Not offered.

Other Money-Saving Options Accelerated degree, co-op program. *Payment Plan:* guaranteed tuition. *Waivers:* full or partial for employees or children of employees.

Contact Financial Aid Office, Denver Technical College, 925 South Niagara Street, Denver, CO 80224-1658, 303-329-3340, fax: 303-321-3412.

DEPAUL UNIVERSITY
Chicago, Illinois

About the Institution Independent/religious, coed. Degrees awarded: B, M, D, P. Offers 98 undergraduate majors. Total enrollment: 17,294. Undergraduates: 10,438 (75% state residents). Freshmen: 1,157.

Undergraduate Expenses (1997–98) Comprehensive fee of $21,296 includes tuition ($13,458 minimum), mandatory fees ($30), and college room and board ($7808). College room only: $3639.

Applications 88% of all full-time undergraduates enrolled in fall 1996 applied for aid; of these, 94% were judged to have need according to Federal Methodology, of whom 95% were aided. *Financial aid deadline (priority):* 4/1. *Financial aid forms:* FAFSA required; CSS Financial Aid PROFILE, state form acceptable. Institutional form required for some. *Regular admission application deadline:* 8/15. Early action deadline: 12/1.

Summary of Aid to Needy Students *From gift & self-help combined:* Average need met: 65%. Average amount awarded: $10,557 (53% gift aid, 47% self-help). *Gift aid:* Total: $28,782,500 (48% from college's own funds, 40% from other college-administered sources, 12% from external sources). 456 Federal Work-Study jobs (averaging $963); 1,513 part-time jobs.

Need-Based Scholarships & Grants Pell, FSEOG, state, college/university.

Loans Perkins, PLUS, Stafford, Unsubsidized Stafford, private.

Non-Need Awards In 1996, a total of 1,479 non-need awards were made. *Academic Interests/Achievement Awards:* 966 ($4,699,569 total): general academic, biological sciences, business, computer science, education. *Creative Arts/Performance Awards:* 298 ($1,049,120 total): art/fine arts, debating, music, performing arts, theater/drama. *Special*

Achievements/Activities Awards: 44 ($182,500 total): community service. *Special Characteristics Awards:* 32 ($408,000 total): children of faculty/staff. *Athletic:* Total: 139 ($1,566,477); Men: 62 ($671,414); Women: 77 ($895,063).

Other Money-Saving Options Accelerated degree, Army ROTC, off-campus living. *Payment Plans:* installment, deferred payment. *Waivers:* full or partial for employees or children of employees.

Contact Ms. Jennifer Sparrow, Admission Officer, DePaul University, 1 East Jackson Boulevard, Suite 9100, Chicago, IL 60604-2287, 312-362-8704, fax: 312-362-5749.

DEPAUW UNIVERSITY
Greencastle, Indiana

About the Institution Independent/religious, coed. Degrees awarded: B. Offers 40 undergraduate majors. Total enrollment: 2,147 (43% state residents). Freshmen: 619.

Undergraduate Expenses (1997–98) Comprehensive fee of $22,666 includes tuition ($16,815), mandatory fees ($235), and college room and board ($5616).

Applications Of all full-time undergraduates enrolled in fall 1996, 81% of those who applied for aid were judged to have need according to Federal Methodology, of whom 100% were aided. *Financial aid deadline (priority):* 2/15. *Financial aid forms:* FAFSA, institutional form required; CSS Financial Aid PROFILE acceptable. *Regular admission application deadline:* 2/15. Early decision deadline: 12/1. Early action deadline: 12/1.

Summary of Aid to Needy Students *From gift & self-help combined:* Average need met: 100%. Average amount awarded: $14,404 (79% gift aid, 21% self-help). *Gift aid:* Total: $12,629,593 (83% from college's own funds, 11% from other college-administered sources, 6% from external sources). 779 Federal Work-Study jobs (averaging $1035); 158 part-time jobs.

Need-Based Scholarships & Grants Pell, FSEOG, state, private, college/university.

Loans Perkins, PLUS, Stafford, Unsubsidized Stafford, private, college/university long-term loans ($2105 average).

Non-Need Awards In 1996, a total of 1,526 non-need awards were made. *Academic Interests/Achievement Awards:* 1,156 ($5,396,396 total): general academic, biological sciences, business, communication, computer science, humanities, mathematics, physical sciences. *Creative Arts/Performance Awards:* 5 ($25,000 total): art/fine arts, cinema/film/broadcasting, journalism/publications, music, theater/drama. *Special Achievements/Activities Awards:* 179 ($734,556 total): community service, leadership. *Special Characteristics Awards:* 186 ($1,138,549 total): children and siblings of alumni, children of faculty/staff, ethnic background, international students, members of minorities, relatives of clergy, religious affiliation.

Other Money-Saving Options Cooperative Army ROTC, cooperative Air Force ROTC. *Payment Plans:* tuition prepayment, installment, deferred payment. *Waivers:* full or partial for employees or children of employees.

Contact Ms. Joanne L. Haymaker, Associate Director of Financial Aid, DePauw University, 313 South Locust, Greencastle, IN 46135-1772, 317-658-4030, fax: 317-658-4177.

DESIGN INSTITUTE OF SAN DIEGO
San Diego, California

About the Institution Proprietary, coed. Degrees awarded: B. Offers 1 undergraduate major. Total enrollment: 215. Freshmen: 40.

Undergraduate Expenses (1996–97) Tuition: $9000.

Applications Of all full-time undergraduates enrolled in fall 1996, 100% of those who applied for aid were judged to have need according to Federal Methodology, of whom 100% were aided. *Financial aid deadline:* continuous. *Financial aid forms:* FAFSA required. State form required for some. *Admission application deadline:* rolling.

Summary of Aid to Needy Students *From gift & self-help combined:* Average need met: 90%. Average amount awarded: $8500. 25 Federal Work-Study jobs.

Need-Based Scholarships & Grants Pell, FSEOG, state.

Loans Perkins, PLUS, Stafford, Unsubsidized Stafford.

Non-Need Awards Not offered.

Another Money-Saving Option *Payment Plan:* installment.

Contact Ms. Jackie Brewer, Director of Financial Aid, Design Institute of San Diego, San Diego, CA 92121-2685, 619-566-1200.

DETROIT COLLEGE OF BUSINESS
Dearborn, Michigan

About the Institution Independent, coed. Degrees awarded: A, B. Offers 12 undergraduate majors. Total enrollment: 3,374 (99% state residents). Freshmen: 816.

Undergraduate Expenses (1997–98) Tuition: $8526.

Applications *Financial aid deadline (priority):* 3/21. *Financial aid forms:* FAFSA, institutional form required. *Admission application deadline:* rolling.

Summary of Aid to Needy Students *From gift & self-help combined:* Average need met: 42%. Average amount awarded: $6367 (38% gift aid, 62% self-help). *Gift aid:* Total: $8,448,617 (10% from college's own funds, 8% from other college-administered sources, 82% from external sources). Federal Work-Study jobs; 22 part-time jobs.

Need-Based Scholarships & Grants Pell, FSEOG, state, college/university.

Loans PLUS, Stafford, Unsubsidized Stafford.

Non-Need Awards *Academic Interests/Achievement Awards:* general academic. *Special Characteristics Awards:* general special characteristics, adult students, children and siblings of alumni, children of public servants, local/state students.

Other Money-Saving Options Co-op program. *Payment Plans:* installment, deferred payment. *Waivers:* full or partial for children of alumni and employees or children of employees.

Contact Ms. Jacqueline Durant, Director of Financial Aid, Detroit College of Business, Dearborn, MI 48126-3799, 313-581-4400.

DETROIT COLLEGE OF BUSINESS–FLINT
Flint, Michigan

About the Institution Independent, coed. Degrees awarded: A, B. Offers 6 undergraduate majors. Total enrollment: 943 (100% state residents). Freshmen: 192.

Undergraduate Expenses (1997–98) Tuition: $6321.

Applications *Financial aid deadline (priority):* 8/1. *Financial aid forms:* FAFSA, institutional form required; CSS Financial Aid PROFILE acceptable. *Admission application deadline:* rolling.

Summary of Aid to Needy Students *From gift & self-help combined:* Average need met: 41%. Average amount awarded: $6216 (74% gift aid, 26% self-help). *Gift aid:* Total: $3,468,455 (4% from college's own funds, 1% from other college-administered sources, 95% from external sources). 15 Federal Work-Study jobs (averaging $3000); 19 part-time jobs.

Need-Based Scholarships & Grants Pell, FSEOG, state, college/university.

Loans PLUS, Stafford, Unsubsidized Stafford.

Non-Need Awards In 1996, a total of 94 non-need awards were made. *Academic Interests/Achievement Awards:* 2 ($3909 total): general academic, business. *Special Characteristics Awards:* 92 ($133,709 total): general special characteristics, adult students, children and siblings of alumni, ethnic background, local/state students.

Other Money-Saving Options Co-op program. *Payment Plans:* installment, deferred payment. *Waivers:* full or partial for children of alumni and employees or children of employees.

Contact Ms. Rita Miller, Financial Aid Coordinator, Detroit College of Business–Flint, 3488 North Jennings Road, Flint, MI 48504-1700, 810-789-2200, fax: 810-789-2266.

DETROIT COLLEGE OF BUSINESS, WARREN CAMPUS
Warren, Michigan

About the Institution Independent, coed. Degrees awarded: A, B. Offers 9 undergraduate majors. Total enrollment: 2,041 (100% state residents). Freshmen: 502.

Undergraduate Expenses (1997–98) Tuition: $8526.

Applications *Financial aid deadline (priority):* 3/21. *Financial aid forms:* FAFSA, institutional form required. *Admission application deadline:* rolling.

Summary of Aid to Needy Students *From gift & self-help combined:* Average need met: 38%. Average amount awarded: $7102 (37% gift aid, 63% self-help). *Gift aid:* Total: $4,696,814 (8% from college's own funds, 9% from other college-administered sources, 83% from external sources). Federal Work-Study jobs; 4 part-time jobs.

Need-Based Scholarships & Grants Pell, FSEOG, state, college/university.

Loans PLUS, Stafford, Unsubsidized Stafford.

Non-Need Awards *Academic Interests/Achievement Awards:* general academic. *Special Characteristics Awards:* general special characteristics, children of public servants.

Other Money-Saving Options Co-op program. *Payment Plans:* installment, deferred payment. *Waivers:* full or partial for children of alumni and employees or children of employees.

Contact Ms. Lonnie Palarchio, Financial Aid Director, Detroit College of Business, Warren Campus, 27500 Dequindre, Warren, MI 48092-5209, 810-558-8700.

DEVRY INSTITUTE OF TECHNOLOGY
Phoenix, Arizona

About the Institution Proprietary, coed. Degrees awarded: A, B. Offers 5 undergraduate majors. Total enrollment: 2,862 (57% state residents). Freshmen: 773.

Undergraduate Expenses (1997–98) Tuition: $6968.

Applications *Financial aid deadline (priority):* 10/28. *Financial aid forms:* FAFSA required. *Admission application deadline:* rolling.

Summary of Aid to Needy Students *From gift & self-help combined:* Average need met: 82%. Average amount awarded: $4099 (12% gift aid, 88% self-help). *Gift aid:* Total: $1,182,492. Federal Work-Study jobs; part-time jobs.

Need-Based Scholarships & Grants Pell, FSEOG, state.

Loans Perkins, PLUS, Stafford, Unsubsidized Stafford, college/university long-term loans.

Non-Need Awards In 1996, a total of 28 non-need awards were made. *Academic Interests/Achievement Awards:* 28 ($508,410 total): general academic.

Other Money-Saving Options Accelerated degree, co-op program. *Payment Plans:* installment, deferred payment. *Waivers:* full or partial for employees or children of employees.

Contact Department of Financial Aid, DeVry Institute of Technology, Phoenix, AZ 85021-2995, 602-870-9222.

DEVRY INSTITUTE OF TECHNOLOGY
Long Beach, California

About the Institution Proprietary, coed. Degrees awarded: A, B. Offers 7 undergraduate majors. Total enrollment: 1,366 (82% state residents). Freshmen: 436.

Undergraduate Expenses (1997–98) Tuition: $6968.

Applications *Financial aid deadline:* 11/3. *Financial aid forms:* FAFSA required. *Admission application deadline:* rolling.

Summary of Aid to Needy Students *From gift & self-help combined:* Average need met: 82%. Federal Work-Study jobs.

Need-Based Scholarships & Grants Pell, FSEOG, state.

Loans Perkins, PLUS, Stafford, Unsubsidized Stafford, college/university long-term loans.

Non-Need Awards In 1996, a total of 8 non-need awards were made. *Academic Interests/Achievement Awards:* 8 ($146,905 total): general academic.

Other Money-Saving Options *Payment Plan:* installment. *Waivers:* full or partial for employees or children of employees.

Contact Department of Financial Aid, DeVry Institute of Technology, Long Beach, CA 90806, 310-427-0861.

DEVRY INSTITUTE OF TECHNOLOGY
Pomona, California

About the Institution Proprietary, coed. Degrees awarded: A, B. Offers 6 undergraduate majors. Total enrollment: 3,037 (91% state residents). Freshmen: 710.

Undergraduate Expenses (1997–98) Tuition: $6968.

Applications *Financial aid deadline (priority):* 10/28. *Financial aid forms:* FAFSA required. State form required for some. *Admission application deadline:* rolling.

Summary of Aid to Needy Students *From gift & self-help combined:* Average need met: 82%. Average amount awarded: $5909 (19% gift aid, 81% self-help). *Gift aid:* Total: $2,842,433. Federal Work-Study jobs; part-time jobs.

Need-Based Scholarships & Grants Pell, FSEOG, state.

Loans Perkins, PLUS, Stafford, Unsubsidized Stafford, college/university long-term loans.

Non-Need Awards In 1996, a total of 4 non-need awards were made. *Academic Interests/Achievement Awards:* 4 ($72,630 total): general academic.

Other Money-Saving Options Accelerated degree, co-op program. *Payment Plans:* installment, deferred payment. *Waivers:* full or partial for employees or children of employees.

Contact Department of Financial Aid, DeVry Institute of Technology, Pomona, CA 91768-2642, 909-622-8866.

DEVRY INSTITUTE OF TECHNOLOGY
Decatur, Georgia

About the Institution Proprietary, coed. Degrees awarded: A, B. Offers 6 undergraduate majors. Total enrollment: 3,109 (62% state residents). Freshmen: 853.

Undergraduate Expenses (1997–98) Tuition: $6968.

Applications *Financial aid deadline (priority):* 11/4. *Financial aid forms:* FAFSA required. *Admission application deadline:* rolling.

Summary of Aid to Needy Students *From gift & self-help combined:* Average need met: 82%. Average amount awarded: $3599 (31% gift aid, 69% self-help). *Gift aid:* Total: $2,957,132. Federal Work-Study jobs; part-time jobs.

Need-Based Scholarships & Grants Pell, FSEOG, state.

Loans Perkins, PLUS, Stafford, Unsubsidized Stafford, college/university long-term loans.

Non-Need Awards In 1996, a total of 8 non-need awards were made. *Academic Interests/Achievement Awards:* 8 ($145,080 total): general academic, business, computer science, engineering/technologies.

Other Money-Saving Options Accelerated degree, co-op program. *Payment Plans:* installment, deferred payment. *Waivers:* full or partial for employees or children of employees.

Contact Department of Financial Aid, DeVry Institute of Technology, Decatur, GA 30030-2198, 404-292-7900.

DEVRY INSTITUTE OF TECHNOLOGY
Addison, Illinois

About the Institution Proprietary, coed. Degrees awarded: A, B. Offers 6 undergraduate majors. Total enrollment: 3,468 (80% state residents). Freshmen: 852.

Undergraduate Expenses (1997–98) Tuition: $6968.

Applications *Financial aid deadline (priority):* 10/28. *Financial aid forms:* FAFSA required. *Admission application deadline:* rolling.

Summary of Aid to Needy Students *From gift & self-help combined:* Average need met: 82%. Average amount awarded: $2690 (9% gift aid, 91% self-help). *Gift aid:* Total: $752,613. Federal Work-Study jobs; part-time jobs.

Need-Based Scholarships & Grants Pell, FSEOG, state.

Loans Perkins, PLUS, Stafford, Unsubsidized Stafford, college/university long-term loans.

Non-Need Awards In 1996, a total of 16 non-need awards were made. *Academic Interests/Achievement Awards:* 16 ($287,230 total): general academic.

Other Money-Saving Options Accelerated degree, co-op program, cooperative Army ROTC. *Payment Plans:* installment, deferred payment. *Waivers:* full or partial for employees or children of employees.

Contact Department of Financial Aid, DeVry Institute of Technology, Addison, IL 60101-6106, 630-953-1300.

DEVRY INSTITUTE OF TECHNOLOGY
Chicago, Illinois

About the Institution Proprietary, coed. Degrees awarded: A, B. Offers 5 undergraduate majors. Total enrollment: 3,192 (83% state residents).

Undergraduate Expenses (1997–98) Tuition: $6968.

Applications *Financial aid deadline (priority):* 10/28. *Financial aid forms:* FAFSA required. *Admission application deadline:* rolling.

Summary of Aid to Needy Students *From gift & self-help combined:* Average need met: 82%. Average amount awarded: $3041 (18% gift aid, 82% self-help). *Gift aid:* Total: $1,465,828. Federal Work-Study jobs; part-time jobs.

Need-Based Scholarships & Grants Pell, FSEOG, state.

Loans Perkins, PLUS, Stafford, Unsubsidized Stafford, college/university long-term loans.

Non-Need Awards In 1996, a total of 3 non-need awards were made. *Academic Interests/Achievement Awards:* 3 ($59,420 total): general academic.

Other Money-Saving Options Accelerated degree, co-op program. *Payment Plans:* installment, deferred payment. *Waivers:* full or partial for employees or children of employees.

Contact Department of Financial Aid, DeVry Institute of Technology, Chicago, IL 60618-5994, 773-929-8500.

DEVRY INSTITUTE OF TECHNOLOGY
Kansas City, Missouri

About the Institution Proprietary, coed. Degrees awarded: A, B. Offers 6 undergraduate majors. Total enrollment: 2,130 (50% state residents). Freshmen: 511.

Undergraduate Expenses (1997–98) Tuition: $6968.

Applications *Financial aid deadline (priority):* 10/28. *Financial aid forms:* FAFSA required. *Admission application deadline:* rolling.

Summary of Aid to Needy Students *From gift & self-help combined:* Average need met: 82%. Average amount awarded: $3321 (13% gift aid, 87% self-help). *Gift aid:* Total: $778,089. Federal Work-Study jobs; part-time jobs.

Need-Based Scholarships & Grants Pell, FSEOG, state.

Loans Perkins, PLUS, Stafford, Unsubsidized Stafford, college/university long-term loans.

Non-Need Awards In 1996, a total of 16 non-need awards were made. *Academic Interests/Achievement Awards:* 16 ($295,455 total): general academic.

Other Money-Saving Options Accelerated degree, co-op program. *Payment Plans:* installment, deferred payment. *Waivers:* full or partial for employees or children of employees.

Contact Department of Financial Aid, DeVry Institute of Technology, Kansas City, MO 64131-3698, 816-941-0430.

DEVRY INSTITUTE OF TECHNOLOGY
Columbus, Ohio

About the Institution Proprietary, coed. Degrees awarded: A, B. Offers 5 undergraduate majors. Total enrollment: 2,647 (63% state residents). Freshmen: 761.

Undergraduate Expenses (1997–98) Tuition: $6968.

Applications *Financial aid deadline (priority):* 10/28. *Financial aid forms:* FAFSA required. State form required for some. *Admission application deadline:* rolling.

Summary of Aid to Needy Students *From gift & self-help combined:* Average need met: 82%. Average amount awarded: $3285 (23% gift aid, 77% self-help). *Gift aid:* Total: $1,687,806. Federal Work-Study jobs; part-time jobs.

Need-Based Scholarships & Grants Pell, FSEOG, state.

Loans Perkins, PLUS, Stafford, Unsubsidized Stafford, college/university long-term loans.

Non-Need Awards In 1996, a total of 28 non-need awards were made. *Academic Interests/Achievement Awards:* 28 ($505,120 total): general academic.

Other Money-Saving Options Accelerated degree, co-op program, cooperative Army ROTC. *Payment Plans:* installment, deferred payment. *Waivers:* full or partial for employees or children of employees.

Contact Department of Financial Aid, DeVry Institute of Technology, Columbus, OH 43209-2764, 614-253-7291.

DEVRY INSTITUTE OF TECHNOLOGY
Irving, Texas

About the Institution Proprietary, coed. Degrees awarded: A, B. Offers 6 undergraduate majors. Total enrollment: 2,419 (82% state residents).

Undergraduate Expenses (1997–98) Tuition: $6968.

Applications *Financial aid deadline (priority):* 10/28. *Financial aid forms:* FAFSA required. *Admission application deadline:* rolling.

Summary of Aid to Needy Students *From gift & self-help combined:* Average need met: 82%. Average amount awarded: $3585 (14% gift aid, 86% self-help). *Gift aid:* Total: $1,015,374. Federal Work-Study jobs; part-time jobs.

Need-Based Scholarships & Grants Pell, FSEOG, state.

Loans Perkins, PLUS, Stafford, Unsubsidized Stafford, college/university long-term loans.

Non-Need Awards In 1996, a total of 4 non-need awards were made. *Academic Interests/Achievement Awards:* 4 ($69,340 total): general academic.

Other Money-Saving Options Accelerated degree, co-op program. *Payment Plans:* installment, deferred payment. *Waivers:* full or partial for employees or children of employees.

Contact Department of Financial Aid, DeVry Institute of Technology, Irving, TX 75063-2440, 214-929-6777.

DICKINSON COLLEGE
Carlisle, Pennsylvania

About the Institution Independent, coed. Degrees awarded: B. Offers 40 undergraduate majors. Total enrollment: 1,709 (43% state residents). Freshmen: 491.

Undergraduate Expenses (1997–98) Comprehensive fee of $27,440 includes tuition ($21,450), mandatory fees ($150), and college room and board ($5840). College room only: $3000.

Applications Of all full-time undergraduates enrolled in fall 1996, 91% of those who applied for aid were judged to have need according to Federal Methodology, of whom 100% were aided. *Financial aid deadline (priority):* 2/15. *Financial aid forms:* FAFSA, CSS Financial Aid PROFILE required. State form required for some. *Regular admission application deadline:* 2/15. Early decision deadline: 2/1.

Summary of Aid to Needy Students *From gift & self-help combined:* Average need met: 81%. Average amount awarded: $17,346 (70% gift aid, 30% self-help). *Gift aid:* Total: $13,672,788 (83% from college's own funds, 2% from other college-administered sources, 15% from external sources). 935 Federal Work-Study jobs (averaging $1300); 385 part-time jobs.

Need-Based Scholarships & Grants Pell, FSEOG, state, private, college/university.

Loans Perkins, PLUS, Stafford, Unsubsidized Stafford, state, private, college/university long-term loans ($653 average).

Non-Need Awards In 1996, a total of 174 non-need awards were made. *Academic Interests/Achievement Awards:* 123 ($29,388 total): general academic. *Creative Arts/Performance Awards:* 7 ($2550 total): music. *Special Characteristics Awards:* 44 ($702,910 total): children of faculty/staff, ROTC participants.

Other Money-Saving Options Accelerated degree, Army ROTC, off-campus living (after freshman year). *Payment Plan:* installment. *Waivers:* full or partial for employees or children of employees.

Contact Mr. Donald V. Raley, Director of Financial Aid, Dickinson College, PO Box 1773, Carlisle, PA 17013-2896, 717-245-1308, fax: 717-245-1972.

DICKINSON STATE UNIVERSITY
Dickinson, North Dakota

About the Institution State-supported, coed. Degrees awarded: A, B. Offers 45 undergraduate majors. Total enrollment: 1,701 (75% state residents). Freshmen: 429.

Undergraduate Expenses (1996–97) State resident tuition: $1680. Nonresident tuition: $4486. Mandatory fees: $290. College room and board: $2328.

Applications Of all full-time undergraduates enrolled in fall 1996, 100% of those judged to have need according to Federal Methodology were aided. *Financial aid deadline (priority):* 4/15. *Financial aid forms:* FAFSA, institutional form required. State form required for some. *Admission application deadline:* 8/19.

Summary of Aid to Needy Students *From gift & self-help combined:* Average amount awarded: $3305 (27% gift aid, 73% self-help). *Gift aid:* Total: $1,360,989. Federal Work-Study jobs; 142 part-time jobs.

Need-Based Scholarships & Grants Pell, FSEOG, state, college/university.

Loans Perkins, PLUS, Stafford, Unsubsidized Stafford, state, college/university long-term loans ($500 average), Alaska Loans, Teacher School Loans.

Non-Need Awards *Academic Interests/Achievement Awards:* general academic. *Creative Arts/Performance Awards:* music. *Special Achievements/Activities Awards:* leadership, rodeo. *Special Characteristics Awards:* general special characteristics, ethnic background, international students. *Athletic:* available.

Other Money-Saving Options Co-op program, off-campus living (after sophomore year). *Waivers:* full or partial for minority students and senior citizens.

Contact Ms. Sandy Klein, Director of Financial Aid, Dickinson State University, Dickinson, ND 58601-4896, 701-227-2371, fax: 701-227-2006.

DILLARD UNIVERSITY
New Orleans, Louisiana

About the Institution Independent/religious, coed. Degrees awarded: B. Offers 44 undergraduate majors. Total enrollment: 1,563 (62% state residents). Freshmen: 433.

Undergraduate Expenses (1996–97) Comprehensive fee of $11,450 includes tuition ($7500) and college room and board ($3950).

Applications 90% of all full-time undergraduates enrolled in fall 1996 applied for aid; of these, 90% were judged to have need according to Federal Methodology, of whom 100% were aided. *Financial aid deadline (priority):* 3/1. *Financial aid forms:* FAFSA required. *Admission application deadline:* 7/15.

Summary of Aid to Needy Students *From gift & self-help combined:* Average need met: 87%. Average amount awarded: $9630 (49% gift aid, 51% self-help). *Gift aid:* Total: $5,700,000 (53% from college's own funds, 7% from other college-administered sources, 40% from external sources). 130 Federal Work-Study jobs (averaging $2000); 150 part-time jobs.

Need-Based Scholarships & Grants Pell, FSEOG, state, private.

Loans Perkins, PLUS, Stafford, Unsubsidized Stafford, private.

Non-Need Awards In 1996, a total of 920 non-need awards were made. *Academic Interests/Achievement Awards:* 816 ($2,100,000 total): general academic. *Special Characteristics Awards:* 73 ($280,151 total): children of faculty/staff, religious affiliation. *Athletic:* Total: 31 ($254,505).

Other Money-Saving Options Accelerated degree, Army ROTC, cooperative Naval ROTC, cooperative Air Force ROTC, off-campus living. *Payment Plan:* installment.

Contact Ms. Rosie C. Toney, Director of Financial Aid, Dillard University, New Orleans, LA 70122-3097, 504-286-4677.

DOANE COLLEGE
Crete, Nebraska

About the Institution Independent/religious, coed. Degrees awarded: B, M. Offers 37 undergraduate majors. Total enrollment: 1,795. Undergraduates: 902 (80% state residents). Freshmen: 274.

Undergraduate Expenses (1997–98) Comprehensive fee of $14,920 includes tuition ($11,180), mandatory fees ($270), and college room and board ($3470).

Applications 87% of all full-time undergraduates enrolled in fall 1996 applied for aid; of these, 91% were judged to have need according to Federal Methodology, of whom 100% were aided. *Financial aid deadline (priority):* 3/15. *Financial aid forms:* institutional form required; CSS Financial Aid PROFILE acceptable. FAFSA required for some. *Admission application deadline:* 8/1.

Summary of Aid to Needy Students *From gift & self-help combined:* Average need met: 82%. Average amount awarded: $9490 (63% gift aid, 37% self-help). *Gift aid:* Total: $4,444,172 (76% from college's own funds, 6% from other college-administered sources, 18% from external sources). 381 Federal Work-Study jobs; 89 part-time jobs.

Need-Based Scholarships & Grants Pell, FSEOG, state, private, college/university.

Loans Perkins, PLUS, Stafford, Unsubsidized Stafford.

Non-Need Awards In 1996, a total of 1,637 non-need awards were made. *Academic Interests/Achievement Awards:* 988 ($1,157,865 total): general academic, business, communication, education, humanities, physical sciences, social sciences. *Creative Arts/Performance Awards:* 171 ($173,965 total): art/fine arts, music, theater/drama. *Special Characteristics Awards:* 100 ($72,750 total): religious affiliation, siblings of current students. *Athletic:* Total: 378 ($722,960).

Other Money-Saving Options Accelerated degree, co-op program, cooperative Army ROTC, cooperative Air Force ROTC, off-campus living (after junior year). *Payment Plan:* installment. *Waivers:* full or partial for employees or children of employees and senior citizens.

Contact Ms. Janet Dodson, Director of Financial Aid, Doane College, 1014 Boswell Avenue, Crete, NE 68333-2430, 402-826-8625.

DR. MARTIN LUTHER COLLEGE
New Ulm, Minnesota

See Martin Luther College

DOMINICAN COLLEGE OF BLAUVELT
Orangeburg, New York

About the Institution Independent, coed. Degrees awarded: A, B, M. Offers 31 undergraduate majors. Total enrollment: 1,811 (75% state residents). Freshmen: 102.

Undergraduate Expenses (1997–98) Comprehensive fee of $15,008 includes tuition ($8496), mandatory fees ($262), and college room and board ($6250).

Applications 96% of all full-time undergraduates enrolled in fall 1996 applied for aid; of these, 97% were judged to have need according to Federal Methodology, of whom 100% were aided. *Financial aid deadline (priority):* 5/1. *Financial aid forms:* FAFSA, institutional form required. State form required for some. *Admission application deadline:* rolling.

Summary of Aid to Needy Students *From gift & self-help combined:* Average need met: 90%. Average amount awarded: $6272 (33% gift aid, 67% self-help). *Gift aid:* Total: $2,132,000 (44% from college's own funds, 9% from other college-administered sources, 47% from external sources). 35 Federal Work-Study jobs (averaging $1139); 16 part-time jobs.

Need-Based Scholarships & Grants Pell, FSEOG, state, private, college/university.

Loans Perkins, PLUS, Stafford, Unsubsidized Stafford, Federal Nursing.

Non-Need Awards In 1996, a total of 190 non-need awards were made. *Academic Interests/Achievement Awards:* 30 ($78,000 total): general academic. *Special Achievements/Activities Awards:* 35 ($35,000 total): leadership. *Special Characteristics Awards:* 10 ($65,000 total): relatives of clergy. *Athletic:* Total: 115 ($360,000); Men: 60 ($200,000); Women: 55 ($160,000).

Other Money-Saving Options Accelerated degree, co-op program, cooperative Army ROTC, off-campus living. *Payment Plans:* guaranteed tuition, installment. *Waivers:* full or partial for employees or children of employees and senior citizens.

Contact Ms. Catherine Kelleher, Assistant Director of Financial Aid, Dominican College of Blauvelt, Orangeburg, NY 10962-1210, 914-359-7800 Ext. 226, fax: 914-359-2313.

DOMINICAN COLLEGE OF SAN RAFAEL
San Rafael, California

About the Institution Independent/religious, coed. Degrees awarded: B, M. Offers 21 undergraduate majors. Total enrollment: 1,417. Undergraduates: 1,025 (95% state residents). Freshmen: 67.

Undergraduate Expenses (1996–97) Comprehensive fee of $21,040 includes tuition ($14,380), mandatory fees ($290), and college room and board ($6370).

Applications 84% of all full-time undergraduates enrolled in fall 1996 applied for aid; of these, 97% were judged to have need according to Federal Methodology, of whom 100% were aided. *Financial aid deadline (priority):* 3/2. *Financial aid forms:* FAFSA, state form, institutional form required. *Admission application deadline:* rolling.

Summary of Aid to Needy Students *From gift & self-help combined:* Average need met: 78%. Average amount awarded: $14,842 (60% gift aid, 40% self-help). *Gift aid:* Total: $3,781,468 (68% from college's own funds, 2% from other college-administered sources, 30% from external sources). Federal Work-Study jobs; 310 part-time jobs.

Need-Based Scholarships & Grants Pell, FSEOG, state, private, college/university.

Loans Perkins, PLUS, Stafford, Unsubsidized Stafford, Federal Nursing, private.

Non-Need Awards In 1996, a total of 279 non-need awards were made. *Academic Interests/Achievement Awards:* 65 ($522,056 total): general academic. *Creative Arts/Performance Awards:* 4 ($7095 total): music. *Special Achievements/Activities Awards:* 6 ($12,000 total): community service. *Special Characteristics Awards:* 145 ($630,690 total): children and siblings of alumni, local/state students. *Athletic:* Total: 59 ($243,734); Men: 26 ($116,094); Women: 33 ($127,640).

Other Money-Saving Options Cooperative Army ROTC, cooperative Naval ROTC, cooperative Air Force ROTC, off-campus living. *Payment Plans:* guaranteed tuition, installment, deferred payment. *Waivers:* full or partial for employees or children of employees.

Contact Office of Financial Aid, Dominican College of San Rafael, 50 Acacia Avenue, San Rafael, CA 94901-2298, 415-457-4440.

DOMINICAN UNIVERSITY
River Forest, Illinois

About the Institution Independent/religious, coed. Degrees awarded: B, M. Offers 44 undergraduate majors. Total enrollment: 1,818. Undergraduates: 904 (90% state residents). Freshmen: 153.

Undergraduate Expenses (1997–98) Comprehensive fee of $17,830 includes tuition ($12,850), mandatory fees ($100), and college room and board ($4880).

Applications 78% of all full-time undergraduates enrolled in fall 1996 applied for aid; of these, 85% were judged to have need according to Federal Methodology, of whom 100% were aided. *Financial aid deadline (priority):* 6/1. *Financial aid forms:* FAFSA required. *Admission application deadline:* rolling.

Summary of Aid to Needy Students *From gift & self-help combined:* Average need met: 95%. Average amount awarded: $12,079 (63% gift aid, 37% self-help). *Gift aid:* Total: $3,294,328 (49% from college's own funds, 7% from other college-administered sources, 44% from external sources). 156 Federal Work-Study jobs (averaging $1500); 76 part-time jobs.

Need-Based Scholarships & Grants Pell, FSEOG, state, private, college/university.

Loans Perkins, PLUS, Stafford, Unsubsidized Stafford.

Non-Need Awards In 1996, a total of 353 non-need awards were made. *Academic Interests/Achievement Awards:* 139 ($529,300 total): general academic. *Special Achievements/Activities Awards:* 174 ($159,500 total): community service, religious involvement. *Special Characteristics Awards:* 40 ($50,000 total): children and siblings of alumni, international students, siblings of current students, spouses of current students, twins.

Other Money-Saving Options Off-campus living. *Payment Plan:* installment. *Waivers:* full or partial for employees or children of employees.

Contact Mr. Howard Florine, Director of Financial Aid, Dominican University, 7900 West Division, River Forest, IL 60305-1099, 708-524-6809, fax: 708-366-5360.

DORDT COLLEGE
Sioux Center, Iowa

About the Institution Independent/religious, coed. Degrees awarded: A, B, M. Offers 50 undergraduate majors. Total enrollment: 1,269 (35% state residents). Freshmen: 389.

Undergraduate Expenses (1996–97) Comprehensive fee of $13,800 includes tuition ($10,800), mandatory fees ($100), and college room and board ($2900). College room only: $1350.

Applications 91% of all full-time undergraduates enrolled in fall 1996 applied for aid; of these, 95% were judged to have need according to Federal Methodology, of whom 100% were aided. *Financial aid deadline (priority):* 4/01. *Financial aid forms:* institutional form required; FAFSA, CSS Financial Aid PROFILE acceptable. *Admission application deadline:* 8/1.

Summary of Aid to Needy Students *From gift & self-help combined.* Average need met: 90%. Average amount awarded: $10,727 (49% gift aid, 51% self-help). *Gift aid:* Total: $5,648,488 (62% from college's own funds, 7% from other college-administered sources, 31% from external sources). 600 Federal Work-Study jobs (averaging $1000); 200 part-time jobs.

Need-Based Scholarships & Grants Pell, FSEOG, state, private, college/university.

Loans Perkins, PLUS, Stafford, Unsubsidized Stafford, private, college/university long-term loans ($1000 average).

Non-Need Awards In 1996, a total of 3,767 non-need awards were made. *Academic Interests/Achievement Awards:* 996 ($1,101,987 total): general academic, agriculture, business, communication, computer science, education, engineering/technologies, English, foreign languages, humanities, mathematics, physical sciences, premedicine, religion/biblical studies, social sciences. *Creative Arts/Performance Awards:* 109 ($77,820 total): journalism/publications, music, theater/drama. *Special Achievements/Activities Awards:* 32 ($29,000 total): general special achievements/activities, leadership. *Special Characteristics Awards:* 2,527 ($1,067,810 total): general special characteristics, children and siblings of alumni, children of faculty/staff, international students, local/state students, out-of-state students, religious affiliation. *Athletic:* Total: 103 ($86,344); Men: 59 ($52,775); Women: 44 ($33,569).

Other Money-Saving Options Off-campus living (after freshman year). *Payment Plan:* installment. *Waivers:* full or partial for children of alumni, employees or children of employees, senior citizens.

Contact Ms. Barbara Schaap, Coordinator of Scholarships, Dordt College, 498 4th Avenue NE, Sioux Center, IA 51250-1697, 712-722-6084, fax: 712-722-1967.

DOUGLASS COLLEGE
New Brunswick, New Jersey

See Rutgers, The State University of New Jersey, Douglass College

DOWLING COLLEGE
Oakdale, New York

About the Institution Independent, coed. Degrees awarded: B, M. Offers 41 undergraduate majors. Total enrollment: 6,046. Undergraduates: 3,812 (95% state residents). Freshmen: 320.

Undergraduate Expenses (1996–97) Tuition: $10,980. Mandatory fees: $690. College room only: $3350.

Applications *Financial aid deadline (priority):* 6/1. *Financial aid forms:* FAFSA, state form, institutional form required; CSS Financial Aid PROFILE acceptable. *Admission application deadline:* rolling.

Summary of Aid to Needy Students *From gift & self-help combined:* Average need met: 85%. Average amount awarded: $6910 (55% gift aid, 45% self-help). *Gift aid:* Total: $7,078,302 (43% from college's own funds, 3% from other college-administered sources, 54% from external sources). 134 Federal Work-Study jobs (averaging $1157); 150 part-time jobs.

Need-Based Scholarships & Grants Pell, FSEOG, state, private, college/university.

Loans Perkins, PLUS, Stafford, Unsubsidized Stafford, private.

Non-Need Awards *Academic Interests/Achievement Awards:* 697 ($1,240,759 total): general academic. *Special Characteristics Awards:* children and siblings of alumni, children of faculty/staff, children of union members/company employees, children of workers in trades, first-generation college students, local/state students. *Athletic:* Total: 114 ($622,681).

Other Money-Saving Options Accelerated degree, co-op program, Air Force ROTC, cooperative Army ROTC, off-campus living. *Payment Plans:* guaranteed tuition, installment, deferred payment. *Waivers:* full or partial for minority students, children of alumni, employees or children of employees, adult students, senior citizens.

Contact Ms. Nancy Brewer, Director of Financial Aid, Dowling College, Idle Hour Boulevard, Oakdale, NY 11769-1999, 516-244-3036, fax: 516-563-3827.

DRAKE UNIVERSITY
Des Moines, Iowa

About the Institution Independent, coed. Degrees awarded: B, M, D, P. Offers 81 undergraduate majors. Total enrollment: 5,376. Undergraduates: 3,630 (35% state residents). Freshmen: 744.

Undergraduate Expenses (1997–98) Comprehensive fee of $19,750 includes tuition ($14,880 minimum) and college room and board ($4870 minimum). College room only: $2570 (minimum).

Applications 73% of all full-time undergraduates enrolled in fall 1996 applied for aid; of these, 91% were judged to have need according to Federal Methodology, of whom 100% were aided. *Financial aid deadline (priority):* 3/1. *Financial aid forms:* FAFSA required. Institutional form required for some. *Admission application deadline:* rolling.

Summary of Aid to Needy Students *From gift & self-help combined:* Average need met: 89%. Average amount awarded: $13,710 (54% gift aid, 46% self-help). *Gift aid:* Total: $15,573,000 (75% from college's

own funds, 4% from other college-administered sources, 21% from external sources). 2,100 Federal Work-Study jobs (averaging $1600); 500 part-time jobs.

Need-Based Scholarships & Grants Pell, FSEOG, state, college/ university.

Loans Perkins, PLUS, Stafford, Unsubsidized Stafford, private, college/ university short-term loans ($200 average), college/university long-term loans ($500 average).

Non-Need Awards In 1996, a total of 4,920 non-need awards were made. *Academic Interests/Achievement Awards:* 3,924 ($15,457,000 total): general academic. *Creative Arts/Performance Awards:* 290 ($570,000 total): art/fine arts, music, theater/drama. *Special Characteristics Awards:* 554 ($2,200,000 total): ethnic background, international students, members of minorities, ROTC participants. *Athletic:* Total: 152 ($2,316,000); Men: 78 ($922,000); Women: 74 ($1,394,000).

Other Money-Saving Options Accelerated degree, co-op program, Army ROTC, cooperative Air Force ROTC, off-campus living (after sophomore year). *Payment Plan:* installment. *Waivers:* full or partial for employees or children of employees and senior citizens.

Contact Office of Student Financial Planning, Drake University, 2507 University Avenue, Des Moines, IA 50311-4516, 800-44-DRAKE.

DREW UNIVERSITY
Madison, New Jersey

About the Institution Independent/religious, coed. Degrees awarded: B, M, D, P. Offers 33 undergraduate majors. Total enrollment: 2,174. Undergraduates: 1,475 (57% state residents). Freshmen: 372.

Undergraduate Expenses (1997–98) Comprehensive fee of $27,510 includes tuition ($20,866), mandatory fees ($530), and college room and board ($6114). College room only: $3576.

Applications 68% of all full-time undergraduates enrolled in fall 1996 applied for aid; of these, 88% were judged to have need according to Federal Methodology, of whom 99% were aided. *Financial aid deadline:* 3/1. *Financial aid forms:* CSS Financial Aid PROFILE required. *Regular admission application deadline:* 2/15. Early decision deadline: 1/15.

Summary of Aid to Needy Students *From gift & self-help combined:* Average need met: 83%. Average amount awarded: $16,010 (73% gift aid, 27% self-help). *Gift aid:* Total: $9,833,546 (76% from college's own funds, 2% from other college-administered sources, 22% from external sources). 458 Federal Work-Study jobs (averaging $1264); 324 part-time jobs.

Need-Based Scholarships & Grants Pell, FSEOG, state, college/ university.

Loans Perkins, PLUS, Stafford, Unsubsidized Stafford, private, college/ university long-term loans.

Non-Need Awards In 1996, a total of 783 non-need awards were made. *Academic Interests/Achievement Awards:* 769 ($6,189,775 total): general academic. *Creative Arts/Performance Awards:* 14 ($135,000 total): general creative.

Other Money-Saving Options Cooperative Army ROTC, off-campus living (after freshman year). *Payment Plans:* tuition prepayment, installment, deferred payment. *Waivers:* full or partial for employees or children of employees and senior citizens.

Contact Office of Financial Aid, Drew University, 36 Madison Avenue, Madison, NJ 07940-1493, 973-408-3000.

DREXEL UNIVERSITY
Philadelphia, Pennsylvania

About the Institution Independent, coed. Degrees awarded: B, M, D. Offers 61 undergraduate majors. Total enrollment: 9,590. Undergraduates: 6,805 (67% state residents). Freshmen: 1,305.

Undergraduate Expenses (1996–97) Comprehensive fee of $21,381 includes tuition ($13,680 minimum), mandatory fees ($792), and college room and board ($6909). College room only: $4085 (minimum).

Applications *Financial aid deadline (priority):* 5/1. *Financial aid forms:* FAFSA, state form, institutional form required. *Regular admission application deadline:* 3/1. Early action deadline: 11/15.

Summary of Aid to Needy Students Federal Work-Study jobs.

Need-Based Scholarships & Grants Pell, FSEOG, state, private, college/ university.

Loans Perkins, PLUS, Stafford, Unsubsidized Stafford, state, private, college/university short-term loans, college/university long-term loans ($759 average).

Non-Need Awards *Academic Interests/Achievement Awards:* general academic. *Creative Arts/Performance Awards:* dance, music, theater/ drama. *Special Characteristics Awards:* ROTC participants. *Athletic:* available.

Other Money-Saving Options Co-op program, Army ROTC, cooperative Naval ROTC, cooperative Air Force ROTC, off-campus living (after freshman year). *Payment Plans:* installment, deferred payment. *Waivers:* full or partial for employees or children of employees and senior citizens.

Contact Mr. Nicholas A. Flocco, Director of Financial Aid, Drexel University, 3141 Chestnut Street, Philadelphia, PA 19104-2875, 215-895-2537.

DRURY COLLEGE
Springfield, Missouri

About the Institution Independent, coed. Degrees awarded: B, M. Offers 39 undergraduate majors. Total enrollment: 1,620. Undergraduates: 1,325 (81% state residents). Freshmen: 350.

Undergraduate Expenses (1997–98 estimated) Comprehensive fee of $13,916 includes tuition ($9750), mandatory fees ($310), and college room and board ($3856).

Applications 92% of all full-time undergraduates enrolled in fall 1996 applied for aid; of these, 91% were judged to have need according to Federal Methodology, of whom 100% were aided. *Financial aid deadline (priority):* 2/15. *Financial aid forms:* FAFSA, institutional form required; CSS Financial Aid PROFILE, state form acceptable. *Admission application deadline:* rolling.

Summary of Aid to Needy Students *From gift & self-help combined:* Average need met: 95%. Average amount awarded: $8643 (49% gift aid, 51% self-help). *Gift aid:* Total: $4,626,129 (60% from college's own funds, 3% from other college-administered sources, 37% from external sources). 293 Federal Work-Study jobs (averaging $1500); 113 part-time jobs.

Need-Based Scholarships & Grants Pell, FSEOG, state, private, college/ university.

Loans Perkins, PLUS, Stafford, Unsubsidized Stafford.

Non-Need Awards In 1996, a total of 2,284 non-need awards were made. *Academic Interests/Achievement Awards:* 1,321 ($2,469,244 total): general academic, architecture, business, education, English, mathematics, premedicine, social sciences. *Creative Arts/Performance Awards:* 143 ($99,827 total): art/fine arts, music, theater/drama. *Special Achievements/Activities Awards:* 719 ($259,420 total): cheerleading/ drum major, leadership, religious involvement. *Special Characteristics Awards:* 18 ($20,980 total): children and siblings of alumni, relatives of clergy. *Athletic:* Total: 83 ($399,090); Men: 47 ($201,400); Women: 36 ($197,690).

Other Money-Saving Options Accelerated degree, cooperative Army ROTC, off-campus living (after freshman year). *Payment Plans:* tuition prepayment, installment, deferred payment. *Waivers:* full or partial for employees or children of employees, adult students, senior citizens.

Contact Office of Financial Aid, Drury College, 900 North Benton Avenue, Springfield, MO 65802-3791, 417-873-7879.

DUKE UNIVERSITY
Durham, North Carolina

About the Institution Independent/religious, coed. Degrees awarded: B, M, D, P. Offers 47 undergraduate majors. Total enrollment: 11,589. Undergraduates: 6,326 (14% state residents). Freshmen: 1,653.

Undergraduate Expenses (1997–98) Comprehensive fee of $28,616 includes tuition ($21,550 minimum), mandatory fees ($523), and college room and board ($6543 minimum). College room only: $3553 (minimum).

Applications Of all full-time undergraduates enrolled in fall 1996, 71% of those who applied for aid were judged to have need according to Federal Methodology, of whom 100% were aided. *Financial aid deadline (priority):* 2/1. *Financial aid forms:* FAFSA, CSS Financial Aid PROFILE required. *Regular admission application deadline:* 1/2. Early decision deadline: 11/1.

Summary of Aid to Needy Students *From gift & self-help combined:* Average need met: 100%. Average amount awarded: $18,373 (74% gift aid, 26% self-help). *Gift aid:* Total: $32,020,390 (82% from college's own funds, 4% from other college-administered sources, 14% from external sources). 2,000 Federal Work-Study jobs (averaging $1700); 450 part-time jobs.

Need-Based Scholarships & Grants Pell, FSEOG, state, private, college/university.

Loans Perkins, PLUS, Stafford, Unsubsidized Stafford, college/university short-term loans ($500 average), college/university long-term loans ($1256 average).

Non-Need Awards *Academic Interests/Achievement Awards:* 120 ($1,847,227 total): general academic, mathematics. *Athletic:* available.

Other Money-Saving Options Accelerated degree, Army ROTC, Naval ROTC, Air Force ROTC, off-campus living (after freshman year). *Payment Plans:* tuition prepayment, installment, deferred payment. *Waivers:* full or partial for employees or children of employees.

Contact Ms. Lori Crooks, Financial Aid Counselor, Duke University, 2106 Campus Drive, Durham, NC 27708-0586, 919-684-6225, fax: 919-660-9811.

DUQUESNE UNIVERSITY
Pittsburgh, Pennsylvania

About the Institution Independent/religious, coed. Degrees awarded: B, M, D, P. Offers 75 undergraduate majors. Total enrollment: 9,400. Undergraduates: 5,751 (81% state residents). Freshmen: 1,238.

Undergraduate Expenses (1996–97) Comprehensive fee of $19,199 includes tuition ($12,420), mandatory fees ($976), and college room and board ($5803). College room only: $3151.

Applications 85% of all full-time undergraduates enrolled in fall 1996 applied for aid; of these, 81% were judged to have need according to Federal Methodology, of whom 99% were aided. *Financial aid deadline:* Applications processed continuously. *Financial aid forms:* institutional form required. FAFSA required for some. *Regular admission application deadline:* 7/1. Early decision deadline: 11/15.

Summary of Aid to Needy Students *From gift & self-help combined:* Average need met: 80%. Average amount awarded: $11,455 (54% gift aid, 46% self-help). *Gift aid:* Total: $20,715,745 (63% from college's own funds, 3% from other college-administered sources, 34% from external sources). 500 Federal Work-Study jobs (averaging $1920); part-time jobs.

Need-Based Scholarships & Grants Pell, FSEOG, state, private, college/university.

Loans Perkins, PLUS, Stafford, Unsubsidized Stafford, Federal Nursing, private, college/university long-term loans ($595 average), Health Professions Loans.

Non-Need Awards In 1996, a total of 2,286 non-need awards were made. *Academic Interests/Achievement Awards:* 1,481 ($5,043,120 total): general academic. *Creative Arts/Performance Awards:* 240 ($878,555 total): dance, music. *Special Characteristics Awards:* 361 ($1,805,986 total): children of faculty/staff, international students, members of minorities. *Athletic:* Total: 204 ($1,596,155); Men: 111 ($833,783); Women: 93 ($762,372).

Other Money-Saving Options Accelerated degree, co-op program, Army ROTC, cooperative Air Force ROTC, off-campus living (after freshman year). *Payment Plans:* installment, deferred payment. *Waivers:* full or partial for employees or children of employees and senior citizens.

Contact Office of Financial Aid, Duquesne University, 600 Forbes Avenue, Pittsburgh, PA 15282-0299, 412-396-6000.

DYKE COLLEGE
Cleveland, Ohio

See David N. Myers College

D'YOUVILLE COLLEGE
Buffalo, New York

About the Institution Independent, coed. Degrees awarded: B, M. Offers 28 undergraduate majors. Total enrollment: 1,915. Undergraduates: 1,445 (68% state residents). Freshmen: 238.

Undergraduate Expenses (1996–97) Comprehensive fee of $14,300 includes tuition ($9510), mandatory fees ($190), and college room and board ($4600).

Applications Of all full-time undergraduates enrolled in fall 1996, 99% of those who applied for aid were judged to have need according to Federal Methodology, of whom 99% were aided. *Financial aid deadline (priority):* 4/15. *Financial aid forms:* FAFSA required. State form, financial aid transcript (for transfers) required for some. *Admission application deadline:* rolling.

Summary of Aid to Needy Students *From gift & self-help combined:* Average need met: 85%. Average amount awarded: $7918 (52% gift aid, 48% self-help). *Gift aid:* Total: $3,715,251 (42% from college's own funds, 6% from other college-administered sources, 52% from external sources). 207 Federal Work-Study jobs (averaging $800); 111 part-time jobs.

Need-Based Scholarships & Grants Pell, FSEOG, state, private, college/university.

Loans Perkins, PLUS, Stafford, Unsubsidized Stafford, Federal Nursing, private, college/university short-term loans ($1000 average), college/university long-term loans ($1000 average).

Non-Need Awards In 1996, a total of 125 non-need awards were made. *Academic Interests/Achievement Awards:* 100 ($168,635 total): general academic. *Athletic:* Total: 25 ($20,000).

Other Money-Saving Options Cooperative Army ROTC, off-campus living (after sophomore year). *Payment Plans:* installment, deferred payment. *Waivers:* full or partial for minority students, children of alumni, employees or children of employees, adult students, senior citizens.

Contact Ms. Lorraine A. Metz, Director of Financial Aid, D'Youville College, 320 Porter Avenue, Buffalo, NY 14201-1084, 716-881-7691, fax: 716-881-7790.

EARLHAM COLLEGE
Richmond, Indiana

About the Institution Independent/religious, coed. Degrees awarded: B. Offers 42 undergraduate majors. Total enrollment: 1,005 (22% state residents). Freshmen: 280.

Undergraduate Expenses (1997–98) Comprehensive fee of $23,162 includes tuition ($18,056), mandatory fees ($562), and college room and board ($4544). College room only: $2172.

Applications *Financial aid deadline (priority):* 3/1. *Financial aid forms:* FAFSA, institutional form required. State form required for some. *Regular admission application deadline:* 2/15. Early decision deadline: 12/1. Early action deadline: 1/15.

Summary of Aid to Needy Students *From gift & self-help combined:* Average need met: 97%. Average amount awarded: $12,000 (72% gift aid, 28% self-help). *Gift aid:* Total: $7,349,000 (85% from college's own funds, 10% from other college-administered sources, 5% from external sources). 500 Federal Work-Study jobs (averaging $1400); 30 part-time jobs.

Need-Based Scholarships & Grants Pell, FSEOG, state, private, college/university.

Loans Perkins, PLUS, Stafford, Unsubsidized Stafford, private, college/university long-term loans ($1400 average).

Non-Need Awards *Academic Interests/Achievement Awards:* general academic, physical sciences. *Special Achievements/Activities Awards:* community service. *Special Characteristics Awards:* religious affiliation.

Other Money-Saving Options Accelerated degree. *Payment Plans:* installment, deferred payment. *Waivers:* full or partial for employees or children of employees.

Contact Ms. Nancy Sinex, Dean of Admissions, Earlham College, National Road West, Richmond, IN 47374-4095, 765-983-1600.

EAST CAROLINA UNIVERSITY
Greenville, North Carolina

About the Institution State-supported, coed. Degrees awarded: B, M, D, P. Offers 80 undergraduate majors. Total enrollment: 16,805. Undergraduates: 14,313 (86% state residents). Freshmen: 2,807.

Undergraduate Expenses (1996–97) State resident tuition: $874. Nonresident tuition: $8028. Mandatory fees: $878. College room and board: $3480. College room only: $1660.

Applications Of all full-time undergraduates enrolled in fall 1996, 85% of those who applied for aid were judged to have need according to Federal Methodology, of whom 90% were aided. *Financial aid deadline (priority):* 4/15. *Financial aid forms:* FAFSA required; CSS Financial Aid PROFILE, state form acceptable. *Admission application deadline:* 3/15.

Summary of Aid to Needy Students *From gift & self-help combined:* Average need met: 90%. *Gift aid:* Total: $12,167,503 (8% from college's own funds, 28% from other college-administered sources, 64% from external sources). 611 Federal Work-Study jobs (averaging $789); part-time jobs.

Need-Based Scholarships & Grants Pell, FSEOG, state, private, college/university.

Loans Perkins, PLUS, Stafford, Unsubsidized Stafford, Federal Nursing, Primary Care, private, college/university short-term loans ($300 average).

Non-Need Awards *Academic Interests/Achievement Awards:* general academic. *Creative Arts/Performance Awards:* applied art and design, art/fine arts, music. *Special Achievements/Activities Awards:* leadership. *Special Characteristics Awards:* adult students, children of faculty/

staff, handicapped students, local/state students, ROTC participants. *Athletic:* Total: 320 ($2,044,280); Men: 214 ($1,395,323); Women: 106 ($648,957).

Other Money-Saving Options Accelerated degree, co-op program, Army ROTC, Air Force ROTC, off-campus living. *Payment Plan:* deferred payment. *Waivers:* full or partial for employees or children of employees and senior citizens.

Contact Ms. Rose Mary Stelma, Director of Financial Aid, East Carolina University, Greenville, NC 27858-4353, 919-328-6610.

EAST CENTRAL UNIVERSITY
Ada, Oklahoma

About the Institution State-supported, coed. Degrees awarded: B, M. Offers 53 undergraduate majors. Total enrollment: 4,369. Undergraduates: 3,670 (98% state residents). Freshmen: 591.

Undergraduate Expenses (1996–97) State resident tuition: $1714 (minimum). Nonresident tuition: $3993 (minimum). Mandatory fees: $10. College room and board: $1832 (minimum). College room only: $660.

Applications 70% of all full-time undergraduates enrolled in fall 1996 applied for aid; of these, 87% were judged to have need according to Federal Methodology, of whom 99% were aided. *Financial aid deadline (priority):* 7/1. *Financial aid forms:* FAFSA, state form, institutional form required. *Admission application deadline:* 8/21.

Summary of Aid to Needy Students *From gift & self-help combined:* Average amount awarded: $4014 (75% gift aid, 25% self-help). *Gift aid:* Total: $5,034,539 (20% from college's own funds, 2% from other college-administered sources, 78% from external sources). 310 Federal Work-Study jobs (averaging $1265); 582 part-time jobs.

Need-Based Scholarships & Grants Pell, FSEOG, state, private, college/university.

Loans Perkins, PLUS, Stafford, Unsubsidized Stafford, college/university short-term loans ($94 average).

Non-Need Awards *Academic Interests/Achievement Awards:* general academic, communication, military science. *Creative Arts/Performance Awards:* music, performing arts. *Special Achievements/Activities Awards:* cheerleading/drum major. *Special Characteristics Awards:* members of minorities, ROTC participants, veterans, veterans' children. *Athletic:* available.

Other Money-Saving Options Accelerated degree, Army ROTC, off-campus living. *Waivers:* full or partial for senior citizens.

Contact Office of Financial Aid, East Central University, 14th and Francis Streets, Ada, OK 74820-6899, 405-332-8000 Ext. 243, fax: 405-436-5612.

EAST COAST BIBLE COLLEGE
Charlotte, North Carolina

About the Institution Independent/religious, coed. Degrees awarded: A, B. Offers 6 undergraduate majors. Total enrollment: 182 (61% state residents). Freshmen: 30.

Undergraduate Expenses (1997–98) Comprehensive fee of $7780 includes tuition ($4920), mandatory fees ($260), and college room and board ($2600).

Applications 85% of all full-time undergraduates enrolled in fall 1996 applied for aid; of these, 93% were judged to have need according to Federal Methodology, of whom 97% were aided. *Financial aid deadline (priority):* 5/1. *Financial aid forms:* FAFSA, institutional form required. *Admission application deadline:* rolling.

Summary of Aid to Needy Students *From gift & self-help combined:* Average need met: 57%. Average amount awarded: $5328 (39% gift aid, 61% self-help). *Gift aid:* Total: $217,183 (36% from college's own

funds, 10% from other college-administered sources, 54% from external sources). 14 Federal Work-Study jobs (averaging $1485); 15 part-time jobs.

Need-Based Scholarships & Grants Pell, FSEOG, college/university.

Loans PLUS, Stafford, Unsubsidized Stafford, college/university short-term loans ($200 average).

Non-Need Awards In 1996, a total of 72 non-need awards were made. *Academic Interests/Achievement Awards:* 7 ($32,760 total): general academic. *Creative Arts/Performance Awards:* 24 ($17,410 total): music, performing arts, theater/drama. *Special Achievements/Activities Awards:* 23 ($13,840 total): general special achievements/activities, leadership. *Special Characteristics Awards:* 18 ($30,645 total): children of faculty/staff, religious affiliation, siblings of current students, spouses of current students.

Other Money-Saving Options *Payment Plan:* deferred payment. *Waivers:* full or partial for employees or children of employees.

Contact Mr. Vince Welch, Director of Financial Aid, East Coast Bible College, 6900 Wilkinson Boulevard, Charlotte, NC 28214-3152, 704-394-2307, fax: 704-393-3689.

EASTERN COLLEGE
St. Davids, Pennsylvania

About the Institution Independent/religious, coed. Degrees awarded: A, B, M. Offers 36 undergraduate majors. Total enrollment: 2,348. Undergraduates: 1,594 (66% state residents). Freshmen: 250.

Undergraduate Expenses (1997–98) Comprehensive fee of $18,140 includes tuition ($12,700) and college room and board ($5440). College room only: $2660.

Applications 92% of all full-time undergraduates enrolled in fall 1996 applied for aid; of these, 93% were judged to have need according to Federal Methodology, of whom 100% were aided. *Financial aid deadline:* continuous. *Financial aid forms:* FAFSA, institutional form, financial aid transcript (for transfers) required. *Admission application deadline:* rolling.

Summary of Aid to Needy Students *From gift & self-help combined:* Average need met: 90%. Average amount awarded: $13,800 (66% gift aid, 34% self-help). *Gift aid:* Total: $5,339,505 (73% from college's own funds, 3% from other college-administered sources, 24% from external sources). 200 Federal Work-Study jobs (averaging $1200); 75 part-time jobs.

Need-Based Scholarships & Grants Pell, FSEOG, state, private, college/university.

Loans Perkins, PLUS, Stafford, Unsubsidized Stafford.

Non-Need Awards In 1996, a total of 596 non-need awards were made. *Academic Interests/Achievement Awards:* 444 ($1,586,050 total): general academic. *Creative Arts/Performance Awards:* 21 ($42,000 total): music. *Special Achievements/Activities Awards:* 47 ($84,000 total): leadership. *Special Characteristics Awards:* 84 ($42,150 total): relatives of clergy.

Other Money-Saving Options Accelerated degree, cooperative Army ROTC, cooperative Air Force ROTC. *Payment Plan:* installment. *Waivers:* full or partial for employees or children of employees.

Contact Financial Aid Office, Eastern College, 1300 Eagle Road, St. Davids, PA 19087-3696, 610-341-5842, fax: 610-341-1723.

EASTERN CONNECTICUT STATE UNIVERSITY
Willimantic, Connecticut

About the Institution State-supported, coed. Degrees awarded: A, B, M. Offers 32 undergraduate majors. Total enrollment: 4,590. Undergraduates: 4,312 (90% state residents). Freshmen: 695.

Undergraduate Expenses (1997–98) State resident tuition: $2062. Nonresident tuition: $6674. Mandatory fees: $1532 (minimum). College room and board: $5048. College room only: $3500.

Applications Of all full-time undergraduates enrolled in fall 1996, 64% of those who applied for aid were judged to have need according to Federal Methodology, of whom 70% were aided. *Financial aid deadline (priority):* 3/15. *Financial aid forms:* FAFSA, institutional form required. *Admission application deadline:* 5/1.

Summary of Aid to Needy Students *From gift & self-help combined:* Average need met: 90%. Average amount awarded: $5768 (59% gift aid, 41% self-help). *Gift aid:* Total: $6,600,000 (29% from college's own funds, 53% from other college-administered sources, 18% from external sources). 152 Federal Work-Study jobs (averaging $1400); 569 part-time jobs.

Need-Based Scholarships & Grants Pell, FSEOG, state, private, college/university.

Loans Perkins, PLUS, Stafford, Unsubsidized Stafford, state, private, college/university short-term loans ($200 average).

Non-Need Awards In 1996, a total of 182 non-need awards were made. *Academic Interests/Achievement Awards:* 130 ($251,460 total): general academic, area/ethnic studies, education, physical sciences. *Creative Arts/Performance Awards:* 3 ($850 total): music, theater/drama. *Special Achievements/Activities Awards:* 21 ($16,350 total): memberships. *Special Characteristics Awards:* 28 ($21,250 total): international students, local/state students, members of minorities, previous college experience.

Other Money-Saving Options Accelerated degree, co-op program, cooperative Army ROTC, cooperative Air Force ROTC, off-campus living. *Payment Plans:* installment, deferred payment. *Waivers:* full or partial for senior citizens.

Contact Mr. Neville Brown, Assistant to the Director of Financial Aid, Eastern Connecticut State University, 83 Windham Street, Willimantic, CT 06226-2295, 860-465-4428, fax: 860-465-4440.

EASTERN ILLINOIS UNIVERSITY
Charleston, Illinois

About the Institution State-supported, coed. Degrees awarded: B, M. Offers 68 undergraduate majors. Total enrollment: 11,711. Undergraduates: 10,106 (97% state residents). Freshmen: 1,739.

Undergraduate Expenses (1997–98 estimated) State resident tuition: $2124. Nonresident tuition: $6372. Mandatory fees: $792. College room and board: $3362.

Applications Of all full-time undergraduates enrolled in fall 1996, 81% of those who applied for aid were judged to have need according to Federal Methodology, of whom 75% were aided. *Financial aid deadline (priority):* 4/15. *Financial aid forms:* FAFSA required. *Admission application deadline:* rolling.

Summary of Aid to Needy Students *From gift & self-help combined:* Average amount awarded: $5198 (49% gift aid, 51% self-help). *Gift aid:* Total: $11,039,285 (16% from college's own funds, 3% from other college-administered sources, 81% from external sources). 350 Federal Work-Study jobs (averaging $800); 3,200 part-time jobs.

Need-Based Scholarships & Grants Pell, FSEOG, state, private, college/university.

Loans Perkins, PLUS, Stafford, Unsubsidized Stafford, college/university short-term loans ($100 average), college/university long-term loans ($575 average).

Non-Need Awards In 1996, a total of 105 non-need awards were made. *Special Characteristics Awards:* 105 ($91,600 total): general special characteristics, handicapped students, members of minorities.

Other Money-Saving Options Army ROTC, off-campus living (after freshman year). *Payment Plan:* installment. *Waivers:* full or partial for employees or children of employees.

Contact Ms. Betty Armstrong, Assistant Director of Financial Aid, Eastern Illinois University, 600 Lincoln Avenue, Charleston, IL 61920-3099, 217-581-3712, fax: 217-581-6422.

EASTERN KENTUCKY UNIVERSITY
Richmond, Kentucky

About the Institution State-supported, coed. Degrees awarded: A, B, M. Offers 133 undergraduate majors. Total enrollment: 16,060. Undergraduates: 14,154 (90% state residents). Freshmen: 2,351.

Undergraduate Expenses (1996–97) State resident tuition: $1740. Nonresident tuition: $5220. Mandatory fees: $230. College room and board: $2706 (minimum). College room only: $1296 (minimum).

Applications *Financial aid deadline (priority):* 4/1. *Financial aid forms:* FAFSA, institutional form required. *Admission application deadline:* rolling.

Summary of Aid to Needy Students Federal Work-Study jobs; 700 part-time jobs.

Need-Based Scholarships & Grants Pell, FSEOG, state.

Loans Perkins, PLUS, Stafford, Unsubsidized Stafford, college/university short-term loans ($100 average).

Non-Need Awards *Academic Interests/Achievement Awards:* general academic. *Creative Arts/Performance Awards:* music. *Special Characteristics Awards:* international students, out-of-state students. *Athletic:* Total: 229 ($1,148,562).

Other Money-Saving Options Accelerated degree, co-op program, Army ROTC, cooperative Air Force ROTC.

Contact Ms. Susan Luhman, Director of Student Financial Aid, Eastern Kentucky University, Richmond, KY 40475-3101, 606-622-2361.

EASTERN MENNONITE UNIVERSITY
Harrisonburg, Virginia

About the Institution Independent/religious, coed. Degrees awarded: A, B, M, P. Offers 48 undergraduate majors. Total enrollment: 1,150. Undergraduates: 989 (40% state residents). Freshmen: 231.

Undergraduate Expenses (1997–98 estimated) Comprehensive fee of $16,620 includes tuition ($12,000), mandatory fees ($120), and college room and board ($4500). College room only: $2250.

Applications 95% of all full-time undergraduates enrolled in fall 1996 applied for aid; of these, 76% were judged to have need according to Federal Methodology, of whom 100% were aided. *Financial aid deadline (priority):* 3/15. *Financial aid forms:* FAFSA, institutional form required; CSS Financial Aid PROFILE acceptable. State form required for some. *Admission application deadline:* 8/1.

Summary of Aid to Needy Students *From gift & self-help combined:* Average need met: 94%. Average amount awarded: $14,769 (51% gift aid, 49% self-help). *Gift aid:* Total: $3,029,562 (43% from college's own funds, 17% from other college-administered sources, 40% from external sources). 345 Federal Work-Study jobs (averaging $1100); 58 part-time jobs.

Need-Based Scholarships & Grants Pell, FSEOG, state, private, college/university.

Loans Perkins, PLUS, Stafford, Unsubsidized Stafford, Federal Nursing, private.

Non-Need Awards In 1996, a total of 1,036 non-need awards were made. *Academic Interests/Achievement Awards:* 491 ($1,114,470 total): general academic, biological sciences, business, education, English, foreign languages, humanities, mathematics, physical sciences, premedicine, religion/biblical studies, social sciences. *Creative Arts/Performance Awards:* 10 ($7300 total): art/fine arts, music. *Special Characteristics Awards:* 535 ($1,005,950 total): general special

characteristics, children and siblings of alumni, children of faculty/staff, ethnic background, international students, local/state students, religious affiliation.

Other Money-Saving Options Off-campus living (after junior year). *Payment Plan:* installment. *Waivers:* full or partial for employees or children of employees.

Contact Mr. David Schrock, Associate Director of Financial Aid, Eastern Mennonite University, 1200 Park Road, Harrisonburg, VA 22801-2462, 540-432-4137.

EASTERN MICHIGAN UNIVERSITY
Ypsilanti, Michigan

About the Institution State-supported, coed. Degrees awarded: B, M, D. Offers 159 undergraduate majors. Total enrollment: 22,541. Undergraduates: 17,732 (90% state residents). Freshmen: 2,400.

Undergraduate Expenses (1996–97) State resident tuition: $2813 (minimum). Nonresident tuition: $7350 (minimum). Mandatory fees: $480. College room and board: $4400. College room only: $2045.

Applications Of all full-time undergraduates enrolled in fall 1996, 70% of those who applied for aid were judged to have need according to Federal Methodology, of whom 100% were aided. *Financial aid deadline (priority):* 3/15. *Financial aid forms:* FAFSA required; CSS Financial Aid PROFILE acceptable. State form required for some. *Admission application deadline:* 7/31.

Summary of Aid to Needy Students *From gift & self-help combined:* Average need met: 85%. Average amount awarded: $7887 (28% gift aid, 72% self-help). *Gift aid:* Total: $9,867,805 (26% from college's own funds, 16% from other college-administered sources, 58% from external sources). 637 Federal Work-Study jobs (averaging $1668); 3,000 part-time jobs.

Need-Based Scholarships & Grants Pell, FSEOG, state, college/university.

Loans Perkins, PLUS, Stafford, Unsubsidized Stafford, state, college/university short-term loans ($350 average).

Non-Need Awards *Academic Interests/Achievement Awards:* 350 ($314,820 total): general academic, agriculture, architecture, biological sciences, business, communication, computer science, education, engineering/technologies, English, foreign languages, health fields, home economics, humanities, mathematics, physical sciences, religion/biblical studies, social sciences. *Creative Arts/Performance Awards:* 153 ($138,146 total): applied art and design, art/fine arts, debating, music, theater/drama. *Special Achievements/Activities Awards:* 306 ($153,000 total): leadership. *Special Characteristics Awards:* 133 ($487,425 total): children and siblings of alumni, international students, out-of-state students. *Athletic:* available.

Other Money-Saving Options Accelerated degree, co-op program, Army ROTC, cooperative Naval ROTC, cooperative Air Force ROTC, off-campus living (after sophomore year). *Payment Plan:* installment. *Waivers:* full or partial for employees or children of employees.

Contact Office of Financial Aid, Eastern Michigan University, 403 Pierce Hall, Ypsilanti, MI 48197, 313-487-0455, fax: 313-487-1484.

EASTERN NAZARENE COLLEGE
Quincy, Massachusetts

About the Institution Independent/religious, coed. Degrees awarded: A, B, M. Offers 54 undergraduate majors. Total enrollment: 844. Undergraduates: 709 (44% state residents). Freshmen: 208.

Undergraduate Expenses (1997–98) Comprehensive fee of $15,415 includes tuition ($10,715), mandatory fees ($725), and college room and board ($3975).

Applications 97% of all full-time undergraduates enrolled in fall 1996 applied for aid; of these, 95% were judged to have need according to Federal Methodology, of whom 98% were aided. *Financial aid deadline (priority):* 3/1. *Financial aid forms:* FAFSA, institutional form required. *Admission application deadline:* rolling.

Summary of Aid to Needy Students *From gift & self-help combined:* Average need met: 80%. Average amount awarded: $15,282 (62% gift aid, 38% self-help). *Gift aid:* Total: $5,611,112 (39% from college's own funds, 51% from other college-administered sources, 10% from external sources). Federal Work-Study jobs; 100 part-time jobs.

Need-Based Scholarships & Grants Pell, FSEOG, state, private, college/university.

Loans Perkins, PLUS, Stafford, Unsubsidized Stafford, state, private, college/university short-term loans ($400 average).

Non-Need Awards *Academic Interests/Achievement Awards:* general academic. *Special Achievements/Activities Awards:* community service, leadership. *Special Characteristics Awards:* children and siblings of alumni, relatives of clergy, siblings of current students.

Other Money-Saving Options Accelerated degree. *Waivers:* full or partial for employees or children of employees.

Contact Financial Aid Department, Eastern Nazarene College, Quincy, MA 02170-2999, 617-745-3000.

EASTERN NEW MEXICO UNIVERSITY
Portales, New Mexico

About the Institution State-supported, coed. Degrees awarded: A, B, M. Offers 70 undergraduate majors. Total enrollment: 3,617. Undergraduates: 3,084 (76% state residents). Freshmen: 472.

Undergraduate Expenses (1996–97) State resident tuition: $1116. Nonresident tuition: $5616. Mandatory fees: $538. College room and board: $2810. College room only: $1280.

Applications Of all full-time undergraduates enrolled in fall 1996, 84% of those who applied for aid were judged to have need according to Federal Methodology. *Financial aid deadline (priority):* 3/1. *Financial aid forms:* FAFSA required. State form required for some. *Admission application deadline:* rolling.

Summary of Aid to Needy Students *From gift & self-help combined:* Average need met: 52%. Average amount awarded: $4540 (52% gift aid, 48% self-help). *Gift aid:* Total: $6,754,201 (53% from college-administered sources, 47% from external sources). 444 Federal Work-Study jobs (averaging $2040); 1,717 part-time jobs.

Need-Based Scholarships & Grants Pell, FSEOG, state, private, college/university.

Loans Perkins, PLUS, Stafford, Unsubsidized Stafford, state, college/university short-term loans ($250 average), college/university long-term loans ($250 average).

Non-Need Awards *Academic Interests/Achievement Awards:* ($465,316 total): general academic, agriculture, biological sciences, business, communication, computer science, education, engineering/technologies, English, foreign languages, health fields, home economics, humanities, mathematics, military science, physical sciences, premedicine, religion/ biblical studies, social sciences. *Creative Arts/Performance Awards:* ($56,850 total): general creative, applied art and design, art/fine arts, cinema/film/broadcasting, creative writing, dance, debating, journalism/ publications, music, performing arts, theater/drama. *Special Achievements/ Activities Awards:* ($27,630 total): general special achievements/ activities, community service, hobbies/interest, leadership, memberships, rodeo. *Special Characteristics Awards:* ($2,098,980 total): general special characteristics, children and siblings of alumni, ethnic background, first-generation college students, international students, members of minorities, out-of-state students, ROTC participants, veterans. *Athletic:* Total: 156 ($645,417); Men: 108 ($464,383); Women: 48 ($181,034).

Other Money-Saving Options Accelerated degree, co-op program, Army ROTC, off-campus living. *Payment Plan:* installment. *Waivers:* full or partial for employees or children of employees.

Contact Ms. Nancy Miller, Accountant, Eastern New Mexico University, Station #4, Portales, NM 88130, 505-562-2615, fax: 505-562-2409.

EASTERN OREGON UNIVERSITY
La Grande, Oregon

About the Institution State-supported, coed. Degrees awarded: A, B, M. Offers 31 undergraduate majors. Total enrollment: 1,876. Undergraduates: 1,849 (71% state residents). Freshmen: 378.

Undergraduate Expenses (1996–97) Comprehensive fee of $6977 includes tuition ($2316), mandatory fees ($695), and college room and board ($3966).

Applications Of all full-time undergraduates enrolled in fall 1996, 95% of those judged to have need according to Federal Methodology were aided. *Financial aid deadline (priority):* 1/31. *Financial aid forms:* state form, Institutional Scholarship Applications required; FAFSA acceptable. *Admission application deadline:* 8/1.

Summary of Aid to Needy Students *From gift & self-help combined:* Average need met: 95%. Average amount awarded: $6995 (42% gift aid, 58% self-help). *Gift aid:* Total: $2,352,798 (30% from college's own funds, 5% from other college-administered sources, 65% from external sources). 270 Federal Work-Study jobs (averaging $2000); 75 part-time jobs.

Need-Based Scholarships & Grants Pell, FSEOG, state, private, college/university.

Loans Perkins, PLUS, Stafford, Unsubsidized Stafford, college/university short-term loans ($100 average).

Non-Need Awards *Academic Interests/Achievement Awards:* 103 ($93,500 total): general academic, agriculture, biological sciences, business, education, home economics, mathematics, physical sciences. *Creative Arts/Performance Awards:* music, theater/drama. *Special Achievements/Activities Awards:* community service, leadership, rodeo. *Special Characteristics Awards:* general special characteristics, adult students, international students, members of minorities, out-of-state students.

Other Money-Saving Options Accelerated degree, co-op program, off-campus living. *Payment Plan:* deferred payment.

Contact Mr. Jack L. Johnson, Director of Financial Aid, Eastern Oregon University, 1410 L Avenue, La Grande, OR 97850-2899, 541-962-3665.

EASTERN WASHINGTON UNIVERSITY
Cheney, Washington

About the Institution State-supported, coed. Degrees awarded: B, M. Offers 115 undergraduate majors. Total enrollment: 7,589. Undergraduates: 6,326 (91% state residents). Freshmen: 707.

Undergraduate Expenses (1996–97) State resident tuition: $2430. Nonresident tuition: $8610. Mandatory fees: $15. College room and board: $4294. College room only: $2188.

Applications Of all full-time undergraduates enrolled in fall 1996, 91% of those judged to have need according to Federal Methodology were aided. *Financial aid deadline (priority):* 2/15. *Financial aid forms:* FAFSA required. *Admission application deadline:* 7/1.

Summary of Aid to Needy Students *From gift & self-help combined:* Average need met: 90%. Average amount awarded: $7514 (31% gift aid, 69% self-help). *Gift aid:* Total: $10,692,706 (8% from college's own funds, 37% from other college-administered sources, 55% from external sources). 299 Federal Work-Study jobs (averaging $1895); 1,500 part-time jobs.

Need-Based Scholarships & Grants Pell, FSEOG, state, private, college/university.

Loans Perkins, PLUS, Stafford, Unsubsidized Stafford, college/university short-term loans ($300 average).

Non-Need Awards In 1996, a total of 425 non-need awards were made. *Academic Interests/Achievement Awards:* 116 ($223,650 total): general academic, architecture, business, education, foreign languages, health fields, physical sciences, social sciences. *Creative Arts/Performance Awards:* 4 ($5400 total): journalism/publications, music, theater/drama. *Special Achievements/Activities Awards:* 1 ($500 total): memberships. *Special Characteristics Awards:* 131 ($253,445 total): adult students, children and siblings of alumni, ethnic background, handicapped students, international students, members of minorities, out-of-state students, veterans. *Athletic:* Total: 173 ($1,020,029); Men: 120 ($679,749); Women: 53 ($340,280).

Other Money-Saving Options Accelerated degree, co-op program, Army ROTC, off-campus living. *Waivers:* full or partial for employees or children of employees.

Contact Office of Financial Aid, Eastern Washington University, 127 Showalter Hall MS 142, Cheney, WA 99004-2431, 509-359-6200.

EASTMAN SCHOOL OF MUSIC
Rochester, New York

See University of Rochester

EAST STROUDSBURG UNIVERSITY OF PENNSYLVANIA
East Stroudsburg, Pennsylvania

About the Institution State-supported, coed. Degrees awarded: A, B, M. Offers 45 undergraduate majors. Total enrollment: 5,552. Undergraduates: 4,647 (84% state residents). Freshmen: 902.

Undergraduate Expenses (1996–97) State resident tuition: $3368. Nonresident tuition: $8566. Mandatory fees: $828. College room and board: $3626. College room only: $2200.

Applications 75% of all full-time undergraduates enrolled in fall 1996 applied for aid; of these, 81% were judged to have need according to Federal Methodology, of whom 93% were aided. *Financial aid deadline:* 3/1. *Financial aid forms:* FAFSA required. Institutional form required for some. *Admission application deadline:* 3/1.

Summary of Aid to Needy Students *From gift & self-help combined:* Average amount awarded: $5707 (33% gift aid, 67% self-help). *Gift aid:* Total: $4,199,695 (1% from college's own funds, 57% from other college-administered sources, 42% from external sources). 270 Federal Work-Study jobs (averaging $1425); 660 part-time jobs.

Need-Based Scholarships & Grants Pell, FSEOG, state, private, college/university.

Loans Perkins, PLUS, Stafford, Unsubsidized Stafford.

Non-Need Awards In 1996, a total of 316 non-need awards were made. *Academic Interests/Achievement Awards:* 147 ($109,683 total): general academic, biological sciences, communication, computer science, education, English, foreign languages, health fields, mathematics. *Special Characteristics Awards:* 35 ($93,084 total): adult students, members of minorities. *Athletic:* Total: 134 ($174,764); Men: 72 ($100,739); Women: 62 ($74,025).

Other Money-Saving Options Accelerated degree, cooperative Air Force ROTC, off-campus living (after sophomore year). *Payment Plan:* installment. *Waivers:* full or partial for employees or children of employees and senior citizens.

Contact Ms. Georgia K. Prell, Director of Financial Aid, East Stroudsburg University of Pennsylvania, 200 Prospect Street, East Stroudsburg, PA 18301-2999, 717-422-3340, fax: 717-422-3056.

EAST TENNESSEE STATE UNIVERSITY
Johnson City, Tennessee

About the Institution State-supported, coed. Degrees awarded: A, B, M, D, P. Offers 81 undergraduate majors. Total enrollment: 11,859. Undergraduates: 9,160 (88% state residents). Freshmen: 1,560.

Undergraduate Expenses (1996–97) State resident tuition: $1928. Nonresident tuition: $6264. College room and board: $2430 (minimum).

Applications *Financial aid deadline (priority):* 4/15. *Financial aid forms:* FAFSA required; state form acceptable. Institutional form required for some. *Admission application deadline:* rolling.

Summary of Aid to Needy Students *From gift & self-help combined:* Average amount awarded: $4012 (37% gift aid, 63% self-help). *Gift aid:* Total: $6,628,195. 624 Federal Work-Study jobs (averaging $752); 636 part-time jobs.

Need-Based Scholarships & Grants Pell, FSEOG, state, private.

Loans Perkins, PLUS, Stafford, Unsubsidized Stafford, private, college/university short-term loans ($1140 average), college/university long-term loans ($414 average).

Non-Need Awards In 1996, a total of 1,970 non-need awards were made. *Academic Interests/Achievement Awards:* 1,666 ($1,127,640 total): general academic. *Creative Arts/Performance Awards:* 74 ($140,105 total): music. *Special Characteristics Awards:* 41 ($48,000 total): members of minorities. *Athletic:* Total: 189 ($1,012,446); Men: 135 ($722,515); Women: 54 ($289,931).

Other Money-Saving Options Accelerated degree, co-op program, Army ROTC, off-campus living. *Waivers:* full or partial for employees or children of employees and senior citizens.

Contact Student Financial Aid Counselor, East Tennessee State University, PO Box 70722, Johnson City, TN 37614-0734, 423-439-4300.

EAST TEXAS BAPTIST UNIVERSITY
Marshall, Texas

About the Institution Independent/religious, coed. Degrees awarded: A, B, M. Offers 44 undergraduate majors. Total enrollment: 1,222. Undergraduates: 1,156 (87% state residents). Freshmen: 279.

Undergraduate Expenses (1996–97) Comprehensive fee of $9230 includes tuition ($5940), mandatory fees ($500), and college room and board ($2790). College room only: $1260.

Applications *Financial aid deadline:* Applications processed continuously. *Financial aid forms:* FAFSA, institutional form required; CSS Financial Aid PROFILE acceptable. State form required for some. *Admission application deadline:* rolling.

Summary of Aid to Needy Students Federal Work-Study jobs; part-time jobs.

Loans College/university short-term loans, college/university long-term loans.

Non-Need Awards *Academic Interests/Achievement Awards:* general academic, biological sciences, English, physical sciences, religion/biblical studies. *Creative Arts/Performance Awards:* music. *Special Achievements/Activities Awards:* religious involvement. *Special Characteristics Awards:* international students, religious affiliation. *Athletic:* available.

Other Money-Saving Options Accelerated degree, cooperative Army ROTC. *Payment Plan:* installment. *Waivers:* full or partial for employees or children of employees.

Contact Office of Financial Aid, East Texas Baptist University, Marshall, TX 75670-1498, 903-935-7963.

EAST-WEST UNIVERSITY
Chicago, Illinois

About the Institution Independent, coed. Degrees awarded: A, B. Offers 17 undergraduate majors. Total enrollment: 334 (85% state residents). Freshmen: 176.

Undergraduate Expenses (1997–98) Tuition: $6900. Mandatory fees: $60.

Applications *Financial aid deadline (priority):* 6/15. *Financial aid forms:* institutional form required; FAFSA, CSS Financial Aid PROFILE acceptable. *Admission application deadline:* rolling.

Summary of Aid to Needy Students *From gift & self-help combined:* Average need met: 90%. Average amount awarded: $3709 (99% gift aid, 1% self-help). *Gift aid:* Total: $1,253,463 (5% from college's own funds, 62% from other college-administered sources, 33% from external sources). 24 Federal Work-Study jobs (averaging $143); part-time jobs.

Need-Based Scholarships & Grants Pell, FSEOG, state.

Non-Need Awards In 1996, a total of 13 non-need awards were made. *Academic Interests/Achievement Awards:* 13 ($4620 total): general academic.

Other Money-Saving Options *Payment Plans:* installment, deferred payment. *Waivers:* full or partial for employees or children of employees.

Contact Office of Financial Aid, East-West University, Chicago, IL 60605-2103, 312-939-0111.

ECKERD COLLEGE
St. Petersburg, Florida

About the Institution Independent/religious, coed. Degrees awarded: B. Offers 41 undergraduate majors. Total enrollment: 1,466 (30% state residents). Freshmen: 429.

Undergraduate Expenses (1997–98) Comprehensive fee of $21,790 includes tuition ($16,950), mandatory fees ($180), and college room and board ($4660).

Applications 66% of all full-time undergraduates enrolled in fall 1996 applied for aid; of these, 88% were judged to have need according to Federal Methodology, of whom 100% were aided. *Financial aid deadline (priority):* 3/1. *Financial aid forms:* FAFSA required; CSS Financial Aid PROFILE acceptable. State form required for some. *Admission application deadline:* rolling.

Summary of Aid to Needy Students *From gift & self-help combined:* Average need met: 85%. Average amount awarded: $14,143 (68% gift aid, 32% self-help). *Gift aid:* Total: $8,196,108 (80% from college's own funds, 3% from other college-administered sources, 17% from external sources). 660 Federal Work-Study jobs (averaging $1300); 50 part-time jobs.

Need-Based Scholarships & Grants Pell, FSEOG, state, private, college/university.

Loans Perkins, PLUS, Stafford, Unsubsidized Stafford, private, college/university short-term loans ($250 average), college/university long-term loans ($1000 average).

Non-Need Awards In 1996, a total of 475 non-need awards were made. *Academic Interests/Achievement Awards:* 150 ($1,568,000 total): general academic. *Creative Arts/Performance Awards:* 40 ($200,000 total): art/fine arts, creative writing, music, theater/drama. *Special Achievements/Activities Awards:* 10 ($50,000 total): community service, leadership. *Special Characteristics Awards:* 175 ($875,000 total): international students, local/state students, religious affiliation, ROTC participants. *Athletic:* Total: 100 ($540,180); Men: 62 ($340,016); Women: 38 ($200,164).

Other Money-Saving Options Accelerated degree, cooperative Army ROTC, cooperative Air Force ROTC, off-campus living (after freshman year). *Payment Plan:* installment. *Waivers:* full or partial for employees or children of employees.

Contact Ms. Margaret Morris, Director of Financial Aid, Eckerd College, 4200 54th Avenue, South, St. Petersburg, FL 33711, 813-864-8334, fax: 813-866-2304.

EDGEWOOD COLLEGE
Madison, Wisconsin

About the Institution Independent/religious, coed. Degrees awarded: A, B, M. Offers 41 undergraduate majors. Total enrollment: 2,032. Undergraduates: 1,500 (87% state residents). Freshmen: 218.

Undergraduate Expenses (1997–98) Comprehensive fee of $14,660 includes tuition ($10,100), mandatory fees ($180), and college room and board ($4380). College room only: $2070.

Applications 88% of all full-time undergraduates enrolled in fall 1996 applied for aid; of these, 76% were judged to have need according to Federal Methodology, of whom 97% were aided. *Financial aid deadline (priority):* 4/1. *Financial aid forms:* FAFSA, institutional form required; CSS Financial Aid PROFILE acceptable. *Admission application deadline:* rolling.

Summary of Aid to Needy Students *From gift & self-help combined:* Average need met: 80%. Average amount awarded: $9000 (37% gift aid, 63% self-help). *Gift aid:* Total: $2,841,000 (54% from college's own funds, 25% from other college-administered sources, 21% from external sources). 150 Federal Work-Study jobs (averaging $1600); 75 part-time jobs.

Need-Based Scholarships & Grants Pell, FSEOG, state, private, college/university.

Loans Perkins, PLUS, Stafford, Unsubsidized Stafford, college/university long-term loans ($1100 average).

Non-Need Awards In 1996, a total of 485 non-need awards were made. *Academic Interests/Achievement Awards:* 245 ($732,000 total): general academic. *Creative Arts/Performance Awards:* 60 ($45,000 total): art/fine arts, creative writing, music, performing arts, theater/drama. *Special Achievements/Activities Awards:* 140 ($165,000 total): community service, hobbies/interest, leadership. *Special Characteristics Awards:* 40 ($60,000 total): local/state students, members of minorities, religious affiliation.

Other Money-Saving Options Off-campus living. *Payment Plan:* deferred payment. *Waivers:* full or partial for employees or children of employees.

Contact Mr. Kevin C. Kucera, Dean of Admissions and Financial Aid, Edgewood College, 855 Woodrow Street, Madison, WI 53711-1998, 608-257-4861 Ext. 2306.

EDINBORO UNIVERSITY OF PENNSYLVANIA
Edinboro, Pennsylvania

About the Institution State-supported, coed. Degrees awarded: A, B, M. Offers 99 undergraduate majors. Total enrollment: 7,178. Undergraduates: 6,509 (93% state residents). Freshmen: 1,296.

Undergraduate Expenses (1996–97) State resident tuition: $3368. Nonresident tuition: $8566. Mandatory fees: $700. College room and board: $3616. College room only: $1936.

Applications Of all full-time undergraduates enrolled in fall 1996, 94% of those who applied for aid were judged to have need according to Federal Methodology, of whom 100% were aided. *Financial aid deadline (priority):* 5/1. *Financial aid forms:* FAFSA required. *Admission application deadline:* rolling.

Summary of Aid to Needy Students *From gift & self-help combined:* Average need met: 95%. Average amount awarded: $5295 (48% gift

aid, 52% self-help). *Gift aid:* Total: $12,306,105 (7% from college's own funds, 4% from other college-administered sources, 89% from external sources). 380 Federal Work-Study jobs (averaging $1500); 321 part-time jobs.

Need-Based Scholarships & Grants Pell, FSEOG, state, private, college/university.

Loans Perkins, PLUS, Stafford, Unsubsidized Stafford, Federal Nursing, college/university short-term loans ($100 average), college/university long-term loans ($500 average).

Non-Need Awards In 1996, a total of 1,247 non-need awards were made. *Academic Interests/Achievement Awards:* 209 ($224,990 total): general academic, biological sciences, business, communication, computer science, education, English, health fields, humanities, mathematics, military science, physical sciences, premedicine, social sciences. *Creative Arts/Performance Awards:* 15 ($7900 total): art/fine arts, cinema/film/broadcasting, journalism/publications, music. *Special Characteristics Awards:* 832 ($1,977,588 total): general special characteristics, adult students, children and siblings of alumni, children of faculty/staff, children of union members/company employees, children with a deceased or disabled parent, first-generation college students, handicapped students, international students, local/state students, members of minorities, out-of-state students, religious affiliation, ROTC participants, veterans, veterans' children. *Athletic:* Total: 191 ($576,025); Men: 131 ($387,675); Women: 60 ($188,350).

Other Money-Saving Options Accelerated degree, Army ROTC, off-campus living (after freshman year). *Payment Plan:* installment. *Waivers:* full or partial for employees or children of employees and senior citizens.

Contact Mr. Kenneth Brandt, Director of Financial Aid, Edinboro University of Pennsylvania, McNerney Hall, Edinboro, PA 16444, 814-732-2821, fax: 814-732-2693.

EDWARD WATERS COLLEGE
Jacksonville, Florida

About the Institution Independent/religious, coed. Degrees awarded: B. Offers 19 undergraduate majors.

Undergraduate Expenses (1997–98) Comprehensive fee of $10,060 includes tuition ($4800), mandatory fees ($960), and college room and board ($4300).

Applications *Financial aid deadline:* continuous. *Financial aid forms:* FAFSA, institutional form required; CSS Financial Aid PROFILE acceptable. *Admission application deadline:* rolling.

Summary of Aid to Needy Students Federal Work-Study jobs; part-time jobs.

Non-Need Awards *Athletic:* available.

Other Money-Saving Options Co-op program, cooperative Army ROTC, off-campus living.

Contact Office of Financial Aid, Edward Waters College, Jacksonville, FL 32209-6199, 904-355-3030.

ELECTRONIC DATA PROCESSING COLLEGE OF PUERTO RICO
San Juan, Puerto Rico

About the Institution Proprietary, coed. Degrees awarded: A, B. Offers 4 undergraduate majors. Total enrollment: 850 (99% commonwealth residents). Freshmen: 350.

Undergraduate Expenses (1997–98) Tuition: $3135. Mandatory fees: $96.

Applications *Financial aid deadline (priority):* 9/30. *Financial aid forms:* FAFSA, commonwealth form, institutional form required. *Admission application deadline:* rolling.

Summary of Aid to Needy Students *From gift & self-help combined:* Average need met: 69%. Average amount awarded: $2991 (78% gift aid, 22% self-help). *Gift aid:* Total: $3,455,210 (1% from college's own funds, 10% from other college-administered sources, 89% from external sources). 85 Federal Work-Study jobs (averaging $1425); 13 part-time jobs.

Need-Based Scholarships & Grants Pell, FSEOG, state.

Loans PLUS, Stafford, Unsubsidized Stafford.

Non-Need Awards *Special Achievements/Activities Awards:* 10 ($10,000 total): community service. *Special Characteristics Awards:* ROTC participants, veterans, veterans' children.

Other Money-Saving Options Cooperative Army ROTC, cooperative Air Force ROTC.

Contact Mr. Angel Rivera, Financial Aid Director, Electronic Data Processing College of Puerto Rico, PO Box 192303, San Juan, PR 00919-2303, 787-765-3560 Ext. 4713, fax: 787-765-2650.

ELIZABETH CITY STATE UNIVERSITY
Elizabeth City, North Carolina

About the Institution State-supported, coed. Degrees awarded: B. Offers 36 undergraduate majors. Total enrollment: 2,000 (89% state residents). Freshmen: 390.

Undergraduate Expenses (1996–97) State resident tuition: $1688. Nonresident tuition: $8004. College room and board: $3248.

Applications 93% of all full-time undergraduates enrolled in fall 1996 applied for aid; of these, 89% were judged to have need according to Federal Methodology, of whom 97% were aided. *Financial aid deadline (priority):* 6/1. *Financial aid forms:* FAFSA, institutional form required. *Admission application deadline:* 8/1.

Summary of Aid to Needy Students *From gift & self-help combined:* Average need met: 88%. Average amount awarded: $5858 (58% gift aid, 42% self-help). *Gift aid:* Total: $4,806,869 (6% from college's own funds, 42% from other college-administered sources, 52% from external sources). 557 Federal Work-Study jobs (averaging $700).

Need-Based Scholarships & Grants Pell, FSEOG, state, private, college/university.

Loans Perkins, PLUS, Stafford, Unsubsidized Stafford.

Non-Need Awards *Academic Interests/Achievement Awards:* 755 ($1,643,208 total): general academic. *Creative Arts/Performance Awards:* 29 ($29,988 total): music, performing arts. *Special Achievements/Activities Awards:* available. *Special Characteristics Awards:* 106 ($56,578 total): handicapped students, members of minorities. *Athletic:* Total: 19 ($20,596); Men: 19 ($20,596); Women: 0.

Other Money-Saving Options Co-op program, Army ROTC, off-campus living. *Waivers:* full or partial for senior citizens.

Contact Ms. Dorothy Riddick-Saunders, Financial Aid Assistant, Elizabeth City State University, 1704 Weeksville Road, Campus Box 914, Elizabeth City, NC 27909-7806, 919-335-3717, fax: 919-335-3716.

ELIZABETHTOWN COLLEGE
Elizabethtown, Pennsylvania

About the Institution Independent/religious, coed. Degrees awarded: B. Offers 66 undergraduate majors. Total enrollment: 1,728 (66% state residents). Freshmen: 442.

Undergraduate Expenses (1997–98) Comprehensive fee of $21,830 includes tuition ($16,230), mandatory fees ($700), and college room and board ($4900). College room only: $2400.

Applications 89% of all full-time undergraduates enrolled in fall 1996 applied for aid; of these, 84% were judged to have need according to Federal Methodology, of whom 100% were aided. *Financial aid deadline*

(priority): 4/1. *Financial aid forms:* FAFSA, CSS Financial Aid PROFILE, required. State form required for some. *Admission application deadline:* rolling.

Summary of Aid to Needy Students *From gift & self-help combined:* Average need met: 90%. Average amount awarded: $13,087 (71% gift aid, 29% self-help). *Gift aid:* Total: $10,840,611 (79% from college's own funds, 2% from other college-administered sources, 19% from external sources). 509 Federal Work-Study jobs (averaging $1327); 436 part-time jobs.

Need-Based Scholarships & Grants Pell, FSEOG, state, private, college/university.

Loans Perkins, PLUS, Stafford, Unsubsidized Stafford, private, college/university short-term loans ($1000 average).

Non-Need Awards In 1996, a total of 771 non-need awards were made. *Academic Interests/Achievement Awards:* 639 ($2,963,782 total): general academic, biological sciences, business, communication, computer science, education, engineering/technologies, English, foreign languages, health fields, humanities, international studies, mathematics, physical sciences, religion/biblical studies, social sciences. *Creative Arts/Performance Awards:* 29 ($14,750 total): music. *Special Achievements/Activities Awards:* 1 ($900 total): Junior Miss. *Special Characteristics Awards:* 102 ($778,087 total): children of faculty/staff, international students, local/state students, members of minorities, siblings of current students.

Other Money-Saving Options *Payment Plan:* installment. *Waivers:* full or partial for employees or children of employees.

Contact Mr. M. Clarke Paine, Director of Financial Aid, Elizabethtown College, Elizabethtown, PA 17022-2298, 717-361-1404, fax: 717-361-1485.

ELMHURST COLLEGE
Elmhurst, Illinois

About the Institution Independent/religious, coed. Degrees awarded: B. Offers 54 undergraduate majors. Total enrollment: 2,701 (90% state residents). Freshmen: 232.

Undergraduate Expenses (1997–98) Comprehensive fee of $16,900 includes tuition ($11,820), mandatory fees ($80), and college room and board ($5000). College room only: $2600.

Applications 77% of all full-time undergraduates enrolled in fall 1996 applied for aid; of these, 86% were judged to have need according to Federal Methodology, of whom 100% were aided. *Financial aid deadline (priority):* 4/15. *Financial aid forms:* FAFSA, institutional form required. *Admission application deadline:* 8/1.

Summary of Aid to Needy Students *From gift & self-help combined:* Average need met: 97%. Average amount awarded: $11,813 (60% gift aid, 40% self-help). *Gift aid:* Total: $8,126,000 (51% from college's own funds, 3% from other college-administered sources, 46% from external sources). 300 Federal Work-Study jobs (averaging $1100); 170 part-time jobs.

Need-Based Scholarships & Grants Pell, FSEOG, state, private, college/university.

Loans Perkins, PLUS, Stafford, Unsubsidized Stafford, college/university short-term loans ($50 average).

Non-Need Awards In 1996, a total of 318 non-need awards were made. *Academic Interests/Achievement Awards:* 184 ($722,073 total): general academic, biological sciences, business, communication, health fields, humanities, mathematics, physical sciences, religion/biblical studies, social sciences. *Creative Arts/Performance Awards:* 22 ($24,340 total): music, theater/drama. *Special Characteristics Awards:* 112 ($352,714 total): members of minorities, religious affiliation.

Other Money-Saving Options Accelerated degree, co-op program, cooperative Army ROTC, cooperative Air Force ROTC, off-campus living. *Payment Plans:* installment, deferred payment. *Waivers:* full or partial for employees or children of employees and senior citizens.

Contact Office of Financial Aid, Elmhurst College, Goebel Hall 106A, Elmhurst, IL 60126-3296, 630-617-3500.

ELMIRA COLLEGE
Elmira, New York

About the Institution Independent, coed. Degrees awarded: B, M. Offers 62 undergraduate majors. Total enrollment: 1,117 (53% state residents). Freshmen: 385.

Undergraduate Expenses (1997–98) Comprehensive fee of $25,450 includes tuition ($18,770), mandatory fees ($400), and college room and board ($6280). College room only: $3800.

Applications 89% of all full-time undergraduates enrolled in fall 1996 applied for aid; of these, 84% were judged to have need according to Federal Methodology, of whom 100% were aided. *Financial aid deadline (priority):* 3/1. *Financial aid forms:* FAFSA, CSS Financial Aid PROFILE required. State form required for some. *Regular admission application deadline:* 7/15. Early decision deadline: 1/15.

Summary of Aid to Needy Students *From gift & self-help combined:* Average need met: 90%. Average amount awarded: $15,139 (70% gift aid, 30% self-help). *Gift aid:* Total: $8,988,435 (82% from college's own funds, 1% from other college-administered sources, 17% from external sources). 400 Federal Work-Study jobs (averaging $1200); 100 part-time jobs.

Need-Based Scholarships & Grants Pell, FSEOG, state, private, college/university.

Loans Perkins, PLUS, Stafford, Unsubsidized Stafford, private, college/university short-term loans ($25 average), college/university long-term loans ($5000 average).

Non-Need Awards In 1996, a total of 783 non-need awards were made. *Academic Interests/Achievement Awards:* 446 ($3,623,683 total): general academic. *Special Achievements/Activities Awards:* 223 ($431,500 total): leadership. *Special Characteristics Awards:* 114 ($833,594 total): children of faculty/staff, local/state students, previous college experience, siblings of current students.

Other Money-Saving Options Accelerated degree, cooperative Army ROTC, cooperative Air Force ROTC. *Payment Plans:* tuition prepayment, installment. *Waivers:* full or partial for employees or children of employees.

Contact Mrs. Kathleen L. Cohen, Dean of Financial Aid, Elmira College, One Park Place, Elmira, NY 14901-2099, 607-735-1728, fax: 607-735-1718.

ELMS COLLEGE
Chicopee, Massachusetts

See College of Our Lady of the Elms

ELON COLLEGE
Elon College, North Carolina

About the Institution Independent/religious, coed. Degrees awarded: B, M. Offers 45 undergraduate majors. Total enrollment: 3,588. Undergraduates: 3,427 (30% state residents). Freshmen: 948.

Undergraduate Expenses (1997–98) Comprehensive fee of $15,782 includes tuition ($11,322), mandatory fees ($220), and college room and board ($4240). College room only: $1900.

Applications 53% of all full-time undergraduates enrolled in fall 1996 applied for aid; of these, 79% were judged to have need according to Federal Methodology, of whom 98% were aided. *Financial aid deadline*

(priority): 4/1. *Financial aid forms:* FAFSA, CSS Financial Aid PROFILE, institutional form required. *Regular admission application deadline:* rolling. Early decision deadline: 12/1.

Summary of Aid to Needy Students *From gift & self-help combined:* Average need met: 65%. Average amount awarded: $7284 (53% gift aid, 47% self-help). *Gift aid:* Total: $5,181,067 (59% from college's own funds, 15% from other college-administered sources, 26% from external sources). 200 Federal Work-Study jobs (averaging $1300); 400 part-time jobs.

Need-Based Scholarships & Grants Pell, FSEOG, state, private, college/university.

Loans Perkins, PLUS, Stafford, Unsubsidized Stafford, private, college/university long-term loans ($2012 average).

Non-Need Awards *Academic Interests/Achievement Awards:* 773 ($1,834,859 total): general academic, biological sciences, computer science, education, mathematics, physical sciences, premedicine. *Creative Arts/Performance Awards:* 88 ($80,675 total): art/fine arts, music, performing arts, theater/drama. *Special Achievements/Activities Awards:* 153 ($179,000 total): leadership. *Special Characteristics Awards:* children of faculty/staff, relatives of clergy, ROTC participants. *Athletic:* Total: 211 ($941,258); Men: 132 ($648,676); Women: 79 ($292,582).

Other Money-Saving Options Accelerated degree, co-op program, cooperative Army ROTC, off-campus living (after freshman year). *Payment Plan:* installment. *Waivers:* full or partial for employees or children of employees.

Contact Office of Financial Aid, Elon College, 2700 Campus Box, Elon College, NC 27244, 910-584-9711.

EMBRY-RIDDLE AERONAUTICAL UNIVERSITY
Prescott, Arizona

About the Institution Independent, coed. Degrees awarded: B. Offers 6 undergraduate majors. Total enrollment: 1,435 (22% state residents). Freshmen: 310.

Undergraduate Expenses (1996–97) Comprehensive fee of $12,820 includes tuition ($8610 minimum), mandatory fees ($130), and college room and board ($4080). College room only: $1950.

Applications 66% of all full-time undergraduates enrolled in fall 1996 applied for aid; of these, 90% were judged to have need according to Federal Methodology, of whom 96% were aided. *Financial aid deadline (priority):* 4/15. *Financial aid forms:* state form, institutional form required; CSS Financial Aid PROFILE acceptable. FAFSA required for some. *Admission application deadline:* rolling.

Summary of Aid to Needy Students *From gift & self-help combined:* Average need met: 71%. Average amount awarded: $11,678 (16% gift aid, 84% self-help). *Gift aid:* Total: $1,766,160 (14% from college's own funds, 53% from other college-administered sources, 33% from external sources). 195 Federal Work-Study jobs (averaging $943); 1,134 part-time jobs.

Need-Based Scholarships & Grants Pell, FSEOG, state, private, college/university.

Loans Perkins, PLUS, Stafford, Unsubsidized Stafford, private, college/university long-term loans ($1055 average).

Non-Need Awards In 1996, a total of 646 non-need awards were made. *Academic Interests/Achievement Awards:* 296 ($320,909 total): general academic. *Special Achievements/Activities Awards:* 28 ($33,735 total): leadership. *Special Characteristics Awards:* 304 ($323,219 total): local/state students, ROTC participants, siblings of current students. *Athletic:* Total: 18 ($58,940); Men: 18 ($58,940); Women: 0.

Other Money-Saving Options Co-op program, Army ROTC, Air Force ROTC, off-campus living (after freshman year). *Waivers:* full or partial for employees or children of employees.

Contact Mr. Dan Lupin, Director of Financial Aid, Embry-Riddle Aeronautical University, 3200 North Willow Creek Road, Prescott, AZ 86301-3720, 520-776-3765.

EMBRY-RIDDLE AERONAUTICAL UNIVERSITY
Daytona Beach, Florida

About the Institution Independent, coed. Degrees awarded: A, B, M. Offers 11 undergraduate majors. Total enrollment: 4,135. Undergraduates: 3,930 (40% state residents). Freshmen: 724.

Undergraduate Expenses (1996–97) Comprehensive fee of $12,380 includes tuition ($8610), mandatory fees ($130), and college room and board ($3640). College room only: $2000.

Applications 71% of all full-time undergraduates enrolled in fall 1996 applied for aid; of these, 95% were judged to have need according to Federal Methodology, of whom 97% were aided. *Financial aid deadline (priority):* 4/15. *Financial aid forms:* FAFSA, state form, institutional form required. *Regular admission application deadline:* 3/1. Early decision deadline: 11/15.

Summary of Aid to Needy Students *From gift & self-help combined:* Average need met: 73%. *Gift aid:* Total: $6,510,623 (19% from college's own funds, 24% from other college-administered sources, 57% from external sources). 280 Federal Work-Study jobs (averaging $770); 1,435 part-time jobs.

Need-Based Scholarships & Grants Pell, FSEOG, state, private, college/university.

Loans Perkins, PLUS, Stafford, Unsubsidized Stafford, private, college/university short-term loans ($400 average), college/university long-term loans ($1274 average).

Non-Need Awards In 1996, a total of 2,311 non-need awards were made. *Academic Interests/Achievement Awards:* 780 ($1,022,634 total): general academic, business, computer science, engineering/technologies. *Special Achievements/Activities Awards:* 58 ($36,467 total): general special achievements/activities, leadership. *Special Characteristics Awards:* 1,319 ($2,110,401 total): general special characteristics, local/state students, ROTC participants, siblings of current students. *Athletic:* Total: 154 ($325,485); Men: 142 ($265,085); Women: 12 ($60,400).

Other Money-Saving Options Co-op program, Army ROTC, Air Force ROTC, off-campus living. *Payment Plans:* installment, deferred payment. *Waivers:* full or partial for employees or children of employees.

Contact Mr. Garry F. Vance, Director of Financial Aid, Embry-Riddle Aeronautical University, 600 South Clyde Morris Boulevard, Daytona Beach, FL 32114-3900, 904-226-6300, fax: 904-226-6307.

EMBRY-RIDDLE AERONAUTICAL UNIVERSITY, EXTENDED CAMPUS
Daytona Beach, Florida

About the Institution Independent, coed. Degrees awarded: A, B, M. Offers 5 undergraduate majors. Total enrollment: 11,716. Undergraduates: 6,256. Freshmen: 271.

Applications *Financial aid deadline (priority):* 4/15. *Financial aid forms:* FAFSA, institutional form required. *Admission application deadline:* rolling.

Summary of Aid to Needy Students *From gift & self-help combined:* Average need met: 68%. Average amount awarded: $4481 (22% gift aid, 78% self-help). *Gift aid:* Total: $535,451 (19% from college's own funds, 5% from other college-administered sources, 76% from external sources).

Need-Based Scholarships & Grants Pell, state.

Loans PLUS, Stafford, Unsubsidized Stafford, private.

Non-Need Awards In 1996, a total of 81 non-need awards were made. *Special Achievements/Activities Awards:* 81 ($8430 total): leadership.

Other Money-Saving Options Co-op program. *Waivers:* full or partial for employees or children of employees.

Contact Mr. Garry F. Vance, Director of Financial Aid, Embry-Riddle Aeronautical University, Extended Campus, 600 South Clyde Morris Boulevard, Daytona Beach, FL 32114-3900, 904-226-6300, fax: 904-226-6307.

EMERSON COLLEGE
Boston, Massachusetts

About the Institution Independent, coed. Degrees awarded: B, M, D. Offers 18 undergraduate majors. Total enrollment: 3,441. Undergraduates: 2,550 (38% state residents). Freshmen: 552.

Undergraduate Expenses (1997–98) Comprehensive fee of $26,076 includes tuition ($17,376), mandatory fees ($450), and college room and board ($8250). College room only: $4890.

Applications 72% of all full-time undergraduates enrolled in fall 1996 applied for aid; of these, 74% were judged to have need according to Federal Methodology, of whom 100% were aided. *Financial aid deadline (priority):* 3/1. *Financial aid forms:* FAFSA, CSS Financial Aid PROFILE, institutional form required. *Regular admission application deadline:* 2/1. Early action deadline: 11/15.

Summary of Aid to Needy Students *From gift & self-help combined:* Average amount awarded: $12,312 (60% gift aid, 40% self-help). *Gift aid:* Total: $9,252,481 (85% from college's own funds, 8% from other college-administered sources, 7% from external sources). 400 Federal Work-Study jobs (averaging $1400); 170 part-time jobs.

Need-Based Scholarships & Grants Pell, FSEOG, state, college/university.

Loans Perkins, PLUS, Stafford, Unsubsidized Stafford, state.

Non-Need Awards In 1996, a total of 429 non-need awards were made. *Academic Interests/Achievement Awards:* 363 ($1,746,000 total): general academic. *Creative Arts/Performance Awards:* 66 ($203,500 total): performing arts.

Other Money-Saving Options Off-campus living (after freshman year). *Payment Plans:* tuition prepayment, deferred payment. *Waivers:* full or partial for employees or children of employees.

Contact Mr. Robert F. Loconto, Acting Director of Financial Assistance, Emerson College, 100 Beacon Street, Boston, MA 02116-1511, 617-824-8655, fax: 617-824-8619.

EMMANUEL COLLEGE
Franklin Springs, Georgia

About the Institution Independent/religious, coed. Degrees awarded: A, B. Offers 14 undergraduate majors. Total enrollment: 695 (72% state residents). Freshmen: 283.

Undergraduate Expenses (1997–98) Comprehensive fee of $9480 includes tuition ($6060) and college room and board ($3420). College room only: $1600.

Applications *Financial aid deadline (priority):* 8/1. *Financial aid forms:* FAFSA, CSS Financial Aid PROFILE required. State form required for some. *Admission application deadline:* 8/1.

Summary of Aid to Needy Students Federal Work-Study jobs.

Non-Need Awards *Academic Interests/Achievement Awards:* available. *Creative Arts/Performance Awards:* general creative. *Special Achievements/Activities Awards:* general special achievements/activities, religious involvement. *Special Characteristics Awards:* children of faculty/staff. *Athletic:* available.

Other Money-Saving Options Off-campus living (after sophomore year). *Payment Plan:* installment. *Waivers:* full or partial for employees or children of employees, adult students, senior citizens.

Contact Office of Financial Aid, Emmanuel College, PO Box 129, Franklin Springs, GA 30639-0129, 706-245-7226.

EMMANUEL COLLEGE
Boston, Massachusetts

About the Institution Independent/religious, women. Degrees awarded: B, M. Offers 36 undergraduate majors. Total enrollment: 1,564. Undergraduates: 1,376 (90% state residents). Freshmen: 87.

Undergraduate Expenses (1997–98) Comprehensive fee of $21,335 includes tuition ($14,250), mandatory fees ($300), and college room and board ($6785).

Applications *Financial aid deadline (priority):* 3/1. *Financial aid forms:* FAFSA required. CSS Financial Aid PROFILE, institutional form required for some. *Regular admission application deadline:* rolling. Early decision deadline: 11/1. Early action deadline: 11/1.

Summary of Aid to Needy Students *From gift & self-help combined:* Average need met: 87%. Average amount awarded: $13,200 (45% gift aid, 55% self-help). *Gift aid:* Total: $1,676,653 (51% from college's own funds, 24% from other college-administered sources, 25% from external sources). 242 Federal Work-Study jobs (averaging $1600); 80 part-time jobs.

Need-Based Scholarships & Grants Pell, FSEOG, state, private, college/university.

Loans Perkins, PLUS, Stafford, Unsubsidized Stafford, state, private, college/university short-term loans ($50 average).

Non-Need Awards In 1996, a total of 211 non-need awards were made. *Academic Interests/Achievement Awards:* 140 ($789,715 total): general academic. *Special Characteristics Awards:* 71 ($240,290 total): children and siblings of alumni, children of educators, children of faculty/staff, international students, religious affiliation.

Other Money-Saving Options Accelerated degree, cooperative Army ROTC, off-campus living. *Payment Plans:* installment, deferred payment. *Waivers:* full or partial for employees or children of employees.

Contact Director of Financial Aid, Emmanuel College, 400 The Fenway, Boston, MA 02115, 617-735-9791, fax: 617-735-9877.

EMMAUS BIBLE COLLEGE
Dubuque, Iowa

About the Institution Independent/religious, coed. Degrees awarded: A, B. Offers 9 undergraduate majors. Total enrollment: 236 (19% state residents). Freshmen: 68.

Undergraduate Expenses (1996–97) Comprehensive fee of $6680 includes tuition ($0), mandatory fees ($2170), and college room and board ($4510).

Applications 65% of all full-time undergraduates enrolled in fall 1996 applied for aid; of these, 87% were judged to have need according to Federal Methodology, of whom 100% were aided. *Financial aid deadline (priority):* 8/1. *Financial aid forms:* institutional form required. FAFSA required for some. *Admission application deadline:* 8/1.

Summary of Aid to Needy Students *From gift & self-help combined:* Average need met: 60%. Average amount awarded: $4100 (58% gift aid, 42% self-help). *Gift aid:* Total: $312,000 (29% from college's own funds, 13% from other college-administered sources, 58% from external sources). 95 part-time jobs.

Need-Based Scholarships & Grants Pell, FSEOG, private, college/university.

Loans PLUS, Stafford, Unsubsidized Stafford.

Non-Need Awards In 1996, a total of 296 non-need awards were made. *Academic Interests/Achievement Awards:* 51 ($10,200 total): general academic. *Creative Arts/Performance Awards:* 18 ($2300 total): music. *Special Achievements/Activities Awards:* 173 ($119,000 total): hobbies/interest, leadership, religious involvement. *Special Characteristics Awards:* 54 ($60,000 total): general special characteristics, children of faculty/staff, international students, out-of-state students, spouses of current students.

Other Money-Saving Options Accelerated degree. *Payment Plan:* installment. *Waivers:* full or partial for employees or children of employees and senior citizens.

Contact Mrs. Laurel Rasmussen, Financial Aid Administrator, Emmaus Bible College, 2570 Asbury Road, Dubuque, IA 52001-3097, 319-588-8000, fax: 319-588-1216.

EMORY & HENRY COLLEGE
Emory, Virginia

About the Institution Independent/religious, coed. Degrees awarded: B. Offers 49 undergraduate majors. Total enrollment: 917 (82% state residents). Freshmen: 257.

Undergraduate Expenses (1997–98) Comprehensive fee of $16,372 includes tuition ($11,572) and college room and board ($4800).

Applications Of all full-time undergraduates enrolled in fall 1996, 90% of those who applied for aid were judged to have need according to Federal Methodology, of whom 99% were aided. *Financial aid deadline (priority):* 4/1. *Financial aid forms:* FAFSA, institutional form required; CSS Financial Aid PROFILE acceptable. State form required for some. *Regular admission application deadline:* rolling. Early decision deadline: 12/1.

Summary of Aid to Needy Students *From gift & self-help combined:* Average need met: 92%. Average amount awarded: $11,881 (51% gift aid, 49% self-help). *Gift aid:* Total: $4,051,751 (19% from college's own funds, 50% from other college-administered sources, 31% from external sources). 238 Federal Work-Study jobs (averaging $1000); 75 part-time jobs.

Need-Based Scholarships & Grants Pell, FSEOG, state, private, college/university.

Loans Perkins, PLUS, Stafford, Unsubsidized Stafford.

Non-Need Awards In 1996, a total of 310 non-need awards were made. *Academic Interests/Achievement Awards:* 280 ($997,120 total): general academic. *Special Characteristics Awards:* 30 ($86,460 total): children of faculty/staff, relatives of clergy.

Other Money-Saving Options *Payment Plan:* installment. *Waivers:* full or partial for employees or children of employees.

Contact Office of Financial Aid, Emory & Henry College, Emory, VA 24327-0947, 540-944-4121.

EMORY UNIVERSITY
Atlanta, Georgia

About the Institution Independent/religious, coed. Degrees awarded: B, M, D, P. Offers 51 undergraduate majors. Total enrollment: 11,270. Undergraduates: 5,400 (19% state residents). Freshmen: 1,160.

Undergraduate Expenses (1997–98) Comprehensive fee of $27,142 includes tuition ($20,870), mandatory fees ($250), and college room and board ($6022). College room only: $4222.

Applications 51% of all full-time undergraduates enrolled in fall 1996 applied for aid; of these, 86% were judged to have need according to Federal Methodology, of whom 97% were aided. *Financial aid deadline (priority):* 2/15. *Financial aid forms:* FAFSA, CSS Financial Aid PROFILE required. State form required for some. *Regular admission application deadline:* 1/15. Early decision deadline: 11/1.

Summary of Aid to Needy Students *From gift & self-help combined:* Average need met: 86%. Average amount awarded: $17,132 (70% gift aid, 30% self-help). *Gift aid:* Total: $24,327,899 (80% from college's own funds, 6% from other college-administered sources, 14% from external sources). 1,217 Federal Work-Study jobs (averaging $1325).

Need-Based Scholarships & Grants Pell, FSEOG, state, private, college/university.

Loans Perkins, PLUS, Stafford, Unsubsidized Stafford, Federal Nursing, Primary Care, state, private, college/university short-term loans ($500 average), college/university long-term loans ($8457 average).

Non-Need Awards In 1996, a total of 683 non-need awards were made. *Academic Interests/Achievement Awards:* 331 ($3,989,881 total): general academic. *Creative Arts/Performance Awards:* 18 ($251,355 total): debating, music, performing arts. *Special Characteristics Awards:* 334 ($4,892,657 total): children of faculty/staff, relatives of clergy, religious affiliation.

Other Money-Saving Options Accelerated degree, cooperative Air Force ROTC, off-campus living (after freshman year). *Payment Plans:* tuition prepayment, installment. *Waivers:* full or partial for employees or children of employees.

Contact Mr. Michael Jacubenta, Associate Director of Financial Aid, Emory University, 300 Boisfeuillet Jones Center, Atlanta, GA 30322-1100, 404-727-6039, fax: 404-727-6709.

EMPORIA STATE UNIVERSITY
Emporia, Kansas

About the Institution State-supported, coed. Degrees awarded: B, M, D. Offers 43 undergraduate majors. Total enrollment: 5,772. Undergraduates: 4,276 (93% state residents). Freshmen: 753.

Undergraduate Expenses (1996–97) State resident tuition: $1834. Nonresident tuition: $5934. College room and board: $3320.

Applications *Financial aid deadline (priority):* 3/15. *Financial aid forms:* FAFSA required; CSS Financial Aid PROFILE acceptable. State form required for some. *Admission application deadline:* rolling.

Summary of Aid to Needy Students *From gift & self-help combined:* Average need met: 80%. *Gift aid:* Total: $3,494,506 (18% from college's own funds, 15% from other college-administered sources, 67% from external sources). 361 Federal Work-Study jobs (averaging $1732); 400 part-time jobs.

Need-Based Scholarships & Grants Pell, FSEOG, state, private.

Loans Perkins, PLUS, Stafford, Unsubsidized Stafford, college/university short-term loans ($100 average).

Non-Need Awards In 1996, a total of 1,342 non-need awards were made. *Academic Interests/Achievement Awards:* 755 ($550,869 total): general academic. *Creative Arts/Performance Awards:* 193 ($81,075 total): art/fine arts, debating, music, theater/drama. *Special Achievements/Activities Awards:* 2 ($450 total): cheerleading/drum major. *Special Characteristics Awards:* 219 ($160,469 total): general special characteristics, children and siblings of alumni, children of faculty/staff, children of union members/company employees, ethnic background, handicapped students, international students, local/state students, members of minorities, out-of-state students, religious affiliation, ROTC participants, veterans, veterans' children. *Athletic:* Total: 173 ($503,593); Men: 110 ($367,136); Women: 63 ($136,457).

Other Money-Saving Options Accelerated degree, co-op program, Army ROTC, off-campus living (after freshman year). *Payment Plans:* installment, deferred payment. *Waivers:* full or partial for employees or children of employees and senior citizens.

Contact Mr. Mike Weatherred, Assistant Director of Financial Aid, Emporia State University, 1200 Commercial Street, Box 4038, Emporia, KS 66801-5087, 316-341-5457, fax: 316-341-6088.

ENDICOTT COLLEGE
Beverly, Massachusetts

About the Institution Independent, coed. Degrees awarded: A, B, M. Offers 33 undergraduate majors. Total enrollment: 902 (51% state residents). Freshmen: 406.

Undergraduate Expenses (1997–98) Comprehensive fee of $20,393 includes tuition ($12,970), mandatory fees ($374), and college room and board ($7049). College room only: $4984.

Applications Of all full-time undergraduates enrolled in fall 1996, 95% of those who applied for aid were judged to have need according to Federal Methodology, of whom 100% were aided. *Financial aid deadline (priority):* 3/15. *Financial aid forms:* FAFSA, institutional form required. CSS Financial Aid PROFILE required for some. *Regular admission application deadline:* rolling. Early action deadline: 11/15.

Summary of Aid to Needy Students *From gift & self-help combined:* Average need met: 61%. Average amount awarded: $8727 (58% gift aid, 42% self-help). *Gift aid:* Total: $3,304,289 (68% from college's own funds, 5% from other college-administered sources, 27% from external sources). 174 Federal Work-Study jobs (averaging $1000); 17 part-time jobs.

Need-Based Scholarships & Grants Pell, FSEOG, state, private, college/university.

Loans Perkins, PLUS, Stafford, Unsubsidized Stafford, state, private, college/university long-term loans ($1000 average).

Non-Need Awards *Academic Interests/Achievement Awards:* 31 ($62,000 total): general academic, architecture, biological sciences, business, communication, education, health fields, humanities, social sciences. *Special Characteristics Awards:* children of educators, siblings of current students.

Another Money-Saving Option *Payment Plan:* installment.

Contact Ms. Marcia Toomey, Director of Financial Aid, Endicott College, 376 Hale Street, Beverly, MA 01915-2096, 508-927-0585, fax: 508-927-0084.

ERSKINE COLLEGE
Due West, South Carolina

About the Institution Independent/religious, coed. Degrees awarded: B. Offers 29 undergraduate majors. Total enrollment: 536 (76% state residents). Freshmen: 134.

Undergraduate Expenses (1997–98) Comprehensive fee of $18,662 includes tuition ($12,996), mandatory fees ($811), and college room and board ($4855). College room only: $2277.

Applications *Financial aid deadline (priority):* 4/1. *Financial aid forms:* FAFSA, state form, institutional form required. *Admission application deadline:* rolling.

Summary of Aid to Needy Students *From gift & self-help combined:* Average need met: 94%. Average amount awarded: $12,757 (80% gift aid, 20% self-help). *Gift aid:* Total: $4,194,926 (59% from college's own funds, 2% from other college-administered sources, 39% from external sources). 123 Federal Work-Study jobs (averaging $877); 67 part-time jobs.

Need-Based Scholarships & Grants Pell, FSEOG, state, private, college/university.

Loans Perkins, PLUS, Stafford, Unsubsidized Stafford, state, private, college/university short-term loans ($45 average), college/university long-term loans ($2000 average).

Non-Need Awards *Academic Interests/Achievement Awards:* 232 ($1,094,137 total): general academic. *Creative Arts/Performance Awards:* 40 ($78,300 total): music, theater/drama. *Special Achievements/Activities Awards:* 121 ($175,239 total): general special achievements/activities, leadership, memberships. *Special Characteristics Awards:*

240 ($338,295 total): children and siblings of alumni, children of faculty/staff, children with a deceased or disabled parent, relatives of clergy, religious affiliation, siblings of current students. *Athletic:* available.

Other Money-Saving Options Accelerated degree. *Payment Plan:* installment. *Waivers:* full or partial for children of alumni and employees or children of employees.

Contact Ms. Visian S. Gaylord, Assistant Director of Financial Aid, Erskine College, PO Box 337, Due West, SC 29639, 864-379-8832, fax: 864-379-2167.

ESCUELA DE ARTES PLASTICAS DE PUERTO RICO
San Juan, Puerto Rico

About the Institution Commonwealth-supported, coed. Degrees awarded: B. Offers 6 undergraduate majors. Total enrollment: 248. Freshmen: 98.

Undergraduate Expenses (1996–97) Tuition: $1320. Mandatory fees: $408.

Applications *Financial aid deadline (priority):* 7/11. *Financial aid forms:* FAFSA, commonwealth form, institutional form acceptable. *Admission application deadline:* 4/1.

Summary of Aid to Needy Students *From gift & self-help combined:* Average amount awarded: $2619 (97% gift aid, 3% self-help). *Gift aid:* Total: $197,535 (5% from college's own funds, 2% from other college-administered sources, 93% from external sources). Federal Work-Study jobs.

Need-Based Scholarships & Grants Pell, FSEOG, college/university.

Non-Need Awards In 1996, a total of 12 non-need awards were made. *Creative Arts/Performance Awards:* 12 ($6500 total): art/fine arts.

Other Money-Saving Options Accelerated degree, co-op program. *Payment Plan:* deferred payment. *Waivers:* full or partial for employees or children of employees.

Contact Ms. Marion E. Muñoz, Financial Aid Administrator, Escuela de Artes Plasticas de Puerto Rico, PO Box 1112, PR 00902-1112, 787-725-8120, fax: 787-725-8111.

ETI TECHNICAL COLLEGE
Cleveland, Ohio

See Bryant and Stratton College

EUGENE BIBLE COLLEGE
Eugene, Oregon

About the Institution Independent/religious, coed. Degrees awarded: B. Offers 6 undergraduate majors. Total enrollment: 250 (52% state residents). Freshmen: 89.

Undergraduate Expenses (1996–97) Comprehensive fee of $8025 includes tuition ($4428), mandatory fees ($549), and college room and board ($3048).

Applications Of all full-time undergraduates enrolled in fall 1996, 100% of those judged to have need according to Federal Methodology were aided. *Financial aid deadline (priority):* 4/15. *Financial aid forms:* CSS Financial Aid PROFILE, institutional form required; state form acceptable. FAFSA required for some. *Admission application deadline:* 9/1.

Summary of Aid to Needy Students *From gift & self-help combined:* Average need met: 95%. Average amount awarded: $4446 (36% gift aid, 64% self-help). *Gift aid:* Total: $309,343 (14% from college's own

funds, 12% from other college-administered sources, 74% from external sources). 4 Federal Work-Study jobs (averaging $500); 28 part-time jobs.

Need-Based Scholarships & Grants Pell, FSEOG, private, college/university.

Loans PLUS, Stafford, Unsubsidized Stafford, college/university short-term loans, Key Alternative Loans, US Bank Signature Loans.

Non-Need Awards In 1996, a total of 100 non-need awards were made. *Academic Interests/Achievement Awards:* 25 ($25,000 total): general academic, religion/biblical studies. *Creative Arts/Performance Awards:* 10 ($19,000 total): music. *Special Achievements/Activities Awards:* 15 ($12,000 total): hobbies/interest, religious involvement. *Special Characteristics Awards:* 50 ($37,500 total): general special characteristics, married students, relatives of clergy.

Other Money-Saving Options Off-campus living (after junior year). *Payment Plans:* tuition prepayment, installment. *Waivers:* full or partial for employees or children of employees and senior citizens.

Contact Mr. Keith Mabus, Financial Aid Director, Eugene Bible College, 2155 Bailey Hill Road, Eugene, OR 97405-1194, 541-485-1780, fax: 541-343-5801.

EUGENE LANG COLLEGE, NEW SCHOOL FOR SOCIAL RESEARCH
New York, New York

About the Institution Independent, coed. Degrees awarded: B. Offers 22 undergraduate majors. Total university enrollment: 5,833. Undergraduates: 383 (42% state residents). Freshmen: 80.

Undergraduate Expenses (1996–97) Comprehensive fee of $25,780 includes tuition ($16,580), mandatory fees ($340), and college room and board ($8860). College room only: $6160.

Applications 79% of all full-time undergraduates enrolled in fall 1996 applied for aid; of these, 95% were judged to have need according to Federal Methodology, of whom 96% were aided. *Financial aid deadline (priority):* 4/1. *Financial aid forms:* FAFSA, institutional form required. CSS Financial Aid PROFILE, state form required for some. *Regular admission application deadline:* 2/1. Early decision deadline: 11/15.

Summary of Aid to Needy Students *From gift & self-help combined:* Average need met: 75%. Average amount awarded: $15,000 (95% gift aid, 5% self-help). *Gift aid:* Total: $2,699,242 (85% from college's own funds, 1% from other college-administered sources, 14% from external sources). 38 Federal Work-Study jobs (averaging $1531); 50 part-time jobs.

Need-Based Scholarships & Grants Pell, FSEOG, state, private, college/university.

Loans Perkins, PLUS, Stafford, Unsubsidized Stafford, private.

Non-Need Awards Not offered.

Other Money-Saving Options Accelerated degree, off-campus living. *Payment Plan:* installment. *Waivers:* full or partial for employees or children of employees.

Contact Ms. Lisa Kandell, Associate Director of Financial Aid, Eugene Lang College, New School for Social Research, 66 West 12th Street, New York, NY 10011-8601, 212-229-8930, fax: 212-229-5919.

EUREKA COLLEGE
Eureka, Illinois

About the Institution Independent/religious, coed. Degrees awarded: B. Offers 42 undergraduate majors. Total enrollment: 486 (90% state residents). Freshmen: 128.

Undergraduate Expenses (1997–98) Comprehensive fee of $18,350 includes tuition ($13,800), mandatory fees ($150), and college room and board ($4400). College room only: $2100.

Applications 100% of all full-time undergraduates enrolled in fall 1996 applied for aid; of these, 91% were judged to have need according to Federal Methodology, of whom 100% were aided. *Financial aid deadline (priority):* 5/1. *Financial aid forms:* FAFSA required; CSS Financial Aid PROFILE, state form acceptable. *Admission application deadline:* rolling.

Summary of Aid to Needy Students *From gift & self-help combined:* Average need met: 82%. Average amount awarded: $14,278 (67% gift aid, 33% self-help). *Gift aid:* Total: $3,807,597 (55% from college's own funds, 36% from other college-administered sources, 9% from external sources). 150 Federal Work-Study jobs (averaging $731); 235 part-time jobs.

Need-Based Scholarships & Grants Pell, FSEOG, state, private, college/university.

Loans Perkins, PLUS, Stafford, Unsubsidized Stafford, college/university short-term loans ($50 average).

Non-Need Awards In 1996, a total of 210 non-need awards were made. *Academic Interests/Achievement Awards:* 138 ($693,600 total): general academic, religion/biblical studies. *Creative Arts/Performance Awards:* 23 ($69,000 total): art/fine arts, performing arts. *Special Achievements/Activities Awards:* 19 ($293,104 total): leadership. *Special Characteristics Awards:* 30 ($28,474 total): religious affiliation.

Other Money-Saving Options *Payment Plan:* installment. *Waivers:* full or partial for children of alumni and employees or children of employees.

Contact Ms. Ellen Rigsby, Associate Director of Financial Aid, Eureka College, 310 College Avenue, Eureka, IL 61530-0128, 309-467-6320, fax: 309-467-6576.

EVANGEL COLLEGE
Springfield, Missouri

About the Institution Independent/religious, coed. Degrees awarded: A, B. Offers 47 undergraduate majors. Total enrollment: 1,574 (40% state residents). Freshmen: 405.

Undergraduate Expenses (1997–98) Comprehensive fee of $11,505 includes tuition ($7700), mandatory fees ($365), and college room and board ($3440).

Applications 81% of all full-time undergraduates enrolled in fall 1996 applied for aid; of these, 86% were judged to have need according to Federal Methodology, of whom 99% were aided. *Financial aid deadline (priority):* 4/1. *Financial aid forms:* FAFSA required. *Admission application deadline:* 8/15.

Summary of Aid to Needy Students *From gift & self-help combined:* Average need met: 68%. Average amount awarded: $6572 (47% gift aid, 53% self-help). *Gift aid:* Total: $3,131,984 (54% from college's own funds, 8% from other college-administered sources, 38% from external sources). 377 Federal Work-Study jobs (averaging $1580); 129 part-time jobs.

Need-Based Scholarships & Grants Pell, FSEOG.

Loans Perkins, PLUS, Stafford, Unsubsidized Stafford, college/university long-term loans ($1637 average).

Non-Need Awards *Academic Interests/Achievement Awards:* 502 ($720,000 total): general academic. *Creative Arts/Performance Awards:* 125 ($142,300 total): debating, music. *Special Achievements/Activities Awards:* 240 ($115,049 total): leadership. *Special Characteristics Awards:* children of faculty/staff. *Athletic:* Total: 142 ($377,700); Men: 102 ($242,400); Women: 40 ($135,300).

Other Money-Saving Options Army ROTC. *Payment Plan:* installment. *Waivers:* full or partial for employees or children of employees.

Contact Mr. Samuel A. Ketcher, Financial Aid Director, Evangel College, 1111 North Glenstone, Springfield, MO 65802-2191, 417-865-2811.

236

THE EVERGREEN STATE COLLEGE
Olympia, Washington

About the Institution State-supported, coed. Degrees awarded: B, M. Offers 100 undergraduate majors. Total enrollment: 3,714. Undergraduates: 3,498 (76% state residents). Freshmen: 494.

Undergraduate Expenses (1996–97) State resident tuition: $2439. Nonresident tuition: $8625. Mandatory fees: $105. College room and board: $4470. College room only: $1958 (minimum).

Applications Of all full-time undergraduates enrolled in fall 1996, 90% of those who applied for aid were judged to have need according to Federal Methodology, of whom 98% were aided. *Financial aid deadline (priority):* 2/15. *Financial aid forms:* FAFSA required. Institutional form required for some. *Admission application deadline:* 3/1.

Summary of Aid to Needy Students *From gift & self-help combined:* Average need met: 76%. Average amount awarded: $7016 (38% gift aid, 62% self-help). *Gift aid:* Total: $3,884,343 (23% from college's own funds, 29% from other college-administered sources, 48% from external sources). 390 Federal Work-Study jobs (averaging $2550); 287 part-time jobs.

Need-Based Scholarships & Grants Pell, FSEOG, state, private, college/university.

Loans Perkins, PLUS, Stafford, Unsubsidized Stafford, college/university short-term loans ($300 average).

Non-Need Awards In 1996, a total of 62 non-need awards were made. *Academic Interests/Achievement Awards:* 40 ($97,600 total): general academic. *Creative Arts/Performance Awards:* 5 ($5000 total): applied art and design, art/fine arts, creative writing. *Special Achievements/Activities Awards:* 12 ($13,950 total): community service. *Special Characteristics Awards:* 5 ($10,260 total): members of minorities.

Other Money-Saving Options Co-op program, off-campus living.

Contact Financial Aid Office, The Evergreen State College, Olympia, WA 98512, 360-866-6000 Ext. 6205, fax: 360-866-6680.

FAIRFIELD UNIVERSITY
Fairfield, Connecticut

About the Institution Independent/religious, coed. Degrees awarded: B, M. Offers 32 undergraduate majors. Total enrollment: 5,111. Undergraduates: 3,100 (30% state residents). Freshmen: 876.

Undergraduate Expenses (1997–98) Comprehensive fee of $25,334 includes tuition ($17,900), mandatory fees ($410), and college room and board ($7024).

Applications 60% of all full-time undergraduates enrolled in fall 1996 applied for aid; of these, 80% were judged to have need according to Federal Methodology, of whom 100% were aided. *Financial aid deadline (priority):* 2/15. *Financial aid forms:* FAFSA required. CSS Financial Aid PROFILE, institutional form required for some. *Regular admission application deadline:* 2/15. Early decision deadline: 12/1.

Summary of Aid to Needy Students *From gift & self-help combined:* Average need met: 84%. Average amount awarded: $10,612 (67% gift aid, 33% self-help). *Gift aid:* Total: $11,954,293 (91% from college's own funds, 4% from other college-administered sources, 5% from external sources). 320 Federal Work-Study jobs (averaging $1000); part-time jobs.

Need-Based Scholarships & Grants Pell, FSEOG, state, private, college/university.

Loans Perkins, PLUS, Stafford, Unsubsidized Stafford, Federal Nursing, state, private.

Non-Need Awards In 1996, a total of 823 non-need awards were made. *Academic Interests/Achievement Awards:* 499 ($1,272,500 total): general academic. *Creative Arts/Performance Awards:* 15 ($23,800 total): music, theater/drama. *Special Characteristics Awards:* 164

($845,891 total): children of faculty/staff, siblings of current students. *Athletic:* Total: 145 ($1,483,428); Men: 70 ($694,540); Women: 75 ($788,888).

Other Money-Saving Options *Payment Plan:* installment. *Waivers:* full or partial for employees or children of employees.

Contact Ms. Susan Kadir, Director of Financial Aid, Fairfield University, 315 Bellarmine Hall, Fairfield, CT 06430-5195, 203-254-4125, fax: 203-254-4008.

FAIRLEIGH DICKINSON UNIVERSITY, TEANECK-HACKENSACK AND FLORHAM-MADISON CAMPUSES
Teaneck, New Jersey
Madison, New Jersey

About the Institution Independent, coed. Degrees awarded: A, B, M, D. Offers 68 undergraduate majors. Total enrollment: 6,934. Undergraduates: 3,934 (81% state residents). Freshmen: 708.

Undergraduate Expenses (1997–98) Comprehensive fee of $20,752 includes tuition ($13,996), mandatory fees ($716 minimum), and college room and board ($6040). College room only: $3562.

Applications 80% of all full-time undergraduates enrolled in fall 1996 applied for aid; of these, 90% were judged to have need according to Federal Methodology, of whom 94% were aided. *Financial aid deadline (priority):* 3/15. *Financial aid forms:* FAFSA required. *Regular admission application deadline:* rolling. Early decision deadline: 12/1.

Summary of Aid to Needy Students *From gift & self-help combined:* Average need met: 76%. Average amount awarded: $13,996 (71% gift aid, 29% self-help). *Gift aid:* Total: $16,958,414 (60% from college's own funds, 4% from other college-administered sources, 36% from external sources). 698 Federal Work-Study jobs (averaging $1158); part-time jobs.

Need-Based Scholarships & Grants Pell, FSEOG, state, private, college/university.

Loans Perkins, PLUS, Stafford, Unsubsidized Stafford, Federal Nursing, state, private.

Non-Need Awards In 1996, a total of 833 non-need awards were made. *Academic Interests/Achievement Awards:* 700 ($4,622,921 total): general academic. *Special Achievements/Activities Awards:* 2 ($6000 total): leadership. *Special Characteristics Awards:* 46 ($111,250 total): children and siblings of alumni, international students, parents of current students, siblings of current students, spouses of current students. *Athletic:* Total: 85 ($882,291); Men: 49 ($495,518); Women: 36 ($386,773).

Other Money-Saving Options Accelerated degree, co-op program, cooperative Army ROTC, off-campus living. *Payment Plans:* installment, deferred payment. *Waivers:* full or partial for employees or children of employees and senior citizens.

Contact Office of Financial Aid, Fairleigh Dickinson University, Teaneck–Hackensack, 285 Madison Avenue, Madison, NJ 07940, 201-692-2000.

FAIRMONT STATE COLLEGE
Fairmont, West Virginia

About the Institution State-supported, coed. Degrees awarded: A, B. Offers 63 undergraduate majors. Total enrollment: 6,555 (95% state residents). Freshmen: 1,214.

Undergraduate Expenses (1997–98) State resident tuition: $2040. Nonresident tuition: $4840. College room and board: $3358 (minimum). College room only: $1630 (minimum).

Applications Of all full-time undergraduates enrolled in fall 1996, 57% of those who applied for aid were judged to have need according to

Federal Methodology, of whom 61% were aided. *Financial aid deadline (priority):* 2/14. *Financial aid forms:* FAFSA required. State form required for some. *Admission application deadline:* 6/15.

Summary of Aid to Needy Students *From gift & self-help combined:* Average need met: 90%. *Gift aid:* Total: $4,332,454 (1% from college's own funds, 20% from other college-administered sources, 79% from external sources). 247 Federal Work-Study jobs (averaging $837); 405 part-time jobs.

Need-Based Scholarships & Grants Pell, FSEOG, state, private, college/university.

Loans Perkins, PLUS, Stafford, Unsubsidized Stafford.

Non-Need Awards In 1996, a total of 278 non-need awards were made. *Academic Interests/Achievement Awards:* 181 ($228,466 total): general academic, business, education, engineering/technologies, foreign languages, health fields, humanities, mathematics, physical sciences, social sciences. *Creative Arts/Performance Awards:* 4 ($4560 total): art/fine arts. *Athletic:* Total: 93 ($109,647); Men: 47 ($55,413); Women: 46 ($54,234).

Other Money-Saving Options Accelerated degree, Army ROTC, cooperative Air Force ROTC, off-campus living. *Payment Plan:* deferred payment. *Waivers:* full or partial for employees or children of employees.

Contact Mr. William D. Shaffer, Director of Financial Aid, Fairmont State College, Locust Avenue, Fairmont, WV 26554, 304-367-4213, fax: 304-367-4584.

FAITH BAPTIST BIBLE COLLEGE AND THEOLOGICAL SEMINARY
Ankeny, Iowa

About the Institution Independent/religious, coed. Degrees awarded: A, B, M. Offers 7 undergraduate majors. Total enrollment: 306. Undergraduates: 256 (44% state residents). Freshmen: 68.

Undergraduate Expenses (1997–98) Comprehensive fee of $9970 includes tuition ($6094), mandatory fees ($600), and college room and board ($3276). College room only: $1180.

Applications 86% of all full-time undergraduates enrolled in fall 1996 applied for aid; of these, 97% were judged to have need according to Federal Methodology, of whom 96% were aided. *Financial aid deadline (priority):* 4/1. *Financial aid forms:* FAFSA, CSS Financial Aid PROFILE acceptable. *Admission application deadline:* 8/1.

Summary of Aid to Needy Students *From gift & self-help combined:* Average need met: 59%. Average amount awarded: $5722 (62% gift aid, 38% self-help). *Gift aid:* Total: $665,180 (24% from college's own funds, 4% from other college-administered sources, 72% from external sources). 68 part-time jobs.

Need-Based Scholarships & Grants Pell, state, private, college/university.

Loans PLUS, Stafford, Unsubsidized Stafford.

Non-Need Awards In 1996, a total of 118 non-need awards were made. *Academic Interests/Achievement Awards:* 59 ($12,400 total): general academic. *Creative Arts/Performance Awards:* 2 ($772 total): music. *Special Achievements/Activities Awards:* 1 ($177 total): leadership. *Special Characteristics Awards:* 56 ($132,578 total): children of faculty/staff, relatives of clergy, spouses of current students.

Other Money-Saving Options *Payment Plan:* installment. *Waivers:* full or partial for employees or children of employees.

Contact Mrs. Dorothy Ball, Director of Financial Assistance, Faith Baptist Bible College and Theological Seminary, 1900 Northwest 4th Street, Ankeny, IA 50021-2152, 515-964-0601, fax: 515-964-1638.

FASHION INSTITUTE OF TECHNOLOGY
New York, New York

About the Institution State & locally supported, coed. Degrees awarded: A, B, M. Offers 19 undergraduate majors. Total enrollment: 8,489. Undergraduates: 8,430 (79% state residents). Freshmen: 1,973.

Undergraduate Expenses (1996–97) State resident tuition: $2400 (minimum). Nonresident tuition: $5750 (minimum). Mandatory fees: $210. College room and board: $5340. College room only: $3007.

Applications Of all full-time undergraduates enrolled in fall 1996, 83% of those who applied for aid were judged to have need according to Federal Methodology, of whom 83% were aided. *Financial aid deadline (priority):* 3/15. *Financial aid forms:* FAFSA required. State form, federal income tax form required for some. *Admission application deadline:* rolling.

Summary of Aid to Needy Students *From gift & self-help combined:* Average need met: 69%. Average amount awarded: $5488 (43% gift aid, 57% self-help). *Gift aid:* Total: $5,779,987 (27% from college's own funds, 5% from other college-administered sources, 68% from external sources). 698 Federal Work-Study jobs (averaging $1340); 45 part-time jobs.

Loans Perkins, PLUS, Stafford, Unsubsidized Stafford, college/university long-term loans ($1000 average).

Non-Need Awards Not offered.

Other Money-Saving Options Co-op program, off-campus living. *Payment Plan:* installment. *Waivers:* full or partial for employees or children of employees.

Contact Mr. Barry Fischer, Financial Aid Counselor, Fashion Institute of Technology, Seventh Avenue at 27th Street, New York, NY 10001-5992, 212-760-7684, fax: 212-629-6352.

FAULKNER UNIVERSITY
Montgomery, Alabama

About the Institution Independent/religious, coed. Degrees awarded: A, B, M, P. Offers 49 undergraduate majors. Total enrollment: 2,376. Undergraduates: 1,939 (74% state residents). Freshmen: 220.

Undergraduate Expenses (1997–98) Comprehensive fee of $10,940 includes tuition ($6880), mandatory fees ($560), and college room and board ($3500).

Applications 94% of all full-time undergraduates enrolled in fall 1996 applied for aid; of these, 69% were judged to have need according to Federal Methodology, of whom 89% were aided. *Financial aid deadline (priority):* 6/1. *Financial aid forms:* FAFSA, state form, institutional form required; CSS Financial Aid PROFILE acceptable. *Admission application deadline:* rolling.

Summary of Aid to Needy Students *From gift & self-help combined:* Average need met: 90%. Average amount awarded: $3700 (51% gift aid, 49% self-help). *Gift aid:* Total: $1,476,041 (41% from college's own funds, 26% from other college-administered sources, 33% from external sources). 230 Federal Work-Study jobs (averaging $800).

Need-Based Scholarships & Grants Pell, FSEOG.

Loans Perkins, PLUS, Stafford, Unsubsidized Stafford.

Non-Need Awards In 1996, a total of 489 non-need awards were made. *Academic Interests/Achievement Awards:* 168 ($210,648 total): general academic, religion/biblical studies. *Creative Arts/Performance Awards:* 31 ($10,625 total): journalism/publications, music, theater/drama. *Special Achievements/Activities Awards:* 177 ($46,050 total): cheerleading/drum major, leadership, religious involvement. *Special Characteristics Awards:* 62 ($65,625 total): adult students, children of faculty/staff, international students, relatives of clergy, siblings of current students. *Athletic:* Total: 51 ($132,072); Men: 35 ($91,787); Women: 16 ($40,285).

Other Money-Saving Options Accelerated degree, off-campus living (after junior year). *Payment Plans:* installment, deferred payment. *Waivers:* full or partial for employees or children of employees and adult students.

Contact Office of Financial Aid, Faulkner University, 5345 Atlanta Highway, Montgomery, AL 36109-3398, 334-272-5820.

FAYETTEVILLE STATE UNIVERSITY
Fayetteville, North Carolina

About the Institution State-supported, coed. Degrees awarded: A, B, M, D. Offers 35 undergraduate majors. Total enrollment: 3,951. Undergraduates: 3,192 (90% state residents). Freshmen: 597.

Undergraduate Expenses (1996–97) State resident tuition: $874. Nonresident tuition: $8028. Mandatory fees: $742. College room and board: $3250 (minimum). College room only: $1800 (minimum).

Applications 92% of all full-time undergraduates enrolled in fall 1996 applied for aid; of these, 89% were judged to have need according to Federal Methodology, of whom 91% were aided. *Financial aid deadline (priority):* 4/1. *Financial aid forms:* FAFSA, institutional form required; CSS Financial Aid PROFILE acceptable. *Admission application deadline:* rolling.

Summary of Aid to Needy Students *From gift & self-help combined:* Average need met: 60%. Average amount awarded: $3840 (59% gift aid, 41% self-help). *Gift aid:* Total: $5,422,225 (10% from college's own funds, 14% from other college-administered sources, 76% from external sources). 340 Federal Work-Study jobs (averaging $860); 17 part-time jobs.

Need-Based Scholarships & Grants Pell, FSEOG, state, private.

Loans Perkins, PLUS, Stafford, Unsubsidized Stafford, Federal Nursing, Primary Care, state, private, college/university short-term loans ($300 average).

Non-Need Awards In 1996, a total of 577 non-need awards were made. *Academic Interests/Achievement Awards:* 424 ($1,059,914 total): general academic. *Creative Arts/Performance Awards:* 22 ($18,350 total): music. *Special Characteristics Awards:* 41 ($64,090 total): local/state students. *Athletic:* Total: 90 ($346,264); Men: 71 ($258,697); Women: 19 ($87,567).

Other Money-Saving Options Accelerated degree, co-op program, Air Force ROTC, off-campus living. *Payment Plan:* installment. *Waivers:* full or partial for employees or children of employees and senior citizens.

Contact Office of Financial Aid, Fayetteville State University, 1200 Murchison Road, Fayetteville, NC 28301-4298, 910-486-1325, fax: 910-486-1423.

FELICIAN COLLEGE
Lodi, New Jersey

About the Institution Independent/religious, coed. Degrees awarded: A, B, M. Offers 34 undergraduate majors. Total enrollment: 1,250 (95% state residents). Freshmen: 180.

Undergraduate Expenses (1997–98) Tuition: $9660. Mandatory fees: $272.

Applications 64% of all full-time undergraduates enrolled in fall 1996 applied for aid; of these, 89% were judged to have need according to Federal Methodology, of whom 100% were aided. *Financial aid deadline (priority):* 9/15. *Financial aid forms:* FAFSA, CSS Financial Aid PROFILE, institutional form required. *Admission application deadline:* rolling.

Summary of Aid to Needy Students *From gift & self-help combined:* Average amount awarded: $5059 (67% gift aid, 33% self-help). *Gift aid:* Total: $1,096,000 (7% from college's own funds, 75% from other college-administered sources, 18% from external sources). 30 Federal Work-Study jobs (averaging $1000).

Need-Based Scholarships & Grants Pell, FSEOG, state.

Loans PLUS, Stafford, Unsubsidized Stafford, state.

Non-Need Awards *Academic Interests/Achievement Awards:* 110 ($80,000 total): general academic, biological sciences, education, English, health fields. *Athletic:* available.

Other Money-Saving Options Off-campus living. *Payment Plan:* installment. *Waivers:* full or partial for employees or children of employees and senior citizens.

Contact Ms. Norma Betz, Financial Aid Director, Felician College, 262 South Main Street, Lodi, NJ 07644-2198, 973-778-1190.

FERRIS STATE UNIVERSITY
Big Rapids, Michigan

About the Institution State-supported, coed. Degrees awarded: A, B, M, P. Offers 91 undergraduate majors. Total enrollment: 9,495. Undergraduates: 9,191 (94% state residents). Freshmen: 1,976.

Undergraduate Expenses (1996–97) State resident tuition: $3630. Nonresident tuition: $7364. Mandatory fees: $35. College room and board: $4631.

Applications Of all full-time undergraduates enrolled in fall 1996, 90% of those who applied for aid were judged to have need according to Federal Methodology, of whom 97% were aided. *Financial aid deadline (priority):* 4/1. *Financial aid forms:* FAFSA required. *Admission application deadline:* rolling.

Summary of Aid to Needy Students *From gift & self-help combined:* Average need met: 73%. Average amount awarded: $6270 (46% gift aid, 54% self-help). *Gift aid:* Total: $12,640,409 (18% from college's own funds, 27% from other college-administered sources, 55% from external sources). 556 Federal Work-Study jobs (averaging $1600); 2,162 part-time jobs.

Need-Based Scholarships & Grants Pell, FSEOG, state, private, college/university.

Loans Perkins, PLUS, Stafford, Unsubsidized Stafford, Federal Nursing, state, college/university short-term loans ($350 average), college/university long-term loans ($800 average).

Non-Need Awards In 1996, a total of 812 non-need awards were made. *Academic Interests/Achievement Awards:* 390 ($852,000 total): general academic. *Creative Arts/Performance Awards:* 227 ($73,610 total): debating, journalism/publications, music, theater/drama. *Athletic:* Total: 195 ($736,545); Men: 126 ($478,804); Women: 69 ($257,741).

Other Money-Saving Options Accelerated degree, co-op program, cooperative Army ROTC, off-campus living (after sophomore year). *Payment Plans:* installment, deferred payment. *Waivers:* full or partial for employees or children of employees.

Contact Mr. Dennis Batt, Interim Director of Financial Aid, Ferris State University, 420 Oak Street, Big Rapids, MI 49307-2020, 616-592-2110.

FERRUM COLLEGE
Ferrum, Virginia

About the Institution Independent/religious, coed. Degrees awarded: B. Offers 36 undergraduate majors. Total enrollment: 1,075 (82% state residents). Freshmen: 307.

Undergraduate Expenses (1997–98) Comprehensive fee of $15,600 includes tuition ($10,750) and college room and board ($4850).

Applications 88% of all full-time undergraduates enrolled in fall 1996 applied for aid; of these, 87% were judged to have need according to Federal Methodology, of whom 100% were aided. *Financial aid deadline (priority):* 4/1. *Financial aid forms:* FAFSA, state form required; CSS Financial Aid PROFILE acceptable. *Admission application deadline:* rolling.

Summary of Aid to Needy Students *From gift & self-help combined:* Average need met: 88%. Average amount awarded: $11,389 (51% gift aid, 49% self-help). *Gift aid:* Total: $4,543,445 (53% from college's own funds, 11% from other college-administered sources, 36% from external sources). 244 Federal Work-Study jobs (averaging $1290); 205 part-time jobs.

Need-Based Scholarships & Grants Pell, FSEOG, state, private, college/university.

Loans Perkins, PLUS, Stafford, Unsubsidized Stafford, private, college/university long-term loans ($1065 average).

Non-Need Awards In 1996, a total of 654 non-need awards were made. *Academic Interests/Achievement Awards:* 264 ($436,825 total): general academic. *Creative Arts/Performance Awards:* 26 ($25,450 total): music, performing arts, theater/drama. *Special Achievements/Activities Awards:* 97 ($171,000 total): community service. *Special Characteristics Awards:* 267 ($377,412 total): children of educators, children of faculty/staff, local/state students, out-of-state students, relatives of clergy, religious affiliation, veterans.

Other Money-Saving Options *Payment Plan:* installment. *Waivers:* full or partial for employees or children of employees and senior citizens.

Contact Ms. Judith B. Carter, Director of Financial Aid, Ferrum College, Ferrum, VA 24088-9001, 540-365-4282, fax: 540-365-4203.

FISK UNIVERSITY
Nashville, Tennessee

About the Institution Independent/religious, coed. Degrees awarded: B, M. Offers 24 undergraduate majors. Total enrollment: 900. Undergraduates: 839 (10% state residents). Freshmen: 230.

Undergraduate Expenses (1997–98) Comprehensive fee of $12,054 includes tuition ($7500), mandatory fees ($250), and college room and board ($4304). College room only: $2522.

Applications 90% of all full-time undergraduates enrolled in fall 1996 applied for aid; of these, 85% were judged to have need according to Federal Methodology, of whom 100% were aided. *Financial aid deadline (priority):* 4/1. *Financial aid forms:* FAFSA, CSS Financial Aid PROFILE, state form, institutional form required. *Admission application deadline:* 6/15.

Summary of Aid to Needy Students *From gift & self-help combined:* Average need met: 62%. Average amount awarded: $8350 (49% gift aid, 51% self-help). *Gift aid:* Total: $2,454,383 (25% from college's own funds, 36% from other college-administered sources, 39% from external sources). 189 Federal Work-Study jobs (averaging $1000).

Need-Based Scholarships & Grants Pell, FSEOG, state, college/university.

Loans Perkins, PLUS, Stafford, Unsubsidized Stafford.

Non-Need Awards In 1996, a total of 89 non-need awards were made. *Academic Interests/Achievement Awards:* 80 ($531,611 total): general academic. *Special Characteristics Awards:* 9 ($63,902 total): children of faculty/staff.

Other Money-Saving Options Co-op program, cooperative Army ROTC, cooperative Air Force ROTC.

Contact Office of Financial Aid, Fisk University, 1000 17th Avenue N, Nashville, TN 37208-3051, 615-329-8735, fax: 615-329-8774.

FITCHBURG STATE COLLEGE
Fitchburg, Massachusetts

About the Institution State-supported, coed. Degrees awarded: B, M. Offers 45 undergraduate majors. Total enrollment: 3,701. Undergraduates: 3,153 (96% state residents). Freshmen: 466.

Undergraduate Expenses (1996–97) State resident tuition: $1338. Nonresident tuition: $5726. Mandatory fees: $1908. College room and board: $4110. College room only: $2340.

Applications Of all full-time undergraduates enrolled in fall 1996, 88% of those who applied for aid were judged to have need according to Federal Methodology, of whom 100% were aided. *Financial aid deadline (priority):* 3/1. *Financial aid forms:* FAFSA, institutional form required. *Admission application deadline:* rolling.

Summary of Aid to Needy Students *From gift & self-help combined:* Average need met: 89%. Average amount awarded: $4913 (26% gift aid, 74% self-help). *Gift aid:* Total: $2,488,568 (14% from college's own funds, 24% from other college-administered sources, 62% from external sources). 525 Federal Work-Study jobs (averaging $1100); 144 part-time jobs.

Need-Based Scholarships & Grants Pell, FSEOG, state, private, college/university.

Loans Perkins, PLUS, Stafford, Unsubsidized Stafford, Federal Nursing, state, private, college/university short-term loans ($200 average).

Non-Need Awards *Academic Interests/Achievement Awards:* general academic. *Creative Arts/Performance Awards:* general creative, music. *Special Characteristics Awards:* children and siblings of alumni.

Other Money-Saving Options Accelerated degree, Army ROTC, off-campus living. *Payment Plan:* installment. *Waivers:* full or partial for employees or children of employees and senior citizens.

Contact Ms. Jennifer Porter, Director of Financial Aid, Fitchburg State College, 160 Pearl Street, Fitchburg, MA 01420-2697, 508-665-3156, fax: 508-665-3559.

FIVE TOWNS COLLEGE
Dix Hills, New York

About the Institution Independent, coed. Degrees awarded: A, B. Offers 24 undergraduate majors. Total enrollment: 650 (90% state residents). Freshmen: 240.

Undergraduate Expenses (1997–98) Comprehensive fee of $13,190 includes tuition ($8500), mandatory fees ($300), and college room and board ($4390).

Applications Of all full-time undergraduates enrolled in fall 1996, 89% of those who applied for aid were judged to have need according to Federal Methodology, of whom 96% were aided. *Financial aid deadline (priority):* 4/1. *Financial aid forms:* FAFSA, state form, institutional form required. *Admission application deadline:* rolling.

Summary of Aid to Needy Students *From gift & self-help combined:* Average need met: 40%. 24 Federal Work-Study jobs (averaging $24,580); 10 part-time jobs.

Need-Based Scholarships & Grants Pell, FSEOG, state, private, college/university.

Loans PLUS, Stafford, Unsubsidized Stafford.

Non-Need Awards *Academic Interests/Achievement Awards:* general academic, business, education. *Creative Arts/Performance Awards:* cinema/film/broadcasting, music.

Other Money-Saving Options Co-op program, off-campus living. *Payment Plans:* installment, deferred payment. *Waivers:* full or partial for employees or children of employees and senior citizens.

Contact Office of Financial Aid, Five Towns College, 305 North Service Road, Dix Hills, NY 11746-6055, 516-424-7000.

FLAGLER COLLEGE
St. Augustine, Florida

About the Institution Independent, coed. Degrees awarded: B. Offers 22 undergraduate majors. Total enrollment: 1,526 (56% state residents). Freshmen: 423.

Undergraduate Expenses (1997–98) Comprehensive fee of $9340 includes tuition ($5760) and college room and board ($3580).

Applications 83% of all full-time undergraduates enrolled in fall 1996 applied for aid; of these, 55% were judged to have need according to Federal Methodology, of whom 97% were aided. *Financial aid deadline (priority):* 4/1. *Financial aid forms:* FAFSA, institutional form required. State form required for some. *Regular admission application deadline:* 3/15. Early decision deadline: 1/15.

Summary of Aid to Needy Students *From gift & self-help combined:* Average need met: 85%. Average amount awarded: $5810 (45% gift aid, 55% self-help). *Gift aid:* Total: $1,760,000 (10% from college's own funds, 59% from other college-administered sources, 31% from external sources). 175 Federal Work-Study jobs (averaging $800); 50 part-time jobs.

Need-Based Scholarships & Grants Pell, FSEOG, state, private, college/university.

Loans Perkins, PLUS, Stafford, Unsubsidized Stafford, private.

Non-Need Awards In 1996, a total of 148 non-need awards were made. *Academic Interests/Achievement Awards:* 25 ($115,000 total): general academic, business, communication, education, humanities. *Creative Arts/Performance Awards:* 2 ($800 total): art/fine arts, theater/drama. *Special Achievements/Activities Awards:* 5 ($4400 total): leadership, religious involvement. *Special Characteristics Awards:* 17 ($38,000 total): general special characteristics, children of faculty/staff, local/state students, members of minorities. *Athletic:* Total: 99 ($249,125); Men: 52 ($134,415); Women: 47 ($114,710).

Other Money-Saving Options Off-campus living (after freshman year). *Waivers:* full or partial for employees or children of employees.

Contact Mr. Chris Haffner, Assistant Director of Financial Aid, Flagler College, PO Box 1027, St. Augustine, FL 32085-1027, 904-829-6481 Ext. 225.

FLORIDA AGRICULTURAL AND MECHANICAL UNIVERSITY
Tallahassee, Florida

About the Institution State-supported, coed. Degrees awarded: A, B, M, D, P. Offers 72 undergraduate majors. Total enrollment: 10,448. Undergraduates: 9,251 (75% state residents). Freshmen: 1,494.

Undergraduate Expenses (1997–98) State resident tuition: $1981. Nonresident tuition: $7898. Mandatory fees: $124. College room and board: $3198. College room only: $1954.

Applications *Financial aid deadline (priority):* 4/1. *Financial aid forms:* FAFSA, institutional form required. *Admission application deadline:* 5/1.

Summary of Aid to Needy Students Federal Work-Study jobs; part-time jobs.

Need-Based Scholarships & Grants Pell, FSEOG, state.

Loans Perkins, PLUS, Stafford, Unsubsidized Stafford, college/university short-term loans.

Non-Need Awards *Academic Interests/Achievement Awards:* general academic, agriculture, business, engineering/technologies, health fields. *Creative Arts/Performance Awards:* general creative, art/fine arts, journalism/publications, music. *Special Achievements/Activities Awards:* general special achievements/activities. *Special Characteristics Awards:* general special characteristics, children of union members/company employees, ethnic background, members of minorities, ROTC participants, veterans' children. *Athletic:* available.

Other Money-Saving Options Accelerated degree, co-op program, Army ROTC, Naval ROTC, cooperative Air Force ROTC, off-campus living (after freshman year). *Payment Plans:* tuition prepayment, deferred payment. *Waivers:* full or partial for employees or children of employees and senior citizens.

Contact Student Financial Aid, Florida Agricultural and Mechanical University, FHAC Suite 101, Tallahassee, FL 32307, 904-561-2824, fax: 904-561-2730.

FLORIDA ATLANTIC UNIVERSITY
Boca Raton, Florida

About the Institution State-supported, coed. Degrees awarded: A, B, M, D. Offers 78 undergraduate majors. Total enrollment: 18,362. Undergraduates: 15,995 (92% state residents). Freshmen: 1,010.

Undergraduate Expenses (1996–97) State resident tuition: $1900. Nonresident tuition: $7200. College room and board: $4365. College room only: $2245.

Applications Of all full-time undergraduates enrolled in fall 1996, 52% of those who applied for aid were judged to have need according to Federal Methodology, of whom 97% were aided. *Financial aid deadline (priority):* 4/1. *Financial aid forms:* FAFSA, financial aid transcript (for transfers) required; CSS Financial Aid PROFILE acceptable. *Admission application deadline:* 5/1.

Summary of Aid to Needy Students *From gift & self-help combined:* Average need met: 49%. Average amount awarded: $3388 (41% gift aid, 59% self-help). *Gift aid:* Total: $4,705,082 (28% from college's own funds, 35% from other college-administered sources, 37% from external sources). 126 Federal Work-Study jobs (averaging $1200); 415 part-time jobs.

Need-Based Scholarships & Grants Pell, FSEOG, state, private, college/university.

Loans Perkins, PLUS, Stafford, Unsubsidized Stafford, college/university short-term loans ($300 average), college/university long-term loans ($2500 average).

Non-Need Awards *Academic Interests/Achievement Awards:* general academic, business, engineering/technologies, physical sciences, social sciences. *Special Characteristics Awards:* members of minorities. *Athletic:* Total: 287 ($992,716); Men: 112 ($453,892); Women: 175 ($538,824).

Other Money-Saving Options Accelerated degree, co-op program, off-campus living (after freshman year). *Payment Plans:* installment, deferred payment. *Waivers:* full or partial for employees or children of employees.

Contact Mr. Mark Judd, Associate Director, Florida Atlantic University, 777 Glades Road, Boca Raton, FL 33431-0991, 561-367-2736, fax: 561-367-3517.

FLORIDA BAPTIST THEOLOGICAL COLLEGE
Graceville, Florida

About the Institution Independent/religious, coed. Degrees awarded: A, B. Offers 8 undergraduate majors. Total enrollment: 529 (62% state residents). Freshmen: 55.

Undergraduate Expenses (1997–98) Tuition: $2850. Mandatory fees: $84. College room only: $1500.

Applications Of all full-time undergraduates enrolled in fall 1996, 100% of those judged to have need according to Federal Methodology were aided. *Financial aid deadline (priority):* 4/1. *Financial aid forms:* FAFSA, institutional form required; CSS Financial Aid PROFILE acceptable. *Regular admission application deadline:* rolling. Early action deadline: 8/1.

Summary of Aid to Needy Students *From gift & self-help combined:* Average need met: 54%. Average amount awarded: $2222 (63% gift aid, 37% self-help). *Gift aid:* Total: $592,075 (17% from college's own funds, 35% from other college-administered sources, 48% from external sources). Federal Work-Study jobs; part-time jobs.

Need-Based Scholarships & Grants Pell, FSEOG, state, college/university.

Loans PLUS, Stafford, Unsubsidized Stafford, college/university short-term loans ($180 average).

Non-Need Awards *Academic Interests/Achievement Awards:* available. *Creative Arts/Performance Awards:* available. *Special Characteristics Awards:* religious affiliation.

Other Money-Saving Options Accelerated degree, off-campus living. *Payment Plan:* deferred payment. *Waivers:* full or partial for employees or children of employees.

Contact Office of Financial Aid, Florida Baptist Theological College, PO Box 1306, Graceville, FL 32440-3306, 904-263-3261.

FLORIDA BIBLE COLLEGE
Miramar, Florida

About the Institution Independent/religious, coed. Degrees awarded: A, B. Offers 7 undergraduate majors.

Undergraduate Expenses (1996–97) Tuition: $4640. Mandatory fees: $288. College room only: $2200.

Applications *Admission application deadline:* rolling.

Summary of Aid to Needy Students *From gift & self-help combined:* Average amount awarded: $750. Part-time jobs.

Need-Based Scholarships & Grants Private.

Loans Private.

Non-Need Awards In 1996, a total of 23 non-need awards were made. *Special Characteristics Awards:* 23: children of faculty/staff, relatives of clergy, religious affiliation.

Other Money-Saving Options *Payment Plan:* deferred payment. *Waivers:* full or partial for children of alumni and employees or children of employees.

Contact Mr. Winston Thompson, Academic Dean, Florida Bible College, 9300 Pembroke Road, Miramar, FL 33025, 954-431-6776.

FLORIDA CHRISTIAN COLLEGE
Kissimmee, Florida

About the Institution Independent/religious, coed. Degrees awarded: A, B. Offers 3 undergraduate majors. Total enrollment: 153 (76% state residents). Freshmen: 42.

Undergraduate Expenses (1997–98 estimated) Tuition: $4480. Mandatory fees: $694. College room only: $1240.

Applications Of all full-time undergraduates enrolled in fall 1996, 98% of those judged to have need according to Federal Methodology were aided. *Financial aid deadline (priority):* 4/1. *Financial aid forms:* FAFSA, institutional form required; CSS Financial Aid PROFILE acceptable. *Admission application deadline:* 7/15.

Summary of Aid to Needy Students *From gift & self-help combined:* Average amount awarded: $2923 (46% gift aid, 54% self-help). *Gift aid:* Total: $132,380 (35% from college's own funds, 3% from other college-administered sources, 62% from external sources). 8 Federal Work-Study jobs (averaging $942); 6 part-time jobs.

Need-Based Scholarships & Grants Pell, FSEOG, state, private, college/university.

Loans PLUS, Stafford, Unsubsidized Stafford, college/university short-term loans ($200 average).

Non-Need Awards In 1996, a total of 128 non-need awards were made. *Creative Arts/Performance Awards:* 6 ($6000 total): music. *Special Achievements/Activities Awards:* 7 ($11,480 total): religious involvement. *Special Characteristics Awards:* 115 ($65,834 total): children and siblings of alumni, children of faculty/staff, relatives of clergy, religious affiliation, spouses of current students.

Other Money-Saving Options Off-campus living (after freshman year). *Payment Plan:* installment. *Waivers:* full or partial for employees or children of employees.

Contact Ms. Sandra Peppard, Director of Student Financial Aid, Florida Christian College, 1011 Bill Beck Boulevard, Kissimmee, FL 34744-5301, 407-847-8966 Ext. 317, fax: 407-847-3925.

FLORIDA INSTITUTE OF TECHNOLOGY
Melbourne, Florida

About the Institution Independent, coed. Degrees awarded: B, M, D. Offers 55 undergraduate majors. Total enrollment: 4,185. Undergraduates: 1,885 (29% state residents). Freshmen: 448.

Undergraduate Expenses (1996–97) Comprehensive fee of $19,492 includes tuition ($15,060 minimum), mandatory fees ($40), and college room and board ($4392). College room only: $1846.

Applications *Financial aid deadline (priority):* 2/1. *Financial aid forms:* FAFSA required. State form required for some. *Admission application deadline:* rolling.

Summary of Aid to Needy Students *From gift & self-help combined:* Average amount awarded: $12,736. *Gift aid:* Total: $11,548,871. 387 Federal Work-Study jobs (averaging $1500); part-time jobs.

Need-Based Scholarships & Grants Pell, FSEOG, state, private, college/university.

Loans Perkins, PLUS, Stafford, Unsubsidized Stafford, private, college/university short-term loans, college/university long-term loans.

Non-Need Awards *Academic Interests/Achievement Awards:* general academic, biological sciences, education, engineering/technologies, physical sciences. *Special Achievements/Activities Awards:* leadership. *Special Characteristics Awards:* ROTC participants. *Athletic:* available.

Other Money-Saving Options Accelerated degree, co-op program, Army ROTC, off-campus living (after freshman year). *Payment Plan:* installment. *Waivers:* full or partial for employees or children of employees and senior citizens.

Contact Office of Student Financial Aid, Florida Institute of Technology, 150 West University Boulevard, Melbourne, FL 32901-6975, 407-768-8000 Ext. 8070, fax: 407-724-2778.

FLORIDA INTERNATIONAL UNIVERSITY
Miami, Florida

About the Institution State-supported, coed. Degrees awarded: B, M, D. Offers 82 undergraduate majors. Total enrollment: 24,413. Undergraduates: 20,314 (91% state residents). Freshmen: 1,157.

Undergraduate Expenses (1996–97) State resident tuition: $1783. Nonresident tuition: $7028. Mandatory fees: $92. College room only: $2400 (minimum).

Applications Of all full-time undergraduates enrolled in fall 1996, 91% of those who applied for aid were judged to have need according to Federal Methodology, of whom 94% were aided. *Financial aid deadline (priority):* 3/15. *Financial aid forms:* FAFSA required. *Admission application deadline:* rolling.

Summary of Aid to Needy Students *From gift & self-help combined:* Average need met: 54%. Average amount awarded: $4539 (50% gift aid, 50% self-help). *Gift aid:* Total: $11,352,545 (24% from college's own funds, 29% from other college-administered sources, 47% from external sources). 310 Federal Work-Study jobs (averaging $1880).

Need-Based Scholarships & Grants Pell, FSEOG, state, private, college/university.

Loans Perkins, PLUS, Stafford, Unsubsidized Stafford, private, college/university short-term loans ($525 average).

Non-Need Awards In 1996, a total of 535 non-need awards were made. *Academic Interests/Achievement Awards:* 164 ($170,560 total): general academic, communication. *Creative Arts/Performance Awards:* 99 ($59,286 total): dance, music, performing arts, theater/drama. *Special*

Characteristics Awards: 117 ($140,400 total): members of minorities. *Athletic:* Total: 155 ($417,270); Men: 85 ($183,300); Women: 70 ($233,970).

Other Money-Saving Options Accelerated degree, co-op program, Army ROTC, Air Force ROTC, off-campus living. *Payment Plan:* tuition prepayment. *Waivers:* full or partial for employees or children of employees and senior citizens.

Contact Mr. Paul Majoros, Associate Director, Florida International University, University Park PC 125, Miami, FL 33199, 305-348-2489, fax: 305-348-2346.

FLORIDA MEMORIAL COLLEGE
Miami, Florida

About the Institution Independent/religious, coed. Degrees awarded: B. Offers 22 undergraduate majors. Total enrollment: 1,457 (75% state residents). Freshmen: 377.

Undergraduate Expenses (1996–97) Comprehensive fee of $9086 includes tuition ($4920), mandatory fees ($930), and college room and board ($3236). College room only: $1726.

Applications Of all full-time undergraduates enrolled in fall 1996, 100% of those who applied for aid were judged to have need according to Federal Methodology, of whom 100% were aided. *Financial aid deadline (priority):* 4/14. *Financial aid forms:* FAFSA required. *Admission application deadline:* 7/1.

Summary of Aid to Needy Students *From gift & self-help combined:* Average need met: 95%. Average amount awarded: $6370. Federal Work-Study jobs; part-time jobs.

Need-Based Scholarships & Grants Pell, FSEOG, state, college/university, United Negro College Fund Scholarships.

Loans PLUS, Stafford, Unsubsidized Stafford.

Non-Need Awards Not offered.

Other Money-Saving Options Co-op program, Army ROTC, cooperative Air Force ROTC, off-campus living.

Contact Office of Financial Aid, Florida Memorial College, Miami, FL 33054, 305-626-3742, fax: 305-626-3106.

FLORIDA METROPOLITAN UNIVERSITY– FORT LAUDERDALE COLLEGE
Fort Lauderdale, Florida

About the Institution Proprietary, coed. Degrees awarded: A, B. Offers 9 undergraduate majors.

Applications 57% of all full-time undergraduates enrolled in fall 1996 applied for aid; of these, 96% were judged to have need according to Federal Methodology, of whom 100% were aided. *Financial aid deadline:* continuous. *Financial aid forms:* FAFSA, institutional form required; state form acceptable. *Admission application deadline:* rolling.

Summary of Aid to Needy Students *From gift & self-help combined:* Average need met: 98%. Average amount awarded: $4500 (40% gift aid, 60% self-help). *Gift aid:* Total: $369,766 (69% from college-administered sources, 31% from external sources). Federal Work-Study jobs; part-time jobs.

Need-Based Scholarships & Grants Pell, FSEOG, state.

Loans PLUS, Stafford, Unsubsidized Stafford, private.

Non-Need Awards Not offered.

Other Money-Saving Options Accelerated degree. *Payment Plan:* installment.

Contact Ms. Rose Carnahan, Senior Finance Officer, Florida Metropolitan University–Fort Lauderdale College, 1040 Bayview Drive, Fort Lauderdale, FL 33304-2522, 954-568-1600, fax: 954-568-2008.

FLORIDA METROPOLITAN UNIVERSITY– ORLANDO COLLEGE, MELBOURNE
Melbourne, Florida

About the Institution Proprietary, coed. Degrees awarded: A, B. Offers 7 undergraduate majors. Total enrollment: 270. Undergraduates: 250. Freshmen: 47.

Applications *Financial aid deadline (priority):* 8/15. *Financial aid forms:* FAFSA, CSS Financial Aid PROFILE, institutional form required; state form acceptable. *Admission application deadline:* rolling.

Summary of Aid to Needy Students 7 Federal Work-Study jobs (averaging $4000).

Need-Based Scholarships & Grants Pell, FSEOG, state, private, college/university.

Loans PLUS, Stafford, Unsubsidized Stafford, private, college/university short-term loans ($1700 average), college/university long-term loans ($3700 average).

Non-Need Awards available.

Other Money-Saving Options *Payment Plans:* guaranteed tuition, tuition prepayment, installment, deferred payment. *Waivers:* full or partial for employees or children of employees.

Contact Office of Financial Aid, Florida Metropolitan University–Orlando College, Melbourne, Melbourne, FL 32935-6657, 407-253-2929.

FLORIDA METROPOLITAN UNIVERSITY– ORLANDO COLLEGE, NORTH
Orlando, Florida

About the Institution Proprietary, coed. Degrees awarded: A, B, M. Offers 11 undergraduate majors. Total enrollment: 1,375. Undergraduates: 1,100 (85% state residents). Freshmen: 633.

Undergraduate Expenses (1997–98) Tuition: $4140 (minimum).

Applications 80% of all full-time undergraduates enrolled in fall 1996 applied for aid; of these, 76% were judged to have need according to Federal Methodology, of whom 100% were aided. *Financial aid deadline:* continuous. *Financial aid forms:* FAFSA required. *Admission application deadline:* rolling.

Summary of Aid to Needy Students *From gift & self-help combined:* Average need met: 90%. Average amount awarded: $4500. 40 Federal Work-Study jobs.

Need-Based Scholarships & Grants Pell, FSEOG.

Loans Perkins, PLUS, Stafford, Unsubsidized Stafford, private.

Non-Need Awards *Special Characteristics Awards:* children of faculty/staff.

Other Money-Saving Options Accelerated degree. *Waivers:* full or partial for employees or children of employees.

Contact Ms. Linda Kaisrlik, Director of Financial Aid, Florida Metropolitan University–Orlando College, North, Orlando, FL 32810-5674, 407-628-5870.

FLORIDA METROPOLITAN UNIVERSITY– TAMPA COLLEGE, PINELLAS
Clearwater, Florida

About the Institution Proprietary, coed. Degrees awarded: A, B, M. Offers 7 undergraduate majors. Total enrollment: 724. Undergraduates: 609 (92% state residents). Freshmen: 312.

Undergraduate Expenses (1996–97) Tuition: $4464.

Applications Of all full-time undergraduates enrolled in fall 1996, 86% of those who applied for aid were judged to have need according to

Federal Methodology, of whom 100% were aided. *Financial aid deadline:* continuous. *Financial aid forms:* FAFSA required. *Admission application deadline:* rolling.

Summary of Aid to Needy Students Federal Work-Study jobs.

Need-Based Scholarships & Grants Pell, FSEOG, state, private.

Loans Stafford, Unsubsidized Stafford, private.

Non-Need Awards *Academic Interests/Achievement Awards:* general academic.

Other Money-Saving Options Accelerated degree, co-op program. *Payment Plans:* guaranteed tuition, installment. *Waivers:* full or partial for employees or children of employees.

Contact Ms. Marcia Hutchinson, Director of Financial Aid, Florida Metropolitan University–Tampa College, Pinellas, 2471 McMullen Booth Road, Suite 200, Clearwater, FL 34619, 813-725-2688.

FLORIDA METROPOLITAN UNIVERSITY– TAMPA COLLEGE, LAKELAND
Lakeland, Florida

About the Institution Proprietary, coed. Degrees awarded: A, B, M. Offers 9 undergraduate majors. Total enrollment: 500. Undergraduates: 450 (98% state residents). Freshmen: 350.

Undergraduate Expenses (1997–98) Tuition: $5220.

Applications 94% of all full-time undergraduates enrolled in fall 1996 applied for aid; of these, 79% were judged to have need according to Federal Methodology, of whom 100% were aided. *Financial aid deadline (priority):* 10/1. *Financial aid forms:* FAFSA, institutional form required.

Summary of Aid to Needy Students *From gift & self-help combined:* Average need met: 100%. Average amount awarded: $4500. 3 Federal Work-Study jobs (averaging $3000).

Need-Based Scholarships & Grants Pell, FSEOG, state.

Loans PLUS, Stafford, Unsubsidized Stafford, college/university long-term loans.

Non-Need Awards In 1996, a total of 2 non-need awards were made. *Academic Interests/Achievement Awards:* 2 ($1200 total): business.

Other Money-Saving Options *Payment Plan:* installment. *Waivers:* full or partial for employees or children of employees.

Contact Ms. Linda Wagner, Director of Student Finance, Florida Metropolitan University–Tampa College, Lakeland, 1200 U.S. Highway 98 South, Suite 45, Lakeland, FL 33801-5907, 941-686-1444.

FLORIDA METROPOLITAN UNIVERSITY– TAMPA COLLEGE
Tampa, Florida

About the Institution Proprietary, coed. Degrees awarded: A, B, M. Offers 11 undergraduate majors. Total enrollment: 1,250. Undergraduates: 1,000 (95% state residents). Freshmen: 150.

Undergraduate Expenses (1996–97) Tuition: $5220 (minimum).

Applications *Financial aid deadline:* continuous. *Financial aid forms:* FAFSA, institutional form required. CSS Financial Aid PROFILE required for some. *Admission application deadline:* rolling.

Summary of Aid to Needy Students Federal Work-Study jobs; part-time jobs.

Need-Based Scholarships & Grants Pell, FSEOG.

Loans PLUS, Stafford, Unsubsidized Stafford, college/university.

Non-Need Awards *Academic Interests/Achievement Awards:* general academic.

Other Money-Saving Options Accelerated degree, co-op program. *Payment Plans:* guaranteed tuition, installment. *Waivers:* full or partial for employees or children of employees.

Contact Office of Financial Aid, Florida Metropolitan University–Tampa College, 3319 West Hillsborough Avenue, Tampa, FL 33614-5899, 813-879-6000.

FLORIDA METROPOLITAN UNIVERSITY– TAMPA COLLEGE, BRANDON
Tampa, Florida

About the Institution Proprietary. Degrees awarded: A, B, M. Offers 11 undergraduate majors. Total enrollment: 850. Undergraduates: 780. Freshmen: 130.

Applications 95% of all full-time undergraduates enrolled in fall 1996 applied for aid; of these, 94% were judged to have need according to Federal Methodology, of whom 100% were aided. *Financial aid deadline:* continuous. *Financial aid forms:* FAFSA required.

Summary of Aid to Needy Students *From gift & self-help combined:* Average need met: 100%. Average amount awarded: $5900. Federal Work-Study jobs.

Need-Based Scholarships & Grants Pell, FSEOG, state.

Loans PLUS, Stafford, Unsubsidized Stafford, private.

Non-Need Awards *Academic Interests/Achievement Awards:* general academic.

Other Money-Saving Options *Payment Plan:* installment. *Waivers:* full or partial for employees or children of employees.

Contact Ms. Robin Hall, Director of Financial Aid, Florida Metropolitan University–Tampa College, Brandon, 3924 Coconut Palm Drive, Tampa, FL 33619, 813-621-0041.

FLORIDA SOUTHERN COLLEGE
Lakeland, Florida

About the Institution Independent/religious, coed. Degrees awarded: B, M. Offers 61 undergraduate majors. Total enrollment: 1,964. Undergraduates: 1,908 (73% state residents). Freshmen: 459.

Undergraduate Expenses (1997–98) Comprehensive fee of $16,034 includes tuition ($9818), mandatory fees ($786), and college room and board ($5430). College room only: $2400.

Applications 58% of all full-time undergraduates enrolled in fall 1996 applied for aid; of these, 87% were judged to have need according to Federal Methodology, of whom 100% were aided. *Financial aid deadline:* Applications processed continuously. *Financial aid forms:* FAFSA, institutional form required. *Admission application deadline:* 8/1.

Summary of Aid to Needy Students *From gift & self-help combined:* Average need met: 90%. Average amount awarded: $12,425 (60% gift aid, 40% self-help). *Gift aid:* Total: $6,050,000 (63% from college's own funds, 2% from other college-administered sources, 35% from external sources). 350 Federal Work-Study jobs (averaging $1000); 250 part-time jobs.

Need-Based Scholarships & Grants Pell, FSEOG, state, private, college/university.

Loans Perkins, PLUS, Stafford, Unsubsidized Stafford, state, college/university long-term loans ($1000 average).

Non-Need Awards In 1996, a total of 1,398 non-need awards were made. *Academic Interests/Achievement Awards:* 695 ($2,850,000 total): general academic, agriculture, biological sciences, business, communication, religion/biblical studies, social sciences. *Creative Arts/Performance Awards:* 85 ($275,000 total): art/fine arts, music, theater/drama. *Special Achievements/Activities Awards:* 10 ($39,500 total): general special achievements/activities. *Special Characteristics Awards:* 475 ($800,000 total): general special characteristics, children and siblings of alumni, children of faculty/staff, local/state students, out-of-state students, relatives of clergy, ROTC participants, siblings of current students. *Athletic:* Total: 133 ($805,000); Men: 69 ($453,000); Women: 64 ($352,000).

Other Money-Saving Options Army ROTC, off-campus living (after junior year). *Waivers:* full or partial for employees or children of employees.

Contact Ms. Callie Haynes, Financial Aid Counselor, Florida Southern College, 111 Lake Hollingsworth Drive, Lakeland, FL 33801-5698, 941-680-4140, fax: 941-680-4567.

FLORIDA STATE UNIVERSITY
Tallahassee, Florida

About the Institution State-supported, coed. Degrees awarded: A, B, M, D, P. Offers 145 undergraduate majors. Total enrollment: 30,264. Undergraduates: 22,408 (89% state residents). Freshmen: 3,228.

Undergraduate Expenses (1997–98) State resident tuition: $1988. Nonresident tuition: $7904. College room and board: $4570. College room only: $2540.

Applications 64% of all full-time undergraduates enrolled in fall 1996 applied for aid; of these, 88% were judged to have need according to Federal Methodology, of whom 85% were aided. *Financial aid deadline (priority):* 3/1. *Financial aid forms:* FAFSA, institutional form required. *Admission application deadline:* 3/3.

Summary of Aid to Needy Students *From gift & self-help combined:* Average need met: 100%. Average amount awarded: $8567 (29% gift aid, 71% self-help). *Gift aid:* Total: $24,166,515 (16% from college's own funds, 16% from other college-administered sources, 68% from external sources). 383 Federal Work-Study jobs (averaging $1848); 2,558 part-time jobs.

Need-Based Scholarships & Grants Pell, FSEOG, state, private, college/university.

Loans Perkins, PLUS, Stafford, Unsubsidized Stafford, college/university short-term loans ($1000 average).

Non-Need Awards In 1996, a total of 1,483 non-need awards were made. *Academic Interests/Achievement Awards:* 1,015 ($1,873,320 total): general academic. *Creative Arts/Performance Awards:* 165 ($114,800 total): music. *Special Characteristics Awards:* 3 ($5107 total): local/state students. *Athletic:* Total: 300 ($1,199,340); Men: 180 ($733,454); Women: 120 ($465,886).

Other Money-Saving Options Accelerated degree, co-op program, Army ROTC, Air Force ROTC, cooperative Naval ROTC, off-campus living. *Payment Plans:* tuition prepayment, installment. *Waivers:* full or partial for employees or children of employees and senior citizens.

Contact Office of Financial Aid, Florida State University, 4441 University Center, Tallahassee, FL 32306-1023, 904-644-2525.

FONTBONNE COLLEGE
St. Louis, Missouri

About the Institution Independent/religious, coed. Degrees awarded: B, M. Offers 48 undergraduate majors. Total enrollment: 1,882. Undergraduates: 1,294 (86% state residents). Freshmen: 149.

Undergraduate Expenses (1997–98) Comprehensive fee of $14,550 includes tuition ($10,000), mandatory fees ($150), and college room and board ($4400).

Applications 80% of all full-time undergraduates enrolled in fall 1996 applied for aid; of these, 74% were judged to have need according to Federal Methodology, of whom 100% were aided. *Financial aid deadline (priority):* 4/30. *Financial aid forms:* FAFSA, institutional form, financial aid transcript (for transfers) required; CSS Financial Aid PROFILE acceptable. *Admission application deadline:* 8/1.

Summary of Aid to Needy Students *From gift & self-help combined:* Average need met: 100%. *Gift aid:* Total: $776,660 (57% from college's own funds, 4% from other college-administered sources, 39% from external sources). 150 Federal Work-Study jobs (averaging $1000); 15 part-time jobs.

Need-Based Scholarships & Grants Pell, FSEOG, state, private, college/university.

Loans Perkins, PLUS, Stafford, Unsubsidized Stafford, private, college/university long-term loans ($2600 average).

Non-Need Awards *Academic Interests/Achievement Awards:* general academic, computer science, English. *Creative Arts/Performance Awards:* art/fine arts, creative writing, theater/drama. *Special Achievements/Activities Awards:* general special achievements/activities, leadership. *Special Characteristics Awards:* religious affiliation, siblings of current students.

Other Money-Saving Options Co-op program, cooperative Army ROTC, off-campus living. *Payment Plans:* installment, deferred payment. *Waivers:* full or partial for minority students, employees or children of employees, senior citizens.

Contact Ms. Crystal Girtman, Assistant Director, Financial Aid, Fontbonne College, 6800 Wydown Boulevard, St. Louis, MO 63105-3098, 314-889-1414, fax: 314-889-1450.

FORDHAM UNIVERSITY
New York, New York

About the Institution Independent/religious, coed. Degrees awarded: B, M, D, P. Offers 84 undergraduate majors. Total enrollment: 13,723. Undergraduates: 5,822 (60% state residents). Freshmen: 1,211.

Undergraduate Expenses (1996–97) Comprehensive fee of $23,125 includes tuition ($15,800), mandatory fees ($200), and college room and board ($7125 minimum).

Applications 76% of all full-time undergraduates enrolled in fall 1996 applied for aid; of these, 93% were judged to have need according to Federal Methodology, of whom 99% were aided. *Financial aid deadline (priority):* 2/1. *Financial aid forms:* FAFSA, institutional form required. CSS Financial Aid PROFILE, state form required for some. *Regular admission application deadline:* 2/1. Early decision deadline: 11/1.

Summary of Aid to Needy Students *From gift & self-help combined:* Average need met: 79%. Average amount awarded: $14,153 (73% gift aid, 27% self-help). *Gift aid:* Total: $32,008,203 (77% from college's own funds, 3% from other college-administered sources, 20% from external sources). 191 Federal Work-Study jobs (averaging $1700); 150 part-time jobs.

Need-Based Scholarships & Grants Pell, FSEOG, state, private, college/university.

Loans Perkins, PLUS, Stafford, Unsubsidized Stafford, private.

Non-Need Awards In 1996, a total of 699 non-need awards were made. *Academic Interests/Achievement Awards:* 402 ($3,961,506 total): general academic, communication. *Creative Arts/Performance Awards:* 39 ($65,500 total): music. *Special Characteristics Awards:* 64 ($702,291 total): children and siblings of alumni, children of faculty/staff, children of union members/company employees, handicapped students, ROTC participants. *Athletic:* Total: 194 ($2,258,458); Men: 132 ($1,657,964); Women: 62 ($600,494).

Other Money-Saving Options Accelerated degree, Army ROTC, cooperative Naval ROTC, cooperative Air Force ROTC, off-campus living. *Payment Plans:* tuition prepayment, installment. *Waivers:* full or partial for employees or children of employees.

Contact Ms. Mary Beth Griffin, Senior Assistant Director of Financial Aid, Fordham University, 441 East Fordham Road, New York, NY 10458, 718-817-3800, fax: 718-817-3817.

FORT HAYS STATE UNIVERSITY
Hays, Kansas

About the Institution State-supported, coed. Degrees awarded: A, B, M. Offers 72 undergraduate majors. Total enrollment: 5,540. Undergraduates: 4,208 (92% state residents). Freshmen: 811.

Undergraduate Expenses (1996–97) State resident tuition: $1929. Nonresident tuition: $6029. College room and board: $3398. College room only: $1766.

Applications Of all full-time undergraduates enrolled in fall 1996, 75% of those who applied for aid were judged to have need according to Federal Methodology, of whom 100% were aided. *Financial aid deadline (priority):* 3/15. *Financial aid forms:* FAFSA, institutional form required; CSS Financial Aid PROFILE, state form acceptable. *Admission application deadline:* rolling.

Summary of Aid to Needy Students *From gift & self-help combined:* Average need met: 81%. Average amount awarded: $3157 (36% gift aid, 64% self-help). *Gift aid:* Total: $2,470,946 (47% from college-administered sources, 53% from external sources). 363 Federal Work-Study jobs (averaging $1400); 906 part-time jobs.

Need-Based Scholarships & Grants Pell, FSEOG, state, private, college/university.

Loans Perkins, PLUS, Stafford, Unsubsidized Stafford, college/university short-term loans ($400 average).

Non-Need Awards *Academic Interests/Achievement Awards:* 1,319 ($936,230 total): general academic, agriculture, biological sciences, business, communication, computer science, education, engineering/technologies, English, foreign languages, health fields, humanities, international studies, library science, mathematics, physical sciences, premedicine, social sciences. *Special Characteristics Awards:* 100 ($10,000 total): adult students. *Athletic:* Total: ($251,904).

Other Money-Saving Options Accelerated degree, off-campus living (after freshman year).

Contact Mr. Craig Karlin, Director of Financial Aid, Fort Hays State University, 600 Park Street, Hays, KS 67601-4099, 913-628-4408, fax: 913-628-4014.

FORT LEWIS COLLEGE
Durango, Colorado

About the Institution State-supported, coed. Degrees awarded: A, B. Offers 56 undergraduate majors. Total enrollment: 4,600 (70% state residents). Freshmen: 1,150.

Undergraduate Expenses (1996–97) State resident tuition: $1594. Nonresident tuition: $7424. Mandatory fees: $456. College room and board: $3740 (minimum). College room only: $1890 (minimum).

Applications Of all full-time undergraduates enrolled in fall 1996, 76% of those who applied for aid were judged to have need according to Federal Methodology, of whom 86% were aided. *Financial aid deadline (priority):* 2/15. *Financial aid forms:* FAFSA required. *Admission application deadline:* 7/15.

Summary of Aid to Needy Students *From gift & self-help combined:* Average need met: 89%. Average amount awarded: $4057 (29% gift aid, 71% self-help). *Gift aid:* Total: $2,257,371 (9% from college's own funds, 18% from other college-administered sources, 73% from external sources). 225 Federal Work-Study jobs (averaging $1600); 375 part-time jobs.

Need-Based Scholarships & Grants Pell, FSEOG, state, private, college/university.

Loans Perkins, PLUS, Stafford, Unsubsidized Stafford, private, college/university short-term loans ($200 average).

Non-Need Awards In 1996, a total of 632 non-need awards were made. *Academic Interests/Achievement Awards:* 65 ($46,000 total): general academic, biological sciences, business, communication, computer science, education, engineering/technologies, English, foreign languages, humanities, mathematics, physical sciences, social sciences. *Creative Arts/Performance Awards:* 5 ($9000 total): art/fine arts, music, performing arts, theater/drama. *Special Achievements/Activities Awards:* 5 ($9000 total): general special achievements/activities. *Special Characteristics Awards:* 445 ($795,400 total): ethnic background, first-generation college students, local/state students, members of minorities, out-of-state students. *Athletic:* Total: 112 ($268,213); Men: 68 ($169,247); Women: 44 ($98,966).

Other Money-Saving Options Accelerated degree, co-op program, off-campus living (after freshman year). *Waivers:* full or partial for employees or children of employees.

Contact Mr. Rick Willis, Director of Financial Aid, Fort Lewis College, 1000 Rim Drive, Durango, CO 81301-3999, 970-247-7142, fax: 970-247-7108.

FORT VALLEY STATE UNIVERSITY
Fort Valley, Georgia

About the Institution State-supported, coed. Degrees awarded: A, B, M, P. Offers 34 undergraduate majors. Total enrollment: 3,024. Undergraduates: 2,554 (94% state residents). Freshmen: 584.

Undergraduate Expenses (1996–97) State resident tuition: $2040. Nonresident tuition: $5919. College room and board: $2925. College room only: $1470.

Applications *Financial aid deadline (priority):* 2/15. *Financial aid forms:* FAFSA, CSS Financial Aid PROFILE, institutional form required. *Admission application deadline:* 9/1.

Summary of Aid to Needy Students *From gift & self-help combined:* Average need met: 83%. Average amount awarded: $7181 (29% gift aid, 71% self-help). *Gift aid:* Total: $5,542,201 (9% from college's own funds, 19% from other college-administered sources, 72% from external sources). 740 Federal Work-Study jobs (averaging $1425); 412 part-time jobs.

Need-Based Scholarships & Grants Pell, FSEOG, state, private, college/university.

Loans Perkins, PLUS, Stafford, Unsubsidized Stafford, state, private, college/university short-term loans ($100 average).

Non-Need Awards In 1996, a total of 411 non-need awards were made. *Academic Interests/Achievement Awards:* 103 ($79,300 total): general academic, agriculture, business, home economics, military science, premedicine, social sciences. *Creative Arts/Performance Awards:* 64 ($23,946 total): music. *Special Characteristics Awards:* 87 ($252,382 total): international students, members of minorities, ROTC participants. *Athletic:* Total: 157 ($310,000); Men: 115 ($245,000); Women: 42 ($65,000).

Other Money-Saving Options Co-op program, Army ROTC.

Contact Ms. Jeanette K. Huff, Financial Aid Director, Fort Valley State University, PO Box 4129 Office of Financial Aid, Fort Valley, GA 31030-3298, 912-825-6351, fax: 912-825-6976.

FRAMINGHAM STATE COLLEGE
Framingham, Massachusetts

About the Institution State-supported, coed. Degrees awarded: B, M. Offers 77 undergraduate majors. Total enrollment: 5,155. Undergraduates: 4,296 (90% state residents). Freshmen: 679.

Undergraduate Expenses (1997–98) State resident tuition: $1270. Nonresident tuition: $5950. Mandatory fees: $1880. College room and board: $3833. College room only: $2399.

Applications Of all full-time undergraduates enrolled in fall 1996, 79% of those who applied for aid were judged to have need according to

Federal Methodology, of whom 91% were aided. *Financial aid deadline (priority):* 3/1. *Financial aid forms:* FAFSA, state form required. *Admission application deadline:* 3/15.

Summary of Aid to Needy Students *From gift & self-help combined:* Average need met: 92%. Average amount awarded: $4801 (38% gift aid, 62% self-help). *Gift aid:* Total: $2,355,244 (5% from college's own funds, 32% from other college-administered sources, 63% from external sources). 120 Federal Work-Study jobs (averaging $1000); 120 part-time jobs.

Need-Based Scholarships & Grants Pell, FSEOG, state, private, college/university.

Loans Perkins, PLUS, Stafford, Unsubsidized Stafford, state, college/university short-term loans ($300 average).

Non-Need Awards In 1996, a total of 107 non-need awards were made. *Academic Interests/Achievement Awards:* 70 ($50,612 total): general academic, biological sciences, education, home economics, physical sciences. *Special Characteristics Awards:* 37 ($44,340 total): children of faculty/staff, children of public servants, children of union members/company employees, local/state students, veterans.

Other Money-Saving Options Cooperative Army ROTC, off-campus living. *Payment Plan:* installment. *Waivers:* full or partial for employees or children of employees and senior citizens.

Contact Mr. Richard Dutilly, Director of Financial Aid, Framingham State College, 100 State Street, Framingham, MA 01701-9101, 508-626-4534.

FRANCISCAN UNIVERSITY OF STEUBENVILLE
Steubenville, Ohio

About the Institution Independent/religious, coed. Degrees awarded: A, B, M. Offers 42 undergraduate majors. Total enrollment: 1,927. Undergraduates: 1,521. Freshmen: 240.

Undergraduate Expenses (1997–98) Comprehensive fee of $16,100 includes tuition ($11,090), mandatory fees ($280), and college room and board ($4730).

Applications 82% of all full-time undergraduates enrolled in fall 1996 applied for aid; of these, 92% were judged to have need according to Federal Methodology. *Financial aid deadline (priority):* 3/15. *Financial aid forms:* FAFSA, institutional form required. State form required for some. *Admission application deadline:* 6/30.

Summary of Aid to Needy Students *From gift & self-help combined:* Average need met: 79%. Average amount awarded: $8468 (50% gift aid, 50% self-help). *Gift aid:* Total: $4,336,495 (67% from college's own funds, 15% from other college-administered sources, 18% from external sources). 273 Federal Work-Study jobs (averaging $1200); 647 part-time jobs.

Need-Based Scholarships & Grants Pell, FSEOG, state, private, college/university.

Loans Perkins, PLUS, Stafford, Unsubsidized Stafford, private, college/university long-term loans ($1000 average).

Non-Need Awards In 1996, a total of 551 non-need awards were made. *Academic Interests/Achievement Awards:* 446 ($844,220 total): general academic. *Special Characteristics Awards:* 105 ($459,656 total): children of faculty/staff, international students, local/state students, religious affiliation.

Other Money-Saving Options Accelerated degree, co-op program. *Payment Plan:* installment. *Waivers:* full or partial for employees or children of employees.

Contact Enrollment Services Office, Franciscan University of Steubenville, University Boulevard, Steubenville, OH 43952-6701, 614-283-6211, fax: 614-283-6472.

FRANCIS MARION UNIVERSITY
Florence, South Carolina

About the Institution State-supported, coed. Degrees awarded: B, M. Offers 35 undergraduate majors. Total enrollment: 3,722. Undergraduates: 3,294 (94% state residents). Freshmen: 668.

Undergraduate Expenses (1996–97) State resident tuition: $3010. Nonresident tuition: $6020. Mandatory fees: $90 (minimum). College room and board: $3138.

Applications *Financial aid deadline (priority):* 3/1. *Financial aid forms:* FAFSA, institutional form required. *Admission application deadline:* rolling.

Summary of Aid to Needy Students 164 Federal Work-Study jobs (averaging $800); 505 part-time jobs.

Need-Based Scholarships & Grants Pell, FSEOG, state, private, college/university.

Loans Perkins, PLUS, Stafford, Unsubsidized Stafford, state, private, college/university short-term loans ($100 average).

Non-Need Awards *Academic Interests/Achievement Awards:* general academic, biological sciences, business, education, English, health fields, humanities, mathematics, premedicine, social sciences. *Creative Arts/Performance Awards:* art/fine arts, music, theater/drama. *Special Achievements/Activities Awards:* cheerleading/drum major. *Special Characteristics Awards:* adult students, children and siblings of alumni, children of faculty/staff, handicapped students, international students, out-of-state students, spouses of deceased or disabled public servants, veterans, veterans' children. *Athletic:* available.

Other Money-Saving Options Accelerated degree, co-op program, Army ROTC, off-campus living. *Waivers:* full or partial for employees or children of employees and senior citizens.

Contact Office of Financial Aid, Francis Marion University, PO Box 100547, Florence, SC 29501-0546, 803-661-1362.

FRANKLIN AND MARSHALL COLLEGE
Lancaster, Pennsylvania

About the Institution Independent, coed. Degrees awarded: B. Offers 29 undergraduate majors. Total enrollment: 1,822 (34% state residents). Freshmen: 525.

Undergraduate Expenses (1996–97) Comprehensive fee: $26,400.

Applications Of all full-time undergraduates enrolled in fall 1996, 83% of those who applied for aid were judged to have need according to Federal Methodology, of whom 100% were aided. *Financial aid deadline (priority):* 2/1. *Financial aid forms:* FAFSA, CSS Financial Aid PROFILE, state form, institutional form required. *Regular admission application deadline:* 2/1. Early decision deadline: 1/15.

Summary of Aid to Needy Students *From gift & self-help combined:* Average need met: 98%. Average amount awarded: $17,100 (73% gift aid, 27% self-help). *Gift aid:* Total: $11,555,661 (89% from college's own funds, 3% from other college-administered sources, 8% from external sources). 450 Federal Work-Study jobs (averaging $830); 380 part-time jobs.

Need-Based Scholarships & Grants Pell, FSEOG, state, private, college/university.

Loans Perkins, PLUS, Stafford, Unsubsidized Stafford.

Non-Need Awards In 1996, a total of 206 non-need awards were made. *Academic Interests/Achievement Awards:* 191 ($1,175,700 total): general academic. *Special Characteristics Awards:* 15 ($49,500 total): local/state students.

Other Money-Saving Options Accelerated degree, cooperative Army ROTC, off-campus living (after sophomore year). *Payment Plan:* installment. *Waivers:* full or partial for employees or children of employees.

Contact Ms. Suzanne K. Schlager, Director of Student Aid, Franklin and Marshall College, Lancaster, PA 17604-3003, 717-291-3991, fax: 717-399-4462.

FRANKLIN COLLEGE OF INDIANA
Franklin, Indiana

About the Institution Independent/religious, coed. Degrees awarded: B. Offers 41 undergraduate majors. Total enrollment: 874 (90% state residents). Freshmen: 261.

Undergraduate Expenses (1997–98 estimated) Comprehensive fee of $16,440 includes tuition ($12,210), mandatory fees ($150), and college room and board ($4080).

Applications 96% of all full-time undergraduates enrolled in fall 1996 applied for aid; of these, 96% were judged to have need according to Federal Methodology, of whom 100% were aided. *Financial aid deadline (priority):* 3/1. *Financial aid forms:* FAFSA required; CSS Financial Aid PROFILE acceptable. Institutional form required for some. *Admission application deadline:* 8/1.

Summary of Aid to Needy Students *From gift & self-help combined:* Average need met: 98%. Average amount awarded: $12,103 (61% gift aid, 39% self-help). *Gift aid:* Total: $5,584,486 (68% from college's own funds, 2% from other college-administered sources, 30% from external sources). 106 Federal Work-Study jobs (averaging $735); 172 part-time jobs.

Need-Based Scholarships & Grants Pell, FSEOG, state, private, college/university.

Loans Perkins, PLUS, Stafford, Unsubsidized Stafford, private.

Non-Need Awards In 1996, a total of 471 non-need awards were made. *Academic Interests/Achievement Awards:* 353 ($2,082,965 total): general academic, foreign languages, mathematics. *Creative Arts/Performance Awards:* 13 ($6250 total): music, performing arts, theater/drama. *Special Achievements/Activities Awards:* 4 ($12,000 total): leadership. *Special Characteristics Awards:* 101 ($234,103 total): children and siblings of alumni, children of educators, children of faculty/staff, local/state students, religious affiliation.

Other Money-Saving Options Accelerated degree, cooperative Army ROTC, off-campus living (after junior year). *Payment Plan:* installment. *Waivers:* full or partial for employees or children of employees and senior citizens.

Contact Dr. Charles R. Carothers, Director of Financial Aid, Franklin College of Indiana, 501 East Monroe Street, Franklin, IN 46131-2598, 317-738-8075, fax: 317-738-8274.

FRANKLIN PIERCE COLLEGE
Rindge, New Hampshire

About the Institution Independent, coed. Degrees awarded: A, B. Offers 51 undergraduate majors. Total enrollment: 1,327 (13% state residents). Freshmen: 470.

Undergraduate Expenses (1996–97) Comprehensive fee of $19,940 includes tuition ($14,850), mandatory fees ($160), and college room and board ($4930). College room only: $2680.

Applications Of all full-time undergraduates enrolled in fall 1996, 97% of those who applied for aid were judged to have need according to Federal Methodology, of whom 100% were aided. *Financial aid deadline:* continuous. *Financial aid forms:* FAFSA, state form required. *Admission application deadline:* rolling.

Summary of Aid to Needy Students *From gift & self-help combined:* Average need met: 80%. Average amount awarded: $12,860 (59% gift aid, 41% self-help). *Gift aid:* Total: $8,829,448 (88% from college's own funds, 4% from other college-administered sources, 8% from external sources). 100 Federal Work-Study jobs (averaging $1500); 380 part-time jobs.

Need-Based Scholarships & Grants Pell, FSEOG, state, private, college/university.

Loans Perkins, PLUS, Stafford, Unsubsidized Stafford, private.

Non-Need Awards In 1996, a total of 580 non-need awards were made. *Academic Interests/Achievement Awards:* 480 ($2,616,334 total): general academic. *Special Characteristics Awards:* 55 ($520,311 total): adult students, children of faculty/staff, international students, out-of-state students, siblings of current students. *Athletic:* Total: 45 ($656,000); Men: 23 ($342,000); Women: 22 ($314,000).

Other Money-Saving Options Accelerated degree, cooperative Air Force ROTC. *Payment Plan:* installment. *Waivers:* full or partial for employees or children of employees and senior citizens.

Contact Mr. Bruce Palmer, Director of Financial Aid, Franklin Pierce College, College Road, PO Box 60, Rindge, NH 03461-0060, 603-899-4180, fax: 603-899-4372.

FRANKLIN UNIVERSITY
Columbus, Ohio

About the Institution Independent, coed. Degrees awarded: A, B, M. Offers 10 undergraduate majors. Total enrollment: 4,049. Undergraduates: 3,669. Freshmen: 108.

Undergraduate Expenses (1996–97) Tuition: $4991. Mandatory fees: $75.

Applications 59% of all full-time undergraduates enrolled in fall 1996 applied for aid; of these, 78% were judged to have need according to Federal Methodology, of whom 100% were aided. *Financial aid deadline (priority):* 5/30. *Financial aid forms:* FAFSA, institutional form required. State form required for some. *Admission application deadline:* rolling.

Summary of Aid to Needy Students *Gift aid:* Total: $1,200,000. Federal Work-Study jobs.

Need-Based Scholarships & Grants Pell, FSEOG, state, private, college/university.

Loans Perkins, PLUS, Stafford, Unsubsidized Stafford, private, college/university short-term loans.

Non-Need Awards *Academic Interests/Achievement Awards:* general academic. *Special Achievements/Activities Awards:* leadership. *Special Characteristics Awards:* members of minorities.

Other Money-Saving Options Accelerated degree, cooperative Army ROTC, cooperative Air Force ROTC. *Payment Plans:* installment, deferred payment. *Waivers:* full or partial for employees or children of employees.

Contact Ms. Lisa Harmon, Financial Aid Assistant, Franklin University, 201 South Grant Avenue, Columbus, OH 43215-5399, 614-341-6245, fax: 614-224-8027.

FREED-HARDEMAN UNIVERSITY
Henderson, Tennessee

About the Institution Independent/religious, coed. Degrees awarded: B, M. Offers 55 undergraduate majors. Total enrollment: 1,564. Undergraduates: 1,285 (50% state residents). Freshmen: 328.

Undergraduate Expenses (1997–98) Comprehensive fee of $11,284 includes tuition ($6504), mandatory fees ($1020), and college room and board ($3760).

Applications 79% of all full-time undergraduates enrolled in fall 1996 applied for aid; of these, 92% were judged to have need according to Federal Methodology, of whom 90% were aided. *Financial aid deadline (priority):* 4/1. *Financial aid forms:* FAFSA required. *Admission application deadline:* rolling.

Summary of Aid to Needy Students *From gift & self-help combined:* Average need met: 100%. Average amount awarded: $8500 (61% gift aid, 39% self-help). *Gift aid:* Total: $5,535,097 (67% from college's

own funds, 12% from other college-administered sources, 21% from external sources). 340 Federal Work-Study jobs (averaging $1020); 70 part-time jobs.

Need-Based Scholarships & Grants Pell, FSEOG, state, private, college/university.

Loans Perkins, PLUS, Stafford, Unsubsidized Stafford, Sallie Mae's Signature Education Loan Program.

Non-Need Awards *Academic Interests/Achievement Awards:* 1,004 ($1,272,824 total): general academic. *Creative Arts/Performance Awards:* 40 ($59,272 total): art/fine arts, cinema/film/broadcasting, journalism/publications, music, performing arts, theater/drama. *Special Achievements/Activities Awards:* 18 ($10,000 total): leadership. *Special Characteristics Awards:* adult students, children of faculty/staff. *Athletic:* Total: 100 ($443,584); Men: 51 ($258,878); Women: 49 ($184,706).

Other Money-Saving Options Accelerated degree, co-op program. *Payment Plan:* installment. *Waivers:* full or partial for employees or children of employees and senior citizens.

Contact Ms. Doris Maness, Director of Financial Aid, Freed-Hardeman University, 158 East Main, Henderson, TN 38340-2399, 901-989-6662, fax: 901-989-6775.

FREE WILL BAPTIST BIBLE COLLEGE
Nashville, Tennessee

About the Institution Independent/religious, coed. Degrees awarded: A, B. Offers 15 undergraduate majors. Total enrollment: 340 (19% state residents). Freshmen: 73.

Undergraduate Expenses (1997–98) Comprehensive fee of $8733 includes tuition ($4929), mandatory fees ($206), and college room and board ($3598). College room only: $1480.

Applications 75% of all full-time undergraduates enrolled in fall 1996 applied for aid; of these, 85% were judged to have need according to Federal Methodology, of whom 92% were aided. *Financial aid deadline (priority):* 4/15. *Financial aid forms:* FAFSA, institutional form required; CSS Financial Aid PROFILE acceptable. *Admission application deadline:* rolling.

Summary of Aid to Needy Students *From gift & self-help combined:* Average amount awarded: $3614 (32% gift aid, 68% self-help). *Gift aid:* Total: $202,176 (4% from college's own funds, 8% from other college-administered sources, 88% from external sources). 15 Federal Work-Study jobs (averaging $837); 59 part-time jobs.

Need-Based Scholarships & Grants Pell, FSEOG, private.

Loans College/university short-term loans ($1069 average), college/university long-term loans ($780 average).

Non-Need Awards In 1996, a total of 6 non-need awards were made. *Creative Arts/Performance Awards:* 5 ($2500 total): creative writing, music. *Special Characteristics Awards:* 1 ($5000 total): ROTC participants.

Other Money-Saving Options Cooperative Army ROTC, cooperative Air Force ROTC. *Payment Plans:* installment, deferred payment. *Waivers:* full or partial for employees or children of employees.

Contact Office of Financial Aid, Free Will Baptist Bible College, 3606 West End Avenue, Nashville, TN 37205-2498, 615-383-1340.

FRESNO PACIFIC UNIVERSITY
Fresno, California

About the Institution Independent/religious, coed. Degrees awarded: A, B, M. Offers 39 undergraduate majors. Total enrollment: 1,000. Undergraduates: 715 (95% state residents). Freshmen: 120.

Undergraduate Expenses (1997–98) Comprehensive fee of $16,036 includes tuition ($11,750), mandatory fees ($186), and college room and board ($4100). College room only: $1750.

Applications 96% of all full-time undergraduates enrolled in fall 1996 applied for aid; of these,100% were judged to have need according to Federal Methodology, of whom 100% were aided. *Financial aid deadline (priority):* 3/2. *Financial aid forms:* FAFSA, institutional form required. *Admission application deadline:* rolling.

Summary of Aid to Needy Students *From gift & self-help combined:* Average need met: 72%. Average amount awarded: $10,305 (65% gift aid, 35% self-help). *Gift aid:* Total: $5,350,000. 369 Federal Work-Study jobs (averaging $1296); 250 part-time jobs.

Need-Based Scholarships & Grants Pell, FSEOG, college/university.

Loans Perkins, PLUS, Stafford, Unsubsidized Stafford, college/university short-term loans ($300 average).

Non-Need Awards *Academic Interests/Achievement Awards:* general academic. *Creative Arts/Performance Awards:* music, theater/drama. *Special Achievements/Activities Awards:* community service, leadership. *Special Characteristics Awards:* international students, relatives of clergy, religious affiliation. *Athletic:* Total: ($450,000).

Other Money-Saving Options Off-campus living (after sophomore year). *Payment Plan:* installment. *Waivers:* full or partial for employees or children of employees and senior citizens.

Contact Office of Financial Aid, Fresno Pacific University, 1717 South Chestnut Avenue, Fresno, CA 93702-4709, 209-453-2041, fax: 209-453-2007.

FRIENDS UNIVERSITY
Wichita, Kansas

About the Institution Independent, coed. Degrees awarded: A, B, M. Offers 62 undergraduate majors. Total enrollment: 2,169. Undergraduates: 846 (87% state residents). Freshmen: 212.

Undergraduate Expenses (1997–98) Comprehensive fee of $13,175 includes tuition ($9885), mandatory fees ($90), and college room and board ($3200). College room only: $1400.

Applications 97% of all full-time undergraduates enrolled in fall 1996 applied for aid; of these, 94% were judged to have need according to Federal Methodology, of whom 98% were aided. *Financial aid deadline (priority):* 4/1. *Financial aid forms:* institutional form required; FAFSA, CSS Financial Aid PROFILE acceptable. State form required for some. *Admission application deadline:* rolling.

Summary of Aid to Needy Students *From gift & self-help combined:* Average need met: 76%. *Gift aid:* Total: $3,209,313 (54% from college's own funds, 44% from other college-administered sources, 2% from external sources). 95 Federal Work-Study jobs (averaging $650); 110 part-time jobs.

Need-Based Scholarships & Grants Pell, FSEOG, state.

Loans Perkins, PLUS, Stafford, Unsubsidized Stafford, college/university short-term loans.

Non-Need Awards In 1996, a total of 1,067 non-need awards were made. *Academic Interests/Achievement Awards:* 373 ($118,254 total): general academic, biological sciences, business, education, foreign languages, humanities, mathematics, physical sciences, religion/biblical studies, social sciences. *Creative Arts/Performance Awards:* 277 ($184,355 total): applied art and design, art/fine arts, dance, music, performing arts, theater/drama. *Special Achievements/Activities Awards:* 110 ($54,250 total): leadership. *Special Characteristics Awards:* 45 ($30,800 total): children and siblings of alumni, relatives of clergy, religious affiliation. *Athletic:* Total: 262; Men: 191; Women: 71.

Other Money-Saving Options Accelerated degree, co-op program, off-campus living. *Payment Plan:* installment. *Waivers:* full or partial for employees or children of employees.

Contact Office of Financial Aid, Friends University, 2100 University, Wichita, KS 67213, 316-295-5000.

FROSTBURG STATE UNIVERSITY
Frostburg, Maryland

About the Institution State-supported, coed. Degrees awarded: B, M. Offers 48 undergraduate majors. Total enrollment: 5,418. Undergraduates: 4,543 (87% state residents). Freshmen: 992.

Undergraduate Expenses (1997–98) State resident tuition: $3544. Nonresident tuition: $7530. College room and board: $4786. College room only: $2489.

Applications 59% of all full-time undergraduates enrolled in fall 1996 applied for aid; of these, 72% were judged to have need according to Federal Methodology, of whom 96% were aided. *Financial aid deadline (priority):* 4/1. *Financial aid forms:* FAFSA, institutional form required; CSS Financial Aid PROFILE acceptable. State form required for some. *Admission application deadline:* rolling.

Summary of Aid to Needy Students *From gift & self-help combined:* Average need met: 83%. Average amount awarded: $3065 (44% gift aid, 56% self-help). *Gift aid:* Total: $2,333,247 (24% from college's own funds, 38% from other college-administered sources, 38% from external sources). 299 Federal Work-Study jobs (averaging $800); 355 part-time jobs.

Need-Based Scholarships & Grants Pell, FSEOG, state, private, college/university.

Loans Perkins, PLUS, Stafford, Unsubsidized Stafford, college/university short-term loans ($200 average), college/university long-term loans ($400 average).

Non-Need Awards In 1996, a total of 53 non-need awards were made. *Academic Interests/Achievement Awards:* 35 ($8250 total): general academic, biological sciences, business, communication, education, English, foreign languages, humanities, international studies, mathematics, physical sciences, social sciences. *Creative Arts/Performance Awards:* 7 ($1450 total): art/fine arts, music, theater/drama. *Special Characteristics Awards:* 11 ($2500 total): children and siblings of alumni, children of union members/company employees, handicapped students, local/state students.

Other Money-Saving Options Accelerated degree, Army ROTC, off-campus living. *Payment Plans:* installment, deferred payment. *Waivers:* full or partial for employees or children of employees and senior citizens.

Contact Mrs. Marjorie Robison, Director of Financial Aid, Frostburg State University, Frostburg, MD 21532-1099, 301-687-4301, fax: 301-687-3029.

FURMAN UNIVERSITY
Greenville, South Carolina

About the Institution Independent, coed. Degrees awarded: B, M. Offers 43 undergraduate majors. Total enrollment: 2,734. Undergraduates: 2,461 (30% state residents). Freshmen: 684.

Undergraduate Expenses (1997–98) Comprehensive fee of $20,868 includes tuition ($16,256), mandatory fees ($163), and college room and board ($4449). College room only: $2329 (minimum).

Applications Of all full-time undergraduates enrolled in fall 1996, 87% of those who applied for aid were judged to have need according to Federal Methodology, of whom 100% were aided. *Financial aid deadline (priority):* 2/15. *Financial aid forms:* FAFSA, CSS Financial Aid PROFILE, institutional form required. *Regular admission application deadline:* 2/1. Early decision deadline: 12/1.

Summary of Aid to Needy Students *From gift & self-help combined:* Average need met: 60%. Average amount awarded: $8600 (76% gift aid, 24% self-help). *Gift aid:* Total: $11,271,548 (67% from college's own funds, 22% from other college-administered sources, 11% from external sources). 480 Federal Work-Study jobs (averaging $1500); 425 part-time jobs.

Need-Based Scholarships & Grants Pell, FSEOG, state, private, college/university.

Loans Perkins, PLUS, Stafford, Unsubsidized Stafford, college/university short-term loans ($1500 average).

Non-Need Awards In 1996, a total of 1,030 non-need awards were made. *Academic Interests/Achievement Awards:* 613 ($1,837,214 total): general academic, mathematics. *Creative Arts/Performance Awards:* 128 ($216,693 total): music. *Special Characteristics Awards:* 61 ($154,557 total): relatives of clergy, religious affiliation. *Athletic:* Total: 228 ($2,701,407); Men: 156 ($1,943,253); Women: 72 ($758,154).

Other Money-Saving Options Accelerated degree, co-op program, Army ROTC, off-campus living (after junior year). *Payment Plan:* installment. *Waivers:* full or partial for employees or children of employees.

Contact Ms. Rebecca Pressley, Assistant Director of Financial Aid, Furman University, 3300 Poinsett Highway, Greenville, SC 29613-0688, 864-294-2204, fax: 864-294-3127.

GALLAUDET UNIVERSITY
Washington, District of Columbia

About the Institution Independent, coed. Degrees awarded: A, B, M, D. Offers 59 undergraduate majors. Total enrollment: 2,034. Undergraduates: 1,344 (2% district residents). Freshmen: 293.

Undergraduate Expenses (1996–97) Comprehensive fee of $12,890 includes tuition ($5702), mandatory fees ($480), and college room and board ($6708). College room only: $3824.

Applications Of all full-time undergraduates enrolled in fall 1996, 83% of those who applied for aid were judged to have need according to Federal Methodology, of whom 97% were aided. *Financial aid deadline (priority):* 5/30. *Financial aid forms:* FAFSA, institutional form required. District form required for some. *Admission application deadline:* 5/15.

Summary of Aid to Needy Students *From gift & self-help combined:* Average need met: 73%. Average amount awarded: $9421 (88% gift aid, 12% self-help). *Gift aid:* Total: $7,301,351 (11% from college's own funds, 9% from other college-administered sources, 80% from external sources). 81 Federal Work-Study jobs (averaging $1600); part-time jobs.

Need-Based Scholarships & Grants Pell, FSEOG, state, private, college/university.

Loans Perkins, PLUS, Stafford, Unsubsidized Stafford, college/university short-term loans ($200 average).

Non-Need Awards *Academic Interests/Achievement Awards:* general academic. *Special Characteristics Awards:* children of educators, children of faculty/staff, handicapped students, international students.

Other Money-Saving Options Accelerated degree, co-op program, off-campus living. *Payment Plan:* installment. *Waivers:* full or partial for employees or children of employees.

Contact Mrs. Nancy C. Goodman, Director of Financial Aid, Gallaudet University, 800 Florida Avenue, Washington, DC 20002-3625, 202-651-5290, fax: 202-651-5740.

GANNON UNIVERSITY
Erie, Pennsylvania

About the Institution Independent/religious, coed. Degrees awarded: A, B, M. Offers 59 undergraduate majors. Total enrollment: 3,327. Undergraduates: 2,826 (82% state residents). Freshmen: 491.

Undergraduate Expenses (1996–97) Comprehensive fee of $16,404 includes tuition ($11,410 minimum), mandatory fees ($284), and college room and board ($4710). College room only: $2540.

Applications 89% of all full-time undergraduates enrolled in fall 1996 applied for aid; of these, 88% were judged to have need according to Federal Methodology, of whom 100% were aided. *Financial aid deadline:* Applications processed continuously. *Financial aid forms:* FAFSA required. Institutional form required for some. *Admission application deadline:* rolling.

Summary of Aid to Needy Students *From gift & self-help combined:* Average need met: 80%. Average amount awarded: $10,542 (58% gift aid, 42% self-help). *Gift aid:* Total: $11,574,252 (50% from college's own funds, 5% from other college-administered sources, 45% from external sources). 498 Federal Work-Study jobs (averaging $1200); 100 part-time jobs.

Need-Based Scholarships & Grants Pell, FSEOG, state, private, college/university.

Loans Perkins, PLUS, Stafford, Unsubsidized Stafford, Federal Nursing, private, college/university short-term loans ($2000 average).

Non-Need Awards In 1996, a total of 1,103 non-need awards were made. *Academic Interests/Achievement Awards:* 620 ($1,534,634 total): general academic, biological sciences, business, engineering/technologies, foreign languages, mathematics. *Creative Arts/Performance Awards:* 9 ($13,000 total): theater/drama. *Special Achievements/Activities Awards:* 284 ($451,228 total): leadership. *Athletic:* Total: 190 ($824,670); Men: 87 ($423,725); Women: 103 ($400,945).

Other Money-Saving Options Accelerated degree, co-op program, Army ROTC, off-campus living (after sophomore year). *Payment Plan:* installment. *Waivers:* full or partial for employees or children of employees and senior citizens.

Contact Mr. James Treiber, Director of Financial Aid, Gannon University, University Square, Erie, PA 16541, 814-871-7337.

GARDNER-WEBB UNIVERSITY
Boiling Springs, North Carolina

About the Institution Independent/religious, coed. Degrees awarded: A, B, M. Offers 41 undergraduate majors. Total enrollment: 2,739. Undergraduates: 2,436 (52% state residents). Freshmen: 319.

Undergraduate Expenses (1997–98) Comprehensive fee of $14,250 includes tuition ($9620) and college room and board ($4630). College room only: $2190.

Applications Of all full-time undergraduates enrolled in fall 1996, 100% of those judged to have need according to Federal Methodology were aided. *Financial aid deadline (priority):* 4/1. *Financial aid forms:* FAFSA acceptable. CSS Financial Aid PROFILE, state form required for some. *Admission application deadline:* rolling.

Summary of Aid to Needy Students *From gift & self-help combined:* Average need met: 84%. Average amount awarded: $13,000 (63% gift aid, 37% self-help). *Gift aid:* Total: $8,564,330 (50% from college's own funds, 12% from other college-administered sources, 38% from external sources). Federal Work-Study jobs; 285 part-time jobs.

Need-Based Scholarships & Grants Pell, FSEOG, state, private, college/university.

Loans Perkins, PLUS, Stafford, Unsubsidized Stafford, Federal Nursing, state, private, college/university long-term loans ($1900 average).

Non-Need Awards In 1996, a total of 1,710 non-need awards were made. *Academic Interests/Achievement Awards:* 990 ($1,488,193 total): general academic, health fields, religion/biblical studies. *Creative Arts/Performance Awards:* 33 ($61,275 total): music. *Special Achievements/Activities Awards:* 417 ($271,655 total): cheerleading/drum major, religious involvement. *Special Characteristics Awards:* 52 ($58,490 total): handicapped students, relatives of clergy. *Athletic:* Total: 218 ($874,684); Men: 156 ($628,242); Women: 62 ($246,442).

Another Money-Saving Option Accelerated degree.

Contact Ms. Cindy Wallace, Assistant Director, Financial Planning, Gardner-Webb University, PO Box 955, Boiling Springs, NC 28017, 704-434-4494, fax: 704-434-4488.

GENEVA COLLEGE
Beaver Falls, Pennsylvania

About the Institution Independent/religious, coed. Degrees awarded: A, B, M. Offers 44 undergraduate majors. Total enrollment: 1,782. Undergraduates: 1,656 (77% state residents). Freshmen: 337.

Undergraduate Expenses (1996–97) Comprehensive fee of $15,464 includes tuition ($10,700), mandatory fees ($164), and college room and board ($4600).

Applications Of all full-time undergraduates enrolled in fall 1996, 100% of those judged to have need according to Federal Methodology were aided. *Financial aid deadline (priority):* 4/15. *Financial aid forms:* FAFSA required; CSS Financial Aid PROFILE acceptable. State form required for some. *Admission application deadline:* rolling.

Summary of Aid to Needy Students *From gift & self-help combined:* Average need met: 95%. Average amount awarded: $9611 (62% gift aid, 38% self-help). *Gift aid:* Total: $6,598,365 (56% from college's own funds, 31% from other college-administered sources, 13% from external sources). 205 Federal Work-Study jobs (averaging $800); 343 part-time jobs.

Need-Based Scholarships & Grants Pell, FSEOG, state, private, college/university.

Loans Perkins, Stafford, Unsubsidized Stafford, private, college/university short-term loans ($100 average).

Non-Need Awards In 1996, a total of 886 non-need awards were made. *Academic Interests/Achievement Awards:* 370 ($1,038,863 total): general academic, engineering/technologies. *Creative Arts/Performance Awards:* 25 ($22,000 total): music. *Special Characteristics Awards:* 264 ($855,175 total): children of faculty/staff, relatives of clergy, religious affiliation. *Athletic:* Total: 227 ($596,000); Men: 149 ($425,000); Women: 78 ($171,000).

Other Money-Saving Options Accelerated degree, co-op program. *Payment Plan:* installment. *Waivers:* full or partial for employees or children of employees.

Contact Mr. Steve Bell, Director of Financial Aid, Geneva College, 3200 College Avenue, Beaver Falls, PA 15010-3599, 800-847-8255.

GEORGE FOX UNIVERSITY
Newberg, Oregon

About the Institution Independent/religious, coed. Degrees awarded: B, M, D. Offers 49 undergraduate majors. Total enrollment: 2,188. Undergraduates: 1,612 (61% state residents). Freshmen: 399.

Undergraduate Expenses (1996–97) Comprehensive fee of $19,160 includes tuition ($14,300), mandatory fees ($220), and college room and board ($4640).

Applications 90% of all full-time undergraduates enrolled in fall 1996 applied for aid; of these, 87% were judged to have need according to Federal Methodology, of whom 100% were aided. *Financial aid deadline (priority):* 2/15. *Financial aid forms:* FAFSA required. State form required for some. *Admission application deadline:* 6/1.

Summary of Aid to Needy Students *From gift & self-help combined:* Average need met: 73%. Average amount awarded: $14,980 (63% gift aid, 37% self-help). *Gift aid:* Total: $9,985,570 (84% from college's own funds, 10% from other college-administered sources, 6% from external sources). 856 Federal Work-Study jobs (averaging $1800); 40 part-time jobs.

Need-Based Scholarships & Grants Pell, FSEOG, state, private, college/university.

Loans Perkins, PLUS, Stafford, Unsubsidized Stafford, private.

Non-Need Awards *Academic Interests/Achievement Awards:* general academic, biological sciences, religion/biblical studies. *Creative Arts/Performance Awards:* debating, music, theater/drama. *Special Achievements/Activities Awards:* leadership. *Special Characteristics Awards:* children and siblings of alumni, ethnic background, international students, members of minorities, out-of-state students, relatives of clergy, religious affiliation.

Other Money-Saving Options Accelerated degree, cooperative Air Force ROTC. *Payment Plan:* installment. *Waivers:* full or partial for minority students, employees or children of employees, senior citizens.

Contact Ms. Cathy Sanchez, Assistant Director of Financial Aid, George Fox University, 414 North Meridian, Newberg, OR 97132-2697, 503-538-8383.

GEORGE MASON UNIVERSITY
Fairfax, Virginia

About the Institution State-supported, coed. Degrees awarded: B, M, D, P. Offers 57 undergraduate majors. Total enrollment: 24,368. Undergraduates: 13,832 (91% state residents). Freshmen: 1,953.

Undergraduate Expenses (1996–97) State resident tuition: $4248. Nonresident tuition: $11,952. College room and board: $5100. College room only: $3200.

Applications 75% of all full-time undergraduates enrolled in fall 1996 applied for aid; of these, 84% were judged to have need according to Federal Methodology, of whom 86% were aided. *Financial aid deadline (priority):* 3/1. *Financial aid forms:* FAFSA required. *Regular admission application deadline:* 2/1. Early action deadline: 12/1.

Summary of Aid to Needy Students *From gift & self-help combined:* Average need met: 68%. Average amount awarded: $5553 (38% gift aid, 62% self-help). *Gift aid:* Total: $11,484,654 (13% from college's own funds, 48% from other college-administered sources, 39% from external sources). 273 Federal Work-Study jobs (averaging $1965); part-time jobs.

Need-Based Scholarships & Grants Pell, FSEOG, state, private, college/university.

Loans Perkins, PLUS, Stafford, Unsubsidized Stafford, state, private, college/university short-term loans ($100 average).

Non-Need Awards In 1996, a total of 374 non-need awards were made. *Academic Interests/Achievement Awards:* 172 ($897,844 total): general academic. *Athletic:* Total: 202 ($2,034,892); Men: 114 ($1,097,915); Women: 88 ($936,977).

Other Money-Saving Options Accelerated degree, co-op program, Army ROTC, cooperative Air Force ROTC, off-campus living. *Payment Plans:* installment, deferred payment. *Waivers:* full or partial for employees or children of employees.

Contact Ms. Christine McGuire, Associate Director of Student Aid, George Mason University, Mail Stop 3B5, Fairfax, VA 22030-4444, 703-993-2346, fax: 703-993-2350.

GEORGETOWN COLLEGE
Georgetown, Kentucky

About the Institution Independent/religious, coed. Degrees awarded: B, M. Offers 45 undergraduate majors. Total enrollment: 1,514. Undergraduates: 1,175 (81% state residents). Freshmen: 326.

Undergraduate Expenses (1996–97) Comprehensive fee of $13,790 includes tuition ($9540), mandatory fees ($200), and college room and board ($4050). College room only: $2015.

Applications 71% of all full-time undergraduates enrolled in fall 1996 applied for aid; of these, 87% were judged to have need according to Federal Methodology, of whom 100% were aided. *Financial aid deadline (priority):* 3/1. *Financial aid forms:* FAFSA required. *Regular admission application deadline:* rolling. Early decision deadline: 9/15.

Summary of Aid to Needy Students *From gift & self-help combined:* Average need met: 99%. Average amount awarded: $10,017 (70% gift aid, 30% self-help). *Gift aid:* Total: $4,877,801 (45% from college's own funds, 3% from other college-administered sources, 52% from external sources). 388 Federal Work-Study jobs (averaging $1080); 100 part-time jobs.

Need-Based Scholarships & Grants Pell, FSEOG, state, college/university.

Loans Perkins, PLUS, Stafford, Unsubsidized Stafford, college/university short-term loans ($1000 average), college/university long-term loans ($2500 average).

Non-Need Awards In 1996, a total of 1,075 non-need awards were made. *Academic Interests/Achievement Awards:* 335 ($1,224,742 total): general academic. *Creative Arts/Performance Awards:* 67 ($55,700 total): art/fine arts, music, performing arts, theater/drama. *Special Achievements/Activities Awards:* 256 ($198,086 total): religious involvement. *Special Characteristics Awards:* 302 ($62,600 total): religious affiliation. *Athletic:* Total: 115 ($466,787); Men: 80 ($314,032); Women: 35 ($152,755).

Other Money-Saving Options Accelerated degree, co-op program, Army ROTC, cooperative Air Force ROTC. *Payment Plan:* deferred payment. *Waivers:* full or partial for employees or children of employees.

Contact Ms. Ann Leigh Bisese, Director of Student Financial Planning, Georgetown College, 440 East College Street, Georgetown, KY 40324-1696, 502-863-8027.

GEORGETOWN UNIVERSITY
Washington, District of Columbia

About the Institution Independent/religious, coed. Degrees awarded: B, M, D, P. Offers 38 undergraduate majors. Total enrollment: 12,629. Undergraduates: 6,338 (3% district residents). Freshmen: 1,415.

Undergraduate Expenses (1997–98) Comprehensive fee of $27,069 includes tuition ($21,216), mandatory fees ($189), and college room and board ($5664 minimum). College room only: $4560 (minimum).

Applications Of all full-time undergraduates enrolled in fall 1996, 85% of those who applied for aid were judged to have need according to Federal Methodology, of whom 100% were aided. *Financial aid deadline:* continuous. *Financial aid forms:* CSS Financial Aid PROFILE required. District form required for some. *Regular admission application deadline:* 1/10. Early action deadline: 11/1.

Summary of Aid to Needy Students *From gift & self-help combined:* Average need met: 100%. Average amount awarded: $17,630 (65% gift aid, 35% self-help). *Gift aid:* Total: $29,162,641 (78% from college's own funds, 3% from other college-administered sources, 19% from external sources). 3,769 Federal Work-Study jobs (averaging $2700); 631 part-time jobs.

Need-Based Scholarships & Grants Pell, FSEOG, state, private, college/university.

Loans Perkins, PLUS, Stafford, Unsubsidized Stafford, Federal Nursing, state, private, college/university short-term loans ($400 average).

Non-Need Awards In 1996, a total of 478 non-need awards were made. *Special Characteristics Awards:* 329 ($5,191,106 total): children of faculty/staff, ROTC participants. *Athletic:* Total: 149 ($2,330,088); Men: 83 ($1,256,828); Women: 66 ($1,073,260).

Other Money-Saving Options Army ROTC, cooperative Naval ROTC, cooperative Air Force ROTC, off-campus living (after freshman year). *Payment Plan:* installment. *Waivers:* full or partial for employees or children of employees.

Contact Ms. Patricia A. McWade, Dean of Student Financial Services, Georgetown University, 37th and O Street, NW, Box 1252, Washington, DC 20057, 202-687-4547.

THE GEORGE WASHINGTON UNIVERSITY
Washington, District of Columbia

About the Institution Independent, coed. Degrees awarded: A, B, M, D, P. Offers 80 undergraduate majors. Total enrollment: 18,986. Undergraduates: 6,581 (9% district residents). Freshmen: 1,657.

Undergraduate Expenses (1997–98) Comprehensive fee of $27,250 includes tuition ($19,650), mandatory fees ($990), and college room and board ($6610 minimum). College room only: $4590 (minimum).

Applications 56% of all full-time undergraduates enrolled in fall 1996 applied for aid; of these, 84% were judged to have need according to Federal Methodology, of whom 95% were aided. *Financial aid deadline (priority):* 1/31. *Financial aid forms:* FAFSA, CSS Financial Aid PROFILE required. Institutional form required for some. *Regular admission application deadline:* 2/1. Early decision deadline: 12/1.

Summary of Aid to Needy Students *From gift & self-help combined:* Average need met: 90%. Average amount awarded: $15,755 (67% gift aid, 33% self-help). *Gift aid:* Total: $29,015,166 (92% from college's own funds, 3% from other college-administered sources, 5% from external sources). 868 Federal Work-Study jobs (averaging $1728); 1,500 part-time jobs.

Need-Based Scholarships & Grants Pell, FSEOG, state, private, college/university.

Loans Perkins, PLUS, Stafford, Unsubsidized Stafford, private, college/university short-term loans ($200 average).

Non-Need Awards In 1996, a total of 2,999 non-need awards were made. *Academic Interests/Achievement Awards:* 2,349 ($14,482,380 total): general academic, engineering/technologies, mathematics. *Creative Arts/Performance Awards:* 126 ($581,000 total): debating, music, performing arts, theater/drama. *Special Achievements/Activities Awards:* 29 ($85,500 total): leadership. *Special Characteristics Awards:* 318 ($3,939,940 total): children of faculty/staff, international students, local/state students, ROTC participants, siblings of current students. *Athletic:* Total: 177 ($3,015,081); Men: 89 ($1,411,407); Women: 88 ($1,603,674).

Other Money-Saving Options Accelerated degree, co-op program, Naval ROTC, cooperative Army ROTC, cooperative Air Force ROTC, off-campus living. *Payment Plans:* installment, deferred payment. *Waivers:* full or partial for employees or children of employees.

Contact Mr. Daniel E. Small, Director, Student Financial Assistance, The George Washington University, 2121 I Street, NW, 3rd Floor, Washington, DC 20052, 202-994-6620, fax: 202-994-0906.

GEORGIA BAPTIST COLLEGE OF NURSING
Atlanta, Georgia

About the Institution Independent/religious, women. Degrees awarded: B. Offers 1 undergraduate major. Total enrollment: 334. Freshmen: 35.

Undergraduate Expenses (1997–98 estimated) Tuition: $6900. Mandatory fees: $300. College room only: $1134.

Applications *Financial aid deadline (priority):* 5/1. *Financial aid forms:* FAFSA, state form, institutional form required; CSS Financial Aid PROFILE acceptable. *Admission application deadline:* 4/15.

Summary of Aid to Needy Students Part-time jobs.

Non-Need Awards *Academic Interests/Achievement Awards:* available. *Special Characteristics Awards:* available.

Other Money-Saving Options Off-campus living. *Waivers:* full or partial for children of alumni.

Contact Office of Financial Aid, Georgia Baptist College of Nursing, Atlanta, GA 30312, 404-265-4512.

GEORGIA COLLEGE AND STATE UNIVERSITY
Milledgeville, Georgia

About the Institution State-supported, coed. Degrees awarded: B, M. Offers 46 undergraduate majors. Total enrollment: 5,534. Undergraduates: 4,382 (95% state residents). Freshmen: 697.

Undergraduate Expenses (1996–97) State resident tuition: $1584. Nonresident tuition: $5463. Mandatory fees: $339. College room and board: $3345.

Applications Of all full-time undergraduates enrolled in fall 1996, 90% of those judged to have need according to Federal Methodology were aided. *Financial aid deadline (priority):* 4/15. *Financial aid forms:* FAFSA, institutional form required; CSS Financial Aid PROFILE acceptable. *Admission application deadline:* rolling.

Summary of Aid to Needy Students *Gift aid:* Total: $2,808,411. 200 Federal Work-Study jobs (averaging $1200); 170 part-time jobs.

Need-Based Scholarships & Grants Pell, FSEOG, state, private.

Loans Perkins, PLUS, Stafford, Unsubsidized Stafford, private, college/university short-term loans.

Non-Need Awards *Academic Interests/Achievement Awards:* general academic, business, health fields, international studies. *Creative Arts/Performance Awards:* debating, journalism/publications, music, theater/drama. *Special Achievements/Activities Awards:* general special achievements/activities, cheerleading/drum major. *Special Characteristics Awards:* children of faculty/staff, international students, members of minorities, ROTC participants. *Athletic:* Total: 106 ($235,441); Men: 65 ($130,436); Women: 41 ($105,005).

Other Money-Saving Options Accelerated degree, co-op program, Army ROTC, off-campus living. *Waivers:* full or partial for senior citizens.

Contact Mrs. Kathy Crawley, Associate Director of Financial Aid, Georgia College and State University, Campus Box 30, Milledgeville, GA 31061, 912-453-5149, fax: 912-454-0729.

GEORGIA INSTITUTE OF TECHNOLOGY
Atlanta, Georgia

About the Institution State-supported, coed. Degrees awarded: B, M, D. Offers 33 undergraduate majors. Total enrollment: 12,985. Undergraduates: 9,469. Freshmen: 1,843.

Undergraduate Expenses (1996–97) State resident tuition: $2115. Nonresident tuition: $8376. Mandatory fees: $570. College room and board: $4560. College room only: $2460.

Applications 49% of all full-time undergraduates enrolled in fall 1996 applied for aid; of these, 78% were judged to have need according to Federal Methodology, of whom 97% were aided. *Financial aid deadline (priority):* 3/1. *Financial aid forms:* FAFSA, institutional form required; HOPE alternate application acceptable. *Admission application deadline:* 2/1.

Summary of Aid to Needy Students *From gift & self-help combined:* Average need met: 57%. Average amount awarded: $4700 (41% gift aid, 59% self-help). *Gift aid:* Total: $6,347,537 (23% from college's own funds, 46% from other college-administered sources, 31% from external sources). 150 Federal Work-Study jobs (averaging $2000).

Need-Based Scholarships & Grants Pell, FSEOG, state, private, college/university.

Loans Perkins, PLUS, Stafford, Unsubsidized Stafford, private, college/university short-term loans ($1300 average), college/university long-term loans ($1540 average).

Non-Need Awards *Academic Interests/Achievement Awards:* general academic. *Special Achievements/Activities Awards:* leadership. *Special Characteristics Awards:* general special characteristics, children of faculty/

staff, ethnic background, members of minorities, ROTC participants. *Athletic:* Total: 232 ($2,055,800); Men: 156 ($1,441,049); Women: 76 ($614,751).

Other Money-Saving Options Accelerated degree, co-op program, Army ROTC, Naval ROTC, Air Force ROTC, off-campus living (after freshman year).

Contact Mr. Jerry McTier, Director of Student Financial Planning and Services, Georgia Institute of Technology, Atlanta, GA 30332-0001, 404-894-4160.

GEORGIAN COURT COLLEGE
Lakewood, New Jersey

About the Institution Independent/religious, primarily women. Degrees awarded: B, M. Offers 27 undergraduate majors. Total enrollment: 1,919. Undergraduates: 1,454 (99% state residents). Freshmen: 132.

Undergraduate Expenses (1997–98) Comprehensive fee of $15,866 includes tuition ($10,926), mandatory fees ($190), and college room and board ($4750).

Applications 96% of all full-time undergraduates enrolled in fall 1996 applied for aid; of these, 90% were judged to have need according to Federal Methodology, of whom 100% were aided. *Financial aid deadline (priority):* 6/1. *Financial aid forms:* FAFSA, institutional form, income tax form (parent/student/spouse) required. CSS Financial Aid PROFILE required for some. *Regular admission application deadline:* 8/1. Early action deadline: 11/15.

Summary of Aid to Needy Students *From gift & self-help combined:* Average need met: 82%. Average amount awarded: $8452 (61% gift aid, 39% self-help). *Gift aid:* Total: $5,105,752 (31% from college's own funds, 59% from other college-administered sources, 10% from external sources). 25 Federal Work-Study jobs (averaging $1048); 248 part-time jobs.

Need-Based Scholarships & Grants Pell, FSEOG, state, private, college/university.

Loans Perkins, PLUS, Stafford, Unsubsidized Stafford, state.

Non-Need Awards In 1996, a total of 185 non-need awards were made. *Academic Interests/Achievement Awards:* 127 ($224,536 total): general academic, biological sciences, foreign languages, mathematics. *Creative Arts/Performance Awards:* 12 ($8000 total): art/fine arts, music. *Athletic:* Total: 46 ($238,500).

Other Money-Saving Options Off-campus living. *Payment Plans:* installment, deferred payment. *Waivers:* full or partial for employees or children of employees and senior citizens.

Contact Office of Financial Aid, Georgian Court College, 900 Lakewood Avenue, Lakewood, NJ 08701-2697, 732-364-2200 Ext. 258, fax: 732-367-3920.

GEORGIA SOUTHERN UNIVERSITY
Statesboro, Georgia

About the Institution State-supported, coed. Degrees awarded: A, B, M, D. Offers 84 undergraduate majors. Total enrollment: 14,312. Undergraduates: 12,650 (88% state residents). Freshmen: 4,020.

Undergraduate Expenses (1996–97) State resident tuition: $1584. Nonresident tuition: $5463. Mandatory fees: $471. College room and board: $3675.

Applications Of all full-time undergraduates enrolled in fall 1996, 96% of those who applied for aid were judged to have need according to Federal Methodology, of whom 100% were aided. *Financial aid deadline (priority):* 5/1. *Financial aid forms:* FAFSA required; CSS Financial Aid PROFILE acceptable. *Admission application deadline:* 8/1.

Summary of Aid to Needy Students *From gift & self-help combined:* Average need met: 58%. Average amount awarded: $4359 (38% gift

aid, 62% self-help). *Gift aid:* Total: $13,516,725 (2% from college's own funds, 52% from other college-administered sources, 46% from external sources). 450 Federal Work-Study jobs (averaging $1425); 800 part-time jobs.

Need-Based Scholarships & Grants Pell, FSEOG, state, college/university.

Loans Perkins, PLUS, Stafford, Unsubsidized Stafford, Federal Nursing, state, college/university short-term loans ($90 average).

Non-Need Awards In 1996, a total of 379 non-need awards were made. *Academic Interests/Achievement Awards:* 94 ($167,304 total): general academic. *Creative Arts/Performance Awards:* 36 ($21,350 total): music. *Athletic:* Total: 249 ($851,512); Men: 170 ($628,449); Women: 79 ($223,063).

Other Money-Saving Options Co-op program, Army ROTC, off-campus living. *Waivers:* full or partial for senior citizens.

Contact Ms. Connie Murphey, Associate Director, Georgia Southern University, PO Box 8065, Statesboro, GA 30460-8065, 912-681-5068, fax: 912-681-0573.

GEORGIA SOUTHWESTERN STATE UNIVERSITY
Americus, Georgia

About the Institution State-supported, coed. Degrees awarded: A, B, M. Offers 64 undergraduate majors. Total enrollment: 2,522. Undergraduates: 2,066 (94% state residents). Freshmen: 310.

Undergraduate Expenses (1996–97) State resident tuition: $1584. Nonresident tuition: $5463. Mandatory fees: $441. College room and board: $3033. College room only: $1425.

Applications Of all full-time undergraduates enrolled in fall 1996, 77% of those who applied for aid were judged to have need according to Federal Methodology, of whom 92% were aided. *Financial aid deadline (priority):* 4/1. *Financial aid forms:* FAFSA, institutional form required. *Admission application deadline:* rolling.

Summary of Aid to Needy Students *From gift & self-help combined:* Average need met: 80%. Average amount awarded: $7838 (46% gift aid, 54% self-help). *Gift aid:* Total: $2,789,228 (16% from college's own funds, 29% from other college-administered sources, 55% from external sources). 117 Federal Work-Study jobs (averaging $1521); 101 part-time jobs.

Need-Based Scholarships & Grants Pell, FSEOG, state.

Loans Perkins, PLUS, Stafford, Unsubsidized Stafford, state, private, college/university short-term loans ($750 average), college/university long-term loans ($500 average).

Non-Need Awards In 1996, a total of 225 non-need awards were made. *Academic Interests/Achievement Awards:* 7 ($11,400 total): general academic. *Creative Arts/Performance Awards:* 24 ($23,554 total): art/fine arts, music. *Special Achievements/Activities Awards:* 22 ($35,008 total): leadership. *Special Characteristics Awards:* 85 ($41,250 total): local/state students. *Athletic:* Total: 87 ($274,549); Men: 57 ($166,875); Women: 30 ($107,674).

Other Money-Saving Options Co-op program, off-campus living (after sophomore year). *Waivers:* full or partial for senior citizens.

Contact Ms. Freida Jones, Director of Financial Aid, Georgia Southwestern State University, 800 Wheatley Street, Americus, GA 31709-4693, 912-928-1378.

GEORGIA STATE UNIVERSITY
Atlanta, Georgia

About the Institution State-supported, coed. Degrees awarded: A, B, M, D, P. Offers 65 undergraduate majors. Total enrollment: 23,410. Undergraduates: 16,320 (90% state residents). Freshmen: 1,705.

Undergraduate Expenses (1996–97) State resident tuition: $2124. Nonresident tuition: $8379. Mandatory fees: $261. College room only: $3790.

Applications Of all full-time undergraduates enrolled in fall 1996, 100% of those judged to have need according to Federal Methodology were aided. *Financial aid deadline (priority): 4/15. Financial aid forms:* FAFSA required. State form required for some. *Admission application deadline: 7/1.*

Summary of Aid to Needy Students *From gift & self-help combined:* Average amount awarded: $4451 (39% gift aid, 61% self-help). *Gift aid:* Total: $14,203,019 (2% from college's own funds, 49% from other college-administered sources, 49% from external sources). 218 Federal Work-Study jobs (averaging $1842); 1,500 part-time jobs.

Need-Based Scholarships & Grants Pell, FSEOG, college/university.

Loans Perkins, PLUS, Stafford, Unsubsidized Stafford, private, college/university short-term loans ($300 average).

Non-Need Awards *Academic Interests/Achievement Awards:* general academic, biological sciences, business, communication, computer science, education, health fields, mathematics, physical sciences, social sciences. *Creative Arts/Performance Awards:* applied art and design, art/fine arts, music, performing arts, theater/drama. *Special Achievements/Activities Awards:* community service, leadership, memberships. *Athletic:* Total: 157 ($1,139,815); Men: 86 ($506,461); Women: 71 ($633,354).

Other Money-Saving Options Accelerated degree, co-op program, Army ROTC, cooperative Naval ROTC, cooperative Air Force ROTC, off-campus living. *Waivers:* full or partial for senior citizens.

Contact Student Financial Services Office, Georgia State University, PO Box 4040, Atlanta, GA 30302, 404-651-2227, fax: 404-651-3418.

GETTYSBURG COLLEGE
Gettysburg, Pennsylvania

About the Institution Independent, coed. Degrees awarded: B. Offers 55 undergraduate majors. Total enrollment: 2,000 (25% state residents). Freshmen: 623.

Undergraduate Expenses (1997–98) Comprehensive fee of $26,636 includes tuition ($22,330), mandatory fees ($100), and college room and board ($4206). College room only: $2656.

Applications Of all full-time undergraduates enrolled in fall 1996, 90% of those who applied for aid were judged to have need according to Federal Methodology, of whom 99% were aided. *Financial aid deadline (priority): 2/15. Financial aid forms:* FAFSA, CSS Financial Aid PROFILE, state form required. *Regular admission application deadline: 2/15.* Early decision deadline: 2/1.

Summary of Aid to Needy Students *From gift & self-help combined:* Average need met: 95%. Average amount awarded: $17,665 (77% gift aid, 23% self-help). *Gift aid:* Total: $15,134,200 (89% from college's own funds, 2% from other college-administered sources, 9% from external sources). 650 Federal Work-Study jobs (averaging $1300); part-time jobs.

Need-Based Scholarships & Grants Pell, FSEOG, state, private, college/university.

Loans Perkins, PLUS, Stafford, Unsubsidized Stafford, state, private, college/university long-term loans ($1400 average).

Non-Need Awards In 1996, a total of 136 non-need awards were made. *Academic Interests/Achievement Awards:* 136 ($680,000 total): general academic.

Other Money-Saving Options Accelerated degree, off-campus living (after freshman year). *Payment Plan:* installment.

Contact Office of Financial Aid, Gettysburg College, Eisenhower House, Gettysburg, PA 17325-1411, 717-337-6000.

GLENVILLE STATE COLLEGE
Glenville, West Virginia

About the Institution State-supported, coed. Degrees awarded: A, B. Offers 41 undergraduate majors. Total enrollment: 2,179 (94% state residents). Freshmen: 440.

Undergraduate Expenses (1997–98) State resident tuition: $1956. Nonresident tuition: $4560. College room and board: $3480. College room only: $1600.

Applications Of all full-time undergraduates enrolled in fall 1996, 93% of those who applied for aid were judged to have need according to Federal Methodology, of whom 94% were aided. *Financial aid deadline (priority): 3/1. Financial aid forms:* FAFSA required. State form required for some. *Admission application deadline: 8/1.*

Summary of Aid to Needy Students *From gift & self-help combined:* Average need met: 85%. Average amount awarded: $4771 (45% gift aid, 55% self-help). *Gift aid:* Total: $2,543,120 (4% from college's own funds, 27% from other college-administered sources, 69% from external sources). 125 Federal Work-Study jobs (averaging $750); 195 part-time jobs.

Need-Based Scholarships & Grants Pell, FSEOG, state.

Loans Perkins, PLUS, Stafford, Unsubsidized Stafford, college/university short-term loans ($200 average).

Non-Need Awards In 1996, a total of 290 non-need awards were made. *Academic Interests/Achievement Awards:* 144 ($169,265 total): general academic. *Creative Arts/Performance Awards:* 16 ($15,957 total): music. *Athletic:* Total: 130 ($211,163); Men: 100 ($177,422); Women: 30 ($33,741).

Other Money-Saving Options Accelerated degree, off-campus living (after freshman year). *Payment Plan:* installment.

Contact Office of Financial Aid, Glenville State College, 200 High Street, Glenville, WV 26351-1200, 304-462-7361.

GMI ENGINEERING & MANAGEMENT INSTITUTE
Flint, Michigan

About the Institution Independent, coed. Degrees awarded: B, M. Offers 19 undergraduate majors. Total enrollment: 3,225. Undergraduates: 2,430 (60% state residents). Freshmen: 538.

Undergraduate Expenses (1997–98 estimated) Comprehensive fee of $17,426 includes tuition ($13,576), mandatory fees ($120), and college room and board ($3730). College room only: $2400.

Applications Of all full-time undergraduates enrolled in fall 1996, 99% of those who applied for aid were judged to have need according to Federal Methodology, of whom 100% were aided. *Financial aid deadline (priority): 3/30. Financial aid forms:* FAFSA, state form, institutional form required. *Admission application deadline: rolling.*

Summary of Aid to Needy Students *From gift & self-help combined:* Average amount awarded: $7836 (23% gift aid, 77% self-help). *Gift aid:* Total: $3,258,632 (12% from college's own funds, 67% from other college-administered sources, 21% from external sources). 573 Federal Work-Study jobs (averaging $413); 150 part-time jobs.

Need-Based Scholarships & Grants Pell, FSEOG, state, private, college/university.

Loans PLUS, Stafford, Unsubsidized Stafford, state, private, college/university short-term loans ($3000 average), college/university long-term loans ($3380 average).

Non-Need Awards In 1996, a total of 86 non-need awards were made. *Academic Interests/Achievement Awards:* 76 ($320,000 total). *Special Characteristics Awards:* 10 ($100,000 total): local/state students.

Other Money-Saving Options Co-op program, off-campus living (after freshman year). *Payment Plan:* installment. *Waivers:* full or partial for employees or children of employees.

Contact Ms. Chris Shell, Associate Director of Financial Aid, GMI Engineering & Management Institute, 1700 West Third Avenue, Flint, MI 48504-4898, 800-955-4464.

GODDARD COLLEGE
Plainfield, Vermont

About the Institution Independent, coed. Degrees awarded: B, M. Offers 70 undergraduate majors. Total enrollment: 550. Undergraduates: 300 (19% state residents). Freshmen: 38.

Undergraduate Expenses (1997–98 estimated) Comprehensive fee of $20,734 includes tuition ($15,226), mandatory fees ($424), and college room and board ($5084).

Applications *Financial aid deadline (priority):* 3/15. *Financial aid forms:* CSS Financial Aid PROFILE required; FAFSA acceptable. *Admission application deadline:* rolling.

Summary of Aid to Needy Students Federal Work-Study jobs.

Non-Need Awards *Special Achievements/Activities Awards:* available. *Special Characteristics Awards:* local/state students.

Other Money-Saving Options Co-op program, off-campus living (after sophomore year). *Payment Plan:* installment. *Waivers:* full or partial for employees or children of employees.

Contact Office of Financial Aid, Goddard College, Plainfield, VT 05667, 802-454-8311.

GOD'S BIBLE SCHOOL AND COLLEGE
Cincinnati, Ohio

About the Institution Independent/religious, coed. Degrees awarded: A, B. Offers 11 undergraduate majors. Total enrollment: 176 (36% state residents). Freshmen: 44.

Undergraduate Expenses (1997–98) Comprehensive fee of $6400 includes tuition ($3560), mandatory fees ($290), and college room and board ($2550). College room only: $1000.

Applications *Financial aid deadline (priority):* 4/27. *Financial aid forms:* FAFSA required. Institutional form required for some. *Admission application deadline:* rolling.

Summary of Aid to Needy Students Part-time jobs.

Non-Need Awards *Academic Interests/Achievement Awards:* general academic. *Creative Arts/Performance Awards:* music. *Special Characteristics Awards:* international students.

Contact Office of Financial Aid, God's Bible School and College, 1810 Young Street, Cincinnati, OH 45210-1599, 513-721-7944.

GOLDEN GATE UNIVERSITY
San Francisco, California

About the Institution Independent, coed. Degrees awarded: A, B, M, D, P. Offers 18 undergraduate majors. Total enrollment: 6,119. Undergraduates: 1,853 (80% state residents). Freshmen: 37.

Undergraduate Expenses (1996–97) Tuition: $8190. Mandatory fees: $224 (minimum).

Applications 18% of all full-time undergraduates enrolled in fall 1996 applied for aid; of these, 98% were judged to have need according to Federal Methodology, of whom 100% were aided. *Financial aid deadline:* continuous. *Financial aid forms:* FAFSA, state form, institutional form required. *Admission application deadline:* rolling.

Summary of Aid to Needy Students *From gift & self-help combined:* Average need met: 73%. *Gift aid:* Total: $235,531 (13% from college's

own funds, 83% from other college-administered sources, 4% from external sources). 35 Federal Work-Study jobs (averaging $3000); 70 part-time jobs.

Need-Based Scholarships & Grants Pell, FSEOG, state, college/university.

Loans Perkins, PLUS, Stafford, Unsubsidized Stafford, college/university short-term loans, college/university long-term loans ($1500 average).

Non-Need Awards *Academic Interests/Achievement Awards:* ($128,000 total): general academic. *Special Achievements/Activities Awards:* 5 ($27,500 total): leadership. *Special Characteristics Awards:* ($210,000 total): members of minorities.

Other Money-Saving Options Accelerated degree, co-op program, cooperative Army ROTC, cooperative Naval ROTC, cooperative Air Force ROTC. *Payment Plan:* installment. *Waivers:* full or partial for employees or children of employees.

Contact Office of Financial Aid, Golden Gate University, 536 Mission Street, San Francisco, CA 94105-2968, 415-442-7000.

GOLDEY-BEACOM COLLEGE
Wilmington, Delaware

About the Institution Independent, coed. Degrees awarded: A, B, M. Offers 7 undergraduate majors. Total enrollment: 1,600. Undergraduates: 1,480 (50% state residents). Freshmen: 240.

Undergraduate Expenses (1997–98) Tuition: $7080. Mandatory fees: $120. College room only: $3290.

Applications Of all full-time undergraduates enrolled in fall 1996, 96% of those judged to have need according to Federal Methodology were aided. *Financial aid deadline (priority):* 4/1. *Financial aid forms:* FAFSA required. Institutional form, nontaxable income verification required for some. *Admission application deadline:* rolling.

Summary of Aid to Needy Students *From gift & self-help combined:* Average need met: 83%. Average amount awarded: $4281 (33% gift aid, 67% self-help). *Gift aid:* Total: $844,587 (50% from college's own funds, 18% from other college-administered sources, 32% from external sources). 30 Federal Work-Study jobs (averaging $1200); 20 part-time jobs.

Need-Based Scholarships & Grants Pell, FSEOG, state, private, college/university.

Loans Perkins, PLUS, Stafford, Unsubsidized Stafford.

Non-Need Awards In 1996, a total of 210 non-need awards were made. *Academic Interests/Achievement Awards:* 179 ($225,000 total): business. *Athletic:* Total: 31 ($53,600); Men: 15 ($26,400); Women: 16 ($27,200).

Other Money-Saving Options Accelerated degree, co-op program, off-campus living. *Payment Plans:* installment, deferred payment. *Waivers:* full or partial for employees or children of employees.

Contact Financial Aid Office, Goldey-Beacom College, Wilmington, DE 19808-1999, 302-998-8814 Ext. 262, fax: 302-998-8631.

GONZAGA UNIVERSITY
Spokane, Washington

About the Institution Independent/religious, coed. Degrees awarded: B, M, D, P. Offers 54 undergraduate majors. Total enrollment: 4,479. Undergraduates: 3,235 (45% state residents). Freshmen: 525.

Undergraduate Expenses (1997–98) Comprehensive fee of $20,370 includes tuition ($15,350) and college room and board ($5020).

Applications 70% of all full-time undergraduates enrolled in fall 1996 applied for aid. *Financial aid deadline (priority):* 2/1. *Financial aid forms:* FAFSA required. *Regular admission application deadline:* 4/1. Early action deadline: 12/15.

Summary of Aid to Needy Students *From gift & self-help combined:* Average need met: 83%. Average amount awarded: $13,588 (51% gift aid, 49% self-help). *Gift aid:* Total: $10,770,716 (79% from college's own funds, 4% from other college-administered sources, 17% from external sources). 427 Federal Work-Study jobs (averaging $1864).

Need-Based Scholarships & Grants Pell, FSEOG, state, private, college/university.

Loans Perkins, PLUS, Stafford, Unsubsidized Stafford, private, college/university short-term loans ($150 average), college/university long-term loans ($1972 average).

Non-Need Awards In 1996, a total of 2,411 non-need awards were made. *Academic Interests/Achievement Awards:* 1,912 ($4,846,194 total): general academic, engineering/technologies. *Creative Arts/Performance Awards:* 57 ($59,270 total): debating, music. *Special Characteristics Awards:* 313 ($1,616,297 total): children and siblings of alumni, local/state students, members of minorities, ROTC participants, siblings of current students. *Athletic:* Total: 129 ($1,298,376); Men: 63 ($603,358); Women: 66 ($695,018).

Other Money-Saving Options Accelerated degree, Army ROTC, off-campus living (after sophomore year). *Payment Plan:* installment. *Waivers:* full or partial for employees or children of employees and senior citizens.

Contact Ms. Melissa Thompson, Assistant Director, Gonzaga University, 502 East Boone Avenue, Spokane, WA 99258, 509-328-4220 Ext. 3186, fax: 509-324-5718.

GORDON COLLEGE
Wenham, Massachusetts

About the Institution Independent/religious, coed. Degrees awarded: B, M. Offers 32 undergraduate majors. Total enrollment: 1,259. Undergraduates: 1,224 (31% state residents). Freshmen: 330.

Undergraduate Expenses (1997–98) Comprehensive fee of $19,980 includes tuition ($14,520), mandatory fees ($630), and college room and board ($4830). College room only: $3150.

Applications Of all full-time undergraduates enrolled in fall 1996, 100% of those who applied for aid were judged to have need according to Federal Methodology, of whom 81% were aided. *Financial aid deadline (priority):* 3/15. *Financial aid forms:* FAFSA, CSS Financial Aid PROFILE, state form, institutional form required. *Regular admission application deadline:* rolling. Early decision deadline: 12/1.

Summary of Aid to Needy Students *From gift & self-help combined:* Average need met: 83%. Average amount awarded: $13,319 (69% gift aid, 31% self-help). *Gift aid:* Total: $9,351,504 (71% from college's own funds, 23% from other college-administered sources, 6% from external sources). 750 Federal Work-Study jobs (averaging $1500); 250 part-time jobs.

Need-Based Scholarships & Grants Pell, FSEOG, state, private, college/university.

Loans Perkins, PLUS, Stafford, Unsubsidized Stafford, private, college/university short-term loans ($50 average).

Non-Need Awards In 1996, a total of 1,182 non-need awards were made. *Academic Interests/Achievement Awards:* 843 ($1,900,200 total): general academic. *Creative Arts/Performance Awards:* 43 ($40,000 total): music. *Special Achievements/Activities Awards:* 48 ($384,000 total): leadership. *Special Characteristics Awards:* 248 ($124,000 total): children and siblings of alumni.

Other Money-Saving Options Co-op program, cooperative Air Force ROTC. *Payment Plans:* tuition prepayment, installment. *Waivers:* full or partial for employees or children of employees.

Contact Mr. Seamus Harreys, Director of Financial Aid, Gordon College, 255 Grapevine Road, Wenham, MA 01984-1899, 508-927-2300 Ext. 4035, fax: 508-524-3704.

GOSHEN COLLEGE
Goshen, Indiana

About the Institution Independent/religious, coed. Degrees awarded: B. Offers 50 undergraduate majors. Total enrollment: 1,014 (48% state residents). Freshmen: 211.

Undergraduate Expenses (1997–98) Comprehensive fee of $15,450 includes tuition ($11,450) and college room and board ($4000).

Applications 91% of all full-time undergraduates enrolled in fall 1996 applied for aid; of these, 69% were judged to have need according to Federal Methodology, of whom 100% were aided. *Financial aid deadline (priority):* 3/1. *Financial aid forms:* FAFSA, institutional form required; CSS Financial Aid PROFILE acceptable. State form required for some. *Admission application deadline:* rolling.

Summary of Aid to Needy Students *From gift & self-help combined:* Average need met: 91%. Average amount awarded: $10,962 (61% gift aid, 39% self-help). *Gift aid:* Total: $3,605,582 (58% from college's own funds, 35% from other college-administered sources, 7% from external sources). 407 Federal Work-Study jobs (averaging $1015); 14 part-time jobs.

Need-Based Scholarships & Grants Pell, FSEOG, state, private, college/university.

Loans Perkins, PLUS, Stafford, Unsubsidized Stafford, Federal Nursing, private, college/university long-term loans ($1880 average).

Non-Need Awards In 1996, a total of 390 non-need awards were made. *Academic Interests/Achievement Awards:* 168 ($332,225 total): general academic. *Special Characteristics Awards:* 203 ($386,423 total): general special characteristics. *Athletic:* Total: 19 ($23,500); Men: 9 ($12,000); Women: 10 ($11,500).

Other Money-Saving Options Accelerated degree, co-op program, off-campus living (after junior year). *Waivers:* full or partial for employees or children of employees.

Contact Mr. Galen Graber, Director of Student Financial Aid, Goshen College, 1700 South Main, Goshen, IN 46526-4794, 219-535-7525, fax: 219-535-7654.

GOUCHER COLLEGE
Baltimore, Maryland

About the Institution Independent, coed. Degrees awarded: B, M. Offers 69 undergraduate majors. Total enrollment: 1,303. Undergraduates: 1,020 (40% state residents). Freshmen: 268.

Undergraduate Expenses (1997–98) Comprehensive fee of $25,450 includes tuition ($18,400), mandatory fees ($125), and college room and board ($6925). College room only: $4600.

Applications 84% of all full-time undergraduates enrolled in fall 1996 applied for aid; of these, 73% were judged to have need according to Federal Methodology, of whom 100% were aided. *Financial aid deadline (priority):* 2/15. *Financial aid forms:* FAFSA, state form, institutional form required. CSS Financial Aid PROFILE required for some. *Regular admission application deadline:* 2/1. Early action deadline: 12/1.

Summary of Aid to Needy Students *From gift & self-help combined:* Average need met: 100%. Average amount awarded: $19,646 (78% gift aid, 22% self-help). *Gift aid:* Total: $9,193,891 (87% from college's own funds, 8% from other college-administered sources, 5% from external sources). 484 Federal Work-Study jobs (averaging $1100); 165 part-time jobs.

Need-Based Scholarships & Grants Pell, FSEOG, state, private, college/university.

Loans Perkins, PLUS, Stafford, Unsubsidized Stafford, private, college/university short-term loans ($3000 average), college/university long-term loans ($2500 average).

Non-Need Awards In 1996, a total of 407 non-need awards were made. *Academic Interests/Achievement Awards:* 396 ($3,901,321 total): general academic, biological sciences, business, physical sciences, social sciences. *Creative Arts/Performance Awards:* 11 ($55,000 total): art/fine arts, dance, music, theater/drama.

Other Money-Saving Options Accelerated degree, cooperative Army ROTC, off-campus living (after sophomore year). *Waivers:* full or partial for employees or children of employees.

Contact Office of Financial Aid, Goucher College, 1021 Dulaney Valley Road, Baltimore, MD 21204-2794, 410-337-6000.

GRACE BIBLE COLLEGE
Grand Rapids, Michigan

About the Institution Independent/religious, coed. Degrees awarded: A, B. Offers 13 undergraduate majors. Total enrollment: 143 (59% state residents). Freshmen: 39.

Undergraduate Expenses (1996–97) Comprehensive fee of $9400 includes tuition ($5600), mandatory fees ($200), and college room and board ($3600).

Applications 84% of all full-time undergraduates enrolled in fall 1996 applied for aid; of these, 98% were judged to have need according to Federal Methodology, of whom 100% were aided. *Financial aid deadline (priority):* 2/15. *Financial aid forms:* FAFSA required. *Admission application deadline:* 7/15.

Summary of Aid to Needy Students *From gift & self-help combined:* Average need met: 75%. Average amount awarded: $6875 (68% gift aid, 32% self-help). *Gift aid:* Total: $478,406 (28% from college's own funds, 29% from other college-administered sources, 43% from external sources). 55 Federal Work-Study jobs (averaging $616); 20 part-time jobs.

Need-Based Scholarships & Grants Pell, FSEOG, state, private, college/university.

Loans PLUS, Stafford, Unsubsidized Stafford, state, private.

Non-Need Awards In 1996, a total of 81 non-need awards were made. *Academic Interests/Achievement Awards:* 67 ($30,975 total): general academic. *Creative Arts/Performance Awards:* 9 ($5625 total): music. *Special Characteristics Awards:* 5 ($1250 total): general special characteristics.

Other Money-Saving Options Off-campus living (after sophomore year). *Payment Plan:* installment. *Waivers:* full or partial for employees or children of employees and senior citizens.

Contact Office of Financial Aid, Grace Bible College, 1011 Aldon Street, SW, PO Box 910, Grand Rapids, MI 49509-1921, 616-538-2330.

GRACE COLLEGE
Winona Lake, Indiana

About the Institution Independent/religious, coed. Degrees awarded: A, B. Offers 32 undergraduate majors. Total enrollment: 645 (45% state residents). Freshmen: 135.

Undergraduate Expenses (1997–98) Comprehensive fee of $14,102 includes tuition ($9820) and college room and board ($4282). College room only: $2062.

Applications 96% of all full-time undergraduates enrolled in fall 1996 applied for aid; of these, 80% were judged to have need according to Federal Methodology, of whom 100% were aided. *Financial aid deadline (priority):* 3/1. *Financial aid forms:* FAFSA required; CSS Financial Aid PROFILE acceptable. State form required for some. *Admission application deadline:* 8/1.

Summary of Aid to Needy Students *From gift & self-help combined:* Average need met: 100%. Average amount awarded: $11,864 (55% gift aid, 45% self-help). *Gift aid:* Total: $2,945,078 (61% from college's

own funds, 29% from other college-administered sources, 10% from external sources). 170 Federal Work-Study jobs (averaging $1300); 100 part-time jobs.

Need-Based Scholarships & Grants Pell, FSEOG, state, college/university.

Loans Perkins, PLUS, Stafford, Unsubsidized Stafford.

Non-Need Awards In 1996, a total of 536 non-need awards were made. *Academic Interests/Achievement Awards:* 159 ($402,985 total): general academic. *Creative Arts/Performance Awards:* 68 ($87,123 total): art/fine arts, music, theater/drama. *Special Achievements/Activities Awards:* 52 ($102,247 total): community service, leadership, religious involvement. *Special Characteristics Awards:* 131 ($391,646 total): children of faculty/staff, relatives of clergy. *Athletic:* Total: 126 ($272,000); Men: 58 ($143,140); Women: 68 ($128,860).

Other Money-Saving Options Accelerated degree. *Payment Plan:* installment. *Waivers:* full or partial for employees or children of employees.

Contact Director of Financial Aid, Grace College, Winona Lake, IN 46590-1294, 219-324-5243.

GRACELAND COLLEGE
Lamoni, Iowa

About the Institution Independent/religious, coed. Degrees awarded: B, M. Offers 47 undergraduate majors. Total enrollment: 1,260 (32% state residents). Freshmen: 297.

Undergraduate Expenses (1996–97) Comprehensive fee of $13,650 includes tuition ($10,230), mandatory fees ($110), and college room and board ($3310). College room only: $1240.

Applications 89% of all full-time undergraduates enrolled in fall 1996 applied for aid; of these, 91% were judged to have need according to Federal Methodology, of whom 99% were aided. *Financial aid deadline (priority):* 4/15. *Financial aid forms:* FAFSA required for some. *Admission application deadline:* 5/1.

Summary of Aid to Needy Students *From gift & self-help combined:* Average need met: 91%. Average amount awarded: $13,781 (47% gift aid, 53% self-help). *Gift aid:* Total: $6,092,955 (68% from college's own funds, 6% from other college-administered sources, 26% from external sources). 497 Federal Work-Study jobs (averaging $1481); 197 part-time jobs.

Need-Based Scholarships & Grants Pell, FSEOG, state, college/university.

Loans College/university long-term loans ($2329 average).

Non-Need Awards In 1996, a total of 2,035 non-need awards were made. *Academic Interests/Achievement Awards:* 476 ($889,172 total): general academic. *Creative Arts/Performance Awards:* 287 ($405,981 total): applied art and design, creative writing, debating, music, theater/drama. *Special Achievements/Activities Awards:* 255 ($255,000 total): leadership, religious involvement. *Special Characteristics Awards:* 471 ($1,164,681 total): general special characteristics, children of faculty/staff, children of public servants, international students, local/state students, members of minorities, religious affiliation. *Athletic:* Total: 546 ($1,422,057); Men: 376 ($1,012,507); Women: 170 ($409,550).

Other Money-Saving Options Off-campus living (after sophomore year). *Payment Plan:* installment. *Waivers:* full or partial for employees or children of employees and senior citizens.

Contact Ms. Nancy Wolff, Director of Financial Aid, Graceland College, 700 College Avenue, Lamoni, IA 50140, 515-784-5140, fax: 515-784-5488.

GRACE UNIVERSITY
Omaha, Nebraska

About the Institution Independent/religious, coed. Degrees awarded: A, B, M. Offers 28 undergraduate majors. Total enrollment: 468. Undergraduates: 414. Freshmen: 136.

Undergraduate Expenses (1997–98) Comprehensive fee of $10,714 includes tuition ($7099), mandatory fees ($385), and college room and board ($3230).

Applications *Financial aid deadline (priority):* 2/1. *Financial aid forms:* FAFSA, institutional form required. *Admission application deadline:* rolling.

Summary of Aid to Needy Students *From gift & self-help combined:* Average need met: 67%. Average amount awarded: $4041 (36% gift aid, 64% self-help). *Gift aid:* Total: $499,880. Part-time jobs.

Need-Based Scholarships & Grants Pell, state.

Loans PLUS, Stafford, Unsubsidized Stafford.

Non-Need Awards *Academic Interests/Achievement Awards:* general academic. *Creative Arts/Performance Awards:* music. *Special Characteristics Awards:* general special characteristics, adult students, children and siblings of alumni, children of faculty/staff, relatives of clergy, religious affiliation, siblings of current students.

Other Money-Saving Options Accelerated degree, co-op program. *Payment Plan:* deferred payment. *Waivers:* full or partial for children of alumni, employees or children of employees, senior citizens.

Contact Office of Financial Aid, Grace University, 1311 South 9th Street, Omaha, NE 68108, 402-449-2810.

GRAMBLING STATE UNIVERSITY
Grambling, Louisiana

About the Institution State-supported, coed. Degrees awarded: A, B, M, D. Offers 74 undergraduate majors. Total enrollment: 8,000. Undergraduates: 7,600 (60% state residents). Freshmen: 1,809.

Undergraduate Expenses (1996–97) State resident tuition: $2088. Nonresident tuition: $4038. College room and board: $2636. College room only: $1574.

Applications 98% of all full-time undergraduates enrolled in fall 1996 applied for aid; of these, 97% were judged to have need according to Federal Methodology, of whom 96% were aided. *Financial aid deadline (priority):* 4/30. *Financial aid forms:* FAFSA, institutional form required. *Regular admission application deadline:* 7/15. Early decision deadline: 4/15.

Summary of Aid to Needy Students *From gift & self-help combined:* Average need met: 80%. Average amount awarded: $8500. *Gift aid:* Total: $5,986,591 (22% from college-administered sources, 78% from external sources). Federal Work-Study jobs (averaging $950); 1,300 part-time jobs.

Need-Based Scholarships & Grants Pell, FSEOG, state, private, college/university.

Loans Perkins, PLUS, Stafford, Unsubsidized Stafford, college/university short-term loans ($250 average).

Non-Need Awards *Academic Interests/Achievement Awards:* general academic, biological sciences, business, computer science, education, social sciences. *Creative Arts/Performance Awards:* dance, music. *Special Achievements/Activities Awards:* cheerleading/drum major, leadership. *Special Characteristics Awards:* children and siblings of alumni, children of faculty/staff, veterans. *Athletic:* available.

Other Money-Saving Options Co-op program, Army ROTC, Air Force ROTC. *Payment Plan:* installment. *Waivers:* full or partial for employees or children of employees and senior citizens.

Contact Mrs. Anne Rugege, Assistant Director, Student Financial Aid, Grambling State University, PO Box 629, Grambling, LA 71245, 318-274-6460, fax: 318-274-3358.

GRAND CANYON UNIVERSITY
Phoenix, Arizona

About the Institution Independent/religious, coed. Degrees awarded: B, M. Offers 55 undergraduate majors.

Undergraduate Expenses (1996–97) Comprehensive fee of $11,696 includes tuition ($8576), mandatory fees ($370), and college room and board ($2750 minimum).

Applications 87% of all full-time undergraduates enrolled in fall 1996 applied for aid; of these, 74% were judged to have need according to Federal Methodology, of whom 98% were aided. *Financial aid deadline (priority):* 3/15. *Financial aid forms:* FAFSA, institutional form required; CSS Financial Aid PROFILE, state form acceptable. *Admission application deadline:* 8/15.

Summary of Aid to Needy Students *From gift & self-help combined:* Average need met: 65%. Average amount awarded: $7634 (42% gift aid, 58% self-help). *Gift aid:* Total: $3,161,231 (59% from college's own funds, 6% from other college-administered sources, 35% from external sources). 137 Federal Work-Study jobs (averaging $2114); part-time jobs.

Need-Based Scholarships & Grants Pell, FSEOG, state, private, college/university, Bureau of Indian Affairs Grants.

Loans Perkins, PLUS, Stafford, Unsubsidized Stafford, college/university short-term loans ($300 average).

Non-Need Awards In 1996, a total of 1,163 non-need awards were made. *Academic Interests/Achievement Awards:* 624 ($1,534,170 total): general academic, biological sciences, business, communication, education, English, health fields, humanities, mathematics, military science, physical sciences, premedicine, religion/biblical studies, social sciences. *Creative Arts/Performance Awards:* 106 ($215,350 total): applied art and design, music, theater/drama. *Special Achievements/Activities Awards:* 61 ($24,275 total): leadership, memberships. *Special Characteristics Awards:* 182 ($195,904 total): children and siblings of alumni, children of faculty/staff, ethnic background, members of minorities, out-of-state students, relatives of clergy, religious affiliation, ROTC participants. *Athletic:* Total: 190 ($883,198); Men: 147 ($565,903); Women: 43 ($317,295).

Other Money-Saving Options Accelerated degree, Army ROTC, cooperative Air Force ROTC, off-campus living (after sophomore year). *Payment Plan:* installment. *Waivers:* full or partial for employees or children of employees.

Contact Office of Financial Aid, Grand Canyon University, Phoenix, AZ 85017-3030, 602-589-2885, fax: 602-589-2044.

GRAND VALLEY STATE UNIVERSITY
Allendale, Michigan

About the Institution State-supported, coed. Degrees awarded: B, M. Offers 117 undergraduate majors. Total enrollment: 14,662. Undergraduates: 11,734 (97% state residents). Freshmen: 2,114.

Undergraduate Expenses (1996–97) State resident tuition: $2866. Nonresident tuition: $6650. Mandatory fees: $360. College room and board: $4380.

Applications 77% of all full-time undergraduates enrolled in fall 1996 applied for aid; of these, 78% were judged to have need according to Federal Methodology, of whom 100% were aided. *Financial aid deadline (priority):* 2/1. *Financial aid forms:* FAFSA required. *Admission application deadline:* 7/26.

Summary of Aid to Needy Students *From gift & self-help combined:* Average need met: 98%. Average amount awarded: $5501 (31% gift

aid, 69% self-help). *Gift aid:* Total: $9,295,629 (24% from college's own funds, 35% from other college-administered sources, 41% from external sources). 850 Federal Work-Study jobs (averaging $1500); 900 part-time jobs.

Need-Based Scholarships & Grants Pell, FSEOG, state, private, college/university.

Loans Perkins, PLUS, Stafford, Unsubsidized Stafford, Federal Nursing, state, private, college/university short-term loans ($150 average), college/university long-term loans ($1500 average).

Non-Need Awards In 1996, a total of 2,134 non-need awards were made. *Academic Interests/Achievement Awards:* 1,071 ($1,354,688 total): general academic. *Creative Arts/Performance Awards:* 117 ($60,500 total): art/fine arts, music, theater/drama. *Special Characteristics Awards:* 786 ($1,536,029 total): children of faculty/staff, children of union members/company employees, handicapped students, international students, local/state students, members of minorities, out-of-state students. *Athletic:* Total: 160 ($664,692); Men: 107 ($436,046); Women: 53 ($228,646).

Other Money-Saving Options Accelerated degree, co-op program, off-campus living. *Payment Plans:* installment, deferred payment. *Waivers:* full or partial for employees or children of employees.

Contact Mr. Ken Fridsma, Director of Financial Aid, Grand Valley State University, 100 Student Services Building, Allendale, MI 49401-9403, 616-895-3234, fax: 616-895-3180.

GRAND VIEW COLLEGE
Des Moines, Iowa

About the Institution Independent/religious, coed. Degrees awarded: A, B. Offers 48 undergraduate majors. Total enrollment: 1,468 (95% state residents). Freshmen: 184.

Undergraduate Expenses (1997–98) Comprehensive fee of $15,185 includes tuition ($11,340), mandatory fees ($70), and college room and board ($3775).

Applications 95% of all full-time undergraduates enrolled in fall 1996 applied for aid; of these, 95% were judged to have need according to Federal Methodology, of whom 100% were aided. *Financial aid deadline (priority):* 3/1. *Financial aid forms:* FAFSA, state form, institutional form required; CSS Financial Aid PROFILE acceptable. *Admission application deadline:* rolling.

Summary of Aid to Needy Students *From gift & self-help combined:* Average need met: 90%. Average amount awarded: $7037 (44% gift aid, 56% self-help). *Gift aid:* Total: $2,802,462 (9% from college's own funds, 5% from other college-administered sources, 86% from external sources). 52 Federal Work-Study jobs (averaging $1230); 104 part-time jobs.

Need-Based Scholarships & Grants Pell, FSEOG, state, private, college/university.

Loans Perkins, PLUS, Stafford, Unsubsidized Stafford, private.

Non-Need Awards In 1996, a total of 1,034 non-need awards were made. *Academic Interests/Achievement Awards:* 888 ($2,334,516 total): general academic. *Creative Arts/Performance Awards:* 84 ($46,907 total): art/fine arts, music, theater/drama. *Athletic:* Total: 62 ($181,033); Men: 39 ($120,150); Women: 23 ($60,883).

Other Money-Saving Options Accelerated degree, co-op program, cooperative Army ROTC, cooperative Air Force ROTC, off-campus living. *Payment Plans:* installment, deferred payment. *Waivers:* full or partial for employees or children of employees and senior citizens.

Contact Office of Financial Aid, Grand View College, 1200 Grand View Avenue, Des Moines, IA 50316-1599, 515-263-2800.

GREAT LAKES CHRISTIAN COLLEGE
Lansing, Michigan

About the Institution Independent/religious, coed. Degrees awarded: A, B. Offers 6 undergraduate majors. Total enrollment: 140 (75% state residents). Freshmen: 37.

Undergraduate Expenses (1997–98) Comprehensive fee of $7858 includes tuition ($4440 minimum), mandatory fees ($218), and college room and board ($3200).

Applications *Financial aid deadline (priority):* 6/1. *Financial aid forms:* FAFSA acceptable. State form required for some. *Admission application deadline:* 8/1.

Summary of Aid to Needy Students Federal Work-Study jobs; part-time jobs.

Non-Need Awards *Academic Interests/Achievement Awards:* general academic, religion/biblical studies. *Creative Arts/Performance Awards:* music. *Special Achievements/Activities Awards:* hobbies/interest, religious involvement. *Special Characteristics Awards:* parents of current students, siblings of current students.

Other Money-Saving Options Off-campus living (after freshman year). *Waivers:* full or partial for employees or children of employees.

Contact Office of Financial Aid, Great Lakes Christian College, Lansing, MI 48917-1299, 517-321-0242.

GREEN MOUNTAIN COLLEGE
Poultney, Vermont

About the Institution Independent/religious, coed. Degrees awarded: B. Offers 25 undergraduate majors. Total enrollment: 585. Freshmen: 215.

Undergraduate Expenses (1997–98) Comprehensive fee of $18,460 includes tuition ($14,940), mandatory fees ($200), and college room and board ($3320).

Applications Of all full-time undergraduates enrolled in fall 1996, 92% of those who applied for aid were judged to have need according to Federal Methodology, of whom 100% were aided. *Financial aid deadline (priority):* 2/15. *Financial aid forms:* FAFSA required. State form, institutional form required for some. *Admission application deadline:* rolling.

Summary of Aid to Needy Students *From gift & self-help combined:* Average amount awarded: $12,179. 36 Federal Work-Study jobs (averaging $1300); 150 part-time jobs.

Need-Based Scholarships & Grants Pell, FSEOG, state, private, college/university.

Loans Perkins, PLUS, Stafford, Unsubsidized Stafford, private.

Non-Need Awards *Academic Interests/Achievement Awards:* 222 ($383,526 total): general academic, English. *Creative Arts/Performance Awards:* 31 ($24,500 total): art/fine arts, music, theater/drama. *Special Achievements/Activities Awards:* 377 ($729,282 total): community service, leadership, religious involvement. *Special Characteristics Awards:* children of faculty/staff, local/state students, siblings of current students. *Athletic:* available.

Other Money-Saving Options Accelerated degree, cooperative Army ROTC, cooperative Naval ROTC, cooperative Air Force ROTC, off-campus living (after junior year). *Payment Plan:* installment. *Waivers:* full or partial for employees or children of employees.

Contact Financial Aid Office, Green Mountain College, Poultney, VT 05764-1199, 802-287-8210.

GREENSBORO COLLEGE
Greensboro, North Carolina

About the Institution Independent/religious, coed. Degrees awarded: B. Offers 35 undergraduate majors. Total enrollment: 1,023 (60% state residents). Freshmen: 216.

Undergraduate Expenses (1997–98) Comprehensive fee of $14,690 includes tuition ($9790), mandatory fees ($200), and college room and board ($4700).

Applications 96% of all full-time undergraduates enrolled in fall 1996 applied for aid; of these, 78% were judged to have need according to Federal Methodology, of whom 100% were aided. *Financial aid deadline (priority):* 3/15. *Financial aid forms:* FAFSA, state form required; institutional form acceptable. CSS Financial Aid PROFILE required for some. *Regular admission application deadline:* rolling. Early action deadline: 12/1.

Summary of Aid to Needy Students *From gift & self-help combined:* Average need met: 84%. Average amount awarded: $8491 (52% gift aid, 48% self-help). *Gift aid:* Total: $2,728,474 (55% from college's own funds, 29% from other college-administered sources, 16% from external sources). 235 Federal Work-Study jobs (averaging $886); 103 part-time jobs.

Need-Based Scholarships & Grants Pell, FSEOG, state, private, college/university.

Loans Perkins, PLUS, Stafford, Unsubsidized Stafford, private, college/university long-term loans ($2144 average).

Non-Need Awards In 1996, a total of 245 non-need awards were made. *Academic Interests/Achievement Awards:* 141 ($542,369 total): general academic. *Creative Arts/Performance Awards:* 48 ($137,962 total): art/fine arts, music, theater/drama. *Special Achievements/Activities Awards:* 9 ($24,000 total): community service, leadership. *Special Characteristics Awards:* 47 ($144,265 total): adult students, children and siblings of alumni, children of faculty/staff, international students, relatives of clergy, religious affiliation, siblings of current students, veterans.

Other Money-Saving Options Accelerated degree, cooperative Army ROTC, cooperative Air Force ROTC. *Payment Plan:* installment. *Waivers:* full or partial for employees or children of employees.

Contact Ms. Katharine Bonisolli, Director Student Financial Planning, Greensboro College, 815 West Market Street, Greensboro, NC 27401-1875, 910-272-7102 Ext. 393, fax: 910-378-0154.

GREENVILLE COLLEGE
Greenville, Illinois

About the Institution Independent/religious, coed. Degrees awarded: B. Offers 48 undergraduate majors. Total enrollment: 910 (63% state residents). Freshmen: 248.

Undergraduate Expenses (1997–98) Comprehensive fee of $17,426 includes tuition ($12,576), mandatory fees ($10), and college room and board ($4840). College room only: $2190.

Applications 84% of all full-time undergraduates enrolled in fall 1996 applied for aid; of these, 90% were judged to have need according to Federal Methodology, of whom 100% were aided. *Financial aid deadline (priority):* 8/1. *Financial aid forms:* FAFSA required. *Admission application deadline:* rolling.

Summary of Aid to Needy Students *From gift & self-help combined:* Average need met: 85%. Average amount awarded: $11,740 (62% gift aid, 38% self-help). *Gift aid:* Total: $4,732,424 (56% from college's own funds, 4% from other college-administered sources, 40% from external sources). 324 Federal Work-Study jobs (averaging $1170); part-time jobs.

Need-Based Scholarships & Grants Pell, FSEOG, state, private, college/university.

Loans Perkins, PLUS, Stafford, Unsubsidized Stafford, private, college/university long-term loans ($2200 average).

Non-Need Awards In 1996, a total of 644 non-need awards were made. *Academic Interests/Achievement Awards:* 356 ($1,131,776 total): general academic, biological sciences, engineering/technologies, mathematics, religion/biblical studies. *Creative Arts/Performance Awards:* 55 ($46,350 total): art/fine arts, music, performing arts. *Special Achievements/Activities Awards:* 118 ($168,950 total): leadership. *Special Characteristics Awards:* 115 ($317,949 total): children and siblings of alumni, children of faculty/staff, out-of-state students, relatives of clergy, religious affiliation, siblings of current students.

Other Money-Saving Options Accelerated degree, co-op program. *Payment Plan:* installment. *Waivers:* full or partial for employees or children of employees and senior citizens.

Contact Office of Financial Aid, Greenville College, PO Box 159, Greenville, IL 62246-9913, 618-664-2800.

GRINNELL COLLEGE
Grinnell, Iowa

About the Institution Independent, coed. Degrees awarded: B. Offers 40 undergraduate majors. Total enrollment: 1,314 (14% state residents). Freshmen: 355.

Undergraduate Expenses (1996–97) Comprehensive fee of $22,060 includes tuition ($16,724), mandatory fees ($410), and college room and board ($4926). College room only: $2262.

Applications Of all full-time undergraduates enrolled in fall 1996, 78% of those who applied for aid were judged to have need according to Federal Methodology, of whom 99% were aided. *Financial aid deadline (priority):* 2/1. *Financial aid forms:* FAFSA, institutional form required; CSS Financial Aid PROFILE acceptable. *Regular admission application deadline:* 2/1. Early decision deadline: 11/30.

Summary of Aid to Needy Students *From gift & self-help combined:* Average need met: 100%. Average amount awarded: $14,658 (78% gift aid, 22% self-help). *Gift aid:* Total: $10,745,171 (89% from college's own funds, 2% from other college-administered sources, 9% from external sources). 455 Federal Work-Study jobs (averaging $1000); 285 part-time jobs.

Need-Based Scholarships & Grants Pell, FSEOG, state, private, college/university.

Loans Perkins, PLUS, Stafford, Unsubsidized Stafford, private, college/university short-term loans ($100 average), college/university long-term loans ($1630 average).

Non-Need Awards In 1996, a total of 293 non-need awards were made. *Academic Interests/Achievement Awards:* 293 ($1,204,100 total): general academic.

Other Money-Saving Options Accelerated degree, off-campus living (after sophomore year). *Payment Plans:* tuition prepayment, installment. *Waivers:* full or partial for employees or children of employees.

Contact Ms. Sue Bim, Financial Aid Counselor, Grinnell College, Mears Cottage, Third Floor, Grinnell, IA 50112-0805, 515-269-3250, fax: 515-269-4937.

GROVE CITY COLLEGE
Grove City, Pennsylvania

About the Institution Independent/religious, coed. Degrees awarded: B, M. Offers 39 undergraduate majors. Total enrollment: 2,329. Undergraduates: 2,310 (59% state residents). Freshmen: 626.

Undergraduate Expenses (1997–98) Comprehensive fee of $10,392 includes tuition ($6576 minimum) and college room and board ($3816).

Applications 54% of all full-time undergraduates enrolled in fall 1996 applied for aid; of these, 72% were judged to have need according to

Federal Methodology, of whom 100% were aided. *Financial aid deadline:* 4/15. *Financial aid forms:* institutional form required. *Regular admission application deadline:* 2/15. Early decision deadline: 11/15.

Summary of Aid to Needy Students *From gift & self-help combined:* Average need met: 81%. Average amount awarded: $5120 (47% gift aid, 53% self-help). *Gift aid:* Total: $2,177,991 (49% from college's own funds, 1% from other college-administered sources, 50% from external sources). 875 part-time jobs.

Need-Based Scholarships & Grants State, private, college/university.

Loans State, private, college/university short-term loans ($50 average), college/university long-term loans ($983 average).

Non-Need Awards In 1996, a total of 101 non-need awards were made. *Academic Interests/Achievement Awards:* 46 ($197,091 total): general academic, biological sciences, business, communication, engineering/technologies, foreign languages, physical sciences. *Creative Arts/Performance Awards:* 4 ($3900 total): creative writing, music. *Special Achievements/Activities Awards:* 10 ($21,339 total): leadership. *Special Characteristics Awards:* 41 ($210,090 total): children of faculty/staff, members of minorities.

Another Money-Saving Option *Waivers:* full or partial for employees or children of employees.

Contact Mrs. Anne P. Bowne, Director of Financial Aid, Grove City College, 100 Campus Drive, Grove City, PA 16127-2104, 412-458-2163, fax: 412-458-3368.

GUILFORD COLLEGE
Greensboro, North Carolina

About the Institution Independent/religious, coed. Degrees awarded: B. Offers 43 undergraduate majors. Total enrollment: 1,071 (31% state residents). Freshmen: 276.

Undergraduate Expenses (1997–98) Comprehensive fee of $20,020 includes tuition ($14,180), mandatory fees ($570), and college room and board ($5270). College room only: $2786.

Applications 70% of all full-time undergraduates enrolled in fall 1996 applied for aid; of these, 87% were judged to have need according to Federal Methodology, of whom 100% were aided. *Financial aid deadline:* Applications processed continuously. *Financial aid forms:* FAFSA, CSS Financial Aid PROFILE required. *Regular admission application deadline:* 2/1. Early decision deadline: 12/1.

Summary of Aid to Needy Students *From gift & self-help combined:* Average need met: 95%. Average amount awarded: $13,573 (68% gift aid, 32% self-help). *Gift aid:* Total: $7,019,630 (84% from college's own funds, 9% from other college-administered sources, 7% from external sources). 181 Federal Work-Study jobs (averaging $1350); 401 part-time jobs.

Need-Based Scholarships & Grants Pell, FSEOG, state, private, college/university.

Loans Perkins, PLUS, Stafford, Unsubsidized Stafford, private, college/university short-term loans ($2500 average), college/university long-term loans ($2300 average).

Non-Need Awards *Academic Interests/Achievement Awards:* general academic, biological sciences, education, international studies, mathematics. *Creative Arts/Performance Awards:* art/fine arts, music. *Special Achievements/Activities Awards:* general special achievements/activities, community service. *Special Characteristics Awards:* general special characteristics, children of faculty/staff, ethnic background, members of minorities, religious affiliation.

Other Money-Saving Options Accelerated degree, cooperative Army ROTC, cooperative Air Force ROTC, off-campus living (after junior year). *Payment Plan:* installment. *Waivers:* full or partial for employees or children of employees.

Contact Mr. Anthony E. Gurley, Director of Student Financial Assistance and Planning, Guilford College, 5800 West Friendly Avenue, Greensboro, NC 27410-4173, 910-316-2142 Ext. 142.

GUSTAVUS ADOLPHUS COLLEGE
St. Peter, Minnesota

About the Institution Independent/religious, coed. Degrees awarded: B. Offers 55 undergraduate majors. Total enrollment: 2,376 (69% state residents). Freshmen: 627.

Undergraduate Expenses (1997–98) Comprehensive fee of $20,150 includes tuition ($15,940), mandatory fees ($200), and college room and board ($4010). College room only: $1900.

Applications Of all full-time undergraduates enrolled in fall 1996, 91% of those who applied for aid were judged to have need according to Federal Methodology, of whom 98% were aided. *Financial aid deadline (priority):* 4/15. *Financial aid forms:* FAFSA, institutional form required; CSS Financial Aid PROFILE acceptable. *Regular admission application deadline:* 4/1. Early decision deadline: 11/15.

Summary of Aid to Needy Students *From gift & self-help combined:* Average amount awarded: $12,196 (63% gift aid, 37% self-help). *Gift aid:* Total: $13,101,933 (65% from college's own funds, 5% from other college-administered sources, 30% from external sources). 1,211 Federal Work-Study jobs (averaging $1400); 400 part-time jobs.

Need-Based Scholarships & Grants Pell, FSEOG, state, private, college/university.

Loans Perkins, PLUS, Stafford, Unsubsidized Stafford, Federal Nursing, private, college/university short-term loans ($500 average).

Non-Need Awards In 1996, a total of 431 non-need awards were made. *Academic Interests/Achievement Awards:* 224 ($845,696 total): general academic. *Creative Arts/Performance Awards:* 64 ($148,000 total): music, theater/drama. *Special Achievements/Activities Awards:* 69 ($103,500 total): community service. *Special Characteristics Awards:* 74 ($210,300 total): children and siblings of alumni, ROTC participants.

Other Money-Saving Options Accelerated degree, co-op program, cooperative Army ROTC. *Payment Plans:* tuition prepayment, installment. *Waivers:* full or partial for employees or children of employees and senior citizens.

Contact Mr. Doug Minter, Associate Director of Admission and Financial Aid, Gustavus Adolphus College, 800 West College Avenue, St. Peter, MN 56082-1498, 507-933-7691, fax: 507-933-6270.

GWYNEDD-MERCY COLLEGE
Gwynedd Valley, Pennsylvania

About the Institution Independent/religious, coed. Degrees awarded: A, B, M. Offers 39 undergraduate majors. Total enrollment: 1,721. Undergraduates: 1,521 (95% state residents). Freshmen: 70.

Undergraduate Expenses (1996–97) Comprehensive fee of $17,594 includes tuition ($11,794 minimum) and college room and board ($5800).

Applications Of all full-time undergraduates enrolled in fall 1996, 97% of those who applied for aid were judged to have need according to Federal Methodology, of whom 100% were aided. *Financial aid deadline (priority):* 3/15. *Financial aid forms:* FAFSA, state form, institutional form, federal income tax form required; CSS Financial Aid PROFILE acceptable. *Admission application deadline:* 7/1.

Summary of Aid to Needy Students *From gift & self-help combined:* Average need met: 93%. Average amount awarded: $11,170 (65% gift aid, 35% self-help). *Gift aid:* Total: $3,432,630 (49% from college's own funds, 12% from other college-administered sources, 39% from external sources). 170 Federal Work-Study jobs (averaging $1000); 20 part-time jobs.

Need-Based Scholarships & Grants Pell, FSEOG, state, private, college/university.

Loans Perkins, PLUS, Stafford, Unsubsidized Stafford, Federal Nursing, private, college/university short-term loans ($200 average).

Non-Need Awards In 1996, a total of 306 non-need awards were made. *Academic Interests/Achievement Awards:* 196 ($617,569 total): general academic, biological sciences, business, communication, computer science, education, English, health fields, humanities, mathematics, premedicine, social sciences. *Special Achievements/Activities Awards:* 76 ($51,750 total): general special achievements/activities, community service, leadership. *Special Characteristics Awards:* 34 ($37,471 total): general special characteristics.

Other Money-Saving Options Accelerated degree, co-op program, off-campus living. *Payment Plan:* installment. *Waivers:* full or partial for employees or children of employees.

Contact Sr. Barbara A. Kaufmann, Director, Student Financial Aid, Gwynedd-Mercy College, PO Box 901, Gwynedd Valley, PA 19437-0901, 215-641-5570, fax: 215-542-4604.

HAHNEMANN UNIVERSITY
Philadelphia, Pennsylvania

See Allegheny University of the Health Sciences

HAMILTON COLLEGE
Clinton, New York

About the Institution Independent, coed. Degrees awarded: B. Offers 46 undergraduate majors. Total enrollment: 1,715 (39% state residents). Freshmen: 499.

Undergraduate Expenses (1997–98) Comprehensive fee of $28,350 includes tuition ($22,700) and college room and board ($5650). College room only: $2850.

Applications 50% of all full-time undergraduates enrolled in fall 1996 applied for aid; of these, 89% were judged to have need according to Federal Methodology, of whom 100% were aided. *Financial aid deadline:* 2/1. *Financial aid forms:* FAFSA, CSS Financial Aid PROFILE, institutional form required. *Regular admission application deadline:* 1/15. Early decision deadline: 11/15.

Summary of Aid to Needy Students *From gift & self-help combined:* Average need met: 100%. Average amount awarded: $17,500 (77% gift aid, 23% self-help). *Gift aid:* Total: $11,909,000 (85% from college's own funds, 8% from other college-administered sources, 7% from external sources). 588 Federal Work-Study jobs; part-time jobs.

Need-Based Scholarships & Grants Pell, FSEOG, state, private, college/university.

Loans Perkins, PLUS, Stafford, Unsubsidized Stafford, private, college/university long-term loans ($3500 average).

Non-Need Awards In 1996, a total of 5 non-need awards were made. *Academic Interests/Achievement Awards:* 5 ($50,000 total): general academic.

Other Money-Saving Options Accelerated degree, cooperative Army ROTC, cooperative Air Force ROTC. *Payment Plans:* installment, deferred payment. *Waivers:* full or partial for employees or children of employees and adult students.

Contact Ms. Andrea C. A. Leithner, Associate Director of Admission and Financial Aid, Hamilton College, 198 College Hill Road, Clinton, NY 13323-1218, 315-859-4434, fax: 315-859-4457.

HAMILTON TECHNICAL COLLEGE
Davenport, Iowa

About the Institution Proprietary, coed. Degrees awarded: A, B. Offers 2 undergraduate majors. Total enrollment: 350 (60% state residents). Freshmen: 120.

Undergraduate Expenses (1997–98) Tuition: $5250.

Applications *Financial aid deadline (priority):* 5/1. *Financial aid forms:* FAFSA required. *Admission application deadline:* rolling.

Need-Based Scholarships & Grants Pell.

Loans PLUS, Stafford, Unsubsidized Stafford.

Non-Need Awards Not offered.

Other Money-Saving Options Accelerated degree. *Payment Plan:* guaranteed tuition.

Contact Office of Financial Aid, Hamilton Technical College, 1011 East 53rd Street, Davenport, IA 52807-2653, 319-386-3570.

HAMLINE UNIVERSITY
St. Paul, Minnesota

About the Institution Independent/religious, coed. Degrees awarded: B, M, D, P. Offers 58 undergraduate majors. Total enrollment: 3,335. Undergraduates: 1,655 (72% state residents). Freshmen: 371.

Undergraduate Expenses (1996–97) Comprehensive fee of $18,880 includes tuition ($14,182), mandatory fees ($162), and college room and board ($4536).

Applications 95% of all full-time undergraduates enrolled in fall 1996 applied for aid; of these, 80% were judged to have need according to Federal Methodology, of whom 100% were aided. *Financial aid deadline (priority):* 4/15. *Financial aid forms:* FAFSA required; CSS Financial Aid PROFILE acceptable. State form, institutional form required for some. *Regular admission application deadline:* rolling. Early action deadline: 12/1.

Summary of Aid to Needy Students *From gift & self-help combined:* Average amount awarded: $15,142 (57% gift aid, 43% self-help). *Gift aid:* Total: $9,581,414 (69% from college's own funds, 25% from other college-administered sources, 6% from external sources). 403 Federal Work-Study jobs (averaging $1496); 689 part-time jobs.

Need-Based Scholarships & Grants Pell, FSEOG, state, private, college/university.

Loans Perkins, PLUS, Stafford, Unsubsidized Stafford.

Non-Need Awards In 1996, a total of 145 non-need awards were made. *Academic Interests/Achievement Awards:* 58 ($295,838 total): general academic, biological sciences. *Creative Arts/Performance Awards:* 1 ($2000 total): creative writing. *Special Characteristics Awards:* 86 ($191,570 total): children of faculty/staff, local/state students, out-of-state students, relatives of clergy.

Other Money-Saving Options Co-op program, cooperative Air Force ROTC, off-campus living. *Payment Plan:* installment. *Waivers:* full or partial for employees or children of employees.

Contact Ms. Cheryl Anderson-Dooley, Assistant Director, Admissions/Financial Aid, Hamline University, 1536 Hewitt Avenue, MS C1915, St. Paul, MN 55104-1284, 612-641-2280, fax: 612-641-2458.

HAMPDEN-SYDNEY COLLEGE
Hampden-Sydney, Virginia

About the Institution Independent/religious, men. Degrees awarded: B. Offers 24 undergraduate majors. Total enrollment: 956 (56% state residents). Freshmen: 287.

Undergraduate Expenses (1997–98) Comprehensive fee of $20,631 includes tuition ($14,909), mandatory fees ($165), and college room and board ($5557). College room only: $2321.

Applications 63% of all full-time undergraduates enrolled in fall 1996 applied for aid; of these, 83% were judged to have need according to Federal Methodology, of whom 94% were aided. *Financial aid deadline (priority):* 3/1. *Financial aid forms:* FAFSA, CSS Financial Aid PROFILE required. State form required for some. *Regular admission application deadline:* 3/1. Early decision deadline: 11/15.

Summary of Aid to Needy Students *From gift & self-help combined:* Average need met: 89%. Average amount awarded: $13,120 (56% gift aid, 44% self-help). *Gift aid:* Total: $4,494,984 (78% from college's own funds, 16% from other college-administered sources, 6% from external sources). 268 Federal Work-Study jobs (averaging $1200); 150 part-time jobs.

Need-Based Scholarships & Grants Pell, FSEOG, state, private, college/university.

Loans Perkins, PLUS, Stafford, Unsubsidized Stafford, private, college/university short-term loans ($150 average), college/university long-term loans ($2628 average).

Non-Need Awards *Academic Interests/Achievement Awards:* general academic, religion/biblical studies. *Special Characteristics Awards:* children of faculty/staff, ROTC participants.

Other Money-Saving Options Accelerated degree, cooperative Army ROTC. *Payment Plan:* installment. *Waivers:* full or partial for employees or children of employees.

Contact Mrs. Lynn N. Clements, Financial Aid Counselor, Hampden-Sydney College, PO Box 726, Hampden-Sydney, VA 23943-0667, 804-223-6275, fax: 804-223-6075.

HAMPSHIRE COLLEGE
Amherst, Massachusetts

About the Institution Independent, coed. Degrees awarded: B. Offers 136 undergraduate majors. Total enrollment: 1,068 (18% state residents). Freshmen: 291.

Undergraduate Expenses (1997–98) Comprehensive fee of $30,045 includes tuition ($23,480), mandatory fees ($300), and college room and board ($6265). College room only: $3955.

Applications 78% of all full-time undergraduates enrolled in fall 1996 applied for aid; of these, 83% were judged to have need according to Federal Methodology, of whom 100% were aided. *Financial aid deadline (priority):* 2/1. *Financial aid forms:* FAFSA, CSS Financial Aid PROFILE, institutional form required. *Regular admission application deadline:* 2/1. Early decision deadline: 11/15. Early action deadline: 1/1.

Summary of Aid to Needy Students *From gift & self-help combined:* Average need met: 100%. Average amount awarded: $17,045 (75% gift aid, 25% self-help). *Gift aid:* Total: $8,775,000 (85% from college's own funds, 6% from other college-administered sources, 9% from external sources). 624 Federal Work-Study jobs (averaging $1750); 30 part-time jobs.

Need-Based Scholarships & Grants Pell, FSEOG, state, private, college/university.

Loans Perkins, PLUS, Stafford, Unsubsidized Stafford.

Non-Need Awards In 1996, a total of 98 non-need awards were made. *Academic Interests/Achievement Awards:* 85 ($416,000 total): general academic, international studies, social sciences. *Special Achievements/Activities Awards:* 3 ($5000 total): community service, leadership. *Special Characteristics Awards:* 10 ($214,000 total): children of faculty/staff.

Other Money-Saving Options Cooperative Army ROTC. *Payment Plans:* installment, deferred payment. *Waivers:* full or partial for employees or children of employees.

Contact Ms. Kathleen Methot, Director of Financial Aid, Hampshire College, Amherst, MA 01002, 413-582-5484, fax: 413-582-5587.

HANNIBAL-LAGRANGE COLLEGE
Hannibal, Missouri

About the Institution Independent/religious, coed. Degrees awarded: A, B. Offers 42 undergraduate majors. Total enrollment: 1,050 (80% state residents). Freshmen: 130.

Undergraduate Expenses (1996–97) Comprehensive fee of $9750 includes tuition ($6880), mandatory fees ($260), and college room and board ($2610).

Applications 100% of all full-time undergraduates enrolled in fall 1996 applied for aid; of these, 92% were judged to have need according to Federal Methodology, of whom 100% were aided. *Financial aid deadline (priority):* 7/1. *Financial aid forms:* FAFSA, institutional form required. *Admission application deadline:* rolling.

Summary of Aid to Needy Students *From gift & self-help combined:* Average need met: 81%. *Gift aid:* Total: $2,049,928 (61% from college's own funds, 22% from other college-administered sources, 17% from external sources). 97 Federal Work-Study jobs (averaging $1000); 35 part-time jobs.

Need-Based Scholarships & Grants Pell, FSEOG, state, private, college/university.

Loans Perkins, PLUS, Stafford, Unsubsidized Stafford, private, college/university long-term loans ($2125 average).

Non-Need Awards In 1996, a total of 1,021 non-need awards were made. *Academic Interests/Achievement Awards:* 410 ($659,510 total): general academic. *Creative Arts/Performance Awards:* 72 ($64,356 total): art/fine arts, journalism/publications, music, performing arts, theater/drama. *Special Achievements/Activities Awards:* 428 ($215,132 total): general special achievements/activities, religious involvement. *Special Characteristics Awards:* 34 ($98,944 total): children of educators, children of faculty/staff, public servants, relatives of clergy. *Athletic:* Total: 77 ($213,158); Men: 36 ($108,648); Women: 41 ($104,510).

Other Money-Saving Options Co-op program. *Payment Plan:* deferred payment. *Waivers:* full or partial for employees or children of employees and senior citizens.

Contact Mr. W. Dean Schoonover, Associate Dean for Financial Aid/Dean of Men, Hannibal-LaGrange College, 2800 Palmyra Road, Hannibal, MO 63401-1940, 573-221-3675 Ext. 279, fax: 573-221-6594.

HANOVER COLLEGE
Hanover, Indiana

About the Institution Independent/religious, coed. Degrees awarded: B. Offers 28 undergraduate majors. Total enrollment: 1,051 (64% state residents). Freshmen: 295.

Undergraduate Expenses (1997–98) Comprehensive fee of $14,360 includes tuition ($9750), mandatory fees ($335), and college room and board ($4275). College room only: $2000.

Applications 90% of all full-time undergraduates enrolled in fall 1996 applied for aid; of these, 87% were judged to have need according to Federal Methodology, of whom 100% were aided. *Financial aid deadline (priority):* 2/15. *Financial aid forms:* FAFSA, CSS Financial Aid PROFILE required. *Regular admission application deadline:* 3/1. Early action deadline: 12/1.

Summary of Aid to Needy Students *From gift & self-help combined:* Average need met: 100%. Average amount awarded: $4704 (68% gift aid, 32% self-help). *Gift aid:* Total: $2,682,618 (60% from college's own funds, 26% from other college-administered sources, 14% from external sources). 350 part-time jobs.

Need-Based Scholarships & Grants Pell, state, private, college/university.

Loans PLUS, Stafford, Unsubsidized Stafford, college/university long-term loans ($900 average).

Non-Need Awards In 1996, a total of 415 non-need awards were made. *Academic Interests/Achievement Awards:* 367 ($897,698 total): general academic. *Special Achievements/Activities Awards:* 27 ($110,900 total): leadership. *Special Characteristics Awards:* 21 ($109,050 total): international students, members of minorities.

Other Money-Saving Options Accelerated degree. *Payment Plan:* installment. *Waivers:* full or partial for employees or children of employees.

Contact Ms. Sue A. Allmon, Director of Financial Aid, Hanover College, PO Box 108, Hanover, IN 47243-0108, 812-866-7030, fax: 812-866-7098.

HARDING UNIVERSITY
Searcy, Arkansas

About the Institution Independent/religious, coed. Degrees awarded: A, B, M. Offers 78 undergraduate majors. Total enrollment: 4,081. Undergraduates: 3,540 (31% state residents). Freshmen: 848.

Undergraduate Expenses (1997–98) Comprehensive fee of $11,698 includes tuition ($6528), mandatory fees ($1184), and college room and board ($3986). College room only: $1874.

Applications 93% of all full-time undergraduates enrolled in fall 1996 applied for aid; of these, 66% were judged to have need according to Federal Methodology, of whom 99% were aided. *Financial aid deadline (priority):* 3/1. *Financial aid forms:* FAFSA, institutional form required; CSS Financial Aid PROFILE acceptable. State form required for some. *Admission application deadline:* 7/1.

Summary of Aid to Needy Students *From gift & self-help combined:* Average need met: 88%. Average amount awarded: $9379 (52% gift aid, 48% self-help). *Gift aid:* Total: $6,630,066 (53% from college's own funds, 9% from other college-administered sources, 38% from external sources). 768 Federal Work-Study jobs (averaging $500); 800 part-time jobs.

Need-Based Scholarships & Grants Pell, FSEOG, state, college/university.

Loans Perkins, PLUS, Stafford, Unsubsidized Stafford, Federal Nursing, state, private, college/university short-term loans ($1855 average), college/university long-term loans ($960 average).

Non-Need Awards In 1996, a total of 2,100 non-need awards were made. *Academic Interests/Achievement Awards:* 1,541 ($2,698,598 total): general academic. *Creative Arts/Performance Awards:* 107 ($114,305 total): music. *Special Achievements/Activities Awards:* 170 ($267,456 total): cheerleading/drum major, leadership, religious involvement. *Special Characteristics Awards:* 135 ($802,369 total): children with a deceased or disabled parent, international students, siblings of current students. *Athletic:* Total: 147 ($854,976); Men: 110 ($620,336); Women: 37 ($234,640).

Other Money-Saving Options Accelerated degree, co-op program, cooperative Army ROTC. *Payment Plans:* tuition prepayment, installment. *Waivers:* full or partial for employees or children of employees and senior citizens.

Contact Mr. Zearl D. Watson, Director of Student Financial Services, Harding University, Box 2282, Searcy, AR 72149-0001, 501-279-4257, fax: 501-279-4129.

HARDIN-SIMMONS UNIVERSITY
Abilene, Texas

About the Institution Independent/religious, coed. Degrees awarded: B, M, P. Offers 59 undergraduate majors. Total enrollment: 2,279. Undergraduates: 1,931 (92% state residents). Freshmen: 417.

Undergraduate Expenses (1997–98) Comprehensive fee of $11,776 includes tuition ($7750), mandatory fees ($630), and college room and board ($3396). College room only: $1610.

Applications 95% of all full-time undergraduates enrolled in fall 1996 applied for aid; of these, 60% were judged to have need according to Federal Methodology, of whom 99% were aided. *Financial aid deadline (priority):* 3/15. *Financial aid forms:* FAFSA, institutional form required; CSS Financial Aid PROFILE acceptable. State form required for some. *Admission application deadline:* rolling.

Summary of Aid to Needy Students *From gift & self-help combined:* Average need met: 77%. Average amount awarded: $10,015 (50% gift aid, 50% self-help). *Gift aid:* Total: $4,988,773 (33% from college's own funds, 40% from other college-administered sources, 27% from external sources). 281 Federal Work-Study jobs (averaging $1085); 432 part-time jobs.

Need-Based Scholarships & Grants Pell, FSEOG, private, college/university.

Loans Perkins, PLUS, Stafford, Unsubsidized Stafford.

Non-Need Awards In 1996, a total of 1,791 non-need awards were made. *Academic Interests/Achievement Awards:* 1,228 ($1,836,277 total): general academic, biological sciences, business, education, humanities, mathematics, religion/biblical studies. *Creative Arts/Performance Awards:* 52 ($32,783 total): art/fine arts, music, theater/drama. *Special Achievements/Activities Awards:* 22 ($6196 total): general special achievements/activities, hobbies/interest, leadership. *Special Characteristics Awards:* 489 ($636,547 total): general special characteristics, children of faculty/staff, local/state students, relatives of clergy, religious affiliation.

Other Money-Saving Options Accelerated degree, off-campus living (after freshman year). *Payment Plans:* guaranteed tuition, installment, deferred payment. *Waivers:* full or partial for employees or children of employees.

Contact Ms. Faye Dodson, Enrollment Services Program Specialist, Hardin-Simmons University, PO Box 16050, Abilene, TX 79698-6050, 915-670-1331, fax: 915-670-2115.

HARID CONSERVATORY
Boca Raton, Florida

About the Institution Independent, coed. Degrees awarded: B. Offers 1 undergraduate major. Total enrollment: 50 (6% state residents). Freshmen: 14.

Undergraduate Expenses (1997–98) Tuition: $0.

Applications *Financial aid deadline:* continuous. *Financial aid forms:* institutional form required. *Admission application deadline:* 3/31.

Summary of Aid to Needy Students *From gift & self-help combined:* Average need met: 100%. Part-time jobs.

Need-Based Scholarships & Grants Private.

Non-Need Awards Not offered.

Contact Admissions Office, Harid Conservatory, 2285 Potomac Road, Boca Raton, FL 33431, 561-997-2677.

HARRINGTON INSTITUTE OF INTERIOR DESIGN
Chicago, Illinois

About the Institution Proprietary, coed. Degrees awarded: A, B. Offers 1 undergraduate major. Total enrollment: 330 (91% state residents). Freshmen: 123.

Undergraduate Expenses (1996–97) Tuition: $9920. Mandatory fees: $29.

Applications 58% of all full-time undergraduates enrolled in fall 1996 applied for aid; of these, 96% were judged to have need according to Federal Methodology, of whom 100% were aided. *Financial aid deadline:* continuous. *Financial aid forms:* FAFSA, Stafford Student Loan form required. *Admission application deadline:* rolling.

Summary of Aid to Needy Students *From gift & self-help combined:* Average need met: 80%. Average amount awarded: $3412 (23% gift aid, 77% self-help). *Gift aid:* Total: $75,945 (100% from external sources).

Need-Based Scholarships & Grants Pell.

Loans PLUS, Stafford, Unsubsidized Stafford, EXCEL Loans.

Non-Need Awards Not offered.

Another Money-Saving Option *Payment Plan:* installment.

Contact Ms. Barbara Lerman, Director of Financial Aid, Harrington Institute of Interior Design, 410 South Michigan Avenue, Chicago, IL 60605-1496, 312-939-4975.

HARTWICK COLLEGE
Oneonta, New York

About the Institution Independent, coed. Degrees awarded: B. Offers 32 undergraduate majors. Total enrollment: 1,494 (59% state residents). Freshmen: 480.

Undergraduate Expenses (1997–98) Comprehensive fee of $28,085 includes tuition ($21,910), mandatory fees ($325), and college room and board ($5850). College room only: $2930.

Applications Of all full-time undergraduates enrolled in fall 1996, 98% of those who applied for aid were judged to have need according to Federal Methodology, of whom 100% were aided. *Financial aid deadline:* 2/1. *Financial aid forms:* FAFSA, CSS Financial Aid PROFILE, institutional form required. State form required for some. *Regular admission application deadline:* 2/15. Early decision deadline: 12/1.

Summary of Aid to Needy Students *From gift & self-help combined:* Average need met: 96%. Average amount awarded: $14,200 (64% gift aid, 36% self-help). *Gift aid:* Total: $13,801,700 (86% from college's own funds, 10% from other college-administered sources, 4% from external sources). 765 Federal Work-Study jobs (averaging $1100); 625 part-time jobs.

Need-Based Scholarships & Grants Pell, FSEOG, state, private, college/university.

Loans Perkins, PLUS, Stafford, Unsubsidized Stafford, Primary Care, college/university long-term loans ($3760 average).

Non-Need Awards In 1996, a total of 406 non-need awards were made. *Academic Interests/Achievement Awards:* 237 ($1,600,000 total): general academic. *Creative Arts/Performance Awards:* 14 ($39,200 total): music. *Special Achievements/Activities Awards:* 89 ($249,000 total): general special achievements/activities. *Special Characteristics Awards:* 54 ($361,179 total): children of faculty/staff, siblings of current students. *Athletic:* Total: 12 ($217,072); Men: 12 ($217,072); Women: 0.

Other Money-Saving Options Accelerated degree, off-campus living (after junior year). *Payment Plan:* installment. *Waivers:* full or partial for employees or children of employees.

Contact Financial Aid Department, Hartwick College, Oneonta, NY 13820-4020, 607-431-4130.

HARVARD UNIVERSITY
Cambridge, Massachusetts

About the Institution Independent, coed. Degrees awarded: B, M, D, P. Offers 149 undergraduate majors. Total enrollment: 18,310. Undergraduates: 6,634 (14% state residents). Freshmen: 1,617.

Undergraduate Expenses (1997–98) Comprehensive fee of $30,080 includes tuition ($20,600), mandatory fees ($2202), and college room and board ($7278). College room only: $3808.

Applications *Financial aid deadline (priority):* 2/01. *Financial aid forms:* FAFSA, CSS Financial Aid PROFILE required. *Regular admission application deadline:* 1/1. Early action deadline: 11/1.

Summary of Aid to Needy Students *From gift & self-help combined:* Average need met: 100%. Average amount awarded: $20,300 (68% gift aid, 32% self-help). *Gift aid:* Total: $46,190,000 (84% from college's own funds, 3% from other college-administered sources, 13% from external sources). 1,675 Federal Work-Study jobs (averaging $1840); 3,000 part-time jobs.

Need-Based Scholarships & Grants Pell, FSEOG, state, private, college/university.

Loans Perkins, PLUS, Stafford, Unsubsidized Stafford, college/university long-term loans ($3000 average).

Non-Need Awards Not offered.

Other Money-Saving Options Accelerated degree, cooperative Army ROTC, cooperative Naval ROTC, cooperative Air Force ROTC, off-campus living (after freshman year). *Payment Plans:* tuition prepayment, installment.

Contact Financial Aid Office, Harvard University, 312 Byerly Hall, 8 Garden Street, Cambridge, MA 02138, 617-495-1581, fax: 617-496-0256.

HARVEY MUDD COLLEGE
Claremont, California

About the Institution Independent, coed. Degrees awarded: B, M. Offers 6 undergraduate majors. Total enrollment: 648. Undergraduates: 643 (39% state residents). Freshmen: 177.

Undergraduate Expenses (1997–98) Comprehensive fee of $27,846 includes tuition ($19,860), mandatory fees ($465), and college room and board ($7521). College room only: $3750.

Applications 66% of all full-time undergraduates enrolled in fall 1996 applied for aid; of these, 84% were judged to have need according to Federal Methodology, of whom 100% were aided. *Financial aid deadline (priority):* 2/1. *Financial aid forms:* FAFSA, CSS Financial Aid PROFILE, state form, institutional form required. *Regular admission application deadline:* 1/15. Early decision deadline: 11/15.

Summary of Aid to Needy Students *From gift & self-help combined:* Average need met: 100%. Average amount awarded: $16,421 (70% gift aid, 30% self-help). *Gift aid:* Total: $4,178,297 (70% from college's own funds, 12% from other college-administered sources, 18% from external sources). 323 Federal Work-Study jobs (averaging $1128); 186 part-time jobs.

Need-Based Scholarships & Grants College/university.

Loans College/university short-term loans ($300 average), college/university long-term loans ($2500 average).

Non-Need Awards *Academic Interests/Achievement Awards:* general academic.

Other Money-Saving Options Air Force ROTC, cooperative Army ROTC, off-campus living (after freshman year). *Payment Plan:* installment. *Waivers:* full or partial for employees or children of employees.

Contact Office of Financial Aid, Harvey Mudd College, 301 East 12th Street, Claremont, CA 91711-5994, 909-621-8055.

HASTINGS COLLEGE
Hastings, Nebraska

About the Institution Independent/religious, coed. Degrees awarded: B, M. Offers 57 undergraduate majors. Total enrollment: 1,107. Undergraduates: 1,076 (67% state residents). Freshmen: 270.

Undergraduate Expenses (1997–98) Comprehensive fee of $15,126 includes tuition ($10,908), mandatory fees ($460), and college room and board ($3758). College room only: $1584.

Applications *Financial aid deadline (priority):* 5/1. *Financial aid forms:* FAFSA, institutional form required; CSS Financial Aid PROFILE acceptable. *Admission application deadline:* 7/15.

Summary of Aid to Needy Students *From gift & self-help combined:* Average need met: 88%. Average amount awarded: $8978 (61% gift aid, 39% self-help). *Gift aid:* Total: $4,123,978 (78% from college's own funds, 7% from other college-administered sources, 15% from external sources). Federal Work-Study jobs (averaging $600); part-time jobs.

Need-Based Scholarships & Grants Pell, FSEOG, state, private, college/university.

Loans Perkins, PLUS, Stafford, Unsubsidized Stafford, private, college/university short-term loans ($150 average), college/university long-term loans ($1200 average).

Non-Need Awards In 1996, a total of 1,472 non-need awards were made. *Academic Interests/Achievement Awards:* 732 ($1,903,542 total): general academic. *Creative Arts/Performance Awards:* 220 ($229,775 total): art/fine arts, debating, music, performing arts, theater/drama. *Special Characteristics Awards:* 186 ($206,919 total): adult students, children of educators, children of faculty/staff, relatives of clergy, religious affiliation, siblings of current students. *Athletic:* Total: 334 ($982,757).

Other Money-Saving Options Accelerated degree, co-op program, off-campus living (after sophomore year). *Payment Plans:* installment, deferred payment. *Waivers:* full or partial for employees or children of employees and adult students.

Contact Office of Financial Aid, Hastings College, Hastings, NE 68902-0269, 402-463-2402.

HAVERFORD COLLEGE
Haverford, Pennsylvania

About the Institution Independent, coed. Degrees awarded: B. Offers 43 undergraduate majors. Total enrollment: 1,137 (14% state residents). Freshmen: 313.

Undergraduate Expenses (1997–98) Comprehensive fee of $29,460 includes tuition ($21,534), mandatory fees ($206), and college room and board ($7720).

Applications 48% of all full-time undergraduates enrolled in fall 1996 applied for aid; of these, 86% were judged to have need according to Federal Methodology, of whom 100% were aided. *Financial aid deadline:* 1/31. *Financial aid forms:* FAFSA, CSS Financial Aid PROFILE, state form required for some. *Regular admission application deadline:* 1/15. Early decision deadline: 11/15.

Summary of Aid to Needy Students *From gift & self-help combined:* Average need met: 100%. Average amount awarded: $17,443 (75% gift aid, 25% self-help). *Gift aid:* Total: $6,211,952 (89% from college's own funds, 2% from other college-administered sources, 9% from external sources). Federal Work-Study jobs; part-time jobs.

Need-Based Scholarships & Grants Pell, FSEOG, state, private, college/university.

Loans Perkins, PLUS, Stafford, Unsubsidized Stafford, private.

Non-Need Awards Not offered.

Other Money-Saving Options Accelerated degree, off-campus living (after freshman year). *Payment Plan:* installment. *Waivers:* full or partial for employees or children of employees.

Contact Office of Financial Aid, Haverford College, Haverford, PA 19041-1392, 610-896-1000.

HAWAII PACIFIC UNIVERSITY
Honolulu, Hawaii

About the Institution Independent, coed. Degrees awarded: A, B, M. Offers 49 undergraduate majors. Total enrollment: 8,270. Undergraduates: 7,158 (39% state residents). Freshmen: 816.

Undergraduate Expenses (1997–98) Comprehensive fee of $15,300 includes tuition ($7500) and college room and board ($7800).

Applications 27% of all full-time undergraduates enrolled in fall 1996 applied for aid; of these, 99% were judged to have need according to Federal Methodology, of whom 100% were aided. *Financial aid deadline (priority):* 3/1. *Financial aid forms:* FAFSA, institutional form required. *Admission application deadline:* rolling.

Summary of Aid to Needy Students *From gift & self-help combined:* Average need met: 87%. Average amount awarded: $10,401 (46% gift aid, 54% self-help). *Gift aid:* Total: $6,886,168 (9% from college's own funds, 48% from other college-administered sources, 43% from external sources). 110 Federal Work-Study jobs (averaging $2831); 207 part-time jobs.

Need-Based Scholarships & Grants Pell, FSEOG, state, private, college/university.

Loans Perkins, PLUS, Stafford, Unsubsidized Stafford, Federal Nursing.

Non-Need Awards In 1996, a total of 402 non-need awards were made. *Academic Interests/Achievement Awards:* 33 ($145,700 total): general academic. *Creative Arts/Performance Awards:* 55 ($348,692 total): dance, music. *Special Achievements/Activities Awards:* 94 ($448,025 total): general special achievements/activities, cheerleading/drum major, hobbies/interest, Junior Miss, memberships. *Special Characteristics Awards:* 69 ($172,247 total): children of faculty/staff, relatives of clergy, religious affiliation, ROTC participants. *Athletic:* Total: 151 ($826,940); Men: 79 ($433,252); Women: 72 ($393,688).

Other Money-Saving Options Accelerated degree, co-op program, cooperative Army ROTC, cooperative Air Force ROTC, off-campus living. *Payment Plan:* installment. *Waivers:* full or partial for employees or children of employees.

Contact Ms. Donna Lubong, Director of Financial Aid, Hawaii Pacific University, 1164 Bishop Street, Suite 201, Honolulu, HI 96813-2785, 808-544-0253, fax: 808-544-1136.

HEBREW COLLEGE
Brookline, Massachusetts

About the Institution Independent/religious, coed. Degrees awarded: B, M. Offers 2 undergraduate majors.

Undergraduate Expenses (1997–98) Tuition: $10,500. Mandatory fees: $90.

Applications *Financial aid deadline (priority):* 6/1. *Financial aid forms:* FAFSA, institutional form required. *Regular admission application deadline:* rolling. Early decision deadline: 8/1.

Need-Based Scholarships & Grants College/university.

Loans Stafford, Unsubsidized Stafford.

Non-Need Awards *Academic Interests/Achievement Awards:* education.

Other Money-Saving Options *Payment Plan:* installment. *Waivers:* full or partial for employees or children of employees.

Contact Ms. Norma Frankel, Registrar, Hebrew College, 43 Hawes Street, Brookline, MA 02146-5495, 617-278-4944, fax: 617-264-9264.

HEBREW THEOLOGICAL COLLEGE
Skokie, Illinois

About the Institution Independent/religious, men. Degrees awarded: B. Offers 5 undergraduate majors. Total enrollment: 135. Freshmen: 44.

Undergraduate Expenses (1997–98) Comprehensive fee of $12,010 includes tuition ($6200), mandatory fees ($300), and college room and board ($5510 minimum). College room only: $2500 (minimum).

Applications *Financial aid deadline (priority):* 5/15. *Financial aid forms:* FAFSA, institutional form required. *Admission application deadline:* rolling.

Summary of Aid to Needy Students Federal Work-Study jobs; part-time jobs.

Need-Based Scholarships & Grants Pell, state.

Non-Need Awards Not offered.

Other Money-Saving Options Accelerated degree, off-campus living. *Payment Plan:* installment.

Contact Ms. Rhoda Morris, Financial Aid Administrator, Hebrew Theological College, 7135 Carpenter Road, Skokie, IL 60077-3263, 847-982-2500, fax: 847-674-6381.

HEIDELBERG COLLEGE
Tiffin, Ohio

About the Institution Independent/religious, coed. Degrees awarded: B, M. Offers 44 undergraduate majors. Total enrollment: 1,386. Undergraduates: 1,149 (88% state residents). Freshmen: 312.

Undergraduate Expenses (1997–98 estimated) Comprehensive fee of $20,579 includes tuition ($15,594) and college room and board ($4985). College room only: $2266.

Applications 92% of all full-time undergraduates enrolled in fall 1996 applied for aid; of these, 94% were judged to have need according to Federal Methodology, of whom 100% were aided. *Financial aid deadline (priority):* 3/1. *Financial aid forms:* FAFSA required. *Regular admission application deadline:* 8/1. Early action deadline: 9/1.

Summary of Aid to Needy Students *From gift & self-help combined:* Average amount awarded: $13,804 (66% gift aid, 34% self-help). *Gift aid:* Total: $6,969,120 (78% from college's own funds, 16% from other college-administered sources, 6% from external sources). 408 Federal Work-Study jobs (averaging $937); 176 part-time jobs.

Need-Based Scholarships & Grants Pell, FSEOG, state, private, college/university.

Loans Perkins, PLUS, Stafford, Unsubsidized Stafford, state, private.

Non-Need Awards In 1996, a total of 682 non-need awards were made. *Academic Interests/Achievement Awards:* 341 ($1,077,300 total): general academic, mathematics, physical sciences. *Creative Arts/Performance Awards:* 72 ($122,250 total): music. *Special Achievements/Activities Awards:* 127 ($125,500 total): leadership. *Special Characteristics Awards:* 142 ($106,065 total): local/state students, religious affiliation.

Other Money-Saving Options Accelerated degree. *Payment Plans:* installment, deferred payment. *Waivers:* full or partial for employees or children of employees.

Contact Ms. Juli L. Weininger, Director of Financial Aid, Heidelberg College, 310 East Market Street, Tiffin, OH 44883-2462, 419-448-2293, fax: 419-448-2124.

HELLENIC COLLEGE
Brookline, Massachusetts

About the Institution Independent/religious, coed. Degrees awarded: B. Offers 5 undergraduate majors. Total enrollment: 64 (12% state residents). Freshmen: 16.

Undergraduate Expenses (1997–98) Comprehensive fee of $13,800 includes tuition ($7600), mandatory fees ($300), and college room and board ($5900).

Applications Of all full-time undergraduates enrolled in fall 1996, 89% of those who applied for aid were judged to have need according to Federal Methodology, of whom 100% were aided. *Financial aid deadline (priority):* 5/1. *Financial aid forms:* FAFSA, institutional form required. *Admission application deadline:* rolling.

Summary of Aid to Needy Students *From gift & self-help combined:* Average need met: 75%. *Gift aid:* Total: $86,580. Federal Work-Study jobs; 15 part-time jobs.

Need-Based Scholarships & Grants Pell, FSEOG, state, college/university.

Loans PLUS, Stafford, Unsubsidized Stafford.

Non-Need Awards *Academic Interests/Achievement Awards:* general academic.

Other Money-Saving Options *Waivers:* full or partial for children of alumni and employees or children of employees.

Contact Ms. Alexandra McInnis, Financial Aid Officer, Hellenic College, 50 Goddard Avenue, Brookline, MA 02146-7496, 617-731-3500.

HENDERSON STATE UNIVERSITY
Arkadelphia, Arkansas

About the Institution State-supported, coed. Degrees awarded: A, B, M. Offers 47 undergraduate majors. Total enrollment: 3,527. Undergraduates: 3,252 (94% state residents). Freshmen: 588.

Undergraduate Expenses (1997–98) State resident tuition: $1980. Nonresident tuition: $3960. Mandatory fees: $186. College room and board: $2816 (minimum).

Applications 55% of all full-time undergraduates enrolled in fall 1996 applied for aid; of these, 97% were judged to have need according to Federal Methodology, of whom 76% were aided. *Financial aid deadline (priority):* 3/15. *Financial aid forms:* FAFSA, institutional form required. *Admission application deadline:* rolling.

Summary of Aid to Needy Students *From gift & self-help combined:* Average need met: 84%. Average amount awarded: $3391 (53% gift aid, 47% self-help). *Gift aid:* Total: $2,138,424 (26% from college's own funds, 19% from other college-administered sources, 55% from external sources). 472 Federal Work-Study jobs (averaging $1127); 93 part-time jobs.

Need-Based Scholarships & Grants Pell, FSEOG, state, private, college/university.

Loans Perkins, PLUS, Stafford, Unsubsidized Stafford, private, college/university short-term loans ($300 average).

Non-Need Awards In 1996, a total of 896 non-need awards were made. *Academic Interests/Achievement Awards:* 364 ($529,350 total): general academic. *Creative Arts/Performance Awards:* 180 ($173,798 total): cinema/film/broadcasting, debating, journalism/publications, music, theater/drama. *Special Characteristics Awards:* 200 ($217,003 total): children of faculty/staff, international students, out-of-state students. *Athletic:* Total: 152 ($364,837); Men: 101 ($231,040); Women: 51 ($133,797).

Other Money-Saving Options Accelerated degree, off-campus living (after freshman year). *Waivers:* full or partial for employees or children of employees and senior citizens.

Contact Ms. Jo Holland, Director of Financial Aid, Henderson State University, Box 7812, Arkadelphia, AR 71999-0001, 870-230-5094, fax: 870-230-5144.

HENDRIX COLLEGE
Conway, Arkansas

About the Institution Independent/religious, coed. Degrees awarded: B. Offers 31 undergraduate majors. Total enrollment: 982 (73% state residents). Freshmen: 307.

Undergraduate Expenses (1997–98) Comprehensive fee of $14,438 includes tuition ($10,280), mandatory fees ($155), and college room and board ($4003).

Applications *Financial aid deadline (priority):* 3/1. *Financial aid forms:* FAFSA, institutional form required; CSS Financial Aid PROFILE acceptable. State form required for some. *Admission application deadline:* rolling.

Summary of Aid to Needy Students Federal Work-Study jobs; part-time jobs.

Non-Need Awards *Academic Interests/Achievement Awards:* general academic. *Creative Arts/Performance Awards:* art/fine arts, music, theater/drama. *Special Achievements/Activities Awards:* leadership, religious involvement. *Special Characteristics Awards:* children of faculty/staff, international students, members of minorities, previous college experience, relatives of clergy.

Other Money-Saving Options Cooperative Army ROTC. *Payment Plan:* installment. *Waivers:* full or partial for employees or children of employees.

Contact Office of Financial Aid, Hendrix College, 1601 Harkrider Street, Conway, AR 72032-3080, 501-329-6811.

HENRY COGSWELL COLLEGE
Everett, Washington

About the Institution Independent, coed. Degrees awarded: B. Offers 6 undergraduate majors. Total enrollment: 170 (100% state residents). Freshmen: 2.

Undergraduate Expenses (1997–98) Tuition: $9360.

Applications 11% of all full-time undergraduates enrolled in fall 1996 applied for aid; of these,100% were judged to have need according to Federal Methodology, of whom 100% were aided. *Financial aid deadline (priority):* 7/31. *Financial aid forms:* FAFSA, institutional form required. *Admission application deadline:* 5/1.

Summary of Aid to Needy Students *From gift & self-help combined:* Average need met: 100%. *Gift aid:* Total: $14,490 (48% from college's own funds, 52% from external sources). 1 part-time job.

Need-Based Scholarships & Grants Pell, FSEOG.

Loans PLUS, Stafford, Unsubsidized Stafford.

Non-Need Awards In 1996, a total of 16 non-need awards were made. *Academic Interests/Achievement Awards:* 15 ($43,000 total): general academic. *Special Characteristics Awards:* 1 ($12,470 total): international students.

Other Money-Saving Options *Payment Plans:* installment, deferred payment. *Waivers:* full or partial for employees or children of employees.

Contact Ms. Caroline C. Moye, Financial Aid Administrator, Henry Cogswell College, Everett, WA 98201, 206-258-3351.

HERITAGE BIBLE COLLEGE
Dunn, North Carolina

About the Institution Independent/religious, coed. Degrees awarded: A, B. Offers 1 undergraduate major. Total enrollment: 93 (1% state residents). Freshmen: 30.

Undergraduate Expenses (1997–98) Comprehensive fee of $4885 includes tuition ($2850) and college room and board ($2035). College room only: $1320.

Applications 77% of all full-time undergraduates enrolled in fall 1996 applied for aid; of these, 85% were judged to have need according to Federal Methodology, of whom 100% were aided. *Financial aid deadline (priority):* 5/30. *Financial aid forms:* FAFSA, institutional form, verification documents required.

Summary of Aid to Needy Students *From gift & self-help combined:* Average need met: 68%. *Gift aid:* Total: $87,645 (3% from college's own funds, 10% from other college-administered sources, 87% from external sources). 11 Federal Work-Study jobs (averaging $503); part-time jobs.

Need-Based Scholarships & Grants Pell, FSEOG, private, college/university.

Loans PLUS, Stafford, Unsubsidized Stafford.

Non-Need Awards Not offered.

Other Money-Saving Options Off-campus living (after freshman year). *Payment Plans:* installment, deferred payment.

Contact Ms. Lori Filban, Director of Financial Aid, Heritage Bible College, Box 1628, Dunn, NC 28335, 910-892-4268, fax: 910-891-1660.

HERITAGE COLLEGE
Toppenish, Washington

About the Institution Independent, coed. Degrees awarded: A, B, M. Offers 26 undergraduate majors. Total enrollment: 1,187. Undergraduates: 644. Freshmen: 44.

Undergraduate Expenses (1996–97) Tuition: $6450. Mandatory fees: $20.

Applications 93% of all full-time undergraduates enrolled in fall 1996 applied for aid; of these, 97% were judged to have need according to Federal Methodology, of whom 97% were aided. *Financial aid deadline (priority):* 2/10. *Financial aid forms:* FAFSA, institutional form required; CSS Financial Aid PROFILE acceptable. *Admission application deadline:* rolling.

Summary of Aid to Needy Students *From gift & self-help combined:* Average need met: 80%. *Gift aid:* Total: $1,319,036 (13% from college's own funds, 35% from other college-administered sources, 52% from external sources). Federal Work-Study jobs.

Need-Based Scholarships & Grants Pell, FSEOG, state, private, college/university.

Loans Perkins, PLUS, Stafford, Unsubsidized Stafford, private, college/university short-term loans ($100 average).

Non-Need Awards *Academic Interests/Achievement Awards:* general academic, biological sciences, business, communication, computer science, education, physical sciences, social sciences.

Other Money-Saving Options Co-op program. *Payment Plans:* installment, deferred payment. *Waivers:* full or partial for employees or children of employees and senior citizens.

Contact Ms. Becky Cochran, Coordinator of Student Grants, Heritage College, 3240 Fort Road, Toppenish, WA 98948-9599, 509-865-2244, fax: 509-865-4469.

HIGH POINT UNIVERSITY
High Point, North Carolina

About the Institution Independent/religious, coed. Degrees awarded: B, M. Offers 44 undergraduate majors. Total enrollment: 2,596. Undergraduates: 2,489 (66% state residents). Freshmen: 393.

Undergraduate Expenses (1997–98) Comprehensive fee of $15,480 includes tuition ($9390), mandatory fees ($1030), and college room and board ($5060). College room only: $2050.

Applications Of all full-time undergraduates enrolled in fall 1996, 95% of those who applied for aid were judged to have need according to Federal Methodology, of whom 100% were aided. *Financial aid deadline (priority):* 3/1. *Financial aid forms:* FAFSA, state form required; CSS Financial Aid PROFILE acceptable. *Admission application deadline:* rolling.

Summary of Aid to Needy Students *From gift & self-help combined:* Average need met: 85%. Average amount awarded: $10,250 (58% gift aid, 42% self-help). *Gift aid:* Total: $6,422,735 (53% from college's own funds, 37% from other college-administered sources, 10% from external sources). 95 Federal Work-Study jobs (averaging $725); 290 part-time jobs.

Need-Based Scholarships & Grants Pell, FSEOG, state, private, college/university.

Loans Perkins, PLUS, Stafford, Unsubsidized Stafford, private.

Non-Need Awards *Academic Interests/Achievement Awards:* 187 ($662,300 total): general academic, biological sciences, business, education, English, foreign languages, humanities, international studies, mathematics, physical sciences, premedicine, religion/biblical studies. *Special Characteristics Awards:* relatives of clergy. *Athletic:* available.

Other Money-Saving Options Accelerated degree, co-op program, cooperative Army ROTC, cooperative Air Force ROTC. *Waivers:* full or partial for employees or children of employees.

Contact Office of Financial Aid, High Point University, Box 3352, University Station, Montlieu Avenue, High Point, NC 27265, 910-841-9124.

HILBERT COLLEGE
Hamburg, New York

About the Institution Independent, coed. Degrees awarded: A, B. Offers 11 undergraduate majors. Total enrollment: 807 (99% state residents). Freshmen: 123.

Undergraduate Expenses (1997–98) Comprehensive fee of $13,950 includes tuition ($8950), mandatory fees ($550), and college room and board ($4450). College room only: $1750.

Applications 96% of all full-time undergraduates enrolled in fall 1996 applied for aid; of these, 91% were judged to have need according to Federal Methodology, of whom 100% were aided. *Financial aid deadline (priority):* 4/28. *Financial aid forms:* FAFSA, state form required; CSS Financial Aid PROFILE acceptable. Institutional form, nontaxable income verification required for some. *Admission application deadline:* 9/1.

Summary of Aid to Needy Students *From gift & self-help combined:* Average need met: 64%. Average amount awarded: $2877 (39% gift aid, 61% self-help). *Gift aid:* Total: $478,647 (40% from college's own funds, 11% from other college-administered sources, 49% from external sources). 37 Federal Work-Study jobs (averaging $1200); part-time jobs.

Need-Based Scholarships & Grants Pell, FSEOG, state, private, college/university.

Loans Perkins, PLUS, Stafford, Unsubsidized Stafford, private.

Non-Need Awards In 1996, a total of 94 non-need awards were made. *Academic Interests/Achievement Awards:* 70 ($52,500 total): general academic. *Special Achievements/Activities Awards:* 8 ($6000 total): leadership. *Special Characteristics Awards:* 16 ($16,300 total): children of educators, members of minorities.

Other Money-Saving Options Co-op program, off-campus living. *Payment Plans:* installment, deferred payment. *Waivers:* full or partial for employees or children of employees and senior citizens.

Contact Ms. Kim M. Downs, Director of Financial Aid, Hilbert College, Hamburg, NY 14075-1597, 716-649-7900 Ext. 208, fax: 716-649-0702.

HILLSDALE COLLEGE
Hillsdale, Michigan

About the Institution Independent, coed. Degrees awarded: B. Offers 38 undergraduate majors. Total enrollment: 1,163 (52% state residents). Freshmen: 359.

Undergraduate Expenses (1997–98) Comprehensive fee of $18,110 includes tuition ($12,470), mandatory fees ($210), and college room and board ($5430). College room only: $2430.

Applications 87% of all full-time undergraduates enrolled in fall 1996 applied for aid; of these, 94% were judged to have need according to Federal Methodology, of whom 100% were aided. *Financial aid deadline (priority):* 3/15. *Financial aid forms:* CSS Financial Aid PROFILE required. FAFSA required for some. *Admission application deadline:* rolling.

Summary of Aid to Needy Students *From gift & self-help combined:* Average need met: 85%. Average amount awarded: $10,276 (78% gift aid, 22% self-help). *Gift aid:* Total: $7,524,090 (90% from college's own funds, 10% from other college-administered sources). 625 part-time jobs.

Need-Based Scholarships & Grants State, private, college/university.

Loans Private, college/university short-term loans ($1000 average), college/university long-term loans ($3500 average).

Non-Need Awards In 1996, a total of 1,125 non-need awards were made. *Academic Interests/Achievement Awards:* 645 ($1,327,254 total): general academic, biological sciences, business, education, English, foreign languages, health fields, humanities, international studies, mathematics, physical sciences, premedicine, religion/biblical studies. *Creative Arts/Performance Awards:* 42 ($69,178 total): art/fine arts, music. *Special Achievements/Activities Awards:* 193 ($811,716 total): general special achievements/activities, community service, leadership. *Special Characteristics Awards:* 53 ($393,406 total): children of faculty/staff, international students. *Athletic:* Total: 192 ($1,307,472); Men: 114 ($878,334); Women: 78 ($429,138).

Other Money-Saving Options Accelerated degree, cooperative Army ROTC, cooperative Naval ROTC, cooperative Air Force ROTC, off-campus living (after sophomore year). *Waivers:* full or partial for employees or children of employees.

Contact Mrs. Connie Bricker, Director of Student Financial Aid, Hillsdale College, 33 East College Street, Hillsdale, MI 49242-1298, 517-437-7341, fax: 517-437-0190.

HIRAM COLLEGE
Hiram, Ohio

About the Institution Independent/religious, coed. Degrees awarded: B. Offers 35 undergraduate majors. Total enrollment: 800 (77% state residents). Freshmen: 234.

Undergraduate Expenses (1997–98) Comprehensive fee of $21,606 includes tuition ($16,224), mandatory fees ($290), and college room and board ($5092). College room only: $2300.

Applications 97% of all full-time undergraduates enrolled in fall 1996 applied for aid; of these, 95% were judged to have need according to Federal Methodology, of whom 100% were aided. *Financial aid deadline (priority):* 3/1. *Financial aid forms:* FAFSA, institutional form required; CSS Financial Aid PROFILE, state form acceptable. *Admission application deadline:* 3/15.

Summary of Aid to Needy Students *From gift & self-help combined:* Average need met: 93%. Average amount awarded: $13,580 (65% gift aid, 35% self-help). *Gift aid:* Total: $6,498,000 (75% from college's own funds, 17% from other college-administered sources, 8% from external sources). 522 Federal Work-Study jobs (averaging $1325); 100 part-time jobs.

Need-Based Scholarships & Grants Pell, FSEOG, state, private, college/university.

Loans Perkins, PLUS, Stafford, Unsubsidized Stafford, state, private, college/university short-term loans ($1500 average).

Non-Need Awards In 1996, a total of 482 non-need awards were made. *Academic Interests/Achievement Awards:* 396 ($1,737,000 total): general academic, physical sciences, religion/biblical studies, social sciences. *Creative Arts/Performance Awards:* 38 ($41,820 total): music. *Special Achievements/Activities Awards:* 3 ($5000 total): leadership. *Special Characteristics Awards:* 45 ($146,500 total): children and siblings of alumni, religious affiliation.

Other Money-Saving Options Accelerated degree, off-campus living (after freshman year). *Payment Plan:* installment. *Waivers:* full or partial for employees or children of employees.

Contact Office of Student Financial Aid, Hiram College, Box 67, Hiram, OH 44234-0067, 330-569-5107, fax: 330-569-5290.

HOBART AND WILLIAM SMITH COLLEGES
Geneva, New York

About the Institution Independent, coed. Degrees awarded: B. Offers 49 undergraduate majors. Total enrollment: 1,794 (49% state residents). Freshmen: 532.

Undergraduate Expenses (1997–98) Comprehensive fee of $28,944 includes tuition ($21,927), mandatory fees ($453), and college room and board ($6564). College room only: $3333.

Applications 69% of all full-time undergraduates enrolled in fall 1996 applied for aid; of these, 95% were judged to have need according to Federal Methodology, of whom 100% were aided. *Financial aid deadline (priority):* 2/15. *Financial aid forms:* FAFSA, CSS Financial Aid PROFILE required. State form required for some. *Regular admission application deadline:* 2/1. Early decision deadline: 11/15.

Summary of Aid to Needy Students *From gift & self-help combined:* Average need met: 82%. Average amount awarded: $18,667 (78% gift aid, 22% self-help). *Gift aid:* Total: $17,244,749 (84% from college's own funds, 2% from other college-administered sources, 14% from external sources). 900 Federal Work-Study jobs (averaging $1000); 80 part-time jobs.

Need-Based Scholarships & Grants Pell, FSEOG, state, college/university.

Loans Perkins, PLUS, Stafford, Unsubsidized Stafford, private.

Non-Need Awards In 1996, a total of 55 non-need awards were made. *Academic Interests/Achievement Awards:* 30 ($300,000 total): general academic. *Creative Arts/Performance Awards:* 25 ($125,000 total): art/fine arts, creative writing, dance, music, performing arts, theater/drama.

Other Money-Saving Options Accelerated degree. *Payment Plans:* tuition prepayment, installment, deferred payment. *Waivers:* full or partial for employees or children of employees.

Contact Mr. Robert Freeman, Director of Financial Aid, Hobart and William Smith Colleges, Geneva, NY 14456-3397, 315-781-3316.

HOBE SOUND BIBLE COLLEGE
Hobe Sound, Florida

About the Institution Independent/religious, coed. Degrees awarded: A, B. Offers 8 undergraduate majors. Total enrollment: 118 (23% state residents). Freshmen: 22.

Undergraduate Expenses (1997–98) Comprehensive fee of $6460 includes tuition ($3940), mandatory fees ($200), and college room and board ($2320). College room only: $760.

Applications 96% of all full-time undergraduates enrolled in fall 1996 applied for aid; of these,100% were judged to have need according to Federal Methodology, of whom 100% were aided. *Financial aid deadline (priority):* 9/1. *Financial aid forms:* FAFSA required. State form, institutional form required for some. *Admission application deadline:* rolling.

Summary of Aid to Needy Students *From gift & self-help combined:* Average need met: 50%. Average amount awarded: $5000 (98% gift aid, 2% self-help). *Gift aid:* Total: $347,000 (57% from college's own funds, 24% from other college-administered sources, 19% from external sources). 3 Federal Work-Study jobs (averaging $2400); 30 part-time jobs.

Need-Based Scholarships & Grants Pell, FSEOG, state, college/university.

Loans PLUS, Stafford, Unsubsidized Stafford.

Non-Need Awards In 1996, a total of 37 non-need awards were made. *Academic Interests/Achievement Awards:* 37 ($38,000 total): general academic.

Other Money-Saving Options *Payment Plan:* installment. *Waivers:* full or partial for employees or children of employees.

Contact Office of Financial Aid, Hobe Sound Bible College, PO Box 1065, Hobe Sound, FL 33475-1065, 561-546-5534, fax: 561-545-1422.

HOFSTRA UNIVERSITY
Hempstead, New York

About the Institution Independent, coed. Degrees awarded: B, M, D, P. Offers 72 undergraduate majors. Total enrollment: 12,279. Undergraduates: 7,149 (83% state residents). Freshmen: 1,746.

Undergraduate Expenses (1996–97) Tuition: $12,240. Mandatory fees: $526. College room only: $4600 (minimum).

Applications Of all full-time undergraduates enrolled in fall 1996, 81% of those who applied for aid were judged to have need according to Federal Methodology, of whom 100% were aided. *Financial aid deadline (priority):* 3/1. *Financial aid forms:* FAFSA, CSS Financial Aid PROFILE required. Institutional form required for some. *Regular admission application deadline:* rolling. Early decision deadline: 12/1.

Summary of Aid to Needy Students *From gift & self-help combined:* Average need met: 57%. Average amount awarded: $7249 (70% gift aid, 30% self-help). *Gift aid:* Total: $21,890,955 (50% from college's own funds, 2% from other college-administered sources, 48% from external sources). 1,253 Federal Work-Study jobs (averaging $1910); 900 part-time jobs.

Need-Based Scholarships & Grants Pell, FSEOG, state, private, college/university.

Loans Perkins, PLUS, Stafford, Unsubsidized Stafford, state, private, college/university short-term loans ($50 average), college/university long-term loans ($2700 average).

Non-Need Awards In 1996, a total of 2,249 non-need awards were made. *Academic Interests/Achievement Awards:* 1,631 ($3,863,134 total): general academic. *Creative Arts/Performance Awards:* 144 ($222,998 total): art/fine arts, dance, music, theater/drama. *Special Achievements/Activities Awards:* 42 ($20,000 total): leadership. *Special Characteristics Awards:* 155 ($1,563,254 total): general special characteristics. *Athletic:* Total: 277 ($3,041,910); Men: 175 ($1,914,229); Women: 102 ($1,127,681).

Other Money-Saving Options Accelerated degree, Army ROTC, off-campus living. *Payment Plans:* installment, deferred payment. *Waivers:* full or partial for employees or children of employees and senior citizens.

Contact Mr. Jerry Trombella, Associate Director of Financial Aid, Hofstra University, 126 Hofstra University, Hempstead, NY 11550-1090, 516-463-6526, fax: 516-463-4936.

HOLLINS COLLEGE
Roanoke, Virginia

About the Institution Independent, women. Degrees awarded: B, M. Offers 40 undergraduate majors. Total enrollment: 1,030. Undergraduates: 844 (37% state residents). Freshmen: 193.

Undergraduate Expenses (1997–98) Comprehensive fee of $21,295 includes tuition ($15,070), mandatory fees ($250), and college room and board ($5975). College room only: $3490.

Applications 67% of all full-time undergraduates enrolled in fall 1996 applied for aid; of these, 87% were judged to have need according to Federal Methodology, of whom 100% were aided. *Financial aid deadline*

(priority): 3/1. *Financial aid forms:* FAFSA required. State form required for some. *Regular admission application deadline:* 2/15. Early decision deadline: 12/1.

Summary of Aid to Needy Students *From gift & self-help combined:* Average need met: 95%. Average amount awarded: $15,711 (69% gift aid, 31% self-help). *Gift aid:* Total: $4,913,572 (86% from college's own funds, 6% from other college-administered sources, 8% from external sources). 298 Federal Work-Study jobs (averaging $1650); 48 part-time jobs.

Need-Based Scholarships & Grants Pell, FSEOG, state, private, college/university.

Loans Perkins, PLUS, Stafford, Unsubsidized Stafford, private, Key Alternative Loans, Plato Loans.

Non-Need Awards In 1996, a total of 87 non-need awards were made. *Academic Interests/Achievement Awards:* 37 ($102,000 total): general academic. *Creative Arts/Performance Awards:* 16 ($40,000 total): music. *Special Achievements/Activities Awards:* 17 ($43,500 total): leadership. *Special Characteristics Awards:* 17 ($42,500 total): local/state students.

Other Money-Saving Options Accelerated degree. *Payment Plans:* tuition prepayment, installment, deferred payment. *Waivers:* full or partial for employees or children of employees.

Contact Office of Financial Aid, Hollins College, PO Box 9718, Roanoke, VA 24020-1688, 540-362-6000.

HOLY APOSTLES COLLEGE AND SEMINARY
Cromwell, Connecticut

About the Institution Independent/religious, coed. Degrees awarded: A, B, M. Offers 6 undergraduate majors. Total enrollment: 125. Undergraduates: 21 (100% state residents).

Undergraduate Expenses (1997–98) Comprehensive fee of $11,430 includes tuition ($4950), mandatory fees ($80), and college room and board ($6400).

Applications *Financial aid deadline (priority):* 8/15. *Financial aid forms:* FAFSA, institutional form required. *Admission application deadline:* rolling.

Summary of Aid to Needy Students *From gift & self-help combined:* Average need met: 82%. Average amount awarded: $11,981 (32% gift aid, 68% self-help). *Gift aid:* Total: $11,660 (100% from college-administered sources). 2 part-time jobs.

Need-Based Scholarships & Grants Pell, FSEOG, state, college/university.

Loans PLUS, Stafford, Unsubsidized Stafford.

Non-Need Awards Not offered.

Other Money-Saving Options Accelerated degree. *Payment Plan:* installment. *Waivers:* full or partial for employees or children of employees.

Contact Ms. Marilyn Mancarella, Financial Aid Counselor, Holy Apostles College and Seminary, 33 Prospect Hill Road, Cromwell, CT 06416-2005, 860-632-8120, fax: 860-632-0176.

HOLY FAMILY COLLEGE
Philadelphia, Pennsylvania

About the Institution Independent/religious, coed. Degrees awarded: A, B, M. Offers 42 undergraduate majors. Total enrollment: 2,590. Undergraduates: 2,124 (91% state residents). Freshmen: 180.

Undergraduate Expenses (1996–97) Tuition: $9800 (minimum). Mandatory fees: $320.

Applications Of all full-time undergraduates enrolled in fall 1996, 88% of those who applied for aid were judged to have need according to Federal Methodology, of whom 100% were aided. *Financial aid deadline*

(priority): 5/31. *Financial aid forms:* FAFSA, institutional form, W-2 forms, copy of parent and student tax returns required. *Admission application deadline:* rolling.

Summary of Aid to Needy Students *From gift & self-help combined:* Average need met: 86%. *Gift aid:* Total: $3,300,000 (18% from college's own funds, 61% from other college-administered sources, 21% from external sources). 94 Federal Work-Study jobs (averaging $500); part-time jobs.

Need-Based Scholarships & Grants Pell, FSEOG, state, college/university.

Loans Perkins, PLUS, Stafford, Unsubsidized Stafford, Federal Nursing.

Non-Need Awards *Academic Interests/Achievement Awards:* general academic. *Special Characteristics Awards:* children of faculty/staff. *Athletic:* available.

Other Money-Saving Options Accelerated degree, co-op program. *Payment Plan:* installment. *Waivers:* full or partial for employees or children of employees.

Contact Ms. Anna M. Raffaele, Director of Financial Aid, Holy Family College, Philadelphia, PA 19114-2094, 215-637-7700 Ext. 3234.

HOLY NAMES COLLEGE
Oakland, California

About the Institution Independent/religious, coed. Degrees awarded: B, M. Offers 22 undergraduate majors. Total enrollment: 923. Undergraduates: 634 (87% state residents). Freshmen: 43.

Undergraduate Expenses (1997–98) Comprehensive fee of $19,660 includes tuition ($13,870) and college room and board ($5790 minimum). College room only: $2440 (minimum).

Applications Of all full-time undergraduates enrolled in fall 1996, 100% of those judged to have need according to Federal Methodology were aided. *Financial aid deadline (priority):* 3/2. *Financial aid forms:* FAFSA, institutional form required. State form required for some. *Admission application deadline:* 8/1.

Summary of Aid to Needy Students *Gift aid:* Total: $1,878,337 (53% from college's own funds, 33% from other college-administered sources, 14% from external sources). Federal Work-Study jobs; 52 part-time jobs.

Need-Based Scholarships & Grants Pell, FSEOG, state, private, college/university.

Loans Perkins, PLUS, Stafford, Unsubsidized Stafford, college/university short-term loans ($100 average).

Non-Need Awards In 1996, a total of 51 non-need awards were made. *Academic Interests/Achievement Awards:* 4 ($4600 total): general academic, biological sciences, business, education, English, foreign languages, health fields. *Creative Arts/Performance Awards:* 12 ($10,817 total): art/fine arts, music. *Special Characteristics Awards:* 4 ($3500 total): children and siblings of alumni. *Athletic:* Total: 31 ($186,298); Men: 13 ($76,126); Women: 18 ($110,172).

Other Money-Saving Options Cooperative Army ROTC, cooperative Air Force ROTC, off-campus living (after freshman year). *Payment Plans:* installment, deferred payment. *Waivers:* full or partial for employees or children of employees.

Contact Financial Aid Office, Holy Names College, 3500 Mountain Boulevard, Oakland, CA 94619-1699, 510-436-1327.

HOOD COLLEGE
Frederick, Maryland

About the Institution Independent/religious, primarily women. Degrees awarded: B, M. Offers 53 undergraduate majors. Total enrollment: 1,870. Undergraduates: 1,034 (58% state residents). Freshmen: 129.

Undergraduate Expenses (1997–98) Comprehensive fee of $23,010 includes tuition ($16,218), mandatory fees ($200), and college room and board ($6592). College room only: $3564.

Applications 92% of all full-time undergraduates enrolled in fall 1996 applied for aid; of these, 84% were judged to have need according to Federal Methodology, of whom 100% were aided. *Financial aid deadline (priority):* 3/1. *Financial aid forms:* FAFSA, CSS Financial Aid PROFILE, state form required. Institutional form required for some. *Regular admission application deadline:* 3/31. Early action deadline: 11/15.

Summary of Aid to Needy Students *From gift & self-help combined:* Average need met: 98%. Average amount awarded: $14,467 (65% gift aid, 35% self-help). *Gift aid:* Total: $4,246,578 (70% from college's own funds, 22% from other college-administered sources, 8% from external sources). 207 Federal Work-Study jobs (averaging $1500); 100 part-time jobs.

Need-Based Scholarships & Grants Pell, FSEOG, state, private, college/university.

Loans Perkins, PLUS, Stafford, Unsubsidized Stafford, college/university long-term loans ($3600 average).

Non-Need Awards *Academic Interests/Achievement Awards:* general academic. *Creative Arts/Performance Awards:* creative writing. *Special Achievements/Activities Awards:* leadership, memberships.

Other Money-Saving Options Accelerated degree, co-op program, cooperative Army ROTC, off-campus living (after sophomore year). *Payment Plans:* tuition prepayment, installment, deferred payment. *Waivers:* full or partial for employees or children of employees and senior citizens.

Contact Ms. Richelle Emerick, Director of Financial Aid, Hood College, 401 Rosemont Avenue, Frederick, MD 21701-8575, 301-696-3411.

HOPE COLLEGE
Holland, Michigan

About the Institution Independent/religious, coed. Degrees awarded: B. Offers 54 undergraduate majors. Total enrollment: 2,849 (79% state residents). Freshmen: 673.

Undergraduate Expenses (1997–98) Comprehensive fee of $19,412 includes tuition ($14,788), mandatory fees ($90), and college room and board ($4534). College room only: $2142.

Applications 72% of all full-time undergraduates enrolled in fall 1996 applied for aid; of these, 86% were judged to have need according to Federal Methodology, of whom 99% were aided. *Financial aid deadline (priority):* 2/1. *Financial aid forms:* FAFSA, CSS Financial Aid PROFILE required. *Admission application deadline:* rolling.

Summary of Aid to Needy Students *From gift & self-help combined:* Average need met: 88%. Average amount awarded: $11,981 (66% gift aid, 34% self-help). *Gift aid:* Total: $12,486,701 (68% from college's own funds, 3% from other college-administered sources, 29% from external sources). 297 Federal Work-Study jobs (averaging $1200); 335 part-time jobs.

Need-Based Scholarships & Grants Pell, FSEOG, state, private, college/university.

Loans Perkins, PLUS, Stafford, Unsubsidized Stafford, state.

Non-Need Awards In 1996, a total of 1,353 non-need awards were made. *Academic Interests/Achievement Awards:* 1,268 ($5,637,529 total): general academic, physical sciences. *Creative Arts/Performance Awards:* 85 ($216,432 total): dance, performing arts, theater/drama.

Other Money-Saving Options Off-campus living (after junior year). *Payment Plan:* installment. *Waivers:* full or partial for employees or children of employees.

Contact Ms. Phyllis Hooyman, Director of Financial Aid, Hope College, 141 East 12th Street, PO Box 9000, Holland, MI 49422-9000, 616-395-7765, fax: 616-395-7160.

HOPE INTERNATIONAL UNIVERSITY
Fullerton, California

About the Institution Independent/religious, coed. Degrees awarded: A, B, M. Offers 19 undergraduate majors. Total enrollment: 841. Undergraduates: 702 (55% state residents). Freshmen: 107.

Undergraduate Expenses (1997–98) Comprehensive fee of $12,884 includes tuition ($8950), mandatory fees ($315), and college room and board ($3619).

Applications Of all full-time undergraduates enrolled in fall 1996, 100% of those judged to have need according to Federal Methodology were aided. *Financial aid deadline (priority):* 3/2. *Financial aid forms:* FAFSA, institutional form required. State form required for some. *Admission application deadline:* 7/1.

Summary of Aid to Needy Students *From gift & self-help combined:* Average need met: 75%. Average amount awarded: $6754 (21% gift aid, 79% self-help). *Gift aid:* Total: $774,789 (22% from college's own funds, 40% from other college-administered sources, 38% from external sources). 21 Federal Work-Study jobs (averaging $1225); 24 part-time jobs.

Need-Based Scholarships & Grants Pell, FSEOG, state.

Loans Perkins, PLUS, Stafford, Unsubsidized Stafford, college/university long-term loans ($2000 average).

Non-Need Awards In 1996, a total of 345 non-need awards were made. *Academic Interests/Achievement Awards:* 49 ($152,616 total): general academic. *Creative Arts/Performance Awards:* 9 ($15,877 total): music. *Special Achievements/Activities Awards:* 82 ($208,501 total): leadership, religious involvement. *Special Characteristics Awards:* 144 ($292,927 total): children and siblings of alumni, children of faculty/staff, international students, local/state students, relatives of clergy, siblings of current students, spouses of current students, veterans, veterans' children. *Athletic:* Total: 61 ($176,373); Men: 32 ($103,457); Women: 29 ($72,916).

Other Money-Saving Options Accelerated degree, off-campus living (after sophomore year). *Payment Plan:* installment. *Waivers:* full or partial for employees or children of employees and senior citizens.

Contact Mr. Mai Bui, Director of Financial Aid Services, Hope International University, 2500 East Nutwood Avenue, Fullerton, CA 92831-3138, 714-879-3901 Ext. 231, fax: 714-526-0231.

HOUGHTON COLLEGE
Houghton, New York

About the Institution Independent/religious, coed. Degrees awarded: A, B. Offers 51 undergraduate majors. Total enrollment: 1,249 (60% state residents). Freshmen: 282.

Undergraduate Expenses (1996–97) Comprehensive fee of $16,058 includes tuition ($11,700), mandatory fees ($360), and college room and board ($3998). College room only: $1998.

Applications 89% of all full-time undergraduates enrolled in fall 1996 applied for aid; of these, 90% were judged to have need according to Federal Methodology, of whom 100% were aided. *Financial aid deadline (priority):* 3/15. *Financial aid forms:* FAFSA, institutional form required; CSS Financial Aid PROFILE acceptable. State form required for some. *Admission application deadline:* 3/1.

Summary of Aid to Needy Students *From gift & self-help combined:* Average need met: 83%. Average amount awarded: $11,959 (61% gift aid, 39% self-help). *Gift aid:* Total: $7,158,659 (64% from college's own funds, 8% from other college-administered sources, 28% from external sources). 550 Federal Work-Study jobs (averaging $900); 150 part-time jobs.

Need-Based Scholarships & Grants Pell, FSEOG, state, private, college/university.

Loans Perkins, PLUS, Stafford, Unsubsidized Stafford, college/university short-term loans ($500 average).

Non-Need Awards In 1996, a total of 1,235 non-need awards were made. *Academic Interests/Achievement Awards:* 534 ($1,050,000 total): general academic. *Creative Arts/Performance Awards:* 58 ($72,000 total): art/fine arts, music. *Special Achievements/Activities Awards:* 14 ($16,150 total): religious involvement. *Special Characteristics Awards:* 514 ($579,857 total): parents of current students, relatives of clergy, religious affiliation, siblings of current students. *Athletic:* Total: 115 ($286,900); Men: 48 ($134,200); Women: 67 ($152,700).

Other Money-Saving Options Cooperative Army ROTC, off-campus living (after sophomore year). *Payment Plan:* installment. *Waivers:* full or partial for employees or children of employees.

Contact Office of Financial Aid, Houghton College, One Willard Avenue, Houghton, NY 14744, 716-567-9200.

HOUSTON BAPTIST UNIVERSITY
Houston, Texas

About the Institution Independent/religious, coed. Degrees awarded: A, B, M. Offers 52 undergraduate majors. Total enrollment: 2,243. Undergraduates: 1,660 (94% state residents). Freshmen: 234.

Undergraduate Expenses (1996–97) Comprehensive fee of $11,385 includes tuition ($8580), mandatory fees ($175), and college room and board ($2630). College room only: $1200.

Applications *Financial aid deadline (priority):* 4/1. *Financial aid forms:* FAFSA, institutional form required. *Admission application deadline:* rolling.

Summary of Aid to Needy Students *From gift & self-help combined:* Average amount awarded: $6961 (31% gift aid, 69% self-help). *Gift aid:* Total: $3,172,266 (43% from college's own funds, 29% from other college-administered sources, 28% from external sources). 157 Federal Work-Study jobs (averaging $1108); 50 part-time jobs.

Loans PLUS, Stafford, Unsubsidized Stafford, college/university long-term loans ($500 average).

Non-Need Awards In 1996, a total of 686 non-need awards were made. *Academic Interests/Achievement Awards:* 335 ($467,000 total): general academic, health fields, religion/biblical studies. *Creative Arts/Performance Awards:* 101 ($218,590 total): music. *Special Achievements/Activities Awards:* 162 ($277,026 total): general special achievements/activities. *Special Characteristics Awards:* 18 ($60,000 total): general special characteristics. *Athletic:* Total: 70 ($329,566); Men: 45 ($217,598); Women: 25 ($111,968).

Other Money-Saving Options Cooperative Army ROTC, cooperative Naval ROTC, off-campus living. *Payment Plans:* installment, deferred payment. *Waivers:* full or partial for employees or children of employees and senior citizens.

Contact Ms. Carolyn Paget, Director of Financial Aid, Houston Baptist University, 7502 Fondren Road, Houston, TX 77074-3298, 281-649-3204, fax: 281-649-3474.

HOWARD PAYNE UNIVERSITY
Brownwood, Texas

About the Institution Independent/religious, coed. Degrees awarded: B. Offers 66 undergraduate majors. Total enrollment: 1,468 (96% state residents). Freshmen: 317.

Undergraduate Expenses (1996–97) Comprehensive fee of $9900 includes tuition ($6000 minimum), mandatory fees ($450), and college room and board ($3450 minimum). College room only: $1600 (minimum).

Applications *Financial aid deadline (priority):* 4/1. *Financial aid forms:* FAFSA, institutional form required. State form required for some. *Admission application deadline:* rolling.

Summary of Aid to Needy Students Federal Work-Study jobs; 125 part-time jobs.

Need-Based Scholarships & Grants Pell, FSEOG, state.

Loans Perkins, PLUS, Stafford, Unsubsidized Stafford, state.

Non-Need Awards *Academic Interests/Achievement Awards:* general academic. *Creative Arts/Performance Awards:* art/fine arts, music, theater/drama. *Special Achievements/Activities Awards:* community service, leadership, religious involvement. *Special Characteristics Awards:* children and siblings of alumni, children of faculty/staff, relatives of clergy, religious affiliation.

Other Money-Saving Options Cooperative Army ROTC, off-campus living (after freshman year). *Waivers:* full or partial for employees or children of employees and senior citizens.

Contact Mrs. Glenda Huff, Director of Student Aid, Howard Payne University, HPU Station, Box 285, Brownwood, TX 76801-2794, 915-649-8015, fax: 915-649-8901.

HOWARD UNIVERSITY
Washington, District of Columbia

About the Institution Independent, coed. Degrees awarded: B, M, D, P. Offers 73 undergraduate majors. Total enrollment: 10,332. Undergraduates: 7,668. Freshmen: 1,410.

Undergraduate Expenses (1997–98) Comprehensive fee of $13,147 includes tuition ($8580), mandatory fees ($405), and college room and board ($4162). College room only: $2364 (minimum).

Applications *Financial aid deadline (priority):* 4/1. *Financial aid forms:* FAFSA, CSS Financial Aid PROFILE required. *Admission application deadline:* 4/1.

Summary of Aid to Needy Students Federal Work-Study jobs; part-time jobs.

Loans College/university short-term loans.

Non-Need Awards *Academic Interests/Achievement Awards:* general academic. *Creative Arts/Performance Awards:* art/fine arts, music, theater/drama. *Special Characteristics Awards:* children and siblings of alumni. *Athletic:* available.

Other Money-Saving Options Co-op program, Army ROTC, Air Force ROTC, cooperative Naval ROTC, off-campus living (after sophomore year).

Contact Office of Financial Aid, Howard University, 2400 Sixth Street, NW, Room 205, Washington, DC 20059-0002, 202-806-6100.

HUMBOLDT STATE UNIVERSITY
Arcata, California

About the Institution State-supported, coed. Degrees awarded: B, M. Offers 76 undergraduate majors. Total enrollment: 7,686. Undergraduates: 6,862 (98% state residents). Freshmen: 842.

Undergraduate Expenses (1996–97) State resident tuition: $0. Nonresident tuition: $7380. Mandatory fees: $1956. College room and board: $5710. College room only: $2955.

Applications Of all full-time undergraduates enrolled in fall 1996, 87% of those who applied for aid were judged to have need according to Federal Methodology, of whom 95% were aided. *Financial aid deadline (priority):* 3/2. *Financial aid forms:* FAFSA required; CSS Financial Aid PROFILE acceptable. State form required for some. *Admission application deadline:* 11/30.

Summary of Aid to Needy Students *From gift & self-help combined:* Average need met: 70%. Average amount awarded: $5957 (45% gift aid, 55% self-help). *Gift aid:* Total: $8,710,660 (36% from college-administered sources, 64% from external sources). Federal Work-Study jobs; 40 part-time jobs.

Need-Based Scholarships & Grants Pell, FSEOG, state, private, college/university.

Loans Perkins, PLUS, Stafford, Unsubsidized Stafford, college/university short-term loans ($160 average), college/university long-term loans ($1328 average).

Non-Need Awards In 1996, a total of 1 non-need award was made. *Academic Interests/Achievement Awards:* 1 ($500 total): mathematics.

Other Money-Saving Options Accelerated degree, co-op program, off-campus living. *Payment Plan:* installment. *Waivers:* full or partial for employees or children of employees and senior citizens.

Contact Ms. Elizabeth Mikles, Financial Aid Associate Director, Humboldt State University, Arcata, CA 95521-8299, 707-826-5373, fax: 707-826-5360.

HUMPHREYS COLLEGE
Stockton, California

About the Institution Independent, coed. Degrees awarded: A, B, P. Offers 13 undergraduate majors. Total enrollment: 1,083. Undergraduates: 900 (94% state residents). Freshmen: 73.

Undergraduate Expenses (1997–98) Comprehensive fee of $10,918 includes tuition ($6258) and college room and board ($4660). College room only: $1575.

Applications 100% of all full-time undergraduates enrolled in fall 1996 applied for aid; of these, 89% were judged to have need according to Federal Methodology, of whom 83% were aided. *Financial aid deadline (priority):* 3/1. *Financial aid forms:* FAFSA required. State form required for some. *Admission application deadline:* rolling.

Summary of Aid to Needy Students *From gift & self-help combined:* Average need met: 89%. Average amount awarded: $9029. *Gift aid:* Total: $4,618,016 (1% from college's own funds, 22% from other college-administered sources, 77% from external sources). Federal Work-Study jobs; 10 part-time jobs.

Need-Based Scholarships & Grants Pell, FSEOG, college/university.

Loans PLUS, Stafford, Unsubsidized Stafford.

Non-Need Awards In 1996, a total of 25 non-need awards were made. *Academic Interests/Achievement Awards:* 25 ($12,500 total): general academic, business.

Other Money-Saving Options Accelerated degree, co-op program, off-campus living. *Payment Plans:* tuition prepayment, installment. *Waivers:* full or partial for employees or children of employees.

Contact Ms. Rita Franco, Financial Aid Adviser, Humphreys College, 6650 Inglewood Avenue, Stockton, CA 95207-3896, 209-478-0800, fax: 209-478-8721.

HUNTER COLLEGE OF THE CITY UNIVERSITY OF NEW YORK
New York, New York

About the Institution State & locally supported, coed. Degrees awarded: B, M. Offers 56 undergraduate majors. Total enrollment: 18,250. Undergraduates: 13,980 (93% state residents). Freshmen: 1,186.

Undergraduate Expenses (1996–97) State resident tuition: $3200. Nonresident tuition: $6800. Mandatory fees: $118. College room only: $1400 (minimum).

Applications *Financial aid deadline (priority):* 5/1. *Financial aid forms:* FAFSA, state form, institutional form required. *Admission application deadline:* 1/15.

Summary of Aid to Needy Students Federal Work-Study jobs.

Loans College/university short-term loans.

Non-Need Awards *Academic Interests/Achievement Awards:* general academic.

Other Money-Saving Options Off-campus living. *Payment Plan:* deferred payment. *Waivers:* full or partial for senior citizens.

Contact Office of Financial Aid, Hunter College of the City University of New York, 695 Park Avenue, New York, NY 10021-5085, 212-772-4000.

HUNTINGDON COLLEGE
Montgomery, Alabama

About the Institution Independent/religious, coed. Degrees awarded: A, B. Offers 59 undergraduate majors. Total enrollment: 646 (70% state residents). Freshmen: 170.

Undergraduate Expenses (1997–98 estimated) Comprehensive fee of $15,250 includes tuition ($9710), mandatory fees ($890), and college room and board ($4650). College room only: $1690.

Applications 76% of all full-time undergraduates enrolled in fall 1996 applied for aid; of these, 86% were judged to have need according to Federal Methodology, of whom 100% were aided. *Financial aid deadline (priority):* 5/1. *Financial aid forms:* FAFSA, institutional form required; CSS Financial Aid PROFILE acceptable. State form required for some. *Admission application deadline:* rolling.

Summary of Aid to Needy Students *From gift & self-help combined:* Average need met: 93%. Average amount awarded: $9496 (73% gift aid, 27% self-help). *Gift aid:* Total: $2,544,181 (69% from college's own funds, 18% from other college-administered sources, 13% from external sources). 120 Federal Work-Study jobs (averaging $1275); 20 part-time jobs.

Need-Based Scholarships & Grants Pell, FSEOG, private, college/university.

Loans Perkins, PLUS, Stafford, Unsubsidized Stafford.

Non-Need Awards In 1996, a total of 337 non-need awards were made. *Academic Interests/Achievement Awards:* 122 ($582,273 total): general academic. *Creative Arts/Performance Awards:* 12 ($53,190 total): applied art and design, dance, music, theater/drama. *Special Achievements/Activities Awards:* 53 ($85,125 total): Junior Miss, leadership. *Special Characteristics Awards:* 91 ($91,175 total): relatives of clergy. *Athletic:* Total: 59 ($432,463); Men: 34 ($252,068); Women: 25 ($180,395).

Other Money-Saving Options Accelerated degree, co-op program, cooperative Army ROTC, cooperative Air Force ROTC. *Payment Plan:* deferred payment. *Waivers:* full or partial for employees or children of employees.

Contact Mr. Thomas G. Dismukes Jr., Director of Student Financial Aid, Huntingdon College, 1500 East Fairview Avenue, Montgomery, AL 36106-2148, 334-833-4519, fax: 334-833-4347.

HUNTINGTON COLLEGE
Huntington, Indiana

About the Institution Independent/religious, coed. Degrees awarded: A, B, M. Offers 45 undergraduate majors. Total enrollment: 726. Undergraduates: 634 (59% state residents). Freshmen: 200.

Undergraduate Expenses (1997–98) Comprehensive fee of $16,750 includes tuition ($11,700), mandatory fees ($480), and college room and board ($4570).

Applications Of all full-time undergraduates enrolled in fall 1996, 80% of those who applied for aid were judged to have need according to Federal Methodology, of whom 100% were aided. *Financial aid deadline (priority):* 3/1. *Financial aid forms:* FAFSA, institutional form required. *Admission application deadline:* 8/15.

Summary of Aid to Needy Students *From gift & self-help combined:* Average need met: 82%. Average amount awarded: $8000 (40% gift aid, 60% self-help). *Gift aid:* Total: $1,684,282 (56% from college's

own funds, 30% from other college-administered sources, 14% from external sources). Federal Work-Study jobs; 100 part-time jobs.

Need-Based Scholarships & Grants Pell, FSEOG, state, private, college/university.

Loans Perkins, PLUS, Stafford, Unsubsidized Stafford, private.

Non-Need Awards *Academic Interests/Achievement Awards:* general academic, education. *Creative Arts/Performance Awards:* art/fine arts, journalism/publications, music, theater/drama. *Special Achievements/ Activities Awards:* leadership. *Special Characteristics Awards:* children of current students, children of faculty/staff, international students, members of minorities, parents of current students, religious affiliation, siblings of current students. *Athletic:* available.

Other Money-Saving Options Accelerated degree, off-campus living (after junior year). *Payment Plans:* guaranteed tuition, installment. *Waivers:* full or partial for minority students, children of alumni, employees or children of employees, adult students, senior citizens.

Contact Financial Aid Department, Huntington College, Huntington, IN 46750-1299, 219-359-4015.

HURON UNIVERSITY
Huron, South Dakota

About the Institution Proprietary, coed. Degrees awarded: A, B, M. Offers 23 undergraduate majors. Total enrollment: 476. Undergraduates: 418 (48% state residents). Freshmen: 138.

Undergraduate Expenses (1996–97) Comprehensive fee of $11,348 includes tuition ($7878) and college room and board ($3470 minimum).

Applications Of all full-time undergraduates enrolled in fall 1996, 91% of those who applied for aid were judged to have need according to Federal Methodology, of whom 100% were aided. *Financial aid deadline (priority):* 5/15. *Financial aid forms:* FAFSA, institutional form required; CSS Financial Aid PROFILE, state form acceptable. *Admission application deadline:* rolling.

Summary of Aid to Needy Students *From gift & self-help combined:* Average need met: 65%. Average amount awarded: $4090 (52% gift aid, 48% self-help). *Gift aid:* Total: $537,926 (66% from college's own funds, 13% from other college-administered sources, 21% from external sources). 75 Federal Work-Study jobs (averaging $1600); 10 part-time jobs.

Need-Based Scholarships & Grants Pell, FSEOG, college/university.

Loans Perkins, PLUS, Stafford, Unsubsidized Stafford.

Non-Need Awards In 1996, a total of 179 non-need awards were made. *Academic Interests/Achievement Awards:* 71 ($71,480 total): general academic. *Special Achievements/Activities Awards:* 7 ($7000 total): cheerleading/drum major. *Special Characteristics Awards:* 1 ($500 total): children and siblings of alumni. *Athletic:* Total: 100 ($208,208).

Other Money-Saving Options Accelerated degree, co-op program.

Contact Ms. Melissa Smith Hofer, Director of Financial Aid, Huron University, Huron, SD 57350-2798, 605-352-8721.

HUSSON COLLEGE
Bangor, Maine

About the Institution Independent, coed. Degrees awarded: A, B, M. Offers 15 undergraduate majors. Total enrollment: 1,946. Undergraduates: 1,717 (81% state residents). Freshmen: 321.

Undergraduate Expenses (1997–98) Comprehensive fee of $13,540 includes tuition ($8700), mandatory fees ($100), and college room and board ($4740).

Applications 84% of all full-time undergraduates enrolled in fall 1996 applied for aid; of these, 98% were judged to have need according to Federal Methodology, of whom 100% were aided. *Financial aid deadline*

(priority): 4/15. *Financial aid forms:* FAFSA required. *Regular admission application deadline:* 9/1. Early decision deadline: 12/15.

Summary of Aid to Needy Students *From gift & self-help combined:* Average need met: 85%. Average amount awarded: $8560 (53% gift aid, 47% self-help). *Gift aid:* Total: $3,278,571 (41% from college's own funds, 31% from other college-administered sources, 28% from external sources). 246 Federal Work-Study jobs (averaging $1419); 60 part-time jobs.

Need-Based Scholarships & Grants Pell, FSEOG, state, private, college/university.

Loans Perkins, PLUS, Stafford, Unsubsidized Stafford.

Non-Need Awards In 1996, a total of 69 non-need awards were made. *Academic Interests/Achievement Awards:* 69 ($32,050 total): general academic, business, education.

Other Money-Saving Options Co-op program, cooperative Army ROTC, cooperative Naval ROTC. *Payment Plans:* tuition prepayment, installment. *Waivers:* full or partial for employees or children of employees and senior citizens.

Contact Office of Financial Aid, Husson College, One College Circle, Bangor, ME 04401-2999, 207-941-7000.

HUSTON-TILLOTSON COLLEGE
Austin, Texas

About the Institution Independent/religious, coed. Degrees awarded: B. Offers 18 undergraduate majors. Total enrollment: 701 (79% state residents). Freshmen: 158.

Undergraduate Expenses (1997–98) Comprehensive fee of $10,262 includes tuition ($5250), mandatory fees ($780), and college room and board ($4232). College room only: $1932.

Applications *Financial aid deadline (priority):* 5/1. *Financial aid forms:* FAFSA, institutional form required. *Admission application deadline:* 5/1.

Summary of Aid to Needy Students Federal Work-Study jobs; 20 part-time jobs.

Need-Based Scholarships & Grants Pell, FSEOG, state, private.

Loans Perkins, PLUS, Stafford, Unsubsidized Stafford, state, private, college/university short-term loans ($500 average), college/university long-term loans.

Non-Need Awards *Academic Interests/Achievement Awards:* general academic. *Creative Arts/Performance Awards:* music. *Special Characteristics Awards:* general special characteristics. *Athletic:* available.

Other Money-Saving Options Accelerated degree, co-op program, off-campus living (after freshman year). *Payment Plan:* installment. *Waivers:* full or partial for employees or children of employees.

Contact Ms. Jackie Wilson, Director of Financial Aid, Huston-Tillotson College, Austin, TX 78702-2795, 512-505-3028.

IDAHO STATE UNIVERSITY
Pocatello, Idaho

About the Institution State-supported, coed. Degrees awarded: A, B, M, D, P. Offers 95 undergraduate majors. Total enrollment: 12,154. Undergraduates: 10,126 (92% state residents). Freshmen: 1,683.

Undergraduate Expenses (1996–97) State resident tuition: $0. Nonresident tuition: $5674. Mandatory fees: $1726. College room and board: $3398. College room only: $1428.

Applications 77% of all full-time undergraduates enrolled in fall 1996 applied for aid; of these, 100% were judged to have need according to Federal Methodology, of whom 100% were aided. *Financial aid deadline (priority):* 3/1. *Financial aid forms:* FAFSA, CSS Financial Aid PROFILE, institutional form required. *Admission application deadline:* 8/1.

Summary of Aid to Needy Students *From gift & self-help combined:* Average amount awarded: $8868 (31% gift aid, 69% self-help). *Gift aid:* Total: $15,317,310 (46% from college's own funds, 3% from other college-administered sources, 51% from external sources). 3,191 Federal Work-Study jobs (averaging $1754); 2,453 part-time jobs.

Need-Based Scholarships & Grants Pell, FSEOG, state, private, college/university.

Loans Perkins, PLUS, Stafford, Unsubsidized Stafford, college/university short-term loans ($300 average).

Non-Need Awards In 1996, a total of 1,969 non-need awards were made. *Academic Interests/Achievement Awards:* 1,357 ($1,490,100 total): general academic, biological sciences, business, communication, computer science, education, engineering/technologies, English, foreign languages, health fields, home economics, humanities, international studies, mathematics, physical sciences, premedicine, religion/biblical studies, social sciences. *Creative Arts/Performance Awards:* 149 ($48,933 total): art/fine arts, music, performing arts, theater/drama. *Special Achievements/Activities Awards:* 134 ($36,931 total): general special achievements/activities, Junior Miss, leadership, memberships, rodeo. *Special Characteristics Awards:* 116 ($137,360 total): children and siblings of alumni, children of faculty/staff, first-generation college students, handicapped students, local/state students, members of minorities, out-of-state students. *Athletic:* Total: 213 ($1,395,025); Men: 133 ($894,613); Women: 80 ($500,412).

Other Money-Saving Options Cooperative Army ROTC, off-campus living. *Payment Plan:* deferred payment. *Waivers:* full or partial for senior citizens.

Contact Mr. Doug Severs, Director of Financial Aid, Idaho State University, Campus Box 8077, Pocatello, ID 83209, 208-236-2981.

ILLINOIS BENEDICTINE COLLEGE
Lisle, Illinois

See Benedictine University

ILLINOIS COLLEGE
Jacksonville, Illinois

About the Institution Independent/religious, coed. Degrees awarded: B. Offers 41 undergraduate majors. Total enrollment: 905 (94% state residents). Freshmen: 200.

Undergraduate Expenses (1997–98) Comprehensive fee of $13,700 includes tuition ($9500) and college room and board ($4200).

Applications Of all full-time undergraduates enrolled in fall 1996, 87% of those who applied for aid were judged to have need according to Federal Methodology, of whom 100% were aided. *Financial aid deadline (priority):* 6/1. *Financial aid forms:* FAFSA required; state form acceptable. *Admission application deadline:* 8/15.

Summary of Aid to Needy Students *From gift & self-help combined:* Average need met: 90%. Average amount awarded: $9829 (56% gift aid, 44% self-help). *Gift aid:* Total: $3,715,614 (39% from college's own funds, 2% from other college-administered sources, 59% from external sources). 520 Federal Work-Study jobs (averaging $1050); 167 part-time jobs.

Need-Based Scholarships & Grants Pell, FSEOG, state, private, college/university.

Loans Perkins, PLUS, Stafford, Unsubsidized Stafford.

Non-Need Awards In 1996, a total of 1,526 non-need awards were made. *Academic Interests/Achievement Awards:* 835 ($1,596,104 total): general academic. *Creative Arts/Performance Awards:* 27 ($14,000 total): art/fine arts, debating, music. *Special Characteristics Awards:* 664 ($2,224,641 total): children of educators, children of faculty/staff, local/state students, members of minorities, previous college experience, relatives of clergy.

Other Money-Saving Options Accelerated degree, off-campus living (after sophomore year). *Payment Plans:* installment, deferred payment. *Waivers:* full or partial for employees or children of employees.

Contact Office of Financial Aid, Illinois College, 1101 West College Avenue, Jacksonville, IL 62650-2299, 217-245-3035, fax: 217-245-3034.

THE ILLINOIS INSTITUTE OF ART
Chicago, Illinois

About the Institution Proprietary, coed. Degrees awarded: A, B. Offers 5 undergraduate majors. Total enrollment: 600 (85% state residents). Freshmen: 343.

Undergraduate Expenses (1997–98) Tuition: $9984.

Applications *Financial aid deadline (priority):* 8/1. *Financial aid forms:* FAFSA, institutional form required. *Admission application deadline:* rolling.

Summary of Aid to Needy Students *From gift & self-help combined:* Average need met: 70%. Average amount awarded: $7700 (21% gift aid, 79% self-help). *Gift aid:* Total: $600,000. Federal Work-Study jobs; 15 part-time jobs.

Need-Based Scholarships & Grants Pell, FSEOG.

Loans PLUS, Stafford, Unsubsidized Stafford.

Non-Need Awards *Academic Interests/Achievement Awards:* general academic. *Creative Arts/Performance Awards:* general creative.

Other Money-Saving Options Accelerated degree, co-op program. *Payment Plan:* installment. *Waivers:* full or partial for employees or children of employees.

Contact Mr. Joseph Payne, Director of Student Financial Services, The Illinois Institute of Art, 1051 Perimeter Drive, Schaumburg, IL 60173, 800-314-3450.

ILLINOIS INSTITUTE OF TECHNOLOGY
Chicago, Illinois

About the Institution Independent, coed. Degrees awarded: B, M, D, P. Offers 22 undergraduate majors. Total enrollment: 6,287. Undergraduates: 1,959 (63% state residents). Freshmen: 245.

Undergraduate Expenses (1997–98 estimated) Comprehensive fee of $21,080 includes tuition ($16,400), mandatory fees ($60), and college room and board ($4620 minimum).

Applications 76% of all full-time undergraduates enrolled in fall 1996 applied for aid; of these, 88% were judged to have need according to Federal Methodology, of whom 99% were aided. *Financial aid deadline (priority):* 3/15. *Financial aid forms:* FAFSA required; CSS Financial Aid PROFILE, state form acceptable. *Admission application deadline:* rolling.

Summary of Aid to Needy Students *From gift & self-help combined:* Average need met: 91%. Average amount awarded: $16,128 (73% gift aid, 27% self-help). *Gift aid:* Total: $11,193,024 (46% from college's own funds, 16% from other college-administered sources, 38% from external sources). 292 Federal Work-Study jobs (averaging $1495); part-time jobs.

Need-Based Scholarships & Grants Pell, FSEOG, state, private, college/university.

Loans Perkins, PLUS, Stafford, Unsubsidized Stafford, private, college/university long-term loans ($1982 average).

Non-Need Awards In 1996, a total of 863 non-need awards were made. *Academic Interests/Achievement Awards:* 294 ($1,770,992 total): general academic, architecture, biological sciences, computer science, engineering/technologies, mathematics, physical sciences, premedicine, social sciences. *Special Achievements/Activities Awards:* 13 ($165,608 total): general special achievements/activities, community service, leadership, memberships. *Special Characteristics Awards:* 476 ($3,647,350 total): general special characteristics, children and siblings of alumni, children of faculty/staff, ethnic background, international students, local/state students, members of minorities, out-of-state students, previous college experience, ROTC participants, siblings of current students, spouses of current students. *Athletic:* Total: 80 ($328,627); Men: 47 ($192,802); Women: 33 ($135,825).

Other Money-Saving Options Accelerated degree, co-op program, Army ROTC, Naval ROTC, Air Force ROTC, off-campus living (after freshman year). *Payment Plan:* installment. *Waivers:* full or partial for children of alumni and employees or children of employees.

Contact Office of Financial Aid, Illinois Institute of Technology, 3300 South Federal Street, Chicago, IL 60616, 312-567-3000.

ILLINOIS STATE UNIVERSITY
Normal, Illinois

About the Institution State-supported, coed. Degrees awarded: B, M, D. Offers 55 undergraduate majors. Total enrollment: 19,409. Undergraduates: 16,763 (98% state residents). Freshmen: 2,896.

Undergraduate Expenses (1997–98) State resident tuition: $2952. Nonresident tuition: $8856. Mandatory fees: $1052. College room and board: $3996. College room only: $2118.

Applications 64% of all full-time undergraduates enrolled in fall 1996 applied for aid; of these, 79% were judged to have need according to Federal Methodology, of whom 96% were aided. *Financial aid deadline (priority):* 3/1. *Financial aid forms:* FAFSA required.

Summary of Aid to Needy Students *From gift & self-help combined:* Average need met: 93%. Average amount awarded: $7016 (48% gift aid, 52% self-help). *Gift aid:* Total: $24,985,960 (5% from college's own funds, 72% from other college-administered sources, 23% from external sources). 939 Federal Work-Study jobs (averaging $1599); part-time jobs.

Need-Based Scholarships & Grants Pell, FSEOG, state, private, college/university.

Loans Perkins, PLUS, Stafford, Unsubsidized Stafford, college/university short-term loans ($500 average).

Non-Need Awards *Academic Interests/Achievement Awards:* general academic, agriculture, biological sciences, business, communication, computer science, education, engineering/technologies, English, foreign languages, health fields, home economics, humanities, international studies, library science, mathematics, military science, physical sciences, premedicine, social sciences. *Creative Arts/Performance Awards:* general creative, applied art and design, art/fine arts, cinema/film/broadcasting, creative writing, debating, music, performing arts, theater/drama. *Special Achievements/Activities Awards:* general special achievements/activities, community service, hobbies/interest, leadership. *Special Characteristics Awards:* general special characteristics, children of faculty/staff, children of union members/company employees, children with a deceased or disabled parent, first-generation college students, handicapped students, local/state students, members of minorities, previous college experience, ROTC participants, veterans, veterans' children. *Athletic:* Total: 272 ($966,881); Men: 141 ($514,348); Women: 131 ($452,533).

Other Money-Saving Options Accelerated degree, co-op program, Army ROTC, off-campus living (after sophomore year). *Payment Plan:* installment. *Waivers:* full or partial for employees or children of employees and senior citizens.

Contact Mr. Bryan Terry, Assistant Director of Financial Aid, Illinois State University, Campus Box 2320, Normal, IL 61790-2320, 309-438-2231, fax: 309-438-3755.

ILLINOIS WESLEYAN UNIVERSITY
Bloomington, Illinois

About the Institution Independent, coed. Degrees awarded: B. Offers 51 undergraduate majors. Total enrollment: 1,928 (84% state residents). Freshmen: 592.

Undergraduate Expenses (1997–98) Comprehensive fee of $22,080 includes tuition ($17,380), mandatory fees ($110), and college room and board ($4590). College room only: $2640.

Applications 86% of all full-time undergraduates enrolled in fall 1996 applied for aid; of these, 75% were judged to have need according to Federal Methodology, of whom 100% were aided. *Financial aid deadline (priority):* 3/1. *Financial aid forms:* FAFSA required; institutional form acceptable. CSS Financial Aid PROFILE required for some. *Admission application deadline:* rolling.

Summary of Aid to Needy Students *From gift & self-help combined:* Average need met: 100%. Average amount awarded: $13,577 (64% gift aid, 36% self-help). *Gift aid:* Total: $10,892,833 (64% from college's own funds, 3% from other college-administered sources, 33% from external sources). 372 Federal Work-Study jobs (averaging $1443); 657 part-time jobs.

Need-Based Scholarships & Grants Pell, FSEOG, state, private, college/university.

Loans Perkins, PLUS, Stafford, Unsubsidized Stafford, Federal Nursing, private, college/university short-term loans ($150 average), college/university long-term loans ($1196 average).

Non-Need Awards In 1996, a total of 453 non-need awards were made. *Academic Interests/Achievement Awards:* 309 ($1,585,853 total): general academic. *Creative Arts/Performance Awards:* 109 ($439,400 total): art/fine arts, music, theater/drama. *Special Achievements/Activities Awards:* 35 ($148,080 total): hobbies/interest.

Other Money-Saving Options Accelerated degree, cooperative Army ROTC. *Payment Plan:* installment. *Waivers:* full or partial for employees or children of employees.

Contact Mr. Lynn Nichelson, Director of Financial Aid, Illinois Wesleyan University, 1312 North Park Street, PO Box 2900, Bloomington, IL 61702-2900, 309-556-3096, fax: 309-556-3411.

IMMACULATA COLLEGE
Immaculata, Pennsylvania

About the Institution Independent/religious, primarily women. Degrees awarded: A, B, M, D. Offers 51 undergraduate majors. Total enrollment: 2,391. Undergraduates: 1,626 (76% state residents). Freshmen: 104.

Undergraduate Expenses (1997–98) Comprehensive fee of $17,971 includes tuition ($11,900), mandatory fees ($215), and college room and board ($5856). College room only: $3120.

Applications Of all full-time undergraduates enrolled in fall 1996, 85% of those who applied for aid were judged to have need according to Federal Methodology, of whom 100% were aided. *Financial aid deadline (priority):* 3/1. *Financial aid forms:* FAFSA required. Institutional form required for some. *Admission application deadline:* rolling.

Summary of Aid to Needy Students *From gift & self-help combined:* Average need met: 90%. Average amount awarded: $13,998 (73% gift aid, 27% self-help). *Gift aid:* Total: $2,662,455 (66% from college's own funds, 23% from other college-administered sources, 11% from external sources). 175 Federal Work-Study jobs (averaging $1000); 45 part-time jobs.

Need-Based Scholarships & Grants Pell, FSEOG, state, private, college/university.

Loans Perkins, PLUS, Stafford, Unsubsidized Stafford, private.

Non-Need Awards In 1996, a total of 187 non-need awards were made. *Academic Interests/Achievement Awards:* 68 ($450,000 total):

general academic. *Creative Arts/Performance Awards:* 17 ($58,000 total): music. *Special Achievements/Activities Awards:* 38 ($57,000 total): community service, leadership, memberships, religious involvement. *Special Characteristics Awards:* 64 ($159,963 total): children of faculty/staff, relatives of clergy, siblings of current students.

Other Money-Saving Options Accelerated degree, off-campus living. *Payment Plan:* installment. *Waivers:* full or partial for employees or children of employees and senior citizens.

Contact Mr. Christopher K. Hanlon, Director of Financial Aid, Immaculata College, Immaculata, PA 19345-0900, 610-647-4400 Ext. 3028, fax: 610-251-1668.

INDIANA INSTITUTE OF TECHNOLOGY
Fort Wayne, Indiana

About the Institution Independent, coed. Degrees awarded: A, B. Offers 17 undergraduate majors. Total enrollment: 1,321 (30% state residents). Freshmen: 210.

Undergraduate Expenses (1997–98) Comprehensive fee of $15,150 includes tuition ($10,850) and college room and board ($4300).

Applications *Financial aid deadline (priority):* 3/1. *Financial aid forms:* FAFSA, CSS Financial Aid PROFILE, institutional form required. State form required for some. *Admission application deadline:* 8/1.

Summary of Aid to Needy Students Federal Work-Study jobs; part-time jobs.

Non-Need Awards *Academic Interests/Achievement Awards:* general academic. *Special Characteristics Awards:* local/state students, out-of-state students, siblings of current students. *Athletic:* available.

Another Money-Saving Option Off-campus living (after sophomore year).

Contact Office of Financial Aid, Indiana Institute of Technology, 1600 East Washington Boulevard, Fort Wayne, IN 46803-1297, 219-422-5561.

INDIANA STATE UNIVERSITY
Terre Haute, Indiana

About the Institution State-supported, coed. Degrees awarded: A, B, M, D. Offers 152 undergraduate majors. Total enrollment: 10,934. Undergraduates: 9,490 (90% state residents). Freshmen: 1,921.

Undergraduate Expenses (1996–97) State resident tuition: $3072. Nonresident tuition: $7604. College room and board: $3995.

Applications 72% of all full-time undergraduates enrolled in fall 1996 applied for aid; of these, 87% were judged to have need according to Federal Methodology, of whom 98% were aided. *Financial aid deadline (priority):* 3/1. *Financial aid forms:* CSS Financial Aid PROFILE, institutional form required. FAFSA required for some. *Admission application deadline:* 8/15.

Summary of Aid to Needy Students *From gift & self-help combined:* Average need met: 49%. Average amount awarded: $3531 (43% gift aid, 57% self-help). *Gift aid:* Total: $5,832,200 (31% from college's own funds, 41% from other college-administered sources, 28% from external sources). 334 Federal Work-Study jobs (averaging $835); 1,316 part-time jobs.

Need-Based Scholarships & Grants Pell, FSEOG, state, private, college/university.

Loans Perkins, PLUS, Stafford, Unsubsidized Stafford, college/university short-term loans ($533 average).

Non-Need Awards In 1996, a total of 1,959 non-need awards were made. *Academic Interests/Achievement Awards:* 531 ($807,000 total): general academic. *Creative Arts/Performance Awards:* 85 ($96,700 total): art/fine arts, performing arts. *Special Characteristics Awards:* 283 ($218,045 total): children and siblings of alumni, children of faculty/staff, children with a deceased or disabled parent, members of minorities, veterans' children. *Athletic:* Total: 1,060 ($1,401,580); Men: 692 ($851,579); Women: 368 ($550,001).

Other Money-Saving Options Accelerated degree, co-op program, Army ROTC, Air Force ROTC, off-campus living (after sophomore year). *Payment Plans:* installment, deferred payment. *Waivers:* full or partial for employees or children of employees.

Contact Mr. Bradley Laubert, Assistant Director, Indiana State University, Tirey Hall, Room 150, Terre Haute, IN 47809-1401, 812-237-7717, fax: 812-237-4330.

INDIANA UNIVERSITY BLOOMINGTON
Bloomington, Indiana

About the Institution State-supported, coed. Degrees awarded: A, B, M, D, P. Offers 151 undergraduate majors. Total enrollment: 34,700. Undergraduates: 25,451 (73% state residents). Freshmen: 5,837.

Undergraduate Expenses (1996–97) State resident tuition: $3320. Nonresident tuition: $10,868. Mandatory fees: $431. College room and board: $4220.

Applications Of all full-time undergraduates enrolled in fall 1996, 78% of those who applied for aid were judged to have need according to Federal Methodology, of whom 94% were aided. *Financial aid deadline (priority):* 3/1. *Financial aid forms:* FAFSA, institutional form required; CSS Financial Aid PROFILE acceptable. *Admission application deadline:* 2/15.

Summary of Aid to Needy Students *From gift & self-help combined:* Average need met: 66%. Average amount awarded: $5684 (42% gift aid, 58% self-help). *Gift aid:* Total: $23,424,311 (24% from college's own funds, 7% from other college-administered sources, 69% from external sources). 1,462 Federal Work-Study jobs (averaging $1421); part-time jobs.

Need-Based Scholarships & Grants Pell, FSEOG, state, private, college/university.

Loans Perkins, PLUS, Stafford, Unsubsidized Stafford, Federal Nursing, private, college/university short-term loans, college/university long-term loans.

Non-Need Awards In 1996, a total of 3,979 non-need awards were made. *Academic Interests/Achievement Awards:* general academic. *Creative Arts/Performance Awards:* available. *Special Achievements/Activities Awards:* available. *Special Characteristics Awards:* available. *Athletic:* Total: 339 ($2,490,270); Men: 209 ($1,449,710); Women: 130 ($1,040,560).

Other Money-Saving Options Accelerated degree, co-op program, Army ROTC, Air Force ROTC, off-campus living. *Payment Plan:* deferred payment. *Waivers:* full or partial for employees or children of employees.

Contact Office of Financial Aid, Indiana University Bloomington, 208 Franklin Hall, Bloomington, IN 47405-2801, 812-855-4848.

INDIANA UNIVERSITY EAST
Richmond, Indiana

About the Institution State-supported, coed. Degrees awarded: A, B. Offers 23 undergraduate majors. Total enrollment: 2,302 (95% state residents). Freshmen: 674.

Undergraduate Expenses (1996–97) State resident tuition: $2612. Nonresident tuition: $6773. Mandatory fees: $116.

Applications 79% of all full-time undergraduates enrolled in fall 1996 applied for aid; of these, 90% were judged to have need according to

Federal Methodology, of whom 99% were aided. *Financial aid deadline (priority):* 3/1. *Financial aid forms:* FAFSA, institutional form required; CSS Financial Aid PROFILE acceptable. *Admission application deadline:* rolling.

Summary of Aid to Needy Students *From gift & self-help combined:* Average need met: 55%. Average amount awarded: $4706 (57% gift aid, 43% self-help). *Gift aid:* Total: $1,832,061 (4% from college's own funds, 6% from other college-administered sources, 90% from external sources). 64 Federal Work-Study jobs (averaging $2688).

Need-Based Scholarships & Grants Pell, FSEOG, state, private, college/university.

Loans Perkins, PLUS, Stafford, Unsubsidized Stafford, Federal Nursing, private, college/university short-term loans.

Non-Need Awards In 1996, a total of 294 non-need awards were made. *Academic Interests/Achievement Awards:* available. *Athletic:* available.

Other Money-Saving Options *Payment Plan:* deferred payment. *Waivers:* full or partial for employees or children of employees.

Contact Office of Financial Aid, Indiana University East, 2325 Chester Boulevard, Richmond, IN 47374-1289, 765-973-8200.

INDIANA UNIVERSITY KOKOMO
Kokomo, Indiana

About the Institution State-supported, coed. Degrees awarded: A, B, M. Offers 24 undergraduate majors. Total enrollment: 2,965. Undergraduates: 2,433 (97% state residents). Freshmen: 579.

Undergraduate Expenses (1996–97) State resident tuition: $2612. Nonresident tuition: $6773. Mandatory fees: $40.

Applications 54% of all full-time undergraduates enrolled in fall 1996 applied for aid; of these, 76% were judged to have need according to Federal Methodology, of whom 95% were aided. *Financial aid deadline (priority):* 3/1. *Financial aid forms:* FAFSA, institutional form required; CSS Financial Aid PROFILE acceptable. *Admission application deadline:* 8/5.

Summary of Aid to Needy Students *From gift & self-help combined:* Average need met: 56%. Average amount awarded: $3858 (61% gift aid, 39% self-help). *Gift aid:* Total: $1,068,435 (4% from college's own funds, 6% from other college-administered sources, 90% from external sources). 22 Federal Work-Study jobs (averaging $918); part-time jobs.

Need-Based Scholarships & Grants Pell, FSEOG, state, private, college/university.

Loans Perkins, PLUS, Stafford, Unsubsidized Stafford, Federal Nursing, private, college/university short-term loans.

Non-Need Awards In 1996, a total of 130 non-need awards were made. *Academic Interests/Achievement Awards:* available. *Creative Arts/Performance Awards:* available. *Special Achievements/Activities Awards:* available. *Special Characteristics Awards:* available.

Contact Office of Financial Aid, Indiana University Kokomo, Kokomo, IN 46904-9003, 765-453-2000.

INDIANA UNIVERSITY NORTHWEST
Gary, Indiana

About the Institution State-supported, coed. Degrees awarded: A, B, M. Offers 42 undergraduate majors. Total enrollment: 5,149. Undergraduates: 4,620 (99% state residents). Freshmen: 723.

Undergraduate Expenses (1996–97) State resident tuition: $2612. Nonresident tuition: $6773. Mandatory fees: $156.

Applications Of all full-time undergraduates enrolled in fall 1996, 85% of those who applied for aid were judged to have need according to Federal Methodology, of whom 98% were aided. *Financial aid deadline*

(priority): 3/1. *Financial aid forms:* FAFSA, institutional form required; CSS Financial Aid PROFILE acceptable. *Admission application deadline:* rolling.

Summary of Aid to Needy Students *From gift & self-help combined:* Average need met: 61%. Average amount awarded: $4541 (61% gift aid, 39% self-help). *Gift aid:* Total: $3,530,153 (3% from college's own funds, 3% from other college-administered sources, 94% from external sources). 150 Federal Work-Study jobs (averaging $1428).

Need-Based Scholarships & Grants Pell, FSEOG, state, private, college/university.

Loans Perkins, PLUS, Stafford, Unsubsidized Stafford, Federal Nursing, private.

Non-Need Awards In 1996, a total of 249 non-need awards were made. *Academic Interests/Achievement Awards:* available. *Special Achievements/Activities Awards:* available. *Special Characteristics Awards:* available.

Other Money-Saving Options Accelerated degree, co-op program, Army ROTC. *Payment Plans:* tuition prepayment, deferred payment. *Waivers:* full or partial for employees or children of employees and senior citizens.

Contact Office of Financial Aid, Indiana University Northwest, 3400 Broadway Street, Gary, IN 46408-1197, 219-980-6500.

INDIANA UNIVERSITY OF PENNSYLVANIA
Indiana, Pennsylvania

About the Institution State-supported, coed. Degrees awarded: A, B, M, D. Offers 90 undergraduate majors. Total enrollment: 13,680. Undergraduates: 12,144 (96% state residents). Freshmen: 1,928.

Undergraduate Expenses (1996–97) State resident tuition: $3368. Nonresident tuition: $8566. Mandatory fees: $696. College room and board: $3332. College room only: $1876.

Applications 91% of all full-time undergraduates enrolled in fall 1996 applied for aid; of these, 70% were judged to have need according to Federal Methodology, of whom 86% were aided. *Financial aid deadline:* Applications processed continuously. *Financial aid forms:* FAFSA required. *Regular admission application deadline:* rolling. Early action deadline: 10/15.

Summary of Aid to Needy Students *From gift & self-help combined:* Average need met: 75%. Average amount awarded: $5355 (50% gift aid, 50% self-help). *Gift aid:* Total: $16,700,000 (9% from college's own funds, 11% from other college-administered sources, 80% from external sources). 2,000 Federal Work-Study jobs (averaging $1400); 2,000 part-time jobs.

Need-Based Scholarships & Grants Pell, FSEOG, state, private, college/university.

Loans Perkins, PLUS, Stafford, Unsubsidized Stafford, college/university short-term loans ($300 average).

Non-Need Awards In 1996, a total of 2,073 non-need awards were made. *Academic Interests/Achievement Awards:* 1,267 ($2,124,859 total): general academic, area/ethnic studies, biological sciences, business, communication, computer science, education, engineering/technologies, English, foreign languages, health fields, home economics, humanities, international studies, mathematics, physical sciences, premedicine, social sciences. *Creative Arts/Performance Awards:* 325 ($440,134 total): general creative, applied art and design, art/fine arts, dance, journalism/publications, music, performing arts, theater/drama. *Special Achievements/Activities Awards:* 186 ($167,400 total): general special achievements/activities, community service, hobbies/interest, leadership. *Special Characteristics Awards:* 110 ($199,910 total): adult students, ethnic background. *Athletic:* Total: 185 ($456,179); Men: 110 ($319,147); Women: 75 ($137,032).

Other Money-Saving Options Accelerated degree, co-op program, Army ROTC, off-campus living (after freshman year). *Payment Plans:* installment, deferred payment. *Waivers:* full or partial for minority students and employees or children of employees.

Contact Mr. Frederick A. Joseph, Director of Financial Aid, Indiana University of Pennsylvania, 308 Pratt Hall, Indiana, PA 15705, 412-357-2218.

INDIANA UNIVERSITY–PURDUE UNIVERSITY FORT WAYNE
Fort Wayne, Indiana

About the Institution State-supported, coed. Degrees awarded: A, B, M. Offers 76 undergraduate majors. Total enrollment: 10,749. Undergraduates: 9,889 (94% state residents). Freshmen: 2,308.

Undergraduate Expenses (1997–98) State resident tuition: $3026. Nonresident tuition: $7311. Mandatory fees: $295.

Applications *Financial aid deadline (priority):* 4/30. *Financial aid forms:* FAFSA required. *Admission application deadline:* 8/1.

Summary of Aid to Needy Students *Gift aid:* Total: $5,600,000. Federal Work-Study jobs; part-time jobs.

Need-Based Scholarships & Grants Pell, FSEOG, state.

Loans Perkins, PLUS, Stafford, Unsubsidized Stafford.

Non-Need Awards *Academic Interests/Achievement Awards:* general academic, business, education, engineering/technologies. *Creative Arts/Performance Awards:* art/fine arts, music, theater/drama. *Special Characteristics Awards:* children of faculty/staff, children with a deceased or disabled parent, handicapped students, local/state students. *Athletic:* available.

Another Money-Saving Option Co-op program.

Contact Mr. Robert M. Zellers, Director of Financial Aid, Indiana University–Purdue University Fort Wayne, 2101 East Coliseum Boulevard, Fort Wayne, IN 46805-1499, 219-481-6130.

INDIANA UNIVERSITY–PURDUE UNIVERSITY INDIANAPOLIS
Indianapolis, Indiana

About the Institution State-supported, coed. Degrees awarded: A, B, M, D, P. Offers 88 undergraduate majors. Total enrollment: 27,011. Undergraduates: 19,950 (98% state residents). Freshmen: 2,840.

Undergraduate Expenses (1997–98) State resident tuition: $3188. Nonresident tuition: $9780. Mandatory fees: $253. College room and board: $3800.

Applications 63% of all full-time undergraduates enrolled in fall 1996 applied for aid; of these, 90% were judged to have need according to Federal Methodology, of whom 95% were aided. *Financial aid deadline (priority):* 3/1. *Financial aid forms:* FAFSA, institutional form required; CSS Financial Aid PROFILE acceptable. *Admission application deadline:* rolling.

Summary of Aid to Needy Students *From gift & self-help combined:* Average need met: 53%. Average amount awarded: $5224 (46% gift aid, 54% self-help). *Gift aid:* Total: $13,984,829 (8% from college's own funds, 3% from other college-administered sources, 89% from external sources). 224 Federal Work-Study jobs (averaging $2839); part-time jobs.

Need-Based Scholarships & Grants Pell, FSEOG, state, private, college/university.

Loans Perkins, PLUS, Stafford, Unsubsidized Stafford, Federal Nursing, private, college/university short-term loans.

Non-Need Awards In 1996, a total of 1,535 non-need awards were made. *Academic Interests/Achievement Awards:* available. *Creative Arts/*

Performance Awards: available. *Special Achievements/Activities Awards:* available. *Special Characteristics Awards:* available. *Athletic:* available.

Other Money-Saving Options Accelerated degree, co-op program, Army ROTC, cooperative Air Force ROTC, off-campus living. *Payment Plans:* installment, deferred payment. *Waivers:* full or partial for employees or children of employees.

Contact Office of Financial Aid, Indiana University–Purdue University Indianapolis, 425 North University Boulevard #103, Indianapolis, IN 46202-5145, 317-274-5555.

INDIANA UNIVERSITY SOUTH BEND
South Bend, Indiana

About the Institution State-supported, coed. Degrees awarded: A, B, M. Offers 58 undergraduate majors. Total enrollment: 7,544. Undergraduates: 5,120 (97% state residents). Freshmen: 1,142.

Undergraduate Expenses (1996–97) State resident tuition: $2658. Nonresident tuition: $7271. Mandatory fees: $180 (minimum).

Applications Of all full-time undergraduates enrolled in fall 1996, 90% of those who applied for aid were judged to have need according to Federal Methodology, of whom 86% were aided. *Financial aid deadline (priority):* 3/1. *Financial aid forms:* FAFSA, institutional form required; CSS Financial Aid PROFILE acceptable. *Admission application deadline:* 7/1.

Summary of Aid to Needy Students *From gift & self-help combined:* Average need met: 49%. Average amount awarded: $3878 (47% gift aid, 53% self-help). *Gift aid:* Total: $2,607,725 (5% from college's own funds, 5% from other college-administered sources, 90% from external sources). 43 Federal Work-Study jobs (averaging $1906).

Need-Based Scholarships & Grants Pell, FSEOG, state, private, college/university.

Loans Perkins, PLUS, Stafford, Unsubsidized Stafford, Federal Nursing, private, college/university short-term loans.

Non-Need Awards In 1996, a total of 199 non-need awards were made. *Academic Interests/Achievement Awards:* available. *Creative Arts/Performance Awards:* available. *Special Achievements/Activities Awards:* available. *Special Characteristics Awards:* available. *Athletic:* available.

Other Money-Saving Options Accelerated degree, cooperative Army ROTC, cooperative Naval ROTC, cooperative Air Force ROTC. *Payment Plans:* installment, deferred payment. *Waivers:* full or partial for employees or children of employees.

Contact Office of Financial Aid, Indiana University South Bend, South Bend, IN 46634-7111, 219-237-4111.

INDIANA UNIVERSITY SOUTHEAST
New Albany, Indiana

About the Institution State-supported, coed. Degrees awarded: A, B, M. Offers 37 undergraduate majors. Total enrollment: 5,396. Undergraduates: 4,854 (98% state residents).

Undergraduate Expenses (1996–97) State resident tuition: $2612. Nonresident tuition: $6773. Mandatory fees: $106.

Applications Of all full-time undergraduates enrolled in fall 1996, 86% of those who applied for aid were judged to have need according to Federal Methodology, of whom 93% were aided. *Financial aid deadline (priority):* 3/1. *Financial aid forms:* FAFSA, institutional form required; CSS Financial Aid PROFILE acceptable. *Admission application deadline:* rolling.

Summary of Aid to Needy Students *From gift & self-help combined:* Average need met: 49%. Average amount awarded: $3713 (63% gift aid, 37% self-help). *Gift aid:* Total: $3,111,603 (9% from college's own funds, 3% from other college-administered sources, 88% from external sources). 95 Federal Work-Study jobs (averaging $1644); part-time jobs.

Need-Based Scholarships & Grants Pell, FSEOG, state, private, college/university.

Loans Perkins, PLUS, Stafford, Unsubsidized Stafford, Federal Nursing, private, college/university short-term loans.

Non-Need Awards In 1996, a total of 589 non-need awards were made. *Academic Interests/Achievement Awards:* available. *Creative Arts/Performance Awards:* available. *Special Characteristics Awards:* available. *Athletic:* available.

Other Money-Saving Options Accelerated degree, cooperative Army ROTC, cooperative Air Force ROTC.

Contact Office of Financial Aid, Indiana University Southeast, 4201 Grant Line Road, New Albany, IN 47150-6405, 812-941-2000.

INDIANA WESLEYAN UNIVERSITY
Marion, Indiana

About the Institution Independent/religious, coed. Degrees awarded: A, B, M. Offers 54 undergraduate majors. Total enrollment: 5,069. Undergraduates: 3,899 (61% state residents). Freshmen: 396.

Undergraduate Expenses (1997–98) Comprehensive fee of $14,880 includes tuition ($10,722) and college room and board ($4158). College room only: $1752.

Applications 90% of all full-time undergraduates enrolled in fall 1996 applied for aid; of these, 95% were judged to have need according to Federal Methodology, of whom 100% were aided. *Financial aid deadline (priority):* 3/1. *Financial aid forms:* FAFSA, institutional form required. *Admission application deadline:* rolling.

Summary of Aid to Needy Students *From gift & self-help combined:* Average amount awarded: $10,500. 320 Federal Work-Study jobs (averaging $1200); 200 part-time jobs.

Need-Based Scholarships & Grants Pell, FSEOG, state, private, college/university.

Loans Perkins, PLUS, Stafford, Unsubsidized Stafford, private, college/university long-term loans ($2500 average).

Non-Need Awards In 1996, a total of 1,346 non-need awards were made. *Academic Interests/Achievement Awards:* 333 ($925,559 total): general academic. *Creative Arts/Performance Awards:* 55 ($50,850 total): art/fine arts, music. *Special Characteristics Awards:* 786 ($920,100 total): children and siblings of alumni, relatives of clergy, religious affiliation, siblings of current students. *Athletic:* Total: 172 ($390,000); Men: 90 ($200,000); Women: 82 ($190,000).

Other Money-Saving Options Accelerated degree, off-campus living (after junior year). *Payment Plan:* installment. *Waivers:* full or partial for employees or children of employees.

Contact Financial Aid Office, Indiana Wesleyan University, Marion, IN 46953-4999, 765-677-2114.

INTER AMERICAN UNIVERSITY OF PUERTO RICO, AGUADILLA CAMPUS
Aguadilla, Puerto Rico

About the Institution Independent, coed. Degrees awarded: A, B. Offers 10 undergraduate majors. Total enrollment: 3,629 (100% commonwealth residents). Freshmen: 849.

Undergraduate Expenses (1996–97) Tuition: $2280. Mandatory fees: $220.

Applications Of all full-time undergraduates enrolled in fall 1996, 100% of those judged to have need according to Federal Methodology were aided. *Financial aid deadline (priority):* 4/30. *Financial aid forms:* FAFSA, institutional form required. Commonwealth form required for some. *Admission application deadline:* rolling.

Summary of Aid to Needy Students *From gift & self-help combined:* Average need met: 85%. *Gift aid:* Total: $5,273,790 (4% from college's

own funds, 19% from other college-administered sources, 77% from external sources). Federal Work-Study jobs.

Need-Based Scholarships & Grants Pell, FSEOG, state, college/university.

Loans Perkins, Stafford, Unsubsidized Stafford.

Non-Need Awards *Academic Interests/Achievement Awards:* 95 ($30,506 total): general academic, biological sciences, business, computer science, education. *Creative Arts/Performance Awards:* 21 ($1995 total): music. *Special Characteristics Awards:* children of faculty/staff, veterans, veterans' children. *Athletic:* Total: 10 ($4102).

Contact Mr. Juan Gonzalez, Director of Financial Aid, Inter American University of Puerto Rico, Aguadilla Campus, PO Box 20000, Aguadilla, PR 00605, 787-891-0925 Ext. 2108, fax: 787-882-3020.

INTER AMERICAN UNIVERSITY OF PUERTO RICO, ARECIBO CAMPUS
Arecibo, Puerto Rico

About the Institution Independent, coed. Degrees awarded: A, B. Offers 17 undergraduate majors. Total enrollment: 4,220 (100% commonwealth residents). Freshmen: 754.

Undergraduate Expenses (1996–97) Comprehensive fee of $5766 includes tuition ($2280), mandatory fees ($220), and college room and board ($3266). College room only: $1250.

Applications *Financial aid deadline:* 4/30. *Financial aid forms:* FAFSA, institutional form required. *Admission application deadline:* rolling.

Summary of Aid to Needy Students Federal Work-Study jobs.

Other Money-Saving Options Co-op program, cooperative Army ROTC. *Payment Plan:* guaranteed tuition. *Waivers:* full or partial for employees or children of employees.

Contact Office of Financial Aid, Inter American University of Puerto Rico, Arecibo Campus, Arecibo, PR 00614-4050, 787-878-5475.

INTER AMERICAN UNIVERSITY OF PUERTO RICO, BARRANQUITAS CAMPUS
Barranquitas, Puerto Rico

About the Institution Independent, coed. Degrees awarded: A, B. Offers 8 undergraduate majors. Total enrollment: 1,687 (100% commonwealth residents).

Undergraduate Expenses (1996–97) Tuition: $2280. Mandatory fees: $110.

Applications *Financial aid deadline:* Applications processed continuously. *Financial aid forms:* FAFSA, institutional form required. *Admission application deadline:* rolling.

Summary of Aid to Needy Students *From gift & self-help combined:* Average need met: 98%. *Gift aid:* Total: $4,051,006 (4% from college's own funds, 9% from other college-administered sources, 87% from external sources). 315 Federal Work-Study jobs.

Need-Based Scholarships & Grants Pell, FSEOG, state.

Loans Perkins, Stafford.

Non-Need Awards In 1996, a total of 498 non-need awards were made. *Special Characteristics Awards:* 496 ($1,100,000 total): adult students, veterans. *Athletic:* Total: 2 ($750); Men: 2 ($750); Women: 0.

Other Money-Saving Options *Payment Plans:* guaranteed tuition, deferred payment. *Waivers:* full or partial for minority students.

Contact Mr. Eduardo Fontánez Colón, Director of Financial Aid, Inter American University of Puerto Rico, Barranquitas Campus, Box 517, Barranquitas, PR 00794, 787-857-3600 Ext. 2049, fax: 787-857-2244.

INTER AMERICAN UNIVERSITY OF PUERTO RICO, FAJARDO CAMPUS
Fajardo, Puerto Rico

About the Institution Independent, coed. Degrees awarded: A, B. Offers 26 undergraduate majors. Total enrollment: 1,964 (100% commonwealth residents).

Undergraduate Expenses (1996–97) Tuition: $2280. Mandatory fees: $220.

Applications *Financial aid deadline:* Applications processed continuously. *Financial aid forms:* FAFSA, institutional form required. *Admission application deadline:* rolling.

Summary of Aid to Needy Students Federal Work-Study jobs.

Another Money-Saving Option *Payment Plan:* deferred payment.

Contact Office of Financial Aid, Inter American University of Puerto Rico, Fajardo Campus, Fajardo, PR 00738-7003, 787-863-2390.

INTER AMERICAN UNIVERSITY OF PUERTO RICO, GUAYAMA CAMPUS
Guayama, Puerto Rico

About the Institution Independent, coed. Degrees awarded: A, B. Offers 9 undergraduate majors. Total enrollment: 2,027 (100% commonwealth residents). Freshmen: 325.

Undergraduate Expenses (1996–97) Tuition: $2280. Mandatory fees: $220.

Applications *Financial aid deadline (priority):* 4/30. *Financial aid forms:* FAFSA, institutional form required. *Admission application deadline:* 8/1.

Summary of Aid to Needy Students 422 Federal Work-Study jobs (averaging $400).

Need-Based Scholarships & Grants Pell, FSEOG, state, college/university.

Loans Perkins, PLUS, Stafford, Unsubsidized Stafford, Federal Nursing.

Non-Need Awards *Athletic:* Total: 1 ($700); Men: 1 ($700); Women: 0.

Other Money-Saving Options Cooperative Army ROTC. *Payment Plan:* deferred payment. *Waivers:* full or partial for employees or children of employees.

Contact Office of Financial Aid, Inter American University of Puerto Rico, Guayama Campus, Guayama, PR 00785, 787-864-2222.

INTER AMERICAN UNIVERSITY OF PUERTO RICO, METROPOLITAN CAMPUS
Hato Rey, Puerto Rico

About the Institution Independent, coed. Degrees awarded: A, B, M. Offers 64 undergraduate majors. Total enrollment: 13,910. Undergraduates: 12,098 (90% commonwealth residents). Freshmen: 2,110.

Undergraduate Expenses (1996–97) Tuition: $2280. Mandatory fees: $220.

Applications *Financial aid deadline:* Applications processed continuously. *Financial aid forms:* FAFSA, institutional form required. *Admission application deadline:* rolling.

Summary of Aid to Needy Students Federal Work-Study jobs; part-time jobs.

Need-Based Scholarships & Grants Pell, FSEOG, state, college/university.

Loans Perkins, PLUS, Stafford, Unsubsidized Stafford.

Non-Need Awards Not offered.

Other Money-Saving Options Accelerated degree, co-op program, cooperative Army ROTC, cooperative Naval ROTC, cooperative Air Force ROTC.

Contact Office of Financial Aid, Inter American University of Puerto Rico, Metropolitan Campus, Hato Rey, PR 00919, 787-758-2891.

INTER AMERICAN UNIVERSITY OF PUERTO RICO, PONCE CAMPUS
Mercedita, Puerto Rico

About the Institution Independent, coed. Degrees awarded: A, B. Offers 16 undergraduate majors. Total enrollment: 3,503. Freshmen: 409.

Undergraduate Expenses (1996–97) Tuition: $2280. Mandatory fees: $220.

Applications *Financial aid deadline (priority):* 4/15. *Financial aid forms:* FAFSA required. *Admission application deadline:* 8/1.

Summary of Aid to Needy Students Federal Work-Study jobs.

Non-Need Awards Not offered.

Contact Office of Financial Aid, Inter American University of Puerto Rico, Ponce Campus, Carr. 1 KM 123.2 (Interior), Mercedita, PR 00715-2201, 787-284-1912.

INTER AMERICAN UNIVERSITY OF PUERTO RICO, SAN GERMÁN CAMPUS
San Germán, Puerto Rico

About the Institution Independent, coed. Degrees awarded: A, B, M. Offers 60 undergraduate majors. Total enrollment: 6,286. Undergraduates: 5,357 (98% commonwealth residents). Freshmen: 921.

Undergraduate Expenses (1996–97) Comprehensive fee of $4700 includes tuition ($2280), mandatory fees ($220), and college room and board ($2200). College room only: $900.

Applications 89% of all full-time undergraduates enrolled in fall 1996 applied for aid; of these, 100% were judged to have need according to Federal Methodology, of whom 94% were aided. *Financial aid deadline:* Applications processed continuously. *Financial aid forms:* FAFSA, institutional form required. *Admission application deadline:* 8/1.

Summary of Aid to Needy Students *From gift & self-help combined:* Average need met: 90%. Average amount awarded: $2925 (64% gift aid, 36% self-help). *Gift aid:* Total: $7,038,400 (3% from college's own funds, 4% from other college-administered sources, 93% from external sources). Federal Work-Study jobs.

Need-Based Scholarships & Grants Pell, FSEOG, state, college/university.

Loans Perkins, PLUS, Stafford, Unsubsidized Stafford.

Non-Need Awards Not offered.

Other Money-Saving Options Cooperative Army ROTC, cooperative Naval ROTC, cooperative Air Force ROTC, off-campus living. *Payment Plan:* deferred payment. *Waivers:* full or partial for employees or children of employees.

Contact Ms. María I. Lugo, Financial Aid Director, Inter American University of Puerto Rico, San Germán Campus, Call Box 5100, San Germán, PR 00683-5008, 787-264-1912 Ext. 7252, fax: 787-893-6350.

INTERNATIONAL ACADEMY OF MERCHANDISING & DESIGN, INC.
Tampa, Florida

About the Institution Proprietary, coed. Degrees awarded: A, B. Offers 6 undergraduate majors. Total enrollment: 500 (85% state residents). Freshmen: 160.

Undergraduate Expenses (1997–98) Tuition: $9270 (minimum).

Applications *Financial aid deadline (priority):* 9/1. *Financial aid forms:* institutional form required; CSS Financial Aid PROFILE acceptable. State form required for some. *Admission application deadline:* rolling.

Summary of Aid to Needy Students *From gift & self-help combined:* Average need met: 93%. Average amount awarded: $6660 (12% gift aid, 88% self-help). *Gift aid:* Total: $116,975 (5% from college's own funds, 29% from other college-administered sources, 66% from external sources). Federal Work-Study jobs; 24 part-time jobs.

Need-Based Scholarships & Grants Pell, FSEOG, state.

Loans PLUS, Stafford, Unsubsidized Stafford, private.

Non-Need Awards In 1996, a total of 2 non-need awards were made. *Academic Interests/Achievement Awards:* 2 ($3500 total): general academic. *Creative Arts/Performance Awards:* 0: applied art and design.

Other Money-Saving Options Accelerated degree, co-op program. *Payment Plans:* installment, deferred payment.

Contact Office of Financial Aid, International Academy of Merchandising & Design, Inc., 5225 Memorial Highway, Tampa, FL 33634-7350, 813-881-0007.

INTERNATIONAL ACADEMY OF MERCHANDISING & DESIGN, LTD.
Chicago, Illinois

About the Institution Proprietary, coed. Degrees awarded: A, B. Offers 6 undergraduate majors. Total enrollment: 758 (90% state residents). Freshmen: 238.

Undergraduate Expenses (1996–97) Tuition: $9270 (minimum).

Applications 92% of all full-time undergraduates enrolled in fall 1996 applied for aid; of these, 94% were judged to have need according to Federal Methodology, of whom 94% were aided. *Financial aid deadline (priority):* 9/1. *Financial aid forms:* FAFSA, institutional form required. *Admission application deadline:* rolling.

Summary of Aid to Needy Students *From gift & self-help combined:* Average amount awarded: $5030 (30% gift aid, 70% self-help). *Gift aid:* Total: $339,011 (19% from college-administered sources, 81% from external sources). 18 Federal Work-Study jobs (averaging $4000); 4 part-time jobs.

Need-Based Scholarships & Grants Pell, FSEOG, private.

Loans PLUS, Stafford, Unsubsidized Stafford, private.

Non-Need Awards Not offered.

Other Money-Saving Options *Payment Plans:* installment, deferred payment. *Waivers:* full or partial for employees or children of employees.

Contact Office of Financial Aid, International Academy of Merchandising & Design, Ltd., 1 North State, Suite 400, Chicago, IL 60602-3300, 312-541-3910, fax: 312-541-3929.

INTERNATIONAL BAPTIST COLLEGE
Tempe, Arizona

About the Institution Independent/religious. Degrees awarded: A, B, M.

Undergraduate Expenses (1996–97) Comprehensive fee of $6140 includes tuition ($3360), mandatory fees ($180), and college room and board ($2600).

Applications *Financial aid forms:* institutional form required.

Need-Based Scholarships & Grants Private, college/university.

Non-Need Awards Not offered.

Contact Mr. Jerry Petreau, College President, International Baptist College, Tempe, AZ 85282, 602-838-7070.

INTERNATIONAL BIBLE COLLEGE
Florence, Alabama

About the Institution Independent/religious, coed. Degrees awarded: A, B. Offers 1 undergraduate major. Total enrollment: 155 (26% state residents). Freshmen: 5.

Undergraduate Expenses (1997–98) Tuition: $4768. Mandatory fees: $452. College room only: $1200.

Applications 64% of all full-time undergraduates enrolled in fall 1996 applied for aid; of these,100% were judged to have need according to Federal Methodology, of whom 96% were aided. *Financial aid deadline (priority):* 6/1. *Financial aid forms:* FAFSA, federal income tax forms required. *Admission application deadline:* rolling.

Summary of Aid to Needy Students *From gift & self-help combined:* Average amount awarded: $4703 (29% gift aid, 71% self-help). *Gift aid:* Total: $72,320. 5 Federal Work-Study jobs (averaging $647); part-time jobs.

Need-Based Scholarships & Grants Pell, FSEOG, college/university.

Loans Stafford, Unsubsidized Stafford.

Non-Need Awards In 1996, a total of 2 non-need awards were made. *Academic Interests/Achievement Awards:* 2 ($200 total): general academic.

Other Money-Saving Options Accelerated degree. *Payment Plans:* installment, deferred payment. *Waivers:* full or partial for employees or children of employees.

Contact Ms. Angie Horton, Financial Aid Counselor, International Bible College, PO Box IBC, Florence, AL 35630, 800-367-3565, fax: 205-760-0981.

INTERNATIONAL COLLEGE
Naples, Florida

About the Institution Independent, coed. Degrees awarded: A, B. Offers 6 undergraduate majors. Total enrollment: 600. Freshmen: 116.

Undergraduate Expenses (1996–97) Tuition: $6600. Mandatory fees: $135.

Applications 83% of all full-time undergraduates enrolled in fall 1996 applied for aid; of these, 98% were judged to have need according to Federal Methodology, of whom 98% were aided. *Financial aid deadline:* continuous. *Financial aid forms:* FAFSA required. *Admission application deadline:* rolling.

Summary of Aid to Needy Students *From gift & self-help combined:* Average need met: 100%. Average amount awarded: $7450 (30% gift aid, 70% self-help). *Gift aid:* Total: $654,000 (1% from college's own funds, 99% from external sources).

Need-Based Scholarships & Grants Pell, state, private, college/university.

Loans PLUS, Stafford, Unsubsidized Stafford.

Non-Need Awards Not offered.

Other Money-Saving Options Accelerated degree, co-op program. *Payment Plan:* installment. *Waivers:* full or partial for employees or children of employees.

Contact Mr. Joe Gilchrist, Director of Financial Aid, International College, 2654 East Tamiami Trail, Naples, FL 34112, 941-774-4700.

IONA COLLEGE
New Rochelle, New York

About the Institution Independent, coed. Degrees awarded: A, B, M. Offers 62 undergraduate majors. Total enrollment: 5,588. Undergraduates: 4,079 (91% state residents). Freshmen: 646.

Undergraduate Expenses (1996–97) Comprehensive fee of $20,040 includes tuition ($12,200), mandatory fees ($320), and college room and board ($7520).

Applications Of all full-time undergraduates enrolled in fall 1996, 90% of those who applied for aid were judged to have need according to Federal Methodology, of whom 90% were aided. *Financial aid deadline (priority):* 4/15. *Financial aid forms:* FAFSA, institutional form required. State form required for some. *Admission application deadline:* 3/15.

Summary of Aid to Needy Students *From gift & self-help combined:* Average need met: 72%. Average amount awarded: $11,400 (58% gift aid, 42% self-help). *Gift aid:* Total: $18,821,868 (36% from college's own funds, 39% from other college-administered sources, 25% from external sources). 331 Federal Work-Study jobs (averaging $1059); 177 part-time jobs.

Need-Based Scholarships & Grants Pell, FSEOG, state, private, college/university.

Loans Perkins, PLUS, Stafford, Unsubsidized Stafford, private.

Non-Need Awards In 1996, a total of 1,210 non-need awards were made. *Academic Interests/Achievement Awards:* 1,072 ($4,378,897 total): general academic. *Creative Arts/Performance Awards:* 16 ($71,608 total): music. *Athletic:* Total: 122 ($578,677); Men: 72 ($346,063); Women: 50 ($232,614).

Other Money-Saving Options Accelerated degree, cooperative Army ROTC, off-campus living. *Payment Plans:* installment, deferred payment. *Waivers:* full or partial for employees or children of employees and senior citizens.

Contact Mrs. Norma Abrams-McNerney, Director of Financial Aid, Iona College, 715 North Avenue, New Rochelle, NY 10801-1890, 914-633-2497.

IOWA STATE UNIVERSITY OF SCIENCE AND TECHNOLOGY
Ames, Iowa

About the Institution State-supported, coed. Degrees awarded: B, M, D, P. Offers 116 undergraduate majors. Total enrollment: 24,899. Undergraduates: 20,503 (77% state residents). Freshmen: 3,610.

Undergraduate Expenses (1996–97) State resident tuition: $2470. Nonresident tuition: $8204. Mandatory fees: $196 (minimum). College room and board: $3508. College room only: $1770.

Applications 70% of all full-time undergraduates enrolled in fall 1996 applied for aid; of these, 82% were judged to have need according to Federal Methodology, of whom 100% were aided. *Financial aid deadline (priority):* 3/1. *Financial aid forms:* FAFSA required. *Admission application deadline:* rolling.

Summary of Aid to Needy Students *From gift & self-help combined:* Average need met: 100%. Average amount awarded: $6093 (23% gift aid, 77% self-help). *Gift aid:* Total: $15,000,000 (13% from college's own funds, 23% from other college-administered sources, 64% from external sources). 1,096 Federal Work-Study jobs (averaging $1006); 3,178 part-time jobs.

Need-Based Scholarships & Grants Pell, FSEOG, state, private, college/university.

Loans Perkins, PLUS, Stafford, Unsubsidized Stafford, private, college/university short-term loans ($600 average), college/university long-term loans ($1200 average).

Non-Need Awards In 1996, a total of 8,802 non-need awards were made. *Academic Interests/Achievement Awards:* 7,496 ($10,626,101 total): general academic, agriculture, architecture, area/ethnic studies, biological sciences, business, communication, computer science, education, engineering/technologies, English, foreign languages, health fields, home economics, humanities, international studies, library science, mathematics, physical sciences, premedicine, social sciences. *Creative Arts/Performance Awards:* 56 ($41,200 total): music. *Special Achievements/*

Activities Awards: 32 ($32,000 total): community service, leadership. *Special Characteristics Awards:* 843 ($2,781,024 total): adult students, ethnic background, first-generation college students, international students, members of minorities, out-of-state students, ROTC participants. *Athletic:* Total: 375 ($2,369,956); Men: 234 ($922,186); Women: 141 ($1,447,770).

Other Money-Saving Options Accelerated degree, co-op program, Army ROTC, Naval ROTC, Air Force ROTC, off-campus living. *Payment Plan:* installment.

Contact Mr. Earl E. Dowling, Director of Financial Aid, Iowa State University of Science and Technology, 12 Beardshear Hall, Ames, IA 50011, 515-294-2223, fax: 515-294-0851.

IOWA WESLEYAN COLLEGE
Mount Pleasant, Iowa

About the Institution Independent/religious, coed. Degrees awarded: B. Offers 43 undergraduate majors. Total enrollment: 794 (79% state residents). Freshmen: 103.

Undergraduate Expenses (1996–97) Comprehensive fee of $15,140 includes tuition ($11,300) and college room and board ($3840). College room only: $1700.

Applications 98% of all full-time undergraduates enrolled in fall 1996 applied for aid; of these, 97% were judged to have need according to Federal Methodology, of whom 100% were aided. *Financial aid deadline (priority):* 4/1. *Financial aid forms:* FAFSA required. *Admission application deadline:* 8/15.

Summary of Aid to Needy Students *From gift & self-help combined:* Average need met: 85%. Average amount awarded: $12,300 (61% gift aid, 39% self-help). *Gift aid:* Total: $3,305,255 (60% from college's own funds, 4% from other college-administered sources, 36% from external sources). 152 Federal Work-Study jobs (averaging $900); 41 part-time jobs.

Need-Based Scholarships & Grants Pell, FSEOG, state, private, college/university.

Loans Perkins, PLUS, Stafford, Unsubsidized Stafford, private, college/university long-term loans ($1400 average).

Non-Need Awards In 1996, a total of 459 non-need awards were made. *Academic Interests/Achievement Awards:* 130 ($134,446 total): general academic, biological sciences, communication. *Creative Arts/Performance Awards:* 16 ($38,800 total): art/fine arts, music. *Special Achievements/Activities Awards:* 8 ($3500 total): cheerleading/drum major. *Special Characteristics Awards:* 79 ($227,950 total): children of faculty/staff, ethnic background, international students, members of minorities, relatives of clergy, religious affiliation. *Athletic:* Total: 226 ($544,085); Men: 139 ($329,218); Women: 87 ($214,867).

Other Money-Saving Options Off-campus living (after junior year). *Payment Plans:* installment, deferred payment. *Waivers:* full or partial for employees or children of employees.

Contact Ms. Marsha Boender, Director of Enrollment Services, Iowa Wesleyan College, 601 North Main Street, Mount Pleasant, IA 52641-1398, 319-385-6242, fax: 319-385-6296.

ITHACA COLLEGE
Ithaca, New York

About the Institution Independent, coed. Degrees awarded: B, M. Offers 73 undergraduate majors. Total enrollment: 5,683. Undergraduates: 5,460 (49% state residents). Freshmen: 1,426.

Undergraduate Expenses (1997–98) Comprehensive fee of $24,240 includes tuition ($16,900) and college room and board ($7340). College room only: $3682.

Applications 73% of all full-time undergraduates enrolled in fall 1996 applied for aid; of these, 91% were judged to have need according to

Federal Methodology, of whom 99% were aided. *Financial aid deadline (priority):* 3/1. *Financial aid forms:* FAFSA required. Institutional form, W-2 forms required for some. *Regular admission application deadline:* 3/1. Early decision deadline: 11/1.

Summary of Aid to Needy Students *From gift & self-help combined:* Average need met: 80%. Average amount awarded: $13,667 (67% gift aid, 33% self-help). *Gift aid:* Total: $33,281,860 (83% from college's own funds, 2% from other college-administered sources, 15% from external sources). 293 Federal Work-Study jobs (averaging $1400); 1,894 part-time jobs.

Need-Based Scholarships & Grants Pell, FSEOG, state, private, college/university.

Loans Perkins, PLUS, Stafford, Unsubsidized Stafford, private, college/university long-term loans ($7039 average).

Non-Need Awards In 1996, a total of 1,122 non-need awards were made. *Academic Interests/Achievement Awards:* 1,053 ($4,802,450 total): general academic. *Creative Arts/Performance Awards:* 69 ($268,500 total): music, theater/drama.

Other Money-Saving Options Accelerated degree, cooperative Army ROTC, cooperative Air Force ROTC. *Payment Plan:* installment. *Waivers:* full or partial for employees or children of employees.

Contact Office of Financial Aid, Ithaca College, 330 Egbert Hall, Ithaca, NY 14850-7130, 607-274-3011.

ITT TECHNICAL INSTITUTE
Maitland, Florida

About the Institution Proprietary, coed. Degrees awarded: A, B. Offers 3 undergraduate majors.

Applications 100% of all full-time undergraduates enrolled in fall 1996 applied for aid; of these,100% were judged to have need according to Federal Methodology, of whom 100% were aided. *Financial aid deadline:* Applications processed continuously. *Financial aid forms:* FAFSA, institutional form required; CSS Financial Aid PROFILE, state form acceptable. *Admission application deadline:* rolling.

Summary of Aid to Needy Students *From gift & self-help combined:* Average need met: 76%. *Gift aid:* Total: $400,000 (100% from external sources). Federal Work-Study jobs.

Need-Based Scholarships & Grants Pell.

Loans PLUS, Stafford, Unsubsidized Stafford.

Non-Need Awards In 1996, a total of 2 non-need awards were made. *Academic Interests/Achievement Awards:* 2 ($22,000 total): engineering/technologies.

Other Money-Saving Options Accelerated degree, co-op program. *Payment Plan:* guaranteed tuition. *Waivers:* full or partial for employees or children of employees.

Contact Office of Financial Aid, ITT Technical Institute, Maitland, FL 32751-7234, 407-660-2900.

JACKSON STATE UNIVERSITY
Jackson, Mississippi

About the Institution State-supported, coed. Degrees awarded: B, M, D. Offers 51 undergraduate majors. Total enrollment: 6,218. Undergraduates: 5,144 (73% state residents). Freshmen: 1,275.

Undergraduate Expenses (1996–97) State resident tuition: $2380. Nonresident tuition: $4974. College room and board: $3138. College room only: $1792.

Applications Of all full-time undergraduates enrolled in fall 1996, 98% of those who applied for aid were judged to have need according to Federal Methodology, of whom 91% were aided. *Financial aid deadline (priority):* 4/1. *Financial aid forms:* FAFSA, state form, institutional form required; CSS Financial Aid PROFILE acceptable. *Admission application deadline:* 8/1.

Summary of Aid to Needy Students *From gift & self-help combined:* Average need met: 80%. Average amount awarded: $7502 (98% gift aid, 2% self-help). *Gift aid:* Total: $25,650,345 (1% from college's own funds, 16% from other college-administered sources, 83% from external sources). 1,780 Federal Work-Study jobs (averaging $1688); 235 part-time jobs.

Need-Based Scholarships & Grants Pell, FSEOG, state, private, college/university.

Loans Perkins, PLUS, Stafford, Unsubsidized Stafford, college/university short-term loans ($75 average).

Non-Need Awards In 1996, a total of 291 non-need awards were made. *Academic Interests/Achievement Awards:* 89 ($436,102 total): general academic. *Creative Arts/Performance Awards:* 40 ($134,569 total): music. *Special Characteristics Awards:* 141 ($161,878 total): children of faculty/staff, children of public servants. *Athletic:* Total: 21 ($53,405); Men: 11 ($36,350); Women: 10 ($17,055).

Other Money-Saving Options Accelerated degree, co-op program, Army ROTC, off-campus living. *Payment Plans:* installment, deferred payment. *Waivers:* full or partial for employees or children of employees.

Contact Mr. Gene Blakley, Director of Financial Aid, Jackson State University, 1400 J.R. Lynch Street, PO Box 17147, Jackson, MS 39217, 601-968-2227, fax: 601-968-2237.

JACKSONVILLE STATE UNIVERSITY
Jacksonville, Alabama

About the Institution State-supported, coed. Degrees awarded: B, M. Offers 60 undergraduate majors. Total enrollment: 7,688. Undergraduates: 6,548 (85% state residents). Freshmen: 950.

Undergraduate Expenses (1996–97) State resident tuition: $1940. Nonresident tuition: $2910. College room and board: $2870. College room only: $1300.

Applications 86% of all full-time undergraduates enrolled in fall 1996 applied for aid; of these, 95% were judged to have need according to Federal Methodology, of whom 93% were aided. *Financial aid deadline (priority):* 4/1. *Financial aid forms:* FAFSA, state form, institutional form required; CSS Financial Aid PROFILE acceptable. *Admission application deadline:* rolling.

Summary of Aid to Needy Students *From gift & self-help combined:* Average need met: 80%. Average amount awarded: $6500 (42% gift aid, 58% self-help). *Gift aid:* Total: $6,310,888 (35% from college's own funds, 5% from other college-administered sources, 60% from external sources). 400 Federal Work-Study jobs (averaging $1800); 500 part-time jobs.

Need-Based Scholarships & Grants Pell, FSEOG, state, private, college/university.

Loans Perkins, PLUS, Stafford, Unsubsidized Stafford, college/university short-term loans ($100 average), college/university long-term loans ($700 average).

Non-Need Awards *Academic Interests/Achievement Awards:* general academic, biological sciences, business, communication, computer science, education, English, health fields, home economics, humanities, mathematics, military science, physical sciences, social sciences. *Creative Arts/Performance Awards:* art/fine arts, music, theater/drama. *Special Achievements/Activities Awards:* general special achievements/activities, cheerleading/drum major, leadership. *Athletic:* Total: 219 ($873,977); Men: 137 ($531,553); Women: 82 ($342,424).

Other Money-Saving Options Accelerated degree, co-op program, Army ROTC, off-campus living. *Waivers:* full or partial for employees or children of employees and senior citizens.

Contact Mr. Larry Smith, Director of Financial Aid, Jacksonville State University, Pelham Road, Jacksonville, AL 36265-9982, 205-782-5006.

JACKSONVILLE UNIVERSITY
Jacksonville, Florida

About the Institution Independent, coed. Degrees awarded: B, M. Offers 58 undergraduate majors. Total enrollment: 2,321. Undergraduates: 2,019 (65% state residents). Freshmen: 370.

Undergraduate Expenses (1997–98) Comprehensive fee of $18,800 includes tuition ($13,360), mandatory fees ($540), and college room and board ($4900). College room only: $2260.

Applications Of all full-time undergraduates enrolled in fall 1996, 100% of those judged to have need according to Federal Methodology were aided. *Financial aid deadline (priority):* 3/15. *Financial aid forms:* FAFSA, institutional form, W-2 forms, federal income tax form required; CSS Financial Aid PROFILE acceptable. *Admission application deadline:* 8/1.

Summary of Aid to Needy Students *From gift & self-help combined:* Average amount awarded: $12,234 (76% gift aid, 24% self-help). *Gift aid:* Total: $11,549,875 (67% from college's own funds, 1% from other college-administered sources, 32% from external sources). 231 Federal Work-Study jobs (averaging $1313); 150 part-time jobs.

Need-Based Scholarships & Grants Pell, FSEOG, state, college/university.

Loans Perkins, PLUS, Stafford, Unsubsidized Stafford, private, college/university short-term loans ($500 average), college/university long-term loans ($4000 average).

Non-Need Awards In 1996, a total of 1,226 non-need awards were made. *Academic Interests/Achievement Awards:* 792 ($3,427,654 total): general academic, business, physical sciences. *Creative Arts/Performance Awards:* 136 ($238,941 total): art/fine arts, dance, music, theater/drama. *Special Characteristics Awards:* 107 ($991,102 total): children of current students, children of faculty/staff, ROTC participants, siblings of current students, spouses of current students. *Athletic:* Total: 191 ($1,116,280); Men: 123 ($684,068); Women: 68 ($432,212).

Other Money-Saving Options Accelerated degree, co-op program, Naval ROTC, off-campus living (after junior year). *Payment Plan:* installment. *Waivers:* full or partial for employees or children of employees.

Contact Financial Aid Office, Jacksonville University, 2800 University Boulevard North, Jacksonville, FL 32211-3394, 904-745-7060, fax: 904-745-7148.

JAMES MADISON UNIVERSITY
Harrisonburg, Virginia

About the Institution State-supported, coed. Degrees awarded: B, M, D. Offers 54 undergraduate majors. Total enrollment: 12,963. Undergraduates: 11,643 (68% state residents). Freshmen: 3,258.

Undergraduate Expenses (1997–98) State resident tuition: $4148. Nonresident tuition: $8816. College room and board: $4846. College room only: $2612.

Applications *Financial aid deadline (priority):* 2/15. *Financial aid forms:* FAFSA required; CSS Financial Aid PROFILE acceptable. Financial aid transcript (for transfers) required for some. *Regular admission application deadline:* 1/15. Early action deadline: 12/1.

Summary of Aid to Needy Students *From gift & self-help combined:* Average need met: 70%. Average amount awarded: $4930 (18% gift aid, 82% self-help). *Gift aid:* Total: $5,162,224 (7% from college's own funds, 60% from other college-administered sources, 33% from external sources). 300 Federal Work-Study jobs (averaging $1190); 3,000 part-time jobs.

Need-Based Scholarships & Grants Pell, FSEOG, state, private, college/university.

Loans Perkins, PLUS, Stafford, Unsubsidized Stafford, Federal Nursing, college/university short-term loans ($600 average), college/university long-term loans.

Non-Need Awards In 1996, a total of 790 non-need awards were made. *Academic Interests/Achievement Awards:* 169 ($146,145 total): general academic, architecture, biological sciences, business, education, English, health fields, humanities, international studies, mathematics, military science, physical sciences, premedicine, religion/biblical studies, social sciences. *Creative Arts/Performance Awards:* 136 ($89,100 total): art/fine arts, dance, journalism/publications, music, theater/drama. *Special Achievements/Activities Awards:* 27 ($25,500 total): cheerleading/drum major, leadership. *Special Characteristics Awards:* 109 ($313,825 total): children and siblings of alumni, children of educators, children of faculty/staff, international students, members of minorities, ROTC participants, siblings of current students. *Athletic:* Total: 349 ($2,291,574); Men: 212 ($1,394,390); Women: 137 ($897,184).

Other Money-Saving Options Accelerated degree, Army ROTC, off-campus living (after freshman year). *Payment Plan:* installment. *Waivers:* full or partial for employees or children of employees and senior citizens.

Contact Mr. John H. Sellers, Director of Financial Aid and Scholarships, James Madison University, Harrisonburg, VA 22807, 540-568-7820.

JAMESTOWN COLLEGE
Jamestown, North Dakota

About the Institution Independent/religious, coed. Degrees awarded: B. Offers 22 undergraduate majors. Total enrollment: 1,094 (63% state residents). Freshmen: 291.

Undergraduate Expenses (1997–98) Comprehensive fee of $11,850 includes tuition ($8770) and college room and board ($3080). College room only: $1400.

Applications 75% of all full-time undergraduates enrolled in fall 1996 applied for aid. *Financial aid deadline (priority):* 8/27. *Financial aid forms:* CSS Financial Aid PROFILE acceptable. FAFSA, state form required for some. *Admission application deadline:* rolling.

Summary of Aid to Needy Students 317 Federal Work-Study jobs (averaging $740); 141 part-time jobs.

Need-Based Scholarships & Grants Pell, FSEOG, state, private, college/university.

Loans Perkins, PLUS, Stafford, Unsubsidized Stafford, Federal Nursing, private, college/university long-term loans ($1000 average).

Non-Need Awards *Academic Interests/Achievement Awards:* 956 ($4,175,494 total): general academic. *Special Achievements/Activities Awards:* 58 ($403,660 total): leadership. *Special Characteristics Awards:* 7 ($58,940 total): children of faculty/staff. *Athletic:* available.

Other Money-Saving Options Accelerated degree, co-op program, off-campus living (after sophomore year). *Payment Plan:* installment. *Waivers:* full or partial for employees or children of employees.

Contact Office of Financial Aid, Jamestown College, 6085 College Lane, Jamestown, ND 58405, 701-252-3467.

JARVIS CHRISTIAN COLLEGE
Hawkins, Texas

About the Institution Independent/religious, coed. Degrees awarded: B. Offers 23 undergraduate majors. Total enrollment: 557 (81% state residents). Freshmen: 209.

Undergraduate Expenses (1997–98) Comprehensive fee of $10,444 includes tuition ($6694) and college room and board ($3750). College room only: $1610.

Applications 98% of all full-time undergraduates enrolled in fall 1996 applied for aid; of these, 96% were judged to have need according to Federal Methodology, of whom 95% were aided. *Financial aid deadline (priority):* 7/15. *Financial aid forms:* FAFSA, institutional form required; state form acceptable. *Admission application deadline:* rolling.

Summary of Aid to Needy Students *From gift & self-help combined:* Average need met: 82%. *Gift aid:* Total: $3,551,098 (30% from college's own funds, 45% from other college-administered sources, 25% from external sources). 205 Federal Work-Study jobs (averaging $1200); 10 part-time jobs.

Need-Based Scholarships & Grants Pell, FSEOG, state, college/university, United Negro College Fund Scholarships.

Loans Perkins, PLUS, Stafford, Unsubsidized Stafford.

Non-Need Awards In 1996, a total of 449 non-need awards were made. *Academic Interests/Achievement Awards:* 375 ($985,000 total): general academic. *Special Characteristics Awards:* 19 ($21,000 total): local/state students, religious affiliation. *Athletic:* Total: 55 ($267,773); Men: 35 ($186,981); Women: 20 ($80,792).

Other Money-Saving Options Co-op program. *Payment Plans:* tuition prepayment, deferred payment. *Waivers:* full or partial for employees or children of employees.

Contact Mr. Eric King, Assistant Director of Financial Aid, Jarvis Christian College, PO Drawer G, Hawkins, TX 75765-9989, 903-769-5743, fax: 903-769-4842.

JERSEY CITY STATE COLLEGE
Jersey City, New Jersey

About the Institution State-supported, coed. Degrees awarded: B, M. Offers 66 undergraduate majors. Total enrollment: 7,450. Undergraduates: 6,213 (95% state residents). Freshmen: 760.

Undergraduate Expenses (1996–97) State resident tuition: $2610. Nonresident tuition: $4080. Mandatory fees: $918. College room and board: $5000. College room only: $3000.

Applications 72% of all full-time undergraduates enrolled in fall 1996 applied for aid; of these, 84% were judged to have need according to Federal Methodology, of whom 98% were aided. *Financial aid deadline (priority):* 4/15. *Financial aid forms:* FAFSA, state form required. Institutional form required for some. *Admission application deadline:* 4/1.

Summary of Aid to Needy Students *From gift & self-help combined:* Average need met: 81%. Average amount awarded: $5495 (59% gift aid, 41% self-help). *Gift aid:* Total: $7,860,966 (1% from college's own funds, 7% from other college-administered sources, 92% from external sources). 519 Federal Work-Study jobs (averaging $1741); 292 part-time jobs.

Need-Based Scholarships & Grants Pell, FSEOG, state, private, college/university.

Loans Perkins, PLUS, Stafford, Unsubsidized Stafford, state, private, college/university short-term loans ($100 average), college/university long-term loans ($1848 average).

Non-Need Awards In 1996, a total of 113 non-need awards were made. *Academic Interests/Achievement Awards:* 68 ($363,893 total): general academic, biological sciences, business, communication, education, mathematics. *Creative Arts/Performance Awards:* 45 ($32,200 total): art/fine arts, dance, music.

Other Money-Saving Options Accelerated degree, co-op program, cooperative Army ROTC, cooperative Naval ROTC, cooperative Air Force ROTC, off-campus living. *Payment Plan:* deferred payment. *Waivers:* full or partial for employees or children of employees and senior citizens.

Contact Mr. Robert J. McBride, Director of Financial Aid, Jersey City State College, 2039 Kennedy Boulevard, Jersey City, NJ 07305-1957, 201-200-3173, fax: 201-200-3181.

JEWISH HOSPITAL COLLEGE OF NURSING AND ALLIED HEALTH
St. Louis, Missouri

About the Institution Independent, primarily women. Degrees awarded: A, B, M. Offers 3 undergraduate majors. Total enrollment: 449. Undergraduates: 401 (58% state residents). Freshmen: 141.

Undergraduate Expenses (1997–98) Tuition: $8480. Mandatory fees: $200. College room only: $1856 (minimum).

Applications *Financial aid deadline (priority):* 4/15. *Financial aid forms:* FAFSA required; CSS Financial Aid PROFILE acceptable. Institutional form required for some. *Regular admission application deadline:* rolling. Early decision deadline: 11/1.

Summary of Aid to Needy Students 10 Federal Work-Study jobs (averaging $1000).

Need-Based Scholarships & Grants Pell, FSEOG, state, college/university.

Loans PLUS, Stafford, Unsubsidized Stafford, college/university long-term loans ($1000 average).

Non-Need Awards available.

Other Money-Saving Options Off-campus living. *Payment Plans:* installment, deferred payment.

Contact Office of Financial Aid, Jewish Hospital College of Nursing and Allied Health, St. Louis, MO 63110-1091, 314-454-7055.

JEWISH THEOLOGICAL SEMINARY OF AMERICA
New York, New York

About the Institution Independent/religious, coed. Degrees awarded: B, M, D. Offers 8 undergraduate majors. Total enrollment: 560. Undergraduates: 138 (25% state residents). Freshmen: 43.

Undergraduate Expenses (1996–97) Tuition: $7190. Mandatory fees: $300. College room only: $4150.

Applications *Financial aid deadline:* Applications processed continuously. *Financial aid forms:* FAFSA, CSS Financial Aid PROFILE, institutional form required. State form required for some. *Regular admission application deadline:* 2/15. Early decision deadline: 11/15.

Summary of Aid to Needy Students Part-time jobs.

Non-Need Awards *Academic Interests/Achievement Awards:* general academic.

Other Money-Saving Options Off-campus living. *Payment Plan:* installment. *Waivers:* full or partial for employees or children of employees and senior citizens.

Contact Office of Financial Aid, Jewish Theological Seminary of America, 3080 Broadway, New York, NY 10027-4649, 212-678-8000.

JOHN BROWN UNIVERSITY
Siloam Springs, Arkansas

About the Institution Independent/religious, coed. Degrees awarded: A, B, M. Offers 60 undergraduate majors. Total enrollment: 1,379. Undergraduates: 1,295 (24% state residents). Freshmen: 280.

Undergraduate Expenses (1997–98) Comprehensive fee of $13,510 includes tuition ($8860), mandatory fees ($260), and college room and board ($4390).

Applications 64% of all full-time undergraduates enrolled in fall 1996 applied for aid; of these, 91% were judged to have need according to Federal Methodology, of whom 100% were aided. *Financial aid deadline (priority):* 3/1. *Financial aid forms:* FAFSA required; CSS Financial Aid PROFILE acceptable. State form required for some. *Admission application deadline:* 3/1.

Summary of Aid to Needy Students *From gift & self-help combined:* Average need met: 60%. Average amount awarded: $7165 (58% gift aid, 42% self-help). *Gift aid:* Total: $2,863,014 (68% from college's own funds, 4% from other college-administered sources, 28% from external sources). 175 Federal Work-Study jobs (averaging $1400); 280 part-time jobs.

Need-Based Scholarships & Grants Pell, FSEOG, state, private, college/university.

Loans Perkins, PLUS, Stafford, Unsubsidized Stafford.

Non-Need Awards In 1996, a total of 1,126 non-need awards were made. *Academic Interests/Achievement Awards:* 449 ($837,806 total): general academic. *Creative Arts/Performance Awards:* 78 ($85,170 total): journalism/publications, music. *Special Achievements/Activities Awards:* 312 ($389,750 total): leadership. *Special Characteristics Awards:* 192 ($454,801 total): children of educators, children of faculty/staff, international students, relatives of clergy. *Athletic:* Total: 95 ($500,646); Men: 52 ($287,598); Women: 43 ($213,048).

Other Money-Saving Options Cooperative Army ROTC, cooperative Air Force ROTC, off-campus living (after junior year). *Payment Plan:* installment. *Waivers:* full or partial for employees or children of employees, adult students, senior citizens.

Contact Ms. Judy Blank, Assistant Director of Student Financial Aid, John Brown University, 2000 West University, Siloam Springs, AR 72761-2121, 501-524-7115, fax: 501-524-4196.

JOHN CARROLL UNIVERSITY
University Heights, Ohio

About the Institution Independent/religious, coed. Degrees awarded: B, M. Offers 51 undergraduate majors. Total enrollment: 4,197. Undergraduates: 3,390 (66% state residents). Freshmen: 778.

Undergraduate Expenses (1997–98) Comprehensive fee of $19,545 includes tuition ($13,883) and college room and board ($5662).

Applications 77% of all full-time undergraduates enrolled in fall 1996 applied for aid; of these, 87% were judged to have need according to Federal Methodology, of whom 100% were aided. *Financial aid deadline (priority):* 3/1. *Financial aid forms:* FAFSA required. State form, institutional form required for some. *Admission application deadline:* rolling.

Summary of Aid to Needy Students *From gift & self-help combined:* Average need met: 87%. Average amount awarded: $11,617 (67% gift aid, 33% self-help). *Gift aid:* Total: $16,369,353. 309 Federal Work-Study jobs (averaging $963); 645 part-time jobs.

Need-Based Scholarships & Grants Pell, FSEOG, state, private, college/university, American Values Scholarships.

Loans Perkins, PLUS, Stafford, Unsubsidized Stafford, state, private.

Non-Need Awards *Academic Interests/Achievement Awards:* general academic, biological sciences, foreign languages, humanities, physical sciences. *Special Characteristics Awards:* children of faculty/staff, local/state students, ROTC participants.

Other Money-Saving Options Accelerated degree, co-op program, Army ROTC, off-campus living. *Payment Plan:* installment. *Waivers:* full or partial for employees or children of employees.

Contact Financial Aid Counselor, John Carroll University, 20700 North Park Boulevard, University Heights, OH 44118-4581, 216-397-4248, fax: 216-397-3098.

JOHN F. KENNEDY UNIVERSITY
Orinda, California

About the Institution Independent, coed. Degrees awarded: B, M, D, P. Offers 6 undergraduate majors. Total enrollment: 1,859. Undergraduates: 368 (94% state residents).

Undergraduate Expenses (1997–98) Tuition: $9225. Mandatory fees: $27.

Applications 69% of all full-time undergraduates enrolled in fall 1996 applied for aid; of these, 96% were judged to have need according to Federal Methodology, of whom 100% were aided. *Financial aid deadline (priority):* 3/2. *Financial aid forms:* FAFSA, institutional form required; CSS Financial Aid PROFILE acceptable.

Summary of Aid to Needy Students *Gift aid:* Total: $67,930 (1% from college's own funds, 63% from other college-administered sources, 36% from external sources).

Need-Based Scholarships & Grants Pell, FSEOG, state, college/university.

Loans Perkins, PLUS, Stafford, Unsubsidized Stafford, college/university short-term loans ($80 average), college/university long-term loans ($3000 average).

Non-Need Awards Not offered.

Another Money-Saving Option *Waivers:* full or partial for employees or children of employees.

Contact Financial Aid Office, John F. Kennedy University, 12 Altarinda Road, Orinda, CA 94563-2689, 510-253-4385, fax: 510-253-2266.

JOHN JAY COLLEGE OF CRIMINAL JUSTICE, THE CITY UNIVERSITY OF NEW YORK
New York, New York

About the Institution State & locally supported, coed. Degrees awarded: A, B, M. Offers 12 undergraduate majors. Total enrollment: 10,724. Undergraduates: 9,790 (97% state residents). Freshmen: 1,812.

Undergraduate Expenses (1996–97) State resident tuition: $2950 (minimum). Nonresident tuition: $6550 (minimum). Mandatory fees: $109.

Applications *Financial aid deadline (priority):* 6/30. *Financial aid forms:* FAFSA required. *Admission application deadline:* rolling.

Summary of Aid to Needy Students *From gift & self-help combined:* Average need met: 85%. *Gift aid:* Total: $24,976,376. 408 Federal Work Study jobs (averaging $805).

Need-Based Scholarships & Grants Pell, FSEOG, state, college/university.

Loans Perkins, PLUS, Stafford, Unsubsidized Stafford.

Non-Need Awards *Academic Interests/Achievement Awards:* general academic.

Other Money-Saving Options Co-op program, cooperative Naval ROTC, cooperative Air Force ROTC.

Contact Mr. John H. Emmons, Director of Financial Aid, John Jay College of Criminal Justice, the City University of New York, 445 West 59th Street, New York, NY 10019-1093, 212-237-8150.

JOHNS HOPKINS UNIVERSITY
Baltimore, Maryland

About the Institution Independent, coed. Degrees awarded: B, M, D. Offers 55 undergraduate majors. Total enrollment: 4,979. Undergraduates: 3,606 (14% state residents). Freshmen: 1,018.

Undergraduate Expenses (1997–98 estimated) Comprehensive fee of $29,075 includes tuition ($21,675) and college room and board ($7400).

Applications 69% of all full-time undergraduates enrolled in fall 1996 applied for aid; of these, 92% were judged to have need according to Federal Methodology, of whom 100% were aided. *Financial aid deadline (priority):* 2/1. *Financial aid forms:* FAFSA, institutional form, federal income tax form required; CSS Financial Aid PROFILE acceptable. State form required for some. *Regular admission application deadline:* 1/1. Early decision deadline: 11/15.

Summary of Aid to Needy Students *From gift & self-help combined:* Average need met: 95%. Average amount awarded: $19,490 (69% gift aid, 31% self-help). *Gift aid:* Total: $18,425,498 (86% from college's own funds, 10% from other college-administered sources, 4% from external sources). 1,342 Federal Work-Study jobs (averaging $1900); 1,200 part-time jobs.

Need-Based Scholarships & Grants Pell, FSEOG, state, private, college/university.

Loans Perkins, PLUS, Stafford, Unsubsidized Stafford, private, college/university short-term loans ($300 average), college/university long-term loans ($2200 average).

Non-Need Awards *Academic Interests/Achievement Awards:* 80 ($960,000 total): general academic. *Special Characteristics Awards:* children of faculty/staff. *Athletic:* Total: 22 ($387,000); Men: 22 ($387,000); Women: 0.

Other Money-Saving Options Accelerated degree, co-op program, Army ROTC, cooperative Air Force ROTC, off-campus living (after sophomore year). *Payment Plans:* tuition prepayment, installment. *Waivers:* full or partial for employees or children of employees.

Contact Office of Financial Aid, Johns Hopkins University, 146 Garland Hall, 3400 N. Charles, Baltimore, MD 21218-2699, 410-516-8000.

JOHNSON & WALES UNIVERSITY
North Miami, Florida

About the Institution Independent, coed. Degrees awarded: A, B. Offers 11 undergraduate majors. Total enrollment: 875 (69% state residents). Freshmen: 386.

Undergraduate Expenses (1997–98) Tuition: $11,526 (minimum). Mandatory fees: $426. College room only: $3180.

Applications 78% of all full-time undergraduates enrolled in fall 1996 applied for aid; of these, 91% were judged to have need according to Federal Methodology, of whom 98% were aided. *Financial aid deadline (priority):* 5/1. *Financial aid forms:* FAFSA required. *Admission application deadline:* rolling.

Summary of Aid to Needy Students *From gift & self-help combined:* Average need met: 67%. Average amount awarded: $10,041 (47% gift aid, 53% self-help). *Gift aid:* Total: $2,511,170 (70% from college's own funds, 6% from other college-administered sources, 24% from external sources). 192 Federal Work-Study jobs (averaging $1701); 7 part-time jobs.

Need-Based Scholarships & Grants Pell, FSEOG, state, college/university.

Loans Perkins, PLUS, Stafford, Unsubsidized Stafford, college/university long-term loans ($1835 average).

Non-Need Awards In 1996, a total of 117 non-need awards were made. *Academic Interests/Achievement Awards:* 59 ($106,083 total): general academic. *Special Achievements/Activities Awards:* 56 ($71,034 total): Junior Miss, leadership, memberships. *Special Characteristics Awards:* 2 ($2000 total): children of current students, previous college experience, siblings of current students, spouses of current students.

Other Money-Saving Options Accelerated degree, co-op program, off-campus living. *Payment Plan:* installment. *Waivers:* full or partial for employees or children of employees.

Contact Ms. Deborah Machowski, Director of Financial Aid, Johnson & Wales University, Abbott Park Place, Providence, RI 02903-3703, 401-598-4648, fax: 401-598-1040.

JOHNSON & WALES UNIVERSITY
Providence, Rhode Island

About the Institution Independent, coed. Degrees awarded: A, B, M, D. Offers 40 undergraduate majors. Total enrollment: 7,851. Undergraduates: 7,266 (16% state residents). Freshmen: 2,310.

Undergraduate Expenses (1997–98) Comprehensive fee of $17,289 includes tuition ($11,526 minimum), mandatory fees ($426), and college room and board ($5337 minimum).

Applications 74% of all full-time undergraduates enrolled in fall 1996 applied for aid; of these, 91% were judged to have need according to Federal Methodology, of whom 98% were aided. *Financial aid deadline (priority):* 5/1. *Financial aid forms:* FAFSA required. *Admission application deadline:* rolling.

Summary of Aid to Needy Students *From gift & self-help combined:* Average need met: 65%. Average amount awarded: $8877 (42% gift aid, 58% self-help). *Gift aid:* Total: $15,453,460 (63% from college's own funds, 7% from other college-administered sources, 30% from external sources). 1,001 Federal Work-Study jobs (averaging $1770); 415 part-time jobs.

Need-Based Scholarships & Grants Pell, FSEOG, state, college/university.

Loans Perkins, PLUS, Stafford, Unsubsidized Stafford, college/university long-term loans ($1885 average).

Non-Need Awards In 1996, a total of 1,836 non-need awards were made. *Academic Interests/Achievement Awards:* 326 ($400,001 total): general academic, business. *Special Achievements/Activities Awards:* 1,422 ($2,174,463 total): Junior Miss, leadership, memberships. *Special Characteristics Awards:* 88 ($81,198 total): children of current students, previous college experience, siblings of current students, spouses of current students.

Other Money-Saving Options Accelerated degree, co-op program, cooperative Army ROTC, off-campus living (after freshman year). *Payment Plan:* installment. *Waivers:* full or partial for minority students and employees or children of employees.

Contact Ms. Deborah Machowski, Director of Financial Aid, Johnson & Wales University, Abbott Park Place, Providence, RI 02903-3703, 401-598-4648, fax: 401-598-1040.

JOHNSON & WALES UNIVERSITY
Charleston, South Carolina

About the Institution Independent, coed. Degrees awarded: A, B. Offers 6 undergraduate majors. Total enrollment: 1,246 (25% state residents). Freshmen: 445.

Undergraduate Expenses (1997–98) Tuition: $10,410 (minimum). Mandatory fees: $426 (minimum). College room only: $3414.

Applications Of all full-time undergraduates enrolled in fall 1996, 90% of those who applied for aid were judged to have need according to Federal Methodology, of whom 98% were aided. *Financial aid deadline (priority):* 5/1. *Financial aid forms:* FAFSA required. *Admission application deadline:* rolling.

Summary of Aid to Needy Students *From gift & self-help combined:* Average need met: 62%. Average amount awarded: $7549 (37% gift aid, 63% self-help). *Gift aid:* Total: $2,422,567 (53% from college's own funds, 8% from other college-administered sources, 39% from external sources). 206 Federal Work-Study jobs (averaging $1741); 18 part-time jobs.

Need-Based Scholarships & Grants Pell, FSEOG, state, college/university.

Loans Perkins, PLUS, Stafford, Unsubsidized Stafford, college/university long-term loans ($1464 average).

Non-Need Awards In 1996, a total of 233 non-need awards were made. *Academic Interests/Achievement Awards:* 61 ($50,000 total): general academic. *Special Achievements/Activities Awards:* 163 ($216,193 total): Junior Miss, leadership, memberships. *Special Characteristics Awards:* 9 ($9000 total): children of current students, siblings of current students, spouses of current students.

Other Money-Saving Options Accelerated degree, co-op program, off-campus living. *Payment Plans:* tuition prepayment, installment. *Waivers:* full or partial for employees or children of employees.

Contact Ms. Deborah Machowski, Director of Financial Aid, Johnson & Wales University, Abbott Park Place, Providence, RI 02903-3703, 401-598-4648, fax: 401-598-1040.

JOHNSON BIBLE COLLEGE
Knoxville, Tennessee

About the Institution Independent/religious, coed. Degrees awarded: A, B, M. Offers 4 undergraduate majors. Total enrollment: 460. Undergraduates: 388 (21% state residents). Freshmen: 85.

Undergraduate Expenses (1997–98) Comprehensive fee of $8270 includes tuition ($4600), mandatory fees ($400), and college room and board ($3270).

Applications 96% of all full-time undergraduates enrolled in fall 1996 applied for aid; of these, 90% were judged to have need according to Federal Methodology, of whom 100% were aided. *Financial aid deadline (priority):* 7/1. *Financial aid forms:* institutional form required; FAFSA acceptable. State form required for some. *Admission application deadline:* rolling.

Summary of Aid to Needy Students *From gift & self-help combined:* Average need met: 65%. Average amount awarded: $2808 (46% gift aid, 54% self-help). *Gift aid:* Total: $440,950 (53% from college's own funds, 10% from other college-administered sources, 37% from external sources). 140 Federal Work-Study jobs (averaging $705); 160 part-time jobs.

Need-Based Scholarships & Grants Pell, FSEOG, state, college/university.

Loans PLUS, Stafford, Unsubsidized Stafford, college/university short-term loans ($300 average), college/university long-term loans ($800 average).

Non-Need Awards In 1996, a total of 372 non-need awards were made. *Academic Interests/Achievement Awards:* 179 ($81,725 total): general academic. *Special Achievements/Activities Awards:* 44 ($27,425 total): general special achievements/activities, community service, leadership, religious involvement. *Special Characteristics Awards:* 149 ($65,525 total): general special characteristics, children of current students, children of faculty/staff, ethnic background, international students, members of minorities, parents of current students, relatives of clergy, religious affiliation, siblings of current students, spouses of current students.

Other Money-Saving Options *Payment Plan:* installment. *Waivers:* full or partial for employees or children of employees.

Contact Mrs. Janette Overton, Financial Aid Director, Johnson Bible College, 7900 Johnson Drive, Knoxville, TN 37998-0001, 423-573-4517.

JOHNSON C. SMITH UNIVERSITY
Charlotte, North Carolina

About the Institution Independent, coed. Degrees awarded: B. Offers 30 undergraduate majors. Total enrollment: 1,427 (19% state residents). Freshmen: 394.

Undergraduate Expenses (1997–98) Comprehensive fee of $11,797 includes tuition ($7702), mandatory fees ($767), and college room and board ($3328).

Applications *Financial aid deadline (priority):* 5/1. *Financial aid forms:* FAFSA required. *Admission application deadline:* 8/1.

Summary of Aid to Needy Students *From gift & self-help combined:* Average need met: 100%. Average amount awarded: $6200 (33% gift aid, 67% self-help). *Gift aid:* Total: $3,301,609. Federal Work-Study jobs (averaging $1000); 32 part-time jobs.

Need-Based Scholarships & Grants Pell, FSEOG, state, private, college/university.

Loans Perkins, PLUS, Stafford, Unsubsidized Stafford, college/university short-term loans ($100 average).

Non-Need Awards In 1996, a total of 249 non-need awards were made. *Academic Interests/Achievement Awards:* 130 ($450,000 total): general academic. *Creative Arts/Performance Awards:* 21 ($21,000 total): music. *Special Achievements/Activities Awards:* 3 ($10,150 total). *Athletic:* Total: 95 ($353,000); Men: 82 ($311,000); Women: 13 ($42,000).

Other Money-Saving Options Accelerated degree, co-op program, cooperative Army ROTC, cooperative Air Force ROTC, off-campus living (after freshman year). *Waivers:* full or partial for employees or children of employees.

Contact Office of Financial Aid, Johnson C. Smith University, 100 Beatties Ford Road, Charlotte, NC 28216, 704-378-1000.

JOHNSON STATE COLLEGE
Johnson, Vermont

About the Institution State-supported, coed. Degrees awarded: A, B, M. Offers 48 undergraduate majors. Total enrollment: 1,591. Undergraduates: 1,313 (72% state residents). Freshmen: 273.

Undergraduate Expenses (1996–97) State resident tuition: $3620. Nonresident tuition: $8380. Mandatory fees: $720. College room and board: $4936. College room only: $2844.

Applications 93% of all full-time undergraduates enrolled in fall 1996 applied for aid; of these, 95% were judged to have need according to Federal Methodology, of whom 100% were aided. *Financial aid deadline (priority):* 3/1. *Financial aid forms:* FAFSA required; state form acceptable. *Admission application deadline:* rolling.

Summary of Aid to Needy Students *From gift & self-help combined:* Average need met: 73%. Average amount awarded: $5197 (34% gift aid, 66% self-help). *Gift aid:* Total: $1,643,985 (10% from college's own funds, 14% from other college-administered sources, 76% from external sources). 393 Federal Work-Study jobs (averaging $1353); part-time jobs.

Need-Based Scholarships & Grants Pell, FSEOG, state.

Loans Perkins, PLUS, Stafford, Unsubsidized Stafford.

Non-Need Awards In 1996, a total of 173 non-need awards were made. *Academic Interests/Achievement Awards:* 118 ($117,575 total): general academic, business, mathematics. *Creative Arts/Performance Awards:* 8 ($3900 total): art/fine arts, dance, music, performing arts, theater/drama. *Special Achievements/Activities Awards:* 35 ($27,000 total): general special achievements/activities, community service, leadership, memberships. *Special Characteristics Awards:* 12 ($8600 total): general special characteristics, local/state students, members of minorities.

Other Money-Saving Options Accelerated degree, off-campus living (after sophomore year). *Payment Plan:* deferred payment. *Waivers:* full or partial for employees or children of employees and senior citizens.

Contact Ms. Kimberly Goodell, Records Specialist III, Johnson State College, RR #2 Box 75, Johnson, VT 05656-9405, 802-635-2356, fax: 802-635-1248.

JOHN WESLEY COLLEGE
High Point, North Carolina

About the Institution Independent/religious, coed. Degrees awarded: A, B. Offers 10 undergraduate majors. Total enrollment: 161 (96% state residents). Freshmen: 15.

Undergraduate Expenses (1997–98) Tuition: $4648. Mandatory fees: $192. College room only: $1600.

Applications Of all full-time undergraduates enrolled in fall 1996, 100% of those who applied for aid were judged to have need according to Federal Methodology, of whom 100% were aided. *Financial aid deadline (priority):* 8/1. *Financial aid forms:* FAFSA required. Institutional form required for some. *Admission application deadline:* 8/1.

Summary of Aid to Needy Students *From gift & self-help combined:* Average amount awarded: $3011 (35% gift aid, 65% self-help). *Gift aid:* Total: $105,321 (34% from college's own funds, 8% from other college-administered sources, 58% from external sources). 4 Federal Work-Study jobs (averaging $2000).

Need-Based Scholarships & Grants Pell, FSEOG, state, private, college/university.

Loans PLUS, Stafford, Unsubsidized Stafford, private, college/university short-term loans ($2000 average), college/university long-term loans.

Non-Need Awards In 1996, a total of 16 non-need awards were made. *Academic Interests/Achievement Awards:* 4 ($1000 total): general academic, education, religion/biblical studies. *Creative Arts/Performance Awards:* 0: music. *Special Achievements/Activities Awards:* 0: religious involvement. *Special Characteristics Awards:* 12 ($7400 total): general special characteristics, children of faculty/staff, married students, relatives of clergy, religious affiliation, spouses of current students, veterans, veterans' children.

Other Money-Saving Options *Payment Plan:* installment. *Waivers:* full or partial for employees or children of employees.

Contact Mrs. Terry Young, Director of Financial Aid, John Wesley College, 2314 North Centennial Street, High Point, NC 27265-3197, 910-889-2262, fax: 910-889-2261.

JONES COLLEGE
Jacksonville, Florida

About the Institution Independent, coed. Degrees awarded: A, B. Offers 6 undergraduate majors. Total enrollment: 860 (96% state residents). Freshmen: 250.

Undergraduate Expenses (1996–97) Tuition: $4350.

Applications Of all full-time undergraduates enrolled in fall 1996, 100% of those who applied for aid were judged to have need according to Federal Methodology, of whom 100% were aided. *Financial aid deadline:* continuous. *Financial aid forms:* FAFSA required. *Admission application deadline:* rolling.

Summary of Aid to Needy Students *From gift & self-help combined:* Average need met: 80%. Average amount awarded: $2500 (45% gift aid, 55% self-help). *Gift aid:* Total: $522,227 (3% from college's own funds, 37% from other college-administered sources, 60% from external sources). Federal Work-Study jobs.

Need-Based Scholarships & Grants Pell, FSEOG, state, private.

Loans Perkins, PLUS, Stafford, Unsubsidized Stafford, college/university short-term loans.

Non-Need Awards In 1996, a total of 11 non-need awards were made. *Academic Interests/Achievement Awards:* 11 ($14,795 total): general academic, business, health fields.

Another Money-Saving Option Accelerated degree.

Contact Mrs. Denise Wendle, Director of Financial Aid, Jones College, 5353 Arlington Expressway, Jacksonville, FL 32211-5540, 904-743-1122, fax: 904-743-4446.

JUDSON COLLEGE
Marion, Alabama

About the Institution Independent/religious, women. Degrees awarded: B. Offers 27 undergraduate majors. Total enrollment: 331 (72% state residents). Freshmen: 120.

Undergraduate Expenses (1997–98) Comprehensive fee of $10,924 includes tuition ($6700) and college room and board ($4224).

Applications 98% of all full-time undergraduates enrolled in fall 1996 applied for aid; of these, 74% were judged to have need according to Federal Methodology, of whom 100% were aided. *Financial aid deadline:* Applications processed continuously. *Financial aid forms:* institutional form required; FAFSA, state form acceptable. *Admission application deadline:* rolling.

Summary of Aid to Needy Students *From gift & self-help combined:* Average need met: 84%. Average amount awarded: $8192 (54% gift aid, 46% self-help). *Gift aid:* Total: $791,132 (53% from college's own funds, 6% from other college-administered sources, 41% from external sources). 47 Federal Work-Study jobs (averaging $816); 72 part-time jobs.

Loans College/university long-term loans ($1260 average).

Non-Need Awards *Academic Interests/Achievement Awards:* available. *Creative Arts/Performance Awards:* available. *Special Achievements/Activities Awards:* available. *Special Characteristics Awards:* relatives of clergy, religious affiliation. *Athletic:* available.

Other Money-Saving Options Accelerated degree, cooperative Army ROTC. *Payment Plan:* installment. *Waivers:* full or partial for employees or children of employees.

Contact Office of Financial Aid, Judson College, PO Box 120, Marion, AL 36756, 334-683-5100.

JUDSON COLLEGE
Elgin, Illinois

About the Institution Independent/religious, coed. Degrees awarded: B. Offers 46 undergraduate majors. Total enrollment: 933 (72% state residents). Freshmen: 191.

Undergraduate Expenses (1997–98) Comprehensive fee of $16,130 includes tuition ($10,900), mandatory fees ($450), and college room and board ($4780).

Applications Of all full-time undergraduates enrolled in fall 1996, 80% of those who applied for aid were judged to have need according to Federal Methodology, of whom 98% were aided. *Financial aid deadline (priority):* 5/1. *Financial aid forms:* institutional form required; FAFSA acceptable. *Admission application deadline:* 8/15.

Summary of Aid to Needy Students *From gift & self-help combined:* Average need met: 66%. Average amount awarded: $13,547 (61% gift aid, 39% self-help). *Gift aid:* Total: $4,906,093 (51% from college's own funds, 31% from other college-administered sources, 18% from external sources). 186 Federal Work-Study jobs (averaging $800); 60 part-time jobs.

Need-Based Scholarships & Grants Pell, FSEOG, state, private, college/university.

Loans Perkins, PLUS, Stafford, Unsubsidized Stafford, college/university long-term loans ($3500 average).

Non-Need Awards *Academic Interests/Achievement Awards:* 289 ($541,440 total): general academic. *Creative Arts/Performance Awards:* 158 ($155,888 total): art/fine arts, cinema/film/broadcasting, journalism/publications. *Special Achievements/Activities Awards:* 270 ($474,318 total): general special achievements/activities, religious involvement. *Special Characteristics Awards:* 495 ($800,000 total): children of faculty/staff, international students, local/state students, out-of-state students, religious affiliation, siblings of current students. *Athletic:* Total: 0 ($528,354); Men: 126 ($276,634); Women: 0 ($251,720).

Other Money-Saving Options Accelerated degree, cooperative Army ROTC. *Payment Plan:* installment.

Contact Mr. William W. Dean, Assistant Director of Financial Aid, Judson College, 1151 North State Street, Elgin, IL 60123-1498, 847-695-2500 Ext. 2331, fax: 847-695-0216.

THE JUILLIARD SCHOOL
New York, New York

About the Institution Independent, coed. Degrees awarded: B, M, D. Offers 8 undergraduate majors. Total enrollment: 851. Undergraduates: 490 (21% state residents). Freshmen: 104.

Undergraduate Expenses (1997–98) Comprehensive fee of $21,500 includes tuition ($14,400), mandatory fees ($600), and college room and board ($6500 minimum).

Applications *Financial aid deadline:* continuous. *Financial aid forms:* FAFSA, institutional form, federal income tax form required. *Admission application deadline:* 1/8.

Summary of Aid to Needy Students Federal Work-Study jobs.

Loans Perkins, PLUS, Stafford, Unsubsidized Stafford, college/university short-term loans, college/university long-term loans.

Non-Need Awards Not offered.

Other Money-Saving Options Accelerated degree, off-campus living (after freshman year). *Payment Plan:* installment. *Waivers:* full or partial for employees or children of employees.

Contact Admissions Office, The Juilliard School, New York, NY 10023-6588, 212-799-5000 Ext. 223.

JUNIATA COLLEGE
Huntingdon, Pennsylvania

About the Institution Independent, coed. Degrees awarded: B. Offers 89 undergraduate majors. Total enrollment: 1,161 (79% state residents). Freshmen: 354.

Undergraduate Expenses (1997–98) Comprehensive fee of $22,080 includes tuition ($16,980), mandatory fees ($280), and college room and board ($4820).

Applications 88% of all full-time undergraduates enrolled in fall 1996 applied for aid; of these, 93% were judged to have need according to Federal Methodology, of whom 100% were aided. *Financial aid deadline (priority):* 3/1. *Financial aid forms:* FAFSA required. CSS Financial Aid PROFILE required for some. *Regular admission application deadline:* rolling. Early decision deadline: 11/15.

Summary of Aid to Needy Students *From gift & self-help combined:* Average need met: 94%. Average amount awarded: $15,307 (69% gift aid, 31% self-help). *Gift aid:* Total: $9,904,000 (78% from college's own funds, 2% from other college-administered sources, 20% from external sources). Federal Work-Study jobs (averaging $1182); 350 part-time jobs.

Need-Based Scholarships & Grants Pell, FSEOG, state, private, college/university.

Loans Perkins, PLUS, Stafford, Unsubsidized Stafford, college/university short-term loans ($1500 average), college/university long-term loans ($3000 average).

Non-Need Awards In 1996, a total of 494 non-need awards were made. *Academic Interests/Achievement Awards:* 277 ($1,542,000 total): general academic, biological sciences, business, education, humanities, international studies, physical sciences, social sciences. *Special Achievements/Activities Awards:* 3 ($49,440 total): general special achievements/activities, community service, leadership. *Special Characteristics Awards:* 214 ($716,000 total): adult students, children of educators, children of faculty/staff, out-of-state students.

Other Money-Saving Options Accelerated degree. *Payment Plan:* installment. *Waivers:* full or partial for employees or children of employees and adult students.

Contact Office of Financial Aid, Juniata College, 1700 Moore Street, Huntingdon, PA 16652-2119, 814-641-3000.

KALAMAZOO COLLEGE
Kalamazoo, Michigan

About the Institution Independent, coed. Degrees awarded: B. Offers 52 undergraduate majors. Total enrollment: 1,302 (69% state residents). Freshmen: 361.

Undergraduate Expenses (1997–98) Comprehensive fee of $23,541 includes tuition ($17,976) and college room and board ($5565).

Applications 64% of all full-time undergraduates enrolled in fall 1996 applied for aid; of these, 88% were judged to have need according to Federal Methodology, of whom 100% were aided. *Financial aid deadline (priority):* 2/15. *Financial aid forms:* FAFSA, CSS Financial Aid PROFILE required. *Admission application deadline:* 2/15.

Summary of Aid to Needy Students *From gift & self-help combined:* Average amount awarded: $14,358 (75% gift aid, 25% self-help). *Gift aid:* Total: $7,758,511 (76% from college's own funds, 5% from other college-administered sources, 19% from external sources). 375 Federal Work-Study jobs (averaging $1100); part-time jobs.

Need-Based Scholarships & Grants Pell, FSEOG, state, private, college/university.

Loans Perkins, PLUS, Stafford, Unsubsidized Stafford, state, private.

Non-Need Awards *Academic Interests/Achievement Awards:* general academic, biological sciences, English, foreign languages, mathematics, physical sciences, social sciences. *Creative Arts/Performance Awards:* 14 ($29,500 total): art/fine arts, cinema/film/broadcasting, music, theater/drama. *Special Characteristics Awards:* 64 ($198,718 total): children of faculty/staff, international students, members of minorities.

Other Money-Saving Options Co-op program, cooperative Army ROTC. *Payment Plans:* installment, deferred payment. *Waivers:* full or partial for employees or children of employees.

Contact Mr. Craig Schmidt, Assistant Director of Financial Aid, Kalamazoo College, 120 Academy Street, Kalamazoo, MI 49006-3295, 616-337-7192, fax: 616-337-7390.

KANSAS CITY ART INSTITUTE
Kansas City, Missouri

About the Institution Independent, coed. Degrees awarded: B. Offers 9 undergraduate majors. Total enrollment: 598 (24% state residents). Freshmen: 146.

Undergraduate Expenses (1997–98) Comprehensive fee of $21,015 includes tuition ($16,320) and college room and board ($4695).

Applications 95% of all full-time undergraduates enrolled in fall 1996 applied for aid; of these, 84% were judged to have need according to Federal Methodology, of whom 100% were aided. *Financial aid deadline (priority):* 2/15. *Financial aid forms:* FAFSA required. *Regular admission application deadline:* rolling. Early action deadline: 12/15.

Summary of Aid to Needy Students *From gift & self-help combined:* Average amount awarded: $10,168 (42% gift aid, 58% self-help). *Gift aid:* Total: $3,512,703 (81% from college's own funds, 10% from other college-administered sources, 9% from external sources). 198 Federal Work-Study jobs (averaging $1000); 35 part-time jobs.

Need-Based Scholarships & Grants Pell, FSEOG, state, college/university.

Loans Perkins, PLUS, Stafford, Unsubsidized Stafford, private, college/university short-term loans ($300 average).

Non-Need Awards In 1996, a total of 145 non-need awards were made. *Creative Arts/Performance Awards:* 145 ($873,750 total): art/fine arts.

Other Money-Saving Options Co-op program, off-campus living.

Contact Ms. Teresa Potts, Director of Financial Aid, Kansas City Art Institute, 4415 Warwick Boulevard, Kansas City, MO 64111-9738, 816-561-4852, fax: 816-561-3405.

KANSAS NEWMAN COLLEGE
Wichita, Kansas

About the Institution Independent/religious, coed. Degrees awarded: A, B, M. Offers 38 undergraduate majors. Total enrollment: 1,989. Undergraduates: 1,930 (91% state residents). Freshmen: 128.

Undergraduate Expenses (1997–98) Comprehensive fee of $12,626 includes tuition ($9000) and college room and board ($3626 minimum). College room only: $1654 (minimum).

Applications Of all full-time undergraduates enrolled in fall 1996, 100% of those judged to have need according to Federal Methodology were aided. *Financial aid deadline (priority):* 3/15. *Financial aid forms:* FAFSA required. *Admission application deadline:* rolling.

Summary of Aid to Needy Students *From gift & self-help combined:* Average amount awarded: $9000. Federal Work-Study jobs; part-time jobs.

Need-Based Scholarships & Grants Pell, FSEOG, state, private, college/university.

Loans Perkins, PLUS, Stafford, Unsubsidized Stafford.

Non-Need Awards *Academic Interests/Achievement Awards:* general academic. *Creative Arts/Performance Awards:* debating, music, theater/drama. *Special Achievements/Activities Awards:* leadership, memberships, religious involvement. *Special Characteristics Awards:* children and siblings of alumni, out-of-state students, previous college experience, religious affiliation, siblings of current students. *Athletic:* available.

Other Money-Saving Options Accelerated degree, co-op program, off-campus living (after sophomore year). *Payment Plans:* installment, deferred payment. *Waivers:* full or partial for minority students, children of alumni, employees or children of employees, senior citizens.

Contact Financial Aid Office, Kansas Newman College, 3100 McCormick Avenue, Wichita, KS 67213-2084, 316-942-4291 Ext. 103, fax: 316-942-4483.

KANSAS STATE UNIVERSITY
Manhattan, Kansas

About the Institution State-supported, coed. Degrees awarded: A, B, M, D, P. Offers 108 undergraduate majors. Total enrollment: 20,325. Undergraduates: 16,935 (89% state residents). Freshmen: 2,985.

Undergraduate Expenses (1996–97) State resident tuition: $1890. Nonresident tuition: $7950. Mandatory fees: $483. College room and board: $3490.

Applications Of all full-time undergraduates enrolled in fall 1996, 54% of those who applied for aid were judged to have need according to Federal Methodology, of whom 92% were aided. *Financial aid deadline (priority):* 3/1. *Financial aid forms:* FAFSA required. State form required for some. *Admission application deadline:* rolling.

Summary of Aid to Needy Students *From gift & self-help combined:* Average need met: 89%. Average amount awarded: $5955 (37% gift aid, 63% self-help). *Gift aid:* Total: $15,583,194 (32% from college's own funds, 14% from other college-administered sources, 54% from external sources). 965 Federal Work-Study jobs (averaging $984); part-time jobs.

Need-Based Scholarships & Grants Pell, FSEOG, state.

Loans Perkins, PLUS, Stafford, Unsubsidized Stafford, private, college/university short-term loans ($400 average), college/university long-term loans ($500 average).

Non-Need Awards *Academic Interests/Achievement Awards:* general academic. *Creative Arts/Performance Awards:* art/fine arts, debating, music, theater/drama. *Special Achievements/Activities Awards:* leadership. *Athletic:* available.

Other Money-Saving Options Accelerated degree, co-op program, Army ROTC, Air Force ROTC, off-campus living. *Payment Plans:* installment, deferred payment.

Contact Mr. Larry Moeder, Director of Student Financial Assistance, Kansas State University, 104 Fairchild Hall, Manhattan, KS 66506, 913-532-6420, fax: 913-532-7628.

KANSAS WESLEYAN UNIVERSITY
Salina, Kansas

About the Institution Independent/religious, coed. Degrees awarded: A, B, M. Offers 40 undergraduate majors. Total enrollment: 700. Undergraduates: 675 (82% state residents). Freshmen: 83.

Undergraduate Expenses (1997–98) Comprehensive fee of $13,900 includes tuition ($10,400) and college room and board ($3500 minimum).

Applications 99% of all full-time undergraduates enrolled in fall 1996 applied for aid; of these, 92% were judged to have need according to Federal Methodology, of whom 100% were aided. *Financial aid deadline (priority):* 3/15. *Financial aid forms:* FAFSA required; CSS Financial Aid PROFILE, institutional form acceptable. State form required for some. *Admission application deadline:* rolling.

Summary of Aid to Needy Students *From gift & self-help combined:* Average need met: 100%. Average amount awarded: $10,637 (60% gift aid, 40% self-help). *Gift aid:* Total: $2,790,000 (55% from college's own funds, 18% from other college-administered sources, 27% from external sources). 150 Federal Work-Study jobs (averaging $800); 65 part-time jobs.

Need-Based Scholarships & Grants Pell, FSEOG, state, private, college/university.

Loans Perkins, PLUS, Stafford, Unsubsidized Stafford, Federal Nursing.

Non-Need Awards In 1996, a total of 559 non-need awards were made. *Academic Interests/Achievement Awards:* 303 ($462,000 total): general academic. *Creative Arts/Performance Awards:* 16 ($17,000 total): dance, music, theater/drama. *Special Achievements/Activities Awards:* 4 ($6700 total): cheerleading/drum major. *Special Characteristics Awards:* 34 ($59,000 total): children and siblings of alumni, children of faculty/staff, siblings of current students, twins. *Athletic:* Total: 202 ($454,000); Men: 137 ($341,000); Women: 65 ($113,000).

Other Money-Saving Options Accelerated degree, off-campus living (after sophomore year). *Payment Plan:* installment. *Waivers:* full or partial for children of alumni, employees or children of employees, senior citizens.

Contact Office of Financial Aid, Kansas Wesleyan University, 100 East Claflin, Salina, KS 67401-6196, 913-827-5541.

KEAN COLLEGE OF NEW JERSEY
Union, New Jersey

About the Institution State-supported, coed. Degrees awarded: B, M. Offers 70 undergraduate majors. Total enrollment: 10,404. Undergraduates: 9,134 (98% state residents). Freshmen: 1,064.

Undergraduate Expenses (1996–97) State resident tuition: $2626. Nonresident tuition: $3945. Mandatory fees: $741. College room and board: $4970.

Applications 64% of all full-time undergraduates enrolled in fall 1996 applied for aid; of these, 83% were judged to have need according to Federal Methodology, of whom 87% were aided. *Financial aid deadline (priority):* 5/1. *Financial aid forms:* FAFSA, CSS Financial Aid PROFILE, institutional form required. Federal work study application, parent PLUS loan data sheet required for some. *Admission application deadline:* 6/15.

Summary of Aid to Needy Students *From gift & self-help combined:* Average need met: 68%. Average amount awarded: $3175 (48% gift aid, 52% self-help). *Gift aid:* Total: $3,946,174 (3% from college's own funds, 5% from other college-administered sources, 92% from external sources). 159 Federal Work-Study jobs (averaging $1480); 440 part-time jobs.

Need-Based Scholarships & Grants Pell, FSEOG, state, private, college/university.

Loans Perkins, PLUS, Stafford, Unsubsidized Stafford, state, college/university short-term loans ($75 average).

Non-Need Awards *Academic Interests/Achievement Awards:* general academic, business, education, health fields, humanities. *Creative Arts/Performance Awards:* music. *Special Achievements/Activities Awards:* community service, leadership. *Special Characteristics Awards:* local/state students, members of minorities.

Other Money-Saving Options Accelerated degree, co-op program, cooperative Army ROTC, cooperative Air Force ROTC, off-campus living. *Waivers:* full or partial for senior citizens.

Contact Mr. Larry B. Eadie, Acting Director of Financial Aid, Kean College of New Jersey, 1000 Morris Avenue, Union, NJ 07083, 908-527-2050.

KEENE STATE COLLEGE
Keene, New Hampshire

About the Institution State-supported, coed. Degrees awarded: A, B, M. Offers 55 undergraduate majors. Total enrollment: 4,021. Undergraduates: 3,924 (60% state residents). Freshmen: 846.

Undergraduate Expenses (1996–97) State resident tuition: $2850. Nonresident tuition: $8510. Mandatory fees: $944. College room and board: $4508. College room only: $2992.

Applications Of all full-time undergraduates enrolled in fall 1996, 79% of those who applied for aid were judged to have need according to Federal Methodology, of whom 96% were aided. *Financial aid deadline (priority):* 3/1. *Financial aid forms:* FAFSA required. *Admission application deadline:* 3/1.

Summary of Aid to Needy Students *From gift & self-help combined:* Average need met: 87%. Average amount awarded: $6668 (24% gift aid, 76% self-help). *Gift aid:* Total: $3,125,829 (49% from college's own funds, 16% from other college-administered sources, 35% from external sources). 639 Federal Work-Study jobs (averaging $718); 350 part-time jobs.

Need-Based Scholarships & Grants Pell, FSEOG, state, private, college/university.

Loans Perkins, PLUS, Stafford, Unsubsidized Stafford, state, private, college/university short-term loans ($392 average), college/university long-term loans ($881 average).

Non-Need Awards In 1996, a total of 91 non-need awards were made. *Academic Interests/Achievement Awards:* 73 ($239,502 total): general academic. *Creative Arts/Performance Awards:* 18 ($41,440 total): art/fine arts, music, theater/drama.

Other Money-Saving Options Accelerated degree, co-op program, cooperative Army ROTC, cooperative Air Force ROTC, off-campus living. *Payment Plan:* installment. *Waivers:* full or partial for employees or children of employees and senior citizens.

Contact Office of Financial Aid, Keene State College, 229 Main Street, Keene, NH 03435-2606, 603-352-1909.

KEHILATH YAKOV RABBINICAL SEMINARY
Brooklyn, New York

About the Institution Independent/religious, men. Total enrollment: 150. Undergraduates: 130. Freshmen: 30.

Undergraduate Expenses (1996–97) Comprehensive fee of $6000 includes tuition ($4000) and college room and board ($2000).

Applications 53% of all full-time undergraduates enrolled in fall 1996 applied for aid; of these,100% were judged to have need according to Federal Methodology, of whom 100% were aided. *Financial aid deadline:* continuous. *Financial aid forms:* FAFSA required.

Summary of Aid to Needy Students *From gift & self-help combined:* Average need met: 65%. Average amount awarded: $3000. Federal Work-Study jobs.

Need-Based Scholarships & Grants Pell, FSEOG, college/university.

Non-Need Awards Not offered.

Contact Financial Aid Office, Kehilath Yakov Rabbinical Seminary, Brooklyn, NY 11211-7207, 718-963-1212.

KENDALL COLLEGE
Evanston, Illinois

About the Institution Independent/religious, coed. Degrees awarded: A, B. Offers 21 undergraduate majors. Total enrollment: 500 (85% state residents). Freshmen: 52.

Undergraduate Expenses (1997–98) Comprehensive fee of $15,219 includes tuition ($10,128 minimum) and college room and board ($5091).

Applications Of all full-time undergraduates enrolled in fall 1996, 100% of those judged to have need according to Federal Methodology were aided. *Financial aid deadline (priority):* 4/1. *Financial aid forms:* FAFSA, institutional form required. *Admission application deadline:* rolling.

Summary of Aid to Needy Students *From gift & self-help combined:* Average need met: 50%. Average amount awarded: $8728 (24% gift aid, 76% self-help). *Gift aid:* Total: $681,784 (64% from college's own funds, 13% from other college-administered sources, 23% from external sources). 200 Federal Work-Study jobs (averaging $1500); 100 part-time jobs.

Need-Based Scholarships & Grants Pell, FSEOG, state, private, college/university.

Loans Perkins, PLUS, Stafford, Unsubsidized Stafford, private.

Non-Need Awards *Academic Interests/Achievement Awards:* general academic. *Special Achievements/Activities Awards:* general special achievements/activities, leadership. *Special Characteristics Awards:* children of faculty/staff, international students, members of minorities.

Other Money-Saving Options Co-op program, off-campus living. *Payment Plan:* installment. *Waivers:* full or partial for employees or children of employees.

Contact Ms. Marie Y. Ortiz, Director of Financial Aid, Kendall College, Evanston, IL 60201-2899, 847-866-1349.

KENDALL COLLEGE OF ART AND DESIGN
Grand Rapids, Michigan

About the Institution Independent, coed. Degrees awarded: B. Offers 7 undergraduate majors. Total enrollment: 527 (91% state residents). Freshmen: 88.

Undergraduate Expenses (1997–98 estimated) Tuition: $10,500. Mandatory fees: $50.

Applications 89% of all full-time undergraduates enrolled in fall 1996 applied for aid; of these, 80% were judged to have need according to

Federal Methodology, of whom 100% were aided. *Financial aid deadline (priority):* 2/21. *Financial aid forms:* FAFSA required; CSS Financial Aid PROFILE acceptable. State form required for some. *Admission application deadline:* rolling.

Summary of Aid to Needy Students *From gift & self-help combined:* Average need met: 74%. Average amount awarded: $9056 (45% gift aid, 55% self-help). *Gift aid:* Total: $1,032,936 (27% from college's own funds, 5% from other college-administered sources, 68% from external sources). 31 Federal Work-Study jobs (averaging $1625); 5 part-time jobs.

Need-Based Scholarships & Grants Pell, FSEOG, state, private, college/university.

Loans Perkins, PLUS, Stafford, Unsubsidized Stafford, state, private.

Non-Need Awards In 1996, a total of 183 non-need awards were made. *Creative Arts/Performance Awards:* 183 ($355,000 total): applied art and design, art/fine arts.

Other Money-Saving Options Co-op program. *Payment Plans:* tuition prepayment, installment, deferred payment. *Waivers:* full or partial for employees or children of employees.

Contact Ms. Sandy K. Britton, Director of Student Business Affairs, Kendall College of Art and Design, 111 Division Avenue North, Grand Rapids, MI 49503, 800-676-2787, fax: 616-451-9867.

KENNESAW STATE UNIVERSITY
Kennesaw, Georgia

About the Institution State-supported, coed. Degrees awarded: B, M. Offers 49 undergraduate majors. Total enrollment: 12,537. Undergraduates: 11,342 (95% state residents). Freshmen: 1,090.

Undergraduate Expenses (1996–97) State resident tuition: $1584. Nonresident tuition: $5463. Mandatory fees: $240.

Applications 61% of all full-time undergraduates enrolled in fall 1996 applied for aid; of these, 65% were judged to have need according to Federal Methodology, of whom 93% were aided. *Financial aid deadline (priority):* 3/31. *Financial aid forms:* FAFSA required. State form required for some. *Admission application deadline:* 8/15.

Summary of Aid to Needy Students *From gift & self-help combined:* Average need met: 54%. Average amount awarded: $3831 (26% gift aid, 74% self-help). *Gift aid:* Total: $2,388,699 (2% from college's own funds, 6% from other college-administered sources, 92% from external sources). 40 Federal Work-Study jobs (averaging $2000); 500 part-time jobs.

Need-Based Scholarships & Grants Pell, FSEOG, state, private, college/university, Georgia HOPE Scholarships.

Loans Perkins, PLUS, Stafford, Unsubsidized Stafford, state, private, college/university short-term loans ($400 average).

Non-Need Awards In 1996, a total of 1,984 non-need awards were made. *Academic Interests/Achievement Awards:* 1,854 ($3,401,435 total): general academic, biological sciences, business, English, health fields, mathematics, physical sciences, premedicine, social sciences. *Creative Arts/Performance Awards:* 13 ($9345 total): art/fine arts, music, performing arts. *Special Achievements/Activities Awards:* 1 ($800 total): community service. *Special Characteristics Awards:* 4 ($3766 total): local/state students, members of minorities. *Athletic:* Total: 112 ($546,985); Men: 62 ($293,862); Women: 50 ($253,123).

Other Money-Saving Options Co-op program, cooperative Army ROTC. *Payment Plan:* deferred payment. *Waivers:* full or partial for senior citizens.

Contact Office of Student Financial Aid, Kennesaw State University, 1000 Chastain Road, Kennesaw, GA 30144-5591, 770-423-6074, fax: 770-423-6708.

KENT STATE UNIVERSITY
Kent, Ohio

About the Institution State-supported, coed. Degrees awarded: B, M, D. Offers 129 undergraduate majors. Total enrollment: 20,600. Undergraduates: 15,958 (92% state residents). Freshmen: 2,811.

Undergraduate Expenses (1996–97) State resident tuition: $4288. Nonresident tuition: $8576. College room and board: $4030.

Applications 84% of all full-time undergraduates enrolled in fall 1996 applied for aid. *Financial aid deadline (priority):* 2/15. *Financial aid forms:* FAFSA, state form required. Summer aid application required for some. *Admission application deadline:* 3/15.

Summary of Aid to Needy Students Federal Work-Study jobs; 4,000 part-time jobs.

Need-Based Scholarships & Grants Pell, FSEOG, state, college/university.

Loans Perkins, PLUS, Stafford, Unsubsidized Stafford, Federal Nursing, college/university short-term loans ($200 average), college/university long-term loans.

Non-Need Awards In 1996, a total of 4,384 non-need awards were made. *Academic Interests/Achievement Awards:* 3,232 ($1,661,854 total): general academic, architecture, area/ethnic studies, biological sciences, business, communication, education, English, health fields, international studies, library science, mathematics, military science, physical sciences, social sciences. *Creative Arts/Performance Awards:* 153 ($64,250 total): art/fine arts, journalism/publications, music. *Special Characteristics Awards:* 674 ($1,304,474 total): children and siblings of alumni, members of minorities, out-of-state students. *Athletic:* Total: 325 ($2,155,082); Men: 201 ($1,345,220); Women: 124 ($809,862).

Other Money-Saving Options Co-op program, Army ROTC, Air Force ROTC, off-campus living (after sophomore year). *Payment Plan:* installment. *Waivers:* full or partial for employees or children of employees.

Contact Mr. Craig Cornell, Coordinator, Quality Assurance and Compliance, Kent State University, 103 Michael Schwartz Center, Kent, OH 44242-0001, 330-672-2972, fax: 330-672-4014.

KENTUCKY CHRISTIAN COLLEGE
Grayson, Kentucky

About the Institution Independent/religious, coed. Degrees awarded: A, B. Offers 13 undergraduate majors. Total enrollment: 529 (29% state residents). Freshmen: 122.

Undergraduate Expenses (1997–98) Comprehensive fee of $9748 includes tuition ($5984) and college room and board ($3764).

Applications 94% of all full-time undergraduates enrolled in fall 1996 applied for aid; of these, 87% were judged to have need according to Federal Methodology, of whom 99% were aided. *Financial aid deadline (priority):* 4/1. *Financial aid forms:* FAFSA, institutional form required; CSS Financial Aid PROFILE acceptable. *Admission application deadline:* 8/1.

Summary of Aid to Needy Students *From gift & self-help combined:* Average need met: 67%. Average amount awarded: $6536 (43% gift aid, 57% self-help). *Gift aid:* Total: $1,197,937 (28% from college's own funds, 14% from other college-administered sources, 58% from external sources). 232 Federal Work-Study jobs (averaging $1258); 56 part-time jobs.

Need-Based Scholarships & Grants Pell, FSEOG, state, private, college/university.

Loans Perkins, PLUS, Stafford, Unsubsidized Stafford, private.

Non-Need Awards In 1996, a total of 269 non-need awards were made. *Academic Interests/Achievement Awards:* 86 ($188,702 total): general academic, business, religion/biblical studies. *Creative Arts/Performance Awards:* 26 ($85,000 total): debating, music, performing arts, theater/drama. *Special Achievements/Activities Awards:* 25 ($15,650 total): general special achievements/activities, community service, leadership, religious involvement. *Special Characteristics Awards:* 132 ($255,745 total): general special characteristics, children and siblings of alumni, children of faculty/staff, international students, members of minorities, out-of-state students, religious affiliation.

Other Money-Saving Options *Payment Plans:* tuition prepayment, installment. *Waivers:* full or partial for minority students and employees or children of employees.

Contact Office of Financial Aid, Kentucky Christian College, 100 Academic Parkway, Grayson, KY 41143-2205, 606-474-3000.

KENTUCKY MOUNTAIN BIBLE COLLEGE
Vancleve, Kentucky

About the Institution Independent/religious, coed. Degrees awarded: A, B. Offers 5 undergraduate majors. Total enrollment: 61. Freshmen: 10.

Undergraduate Expenses (1996–97) Comprehensive fee of $5820 includes tuition ($3000), mandatory fees ($50), and college room and board ($2770). College room only: $730.

Applications 73% of all full-time undergraduates enrolled in fall 1996 applied for aid; of these, 80% were judged to have need according to Federal Methodology, of whom 100% were aided. *Financial aid deadline (priority):* 4/1. *Financial aid forms:* FAFSA required. *Admission application deadline:* rolling.

Summary of Aid to Needy Students *From gift & self-help combined:* Average need met: 66%. Average amount awarded: $4136 (37% gift aid, 63% self-help). *Gift aid:* Total: $71,800 (17% from college's own funds, 4% from other college-administered sources, 79% from external sources). Federal Work-Study jobs; part-time jobs.

Need-Based Scholarships & Grants Pell, FSEOG, private, college/university.

Loans Stafford, Unsubsidized Stafford, college/university short-term loans ($600 average).

Non-Need Awards In 1996, a total of 16 non-need awards were made. *Academic Interests/Achievement Awards:* 10 ($7500 total): general academic. *Creative Arts/Performance Awards:* 6 ($15,000 total): music.

Contact Mrs. Jewel MacGregor, Director of Financial Aid, Kentucky Mountain Bible College, 855 Kentucky Highway 541, PO Box 10, Vancleve, KY 41385, 800-666-5622.

KENTUCKY STATE UNIVERSITY
Frankfort, Kentucky

About the Institution State-related, coed. Degrees awarded: A, B, M. Offers 36 undergraduate majors. Total enrollment: 2,356. Undergraduates: 2,280 (74% state residents). Freshmen: 390.

Undergraduate Expenses (1996–97) State resident tuition: $1740. Nonresident tuition: $5220. Mandatory fees: $210. College room and board: $3088. College room only: $1676.

Applications 79% of all full-time undergraduates enrolled in fall 1996 applied for aid; of these, 94% were judged to have need according to Federal Methodology, of whom 98% were aided. *Financial aid deadline (priority):* 4/15. *Financial aid forms:* FAFSA, institutional form required. *Admission application deadline:* rolling.

Summary of Aid to Needy Students *From gift & self-help combined:* Average need met: 70%. *Gift aid:* Total: $5,581,278. 1,000 Federal Work-Study jobs; 200 part-time jobs.

Need-Based Scholarships & Grants Pell, FSEOG, state, private, college/university.

Loans Perkins, PLUS, Stafford, Unsubsidized Stafford.

Non-Need Awards *Academic Interests/Achievement Awards:* general academic. *Creative Arts/Performance Awards:* music. *Special Characteristics Awards:* adult students, children with a deceased or disabled parent, handicapped students. *Athletic:* available.

Other Money-Saving Options Accelerated degree, co-op program, cooperative Air Force ROTC, off-campus living. *Payment Plans:* installment, deferred payment. *Waivers:* full or partial for employees or children of employees and senior citizens.

Contact Office of Financial Aid, Kentucky State University, Frankfort, KY 40601, 502-227-5960.

KENTUCKY WESLEYAN COLLEGE
Owensboro, Kentucky

About the Institution Independent/religious, coed. Degrees awarded: A, B. Offers 34 undergraduate majors. Total enrollment: 714 (78% state residents). Freshmen: 179.

Undergraduate Expenses (1997–98) Comprehensive fee of $13,870 includes tuition ($9220), mandatory fees ($150), and college room and board ($4500). College room only: $2060.

Applications 84% of all full-time undergraduates enrolled in fall 1996 applied for aid; of these, 87% were judged to have need according to Federal Methodology, of whom 100% were aided. *Financial aid deadline (priority):* 3/1. *Financial aid forms:* FAFSA, institutional form required; CSS Financial Aid PROFILE acceptable. *Admission application deadline:* rolling.

Summary of Aid to Needy Students *From gift & self-help combined:* Average need met: 75%. Average amount awarded: $11,990 (71% gift aid, 29% self-help). *Gift aid:* Total: $4,705,026 (77% from college's own funds, 14% from other college-administered sources, 9% from external sources). 215 Federal Work-Study jobs (averaging $1000); 97 part-time jobs.

Need-Based Scholarships & Grants Pell, FSEOG, state, private, college/university.

Loans Perkins, PLUS, Stafford, Unsubsidized Stafford.

Non-Need Awards In 1996, a total of 853 non-need awards were made. *Academic Interests/Achievement Awards:* 298 ($977,216 total): general academic. *Creative Arts/Performance Awards:* 56 ($56,108 total): art/fine arts, music, theater/drama. *Special Achievements/Activities Awards:* 48 ($127,000 total): leadership. *Special Characteristics Awards:* 333 ($312,753 total): general special characteristics, children and siblings of alumni, religious affiliation. *Athletic:* Total: 118 ($474,780); Men: 67 ($259,303); Women: 51 ($215,477).

Other Money-Saving Options Off-campus living (after junior year). *Payment Plans:* installment, deferred payment. *Waivers:* full or partial for children of alumni, employees or children of employees, senior citizens.

Contact Ms. Dotty Benningfield, Director of Financial Aid, Kentucky Wesleyan College, 3000 Frederick Street, Owensboro, KY 42301, 502-926-3111.

KENYON COLLEGE
Gambier, Ohio

About the Institution Independent, coed. Degrees awarded: B. Offers 45 undergraduate majors. Total enrollment: 1,547 (24% state residents). Freshmen: 425.

Undergraduate Expenses (1997–98) Comprehensive fee of $26,840 includes tuition ($22,200), mandatory fees ($650), and college room and board ($3990). College room only: $1730.

Applications Of all full-time undergraduates enrolled in fall 1996, 80% of those who applied for aid were judged to have need according to Federal Methodology, of whom 98% were aided. *Financial aid deadline:*

2/15. *Financial aid forms:* FAFSA, CSS Financial Aid PROFILE required. *Regular admission application deadline:* 2/15. Early decision deadline: 12/1.

Summary of Aid to Needy Students *From gift & self-help combined:* Average need met: 95%. Average amount awarded: $16,600 (77% gift aid, 23% self-help). *Gift aid:* Total: $7,650,857 (94% from college's own funds, 3% from other college-administered sources, 3% from external sources). 228 Federal Work-Study jobs (averaging $843); 475 part-time jobs.

Need-Based Scholarships & Grants Pell, FSEOG, state, college/university.

Loans Perkins, PLUS, Stafford, Unsubsidized Stafford, college/university short-term loans ($200 average), college/university long-term loans ($1344 average).

Non-Need Awards In 1996, a total of 283 non-need awards were made. *Academic Interests/Achievement Awards:* 283 ($2,044,885 total): general academic.

Other Money-Saving Options *Payment Plan:* installment. *Waivers:* full or partial for employees or children of employees.

Contact Financial Aid Office, Kenyon College, Stephens Hall, Gambier, OH 43022-9623, 614-427-5430.

KEUKA COLLEGE
Keuka Park, New York

About the Institution Independent/religious, coed. Degrees awarded: B. Offers 32 undergraduate majors. Total enrollment: 938 (94% state residents). Freshmen: 326.

Undergraduate Expenses (1997–98) Comprehensive fee of $16,824 includes tuition ($11,040), mandatory fees ($360), and college room and board ($5424).

Applications Of all full-time undergraduates enrolled in fall 1996, 100% of those judged to have need according to Federal Methodology were aided. *Financial aid deadline (priority):* 2/1. *Financial aid forms:* FAFSA, institutional form required; CSS Financial Aid PROFILE acceptable. State form required for some. *Admission application deadline:* rolling.

Summary of Aid to Needy Students *From gift & self-help combined:* Average need met: 87%. Average amount awarded: $10,853 (51% gift aid, 49% self-help). *Gift aid:* Total: $4,219,594. Federal Work-Study jobs; part-time jobs.

Need-Based Scholarships & Grants Pell, FSEOG, state, private, college/university.

Loans Perkins, PLUS, Stafford, Unsubsidized Stafford, private, college/university short-term loans.

Non-Need Awards *Academic Interests/Achievement Awards:* general academic. *Special Achievements/Activities Awards:* leadership.

Other Money-Saving Options Cooperative Army ROTC. *Payment Plan:* installment. *Waivers:* full or partial for employees or children of employees.

Contact Mr. Roger Michaud, Director of Financial Aid, Keuka College, Financial Aid Office, Keuka Park, NY 14478-0098, 315-536-5232.

KING COLLEGE
Bristol, Tennessee

About the Institution Independent/religious, coed. Degrees awarded: B. Offers 29 undergraduate majors. Total enrollment: 589 (41% state residents). Freshmen: 164.

Undergraduate Expenses (1997–98) Comprehensive fee of $13,994 includes tuition ($9830), mandatory fees ($720), and college room and board ($3444). College room only: $1708.

Applications 85% of all full-time undergraduates enrolled in fall 1996 applied for aid; of these, 94% were judged to have need according to Federal Methodology, of whom 100% were aided. *Financial aid deadline (priority):* 3/1. *Financial aid forms:* FAFSA, institutional form required. Financial aid transcript (for transfers) required for some. *Admission application deadline:* rolling.

Summary of Aid to Needy Students *From gift & self-help combined:* Average need met: 80%. Average amount awarded: $10,553 (68% gift aid, 32% self-help). *Gift aid:* Total: $2,654,424 (73% from college's own funds, 3% from other college-administered sources, 24% from external sources). 82 Federal Work-Study jobs (averaging $1074); 238 part-time jobs.

Need-Based Scholarships & Grants Pell, FSEOG, state, private, college/university.

Loans Perkins, PLUS, Stafford, Unsubsidized Stafford, state, college/university long-term loans ($1300 average).

Non-Need Awards In 1996, a total of 331 non-need awards were made. *Academic Interests/Achievement Awards:* 165 ($496,019 total): general academic. *Creative Arts/Performance Awards:* 15 ($15,000 total): music, performing arts, theater/drama. *Special Achievements/Activities Awards:* 30 ($52,900 total): religious involvement. *Special Characteristics Awards:* 58 ($97,089 total): children of faculty/staff, relatives of clergy. *Athletic:* Total: 63 ($275,095); Men: 40 ($178,170); Women: 23 ($96,925).

Other Money-Saving Options Cooperative Army ROTC. *Payment Plan:* installment. *Waivers:* full or partial for employees or children of employees.

Contact Mrs. Mildred B. Greeson, Director of Financial Aid, King College, 1350 King College Road, Bristol, TN 37620-2699, 423-652-4725, fax: 423-652-4727.

KING'S COLLEGE
Wilkes-Barre, Pennsylvania

About the Institution Independent/religious, coed. Degrees awarded: A, B, M. Offers 42 undergraduate majors. Total enrollment: 2,279. Undergraduates: 2,151 (77% state residents). Freshmen: 439.

Undergraduate Expenses (1997–98) Comprehensive fee of $20,120 includes tuition ($13,390), mandatory fees ($610), and college room and board ($6120). College room only: $2860.

Applications 91% of all full-time undergraduates enrolled in fall 1996 applied for aid; of these, 91% were judged to have need according to Federal Methodology, of whom 96% were aided. *Financial aid deadline:* Applications processed continuously. *Financial aid forms:* FAFSA, institutional form required; CSS Financial Aid PROFILE, state form acceptable. *Admission application deadline:* rolling.

Summary of Aid to Needy Students *From gift & self-help combined:* Average need met: 85%. Average amount awarded: $9092 (68% gift aid, 32% self-help). *Gift aid:* Total: $8,839,108 (68% from college's own funds, 2% from other college-administered sources, 30% from external sources). 246 Federal Work-Study jobs (averaging $1200); 175 part-time jobs.

Need-Based Scholarships & Grants Pell, FSEOG, state, private, college/university.

Loans Perkins, PLUS, Stafford, Unsubsidized Stafford, state, private.

Non-Need Awards In 1996, a total of 296 non-need awards were made. *Academic Interests/Achievement Awards:* 180 ($772,150 total): general academic, biological sciences, business, communication, computer science, education, English, foreign languages, health fields, humanities, mathematics, physical sciences, premedicine, religion/biblical studies, social sciences. *Creative Arts/Performance Awards:* 6 ($10,000 total): debating. *Special Achievements/Activities Awards:* 10 ($25,000 total): leadership. *Special Characteristics Awards:* 100

($557,500 total): children of faculty/staff, international students, relatives of clergy, ROTC participants, siblings of current students.

Other Money-Saving Options Co-op program, Army ROTC, cooperative Air Force ROTC, off-campus living (after sophomore year). *Payment Plans:* installment, deferred payment. *Waivers:* full or partial for employees or children of employees and senior citizens.

Contact Mr. Henry L. Chance, Director of Financial Aid, King's College, 133 North River Street, Wilkes-Barre, PA 18711-0801, 717-826-5868.

KNOX COLLEGE
Galesburg, Illinois

About the Institution Independent, coed. Degrees awarded: B. Offers 41 undergraduate majors. Total enrollment: 1,134 (52% state residents). Freshmen: 307.

Undergraduate Expenses (1997–98) Comprehensive fee of $23,289 includes tuition ($18,186), mandatory fees ($207), and college room and board ($4896). College room only: $2178.

Applications 90% of all full-time undergraduates enrolled in fall 1996 applied for aid; of these, 83% were judged to have need according to Federal Methodology, of whom 100% were aided. *Financial aid deadline (priority):* 3/1. *Financial aid forms:* FAFSA, institutional form required; CSS Financial Aid PROFILE acceptable. State form required for some. *Regular admission application deadline:* 2/15. Early action deadline: 12/1.

Summary of Aid to Needy Students *From gift & self-help combined:* Average need met: 95%. Average amount awarded: $17,161 (74% gift aid, 26% self-help). *Gift aid:* Total: $10,324,306 (78% from college's own funds, 1% from other college-administered sources, 21% from external sources). 790 Federal Work-Study jobs (averaging $1188); 64 part-time jobs.

Need-Based Scholarships & Grants Pell, FSEOG, state, private, college/university.

Loans Perkins, PLUS, Stafford, Unsubsidized Stafford, college/university long-term loans ($1477 average).

Non-Need Awards In 1996, a total of 615 non-need awards were made. *Academic Interests/Achievement Awards:* 437 ($2,647,685 total): general academic, mathematics. *Creative Arts/Performance Awards:* 171 ($242,943 total): art/fine arts, creative writing, music, theater/drama. *Special Achievements/Activities Awards:* 7 ($12,500 total): general special achievements/activities, community service.

Other Money-Saving Options *Payment Plans:* tuition prepayment, deferred payment. *Waivers:* full or partial for employees or children of employees.

Contact Ms. Teresa K. Jackson, Director of Financial Aid, Knox College, 2 East South Street, Galesburg, IL 61401, 309-341-7130, fax: 309-341-7070.

KNOXVILLE COLLEGE
Knoxville, Tennessee

About the Institution Independent/religious, coed. Degrees awarded: A, B. Offers 25 undergraduate majors. Total enrollment: 433. Freshmen: 164.

Undergraduate Expenses (1996–97) Comprehensive fee of $9242 includes tuition ($5400), mandatory fees ($392), and college room and board ($3450). College room only: $1900.

Applications *Financial aid deadline (priority):* 6/1. *Financial aid forms:* FAFSA, institutional form required; CSS Financial Aid PROFILE acceptable. State form required for some. *Admission application deadline:* rolling.

Summary of Aid to Needy Students Federal Work-Study jobs; part-time jobs.

Non-Need Awards *Academic Interests/Achievement Awards:* general academic. *Special Achievements/Activities Awards:* leadership. *Special Characteristics Awards:* children of faculty/staff, siblings of current students.

Other Money-Saving Options Co-op program, Army ROTC, Air Force ROTC, off-campus living.

Contact Office of Financial Aid, Knoxville College, Knoxville, TN 37921-4799, 423-524-6500.

KOL YAAKOV TORAH CENTER
Monsey, New York

About the Institution Independent/religious, men. Offers 2 undergraduate majors. Total enrollment: 40. Freshmen: 2.

Undergraduate Expenses (1996–97) Comprehensive fee of $6200 includes tuition ($3300) and college room and board ($2900).

Applications 25% of all full-time undergraduates enrolled in fall 1996 applied for aid; of these,100% were judged to have need according to Federal Methodology, of whom 100% were aided. *Financial aid deadline (priority):* 10/1. *Financial aid forms:* institutional form required. FAFSA required for some. *Admission application deadline:* rolling.

Summary of Aid to Needy Students *From gift & self-help combined:* Average need met: 100%. Average amount awarded: $3500. Federal Work-Study jobs; part-time jobs.

Need-Based Scholarships & Grants Pell, FSEOG, private, college/university.

Non-Need Awards Not offered.

Other Money-Saving Options Co-op program, off-campus living.

Contact Office of Financial Aid, Kol Yaakov Torah Center, 29 West Maple Avenue, Monsey, NY 10952-2954, 914-425-3863.

KUTZTOWN UNIVERSITY OF PENNSYLVANIA
Kutztown, Pennsylvania

About the Institution State supported, coed. Degrees awarded: B, M. Offers 57 undergraduate majors. Total enrollment: 7,843. Undergraduates: 6,925 (91% state residents). Freshmen: 1,411.

Undergraduate Expenses (1996–97) State resident tuition: $3368. Nonresident tuition: $8566. Mandatory fees: $730. College room and board: $3258. College room only: $2240.

Applications Of all full-time undergraduates enrolled in fall 1996, 80% of those who applied for aid were judged to have need according to Federal Methodology, of whom 80% were aided. *Financial aid deadline (priority):* 3/15. *Financial aid forms:* FAFSA required. *Regular admission application deadline:* rolling. Early action deadline: 11/15.

Summary of Aid to Needy Students *From gift & self-help combined:* Average need met: 75%. Average amount awarded: $4189 (42% gift aid, 58% self-help). *Gift aid:* Total: $5,673,885 (2% from college's own funds, 4% from other college-administered sources, 94% from external sources). 147 Federal Work-Study jobs; 1,000 part-time jobs.

Need-Based Scholarships & Grants Pell, FSEOG, state, private, college/university.

Loans Perkins, PLUS, Stafford, Unsubsidized Stafford, college/university short-term loans ($75 average).

Non-Need Awards In 1996, a total of 711 non-need awards were made. *Academic Interests/Achievement Awards:* 401 ($141,246 total): general academic. *Creative Arts/Performance Awards:* 18 ($16,950 total): applied art and design, music. *Special Characteristics Awards:* 35 ($112,590 total): children of faculty/staff. *Athletic:* Total: 257 ($212,144); Men: 133 ($121,834); Women: 124 ($90,310).

Other Money-Saving Options Accelerated degree, cooperative Army ROTC, off-campus living. *Payment Plans:* installment, deferred payment. *Waivers:* full or partial for employees or children of employees.

Contact Ms. Anita Faust, Director of Financial Aid, Kutztown University of Pennsylvania, Box 730, Kutztown, PA 19530-0730, 610-683-4077, fax: 610-683-1380.

LABORATORY INSTITUTE OF MERCHANDISING
New York, New York

About the Institution Proprietary, coed. Degrees awarded: A, B. Offers 1 undergraduate major. Total enrollment: 184 (50% state residents). Freshmen: 48.

Undergraduate Expenses (1997–98 estimated) Tuition: $11,300. Mandatory fees: $150.

Applications 86% of all full-time undergraduates enrolled in fall 1996 applied for aid; of these,100% were judged to have need according to Federal Methodology, of whom 100% were aided. *Financial aid deadline (priority):* 4/1. *Financial aid forms:* FAFSA, institutional form required; state form acceptable. *Admission application deadline:* rolling.

Summary of Aid to Needy Students *From gift & self-help combined:* Average need met: 63%. Average amount awarded: $8600 (66% gift aid, 34% self-help). *Gift aid:* Total: $565,555 (18% from college's own funds, 40% from other college-administered sources, 42% from external sources). 30 part-time jobs.

Need-Based Scholarships & Grants Pell, FSEOG, state, college/university.

Loans Perkins, PLUS, Stafford, Unsubsidized Stafford.

Non-Need Awards In 1996, a total of 151 non-need awards were made. *Academic Interests/Achievement Awards:* 80 ($117,000 total): business. *Special Characteristics Awards:* 71 ($183,717 total): local/state students.

Other Money-Saving Options Co-op program. *Payment Plan:* installment.

Contact Ms. Linda Graham, Assistant to the Director of Financial Aid, Laboratory Institute of Merchandising, 12 East 53rd Street, New York, NY 10022-5268, 212-752-1530, fax: 212-832-6708.

LAFAYETTE COLLEGE
Easton, Pennsylvania

About the Institution Independent/religious, coed. Degrees awarded: B. Offers 34 undergraduate majors. Total enrollment: 2,185 (31% state residents). Freshmen: 577.

Undergraduate Expenses (1996–97) Comprehensive fee of $26,718 includes tuition ($20,308), mandatory fees ($75), and college room and board ($6335). College room only: $3375.

Applications Of all full-time undergraduates enrolled in fall 1996, 88% of those who applied for aid were judged to have need according to Federal Methodology, of whom 94% were aided. *Financial aid deadline (priority):* 2/1. *Financial aid forms:* FAFSA, CSS Financial Aid PROFILE, state form required. Institutional form, Divorced/Separated Parents' Statement, Business/Farm Supplement required for some. *Regular admission application deadline:* 1/1. Early decision deadline:

Summary of Aid to Needy Students *From gift & self-help combined:* Average need met: 82%. Average amount awarded: $16,436 (77% gift aid, 23% self-help). *Gift aid:* Total: $12,842,554 (89% from college's own funds, 2% from other college-administered sources, 9% from external sources). 118 Federal Work-Study jobs (averaging $970); 50 part-time jobs.

Need-Based Scholarships & Grants Pell, FSEOG, state, private, college/university.

Loans Perkins, PLUS, Stafford, Unsubsidized Stafford, state, private, college/university short-term loans ($200 average), college/university long-term loans ($2150 average), Parent loans.

Non-Need Awards In 1996, a total of 29 non-need awards were made. *Academic Interests/Achievement Awards:* 20 ($196,850 total): general academic. *Special Characteristics Awards:* 9 ($156,536 total): ROTC participants.

Other Money-Saving Options Accelerated degree, cooperative Army ROTC. *Payment Plans:* tuition prepayment, deferred payment. *Waivers:* full or partial for employees or children of employees.

Contact Mr. Barry W. McCarty, Director, Lafayette College, 107 Markle Hall, Easton, PA 18042-1777, 610-250-5055, fax: 610-250-5355.

LAGRANGE COLLEGE
LaGrange, Georgia

About the Institution Independent/religious, coed. Degrees awarded: A, B, M. Offers 36 undergraduate majors. Total enrollment: 984. Undergraduates: 932 (84% state residents). Freshmen: 193.

Undergraduate Expenses (1997–98) Comprehensive fee of $13,443 includes tuition ($8928), mandatory fees ($240), and college room and board ($4275).

Applications 78% of all full-time undergraduates enrolled in fall 1996 applied for aid; of these, 87% were judged to have need according to Federal Methodology, of whom 100% were aided. *Financial aid deadline (priority):* 5/1. *Financial aid forms:* FAFSA, state form, institutional form required; CSS Financial Aid PROFILE, SINGLEFILE Form of United Student Aid Funds acceptable. *Admission application deadline:* 8/15.

Summary of Aid to Needy Students *From gift & self-help combined:* Average need met: 82%. Average amount awarded: $9600 (67% gift aid, 33% self-help). *Gift aid:* Total: $3,614,853 (39% from college's own funds, 5% from other college-administered sources, 56% from external sources). 83 Federal Work-Study jobs (averaging $765); 153 part-time jobs.

Need-Based Scholarships & Grants Pell, FSEOG.

Loans Perkins, PLUS, Stafford, Unsubsidized Stafford, state, private.

Non-Need Awards *Academic Interests/Achievement Awards:* general academic, English, mathematics, physical sciences, social sciences. *Creative Arts/Performance Awards:* art/fine arts, music, theater/drama.

Other Money-Saving Options Off-campus living (after junior year). *Payment Plan:* installment. *Waivers:* full or partial for employees or children of employees.

Contact Mrs. Kathryn Fincher, Financial Aid Counselor, LaGrange College, LaGrange, GA 30240-2999, 706-812-7241.

LAKE ERIE COLLEGE
Painesville, Ohio

About the Institution Independent, coed. Degrees awarded: B, M. Offers 32 undergraduate majors. Total enrollment: 622. Undergraduates: 512 (87% state residents). Freshmen: 70.

Undergraduate Expenses (1997–98) Comprehensive fee of $18,690 includes tuition ($13,250), mandatory fees ($500), and college room and board ($4940). College room only: $2540.

Applications Of all full-time undergraduates enrolled in fall 1996, 98% of those who applied for aid were judged to have need according to Federal Methodology, of whom 100% were aided. *Financial aid deadline (priority):* 3/1. *Financial aid forms:* FAFSA, institutional form required. *Admission application deadline:* 8/1.

Summary of Aid to Needy Students *From gift & self-help combined:* Average need met: 77%. Average amount awarded: $13,194 (57% gift aid, 43% self-help). *Gift aid:* Total: $1,905,947 (64% from college's

own funds, 4% from other college-administered sources, 32% from external sources). 18 Federal Work-Study jobs (averaging $2103); 94 part-time jobs.

Need-Based Scholarships & Grants Pell, FSEOG, state, private, college/university.

Loans Perkins, PLUS, Stafford, Unsubsidized Stafford, state.

Non-Need Awards *Academic Interests/Achievement Awards:* general academic. *Creative Arts/Performance Awards:* general creative, art/fine arts. *Special Achievements/Activities Awards:* hobbies/interest. *Special Characteristics Awards:* children of faculty/staff, local/state students, twins.

Other Money-Saving Options Accelerated degree. *Payment Plan:* installment. *Waivers:* full or partial for employees or children of employees and senior citizens.

Contact Financial Aid Office, Lake Erie College, Painesville, OH 44077-3389, 216-639-7815.

LAKE FOREST COLLEGE
Lake Forest, Illinois

About the Institution Independent, coed. Degrees awarded: B, M. Offers 44 undergraduate majors. Total enrollment: 1,106. Undergraduates: 1,093 (43% state residents). Freshmen: 324.

Undergraduate Expenses (1997–98) Comprehensive fee of $24,110 includes tuition ($19,300), mandatory fees ($260), and college room and board ($4550). College room only: $2550.

Applications 73% of all full-time undergraduates enrolled in fall 1996 applied for aid; of these, 98% were judged to have need according to Federal Methodology, of whom 100% were aided. *Financial aid deadline (priority):* 3/1. *Financial aid forms:* FAFSA, institutional form, federal income tax returns required. *Regular admission application deadline:* 3/1. Early decision deadline: 1/1.

Summary of Aid to Needy Students *From gift & self-help combined:* Average need met: 100%. Average amount awarded: $18,161 (79% gift aid, 21% self-help). *Gift aid:* Total: $11,134,835 (80% from college's own funds, 4% from other college-administered sources, 16% from external sources). 700 Federal Work-Study jobs (averaging $1600); 68 part-time jobs.

Need-Based Scholarships & Grants Pell, FSEOG, state, private, college/university.

Loans Perkins, PLUS, Stafford, Unsubsidized Stafford, state, private, college/university short-term loans ($300 average).

Non-Need Awards In 1996, a total of 56 non-need awards were made. *Academic Interests/Achievement Awards:* 31 ($311,625 total): general academic. *Creative Arts/Performance Awards:* 10 ($52,500 total): art/fine arts, music, theater/drama. *Special Achievements/Activities Awards:* 6 ($40,500 total): leadership. *Special Characteristics Awards:* 9 ($103,125 total): children and siblings of alumni, previous college experience.

Other Money-Saving Options Accelerated degree, off-campus living (after freshman year). *Payment Plan:* installment. *Waivers:* full or partial for employees or children of employees.

Contact Office of Financial Aid, Lake Forest College, 555 North Sheridan Road, Lake Forest, IL 60045-2399, 847-234-3100.

LAKELAND COLLEGE
Sheboygan, Wisconsin

About the Institution Independent/religious, coed. Degrees awarded: B, M. Offers 46 undergraduate majors. Total enrollment: 928. Undergraduates: 814 (77% state residents). Freshmen: 193.

Undergraduate Expenses (1997–98) Comprehensive fee of $15,610 includes tuition ($10,770), mandatory fees ($460), and college room and board ($4380). College room only: $2105.

Applications *Financial aid deadline (priority):* 7/1. *Financial aid forms:* FAFSA, institutional form required. *Admission application deadline:* rolling.

Summary of Aid to Needy Students 245 Federal Work-Study jobs (averaging $1225); 47 part-time jobs.

Need-Based Scholarships & Grants Pell, FSEOG.

Loans Perkins, PLUS, Stafford, Unsubsidized Stafford.

Non-Need Awards In 1996, a total of 282 non-need awards were made. *Academic Interests/Achievement Awards:* 227 ($696,375 total): general academic, business, engineering/technologies. *Creative Arts/Performance Awards:* 1 ($2000 total): journalism/publications. *Special Characteristics Awards:* 54 ($89,025 total): religious affiliation, siblings of current students.

Other Money-Saving Options *Payment Plan:* installment. *Waivers:* full or partial for employees or children of employees and senior citizens.

Contact Mr. Don Seymour, Director of Financial Aid, Lakeland College, PO Box 359, Sheboygan, WI 53082-0359, 414-565-1214, fax: 414-565-1206.

LAMAR UNIVERSITY
Beaumont, Texas

About the Institution State-supported, coed. Degrees awarded: A, B, M, D. Offers 103 undergraduate majors. Total enrollment: 8,418. Undergraduates: 7,851 (95% state residents). Freshmen: 1,088.

Undergraduate Expenses (1996–97) State resident tuition: $960. Nonresident tuition: $7380. Mandatory fees: $836. College room and board: $3280. College room only: $1726.

Applications *Financial aid deadline (priority):* 4/1. *Financial aid forms:* FAFSA, institutional form required. *Admission application deadline:* 8/1.

Summary of Aid to Needy Students *From gift & self-help combined:* Average need met: 48%. Average amount awarded: $2592 (65% gift aid, 35% self-help). *Gift aid:* Total: $8,568,000 (32% from college's own funds, 24% from other college-administered sources, 44% from external sources). Federal Work-Study jobs; part-time jobs.

Need-Based Scholarships & Grants Pell, FSEOG, state.

Loans Perkins, PLUS, Stafford, Unsubsidized Stafford, college/university short-term loans ($450 average).

Non-Need Awards *Academic Interests/Achievement Awards:* general academic. *Creative Arts/Performance Awards:* general creative. *Special Achievements/Activities Awards:* general special achievements/activities. *Athletic:* available.

Other Money-Saving Options Accelerated degree, co-op program, off-campus living. *Payment Plan:* installment. *Waivers:* full or partial for senior citizens.

Contact Financial Aid Department, Lamar University, Beaumont, TX 77710, 409-880-8450.

LAMBUTH UNIVERSITY
Jackson, Tennessee

About the Institution Independent/religious, coed. Degrees awarded: B. Offers 53 undergraduate majors. Total enrollment: 1,036 (75% state residents). Freshmen: 228.

Undergraduate Expenses (1997–98) Comprehensive fee of $10,144 includes tuition ($5924), mandatory fees ($270), and college room and board ($3950). College room only: $1780.

Applications 89% of all full-time undergraduates enrolled in fall 1996 applied for aid; of these, 75% were judged to have need according to Federal Methodology, of whom 100% were aided. *Financial aid deadline (priority):* 7/1. *Financial aid forms:* institutional form required. FAFSA required for some. *Admission application deadline:* rolling.

Summary of Aid to Needy Students *From gift & self-help combined:* Average need met: 80%. Average amount awarded: $5913 (65% gift aid, 35% self-help). *Gift aid:* Total: $3,101,967 (66% from college's own funds, 15% from other college-administered sources, 19% from external sources). 139 Federal Work-Study jobs (averaging $978); 80 part-time jobs.

Need-Based Scholarships & Grants Pell, FSEOG, state, private, college/university.

Loans Perkins, PLUS, Stafford, Unsubsidized Stafford, United Methodist Student Loan.

Non-Need Awards In 1996, a total of 879 non-need awards were made. *Academic Interests/Achievement Awards:* 434 ($886,364 total): general academic. *Creative Arts/Performance Awards:* 99 ($111,450 total): dance, music, theater/drama. *Special Achievements/Activities Awards:* 4 ($1250 total): cheerleading/drum major. *Special Characteristics Awards:* 171 ($50,400 total): religious affiliation. *Athletic:* Total: 171 ($545,664); Men: 100 ($325,692); Women: 71 ($219,972).

Other Money-Saving Options Accelerated degree. *Payment Plans:* installment, deferred payment. *Waivers:* full or partial for employees or children of employees, adult students, senior citizens.

Contact Ms. Lisa A. Warmath, Director of Scholarships and Financial Aid, Lambuth University, 705 Lambuth Boulevard, Jackson, TN 38301, 901-425-3330, fax: 901-988-4600.

LANCASTER BIBLE COLLEGE
Lancaster, Pennsylvania

About the Institution Independent/religious, coed. Degrees awarded: A, B, M. Offers 3 undergraduate majors. Total enrollment: 682. Undergraduates: 650 (77% state residents). Freshmen: 106.

Undergraduate Expenses (1997–98) Comprehensive fee of $12,400 includes tuition ($8250), mandatory fees ($300), and college room and board ($3850). College room only: $1550.

Applications 67% of all full-time undergraduates enrolled in fall 1996 applied for aid; of these, 98% were judged to have need according to Federal Methodology, of whom 99% were aided. *Financial aid deadline (priority):* 5/1. *Financial aid forms:* FAFSA, state form required; CSS Financial Aid PROFILE acceptable. *Admission application deadline:* rolling.

Summary of Aid to Needy Students *From gift & self-help combined:* Average need met: 71%. Average amount awarded: $8252 (60% gift aid, 40% self-help). *Gift aid:* Total: $1,579,980 (51% from college's own funds, 30% from other college-administered sources, 19% from external sources). 105 Federal Work-Study jobs (averaging $1375); 45 part-time jobs.

Need-Based Scholarships & Grants Pell, FSEOG, state, private, college/university, Office of Vocational Rehabilitation, Blindness and Visual Services Awards.

Loans Perkins, PLUS, Stafford, Unsubsidized Stafford, private.

Non-Need Awards In 1996, a total of 354 non-need awards were made. *Academic Interests/Achievement Awards:* 90 ($53,000 total): general academic. *Creative Arts/Performance Awards:* 3 ($2500 total): music. *Special Achievements/Activities Awards:* 61 ($41,750 total): leadership, religious involvement. *Special Characteristics Awards:* 200 ($526,700 total): children and siblings of alumni, children of faculty/staff, international students, relatives of clergy, religious affiliation, siblings of current students, spouses of current students.

Other Money-Saving Options *Payment Plan:* installment. *Waivers:* full or partial for children of alumni, employees or children of employees, adult students, senior citizens.

Contact Ms. Beth Kachel, Assistant Director of Financial Aid, Lancaster Bible College, 901 Eden Road, Lancaster, PA 17601-5036, 717-569-7071 Ext. 354, fax: 717-560-8213.

LANDER UNIVERSITY
Greenwood, South Carolina

About the Institution State-supported, coed. Degrees awarded: B; M. Offers 34 undergraduate majors. Total enrollment: 2,722. Undergraduates: 2,536 (94% state residents). Freshmen: 451.

Undergraduate Expenses (1997–98) State resident tuition: $3600. Nonresident tuition: $5832. College room and board: $3560.

Applications 88% of all full-time undergraduates enrolled in fall 1996 applied for aid; of these, 87% were judged to have need according to Federal Methodology, of whom 89% were aided. *Financial aid deadline (priority):* 4/15. *Financial aid forms:* FAFSA required. *Admission application deadline:* rolling.

Summary of Aid to Needy Students *From gift & self-help combined:* Average need met: 70%. Average amount awarded: $6157 (25% gift aid, 75% self-help). *Gift aid:* Total: $2,121,200 (5% from college's own funds, 26% from other college-administered sources, 69% from external sources). Federal Work-Study jobs; 209 part-time jobs.

Need-Based Scholarships & Grants Pell, FSEOG, state, private, college/university.

Loans Perkins, PLUS, Stafford, Unsubsidized Stafford, college/university short-term loans ($150 average).

Non-Need Awards In 1996, a total of 285 non-need awards were made. *Academic Interests/Achievement Awards:* 125 ($200,000 total): general academic, biological sciences, business, computer science, education, health fields, humanities, mathematics, physical sciences. *Creative Arts/Performance Awards:* 47 ($13,000 total): art/fine arts, music, theater/drama. *Special Achievements/Activities Awards:* 10 ($27,000 total): leadership. *Special Characteristics Awards:* 20 ($35,000 total): members of minorities, out-of-state students. *Athletic:* Total: 83 ($246,654); Men: 44 ($125,569); Women: 39 ($121,085).

Other Money-Saving Options Accelerated degree, co-op program, Army ROTC, off-campus living. *Payment Plan:* installment. *Waivers:* full or partial for senior citizens.

Contact Financial Aid Office, Lander University, Greenwood, SC 29649-2099, 864-388-8340.

LANE COLLEGE
Jackson, Tennessee

About the Institution Independent/religious, coed. Degrees awarded: B. Offers 17 undergraduate majors.

Undergraduate Expenses (1996–97) Comprehensive fee of $8800 includes tuition ($5000), mandatory fees ($400), and college room and board ($3400).

Applications 88% of all full-time undergraduates enrolled in fall 1996 applied for aid; of these, 90% were judged to have need according to Federal Methodology, of whom 100% were aided. *Financial aid deadline (priority):* 4/1. *Financial aid forms:* FAFSA required. *Admission application deadline:* rolling.

Summary of Aid to Needy Students *From gift & self-help combined:* Average need met: 80%. Average amount awarded: $9169 (49% gift aid, 51% self-help). *Gift aid:* Total: $2,799,639. Federal Work-Study jobs; part-time jobs.

Need-Based Scholarships & Grants Pell, FSEOG, state, private.

Loans PLUS, Stafford, Unsubsidized Stafford.

Non-Need Awards *Academic Interests/Achievement Awards:* general academic. *Special Characteristics Awards:* children of faculty/staff. *Athletic:* available.

Other Money-Saving Options Co-op program, off-campus living. *Payment Plans:* installment, deferred payment. *Waivers:* full or partial for employees or children of employees.

Contact Financial Aid Office, Lane College, 545 Lane Avenue, Jackson, TN 38301-4598, 901-426-7535, fax: 901-426-7652.

LANGSTON UNIVERSITY
Langston, Oklahoma

About the Institution State-supported, coed. Degrees awarded: A, B, M. Offers 56 undergraduate majors. Total enrollment: 4,008 (80% state residents). Freshmen: 494.

Undergraduate Expenses (1996–97) State resident tuition: $1212. Nonresident tuition: $3274. Mandatory fees: $270. College room and board: $2580.

Applications Of all full-time undergraduates enrolled in fall 1996, 78% of those who applied for aid were judged to have need according to Federal Methodology, of whom 100% were aided. *Financial aid deadline (priority):* 5/1. *Financial aid forms:* FAFSA, institutional form required; state form acceptable. *Admission application deadline:* rolling.

Summary of Aid to Needy Students *From gift & self-help combined:* Average need met: 90%. Federal Work-Study jobs; 350 part-time jobs.

Loans PLUS, Stafford, Unsubsidized Stafford, college/university short-term loans ($250 average).

Non-Need Awards *Academic Interests/Achievement Awards:* general academic. *Creative Arts/Performance Awards:* music. *Athletic:* available.

Other Money-Saving Options Accelerated degree, co-op program, cooperative Army ROTC, off-campus living (after sophomore year).

Contact Office of Financial Aid, Langston University, PO Box 668, Langston, OK 73050-0838, 405-466-3282.

LA ROCHE COLLEGE
Pittsburgh, Pennsylvania

About the Institution Independent/religious, coed. Degrees awarded: B, M. Offers 49 undergraduate majors. Total enrollment: 1,641. Undergraduates: 1,340 (90% state residents). Freshmen: 151.

Undergraduate Expenses (1996–97) Comprehensive fee of $15,110 includes tuition ($9712), mandatory fees ($200), and college room and board ($5198).

Applications 89% of all full-time undergraduates enrolled in fall 1996 applied for aid; of these, 91% were judged to have need according to Federal Methodology, of whom 100% were aided. *Financial aid deadline (priority):* 5/1. *Financial aid forms:* FAFSA, state form, institutional form required. *Regular admission application deadline:* rolling. Early action deadline: 6/30.

Summary of Aid to Needy Students *From gift & self-help combined:* Average need met: 92%. Average amount awarded: $9650 (55% gift aid, 45% self-help). *Gift aid:* Total: $2,804,870 (52% from college's own funds, 33% from other college-administered sources, 15% from external sources). 320 Federal Work-Study jobs (averaging $1500); 1 part-time job.

Need-Based Scholarships & Grants Pell, FSEOG, private, college/university.

Loans Perkins, PLUS, Stafford, Unsubsidized Stafford.

Non-Need Awards In 1996, a total of 225 non-need awards were made. *Academic Interests/Achievement Awards:* 223 ($650,000 total): general academic. *Creative Arts/Performance Awards:* 2 ($2000 total): applied art and design.

Other Money-Saving Options Co-op program, cooperative Army ROTC, cooperative Air Force ROTC, off-campus living. *Payment Plan:* installment. *Waivers:* full or partial for employees or children of employees.

Contact Mr. Michael J. Bertonaschi, Director of Financial Aid, La Roche College, 9000 Babcock Boulevard, Pittsburgh, PA 15237-5898, 412-367-9256.

LA SALLE UNIVERSITY
Philadelphia, Pennsylvania

About the Institution Independent/religious, coed. Degrees awarded: A, B, M. Offers 78 undergraduate majors. Total enrollment: 5,130. Undergraduates: 3,810 (64% state residents). Freshmen: 648.

Undergraduate Expenses (1997–98) Comprehensive fee of $21,020 includes tuition ($14,470), mandatory fees ($380), and college room and board ($6170). College room only: $3390.

Applications 86% of all full-time undergraduates enrolled in fall 1996 applied for aid; of these, 89% were judged to have need according to Federal Methodology, of whom 100% were aided. *Financial aid deadline (priority):* 2/15. *Financial aid forms:* FAFSA, state form required. *Admission application deadline:* 4/1.

Summary of Aid to Needy Students *From gift & self-help combined:* Average need met: 76%. Average amount awarded: $12,421 (55% gift aid, 45% self-help). *Gift aid:* Total: $17,647,128 (77% from college's own funds, 16% from other college-administered sources, 7% from external sources). 910 Federal Work-Study jobs (averaging $1800); 500 part-time jobs.

Need-Based Scholarships & Grants Pell, FSEOG, state, private, college/university.

Loans Perkins, PLUS, Stafford, Unsubsidized Stafford, state, private.

Non-Need Awards *Academic Interests/Achievement Awards:* general academic. *Special Achievements/Activities Awards:* 20 ($7000 total): community service. *Special Characteristics Awards:* children of faculty/staff, members of minorities. *Athletic:* Total: 180 ($1,670,260); Men: ($770,260); Women: ($900,000).

Other Money-Saving Options Accelerated degree, co-op program, cooperative Army ROTC, cooperative Naval ROTC, cooperative Air Force ROTC, off-campus living. *Payment Plans:* installment, deferred payment *Waivers:* full or partial for minority students, children of alumni, employees or children of employees.

Contact Ms. Wendy McLaughlin, Director of Financial Aid, La Salle University, 1900 West Olney Avenue, Philadelphia, PA 19141-1199, 215-951-1070.

LASELL COLLEGE
Newton, Massachusetts

About the Institution Independent, women. Degrees awarded: A, B. Offers 25 undergraduate majors. Total enrollment: 679 (64% state residents). Freshmen: 121.

Undergraduate Expenses (1997–98) Comprehensive fee of $21,000 includes tuition ($13,400), mandatory fees ($600), and college room and board ($7000).

Applications 84% of all full-time undergraduates enrolled in fall 1996 applied for aid; of these, 95% were judged to have need according to Federal Methodology, of whom 100% were aided. *Financial aid deadline (priority):* 4/1. *Financial aid forms:* FAFSA required; CSS Financial Aid PROFILE, institutional form acceptable. State form required for some. *Admission application deadline:* rolling.

Summary of Aid to Needy Students *From gift & self-help combined:* Average amount awarded: $10,542 (59% gift aid, 41% self-help). *Gift aid:* Total: $2,783,018 (78% from college's own funds, 6% from other college-administered sources, 16% from external sources). 168 Federal Work-Study jobs (averaging $545); 85 part-time jobs.

Need-Based Scholarships & Grants Pell, FSEOG, state, college/university.

Loans Perkins, PLUS, Stafford, Unsubsidized Stafford, state, private.

Non-Need Awards In 1996, a total of 39 non-need awards were made. *Academic Interests/Achievement Awards:* 33 ($75,000 total): general academic. *Special Characteristics Awards:* 6 ($41,910 total): children of current students, children of faculty/staff, siblings of current students, twins.

Other Money-Saving Options Off-campus living. *Payment Plan:* installment. *Waivers:* full or partial for employees or children of employees.

Contact Office of Financial Aid, Lasell College, 1844 Commonwealth Avenue, Newton, MA 02166-2709, 617-243-2000.

LA SIERRA UNIVERSITY
Riverside, California

About the Institution Independent/religious, coed. Degrees awarded: A, B, M, D. Offers 52 undergraduate majors. Total enrollment: 1,607. Undergraduates: 1,507 (89% state residents). Freshmen: 341.

Undergraduate Expenses (1997–98) Comprehensive fee of $17,970 includes tuition ($13,800), mandatory fees ($105), and college room and board ($4065). College room only: $2370.

Applications *Financial aid deadline (priority):* 3/2. *Financial aid forms:* FAFSA, state form, financial aid transcript (for transfers) required. *Admission application deadline:* rolling.

Summary of Aid to Needy Students *From gift & self-help combined:* Average need met: 75%. Average amount awarded: $13,000 (48% gift aid, 52% self-help). *Gift aid:* Total: $4,800,000. Federal Work-Study jobs (averaging $2000); 400 part-time jobs.

Need-Based Scholarships & Grants Pell, FSEOG, state, private.

Loans Perkins, PLUS, Stafford, Unsubsidized Stafford, private, college/university short-term loans ($100 average), college/university long-term loans ($1500 average).

Non-Need Awards *Academic Interests/Achievement Awards:* general academic. *Creative Arts/Performance Awards:* music, theater/drama. *Special Achievements/Activities Awards:* leadership. *Special Characteristics Awards:* adult students, children of faculty/staff, relatives of clergy, religious affiliation, siblings of current students. *Athletic:* available.

Other Money-Saving Options Accelerated degree. *Payment Plan:* installment. *Waivers:* full or partial for employees or children of employees.

Contact Ms. B. Marilyn Dietel, Director of Financial Aid, La Sierra University, 4700 Pierce Street, Riverside, CA 92515, 909-785-2175, fax: 909-785-2942.

LAWRENCE TECHNOLOGICAL UNIVERSITY
Southfield, Michigan

About the Institution Independent, coed. Degrees awarded: A, B, M. Offers 29 undergraduate majors. Total enrollment: 3,916. Undergraduates: 3,310. Freshmen: 315.

Undergraduate Expenses (1997–98) Tuition: $8940 (minimum). Mandatory fees: $200. College room only: $2457 (minimum).

Applications Of all full-time undergraduates enrolled in fall 1996, 82% of those who applied for aid were judged to have need according to Federal Methodology, of whom 97% were aided. *Financial aid deadline (priority):* 5/1. *Financial aid forms:* FAFSA required; CSS Financial Aid PROFILE acceptable. *Admission application deadline:* 8/11.

Summary of Aid to Needy Students *From gift & self-help combined:* Average need met: 90%. Average amount awarded: $5373 (37% gift aid, 63% self-help). *Gift aid:* Total: $1,703,124 (25% from college's own funds, 59% from other college-administered sources, 16% from external sources). 65 Federal Work-Study jobs (averaging $1600); 159 part-time jobs.

Need-Based Scholarships & Grants Pell, FSEOG, state, private, college/university.

Loans Perkins, PLUS, Stafford, Unsubsidized Stafford, private.

Non-Need Awards In 1996, a total of 457 non-need awards were made. *Academic Interests/Achievement Awards:* 402 ($281,137 total): general academic, architecture, business, computer science, engineering/technologies, humanities, mathematics, physical sciences. *Special Achievements/Activities Awards:* 0: general special achievements/activities, hobbies/interest. *Special Characteristics Awards:* 55 ($145,754 total): general special characteristics, children of faculty/staff.

Other Money-Saving Options Co-op program, cooperative Army ROTC, cooperative Air Force ROTC, off-campus living. *Waivers:* full or partial for employees or children of employees.

Contact Mr. Paul F. Kinder, Director of Financial Aid, Lawrence Technological University, 21000 West Ten Mile Road, Southfield, MI 48075-1058, 810-204-2120, fax: 810-204-3727.

LAWRENCE UNIVERSITY
Appleton, Wisconsin

About the Institution Independent, coed. Degrees awarded: B. Offers 44 undergraduate majors. Total enrollment: 1,218 (46% state residents). Freshmen: 317.

Undergraduate Expenses (1997–98) Comprehensive fee of $23,961 includes tuition ($19,494), mandatory fees ($126), and college room and board ($4341).

Applications Of all full-time undergraduates enrolled in fall 1996, 92% of those who applied for aid were judged to have need according to Federal Methodology, of whom 100% were aided. *Financial aid deadline (priority):* 3/15. *Financial aid forms:* FAFSA, institutional form required; CSS Financial Aid PROFILE acceptable. *Regular admission application deadline:* 2/1. Early decision deadline: 11/15.

Summary of Aid to Needy Students *From gift & self-help combined:* Average need met: 100%. Average amount awarded: $17,138 (72% gift aid, 28% self-help). *Gift aid:* Total: $9,192,216 (81% from college's own funds, 16% from external sources). 592 Federal Work-Study jobs (averaging $1520); 136 part-time jobs.

Need-Based Scholarships & Grants Pell, FSEOG, state, private, college/university.

Loans Perkins, PLUS, Stafford, Unsubsidized Stafford, private, college/university short-term loans ($50 average), college/university long-term loans ($3120 average).

Non-Need Awards In 1996, a total of 639 non-need awards were made. *Academic Interests/Achievement Awards:* 376 ($2,563,000 total): general academic. *Creative Arts/Performance Awards:* 119 ($451,000 total): music. *Special Characteristics Awards:* 144 ($1,216,986 total): international students, local/state students, members of minorities.

Other Money-Saving Options *Payment Plan:* installment. *Waivers:* full or partial for employees or children of employees.

Contact Ms. Cheryl Schaffer, Director of Financial Aid, Lawrence University, PO Box 599, Appleton, WI 54912-0599, 414-832-6583, fax: 414-832-6582.

LEBANON VALLEY COLLEGE
Annville, Pennsylvania

About the Institution Independent/religious, coed. Degrees awarded: A, B, M. Offers 46 undergraduate majors. Total enrollment: 1,879. Undergraduates: 1,682 (88% state residents). Freshmen: 287.

Undergraduate Expenses (1997–98) Comprehensive fee of $21,090 includes tuition ($15,490), mandatory fees ($446), and college room and board ($5154).

Applications 85% of all full-time undergraduates enrolled in fall 1996 applied for aid; of these, 93% were judged to have need according to Federal Methodology, of whom 100% were aided. *Financial aid deadline (priority):* 3/1. *Financial aid forms:* FAFSA, institutional form, financial aid transcript (for transfers) required. *Admission application deadline:* rolling.

Summary of Aid to Needy Students *From gift & self-help combined:* Average need met: 85%. Average amount awarded: $12,240 (66% gift aid, 34% self-help). *Gift aid:* Total: $7,759,259 (72% from college's own funds, 19% from other college-administered sources, 9% from external sources). 428 Federal Work-Study jobs (averaging $1094); 12 part-time jobs.

Need-Based Scholarships & Grants Pell, FSEOG, state, private, college/university.

Loans Perkins, PLUS, Stafford, Unsubsidized Stafford, private, college/university long-term loans ($1225 average).

Non-Need Awards In 1996, a total of 828 non-need awards were made. *Academic Interests/Achievement Awards:* 798 ($4,626,347 total): general academic, biological sciences. *Creative Arts/Performance Awards:* 26 ($26,000 total): music. *Special Characteristics Awards:* 4 ($13,400 total): handicapped students.

Other Money-Saving Options Accelerated degree, cooperative Army ROTC. *Waivers:* full or partial for employees or children of employees.

Contact Ms. Karin Right-Nolan, Director of Financial Aid, Lebanon Valley College, 101 North College Avenue, Annville, PA 17003-0501, 800-445-6181.

LEES-MCRAE COLLEGE
Banner Elk, North Carolina

About the Institution Independent/religious, coed. Degrees awarded: B. Offers 31 undergraduate majors. Total enrollment: 453 (58% state residents). Freshmen: 125.

Undergraduate Expenses (1997–98) Comprehensive fee of $13,800 includes tuition ($10,080), mandatory fees ($50), and college room and board ($3670). College room only: $1680.

Applications Of all full-time undergraduates enrolled in fall 1996, 88% of those who applied for aid were judged to have need according to Federal Methodology, of whom 100% were aided. *Financial aid deadline (priority):* 3/15. *Financial aid forms:* FAFSA required. State form, institutional form required for some. *Admission application deadline:* 8/1.

Summary of Aid to Needy Students *From gift & self-help combined:* Average need met: 89%. Average amount awarded: $9344 (70% gift aid, 30% self-help). *Gift aid:* Total: $1,702,025 (55% from college's own funds, 10% from other college-administered sources, 35% from external sources). 48 Federal Work-Study jobs (averaging $823); 120 part-time jobs.

Need-Based Scholarships & Grants Pell, FSEOG, state, private, college/university.

Loans Perkins, PLUS, Stafford, Unsubsidized Stafford.

Non-Need Awards In 1996, a total of 387 non-need awards were made. *Academic Interests/Achievement Awards:* 124 ($360,565 total): general academic. *Creative Arts/Performance Awards:* 53 ($68,919 total): dance, journalism/publications, performing arts, theater/drama. *Special Achievements/Activities Awards:* 20 ($34,230 total): general special achievements/activities, cheerleading/drum major, leadership. *Special Characteristics Awards:* 71 ($150,143 total): children of educators, children of faculty/staff, children with a deceased or disabled parent, international students, local/state students, previous college experience, relatives of clergy, religious affiliation, veterans. *Athletic:* Total: 119 ($340,748); Men: 56 ($153,783); Women: 63 ($186,965).

Other Money-Saving Options Accelerated degree, cooperative Army ROTC, off-campus living (after junior year). *Payment Plan:* installment. *Waivers:* full or partial for employees or children of employees.

Contact Mr. Tony D. Carter, Director of Financial Aid, Lees-McRae College, PO Box 128, Banner Elk, NC 28604-0128, 704-898-5241 Ext. 8329, fax: 704-898-8814.

LEE UNIVERSITY
Cleveland, Tennessee

About the Institution Independent/religious, coed. Degrees awarded: B. Offers 35 undergraduate majors.

Undergraduate Expenses (1996–97) Comprehensive fee of $8912 includes tuition ($5232), mandatory fees ($140), and college room and board ($3540). College room only: $1780.

Applications 70% of all full-time undergraduates enrolled in fall 1996 applied for aid; of these, 90% were judged to have need according to Federal Methodology, of whom 90% were aided. *Financial aid deadline (priority):* 4/15. *Financial aid forms:* FAFSA, institutional form required. *Admission application deadline:* rolling.

Summary of Aid to Needy Students *From gift & self-help combined:* Average amount awarded: $6020 (40% gift aid, 60% self-help). *Gift aid:* Total: $3,654,927 (43% from college's own funds, 12% from other college-administered sources, 45% from external sources). 220 Federal Work-Study jobs (averaging $1203); part-time jobs.

Need-Based Scholarships & Grants Pell, FSEOG, state, private, college/university.

Loans Perkins, PLUS, Stafford, Unsubsidized Stafford, college/university short-term loans ($200 average), alternative loans.

Non-Need Awards In 1996, a total of 701 non-need awards were made. *Academic Interests/Achievement Awards:* 419 ($942,000 total): general academic, biological sciences, business, communication, education, English, health fields, mathematics, physical sciences, religion/biblical studies. *Creative Arts/Performance Awards:* 85 ($64,646 total): cinema/film/broadcasting, journalism/publications, music, theater/drama. *Special Achievements/Activities Awards:* 11 ($19,464 total): general special achievements/activities, leadership. *Special Characteristics Awards:* 117 ($163,051 total): children of faculty/staff, siblings of current students, spouses of current students. *Athletic:* Total: 69 ($172,652); Men: 39 ($100,490); Women: 30 ($72,162).

Other Money-Saving Options Co-op program, off-campus living (after junior year). *Payment Plan:* installment. *Waivers:* full or partial for employees or children of employees and senior citizens.

Contact Financial Aid Office, Lee University, 1120 North Ocoee Street, PO Box 3450, Cleveland, TN 37311-4475, 800-533-9930, fax: 423-614-8016.

LEHIGH UNIVERSITY
Bethlehem, Pennsylvania

About the Institution Independent, coed. Degrees awarded: B, M, D. Offers 64 undergraduate majors. Total enrollment: 6,275. Undergraduates: 4,436 (31% state residents). Freshmen: 1,101.

Undergraduate Expenses (1997–98) Comprehensive fee of $27,180 includes tuition ($21,350) and college room and board ($5830 minimum). College room only: $3090 (minimum).

Applications Of all full-time undergraduates enrolled in fall 1996, 89% of those who applied for aid were judged to have need according to Federal Methodology, of whom 100% were aided. *Financial aid deadline*

(priority): 2/15. *Financial aid forms:* FAFSA, CSS Financial Aid PROFILE required. Institutional form required for some. *Regular admission application deadline:* 1/15. Early decision deadline: 12/1.

Summary of Aid to Needy Students *From gift & self-help combined:* Average need met: 97%. Average amount awarded: $16,883 (73% gift aid, 27% self-help). *Gift aid:* Total: $28,383,600 (89% from college's own funds, 3% from other college-administered sources, 8% from external sources). 1,250 Federal Work-Study jobs (averaging $1260); 125 part-time jobs.

Need-Based Scholarships & Grants Pell, FSEOG, state, private, college/university.

Loans Perkins, PLUS, Stafford, Unsubsidized Stafford, college/university short-term loans ($350 average), college/university long-term loans ($2000 average).

Non-Need Awards In 1996, a total of 193 non-need awards were made. *Academic Interests/Achievement Awards:* 106 ($599,374 total): general academic. *Creative Arts/Performance Awards:* 9 ($24,250 total): general creative. *Special Characteristics Awards:* 65 ($991,892 total): children of faculty/staff, ROTC participants. *Athletic:* Total: 13 ($164,645); Men: 13 ($164,645); Women: 0.

Other Money-Saving Options Accelerated degree, co-op program, Army ROTC, off-campus living. *Payment Plans:* tuition prepayment, installment, deferred payment.

Contact Ms. Deborah Feldman, Software Support Administrator, Lehigh University, 218 West Packer Avenue, Bethlehem, PA 18015-3094, 610-758-3183, fax: 610-758-6211.

LEHMAN COLLEGE OF THE CITY UNIVERSITY OF NEW YORK
Bronx, New York

About the Institution State & locally supported, coed. Degrees awarded: B, M. Offers 50 undergraduate majors. Total enrollment: 9,413. Undergraduates: 7,698 (98% state residents). Freshmen: 677.

Undergraduate Expenses (1996–97) State resident tuition: $3200. Nonresident tuition: $6800. Mandatory fees: $120.

Applications Of all full-time undergraduates enrolled in fall 1996, 97% of those who applied for aid were judged to have need according to Federal Methodology, of whom 78% were aided. *Financial aid deadline (priority):* 7/1. *Financial aid forms:* FAFSA, state form, institutional form required. *Admission application deadline:* rolling.

Summary of Aid to Needy Students *From gift & self-help combined:* Average need met: 70%. Average amount awarded: $5000 (79% gift aid, 21% self-help). *Gift aid:* Total: $8,256,930 (3% from college-administered sources, 97% from external sources). 681 Federal Work-Study jobs (averaging $900).

Need-Based Scholarships & Grants Pell, FSEOG, state.

Loans Perkins, PLUS, Stafford, Unsubsidized Stafford, college/university short-term loans ($150 average).

Non-Need Awards Not offered.

Other Money-Saving Options Co-op program, cooperative Army ROTC.

Contact Mr. Irwin I. Rofman, Director of Financial Aid, Lehman College of the City University of New York, Bronx, NY 10468-1589, 718-960-8545.

LE MOYNE COLLEGE
Syracuse, New York

About the Institution Independent/religious, coed. Degrees awarded: B, M. Offers 43 undergraduate majors. Total enrollment: 2,713. Undergraduates: 1,908 (94% state residents). Freshmen: 441.

Undergraduate Expenses (1997–98) Comprehensive fee of $18,980 includes tuition ($13,120), mandatory fees ($270), and college room and board ($5590). College room only: $3460.

Applications 94% of all full-time undergraduates enrolled in fall 1996 applied for aid; of these, 94% were judged to have need according to Federal Methodology, of whom 100% were aided. *Financial aid deadline (priority):* 2/15. *Financial aid forms:* FAFSA required. State form, institutional form, financial aid transcript (for transfers) required for some. *Regular admission application deadline:* 3/15. Early action deadline: 12/1.

Summary of Aid to Needy Students *From gift & self-help combined:* Average need met: 85%. Average amount awarded: $11,232 (54% gift aid, 46% self-help). *Gift aid:* Total: $9,334,692 (65% from college's own funds, 23% from other college-administered sources, 12% from external sources). 388 Federal Work-Study jobs (averaging $953); 305 part-time jobs.

Need-Based Scholarships & Grants Pell, FSEOG, state, private, college/university.

Loans Perkins, PLUS, Stafford, Unsubsidized Stafford.

Non-Need Awards In 1996, a total of 703 non-need awards were made. *Academic Interests/Achievement Awards:* 34 ($315,153 total): general academic. *Special Achievements/Activities Awards:* 417 ($874,352 total): leadership. *Special Characteristics Awards:* 163 ($1,119,693 total): members of minorities. *Athletic:* Total: 89 ($543,460); Men: 50 ($347,170); Women: 39 ($196,290).

Other Money-Saving Options Accelerated degree, cooperative Army ROTC, cooperative Air Force ROTC. *Payment Plan:* installment. *Waivers:* full or partial for employees or children of employees.

Contact Mr. William Cheetham, Director of Financial Aid, Le Moyne College, Financial Aid Office, Syracuse, NY 13214-1399, 315-445-4400, fax: 315-445-4182.

LEMOYNE-OWEN COLLEGE
Memphis, Tennessee

About the Institution Independent/religious, coed. Degrees awarded: B, M. Offers 21 undergraduate majors. Total enrollment: 1,104. Undergraduates: 1,090 (84% state residents). Freshmen: 330.

Undergraduate Expenses (1996–97) Comprehensive fee of $9916 includes tuition ($6000) and college room and board ($3916).

Applications 93% of all full-time undergraduates enrolled in fall 1996 applied for aid; of these, 92% were judged to have need according to Federal Methodology, of whom 98% were aided. *Financial aid deadline (priority):* 4/1. *Financial aid forms:* FAFSA, institutional form required; CSS Financial Aid PROFILE acceptable. State form required for some. *Admission application deadline:* 8/1.

Summary of Aid to Needy Students *From gift & self-help combined:* Average need met: 54%. Average amount awarded: $7334 (50% gift aid, 50% self-help). *Gift aid:* Total: $2,879,424 (12% from college's own funds, 21% from other college-administered sources, 67% from external sources). 305 Federal Work-Study jobs (averaging $1172).

Need-Based Scholarships & Grants Pell, FSEOG, state, private, college/university.

Loans Perkins, Stafford, Unsubsidized Stafford.

Non-Need Awards In 1996, a total of 80 non-need awards were made. *Academic Interests/Achievement Awards:* 17 ($38,586 total): general academic. *Creative Arts/Performance Awards:* 14 ($28,009 total): music. *Athletic:* Total: 49 ($278,322); Men: 27 ($131,505); Women: 22 ($146,817).

Other Money-Saving Options Accelerated degree, co-op program, cooperative Army ROTC, cooperative Air Force ROTC, off-campus living. *Payment Plans:* tuition prepayment, installment, deferred payment. *Waivers:* full or partial for employees or children of employees.

Contact Office of Financial Aid, LeMoyne-Owen College, 807 Walker Avenue, Memphis, TN 38126-6595, 901-774-9090.

LENOIR-RHYNE COLLEGE
Hickory, North Carolina

About the Institution Independent/religious, coed. Degrees awarded: B, M. Offers 52 undergraduate majors. Total enrollment: 1,579. Undergraduates: 1,464 (63% state residents). Freshmen: 230.

Undergraduate Expenses (1997–98) Comprehensive fee of $16,436 includes tuition ($12,036) and college room and board ($4400).

Applications Of all full-time undergraduates enrolled in fall 1996, 78% of those who applied for aid were judged to have need according to Federal Methodology, of whom 97% were aided. *Financial aid deadline (priority):* 3/1. *Financial aid forms:* FAFSA, institutional form required. State form required for some. *Admission application deadline:* rolling.

Summary of Aid to Needy Students *From gift & self-help combined:* Average need met: 76%. Average amount awarded: $9333 (70% gift aid, 30% self-help). *Gift aid:* Total: $6,016,763 (61% from college's own funds, 22% from other college-administered sources, 17% from external sources). Federal Work-Study jobs; part-time jobs.

Need-Based Scholarships & Grants Pell, FSEOG, state, college/university.

Loans Perkins, PLUS, Stafford, Unsubsidized Stafford.

Non-Need Awards In 1996, a total of 723 non-need awards were made. *Academic Interests/Achievement Awards:* 185 ($765,324 total): general academic. *Creative Arts/Performance Awards:* 23 ($54,115 total): music. *Special Achievements/Activities Awards:* 154 ($79,685 total): leadership. *Special Characteristics Awards:* 222 ($517,846 total): children and siblings of alumni, children of faculty/staff, ethnic background, local/state students, members of minorities, relatives of clergy, religious affiliation, siblings of current students. *Athletic:* Total: 139 ($673,142); Men: 91 ($490,082); Women: 48 ($183,060).

Other Money-Saving Options Accelerated degree, cooperative Army ROTC, cooperative Air Force ROTC, off-campus living (after sophomore year). *Payment Plans:* installment, deferred payment. *Waivers:* full or partial for employees or children of employees.

Contact Office of Financial Aid, Lenoir-Rhyne College, Box 7419, Hickory, NC 28603, 704-328-1741.

LESLEY COLLEGE
Cambridge, Massachusetts

About the Institution Independent, women. Degrees awarded: A, B, M, D. Offers 13 undergraduate majors. Total enrollment: 6,166. Undergraduates: 490 (65% state residents). Freshmen: 103.

Undergraduate Expenses (1997–98) Comprehensive fee of $21,306 includes tuition ($14,300), mandatory fees ($306), and college room and board ($6700). College room only: $4050.

Applications Of all full-time undergraduates enrolled in fall 1996, 89% of those who applied for aid were judged to have need according to Federal Methodology, of whom 100% were aided. *Financial aid deadline (priority):* 2/1. *Financial aid forms:* FAFSA, state form, institutional form, financial aid transcript (for transfers) required. *Regular admission application deadline:* 3/15. Early decision deadline: 12/1.

Summary of Aid to Needy Students *From gift & self-help combined:* Average amount awarded: $14,365 (51% gift aid, 49% self-help). *Gift aid:* Total: $2,566,535 (76% from college's own funds, 6% from other college-administered sources, 18% from external sources). 264 Federal Work-Study jobs (averaging $1686); 50 part-time jobs.

Need-Based Scholarships & Grants Pell, FSEOG, state, college/university.

Loans Perkins, PLUS, Stafford, Unsubsidized Stafford, state, private.

Non-Need Awards In 1996, a total of 84 non-need awards were made. *Academic Interests/Achievement Awards:* 51 ($139,750 total): general academic, education. *Special Characteristics Awards:* 33 ($438,025 total): local/state students, members of minorities.

Other Money-Saving Options Off-campus living. *Payment Plan:* installment. *Waivers:* full or partial for employees or children of employees.

Contact Loida Chi, Counselor, Lesley College, 29 Everett Street, Cambridge, MA 02138-2790, 617-349-8711, fax: 617-349-8717.

LETOURNEAU UNIVERSITY
Longview, Texas

About the Institution Independent/religious, coed. Degrees awarded: A, B, M. Offers 41 undergraduate majors. Total enrollment: 2,059. Undergraduates: 1,848 (67% state residents). Freshmen: 164.

Undergraduate Expenses (1996–97) Comprehensive fee of $14,850 includes tuition ($10,090), mandatory fees ($130), and college room and board ($4630).

Applications 91% of all full-time undergraduates enrolled in fall 1996 applied for aid; of these, 83% were judged to have need according to Federal Methodology, of whom 100% were aided. *Financial aid deadline (priority):* 2/15. *Financial aid forms:* FAFSA required; CSS Financial Aid PROFILE acceptable. *Admission application deadline:* 8/15.

Summary of Aid to Needy Students *From gift & self-help combined:* Average need met: 68%. Average amount awarded: $9310 (54% gift aid, 46% self-help). *Gift aid:* Total: $3,237,172 (65% from college's own funds, 1% from other college-administered sources, 34% from external sources). 326 Federal Work-Study jobs (averaging $1742); 81 part-time jobs.

Need-Based Scholarships & Grants Pell, FSEOG, state, college/university.

Loans Perkins, PLUS, Stafford, Unsubsidized Stafford, state, private, college/university short-term loans ($300 average).

Non-Need Awards In 1996, a total of 700 non-need awards were made. *Academic Interests/Achievement Awards:* 410 ($686,928 total): general academic. *Creative Arts/Performance Awards:* 29 ($22,090 total): journalism/publications, music. *Special Characteristics Awards:* 214 ($449,910 total): children of faculty/staff, international students, local/state students, relatives of clergy, spouses of current students. *Athletic:* Total: 47 ($209,969); Men: 34 ($124,714); Women: 13 ($85,255).

Other Money-Saving Options Co-op program. *Payment Plan:* installment. *Waivers:* full or partial for employees or children of employees.

Contact Ms. Brenda Lassater, Financial Aid Counselor, LeTourneau University, PO Box 7001, Longview, TX 75607-7001, 903-233-3430, fax: 903-233-3411.

LEWIS & CLARK COLLEGE
Portland, Oregon

About the Institution Independent, coed. Degrees awarded: B, M, P. Offers 31 undergraduate majors. Total enrollment: 3,074. Undergraduates: 1,842 (29% state residents). Freshmen: 450.

Undergraduate Expenses (1996–97) Comprehensive fee of $23,520 includes tuition ($17,560), mandatory fees ($180), and college room and board ($5780). College room only: $2850.

Applications 76% of all full-time undergraduates enrolled in fall 1996 applied for aid; of these, 72% were judged to have need according to Federal Methodology, of whom 99% were aided. *Financial aid deadline (priority):* 2/15. *Financial aid forms:* FAFSA, institutional form required. *Regular admission application deadline:* 2/1. Early decision deadline: 11/15. Early action deadline: 12/15.

Summary of Aid to Needy Students *From gift & self-help combined:* Average need met: 97%. Average amount awarded: $15,831 (69% gift aid, 31% self-help). *Gift aid:* Total: $10,291,508 (85% from college's own funds, 3% from other college-administered sources, 12% from external sources). 777 Federal Work-Study jobs (averaging $1130); 398 part-time jobs.

Need-Based Scholarships & Grants Pell, FSEOG, state, private, college/university.

Loans Perkins, PLUS, Stafford, Unsubsidized Stafford, state, private, college/university short-term loans ($150 average).

Non-Need Awards *Academic Interests/Achievement Awards:* general academic. *Creative Arts/Performance Awards:* debating, music.

Other Money-Saving Options Accelerated degree, off-campus living (after sophomore year). *Payment Plan:* installment. *Waivers:* full or partial for employees or children of employees.

Contact Mr. J. Ron Elmore, Director of Student Financial Services, Lewis & Clark College, 0615 Southwest Palatine Hill Road, Portland, OR 97219-7899, 503-768-7090.

LEWIS-CLARK STATE COLLEGE
Lewiston, Idaho

About the Institution State-supported, coed. Degrees awarded: A, B. Offers 50 undergraduate majors. Total enrollment: 2,978 (83% state residents). Freshmen: 421.

Undergraduate Expenses (1997–98) State resident tuition: $0. Nonresident tuition: $4962. Mandatory fees: $1868. College room and board: $3210.

Applications Of all full-time undergraduates enrolled in fall 1996, 84% of those who applied for aid were judged to have need according to Federal Methodology, of whom 93% were aided. *Financial aid deadline (priority):* 3/1. *Financial aid forms:* FAFSA required. *Admission application deadline:* rolling.

Summary of Aid to Needy Students *From gift & self-help combined:* Average need met: 84%. Average amount awarded: $6931 (25% gift aid, 75% self-help). *Gift aid:* Total: $2,031,292 (1% from college's own funds, 5% from other college-administered sources, 94% from external sources). 84 Federal Work-Study jobs (averaging $1700); part-time jobs.

Need-Based Scholarships & Grants Pell, FSEOG, state, private, college/university.

Loans Perkins, PLUS, Stafford, Unsubsidized Stafford, Federal Nursing, college/university short-term loans ($250 average).

Non-Need Awards In 1996, a total of 333 non-need awards were made. *Academic Interests/Achievement Awards:* 181 ($213,070 total): general academic, education, health fields. *Creative Arts/Performance Awards:* 5 ($900 total): music. *Special Achievements/Activities Awards:* 28 ($7000 total): Junior Miss, leadership. *Special Characteristics Awards:* 32 ($119,362 total): out-of-state students. *Athletic:* Total: 87 ($243,893); Men: 43 ($139,191); Women: 44 ($104,702).

Other Money-Saving Options Accelerated degree, co-op program, Army ROTC, cooperative Naval ROTC, cooperative Air Force ROTC, off-campus living. *Payment Plan:* deferred payment. *Waivers:* full or partial for employees or children of employees and senior citizens.

Contact Ms. Tonya Kennedy, Senior Secretary, Lewis-Clark State College, 500 8th Avenue, Lewiston, ID 83501-2698, 208-799-2473, fax: 208-799-2063.

LEWIS UNIVERSITY
Romeoville, Illinois

About the Institution Independent/religious, coed. Degrees awarded: A, B, M. Offers 48 undergraduate majors. Total enrollment: 4,310. Undergraduates: 3,563 (97% state residents). Freshmen: 317.

Undergraduate Expenses (1997–98) Comprehensive fee of $17,616 includes tuition ($12,416) and college room and board ($5200 minimum).

Applications *Financial aid deadline (priority):* 4/1. *Financial aid forms:* CSS Financial Aid PROFILE required; FAFSA acceptable. Institutional form required for some. *Admission application deadline:* rolling.

Summary of Aid to Needy Students Federal Work-Study jobs; part-time jobs.

Non-Need Awards *Academic Interests/Achievement Awards:* general academic. *Creative Arts/Performance Awards:* dance, theater/drama. *Special Achievements/Activities Awards:* general special achievements/activities, community service. *Special Characteristics Awards:* children and siblings of alumni. *Athletic:* available.

Other Money-Saving Options Accelerated degree, Army ROTC, cooperative Air Force ROTC, off-campus living. *Payment Plan:* installment. *Waivers:* full or partial for children of alumni and employees or children of employees.

Contact Office of Financial Aid, Lewis University, Romeoville, IL 60446, 815-838-0500.

LEXINGTON BAPTIST COLLEGE
Lexington, Kentucky

About the Institution Independent/religious, coed. Degrees awarded: A, B. Offers 1 undergraduate major. Total enrollment: 82 (46% state residents). Freshmen: 22.

Undergraduate Expenses (1996–97) Tuition: $2280. Mandatory fees: $200.

Applications 98% of all full-time undergraduates enrolled in fall 1996 applied for aid; of these, 100% were judged to have need according to Federal Methodology, of whom 100% were aided. *Financial aid deadline (priority):* 3/31. *Financial aid forms:* FAFSA required. Institutional form required for some. *Admission application deadline:* rolling.

Summary of Aid to Needy Students *From gift & self-help combined:* Average amount awarded: $952 (43% gift aid, 57% self-help). *Gift aid:* Total: $26,125 (5% from college's own funds, 52% from other college-administered sources, 43% from external sources). 4 Federal Work-Study jobs (averaging $952).

Need-Based Scholarships & Grants Pell, FSEOG, private.

Loans PLUS, Stafford, Unsubsidized Stafford.

Non-Need Awards In 1996, a total of 8 non-need awards were made. *Special Achievements/Activities Awards:* 6 ($5220 total): leadership. *Special Characteristics Awards:* 2 ($2280 total): religious affiliation.

Another Money-Saving Option *Waivers:* full or partial for employees or children of employees.

Contact Mr. Tim Parsons, Director of Financial Aid, Lexington Baptist College, 147 Walton Avenue, Lexington, KY 40508, 606-252-1130, fax: 606-252-5649.

LIFE BIBLE COLLEGE
San Dimas, California

About the Institution Independent/religious, coed. Degrees awarded: A, B. Offers 11 undergraduate majors. Total enrollment: 411. Freshmen: 72.

Undergraduate Expenses (1997–98) Comprehensive fee of $7880 includes tuition ($4680), mandatory fees ($200), and college room and board ($3000).

Applications Of all full-time undergraduates enrolled in fall 1996, 48% of those who applied for aid were judged to have need according to Federal Methodology, of whom 100% were aided. *Financial aid deadline*

(priority): 8/1. *Financial aid forms:* FAFSA required; CSS Financial Aid PROFILE acceptable. State form, institutional form required for some. *Admission application deadline:* 7/15.

Summary of Aid to Needy Students *From gift & self-help combined:* Average need met: 68%. Average amount awarded: $750 (95% gift aid, 5% self-help). *Gift aid:* Total: $244,552 (18% from college's own funds, 42% from other college-administered sources, 40% from external sources). 12 Federal Work-Study jobs (averaging $1150); 57 part-time jobs.

Need-Based Scholarships & Grants Pell, FSEOG, state, private, college/university.

Loans Private.

Non-Need Awards Not offered.

Other Money-Saving Options Off-campus living (after freshman year). *Payment Plan:* installment. *Waivers:* full or partial for children of alumni and employees or children of employees.

Contact Mr. Roy Pattillo, Director of Financial Aid, LIFE Bible College, San Dimas, CA 91773-3298, 909-599-5433, fax: 909-599-6690.

LIMESTONE COLLEGE
Gaffney, South Carolina

About the Institution Independent, coed. Degrees awarded: A, B. Offers 28 undergraduate majors. Total enrollment: 366 (66% state residents). Freshmen: 96.

Undergraduate Expenses (1997–98) Comprehensive fee of $12,500 includes tuition ($8600) and college room and board ($3900).

Applications 98% of all full-time undergraduates enrolled in fall 1996 applied for aid; of these, 83% were judged to have need according to Federal Methodology, of whom 100% were aided. *Financial aid deadline (priority):* 5/1. *Financial aid forms:* FAFSA, institutional form required. CSS Financial Aid PROFILE, state form required for some. *Admission application deadline:* rolling.

Summary of Aid to Needy Students *From gift & self-help combined:* Average need met: 98%. Average amount awarded: $8509 (68% gift aid, 32% self-help). *Gift aid:* Total: $1,646,662 (60% from college's own funds, 24% from other college-administered sources, 16% from external sources). 69 Federal Work-Study jobs (averaging $1030); 29 part-time jobs.

Need-Based Scholarships & Grants Pell, FSEOG, state, private, college/university.

Loans Perkins, PLUS, Stafford, Unsubsidized Stafford, private.

Non-Need Awards In 1996, a total of 710 non-need awards were made. *Academic Interests/Achievement Awards:* 88 ($118,675 total): general academic, biological sciences, business, communication, computer science, education, English, humanities, mathematics, religion/biblical studies, social sciences. *Creative Arts/Performance Awards:* 63 ($84,130 total): art/fine arts, music, performing arts. *Special Achievements/Activities Awards:* 29 ($21,400 total): leadership, religious involvement. *Special Characteristics Awards:* 345 ($552,568 total): general special characteristics, children of faculty/staff, local/state students, out-of-state students, ROTC participants, siblings of current students. *Athletic:* Total: 185 ($334,529); Men: 121 ($231,258); Women: 64 ($103,271).

Other Money-Saving Options Accelerated degree, cooperative Army ROTC, off-campus living (after junior year). *Payment Plan:* installment. *Waivers:* full or partial for employees or children of employees.

Contact Ms. Joanne Rogers, Assistant Director of Financial Aid, Limestone College, 1115 College Drive, Gaffney, SC 29340-3798, 864-489-7151 Ext. 597, fax: 864-487-8706.

LINCOLN CHRISTIAN COLLEGE
Lincoln, Illinois

About the Institution Independent/religious, coed. Degrees awarded: A, B. Offers 13 undergraduate majors. Total enrollment: 580 (74% state residents). Freshmen: 152.

Undergraduate Expenses (1996–97) Comprehensive fee of $8460 includes tuition ($4640), mandatory fees ($500), and college room and board ($3320). College room only: $1382.

Applications 89% of all full-time undergraduates enrolled in fall 1996 applied for aid; of these, 90% were judged to have need according to Federal Methodology, of whom 92% were aided. *Financial aid deadline (priority):* 8/15. *Financial aid forms:* FAFSA, state form, institutional form required; CSS Financial Aid PROFILE acceptable. *Admission application deadline:* rolling.

Summary of Aid to Needy Students *From gift & self-help combined:* Average need met: 92%. Average amount awarded: $4369 (49% gift aid, 51% self-help). *Gift aid:* Total: $749,986 (18% from college's own funds, 56% from other college-administered sources, 26% from external sources). Federal Work-Study jobs; 15 part-time jobs.

Need-Based Scholarships & Grants Pell, FSEOG, state.

Loans Perkins, PLUS, Stafford, Unsubsidized Stafford, college/university short-term loans ($300 average).

Non-Need Awards In 1996, a total of 105 non-need awards were made. *Academic Interests/Achievement Awards:* 105 ($60,000 total): general academic.

Other Money-Saving Options *Payment Plans:* installment, deferred payment. *Waivers:* full or partial for employees or children of employees.

Contact Mr. Jack A. Getchel, Director of Financial Aid, Lincoln Christian College, 100 Campus View Drive, Lincoln, IL 62656-2167, 217-732-3168.

LINCOLN MEMORIAL UNIVERSITY
Harrogate, Tennessee

About the Institution Independent, coed. Degrees awarded: A, B, M. Offers 38 undergraduate majors. Total enrollment: 2,003. Undergraduates: 1,581 (43% state residents). Freshmen: 292.

Undergraduate Expenses (1997–98) Comprehensive fee of $10,650 includes tuition ($7200), mandatory fees ($150), and college room and board ($3300 minimum). College room only: $1500.

Applications 94% of all full-time undergraduates enrolled in fall 1996 applied for aid; of these, 95% were judged to have need according to Federal Methodology, of whom 100% were aided. *Financial aid deadline (priority):* 4/1. *Financial aid forms:* FAFSA, institutional form required; CSS Financial Aid PROFILE acceptable. State form required for some. *Admission application deadline:* rolling.

Summary of Aid to Needy Students *From gift & self-help combined:* Average need met: 85%. Average amount awarded: $6438 (72% gift aid, 28% self-help). *Gift aid:* Total: $2,689,407 (74% from college's own funds, 9% from other college-administered sources, 17% from external sources). 124 Federal Work-Study jobs (averaging $1200); 22 part-time jobs.

Need-Based Scholarships & Grants Pell, FSEOG, state, private, college/university.

Loans Perkins, PLUS, Stafford, Unsubsidized Stafford.

Non-Need Awards In 1996, a total of 558 non-need awards were made. *Academic Interests/Achievement Awards:* 320 ($825,413 total): general academic. *Creative Arts/Performance Awards:* 30 ($15,000 total): music. *Special Achievements/Activities Awards:* 10 ($5000 total): cheerleading/drum major. *Special Characteristics Awards:* 71 ($203,841 total): children of faculty/staff. *Athletic:* Total: 127 ($653,796); Men: 63 ($340,910); Women: 64 ($312,886).

Other Money-Saving Options Accelerated degree, off-campus living. *Payment Plan:* installment. *Waivers:* full or partial for employees or children of employees and senior citizens.

Contact Office of Financial Aid, Lincoln Memorial University, Cumberland Gap Parkway, TN 37752-1901, 423-869-6336.

LINCOLN UNIVERSITY
Jefferson City, Missouri

About the Institution State-supported, coed. Degrees awarded: A, B, M. Offers 40 undergraduate majors. Total enrollment: 2,979. Undergraduates: 2,635 (89% state residents). Freshmen: 489.

Undergraduate Expenses (1997–98) State resident tuition: $2016. Nonresident tuition: $4032. Mandatory fees: $60. College room and board: $3276.

Applications Of all full-time undergraduates enrolled in fall 1996, 60% of those who applied for aid were judged to have need according to Federal Methodology, of whom 80% were aided. *Financial aid deadline (priority):* 3/1. *Financial aid forms:* FAFSA required. *Admission application deadline:* 8/1.

Summary of Aid to Needy Students *From gift & self-help combined:* Average amount awarded: $7970. 150 Federal Work-Study jobs (averaging $1869); 115 part-time jobs.

Need-Based Scholarships & Grants Pell, FSEOG, state.

Loans PLUS, Stafford, Unsubsidized Stafford.

Non-Need Awards *Academic Interests/Achievement Awards:* general academic, biological sciences, education, physical sciences. *Creative Arts/Performance Awards:* art/fine arts, music. *Special Achievements/ Activities Awards:* memberships. *Special Characteristics Awards:* general special characteristics, children of faculty/staff. *Athletic:* available.

Other Money-Saving Options Accelerated degree, co-op program, Army ROTC, off-campus living (after sophomore year). *Payment Plan:* deferred payment. *Waivers:* full or partial for employees or children of employees and senior citizens.

Contact Mr. Phillip Rodgers, Director of Financial Aid, Lincoln University, 820 Chestnut Street, Jefferson City, MO 65102-0029, 573-681-6156, fax: 573-681-5871.

LINCOLN UNIVERSITY
Lincoln University, Pennsylvania

About the Institution State-related, coed. Degrees awarded: B, M. Offers 42 undergraduate majors. Total enrollment: 1,810. Undergraduates: 1,443 (47% state residents). Freshmen: 568.

Undergraduate Expenses (1996–97) State resident tuition: $3300. Nonresident tuition: $5280. Mandatory fees: $880. College room and board: $4060.

Applications Of all full-time undergraduates enrolled in fall 1996, 100% of those judged to have need according to Federal Methodology were aided. *Financial aid deadline (priority):* 3/15. *Financial aid forms:* FAFSA, state form, institutional form required; CSS Financial Aid PROFILE acceptable. *Admission application deadline:* rolling.

Summary of Aid to Needy Students *From gift & self-help combined:* Average need met: 95%. Average amount awarded: $11,120 (53% gift aid, 47% self-help). *Gift aid:* Total: $4,437,521 (38% from college's own funds, 31% from other college-administered sources, 31% from external sources). Federal Work-Study jobs (averaging $1000); part-time jobs.

Need-Based Scholarships & Grants Pell, FSEOG, state, college/ university.

Loans Perkins, PLUS, Stafford, Unsubsidized Stafford, college/university long-term loans ($1500 average).

Non-Need Awards *Academic Interests/Achievement Awards:* general academic, biological sciences, business, communication, computer science, education, humanities, mathematics, physical sciences. *Creative Arts/Performance Awards:* 12 ($7100 total): music.

Other Money-Saving Options Accelerated degree, co-op program, cooperative Air Force ROTC, off-campus living (after freshman year). *Waivers:* full or partial for employees or children of employees.

Contact Ms. Cheryl Browning, Director of Financial Aid, Lincoln University, 101 Lincoln Hall, Lincoln University, PA 19352, 610-932-8300 Ext. 3565.

LINDENWOOD COLLEGE
St. Charles, Missouri

About the Institution Independent/religious, coed. Degrees awarded: B, M. Offers 61 undergraduate majors. Total enrollment: 4,293. Undergraduates: 2,891 (83% state residents). Freshmen: 522.

Undergraduate Expenses (1997–98) Comprehensive fee of $15,350 includes tuition ($9950), mandatory fees ($200), and college room and board ($5200). College room only: $2700.

Applications *Financial aid deadline (priority):* 3/15. *Financial aid forms:* FAFSA required; CSS Financial Aid PROFILE acceptable. State form, institutional form required for some. *Admission application deadline:* rolling.

Summary of Aid to Needy Students 160 Federal Work-Study jobs (averaging $1500); 970 part-time jobs.

Need-Based Scholarships & Grants Pell, FSEOG, state, private, college/ university.

Loans Perkins, PLUS, Stafford, Unsubsidized Stafford.

Non-Need Awards *Academic Interests/Achievement Awards:* general academic. *Creative Arts/Performance Awards:* performing arts. *Special Achievements/Activities Awards:* general special achievements/activities. *Special Characteristics Awards:* children of faculty/staff.

Other Money-Saving Options Accelerated degree, co-op program, cooperative Army ROTC, off-campus living. *Payment Plans:* installment, deferred payment. *Waivers:* full or partial for employees or children of employees and senior citizens.

Contact Dr. David R. Williams, Dean of the College, Lindenwood College, 209 South Kingshighway, St. Charles, MO 63301-1695, 314-949-4902, fax: 314-949-4910.

LINDSEY WILSON COLLEGE
Columbia, Kentucky

About the Institution Independent/religious, coed. Degrees awarded: A, B, M. Offers 26 undergraduate majors. Total enrollment: 1,317. Undergraduates: 1,267 (89% state residents). Freshmen: 440.

Undergraduate Expenses (1997–98) Comprehensive fee of $12,510 includes tuition ($8160), mandatory fees ($120), and college room and board ($4230). College room only: $1630.

Applications Of all full-time undergraduates enrolled in fall 1996, 92% of those who applied for aid were judged to have need according to Federal Methodology, of whom 100% were aided. *Financial aid deadline (priority):* 4/1. *Financial aid forms:* FAFSA, institutional form required. State form required for some. *Admission application deadline:* rolling.

Summary of Aid to Needy Students *From gift & self-help combined:* Average need met: 92%. Average amount awarded: $9322 (76% gift aid, 24% self-help). *Gift aid:* Total: $6,408,000 (55% from college's own funds, 25% from other college-administered sources, 20% from external sources). Federal Work-Study jobs (averaging $1500); part-time jobs.

Need-Based Scholarships & Grants Pell, FSEOG, state, private, college/ university.

Loans Perkins, PLUS, Stafford, Unsubsidized Stafford, private, college/university short-term loans, college/university long-term loans.

Non-Need Awards *Academic Interests/Achievement Awards:* ($374,242 total): general academic. *Creative Arts/Performance Awards:* ($79,172 total): art/fine arts, music. *Special Achievements/Activities Awards:* ($96,600 total): Junior Miss, leadership, religious involvement. *Special Characteristics Awards:* ($238,552 total): children of faculty/staff, international students, relatives of clergy, religious affiliation. *Athletic:* Total: ($501,341); Men: ($339,191); Women: ($162,150).

Other Money-Saving Options Accelerated degree, co-op program, cooperative Army ROTC. *Payment Plan:* installment. *Waivers:* full or partial for employees or children of employees.

Contact Ms. Marilyn D. Radford, Assistant Director of Student Financial Services, Lindsey Wilson College, 210 Lindsey Wilson Street, Columbia, KY 42728-1298, 502-384-8022, fax: 502-384-8200.

LINFIELD COLLEGE
McMinnville, Oregon

About the Institution Independent/religious, coed. Degrees awarded: B. Offers 57 undergraduate majors. Total enrollment: 1,594. Undergraduates: 1,582 (59% state residents). Freshmen: 454.

Undergraduate Expenses (1997–98) Comprehensive fee of $21,304 includes tuition ($15,874), mandatory fees ($139), and college room and board ($5291). College room only: $2254.

Applications Of all full-time undergraduates enrolled in fall 1996, 77% of those who applied for aid were judged to have need according to Federal Methodology, of whom 100% were aided. *Financial aid deadline (priority):* 2/1. *Financial aid forms:* FAFSA, institutional form required. *Regular admission application deadline:* 2/15. Early decision deadline: 12/1.

Summary of Aid to Needy Students *From gift & self-help combined:* Average need met: 84%. Average amount awarded: $12,270 (59% gift aid, 41% self-help). *Gift aid:* Total: $7,860,615 (81% from college's own funds, 3% from other college-administered sources, 16% from external sources). 879 Federal Work-Study jobs (averaging $900).

Need-Based Scholarships & Grants Pell, FSEOG, state, private, college/university.

Loans Perkins, PLUS, Stafford, Unsubsidized Stafford, private, college/university short-term loans ($600 average), college/university long-term loans ($1449 average).

Non-Need Awards In 1996, a total of 747 non-need awards were made. *Academic Interests/Achievement Awards:* 684 ($1,390,480 total): general academic. *Creative Arts/Performance Awards:* 31 ($63,100 total): music. *Special Characteristics Awards:* 32 ($469,356 total): children of faculty/staff, siblings of current students.

Other Money-Saving Options Accelerated degree, cooperative Air Force ROTC, off-campus living (after junior year). *Payment Plan:* installment. *Waivers:* full or partial for employees or children of employees.

Contact Office of Financial Aid, Linfield College, 900 Southeast Baker Street, McMinnville, OR 97128-6894, 503-434-2200.

LIPSCOMB UNIVERSITY
Nashville, Tennessee

See David Lipscomb University

LIST COLLEGE OF JEWISH STUDIES
New York, New York

See Jewish Theological Seminary of America

LIVINGSTON COLLEGE
New Brunswick, New Jersey

See Rutgers, The State University of New Jersey, Livingston College

LIVINGSTONE COLLEGE
Salisbury, North Carolina

About the Institution Independent/religious, coed. Degrees awarded: B. Offers 25 undergraduate majors. Total enrollment: 689 (44% state residents). Freshmen: 158.

Undergraduate Expenses (1996–97) Comprehensive fee of $9540 includes tuition ($5240), mandatory fees ($850), and college room and board ($3450). College room only: $2050.

Applications 86% of all full-time undergraduates enrolled in fall 1996 applied for aid; of these, 88% were judged to have need according to Federal Methodology, of whom 93% were aided. *Financial aid deadline (priority):* 5/15. *Financial aid forms:* FAFSA, institutional form required. State form required for some. *Admission application deadline:* rolling.

Summary of Aid to Needy Students *From gift & self-help combined:* Average need met: 70%. Average amount awarded: $6486 (40% gift aid, 60% self-help). *Gift aid:* Total: $1,198,795 (14% from college's own funds, 15% from other college-administered sources, 71% from external sources). 132 Federal Work-Study jobs (averaging $1149).

Need-Based Scholarships & Grants Pell, FSEOG, state.

Loans PLUS, Stafford, Unsubsidized Stafford.

Non-Need Awards In 1996, a total of 368 non-need awards were made. *Academic Interests/Achievement Awards:* 212 ($526,957 total): general academic, education. *Creative Arts/Performance Awards:* 31 ($53,400 total): music. *Special Characteristics Awards:* 6 ($12,022 total): members of minorities. *Athletic:* Total: 119 ($584,764); Men: 82 ($432,690); Women: 37 ($152,074).

Other Money-Saving Options Co-op program, Army ROTC. *Payment Plan:* installment. *Waivers:* full or partial for employees or children of employees.

Contact Mrs. Daisy Henry, Financial Aid Director, Livingstone College, 701 West Monroe Street, Salisbury, NC 20144-5298, 704-638-5561, fax: 704-638-5560.

LIVINGSTON UNIVERSITY
Livingston, Alabama

See University of West Alabama

LOCK HAVEN UNIVERSITY OF PENNSYLVANIA
Lock Haven, Pennsylvania

About the Institution State-supported, coed. Degrees awarded: A, B, M. Offers 76 undergraduate majors. Total enrollment: 3,549. Undergraduates: 3,490 (89% state residents). Freshmen: 820.

Undergraduate Expenses (1996–97) State resident tuition: $3368. Nonresident tuition: $8566. Mandatory fees: $620. College room and board: $3784.

Applications Of all full-time undergraduates enrolled in fall 1996, 90% of those who applied for aid were judged to have need according to Federal Methodology, of whom 100% were aided. *Financial aid deadline (priority):* 4/15. *Financial aid forms:* FAFSA, institutional form required. State form required for some. *Admission application deadline:* rolling.

Summary of Aid to Needy Students *From gift & self-help combined:* Average need met: 75%. Average amount awarded: $4259 (37% gift aid, 63% self-help). *Gift aid:* Total: $3,801,073. Federal Work-Study jobs; 500 part-time jobs.

Need-Based Scholarships & Grants Pell, FSEOG, state, college/university.

Loans Perkins, PLUS, Stafford, Unsubsidized Stafford, college/university short-term loans ($125 average), college/university long-term loans.

Non-Need Awards *Academic Interests/Achievement Awards:* general academic. *Creative Arts/Performance Awards:* music. *Special Achievements/Activities Awards:* memberships. *Special Characteristics Awards:* members of minorities. *Athletic:* Total: 198 ($374,000).

Other Money-Saving Options Accelerated degree, Army ROTC, off-campus living (after sophomore year). *Waivers:* full or partial for minority students and employees or children of employees.

Contact Office of Student Financial Aid, Lock Haven University of Pennsylvania, Lock Haven, PA 17745-2390, 717-893-2344, fax: 717-893-2432.

LONG ISLAND UNIVERSITY, BROOKLYN CAMPUS
Brooklyn, New York

About the Institution Independent, coed. Degrees awarded: A, B, M, D, P. Offers 57 undergraduate majors. Total enrollment: 8,264. Undergraduates: 6,319 (91% state residents). Freshmen: 1,957.

Undergraduate Expenses (1996–97) Comprehensive fee of $18,686 includes tuition ($13,056), mandatory fees ($540), and college room and board ($5090). College room only: $3090.

Applications Of all full-time undergraduates enrolled in fall 1996, 100% of those judged to have need according to Federal Methodology were aided. *Financial aid deadline:* Applications processed continuously. *Financial aid forms:* CSS Financial Aid PROFILE required; FAFSA acceptable. *Admission application deadline:* rolling.

Summary of Aid to Needy Students *From gift & self-help combined:* Average need met: 60%. Average amount awarded: $10,350 (61% gift aid, 39% self-help). *Gift aid:* Total: $32,043,322 (29% from college's own funds, 11% from other college-administered sources, 60% from external sources). 510 Federal Work-Study jobs (averaging $1080); 50 part-time jobs.

Need-Based Scholarships & Grants Pell, FSEOG, college/university, Scholarships for Disadvantaged Students (Nursing and Pharmacy).

Loans Perkins, PLUS, Stafford, Unsubsidized Stafford, college/university long-term loans ($1000 average), Federal Health Professions Student Loan.

Non-Need Awards In 1996, a total of 4,019 non-need awards were made. *Academic Interests/Achievement Awards:* 588 ($2,336,011 total): general academic, health fields. *Creative Arts/Performance Awards:* 55 ($274,293 total): art/fine arts, cinema/film/broadcasting, dance, music. *Special Achievements/Activities Awards:* 86 ($317,120 total): cheerleading/drum major, leadership. *Special Characteristics Awards:* 3,190 ($4,998,020 total): general special characteristics, children and siblings of alumni, children of faculty/staff, ethnic background, first-generation college students, international students. *Athletic:* Total: 100 ($1,214,751); Men: 52 ($631,671); Women: 48 ($583,080).

Other Money-Saving Options Accelerated degree, co-op program, cooperative Army ROTC, off-campus living. *Waivers:* full or partial for employees or children of employees and senior citizens.

Contact Ms. Rose Iannicelli, Dean of Financial Aid, Long Island University, Brooklyn Campus, 1 University Plaza, Brooklyn, NY 11201-8423, 718-488-1037.

LONG ISLAND UNIVERSITY, C.W. POST CAMPUS
Brookville, New York

About the Institution Independent, coed. Degrees awarded: A, B, M, D. Offers 82 undergraduate majors. Total enrollment: 9,172. Undergraduates: 4,670 (89% state residents). Freshmen: 729.

Undergraduate Expenses (1996–97) Comprehensive fee of $19,640 includes tuition ($13,120), mandatory fees ($570), and college room and board ($5950). College room only: $3650.

Applications 85% of all full-time undergraduates enrolled in fall 1996 applied for aid; of these, 94% were judged to have need according to Federal Methodology, of whom 100% were aided. *Financial aid deadline:* Applications processed continuously. *Financial aid forms:* FAFSA, state form required. CSS Financial Aid PROFILE required for some. *Admission application deadline:* rolling.

Summary of Aid to Needy Students *From gift & self-help combined:* Average need met: 75%. Average amount awarded: $8453 (60% gift aid, 40% self-help). *Gift aid:* Total: $14,588,250 (57% from college's own funds, 5% from other college-administered sources, 38% from external sources). 288 Federal Work-Study jobs (averaging $1500); 397 part-time jobs.

Need-Based Scholarships & Grants Pell, FSEOG, state, private, college/university.

Loans Perkins, PLUS, Stafford, Unsubsidized Stafford, private, college/university short-term loans ($100 average).

Non-Need Awards In 1996, a total of 977 non-need awards were made. *Academic Interests/Achievement Awards:* 537 ($2,820,825 total): general academic. *Creative Arts/Performance Awards:* 118 ($229,025 total): art/fine arts, cinema/film/broadcasting, dance, music, theater/drama. *Special Achievements/Activities Awards:* 52 ($40,000 total): general special achievements/activities. *Special Characteristics Awards:* 84 ($597,838 total): adult students, children of faculty/staff, international students. *Athletic:* Total: 186 ($931,500); Men: 123 ($606,320); Women: 63 ($325,180).

Other Money-Saving Options Accelerated degree, co-op program, cooperative Army ROTC, cooperative Air Force ROTC, off-campus living. *Payment Plans:* installment, deferred payment. *Waivers:* full or partial for employees or children of employees and senior citizens.

Contact Ms. Michele Siskind, Associate Director of Financial Aid, Long Island University, C.W. Post Campus, 720 Northern Boulevard, Brookville, NY 11548-1300, 516-299-2338, fax: 516-229-3833.

LONG ISLAND UNIVERSITY, SOUTHAMPTON COLLEGE
Southampton, New York

About the Institution Independent, coed. Degrees awarded: B, M. Offers 38 undergraduate majors. Total enrollment: 1,491. Undergraduates: 1,339 (74% state residents). Freshmen: 328.

Undergraduate Expenses (1996–97) Comprehensive fee of $20,310 includes tuition ($13,120), mandatory fees ($640), and college room and board ($6550). College room only: $3660.

Applications 92% of all full-time undergraduates enrolled in fall 1996 applied for aid; of these, 88% were judged to have need according to Federal Methodology, of whom 98% were aided. *Financial aid deadline (priority):* 6/15. *Financial aid forms:* FAFSA, institutional form required. State form required for some. *Admission application deadline:* rolling.

Summary of Aid to Needy Students *From gift & self-help combined:* Average need met: 78%. Average amount awarded: $14,509 (70% gift aid, 30% self-help). *Gift aid:* Total: $8,346,372 (70% from college's

own funds, 6% from other college-administered sources, 24% from external sources). 184 Federal Work-Study jobs (averaging $1100); 63 part-time jobs.

Need-Based Scholarships & Grants Pell, FSEOG, state, private, college/university.

Loans Perkins, PLUS, Stafford, Unsubsidized Stafford, college/university short-term loans.

Non-Need Awards *Academic Interests/Achievement Awards:* 793 ($2,335,193 total): general academic, business, education, humanities, physical sciences, social sciences. *Creative Arts/Performance Awards:* 80 ($180,943 total): art/fine arts, creative writing. *Special Characteristics Awards:* children and siblings of alumni, children of faculty/staff, ethnic background, siblings of current students. *Athletic:* Total: 100 ($620,035); Men: 59 ($358,135); Women: 41 ($261,900).

Other Money-Saving Options Accelerated degree, co-op program, cooperative Army ROTC, off-campus living (after freshman year). *Payment Plan:* installment. *Waivers:* full or partial for employees or children of employees and senior citizens.

Contact Ms. Susan M. Taylor, Director of Financial Aid, Long Island University, Southampton College, 239 Montauk Highway, Southampton, NY 11968-9822, 516-283-4000 Ext. 321, fax: 516-283-4081.

LONGWOOD COLLEGE
Farmville, Virginia

About the Institution State-supported, coed. Degrees awarded: B, M. Offers 80 undergraduate majors. Total enrollment: 3,023. Undergraduates: 2,891 (87% state residents). Freshmen: 786.

Undergraduate Expenses (1997–98) State resident tuition: $2684. Nonresident tuition: $8156. Mandatory fees: $1732. College room and board: $4204. College room only: $2506.

Applications Of all full-time undergraduates enrolled in fall 1996, 81% of those who applied for aid were judged to have need according to Federal Methodology, of whom 98% were aided. *Financial aid deadline (priority):* 2/15. *Financial aid forms:* FAFSA required. *Regular admission application deadline:* 2/15. Early action deadline: 12/1.

Summary of Aid to Needy Students *From gift & self-help combined:* Average need met: 82%. Average amount awarded: $6192 (43% gift aid, 57% self-help). *Gift aid:* Total: $3,803,768 (16% from college's own funds, 54% from other college-administered sources, 30% from external sources). 596 Federal Work-Study jobs (averaging $1369); 289 part-time jobs.

Need-Based Scholarships & Grants Pell, FSEOG, state, college/university.

Loans Perkins, PLUS, Stafford, Unsubsidized Stafford, college/university short-term loans ($300 average), college/university long-term loans ($1492 average).

Non-Need Awards In 1996, a total of 409 non-need awards were made. *Academic Interests/Achievement Awards:* 216 ($218,746 total): general academic, business, computer science, education, English, humanities, mathematics. *Creative Arts/Performance Awards:* 53 ($18,800 total): art/fine arts, music, theater/drama. *Special Achievements/Activities Awards:* 14 ($13,491 total): memberships. *Special Characteristics Awards:* 36 ($56,527 total): general special characteristics, children and siblings of alumni, local/state students. *Athletic:* Total: 90 ($280,631); Men: 49 ($137,274); Women: 41 ($143,357).

Other Money-Saving Options Accelerated degree, Army ROTC. *Payment Plan:* installment. *Waivers:* full or partial for employees or children of employees and senior citizens.

Contact Ms. Lisa Tumer, Director of Financial Aid, Longwood College, 201 High Street, Farmville, VA 23909-1898, 804-395-2077, fax: 804-395-2829.

LORAS COLLEGE
Dubuque, Iowa

About the Institution Independent/religious, coed. Degrees awarded: A, B, M. Offers 68 undergraduate majors. Total enrollment: 1,815. Undergraduates: 1,736 (55% state residents). Freshmen: 355.

Undergraduate Expenses (1996–97) Comprehensive fee of $17,205 includes tuition ($12,660) and college room and board ($4545).

Applications Of all full-time undergraduates enrolled in fall 1996, 100% of those judged to have need according to Federal Methodology were aided. *Financial aid deadline (priority):* 4/15. *Financial aid forms:* FAFSA required; CSS Financial Aid PROFILE acceptable. *Admission application deadline:* rolling.

Summary of Aid to Needy Students *From gift & self-help combined:* Average need met: 94%. Average amount awarded: $9640 (58% gift aid, 42% self-help). *Gift aid:* Total: $6,912,104 (64% from college's own funds, 28% from other college-administered sources, 8% from external sources). 867 Federal Work-Study jobs (averaging $891); 171 part-time jobs.

Need-Based Scholarships & Grants Pell, FSEOG, state, college/university.

Loans Perkins, PLUS, Stafford, Unsubsidized Stafford, private, college/university long-term loans ($1000 average).

Non-Need Awards In 1996, a total of 1,583 non-need awards were made. *Academic Interests/Achievement Awards:* 834 ($3,330,217 total): general academic. *Special Achievements/Activities Awards:* 579 ($579,040 total): community service, memberships, religious involvement. *Special Characteristics Awards:* 170 ($165,700 total): children and siblings of alumni, siblings of current students.

Other Money-Saving Options Accelerated degree, off-campus living (after junior year). *Payment Plan:* installment. *Waivers:* full or partial for children of alumni, employees or children of employees, senior citizens.

Contact Ms. Julie A. Dunn, Associate Director of Financial Planning, Loras College, 1450 Alta Vista Street, Dubuque, IA 52001, 319-588-7339, fax: 319-588-7964.

LOUISE SALINGER ACADEMY OF FASHION
San Francisco, California

About the Institution Independent, coed. Degrees awarded: A, B. Offers 4 undergraduate majors. Total enrollment: 200 (50% state residents). Freshmen: 35.

Undergraduate Expenses (1996–97) Tuition: $12,240. Mandatory fees: $300.

Applications *Financial aid deadline (priority):* 7/1. *Financial aid forms:* FAFSA, CSS Financial Aid PROFILE, institutional form required. State form required for some. *Admission application deadline:* rolling.

Summary of Aid to Needy Students Federal Work-Study jobs.

Need-Based Scholarships & Grants Pell, FSEOG, state.

Loans PLUS, Stafford, Unsubsidized Stafford.

Non-Need Awards Not offered.

Other Money-Saving Options Accelerated degree. *Payment Plan:* installment. *Waivers:* full or partial for employees or children of employees.

Contact Office of Financial Aid, Louise Salinger Academy of Fashion, 101 Jessie Street, San Francisco, CA 94105-3507, 415-974-6666.

LOUISIANA COLLEGE
Pineville, Louisiana

About the Institution Independent/religious, coed. Degrees awarded: A, B. Offers 65 undergraduate majors. Total enrollment: 959 (95% state residents). Freshmen: 206.

Undergraduate Expenses (1997–98) Comprehensive fee of $9799 includes tuition ($6272), mandatory fees ($491), and college room and board ($3036).

Applications *Financial aid deadline (priority):* 5/1. *Financial aid forms:* FAFSA, state form, institutional form required; CSS Financial Aid PROFILE acceptable. *Admission application deadline:* 8/1.

Summary of Aid to Needy Students *From gift & self-help combined:* Average need met: 55%. Average amount awarded: $4600 (33% gift aid, 67% self-help). *Gift aid:* Total: $1,514,900 (40% from college's own funds, 11% from other college-administered sources, 49% from external sources). 75 Federal Work-Study jobs (averaging $1500); 65 part-time jobs.

Need-Based Scholarships & Grants Pell, FSEOG, private, college/university.

Loans Perkins, PLUS, Stafford, Unsubsidized Stafford, college/university short-term loans ($400 average), college/university long-term loans ($1000 average).

Non-Need Awards In 1996, a total of 583 non-need awards were made. *Academic Interests/Achievement Awards:* 323 ($491,278 total): general academic, health fields, religion/biblical studies. *Creative Arts/Performance Awards:* 32 ($53,200 total): music, performing arts, theater/drama. *Special Achievements/Activities Awards:* 160 ($420,000 total): leadership. *Special Characteristics Awards:* 16 ($83,028 total): children of faculty/staff. *Athletic:* Total: 52 ($256,084); Men: 34 ($170,348); Women: 18 ($85,736).

Other Money-Saving Options Accelerated degree. *Waivers:* full or partial for employees or children of employees.

Contact Financial Aid Office, Louisiana College, Pineville, LA 71359-0001, 318-487-7386.

LOUISIANA STATE UNIVERSITY AND AGRICULTURAL AND MECHANICAL COLLEGE
Baton Rouge, Louisiana

About the Institution State-supported, coed. Degrees awarded: B, M, D, P. Offers 105 undergraduate majors. Total enrollment: 26,842. Undergraduates: 21,413 (87% state residents). Freshmen: 4,025.

Undergraduate Expenses (1996–97) State resident tuition: $2687. Nonresident tuition: $5987. College room and board: $3570. College room only: $1920.

Applications 46% of all full-time undergraduates enrolled in fall 1996 applied for aid; of these, 81% were judged to have need according to Federal Methodology, of whom 100% were aided. *Financial aid deadline (priority):* 3/1. *Financial aid forms:* FAFSA required. *Admission application deadline:* 6/1.

Summary of Aid to Needy Students *From gift & self-help combined:* Average amount awarded: $5875 (39% gift aid, 61% self-help). *Gift aid:* Total: $14,571,375 (23% from college's own funds, 3% from other college-administered sources, 74% from external sources). 720 Federal Work-Study jobs (averaging $1240); 5,103 part-time jobs.

Need-Based Scholarships & Grants Pell, FSEOG, state, private, college/university.

Loans Perkins, PLUS, Stafford, Unsubsidized Stafford, private, college/university short-term loans ($100 average).

Non-Need Awards *Academic Interests/Achievement Awards:* general academic, agriculture, architecture, biological sciences, business, communication, computer science, education, engineering/technologies, foreign languages, home economics, mathematics, military science, physical sciences, premedicine. *Creative Arts/Performance Awards:* applied art and design, art/fine arts, creative writing, journalism/publications, music, performing arts, theater/drama. *Special Achievements/Activities Awards:* hobbies/interest, leadership. *Special Characteristics*

Awards: general special characteristics, children and siblings of alumni, children of public servants, children with a deceased or disabled parent, ROTC participants. *Athletic:* Total: 423 ($2,237,272); Men: 264 ($1,402,469); Women: 159 ($834,803).

Other Money-Saving Options Co-op program, Army ROTC, Air Force ROTC, cooperative Naval ROTC, off-campus living. *Payment Plan:* deferred payment. *Waivers:* full or partial for children of alumni, employees or children of employees, senior citizens.

Contact Office of Financial Aid, Louisiana State University and Agricultural and Mechanical College, LSU 202 Himes Hall, Baton Rouge, LA 70803-3103, 504-388-3113.

LOUISIANA STATE UNIVERSITY IN SHREVEPORT
Shreveport, Louisiana

About the Institution State-supported, coed. Degrees awarded: B, M. Offers 44 undergraduate majors. Total enrollment: 3,945. Undergraduates: 3,354 (82% state residents). Freshmen: 415.

Undergraduate Expenses (1996–97) State resident tuition: $2080. Nonresident tuition: $5010. Mandatory fees: $130.

Applications *Financial aid deadline (priority):* 4/1. *Financial aid forms:* FAFSA, institutional form required; CSS Financial Aid PROFILE acceptable. *Admission application deadline:* 8/5.

Summary of Aid to Needy Students 50 Federal Work-Study jobs (averaging $1800); 250 part-time jobs.

Need-Based Scholarships & Grants Pell, FSEOG, state, private.

Loans PLUS, Stafford, Unsubsidized Stafford.

Non-Need Awards In 1996, a total of 87 non-need awards were made. *Academic Interests/Achievement Awards:* 70 ($55,000 total): general academic, biological sciences, business, computer science, education, English, premedicine. *Athletic:* Total: 17 ($11,000); Men: 13 ($8000); Women: 4 ($3000).

Other Money-Saving Options Accelerated degree, co-op program, Army ROTC. *Payment Plan:* deferred payment. *Waivers:* full or partial for employees or children of employees and senior citizens.

Contact Mr. Edgar L. Chase, Director of Financial Aid, Louisiana State University in Shreveport, Shreveport, LA 71115-2399, 318-797-5363.

LOUISIANA TECH UNIVERSITY
Ruston, Louisiana

About the Institution State-supported, coed. Degrees awarded: A, B, M, D. Offers 94 undergraduate majors. Total enrollment: 9,313. Undergraduates: 7,882 (85% state residents). Freshmen: 1,360.

Undergraduate Expenses (1996–97) State resident tuition: $2352. Nonresident tuition: $4347. College room and board: $2595. College room only: $1425.

Applications 59% of all full-time undergraduates enrolled in fall 1996 applied for aid; of these, 87% were judged to have need according to Federal Methodology, of whom 95% were aided. *Financial aid deadline (priority):* 5/2. *Financial aid forms:* FAFSA, institutional form required; CSS Financial Aid PROFILE acceptable. *Admission application deadline:* rolling.

Summary of Aid to Needy Students *From gift & self-help combined:* Average need met: 95%. Average amount awarded: $7655 (54% gift aid, 46% self-help). *Gift aid:* Total: $12,197,839 (43% from college's own funds, 22% from other college-administered sources, 35% from external sources). 308 Federal Work-Study jobs (averaging $2024); 1,500 part-time jobs.

Need-Based Scholarships & Grants Pell, FSEOG, state, private.

Loans Perkins, PLUS, Stafford, Unsubsidized Stafford.

Non-Need Awards In 1996, a total of 1,251 non-need awards were made. *Academic Interests/Achievement Awards:* 1,064 ($1,673,659 total): general academic, agriculture, business, education, engineering/technologies, home economics, humanities, premedicine. *Creative Arts/Performance Awards:* 66 ($50,325 total): debating, journalism/publications, music, performing arts, theater/drama. *Special Achievements/Activities Awards:* 7 ($5050 total): cheerleading/drum major. *Special Characteristics Awards:* 49 ($64,995 total): children of faculty/staff. *Athletic:* Total: 65 ($296,568); Men: 51 ($236,687); Women: 14 ($59,881).

Other Money-Saving Options Co-op program, Air Force ROTC, off-campus living (after sophomore year). *Waivers:* full or partial for children of alumni, employees or children of employees, senior citizens.

Contact Financial Aid Office, Louisiana Tech University, PO Box 7925, Tech Station, Ruston, LA 71272, 318-257-2641.

LOURDES COLLEGE
Sylvania, Ohio

About the Institution Independent/religious, coed. Degrees awarded: A, B. Offers 22 undergraduate majors. Total enrollment: 1,540 (91% state residents). Freshmen: 50.

Undergraduate Expenses (1997–98) Tuition: $7860. Mandatory fees: $240.

Applications 89% of all full-time undergraduates enrolled in fall 1996 applied for aid; of these, 81% were judged to have need according to Federal Methodology, of whom 97% were aided. *Financial aid deadline (priority):* 8/1. *Financial aid forms:* FAFSA, institutional form required. *Admission application deadline:* rolling.

Summary of Aid to Needy Students *From gift & self-help combined:* Average amount awarded: $8969. 24 Federal Work-Study jobs (averaging $850); 22 part-time jobs.

Need-Based Scholarships & Grants Pell, FSEOG, state, private, college/university.

Loans Perkins, PLUS, Stafford, Unsubsidized Stafford, Federal Nursing, state, college/university long-term loans ($1000 average).

Non-Need Awards In 1996, a total of 5 non-need awards were made. *Special Characteristics Awards:* 5 ($12,000 total): local/state students, members of minorities.

Other Money-Saving Options Accelerated degree, co-op program, cooperative Army ROTC. *Payment Plans:* installment, deferred payment. *Waivers:* full or partial for employees or children of employees and senior citizens.

Contact Ms. Pamela Curavo, Director of Financial Aid, Lourdes College, 6832 Convent Boulevard, Sylvania, OH 43560-2898, 419-885-3211, fax: 419-882-3987.

LOYOLA COLLEGE
Baltimore, Maryland

About the Institution Independent/religious, coed. Degrees awarded: B, M, D. Offers 51 undergraduate majors. Total enrollment: 6,245. Undergraduates: 3,205 (31% state residents). Freshmen: 822.

Undergraduate Expenses (1996–97) Comprehensive fee of $21,990 includes tuition ($15,200), mandatory fees ($510), and college room and board ($6280 minimum). College room only: $4450.

Applications Of all full-time undergraduates enrolled in fall 1996, 91% of those who applied for aid were judged to have need according to Federal Methodology, of whom 97% were aided. *Financial aid deadline:* 2/1. *Financial aid forms:* FAFSA, CSS Financial Aid PROFILE required. State form required for some. *Admission application deadline:* 1/15.

Summary of Aid to Needy Students *From gift & self-help combined:* Average need met: 95%. Average amount awarded: $10,200 (63% gift

aid, 37% self-help). *Gift aid:* Total: $9,725,815 (78% from college's own funds, 4% from other college-administered sources, 18% from external sources). 327 Federal Work-Study jobs (averaging $1400); 225 part-time jobs.

Need-Based Scholarships & Grants Pell, FSEOG, state, private, college/university.

Loans Perkins, PLUS, Stafford, Unsubsidized Stafford, private.

Non-Need Awards In 1996, a total of 879 non-need awards were made. *Academic Interests/Achievement Awards:* 579 ($3,363,000 total): general academic. *Special Characteristics Awards:* 169 ($820,900 total): local/state students, members of minorities, ROTC participants, siblings of current students. *Athletic:* Total: 131 ($1,734,110); Men: 66 ($906,950); Women: 65 ($827,160).

Other Money-Saving Options Army ROTC, cooperative Air Force ROTC, off-campus living (after freshman year). *Waivers:* full or partial for employees or children of employees.

Contact Office of Financial Aid, Loyola College, 4501 North Charles Street, Baltimore, MD 21210-2699, 410-617-2000.

LOYOLA MARYMOUNT UNIVERSITY
Los Angeles, California

About the Institution Independent/religious, coed. Degrees awarded: B, M, P. Offers 39 undergraduate majors. Total enrollment: 6,729. Undergraduates: 4,164 (79% state residents). Freshmen: 828.

Undergraduate Expenses (1997–98) Comprehensive fee of $23,231 includes tuition ($16,296), mandatory fees ($199), and college room and board ($6736). College room only: $3780 (minimum).

Applications 76% of all full-time undergraduates enrolled in fall 1996 applied for aid; of these, 86% were judged to have need according to Federal Methodology, of whom 98% were aided. *Financial aid deadline (priority):* 2/15. *Financial aid forms:* FAFSA, CSS Financial Aid PROFILE required. State form, institutional form required for some. *Admission application deadline:* 2/1.

Summary of Aid to Needy Students *From gift & self-help combined:* Average need met: 90%. Average amount awarded: $16,019 (77% gift aid, 23% self-help). *Gift aid:* Total: $16,683,166 (52% from college's own funds, 37% from other college-administered sources, 11% from external sources). 1,682 Federal Work-Study jobs (averaging $2400); 1,036 part-time jobs.

Need-Based Scholarships & Grants Pell, FSEOG, state, private, college/university.

Loans Perkins, PLUS, Stafford, Unsubsidized Stafford, private, college/university short-term loans ($500 average), college/university long-term loans ($5700 average).

Non-Need Awards *Academic Interests/Achievement Awards:* general academic. *Creative Arts/Performance Awards:* debating, music. *Special Achievements/Activities Awards:* community service, religious involvement. *Special Characteristics Awards:* children and siblings of alumni, children of faculty/staff, ROTC participants. *Athletic:* Total: 158 ($1,597,860); Men: 66 ($677,293); Women: 92 ($920,567).

Other Money-Saving Options Accelerated degree, Air Force ROTC, cooperative Army ROTC, cooperative Naval ROTC, off-campus living. *Payment Plan:* installment. *Waivers:* full or partial for employees or children of employees.

Contact Ms. Darlene Wilson, Financial Aid Counselor, Loyola Marymount University, 7900 Loyola Boulevard, Los Angeles, CA 90045-8350, 310-338-2753, fax: 310-338-2793.

LOYOLA UNIVERSITY CHICAGO
Chicago, Illinois

About the Institution Independent/religious, coed. Degrees awarded: B, M, D, P. Offers 45 undergraduate majors. Total enrollment: 13,759. Undergraduates: 7,669 (83% state residents). Freshmen: 1,063.

Undergraduate Expenses (1997–98) Comprehensive fee of $22,534 includes tuition ($15,654), mandatory fees ($400), and college room and board ($6480).

Applications *Financial aid deadline (priority):* 3/1. *Financial aid forms:* FAFSA required. CSS Financial Aid PROFILE required for some. *Admission application deadline:* 4/1.

Summary of Aid to Needy Students Federal Work-Study jobs; part-time jobs.

Non-Need Awards *Academic Interests/Achievement Awards:* general academic, foreign languages, health fields, physical sciences. *Creative Arts/Performance Awards:* debating, theater/drama. *Special Achievements/ Activities Awards:* general special achievements/activities, memberships. *Special Characteristics Awards:* religious affiliation. *Athletic:* available.

Other Money-Saving Options Accelerated degree, cooperative Army ROTC, cooperative Naval ROTC, cooperative Air Force ROTC, off-campus living. *Payment Plan:* installment. *Waivers:* full or partial for employees or children of employees.

Contact Office of Financial Aid, Loyola University Chicago, 6525 N Sheridan Rd, Granada Ctr 360, Chicago, IL 60626, 312-915-6000.

LOYOLA UNIVERSITY NEW ORLEANS
New Orleans, Louisiana

About the Institution Independent/religious, coed. Degrees awarded: B, M, P. Offers 50 undergraduate majors. Total enrollment: 5,203. Undergraduates: 3,375 (61% state residents). Freshmen: 530.

Undergraduate Expenses (1997–98) Comprehensive fee of $19,096 includes tuition ($12,950), mandatory fees ($316), and college room and board ($5830). College room only: $3260.

Applications 62% of all full-time undergraduates enrolled in fall 1996 applied for aid; of these, 66% were judged to have need according to Federal Methodology, of whom 98% were aided. *Financial aid deadline (priority):* 5/1. *Financial aid forms:* FAFSA required; state form acceptable. *Admission application deadline:* rolling.

Summary of Aid to Needy Students *From gift & self-help combined:* Average need met: 95%. Average amount awarded: $12,202 (58% gift aid, 42% self-help). *Gift aid:* Total: $7,394,888 (78% from college's own funds, 6% from other college-administered sources, 16% from external sources). 700 Federal Work-Study jobs (averaging $1800).

Need-Based Scholarships & Grants Pell, FSEOG, college/university.

Loans Perkins, PLUS, Stafford, Unsubsidized Stafford.

Non-Need Awards *Academic Interests/Achievement Awards:* 1,449 ($12,997,385 total). *Creative Arts/Performance Awards:* 427 ($1,873,559 total). *Special Characteristics Awards:* ROTC participants.

Other Money-Saving Options Accelerated degree, Army ROTC, cooperative Naval ROTC, cooperative Air Force ROTC, off-campus living (after freshman year). *Payment Plan:* installment. *Waivers:* full or partial for employees or children of employees.

Contact Dr. E. P. Seybold Jr., Director of Financial Aid, Loyola University New Orleans, 6363 Saint Charles Avenue, Box 206, New Orleans, LA 70118-6195, 504-865-3523, fax: 504-865-3233.

LUBBOCK CHRISTIAN UNIVERSITY
Lubbock, Texas

About the Institution Independent/religious, coed. Degrees awarded: B, M. Offers 32 undergraduate majors. Total enrollment: 1,232. Undergraduates: 1,210 (64% state residents). Freshmen: 226.

Undergraduate Expenses (1996–97) Comprehensive fee of $11,726 includes tuition ($7750), mandatory fees ($386), and college room and board ($3590).

Applications *Financial aid deadline (priority):* 7/1. *Financial aid forms:* FAFSA, CSS Financial Aid PROFILE acceptable. *Admission application deadline:* rolling.

Summary of Aid to Needy Students Federal Work-Study jobs; part-time jobs.

Non-Need Awards *Academic Interests/Achievement Awards:* available. *Creative Arts/Performance Awards:* available. *Special Achievements/ Activities Awards:* available. *Special Characteristics Awards:* available. *Athletic:* available.

Other Money-Saving Options Accelerated degree, cooperative Army ROTC, cooperative Naval ROTC, cooperative Air Force ROTC, off-campus living (after sophomore year). *Payment Plan:* installment.

Contact Office of Financial Aid, Lubbock Christian University, Lubbock, TX 79407-2099, 806-796-8800.

LUTHERAN BIBLE INSTITUTE OF SEATTLE
Issaquah, Washington

About the Institution Independent/religious, coed. Degrees awarded: A, B. Offers 4 undergraduate majors. Total enrollment: 167 (50% state residents). Freshmen: 24.

Undergraduate Expenses (1997–98) Comprehensive fee of $9655 includes tuition ($4600), mandatory fees ($710), and college room and board ($4345).

Applications 68% of all full-time undergraduates enrolled in fall 1996 applied for aid; of these, 65% were judged to have need according to Federal Methodology, of whom 92% were aided. *Financial aid deadline (priority):* 5/1. *Financial aid forms:* institutional form required; FAFSA, CSS Financial Aid PROFILE acceptable. *Admission application deadline:* 8/15.

Summary of Aid to Needy Students *From gift & self-help combined:* Average need met: 75%. Average amount awarded: $7328 (52% gift aid, 48% self-help). *Gift aid:* Total: $228,227 (50% from college's own funds, 20% from other college-administered sources, 30% from external sources). 35 Federal Work-Study jobs (averaging $1500); 25 part-time jobs.

Need-Based Scholarships & Grants Pell, FSEOG, college/university.

Loans PLUS, Stafford, Unsubsidized Stafford, college/university short-term loans ($500 average), college/university long-term loans ($500 average).

Non-Need Awards In 1996, a total of 27 non-need awards were made. *Special Characteristics Awards:* 27 ($29,846 total): international students, relatives of clergy, religious affiliation.

Other Money-Saving Options *Payment Plan:* installment. *Waivers:* full or partial for employees or children of employees.

Contact Ms. Susan Dalgleish, Director of Financial Aid, Lutheran Bible Institute of Seattle, 4221 228th Avenue Southeast, Issaquah, WA 98029-9299, 206-392-0400, fax: 206-392-0404.

LUTHER COLLEGE
Decorah, Iowa

About the Institution Independent/religious, coed. Degrees awarded: B. Offers 62 undergraduate majors. Total enrollment: 2,409 (36% state residents). Freshmen: 617.

Undergraduate Expenses (1996–97) Comprehensive fee of $18,550 includes tuition ($14,900) and college room and board ($3650). College room only: $1750.

Applications Of all full-time undergraduates enrolled in fall 1996, 67% of those who applied for aid were judged to have need according to Federal Methodology, of whom 100% were aided. *Financial aid deadline (priority):* 3/1. *Financial aid forms:* FAFSA, institutional form required; CSS Financial Aid PROFILE acceptable. State form required for some. *Admission application deadline:* 6/1.

Summary of Aid to Needy Students *From gift & self-help combined:* Average need met: 94%. Average amount awarded: $10,475 (64% gift aid, 36% self-help). *Gift aid:* Total: $11,562,200 (76% from college's own funds, 18% from other college-administered sources, 6% from external sources). 800 Federal Work-Study jobs (averaging $1350); 400 part-time jobs.

Need-Based Scholarships & Grants Pell, FSEOG, state, private, college/university.

Loans Perkins, PLUS, Stafford, Unsubsidized Stafford, private, college/university short-term loans ($100 average), college/university long-term loans ($1500 average).

Non-Need Awards In 1996, a total of 2,085 non-need awards were made. *Academic Interests/Achievement Awards:* 1,168 ($4,191,790 total): general academic. *Creative Arts/Performance Awards:* 460 ($372,750 total): music. *Special Characteristics Awards:* 457 ($155,350 total): religious affiliation.

Other Money-Saving Options *Payment Plans:* guaranteed tuition, installment. *Waivers:* full or partial for employees or children of employees.

Contact Ms. Sally J. Harris, Assistant Dean of Enrollment and Financial Aid, Luther College, Decorah, IA 52101-1045, 319-387-1018.

LUTHER RICE BIBLE COLLEGE AND SEMINARY
Lithonia, Georgia

About the Institution Independent/religious, primarily men. Degrees awarded: B, M, D. Offers 2 undergraduate majors. Total enrollment: 1,285. Undergraduates: 462 (30% state residents). Freshmen: 200.

Undergraduate Expenses (1996–97) Tuition: $2352. Mandatory fees: $160.

Applications *Financial aid forms:* institutional form required. *Admission application deadline:* rolling.

Need-Based Scholarships & Grants College/university.

Non-Need Awards Not offered.

Other Money-Saving Options *Payment Plan:* installment. *Waivers:* full or partial for employees or children of employees.

Contact Dr. Dennis Vines, Director of Financial Aid, Luther Rice Bible College and Seminary, Lithonia, GA 30038-2418, 770-484-1204.

LYCOMING COLLEGE
Williamsport, Pennsylvania

About the Institution Independent/religious, coed. Degrees awarded: B. Offers 50 undergraduate majors. Total enrollment: 1,489 (77% state residents). Freshmen: 390.

Undergraduate Expenses (1997–98 estimated) Comprehensive fee of $20,760 includes tuition ($16,000), mandatory fees ($160), and college room and board ($4600).

Applications Of all full-time undergraduates enrolled in fall 1996, 91% of those who applied for aid were judged to have need according to Federal Methodology, of whom 98% were aided. *Financial aid deadline (priority):* 4/15. *Financial aid forms:* FAFSA, institutional form required. State form required for some. *Admission application deadline:* 4/1.

Summary of Aid to Needy Students *From gift & self-help combined:* Average need met: 83%. Average amount awarded: $13,343 (70% gift aid, 30% self-help). *Gift aid:* Total: $11,252,239 (76% from college's own funds, 2% from other college-administered sources, 22% from external sources). 234 Federal Work-Study jobs (averaging $575); 275 part-time jobs.

Need-Based Scholarships & Grants Pell, FSEOG, state, college/university.

Loans Perkins, PLUS, Stafford, Unsubsidized Stafford, college/university long-term loans ($1924 average).

Non-Need Awards In 1996, a total of 538 non-need awards were made. *Academic Interests/Achievement Awards:* 415 ($2,005,737 total): general academic. *Creative Arts/Performance Awards:* 96 ($145,500 total): art/fine arts, music. *Special Achievements/Activities Awards:* 0: hobbies/interest. *Special Characteristics Awards:* 27 ($292,347 total): children of educators, children of faculty/staff, relatives of clergy.

Other Money-Saving Options Accelerated degree, cooperative Army ROTC. *Payment Plan:* installment. *Waivers:* full or partial for employees or children of employees.

Contact Mr. Benjamin H. Comfort III, Director of Financial Aid, Lycoming College, 700 College Place, Long Hall, Williamsport, PA 17701-5192, 717-321-4040, fax: 717-321-4137.

LYME ACADEMY OF FINE ARTS
Old Lyme, Connecticut

About the Institution Independent, coed. Degrees awarded: B. Offers 3 undergraduate majors. Total enrollment: 67 (75% state residents). Freshmen: 20.

Undergraduate Expenses (1997–98) Tuition: $8640. Mandatory fees: $50.

Applications 52% of all full-time undergraduates enrolled in fall 1996 applied for aid; of these,100% were judged to have need according to Federal Methodology, of whom 100% were aided. *Financial aid deadline:* Applications processed continuously. *Financial aid forms:* CSS Financial Aid PROFILE, institutional form required. FAFSA required for some. *Admission application deadline:* rolling.

Summary of Aid to Needy Students *From gift & self-help combined:* Average need met: 36%. Average amount awarded: $2804 (95% gift aid, 5% self-help). *Gift aid:* Total: $66,490 (26% from college's own funds, 54% from other college-administered sources, 20% from external sources). 2 Federal Work-Study jobs (averaging $1804); 25 part-time jobs.

Need-Based Scholarships & Grants Pell, FSEOG, state, private, college/university.

Loans Private.

Non-Need Awards In 1996, a total of 18 non-need awards were made. *Creative Arts/Performance Awards:* 18 ($17,241 total): art/fine arts.

Other Money-Saving Options *Payment Plan:* installment. *Waivers:* full or partial for employees or children of employees.

Contact Office of Financial Aid, Lyme Academy of Fine Arts, 84 Lyme Street, Old Lyme, CT 06371, 860-434-5232.

LYNCHBURG COLLEGE
Lynchburg, Virginia

About the Institution Independent/religious, coed. Degrees awarded: B, M. Offers 53 undergraduate majors. Total enrollment: 1,842. Undergraduates: 1,413 (59% state residents). Freshmen: 287.

Undergraduate Expenses (1997–98) Comprehensive fee of $20,315 includes tuition ($15,490), mandatory fees ($125), and college room and board ($4700). College room only: $2600.

Applications 73% of all full-time undergraduates enrolled in fall 1996 applied for aid; of these, 88% were judged to have need according to Federal Methodology, of whom 99% were aided. *Financial aid deadline (priority):* 3/1. *Financial aid forms:* FAFSA required; CSS Financial Aid PROFILE acceptable. State form required for some. *Regular admission application deadline:* rolling. Early decision deadline: 11/15.

Summary of Aid to Needy Students *From gift & self-help combined:* Average need met: 97%. Average amount awarded: $13,999 (52% gift aid, 48% self-help). *Gift aid:* Total: $5,624,079 (72% from college's own funds, 17% from other college-administered sources, 11% from external sources). 290 Federal Work-Study jobs (averaging $1000); 170 part-time jobs.

Need-Based Scholarships & Grants Pell, FSEOG, state, private, college/university.

Loans Perkins, PLUS, Stafford, Unsubsidized Stafford, private.

Non-Need Awards In 1996, a total of 736 non-need awards were made. *Academic Interests/Achievement Awards:* 418 ($2,177,462 total): general academic, health fields. *Creative Arts/Performance Awards:* 12 ($27,100 total): music. *Special Achievements/Activities Awards:* 70 ($343,600 total): leadership, religious involvement. *Special Characteristics Awards:* 236 ($525,710 total): children of faculty/staff, international students, local/state students, members of minorities, relatives of clergy, religious affiliation.

Other Money-Saving Options Accelerated degree, off-campus living (after junior year). *Payment Plan:* installment. *Waivers:* full or partial for employees or children of employees, adult students, senior citizens.

Contact Mr. Kenneth J. Eiker, Associate Director of Financial Aid, Lynchburg College, 1501 Lakeside Drive, Lynchburg, VA 24501-3199, 804-544-8228, fax: 804-544-8653.

LYNDON STATE COLLEGE
Lyndonville, Vermont

About the Institution State-supported, coed. Degrees awarded: A, B, M. Offers 38 undergraduate majors. Total enrollment: 1,137. Undergraduates: 1,108 (57% state residents). Freshmen: 383.

Undergraduate Expenses (1996–97) State resident tuition: $3620. Nonresident tuition: $8380. Mandatory fees: $720. College room and board: $4936.

Applications 87% of all full-time undergraduates enrolled in fall 1996 applied for aid; of these, 91% were judged to have need according to Federal Methodology, of whom 100% were aided. *Financial aid deadline (priority):* 3/15. *Financial aid forms:* FAFSA required; CSS Financial Aid PROFILE acceptable. State form, financial aid transcript (for transfers) required for some. *Regular admission application deadline:* rolling. Early decision deadline: 11/1.

Summary of Aid to Needy Students *From gift & self-help combined:* Average need met: 74%. Average amount awarded: $11,451 (39% gift aid, 61% self-help). *Gift aid:* Total: $1,896,157 (6% from college's own funds, 27% from other college-administered sources, 67% from external sources). 199 Federal Work-Study jobs (averaging $15); part-time jobs.

Need-Based Scholarships & Grants Pell, FSEOG, state, private, college/university, Child-Care Grant Program, Faculty-Staff Awards.

Loans Perkins, PLUS, Stafford, Unsubsidized Stafford, private.

Non-Need Awards *Academic Interests/Achievement Awards:* general academic, business, education, humanities. *Special Achievements/Activities Awards:* community service, leadership. *Special Characteristics Awards:* adult students, children of faculty/staff, first-generation college students, siblings of current students.

Other Money-Saving Options Co-op program, Air Force ROTC, off-campus living (after sophomore year). *Waivers:* full or partial for employees or children of employees and senior citizens.

Contact Ms. Terry Van Zile, Assistant Director of Financial Aid, Lyndon State College, Vail Hill, Lyndonville, VT 05851, 802-626-6217, fax: 802-626-9770.

LYNN UNIVERSITY
Boca Raton, Florida

About the Institution Independent, coed. Degrees awarded: A, B, M. Offers 44 undergraduate majors. Total enrollment: 1,652. Undergraduates: 1,508 (30% state residents). Freshmen: 264.

Undergraduate Expenses (1997–98) Comprehensive fee of $22,950 includes tuition ($16,300), mandatory fees ($400), and college room and board ($6250).

Applications 77% of all full-time undergraduates enrolled in fall 1996 applied for aid; of these, 43% were judged to have need according to Federal Methodology, of whom 100% were aided. *Financial aid deadline (priority):* 5/1. *Financial aid forms:* FAFSA required; CSS Financial Aid PROFILE, state form acceptable. *Admission application deadline:* 8/15.

Summary of Aid to Needy Students *From gift & self-help combined:* Average need met: 100%. Average amount awarded: $11,786 (58% gift aid, 42% self-help). *Gift aid:* Total: $2,411,596 (67% from college's own funds, 18% from other college-administered sources, 15% from external sources). 138 Federal Work-Study jobs (averaging $1200); 10 part-time jobs.

Need-Based Scholarships & Grants Pell, FSEOG, state, private, college/university.

Loans Perkins, PLUS, Stafford, Unsubsidized Stafford, private.

Non-Need Awards In 1996, a total of 305 non-need awards were made. *Academic Interests/Achievement Awards:* 166 ($921,095 total): general academic, health fields. *Creative Arts/Performance Awards:* 7 ($3500 total): music. *Special Characteristics Awards:* 56 ($204,355 total): children of faculty/staff. *Athletic:* Total: 76 ($1,102,658); Men: 41 ($619,127); Women: 35 ($483,531).

Other Money-Saving Options Off-campus living (after sophomore year). *Payment Plans:* installment, deferred payment. *Waivers:* full or partial for employees or children of employees.

Contact Ms. Barrie Tripp, New Student Financial Services Counselor, Lynn University, 3601 North Military Trail, Boca Raton, FL 33431-5598, 561-994-0770 Ext. 114, fax: 561-995-0692.

LYON COLLEGE
Batesville, Arkansas

About the Institution Independent/religious, coed. Degrees awarded: B. Offers 20 undergraduate majors. Total enrollment: 559 (76% state residents). Freshmen: 129.

Undergraduate Expenses (1996–97) Comprehensive fee of $13,708 includes tuition ($9350), mandatory fees ($120), and college room and board ($4238). College room only: $1670.

Applications 81% of all full-time undergraduates enrolled in fall 1996 applied for aid; of these, 90% were judged to have need according to Federal Methodology, of whom 100% were aided. *Financial aid deadline (priority):* 4/1. *Financial aid forms:* FAFSA required; CSS Financial Aid PROFILE, institutional form acceptable. State form required for some. *Regular admission application deadline:* rolling. Early decision deadline: 12/1.

Summary of Aid to Needy Students *From gift & self-help combined:* Average need met: 99%. Average amount awarded: $10,363 (75% gift aid, 25% self-help). *Gift aid:* Total: $2,664,285 (81% from college's own funds, 9% from other college-administered sources, 10% from external sources). 101 Federal Work-Study jobs (averaging $1201); 129 part-time jobs.

Need-Based Scholarships & Grants Pell, FSEOG, state, private, college/university.

Loans Perkins, PLUS, Stafford, Unsubsidized Stafford.

Non-Need Awards In 1996, a total of 441 non-need awards were made. *Academic Interests/Achievement Awards:* 320 ($1,877,854 total): general academic. *Creative Arts/Performance Awards:* 4 ($17,944 total): dance, performing arts. *Special Achievements/Activities Awards:* 42 ($115,500 total): leadership. *Athletic:* Total: 75 ($372,509); Men: 48 ($219,496); Women: 27 ($153,013).

Other Money-Saving Options *Payment Plan:* installment. *Waivers:* full or partial for employees or children of employees.

Contact Financial Aid Office, Lyon College, 2300 Highland Road, Batesville, AR 72501, 501-793-9813, fax: 501-698-4622.

MACALESTER COLLEGE
St. Paul, Minnesota

About the Institution Independent/religious, coed. Degrees awarded: B. Offers 39 undergraduate majors. Total enrollment: 1,797 (23% state residents). Freshmen: 491.

Undergraduate Expenses (1997–98) Comprehensive fee of $24,188 includes tuition ($18,630), mandatory fees ($128), and college room and board ($5430).

Applications *Financial aid deadline (priority):* 2/8. *Financial aid forms:* FAFSA, CSS Financial Aid PROFILE, W-2 forms, federal income tax forms required. *Regular admission application deadline:* 1/15. Early decision deadline: 11/15.

Summary of Aid to Needy Students Federal Work-Study jobs.

Non-Need Awards *Academic Interests/Achievement Awards:* general academic. *Special Achievements/Activities Awards:* hobbies/interest.

Other Money-Saving Options Cooperative Naval ROTC, cooperative Air Force ROTC, off-campus living (after sophomore year). *Payment Plan:* installment. *Waivers:* full or partial for employees or children of employees.

Contact Office of Financial Aid, Macalester College, St. Paul, MN 55105-1899, 612-696-6000.

MACHZIKEI HADATH RABBINICAL COLLEGE
Brooklyn, New York

About the Institution Independent/religious, men. Offers 2 undergraduate majors. Total enrollment: 150. Undergraduates: 125 (90% state residents). Freshmen: 35.

Undergraduate Expenses (1996–97) Comprehensive fee of $7000 includes tuition ($5200) and college room and board ($1800).

Applications Of all full-time undergraduates enrolled in fall 1996, 88% of those who applied for aid were judged to have need according to Federal Methodology, of whom 100% were aided. *Financial aid deadline:* Applications processed continuously. *Financial aid forms:* FAFSA, federal income tax return required. *Admission application deadline:* rolling.

Summary of Aid to Needy Students Federal Work-Study jobs.

Need-Based Scholarships & Grants Pell, FSEOG.

Non-Need Awards Not offered.

Other Money-Saving Options Off-campus living. *Payment Plans:* installment, deferred payment. *Waivers:* full or partial for employees or children of employees.

Contact Rabbi Baruch Rozmarin, Director of Financial Aid, Machzikei Hadath Rabbinical College, Brooklyn, NY 11204-1805, 718-854-8777.

MACMURRAY COLLEGE
Jacksonville, Illinois

About the Institution Independent/religious, coed. Degrees awarded: A, B. Offers 38 undergraduate majors. Total enrollment: 669 (84% state residents). Freshmen: 158.

Undergraduate Expenses (1997–98) Comprehensive fee of $15,530 includes tuition ($11,400) and college room and board ($4130). College room only: $1850.

Applications 99% of all full-time undergraduates enrolled in fall 1996 applied for aid; of these, 93% were judged to have need according to Federal Methodology, of whom 100% were aided. *Financial aid deadline (priority):* 5/1. *Financial aid forms:* FAFSA required. *Admission application deadline:* 7/15.

Summary of Aid to Needy Students *From gift & self-help combined:* Average need met: 65%. Average amount awarded: $11,009 (58% gift aid, 42% self-help). *Gift aid:* Total: $3,704,573 (39% from college's own funds, 48% from other college-administered sources, 13% from external sources). 172 Federal Work-Study jobs (averaging $867); 205 part-time jobs.

Need-Based Scholarships & Grants Pell, FSEOG, state, private, college/university.

Loans Perkins, PLUS, Stafford, Unsubsidized Stafford, private, college/university short-term loans ($100 average), college/university long-term loans ($1500 average).

Non-Need Awards In 1996, a total of 303 non-need awards were made. *Academic Interests/Achievement Awards:* 130 ($460,840 total): general academic, biological sciences, English, foreign languages, health fields, physical sciences, religion/biblical studies, social sciences. *Creative Arts/Performance Awards:* 25 ($36,760 total): art/fine arts, music. *Special Achievements/Activities Awards:* 11 ($71,640 total): leadership, religious involvement. *Special Characteristics Awards:* 137 ($191,750 total): children and siblings of alumni, children of faculty/staff, international students, out-of-state students, previous college experience, religious affiliation.

Other Money-Saving Options *Payment Plan:* installment. *Waivers:* full or partial for children of alumni, employees or children of employees, senior citizens.

Contact Mrs. Lori A. Hall, Director of Financial Aid, MacMurray College, 447 East College, Jacksonville, IL 62650, 217-479-7041.

MADONNA UNIVERSITY
Livonia, Michigan

About the Institution Independent/religious, coed. Degrees awarded: A, B, M. Offers 65 undergraduate majors. Total enrollment: 3,972. Undergraduates: 3,412 (98% state residents). Freshmen: 188.

Undergraduate Expenses (1997–98) Comprehensive fee of $10,220 includes tuition ($5940) and college room and board ($4280 minimum). College room only: $1986 (minimum).

Applications 59% of all full-time undergraduates enrolled in fall 1996 applied for aid; of these, 96% were judged to have need according to Federal Methodology, of whom 99% were aided. *Financial aid deadline (priority):* 2/21. *Financial aid forms:* FAFSA, state form, institutional form required. *Admission application deadline:* rolling.

Summary of Aid to Needy Students *From gift & self-help combined:* Average need met: 90%. Average amount awarded: $7148 (55% gift aid, 45% self-help). *Gift aid:* Total: $2,904,223 (5% from college's own funds, 66% from other college-administered sources, 29% from external sources). Federal Work-Study jobs (averaging $2850); 75 part-time jobs.

Need-Based Scholarships & Grants Pell, FSEOG, state, private, college/university.

Loans Perkins, PLUS, Stafford, Unsubsidized Stafford, college/university short-term loans ($400 average).

Non-Need Awards In 1996, a total of 219 non-need awards were made. *Academic Interests/Achievement Awards:* 124 ($122,858 total): general academic, business, communication, computer science, education, humanities. *Athletic:* Total: 95 ($153,705); Men: 56 ($78,262); Women: 39 ($75,443).

Other Money-Saving Options Accelerated degree, co-op program, off-campus living. *Payment Plan:* deferred payment. *Waivers:* full or partial for employees or children of employees.

Contact Ms. Cathy Durham, Secretary, Madonna University, 36600 Schoolcraft Road, Livonia, MI 48150-1173, 313-432-5663, fax: 313-432-5405.

MAGNOLIA BIBLE COLLEGE
Kosciusko, Mississippi

About the Institution Independent/religious, primarily men. Degrees awarded: B. Offers 1 undergraduate major. Total enrollment: 70 (68% state residents). Freshmen: 5.

Undergraduate Expenses (1997–98) Comprehensive fee of $4950 includes tuition ($4000), mandatory fees ($20), and college room and board ($930). College room only: $600.

Applications 77% of all full-time undergraduates enrolled in fall 1996 applied for aid; of these, 85% were judged to have need according to Federal Methodology, of whom 100% were aided. *Financial aid deadline (priority):* 8/1. *Financial aid forms:* CSS Financial Aid PROFILE acceptable. FAFSA required for some. *Admission application deadline:* 8/31.

Summary of Aid to Needy Students *From gift & self-help combined:* Average need met: 46%. Average amount awarded: $4237 (78% gift aid, 22% self-help). *Gift aid:* Total: $39,731 (47% from college's own funds, 16% from other college-administered sources, 37% from external sources). 4 Federal Work-Study jobs (averaging $2030); 2 part-time jobs.

Need-Based Scholarships & Grants Pell, FSEOG, state, college/university.

Loans PLUS, Stafford, Unsubsidized Stafford.

Non-Need Awards In 1996, a total of 11 non-need awards were made. *Academic Interests/Achievement Awards:* 6 ($18,126 total): general academic. *Creative Arts/Performance Awards:* 3 ($5626 total): music. *Special Characteristics Awards:* 2 ($1125 total): general special characteristics, spouses of current students.

Other Money-Saving Options Off-campus living (after sophomore year). *Payment Plan:* deferred payment. *Waivers:* full or partial for employees or children of employees.

Contact Mr. Allen Coker, Admissions Counselor, Magnolia Bible College, Kosciusko, MS 39090-1109, 601-289-2896, fax: 601-289-1850.

MAHARISHI UNIVERSITY OF MANAGEMENT
Fairfield, Iowa

About the Institution Independent, coed. Degrees awarded: A, B, M, D. Offers 14 undergraduate majors. Total enrollment: 1,025. Undergraduates: 813 (20% state residents). Freshmen: 45.

Undergraduate Expenses (1996–97) Comprehensive fee of $18,776 includes tuition ($13,760), mandatory fees ($216), and college room and board ($4800). College room only: $2512.

Applications 90% of all full-time undergraduates enrolled in fall 1996 applied for aid; of these, 97% were judged to have need according to Federal Methodology, of whom 100% were aided. *Financial aid deadline (priority):* 4/10. *Financial aid forms:* FAFSA required; state form acceptable. Institutional form required for some. *Admission application deadline:* 8/1.

Summary of Aid to Needy Students *From gift & self-help combined:* Average need met: 92%. Average amount awarded: $18,774 (65% gift aid, 35% self-help). *Gift aid:* Total: $1,143,752 (65% from college's own funds, 13% from other college-administered sources, 22% from external sources). 90 Federal Work-Study jobs (averaging $1400).

Need-Based Scholarships & Grants Pell, FSEOG, state, private, college/university.

Loans Perkins, PLUS, Stafford, Unsubsidized Stafford, private, college/university long-term loans ($1000 average).

Non-Need Awards In 1996, a total of 123 non-need awards were made. *Academic Interests/Achievement Awards:* 2 ($8000 total): general academic. *Creative Arts/Performance Awards:* 4 ($10,000 total): general creative, creative writing, music. *Special Characteristics Awards:* 117 ($766,892 total): children and siblings of alumni, children of faculty/staff, ethnic background, international students, local/state students, veterans, veterans' children.

Other Money-Saving Options Co-op program. *Payment Plan:* installment. *Waivers:* full or partial for employees or children of employees.

Contact Mr. Bill Christensen, Associate Director of Financial Aid, Maharishi University of Management, Fairfield, IA 52557, 515-472-1156, fax: 515-472-1133.

MAINE COLLEGE OF ART
Portland, Maine

About the Institution Independent, coed. Degrees awarded: B. Offers 7 undergraduate majors. Total enrollment: 316 (46% state residents). Freshmen: 125.

Undergraduate Expenses (1997–98) Comprehensive fee of $20,799 includes tuition ($14,850), mandatory fees ($155), and college room and board ($5794). College room only: $3598 (minimum).

Applications 84% of all full-time undergraduates enrolled in fall 1996 applied for aid; of these, 94% were judged to have need according to Federal Methodology, of whom 100% were aided. *Financial aid deadline (priority):* 3/1. *Financial aid forms:* FAFSA required. *Admission application deadline:* rolling.

Summary of Aid to Needy Students *From gift & self-help combined:* Average need met: 55%. Average amount awarded: $10,116 (57% gift aid, 43% self-help). *Gift aid:* Total: $1,360,688 (72% from college's own funds, 14% from other college-administered sources, 14% from external sources). 100 Federal Work-Study jobs (averaging $1000); 3 part-time jobs.

Need-Based Scholarships & Grants Pell, FSEOG, state, private, college/university.

Loans Perkins, PLUS, Stafford, Unsubsidized Stafford, private, college/university short-term loans ($100 average).

Non-Need Awards In 1996, a total of 8 non-need awards were made. *Creative Arts/Performance Awards:* 8 ($76,230 total): art/fine arts.

Other Money-Saving Options Co-op program, off-campus living. *Payment Plans:* installment, deferred payment.

Contact Ms. Eva Giles, Director of Financial Aid, Maine College of Art, 97 Spring Street, Portland, ME 04101-3987, 207-772-3052, fax: 207-772-5069.

MAINE MARITIME ACADEMY
Castine, Maine

About the Institution State-supported, coed. Degrees awarded: A, B, M. Offers 9 undergraduate majors. Total enrollment: 665. Undergraduates: 615 (60% state residents). Freshmen: 190.

Undergraduate Expenses (1997–98) State resident tuition: $4206. Nonresident tuition: $7720. Mandatory fees: $450. College room and board: $5022.

Applications 86% of all full-time undergraduates enrolled in fall 1996 applied for aid; of these, 93% were judged to have need according to Federal Methodology, of whom 100% were aided. *Financial aid deadline (priority):* 4/15. *Financial aid forms:* FAFSA, institutional form required. State form required for some. *Regular admission application deadline:* 7/1. Early decision deadline: 12/20.

Summary of Aid to Needy Students *From gift & self-help combined:* Average need met: 70%. Average amount awarded: $5669 (30% gift aid, 70% self-help). *Gift aid:* Total: $845,137 (20% from college's own funds, 40% from other college-administered sources, 40% from external sources). 264 Federal Work-Study jobs (averaging $1000).

Need-Based Scholarships & Grants Pell, FSEOG, state, private, college/university.

Loans Perkins, PLUS, Stafford, Unsubsidized Stafford, state, private, college/university short-term loans ($500 average), college/university long-term loans ($1500 average).

Non-Need Awards In 1996, a total of 80 non-need awards were made. *Academic Interests/Achievement Awards:* 12 ($6000 total): general academic, biological sciences, engineering/technologies. *Special Characteristics Awards:* 68 ($179,600 total): children of faculty/staff, local/state students, out-of-state students, ROTC participants.

Other Money-Saving Options Co-op program, Naval ROTC. *Waivers:* full or partial for employees or children of employees.

Contact Ms. Gail H. Ryan, Director of Financial Aid, Maine Maritime Academy, Castine, ME 04420, 207-326-4311.

MALONE COLLEGE
Canton, Ohio

About the Institution Independent/religious, coed. Degrees awarded: A, B, M. Offers 47 undergraduate majors. Total enrollment: 2,069. Undergraduates: 1,877 (94% state residents). Freshmen: 407.

Undergraduate Expenses (1997–98) Comprehensive fee of $16,051 includes tuition ($11,501), mandatory fees ($150), and college room and board ($4400 minimum). College room only: $2580 (minimum).

Applications 96% of all full-time undergraduates enrolled in fall 1996 applied for aid; of these, 79% were judged to have need according to Federal Methodology, of whom 99% were aided. *Financial aid deadline (priority):* 3/1. *Financial aid forms:* FAFSA, institutional form required. *Admission application deadline:* 7/1.

Summary of Aid to Needy Students *From gift & self-help combined:* Average need met: 94%. Average amount awarded: $9718 (52% gift aid, 48% self-help). *Gift aid:* Total: $6,338,043 (58% from college's own funds, 27% from other college-administered sources, 15% from external sources). 360 Federal Work-Study jobs (averaging $1300); 61 part-time jobs.

Need-Based Scholarships & Grants Pell, FSEOG, state, private, college/university.

Loans Perkins, PLUS, Stafford, Unsubsidized Stafford, private, college/university long-term loans ($1500 average).

Non-Need Awards In 1996, a total of 1,290 non-need awards were made. *Academic Interests/Achievement Awards:* 532 ($1,795,125 total): general academic, biological sciences, business, communication, computer science, education, English, foreign languages, health fields, humanities, international studies, mathematics, physical sciences, premedicine, religion/biblical studies, social sciences. *Creative Arts/Performance Awards:* 60 ($35,225 total): music. *Special Achievements/Activities Awards:* 188 ($503,185 total): community service, Junior Miss, leadership, religious involvement. *Special Characteristics Awards:* 292 ($537,168 total): children and siblings of alumni, children of faculty/staff, international students, parents of current students, rela-

tives of clergy, religious affiliation, siblings of current students, spouses of current students. *Athletic:* Total: 218 ($441,375); Men: 167 ($350,853); Women: 51 ($90,522).

Other Money-Saving Options Accelerated degree, co-op program, off-campus living (after junior year). *Payment Plan:* installment. *Waivers:* full or partial for employees or children of employees and senior citizens.

Contact Ms. Patricia L. Little, Director of Financial Aid, Malone College, 515 25th Street, NW, Canton, OH 44709-3897, 330-471-8159, fax: 330-471-8478.

MANCHESTER COLLEGE
North Manchester, Indiana

About the Institution Independent/religious, coed. Degrees awarded: A, B, M. Offers 60 undergraduate majors. Total enrollment: 1,054. Undergraduates: 1,035 (76% state residents). Freshmen: 307.

Undergraduate Expenses (1997–98) Comprehensive fee of $17,160 includes tuition ($12,270), mandatory fees ($390), and college room and board ($4500).

Applications 96% of all full-time undergraduates enrolled in fall 1996 applied for aid; of these, 97% were judged to have need according to Federal Methodology, of whom 97% were aided. *Financial aid deadline (priority):* 3/1. *Financial aid forms:* FAFSA required; CSS Financial Aid PROFILE, state form acceptable. Institutional form required for some. *Admission application deadline:* rolling.

Summary of Aid to Needy Students *From gift & self-help combined:* Average need met: 77%. Average amount awarded: $13,390 (72% gift aid, 28% self-help). *Gift aid:* Total: $8,742,000 (48% from college's own funds, 47% from other college-administered sources, 5% from external sources). 810 Federal Work-Study jobs (averaging $785); 568 part-time jobs.

Need-Based Scholarships & Grants Pell, FSEOG, state, private, college/university.

Loans Perkins, PLUS, Stafford, Unsubsidized Stafford, private.

Non-Need Awards *Academic Interests/Achievement Awards:* general academic, English, international studies, religion/biblical studies. *Creative Arts/Performance Awards:* art/fine arts, music, performing arts, theater/drama. *Special Achievements/Activities Awards:* memberships. *Special Characteristics Awards:* children and siblings of alumni, international students, previous college experience, religious affiliation.

Other Money-Saving Options Accelerated degree, co-op program, off-campus living (after junior year). *Payment Plans:* installment, deferred payment. *Waivers:* full or partial for employees or children of employees.

Contact Mr. Steven M. Payne, Director of Financial Aid, Manchester College, North Manchester, IN 46962-1225, 219-982-5066, fax: 219-982-5043.

MANHATTAN CHRISTIAN COLLEGE
Manhattan, Kansas

About the Institution Independent/religious, coed. Degrees awarded: A, B. Offers 7 undergraduate majors. Total enrollment: 281 (64% state residents). Freshmen: 112.

Undergraduate Expenses (1997–98) Comprehensive fee of $8540 includes tuition ($5620) and college room and board ($2920 minimum).

Applications Of all full-time undergraduates enrolled in fall 1996, 100% of those judged to have need according to Federal Methodology were aided. *Financial aid deadline (priority):* 4/1. *Financial aid forms:* CSS Financial Aid PROFILE acceptable. FAFSA, state form, institutional form required for some.

Summary of Aid to Needy Students *From gift & self-help combined:* Average need met: 69%. Average amount awarded: $6550 (47% gift

aid, 53% self-help). *Gift aid:* Total: $566,872 (54% from college's own funds, 16% from other college-administered sources, 30% from external sources). Federal Work-Study jobs; 45 part-time jobs.

Need-Based Scholarships & Grants Pell, FSEOG, state, private.

Loans Perkins, PLUS, Stafford, Unsubsidized Stafford.

Non-Need Awards In 1996, a total of 218 non-need awards were made. *Academic Interests/Achievement Awards:* 202 ($272,349 total): general academic, religion/biblical studies. *Creative Arts/Performance Awards:* 9 ($5000 total): music. *Special Achievements/Activities Awards:* 6 ($21,550 total): leadership, religious involvement. *Special Characteristics Awards:* 1 ($2650 total): general special characteristics, adult students, children of faculty/staff.

Other Money-Saving Options Off-campus living (after sophomore year). *Payment Plan:* installment. *Waivers:* full or partial for employees or children of employees and senior citizens.

Contact Ms. April Wendt, Financial Aid/Admissions Counselor, Manhattan Christian College, 1415 Anderson Avenue, Manhattan, KS 66502-4081, 913-539-3571, fax: 913-539-8032.

MANHATTAN COLLEGE
Riverdale, New York

About the Institution Independent/religious, coed. Degrees awarded: B, M. Offers 66 undergraduate majors. Total enrollment: 3,076. Undergraduates: 2,601 (85% state residents). Freshmen: 564.

Undergraduate Expenses (1996–97) Comprehensive fee of $21,080 includes tuition ($13,800 minimum), mandatory fees ($130), and college room and board ($7150 minimum).

Applications Of all full-time undergraduates enrolled in fall 1996, 74% of those who applied for aid were judged to have need according to Federal Methodology, of whom 100% were aided. *Financial aid deadline (priority):* 2/15. *Financial aid forms:* FAFSA, state form, institutional form required. *Regular admission application deadline:* 3/1. Early decision deadline: 12/1.

Summary of Aid to Needy Students *From gift & self-help combined:* Average need met: 79%. Average amount awarded: $12,477 (68% gift aid, 32% self-help). *Gift aid:* Total: $13,771,483 (63% from college's own funds, 7% from other college-administered sources, 30% from external sources). 364 Federal Work-Study jobs (averaging $1937).

Need-Based Scholarships & Grants Pell, FSEOG, state, private, college/university.

Loans Perkins, PLUS, Stafford, Unsubsidized Stafford, private.

Non-Need Awards In 1996, a total of 570 non-need awards were made. *Academic Interests/Achievement Awards:* 329 ($2,110,240 total): general academic, biological sciences, business, foreign languages, mathematics. *Creative Arts/Performance Awards:* 8 ($13,000 total): music. *Special Achievements/Activities Awards:* 15 ($23,000 total): community service, leadership. *Special Characteristics Awards:* 58 ($619,717 total): children of faculty/staff, ROTC participants. *Athletic:* Total: 160 ($1,452,259); Men: 83 ($686,319); Women: 77 ($765,940).

Other Money-Saving Options Accelerated degree, co-op program, Air Force ROTC, cooperative Army ROTC, off-campus living. *Payment Plan:* installment. *Waivers:* full or partial for employees or children of employees.

Contact Office of Financial Aid, Manhattan College, 4513 Manhattan College Parkway, Riverdale, NY 10471, 718-862-7200, fax: 718-862-8019.

MANHATTAN SCHOOL OF MUSIC
New York, New York

About the Institution Independent, coed. Degrees awarded: B, M, D. Offers 6 undergraduate majors. Total enrollment: 862. Undergraduates: 431 (26% state residents). Freshmen: 88.

Undergraduate Expenses (1997–98) Tuition: $17,300. Mandatory fees: $680. College room only: $4270 (minimum).

Applications Of all full-time undergraduates enrolled in fall 1996, 72% of those who applied for aid were judged to have need according to Federal Methodology, of whom 92% were aided. *Financial aid deadline (priority):* 3/15. *Financial aid forms:* FAFSA, CSS Financial Aid PROFILE, institutional form, verification worksheet required. State form required for some. *Admission application deadline:* 3/15.

Summary of Aid to Needy Students *From gift & self-help combined:* Average need met: 43%. Average amount awarded: $12,088 (66% gift aid, 34% self-help). *Gift aid:* Total: $1,618,302 (75% from college's own funds, 3% from other college-administered sources, 22% from external sources). 86 Federal Work-Study jobs (averaging $1000); 30 part-time jobs.

Need-Based Scholarships & Grants Pell, FSEOG, state, college/university.

Loans Perkins, PLUS, Stafford, Unsubsidized Stafford, private, college/university short-term loans ($150 average).

Non-Need Awards *Creative Arts/Performance Awards:* music.

Other Money-Saving Options Off-campus living (after freshman year). *Payment Plan:* installment. *Waivers:* full or partial for employees or children of employees.

Contact Office of Financial Aid, Manhattan School of Music, New York, NY 10027-4698, 212-749-2802.

MANHATTANVILLE COLLEGE
Purchase, New York

About the Institution Independent, coed. Degrees awarded: B, M. Offers 50 undergraduate majors. Total enrollment: 1,500. Undergraduates: 835 (67% state residents). Freshmen: 274.

Undergraduate Expenses (1997–98) Comprehensive fee of $25,300 includes tuition ($16,760), mandatory fees ($540), and college room and board ($8000).

Applications Of all full-time undergraduates enrolled in fall 1996, 94% of those who applied for aid were judged to have need according to Federal Methodology, of whom 100% were aided. *Financial aid deadline (priority):* 3/1. *Financial aid forms:* FAFSA, CSS Financial Aid PROFILE, state form required. *Admission application deadline:* 3/1.

Summary of Aid to Needy Students *From gift & self-help combined:* Average need met: 95%. Average amount awarded: $18,697 (77% gift aid, 23% self-help). *Gift aid:* Total: $8,574,679 (76% from college's own funds, 2% from other college-administered sources, 22% from external sources). Federal Work-Study jobs; 111 part-time jobs.

Non-Need Awards In 1996, a total of 452 non-need awards were made. *Academic Interests/Achievement Awards:* 452 ($2,689,440 total): general academic.

Other Money-Saving Options Accelerated degree, off-campus living. *Payment Plan:* installment. *Waivers:* full or partial for employees or children of employees.

Contact Mr. Peter Brennan, Director of Financial Aid, Manhattanville College, 2900 Purchase Street, Purchase, NY 10577-2132, 914-323-5357.

MANKATO STATE UNIVERSITY
Mankato, Minnesota

About the Institution State-supported, coed. Degrees awarded: A, B, M. Offers 142 undergraduate majors. Total enrollment: 12,695. Undergraduates: 10,652 (84% state residents). Freshmen: 1,537.

Undergraduate Expenses (1996–97) State resident tuition: $2517. Nonresident tuition: $5625. Mandatory fees: $379. College room and board: $2965.

Applications *Financial aid deadline (priority):* 3/15. *Financial aid forms:* FAFSA required. *Admission application deadline:* rolling.

Summary of Aid to Needy Students *From gift & self-help combined:* Average need met: 70%. Federal Work-Study jobs; 1,300 part-time jobs.

Need-Based Scholarships & Grants Pell, FSEOG, state, college/university.

Loans Perkins, PLUS, Stafford, Unsubsidized Stafford, private, college/university short-term loans ($225 average).

Non-Need Awards *Academic Interests/Achievement Awards:* general academic, business, computer science, engineering/technologies, mathematics, physical sciences. *Creative Arts/Performance Awards:* applied art and design, art/fine arts, creative writing, debating, music, theater/drama. *Special Achievements/Activities Awards:* leadership. *Special Characteristics Awards:* children of union members/company employees, local/state students, out-of-state students. *Athletic:* available.

Other Money-Saving Options Accelerated degree, Army ROTC, off-campus living. *Waivers:* full or partial for employees or children of employees and senior citizens.

Contact Office of Financial Aid, Mankato State University, Mankato, MN 56002-8400, 507-389-1185.

MANNES COLLEGE OF MUSIC, NEW SCHOOL FOR SOCIAL RESEARCH
New York, New York

About the Institution Independent, coed. Degrees awarded: B, M. Offers 7 undergraduate majors. Total university enrollment: 5,833. Total unit enrollment: 288. Undergraduates: 126 (49% state residents). Freshmen: 29.

Undergraduate Expenses (1996–97) Tuition: $14,580. Mandatory fees: $225. College room only: $6500.

Applications Of all full-time undergraduates enrolled in fall 1996, 80% of those who applied for aid were judged to have need according to Federal Methodology, of whom 100% were aided. *Financial aid deadline (priority):* 4/1. *Financial aid forms:* FAFSA, institutional form required. State form required for some. *Admission application deadline:* 7/15.

Summary of Aid to Needy Students *From gift & self-help combined:* Average need met: 85%. Average amount awarded: $13,283 (77% gift aid, 23% self-help). *Gift aid:* Total: $651,312 (75% from college's own funds, 19% from other college-administered sources, 6% from external sources). 2 Federal Work-Study jobs (averaging $2200).

Need-Based Scholarships & Grants Pell, FSEOG, state, private, college/university.

Loans Perkins, PLUS, Stafford, Unsubsidized Stafford, private.

Non-Need Awards In 1996, a total of 10 non-need awards were made. *Creative Arts/Performance Awards:* 10 ($30,000 total): music.

Other Money-Saving Options Accelerated degree, off-campus living. *Payment Plan:* installment. *Waivers:* full or partial for employees or children of employees.

Contact Mr. Ramon Vedejo, Assistant Director of Financial Aid, Mannes College of Music, New School for Social Research, 150 West 85th Street, New York, NY 10024-4402, 212-580-0210 Ext. 248, fax: 212-580-1738.

MANSFIELD UNIVERSITY OF PENNSYLVANIA
Mansfield, Pennsylvania

About the Institution State-supported, coed. Degrees awarded: A, B, M. Offers 75 undergraduate majors. Total enrollment: 2,897. Undergraduates: 2,691 (88% state residents). Freshmen: 595.

Undergraduate Expenses (1996–97) State resident tuition: $3368. Nonresident tuition: $8566. Mandatory fees: $866 (minimum). College room and board: $3612. College room only: $2080.

Applications Of all full-time undergraduates enrolled in fall 1996, 65% of those who applied for aid were judged to have need according to Federal Methodology, of whom 98% were aided. *Financial aid deadline:* Applications processed continuously. *Financial aid forms:* FAFSA, institutional form required. State form required for some.

Summary of Aid to Needy Students *From gift & self-help combined:* Average need met: 85%. Average amount awarded: $7460 (32% gift aid, 68% self-help). *Gift aid:* Total: $3,658,633 (4% from college's own funds, 3% from other college-administered sources, 93% from external sources). 190 Federal Work-Study jobs (averaging $1020); 300 part-time jobs.

Need-Based Scholarships & Grants Pell, FSEOG, state, private, college/university.

Loans Perkins, PLUS, Stafford, Unsubsidized Stafford, private.

Non-Need Awards *Academic Interests/Achievement Awards:* 66 ($61,800 total): general academic, biological sciences, communication, education, health fields, mathematics, physical sciences. *Creative Arts/Performance Awards:* 10 ($14,000 total): art/fine arts, music. *Special Characteristics Awards:* 10 ($7200 total): local/state students, members of minorities. *Athletic:* available.

Other Money-Saving Options Accelerated degree. *Payment Plans:* installment, deferred payment. *Waivers:* full or partial for employees or children of employees.

Contact Mr. Christopher W. Vaughn, Director of Financial Planning, Mansfield University of Pennsylvania, Mansfield, PA 16933, 717-662-4878.

MAPLE SPRINGS BAPTIST BIBLE COLLEGE AND SEMINARY
Capital Heights, Maryland

About the Institution Independent/religious.

Applications *Financial aid deadline (priority):* 4/30. *Financial aid forms:* institutional form required.

Summary of Aid to Needy Students *From gift & self-help combined:* Average need met: 0%. Average amount awarded: $0. 1,000 part-time jobs.

Non-Need Awards *Academic Interests/Achievement Awards:* 4 ($1000 total): religion/biblical studies. *Special Characteristics Awards:* general special characteristics.

Contact Ms. Pamela Smith, Assistant Director of Business Affairs, Maple Springs Baptist Bible College and Seminary, 4130 Belt Road, Capital Heights, MD 20743, 301-736-3631, fax: 301-736-6507.

MARANATHA BAPTIST BIBLE COLLEGE
Watertown, Wisconsin

About the Institution Independent/religious, coed. Degrees awarded: A, B, M. Offers 19 undergraduate majors. Total enrollment: 700. Undergraduates: 675 (30% state residents). Freshmen: 198.

Undergraduate Expenses (1996–97) Comprehensive fee of $8920 includes tuition ($5120), mandatory fees ($550), and college room and board ($3250).

Applications 91% of all full-time undergraduates enrolled in fall 1996 applied for aid; of these, 96% were judged to have need according to Federal Methodology, of whom 94% were aided. *Financial aid deadline (priority):* 5/1. *Financial aid forms:* institutional form required; FAFSA, CSS Financial Aid PROFILE acceptable. *Admission application deadline:* rolling.

Summary of Aid to Needy Students *From gift & self-help combined:* Average need met: 42%. Average amount awarded: $4564 (50% gift aid, 50% self-help). *Gift aid:* Total: $1,158,613 (24% from college's own funds, 76% from external sources). 200 part-time jobs.

Need-Based Scholarships & Grants Pell, state, college/university.

Loans PLUS, Stafford, Unsubsidized Stafford.

Non-Need Awards In 1996, a total of 144 non-need awards were made. *Academic Interests/Achievement Awards:* 19 ($13,500 total): general academic. *Special Characteristics Awards:* 125 ($162,250 total): children and siblings of alumni, relatives of clergy, religious affiliation.

Other Money-Saving Options *Payment Plan:* installment. *Waivers:* full or partial for children of alumni and employees or children of employees.

Contact Office of Financial Aid, Maranatha Baptist Bible College, 745 West Main Street, Watertown, WI 53094, 414-261-9300.

MARIAN COLLEGE
Indianapolis, Indiana

About the Institution Independent/religious, coed. Degrees awarded: A, B. Offers 43 undergraduate majors. Total enrollment: 1,304 (96% state residents). Freshmen: 255.

Undergraduate Expenses (1997–98) Comprehensive fee of $16,560 includes tuition ($12,126), mandatory fees ($332), and college room and board ($4102).

Applications *Financial aid deadline (priority):* 3/1. *Financial aid forms:* FAFSA required. *Admission application deadline:* 8/15.

Summary of Aid to Needy Students Federal Work-Study jobs; part-time jobs.

Need-Based Scholarships & Grants Pell, FSEOG, state, private, college/university.

Loans Perkins, PLUS, Stafford, Unsubsidized Stafford, state, private, college/university long-term loans.

Non-Need Awards *Academic Interests/Achievement Awards:* general academic. *Creative Arts/Performance Awards:* music, performing arts, theater/drama. *Special Characteristics Awards:* members of minorities, religious affiliation. *Athletic:* available.

Other Money-Saving Options Accelerated degree, co-op program, cooperative Army ROTC, cooperative Air Force ROTC. *Payment Plans:* installment, deferred payment. *Waivers:* full or partial for children of alumni, employees or children of employees, senior citizens.

Contact Mr. John E. Shelton, Assistant Dean of Financial Aid, Marian College, 3200 Cold Spring Road, Indianapolis, IN 46222-1997, 317-955-6040, fax: 317-955-6424.

MARIAN COLLEGE OF FOND DU LAC
Fond du Lac, Wisconsin

About the Institution Independent/religious, coed. Degrees awarded: B, M. Offers 45 undergraduate majors. Total enrollment: 2,432. Undergraduates: 1,714 (85% state residents). Freshmen: 201.

Undergraduate Expenses (1997–98) Comprehensive fee of $15,558 includes tuition ($11,190), mandatory fees ($180), and college room and board ($4188). College room only: $1958.

Applications Of all full-time undergraduates enrolled in fall 1996, 97% of those who applied for aid were judged to have need according to Federal Methodology, of whom 93% were aided. *Financial aid deadline (priority):* 3/1. *Financial aid forms:* FAFSA, institutional form required; CSS Financial Aid PROFILE acceptable. *Admission application deadline:* rolling.

Summary of Aid to Needy Students *From gift & self-help combined:* Average need met: 88%. Average amount awarded: $9615 (35% gift aid, 65% self-help). *Gift aid:* Total: $2,388,545 (43% from college's

own funds, 4% from other college-administered sources, 53% from external sources). 67 Federal Work-Study jobs (averaging $800); 160 part-time jobs.

Need-Based Scholarships & Grants Pell, FSEOG, state, private, college/university.

Loans Perkins, PLUS, Stafford, Unsubsidized Stafford, Federal Nursing, private.

Non-Need Awards In 1996, a total of 510 non-need awards were made. *Academic Interests/Achievement Awards:* 439 ($1,038,304 total): general academic. *Creative Arts/Performance Awards:* 25 ($30,300 total): music. *Special Characteristics Awards:* 46 ($179,125 total): general special characteristics, children of faculty/staff, children with a deceased or disabled parent, ROTC participants, siblings of current students.

Other Money-Saving Options Accelerated degree, co-op program, Army ROTC, off-campus living (after sophomore year). *Payment Plan:* installment. *Waivers:* full or partial for employees or children of employees and senior citizens.

Contact Ms. Debra E. McKinney, Director of Financial Aid, Marian College of Fond du Lac, 45 South National Avenue, Fond du Lac, WI 54935-4699, 414-923-7614, fax: 414-923-7154.

MARIETTA COLLEGE
Marietta, Ohio

About the Institution Independent, coed. Degrees awarded: A, B, M. Offers 48 undergraduate majors. Total enrollment: 1,256. Undergraduates: 1,081 (57% state residents). Freshmen: 271.

Undergraduate Expenses (1997–98) Comprehensive fee of $20,736 includes tuition ($15,950), mandatory fees ($200), and college room and board ($4586). College room only: $2450.

Applications 96% of all full-time undergraduates enrolled in fall 1996 applied for aid; of these, 83% were judged to have need according to Federal Methodology, of whom 91% were aided. *Financial aid deadline:* Applications processed continuously. *Financial aid forms:* FAFSA, institutional form required. *Admission application deadline:* 04/15.

Summary of Aid to Needy Students *From gift & self-help combined:* Average need met: 94%. Average amount awarded: $13,734 (63% gift aid, 37% self-help). *Gift aid:* Total: $6,824,281 (81% from college's own funds, 12% from other college-administered sources, 7% from external sources). 730 Federal Work-Study jobs (averaging $1525); part-time jobs.

Need-Based Scholarships & Grants Pell, FSEOG, state, private, college/university.

Loans Perkins, PLUS, Stafford, Unsubsidized Stafford, state, private, college/university short-term loans ($150 average), college/university long-term loans ($3536 average).

Non-Need Awards In 1996, a total of 334 non-need awards were made. *Academic Interests/Achievement Awards:* 317 ($2,081,248 total): general academic. *Creative Arts/Performance Awards:* 17 ($43,150 total): art/fine arts.

Other Money-Saving Options Accelerated degree, cooperative Army ROTC. *Payment Plan:* installment. *Waivers:* full or partial for employees or children of employees.

Contact Mr. James T. Begany, Director of Student Financial Services, Marietta College, 215 Fifth Street, Marietta, OH 45750-4000, 614-376-4714, fax: 614-376-8888.

MARIST COLLEGE
Poughkeepsie, New York

About the Institution Independent, coed. Degrees awarded: B, M. Offers 46 undergraduate majors. Total enrollment: 4,372. Undergraduates: 3,842 (68% state residents). Freshmen: 876.

Undergraduate Expenses (1996–97) Comprehensive fee of $18,990 includes tuition ($12,070), mandatory fees ($320), and college room and board ($6600). College room only: $2100.

Applications Of all full-time undergraduates enrolled in fall 1996, 86% of those who applied for aid were judged to have need according to Federal Methodology, of whom 100% were aided. *Financial aid deadline (priority):* 3/1. *Financial aid forms:* FAFSA required. State form required for some. *Regular admission application deadline:* 3/1. Early action deadline: 12/1.

Summary of Aid to Needy Students *From gift & self-help combined:* Average need met: 65%. Average amount awarded: $8573 (56% gift aid, 44% self-help). *Gift aid:* Total: $10,935,409 (65% from college's own funds, 3% from other college-administered sources, 32% from external sources). 824 Federal Work-Study jobs (averaging $900); 555 part-time jobs.

Need-Based Scholarships & Grants Pell, FSEOG, state, private, college/university.

Loans Perkins, PLUS, Stafford, Unsubsidized Stafford.

Non-Need Awards In 1996, a total of 438 non-need awards were made. *Academic Interests/Achievement Awards:* 368 ($1,221,923 total): general academic. *Creative Arts/Performance Awards:* 10 ($22,000 total): debating, music. *Athletic:* Total: 60 ($574,157); Men: 33 ($315,589); Women: 27 ($258,568).

Other Money-Saving Options Accelerated degree, co-op program, off-campus living. *Payment Plan:* installment. *Waivers:* full or partial for employees or children of employees.

Contact Ms. Leesa Marcinelli, Acting Assistant Director of Financial Aid, Marist College, 290 North Road, Poughkeepsie, NY 12601-1387, 914-575-3230, fax: 914-471-6213.

MARLBORO COLLEGE
Marlboro, Vermont

About the Institution Independent, coed. Degrees awarded: B, M. Offers 100 undergraduate majors. Total enrollment: 282. Undergraduates: 280 (17% state residents). Freshmen: 58.

Undergraduate Expenses (1996–97) Comprehensive fee of $26,327 includes tuition ($19,295), mandatory fees ($587), and college room and board ($6445). College room only: $2760.

Applications 89% of all full-time undergraduates enrolled in fall 1996 applied for aid; of these, 88% were judged to have need according to Federal Methodology, of whom 100% were aided. *Financial aid deadline (priority):* 3/1. *Financial aid forms:* FAFSA, CSS Financial Aid PROFILE required. State form required for some. *Regular admission application deadline:* rolling. Early decision deadline: 11/15. Early action deadline: 1/15.

Summary of Aid to Needy Students *From gift & self-help combined:* Average need met: 95%. Average amount awarded: $16,300 (68% gift aid, 32% self-help). *Gift aid:* Total: $2,628,223 (81% from college's own funds, 4% from other college-administered sources, 15% from external sources). 204 Federal Work-Study jobs (averaging $1930); 10 part-time jobs.

Need-Based Scholarships & Grants Pell, FSEOG, state, private, college/university.

Loans PLUS, Stafford, Unsubsidized Stafford, college/university short-term loans ($50 average), college/university long-term loans ($500 average).

Non-Need Awards *Academic Interests/Achievement Awards:* general academic.

Other Money-Saving Options Accelerated degree, off-campus living (after freshman year). *Payment Plan:* installment. *Waivers:* full or partial for employees or children of employees.

Contact Office of Financial Aid, Marlboro College, South Road, Marlboro, VT 05344, 802-257-4333.

MARQUETTE UNIVERSITY
Milwaukee, Wisconsin

About the Institution Independent/religious, coed. Degrees awarded: A, B, M, D, P. Offers 78 undergraduate majors. Total enrollment: 10,539. Undergraduates: 7,474 (49% state residents). Freshmen: 1,420.

Undergraduate Expenses (1997–98) Comprehensive fee of $18,420 includes tuition ($13,840 minimum), mandatory fees ($224), and college room and board ($4356 minimum).

Applications 66% of all full-time undergraduates enrolled in fall 1996 applied for aid; of these, 88% were judged to have need according to Federal Methodology, of whom 100% were aided. *Financial aid deadline (priority):* 3/1. *Financial aid forms:* FAFSA required. Institutional form required for some. *Admission application deadline:* rolling.

Summary of Aid to Needy Students *From gift & self-help combined:* Average need met: 92%. Average amount awarded: $14,146 (50% gift aid, 50% self-help). *Gift aid:* Total: $29,809,612 (61% from college's own funds, 7% from other college-administered sources, 32% from external sources). 2,064 Federal Work-Study jobs (averaging $1843); 3,600 part-time jobs.

Need-Based Scholarships & Grants Pell, FSEOG, state, private, college/university.

Loans Perkins, PLUS, Stafford, Unsubsidized Stafford, Federal Nursing, private, college/university long-term loans ($1000 average).

Non-Need Awards In 1996, a total of 3,782 non-need awards were made. *Academic Interests/Achievement Awards:* 2,809 ($8,251,261 total): general academic, biological sciences, business, communication, engineering/technologies, foreign languages, health fields, mathematics. *Creative Arts/Performance Awards:* 7 ($9500 total): theater/drama. *Special Achievements/Activities Awards:* 161 ($337,882 total): leadership. *Special Characteristics Awards:* 650 ($977,043 total): ROTC participants, siblings of current students. *Athletic:* Total: 155 ($1,551,838); Men: 80 ($719,361); Women: 75 ($832,477).

Other Money-Saving Options Accelerated degree, co-op program, Army ROTC, Naval ROTC, Air Force ROTC, off-campus living (after sophomore year). *Payment Plans:* tuition prepayment, installment. *Waivers:* full or partial for employees or children of employees and senior citizens.

Contact Mr. Daniel Goyette, Director of Financial Aid, Marquette University, 1212 West Wisconsin Avenue, PO Box 1881, Milwaukee, WI 53201-1881, 414-288-5266.

MARSHALL UNIVERSITY
Huntington, West Virginia

About the Institution State-supported, coed. Degrees awarded: A, B, M, D, P. Offers 87 undergraduate majors. Total enrollment: 11,066. Undergraduates: 8,778 (85% state residents). Freshmen: 1,642.

Undergraduate Expenses (1997–98) State resident tuition: $2184. Nonresident tuition: $6066. College room and board: $4420. College room only: $2266.

Applications Of all full-time undergraduates enrolled in fall 1996, 82% of those who applied for aid were judged to have need according to Federal Methodology, of whom 97% were aided. *Financial aid deadline (priority):* 2/1. *Financial aid forms:* FAFSA required. *Admission application deadline:* rolling.

Summary of Aid to Needy Students *From gift & self-help combined:* Average need met: 83%. Average amount awarded: $5672 (40% gift aid, 60% self-help). *Gift aid:* Total: $7,978,141 (18% from college's own funds, 24% from other college-administered sources, 58% from external sources). Federal Work-Study jobs; part-time jobs.

Need-Based Scholarships & Grants Pell, FSEOG, state.

Loans Perkins, PLUS, Stafford, Unsubsidized Stafford, Federal Nursing, Primary Care, state, private, college/university short-term loans ($200 average), college/university long-term loans.

Non-Need Awards *Academic Interests/Achievement Awards:* general academic. *Creative Arts/Performance Awards:* 63 ($154,545 total): general creative, debating, music, theater/drama. *Special Characteristics Awards:* 1 ($1600 total): veterans' children. *Athletic:* Total: 268 ($1,570,021).

Other Money-Saving Options Accelerated degree, co-op program, Army ROTC, off-campus living (after sophomore year). *Payment Plans:* installment, deferred payment.

Contact Ms. Nadine A. Hamrick, Associate Director, Student Financial Aid, Marshall University, 400 Hal Greer Boulevard, Huntington, WV 25755-2020, 304-696-2277, fax: 304-696-3242.

MARS HILL COLLEGE
Mars Hill, North Carolina

About the Institution Independent/religious, coed. Degrees awarded: B. Offers 63 undergraduate majors. Total enrollment: 1,050 (60% state residents). Freshmen: 391.

Undergraduate Expenses (1997–98) Comprehensive fee of $12,700 includes tuition ($8350), mandatory fees ($550), and college room and board ($3800). College room only: $1700.

Applications Of all full-time undergraduates enrolled in fall 1996, 100% of those judged to have need according to Federal Methodology were aided. *Financial aid deadline (priority):* 4/15. *Financial aid forms:* FAFSA, institutional form required; CSS Financial Aid PROFILE acceptable. *Admission application deadline:* rolling.

Summary of Aid to Needy Students *From gift & self-help combined:* Average need met: 85%. Average amount awarded: $9000 (55% gift aid, 45% self-help). *Gift aid:* Total: $4,749,629 (46% from college's own funds, 36% from other college-administered sources, 18% from external sources). 266 Federal Work-Study jobs (averaging $2200); 300 part-time jobs.

Need-Based Scholarships & Grants Pell, FSEOG, state, private, college/university.

Loans Perkins, PLUS, Stafford, Unsubsidized Stafford, private, college/university long-term loans ($2000 average).

Non-Need Awards In 1996, a total of 923 non-need awards were made. *Academic Interests/Achievement Awards:* 229 ($712,719 total): general academic, religion/biblical studies. *Creative Arts/Performance Awards:* 122 ($118,550 total): dance, music, theater/drama. *Special Achievements/Activities Awards:* 59 ($55,800 total): religious involvement. *Special Characteristics Awards:* 335 ($295,870 total): adult students, children of faculty/staff, local/state students, relatives of clergy, religious affiliation. *Athletic:* Total: 178 ($696,421); Men: 118 ($515,156); Women: 60 ($181,265).

Other Money-Saving Options Accelerated degree, off-campus living (after sophomore year). *Payment Plan:* installment. *Waivers:* full or partial for employees or children of employees.

Contact Office of Financial Aid, Mars Hill College, Mars Hill, NC 28754, 704-689-1201.

MARTIN LUTHER COLLEGE
New Ulm, Minnesota

About the Institution Independent/religious, coed. Degrees awarded: B. Offers 4 undergraduate majors. Total enrollment: 817 (21% state residents). Freshmen: 223.

Undergraduate Expenses (1997–98) Comprehensive fee of $6670 includes tuition ($3990), mandatory fees ($475), and college room and board ($2205). College room only: $525.

Applications 82% of all full-time undergraduates enrolled in fall 1996 applied for aid; of these, 86% were judged to have need according to Federal Methodology, of whom 98% were aided. *Financial aid deadline (priority):* 5/1. *Financial aid forms:* FAFSA, institutional form required. *Admission application deadline:* 5/1.

Summary of Aid to Needy Students *From gift & self-help combined:* Average need met: 99%. Average amount awarded: $4762 (60% gift aid, 40% self-help). *Gift aid:* Total: $1,650,173 (41% from college's own funds, 6% from other college-administered sources, 53% from external sources). 82 Federal Work-Study jobs (averaging $710); 318 part-time jobs.

Need-Based Scholarships & Grants Pell, FSEOG, state, private, college/university.

Loans Perkins, PLUS, Stafford, Unsubsidized Stafford, state, college/university short-term loans ($750 average), college/university long-term loans ($1950 average).

Non-Need Awards In 1996, a total of 230 non-need awards were made. *Academic Interests/Achievement Awards:* 214 ($136,700 total). *Creative Arts/Performance Awards:* 13 ($2450 total): music. *Special Achievements/Activities Awards:* 3 ($1200 total): general special achievements/activities.

Another Money-Saving Option *Payment Plan:* installment.

Contact Mr. Robert Krueger, Director of Financial Aid, Martin Luther College, 1995 Luther Court, New Ulm, MN 56073-3965, 507-354-8221 Ext. 225.

MARTIN METHODIST COLLEGE
Pulaski, Tennessee

About the Institution Independent/religious, coed. Degrees awarded: A, B. Offers 64 undergraduate majors. Total enrollment: 535 (81% state residents). Freshmen: 155.

Undergraduate Expenses (1997–98) Comprehensive fee of $9950 includes tuition ($6900) and college room and board ($3050).

Applications Of all full-time undergraduates enrolled in fall 1996, 70% of those who applied for aid were judged to have need according to Federal Methodology, of whom 100% were aided. *Financial aid deadline (priority):* 3/1. *Financial aid forms:* FAFSA, institutional form required; CSS Financial Aid PROFILE acceptable. *Admission application deadline:* 8/30.

Summary of Aid to Needy Students *From gift & self-help combined:* Average need met: 76%. Average amount awarded: $5891 (68% gift aid, 32% self-help). *Gift aid:* Total: $1,480,175 (38% from college's own funds, 43% from other college-administered sources, 19% from external sources). 38 Federal Work-Study jobs (averaging $1000); 52 part-time jobs.

Need-Based Scholarships & Grants Pell, FSEOG, state, private, college/university.

Loans PLUS, Stafford, Unsubsidized Stafford, private.

Non-Need Awards In 1996, a total of 298 non-need awards were made. *Academic Interests/Achievement Awards:* 59 ($57,375 total): general academic. *Creative Arts/Performance Awards:* 31 ($24,955 total): art/fine arts, music, theater/drama. *Special Characteristics Awards:* 163 ($95,765 total): local/state students, religious affiliation. *Athletic:* Total: 45 ($418,500).

Other Money-Saving Options Off-campus living (after sophomore year). *Payment Plan:* installment. *Waivers:* full or partial for employees or children of employees.

Contact Ms. Anita Beecham, Financial Aid Assistant, Martin Methodist College, 433 West Madison Street, Pulaski, TN 38478-2716, 615-363-9808, fax: 615-363-9818.

MARTIN UNIVERSITY
Indianapolis, Indiana

About the Institution Independent, coed. Degrees awarded: B, M. Offers 29 undergraduate majors. Total enrollment: 649. Undergraduates: 452 (98% state residents). Freshmen: 47.

Undergraduate Expenses (1997–98) Tuition: $8250. Mandatory fees: $120.

Applications *Financial aid deadline (priority):* 3/1. *Financial aid forms:* FAFSA required; CSS Financial Aid PROFILE, state form, institutional form acceptable. *Admission application deadline:* rolling.

Summary of Aid to Needy Students 4 Federal Work-Study jobs (averaging $942).

Need-Based Scholarships & Grants Pell, FSEOG, state, private, college/university.

Loans PLUS, Stafford, Unsubsidized Stafford, college/university short-term loans ($600 average), college/university long-term loans ($200 average).

Non-Need Awards In 1996, a total of 2 non-need awards were made. *Creative Arts/Performance Awards:* 2: music.

Other Money-Saving Options Accelerated degree. *Payment Plans:* installment, deferred payment. *Waivers:* full or partial for employees or children of employees.

Contact Mrs. Yvette C. Ellis, Director of Financial Aid, Martin University, Indianapolis, IN 46218-3867, 317-543-3258.

MARY BALDWIN COLLEGE
Staunton, Virginia

About the Institution Independent/religious, primarily women. Degrees awarded: B, M. Offers 32 undergraduate majors. Total enrollment: 2,132. Undergraduates: 2,062 (58% state residents). Freshmen: 286.

Undergraduate Expenses (1997–98) Comprehensive fee of $20,360 includes tuition ($13,200), mandatory fees ($160), and college room and board ($7000).

Applications 73% of all full-time undergraduates enrolled in fall 1996 applied for aid; of these, 87% were judged to have need according to Federal Methodology, of whom 100% were aided. *Financial aid deadline (priority):* 5/15. *Financial aid forms:* FAFSA required. State form required for some. *Admission application deadline:* rolling.

Summary of Aid to Needy Students *From gift & self-help combined:* Average need met: 81%. Average amount awarded: $12,533 (67% gift aid, 33% self-help). *Gift aid:* Total: $5,512,146 (67% from college's own funds, 26% from other college-administered sources, 7% from external sources). 293 Federal Work-Study jobs (averaging $1300); 94 part-time jobs.

Need-Based Scholarships & Grants Pell, FSEOG, state, private, college/university.

Loans Perkins, PLUS, Stafford, Unsubsidized Stafford, college/university short-term loans ($50 average).

Non-Need Awards In 1996, a total of 870 non-need awards were made. *Academic Interests/Achievement Awards:* 726 ($3,006,779 total): general academic. *Special Characteristics Awards:* 144 ($344,956 total): children of faculty/staff, members of minorities, relatives of clergy, siblings of current students.

Other Money-Saving Options Accelerated degree, cooperative Army ROTC, cooperative Naval ROTC, cooperative Air Force ROTC. *Payment Plan:* installment. *Waivers:* full or partial for employees or children of employees.

Contact Office of Financial Aid, Mary Baldwin College, Financial Aid Office, Staunton, VA 24401, 540-887-7000.

MARYCREST INTERNATIONAL UNIVERSITY
Davenport, Iowa

About the Institution Independent, coed. Degrees awarded: A, B, M. Offers 39 undergraduate majors. Total enrollment: 905. Undergraduates: 564 (60% state residents). Freshmen: 63.

Undergraduate Expenses (1997–98) Comprehensive fee of $15,898 includes tuition ($11,226), mandatory fees ($210), and college room and board ($4462). College room only: $1800.

Applications *Financial aid deadline (priority):* 4/1. *Financial aid forms:* CSS Financial Aid PROFILE, state form, institutional form acceptable. FAFSA required for some. *Admission application deadline:* rolling.

Summary of Aid to Needy Students *From gift & self-help combined:* Average need met: 75%. Average amount awarded: $6245 (44% gift aid, 56% self-help). *Gift aid:* Total: $847,413 (54% from college's own funds, 29% from other college-administered sources, 17% from external sources). Federal Work-Study jobs; 9 part-time jobs.

Loans Perkins, PLUS, Stafford, Unsubsidized Stafford.

Non-Need Awards *Academic Interests/Achievement Awards:* available. *Creative Arts/Performance Awards:* journalism/publications, performing arts. *Special Achievements/Activities Awards:* leadership. *Special Characteristics Awards:* general special characteristics, out-of-state students. *Athletic:* Total: 101 ($136,565); Men: 63 ($93,765); Women: 38 ($42,800).

Other Money-Saving Options Co-op program, off-campus living. *Payment Plan:* deferred payment. *Waivers:* full or partial for employees or children of employees.

Contact Ms. Judith Stark, Director of Financial Aid, Marycrest International University, 1607 West 12th Street, Davenport, IA 52804-4096, 319-326-9363, fax: 319-327-9606.

MARYGROVE COLLEGE
Detroit, Michigan

About the Institution Independent/religious, primarily women. Degrees awarded: A, B, M. Offers 30 undergraduate majors. Total enrollment: 2,510. Undergraduates: 1,087 (99% state residents). Freshmen: 262.

Undergraduate Expenses (1996–97) Comprehensive fee of $13,216 includes tuition ($8836), mandatory fees ($220), and college room and board ($4160).

Applications 94% of all full-time undergraduates enrolled in fall 1996 applied for aid; of these,100% were judged to have need according to Federal Methodology, of whom 100% were aided. *Financial aid deadline (priority):* 3/1. *Financial aid forms:* FAFSA, institutional form, nontaxable income verification, independent student verification required; CSS Financial Aid PROFILE, state form acceptable. *Admission application deadline:* 8/15.

Summary of Aid to Needy Students *From gift & self-help combined:* Average need met: 75%. Average amount awarded: $13,000 (55% gift aid, 45% self-help). *Gift aid:* Total: $1,755,000 (24% from college's own funds, 47% from other college-administered sources, 29% from external sources). 95 Federal Work-Study jobs (averaging $1700); 25 part-time jobs.

Need-Based Scholarships & Grants Pell, FSEOG, state, private, college/university.

Loans Perkins, PLUS, Stafford, Unsubsidized Stafford, state, private.

Non-Need Awards In 1996, a total of 239 non-need awards were made. *Academic Interests/Achievement Awards:* 77 ($188,000 total): general academic, business, computer science, education, health fields, physical sciences, social sciences. *Creative Arts/Performance Awards:* 15 ($35,000 total): cinema/film/broadcasting, dance, performing arts. *Special Achievements/Activities Awards:* 2 ($4000 total): leadership.

Special Characteristics Awards: 145 ($145,000 total): adult students, handicapped students, local/state students, out-of-state students, previous college experience.

Other Money-Saving Options Co-op program, off-campus living. *Payment Plan:* installment. *Waivers:* full or partial for employees or children of employees and senior citizens.

Contact Mr. Donald Hurt, Director of Financial Aid, Marygrove College, Detroit, MI 48221-2599, 313-862-8000 Ext. 436.

MARYLAND INSTITUTE, COLLEGE OF ART
Baltimore, Maryland

About the Institution Independent, coed. Degrees awarded: B, M. Offers 14 undergraduate majors. Total enrollment: 1,064. Undergraduates: 926 (28% state residents). Freshmen: 246.

Undergraduate Expenses (1997–98) Comprehensive fee of $21,960 includes tuition ($16,590), mandatory fees ($170), and college room and board ($5200). College room only: $4100 (minimum).

Applications 79% of all full-time undergraduates enrolled in fall 1996 applied for aid; of these, 82% were judged to have need according to Federal Methodology, of whom 100% were aided. *Financial aid deadline (priority):* 3/1. *Financial aid forms:* FAFSA, institutional form required. *Regular admission application deadline:* rolling. Early decision deadline: 11/15.

Summary of Aid to Needy Students *From gift & self-help combined:* Average need met: 73%. Average amount awarded: $11,500 (64% gift aid, 36% self-help). *Gift aid:* Total: $4,483,438 (71% from college's own funds, 5% from other college-administered sources, 24% from external sources). 150 Federal Work-Study jobs (averaging $1100); 200 part-time jobs.

Need-Based Scholarships & Grants Pell, FSEOG, state, private, college/university.

Loans Perkins, PLUS, Stafford, Unsubsidized Stafford, private.

Non-Need Awards In 1996, a total of 236 non-need awards were made. *Academic Interests/Achievement Awards:* 23 ($43,875 total): general academic. *Creative Arts/Performance Awards:* 196 ($305,975 total): art/fine arts. *Special Characteristics Awards:* 17 ($60,890 total): children of faculty/staff, international students, local/state students, religious affiliation.

Other Money-Saving Options Cooperative Army ROTC, off-campus living. *Payment Plan:* installment. *Waivers:* full or partial for employees or children of employees.

Contact Ms. Diane Prengaman, Director of Financial Aid, Maryland Institute, College of Art, 1300 Mount Royal Avenue, Baltimore, MD 21217-4192, 410-225-2285, fax: 410-669-9206.

MARYMOUNT COLLEGE
Tarrytown, New York

About the Institution Independent, primarily women. Degrees awarded: B. Offers 56 undergraduate majors. Total enrollment: 947 (80% state residents). Freshmen: 131.

Undergraduate Expenses (1997–98) Comprehensive fee of $21,015 includes tuition ($13,370), mandatory fees ($445), and college room and board ($7200).

Applications *Financial aid deadline (priority):* 4/15. *Financial aid forms:* FAFSA, institutional form required. State form required for some. *Admission application deadline:* 4/15.

Summary of Aid to Needy Students *From gift & self-help combined:* Average need met: 84%. Average amount awarded: $10,922 (64% gift aid, 36% self-help). *Gift aid:* Total: $6,296,204 (33% from college's own funds, 56% from other college-administered sources, 11% from external sources). 300 Federal Work-Study jobs (averaging $1200); 15 part-time jobs.

Need-Based Scholarships & Grants Pell, FSEOG, state, private, college/university.

Loans Perkins, PLUS, Stafford, Unsubsidized Stafford, private.

Non-Need Awards In 1996, a total of 396 non-need awards were made. *Academic Interests/Achievement Awards:* general academic. *Creative Arts/Performance Awards:* art/fine arts. *Special Achievements/Activities Awards:* community service, leadership. *Special Characteristics Awards:* general special characteristics.

Other Money-Saving Options Off-campus living. *Payment Plans:* installment, deferred payment. *Waivers:* full or partial for employees or children of employees.

Contact Financial Aid Office, Marymount College, Tarrytown, NY 10591-3796, 914-332-8345.

MARYMOUNT MANHATTAN COLLEGE
New York, New York

About the Institution Independent, coed. Degrees awarded: B. Offers 18 undergraduate majors. Total enrollment: 2,015 (74% state residents). Freshmen: 288.

Undergraduate Expenses (1996–97) Comprehensive fee of $17,500 includes tuition ($11,650), mandatory fees ($250), and college room and board ($5600).

Applications 72% of all full-time undergraduates enrolled in fall 1996 applied for aid; of these, 90% were judged to have need according to Federal Methodology, of whom 100% were aided. *Financial aid deadline (priority):* 2/15. *Financial aid forms:* FAFSA required. State form required for some. *Regular admission application deadline:* rolling. Early decision deadline: 11/1.

Summary of Aid to Needy Students *From gift & self-help combined:* Average need met: 80%. Average amount awarded: $10,638 (69% gift aid, 31% self-help). *Gift aid:* Total: $5,533,535 (55% from college's own funds, 6% from other college-administered sources, 39% from external sources). 60 Federal Work-Study jobs (averaging $2027); 160 part-time jobs.

Need-Based Scholarships & Grants Pell, FSEOG, state, private, college/university.

Loans PLUS, Stafford, Unsubsidized Stafford.

Non-Need Awards In 1996, a total of 847 non-need awards were made. *Academic Interests/Achievement Awards:* 601 ($2,802,314 total): general academic. *Creative Arts/Performance Awards:* 157 ($389,050 total): art/fine arts, dance, theater/drama. *Special Achievements/Activities Awards:* 42 ($318,251 total): leadership. *Special Characteristics Awards:* 47 ($335,529 total): children and siblings of alumni, international students.

Other Money-Saving Options Accelerated degree, off-campus living. *Payment Plan:* deferred payment.

Contact Ms. Michele Boracci, Director of Financial Aid, Marymount Manhattan College, 221 East 71st Street, New York, NY 10021-4597, 212-517-0463, fax: 212-517-0413.

MARYMOUNT UNIVERSITY
Arlington, Virginia

About the Institution Independent/religious, coed. Degrees awarded: A, B, M. Offers 30 undergraduate majors. Total enrollment: 3,845. Undergraduates: 1,940 (56% state residents). Freshmen: 234.

Undergraduate Expenses (1997–98) Comprehensive fee of $18,580 includes tuition ($12,770) and college room and board ($5810).

Applications 82% of all full-time undergraduates enrolled in fall 1996 applied for aid; of these, 76% were judged to have need according to Federal Methodology, of whom 98% were aided. *Financial aid deadline*

(priority): 3/1. *Financial aid forms:* FAFSA, institutional form required. State form required for some. *Admission application deadline:* rolling.

Summary of Aid to Needy Students *From gift & self-help combined:* Average need met: 84%. Average amount awarded: $11,746 (66% gift aid, 34% self-help). *Gift aid:* Total: $5,768,908 (72% from college's own funds, 16% from other college-administered sources, 12% from external sources). 100 Federal Work-Study jobs (averaging $1600); 300 part-time jobs.

Need-Based Scholarships & Grants Pell, FSEOG.

Loans Perkins, PLUS, Stafford, Unsubsidized Stafford, Federal Nursing.

Non-Need Awards In 1996, a total of 349 non-need awards were made. *Academic Interests/Achievement Awards:* 287 ($951,750 total): general academic, business. *Special Achievements/Activities Awards:* 40 ($17,900 total): general special achievements/activities, leadership. *Special Characteristics Awards:* 22 ($72,260 total): children and siblings of alumni, children of faculty/staff, international students, ROTC participants, siblings of current students.

Other Money-Saving Options Accelerated degree, cooperative Army ROTC, off-campus living (after sophomore year). *Payment Plans:* installment, deferred payment. *Waivers:* full or partial for children of alumni, employees or children of employees, senior citizens.

Contact Ms. Debbie A. Raines, Director of Financial Aid, Marymount University, 2807 North Glebe Road, Arlington, VA 22207-4299, 703-284-1530, fax: 703-516-4771.

MARYVILLE COLLEGE
Maryville, Tennessee

About the Institution Independent/religious, coed. Degrees awarded: B. Offers 42 undergraduate majors. Total enrollment: 927 (66% state residents). Freshmen: 259.

Undergraduate Expenses (1996–97) Comprehensive fee of $17,755 includes tuition ($13,030), mandatory fees ($225), and college room and board ($4500). College room only: $2140.

Applications *Financial aid deadline (priority):* 3/1. *Financial aid forms:* FAFSA required. *Admission application deadline:* 3/1.

Summary of Aid to Needy Students *From gift & self-help combined:* Average need met: 76%. Average amount awarded: $13,365 (57% gift aid, 43% self-help). *Gift aid:* Total: $3,139,846 (60% from college's own funds, 19% from other college-administered sources, 21% from external sources). 181 Federal Work-Study jobs (averaging $1000); 75 part-time jobs.

Need-Based Scholarships & Grants Pell, FSEOG, state, private, college/university.

Loans Perkins, PLUS, Stafford, Unsubsidized Stafford, state, college/university long-term loans ($1000 average).

Non-Need Awards In 1996, a total of 1,102 non-need awards were made. *Academic Interests/Achievement Awards:* 666 ($2,493,541 total): general academic. *Creative Arts/Performance Awards:* 96 ($210,250 total): art/fine arts, music, theater/drama. *Special Achievements/Activities Awards:* 155 ($181,430 total): community service. *Special Characteristics Awards:* 185 ($212,500 total): local/state students, relatives of clergy, religious affiliation.

Other Money-Saving Options *Payment Plans:* installment, deferred payment. *Waivers:* full or partial for employees or children of employees.

Contact Ms. Venita Jones, Director of Financial Aid, Maryville College, 520 East Lamar Alexander Parkway, Maryville, TN 37804-5907, 423-981-8100, fax: 423-981-8010.

MARYVILLE UNIVERSITY OF SAINT LOUIS
St. Louis, Missouri

About the Institution Independent, coed. Degrees awarded: B, M. Offers 41 undergraduate majors. Total enrollment: 3,196. Undergraduates: 2,706 (81% state residents). Freshmen: 215.

Undergraduate Expenses (1997–98) Comprehensive fee of $15,910 includes tuition ($10,850), mandatory fees ($60), and college room and board ($5000).

Applications 85% of all full-time undergraduates enrolled in fall 1996 applied for aid; of these, 88% were judged to have need according to Federal Methodology, of whom 100% were aided. *Financial aid deadline (priority):* 2/1. *Financial aid forms:* FAFSA, institutional form required; CSS Financial Aid PROFILE acceptable. *Admission application deadline:* rolling.

Summary of Aid to Needy Students *From gift & self-help combined:* Average need met: 64%. Average amount awarded: $9188 (38% gift aid, 62% self-help). *Gift aid:* Total: $3,211,979 (73% from college's own funds, 17% from other college-administered sources, 10% from external sources). 103 Federal Work-Study jobs (averaging $1350); 95 part-time jobs.

Need-Based Scholarships & Grants Pell, FSEOG, state, private, college/university, Vocational Rehabilitation Grants, Teacher Discount.

Loans Perkins, PLUS, Federal Nursing, Federal Ford Subsidized and Unsubsidized Loans.

Non-Need Awards In 1996, a total of 678 non-need awards were made. *Academic Interests/Achievement Awards:* 445 ($1,387,967 total): general academic, education. *Creative Arts/Performance Awards:* 6 ($25,500 total): applied art and design, art/fine arts. *Special Achievements/Activities Awards:* 161 ($279,700 total): general special achievements/activities, community service, leadership. *Special Characteristics Awards:* 66 ($199,027 total): children of current students, members of minorities, parents of current students, religious affiliation, siblings of current students, spouses of current students, twins.

Other Money-Saving Options Accelerated degree, co-op program, cooperative Army ROTC, off-campus living. *Payment Plans:* installment, deferred payment. *Waivers:* full or partial for employees or children of employees and senior citizens.

Contact Ms. Martha Harbaugh, Director of Financial Aid, Maryville University of Saint Louis, 13550 Conway Road, Gander Hall, St. Louis, MO 63141-7299, 314-529-9360, fax: 314-542-9085.

MARY WASHINGTON COLLEGE
Fredericksburg, Virginia

About the Institution State-supported, coed. Degrees awarded: B, M. Offers 40 undergraduate majors. Total enrollment: 3,745. Undergraduates: 3,694 (70% state residents). Freshmen: 736.

Undergraduate Expenses (1997–98) State resident tuition: $3556. Nonresident tuition: $8516. College room and board: $5080.

Applications 74% of all full-time undergraduates enrolled in fall 1996 applied for aid; of these, 65% were judged to have need according to Federal Methodology, of whom 99% were aided. *Financial aid deadline:* Applications processed continuously. *Financial aid forms:* FAFSA required. *Regular admission application deadline:* 2/1. Early decision deadline: 11/1. Early action deadline: 1/15.

Summary of Aid to Needy Students *From gift & self-help combined:* Average amount awarded: $3343 (28% gift aid, 72% self-help). *Gift aid:* Total: $1,390,000 (26% from college's own funds, 54% from other college-administered sources, 20% from external sources). 70 Federal Work-Study jobs (averaging $700); 775 part-time jobs.

Need-Based Scholarships & Grants Pell, FSEOG, state, college/university.

Loans Perkins, PLUS, Stafford, Unsubsidized Stafford, college/university short-term loans ($150 average).

Non-Need Awards In 1996, a total of 405 non-need awards were made. *Academic Interests/Achievement Awards:* 220 ($229,000 total): general academic. *Creative Arts/Performance Awards:* 25 ($32,600 total): art/fine arts, dance, journalism/publications, music, theater/drama. *Special Characteristics Awards:* 160 ($200,000 total): adult students, children and siblings of alumni, children of faculty/staff, local/state students, members of minorities.

Other Money-Saving Options Accelerated degree, co-op program, off-campus living. *Payment Plan:* installment. *Waivers:* full or partial for minority students.

Contact Mr. Robert U. MacDonald, Associate Dean for Financial Aid, Mary Washington College, 1301 College Avenue, Fredericksburg, VA 22401-5358, 540-654-2468, fax: 540-654-1858.

MARYWOOD UNIVERSITY
Scranton, Pennsylvania

About the Institution Independent/religious, coed. Degrees awarded: A, B, M, D. Offers 79 undergraduate majors. Total enrollment: 2,926. Undergraduates: 1,758 (77% state residents). Freshmen: 273.

Undergraduate Expenses (1997–98) Comprehensive fee of $19,349 includes tuition ($12,989), mandatory fees ($660), and college room and board ($5700).

Applications 97% of all full-time undergraduates enrolled in fall 1996 applied for aid; of these, 80% were judged to have need according to Federal Methodology, of whom 100% were aided. *Financial aid deadline (priority):* 2/15. *Financial aid forms:* FAFSA, institutional form required. *Admission application deadline:* rolling.

Summary of Aid to Needy Students *From gift & self-help combined:* Average need met: 77%. Average amount awarded: $12,047 (57% gift aid, 43% self-help). *Gift aid:* Total: $7,564,134 (64% from college's own funds, 2% from other college-administered sources, 34% from external sources). 497 Federal Work-Study jobs (averaging $900).

Need-Based Scholarships & Grants Pell, FSEOG, state, private, college/university.

Loans Perkins, PLUS, Stafford, Unsubsidized Stafford, state, private.

Non-Need Awards In 1996, a total of 698 non-need awards were made. *Academic Interests/Achievement Awards:* 264 ($1,470,892 total): general academic. *Creative Arts/Performance Awards:* 91 ($98,800 total): art/fine arts, music, theater/drama. *Special Characteristics Awards:* 343 ($293,625 total): international students, local/state students, religious affiliation, ROTC participants.

Other Money-Saving Options Accelerated degree, cooperative Army ROTC, cooperative Air Force ROTC, off-campus living (after freshman year). *Payment Plans:* installment, deferred payment. *Waivers:* full or partial for employees or children of employees and senior citizens.

Contact Mr. Stanley F. Skrutski, Director of Financial Aid, Marywood University, 2300 Adams Avenue, Scranton, PA 18509-1598, 717-348-6225, fax: 717-961-4739.

MASON GROSS SCHOOL OF THE ARTS
New Brunswick, New Jersey

See Rutgers, The State University of New Jersey, Mason Gross School of the Arts

---

MASSACHUSETTS COLLEGE OF ART
Boston, Massachusetts

About the Institution State-supported, coed. Degrees awarded: B, M. Offers 20 undergraduate majors. Total enrollment: 1,487. Undergraduates: 1,378 (78% state residents). Freshmen: 218.

Undergraduate Expenses (1996–97) State resident tuition: $1390. Nonresident tuition: $6634. Mandatory fees: $2644. College room and board: $5588.

Applications 66% of all full-time undergraduates enrolled in fall 1996 applied for aid; of these, 91% were judged to have need according to Federal Methodology, of whom 98% were aided. *Financial aid deadline:* continuous. *Financial aid forms:* FAFSA required. Financial aid transcripts, verification worksheet required for some. *Regular admission application deadline:* 3/1. Early decision deadline: 12/1.

Summary of Aid to Needy Students *From gift & self-help combined:* Average need met: 65%. Average amount awarded: $4467 (26% gift aid, 74% self-help). *Gift aid:* Total: $809,728 (2% from college's own funds, 23% from other college-administered sources, 75% from external sources). 100 Federal Work-Study jobs (averaging $800).

Need-Based Scholarships & Grants Pell, FSEOG, state.

Loans Perkins, PLUS, Stafford, Unsubsidized Stafford, state, private, college/university short-term loans ($100 average), college/university long-term loans ($1200 average).

Non-Need Awards Not offered.

Other Money-Saving Options Co-op program, off-campus living. *Payment Plan:* installment. *Waivers:* full or partial for employees or children of employees and senior citizens.

Contact Ms. Laura M. Hofeldt, Assistant Director of Financial Aid, Massachusetts College of Art, 621 Huntington Avenue, Boston, MA 02115-5882, 617-232-1555 Ext. 524, fax: 617-566-4034.

MASSACHUSETTS COLLEGE OF PHARMACY AND ALLIED HEALTH SCIENCES
Boston, Massachusetts

About the Institution Independent, coed. Degrees awarded: A, B, M, D, P. Offers 7 undergraduate majors. Total enrollment: 1,451. Undergraduates: 1,235 (55% state residents). Freshmen: 131.

Undergraduate Expenses (1997–98) Comprehensive fee of $22,008 includes tuition ($14,208), mandatory fees ($300), and college room and board ($7500).

Applications Of all full-time undergraduates enrolled in fall 1996, 96% of those who applied for aid were judged to have need according to Federal Methodology, of whom 100% were aided. *Financial aid deadline (priority):* 4/1. *Financial aid forms:* FAFSA, CSS Financial Aid PROFILE, institutional form required; state form acceptable. *Regular admission application deadline:* 3/1. Early action deadline: 11/1.

Summary of Aid to Needy Students *From gift & self-help combined:* Average need met: 72%. Average amount awarded: $8731 (39% gift aid, 61% self-help). *Gift aid:* Total: $3,347,290 (62% from college's own funds, 18% from other college-administered sources, 20% from external sources). 66 Federal Work-Study jobs (averaging $2100); part-time jobs.

Need-Based Scholarships & Grants Pell, FSEOG, state, private, college/university.

Loans Perkins, PLUS, Stafford, Unsubsidized Stafford, private, college/university short-term loans ($500 average), college/university long-term loans ($2400 average).

Non-Need Awards In 1996, a total of 15 non-need awards were made. *Academic Interests/Achievement Awards:* 15 ($75,000 total): general academic, biological sciences, health fields.

Other Money-Saving Options Cooperative Army ROTC, off-campus living. *Waivers:* full or partial for employees or children of employees.

Contact Ms. Julie J. Donlon, Associate Director of Financial Aid, Massachusetts College of Pharmacy and Allied Health Sciences, 179 Longwood Avenue, Boston, MA 02115-5896, 617-732-2864, fax: 617-732-2801.

MASSACHUSETTS INSTITUTE OF TECHNOLOGY
Cambridge, Massachusetts

About the Institution Independent, coed. Degrees awarded: B, M, D. Offers 120 undergraduate majors. Total enrollment: 9,947. Undergraduates: 4,429 (9% state residents). Freshmen: 1,068.

Undergraduate Expenses (1997–98) Comprehensive fee of $28,710 includes tuition ($23,100) and college room and board ($5610). College room only: $2610 (minimum).

Applications Of all full-time undergraduates enrolled in fall 1996, 93% of those who applied for aid were judged to have need according to Federal Methodology, of whom 100% were aided. *Financial aid deadline (priority):* 1/17. *Financial aid forms:* FAFSA, CSS Financial Aid PROFILE, institutional form required. *Regular admission application deadline:* 1/1. Early action deadline: 11/15.

Summary of Aid to Needy Students *From gift & self-help combined:* Average need met: 100%. Average amount awarded: $20,673 (63% gift aid, 37% self-help). *Gift aid:* Total: $33,735,367 (77% from college's own funds, 8% from other college-administered sources, 15% from external sources). 1,945 Federal Work-Study jobs (averaging $1971); 206 part-time jobs.

Need-Based Scholarships & Grants Pell, FSEOG, state, private, college/university.

Loans Perkins, PLUS, Stafford, Unsubsidized Stafford, state, private, college/university short-term loans ($1285 average), college/university long-term loans ($2897 average).

Non-Need Awards Not offered.

Other Money-Saving Options Accelerated degree, co-op program, Army ROTC, Naval ROTC, Air Force ROTC, off-campus living (after freshman year). *Payment Plan:* deferred payment. *Waivers:* full or partial for employees or children of employees.

Contact Mr. Collins Mikesell, Manager, Research and Information Systems, Massachusetts Institute of Technology, 77 Massachusetts Avenue, Cambridge, MA 02139-4307, 617-258-5608, fax: 617-258-8301.

MASSACHUSETTS MARITIME ACADEMY
Buzzards Bay, Massachusetts

About the Institution State-supported, coed. Degrees awarded: B. Offers 5 undergraduate majors. Total enrollment: 750 (71% state residents). Freshmen: 240.

Undergraduate Expenses (1996–97) State resident tuition: $1390. Nonresident tuition: $6634. Mandatory fees: $1703. College room and board: $3900.

Applications Of all full-time undergraduates enrolled in fall 1996, 80% of those who applied for aid were judged to have need according to Federal Methodology, of whom 90% were aided. *Financial aid deadline (priority):* 3/14. *Financial aid forms:* FAFSA, institutional form required. *Regular admission application deadline:* rolling. Early decision deadline: 11/1.

Summary of Aid to Needy Students *From gift & self-help combined:* Average need met: 87%. Average amount awarded: $6300 (28% gift aid, 72% self-help). *Gift aid:* Total: $519,433 (4% from college's own funds, 35% from other college-administered sources, 61% from external sources). 110 Federal Work-Study jobs (averaging $1000).

Need-Based Scholarships & Grants Pell, FSEOG, state, private.

Loans Perkins, PLUS, Stafford, Unsubsidized Stafford, state, private.

Non-Need Awards In 1996, a total of 21 non-need awards were made. *Academic Interests/Achievement Awards:* 21 ($41,500 total): general academic.

Other Money-Saving Options Co-op program, cooperative Army ROTC.

Contact Mr. Michael Cuff, Director of Financial Aid, Massachusetts Maritime Academy, 101 Academy Drive, Buzzards Bay, MA 02532-3400, 508-830-5087.

THE MASTER'S COLLEGE AND SEMINARY
Santa Clarita, California

About the Institution Independent/religious, coed. Degrees awarded: B, M. Offers 44 undergraduate majors. Total enrollment: 793 (96% state residents). Freshmen: 160.

Undergraduate Expenses (1997–98) Comprehensive fee of $16,978 includes tuition ($11,980), mandatory fees ($200), and college room and board ($4798). College room only: $2922.

Applications 94% of all full-time undergraduates enrolled in fall 1996 applied for aid; of these, 97% were judged to have need according to Federal Methodology, of whom 100% were aided. *Financial aid deadline:* Applications processed continuously. *Financial aid forms:* FAFSA, CSS Financial Aid PROFILE, state form, institutional form required. *Admission application deadline:* rolling.

Summary of Aid to Needy Students *From gift & self-help combined:* Average need met: 88%. Average amount awarded: $7134 (43% gift aid, 57% self-help). *Gift aid:* Total: $1,869,747 (35% from college's own funds, 45% from other college-administered sources, 20% from external sources). 300 Federal Work-Study jobs (averaging $2250); part-time jobs.

Need-Based Scholarships & Grants Pell, FSEOG, state, college/university.

Loans Perkins, PLUS, Stafford, Unsubsidized Stafford.

Non-Need Awards In 1996, a total of 527 non-need awards were made. *Academic Interests/Achievement Awards:* 337 ($584,761 total): general academic, biological sciences, business, education, physical sciences, religion/biblical studies. *Creative Arts/Performance Awards:* 35 ($67,700 total): music. *Special Achievements/Activities Awards:* 40 ($40,000 total): general special achievements/activities. *Special Characteristics Awards:* 25 ($247,845 total): children of faculty/staff. *Athletic:* Total: 90 ($485,000); Men: 61 ($414,500); Women: 29 ($70,500).

Other Money-Saving Options Accelerated degree, off-campus living (after sophomore year). *Payment Plans:* installment, deferred payment. *Waivers:* full or partial for employees or children of employees.

Contact Ms. Sharon Shook, Director of Financial Aid, The Master's College and Seminary, 21726 West Placerita Canyon Road, Santa Clarita, CA 91321-1200, 805-259-3540 Ext. 371.

MAYO SCHOOL OF HEALTH-RELATED SCIENCES
Rochester, Minnesota

About the Institution Independent. Degrees awarded: A, B, M. Total enrollment: 307.

Undergraduate Expenses (1996–97) Tuition: $1000 (minimum).

Applications 43% of all full-time undergraduates enrolled in fall 1996 applied for aid; of these, 100% were judged to have need according to Federal Methodology, of whom 100% were aided. *Financial aid deadline:* continuous. *Financial aid forms:* FAFSA, institutional form required.

Summary of Aid to Needy Students *From gift & self-help combined:* Average need met: 100%. *Gift aid:* Total: $138,674 (24% from college's own funds, 73% from other college-administered sources, 3% from external sources).

Need-Based Scholarships & Grants Pell, state, private, college/university.

Loans PLUS, Stafford, Unsubsidized Stafford, state, private, college/university short-term loans ($500 average).

Non-Need Awards In 1996, a total of 14 non-need awards were made. *Special Characteristics Awards:* 14 ($82,867 total): members of minorities.

Contact Ms. Sandra Putnam, Assistant Financial Aid Director, Mayo School of Health-Related Sciences, 200 First Street, SW, Rochester, MN 55905, 507-284-4839, fax: 507-284-2634.

MAYVILLE STATE UNIVERSITY
Mayville, North Dakota

About the Institution State-supported, coed. Degrees awarded: A, B. Offers 23 undergraduate majors. Total enrollment: 680 (74% state residents). Freshmen: 217.

Undergraduate Expenses (1997–98) State resident tuition: $1680. Nonresident tuition: $4486. Mandatory fees: $240. College room and board: $2382.

Applications Of all full-time undergraduates enrolled in fall 1996, 65% of those who applied for aid were judged to have need according to Federal Methodology, of whom 99% were aided. *Financial aid deadline:* continuous. *Financial aid forms:* FAFSA, institutional form required. *Admission application deadline:* rolling.

Summary of Aid to Needy Students *From gift & self-help combined:* Average need met: 80%. Average amount awarded: $6000 (36% gift aid, 64% self-help). *Gift aid:* Total: $400,900 (30% from college's own funds, 10% from other college-administered sources, 60% from external sources). 65 Federal Work-Study jobs (averaging $1200); 117 part-time jobs.

Need-Based Scholarships & Grants Pell, FSEOG, state.

Loans Perkins, PLUS, Stafford, Unsubsidized Stafford, college/university short-term loans ($300 average).

Non-Need Awards In 1996, a total of 316 non-need awards were made. *Academic Interests/Achievement Awards:* 123 ($52,825 total): general academic, biological sciences, business, education, English, library science, mathematics, physical sciences. *Special Characteristics Awards:* 64 ($48,123 total): children of union members/company employees, international students, local/state students, members of minorities. *Athletic:* Total: 129 ($67,576); Men: 94 ($49,321); Women: 35 ($18,255).

Other Money-Saving Options Co-op program, cooperative Army ROTC, off-campus living (after sophomore year).

Contact Mr. Brian Larson, Assistant Director, Student Financial Aid, Mayville State University, 330 3rd Street NE, Mayville, ND 58257-1299, 701-786-4768, fax: 701-786-4748.

MCKENDREE COLLEGE
Lebanon, Illinois

About the Institution Independent/religious, coed. Degrees awarded: B. Offers 38 undergraduate majors. Total enrollment: 1,787 (93% state residents). Freshmen: 315.

Undergraduate Expenses (1997–98) Comprehensive fee of $15,000 includes tuition ($10,400) and college room and board ($4600).

Applications 71% of all full-time undergraduates enrolled in fall 1996 applied for aid; of these, 92% were judged to have need according to Federal Methodology, of whom 100% were aided. *Financial aid deadline*

(priority): 6/1. *Financial aid forms:* FAFSA, institutional form required; CSS Financial Aid PROFILE acceptable. State form required for some. *Admission application deadline:* rolling.

Summary of Aid to Needy Students *From gift & self-help combined:* Average amount awarded: $5156 (66% gift aid, 34% self-help). *Gift aid:* Total: $2,506,383 (45% from college's own funds, 42% from other college-administered sources, 13% from external sources). 395 Federal Work-Study jobs (averaging $1454); 96 part-time jobs.

Need-Based Scholarships & Grants Pell, FSEOG, state, private.

Loans Perkins, PLUS, Stafford, Unsubsidized Stafford.

Non-Need Awards In 1996, a total of 989 non-need awards were made. *Academic Interests/Achievement Awards:* 38 ($53,850 total): general academic, biological sciences, business, mathematics, physical sciences, religion/biblical studies. *Creative Arts/Performance Awards:* 5 ($4000 total): music. *Special Achievements/Activities Awards:* 344 ($467,819 total): community service, leadership. *Special Characteristics Awards:* 292 ($297,558 total): general special characteristics, children of faculty/staff, out-of-state students, religious affiliation. *Athletic:* Total: 310 ($446,734); Men: 214 ($291,592); Women: 96 ($155,142).

Other Money-Saving Options Accelerated degree, cooperative Army ROTC, cooperative Air Force ROTC, off-campus living (after junior year). *Payment Plans:* installment, deferred payment. *Waivers:* full or partial for employees or children of employees.

Contact Office of Financial Aid, McKendree College, 701 College Road, Lebanon, IL 62254-1299, 618-537-4481.

MCMURRY UNIVERSITY
Abilene, Texas

About the Institution Independent/religious, coed. Degrees awarded: B. Offers 52 undergraduate majors. Total enrollment: 1,400 (91% state residents). Freshmen: 261.

Undergraduate Expenses (1996–97) Comprehensive fee of $11,450 includes tuition ($7200), mandatory fees ($750), and college room and board ($3500 minimum).

Applications 92% of all full-time undergraduates enrolled in fall 1996 applied for aid; of these, 86% were judged to have need according to Federal Methodology, of whom 99% were aided. *Financial aid deadline* (priority): 3/15. *Financial aid forms:* FAFSA, institutional form required; CSS Financial Aid PROFILE, state form acceptable. *Admission application deadline:* 8/15.

Summary of Aid to Needy Students *From gift & self-help combined:* Average need met: 89%. Average amount awarded: $8533 (55% gift aid, 45% self-help). *Gift aid:* Total: $3,620,331 (47% from college's own funds, 31% from other college-administered sources, 22% from external sources). 233 Federal Work-Study jobs (averaging $1000); 118 part-time jobs.

Need-Based Scholarships & Grants Pell, FSEOG, state, private, college/university.

Loans Perkins, PLUS, Stafford, Unsubsidized Stafford, state, private.

Non-Need Awards In 1996, a total of 1,279 non-need awards were made. *Academic Interests/Achievement Awards:* 408 ($1,093,826 total): general academic, religion/biblical studies. *Creative Arts/Performance Awards:* 127 ($107,895 total): art/fine arts, music, theater/drama. *Special Achievements/Activities Awards:* 5 ($5000 total): general special achievements/activities, Junior Miss. *Special Characteristics Awards:* 739 ($1,863,818 total): children of faculty/staff, international students, local/state students, previous college experience, relatives of clergy, religious affiliation.

Other Money-Saving Options Off-campus living (after sophomore year). *Payment Plans:* guaranteed tuition, installment. *Waivers:* full or partial for employees or children of employees.

Contact Office of Financial Aid, McMurry University, Box 908, McMurry Station, Abilene, TX 79697, 915-691-6200.

MCNEESE STATE UNIVERSITY
Lake Charles, Louisiana

About the Institution State-supported, coed. Degrees awarded: A, B, M. Offers 53 undergraduate majors. Total enrollment: 8,059. Undergraduates: 7,057 (99% state residents). Freshmen: 1,458.

Undergraduate Expenses (1997–98) State resident tuition: $2012. Nonresident tuition: $6452. College room and board: $2310 (minimum).

Applications 83% of all full-time undergraduates enrolled in fall 1996 applied for aid; of these, 70% were judged to have need according to Federal Methodology, of whom 93% were aided. *Financial aid deadline (priority):* 5/1. *Financial aid forms:* FAFSA, institutional form required. Nontaxable income verification required for some. *Admission application deadline:* 7/15.

Summary of Aid to Needy Students *From gift & self-help combined:* Average need met: 62%. Average amount awarded: $4221 (32% gift aid, 68% self-help). *Gift aid:* Total: $4,261,341 (2% from college's own funds, 8% from other college-administered sources, 90% from external sources). 302 Federal Work-Study jobs (averaging $1098); 414 part-time jobs.

Need-Based Scholarships & Grants Pell, FSEOG, state.

Loans Perkins, PLUS, Stafford, Unsubsidized Stafford, college/university short-term loans ($85 average).

Non-Need Awards *Academic Interests/Achievement Awards:* 964 ($1,356,400 total): general academic, agriculture, biological sciences, business, communication, computer science, education, engineering/technologies, English, foreign languages, health fields, home economics, humanities, mathematics, physical sciences, premedicine, social sciences. *Creative Arts/Performance Awards:* 244 ($335,900 total): art/fine arts, debating, music, theater/drama. *Special Achievements/Activities Awards:* 91 ($45,600 total): cheerleading/drum major, memberships, rodeo. *Special Characteristics Awards:* 218 ($158,000 total): general special characteristics, children and siblings of alumni, children of faculty/staff, international students, local/state students, members of minorities, out-of-state students. *Athletic:* available.

Other Money-Saving Options Accelerated degree, co-op program, Army ROTC, off-campus living (after freshman year). *Payment Plan:* installment. *Waivers:* full or partial for employees or children of employees and senior citizens.

Contact Office of Financial Aid, McNeese State University, Lake Charles, LA 70609-3260, 318-475-5065, fax: 318-475-5068.

MCPHERSON COLLEGE
McPherson, Kansas

About the Institution Independent/religious, coed. Degrees awarded: A, B. Offers 45 undergraduate majors. Total enrollment: 474 (62% state residents). Freshmen: 114.

Undergraduate Expenses (1997–98) Comprehensive fee of $13,700 includes tuition ($9820), mandatory fees ($150), and college room and board ($3730 minimum).

Applications 92% of all full-time undergraduates enrolled in fall 1996 applied for aid; of these, 100% were judged to have need according to Federal Methodology, of whom 100% were aided. *Financial aid deadline (priority):* 4/1. *Financial aid forms:* FAFSA required. *Admission application deadline:* rolling.

Summary of Aid to Needy Students *From gift & self-help combined:* Average amount awarded: $11,036 (55% gift aid, 45% self-help). *Gift aid:* Total: $1,831,800 (70% from college's own funds, 15% from other college-administered sources, 15% from external sources). 164 Federal Work-Study jobs (averaging $1346); part-time jobs.

Need-Based Scholarships & Grants Pell, FSEOG, state, private, college/university.

Loans Perkins, PLUS, Stafford, Unsubsidized Stafford, private.

Non-Need Awards In 1996, a total of 345 non-need awards were made. *Academic Interests/Achievement Awards:* 345 ($1,027,201 total): general academic.

Contact Mr. Fred Schmidt, Director of Financial Aid and Admissions, McPherson College, PO Box 1402, McPherson, KS 67460-3899, 316-241-0731 Ext. 1270.

MEDAILLE COLLEGE
Buffalo, New York

About the Institution Independent, coed. Degrees awarded: A, B. Offers 31 undergraduate majors. Total enrollment: 878 (92% state residents). Freshmen: 127.

Undergraduate Expenses (1997–98) Comprehensive fee of $15,170 includes tuition ($10,230), mandatory fees ($240), and college room and board ($4700 minimum). College room only: $3000 (minimum).

Applications 75% of all full-time undergraduates enrolled in fall 1996 applied for aid; of these, 92% were judged to have need according to Federal Methodology, of whom 100% were aided. *Financial aid deadline (priority):* 3/15. *Financial aid forms:* FAFSA, state form, institutional form required. *Admission application deadline:* rolling.

Summary of Aid to Needy Students *From gift & self-help combined:* Average need met: 80%. Average amount awarded: $9159 (42% gift aid, 58% self-help). *Gift aid:* Total: $1,459,590 (29% from college's own funds, 8% from other college-administered sources, 63% from external sources). 148 Federal Work-Study jobs (averaging $1500).

Need-Based Scholarships & Grants Pell, FSEOG, state, private, college/university.

Loans PLUS, Stafford, Unsubsidized Stafford, private, college/university short-term loans ($25 average).

Non-Need Awards *Academic Interests/Achievement Awards:* 22 ($43,500 total): general academic. *Special Characteristics Awards:* adult students.

Other Money-Saving Options Accelerated degree, cooperative Army ROTC. *Payment Plan:* installment. *Waivers:* full or partial for employees or children of employees, adult students, senior citizens.

Contact Ms. Jacqueline Mathane, Admissions Officer, Medaille College, 18 Agassiz Circle, Buffalo, NY 14214-2695, 716-884-3281.

MEDGAR EVERS COLLEGE OF THE CITY UNIVERSITY OF NEW YORK
Brooklyn, New York

About the Institution State & locally supported, coed. Degrees awarded: A, B. Offers 15 undergraduate majors. Total enrollment: 5,402 (95% state residents). Freshmen: 762.

Undergraduate Expenses (1996–97) State resident tuition: $3200. Nonresident tuition: $6800. Mandatory fees: $40.

Applications *Financial aid deadline (priority):* 8/15. *Financial aid forms:* City University Application for Federal and State Aid required; FAFSA, CSS Financial Aid PROFILE, state form, institutional form acceptable. *Admission application deadline:* rolling.

Summary of Aid to Needy Students *From gift & self-help combined:* Average amount awarded: $2299 (76% gift aid, 24% self-help). *Gift aid:* Total: $5,822,239 (51% from college-administered sources, 49% from external sources). 553 Federal Work-Study jobs (averaging $476); part-time jobs.

Need-Based Scholarships & Grants Pell, FSEOG, state, private, college/university.

Loans Perkins, PLUS, Stafford, Unsubsidized Stafford.

Non-Need Awards Not offered.

Another Money-Saving Option Co-op program.

Contact Mr. Conley James, Director of Financial Aid, Medgar Evers College of the City University of New York, 1150 Carroll Street, Brooklyn, NY 11225-2298, 718-270-6038.

MEDICAL COLLEGE OF GEORGIA
Augusta, Georgia

About the Institution State-supported, coed. Degrees awarded: A, B, M, D, P. Offers 9 undergraduate majors. Total enrollment: 2,048. Undergraduates: 832 (93% state residents). Freshmen: 26.

Undergraduate Expenses (1996–97) State resident tuition: $2115. Nonresident tuition: $7296. Mandatory fees: $249. College room only: $1305.

Applications 80% of all full-time undergraduates enrolled in fall 1996 applied for aid; of these, 73% were judged to have need according to Federal Methodology, of whom 97% were aided. *Financial aid deadline (priority):* 2/15. *Financial aid forms:* FAFSA, institutional form, financial aid transcript (for mid-year transfers) required. *Admission application deadline:* 11/15.

Summary of Aid to Needy Students *From gift & self-help combined:* Average need met: 97%. Average amount awarded: $6225 (36% gift aid, 64% self-help). *Gift aid:* Total: $985,759 (23% from college's own funds, 34% from other college-administered sources, 43% from external sources). 26 Federal Work-Study jobs (averaging $1015); part-time jobs.

Need-Based Scholarships & Grants Pell, FSEOG, state, college/university.

Loans Perkins, PLUS, Stafford, Unsubsidized Stafford, Federal Nursing, state, college/university short-term loans ($300 average), college/university long-term loans ($2000 average).

Non-Need Awards In 1996, a total of 265 non-need awards were made. *Academic Interests/Achievement Awards:* 265 ($581,429 total): general academic.

Other Money-Saving Options Off-campus living. *Waivers:* full or partial for senior citizens.

Contact Office of Student Financial Aid, Medical College of Georgia, Augusta, GA 30912-1003, 706-721-4901.

MEDICAL COLLEGE OF PENNSYLVANIA AND HAHNEMANN UNIVERSITY
Philadelphia, Pennsylvania

See Allegheny University of the Health Sciences

MEMPHIS COLLEGE OF ART
Memphis, Tennessee

About the Institution Independent, coed. Degrees awarded: B, M. Offers 15 undergraduate majors. Total enrollment: 291. Undergraduates: 239 (60% state residents). Freshmen: 72.

Undergraduate Expenses (1997–98) Tuition: $10,900. Mandatory fees: $50. College room only: $3050.

Applications 100% of all full-time undergraduates enrolled in fall 1996 applied for aid; of these, 80% were judged to have need according to Federal Methodology, of whom 100% were aided. *Financial aid deadline (priority):* 4/1. *Financial aid forms:* FAFSA, institutional form required; CSS Financial Aid PROFILE acceptable. State form required for some. *Admission application deadline:* rolling.

Summary of Aid to Needy Students *From gift & self-help combined:* Average need met: 56%. Average amount awarded: $8261 (55% gift aid, 45% self-help). *Gift aid:* Total: $786,652 (67% from college's own

funds, 5% from other college-administered sources, 28% from external sources). 30 Federal Work-Study jobs (averaging $500); 135 part-time jobs.

Need-Based Scholarships & Grants Pell, FSEOG, state.

Loans Perkins, PLUS, Stafford, Unsubsidized Stafford, college/university short-term loans ($25 average).

Non-Need Awards In 1996, a total of 210 non-need awards were made. *Academic Interests/Achievement Awards:* 153 ($361,582 total): general academic. *Creative Arts/Performance Awards:* 57 ($95,000 total): art/fine arts.

Other Money-Saving Options Off-campus living. *Payment Plans:* tuition prepayment, installment, deferred payment. *Waivers:* full or partial for employees or children of employees.

Contact Ms. Donna L. O'Quinn, Director of Financial Aid, Memphis College of Art, 1930 Poplar Avenue, Memphis, TN 38104-2764, 901-726-4085 Ext. 52.

MENLO COLLEGE
Atherton, California

About the Institution Independent, coed. Degrees awarded: B. Offers 3 undergraduate majors. Total enrollment: 516 (80% state residents). Freshmen: 88.

Undergraduate Expenses (1997–98) Comprehensive fee of $22,680 includes tuition ($15,980), mandatory fees ($200), and college room and board ($6500).

Applications *Financial aid deadline (priority):* 3/2. *Financial aid forms:* FAFSA required. State form required for some. *Regular admission application deadline:* rolling. Early decision deadline: 12/1.

Summary of Aid to Needy Students *From gift & self-help combined:* Average amount awarded: $15,040 (54% gift aid, 46% self-help). *Gift aid:* Total: $2,500,000. Part-time jobs.

Need-Based Scholarships & Grants Pell, FSEOG, state, college/university.

Loans PLUS, Stafford, Unsubsidized Stafford, private.

Non-Need Awards *Academic Interests/Achievement Awards:* general academic. *Special Achievements/Activities Awards:* leadership.

Other Money-Saving Options Accelerated degree, cooperative Army ROTC, off-campus living (after junior year). *Payment Plan:* installment.

Contact Financial Aid Office, Menlo College, 1000 El Camino Real, CA 94027-4301, 415-688-3880.

MERCER UNIVERSITY
Macon, Georgia

About the Institution Independent/religious, coed. Degrees awarded: B, M, P. Offers 63 undergraduate majors. Total enrollment: 6,960. Undergraduates: 4,175 (73% state residents). Freshmen: 582.

Undergraduate Expenses (1996–97) Comprehensive fee of $18,111 includes tuition ($13,896) and college room and board ($4215 minimum). College room only: $2085 (minimum).

Applications 87% of all full-time undergraduates enrolled in fall 1996 applied for aid; of these, 76% were judged to have need according to Federal Methodology, of whom 100% were aided. *Financial aid deadline (priority):* 4/1. *Financial aid forms:* FAFSA, institutional form required. State form required for some. *Regular admission application deadline:* rolling. Early decision deadline: 12/1.

Summary of Aid to Needy Students *From gift & self-help combined:* Average need met: 100%. Average amount awarded: $13,130 (73% gift aid, 27% self-help). *Gift aid:* Total: $14,542,458 (58% from college's own funds, 32% from other college-administered sources, 10% from external sources). 432 Federal Work-Study jobs (averaging $1232); 300 part-time jobs.

Need-Based Scholarships & Grants Pell, FSEOG, state, private, college/university.

Loans Perkins, PLUS, Stafford, Unsubsidized Stafford, state, private, college/university short-term loans ($675 average), college/university long-term loans ($1890 average).

Non-Need Awards In 1996, a total of 3,321 non-need awards were made. *Academic Interests/Achievement Awards:* 1,494 ($7,607,776 total): international studies, military science, physical sciences, religion/biblical studies. *Creative Arts/Performance Awards:* 59 ($82,683 total): general creative, debating, music, theater/drama. *Special Achievements/Activities Awards:* 3 ($2500 total): general special achievements/activities. *Special Characteristics Awards:* 1,630 ($3,757,956 total): general special characteristics, children of faculty/staff, international students, local/state students, relatives of clergy, religious affiliation, ROTC participants, siblings of current students. *Athletic:* Total: 135 ($1,265,854); Men: 64 ($685,786); Women: 71 ($580,068).

Other Money-Saving Options Co-op program, cooperative Army ROTC, off-campus living (after sophomore year). *Payment Plan:* installment. *Waivers:* full or partial for employees or children of employees.

Contact Mr. James Schrimshire, Senior Associate Director of Financial Aid, Mercer University, 1400 Coleman Avenkue, Macon, GA 31207-0003, 912-752-2670.

MERCYHURST COLLEGE
Erie, Pennsylvania

About the Institution Independent/religious, coed. Degrees awarded: A, B, M. Offers 97 undergraduate majors. Total enrollment: 2,712. Undergraduates: 2,635 (64% state residents). Freshmen: 456.

Undergraduate Expenses (1997–98) Comprehensive fee of $17,640 includes tuition ($12,192), mandatory fees ($750), and college room and board ($4698).

Applications *Financial aid deadline (priority):* 5/1. *Financial aid forms:* FAFSA, institutional form required; CSS Financial Aid PROFILE acceptable. State form required for some. *Admission application deadline:* rolling.

Summary of Aid to Needy Students *From gift & self-help combined:* Average need met: 85%. Average amount awarded: $7428 (63% gift aid, 37% self-help). *Gift aid:* Total: $9,979,031 (61% from college's own funds, 27% from other college-administered sources, 12% from external sources). 354 Federal Work-Study jobs (averaging $750); 875 part-time jobs.

Need-Based Scholarships & Grants Pell, FSEOG, state, private, college/university.

Loans Perkins, PLUS, Stafford, Unsubsidized Stafford, college/university short-term loans ($750 average).

Non-Need Awards In 1996, a total of 1,617 non-need awards were made. *Academic Interests/Achievement Awards:* 430 ($1,038,565 total). *Creative Arts/Performance Awards:* 97 ($304,289 total): art/fine arts, dance, music. *Special Achievements/Activities Awards:* 760 ($1,162,128 total): community service, religious involvement. *Special Characteristics Awards:* 142 ($658,006 total): children of faculty/staff, local/state students, members of minorities, siblings of current students. *Athletic:* Total: 188 ($816,402); Men: 109 ($507,825); Women: 79 ($308,577).

Other Money-Saving Options Accelerated degree, co-op program, cooperative Army ROTC, off-campus living (after sophomore year). *Payment Plan:* installment. *Waivers:* full or partial for employees or children of employees.

Contact Mrs. Sheila W. Richter, Director of Financial Aid, Mercyhurst College, 501 East 58th Street, Erie, PA 16546, 814-824-2288, fax: 814-824-2071.

MEREDITH COLLEGE
Raleigh, North Carolina

About the Institution Independent/religious, women. Degrees awarded: B, M. Offers 56 undergraduate majors. Total enrollment: 2,574. Undergraduates: 2,052 (85% state residents). Freshmen: 377.

Undergraduate Expenses (1997–98) Comprehensive fee of $12,240 includes tuition ($8490) and college room and board ($3750).

Applications Of all full-time undergraduates enrolled in fall 1996, 67% of those who applied for aid were judged to have need according to Federal Methodology, of whom 100% were aided. *Financial aid deadline (priority):* 2/15. *Financial aid forms:* FAFSA, institutional form required. *Regular admission application deadline:* 2/15. Early decision deadline: 10/15.

Summary of Aid to Needy Students *From gift & self-help combined:* Average need met: 73%. Average amount awarded: $9490 (40% gift aid, 60% self-help). *Gift aid:* Total: $3,090,903 (28% from college's own funds, 48% from other college-administered sources, 24% from external sources). 318 Federal Work-Study jobs (averaging $1148); 181 part-time jobs.

Need-Based Scholarships & Grants Pell, FSEOG, state, college/university.

Loans Perkins, PLUS, Stafford, Unsubsidized Stafford.

Non-Need Awards In 1996, a total of 268 non-need awards were made. *Academic Interests/Achievement Awards:* 141 ($562,045 total): general academic, education, English, mathematics. *Creative Arts/Performance Awards:* 38 ($54,235 total): applied art and design, art/fine arts, music. *Special Achievements/Activities Awards:* 86 ($92,500 total): leadership. *Special Characteristics Awards:* 3 ($2300 total): local/state students.

Other Money-Saving Options Accelerated degree, co-op program, cooperative Army ROTC, cooperative Air Force ROTC, off-campus living (after sophomore year). *Payment Plan:* installment. *Waivers:* full or partial for employees or children of employees.

Contact Mr. Philip D. Roof, Director of Financial Assistance, Meredith College, 3800 Hillsborough Street, Raleigh, NC 27607-5298, 919-829-8565, fax: 919-829-2373.

MERRIMACK COLLEGE
North Andover, Massachusetts

About the Institution Independent/religious, coed. Degrees awarded: A, B. Offers 45 undergraduate majors. Total enrollment: 2,804 (75% state residents). Freshmen: 485.

Undergraduate Expenses (1997–98) Comprehensive fee of $21,530 includes tuition ($14,530) and college room and board ($7000). College room only: $3900 (minimum).

Applications Of all full-time undergraduates enrolled in fall 1996, 94% of those who applied for aid were judged to have need according to Federal Methodology, of whom 99% were aided. *Financial aid deadline (priority):* 2/15. *Financial aid forms:* FAFSA, CSS Financial Aid PROFILE required. *Regular admission application deadline:* 3/1. Early decision deadline: 11/30.

Summary of Aid to Needy Students *From gift & self-help combined:* Average need met: 80%. Average amount awarded: $11,975 (61% gift aid, 39% self-help). *Gift aid:* Total: $10,519,025 (86% from college's own funds, 2% from other college-administered sources, 12% from external sources). 250 Federal Work-Study jobs (averaging $1200); 250 part-time jobs.

Need-Based Scholarships & Grants Pell, FSEOG, state, college/university.

Loans Perkins, PLUS, Stafford, Unsubsidized Stafford, state, college/university long-term loans ($1500 average).

Non-Need Awards In 1996, a total of 286 non-need awards were made. *Academic Interests/Achievement Awards:* 50 ($300,000 total): general academic. *Creative Arts/Performance Awards:* 4 ($58,120 total): art/fine arts, theater/drama. *Special Achievements/Activities Awards:* 50 ($375,000 total): leadership. *Special Characteristics Awards:* 102 ($498,320 total): children and siblings of alumni, children of faculty/staff, international students, relatives of clergy, siblings of current students. *Athletic:* Total: 80 ($978,314); Men: 29 ($600,220); Women: 51 ($378,094).

Other Money-Saving Options Co-op program, cooperative Air Force ROTC, off-campus living. *Payment Plans:* installment, deferred payment. *Waivers:* full or partial for minority students, employees or children of employees, senior citizens.

Contact Office of Financial Aid, Merrimack College, 315 Turnpike Street, North Andover, MA 01845-5800, 508-837-5000.

MESA STATE COLLEGE
Grand Junction, Colorado

About the Institution State-supported, coed. Degrees awarded: A, B. Offers 71 undergraduate majors. Total enrollment: 4,724 (91% state residents). Freshmen: 933.

Undergraduate Expenses (1996–97) State resident tuition: $1500. Nonresident tuition: $5460. Mandatory fees: $433. College room and board: $4100. College room only: $1940 (minimum).

Applications Of all full-time undergraduates enrolled in fall 1996, 90% of those who applied for aid were judged to have need according to Federal Methodology, of whom 100% were aided. *Financial aid deadline (priority):* 3/1. *Financial aid forms:* FAFSA required. State form required for some. *Admission application deadline:* 8/15.

Summary of Aid to Needy Students *From gift & self-help combined:* Average need met: 90%. Average amount awarded: $5667 (34% gift aid, 66% self-help). *Gift aid:* Total: $5,005,868 (18% from college's own funds, 25% from other college-administered sources, 57% from external sources). 157 Federal Work-Study jobs (averaging $1069); 407 part-time jobs.

Need-Based Scholarships & Grants Pell, FSEOG, state.

Loans Perkins, PLUS, Stafford, Unsubsidized Stafford, college/university short-term loans ($250 average).

Non-Need Awards In 1996, a total of 926 non-need awards were made. *Academic Interests/Achievement Awards:* 200 ($353,157 total): general academic, biological sciences, business, communication, computer science, education, engineering/technologies, English, health fields, humanities, mathematics, physical sciences, social sciences. *Creative Arts/Performance Awards:* 39 ($17,040 total): art/fine arts, creative writing, journalism/publications, music, theater/drama. *Special Achievements/Activities Awards:* 159 ($107,110 total): general special achievements/activities, hobbies/interest. *Special Characteristics Awards:* 360 ($646,837 total): local/state students, members of minorities, out-of-state students. *Athletic:* Total: 168 ($352,833); Men: 92 ($194,837); Women: 76 ($157,996).

Other Money-Saving Options Accelerated degree, off-campus living (after sophomore year). *Waivers:* full or partial for senior citizens.

Contact Office of Financial Aid, Mesa State College, PO Box 2647, Grand Junction, CO 81502-2647, 970-248-1020.

MESIVTA OF EASTERN PARKWAY RABBINICAL SEMINARY
Brooklyn, New York

About the Institution Independent/religious, men. Offers 4 undergraduate majors.

Applications *Financial aid deadline (priority):* 6/1. *Financial aid forms:* FAFSA required; institutional form acceptable. *Admission application deadline:* rolling.

Summary of Aid to Needy Students *From gift & self-help combined:* Average need met: 90%. Average amount awarded: $4500. Federal Work-Study jobs.

Need-Based Scholarships & Grants Pell.

Loans Perkins, Stafford, Unsubsidized Stafford.

Non-Need Awards *Academic Interests/Achievement Awards:* religion/biblical studies. *Special Achievements/Activities Awards:* religious involvement.

Another Money-Saving Option Off-campus living.

Contact Rabbi Joseph Halberstadt, Dean, Mesivta of Eastern Parkway Rabbinical Seminary, Brooklyn, NY 11218-5559, 718-438-1002.

MESIVTA TIFERETH JERUSALEM OF AMERICA
New York, New York

About the Institution Independent/religious, men.

Applications *Financial aid forms:* FAFSA required.

Summary of Aid to Needy Students *From gift & self-help combined:* Average need met: 46%. Average amount awarded: $3500. Federal Work-Study jobs.

Need-Based Scholarships & Grants Pell, FSEOG, college/university.

Non-Need Awards Not offered.

Contact Rabbi Dickstein, Director of Financial Aid, Mesivta Tifereth Jerusalem of America, New York, NY 10002-6301, 212-964-2830.

MESIVTA TORAH VODAATH SEMINARY
Brooklyn, New York

About the Institution Independent/religious, men. Offers 1 undergraduate major.

Applications 25% of all full-time undergraduates enrolled in fall 1996 applied for aid; of these, 95% were judged to have need according to Federal Methodology, of whom 100% were aided. *Financial aid deadline (priority):* 8/1. *Financial aid forms:* FAFSA required. Institutional form required for some. *Admission application deadline:* rolling.

Summary of Aid to Needy Students *From gift & self-help combined:* Average need met: 50%. Average amount awarded: $3000. 80 Federal Work-Study jobs (averaging $1200).

Need-Based Scholarships & Grants Pell, FSEOG, private, college/university.

Loans Stafford, Unsubsidized Stafford, college/university.

Non-Need Awards *Academic Interests/Achievement Awards:* general academic.

Another Money-Saving Option Off-campus living.

Contact Mrs. Kayla Goldring, Director of Financial Aid, Mesivta Torah Vodaath Seminary, Brooklyn, NY 11218-5209, 718-941-8000.

MESSENGER COLLEGE
Joplin, Missouri

About the Institution Independent/religious, coed. Degrees awarded: A, B. Offers 4 undergraduate majors. Total enrollment: 93 (22% state residents). Freshmen: 33.

Undergraduate Expenses (1997–98) Tuition: $2880.

Applications *Financial aid forms:* FAFSA, institutional form required. *Admission application deadline:* 9/1.

Summary of Aid to Needy Students Federal Work-Study jobs; part-time jobs.

Need-Based Scholarships & Grants Pell, FSEOG, private.

Loans PLUS, Stafford, Unsubsidized Stafford.

Non-Need Awards *Special Characteristics Awards:* religious affiliation.

Contact Ms. Carole Terherst, Financial Aid Counselor, Messenger College, 300 East 50th Street, Joplin, MO 64803, 417-624-7070 Ext. 308.

MESSIAH COLLEGE
Grantham, Pennsylvania

About the Institution Independent/religious, coed. Degrees awarded: B. Offers 73 undergraduate majors. Total enrollment: 2,517 (51% state residents). Freshmen: 672.

Undergraduate Expenses (1997–98) Comprehensive fee of $18,490 includes tuition ($12,900), mandatory fees ($90), and college room and board ($5500). College room only: $2800.

Applications 79% of all full-time undergraduates enrolled in fall 1996 applied for aid; of these, 92% were judged to have need according to Federal Methodology, of whom 97% were aided. *Financial aid deadline (priority):* 4/1. *Financial aid forms:* FAFSA, institutional form required; CSS Financial Aid PROFILE acceptable. State form required for some. *Admission application deadline:* rolling.

Summary of Aid to Needy Students *From gift & self-help combined:* Average need met: 80%. Average amount awarded: $10,064 (61% gift aid, 39% self-help). *Gift aid:* Total: $10,973,512 (71% from college's own funds, 22% from other college-administered sources, 7% from external sources). 1,083 Federal Work-Study jobs (averaging $1439); 394 part-time jobs.

Need-Based Scholarships & Grants Pell, FSEOG, state, private, college/university.

Loans Perkins, PLUS, Stafford, Unsubsidized Stafford, Federal Nursing, private.

Non-Need Awards In 1996, a total of 2,003 non-need awards were made. *Academic Interests/Achievement Awards:* 1,117 ($2,183,730 total): general academic. *Creative Arts/Performance Awards:* 12 ($17,500 total): art/fine arts, music. *Special Achievements/Activities Awards:* 261 ($271,420 total): leadership *Special Characteristics Awards:* 613 ($230,016 total): relatives of clergy, religious affiliation, siblings of current students.

Other Money-Saving Options Accelerated degree. *Payment Plan:* installment. *Waivers:* full or partial for employees or children of employees and senior citizens.

Contact Mr. Michael Strite, Assistant Director of Financial Aid, Messiah College, Grantham, PA 17027, 717-691-6007, fax: 717-691-6002.

METHODIST COLLEGE
Fayetteville, North Carolina

About the Institution Independent/religious, coed. Degrees awarded: A, B. Offers 55 undergraduate majors. Total enrollment: 1,736 (66% state residents). Freshmen: 390.

Undergraduate Expenses (1997–98) Comprehensive fee of $15,650 includes tuition ($11,250) and college room and board ($4400). College room only: $2000.

Applications 98% of all full-time undergraduates enrolled in fall 1996 applied for aid; of these, 97% were judged to have need according to Federal Methodology, of whom 100% were aided. *Financial aid deadline (priority):* 5/1. *Financial aid forms:* FAFSA required. State form required for some. *Admission application deadline:* rolling.

Summary of Aid to Needy Students *From gift & self-help combined:* Average need met: 85%. Average amount awarded: $6000 (68% gift aid, 32% self-help). *Gift aid:* Total: $7,159,783 (57% from college's

own funds, 12% from other college-administered sources, 31% from external sources). 200 Federal Work-Study jobs (averaging $100); part-time jobs.

Need-Based Scholarships & Grants Pell, FSEOG, state, college/university.

Loans Perkins, PLUS, Stafford, Unsubsidized Stafford, college/university short-term loans ($4500 average).

Non-Need Awards In 1996, a total of 235 non-need awards were made. *Academic Interests/Achievement Awards:* 210 ($732,150 total): general academic. *Creative Arts/Performance Awards:* 25 ($52,000 total): music, theater/drama.

Other Money-Saving Options Accelerated degree, Army ROTC, cooperative Air Force ROTC, off-campus living (after freshman year). *Payment Plans:* installment, deferred payment. *Waivers:* full or partial for employees or children of employees and senior citizens.

Contact Office of Financial Aid, Methodist College, 5400 Ramsey Street, Fayetteville, NC 28311-1420, 910-630-7192.

METROPOLITAN STATE COLLEGE OF DENVER
Denver, Colorado

About the Institution State-supported, coed. Degrees awarded: B. Offers 51 undergraduate majors. Total enrollment: 17,177 (98% state residents). Freshmen: 1,616.

Undergraduate Expenses (1996–97) State resident tuition: $1673. Nonresident tuition: $6630. Mandatory fees: $287.

Applications *Financial aid deadline (priority):* 3/15. *Financial aid forms:* FAFSA required; CSS Financial Aid PROFILE, SINGLEFILE Form of United Student Aid Funds acceptable. *Admission application deadline:* 7/21.

Summary of Aid to Needy Students *From gift & self-help combined:* Average need met: 70%. *Gift aid:* Total: $39,566,098 (1% from college's own funds, 83% from other college-administered sources, 16% from external sources). 140 Federal Work-Study jobs (averaging $273); 398 part-time jobs.

Need-Based Scholarships & Grants Pell, FSEOG, state, private.

Loans Perkins, PLUS, Stafford, Unsubsidized Stafford, college/university short-term loans ($200 average).

Non-Need Awards In 1996, a total of 705 non-need awards were made. *Academic Interests/Achievement Awards:* 529 ($654,000 total): general academic. *Creative Arts/Performance Awards:* 77 ($77,000 total): general creative, music. *Athletic:* Total: 99 ($176,988); Men: 45 ($85,943); Women: 54 ($91,045).

Other Money-Saving Options Accelerated degree, co-op program, Army ROTC, cooperative Air Force ROTC. *Payment Plan:* deferred payment. *Waivers:* full or partial for employees or children of employees and senior citizens.

Contact Office of Financial Aid, Metropolitan State College of Denver, Denver, CO 80217-3362, 303-573-2660.

METROPOLITAN STATE UNIVERSITY
St. Paul, Minnesota

About the Institution State-supported, coed. Degrees awarded: B, M. Offers 24 undergraduate majors. Total enrollment: 5,245. Undergraduates: 4,994 (98% state residents).

Undergraduate Expenses (1996–97) State resident tuition: $2544. Nonresident tuition: $5630. Mandatory fees: $26.

Applications 72% of all full-time undergraduates enrolled in fall 1996 applied for aid; of these, 87% were judged to have need according to

Federal Methodology, of whom 71% were aided. *Financial aid deadline (priority):* 8/1. *Financial aid forms:* FAFSA, institutional form required. *Admission application deadline:* rolling.

Summary of Aid to Needy Students *From gift & self-help combined:* Average need met: 50%. *Gift aid:* Total: $1,645,000 (7% from college's own funds, 14% from other college-administered sources, 79% from external sources). 30 Federal Work-Study jobs (averaging $1800); 35 part-time jobs.

Need-Based Scholarships & Grants Pell, FSEOG, state, private, college/university.

Loans PLUS, Stafford, Unsubsidized Stafford, state, private.

Non-Need Awards Not offered.

Other Money-Saving Options *Waivers:* full or partial for employees or children of employees and senior citizens.

Contact Mr. R. D. Cleaveland, Director, Financial Aid, Metropolitan State University, 700 East 7th Street, St. Paul, MN 55106-5000, 612-772-7670, fax: 612-772-3716.

MIAMI UNIVERSITY
Oxford, Ohio

About the Institution State-related, coed. Degrees awarded: B, M, D. Offers 93 undergraduate majors. Total enrollment: 16,103. Undergraduates: 14,523 (73% state residents). Freshmen: 3,383.

Undergraduate Expenses (1996–97) State resident tuition: $4210. Nonresident tuition: $9966. Mandatory fees: $962. College room and board: $4440. College room only: $2020.

Applications Of all full-time undergraduates enrolled in fall 1996, 71% of those who applied for aid were judged to have need according to Federal Methodology, of whom 98% were aided. *Financial aid deadline (priority):* 2/15. *Financial aid forms:* FAFSA required. State form required for some. *Regular admission application deadline:* 1/31. Early decision deadline: 11/1. Early action deadline: 12/1.

Summary of Aid to Needy Students *From gift & self-help combined:* Average need met: 91%. Average amount awarded: $6833 (28% gift aid, 72% self-help). *Gift aid:* Total: $8,549,242 (16% from college's own funds, 34% from other college-administered sources, 50% from external sources). 775 Federal Work-Study jobs (averaging $1372); 3,100 part-time jobs.

Need-Based Scholarships & Grants Pell, FSEOG, state, private, college/university.

Loans Perkins, PLUS, Stafford, Unsubsidized Stafford, state, private, college/university short-term loans ($688 average), college/university long-term loans ($2527 average).

Non-Need Awards In 1996, a total of 2,054 non-need awards were made. *Academic Interests/Achievement Awards:* 1,271 ($2,074,949 total): general academic, education, engineering/technologies. *Creative Arts/Performance Awards:* 35 ($30,250 total): art/fine arts, music, theater/drama. *Special Characteristics Awards:* 422 ($1,263,448 total): local/state students, members of minorities, out-of-state students. *Athletic:* Total: 326 ($1,914,377); Men: 224 ($1,298,749); Women: 102 ($615,628).

Other Money-Saving Options Accelerated degree, co-op program, Naval ROTC, Air Force ROTC, cooperative Army ROTC, off-campus living (after freshman year). *Payment Plan:* installment. *Waivers:* full or partial for employees or children of employees.

Contact Mr. Chuck Knepfle, Associate Director, Miami University, 301 South Campus Avenue, Oxford, OH 45056, 513-529-8714, fax: 513-529-8713.

MICHIGAN CHRISTIAN COLLEGE
Rochester Hills, Michigan

About the Institution Independent/religious, coed. Degrees awarded: A, B. Offers 15 undergraduate majors. Total enrollment: 363 (78% state residents). Freshmen: 122.

Undergraduate Expenses (1996–97) Comprehensive fee of $9820 includes tuition ($6020), mandatory fees ($100), and college room and board ($3700).

Applications 95% of all full-time undergraduates enrolled in fall 1996 applied for aid; of these, 88% were judged to have need according to Federal Methodology, of whom 99% were aided. *Financial aid deadline (priority):* 6/1. *Financial aid forms:* FAFSA, institutional form required; CSS Financial Aid PROFILE acceptable. *Admission application deadline:* rolling.

Summary of Aid to Needy Students *From gift & self-help combined:* Average need met: 60%. Average amount awarded: $6833 (56% gift aid, 44% self-help). *Gift aid:* Total: $976,245 (50% from college's own funds, 9% from other college-administered sources, 41% from external sources). 82 Federal Work-Study jobs (averaging $1000); 128 part-time jobs.

Need-Based Scholarships & Grants Pell, FSEOG, state.

Loans Perkins, PLUS, Stafford, Unsubsidized Stafford.

Non-Need Awards *Academic Interests/Achievement Awards:* general academic, religion/biblical studies. *Creative Arts/Performance Awards:* 44 ($13,725 total): music, theater/drama. *Special Achievements/Activities Awards:* 52 ($29,129 total): leadership. *Special Characteristics Awards:* general special characteristics, adult students, children and siblings of alumni, children of faculty/staff, out-of-state students, siblings of current students. *Athletic:* Total: 68 ($54,831); Men: 42 ($32,800); Women: 26 ($22,031).

Other Money-Saving Options Accelerated degree, off-campus living (after sophomore year). *Payment Plan:* installment. *Waivers:* full or partial for children of alumni, employees or children of employees, senior citizens.

Contact Ms. Lora Cuthbertson, Director of Financial Aid, Michigan Christian College, 800 West Avon Road, Rochester Hills, MI 48307-2764, 810-650-6018, fax: 810-650-6060.

MICHIGAN STATE UNIVERSITY
East Lansing, Michigan

About the Institution State-supported, coed. Degrees awarded: B, M, D, P. Offers 122 undergraduate majors. Total enrollment: 41,545. Undergraduates: 32,318 (91% state residents). Freshmen: 6,806.

Undergraduate Expenses (1996–97) State resident tuition: $4103 (minimum). Nonresident tuition: $11,168 (minimum). Mandatory fees: $552. College room and board: $3972.

Applications 58% of all full-time undergraduates enrolled in fall 1996 applied for aid; of these, 77% were judged to have need according to Federal Methodology, of whom 99% were aided. *Financial aid deadline:* continuous. *Financial aid forms:* FAFSA required. *Regular admission application deadline:* 7/30. Early action deadline: 10/1.

Summary of Aid to Needy Students *From gift & self-help combined:* Average need met: 100%. Average amount awarded: $9633 (30% gift aid, 70% self-help). *Gift aid:* Total: $35,265,242 (46% from college's own funds, 5% from other college-administered sources, 49% from external sources). 3,935 Federal Work-Study jobs (averaging $2635); 7,618 part-time jobs.

Need-Based Scholarships & Grants Pell, FSEOG, state, private, college/university.

Loans Perkins, PLUS, Stafford, Unsubsidized Stafford, Primary Care, state, college/university short-term loans ($645 average).

Non-Need Awards In 1996, a total of 1,938 non-need awards were made. *Academic Interests/Achievement Awards:* 362 ($1,264,033 total): general academic, agriculture, architecture, biological sciences, business, computer science, education, engineering/technologies, military science, social sciences. *Creative Arts/Performance Awards:* 155 ($366,040 total): creative writing, debating, journalism/publications, music, performing arts, theater/drama. *Special Achievements/Activities Awards:* 294 ($470,605 total): community service, hobbies/interest, Junior Miss, leadership, memberships, religious involvement. *Special Characteristics Awards:* 732 ($1,849,647 total): children and siblings of alumni, children of faculty/staff, children of union members/company employees, ethnic background, first-generation college students, members of minorities, out-of-state students, public servants, religious affiliation, ROTC participants, spouses of deceased or disabled public servants, veterans, veterans' children. *Athletic:* Total: 395 ($3,054,885); Men: 240 ($1,778,515); Women: 155 ($1,276,370).

Other Money-Saving Options Co-op program, Army ROTC, Air Force ROTC, off-campus living (after freshman year). *Payment Plan:* deferred payment. *Waivers:* full or partial for employees or children of employees.

Contact Ms. Pam Shaw, Michigan State University, 265 Student Services Building, East Lansing, MI 48824-1113, 517-353-5940, fax: 517-432-1155.

MICHIGAN TECHNOLOGICAL UNIVERSITY
Houghton, Michigan

About the Institution State-supported, coed. Degrees awarded: A, B, M, D. Offers 63 undergraduate majors. Total enrollment: 6,195. Undergraduates: 5,541 (78% state residents). Freshmen: 1,076.

Undergraduate Expenses (1996–97) State resident tuition: $3822. Nonresident tuition: $9105. Mandatory fees: $126. College room and board: $4284.

Applications Of all full-time undergraduates enrolled in fall 1996, 53% of those who applied for aid were judged to have need according to Federal Methodology, of whom 97% were aided. *Financial aid deadline (priority):* 3/1. *Financial aid forms:* FAFSA required. Institutional form required for some. *Admission application deadline:* rolling.

Summary of Aid to Needy Students *From gift & self-help combined:* Average need met: 78%. Average amount awarded: $6975 (47% gift aid, 53% self-help). *Gift aid:* Total: $8,480,970 (60% from college's own funds, 10% from other college-administered sources, 30% from external sources). 204 Federal Work-Study jobs (averaging $1300); 2,646 part-time jobs.

Need-Based Scholarships & Grants Pell, FSEOG, state, private, college/university.

Loans Perkins, PLUS, Stafford, Unsubsidized Stafford, state, college/university long-term loans ($1850 average).

Non-Need Awards In 1996, a total of 2,654 non-need awards were made. *Academic Interests/Achievement Awards:* 1,586 ($2,767,109 total): general academic, biological sciences, business, computer science, engineering/technologies, mathematics, physical sciences, social sciences. *Special Achievements/Activities Awards:* 47 ($10,011 total): leadership. *Special Characteristics Awards:* 865 ($4,322,872 total): general special characteristics, children and siblings of alumni, international students, members of minorities, out-of-state students, previous college experience. *Athletic:* Total: 156 ($738,361); Men: 125 ($569,692); Women: 31 ($168,669).

Other Money-Saving Options Co-op program, Army ROTC, Air Force ROTC, off-campus living (after freshman year). *Payment Plan:* installment. *Waivers:* full or partial for employees or children of employees and senior citizens.

Contact Adrene Remali, System Administrator, Michigan Technological University, Houghton, MI 49931-1295, 906-487-3222, fax: 906-487-3343.

MID-AMERICA BIBLE COLLEGE
Oklahoma City, Oklahoma

About the Institution Independent/religious, coed. Degrees awarded: A, B. Offers 15 undergraduate majors. Total enrollment: 512 (49% state residents). Freshmen: 106.

Undergraduate Expenses (1997–98) Comprehensive fee of $7782 includes tuition ($4316), mandatory fees ($368), and college room and board ($3098). College room only: $1598.

Applications 81% of all full-time undergraduates enrolled in fall 1996 applied for aid; of these, 94% were judged to have need according to Federal Methodology, of whom 96% were aided. *Financial aid deadline (priority):* 5/1. *Financial aid forms:* FAFSA required. Institutional form required for some. *Admission application deadline:* rolling.

Summary of Aid to Needy Students *From gift & self-help combined:* Average amount awarded: $5300 (47% gift aid, 53% self-help). *Gift aid:* Total: $1,241,104 (56% from college's own funds, 3% from other college-administered sources, 41% from external sources). 41 Federal Work-Study jobs (averaging $2000); 25 part-time jobs.

Need-Based Scholarships & Grants Pell, FSEOG, state.

Loans Perkins, PLUS, Stafford, Unsubsidized Stafford, college/university short-term loans ($25 average).

Non-Need Awards In 1996, a total of 369 non-need awards were made. *Academic Interests/Achievement Awards:* 85 ($150,977 total): general academic. *Creative Arts/Performance Awards:* 12 ($9250 total): music. *Special Achievements/Activities Awards:* 95 ($43,950 total): general special achievements/activities, community service, leadership, memberships, religious involvement. *Special Characteristics Awards:* 177 ($293,999 total): general special characteristics, children of faculty/staff, international students, members of minorities, religious affiliation, spouses of current students.

Other Money-Saving Options Accelerated degree. *Payment Plan:* installment. *Waivers:* full or partial for employees or children of employees.

Contact Ms. Shannon Montgomery, Director of Financial Aid, Mid-America Bible College, 3500 SW 119th Street, Oklahoma City, OK 73170-4504, 405-691-3800, fax: 405-692-3165.

MIDAMERICA NAZARENE UNIVERSITY
Olathe, Kansas

About the Institution Independent/religious, coed. Degrees awarded: A, B, M. Offers 38 undergraduate majors. Total enrollment: 1,394. Undergraduates: 1,266 (61% state residents). Freshmen: 240.

Undergraduate Expenses (1997–98) Comprehensive fee of $13,752 includes tuition ($8790), mandatory fees ($466 minimum), and college room and board ($4496). College room only: $2258.

Applications 73% of all full-time undergraduates enrolled in fall 1996 applied for aid; of these, 96% were judged to have need according to Federal Methodology, of whom 99% were aided. *Financial aid deadline (priority):* 3/1. *Financial aid forms:* FAFSA, institutional form required; CSS Financial Aid PROFILE acceptable. State form required for some. *Admission application deadline:* 8/1.

Summary of Aid to Needy Students *From gift & self-help combined:* Average need met: 51%. Average amount awarded: $7132 (46% gift aid, 54% self-help). *Gift aid:* Total: $2,525,918 (57% from college's own funds, 5% from other college-administered sources, 38% from external sources). 100 Federal Work-Study jobs (averaging $1744); part-time jobs.

Need-Based Scholarships & Grants Pell, FSEOG, state, private, college/university.

Loans Perkins, PLUS, Stafford, Unsubsidized Stafford, Federal Nursing, private.

Non-Need Awards In 1996, a total of 1,391 non-need awards were made. *Academic Interests/Achievement Awards:* 460 ($631,754 total): general academic, agriculture, health fields. *Creative Arts/Performance Awards:* 99 ($54,166 total): music. *Special Achievements/Activities Awards:* 35 ($38,630 total): cheerleading/drum major, leadership. *Special Characteristics Awards:* 518 ($786,396 total): general special characteristics, children of faculty/staff, relatives of clergy, religious affiliation. *Athletic:* Total: 279 ($410,686); Men: 184 ($297,104); Women: 95 ($113,582).

Other Money-Saving Options Accelerated degree, cooperative Army ROTC, cooperative Air Force ROTC. *Payment Plan:* installment. *Waivers:* full or partial for employees or children of employees and senior citizens.

Contact Ms. Sharon Williams, Director of Student Financial Services, MidAmerica Nazarene University, 2030 College Way, Olathe, KS 66062-1899, 913-791-3298, fax: 913-791-3481.

MID-CONTINENT BAPTIST BIBLE COLLEGE
Mayfield, Kentucky

About the Institution Independent/religious, coed. Degrees awarded: B. Offers 2 undergraduate majors. Total enrollment: 115 (70% state residents). Freshmen: 24.

Undergraduate Expenses (1997–98) Comprehensive fee of $5792 includes tuition ($3200), mandatory fees ($60), and college room and board ($2532). College room only: $1312.

Applications 75% of all full-time undergraduates enrolled in fall 1996 applied for aid; of these, 73% were judged to have need according to Federal Methodology, of whom 100% were aided. *Financial aid deadline (priority):* 5/1. *Financial aid forms:* FAFSA, institutional form required; CSS Financial Aid PROFILE acceptable. *Admission application deadline:* rolling.

Summary of Aid to Needy Students *From gift & self-help combined:* Average need met: 85%. Average amount awarded: $2860 (52% gift aid, 48% self-help). *Gift aid:* Total: $40,425 (16% from college's own funds, 84% from external sources). 9 part-time jobs.

Need-Based Scholarships & Grants Pell, private, college/university.

Loans PLUS, Stafford, Unsubsidized Stafford.

Non-Need Awards In 1996, a total of 10 non-need awards were made. *Academic Interests/Achievement Awards:* 10 ($6500 total): general academic.

Other Money-Saving Options Off-campus living. *Payment Plan:* installment. *Waivers:* full or partial for employees or children of employees and senior citizens.

Contact Mrs. Mary Ann Morgan, Director of Financial Aid, Mid-Continent Baptist Bible College, 99 Powell Road East, Mayfield, KY 42066, 502-247-8521 Ext. 12, fax: 502-247-3115.

MIDDLEBURY COLLEGE
Middlebury, Vermont

About the Institution Independent, coed. Degrees awarded: B, M, D. Offers 59 undergraduate majors. Total enrollment: 2,097. Freshmen: 519.

Undergraduate Expenses (1997–98) Comprehensive fee: $29,340.

Applications 48% of all full-time undergraduates enrolled in fall 1996 applied for aid; of these, 95% were judged to have need according to Federal Methodology, of whom 99% were aided. *Financial aid deadline (priority):* 11/15. *Financial aid forms:* FAFSA required. CSS Financial Aid PROFILE, state form, institutional form required for some. *Regular admission application deadline:* 12/31. Early decision deadline: 11/15.

Summary of Aid to Needy Students *From gift & self-help combined:* Average need met: 100%. Average amount awarded: $20,909 (72% gift aid, 28% self-help). *Gift aid:* Total: $12,868,806 (90% from col-

lege's own funds, 4% from other college-administered sources, 6% from external sources). Federal Work-Study jobs; part-time jobs.

Need-Based Scholarships & Grants Pell, FSEOG, state, college/university.

Loans Perkins, PLUS, Stafford, Unsubsidized Stafford, college/university short-term loans, college/university long-term loans.

Non-Need Awards Not offered.

Other Money-Saving Options *Payment Plans:* tuition prepayment, installment, deferred payment. *Waivers:* full or partial for minority students, children of alumni, employees or children of employees, adult students, senior citizens.

Contact Office of Financial Aid, Middlebury College, The Emma Willard House, Middlebury, VT 05753-6002, 802-443-5158, fax: 802-443-2065.

MIDDLE TENNESSEE STATE UNIVERSITY
Murfreesboro, Tennessee

About the Institution State-supported, coed. Degrees awarded: A, B, M, D. Offers 135 undergraduate majors. Total enrollment: 17,924. Undergraduates: 15,890 (94% state residents). Freshmen: 2,292.

Undergraduate Expenses (1996–97) State resident tuition: $1714. Nonresident tuition: $6050. Mandatory fees: $300. College room and board: $2558. College room only: $1580.

Applications 66% of all full-time undergraduates enrolled in fall 1996 applied for aid; of these, 82% were judged to have need according to Federal Methodology, of whom 96% were aided. *Financial aid deadline (priority):* 3/15. *Financial aid forms:* FAFSA required. Institutional form required for some. *Admission application deadline:* rolling.

Summary of Aid to Needy Students *From gift & self-help combined:* Average need met: 60%. Average amount awarded: $6276 (27% gift aid, 73% self-help). *Gift aid:* Total: $11,302,033 (36% from college's own funds, 3% from other college-administered sources, 61% from external sources). 203 Federal Work-Study jobs (averaging $1966); 1,500 part-time jobs.

Need-Based Scholarships & Grants Pell, FSEOG, state.

Loans Perkins, PLUS, Stafford, Unsubsidized Stafford, college/university short-term loans ($150 average).

Non-Need Awards In 1996, a total of 1,512 non-need awards were made. *Academic Interests/Achievement Awards:* 842 ($1,956,089 total): general academic. *Creative Arts/Performance Awards:* 90 ($79,824 total): music. *Special Achievements/Activities Awards:* 44 ($83,366 total): general special achievements/activities, leadership. *Special Characteristics Awards:* 269 ($648,113 total): members of minorities. *Athletic:* Total: 267 ($1,277,200); Men: 178 ($895,092); Women: 89 ($382,108).

Other Money-Saving Options Accelerated degree, co-op program, Army ROTC, cooperative Air Force ROTC, off-campus living. *Waivers:* full or partial for employees or children of employees and senior citizens.

Contact Ms. Beth Parker, Assistant Director of Student Financial Aid, Middle Tennessee State University, Murfreesboro, TN 37132, 615-898-2830, fax: 615-898-5167.

MIDLAND LUTHERAN COLLEGE
Fremont, Nebraska

About the Institution Independent/religious, coed. Degrees awarded: A, B. Offers 58 undergraduate majors. Total enrollment: 1,062 (73% state residents). Freshmen: 284.

Undergraduate Expenses (1997–98 estimated) Comprehensive fee of $15,450 includes tuition ($12,250) and college room and board ($3200). College room only: $1300.

Applications 99% of all full-time undergraduates enrolled in fall 1996 applied for aid; of these, 86% were judged to have need according to Federal Methodology, of whom 100% were aided. *Financial aid deadline:* continuous. *Financial aid forms:* FAFSA, institutional form required. *Admission application deadline:* rolling.

Summary of Aid to Needy Students *From gift & self-help combined:* Average need met: 88%. Average amount awarded: $10,806 (53% gift aid, 47% self-help). *Gift aid:* Total: $4,614,993 (78% from college's own funds, 9% from other college-administered sources, 13% from external sources). 272 Federal Work-Study jobs (averaging $983); 100 part-time jobs.

Need-Based Scholarships & Grants Pell, FSEOG, state, private, college/university.

Loans Perkins, PLUS, Stafford, Unsubsidized Stafford, college/university short-term loans ($1000 average).

Non-Need Awards *Academic Interests/Achievement Awards:* general academic. *Creative Arts/Performance Awards:* art/fine arts, debating, journalism/publications, music, theater/drama. *Special Achievements/Activities Awards:* general special achievements/activities, community service, religious involvement. *Special Characteristics Awards:* handicapped students, international students, members of minorities, religious affiliation, siblings of current students. *Athletic:* available.

Other Money-Saving Options Off-campus living (after junior year). *Payment Plan:* installment. *Waivers:* full or partial for employees or children of employees and senior citizens.

Contact Office of Financial Aid, Midland Lutheran College, 900 North Clarkson Street, Fremont, NE 68025-4200, 402-721-5480.

MIDWAY COLLEGE
Midway, Kentucky

About the Institution Independent/religious, women. Degrees awarded: A, B. Offers 27 undergraduate majors. Total enrollment: 930 (84% state residents). Freshmen: 184.

Undergraduate Expenses (1996–97) Comprehensive fee of $12,410 includes tuition ($8100), mandatory fees ($60), and college room and board ($4250). College room only: $2050.

Applications *Financial aid deadline (priority):* 8/1. *Financial aid forms:* FAFSA, institutional form required. *Admission application deadline:* rolling.

Summary of Aid to Needy Students *From gift & self-help combined:* Average amount awarded: $4293 (48% gift aid, 52% self-help). *Gift aid:* Total: $898,607 (47% from college's own funds, 3% from other college-administered sources, 50% from external sources). 93 Federal Work-Study jobs (averaging $1200); 40 part-time jobs.

Need-Based Scholarships & Grants Pell, FSEOG, state, private, college/university.

Loans Perkins, PLUS, Stafford, Unsubsidized Stafford, private, college/university short-term loans ($300 average), college/university long-term loans ($670 average).

Non-Need Awards In 1996, a total of 217 non-need awards were made. *Academic Interests/Achievement Awards:* 74 ($157,373 total): general academic. *Creative Arts/Performance Awards:* 19 ($6975 total): art/fine arts, music. *Special Characteristics Awards:* 16 ($21,201 total): children and siblings of alumni, children of faculty/staff, members of minorities, relatives of clergy, religious affiliation. *Athletic:* Total: 108 ($104,667); Women: 108 ($104,667).

Other Money-Saving Options Accelerated degree, cooperative Army ROTC, off-campus living (after sophomore year).

Contact Ms. Laura Keown, Director of Financial Aid, Midway College, 512 East Stephens Street, Midway, KY 40347-1120, 606-846-5410; fax: 606-846-5349.

MIDWESTERN STATE UNIVERSITY
Wichita Falls, Texas

About the Institution State-supported, coed. Degrees awarded: A, B, M. Offers 50 undergraduate majors. Total enrollment: 5,643. Undergraduates: 4,956 (88% state residents). Freshmen: 724.

Undergraduate Expenses (1996–97) State resident tuition: $992. Nonresident tuition: $7626. Mandatory fees: $896. College room and board: $3366 (minimum). College room only: $1700 (minimum).

Applications Of all full-time undergraduates enrolled in fall 1996, 74% of those who applied for aid were judged to have need according to Federal Methodology, of whom 100% were aided. *Financial aid deadline (priority):* 4/4. *Financial aid forms:* FAFSA, CSS Financial Aid PROFILE, state form, SINGLEFILE Form of United Student Aid Funds acceptable. Institutional form required for some. *Admission application deadline:* 8/7.

Summary of Aid to Needy Students *From gift & self-help combined:* Average need met: 100%. Average amount awarded: $1833 (37% gift aid, 63% self-help). *Gift aid:* Total: $1,226,929 (1% from college's own funds, 26% from other college-administered sources, 73% from external sources). Federal Work-Study jobs; part-time jobs.

Loans College/university short-term loans.

Non-Need Awards In 1996, a total of 1,126 non-need awards were made. *Academic Interests/Achievement Awards:* 659 ($344,079 total): general academic. *Creative Arts/Performance Awards:* 122 ($63,523 total). *Special Achievements/Activities Awards:* 122 ($63,523 total): leadership. *Special Characteristics Awards:* 111 ($58,228 total). *Athletic:* Total: 112 ($120,861); Men: 68 ($72,394); Women: 44 ($48,467).

Other Money-Saving Options Accelerated degree, off-campus living (after sophomore year). *Payment Plan:* installment. *Waivers:* full or partial for employees or children of employees.

Contact Office of Financial Aid, Midwestern State University, 3410 Taft Boulevard, Wichita Falls, TX 76308-2096, 817-689-4000.

MILES COLLEGE
Birmingham, Alabama

About the Institution Independent/religious, coed. Degrees awarded: B. Offers 15 undergraduate majors. Total enrollment: 1,234 (86% state residents). Freshmen: 375.

Undergraduate Expenses (1997–98) Comprehensive fee of $6900 includes tuition ($4150) and college room and board ($2750). College room only: $1250.

Applications Of all full-time undergraduates enrolled in fall 1996, 100% of those judged to have need according to Federal Methodology were aided. *Financial aid deadline (priority):* 3/15. *Financial aid forms:* FAFSA required. State form required for some. *Admission application deadline:* rolling.

Summary of Aid to Needy Students *From gift & self-help combined:* Average need met: 85%. Average amount awarded: $6800 (38% gift aid, 62% self-help). *Gift aid:* Total: $2,861,846 (4% from college's own funds, 33% from other college-administered sources, 63% from external sources). 250 Federal Work-Study jobs (averaging $1000).

Need-Based Scholarships & Grants Pell, FSEOG, state.

Loans Perkins, PLUS, Stafford, Unsubsidized Stafford.

Non-Need Awards *Academic Interests/Achievement Awards:* general academic. *Creative Arts/Performance Awards:* 30 ($50,000 total): music. *Special Achievements/Activities Awards:* 1 ($1000 total): community service. *Special Characteristics Awards:* handicapped students. *Athletic:* Total: 90 ($197,665); Men: 72 ($166,965); Women: 18 ($30,700).

Other Money-Saving Options Accelerated degree, co-op program, cooperative Army ROTC, cooperative Air Force ROTC, off-campus living.

Contact Financial Aid Office, Miles College, Birmingham, AL 35208, 205-929-1665.

MILLERSVILLE UNIVERSITY OF PENNSYLVANIA
Millersville, Pennsylvania

About the Institution State-supported, coed. Degrees awarded: A, B, M. Offers 79 undergraduate majors. Total enrollment: 7,474. Undergraduates: 6,746 (95% state residents). Freshmen: 1,043.

Undergraduate Expenses (1996–97) State resident tuition: $3368. Nonresident tuition: $8566. Mandatory fees: $900. College room and board: $4300.

Applications Of all full-time undergraduates enrolled in fall 1996, 57% of those who applied for aid were judged to have need according to Federal Methodology, of whom 98% were aided. *Financial aid deadline:* Applications processed continuously. *Financial aid forms:* FAFSA, state form, institutional form required. *Admission application deadline:* rolling.

Summary of Aid to Needy Students *Gift aid:* Total: $1,809,782 (31% from college's own funds, 43% from other college-administered sources, 26% from external sources). 350 Federal Work-Study jobs (averaging $716); 1,185 part-time jobs.

Need-Based Scholarships & Grants Pell, FSEOG, state, private, college/university.

Loans Perkins, PLUS, Stafford, Unsubsidized Stafford, private, college/university short-term loans ($100 average), college/university long-term loans ($1500 average).

Non-Need Awards *Academic Interests/Achievement Awards:* 121 ($264,407 total): general academic. *Creative Arts/Performance Awards:* art/fine arts, performing arts. *Special Achievements/Activities Awards:* available. *Athletic:* Total: 220 ($237,723); Men: 105 ($132,216); Women: 115 ($105,507).

Other Money-Saving Options Co-op program, off-campus living (after sophomore year). *Payment Plan:* installment. *Waivers:* full or partial for employees or children of employees.

Contact Office of Financial Aid, Millersville University of Pennsylvania, PO Box 1002, Millersville, PA 17551-0302, 717-872-3024.

MILLIGAN COLLEGE
Milligan College, Tennessee

About the Institution Independent/religious, coed. Degrees awarded: A, B, M. Offers 56 undergraduate majors. Total enrollment: 836. Undergraduates: 796 (40% state residents). Freshmen: 186.

Undergraduate Expenses (1996–97) Comprehensive fee of $12,940 includes tuition ($9200), mandatory fees ($300), and college room and board ($3440). College room only: $1600.

Applications Of all full-time undergraduates enrolled in fall 1996, 89% of those who applied for aid were judged to have need according to Federal Methodology, of whom 100% were aided. *Financial aid deadline (priority):* 3/1. *Financial aid forms:* institutional form required; CSS Financial Aid PROFILE acceptable. FAFSA, state form required for some. *Admission application deadline:* rolling.

Summary of Aid to Needy Students *From gift & self-help combined:* Average need met: 81%. Average amount awarded: $7793 (46% gift aid, 54% self-help). *Gift aid:* Total: $1,872,629 (65% from college's own funds, 10% from other college-administered sources, 25% from external sources). 66 Federal Work-Study jobs (averaging $1275); 281 part-time jobs.

Need-Based Scholarships & Grants Pell, FSEOG, state, college/university.

Loans Perkins, PLUS, Stafford, Unsubsidized Stafford, Norwest Collegiate Loans, Signature Loans.

Non-Need Awards In 1996, a total of 575 non-need awards were made. *Academic Interests/Achievement Awards:* 351 ($932,766 total): general academic, communication, English, health fields, religion/biblical studies. *Creative Arts/Performance Awards:* 37 ($54,090 total): art/fine arts, music, theater/drama. *Special Achievements/Activities Awards:* 75 ($23,225 total): general special achievements/activities. *Special Characteristics Awards:* 15 ($98,558 total): children of faculty/staff. *Athletic:* Total: 97 ($353,978); Men: 57 ($201,328); Women: 40 ($152,650).

Other Money-Saving Options Accelerated degree, co-op program, cooperative Army ROTC. *Payment Plan:* installment. *Waivers:* full or partial for employees or children of employees.

Contact Mrs. Nancy M. Beverly, Director of Financial Aid, Milligan College, PO Box 250, Milligan College, TN 37682, 423-461-8949, fax: 423-461-8755.

MILLIKIN UNIVERSITY
Decatur, Illinois

About the Institution Independent/religious, coed. Degrees awarded: B. Offers 66 undergraduate majors. Total enrollment: 1,930 (87% state residents). Freshmen: 496.

Undergraduate Expenses (1997–98 estimated) Comprehensive fee of $19,149 includes tuition ($13,988), mandatory fees ($91), and college room and board ($5070). College room only: $2638.

Applications 88% of all full-time undergraduates enrolled in fall 1996 applied for aid; of these, 92% were judged to have need according to Federal Methodology, of whom 100% were aided. *Financial aid deadline (priority):* 8/1. *Financial aid forms:* FAFSA, institutional form required; CSS Financial Aid PROFILE acceptable. *Admission application deadline:* rolling.

Summary of Aid to Needy Students *From gift & self-help combined:* Average need met: 100%. Average amount awarded: $16,676 (61% gift aid, 39% self-help). *Gift aid:* Total: $15,441,224 (54% from college's own funds, 14% from other college-administered sources, 32% from external sources). 639 Federal Work-Study jobs (averaging $1236); 441 part-time jobs.

Need-Based Scholarships & Grants Pell, FSEOG, state, private, college/university.

Loans Perkins, PLUS, Stafford, Unsubsidized Stafford, college/university short-term loans ($300 average), signature loans, alternative loans.

Non-Need Awards In 1996, a total of 324 non-need awards were made. *Academic Interests/Achievement Awards:* 231 ($948,146 total): general academic. *Creative Arts/Performance Awards:* 76 ($167,055 total): art/fine arts, music, theater/drama. *Special Characteristics Awards:* 17 ($102,800 total): international students, relatives of clergy.

Other Money-Saving Options Off-campus living (after junior year). *Payment Plan:* installment. *Waivers:* full or partial for employees or children of employees.

Contact Ms. Jeanne Puckett, Director of Financial Aid, Millikin University, 1184 West Main Street, Decatur, IL 62522-2084, 217-424-6343, fax: 217-425-4669.

MILLSAPS COLLEGE
Jackson, Mississippi

About the Institution Independent/religious, coed. Degrees awarded: B, M. Offers 30 undergraduate majors. Total enrollment: 1,377. Undergraduates: 1,225 (60% state residents). Freshmen: 293.

Undergraduate Expenses (1996–97) Comprehensive fee of $17,990 includes tuition ($12,448), mandatory fees ($640), and college room and board ($4902 minimum). College room only: $2678 (minimum).

Applications 81% of all full-time undergraduates enrolled in fall 1996 applied for aid; of these, 73% were judged to have need according to Federal Methodology, of whom 100% were aided. *Financial aid deadline (priority):* 3/1. *Financial aid forms:* institutional form required; FAFSA, CSS Financial Aid PROFILE acceptable. *Regular admission application deadline:* 3/1. Early decision deadline: 11/15. Early action deadline: 12/1.

Summary of Aid to Needy Students *From gift & self-help combined:* Average need met: 100%. Average amount awarded: $10,461 (66% gift aid, 34% self-help). *Gift aid:* Total: $4,745,331 (81% from college's own funds, 13% from other college-administered sources, 6% from external sources). 218 Federal Work-Study jobs (averaging $1100); 300 part-time jobs.

Need-Based Scholarships & Grants Pell, FSEOG, state, private, college/university, foundation, civic group, and church-sponsored scholarships and grants.

Loans Perkins, PLUS, Stafford, Unsubsidized Stafford, state, private, college/university long-term loans ($1300 average).

Non-Need Awards *Academic Interests/Achievement Awards:* 728 ($4,265,264 total): general academic. *Creative Arts/Performance Awards:* 15 ($30,000 total): art/fine arts, music, theater/drama. *Special Achievements/Activities Awards:* 10 ($20,000 total): community service, leadership. *Special Characteristics Awards:* adult students, children of faculty/staff, religious affiliation.

Other Money-Saving Options Cooperative Army ROTC, off-campus living (after freshman year). *Payment Plan:* installment. *Waivers:* full or partial for employees or children of employees.

Contact Mr. Jack L. Woodward, Dean of Student Aid/Financial Planning, Millsaps College, Jackson, MS 39210-0001, 601-974-1220.

MILLS COLLEGE
Oakland, California

About the Institution Independent, women. Degrees awarded: B, M. Offers 40 undergraduate majors. Total enrollment: 1,182. Undergraduates: 866 (77% state residents). Freshmen: 151.

Undergraduate Expenses (1997–98) Comprehensive fee of $22,552 includes tuition ($16,030), mandatory fees ($492), and college room and board ($6030 minimum).

Applications *Financial aid deadline (priority):* 2/15. *Financial aid forms:* FAFSA, state form, institutional form required. Foreign Student Financial Aid Application required for some. *Admission application deadline:* rolling.

Summary of Aid to Needy Students Federal Work-Study jobs; part-time jobs.

Loans College/university long-term loans.

Non-Need Awards *Academic Interests/Achievement Awards:* general academic, biological sciences, mathematics, physical sciences. *Creative Arts/Performance Awards:* music. *Special Achievements/Activities Awards:* leadership.

Other Money-Saving Options Accelerated degree, co-op program, off-campus living. *Payment Plan:* installment. *Waivers:* full or partial for employees or children of employees.

Contact Office of Financial Aid, Mills College, Oakland, CA 94613-1000, 510-430-2255.

MILWAUKEE INSTITUTE OF ART AND DESIGN
Milwaukee, Wisconsin

About the Institution Independent, coed. Degrees awarded: B. Offers 9 undergraduate majors. Total enrollment: 518 (80% state residents). Freshmen: 112.

Undergraduate Expenses (1996–97) Comprehensive fee of $20,100 includes tuition ($13,700), mandatory fees ($400), and college room and board ($6000).

Applications Of all full-time undergraduates enrolled in fall 1996, 95% of those who applied for aid were judged to have need according to Federal Methodology, of whom 100% were aided. *Financial aid deadline (priority):* 3/1. *Financial aid forms:* FAFSA, institutional form required; CSS Financial Aid PROFILE acceptable. *Admission application deadline:* rolling.

Summary of Aid to Needy Students *From gift & self-help combined:* Average need met: 72%. Average amount awarded: $8212 (60% gift aid, 40% self-help). *Gift aid:* Total: $2,070,000 (63% from college's own funds, 23% from other college-administered sources, 14% from external sources). 50 Federal Work-Study jobs (averaging $1800); 50 part-time jobs.

Need-Based Scholarships & Grants Pell, FSEOG, state, private, college/university.

Loans PLUS, Stafford, Unsubsidized Stafford, private, college/university short-term loans ($300 average).

Non-Need Awards In 1996, a total of 488 non-need awards were made. *Academic Interests/Achievement Awards:* 112 ($360,100 total): general academic. *Creative Arts/Performance Awards:* 145 ($320,000 total): applied art and design, art/fine arts. *Special Characteristics Awards:* 231 ($465,156 total): children of faculty/staff, ethnic background, local/state students, members of minorities.

Other Money-Saving Options Off-campus living (after freshman year). *Payment Plan:* deferred payment. *Waivers:* full or partial for employees or children of employees.

Contact Mr. Lloyd Mueller, Director of Financial Aid, Milwaukee Institute of Art and Design, 273 East Erie Street, Milwaukee, WI 53202-6003, 414-291-3272, fax: 414-291-8077.

MILWAUKEE SCHOOL OF ENGINEERING
Milwaukee, Wisconsin

About the Institution Independent, coed. Degrees awarded: A, B, M. Offers 12 undergraduate majors. Total enrollment: 2,957. Undergraduates: 2,537 (61% state residents). Freshmen: 538.

Undergraduate Expenses (1996–97) Comprehensive fee of $16,920 includes tuition ($13,305) and college room and board ($3615). College room only: $2280.

Applications 81% of all full-time undergraduates enrolled in fall 1996 applied for aid; of these, 94% were judged to have need according to Federal Methodology, of whom 100% were aided. *Financial aid deadline (priority):* 3/15. *Financial aid forms:* FAFSA required. *Admission application deadline:* rolling.

Summary of Aid to Needy Students *From gift & self-help combined:* Average need met: 80%. Average amount awarded: $11,341 (59% gift aid, 41% self-help). *Gift aid:* Total: $8,963,741 (73% from college's own funds, 2% from other college-administered sources, 25% from external sources). 147 Federal Work-Study jobs (averaging $1800); 10 part-time jobs.

Need-Based Scholarships & Grants Pell, FSEOG, state, private, college/university.

Loans Perkins, PLUS, Stafford, Unsubsidized Stafford, college/university short-term loans, college/university long-term loans ($2500 average).

Non-Need Awards *Academic Interests/Achievement Awards:* 1,200 ($4,920,982 total). *Special Characteristics Awards:* children and siblings of alumni, children of faculty/staff, international students, ROTC participants.

Other Money-Saving Options Cooperative Army ROTC, cooperative Air Force ROTC, off-campus living (after sophomore year). *Payment Plan:* installment. *Waivers:* full or partial for employees or children of employees.

Contact Ms. Sue Minzlaff, Assistant Director of Financial Aid, Milwaukee School of Engineering, 1025 North Broadway Street, Milwaukee, WI 53202-3109, 414-277-7222, fax: 414-277-6952.

MINNEAPOLIS COLLEGE OF ART AND DESIGN
Minneapolis, Minnesota

About the Institution Independent, coed. Degrees awarded: B, M. Offers 11 undergraduate majors. Total enrollment: 567. Undergraduates: 541 (53% state residents). Freshmen: 108.

Undergraduate Expenses (1997–98) Tuition: $15,730. Mandatory fees: $80. College room only: $1900 (minimum).

Applications *Financial aid deadline (priority):* 4/20. *Financial aid forms:* FAFSA, institutional form, federal income tax form required. *Admission application deadline:* rolling.

Summary of Aid to Needy Students *From gift & self-help combined:* Average need met: 58%. Average amount awarded: $8413 (49% gift aid, 51% self-help). *Gift aid:* Total: $1,814,422 (63% from college's own funds, 26% from other college-administered sources, 11% from external sources). 122 Federal Work-Study jobs (averaging $1800); part-time jobs.

Need-Based Scholarships & Grants Pell, FSEOG, state, private, college/university.

Loans Perkins, PLUS, Stafford, Unsubsidized Stafford, state, private, college/university short-term loans ($100 average).

Non-Need Awards In 1996, a total of 535 non-need awards were made. *Creative Arts/Performance Awards:* 535 ($1,944,323 total): general creative, applied art and design.

Other Money-Saving Options Co-op program, off-campus living. *Payment Plan:* installment. *Waivers:* full or partial for employees or children of employees.

Contact Ms. Susan Neppl, Financial Aid Director, Minneapolis College of Art and Design, Minneapolis, MN 55404-4347, 612-873-3783.

MINNESOTA BIBLE COLLEGE
Rochester, Minnesota

About the Institution Independent/religious, coed. Degrees awarded: A, B. Offers 4 undergraduate majors. Total enrollment: 116 (60% state residents). Freshmen: 26.

Undergraduate Expenses (1996–97) Tuition: $5168. Mandatory fees: $71. College room only: $1440.

Applications 81% of all full-time undergraduates enrolled in fall 1996 applied for aid; of these, 93% were judged to have need according to Federal Methodology, of whom 100% were aided. *Financial aid deadline (priority):* 6/15. *Financial aid forms:* CSS Financial Aid PROFILE acceptable. FAFSA, state form, institutional form required for some. *Admission application deadline:* 8/15.

Summary of Aid to Needy Students *From gift & self-help combined:* Average need met: 63%. Average amount awarded: $5928 (50% gift aid, 50% self-help). *Gift aid:* Total: $214,140 (31% from college's own funds, 28% from other college-administered sources, 41% from external sources). 15 Federal Work-Study jobs (averaging $600); 11 part-time jobs.

Need-Based Scholarships & Grants Pell, FSEOG, state, college/university.

Loans Stafford, Unsubsidized Stafford, state, private, college/university short-term loans ($500 average).

Non-Need Awards In 1996, a total of 98 non-need awards were made. *Academic Interests/Achievement Awards:* 20 ($18,588 total): general academic, religion/biblical studies. *Creative Arts/Performance Awards:* 3 ($1300 total): art/fine arts, music. *Special Achievements/Activities*

Awards: 52 ($33,572 total): leadership, religious involvement. *Special Characteristics Awards:* 23 ($24,562 total): general special characteristics, children of faculty/staff, international students, religious affiliation, siblings of current students, spouses of current students.

Other Money-Saving Options *Payment Plan:* installment. *Waivers:* full or partial for employees or children of employees and senior citizens.

Contact Office of Financial Aid, Minnesota Bible College, 920 Mayowood Road, Rochester, MN 55902-2275, 507-288-4563.

MINOT STATE UNIVERSITY
Minot, North Dakota

About the Institution State-supported, coed. Degrees awarded: B, M. Offers 46 undergraduate majors. Total enrollment: 3,602. Undergraduates: 3,445 (79% state residents). Freshmen: 485.

Undergraduate Expenses (1996–97) State resident tuition: $2044. Nonresident tuition: $5018. Mandatory fees: $180. College room and board: $2049. College room only: $800.

Applications *Financial aid deadline:* Applications processed continuously. *Financial aid forms:* FAFSA required; CSS Financial Aid PROFILE, state form, institutional form acceptable. *Admission application deadline:* rolling.

Summary of Aid to Needy Students *From gift & self-help combined:* Average need met: 92%. Average amount awarded: $5057 (36% gift aid, 64% self-help). *Gift aid:* Total: $4,023,513 (4% from college's own funds, 6% from other college-administered sources, 90% from external sources). 114 Federal Work-Study jobs (averaging $1000); 100 part-time jobs.

Need-Based Scholarships & Grants Pell, FSEOG, state, private, college/university.

Loans Perkins, PLUS, Stafford, Unsubsidized Stafford, Federal Nursing, college/university short-term loans ($200 average).

Non-Need Awards *Academic Interests/Achievement Awards:* general academic, business, communication, computer science, education, English, health fields, humanities, mathematics, social sciences. *Creative Arts/Performance Awards:* music, theater/drama. *Special Characteristics Awards:* ethnic background, international students, local/state students, members of minorities, parents of current students, veterans. *Athletic:* Total: 117 ($86,016); Men: 81 ($60,350); Women: 36 ($25,666).

Other Money-Saving Options Accelerated degree, co-op program, off-campus living. *Waivers:* full or partial for minority students.

Contact Mr. Dale Gehring, Director of Financial Aid, Minot State University, 500 University Avenue, West, Minot, ND 58707-0002, 701-858-3862, fax: 701-839-6933.

MIRRER YESHIVA
Brooklyn, New York

About the Institution Independent/religious, men.

Applications *Financial aid forms:* FAFSA required.

Summary of Aid to Needy Students *From gift & self-help combined:* Average need met: 50%. Average amount awarded: $5000. Federal Work-Study jobs.

Need-Based Scholarships & Grants Pell, FSEOG, college/university.

Loans Perkins, PLUS, Stafford, Unsubsidized Stafford.

Non-Need Awards *Academic Interests/Achievement Awards:* general academic. *Special Characteristics Awards:* religious affiliation.

Contact Financial Aid Office, Mirrer Yeshiva, Brooklyn, NY 11223-2010, 718-645-0536.

MISSISSIPPI COLLEGE
Clinton, Mississippi

About the Institution Independent/religious, coed. Degrees awarded: B, M, P. Offers 55 undergraduate majors. Total enrollment: 3,321. Undergraduates: 2,092 (87% state residents). Freshmen: 378.

Undergraduate Expenses (1997–98) Comprehensive fee of $11,200 includes tuition ($7200), mandatory fees ($450), and college room and board ($3550).

Applications *Financial aid deadline (priority):* 3/1. *Financial aid forms:* FAFSA, state form, institutional form required for some. *Admission application deadline:* rolling.

Summary of Aid to Needy Students *From gift & self-help combined:* Average amount awarded: $7741 (44% gift aid, 56% self-help). *Gift aid:* Total: $5,612,746 (55% from college's own funds, 19% from other college-administered sources, 26% from external sources). 93 Federal Work-Study jobs (averaging $1385); 250 part-time jobs.

Need-Based Scholarships & Grants Pell, FSEOG, state, private.

Loans Perkins, PLUS, Stafford, Unsubsidized Stafford, Federal Nursing, college/university short-term loans ($100 average), college/university long-term loans ($1500 average).

Non-Need Awards In 1996, a total of 2,302 non-need awards were made. *Academic Interests/Achievement Awards:* 811 ($1,992,606 total): general academic, biological sciences, communication, education, health fields, humanities, mathematics, physical sciences, religion/biblical studies. *Creative Arts/Performance Awards:* 220 ($277,505 total): applied art and design, art/fine arts, music. *Special Achievements/Activities Awards:* 886 ($1,552,538 total): cheerleading/drum major, Junior Miss, leadership, memberships, religious involvement. *Special Characteristics Awards:* 385 ($935,562 total): general special characteristics, children and siblings of alumni, children of faculty/staff, members of minorities, previous college experience, relatives of clergy.

Other Money-Saving Options Accelerated degree, co-op program, cooperative Army ROTC. *Payment Plans:* installment, deferred payment. *Waivers:* full or partial for employees or children of employees.

Contact Ms. Mary Givhan, Director of Financial Aid, Mississippi College, PO Box 4066, Clinton, MS 39058, 601-925-3319, fax: 601-925-3950.

MISSISSIPPI STATE UNIVERSITY
Mississippi State, Mississippi

About the Institution State-supported, coed. Degrees awarded: B, M, D, P. Offers 71 undergraduate majors. Total enrollment: 14,064. Undergraduates: 11,548 (81% state residents). Freshmen: 1,813.

Undergraduate Expenses (1996–97) State resident tuition: $1996. Nonresident tuition: $4816. Mandatory fees: $595. College room and board: $3215. College room only: $1400.

Applications 79% of all full-time undergraduates enrolled in fall 1996 applied for aid; of these, 64% were judged to have need according to Federal Methodology, of whom 96% were aided. *Financial aid deadline (priority):* 4/1. *Financial aid forms:* FAFSA, institutional form required. State form, scholarship application required for some. *Admission application deadline:* 7/26.

Summary of Aid to Needy Students *From gift & self-help combined:* Average need met: 87%. Average amount awarded: $5754 (41% gift aid, 59% self-help). *Gift aid:* Total: $11,384,587 (34% from college's own funds, 24% from other college-administered sources, 42% from external sources). 800 Federal Work-Study jobs (averaging $2167); part-time jobs.

Need-Based Scholarships & Grants Pell, FSEOG, state, private, college/university.

Loans Perkins, PLUS, Stafford, Unsubsidized Stafford, state, private, college/university short-term loans ($100 average), college/university long-term loans.

Non-Need Awards *Academic Interests/Achievement Awards:* general academic, agriculture, architecture, area/ethnic studies, biological sciences, business, communication, computer science, education, engineering/technologies, English, foreign languages, health fields, home economics, humanities, international studies, library science, mathematics, military science, physical sciences, premedicine, religion/biblical studies, social sciences. *Creative Arts/Performance Awards:* general creative, applied art and design, art/fine arts, cinema/film/broadcasting, creative writing, dance, debating, journalism/publications, music, performing arts, theater/drama. *Special Achievements/Activities Awards:* general special achievements/activities, cheerleading/drum major, leadership, memberships. *Special Characteristics Awards:* adult students, children and siblings of alumni, children of educators, children of faculty/staff, children of public servants, first-generation college students, handicapped students, local/state students, out-of-state students, previous college experience, ROTC participants, spouses of deceased or disabled public servants. *Athletic:* Total: 230 ($1,812,981); Men: 149 ($1,192,349); Women: 81 ($620,632).

Other Money-Saving Options Accelerated degree, co-op program, Army ROTC, Air Force ROTC, off-campus living. *Payment Plan:* deferred payment. *Waivers:* full or partial for employees or children of employees and senior citizens.

Contact Ms. Audrey S. Lambert, Director of Financial Aid, Mississippi State University, Box 9501, 106 Magruder Hall, Mississippi State, MS 39762, 601-325-3990, fax: 601-352-0702.

MISSISSIPPI UNIVERSITY FOR WOMEN
Columbus, Mississippi

About the Institution State-supported, primarily women. Degrees awarded: A, B, M. Offers 46 undergraduate majors. Total enrollment: 3,278. Undergraduates: 3,023 (90% state residents). Freshmen: 388.

Undergraduate Expenses (1996–97) State resident tuition: $2244. Nonresident tuition: $4746. Mandatory fees: $505. College room and board: $2557. College room only: $1260.

Applications Of all full-time undergraduates enrolled in fall 1996, 79% of those who applied for aid were judged to have need according to Federal Methodology, of whom 100% were aided. *Financial aid deadline (priority):* 4/1. *Financial aid forms:* FAFSA, state form required. *Admission application deadline:* 9/6.

Summary of Aid to Needy Students *From gift & self-help combined:* Average need met: 95%. Average amount awarded: $4723 (61% gift aid, 39% self-help). *Gift aid:* Total: $4,255,658 (50% from college's own funds, 15% from other college-administered sources, 35% from external sources). 182 Federal Work-Study jobs (averaging $922); 97 part-time jobs.

Need-Based Scholarships & Grants Pell, FSEOG, state.

Loans Perkins, PLUS, Stafford, Unsubsidized Stafford.

Non-Need Awards *Academic Interests/Achievement Awards:* ($1,543,904 total): general academic. *Creative Arts/Performance Awards:* ($21,200 total): art/fine arts, dance, music, performing arts, theater/drama. *Special Achievements/Activities Awards:* ($5250 total): Junior Miss. *Special Characteristics Awards:* ($258,724 total): adult students, children and siblings of alumni, children of faculty/staff, ethnic background, members of minorities, out-of-state students. *Athletic:* Total: 43 ($211,522); Men: 0; Women: 43 ($211,522).

Other Money-Saving Options Accelerated degree, co-op program, cooperative Army ROTC, cooperative Air Force ROTC, off-campus living. *Payment Plans:* installment, deferred payment. *Waivers:* full or partial for minority students, children of alumni, employees or children of employees, adult students.

Contact Mr. W. G. Wyckoff, Director of Financial Aid, Mississippi University for Women, Box W-1614, Columbus, MS 39701-9998, 601-329-7114, fax: 601-241-7481.

MISSISSIPPI VALLEY STATE UNIVERSITY
Itta Bena, Mississippi

About the Institution State-supported, coed. Degrees awarded: B, M. Offers 23 undergraduate majors. Total enrollment: 2,200. Undergraduates: 2,115 (86% state residents). Freshmen: 347.

Undergraduate Expenses (1996–97) State resident tuition: $2278. Nonresident tuition: $4780. College room and board: $2384.

Applications *Financial aid deadline (priority):* 4/1. *Financial aid forms:* FAFSA, institutional form required. *Admission application deadline:* rolling.

Summary of Aid to Needy Students *From gift & self-help combined:* Average need met: 95%. Average amount awarded: $4700 (64% gift aid, 36% self-help). *Gift aid:* Total: $2,887,559 (24% from college's own funds, 7% from other college-administered sources, 69% from external sources). 513 Federal Work-Study jobs.

Need-Based Scholarships & Grants Pell, FSEOG, state, private.

Loans Perkins, PLUS, Stafford, Unsubsidized Stafford.

Non-Need Awards In 1996, a total of 436 non-need awards were made. *Academic Interests/Achievement Awards:* 125 ($330,000 total): general academic. *Creative Arts/Performance Awards:* 134 ($384,000 total): art/fine arts, journalism/publications, music. *Athletic:* Total: 177 ($567,000); Men: 134 ($431,000); Women: 43 ($136,000).

Other Money-Saving Options Co-op program, Army ROTC, Air Force ROTC, off-campus living. *Payment Plan:* installment. *Waivers:* full or partial for children of alumni and employees or children of employees.

Contact Mr. Darrell G. Boyd, Director of Student Financial Aid, Mississippi Valley State University, 14000 Highway 82W #7268, Itta Bena, MS 38941-1400, 601-254-3335, fax: 601-254-7900.

MISSOURI BAPTIST COLLEGE
St. Louis, Missouri

About the Institution Independent/religious, coed. Degrees awarded: A, B. Offers 47 undergraduate majors. Total enrollment: 2,423 (95% state residents). Freshmen: 131.

Undergraduate Expenses (1997–98) Comprehensive fee of $12,450 includes tuition ($8180), mandatory fees ($270), and college room and board ($4000).

Applications 97% of all full-time undergraduates enrolled in fall 1996 applied for aid; of these,100% were judged to have need according to Federal Methodology, of whom 100% were aided. *Financial aid deadline (priority):* 5/1. *Financial aid forms:* FAFSA, institutional form required; CSS Financial Aid PROFILE acceptable. State form required for some. *Admission application deadline:* rolling.

Summary of Aid to Needy Students *From gift & self-help combined:* Average need met: 70%. Average amount awarded: $6434 (74% gift aid, 26% self-help). *Gift aid:* Total: $3,483,484 (79% from college's own funds, 6% from other college-administered sources, 15% from external sources). 8 Federal Work-Study jobs (averaging $1645); 56 part-time jobs.

Need-Based Scholarships & Grants Pell, FSEOG, state, private, college/university.

Loans PLUS, Stafford, Unsubsidized Stafford, college/university short-term loans ($500 average).

Non-Need Awards In 1996, a total of 1,190 non-need awards were made. *Academic Interests/Achievement Awards:* 463 ($1,156,667 total): general academic, religion/biblical studies. *Creative Arts/Performance Awards:* 49 ($109,541 total): music. *Special Achievements/Activities*

Awards: 98 ($133,995 total): cheerleading/drum major, religious involvement. *Special Characteristics Awards:* 441 ($508,957 total): children and siblings of alumni, children of faculty/staff, public servants, relatives of clergy, religious affiliation, siblings of current students. *Athletic:* Total: 139 ($598,847); Men: 75 ($304,345); Women: 64 ($294,502).

Other Money-Saving Options Accelerated degree, co-op program, cooperative Army ROTC, off-campus living. *Payment Plan:* installment. *Waivers:* full or partial for children of alumni, employees or children of employees, senior citizens.

Contact Mr. David Rice, Associate Director of Admissions, Missouri Baptist College, One College Park Drive, St. Louis, MO 63141-8698, 314-434-1115, fax: 314-434-7596.

MISSOURI SOUTHERN STATE COLLEGE
Joplin, Missouri

About the Institution State-supported, coed. Degrees awarded: A, B. Offers 54 undergraduate majors. Total enrollment: 5,258 (93% state residents). Freshmen: 746.

Undergraduate Expenses (1997–98) State resident tuition: $2304. Nonresident tuition: $4608. Mandatory fees: $80. College room and board: $3240.

Applications *Financial aid deadline (priority):* 2/15. *Financial aid forms:* FAFSA required; state form, institutional form, acceptable. *Admission application deadline:* 8/16.

Summary of Aid to Needy Students *From gift & self-help combined:* Average need met: 100%. Average amount awarded: $3998 (56% gift aid, 44% self-help). *Gift aid:* Total: $7,041,347 (28% from college's own funds, 28% from other college-administered sources, 44% from external sources). 175 Federal Work-Study jobs (averaging $1500); 100 part-time jobs.

Need-Based Scholarships & Grants Pell, FSEOG.

Loans Perkins, PLUS, Stafford, Unsubsidized Stafford.

Non-Need Awards In 1996, a total of 825 non-need awards were made. *Academic Interests/Achievement Awards:* 498 ($396,675 total): general academic. *Creative Arts/Performance Awards:* 138 ($67,249 total): art/fine arts, debating, journalism/publications, music, theater/drama. *Special Characteristics Awards:* 65 ($27,794 total): children of faculty/staff. *Athletic:* Total: 124 ($229,697); Men: 111 ($169,630); Women: 13 ($60,067).

Other Money-Saving Options Accelerated degree, co-op program, off-campus living (after sophomore year). *Payment Plan:* deferred payment. *Waivers:* full or partial for employees or children of employees and senior citizens.

Contact Mr. James E. Gilbert, Director of Financial Aid, Missouri Southern State College, 3950 East Newman Road, Joplin, MO 64801-1595, 417-625-9235.

MISSOURI TECHNICAL SCHOOL
St. Louis, Missouri

About the Institution Proprietary, coed. Degrees awarded: A, B. Offers 2 undergraduate majors. Total enrollment: 231. Freshmen: 55.

Undergraduate Expenses (1997–98) Tuition: $7396.

Applications 100% of all full-time undergraduates enrolled in fall 1996 applied for aid; of these,100% were judged to have need according to Federal Methodology, of whom 100% were aided. *Financial aid deadline:* continuous. *Financial aid forms:* FAFSA required. *Admission application deadline:* rolling.

Summary of Aid to Needy Students *From gift & self-help combined:* Average need met: 70%. Average amount awarded: $7500 (13% gift aid, 87% self-help). *Gift aid:* Total: $235,000 (21% from college's own funds, 79% from external sources).

Need-Based Scholarships & Grants Pell.

Loans PLUS, Stafford, Unsubsidized Stafford.

Non-Need Awards *Academic Interests/Achievement Awards:* general academic.

Another Money-Saving Option Accelerated degree.

Contact Mr. Emdad Khondaker, Director of Financial Aid, Missouri Technical School, St. Louis, MO 63132-1716, 314-569-3600.

MISSOURI VALLEY COLLEGE
Marshall, Missouri

About the Institution Independent/religious, coed. Degrees awarded: A, B. Offers 37 undergraduate majors. Total enrollment: 1,214 (62% state residents). Freshmen: 458.

Undergraduate Expenses (1997–98) Comprehensive fee of $15,300 includes tuition ($10,000), mandatory fees ($300), and college room and board ($5000).

Applications 98% of all full-time undergraduates enrolled in fall 1996 applied for aid; of these, 80% were judged to have need according to Federal Methodology, of whom 100% were aided. *Financial aid deadline (priority):* 8/15. *Financial aid forms:* FAFSA required; CSS Financial Aid PROFILE acceptable. State form required for some. *Admission application deadline:* rolling.

Summary of Aid to Needy Students *From gift & self-help combined:* Average need met: 82%. Average amount awarded: $11,925 (40% gift aid, 60% self-help). *Gift aid:* Total: $7,218,730 (75% from college's own funds, 12% from other college-administered sources, 13% from external sources). 55 Federal Work-Study jobs (averaging $1500); 800 part-time jobs.

Need-Based Scholarships & Grants Pell, FSEOG, state, private, college/university.

Loans Perkins, PLUS, Stafford, Unsubsidized Stafford.

Non-Need Awards In 1996, a total of 230 non-need awards were made. *Special Achievements/Activities Awards:* 230 ($7800 total): general special achievements/activities.

Other Money-Saving Options Accelerated degree, co-op program, off-campus living. *Payment Plan:* installment. *Waivers:* full or partial for children of alumni and employees or children of employees.

Contact Office of Financial Aid, Missouri Valley College, 500 East College, Marshall, MO 65340-3197, 816-831-4000.

MISSOURI WESTERN STATE COLLEGE
St. Joseph, Missouri

About the Institution State-supported, coed. Degrees awarded: A, B. Offers 49 undergraduate majors. Total enrollment: 5,109 (92% state residents). Freshmen: 1,053.

Undergraduate Expenses (1996–97) State resident tuition: $2276. Nonresident tuition: $4219. Mandatory fees: $138. College room and board: $2726 (minimum).

Applications 90% of all full-time undergraduates enrolled in fall 1996 applied for aid; of these, 84% were judged to have need according to Federal Methodology, of whom 100% were aided. *Financial aid deadline (priority):* 4/1. *Financial aid forms:* FAFSA required. Institutional form required for some. *Admission application deadline:* 7/30.

Summary of Aid to Needy Students *From gift & self-help combined:* Average need met: 90%. Average amount awarded: $4600 (39% gift aid, 61% self-help). *Gift aid:* Total: $5,839,000 (35% from college's own funds, 5% from other college-administered sources, 60% from external sources). 482 Federal Work-Study jobs (averaging $1600); 364 part-time jobs.

Need-Based Scholarships & Grants Pell, FSEOG, state, private, college/university.

Loans Perkins, PLUS, Stafford, Unsubsidized Stafford, college/university short-term loans ($300 average).

Non-Need Awards *Academic Interests/Achievement Awards:* general academic, biological sciences, business, communication, computer science, education, engineering/technologies, English, health fields, humanities, mathematics, military science, physical sciences, social sciences. *Creative Arts/Performance Awards:* dance, music. *Special Achievements/Activities Awards:* general special achievements/activities, cheerleading/drum major, community service. *Special Characteristics Awards:* members of minorities, out-of-state students, ROTC participants. *Athletic:* Total: 242 ($421,516).

Other Money-Saving Options Accelerated degree, Army ROTC, off-campus living. *Payment Plans:* installment, deferred payment. *Waivers:* full or partial for employees or children of employees and senior citizens.

Contact Financial Aid Department, Missouri Western State College, St. Joseph, MO 64507-2294, 816-271-4361.

MOLLOY COLLEGE
Rockville Centre, New York

About the Institution Independent, coed. Degrees awarded: A, B, M. Offers 44 undergraduate majors. Total enrollment: 2,346. Undergraduates: 2,148 (97% state residents). Freshmen: 152.

Undergraduate Expenses (1996–97) Tuition: $9600. Mandatory fees: $394.

Applications 90% of all full-time undergraduates enrolled in fall 1996 applied for aid; of these, 87% were judged to have need according to Federal Methodology, of whom 100% were aided. *Financial aid deadline (priority):* 3/1. *Financial aid forms:* FAFSA, CSS Financial Aid PROFILE, institutional form required. State form required for some. *Regular admission application deadline:* rolling. Early decision deadline: 11/1.

Summary of Aid to Needy Students *From gift & self-help combined:* Average need met: 75%. Average amount awarded: $9775 (62% gift aid, 38% self-help). *Gift aid:* Total: $11,134,550 (7% from college's own funds, 4% from other college-administered sources, 89% from external sources). 102 Federal Work-Study jobs (averaging $1600).

Need-Based Scholarships & Grants Pell, FSEOG, state, private, college/university.

Loans Perkins, PLUS, Stafford, Unsubsidized Stafford, Federal Nursing, private.

Non-Need Awards *Academic Interests/Achievement Awards:* general academic. *Creative Arts/Performance Awards:* art/fine arts, music, performing arts. *Special Characteristics Awards:* ethnic background, siblings of current students. *Athletic:* available.

Other Money-Saving Options Co-op program, cooperative Army ROTC, cooperative Air Force ROTC. *Payment Plan:* installment. *Waivers:* full or partial for minority students, children of alumni, employees or children of employees, senior citizens.

Contact Financial Aid Office, Molloy College, Rockville Centre, NY 11571-5002, 516-256-2217.

MONMOUTH COLLEGE
Monmouth, Illinois

About the Institution Independent/religious, coed. Degrees awarded: B. Offers 36 undergraduate majors. Total enrollment: 998 (85% state residents). Freshmen: 282.

Undergraduate Expenses (1997–98) Comprehensive fee of $18,980 includes tuition ($14,420), mandatory fees ($210), and college room and board ($4350). College room only: $2350.

Applications Of all full-time undergraduates enrolled in fall 1996, 96% of those who applied for aid were judged to have need according to

Federal Methodology, of whom 100% were aided. *Financial aid deadline (priority):* 4/15. *Financial aid forms:* FAFSA required; CSS Financial Aid PROFILE acceptable. State form, institutional form required for some. *Admission application deadline:* 5/1.

Summary of Aid to Needy Students *From gift & self-help combined:* Average need met: 100%. Average amount awarded: $14,120 (79% gift aid, 21% self-help). *Gift aid:* Total: $11,051,700 (4% from external sources). 192 Federal Work-Study jobs (averaging $950); 42 part-time jobs.

Need-Based Scholarships & Grants Pell, FSEOG, state, private, college/university.

Loans Perkins, PLUS, Stafford, Unsubsidized Stafford.

Non-Need Awards In 1996, a total of 75 non-need awards were made. *Academic Interests/Achievement Awards:* 60 ($75,000 total): general academic. *Creative Arts/Performance Awards:* 15 ($18,750 total): art/fine arts, music, theater/drama.

Other Money-Saving Options Cooperative Army ROTC. *Payment Plan:* installment. *Waivers:* full or partial for employees or children of employees.

Contact Ms. Jayne Whiteside, Director of Student Financial Services, Monmouth College, 700 East Broadway, Monmouth, IL 61462-1998, 309-457-2129, fax: 309-457-2152.

MONMOUTH UNIVERSITY
West Long Branch, New Jersey

About the Institution Independent, coed. Degrees awarded: A, B, M. Offers 47 undergraduate majors. Total enrollment: 5,110. Undergraduates: 3,875 (93% state residents). Freshmen: 799.

Undergraduate Expenses (1996–97) Comprehensive fee of $19,608 includes tuition ($13,270), mandatory fees ($530), and college room and board ($5808). College room only: $2958 (minimum).

Applications 92% of all full-time undergraduates enrolled in fall 1996 applied for aid; of these, 76% were judged to have need according to Federal Methodology, of whom 100% were aided. *Financial aid deadline (priority):* 5/1. *Financial aid forms:* FAFSA required. *Admission application deadline:* 4/1.

Summary of Aid to Needy Students *From gift & self-help combined:* Average need met: 60%. Average amount awarded: $11,332 (68% gift aid, 32% self-help). *Gift aid:* Total: $17,401,192 (61% from college's own funds, 3% from other college-administered sources, 36% from external sources). 200 Federal Work-Study jobs (averaging $1000); 200 part-time jobs.

Need-Based Scholarships & Grants Pell, FSEOG, state, private, college/university.

Loans Perkins, PLUS, Stafford, Unsubsidized Stafford, state, college/university long-term loans ($1300 average).

Non-Need Awards In 1996, a total of 347 non-need awards were made. *Academic Interests/Achievement Awards:* 117 ($341,977 total): general academic. *Special Characteristics Awards:* 149 ($801,821 total): general special characteristics. *Athletic:* Total: 81 ($1,156,977); Men: 38 ($520,640); Women: 43 ($636,337).

Other Money-Saving Options Accelerated degree, co-op program, off-campus living. *Payment Plan:* installment. *Waivers:* full or partial for employees or children of employees and senior citizens.

Contact Ms. Lisa Ferguson, Assistant Director of Financial Aid, Monmouth University, West Long Branch, NJ 07764-1898, 732-571-7552.

MONTANA STATE UNIVERSITY–BILLINGS
Billings, Montana

About the Institution State-supported, coed. Degrees awarded: A, B, M. Offers 51 undergraduate majors. Total enrollment: 4,006. Undergraduates: 3,624 (93% state residents). Freshmen: 690.

Undergraduate Expenses (1996–97) State resident tuition: $2388. Nonresident tuition: $6559. College room and board: $3000 (minimum).

Applications *Financial aid deadline (priority):* 3/1. *Financial aid forms:* FAFSA, institutional form required; CSS Financial Aid PROFILE acceptable. Federal income tax form required for some. *Admission application deadline:* 7/1.

Summary of Aid to Needy Students *From gift & self-help combined:* Average need met: 72%. Average amount awarded: $3167 (28% gift aid, 72% self-help). *Gift aid:* Total: $3,880,853. Federal Work-Study jobs; 210 part-time jobs.

Need-Based Scholarships & Grants Pell, FSEOG, state, college/university.

Loans Perkins, PLUS, Stafford, Unsubsidized Stafford, college/university long-term loans.

Non-Need Awards *Academic Interests/Achievement Awards:* 500 ($373,000 total): general academic, business, English, humanities. *Special Achievements/Activities Awards:* general special achievements/activities. *Special Characteristics Awards:* children and siblings of alumni, local/state students. *Athletic:* available.

Other Money-Saving Options Accelerated degree, co-op program, Army ROTC, off-campus living (after freshman year). *Waivers:* full or partial for employees or children of employees and senior citizens.

Contact Office of Financial Aid, Montana State University–Billings, 1500 North 30th Street, Billings, MT 59101, 406-657-2011.

MONTANA STATE UNIVERSITY–BOZEMAN
Bozeman, Montana

About the Institution State-supported, coed. Degrees awarded: B, M, D. Offers 97 undergraduate majors. Total enrollment: 11,611. Undergraduates: 10,462 (73% state residents). Freshmen: 1,933.

Undergraduate Expenses (1996–97) State resident tuition: $1831. Nonresident tuition: $6468. Mandatory fees: $673 (minimum). College room and board: $4034.

Applications 63% of all full-time undergraduates enrolled in fall 1996 applied for aid; of these, 87% were judged to have need according to Federal Methodology, of whom 70% were aided. *Financial aid deadline (priority):* 3/1. *Financial aid forms:* FAFSA required; CSS Financial Aid PROFILE, state form, institutional form acceptable. *Admission application deadline:* 7/1.

Summary of Aid to Needy Students *From gift & self-help combined:* Average need met: 85%. Average amount awarded: $7000 (30% gift aid, 70% self-help). *Gift aid:* Total: $7,400,000 (46% from college-administered sources, 54% from external sources). 677 Federal Work-Study jobs (averaging $1523); 1,000 part-time jobs.

Need-Based Scholarships & Grants Pell, FSEOG, state, private, college/university.

Loans Perkins, PLUS, Stafford, Unsubsidized Stafford, Federal Nursing, private, college/university short-term loans ($745 average), college/university long-term loans ($1612 average), Freeborn Loans.

Non-Need Awards *Academic Interests/Achievement Awards:* general academic, agriculture, architecture, area/ethnic studies, biological sciences, business, communication, computer science, education, engineering/technologies, English, foreign languages, health fields, home economics, humanities, mathematics, military science, physical sciences, social sciences. *Creative Arts/Performance Awards:* art/fine arts, cinema/film/broadcasting, dance, music, theater/drama. *Athletic:* Total: 288; Men: 194; Women: 94.

Other Money-Saving Options Accelerated degree, Army ROTC, Air Force ROTC, off-campus living (after freshman year). *Payment Plans:* installment, deferred payment. *Waivers:* full or partial for minority students, employees or children of employees, senior citizens.

Contact Mr. James Craig, Director of Financial Aid Services, Montana State University–Bozeman, #135 Strand Union Building, PO Box 174160, Bozeman, MT 59717-4160, 406-994-2845.

MONTANA STATE UNIVERSITY–NORTHERN
Havre, Montana

About the Institution State-supported, coed. Degrees awarded: A, B, M. Offers 29 undergraduate majors. Total enrollment: 1,702. Undergraduates: 1,529 (95% state residents). Freshmen: 390.

Undergraduate Expenses (1996–97) State resident tuition: $2350. Nonresident tuition: $6662. College room and board: $3600.

Applications 87% of all full-time undergraduates enrolled in fall 1996 applied for aid; of these, 81% were judged to have need according to Federal Methodology, of whom 96% were aided. *Financial aid deadline (priority):* 3/1. *Financial aid forms:* FAFSA, institutional form required. *Admission application deadline:* rolling.

Summary of Aid to Needy Students *From gift & self-help combined:* Average need met: 65%. Average amount awarded: $3336 (44% gift aid, 56% self-help). *Gift aid:* Total: $1,118,465 (24% from college's own funds, 4% from other college-administered sources, 72% from external sources). 300 Federal Work-Study jobs (averaging $1000); 300 part-time jobs.

Need-Based Scholarships & Grants Pell, FSEOG, state, private, college/university.

Loans Perkins, PLUS, Stafford, Unsubsidized Stafford, Federal Nursing, college/university short-term loans ($300 average).

Non-Need Awards In 1996, a total of 242 non-need awards were made. *Academic Interests/Achievement Awards:* 45 ($40,000 total): general academic. *Creative Arts/Performance Awards:* 5 ($2000 total): art/fine arts. *Special Achievements/Activities Awards:* 25 ($20,000 total): general special achievements/activities, community service, hobbies/interest, memberships, rodeo. *Special Characteristics Awards:* 115 ($120,000 total): general special characteristics, adult students, children and siblings of alumni, international students, members of minorities, out-of-state students, veterans. *Athletic:* Total: 52 ($135,000); Men: 22 ($60,000); Women: 30 ($75,000).

Other Money-Saving Options Co-op program, off-campus living (after freshman year). *Payment Plan:* deferred payment. *Waivers:* full or partial for minority students, employees or children of employees, senior citizens.

Contact Mr. Steven F. Jamruszka, Director of Financial Aid, Montana State University–Northern, Box 7751, Havre, MT 59501-7751, 406-265-3787.

MONTANA TECH OF THE UNIVERSITY OF MONTANA
Butte, Montana

About the Institution State-supported, coed. Degrees awarded: A, B, M. Offers 33 undergraduate majors. Total enrollment: 1,860. Undergraduates: 1,755 (86% state residents). Freshmen: 298.

Undergraduate Expenses (1996–97) State resident tuition: $2373 (minimum). Nonresident tuition: $6777 (minimum). College room and board: $3560.

Applications Of all full-time undergraduates enrolled in fall 1996, 95% of those who applied for aid were judged to have need according to Federal Methodology, of whom 100% were aided. *Financial aid deadline (priority):* 4/1. *Financial aid forms:* FAFSA, institutional form required; CSS Financial Aid PROFILE acceptable. *Admission application deadline:* 7/1.

Summary of Aid to Needy Students *From gift & self-help combined:* Average need met: 70%. Average amount awarded: $2179 (28% gift aid, 72% self-help). *Gift aid:* Total: $570,000 (2% from college's own funds, 11% from other college-administered sources, 87% from external sources). 88 Federal Work-Study jobs (averaging $1500); 400 part-time jobs.

Need-Based Scholarships & Grants Pell, FSEOG, state.

Loans Perkins, PLUS, Stafford, Unsubsidized Stafford, college/university short-term loans ($200 average).

Non-Need Awards *Academic Interests/Achievement Awards:* 225 ($400,000 total): general academic, business, computer science, engineering/technologies, health fields, mathematics, physical sciences. *Special Achievements/Activities Awards:* general special achievements/activities. *Special Characteristics Awards:* general special characteristics. *Athletic:* Total: 95 ($185,526); Men: 65 ($126,954); Women: 30 ($58,572).

Other Money-Saving Options Co-op program, off-campus living (after freshman year). *Payment Plan:* deferred payment. *Waivers:* full or partial for minority students, employees or children of employees, senior citizens.

Contact Financial Aid Office, Montana Tech of The University of Montana, West Park Street, Butte, MT 59701-8997, 406-496-4212.

MONTCLAIR STATE UNIVERSITY
Upper Montclair, New Jersey

About the Institution State-supported, coed. Degrees awarded: B, M. Offers 78 undergraduate majors. Total enrollment: 12,993. Undergraduates: 9,640 (96% state residents). Freshmen: 1,350.

Undergraduate Expenses (1997–98) State resident tuition: $2912. Nonresident tuition: $4432. Mandatory fees: $782. College room and board: $5546. College room only: $3860.

Applications 82% of all full-time undergraduates enrolled in fall 1996 applied for aid; of these, 91% were judged to have need according to Federal Methodology, of whom 90% were aided. *Financial aid deadline (priority):* 3/1. *Financial aid forms:* FAFSA required. *Admission application deadline:* 3/1.

Summary of Aid to Needy Students *From gift & self-help combined:* Average need met: 90%. Average amount awarded: $5068 (42% gift aid, 58% self-help). *Gift aid:* Total: $9,963,000 (10% from college's own funds, 57% from other college-administered sources, 33% from external sources). 400 Federal Work-Study jobs (averaging $800); 250 part-time jobs.

Need-Based Scholarships & Grants Pell, FSEOG, state, college/university.

Loans Perkins, PLUS, Stafford, Unsubsidized Stafford.

Non-Need Awards In 1996, a total of 295 non-need awards were made. *Academic Interests/Achievement Awards:* 295 ($656,000 total): general academic.

Other Money-Saving Options Accelerated degree, co-op program, off-campus living. *Payment Plan:* installment. *Waivers:* full or partial for employees or children of employees and senior citizens.

Contact Dr. Randall W. Richards III, Director of Financial Aid, Montclair State University, Valley Road and Normal Avenue, Upper Montclair, NJ 07043-1624, 973-655-4461, fax: 973-655-5455.

MONTREAT COLLEGE
Montreat, North Carolina

About the Institution Independent/religious, coed. Degrees awarded: A, B, M. Offers 37 undergraduate majors. Total enrollment: 1,000 (78% state residents). Freshmen: 97.

Undergraduate Expenses (1997–98) Comprehensive fee of $13,982 includes tuition ($10,042) and college room and board ($3940).

Applications 93% of all full-time undergraduates enrolled in fall 1996 applied for aid; of these, 81% were judged to have need according to Federal Methodology, of whom 100% were aided. *Financial aid deadline (priority):* 4/15. *Financial aid forms:* FAFSA, institutional form required. State form required for some. *Admission application deadline:* 8/20.

Summary of Aid to Needy Students *From gift & self-help combined:* Average need met: 86%. Average amount awarded: $9294 (63% gift aid, 37% self-help). *Gift aid:* Total: $1,599,214 (48% from college's own funds, 30% from other college-administered sources, 22% from external sources). 91 Federal Work-Study jobs (averaging $1200); 17 part-time jobs.

Need-Based Scholarships & Grants Pell, FSEOG, state, private, college/university.

Loans Perkins, PLUS, Stafford, Unsubsidized Stafford, private.

Non-Need Awards In 1996, a total of 295 non-need awards were made. *Academic Interests/Achievement Awards:* 129 ($324,156 total). *Creative Arts/Performance Awards:* 27 ($12,621 total): music, theater/drama. *Special Characteristics Awards:* 22 ($96,758 total): children of faculty/staff, international students, local/state students, relatives of clergy. *Athletic:* Total: 117 ($241,041); Men: 65 ($132,572); Women: 52 ($108,469).

Other Money-Saving Options Co-op program, off-campus living (after sophomore year). *Payment Plan:* installment. *Waivers:* full or partial for employees or children of employees and senior citizens.

Contact Ms. Wanda M. Olsen, Assistant Director of Financial Aid, Montreat College, PO Box 1267, Montreat, NC 28757-1267, 704-669-8012 Ext. 3795, fax: 704-669-0120.

MONTSERRAT COLLEGE OF ART
Beverly, Massachusetts

About the Institution Independent, coed. Degrees awarded: B. Offers 10 undergraduate majors. Total enrollment: 320 (52% state residents). Freshmen: 85.

Undergraduate Expenses (1997–98 estimated) Tuition: $11,300. Mandatory fees: $375. College room only: $3200.

Applications Of all full-time undergraduates enrolled in fall 1996, 95% of those who applied for aid were judged to have need according to Federal Methodology, of whom 100% were aided. *Financial aid deadline (priority):* 3/1. *Financial aid forms:* FAFSA required. Institutional form required for some. *Admission application deadline:* 7/15.

Summary of Aid to Needy Students *From gift & self-help combined:* Average need met: 60%. Average amount awarded: $5814 (40% gift aid, 60% self-help). *Gift aid:* Total: $580,600 (41% from college's own funds, 30% from other college-administered sources, 29% from external sources). 16 Federal Work-Study jobs (averaging $700); 10 part-time jobs.

Need-Based Scholarships & Grants Pell, FSEOG, state, college/university.

Loans PLUS, Stafford, Unsubsidized Stafford, state.

Non-Need Awards In 1996, a total of 39 non-need awards were made. *Creative Arts/Performance Awards:* 39 ($86,000 total): applied art and design, art/fine arts.

Other Money-Saving Options Off-campus living. *Payment Plan:* installment. *Waivers:* full or partial for employees or children of employees.

Contact Ms. Ellen Kayser, Director of Financial Aid, Montserrat College of Art, 23 Essex Street, PO Box 26, Beverly, MA 01915, 508-922-8222, fax: 508-922-4268.

MOODY BIBLE INSTITUTE
Chicago, Illinois

About the Institution Independent/religious, coed. Degrees awarded: B, M. Offers 13 undergraduate majors. Total enrollment: 1,553. Undergraduates: 1,483 (27% state residents). Freshmen: 255.

Undergraduate Expenses (1997–98) Comprehensive fee of $5310 includes tuition ($0), mandatory fees ($830), and college room and board ($4480).

Applications 12% of all full-time undergraduates enrolled in fall 1996 applied for aid. *Financial aid deadline:* continuous. *Financial aid forms:* institutional form required for some. *Regular admission application deadline:* 3/1. Early decision deadline: 12/1.

Summary of Aid to Needy Students *From gift & self-help combined:* Average need met: 70%. Average amount awarded: $750. 400 part-time jobs.

Loans College/university short-term loans ($1700 average).

Non-Need Awards In 1996, a total of 16 non-need awards were made. *Special Achievements/Activities Awards:* 16 ($15,200 total): leadership.

Other Money-Saving Options *Payment Plan:* installment. *Waivers:* full or partial for employees or children of employees.

Contact Mr. Joe M. Gonzales Jr., Financial Aid Administrator, Moody Bible Institute, 820 North LaSalle Boulevard, Chicago, IL 60610-3284, 312-329-4202, fax: 312-329-4197.

MOORE COLLEGE OF ART AND DESIGN
Philadelphia, Pennsylvania

About the Institution Independent, women. Degrees awarded: B. Offers 15 undergraduate majors. Total enrollment: 385 (70% state residents). Freshmen: 102.

Undergraduate Expenses (1996–97) Comprehensive fee of $20,026 includes tuition ($14,097), mandatory fees ($325), and college room and board ($5604). College room only: $3357.

Applications Of all full-time undergraduates enrolled in fall 1996, 89% of those who applied for aid were judged to have need according to Federal Methodology, of whom 100% were aided. *Financial aid deadline (priority):* 4/1. *Financial aid forms:* FAFSA required. *Admission application deadline:* rolling.

Summary of Aid to Needy Students *From gift & self-help combined:* Average need met: 78%. *Gift aid:* Total: $2,180,000 (82% from college's own funds, 7% from other college-administered sources, 11% from external sources). Federal Work-Study jobs.

Need-Based Scholarships & Grants Pell, FSEOG, state, college/university.

Loans Perkins, PLUS, Stafford, Unsubsidized Stafford.

Non-Need Awards *Academic Interests/Achievement Awards:* general academic. *Creative Arts/Performance Awards:* art/fine arts.

Other Money-Saving Options Co-op program, off-campus living. *Payment Plan:* installment. *Waivers:* full or partial for employees or children of employees.

Contact Mr. Norman Rahn, Director of Financial Aid, Moore College of Art and Design, 20th and the Parkway, Philadelphia, PA 19103-1179, 215-568-4515 Ext. 1138.

MOORHEAD STATE UNIVERSITY
Moorhead, Minnesota

About the Institution State-supported, coed. Degrees awarded: A, B, M. Offers 78 undergraduate majors. Total enrollment: 6,194. Undergraduates: 5,917 (59% state residents). Freshmen: 1,026.

Undergraduate Expenses (1996–97) State resident tuition: $2474. Nonresident tuition: $5573. Mandatory fees: $407. College room and board: $3078. College room only: $2084.

Applications 73% of all full-time undergraduates enrolled in fall 1996 applied for aid; of these, 88% were judged to have need according to Federal Methodology, of whom 100% were aided. *Financial aid deadline (priority):* 6/15. *Financial aid forms:* FAFSA, institutional form required. *Admission application deadline:* 8/7.

Summary of Aid to Needy Students *From gift & self-help combined:* Average amount awarded: $5282 (33% gift aid, 67% self-help). *Gift aid:* Total: $4,575,659 (12% from college-administered sources, 88% from external sources). 356 Federal Work-Study jobs (averaging $1476); 727 part-time jobs.

Need-Based Scholarships & Grants Pell, FSEOG, state, private.

Loans Perkins, PLUS, Stafford, Unsubsidized Stafford, state, private, college/university short-term loans ($300 average).

Non-Need Awards In 1996, a total of 575 non-need awards were made. *Academic Interests/Achievement Awards:* 391 ($307,945 total): general academic. *Creative Arts/Performance Awards:* art/fine arts, music, theater/drama. *Special Characteristics Awards:* members of minorities. *Athletic:* Total: 184 ($122,000); Men: 108 ($64,200); Women: 76 ($57,800).

Other Money-Saving Options Cooperative Army ROTC, cooperative Air Force ROTC, off-campus living. *Payment Plan:* deferred payment. *Waivers:* full or partial for employees or children of employees and senior citizens.

Contact Ms. Carolyn Zehren, Assistant Director, Moorhead State University, 1104 7th Avenue South, Moorhead, MN 56563-0002, 218-236-2251, fax: 218-236-2058.

MORAVIAN COLLEGE
Bethlehem, Pennsylvania

About the Institution Independent/religious, coed. Degrees awarded: B, M. Offers 48 undergraduate majors. Total enrollment: 1,952. Undergraduates: 1,734 (50% state residents). Freshmen: 290.

Undergraduate Expenses (1996–97) Comprehensive fee of $21,846 includes tuition ($16,500), mandatory fees ($121), and college room and board ($5225). College room only: $2890.

Applications 87% of all full-time undergraduates enrolled in fall 1996 applied for aid. *Financial aid deadline (priority):* 2/15. *Financial aid forms:* FAFSA, CSS Financial Aid PROFILE, state form required. *Regular admission application deadline:* 3/1. Early decision deadline: 1/15.

Summary of Aid to Needy Students *Gift aid:* Total: $9,003,000 (79% from college's own funds, 14% from other college-administered sources, 7% from external sources). 568 Federal Work-Study jobs (averaging $1038); 366 part-time jobs.

Need-Based Scholarships & Grants Pell, FSEOG, state, private, college/university.

Loans Perkins, PLUS, Stafford, Unsubsidized Stafford, private.

Non-Need Awards *Academic Interests/Achievement Awards:* 281 ($717,205 total): general academic, foreign languages, physical sciences. *Special Achievements/Activities Awards:* religious involvement. *Special Characteristics Awards:* 53 ($203,207 total): children and siblings of alumni, relatives of clergy.

Other Money-Saving Options Accelerated degree, cooperative Army ROTC, off-campus living (after freshman year). *Payment Plan:* installment. *Waivers:* full or partial for employees or children of employees.

Contact Office of Financial Aid, Moravian College, 1200 Main Street, Bethlehem, PA 18018-6650, 610-861-1300.

MOREHEAD STATE UNIVERSITY
Morehead, Kentucky

About the Institution State-supported, coed. Degrees awarded: A, B, M. Offers 100 undergraduate majors. Total enrollment: 8,344. Undergraduates: 6,823 (88% state residents). Freshmen: 1,277.

Undergraduate Expenses (1997–98) State resident tuition: $2090. Nonresident tuition: $5570. College room and board: $2950. College room only: $1418 (minimum).

Applications Of all full-time undergraduates enrolled in fall 1996, 74% of those who applied for aid were judged to have need according to Federal Methodology, of whom 98% were aided. *Financial aid deadline (priority):* 4/1. *Financial aid forms:* FAFSA, institutional form, financial aid transcript (for transfers) required. *Admission application deadline:* rolling.

Summary of Aid to Needy Students *From gift & self-help combined:* Average need met: 77%. Average amount awarded: $4792 (59% gift aid, 41% self-help). *Gift aid:* Total: $10,856,552 (32% from college's own funds, 3% from other college-administered sources, 65% from external sources). 810 Federal Work-Study jobs (averaging $1302); 350 part-time jobs.

Need-Based Scholarships & Grants Pell, FSEOG, state, private, college/university.

Loans Perkins, PLUS, Stafford, Unsubsidized Stafford, college/university short-term loans ($30 average), college/university long-term loans ($900 average).

Non-Need Awards In 1996, a total of 2,002 non-need awards were made. *Academic Interests/Achievement Awards:* 1,141 ($1,869,362 total): general academic, agriculture, business, physical sciences. *Creative Arts/Performance Awards:* 112 ($74,460 total): art/fine arts, journalism/publications, music, theater/drama. *Special Achievements/Activities Awards:* 225 ($130,920 total): cheerleading/drum major, leadership. *Special Characteristics Awards:* 268 ($484,147 total): adult students, children and siblings of alumni, local/state students, members of minorities, out-of-state students. *Athletic:* Total: 256 ($687,629); Men: 159 ($417,952); Women: 97 ($269,677).

Other Money-Saving Options Accelerated degree, co-op program, Army ROTC, off-campus living (after sophomore year). *Payment Plans:* installment, deferred payment. *Waivers:* full or partial for employees or children of employees and senior citizens.

Contact Mr. Tim P. Rhodes, Director of Financial Aid, Morehead State University, 305 HM, Morehead, KY 40351, 606-783-2011.

MOREHOUSE COLLEGE
Atlanta, Georgia

About the Institution Independent, men. Degrees awarded: B. Offers 38 undergraduate majors. Total enrollment: 2,926 (23% state residents). Freshmen: 771.

Undergraduate Expenses (1996–97) Comprehensive fee of $15,230 includes tuition ($7700), mandatory fees ($1554), and college room and board ($5976). College room only: $3418.

Applications Of all full-time undergraduates enrolled in fall 1996, 100% of those judged to have need according to Federal Methodology were aided. *Financial aid deadline:* 4/1. *Financial aid forms:* FAFSA, CSS Financial Aid PROFILE, state form, institutional form required. *Regular admission application deadline:* 2/15. Early action deadline: 10/15.

Summary of Aid to Needy Students *From gift & self-help combined:* Average need met: 65%. Average amount awarded: $10,000. 400 Federal Work-Study jobs (averaging $1800); part-time jobs.

Need-Based Scholarships & Grants Pell, FSEOG, state.

Loans Perkins, PLUS, Stafford, Unsubsidized Stafford, Resource Loans.

Non-Need Awards In 1996, a total of 960 non-need awards were made. *Academic Interests/Achievement Awards:* 615 ($913,000 total): general academic, business, military science. *Creative Arts/Performance Awards:* 108 ($111,000 total): music. *Special Achievements/Activities Awards:* 53 ($11,000 total): community service. *Special Characteristics Awards:* 69 ($250,000 total): children of faculty/staff, ROTC participants. *Athletic:* Total: 115 ($484,721).

Other Money-Saving Options Co-op program, Army ROTC, Naval ROTC, cooperative Air Force ROTC, off-campus living. *Payment Plan:* installment.

Contact Office of Financial Aid, Morehouse College, 830 Westview Drive, SW, Atlanta, GA 30314, 404-681-2800.

MORGAN STATE UNIVERSITY
Baltimore, Maryland

About the Institution State-supported, coed. Degrees awarded: B, M, D. Offers 56 undergraduate majors. Total enrollment: 5,889. Undergraduates: 5,552 (61% state residents). Freshmen: 1,089.

Undergraduate Expenses (1997–98) State resident tuition: $3412. Nonresident tuition: $7992. College room and board: $5090. College room only: $3150.

Applications *Financial aid deadline (priority):* 4/1. *Financial aid forms:* FAFSA, CSS Financial Aid PROFILE, institutional form required. *Admission application deadline:* rolling.

Summary of Aid to Needy Students Federal Work-Study jobs; part-time jobs.

Non-Need Awards *Academic Interests/Achievement Awards:* general academic. *Creative Arts/Performance Awards:* music. *Athletic:* available.

Other Money-Saving Options Accelerated degree, co-op program, Army ROTC, off-campus living. *Payment Plans:* installment, deferred payment. *Waivers:* full or partial for employees or children of employees and senior citizens.

Contact Office of Financial Aid, Morgan State University, Baltimore, MD 21251, 410-319-3333.

MORNINGSIDE COLLEGE
Sioux City, Iowa

About the Institution Independent/religious, coed. Degrees awarded: A, B, M. Offers 59 undergraduate majors. Total enrollment: 1,137. Undergraduates: 1,041 (77% state residents). Freshmen: 208.

Undergraduate Expenses (1997–98) Comprehensive fee of $16,140 includes tuition ($11,436), mandatory fees ($176), and college room and board ($4528). College room only: $2230.

Applications 89% of all full-time undergraduates enrolled in fall 1996 applied for aid; of these, 95% were judged to have need according to Federal Methodology, of whom 100% were aided. *Financial aid deadline (priority):* 3/1. *Financial aid forms:* FAFSA required. *Admission application deadline:* rolling.

Summary of Aid to Needy Students *From gift & self-help combined:* Average need met: 99%. Average amount awarded: $11,988 (67% gift aid, 33% self-help). *Gift aid:* Total: $5,948,310 (56% from college's own funds, 5% from other college-administered sources, 39% from external sources). 360 Federal Work-Study jobs (averaging $1500); 94 part-time jobs.

Need-Based Scholarships & Grants Pell, FSEOG, state, private.

Loans Perkins, PLUS, Stafford, Unsubsidized Stafford, private, college/university short-term loans ($100 average), college/university long-term loans ($1063 average).

Non-Need Awards In 1996, a total of 986 non-need awards were made. *Academic Interests/Achievement Awards:* 411 ($1,018,536 total): general academic. *Creative Arts/Performance Awards:* 87 ($187,109 total): art/fine arts, cinema/film/broadcasting, journalism/publications, music, theater/drama. *Special Characteristics Awards:* 333 ($540,625 total): children and siblings of alumni, children of faculty/staff, first-generation college students, local/state students, relatives of clergy, religious affiliation. *Athletic:* Total: 155 ($1,178,565); Men: 99 ($764,194); Women: 56 ($414,371).

Other Money-Saving Options Accelerated degree, off-campus living (after junior year). *Payment Plan:* installment. *Waivers:* full or partial for children of alumni, employees or children of employees, senior citizens.

Contact Office of Financial Aid, Morningside College, 1501 Morningside Avenue, Sioux City, IA 51106-1751, 712-274-5000.

MORRIS COLLEGE
Sumter, South Carolina

About the Institution Independent/religious, coed. Degrees awarded: B. Offers 27 undergraduate majors. Total enrollment: 911 (91% state residents). Freshmen: 248.

Undergraduate Expenses (1996–97) Comprehensive fee of $7796 includes tuition ($4990), mandatory fees ($115), and college room and board ($2691). College room only: $1131.

Applications Of all full-time undergraduates enrolled in fall 1996, 100% of those judged to have need according to Federal Methodology were aided. *Financial aid deadline (priority):* 3/30. *Financial aid forms:* FAFSA, institutional form required. State form, state income tax form required for some. *Admission application deadline:* rolling.

Summary of Aid to Needy Students *From gift & self-help combined:* Average need met: 76%. Average amount awarded: $4000 (55% gift aid, 45% self-help). *Gift aid:* Total: $1,489,507 (1% from college's own funds, 49% from other college-administered sources, 50% from external sources). 425 Federal Work-Study jobs (averaging $1000); part-time jobs.

Need-Based Scholarships & Grants Pell, FSEOG, state, private, college/university.

Loans Perkins, PLUS, Stafford, Unsubsidized Stafford.

Non-Need Awards In 1996, a total of 106 non-need awards were made. *Academic Interests/Achievement Awards:* 40 ($25,000 total): general academic. *Athletic:* Total: 66 ($18,000); Men: 34 ($9200); Women: 32 ($8800).

Other Money-Saving Options Accelerated degree, co-op program, Army ROTC, off-campus living (after freshman year). *Payment Plan:* installment.

Contact Office of Financial Aid, Morris College, Sumter, SC 29150-3599, 803-775-9371.

MORRISON COLLEGE
Reno, Nevada

About the Institution Proprietary, coed. Degrees awarded: A, B. Offers 9 undergraduate majors. Total enrollment: 290 (93% state residents). Freshmen: 225.

Applications Of all full-time undergraduates enrolled in fall 1996, 96% of those who applied for aid were judged to have need according to Federal Methodology, of whom 85% were aided. *Financial aid deadline:* Applications processed continuously. *Financial aid forms:* FAFSA required; CSS Financial Aid PROFILE acceptable.

Summary of Aid to Needy Students *From gift & self-help combined:* Average need met: 90%. Average amount awarded: $1166. *Gift aid:* Total: $208,610 (1% from college's own funds, 4% from other college-administered sources, 95% from external sources). 10 part-time jobs.

Need-Based Scholarships & Grants Pell, state.

Loans PLUS, Stafford, Unsubsidized Stafford, college/university long-term loans ($500 average).

Non-Need Awards *Academic Interests/Achievement Awards:* business. *Special Characteristics Awards:* general special characteristics.

Other Money-Saving Options Accelerated degree. *Payment Plans:* guaranteed tuition, installment. *Waivers:* full or partial for employees or children of employees.

Contact Ms. Linda M. Kuchenbecker, Director of Financial Aid, Morrison College, Reno, NV 89503-5600, 702-323-4145.

MOUNT ALOYSIUS COLLEGE
Cresson, Pennsylvania

About the Institution Independent/religious, coed. Degrees awarded: A, B. Offers 19 undergraduate majors. Total enrollment: 1,012 (91% state residents). Freshmen: 501.

Undergraduate Expenses (1996–97) Comprehensive fee of $12,700 includes tuition ($8780 minimum) and college room and board ($3920 minimum). College room only: $1670.

Applications Of all full-time undergraduates enrolled in fall 1996, 89% of those judged to have need according to Federal Methodology were aided. *Financial aid deadline (priority):* 5/1. *Financial aid forms:* FAFSA, state form required. *Admission application deadline:* rolling.

Summary of Aid to Needy Students *From gift & self-help combined:* Average need met: 62%. Average amount awarded: $5032 (57% gift aid, 43% self-help). *Gift aid:* Total: $1,590,938 (16% from college's own funds, 9% from other college-administered sources, 75% from external sources). 207 Federal Work-Study jobs (averaging $438).

Need-Based Scholarships & Grants Pell, FSEOG, state, private, college/university.

Loans Perkins, PLUS, Stafford, Unsubsidized Stafford, Federal Nursing.

Non-Need Awards In 1996, a total of 14 non-need awards were made. *Academic Interests/Achievement Awards:* 2 ($15,580 total): general academic. *Athletic:* Total: 12 ($41,120); Men: 12 ($41,120); Women: 0.

Other Money-Saving Options Off-campus living. *Waivers:* full or partial for employees or children of employees.

Contact Ms. Stacy L. Klinehans, Director of Financial Aid, Mount Aloysius College, 7373 Admiral Peary Highway, Cresson, PA 16630-1900, 814-886-6357.

MOUNT ANGEL SEMINARY
Saint Benedict, Oregon

About the Institution Independent/religious, men. Degrees awarded: B, M, P. Offers 3 undergraduate majors. Total enrollment: 144. Undergraduates: 53 (21% state residents). Freshmen: 11.

Undergraduate Expenses (1997–98) Comprehensive fee of $12,900 includes tuition ($6900), mandatory fees ($1500), and college room and board ($4500).

Applications *Financial aid deadline (priority):* 8/1. *Financial aid forms:* FAFSA required. *Admission application deadline:* 7/15.

Summary of Aid to Needy Students *From gift & self-help combined:* Average amount awarded: $10,000. 30 part-time jobs.

Need-Based Scholarships & Grants Pell, state.

Loans Stafford, Unsubsidized Stafford.

Non-Need Awards *Academic Interests/Achievement Awards:* general academic. *Special Achievements/Activities Awards:* community service.

Contact Financial Aid Office, Mount Angel Seminary, Saint Benedict, OR 97373, 503-845-3356.

MOUNT CARMEL COLLEGE OF NURSING
Columbus, Ohio

About the Institution Independent. Degrees awarded: B.

Undergraduate Expenses (1996–97) Tuition: $6026 (minimum). College room only: $2312.

Applications 90% of all full-time undergraduates enrolled in fall 1996 applied for aid; of these, 78% were judged to have need according to Federal Methodology, of whom 100% were aided. *Financial aid deadline (priority):* 3/1. *Financial aid forms:* FAFSA, institutional form required.

Summary of Aid to Needy Students *From gift & self-help combined:* Average amount awarded: $6200 (36% gift aid, 64% self-help). *Gift aid:* Total: $510,000. Part-time jobs.

Need-Based Scholarships & Grants Pell, FSEOG, state, college/university.

Loans Perkins, PLUS, Stafford, Unsubsidized Stafford, Federal Nursing, state, private, college/university long-term loans.

Non-Need Awards In 1996, a total of 53 non-need awards were made. *Academic Interests/Achievement Awards:* 49 ($27,750 total): general academic. *Special Achievements/Activities Awards:* 3 ($3000 total): community service. *Special Characteristics Awards:* 1 ($1000 total): members of minorities.

Contact Financial Aid Office, Mount Carmel College of Nursing, 127 South Davis Avenue, Columbus, OH 43222, 614-234-5800.

MOUNT HOLYOKE COLLEGE
South Hadley, Massachusetts

About the Institution Independent, women. Degrees awarded: B, M. Offers 49 undergraduate majors. Total enrollment: 1,898. Undergraduates: 1,889 (20% state residents). Freshmen: 482.

Undergraduate Expenses (1997–98) Comprehensive fee of $28,865 includes tuition ($22,200), mandatory fees ($140), and college room and board ($6525).

Applications 84% of all full-time undergraduates enrolled in fall 1996 applied for aid; of these, 94% were judged to have need according to Federal Methodology, of whom 100% were aided. *Financial aid deadline:* 2/1. *Financial aid forms:* FAFSA, CSS Financial Aid PROFILE required. Institutional form required for some. *Regular admission application deadline:* 1/15. Early decision deadline: 12/1.

Summary of Aid to Needy Students *From gift & self-help combined:* Average need met: 100%. Average amount awarded: $19,300 (77% gift aid, 23% self-help). *Gift aid:* Total: $22,942,530 (92% from college's own funds, 2% from other college-administered sources, 6% from external sources). 900 Federal Work-Study jobs (averaging $1450); 360 part-time jobs.

Need-Based Scholarships & Grants Pell, FSEOG, state, private, college/university.

Loans Perkins, PLUS, Stafford, Unsubsidized Stafford, state, private, college/university long-term loans ($4000 average).

Non-Need Awards Not offered.

Other Money-Saving Options Accelerated degree, cooperative Army ROTC, cooperative Air Force ROTC. *Payment Plans:* tuition prepayment, installment. *Waivers:* full or partial for employees or children of employees.

Contact Office of Financial Aid, Mount Holyoke College, 50 College Street, South Hadley, MA 01075-1492, 413-538-2000.

MOUNT MARTY COLLEGE
Yankton, South Dakota

About the Institution Independent/religious, coed. Degrees awarded: A, B, M. Offers 30 undergraduate majors. Total enrollment: 936. Undergraduates: 895 (73% state residents). Freshmen: 119.

Undergraduate Expenses (1997–98) Comprehensive fee of $12,812 includes tuition ($8388), mandatory fees ($780), and college room and board ($3644).

Applications 93% of all full-time undergraduates enrolled in fall 1996 applied for aid; of these, 94% were judged to have need according to Federal Methodology, of whom 99% were aided. *Financial aid deadline (priority):* 3/1. *Financial aid forms:* FAFSA required for some. *Admission application deadline:* 8/15.

Summary of Aid to Needy Students *From gift & self-help combined:* Average need met: 86%. Average amount awarded: $8661 (54% gift aid, 46% self-help). *Gift aid:* Total: $1,962,159 (63% from college's own funds, 9% from other college-administered sources, 28% from external sources). 209 Federal Work-Study jobs (averaging $800); 60 part-time jobs.

Need-Based Scholarships & Grants Pell, FSEOG, state, private, college/university.

Loans Perkins, PLUS, Stafford, Unsubsidized Stafford, Federal Nursing, private.

Non-Need Awards In 1996, a total of 535 non-need awards were made. *Academic Interests/Achievement Awards:* 266 ($360,000 total): general academic. *Creative Arts/Performance Awards:* 49 ($14,750 total): music, theater/drama. *Special Achievements/Activities Awards:* 96 ($69,524 total): leadership, religious involvement. *Special Characteristics Awards:* 37 ($70,877 total): children of faculty/staff, international students, religious affiliation, siblings of current students. *Athletic:* Total: 87 ($227,310); Men: 49 ($137,718); Women: 38 ($89,592).

Other Money-Saving Options Accelerated degree, co-op program, cooperative Army ROTC. *Payment Plan:* installment. *Waivers:* full or partial for employees or children of employees.

Contact Mr. Ken Kocer, Director of Financial Assistance, Mount Marty College, 1105 West 8th Street, Yankton, SD 57078-3724, 605-668-1589, fax: 605-668-1607.

MOUNT MARY COLLEGE
Milwaukee, Wisconsin

About the Institution Independent/religious, women. Degrees awarded: B, M. Offers 45 undergraduate majors. Total enrollment: 1,287. Undergraduates: 1,160 (62% state residents). Freshmen: 88.

Undergraduate Expenses (1997–98) Comprehensive fee of $13,420 includes tuition ($10,740) and college room and board ($2680 minimum).

Applications Of all full-time undergraduates enrolled in fall 1996, 95% of those who applied for aid were judged to have need according to Federal Methodology, of whom 94% were aided. *Financial aid deadline (priority):* 3/15. *Financial aid forms:* FAFSA, institutional form required; CSS Financial Aid PROFILE acceptable. *Admission application deadline:* 8/15.

Summary of Aid to Needy Students *From gift & self-help combined:* Average need met: 91%. Average amount awarded: $8965 (50% gift aid, 50% self-help). *Gift aid:* Total: $2,765,044 (60% from college's own funds, 23% from other college-administered sources, 17% from external sources). 70 Federal Work-Study jobs (averaging $200); 60 part-time jobs.

Need-Based Scholarships & Grants Pell, FSEOG, state, private, college/university, Metropolitan Milwaukee Association of Commerce Awards.

Loans Perkins, PLUS, Stafford, Unsubsidized Stafford, private.

Non-Need Awards In 1996, a total of 326 non-need awards were made. *Academic Interests/Achievement Awards:* 275 ($693,780 total): general academic, business, communication, education, English, home economics, humanities, mathematics, physical sciences, social sciences. *Creative Arts/Performance Awards:* 14 ($26,650 total): applied art and design, art/fine arts, music. *Special Achievements/Activities Awards:* 11 ($28,730 total): general special achievements/activities, leadership. *Special Characteristics Awards:* 26 ($12,250 total): international students, parents of current students, siblings of current students.

Other Money-Saving Options Accelerated degree, cooperative Army ROTC, off-campus living. *Payment Plan:* installment. *Waivers:* full or partial for employees or children of employees.

Contact Mr. John Rdzak, Director of Financial Aid, Mount Mary College, Milwaukee, WI 53222-4597, 414-258-4810 Ext. 258.

MOUNT MERCY COLLEGE
Cedar Rapids, Iowa

About the Institution Independent/religious, coed. Degrees awarded: B. Offers 36 undergraduate majors. Total enrollment: 1,131 (95% state residents). Freshmen: 148.

Undergraduate Expenses (1997–98) Comprehensive fee of $15,805 includes tuition ($11,860) and college room and board ($3945).

Applications 94% of all full-time undergraduates enrolled in fall 1996 applied for aid; of these, 71% were judged to have need according to Federal Methodology, of whom 100% were aided. *Financial aid deadline (priority):* 3/1. *Financial aid forms:* FAFSA required for some. *Admission application deadline:* 8/15.

Summary of Aid to Needy Students *From gift & self-help combined:* Average need met: 68%. Average amount awarded: $15,350 (63% gift aid, 37% self-help). *Gift aid:* Total: $4,253,180 (61% from college's own funds, 3% from other college-administered sources, 36% from external sources). 278 Federal Work-Study jobs (averaging $1000); 120 part-time jobs.

Need-Based Scholarships & Grants Pell, FSEOG, state, college/university.

Loans Perkins, PLUS, Stafford, Unsubsidized Stafford, Federal Nursing, college/university long-term loans ($2000 average).

Non-Need Awards In 1996, a total of 1,142 non-need awards were made. *Academic Interests/Achievement Awards:* 927 ($2,374,842 total): general academic. *Creative Arts/Performance Awards:* 60 ($93,475 total): art/fine arts, music, theater/drama. *Special Achievements/Activities Awards:* 155 ($227,624 total): leadership.

Other Money-Saving Options Accelerated degree, off-campus living. *Payment Plan:* installment. *Waivers:* full or partial for employees or children of employees.

Contact Office of Financial Aid, Mount Mercy College, 1330 Elmhurst Drive, NE, Cedar Rapids, IA 52402-4797, 319-368-6467, fax: 319-363-5270.

MOUNT OLIVE COLLEGE
Mount Olive, North Carolina

About the Institution Independent/religious, coed. Degrees awarded: A, B. Offers 17 undergraduate majors. Total enrollment: 1,341 (95% state residents). Freshmen: 141.

Undergraduate Expenses (1997–98) Comprehensive fee of $11,815 includes tuition ($8400), mandatory fees ($90), and college room and board ($3325). College room only: $1400.

Applications Of all full-time undergraduates enrolled in fall 1996, 89% of those who applied for aid were judged to have need according to

Federal Methodology, of whom 91% were aided. *Financial aid deadline (priority):* 3/1. *Financial aid forms:* FAFSA, state form, institutional form required. *Admission application deadline:* rolling.

Summary of Aid to Needy Students *From gift & self-help combined:* Average need met: 85%. Average amount awarded: $5620 (80% gift aid, 20% self-help). *Gift aid:* Total: $2,389,361 (39% from college's own funds, 40% from other college-administered sources, 21% from external sources). 114 Federal Work-Study jobs (averaging $528).

Need-Based Scholarships & Grants Pell, FSEOG, state, college/university.

Loans Perkins, PLUS, Stafford, Unsubsidized Stafford.

Non-Need Awards In 1996, a total of 452 non-need awards were made. *Academic Interests/Achievement Awards:* 101 ($329,935 total): general academic. *Creative Arts/Performance Awards:* 87 ($103,900 total): art/fine arts, music. *Special Achievements/Activities Awards:* 131 ($238,174 total): leadership. *Athletic:* Total: 133 ($387,336); Men: 72 ($213,671); Women: 61 ($173,665).

Other Money-Saving Options Accelerated degree, co-op program, off-campus living. *Payment Plan:* installment. *Waivers:* full or partial for employees or children of employees and senior citizens.

Contact Ms. Diane H. Graham, Financial Aid Secretary, Mount Olive College, 634 Henderson Street, Mount Olive, NC 28365, 919-658-2502, fax: 919-658-7180.

MOUNT ST. CLARE COLLEGE
Clinton, Iowa

About the Institution Independent/religious, coed. Degrees awarded: A, B. Offers 43 undergraduate majors. Total enrollment: 515 (49% state residents). Freshmen: 97.

Undergraduate Expenses (1997–98) Comprehensive fee of $15,660 includes tuition ($11,500), mandatory fees ($140), and college room and board ($4020 minimum). College room only: $1820.

Applications 93% of all full-time undergraduates enrolled in fall 1996 applied for aid; of these, 91% were judged to have need according to Federal Methodology, of whom 100% were aided. *Financial aid deadline (priority):* 3/1. *Financial aid forms:* FAFSA, institutional form required. State form required for some. *Admission application deadline:* 8/15.

Summary of Aid to Needy Students *From gift & self-help combined:* Average need met: 95%. *Gift aid:* Total: $2,498,000 (68% from college's own funds, 21% from other college-administered sources, 11% from external sources). 115 Federal Work-Study jobs (averaging $750); 60 part-time jobs.

Need-Based Scholarships & Grants Pell, FSEOG, state, private, college/university.

Loans Perkins, PLUS, Stafford, Unsubsidized Stafford.

Non-Need Awards *Academic Interests/Achievement Awards:* general academic, biological sciences, business, communication, computer science, education, English, foreign languages, health fields, humanities, mathematics, physical sciences, premedicine, social sciences. *Creative Arts/Performance Awards:* music. *Special Achievements/Activities Awards:* community service, memberships, religious involvement. *Special Characteristics Awards:* children and siblings of alumni, children of current students, children of faculty/staff, international students, parents of current students, siblings of current students, spouses of current students, twins. *Athletic:* Total: 136 ($273,538); Men: 78 ($145,798); Women: 58 ($127,740).

Other Money-Saving Options Off-campus living (after sophomore year). *Payment Plan:* installment. *Waivers:* full or partial for employees or children of employees and senior citizens.

Contact Financial Aid Office, Mount St. Clare College, Clinton, IA 52732-3998, 319-242-4023.

MOUNT SAINT MARY COLLEGE
Newburgh, New York

About the Institution Independent, coed. Degrees awarded: B, M. Offers 34 undergraduate majors. Total enrollment: 1,978. Undergraduates: 1,587 (92% state residents). Freshmen: 273.

Undergraduate Expenses (1996–97) Comprehensive fee of $14,480 includes tuition ($9150), mandatory fees ($330), and college room and board ($5000 minimum).

Applications Of all full-time undergraduates enrolled in fall 1996, 91% of those who applied for aid were judged to have need according to Federal Methodology, of whom 100% were aided. *Financial aid deadline (priority):* 3/15. *Financial aid forms:* FAFSA, institutional form required. State form required for some. *Admission application deadline:* rolling.

Summary of Aid to Needy Students *From gift & self-help combined:* Average need met: 70%. Average amount awarded: $7162 (50% gift aid, 50% self-help). *Gift aid:* Total: $3,234,908 (36% from college's own funds, 43% from other college-administered sources, 21% from external sources). 125 Federal Work-Study jobs (averaging $950); 46 part-time jobs.

Need-Based Scholarships & Grants Pell, FSEOG, state, private, college/university.

Loans Perkins, PLUS, Stafford, Unsubsidized Stafford, Federal Nursing, private.

Non-Need Awards In 1996, a total of 299 non-need awards were made. *Academic Interests/Achievement Awards:* 284 ($588,250 total): general academic. *Special Characteristics Awards:* 15 ($135,200 total): children of faculty/staff.

Other Money-Saving Options Accelerated degree, co-op program, cooperative Army ROTC, off-campus living. *Payment Plan:* installment. *Waivers:* full or partial for employees or children of employees.

Contact Ms. Harlene Mehr, Director of Financial Aid, Mount Saint Mary College, 330 Powell Avenue, Newburgh, NY 12550-3494, 914-569-3194, fax: 914-562-6762.

MOUNT ST. MARY'S COLLEGE
Los Angeles, California

About the Institution Independent/religious, primarily women. Degrees awarded: A, B, M. Offers 40 undergraduate majors. Total enrollment: 1,411. Undergraduates: 1,054 (97% state residents). Freshmen: 107.

Undergraduate Expenses (1997–98) Comprehensive fee of $20,554 includes tuition ($14,716), mandatory fees ($500), and college room and board ($5338 minimum).

Applications 89% of all full-time undergraduates enrolled in fall 1996 applied for aid; of these, 91% were judged to have need according to Federal Methodology, of whom 100% were aided. *Financial aid deadline (priority):* 3/1. *Financial aid forms:* FAFSA, state form, institutional form required; CSS Financial Aid PROFILE acceptable. *Admission application deadline:* rolling.

Summary of Aid to Needy Students *Gift aid:* Total: $7,400,000 (69% from college's own funds, 15% from other college-administered sources, 16% from external sources). 300 Federal Work-Study jobs (averaging $2000); part-time jobs.

Need-Based Scholarships & Grants Pell, FSEOG, state, private, college/university.

Loans PLUS, Stafford, Unsubsidized Stafford, college/university short-term loans ($100 average), college/university long-term loans ($2000 average).

Non-Need Awards *Academic Interests/Achievement Awards:* general academic, education. *Special Achievements/Activities Awards:* community service, leadership.

Other Money-Saving Options Cooperative Army ROTC, cooperative Naval ROTC, cooperative Air Force ROTC, off-campus living. *Payment Plan:* deferred payment. *Waivers:* full or partial for employees or children of employees.

Contact Mr. Jim Whitaker, Financial Aid Director, Mount St. Mary's College, 12001 Chalon Road, Los Angeles, CA 90049-1597, 310-954-4190.

MOUNT SAINT MARY'S COLLEGE AND SEMINARY
Emmitsburg, Maryland

About the Institution Independent/religious, coed. Degrees awarded: B, M, P. Offers 31 undergraduate majors. Total enrollment: 1,884. Undergraduates: 1,476 (50% state residents). Freshmen: 368.

Undergraduate Expenses (1997–98) Comprehensive fee of $22,100 includes tuition ($15,450), mandatory fees ($200), and college room and board ($6450). College room only: $3225.

Applications 68% of all full-time undergraduates enrolled in fall 1996 applied for aid; of these, 89% were judged to have need according to Federal Methodology, of whom 99% were aided. *Financial aid deadline (priority):* 3/15. *Financial aid forms:* FAFSA, CSS Financial Aid PROFILE required. *Regular admission application deadline:* 3/1. Early action deadline: 12/1.

Summary of Aid to Needy Students *From gift & self-help combined:* Average need met: 83%. Average amount awarded: $11,247 (71% gift aid, 29% self-help). *Gift aid:* Total: $6,520,289 (82% from college's own funds, 12% from other college-administered sources, 6% from external sources). 197 Federal Work-Study jobs (averaging $1200); 300 part-time jobs.

Need-Based Scholarships & Grants Pell, FSEOG, state, private, college/university.

Loans Perkins, PLUS, Stafford, Unsubsidized Stafford, state, private.

Non-Need Awards In 1996, a total of 1,062 non-need awards were made. *Academic Interests/Achievement Awards:* 842 ($4,854,467 total): general academic. *Special Characteristics Awards:* 80 ($365,375 total): members of minorities, siblings of current students. *Athletic:* Total: 140 ($1,098,316); Men: 69 ($570,197); Women: 71 ($528,119).

Other Money-Saving Options Co-op program, Army ROTC, off-campus living (after freshman year). *Payment Plans:* tuition prepayment, installment. *Waivers:* full or partial for employees or children of employees.

Contact Office of Financial Aid, Mount Saint Mary's College and Seminary, Emmitsburg, MD 21727-7799, 301-447-6122.

MOUNT SENARIO COLLEGE
Ladysmith, Wisconsin

About the Institution Independent, coed. Degrees awarded: A, B. Offers 25 undergraduate majors. Total enrollment: 431 (92% state residents). Freshmen: 160.

Undergraduate Expenses (1996–97) Comprehensive fee of $12,230 includes tuition ($8860), mandatory fees ($120), and college room and board ($3250).

Applications *Financial aid deadline (priority):* 5/15. *Financial aid forms:* FAFSA required. *Admission application deadline:* 8/20.

Summary of Aid to Needy Students *From gift & self-help combined:* Average amount awarded: $5693 (60% gift aid, 40% self-help). *Gift aid:* Total: $1,293,065 (42% from college's own funds, 31% from other college-administered sources, 27% from external sources). 270 Federal Work-Study jobs (averaging $1000).

Need-Based Scholarships & Grants Pell, FSEOG, state, private, college/university.

Loans Perkins, PLUS, Stafford, Unsubsidized Stafford.

Non-Need Awards In 1996, a total of 150 non-need awards were made. *Academic Interests/Achievement Awards:* 88 ($53,430 total): general academic. *Special Characteristics Awards:* 62 ($76,903 total): children and siblings of alumni, children of faculty/staff, local/state students, previous college experience.

Other Money-Saving Options Accelerated degree, co-op program, off-campus living (after freshman year). *Payment Plan:* installment. *Waivers:* full or partial for employees or children of employees.

Contact Ms. Pam Vacho, Director of Financial Aid, Mount Senario College, 1500 College Avenue, Ladysmith, WI 54848-2128, 715-532-5511 Ext. 115.

MOUNT UNION COLLEGE
Alliance, Ohio

About the Institution Independent/religious, coed. Degrees awarded: B. Offers 47 undergraduate majors. Total enrollment: 1,731 (87% state residents). Freshmen: 565.

Undergraduate Expenses (1997–98) Comprehensive fee of $18,160 includes tuition ($13,520), mandatory fees ($770), and college room and board ($3870). College room only: $1540.

Applications 79% of all full-time undergraduates enrolled in fall 1996 applied for aid; of these, 99% were judged to have need according to Federal Methodology, of whom 100% were aided. *Financial aid deadline (priority):* 5/1. *Financial aid forms:* FAFSA required. *Admission application deadline:* rolling.

Summary of Aid to Needy Students *From gift & self-help combined:* Average amount awarded: $13,610 (65% gift aid, 35% self-help). *Gift aid:* Total: $10,842,400 (77% from college's own funds, 15% from other college-administered sources, 8% from external sources). 871 Federal Work-Study jobs (averaging $1146); 120 part-time jobs.

Need-Based Scholarships & Grants Pell, FSEOG, state, private, college/university.

Loans Perkins, PLUS, Stafford, Unsubsidized Stafford.

Non-Need Awards In 1996, a total of 613 non-need awards were made. *Academic Interests/Achievement Awards:* 498 ($2,420,247 total): general academic. *Creative Arts/Performance Awards:* 77 ($153,950 total): art/fine arts, cinema/film/broadcasting, debating, journalism/publications, music, theater/drama. *Special Characteristics Awards:* 38 ($249,580 total): children and siblings of alumni, children of faculty/staff, relatives of clergy, siblings of current students.

Other Money-Saving Options Accelerated degree, co-op program, cooperative Army ROTC, cooperative Air Force ROTC, off-campus living (after freshman year). *Payment Plans:* tuition prepayment, installment. *Waivers:* full or partial for children of alumni and employees or children of employees.

Contact Mrs. Sandra S. Pittenger, Director of Student Financial Services, Mount Union College, 1972 Clark Avenue, Alliance, OH 44601-3993, 330-823-2674.

MOUNT VERNON COLLEGE
Washington, District of Columbia

About the Institution Independent, women. Degrees awarded: A, B, M. Offers 21 undergraduate majors. Total enrollment: 600. Undergraduates: 434 (17% district residents). Freshmen: 123.

Undergraduate Expenses (1997–98) Comprehensive fee of $24,140 includes tuition ($15,870), mandatory fees ($540), and college room and board ($7730).

Applications Of all full-time undergraduates enrolled in fall 1996, 64% of those who applied for aid were judged to have need according to Federal Methodology, of whom 100% were aided. *Financial aid deadline*

(priority): 4/1. *Financial aid forms:* FAFSA required; CSS Financial Aid PROFILE acceptable. District form, institutional form required for some. *Admission application deadline:* rolling.

Summary of Aid to Needy Students *From gift & self-help combined:* Average need met: 80%. Average amount awarded: $11,175 (73% gift aid, 27% self-help). *Gift aid:* Total: $1,601,810 (84% from college's own funds, 3% from other college-administered sources, 13% from external sources). 200 Federal Work-Study jobs (averaging $1800).

Need-Based Scholarships & Grants Pell, FSEOG, state.

Loans PLUS, Stafford, Unsubsidized Stafford.

Non-Need Awards *Academic Interests/Achievement Awards:* general academic. *Special Characteristics Awards:* international students.

Other Money-Saving Options Accelerated degree, co-op program, off-campus living (after freshman year). *Payment Plan:* installment. *Waivers:* full or partial for employees or children of employees.

Contact Office of Financial Aid, Mount Vernon College, 2100 Foxhall Road, NW, Washington, DC 20007, 202-625-4682.

MOUNT VERNON NAZARENE COLLEGE
Mount Vernon, Ohio

About the Institution Independent/religious, coed. Degrees awarded: A, B, M. Offers 62 undergraduate majors. Total enrollment: 1,685. Undergraduates: 1,631 (86% state residents). Freshmen: 393.

Undergraduate Expenses (1997–98) Comprehensive fee of $13,820 includes tuition ($9430), mandatory fees ($547), and college room and board ($3843). College room only: $2178.

Applications 99% of all full-time undergraduates enrolled in fall 1996 applied for aid; of these, 78% were judged to have need according to Federal Methodology, of whom 100% were aided. *Financial aid deadline (priority):* 4/30. *Financial aid forms:* FAFSA, institutional form required. State form required for some. *Admission application deadline:* 6/15.

Summary of Aid to Needy Students *From gift & self-help combined:* Average need met: 84%. Average amount awarded: $9142 (83% gift aid, 17% self-help). *Gift aid:* Total: $3,979,411 (46% from college's own funds, 30% from other college-administered sources, 24% from external sources). 140 Federal Work-Study jobs (averaging $1200); 380 part-time jobs.

Need-Based Scholarships & Grants Pell, FSEOG, state, college/university.

Loans Perkins, PLUS, Stafford, Unsubsidized Stafford, state, private.

Non-Need Awards In 1996, a total of 3,096 non-need awards were made. *Academic Interests/Achievement Awards:* 572 ($869,326 total): general academic. *Creative Arts/Performance Awards:* 10 ($6700 total): music. *Special Achievements/Activities Awards:* 122 ($40,600 total): general special achievements/activities, Junior Miss, religious involvement. *Special Characteristics Awards:* 2,317 ($1,845,188 total): children of faculty/staff, international students, local/state students, relatives of clergy, religious affiliation, siblings of current students, spouses of current students, veterans, veterans' children. *Athletic:* Total: 75 ($197,200); Men: 42 ($115,950); Women: 33 ($81,250).

Another Money-Saving Option *Waivers:* full or partial for employees or children of employees.

Contact Mrs. Joanne E. Bowman, Director of Student Financial Planning, Mount Vernon Nazarene College, 800 Martinsburg Road, Mount Vernon, OH 43050-9500, 614-397-1244 Ext. 4520, fax: 614-393-0511.

MUHLENBERG COLLEGE
Allentown, Pennsylvania

About the Institution Independent/religious, coed. Degrees awarded: B. Offers 45 undergraduate majors. Total enrollment: 1,953 (34% state residents). Freshmen: 532.

Undergraduate Expenses (1996–97) Comprehensive fee of $22,970 includes tuition ($17,955), mandatory fees ($145), and college room and board ($4870). College room only: $2520.

Applications 72% of all full-time undergraduates enrolled in fall 1996 applied for aid; of these, 86% were judged to have need according to Federal Methodology, of whom 100% were aided. *Financial aid deadline (priority):* 2/15. *Financial aid forms:* FAFSA, CSS Financial Aid PROFILE, institutional form required. State form required for some. *Regular admission application deadline:* 2/15. Early decision deadline: 1/15.

Summary of Aid to Needy Students *From gift & self-help combined:* Average need met: 95%. Average amount awarded: $11,959 (74% gift aid, 26% self-help). *Gift aid:* Total: $10,072,037 (86% from college's own funds, 4% from other college-administered sources, 10% from external sources). 125 Federal Work-Study jobs (averaging $1250); 295 part-time jobs.

Need-Based Scholarships & Grants Pell, FSEOG, state, private, college/university.

Loans Perkins, PLUS, Stafford, Unsubsidized Stafford, private.

Non-Need Awards *Academic Interests/Achievement Awards:* general academic. *Creative Arts/Performance Awards:* dance, music, performing arts, theater/drama. *Special Achievements/Activities Awards:* leadership, memberships. *Special Characteristics Awards:* relatives of clergy.

Other Money-Saving Options Accelerated degree, cooperative Army ROTC, off-campus living (after freshman year). *Payment Plan:* installment. *Waivers:* full or partial for employees or children of employees and adult students.

Contact Mr. Greg Mitton, Director of Financial Aid, Muhlenberg College, 2400 Chew Street, Allentown, PA 18104-5586, 610-821-3175, fax: 610-821-3234.

MULTNOMAH BIBLE COLLEGE AND BIBLICAL SEMINARY
Portland, Oregon

About the Institution Independent/religious, coed. Degrees awarded: B, M, P. Offers 11 undergraduate majors. Total enrollment: 750. Undergraduates: 534 (42% state residents). Freshmen: 216.

Undergraduate Expenses (1996–97) Comprehensive fee of $10,090 includes tuition ($7100) and college room and board ($2990). College room only: $1530.

Applications Of all full-time undergraduates enrolled in fall 1996, 100% of those judged to have need according to Federal Methodology were aided. *Financial aid deadline (priority):* 3/1. *Financial aid forms:* FAFSA, institutional form required. *Admission application deadline:* 7/15.

Summary of Aid to Needy Students *From gift & self-help combined:* Average need met: 75%. Average amount awarded: $5709 (42% gift aid, 58% self-help). *Gift aid:* Total: $940,119 (48% from college's own funds, 8% from other college-administered sources, 44% from external sources). 50 Federal Work-Study jobs (averaging $1300); 120 part-time jobs.

Need-Based Scholarships & Grants Pell, FSEOG, private, college/university.

Loans PLUS, Stafford, Unsubsidized Stafford, college/university short-term loans ($100 average).

Non-Need Awards In 1996, a total of 49 non-need awards were made. *Academic Interests/Achievement Awards:* 27 ($80,000 total): general academic, religion/biblical studies. *Special Characteristics Awards:* 22 ($22,000 total): international students, religious affiliation, siblings of current students.

Other Money-Saving Options *Payment Plan:* installment. *Waivers:* full or partial for employees or children of employees.

Contact Mr. David Allen, Director of Financial Aid, Multnomah Bible College and Biblical Seminary, 8435 Northeast Glisan Street, Portland, OR 97220-5898, 503-251-5336, fax: 503-254-1268.

MURRAY STATE UNIVERSITY
Murray, Kentucky

About the Institution State-supported, coed. Degrees awarded: A, B, M. Offers 90 undergraduate majors. Total enrollment: 8,636. Undergraduates: 7,120 (75% state residents). Freshmen: 1,496.

Undergraduate Expenses (1997–98) State resident tuition: $1800. Nonresident tuition: $5400. Mandatory fees: $320. College room and board: $3410. College room only: $1470.

Applications 79% of all full-time undergraduates enrolled in fall 1996 applied for aid; of these, 71% were judged to have need according to Federal Methodology, of whom 97% were aided. *Financial aid deadline (priority):* 4/1. *Financial aid forms:* FAFSA, institutional form, financial aid transcript (for transfers) required. *Regular admission application deadline:* rolling. Nonresident deadline: 8/01.

Summary of Aid to Needy Students *From gift & self-help combined:* Average need met: 90%. Average amount awarded: $4516 (50% gift aid, 50% self-help). *Gift aid:* Total: $7,698,693 (40% from college's own funds, 14% from other college-administered sources, 46% from external sources). 507 Federal Work-Study jobs (averaging $1102); 2,029 part-time jobs.

Need-Based Scholarships & Grants Pell, FSEOG, state, private, college/university.

Loans Perkins, PLUS, Stafford, Unsubsidized Stafford, Federal Nursing, college/university short-term loans ($502 average).

Non-Need Awards *Academic Interests/Achievement Awards:* general academic, agriculture, biological sciences, business, communication, computer science, education, English, foreign languages, health fields, home economics, mathematics, physical sciences, premedicine, social sciences. *Creative Arts/Performance Awards:* general creative, applied art and design, art/fine arts, creative writing, dance, debating, journalism/publications, music, theater/drama. *Special Achievements/Activities Awards:* general special achievements/activities, Junior Miss, leadership, rodeo. *Special Characteristics Awards:* general special characteristics, adult students, children and siblings of alumni, children of faculty/staff, handicapped students, international students, local/state students, members of minorities. *Athletic:* Total: 149 ($1,254,130); Men: 106 ($909,470); Women: 43 ($344,660).

Other Money-Saving Options Accelerated degree, co-op program, Army ROTC, off-campus living (after sophomore year). *Payment Plans:* installment, deferred payment. *Waivers:* full or partial for children of alumni, employees or children of employees, senior citizens.

Contact Mr. Johnny McDougal, Director of Student Financial Aid, Murray State University, PO Box 9, Murray, KY 42071-0009, 502-762-2546.

MUSICIANS INSTITUTE
Hollywood, California

About the Institution Proprietary, coed. Degrees awarded: A, B. Offers 1 undergraduate major.

Undergraduate Expenses (1997–98) Tuition: $12,000.

Applications 25% of all full-time undergraduates enrolled in fall 1996 applied for aid. *Financial aid deadline (priority):* 8/31. *Financial aid forms:* FAFSA, institutional form required. *Admission application deadline:* rolling.

Summary of Aid to Needy Students *Gift aid:* Total: $250,000. Federal Work-Study jobs; part-time jobs.

Need-Based Scholarships & Grants Pell, FSEOG.

Loans PLUS, Stafford, Unsubsidized Stafford.

Non-Need Awards Not offered.

Contact Office of Financial Aid, Musicians Institute, 1655 North McCadden Place, CA 90028, 213-462-1384.

MUSKINGUM COLLEGE
New Concord, Ohio

About the Institution Independent/religious, coed. Degrees awarded: B, M. Offers 52 undergraduate majors. Total enrollment: 1,411. Undergraduates: 1,302 (85% state residents). Freshmen: 394.

Undergraduate Expenses (1997–98) Comprehensive fee of $15,285 includes tuition ($10,450 minimum), mandatory fees ($335), and college room and board ($4500). College room only: $2130.

Applications 86% of all full-time undergraduates enrolled in fall 1996 applied for aid; of these, 95% were judged to have need according to Federal Methodology, of whom 100% were aided. *Financial aid deadline (priority):* 3/15. *Financial aid forms:* FAFSA, institutional form required; CSS Financial Aid PROFILE acceptable. State form required for some. *Admission application deadline:* 6/1.

Summary of Aid to Needy Students *From gift & self-help combined:* Average need met: 91%. Average amount awarded: $12,688 (69% gift aid, 31% self-help). *Gift aid:* Total: $8,723,000 (73% from college's own funds, 17% from other college-administered sources, 10% from external sources). 535 Federal Work-Study jobs (averaging $800); 40 part-time jobs.

Need-Based Scholarships & Grants Pell, FSEOG, state, private, college/university.

Loans Perkins, PLUS, Stafford, Unsubsidized Stafford, state, private, college/university short-term loans ($500 average), college/university long-term loans ($1000 average).

Non-Need Awards In 1996, a total of 1,495 non-need awards were made. *Academic Interests/Achievement Awards:* 373 ($1,727,000 total). *Creative Arts/Performance Awards:* 152 ($207,000 total): art/fine arts, cinema/film/broadcasting, debating, music, theater/drama. *Special Achievements/Activities Awards:* 51 ($48,000 total): leadership, religious involvement. *Special Characteristics Awards:* 919 ($1,270,000 total): children and siblings of alumni, local/state students, members of minorities, religious affiliation, siblings of current students.

Other Money-Saving Options Accelerated degree, off-campus living (after junior year). *Payment Plan:* installment. *Waivers:* full or partial for employees or children of employees and senior citizens.

Contact Office of Financial Aid, Muskingum College, 163 Stormont, New Concord, OH 43762, 614-826-8211.

NAES COLLEGE
Chicago, Illinois

About the Institution Independent, coed. Degrees awarded: B. Offers 1 undergraduate major. Total enrollment: 87 (100% state residents). Freshmen: 5.

Undergraduate Expenses (1997–98) Tuition: $4200. Mandatory fees: $140.

Applications *Financial aid deadline (priority):* 7/1. *Financial aid forms:* FAFSA, CSS Financial Aid PROFILE, institutional form, Bureau of Indian Affairs form required. *Admission application deadline:* rolling.

Summary of Aid to Needy Students *From gift & self-help combined:* Average need met: 75%. Average amount awarded: $2420. *Gift aid:* Total: $150,053 (9% from college's own funds, 70% from other college-administered sources, 21% from external sources). Federal Work-Study jobs.

Need-Based Scholarships & Grants Pell, FSEOG, state, private, tribal scholarships.

Non-Need Awards Not offered.

Other Money-Saving Options Accelerated degree. *Payment Plan:* tuition prepayment.

Contact Mr. Timothy Murphy, Financial Aid Officer, NAES College, 2838 West Peterson Avenue, Chicago, IL 60659-3813, 773-761-5000, fax: 773-761-3808.

NATIONAL AMERICAN UNIVERSITY
Denver, Colorado

About the Institution Proprietary, coed. Degrees awarded: A, B. Offers 4 undergraduate majors. Total enrollment: 350 (83% state residents). Freshmen: 55.

Undergraduate Expenses (1996–97) Tuition: $7920.

Applications *Financial aid deadline (priority):* 8/16. *Financial aid forms:* FAFSA, institutional form required. State form required for some. *Admission application deadline:* rolling.

Summary of Aid to Needy Students Federal Work-Study jobs; part-time jobs.

Non-Need Awards *Academic Interests/Achievement Awards:* general academic.

Other Money-Saving Options Accelerated degree. *Payment Plan:* installment. *Waivers:* full or partial for employees or children of employees and senior citizens.

Contact Office of Financial Aid, National American University, 321 Kansas City Street, Rapid City, SD 57701, 303-758-6700.

NATIONAL COLLEGE
Colorado Springs, Colorado

About the Institution Proprietary, coed. Degrees awarded: A, B. Offers 5 undergraduate majors. Total enrollment: 350 (50% state residents). Freshmen: 85.

Undergraduate Expenses (1996–97) Tuition: $7920. Mandatory fees: $75.

Applications *Financial aid deadline:* Applications processed continuously. *Financial aid forms:* FAFSA, institutional form required. *Admission application deadline:* rolling.

Summary of Aid to Needy Students Federal Work-Study jobs.

Non-Need Awards *Academic Interests/Achievement Awards:* general academic.

Another Money-Saving Option Accelerated degree.

Contact Office of Financial Aid, National College, 321 Kansas City Street, Rapid City, SD 57701, 719-471-4205.

NATIONAL COLLEGE
Kansas City, Missouri

About the Institution Proprietary, coed. Degrees awarded: A, B. Offers 5 undergraduate majors. Total enrollment: 156 (75% state residents). Freshmen: 42.

Undergraduate Expenses (1997–98) Tuition: $8400.

Applications *Financial aid deadline:* Applications processed continuously. *Financial aid forms:* FAFSA required. Institutional form required for some. *Admission application deadline:* rolling.

Summary of Aid to Needy Students Federal Work-Study jobs.

Non-Need Awards *Academic Interests/Achievement Awards:* general academic.

Other Money-Saving Options Co-op program. *Payment Plan:* installment.

Contact Office of Financial Aid, National College, Kansas City, MO 64133-1612, 816-353-4554.

NATIONAL COLLEGE
Albuquerque, New Mexico

About the Institution Proprietary, coed. Degrees awarded: A, B. Offers 7 undergraduate majors. Total enrollment: 294.

Undergraduate Expenses (1997–98) Tuition: $8160. Mandatory fees: $50.

Applications *Financial aid deadline:* continuous. *Financial aid forms:* FAFSA, state form acceptable. *Admission application deadline:* rolling.

Non-Need Awards *Academic Interests/Achievement Awards:* general academic.

Other Money-Saving Options Accelerated degree, co-op program.

Contact Office of Financial Aid, National College, 321 Kansas City Street, Rapid City, SD 57701, 505-265-7517.

NATIONAL COLLEGE
Rapid City, South Dakota

About the Institution Proprietary, coed. Degrees awarded: A, B. Offers 15 undergraduate majors. Total enrollment: 621 (75% state residents). Freshmen: 240.

Undergraduate Expenses (1997–98) Comprehensive fee of $11,835 includes tuition ($8400), mandatory fees ($75), and college room and board ($3360). College room only: $1530.

Applications *Financial aid deadline (priority):* 4/15. *Financial aid forms:* FAFSA, institutional form required. State form required for some. *Admission application deadline:* rolling.

Summary of Aid to Needy Students Federal Work-Study jobs; part-time jobs.

Loans College/university long-term loans.

Non-Need Awards *Academic Interests/Achievement Awards:* general academic. *Special Characteristics Awards:* local/state students. *Athletic:* available.

Other Money-Saving Options Accelerated degree, co-op program, cooperative Army ROTC, off-campus living (after freshman year). *Payment Plan:* installment. *Waivers:* full or partial for employees or children of employees.

Contact Office of Financial Aid, National College, 321 Kansas City Street, Rapid City, SD 57701, 605-394-4800.

NATIONAL COLLEGE–ST. PAUL CAMPUS
St. Paul, Minnesota

About the Institution Proprietary, coed. Degrees awarded: A, B. Offers 6 undergraduate majors. Total enrollment: 310 (70% state residents).

Undergraduate Expenses (1996–97) Tuition: $8160.

Applications *Financial aid deadline:* Applications processed continuously. *Financial aid forms:* FAFSA, institutional form required. State form required for some. *Admission application deadline:* rolling.

Summary of Aid to Needy Students *From gift & self-help combined:* Average need met: 95%. Federal Work-Study jobs.

Need-Based Scholarships & Grants Pell, FSEOG, state, college/university.

Loans Perkins, PLUS, Stafford, Unsubsidized Stafford, state, college/university short-term loans, college/university long-term loans.

Non-Need Awards *Academic Interests/Achievement Awards:* general academic.

Other Money-Saving Options Accelerated degree, co-op program. *Payment Plans:* installment, deferred payment. *Waivers:* full or partial for employees or children of employees and senior citizens.

Contact Ms. Barbara Early, Financial Aid Coordinator, National College–St. Paul Campus, St. Paul, MN 55108-9952, 612-644-1265.

NATIONAL COLLEGE–SIOUX FALLS BRANCH
Sioux Falls, South Dakota

About the Institution Proprietary, coed. Degrees awarded: A, B. Offers 9 undergraduate majors. Total enrollment: 326 (95% state residents). Freshmen: 80.

Undergraduate Expenses (1996–97) Tuition: $7680.

Applications *Financial aid deadline:* Applications processed continuously. *Financial aid forms:* FAFSA, institutional form required. *Admission application deadline:* rolling.

Summary of Aid to Needy Students *From gift & self-help combined:* Average need met: 95%. Federal Work-Study jobs; 15 part-time jobs.

Need-Based Scholarships & Grants Pell, FSEOG, state, college/ university.

Loans Perkins, PLUS, Stafford, Unsubsidized Stafford.

Non-Need Awards *Academic Interests/Achievement Awards:* general academic. *Special Characteristics Awards:* siblings of current students, spouses of current students.

Other Money-Saving Options Accelerated degree, co-op program. *Payment Plan:* guaranteed tuition.

Contact Ms. Jan Hegemeyer, Director of Financial Aid, National College– Sioux Falls Branch, Sioux Falls, SD 57105-4293, 605-334-5430.

THE NATIONAL HISPANIC UNIVERSITY
San Jose, California

About the Institution Independent, coed. Degrees awarded: A, B. Offers 5 undergraduate majors. Total enrollment: 300 (85% state residents). Freshmen: 146.

Undergraduate Expenses (1997–98) Tuition: $3875.

Applications 49% of all full-time undergraduates enrolled in fall 1996 applied for aid; of these, 94% were judged to have need according to Federal Methodology, of whom 93% were aided. *Financial aid deadline (priority):* 8/15. *Financial aid forms:* FAFSA required. State form, institutional form required for some. *Admission application deadline:* 8/15.

Summary of Aid to Needy Students *From gift & self-help combined:* Average need met: 91%. Average amount awarded: $1368 (95% gift aid, 5% self-help). *Gift aid:* Total: $40,100 (23% from college's own funds, 14% from other college-administered sources, 63% from external sources). 15 Federal Work-Study jobs (averaging $500); 5 part-time jobs.

Need-Based Scholarships & Grants Pell, FSEOG, state, private, college/ university.

Loans PLUS, Stafford, Unsubsidized Stafford, private.

Non-Need Awards Not offered.

Other Money-Saving Options Accelerated degree, co-op program.

Contact Ms. Pilar Diaz, Financial Aid Administrator, The National Hispanic University, 14271 Story Road, San Jose, CA 95127-3823, 408-254-6900, fax: 408-254-1369.

NATIONAL-LOUIS UNIVERSITY
Evanston, Illinois

About the Institution Independent, coed. Degrees awarded: B, M, D. Offers 26 undergraduate majors. Total enrollment: 7,430. Undergraduates: 3,076 (95% state residents). Freshmen: 231.

Undergraduate Expenses (1996–97) Comprehensive fee of $15,990 includes tuition ($11,250) and college room and board ($4740 minimum).

Applications *Financial aid deadline (priority):* 7/15. *Financial aid forms:* FAFSA, institutional form, federal income tax forms required; CSS Financial Aid PROFILE acceptable. State form required for some. *Admission application deadline:* rolling.

Summary of Aid to Needy Students *From gift & self-help combined:* Average need met: 88%. Average amount awarded: $7306 (77% gift aid, 23% self-help). *Gift aid:* Total: $12,232,000 (43% from college's own funds, 43% from other college-administered sources, 14% from external sources). Federal Work-Study jobs; part-time jobs.

Need-Based Scholarships & Grants Pell, FSEOG, state, private, college/ university.

Loans Perkins, PLUS, Stafford, Unsubsidized Stafford.

Non-Need Awards *Academic Interests/Achievement Awards:* general academic. *Creative Arts/Performance Awards:* theater/drama.

Other Money-Saving Options Accelerated degree, off-campus living. *Payment Plan:* installment. *Waivers:* full or partial for employees or children of employees.

Contact Financial Aid Office, National-Louis University, Evanston, IL 60201-1730, 800-443-5522.

NATIONAL UNIVERSITY
La Jolla, California

About the Institution Independent, coed. Degrees awarded: A, B, M. Offers 25 undergraduate majors.

Undergraduate Expenses (1996–97) Tuition: $6660.

Applications *Financial aid deadline (priority):* 7/1. *Financial aid forms:* FAFSA, institutional form required. State form required for some. *Admission application deadline:* rolling.

Summary of Aid to Needy Students *From gift & self-help combined:* Average need met: 80%. Average amount awarded: $6000 (27% gift aid, 73% self-help). *Gift aid:* Total: $1,925,089 (19% from college's own funds, 19% from other college-administered sources, 62% from external sources). Federal Work-Study jobs; 200 part-time jobs.

Need-Based Scholarships & Grants Pell, FSEOG, state, college/ university.

Loans Perkins, PLUS, Stafford, Unsubsidized Stafford, college/university long-term loans.

Non-Need Awards In 1996, a total of 1,570 non-need awards were made. *Academic Interests/Achievement Awards:* 330 ($171,100 total): general academic. *Special Achievements/Activities Awards:* 1,240 ($890,285 total): leadership.

Other Money-Saving Options Accelerated degree, cooperative Army ROTC, cooperative Air Force ROTC. *Payment Plan:* tuition prepayment.

Contact Ms. Cara Hartinger, Financial Aid Officer, National University, 11255 North Torrey Pines Road, La Jolla, CA 92037-1011, 619-642-8509, fax: 619-642-8720.

NAZARENE BIBLE COLLEGE
Colorado Springs, Colorado

About the Institution Independent/religious, coed. Degrees awarded: A, B. Offers 5 undergraduate majors. Total enrollment: 426. Freshmen: 117.

Undergraduate Expenses (1997–98) Tuition: $4890. Mandatory fees: $165.

Applications 88% of all full-time undergraduates enrolled in fall 1996 applied for aid; of these, 98% were judged to have need according to Federal Methodology, of whom 99% were aided. *Financial aid deadline:* continuous. *Financial aid forms:* FAFSA required. Institutional form required for some. *Admission application deadline:* 8/31.

Summary of Aid to Needy Students *From gift & self-help combined:* Average need met: 48%. Average amount awarded: $5529 (44% gift

aid, 56% self-help). *Gift aid:* Total: $460,323 (17% from college's own funds, 8% from other college-administered sources, 75% from external sources). Federal Work-Study jobs; 10 part-time jobs.

Need-Based Scholarships & Grants Pell, FSEOG, college/university.

Loans Perkins, PLUS, Stafford, Unsubsidized Stafford, college/university short-term loans ($300 average).

Non-Need Awards Not offered.

Another Money-Saving Option *Waivers:* full or partial for employees or children of employees.

Contact Mr. Malcolm Britton, Director of Financial Aid, Nazarene Bible College, 1111 Academy Park Loop, Colorado Springs, CO 80910-3717, 719-550-5110, fax: 719-550-9437.

NAZARENE INDIAN BIBLE COLLEGE
Albuquerque, New Mexico

About the Institution Independent/religious, coed. Degrees awarded: A, B. Offers 4 undergraduate majors. Total enrollment: 46. Freshmen: 12.

Undergraduate Expenses (1997–98 estimated) Tuition: $4050. Mandatory fees: $120. College room only: $900 (minimum).

Applications 86% of all full-time undergraduates enrolled in fall 1996 applied for aid; of these,100% were judged to have need according to Federal Methodology, of whom 100% were aided. *Financial aid deadline:* continuous. *Financial aid forms:* FAFSA required. *Admission application deadline:* rolling.

Summary of Aid to Needy Students *From gift & self-help combined:* Average amount awarded: $3784 (68% gift aid, 32% self-help). *Gift aid:* Total: $49,138 (7% from college's own funds, 93% from external sources). 11 part-time jobs.

Need-Based Scholarships & Grants Pell, private, college/university, Tribal Awards.

Loans Stafford, Unsubsidized Stafford.

Non-Need Awards In 1996, a total of 7 non-need awards were made. *Academic Interests/Achievement Awards:* 7 ($3460 total): general academic, religion/biblical studies.

Contact Financial Aid Department, Nazarene Indian Bible College, Albuquerque, NM 87105, 505-877-0240.

NAZARETH COLLEGE OF ROCHESTER
Rochester, New York

About the Institution Independent, coed. Degrees awarded: B, M. Offers 63 undergraduate majors. Total enrollment: 2,761. Undergraduates: 1,764 (98% state residents). Freshmen: 337.

Undergraduate Expenses (1996–97) Comprehensive fee of $17,454 includes tuition ($11,926), mandatory fees ($204), and college room and board ($5324 minimum). College room only: $3256.

Applications Of all full-time undergraduates enrolled in fall 1996, 91% of those who applied for aid were judged to have need according to Federal Methodology, of whom 99% were aided. *Financial aid deadline (priority):* 2/15. *Financial aid forms:* FAFSA, CSS Financial Aid PROFILE required. State form required for some. *Regular admission application deadline:* 3/1. Early decision deadline: 12/1.

Summary of Aid to Needy Students *From gift & self-help combined:* Average need met: 82%. Average amount awarded: $11,422 (57% gift aid, 43% self-help). *Gift aid:* Total: $6,986,415 (65% from college's own funds, 2% from other college-administered sources, 33% from external sources). 469 Federal Work-Study jobs (averaging $738); 236 part-time jobs.

Need-Based Scholarships & Grants Pell, FSEOG, state, private, college/university.

Loans Perkins, PLUS, Stafford, Unsubsidized Stafford, private.

Non-Need Awards In 1996, a total of 346 non-need awards were made. *Academic Interests/Achievement Awards:* 236 ($1,074,274 total): general academic. *Creative Arts/Performance Awards:* 42 ($57,825 total): art/fine arts, music, theater/drama. *Special Characteristics Awards:* 68 ($287,171 total): children and siblings of alumni, children of faculty/staff, siblings of current students.

Other Money-Saving Options Accelerated degree, co-op program, cooperative Air Force ROTC, off-campus living. *Payment Plan:* installment. *Waivers:* full or partial for employees or children of employees.

Contact Dr. Bruce C. Woolley, Director of Financial Aid, Nazareth College of Rochester, 4245 East Avenue, Rochester, NY 14618-3790, 716-389-2310, fax: 716-586-2452.

NEBRASKA CHRISTIAN COLLEGE
Norfolk, Nebraska

About the Institution Independent/religious, coed. Degrees awarded: A, B. Offers 10 undergraduate majors. Total enrollment: 141. Freshmen: 60.

Undergraduate Expenses (1997–98) Comprehensive fee of $7200 includes tuition ($4160), mandatory fees ($350), and college room and board ($2690). College room only: $1210.

Applications 100% of all full-time undergraduates enrolled in fall 1996 applied for aid; of these, 76% were judged to have need according to Federal Methodology, of whom 100% were aided. *Financial aid deadline (priority):* 6/1. *Financial aid forms:* FAFSA, institutional form required. *Admission application deadline:* rolling.

Summary of Aid to Needy Students *From gift & self-help combined:* Average need met: 64%. Average amount awarded: $6260 (58% gift aid, 42% self-help). *Gift aid:* Total: $356,522 (36% from college's own funds, 12% from other college-administered sources, 52% from external sources). 8 Federal Work-Study jobs (averaging $1445); 16 part-time jobs.

Need-Based Scholarships & Grants Pell, FSEOG, state, private, college/university.

Loans PLUS, Stafford, Unsubsidized Stafford.

Non-Need Awards In 1996, a total of 113 non-need awards were made. *Academic Interests/Achievement Awards:* 86 ($116,258 total): general academic, education, religion/biblical studies. *Creative Arts/Performance Awards:* 4 ($3800 total): music. *Special Characteristics Awards:* 23 ($11,750 total): children of faculty/staff, international students, relatives of clergy.

Another Money-Saving Option *Waivers:* full or partial for employees or children of employees.

Contact Ms. Merelyn Stites, Financial Aid Officer, Nebraska Christian College, 1800 Syracuse, Norfolk, NE 68701-2458, 402-371-5960, fax: 402-371-5967.

NEBRASKA METHODIST COLLEGE OF NURSING AND ALLIED HEALTH
Omaha, Nebraska

About the Institution Independent, primarily women. Degrees awarded: A, B. Offers 3 undergraduate majors. Total enrollment: 380 (80% state residents). Freshmen: 30.

Undergraduate Expenses (1996–97) Comprehensive fee of $10,320 includes tuition ($7776), mandatory fees ($544), and college room and board ($2000). College room only: $1420.

Applications 81% of all full-time undergraduates enrolled in fall 1996 applied for aid; of these, 87% were judged to have need according to Federal Methodology, of whom 100% were aided. *Financial aid deadline (priority):* 5/1. *Financial aid forms:* FAFSA, institutional form required. *Admission application deadline:* 4/1.

Summary of Aid to Needy Students *From gift & self-help combined:* Average need met: 97%. Average amount awarded: $4704 (37% gift aid, 63% self-help). *Gift aid:* Total: $276,100 (58% from college's own funds, 3% from other college-administered sources, 39% from external sources). 2 part-time jobs.

Need-Based Scholarships & Grants Pell, FSEOG, state, private, college/university.

Loans Perkins, PLUS, Stafford, Unsubsidized Stafford, Federal Nursing, college/university short-term loans ($2000 average).

Non-Need Awards In 1996, a total of 115 non-need awards were made. *Academic Interests/Achievement Awards:* 115 ($104,000 total): general academic.

Other Money-Saving Options Cooperative Army ROTC, cooperative Naval ROTC, cooperative Air Force ROTC, off-campus living.

Contact Ms. Brenda Boyd, Financial Aid Coordinator, Nebraska Methodist College of Nursing and Allied Health, 8501 West Dodge Road, Omaha, NE 68114-3426, 402-354-4874, fax: 402-354-8875.

NEBRASKA WESLEYAN UNIVERSITY
Lincoln, Nebraska

About the Institution Independent/religious, coed. Degrees awarded: B. Offers 39 undergraduate majors. Total enrollment: 1,562 (93% state residents). Freshmen: 387.

Undergraduate Expenses (1996–97) Comprehensive fee of $14,234 includes tuition ($10,284), mandatory fees ($430), and college room and board ($3520 minimum).

Applications 77% of all full-time undergraduates enrolled in fall 1996 applied for aid; of these, 92% were judged to have need according to Federal Methodology, of whom 99% were aided. *Financial aid deadline (priority):* 7/15. *Financial aid forms:* CSS Financial Aid PROFILE acceptable. FAFSA, institutional form required for some. *Regular admission application deadline:* 3/15. Early decision deadline: 11/15.

Summary of Aid to Needy Students *From gift & self-help combined:* Average need met: 72%. Average amount awarded: $8119 (57% gift aid, 43% self-help). *Gift aid:* Total: $4,586,448 (79% from college's own funds, 6% from other college-administered sources, 15% from external sources). 130 Federal Work-Study jobs (averaging $775); 270 part-time jobs.

Need-Based Scholarships & Grants Pell, FSEOG, state, private, college/university.

Loans Perkins, PLUS, Stafford, Unsubsidized Stafford, private.

Non-Need Awards In 1996, a total of 1,319 non-need awards were made. *Academic Interests/Achievement Awards:* 1,053 ($1,538,984 total): general academic. *Creative Arts/Performance Awards:* 127 ($99,400 total): art/fine arts, music, theater/drama. *Special Characteristics Awards:* 139 ($261,305 total): relatives of clergy, siblings of current students.

Other Money-Saving Options Cooperative Army ROTC, cooperative Air Force ROTC, off-campus living (after sophomore year). *Payment Plan:* installment. *Waivers:* full or partial for employees or children of employees, adult students, senior citizens.

Contact Office of Financial Aid, Nebraska Wesleyan University, 5000 Saint Paul Avenue, Lincoln, NE 68504-2796, 402-466-2371.

NER ISRAEL RABBINICAL COLLEGE
Baltimore, Maryland

About the Institution Independent/religious, men. Degrees awarded: B, M. Offers 4 undergraduate majors.

Applications *Financial aid deadline:* continuous. *Financial aid forms:* FAFSA, institutional form required. *Admission application deadline:* rolling.

Summary of Aid to Needy Students 30 part-time jobs.

Need-Based Scholarships & Grants Pell, state.

Loans Perkins, Stafford, Unsubsidized Stafford.

Non-Need Awards *Academic Interests/Achievement Awards:* general academic. *Special Characteristics Awards:* children of faculty/staff.

Contact Mr. Moshe Pelberg, Financial Aid Administrator, Ner Israel Rabbinical College, 400 Mount Wilson Lane, Baltimore, MD 21208, 410-484-7200.

NEUMANN COLLEGE
Aston, Pennsylvania

About the Institution Independent/religious, coed. Degrees awarded: A, B, M. Offers 17 undergraduate majors. Total enrollment: 1,142. Undergraduates: 1,040 (79% state residents). Freshmen: 216.

Undergraduate Expenses (1997–98) Tuition: $12,400 (minimum). Mandatory fees: $470.

Applications 90% of all full-time undergraduates enrolled in fall 1996 applied for aid; of these, 94% were judged to have need according to Federal Methodology, of whom 100% were aided. *Financial aid deadline (priority):* 5/1. *Financial aid forms:* FAFSA, state form required; CSS Financial Aid PROFILE acceptable. *Admission application deadline:* rolling.

Summary of Aid to Needy Students *From gift & self-help combined:* Average need met: 90%. Average amount awarded: $9321 (44% gift aid, 56% self-help). *Gift aid:* Total: $1,805,001 (73% from college's own funds, 6% from other college-administered sources, 21% from external sources). 191 Federal Work-Study jobs (averaging $1347); part-time jobs.

Need-Based Scholarships & Grants Pell, FSEOG, state, private, college/university.

Loans PLUS, Stafford, Unsubsidized Stafford, Federal Nursing.

Non-Need Awards In 1996, a total of 279 non-need awards were made. *Academic Interests/Achievement Awards:* 255 ($749,750 total): general academic. *Special Achievements/Activities Awards:* 3 ($7200 total): religious involvement. *Special Characteristics Awards:* 21 ($80,889 total): children of faculty/staff, religious affiliation.

Other Money-Saving Options Co-op program, Army ROTC. *Payment Plans:* installment, deferred payment. *Waivers:* full or partial for employees or children of employees.

Contact Office of Financial Aid, Neumann College, Concord Road, Aston, PA 19014-1298, 610-459-0905.

NEWARK COLLEGE OF ARTS AND SCIENCES
Newark, New Jersey

See Rutgers, The State University of New Jersey, Newark College of Arts and Sciences

---

NEWBERRY COLLEGE
Newberry, South Carolina

About the Institution Independent/religious, coed. Degrees awarded: B. Offers 41 undergraduate majors. Total enrollment: 700 (84% state residents). Freshmen: 235.

Undergraduate Expenses (1997–98) Comprehensive fee of $15,544 includes tuition ($11,996), mandatory fees ($330), and college room and board ($3218). College room only: $1364.

Applications 92% of all full-time undergraduates enrolled in fall 1996 applied for aid; of these, 84% were judged to have need according to

Federal Methodology, of whom 100% were aided. *Financial aid deadline (priority):* 5/1. *Financial aid forms:* FAFSA, institutional form required. *Admission application deadline:* rolling.

Summary of Aid to Needy Students *From gift & self-help combined:* Average need met: 87%. Average amount awarded: $8034 (73% gift aid, 27% self-help). *Gift aid:* Total: $4,070,965 (59% from college's own funds, 2% from other college-administered sources, 39% from external sources). 89 Federal Work-Study jobs (averaging $800); 76 part-time jobs.

Need-Based Scholarships & Grants Pell, FSEOG, state, private, college/university.

Loans Perkins, PLUS, Stafford, Unsubsidized Stafford, private, college/university long-term loans ($1500 average).

Non-Need Awards In 1996, a total of 789 non-need awards were made. *Academic Interests/Achievement Awards:* 277 ($1,293,659 total): general academic. *Creative Arts/Performance Awards:* 66 ($71,048 total): music, theater/drama. *Special Achievements/Activities Awards:* 17 ($2000 total): cheerleading/drum major. *Special Characteristics Awards:* 217 ($336,797 total): children of faculty/staff, local/state students, relatives of clergy, religious affiliation. *Athletic:* Total: 212 ($878,823); Men: 139 ($650,684); Women: 73 ($228,139).

Other Money-Saving Options Accelerated degree, Army ROTC, off-campus living (after sophomore year).

Contact Ms. Catherine Flaherty, Director of Financial Aid, Newberry College, 2100 College Street, Newberry, SC 29108-2197, 803-321-5020, fax: 803-321-5627.

NEW COLLEGE OF CALIFORNIA
San Francisco, California

About the Institution Independent, coed. Degrees awarded: A, B, M, P. Offers 1 undergraduate major. Total enrollment: 1,600. Undergraduates: 900 (85% state residents). Freshmen: 20.

Undergraduate Expenses (1996–97) Tuition: $8276. Mandatory fees: $50.

Applications *Financial aid deadline (priority):* 5/1. *Financial aid forms:* FAFSA, institutional form required; CSS Financial Aid PROFILE acceptable. CSS Financial Aid PROFILE, state form required for some. *Admission application deadline:* rolling.

Summary of Aid to Needy Students Federal Work-Study jobs; part-time jobs.

Other Money-Saving Options Accelerated degree, co-op program.

Contact Office of Financial Aid, New College of California, San Francisco, CA 94102-5206, 415-241-1300.

NEW COLLEGE OF THE UNIVERSITY OF SOUTH FLORIDA
Sarasota, Florida

About the Institution State-supported, coed. Degrees awarded: B. Offers 55 undergraduate majors. Total enrollment: 596 (58% state residents). Freshmen: 155.

Undergraduate Expenses (1997–98) State resident tuition: $2033 (minimum). Nonresident tuition: $8344 (minimum). College room and board: $4117. College room only: $2350.

Applications *Financial aid deadline (priority):* 2/1. *Financial aid forms:* FAFSA required; CSS Financial Aid PROFILE acceptable. State form required for some. *Admission application deadline:* rolling.

Summary of Aid to Needy Students Federal Work-Study jobs; part-time jobs.

Loans College/university long-term loans.

Non-Need Awards *Academic Interests/Achievement Awards:* general academic.

Other Money-Saving Options Accelerated degree, cooperative Army ROTC, cooperative Air Force ROTC, off-campus living (after freshman year). *Payment Plans:* tuition prepayment, installment. *Waivers:* full or partial for employees or children of employees.

Contact Office of Financial Aid, New College of the University of South Florida, 4202 East Fowler Avenue, SVC 1102, Sarasota, FL 34243-2197, 941-359-4200.

NEW ENGLAND COLLEGE
Henniker, New Hampshire

About the Institution Independent, coed. Degrees awarded: B, M. Offers 33 undergraduate majors. Total enrollment: 800. Undergraduates: 700 (15% state residents). Freshmen: 200.

Undergraduate Expenses (1997–98) Comprehensive fee of $21,704 includes tuition ($15,784) and college room and board ($5920).

Applications 70% of all full-time undergraduates enrolled in fall 1996 applied for aid; of these, 88% were judged to have need according to Federal Methodology, of whom 100% were aided. *Financial aid deadline (priority):* 3/1. *Financial aid forms:* FAFSA, institutional form required. *Regular admission application deadline:* rolling. Early action deadline: 12/06.

Summary of Aid to Needy Students *From gift & self-help combined:* Average need met: 88%. Average amount awarded: $13,200 (36% gift aid, 64% self-help). *Gift aid:* Total: $3,341,442 (84% from college's own funds, 9% from other college-administered sources, 7% from external sources). 376 Federal Work-Study jobs (averaging $1250); 40 part-time jobs.

Need-Based Scholarships & Grants Pell, FSEOG, state, private, college/university.

Loans Perkins, PLUS, Stafford, Unsubsidized Stafford, state, private.

Non-Need Awards *Academic Interests/Achievement Awards:* 49 ($162,000 total): general academic. *Creative Arts/Performance Awards:* 3 ($4500 total): art/fine arts. *Special Achievements/Activities Awards:* 52 ($75,750 total): community service, leadership. *Special Characteristics Awards:* children of educators, children of faculty/staff, local/state students, siblings of current students.

Other Money-Saving Options Cooperative Army ROTC, cooperative Air Force ROTC, off-campus living (after sophomore year). *Payment Plan:* installment. *Waivers:* full or partial for employees or children of employees.

Contact Mr. Corey W. Hah, Financial Aid Counselor, New England College, 7 Main Street, Henniker, NH 03242-3293, 603-428-2414, fax: 603-428-2266.

NEW ENGLAND CONSERVATORY OF MUSIC
Boston, Massachusetts

About the Institution Independent, coed. Degrees awarded: B, M, D. Offers 9 undergraduate majors. Total enrollment: 792. Undergraduates: 371. Freshmen: 105.

Undergraduate Expenses (1997–98) Comprehensive fee of $26,375 includes tuition ($17,900), mandatory fees ($100), and college room and board ($8375 minimum).

Applications Of all full-time undergraduates enrolled in fall 1996, 90% of those who applied for aid were judged to have need according to Federal Methodology, of whom 91% were aided. *Financial aid deadline (priority):* 3/1. *Financial aid forms:* FAFSA, institutional form required. *Admission application deadline:* 1/3.

Summary of Aid to Needy Students *From gift & self-help combined:* Average need met: 53%. Average amount awarded: $13,776 (50% gift

aid, 50% self-help). *Gift aid:* Total: $1,482,898 (85% from college's own funds, 9% from other college-administered sources, 6% from external sources). Federal Work-Study jobs; part-time jobs.

Need-Based Scholarships & Grants Pell, FSEOG, state, private, college/university.

Loans Perkins, PLUS, Stafford, Unsubsidized Stafford, state.

Non-Need Awards Not offered.

Another Money-Saving Option Off-campus living (after freshman year).

Contact Ms. Patricia K. Harden, Director of Financial Aid, New England Conservatory of Music, 290 Huntington Avenue, Boston, MA 02115-5000, 617-262-1120 Ext. 440.

THE NEW ENGLAND SCHOOL OF ART AND DESIGN AT SUFFOLK UNIVERSITY
Boston, Massachusetts
See Suffolk University

NEW HAMPSHIRE COLLEGE
Manchester, New Hampshire

About the Institution Independent, coed. Degrees awarded: A, B, M. Offers 28 undergraduate majors. Total enrollment: 5,614. Undergraduates: 1,278 (30% state residents). Freshmen: 314.

Undergraduate Expenses (1997–98) Comprehensive fee of $18,736 includes tuition ($12,400), mandatory fees ($580), and college room and board ($5756 minimum).

Applications Of all full-time undergraduates enrolled in fall 1996, 77% of those who applied for aid were judged to have need according to Federal Methodology, of whom 100% were aided. *Financial aid deadline (priority):* 3/15. *Financial aid forms:* FAFSA, CSS Financial Aid PROFILE required. *Regular admission application deadline:* rolling. Early action deadline: 11/15.

Summary of Aid to Needy Students *From gift & self-help combined:* Average need met: 75%. Average amount awarded: $8500 (45% gift aid, 55% self-help). *Gift aid:* Total: $3,244,634 (66% from college's own funds, 8% from other college-administered sources, 26% from external sources). 243 Federal Work-Study jobs (averaging $1850); 218 part-time jobs.

Need-Based Scholarships & Grants Pell, FSEOG, state.

Loans Perkins, PLUS, Stafford, Unsubsidized Stafford.

Non-Need Awards In 1996, a total of 316 non-need awards were made. *Academic Interests/Achievement Awards:* 247 ($292,750 total): general academic. *Special Characteristics Awards:* 16 ($115,905 total): general special characteristics, children of faculty/staff, local/state students. *Athletic:* Total: 53 ($617,736); Men: 27 ($337,140); Women: 26 ($280,596).

Other Money-Saving Options Accelerated degree, co-op program, cooperative Army ROTC, cooperative Air Force ROTC, off-campus living (after freshman year). *Payment Plan:* installment. *Waivers:* full or partial for employees or children of employees and senior citizens.

Contact Office of Financial Aid, New Hampshire College, 2500 North River Road, Manchester, NH 03106-1045, 603-668-2211.

NEW JERSEY INSTITUTE OF TECHNOLOGY
Newark, New Jersey

About the Institution State-supported, coed. Degrees awarded: B, M, D. Offers 33 undergraduate majors. Total enrollment: 7,837. Undergraduates: 5,007 (90% state residents). Freshmen: 624.

Undergraduate Expenses (1997–98 estimated) State resident tuition: $4638. Nonresident tuition: $8982. Mandatory fees: $828. College room and board: $5210 (minimum). College room only: $3550 (minimum).

Applications 76% of all full-time undergraduates enrolled in fall 1996 applied for aid; of these, 79% were judged to have need according to Federal Methodology, of whom 100% were aided. *Financial aid deadline (priority):* 3/15. *Financial aid forms:* FAFSA required. State form, institutional form required for some. *Regular admission application deadline:* 4/1. Early decision deadline: 12/1.

Summary of Aid to Needy Students *From gift & self-help combined:* Average need met: 91%. Average amount awarded: $9915 (46% gift aid, 54% self-help). *Gift aid:* Total: $9,432,812 (12% from college's own funds, 14% from other college-administered sources, 74% from external sources). 823 Federal Work-Study jobs (averaging $1791); 545 part-time jobs.

Need-Based Scholarships & Grants Pell, FSEOG, state, private, college/university.

Loans Perkins, PLUS, Stafford, Unsubsidized Stafford, state, college/university long-term loans ($4828 average).

Non-Need Awards In 1996, a total of 933 non-need awards were made. *Academic Interests/Achievement Awards:* 933 ($2,286,430 total): general academic.

Other Money-Saving Options Co-op program, Air Force ROTC, off-campus living. *Payment Plans:* installment, deferred payment. *Waivers:* full or partial for employees or children of employees.

Contact Mr. William Anderson, Associate Vice-President for Enrollment Planning, New Jersey Institute of Technology, University Heights, Newark, NJ 07102-1982, 973-596-3479, fax: 973-596-6471.

NEW MEXICO HIGHLANDS UNIVERSITY
Las Vegas, New Mexico

About the Institution State-supported, coed. Degrees awarded: A, B, M. Offers 45 undergraduate majors. Total enrollment: 2,751. Undergraduates: 1,946 (89% state residents). Freshmen: 418.

Undergraduate Expenses (1997–98) State resident tuition: $1602. Nonresident tuition: $6786. Mandatory fees: $60. College room and board: $2706 (minimum). College room only: $1320 (minimum).

Applications *Financial aid deadline (priority):* 3/1. *Financial aid forms:* FAFSA, institutional form required. *Admission application deadline:* rolling.

Summary of Aid to Needy Students *From gift & self-help combined:* Average amount awarded: $4328 (36% gift aid, 64% self-help). *Gift aid:* Total: $2,400,000. Federal Work-Study jobs; 260 part-time jobs.

Need-Based Scholarships & Grants Pell, FSEOG, state, college/university.

Loans Perkins, Stafford, Unsubsidized Stafford.

Non-Need Awards *Academic Interests/Achievement Awards:* general academic. *Creative Arts/Performance Awards:* art/fine arts, music, theater/drama. *Special Characteristics Awards:* local/state students, members of minorities. *Athletic:* available.

Other Money-Saving Options Accelerated degree, co-op program, off-campus living. *Payment Plan:* deferred payment. *Waivers:* full or partial for employees or children of employees and senior citizens.

Contact Office of Financial Aid, New Mexico Highlands University, University Avenue, Las Vegas, NM 87701, 505-454-3318.

NEW MEXICO INSTITUTE OF MINING AND TECHNOLOGY
Socorro, New Mexico

About the Institution State-supported, coed. Degrees awarded: A, B, M, D. Offers 38 undergraduate majors. Total enrollment: 1,461. Undergraduates: 1,217 (54% state residents). Freshmen: 222.

Undergraduate Expenses (1997–98) State resident tuition: $1450. Nonresident tuition: $5988. Mandatory fees: $624. College room and board: $3308.

Applications 91% of all full-time undergraduates enrolled in fall 1996 applied for aid; of these, 47% were judged to have need according to Federal Methodology, of whom 100% were aided. *Financial aid deadline (priority):* 3/1. *Financial aid forms:* FAFSA, institutional form required. *Admission application deadline:* 8/1.

Summary of Aid to Needy Students *From gift & self-help combined:* Average need met: 92%. Average amount awarded: $7441 (50% gift aid, 50% self-help). *Gift aid:* Total: $1,628,610 (36% from college's own funds, 24% from other college-administered sources, 40% from external sources). 235 Federal Work-Study jobs (averaging $1400); 456 part-time jobs.

Need-Based Scholarships & Grants Pell, FSEOG, state, New Mexico Scholar Program, Legislative Endowment Scholarships.

Loans Perkins, PLUS, Stafford, Unsubsidized Stafford, state, private, college/university short-term loans ($650 average).

Non-Need Awards In 1996, a total of 749 non-need awards were made. *Academic Interests/Achievement Awards:* 749 ($1,445,309 total): general academic, communication, engineering/technologies, physical sciences.

Other Money-Saving Options Co-op program, off-campus living. *Payment Plan:* deferred payment. *Waivers:* full or partial for employees or children of employees.

Contact Office of Financial Aid, New Mexico Institute of Mining and Technology, 801 Leroy Place, Socorro, NM 87801, 505-835-5011.

NEW MEXICO STATE UNIVERSITY
Las Cruces, New Mexico

About the Institution State-supported, coed. Degrees awarded: A, B, M, D. Offers 125 undergraduate majors. Total enrollment: 14,748. Undergraduates: 11,872 (80% state residents). Freshmen: 1,520.

Undergraduate Expenses (1997–98 estimated) State resident tuition: $2196. Nonresident tuition: $7152. College room and board: $3288 (minimum). College room only: $1650 (minimum).

Applications *Financial aid deadline (priority):* 3/1. *Financial aid forms:* FAFSA, institutional form required. *Admission application deadline:* 8/14.

Summary of Aid to Needy Students *From gift & self-help combined:* Average need met: 80%. Average amount awarded: $3228 (53% gift aid, 47% self-help). *Gift aid:* Total: $14,603,625 (1% from college's own funds, 58% from other college-administered sources, 41% from external sources). 406 Federal Work-Study jobs (averaging $1349); part-time jobs.

Need-Based Scholarships & Grants Pell, FSEOG, state, private, college/university.

Loans Perkins, PLUS, Stafford, Unsubsidized Stafford, state, college/university short-term loans ($100 average), college/university long-term loans ($500 average).

Non-Need Awards *Academic Interests/Achievement Awards:* general academic, agriculture, biological sciences, business, communication, computer science, education, engineering/technologies, English, foreign languages, health fields, home economics, humanities, mathematics, military science, physical sciences, social sciences. *Creative Arts/*

Performance Awards: general creative, applied art and design, art/fine arts, journalism/publications, music, performing arts, theater/drama. *Special Achievements/Activities Awards:* leadership, rodeo. *Special Characteristics Awards:* adult students, children and siblings of alumni, children of faculty/staff, local/state students, married students, members of minorities, out-of-state students, previous college experience, ROTC participants, spouses of current students, veterans' children. *Athletic:* Total: 254 ($407,139); Men: 148 ($266,680); Women: 106 ($140,459).

Other Money-Saving Options Accelerated degree, co-op program, Army ROTC, Air Force ROTC, off-campus living. *Payment Plan:* deferred payment. *Waivers:* full or partial for senior citizens.

Contact Office of Financial Aid, New Mexico State University, Box 30001, Department 5100, Las Cruces, NM 88003-8001, 505-646-0111.

NEW ORLEANS BAPTIST THEOLOGICAL SEMINARY
New Orleans, Louisiana

About the Institution Independent/religious, coed. Degrees awarded: A, B, M, D, P. Offers 1 undergraduate major. Total enrollment: 1,822. Undergraduates: 778 (30% state residents). Freshmen: 102.

Undergraduate Expenses (1996–97) Tuition: $1600. Mandatory fees: $200. College room only: $1125 (minimum).

Applications *Financial aid deadline (priority):* 6/1. *Financial aid forms:* institutional form required. *Admission application deadline:* 8/9.

Summary of Aid to Needy Students *From gift & self-help combined:* Average need met: 85%. *Gift aid:* Total: $696,000.

Need-Based Scholarships & Grants Private.

Loans College/university short-term loans.

Non-Need Awards Not offered.

Other Money-Saving Options Off-campus living. *Payment Plan:* deferred payment.

Contact Financial Aid Office, New Orleans Baptist Theological Seminary, New Orleans, LA 70126-4858, 504-282-4455 Ext. 3348.

NEW SCHOOL FOR SOCIAL RESEARCH, EUGENE LANG COLLEGE
New York, New York

See Eugene Lang College, New School for Social Research

NEW SCHOOL FOR SOCIAL RESEARCH, MANNES COLLEGE OF MUSIC
New York, New York

See Mannes College of Music, New School for Social Research

NEW SCHOOL FOR SOCIAL RESEARCH, PARSONS SCHOOL OF DESIGN
New York, New York

See Parsons School of Design, New School for Social Research

NEWSCHOOL OF ARCHITECTURE
San Diego, California

About the Institution Proprietary, coed. Degrees awarded: A, B, M, P. Offers 6 undergraduate majors. Total enrollment: 93. Undergraduates: 72 (70% state residents). Freshmen: 11.

Undergraduate Expenses (1997–98) Comprehensive fee of $16,080 includes tuition ($10,080 minimum) and college room and board ($6000).

Applications Of all full-time undergraduates enrolled in fall 1996, 92% of those who applied for aid were judged to have need according to Federal Methodology, of whom 100% were aided. *Financial aid deadline:* Applications processed continuously. *Financial aid forms:* FAFSA, CSS Financial Aid PROFILE, institutional form required. State form required for some. *Regular admission application deadline:* 8/15. Nonresident deadline: 8/1.

Summary of Aid to Needy Students *From gift & self-help combined:* Average need met: 100%. Average amount awarded: $10,688 (25% gift aid, 75% self-help). *Gift aid:* Total: $132,488 (11% from college's own funds, 37% from other college-administered sources, 52% from external sources). 5 Federal Work-Study jobs (averaging $2000); 5 part-time jobs.

Need-Based Scholarships & Grants Pell, FSEOG, state.

Loans PLUS, Stafford, Unsubsidized Stafford, college/university short-term loans ($500 average), college/university long-term loans ($400 average).

Non-Need Awards *Academic Interests/Achievement Awards:* 6 ($10,000 total): general academic, architecture. *Creative Arts/Performance Awards:* applied art and design. *Special Characteristics Awards:* general special characteristics.

Other Money-Saving Options Co-op program, off-campus living. *Payment Plans:* tuition prepayment, installment, deferred payment. *Waivers:* full or partial for employees or children of employees.

Contact Ms. Pamela B. Palermo, Director of Financial Aid, Newschool of Architecture, 1249 F Street, San Diego, CA 92101-6634, 619-235-4100 Ext. 103, fax: 619-235-4651.

NEW YORK INSTITUTE OF TECHNOLOGY
Old Westbury, New York

About the Institution Independent, coed. Degrees awarded: A, B, M, P. Offers 59 undergraduate majors. Total enrollment: 9,396. Undergraduates: 5,635 (83% state residents). Freshmen: 648.

Undergraduate Expenses (1996–97) Comprehensive fee of $17,120 includes tuition ($10,180 minimum), mandatory fees ($880), and college room and board ($6060). College room only: $3260.

Applications *Financial aid deadline (priority):* 1/1. *Financial aid forms:* FAFSA, institutional form required. *Admission application deadline:* rolling.

Summary of Aid to Needy Students *From gift & self-help combined:* Average need met: 72%. Average amount awarded: $7000 (64% gift aid, 36% self-help). *Gift aid:* Total: $11,205,426 (35% from college's own funds, 41% from other college-administered sources, 24% from external sources). Federal Work-Study jobs; part-time jobs.

Need-Based Scholarships & Grants Pell, FSEOG, state, private, college/university.

Loans Perkins, PLUS, Stafford, Unsubsidized Stafford, private.

Non-Need Awards In 1996, a total of 3,186 non-need awards were made. *Academic Interests/Achievement Awards:* 1,865 ($3,066,618 total): general academic. *Special Characteristics Awards:* 1,158 ($1,837,507 total): children of educators, children of faculty/staff, children of public servants, local/state students, public servants, spouses of deceased or disabled public servants. *Athletic:* Total: 163 ($885,154); Men: 115 ($592,598); Women: 48 ($292,556).

Other Money-Saving Options Accelerated degree, co-op program, Air Force ROTC, off-campus living. *Payment Plan:* installment. *Waivers:* full or partial for employees or children of employees and senior citizens.

Contact Financial Aid Office, New York Institute of Technology, Old Westbury, NY 11568-8000, 516-686-7680.

NEW YORK SCHOOL OF INTERIOR DESIGN
New York, New York

About the Institution Independent, coed. Degrees awarded: A, B. Offers 1 undergraduate major. Total enrollment: 695 (85% state residents). Freshmen: 177.

Undergraduate Expenses (1997–98) Tuition: $12,750. Mandatory fees: $50.

Applications Of all full-time undergraduates enrolled in fall 1996, 64% of those who applied for aid were judged to have need according to Federal Methodology, of whom 100% were aided. *Financial aid deadline:* Applications processed continuously. *Financial aid forms:* FAFSA, institutional form required. State form required for some.

Summary of Aid to Needy Students *From gift & self-help combined:* Average need met: 80%. Average amount awarded: $6726. 10 Federal Work-Study jobs (averaging $1500).

Need-Based Scholarships & Grants Pell, FSEOG, state, college/university.

Loans PLUS, Stafford, Unsubsidized Stafford, private.

Non-Need Awards In 1996, a total of 5 non-need awards were made. *Academic Interests/Achievement Awards:* 5 ($10,000 total): general academic.

Other Money-Saving Options *Payment Plans:* installment, deferred payment. *Waivers:* full or partial for employees or children of employees.

Contact Mr. A. Thomas Zarkos, Financial Aid Administrator, New York School of Interior Design, 170 East 70th Street, New York, NY 10021-5110, 212-472-1500 Ext. 18, fax: 212-472-3800.

NEW YORK STATE COLLEGE OF CERAMICS
Alfred, New York

See Alfred University

NEW YORK UNIVERSITY
New York, New York

About the Institution Independent, coed. Degrees awarded: A, B, M, D, P. Offers 141 undergraduate majors. Total enrollment: 36,056. Undergraduates: 17,063 (59% state residents). Freshmen: 3,090.

Undergraduate Expenses (1997–98) Comprehensive fee of $29,900 includes tuition ($21,730 minimum) and college room and board ($8170).

Applications 70% of all full-time undergraduates enrolled in fall 1996 applied for aid; of these, 91% were judged to have need according to Federal Methodology, of whom 98% were aided. *Financial aid deadline (priority):* 2/15. *Financial aid forms:* FAFSA required. State form required for some. *Regular admission application deadline:* 1/15. Early decision deadline: 11/15.

Summary of Aid to Needy Students *From gift & self-help combined:* Average need met: 67%. Average amount awarded: $13,498 (66% gift aid, 34% self-help). *Gift aid:* Total: $80,629,024 (70% from college's own funds, 4% from other college-administered sources, 26% from external sources). 1,657 Federal Work-Study jobs (averaging $2298); 2,700 part-time jobs.

Need-Based Scholarships & Grants Pell, FSEOG, state, private, college/university.

Loans Perkins, PLUS, Stafford, Unsubsidized Stafford, Federal Nursing, state, private, college/university short-term loans ($300 average), college/university long-term loans ($1140 average).

Non-Need Awards In 1996, a total of 2,425 non-need awards were made. *Academic Interests/Achievement Awards:* 2,425 ($20,841,738 total): general academic, business.

Other Money-Saving Options Cooperative Air Force ROTC, off-campus living. *Payment Plans:* tuition prepayment, installment, deferred payment. *Waivers:* full or partial for employees or children of employees.

Contact Financial Aid Office, New York University, 25 West Fourth Street, New York, NY 10012-1019, 212-998-4444, fax: 212-995-4661.

NIAGARA UNIVERSITY
Niagara Falls, New York

About the Institution Independent, coed. Degrees awarded: A, B, M. Offers 45 undergraduate majors. Total enrollment: 2,935. Undergraduates: 2,291 (88% state residents). Freshmen: 557.

Undergraduate Expenses (1996–97) Comprehensive fee of $17,644 includes tuition ($11,800), mandatory fees ($456), and college room and board ($5388).

Applications 94% of all full-time undergraduates enrolled in fall 1996 applied for aid; of these, 98% were judged to have need according to Federal Methodology, of whom 100% were aided. *Financial aid deadline (priority):* 2/15. *Financial aid forms:* FAFSA, state form required. *Admission application deadline:* 8/1.

Summary of Aid to Needy Students *From gift & self-help combined:* Average need met: 99%. Average amount awarded: $11,264 (67% gift aid, 33% self-help). *Gift aid:* Total: $13,795,346 (68% from college's own funds, 2% from other college-administered sources, 30% from external sources). 435 Federal Work-Study jobs (averaging $2140); 34 part-time jobs.

Need-Based Scholarships & Grants Pell, FSEOG, state, private, college/university.

Loans Perkins, PLUS, Stafford, Unsubsidized Stafford, Federal Nursing, college/university short-term loans ($75 average).

Non-Need Awards In 1996, a total of 1,265 non-need awards were made. *Academic Interests/Achievement Awards:* 994 ($5,074,471 total): general academic. *Creative Arts/Performance Awards:* 25 ($65,200 total): theater/drama. *Special Characteristics Awards:* 43 ($434,337 total): children of faculty/staff, relatives of clergy. *Athletic:* Total: 203 ($1,265,216); Men: 119 ($760,577); Women: 84 ($504,639).

Other Money-Saving Options Accelerated degree, co-op program, Army ROTC, off-campus living (after sophomore year). *Payment Plans:* installment, deferred payment. *Waivers:* full or partial for employees or children of employees.

Contact Mrs. Maureen E. Salfi, Director of Financial Aid, Niagara University, Financial Aid Office, Niagara University, NY 14109, 716-286-8686, fax: 716-286-8733.

NICHOLLS STATE UNIVERSITY
Thibodaux, Louisiana

About the Institution State-supported, coed. Degrees awarded: A, B, M. Offers 59 undergraduate majors. Total enrollment: 7,210. Undergraduates: 6,355 (97% state residents). Freshmen: 1,362.

Undergraduate Expenses (1996–97) State resident tuition: $2017. Nonresident tuition: $4609. College room and board: $2700. College room only: $1150.

Applications *Financial aid deadline (priority):* 3/29. *Financial aid forms:* FAFSA, institutional form required. *Admission application deadline:* rolling.

Summary of Aid to Needy Students 240 Federal Work-Study jobs (averaging $1462); 430 part-time jobs.

Need-Based Scholarships & Grants Pell, FSEOG, state, private.

Loans Perkins, PLUS, Stafford, Unsubsidized Stafford.

Non-Need Awards *Academic Interests/Achievement Awards:* general academic, agriculture. *Creative Arts/Performance Awards:* music. *Special*

Achievements/Activities Awards: leadership. *Special Characteristics Awards:* children of public servants, children with a deceased or disabled parent. *Athletic:* available.

Other Money-Saving Options Accelerated degree, co-op program, off-campus living (after freshman year). *Waivers:* full or partial for employees or children of employees and senior citizens.

Contact Financial Aid Department, Nicholls State University, Thibodaux, LA 70310, 504-448-4048.

NICHOLS COLLEGE
Dudley, Massachusetts

About the Institution Independent, coed. Degrees awarded: B, M. Offers 13 undergraduate majors. Total enrollment: 1,501. Undergraduates: 1,247 (61% state residents). Freshmen: 234.

Undergraduate Expenses (1997–98) Comprehensive fee of $17,495 includes tuition ($11,170), mandatory fees ($125), and college room and board ($6200).

Applications 99% of all full-time undergraduates enrolled in fall 1996 applied for aid; of these, 96% were judged to have need according to Federal Methodology, of whom 100% were aided. *Financial aid deadline (priority):* 03/01. *Financial aid forms:* FAFSA required. *Admission application deadline:* rolling.

Summary of Aid to Needy Students *From gift & self-help combined:* Average amount awarded: $13,068 (43% gift aid, 57% self-help). *Gift aid:* Total: $3,113,880 (78% from college's own funds, 5% from other college-administered sources, 17% from external sources). 325 Federal Work-Study jobs (averaging $1500); 160 part-time jobs.

Need-Based Scholarships & Grants Pell, FSEOG, state, private, college/university.

Loans PLUS, Stafford, Unsubsidized Stafford, state, private.

Non-Need Awards In 1996, a total of 462 non-need awards were made. *Academic Interests/Achievement Awards:* 432 ($1,435,585 total): general academic. *Special Achievements/Activities Awards:* 25 ($32,450 total): general special achievements/activities. *Special Characteristics Awards:* 5 ($33,082 total): children of faculty/staff.

Other Money-Saving Options Army ROTC. *Payment Plan:* installment. *Waivers:* full or partial for employees or children of employees and senior citizens.

Contact Ms. Diane L. Gillespie, Associate Director of Financial Aid, Nichols College, PO Box 5000, Dudley, MA 01571, 508-943-2055, fax: 508-943-9885.

NORFOLK STATE UNIVERSITY
Norfolk, Virginia

About the Institution State-supported, coed. Degrees awarded: A, B, M, D. Offers 48 undergraduate majors. Total enrollment: 8,352. Undergraduates: 7,241 (66% state residents). Freshmen: 1,244.

Undergraduate Expenses (1997–98) State resident tuition: $3000. Nonresident tuition: $6802. College room and board: $4166.

Applications Of all full-time undergraduates enrolled in fall 1996, 89% of those who applied for aid were judged to have need according to Federal Methodology, of whom 90% were aided. *Financial aid deadline (priority):* 3/15. *Financial aid forms:* FAFSA, institutional form required; CSS Financial Aid PROFILE acceptable. *Admission application deadline:* rolling.

Summary of Aid to Needy Students *From gift & self-help combined:* Average need met: 90%. Average amount awarded: $6064 (40% gift aid, 60% self-help). *Gift aid:* Total: $16,237,703 (20% from college's own funds, 37% from other college-administered sources, 43% from external sources). 322 Federal Work-Study jobs (averaging $1600); 272 part-time jobs.

Need-Based Scholarships & Grants Pell, FSEOG, state, private, college/university.

Loans Perkins, PLUS, Stafford, Unsubsidized Stafford, state, private.

Non-Need Awards In 1996, a total of 538 non-need awards were made. *Academic Interests/Achievement Awards:* 95 ($837,620 total): general academic, biological sciences, computer science, mathematics. *Creative Arts/Performance Awards:* 61 ($54,263 total): music, performing arts. *Special Achievements/Activities Awards:* 217 ($397,519 total): general special achievements/activities. *Athletic:* Total: 165 ($1,614,299); Men: 112 ($937,606); Women: 53 ($676,693).

Other Money-Saving Options Accelerated degree, co-op program, Army ROTC, Naval ROTC, off-campus living.

Contact Mrs. Estherine Harding, Director of Financial Aid, Norfolk State University, 2401 Corprew Avenue, Norfolk, VA 23504-3907, 757-683-8381.

NORTH ADAMS STATE COLLEGE
North Adams, Massachusetts

About the Institution State-supported, coed. Degrees awarded: B, M. Offers 43 undergraduate majors. Total enrollment: 1,745. Undergraduates: 1,617 (80% state residents). Freshmen: 333.

Undergraduate Expenses (1997–98) State resident tuition: $1270. Nonresident tuition: $5850. Mandatory fees: $2167. College room and board: $4901 (minimum). College room only: $2660 (minimum).

Applications 84% of all full-time undergraduates enrolled in fall 1996 applied for aid; of these, 86% were judged to have need according to Federal Methodology, of whom 100% were aided. *Financial aid deadline (priority):* 4/1. *Financial aid forms:* FAFSA, institutional form required. *Regular admission application deadline:* rolling. Early action deadline: 12/1.

Summary of Aid to Needy Students *From gift & self-help combined:* Average need met: 78%. Average amount awarded: $5807 (38% gift aid, 62% self-help). *Gift aid:* Total: $2,024,294 (10% from college's own funds, 45% from other college-administered sources, 45% from external sources). 266 Federal Work-Study jobs (averaging $1043); 95 part-time jobs.

Need-Based Scholarships & Grants Pell, FSEOG, state, college/university.

Loans Perkins, PLUS, Stafford, Unsubsidized Stafford, state, private.

Non-Need Awards In 1996, a total of 65 non-need awards were made. *Academic Interests/Achievement Awards:* 65 ($94,500 total): general academic.

Other Money-Saving Options Off-campus living (after sophomore year). *Payment Plan:* installment. *Waivers:* full or partial for employees or children of employees.

Contact Office of Financial Aid, North Adams State College, Church Street, North Adams, MA 01247-4100, 413-662-5000.

NORTH CAROLINA AGRICULTURAL AND TECHNICAL STATE UNIVERSITY
Greensboro, North Carolina

About the Institution State-supported, coed. Degrees awarded: B, M, D. Offers 60 undergraduate majors. Total enrollment: 7,533. Undergraduates: 6,598 (73% state residents). Freshmen: 1,324.

Undergraduate Expenses (1996–97) State resident tuition: $1561. Nonresident tuition: $8715. College room and board: $3410.

Applications 72% of all full-time undergraduates enrolled in fall 1996 applied for aid; of these, 87% were judged to have need according to Federal Methodology, of whom 94% were aided. *Financial aid deadline (priority):* 5/15. *Financial aid forms:* FAFSA required. *Regular admission application deadline:* 6/1. Early action deadline: 11/1.

Summary of Aid to Needy Students *From gift & self-help combined:* Average need met: 63%. Average amount awarded: $5265 (46% gift aid, 54% self-help). *Gift aid:* Total: $7,375,496 (8% from college's own funds, 19% from other college-administered sources, 73% from external sources). 480 Federal Work-Study jobs (averaging $1288); 835 part-time jobs.

Non-Need Awards In 1996, a total of 1,087 non-need awards were made. *Academic Interests/Achievement Awards:* 691 ($1,390,634 total): general academic, biological sciences, business, engineering/technologies, health fields, military science. *Creative Arts/Performance Awards:* 15 ($5100 total): music, theater/drama. *Special Achievements/Activities Awards:* 15 ($14,471 total): general special achievements/activities, memberships, religious involvement. *Special Characteristics Awards:* 213 ($288,719 total): ethnic background, handicapped students, members of minorities, ROTC participants. *Athletic:* Total: 153 ($657,965); Men: 94 ($391,141); Women: 59 ($266,824).

Other Money-Saving Options Co-op program, Army ROTC, Air Force ROTC, off-campus living. *Payment Plan:* deferred payment.

Contact Office of Financial Aid, North Carolina Agricultural and Technical State University, Dowdy Administration Building, Greensboro, NC 27411, 910-334-7973.

NORTH CAROLINA CENTRAL UNIVERSITY
Durham, North Carolina

About the Institution State-supported, coed. Degrees awarded: B, M, P. Offers 55 undergraduate majors. Total enrollment: 5,400. Undergraduates: 3,898 (86% state residents). Freshmen: 706.

Undergraduate Expenses (1996–97) State resident tuition: $1789. Nonresident tuition: $8028. Mandatory fees: $721. College room and board: $3270. College room only: $1838.

Applications *Financial aid deadline (priority):* 4/1. *Financial aid forms:* FAFSA, institutional form required. State form required for some. *Admission application deadline:* 7/1.

Summary of Aid to Needy Students *From gift & self-help combined:* Average need met: 75%. Average amount awarded: $6690 (26% gift aid, 74% self-help). *Gift aid:* Total: $7,082,000 (20% from college's own funds, 38% from other college-administered sources, 42% from external sources). 300 Federal Work-Study jobs (averaging $1000); part-time jobs.

Need-Based Scholarships & Grants Pell, FSEOG, state, private, college/university.

Loans Perkins, PLUS, Stafford, Unsubsidized Stafford, state, private.

Non-Need Awards *Academic Interests/Achievement Awards:* general academic, biological sciences, physical sciences, social sciences. *Creative Arts/Performance Awards:* theater/drama. *Special Characteristics Awards:* general special characteristics. *Athletic:* Total: ($351,933); Men: ($254,729); Women: ($97,204).

Other Money-Saving Options Co-op program, cooperative Army ROTC, cooperative Naval ROTC, cooperative Air Force ROTC, off-campus living.

Contact Ms. Sharon Oliver, Assistant Vice Chancellor for Scholarships and Student Aid, North Carolina Central University, PO Box 19496, Shepard Station, Durham, NC 27707-3129, 919-560-6202.

NORTH CAROLINA SCHOOL OF THE ARTS
Winston-Salem, North Carolina

About the Institution State-supported, coed. Degrees awarded: B, M. Offers 7 undergraduate majors. Total enrollment: 716. Undergraduates: 656 (51% state residents). Freshmen: 143.

Undergraduate Expenses (1996–97) State resident tuition: $1359. Nonresident tuition: $9570. Mandatory fees: $870. College room and board: $3798. College room only: $1978.

Applications 61% of all full-time undergraduates enrolled in fall 1996 applied for aid; of these, 85% were judged to have need according to Federal Methodology, of whom 100% were aided. *Financial aid deadline (priority):* 3/1. *Financial aid forms:* FAFSA required; state form acceptable. *Admission application deadline:* rolling.

Summary of Aid to Needy Students *From gift & self-help combined:* Average need met: 65%. Average amount awarded: $6844 (45% gift aid, 55% self-help). *Gift aid:* Total: $1,062,886 (52% from college's own funds, 20% from other college-administered sources, 28% from external sources). 110 Federal Work-Study jobs (averaging $381); 100 part-time jobs.

Need-Based Scholarships & Grants Pell, FSEOG, state, private, college/university.

Loans Perkins, PLUS, Stafford, Unsubsidized Stafford, private.

Non-Need Awards In 1996, a total of 237 non-need awards were made. *Creative Arts/Performance Awards:* 237 ($251,199 total): applied art and design, cinema/film/broadcasting, dance, music, theater/drama.

Another Money-Saving Option *Payment Plan:* installment.

Contact Office of Financial Aid, North Carolina School of the Arts, 200 Waughtown Street, Winston-Salem, NC 27127, 910-770-3399.

NORTH CAROLINA STATE UNIVERSITY
Raleigh, North Carolina

About the Institution State-supported, coed. Degrees awarded: A, B, M, D. Offers 100 undergraduate majors. Total enrollment: 27,169. Undergraduates: 18,965 (82% state residents). Freshmen: 3,535.

Undergraduate Expenses (1997–98 estimated) State resident tuition: $2200. Nonresident tuition: $10,732. College room and board: $3350. College room only: $1850.

Applications Of all full-time undergraduates enrolled in fall 1996, 77% of those who applied for aid were judged to have need according to Federal Methodology, of whom 73% were aided. *Financial aid deadline (priority):* 3/1. *Financial aid forms:* FAFSA, institutional form required. *Regular admission application deadline:* 2/1. Early action deadline: 11/1.

Summary of Aid to Needy Students *From gift & self-help combined:* Average need met: 72%. Average amount awarded: $6237 (30% gift aid, 70% self-help). *Gift aid:* Total: $11,487,383 (12% from college's own funds, 26% from other college-administered sources, 62% from external sources). 675 Federal Work-Study jobs (averaging $1000); 3,390 part-time jobs.

Need-Based Scholarships & Grants Pell, FSEOG, state, college/university.

Loans Perkins, PLUS, Stafford, Unsubsidized Stafford, state, private, college/university short-term loans ($100 average), college/university long-term loans ($1000 average).

Non-Need Awards In 1996, a total of 1,552 non-need awards were made. *Academic Interests/Achievement Awards:* 1,150 ($2,750,226 total): general academic, agriculture, biological sciences, business, education, engineering/technologies, humanities, mathematics, physical sciences, social sciences. *Athletic:* Total: 402 ($3,105,751); Men: 272 ($2,047,637); Women: 130 ($1,058,114).

Other Money-Saving Options Co-op program, Army ROTC, Naval ROTC, Air Force ROTC, off-campus living. *Waivers:* full or partial for senior citizens.

Contact Ms. Julia Rice Mallette, Director of Financial Aid, North Carolina State University, 2005 Harris Hall, Box 7302, Raleigh, NC 27695-7302, 919-515-2334, fax: 919-515-8422.

NORTH CAROLINA WESLEYAN COLLEGE
Rocky Mount, North Carolina

About the Institution Independent/religious, coed. Degrees awarded: B. Offers 26 undergraduate majors. Total enrollment: 610 (49% state residents). Freshmen: 186.

Undergraduate Expenses (1997–98 estimated) Comprehensive fee of $12,260 includes tuition ($6850), mandatory fees ($580), and college room and board ($4830). College room only: $2000.

Applications 92% of all full-time undergraduates enrolled in fall 1996 applied for aid; of these, 89% were judged to have need according to Federal Methodology, of whom 100% were aided. *Financial aid deadline (priority):* 3/1. *Financial aid forms:* FAFSA required; CSS Financial Aid PROFILE acceptable. State form required for some. *Admission application deadline:* rolling.

Summary of Aid to Needy Students *From gift & self-help combined:* Average need met: 72%. Average amount awarded: $6059 (53% gift aid, 47% self-help). *Gift aid:* Total: $1,173,014 (19% from college's own funds, 52% from other college-administered sources, 29% from external sources). 131 Federal Work-Study jobs (averaging $856); 100 part-time jobs.

Need-Based Scholarships & Grants Pell, FSEOG, state, private.

Loans Perkins, PLUS, Stafford, Unsubsidized Stafford.

Non-Need Awards *Academic Interests/Achievement Awards:* general academic.

Other Money-Saving Options Co-op program, off-campus living (after sophomore year). *Payment Plan:* installment. *Waivers:* full or partial for employees or children of employees and senior citizens.

Contact Ms. Vickie Edwards, Director of Financial Aid, North Carolina Wesleyan College, Rocky Mount, NC 27804-8677, 919-985-5291, fax: 919-985-5295.

NORTH CENTRAL BIBLE COLLEGE
Minneapolis, Minnesota

About the Institution Independent/religious, coed. Degrees awarded: A, B. Offers 26 undergraduate majors. Total enrollment: 1,008 (31% state residents). Freshmen: 195.

Undergraduate Expenses (1996–97) Comprehensive fee of $10,580 includes tuition ($6360), mandatory fees ($670), and college room and board ($3550). College room only: $1710.

Applications *Financial aid deadline (priority):* 4/30. *Financial aid forms:* institutional form required; FAFSA acceptable. State form required for some. *Admission application deadline:* rolling.

Summary of Aid to Needy Students *Gift aid:* Total: $2,076,846 (53% from college's own funds, 23% from other college-administered sources, 24% from external sources). 60 Federal Work-Study jobs (averaging $1817); part-time jobs.

Need-Based Scholarships & Grants Pell, FSEOG, state, private, college/university.

Loans Perkins, PLUS, Stafford, Unsubsidized Stafford, state, private.

Non-Need Awards In 1996, a total of 894 non-need awards were made. *Academic Interests/Achievement Awards:* 112 ($143,532 total): general academic. *Creative Arts/Performance Awards:* 94 ($99,912 total): art/fine arts, music, theater/drama. *Special Achievements/Activities Awards:* 122 ($123,300 total): religious involvement. *Special Characteristics Awards:* 566: general special characteristics, children of current students, children of faculty/staff, international students, married students, relatives of clergy, religious affiliation, siblings of current students.

Other Money-Saving Options Co-op program, cooperative Army ROTC, cooperative Air Force ROTC. *Payment Plan:* installment. *Waivers:* full or partial for employees or children of employees and senior citizens.

Contact Office of Financial Aid, North Central Bible College, 910 Elliot Avenue South, Minneapolis, MN 55404-1322, 612-332-3491.

NORTH CENTRAL COLLEGE
Naperville, Illinois

About the Institution Independent/religious, coed. Degrees awarded: B, M. Offers 59 undergraduate majors. Total enrollment: 2,623. Undergraduates: 1,759 (87% state residents). Freshmen: 314.

Undergraduate Expenses (1997–98) Comprehensive fee of $18,915 includes tuition ($13,725), mandatory fees ($120), and college room and board ($5070).

Applications 74% of all full-time undergraduates enrolled in fall 1996 applied for aid; of these, 92% were judged to have need according to Federal Methodology, of whom 99% were aided. *Financial aid deadline:* continuous. *Financial aid forms:* FAFSA, institutional form, federal income tax forms (student and parent) required; CSS Financial Aid PROFILE, state form acceptable. *Admission application deadline:* rolling.

Summary of Aid to Needy Students *From gift & self-help combined:* Average need met: 85%. Average amount awarded: $11,987 (71% gift aid, 29% self-help). *Gift aid:* Total: $8,294,552 (67% from college's own funds, 1% from other college-administered sources, 32% from external sources). 123 Federal Work-Study jobs (averaging $717); part-time jobs.

Need-Based Scholarships & Grants Pell, FSEOG, state, private, college/university.

Loans Perkins, PLUS, Stafford, Unsubsidized Stafford, state, private, college/university long-term loans ($1388 average).

Non-Need Awards In 1996, a total of 980 non-need awards were made. *Academic Interests/Achievement Awards:* 742 ($3,667,471 total): general academic, education. *Creative Arts/Performance Awards:* 157 ($172,488 total): art/fine arts, cinema/film/broadcasting, debating, music, theater/drama. *Special Achievements/Activities Awards:* 55 ($37,309 total): religious involvement. *Special Characteristics Awards:* 26 ($212,489 total): adult students, children of faculty/staff, relatives of clergy.

Other Money-Saving Options Accelerated degree, co-op program, cooperative Army ROTC, cooperative Naval ROTC, cooperative Air Force ROTC, off-campus living. *Payment Plan:* installment. *Waivers:* full or partial for employees or children of employees and senior citizens.

Contact Ms. Katherine A. Edmunds, Director of Financial Aid, North Central College, 30 North Brainard Street, PO Box 3063, Naperville, IL 60566-7063, 630-637-5600, fax: 630-637-5819.

NORTH DAKOTA STATE UNIVERSITY
Fargo, North Dakota

About the Institution State-supported, coed. Degrees awarded: B, M, D, P. Offers 114 undergraduate majors. Total enrollment: 9,688. Undergraduates: 8,627 (58% state residents). Freshmen: 1,643.

Undergraduate Expenses (1996–97) State resident tuition: $2110. Nonresident tuition: $5634. Mandatory fees: $300. College room and board: $2968. College room only: $1120.

Applications Of all full-time undergraduates enrolled in fall 1996, 59% of those who applied for aid were judged to have need according to Federal Methodology, of whom 98% were aided. *Financial aid deadline:* Applications processed continuously. *Financial aid forms:* FAFSA required. Institutional form required for some. *Admission application deadline:* rolling.

Summary of Aid to Needy Students *From gift & self-help combined:* Average need met: 85%. Average amount awarded: $4620 (27% gift aid, 73% self-help). *Gift aid:* Total: $4,806,040 (14% from college's

own funds, 21% from other college-administered sources, 65% from external sources). 675 Federal Work-Study jobs (averaging $1152); 1,300 part-time jobs.

Need-Based Scholarships & Grants Pell, FSEOG, state, private, college/university, Diversity Waivers.

Loans Perkins, PLUS, Stafford, Unsubsidized Stafford, Federal Nursing, state, private, college/university short-term loans ($350 average).

Non-Need Awards In 1996, a total of 827 non-need awards were made. *Academic Interests/Achievement Awards:* 562 ($884,441 total): general academic, agriculture, architecture, business, education, engineering/technologies, home economics, humanities, social sciences. *Creative Arts/Performance Awards:* 63 ($34,840 total): art/fine arts, music. *Athletic:* Total: 202 ($487,247); Men: 146 ($348,439); Women: 56 ($138,808).

Other Money-Saving Options Accelerated degree, co-op program, Army ROTC, Air Force ROTC, off-campus living (after freshman year). *Payment Plan:* installment.

Contact Office of Financial Aid, North Dakota State University, PO Box 5315, Fargo, ND 58105, 701-231-8011.

NORTHEASTERN ILLINOIS UNIVERSITY
Chicago, Illinois

About the Institution State-supported, coed. Degrees awarded: B, M. Offers 36 undergraduate majors. Total enrollment: 10,035. Undergraduates: 7,179 (98% state residents). Freshmen: 884.

Undergraduate Expenses (1996–97) State resident tuition: $2352. Nonresident tuition: $6432. Mandatory fees: $305.

Applications 64% of all full-time undergraduates enrolled in fall 1996 applied for aid; of these, 92% were judged to have need according to Federal Methodology, of whom 91% were aided. *Financial aid deadline (priority):* 4/1. *Financial aid forms:* FAFSA, institutional form required. *Admission application deadline:* 7/1.

Summary of Aid to Needy Students *From gift & self-help combined:* Average need met: 67%. Average amount awarded: $4750 (69% gift aid, 31% self-help). *Gift aid:* Total: $10,383,100 (10% from college's own funds, 12% from other college-administered sources, 78% from external sources). 270 Federal Work-Study jobs; 500 part-time jobs.

Need-Based Scholarships & Grants Pell, FSEOG, state, private, college/university.

Loans Perkins, PLUS, Stafford, Unsubsidized Stafford, college/university short-term loans.

Non-Need Awards *Academic Interests/Achievement Awards:* general academic. *Creative Arts/Performance Awards:* applied art and design, art/fine arts, dance, music, theater/drama. *Special Achievements/Activities Awards:* general special achievements/activities. *Special Characteristics Awards:* general special characteristics, children of faculty/staff, members of minorities. *Athletic:* Total: 80 ($120,000).

Other Money-Saving Options Co-op program, cooperative Army ROTC, cooperative Air Force ROTC. *Payment Plan:* deferred payment. *Waivers:* full or partial for employees or children of employees and senior citizens.

Contact Financial Aid Office, Northeastern Illinois University, Chicago, IL 60625-4699, 773-794-2900.

NORTHEASTERN STATE UNIVERSITY
Tahlequah, Oklahoma

About the Institution State-supported, coed. Degrees awarded: B, M, D. Offers 72 undergraduate majors. Total enrollment: 8,735. Undergraduates: 7,851 (96% state residents). Freshmen: 918.

Undergraduate Expenses (1996–97) State resident tuition: $1605 (minimum). Nonresident tuition: $3810 (minimum). Mandatory fees: $45. College room and board: $2520 (minimum). College room only: $1084.

Applications *Financial aid deadline (priority):* 4/1. *Financial aid forms:* FAFSA, CSS Financial Aid PROFILE, state form required. *Admission application deadline:* 8/1.

Summary of Aid to Needy Students *From gift & self-help combined:* Average amount awarded: $3425 (44% gift aid, 56% self-help). *Gift aid:* Total: $9,788,261 (11% from college's own funds, 3% from other college-administered sources, 86% from external sources). 526 Federal Work-Study jobs (averaging $2040); 708 part-time jobs.

Need-Based Scholarships & Grants Pell, FSEOG, state, private, college/university.

Loans Perkins, PLUS, Stafford, Unsubsidized Stafford, college/university short-term loans ($100 average).

Non-Need Awards In 1996, a total of 556 non-need awards were made. *Academic Interests/Achievement Awards:* 244 ($276,425 total): general academic, biological sciences, business, communication, computer science, education, English, foreign languages, health fields, home economics, humanities, library science, mathematics, physical sciences, premedicine, social sciences. *Creative Arts/Performance Awards:* 105 ($105,000 total): applied art and design, art/fine arts, dance, debating, journalism/publications, music, performing arts, theater/drama. *Special Achievements/Activities Awards:* 25 ($20,000 total): cheerleading/drum major, hobbies/interest, Junior Miss. *Athletic:* Total: 182 ($325,000); Men: 120 ($230,000); Women: 62 ($95,000).

Another Money-Saving Option Off-campus living (after sophomore year).

Contact Ms. Peggy S. Carey, Director, Office of Student Financial Services, Northeastern State University, 600 North Grand, Tahlequah, OK 74464-2399, 918-456-5511 Ext. 3456, fax: 918-458-2150.

NORTHEASTERN UNIVERSITY
Boston, Massachusetts

About the Institution Independent, coed. Degrees awarded: A, B, M, D, P. Offers 91 undergraduate majors. Total enrollment: 24,579. Undergraduates: 19,780 (61% state residents). Freshmen: 2,975.

Undergraduate Expenses (1996–97) Comprehensive fee of $21,402 includes tuition ($13,370 minimum), mandatory fees ($127), and college room and board ($7905). College room only: $4185.

Applications 71% of all full-time undergraduates enrolled in fall 1996 applied for aid; of these, 95% were judged to have need according to Federal Methodology, of whom 100% were aided. *Financial aid deadline (priority):* 3/1. *Financial aid forms:* FAFSA, state form required. CSS Financial Aid PROFILE, institutional form required for some. *Admission application deadline:* rolling.

Summary of Aid to Needy Students *From gift & self-help combined:* Average need met: 60%. Average amount awarded: $10,824 (52% gift aid, 48% self-help). *Gift aid:* Total: $44,903,852 (64% from college's own funds, 12% from other college-administered sources, 24% from external sources). 3,345 Federal Work-Study jobs (averaging $1722).

Need-Based Scholarships & Grants Pell, FSEOG, state, private, college/university.

Loans Perkins, PLUS, Stafford, Unsubsidized Stafford, Federal Nursing, state, private, college/university long-term loans ($1662 average).

Non-Need Awards In 1996, a total of 602 non-need awards were made. *Academic Interests/Achievement Awards:* 276 ($5,186,722 total): general academic. *Special Characteristics Awards:* 110 ($943,355 total): local/state students. *Athletic:* Total: 216 ($3,164,123); Men: 121 ($1,888,033); Women: 95 ($1,276,090).

Other Money-Saving Options Co-op program, Army ROTC, cooperative Naval ROTC, cooperative Air Force ROTC, off-campus living. *Pay-*ment *Plans:* installment, deferred payment. *Waivers:* full or partial for employees or children of employees and senior citizens.

Contact Office of Financial Aid, Northeastern University, PO Box 75, Boston, MA 02117, 617-373-2000.

NORTHEAST LOUISIANA UNIVERSITY
Monroe, Louisiana

About the Institution State-supported, coed. Degrees awarded: A, B, M, D. Offers 60 undergraduate majors. Total enrollment: 11,116. Undergraduates: 9,994 (94% state residents). Freshmen: 1,884.

Undergraduate Expenses (1996–97) State resident tuition: $1926. Nonresident tuition: $4326. College room and board: $2160.

Applications Of all full-time undergraduates enrolled in fall 1996, 71% of those who applied for aid were judged to have need according to Federal Methodology, of whom 82% were aided. *Financial aid deadline (priority):* 4/1. *Financial aid forms:* FAFSA, institutional form required; CSS Financial Aid PROFILE acceptable. *Admission application deadline:* rolling.

Summary of Aid to Needy Students *From gift & self-help combined:* Average need met: 83%. Average amount awarded: $3036 (53% gift aid, 47% self-help). *Gift aid:* Total: $7,204,159 (10% from college's own funds, 43% from other college-administered sources, 47% from external sources). 557 Federal Work-Study jobs (averaging $1415); 793 part-time jobs.

Need-Based Scholarships & Grants Pell, FSEOG, state, private, college/university.

Loans Perkins, PLUS, Stafford, Unsubsidized Stafford, college/university short-term loans ($692 average), college/university long-term loans ($1793 average).

Non-Need Awards In 1996, a total of 1,827 non-need awards were made. *Academic Interests/Achievement Awards:* 888 ($1,110,208 total): general academic, agriculture, biological sciences, business, communication, computer science, education, English, foreign languages, health fields, home economics, library science, mathematics, military science, physical sciences, social sciences. *Creative Arts/Performance Awards:* 287 ($258,179 total): art/fine arts, creative writing, debating, journalism/publications, music, performing arts, theater/drama. *Special Achievements/Activities Awards:* 93 ($119,524 total): cheerleading/drum major, community service, leadership. *Special Characteristics Awards:* 311 ($533,876 total): children of faculty/staff, children with a deceased or disabled parent, international students, out-of-state students, ROTC participants. *Athletic:* Total: 248 ($919,034); Men: 168 ($650,658); Women: 80 ($268,376).

Other Money-Saving Options Accelerated degree, co-op program, Army ROTC. *Waivers:* full or partial for employees or children of employees and senior citizens.

Contact Jerry L. Futch, Associate Director, Fiscal Operations, Northeast Louisiana University, 700 University Avenue, Monroe, LA 71209-1120, 318-342-5329, fax: 318-342-3539.

NORTHEAST MISSOURI STATE UNIVERSITY
Kirksville, Missouri

See Truman State University

NORTHERN ARIZONA UNIVERSITY
Flagstaff, Arizona

About the Institution State-supported, coed. Degrees awarded: B, M, D. Offers 120 undergraduate majors. Total enrollment: 19,605. Undergraduates: 14,250 (81% state residents). Freshmen: 2,262.

Undergraduate Expenses (1996–97) State resident tuition: $2010. Nonresident tuition: $7526. Mandatory fees: $70. College room and board: $3390. College room only: $1636.

Applications 73% of all full-time undergraduates enrolled in fall 1996 applied for aid; of these, 82% were judged to have need according to Federal Methodology, of whom 95% were aided. *Financial aid deadline (priority):* 4/15. *Financial aid forms:* proof of Selective Service registration (for men), Statement of Educational Purpose required; FAFSA acceptable. Institutional form required for some. *Admission application deadline:* 7/15.

Summary of Aid to Needy Students *From gift & self-help combined:* Average need met: 84%. Average amount awarded: $7229 (36% gift aid, 64% self-help). *Gift aid:* Total: $16,426,397 (40% from college's own funds, 3% from other college-administered sources, 57% from external sources). 655 Federal Work-Study jobs (averaging $1053); 2,575 part-time jobs.

Need-Based Scholarships & Grants Pell, FSEOG, private, college/university.

Loans Perkins, PLUS, Stafford, Unsubsidized Stafford, Federal Nursing, private, college/university short-term loans ($200 average), college/university long-term loans ($1350 average).

Non-Need Awards In 1996, a total of 3,616 non-need awards were made. *Academic Interests/Achievement Awards:* 3,004 ($4,303,808 total): general academic. *Creative Arts/Performance Awards:* 350 ($462,587 total): art/fine arts, cinema/film/broadcasting, debating, journalism/publications, music, theater/drama. *Special Characteristics Awards:* 82 ($195,294 total): children and siblings of alumni, handicapped students, international students, members of minorities, ROTC participants. *Athletic:* Total: 180 ($593,292); Men: 112 ($374,270); Women: 68 ($219,022).

Other Money-Saving Options Accelerated degree, co-op program, Army ROTC, Air Force ROTC, off-campus living. *Waivers:* full or partial for employees or children of employees.

Contact Mr. Thurburn H. Barker Jr., Senior Management Analyst, Northern Arizona University, Box 4108, Flagstaff, AZ 86011, 520-523-5699, fax: 520-523-1551.

NORTHERN ILLINOIS UNIVERSITY
De Kalb, Illinois

About the Institution State-supported, coed. Degrees awarded: B, M, D, P. Offers 89 undergraduate majors. Total enrollment: 21,609. Undergraduates: 15,387 (97% state residents). Freshmen: 2,451.

Undergraduate Expenses (1996–97) State resident tuition: $2276 (minimum). Nonresident tuition: $6830 (minimum). Mandatory fees: $1102. College room and board: $3600.

Applications 65% of all full-time undergraduates enrolled in fall 1996 applied for aid; of these, 79% were judged to have need according to Federal Methodology, of whom 92% were aided. *Financial aid deadline (priority):* 3/1. *Financial aid forms:* FAFSA, institutional form required. *Admission application deadline:* 8/1.

Summary of Aid to Needy Students *From gift & self-help combined:* Average need met: 72%. Average amount awarded: $7000 (44% gift aid, 56% self-help). *Gift aid:* Total: $26,516,239 (1% from college's own funds, 22% from other college-administered sources, 77% from external sources). 592 Federal Work-Study jobs (averaging $1000); 3,861 part-time jobs.

Need-Based Scholarships & Grants Pell, FSEOG, state, private, college/university.

Loans Perkins, PLUS, Stafford, Unsubsidized Stafford, state, college/university short-term loans ($150 average).

Non-Need Awards *Academic Interests/Achievement Awards:* general academic. *Creative Arts/Performance Awards:* art/fine arts, music, performing arts, theater/drama. *Special Characteristics Awards:* children

of faculty/staff, international students, members of minorities, ROTC participants, veterans. *Athletic:* Total: 249 ($568,526); Men: 152 ($333,937); Women: 97 ($234,589).

Other Money-Saving Options Accelerated degree, co-op program, Army ROTC, cooperative Air Force ROTC, off-campus living (after freshman year). *Payment Plan:* installment. *Waivers:* full or partial for minority students and employees or children of employees.

Contact Ms. Kathleen D. Brunson, Associate Director of Financial Aid, Northern Illinois University, Swen Parson Building, Room 245, De Kalb, IL 60115-2854, 815-753-1300, fax: 815-753-9475.

NORTHERN KENTUCKY UNIVERSITY
Highland Heights, Kentucky

About the Institution State-supported, coed. Degrees awarded: A, B, M, P. Offers 60 undergraduate majors. Total enrollment: 11,505. Undergraduates: 10,283 (75% state residents). Freshmen: 1,628.

Undergraduate Expenses (1997–98) State resident tuition: $2020. Nonresident tuition: $5500. College room and board: $3164 (minimum). College room only: $1530 (minimum).

Applications Of all full-time undergraduates enrolled in fall 1996, 89% of those who applied for aid were judged to have need according to Federal Methodology, of whom 97% were aided. *Financial aid deadline (priority):* 4/1. *Financial aid forms:* FAFSA, institutional form required. *Admission application deadline:* rolling.

Summary of Aid to Needy Students *From gift & self-help combined:* Average need met: 80%. Average amount awarded: $5645 (25% gift aid, 75% self-help). *Gift aid:* Total: $7,276,086 (42% from college's own funds, 15% from other college-administered sources, 43% from external sources). 338 Federal Work-Study jobs (averaging $1285); 1,033 part-time jobs.

Need-Based Scholarships & Grants Pell, FSEOG, state, private.

Loans Perkins, PLUS, Stafford, Unsubsidized Stafford, private.

Non-Need Awards In 1996, a total of 2,241 non-need awards were made. *Academic Interests/Achievement Awards:* 2,019 ($3,024,130 total): general academic. *Creative Arts/Performance Awards:* 81 ($68,520 total): art/fine arts. *Special Characteristics Awards:* 31 ($157,096 total): members of minorities. *Athletic:* Total: 110 ($278,572); Men: 62 ($140,022); Women: 48 ($138,550).

Other Money-Saving Options Co-op program, cooperative Army ROTC, cooperative Air Force ROTC, off-campus living. *Payment Plan:* installment. *Waivers:* full or partial for employees or children of employees and senior citizens.

Contact Mr. Robert F. Sprague, Director of Financial Aid, Northern Kentucky University, 412 Administrative Center, Nunn Drive, Highland Heights, KY 41099-7101, 606-572-5144, fax: 606-572-6997.

NORTHERN MICHIGAN UNIVERSITY
Marquette, Michigan

About the Institution State-supported, coed. Degrees awarded: A, B, M. Offers 121 undergraduate majors. Total enrollment: 8,034. Undergraduates: 7,145 (95% state residents). Freshmen: 1,080.

Undergraduate Expenses (1996–97) State resident tuition: $2768. Nonresident tuition: $5118. Mandatory fees: $171. College room and board: $4141. College room only: $1969.

Applications 99% of all full-time undergraduates enrolled in fall 1996 applied for aid; of these, 57% were judged to have need according to Federal Methodology, of whom 100% were aided. *Financial aid deadline (priority):* 2/1. *Financial aid forms:* FAFSA required. *Admission application deadline:* rolling.

Summary of Aid to Needy Students *From gift & self-help combined:* Average need met: 98%. Average amount awarded: $6097 (39% gift

aid, 61% self-help). *Gift aid:* Total: $7,993,915 (26% from college's own funds, 18% from other college-administered sources, 56% from external sources). 1,200 Federal Work-Study jobs (averaging $800); 1,600 part-time jobs.

Need-Based Scholarships & Grants Pell, FSEOG, state, private, college/university.

Loans Perkins, PLUS, Stafford, Unsubsidized Stafford, college/university short-term loans ($100 average).

Non-Need Awards *Academic Interests/Achievement Awards:* 500 ($500,000 total): general academic, business, engineering/technologies, health fields, premedicine. *Creative Arts/Performance Awards:* 50 ($50,000 total): applied art and design, music, theater/drama. *Special Achievements/Activities Awards:* 25 ($25,000 total): leadership. *Special Characteristics Awards:* 100 ($50,000 total): members of minorities. *Athletic:* available.

Other Money-Saving Options Accelerated degree, Army ROTC, off-campus living (after sophomore year). *Payment Plan:* installment. *Waivers:* full or partial for children of alumni, employees or children of employees, senior citizens.

Contact Mr. Robert L. Pecotte, Director of Financial Aid, Northern Michigan University, Presque Isle Avenue, Marquette, MI 49855-5301, 906-227-2327, fax: 906-227-2321.

NORTHERN STATE UNIVERSITY
Aberdeen, South Dakota

About the Institution State-supported, coed. Degrees awarded: A, B, M. Offers 54 undergraduate majors. Total enrollment: 2,634. Undergraduates: 2,496 (84% state residents). Freshmen: 571.

Undergraduate Expenses (1996–97) State resident tuition: $1646. Nonresident tuition: $4832. Mandatory fees: $844. College room and board: $2672. College room only: $1196.

Applications Of all full-time undergraduates enrolled in fall 1996, 69% of those who applied for aid were judged to have need according to Federal Methodology, of whom 100% were aided. *Financial aid deadline (priority):* 3/1. *Financial aid forms:* FAFSA required; CSS Financial Aid PROFILE acceptable. *Admission application deadline:* 9/1.

Summary of Aid to Needy Students *From gift & self-help combined:* Average need met: 100%. Average amount awarded: $5861 (31% gift aid, 69% self-help). *Gift aid:* Total: $2,319,614 (19% from college's own funds, 9% from other college-administered sources, 72% from external sources). 469 Federal Work-Study jobs (averaging $990); 349 part-time jobs.

Need-Based Scholarships & Grants Pell, FSEOG, state, private.

Loans Perkins, PLUS, Stafford, Unsubsidized Stafford, state, private, college/university short-term loans ($100 average), SELF Loans, Norwest Collegiate Loans.

Non-Need Awards In 1996, a total of 719 non-need awards were made. *Academic Interests/Achievement Awards:* 407 ($216,077 total): general academic. *Creative Arts/Performance Awards:* 57 ($23,515 total): art/fine arts, music, theater/drama. *Special Achievements/Activities Awards:* 21 ($8240 total): leadership. *Athletic:* Total: 234 ($188,350); Men: 135 ($108,350); Women: 99 ($80,000).

Other Money-Saving Options Accelerated degree, co-op program, off-campus living (after sophomore year). *Payment Plan:* installment. *Waivers:* full or partial for children of alumni.

Contact Ms. Sharon Kienow, Director of Financial Assistance, Northern State University, 1200 South Jay Street, Aberdeen, SD 57401-7198, 605-626-2640, fax: 605-626-3022.

NORTH GEORGIA COLLEGE & STATE UNIVERSITY
Dahlonega, Georgia

About the Institution State-supported, coed. Degrees awarded: A, B, M. Offers 36 undergraduate majors. Total enrollment: 3,198. Undergraduates: 2,784 (96% state residents). Freshmen: 450.

Undergraduate Expenses (1996–97) State resident tuition: $1584. Nonresident tuition: $5463. Mandatory fees: $372. College room and board: $3057.

Applications *Financial aid deadline (priority):* 5/1. *Financial aid forms:* FAFSA, institutional form required. *Admission application deadline:* 8/15.

Summary of Aid to Needy Students Federal Work-Study jobs; part-time jobs.

Loans College/university short-term loans, college/university long-term loans.

Non-Need Awards *Academic Interests/Achievement Awards:* general academic. *Creative Arts/Performance Awards:* general creative. *Special Achievements/Activities Awards:* leadership. *Special Characteristics Awards:* ROTC participants. *Athletic:* available.

Other Money-Saving Options Co-op program, Army ROTC, off-campus living (after sophomore year). *Waivers:* full or partial for senior citizens.

Contact Office of Financial Aid, North Georgia College & State University, Dahlonega, GA 30597-1001, 706-864-1400.

NORTH GREENVILLE COLLEGE
Tigerville, South Carolina

About the Institution Independent/religious, coed. Degrees awarded: A, B. Offers 24 undergraduate majors. Total enrollment: 942 (89% state residents). Freshmen: 318.

Undergraduate Expenses (1997–98) Comprehensive fee of $10,980 includes tuition ($6900) and college room and board ($4080).

Applications 96% of all full-time undergraduates enrolled in fall 1996 applied for aid; of these, 97% were judged to have need according to Federal Methodology, of whom 100% were aided. *Financial aid deadline (priority):* 6/1. *Financial aid forms:* FAFSA required; CSS Financial Aid PROFILE acceptable. State form required for some. *Admission application deadline:* 8/27.

Summary of Aid to Needy Students *From gift & self-help combined:* Average need met: 71%. Average amount awarded: $7676 (70% gift aid, 30% self-help). *Gift aid:* Total: $4,742,783 (48% from college's own funds, 36% from other college-administered sources, 16% from external sources). 74 Federal Work-Study jobs (averaging $1000); 26 part-time jobs.

Need-Based Scholarships & Grants Pell, FSEOG, state, private, college/university.

Loans PLUS, Stafford, Unsubsidized Stafford, state, private.

Non-Need Awards In 1996, a total of 916 non-need awards were made. *Academic Interests/Achievement Awards:* 600 ($390,000 total): general academic, military science, religion/biblical studies. *Creative Arts/Performance Awards:* 60 ($40,000 total): art/fine arts, journalism/publications, music, theater/drama. *Special Achievements/Activities Awards:* 20 ($15,000 total): cheerleading/drum major, Junior Miss, religious involvement. *Special Characteristics Awards:* 25 ($25,000 total): children of faculty/staff, siblings of current students. *Athletic:* Total: 211 ($341,632); Men: 137 ($201,280); Women: 74 ($140,352).

Other Money-Saving Options Accelerated degree, Army ROTC, off-campus living. *Payment Plan:* installment. *Waivers:* full or partial for employees or children of employees.

Contact Ms. Shirley Eskew, Assistant Director of Financial Aid, North Greenville College, PO Box 1892, Tigerville, SC 29688-1892, 864-977-7057, fax: 864-977-7177.

NORTHLAND COLLEGE
Ashland, Wisconsin

About the Institution Independent/religious, coed. Degrees awarded: B. Offers 57 undergraduate majors. Total enrollment: 879 (35% state residents). Freshmen: 242.

Undergraduate Expenses (1997–98) Comprehensive fee of $16,580 includes tuition ($12,125), mandatory fees ($240), and college room and board ($4215). College room only: $1755.

Applications Of all full-time undergraduates enrolled in fall 1996, 92% of those who applied for aid were judged to have need according to Federal Methodology, of whom 100% were aided. *Financial aid deadline:* continuous. *Financial aid forms:* FAFSA, institutional form required; CSS Financial Aid PROFILE acceptable. *Regular admission application deadline:* 8/1. Early decision deadline: 11/22.

Summary of Aid to Needy Students *From gift & self-help combined:* Average need met: 85%. Average amount awarded: $10,586 (56% gift aid, 44% self-help). *Gift aid:* Total: $4,095,178 (73% from college's own funds, 12% from other college-administered sources, 15% from external sources). 488 Federal Work-Study jobs (averaging $1403); 209 part-time jobs.

Need-Based Scholarships & Grants Pell, FSEOG, state, college/university.

Loans Perkins, PLUS, Stafford, Unsubsidized Stafford.

Non-Need Awards In 1996, a total of 292 non-need awards were made. *Academic Interests/Achievement Awards:* 167 ($413,750 total): general academic. *Creative Arts/Performance Awards:* 24 ($8975 total): music. *Special Achievements/Activities Awards:* 46 ($55,250 total): leadership. *Special Characteristics Awards:* 24 ($23,000 total): ethnic background. *Athletic:* Total: 31 ($39,325); Men: 20 ($22,625); Women: 11 ($16,700).

Other Money-Saving Options Accelerated degree, co-op program, off-campus living (after sophomore year). *Payment Plans:* tuition prepayment, installment. *Waivers:* full or partial for employees or children of employees.

Contact Ms. Susan Bradford, Assistant Director of Financial Aid, Northland College, 1411 Ellis Avenue, Ashland, WI 54806-3925, 715-682-1269.

NORTH PARK UNIVERSITY
Chicago, Illinois

About the Institution Independent/religious, coed. Degrees awarded: B, M, D, P. Offers 56 undergraduate majors. Total enrollment: 1,815. Undergraduates: 1,437 (64% state residents). Freshmen: 294.

Undergraduate Expenses (1997–98 estimated) Comprehensive fee of $18,810 includes tuition ($13,990) and college room and board ($4820). College room only: $2680.

Applications 80% of all full-time undergraduates enrolled in fall 1996 applied for aid; of these, 92% were judged to have need according to Federal Methodology, of whom 99% were aided. *Financial aid deadline (priority):* 5/1. *Financial aid forms:* CSS Financial Aid PROFILE, institutional form required. FAFSA, state form required for some. *Admission application deadline:* rolling.

Summary of Aid to Needy Students *From gift & self-help combined:* Average need met: 70%. Average amount awarded: $10,953 (93% gift aid, 7% self-help). *Gift aid:* Total: $6,639,386 (63% from college's own funds, 37% from external sources). 195 Federal Work-Study jobs (averaging $1245); 150 part-time jobs.

Need-Based Scholarships & Grants Pell, FSEOG, state, private, college/university.

Loans Perkins, PLUS, Stafford, Unsubsidized Stafford, Federal Nursing, private.

Non-Need Awards *Academic Interests/Achievement Awards:* general academic. *Creative Arts/Performance Awards:* 59 ($94,350 total): art/fine arts, music, theater/drama.

Other Money-Saving Options Accelerated degree, off-campus living (after junior year). *Payment Plan:* installment. *Waivers:* full or partial for employees or children of employees and adult students.

Contact Dr. Lucy Shaker, Director of Financial Aid, North Park University, 3225 West Foster Avenue, Chicago, IL 60625-4895, 773-244-5526, fax: 773-244-4953.

NORTHWEST CHRISTIAN COLLEGE
Eugene, Oregon

About the Institution Independent/religious, coed. Degrees awarded: A, B, M. Offers 26 undergraduate majors. Total enrollment: 408. Undergraduates: 325 (85% state residents). Freshmen: 57.

Undergraduate Expenses (1996–97) Comprehensive fee of $14,620 includes tuition ($9990), mandatory fees ($320), and college room and board ($4310).

Applications 88% of all full-time undergraduates enrolled in fall 1996 applied for aid; of these, 96% were judged to have need according to Federal Methodology, of whom 100% were aided. *Financial aid deadline (priority):* 3/1. *Financial aid forms:* FAFSA, institutional form required. State form required for some. *Admission application deadline:* rolling.

Summary of Aid to Needy Students *From gift & self-help combined:* Average need met: 87%. Average amount awarded: $14,958 (48% gift aid, 52% self-help). *Gift aid:* Total: $1,617,154 (56% from college's own funds, 6% from other college-administered sources, 38% from external sources). 22 Federal Work-Study jobs (averaging $1500); 110 part-time jobs.

Need-Based Scholarships & Grants Pell, FSEOG, state, private, college/university.

Loans Perkins, PLUS, Stafford, Unsubsidized Stafford, private.

Non-Need Awards In 1996, a total of 216 non-need awards were made. *Academic Interests/Achievement Awards:* 132 ($290,825 total): general academic. *Creative Arts/Performance Awards:* 8 ($54,168 total): general creative. *Special Characteristics Awards:* 76 ($94,800 total): relatives of clergy, religious affiliation.

Other Money-Saving Options Co-op program, cooperative Army ROTC, off-campus living (after junior year). *Payment Plans:* installment, deferred payment. *Waivers:* full or partial for employees or children of employees.

Contact Ms. Charlotte Long, Financial Aid Counselor, Northwest Christian College, 828 East 11th Avenue, Eugene, OR 97401-3727, 541-684-7203, fax: 541-343-9159.

NORTHWEST COLLEGE OF ART
Poulsbo, Washington

About the Institution Proprietary, coed. Degrees awarded: B. Offers 4 undergraduate majors.

Undergraduate Expenses (1997–98) Tuition: $7500. Mandatory fees: $100.

Applications 66% of all full-time undergraduates enrolled in fall 1996 applied for aid; of these, 100% were judged to have need according to Federal Methodology, of whom 100% were aided. *Financial aid deadline (priority):* 6/1. *Financial aid forms:* FAFSA required. *Admission application deadline:* 7/15.

Summary of Aid to Needy Students *From gift & self-help combined:* Average need met: 70%. Average amount awarded: $4137 (21% gift aid, 79% self-help). *Gift aid:* Total: $45,410 (21% from college's own funds, 79% from external sources).

Need-Based Scholarships & Grants Pell.

Loans PLUS, Stafford, Unsubsidized Stafford, private.

Non-Need Awards *Creative Arts/Performance Awards:* applied art and design , art/fine arts.

Other Money-Saving Options Accelerated degree. *Payment Plan:* installment.

Contact Ms. Kim Y. Perigard, Director of Financial Aid, Northwest College of Art, 16464 State Highway 305, Poulsbo, WA 98370, 360-779-9993, fax: 360-779-9933.

NORTHWEST COLLEGE OF THE ASSEMBLIES OF GOD
Kirkland, Washington

About the Institution Independent/religious, coed. Degrees awarded: A, B. Offers 26 undergraduate majors. Total enrollment: 802 (66% state residents). Freshmen: 140.

Undergraduate Expenses (1997–98) Comprehensive fee of $13,250 includes tuition ($8250), mandatory fees ($690), and college room and board ($4310).

Applications 87% of all full-time undergraduates enrolled in fall 1996 applied for aid; of these, 81% were judged to have need according to Federal Methodology, of whom 100% were aided. *Financial aid deadline (priority):* 3/1. *Financial aid forms:* FAFSA, institutional form required. *Regular admission application deadline:* 8/1. Early action deadline: 11/15.

Summary of Aid to Needy Students *From gift & self-help combined:* Average need met: 72%. Average amount awarded: $7190 (43% gift aid, 57% self-help). *Gift aid:* Total: $1,681,074 (53% from college's own funds, 15% from other college-administered sources, 32% from external sources). 66 Federal Work-Study jobs (averaging $1500); 110 part-time jobs.

Need-Based Scholarships & Grants Pell, FSEOG, state, college/university.

Loans Perkins, PLUS, Stafford, Unsubsidized Stafford, private, college/university short-term loans.

Non-Need Awards In 1996, a total of 515 non-need awards were made. *Academic Interests/Achievement Awards:* 182 ($433,533 total): general academic, religion/biblical studies. *Creative Arts/Performance Awards:* 81 ($62,750 total): art/fine arts. *Special Characteristics Awards:* 219 ($416,919 total): general special characteristics, children of faculty/staff, international students, relatives of clergy, religious affiliation, siblings of current students, spouses of current students. *Athletic:* Total: 33 ($54,500); Men: 13 ($24,625); Women: 20 ($29,875).

Other Money-Saving Options Accelerated degree, off-campus living (after junior year). *Payment Plans:* tuition prepayment, installment, deferred payment. *Waivers:* full or partial for employees or children of employees and senior citizens.

Contact Ms. Lana J. Walter, Financial Planning Coordinator, Northwest College of the Assemblies of God, PO Box 579, Kirkland, WA 98083-0579, 206-889-5336, fax: 206-827-0148.

NORTHWESTERN COLLEGE
Orange City, Iowa

About the Institution Independent/religious, coed. Degrees awarded: A, B. Offers 35 undergraduate majors. Total enrollment: 1,160 (63% state residents). Freshmen: 354.

Undergraduate Expenses (1996–97) Comprehensive fee of $14,100 includes tuition ($10,850) and college room and board ($3250). College room only: $1375.

Applications 91% of all full-time undergraduates enrolled in fall 1996 applied for aid; of these, 85% were judged to have need according to Federal Methodology, of whom 100% were aided. *Financial aid deadline (priority):* 4/1. *Financial aid forms:* institutional form required. FAFSA required for some. *Admission application deadline:* rolling.

Summary of Aid to Needy Students *From gift & self-help combined:* Average need met: 94%. Average amount awarded: $11,838 (57% gift aid, 43% self-help). *Gift aid:* Total: $5,986,750 (48% from college's own funds, 4% from other college-administered sources, 48% from external sources). 562 Federal Work-Study jobs (averaging $700); 235 part-time jobs.

Need-Based Scholarships & Grants Pell, FSEOG, state, private, college/university.

Loans Perkins, PLUS, Stafford, Unsubsidized Stafford, state, private, college/university long-term loans ($1425 average).

Non-Need Awards In 1996, a total of 1,817 non-need awards were made. *Academic Interests/Achievement Awards:* 631 ($1,622,556 total). *Creative Arts/Performance Awards:* 207 ($193,437 total): art/fine arts, journalism/publications, music, theater/drama. *Special Characteristics Awards:* 626 ($759,350 total): adult students, children and siblings of alumni, children of faculty/staff, international students, religious affiliation, siblings of current students. *Athletic:* Total: 353 ($437,290); Men: 247 ($296,440); Women: 106 ($140,850).

Other Money-Saving Options Accelerated degree, co-op program. *Payment Plan:* installment. *Waivers:* full or partial for employees or children of employees.

Contact Mrs. Carol Bogaard, Director of Financial Aid, Northwestern College, 101 Seventh Street, SW, Orange City, IA 51041-1996, 712-737-7131, fax: 712-737-7164.

NORTHWESTERN COLLEGE
St. Paul, Minnesota

About the Institution Independent/religious, coed. Degrees awarded: A, B. Offers 39 undergraduate majors. Total enrollment: 1,362 (56% state residents). Freshmen: 350.

Undergraduate Expenses (1997–98) Comprehensive fee of $17,160 includes tuition ($13,140) and college room and board ($4020). College room only: $2325.

Applications Of all full-time undergraduates enrolled in fall 1996, 83% of those who applied for aid were judged to have need according to Federal Methodology, of whom 100% were aided. *Financial aid deadline (priority):* 3/1. *Financial aid forms:* FAFSA required; CSS Financial Aid PROFILE acceptable. Institutional form required for some. *Admission application deadline:* 8/15.

Summary of Aid to Needy Students *From gift & self-help combined:* Average need met: 71%. Average amount awarded: $11,089 (56% gift aid, 44% self-help). *Gift aid:* Total: $6,830,509 (64% from college's own funds, 26% from other college-administered sources, 10% from external sources). 164 Federal Work-Study jobs (averaging $1556); 256 part-time jobs.

Need-Based Scholarships & Grants Pell, FSEOG, state, private, college/university.

Loans Perkins, PLUS, Stafford, Unsubsidized Stafford, state, private.

Non-Need Awards In 1996, a total of 2,805 non-need awards were made. *Academic Interests/Achievement Awards:* 2,113 ($2,094,268 total): general academic. *Creative Arts/Performance Awards:* 124 ($79,619 total): music. *Special Characteristics Awards:* 568 ($971,348 total): children of faculty/staff, out-of-state students, relatives of clergy, siblings of current students.

Other Money-Saving Options Cooperative Army ROTC, cooperative Air Force ROTC, off-campus living (after sophomore year). *Waivers:* full or partial for employees or children of employees and senior citizens.

Contact Mr. Bryan F. Knowles, Assistant Director, Financial Aid Programs, Northwestern College, 3003 Snelling Avenue North, St. Paul, MN 55113-1598, 612-631-5294, fax: 612-628-3332.

NORTHWESTERN OKLAHOMA STATE UNIVERSITY
Alva, Oklahoma

About the Institution State-supported, coed. Degrees awarded: B, M. Offers 41 undergraduate majors. Total enrollment: 1,790. Undergraduates: 1,485 (84% state residents). Freshmen: 275.

Undergraduate Expenses (1996–97) State resident tuition: $1620. Nonresident tuition: $3898. Mandatory fees: $30. College room and board: $1932 (minimum).

Applications Of all full-time undergraduates enrolled in fall 1996, 83% of those who applied for aid were judged to have need according to Federal Methodology, of whom 100% were aided. *Financial aid deadline (priority):* 6/1. *Financial aid forms:* FAFSA, institutional form required; CSS Financial Aid PROFILE, state form acceptable. *Admission application deadline:* rolling.

Summary of Aid to Needy Students *From gift & self-help combined:* Average need met: 95%. Average amount awarded: $2300 (51% gift aid, 49% self-help). *Gift aid:* Total: $978,400 (13% from college's own funds, 18% from other college-administered sources, 69% from external sources). 120 Federal Work-Study jobs (averaging $1800); 120 part-time jobs.

Need-Based Scholarships & Grants Pell, FSEOG, state, college/university.

Loans Perkins, PLUS, Stafford, Unsubsidized Stafford, college/university short-term loans ($100 average).

Non-Need Awards In 1996, a total of 221 non-need awards were made. *Academic Interests/Achievement Awards:* 90 ($32,300 total): general academic, agriculture, biological sciences, business, communication, computer science, education, English, foreign languages, humanities, library science, mathematics, premedicine, social sciences. *Creative Arts/Performance Awards:* 5 ($1500 total): general creative, music, theater/drama. *Special Achievements/Activities Awards:* 4 ($1200 total): cheerleading/drum major, memberships, rodeo. *Athletic:* Total: 122 ($95,500); Men: 109 ($76,500); Women: 13 ($19,000).

Other Money-Saving Options Off-campus living. *Waivers:* full or partial for employees or children of employees and senior citizens.

Contact Mr. David Pecha, Director of Financial Aid, Northwestern Oklahoma State University, 709 Oklahoma Boulevard, Alva, OK 73717-2799, 405-327-1700 Ext. 8542, fax: 405-327-8674.

NORTHWESTERN STATE UNIVERSITY OF LOUISIANA
Natchitoches, Louisiana

About the Institution State-supported, coed. Degrees awarded: A, B, M, D. Offers 60 undergraduate majors. Total enrollment: 9,037. Undergraduates: 8,173 (76% state residents). Freshmen: 1,702.

Undergraduate Expenses (1997–98) State resident tuition: $1880. Nonresident tuition: $5216. Mandatory fees: $179. College room and board: $2292 (minimum). College room only: $1180 (minimum).

Applications 74% of all full-time undergraduates enrolled in fall 1996 applied for aid; of these, 99% were judged to have need according to

Federal Methodology, of whom 92% were aided. *Financial aid deadline (priority):* 5/1. *Financial aid forms:* FAFSA required. *Admission application deadline:* rolling.

Summary of Aid to Needy Students *From gift & self-help combined:* Average need met: 44%. Average amount awarded: $4701 (41% gift aid, 59% self-help). *Gift aid:* Total: $8,162,233 (3% from college's own funds, 26% from other college-administered sources, 71% from external sources). 170 Federal Work-Study jobs (averaging $1319); 94 part-time jobs.

Need-Based Scholarships & Grants Pell, FSEOG.

Loans Perkins, PLUS, Stafford, Unsubsidized Stafford.

Non-Need Awards *Academic Interests/Achievement Awards:* 1,934 ($3,282,755 total): general academic. *Creative Arts/Performance Awards:* dance, debating, music, theater/drama. *Special Achievements/Activities Awards:* cheerleading/drum major, leadership. *Special Characteristics Awards:* adult students, children and siblings of alumni. *Athletic:* Total: 210 ($621,641); Men: 137 ($394,621); Women: 73 ($227,020).

Other Money-Saving Options Co-op program, Army ROTC, off-campus living (after junior year). *Payment Plan:* installment. *Waivers:* full or partial for children of alumni and employees or children of employees.

Contact Mr. Gil Gilson, Director of Financial Aid, Northwestern State University of Louisiana, Natchitoches, LA 71497, 318-357-5961.

NORTHWESTERN UNIVERSITY
Evanston, Illinois

About the Institution Independent, coed. Degrees awarded: B, M, D, P. Offers 90 undergraduate majors. Total enrollment: 12,213. Undergraduates: 7,645 (25% state residents). Freshmen: 1,948.

Undergraduate Expenses (1997–98) Comprehensive fee of $25,668 includes tuition ($19,152), mandatory fees ($66), and college room and board ($6450).

Applications Of all full-time undergraduates enrolled in fall 1996, 88% of those who applied for aid were judged to have need according to Federal Methodology, of whom 100% were aided. *Financial aid deadline (priority):* 2/21. *Financial aid forms:* FAFSA, CSS Financial Aid PROFILE required. Institutional form, federal income tax return required for some. *Regular admission application deadline:* 1/1. Early decision deadline: 11/1.

Summary of Aid to Needy Students *From gift & self-help combined:* Average need met: 100%. Average amount awarded: $15,480 (71% gift aid, 29% self-help). *Gift aid:* Total: $40,510,982 (76% from college's own funds, 6% from other college-administered sources, 18% from external sources). 2,400 Federal Work-Study jobs (averaging $1590); 399 part-time jobs.

Need-Based Scholarships & Grants Pell, FSEOG, state, private, college/university.

Loans Perkins, PLUS, Stafford, Unsubsidized Stafford, private, college/university short-term loans ($100 average), college/university long-term loans ($3100 average).

Non-Need Awards *Athletic:* available.

Other Money-Saving Options Accelerated degree, co-op program, Naval ROTC, cooperative Army ROTC, cooperative Air Force ROTC, off-campus living. *Payment Plan:* installment. *Waivers:* full or partial for employees or children of employees.

Contact Mr. Allen Lentino, Associate Director of Admission and Aid, Northwestern University, 1801 Hinman Avenue, Evanston, IL 60208, 847-491-8000.

NORTHWEST MISSOURI STATE UNIVERSITY
Maryville, Missouri

About the Institution State-supported, coed. Degrees awarded: B, M. Offers 117 undergraduate majors. Total enrollment: 6,154. Undergraduates: 5,172 (65% state residents). Freshmen: 1,280.

Undergraduate Expenses (1997–98) State resident tuition: $2620. Nonresident tuition: $4580. Mandatory fees: $93. College room and board: $3780 (minimum).

Applications *Financial aid deadline (priority):* 3/30. *Financial aid forms:* FAFSA required. *Admission application deadline:* rolling.

Summary of Aid to Needy Students *From gift & self-help combined:* Average need met: 88%. Average amount awarded: $5360 (38% gift aid, 62% self-help). *Gift aid:* Total: $5,303,657 (35% from college's own funds, 3% from other college-administered sources, 62% from external sources). 328 Federal Work-Study jobs (averaging $1690); 600 part-time jobs.

Need-Based Scholarships & Grants Pell, FSEOG, college/university.

Loans Perkins, PLUS, Stafford, Unsubsidized Stafford, college/university short-term loans ($300 average).

Non-Need Awards In 1996, a total of 2,329 non-need awards were made. *Academic Interests/Achievement Awards:* 1,494 ($1,326,032 total): general academic, agriculture, biological sciences, business, computer science, education, English, foreign languages, health fields, home economics, mathematics, physical sciences, social sciences. *Creative Arts/Performance Awards:* 186 ($121,538 total): art/fine arts, debating, journalism/publications, music, theater/drama. *Special Achievements/Activities Awards:* 187 ($98,939 total): general special achievements/activities, cheerleading/drum major, leadership, memberships. *Special Characteristics Awards:* 264 ($183,248 total): general special characteristics, members of minorities. *Athletic:* Total: 198 ($542,268); Men: 131 ($382,170); Women: 67 ($160,098).

Other Money-Saving Options Accelerated degree, off-campus living (after freshman year). *Payment Plan:* installment. *Waivers:* full or partial for employees or children of employees and senior citizens.

Contact Office of Financial Aid, Northwest Missouri State University, 800 University Drive, Maryville, MO 64468 6001, 816-562-1212.

NORTHWOOD UNIVERSITY
Midland, Michigan

About the Institution Independent, coed. Degrees awarded: A, B, M. Offers 17 undergraduate majors. Total enrollment: 1,549. Undergraduates: 1,386 (80% state residents). Freshmen: 372.

Undergraduate Expenses (1997–98) Comprehensive fee of $15,767 includes tuition ($10,889) and college room and board ($4878).

Applications Of all full-time undergraduates enrolled in fall 1996, 88% of those who applied for aid were judged to have need according to Federal Methodology, of whom 99% were aided. *Financial aid deadline (priority):* 4/15. *Financial aid forms:* FAFSA required. *Admission application deadline:* rolling.

Summary of Aid to Needy Students *From gift & self-help combined:* Average need met: 92%. Average amount awarded: $11,909 (67% gift aid, 33% self-help). *Gift aid:* Total: $5,319,644 (57% from college's own funds, 7% from other college-administered sources, 36% from external sources). 115 Federal Work-Study jobs (averaging $1800); part-time jobs.

Need-Based Scholarships & Grants Pell, FSEOG, state, private, college/university.

Loans PLUS, Stafford, Unsubsidized Stafford, state, private.

Non-Need Awards In 1996, a total of 980 non-need awards were made. *Academic Interests/Achievement Awards:* 655 ($2,114,448 total): general academic, business. *Special Characteristics Awards:* 112 ($316,225 total): children and siblings of alumni, children of faculty/staff, siblings of current students. *Athletic:* Total: 213 ($1,123,556); Men: 150 ($720,825); Women: 63 ($402,731).

Other Money-Saving Options Accelerated degree, off-campus living (after freshman year).

Contact Mrs. Diane Todd Sprague, Director of Financial Aid, Northwood University, Midland, MI 48640-2398, 517-837-4230.

NORTHWOOD UNIVERSITY, FLORIDA CAMPUS
West Palm Beach, Florida

About the Institution Independent, coed. Degrees awarded: A, B. Offers 12 undergraduate majors. Total enrollment: 760 (60% state residents). Freshmen: 175.

Undergraduate Expenses (1997–98) Comprehensive fee of $16,887 includes tuition ($10,659), mandatory fees ($215), and college room and board ($6013).

Applications 46% of all full-time undergraduates enrolled in fall 1996 applied for aid; of these, 77% were judged to have need according to Federal Methodology, of whom 96% were aided. *Financial aid deadline (priority):* 3/15. *Financial aid forms:* FAFSA required; CSS Financial Aid PROFILE acceptable. *Admission application deadline:* rolling.

Summary of Aid to Needy Students *From gift & self-help combined:* Average need met: 83%. Average amount awarded: $10,439 (62% gift aid, 38% self-help). *Gift aid:* Total: $1,381,080 (76% from college's own funds, 6% from other college-administered sources, 18% from external sources). 20 Federal Work-Study jobs (averaging $1800); 74 part-time jobs.

Need-Based Scholarships & Grants Pell, FSEOG, private, college/university.

Loans PLUS, Stafford, Unsubsidized Stafford, private.

Non-Need Awards In 1996, a total of 470 non-need awards were made. *Academic Interests/Achievement Awards:* 179 ($477,833 total): general academic, business. *Special Achievements/Activities Awards:* 6 ($7667 total): memberships. *Special Characteristics Awards:* 163 ($201,863 total): children and siblings of alumni, children of faculty/staff, children of union members/company employees, local/state students, siblings of current students. *Athletic:* Total: 122 ($221,985); Men: 80 ($150,752); Women: 42 ($71,233).

Other Money-Saving Options Accelerated degree, off-campus living (after sophomore year). *Payment Plan:* installment. *Waivers:* full or partial for employees or children of employees.

Contact Office of Financial Aid, Northwood University, Florida Campus, 2600 North Military Trail, West Palm Beach, FL 33409-2999, 561-478-5500.

NORTHWOOD UNIVERSITY, TEXAS CAMPUS
Cedar Hill, Texas

About the Institution Independent, coed. Degrees awarded: A, B. Offers 9 undergraduate majors. Total enrollment: 354 (86% state residents). Freshmen: 119.

Undergraduate Expenses (1996–97) Comprehensive fee of $15,239 includes tuition ($10,350), mandatory fees ($180), and college room and board ($4709). College room only: $1926.

Applications Of all full-time undergraduates enrolled in fall 1996, 97% of those judged to have need according to Federal Methodology were aided. *Financial aid deadline:* continuous. *Financial aid forms:* FAFSA, CSS Financial Aid PROFILE, institutional form required. *Admission application deadline:* 9/1.

Summary of Aid to Needy Students *From gift & self-help combined:* Average need met: 92%. Average amount awarded: $10,528 (66% gift aid, 34% self-help). *Gift aid:* Total: $1,878,373 (79% from college's own funds, 7% from other college-administered sources, 14% from external sources). 20 Federal Work-Study jobs (averaging $1500); 12 part-time jobs.

Need-Based Scholarships & Grants Pell, FSEOG, private, college/university.

Loans Perkins, PLUS, Stafford, Unsubsidized Stafford.

Non-Need Awards In 1996, a total of 508 non-need awards were made. *Academic Interests/Achievement Awards:* 158 ($523,934 total). *Special Achievements/Activities Awards:* 43 ($45,000 total). *Special Characteristics Awards:* 239 ($359,600 total): general special characteristics, children and siblings of alumni, children of faculty/staff, local/state students, siblings of current students. *Athletic:* Total: 68 ($234,055); Men: 47 ($150,555); Women: 21 ($83,500).

Other Money-Saving Options Co-op program, off-campus living (after freshman year). *Payment Plan:* installment. *Waivers:* full or partial for employees or children of employees.

Contact Ms. Cynthia Butler, Assistant Director of Financial Aid, Northwood University, Texas Campus, PO Box 58- 1114 West FM 1382, Cedar Hill, TX 75014-0058, 972-293-5430.

NORWICH UNIVERSITY
Northfield, Vermont

About the Institution Independent, coed. Degrees awarded: A, B, M. Offers 37 undergraduate majors. Total enrollment: 2,556. Undergraduates: 1,500 (22% state residents). Freshmen: 524.

Undergraduate Expenses (1997–98) Comprehensive fee of $20,580 includes tuition ($14,926), mandatory fees ($24), and college room and board ($5630).

Applications *Financial aid deadline:* continuous. *Financial aid forms:* CSS Financial Aid PROFILE required; FAFSA acceptable. State form required for some. *Regular admission application deadline:* rolling. Early decision deadline: 11/15.

Summary of Aid to Needy Students Federal Work-Study jobs.

Loans College/university long-term loans.

Non-Need Awards *Academic Interests/Achievement Awards:* available. *Special Characteristics Awards:* general special characteristics, ROTC participants.

Other Money-Saving Options Co-op program, Army ROTC, Naval ROTC, Air Force ROTC.

Contact Office of Financial Aid, Norwich University, Northfield, VT 05663, 802-485-2000.

NOTRE DAME COLLEGE
Manchester, New Hampshire

About the Institution Independent/religious, coed. Degrees awarded: A, B, M. Offers 21 undergraduate majors. Total enrollment: 1,017. Undergraduates: 750 (68% state residents). Freshmen: 115.

Undergraduate Expenses (1996–97) Comprehensive fee of $17,135 includes tuition ($11,440), mandatory fees ($400), and college room and board ($5295).

Applications *Financial aid deadline (priority):* 3/15. *Financial aid forms:* FAFSA, CSS Financial Aid PROFILE, institutional form required. *Admission application deadline:* rolling.

Summary of Aid to Needy Students *From gift & self-help combined:* Average need met: 85%. Average amount awarded: $8200 (32% gift aid, 68% self-help). *Gift aid:* Total: $1,383,164 (73% from college's

own funds, 11% from other college-administered sources, 16% from external sources). 120 Federal Work-Study jobs (averaging $1000); 50 part-time jobs.

Need-Based Scholarships & Grants Pell, FSEOG, state, private, college/university.

Loans Perkins, PLUS, Stafford, Unsubsidized Stafford, private.

Non-Need Awards *Academic Interests/Achievement Awards:* 20 ($35,000 total): general academic. *Special Characteristics Awards:* children and siblings of alumni, siblings of current students. *Athletic:* Total: 43 ($117,650); Men: 23 ($72,650); Women: 20 ($45,000).

Other Money-Saving Options Accelerated degree, cooperative Air Force ROTC, off-campus living. *Payment Plan:* installment. *Waivers:* full or partial for children of alumni, employees or children of employees, senior citizens.

Contact Office of Financial Aid, Notre Dame College, Manchester, NH 03104-2299, 603-669-4298.

NOTRE DAME COLLEGE OF OHIO
South Euclid, Ohio

About the Institution Independent/religious, women. Degrees awarded: A, B, M. Offers 42 undergraduate majors. Total enrollment: 644. Undergraduates: 611 (97% state residents). Freshmen: 60.

Undergraduate Expenses (1997–98) Comprehensive fee of $17,150 includes tuition ($12,000), mandatory fees ($150), and college room and board ($5000).

Applications *Financial aid deadline:* continuous. *Financial aid forms:* FAFSA required; CSS Financial Aid PROFILE acceptable. *Admission application deadline:* rolling.

Summary of Aid to Needy Students *From gift & self-help combined:* Average need met: 100%. Average amount awarded: $6478 (56% gift aid, 44% self-help). *Gift aid:* Total: $1,450,665 (61% from college's own funds, 23% from other college-administered sources, 16% from external sources). 17 Federal Work-Study jobs (averaging $1500); 35 part-time jobs.

Need-Based Scholarships & Grants Pell, FSEOG, state, private, college/university.

Loans Perkins, PLUS, Stafford, Unsubsidized Stafford, state, private.

Non-Need Awards In 1996, a total of 204 non-need awards were made. *Academic Interests/Achievement Awards:* 194 ($624,834 total): general academic. *Special Characteristics Awards:* 10 ($5000 total): children and siblings of alumni, children of faculty/staff, relatives of clergy.

Other Money-Saving Options Accelerated degree, co-op program, off-campus living (after junior year). *Payment Plan:* installment. *Waivers:* full or partial for employees or children of employees.

Contact Ms. Mary E. McCrystal, Financial Aid Director, Notre Dame College of Ohio, South Euclid, OH 44121-4293, 216-381-1680 Ext. 263.

NOVA SOUTHEASTERN UNIVERSITY
Fort Lauderdale, Florida

About the Institution Independent, coed. Degrees awarded: B, M, D, P. Offers 22 undergraduate majors. Total enrollment: 14,951. Freshmen: 170.

Undergraduate Expenses (1997–98) Comprehensive fee of $16,018 includes tuition ($10,350), mandatory fees ($70), and college room and board ($5598 minimum). College room only: $3298 (minimum).

Applications 88% of all full-time undergraduates enrolled in fall 1996 applied for aid; of these, 97% were judged to have need according to Federal Methodology, of whom 100% were aided. *Financial aid deadline*

(priority): 4/1. *Financial aid forms:* FAFSA, institutional form required; CSS Financial Aid PROFILE acceptable. State form required for some. *Admission application deadline:* rolling.

Summary of Aid to Needy Students *From gift & self-help combined:* Average need met: 50%. Average amount awarded: $11,560 (27% gift aid, 73% self-help). *Gift aid:* Total: $7,477,824 (23% from college's own funds, 13% from other college-administered sources, 64% from external sources). 350 Federal Work-Study jobs (averaging $1600); 396 part-time jobs.

Need-Based Scholarships & Grants Pell, FSEOG, state, private, college/university.

Loans Perkins, PLUS, Stafford, Unsubsidized Stafford, private, college/university long-term loans ($2200 average).

Non-Need Awards In 1996, a total of 463 non-need awards were made. *Academic Interests/Achievement Awards:* 327 ($1,122,991 total): general academic. *Special Achievements/Activities Awards:* 4 ($6400 total): community service. *Special Characteristics Awards:* 35 ($36,852 total): children of faculty/staff, local/state students. *Athletic:* Total: 97 ($417,421); Men: 54 ($221,183); Women: 43 ($196,238).

Other Money-Saving Options Accelerated degree, co-op program, off-campus living (after freshman year). *Payment Plan:* installment. *Waivers:* full or partial for employees or children of employees.

Contact Office of Financial Aid, Nova Southeastern University, 3301 College Avenue, Fort Lauderdale, FL 33314-7721, 954-262-7300.

NYACK COLLEGE
Nyack, New York

About the Institution Independent/religious, coed. Degrees awarded: A, B, M. Offers 25 undergraduate majors. Total enrollment: 1,312. Undergraduates: 1,010 (64% state residents). Freshmen: 209.

Undergraduate Expenses (1997–98) Comprehensive fee of $15,960 includes tuition ($10,400), mandatory fees ($700), and college room and board ($4860).

Applications 95% of all full-time undergraduates enrolled in fall 1996 applied for aid; of these, 79% were judged to have need according to Federal Methodology, of whom 97% were aided. *Financial aid deadline (priority):* 5/15. *Financial aid forms:* FAFSA, institutional form required. State form required for some. *Admission application deadline:* 9/11.

Summary of Aid to Needy Students *From gift & self-help combined:* Average need met: 75%. Average amount awarded: $11,428 (52% gift aid, 48% self-help). *Gift aid:* Total: $4,142,800 (49% from college's own funds, 29% from other college-administered sources, 22% from external sources). 200 Federal Work-Study jobs (averaging $400); 260 part-time jobs.

Need-Based Scholarships & Grants Pell, FSEOG, state, private, college/university.

Loans Perkins, PLUS, Stafford, Unsubsidized Stafford.

Non-Need Awards In 1996, a total of 620 non-need awards were made. *Academic Interests/Achievement Awards:* 109 ($196,000 total): general academic. *Creative Arts/Performance Awards:* 30 ($40,000 total): journalism/publications, music, performing arts, theater/drama. *Special Achievements/Activities Awards:* 80 ($65,000 total): general special achievements/activities, leadership, religious involvement. *Special Characteristics Awards:* 280 ($574,000 total): children and siblings of alumni, children of current students, children of faculty/staff, international students, out-of-state students, relatives of clergy, religious affiliation. *Athletic:* Total: 121 ($375,000).

Other Money-Saving Options *Payment Plan:* installment. *Waivers:* full or partial for employees or children of employees.

Contact Financial Aid Office, Nyack College, Nyack, NY 10960-3698, 914-358-1710 Ext. 151.

OAK HILLS BIBLE COLLEGE
Bemidji, Minnesota

About the Institution Independent/religious, coed. Degrees awarded: A, B. Offers 4 undergraduate majors. Total enrollment: 174 (64% state residents). Freshmen: 49.

Undergraduate Expenses (1997–98) Comprehensive fee of $10,155 includes tuition ($7170), mandatory fees ($510), and college room and board ($2475). College room only: $975.

Applications 89% of all full-time undergraduates enrolled in fall 1996 applied for aid; of these, 94% were judged to have need according to Federal Methodology, of whom 100% were aided. *Financial aid deadline (priority):* 8/1. *Financial aid forms:* FAFSA required; state form acceptable. Institutional form required for some.

Summary of Aid to Needy Students *From gift & self-help combined:* Average need met: 64%. Average amount awarded: $7478 (64% gift aid, 36% self-help). *Gift aid:* Total: $538,101 (30% from college's own funds, 45% from other college-administered sources, 25% from external sources). 12 Federal Work-Study jobs (averaging $640); 35 part-time jobs.

Need-Based Scholarships & Grants Pell, FSEOG, state, private, college/university.

Loans PLUS, Stafford, Unsubsidized Stafford, state, college/university short-term loans ($500 average).

Non-Need Awards In 1996, a total of 21 non-need awards were made. *Special Characteristics Awards:* 21 ($76,264 total): children of faculty/staff, international students, siblings of current students, spouses of current students.

Other Money-Saving Options Off-campus living. *Payment Plan:* installment. *Waivers:* full or partial for employees or children of employees.

Contact Mr. Daniel Hovestol, Financial Aid Director, Oak Hills Bible College, 1600 Oak Hills Road, SW, Bemidji, MN 56601-8832, 218-751-8670 Ext. 220, fax: 218-751-8825.

OAKLAND CITY UNIVERSITY
Oakland City, Indiana

About the Institution Independent/religious, coed. Degrees awarded: A, B, M. Offers 42 undergraduate majors. Total enrollment: 1,087. Undergraduates: 1,030 (85% state residents). Freshmen: 218.

Undergraduate Expenses (1996–97) Comprehensive fee of $11,112 includes tuition ($7800), mandatory fees ($166), and college room and board ($3146).

Applications 95% of all full-time undergraduates enrolled in fall 1996 applied for aid. *Financial aid deadline (priority):* 4/1. *Financial aid forms:* FAFSA, institutional form required. *Admission application deadline:* rolling.

Summary of Aid to Needy Students *From gift & self-help combined:* Average need met: 95%. Average amount awarded: $5500 (75% gift aid, 25% self-help). *Gift aid:* Total: $4,550,000 (37% from college's own funds, 51% from other college-administered sources, 12% from external sources). Federal Work-Study jobs; part-time jobs.

Need-Based Scholarships & Grants Pell, FSEOG, state.

Loans Perkins, PLUS, Stafford, Unsubsidized Stafford.

Non-Need Awards *Academic Interests/Achievement Awards:* general academic. *Creative Arts/Performance Awards:* art/fine arts, music. *Special Achievements/Activities Awards:* religious involvement. *Special Characteristics Awards:* religious affiliation. *Athletic:* available.

Other Money-Saving Options Accelerated degree, off-campus living (after freshman year). *Payment Plans:* installment, deferred payment. *Waivers:* full or partial for minority students and employees or children of employees.

Contact Ms. Caren K. Richeson, Director of Financial Aid, Oakland City University, Oakland City, IN 47660-1099, 812-749-1224.

OAKLAND UNIVERSITY
Rochester, Michigan

About the Institution State-supported, coed. Degrees awarded: B, M, D. Offers 77 undergraduate majors. Total enrollment: 13,965. Undergraduates: 10,886 (96% state residents). Freshmen: 1,411.

Undergraduate Expenses (1996–97) State resident tuition: $3448 (minimum). Nonresident tuition: $10,160 (minimum). Mandatory fees: $254. College room and board: $4250.

Applications Of all full-time undergraduates enrolled in fall 1996, 81% of those who applied for aid were judged to have need according to Federal Methodology, of whom 98% were aided. *Financial aid deadline (priority):* 4/1. *Financial aid forms:* FAFSA, institutional form required; CSS Financial Aid PROFILE acceptable. *Admission application deadline:* 8/1.

Summary of Aid to Needy Students *From gift & self-help combined:* Average need met: 74%. Average amount awarded: $4669 (38% gift aid, 62% self-help). *Gift aid:* Total: $4,652,061 (30% from college's own funds, 8% from other college-administered sources, 62% from external sources). 350 Federal Work-Study jobs (averaging $2100); 1,200 part-time jobs.

Need-Based Scholarships & Grants Pell, FSEOG, state, college/university.

Loans Perkins, PLUS, Stafford, Unsubsidized Stafford, college/university short-term loans ($250 average).

Non-Need Awards In 1996, a total of 784 non-need awards were made. *Academic Interests/Achievement Awards:* 369 ($805,000 total): general academic, biological sciences, engineering/technologies. *Creative Arts/Performance Awards:* 61 ($61,000 total): music, performing arts. *Special Achievements/Activities Awards:* 189 ($217,500 total): leadership. *Special Characteristics Awards:* 34 ($185,000 total): children of union members/company employees, out-of-state students. *Athletic:* Total: 131 ($521,000); Men: 71 ($304,000); Women: 60 ($217,000).

Other Money-Saving Options Accelerated degree, co-op program, off-campus living (after sophomore year). *Payment Plan:* installment. *Waivers:* full or partial for employees or children of employees.

Contact Mr. Robert E. Johnson, Associate Vice President for Enrollment Management, Oakland University, 101 North Foundation Hall, Rochester, MI 48309-4401, 810-370-3360, fax: 810-370-4462.

OAKWOOD COLLEGE
Huntsville, Alabama

About the Institution Independent/religious, coed. Degrees awarded: A, B. Offers 41 undergraduate majors. Total enrollment: 1,666 (23% state residents). Freshmen: 375.

Undergraduate Expenses (1997–98) Comprehensive fee of $12,128 includes tuition ($7468), mandatory fees ($160), and college room and board ($4500).

Applications Of all full-time undergraduates enrolled in fall 1996, 84% of those who applied for aid were judged to have need according to Federal Methodology, of whom 99% were aided. *Financial aid deadline (priority):* 3/31. *Financial aid forms:* FAFSA, institutional form required; state form acceptable. *Admission application deadline:* rolling.

Summary of Aid to Needy Students *From gift & self-help combined:* Average need met: 90%. Average amount awarded: $9741 (23% gift aid, 77% self-help). *Gift aid:* Total: $1,961,475 (8% from college's own funds, 14% from other college-administered sources, 78% from external sources). 90 Federal Work-Study jobs (averaging $2796); 674 part-time jobs.

Need-Based Scholarships & Grants Pell, FSEOG, state, private, college/university.

Loans PLUS, Stafford, Unsubsidized Stafford, private.

Non-Need Awards In 1996, a total of 86 non-need awards were made. *Academic Interests/Achievement Awards:* 25 ($64,742 total): general academic. *Special Characteristics Awards:* 61 ($277,461 total): general special characteristics, relatives of clergy.

Other Money-Saving Options Accelerated degree, co-op program.

Contact Office of Financial Aid, Oakwood College, Oakwood Road, NW, Huntsville, AL 35896, 205-726-7000.

OBERLIN COLLEGE
Oberlin, Ohio

About the Institution Independent, coed. Degrees awarded: B. Offers 53 undergraduate majors. Total enrollment: 2,861 (9% state residents). Freshmen: 671.

Undergraduate Expenses (1997–98) Comprehensive fee of $28,796 includes tuition ($22,282), mandatory fees ($156), and college room and board ($6358). College room only: $3166.

Applications 69% of all full-time undergraduates enrolled in fall 1996 applied for aid; of these, 84% were judged to have need according to Federal Methodology, of whom 100% were aided. *Financial aid deadline:* Applications processed continuously. *Financial aid forms:* FAFSA, CSS Financial Aid PROFILE, institutional form required. State form required for some. *Regular admission application deadline:* 1/15. Early decision deadline: 11/15.

Summary of Aid to Needy Students *From gift & self-help combined:* Average need met: 100%. Average amount awarded: $18,942 (73% gift aid, 27% self-help). *Gift aid:* Total: $22,784,711 (89% from college's own funds, 4% from other college-administered sources, 7% from external sources). 1,229 Federal Work-Study jobs (averaging $1415); 152 part-time jobs.

Need-Based Scholarships & Grants Pell, FSEOG, state, private, college/university.

Loans Perkins, PLUS, Stafford, Unsubsidized Stafford, private, college/university short-term loans ($200 average), college/university long-term loans ($4000 average).

Non-Need Awards In 1996, a total of 170 non-need awards were made. *Academic Interests/Achievement Awards:* 83 ($323,662 total): general academic. *Creative Arts/Performance Awards:* 87 ($559,148 total): music.

Other Money-Saving Options Accelerated degree, off-campus living (after sophomore year). *Payment Plan:* installment. *Waivers:* full or partial for employees or children of employees.

Contact Mr. Howard Thomas, Director of Financial Aid, Oberlin College, 52 West Lorain Street, Oberlin, OH 44074-1090, 800-693-3173.

OCCIDENTAL COLLEGE
Los Angeles, California

About the Institution Independent, coed. Degrees awarded: B, M. Offers 61 undergraduate majors. Total enrollment: 1,534. Undergraduates: 1,477 (69% state residents). Freshmen: 353.

Undergraduate Expenses (1997–98) Comprehensive fee of $25,864 includes tuition ($19,800), mandatory fees ($174), and college room and board ($5890). College room only: $3230.

Applications 71% of all full-time undergraduates enrolled in fall 1996 applied for aid; of these, 93% were judged to have need according to Federal Methodology, of whom 99% were aided. *Financial aid deadline:* 2/1. *Financial aid forms:* FAFSA, state form required. CSS Financial Aid

PROFILE, institutional form, Divorced/Separated Parents' Statement, Business Supplement required for some. *Regular admission application deadline:* 1/15. Early decision deadline: 11/15.

Summary of Aid to Needy Students *From gift & self-help combined:* Average need met: 100%. Average amount awarded: $20,917 (64% gift aid, 36% self-help). *Gift aid:* Total: $12,756,458 (72% from college's own funds, 19% from other college-administered sources, 9% from external sources). 134 Federal Work-Study jobs (averaging $1845); 623 part-time jobs.

Need-Based Scholarships & Grants Pell, FSEOG, state, college/university.

Loans Perkins, PLUS, Stafford, Unsubsidized Stafford, private, college/university short-term loans ($500 average), college/university long-term loans ($3654 average).

Non-Need Awards In 1996, a total of 474 non-need awards were made. *Academic Interests/Achievement Awards:* 473 ($3,585,114 total): general academic. *Creative Arts/Performance Awards:* 1 ($1000 total): music.

Other Money-Saving Options Accelerated degree, cooperative Army ROTC, cooperative Naval ROTC, cooperative Air Force ROTC, off-campus living (after freshman year). *Payment Plans:* tuition prepayment, installment. *Waivers:* full or partial for employees or children of employees.

Contact Mrs. Gilma Lopez, Interim Financial Aid Director, Occidental College, 1600 Campus Road, Los Angeles, CA 90041-3392, 213-259-2548, fax: 213-341-4961.

OGLALA LAKOTA COLLEGE
Kyle, South Dakota

About the Institution State & locally supported, coed. Degrees awarded: A, B, M. Offers 23 undergraduate majors.

Applications 59% of all full-time undergraduates enrolled in fall 1996 applied for aid; of these, 97% were judged to have need according to Federal Methodology, of whom 100% were aided. *Financial aid deadline (priority):* 4/1. *Financial aid forms:* FAFSA required. Bureau of Indian Affairs form required for some. *Admission application deadline:* rolling.

Summary of Aid to Needy Students *From gift & self-help combined:* Average need met: 50%. Average amount awarded: $4075. Federal Work-Study jobs.

Need-Based Scholarships & Grants Pell, FSEOG, state, private, college/university.

Non-Need Awards In 1996, a total of 10 non-need awards were made. *Academic Interests/Achievement Awards:* 10 ($20,000 total): business.

Other Money-Saving Options Accelerated degree, co-op program. *Payment Plan:* installment. *Waivers:* full or partial for employees or children of employees.

Contact Ms. Verola Mills, Financial Aid Assistant, Oglala Lakota College, Box 490, Kyle, SD 57752-0490, 605-455-2321 Ext. 245, fax: 605-455-2787.

OGLETHORPE UNIVERSITY
Atlanta, Georgia

About the Institution Independent, coed. Degrees awarded: B, M. Offers 33 undergraduate majors. Total enrollment: 1,227. Undergraduates: 1,145 (53% state residents). Freshmen: 156.

Undergraduate Expenses (1997–98) Comprehensive fee of $20,520 includes tuition ($15,820), mandatory fees ($100), and college room and board ($4600 minimum).

Applications 75% of all full-time undergraduates enrolled in fall 1996 applied for aid; of these, 89% were judged to have need according to Federal Methodology, of whom 96% were aided. *Financial aid deadline (priority):* 3/1. *Financial aid forms:* FAFSA, institutional form required. State form required for some. *Regular admission application deadline:* 8/1. Early decision deadline: 12/1.

Summary of Aid to Needy Students *From gift & self-help combined:* Average need met: 81%. Average amount awarded: $14,086 (72% gift aid, 28% self-help). *Gift aid:* Total: $4,722,477 (76% from college's own funds, 18% from other college-administered sources, 6% from external sources). 322 Federal Work-Study jobs (averaging $1200); 20 part-time jobs.

Need-Based Scholarships & Grants Pell, FSEOG, state, private, college/university.

Loans Perkins, PLUS, Stafford, Unsubsidized Stafford, private, college/university short-term loans ($200 average), college/university long-term loans ($1200 average).

Non-Need Awards In 1996, a total of 561 non-need awards were made. *Academic Interests/Achievement Awards:* 517 ($2,966,693 total): general academic. *Creative Arts/Performance Awards:* 28 ($25,300 total): journalism/publications, music, performing arts, theater/drama. *Special Achievements/Activities Awards:* 11 ($14,500 total): community service, religious involvement. *Special Characteristics Awards:* 5 ($49,295 total): children of faculty/staff, siblings of current students.

Other Money-Saving Options Accelerated degree, co-op program, cooperative Army ROTC, cooperative Air Force ROTC, off-campus living. *Payment Plans:* tuition prepayment, installment. *Waivers:* full or partial for employees or children of employees.

Contact Ms. Pam Beaird, Director of Financial Aid, Oglethorpe University, 4484 Peachtree Road, NE, Atlanta, GA 30319-2797, 404-364-8354, fax: 404-364-8500.

OHIO DOMINICAN COLLEGE
Columbus, Ohio

About the Institution Independent/religious, coed. Degrees awarded: A, B. Offers 37 undergraduate majors. Total enrollment: 1,883 (91% state residents). Freshmen: 197.

Undergraduate Expenses (1997–98) Comprehensive fee of $14,070 includes tuition ($9350) and college room and board ($4720).

Applications 87% of all full-time undergraduates enrolled in fall 1996 applied for aid; of these, 95% were judged to have need according to Federal Methodology, of whom 100% were aided. *Financial aid deadline (priority):* 5/1. *Financial aid forms:* FAFSA required. *Admission application deadline:* rolling.

Summary of Aid to Needy Students *From gift & self-help combined:* Average need met: 89%. Average amount awarded: $6446 (51% gift aid, 49% self-help). *Gift aid:* Total: $3,251,381 (43% from college's own funds, 36% from other college-administered sources, 21% from external sources). 130 Federal Work-Study jobs (averaging $1100); 46 part-time jobs.

Need-Based Scholarships & Grants Pell, FSEOG, state, private, college/university.

Loans Perkins, PLUS, Stafford, Unsubsidized Stafford.

Non-Need Awards In 1996, a total of 310 non-need awards were made. *Academic Interests/Achievement Awards:* 220 ($407,079 total): general academic. *Athletic:* Total: 90 ($178,045); Men: 47 ($95,245); Women: 43 ($82,800).

Other Money-Saving Options Cooperative Army ROTC, cooperative Air Force ROTC, off-campus living (after junior year). *Payment Plan:* installment. *Waivers:* full or partial for employees or children of employees.

Contact Financial Aid Office, Ohio Dominican College, 1216 Sunbury Road, Columbus, OH 43219-2099, 614-251-4640, fax: 614-252-0776.

OHIO NORTHERN UNIVERSITY
Ada, Ohio

About the Institution Independent/religious, coed. Degrees awarded: B, P. Offers 49 undergraduate majors. Total enrollment: 2,931. Undergraduates: 2,589 (86% state residents). Freshmen: 636.

Undergraduate Expenses (1997–98) Comprehensive fee of $23,535 includes tuition ($18,870 minimum) and college room and board ($4665). College room only: $2040.

Applications Of all full-time undergraduates enrolled in fall 1996, 84% of those who applied for aid were judged to have need according to Federal Methodology, of whom 100% were aided. *Financial aid deadline (priority):* 5/1. *Financial aid forms:* FAFSA, institutional form required; CSS Financial Aid PROFILE acceptable. State form required for some. *Admission application deadline:* 8/15.

Summary of Aid to Needy Students *From gift & self-help combined:* Average need met: 97%. Average amount awarded: $15,356 (71% gift aid, 29% self-help). *Gift aid:* Total: $21,485,415 (78% from college's own funds, 2% from other college-administered sources, 20% from external sources). 1,870 Federal Work-Study jobs (averaging $1000); 550 part-time jobs.

Need-Based Scholarships & Grants Pell, FSEOG, state, private, college/university.

Loans Perkins, PLUS, Stafford, Unsubsidized Stafford, state, private, college/university short-term loans ($1400 average), college/university long-term loans ($1230 average).

Non-Need Awards In 1996, a total of 1,764 non-need awards were made. *Academic Interests/Achievement Awards:* 1,361 ($6,525,235 total): general academic. *Creative Arts/Performance Awards:* 120 ($513,719 total): art/fine arts, music, theater/drama. *Special Achievements/Activities Awards:* 2 ($5000 total): Junior Miss. *Special Characteristics Awards:* 281 ($1,755,345 total): children of faculty/staff, relatives of clergy, religious affiliation, siblings of current students.

Other Money-Saving Options Co-op program, cooperative Army ROTC, cooperative Air Force ROTC, off-campus living (after junior year). *Payment Plan:* installment. *Waivers:* full or partial for employees or children of employees.

Contact Mr. Wendell Schick, Director of Financial Aid, Ohio Northern University, 525 South Main Street, Ada, OH 45810-1599, 419-772-2272, fax: 419-772-2313.

THE OHIO STATE UNIVERSITY
Columbus, Ohio

About the Institution State-supported, coed. Degrees awarded: B, M, D, P. Offers 179 undergraduate majors. Total enrollment: 48,352. Undergraduates: 35,486 (90% state residents). Freshmen: 5,976.

Undergraduate Expenses (1996–97) State resident tuition: $3468. Nonresident tuition: $10,335. College room and board: $4907.

Applications Of all full-time undergraduates enrolled in fall 1996, 66% of those who applied for aid were judged to have need according to Federal Methodology, of whom 81% were aided. *Financial aid deadline:* continuous. *Financial aid forms:* FAFSA required; CSS Financial Aid PROFILE, state form acceptable. Institutional form required for some. *Admission application deadline:* 2/15.

Summary of Aid to Needy Students *From gift & self-help combined:* Average need met: 82%. Average amount awarded: $7460 (36% gift aid, 64% self-help). *Gift aid:* Total: $43,071,000 (51% from college's own funds, 5% from other college-administered sources, 44% from external sources). 4,794 Federal Work-Study jobs (averaging $1500); part-time jobs.

Need-Based Scholarships & Grants Pell, FSEOG, state, private, college/university.

Loans Perkins, PLUS, Stafford, Unsubsidized Stafford, Federal Nursing, Primary Care, state, private, college/university short-term loans ($300 average), college/university long-term loans ($650 average).

Non-Need Awards In 1996, a total of 18,437 non-need awards were made. *Academic Interests/Achievement Awards:* 14,390 ($8,297,100 total): general academic, agriculture, architecture, area/ethnic studies, biological sciences, business, communication, computer science, education, engineering/technologies, English, foreign languages, health fields, home economics, humanities, international studies, mathematics, military science, physical sciences, premedicine, social sciences. *Creative Arts/Performance Awards:* 398 ($358,900 total): creative writing, dance, journalism/publications, music, performing arts, theater/drama. *Special Achievements/Activities Awards:* 31 ($28,000 total): cheerleading/drum major, hobbies/interest, leadership, memberships. *Special Characteristics Awards:* 3,211 ($8,953,100 total): adult students, children and siblings of alumni, children of faculty/staff, children of public servants, children of union members/company employees, children of workers in trades, children with a deceased or disabled parent, ethnic background, handicapped students, international students, members of minorities, out-of-state students, previous college experience, ROTC participants. *Athletic:* Total: 407 ($3,875,800); Men: 246 ($2,145,400); Women: 161 ($1,730,400).

Other Money-Saving Options Accelerated degree, co-op program, Army ROTC, Naval ROTC, Air Force ROTC, off-campus living (after freshman year). *Payment Plan:* installment. *Waivers:* full or partial for employees or children of employees and senior citizens.

Contact Mr. Roger A. Meyer, Associate Director of Student Financial Aid, The Ohio State University, 440 Lincoln Tower, 1800 Cannon Drive, Columbus, OH 43210-1230, 614-292-8284, fax: 614-292-7828.

OHIO UNIVERSITY
Athens, Ohio

About the Institution State-supported, coed. Degrees awarded: A, B, M, D, P. Offers 164 undergraduate majors. Total enrollment: 18,997. Undergraduates: 16,075 (89% state residents). Freshmen: 3,191.

Undergraduate Expenses (1996–97) State resident tuition: $4080. Nonresident tuition: $8574. College room and board: $4473. College room only: $2199.

Applications Of all full-time undergraduates enrolled in fall 1996, 62% of those who applied for aid were judged to have need according to Federal Methodology, of whom 92% were aided. *Financial aid deadline (priority):* 3/15. *Financial aid forms:* FAFSA required. *Admission application deadline:* 2/1.

Summary of Aid to Needy Students *From gift & self-help combined:* Average need met: 97%. Average amount awarded: $7652 (23% gift aid, 77% self-help). *Gift aid:* Total: $11,734,529 (9% from college's own funds, 18% from other college-administered sources, 73% from external sources). 1,020 Federal Work-Study jobs (averaging $914); 2,500 part-time jobs.

Need-Based Scholarships & Grants Pell, FSEOG, state, private, college/university.

Loans Perkins, PLUS, Stafford, Unsubsidized Stafford, private, college/university short-term loans ($489 average), college/university long-term loans ($871 average).

Non-Need Awards *Academic Interests/Achievement Awards:* general academic, area/ethnic studies, biological sciences, business, communication, computer science, education, engineering/technologies, English, foreign languages, health fields, home economics, humanities, international studies, mathematics, military science, physical sciences, premedicine, social sciences. *Creative Arts/Performance Awards:* applied art and design, art/fine arts, cinema/film/broadcasting, dance, journalism/publications, music, performing arts, theater/drama. *Special Characteristics Awards:* children of faculty/staff, ROTC participants. *Athletic:* Total: 306 ($726,596); Men: 192 ($460,346); Women: 114 ($266,250).

Other Money-Saving Options Accelerated degree, co-op program, Army ROTC, Air Force ROTC, off-campus living (after sophomore year). *Payment Plan:* installment. *Waivers:* full or partial for employees or children of employees.

Contact Ms. Carolyn Sabatino, Director of Financial Aid, Ohio University, 020 Chubb Hall, Athens, OH 45701-2979, 614-593-4141.

OHIO UNIVERSITY–CHILLICOTHE
Chillicothe, Ohio

About the Institution State-supported, coed. Degrees awarded: A, B. Offers 12 undergraduate majors. Total enrollment: 1,565 (99% state residents). Freshmen: 345.

Undergraduate Expenses (1996–97) State resident tuition: $3021. Nonresident tuition: $7383.

Applications *Financial aid deadline (priority):* 4/1. *Financial aid forms:* FAFSA, institutional form required. *Admission application deadline:* 9/1.

Summary of Aid to Needy Students Federal Work-Study jobs; part-time jobs.

Loans College/university short-term loans.

Non-Need Awards *Academic Interests/Achievement Awards:* general academic. *Creative Arts/Performance Awards:* applied art and design, art/fine arts. *Special Characteristics Awards:* local/state students, members of minorities.

Other Money-Saving Options Accelerated degree, Army ROTC, cooperative Air Force ROTC. *Waivers:* full or partial for employees or children of employees and senior citizens.

Contact Office of Financial Aid, Ohio University–Chillicothe, Chillicothe, OH 45601-0629, 614-774-7200.

OHIO UNIVERSITY–EASTERN
St. Clairsville, Ohio

About the Institution State-supported, coed. Degrees awarded: A, B. Offers 77 undergraduate majors. Total enrollment: 1,050. Undergraduates: 1,000 (95% state residents). Freshmen: 300.

Undergraduate Expenses (1996–97) State resident tuition: $3021. Nonresident tuition: $7383.

Applications *Financial aid deadline (priority):* 4/1. *Financial aid forms:* FAFSA required. *Admission application deadline:* rolling.

Summary of Aid to Needy Students Federal Work-Study jobs; part-time jobs.

Loans College/university short-term loans.

Non-Need Awards *Academic Interests/Achievement Awards:* general academic. *Special Characteristics Awards:* children and siblings of alumni.

Another Money-Saving Option Accelerated degree.

Contact Office of Financial Aid, Ohio University–Eastern, St. Clairsville, OH 43950-9724, 614-695-1720.

OHIO UNIVERSITY–LANCASTER
Lancaster, Ohio

About the Institution State-supported, coed. Degrees awarded: A, B, M. Offers 21 undergraduate majors. Total enrollment: 1,500 (99% state residents). Freshmen: 340.

Undergraduate Expenses (1996–97) State resident tuition: $3021. Nonresident tuition: $7383.

Applications Of all full-time undergraduates enrolled in fall 1996, 100% of those judged to have need according to Federal Methodology were aided. *Financial aid deadline (priority):* 2/15. *Financial aid forms:*

FAFSA, CSS Financial Aid PROFILE, institutional form required. State form required for some. *Admission application deadline:* rolling.

Summary of Aid to Needy Students *From gift & self-help combined:* Average amount awarded: $3553 (70% gift aid, 30% self-help). *Gift aid:* Total: $1,900,000. Federal Work-Study jobs; 30 part-time jobs.

Need-Based Scholarships & Grants Pell, FSEOG, state, college/university.

Loans Perkins, PLUS, Stafford, Unsubsidized Stafford, college/university short-term loans.

Non-Need Awards *Academic Interests/Achievement Awards:* general academic. *Creative Arts/Performance Awards:* art/fine arts. *Special Characteristics Awards:* adult students.

Other Money-Saving Options Accelerated degree, cooperative Army ROTC, cooperative Air Force ROTC.

Contact Ms. Pat Fox, Financial Aid Coordinator, Ohio University–Lancaster, Lancaster, OH 43130-1097, 614-654-6711 Ext. 209.

OHIO UNIVERSITY–ZANESVILLE
Zanesville, Ohio

About the Institution State-supported, coed. Degrees awarded: A, B, M. Offers 8 undergraduate majors. Total enrollment: 1,195. Undergraduates: 1,078 (99% state residents). Freshmen: 209.

Undergraduate Expenses (1996–97) State resident tuition: $3036. Nonresident tuition: $7383. Mandatory fees: $15.

Applications *Financial aid deadline (priority):* 2/15. *Financial aid forms:* FAFSA required; CSS Financial Aid PROFILE acceptable. State form, institutional form required for some. *Admission application deadline:* rolling.

Summary of Aid to Needy Students Federal Work-Study jobs; part-time jobs.

Loans College/university short-term loans.

Non-Need Awards *Academic Interests/Achievement Awards:* general academic. *Special Characteristics Awards:* available.

Other Money-Saving Options *Waivers:* full or partial for employees or children of employees and senior citizens.

Contact Office of Financial Aid, Ohio University–Zanesville, Zanesville, OH 43701-2695, 614-453-0762.

OHIO WESLEYAN UNIVERSITY
Delaware, Ohio

About the Institution Independent/religious, coed. Degrees awarded: B. Offers 61 undergraduate majors. Total enrollment: 1,815 (49% state residents). Freshmen: 674.

Undergraduate Expenses (1997–98) Comprehensive fee of $25,320 includes tuition ($19,140) and college room and board ($6180). College room only: $3130.

Applications Of all full-time undergraduates enrolled in fall 1996, 92% of those who applied for aid were judged to have need according to Federal Methodology, of whom 100% were aided. *Financial aid deadline (priority):* 3/1. *Financial aid forms:* FAFSA, institutional form required; CSS Financial Aid PROFILE acceptable. State form required for some. *Regular admission application deadline:* 3/1. Early decision deadline: 12/1. Early action deadline: 12/1.

Summary of Aid to Needy Students *From gift & self-help combined:* Average need met: 93%. Average amount awarded: $17,061 (74% gift aid, 26% self-help). *Gift aid:* Total: $12,972,372 (85% from college's own funds, 3% from other college-administered sources, 12% from external sources). 718 Federal Work-Study jobs (averaging $908); 200 part-time jobs.

Need-Based Scholarships & Grants Pell, FSEOG, state, private, college/university.

Loans Perkins, PLUS, Stafford, Unsubsidized Stafford, state, private, college/university short-term loans ($150 average), college/university long-term loans ($2000 average).

Non-Need Awards In 1996, a total of 1,116 non-need awards were made. *Academic Interests/Achievement Awards:* 762 ($5,473,633 total): general academic, biological sciences, computer science, English, mathematics. *Creative Arts/Performance Awards:* 40 ($328,965 total): art/fine arts, music, theater/drama. *Special Achievements/Activities Awards:* 74 ($240,250 total): community service. *Special Characteristics Awards:* 240 ($2,227,729 total): children and siblings of alumni, children of faculty/staff, international students, members of minorities, out-of-state students, relatives of clergy, religious affiliation, twins.

Other Money-Saving Options *Payment Plan:* installment. *Waivers:* full or partial for employees or children of employees.

Contact Ms. Nancy Sanford, Associate Director of Financial Aid, Ohio Wesleyan University, 61 South Sandusky Street, Delaware, OH 43015, 614-368-3050, fax: 614-368-3314.

OHR SOMAYACH/JOSEPH TANENBAUM EDUCATIONAL CENTER
Monsey, New York

About the Institution Independent/religious, men. Offers 1 undergraduate major.

Applications *Financial aid deadline (priority):* 7/31. *Financial aid forms:* FAFSA, CSS Financial Aid PROFILE acceptable. *Admission application deadline:* rolling.

Summary of Aid to Needy Students Part-time jobs.

Another Money-Saving Option Off-campus living.

Contact Office of Financial Aid, Ohr Somayach/Joseph Tanenbaum Educational Center, Monsey, NY 10952-0334, 914-425-1370.

OKLAHOMA BAPTIST UNIVERSITY
Shawnee, Oklahoma

About the Institution Independent/religious, coed. Degrees awarded: B, M. Offers 80 undergraduate majors. Total enrollment: 2,361. Undergraduates: 2,322 (64% state residents). Freshmen: 499.

Undergraduate Expenses (1997–98 estimated) Comprehensive fee of $10,836 includes tuition ($7090), mandatory fees ($566), and college room and board ($3180). College room only: $1450.

Applications 84% of all full-time undergraduates enrolled in fall 1996 applied for aid; of these, 80% were judged to have need according to Federal Methodology, of whom 100% were aided. *Financial aid deadline (priority):* 3/1. *Financial aid forms:* FAFSA, institutional form required. State form required for some. *Admission application deadline:* 8/1.

Summary of Aid to Needy Students *From gift & self-help combined:* Average need met: 85%. Average amount awarded: $6595 (63% gift aid, 37% self-help). *Gift aid:* Total: $4,885,914 (68% from college's own funds, 3% from other college-administered sources, 29% from external sources). 225 Federal Work-Study jobs (averaging $844); 400 part-time jobs.

Need-Based Scholarships & Grants Pell, FSEOG, state.

Loans Perkins, PLUS, Stafford, Unsubsidized Stafford, college/university long-term loans ($1000 average).

Non-Need Awards In 1996, a total of 3,038 non-need awards were made. *Academic Interests/Achievement Awards:* 1,068 ($1,430,784 total): general academic, religion/biblical studies. *Creative Arts/Performance Awards:* 168 ($106,550 total): art/fine arts, creative writing, journalism/publications, music. *Special Achievements/Activities Awards:* 154 ($72,400 total): hobbies/interest, leadership, religious involvement. *Special Characteristics Awards:* 1,540 ($783,155 total): general special characteristics, children and siblings of alumni, children

of faculty/staff, local/state students, out-of-state students, relatives of clergy, religious affiliation. *Athletic:* Total: 108 ($459,954); Men: 66 ($286,213); Women: 42 ($173,741).

Other Money-Saving Options Co-op program, cooperative Air Force ROTC, off-campus living (after junior year). *Payment Plan:* installment. *Waivers:* full or partial for employees or children of employees and senior citizens.

Contact Student Financial Services, Oklahoma Baptist University, 200 Thurmond Hall, Shawnee, OK 74801-2558, 405-878-2016.

OKLAHOMA CHRISTIAN UNIVERSITY OF SCIENCE AND ARTS
Oklahoma City, Oklahoma

About the Institution Independent/religious, coed. Degrees awarded: B, M. Offers 62 undergraduate majors. Total enrollment: 1,562. Undergraduates: 1,534 (46% state residents). Freshmen: 387.

Undergraduate Expenses (1996–97) Comprehensive fee of $11,318 includes tuition ($7000), mandatory fees ($478), and college room and board ($3840).

Applications 81% of all full-time undergraduates enrolled in fall 1996 applied for aid; of these, 91% were judged to have need according to Federal Methodology, of whom 100% were aided. *Financial aid deadline (priority):* 4/15. *Financial aid forms:* FAFSA, institutional form required; CSS Financial Aid PROFILE acceptable. State form required for some. *Admission application deadline:* rolling.

Summary of Aid to Needy Students *From gift & self-help combined:* Average need met: 78%. Average amount awarded: $7314 (62% gift aid, 38% self-help). *Gift aid:* Total: $4,700,000 (81% from college's own funds, 7% from other college-administered sources, 12% from external sources). 230 Federal Work-Study jobs (averaging $1200); 100 part-time jobs.

Need-Based Scholarships & Grants Pell, FSEOG, state, private, college/university.

Loans Perkins, PLUS, Stafford, Unsubsidized Stafford.

Non-Need Awards In 1996, a total of 1,388 non-need awards were made. *Academic Interests/Achievement Awards:* 839 ($1,000,000 total): general academic, business, communication, computer science, education, engineering/technologies, religion/biblical studies. *Creative Arts/Performance Awards:* 91 ($194,000 total): art/fine arts, journalism/publications, music, performing arts, theater/drama. *Special Achievements/Activities Awards:* 44 ($33,000 total): leadership, religious involvement. *Special Characteristics Awards:* 283 ($521,000 total): general special characteristics, children and siblings of alumni, children of current students, children of educators, children of faculty/staff, international students, parents of current students, ROTC participants, siblings of current students, spouses of current students. *Athletic:* Total: 131 ($786,000); Men: 79 ($489,000); Women: 52 ($297,000).

Other Money-Saving Options Accelerated degree, cooperative Army ROTC, cooperative Air Force ROTC. *Payment Plan:* tuition prepayment. *Waivers:* full or partial for employees or children of employees.

Contact Office of Financial Aid, Oklahoma Christian University of Science and Arts, Box 11000, Oklahoma City, OK 73136-1100, 405-425-5000.

OKLAHOMA CITY UNIVERSITY
Oklahoma City, Oklahoma

About the Institution Independent/religious, coed. Degrees awarded: A, B, M, P. Offers 68 undergraduate majors. Total enrollment: 4,696. Undergraduates: 2,421 (74% state residents). Freshmen: 317.

Undergraduate Expenses (1996–97) Comprehensive fee of $12,125 includes tuition ($8050), mandatory fees ($85), and college room and board ($3990). College room only: $1820.

Applications 72% of all full-time undergraduates enrolled in fall 1996 applied for aid; of these, 63% were judged to have need according to Federal Methodology, of whom 100% were aided. *Financial aid deadline (priority):* 3/1. *Financial aid forms:* FAFSA, institutional form required. *Admission application deadline:* rolling.

Summary of Aid to Needy Students *Gift aid:* Total: $2,889,086. 165 Federal Work-Study jobs (averaging $1833); 105 part-time jobs.

Need-Based Scholarships & Grants Pell, FSEOG, state, private, college/university.

Loans Perkins, PLUS, Stafford, Unsubsidized Stafford, private, college/university short-term loans ($400 average).

Non-Need Awards *Academic Interests/Achievement Awards:* general academic, religion/biblical studies. *Creative Arts/Performance Awards:* dance, music, performing arts. *Special Achievements/Activities Awards:* general special achievements/activities, cheerleading/drum major, Junior Miss, leadership, religious involvement. *Special Characteristics Awards:* children of faculty/staff, relatives of clergy. *Athletic:* Total: 127 ($467,601); Men: 77 ($260,456); Women: 50 ($207,145).

Other Money-Saving Options Co-op program, cooperative Army ROTC, cooperative Air Force ROTC. *Payment Plans:* installment, deferred payment. *Waivers:* full or partial for employees or children of employees.

Contact Financial Aid Office, Oklahoma City University, 2501 North Blackwelder, Oklahoma City, OK 73106-1402, 405-521-5211.

OKLAHOMA PANHANDLE STATE UNIVERSITY
Goodwell, Oklahoma

About the Institution State-supported, coed. Degrees awarded: A, B. Offers 32 undergraduate majors. Total enrollment: 1,366 (50% state residents). Freshmen: 225.

Undergraduate Expenses (1996–97) State resident tuition: $1333 (minimum). Nonresident tuition: $3612 (minimum). Mandatory fees: $320. College room and board: $2070 (minimum). College room only: $670.

Applications *Financial aid deadline (priority):* 8/25. *Financial aid forms:* FAFSA required; CSS Financial Aid PROFILE acceptable. *Admission application deadline:* rolling.

Summary of Aid to Needy Students Federal Work-Study jobs; part-time jobs.

Loans College/university short-term loans, college/university long-term loans.

Non-Need Awards *Academic Interests/Achievement Awards:* general academic. *Creative Arts/Performance Awards:* cinema/film/broadcasting, debating, music, theater/drama. *Special Achievements/Activities Awards:* general special achievements/activities, cheerleading/drum major, rodeo. *Special Characteristics Awards:* general special characteristics. *Athletic:* available.

Other Money-Saving Options Accelerated degree, co-op program, off-campus living (after freshman year). *Waivers:* full or partial for employees or children of employees.

Contact Office of Financial Aid, Oklahoma Panhandle State University, PO Box 430, Goodwell, OK 73939-0430, 405-349-2611.

OKLAHOMA STATE UNIVERSITY
Stillwater, Oklahoma

About the Institution State-supported, coed. Degrees awarded: B, M, D, P. Offers 139 undergraduate majors. Total enrollment: 19,201. Undergraduates: 14,640 (82% state residents). Freshmen: 2,442.

Undergraduate Expenses (1996–97) State resident tuition: $1248 (minimum). Nonresident tuition: $4020 (minimum). Mandatory fees: $460 (minimum). College room and board: $4160 (minimum). College room only: $1904 (minimum).

Applications Of all full-time undergraduates enrolled in fall 1996, 68% of those who applied for aid were judged to have need according to Federal Methodology, of whom 99% were aided. *Financial aid deadline (priority):* 3/1. *Financial aid forms:* FAFSA required. *Admission application deadline:* rolling.

Summary of Aid to Needy Students *From gift & self-help combined:* Average need met: 85%. Average amount awarded: $8057 (32% gift aid, 68% self-help). *Gift aid:* Total: $15,879,000 (37% from college's own funds, 4% from other college-administered sources, 59% from external sources). 700 Federal Work-Study jobs (averaging $1875); 2,300 part-time jobs.

Need-Based Scholarships & Grants Pell, FSEOG, state, private, college/university.

Loans Perkins, PLUS, Stafford, Unsubsidized Stafford, college/university short-term loans ($300 average), college/university long-term loans ($1550 average).

Non-Need Awards In 1996, a total of 7,518 non-need awards were made. *Academic Interests/Achievement Awards:* 5,300 ($4,668,600 total): general academic, agriculture, architecture, area/ethnic studies, biological sciences, business, communication, computer science, education, engineering/technologies, English, foreign languages, home economics, humanities, international studies, mathematics, military science, physical sciences, premedicine, social sciences. *Creative Arts/Performance Awards:* 300 ($188,800 total): music. *Special Characteristics Awards:* 1,000 ($2,719,900 total): adult students, children and siblings of alumni, members of minorities, out-of-state students, ROTC participants. *Athletic:* Total: 918 ($1,583,500); Men: 642 ($1,138,600); Women: 276 ($444,900).

Other Money-Saving Options Accelerated degree, co-op program, Army ROTC, Air Force ROTC, off-campus living (after freshman year). *Payment Plans:* installment, deferred payment. *Waivers:* full or partial for minority students and children of alumni.

Contact Office of Student Financial Aid, Oklahoma State University, 101 Hanner Hall, Stillwater, OK 74078, 405-744-6604, fax: 405-744-6438.

OLD DOMINION UNIVERSITY
Norfolk, Virginia

About the Institution State-supported, coed. Degrees awarded: B, M, D. Offers 97 undergraduate majors. Total enrollment: 11,400. Undergraduates: 7,686 (91% state residents). Freshmen: 1,540.

Undergraduate Expenses (1997–98) State resident tuition: $4110. Nonresident tuition: $10,650. Mandatory fees: $140. College room and board: $4866.

Applications *Financial aid deadline (priority):* 4/1. *Financial aid forms:* FAFSA required. State form, institutional form required for some. *Admission application deadline:* 5/1.

Summary of Aid to Needy Students *From gift & self-help combined:* Average need met: 70%. Average amount awarded: $6821 (40% gift aid, 60% self-help). *Gift aid:* Total: $15,435,936 (18% from college's own funds, 39% from other college-administered sources, 43% from external sources). 338 Federal Work-Study jobs (averaging $2000); 1,000 part-time jobs.

Need-Based Scholarships & Grants Pell, FSEOG, state, private, college/university.

Loans Perkins, PLUS, Stafford, Unsubsidized Stafford, Federal Nursing, state, private.

Non-Need Awards In 1996, a total of 514 non-need awards were made. *Academic Interests/Achievement Awards:* 53 ($33,054 total):

general academic, biological sciences, business, computer science, engineering/technologies, English, health fields, humanities, mathematics, physical sciences. *Creative Arts/Performance Awards:* 61 ($38,123 total): art/fine arts, dance, music, performing arts, theater/drama. *Special Achievements/Activities Awards:* 17 ($32,530 total): community service, leadership, memberships, religious involvement. *Special Characteristics Awards:* 204 ($495,171 total): adult students, children of faculty/staff, handicapped students, international students, local/state students, members of minorities, out-of-state students, previous college experience, ROTC participants. *Athletic:* Total: 179 ($1,372,808); Men: 89 ($627,202); Women: 90 ($745,606).

Other Money-Saving Options Accelerated degree, co-op program, Army ROTC, Naval ROTC, off-campus living. *Payment Plans:* installment, deferred payment. *Waivers:* full or partial for employees or children of employees and senior citizens.

Contact Ms. Karen Rostov, Scholarship Coordinator, Old Dominion University, 121 Rollins Hall, Norfolk, VA 23529-0052, 757-683-5524, fax: 757-683-5920.

OLIVET COLLEGE
Olivet, Michigan

About the Institution Independent/religious, coed. Degrees awarded: B. Offers 37 undergraduate majors. Total enrollment: 831 (83% state residents). Freshmen: 241.

Undergraduate Expenses (1997–98) Comprehensive fee of $16,698 includes tuition ($12,524), mandatory fees ($136), and college room and board ($4038). College room only: $2164.

Applications 95% of all full-time undergraduates enrolled in fall 1996 applied for aid; of these, 98% were judged to have need according to Federal Methodology, of whom 100% were aided. *Financial aid deadline (priority):* 3/15. *Financial aid forms:* FAFSA required. *Admission application deadline:* 9/1.

Summary of Aid to Needy Students *From gift & self-help combined:* Average need met: 93%. Average amount awarded: $12,556 (61% gift aid, 39% self-help). *Gift aid:* Total: $5,427,396 (63% from college's own funds, 25% from other college-administered sources, 12% from external sources). 105 Federal Work-Study jobs (averaging $1300); 424 part-time jobs.

Need-Based Scholarships & Grants Pell, FSEOG, state, college/university.

Loans Perkins, PLUS, Stafford, Unsubsidized Stafford, state.

Non-Need Awards In 1996, a total of 126 non-need awards were made. *Academic Interests/Achievement Awards:* 19 ($50,475 total): general academic. *Creative Arts/Performance Awards:* 14 ($15,500 total): music. *Special Achievements/Activities Awards:* 93 ($299,455 total): community service, leadership.

Other Money-Saving Options Accelerated degree, off-campus living (after junior year). *Payment Plan:* installment. *Waivers:* full or partial for employees or children of employees.

Contact Mr. Bernie McConnell, Director of Admissions, Olivet College, 320 South Main, Olivet, MI 49076-9701, 800-456-7189, fax: 616-749-3821.

OLIVET NAZARENE UNIVERSITY
Kankakee, Illinois

About the Institution Independent/religious, coed. Degrees awarded: A, B, M. Offers 85 undergraduate majors. Total enrollment: 2,256. Undergraduates: 1,593 (40% state residents). Freshmen: 389.

Undergraduate Expenses (1996–97) Comprehensive fee of $14,626 includes tuition ($10,026), mandatory fees ($140), and college room and board ($4460). College room only: $2230.

Applications Of all full-time undergraduates enrolled in fall 1996, 91% of those who applied for aid were judged to have need according to Federal Methodology, of whom 99% were aided. *Financial aid deadline (priority):* 3/1. *Financial aid forms:* FAFSA, institutional form required. *Admission application deadline:* 8/1.

Summary of Aid to Needy Students *From gift & self-help combined:* Average need met: 97%. Average amount awarded: $11,077 (66% gift aid, 34% self-help). *Gift aid:* Total: $7,925,494 (60% from college's own funds, 25% from other college-administered sources, 15% from external sources). 282 Federal Work-Study jobs (averaging $892); 262 part-time jobs.

Need-Based Scholarships & Grants Pell, FSEOG, state, private, college/university.

Loans Perkins, PLUS, Stafford, Unsubsidized Stafford, private.

Non-Need Awards In 1996, a total of 2,402 non-need awards were made. *Academic Interests/Achievement Awards:* 653 ($1,482,857 total): general academic. *Creative Arts/Performance Awards:* 58 ($45,825 total): art/fine arts, music. *Special Achievements/Activities Awards:* 704 ($702,917 total): religious involvement. *Special Characteristics Awards:* 910 ($1,942,247 total): general special characteristics, children of current students, children of faculty/staff, international students, parents of current students, relatives of clergy, religious affiliation, ROTC participants, siblings of current students, spouses of current students. *Athletic:* Total: 77 ($784,590); Men: 52 ($548,258); Women: 25 ($236,332).

Other Money-Saving Options Accelerated degree, co-op program, cooperative Army ROTC. *Payment Plan:* installment. *Waivers:* full or partial for employees or children of employees.

Contact Mr. Greg Bruner, Assistant Director of Financial Aid, Olivet Nazarene University, PO Box 592, Kankakee, IL 60901-0592, 815-939-5249, fax: 815-939-5074.

O'MORE COLLEGE OF DESIGN
Franklin, Tennessee

About the Institution Independent, primarily women. Degrees awarded: A, B. Offers 4 undergraduate majors. Total enrollment: 151 (80% state residents). Freshmen: 60.

Undergraduate Expenses (1997–98) Tuition: $7950. Mandatory fees: $5.

Applications 63% of all full-time undergraduates enrolled in fall 1996 applied for aid; of these, 100% were judged to have need according to Federal Methodology, of whom 100% were aided. *Financial aid deadline (priority):* 7/1. *Financial aid forms:* FAFSA, institutional form required. *Admission application deadline:* 8/1.

Summary of Aid to Needy Students *From gift & self-help combined:* Average need met: 65%. Average amount awarded: $5000. Part-time jobs.

Need-Based Scholarships & Grants Pell, college/university.

Loans PLUS, Stafford, Unsubsidized Stafford.

Non-Need Awards In 1996, a total of 6 non-need awards were made. *Academic Interests/Achievement Awards:* 6 ($15,000 total): general academic.

Contact Office of Financial Aid, O'More College of Design, Franklin, TN 37064-2816, 615-794-4254.

ORAL ROBERTS UNIVERSITY
Tulsa, Oklahoma

About the Institution Independent/religious, coed. Degrees awarded: B, M, D. Offers 79 undergraduate majors. Total enrollment: 3,761. Undergraduates: 3,001 (14% state residents). Freshmen: 564.

Undergraduate Expenses (1997–98) Comprehensive fee of $14,658 includes tuition ($9674), mandatory fees ($260), and college room and board ($4724). College room only: $2208.

Applications 72% of all full-time undergraduates enrolled in fall 1996 applied for aid; of these, 94% were judged to have need according to Federal Methodology, of whom 99% were aided. *Financial aid deadline (priority):* 3/1. *Financial aid forms:* FAFSA required. *Regular admission application deadline:* rolling. Early action deadline: 9/1.

Summary of Aid to Needy Students *From gift & self-help combined:* Average need met: 80%. Average amount awarded: $12,632 (37% gift aid, 63% self-help). *Gift aid:* Total: $8,559,842 (69% from college's own funds, 4% from other college-administered sources, 27% from external sources). 500 Federal Work-Study jobs (averaging $1400); 750 part-time jobs.

Need-Based Scholarships & Grants Pell, FSEOG, state, private, college/university.

Loans Perkins, PLUS, Stafford, Unsubsidized Stafford, college/university short-term loans, college/university long-term loans ($1750 average).

Non-Need Awards In 1996, a total of 3,136 non-need awards were made. *Academic Interests/Achievement Awards:* 1,526 ($1,988,996 total): general academic, engineering/technologies, health fields. *Creative Arts/Performance Awards:* 306 ($268,791 total): art/fine arts, cinema/film/broadcasting, journalism/publications, music. *Special Achievements/Activities Awards:* 526 ($404,640 total): cheerleading/drum major, community service, leadership, memberships, religious involvement. *Special Characteristics Awards:* 596 ($496,080 total): children and siblings of alumni, children of faculty/staff, international students, relatives of clergy, siblings of current students. *Athletic:* Total: 182 ($1,177,881); Men: 98 ($764,181); Women: 84 ($413,700).

Other Money-Saving Options Accelerated degree. *Payment Plan:* installment. *Waivers:* full or partial for employees or children of employees.

Contact Mr. Mike Watson, Computer Coordinator, Oral Roberts University, PO Box 700540, Tulsa, OK 76170, 918-495-6513, fax: 918-495-6803.

OREGON COLLEGE OF ART AND CRAFT
Portland, Oregon

About the Institution Independent, coed. Degrees awarded: B. Offers 3 undergraduate majors. Total enrollment: 91 (44% state residents). Freshmen: 33.

Undergraduate Expenses (1996–97) Tuition: $9828. Mandatory fees: $90.

Applications 66% of all full-time undergraduates enrolled in fall 1996 applied for aid; of these, 95% were judged to have need according to Federal Methodology, of whom 86% were aided. *Financial aid deadline (priority):* 4/15. *Financial aid forms:* FAFSA, institutional form required.

Summary of Aid to Needy Students *From gift & self-help combined:* Average need met: 40%. Average amount awarded: $7617 (38% gift aid, 62% self-help). *Gift aid:* Total: $57,738 (46% from college's own funds, 6% from other college-administered sources, 48% from external sources). 5 Federal Work-Study jobs (averaging $1206); 35 part-time jobs.

Need-Based Scholarships & Grants Pell, FSEOG, state, college/university.

Loans PLUS, Stafford, Unsubsidized Stafford.

Non-Need Awards Not offered.

Another Money-Saving Option *Payment Plan:* installment.

Contact Mr. Paul Krull, Director of Financial Aid, Oregon College of Art and Craft, 8245 Southwest Barnes Road, Portland, OR 97225, 503-297-5544, fax: 503-297-9651.

OREGON INSTITUTE OF TECHNOLOGY
Klamath Falls, Oregon

About the Institution State-supported, coed. Degrees awarded: A, B, M. Offers 20 undergraduate majors. Total enrollment: 2,339 (87% state residents). Freshmen: 302.

Undergraduate Expenses (1996–97) State resident tuition: $3144. Nonresident tuition: $10,083. College room and board: $3910.

Applications Of all full-time undergraduates enrolled in fall 1996, 96% of those who applied for aid were judged to have need according to Federal Methodology, of whom 75% were aided. *Financial aid deadline (priority):* 3/1. *Financial aid forms:* FAFSA, CSS Financial Aid PROFILE acceptable. State form required for some. *Admission application deadline:* 6/1.

Summary of Aid to Needy Students *From gift & self-help combined:* Average need met: 92%. Average amount awarded: $7969 (48% gift aid, 52% self-help). *Gift aid:* Total: $4,157,721 (31% from college's own funds, 7% from other college-administered sources, 62% from external sources). 366 Federal Work-Study jobs (averaging $1350); 400 part-time jobs.

Need-Based Scholarships & Grants Pell, FSEOG, state, private, college/university.

Loans Perkins, PLUS, Stafford, Unsubsidized Stafford, college/university short-term loans ($100 average), college/university long-term loans ($1000 average).

Non-Need Awards In 1996, a total of 168 non-need awards were made. *Academic Interests/Achievement Awards:* 74 ($97,800 total): general academic. *Special Characteristics Awards:* 50 ($159,804 total): ethnic background, members of minorities. *Athletic:* Total: 44 ($94,645); Men: 28 ($60,403); Women: 16 ($34,242).

Other Money-Saving Options Co-op program, off-campus living. *Payment Plans:* installment, deferred payment. *Waivers:* full or partial for employees or children of employees.

Contact Financial Aid Office, Oregon Institute of Technology, Klamath Falls, OR 97601-8801, 541-885-1280.

OREGON SCHOOL OF ART AND CRAFT
Portland, Oregon

See Oregon College of Art and Craft

OREGON STATE UNIVERSITY
Corvallis, Oregon

About the Institution State-supported, coed. Degrees awarded: B, M, D, P. Offers 124 undergraduate majors. Total enrollment: 13,784. Undergraduates: 11,096 (82% state residents). Freshmen: 1,975.

Undergraduate Expenses (1996–97) State resident tuition: $2694. Nonresident tuition: $10,332. Mandatory fees: $753. College room and board: $4587.

Applications *Financial aid deadline (priority):* 2/1. *Financial aid forms:* FAFSA required. *Admission application deadline:* 3/1.

Summary of Aid to Needy Students Federal Work-Study jobs; part-time jobs.

Need-Based Scholarships & Grants Pell, FSEOG, state, private, college/university.

Loans Perkins, PLUS, Stafford, Unsubsidized Stafford, college/university short-term loans ($300 average), college/university long-term loans ($1000 average).

Non-Need Awards *Academic Interests/Achievement Awards:* general academic. *Creative Arts/Performance Awards:* music. *Special Characteristics Awards:* general special characteristics. *Athletic:* Total: 360 ($2,300,000).

Other Money-Saving Options Co-op program, Army ROTC, Naval ROTC, Air Force ROTC, off-campus living. *Payment Plan:* deferred payment.

Contact Financial Aid Office, Oregon State University, 218 Kerr Administration Building, Corvallis, OR 97331-2120, 541-737-2241.

OTIS COLLEGE OF ART AND DESIGN
Los Angeles, California

About the Institution Independent, coed. Degrees awarded: B, M. Offers 13 undergraduate majors. Total enrollment: 771. Undergraduates: 752 (61% state residents). Freshmen: 240.

Undergraduate Expenses (1996–97) Tuition: $14,900. Mandatory fees: $450.

Applications 59% of all full-time undergraduates enrolled in fall 1996 applied for aid; of these, 98% were judged to have need according to Federal Methodology, of whom 100% were aided. *Financial aid deadline (priority):* 3/1. *Financial aid forms:* FAFSA, CSS Financial Aid PROFILE, institutional form required. *Admission application deadline:* rolling.

Summary of Aid to Needy Students *From gift & self-help combined:* Average amount awarded: $12,395 (60% gift aid, 40% self-help). *Gift aid:* Total: $2,958,340 (65% from college's own funds, 20% from other college-administered sources, 15% from external sources). 64 Federal Work-Study jobs (averaging $1000); 75 part-time jobs.

Need-Based Scholarships & Grants Pell, FSEOG, state, college/university.

Loans Perkins, PLUS, Stafford, Unsubsidized Stafford, private.

Non-Need Awards *Creative Arts/Performance Awards:* applied art and design , art/fine arts.

Another Money-Saving Option Co-op program.

Contact Ms. Jaris A. Wise, Director of Financial Aid, Otis College of Art and Design, 9045 Lincoln Boulevard, Los Angeles, CA 90045-9785, 310-665-6880, fax: 310-665-6805.

OTTAWA UNIVERSITY
Ottawa, Kansas

About the Institution Independent/religious, coed. Degrees awarded: B, M. Offers 22 undergraduate majors. Total enrollment: 575 (67% state residents). Freshmen: 129.

Undergraduate Expenses (1996–97) Comprehensive fee of $12,910 includes tuition ($8850), mandatory fees ($140), and college room and board ($3920 minimum). College room only: $1500 (minimum).

Applications Of all full-time undergraduates enrolled in fall 1996, 89% of those who applied for aid were judged to have need according to Federal Methodology, of whom 100% were aided. *Financial aid deadline (priority):* 8/1. *Financial aid forms:* FAFSA, institutional form required; CSS Financial Aid PROFILE acceptable. State form required for some. *Admission application deadline:* rolling.

Summary of Aid to Needy Students *From gift & self-help combined:* Average need met: 90%. Average amount awarded: $10,600 (51% gift aid, 49% self-help). *Gift aid:* Total: $2,532,332 (67% from college's own funds, 16% from other college-administered sources, 17% from external sources). 200 Federal Work-Study jobs (averaging $1360); 100 part-time jobs.

Need-Based Scholarships & Grants Pell, FSEOG, state, private, college/university.

Loans Perkins, PLUS, Stafford, Unsubsidized Stafford, college/university short-term loans ($411 average), college/university long-term loans ($3500 average).

Non-Need Awards *Academic Interests/Achievement Awards:* 260 ($775,000 total): general academic, biological sciences, business, communication, education, English, foreign languages, health fields, humanities, international studies, mathematics, physical sciences, premedicine, religion/biblical studies, social sciences. *Creative Arts/Performance Awards:* 40 ($100,000 total): art/fine arts, music, theater/drama. *Special Achievements/Activities Awards:* 56 ($140,000 total): general special achievements/activities, cheerleading/drum major, Junior Miss, religious involvement. *Special Characteristics Awards:* 72 ($180,000 total): children and siblings of alumni, children of faculty/staff, local/state students, religious affiliation. *Athletic:* available.

Other Money-Saving Options Accelerated degree, off-campus living (after junior year). *Payment Plans:* installment, deferred payment. *Waivers:* full or partial for employees or children of employees.

Contact Mr. Ronald C. Yingling, Financial Aid Administrator, Ottawa University, 1001 South Cedar, Ottawa, KS 66067-3399, 913-242-5200 Ext. 5570, fax: 913-242-7429.

OTTERBEIN COLLEGE
Westerville, Ohio

About the Institution Independent/religious, coed. Degrees awarded: B, M. Offers 63 undergraduate majors. Total enrollment: 2,526. Undergraduates: 2,370 (86% state residents). Freshmen: 473.

Undergraduate Expenses (1997–98) Comprehensive fee of $19,747 includes tuition ($14,997) and college room and board ($4750). College room only: $2100.

Applications Of all full-time undergraduates enrolled in fall 1996, 92% of those who applied for aid were judged to have need according to Federal Methodology, of whom 98% were aided. *Financial aid deadline (priority):* 4/1. *Financial aid forms:* FAFSA required. Institutional form required for some. *Admission application deadline:* 4/20.

Summary of Aid to Needy Students *From gift & self-help combined:* Average need met: 80%. Average amount awarded: $13,638 (65% gift aid, 35% self-help). *Gift aid:* Total: $9,081,120 (74% from college's own funds, 18% from other college-administered sources, 8% from external sources). 775 Federal Work-Study jobs (averaging $1000); 109 part-time jobs.

Need-Based Scholarships & Grants Pell, FSEOG, state, private, college/university.

Loans Perkins, PLUS, Stafford, Unsubsidized Stafford, Federal Nursing, private, college/university long-term loans ($750 average).

Non-Need Awards In 1996, a total of 1,250 non-need awards were made. *Academic Interests/Achievement Awards:* 668 ($3,046,554 total): general academic. *Creative Arts/Performance Awards:* 253 ($354,226 total): art/fine arts, music, theater/drama. *Special Achievements/Activities Awards:* 64 ($62,533 total): community service, leadership. *Special Characteristics Awards:* 265 ($629,994 total): general special characteristics, children and siblings of alumni, children of faculty/staff, international students, members of minorities, previous college experience, relatives of clergy, siblings of current students.

Other Money-Saving Options Accelerated degree, cooperative Army ROTC, cooperative Air Force ROTC, off-campus living (after sophomore year). *Payment Plan:* installment. *Waivers:* full or partial for employees or children of employees.

Contact Mr. Thomas V. Yarnell, Director of Financial Aid, Otterbein College, Westerville, OH 43081, 614-823-1502, fax: 614-823-1200.

OUACHITA BAPTIST UNIVERSITY
Arkadelphia, Arkansas

About the Institution Independent/religious, coed. Degrees awarded: B. Offers 50 undergraduate majors. Total enrollment: 1,604 (65% state residents). Freshmen: 451.

Undergraduate Expenses (1997–98) Comprehensive fee of $11,010 includes tuition ($7970), mandatory fees ($120), and college room and board ($2920). College room only: $1390.

Applications 63% of all full-time undergraduates enrolled in fall 1996 applied for aid; of these, 84% were judged to have need according to Federal Methodology, of whom 99% were aided. *Financial aid deadline:* Applications processed continuously. *Financial aid forms:* FAFSA, institutional form required. State form required for some. *Admission application deadline:* 8/15.

Summary of Aid to Needy Students *From gift & self-help combined:* Average need met: 100%. Average amount awarded: $8200 (59% gift aid, 41% self-help). *Gift aid:* Total: $3,841,357 (63% from college's own funds, 4% from other college-administered sources, 33% from external sources). 550 Federal Work-Study jobs (averaging $1400); 200 part-time jobs.

Need-Based Scholarships & Grants Pell, FSEOG, state, private, college/university.

Loans Perkins, PLUS, Stafford, Unsubsidized Stafford, college/university short-term loans ($500 average).

Non-Need Awards In 1996, a total of 1,332 non-need awards were made. *Academic Interests/Achievement Awards:* 678 ($1,709,750 total): general academic, religion/biblical studies. *Creative Arts/Performance Awards:* 146 ($374,500 total): music. *Special Achievements/Activities Awards:* 177 ($261,800 total): community service, leadership, religious involvement. *Special Characteristics Awards:* 214 ($1,117,000 total): children of faculty/staff, international students, relatives of clergy, religious affiliation. *Athletic:* Total: 117 ($686,567); Men: 87 ($475,000); Women: 30 ($211,567).

Other Money-Saving Options Accelerated degree, co-op program. *Payment Plan:* installment. *Waivers:* full or partial for employees or children of employees.

Contact Mrs. Susan Hurst, Director of Financial Aid, Ouachita Baptist University, Box 3774, Arkadelphia, AR 71998-0001, 501-245-5570, fax: 501-245-5500.

OUR LADY OF HOLY CROSS COLLEGE
New Orleans, Louisiana

About the Institution Independent/religious, coed. Degrees awarded: A, B, M. Offers 22 undergraduate majors. Total enrollment: 1,316. Undergraduates: 1,182 (98% state residents). Freshmen: 266.

Undergraduate Expenses (1996–97) Tuition: $4800. Mandatory fees: $312.

Applications *Financial aid deadline (priority):* 4/15. *Financial aid forms:* FAFSA, institutional form required. *Admission application deadline:* rolling.

Summary of Aid to Needy Students *From gift & self-help combined:* Average need met: 50%. Average amount awarded: $4816 (23% gift aid, 77% self-help). *Gift aid:* Total: $751,850 (8% from college's own funds, 12% from other college-administered sources, 80% from external sources). 8 Federal Work-Study jobs (averaging $3812); 10 part-time jobs.

Need-Based Scholarships & Grants Pell, FSEOG, state.

Loans PLUS, Stafford, Unsubsidized Stafford, private.

Non-Need Awards In 1996, a total of 17 non-need awards were made. *Academic Interests/Achievement Awards:* 17 ($60,608 total): general academic.

Other Money-Saving Options Co-op program, cooperative Army ROTC, cooperative Naval ROTC, cooperative Air Force ROTC. *Waivers:* full or partial for employees or children of employees.

Contact Mr. Frank Candalisa, Director of Financial Aid, Our Lady of Holy Cross College, 4123 Woodland Drive, New Orleans, LA 70131-7399, 504-394-7744, fax: 504-391-2421.

OUR LADY OF THE LAKE UNIVERSITY OF SAN ANTONIO
San Antonio, Texas

About the Institution Independent/religious, coed. Degrees awarded: B, M, D. Offers 38 undergraduate majors. Total enrollment: 3,468. Undergraduates: 2,365 (98% state residents). Freshmen: 358.

Undergraduate Expenses (1996–97) Comprehensive fee of $13,094 includes tuition ($9540), mandatory fees ($254), and college room and board ($3300 minimum). College room only: $1900 (minimum).

Applications 93% of all full-time undergraduates enrolled in fall 1996 applied for aid; of these, 95% were judged to have need according to Federal Methodology, of whom 100% were aided. *Financial aid deadline:* continuous. *Financial aid forms:* FAFSA required. *Admission application deadline:* rolling.

Summary of Aid to Needy Students *From gift & self-help combined:* Average amount awarded: $11,863 (45% gift aid, 55% self-help). *Gift aid:* Total: $5,728,807 (44% from college's own funds, 26% from other college-administered sources, 30% from external sources). 250 Federal Work-Study jobs (averaging $1600); part-time jobs.

Need-Based Scholarships & Grants Pell, FSEOG, state, college/university.

Loans Perkins, PLUS, Stafford, Unsubsidized Stafford, state, private.

Non-Need Awards *Academic Interests/Achievement Awards:* 401 ($1,500,000 total): general academic. *Creative Arts/Performance Awards:* music. *Special Characteristics Awards:* children of faculty/staff.

Other Money-Saving Options Accelerated degree, co-op program, cooperative Army ROTC, cooperative Air Force ROTC, off-campus living. *Payment Plan:* installment. *Waivers:* full or partial for employees or children of employees.

Contact Mr. Jeff R. Scofield, Director of Financial Aid, Our Lady of the Lake University of San Antonio, San Antonio, TX 78207-4689, 210-434-6711 Ext. 320.

OZARK CHRISTIAN COLLEGE
Joplin, Missouri

About the Institution Independent/religious, coed. Degrees awarded: A, B. Offers 7 undergraduate majors. Total enrollment: 661 (30% state residents). Freshmen: 181.

Undergraduate Expenses (1997–98) Comprehensive fee of $7245 includes tuition ($3520), mandatory fees ($505), and college room and board ($3220). College room only: $1540.

Applications *Financial aid deadline (priority):* 4/15. *Financial aid forms:* FAFSA, institutional form required. *Admission application deadline:* 8/15.

Summary of Aid to Needy Students *Gift aid:* Total: $517,787 (12% from college's own funds, 4% from other college-administered sources, 84% from external sources). 30 Federal Work-Study jobs (averaging $1200); 200 part-time jobs.

Need-Based Scholarships & Grants Pell, FSEOG, private, college/university.

Loans PLUS, Stafford, Unsubsidized Stafford, college/university long-term loans ($500 average).

Non-Need Awards *Academic Interests/Achievement Awards:* general academic, religion/biblical studies. *Creative Arts/Performance Awards:* music. *Special Achievements/Activities Awards:* religious involvement. *Special Characteristics Awards:* children of faculty/staff, religious affiliation.

Other Money-Saving Options *Payment Plans:* installment, deferred payment. *Waivers:* full or partial for employees or children of employees and senior citizens.

Contact Ms. Carol Perry, Director of Financial Aid, Ozark Christian College, 1111 North Main Street, Joplin, MO 64801-4804, 417-624-2518 Ext. 2032, fax: 417-624-0090.

PACE UNIVERSITY
New York, New York

About the Institution Independent, coed. Degrees awarded: A, B, M, D, P. Offers 70 undergraduate majors. Total enrollment: 11,915. Undergraduates: 7,901 (75% state residents). Freshmen: 1,370.

Undergraduate Expenses (1996–97) Comprehensive fee of $18,370 includes tuition ($12,710), mandatory fees ($320), and college room and board ($5340). College room only: $3900.

Applications Of all full-time undergraduates enrolled in fall 1996, 53% of those who applied for aid were judged to have need according to Federal Methodology, of whom 99% were aided. *Financial aid deadline (priority):* 2/8. *Financial aid forms:* FAFSA required; CSS Financial Aid PROFILE acceptable. State form required for some. *Regular admission application deadline:* 8/15. Early action deadline: 11/1.

Summary of Aid to Needy Students *From gift & self-help combined:* Average need met: 66%. Average amount awarded: $8350 (83% gift aid, 17% self-help). *Gift aid:* Total: $18,973,796 (34% from college's own funds, 4% from other college-administered sources, 62% from external sources). 258 Federal Work-Study jobs (averaging $2500); 650 part-time jobs.

Need-Based Scholarships & Grants Pell, FSEOG, state, private, college/university.

Loans Perkins, PLUS, Stafford, Unsubsidized Stafford, Federal Nursing, private, college/university short-term loans ($50 average).

Non-Need Awards *Academic Interests/Achievement Awards:* general academic. *Special Achievements/Activities Awards:* leadership. *Special Characteristics Awards:* out-of-state students. *Athletic:* available.

Other Money-Saving Options Accelerated degree, co-op program, cooperative Air Force ROTC, off-campus living. *Payment Plan:* installment. *Waivers:* full or partial for employees or children of employees.

Contact Ms. Regina K. Robinson, University Director of Financial Aid, Pace University, 1 Pace Plaza, New York, NY 10038, 212-346-1305, fax: 212-346-1750.

PACE UNIVERSITY, PLEASANTVILLE/ BRIARCLIFF CAMPUS
Pleasantville, New York

See Pace University (New York City)

PACE UNIVERSITY, WHITE PLAINS CAMPUS
White Plains, New York

See Pace University (New York City)

PACIFIC CHRISTIAN COLLEGE
Fullerton, California

See Hope International University

PACIFIC LUTHERAN UNIVERSITY
Tacoma, Washington

About the Institution Independent/religious, coed. Degrees awarded: B, M. Offers 77 undergraduate majors. Total enrollment: 3,463. Undergraduates: 3,087 (72% state residents). Freshmen: 617.

Undergraduate Expenses (1997–98) Comprehensive fee of $19,950 includes tuition ($15,136) and college room and board ($4814). College room only: $2390.

Applications Of all full-time undergraduates enrolled in fall 1996, 90% of those who applied for aid were judged to have need according to Federal Methodology, of whom 99% were aided. *Financial aid deadline (priority):* 3/1. *Financial aid forms:* CSS Financial Aid PROFILE acceptable. FAFSA, institutional form required for some. *Regular admission application deadline:* rolling. Early action deadline: 11/15.

Summary of Aid to Needy Students *From gift & self-help combined:* Average need met: 83%. Average amount awarded: $13,553 (55% gift aid, 45% self-help). *Gift aid:* Total: $15,553,182 (76% from college's own funds, 10% from other college-administered sources, 14% from external sources). 677 Federal Work-Study jobs (averaging $1200); 778 part-time jobs.

Need-Based Scholarships & Grants Pell, FSEOG, state, private, college/ university.

Loans Perkins, PLUS, Stafford, Unsubsidized Stafford, Federal Nursing, state, private, college/university short-term loans ($250 average).

Non-Need Awards In 1996, a total of 1,569 non-need awards were made. *Academic Interests/Achievement Awards:* 985 ($3,838,428 total): general academic. *Special Achievements/Activities Awards:* 51 ($91,300 total): leadership. *Special Characteristics Awards:* 533 ($1,379,920 total): children and siblings of alumni, children of educators, children of faculty/staff, international students, previous college experience, relatives of clergy, ROTC participants.

Other Money-Saving Options Accelerated degree, co-op program, Army ROTC, off-campus living (after junior year). *Payment Plan:* installment. *Waivers:* full or partial for employees or children of employees and senior citizens.

Contact Ms. Joan Riley, Assistant Director, Pacific Lutheran University, Tacoma, WA 98447, 253-535-7168, fax: 253-535-8320.

PACIFIC NORTHWEST COLLEGE OF ART
Portland, Oregon

About the Institution Independent, coed. Degrees awarded: B. Offers 8 undergraduate majors. Total enrollment: 257 (70% state residents). Freshmen: 20.

Undergraduate Expenses (1997–98) Tuition: $10,374. Mandatory fees: $358.

Applications 87% of all full-time undergraduates enrolled in fall 1996 applied for aid; of these, 86% were judged to have need according to Federal Methodology, of whom 100% were aided. *Financial aid deadline (priority):* 4/1. *Financial aid forms:* FAFSA, institutional form required. *Admission application deadline:* 8/1.

Summary of Aid to Needy Students *From gift & self-help combined:* Average need met: 79%. *Gift aid:* Total: $521,616 (47% from college's own funds, 27% from other college-administered sources, 26% from external sources). 38 Federal Work-Study jobs (averaging $931); 25 part-time jobs.

Need-Based Scholarships & Grants Pell, FSEOG, state, private, college/ university.

Loans PLUS, Stafford, Unsubsidized Stafford, college/university short-term loans ($100 average).

Non-Need Awards In 1996, a total of 102 non-need awards were made. *Creative Arts/Performance Awards:* 102 ($77,795 total): art/fine arts.

Other Money-Saving Options *Payment Plan:* installment. *Waivers:* full or partial for employees or children of employees.

Contact Mrs. Laurie Radford, Financial Aid Counselor, Pacific Northwest College of Art, PO Box 2725, Portland, OR 97208-2725, 503-226-4391 Ext. 267, fax: 503-226-3587.

PACIFIC UNIVERSITY
Forest Grove, Oregon

About the Institution Independent, coed. Degrees awarded: B, M, P. Offers 49 undergraduate majors. Total enrollment: 1,750. Undergraduates: 1,019 (53% state residents). Freshmen: 269.

Undergraduate Expenses (1997–98) Comprehensive fee of $20,933 includes tuition ($15,830), mandatory fees ($390), and college room and board ($4713). College room only: $2140.

Applications Of all full-time undergraduates enrolled in fall 1996, 87% of those who applied for aid were judged to have need according to Federal Methodology, of whom 99% were aided. *Financial aid deadline (priority):* 3/1. *Financial aid forms:* institutional form required; CSS Financial Aid PROFILE acceptable. FAFSA required for some. *Regular admission application deadline:* 2/15. Early decision deadline: 11/15.

Summary of Aid to Needy Students *From gift & self-help combined:* Average need met: 81%. Average amount awarded: $12,921 (66% gift aid, 34% self-help). *Gift aid:* Total: $6,332,076 (76% from college's own funds, 4% from other college-administered sources, 20% from external sources). 415 Federal Work-Study jobs (averaging $1155); 68 part-time jobs.

Need-Based Scholarships & Grants Pell, FSEOG, state, private, college/university.

Loans Perkins, PLUS, Stafford, Unsubsidized Stafford, private, college/university short-term loans ($500 average), college/university long-term loans ($1500 average).

Non-Need Awards In 1996, a total of 570 non-need awards were made. *Academic Interests/Achievement Awards:* 448 ($2,146,647 total): general academic. *Creative Arts/Performance Awards:* 81 ($185,535 total): debating, music. *Special Characteristics Awards:* 41 ($130,972 total): international students, local/state students, religious affiliation.

Other Money-Saving Options Accelerated degree, cooperative Army ROTC, off-campus living (after sophomore year). *Payment Plans:* installment, deferred payment. *Waivers:* full or partial for employees or children of employees.

Contact Ms. Glendi Gaddis, Director of Financial Aid, Pacific University, 2043 College Way, Forest Grove, OR 97116-1797, 503-359-2222, fax: 503-359-2950.

PAIER COLLEGE OF ART, INC.
Hamden, Connecticut

About the Institution Proprietary, coed. Degrees awarded: A, B. Offers 6 undergraduate majors. Total enrollment: 259 (93% state residents). Freshmen: 98.

Undergraduate Expenses (1997–98) Tuition: $10,260. Mandatory fees: $335.

Applications 76% of all full-time undergraduates enrolled in fall 1996 applied for aid; of these, 80% were judged to have need according to Federal Methodology, of whom 95% were aided. *Financial aid deadline (priority):* 5/15. *Financial aid forms:* FAFSA required; state form acceptable. *Admission application deadline:* rolling.

Summary of Aid to Needy Students *From gift & self-help combined:* Average need met: 53%. Average amount awarded: $5550 (35% gift aid, 65% self-help). *Gift aid:* Total: $281,154 (2% from college's own funds, 70% from other college-administered sources, 28% from external sources). 9 part-time jobs.

Need-Based Scholarships & Grants Pell, FSEOG, state, private, college/university.

Loans Perkins, PLUS, Stafford, Unsubsidized Stafford.

Non-Need Awards Not offered.

Other Money-Saving Options *Payment Plan:* installment. *Waivers:* full or partial for employees or children of employees and senior citizens.

Contact Mr. John DeRose, Director of Financial Aid, Paier College of Art, Inc., 20 Gorham Avenue, Hamden, CT 06514-3902, 203-287-3034.

PAINE COLLEGE
Augusta, Georgia

About the Institution Independent/religious, coed. Degrees awarded: B. Offers 18 undergraduate majors. Total enrollment: 915 (72% state residents). Freshmen: 179.

Undergraduate Expenses (1997–98) Comprehensive fee of $9980 includes tuition ($6470), mandatory fees ($440), and college room and board ($3070). College room only: $1300.

Applications *Financial aid deadline (priority):* 9/1. *Financial aid forms:* FAFSA, CSS Financial Aid PROFILE, institutional form required. State form required for some. *Admission application deadline:* 8/1.

Summary of Aid to Needy Students *From gift & self-help combined:* Average need met: 70%. Average amount awarded: $8500 (53% gift aid, 47% self-help). *Gift aid:* Total: $2,300,000 (9% from college's own funds, 39% from other college-administered sources, 52% from external sources). Federal Work-Study jobs.

Need-Based Scholarships & Grants Pell, FSEOG, college/university.

Loans PLUS, Stafford, Unsubsidized Stafford.

Non-Need Awards *Academic Interests/Achievement Awards:* general academic. *Creative Arts/Performance Awards:* music. *Special Characteristics Awards:* children of faculty/staff, religious affiliation, siblings of current students. *Athletic:* Total: 90 ($125,000); Men: 45 ($62,500); Women: 45 ($62,500).

Other Money-Saving Options Accelerated degree, co-op program, cooperative Army ROTC, off-campus living. *Payment Plan:* installment. *Waivers:* full or partial for children of alumni and employees or children of employees.

Contact Mr. Mark Adkins, Director of Financial Aid, Paine College, Augusta, GA 30901-3182, 706-821-8262.

PALM BEACH ATLANTIC COLLEGE
West Palm Beach, Florida

About the Institution Independent/religious, coed. Degrees awarded: B, M. Offers 35 undergraduate majors. Total enrollment: 1,830. Undergraduates: 1,543 (80% state residents). Freshmen: 257.

Undergraduate Expenses (1997–98) Comprehensive fee of $13,550 includes tuition ($9900) and college room and board ($3650 minimum). College room only: $1890 (minimum).

Applications 79% of all full-time undergraduates enrolled in fall 1996 applied for aid; of these, 87% were judged to have need according to Federal Methodology, of whom 98% were aided. *Financial aid deadline (priority):* 5/1. *Financial aid forms:* FAFSA, state form, institutional form required for some. *Admission application deadline:* 8/1.

Summary of Aid to Needy Students *From gift & self-help combined:* Average need met: 85%. Average amount awarded: $11,500 (36% gift aid, 64% self-help). *Gift aid:* Total: $1,833,000 (18% from college-administered sources, 82% from external sources). 222 Federal Work-Study jobs (averaging $1300); 25 part-time jobs.

Need-Based Scholarships & Grants Pell, FSEOG, state, private, college/university.

Loans Perkins, PLUS, Stafford, Unsubsidized Stafford, private, college/university long-term loans ($750 average).

Non-Need Awards In 1996, a total of 1,566 non-need awards were made. *Academic Interests/Achievement Awards:* 356 ($804,717 total): general academic. *Creative Arts/Performance Awards:* 96 ($162,700 total): debating, music, theater/drama. *Special Achievements/Activities Awards:* 810 ($886,000 total): leadership, religious involvement. *Special Characteristics Awards:* 222 ($169,450 total): children of current students, relatives of clergy, siblings of current students, spouses of current students. *Athletic:* Total: 82 ($142,550); Men: 47 ($78,075); Women: 35 ($64,475).

Other Money-Saving Options Off-campus living (after sophomore year). *Payment Plan:* installment. *Waivers:* full or partial for employees or children of employees and senior citizens.

Contact Ms. Kathy Fruge, Director of Student Financial Planning, Palm Beach Atlantic College, PO Box 24708, West Palm Beach, FL 33416-4708, 561-803-2126.

PALMER COLLEGE OF CHIROPRACTIC
Davenport, Iowa

About the Institution Independent, coed. Degrees awarded: A, B, M, P. Offers 2 undergraduate majors. Total enrollment: 1,922. Undergraduates: 1,906 (16% state residents). Freshmen: 232.

Undergraduate Expenses (1996–97) Tuition: $13,905.

Applications 100% of all full-time undergraduates enrolled in fall 1996 applied for aid; of these,100% were judged to have need according to Federal Methodology, of whom 98% were aided. *Financial aid deadline (priority):* 4/1. *Financial aid forms:* FAFSA, institutional form required. *Admission application deadline:* rolling.

Summary of Aid to Needy Students *From gift & self-help combined:* Average need met: 90%. *Gift aid:* Total: $255,000 (12% from college's own funds, 24% from other college-administered sources, 64% from external sources). 250 Federal Work-Study jobs (averaging $900); 300 part-time jobs.

Need-Based Scholarships & Grants Pell, FSEOG, state, private, college/university.

Loans Perkins, PLUS, Stafford, Unsubsidized Stafford, college/university short-term loans ($410 average).

Non-Need Awards In 1996, a total of 240 non-need awards were made. *Academic Interests/Achievement Awards:* 200 ($420,000 total): general academic, biological sciences, health fields. *Athletic:* Total: 40 ($200,000); Men: 40 ($200,000); Women: 0.

Other Money-Saving Options *Payment Plan:* deferred payment. *Waivers:* full or partial for employees or children of employees.

Contact Financial Planning Office, Palmer College of Chiropractic, 1000 Brady Street, Davenport, IA 52803-5287, 319-326-9889, fax: 319-326-8414.

PARK COLLEGE
Parkville, Missouri

About the Institution Independent/religious, coed. Degrees awarded: A, B, M. Offers 35 undergraduate majors. Total enrollment: 1,207. Undergraduates: 1,059 (79% state residents). Freshmen: 121.

Undergraduate Expenses (1997–98) Comprehensive fee of $8840 includes tuition ($4410) and college room and board ($4430).

Applications Of all full-time undergraduates enrolled in fall 1996, 100% of those judged to have need according to Federal Methodology were aided. *Financial aid deadline (priority):* 4/1. *Financial aid forms:* institutional form required; CSS Financial Aid PROFILE acceptable. *Admission application deadline:* 8/1.

Summary of Aid to Needy Students *From gift & self-help combined:* Average amount awarded: $6766 (43% gift aid, 57% self-help). *Gift aid:* Total: $1,477,076 (39% from college's own funds, 22% from other college-administered sources, 39% from external sources). 165 Federal Work-Study jobs (averaging $1798); 129 part-time jobs.

Need-Based Scholarships & Grants Pell, FSEOG, state.

Loans Perkins, PLUS, Stafford, Unsubsidized Stafford, college/university short-term loans ($500 average), college/university long-term loans ($2000 average).

Non-Need Awards In 1996, a total of 338 non-need awards were made. *Academic Interests/Achievement Awards:* 141 ($168,858 total): general academic. *Creative Arts/Performance Awards:* 22 ($9829 total): art/fine arts, theater/drama. *Special Characteristics Awards:* 43 ($79,987 total): children of faculty/staff, public servants, religious affiliation. *Athletic:* Total: 132 ($307,245); Men: 64 ($163,365); Women: 68 ($143,880).

Other Money-Saving Options Army ROTC, off-campus living (after junior year). *Payment Plan:* installment. *Waivers:* full or partial for employees or children of employees and senior citizens.

Contact Ms. Cathy Colapietro, Associate Director of Student Financial Services, Park College, 8700 NW River Park Drive, Parkville, MO 64152-3795, 816-741-2000 Ext. 6728, fax: 816-741-9668.

PARSONS SCHOOL OF DESIGN, NEW SCHOOL FOR SOCIAL RESEARCH
New York, New York

About the Institution Independent, coed. Degrees awarded: A, B, M. Offers 17 undergraduate majors. Total university enrollment: 5,833. Total unit enrollment: 1,881. Undergraduates: 1,751 (50% state residents). Freshmen: 375.

Undergraduate Expenses (1997–98) Comprehensive fee of $27,095 includes tuition ($18,200), mandatory fees ($340), and college room and board ($8555). College room only: $6035.

Applications Of all full-time undergraduates enrolled in fall 1996, 96% of those who applied for aid were judged to have need according to Federal Methodology, of whom 97% were aided. *Financial aid deadline (priority):* 4/1. *Financial aid forms:* FAFSA, institutional form required. CSS Financial Aid PROFILE, state form required for some. *Admission application deadline:* rolling.

Summary of Aid to Needy Students *From gift & self-help combined:* Average need met: 65%. Average amount awarded: $11,500 (53% gift aid, 47% self-help). *Gift aid:* Total: $7,659,590 (72% from college's own funds, 3% from other college-administered sources, 25% from external sources). 150 Federal Work-Study jobs (averaging $2000); 100 part-time jobs.

Need-Based Scholarships & Grants Pell, FSEOG, state, private, college/university.

Loans Perkins, PLUS, Stafford, Unsubsidized Stafford, private, college/university short-term loans ($200 average).

Non-Need Awards *Creative Arts/Performance Awards:* art/fine arts.

Other Money-Saving Options Off-campus living. *Payment Plan:* installment. *Waivers:* full or partial for employees or children of employees.

Contact Office of Financial Aid, Parsons School of Design, New School for Social Research, 66 West 12th Street, New York, NY 10011-8878, 212-229-8900.

PATTEN COLLEGE
Oakland, California

About the Institution Independent/religious, coed. Degrees awarded: A, B. Offers 7 undergraduate majors. Total enrollment: 627 (95% state residents). Freshmen: 65.

Undergraduate Expenses (1997–98) Tuition: $7008. College room only: $2350.

Applications *Financial aid deadline (priority):* 5/31. *Financial aid forms:* FAFSA, state form, institutional form required. *Admission application deadline:* 7/15.

Summary of Aid to Needy Students *From gift & self-help combined:* Average amount awarded: $6000 (52% gift aid, 48% self-help). *Gift aid:* Total: $730,000. 20 Federal Work-Study jobs (averaging $1200); 20 part-time jobs.

Need-Based Scholarships & Grants Pell, FSEOG, state, college/university.

Loans Perkins, Stafford, Unsubsidized Stafford.

Non-Need Awards *Special Achievements/Activities Awards:* leadership, religious involvement. *Special Characteristics Awards:* religious affiliation. *Athletic:* available.

Other Money-Saving Options Accelerated degree, off-campus living. *Payment Plan:* installment. *Waivers:* full or partial for employees or children of employees.

Contact Mr. Robert Olivera, Dean of Enrollment Services, Patten College, Oakland, CA 94601-2699, 510-533-8300.

PAUL QUINN COLLEGE
Dallas, Texas

About the Institution Independent/religious, coed. Degrees awarded: B. Offers 18 undergraduate majors. Total enrollment: 700 (60% state residents). Freshmen: 250.

Undergraduate Expenses (1997–98) Comprehensive fee of $8135 includes tuition ($3900), mandatory fees ($785), and college room and board ($3450). College room only: $1300.

Applications *Financial aid deadline (priority):* 4/30. *Financial aid forms:* FAFSA, institutional form required. *Admission application deadline:* 6/1.

Summary of Aid to Needy Students *From gift & self-help combined:* Average need met: 80%. 200 Federal Work-Study jobs (averaging $1000).

Need-Based Scholarships & Grants Pell, FSEOG, state, private, college/university.

Loans Stafford, Unsubsidized Stafford.

Non-Need Awards *Academic Interests/Achievement Awards:* general academic. *Special Achievements/Activities Awards:* religious involvement. *Athletic:* available.

Other Money-Saving Options Accelerated degree, co-op program, off-campus living (after sophomore year). *Payment Plan:* installment.

Contact Mr. Rickey Eddie, Director of Student Financial Aid, Paul Quinn College, 3837 Simpson-Stuart Road, Dallas, TX 75241-4331, 214-302-3530.

PEABODY CONSERVATORY OF MUSIC OF THE JOHNS HOPKINS UNIVERSITY
Baltimore, Maryland

About the Institution Independent, coed. Degrees awarded: B, M, D. Offers 7 undergraduate majors. Total enrollment: 637. Undergraduates: 278 (19% state residents). Freshmen: 85.

Undergraduate Expenses (1996–97) Comprehensive fee of $23,460 includes tuition ($16,520 minimum) and college room and board ($6940).

Applications 65% of all full-time undergraduates enrolled in fall 1996 applied for aid; of these, 89% were judged to have need according to Federal Methodology, of whom 100% were aided. *Financial aid deadline (priority):* 2/1. *Financial aid forms:* FAFSA, institutional form required. *Admission application deadline:* 2/1.

Summary of Aid to Needy Students *From gift & self-help combined:* Average need met: 52%. Average amount awarded: $14,000 (58% gift aid, 42% self-help). *Gift aid:* Total: $1,278,000 (77% from college's own funds, 13% from other college-administered sources, 10% from external sources). 118 Federal Work-Study jobs (averaging $1500); 100 part-time jobs.

Need-Based Scholarships & Grants Pell, FSEOG, state, private, college/university.

Loans Perkins, PLUS, Stafford, Unsubsidized Stafford, private, college/university short-term loans ($300 average), college/university long-term loans ($8000 average).

Non-Need Awards In 1996, a total of 182 non-need awards were made. *Creative Arts/Performance Awards:* 182 ($941,000 total): music.

Other Money-Saving Options Accelerated degree, off-campus living (after sophomore year). *Waivers:* full or partial for employees or children of employees.

Contact Financial Aid Office, Peabody Conservatory of Music of The Johns Hopkins University, 1 East Mount Vernon Place, Baltimore, MD 21202-2397, 410-659-8171.

PEMBROKE STATE UNIVERSITY
Pembroke, North Carolina

See University of North Carolina at Pembroke

PENNSYLVANIA STATE UNIVERSITY ABINGTON COLLEGE
Abington, Pennsylvania

About the Institution State-related, coed. Degrees awarded: A, B. Offers 10 undergraduate majors. Total enrollment: 3,262. Undergraduates: 3,238 (98% state residents). Freshmen: 852.

Undergraduate Expenses (1996–97) State resident tuition: $5262. Nonresident tuition: $8178. Mandatory fees: $190.

Applications *Financial aid deadline (priority):* 2/15. *Financial aid forms:* FAFSA required. *Admission application deadline:* rolling.

Summary of Aid to Needy Students Federal Work-Study jobs; part-time jobs.

Need-Based Scholarships & Grants Pell, FSEOG, state, private, college/university.

Loans Perkins, PLUS, Stafford, Unsubsidized Stafford, private, college/university long-term loans ($1500 average).

Non-Need Awards available.

Other Money-Saving Options Army ROTC, cooperative Air Force ROTC. *Payment Plan:* deferred payment. *Waivers:* full or partial for employees or children of employees and senior citizens.

Contact Office of Financial Aid, Pennsylvania State University Abington College, Abington, PA 19001-3918, 215-881-7300.

PENNSYLVANIA STATE UNIVERSITY ALTOONA COLLEGE
Altoona, Pennsylvania

About the Institution State-related, coed. Degrees awarded: A, B. Offers 10 undergraduate majors. Total enrollment: 3,475. Undergraduates: 3,463 (91% state residents). Freshmen: 1,463.

Undergraduate Expenses (1996–97) State resident tuition: $5262. Nonresident tuition: $8178. Mandatory fees: $190. College room and board: $4170.

Applications *Financial aid deadline (priority):* 2/15. *Financial aid forms:* FAFSA required. *Admission application deadline:* rolling.

Summary of Aid to Needy Students Federal Work-Study jobs; part-time jobs.

Need-Based Scholarships & Grants Pell, FSEOG, state, private, college/university.

Loans Perkins, PLUS, Stafford, Unsubsidized Stafford, private, college/university long-term loans ($1500 average).

Non-Need Awards available.

Other Money-Saving Options Army ROTC, off-campus living. *Payment Plan:* deferred payment. *Waivers:* full or partial for employees or children of employees and senior citizens.

Contact Office of Financial Aid, Pennsylvania State University Altoona College, Altoona, PA 16601-3760, 814-949-5000.

PENNSYLVANIA STATE UNIVERSITY AT ERIE, THE BEHREND COLLEGE
Erie, Pennsylvania

About the Institution State-related, coed. Degrees awarded: A, B, M. Offers 21 undergraduate majors. Total enrollment: 3,207. Undergraduates: 3,061 (94% state residents). Freshmen: 684.

Undergraduate Expenses (1996–97) State resident tuition: $5434. Nonresident tuition: $11,774. Mandatory fees: $190. College room and board: $4170.

Applications *Financial aid deadline (priority):* 2/15. *Financial aid forms:* FAFSA required. *Admission application deadline:* rolling.

Summary of Aid to Needy Students Federal Work-Study jobs; part-time jobs.

Need-Based Scholarships & Grants Pell, FSEOG, state, private, college/university.

Loans Perkins, PLUS, Stafford, Unsubsidized Stafford, private, college/university long-term loans ($1500 average).

Non-Need Awards *Academic Interests/Achievement Awards:* available. *Creative Arts/Performance Awards:* available. *Special Achievements/Activities Awards:* available. *Special Characteristics Awards:* available.

Other Money-Saving Options Off-campus living. *Payment Plan:* deferred payment. *Waivers:* full or partial for employees or children of employees and senior citizens.

Contact Ms. Jane Brady, Assistant Director of Admissions & Graduate Admissions, Pennsylvania State University at Erie, The Behrend College, 200 Glenhill Farmhouse, Erie, PA 16563, 814-898-6162.

PENNSYLVANIA STATE UNIVERSITY BERKS–LEHIGH VALLEY COLLEGE
Reading, Pennsylvania

About the Institution State-related, coed. Degrees awarded: A, B. Offers 10 undergraduate majors. Total enrollment: 2,423. Undergraduates: 2,367 (94% state residents). Freshmen: 883.

Undergraduate Expenses (1996–97) State resident tuition: $5262. Nonresident tuition: $8178. Mandatory fees: $190. College room and board: $4170 (minimum).

Applications *Financial aid deadline (priority):* 2/15. *Financial aid forms:* FAFSA required. *Admission application deadline:* rolling.

Summary of Aid to Needy Students Federal Work-Study jobs; part-time jobs.

Need-Based Scholarships & Grants Pell, FSEOG, state, private, college/university.

Loans Perkins, PLUS, Stafford, Unsubsidized Stafford, private, college/university long-term loans ($1500 average).

Non-Need Awards available.

Other Money-Saving Options Army ROTC, off-campus living. *Payment Plan:* deferred payment. *Waivers:* full or partial for employees or children of employees and senior citizens.

Contact Office of Financial Aid, Pennsylvania State University Berks–Lehigh Valley College, Reading, PA 19610-6009, 610-320-4800.

PENNSYLVANIA STATE UNIVERSITY HARRISBURG CAMPUS OF THE CAPITAL COLLEGE
Middletown, Pennsylvania

About the Institution State-related, coed. Degrees awarded: A, B, M, D. Offers 26 undergraduate majors. Total enrollment: 3,417. Undergraduates: 2,069 (98% state residents). Freshmen: 373.

Undergraduate Expenses (1996–97) State resident tuition: $5434. Nonresident tuition: $11,774. Mandatory fees: $190. College room and board: $4170.

Applications *Financial aid deadline (priority):* 2/15. *Financial aid forms:* FAFSA required.

Summary of Aid to Needy Students Federal Work-Study jobs; part-time jobs.

Need-Based Scholarships & Grants Pell, FSEOG, state, private, college/university.

Loans Perkins, PLUS, Stafford, Unsubsidized Stafford, private, college/university long-term loans ($1500 average).

Non-Need Awards *Academic Interests/Achievement Awards:* available. *Creative Arts/Performance Awards:* available. *Special Achievements/Activities Awards:* available. *Special Characteristics Awards:* available.

Other Money-Saving Options Cooperative Army ROTC, off-campus living. *Payment Plan:* deferred payment. *Waivers:* full or partial for employees or children of employees and senior citizens.

Contact Ms. Carolyn Bryan, Student Aid Adviser, Pennsylvania State University Harrisburg Campus of the Capital College, W112 Olmstead, Middletown, PA 17057-4898, 717-948-6307.

PENNSYLVANIA STATE UNIVERSITY SCHUYLKILL CAMPUS OF THE CAPITAL COLLEGE
Schuylkill Haven, Pennsylvania

About the Institution State-related, coed. Degrees awarded: A, B. Offers 12 undergraduate majors. Total enrollment: 988 (94% state residents). Freshmen: 241.

Undergraduate Expenses (1996–97) State resident tuition: $5262. Nonresident tuition: $8178. Mandatory fees: $190. College room and board: $4170. College room only: $3480.

Applications *Financial aid deadline (priority):* 2/15. *Financial aid forms:* FAFSA required. *Admission application deadline:* rolling.

Summary of Aid to Needy Students Federal Work-Study jobs; part-time jobs.

Need-Based Scholarships & Grants Pell, FSEOG, state, private, college/university.

Loans Perkins, PLUS, Stafford, Unsubsidized Stafford, private, college/university long-term loans ($1500 average).

Non-Need Awards available.

Other Money-Saving Options Army ROTC, off-campus living. *Payment Plan:* deferred payment. *Waivers:* full or partial for employees or children of employees and senior citizens.

Contact Office of Financial Aid, Pennsylvania State University Schuylkill Campus of the Capital College, Schuylkill Haven, PA 17972-2208, 717-385-6000.

PENNSYLVANIA STATE UNIVERSITY
UNIVERSITY PARK CAMPUS
State College, Pennsylvania

About the Institution State-related, coed. Degrees awarded: A, B, M, D. Offers 126 undergraduate majors. Total enrollment: 39,782. Undergraduates: 33,163 (81% state residents). Freshmen: 3,535.

Undergraduate Expenses (1996–97) State resident tuition: $5434. Nonresident tuition: $11,774. Mandatory fees: $190. College room and board: $4170.

Applications *Financial aid deadline (priority):* 2/15. *Financial aid forms:* FAFSA required. *Admission application deadline:* rolling.

Summary of Aid to Needy Students Federal Work-Study jobs; part-time jobs.

Need-Based Scholarships & Grants Pell, FSEOG, state, private, college/university.

Loans Perkins, PLUS, Stafford, Unsubsidized Stafford, state, private, college/university short-term loans, college/university long-term loans ($1500 average).

Non-Need Awards *Academic Interests/Achievement Awards:* available. *Creative Arts/Performance Awards:* available. *Special Achievements/Activities Awards:* available. *Special Characteristics Awards:* available. *Athletic:* available.

Other Money-Saving Options Co-op program, Army ROTC, Naval ROTC, Air Force ROTC, off-campus living (after freshman year). *Payment Plan:* deferred payment. *Waivers:* full or partial for employees or children of employees and senior citizens.

Contact Office of Financial Aid, Pennsylvania State University University Park Campus, 314 Shields Building, University Park, PA 16802-1503, 814-865-4700.

PEPPERDINE UNIVERSITY
Malibu, California

About the Institution Independent/religious, coed. Degrees awarded: B, M, D, P. Offers 43 undergraduate majors. Total enrollment: 7,896. Undergraduates: 3,534 (60% state residents). Freshmen: 673.

Undergraduate Expenses (1996–97) Comprehensive fee of $27,070 includes tuition ($20,140), mandatory fees ($70), and college room and board ($6860). College room only: $4030.

Applications 69% of all full-time undergraduates enrolled in fall 1996 applied for aid; of these, 64% were judged to have need according to Federal Methodology, of whom 98% were aided. *Financial aid deadline (priority):* 2/15. *Financial aid forms:* FAFSA, CSS Financial Aid PROFILE, institutional form, W-2 forms required. State form required for some. *Regular admission application deadline:* 2/1. Early action deadline: 11/15.

Summary of Aid to Needy Students *From gift & self-help combined:* Average need met: 87%. Average amount awarded: $19,126 (50% gift aid, 50% self-help). *Gift aid:* Total: $17,256,280 (73% from college's own funds, 22% from other college-administered sources, 5% from external sources). 453 Federal Work-Study jobs (averaging $1500); 744 part-time jobs.

Need-Based Scholarships & Grants Pell, FSEOG, state, private, college/university.

Loans Perkins, PLUS, Stafford, Unsubsidized Stafford, state, private, college/university short-term loans ($200 average), college/university long-term loans ($2500 average).

Non-Need Awards In 1996, a total of 1,372 non-need awards were made. *Academic Interests/Achievement Awards:* 477 ($3,540,829 total): general academic, biological sciences, business, communication, education, humanities, international studies, religion/biblical studies, social sciences. *Creative Arts/Performance Awards:* 129 ($650,247 total):

art/fine arts, journalism/publications, music, performing arts, theater/drama. *Special Characteristics Awards:* 650 ($1,414,861 total): children of faculty/staff, religious affiliation. *Athletic:* Total: 116 ($1,986,596); Men: 55 ($989,729); Women: 61 ($996,867).

Other Money-Saving Options Accelerated degree, cooperative Army ROTC, cooperative Naval ROTC, cooperative Air Force ROTC, off-campus living (after sophomore year). *Payment Plans:* tuition prepayment, installment, deferred payment. *Waivers:* full or partial for employees or children of employees.

Contact Ms. Edna Powell, Director of Financial Assistance, Pepperdine University, 24255 Pacific Coast Highway, Malibu, CA 90263-0001, 310-456-4301.

PERU STATE COLLEGE
Peru, Nebraska

About the Institution State-supported, coed. Degrees awarded: B, M. Offers 50 undergraduate majors. Total enrollment: 1,800. Undergraduates: 1,635 (89% state residents). Freshmen: 229.

Undergraduate Expenses (1996–97) State resident tuition: $1650. Nonresident tuition: $3300. Mandatory fees: $286. College room and board: $2966. College room only: $1456.

Applications *Financial aid deadline (priority):* 3/1. *Financial aid forms:* institutional form required; CSS Financial Aid PROFILE, state form acceptable. FAFSA required for some. *Admission application deadline:* rolling.

Summary of Aid to Needy Students *From gift & self-help combined:* Average need met: 80%. Average amount awarded: $3900 (35% gift aid, 65% self-help). *Gift aid:* Total: $1,260,000 (18% from college's own funds, 5% from other college-administered sources, 77% from external sources). 133 Federal Work-Study jobs (averaging $900); part-time jobs.

Need-Based Scholarships & Grants Pell, FSEOG, state, college/university.

Loans Perkins, PLUS, Stafford, Unsubsidized Stafford, college/university short-term loans ($400 average).

Non-Need Awards In 1996, a total of 374 non-need awards were made. *Academic Interests/Achievement Awards:* 60 ($48,000 total): general academic, biological sciences, business, computer science, education, English, humanities, mathematics, physical sciences, premedicine, social sciences. *Creative Arts/Performance Awards:* 54 ($34,000 total): art/fine arts, music, theater/drama. *Special Achievements/Activities Awards:* 140 ($150,000 total): leadership, memberships. *Athletic:* Total: 120 ($77,000); Men: 84 ($49,000); Women: 36 ($28,000).

Other Money-Saving Options Co-op program, off-campus living (after sophomore year). *Waivers:* full or partial for employees or children of employees.

Contact Mr. Dwight Garman, Director of Financial Aid, Peru State College, Peru, NE 68421, 402-872-3815.

PFEIFFER UNIVERSITY
Misenheimer, North Carolina

About the Institution Independent/religious, coed. Degrees awarded: B, M. Offers 36 undergraduate majors. Total enrollment: 1,534. Undergraduates: 847 (73% state residents). Freshmen: 120.

Undergraduate Expenses (1997–98) Comprehensive fee of $13,816 includes tuition ($9816) and college room and board ($4000).

Applications Of all full-time undergraduates enrolled in fall 1996, 91% of those who applied for aid were judged to have need according to Federal Methodology, of whom 99% were aided. *Financial aid deadline (priority):* 3/15. *Financial aid forms:* FAFSA required; CSS Financial Aid PROFILE acceptable. State form required for some. *Admission application deadline:* rolling.

Summary of Aid to Needy Students *Gift aid:* Total: $711,629 (46% from college-administered sources, 54% from external sources). 136 Federal Work-Study jobs (averaging $750); 13 part-time jobs.

Need-Based Scholarships & Grants Pell, FSEOG, state, private, United Methodist Board of Higher Education and Ministry Scholarships.

Loans Perkins, PLUS, Stafford, Unsubsidized Stafford, United Methodist Board of Higher Education and Ministry Loans.

Non-Need Awards In 1996, a total of 377 non-need awards were made. *Academic Interests/Achievement Awards:* 213 ($492,740 total): general academic, international studies. *Athletic:* Total: 164 ($509,866); Men: 89 ($271,725); Women: 75 ($238,141).

Other Money-Saving Options Accelerated degree, co-op program, cooperative Army ROTC. *Payment Plans:* installment, deferred payment. *Waivers:* full or partial for employees or children of employees.

Contact Financial Aid Office, Pfeiffer University, Highway 52 North, Misenheimer, NC 28109-0960, 704-463-1360, fax: 704-463-1363.

PHILADELPHIA COLLEGE OF BIBLE
Langhorne, Pennsylvania

About the Institution Independent/religious, coed. Degrees awarded: A, B, M. Offers 14 undergraduate majors. Total enrollment: 1,187. Undergraduates: 926 (43% state residents). Freshmen: 181.

Undergraduate Expenses (1997–98) Comprehensive fee of $13,940 includes tuition ($8850), mandatory fees ($270), and college room and board ($4820 minimum). College room only: $2220.

Applications Of all full-time undergraduates enrolled in fall 1996, 91% of those who applied for aid were judged to have need according to Federal Methodology, of whom 94% were aided. *Financial aid deadline (priority):* 3/15. *Financial aid forms:* FAFSA, state form required; CSS Financial Aid PROFILE acceptable. International Student Aid form required for some. *Admission application deadline:* rolling.

Summary of Aid to Needy Students *From gift & self-help combined:* Average need met: 73%. Average amount awarded: $7462 (58% gift aid, 42% self-help). *Gift aid:* Total: $1,883,015 (52% from college's own funds, 24% from other college-administered sources, 24% from external sources). 75 Federal Work-Study jobs (averaging $1000); 215 part-time jobs.

Need-Based Scholarships & Grants Pell, FSEOG, state, private, college/university.

Loans PLUS, Stafford, Unsubsidized Stafford, private.

Non-Need Awards In 1996, a total of 929 non-need awards were made. *Academic Interests/Achievement Awards:* 199 ($291,550 total): general academic. *Creative Arts/Performance Awards:* 50 ($52,000 total): music. *Special Achievements/Activities Awards:* 445 ($367,700 total): general special achievements/activities, leadership, religious involvement. *Special Characteristics Awards:* 235 ($39,549 total): children and siblings of alumni, children of faculty/staff, international students, relatives of clergy, siblings of current students.

Other Money-Saving Options *Payment Plan:* installment. *Waivers:* full or partial for children of alumni and employees or children of employees.

Contact Mr. Travis S. Roy, Financial Aid Administrator, Philadelphia College of Bible, 200 Manor Avenue, Langhorne, PA 19047-2990, 215-702-4246, fax: 215-702-4248.

PHILADELPHIA COLLEGE OF PHARMACY AND SCIENCE
Philadelphia, Pennsylvania

About the Institution Independent, coed. Degrees awarded: B, M, D, P. Offers 12 undergraduate majors. Total enrollment: 2,021. Undergraduates: 1,918 (66% state residents). Freshmen: 373.

Undergraduate Expenses (1996–97) Comprehensive fee of $17,420 includes tuition ($12,000), mandatory fees ($330), and college room and board ($5090). College room only: $3180.

Applications 76% of all full-time undergraduates enrolled in fall 1996 applied for aid; of these, 94% were judged to have need according to Federal Methodology, of whom 97% were aided. *Financial aid deadline (priority):* 3/15. *Financial aid forms:* FAFSA, institutional form, federal income tax form, W-2 form required. State form required for some. *Admission application deadline:* rolling.

Summary of Aid to Needy Students *From gift & self-help combined:* Average need met: 75%. Average amount awarded: $9679 (33% gift aid, 67% self-help). *Gift aid:* Total: $4,262,509 (32% from college's own funds, 20% from other college-administered sources, 48% from external sources). 239 Federal Work-Study jobs (averaging $600); 150 part-time jobs.

Need-Based Scholarships & Grants Pell, FSEOG, state, college/university, scholarships for disadvantaged students.

Loans Perkins, PLUS, Stafford, Unsubsidized Stafford, college/university short-term loans ($1500 average).

Non-Need Awards *Academic Interests/Achievement Awards:* 65 ($340,000 total): general academic. *Special Characteristics Awards:* 119 ($177,900 total): children of union members/company employees, local/state students, members of minorities. *Athletic:* available.

Other Money-Saving Options Cooperative Army ROTC, off-campus living (after sophomore year). *Payment Plans:* installment, deferred payment. *Waivers:* full or partial for employees or children of employees.

Contact Ms. Linda Stanley, Director of Financial Aid, Philadelphia College of Pharmacy and Science, 600 South 43rd Street, Philadelphia, PA 19104-4495, 215-596-8894, fax: 215-895-1100.

PHILADELPHIA COLLEGE OF TEXTILES AND SCIENCE
Philadelphia, Pennsylvania

About the Institution Independent, coed. Degrees awarded: B, M. Offers 31 undergraduate majors. Total enrollment: 3,402. Undergraduates: 2,802 (67% state residents). Freshmen: 542.

Undergraduate Expenses (1997–98) Comprehensive fee of $19,356 includes tuition ($13,466 minimum) and college room and board ($5890). College room only: $2960.

Applications 81% of all full-time undergraduates enrolled in fall 1996 applied for aid; of these, 89% were judged to have need according to Federal Methodology, of whom 98% were aided. *Financial aid deadline:* Applications processed continuously. *Financial aid forms:* FAFSA required. *Admission application deadline:* rolling.

Summary of Aid to Needy Students *From gift & self-help combined:* Average need met: 74%. Average amount awarded: $11,009 (51% gift aid, 49% self-help). *Gift aid:* Total: $7,871,640 (66% from college's own funds, 3% from other college-administered sources, 31% from external sources). 668 Federal Work-Study jobs (averaging $1400); 75 part-time jobs.

Need-Based Scholarships & Grants Pell, FSEOG, state, college/university.

Loans Perkins, PLUS, Stafford, Unsubsidized Stafford, private.

Non-Need Awards In 1996, a total of 1,227 non-need awards were made. *Academic Interests/Achievement Awards:* 1,089 ($4,283,837 total): general academic. *Athletic:* Total: 138 ($693,894); Men: 48 ($365,911); Women: 90 ($327,983).

Other Money-Saving Options Accelerated degree, co-op program, off-campus living. *Payment Plans:* installment, deferred payment. *Waivers:* full or partial for employees or children of employees.

Contact Ms. Lisa J. Cooper, Director of Financial Aid, Philadelphia College of Textiles and Science, Schoolhouse Lane and Henry Avenue, Philadelphia, PA 19144-5497, 215-951-2940, fax: 215-951-2907.

PHILANDER SMITH COLLEGE
Little Rock, Arkansas

About the Institution Independent/religious, coed. Degrees awarded: B. Offers 25 undergraduate majors. Total enrollment: 925 (80% state residents). Freshmen: 180.

Undergraduate Expenses (1997–98) Comprehensive fee of $6034 includes tuition ($3288) and college room and board ($2746). College room only: $1334.

Applications *Financial aid deadline (priority):* 6/15. *Admission application deadline:* rolling.

Summary of Aid to Needy Students Federal Work-Study jobs; part-time jobs.

Loans College/university short-term loans.

Non-Need Awards *Academic Interests/Achievement Awards:* general academic. *Creative Arts/Performance Awards:* music.

Other Money-Saving Options Co-op program, Army ROTC, off-campus living (after freshman year).

Contact Office of Financial Aid, Philander Smith College, 812 West 13th Street, Little Rock, AR 72202-3799, 501-375-9845.

PHILLIPS UNIVERSITY
Enid, Oklahoma

About the Institution Independent/religious, coed. Degrees awarded: A, B, M. Offers 55 undergraduate majors. Total enrollment: 613. Undergraduates: 519 (57% state residents). Freshmen: 162.

Undergraduate Expenses (1997–98) Comprehensive fee of $11,009 includes tuition ($6490), mandatory fees ($615), and college room and board ($3904). College room only: $1700.

Applications Of all full-time undergraduates enrolled in fall 1996, 86% of those who applied for aid were judged to have need according to Federal Methodology, of whom 100% were aided. *Financial aid deadline (priority):* 4/30. *Financial aid forms:* FAFSA required for some. *Admission application deadline:* rolling.

Summary of Aid to Needy Students *From gift & self-help combined:* Average need met: 77%. Average amount awarded: $10,244 (45% gift aid, 55% self-help). *Gift aid:* Total: $1,319,571 (53% from college's own funds, 21% from other college-administered sources, 26% from external sources). 119 Federal Work-Study jobs (averaging $1127); 120 part-time jobs.

Need-Based Scholarships & Grants Pell, FSEOG, state, private, college/university.

Loans Perkins, PLUS, Stafford, Unsubsidized Stafford, college/university short-term loans ($50 average), college/university long-term loans ($1678 average).

Non-Need Awards In 1996, a total of 500 non-need awards were made. *Academic Interests/Achievement Awards:* 345 ($474,486 total): general academic. *Creative Arts/Performance Awards:* 37 ($47,770 total): music. *Special Achievements/Activities Awards:* 19 ($15,800 total): religious involvement. *Special Characteristics Awards:* 21 ($48,830 total): children of faculty/staff. *Athletic:* Total: 78 ($356,556); Men: 45 ($200,133); Women: 33 ($156,423).

Other Money-Saving Options Accelerated degree, co-op program. *Payment Plans:* installment, deferred payment. *Waivers:* full or partial for employees or children of employees and senior citizens.

Contact Ms. Nancy Moats, Director of Student Financial Aid, Phillips University, 100 South University Avenue, Enid, OK 73701-6439, 405-237-4433, fax: 405-237-1607.

PIEDMONT BIBLE COLLEGE
Winston-Salem, North Carolina

About the Institution Independent/religious, coed. Degrees awarded: A, B, M. Offers 15 undergraduate majors. Total enrollment: 270. Undergraduates: 249 (61% state residents). Freshmen: 63.

Undergraduate Expenses (1997–98) Comprehensive fee of $8340 includes tuition ($4790), mandatory fees ($460), and college room and board ($3090).

Applications Of all full-time undergraduates enrolled in fall 1996, 92% of those judged to have need according to Federal Methodology were aided. *Financial aid deadline (priority):* 5/15. *Financial aid forms:* FAFSA, institutional form required; CSS Financial Aid PROFILE acceptable. *Regular admission application deadline:* rolling. Early action deadline: 11/1.

Summary of Aid to Needy Students *From gift & self-help combined:* Average need met: 49%. Average amount awarded: $6463 (27% gift aid, 73% self-help). *Gift aid:* Total: $294,097 (28% from college's own funds, 8% from other college-administered sources, 64% from external sources). 5 Federal Work-Study jobs (averaging $2200); 50 part-time jobs.

Need-Based Scholarships & Grants Pell, FSEOG, college/university.

Loans PLUS, Stafford, Unsubsidized Stafford, state.

Non-Need Awards In 1996, a total of 129 non-need awards were made. *Academic Interests/Achievement Awards:* 74 ($66,410 total): general academic. *Special Characteristics Awards:* 55 ($84,485 total): children of faculty/staff, relatives of clergy, spouses of current students, veterans.

Other Money-Saving Options *Payment Plan:* installment. *Waivers:* full or partial for children of alumni, employees or children of employees, adult students.

Contact Mr. Erich Richter, Director of Financial Aid, Piedmont Bible College, 716 Franklin Street, Winston-Salem, NC 27101-5197, 910-725-8344 Ext. 272, fax: 910-725-5522.

PIEDMONT COLLEGE
Demorest, Georgia

About the Institution Independent/religious, coed. Degrees awarded: B, M. Offers 38 undergraduate majors. Total enrollment: 1,128. Undergraduates: 891 (96% state residents). Freshmen: 119.

Undergraduate Expenses (1997–98) Comprehensive fee of $11,130 includes tuition ($7200) and college room and board ($3930). College room only: $1980.

Applications 95% of all full-time undergraduates enrolled in fall 1996 applied for aid; of these, 81% were judged to have need according to Federal Methodology, of whom 98% were aided. *Financial aid deadline (priority):* 6/1. *Financial aid forms:* FAFSA, state form, institutional form required; CSS Financial Aid PROFILE acceptable. *Admission application deadline:* rolling.

Summary of Aid to Needy Students *From gift & self-help combined:* Average need met: 86%. Average amount awarded: $6420 (61% gift aid, 39% self-help). *Gift aid:* Total: $2,295,600 (19% from college's own funds, 44% from other college-administered sources, 37% from external sources). 17 Federal Work-Study jobs (averaging $1050); 91 part-time jobs.

Need-Based Scholarships & Grants Pell, FSEOG, state, private, college/university.

Loans Perkins, PLUS, Stafford, Unsubsidized Stafford, state, private, college/university short-term loans ($500 average), college/university long-term loans ($1000 average).

Non-Need Awards In 1996, a total of 333 non-need awards were made. *Academic Interests/Achievement Awards:* 102 ($318,330 total):

general academic, biological sciences, education, English, foreign languages, health fields, humanities, mathematics, premedicine, religion/biblical studies. *Creative Arts/Performance Awards:* 41 ($33,000 total): art/fine arts, music, theater/drama. *Special Achievements/Activities Awards:* 94 ($146,080 total): leadership. *Special Characteristics Awards:* 4 ($10,000 total): members of minorities. *Athletic:* Total: 92 ($252,000); Men: 50 ($123,300); Women: 42 ($128,700).

Other Money-Saving Options Accelerated degree, off-campus living (after sophomore year). *Payment Plan:* installment. *Waivers:* full or partial for employees or children of employees and senior citizens.

Contact Office of Financial Aid, Piedmont College, PO Box 10, Demorest, GA 30535-0010, 706-778-3000.

PIKEVILLE COLLEGE
Pikeville, Kentucky

About the Institution Independent/religious, coed. Degrees awarded: A, B. Offers 26 undergraduate majors. Total enrollment: 824 (92% state residents). Freshmen: 219.

Undergraduate Expenses (1996–97) Comprehensive fee of $9550 includes tuition ($6500) and college room and board ($3050). College room only: $1500.

Applications *Financial aid deadline (priority):* 4/1. *Financial aid forms:* FAFSA, institutional form required; CSS Financial Aid PROFILE acceptable. *Admission application deadline:* 9/4.

Summary of Aid to Needy Students *From gift & self-help combined:* Average need met: 81%. Average amount awarded: $9195 (60% gift aid, 40% self-help). 26 Federal Work-Study jobs (averaging $1300); 15 part-time jobs.

Need-Based Scholarships & Grants Pell, FSEOG, state, private, college/university.

Loans Perkins, PLUS, Stafford, Unsubsidized Stafford, college/university long-term loans ($1450 average).

Non-Need Awards In 1996, a total of 378 non-need awards were made. *Academic Interests/Achievement Awards:* 312 ($858,280 total): general academic. *Athletic:* Total: 66 ($237,430); Men: 36 ($148,300); Women: 30 ($89,130).

Other Money-Saving Options Accelerated degree, off-campus living. *Payment Plan:* installment. *Waivers:* full or partial for employees or children of employees.

Contact Ms. Teresa L. Jones, Assistant Director of Financial Aid, Pikeville College, 214 Sycamore Street, Pikeville, KY 41501, 606-432-9386, fax: 606-432-9328.

PILLSBURY BAPTIST BIBLE COLLEGE
Owatonna, Minnesota

About the Institution Independent/religious, coed. Degrees awarded: A, B. Offers 18 undergraduate majors.

Applications 100% of all full-time undergraduates enrolled in fall 1996 applied for aid; of these, 73% were judged to have need according to Federal Methodology, of whom 100% were aided. *Financial aid deadline (priority):* 12/10. *Financial aid forms:* FAFSA, institutional form required; CSS Financial Aid PROFILE acceptable. State form required for some. *Admission application deadline:* 8/27.

Summary of Aid to Needy Students *From gift & self-help combined:* Average need met: 49%. Average amount awarded: $5660 (49% gift aid, 51% self-help). *Gift aid:* Total: $209,568 (49% from college's own funds, 49% from other college-administered sources, 2% from external sources). 83 part-time jobs.

Need-Based Scholarships & Grants State, private, college/university.

Loans State, private.

Non-Need Awards In 1996, a total of 30 non-need awards were made. *Academic Interests/Achievement Awards:* general academic, business, education, home economics, mathematics, religion/biblical studies. *Special Characteristics Awards:* children and siblings of alumni, children of faculty/staff, members of minorities, relatives of clergy, religious affiliation. *Athletic:* Total: 2 ($800); Men: 1 ($400); Women: 1 ($400).

Other Money-Saving Options Accelerated degree. *Payment Plan:* installment. *Waivers:* full or partial for employees or children of employees.

Contact Dr. Arlene A. Orton, Financial Aid Administrator, Pillsbury Baptist Bible College, 315 South Grove Street, Owatonna, MN 55060-3097, 507-451-2710 Ext. 276, fax: 507-451-6459.

PINE MANOR COLLEGE
Chestnut Hill, Massachusetts

About the Institution Independent, women. Degrees awarded: A, B, M. Offers 29 undergraduate majors. Total enrollment: 300. Undergraduates: 280 (38% state residents). Freshmen: 75.

Undergraduate Expenses (1997–98) State resident tuition: $10,000. Nonresident tuition: $16,000. Mandatory fees: $700. College room and board: $6900. College room only: $3450.

Applications 56% of all full-time undergraduates enrolled in fall 1996 applied for aid; of these, 86% were judged to have need according to Federal Methodology, of whom 100% were aided. *Financial aid deadline:* continuous. *Financial aid forms:* FAFSA, CSS Financial Aid PROFILE required. State form required for some. *Regular admission application deadline:* rolling. Early decision deadline: 11/15.

Summary of Aid to Needy Students *From gift & self-help combined:* Average need met: 90%. Average amount awarded: $13,269 (71% gift aid, 29% self-help). *Gift aid:* Total: $1,212,300 (79% from college's own funds, 12% from other college-administered sources, 9% from external sources). 57 Federal Work-Study jobs (averaging $1350).

Need-Based Scholarships & Grants Pell, FSEOG, state, private, college/university.

Loans PLUS, Stafford, Unsubsidized Stafford, state, private.

Non-Need Awards *Academic Interests/Achievement Awards:* 81 ($31,800 total): general academic, biological sciences, education. *Special Characteristics Awards:* children and siblings of alumni, ethnic background, international students, local/state students, members of minorities, siblings of current students.

Other Money-Saving Options Accelerated degree, off-campus living (after sophomore year). *Payment Plans:* tuition prepayment, installment. *Waivers:* full or partial for children of alumni, employees or children of employees, adult students.

Contact Office of Financial Aid, Pine Manor College, 400 Heath Street, Chestnut Hill, MA 02167-2332, 617-731-7000.

PITTSBURG STATE UNIVERSITY
Pittsburg, Kansas

About the Institution State-supported, coed. Degrees awarded: A, B, M. Offers 96 undergraduate majors. Total enrollment: 6,426. Undergraduates: 4,879 (84% state residents). Freshmen: 803.

Undergraduate Expenses (1996–97) State resident tuition: $1876. Nonresident tuition: $5976. College room and board: $3188.

Applications Of all full-time undergraduates enrolled in fall 1996, 89% of those who applied for aid were judged to have need according to Federal Methodology, of whom 95% were aided. *Financial aid deadline (priority):* 3/1. *Financial aid forms:* FAFSA required; CSS Financial Aid PROFILE acceptable. State form required for some. *Admission application deadline:* rolling.

Summary of Aid to Needy Students *From gift & self-help combined:* Average need met: 86%. Average amount awarded: $4442 (39% gift

aid, 61% self-help). *Gift aid:* Total: $4,010,277 (9% from college's own funds, 13% from other college-administered sources, 78% from external sources). 425 Federal Work-Study jobs (averaging $2200); 679 part-time jobs.

Need-Based Scholarships & Grants Pell, FSEOG, state, private, college/university.

Loans Perkins, PLUS, Stafford, Unsubsidized Stafford, Federal Nursing, college/university short-term loans ($300 average).

Non-Need Awards In 1996, a total of 1,071 non-need awards were made. *Academic Interests/Achievement Awards:* 581 ($475,418 total): general academic, biological sciences, business, communication, computer science, education, engineering/technologies, English, foreign languages, health fields, home economics, mathematics, military science, physical sciences, social sciences. *Creative Arts/Performance Awards:* 163 ($78,276 total): music. *Special Characteristics Awards:* 31 ($114,526 total): ROTC participants. *Athletic:* Total: 296 ($525,465); Men: 187 ($369,236); Women: 109 ($156,229).

Other Money-Saving Options Co-op program, Army ROTC, off-campus living (after freshman year). *Payment Plan:* deferred payment. *Waivers:* full or partial for employees or children of employees.

Contact Ms. Marilyn Haverly, Assistant Director, Student Financial Aid, Pittsburg State University, 1701 South Broadway, Pittsburg, KS 66762-5880, 316-235-4238, fax: 316-235-4078.

PITZER COLLEGE
Claremont, California

About the Institution Independent, coed. Degrees awarded: B. Offers 40 undergraduate majors. Total enrollment: 869 (60% state residents). Freshmen: 216.

Undergraduate Expenses (1997–98) Comprehensive fee of $28,202 includes tuition ($20,088), mandatory fees ($1792), and college room and board ($6322 minimum). College room only: $3624 (minimum).

Applications 53% of all full-time undergraduates enrolled in fall 1996 applied for aid; of these, 95% were judged to have need according to Federal Methodology, of whom 99% were aided. *Financial aid deadline:* 2/1. *Financial aid forms:* FAFSA, CSS Financial Aid PROFILE required. State form required for some. *Regular admission application deadline:* 2/1. Early action deadline: 12/1.

Summary of Aid to Needy Students *From gift & self-help combined:* Average need met: 100%. Average amount awarded: $19,043 (70% gift aid, 30% self-help). *Gift aid:* Total: $6,123,404 (80% from college's own funds, 4% from other college-administered sources, 16% from external sources). 335 Federal Work-Study jobs (averaging $2401).

Need-Based Scholarships & Grants Pell, FSEOG, state, private, college/university.

Loans Perkins, PLUS, Stafford, Unsubsidized Stafford, college/university short-term loans ($100 average), college/university long-term loans ($5385 average).

Non-Need Awards Not offered.

Other Money-Saving Options Co-op program, off-campus living (after junior year). *Payment Plans:* installment, deferred payment. *Waivers:* full or partial for employees or children of employees.

Contact Ms. Abigail W. Parsons, Director of Financial Aid, Pitzer College, 1050 North Mills Avenue, Claremont, CA 91711-6101, 909-621-8208, fax: 909-607-1205.

PLYMOUTH STATE COLLEGE OF THE UNIVERSITY SYSTEM OF NEW HAMPSHIRE
Plymouth, New Hampshire

About the Institution State-supported, coed. Degrees awarded: A, B, M. Offers 73 undergraduate majors. Total enrollment: 4,000. Undergraduates: 3,500 (60% state residents). Freshmen: 904.

Undergraduate Expenses (1996–97) State resident tuition: $2850. Nonresident tuition: $8510. Mandatory fees: $1076. College room and board: $4000 (minimum).

Applications Of all full-time undergraduates enrolled in fall 1996, 85% of those who applied for aid were judged to have need according to Federal Methodology, of whom 96% were aided. *Financial aid deadline (priority):* 3/1. *Financial aid forms:* FAFSA required. *Admission application deadline:* 4/1.

Summary of Aid to Needy Students *From gift & self-help combined:* Average need met: 95%. Average amount awarded: $8155 (24% gift aid, 76% self-help). *Gift aid:* Total: $4,148,065 (37% from college's own funds, 17% from other college-administered sources, 46% from external sources). 1,019 Federal Work-Study jobs (averaging $1345); part-time jobs.

Need-Based Scholarships & Grants Pell, FSEOG, state, private, college/university.

Loans Perkins, PLUS, Stafford, Unsubsidized Stafford, private.

Non-Need Awards In 1996, a total of 77 non-need awards were made. *Academic Interests/Achievement Awards:* 65 ($65,500 total): general academic. *Creative Arts/Performance Awards:* 12 ($22,346 total): creative writing, music, theater/drama. *Special Characteristics Awards:* 0: children of faculty/staff, international students, ROTC participants.

Other Money-Saving Options Accelerated degree, cooperative Army ROTC, cooperative Air Force ROTC, off-campus living (after sophomore year). *Waivers:* full or partial for minority students and employees or children of employees.

Contact Mr. Robert A. Tuveson, Director of Financial Aid, Plymouth State College of the University System of New Hampshire, Plymouth, NH 03264-1595, 603-535-2338.

POINT LOMA NAZARENE COLLEGE
San Diego, California

About the Institution Independent/religious, coed. Degrees awarded: B, M. Offers 53 undergraduate majors. Total enrollment: 2,491. Undergraduates: 2,142 (80% state residents). Freshmen: 515.

Undergraduate Expenses (1997–98) Comprehensive fee of $17,434 includes tuition ($12,224), mandatory fees ($240), and college room and board ($4970).

Applications Of all full-time undergraduates enrolled in fall 1996, 84% of those who applied for aid were judged to have need according to Federal Methodology, of whom 97% were aided. *Financial aid deadline (priority):* 4/15. *Financial aid forms:* FAFSA, institutional form required. *Admission application deadline:* 8/1.

Summary of Aid to Needy Students *From gift & self-help combined:* Average need met: 88%. Average amount awarded: $6439. 190 Federal Work-Study jobs (averaging $1500); 100 part-time jobs.

Need-Based Scholarships & Grants Pell, FSEOG, state, private, college/university.

Loans Perkins, PLUS, Stafford, Unsubsidized Stafford, Federal Nursing, private.

Non-Need Awards In 1996, a total of 2,959 non-need awards were made. *Academic Interests/Achievement Awards:* 1,045 ($2,194,581 total): general academic, biological sciences, business, communication, education, engineering/technologies, health fields, home economics, humanities, mathematics, religion/biblical studies, social sciences.

Creative Arts/Performance Awards: 96 ($136,947 total): art/fine arts, debating, music, theater/drama. *Special Characteristics Awards:* 1,659 ($2,205,932 total): children of faculty/staff, local/state students, relatives of clergy, religious affiliation, ROTC participants, siblings of current students. *Athletic:* Total: 159 ($526,159); Men: 96 ($302,892); Women: 63 ($223,267).

Other Money-Saving Options Accelerated degree, cooperative Army ROTC, cooperative Naval ROTC, cooperative Air Force ROTC, off-campus living (after junior year). *Payment Plan:* installment. *Waivers:* full or partial for employees or children of employees and senior citizens.

Contact Ms. Susan R. Tornquist, Director, Financial Aid, Point Loma Nazarene College, 3900 Lomaland Drive, San Diego, CA 92106-2899, 619-849-2296, fax: 619-849-2579.

POINT PARK COLLEGE
Pittsburgh, Pennsylvania

About the Institution Independent, coed. Degrees awarded: A, B, M. Offers 49 undergraduate majors. Total enrollment: 2,297. Undergraduates: 2,221 (80% state residents). Freshmen: 203.

Undergraduate Expenses (1997–98) Comprehensive fee of $16,118 includes tuition ($11,050), mandatory fees ($356), and college room and board ($4712 minimum). College room only: $2292 (minimum).

Applications Of all full-time undergraduates enrolled in fall 1996, 92% of those who applied for aid were judged to have need according to Federal Methodology, of whom 100% were aided. *Financial aid deadline (priority):* 4/16. *Financial aid forms:* FAFSA, institutional form required. *Admission application deadline:* rolling.

Summary of Aid to Needy Students *From gift & self-help combined:* Average need met: 95%. Average amount awarded: $10,500. *Gift aid:* Total: $4,600,000. 781 Federal Work-Study jobs (averaging $1129); 29 part-time jobs.

Need-Based Scholarships & Grants Pell, FSEOG, state, college/university.

Loans Perkins, Stafford, Unsubsidized Stafford.

Non-Need Awards *Academic Interests/Achievement Awards:* general academic. *Creative Arts/Performance Awards:* dance, journalism/publications, performing arts, theater/drama. *Athletic:* available.

Other Money-Saving Options Accelerated degree, co-op program, cooperative Army ROTC, cooperative Air Force ROTC, off-campus living. *Payment Plans:* installment, deferred payment. *Waivers:* full or partial for employees or children of employees and senior citizens.

Contact Mr. Robert Reddy, Associate Director of Financial Aid, Point Park College, 201 Wood Street, Pittsburgh, PA 15222-1984, 412-392-3930.

POLYTECHNIC UNIVERSITY, BROOKLYN CAMPUS
Brooklyn, New York

About the Institution Independent, coed. Degrees awarded: B, M, D. Offers 20 undergraduate majors. Total enrollment: 2,219. Undergraduates: 1,199 (92% state residents). Freshmen: 254.

Undergraduate Expenses (1996–97) Comprehensive fee of $22,590 includes tuition ($17,890), mandatory fees ($460), and college room and board ($4240 minimum).

Applications 96% of all full-time undergraduates enrolled in fall 1996 applied for aid; of these, 93% were judged to have need according to Federal Methodology, of whom 100% were aided. *Financial aid deadline (priority):* 3/1. *Financial aid forms:* FAFSA, CSS Financial Aid PROFILE, institutional form required. *Admission application deadline:* rolling.

Summary of Aid to Needy Students *From gift & self-help combined:* Average need met: 81%. Average amount awarded: $9527 (71% gift aid, 29% self-help). *Gift aid:* Total: $6,160,277 (52% from college's own funds, 8% from other college-administered sources, 40% from external sources). 358 Federal Work-Study jobs (averaging $1392); 381 part-time jobs.

Need-Based Scholarships & Grants Pell, FSEOG, college/university.

Loans Perkins, Stafford, Unsubsidized Stafford, college/university long-term loans ($1567 average).

Non-Need Awards *Academic Interests/Achievement Awards:* general academic, computer science, engineering/technologies.

Other Money-Saving Options Accelerated degree, co-op program, Army ROTC, cooperative Air Force ROTC, off-campus living. *Payment Plans:* tuition prepayment, deferred payment. *Waivers:* full or partial for minority students and employees or children of employees.

Contact Office of Financial Aid Services, Polytechnic University, Brooklyn Campus, 333 Jay Street, Brooklyn, NY 11201-2990, 718-260-3300, fax: 718-260-3052.

POLYTECHNIC UNIVERSITY, FARMINGDALE CAMPUS
Farmingdale, New York

About the Institution Independent, coed. Degrees awarded: B, M, D. Offers 12 undergraduate majors. Total enrollment: 697. Undergraduates: 389 (85% state residents). Freshmen: 112.

Undergraduate Expenses (1996–97) Comprehensive fee of $22,750 includes tuition ($17,890), mandatory fees ($460), and college room and board ($4400 minimum).

Applications 95% of all full-time undergraduates enrolled in fall 1996 applied for aid; of these, 78% were judged to have need according to Federal Methodology, of whom 100% were aided. *Financial aid deadline (priority):* 3/1. *Financial aid forms:* FAFSA, CSS Financial Aid PROFILE, institutional form required. *Admission application deadline:* rolling.

Summary of Aid to Needy Students *From gift & self-help combined:* Average need met: 79%. Average amount awarded: $9274 (73% gift aid, 27% self-help). *Gift aid:* Total: $1,775,296 (74% from college's own funds, 8% from other college-administered sources, 18% from external sources). 60 Federal Work-Study jobs (averaging $1107); 47 part-time jobs.

Need-Based Scholarships & Grants Pell, FSEOG, college/university.

Loans Perkins, Stafford, Unsubsidized Stafford, college/university long-term loans ($1535 average).

Non-Need Awards *Academic Interests/Achievement Awards:* general academic , engineering/technologies.

Other Money-Saving Options Accelerated degree, co-op program, Army ROTC, cooperative Air Force ROTC, off-campus living. *Payment Plans:* tuition prepayment, deferred payment. *Waivers:* full or partial for minority students and employees or children of employees.

Contact Financial Aid Office, Polytechnic University, Farmingdale Campus, 333 Jay Street, Brooklyn, NY 11201-9210, 718-260-3541.

POLYTECHNIC UNIVERSITY OF PUERTO RICO
Hato Rey, Puerto Rico

About the Institution Independent, coed. Degrees awarded: B, M. Offers 8 undergraduate majors. Total enrollment: 4,461. Undergraduates: 4,338 (98% commonwealth residents). Freshmen: 894.

Undergraduate Expenses (1996–97) Tuition: $3420. Mandatory fees: $720.

Applications Of all full-time undergraduates enrolled in fall 1996, 100% of those who applied for aid were judged to have need according to Federal Methodology, of whom 100% were aided. *Financial aid deadline (priority): 6/30. Financial aid forms:* FAFSA, institutional form required. Territory of Puerto Rico income tax form required for some. *Admission application deadline:* 8/15.

Summary of Aid to Needy Students *From gift & self-help combined:* Average need met: 70%. Average amount awarded: $3267 (71% gift aid, 29% self-help). *Gift aid:* Total: $5,558,931 (1% from college's own funds, 15% from other college-administered sources, 84% from external sources). 40 Federal Work-Study jobs (averaging $1692); 60 part-time jobs.

Need-Based Scholarships & Grants Pell, FSEOG, state.

Loans PLUS, Stafford, Unsubsidized Stafford.

Non-Need Awards In 1996, a total of 60 non-need awards were made. *Academic Interests/Achievement Awards:* 60 ($6000 total).

Other Money-Saving Options Cooperative Army ROTC. *Payment Plan:* deferred payment. *Waivers:* full or partial for employees or children of employees.

Contact Sra. Carmen E. Rivera, Director of Financial Aid, Polytechnic University of Puerto Rico, Hato Rey, PR 00919, 787-754-8000 Ext. 253.

POMONA COLLEGE
Claremont, California

About the Institution Independent, coed. Degrees awarded: B. Offers 56 undergraduate majors. Total enrollment: 1,420 (44% state residents). Freshmen: 399.

Undergraduate Expenses (1997–98) Comprehensive fee of $28,860 includes tuition ($20,500), mandatory fees ($180), and college room and board ($8180).

Applications Of all full-time undergraduates enrolled in fall 1996, 92% of those who applied for aid were judged to have need according to Federal Methodology, of whom 100% were aided. *Financial aid deadline:* 2/11. *Financial aid forms:* FAFSA, CSS Financial Aid PROFILE, state form required. *Regular admission application deadline:* 1/1. Early decision deadline: 11/15.

Summary of Aid to Needy Students *From gift & self-help combined:* Average need met: 100%. Average amount awarded: $20,600 (72% gift aid, 28% self-help). *Gift aid:* Total: $12,457,957 (83% from college's own funds, 11% from other college-administered sources, 6% from external sources). 206 Federal Work-Study jobs (averaging $2110); 565 part-time jobs.

Need-Based Scholarships & Grants Pell, FSEOG, state, private, college/university.

Loans Perkins, PLUS, Stafford, Unsubsidized Stafford, private, college/university short-term loans ($150 average), college/university long-term loans ($3500 average).

Non-Need Awards Not offered.

Other Money-Saving Options Off-campus living (after sophomore year). *Payment Plan:* installment. *Waivers:* full or partial for employees or children of employees.

Contact Ms. Colleen MacDonald, Assistant Director of Financial Aid, Pomona College, 550 North College Avenue, #117, Claremont, CA 91711, 909-621-8205, fax: 909-621-8403.

PONTIFICAL CATHOLIC UNIVERSITY OF PUERTO RICO
Ponce, Puerto Rico

About the Institution Independent/religious, coed. Degrees awarded: A, B, M. Offers 46 undergraduate majors. Total enrollment: 11,470. Undergraduates: 10,155 (99% commonwealth residents). Freshmen: 1,791.

Undergraduate Expenses (1996–97) Comprehensive fee of $6174 includes tuition ($3040), mandatory fees ($474), and college room and board ($2660). College room only: $900.

Applications *Financial aid deadline (priority):* 6/15. *Financial aid forms:* FAFSA, institutional form required. *Admission application deadline:* 7/15.

Summary of Aid to Needy Students *From gift & self-help combined:* Average need met: 30%. Average amount awarded: $3300. Federal Work-Study jobs; 500 part-time jobs.

Need-Based Scholarships & Grants Pell, FSEOG, state, private, college/university, Federal Nursing Grants for Disadvantaged Students.

Loans Perkins, PLUS, Stafford, Unsubsidized Stafford.

Non-Need Awards *Academic Interests/Achievement Awards:* available. *Creative Arts/Performance Awards:* available. *Special Characteristics Awards:* spouses of current students. *Athletic:* available.

Other Money-Saving Options Accelerated degree, cooperative Army ROTC, cooperative Air Force ROTC, off-campus living. *Waivers:* full or partial for employees or children of employees.

Contact Financial Aid Office, Pontifical Catholic University of Puerto Rico, Ponce, PR 00731-6382, 787-841-2000 Ext. 442.

PONTIFICAL COLLEGE JOSEPHINUM
Columbus, Ohio

About the Institution Independent/religious, primarily men. Degrees awarded: B, M. Offers 7 undergraduate majors. Total enrollment: 130. Undergraduates: 42 (27% state residents). Freshmen: 6.

Undergraduate Expenses (1997–98) Comprehensive fee of $11,690 includes tuition ($6870), mandatory fees ($300), and college room and board ($4520). College room only: $2260.

Applications 86% of all full-time undergraduates enrolled in fall 1996 applied for aid; of these, 73% were judged to have need according to Federal Methodology, of whom 100% were aided. *Financial aid deadline (priority):* 7/15. *Financial aid forms:* FAFSA, institutional form required; CSS Financial Aid PROFILE acceptable. State form required for some. *Admission application deadline:* rolling.

Summary of Aid to Needy Students *Gift aid:* Total: $232,971 (19% from college's own funds, 33% from other college-administered sources, 48% from external sources). Federal Work-Study jobs; part-time jobs.

Need-Based Scholarships & Grants Pell, FSEOG, state, private, college/university.

Loans Perkins, PLUS, Stafford, Unsubsidized Stafford, private.

Non-Need Awards *Special Characteristics Awards:* local/state students.

Other Money-Saving Options *Payment Plans:* installment, deferred payment.

Contact Mrs. Linda Bryant, Director of Financial Aid, Pontifical College Josephinum, 7625 North High Street, Columbus, OH 43235-1498, 614-885-5585.

PORTLAND STATE UNIVERSITY
Portland, Oregon

About the Institution State-supported, coed. Degrees awarded: B, M, D. Offers 58 undergraduate majors. Total enrollment: 14,768. Undergraduates: 10,368 (87% state residents). Freshmen: 910.

Undergraduate Expenses (1996–97) State resident tuition: $2694. Nonresident tuition: $9960. Mandatory fees: $486. College room and board: $4500. College room only: $2007 (minimum).

Applications Of all full-time undergraduates enrolled in fall 1996, 84% of those who applied for aid were judged to have need according to Federal Methodology, of whom 90% were aided. *Financial aid deadline:* Applications processed continuously. *Financial aid forms:* FAFSA, institutional form required. *Admission application deadline:* 6/1.

Summary of Aid to Needy Students *From gift & self-help combined:* Average need met: 68%. Average amount awarded: $5646 (32% gift aid, 68% self-help). *Gift aid:* Total: $7,569,517 (3% from college's own funds, 32% from other college-administered sources, 65% from external sources). 627 Federal Work-Study jobs (averaging $2643); 700 part-time jobs.

Need-Based Scholarships & Grants Pell, FSEOG, state, private, college/university.

Loans Perkins, PLUS, Stafford, Unsubsidized Stafford, private, college/university short-term loans ($300 average).

Non-Need Awards *Academic Interests/Achievement Awards:* available. *Creative Arts/Performance Awards:* 47 ($40,280 total): art/fine arts, music, theater/drama. *Special Achievements/Activities Awards:* community service, memberships. *Special Characteristics Awards:* 220 ($698,708 total): members of minorities. *Athletic:* Total: 179 ($1,159,469); Men: 123 ($845,974); Women: 56 ($313,495).

Other Money-Saving Options Accelerated degree, co-op program, Army ROTC, cooperative Air Force ROTC, off-campus living. *Payment Plans:* installment, deferred payment. *Waivers:* full or partial for minority students, employees or children of employees, senior citizens.

Contact Mr. Samuel Collie, Director of Student Financial Aid, Portland State University, PO Box 751, Portland, OR 97207-0751, 503-725-5448.

PRACTICAL BIBLE COLLEGE
Bible School Park, New York

About the Institution Independent/religious, coed. Degrees awarded: A, B. Offers 1 undergraduate major. Total enrollment: 240 (83% state residents). Freshmen: 45.

Undergraduate Expenses (1996–97) Comprehensive fee of $8350 includes tuition ($4500), mandatory fees ($500), and college room and board ($3350).

Applications 88% of all full-time undergraduates enrolled in fall 1996 applied for aid; of these, 98% were judged to have need according to Federal Methodology, of whom 95% were aided. *Financial aid deadline (priority):* 7/15. *Financial aid forms:* FAFSA required. State form, institutional form required for some. *Admission application deadline:* rolling.

Summary of Aid to Needy Students *From gift & self-help combined:* Average need met: 73%. Average amount awarded: $6558 (73% gift aid, 27% self-help). *Gift aid:* Total: $717,522 (28% from college's own funds, 27% from other college-administered sources, 45% from external sources). 30 part-time jobs.

Need-Based Scholarships & Grants Pell, state, private, college/university.

Loans PLUS, Stafford, Unsubsidized Stafford, private, college/university short-term loans ($1000 average), college/university long-term loans ($1000 average).

Non-Need Awards In 1996, a total of 50 non-need awards were made. *Academic Interests/Achievement Awards:* 3 ($3000 total): general academic. *Creative Arts/Performance Awards:* 6 ($13,500 total): music. *Special Achievements/Activities Awards:* 6 ($1000 total): leadership. *Special Characteristics Awards:* 35 ($65,000 total): children and siblings of alumni, children of educators, children of faculty/staff, international students, relatives of clergy, spouses of current students.

Other Money-Saving Options Off-campus living (after freshman year). *Payment Plan:* installment. *Waivers:* full or partial for children of alumni and employees or children of employees.

Contact Mr. Randy Carman, Financial Aid Director, Practical Bible College, PO Box 601, Bible School Park, NY 13737-0601, 607-729-1581 Ext. 332, fax: 607-729-2962.

PRAIRIE VIEW A&M UNIVERSITY
Prairie View, Texas

About the Institution State-supported, coed. Degrees awarded: B, M. Offers 58 undergraduate majors. Total enrollment: 5,999. Undergraduates: 4,929 (87% state residents). Freshmen: 1,069.

Undergraduate Expenses (1996–97) State resident tuition: $900. Nonresident tuition: $6660. Mandatory fees: $1000. College room and board: $3620.

Applications *Financial aid deadline (priority):* 4/1. *Financial aid forms:* FAFSA, CSS Financial Aid PROFILE, institutional form required. *Admission application deadline:* rolling.

Summary of Aid to Needy Students *From gift & self-help combined:* Average need met: 70%. Average amount awarded: $4500. 558 Federal Work-Study jobs (averaging $2500); 438 part-time jobs.

Need-Based Scholarships & Grants Pell, FSEOG, state, private, college/university.

Loans Perkins, PLUS, Stafford, Unsubsidized Stafford, state, private.

Non-Need Awards *Academic Interests/Achievement Awards:* 325 ($1,300,000 total): general academic, agriculture, architecture. *Creative Arts/Performance Awards:* 30 ($90,000 total): art/fine arts, music, performing arts. *Special Characteristics Awards:* ethnic background. *Athletic:* Total: 49 ($114,000); Men: 35 ($75,000); Women: 14 ($39,000).

Other Money-Saving Options Accelerated degree, co-op program, Army ROTC, Naval ROTC, off-campus living (after sophomore year). *Payment Plan:* installment. *Waivers:* full or partial for minority students and employees or children of employees.

Contact Mr. A. D. James Jr., Director of Financial Aid, Prairie View A&M University, PO Box 2967, Prairie View, TX 77446-2967, 409-857-2423, fax: 409-857-2425.

PRATT INSTITUTE
Brooklyn, New York

About the Institution Independent, coed. Degrees awarded: A, B, M. Offers 23 undergraduate majors. Total enrollment: 3,363. Undergraduates: 1,972 (45% state residents). Freshmen: 420.

Undergraduate Expenses (1997–98) Comprehensive fee of $24,304 includes tuition ($16,601), mandatory fees ($550), and college room and board ($7153 minimum). College room only: $4199 (minimum).

Applications Of all full-time undergraduates enrolled in fall 1996, 89% of those who applied for aid were judged to have need according to Federal Methodology, of whom 100% were aided. *Financial aid deadline (priority):* 2/1. *Financial aid forms:* FAFSA, institutional form required. State form required for some. *Regular admission application deadline:* rolling. Early action deadline: 11/1.

Summary of Aid to Needy Students *From gift & self-help combined:* Average need met: 59%. Average amount awarded: $12,730 (64% gift aid, 36% self-help). *Gift aid:* Total: $10,792,956 (70% from college's

own funds, 4% from other college-administered sources, 26% from external sources). 430 Federal Work-Study jobs (averaging $2250); 100 part-time jobs.

Need-Based Scholarships & Grants Pell, FSEOG, state, college/university.

Loans Perkins, PLUS, Stafford, Unsubsidized Stafford, college/university short-term loans ($300 average).

Non-Need Awards In 1996, a total of 785 non-need awards were made. *Academic Interests/Achievement Awards:* 190 ($480,750 total): architecture. *Creative Arts/Performance Awards:* 595 ($1,839,736 total): applied art and design.

Other Money-Saving Options Co-op program, cooperative Army ROTC, off-campus living. *Payment Plans:* installment, deferred payment. *Waivers:* full or partial for employees or children of employees.

Contact Office of Financial Aid, Pratt Institute, 200 Willoughby Avenue, Brooklyn, NY 11205-3899, 718-636-3600.

PRESBYTERIAN COLLEGE
Clinton, South Carolina

About the Institution Independent/religious, coed. Degrees awarded: B. Offers 31 undergraduate majors. Total enrollment: 1,153 (48% state residents). Freshmen: 287.

Undergraduate Expenses (1997–98) Comprehensive fee of $19,022 includes tuition ($13,716), mandatory fees ($1090), and college room and board ($4216). College room only: $1990.

Applications 67% of all full-time undergraduates enrolled in fall 1996 applied for aid; of these, 89% were judged to have need according to Federal Methodology, of whom 100% were aided. *Financial aid deadline (priority):* 3/1. *Financial aid forms:* FAFSA, institutional form required; CSS Financial Aid PROFILE acceptable. State form required for some. *Regular admission application deadline:* 4/1. Early decision deadline: 12/5.

Summary of Aid to Needy Students *From gift & self-help combined:* Average need met: 98%. Average amount awarded: $12,329 (84% gift aid, 16% self-help). *Gift aid:* Total: $6,994,633 (73% from college's own funds, 1% from other college-administered sources, 26% from external sources). Federal Work-Study jobs (averaging $1000); 150 part-time jobs.

Need-Based Scholarships & Grants Pell, FSEOG, state, private, college/university.

Loans Perkins, PLUS, Stafford, Unsubsidized Stafford, college/university long-term loans ($2500 average).

Non-Need Awards In 1996, a total of 451 non-need awards were made. *Academic Interests/Achievement Awards:* 146 ($647,250 total): general academic. *Creative Arts/Performance Awards:* 45 ($63,150 total): music. *Special Achievements/Activities Awards:* 53 ($135,000 total): leadership. *Special Characteristics Awards:* 34 ($34,000 total): relatives of clergy. *Athletic:* Total: 173 ($874,799); Men: 123 ($669,469); Women: 50 ($205,330).

Other Money-Saving Options Accelerated degree, Army ROTC, off-campus living (after junior year). *Payment Plans:* tuition prepayment, installment. *Waivers:* full or partial for employees or children of employees and senior citizens.

Contact Ms. Judi Gillespie, Director of Financial Aid, Presbyterian College, 503 South Broad Street, Clinton, SC 29325, 864-833-8287, fax: 864-833-8481.

PRESCOTT COLLEGE
Prescott, Arizona

About the Institution Independent, coed. Degrees awarded: B, M.

Applications *Financial aid deadline (priority):* 4/15. *Financial aid forms:* FAFSA, institutional form required; CSS Financial Aid PROFILE, state form acceptable. *Admission application deadline:* 2/1.

Need-Based Scholarships & Grants Pell, FSEOG, private, college/university.

Loans Perkins, PLUS, Stafford, Unsubsidized Stafford.

Non-Need Awards Not offered.

Other Money-Saving Options Accelerated degree. *Payment Plan:* installment. *Waivers:* full or partial for employees or children of employees.

Contact Ms. Donna Endresen, Director of Financial Aid, Prescott College, 220 Grove Avenue, Prescott, AZ 86301-2990, 520-776-5168, fax: 520-776-5175.

PRESENTATION COLLEGE
Aberdeen, South Dakota

About the Institution Independent/religious, primarily women. Degrees awarded: A, B. Offers 19 undergraduate majors. Total enrollment: 422 (81% state residents). Freshmen: 70.

Undergraduate Expenses (1996–97) Comprehensive fee of $10,136 includes tuition ($6690), mandatory fees ($400), and college room and board ($3046).

Applications *Financial aid deadline (priority):* 4/1. *Financial aid forms:* FAFSA required. *Admission application deadline:* rolling.

Summary of Aid to Needy Students *From gift & self-help combined:* Average amount awarded: $6484 (37% gift aid, 63% self-help). *Gift aid:* Total: $833,853 (46% from college's own funds, 9% from other college-administered sources, 45% from external sources). 52 Federal Work-Study jobs (averaging $1000); 13 part-time jobs.

Need-Based Scholarships & Grants Pell, FSEOG, private, college/university.

Loans Perkins, PLUS, Stafford, Unsubsidized Stafford, private, college/university long-term loans ($1000 average).

Non-Need Awards *Academic Interests/Achievement Awards:* general academic, business, communication, computer science, health fields, religion/biblical studies. *Special Characteristics Awards:* children and siblings of alumni, children of current students, children of faculty/staff, parents of current students, siblings of current students, spouses of current students.

Other Money-Saving Options Co-op program, cooperative Army ROTC, off-campus living (after freshman year). *Waivers:* full or partial for employees or children of employees and senior citizens.

Contact Ms. Brenda Schmitt, Director of Financial Aid and Admissions, Presentation College, Aberdeen, SD 57401-1299, 605-229-8429, fax: 605-229-8430.

PRINCETON UNIVERSITY
Princeton, New Jersey

About the Institution Independent, coed. Degrees awarded: B, M, D. Offers 37 undergraduate majors. Total enrollment: 6,340. Undergraduates: 4,593 (14% state residents). Freshmen: 1,129.

Undergraduate Expenses (1997–98) Comprehensive fee of $29,435 includes tuition ($22,920) and college room and board ($6515). College room only: $2987.

Applications 49% of all full-time undergraduates enrolled in fall 1996 applied for aid; of these, 87% were judged to have need according to Federal Methodology, of whom 100% were aided. *Financial aid deadline (priority):* 2/1. *Financial aid forms:* FAFSA, CSS Financial Aid PROFILE, institutional form required. *Regular admission application deadline:* 1/2. Early decision deadline: 11/1.

Summary of Aid to Needy Students *From gift & self-help combined:* Average need met: 100%. Average amount awarded: $18,434 (76% gift aid, 24% self-help). *Gift aid:* Total: $28,131,000 (85% from college's own funds, 4% from other college-administered sources, 11% from external sources). 1,000 Federal Work-Study jobs (averaging $1200); 1,500 part-time jobs.

Need-Based Scholarships & Grants Pell, FSEOG, state, private, college/university.

Loans Perkins, PLUS, Stafford, Unsubsidized Stafford, college/university long-term loans ($3600 average).

Non-Need Awards Not offered.

Other Money-Saving Options Accelerated degree, Army ROTC, cooperative Air Force ROTC, off-campus living (after sophomore year). *Payment Plans:* installment, deferred payment. *Waivers:* full or partial for employees or children of employees.

Contact Office of Financial Aid, Princeton University, Box 591, Princeton, NJ 08544-1019, 609-258-3000.

PRINCIPIA COLLEGE
Elsah, Illinois

About the Institution Independent/religious, coed. Degrees awarded: B. Offers 34 undergraduate majors. Total enrollment: 533 (3% state residents). Freshmen: 118.

Undergraduate Expenses (1997–98 estimated) Comprehensive fee of $19,698 includes tuition ($13,866), mandatory fees ($246), and college room and board ($5586). College room only: $2874.

Applications *Financial aid deadline (priority):* 3/1. *Financial aid forms:* CSS Financial Aid PROFILE, institutional form required; state form acceptable. *Admission application deadline:* 5/1.

Summary of Aid to Needy Students 378 part-time jobs.

Need-Based Scholarships & Grants Private, college/university.

Loans State, private, college/university long-term loans ($2445 average).

Non-Need Awards *Academic Interests/Achievement Awards:* general academic. *Special Characteristics Awards:* children and siblings of alumni, local/state students.

Other Money-Saving Options Accelerated degree. *Payment Plan:* installment. *Waivers:* full or partial for employees or children of employees.

Contact Mr. Brooks F. Benjamin, Director of Financial Aid, Principia College, Elsah, IL 62028-9799, 618-374-5186.

PROVIDENCE COLLEGE
Providence, Rhode Island

About the Institution Independent/religious, coed. Degrees awarded: A, B, M, D. Offers 44 undergraduate majors. Total enrollment: 5,621. Undergraduates: 3,589 (15% state residents). Freshmen: 937.

Undergraduate Expenses (1997–98) Comprehensive fee of $23,574 includes tuition ($16,350), mandatory fees ($220), and college room and board ($7004). College room only: $3485.

Applications Of all full-time undergraduates enrolled in fall 1996, 100% of those judged to have need according to Federal Methodology were aided. *Financial aid deadline (priority):* 2/1. *Financial aid forms:*

FAFSA, state form required. CSS Financial Aid PROFILE required for some. *Regular admission application deadline:* 1/15. Early action deadline: 11/15.

Summary of Aid to Needy Students *From gift & self-help combined:* Average need met: 80%. Average amount awarded: $13,808 (64% gift aid, 36% self-help). *Gift aid:* Total: $16,759,000 (80% from college's own funds, 8% from other college-administered sources, 12% from external sources). 918 Federal Work-Study jobs (averaging $1600); 700 part-time jobs.

Need-Based Scholarships & Grants Pell, FSEOG, state, private, college/university.

Loans Perkins, PLUS, Stafford, Unsubsidized Stafford.

Non-Need Awards *Academic Interests/Achievement Awards:* general academic, business, military science, premedicine. *Special Achievements/Activities Awards:* community service. *Athletic:* available.

Other Money-Saving Options Army ROTC, off-campus living (after sophomore year). *Payment Plan:* installment. *Waivers:* full or partial for employees or children of employees.

Contact Mr. Herbert J. D'Arcy, Executive Director of Financial Aid, Providence College, Providence, RI 02918, 401-865-2286.

PUGET SOUND CHRISTIAN COLLEGE
Edmonds, Washington

About the Institution Independent/religious, coed. Degrees awarded: A, B. Offers 10 undergraduate majors. Total enrollment: 166 (76% state residents). Freshmen: 37.

Undergraduate Expenses (1997–98) Comprehensive fee of $9945 includes tuition ($5550), mandatory fees ($525), and college room and board ($3870).

Applications 84% of all full-time undergraduates enrolled in fall 1996 applied for aid; of these, 98% were judged to have need according to Federal Methodology, of whom 100% were aided. *Financial aid deadline (priority):* 9/1. *Financial aid forms:* FAFSA, institutional form required. *Admission application deadline:* 9/15.

Summary of Aid to Needy Students *From gift & self-help combined:* Average need met: 80%. Average amount awarded: $6894 (45% gift aid, 55% self-help). *Gift aid:* Total: $390,390 (50% from college's own funds, 2% from other college-administered sources, 48% from external sources). 16 Federal Work-Study jobs (averaging $1928); 10 part-time jobs.

Need-Based Scholarships & Grants Pell, FSEOG, private, college/university.

Loans PLUS, Stafford, Unsubsidized Stafford, college/university short-term loans ($50 average).

Non-Need Awards *Academic Interests/Achievement Awards:* general academic, religion/biblical studies. *Special Characteristics Awards:* 41 ($177,716 total): children of faculty/staff, relatives of clergy, spouses of current students, veterans.

Other Money-Saving Options Off-campus living (after sophomore year). *Payment Plans:* tuition prepayment, installment. *Waivers:* full or partial for employees or children of employees and senior citizens.

Contact Office of Financial Aid, Puget Sound Christian College, 410 4th Avenue North, Edmonds, WA 98020-3171, 206-775-8686, fax: 206-775-8688.

PURCHASE COLLEGE, STATE UNIVERSITY OF NEW YORK
Purchase, New York

About the Institution State-supported, coed. Degrees awarded: B, M. Offers 22 undergraduate majors. Total enrollment: 2,396. Undergraduates: 2,317 (86% state residents). Freshmen: 410.

Undergraduate Expenses (1996–97) State resident tuition: $3400. Nonresident tuition: $8300. Mandatory fees: $465. College room and board: $5096. College room only: $3240.

Applications 78% of all full-time undergraduates enrolled in fall 1996 applied for aid; of these, 66% were judged to have need according to Federal Methodology, of whom 100% were aided. *Financial aid deadline (priority):* 2/15. *Financial aid forms:* FAFSA, institutional form required. State form required for some. *Admission application deadline:* rolling.

Summary of Aid to Needy Students *From gift & self-help combined:* Average need met: 72%. Average amount awarded: $9355 (47% gift aid, 53% self-help). *Gift aid:* Total: $4,842,229 (10% from college's own funds, 40% from other college-administered sources, 50% from external sources). 251 Federal Work-Study jobs (averaging $1000); 350 part-time jobs.

Need-Based Scholarships & Grants Pell, FSEOG, state, private, college/university.

Loans Perkins, PLUS, Stafford, Unsubsidized Stafford, private, college/university short-term loans ($200 average).

Non-Need Awards In 1996, a total of 259 non-need awards were made. *Academic Interests/Achievement Awards:* 87 ($124,175 total): general academic, biological sciences. *Creative Arts/Performance Awards:* 172 ($255,602 total): general creative, art/fine arts, cinema/film/broadcasting, dance, music, performing arts, theater/drama.

Other Money-Saving Options Off-campus living. *Payment Plan:* installment. *Waivers:* full or partial for employees or children of employees and senior citizens.

Contact Ms. Emilie B. Devine, Director Financial Aid, Purchase College, State University of New York, 735 Anderson Hill Road, Purchase, NY 10577-1400, 914-251-6355, fax: 914-251-6356.

PURDUE UNIVERSITY
West Lafayette, Indiana

About the Institution State-supported, coed. Degrees awarded: A, B, M, D, P. Offers 210 undergraduate majors. Total enrollment: 35,156. Undergraduates: 28,567 (74% state residents). Freshmen: 6,241.

Undergraduate Expenses (1997–98) State resident tuition: $3352. Nonresident tuition: $11,184. College room and board: $4800.

Applications Of all full-time undergraduates enrolled in fall 1996, 69% of those who applied for aid were judged to have need according to Federal Methodology, of whom 93% were aided. *Financial aid deadline (priority):* 3/1. *Financial aid forms:* FAFSA required. *Admission application deadline:* rolling.

Summary of Aid to Needy Students *From gift & self-help combined:* Average need met: 100%. Average amount awarded: $8127 (29% gift aid, 71% self-help). *Gift aid:* Total: $25,290,416 (26% from college's own funds, 6% from other college-administered sources, 68% from external sources). 1,395 Federal Work-Study jobs (averaging $1591); 1,600 part-time jobs.

Need-Based Scholarships & Grants Pell, FSEOG, state, private, college/university.

Loans Perkins, PLUS, Stafford, Unsubsidized Stafford, private, college/university long-term loans ($972 average).

Non-Need Awards *Academic Interests/Achievement Awards:* agriculture, biological sciences, business, education, engineering/technologies, physical sciences. *Special Characteristics Awards:* children of faculty/staff, international students, out-of-state students, ROTC participants. *Athletic:* Total: 311 ($2,906,402); Men: 204 ($1,905,519); Women: 107 ($1,000,883).

Other Money-Saving Options Accelerated degree, co-op program, Army ROTC, Naval ROTC, Air Force ROTC, off-campus living. *Payment Plan:* installment. *Waivers:* full or partial for employees or children of employees.

Contact Division of Financial Aid, Purdue University, Schleman Hall, Room 305, West Lafayette, IN 47907-1968, 765-494-5050.

PURDUE UNIVERSITY CALUMET
Hammond, Indiana

About the Institution State-supported, coed. Degrees awarded: A, B, M. Offers 78 undergraduate majors. Total enrollment: 9,402. Undergraduates: 8,974 (95% state residents).

Undergraduate Expenses (1997–98) State resident tuition: $2806. Nonresident tuition: $7060. Mandatory fees: $282.

Applications Of all full-time undergraduates enrolled in fall 1996, 100% of those judged to have need according to Federal Methodology were aided. *Financial aid deadline (priority):* 3/1. *Financial aid forms:* FAFSA required. *Admission application deadline:* rolling.

Summary of Aid to Needy Students *From gift & self-help combined:* Average need met: 100%. Average amount awarded: $4100 (41% gift aid, 59% self-help). *Gift aid:* Total: $5,560,000 (6% from college's own funds, 37% from other college-administered sources, 57% from external sources). 100 Federal Work-Study jobs (averaging $1800).

Need-Based Scholarships & Grants Pell, FSEOG, state, private, college/university.

Loans Perkins, PLUS, Stafford, Unsubsidized Stafford.

Non-Need Awards In 1996, a total of 294 non-need awards were made. *Academic Interests/Achievement Awards:* 250 ($250,000 total): general academic. *Athletic:* Total: 44 ($46,273); Men: 24 ($21,950); Women: 20 ($24,323).

Other Money-Saving Options Co-op program, cooperative Army ROTC. *Payment Plan:* deferred payment. *Waivers:* full or partial for employees or children of employees and senior citizens.

Contact Office of Financial Aid, Purdue University Calumet, 2200 169th Street, Hammond, IN 46323-2094, 219-989-2660, fax: 219-989-2771.

PURDUE UNIVERSITY NORTH CENTRAL
Westville, Indiana

About the Institution State-supported, coed. Degrees awarded: A, B, M. Offers 25 undergraduate majors. Total enrollment: 3,399. Undergraduates: 3,355 (99% state residents). Freshmen: 1,046.

Undergraduate Expenses (1997–98) State resident tuition: $2715. Nonresident tuition: $6899. Mandatory fees: $264.

Applications Of all full-time undergraduates enrolled in fall 1996, 68% of those who applied for aid were judged to have need according to Federal Methodology, of whom 85% were aided. *Financial aid deadline (priority):* 3/1. *Financial aid forms:* FAFSA, state form, institutional form required. *Admission application deadline:* 8/6.

Summary of Aid to Needy Students *From gift & self-help combined:* Average need met: 65%. Average amount awarded: $3127 (51% gift aid, 49% self-help). *Gift aid:* Total: $1,150,700 (2% from college's own funds, 43% from other college-administered sources, 55% from external sources). 50 Federal Work-Study jobs (averaging $1600); 30 part-time jobs.

Need-Based Scholarships & Grants Pell, FSEOG, state, private, college/university.

Loans Perkins, PLUS, Stafford, Unsubsidized Stafford, college/university short-term loans ($100 average).

Non-Need Awards In 1996, a total of 197 non-need awards were made. *Special Achievements/Activities Awards:* 17 ($20,000 total): general special achievements/activities, leadership. *Special Characteristics Awards:* 180 ($65,000 total): adult students, children of faculty/staff, veterans' children.

Other Money-Saving Options Co-op program. *Waivers:* full or partial for senior citizens.

Contact Financial Aid Office, Purdue University North Central, Westville, IN 46391-9543, 219-785-5279, fax: 219-785-5538.

QUEENS COLLEGE
Charlotte, North Carolina

About the Institution Independent/religious, coed. Degrees awarded: B, M. Offers 37 undergraduate majors. Total enrollment: 1,564. Undergraduates: 1,110 (70% state residents). Freshmen: 160.

Undergraduate Expenses (1997–98) Comprehensive fee of $18,580 includes tuition ($12,980) and college room and board ($5600).

Applications *Financial aid deadline (priority):* 3/1. *Financial aid forms:* FAFSA required. *Admission application deadline:* rolling.

Summary of Aid to Needy Students *From gift & self-help combined:* Average amount awarded: $12,002 (70% gift aid, 30% self-help). *Gift aid:* Total: $3,304,471 (77% from college's own funds, 12% from other college-administered sources, 11% from external sources). 83 Federal Work-Study jobs (averaging $1500); 126 part-time jobs.

Need-Based Scholarships & Grants Pell, FSEOG, state, private, college/university.

Loans Perkins, PLUS, Stafford, Unsubsidized Stafford.

Non-Need Awards *Academic Interests/Achievement Awards:* general academic. *Creative Arts/Performance Awards:* art/fine arts, music. *Special Achievements/Activities Awards:* general special achievements/activities, community service, leadership. *Special Characteristics Awards:* adult students, children of current students, international students, local/state students, members of minorities, previous college experience, relatives of clergy, siblings of current students. *Athletic:* Total: 91 ($490,075).

Other Money-Saving Options Cooperative Army ROTC, cooperative Air Force ROTC. *Payment Plans:* installment, deferred payment. *Waivers:* full or partial for employees or children of employees.

Contact Ms. Amanda Fagg, Assistant Director of Financial Aid, Queens College, 1900 Selwyn Avenue, Charlotte, NC 28274-0002, 704-337-2225, fax: 704-337-2403.

QUEENS COLLEGE OF THE CITY UNIVERSITY OF NEW YORK
Flushing, New York

About the Institution State & locally supported, coed. Degrees awarded: B, M. Offers 93 undergraduate majors. Total enrollment: 17,073. Undergraduates: 13,442 (96% state residents). Freshmen: 1,183.

Undergraduate Expenses (1996–97) State resident tuition: $3200. Nonresident tuition: $6800. Mandatory fees: $187.

Applications *Financial aid deadline (priority):* 5/31. *Financial aid forms:* FAFSA, institutional form required. *Admission application deadline:* 1/15.

Summary of Aid to Needy Students *From gift & self-help combined:* Average need met: 80%. *Gift aid:* Total: $16,300,000. Federal Work-Study jobs.

Need-Based Scholarships & Grants Pell, FSEOG.

Loans Perkins, Stafford, Unsubsidized Stafford.

Non-Need Awards *Academic Interests/Achievement Awards:* general academic. *Athletic:* available.

Other Money-Saving Options Accelerated degree, co-op program. *Payment Plan:* installment. *Waivers:* full or partial for employees or children of employees.

Contact Office of Financial Aid, Queens College of the City University of New York, 65-30 Kissena Boulevard, Flushing, NY 11367-1597, 718-997-5100.

QUINCY UNIVERSITY
Quincy, Illinois

About the Institution Independent/religious, coed. Degrees awarded: A, B, M. Offers 49 undergraduate majors. Total enrollment: 1,141. Undergraduates: 1,050 (67% state residents). Freshmen: 283.

Undergraduate Expenses (1997–98) Comprehensive fee of $16,830 includes tuition ($12,080), mandatory fees ($330), and college room and board ($4420). College room only: $1800.

Applications 89% of all full-time undergraduates enrolled in fall 1996 applied for aid; of these, 94% were judged to have need according to Federal Methodology, of whom 100% were aided. *Financial aid deadline:* continuous. *Financial aid forms:* FAFSA, institutional form required. *Admission application deadline:* rolling.

Summary of Aid to Needy Students *From gift & self-help combined:* Average need met: 96%. Average amount awarded: $12,503 (72% gift aid, 28% self-help). *Gift aid:* Total: $7,543,977 (69% from college's own funds, 23% from other college-administered sources, 8% from external sources). 374 Federal Work-Study jobs (averaging $1200); 56 part-time jobs.

Need-Based Scholarships & Grants Pell, FSEOG, state, private, college/university.

Loans Perkins, PLUS, Stafford, Unsubsidized Stafford, private, college/university short-term loans ($150 average).

Non-Need Awards In 1996, a total of 1,008 non-need awards were made. *Academic Interests/Achievement Awards:* 640 ($1,665,671 total): general academic, biological sciences, business, education, English, health fields, international studies, mathematics, religion/biblical studies, social sciences. *Creative Arts/Performance Awards:* 71 ($87,335 total): art/fine arts, cinema/film/broadcasting, music. *Special Achievements/Activities Awards:* 19 ($24,475 total): community service, leadership. *Special Characteristics Awards:* 99 ($167,402 total): children and siblings of alumni, children of faculty/staff, relatives of clergy, siblings of current students. *Athletic:* Total: 179 ($968,729); Men: 126 ($618,179); Women: 53 ($350,550).

Other Money-Saving Options Accelerated degree, off-campus living (after junior year). *Payment Plans:* guaranteed tuition, installment. *Waivers:* full or partial for employees or children of employees and senior citizens.

Contact Ms. Briget A. Biernat, Director of Financial Aid, Quincy University, 1800 College Avenue, Quincy, IL 62301-2699, 217-228-5260, fax: 217-228-5479.

QUINNIPIAC COLLEGE
Hamden, Connecticut

About the Institution Independent, coed. Degrees awarded: B, M, P. Offers 60 undergraduate majors. Total enrollment: 5,117. Undergraduates: 3,814 (38% state residents). Freshmen: 959.

Undergraduate Expenses (1997–98) Comprehensive fee of $22,070 includes tuition ($14,160), mandatory fees ($720), and college room and board ($7190).

Applications Of all full-time undergraduates enrolled in fall 1996, 88% of those who applied for aid were judged to have need according to Federal Methodology, of whom 99% were aided. *Financial aid deadline (priority):* 3/1. *Financial aid forms:* FAFSA, institutional form required; state form acceptable. *Admission application deadline:* 2/15.

Summary of Aid to Needy Students *From gift & self-help combined:* Average need met: 65%. Average amount awarded: $9358 (56% gift aid, 44% self-help). *Gift aid:* Total: $12,014,531 (70% from college's own funds, 18% from other college-administered sources, 12% from external sources). 266 Federal Work-Study jobs (averaging $1500); part-time jobs.

Need-Based Scholarships & Grants Pell, FSEOG, state, private, college/university.

Loans Perkins, PLUS, Stafford, Unsubsidized Stafford, Federal Nursing, private, college/university short-term loans ($100 average), college/university long-term loans ($650 average).

Non-Need Awards In 1996, a total of 672 non-need awards were made. *Academic Interests/Achievement Awards:* 497 ($1,222,150 total): general academic. *Special Achievements/Activities Awards:* 23 ($82,500 total): leadership. *Special Characteristics Awards:* 20 ($164,620 total): children of faculty/staff, local/state students, veterans. *Athletic:* Total: 132 ($776,209); Men: 63 ($379,090); Women: 69 ($397,119).

Other Money-Saving Options Accelerated degree, cooperative Army ROTC, cooperative Air Force ROTC, off-campus living. *Payment Plan:* installment. *Waivers:* full or partial for employees or children of employees and senior citizens.

Contact Office of Financial Aid, Quinnipiac College, Mount Carmel Avenue, Hamden, CT 06518-1904, 203-288-5251.

RABBINICAL ACADEMY MESIVTA RABBI CHAIM BERLIN
Brooklyn, New York

About the Institution Independent/religious, men. Offers 4 undergraduate majors. Total enrollment: 375. Undergraduates: 275 (95% state residents). Freshmen: 40.

Undergraduate Expenses (1996–97) Comprehensive fee of $7650 includes tuition ($4750) and college room and board ($2900).

Applications *Financial aid deadline (priority):* 10/15. *Financial aid forms:* FAFSA required.

Summary of Aid to Needy Students Federal Work-Study jobs.

Contact Office of Financial Aid, Rabbinical Academy Mesivta Rabbi Chaim Berlin, Brooklyn, NY 11230-4715, 718-377-0777.

RABBINICAL COLLEGE BOBOVER YESHIVA B'NEI ZION
Brooklyn, New York

About the Institution Independent/religious, men. Offers 1 undergraduate major.

Applications *Financial aid deadline:* continuous. *Financial aid forms:* FAFSA required.

Summary of Aid to Needy Students Federal Work-Study jobs; part-time jobs.

Need-Based Scholarships & Grants Pell, FSEOG, private, college/university.

Non-Need Awards Not offered.

Another Money-Saving Option Off-campus living.

Contact Financial Aid Office, Rabbinical College Bobover Yeshiva B'nei Zion, Brooklyn, NY 11219, 718-438-2018.

RABBINICAL COLLEGE OF AMERICA
Morristown, New Jersey

About the Institution Independent/religious, men. Degrees awarded: B. Offers 1 undergraduate major.

Applications *Financial aid deadline (priority):* 9/1. *Financial aid forms:* FAFSA required. *Admission application deadline:* rolling.

Summary of Aid to Needy Students *From gift & self-help combined:* Average amount awarded: $4000. Federal Work-Study jobs.

Need-Based Scholarships & Grants Pell, FSEOG, college/university.

Loans Stafford.

Non-Need Awards Not offered.

Other Money-Saving Options Accelerated degree. *Payment Plan:* installment.

Contact Financial Aid Office, Rabbinical College of America, 226 Sussex Avenue, Morristown, NJ 07960, 973-267-9404, fax: 973-267-5208.

RABBINICAL COLLEGE OF LONG ISLAND
Long Beach, New York

About the Institution Independent/religious, men.

Applications Of all full-time undergraduates enrolled in fall 1996, 66% of those who applied for aid were judged to have need according to Federal Methodology, of whom 100% were aided. *Financial aid deadline:* continuous. *Financial aid forms:* FAFSA required.

Summary of Aid to Needy Students Federal Work-Study jobs; part-time jobs.

Need-Based Scholarships & Grants Pell, FSEOG, private.

Non-Need Awards Not offered.

Contact Rabbi Cone, Financial Aid Administrator, Rabbinical College of Long Island, Long Beach, NY 11561-3305, 516-431-7414.

RABBINICAL SEMINARY ADAS YEREIM
Brooklyn, New York

About the Institution Independent/religious, men.

Applications 64% of all full-time undergraduates enrolled in fall 1996 applied for aid; of these, 90% were judged to have need according to Federal Methodology, of whom 100% were aided. *Financial aid deadline:* 5/1. *Financial aid forms:* FAFSA, federal income tax form required.

Summary of Aid to Needy Students *From gift & self-help combined:* Average need met: 75%. Federal Work-Study jobs.

Need-Based Scholarships & Grants Pell, FSEOG, college/university.

Non-Need Awards *Academic Interests/Achievement Awards:* religion/biblical studies.

Contact Mr. Israel Weingarten, Financial Aid Administrator, Rabbinical Seminary Adas Yereim, 185 Wilson Street, Brooklyn, NY 11211-7206, 718-388-1751.

RABBINICAL SEMINARY OF AMERICA
Forest Hills, New York

About the Institution Independent/religious, men. Degrees awarded: P. Offers 2 undergraduate majors.

Applications *Financial aid deadline (priority):* 1/1. *Financial aid forms:* CSS Financial Aid PROFILE required. *Admission application deadline:* 12/1.

Summary of Aid to Needy Students 23 Federal Work-Study jobs.

Need-Based Scholarships & Grants Pell, FSEOG, college/university.

Non-Need Awards *Academic Interests/Achievement Awards:* general academic. *Special Achievements/Activities Awards:* religious involvement. *Special Characteristics Awards:* religious affiliation.

Other Money-Saving Options *Payment Plan:* installment. *Waivers:* full or partial for employees or children of employees.

Contact Ms. Leah Eisenstein, Director of Financial Aid, Rabbinical Seminary of America, Forest Hills, NY 11375, 718-268-4700, fax: 718-268-4684.

RADCLIFFE COLLEGE
Cambridge, Massachusetts

See Harvard University

RADFORD UNIVERSITY
Radford, Virginia

About the Institution State-supported, coed. Degrees awarded: B, M. Offers 85 undergraduate majors. Total enrollment: 8,270. Undergraduates: 7,262 (87% state residents). Freshmen: 1,429.

Undergraduate Expenses (1997–98) State resident tuition: $3180. Nonresident tuition: $7952. Mandatory fees: $1164. College room and board: $4416. College room only: $2448.

Applications 55% of all full-time undergraduates enrolled in fall 1996 applied for aid; of these, 76% were judged to have need according to Federal Methodology, of whom 95% were aided. *Financial aid deadline (priority):* 3/01. *Financial aid forms:* FAFSA required. *Admission application deadline:* 4/1.

Summary of Aid to Needy Students *From gift & self-help combined:* Average need met: 79%. Average amount awarded: $5368 (41% gift aid, 59% self-help). *Gift aid:* Total: $5,952,494 (10% from college's own funds, 45% from other college-administered sources, 45% from external sources). 473 Federal Work-Study jobs (averaging $1125); 943 part-time jobs.

Need-Based Scholarships & Grants Pell, FSEOG, state, private, college/university.

Loans Perkins, PLUS, Stafford, Unsubsidized Stafford, Federal Nursing, state, private, college/university short-term loans ($200 average).

Non-Need Awards In 1996, a total of 504 non-need awards were made. *Academic Interests/Achievement Awards:* 220 ($430,990 total): general academic, biological sciences, business, education, English, health fields, humanities, library science, mathematics, military science, physical sciences, premedicine. *Creative Arts/Performance Awards:* 40 ($37,635 total): applied art and design, art/fine arts, cinema/film/broadcasting, dance, music, theater/drama. *Special Achievements/Activities Awards:* 2 ($2550 total): leadership. *Special Characteristics Awards:* 60 ($248,558 total): members of minorities, ROTC participants. *Athletic:* Total: 182 ($850,316); Men: 84 ($384,583); Women: 98 ($465,733).

Other Money-Saving Options Accelerated degree, Army ROTC, off-campus living (after freshman year). *Payment Plan:* installment. *Waivers:* full or partial for employees or children of employees.

Contact Ms. Barbara Porter, Associate Director of Financial Aid, Radford University, PO Box 6905, Radford, VA 24142, 540-831-5408, fax: 540-831-5138.

RAMAPO COLLEGE OF NEW JERSEY
Mahwah, New Jersey

About the Institution State-supported, coed. Degrees awarded: B, M. Offers 40 undergraduate majors. Total enrollment: 4,001. Undergraduates: 3,947 (81% state residents). Freshmen: 430.

Undergraduate Expenses (1996–97) State resident tuition: $3752. Nonresident tuition: $5496. College room and board: $5678. College room only: $3714 (minimum).

Applications Of all full-time undergraduates enrolled in fall 1996, 84% of those who applied for aid were judged to have need according to Federal Methodology, of whom 72% were aided. *Financial aid deadline (priority):* 3/15. *Financial aid forms:* FAFSA required. *Admission application deadline:* 3/15.

Summary of Aid to Needy Students *From gift & self-help combined:* Average need met: 41%. Average amount awarded: $5092 (58% gift aid, 42% self-help). *Gift aid:* Total: $3,818,103 (9% from college's own funds, 4% from other college-administered sources, 87% from external sources). 150 Federal Work-Study jobs (averaging $1500); 250 part-time jobs.

Need-Based Scholarships & Grants Pell, FSEOG, state, private, college/university.

Loans Perkins, PLUS, Stafford, Unsubsidized Stafford, state.

Non-Need Awards In 1996, a total of 522 non-need awards were made. *Academic Interests/Achievement Awards:* 136 ($301,705 total): general academic. *Special Characteristics Awards:* 386 ($400,407 total): international students, out-of-state students, veterans.

Other Money-Saving Options Accelerated degree, co-op program, cooperative Army ROTC, off-campus living. *Payment Plan:* installment. *Waivers:* full or partial for employees or children of employees and senior citizens.

Contact Mr. Frank Cuozzo, Associate Director, Ramapo College of New Jersey, 505 Ramapo Valley Road, Mahwah, NJ 07430-1680, 201-529-6473, fax: 201-529-7508.

RANDOLPH-MACON COLLEGE
Ashland, Virginia

About the Institution Independent/religious, coed. Degrees awarded: B. Offers 31 undergraduate majors. Total enrollment: 1,101 (58% state residents). Freshmen: 324.

Undergraduate Expenses (1997–98) Comprehensive fee of $20,415 includes tuition ($15,865), mandatory fees ($125), and college room and board ($4425). College room only: $2380.

Applications 61% of all full-time undergraduates enrolled in fall 1996 applied for aid; of these, 76% were judged to have need according to Federal Methodology, of whom 100% were aided. *Financial aid deadline (priority):* 3/1. *Financial aid forms:* FAFSA, institutional form required. State form required for some. *Regular admission application deadline:* 3/1. Early decision deadline: 12/1.

Summary of Aid to Needy Students *From gift & self-help combined:* Average need met: 89%. Average amount awarded: $13,773 (54% gift aid, 46% self-help). *Gift aid:* Total: $3,800,000 (74% from college's own funds, 5% from other college-administered sources, 21% from external sources). 211 Federal Work-Study jobs (averaging $900); 200 part-time jobs.

Need-Based Scholarships & Grants Pell, FSEOG, state, private, college/university.

Loans Perkins, PLUS, Stafford, Unsubsidized Stafford, private, college/university long-term loans ($1400 average).

Non-Need Awards In 1996, a total of 230 non-need awards were made. *Academic Interests/Achievement Awards:* 195 ($960,000 total): general academic. *Special Characteristics Awards:* 35 ($190,000 total): relatives of clergy, siblings of current students.

Other Money-Saving Options Accelerated degree, cooperative Army ROTC, off-campus living (after junior year). *Payment Plan:* installment. *Waivers:* full or partial for employees or children of employees.

Contact Ms. Mary Neal, Director of Financial Aid, Randolph-Macon College, PO Box 5005, Ashland, VA 23005-5505, 804-752-7259, fax: 804-752-3719.

RANDOLPH-MACON WOMAN'S COLLEGE
Lynchburg, Virginia

About the Institution Independent/religious, women. Degrees awarded: B. Offers 36 undergraduate majors. Total enrollment: 698 (35% state residents). Freshmen: 189.

Undergraduate Expenses (1997–98) Comprehensive fee of $22,950 includes tuition ($15,880), mandatory fees ($350), and college room and board ($6720).

Applications 76% of all full-time undergraduates enrolled in fall 1996 applied for aid; of these, 84% were judged to have need according to Federal Methodology, of whom 100% were aided. *Financial aid deadline (priority):* 3/1. *Financial aid forms:* FAFSA, institutional form required. State form required for some. *Regular admission application deadline:* 3/1. Early decision deadline: 11/15.

Summary of Aid to Needy Students *From gift & self-help combined:* Average need met: 97%. Average amount awarded: $14,662 (66% gift aid, 34% self-help). *Gift aid:* Total: $3,535,656 (85% from college's own funds, 8% from other college-administered sources, 7% from external sources). 351 Federal Work-Study jobs (averaging $1550); 105 part-time jobs.

Need-Based Scholarships & Grants Pell, FSEOG, state, private, college/university.

Loans Perkins, PLUS, Stafford, Unsubsidized Stafford, college/university long-term loans ($8020 average).

Non-Need Awards In 1996, a total of 693 non-need awards were made. *Academic Interests/Achievement Awards:* 405 ($2,030,033 total): general academic. *Special Characteristics Awards:* 288 ($1,079,932 total): adult students, children of faculty/staff, international students, local/state students, relatives of clergy.

Other Money-Saving Options Accelerated degree. *Payment Plan:* installment. *Waivers:* full or partial for employees or children of employees and adult students.

Contact Mrs. Brantley R. Townes, Director of Financial Planning and Assistance, Randolph-Macon Woman's College, 2500 Rivermont Avenue, Lynchburg, VA 24503-1526, 804-947-8128.

REED COLLEGE
Portland, Oregon

About the Institution Independent, coed. Degrees awarded: B, M. Offers 33 undergraduate majors. Total enrollment: 1,325. Undergraduates: 1,306 (15% state residents). Freshmen: 361.

Undergraduate Expenses (1996–97) Comprehensive fee of $27,490 includes tuition ($21,330), mandatory fees ($160), and college room and board ($6000). College room only: $3000.

Applications 54% of all full-time undergraduates enrolled in fall 1996 applied for aid; of these, 92% were judged to have need according to Federal Methodology, of whom 94% were aided. *Financial aid deadline:* 3/1. *Financial aid forms:* FAFSA, CSS Financial Aid PROFILE required. Institutional form required for some. *Regular admission application deadline:* 2/1. Early decision deadline: 12/1.

Summary of Aid to Needy Students *From gift & self-help combined:* Average amount awarded: $17,256 (82% gift aid, 18% self-help). *Gift aid:* Total: $8,361,583 (88% from college's own funds, 3% from other college-administered sources, 9% from external sources). 198 Federal Work-Study jobs (averaging $639); part-time jobs.

Need-Based Scholarships & Grants Pell, FSEOG, state, college/university.

Loans Perkins, PLUS, Stafford, Unsubsidized Stafford, college/university short-term loans ($100 average), college/university long-term loans ($2800 average).

Non-Need Awards Not offered.

Other Money-Saving Options Accelerated degree, cooperative Army ROTC, off-campus living. *Payment Plan:* installment. *Waivers:* full or partial for employees or children of employees.

Contact Office of Financial Aid, Reed College, 3203 Southeast Woodstock Boulevard, Portland, OR 97202-8199, 503-771-1112.

REFORMED BIBLE COLLEGE
Grand Rapids, Michigan

About the Institution Independent/religious, coed. Degrees awarded: A, B. Offers 12 undergraduate majors. Total enrollment: 181 (53% state residents). Freshmen: 30.

Undergraduate Expenses (1996–97) Comprehensive fee of $10,086 includes tuition ($6600), mandatory fees ($136), and college room and board ($3350).

Applications Of all full-time undergraduates enrolled in fall 1996, 92% of those who applied for aid were judged to have need according to Federal Methodology, of whom 100% were aided. *Financial aid deadline (priority):* 4/15. *Financial aid forms:* FAFSA, institutional form required. *Admission application deadline:* rolling.

Summary of Aid to Needy Students *From gift & self-help combined:* Average need met: 55%. Average amount awarded: $6484 (60% gift aid, 40% self-help). *Gift aid:* Total: $343,434 (21% from college's own funds, 10% from other college-administered sources, 69% from external sources). 28 Federal Work-Study jobs (averaging $1100); 19 part-time jobs.

Need-Based Scholarships & Grants Pell, FSEOG, state, college/university.

Loans PLUS, Stafford, Unsubsidized Stafford, college/university long-term loans ($1808 average).

Non-Need Awards In 1996, a total of 48 non-need awards were made. *Academic Interests/Achievement Awards:* 29 ($17,825 total): general academic. *Special Achievements/Activities Awards:* 4 ($6000 total): leadership, religious involvement. *Special Characteristics Awards:* 15 ($148,300 total): children of faculty/staff, international students, spouses of current students.

Other Money-Saving Options Accelerated degree, co-op program, off-campus living (after sophomore year). *Payment Plan:* deferred payment. *Waivers:* full or partial for employees or children of employees.

Contact Ms. Agnes Russell, Financial Aid Administrator, Reformed Bible College, 3333 East Beltline NE, Grand Rapids, MI 49505-9749, 616-222-3000 Ext. 156, fax: 616-222-3045.

REGENTS COLLEGE
Albany, New York

See University of the State of New York, Regents College

REGIS COLLEGE
Weston, Massachusetts

About the Institution Independent/religious, women. Degrees awarded: B, M. Offers 18 undergraduate majors. Total enrollment: 1,401. Undergraduates: 1,206 (83% state residents). Freshmen: 207.

Undergraduate Expenses (1997–98) Comprehensive fee of $22,150 includes tuition ($15,250) and college room and board ($6900).

Applications 75% of all full-time undergraduates enrolled in fall 1996 applied for aid; of these, 94% were judged to have need according to Federal Methodology, of whom 99% were aided. *Financial aid deadline (priority):* 2/15. *Financial aid forms:* FAFSA, state form, institutional form required. CSS Financial Aid PROFILE required for some. *Admission application deadline:* rolling.

Summary of Aid to Needy Students *From gift & self-help combined:* Average need met: 83%. Average amount awarded: $15,290 (62% gift aid, 38% self-help). *Gift aid:* Total: $4,999,186 (71% from college's own funds, 13% from other college-administered sources, 16% from external sources). 275 Federal Work-Study jobs (averaging $890); 75 part-time jobs.

Need-Based Scholarships & Grants Pell, FSEOG, state, private, college/university.

Loans Perkins, PLUS, Stafford, Unsubsidized Stafford, state, private, college/university long-term loans ($1820 average).

Non-Need Awards In 1996, a total of 142 non-need awards were made. *Academic Interests/Achievement Awards:* 76 ($281,250 total): general academic. *Special Achievements/Activities Awards:* 66 ($130,000 total): community service, leadership.

Other Money-Saving Options Off-campus living. *Payment Plans:* tuition prepayment, installment, deferred payment. *Waivers:* full or partial for employees or children of employees.

Contact Office of Financial Aid, Regis College, Box 81, 235 Wellesley Street, Weston, MA 02193-1571, 617-768-7180, fax: 617-768-8339.

REGIS UNIVERSITY
Denver, Colorado

About the Institution Independent/religious, coed. Degrees awarded: B, M. Offers 32 undergraduate majors. Total enrollment: 7,039. Undergraduates: 1,160 (62% state residents). Freshmen: 224.

Undergraduate Expenses (1997–98) Comprehensive fee of $20,870 includes tuition ($14,900), mandatory fees ($70), and college room and board ($5900). College room only: $3200.

Applications 74% of all full-time undergraduates enrolled in fall 1996 applied for aid; of these, 85% were judged to have need according to Federal Methodology, of whom 98% were aided. *Financial aid deadline (priority):* 3/5. *Financial aid forms:* FAFSA required. State form, institutional form required for some. *Admission application deadline:* 8/15.

Summary of Aid to Needy Students *From gift & self-help combined:* Average need met: 79%. Average amount awarded: $13,437 (59% gift aid, 41% self-help). *Gift aid:* Total: $5,514,345 (70% from college's own funds, 22% from other college-administered sources, 8% from external sources). 156 Federal Work-Study jobs (averaging $2216); 394 part-time jobs.

Need-Based Scholarships & Grants Pell, FSEOG, state, college/university.

Loans Perkins, PLUS, Stafford, Unsubsidized Stafford, Federal Nursing, private.

Non-Need Awards In 1996, a total of 997 non-need awards were made. *Academic Interests/Achievement Awards:* 421 ($1,976,627 total): physical sciences. *Creative Arts/Performance Awards:* 9 ($59,925 total): debating. *Special Characteristics Awards:* 430 ($1,349,593 total): children of faculty/staff, ethnic background, local/state students, members of minorities, ROTC participants. *Athletic:* Total: 137 ($1,066,675); Men: 68 ($519,215); Women: 69 ($547,460).

Other Money-Saving Options Accelerated degree, co-op program, cooperative Air Force ROTC, off-campus living (after sophomore year). *Payment Plan:* deferred payment. *Waivers:* full or partial for employees or children of employees, adult students, senior citizens.

Contact Ms. Lydia MacMillan, Director of Financial Aid, Regis University, 3333 Regis Boulevard, A-8, Denver, CO 80221-1099, 303-458-4066, fax: 303-964-5534.

REINHARDT COLLEGE
Waleska, Georgia

About the Institution Independent/religious, coed. Degrees awarded: A, B. Offers 19 undergraduate majors. Total enrollment: 959 (95% state residents). Freshmen: 271.

Undergraduate Expenses (1997–98) Comprehensive fee of $11,235 includes tuition ($6762) and college room and board ($4473).

Applications 95% of all full-time undergraduates enrolled in fall 1996 applied for aid. *Financial aid deadline (priority):* 5/1. *Financial aid forms:* state form, institutional form required; CSS Financial Aid PROFILE acceptable. FAFSA required for some. *Regular admission application deadline:* rolling. Early action deadline: 12/31.

Summary of Aid to Needy Students *From gift & self-help combined:* Average need met: 100%. Average amount awarded: $5300 (83% gift aid, 17% self-help). *Gift aid:* Total: $3,119,499 (27% from college's

own funds, 60% from other college-administered sources, 13% from external sources). 50 Federal Work-Study jobs (averaging $1100); 132 part-time jobs.

Need-Based Scholarships & Grants Pell, FSEOG, state, private, college/university.

Loans PLUS, Stafford, Unsubsidized Stafford, private.

Non-Need Awards In 1996, a total of 150 non-need awards were made. *Academic Interests/Achievement Awards:* 15 ($1500 total): biological sciences, business, education, English, health fields, humanities, mathematics, social sciences. *Creative Arts/Performance Awards:* 15 ($20,000 total): art/fine arts, music, performing arts. *Special Achievements/Activities Awards:* 10 ($10,000 total): leadership. *Special Characteristics Awards:* 40 ($50,000 total): adult students, children and siblings of alumni, children of educators, children of faculty/staff, local/state students, relatives of clergy, religious affiliation. *Athletic:* Total: 70 ($100,000); Men: 35 ($50,000); Women: 35 ($50,000).

Other Money-Saving Options Off-campus living (after sophomore year). *Payment Plan:* installment. *Waivers:* full or partial for children of alumni, employees or children of employees, senior citizens.

Contact Ms. Amy Moser, Director of Financial Aid, Reinhardt College, 7300 Reinhardt College Parkway, Waleska, GA 30183-0128, 770-720-5603, fax: 770-720-5602.

RENSSELAER POLYTECHNIC INSTITUTE
Troy, New York

About the Institution Independent, coed. Degrees awarded: B, M, D. Offers 50 undergraduate majors. Total enrollment: 6,250. Undergraduates: 4,149 (41% state residents). Freshmen: 899.

Undergraduate Expenses (1997–98) Comprehensive fee of $27,386 includes tuition ($20,030), mandatory fees ($570), and college room and board ($6786).

Applications *Financial aid deadline (priority):* 2/15. *Financial aid forms:* FAFSA required. State form, institutional form required for some. *Regular admission application deadline:* 1/1. Early decision deadline: 12/1.

Summary of Aid to Needy Students *From gift & self-help combined:* Average amount awarded: $15,423 (72% gift aid, 28% self-help). *Gift aid:* Total: $38,451,000 (73% from college's own funds, 23% from other college-administered sources, 4% from external sources). 1,150 Federal Work-Study jobs (averaging $700).

Need-Based Scholarships & Grants Pell, FSEOG, state, private, college/university.

Loans Perkins, PLUS, Stafford, Unsubsidized Stafford, private, college/university long-term loans ($1230 average).

Non-Need Awards *Academic Interests/Achievement Awards:* ($2,806,000 total). *Special Characteristics Awards:* ($854,000 total): international students, local/state students, ROTC participants. *Athletic:* Total: 18 ($4,161,000); Men: 18 ($461,000).

Other Money-Saving Options Accelerated degree, co-op program, Army ROTC, Naval ROTC, Air Force ROTC, off-campus living (after freshman year). *Payment Plan:* installment. *Waivers:* full or partial for employees or children of employees.

Contact Office of Financial Aid, Rensselaer Polytechnic Institute, Admissions and Financial Aid Bldg, Troy, NY 12180-3590, 518-276-6000.

RESEARCH COLLEGE OF NURSING– ROCKHURST COLLEGE
Kansas City, Missouri

About the Institution Independent, coed. Degrees awarded: B, M. Offers 1 undergraduate major. Total enrollment: 274. Undergraduates: 268 (98% state residents). Freshmen: 25.

Undergraduate Expenses (1997–98) Comprehensive fee of $17,150 includes tuition ($11,550), mandatory fees ($600), and college room and board ($5000).

Applications 92% of all full-time undergraduates enrolled in fall 1996 applied for aid; of these, 98% were judged to have need according to Federal Methodology, of whom 100% were aided. *Financial aid deadline (priority):* 4/1. *Financial aid forms:* institutional form required; FAFSA, CSS Financial Aid PROFILE acceptable. *Admission application deadline:* 6/30.

Summary of Aid to Needy Students *From gift & self-help combined:* Average need met: 80%. Average amount awarded: $11,324 (49% gift aid, 51% self-help). *Gift aid:* Total: $669,450 (54% from college's own funds, 8% from other college-administered sources, 38% from external sources). 8 Federal Work-Study jobs (averaging $1500); 20 part-time jobs.

Need-Based Scholarships & Grants Pell, FSEOG, state, private, college/university.

Loans Perkins, PLUS, Stafford, Unsubsidized Stafford, Federal Nursing, private, college/university short-term loans ($500 average), college/university long-term loans ($1500 average).

Non-Need Awards In 1996, a total of 24 non-need awards were made. *Academic Interests/Achievement Awards:* 23 ($107,000 total): health fields. *Athletic:* Total: 1 ($5000); Men: 0; Women: 1 ($5000).

Other Money-Saving Options Cooperative Army ROTC, off-campus living (after freshman year). *Payment Plans:* guaranteed tuition, installment, deferred payment. *Waivers:* full or partial for employees or children of employees and senior citizens.

Contact Ms. Martha Harrison, Financial Aid Director, Research College of Nursing–Rockhurst College, Kansas City, MO 64132, 816-276-4732.

RHODE ISLAND COLLEGE
Providence, Rhode Island

About the Institution State-supported, coed. Degrees awarded: B, M. Offers 65 undergraduate majors. Total enrollment: 7,150. Undergraduates: 6,331 (93% state residents). Freshmen: 918.

Undergraduate Expenses (1996–97) State resident tuition: $2476. Nonresident tuition: $6996. Mandatory fees: $523. College room and board: $5367.

Applications Of all full-time undergraduates enrolled in fall 1996, 86% of those who applied for aid were judged to have need according to Federal Methodology, of whom 84% were aided. *Financial aid deadline (priority):* 3/1. *Financial aid forms:* FAFSA required. CSS Financial Aid PROFILE required for some. *Admission application deadline:* 5/1.

Summary of Aid to Needy Students *From gift & self-help combined:* Average need met: 76%. Average amount awarded: $5202 (40% gift aid, 60% self-help). *Gift aid:* Total: $6,301,791 (29% from college's own funds, 12% from other college-administered sources, 59% from external sources). 544 Federal Work-Study jobs (averaging $1313); 520 part-time jobs.

Need-Based Scholarships & Grants Pell, FSEOG, state, private, college/university.

Loans Perkins, PLUS, Stafford, Unsubsidized Stafford, state, college/university short-term loans ($180 average).

Non-Need Awards *Academic Interests/Achievement Awards:* 59 ($106,880 total): general academic. *Creative Arts/Performance Awards:* 103 ($61,120 total): art/fine arts, dance, debating, journalism/publications, music, theater/drama. *Special Achievements/Activities Awards:* 4 ($5100 total): hobbies/interest. *Special Characteristics Awards:* children of union members/company employees.

Other Money-Saving Options Accelerated degree, cooperative Army ROTC, off-campus living. *Payment Plan:* installment. *Waivers:* full or partial for employees or children of employees and senior citizens.

Contact Office of Financial Aid, Rhode Island College, 600 Mount Pleasant Avenue, Providence, RI 02908-1924, 401-456-8684.

RHODE ISLAND SCHOOL OF DESIGN
Providence, Rhode Island

About the Institution Independent, coed. Degrees awarded: B, M. Offers 17 undergraduate majors. Total enrollment: 2,003. Undergraduates: 1,818 (11% state residents). Freshmen: 384.

Undergraduate Expenses (1997–98) Comprehensive fee of $26,060 includes tuition ($19,340), mandatory fees ($330), and college room and board ($6390). College room only: $3390.

Applications 45% of all full-time undergraduates enrolled in fall 1996 applied for aid; of these, 94% were judged to have need according to Federal Methodology, of whom 98% were aided. *Financial aid deadline (priority):* 2/15. *Financial aid forms:* FAFSA, CSS Financial Aid PROFILE required. *Regular admission application deadline:* 2/15. Early action deadline: 12/15.

Summary of Aid to Needy Students *From gift & self-help combined:* Average amount awarded: $15,722 (45% gift aid, 55% self-help). *Gift aid:* Total: $5,588,918 (82% from college's own funds, 11% from other college-administered sources, 7% from external sources). 689 Federal Work-Study jobs (averaging $1350); 503 part-time jobs.

Need-Based Scholarships & Grants Pell, FSEOG, state, private, college/university.

Loans Perkins, PLUS, Stafford, Unsubsidized Stafford, college/university short-term loans ($25 average), college/university long-term loans ($1730 average).

Non-Need Awards *Academic Interests/Achievement Awards:* 31 ($65,000 total): general academic. *Creative Arts/Performance Awards:* applied art and design, art/fine arts. *Special Characteristics Awards:* children of faculty/staff.

Other Money-Saving Options Off-campus living (after freshman year). *Payment Plan:* installment. *Waivers:* full or partial for employees or children of employees.

Contact Mr. Peter R. Riefler, Director of Financial Aid, Rhode Island School of Design, 2 College Street, Providence, RI 02903-2784, 401-454-6636, fax: 401-454-6412.

RHODES COLLEGE
Memphis, Tennessee

About the Institution Independent/religious, coed. Degrees awarded: B, M. Offers 35 undergraduate majors. Total enrollment: 1,425. Undergraduates: 1,419 (31% state residents). Freshmen: 375.

Undergraduate Expenses (1997–98) Comprehensive fee of $22,628 includes tuition ($17,360), mandatory fees ($158), and college room and board ($5110 minimum). College room only: $2890 (minimum).

Applications 48% of all full-time undergraduates enrolled in fall 1996 applied for aid; of these, 84% were judged to have need according to Federal Methodology, of whom 99% were aided. *Financial aid deadline (priority):* 3/1. *Financial aid forms:* FAFSA, institutional form required. *Regular admission application deadline:* 2/1. Early decision deadline: 11/15.

Summary of Aid to Needy Students *From gift & self-help combined:* Average need met: 93%. Average amount awarded: $14,084 (72% gift aid, 28% self-help). *Gift aid:* Total: $5,676,081 (84% from college's own funds, 2% from other college-administered sources, 14% from external sources). 200 Federal Work-Study jobs (averaging $1265); 181 part-time jobs.

Need-Based Scholarships & Grants Pell, FSEOG, state, private, college/university.

Loans Perkins, PLUS, Stafford, Unsubsidized Stafford, private.

Non-Need Awards In 1996, a total of 676 non-need awards were made. *Academic Interests/Achievement Awards:* 537 ($3,916,533 total): general academic. *Creative Arts/Performance Awards:* 36 ($341,500 total): art/fine arts, music, theater/drama. *Special Achievements/Activities Awards:* 77 ($86,500 total): general special achievements/activities, hobbies/interest, memberships. *Special Characteristics Awards:* 26 ($297,206 total): children of faculty/staff, ethnic background, relatives of clergy, religious affiliation.

Other Money-Saving Options Accelerated degree, cooperative Army ROTC, cooperative Air Force ROTC, off-campus living. *Payment Plan:* installment. *Waivers:* full or partial for employees or children of employees.

Contact Office of Financial Aid, Rhodes College, 2000 North Parkway, Memphis, TN 38112-1690, 901-843-3000.

RICE UNIVERSITY
Houston, Texas

About the Institution Independent, coed. Degrees awarded: B, M, D, P. Offers 43 undergraduate majors. Total enrollment: 4,225. Undergraduates: 2,631 (47% state residents). Freshmen: 675.

Undergraduate Expenses (1996–97) Comprehensive fee of $19,200 includes tuition ($12,800), mandatory fees ($400), and college room and board ($6000).

Applications Of all full-time undergraduates enrolled in fall 1996, 74% of those who applied for aid were judged to have need according to Federal Methodology, of whom 98% were aided. *Financial aid deadline:* continuous. *Financial aid forms:* FAFSA, institutional form required. State form required for some. *Regular admission application deadline:* 1/2. Early decision deadline: 11/1. Early action deadline: 12/1.

Summary of Aid to Needy Students *From gift & self-help combined:* Average need met: 100%. Average amount awarded: $14,124 (75% gift aid, 25% self-help). *Gift aid:* Total: $11,056,516 (72% from college's own funds, 12% from other college-administered sources, 16% from external sources). 366 Federal Work-Study jobs (averaging $1284); part-time jobs.

Need-Based Scholarships & Grants Pell, FSEOG, state, private, college/university.

Loans Perkins, PLUS, Stafford, Unsubsidized Stafford, state, college/university short-term loans ($300 average).

Non-Need Awards In 1996, a total of 1,546 non-need awards were made. *Academic Interests/Achievement Awards:* 1,117 ($1,235,683 total): general academic, engineering/technologies. *Creative Arts/Performance Awards:* 57 ($220,564 total): music. *Special Characteristics Awards:* 78 ($947,795 total): children of faculty/staff, ROTC participants. *Athletic:* Total: 294 ($4,058,926); Men: 203 ($2,739,705); Women: 91 ($1,319,221).

Other Money-Saving Options Accelerated degree, Naval ROTC, cooperative Army ROTC, off-campus living. *Payment Plan:* installment. *Waivers:* full or partial for employees or children of employees.

Contact Office of Financial Aid, Rice University, 6100 South Main, MS 12, Houston, TX 77005-1892, 713-527-8101.

THE RICHARD STOCKTON COLLEGE OF NEW JERSEY
Pomona, New Jersey

About the Institution State-supported, coed. Degrees awarded: B, M. Offers 60 undergraduate majors. Total enrollment: 5,512 (96% state residents). Freshmen: 742.

Undergraduate Expenses (1996–97) State resident tuition: $2624. Nonresident tuition: $4224. Mandatory fees: $848. College room and board: $4487. College room only: $2925.

Applications 63% of all full-time undergraduates enrolled in fall 1996 applied for aid; of these, 79% were judged to have need according to Federal Methodology, of whom 95% were aided. *Financial aid deadline (priority):* 3/1. *Financial aid forms:* FAFSA required. *Admission application deadline:* 5/1.

Summary of Aid to Needy Students *From gift & self-help combined:* Average need met: 95%. Average amount awarded: $5171 (48% gift aid, 52% self-help). *Gift aid:* Total: $5,582,711 (6% from college's own funds, 8% from other college-administered sources, 86% from external sources). 179 Federal Work-Study jobs (averaging $1564); 365 part-time jobs.

Need-Based Scholarships & Grants Pell, FSEOG, state, college/university.

Loans Perkins, PLUS, Stafford, Unsubsidized Stafford, state.

Non-Need Awards In 1996, a total of 247 non-need awards were made. *Academic Interests/Achievement Awards:* 183 ($260,500 total): general academic, area/ethnic studies, biological sciences, business, computer science, education, health fields, humanities, mathematics, physical sciences, social sciences. *Creative Arts/Performance Awards:* 9 ($18,500 total): applied art and design, art/fine arts, creative writing, dance, journalism/publications, music, performing arts, theater/drama. *Special Achievements/Activities Awards:* 3 ($2000 total): general special achievements/activities, leadership. *Special Characteristics Awards:* 52 ($42,000 total): general special characteristics, adult students, children of faculty/staff, ethnic background, international students, local/state students, members of minorities, previous college experience.

Other Money-Saving Options Accelerated degree, cooperative Army ROTC, off-campus living. *Payment Plan:* installment. *Waivers:* full or partial for employees or children of employees and senior citizens.

Contact Office of Financial Aid, The Richard Stockton College of New Jersey, Jim Leeds Road, Pomona, NJ 08240-9988, 609-652-1776.

RIDER UNIVERSITY
Lawrenceville, New Jersey

About the Institution Independent, coed. Degrees awarded: B, M. Offers 55 undergraduate majors. Total enrollment: 4,640. Undergraduates: 3,633 (78% state residents). Freshmen: 696.

Undergraduate Expenses (1997–98) Comprehensive fee of $21,680 includes tuition ($15,120), mandatory fees ($290), and college room and board ($6270). College room only: $3370.

Applications Of all full-time undergraduates enrolled in fall 1996, 100% of those judged to have need according to Federal Methodology were aided. *Financial aid deadline (priority):* 3/1. *Financial aid forms:* FAFSA required. *Admission application deadline:* rolling.

Summary of Aid to Needy Students *From gift & self-help combined:* Average need met: 96%. Average amount awarded: $14,490 (63% gift aid, 37% self-help). *Gift aid:* Total: $18,026,295 (58% from college's own funds, 4% from other college-administered sources, 38% from external sources). 1,386 Federal Work-Study jobs (averaging $962); part-time jobs.

Need-Based Scholarships & Grants Pell, FSEOG, state, private, college/university.

Loans Perkins, PLUS, Stafford, Unsubsidized Stafford, state, private, college/university short-term loans ($50 average), college/university long-term loans ($1400 average).

Non-Need Awards In 1996, a total of 570 non-need awards were made. *Academic Interests/Achievement Awards:* 336 ($2,078,598 total): general academic. *Creative Arts/Performance Awards:* 7 ($97,150 total): art/fine arts, theater/drama. *Special Characteristics Awards:* 29 ($236,225 total): members of minorities, ROTC participants. *Athletic:* Total: 198 ($1,351,363); Men: 103 ($689,195); Women: 95 ($662,168).

Other Money-Saving Options Army ROTC, cooperative Air Force ROTC, off-campus living. *Waivers:* full or partial for employees or children of employees.

Contact Mr. John J. Williams, Director of Financial Aid, Rider University, 2083 Lawrenceville Road, Lawrenceville, NJ 08648-3001, 609-896-5360.

RINGLING SCHOOL OF ART AND DESIGN
Sarasota, Florida

About the Institution Independent, coed. Degrees awarded: B. Offers 7 undergraduate majors. Total enrollment: 830 (45% state residents). Freshmen: 218.

Undergraduate Expenses (1997–98) Comprehensive fee of $19,942 includes tuition ($13,050), mandatory fees ($200), and college room and board ($6692).

Applications 87% of all full-time undergraduates enrolled in fall 1996 applied for aid; of these, 91% were judged to have need according to Federal Methodology, of whom 96% were aided. *Financial aid deadline (priority):* 3/1. *Financial aid forms:* FAFSA, CSS Financial Aid PROFILE, institutional form required. State form required for some. *Admission application deadline:* rolling.

Summary of Aid to Needy Students *From gift & self-help combined:* Average need met: 73%. Average amount awarded: $7563 (33% gift aid, 67% self-help). *Gift aid:* Total: $1,488,431 (14% from college's own funds, 6% from other college-administered sources, 80% from external sources). 20 Federal Work-Study jobs (averaging $2200); 40 part-time jobs.

Need-Based Scholarships & Grants Pell, FSEOG, state, private.

Loans PLUS, Stafford, Unsubsidized Stafford, private.

Non-Need Awards In 1996, a total of 12 non-need awards were made. *Creative Arts/Performance Awards:* 12 ($21,000 total): applied art and design, art/fine arts.

Other Money-Saving Options Off-campus living. *Payment Plan:* installment. *Waivers:* full or partial for employees or children of employees.

Contact Office of Financial Aid, Ringling School of Art and Design, 2700 North Tamiami Trail, Sarasota, FL 34234-5895, 941-351-5100.

RIPON COLLEGE
Ripon, Wisconsin

About the Institution Independent, coed. Degrees awarded: B. Offers 40 undergraduate majors. Total enrollment: 734 (61% state residents). Freshmen: 169.

Undergraduate Expenses (1997–98) Comprehensive fee of $21,980 includes tuition ($17,350), mandatory fees ($230), and college room and board ($4400). College room only: $2000.

Applications 90% of all full-time undergraduates enrolled in fall 1996 applied for aid; of these, 98% were judged to have need according to Federal Methodology, of whom 100% were aided. *Financial aid deadline (priority):* 3/1. *Financial aid forms:* FAFSA required. Institutional form required for some. *Regular admission application deadline:* 3/15. Early decision deadline: 12/1.

Summary of Aid to Needy Students *From gift & self-help combined:* Average need met: 96%. Average amount awarded: $16,086 (69% gift aid, 31% self-help). *Gift aid:* Total: $6,694,119 (80% from college's own funds, 4% from other college-administered sources, 16% from external sources). 168 Federal Work-Study jobs (averaging $1080); 272 part-time jobs.

Need-Based Scholarships & Grants Pell, FSEOG, state, private, college/university.

Loans Perkins, PLUS, Stafford, Unsubsidized Stafford, private, college/university short-term loans ($50 average).

Non-Need Awards In 1996, a total of 473 non-need awards were made. *Academic Interests/Achievement Awards:* 296 ($1,035,062 total): general academic. *Creative Arts/Performance Awards:* 60 ($71,240 total): debating, music, theater/drama. *Special Achievements/Activities Awards:* 74 ($138,650 total): leadership, memberships. *Special Characteristics Awards:* 43 ($243,585 total): children and siblings of alumni, children of faculty/staff.

Other Money-Saving Options Accelerated degree, Army ROTC. *Payment Plan:* installment. *Waivers:* full or partial for children of alumni and employees or children of employees.

Contact Ms. Karri V. Michell, Director of Financial Aid, Ripon College, 300 Seward Street, Ripon, WI 54971, 414-748-8101, fax: 414-748-7243.

RIVIER COLLEGE
Nashua, New Hampshire

About the Institution Independent/religious, coed. Degrees awarded: A, B, M. Offers 40 undergraduate majors. Total enrollment: 2,798. Undergraduates: 1,726 (78% state residents). Freshmen: 124.

Undergraduate Expenses (1997–98) Comprehensive fee of $17,880 includes tuition ($12,300), mandatory fees ($200), and college room and board ($5380).

Applications *Financial aid deadline (priority):* 4/1. *Financial aid forms:* FAFSA required. State form required for some. *Regular admission application deadline:* rolling. Early action deadline: 11/15.

Summary of Aid to Needy Students *From gift & self-help combined:* Average need met: 85%. Average amount awarded: $8100. 200 Federal Work-Study jobs (averaging $1000); 52 part-time jobs.

Need-Based Scholarships & Grants Pell, FSEOG, state, private, college/university.

Loans Perkins, PLUS, Stafford, Unsubsidized Stafford, college/university short-term loans ($1000 average), college/university long-term loans ($1000 average).

Non-Need Awards *Academic Interests/Achievement Awards:* general academic.

Other Money-Saving Options Cooperative Air Force ROTC, off-campus living. *Payment Plans:* installment, deferred payment. *Waivers:* full or partial for employees or children of employees and senior citizens.

Contact Mr. Paul Henderson, Director of Financial Aid, Rivier College, 420 Main Street, Nashua, NH 03060-5086, 603-888-1311 Ext. 8534, fax: 603-891-1799.

ROANOKE BIBLE COLLEGE
Elizabeth City, North Carolina

About the Institution Independent/religious, coed. Degrees awarded: A, B. Offers 4 undergraduate majors. Total enrollment: 161 (52% state residents). Freshmen: 37.

Undergraduate Expenses (1997–98) Comprehensive fee of $8220 includes tuition ($4480), mandatory fees ($540), and college room and board ($3200 minimum). College room only: $1400 (minimum).

Applications 100% of all full-time undergraduates enrolled in fall 1996 applied for aid; of these, 78% were judged to have need according to Federal Methodology, of whom 100% were aided. *Financial aid deadline (priority):* 3/1. *Financial aid forms:* FAFSA, institutional form required; CSS Financial Aid PROFILE, state form acceptable. *Admission application deadline:* 8/1.

Summary of Aid to Needy Students *From gift & self-help combined:* Average need met: 90%. Average amount awarded: $3494 (58% gift aid, 42% self-help). *Gift aid:* Total: $144,941 (53% from college's own funds, 3% from other college-administered sources, 44% from external sources). Part-time jobs.

Need-Based Scholarships & Grants Pell, FSEOG, college/university.

Loans PLUS, Stafford, Unsubsidized Stafford.

Non-Need Awards In 1996, a total of 177 non-need awards were made. *Academic Interests/Achievement Awards:* 22 ($61,748 total): general academic, communication, international studies, religion/biblical studies. *Special Characteristics Awards:* 155 ($68,200 total): general special characteristics, children of faculty/staff, international students, spouses of current students, veterans' children.

Other Money-Saving Options *Payment Plans:* installment, deferred payment. *Waivers:* full or partial for employees or children of employees and senior citizens.

Contact Office of Financial Aid, Roanoke Bible College, 714 First Street, Elizabeth City, NC 27909-3926, 919-338-5191.

ROANOKE COLLEGE
Salem, Virginia

About the Institution Independent/religious, coed. Degrees awarded: B. Offers 24 undergraduate majors. Total enrollment: 1,694 (53% state residents). Freshmen: 438.

Undergraduate Expenses (1997–98) Comprehensive fee of $20,660 includes tuition ($15,380), mandatory fees ($190), and college room and board ($5090). College room only: $2470.

Applications 69% of all full-time undergraduates enrolled in fall 1996 applied for aid; of these, 88% were judged to have need according to Federal Methodology, of whom 99% were aided. *Financial aid deadline (priority):* 3/1. *Financial aid forms:* FAFSA required. State form required for some. *Regular admission application deadline:* 3/1. Early decision deadline: 11/15. Early action deadline: 9/15.

Summary of Aid to Needy Students *From gift & self-help combined:* Average need met: 94%. Average amount awarded: $13,834 (70% gift aid, 30% self-help). *Gift aid:* Total: $7,680,097 (79% from college's own funds, 16% from other college-administered sources, 5% from external sources). 361 Federal Work-Study jobs (averaging $1500); 400 part-time jobs.

Need-Based Scholarships & Grants Pell, FSEOG, state, private, college/university.

Loans Perkins, PLUS, Stafford, Unsubsidized Stafford, college/university long-term loans ($1600 average).

Non-Need Awards In 1996, a total of 3,578 non-need awards were made. *Academic Interests/Achievement Awards:* 2,461 ($6,981,023 total): general academic. *Creative Arts/Performance Awards:* 17 ($20,450 total): art/fine arts, music. *Special Characteristics Awards:* 1,100 ($1,635,300 total): local/state students, members of minorities, religious affiliation.

Other Money-Saving Options Accelerated degree. *Waivers:* full or partial for employees or children of employees and senior citizens.

Contact Mr. Thomas S. Blair Jr., Director of Financial Aid, Roanoke College, 221 College Lane, Salem, VA 24153-3794, 540-375-2235.

ROBERT MORRIS COLLEGE
Chicago, Illinois

About the Institution Independent, coed. Degrees awarded: A, B. Offers 14 undergraduate majors. Total enrollment: 3,734 (95% state residents). Freshmen: 1,979.

Undergraduate Expenses (1996–97) Tuition: $9750.

Applications 97% of all full-time undergraduates enrolled in fall 1996 applied for aid; of these, 91% were judged to have need according to Federal Methodology, of whom 96% were aided. *Financial aid deadline (priority):* 4/1. *Financial aid forms:* FAFSA required. State form, institutional form required for some. *Admission application deadline:* rolling.

Summary of Aid to Needy Students *From gift & self-help combined:* Average need met: 87%. Average amount awarded: $9761 (69% gift aid, 31% self-help). *Gift aid:* Total: $15,990,130 (23% from college's own funds, 55% from other college-administered sources, 22% from external sources). 325 Federal Work-Study jobs (averaging $764); 35 part-time jobs.

Need-Based Scholarships & Grants Pell, FSEOG, state, college/university.

Loans Perkins, PLUS, Stafford, Unsubsidized Stafford.

Non-Need Awards In 1996, a total of 539 non-need awards were made. *Academic Interests/Achievement Awards:* 265 ($472,643 total): general academic. *Special Achievements/Activities Awards:* 41 ($65,500 total): general special achievements/activities, community service. *Special Characteristics Awards:* 132 ($204,550 total): general special characteristics, children of faculty/staff, out-of-state students, veterans. *Athletic:* Total: 101 ($736,042); Men: 51 ($294,026); Women: 50 ($442,016).

Other Money-Saving Options Co-op program. *Payment Plan:* installment. *Waivers:* full or partial for employees or children of employees.

Contact Ms. Pamela Mills, Associate Director of Financial Services, Robert Morris College, 180 North LaSalle, Chicago, IL 60601-2592, 312-836-6271, fax: 312-836-9020.

ROBERT MORRIS COLLEGE
Moon Township, Pennsylvania

About the Institution Independent, coed. Degrees awarded: A, B, M. Offers 23 undergraduate majors. Total enrollment: 4,907. Undergraduates: 3,998 (91% state residents). Freshmen: 459.

Undergraduate Expenses (1997–98) Comprehensive fee of $13,273 includes tuition ($7905), mandatory fees ($434), and college room and board ($4934). College room only: $2868.

Applications 84% of all full-time undergraduates enrolled in fall 1996 applied for aid; of these, 96% were judged to have need according to Federal Methodology, of whom 93% were aided. *Financial aid deadline:* Applications processed continuously. *Financial aid forms:* FAFSA, state form, institutional form required. *Admission application deadline:* rolling.

Summary of Aid to Needy Students *From gift & self-help combined:* Average need met: 85%. Average amount awarded: $3776 (42% gift aid, 58% self-help). *Gift aid:* Total: $5,138,284 (19% from college's own funds, 54% from other college-administered sources, 27% from external sources). 450 Federal Work-Study jobs (averaging $1200); 150 part-time jobs.

Need-Based Scholarships & Grants Pell, FSEOG, state, private, college/university.

Loans Perkins, PLUS, Stafford, Unsubsidized Stafford, state, private, college/university long-term loans ($2300 average).

Non-Need Awards In 1996, a total of 695 non-need awards were made. *Academic Interests/Achievement Awards:* 311 ($615,116 total): general academic, business, communication, international studies. *Special Achievements/Activities Awards:* 156 ($398,773 total): hobbies/interest, leadership. *Special Characteristics Awards:* 81 ($196,864 total): children of faculty/staff, ethnic background, members of minorities, out-of-state students. *Athletic:* Total: 147 ($802,230); Men: 69 ($383,052); Women: 78 ($419,178).

Other Money-Saving Options Accelerated degree, co-op program, cooperative Army ROTC, cooperative Air Force ROTC, off-campus living. *Payment Plans:* installment, deferred payment. *Waivers:* full or partial for employees or children of employees and senior citizens.

Contact Mrs. Janet L. Lawson, Manager of Financial Aid, Robert Morris College, 881 Narrows Run Road, Moon Township, PA 15108-1189, 412-262-8267, fax: 412-262-8619.

ROBERTS WESLEYAN COLLEGE
Rochester, New York

About the Institution Independent/religious, coed. Degrees awarded: A, B, M. Offers 37 undergraduate majors. Total enrollment: 1,337. Undergraduates: 1,134 (81% state residents). Freshmen: 173.

Undergraduate Expenses (1997–98) Comprehensive fee of $16,570 includes tuition ($11,930), mandatory fees ($470), and college room and board ($4170). College room only: $2890.

Applications 79% of all full-time undergraduates enrolled in fall 1996 applied for aid; of these, 96% were judged to have need according to Federal Methodology, of whom 99% were aided. *Financial aid deadline (priority):* 3/15. *Financial aid forms:* FAFSA, institutional form required; CSS Financial Aid PROFILE acceptable. State form required for some. *Admission application deadline:* rolling.

Summary of Aid to Needy Students *From gift & self-help combined:* Average need met: 91%. Average amount awarded: $10,652 (59% gift aid, 41% self-help). *Gift aid:* Total: $4,549,920 (55% from college's own funds, 28% from other college-administered sources, 17% from external sources). 360 Federal Work-Study jobs (averaging $958); 232 part-time jobs.

Need-Based Scholarships & Grants Pell, FSEOG, state, private, college/university.

Loans Perkins, PLUS, Stafford, Unsubsidized Stafford, private.

Non-Need Awards *Academic Interests/Achievement Awards:* 372 ($1,011,991 total): general academic. *Creative Arts/Performance Awards:* 166 ($219,225 total): art/fine arts, music. *Special Achievements/ Activities Awards:* 259 ($214,577 total): community service, Junior Miss, leadership, religious involvement. *Special Characteristics Awards:* children of faculty/staff, international students, religious affiliation. *Athletic:* Total: 98 ($349,200); Men: 49 ($181,700); Women: 49 ($167,500).

Other Money-Saving Options Co-op program, cooperative Army ROTC, cooperative Air Force ROTC. *Payment Plan:* installment. *Waivers:* full or partial for employees or children of employees.

Contact Mr. Stephen Field, Director of Financial Aid, Roberts Wesleyan College, 2301 Westside Drive, Rochester, NY 14624-1997, 716-594-6150, fax: 716-594-6036.

ROCHESTER INSTITUTE OF TECHNOLOGY
Rochester, New York

About the Institution Independent, coed. Degrees awarded: A, B, M, D. Offers 91 undergraduate majors. Total enrollment: 12,933. Undergraduates: 10,755 (60% state residents). Freshmen: 1,774.

Undergraduate Expenses (1997–98) Comprehensive fee of $22,776 includes tuition ($16,083), mandatory fees ($276), and college room and board ($6417). College room only: $3486.

Applications 71% of all full-time undergraduates enrolled in fall 1996 applied for aid; of these, 95% were judged to have need according to Federal Methodology, of whom 100% were aided. *Financial aid deadline (priority):* 3/15. *Financial aid forms:* FAFSA required. State form, institutional form required for some. *Regular admission application deadline:* 7/1. Early decision deadline: 12/15.

Summary of Aid to Needy Students *From gift & self-help combined:* Average amount awarded: $14,428 (59% gift aid, 41% self-help). *Gift aid:* Total: $42,637,000 (69% from college's own funds, 6% from other college-administered sources, 25% from external sources). 2,000 Federal Work-Study jobs (averaging $2000); 2,600 part-time jobs.

Need-Based Scholarships & Grants Pell, FSEOG, state, private, college/university.

Loans Perkins, PLUS, Stafford, Unsubsidized Stafford, state, private, college/university short-term loans ($100 average).

Non-Need Awards In 1996, a total of 1,840 non-need awards were made. *Academic Interests/Achievement Awards:* 1,550 ($5,273,500 total): general academic, biological sciences, business, communication, computer science, engineering/technologies, health fields, mathematics, physical sciences, premedicine, social sciences. *Creative Arts/ Performance Awards:* 75 ($262,500 total): applied art and design, art/fine arts. *Special Characteristics Awards:* 215 ($751,580 total): international students, members of minorities, ROTC participants.

Other Money-Saving Options Co-op program, Army ROTC, Air Force ROTC, cooperative Naval ROTC, off-campus living (after sophomore year). *Payment Plans:* tuition prepayment, installment, deferred payment. *Waivers:* full or partial for employees or children of employees.

Contact Mrs. Verna Hazen, Director of Financial Aid, Rochester Institute of Technology, 56 Lomb Memorial Drive, Rochester, NY 14623-5604, 716-475-2186, fax: 716-475-7270.

ROCKFORD COLLEGE
Rockford, Illinois

About the Institution Independent, coed. Degrees awarded: B, M. Offers 50 undergraduate majors. Total enrollment: 1,309. Undergraduates: 1,036 (84% state residents). Freshmen: 97.

Undergraduate Expenses (1997–98) Comprehensive fee of $19,550 includes tuition ($14,750) and college room and board ($4800). College room only: $2900.

Applications Of all full-time undergraduates enrolled in fall 1996, 93% of those who applied for aid were judged to have need according to Federal Methodology, of whom 100% were aided. *Financial aid deadline (priority):* 4/15. *Financial aid forms:* FAFSA, institutional form required. *Admission application deadline:* rolling.

Summary of Aid to Needy Students *From gift & self-help combined:* Average need met: 90%. Average amount awarded: $14,686 (70% gift aid, 30% self-help). *Gift aid:* Total: $5,883,700 (47% from college's own funds, 29% from other college-administered sources, 24% from external sources). 253 Federal Work-Study jobs (averaging $1642); 18 part-time jobs.

Need-Based Scholarships & Grants Pell, FSEOG, state, private, college/university.

Loans Perkins, PLUS, Stafford, Unsubsidized Stafford, college/university long-term loans ($1251 average).

Non-Need Awards In 1996, a total of 274 non-need awards were made. *Academic Interests/Achievement Awards:* 7 ($2675 total): general academic, biological sciences, business, education, English, mathematics, physical sciences, premedicine. *Creative Arts/Performance Awards:* 4 ($7500 total): dance, music, theater/drama. *Special Characteristics Awards:* 263 ($854,647 total): general special characteristics, children and siblings of alumni, children of current students, children of educators, children of faculty/staff, children of workers in trades, handicapped students, international students, out-of-state students, parents of current students, relatives of clergy, siblings of current students.

Other Money-Saving Options Cooperative Army ROTC. *Payment Plans:* installment, deferred payment. *Waivers:* full or partial for employees or children of employees.

Contact Ms. Judy Seebach, Director of Financial Aid, Rockford College, 5050 East State Street, Rockford, IL 61103, 815-226-4050, fax: 815-226-4119.

ROCKHURST COLLEGE
Kansas City, Missouri

About the Institution Independent/religious, coed. Degrees awarded: B, M. Offers 32 undergraduate majors. Total enrollment: 2,866. Undergraduates: 2,157 (69% state residents). Freshmen: 368.

Undergraduate Expenses (1997–98 estimated) Comprehensive fee of $16,550 includes tuition ($11,550), mandatory fees ($240), and college room and board ($4760).

Applications *Financial aid deadline (priority):* 4/1. *Financial aid forms:* institutional form required; FAFSA, CSS Financial Aid PROFILE acceptable. State form required for some. *Admission application deadline:* rolling.

Summary of Aid to Needy Students Federal Work-Study jobs; part-time jobs.

Loans College/university short-term loans, college/university long-term loans.

Non-Need Awards *Academic Interests/Achievement Awards:* general academic, health fields. *Creative Arts/Performance Awards:* creative writing, performing arts. *Special Achievements/Activities Awards:* community service, leadership. *Special Characteristics Awards:* children and siblings of alumni, children of faculty/staff, religious affiliation, siblings of current students. *Athletic:* available.

Other Money-Saving Options Accelerated degree, co-op program, cooperative Army ROTC, off-campus living (after junior year). *Payment Plans:* installment, deferred payment. *Waivers:* full or partial for minority students, children of alumni, employees or children of employees, adult students, senior citizens.

Contact Office of Financial Aid, Rockhurst College, 1100 Rockhurst Road, Kansas City, MO 64110-2561, 816-501-4000.

ROCKY MOUNTAIN COLLEGE
Billings, Montana

About the Institution Independent/religious, coed. Degrees awarded: A, B. Offers 50 undergraduate majors. Total enrollment: 744 (67% state residents). Freshmen: 122.

Undergraduate Expenses (1996–97) Comprehensive fee of $13,921 includes tuition ($9994), mandatory fees ($105), and college room and board ($3822).

Applications 89% of all full-time undergraduates enrolled in fall 1996 applied for aid; of these, 78% were judged to have need according to Federal Methodology, of whom 100% were aided. *Financial aid deadline (priority):* 4/1. *Financial aid forms:* FAFSA, state form, institutional form required; CSS Financial Aid PROFILE acceptable. *Admission application deadline:* rolling.

Summary of Aid to Needy Students *From gift & self-help combined:* Average need met: 87%. Average amount awarded: $7305 (53% gift aid, 47% self-help). *Gift aid:* Total: $1,754,847 (68% from college's own funds, 20% from other college-administered sources, 12% from external sources). 212 Federal Work-Study jobs (averaging $1060); 111 part-time jobs.

Need-Based Scholarships & Grants Pell, FSEOG, state, private, college/university.

Loans Perkins, PLUS, Stafford, Unsubsidized Stafford, private.

Non-Need Awards In 1996, a total of 502 non-need awards were made. *Academic Interests/Achievement Awards:* 254 ($370,842 total): general academic. *Creative Arts/Performance Awards:* 89 ($103,450 total): general creative, art/fine arts, debating, music, theater/drama. *Special Characteristics Awards:* 58 ($199,068 total): children and siblings of alumni, children of faculty/staff, religious affiliation. *Athletic:* Total: 101 ($559,344); Men: 63 ($350,834); Women: 38 ($208,510).

Other Money-Saving Options Accelerated degree, co-op program, off-campus living (after sophomore year). *Payment Plan:* installment. *Waivers:* full or partial for employees or children of employees.

Contact Financial Aid Office, Rocky Mountain College, Billings, MT 59102-1796, 406-657-1031.

ROCKY MOUNTAIN COLLEGE OF ART & DESIGN
Denver, Colorado

About the Institution Proprietary, coed. Degrees awarded: B. Offers 5 undergraduate majors. Total enrollment: 459 (60% state residents). Freshmen: 95.

Undergraduate Expenses (1996–97) Tuition: $6810. Mandatory fees: $30.

Applications 95% of all full-time undergraduates enrolled in fall 1996 applied for aid; of these, 40% were judged to have need according to Federal Methodology, of whom 100% were aided. *Financial aid deadline (priority):* 8/1. *Financial aid forms:* FAFSA, institutional form required; CSS Financial Aid PROFILE, state form acceptable. *Admission application deadline:* rolling.

Summary of Aid to Needy Students *From gift & self-help combined:* Average need met: 100%. *Gift aid:* Total: $160,682 (6% from college's own funds, 38% from other college-administered sources, 56% from external sources). Federal Work-Study jobs; part-time jobs.

Need-Based Scholarships & Grants Pell, FSEOG, state, college/university.

Loans Perkins, PLUS, Stafford, Unsubsidized Stafford.

Non-Need Awards In 1996, a total of 47 non-need awards were made. *Academic Interests/Achievement Awards:* 10 ($70,763 total). *Creative Arts/Performance Awards:* 37 ($87,937 total): applied art and design, art/fine arts.

Other Money-Saving Options *Payment Plan:* installment. *Waivers:* full or partial for employees or children of employees.

Contact Financial Aid Department, Rocky Mountain College of Art & Design, Denver, CO 80224-2329, 303-753-6046.

ROGER WILLIAMS UNIVERSITY
Bristol, Rhode Island

About the Institution Independent, coed. Degrees awarded: A, B, P. Offers 41 undergraduate majors. Total enrollment: 3,875. Undergraduates: 3,364 (15% state residents). Freshmen: 448.

Undergraduate Expenses (1996–97) Comprehensive fee of $21,960 includes tuition ($14,520), mandatory fees ($580), and college room and board ($6860). College room only: $3620.

Applications 76% of all full-time undergraduates enrolled in fall 1996 applied for aid; of these, 69% were judged to have need according to Federal Methodology, of whom 100% were aided. *Financial aid deadline (priority):* 3/1. *Financial aid forms:* FAFSA, institutional form required. *Regular admission application deadline:* rolling. Early decision deadline: 12/1.

Summary of Aid to Needy Students *From gift & self-help combined:* Average need met: 80%. Average amount awarded: $15,091 (47% gift aid, 53% self-help). *Gift aid:* Total: $7,160,000 (79% from college's own funds, 11% from other college-administered sources, 10% from external sources). 1,132 Federal Work-Study jobs (averaging $1813); 100 part-time jobs.

Need-Based Scholarships & Grants Pell, FSEOG, state, private, college/university.

Loans Perkins, PLUS, Stafford, Unsubsidized Stafford, state, private.

Non-Need Awards In 1996, a total of 269 non-need awards were made. *Academic Interests/Achievement Awards:* 265 ($1,505,000 total): general academic. *Special Characteristics Awards:* 4 ($60,600 total): local/state students.

Other Money-Saving Options Accelerated degree, co-op program, cooperative Army ROTC, off-campus living (after sophomore year). *Payment Plans:* installment, deferred payment. *Waivers:* full or partial for employees or children of employees.

Contact Mr. John Lawton, Director of Financial Aid, Roger Williams University, One Old Ferry Road, Bristol, RI 02809, 401-254-3100.

ROLLINS COLLEGE
Winter Park, Florida

About the Institution Independent, coed. Degrees awarded: B, M. Offers 34 undergraduate majors. Total enrollment: 3,297. Undergraduates: 1,424 (45% state residents). Freshmen: 418.

Undergraduate Expenses (1997–98) Comprehensive fee of $26,350 includes tuition ($19,450), mandatory fees ($560), and college room and board ($6340). College room only: $3515.

Applications Of all full-time undergraduates enrolled in fall 1996, 92% of those who applied for aid were judged to have need according to Federal Methodology, of whom 100% were aided. *Financial aid deadline (priority):* 3/1. *Financial aid forms:* FAFSA, institutional form required. *Regular admission application deadline:* 2/15. Early decision deadline: 11/15.

Summary of Aid to Needy Students *From gift & self-help combined:* Average need met: 86%. Average amount awarded: $18,821 (72% gift aid, 28% self-help). *Gift aid:* Total: $8,610,169 (80% from college's own funds, 4% from other college-administered sources, 16% from external sources). 135 Federal Work-Study jobs (averaging $1500); 91 part-time jobs.

Need-Based Scholarships & Grants Pell, FSEOG, state, private, college/university.

Loans Perkins, PLUS, Stafford, Unsubsidized Stafford, private, college/university short-term loans ($200 average), college/university long-term loans ($1000 average).

Non-Need Awards In 1996, a total of 463 non-need awards were made. *Academic Interests/Achievement Awards:* 319 ($1,898,373 total): general academic, computer science, engineering/technologies, mathematics, physical sciences. *Creative Arts/Performance Awards:* 48 ($116,732 total): art/fine arts, music, theater/drama. *Athletic:* Total: 96 ($1,210,956); Men: 55 ($681,505); Women: 41 ($529,451).

Other Money-Saving Options Accelerated degree, off-campus living. *Payment Plans:* tuition prepayment, installment. *Waivers:* full or partial for employees or children of employees.

Contact Office of Financial Aid, Rollins College, 1000 Holt Avenue-2721, Winter Park, FL 32789-4499, 407-646-2000.

ROSARY COLLEGE
River Forest, Illinois

See Dominican University

ROSE-HULMAN INSTITUTE OF TECHNOLOGY
Terre Haute, Indiana

About the Institution Independent, coed. Degrees awarded: B, M. Offers 11 undergraduate majors. Total enrollment: 1,574. Undergraduates: 1,442 (55% state residents). Freshmen: 386.

Undergraduate Expenses (1997–98 estimated) Comprehensive fee of $21,924 includes tuition ($16,863), mandatory fees ($105), and college room and board ($4956).

Applications Of all full-time undergraduates enrolled in fall 1996, 92% of those who applied for aid were judged to have need according to Federal Methodology, of whom 100% were aided. *Financial aid deadline (priority):* 3/1. *Financial aid forms:* FAFSA required. *Admission application deadline:* rolling.

Summary of Aid to Needy Students *From gift & self-help combined:* Average need met: 79%. Average amount awarded: $11,709 (58% gift

aid, 42% self-help). *Gift aid:* Total: $7,843,559 (52% from college's own funds, 26% from other college-administered sources, 22% from external sources). 965 Federal Work-Study jobs (averaging $1200); 150 part-time jobs.

Need-Based Scholarships & Grants Pell, FSEOG, state, private, college/university.

Loans Perkins, PLUS, Stafford, Unsubsidized Stafford, college/university short-term loans ($200 average).

Non-Need Awards In 1996, a total of 976 non-need awards were made. *Academic Interests/Achievement Awards:* 913 ($1,801,414 total): general academic, computer science, engineering/technologies, mathematics, physical sciences. *Special Characteristics Awards:* 63 ($88,380 total): members of minorities, ROTC participants.

Other Money-Saving Options Co-op program, Army ROTC, Air Force ROTC, off-campus living (after freshman year). *Payment Plans:* tuition prepayment, installment. *Waivers:* full or partial for employees or children of employees.

Contact Office of Financial Aid, Rose-Hulman Institute of Technology, 5500 Wabash Avenue, Terre Haute, IN 47803-3920, 812-877-1511.

ROSEMONT COLLEGE
Rosemont, Pennsylvania

About the Institution Independent/religious, women. Degrees awarded: B, M. Offers 26 undergraduate majors. Total enrollment: 846. Undergraduates: 736 (56% state residents). Freshmen: 110.

Undergraduate Expenses (1997–98) Comprehensive fee of $19,840 includes tuition ($12,960), mandatory fees ($380), and college room and board ($6500).

Applications 75% of all full-time undergraduates enrolled in fall 1996 applied for aid; of these, 96% were judged to have need according to Federal Methodology, of whom 100% were aided. *Financial aid deadline (priority):* 3/15. *Financial aid forms:* FAFSA required. State form required for some. *Regular admission application deadline:* rolling. Early action deadline: 12/15.

Summary of Aid to Needy Students *From gift & self-help combined:* Average need met: 80%. Average amount awarded: $8900 (47% gift aid, 53% self-help). *Gift aid:* Total: $903,855 (52% from college's own funds, 32% from other college-administered sources, 16% from external sources). Federal Work-Study jobs; 85 part-time jobs.

Need-Based Scholarships & Grants Pell, FSEOG, state, college/university.

Loans Perkins, PLUS, Stafford, Unsubsidized Stafford.

Non-Need Awards In 1996, a total of 169 non-need awards were made. *Academic Interests/Achievement Awards:* 154 ($713,558 total): general academic. *Creative Arts/Performance Awards:* 5 ($34,265 total): art/fine arts. *Special Characteristics Awards:* 10 ($33,463 total): children of educators, siblings of current students.

Other Money-Saving Options Accelerated degree, off-campus living (after junior year). *Payment Plan:* installment. *Waivers:* full or partial for employees or children of employees and senior citizens.

Contact Office of Financial Aid, Rosemont College, 1400 Montgomery Avenue, Rosemont, PA 19010-1699, 610-527-0200.

ROWAN UNIVERSITY
Glassboro, New Jersey

About the Institution State-supported, coed. Degrees awarded: B, M. Offers 56 undergraduate majors. Total enrollment: 9,213. Undergraduates: 7,600 (98% state residents). Freshmen: 1,142.

Undergraduate Expenses (1996–97) State resident tuition: $2740. Nonresident tuition: $5480. Mandatory fees: $1011. College room and board: $4768. College room only: $3168.

Applications *Financial aid deadline (priority):* 4/30. *Financial aid forms:* FAFSA, CSS Financial Aid PROFILE, state form, institutional form required. *Admission application deadline:* 3/15.

Summary of Aid to Needy Students *From gift & self-help combined:* Average need met: 95%. Average amount awarded: $4283 (48% gift aid, 52% self-help). *Gift aid:* Total: $7,272,409 (7% from college's own funds, 57% from other college-administered sources, 36% from external sources). 337 Federal Work-Study jobs (averaging $850); 400 part-time jobs.

Need-Based Scholarships & Grants Pell, FSEOG, state, private, college/university.

Loans Perkins, PLUS, Stafford, Unsubsidized Stafford.

Non-Need Awards In 1996, a total of 202 non-need awards were made. *Academic Interests/Achievement Awards:* 117 ($82,993 total): general academic, biological sciences, business, communication, computer science, education, engineering/technologies, humanities, physical sciences, social sciences. *Creative Arts/Performance Awards:* 41 ($70,394 total): general creative, art/fine arts, music, performing arts. *Special Characteristics Awards:* 44 ($378,591 total): handicapped students, international students, members of minorities.

Other Money-Saving Options Accelerated degree, co-op program, Army ROTC, off-campus living (after freshman year). *Payment Plan:* deferred payment. *Waivers:* full or partial for employees or children of employees.

Contact Mr. William Murphy, Director of Financial Aid, Rowan University, Glassboro, NJ 08028-1701, 609-256-4250.

RUSSELL SAGE COLLEGE
Troy, New York

About the Institution Independent, women. Degrees awarded: B. Offers 27 undergraduate majors. Total enrollment: 1,038 (83% state residents). Freshmen: 149.

Undergraduate Expenses (1997–98) Comprehensive fee of $20,190 includes tuition ($13,950), mandatory fees ($280), and college room and board ($5960). College room only: $2770.

Applications 91% of all full-time undergraduates enrolled in fall 1996 applied for aid; of these, 97% were judged to have need according to Federal Methodology, of whom 100% were aided. *Financial aid deadline (priority):* 3/1. *Financial aid forms:* FAFSA required; CSS Financial Aid PROFILE acceptable. State form required for some. *Regular admission application deadline:* 8/1. Early decision deadline: 12/1.

Summary of Aid to Needy Students *From gift & self-help combined:* Average need met: 75%. Average amount awarded: $7000 (56% gift aid, 44% self-help). *Gift aid:* Total: $3,381,030 (71% from college's own funds, 18% from other college-administered sources, 11% from external sources). 243 Federal Work-Study jobs (averaging $1200); 66 part-time jobs.

Need-Based Scholarships & Grants Pell, FSEOG, state, college/university.

Loans Perkins, PLUS, Stafford, Unsubsidized Stafford, college/university short-term loans ($500 average), college/university long-term loans ($1200 average).

Non-Need Awards In 1996, a total of 180 non-need awards were made. *Academic Interests/Achievement Awards:* 180 ($975,747 total): general academic, health fields.

Other Money-Saving Options Accelerated degree, co-op program, cooperative Army ROTC, cooperative Air Force ROTC. *Waivers:* full or partial for employees or children of employees.

Contact Ms. Lisa Bonaquist, Director of Financial Aid, Russell Sage College, 45 Ferry Street, Troy, NY 12180-4115, 518-270-2341, fax: 518-270-2460.

RUST COLLEGE
Holly Springs, Mississippi

About the Institution Independent/religious, coed. Degrees awarded: A, B. Offers 25 undergraduate majors. Total enrollment: 937 (67% state residents). Freshmen: 249.

Undergraduate Expenses (1997–98) Comprehensive fee of $7300 includes tuition ($5025) and college room and board ($2275).

Applications 98% of all full-time undergraduates enrolled in fall 1996 applied for aid; of these, 98% were judged to have need according to Federal Methodology, of whom 100% were aided. *Financial aid deadline (priority):* 4/1. *Financial aid forms:* FAFSA, institutional form required. State form required for some. *Admission application deadline:* rolling.

Summary of Aid to Needy Students *From gift & self-help combined:* Average need met: 87%. Average amount awarded: $6155 (55% gift aid, 45% self-help). *Gift aid:* Total: $2,395,053 (27% from college's own funds, 22% from other college-administered sources, 51% from external sources). 475 Federal Work-Study jobs (averaging $736).

Need-Based Scholarships & Grants Pell, FSEOG, state, private, college/university.

Loans Perkins, PLUS, Stafford, Unsubsidized Stafford, United Methodist Student Loans.

Non-Need Awards In 1996, a total of 613 non-need awards were made. *Academic Interests/Achievement Awards:* 256 ($100,023 total): general academic. *Creative Arts/Performance Awards:* 59 ($39,134 total): music. *Special Characteristics Awards:* 298 ($321,033 total): children of faculty/staff, ethnic background, international students, local/state students, members of minorities, religious affiliation, veterans.

Other Money-Saving Options Accelerated degree, co-op program, off-campus living. *Payment Plan:* installment. *Waivers:* full or partial for employees or children of employees.

Contact Office of Financial Aid, Rust College, 150 Rust Avenue, Holly Springs, MS 38635-2328, 601-252-8000.

RUTGERS, THE STATE UNIVERSITY OF NEW JERSEY, CAMDEN COLLEGE OF ARTS AND SCIENCES
Camden, New Jersey

About the Institution State-supported, coed. Degrees awarded: B. Offers 47 undergraduate majors. Total university enrollment: 47,812. Undergraduates: 2,223 (97% state residents). Freshmen: 189.

Undergraduate Expenses (1996–97) State resident tuition: $4028. Nonresident tuition: $8200. Mandatory fees: $920. College room and board: $5134.

Applications Of all full-time undergraduates enrolled in fall 1996, 86% of those who applied for aid were judged to have need according to Federal Methodology, of whom 97% were aided. *Financial aid deadline (priority):* 3/1. *Financial aid forms:* FAFSA, financial aid transcript (for transfers) required. State form required for some. *Admission application deadline:* 12/15.

Summary of Aid to Needy Students *From gift & self-help combined:* Average need met: 90%. Average amount awarded: $8347 (59% gift aid, 41% self-help). *Gift aid:* Total: $4,668,314 (8% from college's own funds, 7% from other college-administered sources, 85% from external sources). 164 Federal Work-Study jobs (averaging $1186).

Need-Based Scholarships & Grants Pell, FSEOG, state, college/university.

Loans Perkins, PLUS, Stafford, Unsubsidized Stafford, state, private, college/university short-term loans ($400 average), college/university long-term loans ($1194 average).

Non-Need Awards In 1996, a total of 94 non-need awards were made. *Academic Interests/Achievement Awards:* 86 ($224,767 total): general academic. *Special Characteristics Awards:* 8 ($32,224 total): children of faculty/staff.

Other Money-Saving Options Cooperative Army ROTC, cooperative Naval ROTC, cooperative Air Force ROTC, off-campus living. *Payment Plan:* installment. *Waivers:* full or partial for employees or children of employees.

Contact Ms. Marlene Martin, Assistant Funds Manager, Rutgers, The State University of New Jersey, Camden College of Arts and Sciences, Records Hall, Room 140, New Brunswick, NJ 08903, 732-932-7868, fax: 732-932-7385.

RUTGERS, THE STATE UNIVERSITY OF NEW JERSEY, COLLEGE OF ENGINEERING
Piscataway, New Jersey

About the Institution State-supported, coed. Degrees awarded: B. Offers 11 undergraduate majors. Total university enrollment: 47,812. Undergraduates: 2,156 (87% state residents). Freshmen: 497.

Undergraduate Expenses (1996–97) State resident tuition: $4472. Nonresident tuition: $9098. Mandatory fees: $1052 (minimum). College room and board: $5134. College room only: $3006.

Applications Of all full-time undergraduates enrolled in fall 1996, 82% of those who applied for aid were judged to have need according to Federal Methodology, of whom 98% were aided. *Financial aid deadline (priority):* 3/1. *Financial aid forms:* FAFSA, financial aid transcript (for transfers) required. State form required for some. *Admission application deadline:* 12/15.

Summary of Aid to Needy Students *From gift & self-help combined:* Average need met: 82%. Average amount awarded: $8204 (58% gift aid, 42% self-help). *Gift aid:* Total: $4,708,020 (16% from college's own funds, 6% from other college-administered sources, 78% from external sources). 202 Federal Work-Study jobs (averaging $1179).

Need-Based Scholarships & Grants Pell, FSEOG, state, college/university.

Loans Perkins, PLUS, Stafford, Unsubsidized Stafford, state, private, college/university short-term loans ($400 average), college/university long-term loans ($1290 average).

Non-Need Awards In 1996, a total of 369 non-need awards were made. *Academic Interests/Achievement Awards:* 334 ($770,499 total): general academic, engineering/technologies. *Special Characteristics Awards:* 20 ($94,066 total): children of faculty/staff. *Athletic:* Total: 15 ($53,150); Men: 11 ($44,600); Women: 4 ($8550).

Other Money-Saving Options Army ROTC, Air Force ROTC, off-campus living. *Payment Plan:* installment. *Waivers:* full or partial for employees or children of employees.

Contact Ms. Marlene Martin, Assistant Funds Manager, Rutgers, The State University of New Jersey, College of Engineering, Records Hall, Room 140, New Brunswick, NJ 08903, 732-932-7868, fax: 732-932-7385.

RUTGERS, THE STATE UNIVERSITY OF NEW JERSEY, COLLEGE OF NURSING
Newark, New Jersey

About the Institution State-supported, coed. Degrees awarded: B, M, D. Offers 1 undergraduate major. Total university enrollment: 47,812. Undergraduates: 370 (96% state residents). Freshmen: 50.

Undergraduate Expenses (1996–97) State resident tuition: $4028. Nonresident tuition: $8200. Mandatory fees: $852. College room and board: $5134. College room only: $3006.

Applications 71% of all full-time undergraduates enrolled in fall 1996 applied for aid; of these, 88% were judged to have need according to Federal Methodology, of whom 96% were aided. *Financial aid deadline (priority):* 3/1. *Financial aid forms:* FAFSA, financial aid transcript (for transfers) required. State form required for some. *Admission application deadline:* 12/15.

Summary of Aid to Needy Students *From gift & self-help combined:* Average need met: 87%. Average amount awarded: $8990 (65% gift aid, 35% self-help). *Gift aid:* Total: $1,088,389 (23% from college's own funds, 8% from other college-administered sources, 69% from external sources). 32 Federal Work-Study jobs (averaging $1153).

Need-Based Scholarships & Grants Pell, FSEOG, state, college/university.

Loans Perkins, PLUS, Stafford, Unsubsidized Stafford, state, private, college/university short-term loans ($400 average), college/university long-term loans ($1184 average).

Non-Need Awards In 1996, a total of 34 non-need awards were made. *Academic Interests/Achievement Awards:* 33 ($96,103 total): general academic. *Special Characteristics Awards:* 1 ($4028 total): children of faculty/staff.

Other Money-Saving Options Cooperative Army ROTC, cooperative Air Force ROTC, off-campus living. *Payment Plan:* installment. *Waivers:* full or partial for employees or children of employees.

Contact Ms. Marlene Martin, Assistant Funds Manager, Rutgers, The State University of New Jersey, College of Nursing, Records Hall, Room 140, New Brunswick, NJ 08903, 732-932-7868, fax: 732-932-7385.

RUTGERS, THE STATE UNIVERSITY OF NEW JERSEY, COLLEGE OF PHARMACY
Piscataway, New Jersey

About the Institution State-supported, coed. Degrees awarded: B, D. Offers 1 undergraduate major. Total university enrollment: 47,812. Total unit enrollment: 986. Undergraduates: 899 (84% state residents). Freshmen: 187.

Undergraduate Expenses (1996–97) State resident tuition: $4472. Nonresident tuition: $9098. Mandatory fees: $1052 (minimum). College room and board: $5134. College room only: $3006.

Applications 63% of all full-time undergraduates enrolled in fall 1996 applied for aid; of these, 85% were judged to have need according to Federal Methodology, of whom 99% were aided. *Financial aid deadline (priority):* 3/1. *Financial aid forms:* FAFSA, financial aid transcript (for transfers) required. State form required for some. *Admission application deadline:* 12/15.

Summary of Aid to Needy Students *From gift & self-help combined:* Average need met: 81%. Average amount awarded: $8544 (58% gift aid, 42% self-help). *Gift aid:* Total: $2,229,451 (14% from college's own funds, 7% from other college-administered sources, 79% from external sources). 74 Federal Work-Study jobs (averaging $1197).

Need-Based Scholarships & Grants Pell, FSEOG, state, college/university.

Loans Perkins, PLUS, Stafford, Unsubsidized Stafford, state, private, college/university short-term loans ($400 average), college/university long-term loans ($1385 average).

Non-Need Awards In 1996, a total of 91 non-need awards were made. *Academic Interests/Achievement Awards:* 84 ($246,124 total): general academic. *Special Characteristics Awards:* 2 ($8944 total): children of faculty/staff. *Athletic:* Total: 5 ($22,000); Men: 0; Women: 5 ($22,000).

Other Money-Saving Options Army ROTC, Air Force ROTC, off-campus living. *Payment Plan:* installment. *Waivers:* full or partial for employees or children of employees.

Contact Ms. Marlene Martin, Assistant Funds Manager, Rutgers, The State University of New Jersey, College of Pharmacy, Records Hall, Room 140, New Brunswick, NJ 08903, 732-932-7868, fax: 732-932-7385.

RUTGERS, THE STATE UNIVERSITY OF NEW JERSEY, COOK COLLEGE
New Brunswick, New Jersey

About the Institution State-supported, coed. Degrees awarded: B. Offers 62 undergraduate majors. Total university enrollment: 47,812. Undergraduates: 3,160 (90% state residents). Freshmen: 629.

Undergraduate Expenses (1996–97) State resident tuition: $4472. Nonresident tuition: $9098. Mandatory fees: $1056. College room and board: $5134. College room only: $3006.

Applications Of all full-time undergraduates enrolled in fall 1996, 83% of those who applied for aid were judged to have need according to Federal Methodology, of whom 98% were aided. *Financial aid deadline (priority):* 3/1. *Financial aid forms:* FAFSA, financial aid transcript (for transfers) required. State form required for some. *Admission application deadline:* 12/15.

Summary of Aid to Needy Students *From gift & self-help combined:* Average need met: 85%. Average amount awarded: $8195 (54% gift aid, 46% self-help). *Gift aid:* Total: $5,864,596 (17% from college's own funds, 6% from other college-administered sources, 77% from external sources). 297 Federal Work-Study jobs (averaging $1185); part-time jobs.

Need-Based Scholarships & Grants Pell, FSEOG, state, college/university.

Loans Perkins, PLUS, Stafford, Unsubsidized Stafford, state, private, college/university short-term loans ($400 average), college/university long-term loans ($1275 average).

Non-Need Awards In 1996, a total of 533 non-need awards were made. *Academic Interests/Achievement Awards:* 425 ($1,077,466 total): general academic, biological sciences. *Special Characteristics Awards:* 45 ($203,630 total): children of faculty/staff. *Athletic:* Total: 63 ($390,827); Men: 36 ($302,649); Women: 27 ($88,178).

Other Money-Saving Options Co-op program, Army ROTC, Air Force ROTC, off-campus living. *Payment Plan:* installment. *Waivers:* full or partial for employees or children of employees.

Contact Ms. Marlene Martin, Assistant Funds Manager, Rutgers, The State University of New Jersey, Cook College, Records Hall, Room 140, New Brunswick, NJ 08903-0231, 732-932-7868, fax: 732-932-7385.

RUTGERS, THE STATE UNIVERSITY OF NEW JERSEY, DOUGLASS COLLEGE
New Brunswick, New Jersey

About the Institution State-supported, women. Degrees awarded: B. Offers 81 undergraduate majors. Total university enrollment: 47,812. Undergraduates: 2,965 (94% state residents). Freshmen: 623.

Undergraduate Expenses (1996–97) State resident tuition: $4028. Nonresident tuition: $8200. Mandatory fees: $1052. College room and board: $5134. College room only: $3006.

Applications Of all full-time undergraduates enrolled in fall 1996, 84% of those who applied for aid were judged to have need according to Federal Methodology, of whom 98% were aided. *Financial aid deadline (priority):* 3/1. *Financial aid forms:* FAFSA, financial aid transcript (for transfers) required. State form required for some. *Admission application deadline:* 12/15.

Summary of Aid to Needy Students *From gift & self-help combined:* Average need met: 85%. Average amount awarded: $8157 (54% gift aid, 46% self-help). *Gift aid:* Total: $6,078,351 (15% from college's own funds, 8% from other college-administered sources, 77% from external sources). 349 Federal Work-Study jobs (averaging $1180).

Need-Based Scholarships & Grants Pell, FSEOG, state, college/university.

Loans Perkins, PLUS, Stafford, Unsubsidized Stafford, state, private, college/university short-term loans ($400 average), college/university long-term loans ($1275 average).

Non-Need Awards In 1996, a total of 629 non-need awards were made. *Academic Interests/Achievement Awards:* 548 ($1,049,353 total): general academic. *Special Characteristics Awards:* 57 ($240,098 total): children of faculty/staff. *Athletic:* Total: 24 ($103,400).

Other Money-Saving Options Army ROTC, Air Force ROTC, off-campus living (after freshman year). *Payment Plan:* installment. *Waivers:* full or partial for employees or children of employees.

Contact Ms. Marlene Martin, Assistant Funds Manager, Rutgers, The State University of New Jersey, Douglass College, Records Hall, Room 140, New Brunswick, NJ 08903-0270, 732-932-7868, fax: 732-932-7385.

RUTGERS, THE STATE UNIVERSITY OF NEW JERSEY, LIVINGSTON COLLEGE
New Brunswick, New Jersey

About the Institution State-supported, coed. Degrees awarded: B. Offers 81 undergraduate majors. Total university enrollment: 47,812. Undergraduates: 3,032 (90% state residents). Freshmen: 659.

Undergraduate Expenses (1996–97) State resident tuition: $4028. Nonresident tuition: $8200. Mandatory fees: $1102. College room and board: $5134. College room only: $3006.

Applications Of all full-time undergraduates enrolled in fall 1996, 84% of those who applied for aid were judged to have need according to Federal Methodology, of whom 98% were aided. *Financial aid deadline (priority):* 3/1. *Financial aid forms:* FAFSA, financial aid transcript (for transfers) required. State form required for some. *Admission application deadline:* 12/15.

Summary of Aid to Needy Students *From gift & self-help combined:* Average need met: 76%. Average amount awarded: $8244 (54% gift aid, 46% self-help). *Gift aid:* Total: $6,396,078 (14% from college's own funds, 9% from other college-administered sources, 77% from external sources). 415 Federal Work-Study jobs (averaging $1215).

Need-Based Scholarships & Grants Pell, FSEOG, state, college/university.

Loans Perkins, PLUS, Stafford, Unsubsidized Stafford, state, private, college/university short-term loans ($400 average), college/university long-term loans ($1213 average).

Non-Need Awards In 1996, a total of 296 non-need awards were made. *Academic Interests/Achievement Awards:* 213 ($874,330 total): general academic. *Special Characteristics Awards:* 24 ($103,002 total): children of faculty/staff. *Athletic:* Total: 59 ($489,428); Men: 45 ($400,331); Women: 14 ($89,097).

Other Money-Saving Options Army ROTC, Air Force ROTC, off-campus living. *Payment Plan:* installment. *Waivers:* full or partial for employees or children of employees.

Contact Ms. Marlene Martin, Assistant Funds Manager, Rutgers, The State University of New Jersey, Livingston College, Records Hall, Room 140, New Brunswick, NJ 08903, 732-932-7868, fax: 732-932-7385.

RUTGERS, THE STATE UNIVERSITY OF NEW JERSEY, MASON GROSS SCHOOL OF THE ARTS
New Brunswick, New Jersey

About the Institution State-supported, coed. Degrees awarded: B, M, D. Offers 13 undergraduate majors. Total university enrollment: 47,812. Total unit enrollment: 725. Undergraduates: 499 (84% state residents). Freshmen: 120.

Undergraduate Expenses (1996–97) State resident tuition: $4028. Nonresident tuition: $8200. Mandatory fees: $1052 (minimum). College room and board: $5134. College room only: $3006.

Applications Of all full-time undergraduates enrolled in fall 1996, 82% of those who applied for aid were judged to have need according to Federal Methodology, of whom 98% were aided. *Financial aid deadline (priority):* 3/1. *Financial aid forms:* FAFSA, financial aid transcript (for transfers) required. State form required for some. *Admission application deadline:* 12/15.

Summary of Aid to Needy Students *From gift & self-help combined:* Average need met: 81%. Average amount awarded: $7876 (50% gift aid, 50% self-help). *Gift aid:* Total: $886,057 (16% from college's own funds, 6% from other college-administered sources, 78% from external sources). 45 Federal Work-Study jobs (averaging $1221).

Need-Based Scholarships & Grants Pell, FSEOG, state, college/university.

Loans Perkins, PLUS, Stafford, Unsubsidized Stafford, state, private, college/university short-term loans ($400 average), college/university long-term loans ($1472 average).

Non-Need Awards In 1996, a total of 83 non-need awards were made. *Academic Interests/Achievement Awards:* 74 ($128,983 total): general academic. *Special Characteristics Awards:* 7 ($28,196 total): children of faculty/staff. *Athletic:* Total: 2 ($6000); Men: 1 ($4000); Women: 1 ($2000).

Other Money-Saving Options Army ROTC, Air Force ROTC, off-campus living. *Payment Plan:* installment. *Waivers:* full or partial for employees or children of employees.

Contact Ms. Marlene Martin, Assistant Funds Manager, Rutgers, The State University of New Jersey, Mason Gross School of the Arts, Records Hall, room 140, New Brunswick, NJ 08903-0270, 732-932-7868, fax: 732-932-7385.

RUTGERS, THE STATE UNIVERSITY OF NEW JERSEY, NEWARK COLLEGE OF ARTS AND SCIENCES
Newark, New Jersey

About the Institution State-supported, coed. Degrees awarded: B. Offers 48 undergraduate majors. Total university enrollment: 47,812. Undergraduates: 3,684 (94% state residents). Freshmen: 454.

Undergraduate Expenses (1996–97) State resident tuition: $4028. Nonresident tuition: $8200. Mandatory fees: $874. College room and board: $5134.

Applications Of all full-time undergraduates enrolled in fall 1996, 91% of those who applied for aid were judged to have need according to Federal Methodology, of whom 96% were aided. *Financial aid deadline (priority):* 3/1. *Financial aid forms:* FAFSA, financial aid transcript (for transfers) required. State form required for some. *Admission application deadline:* 12/15.

Summary of Aid to Needy Students *From gift & self-help combined:* Average need met: 76%. Average amount awarded: $7329 (65% gift aid, 35% self-help). *Gift aid:* Total: $8,523,840 (7% from college's own funds, 7% from other college-administered sources, 86% from external sources). 301 Federal Work-Study jobs (averaging $1248).

Need-Based Scholarships & Grants Pell, FSEOG, state, college/university.

Loans Perkins, PLUS, Stafford, Unsubsidized Stafford, state, private, college/university short-term loans ($400 average), college/university long-term loans ($1379 average).

Non-Need Awards In 1996, a total of 154 non-need awards were made. *Academic Interests/Achievement Awards:* 145 ($408,151 total): general academic. *Special Characteristics Awards:* 9 ($36,252 total): children of faculty/staff.

Other Money-Saving Options Cooperative Army ROTC, cooperative Air Force ROTC, off-campus living. *Payment Plan:* installment. *Waivers:* full or partial for employees or children of employees.

Contact Ms. Marlene Martin, Assistant Funds Manager, Rutgers, The State University of New Jersey, Newark College of Arts and Sciences, Records Hall, Room 140, New Brunswick, NJ 08903, 732-932-7868, fax: 732-932-7385.

RUTGERS, THE STATE UNIVERSITY OF NEW JERSEY, RUTGERS COLLEGE
New Brunswick, New Jersey

About the Institution State-supported, coed. Degrees awarded: B. Offers 78 undergraduate majors. Total university enrollment: 47,812. Undergraduates: 10,317 (88% state residents). Freshmen: 2,273.

Undergraduate Expenses (1996–97) State resident tuition: $4028. Nonresident tuition: $8200. Mandatory fees: $1098. College room and board: $5134. College room only: $3006.

Applications Of all full-time undergraduates enrolled in fall 1996, 82% of those who applied for aid were judged to have need according to Federal Methodology, of whom 98% were aided. *Financial aid deadline (priority):* 3/1. *Financial aid forms:* FAFSA, financial aid transcript (for transfers) required. State form required for some. *Admission application deadline:* 12/15.

Summary of Aid to Needy Students *From gift & self-help combined:* Average need met: 84%. Average amount awarded: $8093 (55% gift aid, 45% self-help). *Gift aid:* Total: $20,438,524 (16% from college's own funds, 8% from other college-administered sources, 76% from external sources). 1,083 Federal Work-Study jobs (averaging $1193).

Need-Based Scholarships & Grants Pell, FSEOG, state, college/university.

Loans Perkins, PLUS, Stafford, Unsubsidized Stafford, state, private, college/university short-term loans ($400 average), college/university long-term loans ($1288 average).

Non-Need Awards In 1996, a total of 1,689 non-need awards were made. *Academic Interests/Achievement Awards:* 1,344 ($4,055,524 total): general academic. *Special Characteristics Awards:* 97 ($401,362 total): children of faculty/staff. *Athletic:* Total: 248 ($1,528,207); Men: 129 ($874,773); Women: 119 ($653,434).

Other Money-Saving Options Army ROTC, Air Force ROTC, off-campus living. *Payment Plan:* installment. *Waivers:* full or partial for employees or children of employees.

Contact Ms. Marlene Martin, Assistant Funds Manager, Rutgers, The State University of New Jersey, Rutgers College, Records Hall, Room 140, New Brunswick, NJ 08903-2101, 732-932-7868, fax: 732-932-7385.

RUTGERS, THE STATE UNIVERSITY OF NEW JERSEY, UNIVERSITY COLLEGE–CAMDEN
Camden, New Jersey

About the Institution State-supported, coed. Degrees awarded: B. Offers 47 undergraduate majors. Total university enrollment: 47,812. Undergraduates: 714 (98% state residents). Freshmen: 64.

Applications Of all full-time undergraduates enrolled in fall 1996, 82% of those who applied for aid were judged to have need according to Federal Methodology, of whom 98% were aided. *Financial aid deadline (priority):* 3/1. *Financial aid forms:* FAFSA, CSS Financial Aid PROFILE, financial aid transcript (for transfers) required. State form required for some. *Admission application deadline:* 12/15.

Summary of Aid to Needy Students *From gift & self-help combined:* Average need met: 94%. Average amount awarded: $7458 (61% gift aid, 39% self-help). *Gift aid:* Total: $693,874 (4% from college's own funds, 4% from other college-administered sources, 92% from external sources). 13 Federal Work-Study jobs (averaging $1157).

Need-Based Scholarships & Grants Pell, FSEOG, state, college/university.

Loans Perkins, PLUS, Stafford, Unsubsidized Stafford, state, private, college/university short-term loans ($400 average), college/university long-term loans ($1100 average).

Non-Need Awards In 1996, a total of 19 non-need awards were made. *Academic Interests/Achievement Awards:* 17 ($18,570 total): general academic. *Special Characteristics Awards:* 2 ($7818 total): children of faculty/staff.

Other Money-Saving Options Cooperative Army ROTC, cooperative Naval ROTC, cooperative Air Force ROTC. *Payment Plan:* installment. *Waivers:* full or partial for employees or children of employees.

Contact Ms. Marlene Martin, Assistant Funds Manager, Rutgers, The State University of New Jersey, University College–Camden, Records Hall, Room 140, New Brunswick, NJ 08903, 732-932-7868, fax: 732-932-7385.

RUTGERS, THE STATE UNIVERSITY OF NEW JERSEY, UNIVERSITY COLLEGE–NEWARK
Newark, New Jersey

About the Institution State-supported, coed. Degrees awarded: B. Offers 17 undergraduate majors. Total university enrollment: 47,812. Undergraduates: 1,776 (98% state residents). Freshmen: 101.

Applications Of all full-time undergraduates enrolled in fall 1996, 91% of those who applied for aid were judged to have need according to Federal Methodology, of whom 97% were aided. *Financial aid deadline (priority):* 3/1. *Financial aid forms:* FAFSA, financial aid transcript (for transfers) required. State form required for some. *Admission application deadline:* 12/15.

Summary of Aid to Needy Students *From gift & self-help combined:* Average need met: 82%. Average amount awarded: $7641 (62% gift aid, 38% self-help). *Gift aid:* Total: $1,828,136 (5% from college's own funds, 5% from other college-administered sources, 90% from external sources). 33 Federal Work-Study jobs (averaging $1302).

Need-Based Scholarships & Grants Pell, FSEOG, state, college/university.

Loans Perkins, PLUS, Stafford, Unsubsidized Stafford, state, private, college/university short-term loans ($400 average), college/university long-term loans ($1192 average).

Non-Need Awards In 1996, a total of 12 non-need awards were made. *Academic Interests/Achievement Awards:* 10 ($19,143 total): general academic. *Special Characteristics Awards:* 2 ($6643 total): children of faculty/staff.

Other Money-Saving Options Cooperative Army ROTC, cooperative Air Force ROTC. *Payment Plan:* installment. *Waivers:* full or partial for employees or children of employees.

Contact Ms. Marlene Martin, Assistant Funds Manager, Rutgers, The State University of New Jersey, University College–Newark, Records Hall, Room 140, New Brunswick, NJ 08903, 732-932-7868, fax: 732-932-7385.

RUTGERS, THE STATE UNIVERSITY OF NEW JERSEY, UNIVERSITY COLLEGE–NEW BRUNSWICK
New Brunswick, New Jersey

About the Institution State-supported, coed. Degrees awarded: B. Offers 75 undergraduate majors. Total university enrollment: 47,812. Undergraduates: 2,911 (99% state residents). Freshmen: 26.

Applications Of all full-time undergraduates enrolled in fall 1996, 90% of those who applied for aid were judged to have need according to Federal Methodology, of whom 98% were aided. *Financial aid deadline (priority):* 3/1. *Financial aid forms:* FAFSA, financial aid transcript (for transfers) required. State form required for some. *Admission application deadline:* 7/19.

Summary of Aid to Needy Students *From gift & self-help combined:* Average need met: 87%. Average amount awarded: $8550 (49% gift aid, 51% self-help). *Gift aid:* Total: $1,132,824 (4% from college's own funds, 5% from other college-administered sources, 91% from external sources). 7 Federal Work-Study jobs (averaging $1083).

Need-Based Scholarships & Grants Pell, FSEOG, state, college/university.

Loans Perkins, PLUS, Stafford, Unsubsidized Stafford, state, private, college/university short-term loans ($400 average), college/university long-term loans ($1443 average).

Non-Need Awards In 1996, a total of 11 non-need awards were made. *Academic Interests/Achievement Awards:* 10 ($12,008 total): general academic. *Special Characteristics Awards:* 1 ($3908 total): children of faculty/staff.

Other Money-Saving Options Army ROTC, Air Force ROTC. *Payment Plan:* installment. *Waivers:* full or partial for employees or children of employees.

Contact Ms. Marlene Martin, Assistant Funds Manager, Rutgers, The State University of New Jersey, University College–New Brunswick, Records Hall, Room 140, New Brunswick, NJ 08903, 732-932-7868, fax: 732-932-7385.

SACRED HEART MAJOR SEMINARY
Detroit, Michigan

About the Institution Independent/religious, coed. Degrees awarded: A, B, M, P. Offers 2 undergraduate majors. Total enrollment: 92. Undergraduates: 24 (99% state residents). Freshmen: 3.

Undergraduate Expenses (1997–98) Comprehensive fee of $9421 includes tuition ($5150), mandatory fees ($30), and college room and board ($4241).

Applications 36% of all full-time undergraduates enrolled in fall 1996 applied for aid; of these, 87% were judged to have need according to Federal Methodology, of whom 85% were aided. *Financial aid deadline (priority):* 2/15. *Financial aid forms:* FAFSA, institutional form required; CSS Financial Aid PROFILE acceptable. *Admission application deadline:* 7/31.

Summary of Aid to Needy Students *From gift & self-help combined:* Average amount awarded: $5050 (60% gift aid, 40% self-help). *Gift aid:* Total: $18,300 (27% from college's own funds, 7% from other college-administered sources, 66% from external sources). 4 Federal Work-Study jobs (averaging $400); 20 part-time jobs.

Need-Based Scholarships & Grants Pell, FSEOG, state, private, college/university.

Loans Stafford, Unsubsidized Stafford, private, college/university long-term loans ($1500 average).

Non-Need Awards *Special Characteristics Awards:* local/state students , religious affiliation.

Other Money-Saving Options *Payment Plans:* installment, deferred payment. *Waivers:* full or partial for minority students and employees or children of employees.

Contact Office of the Registrar and Financial Aid, Sacred Heart Major Seminary, 2701 Chicago Boulevard, Detroit, MI 48206-1799, 313-883-8512.

SACRED HEART UNIVERSITY
Fairfield, Connecticut

About the Institution Independent/religious, coed. Degrees awarded: A, B, M. Offers 67 undergraduate majors. Total enrollment: 5,545. Undergraduates: 2,122 (52% state residents). Freshmen: 632.

Undergraduate Expenses (1996–97) Comprehensive fee of $19,092 includes tuition ($12,212), mandatory fees ($500), and college room and board ($6380). College room only: $4490.

Applications Of all full-time undergraduates enrolled in fall 1996, 87% of those who applied for aid were judged to have need according to Federal Methodology, of whom 100% were aided. *Financial aid deadline (priority):* 3/1. *Financial aid forms:* FAFSA required. CSS Financial Aid PROFILE, institutional form required for some. *Regular admission application deadline:* 4/15. Early decision deadline: 12/7.

Summary of Aid to Needy Students *From gift & self-help combined:* Average need met: 74%. Average amount awarded: $9056 (58% gift aid, 42% self-help). *Gift aid:* Total: $9,529,429 (67% from college's own funds, 23% from other college-administered sources, 10% from external sources). 500 Federal Work-Study jobs (averaging $1000); 20 part-time jobs.

Need-Based Scholarships & Grants Pell, FSEOG, state, college/university.

Loans Perkins, PLUS, Stafford, Unsubsidized Stafford.

Non-Need Awards In 1996, a total of 697 non-need awards were made. *Academic Interests/Achievement Awards:* 575 ($2,372,864 total): general academic. *Special Achievements/Activities Awards:* 122 ($144,210 total): hobbies/interest, leadership.

Other Money-Saving Options Accelerated degree, co-op program, cooperative Army ROTC, off-campus living. *Payment Plans:* installment, deferred payment. *Waivers:* full or partial for employees or children of employees and senior citizens.

Contact Ms. Julie B. Savino, Director of Financial Aid, Sacred Heart University, 5151 Park Avenue, Fairfield, CT 06432-1000, 203-371-7981.

SAGINAW VALLEY STATE UNIVERSITY
University Center, Michigan

About the Institution State-supported, coed. Degrees awarded: B, M. Offers 48 undergraduate majors. Total enrollment: 7,338. Undergraduates: 6,407 (99% state residents). Freshmen: 784.

Undergraduate Expenses (1996–97) State resident tuition: $3092. Nonresident tuition: $6470. Mandatory fees: $257. College room and board: $4140.

Applications 78% of all full-time undergraduates enrolled in fall 1996 applied for aid; of these, 70% were judged to have need according to Federal Methodology, of whom 100% were aided. *Financial aid deadline:* continuous. *Financial aid forms:* FAFSA acceptable. CSS Financial Aid PROFILE required for some. *Admission application deadline:* rolling.

Summary of Aid to Needy Students *From gift & self-help combined:* Average need met: 91%. Average amount awarded: $7302 (27% gift aid, 73% self-help). *Gift aid:* Total: $3,966,664 (11% from college's own funds, 21% from other college-administered sources, 68% from external sources). 178 Federal Work-Study jobs (averaging $1600); 699 part-time jobs.

Need-Based Scholarships & Grants Pell, FSEOG, state, private.

Loans PLUS, Stafford, Unsubsidized Stafford, state, private.

Non-Need Awards In 1996, a total of 1,848 non-need awards were made. *Academic Interests/Achievement Awards:* 1,574 ($1,555,988 total): general academic, biological sciences, business, computer science, education, health fields, international studies, mathematics, social sciences. *Creative Arts/Performance Awards:* 80 ($28,854 total): music. *Special Characteristics Awards:* 5 ($2000 total): international students. *Athletic:* Total: 189 ($501,393); Men: 135 ($378,551); Women: 54 ($122,842).

Other Money-Saving Options Accelerated degree, co-op program, off-campus living. *Waivers:* full or partial for employees or children of employees and senior citizens.

Contact Mr. William Healy, Director of Scholarships and Financial Aid, Saginaw Valley State University, 7400 Bay Road, University Center, MI 48710, 517-790-4103.

ST. AMBROSE UNIVERSITY
Davenport, Iowa

About the Institution Independent/religious, coed. Degrees awarded: B, M. Offers 56 undergraduate majors. Total enrollment: 2,680. Undergraduates: 1,820 (69% state residents). Freshmen: 306.

Undergraduate Expenses (1997–98 estimated) Comprehensive fee of $16,700 includes tuition ($12,300) and college room and board ($4400 minimum).

Applications Of all full-time undergraduates enrolled in fall 1996, 89% of those who applied for aid were judged to have need according to Federal Methodology, of whom 100% were aided. *Financial aid deadline (priority):* 3/15. *Financial aid forms:* FAFSA, institutional form required. State form required for some. *Admission application deadline:* rolling.

Summary of Aid to Needy Students *From gift & self-help combined:* Average need met: 90%. Average amount awarded: $10,500 (41% gift aid, 59% self-help). *Gift aid:* Total: $8,150,675 (70% from college's own funds, 23% from other college-administered sources, 7% from external sources). 352 Federal Work-Study jobs (averaging $1680); 186 part-time jobs.

Need-Based Scholarships & Grants Pell, FSEOG, state, private, college/university.

Loans Perkins, PLUS, Stafford, Unsubsidized Stafford, private, college/university long-term loans ($1400 average).

Non-Need Awards *Academic Interests/Achievement Awards:* general academic, biological sciences, business, communication, computer science, education, engineering/technologies, English, foreign languages, health fields, mathematics, physical sciences, premedicine, religion/biblical studies, social sciences. *Creative Arts/Performance Awards:* art/fine arts, music, theater/drama. *Special Characteristics Awards:* general special characteristics, adult students, children and siblings of alumni, children of educators, children of faculty/staff, international students, relatives of clergy, religious affiliation, siblings of current students. *Athletic:* Total: 291 ($1,028,365); Men: 192 ($733,290); Women: 99 ($295,075).

Other Money-Saving Options Accelerated degree, co-op program, off-campus living (after sophomore year). *Payment Plan:* installment. *Waivers:* full or partial for employees or children of employees.

Contact Office of Financial Aid, St. Ambrose University, 518 West Locust Street, Davenport, IA 52803-2898, 319-333-6000.

ST. ANDREWS PRESBYTERIAN COLLEGE
Laurinburg, North Carolina

About the Institution Independent/religious, coed. Degrees awarded: B. Offers 37 undergraduate majors. Total enrollment: 662 (34% state residents). Freshmen: 165.

Undergraduate Expenses (1997–98 estimated) Comprehensive fee of $17,497 includes tuition ($12,042), mandatory fees ($140), and college room and board ($5315). College room only: $2121.

Applications 79% of all full-time undergraduates enrolled in fall 1996 applied for aid; of these, 98% were judged to have need according to Federal Methodology, of whom 100% were aided. *Financial aid deadline (priority):* 3/15. *Financial aid forms:* FAFSA required. Institutional Scholarship Application required for some. *Regular admission application deadline:* rolling. Early decision deadline: 12/1.

Summary of Aid to Needy Students *From gift & self-help combined:* Average need met: 80%. Average amount awarded: $5300 (67% gift aid, 33% self-help). *Gift aid:* Total: $3,653,139 (82% from college's own funds, 12% from other college-administered sources, 6% from external sources). 164 Federal Work-Study jobs (averaging $1800); 52 part-time jobs.

Need-Based Scholarships & Grants Pell, FSEOG, state, private, college/university.

Loans Perkins, PLUS, Stafford, Unsubsidized Stafford.

Non-Need Awards *Academic Interests/Achievement Awards:* general academic. *Creative Arts/Performance Awards:* art/fine arts, creative writing, music. *Special Achievements/Activities Awards:* general special achievements/activities, leadership, memberships, religious involvement. *Special Characteristics Awards:* general special characteristics. *Athletic:* available.

Other Money-Saving Options Accelerated degree. *Payment Plan:* installment. *Waivers:* full or partial for employees or children of employees.

Contact Financial Aid Department, St. Andrews Presbyterian College, Laurinburg, NC 28352-5598, 910-277-5560.

SAINT ANSELM COLLEGE
Manchester, New Hampshire

About the Institution Independent/religious, coed. Degrees awarded: B. Offers 32 undergraduate majors. Total enrollment: 1,928 (19% state residents). Freshmen: 580.

Undergraduate Expenses (1996–97) Comprehensive fee of $20,660 includes tuition ($14,550), mandatory fees ($400), and college room and board ($5710).

Applications Of all full-time undergraduates enrolled in fall 1996, 98% of those who applied for aid were judged to have need according to Federal Methodology, of whom 100% were aided. *Financial aid deadline (priority):* 3/15. *Financial aid forms:* FAFSA, CSS Financial Aid PROFILE required. *Regular admission application deadline:* rolling. Early decision deadline: 12/1.

Summary of Aid to Needy Students *From gift & self-help combined:* Average need met: 79%. Average amount awarded: $11,927 (64% gift aid, 36% self-help). *Gift aid:* Total: $11,500,959 (91% from college's own funds, 4% from other college-administered sources, 5% from external sources). 822 Federal Work-Study jobs (averaging $800); 290 part-time jobs.

Need-Based Scholarships & Grants Pell, FSEOG, state, private, college/university.

Loans Perkins, PLUS, Stafford, Unsubsidized Stafford, Federal Nursing, GATE Loans.

Non-Need Awards In 1996, a total of 257 non-need awards were made. *Academic Interests/Achievement Awards:* 115 ($814,000 total): general academic. *Creative Arts/Performance Awards:* 6 ($8000 total): debating. *Special Characteristics Awards:* 111 ($732,108 total): children of faculty/staff, members of minorities, siblings of current students. *Athletic:* Total: 25 ($425,090); Men: 10 ($211,970); Women: 15 ($213,120).

Other Money-Saving Options Cooperative Army ROTC, cooperative Air Force ROTC, off-campus living (after freshman year). *Waivers:* full or partial for employees or children of employees and senior citizens.

Contact Office of Financial Aid, Saint Anselm College, 100 Saint Anselm Drive-1735, Manchester, NH 03102-1310, 603-641-7000.

SAINT AUGUSTINE'S COLLEGE
Raleigh, North Carolina

About the Institution Independent/religious, coed. Degrees awarded: B. Offers 50 undergraduate majors. Total enrollment: 1,584 (51% state residents). Freshmen: 412.

Undergraduate Expenses (1997–98 estimated) Comprehensive fee of $10,560 includes tuition ($4680), mandatory fees ($1880), and college room and board ($4000).

Applications *Financial aid deadline (priority):* 8/10. *Financial aid forms:* FAFSA, CSS Financial Aid PROFILE required. *Admission application deadline:* 8/10.

Summary of Aid to Needy Students Federal Work-Study jobs.

Non-Need Awards *Academic Interests/Achievement Awards:* general academic. *Creative Arts/Performance Awards:* music. *Special Achievements/Activities Awards:* general special achievements/activities. *Special Characteristics Awards:* children of faculty/staff, ROTC participants. *Athletic:* available.

Other Money-Saving Options Co-op program, Army ROTC, Air Force ROTC, off-campus living.

Contact Office of Financial Aid, Saint Augustine's College, 1315 Oakwood Avenue, Raleigh, NC 27610-2298, 919-516-4000.

ST. BONAVENTURE UNIVERSITY
St. Bonaventure, New York

About the Institution Independent/religious, coed. Degrees awarded: B, M. Offers 41 undergraduate majors. Total enrollment: 2,723. Undergraduates: 2,045 (77% state residents). Freshmen: 590.

Undergraduate Expenses (1997–98) Comprehensive fee of $18,478 includes tuition ($12,580), mandatory fees ($520), and college room and board ($5378).

Applications Of all full-time undergraduates enrolled in fall 1996, 89% of those who applied for aid were judged to have need according to Federal Methodology, of whom 99% were aided. *Financial aid deadline (priority):* 2/1. *Financial aid forms:* FAFSA, institutional form required. State form required for some. *Admission application deadline:* 3/1.

Summary of Aid to Needy Students *From gift & self-help combined:* Average need met: 84%. Average amount awarded: $11,488 (64% gift aid, 36% self-help). *Gift aid:* Total: $10,604,000 (70% from college's own funds, 18% from other college-administered sources, 12% from external sources). 300 Federal Work-Study jobs (averaging $750); 400 part-time jobs.

Need-Based Scholarships & Grants Pell, FSEOG, state, private, college/university.

Loans Perkins, PLUS, Stafford, Unsubsidized Stafford, college/university short-term loans ($50 average), college/university long-term loans ($1000 average).

Non-Need Awards In 1996, a total of 1,813 non-need awards were made. *Academic Interests/Achievement Awards:* 1,460 ($3,766,000 total): general academic. *Creative Arts/Performance Awards:* 45 ($38,000 total): music. *Special Characteristics Awards:* 160 ($1,363,000 total): children of faculty/staff, local/state students, members of minorities, relatives of clergy, religious affiliation, ROTC participants, siblings of current students. *Athletic:* Total: 148 ($1,204,000); Men: 76 ($576,000); Women: 72 ($628,000).

Other Money-Saving Options Accelerated degree, Army ROTC, off-campus living (after junior year). *Payment Plans:* installment, deferred payment. *Waivers:* full or partial for employees or children of employees and senior citizens.

Contact Ms. Mary K. Piccioli, Director of Financial Aid, St. Bonaventure University, Route 417, St. Bonaventure, NY 14778-2284, 716-375-2528.

ST. CHARLES BORROMEO SEMINARY, OVERBROOK
Wynnewood, Pennsylvania

About the Institution Independent/religious, men. Degrees awarded: B, M, P. Offers 1 undergraduate major. Total enrollment: 515. Undergraduates: 103 (54% state residents). Freshmen: 8.

Undergraduate Expenses (1996–97) Comprehensive fee of $10,950 includes tuition ($6650), mandatory fees ($50), and college room and board ($4250).

Applications 20% of all full-time undergraduates enrolled in fall 1996 applied for aid; of these,100% were judged to have need according to Federal Methodology, of whom 100% were aided. *Financial aid deadline (priority):* 4/15. *Financial aid forms:* FAFSA required; CSS Financial Aid PROFILE, institutional form acceptable. State form required for some. *Admission application deadline:* 7/1.

Summary of Aid to Needy Students *From gift & self-help combined:* Average need met: 100%. *Gift aid:* Total: $196,661 (73% from college's own funds, 3% from other college-administered sources, 24% from external sources). 10 Federal Work-Study jobs (averaging $500); 2 part-time jobs.

Need-Based Scholarships & Grants Pell, FSEOG, state, college/university.

Loans PLUS, Stafford, Unsubsidized Stafford.

Non-Need Awards *Academic Interests/Achievement Awards:* general academic.

Other Money-Saving Options Accelerated degree. *Payment Plan:* installment. *Waivers:* full or partial for employees or children of employees.

Contact Ms. Arlene Dittbrenner, Coordinator of Financial Aid, St. Charles Borromeo Seminary, Overbrook, 100 East Wynnewood Road, Wynnewood, PA 19096, 610-667-3394 Ext. 201, fax: 610-667-3971.

ST. CLOUD STATE UNIVERSITY
St. Cloud, Minnesota

About the Institution State-supported, coed. Degrees awarded: A, B, M, D. Offers 121 undergraduate majors. Total enrollment: 14,048. Undergraduates: 12,958 (90% state residents). Freshmen: 2,114.

Undergraduate Expenses (1996–97) State resident tuition: $2526. Nonresident tuition: $5470. Mandatory fees: $378. College room and board: $3027.

Applications 73% of all full-time undergraduates enrolled in fall 1996 applied for aid; of these, 80% were judged to have need according to Federal Methodology, of whom 100% were aided. *Financial aid deadline (priority):* 4/20. *Financial aid forms:* FAFSA, institutional form required. *Admission application deadline:* 5/1.

Summary of Aid to Needy Students *From gift & self-help combined:* Average need met: 95%. Average amount awarded: $4437 (42% gift aid, 58% self-help). *Gift aid:* Total: $11,571,071 (13% from college's own funds, 7% from other college-administered sources, 80% from external sources). 539 Federal Work-Study jobs (averaging $2400); 1,288 part-time jobs.

Need-Based Scholarships & Grants Pell, FSEOG, state, college/university.

Loans Perkins, PLUS, Stafford, Unsubsidized Stafford, state, college/university short-term loans ($295 average).

Non-Need Awards In 1996, a total of 1,954 non-need awards were made. *Academic Interests/Achievement Awards:* 1,317 ($766,981 total): general academic, biological sciences, business, communication, computer science, education, engineering/technologies, English, international studies, mathematics, physical sciences, social sciences. *Creative Arts/Performance Awards:* 82 ($37,063 total): applied art and design, art/fine arts, cinema/film/broadcasting, journalism/publications, music, performing arts, theater/drama. *Special Characteristics Awards:* 321 ($356,428 total): children of faculty/staff, children of union members/company employees, members of minorities, out-of-state students. *Athletic:* Total: 234 ($515,103); Men: 153 ($365,653); Women: 81 ($149,450).

Other Money-Saving Options Accelerated degree, Army ROTC, off-campus living. *Waivers:* full or partial for employees or children of employees and senior citizens.

Contact Mr. Michael Uran, Assistant Director, St. Cloud State University, 720 4th Avenue South, St. Cloud, MN 56301-4498, 320-255-2047, fax: 320-654-5424.

ST. EDWARD'S UNIVERSITY
Austin, Texas

About the Institution Independent/religious, coed. Degrees awarded: B, M. Offers 39 undergraduate majors. Total enrollment: 3,082. Undergraduates: 2,546 (91% state residents). Freshmen: 373.

Undergraduate Expenses (1996–97) Comprehensive fee of $14,516 includes tuition ($10,400) and college room and board ($4116 minimum).

Applications 69% of all full-time undergraduates enrolled in fall 1996 applied for aid; of these, 92% were judged to have need according to Federal Methodology, of whom 99% were aided. *Financial aid deadline (priority):* 3/1. *Financial aid forms:* FAFSA required; CSS Financial Aid PROFILE acceptable. *Admission application deadline:* rolling.

Summary of Aid to Needy Students *From gift & self-help combined:* Average need met: 62%. Average amount awarded: $10,102 (61% gift aid, 39% self-help). *Gift aid:* Total: $6,641,881 (57% from college's own funds, 25% from other college-administered sources, 18% from external sources). Federal Work-Study jobs; 200 part-time jobs.

Need-Based Scholarships & Grants Pell, FSEOG, state, private, college/university.

Loans Perkins, PLUS, Stafford, Unsubsidized Stafford, state, college/university short-term loans ($100 average).

Non-Need Awards In 1996, a total of 689 non-need awards were made. *Academic Interests/Achievement Awards:* 299 ($760,620 total): general academic, biological sciences, business, education, humanities, physical sciences, social sciences. *Creative Arts/Performance Awards:* 19 ($29,650 total): theater/drama. *Special Achievements/Activities Awards:* 160 ($181,700 total): general special achievements/activities, leadership. *Special Characteristics Awards:* 84 ($211,795 total): adult students, children of faculty/staff, religious affiliation, ROTC participants, spouses of current students. *Athletic:* Total: 127 ($887,839); Men: 67 ($426,397); Women: 60 ($461,442).

Other Money-Saving Options Accelerated degree, co-op program, cooperative Army ROTC, cooperative Naval ROTC, cooperative Air Force ROTC, off-campus living (after freshman year). *Payment Plan:* installment. *Waivers:* full or partial for employees or children of employees.

Contact Financial Aid Office, St. Edward's University, 3001 South Congress Avenue, Austin, TX 78704-6489, 512-448-8523, fax: 512-416-5837.

SAINT FRANCIS COLLEGE
Fort Wayne, Indiana

About the Institution Independent/religious, coed. Degrees awarded: A, B, M. Offers 39 undergraduate majors. Total enrollment: 954. Undergraduates: 746 (84% state residents). Freshmen: 138.

Undergraduate Expenses (1997–98) Comprehensive fee of $14,980 includes tuition ($10,310), mandatory fees ($400), and college room and board ($4270).

Applications Of all full-time undergraduates enrolled in fall 1996, 100% of those judged to have need according to Federal Methodology were aided. *Financial aid deadline (priority):* 3/1. *Financial aid forms:* FAFSA, institutional form required. *Admission application deadline:* rolling.

Summary of Aid to Needy Students *From gift & self-help combined:* Average need met: 90%. Average amount awarded: $8422 (49% gift aid, 51% self-help). *Gift aid:* Total: $2,450,499 (54% from college's own funds, 2% from other college-administered sources, 44% from external sources). 100 Federal Work-Study jobs (averaging $1500); part-time jobs.

Need-Based Scholarships & Grants Pell, FSEOG, state, private, college/university.

Loans Perkins, PLUS, Stafford, Unsubsidized Stafford, college/university short-term loans ($500 average).

Non-Need Awards *Academic Interests/Achievement Awards:* 155 ($311,713 total): general academic, biological sciences, health fields, physical sciences. *Creative Arts/Performance Awards:* 70 ($150,225 total): art/fine arts. *Special Characteristics Awards:* 276 ($182,944 total): adult students, children and siblings of alumni, first-generation college students, out-of-state students, siblings of current students. *Athletic:* Total: ($356,700).

Other Money-Saving Options Co-op program. *Payment Plan:* installment. *Waivers:* full or partial for children of alumni, employees or children of employees, senior citizens.

Contact Ms. Meredith Jester, Director of Financial Aid, Saint Francis College, 2701 Spring Street, Fort Wayne, IN 46808-3994, 219-434-3283.

ST. FRANCIS COLLEGE
Brooklyn Heights, New York

About the Institution Independent, coed. Degrees awarded: A, B. Offers 33 undergraduate majors. Total enrollment: 2,077. Freshmen: 360.

Undergraduate Expenses (1996–97) Tuition: $7520. Mandatory fees: $180.

Applications Of all full-time undergraduates enrolled in fall 1996, 80% of those who applied for aid were judged to have need according to Federal Methodology, of whom 98% were aided. *Financial aid deadline (priority):* 2/15. *Financial aid forms:* FAFSA, state form, institutional form required; CSS Financial Aid PROFILE acceptable. *Admission application deadline:* rolling.

Summary of Aid to Needy Students *From gift & self-help combined:* Average need met: 64%. Average amount awarded: $6888 (63% gift aid, 37% self-help). *Gift aid:* Total: $4,891,000 (17% from college's own funds, 56% from other college-administered sources, 27% from external sources). Federal Work-Study jobs.

Need-Based Scholarships & Grants Pell, FSEOG, state, private, college/university.

Non-Need Awards *Academic Interests/Achievement Awards:* general academic. *Athletic:* Total: 135 ($513,390); Men: 80 ($289,876); Women: 55 ($223,514).

Other Money-Saving Options Accelerated degree, cooperative Army ROTC, cooperative Air Force ROTC. *Payment Plan:* installment. *Waivers:* full or partial for employees or children of employees.

Contact Office of Financial Aid, St. Francis College, 180 Remsen Street, Brooklyn Heights, NY 11201-4398, 718-522-2300.

SAINT FRANCIS COLLEGE
Loretto, Pennsylvania

About the Institution Independent/religious, coed. Degrees awarded: A, B, M. Offers 54 undergraduate majors. Total enrollment: 1,886. Undergraduates: 1,200 (80% state residents). Freshmen: 290.

Undergraduate Expenses (1996–97) Comprehensive fee of $18,888 includes tuition ($12,288), mandatory fees ($950), and college room and board ($5650).

Applications Of all full-time undergraduates enrolled in fall 1996, 89% of those who applied for aid were judged to have need according to Federal Methodology, of whom 99% were aided. *Financial aid deadline (priority):* 5/1. *Financial aid forms:* FAFSA required. State form, institutional form required for some. *Admission application deadline:* rolling.

Summary of Aid to Needy Students *From gift & self-help combined:* Average need met: 85%. Average amount awarded: $11,000 (62% gift aid, 38% self-help). *Gift aid:* Total: $6,291,000 (61% from college's own funds, 28% from other college-administered sources, 11% from external sources). 554 Federal Work-Study jobs (averaging $900); 320 part-time jobs.

Need-Based Scholarships & Grants Pell, FSEOG, state, private, college/university.

Loans Perkins, PLUS, Stafford, Unsubsidized Stafford, private.

Non-Need Awards In 1996, a total of 652 non-need awards were made. *Academic Interests/Achievement Awards:* 403 ($1,027,000 total): general academic. *Creative Arts/Performance Awards:* 3 ($1500 total): art/fine arts, music, theater/drama. *Special Achievements/Activities Awards:* 8 ($8000 total): cheerleading/drum major, Junior Miss. *Special Characteristics Awards:* 63 ($325,736 total): adult students, children of faculty/staff, siblings of current students. *Athletic:* Total: 175 ($1,099,500); Men: 69 ($561,000); Women: 106 ($538,500).

Other Money-Saving Options Accelerated degree, cooperative Army ROTC, off-campus living (after junior year). *Payment Plans:* installment, deferred payment. *Waivers:* full or partial for children of alumni and employees or children of employees.

Contact Mr. Michael D. Price, Director of Student Financial Aid, Saint Francis College, PO Box 600, Loretto, PA 15940-0600, 814-472-3010, fax: 814-472-3356.

ST. JOHN FISHER COLLEGE
Rochester, New York

About the Institution Independent/religious, coed. Degrees awarded: B, M. Offers 44 undergraduate majors. Total enrollment: 2,333. Undergraduates: 2,000 (97% state residents). Freshmen: 293.

Undergraduate Expenses (1997–98) Comprehensive fee of $18,200 includes tuition ($12,300), mandatory fees ($200), and college room and board ($5700 minimum). College room only: $4000 (minimum).

Applications 96% of all full-time undergraduates enrolled in fall 1996 applied for aid; of these, 92% were judged to have need according to Federal Methodology, of whom 100% were aided. *Financial aid deadline (priority):* 3/1. *Financial aid forms:* FAFSA required. State form required for some. *Regular admission application deadline:* rolling. Early action deadline: 11/15.

Summary of Aid to Needy Students *From gift & self-help combined:* Average need met: 93%. Average amount awarded: $10,156 (58% gift aid, 42% self-help). *Gift aid:* Total: $7,920,848 (54% from college's own funds, 11% from other college-administered sources, 35% from external sources). 1,122 Federal Work-Study jobs (averaging $1124); 216 part-time jobs.

Need-Based Scholarships & Grants Pell, FSEOG, state, private, college/university.

Loans Perkins, PLUS, Stafford, Unsubsidized Stafford, private.

Non-Need Awards In 1996, a total of 592 non-need awards were made. *Academic Interests/Achievement Awards:* 526 ($1,814,600 total): humanities, mathematics, physical sciences. *Special Achievements/Activities Awards:* 1 ($3500 total): community service. *Special Characteristics Awards:* 65 ($105,627 total): children and siblings of alumni, ethnic background, local/state students, members of minorities.

Other Money-Saving Options Accelerated degree, cooperative Army ROTC, cooperative Air Force ROTC, off-campus living. *Payment Plans:* installment, deferred payment. *Waivers:* full or partial for employees or children of employees and senior citizens.

Contact Office of Financial Aid, St. John Fisher College, 3690 East Avenue, Rochester, NY 14618-3597, 716-385-8000.

ST. JOHN'S COLLEGE
Annapolis, Maryland

About the Institution Independent, coed. Degrees awarded: B, M. Offers 3 undergraduate majors. Total enrollment: 516. Undergraduates: 438 (16% state residents). Freshmen: 115.

Undergraduate Expenses (1997–98) Comprehensive fee of $27,190 includes tuition ($20,980), mandatory fees ($200), and college room and board ($6010).

Applications 74% of all full-time undergraduates enrolled in fall 1996 applied for aid; of these, 86% were judged to have need according to Federal Methodology, of whom 97% were aided. *Financial aid deadline (priority):* 2/15. *Financial aid forms:* FAFSA, CSS Financial Aid PROFILE required. State form required for some. *Admission application deadline:* rolling.

Summary of Aid to Needy Students *From gift & self-help combined:* Average need met: 90%. Average amount awarded: $17,336 (69% gift aid, 31% self-help). *Gift aid:* Total: $3,315,350 (82% from college's own funds, 8% from other college-administered sources, 10% from external sources). 155 Federal Work-Study jobs (averaging $2050); 20 part-time jobs.

Need-Based Scholarships & Grants Pell, FSEOG, state, college/university.

Loans Perkins, PLUS, Stafford, Unsubsidized Stafford, college/university long-term loans ($4280 average).

Non-Need Awards Not offered.

Other Money-Saving Options Off-campus living (after freshman year). *Payment Plans:* tuition prepayment, installment. *Waivers:* full or partial for employees or children of employees.

Contact Office of Financial Aid, St. John's College, PO Box 2800, Annapolis, MD 21404, 410-263-2371.

ST. JOHN'S COLLEGE
Santa Fe, New Mexico

About the Institution Independent, coed. Degrees awarded: B, M. Offers 5 undergraduate majors. Total enrollment: 472. Undergraduates: 375 (11% state residents). Freshmen: 116.

Undergraduate Expenses (1997–98) Comprehensive fee of $25,816 includes tuition ($19,500), mandatory fees ($200), and college room and board ($6116).

Applications 74% of all full-time undergraduates enrolled in fall 1996 applied for aid; of these, 97% were judged to have need according to Federal Methodology, of whom 100% were aided. *Financial aid deadline (priority):* 2/15. *Financial aid forms:* FAFSA, CSS Financial Aid PROFILE, institutional form required. State form, Divorced/Separated Parents' Statement required for some. *Admission application deadline:* rolling.

Summary of Aid to Needy Students *From gift & self-help combined:* Average need met: 98%. Average amount awarded: $16,279 (68% gift aid, 32% self-help). *Gift aid:* Total: $3,033,560 (87% from college's own funds, 7% from other college-administered sources, 6% from external sources). 185 Federal Work-Study jobs (averaging $2015); 50 part-time jobs.

Need-Based Scholarships & Grants Pell, FSEOG, state, private, college/university.

Loans Perkins, PLUS, Stafford, Unsubsidized Stafford, college/university long-term loans ($3000 average).

Non-Need Awards In 1996, a total of 4 non-need awards were made. *Special Characteristics Awards:* 4 ($37,000 total): children of faculty/staff.

Other Money-Saving Options Off-campus living (after junior year). *Payment Plans:* tuition prepayment, installment. *Waivers:* full or partial for employees or children of employees.

Contact Office of Financial Aid, St. John's College, 1160 Camino de La Cruz Blanca, Santa Fe, NM 87501-4599, 505-984-6000.

ST. JOHN'S SEMINARY COLLEGE
Camarillo, California

About the Institution Independent/religious, men. Degrees awarded: B. Offers 4 undergraduate majors. Total enrollment: 66 (89% state residents). Freshmen: 8.

Undergraduate Expenses (1997–98) Comprehensive fee of $10,103 includes tuition ($6870), mandatory fees ($210), and college room and board ($3023).

Applications 46% of all full-time undergraduates enrolled in fall 1996 applied for aid; of these,100% were judged to have need according to Federal Methodology, of whom 100% were aided. *Financial aid deadline (priority):* 7/15. *Financial aid forms:* FAFSA required; CSS Financial Aid PROFILE, institutional form acceptable. State form required for some. *Admission application deadline:* 7/15.

Summary of Aid to Needy Students *From gift & self-help combined:* Average need met: 75%. Average amount awarded: $11,967 (63% gift aid, 37% self-help). *Gift aid:* Total: $227,544 (34% from college-administered sources, 66% from external sources). 32 Federal Work-Study jobs (averaging $2000); 20 part-time jobs.

Need-Based Scholarships & Grants Pell, state, college/university.

Loans College/university long-term loans ($2000 average).

Non-Need Awards *Academic Interests/Achievement Awards:* available. *Special Characteristics Awards:* religious affiliation, veterans.

Other Money-Saving Options *Payment Plans:* installment, deferred payment.

Contact Mrs. Shirley A. Waynar, Financial Aid Officer, St. John's Seminary College, 5118 Seminary Road, Camarillo, CA 93012-2599, 805-482-2755, fax: 805-484-4074.

SAINT JOHN'S SEMINARY COLLEGE OF LIBERAL ARTS
Brighton, Massachusetts

About the Institution Independent/religious, men. Degrees awarded: A, B. Offers 1 undergraduate major. Total enrollment: 33 (90% state residents). Freshmen: 7.

Undergraduate Expenses (1996–97) Comprehensive fee of $7800 includes tuition ($5200) and college room and board ($2600).

Applications 56% of all full-time undergraduates enrolled in fall 1996 applied for aid; of these, 52% were judged to have need according to Federal Methodology, of whom 100% were aided. *Financial aid deadline (priority):* 5/1. *Financial aid forms:* FAFSA required. CSS Financial Aid PROFILE, state form required for some. *Admission application deadline:* 8/1.

Summary of Aid to Needy Students *From gift & self-help combined:* Average need met: 50%. Average amount awarded: $7120 (71% gift aid, 29% self-help). *Gift aid:* Total: $48,690 (32% from college's own funds, 36% from other college-administered sources, 32% from external sources). Federal Work-Study jobs; 3 part-time jobs.

Need-Based Scholarships & Grants Pell, FSEOG, state.

Loans PLUS, Stafford, Unsubsidized Stafford, college/university short-term loans.

Non-Need Awards In 1996, a total of 11 non-need awards were made. *Academic Interests/Achievement Awards:* 11 ($15,400 total).

Contact Mr. John B. Lynch Jr., Business Manager, Saint John's Seminary College of Liberal Arts, 127 Lake Street, Brighton, MA 02135-4644, 617-254-2610, fax: 617-787-2336.

SAINT JOHN'S UNIVERSITY
Collegeville, Minnesota

About the Institution Independent/religious, men. Degrees awarded: B, M. Offers 54 undergraduate majors. Total enrollment: 1,796. Undergraduates: 1,687 (82% state residents). Freshmen: 426.

Undergraduate Expenses (1996–97) Comprehensive fee of $18,388 includes tuition ($13,858), mandatory fees ($138), and college room and board ($4392). College room only: $2078.

Applications 85% of all full-time undergraduates enrolled in fall 1996 applied for aid; of these, 77% were judged to have need according to Federal Methodology, of whom 100% were aided. *Financial aid deadline (priority):* 3/1. *Financial aid forms:* FAFSA required; CSS Financial Aid PROFILE acceptable. Institutional form required for some. *Admission application deadline:* rolling.

Summary of Aid to Needy Students *From gift & self-help combined:* Average need met: 96%. Average amount awarded: $13,280 (57% gift aid, 43% self-help). *Gift aid:* Total: $8,083,615 (62% from college's own funds, 26% from other college-administered sources, 12% from external sources). 295 Federal Work-Study jobs (averaging $1900); 635 part-time jobs.

Need-Based Scholarships & Grants Pell, FSEOG, state, private, college/university.

Loans Perkins, PLUS, Stafford, Unsubsidized Stafford, private, Student Educational Loan Fund (SELF).

Non-Need Awards In 1996, a total of 301 non-need awards were made. *Academic Interests/Achievement Awards:* 215 ($808,500 total): general academic. *Creative Arts/Performance Awards:* 35 ($26,250 total): art/fine arts, music, theater/drama. *Special Achievements/Activities Awards:* 10 ($20,000 total): leadership. *Special Characteristics Awards:* 41 ($370,263 total): international students, ROTC participants.

Other Money-Saving Options Army ROTC, off-campus living (after sophomore year). *Payment Plans:* tuition prepayment, installment, deferred payment. *Waivers:* full or partial for employees or children of employees.

Contact Ms. Mary Dehler, Associate Director of Financial Aid, Saint John's University, Collegeville, MN 56321-5000, 320-363-3664, fax: 320-363-2115.

ST. JOHN'S UNIVERSITY
Jamaica, New York

About the Institution Independent/religious, coed. Degrees awarded: A, B, M, D, P. Offers 72 undergraduate majors. Total enrollment: 16,804. Undergraduates: 12,108 (96% state residents). Freshmen: 2,260.

Undergraduate Expenses (1997–98) Tuition: $11,800 (minimum). Mandatory fees: $430.

Applications *Financial aid deadline (priority):* 4/1. *Financial aid forms:* FAFSA, CSS Financial Aid PROFILE required. State form required for some. *Admission application deadline:* rolling.

Summary of Aid to Needy Students *From gift & self-help combined:* Average need met: 60%. Average amount awarded: $8038 (56% gift aid, 44% self-help). *Gift aid:* Total: $42,235,852 (44% from college's own funds, 37% from other college-administered sources, 19% from external sources). 325 Federal Work-Study jobs (averaging $2500); 775 part-time jobs.

Need-Based Scholarships & Grants Pell, FSEOG, state, private, college/university.

Loans Perkins, PLUS, Stafford, Unsubsidized Stafford, private, college/university short-term loans ($500 average), Health Professions Loans.

Non-Need Awards In 1996, a total of 2,957 non-need awards were made. *Academic Interests/Achievement Awards:* 2,003 ($7,700,208 total): general academic, biological sciences, computer science, health fields, mathematics, military science. *Creative Arts/Performance Awards:* 154 ($408,240 total): art/fine arts, cinema/film/broadcasting, debating, journalism/publications, music, performing arts, theater/drama. *Special Achievements/Activities Awards:* 191 ($285,250 total): general special achievements/activities, community service, hobbies/interest, leadership, religious involvement. *Special Characteristics Awards:* 358 ($2,877,618 total): general special characteristics, children and siblings of alumni, children of faculty/staff, relatives of clergy, religious affiliation, ROTC participants, siblings of current students, veterans, veterans' children. *Athletic:* Total: 251 ($1,182,832); Men: 162 ($724,880); Women: 89 ($457,952).

Other Money-Saving Options Accelerated degree, Army ROTC. *Payment Plan:* installment. *Waivers:* full or partial for employees or children of employees.

Contact Mr. Jorge Rodriguez, Executive Director of Financial Aid, St. John's University, 8000 Utopia Parkway, Jamaica, NY 11439, 718-990-6403.

ST. JOHN VIANNEY COLLEGE SEMINARY
Miami, Florida

About the Institution Independent/religious. Degrees awarded: B. Offers 1 undergraduate major. Total enrollment: 44 (80% state residents). Freshmen: 4.

Undergraduate Expenses (1996–97) Comprehensive fee of $11,000 includes tuition ($6900), mandatory fees ($100), and college room and board ($4000).

Applications 38% of all full-time undergraduates enrolled in fall 1996 applied for aid; of these, 57% were judged to have need according to Federal Methodology, of whom 100% were aided. *Financial aid deadline*

(priority): 8/1. *Financial aid forms:* FAFSA required; CSS Financial Aid PROFILE, state form acceptable. *Admission application deadline:* rolling.

Summary of Aid to Needy Students *From gift & self-help combined:* Average amount awarded: $4906 (66% gift aid, 34% self-help). *Gift aid:* Total: $49,300 (72% from college-administered sources, 28% from external sources).

Need-Based Scholarships & Grants Pell, state.

Loans Stafford, Unsubsidized Stafford.

Non-Need Awards Not offered.

Another Money-Saving Option *Payment Plan:* installment.

Contact Ms. Bonnie de Angulo, Director of Financial Aid, St. John Vianney College Seminary, 2900 Southwest 87 Avenue, Miami, FL 33165-3244, 305-223-4561 Ext. 10.

SAINT JOSEPH COLLEGE
West Hartford, Connecticut

About the Institution Independent/religious, primarily women. Degrees awarded: B, M. Offers 43 undergraduate majors. Total enrollment: 1,922. Undergraduates: 1,206 (91% state residents). Freshmen: 166.

Undergraduate Expenses (1997–98) Comprehensive fee of $20,215 includes tuition ($14,490) and college room and board ($5725). College room only: $2700.

Applications 97% of all full-time undergraduates enrolled in fall 1996 applied for aid; of these, 95% were judged to have need according to Federal Methodology, of whom 100% were aided. *Financial aid deadline (priority):* 2/14. *Financial aid forms:* FAFSA, institutional form required. *Regular admission application deadline:* 5/1. Early action deadline: 11/15.

Summary of Aid to Needy Students *From gift & self-help combined:* Average need met: 76%. *Gift aid:* Total: $3,311,430 (62% from college's own funds, 34% from other college-administered sources, 4% from external sources). 34 Federal Work-Study jobs (averaging $1200); 168 part-time jobs.

Need-Based Scholarships & Grants Pell, FSEOG, state, private, college/university.

Loans Perkins, PLUS, Stafford, Unsubsidized Stafford, state, private.

Non-Need Awards In 1996, a total of 156 non-need awards were made. *Academic Interests/Achievement Awards:* 126 ($367,638 total): general academic. *Special Characteristics Awards:* 30 ($42,000 total): religious affiliation.

Other Money-Saving Options Accelerated degree, off-campus living. *Payment Plan:* installment. *Waivers:* full or partial for employees or children of employees and senior citizens.

Contact Office of Financial Aid, Saint Joseph College, 1678 Asylum Avenue, West Hartford, CT 06117-2700, 860-232-4571 Ext. 223, fax: 860-233-5695.

SAINT JOSEPH'S COLLEGE
Rensselaer, Indiana

About the Institution Independent/religious, coed. Degrees awarded: A, B, M. Offers 48 undergraduate majors. Total enrollment: 876 (69% state residents). Freshmen: 195.

Undergraduate Expenses (1996–97) Comprehensive fee of $17,230 includes tuition ($12,260), mandatory fees ($330), and college room and board ($4640).

Applications 90% of all full-time undergraduates enrolled in fall 1996 applied for aid; of these, 81% were judged to have need according to Federal Methodology, of whom 100% were aided. *Financial aid deadline (priority):* 5/1. *Financial aid forms:* FAFSA, institutional form required. *Admission application deadline:* rolling.

Summary of Aid to Needy Students *From gift & self-help combined:* Average need met: 90%. Average amount awarded: $11,898 (70% gift aid, 30% self-help). *Gift aid:* Total: $4,422,943 (72% from college's own funds, 3% from other college-administered sources, 25% from external sources). 299 Federal Work-Study jobs (averaging $1335); 140 part-time jobs.

Need-Based Scholarships & Grants Pell, FSEOG, state, college/university.

Loans Perkins, PLUS, Stafford, Unsubsidized Stafford.

Non-Need Awards In 1996, a total of 791 non-need awards were made. *Academic Interests/Achievement Awards:* 230 ($1,552,503 total): general academic. *Special Achievements/Activities Awards:* 158 ($258,400 total): general special achievements/activities, cheerleading/drum major. *Special Characteristics Awards:* 111 ($295,970 total): children and siblings of alumni, children of faculty/staff, members of minorities, siblings of current students. *Athletic:* Total: 292 ($1,405,425); Men: 182 ($917,000); Women: 110 ($488,425).

Other Money-Saving Options Accelerated degree, co-op program. *Payment Plan:* installment. *Waivers:* full or partial for minority students, children of alumni, employees or children of employees.

Contact Ms. Dianne Mickey, Director of Financial Aid, Saint Joseph's College, Box 971, Rensselaer, IN 47978-0850, 219-866-6149, fax: 219-866-6100.

SAINT JOSEPH'S COLLEGE
Standish, Maine

About the Institution Independent/religious, coed. Degrees awarded: A, B, M. Offers 33 undergraduate majors. Total enrollment: 1,105 (55% state residents). Freshmen: 217.

Undergraduate Expenses (1997–98) Comprehensive fee of $17,365 includes tuition ($11,340), mandatory fees ($370), and college room and board ($5655).

Applications 96% of all full-time undergraduates enrolled in fall 1996 applied for aid; of these, 90% were judged to have need according to Federal Methodology, of whom 100% were aided. *Financial aid deadline (priority):* 3/1. *Financial aid forms:* FAFSA required. CSS Financial Aid PROFILE required for some. *Regular admission application deadline:* rolling. Early action deadline: 12/1.

Summary of Aid to Needy Students *From gift & self-help combined:* Average need met: 82%. Average amount awarded: $11,895 (47% gift aid, 53% self-help). *Gift aid:* Total: $3,602,570 (68% from college's own funds, 10% from other college-administered sources, 22% from external sources). 275 Federal Work-Study jobs (averaging $1000); 40 part-time jobs.

Need-Based Scholarships & Grants Pell, FSEOG, state, private, college/university.

Loans Perkins, PLUS, Stafford, Unsubsidized Stafford, Federal Nursing, state, private.

Non-Need Awards In 1996, a total of 412 non-need awards were made. *Academic Interests/Achievement Awards:* 312 ($568,737 total): general academic, biological sciences, business, communication, education, English, health fields, humanities, social sciences. *Special Achievements/Activities Awards:* 30 ($120,200 total): general special achievements/activities, community service, leadership, memberships. *Special Characteristics Awards:* 70 ($248,515 total): children of faculty/staff, international students, members of minorities, ROTC participants, siblings of current students, spouses of current students.

Other Money-Saving Options Accelerated degree, cooperative Army ROTC, off-campus living. *Payment Plan:* installment. *Waivers:* full or partial for employees or children of employees and senior citizens.

Contact Office of Financial Aid, Saint Joseph's College, 278 White's Bridge Road, Standish, ME 04084-5263, 207-893-6612, fax: 207-893-7862.

ST. JOSEPH'S COLLEGE, NEW YORK
Brooklyn, New York

About the Institution Independent, coed. Degrees awarded: B. Offers 35 undergraduate majors. Total enrollment: 1,263 (99% state residents). Freshmen: 94.

Undergraduate Expenses (1997–98) Tuition: $8106. Mandatory fees: $220.

Applications 79% of all full-time undergraduates enrolled in fall 1996 applied for aid; of these, 83% were judged to have need according to Federal Methodology, of whom 100% were aided. *Financial aid deadline (priority):* 2/25. *Financial aid forms:* FAFSA, institutional form required. State form, federal, state income tax forms required for some. *Admission application deadline:* 8/15.

Summary of Aid to Needy Students *From gift & self-help combined:* Average need met: 98%. Average amount awarded: $8240 (56% gift aid, 44% self-help). *Gift aid:* Total: $1,714,500 (37% from college's own funds, 3% from other college-administered sources, 60% from external sources). 40 Federal Work-Study jobs (averaging $1675); 20 part-time jobs.

Need-Based Scholarships & Grants Pell, FSEOG, state, college/university.

Loans Perkins, PLUS, Stafford, Unsubsidized Stafford.

Non-Need Awards In 1996, a total of 216 non-need awards were made. *Academic Interests/Achievement Awards:* 191 ($637,000 total): general academic. *Special Characteristics Awards:* 25 ($32,000 total): children and siblings of alumni, children of faculty/staff.

Other Money-Saving Options *Payment Plans:* installment, deferred payment. *Waivers:* full or partial for employees or children of employees.

Contact Ms. Carol Sullivan, Director of Financial Aid, St. Joseph's College, New York, 245 Clinton Avenue, Brooklyn, NY 11205-3688, 718-636-6800, fax: 718-636-6075.

ST. JOSEPH'S COLLEGE, SUFFOLK CAMPUS
Patchogue, New York

About the Institution Independent, coed. Degrees awarded: B, M. Offers 30 undergraduate majors. Total enrollment: 2,593. Undergraduates: 2,550 (100% state residents). Freshmen: 208.

Undergraduate Expenses (1997–98) Tuition: $8345. Mandatory fees: $352.

Applications 80% of all full-time undergraduates enrolled in fall 1996 applied for aid; of these, 83% were judged to have need according to Federal Methodology, of whom 100% were aided. *Financial aid deadline (priority):* 2/25. *Financial aid forms:* FAFSA, institutional form required. State form required for some. *Admission application deadline:* 8/15.

Summary of Aid to Needy Students *From gift & self-help combined:* Average need met: 100%. Average amount awarded: $6855 (48% gift aid, 52% self-help). *Gift aid:* Total: $3,426,867 (26% from college's own funds, 6% from other college-administered sources, 68% from external sources). 35 Federal Work-Study jobs (averaging $1800); 40 part-time jobs.

Need-Based Scholarships & Grants Pell, FSEOG, college/university.

Loans Perkins, PLUS, Stafford, Unsubsidized Stafford.

Non-Need Awards In 1996, a total of 370 non-need awards were made. *Academic Interests/Achievement Awards:* 370 ($803,283 total): general academic.

Other Money-Saving Options Cooperative Army ROTC, cooperative Air Force ROTC. *Payment Plan:* installment. *Waivers:* full or partial for employees or children of employees and senior citizens.

Contact Ms. Joan Farley, Associate Director of Financial Aid, St. Joseph's College, Suffolk Campus, 155 West Roe Boulevard, Patchogue, NY 11772-2399, 516-447-3214, fax: 516-447-1734.

SAINT JOSEPH SEMINARY COLLEGE
Saint Benedict, Louisiana

About the Institution Independent/religious, primarily men. Degrees awarded: B. Offers 1 undergraduate major.

Undergraduate Expenses (1996–97) Comprehensive fee of $10,330 includes tuition ($5650), mandatory fees ($130), and college room and board ($4550). College room only: $2150.

Applications 54% of all full-time undergraduates enrolled in fall 1996 applied for aid; of these, 96% were judged to have need according to Federal Methodology, of whom 100% were aided. *Financial aid deadline (priority):* 4/30. *Financial aid forms:* FAFSA required; CSS Financial Aid PROFILE, state form, institutional form acceptable. *Admission application deadline:* rolling.

Summary of Aid to Needy Students *From gift & self-help combined:* Average need met: 90%. Average amount awarded: $11,453 (53% gift aid, 47% self-help). *Gift aid:* Total: $171,542 (3% from college's own funds, 7% from other college-administered sources, 90% from external sources). 27 Federal Work-Study jobs (averaging $800); 8 part-time jobs.

Need-Based Scholarships & Grants Pell, FSEOG, private, college/university.

Loans Perkins, PLUS, Stafford, Unsubsidized Stafford.

Non-Need Awards In 1996, a total of 5 non-need awards were made. *Academic Interests/Achievement Awards:* 2 ($2000 total): general academic. *Special Achievements/Activities Awards:* 3 ($3000 total): leadership.

Other Money-Saving Options *Payment Plan:* installment. *Waivers:* full or partial for senior citizens.

Contact Mr. Les Lavergne, Financial Aid Officer, Saint Joseph Seminary College, Saint Benedict, LA 70457, 504-867-2229, fax: 504-867-2270.

SAINT JOSEPH'S UNIVERSITY
Philadelphia, Pennsylvania

About the Institution Independent/religious, coed. Degrees awarded: A, B, M. Offers 38 undergraduate majors. Total enrollment: 6,963. Undergraduates: 4,077 (70% state residents). Freshmen: 827.

Undergraduate Expenses (1997–98) Comprehensive fee of $22,985 includes tuition ($15,700 minimum), mandatory fees ($325), and college room and board ($6960). College room only: $4460.

Applications Of all full-time undergraduates enrolled in fall 1996, 82% of those who applied for aid were judged to have need according to Federal Methodology, of whom 100% were aided. *Financial aid deadline (priority):* 3/1. *Financial aid forms:* FAFSA required. State form, institutional form required for some. *Admission application deadline:* rolling.

Summary of Aid to Needy Students *From gift & self-help combined:* Average need met: 70%. Average amount awarded: $10,462 (66% gift aid, 34% self-help). *Gift aid:* Total: $13,035,954 (77% from college's own funds, 15% from other college-administered sources, 8% from external sources). 232 Federal Work-Study jobs (averaging $1000); part-time jobs.

Need-Based Scholarships & Grants Pell, FSEOG, state, college/university.

Loans Perkins, PLUS, Stafford, Unsubsidized Stafford, private.

Non-Need Awards In 1996, a total of 1,107 non-need awards were made. *Academic Interests/Achievement Awards:* 881 ($5,331,402 total):

general academic. *Creative Arts/Performance Awards:* 25 ($115,300 total): debating, theater/drama. *Athletic:* Total: 201 ($1,787,000); Men: 96 ($857,760); Women: 105 ($929,240).

Other Money-Saving Options Accelerated degree, co-op program, Air Force ROTC, cooperative Army ROTC, cooperative Naval ROTC, off-campus living. *Payment Plans:* installment, deferred payment. *Waivers:* full or partial for employees or children of employees.

Contact Office of Financial Aid, Saint Joseph's University, 5600 City Avenue, Philadelphia, PA 19131-1395, 610-660-1000.

ST. LAWRENCE UNIVERSITY
Canton, New York

About the Institution Independent, coed. Degrees awarded: B, M. Offers 33 undergraduate majors. Total enrollment: 2,096. Undergraduates: 1,999 (47% state residents). Freshmen: 593.

Undergraduate Expenses (1997–98) Comprehensive fee of $27,785 includes tuition ($21,175), mandatory fees ($250), and college room and board ($6360). College room only: $3280.

Applications 70% of all full-time undergraduates enrolled in fall 1996 applied for aid; of these, 95% were judged to have need according to Federal Methodology, of whom 99% were aided. *Financial aid deadline:* 2/15. *Financial aid forms:* FAFSA, CSS Financial Aid PROFILE, institutional form required. State form required for some. *Regular admission application deadline:* 2/15. Early decision deadline: 12/15.

Summary of Aid to Needy Students *From gift & self-help combined:* Average need met: 93%. Average amount awarded: $19,482 (74% gift aid, 26% self-help). *Gift aid:* Total: $18,934,067 (86% from college's own funds, 7% from other college-administered sources, 7% from external sources). 779 Federal Work-Study jobs (averaging $1381); 341 part-time jobs.

Need-Based Scholarships & Grants Pell, FSEOG, state, private, college/university.

Loans Perkins, PLUS, Stafford, Unsubsidized Stafford, college/university short-term loans ($100 average), college/university long-term loans.

Non-Need Awards In 1996, a total of 91 non-need awards were made. *Academic Interests/Achievement Awards:* 77 ($637,500 total): general academic. *Special Achievements/Activities Awards:* 6 ($60,000 total): community service. *Special Characteristics Awards:* 6 ($60,000 total): members of minorities. *Athletic:* Total: 2; Men: 2.

Other Money-Saving Options Accelerated degree, cooperative Air Force ROTC. *Payment Plans:* installment, deferred payment. *Waivers:* full or partial for employees or children of employees.

Contact Office of Financial Aid, St. Lawrence University, Romoda Drive, Canton, NY 13617-1455, 315-379-5011.

SAINT LEO COLLEGE
Saint Leo, Florida

About the Institution Independent/religious, coed. Degrees awarded: A, B, M. Offers 33 undergraduate majors. Total enrollment: 1,651. Undergraduates: 1,463 (83% state residents). Freshmen: 326.

Undergraduate Expenses (1997–98) Comprehensive fee of $16,236 includes tuition ($10,400), mandatory fees ($596), and college room and board ($5240 minimum). College room only: $2660 (minimum).

Applications 99% of all full-time undergraduates enrolled in fall 1996 applied for aid; of these, 96% were judged to have need according to Federal Methodology, of whom 100% were aided. *Financial aid deadline (priority):* 3/1. *Financial aid forms:* FAFSA, institutional form required. State form required for some. *Admission application deadline:* 8/1.

Summary of Aid to Needy Students *From gift & self-help combined:* Average need met: 57%. Average amount awarded: $10,415 (64% gift aid, 36% self-help). *Gift aid:* Total: $4,404,212 (60% from college's

own funds, 29% from other college-administered sources, 11% from external sources). 167 Federal Work-Study jobs (averaging $995); 104 part-time jobs.

Need-Based Scholarships & Grants Pell, FSEOG, state, private, college/university.

Loans Perkins, PLUS, Stafford, Unsubsidized Stafford.

Non-Need Awards In 1996, a total of 172 non-need awards were made. *Academic Interests/Achievement Awards:* 29 ($158,468 total): general academic. *Special Achievements/Activities Awards:* 15 ($7000 total): religious involvement. *Special Characteristics Awards:* 42 ($190,948 total): children of faculty/staff, members of minorities, ROTC participants. *Athletic:* Total: 86 ($606,906); Men: 55 ($395,446); Women: 31 ($211,460).

Other Money-Saving Options Accelerated degree, cooperative Army ROTC, cooperative Air Force ROTC, off-campus living (after junior year). *Payment Plan:* installment. *Waivers:* full or partial for employees or children of employees.

Contact Office of Financial Aid, Saint Leo College, PO Box 6665, Saint Leo, FL 33574-6665, 352-588-8200.

ST. LOUIS CHRISTIAN COLLEGE
Florissant, Missouri

About the Institution Independent/religious, coed. Degrees awarded: A, B. Offers 8 undergraduate majors. Total enrollment: 176 (60% state residents). Freshmen: 55.

Undergraduate Expenses (1996–97) Comprehensive fee of $7450 includes tuition ($4000), mandatory fees ($380), and college room and board ($3070). College room only: $1700.

Applications 66% of all full-time undergraduates enrolled in fall 1996 applied for aid; of these, 86% were judged to have need according to Federal Methodology, of whom 100% were aided. *Financial aid deadline (priority):* 8/1. *Financial aid forms:* FAFSA, institutional form required. *Admission application deadline:* 7/1.

Summary of Aid to Needy Students *From gift & self-help combined:* Average need met: 50%. Average amount awarded: $5694 (49% gift aid, 51% self-help). *Gift aid:* Total: $236,755 (37% from college's own funds, 3% from other college-administered sources, 60% from external sources). 9 Federal Work-Study jobs (averaging $900); 16 part-time jobs.

Need-Based Scholarships & Grants Pell, FSEOG, private, college/university.

Loans PLUS, Stafford, Unsubsidized Stafford, college/university short-term loans ($375 average).

Non-Need Awards In 1996, a total of 73 non-need awards were made. *Academic Interests/Achievement Awards:* 14 ($3200 total): general academic. *Creative Arts/Performance Awards:* 9 ($13,592 total): music. *Special Achievements/Activities Awards:* 25 ($20,000 total): leadership, religious involvement. *Special Characteristics Awards:* 25 ($13,000 total): local/state students, religious affiliation.

Other Money-Saving Options Accelerated degree. *Payment Plan:* installment. *Waivers:* full or partial for employees or children of employees.

Contact Mrs. Catherine Wilhoit, Director of Financial Aid, St. Louis Christian College, 1360 Grandview Drive, Florissant, MO 63033-6499, 314-837-6777, fax: 314-837-8291.

ST. LOUIS COLLEGE OF PHARMACY
St. Louis, Missouri

About the Institution Independent, coed. Degrees awarded: B, M. Offers 1 undergraduate major. Total enrollment: 832. Undergraduates: 795 (49% state residents). Freshmen: 139.

Undergraduate Expenses (1997–98) Comprehensive fee of $16,550 includes tuition ($11,600) and college room and board ($4950).

Applications Of all full-time undergraduates enrolled in fall 1996, 85% of those who applied for aid were judged to have need according to Federal Methodology, of whom 100% were aided. *Financial aid deadline (priority):* 4/1. *Financial aid forms:* FAFSA, institutional form required. *Admission application deadline:* rolling.

Summary of Aid to Needy Students *From gift & self-help combined:* Average amount awarded: $3865 (23% gift aid, 77% self-help). *Gift aid:* Total: $500,237 (28% from college's own funds, 16% from other college-administered sources, 56% from external sources). 95 Federal Work-Study jobs (averaging $1100); 120 part-time jobs.

Need-Based Scholarships & Grants Pell, FSEOG, state, private, college/university.

Loans Perkins, PLUS, Stafford, Unsubsidized Stafford, private, college/university short-term loans ($500 average), college/university long-term loans ($1000 average).

Non-Need Awards *Academic Interests/Achievement Awards:* general academic. *Special Achievements/Activities Awards:* community service, leadership. *Special Characteristics Awards:* children of faculty/staff, local/state students.

Other Money-Saving Options Cooperative Army ROTC, cooperative Air Force ROTC, off-campus living. *Payment Plan:* deferred payment. *Waivers:* full or partial for employees or children of employees.

Contact Ms. Francine Royal, Director of Financial Aid, St. Louis College of Pharmacy, 4588 Parkview Place, St. Louis, MO 63110-1088, 314-367-8700 Ext. 1116, fax: 314-367-2784.

SAINT LOUIS UNIVERSITY
St. Louis, Missouri

About the Institution Independent/religious, coed. Degrees awarded: A, B, M, D, P. Offers 78 undergraduate majors. Total enrollment: 10,572. Undergraduates: 6,038 (53% state residents). Freshmen: 1,070.

Undergraduate Expenses (1997–98) Comprehensive fee of $19,422 includes tuition ($14,940), mandatory fees ($110), and college room and board ($4372 minimum). College room only: $1952 (minimum).

Applications 87% of all full-time undergraduates enrolled in fall 1996 applied for aid; of these, 81% were judged to have need according to Federal Methodology, of whom 100% were aided. *Financial aid deadline (priority):* 4/1. *Financial aid forms:* FAFSA required. State form, institutional form required for some. *Admission application deadline:* rolling.

Summary of Aid to Needy Students *From gift & self-help combined:* Average need met: 48%. Average amount awarded: $13,551 (61% gift aid, 39% self-help). *Gift aid:* Total: $27,148,159 (66% from college's own funds, 15% from other college-administered sources, 19% from external sources). 877 Federal Work-Study jobs (averaging $2624).

Need-Based Scholarships & Grants Pell, FSEOG, state, private, college/university.

Loans Perkins, PLUS, Stafford, Unsubsidized Stafford, Federal Nursing, private, college/university short-term loans ($200 average).

Non-Need Awards In 1996, a total of 3,037 non-need awards were made. *Academic Interests/Achievement Awards:* 1,699 ($9,531,279 total): general academic, health fields. *Creative Arts/Performance Awards:* 44 ($62,500 total): art/fine arts, music, performing arts, theater/drama. *Special Achievements/Activities Awards:* 305 ($1,056,241 total): community service, leadership, memberships. *Special Characteristics Awards:* 831 ($5,395,455 total): general special characteristics, children of faculty/staff, members of minorities, siblings of current students. *Athletic:* Total: 158 ($1,396,764); Men: 73 ($654,958); Women: 85 ($741,806).

Other Money-Saving Options Accelerated degree, Air Force ROTC, cooperative Army ROTC, off-campus living. *Payment Plan:* installment. *Waivers:* full or partial for employees or children of employees.

Contact Office of Financial Aid, Saint Louis University, Room 121, 221 North Grand Boulevard, St. Louis, MO 63103-2097, 314-977-2222.

SAINT MARTIN'S COLLEGE
Lacey, Washington

About the Institution Independent/religious, coed. Degrees awarded: A, B, M. Offers 33 undergraduate majors. Total enrollment: 958. Undergraduates: 674 (81% state residents). Freshmen: 87.

Undergraduate Expenses (1997–98) Comprehensive fee of $17,710 includes tuition ($12,990), mandatory fees ($130), and college room and board ($4590).

Applications *Financial aid deadline (priority):* 3/1. *Financial aid forms:* FAFSA required; CSS Financial Aid PROFILE acceptable. Institutional form required for some. *Admission application deadline:* 8/1.

Summary of Aid to Needy Students *From gift & self-help combined:* Average need met: 90%. Average amount awarded: $9489 (49% gift aid, 51% self-help). *Gift aid:* Total: $2,648,879 (64% from college's own funds, 18% from other college-administered sources, 18% from external sources). 137 Federal Work-Study jobs (averaging $2294); 30 part-time jobs.

Need-Based Scholarships & Grants Pell, FSEOG, state, college/university.

Loans Perkins, PLUS, Stafford, Unsubsidized Stafford, private, college/university short-term loans ($200 average).

Non-Need Awards In 1996, a total of 293 non-need awards were made. *Academic Interests/Achievement Awards:* 127 ($464,300 total). *Creative Arts/Performance Awards:* 3 ($1000 total). *Special Achievements/Activities Awards:* 30 ($53,000 total). *Special Characteristics Awards:* 67 ($171,198 total): local/state students, members of minorities, religious affiliation, siblings of current students, spouses of current students. *Athletic:* Total: 66 ($225,305); Men: 35 ($126,725); Women: 31 ($98,580).

Other Money-Saving Options Accelerated degree, co-op program, cooperative Army ROTC, off-campus living (after sophomore year). *Payment Plan:* installment. *Waivers:* full or partial for employees or children of employees.

Contact Mr. Ronald Noborikawa, Director of Financial Aid, Saint Martin's College, 5300 Pacific Avenue, SE, Lacey, WA 98503-7500, 360-438-4397, fax: 360-459-4124.

SAINT MARY COLLEGE
Leavenworth, Kansas

About the Institution Independent/religious, coed. Degrees awarded: A, B, M. Offers 26 undergraduate majors. Total enrollment: 678. Undergraduates: 504 (69% state residents). Freshmen: 79.

Undergraduate Expenses (1997–98) Comprehensive fee of $14,650 includes tuition ($10,350) and college room and board ($4300).

Applications Of all full-time undergraduates enrolled in fall 1996, 94% of those who applied for aid were judged to have need according to Federal Methodology, of whom 100% were aided. *Financial aid deadline (priority):* 8/1. *Financial aid forms:* FAFSA, CSS Financial Aid PROFILE acceptable. State form, institutional form required for some. *Admission application deadline:* rolling.

Summary of Aid to Needy Students *From gift & self-help combined:* Average amount awarded: $9565 (58% gift aid, 42% self-help). *Gift aid:* Total: $1,266,317 (70% from college's own funds, 18% from other college-administered sources, 12% from external sources). 65 Federal Work-Study jobs (averaging $958); 64 part-time jobs.

Need-Based Scholarships & Grants Pell, FSEOG, state.

Loans Perkins, PLUS, Stafford, Unsubsidized Stafford.

Non-Need Awards In 1996, a total of 405 non-need awards were made. *Academic Interests/Achievement Awards:* 138 ($546,280 total): general academic. *Creative Arts/Performance Awards:* 33 ($17,600 total): art/fine arts, creative writing, music, theater/drama. *Special Achievements/Activities Awards:* 10 ($48,300 total): community service. *Special Characteristics Awards:* 161 ($213,716 total): general special characteristics, children of faculty/staff, out-of-state students, religious affiliation, siblings of current students. *Athletic:* Total: 63 ($60,421); Men: 29 ($27,176); Women: 34 ($33,245).

Other Money-Saving Options Army ROTC. *Payment Plan:* installment. *Waivers:* full or partial for minority students, employees or children of employees, adult students.

Contact Office of Financial Aid, Saint Mary College, 4100 South Fourth Street Trafficway, Leavenworth, KS 66048-5082, 913-682-5151.

SAINT MARY-OF-THE-WOODS COLLEGE
Saint Mary-of-the-Woods, Indiana

About the Institution Independent/religious, women. Degrees awarded: A, B, M. Offers 43 undergraduate majors. Total enrollment: 1,266. Undergraduates: 1,204 (82% state residents). Freshmen: 77.

Undergraduate Expenses (1997–98) Comprehensive fee of $17,775 includes tuition ($12,540), mandatory fees ($435), and college room and board ($4800). College room only: $1830.

Applications *Financial aid deadline (priority):* 3/1. *Financial aid forms:* institutional form required; state form acceptable. FAFSA required for some. *Admission application deadline:* 8/15.

Summary of Aid to Needy Students Federal Work-Study jobs; part-time jobs.

Non-Need Awards *Academic Interests/Achievement Awards:* general academic. *Creative Arts/Performance Awards:* art/fine arts, journalism/publications, music. *Special Achievements/Activities Awards:* general special achievements/activities, leadership. *Special Characteristics Awards:* adult students, children and siblings of alumni, local/state students, out-of-state students, religious affiliation. *Athletic:* available.

Other Money-Saving Options Accelerated degree, cooperative Army ROTC, cooperative Air Force ROTC. *Payment Plan:* installment. *Waivers:* full or partial for minority students, children of alumni, employees or children of employees.

Contact Office of Financial Aid, Saint Mary-of-the-Woods College, Saint Mary-of-the-Woods, IN 47876, 812-535-5151.

SAINT MARY'S COLLEGE
Notre Dame, Indiana

About the Institution Independent/religious, women. Degrees awarded: B. Offers 42 undergraduate majors. Total enrollment: 1,474 (25% state residents). Freshmen: 345.

Undergraduate Expenses (1997–98) Comprehensive fee of $20,849 includes tuition ($14,738), mandatory fees ($914), and college room and board ($5197).

Applications 67% of all full-time undergraduates enrolled in fall 1996 applied for aid; of these, 94% were judged to have need according to Federal Methodology, of whom 94% were aided. *Financial aid deadline (priority):* 3/1. *Financial aid forms:* FAFSA, CSS Financial Aid PROFILE required. *Regular admission application deadline:* 3/1. Early decision deadline: 11/15.

Summary of Aid to Needy Students *From gift & self-help combined:* Average amount awarded: $12,007 (67% gift aid, 33% self-help). *Gift aid:* Total: $6,722,958 (81% from college's own funds, 10% from other college-administered sources, 9% from external sources). 150 Federal Work-Study jobs (averaging $1750); 600 part-time jobs.

Need-Based Scholarships & Grants Pell, FSEOG, state, private, college/university.

Loans Perkins, PLUS, Stafford, Unsubsidized Stafford, private, college/university short-term loans ($150 average), college/university long-term loans ($2500 average).

Non-Need Awards In 1996, a total of 324 non-need awards were made. *Academic Interests/Achievement Awards:* 150 ($827,000 total): general academic. *Creative Arts/Performance Awards:* 0: art/fine arts, music. *Special Characteristics Awards:* 174 ($523,820 total): children of faculty/staff, ROTC participants, siblings of current students.

Other Money-Saving Options Accelerated degree, cooperative Army ROTC, cooperative Naval ROTC, cooperative Air Force ROTC, off-campus living. *Payment Plans:* installment, deferred payment. *Waivers:* full or partial for employees or children of employees, adult students, senior citizens.

Contact Mrs. Mary Nucciarone, Director of Financial Aid, Saint Mary's College, 150 Le Mans Hall, Notre Dame, IN 46556, 219-284-4557, fax: 219-284-4716.

SAINT MARY'S COLLEGE
Orchard Lake, Michigan

About the Institution Independent/religious, coed. Degrees awarded: B. Offers 18 undergraduate majors. Total enrollment: 350 (85% state residents). Freshmen: 80.

Undergraduate Expenses (1996–97) Comprehensive fee of $10,430 includes tuition ($6300), mandatory fees ($30), and college room and board ($4100). College room only: $1900.

Applications 100% of all full-time undergraduates enrolled in fall 1996 applied for aid; of these, 56% were judged to have need according to Federal Methodology, of whom 100% were aided. *Financial aid deadline (priority):* 04/15. *Financial aid forms:* FAFSA, institutional form required. *Admission application deadline:* rolling.

Summary of Aid to Needy Students *From gift & self-help combined:* Average need met: 70%. Average amount awarded: $5828 (66% gift aid, 34% self-help). *Gift aid:* Total: $304,644 (16% from college's own funds, 57% from other college-administered sources, 27% from external sources). 14 Federal Work-Study jobs (averaging $500); 5 part-time jobs.

Need-Based Scholarships & Grants Pell, FSEOG, state, private, college/university.

Loans PLUS, Stafford, Unsubsidized Stafford, private.

Non-Need Awards In 1996, a total of 24 non-need awards were made. *Academic Interests/Achievement Awards:* 24 ($16,500 total): general academic.

Other Money-Saving Options Co-op program, off-campus living. *Payment Plan:* installment. *Waivers:* full or partial for employees or children of employees.

Contact Ms. Carol Sturgis, Assistant Director of Financial Aid, Saint Mary's College, 3535 Indian Trail, Orchard Lake, MI 48324-1623, 810-683-0508, fax: 810-683-0433.

SAINT MARY'S COLLEGE OF CALIFORNIA
Moraga, California

About the Institution Independent/religious, coed. Degrees awarded: B, M. Offers 45 undergraduate majors. Total enrollment: 4,204. Undergraduates: 2,113 (88% state residents). Freshmen: 486.

Undergraduate Expenses (1997–98) Comprehensive fee of $21,848 includes tuition ($15,880), mandatory fees ($118), and college room and board ($5850). College room only: $3600.

Applications 60% of all full-time undergraduates enrolled in fall 1996 applied for aid; of these, 86% were judged to have need according to Federal Methodology, of whom 98% were aided. *Financial aid deadline*

(priority): 3/2. *Financial aid forms:* FAFSA, state form required. *Regular admission application deadline:* 2/1. *Early action deadline:* 11/30.

Summary of Aid to Needy Students *From gift & self-help combined:* Average need met: 68%. Average amount awarded: $11,882 (67% gift aid, 33% self-help). *Gift aid:* Total: $8,377,928 (64% from college's own funds, 27% from other college-administered sources, 9% from external sources). 89 Federal Work-Study jobs (averaging $1997); 250 part-time jobs.

Need-Based Scholarships & Grants Pell, FSEOG, state, college/university.

Loans College/university long-term loans.

Non-Need Awards In 1996, a total of 418 non-need awards were made. *Academic Interests/Achievement Awards:* 196 ($241,250 total): general academic. *Special Characteristics Awards:* 29 ($339,647 total): children and siblings of alumni, children of faculty/staff. *Athletic:* Total: 193 ($1,627,338); Men: 136 ($919,935); Women: 57 ($707,403).

Other Money-Saving Options Cooperative Army ROTC, cooperative Naval ROTC, cooperative Air Force ROTC, off-campus living. *Payment Plans:* tuition prepayment, installment. *Waivers:* full or partial for employees or children of employees.

Contact Ms. Billie C. Jones, Director of Financial Aid, Saint Mary's College of California, PO Box 4530, Moraga, CA 94575, 510-631-4370, fax: 510-376-2965.

ST. MARY'S COLLEGE OF MARYLAND
St. Mary's City, Maryland

About the Institution State-supported, coed. Degrees awarded: B. Offers 22 undergraduate majors. Total enrollment: 1,478 (84% state residents). Freshmen: 312.

Undergraduate Expenses (1997–98) State resident tuition: $5500. Nonresident tuition: $9300. Mandatory fees: $1075. College room and board: $5480. College room only: $2985.

Applications 61% of all full-time undergraduates enrolled in fall 1996 applied for aid; of these, 74% were judged to have need according to Federal Methodology, of whom 97% were aided. *Financial aid deadline (priority):* 3/1. *Financial aid forms:* FAFSA required. State form required for some. *Regular admission application deadline:* 1/15. *Early decision deadline:* 12/1.

Summary of Aid to Needy Students *From gift & self-help combined:* Average need met: 72%. Average amount awarded: $6234 (52% gift aid, 48% self-help). *Gift aid:* Total: $1,949,077 (47% from college's own funds, 15% from other college-administered sources, 38% from external sources). 62 Federal Work-Study jobs (averaging $600); part-time jobs.

Need-Based Scholarships & Grants Pell, FSEOG, state, college/university.

Loans Perkins, PLUS, Stafford, Unsubsidized Stafford, college/university short-term loans ($125 average).

Non-Need Awards In 1996, a total of 119 non-need awards were made. *Academic Interests/Achievement Awards:* 119 ($424,633 total): general academic.

Other Money-Saving Options Off-campus living. *Waivers:* full or partial for employees or children of employees and senior citizens.

Contact Mr. George Bachman, Director of Financial Aid, St. Mary's College of Maryland, St. Mary's City, MD 20686, 301-862-0300, fax: 301-862-0959.

SAINT MARY'S UNIVERSITY OF MINNESOTA
Winona, Minnesota

About the Institution Independent/religious, coed. Degrees awarded: B, M. Offers 59 undergraduate majors. Total enrollment: 9,321. Undergraduates: 1,400 (48% state residents). Freshmen: 385.

Undergraduate Expenses (1997–98) Comprehensive fee of $16,595 includes tuition ($12,150 minimum), mandatory fees ($345), and college room and board ($4100). College room only: $2250.

Applications 70% of all full-time undergraduates enrolled in fall 1996 applied for aid; of these, 95% were judged to have need according to Federal Methodology, of whom 96% were aided. *Financial aid deadline (priority):* 4/15. *Financial aid forms:* FAFSA, institutional form required. *Admission application deadline:* rolling.

Summary of Aid to Needy Students *From gift & self-help combined:* Average need met: 88%. Average amount awarded: $10,317 (56% gift aid, 44% self-help). *Gift aid:* Total: $4,896,000 (63% from college's own funds, 25% from other college-administered sources, 12% from external sources). 584 Federal Work-Study jobs (averaging $930); 202 part-time jobs.

Need-Based Scholarships & Grants Pell, FSEOG, state, college/university.

Loans Perkins, PLUS, Stafford, Unsubsidized Stafford, state.

Non-Need Awards In 1996, a total of 498 non-need awards were made. *Academic Interests/Achievement Awards:* general academic. *Creative Arts/Performance Awards:* debating, music, theater/drama. *Special Achievements/Activities Awards:* leadership, memberships.

Other Money-Saving Options Accelerated degree, off-campus living (after sophomore year). *Payment Plan:* installment. *Waivers:* full or partial for employees or children of employees.

Contact Ms. Jayne P. Wobig, Director of Financial Aid, Saint Mary's University of Minnesota, Winona, MN 55987-1399, 507-457-1437.

ST. MARY'S UNIVERSITY OF SAN ANTONIO
San Antonio, Texas

About the Institution Independent/religious, coed. Degrees awarded: B, M, D, P. Offers 42 undergraduate majors. Total enrollment: 4,096. Undergraduates: 2,560 (91% state residents). Freshmen: 509.

Undergraduate Expenses (1997–98) Comprehensive fee of $14,916 includes tuition ($10,380), mandatory fees ($228), and college room and board ($4308). College room only: $2808 (minimum).

Applications *Financial aid deadline (priority):* 4/1. *Financial aid forms:* FAFSA, state form, verification worksheet required. *Admission application deadline:* 8/15.

Summary of Aid to Needy Students *From gift & self-help combined:* Average need met: 76%. Average amount awarded: $11,424 (55% gift aid, 45% self-help). *Gift aid:* Total: $9,798,000. 829 Federal Work-Study jobs (averaging $1701); 110 part-time jobs.

Need-Based Scholarships & Grants Pell, FSEOG, state, private, college/university.

Loans Perkins, PLUS, Stafford, Unsubsidized Stafford, state, private.

Non-Need Awards In 1996, a total of 1,150 non-need awards were made. *Academic Interests/Achievement Awards:* 792 ($2,400,000 total): general academic. *Creative Arts/Performance Awards:* 30 ($115,000 total): music. *Special Achievements/Activities Awards:* 10 ($10,000 total): cheerleading/drum major. *Special Characteristics Awards:* 112 ($840,000 total): children of faculty/staff, out-of-state students, ROTC participants. *Athletic:* Total: 206 ($760,000); Men: 97 ($366,000); Women: 109 ($394,000).

Other Money-Saving Options Accelerated degree, co-op program, Army ROTC, off-campus living (after freshman year). *Payment Plans:* tuition prepayment, installment, deferred payment. *Waivers:* full or partial for employees or children of employees.

Contact Mr. David R. Krause, Director of Financial Assistance, St. Mary's University of San Antonio, San Antonio, TX 78228-8507, 210-436-3141.

SAINT MICHAEL'S COLLEGE
Colchester, Vermont

About the Institution Independent/religious, coed. Degrees awarded: B, M. Offers 35 undergraduate majors. Total enrollment: 2,641. Undergraduates: 1,817 (20% state residents). Freshmen: 486.

Undergraduate Expenses (1997–98) Comprehensive fee of $22,900 includes tuition ($15,744), mandatory fees ($156), and college room and board ($7000). College room only: $4350.

Applications Of all full-time undergraduates enrolled in fall 1996, 89% of those who applied for aid were judged to have need according to Federal Methodology, of whom 99% were aided. *Financial aid deadline (priority):* 3/15. *Financial aid forms:* FAFSA, institutional form required; CSS Financial Aid PROFILE acceptable. *Regular admission application deadline:* 2/15. Early action deadline: 11/15.

Summary of Aid to Needy Students *From gift & self-help combined:* Average need met: 75%. Average amount awarded: $11,767 (64% gift aid, 36% self-help). *Gift aid:* Total: $9,159,230 (84% from college's own funds, 8% from other college-administered sources, 8% from external sources). 216 Federal Work-Study jobs (averaging $1050); 431 part-time jobs.

Need-Based Scholarships & Grants Pell, FSEOG, state, college/university.

Loans Perkins, PLUS, Stafford, Unsubsidized Stafford.

Non-Need Awards In 1996, a total of 118 non-need awards were made. *Academic Interests/Achievement Awards:* 46 ($253,000 total): general academic. *Creative Arts/Performance Awards:* 1 ($2500 total): art/fine arts. *Special Characteristics Awards:* 51 ($333,250 total): local/state students, members of minorities, religious affiliation, ROTC participants, siblings of current students. *Athletic:* Total: 20 ($423,200); Men: 10 ($211,600); Women: 10 ($211,600).

Other Money-Saving Options Cooperative Army ROTC, cooperative Air Force ROTC. *Payment Plan:* installment. *Waivers:* full or partial for employees or children of employees.

Contact Mrs. Nelberta B. Lunde, Director of Financial Aid, Saint Michael's College, Winooski Park, Colchester, VT 05439, 802-654-3243.

ST. NORBERT COLLEGE
De Pere, Wisconsin

About the Institution Independent/religious, coed. Degrees awarded: B, M. Offers 51 undergraduate majors. Total enrollment: 2,122. Undergraduates: 2,066 (71% state residents). Freshmen: 512.

Undergraduate Expenses (1997–98) Comprehensive fee of $19,554 includes tuition ($14,234), mandatory fees ($200), and college room and board ($5120). College room only: $2675.

Applications Of all full-time undergraduates enrolled in fall 1996, 90% of those who applied for aid were judged to have need according to Federal Methodology, of whom 99% were aided. *Financial aid deadline (priority):* 3/1. *Financial aid forms:* FAFSA, institutional form required; CSS Financial Aid PROFILE acceptable. *Admission application deadline:* rolling.

Summary of Aid to Needy Students *From gift & self-help combined:* Average need met: 98%. Average amount awarded: $13,570 (56% gift aid, 44% self-help). *Gift aid:* Total: $10,236,113 (75% from college's

own funds, 15% from other college-administered sources, 10% from external sources). 517 Federal Work-Study jobs (averaging $1550); 370 part-time jobs.

Need-Based Scholarships & Grants Pell, FSEOG, state, private, college/university.

Loans Perkins, PLUS, Stafford, Unsubsidized Stafford.

Non-Need Awards In 1996, a total of 1,192 non-need awards were made. *Academic Interests/Achievement Awards:* 1,069 ($3,118,644 total): general academic. *Creative Arts/Performance Awards:* 68 ($106,530 total): art/fine arts, music, theater/drama. *Special Characteristics Awards:* 55 ($500,908 total): children of faculty/staff, children with a deceased or disabled parent, ROTC participants.

Other Money-Saving Options Accelerated degree, co-op program, cooperative Army ROTC. *Payment Plans:* guaranteed tuition, installment, deferred payment. *Waivers:* full or partial for employees or children of employees.

Contact Office of Financial Aid, St. Norbert College, 100 Grant Street, De Pere, WI 54115-2099, 414-403-3181.

ST. OLAF COLLEGE
Northfield, Minnesota

About the Institution Independent/religious, coed. Degrees awarded: B. Offers 62 undergraduate majors. Total enrollment: 2,959 (54% state residents). Freshmen: 775.

Undergraduate Expenses (1997–98) Comprehensive fee of $20,520 includes tuition ($16,500) and college room and board ($4020).

Applications 69% of all full-time undergraduates enrolled in fall 1996 applied for aid; of these, 92% were judged to have need according to Federal Methodology, of whom 100% were aided. *Financial aid deadline (priority):* 3/1. *Financial aid forms:* FAFSA, institutional form required; CSS Financial Aid PROFILE acceptable. State form required for some. *Regular admission application deadline:* rolling. Early decision deadline: 11/15.

Summary of Aid to Needy Students *From gift & self-help combined:* Average need met: 100%. Average amount awarded: $13,033 (63% gift aid, 37% self-help). *Gift aid:* Total: $15,108,000 (70% from college's own funds, 5% from other college-administered sources, 25% from external sources). 1,700 Federal Work-Study jobs (averaging $1472); 297 part-time jobs.

Need-Based Scholarships & Grants Pell, FSEOG, state, private, college/university.

Loans Perkins, PLUS, Stafford, Unsubsidized Stafford, Federal Nursing, state, college/university short-term loans ($2500 average), college/university long-term loans ($2500 average).

Non-Need Awards In 1996, a total of 388 non-need awards were made. *Academic Interests/Achievement Awards:* 218 ($518,000 total): general academic. *Creative Arts/Performance Awards:* 90 ($158,000 total): music. *Special Achievements/Activities Awards:* 80 ($120,000 total): community service, religious involvement.

Other Money-Saving Options Accelerated degree. *Payment Plans:* tuition prepayment, installment. *Waivers:* full or partial for employees or children of employees.

Contact Mr. Mark Gelle, Director of Student Financial Services, St. Olaf College, 1520 Saint Olaf Avenue, Northfield, MN 55057-1098, 507-646-3019, fax: 507-646-3832.

SAINT PAUL'S COLLEGE
Lawrenceville, Virginia

About the Institution Independent/religious, coed. Degrees awarded: B. Offers 12 undergraduate majors. Total enrollment: 666 (76% state residents). Freshmen: 133.

Undergraduate Expenses (1997–98) Comprehensive fee of $11,300 includes tuition ($6820), mandatory fees ($440), and college room and board ($4040).

Applications *Financial aid deadline (priority):* 5/16. *Financial aid forms:* FAFSA required.

Summary of Aid to Needy Students Federal Work-Study jobs; 50 part-time jobs.

Need-Based Scholarships & Grants Pell, FSEOG, state, private, college/university.

Loans Perkins, PLUS, Stafford, Unsubsidized Stafford, private.

Non-Need Awards In 1996, a total of 242 non-need awards were made. *Academic Interests/Achievement Awards:* 42 ($101,018 total): general academic, biological sciences. *Special Achievements/Activities Awards:* 127 ($104,205 total): general special achievements/activities. *Special Characteristics Awards:* 1 ($1500 total): general special characteristics. *Athletic:* Total: 72 ($152,659); Men: 44 ($101,135); Women: 28 ($51,524).

Other Money-Saving Options Co-op program, Army ROTC, off-campus living (after sophomore year).

Contact Financial Aid Department, Saint Paul's College, Lawrenceville, VA 23868-1202, 804-848-3111.

SAINT PETER'S COLLEGE
Jersey City, New Jersey

About the Institution Independent/religious, coed. Degrees awarded: A, B, M. Offers 44 undergraduate majors. Total enrollment: 3,863. Undergraduates: 3,437 (86% state residents). Freshmen: 669.

Undergraduate Expenses (1997–98) Comprehensive fee of $19,744 includes tuition ($13,888), mandatory fees ($326), and college room and board ($5530). College room only: $2980 (minimum).

Applications 84% of all full-time undergraduates enrolled in fall 1996 applied for aid; of these, 94% were judged to have need according to Federal Methodology, of whom 96% were aided. *Financial aid deadline (priority):* 3/1. *Financial aid forms:* FAFSA required. *Regular admission application deadline:* rolling. Early action deadline: 12/1.

Summary of Aid to Needy Students *From gift & self-help combined:* Average need met: 65%. Average amount awarded: $10,100 (53% gift aid, 47% self-help). *Gift aid:* Total: $8,536,000 (11% from college's own funds, 68% from other college-administered sources, 21% from external sources). 400 Federal Work-Study jobs (averaging $1500); 168 part-time jobs.

Need-Based Scholarships & Grants Pell, FSEOG, state, college/university.

Loans Perkins, PLUS, Stafford, Unsubsidized Stafford, state, private.

Non-Need Awards In 1996, a total of 760 non-need awards were made. *Academic Interests/Achievement Awards:* 548 ($4,495,000 total): general academic. *Special Achievements/Activities Awards:* 52 ($72,000 total): leadership. *Special Characteristics Awards:* 25 ($252,892 total): general special characteristics, children of faculty/staff, relatives of clergy, religious affiliation. *Athletic:* Total: 135 ($1,671,200); Men: 70 ($751,200); Women: 65 ($920,000).

Other Money-Saving Options Accelerated degree, co-op program, cooperative Army ROTC, cooperative Air Force ROTC, off-campus living. *Payment Plans:* installment, deferred payment. *Waivers:* full or partial for employees or children of employees.

Contact Ms. Carol Anne Zablocki, Director of Financial Aid, Saint Peter's College, 2641 Kennedy Boulevard, Jersey City, NJ 07306-5997, 201-915-9309, fax: 201-434-6878.

ST. THOMAS AQUINAS COLLEGE
Sparkill, New York

About the Institution Independent, coed. Degrees awarded: B, M. Offers 39 undergraduate majors. Total enrollment: 2,100. Undergraduates: 1,500 (68% state residents). Freshmen: 262.

Undergraduate Expenses (1997–98 estimated) Comprehensive fee of $16,900 includes tuition ($10,200), mandatory fees ($200), and college room and board ($6500). College room only: $3600.

Applications *Financial aid deadline (priority):* 2/15. *Financial aid forms:* FAFSA, institutional form required. *Regular admission application deadline:* rolling. Early decision deadline: 11/1. Early action deadline: 12/1.

Summary of Aid to Needy Students *From gift & self-help combined:* Average amount awarded: $4259 (33% gift aid, 67% self-help). *Gift aid:* Total: $1,548,969 (39% from college's own funds, 29% from other college-administered sources, 32% from external sources). 68 Federal Work-Study jobs (averaging $1500); 10 part-time jobs.

Need-Based Scholarships & Grants Pell, FSEOG, state, private, college/university.

Loans Perkins, PLUS, Stafford, Unsubsidized Stafford.

Non-Need Awards *Academic Interests/Achievement Awards:* general academic. *Special Achievements/Activities Awards:* community service, leadership. *Special Characteristics Awards:* spouses of current students. *Athletic:* available.

Other Money-Saving Options Accelerated degree, cooperative Air Force ROTC, off-campus living. *Payment Plans:* installment, deferred payment. *Waivers:* full or partial for employees or children of employees and senior citizens.

Contact Mr. Brian Metcalf, Admissions and Financial Aid Counselor, St. Thomas Aquinas College, 125 Route 340, Sparkill, NY 10976, 914-398-4097.

ST. THOMAS UNIVERSITY
Miami, Florida

About the Institution Independent/religious, coed. Degrees awarded: B, M, P. Offers 28 undergraduate majors. Total enrollment: 2,262. Undergraduates: 1,165 (56% state residents). Freshmen: 200.

Undergraduate Expenses (1997–98) Comprehensive fee of $15,410 includes tuition ($11,400), mandatory fees ($440), and college room and board ($3570).

Applications 82% of all full-time undergraduates enrolled in fall 1996 applied for aid; of these, 65% were judged to have need according to Federal Methodology, of whom 100% were aided. *Financial aid deadline (priority):* 4/1. *Financial aid forms:* FAFSA, institutional form required; CSS Financial Aid PROFILE, state form acceptable. *Admission application deadline:* rolling.

Summary of Aid to Needy Students *From gift & self-help combined:* Average need met: 85%. Average amount awarded: $6805 (52% gift aid, 48% self-help). *Gift aid:* Total: $1,452,507 (42% from college's own funds, 38% from other college-administered sources, 20% from external sources). 102 Federal Work-Study jobs (averaging $2400); 73 part-time jobs.

Need-Based Scholarships & Grants Pell, FSEOG, state, private, college/university.

Loans Perkins, PLUS, Stafford, Unsubsidized Stafford, private.

Non-Need Awards In 1996, a total of 773 non-need awards were made. *Academic Interests/Achievement Awards:* 689 ($1,361,256 total): general academic. *Special Characteristics Awards:* 6 ($54,600 total): members of minorities. *Athletic:* Total: 78 ($474,130); Men: 47 ($287,276); Women: 31 ($186,854).

Other Money-Saving Options Co-op program, cooperative Army ROTC, cooperative Air Force ROTC, off-campus living. *Payment Plan:* installment. *Waivers:* full or partial for minority students, children of alumni, employees or children of employees.

Contact Ms. Tina Jones, Assistant Director of Financial Aid, St. Thomas University, 16400 Northwest 32nd Avenue, Miami, FL 33054-6459, 305-628-6547, fax: 305-628-6754.

SAINT VINCENT COLLEGE
Latrobe, Pennsylvania

About the Institution Independent/religious, coed. Degrees awarded: B. Offers 55 undergraduate majors. Total enrollment: 1,215 (88% state residents). Freshmen: 273.

Undergraduate Expenses (1997–98) Comprehensive fee of $18,103 includes tuition ($13,361), mandatory fees ($100), and college room and board ($4642). College room only: $2266.

Applications 84% of all full-time undergraduates enrolled in fall 1996 applied for aid; of these, 91% were judged to have need according to Federal Methodology, of whom 100% were aided. *Financial aid deadline (priority):* 5/1. *Financial aid forms:* FAFSA required. State form required for some. *Admission application deadline:* rolling.

Summary of Aid to Needy Students *From gift & self-help combined:* Average need met: 81%. Average amount awarded: $10,579 (65% gift aid, 35% self-help). *Gift aid:* Total: $5,619,886 (63% from college's own funds, 27% from other college-administered sources, 10% from external sources). Federal Work-Study jobs; 185 part-time jobs.

Need-Based Scholarships & Grants Pell, FSEOG, state, college/ university.

Loans Perkins, PLUS, Stafford, Unsubsidized Stafford.

Non-Need Awards In 1996, a total of 721 non-need awards were made. *Academic Interests/Achievement Awards:* 312 ($1,062,247 total): general academic, biological sciences, business, computer science, mathematics, physical sciences, social sciences. *Creative Arts/ Performance Awards:* 3 ($6000 total): music. *Special Achievements/ Activities Awards:* 285 ($263,175 total): leadership. *Special Characteristics Awards:* 10 ($47,000 total): international students, members of minorities. *Athletic:* Total: 111 ($380,080); Men: 60 ($206,671); Women: 51 ($173,409).

Other Money-Saving Options Accelerated degree, co-op program, cooperative Air Force ROTC, off-campus living. *Payment Plans:* installment, deferred payment. *Waivers:* full or partial for employees or children of employees.

Contact Ms. Karen G. Squib, Assistant Director of Financial Aid, Saint Vincent College, 300 Fraser Purchase Road, Latrobe, PA 15650, 412-537-4540, fax: 412-537-4554.

SAINT XAVIER UNIVERSITY
Chicago, Illinois

About the Institution Independent/religious, coed. Degrees awarded: B, M. Offers 51 undergraduate majors. Total enrollment: 4,200. Undergraduates: 3,000 (94% state residents). Freshmen: 237.

Undergraduate Expenses (1996–97) Comprehensive fee of $17,065 includes tuition ($11,970), mandatory fees ($110), and college room and board ($4985).

Applications *Financial aid deadline (priority):* 3/1. *Financial aid forms:* FAFSA required. *Admission application deadline:* 8/1.

Summary of Aid to Needy Students *From gift & self-help combined:* Average need met: 100%. Average amount awarded: $10,167 (45% gift aid, 55% self-help). *Gift aid:* Total: $9,025,288 (40% from college's own funds, 5% from other college-administered sources, 55% from external sources). 305 Federal Work-Study jobs (averaging $937); 105 part-time jobs.

Need-Based Scholarships & Grants Pell, FSEOG, state, private, college/ university.

Loans Perkins, PLUS, Stafford, Unsubsidized Stafford, private.

Non-Need Awards In 1996, a total of 556 non-need awards were made. *Academic Interests/Achievement Awards:* 168 ($450,500 total): general academic. *Creative Arts/Performance Awards:* 35 ($70,000 total): music. *Special Achievements/Activities Awards:* 54 ($75,000 total): leadership. *Special Characteristics Awards:* 102 ($511,072 total): children of faculty/staff, international students. *Athletic:* Total: 197 ($794,160); Men: 115 ($575,650); Women: 82 ($218,510).

Other Money-Saving Options Co-op program, cooperative Air Force ROTC, off-campus living. *Payment Plan:* installment. *Waivers:* full or partial for employees or children of employees and senior citizens.

Contact Ms. Susan Swisher, Director of Financial Aid, Saint Xavier University, 3700 West 103rd Street, IL 60655-3105, 773-298-3070, fax: 773-779-9061.

SALEM COLLEGE
Winston-Salem, North Carolina

About the Institution Independent/religious, primarily women. Degrees awarded: B, M. Offers 28 undergraduate majors. Total enrollment: 903. Undergraduates: 787 (53% state residents). Freshmen: 151.

Undergraduate Expenses (1997–98) Comprehensive fee of $19,735 includes tuition ($12,200), mandatory fees ($215), and college room and board ($7320).

Applications *Financial aid deadline (priority):* 3/1. *Financial aid forms:* FAFSA, institutional form required; CSS Financial Aid PROFILE acceptable. State form required for some. *Admission application deadline:* rolling.

Summary of Aid to Needy Students Federal Work-Study jobs; part-time jobs.

Non-Need Awards *Academic Interests/Achievement Awards:* general academic. *Creative Arts/Performance Awards:* music. *Special Achievements/ Activities Awards:* leadership. *Special Characteristics Awards:* children of educators, children of faculty/staff, relatives of clergy.

Other Money-Saving Options Cooperative Army ROTC. *Payment Plan:* installment. *Waivers:* full or partial for employees or children of employees.

Contact Office of Financial Aid, Salem College, PO Box 10548, Winston-Salem, NC 27108-0548, 910-721-2600.

SALEM STATE COLLEGE
Salem, Massachusetts

About the Institution State-supported, coed. Degrees awarded: B, M. Offers 61 undergraduate majors.

Applications 69% of all full-time undergraduates enrolled in fall 1996 applied for aid; of these, 79% were judged to have need according to Federal Methodology, of whom 76% were aided. *Financial aid deadline (priority):* 4/1. *Financial aid forms:* FAFSA required. *Admission application deadline:* 3/1.

Summary of Aid to Needy Students *From gift & self-help combined:* Average need met: 61%. Average amount awarded: $5850 (43% gift aid, 57% self-help). *Gift aid:* Total: $5,614,371 (6% from college's own funds, 39% from other college-administered sources, 55% from external sources). 512 Federal Work-Study jobs (averaging $1100); 600 part-time jobs.

Need-Based Scholarships & Grants Pell, FSEOG, state, private, college/ university.

Loans Perkins, PLUS, Stafford, Unsubsidized Stafford, Federal Nursing, state, private, college/university short-term loans ($500 average).

Non-Need Awards In 1996, a total of 291 non-need awards were made. *Academic Interests/Achievement Awards:* 58 ($20,938 total): general academic. *Creative Arts/Performance Awards:* 21 ($26,091 total): art/fine arts, creative writing, dance, music, performing arts, theater/drama. *Special Achievements/Activities Awards:* 77 ($79,575 total): memberships. *Special Characteristics Awards:* 135 ($123,387 total): children and siblings of alumni, children of faculty/staff, first-generation college students, members of minorities, veterans.

Other Money-Saving Options Off-campus living. *Payment Plan:* deferred payment. *Waivers:* full or partial for minority students, employees or children of employees, senior citizens.

Contact Office of Financial Aid, Salem State College, 352 Lafayette Street, Salem, MA 01970-5353, 508-741-6000.

SALEM-TEIKYO UNIVERSITY
Salem, West Virginia

About the Institution Independent, coed. Degrees awarded: A, B, M. Offers 32 undergraduate majors. Total enrollment: 867. Undergraduates: 756 (26% state residents). Freshmen: 215.

Undergraduate Expenses (1996–97) Comprehensive fee of $16,073 includes tuition ($12,066 minimum), mandatory fees ($55), and college room and board ($3952). College room only: $1600.

Applications 63% of all full-time undergraduates enrolled in fall 1996 applied for aid; of these, 95% were judged to have need according to Federal Methodology, of whom 100% were aided. *Financial aid deadline (priority):* 4/15. *Financial aid forms:* FAFSA required; AFSSA-CSX, SINGLEFILE Form of United Student Aid Funds acceptable. *Admission application deadline:* rolling.

Summary of Aid to Needy Students *From gift & self-help combined:* Average need met: 99%. Average amount awarded: $13,371 (63% gift aid, 37% self-help). *Gift aid:* Total: $3,737,289 (74% from college's own funds, 8% from other college-administered sources, 18% from external sources). 361 Federal Work-Study jobs (averaging $1774); 309 part-time jobs.

Need-Based Scholarships & Grants Pell, FSEOG, state, private, college/university.

Loans Perkins, PLUS, Stafford, Unsubsidized Stafford, college/university long-term loans.

Non-Need Awards In 1996, a total of 557 non-need awards were made. *Academic Interests/Achievement Awards:* 474 ($2,606,014 total): general academic. *Athletic:* Total: 83 ($352,588); Men: 44 ($222,923); Women: 39 ($129,665).

Other Money-Saving Options Accelerated degree, cooperative Army ROTC, cooperative Air Force ROTC, off-campus living (after sophomore year). *Payment Plan:* installment. *Waivers:* full or partial for employees or children of employees and senior citizens.

Contact Ms. Laura V. Miller, Director of Financial Aid, Salem-Teikyo University, 223 West Main Street, Salem, WV 26426-0500, 304-782-5303, fax: 304-782-5395.

SALISBURY STATE UNIVERSITY
Salisbury, Maryland

About the Institution State-supported, coed. Degrees awarded: B, M. Offers 47 undergraduate majors. Total enrollment: 5,308. Undergraduates: 4,839 (75% state residents). Freshmen: 696.

Undergraduate Expenses (1997–98) State resident tuition: $2746. Nonresident tuition: $6498. Mandatory fees: $1096. College room and board: $5060.

Applications Of all full-time undergraduates enrolled in fall 1996, 79% of those who applied for aid were judged to have need according to Federal Methodology, of whom 90% were aided. *Financial aid deadline*

(priority): 3/1. *Financial aid forms:* FAFSA required. *Regular admission application deadline:* 3/1. Early decision deadline: 12/15.

Summary of Aid to Needy Students *From gift & self-help combined:* Average need met: 60%. Average amount awarded: $7500 (30% gift aid, 70% self-help). *Gift aid:* Total: $2,902,994 (3% from college's own funds, 7% from other college-administered sources, 90% from external sources). 60 Federal Work-Study jobs (averaging $1500); 1,100 part-time jobs.

Need-Based Scholarships & Grants Pell, FSEOG, college/university.

Loans Perkins, PLUS, Stafford, Unsubsidized Stafford.

Non-Need Awards In 1996, a total of 428 non-need awards were made. *Academic Interests/Achievement Awards:* 428 ($763,187 total): general academic, biological sciences, business, communication, education, English, foreign languages, humanities, mathematics, physical sciences, premedicine, social sciences.

Other Money-Saving Options Accelerated degree, co-op program, Army ROTC, off-campus living. *Waivers:* full or partial for employees or children of employees and senior citizens.

Contact Ms. Beverly N. Horner, Director of Financial Aid, Salisbury State University, 1101 Camden Avenue, Salisbury, MD 21801-6837, 410-543-6165, fax: 410-543-6138.

SALVE REGINA UNIVERSITY
Newport, Rhode Island

About the Institution Independent/religious, coed. Degrees awarded: A, B, M, D. Offers 44 undergraduate majors. Total enrollment: 1,844. Undergraduates: 1,433 (26% state residents). Freshmen: 393.

Undergraduate Expenses (1997–98) Comprehensive fee of $22,750 includes tuition ($15,450), mandatory fees ($200), and college room and board ($7100).

Applications 80% of all full-time undergraduates enrolled in fall 1996 applied for aid; of these, 89% were judged to have need according to Federal Methodology, of whom 100% were aided. *Financial aid deadline (priority):* 3/1. *Financial aid forms:* FAFSA, CSS Financial Aid PROFILE, state form, institutional form, affidavit of nonsupport required. *Regular admission application deadline:* rolling. Early decision deadline: 11/1.

Summary of Aid to Needy Students *From gift & self-help combined:* Average amount awarded: $9846 (56% gift aid, 44% self-help). *Gift aid:* Total: $5,255,700 (86% from college's own funds, 5% from other college-administered sources, 9% from external sources). 742 Federal Work-Study jobs (averaging $1500); 184 part-time jobs.

Need-Based Scholarships & Grants Pell, FSEOG, state, private, college/university.

Loans Perkins, PLUS, Stafford, Unsubsidized Stafford, Federal Nursing, state, private, college/university short-term loans ($50 average), college/university long-term loans ($1000 average).

Non-Need Awards *Academic Interests/Achievement Awards:* general academic.

Other Money-Saving Options Accelerated degree, Army ROTC, off-campus living. *Waivers:* full or partial for employees or children of employees.

Contact Mrs. Lucile Flanagan, Director of Financial Aid, Salve Regina University, Newport, RI 02840-4192, 401-847-6650.

SAMFORD UNIVERSITY
Birmingham, Alabama

About the Institution Independent/religious, coed. Degrees awarded: A, B, M, P. Offers 70 undergraduate majors. Total enrollment: 4,473. Undergraduates: 2,918 (35% state residents). Freshmen: 652.

Undergraduate Expenses (1997–98) Comprehensive fee of $13,828 includes tuition ($9432) and college room and board ($4396).

Applications 46% of all full-time undergraduates enrolled in fall 1996 applied for aid; of these, 82% were judged to have need according to Federal Methodology, of whom 98% were aided. *Financial aid deadline (priority):* 3/1. *Financial aid forms:* FAFSA required. State form required for some. *Regular admission application deadline:* rolling. Early decision deadline: 12/1.

Summary of Aid to Needy Students *From gift & self-help combined:* Average need met: 82%. Average amount awarded: $8291 (48% gift aid, 52% self-help). *Gift aid:* Total: $2,880,839 (70% from college's own funds, 12% from other college-administered sources, 18% from external sources). 205 Federal Work-Study jobs (averaging $1312); 456 part-time jobs.

Need-Based Scholarships & Grants Pell, FSEOG, state, private, college/university.

Loans Perkins, PLUS, Stafford, Unsubsidized Stafford, private, college/university long-term loans ($2019 average).

Non-Need Awards In 1996, a total of 1,705 non-need awards were made. *Academic Interests/Achievement Awards:* 598 ($1,462,665 total): general academic. *Creative Arts/Performance Awards:* 78 ($86,220 total): music. *Special Achievements/Activities Awards:* 144 ($215,388 total): leadership. *Special Characteristics Awards:* 577 ($2,288,862 total): children of faculty/staff, relatives of clergy, ROTC participants. *Athletic:* Total: 308 ($1,803,472); Men: 209 ($1,259,710); Women: 99 ($543,762).

Other Money-Saving Options Accelerated degree, co-op program, Air Force ROTC, cooperative Army ROTC, off-campus living (after sophomore year). *Waivers:* full or partial for employees or children of employees.

Contact Mr. Clyde Walker, Director of Financial Aid, Samford University, Birmingham, AL 35229-0002, 205-870-2905, fax: 205-870-2171.

SAM HOUSTON STATE UNIVERSITY
Huntsville, Texas

About the Institution State-supported, coed. Degrees awarded: B, M, D. Offers 68 undergraduate majors. Total enrollment: 12,564. Undergraduates: 11,096 (98% state residents). Freshmen: 1,811.

Undergraduate Expenses (1996–97) State resident tuition: $960. Nonresident tuition: $7380. Mandatory fees: $770. College room and board: $3160 (minimum). College room only: $1580 (minimum).

Applications Of all full-time undergraduates enrolled in fall 1996, 78% of those who applied for aid were judged to have need according to Federal Methodology, of whom 99% were aided. *Financial aid deadline (priority):* 5/31. *Financial aid forms:* FAFSA required. *Admission application deadline:* rolling.

Summary of Aid to Needy Students *From gift & self-help combined:* Average amount awarded: $5255 (33% gift aid, 67% self-help). *Gift aid:* Total: $3,285,823 (18% from college's own funds, 19% from other college-administered sources, 63% from external sources). 158 Federal Work-Study jobs; 25 part-time jobs.

Need-Based Scholarships & Grants Pell, FSEOG, state, college/university.

Loans Perkins, PLUS, Stafford, Unsubsidized Stafford, state, college/university short-term loans ($200 average), college/university long-term loans.

Non-Need Awards In 1996, a total of 737 non-need awards were made. *Academic Interests/Achievement Awards:* 266 ($100,240 total): general academic, agriculture, biological sciences, business, communication, computer science, education, engineering/technologies, English, foreign languages, home economics, humanities, library science, mathematics, military science, physical sciences, social sciences. *Creative Arts/Performance Awards:* 190 ($57,802 total): art/fine arts, cinema/film/broadcasting, dance, journalism/publications, music, performing arts, theater/drama. *Special Achievements/Activities Awards:* 130

($47,713 total): general special achievements/activities, cheerleading/drum major, leadership, rodeo. *Special Characteristics Awards:* 0: general special characteristics, handicapped students, ROTC participants. *Athletic:* Total: 151 ($377,500); Men: 101 ($252,500); Women: 50 ($125,000).

Other Money-Saving Options Accelerated degree, co-op program, Army ROTC, off-campus living (after freshman year). *Payment Plan:* installment.

Contact Office of Financial Aid, Sam Houston State University, PO Box 2328, Huntsville, TX 77341, 409-294-1111.

SAMUEL MERRITT COLLEGE
Oakland, California

About the Institution Independent, coed. Degrees awarded: B, M. Offers 1 undergraduate major. Total enrollment: 677. Undergraduates: 309 (98% state residents). Freshmen: 9.

Undergraduate Expenses (1997–98) Tuition: $14,560. Mandatory fees: $65. College room only: $3330.

Applications Of all full-time undergraduates enrolled in fall 1996, 95% of those judged to have need according to Federal Methodology were aided. *Financial aid deadline (priority):* 3/2. *Financial aid forms:* FAFSA required; CSS Financial Aid PROFILE acceptable. State form, institutional form required for some. *Admission application deadline:* rolling.

Summary of Aid to Needy Students *From gift & self-help combined:* Average need met: 80%. Average amount awarded: $14,000 (36% gift aid, 64% self-help). *Gift aid:* Total: $880,734 (31% from college's own funds, 20% from other college-administered sources, 49% from external sources). 45 Federal Work-Study jobs (averaging $1000); 65 part-time jobs.

Need-Based Scholarships & Grants Pell, FSEOG, state, private, college/university.

Loans PLUS, Stafford, Unsubsidized Stafford, Federal Nursing, private, college/university short-term loans ($300 average), college/university long-term loans ($3200 average).

Non-Need Awards In 1996, a total of 146 non-need awards were made. *Academic Interests/Achievement Awards:* 146 ($254,897 total): general academic.

Other Money-Saving Options Accelerated degree, cooperative Army ROTC, cooperative Naval ROTC, cooperative Air Force ROTC, off-campus living. *Payment Plans:* installment, deferred payment.

Contact Ms. Mary E. Robinson, Financial Aid Director, Samuel Merritt College, 370 Hawthorne Avenue, Oakland, CA 94609-3108, 510-869-6131.

SAN DIEGO STATE UNIVERSITY
San Diego, California

About the Institution State-supported, coed. Degrees awarded: B, M, D. Offers 108 undergraduate majors. Total enrollment: 29,331. Undergraduates: 23,847 (93% state residents). Freshmen: 3,254.

Undergraduate Expenses (1996–97) State resident tuition: $0. Nonresident tuition: $7380. Mandatory fees: $1902. College room and board: $6192. College room only: $3736.

Applications 63% of all full-time undergraduates enrolled in fall 1996 applied for aid; of these, 88% were judged to have need according to Federal Methodology, of whom 95% were aided. *Financial aid deadline (priority):* 3/1. *Financial aid forms:* FAFSA, state form required; CSS Financial Aid PROFILE acceptable. *Admission application deadline:* rolling.

Summary of Aid to Needy Students *From gift & self-help combined:* Average need met: 87%. Average amount awarded: $7458 (36% gift aid, 64% self-help). *Gift aid:* Total: $27,730,741 (31% from college's

own funds, 8% from other college-administered sources, 61% from external sources). 554 Federal Work-Study jobs (averaging $2400); 259 part-time jobs.

Need-Based Scholarships & Grants Pell, FSEOG, state, private, college/university.

Loans Perkins, PLUS, Stafford, Unsubsidized Stafford, college/university short-term loans ($300 average), college/university long-term loans ($1875 average).

Non-Need Awards In 1996, a total of 1,353 non-need awards were made. *Academic Interests/Achievement Awards:* 1,101 ($867,406 total): general academic. *Special Achievements/Activities Awards:* 12 ($3200 total): community service, leadership. *Special Characteristics Awards:* 25 ($45,000 total): handicapped students, members of minorities. *Athletic:* Total: 215 ($1,731,822); Men: 123 ($990,810); Women: 92 ($741,012).

Other Money-Saving Options Accelerated degree, Army ROTC, Naval ROTC, Air Force ROTC, off-campus living. *Payment Plan:* installment. *Waivers:* full or partial for employees or children of employees and senior citizens.

Contact Office of Financial Aid, San Diego State University, 5500 Campanile Drive, SSW 3605, San Diego, CA 92182-7436, 619-594-5200.

SAN FRANCISCO ART INSTITUTE
San Francisco, California

About the Institution Independent, coed. Degrees awarded: B, M. Offers 7 undergraduate majors. Total enrollment: 681. Undergraduates: 533 (66% state residents). Freshmen: 50.

Undergraduate Expenses (1997–98) Tuition: $17,400.

Applications Of all full-time undergraduates enrolled in fall 1996, 91% of those who applied for aid were judged to have need according to Federal Methodology, of whom 100% were aided. *Financial aid deadline (priority):* 9/1. *Financial aid forms:* FAFSA required. *Admission application deadline:* rolling.

Summary of Aid to Needy Students *From gift & self-help combined:* Average need met: 92%. *Gift aid:* Total: $3,680,410 (80% from college's own funds, 3% from other college-administered sources, 17% from external sources). 297 Federal Work-Study jobs (averaging $1933).

Need-Based Scholarships & Grants Pell, FSEOG, state, college/university.

Loans PLUS, Stafford, Unsubsidized Stafford.

Non-Need Awards In 1996, a total of 150 non-need awards were made. *Creative Arts/Performance Awards:* 150 ($530,597 total): art/fine arts.

Other Money-Saving Options *Payment Plan:* installment. *Waivers:* full or partial for employees or children of employees.

Contact Mr. Dennis Tominaga, Director of Financial Aid, San Francisco Art Institute, 800 Chestnut Street, San Francisco, CA 94133-2299, 415-749-4520, fax: 415-749-4592.

SAN FRANCISCO CONSERVATORY OF MUSIC
San Francisco, California

About the Institution Independent, coed. Degrees awarded: B, M. Offers 6 undergraduate majors. Total enrollment: 270. Undergraduates: 156 (50% state residents). Freshmen: 29.

Undergraduate Expenses (1997–98) Tuition: $16,300. Mandatory fees: $250.

Applications 70% of all full-time undergraduates enrolled in fall 1996 applied for aid; of these, 92% were judged to have need according to

Federal Methodology, of whom 97% were aided. *Financial aid deadline (priority):* 3/1. *Financial aid forms:* FAFSA, institutional form required. *Admission application deadline:* 3/1.

Summary of Aid to Needy Students *From gift & self-help combined:* Average need met: 75%. Average amount awarded: $10,244 (66% gift aid, 34% self-help). *Gift aid:* Total: $653,700 (78% from college's own funds, 12% from other college-administered sources, 10% from external sources). 7 Federal Work-Study jobs (averaging $1800); 30 part-time jobs.

Need-Based Scholarships & Grants Pell, FSEOG, state, college/university.

Loans Perkins, PLUS, Stafford, Unsubsidized Stafford, college/university long-term loans ($1000 average).

Non-Need Awards In 1996, a total of 1 non-need award was made. *Creative Arts/Performance Awards:* 1 ($2000 total): performing arts.

Other Money-Saving Options Accelerated degree. *Payment Plan:* installment. *Waivers:* full or partial for employees or children of employees.

Contact Ms. Colleen Katzowitz, Director of Student Services, San Francisco Conservatory of Music, 1201 Ortega Street, San Francisco, CA 94122-4411, 415-759-3422, fax: 415-759-3499.

SAN FRANCISCO STATE UNIVERSITY
San Francisco, California

About the Institution State-supported, coed. Degrees awarded: B, M. Offers 92 undergraduate majors. Total enrollment: 27,420. Undergraduates: 21,049 (95% state residents). Freshmen: 1,960.

Undergraduate Expenses (1996–97) State resident tuition: $0. Nonresident tuition: $7380. Mandatory fees: $1982. College room and board: $5600.

Applications 63% of all full-time undergraduates enrolled in fall 1996 applied for aid; of these, 93% were judged to have need according to Federal Methodology, of whom 99% were aided. *Financial aid deadline (priority):* 3/1. *Financial aid forms:* FAFSA required. *Admission application deadline:* 11/30.

Summary of Aid to Needy Students *From gift & self-help combined:* Average need met: 80%. Average amount awarded: $7429 (46% gift aid, 54% self-help). *Gift aid:* Total: $28,311,207 (1% from college's own funds, 81% from other college-administered sources, 18% from external sources). 3,942 Federal Work-Study jobs (averaging $818); part-time jobs.

Need-Based Scholarships & Grants Pell, FSEOG, state, college/university.

Loans Perkins, PLUS, Stafford, Unsubsidized Stafford, college/university short-term loans ($400 average), college/university long-term loans ($1416 average).

Non-Need Awards *Academic Interests/Achievement Awards:* general academic.

Other Money-Saving Options Accelerated degree, co-op program, cooperative Army ROTC, cooperative Naval ROTC, cooperative Air Force ROTC, off-campus living. *Waivers:* full or partial for employees or children of employees.

Contact Mr. Marlew Haskins, Assistant Director, San Francisco State University, 1600 Holloway Avenue, San Francisco, CA 94132-1722, 415-338-2592.

SAN JOSE CHRISTIAN COLLEGE
San Jose, California

About the Institution Independent/religious, coed. Degrees awarded: A, B. Offers 7 undergraduate majors. Total enrollment: 338 (83% state residents). Freshmen: 23.

Undergraduate Expenses (1997–98) Comprehensive fee of $10,578 includes tuition ($6672), mandatory fees ($342), and college room and board ($3564).

Applications 73% of all full-time undergraduates enrolled in fall 1996 applied for aid; of these,100% were judged to have need according to Federal Methodology, of whom 100% were aided. *Financial aid deadline (priority):* 3/2. *Financial aid forms:* FAFSA, institutional form required. State form required for some. *Admission application deadline:* 8/1.

Summary of Aid to Needy Students *Gift aid:* Total: $580,000. 6 Federal Work-Study jobs (averaging $1500); 20 part-time jobs.

Need-Based Scholarships & Grants Pell, FSEOG, private, college/university.

Loans PLUS, Stafford, Unsubsidized Stafford.

Non-Need Awards Not offered.

Other Money-Saving Options Off-campus living (after freshman year). *Payment Plan:* deferred payment. *Waivers:* full or partial for employees or children of employees.

Contact Ms. Elissa Salter, Financial Aid Administrator, San Jose Christian College, 790 South Twelfth Street, San Jose, CA 95112-2381, 408-293-9058.

SAN JOSE STATE UNIVERSITY
San Jose, California

About the Institution State-supported, coed. Degrees awarded: B, M. Offers 135 undergraduate majors. Total enrollment: 25,874. Undergraduates: 20,993 (96% state residents). Freshmen: 1,696.

Undergraduate Expenses (1996–97) State resident tuition: $0. Nonresident tuition: $7626. Mandatory fees: $2004. College room and board: $4875 (minimum).

Applications Of all full-time undergraduates enrolled in fall 1996, 84% of those who applied for aid were judged to have need according to Federal Methodology, of whom 98% were aided. *Financial aid deadline (priority):* 3/2. *Financial aid forms:* FAFSA, state form required; CSS Financial Aid PROFILE, institutional form acceptable. *Admission application deadline:* rolling.

Summary of Aid to Needy Students *From gift & self-help combined:* Average need met: 68%. Average amount awarded: $3193 (53% gift aid, 47% self-help). *Gift aid:* Total: $17,702,291. 706 Federal Work-Study jobs (averaging $1941).

Need-Based Scholarships & Grants Pell, FSEOG, state, private, college/university.

Loans Perkins, PLUS, Stafford, Unsubsidized Stafford, private, college/university short-term loans ($250 average), college/university long-term loans ($1000 average).

Non-Need Awards In 1996, a total of 284 non-need awards were made. *Special Characteristics Awards:* 5 ($8496 total): ROTC participants. *Athletic:* Total: 279 ($1,519,029); Men: 158 ($926,109); Women: 121 ($592,920).

Other Money-Saving Options Accelerated degree, co-op program, Army ROTC, Air Force ROTC, cooperative Naval ROTC, off-campus living. *Waivers:* full or partial for employees or children of employees and senior citizens.

Contact Mr. Donald R. Ryan, Director of Financial Aid, San Jose State University, One Washington Square, San Jose, CA 95192-0036, 408-924-6060.

SANTA CLARA UNIVERSITY
Santa Clara, California

About the Institution Independent/religious, coed. Degrees awarded: B, M, D, P. Offers 48 undergraduate majors. Total enrollment: 7,863. Undergraduates: 4,230 (67% state residents). Freshmen: 1,075.

Undergraduate Expenses (1997–98) Comprehensive fee of $23,661 includes tuition ($16,455), mandatory fees ($180), and college room and board ($7026). College room only: $4446.

Applications 71% of all full-time undergraduates enrolled in fall 1996 applied for aid; of these, 90% were judged to have need according to Federal Methodology, of whom 100% were aided. *Financial aid deadline (priority):* 2/1. *Financial aid forms:* FAFSA, CSS Financial Aid PROFILE required. *Admission application deadline:* 1/15.

Summary of Aid to Needy Students *From gift & self-help combined:* Average need met: 85%. Average amount awarded: $14,105 (61% gift aid, 39% self-help). *Gift aid:* Total: $25,130,151 (71% from college's own funds, 17% from other college-administered sources, 12% from external sources). 250 Federal Work-Study jobs (averaging $1500); 1,200 part-time jobs.

Need-Based Scholarships & Grants Pell, FSEOG, state, private, college/university.

Loans Perkins, PLUS, Stafford, Unsubsidized Stafford, college/university long-term loans ($3000 average).

Non-Need Awards In 1996, a total of 1,381 non-need awards were made. *Academic Interests/Achievement Awards:* 1,158 ($395,432 total): general academic, military science. *Creative Arts/Performance Awards:* 50 ($109,609 total): debating, music, theater/drama. *Special Characteristics Awards:* 95 ($258,827 total): children and siblings of alumni, siblings of current students. *Athletic:* Total: 78 ($1,823,512); Men: 0 ($888,684); Women: 0 ($934,828).

Other Money-Saving Options Co-op program, Army ROTC, cooperative Naval ROTC, cooperative Air Force ROTC, off-campus living. *Payment Plans:* tuition prepayment, installment, deferred payment. *Waivers:* full or partial for employees or children of employees.

Contact Ms. Sandra L. Hayes, Director of Financial Aid, Santa Clara University, 500 El Camino Real, Santa Clara, CA 95053-0001, 408-554-4505, fax: 408-554-2154.

SARAH LAWRENCE COLLEGE
Bronxville, New York

About the Institution Independent, coed. Degrees awarded: B, M. Offers 77 undergraduate majors. Total enrollment: 1,329. Undergraduates: 1,072 (22% state residents). Freshmen: 296.

Undergraduate Expenses (1996–97) Comprehensive fee of $28,878 includes tuition ($21,450), mandatory fees ($526), and college room and board ($6902). College room only: $4870.

Applications 69% of all full-time undergraduates enrolled in fall 1996 applied for aid; of these, 96% were judged to have need according to Federal Methodology, of whom 91% were aided. *Financial aid deadline:* 2/1. *Financial aid forms:* FAFSA, CSS Financial Aid PROFILE required. Divorced/Separated Parents' Statement required for some. *Regular admission application deadline:* 2/1. Early decision deadline: 1/1.

Summary of Aid to Needy Students *From gift & self-help combined:* Average need met: 100%. Average amount awarded: $17,928 (73% gift aid, 27% self-help). *Gift aid:* Total: $7,917,523 (91% from college's own funds, 1% from other college-administered sources, 8% from external sources). 487 Federal Work-Study jobs (averaging $1500); 5 part-time jobs.

Need-Based Scholarships & Grants Pell, FSEOG, state, private, college/university.

Loans Perkins, PLUS, Stafford, Unsubsidized Stafford, private, college/university short-term loans ($100 average).

Non-Need Awards Not offered.

Other Money-Saving Options Off-campus living (after freshman year). *Payment Plans:* installment, deferred payment. *Waivers:* full or partial for employees or children of employees.

Contact Office of Financial Aid, Sarah Lawrence College, 1 Meadway, Bronxville, NY 10708, 914-337-0700.

SAVANNAH COLLEGE OF ART AND DESIGN
Savannah, Georgia

About the Institution Independent, coed. Degrees awarded: B, M. Offers 16 undergraduate majors. Total enrollment: 3,093. Undergraduates: 2,672 (20% state residents). Freshmen: 585.

Undergraduate Expenses (1997–98) Comprehensive fee of $18,300 includes tuition ($12,600) and college room and board ($5700). College room only: $3300.

Applications 61% of all full-time undergraduates enrolled in fall 1996 applied for aid; of these, 85% were judged to have need according to Federal Methodology, of whom 99% were aided. *Financial aid deadline (priority):* 4/1. *Financial aid forms:* FAFSA, institutional form required; CSS Financial Aid PROFILE, state form acceptable. *Admission application deadline:* rolling.

Summary of Aid to Needy Students *From gift & self-help combined:* Average need met: 35%. Average amount awarded: $6500 (46% gift aid, 54% self-help). *Gift aid:* Total: $3,700,000 (56% from college's own funds, 18% from other college-administered sources, 26% from external sources). 120 Federal Work-Study jobs (averaging $400); 150 part-time jobs.

Need-Based Scholarships & Grants Pell, FSEOG, state.

Loans Perkins, PLUS, Stafford, Unsubsidized Stafford.

Non-Need Awards In 1996, a total of 1,115 non-need awards were made. *Academic Interests/Achievement Awards:* 526 ($633,000 total): general academic, architecture. *Creative Arts/Performance Awards:* 553 ($903,000 total): general creative, art/fine arts. *Special Achievements/Activities Awards:* 36 ($39,000 total): general special achievements/activities.

Other Money-Saving Options Off-campus living. *Payment Plan:* installment. *Waivers:* full or partial for employees or children of employees.

Contact Ms. Cindy Bradley, Director of Financial Aid, Savannah College of Art and Design, PO Box 3146, Savannah, GA 31402-3146, 912-238-2400, fax: 912-238-2436.

SAVANNAH STATE UNIVERSITY
Savannah, Georgia

About the Institution State-supported, coed. Degrees awarded: B. Offers 32 undergraduate majors. Total enrollment: 3,211 (80% state residents). Freshmen: 660.

Undergraduate Expenses (1996–97) State resident tuition: $2130. Nonresident tuition: $6009. Mandatory fees: $426. College room and board: $2970.

Applications Of all full-time undergraduates enrolled in fall 1996, 91% of those who applied for aid were judged to have need according to Federal Methodology, of whom 100% were aided. *Financial aid deadline (priority):* 9/1. *Financial aid forms:* CSS Financial Aid PROFILE, institutional form required. FAFSA required for some. *Admission application deadline:* 9/1.

Summary of Aid to Needy Students *From gift & self-help combined:* Average need met: 82%. 450 Federal Work-Study jobs (averaging $1200).

Need-Based Scholarships & Grants Pell, FSEOG, state, private, college/university.

Loans Perkins, PLUS, Stafford, Unsubsidized Stafford, college/university short-term loans ($90 average).

Non-Need Awards *Academic Interests/Achievement Awards:* general academic, biological sciences, physical sciences, social sciences. *Athletic:* Total: 128 ($504,331); Men: 94 ($362,632); Women: 34 ($141,699).

Other Money-Saving Options Accelerated degree, co-op program, Army ROTC, Naval ROTC, off-campus living (after junior year).

Contact Office of Financial Aid, Savannah State University, Savannah, GA 31404, 912-356-2186.

SCHOOL OF THE ART INSTITUTE OF CHICAGO
Chicago, Illinois

About the Institution Independent, coed. Degrees awarded: B, M. Offers 14 undergraduate majors. Total enrollment: 2,012. Undergraduates: 1,485 (32% state residents).

Undergraduate Expenses (1996–97) Tuition: $16,320. College room only: $4980.

Applications 74% of all full-time undergraduates enrolled in fall 1996 applied for aid; of these, 95% were judged to have need according to Federal Methodology, of whom 100% were aided. *Financial aid deadline (priority):* 4/1. *Financial aid forms:* FAFSA, institutional form required; state form acceptable. *Admission application deadline:* rolling.

Summary of Aid to Needy Students *From gift & self-help combined:* Average amount awarded: $14,223 (51% gift aid, 49% self-help). *Gift aid:* Total: $6,509,341 (70% from college's own funds, 2% from other college-administered sources, 28% from external sources). 319 Federal Work-Study jobs (averaging $1567); 90 part-time jobs.

Need-Based Scholarships & Grants Pell, FSEOG, state, private, college/university.

Loans Perkins, PLUS, Stafford, Unsubsidized Stafford, college/university short-term loans ($300 average).

Non-Need Awards In 1996, a total of 318 non-need awards were made. *Creative Arts/Performance Awards:* 318 ($722,827 total): art/fine arts.

Other Money-Saving Options Co-op program, off-campus living. *Payment Plan:* installment. *Waivers:* full or partial for employees or children of employees and senior citizens.

Contact Ms. Kathleen M. Amato, Director of Financial Aid, School of the Art Institute of Chicago, 37 South Wabash, Chicago, IL 60603-3103, 312-899-5106, fax: 312-263-0141.

SCHOOL OF THE MUSEUM OF FINE ARTS
Boston, Massachusetts

About the Institution Independent, coed. Degrees awarded: B, M. Offers 16 undergraduate majors. Total enrollment: 723. Undergraduates: 620 (70% state residents). Freshmen: 173.

Undergraduate Expenses (1996–97) Tuition: $14,765. Mandatory fees: $360.

Applications 51% of all full-time undergraduates enrolled in fall 1996 applied for aid; of these, 85% were judged to have need according to Federal Methodology, of whom 100% were aided. *Financial aid deadline (priority):* 3/15. *Financial aid forms:* FAFSA, CSS Financial Aid PROFILE, institutional form required. State form required for some. *Admission application deadline:* rolling.

Summary of Aid to Needy Students *From gift & self-help combined:* Average need met: 65%. Average amount awarded: $11,186 (57% gift aid, 43% self-help). *Gift aid:* Total: $1,556,171 (77% from college's own funds, 14% from other college-administered sources, 9% from external sources). 60 Federal Work-Study jobs (averaging $1500); 40 part-time jobs.

Need-Based Scholarships & Grants Pell, FSEOG, state, private, college/university.

Loans PLUS, Stafford, Unsubsidized Stafford, state.

Non-Need Awards Not offered.

Other Money-Saving Options *Payment Plan:* installment. *Waivers:* full or partial for employees or children of employees.

Contact Ms. Elizabeth Goreham, Director of Financial Aid, School of the Museum of Fine Arts, 230 The Fenway, Boston, MA 02115, 617-369-3684, fax: 617-424-6271.

SCHOOL OF VISUAL ARTS
New York, New York

About the Institution Proprietary, coed. Degrees awarded: B, M. Offers 16 undergraduate majors. Total enrollment: 3,047. Undergraduates: 2,761 (49% state residents). Freshmen: 393.

Undergraduate Expenses (1997–98) Tuition: $13,650. Mandatory fees: $240. College room only: $5800 (minimum).

Applications Of all full-time undergraduates enrolled in fall 1996, 91% of those who applied for aid were judged to have need according to Federal Methodology, of whom 93% were aided. *Financial aid deadline (priority):* 3/1. *Financial aid forms:* FAFSA required. State form required for some. *Regular admission application deadline:* rolling. Early decision deadline: 12/18.

Summary of Aid to Needy Students *From gift & self-help combined:* Average need met: 76%. Average amount awarded: $7900 (69% gift aid, 31% self-help). *Gift aid:* Total: $6,605,000 (44% from college's own funds, 32% from other college-administered sources, 24% from external sources). 70 Federal Work-Study jobs (averaging $1500); 160 part-time jobs.

Need-Based Scholarships & Grants Pell, FSEOG, state, private, college/university.

Loans Perkins, PLUS, Stafford, Unsubsidized Stafford, state, private.

Non-Need Awards In 1996, a total of 267 non-need awards were made. *Creative Arts/Performance Awards:* 267 ($937,000 total): applied art and design, art/fine arts.

Other Money-Saving Options Off-campus living. *Payment Plan:* installment. *Waivers:* full or partial for employees or children of employees.

Contact Mr. Howard Leslie, Director of Student Financial Services, School of Visual Arts, 209 East 23rd Street, New York, NY 10010-3994, 212-592-2031, fax: 212-592-2029.

SCRIPPS COLLEGE
Claremont, California

About the Institution Independent, women. Degrees awarded: B. Offers 54 undergraduate majors. Total enrollment: 704 (54% state residents). Freshmen: 191.

Undergraduate Expenses (1997–98) Comprehensive fee of $27,230 includes tuition ($19,356), mandatory fees ($124), and college room and board ($7750). College room only: $3900.

Applications 66% of all full-time undergraduates enrolled in fall 1996 applied for aid; of these, 95% were judged to have need according to Federal Methodology, of whom 100% were aided. *Financial aid deadline (priority):* 2/1. *Financial aid forms:* FAFSA, CSS Financial Aid PROFILE required. *Regular admission application deadline:* 2/1. Early decision deadline: 11/15.

Summary of Aid to Needy Students *From gift & self-help combined:* Average need met: 96%. Average amount awarded: $19,502 (72% gift aid, 28% self-help). *Gift aid:* Total: $6,105,846 (84% from college's own funds, 12% from other college-administered sources, 4% from external sources). 303 Federal Work-Study jobs (averaging $1600); 120 part-time jobs.

Need-Based Scholarships & Grants Pell, FSEOG, state, private, college/university.

Loans Perkins, PLUS, Stafford, Unsubsidized Stafford, private, college/university short-term loans ($500 average), college/university long-term loans ($4000 average).

Non-Need Awards *Academic Interests/Achievement Awards:* available. *Creative Arts/Performance Awards:* music.

Other Money-Saving Options Cooperative Army ROTC, cooperative Air Force ROTC, off-campus living (after freshman year). *Payment Plan:* installment. *Waivers:* full or partial for employees or children of employees.

Contact Ms. Pati Pineiro-Goodenberger, Associate Director of Financial Aid, Scripps College, 1030 Columbia Avenue, Claremont, CA 91711-3948, 909-621-8275, fax: 909-621-8232.

SEATTLE PACIFIC UNIVERSITY
Seattle, Washington

About the Institution Independent/religious, coed. Degrees awarded: B, M, D. Offers 48 undergraduate majors. Total enrollment: 3,293. Undergraduates: 2,506 (64% state residents). Freshmen: 478.

Undergraduate Expenses (1997–98) Comprehensive fee of $19,548 includes tuition ($14,130) and college room and board ($5418).

Applications Of all full-time undergraduates enrolled in fall 1996, 91% of those who applied for aid were judged to have need according to Federal Methodology, of whom 99% were aided. *Financial aid deadline (priority):* 1/1. *Financial aid forms:* FAFSA required. *Regular admission application deadline:* 9/1. Early action deadline: 12/1.

Summary of Aid to Needy Students *From gift & self-help combined:* Average need met: 89%. Average amount awarded: $13,852 (49% gift aid, 51% self-help). *Gift aid:* Total: $10,320,645 (77% from college's own funds, 15% from other college-administered sources, 8% from external sources). 288 Federal Work-Study jobs (averaging $2291).

Need-Based Scholarships & Grants Pell, FSEOG, state, private, college/university.

Loans Perkins, PLUS, Stafford, Unsubsidized Stafford, Federal Nursing, private, college/university short-term loans ($200 average), college/university long-term loans ($2325 average).

Non-Need Awards In 1996, a total of 1,315 non-need awards were made. *Academic Interests/Achievement Awards:* 541 ($1,667,407 total): general academic. *Creative Arts/Performance Awards:* 133 ($218,811 total): art/fine arts, performing arts. *Special Achievements/Activities Awards:* 2 ($7000 total): leadership. *Special Characteristics Awards:* 558 ($443,037 total): general special characteristics, children and siblings of alumni, relatives of clergy, religious affiliation, ROTC participants. *Athletic:* Total: 81 ($684,542); Men: 33 ($341,702); Women: 48 ($342,840).

Other Money-Saving Options Co-op program, cooperative Army ROTC, cooperative Naval ROTC, cooperative Air Force ROTC. *Payment Plan:* installment. *Waivers:* full or partial for employees or children of employees and senior citizens.

Contact Ms. Vickie Rekow, Director of Student Financial Services, Seattle Pacific University, 3307 Third Avenue West, Seattle, WA 98119-1997, 206-281-2469, fax: 206-281-2835.

SEATTLE UNIVERSITY
Seattle, Washington

About the Institution Independent/religious, coed. Degrees awarded: B, M, D, P. Offers 59 undergraduate majors. Total enrollment: 5,990. Undergraduates: 3,272 (57% state residents). Freshmen: 580.

Undergraduate Expenses (1997–98) Comprehensive fee of $20,298 includes tuition ($14,805) and college room and board ($5493 minimum). College room only: $3570 (minimum).

Applications *Financial aid deadline (priority):* 2/1. *Financial aid forms:* FAFSA required. *Admission application deadline:* 3/1.

Summary of Aid to Needy Students *From gift & self-help combined:* Average amount awarded: $15,490 (20% gift aid, 80% self-help). *Gift* *aid:* Total: $9,585,521 (55% from college's own funds, 33% from other college-administered sources, 12% from external sources). 904 Federal Work-Study jobs (averaging $3385).

Need-Based Scholarships & Grants Pell, FSEOG, state, college/university.

Loans Perkins, PLUS, Stafford, Unsubsidized Stafford, Federal Nursing, private.

Non-Need Awards In 1996, a total of 914 non-need awards were made. *Academic Interests/Achievement Awards:* 585 ($3,702,053 total): general academic, biological sciences, business, communication, computer science, education, engineering/technologies, English, foreign languages, health fields, humanities, international studies, mathematics, military science, religion/biblical studies, social sciences. *Creative Arts/Performance Awards:* 7 ($12,000 total): music. *Special Achievements/Activities Awards:* 21 ($419,388 total): leadership. *Special Characteristics Awards:* 301 ($1,083,570 total): children and siblings of alumni, children of educators, children of faculty/staff, members of minorities, ROTC participants.

Other Money-Saving Options Accelerated degree, Army ROTC, cooperative Naval ROTC, cooperative Air Force ROTC, off-campus living (after freshman year). *Payment Plan:* installment. *Waivers:* full or partial for employees or children of employees.

Contact Mr. James White, Director of Financial Aid, Seattle University, Broadway & Madison, Seattle, WA 98122-4460, 206-296-5656, fax: 206-296-5656.

SETON HALL UNIVERSITY
South Orange, New Jersey

About the Institution Independent/religious, coed. Degrees awarded: B, M, D, P. Offers 50 undergraduate majors. Total enrollment: 8,518. Undergraduates: 4,717 (85% state residents). Freshmen: 973.

Undergraduate Expenses (1997–98) Comprehensive fee of $21,258 includes tuition ($13,920), mandatory fees ($550), and college room and board ($6788).

Applications 76% of all full-time undergraduates enrolled in fall 1996 applied for aid; of these, 91% were judged to have need according to Federal Methodology, of whom 99% were aided. *Financial aid deadline:* continuous. *Financial aid forms:* FAFSA required. *Admission application deadline:* 3/1.

Summary of Aid to Needy Students *From gift & self-help combined:* Average need met: 82%. Average amount awarded: $13,886 (52% gift aid, 48% self-help). *Gift aid:* Total: $20,616,392 (42% from college's own funds, 6% from other college-administered sources, 52% from external sources). 650 Federal Work-Study jobs (averaging $1000); 1,318 part-time jobs.

Need-Based Scholarships & Grants Pell, FSEOG, state, private, college/university.

Loans Perkins, PLUS, Stafford, Unsubsidized Stafford, Federal Nursing, state, private, college/university long-term loans ($1500 average).

Non-Need Awards In 1996, a total of 987 non-need awards were made. *Academic Interests/Achievement Awards:* 473 ($2,605,025 total): general academic, biological sciences, education, health fields, military science, physical sciences, premedicine. *Creative Arts/Performance Awards:* 45 ($76,263 total): art/fine arts, cinema/film/broadcasting, debating, journalism/publications, music. *Special Achievements/Activities Awards:* 10 ($8950 total): leadership. *Special Characteristics Awards:* 273 ($1,238,074 total): children of faculty/staff, relatives of clergy, siblings of current students. *Athletic:* Total: 186 ($2,386,177); Men: 104 ($1,230,790); Women: 82 ($1,155,387).

Other Money-Saving Options Accelerated degree, co-op program, Army ROTC, cooperative Air Force ROTC, off-campus living. *Payment Plans:* installment, deferred payment. *Waivers:* full or partial for employees or children of employees and senior citizens.

Contact Mr. Michael Menendez, Director of Financial Aid, Seton Hall University, 400 South Orange Avenue, South Orange, NJ 07079-2697, 973-761-9350, fax: 973-761-7654.

SETON HILL COLLEGE
Greensburg, Pennsylvania

About the Institution Independent/religious, primarily women. Degrees awarded: B, M. Offers 85 undergraduate majors. Total enrollment: 929. Undergraduates: 893 (85% state residents). Freshmen: 114.

Undergraduate Expenses (1997–98) Comprehensive fee of $17,370 includes tuition ($12,640) and college room and board ($4730).

Applications Of all full-time undergraduates enrolled in fall 1996, 100% of those judged to have need according to Federal Methodology were aided. *Financial aid deadline (priority):* 7/1. *Financial aid forms:* institutional form required; CSS Financial Aid PROFILE acceptable. FAFSA, state form required for some. *Admission application deadline:* 8/1.

Summary of Aid to Needy Students *From gift & self-help combined:* Average need met: 88%. Average amount awarded: $8854 (63% gift aid, 37% self-help). *Gift aid:* Total: $3,796,701 (52% from college's own funds, 8% from other college-administered sources, 40% from external sources). 350 Federal Work-Study jobs (averaging $1100); 72 part-time jobs.

Need-Based Scholarships & Grants Pell, FSEOG, state, private, college/university.

Loans Perkins, PLUS, Stafford, Unsubsidized Stafford, college/university long-term loans ($1500 average).

Non-Need Awards In 1996, a total of 288 non-need awards were made. *Academic Interests/Achievement Awards:* 176 ($736,588 total): general academic, biological sciences, English, home economics, mathematics, physical sciences, religion/biblical studies. *Creative Arts/Performance Awards:* 28 ($22,060 total): art/fine arts, music, theater/drama. *Special Characteristics Awards:* 31 ($77,332 total): children and siblings of alumni, children of faculty/staff, international students, parents of current students, siblings of current students. *Athletic:* Total: 53 ($170,625); Men: 0; Women: 53 ($170,625).

Other Money-Saving Options Accelerated degree, co-op program, cooperative Army ROTC, off-campus living. *Payment Plan:* installment. *Waivers:* full or partial for employees or children of employees.

Contact Sr. Mary Philip Aaron, Director of Financial Aid, Seton Hill College, Seton Hill Drive, Greensburg, PA 15601, 412-838-4293, fax: 412-830-4611.

SHASTA BIBLE COLLEGE
Redding, California

About the Institution Independent/religious. Degrees awarded: A, B. Offers 3 undergraduate majors. Total enrollment: 175. Freshmen: 25.

Undergraduate Expenses (1996–97) Tuition: $3300. Mandatory fees: $130. College room only: $1107 (minimum).

Applications *Financial aid deadline:* continuous. *Financial aid forms:* FAFSA required.

Summary of Aid to Needy Students Part-time jobs.

Need-Based Scholarships & Grants Pell, FSEOG, state, private.

Loans PLUS, Stafford, Unsubsidized Stafford.

Non-Need Awards Not offered.

Contact Dr. Sam Rodriguez, Dean of Professional Education, Shasta Bible College, 2980 Hartnell Avenue, Redding, CA 96002, 916-221-4275.

SHAWNEE STATE UNIVERSITY
Portsmouth, Ohio

About the Institution State-supported, coed. Degrees awarded: A, B. Offers 55 undergraduate majors. Total enrollment: 3,505 (90% state residents). Freshmen: 1,083.

Undergraduate Expenses (1996–97) State resident tuition: $2445. Nonresident tuition: $4620. Mandatory fees: $531. College room and board: $3945. College room only: $2625.

Applications 96% of all full-time undergraduates enrolled in fall 1996 applied for aid. *Financial aid deadline (priority):* 3/1. *Financial aid forms:* FAFSA required. *Admission application deadline:* rolling.

Summary of Aid to Needy Students *Gift aid:* Total: $4,376,865 (10% from college-administered sources, 90% from external sources). Federal Work-Study jobs; part-time jobs.

Need-Based Scholarships & Grants Pell, FSEOG, state, private, college/university.

Loans PLUS, Stafford, Unsubsidized Stafford, college/university short-term loans ($50 average).

Non-Need Awards In 1996, a total of 185 non-need awards were made. *Academic Interests/Achievement Awards:* 173 ($513,656 total): general academic. *Creative Arts/Performance Awards:* 1 ($2300 total): performing arts. *Special Achievements/Activities Awards:* 1 ($1323 total): memberships. *Special Characteristics Awards:* 10 ($24,370 total): local/state students, members of minorities.

Other Money-Saving Options Off-campus living (after sophomore year). *Waivers:* full or partial for employees or children of employees and senior citizens.

Contact Ms. Audrey Clay, Director of Financial Aid, Shawnee State University, Portsmouth, OH 45662-4344, 614-355-2237.

SHAW UNIVERSITY
Raleigh, North Carolina

About the Institution Independent/religious, coed. Degrees awarded: Λ, B. Offers 31 undergraduate majors. Total enrollment: 2,262 (62% state residents). Freshmen: 386.

Undergraduate Expenses (1997–98) Comprehensive fee of $10,356 includes tuition ($6304) and college room and board ($4052). College room only: $1642.

Applications *Financial aid deadline (priority):* 6/1. *Financial aid forms:* FAFSA, institutional form required; CSS Financial Aid PROFILE acceptable. State form required for some. *Admission application deadline:* 8/10.

Summary of Aid to Needy Students *From gift & self-help combined:* Average need met: 85%. Average amount awarded: $10,500 (65% gift aid, 35% self-help). *Gift aid:* Total: $3,522,767 (9% from college's own funds, 48% from other college-administered sources, 43% from external sources). 260 Federal Work-Study jobs (averaging $800); 15 part-time jobs.

Need-Based Scholarships & Grants Pell, FSEOG, state, private, college/university.

Loans Perkins, PLUS, Stafford, Unsubsidized Stafford.

Non-Need Awards In 1996, a total of 284 non-need awards were made. *Academic Interests/Achievement Awards:* 143 ($613,190 total): general academic, education, engineering/technologies, mathematics. *Creative Arts/Performance Awards:* 52 ($157,845 total): music. *Special Characteristics Awards:* 14 ($63,556 total): children of faculty/staff, ROTC participants. *Athletic:* Total: 75 ($413,628); Men: 43 ($193,818); Women: 32 ($219,810).

Other Money-Saving Options Army ROTC, cooperative Air Force ROTC, off-campus living (after freshman year). *Payment Plan:* installment. *Waivers:* full or partial for employees or children of employees.

Contact Ms. Bebe Tyson, Interim Director of Financial Aid, Shaw University, 118 East South Street, Raleigh, NC 27601-2399, 919-546-8264, fax: 919-546-8356.

SHELDON JACKSON COLLEGE
Sitka, Alaska

About the Institution Independent/religious, coed. Degrees awarded: A, B. Offers 25 undergraduate majors. Total enrollment: 223 (40% state residents). Freshmen: 35.

Undergraduate Expenses (1997–98 estimated) Comprehensive fee of $14,100 includes tuition ($9000), mandatory fees ($300), and college room and board ($4800). College room only: $2100.

Applications Of all full-time undergraduates enrolled in fall 1996, 95% of those who applied for aid were judged to have need according to Federal Methodology, of whom 100% were aided. *Financial aid deadline (priority):* 6/1. *Financial aid forms:* FAFSA, institutional form required; CSS Financial Aid PROFILE acceptable. State form required for some. *Admission application deadline:* rolling.

Summary of Aid to Needy Students *From gift & self-help combined:* Average need met: 79%. Average amount awarded: $12,854 (38% gift aid, 62% self-help). *Gift aid:* Total: $739,850 (68% from college's own funds, 6% from other college-administered sources, 26% from external sources). 115 Federal Work-Study jobs (averaging $1500); 15 part-time jobs.

Need-Based Scholarships & Grants Pell, FSEOG, state, college/university.

Loans Perkins, PLUS, Stafford, Unsubsidized Stafford, state.

Non-Need Awards In 1996, a total of 95 non-need awards were made. *Academic Interests/Achievement Awards:* 89 ($69,900 total): general academic. *Creative Arts/Performance Awards:* 6 ($8000 total): music, theater/drama.

Other Money-Saving Options Off-campus living (after sophomore year). *Payment Plan:* installment.

Contact Office of Financial Aid, Sheldon Jackson College, 801 Lincoln Street, Sitka, AK 99835-7699, 907-747-5222.

SHENANDOAH UNIVERSITY
Winchester, Virginia

About the Institution Independent/religious, coed. Degrees awarded: A, B, M, D, P. Offers 46 undergraduate majors. Total enrollment: 1,871. Undergraduates: 1,261 (58% state residents). Freshmen: 306.

Undergraduate Expenses (1997–98) Comprehensive fee of $19,450 includes tuition ($14,400) and college room and board ($5050).

Applications *Financial aid deadline (priority):* 2/15. *Financial aid forms:* FAFSA, institutional form required. State form required for some. *Admission application deadline:* rolling.

Summary of Aid to Needy Students 180 Federal Work-Study jobs (averaging $1300); 41 part-time jobs.

Need-Based Scholarships & Grants Pell, FSEOG, college/university.

Loans Perkins, PLUS, Stafford, Unsubsidized Stafford, Federal Nursing, college/university long-term loans ($2000 average).

Non-Need Awards *Academic Interests/Achievement Awards:* general academic, business. *Creative Arts/Performance Awards:* dance, music, performing arts, theater/drama. *Special Characteristics Awards:* children of educators, handicapped students, local/state students, relatives of clergy, religious affiliation.

Other Money-Saving Options Accelerated degree. *Payment Plan:* deferred payment. *Waivers:* full or partial for employees or children of employees.

Contact Office of Financial Aid, Shenandoah University, 1460 University Drive, Winchester, VA 22601-5195, 540-665-4538.

SHEPHERD COLLEGE
Shepherdstown, West Virginia

About the Institution State-supported, coed. Degrees awarded: A, B. Offers 102 undergraduate majors. Total enrollment: 3,845 (70% state residents). Freshmen: 662.

Undergraduate Expenses (1997–98) State resident tuition: $2228. Nonresident tuition: $5348. College room and board: $4139.

Applications 66% of all full-time undergraduates enrolled in fall 1996 applied for aid; of these, 57% were judged to have need according to Federal Methodology, of whom 94% were aided. *Financial aid deadline:* Applications processed continuously. *Financial aid forms:* FAFSA, institutional form required. *Regular admission application deadline:* 2/1. Early action deadline: 11/15.

Summary of Aid to Needy Students *From gift & self-help combined:* Average need met: 80%. Average amount awarded: $5616 (31% gift aid, 69% self-help). *Gift aid:* Total: $1,531,283 (22% from college's own funds, 22% from other college-administered sources, 56% from external sources). 156 Federal Work-Study jobs (averaging $1203); 125 part-time jobs.

Need-Based Scholarships & Grants Pell, FSEOG, private, college/university.

Loans Perkins, PLUS, Stafford, Unsubsidized Stafford, Federal Nursing, college/university short-term loans ($250 average).

Non-Need Awards In 1996, a total of 422 non-need awards were made. *Academic Interests/Achievement Awards:* 293 ($521,461 total): general academic, biological sciences, business, communication, computer science, education, engineering/technologies, English, foreign languages, health fields, home economics, humanities, mathematics, physical sciences, premedicine, social sciences. *Creative Arts/Performance Awards:* 18 ($14,061 total): applied art and design, art/fine arts, music, performing arts. *Special Achievements/Activities Awards:* 8 ($7000 total): leadership. *Special Characteristics Awards:* 25 ($65,873 total): ethnic background, members of minorities. *Athletic:* Total: 78 ($264,449); Men: 58 ($200,047); Women: 20 ($64,402).

Other Money-Saving Options Accelerated degree, co-op program, cooperative Army ROTC, cooperative Air Force ROTC. *Payment Plan:* installment. *Waivers:* full or partial for minority students and employees or children of employees.

Contact Ms. Danette L. Miller, Director/Team Manager of Student Financial Aid, Shepherd College, 301 North King Street, Shepherdstown, WV 25443-3210, 304-876-5283, fax: 304-876-5238.

SHIMER COLLEGE
Waukegan, Illinois

About the Institution Independent, coed. Degrees awarded: B. Offers 5 undergraduate majors. Total enrollment: 130 (60% state residents). Freshmen: 26.

Undergraduate Expenses (1997–98 estimated) Tuition: $13,400. Mandatory fees: $400. College room only: $1725.

Applications 87% of all full-time undergraduates enrolled in fall 1996 applied for aid; of these, 95% were judged to have need according to Federal Methodology, of whom 100% were aided. *Financial aid deadline (priority):* 7/1. *Financial aid forms:* FAFSA, CSS Financial Aid PROFILE, institutional form required. *Admission application deadline:* 8/10.

Summary of Aid to Needy Students *From gift & self-help combined:* Average need met: 77%. *Gift aid:* Total: $1,307,331 (30% from college's own funds, 22% from other college-administered sources, 48% from external sources). 40 Federal Work-Study jobs (averaging $1100); 10 part-time jobs.

Need-Based Scholarships & Grants Pell, FSEOG, state, private, college/university.

Loans Perkins, PLUS, Stafford, Unsubsidized Stafford.

Non-Need Awards *Academic Interests/Achievement Awards:* general academic. *Creative Arts/Performance Awards:* art/fine arts, creative writing, theater/drama. *Special Achievements/Activities Awards:* hobbies/interest. *Special Characteristics Awards:* children and siblings of alumni, out-of-state students.

Other Money-Saving Options Accelerated degree, co-op program, off-campus living. *Payment Plan:* installment. *Waivers:* full or partial for minority students, children of alumni, employees or children of employees, senior citizens.

Contact Office of Financial Aid, Shimer College, PO Box A500, Waukegan, IL 60079-0500, 847-623-8400.

SHIPPENSBURG UNIVERSITY OF PENNSYLVANIA
Shippensburg, Pennsylvania

About the Institution State-supported, coed. Degrees awarded: B, M. Offers 51 undergraduate majors. Total enrollment: 6,683. Undergraduates: 5,657 (92% state residents). Freshmen: 1,277.

Undergraduate Expenses (1996–97) State resident tuition: $3368. Nonresident tuition: $8566. Mandatory fees: $862. College room and board: $3700.

Applications 90% of all full-time undergraduates enrolled in fall 1996 applied for aid; of these, 66% were judged to have need according to Federal Methodology, of whom 97% were aided. *Financial aid deadline:* Applications processed continuously. *Financial aid forms:* FAFSA, state form, institutional form required. *Admission application deadline:* rolling.

Summary of Aid to Needy Students *From gift & self-help combined:* Average amount awarded: $5195 (37% gift aid, 63% self-help). *Gift aid:* Total: $5,299,454 (14% from college's own funds, 3% from other college-administered sources, 83% from external sources). 225 Federal Work-Study jobs; 763 part-time jobs.

Need-Based Scholarships & Grants Pell, FSEOG, state, college/university.

Loans Perkins, PLUS, Stafford, Unsubsidized Stafford, state, private, college/university long-term loans ($2785 average).

Non-Need Awards *Academic Interests/Achievement Awards:* general academic. *Athletic:* available.

Other Money-Saving Options Accelerated degree, Army ROTC, off-campus living (after freshman year). *Waivers:* full or partial for employees or children of employees and senior citizens.

Contact Financial Aid Office, Shippensburg University of Pennsylvania, 1871 Old Main Drive, Shippensburg, PA 17257-2299, 717-532-1131, fax: 717-530-4028.

SHORTER COLLEGE
Rome, Georgia

About the Institution Independent/religious, coed. Degrees awarded: B. Offers 53 undergraduate majors. Total enrollment: 1,577 (87% state residents). Freshmen: 202.

Undergraduate Expenses (1997–98) Comprehensive fee of $12,510 includes tuition ($8150), mandatory fees ($110), and college room and board ($4250).

Applications Of all full-time undergraduates enrolled in fall 1996, 85% of those who applied for aid were judged to have need according to Federal Methodology, of whom 100% were aided. *Financial aid deadline (priority):* 4/15. *Financial aid forms:* FAFSA, state form, institutional form required. *Admission application deadline:* rolling.

Summary of Aid to Needy Students *From gift & self-help combined:* Average need met: 66%. Average amount awarded: $7673 (59% gift aid, 41% self-help). *Gift aid:* Total: $4,124,471 (33% from college's

own funds, 12% from other college-administered sources, 55% from external sources). 99 Federal Work-Study jobs (averaging $965); 20 part-time jobs.

Need-Based Scholarships & Grants Pell, FSEOG, state, private, college/university.

Loans Perkins, PLUS, Stafford, Unsubsidized Stafford, state, private, college/university short-term loans, college/university long-term loans.

Non-Need Awards In 1996, a total of 1,526 non-need awards were made. *Academic Interests/Achievement Awards:* 330 ($773,094 total): general academic. *Creative Arts/Performance Awards:* 93 ($103,645 total): art/fine arts, music, theater/drama. *Special Achievements/Activities Awards:* 112 ($124,994 total): religious involvement. *Special Characteristics Awards:* 913 ($643,856 total): local/state students, religious affiliation, siblings of current students. *Athletic:* Total: 78 ($340,230); Men: 55 ($241,817); Women: 23 ($98,413).

Other Money-Saving Options Accelerated degree. *Payment Plan:* installment. *Waivers:* full or partial for employees or children of employees and senior citizens.

Contact Mr. Rondall H. Day, Director of Financial Aid, Shorter College, 315 Shorter Avenue, Rome, GA 30165-4298, 706-233-7227.

SH'OR YOSHUV RABBINICAL COLLEGE
Far Rockaway, New York

About the Institution Independent/religious, men. Offers 3 undergraduate majors.

Applications *Financial aid deadline (priority):* 4/1. *Financial aid forms:* FAFSA, CSS Financial Aid PROFILE required. Institutional form required for some. *Admission application deadline:* 9/20.

Summary of Aid to Needy Students Federal Work-Study jobs.

Loans College/university short-term loans.

Non-Need Awards available.

Other Money-Saving Options Co-op program, off-campus living.

Contact Office of Financial Aid, Sh'or Yoshuv Rabbinical College, Far Rockaway, NY 11691-4002, 718-327-2048.

SIENA COLLEGE
Loudonville, New York

About the Institution Independent/religious, coed. Degrees awarded: B, M. Offers 26 undergraduate majors. Total enrollment: 3,212. Undergraduates: 3,188 (82% state residents). Freshmen: 570.

Undergraduate Expenses (1997–98) Comprehensive fee of $18,345 includes tuition ($12,400), mandatory fees ($310), and college room and board ($5635). College room only: $3330.

Applications 87% of all full-time undergraduates enrolled in fall 1996 applied for aid; of these, 89% were judged to have need according to Federal Methodology, of whom 100% were aided. *Financial aid deadline (priority):* 2/1. *Financial aid forms:* FAFSA, institutional form required. State form required for some. *Regular admission application deadline:* 3/1. Early decision deadline: 12/1. Early action deadline: 12/1.

Summary of Aid to Needy Students *From gift & self-help combined:* Average need met: 77%. Average amount awarded: $9326 (66% gift aid, 34% self-help). *Gift aid:* Total: $12,320,195 (65% from college's own funds, 20% from other college-administered sources, 15% from external sources). 374 Federal Work-Study jobs (averaging $800); 295 part-time jobs.

Need-Based Scholarships & Grants Pell, FSEOG, state, private, college/university, Siena Grants, Franciscan Community Grants.

Loans Perkins, PLUS, Stafford, Unsubsidized Stafford, private.

Non-Need Awards In 1996, a total of 527 non-need awards were made. *Academic Interests/Achievement Awards:* 430 ($1,295,175 total): general academic, premedicine. *Athletic:* Total: 97 ($898,632); Men: 48 ($426,127); Women: 49 ($472,505).

Other Money-Saving Options Army ROTC, cooperative Air Force ROTC, off-campus living (after freshman year). *Payment Plan:* installment. *Waivers:* full or partial for employees or children of employees and senior citizens.

Contact Ms. Ann D. White, Director of Financial Aid, Siena College, 515 Loudon Road, Loudonville, NY 12211-1462, 518-783-2427.

SIENA HEIGHTS COLLEGE
Adrian, Michigan

About the Institution Independent/religious, coed. Degrees awarded: A, B, M. Offers 33 undergraduate majors. Total enrollment: 2,002. Undergraduates: 1,180 (86% state residents). Freshmen: 189.

Undergraduate Expenses (1997–98) Comprehensive fee of $15,030 includes tuition ($10,450), mandatory fees ($250), and college room and board ($4330 minimum).

Applications 85% of all full-time undergraduates enrolled in fall 1996 applied for aid; of these, 96% were judged to have need according to Federal Methodology, of whom 100% were aided. *Financial aid deadline (priority):* 3/15. *Financial aid forms:* FAFSA required. *Admission application deadline:* rolling.

Summary of Aid to Needy Students *From gift & self-help combined:* Average need met: 98%. *Gift aid:* Total: $11,883,217 (27% from college's own funds, 68% from other college-administered sources, 5% from external sources). Federal Work-Study jobs (averaging $1500).

Need-Based Scholarships & Grants Pell, FSEOG, state, private, college/university.

Loans PLUS, Stafford, Unsubsidized Stafford.

Non-Need Awards In 1996, a total of 1,245 non-need awards were made. *Academic Interests/Achievement Awards:* 699 ($2,448,811 total): general academic, business, computer science, foreign languages, mathematics, physical sciences, social sciences. *Creative Arts/Performance Awards:* 127 ($192,282 total): art/fine arts, music, theater/drama. *Special Achievements/Activities Awards:* 109 ($209,992 total): community service. *Special Characteristics Awards:* 92 ($257,909 total): general special characteristics, children and siblings of alumni, members of minorities, relatives of clergy, religious affiliation. *Athletic:* Total: 218 ($443,778).

Other Money-Saving Options Accelerated degree, co-op program, off-campus living (after sophomore year). *Payment Plan:* deferred payment. *Waivers:* full or partial for employees or children of employees.

Contact Office of Financial Aid, Siena Heights College, Adrian, MI 49221-1796, 517-263-0731.

SIERRA NEVADA COLLEGE
Incline Village, Nevada

About the Institution Independent, coed. Degrees awarded: B. Offers 8 undergraduate majors. Total enrollment: 600 (49% state residents). Freshmen: 70.

Undergraduate Expenses (1997–98) Comprehensive fee of $14,650 includes tuition ($9450) and college room and board ($5200). College room only: $2600.

Applications 93% of all full-time undergraduates enrolled in fall 1996 applied for aid; of these, 95% were judged to have need according to Federal Methodology, of whom 100% were aided. *Financial aid deadline (priority):* 6/1. *Financial aid forms:* FAFSA, institutional form, financial aid transcript (for transfers) required; CSS Financial Aid PROFILE acceptable. *Admission application deadline:* rolling.

Summary of Aid to Needy Students *From gift & self-help combined:* Average need met: 73%. Average amount awarded: $11,134 (20% gift aid, 80% self-help). *Gift aid:* Total: $531,877 (60% from college's own funds, 6% from other college-administered sources, 34% from external sources). Federal Work-Study jobs.

Need-Based Scholarships & Grants Pell, FSEOG, state, private, college/university.

Loans PLUS, Stafford, Unsubsidized Stafford, college/university short-term loans ($100 average).

Non-Need Awards *Academic Interests/Achievement Awards:* general academic, business, education, humanities. *Creative Arts/Performance Awards:* art/fine arts, music. *Special Achievements/Activities Awards:* community service. *Special Characteristics Awards:* children of faculty/staff, ethnic background, local/state students, siblings of current students, spouses of current students. *Athletic:* Total: 8; Men: 4; Women: 4.

Other Money-Saving Options Accelerated degree, cooperative Army ROTC, off-campus living. *Payment Plans:* guaranteed tuition, installment. *Waivers:* full or partial for employees or children of employees.

Contact Ms. Laura Whitelaw, Director of Financial Aid, Sierra Nevada College, PO Box 4269, Incline Village, NV 89450-4269, 702-831-1314.

SILVER LAKE COLLEGE
Manitowoc, Wisconsin

About the Institution Independent/religious, coed. Degrees awarded: A, B, M. Offers 22 undergraduate majors. Total enrollment: 1,144. Undergraduates: 822 (99% state residents). Freshmen: 34.

Undergraduate Expenses (1997–98) Comprehensive fee of $13,720 includes tuition ($9630) and college room and board ($4090). College room only: $2200.

Applications Of all full-time undergraduates enrolled in fall 1996, 92% of those who applied for aid were judged to have need according to Federal Methodology, of whom 97% were aided. *Financial aid deadline (priority):* 4/15. *Financial aid forms:* FAFSA, institutional form required. *Admission application deadline:* 8/31.

Summary of Aid to Needy Students *From gift & self-help combined:* Average amount awarded: $9052 (51% gift aid, 49% self-help). *Gift aid:* Total: $1,030,000 (37% from college's own funds, 11% from other college-administered sources, 52% from external sources). Federal Work-Study jobs.

Need-Based Scholarships & Grants Pell, FSEOG, state, private, college/university.

Loans PLUS, Stafford, Unsubsidized Stafford, college/university short-term loans ($372 average).

Non-Need Awards In 1996, a total of 341 non-need awards were made. *Academic Interests/Achievement Awards:* 166 ($268,956 total): general academic. *Creative Arts/Performance Awards:* 5 ($3500 total): music. *Special Characteristics Awards:* 160 ($230,155 total): local/state students, religious affiliation. *Athletic:* Total: 10 ($20,000); Men: 0; Women: 10 ($20,000).

Other Money-Saving Options Co-op program, off-campus living (after sophomore year). *Payment Plan:* installment. *Waivers:* full or partial for employees or children of employees and senior citizens.

Contact Sr. Mary Beth Kornely, Director of Financial Aid, Silver Lake College, 2406 South Alverno Road, Manitowoc, WI 54220-9319, 414-684-6418.

SIMMONS COLLEGE
Boston, Massachusetts

About the Institution Independent, women. Degrees awarded: B, M, D. Offers 51 undergraduate majors. Total enrollment: 3,740. Undergraduates: 1,397 (61% state residents). Freshmen: 250.

Undergraduate Expenses (1997–98) Comprehensive fee of $25,792 includes tuition ($17,984), mandatory fees ($580), and college room and board ($7228).

Applications Of all full-time undergraduates enrolled in fall 1996, 100% of those judged to have need according to Federal Methodology were aided. *Financial aid deadline:* 2/1. *Financial aid forms:* FAFSA, institutional form required. *Regular admission application deadline:* 2/1. Early decision deadline: 11/15.

Summary of Aid to Needy Students *From gift & self-help combined:* Average need met: 90%. Average amount awarded: $15,026 (62% gift aid, 38% self-help). *Gift aid:* Total: $10,588,225 (82% from college's own funds, 10% from other college-administered sources, 8% from external sources). 871 Federal Work-Study jobs (averaging $1800); 200 part-time jobs.

Need-Based Scholarships & Grants Pell, FSEOG, state, private, college/university.

Loans Perkins, PLUS, Stafford, Unsubsidized Stafford, state, private, college/university short-term loans ($100 average), college/university long-term loans ($1472 average).

Non-Need Awards In 1996, a total of 113 non-need awards were made. *Academic Interests/Achievement Awards:* 113 ($1,513,990 total): general academic.

Other Money-Saving Options Accelerated degree, cooperative Army ROTC, off-campus living. *Payment Plan:* installment. *Waivers:* full or partial for employees or children of employees, adult students, senior citizens.

Contact Ms. Barbara Layne, Assistant Director of Financial Aid, Simmons College, 300 The Fenway, Boston, MA 02115, 617-521-2036, fax: 617-521-3195.

SIMON'S ROCK COLLEGE OF BARD
Great Barrington, Massachusetts

About the Institution Independent, coed. Degrees awarded: A, B. Offers 22 undergraduate majors. Total enrollment: 334 (18% state residents). Freshmen: 154.

Undergraduate Expenses (1997–98) Comprehensive fee of $27,650 includes tuition ($19,250), mandatory fees ($2300), and college room and board ($6100). College room only: $3000.

Applications *Financial aid deadline (priority):* 6/30. *Financial aid forms:* FAFSA, CSS Financial Aid PROFILE required. *Admission application deadline:* 6/15.

Summary of Aid to Needy Students *From gift & self-help combined:* Average need met: 90%. Average amount awarded: $13,000 (58% gift aid, 42% self-help). *Gift aid:* Total: $2,800,000. Federal Work-Study jobs; 30 part-time jobs.

Need-Based Scholarships & Grants Pell, FSEOG, state, private, college/university.

Loans Perkins, PLUS, Stafford, Unsubsidized Stafford, private.

Non-Need Awards *Academic Interests/Achievement Awards:* general academic. *Creative Arts/Performance Awards:* general creative. *Special Achievements/Activities Awards:* general special achievements/activities. *Special Characteristics Awards:* general special characteristics, local/state students.

Other Money-Saving Options Off-campus living (after sophomore year). *Payment Plan:* installment. *Waivers:* full or partial for employees or children of employees.

Contact Ms. Eve Caimano, Assistant Director of Financial Aid, Simon's Rock College of Bard, Great Barrington, MA 01230-9702, 413-528-0771, fax: 413-528-7365.

SIMPSON COLLEGE
Redding, California

About the Institution Independent/religious, coed. Degrees awarded: A, B, M. Offers 20 undergraduate majors. Total enrollment: 1,169. Undergraduates: 844 (72% state residents). Freshmen: 138.

Undergraduate Expenses (1997–98) Comprehensive fee of $13,010 includes tuition ($8200), mandatory fees ($910), and college room and board ($3900).

Applications 87% of all full-time undergraduates enrolled in fall 1996 applied for aid; of these, 91% were judged to have need according to Federal Methodology, of whom 98% were aided. *Financial aid deadline (priority):* 3/2. *Financial aid forms:* FAFSA, institutional form required. State form required for some. *Admission application deadline:* rolling.

Summary of Aid to Needy Students *From gift & self-help combined:* Average need met: 79%. Average amount awarded: $8973 (45% gift aid, 55% self-help). *Gift aid:* Total: $1,959,000 (15% from college's own funds, 3% from other college-administered sources, 82% from external sources). 125 Federal Work-Study jobs (averaging $1000); 35 part-time jobs.

Need-Based Scholarships & Grants Pell, FSEOG, state.

Loans Perkins, PLUS, Stafford, Unsubsidized Stafford, private, college/university long-term loans ($900 average).

Non-Need Awards In 1996, a total of 608 non-need awards were made. *Academic Interests/Achievement Awards:* 169 ($238,000 total): general academic. *Creative Arts/Performance Awards:* 5 ($3250 total): music. *Special Achievements/Activities Awards:* 304 ($200,500 total): leadership, religious involvement. *Special Characteristics Awards:* 130 ($124,150 total): general special characteristics, religious affiliation.

Other Money-Saving Options Off-campus living (after junior year). *Payment Plan:* installment. *Waivers:* full or partial for employees or children of employees.

Contact Mr. Chris Kinnier, Director of Financial Aid, Simpson College, 2211 College View Drive, Redding, CA 96003-8606, 916-224-5600, fax: 916-224-5627.

SIMPSON COLLEGE
Indianola, Iowa

About the Institution Independent/religious, coed. Degrees awarded: B. Offers 45 undergraduate majors. Total enrollment: 1,805 (93% state residents). Freshmen: 323.

Undergraduate Expenses (1996–97) Comprehensive fee of $16,795 includes tuition ($12,530), mandatory fees ($120), and college room and board ($4145).

Applications 98% of all full-time undergraduates enrolled in fall 1996 applied for aid; of these, 88% were judged to have need according to Federal Methodology, of whom 100% were aided. *Financial aid deadline (priority):* 4/20. *Financial aid forms:* institutional form required. FAFSA required for some. *Admission application deadline:* rolling.

Summary of Aid to Needy Students *From gift & self-help combined:* Average need met: 95%. Average amount awarded: $13,840 (64% gift aid, 36% self-help). *Gift aid:* Total: $9,815,067 (63% from college's own funds, 2% from other college-administered sources, 35% from external sources). 271 Federal Work-Study jobs (averaging $642); 384 part-time jobs.

Need-Based Scholarships & Grants Pell, FSEOG, state, private, college/university.

Loans Perkins, PLUS, Stafford, Unsubsidized Stafford, private, college/university short-term loans ($500 average), college/university long-term loans ($1520 average).

Non-Need Awards In 1996, a total of 2,389 non-need awards were made. *Academic Interests/Achievement Awards:* 1,770 ($2,857,385 total): general academic. *Creative Arts/Performance Awards:* 337 ($390,432 total): art/fine arts, music, theater/drama. *Special Characteristics Awards:* 282 ($349,714 total): children and siblings of alumni, children of faculty/staff, international students, members of minorities, relatives of clergy, siblings of current students.

Other Money-Saving Options Accelerated degree, co-op program. *Payment Plan:* installment. *Waivers:* full or partial for employees or children of employees.

Contact Ms. Debbie M. Barger, Director of Financial Assistance, Simpson College, 701 North C Street, Indianola, IA 50125-1297, 515-961-1630, fax: 515-961-1830.

SINTE GLESKA UNIVERSITY
Rosebud, South Dakota

About the Institution Independent, coed. Degrees awarded: A, B, M. Offers 14 undergraduate majors. Total enrollment: 698. Undergraduates: 653 (95% state residents). Freshmen: 156.

Undergraduate Expenses (1997–98) Tuition: $1920. Mandatory fees: $60.

Applications *Financial aid deadline:* continuous. *Financial aid forms:* FAFSA, institutional form required. *Admission application deadline:* 8/20.

Summary of Aid to Needy Students *Gift aid:* Total: $44,456. Federal Work-Study jobs.

Need-Based Scholarships & Grants Pell, FSEOG.

Non-Need Awards *Academic Interests/Achievement Awards:* business, education. *Creative Arts/Performance Awards:* art/fine arts. *Special Achievements/Activities Awards:* general special achievements/activities, rodeo.

Other Money-Saving Options *Payment Plan:* installment. *Waivers:* full or partial for employees or children of employees.

Contact Office of Financial Aid, Sinte Gleska University, Rosebud, SD 57570-0490, 605-747-2263.

SKIDMORE COLLEGE
Saratoga Springs, New York

About the Institution Independent, coed. Degrees awarded: B, M. Offers 36 undergraduate majors. Total enrollment: 2,244. Undergraduates: 2,189 (30% state residents). Freshmen: 705.

Undergraduate Expenses (1996–97) Comprehensive fee of $27,005 includes tuition ($20,670), mandatory fees ($225), and college room and board ($6110). College room only: $3415.

Applications 39% of all full-time undergraduates enrolled in fall 1996 applied for aid; of these, 93% were judged to have need according to Federal Methodology, of whom 100% were aided. *Financial aid deadline:* 2/1. *Financial aid forms:* FAFSA, CSS Financial Aid PROFILE required. State form, Divorced/Separated Parents' Statement required for some. *Regular admission application deadline:* 2/1. Early decision deadline: 12/1.

Summary of Aid to Needy Students *From gift & self-help combined:* Average need met: 97%. Average amount awarded: $18,147 (76% gift aid, 24% self-help). *Gift aid:* Total: $11,160,000 (83% from college's own funds, 4% from other college-administered sources, 13% from external sources). 680 Federal Work-Study jobs (averaging $1700); 425 part-time jobs.

Need-Based Scholarships & Grants Pell, FSEOG, state, college/university.

Loans Perkins, PLUS, Stafford, Unsubsidized Stafford, college/university short-term loans, college/university long-term loans ($14,041 average).

Non-Need Awards In 1996, a total of 16 non-need awards were made. *Creative Arts/Performance Awards:* 16 ($96,000 total): music.

Other Money-Saving Options Accelerated degree, cooperative Army ROTC, cooperative Air Force ROTC, off-campus living (after sophomore year). *Payment Plans:* tuition prepayment, installment. *Waivers:* full or partial for employees or children of employees.

Contact Mr. Robert D. Shorb, Director of Student Aid and Family Finance, Skidmore College, 815 North Broadway, Saratoga Springs, NY 12866-1632, 518-584-5000 Ext. 2145, fax: 518-584-7963.

SLIPPERY ROCK UNIVERSITY OF PENNSYLVANIA
Slippery Rock, Pennsylvania

About the Institution State-supported, coed. Degrees awarded: B, M, D. Offers 64 undergraduate majors. Total enrollment: 7,291. Undergraduates: 6,452 (94% state residents). Freshmen: 1,307.

Undergraduate Expenses (1996–97) State resident tuition: $3368. Nonresident tuition: $8566. Mandatory fees: $751. College room and board: $3552. College room only: $1972.

Applications 88% of all full-time undergraduates enrolled in fall 1996 applied for aid; of these, 87% were judged to have need according to Federal Methodology, of whom 95% were aided. *Financial aid deadline (priority):* 5/1. *Financial aid forms:* FAFSA required. *Admission application deadline:* 5/1.

Summary of Aid to Needy Students *From gift & self-help combined:* Average need met: 82%. Average amount awarded: $4950 (41% gift aid, 59% self-help). *Gift aid:* Total: $8,477,241 (8% from college's own funds, 4% from other college-administered sources, 88% from external sources). 350 Federal Work-Study jobs; 1,000 part-time jobs.

Need-Based Scholarships & Grants Pell, FSEOG, state, private, college/university.

Loans Perkins, PLUS, Stafford, Unsubsidized Stafford, college/university short-term loans ($275 average).

Non-Need Awards *Academic Interests/Achievement Awards:* general academic, biological sciences, business, computer science, education, English, social sciences. *Creative Arts/Performance Awards:* art/fine arts, music. *Special Achievements/Activities Awards:* general special achievements/activities, leadership. *Special Characteristics Awards:* general special characteristics, children of faculty/staff, children of union members/company employees, ethnic background, members of minorities. *Athletic:* Total: 202 ($375,647).

Other Money-Saving Options Accelerated degree, Army ROTC, off-campus living (after freshman year). *Payment Plan:* installment. *Waivers:* full or partial for minority students, employees or children of employees, senior citizens.

Contact Office of Financial Aid, Slippery Rock University of Pennsylvania, 008 Old Main, Slippery Rock, PA 16057, 412-738-0512.

SMITH COLLEGE
Northampton, Massachusetts

About the Institution Independent, women. Degrees awarded: B, M, D. Offers 44 undergraduate majors. Total enrollment: 2,788. Undergraduates: 2,670 (18% state residents). Freshmen: 643.

Undergraduate Expenses (1997–98) Comprehensive fee of $28,762 includes tuition ($21,360), mandatory fees ($152), and college room and board ($7250).

Applications Of all full-time undergraduates enrolled in fall 1996, 92% of those who applied for aid were judged to have need according to Federal Methodology, of whom 100% were aided. *Financial aid deadline:*

2/1. *Financial aid forms:* FAFSA, CSS Financial Aid PROFILE, institutional form required. State form required for some. *Regular admission application deadline:* 1/15. Early decision deadline: 11/15.

Summary of Aid to Needy Students *From gift & self-help combined:* Average need met: 100%. Average amount awarded: $18,601 (69% gift aid, 31% self-help). *Gift aid:* Total: $21,313,906 (89% from college's own funds, 3% from other college-administered sources, 8% from external sources). 1,261 Federal Work-Study jobs (averaging $1701); 142 part-time jobs.

Need-Based Scholarships & Grants Pell, FSEOG, state, college/university.

Loans College/university short-term loans ($35 average), college/university long-term loans ($2568 average).

Non-Need Awards Not offered.

Other Money-Saving Options Accelerated degree, cooperative Army ROTC, cooperative Air Force ROTC. *Payment Plans:* tuition prepayment, installment. *Waivers:* full or partial for employees or children of employees.

Contact Ms. Myra Baas Smith, Director of Financial Aid, Smith College, College Hall, Northampton, MA 01063, 413-585-2530, fax: 413-585-2566.

SOJOURNER-DOUGLASS COLLEGE
Baltimore, Maryland

About the Institution Independent, coed. Degrees awarded: B. Offers 18 undergraduate majors. Total enrollment: 433 (99% state residents). Freshmen: 113.

Undergraduate Expenses (1997–98) Tuition: $3980. Mandatory fees: $110.

Applications Of all full-time undergraduates enrolled in fall 1996, 96% of those who applied for aid were judged to have need according to Federal Methodology, of whom 100% were aided. *Financial aid deadline (priority):* 8/15. *Financial aid forms:* FAFSA, institutional form required. *Admission application deadline:* rolling.

Summary of Aid to Needy Students *From gift & self-help combined:* Average need met: 75%. Average amount awarded: $3000 (60% gift aid, 40% self-help). *Gift aid:* Total: $615,876 (8% from college's own funds, 19% from other college-administered sources, 73% from external sources). Federal Work-Study jobs.

Need-Based Scholarships & Grants Pell, FSEOG, state.

Loans PLUS, Stafford, Unsubsidized Stafford, college/university short-term loans ($70 average).

Non-Need Awards Not offered.

Other Money-Saving Options Accelerated degree. *Payment Plans:* installment, deferred payment. *Waivers:* full or partial for employees or children of employees.

Contact Ms. Rebecca Chalk, Financial Aid Director, Sojourner-Douglass College, Baltimore, MD 21205-1814, 410-276-0306.

SONOMA STATE UNIVERSITY
Rohnert Park, California

About the Institution State-supported, coed. Degrees awarded: B, M. Offers 60 undergraduate majors. Total enrollment: 6,999. Undergraduates: 5,872 (96% state residents). Freshmen: 816.

Undergraduate Expenses (1996–97) State resident tuition: $0. Nonresident tuition: $7380. Mandatory fees: $2130. College room and board: $5328. College room only: $3456.

Applications 57% of all full-time undergraduates enrolled in fall 1996 applied for aid; of these, 83% were judged to have need according to

Federal Methodology, of whom 99% were aided. *Financial aid deadline (priority):* 3/2. *Financial aid forms:* FAFSA required. *Admission application deadline:* 1/30.

Summary of Aid to Needy Students *From gift & self-help combined:* Average need met: 79%. Average amount awarded: $6244 (40% gift aid, 60% self-help). *Gift aid:* Total: $5,860,309 (2% from college's own funds, 35% from other college-administered sources, 63% from external sources). 263 Federal Work-Study jobs (averaging $1706); 400 part-time jobs.

Need-Based Scholarships & Grants Pell, FSEOG, state, private.

Loans Perkins, PLUS, Stafford, Unsubsidized Stafford, Federal Nursing, college/university short-term loans ($150 average).

Non-Need Awards In 1996, a total of 312 non-need awards were made. *Academic Interests/Achievement Awards:* 200 ($200,000 total): general academic, area/ethnic studies, biological sciences, business, communication, computer science, education, English, foreign languages, health fields, humanities, international studies, mathematics, physical sciences, premedicine, social sciences. *Creative Arts/Performance Awards:* 61 ($19,000 total): applied art and design, art/fine arts, cinema/film/broadcasting, creative writing, dance, journalism/publications, music, performing arts, theater/drama. *Special Characteristics Awards:* 60 ($60,000 total): adult students, children and siblings of alumni, children of educators, children of faculty/staff, children of public servants, children of union members/company employees, ethnic background, first-generation college students, handicapped students, international students, members of minorities, previous college experience, veterans.

Other Money-Saving Options Cooperative Army ROTC, cooperative Naval ROTC, cooperative Air Force ROTC, off-campus living. *Waivers:* full or partial for employees or children of employees.

Contact Financial Aid Representative, Sonoma State University, 1801 East Cotati Avenue, Rohnert Park, CA 94928-3609, 707-664-2389, fax: 707-664-4242.

SOUTHAMPTON CAMPUS OF LONG ISLAND UNIVERSITY
Southampton, New York

See Long Island University, Southampton College

SOUTH COLLEGE
Savannah, Georgia

About the Institution Proprietary, coed. Degrees awarded: A, B. Offers 7 undergraduate majors. Total enrollment: 427 (99% state residents). Freshmen: 109.

Undergraduate Expenses (1996–97) Tuition: $5685. Mandatory fees: $25.

Applications *Financial aid deadline (priority):* 10/3. *Financial aid forms:* FAFSA required. *Admission application deadline:* rolling.

Summary of Aid to Needy Students 28 Federal Work-Study jobs (averaging $3060).

Need-Based Scholarships & Grants Pell, FSEOG.

Loans Perkins, PLUS, Stafford, Unsubsidized Stafford, college/university short-term loans ($300 average), college/university long-term loans ($750 average).

Non-Need Awards In 1996, a total of 5 non-need awards were made. *Academic Interests/Achievement Awards:* 5 ($10,000 total): general academic.

Another Money-Saving Option *Waivers:* full or partial for employees or children of employees.

Contact Ms. Cynthia A. Morris, Director of Financial Aid, South College, Savannah, GA 31406-4881, 912-651-8107.

SOUTH DAKOTA SCHOOL OF MINES AND TECHNOLOGY
Rapid City, South Dakota

About the Institution State-supported, coed. Degrees awarded: B, M, D. Offers 15 undergraduate majors. Total enrollment: 2,218. Undergraduates: 1,994 (72% state residents). Freshmen: 373.

Undergraduate Expenses (1997–98) State resident tuition: $1728. Nonresident tuition: $5496. Mandatory fees: $1650. College room and board: $2910.

Applications Of all full-time undergraduates enrolled in fall 1996, 83% of those who applied for aid were judged to have need according to Federal Methodology, of whom 100% were aided. *Financial aid deadline (priority):* 4/15. *Financial aid forms:* FAFSA required; CSS Financial Aid PROFILE acceptable. State form, institutional form required for some. *Admission application deadline:* rolling.

Summary of Aid to Needy Students *From gift & self-help combined:* Average need met: 95%. Average amount awarded: $6966 (22% gift aid, 78% self-help). *Gift aid:* Total: $1,682,606 (14% from college's own funds, 5% from other college-administered sources, 81% from external sources). 203 Federal Work-Study jobs (averaging $1020); 648 part-time jobs.

Need-Based Scholarships & Grants Pell, FSEOG, state, private.

Loans Perkins, PLUS, Stafford, Unsubsidized Stafford, college/university short-term loans ($510 average).

Non-Need Awards *Academic Interests/Achievement Awards:* 547 ($228,421 total): general academic, biological sciences, computer science, engineering/technologies, mathematics, physical sciences. *Special Characteristics Awards:* general special characteristics. *Athletic:* available.

Other Money-Saving Options Co-op program, Army ROTC, off-campus living (after sophomore year). *Payment Plan:* installment. *Waivers:* full or partial for children of alumni and senior citizens.

Contact Office of Financial Aid, South Dakota School of Mines and Technology, 501 East Saint Joseph, Rapid City, SD 57701, 605-394-2511.

SOUTH DAKOTA STATE UNIVERSITY
Brookings, South Dakota

About the Institution State-supported, coed. Degrees awarded: A, B, M, D. Offers 75 undergraduate majors. Total enrollment: 8,350. Undergraduates: 7,356 (65% state residents). Freshmen: 1,496.

Undergraduate Expenses (1996–97) State resident tuition: $1696. Nonresident tuition: $5376. Mandatory fees: $1088. College room and board: $2344 (minimum). College room only: $1244.

Applications Of all full-time undergraduates enrolled in fall 1996, 89% of those who applied for aid were judged to have need according to Federal Methodology, of whom 100% were aided. *Financial aid deadline (priority):* 3/15. *Financial aid forms:* FAFSA, financial aid transcript (for transfers) required. State form required for some. *Admission application deadline:* rolling.

Summary of Aid to Needy Students *From gift & self-help combined:* Average need met: 92%. Average amount awarded: $4974 (25% gift aid, 75% self-help). *Gift aid:* Total: $6,334,091 (21% from college's own funds, 26% from other college-administered sources, 53% from external sources). 752 Federal Work-Study jobs (averaging $1055); 1,820 part-time jobs.

Need-Based Scholarships & Grants Pell, FSEOG, state, private, college/university.

Loans Perkins, PLUS, Stafford, Unsubsidized Stafford, Federal Nursing, state, private, college/university short-term loans ($500 average), college/university long-term loans ($1000 average).

Non-Need Awards In 1996, a total of 1,766 non-need awards were made. *Academic Interests/Achievement Awards:* 984 ($864,616 total): general academic, agriculture, area/ethnic studies, biological sciences, business, communication, computer science, education, engineering/technologies, English, foreign languages, health fields, home economics, humanities, international studies, mathematics, military science, physical sciences, premedicine, social sciences. *Creative Arts/Performance Awards:* 184 ($136,528 total): general creative, art/fine arts, debating, journalism/publications, music, performing arts, theater/drama. *Special Achievements/Activities Awards:* 64 ($79,360 total): general special achievements/activities, Junior Miss, leadership, memberships, rodeo. *Special Characteristics Awards:* 62 ($52,514 total): general special characteristics, children of workers in trades, handicapped students, international students, members of minorities, ROTC participants, veterans, veterans' children. *Athletic:* Total: 472 ($506,719); Men: 288 ($350,744); Women: 184 ($155,975).

Other Money-Saving Options Accelerated degree, co-op program, Army ROTC, Air Force ROTC, off-campus living (after sophomore year). *Payment Plans:* installment, deferred payment. *Waivers:* full or partial for employees or children of employees and senior citizens.

Contact Mr. Jay Larsen, Director of Financial Aid, South Dakota State University, Administration 106, Brookings, SD 57007, 605-688-4703, fax: 605-688-6384.

SOUTHEASTERN BAPTIST COLLEGE
Laurel, Mississippi

About the Institution Independent/religious, coed. Degrees awarded: A, B. Offers 5 undergraduate majors. Total enrollment: 69 (96% state residents). Freshmen: 16.

Undergraduate Expenses (1996–97) Comprehensive fee of $4020 includes tuition ($2040), mandatory fees ($180), and college room and board ($1800).

Applications 100% of all full-time undergraduates enrolled in fall 1996 applied for aid; of these, 74% were judged to have need according to Federal Methodology, of whom 100% were aided. *Financial aid deadline (priority):* 8/1. *Financial aid forms:* FAFSA, institutional form required. *Admission application deadline:* rolling.

Summary of Aid to Needy Students *From gift & self-help combined:* Average need met: 80%. Average amount awarded: $1574. *Gift aid:* Total: $36,207 (31% from college's own funds, 69% from external sources). 1 part-time job.

Need-Based Scholarships & Grants Pell, private, college/university.

Non-Need Awards In 1996, a total of 36 non-need awards were made. *Academic Interests/Achievement Awards:* 3 ($1785 total): general academic. *Creative Arts/Performance Awards:* 12 ($1200 total): music. *Special Achievements/Activities Awards:* 21 ($11,454 total): religious involvement. *Special Characteristics Awards:* 0: children of faculty/staff.

Other Money-Saving Options Off-campus living. *Payment Plan:* installment.

Contact Financial Aid Officer, Southeastern Baptist College, 4229 Highway 15 North, Laurel, MS 39440-1096, 601-426-6346, fax: 601-426-6347.

SOUTHEASTERN BIBLE COLLEGE
Birmingham, Alabama

About the Institution Independent/religious, coed. Degrees awarded: A, B. Offers 14 undergraduate majors.

Undergraduate Expenses (1996–97) Comprehensive fee of $7980 includes tuition ($4640), mandatory fees ($400), and college room and board ($2940).

Applications 84% of all full-time undergraduates enrolled in fall 1996 applied for aid; of these, 98% were judged to have need according to Federal Methodology, of whom 100% were aided. *Financial aid deadline (priority):* 5/1. *Financial aid forms:* FAFSA required. Institutional form required for some. *Admission application deadline:* rolling.

Summary of Aid to Needy Students *From gift & self-help combined:* Average need met: 85%. Average amount awarded: $5807 (48% gift aid, 52% self-help). *Gift aid:* Total: $323,368 (33% from college's own funds, 19% from other college-administered sources, 48% from external sources). 10 Federal Work-Study jobs (averaging $800); 20 part-time jobs.

Need-Based Scholarships & Grants Pell, FSEOG, college/university.

Loans PLUS, Stafford, Unsubsidized Stafford.

Non-Need Awards In 1996, a total of 29 non-need awards were made. *Academic Interests/Achievement Awards:* 3 ($10,000 total): general academic, religion/biblical studies. *Creative Arts/Performance Awards:* 2 ($2000 total): music. *Special Characteristics Awards:* 24 ($30,000 total): children of faculty/staff, local/state students, relatives of clergy, spouses of current students, veterans.

Other Money-Saving Options *Payment Plan:* installment. *Waivers:* full or partial for children of alumni and employees or children of employees.

Contact Ms. Joanne Belin, Financial Aid Administrator, Southeastern Bible College, 3001 Highway 280 East, Birmingham, AL 35243-4181, 205-970-9215, fax: 205-970-9207.

SOUTHEASTERN COLLEGE OF THE ASSEMBLIES OF GOD
Lakeland, Florida

About the Institution Independent/religious, coed. Degrees awarded: B. Offers 13 undergraduate majors. Total enrollment: 1,090 (46% state residents). Freshmen: 194.

Undergraduate Expenses (1996–97) Comprehensive fee of $7850 includes tuition ($4170), mandatory fees ($634), and college room and board ($3046).

Applications 88% of all full-time undergraduates enrolled in fall 1996 applied for aid; of these, 85% were judged to have need according to Federal Methodology, of whom 94% were aided. *Financial aid deadline (priority):* 5/1. *Financial aid forms:* FAFSA, institutional form required. State form required for some. *Admission application deadline:* 8/1.

Summary of Aid to Needy Students *From gift & self-help combined:* Average amount awarded: $6520 (26% gift aid, 74% self-help). *Gift aid:* Total: $1,252,800 (16% from college's own funds, 35% from other college-administered sources, 49% from external sources). 117 Federal Work-Study jobs (averaging $1350); part-time jobs.

Need-Based Scholarships & Grants Pell, FSEOG, state, private.

Loans Perkins, PLUS, Stafford, Unsubsidized Stafford, private.

Non-Need Awards *Academic Interests/Achievement Awards:* general academic, communication. *Creative Arts/Performance Awards:* music. *Special Achievements/Activities Awards:* religious involvement. *Special Characteristics Awards:* general special characteristics, children of faculty/staff, relatives of clergy, ROTC participants, siblings of current students.

Other Money-Saving Options Accelerated degree, cooperative Army ROTC. *Payment Plan:* installment. *Waivers:* full or partial for employees or children of employees.

Contact Ms. Carol B. Bradley, Financial Aid Director, Southeastern College of the Assemblies of God, 1000 Longfellow Boulevard, Lakeland, FL 33801-6099, 941-667-5000, fax: 941-667-5200.

SOUTHEASTERN LOUISIANA UNIVERSITY
Hammond, Louisiana

About the Institution State-supported, coed. Degrees awarded: A, B, M. Offers 51 undergraduate majors. Total enrollment: 14,592. Undergraduates: 12,840 (98% state residents). Freshmen: 2,451.

Undergraduate Expenses (1996–97) State resident tuition: $1930. Nonresident tuition: $4162. Mandatory fees: $120 (minimum). College room and board: $2320 (minimum). College room only: $1030.

Applications *Financial aid deadline (priority):* 4/1. *Financial aid forms:* FAFSA, institutional form required. *Admission application deadline:* 7/15.

Summary of Aid to Needy Students Federal Work-Study jobs; part-time jobs.

Need-Based Scholarships & Grants Pell, FSEOG, state.

Loans Perkins, Stafford, Unsubsidized Stafford, private, college/university short-term loans.

Non-Need Awards *Academic Interests/Achievement Awards:* general academic, agriculture, biological sciences, business, education, engineering/technologies, English, home economics, humanities, mathematics, physical sciences, religion/biblical studies, social sciences. *Creative Arts/Performance Awards:* debating, journalism/publications, music. *Special Achievements/Activities Awards:* cheerleading/drum major. *Special Characteristics Awards:* adult students, children of faculty/staff, handicapped students, members of minorities, religious affiliation, ROTC participants. *Athletic:* available.

Other Money-Saving Options Cooperative Army ROTC, off-campus living (after sophomore year). *Waivers:* full or partial for employees or children of employees and senior citizens.

Contact Ms. Kim Russell, Acting Director of Financial Aid, Southeastern Louisiana University, PO Box 703, Hammond, LA 70402, 504-549-2244.

SOUTHEASTERN OKLAHOMA STATE UNIVERSITY
Durant, Oklahoma

About the Institution State-supported, coed. Degrees awarded: B, M. Offers 66 undergraduate majors. Total enrollment: 3,831. Undergraduates: 3,401 (83% state residents). Freshmen: 562.

Undergraduate Expenses (1996–97) State resident tuition: $1290 (minimum). Nonresident tuition: $3495 (minimum). Mandatory fees: $419. College room and board: $2619. College room only: $888.

Applications *Financial aid deadline (priority):* 4/1. *Financial aid forms:* FAFSA, institutional form required; CSS Financial Aid PROFILE acceptable. *Admission application deadline:* 8/15.

Summary of Aid to Needy Students Federal Work-Study jobs; part-time jobs.

Loans College/university short-term loans.

Non-Need Awards *Academic Interests/Achievement Awards:* general academic, business, education, engineering/technologies. *Creative Arts/Performance Awards:* art/fine arts, music, theater/drama. *Athletic:* available.

Other Money-Saving Options Accelerated degree, off-campus living.

Contact Office of Financial Aid, Southeastern Oklahoma State University, Station A, Box 4113, Durant, OK 74701-0609, 405-924-0121.

SOUTHEASTERN UNIVERSITY
Washington, District of Columbia

About the Institution Independent, coed. Degrees awarded: A, B, M. Offers 13 undergraduate majors. Total enrollment: 610. Undergraduates: 301. Freshmen: 141.

Undergraduate Expenses (1997–98) Tuition: $5550. Mandatory fees: $300 (minimum).

Applications *Financial aid deadline (priority):* 7/15. *Financial aid forms:* FAFSA, institutional form required. *Admission application deadline:* rolling.

Summary of Aid to Needy Students *From gift & self-help combined:* Average need met: 100%. *Gift aid:* Total: $229,360 (17% from college's own funds, 10% from other college-administered sources, 73% from external sources). 15 Federal Work-Study jobs (averaging $2000); 9 part-time jobs.

Need-Based Scholarships & Grants Pell, FSEOG, state, college/university.

Loans PLUS, Stafford, Unsubsidized Stafford, college/university short-term loans ($500 average).

Non-Need Awards In 1996, a total of 18 non-need awards were made. *Academic Interests/Achievement Awards:* 10 ($15,000 total): general academic. *Special Characteristics Awards:* 8 ($6000 total): general special characteristics, local/state students.

Other Money-Saving Options Accelerated degree, co-op program. *Payment Plan:* installment. *Waivers:* full or partial for employees or children of employees.

Contact Toni Hudson, Financial Aid Counselor, Southeastern University, 501 I Street SW, DC 20024-2788, 202-488-8612 Ext. 234, fax: 202-488-8093.

SOUTHEAST MISSOURI STATE UNIVERSITY
Cape Girardeau, Missouri

About the Institution State-supported, coed. Degrees awarded: A, B, M. Offers 92 undergraduate majors. Total enrollment: 8,200. Undergraduates: 7,400 (84% state residents). Freshmen: 1,300.

Undergraduate Expenses (1997–98) State resident tuition: $2892. Nonresident tuition: $5372. Mandatory fees: $208. College room and board: $4000 (minimum). College room only: $2500 (minimum).

Applications 74% of all full-time undergraduates enrolled in fall 1996 applied for aid; of these, 78% were judged to have need according to Federal Methodology, of whom 95% were aided. *Financial aid deadline (priority):* 3/1. *Financial aid forms:* FAFSA required; CSS Financial Aid PROFILE, state form acceptable. *Admission application deadline:* 7/15.

Summary of Aid to Needy Students *From gift & self-help combined:* Average need met: 65%. Average amount awarded: $4417 (29% gift aid, 71% self-help). *Gift aid:* Total: $4,063,926 (29% from college's own funds, 13% from other college-administered sources, 58% from external sources). 749 part-time jobs.

Need-Based Scholarships & Grants Pell, FSEOG, state, private, college/university.

Loans Perkins, PLUS, Stafford, Unsubsidized Stafford, Federal Nursing, college/university long-term loans ($1959 average).

Non-Need Awards In 1996, a total of 1,320 non-need awards were made. *Academic Interests/Achievement Awards:* 991 ($2,863,928 total): general academic, agriculture, biological sciences, business, communication, computer science, education, English, foreign languages, health fields, home economics, humanities, mathematics, military science, physical sciences, social sciences. *Creative Arts/Performance Awards:* 96 ($17,910 total): music, theater/drama. *Special Achievements/*

Activities Awards: 23 ($4600 total): cheerleading/drum major, leadership. *Athletic:* Total: 210 ($1,216,939); Men: 132 ($724,751); Women: 78 ($492,188).

Other Money-Saving Options Accelerated degree, co-op program, Army ROTC, Air Force ROTC, off-campus living (after sophomore year). *Payment Plans:* installment, deferred payment. *Waivers:* full or partial for employees or children of employees and senior citizens.

Contact Office of Financial Aid, Southeast Missouri State University, One University Plaza, Cape Girardeau, MO 63701-4799, 573-651-2000.

SOUTHERN ADVENTIST UNIVERSITY
Collegedale, Tennessee

About the Institution Independent/religious, coed. Degrees awarded: A, B, M. Offers 42 undergraduate majors. Total enrollment: 1,650. Undergraduates: 1,625 (23% state residents). Freshmen: 401.

Undergraduate Expenses (1997–98) Comprehensive fee of $13,364 includes tuition ($9476), mandatory fees ($260), and college room and board ($3628). College room only: $1678.

Applications 52% of all full-time undergraduates enrolled in fall 1996 applied for aid; of these, 96% were judged to have need according to Federal Methodology, of whom 92% were aided. *Financial aid deadline (priority):* 3/1. *Financial aid forms:* FAFSA, institutional form, federal income tax forms, W-2 forms, and supporting documents required; state form acceptable. *Admission application deadline:* rolling.

Summary of Aid to Needy Students *From gift & self-help combined:* Average need met: 77%. Average amount awarded: $7368 (41% gift aid, 59% self-help). *Gift aid:* Total: $1,817,337 (64% from college's own funds, 14% from other college-administered sources, 22% from external sources). 386 Federal Work-Study jobs (averaging $1655); part-time jobs.

Need-Based Scholarships & Grants Pell, FSEOG, state, private, college/university.

Loans Perkins, PLUS, Stafford, Unsubsidized Stafford, Federal Nursing, state, private, college/university short-term loans ($1630 average).

Non-Need Awards In 1996, a total of 1,660 non-need awards were made. *Academic Interests/Achievement Awards:* general academic, business. *Creative Arts/Performance Awards:* art/fine arts, journalism/publications, music, theater/drama. *Special Achievements/Activities Awards:* general special achievements/activities, community service, leadership, religious involvement. *Special Characteristics Awards:* general special characteristics, international students, local/state students, members of minorities, out-of-state students.

Other Money-Saving Options Accelerated degree. *Payment Plans:* tuition prepayment, installment. *Waivers:* full or partial for employees or children of employees, adult students, senior citizens.

Contact Mr. Don E. Tucker, Director of Financial Aid, Southern Adventist University, PO Box 370, Collegedale, TN 37315-0370, 423-238-2834, fax: 423-238-3007.

SOUTHERN ARKANSAS UNIVERSITY– MAGNOLIA
Magnolia, Arkansas

About the Institution State-supported, coed. Degrees awarded: A, B, M. Offers 44 undergraduate majors. Total enrollment: 2,592. Undergraduates: 2,408 (77% state residents). Freshmen: 483.

Undergraduate Expenses (1997–98) State resident tuition: $1848. Nonresident tuition: $2856. Mandatory fees: $48. College room and board: $2530.

Applications 91% of all full-time undergraduates enrolled in fall 1996 applied for aid; of these, 91% were judged to have need according to Federal Methodology, of whom 100% were aided. *Financial aid deadline (priority):* 7/1. *Financial aid forms:* FAFSA, institutional form required. State form required for some. *Admission application deadline:* 8/15.

Summary of Aid to Needy Students *From gift & self-help combined:* Average need met: 100%. Average amount awarded: $5112 (33% gift aid, 67% self-help). *Gift aid:* Total: $2,199,248 (23% from college's own funds, 3% from other college-administered sources, 74% from external sources). Federal Work-Study jobs; 182 part-time jobs.

Need-Based Scholarships & Grants Pell, FSEOG, state, private, college/university.

Loans Perkins, PLUS, Stafford, Unsubsidized Stafford.

Non-Need Awards In 1996, a total of 741 non-need awards were made. *Academic Interests/Achievement Awards:* 186 ($337,166 total): general academic, agriculture. *Creative Arts/Performance Awards:* 91 ($148,416 total): art/fine arts, music, theater/drama. *Special Achievements/Activities Awards:* 64 ($64,563 total): cheerleading/drum major, leadership, rodeo. *Special Characteristics Awards:* 310 ($121,756 total): adult students, children of faculty/staff, out-of-state students. *Athletic:* Total: 90 ($241,362); Men: 68 ($180,422); Women: 22 ($60,940).

Other Money-Saving Options Accelerated degree, off-campus living (after junior year). *Payment Plans:* installment, deferred payment. *Waivers:* full or partial for children of alumni, employees or children of employees, senior citizens.

Contact Ms. Bronwyn C. Sneed, Director of Student Aid, Southern Arkansas University–Magnolia, SAU Box 1344, Magnolia, AR 71753, 870-235-4023, fax: 870-235-5005.

SOUTHERN CALIFORNIA COLLEGE
Costa Mesa, California

About the Institution Independent/religious, coed. Degrees awarded: B, M. Offers 37 undergraduate majors. Total enrollment: 1,226. Undergraduates: 1,084 (77% state residents). Freshmen: 201.

Undergraduate Expenses (1997–98) Comprehensive fee of $16,708 includes tuition ($11,320), mandatory fees ($528), and college room and board ($4860). College room only: $2700.

Applications 90% of all full-time undergraduates enrolled in fall 1996 applied for aid; of these, 87% were judged to have need according to Federal Methodology, of whom 100% were aided. *Financial aid deadline (priority):* 3/2. *Financial aid forms:* FAFSA required. State form required for some. *Admission application deadline:* rolling.

Summary of Aid to Needy Students *From gift & self-help combined:* Average need met: 80%. Average amount awarded: $13,499 (52% gift aid, 48% self-help). *Gift aid:* Total: $5,140,900. Federal Work-Study jobs; 196 part-time jobs.

Need-Based Scholarships & Grants Pell, FSEOG, state, college/university.

Loans Perkins, PLUS, Stafford, Unsubsidized Stafford, private, college/university short-term loans ($200 average).

Non-Need Awards *Academic Interests/Achievement Awards:* general academic. *Creative Arts/Performance Awards:* debating, music. *Special Characteristics Awards:* children of faculty/staff, relatives of clergy, religious affiliation. *Athletic:* Total: 127 ($660,000).

Other Money-Saving Options Accelerated degree, cooperative Army ROTC, cooperative Naval ROTC, cooperative Air Force ROTC. *Payment Plan:* installment. *Waivers:* full or partial for employees or children of employees.

Contact Admissions Office, Southern California College, 55 Fair Drive, Costa Mesa, CA 92626-6597, 800-SCC-6279.

SOUTHERN CALIFORNIA INSTITUTE OF ARCHITECTURE
Los Angeles, California

About the Institution Independent, coed. Degrees awarded: B, M. Offers 1 undergraduate major. Total enrollment: 430. Undergraduates: 218 (50% state residents). Freshmen: 44.

Undergraduate Expenses (1996–97) Tuition: $13,800. Mandatory fees: $190.

Applications Of all full-time undergraduates enrolled in fall 1996, 99% of those who applied for aid were judged to have need according to Federal Methodology, of whom 100% were aided. *Financial aid deadline (priority):* 5/30. *Financial aid forms:* FAFSA, institutional form required. *Admission application deadline:* rolling.

Summary of Aid to Needy Students *From gift & self-help combined:* Average amount awarded: $8195 (32% gift aid, 68% self-help). *Gift aid:* Total: $475,000. Federal Work-Study jobs; 50 part-time jobs.

Need-Based Scholarships & Grants Pell, FSEOG, state, private, college/university.

Loans PLUS, Stafford, Unsubsidized Stafford, private.

Non-Need Awards In 1996, a total of 4 non-need awards were made. *Creative Arts/Performance Awards:* 4 ($2800 total): general creative.

Other Money-Saving Options Co-op program. *Waivers:* full or partial for employees or children of employees.

Contact Financial Aid Office, Southern California Institute of Architecture, Los Angeles, CA 90066-7017, 310-574-1123 Ext. 345.

SOUTHERN CHRISTIAN UNIVERSITY
Montgomery, Alabama

About the Institution Independent/religious, primarily men. Degrees awarded: B, M, D, P. Offers 4 undergraduate majors. Total enrollment: 188. Undergraduates: 57. Freshmen: 40.

Undergraduate Expenses (1997–98) Tuition: $6576. Mandatory fees: $450.

Applications 100% of all full-time undergraduates enrolled in fall 1996 applied for aid; of these, 62% were judged to have need according to Federal Methodology, of whom 100% were aided. *Financial aid deadline (priority):* 7/1. *Financial aid forms:* FAFSA, institutional form required.

Summary of Aid to Needy Students *From gift & self-help combined:* Average need met: 100%. Average amount awarded: $2829 (50% gift aid, 50% self-help). *Gift aid:* Total: $7106 (35% from college's own funds, 14% from other college-administered sources, 51% from external sources). Federal Work-Study jobs.

Need-Based Scholarships & Grants Pell, FSEOG, private, college/university.

Loans Stafford, Unsubsidized Stafford.

Non-Need Awards Not offered.

Contact Ms. Dot Fuller, Director of Financial Aid, Southern Christian University, 1200 Taylor Road, Montgomery, AL 36117, 334-277-2277.

SOUTHERN COLLEGE OF TECHNOLOGY
Marietta, Georgia

See Southern Polytechnic State University

SOUTHERN CONNECTICUT STATE UNIVERSITY
New Haven, Connecticut

About the Institution State-supported, coed. Degrees awarded: A, B, M. Offers 57 undergraduate majors. Total enrollment: 11,412. Undergraduates: 7,568 (92% state residents). Freshmen: 1,009.

Undergraduate Expenses (1997–98) State resident tuition: $2062. Nonresident tuition: $6674. Mandatory fees: $1506 (minimum). College room and board: $5366. College room only: $2774.

Applications *Financial aid deadline:* Applications processed continuously. *Financial aid forms:* FAFSA, institutional form, parent and student federal income tax forms required. *Admission application deadline:* 7/1.

Summary of Aid to Needy Students *From gift & self-help combined:* Average need met: 70%. Average amount awarded: $3963 (35% gift aid, 65% self-help). *Gift aid:* Total: $4,331,491 (42% from college's own funds, 18% from other college-administered sources, 40% from external sources). 150 Federal Work-Study jobs (averaging $1867); 500 part-time jobs.

Need-Based Scholarships & Grants Pell, FSEOG, state, college/university.

Loans Perkins, PLUS, Stafford, Unsubsidized Stafford, state.

Non-Need Awards *Academic Interests/Achievement Awards:* 90 ($276,000 total): general academic. *Special Characteristics Awards:* children of faculty/staff, ROTC participants, veterans. *Athletic:* Total: 62 ($241,000).

Other Money-Saving Options Accelerated degree, co-op program, cooperative Army ROTC, cooperative Air Force ROTC. *Payment Plan:* installment. *Waivers:* full or partial for senior citizens.

Contact Office of Financial Aid, Southern Connecticut State University, 501 Crescent Street, New Haven, CT 06515-1355, 203-392-5200.

SOUTHERN ILLINOIS UNIVERSITY AT CARBONDALE
Carbondale, Illinois

About the Institution State-supported, coed. Degrees awarded: A, B, M, D, P. Offers 155 undergraduate majors. Total enrollment: 21,863. Undergraduates: 17,725 (83% state residents). Freshmen: 2,366.

Undergraduate Expenses (1997–98) State resident tuition: $2700. Nonresident tuition: $8100. Mandatory fees: $560. College room and board: $3472.

Applications Of all full-time undergraduates enrolled in fall 1996, 100% of those judged to have need according to Federal Methodology were aided. *Financial aid deadline (priority):* 4/1. *Financial aid forms:* FAFSA required; state form acceptable. *Admission application deadline:* rolling.

Summary of Aid to Needy Students *From gift & self-help combined:* Average need met: 100%. Average amount awarded: $5800 (50% gift aid, 50% self-help). *Gift aid:* Total: $37,455,000 (10% from college's own funds, 3% from other college-administered sources, 87% from external sources). 3,000 Federal Work-Study jobs (averaging $1200); 5,200 part-time jobs.

Need-Based Scholarships & Grants Pell, FSEOG, state, private, college/university.

Loans Perkins, PLUS, Stafford, Unsubsidized Stafford, college/university short-term loans ($310 average), college/university long-term loans ($2270 average).

Non-Need Awards In 1996, a total of 1,286 non-need awards were made. *Academic Interests/Achievement Awards:* 1,000 ($1,600,000 total): general academic. *Athletic:* Total: 286 ($1,313,000); Men: 178 ($815,000); Women: 108 ($498,000).

Other Money-Saving Options Accelerated degree, co-op program, Army ROTC, Air Force ROTC, off-campus living (after freshman year). *Payment Plan:* installment. *Waivers:* full or partial for employees or children of employees and senior citizens.

Contact Ms. Pamela Britton, Director of Financial Aid, Southern Illinois University at Carbondale, Woody Hall, Third Floor, B-Wing, Carbondale, IL 62901-4702, 618-453-4334.

SOUTHERN ILLINOIS UNIVERSITY AT EDWARDSVILLE
Edwardsville, Illinois

About the Institution State-supported, coed. Degrees awarded: B, M, P. Offers 62 undergraduate majors. Total enrollment: 11,151. Undergraduates: 8,610 (87% state residents). Freshmen: 1,274.

Undergraduate Expenses (1996–97) State resident tuition: $1928. Nonresident tuition: $5785. Mandatory fees: $541. College room and board: $3960. College room only: $2190.

Applications Of all full-time undergraduates enrolled in fall 1996, 75% of those who applied for aid were judged to have need according to Federal Methodology, of whom 92% were aided. *Financial aid deadline (priority):* 3/1. *Financial aid forms:* FAFSA required. *Admission application deadline:* 8/4.

Summary of Aid to Needy Students *From gift & self-help combined:* Average need met: 95%. Average amount awarded: $5939 (43% gift aid, 57% self-help). *Gift aid:* Total: $10,766,701 (6% from college's own funds, 7% from other college-administered sources, 87% from external sources). 478 Federal Work-Study jobs (averaging $1073); 1,800 part-time jobs.

Need-Based Scholarships & Grants Pell, FSEOG, state, private, college/university.

Loans Perkins, PLUS, Stafford, Unsubsidized Stafford, college/university short-term loans ($150 average), college/university long-term loans ($500 average).

Non-Need Awards In 1996, a total of 225 non-need awards were made. *Academic Interests/Achievement Awards:* 105 ($138,492 total): general academic. *Creative Arts/Performance Awards:* 12 ($23,136 total): art/fine arts, music, theater/drama. *Athletic:* Total: 108 ($155,299).

Other Money-Saving Options Accelerated degree, co-op program, Army ROTC, Air Force ROTC, off-campus living. *Payment Plans:* installment, deferred payment. *Waivers:* full or partial for employees or children of employees.

Contact Office of Financial Aid, Southern Illinois University at Edwardsville, Box 1060, Rendleman Hall, Rm. 2308, Edwardsville, IL 62026-0001, 618-692-2000.

SOUTHERN METHODIST UNIVERSITY
Dallas, Texas

About the Institution Independent/religious, coed. Degrees awarded: B, M, D, P. Offers 75 undergraduate majors. Total enrollment: 9,464. Undergraduates: 5,362 (60% state residents). Freshmen: 1,218.

Undergraduate Expenses (1997–98) Comprehensive fee of $26,926 includes tuition ($16,790), mandatory fees ($2400), and college room and board ($7736 minimum). College room only: $3520 (minimum).

Applications Of all full-time undergraduates enrolled in fall 1996, 90% of those who applied for aid were judged to have need according to Federal Methodology, of whom 100% were aided. *Financial aid deadline (priority):* 1/15. *Financial aid forms:* FAFSA required. *Regular admission application deadline:* 4/1. Early action deadline: 11/1.

Summary of Aid to Needy Students *From gift & self-help combined:* Average need met: 40%. Average amount awarded: $7554 (58% gift aid, 42% self-help). *Gift aid:* Total: $15,028,027 (74% from college's own funds, 16% from other college-administered sources, 10% from external sources). 1,315 Federal Work-Study jobs (averaging $1750); 104 part-time jobs.

Need-Based Scholarships & Grants Pell, FSEOG, state, college/university.

Loans Perkins, PLUS, Stafford, Unsubsidized Stafford, state, private, college/university short-term loans ($1802 average), college/university long-term loans ($10,013 average).

Non-Need Awards In 1996, a total of 3,208 non-need awards were made. *Academic Interests/Achievement Awards:* 2,205 ($5,642,086 total): general academic, biological sciences, business, communication, computer science, engineering/technologies, humanities, mathematics, physical sciences. *Creative Arts/Performance Awards:* 591 ($2,501,412 total): art/fine arts, dance, music, theater/drama. *Special Characteristics Awards:* 152 ($1,623,442 total): children of faculty/staff, relatives of clergy. *Athletic:* Total: 260 ($4,033,713); Men: 168 ($2,655,798); Women: 92 ($1,377,915).

Other Money-Saving Options Co-op program, cooperative Army ROTC, cooperative Air Force ROTC, off-campus living (after freshman year). *Payment Plans:* tuition prepayment, installment. *Waivers:* full or partial for employees or children of employees.

Contact Mr. Russ Jeffrey, Associate Director, Southern Methodist University, Box 750196, Dallas, TX 75275, 214-768-3417, fax: 214-768-3878.

SOUTHERN NAZARENE UNIVERSITY
Bethany, Oklahoma

About the Institution Independent/religious, coed. Degrees awarded: A, B, M. Offers 67 undergraduate majors. Total enrollment: 1,828. Undergraduates: 1,578 (65% state residents). Freshmen: 307.

Undergraduate Expenses (1997–98) Comprehensive fee of $12,190 includes tuition ($7860), mandatory fees ($362), and college room and board ($3968). College room only: $1896.

Applications Of all full-time undergraduates enrolled in fall 1996, 91% of those who applied for aid were judged to have need according to Federal Methodology, of whom 100% were aided. *Financial aid deadline (priority):* 3/1. *Financial aid forms:* FAFSA or CSS Financial Aid PROFILE required. *Admission application deadline:* 8/15.

Summary of Aid to Needy Students *From gift & self-help combined:* Average need met: 60%. Average amount awarded: $3500 (49% gift aid, 51% self-help). *Gift aid:* Total: $4,508,315 (60% from college's own funds, 11% from other college-administered sources, 29% from external sources). Federal Work-Study jobs; part-time jobs.

Need-Based Scholarships & Grants Pell, FSEOG, state, private, college/university.

Loans Perkins, PLUS, Stafford, Unsubsidized Stafford.

Non-Need Awards *Academic Interests/Achievement Awards:* general academic. *Creative Arts/Performance Awards:* music, performing arts. *Special Characteristics Awards:* local/state students, religious affiliation. *Athletic:* available.

Other Money-Saving Options Accelerated degree, cooperative Army ROTC. *Payment Plans:* tuition prepayment, installment. *Waivers:* full or partial for employees or children of employees and senior citizens.

Contact Ms. Diana Lee, Director of Financial Assistance, Southern Nazarene University, 6729 Northwest 39 Expressway, Bethany, OK 73008-2694, 405-789-6400.

SOUTHERN OREGON UNIVERSITY
Ashland, Oregon

About the Institution State-supported, coed. Degrees awarded: A, B, M. Offers 38 undergraduate majors. Total enrollment: 4,247. Undergraduates: 4,038 (82% state residents). Freshmen: 870.

Undergraduate Expenses (1996–97) State resident tuition: $3147. Nonresident tuition: $8847. College room and board: $4200.

Applications Of all full-time undergraduates enrolled in fall 1996, 91% of those who applied for aid were judged to have need according to Federal Methodology, of whom 71% were aided. *Financial aid deadline (priority):* 2/1. *Financial aid forms:* FAFSA required. *Admission application deadline:* rolling.

Summary of Aid to Needy Students *From gift & self-help combined:* Average need met: 66%. Average amount awarded: $7478 (43% gift aid, 57% self-help). *Gift aid:* Total: $6,278,942 (23% from college's own funds, 32% from other college-administered sources, 45% from external sources). 500 Federal Work-Study jobs (averaging $1000); 425 part-time jobs.

Need-Based Scholarships & Grants Pell, FSEOG, state, private, college/university.

Loans Perkins, PLUS, Stafford, Unsubsidized Stafford, college/university short-term loans ($200 average), college/university long-term loans ($500 average).

Non-Need Awards In 1996, a total of 607 non-need awards were made. *Academic Interests/Achievement Awards:* 273 ($303,767 total): general academic, biological sciences, business, education, mathematics, physical sciences, social sciences. *Creative Arts/Performance Awards:* 44 ($17,825 total): art/fine arts, music, theater/drama. *Special Achievements/Activities Awards:* 13 ($29,182 total): general special achievements/activities, leadership. *Special Characteristics Awards:* 224 ($803,706 total): general special characteristics, children of faculty/staff, international students, members of minorities, out-of-state students. *Athletic:* Total: 53 ($35,903); Men: 35 ($24,703); Women: 18 ($11,200).

Other Money-Saving Options Accelerated degree, co-op program, off-campus living. *Payment Plan:* deferred payment. *Waivers:* full or partial for minority students.

Contact Ms. Constance Alexander, Director of Financial Aid, Southern Oregon University, 1250 Siskiyou Boulevard, Ashland, OR 97520-5066, 541-552-6161, fax: 541-552-6035.

SOUTHERN POLYTECHNIC STATE UNIVERSITY
Marietta, Georgia

About the Institution State-supported, coed. Degrees awarded: A, B, M. Offers 19 undergraduate majors. Total enrollment: 3,871. Undergraduates: 3,296 (93% state residents). Freshmen: 375.

Undergraduate Expenses (1996–97) State resident tuition: $1584. Nonresident tuition: $5463. Mandatory fees: $267. College room and board: $3930. College room only: $1725 (minimum).

Applications Of all full-time undergraduates enrolled in fall 1996, 70% of those who applied for aid were judged to have need according to Federal Methodology, of whom 84% were aided. *Financial aid deadline (priority):* 3/15. *Financial aid forms:* FAFSA, institutional form required; CSS Financial Aid PROFILE acceptable. *Admission application deadline:* 8/31.

Summary of Aid to Needy Students *From gift & self-help combined:* Average need met: 85%. Average amount awarded: $3645 (34% gift aid, 66% self-help). *Gift aid:* Total: $1,225,978 (1% from college's own funds, 6% from other college-administered sources, 93% from external sources). 45 Federal Work-Study jobs (averaging $1200); 225 part-time jobs.

Need-Based Scholarships & Grants Pell, FSEOG, state, private, college/university.

Loans Perkins, PLUS, Stafford, Unsubsidized Stafford, college/university short-term loans ($500 average).

Non-Need Awards In 1996, a total of 64 non-need awards were made. *Academic Interests/Achievement Awards:* 23 ($36,459 total): general

academic. *Special Achievements/Activities Awards:* 11 ($55,000 total): general special achievements/activities. *Athletic:* Total: 30 ($105,119); Men: 30 ($105,119); Women: 0.

Other Money-Saving Options Accelerated degree, co-op program, cooperative Army ROTC, cooperative Naval ROTC, cooperative Air Force ROTC, off-campus living. *Waivers:* full or partial for senior citizens.

Contact Dr. Emerelle McNair, Director of Financial Aid, Southern Polytechnic State University, 1100 South Marietta Parkway, Marietta, GA 30060-2896, 770-528-7290, fax: 770-528-7301.

SOUTHERN UNIVERSITY AND AGRICULTURAL AND MECHANICAL COLLEGE
Baton Rouge, Louisiana

About the Institution State-supported, coed. Degrees awarded: A, B, M, D, P. Offers 95 undergraduate majors. Total enrollment: 9,800. Undergraduates: 7,300 (75% state residents). Freshmen: 2,000.

Undergraduate Expenses (1996–97) State resident tuition: $2028. Nonresident tuition: $4808. College room and board: $3022.

Applications *Financial aid deadline (priority):* 7/15. *Financial aid forms:* FAFSA required; CSS Financial Aid PROFILE, state form acceptable. *Admission application deadline:* 7/1.

Summary of Aid to Needy Students *From gift & self-help combined:* Average need met: 93%. Average amount awarded: $6500 (39% gift aid, 61% self-help). *Gift aid:* Total: $11,050,740 (6% from college-administered sources, 94% from external sources). Federal Work-Study jobs; part-time jobs.

Need-Based Scholarships & Grants Pell, FSEOG, state, private, college/university.

Loans PLUS, Stafford, Unsubsidized Stafford, college/university short-term loans ($50 average).

Non-Need Awards *Academic Interests/Achievement Awards:* general academic. *Athletic:* available.

Other Money-Saving Options Co-op program, Army ROTC, Naval ROTC, cooperative Air Force ROTC, off-campus living.

Contact Office of Financial Aid, Southern University and Agricultural and Mechanical College, PO Box 9961, Baton Rouge, LA 70813, 504-771-4500.

SOUTHERN UNIVERSITY AT NEW ORLEANS
New Orleans, Louisiana

About the Institution State-supported, coed. Degrees awarded: A, B, M. Offers 20 undergraduate majors.

Applications 85% of all full-time undergraduates enrolled in fall 1996 applied for aid; of these, 90% were judged to have need according to Federal Methodology, of whom 100% were aided. *Financial aid deadline (priority):* 4/15. *Financial aid forms:* FAFSA, state form required; institutional form acceptable. *Admission application deadline:* 7/1.

Summary of Aid to Needy Students 175 Federal Work-Study jobs (averaging $1530); 100 part-time jobs.

Need-Based Scholarships & Grants Pell, FSEOG, state.

Loans Stafford, Unsubsidized Stafford.

Non-Need Awards In 1996, a total of 116 non-need awards were made. *Academic Interests/Achievement Awards:* 40 ($40,000 total): biological sciences, physical sciences. *Creative Arts/Performance Awards:* 30 ($9600 total): music. *Athletic:* Total: 46 ($76,452); Men: 21 ($34,902); Women: 25 ($41,550).

Other Money-Saving Options Cooperative Army ROTC, cooperative Air Force ROTC.

Contact Ms. Ursula J. Shorty, Director of Financial Aid, Southern University at New Orleans, 6400 Press Drive, New Orleans, LA 70126-1009, 504-286-5263, fax: 504-286-5213.

SOUTHERN UTAH UNIVERSITY
Cedar City, Utah

About the Institution State-supported, coed. Degrees awarded: A, B, M. Offers 50 undergraduate majors. Total enrollment: 5,640. Undergraduates: 5,426 (90% state residents). Freshmen: 1,011.

Undergraduate Expenses (1996–97) State resident tuition: $1386. Nonresident tuition: $5238. Mandatory fees: $414. College room and board: $2070 (minimum). College room only: $1440.

Applications *Financial aid deadline (priority):* 8/10. *Financial aid forms:* FAFSA, institutional form required. *Admission application deadline:* 7/1.

Summary of Aid to Needy Students *Gift aid:* Total: $6,197,429 (3% from college's own funds, 6% from other college-administered sources, 91% from external sources). 286 Federal Work-Study jobs (averaging $926); 461 part-time jobs.

Need-Based Scholarships & Grants Pell, FSEOG, state.

Loans Perkins, PLUS, Stafford, Unsubsidized Stafford, college/university short-term loans ($891 average).

Non-Need Awards *Academic Interests/Achievement Awards:* general academic, business, communication, education. *Creative Arts/Performance Awards:* general creative, dance, journalism/publications, music, performing arts, theater/drama. *Special Achievements/Activities Awards:* general special achievements/activities, cheerleading/drum major, leadership. *Special Characteristics Awards:* ethnic background. *Athletic:* available.

Other Money-Saving Options Accelerated degree, co-op program, off-campus living. *Waivers:* full or partial for employees or children of employees.

Contact Mr. Rex Michie, Director of Financial Aid, Southern Utah University, Cedar City, UT 84720-2498, 801-586-7735.

SOUTHERN VERMONT COLLEGE
Bennington, Vermont

About the Institution Independent, coed. Degrees awarded: A, B. Offers 17 undergraduate majors. Total enrollment: 616 (43% state residents). Freshmen: 135.

Undergraduate Expenses (1997–98) Comprehensive fee of $16,234 includes tuition ($11,130), mandatory fees ($170), and college room and board ($4934). College room only: $2394.

Applications 87% of all full-time undergraduates enrolled in fall 1996 applied for aid; of these, 93% were judged to have need according to Federal Methodology, of whom 100% were aided. *Financial aid deadline (priority):* 5/1. *Financial aid forms:* FAFSA, institutional form required; CSS Financial Aid PROFILE acceptable. *Admission application deadline:* rolling.

Summary of Aid to Needy Students *From gift & self-help combined:* Average need met: 100%. Average amount awarded: $12,807 (52% gift aid, 48% self-help). *Gift aid:* Total: $2,045,368 (68% from college's own funds, 5% from other college-administered sources, 27% from external sources). 115 Federal Work-Study jobs (averaging $1500); part-time jobs.

Need-Based Scholarships & Grants Pell, FSEOG, state, private, college/university.

Loans PLUS, Stafford, Unsubsidized Stafford.

Non-Need Awards Not offered.

Other Money-Saving Options Accelerated degree, off-campus living (after freshman year). *Payment Plans:* installment, deferred payment. *Waivers:* full or partial for employees or children of employees.

Contact Ms. Cathleen Seaton, Director of Financial Aid, Southern Vermont College, Monument Avenue, Bennington, VT 05201-2128, 802-447-6330.

SOUTHERN WESLEYAN UNIVERSITY
Central, South Carolina

About the Institution Independent/religious, coed. Degrees awarded: A, B, M. Offers 26 undergraduate majors. Total enrollment: 1,298. Undergraduates: 1,214 (83% state residents). Freshmen: 77.

Undergraduate Expenses (1997–98) Comprehensive fee of $13,720 includes tuition ($9980), mandatory fees ($200), and college room and board ($3540). College room only: $1210.

Applications 84% of all full-time undergraduates enrolled in fall 1996 applied for aid; of these, 96% were judged to have need according to Federal Methodology, of whom 100% were aided. *Financial aid deadline (priority):* 4/15. *Financial aid forms:* institutional form required. FAFSA, state form required for some. *Admission application deadline:* 8/10.

Summary of Aid to Needy Students *From gift & self-help combined:* Average need met: 85%. Average amount awarded: $7119 (26% gift aid, 74% self-help). *Gift aid:* Total: $1,740,267 (48% from college's own funds, 29% from other college-administered sources, 23% from external sources). 101 Federal Work-Study jobs (averaging $800); 28 part-time jobs.

Need-Based Scholarships & Grants Pell, FSEOG, state, private.

Loans Perkins, PLUS, Stafford, Unsubsidized Stafford.

Non-Need Awards In 1996, a total of 480 non-need awards were made. *Academic Interests/Achievement Awards:* 64 ($116,574 total): general academic, education, English, mathematics, religion/biblical studies, social sciences. *Creative Arts/Performance Awards:* 13 ($16,000 total): music, theater/drama. *Special Achievements/Activities Awards:* 83 ($182,000 total): community service, leadership, religious involvement. *Special Characteristics Awards:* 229 ($350,998 total): children of faculty/staff, relatives of clergy, religious affiliation, siblings of current students. *Athletic:* Total: 91 ($361,760); Men: 55 ($249,843); Women: 36 ($111,917).

Other Money-Saving Options Accelerated degree, cooperative Army ROTC, cooperative Air Force ROTC, off-campus living (after junior year). *Payment Plan:* installment. *Waivers:* full or partial for employees or children of employees and senior citizens.

Contact Ms. Wanda Marshall, Financial Aid Assistant, Southern Wesleyan University, One Wesleyan Drive, Central, SC 29630-1020, 800-289-1292, fax: 864-639-1956.

SOUTHWEST BAPTIST UNIVERSITY
Bolivar, Missouri

About the Institution Independent/religious, coed. Degrees awarded: A, B, M. Offers 41 undergraduate majors. Total enrollment: 3,096. Undergraduates: 2,498 (81% state residents). Freshmen: 485.

Undergraduate Expenses (1996–97) Comprehensive fee of $10,495 includes tuition ($7708), mandatory fees ($164), and college room and board ($2623). College room only: $1230.

Applications *Financial aid deadline (priority):* 3/30. *Financial aid forms:* FAFSA, institutional form required; CSS Financial Aid PROFILE acceptable. *Admission application deadline:* 9/6.

Summary of Aid to Needy Students 800 Federal Work-Study jobs (averaging $900); 75 part-time jobs.

Need-Based Scholarships & Grants Pell, FSEOG, state, private, college/university.

Loans Perkins, PLUS, Stafford, Unsubsidized Stafford, college/university short-term loans ($250 average).

Non-Need Awards In 1996, a total of 1,262 non-need awards were made. *Academic Interests/Achievement Awards:* 742 ($547,308 total): general academic, communication. *Creative Arts/Performance Awards:* 145 ($98,600 total): general creative, music, theater/drama. *Special Characteristics Awards:* 205 ($116,125 total): local/state students, relatives of clergy. *Athletic:* Total: 170 ($833,163); Men: 119 ($560,105); Women: 51 ($273,058).

Other Money-Saving Options Accelerated degree, co-op program, cooperative Army ROTC. *Payment Plan:* installment. *Waivers:* full or partial for employees or children of employees and senior citizens.

Contact Mr. Brad Gamble, Associate Director of Student Financial Services, Southwest Baptist University, 1600 University Avenue, Bolivar, MO 65613-2597, 417-326-1823.

SOUTHWESTERN ADVENTIST UNIVERSITY
Keene, Texas

About the Institution Independent/religious, coed. Degrees awarded: A, B, M. Offers 25 undergraduate majors. Total enrollment: 1,030. Undergraduates: 1,016 (54% state residents). Freshmen: 211.

Undergraduate Expenses (1996–97) Comprehensive fee of $12,018 includes tuition ($7992), mandatory fees ($100), and college room and board ($3926).

Applications 78% of all full-time undergraduates enrolled in fall 1996 applied for aid; of these, 94% were judged to have need according to Federal Methodology, of whom 96% were aided. *Financial aid deadline (priority):* 7/15. *Financial aid forms:* FAFSA, CSS Financial Aid PROFILE, institutional form required. *Admission application deadline:* rolling.

Summary of Aid to Needy Students *From gift & self-help combined:* Average need met: 82%. Average amount awarded: $7554 (54% gift aid, 46% self-help). *Gift aid:* Total: $2,067,343 (42% from college's own funds, 15% from other college-administered sources, 43% from external sources). 73 Federal Work-Study jobs (averaging $1685); 330 part-time jobs.

Need-Based Scholarships & Grants Pell, FSEOG, state, private, college/university.

Loans Perkins, PLUS, Stafford, Unsubsidized Stafford, state, private, college/university short-term loans ($3000 average).

Non-Need Awards In 1996, a total of 432 non-need awards were made. *Academic Interests/Achievement Awards:* 176 ($225,828 total): general academic, education, English, humanities, premedicine, religion/biblical studies. *Creative Arts/Performance Awards:* 12 ($2100 total): music, theater/drama. *Special Achievements/Activities Awards:* 188 ($238,331 total): community service, leadership, religious involvement. *Special Characteristics Awards:* 30 ($37,754 total): children of faculty/staff, married students, siblings of current students. *Athletic:* Total: 26 ($18,217); Men: 10 ($7597); Women: 16 ($10,620).

Other Money-Saving Options Accelerated degree, co-op program. *Payment Plan:* installment. *Waivers:* full or partial for employees or children of employees.

Contact Ms. Sandie Adams, Assistant Financial Aid Director, Southwestern Adventist University, PO Box 567, Keene, TX 76059, 817-645-3921 Ext. 595, fax: 817-556-4744.

SOUTHWESTERN ASSEMBLIES OF GOD UNIVERSITY
Waxahachie, Texas

About the Institution Independent/religious, coed. Degrees awarded: A, B. Offers 14 undergraduate majors.

Undergraduate Expenses (1996–97) Comprehensive fee of $7792 includes tuition ($4092), mandatory fees ($310), and college room and board ($3390).

Applications 79% of all full-time undergraduates enrolled in fall 1996 applied for aid; of these, 94% were judged to have need according to Federal Methodology, of whom 94% were aided. *Financial aid deadline (priority):* 3/1. *Financial aid forms:* FAFSA, institutional form, financial aid transcript (for transfers) required. State form required for some. *Admission application deadline:* rolling.

Summary of Aid to Needy Students *From gift & self-help combined:* Average need met: 60%. Average amount awarded: $5802 (32% gift aid, 68% self-help). *Gift aid:* Total: $1,493,909 (20% from college's own funds, 22% from other college-administered sources, 58% from external sources). Federal Work-Study jobs; 36 part-time jobs.

Need-Based Scholarships & Grants Pell, FSEOG, state, private, college/university.

Loans Perkins, PLUS, Stafford, Unsubsidized Stafford, state, private.

Non-Need Awards In 1996, a total of 460 non-need awards were made. *Academic Interests/Achievement Awards:* 76 ($104,442 total): general academic, business, communication, education, foreign languages, religion/biblical studies, social sciences. *Creative Arts/Performance Awards:* 103 ($68,644 total): general creative, art/fine arts, creative writing, journalism/publications, music, performing arts, theater/drama. *Special Achievements/Activities Awards:* 78 ($38,750 total): general special achievements/activities, leadership, religious involvement. *Special Characteristics Awards:* 203 ($169,525 total): children of faculty/staff, relatives of clergy, spouses of current students.

Other Money-Saving Options *Payment Plans:* guaranteed tuition, installment.

Contact Ms. Myrna Wycoff, Director of Financial Aid, Southwestern Assemblies of God University, 1200 Sycamore Street, Waxahachie, TX 75165-2342, 972-937-4010.

SOUTHWESTERN CHRISTIAN COLLEGE
Terrell, Texas

About the Institution Independent/religious, coed. Degrees awarded: A, B. Offers 12 undergraduate majors. Total enrollment: 198 (58% state residents). Freshmen: 95.

Undergraduate Expenses (1997–98 estimated) Comprehensive fee of $8012 includes tuition ($4847), mandatory fees ($303), and college room and board ($2862).

Applications Of all full-time undergraduates enrolled in fall 1996, 96% of those who applied for aid were judged to have need according to Federal Methodology, of whom 100% were aided. *Financial aid deadline (priority):* 7/15. *Financial aid forms:* FAFSA, CSS Financial Aid PROFILE required. *Admission application deadline:* 7/15.

Summary of Aid to Needy Students *From gift & self-help combined:* Average need met: 80%. Average amount awarded: $2961 (56% gift aid, 44% self-help). *Gift aid:* Total: $260,425 (36% from college's own funds, 31% from other college-administered sources, 33% from external sources). 137 Federal Work-Study jobs (averaging $591).

Need-Based Scholarships & Grants Pell, FSEOG, state, private, college/university.

Loans PLUS, Stafford, Unsubsidized Stafford.

Non-Need Awards In 1996, a total of 73 non-need awards were made. *Academic Interests/Achievement Awards:* 3 ($1350 total): general academic. *Creative Arts/Performance Awards:* 15 ($8200 total): music. *Special Characteristics Awards:* 18 ($32,182 total): children of faculty/staff, local/state students. *Athletic:* Total: 37 ($94,394); Men: 22 ($64,759); Women: 15 ($29,635).

Another Money-Saving Option Off-campus living.

Contact Ms. Felicia Robinson, Financial Aid Director, Southwestern Christian College, 200 Bowser Circle, Terrell, TX 75160-0010, 972-524-3341, fax: 972-563-7133.

SOUTHWESTERN COLLEGE
Phoenix, Arizona

About the Institution Independent/religious, coed. Degrees awarded: A, B. Offers 8 undergraduate majors.

Undergraduate Expenses (1996–97) Comprehensive fee of $8950 includes tuition ($6000), mandatory fees ($300), and college room and board ($2650). College room only: $1900.

Applications 90% of all full-time undergraduates enrolled in fall 1996 applied for aid; of these, 95% were judged to have need according to Federal Methodology, of whom 100% were aided. *Financial aid deadline (priority):* 4/15. *Financial aid forms:* FAFSA required. *Admission application deadline:* 8/15.

Summary of Aid to Needy Students *From gift & self-help combined:* Average need met: 90%. Average amount awarded: $4767 (40% gift aid, 60% self-help). *Gift aid:* Total: $328,785. Federal Work-Study jobs; part-time jobs.

Need-Based Scholarships & Grants Pell, FSEOG, state, college/university.

Loans Perkins, PLUS, Stafford, Unsubsidized Stafford.

Non-Need Awards *Academic Interests/Achievement Awards:* general academic. *Creative Arts/Performance Awards:* music. *Special Achievements/Activities Awards:* leadership. *Special Characteristics Awards:* children and siblings of alumni, relatives of clergy, religious affiliation, siblings of current students.

Another Money-Saving Option Accelerated degree.

Contact Ms. Sheri Doerksen, Director of Financial Aid, Southwestern College, 2625 East Cactus Road, Phoenix, AZ 85032-7097, 602-992-6101, fax: 602-404-2159.

SOUTHWESTERN COLLEGE
Winfield, Kansas

About the Institution Independent/religious, coed. Degrees awarded: B, M. Offers 32 undergraduate majors. Total enrollment: 649. Undergraduates: 635 (85% state residents). Freshmen: 103.

Undergraduate Expenses (1997–98) Comprehensive fee of $13,100 includes tuition ($9260) and college room and board ($3840). College room only: $1680.

Applications Of all full-time undergraduates enrolled in fall 1996, 91% of those who applied for aid were judged to have need according to Federal Methodology, of whom 100% were aided. *Financial aid deadline (priority):* 4/1. *Financial aid forms:* institutional form required; CSS Financial Aid PROFILE acceptable. FAFSA, state form required for some. *Admission application deadline:* 8/1.

Summary of Aid to Needy Students *From gift & self-help combined:* Average need met: 86%. Average amount awarded: $11,095 (60% gift aid, 40% self-help). *Gift aid:* Total: $2,681,514 (64% from college's own funds, 17% from other college-administered sources, 19% from external sources). 146 Federal Work-Study jobs (averaging $1100); 85 part-time jobs.

Need-Based Scholarships & Grants Pell, FSEOG, state, college/university.

Loans Perkins, PLUS, Stafford, Unsubsidized Stafford, private.

Non-Need Awards In 1996, a total of 1,012 non-need awards were made. *Academic Interests/Achievement Awards:* 292 ($774,586 total): general academic, biological sciences, business, humanities. *Creative Arts/Performance Awards:* 203 ($218,581 total): cinema/film/broadcasting, debating, journalism/publications, music, theater/drama.

Special Achievements/Activities Awards: 59 ($57,285 total): cheerleading/drum major, community service, leadership, religious involvement. *Special Characteristics Awards:* 136 ($191,320 total): children and siblings of alumni, children of current students, children of faculty/staff, ethnic background, international students, local/state students, members of minorities, relatives of clergy, religious affiliation, siblings of current students. *Athletic:* Total: 322 ($344,476); Men: 227 ($248,126); Women: 95 ($96,350).

Other Money-Saving Options Off-campus living (after sophomore year). *Payment Plan:* installment. *Waivers:* full or partial for employees or children of employees and senior citizens.

Contact Mrs. Margaret Robinson, Director of Financial Aid, Southwestern College, 100 College Street, Winfield, KS 67156-2499, 316-221-8215.

SOUTHWESTERN COLLEGE OF CHRISTIAN MINISTRIES
Bethany, Oklahoma

About the Institution Independent/religious, coed. Degrees awarded: A, B, M. Offers 8 undergraduate majors. Total enrollment: 222. Undergraduates: 160 (72% state residents). Freshmen: 31.

Undergraduate Expenses (1997–98) Comprehensive fee of $7024 includes tuition ($4224), mandatory fees ($100), and college room and board ($2700).

Applications *Financial aid deadline (priority):* 7/1. *Financial aid forms:* FAFSA, institutional form required. *Admission application deadline:* rolling.

Summary of Aid to Needy Students Federal Work-Study jobs.

Loans College/university short-term loans.

Non-Need Awards *Academic Interests/Achievement Awards:* general academic. *Creative Arts/Performance Awards:* music. *Special Characteristics Awards:* relatives of clergy, religious affiliation.

Other Money-Saving Options *Payment Plan:* installment. *Waivers:* full or partial for employees or children of employees.

Contact Office of Financial Aid, Southwestern College of Christian Ministries, PO Box 340, Bethany, OK 73008-0340, 405-789-7661.

SOUTHWESTERN OKLAHOMA STATE UNIVERSITY
Weatherford, Oklahoma

About the Institution State-supported, coed. Degrees awarded: B, M. Offers 50 undergraduate majors. Total enrollment: 4,506. Undergraduates: 4,004 (88% state residents). Freshmen: 753.

Undergraduate Expenses (1996–97) State resident tuition: $1575 (minimum). Nonresident tuition: $3780 (minimum). Mandatory fees: $9. College room and board: $2096 (minimum). College room only: $800.

Applications 73% of all full-time undergraduates enrolled in fall 1996 applied for aid; of these, 83% were judged to have need according to Federal Methodology, of whom 100% were aided. *Financial aid deadline (priority):* 3/15. *Financial aid forms:* FAFSA, institutional form required. *Admission application deadline:* 8/15.

Summary of Aid to Needy Students *From gift & self-help combined:* Average need met: 65%. Average amount awarded: $2631 (43% gift aid, 57% self-help). *Gift aid:* Total: $2,327,473 (20% from college's own funds, 17% from other college-administered sources, 63% from external sources). 144 Federal Work-Study jobs (averaging $1003); 470 part-time jobs.

Need-Based Scholarships & Grants Pell, FSEOG, state, private, college/university.

Loans PLUS, Stafford, Unsubsidized Stafford, private, college/university short-term loans ($200 average).

Non-Need Awards In 1996, a total of 1,635 non-need awards were made. *Academic Interests/Achievement Awards:* 376 ($187,450 total): general academic, foreign languages. *Creative Arts/Performance Awards:* 43 ($16,000 total): art/fine arts, music, theater/drama. *Special Achievements/Activities Awards:* 4 ($1225 total): cheerleading/drum major, rodeo. *Special Characteristics Awards:* 976 ($514,596 total): children and siblings of alumni, local/state students, out-of-state students. *Athletic:* Total: 236 ($102,996); Men: 149 ($66,826); Women: 87 ($36,170).

Other Money-Saving Options Accelerated degree, co-op program, off-campus living. *Payment Plan:* installment. *Waivers:* full or partial for employees or children of employees and senior citizens.

Contact Financial Services Receptionist, Southwestern Oklahoma State University, 100 Campus Drive, Weatherford, OK 73096-3098, 405-774-3786, fax: 405-774-7066.

SOUTHWESTERN UNIVERSITY
Georgetown, Texas

About the Institution Independent/religious, coed. Degrees awarded: B. Offers 39 undergraduate majors. Total enrollment: 1,226 (87% state residents). Freshmen: 309.

Undergraduate Expenses (1996–97) Comprehensive fee of $18,425 includes tuition ($13,400) and college room and board ($5025). College room only: $2590.

Applications Of all full-time undergraduates enrolled in fall 1996, 85% of those who applied for aid were judged to have need according to Federal Methodology, of whom 100% were aided. *Financial aid deadline (priority):* 3/1. *Financial aid forms:* institutional form required. FAFSA, state form required for some. *Regular admission application deadline:* 2/15. Early decision deadline: 11/1.

Summary of Aid to Needy Students *From gift & self-help combined:* Average need met: 100%. Average amount awarded: $12,673 (66% gift aid, 34% self-help). *Gift aid:* Total: $5,845,624 (75% from college's own funds, 15% from other college-administered sources, 10% from external sources). 179 Federal Work-Study jobs (averaging $1320); 318 part-time jobs.

Need-Based Scholarships & Grants Pell, FSEOG, state, private, college/university.

Loans Perkins, PLUS, Stafford, Unsubsidized Stafford, state, private, college/university short-term loans ($250 average), college/university long-term loans ($2291 average).

Non-Need Awards In 1996, a total of 486 non-need awards were made. *Academic Interests/Achievement Awards:* 340 ($1,229,551 total): general academic. *Creative Arts/Performance Awards:* 84 ($101,700 total): dance, music, theater/drama. *Special Characteristics Awards:* 62 ($350,500 total): children and siblings of alumni, children of faculty/staff, relatives of clergy, religious affiliation.

Other Money-Saving Options Accelerated degree, off-campus living (after freshman year). *Payment Plans:* tuition prepayment, installment, deferred payment. *Waivers:* full or partial for employees or children of employees.

Contact Mr. Paul J. Gilroy, Associate Vice President for Financial Aid, Southwestern University, PO Box 770, Georgetown, TX 78627-0770, 512-863-1200, fax: 512-863-9601.

SOUTHWEST MISSOURI STATE UNIVERSITY
Springfield, Missouri

About the Institution State-supported, coed. Degrees awarded: A, B, M. Offers 115 undergraduate majors. Total enrollment: 15,535. Undergraduates: 13,473 (93% state residents). Freshmen: 2,507.

Undergraduate Expenses (1997–98) State resident tuition: $2790. Nonresident tuition: $5580. Mandatory fees: $270. College room and board: $3472 (minimum). College room only: $1966 (minimum).

Applications Of all full-time undergraduates enrolled in fall 1996, 74% of those who applied for aid were judged to have need according to Federal Methodology, of whom 92% were aided. *Financial aid deadline (priority):* 3/31. *Financial aid forms:* FAFSA required. *Admission application deadline:* 8/1.

Summary of Aid to Needy Students *From gift & self-help combined:* Average need met: 70%. Average amount awarded: $7385 (83% gift aid, 17% self-help). *Gift aid:* Total: $18,862,824 (63% from college's own funds, 15% from other college-administered sources, 22% from external sources). 562 Federal Work-Study jobs (averaging $926); 2,854 part-time jobs.

Need-Based Scholarships & Grants Pell, FSEOG, state, college/university.

Loans Perkins, PLUS, Stafford, Unsubsidized Stafford, college/university short-term loans ($90 average), college/university long-term loans ($901 average).

Non-Need Awards In 1996, a total of 7,386 non-need awards were made. *Academic Interests/Achievement Awards:* 1,125 ($1,462,611 total): general academic, agriculture, biological sciences, business, communication, education, foreign languages, mathematics, premedicine, social sciences. *Creative Arts/Performance Awards:* 747 ($334,575 total): general creative, art/fine arts, dance, debating, journalism/publications, music, performing arts, theater/drama. *Special Achievements/Activities Awards:* 1,927 ($3,506,079 total): general special achievements/activities. *Special Characteristics Awards:* 3,306 ($3,898,527 total): adult students, children and siblings of alumni, children of faculty/staff, ethnic background, first-generation college students, handicapped students, members of minorities, out-of-state students, ROTC participants, spouses of deceased or disabled public servants, veterans. *Athletic:* Total: 281 ($1,553,390); Men: 181 ($971,376); Women: 100 ($582,014).

Other Money-Saving Options Accelerated degree, co-op program, Army ROTC, off-campus living (after sophomore year). *Payment Plan:* deferred payment. *Waivers:* full or partial for employees or children of employees and senior citizens.

Contact Mr. David G. King, Assistant Director, Southwest Missouri State University, 901 South National, MO 65804-0095, 417-836-5262, fax: 417-836-8392.

SOUTHWEST STATE UNIVERSITY
Marshall, Minnesota

About the Institution State-supported, coed. Degrees awarded: A, B, M. Offers 42 undergraduate majors. Total enrollment: 2,900. Undergraduates: 2,798 (84% state residents). Freshmen: 420.

Undergraduate Expenses (1996–97) State resident tuition: $2496. Nonresident tuition: $5624. Mandatory fees: $484. College room and board: $2900. College room only: $2012.

Applications Of all full-time undergraduates enrolled in fall 1996, 86% of those who applied for aid were judged to have need according to Federal Methodology, of whom 98% were aided. *Financial aid deadline (priority):* 4/1. *Financial aid forms:* FAFSA, institutional form required. *Admission application deadline:* rolling.

Summary of Aid to Needy Students *From gift & self-help combined:* Average need met: 92%. Average amount awarded: $5385 (45% gift

aid, 55% self-help). *Gift aid:* Total: $2,869,475 (20% from college's own funds, 39% from other college-administered sources, 41% from external sources). 237 Federal Work-Study jobs (averaging $1426); 473 part-time jobs.

Need-Based Scholarships & Grants Pell, FSEOG, state, private, college/university.

Loans Perkins, PLUS, Stafford, Unsubsidized Stafford, state, private, college/university short-term loans ($300 average).

Non-Need Awards *Academic Interests/Achievement Awards:* general academic, biological sciences, mathematics, physical sciences. *Creative Arts/Performance Awards:* music, theater/drama. *Special Achievements/ Activities Awards:* leadership. *Special Characteristics Awards:* members of minorities. *Athletic:* available.

Other Money-Saving Options Accelerated degree, off-campus living. *Payment Plans:* installment, deferred payment. *Waivers:* full or partial for employees or children of employees and senior citizens.

Contact Mr. Scott Crowell, Director of Financial Aid, Southwest State University, 1501 State Street, Marshall, MN 56258-1598, 507-537-6281.

SOUTHWEST TEXAS STATE UNIVERSITY
San Marcos, Texas

About the Institution State-supported, coed. Degrees awarded: B, M, D. Offers 109 undergraduate majors. Total enrollment: 20,776. Undergraduates: 17,677 (97% state residents). Freshmen: 2,472.

Undergraduate Expenses (1996–97) State resident tuition: $960. Nonresident tuition: $7380. Mandatory fees: $1196. College room and board: $3787. College room only: $2264.

Applications Of all full-time undergraduates enrolled in fall 1996, 77% of those who applied for aid were judged to have need according to Federal Methodology, of whom 91% were aided. *Financial aid deadline (priority):* 4/1. *Financial aid forms:* FAFSA required. *Admission application deadline:* 7/1.

Summary of Aid to Needy Students *From gift & self-help combined:* Average need met: 95%. Average amount awarded: $6743 (32% gift aid, 68% self-help). *Gift aid:* Total: $10,370,339 (19% from college's own funds, 20% from other college-administered sources, 61% from external sources). 731 Federal Work-Study jobs (averaging $1168); 3,307 part-time jobs.

Need-Based Scholarships & Grants Pell, FSEOG, state, college/university.

Loans Perkins, PLUS, Stafford, Unsubsidized Stafford, college/university short-term loans ($250 average).

Non-Need Awards In 1996, a total of 1,292 non-need awards were made. *Academic Interests/Achievement Awards:* 830 ($751,086 total): general academic, agriculture, education, international studies. *Creative Arts/Performance Awards:* 189 ($132,155 total): applied art and design, music, theater/drama. *Athletic:* Total: 273 ($1,174,108); Men: 177 ($745,127); Women: 96 ($428,981).

Other Money-Saving Options Accelerated degree, Army ROTC, Air Force ROTC, off-campus living (after sophomore year). *Payment Plan:* installment.

Contact Office of Financial Aid, Southwest Texas State University, 601 University Drive, San Marcos, TX 78666-4602, 512-245-2111.

SPALDING UNIVERSITY
Louisville, Kentucky

About the Institution Independent/religious, coed. Degrees awarded: A, B, M, D. Offers 30 undergraduate majors. Total enrollment: 1,423. Undergraduates: 1,055 (85% state residents). Freshmen: 147.

Undergraduate Expenses (1996–97) Comprehensive fee of $12,376 includes tuition ($9600), mandatory fees ($96), and college room and board ($2680).

Applications 100% of all full-time undergraduates enrolled in fall 1996 applied for aid; of these, 89% were judged to have need according to Federal Methodology, of whom 100% were aided. *Financial aid deadline (priority):* 3/15. *Financial aid forms:* FAFSA, institutional form required. *Admission application deadline:* 8/15.

Summary of Aid to Needy Students *From gift & self-help combined:* Average need met: 77%. Average amount awarded: $9455 (55% gift aid, 45% self-help). *Gift aid:* Total: $3,182,936 (49% from college's own funds, 33% from other college-administered sources, 18% from external sources). 109 Federal Work-Study jobs (averaging $1763).

Need-Based Scholarships & Grants Pell, FSEOG, state, college/university.

Loans Perkins, PLUS, Stafford, Unsubsidized Stafford, Federal Nursing, private, college/university long-term loans ($1246 average).

Non-Need Awards In 1996, a total of 393 non-need awards were made. *Academic Interests/Achievement Awards:* 173 ($553,776 total): general academic. *Creative Arts/Performance Awards:* 4 ($8400 total): applied art and design, art/fine arts. *Special Achievements/Activities Awards:* 33 ($125,360 total): general special achievements/activities, community service, leadership. *Special Characteristics Awards:* 103 ($634,632 total): general special characteristics, children and siblings of alumni, children of faculty/staff, international students, siblings of current students, spouses of current students. *Athletic:* Total: 80 ($444,743); Men: 39 ($187,655); Women: 41 ($257,088).

Other Money-Saving Options Cooperative Army ROTC, cooperative Air Force ROTC, off-campus living. *Payment Plan:* installment. *Waivers:* full or partial for children of alumni, employees or children of employees, senior citizens.

Contact Office of Financial Aid, Spalding University, 851 South Fourth Street, Louisville, KY 40203-2188, 502-585-9911.

SPELMAN COLLEGE
Atlanta, Georgia

About the Institution Independent, women. Degrees awarded: B. Offers 22 undergraduate majors. Total enrollment: 1,961 (21% state residents). Freshmen: 481.

Undergraduate Expenses (1996–97) Comprehensive fee of $15,630 includes tuition ($8150), mandatory fees ($1350), and college room and board ($6130).

Applications *Financial aid deadline (priority):* 4/1. *Financial aid forms:* FAFSA, institutional form required; CSS Financial Aid PROFILE, state form acceptable. *Regular admission application deadline:* 2/1. Early action deadline: 11/15.

Summary of Aid to Needy Students *From gift & self-help combined:* Average need met: 52%. Average amount awarded: $10,800. *Gift aid:* Total: $4,629,349. Federal Work-Study jobs; 40 part-time jobs.

Need-Based Scholarships & Grants Pell, FSEOG, state, private, college/university.

Loans Perkins, PLUS, Stafford, Unsubsidized Stafford, state, private.

Non-Need Awards *Academic Interests/Achievement Awards:* general academic, biological sciences, mathematics, physical sciences. *Creative Arts/Performance Awards:* general creative.

Other Money-Saving Options Accelerated degree, cooperative Army ROTC, cooperative Naval ROTC, cooperative Air Force ROTC, off-campus living. *Payment Plan:* installment. *Waivers:* full or partial for employees or children of employees.

Contact Ms. Vera Brooks, Director, Student Financial Services, Spelman College, 350 Spelman Lane, Southwest, Atlanta, GA 30314-4399, 404-681-3643 Ext. 1470.

SPRING ARBOR COLLEGE
Spring Arbor, Michigan

About the Institution Independent/religious, coed. Degrees awarded: A, B, M. Offers 29 undergraduate majors. Total enrollment: 1,069. Undergraduates: 853 (89% state residents). Freshmen: 171.

Undergraduate Expenses (1997–98) Comprehensive fee of $14,876 includes tuition ($10,580), mandatory fees ($106), and college room and board ($4190).

Applications *Financial aid deadline (priority):* 2/15. *Financial aid forms:* FAFSA required. Institutional form required for some. *Admission application deadline:* rolling.

Summary of Aid to Needy Students *From gift & self-help combined:* Average amount awarded: $6562 (67% gift aid, 33% self-help). *Gift aid:* Total: $5,695,757 (50% from college's own funds, 33% from other college-administered sources, 17% from external sources). 392 Federal Work-Study jobs (averaging $884); 280 part-time jobs.

Need-Based Scholarships & Grants Pell, FSEOG, state.

Loans Perkins, PLUS, Stafford, Unsubsidized Stafford, private.

Non-Need Awards In 1996, a total of 934 non-need awards were made. *Academic Interests/Achievement Awards:* 338 ($771,508 total): general academic, communication, computer science, religion/biblical studies. *Creative Arts/Performance Awards:* 82 ($56,776 total): art/fine arts, music. *Special Characteristics Awards:* 390 ($730,272 total): children of faculty/staff, international students, members of minorities, out-of-state students, relatives of clergy, religious affiliation. *Athletic:* Total: 124 ($270,460); Men: 60 ($137,166); Women: 64 ($133,294).

Other Money-Saving Options *Payment Plans:* installment, deferred payment. *Waivers:* full or partial for employees or children of employees and senior citizens.

Contact Financial Aid Office, Spring Arbor College, 106 Main Street, Spring Arbor, MI 49283-9799, 517-750-6463, fax: 517-750-6620.

SPRINGFIELD COLLEGE
Springfield, Massachusetts

About the Institution Independent, coed. Degrees awarded: B, M, D. Offers 53 undergraduate majors. Total enrollment: 2,923. Undergraduates: 2,011 (33% state residents). Freshmen: 482.

Undergraduate Expenses (1996–97) Comprehensive fee of $18,500 includes tuition ($12,700) and college room and board ($5800). College room only: $2716.

Applications Of all full-time undergraduates enrolled in fall 1996, 93% of those who applied for aid were judged to have need according to Federal Methodology, of whom 100% were aided. *Financial aid deadline (priority):* 3/15. *Financial aid forms:* FAFSA, federal income tax forms required. CSS Financial Aid PROFILE, institutional form required for some. *Regular admission application deadline:* 4/1. Early decision deadline: 12/1.

Summary of Aid to Needy Students *From gift & self-help combined:* Average need met: 80%. Average amount awarded: $10,213 (50% gift aid, 50% self-help). *Gift aid:* Total: $7,775,949 (73% from college's own funds, 5% from other college-administered sources, 22% from external sources). 413 Federal Work-Study jobs (averaging $1250); 450 part-time jobs.

Need-Based Scholarships & Grants Pell, FSEOG, state, private, college/university, Project Spirit.

Loans Perkins, PLUS, Stafford, Unsubsidized Stafford, state, private, college/university short-term loans ($1000 average).

Non-Need Awards *Special Characteristics Awards:* local/state students, members of minorities.

Other Money-Saving Options Accelerated degree, co-op program, cooperative Army ROTC, cooperative Air Force ROTC, off-campus living (after junior year).

Contact Dr. Linda M. Dagradi, Director of Financial Aid, Springfield College, 263 Alden Street, Springfield, MA 01109-3797, 413-748-3108, fax: 413-748-3462.

SPRING HILL COLLEGE
Mobile, Alabama

About the Institution Independent/religious, coed. Degrees awarded: B, M. Offers 43 undergraduate majors. Total enrollment: 1,445. Undergraduates: 1,160 (46% state residents). Freshmen: 201.

Undergraduate Expenses (1997–98) Comprehensive fee of $18,840 includes tuition ($13,040), mandatory fees ($820), and college room and board ($4980). College room only: $2630.

Applications Of all full-time undergraduates enrolled in fall 1996, 100% of those judged to have need according to Federal Methodology were aided. *Financial aid deadline (priority):* 3/1. *Financial aid forms:* FAFSA, institutional form required. State form required for some. *Admission application deadline:* rolling.

Summary of Aid to Needy Students *From gift & self-help combined:* Average need met: 88%. Average amount awarded: $9429 (59% gift aid, 41% self-help). *Gift aid:* Total: $3,360,362 (61% from college's own funds, 14% from other college-administered sources, 25% from external sources). 107 Federal Work-Study jobs (averaging $1260); 116 part-time jobs.

Need-Based Scholarships & Grants Pell, FSEOG, state, private, college/university, Whitehead Scholarships, Bedote Grants.

Loans Perkins, PLUS, Stafford, Unsubsidized Stafford, private, Key Corp Loans, Signature Loans.

Non-Need Awards In 1996, a total of 641 non-need awards were made. *Academic Interests/Achievement Awards:* 339 ($1,533,982 total): general academic. *Special Achievements/Activities Awards:* 125 ($333,063 total): community service. *Special Characteristics Awards:* 45 ($360,856 total): children of faculty/staff, siblings of current students. *Athletic:* Total: 132 ($711,978); Men: 87 ($457,138); Women: 45 ($254,840).

Other Money-Saving Options Accelerated degree, co-op program, Army ROTC, Air Force ROTC, off-campus living (after junior year). *Payment Plan:* deferred payment. *Waivers:* full or partial for employees or children of employees.

Contact Ms. Karen Walker, Director of Financial Aid, Spring Hill College, 4000 Dauphin Street, Mobile, AL 36608-1791, 334-380-3460, fax: 334-460-2176.

STANFORD UNIVERSITY
Stanford, California

About the Institution Independent, coed. Degrees awarded: B, M, D, P. Offers 64 undergraduate majors. Total enrollment: 13,811. Undergraduates: 6,550 (46% state residents). Freshmen: 1,614.

Undergraduate Expenses (1997–98) Comprehensive fee of $29,108 includes tuition ($21,300), mandatory fees ($89), and college room and board ($7719).

Applications 48% of all full-time undergraduates enrolled in fall 1996 applied for aid; of these, 92% were judged to have need according to Federal Methodology, of whom 99% were aided. *Financial aid deadline (priority):* 4/15. *Financial aid forms:* FAFSA, CSS Financial Aid PROFILE required. *Regular admission application deadline:* 12/15. Early decision deadline: 11/1.

Summary of Aid to Needy Students *From gift & self-help combined:* Average need met: 100%. Average amount awarded: $20,900 (74% gift aid, 26% self-help). *Gift aid:* Total: $43,120,000 (81% from college's own funds, 9% from other college-administered sources, 10% from external sources). 175 Federal Work-Study jobs (averaging $1800); 1,500 part-time jobs.

Need-Based Scholarships & Grants Pell, FSEOG, state, private, college/university.

Loans Perkins, PLUS, Stafford, Unsubsidized Stafford, college/university short-term loans ($500 average), college/university long-term loans ($2500 average).

Non-Need Awards In 1996, a total of 371 non-need awards were made. *Athletic:* Total: 371 ($7,325,000); Men: 210 ($4,325,000); Women: 161 ($3,000,000).

Other Money-Saving Options Accelerated degree, cooperative Army ROTC, cooperative Naval ROTC, cooperative Air Force ROTC, off-campus living (after freshman year). *Payment Plans:* installment, deferred payment. *Waivers:* full or partial for employees or children of employees.

Contact Office of Financial Aid, Stanford University, 214 Old Union, Stanford, CA 94305-9991, 415-723-2300.

STATE UNIVERSITY OF NEW YORK AT ALBANY
Albany, New York

See University at Albany, State University of New York

STATE UNIVERSITY OF NEW YORK AT BINGHAMTON
Binghamton, New York

About the Institution State-supported, coed. Degrees awarded: B, M, D. Offers 56 undergraduate majors. Total enrollment: 11,976. Undergraduates: 9,349 (95% state residents). Freshmen: 1,804.

Undergraduate Expenses (1996–97) State resident tuition: $3400. Nonresident tuition: $8300. Mandatory fees: $645. College room and board: $4814.

Applications 70% of all full-time undergraduates enrolled in fall 1996 applied for aid; of these, 92% were judged to have need according to Federal Methodology, of whom 92% were aided. *Financial aid deadline (priority):* 3/1. *Financial aid forms:* FAFSA, state form required. CSS Financial Aid PROFILE required for some. *Regular admission application deadline:* 2/15. Early decision deadline: 11/1.

Summary of Aid to Needy Students *From gift & self-help combined:* Average need met: 63%. Average amount awarded: $6747 (35% gift aid, 65% self-help). *Gift aid:* Total: $12,606,791 (4% from college's own funds, 8% from other college-administered sources, 88% from external sources). 683 Federal Work-Study jobs (averaging $938); 345 part-time jobs.

Need-Based Scholarships & Grants Pell, FSEOG, state, college/university.

Loans Perkins, PLUS, Stafford, Unsubsidized Stafford, Federal Nursing, college/university short-term loans ($200 average).

Non-Need Awards In 1996, a total of 60 non-need awards were made. *Academic Interests/Achievement Awards:* 59 ($163,700 total): general academic, engineering/technologies, physical sciences. *Creative Arts/Performance Awards:* 1 ($500 total): creative writing.

Other Money-Saving Options Accelerated degree, cooperative Air Force ROTC, off-campus living (after freshman year). *Payment Plan:* installment.

Contact Ms. Christina M. Knickerbocker, Director of Student Financial Aid and Employment, State University of New York at Binghamton, PO Box 6011, Binghamton, NY 13902-6011, 607-777-4290, fax: 607-777-6897.

STATE UNIVERSITY OF NEW YORK AT BUFFALO
Buffalo, New York

About the Institution State-supported, coed. Degrees awarded: B, M, D, P. Offers 67 undergraduate majors. Total enrollment: 23,577. Undergraduates: 15,571 (96% state residents). Freshmen: 2,575.

Undergraduate Expenses (1996–97) State resident tuition: $3400. Nonresident tuition: $8300. Mandatory fees: $790. College room and board: $5455. College room only: $3125.

Applications 70% of all full-time undergraduates enrolled in fall 1996 applied for aid; of these, 83% were judged to have need according to Federal Methodology, of whom 98% were aided. *Financial aid deadline (priority):* 3/1. *Financial aid forms:* FAFSA required. State form required for some. *Regular admission application deadline:* rolling. Early decision deadline: 11/1.

Summary of Aid to Needy Students *From gift & self-help combined:* Average need met: 100%. Average amount awarded: $6388 (44% gift aid, 56% self-help). *Gift aid:* Total: $21,548,720 (1% from college's own funds, 14% from other college-administered sources, 85% from external sources). 803 Federal Work-Study jobs (averaging $908); 1,075 part-time jobs.

Need-Based Scholarships & Grants Pell, FSEOG, state, private, college/university.

Loans Perkins, PLUS, Stafford, Unsubsidized Stafford, Federal Nursing, Primary Care, private, college/university short-term loans ($300 average), college/university long-term loans ($831 average).

Non-Need Awards In 1996, a total of 597 non-need awards were made. *Academic Interests/Achievement Awards:* 71 ($27,874 total): general academic. *Creative Arts/Performance Awards:* 1 ($750 total): music. *Special Achievements/Activities Awards:* 258 ($588,838 total): general special achievements/activities. *Special Characteristics Awards:* 28 ($11,890 total): local/state students. *Athletic:* Total: 239 ($1,401,803); Men: 153 ($982,130); Women: 86 ($419,673).

Other Money-Saving Options Cooperative Army ROTC, off-campus living. *Payment Plan:* installment.

Contact Mr. Pablo Gutierrez, Financial Aid Assistant, State University of New York at Buffalo, Hayes Annex C, 3435 Main Street, Buffalo, NY 14260, 716-829-2339, fax: 716-829-2022.

STATE UNIVERSITY OF NEW YORK AT NEW PALTZ
New Paltz, New York

About the Institution State-supported, coed. Degrees awarded: B, M. Offers 76 undergraduate majors. Total enrollment: 7,539. Undergraduates: 6,029 (95% state residents). Freshmen: 886.

Undergraduate Expenses (1996–97) State resident tuition: $3400. Nonresident tuition: $8300. Mandatory fees: $425. College room and board: $5030. College room only: $2990.

Applications Of all full-time undergraduates enrolled in fall 1996, 80% of those who applied for aid were judged to have need according to Federal Methodology, of whom 96% were aided. *Financial aid deadline (priority):* 3/15. *Financial aid forms:* FAFSA required. State form, institutional form required for some. *Regular admission application deadline:* 5/1. Early decision deadline: 11/1.

Summary of Aid to Needy Students *From gift & self-help combined:* Average need met: 75%. Average amount awarded: $6500 (48% gift aid, 52% self-help). *Gift aid:* Total: $10,570,000 (1% from college's own funds, 68% from other college-administered sources, 31% from external sources). 650 Federal Work-Study jobs (averaging $800); 500 part-time jobs.

Need-Based Scholarships & Grants Pell, FSEOG, state, college/university.

Loans Perkins, PLUS, Stafford, Unsubsidized Stafford.

Non-Need Awards *Academic Interests/Achievement Awards:* general academic, computer science, education, engineering/technologies, English, health fields, humanities, mathematics, physical sciences, premedicine. *Creative Arts/Performance Awards:* art/fine arts, creative writing. *Special Achievements/Activities Awards:* community service. *Special Characteristics Awards:* members of minorities.

Other Money-Saving Options Accelerated degree, co-op program, off-campus living (after freshman year). *Payment Plan:* installment.

Contact Mr. Daniel Sistarenik, Director of Financial Aid, State University of New York at New Paltz, 75 South Manheim Boulevard, New Paltz, NY 12561-2499, 914-257-3250, fax: 914-257-3009.

STATE UNIVERSITY OF NEW YORK AT OSWEGO
Oswego, New York

About the Institution State-supported, coed. Degrees awarded: B, M. Offers 56 undergraduate majors. Total enrollment: 8,264. Undergraduates: 7,090 (97% state residents). Freshmen: 1,350.

Undergraduate Expenses (1996–97) State resident tuition: $3400. Nonresident tuition: $8300. Mandatory fees: $487. College room and board: $5460. College room only: $3190.

Applications Of all full-time undergraduates enrolled in fall 1996, 84% of those who applied for aid were judged to have need according to Federal Methodology, of whom 95% were aided. *Financial aid deadline (priority):* 4/1. *Financial aid forms:* FAFSA required; state form acceptable. *Regular admission application deadline:* rolling. Early decision deadline: 11/15.

Summary of Aid to Needy Students *From gift & self-help combined:* Average need met: 75%. Average amount awarded: $6012 (39% gift aid, 61% self-help). *Gift aid:* Total: $9,488,753 (1% from college's own funds, 5% from other college-administered sources, 94% from external sources). 338 Federal Work-Study jobs (averaging $1000); 1,201 part-time jobs.

Need-Based Scholarships & Grants Pell, FSEOG, state, private, college/university.

Loans Perkins, PLUS, Stafford, Unsubsidized Stafford, private, college/university short-term loans ($75 average).

Non-Need Awards In 1996, a total of 119 non-need awards were made. *Academic Interests/Achievement Awards:* 76 ($48,030 total): biological sciences, communication, education, English, humanities, international studies, mathematics, physical sciences, premedicine, social sciences. *Creative Arts/Performance Awards:* 20 ($2525 total): art/fine arts, creative writing, music, theater/drama. *Special Achievements/Activities Awards:* 6 ($2250 total): leadership. *Special Characteristics Awards:* 17 ($13,250 total): adult students, children and siblings of alumni, children of workers in trades, ethnic background, local/state students.

Other Money-Saving Options Co-op program, Army ROTC, off-campus living (after sophomore year). *Payment Plans:* installment, deferred payment.

Contact Office of Financial Aid, State University of New York at Oswego, 206 Culkin Hall, Oswego, NY 13126, 315-341-2500.

STATE UNIVERSITY OF NEW YORK AT STONY BROOK
Stony Brook, New York

About the Institution State-supported, coed. Degrees awarded: B, M, D, P. Offers 52 undergraduate majors. Total enrollment: 17,309. Undergraduates: 11,265 (95% state residents). Freshmen: 1,770.

Undergraduate Expenses (1996–97) State resident tuition: $3400. Nonresident tuition: $8300. Mandatory fees: $479. College room and board: $5594. College room only: $3494.

Applications 70% of all full-time undergraduates enrolled in fall 1996 applied for aid; of these, 88% were judged to have need according to Federal Methodology, of whom 99% were aided. *Financial aid deadline (priority):* 3/1. *Financial aid forms:* FAFSA, state form required. *Admission application deadline:* rolling.

Summary of Aid to Needy Students *From gift & self-help combined:* Average need met: 66%. Average amount awarded: $7896 (41% gift aid, 59% self-help). *Gift aid:* Total: $19,028,339 (2% from college's own funds, 5% from other college-administered sources, 93% from external sources). 689 Federal Work-Study jobs (averaging $1132); 1,419 part-time jobs.

Need-Based Scholarships & Grants Pell, FSEOG, state, private.

Loans Perkins, PLUS, Stafford, Unsubsidized Stafford, Primary Care, private, college/university short-term loans ($418 average).

Non-Need Awards *Academic Interests/Achievement Awards:* 198 ($289,855 total): general academic. *Special Achievements/Activities Awards:* general special achievements/activities. *Athletic:* Total: 38 ($60,178); Men: 16 ($37,778); Women: 22 ($22,400).

Other Money-Saving Options Off-campus living. *Payment Plans:* installment, deferred payment. *Waivers:* full or partial for minority students.

Contact Office of Financial Aid, State University of New York at Stony Brook, Administration 230, Stony Brook, NY 11794, 516-689-6000.

STATE UNIVERSITY OF NEW YORK COLLEGE AT BROCKPORT
Brockport, New York

About the Institution State-supported, coed. Degrees awarded: B, M. Offers 80 undergraduate majors. Total enrollment: 8,723. Undergraduates: 6,854 (98% state residents). Freshmen: 921.

Undergraduate Expenses (1996–97) State resident tuition: $3400. Nonresident tuition: $8300. Mandatory fees: $515. College room and board: $4780. College room only: $2960.

Applications 80% of all full-time undergraduates enrolled in fall 1996 applied for aid; of these, 85% were judged to have need according to Federal Methodology, of whom 96% were aided. *Financial aid deadline (priority):* 5/1. *Financial aid forms:* FAFSA, state form required; CSS Financial Aid PROFILE acceptable. *Regular admission application deadline:* rolling. Early decision deadline: 11/15.

Summary of Aid to Needy Students *From gift & self-help combined:* Average need met: 95%. Average amount awarded: $7277 (30% gift aid, 70% self-help). *Gift aid:* Total: $11,440,858 (1% from college's own funds, 57% from other college-administered sources, 42% from external sources). 909 Federal Work-Study jobs (averaging $1400); 1,470 part-time jobs.

Need-Based Scholarships & Grants Pell, FSEOG, state, private, college/university.

Loans Perkins, PLUS, Stafford, Unsubsidized Stafford, Federal Nursing, private, college/university short-term loans ($50 average), college/university long-term loans ($500 average).

Non-Need Awards In 1996, a total of 146 non-need awards were made. *Academic Interests/Achievement Awards:* 105 ($43,000 total): general academic, biological sciences, education, English, foreign languages, mathematics, physical sciences. *Creative Arts/Performance Awards:* 13 ($5575 total): art/fine arts. *Special Achievements/Activities Awards:* 11 ($2425 total): community service, leadership. *Special Characteristics Awards:* 17 ($23,000 total): local/state students, members of minorities.

Other Money-Saving Options Accelerated degree, co-op program, Army ROTC, cooperative Naval ROTC, cooperative Air Force ROTC, off-campus living (after freshman year). *Payment Plan:* installment. *Waivers:* full or partial for senior citizens.

Contact Mr. J. Scott Atkinson, Director of Financial Aid, State University of New York College at Brockport, 350 New Campus Drive, Brockport, NY 14420-2997, 716-395-2501, fax: 716-395-5445.

STATE UNIVERSITY OF NEW YORK COLLEGE AT BUFFALO
Buffalo, New York

About the Institution State-supported, coed. Degrees awarded: B, M. Offers 68 undergraduate majors. Total enrollment: 11,184. Undergraduates: 9,421 (97% state residents). Freshmen: 1,293.

Undergraduate Expenses (1996–97) State resident tuition: $3400. Nonresident tuition: $8300. Mandatory fees: $391. College room and board: $4460 (minimum). College room only: $2960.

Applications Of all full-time undergraduates enrolled in fall 1996, 100% of those who applied for aid were judged to have need according to Federal Methodology, of whom 100% were aided. *Financial aid deadline (priority):* 3/15. *Financial aid forms:* FAFSA required; CSS Financial Aid PROFILE acceptable. *Regular admission application deadline:* rolling. Early decision deadline: 11/15.

Summary of Aid to Needy Students *From gift & self-help combined:* Average need met: 65%. Average amount awarded: $5778 (47% gift aid, 53% self-help). *Gift aid:* Total: $13,094,816 (1% from college's own funds, 12% from other college-administered sources, 87% from external sources). 440 Federal Work-Study jobs (averaging $1400); 325 part-time jobs.

Need-Based Scholarships & Grants Pell, FSEOG, state.

Loans Perkins, PLUS, Stafford, Unsubsidized Stafford, college/university short-term loans ($50 average), college/university long-term loans ($1569 average).

Non-Need Awards *Academic Interests/Achievement Awards:* general academic.

Other Money-Saving Options Cooperative Army ROTC, off-campus living. *Payment Plan:* installment. *Waivers:* full or partial for employees or children of employees.

Contact Mr. Daniel R. Hunter, Director of Financial Aid, State University of New York College at Buffalo, Buffalo, NY 14222-1095, 716-878-4901.

STATE UNIVERSITY OF NEW YORK COLLEGE AT CORTLAND
Cortland, New York

About the Institution State-supported, coed. Degrees awarded: B, M. Offers 47 undergraduate majors. Total enrollment: 6,278. Undergraduates: 5,046 (97% state residents). Freshmen: 987.

Undergraduate Expenses (1996–97) State resident tuition: $3400. Nonresident tuition: $8300. Mandatory fees: $442. College room and board: $5020. College room only: $2940.

Applications Of all full-time undergraduates enrolled in fall 1996, 100% of those who applied for aid were judged to have need according to Federal Methodology, of whom 94% were aided. *Financial aid deadline (priority):* 5/1. *Financial aid forms:* FAFSA, state form required. *Regular admission application deadline:* 12/1. Early decision deadline: 11/15.

Summary of Aid to Needy Students *From gift & self-help combined:* Average need met: 85%. Average amount awarded: $7814 (32% gift aid, 68% self-help). *Gift aid:* Total: $6,530,500 (3% from college's own funds, 61% from other college-administered sources, 36% from external sources). Federal Work-Study jobs; 500 part-time jobs.

Need-Based Scholarships & Grants Pell, FSEOG, state, private, college/university.

Loans Perkins, Stafford, Unsubsidized Stafford.

Non-Need Awards In 1996, a total of 20 non-need awards were made. *Academic Interests/Achievement Awards:* 12: general academic. *Creative Arts/Performance Awards:* 8: general creative.

Other Money-Saving Options Co-op program, cooperative Army ROTC, cooperative Naval ROTC, cooperative Air Force ROTC, off-campus living (after sophomore year).

Contact Financial Aid Office, State University of New York College at Cortland, Cortland, NY 13045, 607-753-4717.

STATE UNIVERSITY OF NEW YORK COLLEGE AT FREDONIA
Fredonia, New York

About the Institution State-supported, coed. Degrees awarded: B, M. Offers 72 undergraduate majors. Total enrollment: 4,556. Undergraduates: 4,350 (98% state residents). Freshmen: 922.

Undergraduate Expenses (1996–97) State resident tuition: $3400. Nonresident tuition: $8300. Mandatory fees: $613. College room and board: $4900. College room only: $2900.

Applications 77% of all full-time undergraduates enrolled in fall 1996 applied for aid; of these, 79% were judged to have need according to Federal Methodology, of whom 97% were aided. *Financial aid deadline (priority):* 3/15. *Financial aid forms:* FAFSA required; CSS Financial Aid PROFILE acceptable. State form required for some. *Regular admission application deadline:* rolling. Early decision deadline: 11/1.

Summary of Aid to Needy Students *From gift & self-help combined:* Average need met: 89%. Average amount awarded: $5453 (39% gift aid, 61% self-help). *Gift aid:* Total: $5,173,709 (4% from college's own funds, 4% from other college-administered sources, 92% from external sources). 248 Federal Work-Study jobs (averaging $1100); 736 part-time jobs.

Need-Based Scholarships & Grants Pell, FSEOG, state, private, college/university.

Loans Perkins, PLUS, Stafford, Unsubsidized Stafford.

Non-Need Awards In 1996, a total of 250 non-need awards were made. *Academic Interests/Achievement Awards:* 81 ($97,525 total): general academic, biological sciences, business, communication, education, English, foreign languages, physical sciences. *Creative Arts/Performance Awards:* 56 ($42,125 total): applied art and design, music, theater/drama. *Special Achievements/Activities Awards:* 63 ($60,900 total): general special achievements/activities, leadership. *Special Characteristics Awards:* 50 ($18,000 total): general special characteristics, children and siblings of alumni, members of minorities, previous college experience, veterans' children.

Other Money-Saving Options Accelerated degree, cooperative Army ROTC, off-campus living (after sophomore year). *Payment Plan:* installment.

Contact Office of Financial Aid, State University of New York College at Fredonia, Maytum Hall, 215, Fredonia, NY 14063, 716-673-3111.

STATE UNIVERSITY OF NEW YORK COLLEGE AT GENESEO
Geneseo, New York

About the Institution State-supported, coed. Degrees awarded: B, M. Offers 48 undergraduate majors. Total enrollment: 5,564. Undergraduates: 5,252 (98% state residents). Freshmen: 1,183.

Undergraduate Expenses (1996–97) State resident tuition: $3400. Nonresident tuition: $8300. Mandatory fees: $584. College room and board: $4540.

Applications 67% of all full-time undergraduates enrolled in fall 1996 applied for aid; of these, 70% were judged to have need according to Federal Methodology, of whom 99% were aided. *Financial aid deadline (priority):* 2/15. *Financial aid forms:* FAFSA required. *Regular admission application deadline:* 2/15. Early decision deadline: 11/15.

Summary of Aid to Needy Students *From gift & self-help combined:* Average need met: 99%. Average amount awarded: $6304 (29% gift aid, 71% self-help). *Gift aid:* Total: $4,506,297 (5% from college's own funds, 61% from other college-administered sources, 34% from external sources). 400 Federal Work-Study jobs (averaging $1300); 1,600 part-time jobs.

Need-Based Scholarships & Grants Pell, FSEOG, state.

Loans Perkins, PLUS, Stafford, Unsubsidized Stafford, college/university short-term loans ($200 average).

Non-Need Awards In 1996, a total of 413 non-need awards were made. *Academic Interests/Achievement Awards:* 329 ($210,740 total): general academic, area/ethnic studies, biological sciences, business, communication, computer science, education, English, foreign languages, humanities, mathematics, physical sciences, premedicine, social sciences. *Creative Arts/Performance Awards:* 44 ($18,800 total): general creative, applied art and design, art/fine arts, creative writing, dance, journalism/publications, music, performing arts, theater/drama. *Special Achievements/Activities Awards:* 13 ($8570 total): general special achievements/activities, community service, leadership. *Special Characteristics Awards:* 27 ($29,350 total): local/state students, members of minorities.

Other Money-Saving Options Cooperative Army ROTC, cooperative Air Force ROTC, off-campus living (after freshman year). *Payment Plans:* installment, deferred payment.

Contact Office of Financial Aid, State University of New York College at Geneseo, 1 College Circle, Geneseo, NY 14454-1401, 716-245-5211.

STATE UNIVERSITY OF NEW YORK COLLEGE AT OLD WESTBURY
Old Westbury, New York

About the Institution State-supported, coed. Degrees awarded: B. Offers 29 undergraduate majors. Total enrollment: 3,790 (97% state residents). Freshmen: 467.

Undergraduate Expenses (1996–97) State resident tuition: $3400. Nonresident tuition: $8300. Mandatory fees: $331. College room and board: $5407. College room only: $3448.

Applications Of all full-time undergraduates enrolled in fall 1996, 70% of those who applied for aid were judged to have need according to Federal Methodology, of whom 89% were aided. *Financial aid deadline (priority):* 4/23. *Financial aid forms:* FAFSA, state form, institutional form required; CSS Financial Aid PROFILE acceptable. *Admission application deadline:* rolling.

Summary of Aid to Needy Students *From gift & self-help combined:* Average need met: 70%. Average amount awarded: $3450 (57% gift aid, 43% self-help). *Gift aid:* Total: $3,398,380 (1% from college's own funds, 13% from other college-administered sources, 86% from external sources). 190 Federal Work-Study jobs (averaging $1137); 75 part-time jobs.

Need-Based Scholarships & Grants Pell, FSEOG, state, private, college/university.

Loans Perkins, PLUS, Stafford, Unsubsidized Stafford.

Non-Need Awards In 1996, a total of 7 non-need awards were made. *Academic Interests/Achievement Awards:* 7 ($14,672 total): biological sciences, health fields, physical sciences.

Other Money-Saving Options Cooperative Army ROTC, cooperative Air Force ROTC, off-campus living. *Payment Plan:* installment. *Waivers:* full or partial for senior citizens.

Contact Financial Aid Office, State University of New York College at Old Westbury, Old Westbury, NY 11568-0210, 516-876-3222.

STATE UNIVERSITY OF NEW YORK COLLEGE AT ONEONTA
Oneonta, New York

About the Institution State-supported, coed. Degrees awarded: B, M. Offers 61 undergraduate majors. Total enrollment: 5,616. Undergraduates: 5,171 (98% state residents). Freshmen: 1,160.

Undergraduate Expenses (1996–97) State resident tuition: $3400. Nonresident tuition: $8300. Mandatory fees: $358. College room and board: $5590. College room only: $3000.

Applications Of all full-time undergraduates enrolled in fall 1996, 89% of those who applied for aid were judged to have need according to Federal Methodology, of whom 97% were aided. *Financial aid deadline (priority):* 4/15. *Financial aid forms:* FAFSA required. *Regular admission application deadline:* 5/1. Early decision deadline: 12/15.

Summary of Aid to Needy Students *From gift & self-help combined:* Average need met: 90%. Average amount awarded: $5200 (32% gift aid, 68% self-help). *Gift aid:* Total: $5,680,000 (3% from college's own funds, 53% from other college-administered sources, 44% from external sources). 325 Federal Work-Study jobs (averaging $1000); part-time jobs.

Need-Based Scholarships & Grants Pell, FSEOG, state.

Loans Perkins, PLUS, Stafford, Unsubsidized Stafford, private, college/university short-term loans.

Non-Need Awards In 1996, a total of 110 non-need awards were made. *Academic Interests/Achievement Awards:* 50 ($50,000 total): general academic. *Creative Arts/Performance Awards:* 10 ($15,000 total): music. *Special Achievements/Activities Awards:* 50 ($50,000 total).

Another Money-Saving Option Off-campus living (after sophomore year).

Contact Mr. Bill Goodhue, Director of Financial Aid, State University of New York College at Oneonta, Ravine Parkway, Oneonta, NY 13820, 607-436-2441.

STATE UNIVERSITY OF NEW YORK COLLEGE AT PLATTSBURGH
Plattsburgh, New York

About the Institution State-supported, coed. Degrees awarded: B, M. Offers 57 undergraduate majors. Total enrollment: 5,624. Undergraduates: 5,147 (98% state residents). Freshmen: 934.

Undergraduate Expenses (1996–97) State resident tuition: $3400. Nonresident tuition: $8300. Mandatory fees: $437. College room and board: $4250. College room only: $2620.

Applications 74% of all full-time undergraduates enrolled in fall 1996 applied for aid; of these, 83% were judged to have need according to

Federal Methodology, of whom 97% were aided. *Financial aid deadline (priority):* 4/15. *Financial aid forms:* FAFSA, state form required. *Regular admission application deadline:* rolling. Early decision deadline: 11/1.

Summary of Aid to Needy Students *From gift & self-help combined:* Average need met: 60%. Average amount awarded: $6223 (41% gift aid, 59% self-help). *Gift aid:* Total: $7,502,088 (5% from college's own funds, 6% from other college-administered sources, 89% from external sources). 400 Federal Work-Study jobs (averaging $1000); 500 part-time jobs.

Need-Based Scholarships & Grants Pell, FSEOG, state, private, college/university.

Loans Perkins, PLUS, Stafford, Unsubsidized Stafford, Federal Nursing, private, college/university short-term loans ($25 average).

Non-Need Awards In 1996, a total of 348 non-need awards were made. *Academic Interests/Achievement Awards:* 245 ($219,939 total): general academic, biological sciences, business, communication, computer science, education, English, health fields, home economics, humanities, international studies, mathematics, physical sciences, premedicine, social sciences. *Creative Arts/Performance Awards:* 41 ($14,266 total): art/fine arts, music, theater/drama. *Special Achievements/Activities Awards:* 32 ($10,195 total): general special achievements/activities, leadership. *Special Characteristics Awards:* 30 ($13,500 total): members of minorities.

Other Money-Saving Options Co-op program, off-campus living (after sophomore year). *Payment Plan:* installment.

Contact Office of Financial Aid, State University of New York College at Plattsburgh, 101 Broad Street, 401A Kehoe Bldg., Plattsburgh, NY 12901, 518-564-2000.

STATE UNIVERSITY OF NEW YORK COLLEGE AT POTSDAM
Potsdam, New York

About the Institution State-supported, coed. Degrees awarded: B, M. Offers 58 undergraduate majors. Total enrollment: 4,073. Undergraduates: 3,583 (94% state residents). Freshmen: 815.

Undergraduate Expenses (1996–97) State resident tuition: $3400. Nonresident tuition: $8300. Mandatory fees: $339. College room and board: $4900 (minimum). College room only: $3000.

Applications 80% of all full-time undergraduates enrolled in fall 1996 applied for aid; of these, 87% were judged to have need according to Federal Methodology, of whom 96% were aided. *Financial aid deadline:* continuous. *Financial aid forms:* FAFSA required. State form, institutional form required for some. *Regular admission application deadline:* rolling. Early decision deadline: 11/15.

Summary of Aid to Needy Students *From gift & self-help combined:* Average need met: 98%. Average amount awarded: $6410 (41% gift aid, 59% self-help). *Gift aid:* Total: $5,971,252 (3% from college's own funds, 2% from other college-administered sources, 95% from external sources). 310 Federal Work-Study jobs (averaging $800); 1,800 part-time jobs.

Need-Based Scholarships & Grants Pell, FSEOG, state, private, college/university.

Loans Perkins, PLUS, Stafford, Unsubsidized Stafford, private.

Non-Need Awards In 1996, a total of 253 non-need awards were made. *Academic Interests/Achievement Awards:* 132 ($112,130 total): general academic. *Creative Arts/Performance Awards:* 88 ($63,650 total): music. *Special Characteristics Awards:* 33 ($48,000 total): ethnic background.

Other Money-Saving Options Co-op program, cooperative Army ROTC, cooperative Air Force ROTC, off-campus living (after junior year). *Payment Plan:* installment.

Contact Ms. Susan C. Aldrich, Assistant Director of Financial Aid, State University of New York College at Potsdam, 44 Pierrepont Avenue, Potsdam, NY 13676, 315-267-2162, fax: 315-267-3067.

STATE UNIVERSITY OF NEW YORK COLLEGE AT PURCHASE
Purchase, New York

See Purchase College, State University of New York

STATE UNIVERSITY OF NEW YORK COLLEGE OF ENVIRONMENTAL SCIENCE AND FORESTRY
Syracuse, New York

About the Institution State-supported, coed. Degrees awarded: B, M, D. Offers 29 undergraduate majors. Total enrollment: 1,740. Undergraduates: 1,187 (90% state residents). Freshmen: 116.

Undergraduate Expenses (1997–98 estimated) State resident tuition: $3400. Nonresident tuition: $8300. Mandatory fees: $13. College room and board: $6910. College room only: $3760.

Applications Of all full-time undergraduates enrolled in fall 1996, 100% of those judged to have need according to Federal Methodology were aided. *Financial aid deadline (priority):* 3/1. *Financial aid forms:* FAFSA, state form required. *Regular admission application deadline:* rolling. Early decision deadline: 11/15.

Summary of Aid to Needy Students *From gift & self-help combined:* Average need met: 80%. Average amount awarded: $7814 (16% gift aid, 84% self-help). *Gift aid:* Total: $1,200,000 (21% from college's own funds, 49% from other college-administered sources, 30% from external sources). 287 Federal Work-Study jobs (averaging $1000); 340 part-time jobs.

Need-Based Scholarships & Grants Pell, FSEOG, state, private, college/university.

Loans Perkins, PLUS, Stafford, Unsubsidized Stafford, private, college/university short-term loans ($200 average).

Non-Need Awards In 1996, a total of 375 non-need awards were made. *Academic Interests/Achievement Awards:* 300 ($350,000 total): agriculture, biological sciences, engineering/technologies. *Special Characteristics Awards:* 75 ($110,000 total): members of minorities, ROTC participants.

Other Money-Saving Options Cooperative Army ROTC, cooperative Air Force ROTC, off-campus living (after freshman year). *Payment Plan:* deferred payment.

Contact Mr. John E. View, Director of Financial Aid, State University of New York College of Environmental Science and Forestry, 1 Forestry Drive, 115 Bray Hall, Syracuse, NY 13210-2779, 315-470-6670, fax: 315-470-6933.

STATE UNIVERSITY OF NEW YORK HEALTH SCIENCE CENTER AT SYRACUSE
Syracuse, New York

About the Institution State-supported, coed. Degrees awarded: A, B, M, D, P. Offers 7 undergraduate majors. Total enrollment: 1,020. Undergraduates: 301 (96% state residents). Freshmen: 5.

Undergraduate Expenses (1996–97) State resident tuition: $3400. Nonresident tuition: $8300. Mandatory fees: $215. College room only: $3419.

Applications 93% of all full-time undergraduates enrolled in fall 1996 applied for aid; of these, 100% were judged to have need according to Federal Methodology, of whom 100% were aided. *Financial aid deadline*

(priority): 4/1. *Financial aid forms:* FAFSA, state form required. Institutional form required for some. *Admission application deadline:* rolling.

Summary of Aid to Needy Students *From gift & self-help combined:* Average need met: 92%. *Gift aid:* Total: $632,424 (10% from college's own funds, 27% from other college-administered sources, 63% from external sources). 61 Federal Work-Study jobs (averaging $1033).

Need-Based Scholarships & Grants Pell, FSEOG, state, private, college/university.

Loans Perkins, PLUS, Stafford, Unsubsidized Stafford, college/university short-term loans ($300 average), college/university long-term loans ($1700 average).

Non-Need Awards Not offered.

Other Money-Saving Options Off-campus living (after freshman year). *Payment Plan:* installment.

Contact Office of Financial Aid, State University of New York Health Science Center at Syracuse, 155 Elizabeth Blackwell Street, Syracuse, NY 13210-2334, 315-464-4329.

STATE UNIVERSITY OF NEW YORK MARITIME COLLEGE
Throgs Neck, New York

About the Institution State-supported, coed. Degrees awarded: A, B, M. Offers 12 undergraduate majors. Total enrollment: 776. Undergraduates: 636 (72% state residents). Freshmen: 201.

Undergraduate Expenses (1996–97) State resident tuition: $3400. Nonresident tuition: $8300. Mandatory fees: $476. College room and board: $5000.

Applications Of all full-time undergraduates enrolled in fall 1996, 85% of those who applied for aid were judged to have need according to Federal Methodology, of whom 100% were aided. *Financial aid deadline (priority):* 5/1. *Financial aid forms:* FAFSA, institutional form, proof of Selective Service registration (for men) required; CSS Financial Aid PROFILE acceptable. State form required for some. *Regular admission application deadline:* rolling. Early decision deadline: 12/1.

Summary of Aid to Needy Students *From gift & self-help combined:* Average amount awarded: $4720 (44% gift aid, 56% self-help). *Gift aid:* Total: $1,078,443 (16% from college's own funds, 2% from other college-administered sources, 82% from external sources). 75 Federal Work-Study jobs (averaging $1000); 50 part-time jobs.

Need-Based Scholarships & Grants Pell, FSEOG, state, private.

Loans Perkins, PLUS, Stafford, Unsubsidized Stafford, college/university short-term loans ($300 average).

Non-Need Awards *Academic Interests/Achievement Awards:* general academic.

Other Money-Saving Options Naval ROTC, cooperative Air Force ROTC.

Contact Ms. Michele McCarthy, Assistant Director of Financial Aid, State University of New York Maritime College, 6 Pennyfield Avenue, Throgs Neck, NY 10465-4198, 718-409-7268, fax: 718-409-7275.

STEPHEN F. AUSTIN STATE UNIVERSITY
Nacogdoches, Texas

About the Institution State-supported, coed. Degrees awarded: B, M, D. Offers 113 undergraduate majors. Total enrollment: 11,671. Undergraduates: 10,116 (98% state residents). Freshmen: 2,048.

Undergraduate Expenses (1996–97) State resident tuition: $960. Nonresident tuition: $6660. Mandatory fees: $553. College room and board: $3680.

Applications Of all full-time undergraduates enrolled in fall 1996, 79% of those who applied for aid were judged to have need according to Federal Methodology, of whom 92% were aided. *Financial aid deadline (priority):* 4/15. *Financial aid forms:* FAFSA, institutional form required. *Admission application deadline:* rolling.

Summary of Aid to Needy Students *From gift & self-help combined:* Average need met: 92%. Average amount awarded: $2262 (63% gift aid, 37% self-help). *Gift aid:* Total: $5,115,817 (26% from college's own funds, 1% from other college-administered sources, 73% from external sources). 600 Federal Work-Study jobs (averaging $2800); 1,180 part-time jobs.

Need-Based Scholarships & Grants Pell, FSEOG, state, private, college/university.

Loans Perkins, PLUS, Stafford, Unsubsidized Stafford, state, private, college/university short-term loans ($523 average).

Non-Need Awards In 1996, a total of 3,945 non-need awards were made. *Academic Interests/Achievement Awards:* general academic, agriculture, biological sciences, business, communication, computer science, education, health fields, home economics, mathematics, military science, physical sciences, premedicine. *Creative Arts/Performance Awards:* applied art and design, art/fine arts, journalism/publications, music, theater/drama. *Special Achievements/Activities Awards:* general special achievements/activities, cheerleading/drum major, hobbies/interest, leadership, rodeo. *Special Characteristics Awards:* general special characteristics, adult students, children of union members/company employees, first-generation college students, local/state students, previous college experience, religious affiliation, ROTC participants. *Athletic:* Total: 404 ($1,002,156); Men: 234 ($642,368); Women: 170 ($359,788).

Other Money-Saving Options Accelerated degree, Army ROTC, off-campus living (after sophomore year). *Payment Plan:* installment.

Contact Ms. Kim Butler, Accountant, Stephen F. Austin State University, PO Box 13052, SFA Station, Nacogdoches, TX 75964, 409-468-1094, fax: 409-468-1048.

STEPHENS COLLEGE
Columbia, Missouri

About the Institution Independent, women. Degrees awarded: A, B. Offers 36 undergraduate majors. Total enrollment: 789 (30% state residents). Freshmen: 167.

Undergraduate Expenses (1997–98) Comprehensive fee of $20,530 includes tuition ($14,830) and college room and board ($5700). College room only: $2990.

Applications *Financial aid deadline (priority):* 3/15. *Financial aid forms:* FAFSA, CSS Financial Aid PROFILE acceptable. State form, institutional form required for some. *Regular admission application deadline:* 7/31. Early decision deadline: 12/15.

Summary of Aid to Needy Students Federal Work-Study jobs; part-time jobs.

Loans College/university short-term loans, college/university long-term loans.

Non-Need Awards *Academic Interests/Achievement Awards:* general academic. *Creative Arts/Performance Awards:* theater/drama. *Special Characteristics Awards:* local/state students, siblings of current students.

Other Money-Saving Options Accelerated degree, cooperative Army ROTC, cooperative Naval ROTC, cooperative Air Force ROTC. *Payment Plan:* installment. *Waivers:* full or partial for employees or children of employees.

Contact Office of Financial Aid, Stephens College, 1200 East Broadway, Columbia, MO 65215-0002, 573-442-2211.

STERLING COLLEGE
Sterling, Kansas

About the Institution Independent/religious, coed. Degrees awarded: A, B. Offers 44 undergraduate majors. Total enrollment: 674 (85% state residents). Freshmen: 147.

Undergraduate Expenses (1997–98) Comprehensive fee of $14,180 includes tuition ($10,076) and college room and board ($4104).

Applications Of all full-time undergraduates enrolled in fall 1996, 100% of those who applied for aid were judged to have need according to Federal Methodology, of whom 100% were aided. *Financial aid deadline (priority):* 3/15. *Financial aid forms:* FAFSA required; CSS Financial Aid PROFILE acceptable. *Admission application deadline:* rolling.

Summary of Aid to Needy Students *From gift & self-help combined:* Average need met: 79%. Average amount awarded: $10,520 (61% gift aid, 39% self-help). *Gift aid:* Total: $2,434,894 (66% from college's own funds, 16% from other college-administered sources, 18% from external sources). Federal Work-Study jobs (averaging $1100); part-time jobs.

Need-Based Scholarships & Grants Pell, FSEOG, state, private, college/university.

Loans Perkins, PLUS, Stafford, Unsubsidized Stafford, college/university long-term loans ($1000 average).

Non-Need Awards In 1996, a total of 820 non-need awards were made. *Academic Interests/Achievement Awards:* 317 ($294,019 total): general academic. *Creative Arts/Performance Awards:* 199 ($76,658 total): debating, music, theater/drama. *Special Achievements/Activities Awards:* 58 ($25,541 total): cheerleading/drum major, leadership. *Special Characteristics Awards:* 13 ($31,187 total): general special characteristics, twins. *Athletic:* Total: 233 ($282,271); Men: 154 ($196,234); Women: 79 ($86,037).

Other Money-Saving Options *Payment Plan:* installment. *Waivers:* full or partial for employees or children of employees.

Contact Ms. Kay Barnes, Director of Financial Aid, Sterling College, PO Box 98, Sterling, KS 67579-0098, 316-278-2173.

STERN COLLEGE FOR WOMEN
New York, New York

See Yeshiva University

STETSON UNIVERSITY
DeLand, Florida

About the Institution Independent, coed. Degrees awarded: B, M, P. Offers 49 undergraduate majors. Total enrollment: 2,784. Undergraduates: 1,851 (76% state residents). Freshmen: 426.

Undergraduate Expenses (1997–98) Comprehensive fee of $21,477 includes tuition ($15,100), mandatory fees ($665), and college room and board ($5712). College room only: $3103.

Applications 54% of all full-time undergraduates enrolled in fall 1996 applied for aid; of these, 100% were judged to have need according to Federal Methodology, of whom 100% were aided. *Financial aid deadline (priority):* 3/15. *Financial aid forms:* FAFSA, institutional form required; CSS Financial Aid PROFILE acceptable. *Regular admission application deadline:* 3/15. Early decision deadline: 11/15.

Summary of Aid to Needy Students *From gift & self-help combined:* Average need met: 90%. Average amount awarded: $11,241. *Gift aid:* Total: $5,579,820. Federal Work-Study jobs; 562 part-time jobs.

Need-Based Scholarships & Grants Pell, FSEOG, state, private, college/university.

Loans Perkins, PLUS, Stafford, Unsubsidized Stafford, state, private, college/university short-term loans ($300 average), college/university long-term loans ($1113 average).

Non-Need Awards *Academic Interests/Achievement Awards:* general academic, area/ethnic studies, biological sciences, business, communication, computer science, education, English, foreign languages, humanities, mathematics, military science, physical sciences, premedicine, religion/biblical studies, social sciences. *Creative Arts/Performance Awards:* applied art and design, art/fine arts, music, theater/drama. *Special Achievements/Activities Awards:* general special achievements/activities, cheerleading/drum major, community service, leadership, religious involvement. *Special Characteristics Awards:* general special characteristics, children of faculty/staff, local/state students, members of minorities, ROTC participants. *Athletic:* Total: 144 ($1,190,696).

Other Money-Saving Options Accelerated degree, cooperative Army ROTC, off-campus living (after sophomore year). *Payment Plan:* installment. *Waivers:* full or partial for employees or children of employees.

Contact Dr. James Beasley, Vice President for Enrollment Management and Campus Life, Stetson University, DeLand, FL 32720-3781, 904-822-7210.

STEVENS INSTITUTE OF TECHNOLOGY
Hoboken, New Jersey

About the Institution Independent, coed. Degrees awarded: B, M, D. Offers 52 undergraduate majors. Total enrollment: 3,382. Undergraduates: 1,382 (55% state residents). Freshmen: 410.

Undergraduate Expenses (1996–97) Comprehensive fee of $25,060 includes tuition ($18,300), mandatory fees ($270), and college room and board ($6490). College room only: $3266.

Applications 77% of all full-time undergraduates enrolled in fall 1996 applied for aid; of these, 90% were judged to have need according to Federal Methodology, of whom 99% were aided. *Financial aid deadline (priority):* 3/1. *Financial aid forms:* FAFSA, institutional form required. *Regular admission application deadline:* 3/1. Early decision deadline: 12/1.

Summary of Aid to Needy Students *From gift & self-help combined:* Average need met: 95%. Average amount awarded: $17,761 (65% gift aid, 35% self-help). *Gift aid:* Total: $10,966,874 (72% from college's own funds, 2% from other college-administered sources, 26% from external sources). 800 Federal Work-Study jobs (averaging $1400); part-time jobs.

Need-Based Scholarships & Grants Pell, FSEOG, state, private, college/university.

Loans Perkins, PLUS, Stafford, Unsubsidized Stafford, state, private.

Non-Need Awards In 1996, a total of 762 non-need awards were made. *Academic Interests/Achievement Awards:* 720 ($3,922,000 total): general academic, computer science, engineering/technologies, humanities, mathematics, physical sciences, premedicine. *Special Characteristics Awards:* 42 ($278,000 total): children and siblings of alumni, children of faculty/staff, local/state students, members of minorities, ROTC participants.

Other Money-Saving Options Accelerated degree, co-op program, cooperative Army ROTC, cooperative Air Force ROTC, off-campus living. *Payment Plan:* installment. *Waivers:* full or partial for employees or children of employees.

Contact Mr. David Sheridan, Director of Financial Aid, Stevens Institute of Technology, Castle Point on Hudson, Hoboken, NJ 07030, 201-216-5201, fax: 201-216-8348.

STILLMAN COLLEGE
Tuscaloosa, Alabama

About the Institution Independent/religious, coed. Degrees awarded: B. Offers 18 undergraduate majors. Total enrollment: 842 (72% state residents). Freshmen: 226.

Undergraduate Expenses (1997–98) Comprehensive fee of $9149 includes tuition ($5460) and college room and board ($3689).

Applications *Financial aid deadline:* Applications processed continuously. *Financial aid forms:* FAFSA required. State form required for some. *Admission application deadline:* rolling.

Summary of Aid to Needy Students *From gift & self-help combined:* Average need met: 90%. Average amount awarded: $9500 (35% gift aid, 65% self-help). *Gift aid:* Total: $3,000,000. Federal Work-Study jobs; part-time jobs.

Need-Based Scholarships & Grants Pell, FSEOG.

Loans Perkins, Stafford, Unsubsidized Stafford.

Non-Need Awards *Academic Interests/Achievement Awards:* general academic, education. *Creative Arts/Performance Awards:* music. *Special Characteristics Awards:* children of faculty/staff.

Other Money-Saving Options Accelerated degree, cooperative Army ROTC, off-campus living. *Payment Plan:* installment. *Waivers:* full or partial for employees or children of employees.

Contact Mr. Booker T. Crawford, Director of Financial Aid, Stillman College, PO Box 1430, Tuscaloosa, AL 35403-9990, 205-349-4240.

STONEHILL COLLEGE
Easton, Massachusetts

About the Institution Independent/religious, coed. Degrees awarded: B. Offers 32 undergraduate majors. Total enrollment: 2,041 (62% state residents). Freshmen: 551.

Undergraduate Expenses (1997–98) Comprehensive fee of $21,852 includes tuition ($14,406), mandatory fees ($450), and college room and board ($6996).

Applications 82% of all full-time undergraduates enrolled in fall 1996 applied for aid; of these, 86% were judged to have need according to Federal Methodology, of whom 99% were aided. *Financial aid deadline (priority):* 2/1. *Financial aid forms:* FAFSA, CSS Financial Aid PROFILE required. *Regular admission application deadline:* 2/1. Early decision deadline: 11/1.

Summary of Aid to Needy Students *From gift & self-help combined:* Average need met: 86%. Average amount awarded: $13,063 (46% gift aid, 54% self-help). *Gift aid:* Total: $8,653,400 (83% from college's own funds, 8% from other college-administered sources, 9% from external sources). 576 Federal Work-Study jobs (averaging $1118); 135 part-time jobs.

Need-Based Scholarships & Grants Pell, FSEOG, state, college/university.

Loans Perkins, PLUS, Stafford, Unsubsidized Stafford, state, private.

Non-Need Awards *Academic Interests/Achievement Awards:* general academic. *Special Achievements/Activities Awards:* general special achievements/activities, leadership. *Special Characteristics Awards:* general special characteristics, children of faculty/staff, relatives of clergy, siblings of current students. *Athletic:* Total: 22 ($395,506); Men: 10 ($189,818); Women: 12 ($205,688).

Other Money-Saving Options Army ROTC, off-campus living. *Payment Plans:* tuition prepayment, installment. *Waivers:* full or partial for minority students, employees or children of employees, senior citizens.

Contact Office of Financial Aid, Stonehill College, 320 Washington Street, Easton, MA 02357-5510, 508-565-1000.

STRAYER COLLEGE
Washington, District of Columbia

About the Institution Proprietary, coed. Degrees awarded: A, B, M. Offers 6 undergraduate majors. Total enrollment: 8,172. Undergraduates: 7,083 (93% district residents). Freshmen: 1,180.

Undergraduate Expenses (1997–98) Tuition: $7650.

Applications Of all full-time undergraduates enrolled in fall 1996, 74% of those who applied for aid were judged to have need according to Federal Methodology, of whom 100% were aided. *Financial aid deadline (priority):* 8/1. *Financial aid forms:* FAFSA required; CSS Financial Aid PROFILE, district form acceptable. *Admission application deadline:* rolling.

Summary of Aid to Needy Students *From gift & self-help combined:* Average need met: 75%. *Gift aid:* Total: $2,680,328 (3% from college's own funds, 13% from other college-administered sources, 84% from external sources). Federal Work-Study jobs; 8 part-time jobs.

Need-Based Scholarships & Grants Pell, FSEOG, state.

Loans PLUS, Stafford, Unsubsidized Stafford, credit-based loans for tuition and fees.

Non-Need Awards In 1996, a total of 83 non-need awards were made. *Academic Interests/Achievement Awards:* 35 ($42,500 total): general academic, business, computer science. *Special Achievements/Activities Awards:* 48 ($64,000 total): general special achievements/activities.

Other Money-Saving Options Accelerated degree, co-op program. *Payment Plan:* installment. *Waivers:* full or partial for employees or children of employees.

Contact Mr. Michael Williams, Campus Coordinator, Strayer College, 1025 15th Street, NW, Washington, DC 20005-2603, 202-408-2400, fax: 202-289-1831.

SUE BENNETT COLLEGE
London, Kentucky

About the Institution Independent/religious, coed. Degrees awarded: A, B. Offers 7 undergraduate majors. Total enrollment: 404 (81% state residents). Freshmen: 126.

Undergraduate Expenses (1997–98 estimated) Comprehensive fee of $11,675 includes tuition ($7780) and college room and board ($3895). College room only: $1838.

Applications *Financial aid deadline (priority):* 5/1. *Financial aid forms:* FAFSA, CSS Financial Aid PROFILE, institutional form required. State form required for some. *Admission application deadline:* rolling.

Summary of Aid to Needy Students Federal Work-Study jobs; part-time jobs.

Loans College/university long-term loans.

Non-Need Awards *Athletic:* available.

Other Money-Saving Options Off-campus living. *Payment Plan:* installment. *Waivers:* full or partial for employees or children of employees and senior citizens.

Contact Office of Financial Aid, Sue Bennett College, London, KY 40741-2400, 606-864-2238.

SUFFOLK UNIVERSITY
Boston, Massachusetts

About the Institution Independent, coed. Degrees awarded: A, B, M, D, P. Offers 70 undergraduate majors. Total enrollment: 6,401. Undergraduates: 2,986 (77% state residents). Freshmen: 521.

Undergraduate Expenses (1997–98) Comprehensive fee of $21,270 includes tuition ($12,840), mandatory fees ($80), and college room and board ($8350 minimum).

Applications 69% of all full-time undergraduates enrolled in fall 1996 applied for aid; of these, 88% were judged to have need according to Federal Methodology, of whom 98% were aided. *Financial aid deadline (priority):* 3/1. *Financial aid forms:* FAFSA, institutional form, nontaxable income verification required; CSS Financial Aid PROFILE acceptable. *Regular admission application deadline:* rolling. Early action deadline: 11/15.

Summary of Aid to Needy Students *From gift & self-help combined:* Average need met: 86%. Average amount awarded: $11,386 (36% gift aid, 64% self-help). *Gift aid:* Total: $5,701,947 (67% from college's own funds, 15% from other college-administered sources, 18% from external sources). 643 Federal Work-Study jobs (averaging $1200); 56 part-time jobs.

Need-Based Scholarships & Grants Pell, FSEOG, state, private, college/university.

Loans Perkins, PLUS, Stafford, Unsubsidized Stafford, private, college/university short-term loans ($200 average), college/university long-term loans ($2500 average).

Non-Need Awards In 1996, a total of 299 non-need awards were made. *Academic Interests/Achievement Awards:* general academic. *Creative Arts/Performance Awards:* 4 ($6000 total): debating. *Special Characteristics Awards:* 28 ($5876 total): adult students, siblings of current students.

Other Money-Saving Options Accelerated degree, co-op program, cooperative Army ROTC, off-campus living. *Payment Plans:* installment, deferred payment. *Waivers:* full or partial for employees or children of employees and senior citizens.

Contact Ms. Christine A. Perry, Director of Financial Aid, Suffolk University, 8 Ashburton Place, Boston, MA 02108-2770, 617-573-8470, fax: 617-720-3579.

SULLIVAN COLLEGE
Louisville, Kentucky

About the Institution Proprietary, coed. Degrees awarded: A, B, M. Offers 12 undergraduate majors. Total enrollment: 2,321. Undergraduates: 2,296 (83% state residents). Freshmen: 515.

Undergraduate Expenses (1997–98) Tuition: $8904 (minimum). College room only: $2700.

Applications *Financial aid deadline:* Applications processed continuously. *Financial aid forms:* FAFSA, institutional form required. *Admission application deadline:* 9/30.

Summary of Aid to Needy Students Federal Work-Study jobs; part-time jobs.

Loans College/university short-term loans, college/university long-term loans.

Non-Need Awards *Athletic:* available.

Other Money-Saving Options Accelerated degree, off-campus living. *Payment Plans:* installment, deferred payment. *Waivers:* full or partial for employees or children of employees.

Contact Office of Financial Aid, Sullivan College, 3101 Bardstown Road, Louisville, KY 40205, 502-456-6504.

SUL ROSS STATE UNIVERSITY
Alpine, Texas

About the Institution State-supported, coed. Degrees awarded: A, B, M. Offers 35 undergraduate majors. Total enrollment: 2,458. Undergraduates: 1,801 (97% state residents). Freshmen: 382.

Undergraduate Expenses (1997–98) State resident tuition: $1020. Nonresident tuition: $6660. Mandatory fees: $660. College room and board: $3020 (minimum).

Applications Of all full-time undergraduates enrolled in fall 1996, 98% of those who applied for aid were judged to have need according to Federal Methodology, of whom 99% were aided. *Financial aid deadline (priority):* 5/1. *Financial aid forms:* FAFSA, institutional form required; CSS Financial Aid PROFILE acceptable. State form required for some. *Admission application deadline:* rolling.

Summary of Aid to Needy Students *From gift & self-help combined:* Average need met: 73%. Average amount awarded: $5504 (36% gift aid, 64% self-help). *Gift aid:* Total: $2,994,103 (7% from college's own funds, 8% from other college-administered sources, 85% from external sources). 500 Federal Work-Study jobs (averaging $2500); 182 part-time jobs.

Need-Based Scholarships & Grants Pell, FSEOG, state, college/university.

Loans Perkins, PLUS, Stafford, Unsubsidized Stafford, state, college/university short-term loans ($450 average).

Non-Need Awards In 1996, a total of 75 non-need awards were made. *Academic Interests/Achievement Awards:* 45 ($45,000 total): general academic, agriculture, biological sciences, business, education, English, foreign languages, health fields. *Creative Arts/Performance Awards:* 10 ($3000 total): art/fine arts, cinema/film/broadcasting, journalism/publications, music, theater/drama. *Special Achievements/Activities Awards:* 20 ($20,000 total): leadership.

Other Money-Saving Options Off-campus living (after sophomore year). *Payment Plan:* installment.

Contact Mr. Robert Vasquez, Director of Financial Aid, Sul Ross State University, Alpine, TX 79832, 915-837-8055.

SUSQUEHANNA UNIVERSITY
Selinsgrove, Pennsylvania

About the Institution Independent/religious, coed. Degrees awarded: B. Offers 50 undergraduate majors. Total enrollment: 1,568 (59% state residents). Freshmen: 432.

Undergraduate Expenses (1996–97) Comprehensive fee of $22,770 includes tuition ($17,400), mandatory fees ($290), and college room and board ($5080). College room only: $2690.

Applications Of all full-time undergraduates enrolled in fall 1996, 97% of those who applied for aid were judged to have need according to Federal Methodology, of whom 100% were aided. *Financial aid deadline (priority):* 3/1. *Financial aid forms:* FAFSA, CSS Financial Aid PROFILE, state form required. Business/Farm Supplement required for some. *Regular admission application deadline:* 3/1. Early decision deadline: 12/15.

Summary of Aid to Needy Students *From gift & self-help combined:* Average need met: 89%. Average amount awarded: $14,943 (67% gift aid, 33% self-help). *Gift aid:* Total: $10,952,921 (79% from college's own funds, 2% from other college-administered sources, 19% from external sources). 899 Federal Work-Study jobs (averaging $1400); 56 part-time jobs.

Need-Based Scholarships & Grants Pell, FSEOG, state, private, college/university.

Loans Perkins, PLUS, Stafford, Unsubsidized Stafford, private, college/university long-term loans ($2000 average).

Non-Need Awards In 1996, a total of 713 non-need awards were made. *Academic Interests/Achievement Awards:* 414 ($2,406,730 total): general academic, business, mathematics. *Creative Arts/Performance Awards:* 47 ($104,000 total): general creative, music. *Special Achievements/Activities Awards:* 206 ($727,750 total): general special achievements/activities. *Special Characteristics Awards:* 46 ($480,345 total): members of minorities.

Other Money-Saving Options Accelerated degree, cooperative Army ROTC, off-campus living (after junior year). *Payment Plans:* tuition prepayment, installment, deferred payment. *Waivers:* full or partial for employees or children of employees.

Contact Financial Aid Office, Susquehanna University, Selinsgrove, PA 17870-1001, 717-372-4450.

SWARTHMORE COLLEGE
Swarthmore, Pennsylvania

About the Institution Independent, coed. Degrees awarded: B. Offers 43 undergraduate majors. Total enrollment: 1,437 (13% state residents). Freshmen: 411.

Undergraduate Expenses (1997–98) Comprehensive fee of $29,500 includes tuition ($21,792), mandatory fees ($208), and college room and board ($7500). College room only: $3854.

Applications 57% of all full-time undergraduates enrolled in fall 1996 applied for aid; of these, 84% were judged to have need according to Federal Methodology, of whom 100% were aided. *Financial aid deadline (priority):* 2/15. *Financial aid forms:* FAFSA, CSS Financial Aid PROFILE, institutional form, copy of student and parent tax returns required. State form required for some. *Regular admission application deadline:* 1/1. Early decision deadline: 11/15.

Summary of Aid to Needy Students *From gift & self-help combined:* Average need met: 100%. Average amount awarded: $19,650 (81% gift aid, 19% self-help). *Gift aid:* Total: $11,037,916 (91% from college's own funds, 2% from other college-administered sources, 7% from external sources). 626 Federal Work-Study jobs (averaging $1260); 396 part-time jobs.

Need-Based Scholarships & Grants Pell, FSEOG, state, college/university.

Loans Perkins, PLUS, Stafford, Unsubsidized Stafford, college/university short-term loans ($100 average), college/university long-term loans ($3000 average).

Non-Need Awards In 1996, a total of 16 non-need awards were made. *Academic Interests/Achievement Awards:* 16 ($300,000 total): general academic.

Other Money-Saving Options Cooperative Army ROTC, cooperative Naval ROTC, cooperative Air Force ROTC, off-campus living (after freshman year). *Payment Plan:* installment. *Waivers:* full or partial for employees or children of employees.

Contact Ms. Patricia Serianni, Associate Director of Financial Aid, Swarthmore College, 500 College Avenue, Swarthmore, PA 19081-1397, 610-328-8357, fax: 610-328-8673.

SWEET BRIAR COLLEGE
Sweet Briar, Virginia

About the Institution Independent, women. Degrees awarded: B. Offers 33 undergraduate majors. Total enrollment: 734 (32% state residents). Freshmen: 156.

Undergraduate Expenses (1997–98) Comprehensive fee of $22,305 includes tuition ($15,420), mandatory fees ($375), and college room and board ($6510).

Applications 73% of all full-time undergraduates enrolled in fall 1996 applied for aid; of these, 88% were judged to have need according to Federal Methodology, of whom 100% were aided. *Financial aid deadline (priority):* 3/1. *Financial aid forms:* FAFSA, institutional form required. State form, Divorced/Separated Parents' Statement, Business/Farm Supplement required for some. *Regular admission application deadline:* 2/15. Early decision deadline: 12/1.

Summary of Aid to Needy Students *From gift & self-help combined:* Average need met: 87%. Average amount awarded: $14,889 (71% gift aid, 29% self-help). *Gift aid:* Total: $3,731,000 (83% from college's

own funds, 12% from other college-administered sources, 5% from external sources). 55 Federal Work-Study jobs (averaging $961); 362 part-time jobs.

Need-Based Scholarships & Grants Pell, FSEOG, state, private, college/university.

Loans Perkins, PLUS, Stafford, Unsubsidized Stafford, college/university short-term loans ($500 average), college/university long-term loans ($3284 average).

Non-Need Awards In 1996, a total of 303 non-need awards were made. *Academic Interests/Achievement Awards:* 301 ($1,539,000 total): general academic, premedicine. *Special Achievements/Activities Awards:* 2 ($2000 total): leadership.

Other Money-Saving Options Accelerated degree, cooperative Army ROTC. *Payment Plan:* installment. *Waivers:* full or partial for employees or children of employees, adult students, senior citizens.

Contact Mr. Robert Steckel, Director of Financial Aid, Sweet Briar College, Box AS, Sweet Briar, VA 24595, 804-381-6156.

SYRACUSE UNIVERSITY
Syracuse, New York

About the Institution Independent, coed. Degrees awarded: B, M, D, P. Offers 123 undergraduate majors. Total enrollment: 14,719. Undergraduates: 10,289 (42% state residents). Freshmen: 2,665.

Undergraduate Expenses (1997–98) Comprehensive fee of $25,166 includes tuition ($17,550), mandatory fees ($506), and college room and board ($7110). College room only: $3690.

Applications 71% of all full-time undergraduates enrolled in fall 1996 applied for aid; of these, 89% were judged to have need according to Federal Methodology, of whom 100% were aided. *Financial aid deadline (priority):* 2/15. *Financial aid forms:* FAFSA, state form required. *Regular admission application deadline:* 2/1. Early decision deadline: 11/15.

Summary of Aid to Needy Students *From gift & self-help combined:* Average amount awarded: $14,500 (70% gift aid, 30% self-help). *Gift aid:* Total: $66,380,000 (79% from college's own funds, 3% from other college-administered sources, 18% from external sources). Federal Work-Study jobs (averaging $1500); 2,400 part-time jobs.

Need-Based Scholarships & Grants Pell, FSEOG, state, college/university.

Loans Perkins, PLUS, Stafford, Unsubsidized Stafford, Federal Nursing, college/university short-term loans.

Non-Need Awards *Academic Interests/Achievement Awards:* general academic, architecture. *Creative Arts/Performance Awards:* art/fine arts, music. *Special Characteristics Awards:* children of faculty/staff, ROTC participants. *Athletic:* available.

Other Money-Saving Options Accelerated degree, co-op program, Army ROTC, Air Force ROTC, off-campus living (after sophomore year). *Payment Plans:* tuition prepayment, installment. *Waivers:* full or partial for employees or children of employees.

Contact Office of Financial Aid, Syracuse University, 200 Archbold Gymnasium, Syracuse, NY 13244-1140, 315-443-1870.

SYRACUSE UNIVERSITY, UTICA COLLEGE
Utica, New York

See Utica College of Syracuse University

TABOR COLLEGE
Hillsboro, Kansas

About the Institution Independent/religious, coed. Degrees awarded: A, B. Offers 53 undergraduate majors. Total enrollment: 500 (65% state residents). Freshmen: 119.

Undergraduate Expenses (1997–98) Comprehensive fee of $14,560 includes tuition ($10,360), mandatory fees ($200), and college room and board ($4000). College room only: $1570.

Applications 100% of all full-time undergraduates enrolled in fall 1996 applied for aid; of these, 88% were judged to have need according to Federal Methodology, of whom 100% were aided. *Financial aid deadline (priority):* 3/1. *Financial aid forms:* institutional form required; FAFSA acceptable. State form required for some. *Admission application deadline:* rolling.

Summary of Aid to Needy Students *From gift & self-help combined:* Average need met: 84%. Average amount awarded: $8726 (62% gift aid, 38% self-help). *Gift aid:* Total: $2,210,583 (63% from college's own funds, 17% from other college-administered sources, 20% from external sources). 185 Federal Work-Study jobs (averaging $670); 75 part-time jobs.

Need-Based Scholarships & Grants Pell, FSEOG, state, private, college/university.

Loans Perkins, PLUS, Stafford, Unsubsidized Stafford.

Non-Need Awards In 1996, a total of 1,098 non-need awards were made. *Academic Interests/Achievement Awards:* 285 ($752,086 total): general academic. *Creative Arts/Performance Awards:* 124 ($81,126 total): music, performing arts, theater/drama. *Special Achievements/ Activities Awards:* 250 ($121,213 total): cheerleading/drum major, religious involvement. *Special Characteristics Awards:* 207 ($272,595 total): general special characteristics, children and siblings of alumni, children of faculty/staff, international students, relatives of clergy, religious affiliation, siblings of current students, spouses of current students. *Athletic:* Total: 232 ($291,397); Men: 166 ($227,425); Women: 66 ($63,972).

Other Money-Saving Options *Payment Plan:* installment. *Waivers:* full or partial for children of alumni, employees or children of employees, adult students, senior citizens.

Contact Mr. Mark Bandré, Director of Student Financial Assistance, Tabor College, 400 South Jefferson, Hillsboro, KS 67063, 316-947-3121 Ext. 1726, fax: 316-947-2607.

TALLADEGA COLLEGE
Talladega, Alabama

About the Institution Independent, coed. Degrees awarded: B. Offers 24 undergraduate majors. Total enrollment: 642 (60% state residents). Freshmen: 123.

Undergraduate Expenses (1996–97) Comprehensive fee of $9048 includes tuition ($5666), mandatory fees ($418), and college room and board ($2964). College room only: $1424.

Applications Of all full-time undergraduates enrolled in fall 1996, 100% of those judged to have need according to Federal Methodology were aided. *Financial aid deadline (priority):* 5/1. *Financial aid forms:* FAFSA, institutional form required; CSS Financial Aid PROFILE acceptable. *Admission application deadline:* rolling.

Summary of Aid to Needy Students *From gift & self-help combined:* Average need met: 93%. Average amount awarded: $7269 (54% gift aid, 46% self-help). *Gift aid:* Total: $2,376,039 (47% from college's own funds, 14% from other college-administered sources, 39% from external sources). 213 Federal Work-Study jobs (averaging $900); 16 part-time jobs.

Need-Based Scholarships & Grants Pell, FSEOG, state, private, college/university.

Loans Perkins, PLUS, Stafford, Unsubsidized Stafford, college/university short-term loans, college/university long-term loans.

Non-Need Awards In 1996, a total of 205 non-need awards were made. *Academic Interests/Achievement Awards:* 165 ($512,967 total): general academic. *Athletic:* Total: 40 ($292,652); Men: 22 ($152,076); Women: 18 ($140,576).

Other Money-Saving Options Accelerated degree, co-op program, cooperative Army ROTC, off-campus living. *Payment Plan:* installment. *Waivers:* full or partial for employees or children of employees.

Contact Mr. Johnny Byrd, Director of Financial Aid, Talladega College, 627 West Battle Street, Talladega, AL 35160, 205-362-0206 Ext. 235, fax: 205-362-2268.

TALMUDICAL ACADEMY OF NEW JERSEY
Adelphia, New Jersey

About the Institution Independent/religious, men. Degrees awarded: B, M.

Applications *Financial aid deadline:* continuous. *Financial aid forms:* FAFSA required.

Summary of Aid to Needy Students Federal Work-Study jobs.

Need-Based Scholarships & Grants Pell, FSEOG, college/university.

Non-Need Awards *Academic Interests/Achievement Awards:* general academic.

Contact Office of Financial Aid, Talmudical Academy of New Jersey, Adelphia, NJ 07710, 732-431-1600.

TALMUDICAL INSTITUTE OF UPSTATE NEW YORK
Rochester, New York

About the Institution Independent/religious, men. Offers 2 undergraduate majors.

Applications *Financial aid deadline (priority):* 1/31. *Financial aid forms:* FAFSA required. *Admission application deadline:* rolling.

Summary of Aid to Needy Students Federal Work-Study jobs; 7 part-time jobs.

Need-Based Scholarships & Grants Pell, FSEOG.

Non-Need Awards *Academic Interests/Achievement Awards:* religion/biblical studies.

Other Money-Saving Options Off-campus living. *Payment Plan:* installment.

Contact Office of Financial Aid, Talmudical Institute of Upstate New York, 769 Park Avenue, Rochester, NY 14607-3046, 716-473-2810.

TALMUDICAL SEMINARY OHOLEI TORAH
Brooklyn, New York

About the Institution Independent/religious, men. Offers 1 undergraduate major.

Applications *Financial aid deadline (priority):* 2/1. *Financial aid forms:* FAFSA required. *Admission application deadline:* 9/1.

Summary of Aid to Needy Students Federal Work-Study jobs.

Other Money-Saving Options Off-campus living. *Payment Plan:* installment. *Waivers:* full or partial for employees or children of employees.

Contact Office of Financial Aid, Talmudical Seminary Oholei Torah, Brooklyn, NY 11213-3310, 718-774-5050.

TALMUDIC COLLEGE OF FLORIDA
Miami Beach, Florida

About the Institution Independent/religious, men. Degrees awarded: B, M. Offers 4 undergraduate majors.

Applications *Financial aid deadline (priority):* 2/28. *Financial aid forms:* FAFSA, CSS Financial Aid PROFILE, state form acceptable. *Regular admission application deadline:* 9/5. Early action deadline: 3/5.

Summary of Aid to Needy Students Federal Work-Study jobs.

Contact Office of Financial Aid, Talmudic College of Florida, Miami Beach, FL 33139, 305-534-7050.

TARLETON STATE UNIVERSITY
Stephenville, Texas

About the Institution State-supported, coed. Degrees awarded: A, B, M. Offers 52 undergraduate majors. Total enrollment: 6,369. Undergraduates: 5,551 (99% state residents). Freshmen: 903.

Undergraduate Expenses (1996–97) State resident tuition: $960. Nonresident tuition: $7380. Mandatory fees: $978. College room and board: $2324 (minimum).

Applications *Financial aid deadline (priority):* 5/1. *Financial aid forms:* FAFSA, institutional form acceptable. *Admission application deadline:* 8/1.

Summary of Aid to Needy Students *From gift & self-help combined:* Average need met: 90%. Average amount awarded: $8000 (46% gift aid, 54% self-help). *Gift aid:* Total: $3,988,484 (9% from college's own funds, 15% from other college-administered sources, 76% from external sources). 140 Federal Work-Study jobs (averaging $2800); 600 part-time jobs.

Need-Based Scholarships & Grants Pell, FSEOG, state, private, college/university.

Loans Perkins, PLUS, Stafford, Unsubsidized Stafford, college/university short-term loans ($700 average).

Non-Need Awards *Academic Interests/Achievement Awards:* available. *Creative Arts/Performance Awards:* 101 ($59,400 total): music, theater/drama. *Special Achievements/Activities Awards:* 19 ($21,600 total): rodeo. *Special Characteristics Awards:* 176 ($17,600 total): children of faculty/staff. *Athletic:* Total: 143 ($124,635); Men: 92 ($83,011); Women: 51 ($41,624).

Other Money-Saving Options Accelerated degree, co-op program, Army ROTC, off-campus living (after sophomore year). *Payment Plan:* installment. *Waivers:* full or partial for employees or children of employees and senior citizens.

Contact Dr. F. H. Landis, Director of Financial Aid, Tarleton State University, Box T-0310, Stephenville, TX 76402, 817-968-9070, fax: 817-968-9389.

TAYLOR UNIVERSITY
Upland, Indiana

About the Institution Independent/religious, coed. Degrees awarded: A, B. Offers 65 undergraduate majors. Total enrollment: 1,866 (29% state residents). Freshmen: 489.

Undergraduate Expenses (1997–98) Comprehensive fee of $17,894 includes tuition ($13,270), mandatory fees ($214), and college room and board ($4410). College room only: $2100.

Applications 66% of all full-time undergraduates enrolled in fall 1996 applied for aid; of these, 86% were judged to have need according to Federal Methodology, of whom 98% were aided. *Financial aid deadline:* Applications processed continuously. *Financial aid forms:* FAFSA, institutional form required. *Admission application deadline:* rolling.

Summary of Aid to Needy Students *From gift & self-help combined:* Average need met: 85%. Average amount awarded: $10,273 (60% gift aid, 40% self-help). *Gift aid:* Total: $6,344,395 (71% from college's own funds, 4% from other college-administered sources, 25% from external sources). 768 Federal Work-Study jobs (averaging $1379); part-time jobs.

Need-Based Scholarships & Grants Pell, FSEOG, state, private, college/university.

Loans Perkins, PLUS, Stafford, Unsubsidized Stafford, private, college/university short-term loans ($300 average), college/university long-term loans ($1300 average).

Non-Need Awards In 1996, a total of 1,411 non-need awards were made. *Academic Interests/Achievement Awards:* 668 ($1,074,375 total): general academic. *Creative Arts/Performance Awards:* 26 ($38,780 total): music, theater/drama. *Special Achievements/Activities Awards:* 48 ($254,968 total): leadership, religious involvement. *Special Characteristics Awards:* 538 ($1,247,874 total): children and siblings of alumni, children of faculty/staff, ethnic background, international students, religious affiliation. *Athletic:* Total: 131 ($356,646); Men: 93 ($265,176); Women: 38 ($91,470).

Other Money-Saving Options Accelerated degree, off-campus living (after sophomore year). *Payment Plan:* installment. *Waivers:* full or partial for employees or children of employees.

Contact Mr. Timothy A. Nace, Director of Financial Aid, Taylor University, 500 West Reade Avenue, Upland, IN 46989-1001, 317-998-5358, fax: 317-998-4910.

TAYLOR UNIVERSITY, FORT WAYNE CAMPUS
Fort Wayne, Indiana

About the Institution Independent/religious, coed. Degrees awarded: A, B. Offers 16 undergraduate majors. Total enrollment: 404 (62% state residents). Freshmen: 85.

Undergraduate Expenses (1997–98) Comprehensive fee of $15,430 includes tuition ($11,325), mandatory fees ($95), and college room and board ($4010). College room only: $1700.

Applications Of all full-time undergraduates enrolled in fall 1996, 91% of those who applied for aid were judged to have need according to Federal Methodology, of whom 100% were aided. *Financial aid deadline (priority):* 3/1. *Financial aid forms:* FAFSA, institutional form required. *Admission application deadline:* rolling.

Summary of Aid to Needy Students *From gift & self-help combined:* Average need met: 100%. Average amount awarded: $5116 (66% gift aid, 34% self-help). *Gift aid:* Total: $1,171,542 (32% from college's own funds, 36% from other college-administered sources, 32% from external sources). 191 Federal Work-Study jobs (averaging $1250); 50 part-time jobs.

Need-Based Scholarships & Grants Pell, FSEOG, state, private, college/university, endowed-donor scholarships.

Loans Perkins, PLUS, Stafford, Unsubsidized Stafford, college/university long-term loans ($1400 average).

Non-Need Awards In 1996, a total of 14 non-need awards were made. *Academic Interests/Achievement Awards:* 13 ($14,500 total): general academic, communication, social sciences. *Special Characteristics Awards:* 1 ($1550 total): ethnic background, members of minorities, religious affiliation.

Other Money-Saving Options Co-op program, off-campus living (after junior year). *Payment Plan:* installment. *Waivers:* full or partial for employees or children of employees and senior citizens.

Contact Ms. Kim Barnett-Johnson, Director of Financial Aid, Taylor University, Fort Wayne Campus, 1025 West Rudisill Boulevard, Fort Wayne, IN 46807-2197, 219-456-2111.

TEIKYO MARYCREST UNIVERSITY
Davenport, Iowa

See Marycrest International University

TEIKYO POST UNIVERSITY
Waterbury, Connecticut

About the Institution Independent, coed. Degrees awarded: A, B. Offers 21 undergraduate majors. Total enrollment: 1,550 (87% state residents). Freshmen: 113.

Undergraduate Expenses (1997–98) Comprehensive fee of $17,860 includes tuition ($12,000), mandatory fees ($260), and college room and board ($5600).

Applications *Financial aid deadline (priority):* 3/15. *Financial aid forms:* FAFSA, institutional form required. State form required for some. *Admission application deadline:* rolling.

Summary of Aid to Needy Students *From gift & self-help combined:* Average need met: 47%. Average amount awarded: $11,778 (74% gift aid, 26% self-help). *Gift aid:* Total: $3,278,434 (56% from college's own funds, 34% from other college-administered sources, 10% from external sources). 87 Federal Work-Study jobs (averaging $1200); 12 part-time jobs.

Need-Based Scholarships & Grants Pell, FSEOG, state, private, college/university.

Loans Perkins, PLUS, Stafford, Unsubsidized Stafford, state.

Non-Need Awards In 1996, a total of 128 non-need awards were made. *Academic Interests/Achievement Awards:* 15 ($41,315 total): general academic, business, English, international studies, mathematics. *Special Achievements/Activities Awards:* 3 ($500 total): rodeo. *Special Characteristics Awards:* 24 ($180,100 total): general special characteristics, children and siblings of alumni, local/state students, members of minorities, siblings of current students. *Athletic:* Total: 86 ($286,924); Men: 47 ($171,290); Women: 39 ($115,634).

Other Money-Saving Options Accelerated degree, co-op program, cooperative Army ROTC, off-campus living. *Payment Plans:* installment, deferred payment. *Waivers:* full or partial for minority students, children of alumni, employees or children of employees, adult students, senior citizens.

Contact Ms. Heather K. Coulson, Assistant Director of Financial Aid, Teikyo Post University, 800 Country Club Road, Waterbury, CT 06723-2540, 203-596-4528, fax: 203-758-5610.

TEIKYO WESTMAR UNIVERSITY
Le Mars, Iowa

See Westmar University

TELSHE YESHIVA–CHICAGO
Chicago, Illinois

About the Institution Independent/religious, men. Degrees awarded: B, M. Offers 1 undergraduate major.

Applications *Financial aid deadline (priority):* 5/15. *Financial aid forms:* institutional form required. FAFSA required for some.

Summary of Aid to Needy Students Federal Work-Study jobs; part-time jobs.

Non-Need Awards available.

Contact Office of Financial Aid, Telshe Yeshiva–Chicago, Chicago, IL 60625-5598, 773-463-7738.

TEMPLE UNIVERSITY
Philadelphia, Pennsylvania

About the Institution State-related, coed. Degrees awarded: A, B, M, D, P. Offers 105 undergraduate majors. Total enrollment: 25,469. Undergraduates: 16,982 (83% state residents). Freshmen: 2,321.

Undergraduate Expenses (1996–97) State resident tuition: $5628. Nonresident tuition: $10,510. Mandatory fees: $220. College room and board: $5712.

Applications Of all full-time undergraduates enrolled in fall 1996, 87% of those who applied for aid were judged to have need according to Federal Methodology, of whom 96% were aided. *Financial aid deadline (priority):* 3/31. *Financial aid forms:* FAFSA, state form required; CSS Financial Aid PROFILE acceptable. *Admission application deadline:* 5/1.

Summary of Aid to Needy Students *From gift & self-help combined:* Average need met: 70%. Average amount awarded: $8210 (47% gift aid, 53% self-help). *Gift aid:* Total: $35,457,080 (33% from college's own funds, 21% from other college-administered sources, 46% from external sources). 3,528 Federal Work-Study jobs (averaging $1000); 1,200 part-time jobs.

Need-Based Scholarships & Grants Pell, FSEOG, state, college/university.

Loans College/university short-term loans ($200 average), college/university long-term loans ($500 average).

Non-Need Awards In 1996, a total of 892 non-need awards were made. *Academic Interests/Achievement Awards:* 478 ($1,407,662 total): general academic. *Creative Arts/Performance Awards:* 145 ($215,234 total): general creative, music, performing arts. *Special Characteristics Awards:* 59 ($213,924 total): general special characteristics. *Athletic:* Total: 210 ($2,199,579); Men: 118 ($1,341,969); Women: 92 ($857,610).

Other Money-Saving Options Accelerated degree, co-op program, Army ROTC, cooperative Naval ROTC, cooperative Air Force ROTC, off-campus living. *Payment Plan:* installment. *Waivers:* full or partial for employees or children of employees.

Contact Mr. Richard F. McCracken, Associate Director, Temple University, Conwell Hall Second Floor, 1810 North Broad Street, Philadelphia, PA 19122-6096, 215-204-3513, fax: 215-204-5897.

TENNESSEE STATE UNIVERSITY
Nashville, Tennessee

About the Institution State-supported, coed. Degrees awarded: A, B, M, D. Offers 59 undergraduate majors. Total enrollment: 8,643. Undergraduates: 7,013 (71% state residents). Freshmen: 1,095.

Undergraduate Expenses (1996–97) State resident tuition: $1916. Nonresident tuition: $6252. College room and board: $2720. College room only: $1420.

Applications *Financial aid deadline (priority):* 4/1. *Financial aid forms:* FAFSA required. *Admission application deadline:* 8/1.

Summary of Aid to Needy Students *From gift & self-help combined:* Average need met: 77%. Average amount awarded: $4500. 1,000 Federal Work-Study jobs (averaging $2000); 1,200 part-time jobs.

Need-Based Scholarships & Grants Pell, FSEOG, state.

Loans Perkins, PLUS, Stafford, Unsubsidized Stafford, college/university short-term loans, college/university long-term loans.

Non-Need Awards *Academic Interests/Achievement Awards:* general academic. *Creative Arts/Performance Awards:* music. *Special Characteristics Awards:* local/state students, members of minorities. *Athletic:* available.

Other Money-Saving Options Accelerated degree, co-op program, Air Force ROTC, cooperative Army ROTC, cooperative Naval ROTC, off-campus living. *Payment Plan:* deferred payment. *Waivers:* full or partial for minority students.

Contact Financial Aid Office, Tennessee State University, 3500 John Merritt Boulevard, Nashville, TN 37209-1561, 615-963-5701, fax: 615-963-7540.

TENNESSEE TECHNOLOGICAL UNIVERSITY
Cookeville, Tennessee

About the Institution State-supported, coed. Degrees awarded: A, B, M, D. Offers 68 undergraduate majors. Total enrollment: 8,173. Undergraduates: 7,107 (93% state residents). Freshmen: 1,162.

Undergraduate Expenses (1996–97) State resident tuition: $0. Nonresident tuition: $4336. Mandatory fees: $1920. College room and board: $3720. College room only: $1850.

Applications 66% of all full-time undergraduates enrolled in fall 1996 applied for aid; of these, 84% were judged to have need according to Federal Methodology, of whom 82% were aided. *Financial aid deadline (priority):* 3/15. *Financial aid forms:* FAFSA, student and parent tax returns required. *Admission application deadline:* rolling.

Summary of Aid to Needy Students *From gift & self-help combined:* Average need met: 98%. Average amount awarded: $4604 (31% gift aid, 69% self-help). *Gift aid:* Total: $4,070,000 (4% from college's own funds, 8% from other college-administered sources, 88% from external sources). 498 Federal Work-Study jobs (averaging $1200); 1,000 part-time jobs.

Need-Based Scholarships & Grants Pell, FSEOG, state, private, college/university.

Loans Perkins, PLUS, Stafford, Unsubsidized Stafford, private, college/university short-term loans ($275 average).

Non-Need Awards In 1996, a total of 2,247 non-need awards were made. *Academic Interests/Achievement Awards:* 710 ($1,233,406 total): general academic, agriculture, biological sciences, business, education, engineering/technologies, English, health fields, home economics, mathematics, military science. *Creative Arts/Performance Awards:* 155 ($132,320 total): music. *Special Achievements/Activities Awards:* 5 ($2500 total): cheerleading/drum major, memberships. *Special Characteristics Awards:* 1,171 ($631,962 total): children of educators, children of faculty/staff, children of public servants, first-generation college students, members of minorities. *Athletic:* Total: 206 ($1,021,000); Men: 140 ($686,900); Women: 66 ($334,100).

Other Money-Saving Options Accelerated degree, co-op program, Army ROTC, cooperative Air Force ROTC, off-campus living (after sophomore year). *Waivers:* full or partial for employees or children of employees.

Contact Dr. Raymond L. Holbrook, Director of Student Financial Aid, Tennessee Technological University, Box 5076 University Center, Cookeville, TN 38505, 615-372-3073, fax: 615-372-6309.

TENNESSEE TEMPLE UNIVERSITY
Chattanooga, Tennessee

About the Institution Independent/religious, coed. Degrees awarded: A, B, M. Offers 25 undergraduate majors. Total enrollment: 541 (16% state residents). Freshmen: 130.

Undergraduate Expenses (1997–98) Comprehensive fee of $11,020 includes tuition ($5820), mandatory fees ($450), and college room and board ($4750).

Applications *Financial aid deadline (priority):* 6/1. *Financial aid forms:* FAFSA, institutional form required; CSS Financial Aid PROFILE, state form acceptable. *Admission application deadline:* 8/20.

Summary of Aid to Needy Students *From gift & self-help combined:* Average amount awarded: $6895 (67% gift aid, 33% self-help). *Gift aid:* Total: $2,307,810. Federal Work-Study jobs; part-time jobs.

Need-Based Scholarships & Grants Pell, FSEOG, state, private, college/university.

Loans Perkins, PLUS, Stafford, Unsubsidized Stafford.

Non-Need Awards *Academic Interests/Achievement Awards:* general academic. *Creative Arts/Performance Awards:* music. *Special Achievements/*

Activities Awards: leadership. *Special Characteristics Awards:* children and siblings of alumni, relatives of clergy. *Athletic:* available.

Other Money-Saving Options Co-op program. *Payment Plan:* installment. *Waivers:* full or partial for employees or children of employees.

Contact Ms. Louise Sansbury, Director of Financial Aid, Tennessee Temple University, 1815 Union Avenue, Chattanooga, TN 37404-3587, 423-493-4207, fax: 423-493-4497.

TENNESSEE WESLEYAN COLLEGE
Athens, Tennessee

About the Institution Independent/religious, coed. Degrees awarded: B. Offers 35 undergraduate majors. Total enrollment: 738 (82% state residents). Freshmen: 150.

Undergraduate Expenses (1997–98) Comprehensive fee of $10,470 includes tuition ($6500), mandatory fees ($100), and college room and board ($3870).

Applications Of all full-time undergraduates enrolled in fall 1996, 95% of those judged to have need according to Federal Methodology were aided. *Financial aid deadline (priority):* 3/15. *Financial aid forms:* FAFSA, institutional form required; CSS Financial Aid PROFILE acceptable. *Admission application deadline:* rolling.

Summary of Aid to Needy Students *From gift & self-help combined:* Average need met: 75%. Average amount awarded: $7967 (70% gift aid, 30% self-help). *Gift aid:* Total: $2,139,393 (70% from college's own funds, 14% from other college-administered sources, 16% from external sources). 39 Federal Work-Study jobs (averaging $1155); 32 part-time jobs.

Need-Based Scholarships & Grants Pell, FSEOG, state, private.

Loans Perkins, PLUS, Stafford, Unsubsidized Stafford, state, private.

Non-Need Awards In 1996, a total of 651 non-need awards were made. *Academic Interests/Achievement Awards:* 215 ($670,405 total): general academic, religion/biblical studies. *Creative Arts/Performance Awards:* 21 ($41,258 total): music. *Special Achievements/Activities Awards:* 191 ($261,198 total): general special achievements/activities, cheerleading/drum major, Junior Miss, leadership, memberships, religious involvement. *Special Characteristics Awards:* 111 ($216,450 total): general special characteristics, children of faculty/staff, international students, members of minorities, relatives of clergy, religious affiliation. *Athletic:* Total: 113 ($316,131); Men: 60 ($174,581); Women: 53 ($141,550).

Other Money-Saving Options Accelerated degree. *Payment Plan:* deferred payment. *Waivers:* full or partial for minority students and employees or children of employees.

Contact Ms. Bobbie Pennington, Financial Aid Officer, Tennessee Wesleyan College, PO Box 40, Athens, TN 37371-0040, 423-745-7504 Ext. 5215, fax: 423-744-9968.

TEXAS A&M INTERNATIONAL UNIVERSITY
Laredo, Texas

About the Institution State-supported, coed. Degrees awarded: B, M. Offers 22 undergraduate majors. Total enrollment: 2,510. Undergraduates: 1,538 (94% state residents). Freshmen: 344.

Undergraduate Expenses (1996–97) State resident tuition: $992. Nonresident tuition: $7626. Mandatory fees: $955.

Applications Of all full-time undergraduates enrolled in fall 1996, 100% of those who applied for aid were judged to have need according to Federal Methodology, of whom 100% were aided. *Financial aid deadline (priority):* 3/15. *Financial aid forms:* CSS Financial Aid PROFILE, state form, institutional form required; FAFSA acceptable. *Admission application deadline:* 7/1.

Summary of Aid to Needy Students *From gift & self-help combined:* Average amount awarded: $2358 (41% gift aid, 59% self-help). *Gift aid:* Total: $788,190 (7% from college's own funds, 10% from other college-administered sources, 83% from external sources). 67 Federal Work-Study jobs (averaging $827); 114 part-time jobs.

Need-Based Scholarships & Grants Pell, FSEOG, state, college/university.

Loans PLUS, Stafford, Unsubsidized Stafford, college/university short-term loans ($100 average).

Non-Need Awards Not offered.

Other Money-Saving Options *Payment Plan:* installment. *Waivers:* full or partial for employees or children of employees.

Contact Araceli S. Rangel, Director of Financial Aid, Texas A&M International University, 5201 University Boulevard, Laredo, TX 78041-1999, 210-326-2225, fax: 210-326-2224.

TEXAS A&M UNIVERSITY
College Station, Texas

About the Institution State-supported, coed. Degrees awarded: B, M, D, P. Offers 92 undergraduate majors. Total enrollment: 41,892. Undergraduates: 34,342 (86% state residents). Freshmen: 6,387.

Undergraduate Expenses (1996–97) State resident tuition: $1024. Nonresident tuition: $7872. Mandatory fees: $1464. College room and board: $2496 (minimum). College room only: $1590.

Applications Of all full-time undergraduates enrolled in fall 1996, 78% of those who applied for aid were judged to have need according to Federal Methodology, of whom 93% were aided. *Financial aid deadline (priority):* 4/1. *Financial aid forms:* FAFSA, institutional form, financial aid transcript (for transfers) required; CSS Financial Aid PROFILE acceptable. *Admission application deadline:* 3/1.

Summary of Aid to Needy Students *From gift & self-help combined:* Average need met: 70%. Average amount awarded: $5074 (43% gift aid, 57% self-help). *Gift aid:* Total: $24,824,068 (30% from college's own funds, 20% from other college-administered sources, 50% from external sources). 484 Federal Work-Study jobs (averaging $1092); 8,666 part-time jobs.

Need-Based Scholarships & Grants Pell, FSEOG, state, private, college/university.

Loans Perkins, PLUS, Stafford, Unsubsidized Stafford, Primary Care, state, private, college/university short-term loans ($600 average).

Non-Need Awards In 1996, a total of 7,807 non-need awards were made. *Academic Interests/Achievement Awards:* 5,200 ($8,300,000 total): general academic, agriculture, architecture, biological sciences, business, computer science, education, engineering/technologies, health fields, physical sciences. *Creative Arts/Performance Awards:* 30 ($30,000 total): journalism/publications, performing arts, theater/drama. *Special Achievements/Activities Awards:* 1,900 ($2,500,000 total): general special achievements/activities, leadership, memberships, rodeo. *Special Characteristics Awards:* 340 ($1,200,000 total): children of faculty/staff, ROTC participants, veterans, veterans' children. *Athletic:* Total: 337 ($1,347,379); Men: 198 ($627,979); Women: 139 ($719,400).

Other Money-Saving Options Accelerated degree, co-op program, Army ROTC, Naval ROTC, Air Force ROTC, off-campus living. *Payment Plan:* installment.

Contact Mr. Joseph P. Pettibon II, Systems Analyst, Texas A&M University, Student Financial Aid, College Station, TX 77843-1252, 409-845-8260, fax: 409-847-9061.

TEXAS A&M UNIVERSITY AT GALVESTON
Galveston, Texas

About the Institution State-supported, coed. Degrees awarded: B. Offers 8 undergraduate majors. Total enrollment: 1,203 (57% state residents). Freshmen: 336.

Undergraduate Expenses (1996–97) State resident tuition: $960. Nonresident tuition: $7380. Mandatory fees: $1160. College room and board: $3653.

Applications Of all full-time undergraduates enrolled in fall 1996, 62% of those who applied for aid were judged to have need according to Federal Methodology, of whom 100% were aided. *Financial aid deadline (priority):* 4/1. *Financial aid forms:* FAFSA required. *Admission application deadline:* rolling.

Summary of Aid to Needy Students *From gift & self-help combined:* Average need met: 100%. Average amount awarded: $4846 (30% gift aid, 70% self-help). *Gift aid:* Total: $723,000. Federal Work-Study jobs; 50 part-time jobs.

Need-Based Scholarships & Grants Pell, FSEOG, state.

Loans PLUS, Stafford, Unsubsidized Stafford, private, college/university short-term loans ($500 average).

Non-Need Awards *Academic Interests/Achievement Awards:* general academic.

Other Money-Saving Options Accelerated degree, co-op program, Naval ROTC, off-campus living (after sophomore year). *Payment Plan:* installment.

Contact Office of Financial Aid, Texas A&M University at Galveston, Galveston, TX 77553-1675, 409-740-4500.

TEXAS A&M UNIVERSITY–COMMERCE
Commerce, Texas

About the Institution State-supported, coed. Degrees awarded: B, M, D. Offers 68 undergraduate majors. Total enrollment: 7,546. Undergraduates: 4,929 (90% state residents). Freshmen: 670.

Undergraduate Expenses (1996–97) State resident tuition: $992. Nonresident tuition: $7626. Mandatory fees: $1296. College room and board: $3678. College room only: $1968.

Applications *Financial aid deadline (priority):* 5/1. *Financial aid forms:* FAFSA, institutional form required. *Admission application deadline:* 8/1.

Summary of Aid to Needy Students Federal Work-Study jobs; 350 part-time jobs.

Need-Based Scholarships & Grants Pell, FSEOG.

Loans Perkins, PLUS, Stafford, Unsubsidized Stafford.

Non-Need Awards *Academic Interests/Achievement Awards:* general academic, agriculture. *Creative Arts/Performance Awards:* art/fine arts, music, theater/drama. *Special Characteristics Awards:* ethnic background, members of minorities. *Athletic:* Total: 85 ($241,027); Men: 53 ($151,736); Women: 32 ($89,291).

Other Money-Saving Options Accelerated degree, co-op program, off-campus living (after freshman year). *Payment Plan:* installment. *Waivers:* full or partial for senior citizens.

Contact Office of Financial Aid, Texas A&M University–Commerce, Box 3011, Commerce, TX 75429-3011, 903-886-5081.

TEXAS A&M UNIVERSITY–CORPUS CHRISTI
Corpus Christi, Texas

About the Institution State-supported, coed. Degrees awarded: B, M, D. Offers 31 undergraduate majors. Total enrollment: 5,671. Undergraduates: 4,230 (98% state residents). Freshmen: 545.

Undergraduate Expenses (1996–97) State resident tuition: $960. Nonresident tuition: $6660. Mandatory fees: $1026. College room only: $2817.

Applications Of all full-time undergraduates enrolled in fall 1996, 97% of those who applied for aid were judged to have need according to Federal Methodology, of whom 100% were aided. *Financial aid deadline (priority):* 4/1. *Financial aid forms:* FAFSA, institutional form required. State form required for some. *Admission application deadline:* 7/1.

Summary of Aid to Needy Students *From gift & self-help combined:* Average amount awarded: $4631 (27% gift aid, 73% self-help). *Gift aid:* Total: $2,430,000 (5% from college's own funds, 5% from other college-administered sources, 90% from external sources). 66 Federal Work-Study jobs (averaging $2000); 130 part-time jobs.

Need-Based Scholarships & Grants Pell, FSEOG, state, private, college/university.

Loans Perkins, PLUS, Stafford, Unsubsidized Stafford, college/university short-term loans ($700 average).

Non-Need Awards In 1996, a total of 200 non-need awards were made. *Academic Interests/Achievement Awards:* 200 ($314,000 total): general academic.

Other Money-Saving Options Co-op program, Army ROTC, off-campus living. *Payment Plans:* installment, deferred payment. *Waivers:* full or partial for employees or children of employees.

Contact Financial Aid Department, Texas A&M University–Corpus Christi, Corpus Christi, TX 78412-5503, 800-482-6822.

TEXAS A&M UNIVERSITY–KINGSVILLE
Kingsville, Texas

About the Institution State-supported, coed. Degrees awarded: B, M, D. Offers 72 undergraduate majors. Total enrollment: 6,113. Undergraduates: 5,021 (96% state residents). Freshmen: 886.

Undergraduate Expenses (1996–97) State resident tuition: $960. Nonresident tuition: $7380. Mandatory fees: $812. College room and board: $3484. College room only: $1784.

Applications *Financial aid deadline (priority):* 4/15. *Financial aid forms:* FAFSA, CSS Financial Aid PROFILE, institutional form, financial aid transcript (for transfers) required. *Admission application deadline:* rolling.

Summary of Aid to Needy Students *From gift & self-help combined:* Average need met: 62%. 397 Federal Work-Study jobs (averaging $1185); 947 part-time jobs.

Need-Based Scholarships & Grants Pell, FSEOG, state, private, college/university, ethnic minority scholarships.

Loans Perkins, PLUS, Stafford, Unsubsidized Stafford, college/university short-term loans ($800 average).

Non-Need Awards In 1996, a total of 545 non-need awards were made. *Academic Interests/Achievement Awards:* 337 ($357,754 total): general academic, agriculture, biological sciences, business, communication, computer science, education, English, health fields, home economics, mathematics, military science, physical sciences, social sciences. *Creative Arts/Performance Awards:* 61 ($20,140 total): music. *Special Achievements/Activities Awards:* 21 ($21,485 total): rodeo. *Special Characteristics Awards:* 35 ($27,235 total): ROTC participants. *Athletic:* Total: 91 ($200,165); Men: 75 ($167,106); Women: 16 ($33,059).

Other Money-Saving Options Accelerated degree, co-op program, Army ROTC, off-campus living (after sophomore year). *Payment Plan:* installment. *Waivers:* full or partial for employees or children of employees.

Contact Office of Financial Aid, Texas A&M University–Kingsville, Campus Box 115, Kingsville, TX 78363, 512-593-2111.

TEXAS CHRISTIAN UNIVERSITY
Fort Worth, Texas

About the Institution Independent/religious, coed. Degrees awarded: B, M, D, P. Offers 69 undergraduate majors. Total enrollment: 6,961. Undergraduates: 5,810 (70% state residents). Freshmen: 1,238.

Undergraduate Expenses (1996–97) Comprehensive fee of $14,310 includes tuition ($9420), mandatory fees ($1090), and college room and board ($3800).

Applications 47% of all full-time undergraduates enrolled in fall 1996 applied for aid; of these, 81% were judged to have need according to Federal Methodology, of whom 99% were aided. *Financial aid deadline (priority):* 5/1. *Financial aid forms:* FAFSA, institutional form required. *Regular admission application deadline:* 2/15. Early action deadline: 11/15.

Summary of Aid to Needy Students *From gift & self-help combined:* Average amount awarded: $11,736 (47% gift aid, 53% self-help). *Gift aid:* Total: $11,410,222 (61% from college's own funds, 25% from other college-administered sources, 14% from external sources). 463 Federal Work-Study jobs (averaging $1385); 1,134 part-time jobs.

Need-Based Scholarships & Grants Pell, FSEOG, state, private, college/university.

Loans Perkins, PLUS, Stafford, Unsubsidized Stafford, Federal Nursing, state, private, college/university short-term loans ($200 average), college/university long-term loans ($1000 average).

Non-Need Awards In 1996, a total of 1,898 non-need awards were made. *Academic Interests/Achievement Awards:* 925 ($3,116,741 total): general academic. *Creative Arts/Performance Awards:* 207 ($578,740 total): art/fine arts, cinema/film/broadcasting, dance, journalism/publications, music, theater/drama. *Special Achievements/Activities Awards:* 183 ($755,025 total): general special achievements/activities, leadership, religious involvement. *Special Characteristics Awards:* 325 ($1,560,086 total): adult students, children of faculty/staff, children of union members/company employees, first-generation college students, international students, relatives of clergy, religious affiliation, ROTC participants. *Athletic:* Total: 258 ($2,515,159); Men: 187 ($1,789,611); Women: 71 ($725,548).

Other Money-Saving Options Accelerated degree, Army ROTC, Air Force ROTC, off-campus living (after freshman year). *Payment Plan:* installment. *Waivers:* full or partial for employees or children of employees.

Contact Mr. Ruben Chanlatte, Manager Information Systems for Admissions, Financial Aid, Texas Christian University, PO Box 297012, Fort Worth, TX 76129-0002, 817-921-7858, fax: 817-921-7462.

TEXAS LUTHERAN UNIVERSITY
Seguin, Texas

About the Institution Independent/religious, coed. Degrees awarded: B. Offers 31 undergraduate majors. Total enrollment: 1,234 (86% state residents). Freshmen: 210.

Undergraduate Expenses (1997–98) Comprehensive fee of $14,142 includes tuition ($10,300), mandatory fees ($70), and college room and board ($3772). College room only: $1636.

Applications Of all full-time undergraduates enrolled in fall 1996, 66% of those who applied for aid were judged to have need according to Federal Methodology, of whom 100% were aided. *Financial aid deadline*

(priority): 5/1. *Financial aid forms:* institutional form required. FAFSA required for some. *Admission application deadline:* rolling.

Summary of Aid to Needy Students *From gift & self-help combined:* Average need met: 85%. Average amount awarded: $9590 (46% gift aid, 54% self-help). *Gift aid:* Total: $2,538,580 (53% from college's own funds, 26% from other college-administered sources, 21% from external sources). 120 Federal Work-Study jobs (averaging $900); 228 part-time jobs.

Need-Based Scholarships & Grants Pell, FSEOG, state, private, college/university.

Loans Perkins, PLUS, Stafford, Unsubsidized Stafford, state.

Non-Need Awards In 1996, a total of 870 non-need awards were made. *Academic Interests/Achievement Awards:* 413 ($979,400 total): general academic, religion/biblical studies. *Creative Arts/Performance Awards:* 110 ($205,933 total): journalism/publications, music, theater/drama. *Special Achievements/Activities Awards:* 35 ($27,450 total): general special achievements/activities, leadership, religious involvement. *Special Characteristics Awards:* 180 ($205,116 total): first-generation college students, international students, previous college experience, religious affiliation. *Athletic:* Total: 132 ($566,637); Men: 79 ($286,434); Women: 53 ($280,203).

Other Money-Saving Options Accelerated degree, cooperative Air Force ROTC. *Payment Plan:* installment. *Waivers:* full or partial for employees or children of employees.

Contact Ms. Carol Hamilton, Director, Financial Aid, Texas Lutheran University, 1000 West Court Street, Seguin, TX 78155-5999, 210-372-8075, fax: 210-372-8096.

TEXAS SOUTHERN UNIVERSITY
Houston, Texas

About the Institution State-supported, coed. Degrees awarded: B, M, D, P. Offers 76 undergraduate majors. Total enrollment: 9,518. Undergraduates: 7,914 (92% state residents).

Undergraduate Expenses (1997–98) State resident tuition: $1054. Nonresident tuition: $7688. Mandatory fees: $1010. College room and board: $4000.

Applications *Financial aid deadline (priority):* 4/30. *Financial aid forms:* FAFSA, institutional form required. *Admission application deadline:* 8/10.

Summary of Aid to Needy Students *From gift & self-help combined:* Average need met: 80%. Average amount awarded: $10,200 (23% gift aid, 77% self-help). *Gift aid:* Total: $8,000,000. Federal Work-Study jobs; part-time jobs.

Need-Based Scholarships & Grants Pell, FSEOG.

Loans Perkins, PLUS, Stafford, Unsubsidized Stafford.

Non-Need Awards *Academic Interests/Achievement Awards:* general academic. *Athletic:* available.

Other Money-Saving Options Accelerated degree, co-op program, cooperative Army ROTC, cooperative Naval ROTC, off-campus living (after freshman year). *Payment Plan:* installment. *Waivers:* full or partial for minority students.

Contact Financial Aid Office, Texas Southern University, 3100 Cleburne, Houston, TX 77004-4584, 713-313-7011.

TEXAS TECH UNIVERSITY
Lubbock, Texas

About the Institution State-supported, coed. Degrees awarded: B, M, D, P. Offers 123 undergraduate majors. Total enrollment: 24,717. Undergraduates: 20,420 (92% state residents). Freshmen: 3,520.

Undergraduate Expenses (1996–97) State resident tuition: $960. Nonresident tuition: $7380. Mandatory fees: $1366. College room and board: $4084.

Applications *Financial aid deadline (priority):* 5/1. *Financial aid forms:* FAFSA, institutional form required. *Admission application deadline:* rolling.

Summary of Aid to Needy Students *From gift & self-help combined:* Average need met: 90%. *Gift aid:* Total: $50,057,279. 549 Federal Work-Study jobs (averaging $1393); 290 part-time jobs.

Need-Based Scholarships & Grants Pell, FSEOG, state, college/university.

Loans Perkins, PLUS, Stafford, Unsubsidized Stafford, college/university short-term loans ($724 average), college/university long-term loans ($3553 average).

Non-Need Awards In 1996, a total of 4,290 non-need awards were made. *Academic Interests/Achievement Awards:* general academic, agriculture, architecture, biological sciences, business, communication, computer science, education, engineering/technologies, English, foreign languages, home economics, international studies, mathematics, physical sciences, premedicine, social sciences. *Creative Arts/Performance Awards:* applied art and design, art/fine arts, dance, journalism/publications, music, performing arts, theater/drama. *Special Achievements/Activities Awards:* community service, memberships, rodeo. *Special Characteristics Awards:* children of faculty/staff, handicapped students, international students, out-of-state students, ROTC participants, veterans, veterans' children. *Athletic:* Total: 348 ($964,404); Men: 205; Women: 143.

Other Money-Saving Options Accelerated degree, Army ROTC, Air Force ROTC, off-campus living (after freshman year). *Payment Plan:* installment.

Contact Mr. Edwin Earl Hudgins, Director of Financial Aid, Texas Tech University, PO Box 45011, Lubbock, TX 79409-5011, 806-742-3681.

TEXAS WESLEYAN UNIVERSITY
Fort Worth, Texas

About the Institution Independent/religious, coed. Degrees awarded: B, M, P. Offers 62 undergraduate majors. Total enrollment: 2,966. Undergraduates: 1,871 (96% state residents). Freshmen: 273.

Undergraduate Expenses (1996–97) Comprehensive fee of $11,084 includes tuition ($7200), mandatory fees ($400), and college room and board ($3484).

Applications 99% of all full-time undergraduates enrolled in fall 1996 applied for aid; of these, 83% were judged to have need according to Federal Methodology, of whom 100% were aided. *Financial aid deadline (priority):* 4/15. *Financial aid forms:* FAFSA, institutional form required; CSS Financial Aid PROFILE acceptable. State form required for some. *Admission application deadline:* rolling.

Summary of Aid to Needy Students *From gift & self-help combined:* Average need met: 78%. Average amount awarded: $7509 (47% gift aid, 53% self-help). *Gift aid:* Total: $3,798,213 (37% from college's own funds, 35% from other college-administered sources, 28% from external sources). 100 Federal Work-Study jobs (averaging $1700); 82 part-time jobs.

Need-Based Scholarships & Grants Pell, FSEOG, state, private, college/university.

Loans PLUS, Stafford, Unsubsidized Stafford, state, college/university short-term loans ($400 average), college/university long-term loans ($1125 average).

Non-Need Awards *Academic Interests/Achievement Awards:* 1,264 ($2,260,222 total): general academic. *Creative Arts/Performance Awards:* 138 ($296,772 total): general creative, art/fine arts. *Special Achievements/Activities Awards:* 33 ($23,960 total): general special achievements/activities, cheerleading/drum major, leadership, religious involvement

Special Characteristics Awards: relatives of clergy, religious affiliation. *Athletic:* Total: 115 ($631,651); Men: 71 ($342,765); Women: 44 ($288,886).

Other Money-Saving Options Accelerated degree, cooperative Army ROTC, cooperative Air Force ROTC, off-campus living. *Payment Plans:* installment, deferred payment. *Waivers:* full or partial for employees or children of employees.

Contact Office of Financial Aid, Texas Wesleyan University, 1201 Wesleyan Street, Fort Worth, TX 76105-1536, 817-531-4444.

TEXAS WOMAN'S UNIVERSITY
Denton, Texas

About the Institution State-supported, primarily women. Degrees awarded: B, M, D. Offers 53 undergraduate majors. Total enrollment: 9,788. Undergraduates: 5,592 (95% state residents). Freshmen: 442.

Undergraduate Expenses (1996–97) State resident tuition: $1929. Nonresident tuition: $8349. College room and board: $3170. College room only: $1500.

Applications 74% of all full-time undergraduates enrolled in fall 1996 applied for aid; of these, 87% were judged to have need according to Federal Methodology, of whom 100% were aided. *Financial aid deadline (priority):* 4/1. *Financial aid forms:* FAFSA, institutional form required. *Admission application deadline:* 7/15.

Summary of Aid to Needy Students *From gift & self-help combined:* Average need met: 100%. Average amount awarded: $7273 (23% gift aid, 77% self-help). *Gift aid:* Total: $4,114,167 (32% from college's own funds, 14% from other college-administered sources, 54% from external sources). 402 Federal Work-Study jobs (averaging $1720); 551 part-time jobs.

Need-Based Scholarships & Grants Pell, FSEOG, state, private, college/university.

Loans Perkins, PLUS, Stafford, Unsubsidized Stafford, Federal Nursing, state, private, college/university short-term loans ($1344 average), college/university long-term loans ($2674 average).

Non-Need Awards In 1996, a total of 1,102 non-need awards were made. *Academic Interests/Achievement Awards:* 954 ($794,540 total): general academic, biological sciences, business, communication, computer science, education, English, foreign languages, health fields, home economics, humanities, mathematics, physical sciences, premedicine, social sciences. *Creative Arts/Performance Awards:* 89 ($38,373 total): applied art and design, art/fine arts, dance, journalism/publications, music, theater/drama. *Athletic:* Total: 59 ($132,879).

Other Money-Saving Options Accelerated degree, co-op program, off-campus living (after sophomore year). *Payment Plan:* installment. *Waivers:* full or partial for employees or children of employees and senior citizens.

Contact Mr. Governor Jackson, Director of Financial Aid, Texas Woman's University, PO Box 425408, Denton, TX 76204-5408, 817-898-3050, fax: 817-898-3068.

THIEL COLLEGE
Greenville, Pennsylvania

About the Institution Independent/religious, coed. Degrees awarded: A, B. Offers 43 undergraduate majors. Total enrollment: 985 (76% state residents). Freshmen: 256.

Undergraduate Expenses (1997–98) Comprehensive fee of $18,575 includes tuition ($13,160), mandatory fees ($195), and college room and board ($5220). College room only: $2660.

Applications 97% of all full-time undergraduates enrolled in fall 1996 applied for aid; of these,100% were judged to have need according to Federal Methodology, of whom 100% were aided. *Financial aid deadline (priority):* 5/1. *Financial aid forms:* FAFSA, state form required; CSS

Financial Aid PROFILE acceptable. Institutional form required for some. *Regular admission application deadline:* rolling. Early action deadline: 9/1.

Summary of Aid to Needy Students *From gift & self-help combined:* Average need met: 90%. Average amount awarded: $14,000 (60% gift aid, 40% self-help). *Gift aid:* Total: $7,174,356 (64% from college's own funds, 4% from other college-administered sources, 32% from external sources). 55 Federal Work-Study jobs (averaging $1224); 350 part-time jobs.

Need-Based Scholarships & Grants Pell, FSEOG, state, private, college/university.

Loans Perkins, PLUS, Stafford, Unsubsidized Stafford, private, college/university long-term loans ($2500 average).

Non-Need Awards In 1996, a total of 227 non-need awards were made. *Academic Interests/Achievement Awards:* 157 ($903,352 total): general academic. *Special Achievements/Activities Awards:* 20 ($20,000 total): leadership. *Special Characteristics Awards:* 50 ($179,423 total): children of faculty/staff, religious affiliation, siblings of current students.

Other Money-Saving Options Accelerated degree, co-op program, cooperative Army ROTC. *Payment Plan:* installment. *Waivers:* full or partial for employees or children of employees.

Contact Ms. Cynthia H. Farrell, Director of Financial Aid, Thiel College, 75 College Avenue, Greenville, PA 16125-2181, 412-589-2178, fax: 412-589-2850.

THOMAS AQUINAS COLLEGE
Santa Paula, California

About the Institution Independent/religious, coed. Degrees awarded: B. Offers 3 undergraduate majors. Total enrollment: 223 (34% state residents). Freshmen: 70.

Undergraduate Expenses (1996–97) Comprehensive fee of $19,200 includes tuition ($13,900) and college room and board ($5300).

Applications 86% of all full-time undergraduates enrolled in fall 1996 applied for aid; of these, 98% were judged to have need according to Federal Methodology, of whom 100% were aided. *Financial aid deadline:* continuous. *Financial aid forms:* FAFSA, institutional form required; CSS Financial Aid PROFILE acceptable. *Admission application deadline:* rolling.

Summary of Aid to Needy Students *From gift & self-help combined:* Average need met: 93%. Average amount awarded: $14,316 (60% gift aid, 40% self-help). *Gift aid:* Total: $1,644,152 (97% from college's own funds, 3% from external sources). 181 part-time jobs.

Need-Based Scholarships & Grants State, college/university.

Loans PLUS, Stafford, Unsubsidized Stafford, private.

Non-Need Awards Not offered.

Another Money-Saving Option *Payment Plan:* installment.

Contact Mr. Gregory Becher, Director of Financial Aid, Thomas Aquinas College, 10000 North Ojai Road, Santa Paula, CA 93060-9980, 805-525-4419 Ext. 308, fax: 805-525-9342.

THOMAS COLLEGE
Thomasville, Georgia

About the Institution Independent, coed. Degrees awarded: A, B. Offers 29 undergraduate majors. Total enrollment: 827 (93% state residents). Freshmen: 141.

Undergraduate Expenses (1997–98) Tuition: $4950. Mandatory fees: $390.

Applications 100% of all full-time undergraduates enrolled in fall 1996 applied for aid; of these, 40% were judged to have need according to Federal Methodology, of whom 100% were aided. *Financial aid deadline*

(priority): 9/15. *Financial aid forms:* FAFSA, state form, institutional form required; CSS Financial Aid PROFILE, AFSSA-CSX acceptable. *Admission application deadline:* rolling.

Summary of Aid to Needy Students *From gift & self-help combined:* Average need met: 90%. Average amount awarded: $2253 (67% gift aid, 33% self-help). *Gift aid:* Total: $663,433 (9% from college's own funds, 68% from other college-administered sources, 23% from external sources). 6 Federal Work-Study jobs (averaging $1710).

Need-Based Scholarships & Grants Pell, FSEOG, state, private, college/university.

Loans PLUS, Stafford, Unsubsidized Stafford, private, college/university short-term loans ($150 average).

Non-Need Awards In 1996, a total of 90 non-need awards were made. *Academic Interests/Achievement Awards:* 3 ($2700 total): general academic. *Creative Arts/Performance Awards:* 9 ($8100 total): music. *Special Achievements/Activities Awards:* 0: Junior Miss. *Special Characteristics Awards:* 18 ($16,200 total): children of faculty/staff, out-of-state students, ROTC participants, veterans. *Athletic:* Total: 60 ($33,225); Men: 50 ($28,025); Women: 10 ($5200).

Other Money-Saving Options Accelerated degree, co-op program, Army ROTC. *Payment Plan:* installment. *Waivers:* full or partial for employees or children of employees and senior citizens.

Contact Mr. Thomas Silarek, Director of Financial Aid, Thomas College, 1501 Millpond Road, Thomasville, GA 31792-7499, 912-226-1621.

THOMAS COLLEGE
Waterville, Maine

About the Institution Independent, coed. Degrees awarded: A, B, M. Offers 19 undergraduate majors. Total enrollment: 842. Undergraduates: 712 (96% state residents). Freshmen: 144.

Undergraduate Expenses (1997–98 estimated) Comprehensive fee of $17,225 includes tuition ($10,850), mandatory fees ($350), and college room and board ($6025). College room only: $2400.

Applications 95% of all full-time undergraduates enrolled in fall 1996 applied for aid; of these, 97% were judged to have need according to Federal Methodology, of whom 100% were aided. *Financial aid deadline (priority):* 2/15. *Financial aid forms:* FAFSA required. *Admission application deadline:* rolling.

Summary of Aid to Needy Students *From gift & self-help combined:* Average need met: 83%. Average amount awarded: $8862 (51% gift aid, 49% self-help). *Gift aid:* Total: $1,914,193 (46% from college's own funds, 17% from other college-administered sources, 37% from external sources). 95 Federal Work-Study jobs (averaging $1350); 5 part-time jobs.

Need-Based Scholarships & Grants Pell, FSEOG, state, private, college/university.

Loans Perkins, PLUS, Stafford, Unsubsidized Stafford, private.

Non-Need Awards In 1996, a total of 28 non-need awards were made. *Academic Interests/Achievement Awards:* 28 ($171,249 total): international studies.

Other Money-Saving Options Cooperative Army ROTC, off-campus living (after freshman year). *Payment Plan:* installment.

Contact Financial Aid Office, Thomas College, 180 West River Road, Waterville, ME 04901-5097, 207-877-0112.

THOMAS MORE COLLEGE
Crestview Hills, Kentucky

About the Institution Independent/religious, coed. Degrees awarded: A, B, M. Offers 40 undergraduate majors. Total enrollment: 1,345 (68% state residents). Freshmen: 263.

Undergraduate Expenses (1997–98) Comprehensive fee of $15,140 includes tuition ($10,970), mandatory fees ($280), and college room and board ($3890 minimum). College room only: $1900 (minimum).

Applications Of all full-time undergraduates enrolled in fall 1996, 97% of those judged to have need according to Federal Methodology were aided. *Financial aid deadline (priority):* 3/1. *Financial aid forms:* FAFSA, institutional form required; CSS Financial Aid PROFILE acceptable. *Admission application deadline:* 8/15.

Summary of Aid to Needy Students *From gift & self-help combined:* Average need met: 71%. Average amount awarded: $9731 (58% gift aid, 42% self-help). *Gift aid:* Total: $4,069,588 (71% from college's own funds, 3% from other college-administered sources, 26% from external sources). 133 Federal Work-Study jobs (averaging $1000); 75 part-time jobs.

Need-Based Scholarships & Grants Pell, FSEOG, state, private, college/university.

Loans Perkins, PLUS, Stafford, Unsubsidized Stafford, Federal Nursing, private.

Non-Need Awards *Academic Interests/Achievement Awards:* general academic. *Creative Arts/Performance Awards:* art/fine arts, theater/drama. *Special Achievements/Activities Awards:* leadership, religious involvement. *Special Characteristics Awards:* religious affiliation.

Other Money-Saving Options Accelerated degree, co-op program, cooperative Army ROTC, cooperative Air Force ROTC, off-campus living. *Payment Plan:* installment. *Waivers:* full or partial for children of alumni and employees or children of employees.

Contact Ms. Dolores Fink, Assistant Director, Thomas More College, 333 Thomas More Parkway, Crestview Hills, KY 41017-3428, 606-344-3334, fax: 606-344-3638.

THOMAS MORE COLLEGE OF LIBERAL ARTS
Merrimack, New Hampshire

About the Institution Independent/religious, coed. Degrees awarded: B. Offers 3 undergraduate majors. Total enrollment: 63 (15% state residents). Freshmen: 16.

Undergraduate Expenses (1996–97) Comprehensive fee of $14,200 includes tuition ($8200) and college room and board ($6000).

Applications 80% of all full-time undergraduates enrolled in fall 1996 applied for aid; of these, 78% were judged to have need according to Federal Methodology, of whom 100% were aided. *Financial aid deadline (priority):* 9/10. *Financial aid forms:* FAFSA, institutional form required; state form acceptable. *Admission application deadline:* rolling.

Summary of Aid to Needy Students *From gift & self-help combined:* Average need met: 80%. Average amount awarded: $9175 (67% gift aid, 33% self-help). *Gift aid:* Total: $458,744 (49% from college's own funds, 49% from other college-administered sources, 2% from external sources). 22 Federal Work-Study jobs (averaging $2065).

Need-Based Scholarships & Grants Pell, FSEOG, state, college/university.

Loans PLUS, Stafford, Unsubsidized Stafford, private.

Non-Need Awards In 1996, a total of 24 non-need awards were made. *Academic Interests/Achievement Awards:* 24 ($5883 total): general academic.

Other Money-Saving Options *Payment Plans:* installment, deferred payment. *Waivers:* full or partial for employees or children of employees.

Contact Ms. Pam Bernstein, Business Manager, Thomas More College of Liberal Arts, 6 Manchester Street, Merrimack, NH 03054-4818, 603-880-8308 Ext. 18, fax: 603-880-9280.

TIFFIN UNIVERSITY
Tiffin, Ohio

About the Institution Independent, coed. Degrees awarded: A, B, M. Offers 25 undergraduate majors. Total enrollment: 1,151. Undergraduates: 1,073 (94% state residents). Freshmen: 247.

Undergraduate Expenses (1997–98) Comprehensive fee of $13,610 includes tuition ($9210) and college room and board ($4400). College room only: $2250.

Applications 91% of all full-time undergraduates enrolled in fall 1996 applied for aid; of these, 89% were judged to have need according to Federal Methodology, of whom 98% were aided. *Financial aid deadline (priority):* 3/31. *Financial aid forms:* FAFSA required; CSS Financial Aid PROFILE acceptable. State form, institutional form required for some. *Admission application deadline:* rolling.

Summary of Aid to Needy Students *From gift & self-help combined:* Average need met: 57%. Average amount awarded: $8272 (49% gift aid, 51% self-help). *Gift aid:* Total: $2,542,041 (38% from college's own funds, 12% from other college-administered sources, 50% from external sources). 28 Federal Work-Study jobs (averaging $1000); 32 part-time jobs.

Need-Based Scholarships & Grants Pell, FSEOG, state, college/university.

Loans Perkins, PLUS, Stafford, Unsubsidized Stafford, state, college/university short-term loans ($100 average), college/university long-term loans ($1000 average).

Non-Need Awards In 1996, a total of 494 non-need awards were made. *Academic Interests/Achievement Awards:* 103 ($165,000 total): general academic, business. *Creative Arts/Performance Awards:* 7 ($6700 total): music. *Special Characteristics Awards:* 49 ($34,465 total): local/state students, out-of-state students. *Athletic:* Total: 335 ($411,959); Men: 217 ($292,325); Women: 118 ($119,634).

Other Money-Saving Options Accelerated degree, off-campus living (after sophomore year). *Payment Plan:* installment. *Waivers:* full or partial for employees or children of employees.

Contact Ms. Carol McDannell, Director of Financial Aid, Tiffin University, 155 Miami Street, Tiffin, OH 44883-2161, 419-447-6442.

TOCCOA FALLS COLLEGE
Toccoa Falls, Georgia

About the Institution Independent/religious, coed. Degrees awarded: A, B. Offers 33 undergraduate majors. Total enrollment: 892 (28% state residents). Freshmen: 185.

Undergraduate Expenses (1997–98) Comprehensive fee of $11,127 includes tuition ($7254), mandatory fees ($165), and college room and board ($3708).

Applications Of all full-time undergraduates enrolled in fall 1996, 90% of those who applied for aid were judged to have need according to Federal Methodology, of whom 87% were aided. *Financial aid deadline (priority):* 8/1. *Financial aid forms:* FAFSA, CSS Financial Aid PROFILE, institutional form required. State form required for some. *Admission application deadline:* rolling.

Summary of Aid to Needy Students *From gift & self-help combined:* Average need met: 72%. Average amount awarded: $3700 (36% gift aid, 64% self-help). *Gift aid:* Total: $825,263 (24% from college's own funds, 39% from other college-administered sources, 37% from external sources). Federal Work-Study jobs; part-time jobs.

Need-Based Scholarships & Grants Pell, FSEOG, state.

Loans Perkins, PLUS, Stafford, Unsubsidized Stafford, state, college/university short-term loans.

Non-Need Awards In 1996, a total of 227 non-need awards were made. *Academic Interests/Achievement Awards:* 95 ($72,500 total): general academic. *Creative Arts/Performance Awards:* 57 ($57,000 total): music. *Special Characteristics Awards:* 75 ($75,000 total): relatives of clergy.

Other Money-Saving Options Accelerated degree. *Payment Plan:* installment. *Waivers:* full or partial for employees or children of employees and senior citizens.

Contact Mr. Mark A. Gerl, Student Loan Manager, Toccoa Falls College, PO Box 800900, Toccoa Falls, GA 30598-1000, 706-886-6831 Ext. 5233, fax: 706-886-0210.

TOUGALOO COLLEGE
Tougaloo, Mississippi

About the Institution Independent/religious, coed. Degrees awarded: A, B. Offers 21 undergraduate majors. Total enrollment: 982 (83% state residents). Freshmen: 211.

Undergraduate Expenses (1997–98) Comprehensive fee of $9240 includes tuition ($5660), mandatory fees ($500), and college room and board ($3080). College room only: $1930.

Applications *Financial aid deadline (priority):* 4/15. *Financial aid forms:* FAFSA, institutional form required; CSS Financial Aid PROFILE acceptable. State form required for some. *Admission application deadline:* rolling.

Summary of Aid to Needy Students Federal Work-Study jobs; part-time jobs.

Non-Need Awards *Academic Interests/Achievement Awards:* general academic. *Creative Arts/Performance Awards:* music.

Other Money-Saving Options Accelerated degree, co-op program, Army ROTC, off-campus living.

Contact Office of Financial Aid, Tougaloo College, 500 West County Line Road, Tougaloo, MS 39174, 601-977-7700.

TOURO COLLEGE
New York, New York

About the Institution Independent, coed. Degrees awarded: A, B, M, P. Offers 35 undergraduate majors. Total enrollment: 8,876. Undergraduates: 7,676 (95% state residents). Freshmen: 1,138.

Undergraduate Expenses (1996–97) Tuition: $8780. Mandatory fees: $280. College room only: $4500 (minimum).

Applications Of all full-time undergraduates enrolled in fall 1996, 100% of those judged to have need according to Federal Methodology were aided. *Financial aid deadline (priority):* 4/15. *Financial aid forms:* FAFSA required. *Admission application deadline:* 5/15.

Summary of Aid to Needy Students *From gift & self-help combined:* Average need met: 85%. Average amount awarded: $8117 (87% gift aid, 13% self-help). *Gift aid:* Total: $49,300,000. Federal Work-Study jobs.

Need-Based Scholarships & Grants Pell, FSEOG, state, private, college/university.

Loans Perkins, PLUS, Stafford, Unsubsidized Stafford, private.

Non-Need Awards *Academic Interests/Achievement Awards:* general academic. *Special Characteristics Awards:* children of faculty/staff.

Other Money-Saving Options Accelerated degree, off-campus living. *Waivers:* full or partial for employees or children of employees.

Contact Office of Financial Aid, Touro College, 1602 Avenue J, Brooklyn, NY 11230, 718-252-7800.

TOWSON UNIVERSITY
Towson, Maryland

About the Institution State-supported, coed. Degrees awarded: B, M. Offers 97 undergraduate majors. Total enrollment: 15,105. Undergraduates: 13,063 (80% state residents). Freshmen: 1,863.

Undergraduate Expenses (1997–98) State resident tuition: $3080. Nonresident tuition: $8158. Mandatory fees: $1040. College room and board: $4830. College room only: $2700.

Applications Of all full-time undergraduates enrolled in fall 1996, 69% of those who applied for aid were judged to have need according to Federal Methodology, of whom 90% were aided. *Financial aid deadline (priority):* 3/1. *Financial aid forms:* FAFSA required. *Admission application deadline:* 5/1.

Summary of Aid to Needy Students *From gift & self-help combined:* Average need met: 75%. Average amount awarded: $4212 (54% gift aid, 46% self-help). *Gift aid:* Total: $12,786,972 (27% from college's own funds, 56% from other college-administered sources, 17% from external sources). 189 Federal Work-Study jobs (averaging $1252); 1,972 part-time jobs.

Need-Based Scholarships & Grants Pell, FSEOG, state, private, college/university.

Loans Perkins, PLUS, Stafford, Unsubsidized Stafford, private.

Non-Need Awards In 1996, a total of 938 non-need awards were made. *Academic Interests/Achievement Awards:* 654 ($1,417,226 total): general academic. *Creative Arts/Performance Awards:* 53 ($5300 total): art/fine arts, dance, music, theater/drama. *Athletic:* Total: 231 ($1,030,260); Men: 103 ($450,910); Women: 128 ($579,350).

Other Money-Saving Options Accelerated degree, co-op program, cooperative Army ROTC, cooperative Air Force ROTC, off-campus living. *Waivers:* full or partial for employees or children of employees and senior citizens.

Contact Financial Aid Office, Towson University, Towson, MD 21252-0001, 410-830-2061.

TRANSYLVANIA UNIVERSITY
Lexington, Kentucky

About the Institution Independent/religious, coed. Degrees awarded: B. Offers 28 undergraduate majors. Total enrollment: 979 (80% state residents). Freshmen: 329.

Undergraduate Expenses (1997–98) Comprehensive fee of $18,250 includes tuition ($12,750), mandatory fees ($510), and college room and board ($4990).

Applications Of all full-time undergraduates enrolled in fall 1996, 94% of those who applied for aid were judged to have need according to Federal Methodology, of whom 100% were aided. *Financial aid deadline (priority):* 3/15. *Financial aid forms:* FAFSA required; CSS Financial Aid PROFILE acceptable. *Admission application deadline:* 3/1.

Summary of Aid to Needy Students *From gift & self-help combined:* Average need met: 91%. Average amount awarded: $9098 (73% gift aid, 27% self-help). *Gift aid:* Total: $2,806,624 (77% from college's own funds, 17% from other college-administered sources, 6% from external sources). 223 Federal Work-Study jobs (averaging $1782); 37 part-time jobs.

Need-Based Scholarships & Grants Pell, FSEOG, state, college/university.

Loans Perkins, PLUS, Stafford, Unsubsidized Stafford, private, college/university long-term loans ($2223 average).

Non-Need Awards In 1996, a total of 1,243 non-need awards were made. *Academic Interests/Achievement Awards:* 850 ($3,663,342 total): general academic, computer science, education. *Creative Arts/Performance Awards:* 51 ($89,000 total): art/fine arts, music. *Special*

Achievements/Activities Awards: 17 ($7500 total): general special achievements/activities, religious involvement. *Special Characteristics Awards:* 160 ($225,496 total): children of faculty/staff, members of minorities, out-of-state students, relatives of clergy, religious affiliation, ROTC participants. *Athletic:* Total: 165 ($538,270); Men: 77 ($290,680); Women: 88 ($247,590).

Other Money-Saving Options Accelerated degree, cooperative Army ROTC, cooperative Air Force ROTC, off-campus living (after junior year). *Payment Plans:* installment, deferred payment. *Waivers:* full or partial for employees or children of employees.

Contact Mrs. Peggy Fain, Director of Financial Aid, Transylvania University, 300 North Broadway, Lexington, KY 40508-1797, 606-233-8239.

TRENTON STATE COLLEGE
Trenton, New Jersey

See The College of New Jersey

TREVECCA NAZARENE UNIVERSITY
Nashville, Tennessee

About the Institution Independent/religious, coed. Degrees awarded: A, B, M. Offers 38 undergraduate majors. Total enrollment: 1,547. Undergraduates: 1,114 (61% state residents). Freshmen: 195.

Undergraduate Expenses (1997–98) Comprehensive fee of $13,128 includes tuition ($8480), mandatory fees ($610), and college room and board ($4038). College room only: $1750.

Applications Of all full-time undergraduates enrolled in fall 1996, 100% of those judged to have need according to Federal Methodology were aided. *Financial aid deadline (priority):* 4/15. *Financial aid forms:* CSS Financial Aid PROFILE acceptable. FAFSA required for some. *Admission application deadline:* rolling.

Summary of Aid to Needy Students *From gift & self-help combined:* Average need met: 100%. Average amount awarded: $11,500 (43% gift aid, 57% self-help). *Gift aid:* Total: $2,532,164 (60% from college's own funds, 22% from other college-administered sources, 18% from external sources). 850 Federal Work-Study jobs (averaging $1000); 221 part-time jobs.

Need-Based Scholarships & Grants Pell, FSEOG, state, private, college/university.

Loans Perkins, PLUS, Stafford, Unsubsidized Stafford, private.

Non-Need Awards In 1996, a total of 777 non-need awards were made. *Academic Interests/Achievement Awards:* 241 ($533,084 total): general academic. *Creative Arts/Performance Awards:* 26 ($28,252 total): music, theater/drama. *Special Achievements/Activities Awards:* 15 ($7790 total): religious involvement. *Special Characteristics Awards:* 430 ($263,833 total): general special characteristics, children and siblings of alumni, relatives of clergy, religious affiliation. *Athletic:* Total: 65 ($234,802); Men: 31 ($141,570); Women: 34 ($93,232).

Other Money-Saving Options Accelerated degree, co-op program, cooperative Army ROTC, off-campus living (after junior year). *Payment Plan:* installment. *Waivers:* full or partial for employees or children of employees and senior citizens.

Contact Ms. Jeanie Hall, Senior Counselor/Undergraduate Studies, Trevecca Nazarene University, 333 Murfreesboro Road, Nashville, TN 37210-2834, 615-248-1242, fax: 615-248-7728.

TRINITY BAPTIST COLLEGE
Jacksonville, Florida

About the Institution Independent/religious, coed. Degrees awarded: A, B. Offers 10 undergraduate majors. Total enrollment: 310 (18% state residents). Freshmen: 90.

Undergraduate Expenses (1997–98) Comprehensive fee of $6498 includes tuition ($3298), mandatory fees ($400), and college room and board ($2800).

Applications *Financial aid deadline (priority):* 3/15. *Financial aid forms:* FAFSA required.

Summary of Aid to Needy Students Federal Work-Study jobs; part-time jobs.

Need-Based Scholarships & Grants Pell, FSEOG, college/university.

Loans PLUS, Stafford, Unsubsidized Stafford.

Non-Need Awards *Academic Interests/Achievement Awards:* general academic. *Special Achievements/Activities Awards:* leadership, religious involvement. *Special Characteristics Awards:* spouses of current students.

Other Money-Saving Options Accelerated degree. *Payment Plans:* guaranteed tuition, installment. *Waivers:* full or partial for employees or children of employees.

Contact Financial Aid Office, Trinity Baptist College, 426 South McDuff Avenue, Jacksonville, FL 32254, 800-786-2206.

TRINITY BIBLE COLLEGE
Ellendale, North Dakota

About the Institution Independent/religious, coed. Degrees awarded: A, B. Offers 12 undergraduate majors. Total enrollment: 329 (23% state residents). Freshmen: 80.

Undergraduate Expenses (1997–98) Comprehensive fee of $9278 includes tuition ($5408), mandatory fees ($670), and college room and board ($3200).

Applications 94% of all full-time undergraduates enrolled in fall 1996 applied for aid; of these, 96% were judged to have need according to Federal Methodology, of whom 100% were aided. *Financial aid deadline (priority):* 3/1. *Financial aid forms:* FAFSA, state form required; CSS Financial Aid PROFILE acceptable. *Admission application deadline:* rolling.

Summary of Aid to Needy Students *Gift aid:* Total: $830,648 (35% from college's own funds, 14% from other college-administered sources, 51% from external sources). 125 Federal Work-Study jobs (averaging $800).

Need-Based Scholarships & Grants Pell, FSEOG, state, private.

Loans Perkins, PLUS, Stafford, Unsubsidized Stafford, private.

Non-Need Awards In 1996, a total of 315 non-need awards were made. *Academic Interests/Achievement Awards:* 28 ($21,056 total): general academic, education. *Creative Arts/Performance Awards:* 14 ($20,177 total): art/fine arts. *Special Achievements/Activities Awards:* 182 ($170,985 total): general special achievements/activities, leadership, religious involvement. *Special Characteristics Awards:* 91 ($62,821 total): general special characteristics, children of faculty/staff, relatives of clergy, spouses of current students.

Other Money-Saving Options Accelerated degree. *Payment Plans:* installment, deferred payment. *Waivers:* full or partial for employees or children of employees.

Contact Office of Financial Aid, Trinity Bible College, 50 South 6th Avenue, Ellendale, ND 58436-7150, 701-349-3621.

TRINITY CHRISTIAN COLLEGE
Palos Heights, Illinois

About the Institution Independent/religious, coed. Degrees awarded: B. Offers 30 undergraduate majors. Total enrollment: 619 (52% state residents). Freshmen: 150.

Undergraduate Expenses (1997–98 estimated) Comprehensive fee of $16,160 includes tuition ($11,700) and college room and board ($4460). College room only: $2400.

Applications Of all full-time undergraduates enrolled in fall 1996, 95% of those who applied for aid were judged to have need according to Federal Methodology, of whom 95% were aided. *Financial aid deadline (priority):* 2/15. *Financial aid forms:* CSS Financial Aid PROFILE required; FAFSA, institutional form acceptable. State form required for some. *Admission application deadline:* 8/15.

Summary of Aid to Needy Students *From gift & self-help combined:* Average amount awarded: $9114 (52% gift aid, 48% self-help). *Gift aid:* Total: $2,002,864 (57% from college's own funds, 28% from other college-administered sources, 15% from external sources). 165 Federal Work-Study jobs (averaging $1390); 173 part-time jobs.

Need-Based Scholarships & Grants Pell, FSEOG, state, private, college/university.

Loans Perkins, PLUS, Stafford, Unsubsidized Stafford, Federal Nursing, private.

Non-Need Awards *Academic Interests/Achievement Awards:* 350 ($580,657 total): general academic, business, English, health fields, mathematics. *Creative Arts/Performance Awards:* 87 ($104,825 total): journalism/publications, music, theater/drama. *Special Achievements/Activities Awards:* 7 ($9500 total): general special achievements/activities, leadership. *Special Characteristics Awards:* children and siblings of alumni, children of faculty/staff, local/state students, members of minorities, out-of-state students. *Athletic:* Total: 72 ($135,000); Men: 42 ($86,500); Women: 30 ($48,500).

Other Money-Saving Options Off-campus living. *Payment Plan:* installment. *Waivers:* full or partial for employees or children of employees and senior citizens.

Contact Ms. Nancy Rietveld, Director of Financial Aid, Trinity Christian College, 6601 West College Drive, Palos Heights, Il 60463-0929, 708-597-3000 Ext. 4706.

TRINITY COLLEGE
Hartford, Connecticut

About the Institution Independent, coed. Degrees awarded: B, M. Offers 50 undergraduate majors. Total enrollment: 2,134. Undergraduates: 2,004 (28% state residents). Freshmen: 504.

Undergraduate Expenses (1997–98) Comprehensive fee of $28,790 includes tuition ($21,710), mandatory fees ($760), and college room and board ($6320). College room only: $3880.

Applications Of all full-time undergraduates enrolled in fall 1996, 92% of those who applied for aid were judged to have need according to Federal Methodology, of whom 100% were aided. *Financial aid deadline:* 2/1. *Financial aid forms:* FAFSA, CSS Financial Aid PROFILE required. State form required for some. *Regular admission application deadline:* 1/15. Early decision deadline: 11/15.

Summary of Aid to Needy Students *From gift & self-help combined:* Average need met: 100%. Average amount awarded: $18,250 (71% gift aid, 29% self-help). *Gift aid:* Total: $10,462,643 (90% from college's own funds, 5% from other college-administered sources, 5% from external sources). 725 Federal Work-Study jobs (averaging $1500); 150 part-time jobs.

Need-Based Scholarships & Grants Pell, FSEOG, state, private, college/university.

Loans Perkins, PLUS, Stafford, Unsubsidized Stafford, college/university short-term loans ($100 average), college/university long-term loans.

Non-Need Awards In 1996, a total of 3 non-need awards were made. *Academic Interests/Achievement Awards:* 3 ($3000 total): general academic.

Other Money-Saving Options Accelerated degree, cooperative Army ROTC, off-campus living. *Payment Plan:* installment.

Contact Ms. Kelly O'Brien, Director of Financial Aid, Trinity College, 300 Summit Street, Hartford, CT 06106-3100, 860-297-2046.

TRINITY COLLEGE
Washington, District of Columbia

About the Institution Independent/religious, women. Degrees awarded: B, M. Offers 27 undergraduate majors. Total enrollment: 1,453. Undergraduates: 1,040 (35% district residents). Freshmen: 115.

Undergraduate Expenses (1997–98) Comprehensive fee of $19,070 includes tuition ($12,340), mandatory fees ($150), and college room and board ($6580 minimum). College room only: $3050 (minimum).

Applications 96% of all full-time undergraduates enrolled in fall 1996 applied for aid; of these, 96% were judged to have need according to Federal Methodology, of whom 99% were aided. *Financial aid deadline (priority):* 3/15. *Financial aid forms:* FAFSA required; CSS Financial Aid PROFILE acceptable. District form required for some. *Regular admission application deadline:* 3/1. Early decision deadline: 12/15.

Summary of Aid to Needy Students *From gift & self-help combined:* Average need met: 90%. Average amount awarded: $9935 (41% gift aid, 59% self-help). *Gift aid:* Total: $2,850,665 (83% from college's own funds, 4% from other college-administered sources, 13% from external sources). 125 Federal Work-Study jobs (averaging $1000); 55 part-time jobs.

Need-Based Scholarships & Grants Pell, FSEOG, state, private, college/university.

Loans Perkins, PLUS, Stafford, Unsubsidized Stafford, private, college/university short-term loans ($500 average), college/university long-term loans ($1500 average).

Non-Need Awards *Academic Interests/Achievement Awards:* general academic. *Special Achievements/Activities Awards:* leadership. *Special Characteristics Awards:* siblings of current students.

Other Money-Saving Options Accelerated degree, cooperative Army ROTC, cooperative Naval ROTC, cooperative Air Force ROTC, off-campus living (after junior year). *Payment Plans:* installment, deferred payment. *Waivers:* full or partial for employees or children of employees.

Contact Mr. Raymond Brien Krull, Director of Student Financial Services, Trinity College, Washington, DC 20017-1094, 202-884-9530.

TRINITY COLLEGE
Deerfield, Illinois

See Trinity International University

TRINITY COLLEGE OF FLORIDA
New Port Richey, Florida

About the Institution Independent/religious, coed. Degrees awarded: A, B. Offers 4 undergraduate majors. Total enrollment: 170 (71% state residents). Freshmen: 32.

Undergraduate Expenses (1997–98) Comprehensive fee of $5870 includes tuition ($3250), mandatory fees ($220), and college room and board ($2400). College room only: $1800.

Applications *Financial aid deadline (priority):* 7/31. *Financial aid forms:* FAFSA, institutional form required; state form acceptable. *Admission application deadline:* rolling.

Summary of Aid to Needy Students *From gift & self-help combined:* Average need met: 44%. 4 part-time jobs.

Need-Based Scholarships & Grants Pell, private, college/university.

Loans Private.

Non-Need Awards *Academic Interests/Achievement Awards:* general academic.

Other Money-Saving Options *Payment Plan:* deferred payment. *Waivers:* full or partial for employees or children of employees and senior citizens.

Contact Ms. Audrey Ahern, Director of Financial Aid, Trinity College of Florida, 2430 Trinity Oaks Boulevard, New Port Richey, FL 34655, 813-376-6911.

TRINITY COLLEGE OF VERMONT
Burlington, Vermont

About the Institution Independent/religious, primarily women. Degrees awarded: A, B, M. Offers 36 undergraduate majors. Total enrollment: 1,042. Undergraduates: 913 (86% state residents). Freshmen: 106.

Undergraduate Expenses (1997–98) Comprehensive fee of $19,732 includes tuition ($13,080), mandatory fees ($340), and college room and board ($6312). College room only: $3536 (minimum).

Applications *Financial aid deadline (priority):* 3/1. *Financial aid forms:* FAFSA, institutional form required; CSS Financial Aid PROFILE acceptable. State form required for some. *Admission application deadline:* rolling.

Summary of Aid to Needy Students *From gift & self-help combined:* Average need met: 86%. Average amount awarded: $9180 (58% gift aid, 42% self-help). *Gift aid:* Total: $3,275,324 (50% from college's own funds, 37% from other college-administered sources, 13% from external sources). 160 Federal Work-Study jobs (averaging $1150); 22 part-time jobs.

Need-Based Scholarships & Grants Pell, FSEOG, state, college/university.

Loans Perkins, PLUS, Stafford, Unsubsidized Stafford, college/university long-term loans ($650 average).

Non-Need Awards In 1996, a total of 103 non-need awards were made. *Academic Interests/Achievement Awards:* 103 ($359,000 total): general academic.

Other Money-Saving Options Cooperative Air Force ROTC, off-campus living (after junior year). *Payment Plans:* installment, deferred payment. *Waivers:* full or partial for employees or children of employees and senior citizens.

Contact Ms. Elizabeth Cote, Director of Financial Aid, Trinity College of Vermont, 208 Colchester Avenue, Burlington, VT 05401-1470, 802-658-0337.

TRINITY INTERNATIONAL UNIVERSITY
Deerfield, Illinois

About the Institution Independent/religious, coed. Degrees awarded: B, M, D, P. Offers 31 undergraduate majors. Total enrollment: 2,160. Undergraduates: 831 (49% state residents). Freshmen: 144.

Undergraduate Expenses (1997–98) Comprehensive fee of $17,130 includes tuition ($12,390), mandatory fees ($240), and college room and board ($4500 minimum). College room only: $2320 (minimum).

Applications 89% of all full-time undergraduates enrolled in fall 1996 applied for aid; of these, 94% were judged to have need according to Federal Methodology, of whom 100% were aided. *Financial aid deadline (priority):* 5/1. *Financial aid forms:* FAFSA required; CSS Financial Aid PROFILE acceptable. *Admission application deadline:* rolling.

Summary of Aid to Needy Students *From gift & self-help combined:* Average need met: 89%. Average amount awarded: $13,420 (61% gift

aid, 39% self-help). *Gift aid:* Total: $4,143,758 (67% from college's own funds, 25% from other college-administered sources, 8% from external sources). 377 Federal Work-Study jobs (averaging $1540); part-time jobs.

Need-Based Scholarships & Grants Pell, FSEOG, state, private, college/university.

Loans Perkins, PLUS, Stafford, Unsubsidized Stafford, college/university long-term loans ($1650 average).

Non-Need Awards In 1996, a total of 637 non-need awards were made. *Academic Interests/Achievement Awards:* 170 ($290,106 total): general academic. *Creative Arts/Performance Awards:* 86 ($99,880 total): debating, journalism/publications, music. *Special Achievements/Activities Awards:* 41 ($20,250 total): leadership, religious involvement. *Special Characteristics Awards:* 169 ($114,300 total): religious affiliation. *Athletic:* Total: 171 ($590,009); Men: 121 ($438,427); Women: 50 ($151,582).

Other Money-Saving Options Co-op program, off-campus living (after junior year). *Payment Plan:* installment. *Waivers:* full or partial for employees or children of employees.

Contact Mr. Alex Shu, Director of Financial Aid, Trinity International University, 2065 Half Day Road, Deerfield, IL 60015-1284, 847-317-8060, fax: 847-317-7081.

TRINITY INTERNATIONAL UNIVERSITY, SOUTH FLORIDA CAMPUS
Miami, Florida

About the Institution Independent/religious, coed. Degrees awarded: B, M. Offers 9 undergraduate majors. Total enrollment: 423 (97% state residents). Freshmen: 52.

Undergraduate Expenses (1996–97) Tuition: $7590. Mandatory fees: $218.

Applications Of all full-time undergraduates enrolled in fall 1996, 95% of those who applied for aid were judged to have need according to Federal Methodology, of whom 100% were aided. *Financial aid deadline (priority):* 4/1. *Financial aid forms:* FAFSA required. *Admission application deadline:* rolling.

Summary of Aid to Needy Students *From gift & self-help combined:* Average need met: 96%. *Gift aid:* Total: $800,000 (61% from college's own funds, 8% from other college-administered sources, 31% from external sources). Federal Work-Study jobs; 30 part-time jobs.

Need-Based Scholarships & Grants Pell, FSEOG, college/university.

Loans PLUS, Stafford, Unsubsidized Stafford.

Non-Need Awards *Academic Interests/Achievement Awards:* general academic. *Special Achievements/Activities Awards:* leadership. *Special Characteristics Awards:* general special characteristics. *Athletic:* available.

Other Money-Saving Options Accelerated degree. *Payment Plan:* installment. *Waivers:* full or partial for employees or children of employees.

Contact Ms. Lidiette Esquivel, Director of Financial Aid, Trinity International University, South Florida Campus, Miami, FL 33101-9674, 305-577-4600.

TRINITY UNIVERSITY
San Antonio, Texas

About the Institution Independent/religious, coed. Degrees awarded: B, M. Offers 48 undergraduate majors. Total enrollment: 2,495. Undergraduates: 2,251 (67% state residents). Freshmen: 597.

Undergraduate Expenses (1996–97) Comprehensive fee of $19,189 includes tuition ($13,500), mandatory fees ($144), and college room and board ($5545). College room only: $3485.

Applications Of all full-time undergraduates enrolled in fall 1996, 100% of those who applied for aid were judged to have need according to Federal Methodology, of whom 100% were aided. *Financial aid deadline (priority):* 2/1. *Financial aid forms:* CSS Financial Aid PROFILE required. FAFSA, state form, institutional form required for some. *Regular admission application deadline:* 2/1. Early decision deadline: 11/15. Early action deadline: 1/11.

Summary of Aid to Needy Students *From gift & self-help combined:* Average need met: 100%. Average amount awarded: $12,521 (73% gift aid, 27% self-help). *Gift aid:* Total: $8,744,629 (75% from college's own funds, 15% from other college-administered sources, 10% from external sources). 594 Federal Work-Study jobs (averaging $1350); part-time jobs.

Need-Based Scholarships & Grants Pell, FSEOG, state, private, college/university.

Loans Perkins, PLUS, Stafford, Unsubsidized Stafford, state, private, college/university short-term loans, college/university long-term loans ($4000 average).

Non-Need Awards In 1996, a total of 866 non-need awards were made. *Academic Interests/Achievement Awards:* 766 ($3,165,329 total): general academic. *Creative Arts/Performance Awards:* 100 ($94,000 total): music.

Other Money-Saving Options Accelerated degree, cooperative Air Force ROTC, off-campus living (after junior year). *Payment Plans:* tuition prepayment, installment. *Waivers:* full or partial for employees or children of employees.

Contact Ms. Estelle Frerichs, Director of Financial Aid, Trinity University, 715 Stadium Drive, San Antonio, TX 78212-7200, 210-736-8315, fax: 210-736-8316.

TRI-STATE UNIVERSITY
Angola, Indiana

About the Institution Independent, coed. Degrees awarded: A, B. Offers 38 undergraduate majors. Total enrollment: 1,146 (48% state residents). Freshmen: 285.

Undergraduate Expenses (1997–98 estimated) Comprehensive fee of $15,744 includes tuition ($11,100) and college room and board ($4644).

Applications 95% of all full-time undergraduates enrolled in fall 1996 applied for aid; of these, 97% were judged to have need according to Federal Methodology, of whom 100% were aided. *Financial aid deadline (priority):* 3/1. *Financial aid forms:* FAFSA required. State form, institutional form required for some. *Admission application deadline:* 6/1.

Summary of Aid to Needy Students *From gift & self-help combined:* Average need met: 85%. Average amount awarded: $7503 (76% gift aid, 24% self-help). *Gift aid:* Total: $5,908,000 (82% from college's own funds, 12% from other college-administered sources, 6% from external sources). 150 Federal Work-Study jobs (averaging $1500); 50 part-time jobs.

Need-Based Scholarships & Grants Pell, FSEOG, state, private, college/university.

Loans PLUS, Stafford, Unsubsidized Stafford, private, college/university short-term loans ($75 average).

Non-Need Awards In 1996, a total of 816 non-need awards were made. *Academic Interests/Achievement Awards:* 300 ($1,700,000 total): general academic. *Special Characteristics Awards:* 139 ($570,000 total): international students, members of minorities. *Athletic:* Total: 377 ($943,834); Men: 271 ($660,810); Women: 106 ($283,024).

Other Money-Saving Options Accelerated degree, co-op program, off-campus living (after freshman year). *Payment Plan:* installment. *Waivers:* full or partial for employees or children of employees and senior citizens.

Contact Ms. Grace Beltz, Director of Financial Aid, Tri-State University, 1 University Avenue, Angola, IN 46703-1764, 219-665-4175.

TROY STATE UNIVERSITY
Troy, Alabama

About the Institution State-supported, coed. Degrees awarded: A, B, M. Offers 65 undergraduate majors. Total enrollment: 6,211. Undergraduates: 5,126. Freshmen: 811.

Undergraduate Expenses (1996–97) State resident tuition: $1980. Nonresident tuition: $3960. Mandatory fees: $195. College room and board: $3000. College room only: $1350.

Applications Of all full-time undergraduates enrolled in fall 1996, 58% of those who applied for aid were judged to have need according to Federal Methodology, of whom 100% were aided. *Financial aid deadline (priority):* 5/1. *Financial aid forms:* FAFSA, institutional form required; CSS Financial Aid PROFILE acceptable. *Admission application deadline:* rolling.

Summary of Aid to Needy Students *From gift & self-help combined:* Average need met: 68%. Average amount awarded: $5882 (44% gift aid, 56% self-help). *Gift aid:* Total: $5,151,937 (48% from college's own funds, 6% from other college-administered sources, 46% from external sources). 189 Federal Work-Study jobs (averaging $2378); 250 part-time jobs.

Need-Based Scholarships & Grants Pell, FSEOG, state.

Loans Perkins, PLUS, Stafford, Unsubsidized Stafford.

Non-Need Awards In 1996, a total of 2,293 non-need awards were made. *Academic Interests/Achievement Awards:* 1,835 ($1,205,928 total): general academic. *Creative Arts/Performance Awards:* 74 ($210,419 total): journalism/publications, music, performing arts, theater/drama. *Special Characteristics Awards:* 160 ($160,915 total): general special characteristics. *Athletic:* Total: 224 ($1,124,522); Men: 146 ($710,602); Women: 78 ($413,920).

Other Money-Saving Options Accelerated degree, Army ROTC, Air Force ROTC, off-campus living (after freshman year). *Payment Plan:* installment. *Waivers:* full or partial for employees or children of employees.

Contact Ms. Carol Supri, Director of Financial Aid, Troy State University, Adams Administration 141, Troy, AL 36082, 334-670-3186.

TROY STATE UNIVERSITY DOTHAN
Dothan, Alabama

About the Institution State-supported, coed. Degrees awarded: A, B, M. Offers 22 undergraduate majors. Total enrollment: 2,150. Undergraduates: 1,574 (81% state residents). Freshmen: 34.

Undergraduate Expenses (1996–97) State resident tuition: $2100. Nonresident tuition: $4200.

Applications *Financial aid deadline (priority):* 5/1. *Financial aid forms:* FAFSA, institutional form required; CSS Financial Aid PROFILE acceptable. *Admission application deadline:* rolling.

Summary of Aid to Needy Students *Gift aid:* Total: $850,000. Federal Work-Study jobs; part-time jobs.

Need-Based Scholarships & Grants Pell, FSEOG.

Loans Stafford, Unsubsidized Stafford.

Non-Need Awards *Academic Interests/Achievement Awards:* general academic.

Other Money-Saving Options Accelerated degree. *Waivers:* full or partial for employees or children of employees.

Contact Office of Financial Aid, Troy State University Dothan, PO Box 8368, Dothan, AL 36304-8368, 334-983-6556.

TROY STATE UNIVERSITY MONTGOMERY
Montgomery, Alabama

About the Institution State-supported, coed. Degrees awarded: A, B, M. Offers 13 undergraduate majors. Total enrollment: 3,360. Undergraduates: 2,816 (100% state residents). Freshmen: 102.

Undergraduate Expenses (1996–97) State resident tuition: $1980. Nonresident tuition: $3774. Mandatory fees: $45.

Applications 35% of all full-time undergraduates enrolled in fall 1996 applied for aid; of these, 92% were judged to have need according to Federal Methodology, of whom 100% were aided. *Financial aid deadline (priority):* 5/1. *Financial aid forms:* FAFSA, institutional form required. *Admission application deadline:* rolling.

Summary of Aid to Needy Students *From gift & self-help combined:* Average need met: 33%. Average amount awarded: $2946 (58% gift aid, 42% self-help). *Gift aid:* Total: $354,893 (4% from college-administered sources, 96% from external sources). 12 Federal Work-Study jobs (averaging $1950).

Need-Based Scholarships & Grants Pell, FSEOG, state.

Loans Perkins, PLUS, Stafford, Unsubsidized Stafford.

Non-Need Awards Not offered.

Other Money-Saving Options Accelerated degree, cooperative Army ROTC, cooperative Air Force ROTC. *Payment Plan:* deferred payment. *Waivers:* full or partial for employees or children of employees.

Contact Ms. Carol Supri, Director of Financial Aid, Troy State University Montgomery, Adams Administration 141, Troy, AL 36082, 334-670-3182.

TRUMAN STATE UNIVERSITY
Kirksville, Missouri

About the Institution State-supported, coed. Degrees awarded: B, M. Offers 50 undergraduate majors. Total enrollment: 6,261. Undergraduates: 6,017 (70% state residents). Freshmen: 1,482.

Undergraduate Expenses (1997–98) State resident tuition: $3256. Nonresident tuition: $5736. Mandatory fees: $18. College room and board: $3992.

Applications Of all full-time undergraduates enrolled in fall 1996, 75% of those who applied for aid were judged to have need according to Federal Methodology. *Financial aid deadline (priority):* 4/30. *Financial aid forms:* FAFSA required; state form acceptable. *Regular admission application deadline:* 3/1. *Early action deadline:* 11/15.

Summary of Aid to Needy Students 325 Federal Work-Study jobs (averaging $797); 1,663 part-time jobs.

Need-Based Scholarships & Grants Pell, FSEOG, state, private.

Loans Perkins, PLUS, Stafford, Unsubsidized Stafford, Federal Nursing, Primary Care, private, college/university short-term loans ($819 average), college/university long-term loans ($2584 average).

Non-Need Awards In 1996, a total of 3,324 non-need awards were made. *Academic Interests/Achievement Awards:* 2,421 ($4,155,099 total): general academic, biological sciences, business, communication, education, English, foreign languages, mathematics, military science, physical sciences, premedicine, social sciences. *Creative Arts/Performance Awards:* 285 ($624,018 total): art/fine arts, debating, music, theater/drama. *Special Achievements/Activities Awards:* 22 ($9625 total): leadership. *Special Characteristics Awards:* 340 ($791,814 total): children and siblings of alumni, children of faculty/staff, ethnic background, international students, ROTC participants. *Athletic:* Total: 256 ($626,390); Men: 166 ($426,865); Women: 90 ($199,525).

Other Money-Saving Options Accelerated degree, Army ROTC, off-campus living (after freshman year). *Payment Plan:* installment. *Waivers:* full or partial for employees or children of employees and senior citizens.

Contact Office of Financial Aid, Truman State University, 103 McClain Hall, Kirksville, MO 63501-4221, 816-785-4000.

TUFTS UNIVERSITY
Medford, Massachusetts

About the Institution Independent, coed. Degrees awarded: B, M, D, P. Offers 64 undergraduate majors. Total enrollment: 8,183. Undergraduates: 4,504 (26% state residents). Freshmen: 1,181.

Undergraduate Expenses (1997–98) Comprehensive fee of $29,429 includes tuition ($22,230), mandatory fees ($581), and college room and board ($6618). College room only: $3518.

Applications 42% of all full-time undergraduates enrolled in fall 1996 applied for aid; of these, 91% were judged to have need according to Federal Methodology, of whom 100% were aided. *Financial aid deadline (priority):* 1/15. *Financial aid forms:* FAFSA, CSS Financial Aid PROFILE, parent and student federal tax forms required. *Regular admission application deadline:* 1/1. Early decision deadline: 11/15.

Summary of Aid to Needy Students *From gift & self-help combined:* Average need met: 99%. Average amount awarded: $17,827 (72% gift aid, 28% self-help). *Gift aid:* Total: $22,350,429 (87% from college's own funds, 5% from other college-administered sources, 8% from external sources). 1,360 Federal Work-Study jobs (averaging $1650); 10 part-time jobs.

Need-Based Scholarships & Grants Pell, FSEOG, state, private, college/university.

Loans Perkins, PLUS, Stafford, Unsubsidized Stafford, state, private, college/university short-term loans ($2450 average), college/university long-term loans ($893 average).

Non-Need Awards In 1996, a total of 126 non-need awards were made. *Academic Interests/Achievement Awards:* 61 ($86,000 total): general academic. *Special Characteristics Awards:* 65 ($1,350,000 total): children of faculty/staff.

Other Money-Saving Options Cooperative Army ROTC, cooperative Naval ROTC, cooperative Air Force ROTC, off-campus living (after sophomore year). *Payment Plans:* tuition prepayment, installment. *Waivers:* full or partial for employees or children of employees.

Contact Office of Financial Aid, Tufts University, 128 Professors Row, Medford, MA 02155, 617-628-5000.

TULANE UNIVERSITY
New Orleans, Louisiana

About the Institution Independent, coed. Degrees awarded: A, B, M, D, P. Offers 75 undergraduate majors. Total enrollment: 11,246. Undergraduates: 6,402 (35% state residents). Freshmen: 1,323.

Undergraduate Expenses (1997–98) Comprehensive fee of $28,536 includes tuition ($20,490), mandatory fees ($1576), and college room and board ($6470). College room only: $3650.

Applications Of all full-time undergraduates enrolled in fall 1996, 88% of those who applied for aid were judged to have need according to Federal Methodology, of whom 98% were aided. *Financial aid deadline (priority):* 1/15. *Financial aid forms:* FAFSA, CSS Financial Aid PROFILE required. *Regular admission application deadline:* 1/15. Early action deadline: 11/1.

Summary of Aid to Needy Students *From gift & self-help combined:* Average need met: 95%. Average amount awarded: $20,200 (77% gift aid, 23% self-help). *Gift aid:* Total: $38,935,596 (88% from college's own funds, 2% from other college-administered sources, 10% from external sources). 1,365 Federal Work-Study jobs (averaging $1400); 150 part-time jobs.

Need-Based Scholarships & Grants Pell, FSEOG, state, private, college/university.

Loans Perkins, PLUS, Stafford, Unsubsidized Stafford, private, college/university short-term loans ($200 average), college/university long-term loans ($1365 average).

Non-Need Awards *Academic Interests/Achievement Awards:* 868 ($11,520,617 total): general academic. *Special Characteristics Awards:* children of faculty/staff, local/state students, ROTC participants. *Athletic:* Total: 222 ($4,859,769); Men: 156 ($3,477,691); Women: 66 ($1,382,078).

Other Money-Saving Options Accelerated degree, Army ROTC, Naval ROTC, Air Force ROTC, off-campus living (after freshman year). *Payment Plan:* installment. *Waivers:* full or partial for employees or children of employees.

Contact Ms. Elaine Rivera, Director of Financial Aid, Tulane University, New Orleans, LA 70118-5669, 504-865-5723.

TUSCULUM COLLEGE
Greeneville, Tennessee

About the Institution Independent/religious, coed. Degrees awarded: B, M. Offers 29 undergraduate majors. Total enrollment: 1,516. Undergraduates: 1,042 (79% state residents). Freshmen: 165.

Undergraduate Expenses (1997–98) Comprehensive fee of $14,850 includes tuition ($10,900), mandatory fees ($250), and college room and board ($3700).

Applications 70% of all full-time undergraduates enrolled in fall 1996 applied for aid; of these, 77% were judged to have need according to Federal Methodology, of whom 100% were aided. *Financial aid deadline (priority):* 4/1. *Financial aid forms:* FAFSA, institutional form required; CSS Financial Aid PROFILE, state form acceptable. *Admission application deadline:* rolling.

Summary of Aid to Needy Students *From gift & self-help combined:* Average need met: 84%. Average amount awarded: $7881 (57% gift aid, 43% self-help). *Gift aid:* Total: $2,470,741 (67% from college's own funds, 15% from other college-administered sources, 18% from external sources). 149 Federal Work-Study jobs (averaging $802); 171 part-time jobs.

Need-Based Scholarships & Grants Pell, FSEOG, state, private, college/university.

Loans Perkins, PLUS, Stafford, Unsubsidized Stafford, private.

Non-Need Awards *Academic Interests/Achievement Awards:* general academic. *Creative Arts/Performance Awards:* 12 ($7500 total): performing arts. *Special Characteristics Awards:* children of faculty/staff, international students, local/state students. *Athletic:* Total: 205 ($721,469); Men: 133 ($516,999); Women: 72 ($204,470).

Other Money-Saving Options *Payment Plan:* installment. *Waivers:* full or partial for employees or children of employees.

Contact Mr. Anthony P. Jones, Director of Financial Aid, Tusculum College, 5049 Tusculum Station, Greeneville, TN 37743-9997, 423-636-7376, fax: 423-638-5181.

TUSKEGEE UNIVERSITY
Tuskegee, Alabama

About the Institution Independent, coed. Degrees awarded: B, M, P. Offers 45 undergraduate majors. Total enrollment: 3,124. Undergraduates: 2,875 (23% state residents). Freshmen: 759.

Undergraduate Expenses (1996–97) Comprehensive fee of $12,070 includes tuition ($8020) and college room and board ($4050).

Applications Of all full-time undergraduates enrolled in fall 1996, 79% of those who applied for aid were judged to have need according to Federal Methodology, of whom 91% were aided. *Financial aid deadline (priority):* 3/31. *Financial aid forms:* FAFSA, CSS Financial Aid PROFILE, institutional form required. *Admission application deadline:* 4/15.

Summary of Aid to Needy Students *From gift & self-help combined:* Average need met: 75%. Average amount awarded: $7785 (50% gift aid, 50% self-help). *Gift aid:* Total: $7,150,274 (31% from college's own funds, 22% from other college-administered sources, 47% from external sources). 455 Federal Work-Study jobs (averaging $1530); 200 part-time jobs.

Need-Based Scholarships & Grants Pell, FSEOG, state, private, college/university.

Loans Perkins, PLUS, Stafford, Unsubsidized Stafford, Federal Nursing, college/university.

Non-Need Awards *Academic Interests/Achievement Awards:* general academic. *Creative Arts/Performance Awards:* music. *Special Characteristics Awards:* children of faculty/staff, local/state students, ROTC participants. *Athletic:* Total: 56 ($449,120); Men: 46 ($368,920); Women: 10 ($80,200).

Other Money-Saving Options Co-op program, Army ROTC, Air Force ROTC, off-campus living (after sophomore year). *Payment Plan:* installment. *Waivers:* full or partial for employees or children of employees.

Contact Mrs. Barbara Chisholm, Director of Financial Aid, Tuskegee University, Office of Financial Aid Services, Tuskegee, AL 36088, 334-727-8021.

UNION COLLEGE
Barbourville, Kentucky

About the Institution Independent/religious, coed. Degrees awarded: A, B, M. Offers 45 undergraduate majors. Total enrollment: 987. Undergraduates: 663 (71% state residents). Freshmen: 134.

Undergraduate Expenses (1997–98) Comprehensive fee of $12,460 includes tuition ($9340) and college room and board ($3120).

Applications 91% of all full-time undergraduates enrolled in fall 1996 applied for aid; of these, 97% were judged to have need according to Federal Methodology, of whom 100% were aided. *Financial aid deadline (priority):* 3/15. *Financial aid forms:* FAFSA required. *Admission application deadline:* 8/15.

Summary of Aid to Needy Students *From gift & self-help combined:* Average need met: 100%. Average amount awarded: $7759 (64% gift aid, 36% self-help). *Gift aid:* Total: $2,620,050 (53% from college's own funds, 22% from other college-administered sources, 25% from external sources). 185 Federal Work-Study jobs (averaging $1000).

Need-Based Scholarships & Grants Pell, FSEOG, state, college/university.

Loans Perkins, PLUS, Stafford, Unsubsidized Stafford, college/university long-term loans ($1004 average).

Non-Need Awards In 1996, a total of 599 non-need awards were made. *Academic Interests/Achievement Awards:* 238 ($389,708 total): general academic. *Creative Arts/Performance Awards:* 45 ($51,850 total): music. *Special Achievements/Activities Awards:* 16 ($12,500 total): cheerleading/drum major. *Special Characteristics Awards:* 78 ($72,380 total): children and siblings of alumni, religious affiliation. *Athletic:* Total: 222 ($762,207); Men: 142 ($483,297); Women: 80 ($278,910).

Other Money-Saving Options Accelerated degree, co-op program, off-campus living (after sophomore year). *Payment Plan:* installment. *Waivers:* full or partial for children of alumni, employees or children of employees, senior citizens.

Contact Office of Financial Aid, Union College, 310 College Street, Barbourville, KY 40906-1499, 606-546-4151.

UNION COLLEGE
Lincoln, Nebraska

About the Institution Independent/religious, coed. Degrees awarded: A, B. Offers 40 undergraduate majors. Total enrollment: 553 (21% state residents). Freshmen: 142.

Undergraduate Expenses (1997–98) Comprehensive fee of $13,166 includes tuition ($9926) and college room and board ($3240). College room only: $1940.

Applications 59% of all full-time undergraduates enrolled in fall 1996 applied for aid; of these, 94% were judged to have need according to Federal Methodology, of whom 97% were aided. *Financial aid deadline (priority):* 6/15. *Financial aid forms:* FAFSA required; CSS Financial Aid PROFILE acceptable. *Admission application deadline:* rolling.

Summary of Aid to Needy Students *From gift & self-help combined:* Average need met: 55%. Average amount awarded: $7710 (40% gift aid, 60% self-help). *Gift aid:* Total: $766,469 (55% from college's own funds, 19% from other college-administered sources, 26% from external sources). Federal Work-Study jobs; 402 part-time jobs.

Need-Based Scholarships & Grants Pell, FSEOG, state, private, college/university.

Loans Perkins, Stafford, Unsubsidized Stafford, Federal Nursing, college/university short-term loans.

Non-Need Awards *Academic Interests/Achievement Awards:* general academic. *Creative Arts/Performance Awards:* music. *Special Achievements/Activities Awards:* community service, leadership, religious involvement.

Other Money-Saving Options Accelerated degree, co-op program. *Payment Plans:* tuition prepayment, installment. *Waivers:* full or partial for minority students and employees or children of employees.

Contact Mr. Dan Duff, Director of Financial Aid, Union College, 3800 South 48th Street, Lincoln, NE 68506-4300, 402-486-2505.

UNION COLLEGE
Schenectady, New York

About the Institution Independent, coed. Degrees awarded: B, M. Offers 34 undergraduate majors. Total enrollment: 2,335. Undergraduates: 2,088 (50% state residents). Freshmen: 589.

Undergraduate Expenses (1997–98) Comprehensive fee of $28,464 includes tuition ($21,945), mandatory fees ($190), and college room and board ($6329). College room only: $3491.

Applications 63% of all full-time undergraduates enrolled in fall 1996 applied for aid; of these, 94% were judged to have need according to Federal Methodology, of whom 100% were aided. *Financial aid deadline (priority):* 2/1. *Financial aid forms:* FAFSA, CSS Financial Aid PROFILE required. State form, institutional form required for some. *Regular admission application deadline:* 2/1. Early decision deadline: 11/15.

Summary of Aid to Needy Students *From gift & self-help combined:* Average need met: 88%. Average amount awarded: $18,687 (72% gift aid, 28% self-help). *Gift aid:* Total: $16,402,666 (87% from college's own funds, 2% from other college-administered sources, 11% from external sources). 663 Federal Work-Study jobs (averaging $1155); 27 part-time jobs.

Need-Based Scholarships & Grants Pell, FSEOG, state, private, college/university.

Loans Perkins, PLUS, Stafford, Unsubsidized Stafford, private, college/university short-term loans ($200 average), college/university long-term loans ($1800 average).

Non-Need Awards Not offered.

Other Money-Saving Options Accelerated degree, cooperative Army ROTC, cooperative Naval ROTC, cooperative Air Force ROTC, off-campus living (after junior year). *Payment Plan:* installment. *Waivers:* full or partial for employees or children of employees and senior citizens.

Contact Mr. Michael Brown, Director of Financial Aid, Union College, Becker Hall, Schenectady, NY 12308-2311, 518-388-6123.

THE UNION INSTITUTE
Cincinnati, Ohio

About the Institution Independent, coed. Degrees awarded: B, D. Offers 60 undergraduate majors. Total enrollment: 2,016. Undergraduates: 767. Freshmen: 229.

Undergraduate Expenses (1996–97) Tuition: $7296.

Applications 76% of all full-time undergraduates enrolled in fall 1996 applied for aid; of these, 95% were judged to have need according to Federal Methodology, of whom 100% were aided. *Financial aid deadline (priority):* 9/1. *Financial aid forms:* FAFSA, institutional form, federal income tax form required; CSS Financial Aid PROFILE acceptable. State form required for some. *Admission application deadline:* 10/9.

Summary of Aid to Needy Students *From gift & self-help combined:* Average need met: 60%. *Gift aid:* Total: $400,000 (50% from college-administered sources, 50% from external sources). 18 Federal Work-Study jobs (averaging $4500); part-time jobs.

Need-Based Scholarships & Grants Pell, FSEOG, state, private, college/university.

Loans Perkins, PLUS, Stafford, Unsubsidized Stafford, private.

Non-Need Awards Not offered.

Other Money-Saving Options *Payment Plan:* installment. *Waivers:* full or partial for employees or children of employees.

Contact Ms. Rebecca Zackerman, Director of Financial Aid, The Union Institute, 440 East McMillan Street, Cincinnati, OH 45206-1925, 513-861-6400, fax: 513-861-0779.

UNION UNIVERSITY
Jackson, Tennessee

About the Institution Independent/religious, coed. Degrees awarded: B, M. Offers 52 undergraduate majors. Total enrollment: 1,975. Undergraduates: 1,832 (75% state residents). Freshmen: 353.

Undergraduate Expenses (1997–98) Comprehensive fee of $11,185 includes tuition ($7990), mandatory fees ($190), and college room and board ($3005).

Applications 73% of all full-time undergraduates enrolled in fall 1996 applied for aid; of these, 76% were judged to have need according to Federal Methodology, of whom 100% were aided. *Financial aid deadline (priority):* 2/1. *Financial aid forms:* FAFSA, institutional form required. *Admission application deadline:* 2/1.

Summary of Aid to Needy Students *From gift & self-help combined:* Average need met: 80%. Average amount awarded: $6000 (53% gift aid, 47% self-help). *Gift aid:* Total: $2,736,520 (31% from college's own funds, 29% from other college-administered sources, 40% from external sources). 120 Federal Work-Study jobs (averaging $800); 170 part-time jobs.

Need-Based Scholarships & Grants Pell, FSEOG, state, private, college/university.

Loans College/university short-term loans ($300 average), college/university long-term loans ($500 average).

Non-Need Awards In 1996, a total of 1,220 non-need awards were made. *Academic Interests/Achievement Awards:* 647 ($1,378,719 total): general academic. *Creative Arts/Performance Awards:* 65 ($55,000 total): music. *Special Achievements/Activities Awards:* 287 ($251,119 total): leadership. *Special Characteristics Awards:* 149 ($109,330 total): relatives of clergy. *Athletic:* Total: 72 ($444,425); Men: 46 ($259,849); Women: 26 ($184,576).

Other Money-Saving Options Accelerated degree. *Payment Plans:* installment, deferred payment. *Waivers:* full or partial for employees or children of employees.

Contact Office of Financial Aid, Union University, Jackson, TN 38305, 901-668-1818.

UNITED STATES INTERNATIONAL UNIVERSITY
San Diego, California

About the Institution Independent, coed. Degrees awarded: A, B; M, D. Offers 19 undergraduate majors. Total enrollment: 1,873. Undergraduates: 516 (40% state residents). Freshmen: 77.

Undergraduate Expenses (1997–98) Comprehensive fee of $16,545 includes tuition ($11,445), mandatory fees ($300), and college room and board ($4800 minimum).

Applications 67% of all full-time undergraduates enrolled in fall 1996 applied for aid; of these, 93% were judged to have need according to Federal Methodology, of whom 100% were aided. *Financial aid deadline (priority):* 3/2. *Financial aid forms:* FAFSA, institutional form required; CSS Financial Aid PROFILE, state form acceptable. *Admission application deadline:* rolling.

Summary of Aid to Needy Students *From gift & self-help combined:* Average need met: 80%. Average amount awarded: $9500 (56% gift aid, 44% self-help). *Gift aid:* Total: $1,287,233 (38% from college's own funds, 41% from other college-administered sources, 21% from external sources). 130 Federal Work-Study jobs (averaging $4200); 29 part-time jobs.

Need-Based Scholarships & Grants Pell, FSEOG, state, private, college/university.

Loans Perkins, PLUS, Stafford, Unsubsidized Stafford, private.

Non-Need Awards In 1996, a total of 247 non-need awards were made. *Academic Interests/Achievement Awards:* 100 ($290,000 total): general academic, business, communication, education, foreign languages, international studies, social sciences. *Special Achievements/Activities Awards:* 11 ($11,000 total): general special achievements/activities, community service, leadership. *Special Characteristics Awards:* 108 ($279,936 total): children of faculty/staff, ethnic background, international students, local/state students, members of minorities. *Athletic:* Total: 28 ($75,825); Men: 12 ($29,061); Women: 16 ($46,764).

Other Money-Saving Options Accelerated degree, cooperative Army ROTC, off-campus living. *Payment Plan:* deferred payment. *Waivers:* full or partial for employees or children of employees.

Contact Mr. John B. Green, Systems Administrator, United States International University, 10455 Pomerado Road, San Diego, CA 92131-1799, 619-635-4559, fax: 619-635-4848.

UNITED TALMUDICAL SEMINARY
Brooklyn, New York

About the Institution Independent/religious, men.

Applications *Financial aid deadline (priority):* 1/1. *Financial aid forms:* FAFSA required.

Summary of Aid to Needy Students Federal Work-Study jobs.

Need-Based Scholarships & Grants Pell, private.

Non-Need Awards *Academic Interests/Achievement Awards:* general academic.

Contact Financial Aid Office, United Talmudical Seminary, Brooklyn, NY 11211-7900, 718-963-9770 Ext. 309.

UNITY COLLEGE
Unity, Maine

About the Institution Independent, coed. Degrees awarded: A, B. Offers 17 undergraduate majors. Total enrollment: 512 (33% state residents). Freshmen: 188.

Undergraduate Expenses (1997–98) Comprehensive fee of $16,150 includes tuition ($10,750), mandatory fees ($200), and college room and board ($5200).

Applications 89% of all full-time undergraduates enrolled in fall 1996 applied for aid; of these, 90% were judged to have need according to Federal Methodology, of whom 95% were aided. *Financial aid deadline (priority):* 4/15. *Financial aid forms:* FAFSA, state form, institutional form required. *Admission application deadline:* rolling.

Summary of Aid to Needy Students *From gift & self-help combined:* Average need met: 74%. Average amount awarded: $8495 (40% gift aid, 60% self-help). *Gift aid:* Total: $1,354,748 (57% from college's own funds, 21% from other college-administered sources, 22% from external sources). 297 Federal Work-Study jobs (averaging $1916); 25 part-time jobs.

Need-Based Scholarships & Grants Pell, FSEOG, state, private, college/university.

Loans Perkins, PLUS, Stafford, Unsubsidized Stafford, private.

Non-Need Awards In 1996, a total of 139 non-need awards were made. *Academic Interests/Achievement Awards:* 87 ($88,450 total): general academic. *Special Achievements/Activities Awards:* 10 ($6000 total): community service, leadership. *Special Characteristics Awards:* 1 ($1000 total): members of minorities. *Athletic:* Total: 41 ($24,300); Men: 33 ($19,600); Women: 8 ($4700).

Other Money-Saving Options Accelerated degree, co-op program, cooperative Army ROTC, off-campus living (after freshman year). *Payment Plan:* installment. *Waivers:* full or partial for employees or children of employees.

Contact Office of Financial Aid, Unity College, HC 78, Box 1, Unity, ME 04988, 207-948-3131.

UNIVERSIDAD ADVENTISTA DE LAS ANTILLAS
Mayagüez, Puerto Rico

About the Institution Independent/religious, coed. Degrees awarded: A, B. Offers 19 undergraduate majors. Total enrollment: 767 (74% commonwealth residents). Freshmen: 137.

Undergraduate Expenses (1996–97) Comprehensive fee of $5880 includes tuition ($3040), mandatory fees ($690), and college room and board ($2150 minimum). College room only: $650.

Applications 100% of all full-time undergraduates enrolled in fall 1996 applied for aid; of these, 85% were judged to have need according to Federal Methodology, of whom 100% were aided. *Financial aid deadline (priority):* 5/30. *Financial aid forms:* FAFSA required. Commonwealth form, institutional form required for some. *Admission application deadline:* 7/8.

Summary of Aid to Needy Students *From gift & self-help combined:* Average amount awarded: $2400 (57% gift aid, 43% self-help). *Gift aid:* Total: $780,612 (6% from college's own funds, 13% from other college-administered sources, 81% from external sources). 137 Federal Work-Study jobs (averaging $600).

Need-Based Scholarships & Grants Pell, FSEOG, state, college/university.

Loans PLUS, Stafford, Unsubsidized Stafford, college/university.

Non-Need Awards Not offered.

Other Money-Saving Options Co-op program, off-campus living (after freshman year). *Payment Plans:* installment, deferred payment. *Waivers:* full or partial for employees or children of employees.

Contact Office of Financial Aid, Universidad Adventista de las Antillas, Box 118, Mayagüez, PR 00681-0118, 787-834-9595.

UNIVERSIDAD DEL TURABO
Gurabo, Puerto Rico

About the Institution Independent, coed. Degrees awarded: A, B, M. Offers 28 undergraduate majors. Total enrollment: 7,320. Undergraduates: 6,480 (99% commonwealth residents). Freshmen: 1,300.

Undergraduate Expenses (1997–98) Tuition: $2620. Mandatory fees: $240.

Applications *Financial aid deadline (priority):* 6/15. *Financial aid forms:* FAFSA required. *Admission application deadline:* rolling.

Summary of Aid to Needy Students *From gift & self-help combined:* Average need met: 50%. *Gift aid:* Total: $23,837,226 (1% from college's own funds, 6% from other college-administered sources, 93% from external sources). 600 Federal Work-Study jobs (averaging $870).

Need-Based Scholarships & Grants Pell, FSEOG, state, private, college/university.

Loans PLUS, Stafford, Unsubsidized Stafford.

Non-Need Awards Not offered.

Other Money-Saving Options Cooperative Army ROTC, cooperative Air Force ROTC.

Contact Ms. Ivette Vázquez Ríos, Directora Oficina de Asistencia Económica, Universidad del Turabo, Apartado 3030, Gurabo, PR 00778-3030, 787-743-7979 Ext. 4352, fax: 787-743-7979.

UNIVERSIDAD METROPOLITANA
Río Piedras, Puerto Rico

About the Institution Independent, coed. Degrees awarded: A, B, M. Offers 22 undergraduate majors. Total enrollment: 4,700.

Undergraduate Expenses (1997–98) Tuition: $3392. Mandatory fees: $120 (minimum).

Applications *Financial aid deadline (priority):* 5/15. *Financial aid forms:* FAFSA, institutional form required. *Admission application deadline:* 7/30.

Summary of Aid to Needy Students Federal Work-Study jobs.

Non-Need Awards *Academic Interests/Achievement Awards:* biological sciences , physical sciences.

Another Money-Saving Option Co-op program.

Contact Office of Financial Aid, Universidad Metropolitana, Río Piedras, PR 00928-1150, 787-766-1717.

UNIVERSIDAD POLITÉCNICA DE PUERTO RICO
Hato Rey, Puerto Rico

See Polytechnic University of Puerto Rico

UNIVERSITY AT ALBANY, STATE UNIVERSITY OF NEW YORK
Albany, New York

About the Institution State-supported, coed. Degrees awarded: B, M, D. Offers 63 undergraduate majors. Total enrollment: 14,215. Undergraduates: 10,027 (97% state residents). Freshmen: 2,008.

Undergraduate Expenses (1996–97) State resident tuition: $3400. Nonresident tuition: $8300. Mandatory fees: $730. College room and board: $5050. College room only: $3412.

Applications Of all full-time undergraduates enrolled in fall 1996, 80% of those who applied for aid were judged to have need according to Federal Methodology, of whom 95% were aided. *Financial aid deadline (priority):* 3/15. *Financial aid forms:* FAFSA required; CSS Financial Aid PROFILE acceptable. *Regular admission application deadline:* rolling. Early decision deadline: 11/15.

Summary of Aid to Needy Students *From gift & self-help combined:* Average need met: 75%. Average amount awarded: $6464 (41% gift aid, 59% self-help). *Gift aid:* Total: $14,391,508 (2% from college's own funds, 59% from other college-administered sources, 39% from external sources). 1,200 Federal Work-Study jobs (averaging $900); part-time jobs.

Need-Based Scholarships & Grants Pell, FSEOG, state, private, college/university.

Loans Perkins, PLUS, Stafford, Unsubsidized Stafford, private, college/university short-term loans ($300 average).

Non-Need Awards In 1996, a total of 112 non-need awards were made. *Academic Interests/Achievement Awards:* 74 ($212,000 total): general academic. *Athletic:* Total: 38 ($67,116); Men: 15 ($32,000); Women: 23 ($35,116).

Other Money-Saving Options Army ROTC, cooperative Naval ROTC, cooperative Air Force ROTC, off-campus living (after sophomore year). *Payment Plan:* installment. *Waivers:* full or partial for senior citizens.

Contact Mr. Dennis Tillman, Director of Financial Aid, University at Albany, State University of New York, 1400 Washington Avenue, Campus Center B52, Albany, NY 12222-0001, 518-442-5757, fax: 518-442-5295.

UNIVERSITY OF ADVANCING COMPUTER TECHNOLOGY
Phoenix, Arizona

About the Institution Proprietary, coed. Degrees awarded: A, B. Offers 6 undergraduate majors. Total enrollment: 750. Freshmen: 150.

Applications *Financial aid deadline:* continuous. *Financial aid forms:* FAFSA, institutional form required.

Summary of Aid to Needy Students Federal Work-Study jobs; part-time jobs.

Need-Based Scholarships & Grants Pell, FSEOG.

Loans Stafford, Unsubsidized Stafford.

Non-Need Awards *Academic Interests/Achievement Awards:* general academic, computer science. *Special Characteristics Awards:* local/state students, out-of-state students.

Another Money-Saving Option Accelerated degree.

Contact Ms. Gina Myers, Director of Financial Aid, University of Advancing Computer Technology, 4100 East Broadway Road, Suite 180, Phoenix, AZ 85040, 602-437-0405.

THE UNIVERSITY OF AKRON
Akron, Ohio

About the Institution State-supported, coed. Degrees awarded: A, B, M, D, P. Offers 150 undergraduate majors. Total enrollment: 24,252. Undergraduates: 20,037 (98% state residents). Freshmen: 3,065.

Undergraduate Expenses (1997–98) State resident tuition: $3282. Nonresident tuition: $9051. Mandatory fees: $343. College room and board: $4380. College room only: $2710 (minimum).

Applications 61% of all full-time undergraduates enrolled in fall 1996 applied for aid; of these, 84% were judged to have need according to Federal Methodology, of whom 100% were aided. *Financial aid deadline (priority):* 3/1. *Financial aid forms:* FAFSA, state form required. Institutional form required for some. *Admission application deadline:* 08/25.

Summary of Aid to Needy Students *From gift & self-help combined:* Average need met: 100%. Average amount awarded: $6525 (44% gift aid, 56% self-help). *Gift aid:* Total: $16,706,197 (6% from college's own funds, 11% from other college-administered sources, 83% from external sources). 912 Federal Work-Study jobs (averaging $1900); 1,200 part-time jobs.

Need-Based Scholarships & Grants Pell, FSEOG, state, college/university.

Loans Perkins, PLUS, Stafford, Unsubsidized Stafford, Federal Nursing, state, private, college/university short-term loans ($200 average), college/university long-term loans ($500 average).

Non-Need Awards In 1996, a total of 1,856 non-need awards were made. *Academic Interests/Achievement Awards:* 508 ($425,346 total): general academic, biological sciences, business, communication, computer science, education, engineering/technologies, English, foreign languages, health fields, home economics, humanities, international studies, mathematics, military science, physical sciences, premedicine, social sciences. *Creative Arts/Performance Awards:* 210 ($148,000 total): general creative, applied art and design, art/fine arts, creative writing, dance, debating, journalism/publications, music, performing arts, theater/drama. *Special Characteristics Awards:* 875 ($807,576 total): general special characteristics, adult students, handicapped students, local/state students, members of minorities, out-of-state students, ROTC participants. *Athletic:* Total: 263 ($1,798,169); Men: 196 ($1,323,386); Women: 67 ($474,783).

Other Money-Saving Options Accelerated degree, co-op program, Army ROTC, Air Force ROTC, off-campus living. *Payment Plan:* installment. *Waivers:* full or partial for employees or children of employees and senior citizens.

Contact Mr. Doug McNutt, Director of Financial Aid, The University of Akron, Student Financial Aid, Akron, OH 44325-0001, 330-972-6343, fax: 330-972-7139.

THE UNIVERSITY OF ALABAMA AT BIRMINGHAM
Birmingham, Alabama

About the Institution State-supported, coed. Degrees awarded: A, B, M, D, P. Offers 57 undergraduate majors. Total enrollment: 15,274. Undergraduates: 10,692 (94% state residents). Freshmen: 1,131.

Undergraduate Expenses (1996–97) State resident tuition: $2400. Nonresident tuition: $4800. Mandatory fees: $300. College room and board: $6384. College room only: $2742.

Applications Of all full-time undergraduates enrolled in fall 1996, 80% of those who applied for aid were judged to have need according to Federal Methodology, of whom 93% were aided. *Financial aid deadline (priority):* 5/1. *Financial aid forms:* FAFSA, institutional form required; CSS Financial Aid PROFILE acceptable. *Admission application deadline:* 8/1.

Summary of Aid to Needy Students *From gift & self-help combined:* Average need met: 80%. Average amount awarded: $3471 (40% gift aid, 60% self-help). *Gift aid:* Total: $4,703,944 (32% from college's own funds, 21% from other college-administered sources, 47% from external sources). 817 Federal Work-Study jobs (averaging $2500); part-time jobs.

Need-Based Scholarships & Grants Pell, FSEOG, state, private, college/university.

Loans Perkins, PLUS, Stafford, Unsubsidized Stafford, state, private, college/university short-term loans ($150 average), college/university long-term loans ($1000 average).

Non-Need Awards *Academic Interests/Achievement Awards:* ($1,420,871 total): general academic, business, engineering/technologies. *Creative Arts/Performance Awards:* 55 ($27,388 total): art/fine arts, music, performing arts, theater/drama. *Special Achievements/Activities Awards:* 46 ($37,231 total): cheerleading/drum major, leadership, memberships. *Special Characteristics Awards:* 15 ($31,000 total): general special characteristics, adult students, children and siblings of alumni, children of current students, children of educators, children of faculty/staff, children of public servants, children of union members/company employees, children of workers in trades, children with a deceased or disabled parent, ethnic background, first-generation college students, handicapped students, local/state students, married students, out-of-state students, parents of current students, previous college experience, public servants, relatives of clergy, religious affiliation, siblings of current students, spouses of current students, spouses of deceased or disabled public servants, twins, veterans, veterans' children. *Athletic:* Total: 224 ($696,080); Men: 159 ($488,177); Women: 65 ($207,903).

Other Money-Saving Options Accelerated degree, co-op program, Army ROTC, cooperative Air Force ROTC, off-campus living. *Waivers:* full or partial for employees or children of employees.

Contact Ms. Cindy R. Edwards, Assistant Director of Financial Aid, The University of Alabama at Birmingham, 317 Hill, University Center, 1400 University Boulevard, Birmingham, AL 35294-1150, 205-934-8132, fax: 205-934-8941.

THE UNIVERSITY OF ALABAMA IN HUNTSVILLE
Huntsville, Alabama

About the Institution State-supported, coed. Degrees awarded: B, M, D. Offers 37 undergraduate majors. Total enrollment: 4,982. Undergraduates: 3,881 (80% state residents). Freshmen: 442.

Undergraduate Expenses (1996–97) State resident tuition: $2698. Nonresident tuition: $5656. College room and board: $3645. College room only: $2645.

Applications *Financial aid deadline:* continuous. *Financial aid forms:* FAFSA, institutional form required. *Admission application deadline:* 8/15.

Summary of Aid to Needy Students *From gift & self-help combined:* Average amount awarded: $3871 (33% gift aid, 67% self-help). *Gift aid:* Total: $3,400,000 (44% from college's own funds, 7% from other college-administered sources, 49% from external sources). 38 Federal Work-Study jobs (averaging $3500); 500 part-time jobs.

Need-Based Scholarships & Grants Pell, FSEOG, state, private, college/university.

Loans PLUS, Stafford, Unsubsidized Stafford, college/university short-term loans ($250 average).

Non-Need Awards *Academic Interests/Achievement Awards:* general academic, engineering/technologies, health fields, physical sciences. *Creative Arts/Performance Awards:* music. *Special Achievements/Activities Awards:* leadership. *Special Characteristics Awards:* ROTC participants. *Athletic:* Total: 165 ($755,056); Men: 90 ($324,674); Women: 75 ($430,382).

Other Money-Saving Options Co-op program, cooperative Army ROTC, cooperative Air Force ROTC, off-campus living. *Waivers:* full or partial for employees or children of employees.

Contact Mr. Jerry Davis, Drector of Financial Aid, The University of Alabama in Huntsville, 121 University Center, Huntsville, AL 35899, 205-890-6241.

UNIVERSITY OF ALASKA ANCHORAGE
Anchorage, Alaska

About the Institution State-supported, coed. Degrees awarded: A, B, M. Offers 63 undergraduate majors. Total enrollment: 13,049. Undergraduates: 12,397 (95% state residents). Freshmen: 1,208.

Undergraduate Expenses (1996–97) State resident tuition: $2100 (minimum). Nonresident tuition: $6300 (minimum). Mandatory fees: $163. College room only: $2800.

Applications Of all full-time undergraduates enrolled in fall 1996, 99% of those who applied for aid were judged to have need according to Federal Methodology, of whom 90% were aided. *Financial aid deadline (priority):* 4/1. *Financial aid forms:* institutional form required; state form acceptable. FAFSA, verification worksheet, Stafford Student Loan form required for some. *Admission application deadline:* rolling.

Summary of Aid to Needy Students *From gift & self-help combined:* Average need met: 66%. Average amount awarded: $3563 (24% gift aid, 76% self-help). *Gift aid:* Total: $2,663,358 (17% from college's own funds, 38% from other college-administered sources, 45% from external sources). 120 Federal Work-Study jobs (averaging $2074); 480 part-time jobs.

Need-Based Scholarships & Grants Pell, FSEOG, state, private, college/university.

Loans Perkins, PLUS, Stafford, Unsubsidized Stafford, state, private, college/university short-term loans ($188 average).

Non-Need Awards In 1996, a total of 420 non-need awards were made. *Academic Interests/Achievement Awards:* general academic, biological sciences, business, communication, computer science, education, engineering/technologies, English, health fields, humanities, mathematics, social sciences. *Creative Arts/Performance Awards:* art/fine arts, music. *Special Achievements/Activities Awards:* general special achievements/activities. *Special Characteristics Awards:* general special characteristics, children of faculty/staff, ethnic background, international students, members of minorities, spouses of deceased or disabled public servants. *Athletic:* Total: 121 ($324,384).

Other Money-Saving Options Co-op program, off-campus living. *Payment Plan:* deferred payment. *Waivers:* full or partial for minority students, children of alumni, employees or children of employees, adult students, senior citizens.

Contact Ms. Tami Coli, Financial Aid Counselor, University of Alaska Anchorage, Anchorage, AK 99508-8060, 907-786-1586, fax: 907-786-6122.

UNIVERSITY OF ALASKA FAIRBANKS
Fairbanks, Alaska

About the Institution State-supported, coed. Degrees awarded: A, B, M, D. Offers 91 undergraduate majors. Total enrollment: 5,197. Freshmen: 739.

Undergraduate Expenses (1996–97) State resident tuition: $2100. Nonresident tuition: $6300. Mandatory fees: $330. College room and board: $3790. College room only: $1950.

Applications *Financial aid deadline (priority):* 5/15. *Financial aid forms:* FAFSA required; CSS Financial Aid PROFILE acceptable. *Admission application deadline:* 8/1.

Summary of Aid to Needy Students *From gift & self-help combined:* Average need met: 60%. Average amount awarded: $8000 (20% gift aid, 80% self-help). *Gift aid:* Total: $3,000,000 (17% from college's own funds, 17% from other college-administered sources, 66% from external sources). 160 Federal Work-Study jobs (averaging $4000); 951 part-time jobs.

Need-Based Scholarships & Grants Pell, FSEOG, state, private, college/university.

Loans PLUS, Stafford, Unsubsidized Stafford, state, college/university short-term loans ($200 average), college/university long-term loans ($500 average).

Non-Need Awards *Academic Interests/Achievement Awards:* general academic. *Creative Arts/Performance Awards:* creative writing, music, theater/drama. *Special Achievements/Activities Awards:* general special achievements/activities. *Special Characteristics Awards:* general special characteristics. *Athletic:* Total: 68 ($485,793); Men: 43 ($330,589); Women: 25 ($155,204).

Other Money-Saving Options Accelerated degree, Army ROTC, off-campus living. *Payment Plan:* deferred payment. *Waivers:* full or partial for children of alumni, employees or children of employees, senior citizens.

Contact Financial Aid Office, University of Alaska Fairbanks, 101 Eielson Building, PO Box 756360, Fairbanks, AK 99775-6360, 907-474-7256.

UNIVERSITY OF ALASKA SOUTHEAST
Juneau, Alaska

About the Institution State-supported, coed. Degrees awarded: A, B, M. Offers 17 undergraduate majors. Total enrollment: 2,944 (80% state residents). Freshmen: 139.

Undergraduate Expenses (1996–97) State resident tuition: $1680 (minimum). Nonresident tuition: $5040 (minimum). Mandatory fees: $34. College room only: $2900.

Applications *Financial aid deadline (priority):* 5/1. *Financial aid forms:* institutional form required. FAFSA, state form, financial aid transcript (for transfers) required for some. *Admission application deadline:* rolling.

Summary of Aid to Needy Students *From gift & self-help combined:* Average need met: 25%. *Gift aid:* Total: $405,610. Federal Work-Study jobs; part-time jobs.

Need-Based Scholarships & Grants Pell, FSEOG, state, private, college/university.

Loans PLUS, Stafford, Unsubsidized Stafford, state, college/university short-term loans ($200 average).

Non-Need Awards *Academic Interests/Achievement Awards:* general academic. *Special Achievements/Activities Awards:* available. *Special Characteristics Awards:* international students.

Other Money-Saving Options Co-op program, off-campus living. *Payment Plans:* installment, deferred payment. *Waivers:* full or partial for employees or children of employees and senior citizens.

Contact Ms. Barbara Carlson Burnett, Financial Aid Director, University of Alaska Southeast, 11120 Glacier Highway, Juneau, AK 99801-8680, 907-465-6255, fax: 907-465-6365.

UNIVERSITY OF ARIZONA
Tucson, Arizona

About the Institution State-supported, coed. Degrees awarded: B, M, D, P. Offers 145 undergraduate majors. Total enrollment: 33,504. Undergraduates: 25,293 (72% state residents). Freshmen: 4,168.

Undergraduate Expenses (1996–97) State resident tuition: $1940. Nonresident tuition: $8308. Mandatory fees: $69. College room and board: $4410. College room only: $2430.

Applications Of all full-time undergraduates enrolled in fall 1996, 75% of those who applied for aid were judged to have need according to Federal Methodology, of whom 98% were aided. *Financial aid deadline (priority):* 3/1. *Financial aid forms:* FAFSA, CSS Financial Aid PROFILE, institutional form acceptable. *Regular admission application deadline:* 4/1. Early action deadline: 11/1.

Summary of Aid to Needy Students *From gift & self-help combined:* Average need met: 81%. Average amount awarded: $7298 (34% gift aid, 66% self-help). *Gift aid:* Total: $20,293,193. 599 Federal Work-Study jobs (averaging $1903); 4,144 part-time jobs.

Loans Perkins, PLUS, Stafford, Unsubsidized Stafford, Federal Nursing, Primary Care, state, private, college/university short-term loans ($997 average), college/university long-term loans ($1000 average).

Non-Need Awards In 1996, a total of 4,440 non-need awards were made. *Academic Interests/Achievement Awards:* 1,892 ($3,443,190 total). *Creative Arts/Performance Awards:* 205 ($550,534 total). *Special Characteristics Awards:* 2,045 ($4,869,127 total): children of faculty/staff, ethnic background, international students. *Athletic:* Total: 298 ($1,364,444).

Other Money-Saving Options Co-op program, Army ROTC, Naval ROTC, Air Force ROTC, off-campus living. *Waivers:* full or partial for minority students and employees or children of employees.

Contact Office of Financial Aid, University of Arizona, Rm. 203 Admin. Bdg., PO Box 210066, Tucson, AZ 85721-0066, 520-621-2211.

UNIVERSITY OF ARKANSAS
Fayetteville, Arkansas

About the Institution State-supported, coed. Degrees awarded: A, B, M, D, P. Offers 86 undergraduate majors. Total enrollment: 14,577. Undergraduates: 11,991 (87% state residents). Freshmen: 2,313.

Undergraduate Expenses (1996–97) State resident tuition: $2224. Nonresident tuition: $5786. Mandatory fees: $186 (minimum). College room and board: $3780 (minimum).

Applications *Financial aid deadline (priority):* 4/1. *Financial aid forms:* FAFSA required. *Admission application deadline:* 8/15.

Summary of Aid to Needy Students *From gift & self-help combined:* Average amount awarded: $5460 (30% gift aid, 70% self-help). *Gift aid:* Total: $14,750,000. Federal Work-Study jobs.

Need-Based Scholarships & Grants Pell, FSEOG, state, college/university.

Loans Perkins, PLUS, Stafford, Unsubsidized Stafford, state, college/university short-term loans ($300 average), college/university long-term loans ($1732 average).

Non-Need Awards *Academic Interests/Achievement Awards:* general academic. *Creative Arts/Performance Awards:* music. *Athletic:* available.

Other Money-Saving Options Co-op program, Army ROTC, Air Force ROTC, off-campus living (after freshman year). *Payment Plan:* installment. *Waivers:* full or partial for employees or children of employees and senior citizens.

Contact Office of Student Aid, University of Arkansas, 114 Silas H. Hunt Hall, Fayetteville, AR 72701-1201, 501-575-3806.

UNIVERSITY OF ARKANSAS AT LITTLE ROCK
Little Rock, Arkansas

About the Institution State-supported, coed. Degrees awarded: A, B, M, D, P. Offers 48 undergraduate majors. Total enrollment: 10,720. Undergraduates: 8,559 (95% state residents). Freshmen: 893.

Undergraduate Expenses (1996–97) State resident tuition: $2511. Nonresident tuition: $6438. Mandatory fees: $368. College room only: $2410.

Applications 56% of all full-time undergraduates enrolled in fall 1996 applied for aid; of these, 86% were judged to have need according to Federal Methodology, of whom 90% were aided. *Financial aid deadline (priority):* 11/1. *Financial aid forms:* FAFSA required. *Admission application deadline:* rolling.

Summary of Aid to Needy Students *From gift & self-help combined:* Average amount awarded: $992. *Gift aid:* Total: $7,514,830. 196 Federal Work-Study jobs (averaging $604); part-time jobs.

Need-Based Scholarships & Grants Pell, FSEOG, state, private.

Loans PLUS, Stafford, Unsubsidized Stafford, private, college/university short-term loans ($300 average).

Non-Need Awards *Academic Interests/Achievement Awards:* general academic, biological sciences, business, communication, computer science, education, engineering/technologies, English, foreign languages, health fields, humanities, international studies, mathematics, physical sciences, social sciences. *Creative Arts/Performance Awards:* art/fine arts, music, theater/drama. *Special Achievements/Activities Awards:* community service, leadership, memberships. *Special Characteristics Awards:* local/state students. *Athletic:* Total: 140 ($363,051); Men: 71 ($176,863); Women: 69 ($186,188).

Other Money-Saving Options Accelerated degree, co-op program, Army ROTC, off-campus living. *Payment Plan:* deferred payment. *Waivers:* full or partial for employees or children of employees and senior citizens.

Contact Financial Aid Office, University of Arkansas at Little Rock, 2801 South University, Little Rock, AR 72204-1099, 501-569-3130.

UNIVERSITY OF ARKANSAS AT MONTICELLO
Monticello, Arkansas

About the Institution State-supported, coed. Degrees awarded: A, B, M. Offers 34 undergraduate majors. Total enrollment: 2,124. Undergraduates: 2,042 (92% state residents). Freshmen: 478.

Undergraduate Expenses (1996–97) State resident tuition: $1906. Nonresident tuition: $4114. College room and board: $2400 (minimum).

Applications *Financial aid deadline (priority):* 5/1. *Financial aid forms:* FAFSA required. *Admission application deadline:* 8/1.

Summary of Aid to Needy Students Federal Work-Study jobs.

Need-Based Scholarships & Grants Pell, FSEOG, state.

Loans Perkins, PLUS, Stafford, Unsubsidized Stafford.

Non-Need Awards *Academic Interests/Achievement Awards:* general academic. *Creative Arts/Performance Awards:* debating, music. *Special Achievements/Activities Awards:* cheerleading/drum major, leadership. *Special Characteristics Awards:* children of faculty/staff. *Athletic:* available.

Other Money-Saving Options Accelerated degree, off-campus living. *Waivers:* full or partial for employees and children of employees and senior citizens.

Contact Office of Financial Aid, University of Arkansas at Monticello, PO Box 3470, Monticello, AR 71656, 870-460-1050.

UNIVERSITY OF ARKANSAS AT PINE BLUFF
Pine Bluff, Arkansas

About the Institution State-supported, coed. Degrees awarded: A, B, M. Offers 52 undergraduate majors. Total enrollment: 3,242. Undergraduates: 3,182 (87% state residents). Freshmen: 587.

Undergraduate Expenses (1996–97) State resident tuition: $1680. Nonresident tuition: $3888. Mandatory fees: $210. College room and board: $2900 (minimum).

Applications 80% of all full-time undergraduates enrolled in fall 1996 applied for aid; of these, 95% were judged to have need according to Federal Methodology, of whom 92% were aided. *Financial aid deadline (priority):* 4/15. *Financial aid forms:* FAFSA required. *Admission application deadline:* 8/1.

Summary of Aid to Needy Students *From gift & self-help combined:* Average amount awarded: $3480 (53% gift aid, 47% self-help). *Gift aid:* Total: $4,100,000. Federal Work-Study jobs.

Need-Based Scholarships & Grants Pell, FSEOG, state.

Loans Perkins, PLUS, Stafford, Unsubsidized Stafford, state.

Non-Need Awards *Academic Interests/Achievement Awards:* general academic. *Creative Arts/Performance Awards:* art/fine arts, music, performing arts. *Special Characteristics Awards:* children and siblings of alumni, members of minorities, religious affiliation. *Athletic:* available.

Other Money-Saving Options Accelerated degree, co-op program, Army ROTC, off-campus living.

Contact Ms. Caroline Robinson, Financial Aid Officer, University of Arkansas at Pine Bluff, PO Box 4985, Pine Bluff, AR 71601-2799, 501-543-8304.

UNIVERSITY OF BIBLICAL STUDIES AND SEMINARY
Bethany, Oklahoma

About the Institution Independent/religious, coed. Degrees awarded: A, B, M. Offers 2 undergraduate majors. Total enrollment: 1,400. Undergraduates: 1,120 (10% state residents). Freshmen: 336.

Undergraduate Expenses (1997–98) Tuition: $2325.

Applications *Financial aid deadline (priority):* 4/30. *Financial aid forms:* FAFSA required.

Need-Based Scholarships & Grants Pell, college/university.

Loans Stafford, Unsubsidized Stafford.

Non-Need Awards Not offered.

Contact Financial Aid Office, University of Biblical Studies and Seminary, 7045 NW 16th Street, Bethany, OK 73008, 405-495-2526, fax: 405-495-2521.

UNIVERSITY OF BRIDGEPORT
Bridgeport, Connecticut

About the Institution Independent, coed. Degrees awarded: A, B, M, D, P. Offers 52 undergraduate majors. Total enrollment: 2,142. Undergraduates: 1,001 (40% state residents). Freshmen: 136.

Undergraduate Expenses (1997–98) Comprehensive fee of $20,505 includes tuition ($13,000), mandatory fees ($695), and college room and board ($6810). College room only: $3700.

Applications 96% of all full-time undergraduates enrolled in fall 1996 applied for aid; of these, 58% were judged to have need according to Federal Methodology, of whom 100% were aided. *Financial aid deadline (priority):* 4/15. *Financial aid forms:* FAFSA, institutional form required. State form required for some. *Regular admission application deadline:* 4/1. Early action deadline: 1/1.

Summary of Aid to Needy Students *From gift & self-help combined:* Average need met: 95%. Average amount awarded: $14,372 (81% gift aid, 19% self-help). *Gift aid:* Total: $8,160,186 (78% from college's own funds, 9% from other college-administered sources, 13% from external sources). 299 Federal Work-Study jobs (averaging $2000); 154 part-time jobs.

Need-Based Scholarships & Grants Pell, FSEOG, state, private, college/university.

Loans Perkins, PLUS, Stafford, Unsubsidized Stafford, state, private.

Non-Need Awards In 1996, a total of 318 non-need awards were made. *Academic Interests/Achievement Awards:* 233 ($3,771,727 total): general academic. *Creative Arts/Performance Awards:* 10 ($152,194 total): music. *Special Characteristics Awards:* 9 ($60,942 total): children of faculty/staff, parents of current students, siblings of current students, spouses of current students. *Athletic:* Total: 66 ($672,106); Men: 38 ($314,680); Women: 28 ($357,426).

Other Money-Saving Options Accelerated degree, co-op program, Army ROTC, off-campus living (after sophomore year). *Payment Plans:* installment, deferred payment. *Waivers:* full or partial for employees or children of employees and senior citizens.

Contact Mr. Dominic R. Yoia, Director of Financial Aid, University of Bridgeport, 126 Park Avenue, Bridgeport, CT 06601, 203-576-4568, fax: 203-576-4941.

UNIVERSITY OF CALIFORNIA, BERKELEY
Berkeley, California

About the Institution State-supported, coed. Degrees awarded: B, M, D, P. Offers 99 undergraduate majors. Total enrollment: 29,630. Undergraduates: 21,189 (88% state residents). Freshmen: 3,775.

Undergraduate Expenses (1996–97) State resident tuition: $0. Nonresident tuition: $8394. Mandatory fees: $3956. College room and board: $6710.

Applications Of all full-time undergraduates enrolled in fall 1996, 82% of those who applied for aid were judged to have need according to Federal Methodology, of whom 100% were aided. *Financial aid deadline (priority):* 3/2. *Financial aid forms:* FAFSA, state form required. *Admission application deadline:* 11/30.

Summary of Aid to Needy Students *From gift & self-help combined:* Average need met: 100%. Average amount awarded: $9542 (60% gift aid, 40% self-help). *Gift aid:* Total: $64,616,792 (47% from college's own funds, 32% from other college-administered sources, 21% from external sources). 2,249 Federal Work-Study jobs (averaging $1916); part-time jobs.

Need-Based Scholarships & Grants Pell, FSEOG, state, private, college/university.

Loans Perkins, PLUS, Stafford, Unsubsidized Stafford, private, college/university short-term loans ($350 average), college/university long-term loans ($4718 average).

Non-Need Awards *Academic Interests/Achievement Awards:* general academic, engineering/technologies. *Creative Arts/Performance Awards:* available. *Special Achievements/Activities Awards:* available. *Special Characteristics Awards:* available. *Athletic:* available.

Other Money-Saving Options Accelerated degree, co-op program, Army ROTC, Naval ROTC, Air Force ROTC, off-campus living. *Payment Plan:* installment.

Contact Ms. Carol Lynn Stewart, Fiscal/Policy Analyst, University of California, Berkeley, 220 Sproul Hall, Berkeley, CA 94720-1960, 510-642-1699, fax: 510-643-5526.

UNIVERSITY OF CALIFORNIA, DAVIS
Davis, California

About the Institution State-supported, coed. Degrees awarded: B, M, D, P. Offers 111 undergraduate majors. Total enrollment: 23,931. Undergraduates: 18,819 (98% state residents). Freshmen: 3,752.

Undergraduate Expenses (1996–97) State resident tuition: $0. Nonresident tuition: $8394. Mandatory fees: $4230. College room and board: $5468 (minimum).

Applications *Financial aid deadline (priority):* 3/2. *Financial aid forms:* FAFSA required; CSS Financial Aid PROFILE acceptable. State form required for some. *Admission application deadline:* 11/30.

Summary of Aid to Needy Students Federal Work-Study jobs; 5,400 part-time jobs.

Need-Based Scholarships & Grants Pell, FSEOG, state, private, college/university, Bureau of Indian Affairs Grants.

Loans Perkins, PLUS, Stafford, Unsubsidized Stafford, private, college/university short-term loans ($1411 average), college/university long-term loans ($2157 average).

Non-Need Awards *Academic Interests/Achievement Awards:* general academic, agriculture. *Special Characteristics Awards:* international students.

Other Money-Saving Options Army ROTC, cooperative Air Force ROTC, off-campus living. *Waivers:* full or partial for employees or children of employees.

Contact Ms. Rose Mary Miller, Assistant Director, University of California, Davis, Davis, CA 95616, 916-752-7605, fax: 916-752-7339.

UNIVERSITY OF CALIFORNIA, IRVINE
Irvine, California

About the Institution State-supported, coed. Degrees awarded: B, M, D. Offers 46 undergraduate majors. Total enrollment: 17,281. Undergraduates: 13,833 (97% state residents). Freshmen: 2,910.

Undergraduate Expenses (1997–98 estimated) State resident tuition: $0. Nonresident tuition: $8394. Mandatory fees: $4050. College room and board: $5565 (minimum).

Applications Of all full-time undergraduates enrolled in fall 1996, 86% of those who applied for aid were judged to have need according to Federal Methodology, of whom 94% were aided. *Financial aid deadline (priority):* 3/2. *Financial aid forms:* FAFSA, state form required; CSS Financial Aid PROFILE acceptable. *Admission application deadline:* 11/30.

Summary of Aid to Needy Students *From gift & self-help combined:* Average need met: 100%. Average amount awarded: $8324 (59% gift aid, 41% self-help). *Gift aid:* Total: $39,415,546 (33% from college's own funds, 3% from other college-administered sources, 64% from external sources). 1,828 Federal Work-Study jobs (averaging $1265); 2,800 part-time jobs.

Need-Based Scholarships & Grants Pell, FSEOG, state, private, college/university.

Loans Perkins, PLUS, Stafford, Unsubsidized Stafford, college/university short-term loans ($100 average), college/university long-term loans ($2011 average).

Non-Need Awards In 1996, a total of 990 non-need awards were made. *Academic Interests/Achievement Awards:* 837 ($1,838,826 total): general academic. *Athletic:* Total: 153 ($683,934); Men: 80 ($327,082); Women: 73 ($356,852).

Other Money-Saving Options Accelerated degree, cooperative Army ROTC, cooperative Air Force ROTC, off-campus living. *Waivers:* full or partial for employees or children of employees.

Contact Mr. Dean Kalju, Assistant Director, University of California, Irvine, 102 Administration Building, Irvine, CA 92697-2825, 714-824-4885, fax: 714-824-4876.

UNIVERSITY OF CALIFORNIA, LOS ANGELES
Los Angeles, California

About the Institution State-supported, coed. Degrees awarded: B, M, D, P. Offers 91 undergraduate majors. Total enrollment: 34,935. Undergraduates: 23,914 (95% state residents). Freshmen: 3,821.

Undergraduate Expenses (1996–97) State resident tuition: $0. Nonresident tuition: $8394. Mandatory fees: $4006. College room and board: $6147.

Applications 65% of all full-time undergraduates enrolled in fall 1996 applied for aid; of these, 82% were judged to have need according to Federal Methodology, of whom 100% were aided. *Financial aid deadline:* Applications processed continuously. *Financial aid forms:* FAFSA, institutional form required. CSS Financial Aid PROFILE, state form required for some. *Admission application deadline:* 11/30.

Summary of Aid to Needy Students *From gift & self-help combined:* Average need met: 100%. Average amount awarded: $8565 (54% gift aid, 46% self-help). *Gift aid:* Total: $61,412,391 (34% from college's own funds, 40% from other college-administered sources, 26% from external sources). 3,000 Federal Work-Study jobs (averaging $1800); 7,000 part-time jobs.

Need-Based Scholarships & Grants Pell, FSEOG, state, private, college/university, National Merit Scholarships.

Loans Perkins, PLUS, Stafford, Unsubsidized Stafford, Federal Nursing, private, college/university short-term loans ($800 average), college/university long-term loans ($4200 average).

Non-Need Awards In 1996, a total of 544 non-need awards were made. *Academic Interests/Achievement Awards:* 154 ($77,000 total): general academic. *Athletic:* Total: 390 ($3,815,757); Men: 233 ($2,120,478); Women: 157 ($1,695,279).

Other Money-Saving Options Army ROTC, Naval ROTC, Air Force ROTC, off-campus living.

Contact Ms. Yolanda Tan, Administrative Assistant, University of California, Los Angeles, A-129 Murphy Hall, 405 Hilgard Avenue, Los Angeles, CA 90095-1435, 310-206-0404, fax: 310-206-5530.

UNIVERSITY OF CALIFORNIA, RIVERSIDE
Riverside, California

About the Institution State-supported, coed. Degrees awarded: B, M, D. Offers 58 undergraduate majors. Total enrollment: 9,063. Undergraduates: 7,665 (98% state residents). Freshmen: 1,485.

Undergraduate Expenses (1996–97) State resident tuition: $0. Nonresident tuition: $8394. Mandatory fees: $4105. College room and board: $5870.

Applications 76% of all full-time undergraduates enrolled in fall 1996 applied for aid; of these, 87% were judged to have need according to Federal Methodology, of whom 96% were aided. *Financial aid deadline (priority):* 3/2. *Financial aid forms:* FAFSA required. Institutional form, financial aid transcript (for transfers) required for some. *Admission application deadline:* 11/30.

Summary of Aid to Needy Students *From gift & self-help combined:* Average need met: 86%. Average amount awarded: $9218 (51% gift aid, 49% self-help). *Gift aid:* Total: $21,910,582 (34% from college's own funds, 2% from other college-administered sources, 64% from external sources). 783 Federal Work-Study jobs (averaging $1305); 1,020 part-time jobs.

Need-Based Scholarships & Grants Pell, FSEOG, state, private, college/university.

Loans Perkins, PLUS, Stafford, Unsubsidized Stafford, private, college/university short-term loans ($200 average), college/university long-term loans ($3500 average).

Non-Need Awards In 1996, a total of 357 non-need awards were made. *Academic Interests/Achievement Awards:* 277 ($977,201 total): general academic, agriculture, engineering/technologies, premedicine. *Creative Arts/Performance Awards:* 23 ($14,237 total): art/fine arts, creative writing, dance, music, theater/drama. *Athletic:* Total: 57 ($149,340); Men: 33 ($88,368); Women: 24 ($60,972).

Other Money-Saving Options Accelerated degree, co-op program, cooperative Army ROTC, cooperative Air Force ROTC, off-campus living. *Payment Plans:* installment, deferred payment.

Contact Ms. Sheryl Hayes, Director of Financial Aid, University of California, Riverside, Riverside, CA 92521-0209, 909-787-3878.

UNIVERSITY OF CALIFORNIA, SAN DIEGO
La Jolla, California

About the Institution State-supported, coed. Degrees awarded: B, M, D. Offers 70 undergraduate majors. Total enrollment: 18,119. Undergraduates: 14,623 (98% state residents). Freshmen: 2,725.

Undergraduate Expenses (1996–97) State resident tuition: $0. Nonresident tuition: $8394. Mandatory fees: $4198. College room and board: $6837.

Applications Of all full-time undergraduates enrolled in fall 1996, 86% of those who applied for aid were judged to have need according to Federal Methodology, of whom 98% were aided. *Financial aid deadline (priority):* 3/2. *Financial aid forms:* FAFSA, state form required. *Admission application deadline:* 11/30.

Summary of Aid to Needy Students *From gift & self-help combined:* Average need met: 100%. Average amount awarded: $8963 (56% gift aid, 44% self-help). *Gift aid:* Total: $35,074,968 (30% from college's own funds, 43% from other college-administered sources, 27% from external sources). 2,546 Federal Work-Study jobs (averaging $1340); 4,800 part-time jobs.

Need-Based Scholarships & Grants Pell, FSEOG, state, private, college/university.

Loans Perkins, PLUS, Stafford, Unsubsidized Stafford, private, college/university short-term loans ($500 average), college/university long-term loans ($1430 average).

Non-Need Awards In 1996, a total of 547 non-need awards were made. *Academic Interests/Achievement Awards:* 247 ($1,150,690 total): general academic, biological sciences, communication, education, English, humanities, mathematics, premedicine, social sciences. *Special Achievements/Activities Awards:* 4 ($5000 total): community service, leadership. *Special Characteristics Awards:* 296 ($372,217 total): general special characteristics, ethnic background, handicapped students, veterans' children.

Other Money-Saving Options Accelerated degree, off-campus living. *Payment Plan:* deferred payment.

Contact Ms. Maura Richman, Associate Director of Student Financial Services, University of California, San Diego, 9500 Gilman Drive, La Jolla, CA 92093-0013, 619-534-4598, fax: 619-534-5459.

UNIVERSITY OF CALIFORNIA, SANTA BARBARA
Santa Barbara, California

About the Institution State-supported, coed. Degrees awarded: B, M, D. Offers 66 undergraduate majors. Total enrollment: 18,531. Undergraduates: 16,281 (95% state residents). Freshmen: 3,464.

Undergraduate Expenses (1996–97) State resident tuition: $0. Nonresident tuition: $8394. Mandatory fees: $4098. College room and board: $6131.

Applications *Financial aid deadline (priority):* 3/2. *Financial aid forms:* FAFSA required. State form, institutional form required for some. *Admission application deadline:* 11/30.

Summary of Aid to Needy Students 2,948 Federal Work-Study jobs (averaging $1274).

Need-Based Scholarships & Grants Pell, FSEOG, state.

Loans Perkins, PLUS, Stafford, Unsubsidized Stafford, college/university short-term loans ($418 average), college/university long-term loans ($1494 average).

Non-Need Awards *Academic Interests/Achievement Awards:* general academic. *Athletic:* available.

Other Money-Saving Options Accelerated degree, co-op program, Army ROTC, off-campus living.

Contact Office of Financial Aid, University of California, Santa Barbara, Santa Barbara, CA 93106, 805-893-8000.

UNIVERSITY OF CALIFORNIA, SANTA CRUZ
Santa Cruz, California

About the Institution State-supported, coed. Degrees awarded: B, M, D. Offers 71 undergraduate majors. Total enrollment: 10,215. Undergraduates: 9,159 (95% state residents). Freshmen: 1,997.

Undergraduate Expenses (1996–97) State resident tuition: $0. Nonresident tuition: $8394. Mandatory fees: $4136. College room and board: $6222 (minimum).

Applications Of all full-time undergraduates enrolled in fall 1996, 85% of those who applied for aid were judged to have need according to Federal Methodology, of whom 100% were aided. *Financial aid deadline (priority):* 3/2. *Financial aid forms:* FAFSA required. *Admission application deadline:* 11/30.

Summary of Aid to Needy Students *From gift & self-help combined:* Average need met: 100%. Average amount awarded: $8146 (45% gift aid, 55% self-help). *Gift aid:* Total: $21,323,530 (45% from college's own funds, 3% from other college-administered sources, 52% from external sources). 3,748 Federal Work-Study jobs (averaging $953); 2,200 part-time jobs.

Need-Based Scholarships & Grants Pell, FSEOG, state, private, college/university.

Loans Perkins, PLUS, Stafford, Unsubsidized Stafford, college/university short-term loans ($500 average), college/university long-term loans ($1740 average).

Non-Need Awards In 1996, a total of 86 non-need awards were made. *Academic Interests/Achievement Awards:* 86 ($174,184 total): general academic.

Other Money-Saving Options Cooperative Army ROTC, cooperative Air Force ROTC, off-campus living. *Payment Plan:* deferred payment. *Waivers:* full or partial for senior citizens.

Contact Ms. Ann Draper, Associate Director, University of California, Santa Cruz, 201 Hahn Student Services Building, Santa Cruz, CA 95064, 408-459-4358, fax: 408-459-3628.

UNIVERSITY OF CENTRAL ARKANSAS
Conway, Arkansas

About the Institution State-supported, coed. Degrees awarded: A, B, M. Offers 91 undergraduate majors. Total enrollment: 8,994. Undergraduates: 7,952 (94% state residents). Freshmen: 1,679.

Undergraduate Expenses (1997–98) State resident tuition: $1744 (minimum). Nonresident tuition: $3622 (minimum). Mandatory fees: $410. College room and board: $2840 (minimum). College room only: $1590 (minimum).

Applications Of all full-time undergraduates enrolled in fall 1996, 96% of those judged to have need according to Federal Methodology were aided. *Financial aid deadline (priority):* 2/15. *Financial aid forms:* FAFSA, institutional form required. *Admission application deadline:* rolling.

Summary of Aid to Needy Students *From gift & self-help combined:* Average need met: 42%. Average amount awarded: $3790 (26% gift aid, 74% self-help). *Gift aid:* Total: $6,255,548 (14% from college's own funds, 5% from other college-administered sources, 81% from external sources). 250 Federal Work-Study jobs (averaging $1360); 125 part-time jobs.

Need-Based Scholarships & Grants Pell, FSEOG, state, private, college/university, Junior Training Partnership Act, Vocational Rehabilitation Act, Veterans Administration Rehab.

Loans Perkins, PLUS, Stafford, Unsubsidized Stafford, state, private.

Non-Need Awards *Academic Interests/Achievement Awards:* general academic. *Creative Arts/Performance Awards:* cinema/film/broadcasting, music, theater/drama. *Special Achievements/Activities Awards:* cheerleading/drum major, leadership. *Special Characteristics Awards:* children of educators, children of faculty/staff, handicapped students. *Athletic:* Total: 117 ($375,000); Men: 65 ($225,000); Women: 52 ($150,000).

Other Money-Saving Options Accelerated degree, co-op program, Army ROTC, off-campus living (after freshman year). *Payment Plan:* installment. *Waivers:* full or partial for employees or children of employees and senior citizens.

Contact Mr. Jim Brock, Associate Director of Financial Aid, University of Central Arkansas, 201 Bernard Hall, Conway, AR 72035-0001, 501-450-5151, fax: 501-450-5159.

UNIVERSITY OF CENTRAL FLORIDA
Orlando, Florida

About the Institution State-supported, coed. Degrees awarded: A, B, M, D. Offers 85 undergraduate majors. Total enrollment: 27,278. Undergraduates: 21,831 (93% state residents). Freshmen: 2,430.

Undergraduate Expenses (1996–97) State resident tuition: $1830. Nonresident tuition: $7074. Mandatory fees: $95. College room and board: $4240. College room only: $2640.

Applications Of all full-time undergraduates enrolled in fall 1996, 81% of those who applied for aid were judged to have need according to Federal Methodology, of whom 95% were aided. *Financial aid deadline (priority):* 3/1. *Financial aid forms:* FAFSA, institutional form required; CSS Financial Aid PROFILE acceptable. State form required for some. *Admission application deadline:* 7/15.

Summary of Aid to Needy Students *From gift & self-help combined:* Average need met: 60%. Average amount awarded: $4902 (33% gift aid, 67% self-help). *Gift aid:* Total: $11,310,301 (3% from college's own funds, 5% from other college-administered sources, 92% from external sources). 400 Federal Work-Study jobs (averaging $2198); 1,904 part-time jobs.

Need-Based Scholarships & Grants Pell, FSEOG, state, private, college/university.

Loans Perkins, PLUS, Stafford, Unsubsidized Stafford, private, college/university short-term loans ($300 average), college/university long-term loans ($2000 average).

Non-Need Awards In 1996, a total of 4,587 non-need awards were made. *Academic Interests/Achievement Awards:* 3,627 ($3,997,607 total): general academic. *Creative Arts/Performance Awards:* 82 ($57,400 total): music. *Special Achievements/Activities Awards:* 72 ($78,000 total): general special achievements/activities. *Special Characteristics Awards:* 261 ($532,549 total): members of minorities. *Athletic:* Total: 545 ($1,052,771); Men: 345 ($708,585); Women: 200 ($344,186).

Other Money-Saving Options Accelerated degree, co-op program, Army ROTC, Air Force ROTC, off-campus living. *Payment Plan:* deferred payment. *Waivers:* full or partial for employees or children of employees and senior citizens.

Contact Mr. Stanley Rosenberg, Financial Aid Coordinator, University of Central Florida, 4000 Central Florida Boulevard, Orlando, FL 32816, 407-823-5729, fax: 407-823-5241.

UNIVERSITY OF CENTRAL OKLAHOMA
Edmond, Oklahoma

About the Institution State-supported, coed. Degrees awarded: B, M. Offers 86 undergraduate majors. Total enrollment: 14,481. Undergraduates: 11,547 (91% state residents). Freshmen: 1,468.

Undergraduate Expenses (1996–97) State resident tuition: $1290 (minimum). Nonresident tuition: $3495 (minimum). Mandatory fees: $426. College room and board: $2431.

Applications 68% of all full-time undergraduates enrolled in fall 1996 applied for aid; of these, 77% were judged to have need according to Federal Methodology, of whom 100% were aided. *Financial aid deadline (priority):* 4/1. *Financial aid forms:* FAFSA, institutional form required; CSS Financial Aid PROFILE acceptable. *Admission application deadline:* rolling.

Summary of Aid to Needy Students *From gift & self-help combined:* Average need met: 70%. Average amount awarded: $5200 (40% gift aid, 60% self-help). *Gift aid:* Total: $3,048,156 (9% from college's own

funds, 22% from other college-administered sources, 69% from external sources). 858 Federal Work-Study jobs (averaging $1500); 700 part-time jobs.

Need-Based Scholarships & Grants Pell, FSEOG, state, private, college/university.

Loans PLUS, Stafford, Unsubsidized Stafford, college/university short-term loans ($125 average).

Non-Need Awards In 1996, a total of 680 non-need awards were made. *Academic Interests/Achievement Awards:* 97 ($28,840 total): general academic, biological sciences, business, computer science, education, foreign languages, health fields, home economics, mathematics, military science, physical sciences, social sciences. *Creative Arts/Performance Awards:* 116 ($70,468 total): applied art and design, art/fine arts, journalism/publications, music, theater/drama. *Special Achievements/Activities Awards:* 221 ($136,560 total): general special achievements/activities, leadership. *Special Characteristics Awards:* 36 ($17,706 total): ethnic background, members of minorities. *Athletic:* Total: 210 ($233,697); Men: 152 ($155,346); Women: 58 ($78,351).

Other Money-Saving Options Accelerated degree, Army ROTC, cooperative Air Force ROTC, off-campus living. *Waivers:* full or partial for employees or children of employees.

Contact Ms. Becky Garrett, Assistant Director, Technical Services, University of Central Oklahoma, 100 North University Drive, Edmond, OK 73034-5209, 405-341-2980 Ext. 3336, fax: 405-340-7658.

THE UNIVERSITY OF CHARLESTON
Charleston, West Virginia

About the Institution Independent, coed. Degrees awarded: A, B, M. Offers 51 undergraduate majors. Total enrollment: 1,424. Undergraduates: 1,376 (82% state residents). Freshmen: 242.

Undergraduate Expenses (1997–98) Comprehensive fee of $15,640 includes tuition ($11,600) and college room and board ($4040).

Applications 95% of all full-time undergraduates enrolled in fall 1996 applied for aid; of these, 82% were judged to have need according to Federal Methodology, of whom 99% were aided. *Financial aid deadline (priority):* 3/1. *Financial aid forms:* FAFSA, institutional form, financial aid transcript (for transfers) required. State form required for some. *Regular admission application deadline:* rolling. Early decision deadline: 12/15.

Summary of Aid to Needy Students *From gift & self-help combined:* Average need met: 91%. Average amount awarded: $11,016 (50% gift aid, 50% self-help). *Gift aid:* Total: $3,723,000 (82% from college's own funds, 4% from other college-administered sources, 14% from external sources). 250 Federal Work-Study jobs (averaging $1000); 25 part-time jobs.

Need-Based Scholarships & Grants Pell, FSEOG, state, private, college/university, Council of Independent Colleges Tuition Exchange grants, Tuition Exchange Inc. grants.

Loans Perkins, PLUS, Stafford, Unsubsidized Stafford, Federal Nursing, private.

Non-Need Awards In 1996, a total of 965 non-need awards were made. *Academic Interests/Achievement Awards:* 525 ($2,510,000 total): general academic. *Creative Arts/Performance Awards:* 30 ($300,000 total): music. *Special Achievements/Activities Awards:* 100 ($135,000 total): general special achievements/activities, leadership. *Special Characteristics Awards:* 100 ($315,000 total): children of educators, children of faculty/staff, international students, local/state students, ROTC participants. *Athletic:* Total: 210 ($463,000); Men: 126 ($277,800); Women: 84 ($185,200).

Other Money-Saving Options Accelerated degree, Army ROTC, off-campus living (after freshman year). *Payment Plan:* installment. *Waivers:* full or partial for employees or children of employees and senior citizens.

Contact Ms. Janet M. Ruge, Director of Financial Aid, The University of Charleston, 2300 MacCorkle Avenue SE, Charleston, WV 25304-1099, 304-357-4760, fax: 304-357-4715.

UNIVERSITY OF CHICAGO
Chicago, Illinois

About the Institution Independent, coed. Degrees awarded: B, M, D, P. Offers 64 undergraduate majors. Total enrollment: 12,117. Undergraduates: 3,561 (26% state residents). Freshmen: 978.

Undergraduate Expenses (1996–97) Comprehensive fee of $28,575 includes tuition ($20,970), mandatory fees ($330), and college room and board ($7275).

Applications Of all full-time undergraduates enrolled in fall 1996, 88% of those who applied for aid were judged to have need according to Federal Methodology, of whom 100% were aided. *Financial aid deadline (priority):* 2/1. *Financial aid forms:* FAFSA, CSS Financial Aid PROFILE, institutional form required. *Regular admission application deadline:* 1/1. Early action deadline: 11/15.

Summary of Aid to Needy Students *From gift & self-help combined:* Average need met: 100%. *Gift aid:* Total: $30,600,000 (81% from college's own funds, 15% from other college-administered sources, 4% from external sources). Federal Work-Study jobs; 1,072 part-time jobs.

Need-Based Scholarships & Grants Pell, FSEOG, state, college/university.

Loans Perkins, PLUS, Stafford, Unsubsidized Stafford, college/university short-term loans.

Non-Need Awards *Academic Interests/Achievement Awards:* general academic.

Other Money-Saving Options Accelerated degree, cooperative Army ROTC, cooperative Air Force ROTC, off-campus living (after freshman year). *Payment Plans:* tuition prepayment, installment. *Waivers:* full or partial for employees or children of employees.

Contact Office of College Aid, University of Chicago, 1116 East 59th Street, Chicago, IL 60637-1513, 773-702-8666.

UNIVERSITY OF CINCINNATI
Cincinnati, Ohio

About the Institution State-supported, coed. Degrees awarded: A, B, M, D, P. Offers 149 undergraduate majors. Total enrollment: 19,139. Undergraduates: 13,730 (93% state residents). Freshmen: 2,444.

Undergraduate Expenses (1996–97) State resident tuition: $4152. Nonresident tuition: $10,464. Mandatory fees: $169. College room and board: $5049 (minimum).

Applications 60% of all full-time undergraduates enrolled in fall 1996 applied for aid; of these, 84% were judged to have need according to Federal Methodology, of whom 96% were aided. *Financial aid deadline:* continuous. *Financial aid forms:* FAFSA required. *Admission application deadline:* rolling.

Summary of Aid to Needy Students *From gift & self-help combined:* Average need met: 61%. Average amount awarded: $5878 (34% gift aid, 66% self-help). *Gift aid:* Total: $11,226,009 (33% from college's own funds, 8% from other college-administered sources, 59% from external sources). Federal Work-Study jobs; part-time jobs.

Need-Based Scholarships & Grants Pell, FSEOG, state, private, college/university.

Loans Perkins, PLUS, Stafford, Unsubsidized Stafford, Federal Nursing, state, college/university short-term loans, college/university long-term loans.

Non-Need Awards *Academic Interests/Achievement Awards:* general academic, architecture, area/ethnic studies, biological sciences, business, communication, computer science, education, engineering/technologies, English, foreign languages, health fields, humanities, mathematics, military science, physical sciences, premedicine, social sciences. *Creative Arts/Performance Awards:* applied art and design, art/fine arts, music. *Special Characteristics Awards:* children of faculty/staff, members of minorities, out-of-state students, ROTC participants. *Athletic:* available.

Other Money-Saving Options Accelerated degree, co-op program, Army ROTC, Air Force ROTC, off-campus living (after freshman year). *Payment Plan:* installment. *Waivers:* full or partial for employees or children of employees.

Contact Ms. Ann Sexton, Associate Director of Student Financial Aid, University of Cincinnati, 52 Beecher Hall, Cincinnati, OH 45221-0125, 513-556-6994, fax: 513-556-9171.

UNIVERSITY OF COLORADO AT BOULDER
Boulder, Colorado

About the Institution State-supported, coed. Degrees awarded: B, M, D, P. Offers 80 undergraduate majors. Total enrollment: 24,622. Undergraduates: 19,845 (68% state residents). Freshmen: 3,952.

Undergraduate Expenses (1996–97) State resident tuition: $2322 (minimum). Nonresident tuition: $13,914 (minimum). Mandatory fees: $518. College room and board: $4370.

Applications Of all full-time undergraduates enrolled in fall 1996, 63% of those who applied for aid were judged to have need according to Federal Methodology, of whom 100% were aided. *Financial aid deadline (priority):* 4/1. *Financial aid forms:* FAFSA required. *Admission application deadline:* 2/15.

Summary of Aid to Needy Students *From gift & self-help combined:* Average need met: 80%. Average amount awarded: $8285 (38% gift aid, 62% self-help). *Gift aid:* Total: $22,197,584 (33% from college's own funds, 21% from other college-administered sources, 46% from external sources). 1,245 Federal Work-Study jobs (averaging $1580); 2,181 part-time jobs.

Need-Based Scholarships & Grants Pell, FSEOG, state, private, college/university.

Loans Perkins, PLUS, Stafford, Unsubsidized Stafford, private, college/university short-term loans ($500 average), college/university long-term loans ($2699 average).

Non-Need Awards In 1996, a total of 4,374 non-need awards were made. *Academic Interests/Achievement Awards:* 1,904 ($2,445,945 total): general academic, architecture, area/ethnic studies, biological sciences, business, communication, computer science, education, engineering/technologies, English, foreign languages, health fields, humanities, international studies, mathematics, military science, physical sciences, premedicine, religion/biblical studies, social sciences. *Creative Arts/Performance Awards:* 416 ($1,152,629 total): art/fine arts, cinema/film/broadcasting, creative writing, dance, journalism/publications, music, performing arts, theater/drama. *Special Achievements/Activities Awards:* 252 ($242,585 total): general special achievements/activities, leadership. *Special Characteristics Awards:* 1,573 ($4,109,983 total): general special characteristics, ethnic background, first-generation college students, local/state students, members of minorities, ROTC participants. *Athletic:* Total: 229 ($1,500,884); Men: 152 ($1,056,659); Women: 77 ($444,225).

Other Money-Saving Options Accelerated degree, co-op program, Army ROTC, Naval ROTC, Air Force ROTC, off-campus living (after freshman year). *Payment Plan:* deferred payment. *Waivers:* full or partial for senior citizens.

Contact Financial Aid Office, University of Colorado at Boulder, Room 2, Environmental Design Building, Campus Box 106, Boulder, CO 80309, 303-492-5091, fax: 303-492-0838.

UNIVERSITY OF COLORADO AT COLORADO SPRINGS
Colorado Springs, Colorado

About the Institution State-supported, coed. Degrees awarded: B, M, D. Offers 35 undergraduate majors. Total enrollment: 5,840. Undergraduates: 4,157 (88% state residents). Freshmen: 441.

Undergraduate Expenses (1996–97) State resident tuition: $2122 (minimum). Nonresident tuition: $8422 (minimum). Mandatory fees: $371. College room and board: $4700 (minimum).

Applications *Financial aid deadline (priority):* 4/1. *Financial aid forms:* FAFSA required. *Admission application deadline:* 7/1.

Summary of Aid to Needy Students 196 Federal Work-Study jobs (averaging $1918); 470 part-time jobs.

Need-Based Scholarships & Grants Pell, FSEOG, state, private, college/university.

Loans Perkins, PLUS, Stafford, Unsubsidized Stafford, private, college/university short-term loans ($300 average).

Non-Need Awards *Academic Interests/Achievement Awards:* general academic. *Special Achievements/Activities Awards:* community service, leadership. *Special Characteristics Awards:* general special characteristics. *Athletic:* available.

Other Money-Saving Options Accelerated degree, co-op program, Army ROTC, off-campus living. *Payment Plan:* deferred payment. *Waivers:* full or partial for employees or children of employees.

Contact Ms. Lee Ingalls-Noble, Director of Financial Aid, University of Colorado at Colorado Springs, 1420 Austin Bluffs Parkway, Colorado Springs, CO 80933-7150, 719-262-3466.

UNIVERSITY OF COLORADO AT DENVER
Denver, Colorado

About the Institution State-supported, coed. Degrees awarded: B, M, D. Offers 41 undergraduate majors. Total enrollment: 10,844. Undergraduates: 5,933 (95% state residents). Freshmen: 408.

Undergraduate Expenses (1996–97) State resident tuition: $1916 (minimum). Nonresident tuition: $10,064 (minimum). Mandatory fees: $267.

Applications *Financial aid deadline (priority):* 3/31. *Financial aid forms:* FAFSA, institutional form, financial aid transcript (for transfers) required; CSS Financial Aid PROFILE acceptable. *Admission application deadline:* 7/22.

Summary of Aid to Needy Students Federal Work-Study jobs; part-time jobs.

Loans College/university short-term loans.

Non-Need Awards *Academic Interests/Achievement Awards:* general academic.

Other Money-Saving Options Accelerated degree, co-op program, Army ROTC, cooperative Naval ROTC, cooperative Air Force ROTC. *Payment Plans:* installment, deferred payment. *Waivers:* full or partial for employees or children of employees.

Contact Office of Financial Aid, University of Colorado at Denver, Denver, CO 80217-3364, 303-556-2400.

UNIVERSITY OF CONNECTICUT
Storrs, Connecticut

About the Institution State-supported, coed. Degrees awarded: A, B, M, D, P. Offers 101 undergraduate majors. Total enrollment: 15,541. Undergraduates: 11,336 (84% state residents). Freshmen: 2,165.

Undergraduate Expenses (1997–98 estimated) State resident tuition: $4158. Nonresident tuition: $12,676. Mandatory fees: $938. College room and board: $5461.

Applications Of all full-time undergraduates enrolled in fall 1996, 78% of those who applied for aid were judged to have need according to Federal Methodology, of whom 96% were aided. *Financial aid deadline (priority):* 3/1. *Financial aid forms:* FAFSA, institutional form required. *Admission application deadline:* 3/1.

Summary of Aid to Needy Students *From gift & self-help combined:* Average need met: 77%. Average amount awarded: $6942 (42% gift aid, 58% self-help). *Gift aid:* Total: $16,022,880 (55% from college's own funds, 33% from other college-administered sources, 12% from external sources). 1,604 Federal Work-Study jobs (averaging $1300); 3,374 part-time jobs.

Need-Based Scholarships & Grants Pell, FSEOG, state, private, college/university.

Loans Perkins, PLUS, Stafford, Unsubsidized Stafford, college/university short-term loans ($500 average).

Non-Need Awards In 1996, a total of 1,217 non-need awards were made. *Academic Interests/Achievement Awards:* 819 ($2,757,869 total): general academic. *Creative Arts/Performance Awards:* 116 ($146,400 total): art/fine arts, music, theater/drama. *Athletic:* Total: 282 ($3,185,907); Men: 161 ($1,854,546); Women: 121 ($1,331,361).

Other Money-Saving Options Accelerated degree, co-op program, Army ROTC, Air Force ROTC, off-campus living. *Payment Plans:* installment, deferred payment. *Waivers:* full or partial for employees or children of employees and senior citizens.

Contact Mr. Vincent C. Amoroso, Associate Director of Financial Aid, University of Connecticut, 233 Glenbrook Road, U-116, Storrs, CT 06269-4116, 860-486-2819.

UNIVERSITY OF DALLAS
Irving, Texas

About the Institution Independent/religious, coed. Degrees awarded: B, M, D. Offers 26 undergraduate majors. Total enrollment: 2,771. Undergraduates: 1,088 (57% state residents). Freshmen: 258.

Undergraduate Expenses (1997–98 estimated) Comprehensive fee of $16,974 includes tuition ($12,114), mandatory fees ($30), and college room and board ($4830). College room only: $2560.

Applications 76% of all full-time undergraduates enrolled in fall 1996 applied for aid; of these, 91% were judged to have need according to Federal Methodology, of whom 100% were aided. *Financial aid deadline (priority):* 3/1. *Financial aid forms:* FAFSA, institutional form required. *Regular admission application deadline:* 3/1. Early action deadline: 12/1.

Summary of Aid to Needy Students *From gift & self-help combined:* Average need met: 90%. Average amount awarded: $12,824 (58% gift aid, 42% self-help). *Gift aid:* Total: $5,185,206 (67% from college's own funds, 23% from other college-administered sources, 10% from external sources). 153 Federal Work-Study jobs (averaging $2049); 435 part-time jobs.

Need-Based Scholarships & Grants Pell, FSEOG, state, private, college/university.

Loans Perkins, PLUS, Stafford, Unsubsidized Stafford, state, private.

Non-Need Awards In 1996, a total of 582 non-need awards were made. *Academic Interests/Achievement Awards:* 324 ($1,156,983 total): general academic, foreign languages. *Creative Arts/Performance Awards:* 28 ($118,500 total): art/fine arts, performing arts. *Special Achievements/Activities Awards:* 128 ($456,750 total): leadership. *Special Characteristics Awards:* 102 ($132,566 total): children of faculty/staff, members of minorities, siblings of current students.

Other Money-Saving Options Accelerated degree, cooperative Army ROTC, cooperative Air Force ROTC, off-campus living (after junior year). *Payment Plans:* installment, deferred payment. *Waivers:* full or partial for employees or children of employees.

Contact Office of Financial Aid, University of Dallas, 1845 East Northgate Drive, Irving, TX 75062-9991, 972-721-5000.

UNIVERSITY OF DAYTON
Dayton, Ohio

About the Institution Independent/religious, coed. Degrees awarded: B, M, D, P. Offers 78 undergraduate majors. Total enrollment: 10,320. Undergraduates: 6,511 (60% state residents). Freshmen: 1,564.

Undergraduate Expenses (1997–98) Comprehensive fee of $18,920 includes tuition ($13,690), mandatory fees ($490), and college room and board ($4740). College room only: $2370.

Applications 74% of all full-time undergraduates enrolled in fall 1996 applied for aid; of these, 84% were judged to have need according to Federal Methodology, of whom 99% were aided. *Financial aid deadline (priority):* 3/31. *Financial aid forms:* FAFSA required; CSS Financial Aid PROFILE, state form, institutional form acceptable. *Admission application deadline:* rolling.

Summary of Aid to Needy Students *From gift & self-help combined:* Average need met: 93%. Average amount awarded: $13,441 (62% gift aid, 38% self-help). *Gift aid:* Total: $27,118,661 (62% from college's own funds, 20% from other college-administered sources, 18% from external sources). 991 Federal Work-Study jobs (averaging $1200); 2,000 part-time jobs.

Need-Based Scholarships & Grants Pell, FSEOG, state, private, college/university.

Loans Perkins, PLUS, Stafford, Unsubsidized Stafford, state, private, college/university short-term loans ($200 average).

Non-Need Awards In 1996, a total of 3,522 non-need awards were made. *Academic Interests/Achievement Awards:* 3,291 ($13,302,646 total): general academic, business, education, engineering/technologies, humanities. *Creative Arts/Performance Awards:* 74 ($105,050 total): art/fine arts, music. *Special Characteristics Awards:* 8 ($15,000 total): local/state students, religious affiliation. *Athletic:* Total: 149 ($1,244,549); Men: 69 ($529,360); Women: 80 ($715,189).

Other Money-Saving Options Accelerated degree, co-op program, Army ROTC, cooperative Air Force ROTC, off-campus living (after sophomore year). *Payment Plans:* installment, deferred payment. *Waivers:* full or partial for employees or children of employees.

Contact Jameelah Uqdah, Administrative Assistant of Computer Operations, University of Dayton, 300 College Park Drive, Dayton, OH 45469-1611, 800-837-7433, fax: 937-229-4545.

UNIVERSITY OF DELAWARE
Newark, Delaware

About the Institution State-related, coed. Degrees awarded: A, B, M, D. Offers 128 undergraduate majors. Total enrollment: 18,115. Undergraduates: 14,829 (42% state residents). Freshmen: 3,305.

Undergraduate Expenses (1996–97) State resident tuition: $3990. Nonresident tuition: $11,250. Mandatory fees: $440. College room and board: $4590 (minimum).

Applications *Financial aid deadline (priority):* 3/15. *Financial aid forms:* FAFSA required. State form required for some. *Regular admission application deadline:* 3/1. Early decision deadline: 11/15.

Summary of Aid to Needy Students *From gift & self-help combined:* Average amount awarded: $6750. 1,000 Federal Work-Study jobs (averaging $1100); 2,100 part-time jobs.

Need-Based Scholarships & Grants Pell, FSEOG, state, college/university.

Loans Perkins, PLUS, Stafford, Unsubsidized Stafford, Federal Nursing, college/university short-term loans ($100 average).

Non-Need Awards *Academic Interests/Achievement Awards:* general academic, agriculture, biological sciences, business, education, engineering/technologies, home economics, humanities, physical sciences. *Creative Arts/Performance Awards:* art/fine arts, music. *Special Achievements/Activities Awards:* cheerleading/drum major, leadership. *Special Characteristics Awards:* general special characteristics, children and siblings of alumni, children of public servants, local/state students. *Athletic:* available.

Other Money-Saving Options Accelerated degree, co-op program, Army ROTC, Air Force ROTC, off-campus living (after freshman year). *Payment Plans:* tuition prepayment, installment. *Waivers:* full or partial for employees or children of employees and senior citizens.

Contact Office of Financial Aid, University of Delaware, 224 Hullihen Hall, Newark, DE 19716, 302-831-2000.

UNIVERSITY OF DENVER
Denver, Colorado

About the Institution Independent, coed. Degrees awarded: B, M, D, P. Offers 65 undergraduate majors. Total enrollment: 8,714. Undergraduates: 2,949 (41% state residents). Freshmen: 716.

Undergraduate Expenses (1996–97) Comprehensive fee of $27,160 includes tuition ($21,274), mandatory fees ($348), and college room and board ($5538).

Applications Of all full-time undergraduates enrolled in fall 1996, 74% of those who applied for aid were judged to have need according to Federal Methodology, of whom 100% were aided. *Financial aid deadline (priority):* 2/19. *Financial aid forms:* FAFSA required. State form required for some. *Regular admission application deadline:* rolling. Early action deadline: 12/1.

Summary of Aid to Needy Students *From gift & self-help combined:* Average need met: 85%. Average amount awarded: $14,397 (61% gift aid, 39% self-help). *Gift aid:* Total: $13,905,862 (84% from college's own funds, 10% from other college-administered sources, 6% from external sources). 385 Federal Work-Study jobs (averaging $1800); 335 part-time jobs.

Need-Based Scholarships & Grants Pell, FSEOG, state, private, college/university.

Loans Perkins, PLUS, Stafford, Unsubsidized Stafford, private, college/university short-term loans ($150 average), college/university long-term loans ($1348 average).

Non-Need Awards In 1996, a total of 714 non-need awards were made. *Academic Interests/Achievement Awards:* 394 ($1,000,000 total): general academic, biological sciences, business, education, engineering/technologies, humanities, premedicine. *Creative Arts/Performance Awards:* 125 ($694,631 total): art/fine arts, music, theater/drama. *Special Characteristics Awards:* 50 ($837,000 total): general special characteristics, international students, local/state students, members of minorities. *Athletic:* Total: 145 ($2,193,129); Men: 77 ($1,181,061); Women: 68 ($1,012,068).

Other Money-Saving Options Accelerated degree, co-op program, cooperative Army ROTC, cooperative Air Force ROTC, off-campus living (after sophomore year). *Payment Plan:* deferred payment. *Waivers:* full or partial for employees or children of employees.

Contact Mrs. Colleen Hillmeyer, Director of Financial Aid, University of Denver, Office of Financial Aid, MRB 222, Denver, CO 80208, 303-871-2331.

UNIVERSITY OF DETROIT MERCY
Detroit, Michigan

About the Institution Independent/religious, coed. Degrees awarded: A, B, M, D, P. Offers 67 undergraduate majors. Total enrollment: 7,284. Undergraduates: 4,484 (95% state residents). Freshmen: 452.

Undergraduate Expenses (1997–98) Comprehensive fee of $17,506 includes tuition ($12,764 minimum), mandatory fees ($222), and college room and board ($4520 minimum). College room only: $2520 (minimum).

Applications *Financial aid deadline (priority):* 4/1. *Financial aid forms:* FAFSA, institutional form required. *Admission application deadline:* 8/15.

Summary of Aid to Needy Students Federal Work-Study jobs; part-time jobs.

Loans College/university long-term loans.

Non-Need Awards *Academic Interests/Achievement Awards:* general academic. *Special Achievements/Activities Awards:* religious involvement. *Special Characteristics Awards:* children and siblings of alumni, children of faculty/staff, members of minorities. *Athletic:* available.

Other Money-Saving Options Accelerated degree, co-op program, cooperative Army ROTC, off-campus living. *Payment Plans:* installment, deferred payment. *Waivers:* full or partial for children of alumni, employees or children of employees, senior citizens.

Contact Office of Financial Aid, University of Detroit Mercy, PO Box 19900, Detroit, MI 48219-0900, 313-993-1000.

UNIVERSITY OF DUBUQUE
Dubuque, Iowa

About the Institution Independent/religious, coed. Degrees awarded: A, B, M, P. Offers 41 undergraduate majors. Total enrollment: 954. Undergraduates: 672 (55% state residents). Freshmen: 197.

Undergraduate Expenses (1996–97) Comprehensive fee of $16,710 includes tuition ($12,150), mandatory fees ($220), and college room and board ($4340). College room only: $2140.

Applications 92% of all full-time undergraduates enrolled in fall 1996 applied for aid; of these, 98% were judged to have need according to Federal Methodology, of whom 100% were aided. *Financial aid deadline (priority):* 4/1. *Financial aid forms:* FAFSA required; CSS Financial Aid PROFILE acceptable. Institutional form required for some. *Admission application deadline:* 8/15.

Summary of Aid to Needy Students *From gift & self-help combined:* Average need met: 80%. Average amount awarded: $13,393 (56% gift aid, 44% self-help). *Gift aid:* Total: $3,902,100 (71% from college's own funds, 18% from other college-administered sources, 11% from external sources). 260 Federal Work-Study jobs (averaging $1500); 140 part-time jobs.

Need-Based Scholarships & Grants Pell, FSEOG, state, private, college/university.

Loans Perkins, PLUS, Stafford, Unsubsidized Stafford, state, private, college/university long-term loans ($1500 average).

Non-Need Awards In 1996, a total of 344 non-need awards were made. *Academic Interests/Achievement Awards:* 112 ($422,160 total): general academic. *Creative Arts/Performance Awards:* 26 ($40,600 total): music. *Special Characteristics Awards:* 206 ($344,200 total): children and siblings of alumni, children of educators, children of faculty/staff, ethnic background, members of minorities, out-of-state students, relatives of clergy, religious affiliation, siblings of current students.

Other Money-Saving Options Accelerated degree, off-campus living (after junior year). *Payment Plans:* installment, deferred payment. *Waivers:* full or partial for children of alumni, employees or children of employees, senior citizens.

Contact Office of Financial Aid, University of Dubuque, 2000 University Avenue, Dubuque, IA 52001-5050, 319-589-3000.

UNIVERSITY OF EVANSVILLE
Evansville, Indiana

About the Institution Independent/religious, coed. Degrees awarded: A, B, M. Offers 72 undergraduate majors. Total enrollment: 3,185. Undergraduates: 3,091 (55% state residents). Freshmen: 675.

Undergraduate Expenses (1997–98) Comprehensive fee of $18,400 includes tuition ($13,600), mandatory fees ($280), and college room and board ($4520). College room only: $2060.

Applications 80% of all full-time undergraduates enrolled in fall 1996 applied for aid; of these, 79% were judged to have need according to Federal Methodology, of whom 100% were aided. *Financial aid deadline (priority):* 3/1. *Financial aid forms:* FAFSA, institutional form required; CSS Financial Aid PROFILE acceptable. State form required for some. *Regular admission application deadline:* 2/15. Early action deadline: 12/1.

Summary of Aid to Needy Students *From gift & self-help combined:* Average need met: 82%. Average amount awarded: $10,991 (65% gift aid, 35% self-help). *Gift aid:* Total: $12,802,397 (67% from college's own funds, 2% from other college-administered sources, 31% from external sources). 350 Federal Work-Study jobs (averaging $1100); 136 part-time jobs.

Need-Based Scholarships & Grants Pell, FSEOG, state, college/university.

Loans Perkins, PLUS, Stafford, Unsubsidized Stafford, Federal Nursing, private, college/university short-term loans ($400 average).

Non-Need Awards In 1996, a total of 2,120 non-need awards were made. *Academic Interests/Achievement Awards:* 1,204 ($4,529,618 total): general academic, biological sciences, business, communication, computer science, education, engineering/technologies, English, foreign languages, health fields, humanities, international studies, mathematics, physical sciences, premedicine, religion/biblical studies, social sciences. *Creative Arts/Performance Awards:* 180 ($677,230 total): art/fine arts, music, theater/drama. *Special Achievements/Activities Awards:* 298 ($682,408 total): leadership. *Special Characteristics Awards:* 269 ($867,030 total): children and siblings of alumni, international students, religious affiliation, siblings of current students. *Athletic:* Total: 169 ($1,790,826); Men: 81 ($833,289); Women: 88 ($957,537).

Other Money-Saving Options Co-op program, off-campus living (after freshman year). *Payment Plan:* installment. *Waivers:* full or partial for employees or children of employees.

Contact Ms. JoAnn E. Laugel, Co-Director of Financial Aid, University of Evansville, 1800 Lincoln Avenue, Evansville, IN 47722-0002, 812-479-2364, fax: 812-479-2028.

THE UNIVERSITY OF FINDLAY
Findlay, Ohio

About the Institution Independent/religious, coed. Degrees awarded: A, B, M. Offers 54 undergraduate majors. Total enrollment: 3,743. Undergraduates: 3,160 (79% state residents). Freshmen: 583.

Undergraduate Expenses (1996–97) Comprehensive fee of $18,322 includes tuition ($13,000), mandatory fees ($112), and college room and board ($5210). College room only: $2550.

Applications Of all full-time undergraduates enrolled in fall 1996, 100% of those judged to have need according to Federal Methodology

were aided. *Financial aid deadline (priority):* 6/1. *Financial aid forms:* FAFSA required; CSS Financial Aid PROFILE acceptable. State form required for some. *Admission application deadline:* rolling.

Summary of Aid to Needy Students *From gift & self-help combined:* Average need met: 90%. Average amount awarded: $12,000 (64% gift aid, 36% self-help). *Gift aid:* Total: $17,600,000 (65% from college's own funds, 23% from other college-administered sources, 12% from external sources). 400 Federal Work-Study jobs (averaging $800); 100 part-time jobs.

Need-Based Scholarships & Grants Pell, FSEOG, state, college/university.

Loans Perkins, PLUS, Stafford, Unsubsidized Stafford, private, college/university long-term loans ($500 average).

Non-Need Awards *Academic Interests/Achievement Awards:* general academic, foreign languages, physical sciences. *Creative Arts/Performance Awards:* music, theater/drama. *Special Characteristics Awards:* 270: children and siblings of alumni, children of faculty/staff, parents of current students, religious affiliation, siblings of current students. *Athletic:* Total: 332 ($782,000); Men: 214 ($550,000); Women: 118 ($232,000).

Other Money-Saving Options Co-op program, cooperative Air Force ROTC. *Payment Plan:* installment. *Waivers:* full or partial for employees or children of employees and senior citizens.

Contact Mr. Charles Ernst, Financial Aid Counselor, The University of Findlay, 1000 North Main Street, Findlay, OH 45840-3653, 419-424-6935, fax: 419-424-4822.

UNIVERSITY OF FLORIDA
Gainesville, Florida

About the Institution State-supported, coed. Degrees awarded: B, M, D, P. Offers 100 undergraduate majors. Total enrollment: 39,932. Undergraduates: 30,711 (92% state residents). Freshmen: 3,318.

Undergraduate Expenses (1996–97) State resident tuition: $1793. Nonresident tuition: $7038. College room and board: $4500. College room only: $2200.

Applications 66% of all full-time undergraduates enrolled in fall 1996 applied for aid; of these, 58% were judged to have need according to Federal Methodology, of whom 99% were aided. *Financial aid deadline (priority):* 4/15. *Financial aid forms:* FAFSA, institutional form required; CSS Financial Aid PROFILE acceptable. *Admission application deadline:* 2/1.

Summary of Aid to Needy Students *From gift & self-help combined:* Average need met: 88%. Average amount awarded: $8191 (40% gift aid, 60% self-help). *Gift aid:* Total: $33,199,737 (4% from college's own funds, 40% from other college-administered sources, 56% from external sources). 1,238 Federal Work-Study jobs (averaging $1170); 5,098 part-time jobs.

Need-Based Scholarships & Grants Pell, FSEOG, state, private, college/university.

Loans Perkins, PLUS, Stafford, Unsubsidized Stafford, state, private, college/university short-term loans ($600 average), college/university long-term loans ($500 average).

Non-Need Awards In 1996, a total of 1,424 non-need awards were made. *Academic Interests/Achievement Awards:* 743 ($1,897,896 total): general academic. *Special Characteristics Awards:* 350 ($851,782 total): out-of-state students. *Athletic:* Total: 331 ($2,068,534); Men: 200 ($1,082,462); Women: 131 ($986,072).

Other Money-Saving Options Accelerated degree, co-op program, Army ROTC, Naval ROTC, Air Force ROTC, off-campus living. *Payment Plan:* tuition prepayment. *Waivers:* full or partial for employees or children of employees and senior citizens.

Contact Office of Financial Aid, University of Florida, S-107 Criser Hall, PO Box 114025, Gainesville, FL 32611-4025, 352-392-3261.

UNIVERSITY OF GEORGIA
Athens, Georgia

About the Institution State-supported, coed. Degrees awarded: A, B, M, D, P. Offers 151 undergraduate majors. Total enrollment: 29,404. Undergraduates: 22,946 (84% state residents). Freshmen: 3,480.

Undergraduate Expenses (1996–97) State resident tuition: $2115. Nonresident tuition: $7296. Mandatory fees: $579. College room and board: $4045. College room only: $2115.

Applications 71% of all full-time undergraduates enrolled in fall 1996 applied for aid; of these, 56% were judged to have need according to Federal Methodology, of whom 97% were aided. *Financial aid deadline (priority):* 3/1. *Financial aid forms:* FAFSA required. *Admission application deadline:* 2/1.

Summary of Aid to Needy Students *From gift & self-help combined:* Average amount awarded: $4971 (50% gift aid, 50% self-help). *Gift aid:* Total: $20,119,978 (8% from college's own funds, 61% from other college-administered sources, 31% from external sources). 354 Federal Work-Study jobs (averaging $2477); 2,444 part-time jobs.

Need-Based Scholarships & Grants Pell, FSEOG, state, private, college/university.

Loans Perkins, PLUS, Stafford, Unsubsidized Stafford, state, private, college/university short-term loans ($150 average), college/university long-term loans ($1445 average).

Non-Need Awards In 1996, a total of 16,273 non-need awards were made. *Academic Interests/Achievement Awards:* 15,642 ($31,040,231 total): general academic, agriculture, business, education. *Creative Arts/Performance Awards:* 119 ($93,959 total): debating, journalism/publications. *Special Characteristics Awards:* 209 ($167,140 total): local/state students, members of minorities. *Athletic:* Total: 303; Men: 178; Women: 125.

Other Money-Saving Options Accelerated degree, co-op program, Army ROTC, Air Force ROTC, off-campus living. *Waivers:* full or partial for senior citizens.

Contact Mr. D. Ray Tripp, Director of Financial Aid, University of Georgia, 220 Academic Building, Athens, GA 30602, 706-542-8208.

UNIVERSITY OF GREAT FALLS
Great Falls, Montana

About the Institution Independent/religious, coed. Degrees awarded: A, B, M. Offers 38 undergraduate majors. Total enrollment: 1,291. Undergraduates: 1,147 (93% state residents). Freshmen: 242.

Undergraduate Expenses (1997–98) Comprehensive fee of $10,530 includes tuition ($7840), mandatory fees ($260), and college room and board ($2430).

Applications *Financial aid deadline (priority):* 4/1. *Financial aid forms:* FAFSA, institutional form required; CSS Financial Aid PROFILE acceptable. *Admission application deadline:* rolling.

Summary of Aid to Needy Students *From gift & self-help combined:* Average amount awarded: $2465 (34% gift aid, 66% self-help). *Gift aid:* Total: $831,676 (12% from college's own funds, 8% from other college-administered sources, 80% from external sources). 37 Federal Work-Study jobs (averaging $3000); 75 part-time jobs.

Need-Based Scholarships & Grants Pell, FSEOG, state, private, college/university, Junior Training Partnership Act, AFL-CIO Scholarships.

Loans Perkins, PLUS, Stafford, Unsubsidized Stafford, college/university short-term loans ($350 average).

Non-Need Awards *Academic Interests/Achievement Awards:* 108 ($123,000 total): general academic, business, computer science, education, humanities, mathematics, religion/biblical studies, social sciences. *Special Characteristics Awards:* adult students.

Other Money-Saving Options Accelerated degree, co-op program, off-campus living. *Payment Plan:* deferred payment. *Waivers:* full or partial for employees or children of employees and senior citizens.

Contact Ms. Sally Schuman, Director of Financial Aid, University of Great Falls, 1301 20th Street S, Great Falls, MT 59401, 406-791-5235, fax: 406-791-5242.

UNIVERSITY OF GUAM
Mangilao, Guam

About the Institution Territory-supported, coed. Degrees awarded: B, M. Offers 36 undergraduate majors. Total enrollment: 3,654. Undergraduates: 3,307 (96% territory residents). Freshmen: 468.

Undergraduate Expenses (1996–97) Territory resident tuition: $1800. Nonresident tuition: $4920. Mandatory fees: $268. College room and board: $3242. College room only: $1460.

Applications *Financial aid deadline (priority):* 5/31. *Financial aid forms:* FAFSA, institutional form, verification worksheet required. *Admission application deadline:* 7/8.

Summary of Aid to Needy Students Federal Work-Study jobs; part-time jobs.

Need-Based Scholarships & Grants Pell, FSEOG, state.

Loans Stafford, Unsubsidized Stafford, state.

Non-Need Awards *Academic Interests/Achievement Awards:* general academic. *Creative Arts/Performance Awards:* general creative, art/fine arts, journalism/publications. *Special Characteristics Awards:* children of faculty/staff. *Athletic:* available.

Other Money-Saving Options Accelerated degree, Army ROTC, off-campus living. *Payment Plans:* installment, deferred payment. *Waivers:* full or partial for senior citizens.

Contact Office of Financial Aid, University of Guam, 303 University Drive, Mangilao, GU 96923, 671-734-4469.

UNIVERSITY OF HARTFORD
West Hartford, Connecticut

About the Institution Independent, coed. Degrees awarded: A, B, M, D. Offers 91 undergraduate majors. Total enrollment: 7,068. Undergraduates: 5,354 (44% state residents). Freshmen: 1,276.

Undergraduate Expenses (1997–98) Comprehensive fee of $24,210 includes tuition ($16,380), mandatory fees ($940), and college room and board ($6890). College room only: $4250.

Applications 62% of all full-time undergraduates enrolled in fall 1996 applied for aid; of these, 92% were judged to have need according to Federal Methodology, of whom 98% were aided. *Financial aid deadline (priority):* 2/1. *Financial aid forms:* FAFSA, institutional form required. *Admission application deadline:* rolling.

Summary of Aid to Needy Students *From gift & self-help combined:* Average need met: 70%. Average amount awarded: $15,786 (62% gift aid, 38% self-help). *Gift aid:* Total: $22,600,000 (86% from college's own funds, 7% from other college-administered sources, 7% from external sources). 300 Federal Work-Study jobs (averaging $976); 300 part-time jobs.

Need-Based Scholarships & Grants Pell, FSEOG, state, private, college/university.

Loans Perkins, PLUS, Stafford, Unsubsidized Stafford, private.

Non-Need Awards In 1996, a total of 1,035 non-need awards were made. *Academic Interests/Achievement Awards:* 399 ($2,847,000 total): general academic. *Creative Arts/Performance Awards:* 309 ($1,997,000 total): art/fine arts, dance, music, performing arts, theater/drama. *Special Characteristics Awards:* 219 ($1,834,000 total): children of faculty/staff, international students, local/state students, siblings of current students, twins. *Athletic:* Total: 108 ($1,997,000).

Other Money-Saving Options Co-op program, cooperative Army ROTC, cooperative Air Force ROTC, off-campus living. *Payment Plans:* tuition prepayment, installment. *Waivers:* full or partial for employees or children of employees and senior citizens.

Contact Assistant Director of Student Financial Assistance, University of Hartford, 200 Bloomfield Avenue, West Hartford, CT 06117-1599, 860-768-4296, fax: 860-768-4961.

UNIVERSITY OF HAWAII AT HILO
Hilo, Hawaii

About the Institution State-supported, coed. Degrees awarded: B. Offers 33 undergraduate majors. Total enrollment: 2,870 (82% state residents). Freshmen: 445.

Undergraduate Expenses (1997–98 estimated) State resident tuition: $1272 (minimum). Nonresident tuition: $6888 (minimum). Mandatory fees: $50. College room and board: $3480 (minimum). College room only: $1382.

Applications Of all full-time undergraduates enrolled in fall 1996, 100% of those who applied for aid were judged to have need according to Federal Methodology, of whom 100% were aided. *Financial aid deadline (priority):* 3/1. *Financial aid forms:* FAFSA, institutional form required. *Admission application deadline:* 5/15.

Summary of Aid to Needy Students *From gift & self-help combined:* Average need met: 74%. Average amount awarded: $4065 (69% gift aid, 31% self-help). *Gift aid:* Total: $2,566,806 (19% from college-administered sources, 81% from external sources). 160 Federal Work-Study jobs (averaging $1092); 497 part-time jobs.

Need-Based Scholarships & Grants Pell, FSEOG, state, private.

Loans Perkins, PLUS, Stafford, Unsubsidized Stafford, state, college/university short-term loans ($100 average), college/university long-term loans ($1842 average).

Non-Need Awards *Academic Interests/Achievement Awards:* general academic, agriculture, business, computer science, English, health fields, social sciences. *Creative Arts/Performance Awards:* art/fine arts, music, performing arts, theater/drama. *Special Achievements/Activities Awards:* community service, leadership. *Special Characteristics Awards:* local/state students. *Athletic:* available.

Other Money-Saving Options Accelerated degree, off-campus living. *Waivers:* full or partial for senior citizens.

Contact Ms. Jeane Coffman, Financial Aid Coordinator, University of Hawaii at Hilo, 200 West Kawili Street, Hilo, HI 96720-4091, 808-974-7324, fax: 808-974-7691.

UNIVERSITY OF HAWAII AT MANOA
Honolulu, Hawaii

About the Institution State-supported, coed. Degrees awarded: B, M, D, P. Offers 78 undergraduate majors. Total enrollment: 17,023. Undergraduates: 12,216 (87% state residents). Freshmen: 1,435.

Undergraduate Expenses (1997–98 estimated) State resident tuition: $2832. Nonresident tuition: $9312. Mandatory fees: $118. College room and board: $4740. College room only: $2660.

Applications Of all full-time undergraduates enrolled in fall 1996, 79% of those who applied for aid were judged to have need according to Federal Methodology, of whom 100% were aided. *Financial aid deadline (priority):* 3/1. *Financial aid forms:* FAFSA, institutional form required; CSS Financial Aid PROFILE acceptable. Validation form required for some. *Admission application deadline:* 5/1.

Summary of Aid to Needy Students *From gift & self-help combined:* Average need met: 83%. Average amount awarded: $5513 (25% gift aid, 75% self-help). *Gift aid:* Total: $1,917,214 (19% from college's

own funds, 31% from other college-administered sources, 50% from external sources). 205 Federal Work-Study jobs (averaging $1764); part-time jobs.

Need-Based Scholarships & Grants Pell, FSEOG, state, private, college/university.

Loans Perkins, PLUS, Stafford, Unsubsidized Stafford, Federal Nursing, Primary Care, state, college/university short-term loans ($275 average), college/university long-term loans ($2027 average).

Non-Need Awards In 1996, a total of 597 non-need awards were made. *Academic Interests/Achievement Awards:* 85 ($97,920 total): general academic. *Creative Arts/Performance Awards:* 218 ($158,985 total): music. *Athletic:* Total: 294 ($787,025); Men: 174 ($488,069); Women: 120 ($298,956).

Other Money-Saving Options Co-op program, Army ROTC, Air Force ROTC, off-campus living. *Waivers:* full or partial for minority students, employees or children of employees, adult students, senior citizens.

Contact Financial Aid Office, University of Hawaii at Manoa, 2600 Campus Road, Suite 112, Honolulu, HI 96822, 808-956-7251.

UNIVERSITY OF HOUSTON
Houston, Texas

About the Institution State-supported, coed. Degrees awarded: B, M, D, P. Offers 112 undergraduate majors. Total enrollment: 30,774. Undergraduates: 21,522 (93% state residents). Freshmen: 2,433.

Undergraduate Expenses (1996–97) State resident tuition: $960. Nonresident tuition: $7300. Mandatory fees: $766. College room and board: $4405. College room only: $2445.

Applications 77% of all full-time undergraduates enrolled in fall 1996 applied for aid; of these, 87% were judged to have need according to Federal Methodology, of whom 93% were aided. *Financial aid deadline (priority):* 4/1. *Financial aid forms:* FAFSA, institutional form required. *Admission application deadline:* 7/1.

Summary of Aid to Needy Students *From gift & self-help combined:* Average need met: 75%. Average amount awarded: $5058 (35% gift aid, 65% self-help). *Gift aid:* Total: $15,961,632 (35% from college's own funds, 6% from other college-administered sources, 59% from external sources). 867 Federal Work-Study jobs (averaging $2190); 2,200 part-time jobs.

Need-Based Scholarships & Grants Pell, FSEOG, state, private, college/university.

Loans Perkins, PLUS, Stafford, Unsubsidized Stafford, private, college/university short-term loans ($1000 average), college/university long-term loans ($5850 average).

Non-Need Awards *Academic Interests/Achievement Awards:* biological sciences, business, computer science, education, engineering/technologies, English, health fields, humanities, military science, physical sciences, social sciences. *Creative Arts/Performance Awards:* art/fine arts, creative writing, music, theater/drama. *Special Achievements/Activities Awards:* leadership. *Athletic:* Total: 236 ($1,318,095); Men: 153 ($875,977); Women: 83 ($442,118).

Other Money-Saving Options Accelerated degree, co-op program, Army ROTC, cooperative Naval ROTC, off-campus living. *Payment Plan:* installment.

Contact Financial Aid Office, University of Houston, 4800 Calhoun, Houston, TX 77204-2160, 713-743-1010, fax: 713-743-9098.

UNIVERSITY OF HOUSTON–DOWNTOWN
Houston, Texas

About the Institution State-supported, coed. Degrees awarded: B. Offers 29 undergraduate majors. Total enrollment: 7,947 (95% state residents). Freshmen: 927.

Undergraduate Expenses (1997–98) State resident tuition: $1071. Nonresident tuition: $7812. Mandatory fees: $906.

Applications Of all full-time undergraduates enrolled in fall 1996, 100% of those judged to have need according to Federal Methodology were aided. *Financial aid deadline (priority):* 4/1. *Financial aid forms:* FAFSA, institutional form required. *Admission application deadline:* 8/15.

Summary of Aid to Needy Students *From gift & self-help combined:* Average need met: 85%. Average amount awarded: $3469 (66% gift aid, 34% self-help). *Gift aid:* Total: $4,701,885. Federal Work-Study jobs; 40 part-time jobs.

Need-Based Scholarships & Grants Pell, FSEOG, state.

Loans PLUS, Stafford, Unsubsidized Stafford, state, college/university short-term loans ($400 average).

Non-Need Awards *Academic Interests/Achievement Awards:* available. *Special Characteristics Awards:* members of minorities.

Other Money-Saving Options Accelerated degree, co-op program, cooperative Army ROTC, cooperative Naval ROTC. *Payment Plan:* installment.

Contact Ms. Marilyn S. Allen, Director of Financial Aid, University of Houston–Downtown, Houston, TX 77002-1001, 713-221-8163.

UNIVERSITY OF IDAHO
Moscow, Idaho

About the Institution State-supported, coed. Degrees awarded: B, M, D, P. Offers 113 undergraduate majors. Total enrollment: 11,727. Undergraduates: 8,103 (77% state residents). Freshmen: 1,260.

Undergraduate Expenses (1997–98) State resident tuition: $0. Nonresident tuition: $5800. Mandatory fees: $1942. College room and board: $3680.

Applications 64% of all full-time undergraduates enrolled in fall 1996 applied for aid; of these, 84% were judged to have need according to Federal Methodology, of whom 100% were aided. *Financial aid deadline (priority):* 2/15. *Financial aid forms:* FAFSA required. *Admission application deadline:* 8/1.

Summary of Aid to Needy Students *From gift & self-help combined:* Average need met: 80%. Average amount awarded: $6182 (25% gift aid, 75% self-help). *Gift aid:* Total: $6,044,979 (20% from college's own funds, 11% from other college-administered sources, 69% from external sources). 900 Federal Work-Study jobs (averaging $1300); 2,800 part-time jobs.

Need-Based Scholarships & Grants Pell, FSEOG, state, private, college/university.

Loans Perkins, PLUS, Stafford, Unsubsidized Stafford, private, college/university short-term loans ($600 average), college/university long-term loans ($900 average).

Non-Need Awards *Academic Interests/Achievement Awards:* 1,500 ($2,000,000 total): business, communication, computer science, education, engineering/technologies, English, foreign languages, home economics, humanities, mathematics, military science, physical sciences, premedicine, social sciences. *Creative Arts/Performance Awards:* applied art and design, art/fine arts, creative writing, dance, journalism/publications, music, performing arts, theater/drama. *Special Achievements/Activities Awards:* leadership, rodeo. *Special Characteristics Awards:* 400 ($90,000 total): children and siblings of alumni, children of faculty/staff, handicapped students, international students, local/state students, members of minorities, out-of-state students, ROTC participants. *Athletic:* Total: 179 ($1,331,702); Men: 112 ($887,614); Women: 67 ($444,088).

Other Money-Saving Options Accelerated degree, co-op program, Army ROTC, Naval ROTC, cooperative Air Force ROTC, off-campus living. *Payment Plan:* deferred payment. *Waivers:* full or partial for employees or children of employees.

Contact Ms. Harriet Rojas, Associate Director, University of Idaho, Moscow, ID 83844-4140, 208-885-6312, fax: 208-885-5592.

UNIVERSITY OF ILLINOIS AT CHICAGO
Chicago, Illinois

About the Institution State-supported, coed. Degrees awarded: B, M, D, P. Offers 79 undergraduate majors. Total enrollment: 24,583. Undergraduates: 16,190 (96% state residents). Freshmen: 2,807.

Undergraduate Expenses (1996–97) State resident tuition: $2870 (minimum). Nonresident tuition: $8610 (minimum). Mandatory fees: $906. College room and board: $5188. College room only: $3112.

Applications Of all full-time undergraduates enrolled in fall 1996, 96% of those who applied for aid were judged to have need according to Federal Methodology, of whom 100% were aided. *Financial aid deadline (priority):* 3/1. *Financial aid forms:* FAFSA, financial aid transcript (for transfers) required. Institutional form required for some. *Admission application deadline:* 6/9.

Summary of Aid to Needy Students *From gift & self-help combined:* Average need met: 65%. Average amount awarded: $6500 (53% gift aid, 47% self-help). *Gift aid:* Total: $39,000,000 (13% from college's own funds, 2% from other college-administered sources, 85% from external sources). 2,000 Federal Work-Study jobs (averaging $2500); part-time jobs.

Need-Based Scholarships & Grants Pell, FSEOG, state, private, college/university.

Loans Perkins, PLUS, Stafford, Unsubsidized Stafford, Federal Nursing, Primary Care, private, college/university short-term loans ($200 average), college/university long-term loans ($1000 average).

Non-Need Awards In 1996, a total of 2,331 non-need awards were made. *Academic Interests/Achievement Awards:* 200 ($400,000 total): general academic. *Creative Arts/Performance Awards:* 60 ($180,000 total): art/fine arts. *Special Achievements/Activities Awards:* 400 ($280,000 total): general special achievements/activities. *Special Characteristics Awards:* 1,500 ($3,600,000 total): general special characteristics, children of faculty/staff, members of minorities, ROTC participants, veterans. *Athletic:* Total: 171 ($1,224,080); Men: 87 ($646,544); Women: 84 ($577,536).

Other Money-Saving Options Accelerated degree, co-op program, Army ROTC, cooperative Naval ROTC, cooperative Air Force ROTC, off-campus living. *Waivers:* full or partial for employees or children of employees and senior citizens.

Contact Mr. Alex Swenson, Assistant Director of Financial Aid, University of Illinois at Chicago, 1200 West Harrison, M/C 334, Chicago, IL 60607, 312-996-5563, fax: 312-996-3385.

UNIVERSITY OF ILLINOIS AT URBANA–CHAMPAIGN
Champaign, Illinois

About the Institution State-supported, coed. Degrees awarded: B, M, D, P. Offers 156 undergraduate majors. Total enrollment: 36,164. Undergraduates: 26,738 (90% state residents). Freshmen: 5,946.

Undergraduate Expenses (1996–97) State resident tuition: $3150 (minimum). Nonresident tuition: $8580 (minimum). Mandatory fees: $1036. College room and board: $4560.

Applications Of all full-time undergraduates enrolled in fall 1996, 76% of those who applied for aid were judged to have need according to Federal Methodology, of whom 95% were aided. *Financial aid deadline (priority):* 3/15. *Financial aid forms:* FAFSA required. *Admission application deadline:* 1/1.

Summary of Aid to Needy Students *From gift & self-help combined:* Average need met: 75%. Average amount awarded: $7100 (46% gift aid, 54% self-help). *Gift aid:* Total: $45,762,266 (25% from college's own funds, 2% from other college-administered sources, 73% from external sources). 1,084 Federal Work-Study jobs (averaging $749); 12,872 part-time jobs.

Need-Based Scholarships & Grants Pell, FSEOG, state, private, college/university.

Loans Perkins, PLUS, Stafford, Unsubsidized Stafford, private, college/university short-term loans ($200 average), college/university long-term loans ($1450 average).

Non-Need Awards *Academic Interests/Achievement Awards:* available. *Creative Arts/Performance Awards:* available. *Special Achievements/Activities Awards:* available. *Special Characteristics Awards:* available. *Athletic:* Total: 280 ($2,774,365); Men: 184 ($1,765,191); Women: 96 ($1,009,174).

Other Money-Saving Options Accelerated degree, co-op program, Army ROTC, Naval ROTC, Air Force ROTC, off-campus living (after freshman year). *Payment Plan:* installment. *Waivers:* full or partial for minority students, employees or children of employees, senior citizens.

Contact Office of Student Financial Aid, University of Illinois at Urbana–Champaign, 610 East John Street, Champaign, IL 61820-5711, 217-333-0100.

UNIVERSITY OF INDIANAPOLIS
Indianapolis, Indiana

About the Institution Independent/religious, coed. Degrees awarded: A, B, M, D. Offers 72 undergraduate majors. Total enrollment: 3,861. Undergraduates: 2,906 (83% state residents). Freshmen: 449.

Undergraduate Expenses (1997–98) Comprehensive fee of $17,540 includes tuition ($12,990) and college room and board ($4550).

Applications 80% of all full-time undergraduates enrolled in fall 1996 applied for aid; of these, 91% were judged to have need according to Federal Methodology, of whom 99% were aided. *Financial aid deadline (priority):* 3/1. *Financial aid forms:* FAFSA, institutional form required; CSS Financial Aid PROFILE acceptable. *Admission application deadline:* 8/15.

Summary of Aid to Needy Students *From gift & self-help combined:* Average need met: 89%. Average amount awarded: $12,287 (58% gift aid, 42% self-help). *Gift aid:* Total: $7,797,017 (54% from college's own funds, 3% from other college-administered sources, 43% from external sources). 527 Federal Work-Study jobs (averaging $1000); 266 part-time jobs.

Need-Based Scholarships & Grants Pell, FSEOG, state, college/university.

Loans Perkins, PLUS, Stafford, Unsubsidized Stafford.

Non-Need Awards In 1996, a total of 1,289 non-need awards were made. *Academic Interests/Achievement Awards:* 402 ($2,438,392 total): general academic. *Creative Arts/Performance Awards:* 114 ($204,220 total): art/fine arts, music, theater/drama. *Special Achievements/Activities Awards:* 258 ($622,033 total): community service. *Special Characteristics Awards:* 234 ($832,872 total): children of faculty/staff, international students, relatives of clergy, religious affiliation. *Athletic:* Total: 281 ($1,708,233); Men: 179 ($1,129,978); Women: 102 ($578,255).

Other Money-Saving Options Co-op program, cooperative Army ROTC, off-campus living. *Payment Plans:* installment, deferred payment. *Waivers:* full or partial for employees or children of employees and senior citizens.

Contact Office of Financial Aid, University of Indianapolis, 1400 East Hanna Avenue, Indianapolis, IN 46227-3697, 317-788-3368.

THE UNIVERSITY OF IOWA
Iowa City, Iowa

About the Institution State-supported, coed. Degrees awarded: B, M, D, P. Offers 133 undergraduate majors. Total enrollment: 27,921. Undergraduates: 16,566 (69% state residents). Freshmen: 3,535.

Undergraduate Expenses (1996–97) State resident tuition: $2470. Nonresident tuition: $9068. Mandatory fees: $176. College room and board: $3688.

Applications Of all full-time undergraduates enrolled in fall 1996, 90% of those who applied for aid were judged to have need according to Federal Methodology, of whom 94% were aided. *Financial aid deadline:* Applications processed continuously. *Financial aid forms:* FAFSA, institutional form required. *Admission application deadline:* 5/15.

Summary of Aid to Needy Students *Gift aid:* Total: $19,504,911 (42% from college's own funds, 9% from other college-administered sources, 49% from external sources). Federal Work-Study jobs; 8,275 part-time jobs.

Loans College/university short-term loans ($300 average), college/university long-term loans ($1213 average).

Non-Need Awards *Academic Interests/Achievement Awards:* general academic. *Creative Arts/Performance Awards:* music, performing arts, theater/drama. *Special Achievements/Activities Awards:* available. *Athletic:* available.

Other Money-Saving Options Accelerated degree, co-op program, Army ROTC, Air Force ROTC, off-campus living. *Payment Plan:* installment.

Contact Office of Financial Aid, The University of Iowa, 208 Calvin Hall, Iowa City, IA 52242, 319-335-3500.

UNIVERSITY OF KANSAS
Lawrence, Kansas

About the Institution State-supported, coed. Degrees awarded: B, M, D, P. Offers 110 undergraduate majors. Total enrollment: 27,407. Undergraduates: 18,652 (70% state residents). Freshmen: 3,644.

Undergraduate Expenses (1997–98) State resident tuition: $2031. Nonresident tuition: $8545. Mandatory fees: $420. College room and board: $3736.

Applications 48% of all full-time undergraduates enrolled in fall 1996 applied for aid; of these, 81% were judged to have need according to Federal Methodology, of whom 82% were aided. *Financial aid deadline (priority):* 3/1. *Financial aid forms:* FAFSA required. State form required for some. *Regular admission application deadline:* 4/1. Nonresident deadline: 2/1.

Summary of Aid to Needy Students *From gift & self-help combined:* Average need met: 65%. Average amount awarded: $4711 (34% gift aid, 66% self-help). *Gift aid:* Total: $8,567,952 (23% from college's own funds, 20% from other college-administered sources, 57% from external sources). 473 Federal Work-Study jobs (averaging $1096); 2,500 part-time jobs.

Need-Based Scholarships & Grants Pell, FSEOG, state, private, college/university.

Loans Perkins, PLUS, Stafford, Unsubsidized Stafford, college/university long-term loans ($1158 average).

Non-Need Awards In 1996, a total of 5,805 non-need awards were made. *Academic Interests/Achievement Awards:* 2,609 ($2,934,009 total): general academic, architecture, area/ethnic studies, biological sciences, business, communication, computer science, education, engineering/technologies, English, foreign languages, health fields, humanities, international studies, library science, mathematics, military science, physical sciences, premedicine, religion/biblical studies, social sciences. *Creative Arts/Performance Awards:* 381 ($444,172 total): general creative, applied art and design, art/fine arts, cinema/film/broadcasting, creative writing, dance, debating, journalism/publications, music, performing arts, theater/drama. *Special Achievements/Activities Awards:* 272 ($300,000 total): community service, leadership. *Special Characteristics Awards:* 2,174 ($2,428,760 total): general special characteristics, adult students, ethnic background, first-generation college students, international students, local/state students, married students, members of minorities, out-of-state students, ROTC participants. *Athletic:* Total: 369 ($2,511,180); Men: 230 ($1,614,689); Women: 139 ($896,491).

Other Money-Saving Options Accelerated degree, co-op program, Army ROTC, Naval ROTC, Air Force ROTC, off-campus living. *Waivers:* full or partial for employees or children of employees and senior citizens.

Contact Mr. Chris Johnson, Systems Manager, University of Kansas, Office of Student Financial Aid, 50 Strong Hall, Lawrence, KS 66045-1920, 913-864-5494, fax: 913-864-5469.

UNIVERSITY OF KENTUCKY
Lexington, Kentucky

About the Institution State-supported, coed. Degrees awarded: B, M, D, P. Offers 82 undergraduate majors. Total enrollment: 23,431. Undergraduates: 17,036 (83% state residents). Freshmen: 2,637.

Undergraduate Expenses (1997–98 estimated) State resident tuition: $2400. Nonresident tuition: $7200. Mandatory fees: $336. College room and board: $3198.

Applications Of all full-time undergraduates enrolled in fall 1996, 95% of those who applied for aid were judged to have need according to Federal Methodology, of whom 81% were aided. *Financial aid deadline (priority):* 4/1. *Financial aid forms:* FAFSA required. *Admission application deadline:* 6/1.

Summary of Aid to Needy Students *From gift & self-help combined:* Average need met: 43%. Average amount awarded: $6823 (51% gift aid, 49% self-help). *Gift aid:* Total: $12,446,286 (27% from college's own funds, 32% from other college-administered sources, 41% from external sources). 1,144 Federal Work-Study jobs (averaging $1028); part-time jobs.

Need-Based Scholarships & Grants Pell, FSEOG, state, private, college/university.

Loans Perkins, PLUS, Stafford, Unsubsidized Stafford, Federal Nursing, private, college/university short-term loans ($200 average).

Non-Need Awards In 1996, a total of 2,234 non-need awards were made. *Academic Interests/Achievement Awards:* 1,200 ($3,300,000 total): general academic. *Creative Arts/Performance Awards:* 272 ($518,244 total): debating, music. *Special Characteristics Awards:* 466 ($1,408,159 total): members of minorities. *Athletic:* Total: 296 ($3,137,700); Men: 181 ($2,125,700); Women: 115 ($1,012,000).

Other Money-Saving Options Accelerated degree, co-op program, Army ROTC, Air Force ROTC, off-campus living. *Waivers:* full or partial for employees or children of employees and senior citizens.

Contact Ms. Lynda S. George, Director of Financial Aid, University of Kentucky, 128 Funkhouser Building, Lexington, KY 40506-0054, 606-257-3172 Ext. 241, fax: 606-257-4398.

UNIVERSITY OF LA VERNE
La Verne, California

About the Institution Independent, coed. Degrees awarded: A, B, M, D, P. Offers 51 undergraduate majors. Total enrollment: 2,965. Undergraduates: 1,052 (95% state residents). Freshmen: 224.

Undergraduate Expenses (1996–97) Comprehensive fee of $19,040 includes tuition ($14,650), mandatory fees ($60), and college room and board ($4330 minimum). College room only: $2220 (minimum).

Applications 86% of all full-time undergraduates enrolled in fall 1996 applied for aid; of these, 94% were judged to have need according to Federal Methodology, of whom 100% were aided. *Financial aid deadline (priority):* 3/1. *Financial aid forms:* FAFSA, institutional form required. State form required for some. *Admission application deadline:* rolling.

Summary of Aid to Needy Students *From gift & self-help combined:* Average need met: 80%. Average amount awarded: $13,694 (63% gift aid, 37% self-help). *Gift aid:* Total: $7,075,733 (69% from college's own funds, 20% from other college-administered sources, 11% from external sources). 335 Federal Work-Study jobs (averaging $1420); 146 part-time jobs.

Need-Based Scholarships & Grants Pell, FSEOG, state, private, college/university.

Loans Perkins, PLUS, Stafford, Unsubsidized Stafford, private, college/university short-term loans ($75 average), college/university long-term loans ($2391 average).

Non-Need Awards *Academic Interests/Achievement Awards:* general academic. *Creative Arts/Performance Awards:* debating, journalism/publications, theater/drama. *Special Achievements/Activities Awards:* community service, leadership. *Special Characteristics Awards:* general special characteristics, children and siblings of alumni, children of faculty/staff, religious affiliation.

Other Money-Saving Options Accelerated degree, co-op program, cooperative Army ROTC, off-campus living. *Payment Plans:* tuition prepayment, installment, deferred payment. *Waivers:* full or partial for employees or children of employees and adult students.

Contact Financial Aid Office, University of La Verne, 1950 Third Street, La Verne, CA 91750-4443, 909-596-4135, fax: 909-392-2703.

UNIVERSITY OF LOUISVILLE
Louisville, Kentucky

About the Institution State-supported, coed. Degrees awarded: A, B, M, D, P. Offers 65 undergraduate majors. Total enrollment: 21,020. Undergraduates: 14,798 (93% state residents). Freshmen: 1,911.

Undergraduate Expenses (1996–97) State resident tuition: $2570. Nonresident tuition: $7250. College room and board: $3330 (minimum). College room only: $1880 (minimum).

Applications 44% of all full-time undergraduates enrolled in fall 1996 applied for aid; of those, 86% were judged to have need according to Federal Methodology, of whom 96% were aided. *Financial aid deadline (priority):* 3/15. *Financial aid forms:* FAFSA required. Institutional form required for some. *Admission application deadline:* rolling.

Summary of Aid to Needy Students *From gift & self-help combined:* Average amount awarded: $5274 (44% gift aid, 56% self-help). *Gift aid:* Total: $8,364,186 (27% from college's own funds, 8% from other college-administered sources, 65% from external sources). 700 Federal Work-Study jobs (averaging $2200); 447 part-time jobs.

Need-Based Scholarships & Grants Pell, FSEOG, state, private, college/university.

Loans Perkins, PLUS, Stafford, Unsubsidized Stafford, Federal Nursing, Primary Care, college/university short-term loans ($200 average), college/university long-term loans ($1500 average).

Non-Need Awards *Academic Interests/Achievement Awards:* general academic. *Creative Arts/Performance Awards:* performing arts. *Special Achievements/Activities Awards:* general special achievements/activities. *Special Characteristics Awards:* general special characteristics. *Athletic:* available.

Other Money-Saving Options Accelerated degree, co-op program, Army ROTC, Air Force ROTC, off-campus living. *Payment Plan:* installment. *Waivers:* full or partial for employees or children of employees and senior citizens.

Contact Ms. Patricia O. Arauz, Acting Director of Financial Aid, University of Louisville, Louisville, KY 40292-0001, 502-852-6145, fax: 502-852-0182.

UNIVERSITY OF MAINE
Orono, Maine

About the Institution State-supported, coed. Degrees awarded: A, B, M, D. Offers 76 undergraduate majors. Total enrollment: 9,928. Undergraduates: 7,850 (82% state residents). Freshmen: 1,779.

Undergraduate Expenses (1996–97) State resident tuition: $3570. Nonresident tuition: $10,110. Mandatory fees: $569. College room and board: $4842.

Applications *Financial aid deadline (priority):* 3/1. *Financial aid forms:* FAFSA, CSS Financial Aid PROFILE required. *Regular admission application deadline:* 2/1. Early action deadline: 11/30.

Summary of Aid to Needy Students Federal Work-Study jobs; part-time jobs.

Loans College/university short-term loans, college/university long-term loans.

Non-Need Awards *Academic Interests/Achievement Awards:* general academic, engineering/technologies, physical sciences. *Creative Arts/Performance Awards:* art/fine arts, performing arts. *Special Characteristics Awards:* members of minorities. *Athletic:* available.

Other Money-Saving Options Accelerated degree, co-op program, Army ROTC, Naval ROTC, Air Force ROTC, off-campus living (after freshman year). *Payment Plan:* installment. *Waivers:* full or partial for employees or children of employees and senior citizens.

Contact Office of Financial Aid, University of Maine, 5781 Wingate Hall, Orono, ME 04469, 207-581-1110.

UNIVERSITY OF MAINE AT FARMINGTON
Farmington, Maine

About the Institution State-supported, coed. Degrees awarded: B. Offers 39 undergraduate majors. Total enrollment: 2,391 (87% state residents). Freshmen: 489.

Undergraduate Expenses (1996–97) State resident tuition: $3060. Nonresident tuition: $7470. Mandatory fees: $310. College room and board: $4142. College room only: $2224.

Applications *Financial aid deadline (priority):* 3/1. *Financial aid forms:* FAFSA, financial aid transcript (for transfers) required. *Regular admission application deadline:* 4/15. Early action deadline: 12/15.

Summary of Aid to Needy Students 432 Federal Work-Study jobs (averaging $1233); 181 part-time jobs.

Need-Based Scholarships & Grants Pell, FSEOG, college/university.

Loans Perkins, PLUS, Stafford, Unsubsidized Stafford, college/university short-term loans ($175 average), college/university long-term loans ($909 average).

Non-Need Awards *Academic Interests/Achievement Awards:* general academic. *Special Characteristics Awards:* members of minorities.

Other Money-Saving Options Accelerated degree, off-campus living. *Payment Plan:* installment. *Waivers:* full or partial for minority students and employees or children of employees.

Contact Mr. Ronald P. Milliken, Director of Financial Aid, University of Maine at Farmington, Farmington, ME 04938-1911, 207-778-7100.

UNIVERSITY OF MAINE AT FORT KENT
Fort Kent, Maine

About the Institution State-supported, coed. Degrees awarded: A, B. Offers 22 undergraduate majors. Total enrollment: 767 (77% state residents). Freshmen: 94.

Undergraduate Expenses (1996–97) State resident tuition: $2820. Nonresident tuition: $6870. Mandatory fees: $220. College room and board: $3600. College room only: $1825.

Applications 80% of all full-time undergraduates enrolled in fall 1996 applied for aid; of these, 88% were judged to have need according to Federal Methodology, of whom 99% were aided. *Financial aid deadline (priority):* 3/15. *Financial aid forms:* FAFSA required. *Admission application deadline:* rolling.

Summary of Aid to Needy Students *From gift & self-help combined:* Average need met: 81%. Average amount awarded: $5795 (45% gift aid, 55% self-help). *Gift aid:* Total: $677,389 (16% from college's own funds, 17% from other college-administered sources, 67% from external sources). 150 Federal Work-Study jobs (averaging $1000); 45 part-time jobs.

Need-Based Scholarships & Grants Pell, FSEOG, state, private, college/university.

Loans Perkins, PLUS, Stafford, Unsubsidized Stafford, college/university long-term loans ($750 average).

Non-Need Awards *Academic Interests/Achievement Awards:* general academic, business, education, foreign languages. *Special Characteristics Awards:* 42 ($72,039 total): adult students, international students, members of minorities.

Other Money-Saving Options Off-campus living. *Payment Plan:* installment. *Waivers:* full or partial for employees or children of employees and senior citizens.

Contact Mr. John Murphy, Director of Student Financial Aid, University of Maine at Fort Kent, 25 Pleasant Street, Fort Kent, ME 04743-1292, 207-834-7500.

UNIVERSITY OF MAINE AT MACHIAS
Machias, Maine

About the Institution State-supported, coed. Degrees awarded: A, B. Offers 28 undergraduate majors. Total enrollment: 915 (80% state residents). Freshmen: 181.

Undergraduate Expenses (1996–97) State resident tuition: $2820. Nonresident tuition: $6870. Mandatory fees: $175. College room and board: $3895 (minimum).

Applications 79% of all full-time undergraduates enrolled in fall 1996 applied for aid; of these, 89% were judged to have need according to Federal Methodology, of whom 96% were aided. *Financial aid deadline (priority):* 3/1. *Financial aid forms:* FAFSA required. *Regular admission application deadline:* rolling. Early action deadline: 12/15.

Summary of Aid to Needy Students *From gift & self-help combined:* Average need met: 80%. Average amount awarded: $6545 (42% gift aid, 58% self-help). *Gift aid:* Total: $1,037,433 (18% from college's own funds, 32% from other college-administered sources, 50% from external sources). 225 Federal Work-Study jobs (averaging $827); 150 part-time jobs.

Need-Based Scholarships & Grants Pell, FSEOG, state, college/university.

Loans Perkins, PLUS, Stafford, Unsubsidized Stafford, state, college/university short-term loans ($300 average), college/university long-term loans ($450 average).

Non-Need Awards Not offered.

Other Money-Saving Options Accelerated degree, co-op program, off-campus living. *Payment Plans:* installment, deferred payment. *Waivers:* full or partial for employees or children of employees and senior citizens.

Contact Office of Financial Aid, University of Maine at Machias, 9 O'Brien Avenue, Machias, ME 04654-1321, 207-255-1200.

UNIVERSITY OF MAINE AT PRESQUE ISLE
Presque Isle, Maine

About the Institution State-supported, coed. Degrees awarded: A, B. Offers 34 undergraduate majors. Total enrollment: 1,347 (92% state residents). Freshmen: 253.

Undergraduate Expenses (1996–97) State resident tuition: $2820. Nonresident tuition: $6870. Mandatory fees: $240. College room and board: $3704. College room only: $1904.

Applications 76% of all full-time undergraduates enrolled in fall 1996 applied for aid; of these, 86% were judged to have need according to Federal Methodology, of whom 98% were aided. *Financial aid deadline (priority):* 4/1. *Financial aid forms:* FAFSA, institutional form required; state form acceptable. *Admission application deadline:* rolling.

Summary of Aid to Needy Students *From gift & self-help combined:* Average need met: 84%. Average amount awarded: $5329 (56% gift aid, 44% self-help). *Gift aid:* Total: $1,789,606 (21% from college's own funds, 23% from other college-administered sources, 56% from external sources). 275 Federal Work-Study jobs (averaging $1700); 25 part-time jobs.

Need-Based Scholarships & Grants Pell, FSEOG, state, private, college/university.

Loans Perkins, PLUS, Stafford, Unsubsidized Stafford, state, college/university short-term loans ($50 average).

Non-Need Awards In 1996, a total of 31 non-need awards were made. *Academic Interests/Achievement Awards:* 5 ($15,000 total): general academic. *Creative Arts/Performance Awards:* 2 ($5264 total): art/fine arts. *Special Characteristics Awards:* 24 ($101,500 total): children of faculty/staff, international students.

Other Money-Saving Options Accelerated degree, off-campus living. *Payment Plans:* installment, deferred payment. *Waivers:* full or partial for minority students, children of alumni, employees or children of employees, adult students, senior citizens.

Contact Office of Financial Aid, University of Maine at Presque Isle, 181 Main Street, Presque Isle, ME 04769-2888, 207-768-9400.

UNIVERSITY OF MARY
Bismarck, North Dakota

About the Institution Independent/religious, coed. Degrees awarded: A, B, M. Offers 29 undergraduate majors. Total enrollment: 2,016. Undergraduates: 1,718 (92% state residents). Freshmen: 442.

Undergraduate Expenses (1997–98) Comprehensive fee of $10,730 includes tuition ($7590), mandatory fees ($150), and college room and board ($2990). College room only: $1300.

Applications Of all full-time undergraduates enrolled in fall 1996, 100% of those judged to have need according to Federal Methodology were aided. *Financial aid deadline (priority):* 8/1. *Financial aid forms:* institutional form required; FAFSA, CSS Financial Aid PROFILE acceptable. State form required for some. *Admission application deadline:* rolling.

Summary of Aid to Needy Students *From gift & self-help combined:* Average need met: 89%. Average amount awarded: $7718 (52% gift aid, 48% self-help). *Gift aid:* Total: $5,071,938 (58% from college's own funds, 10% from other college-administered sources, 32% from external sources). Federal Work-Study jobs; 10 part-time jobs.

Need-Based Scholarships & Grants Pell, FSEOG, state, private, college/university.

Loans Perkins, PLUS, Stafford, Unsubsidized Stafford, Federal Nursing, private, college/university short-term loans ($150 average).

Non-Need Awards In 1996, a total of 603 non-need awards were made. *Creative Arts/Performance Awards:* 95 ($250,000 total): debat-ing, music, theater/drama. *Special Characteristics Awards:* 8 ($43,400 total): children of faculty/staff. *Athletic:* Total: 500 ($920,000); Men: 330 ($550,000); Women: 170 ($370,000).

Other Money-Saving Options Accelerated degree, co-op program, off-campus living (after sophomore year). *Payment Plan:* installment. *Waivers:* full or partial for employees or children of employees.

Contact Sr. Rosanne Zastoupil, Director of Financial Aid, University of Mary, 7500 University Drive, Bismarck, ND 58504-9652, 701-225-7500 Ext. 383.

UNIVERSITY OF MARY HARDIN-BAYLOR
Belton, Texas

About the Institution Independent/religious, coed. Degrees awarded: B, M. Offers 56 undergraduate majors. Total enrollment: 2,265. Undergraduates: 2,014 (95% state residents). Freshmen: 307.

Undergraduate Expenses (1996–97) Comprehensive fee of $9936 includes tuition ($6510), mandatory fees ($14), and college room and board ($3412).

Applications 81% of all full-time undergraduates enrolled in fall 1996 applied for aid; of these, 90% were judged to have need according to Federal Methodology, of whom 99% were aided. *Financial aid deadline (priority):* 6/1. *Financial aid forms:* FAFSA required. Institutional form required for some. *Admission application deadline:* rolling.

Summary of Aid to Needy Students *From gift & self-help combined:* Average need met: 82%. Average amount awarded: $7264 (39% gift aid, 61% self-help). *Gift aid:* Total: $3,200,062 (23% from college's own funds, 34% from other college-administered sources, 43% from external sources). 169 Federal Work-Study jobs (averaging $1900); 121 part-time jobs.

Need-Based Scholarships & Grants Pell, FSEOG, state, private, college/university.

Loans Perkins, PLUS, Stafford, Unsubsidized Stafford, state, private, college/university long-term loans ($3000 average).

Non-Need Awards In 1996, a total of 788 non-need awards were made. *Academic Interests/Achievement Awards:* 311 ($456,146 total): general academic, biological sciences, business, communication, education, English, foreign languages, health fields, humanities, international studies, mathematics, physical sciences, premedicine, religion/biblical studies, social sciences. *Creative Arts/Performance Awards:* 68 ($50,008 total): art/fine arts, journalism/publications, music. *Special Achievements/Activities Awards:* 75 ($210,494 total): cheerleading/drum major, leadership, religious involvement. *Special Characteristics Awards:* 237 ($278,738 total): general special characteristics, children and siblings of alumni, children of current students, children of faculty/staff, handicapped students, international students, religious affiliation, siblings of current students. *Athletic:* Total: 97 ($444,420); Men: 52 ($227,314); Women: 45 ($217,106).

Other Money-Saving Options Accelerated degree, co-op program, cooperative Air Force ROTC. *Payment Plan:* installment. *Waivers:* full or partial for employees or children of employees.

Contact Mr. Steve Theodore, Associate Director of Financial Aid, University of Mary Hardin-Baylor, Box 8004 UMHB Station, Belton, TX 76513, 817-939-4517, fax: 817-939-4535.

UNIVERSITY OF MARYLAND BALTIMORE COUNTY
Baltimore, Maryland

About the Institution State-supported, coed. Degrees awarded: B, M, D. Offers 45 undergraduate majors. Total enrollment: 9,932. Undergraduates: 8,475 (92% state residents). Freshmen: 1,023.

Undergraduate Expenses (1996–97) State resident tuition: $3400. Nonresident tuition: $8192. Mandatory fees: $736. College room and board: $4746. College room only: $2636.

Applications Of all full-time undergraduates enrolled in fall 1996, 84% of those who applied for aid were judged to have need according to Federal Methodology, of whom 74% were aided. *Financial aid deadline (priority):* 3/1. *Financial aid forms:* FAFSA required. *Regular admission application deadline:* 3/15. Early action deadline: 12/1.

Summary of Aid to Needy Students *From gift & self-help combined:* Average need met: 75%. Average amount awarded: $7542 (37% gift aid, 63% self-help). *Gift aid:* Total: $5,923,464 (13% from college's own funds, 44% from other college-administered sources, 43% from external sources). Federal Work-Study jobs; 1,972 part-time jobs.

Need-Based Scholarships & Grants Pell, FSEOG, state, private, college/university.

Loans Perkins, PLUS, Stafford, Unsubsidized Stafford.

Non-Need Awards In 1996, a total of 1,492 non-need awards were made. *Academic Interests/Achievement Awards:* 1,185 ($3,082,399 total): general academic, humanities. *Creative Arts/Performance Awards:* 107 ($5561 total): art/fine arts, creative writing, dance, music, theater/drama. *Athletic:* Total: 200 ($749,155); Men: 111 ($410,536); Women: 89 ($338,619).

Other Money-Saving Options Accelerated degree, co-op program, cooperative Army ROTC, cooperative Air Force ROTC, off-campus living. *Payment Plan:* installment. *Waivers:* full or partial for employees or children of employees and senior citizens.

Contact Ms. Janice B. Doyle, Director of Financial Aid and Scholarships, University of Maryland Baltimore County, 100 Hilltop Circle, Baltimore, MD 21250, 410-455-2387, fax: 410-455-1094.

UNIVERSITY OF MARYLAND COLLEGE PARK
College Park, Maryland

About the Institution State-supported, coed. Degrees awarded: B, M, D. Offers 147 undergraduate majors. Total enrollment: 31,471. Undergraduates: 23,758 (74% state residents). Freshmen: 3,638.

Undergraduate Expenses (1996–97) State resident tuition: $3494. Nonresident tuition: $9553. Mandatory fees: $675. College room and board: $5442 (minimum).

Applications *Financial aid deadline (priority):* 2/15. *Financial aid forms:* FAFSA required. *Admission application deadline:* 2/15.

Summary of Aid to Needy Students 872 Federal Work-Study jobs (averaging $1300); part-time jobs.

Need-Based Scholarships & Grants Pell, FSEOG, state, college/university.

Loans Perkins, Stafford, college/university short-term loans ($500 average), college/university long-term loans ($1079 average).

Non-Need Awards *Academic Interests/Achievement Awards:* general academic. *Creative Arts/Performance Awards:* art/fine arts, music, theater/drama. *Special Characteristics Awards:* general special characteristics, adult students, children of faculty/staff, handicapped students. *Athletic:* available.

Other Money-Saving Options Accelerated degree, co-op program, Air Force ROTC, cooperative Naval ROTC, off-campus living. *Payment Plan:* deferred payment. *Waivers:* full or partial for employees or children of employees and senior citizens.

Contact Mr. William D. Leith Jr., Director of Financial Aid, University of Maryland College Park, 0102 Lee Building, College Park, MD 20742, 301-314-8279.

UNIVERSITY OF MARYLAND EASTERN SHORE
Princess Anne, Maryland

About the Institution State-supported, coed. Degrees awarded: B, M, D. Offers 54 undergraduate majors. Total enrollment: 3,166. Undergraduates: 2,862 (72% state residents). Freshmen: 774.

Undergraduate Expenses (1996–97) State resident tuition: $3036. Nonresident tuition: $7646. College room and board: $4130. College room only: $2330.

Applications *Financial aid deadline (priority):* 3/1. *Financial aid forms:* FAFSA, institutional form required. *Admission application deadline:* rolling.

Summary of Aid to Needy Students *From gift & self-help combined:* Average need met: 49%. Average amount awarded: $3839. Federal Work-Study jobs; 327 part-time jobs.

Need-Based Scholarships & Grants Pell, FSEOG, state, college/university.

Loans Perkins, PLUS, Stafford, Unsubsidized Stafford.

Non-Need Awards *Academic Interests/Achievement Awards:* general academic, agriculture, business, education, engineering/technologies, English, home economics. *Creative Arts/Performance Awards:* art/fine arts, music, performing arts, theater/drama. *Special Achievements/Activities Awards:* community service, leadership. *Special Characteristics Awards:* children of faculty/staff, first-generation college students, ROTC participants. *Athletic:* Total: 67 ($383,243); Men: 44 ($235,127); Women: 23 ($148,116).

Other Money-Saving Options Accelerated degree, co-op program, cooperative Army ROTC, off-campus living. *Payment Plans:* installment, deferred payment. *Waivers:* full or partial for minority students, employees or children of employees, senior citizens.

Contact Ms. Dorothy L. Body, Director of Financial Aid, University of Maryland Eastern Shore, Princess Anne, MD 21853, 410-651-6172.

UNIVERSITY OF MASSACHUSETTS AMHERST
Amherst, Massachusetts

About the Institution State-supported, coed. Degrees awarded: A, B, M, D. Offers 88 undergraduate majors. Total enrollment: 23,108. Undergraduates: 18,209 (73% state residents). Freshmen: 3,985.

Undergraduate Expenses (1996–97) State resident tuition: $2109. Nonresident tuition: $8842. Mandatory fees: $3304 (minimum). College room and board: $4228. College room only: $2416.

Applications 79% of all full-time undergraduates enrolled in fall 1996 applied for aid; of these, 91% were judged to have need according to Federal Methodology, of whom 88% were aided. *Financial aid deadline:* Applications processed continuously. *Financial aid forms:* FAFSA required. *Admission application deadline:* 2/1.

Summary of Aid to Needy Students *From gift & self-help combined:* Average need met: 81%. Average amount awarded: $7535 (40% gift aid, 60% self-help). *Gift aid:* Total: $28,000,000 (36% from college's own funds, 39% from other college-administered sources, 25% from external sources). 3,100 Federal Work-Study jobs (averaging $1000); 4,160 part-time jobs.

Need-Based Scholarships & Grants Pell, FSEOG, state, private, college/university.

Loans Perkins, PLUS, Stafford, Unsubsidized Stafford, state, private, college/university short-term loans ($200 average).

Non-Need Awards *Academic Interests/Achievement Awards:* general academic, agriculture, architecture, biological sciences, business, communication, computer science, education, engineering/technologies, health fields, humanities, mathematics, military science, physical sciences, premedicine, social sciences. *Creative Arts/Performance Awards:* 157 ($388,000 total): art/fine arts, dance, music, theater/drama. *Special Characteristics Awards:* children and siblings of alumni, children of faculty/staff, handicapped students, ROTC participants, veterans. *Athletic:* Total: 357 ($2,987,258); Men: 205 ($1,454,157); Women: 152 ($1,533,101).

Other Money-Saving Options Co-op program, Army ROTC, Air Force ROTC, off-campus living (after sophomore year). *Payment Plan:* installment. *Waivers:* full or partial for employees or children of employees and senior citizens.

Contact Office of Financial Aid, University of Massachusetts Amherst, 255 Whitmore Administration, Amherst, MA 01003-0001, 413-545-0111.

UNIVERSITY OF MASSACHUSETTS BOSTON
Boston, Massachusetts

About the Institution State-supported, coed. Degrees awarded: B, M, D. Offers 42 undergraduate majors. Total enrollment: 10,216. Undergraduates: 7,821 (94% state residents). Freshmen: 743.

Undergraduate Expenses (1996–97) State resident tuition: $2109. Nonresident tuition: $8842. Mandatory fees: $2239.

Applications *Financial aid deadline (priority):* 3/1. *Financial aid forms:* FAFSA, institutional form required. *Admission application deadline:* 3/1.

Summary of Aid to Needy Students Federal Work-Study jobs; part-time jobs.

Loans College/university short-term loans.

Non-Need Awards *Academic Interests/Achievement Awards:* general academic.

Other Money-Saving Options Accelerated degree, co-op program. *Payment Plan:* installment. *Waivers:* full or partial for employees or children of employees and senior citizens.

Contact Office of Financial Aid, University of Massachusetts Boston, Boston, MA 02125-3393, 617-287-5000.

UNIVERSITY OF MASSACHUSETTS DARTMOUTH
North Dartmouth, Massachusetts

About the Institution State-supported, coed. Degrees awarded: B, M, D. Offers 57 undergraduate majors. Total enrollment: 5,103. Undergraduates: 4,612 (94% state residents). Freshmen: 872.

Undergraduate Expenses (1997–98) State resident tuition: $1744. Nonresident tuition: $7140. Mandatory fees: $2407 (minimum). College room and board: $4718. College room only: $3134 (minimum).

Applications *Financial aid deadline (priority):* 3/1. *Financial aid forms:* FAFSA required. *Regular admission application deadline:* rolling. Early decision deadline: 11/15.

Summary of Aid to Needy Students Federal Work-Study jobs; part-time jobs.

Loans College/university short-term loans.

Non-Need Awards *Academic Interests/Achievement Awards:* general academic.

Other Money-Saving Options Co-op program, Army ROTC, off-campus living. *Payment Plan:* installment. *Waivers:* full or partial for employees or children of employees and senior citizens.

Contact Office of Financial Aid, University of Massachusetts Dartmouth, North Dartmouth, MA 02747-2300, 508-999-8000.

UNIVERSITY OF MASSACHUSETTS LOWELL
Lowell, Massachusetts

About the Institution State-supported, coed. Degrees awarded: A, B, M, D. Offers 46 undergraduate majors. Total enrollment: 12,731. Undergraduates: 6,500 (90% state residents).

Undergraduate Expenses (1997–98) State resident tuition: $1700. Nonresident tuition: $7347. Mandatory fees: $2722. College room and board: $4165 (minimum). College room only: $2580.

Applications Of all full-time undergraduates enrolled in fall 1996, 67% of those who applied for aid were judged to have need according to Federal Methodology, of whom 98% were aided. *Financial aid deadline (priority):* 3/1. *Financial aid forms:* FAFSA required. *Admission application deadline:* rolling.

Summary of Aid to Needy Students *From gift & self-help combined:* Average need met: 94%. Average amount awarded: $6850 (39% gift aid, 61% self-help). *Gift aid:* Total: $8,250,000. 250 Federal Work-Study jobs (averaging $2800); 600 part-time jobs.

Need-Based Scholarships & Grants Pell, FSEOG, state, private, college/university.

Loans Perkins, PLUS, Stafford, Unsubsidized Stafford, state, private.

Non-Need Awards *Academic Interests/Achievement Awards:* general academic. *Creative Arts/Performance Awards:* music. *Special Achievements/Activities Awards:* general special achievements/activities. *Special Characteristics Awards:* general special characteristics. *Athletic:* available.

Other Money-Saving Options Accelerated degree, co-op program, Army ROTC, Air Force ROTC, off-campus living. *Payment Plan:* installment. *Waivers:* full or partial for employees or children of employees.

Contact Ms. Judy Keyes, Director of Student Financial Assistance, University of Massachusetts Lowell, Lowell, MA 01854-2881, 508-934-4232.

THE UNIVERSITY OF MEMPHIS
Memphis, Tennessee

About the Institution State-supported, coed. Degrees awarded: B, M, D, P. Offers 53 undergraduate majors. Total enrollment: 19,271. Undergraduates: 14,298 (87% state residents). Freshmen: 1,642.

Undergraduate Expenses (1996–97) State resident tuition: $2112. Nonresident tuition: $6448. Mandatory fees: $68. College room only: $1680.

Applications 69% of all full-time undergraduates enrolled in fall 1996 applied for aid; of these, 85% were judged to have need according to Federal Methodology, of whom 90% were aided. *Financial aid deadline:* Applications processed continuously. *Financial aid forms:* FAFSA, institutional form required. *Admission application deadline:* 8/1.

Summary of Aid to Needy Students *From gift & self-help combined:* Average need met: 60%. Average amount awarded: $5840 (32% gift aid, 68% self-help). *Gift aid:* Total: $9,970,000 (15% from college's own funds, 5% from other college-administered sources, 80% from external sources). Federal Work-Study jobs; part-time jobs.

Need-Based Scholarships & Grants Pell, FSEOG, state, college/university.

Loans Perkins, PLUS, Stafford, Unsubsidized Stafford, college/university short-term loans ($1100 average), college/university long-term loans ($1500 average).

Non-Need Awards *Academic Interests/Achievement Awards:* general academic, biological sciences, business, communication, education, engineering/technologies, health fields, international studies, military science, premedicine, social sciences. *Creative Arts/Performance Awards:* art/fine arts, cinema/film/broadcasting, journalism/publications, music.

Special Achievements/Activities Awards: general special achievements/activities, cheerleading/drum major, leadership. *Special Characteristics Awards:* adult students, children of educators, children of faculty/staff, children of public servants, handicapped students, members of minorities, public servants, ROTC participants. *Athletic:* available.

Other Money-Saving Options Accelerated degree, Army ROTC, Naval ROTC, Air Force ROTC, off-campus living. *Payment Plan:* installment. *Waivers:* full or partial for employees or children of employees and senior citizens.

Contact Office of Financial Aid, The University of Memphis, Scates Hall 312, Memphis, TN 38152, 901-678-2000.

UNIVERSITY OF MIAMI
Coral Gables, Florida

About the Institution Independent, coed. Degrees awarded: B, M, D, P. Offers 123 undergraduate majors. Total enrollment: 13,677. Undergraduates: 8,377 (58% state residents). Freshmen: 1,708.

Undergraduate Expenses (1997–98 estimated) Comprehensive fee of $26,865 includes tuition ($19,140), mandatory fees ($373), and college room and board ($7352). College room only: $4194.

Applications 64% of all full-time undergraduates enrolled in fall 1996 applied for aid; of these, 94% were judged to have need according to Federal Methodology, of whom 98% were aided. *Financial aid deadline (priority):* 2/15. *Financial aid forms:* FAFSA required; CSS Financial Aid PROFILE acceptable. State form required for some. *Regular admission application deadline:* 3/1. Early decision deadline: 11/15. Early action deadline: 11/15.

Summary of Aid to Needy Students *From gift & self-help combined:* Average need met: 90%. Average amount awarded: $19,706 (61% gift aid, 39% self-help). *Gift aid:* Total: $53,744,390 (73% from college's own funds, 4% from other college-administered sources, 23% from external sources). Federal Work-Study jobs; 700 part-time jobs.

Need-Based Scholarships & Grants Pell, FSEOG, state, private, college/university.

Loans Perkins, PLUS, Stafford, Unsubsidized Stafford, private, college/university short-term loans.

Non-Need Awards In 1996, a total of 3,892 non-need awards were made. *Academic Interests/Achievement Awards:* 2,691 ($19,202,093 total): general academic. *Creative Arts/Performance Awards:* 262 ($1,803,746 total): music. *Special Characteristics Awards:* 46 ($148,871 total): ROTC participants. *Athletic:* Total: 893 ($4,252,709); Men: 608 ($2,891,608); Women: 285 ($1,361,101).

Other Money-Saving Options Accelerated degree, Air Force ROTC, cooperative Army ROTC, off-campus living (after freshman year). *Payment Plans:* tuition prepayment, installment. *Waivers:* full or partial for employees or children of employees.

Contact Office of Financial Aid, University of Miami, 1204 Dickinson Drive, PO Box 248187, Coral Gables, FL 33124-5240, 305-284-2211.

UNIVERSITY OF MICHIGAN
Ann Arbor, Michigan

About the Institution State-supported, coed. Degrees awarded: B, M, D, P. Offers 141 undergraduate majors. Total enrollment: 36,525. Undergraduates: 23,590 (66% state residents). Freshmen: 5,327.

Undergraduate Expenses (1996–97) State resident tuition: $5710 (minimum). Nonresident tuition: $17,916 (minimum). Mandatory fees: $178. College room and board: $5137.

Applications Of all full-time undergraduates enrolled in fall 1996, 81% of those who applied for aid were judged to have need according to Federal Methodology, of whom 100% were aided. *Financial aid deadline (priority):* 2/3. *Financial aid forms:* FAFSA required. Institutional form required for some. *Admission application deadline:* 2/1.

Summary of Aid to Needy Students *Gift aid:* Total: $44,700,000 (68% from college's own funds, 4% from other college-administered sources, 28% from external sources). 3,725 Federal Work-Study jobs (averaging $1850); 7,000 part-time jobs.

Need-Based Scholarships & Grants Pell, FSEOG, state, private, college/university.

Loans Perkins, PLUS, Stafford, Unsubsidized Stafford, Federal Nursing, state, private, college/university short-term loans ($475 average), college/university long-term loans ($600 average), MI-Loan Program.

Non-Need Awards *Academic Interests/Achievement Awards:* 1,100 ($2,400,000 total): general academic, architecture, area/ethnic studies, biological sciences, business, computer science, education, engineering/technologies, English, foreign languages, health fields, humanities, international studies, mathematics, military science, physical sciences, premedicine, social sciences. *Creative Arts/Performance Awards:* theater/drama. *Special Achievements/Activities Awards:* general special achievements/activities. *Special Characteristics Awards:* local/state students, members of minorities, out-of-state students, ROTC participants. *Athletic:* Total: 318 ($5,638,611); Men: 173 ($3,062,323); Women: 145 ($2,576,288).

Other Money-Saving Options Accelerated degree, co-op program, Army ROTC, Naval ROTC, Air Force ROTC, off-campus living. *Payment Plan:* installment. *Waivers:* full or partial for senior citizens.

Contact Financial Aid Counseling and Advising Office, University of Michigan, 2011 Student Activities Building, Ann Arbor, MI 48109-1316, 313-763-6600, fax: 313-647-3081.

UNIVERSITY OF MICHIGAN–DEARBORN
Dearborn, Michigan

About the Institution State-supported, coed. Degrees awarded: B, M. Offers 62 undergraduate majors. Total enrollment: 8,324. Undergraduates: 6,744 (99% state residents). Freshmen: 792.

Undergraduate Expenses (1996–97) State resident tuition: $3820 (minimum). Nonresident tuition: $10,450 (minimum). Mandatory fees: $220.

Applications Of all full-time undergraduates enrolled in fall 1996, 100% of those judged to have need according to Federal Methodology were aided. *Financial aid deadline (priority):* 4/1. *Financial aid forms:* FAFSA required; CSS Financial Aid PROFILE, institutional form acceptable. *Admission application deadline:* rolling.

Summary of Aid to Needy Students *From gift & self-help combined:* Average need met: 80%. *Gift aid:* Total: $4,893,625 (40% from college's own funds, 21% from other college-administered sources, 39% from external sources). Federal Work-Study jobs; part-time jobs.

Need-Based Scholarships & Grants Pell, FSEOG, state, private, college/university.

Loans Perkins, PLUS, Stafford, Unsubsidized Stafford, college/university short-term loans ($174 average).

Non-Need Awards In 1996, a total of 1,254 non-need awards were made. *Academic Interests/Achievement Awards:* 487 ($764,651 total): general academic, biological sciences, computer science, engineering/technologies, international studies, physical sciences. *Special Characteristics Awards:* 741 ($191,081 total): ethnic background. *Athletic:* Total: 26 ($47,060); Men: 8 ($16,390); Women: 18 ($30,670).

Other Money-Saving Options Accelerated degree, co-op program, Army ROTC, cooperative Naval ROTC, cooperative Air Force ROTC. *Payment Plan:* installment. *Waivers:* full or partial for employees or children of employees and senior citizens.

Contact Mr. John A. Mason, Director of Financial Aid, University of Michigan–Dearborn, 4901 Evergreen Road, Dearborn, MI 48128-1491, 313-593-5300, fax: 313-593-5313.

UNIVERSITY OF MICHIGAN–FLINT
Flint, Michigan

About the Institution State-supported, coed. Degrees awarded: B, M. Offers 51 undergraduate majors. Total enrollment: 6,236. Undergraduates: 5,854 (98% state residents). Freshmen: 512.

Undergraduate Expenses (1996–97) State resident tuition: $3309 (minimum). Nonresident tuition: $9823 (minimum). Mandatory fees: $125.

Applications Of all full-time undergraduates enrolled in fall 1996, 93% of those who applied for aid were judged to have need according to Federal Methodology, of whom 100% were aided. *Financial aid deadline (priority):* 4/15. *Financial aid forms:* FAFSA, institutional form required. *Admission application deadline:* 8/21.

Summary of Aid to Needy Students *From gift & self-help combined:* Average need met: 100%. Average amount awarded: $6606 (34% gift aid, 66% self-help). *Gift aid:* Total: $4,841,453 (34% from college's own funds, 19% from other college-administered sources, 47% from external sources). 310 Federal Work-Study jobs (averaging $900); 250 part-time jobs.

Need-Based Scholarships & Grants Pell, FSEOG, state, private, college/university.

Loans Perkins, PLUS, Stafford, Unsubsidized Stafford, Federal Nursing, state, college/university short-term loans ($500 average).

Non-Need Awards In 1996, a total of 284 non-need awards were made. *Academic Interests/Achievement Awards:* 212 ($216,918 total): general academic, business, education. *Creative Arts/Performance Awards:* 52 ($25,500 total): music, theater/drama. *Special Achievements/Activities Awards:* 20 ($20,000 total): community service, leadership.

Other Money-Saving Options Accelerated degree, co-op program. *Payment Plan:* deferred payment. *Waivers:* full or partial for minority students and senior citizens.

Contact Financial Aid Office, University of Michigan–Flint, Room 277 UPAV, Flint, MI 48502-2186, 810-762-3444, fax: 810-766-6757.

UNIVERSITY OF MINNESOTA, CROOKSTON
Crookston, Minnesota

About the Institution State-supported, coed. Degrees awarded: A, B. Offers 32 undergraduate majors. Total enrollment: 937 (65% state residents). Freshmen: 293.

Undergraduate Expenses (1996–97) State resident tuition: $3114 (minimum). Nonresident tuition: $8835 (minimum). Mandatory fees: $1137. College room and board: $3492.

Applications *Financial aid deadline (priority):* 4/1. *Financial aid forms:* FAFSA required. *Admission application deadline:* rolling.

Summary of Aid to Needy Students *From gift & self-help combined:* Average amount awarded: $6885 (48% gift aid, 52% self-help). *Gift aid:* Total: $2,435,401 (20% from college's own funds, 9% from other college-administered sources, 71% from external sources). 258 Federal Work-Study jobs (averaging $1398); 85 part-time jobs.

Need-Based Scholarships & Grants Pell, FSEOG, state, college/university.

Loans Perkins, PLUS, Stafford, Unsubsidized Stafford, college/university short-term loans ($125 average).

Non-Need Awards *Academic Interests/Achievement Awards:* general academic, agriculture, business. *Special Achievements/Activities Awards:* general special achievements/activities, leadership. *Special Characteristics Awards:* general special characteristics, members of minorities, previous college experience. *Athletic:* Total: 76 ($55,356); Men: 55 ($39,822); Women: 21 ($15,534).

Other Money-Saving Options Off-campus living. *Payment Plans:* guaranteed tuition, installment. *Waivers:* full or partial for senior citizens.

Contact Ms. Gayle Schuster, Assistant to Director of Financial Aid, University of Minnesota, Crookston, 4 Hill Hall, Crookston, MN 56716-5001, 218-281-8561, fax: 218-281-8050.

UNIVERSITY OF MINNESOTA, DULUTH
Duluth, Minnesota

About the Institution State-supported, coed. Degrees awarded: B, M. Offers 64 undergraduate majors. Total enrollment: 7,501. Undergraduates: 7,023 (87% state residents). Freshmen: 1,794.

Undergraduate Expenses (1996–97) State resident tuition: $3850. Nonresident tuition: $11,004. Mandatory fees: $337. College room and board: $3774.

Applications Of all full-time undergraduates enrolled in fall 1996, 82% of those who applied for aid were judged to have need according to Federal Methodology, of whom 99% were aided. *Financial aid deadline:* continuous. *Financial aid forms:* FAFSA required. *Admission application deadline:* 2/1.

Summary of Aid to Needy Students *From gift & self-help combined:* Average need met: 96%. Average amount awarded: $6335 (37% gift aid, 63% self-help). *Gift aid:* Total: $9,921,043. 848 Federal Work-Study jobs (averaging $1114); 1,500 part-time jobs.

Need-Based Scholarships & Grants Pell, FSEOG, state, private, college/university.

Loans Perkins, PLUS, Stafford, Unsubsidized Stafford, Primary Care, state, private, college/university short-term loans ($327 average), college/university long-term loans ($1049 average).

Non-Need Awards *Academic Interests/Achievement Awards:* general academic. *Creative Arts/Performance Awards:* art/fine arts, theater/drama. *Special Characteristics Awards:* general special characteristics, ROTC participants. *Athletic:* available.

Other Money-Saving Options Air Force ROTC, off-campus living. *Payment Plan:* installment. *Waivers:* full or partial for employees or children of employees and senior citizens.

Contact Ms. Brenda Herzig, Director of Financial Aid, University of Minnesota, Duluth, Duluth, MN 55812-2496, 218-726-8786.

UNIVERSITY OF MINNESOTA, MORRIS
Morris, Minnesota

About the Institution State-supported, coed. Degrees awarded: B. Offers 35 undergraduate majors. Total enrollment: 1,970 (83% state residents). Freshmen: 550.

Undergraduate Expenses (1996–97) State resident tuition: $4194. Nonresident tuition: $12,020. Mandatory fees: $360. College room and board: $3594. College room only: $1674.

Applications 78% of all full-time undergraduates enrolled in fall 1996 applied for aid; of these, 90% were judged to have need according to Federal Methodology, of whom 100% were aided. *Financial aid deadline (priority):* 4/1. *Financial aid forms:* FAFSA required. *Regular admission application deadline:* 3/15. Early action deadline: 2/1.

Summary of Aid to Needy Students *From gift & self-help combined:* Average need met: 90%. Average amount awarded: $5800 (48% gift aid, 52% self-help). *Gift aid:* Total: $4,909,000 (23% from college's own funds, 40% from other college-administered sources, 37% from external sources). 530 Federal Work-Study jobs (averaging $900); 350 part-time jobs.

Need-Based Scholarships & Grants Pell, FSEOG, state, private, college/university.

Loans Perkins, PLUS, Stafford, Unsubsidized Stafford, state, private, college/university short-term loans ($200 average), college/university long-term loans ($1780 average).

Non-Need Awards *Academic Interests/Achievement Awards:* available. *Creative Arts/Performance Awards:* available. *Special Characteristics Awards:* members of minorities, out-of-state students.

Other Money-Saving Options Accelerated degree, off-campus living. *Payment Plans:* installment, deferred payment. *Waivers:* full or partial for minority students, employees or children of employees, senior citizens.

Contact Ms. Pam Engebretson, Senior Financial Aid Officer, University of Minnesota, Morris, 600 East 4th Street, Morris, MN 56267, 320-589-6035, fax: 320-589-1673.

UNIVERSITY OF MINNESOTA, TWIN CITIES CAMPUS
Minneapolis, Minnesota

About the Institution State-supported, coed. Degrees awarded: B, M, D, P. Offers 135 undergraduate majors. Total enrollment: 37,018. Undergraduates: 23,689 (73% state residents). Freshmen: 4,279.

Undergraduate Expenses (1996–97) State resident tuition: $3620 (minimum). Nonresident tuition: $10,327 (minimum). Mandatory fees: $470. College room and board: $4056.

Applications Of all full-time undergraduates enrolled in fall 1996, 85% of those who applied for aid were judged to have need according to Federal Methodology, of whom 97% were aided. *Financial aid deadline (priority):* 2/15. *Financial aid forms:* FAFSA required. *Admission application deadline:* rolling.

Summary of Aid to Needy Students *From gift & self-help combined:* Average need met: 75%. Average amount awarded: $5993 (42% gift aid, 58% self-help). *Gift aid:* Total: $26,719,915. Federal Work-Study jobs; part-time jobs.

Need-Based Scholarships & Grants Pell, FSEOG, state, private, college/university.

Loans Perkins, PLUS, Stafford, Unsubsidized Stafford, Federal Nursing, Primary Care, state, private, college/university short-term loans, college/university long-term loans.

Non-Need Awards *Academic Interests/Achievement Awards:* general academic, agriculture, architecture, area/ethnic studies, biological sciences, business, communication, computer science, education, engineering/technologies, English, foreign languages, health fields, home economics, humanities, international studies, library science, mathematics, military science, physical sciences, premedicine, religion/biblical studies, social sciences. *Creative Arts/Performance Awards:* general creative. *Special Achievements/Activities Awards:* hobbies/interest. *Special Characteristics Awards:* members of minorities. *Athletic:* Total: 396; Men: 255; Women: 141.

Other Money-Saving Options Accelerated degree, co-op program, Army ROTC, Naval ROTC, Air Force ROTC, off-campus living. *Payment Plans:* guaranteed tuition, installment. *Waivers:* full or partial for employees or children of employees and senior citizens.

Contact Mr. John Kellogg, Analyst, University of Minnesota, Twin Cities Campus, Minneapolis, MN 55455-0213, 612-625-3387, fax: 612-624-6057.

UNIVERSITY OF MISSISSIPPI
Oxford, Mississippi

About the Institution State-supported, coed. Degrees awarded: B, M, D, P. Offers 64 undergraduate majors. Total enrollment: 10,280. Undergraduates: 8,117 (63% state residents). Freshmen: 1,838.

Undergraduate Expenses (1996–97) State resident tuition: $1996. Nonresident tuition: $4816. Mandatory fees: $635. College room only: $1660.

Applications *Financial aid deadline (priority):* 4/1. *Financial aid forms:* FAFSA, institutional form required. *Admission application deadline:* 7/26.

Summary of Aid to Needy Students Federal Work-Study jobs.

Need-Based Scholarships & Grants Pell, FSEOG.

Loans Perkins, Stafford, Unsubsidized Stafford, college/university short-term loans ($300 average), college/university long-term loans ($2000 average).

Non-Need Awards *Academic Interests/Achievement Awards:* general academic. *Creative Arts/Performance Awards:* art/fine arts, music, theater/drama. *Special Achievements/Activities Awards:* leadership. *Special Characteristics Awards:* children and siblings of alumni, local/state students, out-of-state students. *Athletic:* available.

Other Money-Saving Options Accelerated degree, Army ROTC, Naval ROTC, Air Force ROTC, off-campus living (after freshman year). *Payment Plan:* deferred payment. *Waivers:* full or partial for children of alumni, employees or children of employees, senior citizens.

Contact Mr. Larry D. Ridgeway, Director of Financial Aid, University of Mississippi, 25 Old Chemistry Building, University, MS 38677-9702, 601-232-7175.

UNIVERSITY OF MISSOURI–COLUMBIA
Columbia, Missouri

About the Institution State-supported, coed. Degrees awarded: B, M, D, P. Offers 104 undergraduate majors. Total enrollment: 22,483. Undergraduates: 17,165 (87% state residents). Freshmen: 3,737.

Undergraduate Expenses (1996–97) State resident tuition: $3389. Nonresident tuition: $10,129. Mandatory fees: $479. College room and board: $4172.

Applications Of all full-time undergraduates enrolled in fall 1996, 80% of those who applied for aid were judged to have need according to Federal Methodology, of whom 97% were aided. *Financial aid deadline (priority):* 3/1. *Financial aid forms:* FAFSA required for some. *Admission application deadline:* 5/1.

Summary of Aid to Needy Students *From gift & self-help combined:* Average need met: 78%. Average amount awarded: $5993 (52% gift aid, 48% self-help). *Gift aid:* Total: $20,497,851 (43% from college's own funds, 32% from other college-administered sources, 25% from external sources). 940 Federal Work-Study jobs (averaging $1319); part-time jobs.

Need-Based Scholarships & Grants Pell, FSEOG, state, private, college/university.

Loans Perkins, PLUS, Stafford, Unsubsidized Stafford, Federal Nursing, Primary Care, state, private, college/university short-term loans ($783 average), college/university long-term loans ($2014 average).

Non-Need Awards In 1996, a total of 4,145 non-need awards were made. *Academic Interests/Achievement Awards:* 2,843 ($4,962,508 total). *Creative Arts/Performance Awards:* 296 ($231,645 total). *Special Achievements/Activities Awards:* 16 ($28,000 total). *Special Characteristics Awards:* 647 ($3,040,902 total): members of minorities, out-of-state students, ROTC participants. *Athletic:* Total: 343 ($2,650,779); Men: 205 ($1,577,992); Women: 138 ($1,072,787).

Other Money-Saving Options Accelerated degree, co-op program, Army ROTC, Naval ROTC, Air Force ROTC, off-campus living (after freshman year). *Payment Plan:* installment. *Waivers:* full or partial for employees or children of employees.

Contact Mr. Leonard E. Johnsen, Associate Director, Student Financial Aid, University of Missouri–Columbia, 11 Jesse Hall, Columbia, MO 65211, 573-882-3569, fax: 573-884-5335.

UNIVERSITY OF MISSOURI–KANSAS CITY
Kansas City, Missouri

About the Institution State-supported, coed. Degrees awarded: B, M, D, P. Offers 50 undergraduate majors. Total enrollment: 10,298. Undergraduates: 5,632 (78% state residents). Freshmen: 764.

Undergraduate Expenses (1996–97) State resident tuition: $3330. Nonresident tuition: $9954. Mandatory fees: $469. College room and board: $3750.

Applications Of all full-time undergraduates enrolled in fall 1996, 77% of those who applied for aid were judged to have need according to Federal Methodology, of whom 95% were aided. *Financial aid deadline (priority):* 3/1. *Financial aid forms:* FAFSA required. *Admission application deadline:* rolling.

Summary of Aid to Needy Students *From gift & self-help combined:* Average need met: 68%. Average amount awarded: $11,207 (31% gift aid, 69% self-help). *Gift aid:* Total: $8,723,075 (56% from college's own funds, 5% from other college-administered sources, 39% from external sources). 220 Federal Work-Study jobs (averaging $3467); 509 part-time jobs.

Need-Based Scholarships & Grants Pell, FSEOG, state, private, college/university.

Loans Perkins, PLUS, Stafford, Unsubsidized Stafford, Primary Care, private, college/university short-term loans ($500 average), college/university long-term loans ($2332 average).

Non-Need Awards In 1996, a total of 1,294 non-need awards were made. *Academic Interests/Achievement Awards:* 920 ($2,200,031 total): general academic. *Creative Arts/Performance Awards:* 83 ($123,271 total): general creative, debating, music, performing arts. *Special Characteristics Awards:* 119 ($632,029 total): members of minorities. *Athletic:* Total: 172 ($1,209,590).

Other Money-Saving Options Accelerated degree, co-op program, Army ROTC, off-campus living. *Waivers:* full or partial for employees or children of employees.

Contact Ms. Sheryl A. Schmidt, Administrative Associate II, University of Missouri–Kansas City, Administrative Center, 5100 Rockhill Road, Kansas City, MO 64110-2499, 816-235-5446, fax: 816-235-5511.

UNIVERSITY OF MISSOURI–ROLLA
Rolla, Missouri

About the Institution State-supported, coed. Degrees awarded: B, M, D. Offers 31 undergraduate majors. Total enrollment: 5,264. Undergraduates: 4,342 (72% state residents). Freshmen: 803.

Undergraduate Expenses (1996–97) State resident tuition: $3630 (minimum). Nonresident tuition: $10,851 (minimum). Mandatory fees: $583. College room and board: $4026.

Applications 80% of all full-time undergraduates enrolled in fall 1996 applied for aid; of these, 81% were judged to have need according to Federal Methodology, of whom 100% were aided. *Financial aid deadline (priority):* 3/1. *Financial aid forms:* FAFSA acceptable. State form required for some. *Admission application deadline:* 7/1.

Summary of Aid to Needy Students *From gift & self-help combined:* Average need met: 75%. Average amount awarded: $4794 (20% gift aid, 80% self-help). *Gift aid:* Total: $1,850,285 (16% from college-administered sources, 84% from external sources). 268 Federal Work-Study jobs (averaging $1400); 1,193 part-time jobs.

Need-Based Scholarships & Grants Pell, FSEOG, state, college/university.

Loans Perkins, PLUS, Stafford, Unsubsidized Stafford, private, college/university short-term loans ($200 average), college/university long-term loans ($1200 average).

Non-Need Awards *Academic Interests/Achievement Awards:* 1,729 ($5,799,481 total): general academic, education, engineering/technologies, humanities. *Creative Arts/Performance Awards:* 20 ($10,000 total): music, theater/drama. *Special Characteristics Awards:* children and siblings of alumni, members of minorities, out-of-state students. *Athletic:* Total: 185 ($530,391).

Other Money-Saving Options Accelerated degree, co-op program, Army ROTC, Air Force ROTC, off-campus living (after sophomore year). *Payment Plan:* installment. *Waivers:* full or partial for employees or children of employees.

Contact Mr. Robert W. Whites, Associate Director of Admissions/Student Financial Aid, University of Missouri–Rolla, G-1 Parker Hall, Rolla, MO 65409-0250, 573-341-4282, fax: 573-341-4274.

UNIVERSITY OF MISSOURI–ST. LOUIS
St. Louis, Missouri

About the Institution State-supported, coed. Degrees awarded: B, M, D, P. Offers 83 undergraduate majors. Total enrollment: 23,344. Undergraduates: 13,941 (98% state residents). Freshmen: 715.

Undergraduate Expenses (1996–97) State resident tuition: $2904. Nonresident tuition: $8681. Mandatory fees: $479. College room and board: $4341 (minimum). College room only: $2941.

Applications 50% of all full-time undergraduates enrolled in fall 1996 applied for aid; of these, 85% were judged to have need according to Federal Methodology, of whom 98% were aided. *Financial aid deadline (priority):* 4/1. *Financial aid forms:* FAFSA required. *Admission application deadline:* rolling.

Summary of Aid to Needy Students *From gift & self-help combined:* Average need met: 72%. Average amount awarded: $6509 (29% gift aid, 71% self-help). *Gift aid:* Total: $4,095,912 (44% from college's own funds, 14% from other college-administered sources, 42% from external sources). 83 Federal Work-Study jobs (averaging $1776); 500 part-time jobs.

Need-Based Scholarships & Grants Pell, FSEOG, state, private, college/university.

Loans Perkins, PLUS, Stafford, Unsubsidized Stafford, Federal Nursing, college/university short-term loans ($800 average), college/university long-term loans ($500 average).

Non-Need Awards In 1996, a total of 1,301 non-need awards were made. *Academic Interests/Achievement Awards:* 993 ($2,713,258 total): general academic, biological sciences, business, communication, computer science, education, engineering/technologies, English, foreign languages, health fields, humanities, international studies, mathematics. *Creative Arts/Performance Awards:* 80 ($89,735 total): art/fine arts, music. *Special Achievements/Activities Awards:* 2 ($1000 total): memberships. *Special Characteristics Awards:* 87 ($194,910 total): general special characteristics, ethnic background, local/state students, members of minorities. *Athletic:* Total: 139 ($345,713); Men: 77 ($190,400); Women: 62 ($155,313).

Other Money-Saving Options Accelerated degree, co-op program, cooperative Army ROTC, cooperative Air Force ROTC, off-campus living. *Payment Plan:* installment. *Waivers:* full or partial for employees or children of employees.

Contact Dr. Gerard Joseph, Associate Director of Financial Aid, University of Missouri–St. Louis, 8001 Natural Bridge Road, 209 Woods Hall, St. Louis, MO 63121-4499, 314-516-6397, fax: 314-516-5408.

UNIVERSITY OF MOBILE
Mobile, Alabama

About the Institution Independent/religious, coed. Degrees awarded: A, B, M. Offers 39 undergraduate majors. Total enrollment: 2,241. Undergraduates: 1,943 (93% state residents). Freshmen: 255.

Undergraduate Expenses (1997–98) Comprehensive fee of $11,816 includes tuition ($7616), mandatory fees ($120), and college room and board ($4080).

Applications 96% of all full-time undergraduates enrolled in fall 1996 applied for aid; of these, 92% were judged to have need according to Federal Methodology, of whom 100% were aided. *Financial aid deadline (priority):* 3/31. *Financial aid forms:* FAFSA, state form, institutional form required. *Admission application deadline:* rolling.

Summary of Aid to Needy Students *From gift & self-help combined:* Average amount awarded: $11,651 (27% gift aid, 73% self-help). *Gift aid:* Total: $3,976,493 (30% from college-administered sources, 70% from external sources). 95 Federal Work-Study jobs (averaging $1275); 75 part-time jobs.

Need-Based Scholarships & Grants Pell, FSEOG, state, private, college/university.

Loans Perkins, PLUS, Stafford, Unsubsidized Stafford, college/university long-term loans ($1100 average).

Non-Need Awards In 1996, a total of 1,074 non-need awards were made. *Academic Interests/Achievement Awards:* 415 ($1,022,076 total): general academic, religion/biblical studies. *Creative Arts/Performance Awards:* 72 ($193,528 total): general creative, art/fine arts, music. *Special Achievements/Activities Awards:* 157 ($130,791 total): Junior Miss, leadership. *Special Characteristics Awards:* 226 ($379,834 total): out-of-state students, religious affiliation. *Athletic:* Total: 204 ($1,029,512); Men: 84 ($474,384); Women: 120 ($555,128).

Other Money-Saving Options Accelerated degree, cooperative Army ROTC, cooperative Air Force ROTC, off-campus living (after junior year). *Waivers:* full or partial for employees or children of employees.

Contact Ms. Lydia Husley, Director of Financial Aid, University of Mobile, Mobile, AL 36663-0220, 334-675-5940 Ext. 252.

THE UNIVERSITY OF MONTANA–MISSOULA
Missoula, Montana

About the Institution State-supported, coed. Degrees awarded: A, B, M, D, P. Offers 90 undergraduate majors. Total enrollment: 11,886. Undergraduates: 9,853 (65% state residents). Freshmen: 2,009.

Undergraduate Expenses (1996–97) State resident tuition: $2484. Nonresident tuition: $6733. College room and board: $3962.

Applications Of all full-time undergraduates enrolled in fall 1996, 87% of those who applied for aid were judged to have need according to Federal Methodology, of whom 92% were aided. *Financial aid deadline (priority):* 3/1. *Financial aid forms:* FAFSA, CSS Financial Aid PROFILE, institutional form required. *Admission application deadline:* 7/1.

Summary of Aid to Needy Students *From gift & self-help combined:* Average need met: 90%. Average amount awarded: $6637 (30% gift aid, 70% self-help). *Gift aid:* Total: $9,135,764 (15% from college's own funds, 23% from other college-administered sources, 62% from external sources). 900 Federal Work-Study jobs (averaging $1500); 2,000 part-time jobs.

Need-Based Scholarships & Grants Pell, FSEOG, state, private, college/university.

Loans Perkins, PLUS, Stafford, Unsubsidized Stafford, private, college/university short-term loans ($200 average).

Non-Need Awards In 1996, a total of 1,317 non-need awards were made. *Academic Interests/Achievement Awards:* 782 ($795,823 total): general academic, biological sciences, business, computer science, education, English, foreign languages, health fields, humanities, international studies, mathematics, physical sciences, premedicine, social sciences. *Creative Arts/Performance Awards:* 200 ($153,500 total): art/fine arts, journalism/publications, music, performing arts, theater/drama. *Special Achievements/Activities Awards:* 55 ($160,000 total): leadership, rodeo. *Special Characteristics Awards:* 77 ($70,000 total):

children and siblings of alumni, members of minorities. *Athletic:* Total: 203 ($1,536,068); Men: 119 ($912,445); Women: 84 ($623,623).

Other Money-Saving Options Co-op program, Army ROTC, off-campus living (after freshman year). *Payment Plan:* installment. *Waivers:* full or partial for minority students and senior citizens.

Contact Financial Aid Office, The University of Montana–Missoula, Missoula, MT 59812-0002, 406-243-5373, fax: 406-243-4930.

UNIVERSITY OF MONTEVALLO
Montevallo, Alabama

About the Institution State-supported, coed. Degrees awarded: B, M. Offers 49 undergraduate majors. Total enrollment: 3,206. Undergraduates: 2,702 (95% state residents). Freshmen: 505.

Undergraduate Expenses (1997–98) State resident tuition: $3040. Nonresident tuition: $6080. Mandatory fees: $140. College room and board: $3116 (minimum).

Applications Of all full-time undergraduates enrolled in fall 1996, 57% of those who applied for aid were judged to have need according to Federal Methodology, of whom 89% were aided. *Financial aid deadline (priority):* 4/1. *Financial aid forms:* FAFSA, institutional form required for some. *Admission application deadline:* 8/1.

Summary of Aid to Needy Students *From gift & self-help combined:* Average need met: 87%. Average amount awarded: $3536 (43% gift aid, 57% self-help). *Gift aid:* Total: $1,718,312 (26% from college's own funds, 14% from other college-administered sources, 60% from external sources). 137 Federal Work-Study jobs (averaging $1288); 306 part-time jobs.

Need-Based Scholarships & Grants Pell, FSEOG, state, college/university.

Loans Perkins, PLUS, Stafford, Unsubsidized Stafford, college/university short-term loans ($100 average).

Non-Need Awards In 1996, a total of 832 non-need awards were made. *Academic Interests/Achievement Awards:* 575 ($1,093,738 total): general academic, biological sciences, education, physical sciences. *Creative Arts/Performance Awards:* 81 ($102,825 total): art/fine arts, music. *Special Achievements/Activities Awards:* 0: Junior Miss. *Special Characteristics Awards:* 64 ($106,221 total): international students, out-of-state students, veterans, veterans' children. *Athletic:* Total: 112 ($433,212); Men: 63 ($221,083); Women: 49 ($212,129).

Other Money-Saving Options Cooperative Army ROTC, cooperative Air Force ROTC, off-campus living (after freshman year). *Waivers:* full or partial for employees or children of employees and senior citizens.

Contact Mr. Clark Aldridge, Director of Student Financial Services, University of Montevallo, Station 6050, Montevallo, AL 35115, 205-665-6050.

UNIVERSITY OF NEBRASKA AT KEARNEY
Kearney, Nebraska

About the Institution State-supported, coed. Degrees awarded: B, M. Offers 92 undergraduate majors. Total enrollment: 7,620. Undergraduates: 6,467 (94% state residents). Freshmen: 1,407.

Undergraduate Expenses (1996–97) State resident tuition: $1823. Nonresident tuition: $3413. Mandatory fees: $322. College room and board: $4100 (minimum). College room only: $1380 (minimum).

Applications 71% of all full-time undergraduates enrolled in fall 1996 applied for aid; of these, 75% were judged to have need according to Federal Methodology, of whom 81% were aided. *Financial aid deadline (priority):* 3/1. *Financial aid forms:* FAFSA, institutional form, federal income tax returns required. CSS Financial Aid PROFILE required for some. *Admission application deadline:* 8/1.

Summary of Aid to Needy Students *From gift & self-help combined:* Average need met: 90%. Average amount awarded: $3169 (42% gift aid, 58% self-help). *Gift aid:* Total: $3,161,804 (32% from college's own funds, 7% from other college-administered sources, 61% from external sources). 706 Federal Work-Study jobs (averaging $2000); 23 part-time jobs.

Need-Based Scholarships & Grants Pell, FSEOG, state, college/university.

Loans Perkins, PLUS, Stafford, Unsubsidized Stafford, college/university short-term loans ($500 average).

Non-Need Awards In 1996, a total of 1,446 non-need awards were made. *Academic Interests/Achievement Awards:* 46 ($10,500 total): general academic, business, English, foreign languages. *Creative Arts/Performance Awards:* 104 ($45,090 total): applied art and design, art/fine arts, cinema/film/broadcasting, creative writing, dance, debating, journalism/publications, music, theater/drama. *Special Achievements/Activities Awards:* 822 ($889,867 total): general special achievements/activities, cheerleading/drum major, leadership, memberships. *Special Characteristics Awards:* 190 ($239,212 total): children of faculty/staff, international students, out-of-state students, veterans, veterans' children. *Athletic:* Total: 284 ($472,612); Men: 158 ($301,351); Women: 126 ($171,261).

Other Money-Saving Options Co-op program, off-campus living (after freshman year). *Payment Plan:* installment.

Contact Financial Aid Office, University of Nebraska at Kearney, 905 West 25th Street, Kearney, NE 68849-0001, 308-865-8520, fax: 308-865-8096.

UNIVERSITY OF NEBRASKA AT OMAHA
Omaha, Nebraska

About the Institution State-supported, coed. Degrees awarded: A, B, M, D. Offers 83 undergraduate majors. Total enrollment: 15,000. Undergraduates: 12,221 (93% state residents). Freshmen: 1,456.

Undergraduate Expenses (1996–97) State resident tuition: $2124. Nonresident tuition: $5735. Mandatory fees: $204.

Applications 82% of all full-time undergraduates enrolled in fall 1996 applied for aid; of these, 81% were judged to have need according to Federal Methodology, of whom 99% were aided. *Financial aid deadline (priority):* 3/1. *Financial aid forms:* FAFSA required. Institutional form required for some. *Admission application deadline:* rolling.

Summary of Aid to Needy Students *Gift aid:* Total: $9,896,554 (37% from college's own funds, 9% from other college-administered sources, 54% from external sources). 250 Federal Work-Study jobs (averaging $2300); 350 part-time jobs.

Need-Based Scholarships & Grants Pell, FSEOG, state, private, college/university.

Loans Perkins, PLUS, Stafford, Unsubsidized Stafford, college/university short-term loans ($200 average).

Non-Need Awards *Academic Interests/Achievement Awards:* general academic, biological sciences, business, communication, computer science, education, engineering/technologies, English, foreign languages, home economics, mathematics, physical sciences, premedicine, social sciences. *Creative Arts/Performance Awards:* art/fine arts, debating, journalism/publications, music. *Special Achievements/Activities Awards:* general special achievements/activities, leadership, memberships. *Special Characteristics Awards:* children of faculty/staff, international students, out-of-state students, veterans' children. *Athletic:* available.

Other Money-Saving Options Co-op program, Air Force ROTC, cooperative Army ROTC. *Payment Plan:* deferred payment.

Contact Office of Financial Aid, University of Nebraska at Omaha, EAB, 60th and Dodge Streets, Omaha, NE 68182, 402-554-2327.

UNIVERSITY OF NEBRASKA–LINCOLN
Lincoln, Nebraska

About the Institution State-supported, coed. Degrees awarded: A, B, M, D, P. Offers 141 undergraduate majors. Total enrollment: 23,887. Undergraduates: 18,954 (90% state residents). Freshmen: 3,715.

Undergraduate Expenses (1996–97) State resident tuition: $2325. Nonresident tuition: $6324. Mandatory fees: $388. College room and board: $3525. College room only: $1538.

Applications 62% of all full-time undergraduates enrolled in fall 1996 applied for aid; of these, 78% were judged to have need according to Federal Methodology, of whom 95% were aided. *Financial aid deadline:* continuous. *Financial aid forms:* FAFSA required. Institutional form required for some. *Admission application deadline:* 6/30.

Summary of Aid to Needy Students *From gift & self-help combined:* Average need met: 75%. Average amount awarded: $4838 (33% gift aid, 67% self-help). *Gift aid:* Total: $12,463,411 (30% from college's own funds, 9% from other college-administered sources, 61% from external sources). 1,920 Federal Work-Study jobs (averaging $2000); part-time jobs.

Need-Based Scholarships & Grants Pell, FSEOG, state, private, college/university.

Loans College/university short-term loans ($540 average).

Non-Need Awards *Academic Interests/Achievement Awards:* general academic, agriculture, architecture, biological sciences, business, computer science, education, engineering/technologies, English, foreign languages, health fields, home economics, humanities, international studies, mathematics, physical sciences, premedicine, social sciences. *Creative Arts/Performance Awards:* art/fine arts, cinema/film/broadcasting, dance, journalism/publications, music, performing arts, theater/drama. *Special Achievements/Activities Awards:* cheerleading/drum major, leadership. *Special Characteristics Awards:* ethnic background, handicapped students, international students, members of minorities, out-of-state students, ROTC participants, veterans' children. *Athletic:* Total: 413 ($2,603,009); Men: 257 ($1,578,102); Women: 156 ($1,024,907).

Other Money-Saving Options Accelerated degree, co-op program, Army ROTC, Naval ROTC, Air Force ROTC, off-campus living (after freshman year). *Waivers:* full or partial for employees or children of employees.

Contact Ms. Jo Tederman, Assistant Director, University of Nebraska–Lincoln, PO Box 880411, Lincoln, NE 68588-0411, 402-472-0561, fax: 402-472-9826.

UNIVERSITY OF NEVADA, LAS VEGAS
Las Vegas, Nevada

About the Institution State-supported, coed. Degrees awarded: B, M, D. Offers 109 undergraduate majors. Total enrollment: 19,682. Undergraduates: 15,313 (80% state residents). Freshmen: 1,569.

Undergraduate Expenses (1997–98) State resident tuition: $1995. Nonresident tuition: $7430. Mandatory fees: $50. College room and board: $5300.

Applications Of all full-time undergraduates enrolled in fall 1996, 88% of those judged to have need according to Federal Methodology were aided. *Financial aid deadline (priority):* 2/1. *Financial aid forms:* FAFSA required. State form required for some. *Admission application deadline:* 8/15.

Summary of Aid to Needy Students *From gift & self-help combined:* Average amount awarded: $2660 (32% gift aid, 68% self-help). *Gift aid:* Total: $6,185,949 (3% from college's own funds, 42% from other college-administered sources, 55% from external sources). 193 Federal Work-Study jobs (averaging $1600); part-time jobs.

Need-Based Scholarships & Grants Pell, FSEOG, state, private, college/university.

Loans Perkins, PLUS, Stafford, Unsubsidized Stafford, private, college/university short-term loans ($200 average), college/university long-term loans ($1500 average).

Non-Need Awards In 1996, a total of 1,551 non-need awards were made. *Academic Interests/Achievement Awards:* 684 ($959,934 total): general academic, architecture, biological sciences, business, communication, computer science, education, engineering/technologies, English, health fields, humanities, international studies, mathematics, physical sciences, premedicine, social sciences. *Creative Arts/Performance Awards:* 58 ($41,400 total): applied art and design, art/fine arts, cinema/film/broadcasting, dance, journalism/publications, music, performing arts, theater/drama. *Special Achievements/Activities Awards:* 78 ($39,925 total): general special achievements/activities, cheerleading/drum major, community service, hobbies/interest, leadership, memberships, rodeo. *Special Characteristics Awards:* 503 ($593,945 total): general special characteristics, children and siblings of alumni, children of faculty/staff, children of public servants, children of workers in trades, ethnic background, first-generation college students, handicapped students, international students, local/state students, members of minorities, out-of-state students. *Athletic:* Total: 228 ($2,183,288); Men: 156 ($1,433,820); Women: 72 ($749,468).

Other Money-Saving Options Accelerated degree, co-op program, off-campus living (after freshman year). *Payment Plan:* deferred payment. *Waivers:* full or partial for children of alumni, employees or children of employees, senior citizens.

Contact Ms. Cheryl Dedrickson, Assistant Director, Student Financial Services, University of Nevada, Las Vegas, Box 452016, Las Vegas, NV 89154-2016, 702-895-4113, fax: 702-895-1353.

UNIVERSITY OF NEVADA, RENO
Reno, Nevada

About the Institution State-supported, coed. Degrees awarded: B, M, D, P. Offers 71 undergraduate majors. Total enrollment: 11,652. Undergraduates: 8,558 (80% state residents). Freshmen: 1,224.

Undergraduate Expenses (1996–97) State resident tuition: $1920. Nonresident tuition: $7020. Mandatory fees: $114. College room and board: $4695. College room only: $2745.

Applications 84% of all full-time undergraduates enrolled in fall 1996 applied for aid; of these, 95% were judged to have need according to Federal Methodology, of whom 88% were aided. *Financial aid deadline (priority):* 3/1. *Financial aid forms:* FAFSA required. *Admission application deadline:* 3/1.

Summary of Aid to Needy Students *From gift & self-help combined:* Average need met: 73%. Average amount awarded: $2911 (38% gift aid, 62% self-help). *Gift aid:* Total: $5,494,806 (2% from college's own funds, 34% from other college-administered sources, 64% from external sources). 182 Federal Work-Study jobs (averaging $2700); 2,000 part-time jobs.

Need-Based Scholarships & Grants Pell, FSEOG, state, private, college/university.

Loans Perkins, PLUS, Stafford, Unsubsidized Stafford, Federal Nursing, Primary Care, college/university short-term loans ($200 average), college/university long-term loans ($2000 average).

Non-Need Awards In 1996, a total of 2,826 non-need awards were made. *Academic Interests/Achievement Awards:* 1,830 ($1,841,197 total): general academic, agriculture, area/ethnic studies, biological sciences, business, computer science, education, engineering/technologies, English, foreign languages, health fields, humanities, international studies, mathematics, military science, physical sciences, premedicine, social sciences. *Creative Arts/Performance Awards:* 286 ($349,547 total): applied art and design, art/fine arts, dance, debating, journalism/publications, music, theater/drama. *Special Achievements/*

Activities Awards: 86 ($70,801 total): cheerleading/drum major, leadership. *Special Characteristics Awards:* 455 ($548,777 total): children and siblings of alumni, children of faculty/staff, ethnic background, first-generation college students, international students, members of minorities, ROTC participants. *Athletic:* Total: 169 ($2,023,786); Men: 111 ($1,301,197); Women: 58 ($722,589).

Other Money-Saving Options Co-op program, Army ROTC, off-campus living. *Payment Plan:* deferred payment. *Waivers:* full or partial for children of alumni, employees or children of employees, senior citizens.

Contact Dr. Nancee Langley, Director of Student Financial Services, University of Nevada, Reno, 200 Thompson, Mail Stop 076, Reno, NV 89557, 702-784-1288, fax: 702-784-1025.

UNIVERSITY OF NEW ENGLAND
Biddeford, Maine

About the Institution Independent, coed. Degrees awarded: A, B, M, P. Offers 40 undergraduate majors. Total enrollment: 1,892. Undergraduates: 1,000 (53% state residents). Freshmen: 273.

Undergraduate Expenses (1997–98) Comprehensive fee of $19,680 includes tuition ($13,575), mandatory fees ($510), and college room and board ($5595).

Applications Of all full-time undergraduates enrolled in fall 1996, 91% of those who applied for aid were judged to have need according to Federal Methodology, of whom 100% were aided. *Financial aid deadline (priority):* 5/1. *Financial aid forms:* FAFSA, state form, institutional form required; CSS Financial Aid PROFILE acceptable. *Regular admission application deadline:* rolling. Early decision deadline: 11/15.

Summary of Aid to Needy Students *From gift & self-help combined:* Average need met: 65%. Average amount awarded: $9265 (36% gift aid, 64% self-help). *Gift aid:* Total: $2,601,384 (59% from college's own funds, 7% from other college-administered sources, 34% from external sources). 288 Federal Work-Study jobs (averaging $850); 10 part-time jobs.

Need-Based Scholarships & Grants Pell, FSEOG, state, private, college/university.

Loans Perkins, PLUS, Stafford, Unsubsidized Stafford, Federal Nursing, Primary Care, private, college/university short-term loans ($100 average).

Non-Need Awards In 1996, a total of 160 non-need awards were made. *Academic Interests/Achievement Awards:* 93 ($213,400 total): general academic, biological sciences. *Special Achievements/Activities Awards:* 52 ($122,500 total): community service, hobbies/interest, leadership. *Special Characteristics Awards:* 15 ($85,807 total): children of faculty/staff.

Other Money-Saving Options Accelerated degree, co-op program, cooperative Army ROTC, off-campus living (after sophomore year). *Payment Plans:* installment, deferred payment. *Waivers:* full or partial for employees or children of employees.

Contact Financial Aid Office, University of New England, 11 Hills Beach Road, Biddeford, ME 04005-9526, 207-283-0171.

UNIVERSITY OF NEW HAMPSHIRE
Durham, New Hampshire

About the Institution State-supported, coed. Degrees awarded: A, B, M, D. Offers 133 undergraduate majors. Total enrollment: 12,454. Undergraduates: 10,649 (60% state residents). Freshmen: 2,622.

Undergraduate Expenses (1996–97) State resident tuition: $4020. Nonresident tuition: $12,540. Mandatory fees: $1241. College room and board: $4354 (minimum). College room only: $2554.

Applications *Financial aid deadline:* Applications processed continuously. *Financial aid forms:* FAFSA required; prose documentation acceptable. *Regular admission application deadline:* 2/1. Early action deadline: 12/1.

Summary of Aid to Needy Students Federal Work-Study jobs; part-time jobs.

Loans College/university short-term loans, college/university long-term loans.

Non-Need Awards *Academic Interests/Achievement Awards:* general academic. *Creative Arts/Performance Awards:* music. *Athletic:* available.

Other Money-Saving Options Accelerated degree, Army ROTC, Air Force ROTC, off-campus living. *Waivers:* full or partial for minority students, employees or children of employees, senior citizens.

Contact Office of Financial Aid, University of New Hampshire, Stoke Hall, Durham, NH 03824, 603-862-1234.

UNIVERSITY OF NEW HAMPSHIRE AT MANCHESTER
Manchester, New Hampshire

About the Institution State-supported, coed. Degrees awarded: A, B. Offers 14 undergraduate majors. Total enrollment: 719 (98% state residents). Freshmen: 113.

Undergraduate Expenses (1996–97) State resident tuition: $3520. Nonresident tuition: $10,490. Mandatory fees: $46.

Applications Of all full-time undergraduates enrolled in fall 1996, 81% of those who applied for aid were judged to have need according to Federal Methodology, of whom 91% were aided. *Financial aid deadline (priority):* 5/1. *Financial aid forms:* FAFSA required. *Admission application deadline:* 6/15.

Summary of Aid to Needy Students *From gift & self-help combined:* Average need met: 60%. Average amount awarded: $4797 (19% gift aid, 81% self-help). *Gift aid:* Total: $249,994 (3% from college's own funds, 27% from other college-administered sources, 70% from external sources). 83 Federal Work-Study jobs (averaging $1753); 15 part-time jobs.

Need-Based Scholarships & Grants Pell, FSEOG, state, college/university.

Loans Perkins, PLUS, Stafford, Unsubsidized Stafford.

Non-Need Awards *Academic Interests/Achievement Awards:* general academic. *Special Characteristics Awards:* ($22,000 total): children of faculty/staff, ethnic background, members of minorities.

Other Money-Saving Options Cooperative Army ROTC, cooperative Air Force ROTC. *Payment Plan:* installment. *Waivers:* full or partial for employees or children of employees and senior citizens.

Contact Ms. Steffani Stoddard, Assistant Director of Financial Aid, University of New Hampshire at Manchester, 220 Hackett Hill Road, Manchester, NH 03102-8597, 603-668-0700, fax: 603-623-2745.

UNIVERSITY OF NEW HAVEN
West Haven, Connecticut

About the Institution Independent, coed. Degrees awarded: A, B, M, D. Offers 59 undergraduate majors. Total enrollment: 5,438. Undergraduates: 3,004 (74% state residents). Freshmen: 411.

Undergraduate Expenses (1997–98) Comprehensive fee of $18,800 includes tuition ($12,800), mandatory fees ($300), and college room and board ($5700 minimum). College room only: $3600.

Applications 71% of all full-time undergraduates enrolled in fall 1996 applied for aid. *Financial aid deadline (priority):* 3/15. *Financial aid forms:* FAFSA, CSS Financial Aid PROFILE, institutional form required. *Admission application deadline:* 9/1.

Summary of Aid to Needy Students *From gift & self-help combined:* Average amount awarded: $9101 (42% gift aid, 58% self-help). *Gift aid:* Total: $4,335,299 (45% from college's own funds, 41% from other college-administered sources, 14% from external sources). 215 Federal Work-Study jobs (averaging $1200); 170 part-time jobs.

Need-Based Scholarships & Grants Pell, FSEOG, state, private, college/university.

Loans Perkins, PLUS, Stafford, Unsubsidized Stafford, private.

Non-Need Awards In 1996, a total of 284 non-need awards were made. *Academic Interests/Achievement Awards:* 118 ($536,725 total): general academic. *Athletic:* Total: 166 ($1,205,292).

Other Money-Saving Options Co-op program, cooperative Air Force ROTC. *Payment Plan:* installment. *Waivers:* full or partial for employees or children of employees and senior citizens.

Contact Ms. Jane Sangeloty, Director of Financial Aid, University of New Haven, 300 Orange Avenue, West Haven, CT 06516-1916, 203-932-7315, fax: 203-931-6093.

UNIVERSITY OF NEW MEXICO
Albuquerque, New Mexico

About the Institution State-supported, coed. Degrees awarded: A, B, M, D, P. Offers 105 undergraduate majors. Total enrollment: 23,617. Undergraduates: 15,056 (92% state residents). Freshmen: 1,587.

Undergraduate Expenses (1997–98) State resident tuition: $2165. Nonresident tuition: $8174. College room and board: $4314.

Applications 67% of all full-time undergraduates enrolled in fall 1996 applied for aid; of these, 87% were judged to have need according to Federal Methodology, of whom 100% were aided. *Financial aid deadline (priority):* 3/1. *Financial aid forms:* FAFSA, institutional form required. *Admission application deadline:* 7/20.

Summary of Aid to Needy Students *From gift & self-help combined:* Average need met: 76%. Average amount awarded: $6106 (31% gift aid, 69% self-help). *Gift aid:* Total: $18,631,294 (35% from college's own funds, 27% from other college-administered sources, 38% from external sources). 2,583 Federal Work-Study jobs (averaging $3359); 2,189 part-time jobs.

Need-Based Scholarships & Grants Pell, FSEOG, state, private.

Loans Perkins, Stafford, Unsubsidized Stafford, Federal Nursing, Primary Care, private, college/university short-term loans ($500 average).

Non-Need Awards In 1996, a total of 2,776 non-need awards were made. *Academic Interests/Achievement Awards:* 1,405 ($2,726,831 total): general academic, engineering/technologies. *Creative Arts/Performance Awards:* 400 ($320,000 total): art/fine arts, music, theater/drama. *Special Characteristics Awards:* 650 ($1,350,000 total): children of faculty/staff, children of union members/company employees, members of minorities, out-of-state students, ROTC participants, veterans. *Athletic:* Total: 321 ($2,545,999).

Other Money-Saving Options Co-op program, Army ROTC, Air Force ROTC, off-campus living. *Payment Plan:* installment. *Waivers:* full or partial for employees or children of employees and senior citizens.

Contact Office of Financial Aid, University of New Mexico, Mesa Vista North, Albuquerque, NM 87131-2081, 505-277-5017, fax: 505-277-6326.

UNIVERSITY OF NORTH ALABAMA
Florence, Alabama

About the Institution State-supported, coed. Degrees awarded: B, M. Offers 57 undergraduate majors. Total enrollment: 5,529. Undergraduates: 4,960 (88% state residents). Freshmen: 807.

Undergraduate Expenses (1996–97) State resident tuition: $1902. Nonresident tuition: $3804. Mandatory fees: $96. College room and board: $3130. College room only: $1470.

Applications 61% of all full-time undergraduates enrolled in fall 1996 applied for aid; of these, 85% were judged to have need according to Federal Methodology, of whom 93% were aided. *Financial aid deadline (priority):* 4/1. *Financial aid forms:* FAFSA required; CSS Financial Aid PROFILE acceptable. *Admission application deadline:* rolling.

Summary of Aid to Needy Students *From gift & self-help combined:* Average need met: 75%. Average amount awarded: $2029 (44% gift aid, 56% self-help). *Gift aid:* Total: $4,506,431 (33% from college's own funds, 8% from other college-administered sources, 59% from external sources). 215 Federal Work-Study jobs (averaging $2049); 317 part-time jobs.

Need-Based Scholarships & Grants Pell, FSEOG, state, private.

Loans Perkins, PLUS, Stafford, Unsubsidized Stafford, college/university short-term loans ($200 average).

Non-Need Awards In 1996, a total of 963 non-need awards were made. *Academic Interests/Achievement Awards:* 271 ($320,009 total): general academic. *Creative Arts/Performance Awards:* 220 ($134,367 total): journalism/publications, music. *Special Achievements/Activities Awards:* 141 ($136,574 total): general special achievements/activities, cheerleading/drum major, leadership. *Special Characteristics Awards:* 158 ($156,893 total): general special characteristics, children of faculty/staff, first-generation college students, out-of-state students, ROTC participants. *Athletic:* Total: 173 ($421,270); Men: 118 ($288,847); Women: 55 ($132,423).

Other Money-Saving Options Co-op program, Army ROTC, off-campus living. *Waivers:* full or partial for employees or children of employees.

Contact Dr. Jo Weaver, Director of Financial Aid, University of North Alabama, PO Box 5014, Florence, AL 35632-0001, 205-765-4278, fax: 205-765-4920.

UNIVERSITY OF NORTH CAROLINA AT ASHEVILLE
Asheville, North Carolina

About the Institution State-supported, coed. Degrees awarded: B, M. Offers 35 undergraduate majors. Total enrollment: 3,092. Undergraduates: 3,036 (89% state residents). Freshmen: 455.

Undergraduate Expenses (1996–97) State resident tuition: $730. Nonresident tuition: $7046. Mandatory fees: $1043. College room and board: $3650.

Applications 84% of all full-time undergraduates enrolled in fall 1996 applied for aid; of these, 51% were judged to have need according to Federal Methodology, of whom 97% were aided. *Financial aid deadline (priority):* 3/1. *Financial aid forms:* FAFSA, state form required. *Regular admission application deadline:* 4/15. Early action deadline: 10/15.

Summary of Aid to Needy Students *From gift & self-help combined:* Average need met: 80%. Average amount awarded: $5681 (33% gift aid, 67% self-help). *Gift aid:* Total: $1,714,515 (24% from college's own funds, 63% from other college-administered sources, 13% from external sources). 69 Federal Work-Study jobs (averaging $870); 542 part-time jobs.

Need-Based Scholarships & Grants Pell, FSEOG, state, private, college/university.

Loans Perkins, PLUS, Stafford, Unsubsidized Stafford, college/university short-term loans ($2336 average).

Non-Need Awards In 1996, a total of 705 non-need awards were made. *Academic Interests/Achievement Awards:* 339 ($664,471 total): general academic. *Creative Arts/Performance Awards:* 21 ($15,512 total): art/fine arts, music, theater/drama. *Special Characteristics Awards:* 201 ($240,821 total): children of faculty/staff, handicapped students,

---

local/state students, members of minorities, veterans, veterans' children. *Athletic:* Total: 144 ($625,950); Men: 80 ($320,546); Women: 64 ($305,404).

Other Money-Saving Options Accelerated degree, off-campus living (after freshman year). *Payment Plan:* installment. *Waivers:* full or partial for employees or children of employees and senior citizens.

Contact Mrs. V. Carolyn McElrath, Director of Financial Aid, University of North Carolina at Asheville, One University Heights, Asheville, NC 28804-3299, 704-251-6535.

THE UNIVERSITY OF NORTH CAROLINA AT CHAPEL HILL
Chapel Hill, North Carolina

About the Institution State-supported, coed. Degrees awarded: B, M, D, P. Offers 69 undergraduate majors. Total enrollment: 24,141. Undergraduates: 15,363 (82% state residents). Freshmen: 3,278.

Undergraduate Expenses (1996–97) State resident tuition: $1386. Nonresident tuition: $9918. Mandatory fees: $775. College room and board: $4500. College room only: $2110.

Applications Of all full-time undergraduates enrolled in fall 1996, 67% of those who applied for aid were judged to have need according to Federal Methodology, of whom 97% were aided. *Financial aid deadline (priority):* 3/1. *Financial aid forms:* FAFSA, CSS Financial Aid PROFILE required. *Admission application deadline:* 1/15.

Summary of Aid to Needy Students *From gift & self-help combined:* Average need met: 95%. Average amount awarded: $6557 (48% gift aid, 52% self-help). *Gift aid:* Total: $12,969,240 (48% from college's own funds, 7% from other college-administered sources, 45% from external sources). 650 Federal Work-Study jobs (averaging $960); 5,000 part-time jobs.

Need-Based Scholarships & Grants Pell, FSEOG, state, private, college/university.

Loans Perkins, PLUS, Stafford, Unsubsidized Stafford, Primary Care, state, private, college/university short-term loans ($500 average), college/university long-term loans ($1450 average).

Non-Need Awards *Academic Interests/Achievement Awards:* 186 ($705,613 total): general academic. *Athletic:* available.

Other Money-Saving Options Accelerated degree, Army ROTC, Naval ROTC, Air Force ROTC, off-campus living.

Contact Mr. Stuart B. Bethune, Associate Director, office of Scholarships and Student Aid, The University of North Carolina at Chapel Hill, PO Box 1080, Chapel Hill, NC 27514, 919-962-4161, fax: 919-962-2716.

UNIVERSITY OF NORTH CAROLINA AT CHARLOTTE
Charlotte, North Carolina

About the Institution State-supported, coed. Degrees awarded: B, M, D. Offers 50 undergraduate majors. Total enrollment: 15,795. Undergraduates: 13,147 (88% state residents). Freshmen: 1,719.

Undergraduate Expenses (1996–97) State resident tuition: $874. Nonresident tuition: $8028. Mandatory fees: $844. College room and board: $3120 (minimum). College room only: $2040 (minimum).

Applications Of all full-time undergraduates enrolled in fall 1996, 86% of those who applied for aid were judged to have need according to Federal Methodology, of whom 95% were aided. *Financial aid deadline (priority):* 4/1. *Financial aid forms:* FAFSA required. *Regular admission application deadline:* 7/1. Early action deadline: 11/1.

Summary of Aid to Needy Students *From gift & self-help combined:* Average need met: 76%. Average amount awarded: $4776 (25% gift aid, 75% self-help). *Gift aid:* Total: $6,052,355 (5% from college's own funds, 21% from other college-administered sources, 74% from external sources). 380 Federal Work-Study jobs (averaging $1500); 1,800 part-time jobs.

Need-Based Scholarships & Grants Pell, FSEOG, state, private, college/university.

Loans Perkins, PLUS, Stafford, Unsubsidized Stafford, state, private, college/university short-term loans ($500 average), college/university long-term loans ($1950 average).

Non-Need Awards In 1996, a total of 623 non-need awards were made. *Academic Interests/Achievement Awards:* 450 ($618,500 total): general academic, architecture, business, computer science, engineering/technologies, health fields, mathematics. *Special Characteristics Awards:* 10 ($8700 total): adult students. *Athletic:* Total: 163 ($927,029); Men: 93 ($474,235); Women: 70 ($452,794).

Other Money-Saving Options Co-op program, Army ROTC, Air Force ROTC, off-campus living. *Waivers:* full or partial for senior citizens.

Contact Office of Financial Aid, University of North Carolina at Charlotte, 9201 University City Boulevard, Charlotte, NC 28223-0001, 704-547-2000.

UNIVERSITY OF NORTH CAROLINA AT GREENSBORO
Greensboro, North Carolina

About the Institution State-supported, coed. Degrees awarded: B, M, D. Offers 112 undergraduate majors. Total enrollment: 12,323. Undergraduates: 9,694 (90% state residents). Freshmen: 1,567.

Undergraduate Expenses (1996–97) State resident tuition: $986. Nonresident tuition: $9304. Mandatory fees: $957. College room and board: $3505. College room only: $1715.

Applications Of all full-time undergraduates enrolled in fall 1996, 81% of those who applied for aid were judged to have need according to Federal Methodology, of whom 96% were aided. *Financial aid deadline (priority):* 3/1. *Financial aid forms:* FAFSA required. *Admission application deadline:* 8/1.

Summary of Aid to Needy Students *From gift & self-help combined:* Average need met: 67%. Average amount awarded: $5683 (32% gift aid, 68% self-help). *Gift aid:* Total: $6,757,157 (23% from college's own funds, 18% from other college-administered sources, 59% from external sources). 325 Federal Work-Study jobs (averaging $1500); part-time jobs.

Need-Based Scholarships & Grants Pell, FSEOG, state, private, college/university.

Loans Perkins, PLUS, Stafford, Unsubsidized Stafford, college/university short-term loans ($200 average), college/university long-term loans ($1000 average).

Non-Need Awards In 1996, a total of 203 non-need awards were made. *Academic Interests/Achievement Awards:* general academic, biological sciences, business, communication, education, English, foreign languages, health fields, home economics, humanities, library science, mathematics, physical sciences, premedicine, religion/biblical studies, social sciences. *Creative Arts/Performance Awards:* music, performing arts. *Athletic:* Total: 153 ($872,646); Men: 82 ($414,581); Women: 71 ($458,065).

Other Money-Saving Options Accelerated degree, cooperative Army ROTC, cooperative Air Force ROTC, off-campus living. *Waivers:* full or partial for employees or children of employees and senior citizens.

Contact Mr. Eric Locklear, Associate Director of Financial Aid, University of North Carolina at Greensboro, Greensboro, NC 27412-0001, 910-334-4230, fax: 910-334-3010.

UNIVERSITY OF NORTH CAROLINA AT PEMBROKE
Pembroke, North Carolina

About the Institution State-supported, coed. Degrees awarded: B, M. Offers 45 undergraduate majors. Total enrollment: 3,006. Undergraduates: 2,690 (98% state residents). Freshmen: 465.

Undergraduate Expenses (1996–97) State resident tuition: $874. Nonresident tuition: $8028. Mandatory fees: $593. College room and board: $3320. College room only: $1410 (minimum).

Applications 89% of all full-time undergraduates enrolled in fall 1996 applied for aid; of these, 79% were judged to have need according to Federal Methodology, of whom 91% were aided. *Financial aid deadline (priority):* 3/15. *Financial aid forms:* FAFSA, institutional form required. *Admission application deadline:* 7/15.

Summary of Aid to Needy Students *From gift & self-help combined:* Average need met: 77%. Average amount awarded: $3663 (62% gift aid, 38% self-help). *Gift aid:* Total: $2,331,703 (6% from college's own funds, 29% from other college-administered sources, 65% from external sources). 152 Federal Work-Study jobs (averaging $898); 72 part-time jobs.

Need-Based Scholarships & Grants Pell, FSEOG, state, private, college/university.

Loans Perkins, PLUS, Stafford, Unsubsidized Stafford, college/university short-term loans ($300 average), college/university long-term loans ($2547 average).

Non-Need Awards In 1996, a total of 490 non-need awards were made. *Academic Interests/Achievement Awards:* 75 ($130,925 total): general academic, business, communication, education, English, health fields, physical sciences. *Creative Arts/Performance Awards:* 11 ($4375 total): journalism/publications, music. *Special Characteristics Awards:* 281 ($327,879 total): children and siblings of alumni, members of minorities. *Athletic:* Total: 123 ($224,968); Men: 74 ($124,228); Women: 49 ($100,740).

Other Money-Saving Options Accelerated degree, co-op program, Army ROTC, Air Force ROTC, off-campus living. *Payment Plan:* installment. *Waivers:* full or partial for senior citizens.

Contact Ms. Mildred Weber, Program Assistant, University of North Carolina at Pembroke, PO Box 1510, Pembroke, NC 28372-1510, 910-521-6612, fax: 910-521-6497.

UNIVERSITY OF NORTH CAROLINA AT WILMINGTON
Wilmington, North Carolina

About the Institution State-supported, coed. Degrees awarded: B, M. Offers 43 undergraduate majors. Total enrollment: 9,077. Undergraduates: 8,584 (87% state residents). Freshmen: 1,670.

Undergraduate Expenses (1996–97) State resident tuition: $874. Nonresident tuition: $8028. Mandatory fees: $874. College room and board: $3900 (minimum).

Applications Of all full-time undergraduates enrolled in fall 1996, 79% of those who applied for aid were judged to have need according to Federal Methodology, of whom 84% were aided. *Financial aid deadline (priority):* 3/15. *Financial aid forms:* FAFSA, financial aid transcript (for transfers) required; state form acceptable. *Admission application deadline:* rolling.

Summary of Aid to Needy Students *From gift & self-help combined:* Average need met: 97%. Average amount awarded: $2161 (93% gift aid, 7% self-help). *Gift aid:* Total: $2,870,560. Federal Work-Study jobs; 780 part-time jobs.

Need-Based Scholarships & Grants Pell, FSEOG, state, private, college/university.

Loans Perkins, PLUS, Stafford, Unsubsidized Stafford, state, private, college/university short-term loans ($200 average).

Non-Need Awards *Academic Interests/Achievement Awards:* general academic, biological sciences, business, communication, computer science, education, English, foreign languages, health fields, humanities, mathematics, physical sciences, social sciences. *Creative Arts/Performance Awards:* art/fine arts, music. *Special Achievements/Activities Awards:* general special achievements/activities. *Special Characteristics Awards:* local/state students, members of minorities. *Athletic:* Total: 195 ($417,030); Men: 108 ($220,399); Women: 87 ($196,631).

Other Money-Saving Options Accelerated degree, co-op program, off-campus living. *Payment Plan:* installment. *Waivers:* full or partial for employees or children of employees and senior citizens.

Contact Office of Financial Aid, University of North Carolina at Wilmington, Wilmington, NC 28403-3201, 910-962-3177.

UNIVERSITY OF NORTH DAKOTA
Grand Forks, North Dakota

About the Institution State-supported, coed. Degrees awarded: B, M, D, P. Offers 112 undergraduate majors. Total enrollment: 11,300. Undergraduates: 9,351 (56% state residents). Freshmen: 1,654.

Undergraduate Expenses (1996–97) State resident tuition: $2528. Nonresident tuition: $6052. Mandatory fees: $418. College room and board: $2910. College room only: $1122.

Applications 64% of all full-time undergraduates enrolled in fall 1996 applied for aid; of these, 56% were judged to have need according to Federal Methodology, of whom 100% were aided. *Financial aid deadline (priority):* 4/15. *Financial aid forms:* FAFSA required. Institutional form required for some. *Admission application deadline:* 7/1.

Summary of Aid to Needy Students *From gift & self-help combined:* Average need met: 70%. Average amount awarded: $6000 (37% gift aid, 63% self-help). *Gift aid:* Total: $6,095,088 (18% from college's own funds, 21% from other college-administered sources, 61% from external sources). 1,466 Federal Work-Study jobs (averaging $1800); 1,362 part-time jobs.

Need-Based Scholarships & Grants Pell, FSEOG, state, private, college/university.

Loans Perkins, PLUS, Stafford, Unsubsidized Stafford, Federal Nursing, Primary Care, private, college/university short-term loans ($300 average), college/university long-term loans ($1378 average).

Non-Need Awards In 1996, a total of 1,788 non-need awards were made. *Academic Interests/Achievement Awards:* general academic. *Creative Arts/Performance Awards:* art/fine arts, music, theater/drama. *Special Characteristics Awards:* 66 ($101,239 total): members of minorities, ROTC participants. *Athletic:* Total: 235 ($608,914).

Other Money-Saving Options Accelerated degree, co-op program, Army ROTC, off-campus living. *Waivers:* full or partial for employees or children of employees and senior citizens.

Contact Ms. Alice Hoffert, Director, Student Financial Aid, University of North Dakota, Box 8371, Grand Forks, ND 58202, 701-777-3121, fax: 701-777-2040.

UNIVERSITY OF NORTHERN COLORADO
Greeley, Colorado

About the Institution State-supported, coed. Degrees awarded: B, M, D. Offers 68 undergraduate majors. Total enrollment: 10,306. Undergraduates: 8,569 (88% state residents). Freshmen: 1,653.

Undergraduate Expenses (1996–97) State resident tuition: $1914. Nonresident tuition: $8416. Mandatory fees: $464. College room and board: $4270 (minimum).

Applications 77% of all full-time undergraduates enrolled in fall 1996 applied for aid; of these, 69% were judged to have need according to Federal Methodology, of whom 94% were aided. *Financial aid deadline (priority):* 3/1. *Financial aid forms:* FAFSA required. *Admission application deadline:* rolling.

Summary of Aid to Needy Students *From gift & self-help combined:* Average need met: 82%. Average amount awarded: $7709 (23% gift aid, 77% self-help). *Gift aid:* Total: $7,006,082 (11% from college's own funds, 29% from other college-administered sources, 60% from external sources). 264 Federal Work-Study jobs (averaging $2115); 3,106 part-time jobs.

Need-Based Scholarships & Grants Pell, FSEOG, state, private, college/university.

Loans Perkins, PLUS, Stafford, Unsubsidized Stafford, private, college/university short-term loans ($1112 average), college/university long-term loans ($3430 average).

Non-Need Awards In 1996, a total of 2,619 non-need awards were made. *Academic Interests/Achievement Awards:* 907 ($697,381 total): general academic, biological sciences, business, communication, education, English, health fields, home economics, mathematics, military science, physical sciences, social sciences. *Creative Arts/Performance Awards:* 416 ($276,534 total): dance, music, performing arts, theater/drama. *Special Characteristics Awards:* 1,006 ($1,514,210 total): general special characteristics, adult students, children and siblings of alumni, children of faculty/staff, children of union members/company employees, ethnic background, handicapped students, international students, local/state students, members of minorities, out-of-state students, ROTC participants, veterans. *Athletic:* Total: 290 ($538,015).

Other Money-Saving Options Accelerated degree, co-op program, Army ROTC, Air Force ROTC, off-campus living (after freshman year). *Payment Plan:* deferred payment. *Waivers:* full or partial for employees or children of employees.

Contact Ms. Shannon Sheaf, Assistant Director, University of Northern Colorado, Carter Hall 1005, Greeley, CO 80639, 970-351-2502, fax: 970-351-3737.

UNIVERSITY OF NORTHERN IOWA
Cedar Falls, Iowa

About the Institution State-supported, coed. Degrees awarded: B, M, D. Offers 102 undergraduate majors. Total enrollment: 12,957. Undergraduates: 11,587 (94% state residents). Freshmen: 2,051.

Undergraduate Expenses (1996–97) State resident tuition: $2470. Nonresident tuition: $6688. Mandatory fees: $180. College room and board: $3264.

Applications *Financial aid deadline (priority):* 2/15. *Financial aid forms:* FAFSA required; CSS Financial Aid PROFILE acceptable. Institutional form required for some. *Admission application deadline:* rolling.

Summary of Aid to Needy Students *From gift & self-help combined:* Average need met: 100%. Average amount awarded: $9400 (16% gift aid, 84% self-help). *Gift aid:* Total: $10,199,303 (37% from college's own funds, 10% from other college-administered sources, 53% from external sources). 399 Federal Work-Study jobs (averaging $1786); 2,500 part-time jobs.

Need-Based Scholarships & Grants Pell, FSEOG, state, private, college/university.

Loans Perkins, PLUS, Stafford, Unsubsidized Stafford, college/university short-term loans ($300 average).

Non-Need Awards *Academic Interests/Achievement Awards:* general academic, biological sciences, business, education, mathematics, physical sciences, social sciences. *Creative Arts/Performance Awards:* applied art and design, art/fine arts, music, theater/drama. *Special Achievements/Activities Awards:* leadership. *Special Characteristics Awards:* general special characteristics, members of minorities. *Athletic:* Total: 242 ($1,132,681); Men: 149 ($744,039); Women: 93 ($388,642).

Other Money-Saving Options Accelerated degree, co-op program, Army ROTC, off-campus living. *Payment Plan:* installment.

Contact Office of Financial Aid, University of Northern Iowa, 116 Gilchrist Hall, Cedar Falls, IA 50614-0024, 319-273-2311.

UNIVERSITY OF NORTH FLORIDA
Jacksonville, Florida

About the Institution State-supported, coed. Degrees awarded: A, B, M, D. Offers 59 undergraduate majors. Total enrollment: 10,909. Undergraduates: 9,624 (91% state residents). Freshmen: 795.

Undergraduate Expenses (1997–98) State resident tuition: $2006. Nonresident tuition: $7923. College room and board: $2940 (minimum). College room only: $1960 (minimum).

Applications Of all full-time undergraduates enrolled in fall 1996, 64% of those who applied for aid were judged to have need according to Federal Methodology, of whom 96% were aided. *Financial aid deadline (priority):* 4/1. *Financial aid forms:* FAFSA, financial aid transcript (for transfers) required; CSS Financial Aid PROFILE acceptable. State form required for some. *Admission application deadline:* 6/1.

Summary of Aid to Needy Students *From gift & self-help combined:* Average need met: 85%. Average amount awarded: $5780 (37% gift aid, 63% self-help). *Gift aid:* Total: $4,205,262 (21% from college's own funds, 3% from other college-administered sources, 76% from external sources). 68 Federal Work-Study jobs (averaging $1590); 517 part-time jobs.

Need-Based Scholarships & Grants Pell, FSEOG, state, college/university.

Loans Perkins, PLUS, Stafford, Unsubsidized Stafford.

Non-Need Awards In 1996, a total of 834 non-need awards were made. *Academic Interests/Achievement Awards:* 520 ($822,595 total): general academic. *Creative Arts/Performance Awards:* 69 ($62,975 total): music. *Special Achievements/Activities Awards:* 70 ($124,120 total): general special achievements/activities, leadership. *Special Characteristics Awards:* 24 ($22,000 total): members of minorities. *Athletic:* Total: 151 ($360,777); Men: 77 ($200,431); Women: 74 ($160,346).

Other Money-Saving Options Accelerated degree, co-op program, Naval ROTC, off-campus living. *Payment Plan:* deferred payment. *Waivers:* full or partial for senior citizens.

Contact Mrs. Janice Nowak, Director of Financial Aid, University of North Florida, 4567 St. Johns Bluff Road, South, Jacksonville, FL 32224-2645, 904-646-2604, fax: 904-646-2703.

UNIVERSITY OF NORTH TEXAS
Denton, Texas

About the Institution State-supported, coed. Degrees awarded: B, M, D. Offers 93 undergraduate majors. Total enrollment: 24,957. Undergraduates: 18,665 (91% state residents). Freshmen: 2,288.

Undergraduate Expenses (1996–97) State resident tuition: $960. Nonresident tuition: $7380. Mandatory fees: $1084. College room and board: $3767. College room only: $1877.

Applications *Financial aid deadline (priority):* 6/1. *Financial aid forms:* FAFSA required. Financial aid transcript (for transfers) required for some. *Admission application deadline:* 6/15.

Summary of Aid to Needy Students Federal Work-Study jobs; 2,500 part-time jobs.

Need-Based Scholarships & Grants Pell, FSEOG, state.

Loans Perkins, PLUS, Stafford, Unsubsidized Stafford, state, college/university short-term loans ($600 average).

Non-Need Awards *Academic Interests/Achievement Awards:* available. *Creative Arts/Performance Awards:* available. *Athletic:* available.

Other Money-Saving Options Accelerated degree, co-op program, Air Force ROTC, off-campus living (after freshman year). *Payment Plan:* installment. *Waivers:* full or partial for senior citizens.

Contact Financial Aid Office, University of North Texas, Denton, TX 76203-6737, 817-565-2302.

UNIVERSITY OF NOTRE DAME
Notre Dame, Indiana

About the Institution Independent/religious, coed. Degrees awarded: B, M, D, P. Offers 73 undergraduate majors. Total enrollment: 9,927. Undergraduates: 7,700 (9% state residents). Freshmen: 1,922.

Undergraduate Expenses (1997–98) Comprehensive fee of $25,063 includes tuition ($19,800), mandatory fees ($147), and college room and board ($5116).

Applications Of all full-time undergraduates enrolled in fall 1996, 85% of those who applied for aid were judged to have need according to Federal Methodology, of whom 96% were aided. *Financial aid deadline:* Applications processed continuously. *Financial aid forms:* FAFSA, CSS Financial Aid PROFILE required. State form required for some. *Regular admission application deadline:* 1/5. Early action deadline: 11/1.

Summary of Aid to Needy Students *From gift & self-help combined:* Average need met: 84%. Average amount awarded: $12,683 (57% gift aid, 43% self-help). *Gift aid:* Total: $25,778,554 (69% from college's own funds, 7% from other college-administered sources, 24% from external sources). 1,620 Federal Work-Study jobs (averaging $1910); 330 part-time jobs.

Need-Based Scholarships & Grants Pell, FSEOG, state, private, college/university.

Loans Perkins, PLUS, Stafford, Unsubsidized Stafford, private.

Non-Need Awards In 1996, a total of 554 non-need awards were made. *Special Characteristics Awards:* 227 ($3,734,906 total): children of faculty/staff. *Athletic:* Total: 327 ($5,432,040); Men: 209 ($3,589,796); Women: 118 ($1,842,244).

Other Money-Saving Options Accelerated degree, Army ROTC, Naval ROTC, Air Force ROTC, off-campus living (after freshman year). *Payment Plan:* installment. *Waivers:* full or partial for employees or children of employees.

Contact Mr. Joseph A. Russo, Director of Financial Aid, University of Notre Dame, 103 Main Building, Notre Dame, IN 46556, 219-631-6436, fax: 219-631-6899.

UNIVERSITY OF OKLAHOMA
Norman, Oklahoma

About the Institution State-supported, coed. Degrees awarded: B, M, D, P. Offers 106 undergraduate majors. Total enrollment: 20,026. Undergraduates: 15,732 (78% state residents). Freshmen: 2,645.

Undergraduate Expenses (1996–97) State resident tuition: $1940 (minimum). Nonresident tuition: $5405 (minimum). Mandatory fees: $186. College room and board: $3904.

Applications Of all full-time undergraduates enrolled in fall 1996, 90% of those who applied for aid were judged to have need according to Federal Methodology, of whom 90% were aided. *Financial aid deadline (priority):* 3/1. *Financial aid forms:* FAFSA required. *Admission application deadline:* 7/15.

Summary of Aid to Needy Students *From gift & self-help combined:* Average need met: 92%. Average amount awarded: $5805 (42% gift aid, 58% self-help). *Gift aid:* Total: $15,660,211 (37% from college's own funds, 3% from other college-administered sources, 60% from external sources). 600 Federal Work-Study jobs (averaging $2880); 2,000 part-time jobs.

Need-Based Scholarships & Grants Pell, FSEOG, state, private, college/university.

Loans Perkins, PLUS, Stafford, Unsubsidized Stafford, private, college/university short-term loans ($200 average), college/university long-term loans ($1460 average).

Non-Need Awards In 1996, a total of 5,666 non-need awards were made. *Academic Interests/Achievement Awards:* 4,834 ($9,904,802 total): general academic, architecture, area/ethnic studies, biological sciences, business, communication, computer science, education, engineering/technologies, library science, mathematics, military science, physical sciences, social sciences. *Creative Arts/Performance Awards:* 143 ($135,865 total): art/fine arts, dance, journalism/publications, music, performing arts, theater/drama. *Special Achievements/Activities Awards:* 61 ($61,000 total): leadership. *Special Characteristics Awards:* 304 ($740,150 total): children and siblings of alumni, ethnic background, members of minorities, previous college experience. *Athletic:* Total: 324 ($2,169,912); Men: 219 ($1,386,998); Women: 105 ($782,914).

Other Money-Saving Options Accelerated degree, co-op program, Army ROTC, Naval ROTC, Air Force ROTC, off-campus living (after freshman year). *Payment Plan:* installment. *Waivers:* full or partial for children of alumni, employees or children of employees, senior citizens.

Contact Financial Aid Assistant, Office of Financial Aid Services, University of Oklahoma, 731 Elm, Robertson Hall, Norman, OK 73019-0230, 405-325-4521, fax: 405-325-7608.

UNIVERSITY OF OREGON
Eugene, Oregon

About the Institution State-supported, coed. Degrees awarded: B, M, D, P. Offers 85 undergraduate majors. Total enrollment: 17,269. Undergraduates: 13,874 (63% state residents). Freshmen: 2,576.

Undergraduate Expenses (1996–97) State resident tuition: $2694. Nonresident tuition: $10,818. Mandatory fees: $846. College room and board: $4342.

Applications 49% of all full-time undergraduates enrolled in fall 1996 applied for aid; of these, 93% were judged to have need according to Federal Methodology, of whom 96% were aided. *Financial aid deadline (priority):* 3/1. *Financial aid forms:* FAFSA required. *Admission application deadline:* 3/1.

Summary of Aid to Needy Students *From gift & self-help combined:* Average need met: 90%. Average amount awarded: $6764 (25% gift aid, 75% self-help). *Gift aid:* Total: $11,428,663 (37% from college's own funds, 24% from other college-administered sources, 39% from external sources). 1,328 Federal Work-Study jobs (averaging $1074); 3,359 part-time jobs.

Need-Based Scholarships & Grants Pell, FSEOG, state, private, college/university.

Loans Perkins, PLUS, Stafford, Unsubsidized Stafford, college/university short-term loans ($200 average), college/university long-term loans ($1200 average).

Non-Need Awards In 1996, a total of 1,129 non-need awards were made. *Academic Interests/Achievement Awards:* general academic. *Creative Arts/Performance Awards:* art/fine arts, journalism/publications, performing arts. *Special Characteristics Awards:* general special characteristics. *Athletic:* Total: 259 ($2,955,527); Men: 158 ($1,714,206); Women: 101 ($1,241,321).

Other Money-Saving Options Accelerated degree, Army ROTC, cooperative Air Force ROTC, off-campus living. *Payment Plan:* deferred payment. *Waivers:* full or partial for minority students.

Contact Mr. Edmond Vignoul, Director of Financial Aid, University of Oregon, 260 Oregon Hall, Eugene, OR 97403, 541-346-3205, fax: 541-346-1175.

UNIVERSITY OF PENNSYLVANIA
Philadelphia, Pennsylvania

About the Institution Independent, coed. Degrees awarded: A, B, M, D, P. Offers 128 undergraduate majors. Total enrollment: 21,171. Undergraduates: 11,024 (21% state residents). Freshmen: 2,331.

Undergraduate Expenses (1997–98) Comprehensive fee of $29,680 includes tuition ($19,970), mandatory fees ($2280), and college room and board ($7430). College room only: $4230.

Applications 53% of all full-time undergraduates enrolled in fall 1996 applied for aid. *Financial aid deadline (priority):* 2/15. *Financial aid forms:* FAFSA, CSS Financial Aid PROFILE, state form, institutional form required. *Regular admission application deadline:* 1/1. Early decision deadline: 11/1.

Summary of Aid to Needy Students *From gift & self-help combined:* Average need met: 100%. Average amount awarded: $20,231 (67% gift aid, 33% self-help). *Gift aid:* Total: $60,143,419 (83% from college's own funds, 5% from other college-administered sources, 12% from external sources). 4,100 Federal Work-Study jobs (averaging $1975).

Need-Based Scholarships & Grants Pell, FSEOG, state, private, college/university.

Loans Perkins, PLUS, Stafford, Unsubsidized Stafford, Federal Nursing, Primary Care, private, college/university short-term loans ($250 average), college/university long-term loans ($1135 average).

Non-Need Awards Not offered.

Other Money-Saving Options Accelerated degree, Army ROTC, Naval ROTC, cooperative Air Force ROTC, off-campus living. *Payment Plans:* tuition prepayment, installment. *Waivers:* full or partial for employees or children of employees.

Contact Mr. William Schilling, Director of Financial Aid, University of Pennsylvania, 212 Franklin Building, 3451 Walnut Street, Philadelphia, PA 19104-6270, 215-898-6784, fax: 215-573-2208.

UNIVERSITY OF PITTSBURGH
Pittsburgh, Pennsylvania

About the Institution State-related, coed. Degrees awarded: B, M, D, P. Offers 83 undergraduate majors. Total enrollment: 25,479. Undergraduates: 16,049 (87% state residents). Freshmen: 2,202.

Undergraduate Expenses (1996–97) State resident tuition: $5416 (minimum). Nonresident tuition: $11,776 (minimum). Mandatory fees: $454. College room and board: $4964. College room only: $3014.

Applications 75% of all full-time undergraduates enrolled in fall 1996 applied for aid; of these, 85% were judged to have need according to Federal Methodology, of whom 100% were aided. *Financial aid deadline (priority):* 3/1. *Financial aid forms:* FAFSA, institutional form required. State form required for some. *Admission application deadline:* rolling.

Summary of Aid to Needy Students *From gift & self-help combined:* Average need met: 85%. Average amount awarded: $7650 (33% gift aid, 67% self-help). *Gift aid:* Total: $20,162,000 (20% from college's own funds, 53% from other college-administered sources, 27% from external sources). 1,100 Federal Work-Study jobs (averaging $1200); 2,000 part-time jobs.

Need-Based Scholarships & Grants Pell, FSEOG, state, private, college/university.

Loans Perkins, PLUS, Stafford, Unsubsidized Stafford, Federal Nursing, private, college/university short-term loans ($100 average).

Non-Need Awards *Academic Interests/Achievement Awards:* 1,243 ($2,829,000 total): general academic. *Creative Arts/Performance Awards:* 0. *Special Achievements/Activities Awards:* 0. *Special Characteristics Awards:* adult students, children of faculty/staff, members of minorities. *Athletic:* Total: 350 ($3,000,000).

Other Money-Saving Options Co-op program, Army ROTC, Air Force ROTC, cooperative Naval ROTC, off-campus living. *Payment Plans:* installment, deferred payment. *Waivers:* full or partial for employees or children of employees and senior citizens.

Contact Dr. Betsy A. Porter, Director of Admissions and Financial Aid, University of Pittsburgh, Bruce Hall, Second Floor, Pittsburgh, PA 15260, 412-624-7488, fax: 412-648-8815.

UNIVERSITY OF PITTSBURGH AT BRADFORD
Bradford, Pennsylvania

About the Institution State-related, coed. Degrees awarded: A, B. Offers 66 undergraduate majors. Total enrollment: 1,274 (86% state residents). Freshmen: 304.

Undergraduate Expenses (1996–97) State resident tuition: $5416 (minimum). Nonresident tuition: $11,776 (minimum). Mandatory fees: $410. College room and board: $4450 (minimum).

Applications *Financial aid deadline (priority):* 3/1. *Financial aid forms:* FAFSA, state form required. *Admission application deadline:* rolling.

Summary of Aid to Needy Students Federal Work-Study jobs; 150 part-time jobs.

Need-Based Scholarships & Grants Pell, FSEOG, state, private, college/university.

Loans Perkins, PLUS, Stafford, Unsubsidized Stafford, state.

Non-Need Awards *Academic Interests/Achievement Awards:* general academic, biological sciences, humanities, social sciences. *Creative Arts/Performance Awards:* general creative. *Special Characteristics Awards:* out-of-state students, ROTC participants.

Other Money-Saving Options Accelerated degree, Army ROTC, cooperative Air Force ROTC, off-campus living (after sophomore year). *Payment Plans:* installment, deferred payment. *Waivers:* full or partial for employees or children of employees.

Contact Financial Aid Office, University of Pittsburgh at Bradford, 300 Campus Drive, Bradford, PA 16701-2812, 814-362-7550.

UNIVERSITY OF PITTSBURGH AT GREENSBURG
Greensburg, Pennsylvania

About the Institution State-related, coed. Degrees awarded: B. Offers 22 undergraduate majors. Total enrollment: 1,381 (98% state residents). Freshmen: 326.

Undergraduate Expenses (1996–97) State resident tuition: $5184. Nonresident tuition: $11,270. Mandatory fees: $416. College room and board: $3870.

Applications 78% of all full-time undergraduates enrolled in fall 1996 applied for aid; of these, 91% were judged to have need according to Federal Methodology, of whom 93% were aided. *Financial aid deadline:* Applications processed continuously. *Financial aid forms:* FAFSA, state form, institutional form required. *Admission application deadline:* 8/1.

Summary of Aid to Needy Students *From gift & self-help combined:* Average need met: 84%. Average amount awarded: $6994 (38% gift aid, 62% self-help). *Gift aid:* Total: $1,956,300 (5% from college's own funds, 59% from other college-administered sources, 36% from external sources). 80 Federal Work-Study jobs (averaging $1300); 20 part-time jobs.

Need-Based Scholarships & Grants Pell, FSEOG, state, private, college/university.

Loans Perkins, PLUS, Stafford, Unsubsidized Stafford, private, college/university short-term loans ($200 average).

Non-Need Awards In 1996, a total of 50 non-need awards were made. *Academic Interests/Achievement Awards:* 30 ($22,000 total): general academic. *Special Characteristics Awards:* 20 ($20,000 total): general special characteristics.

Other Money-Saving Options Accelerated degree, cooperative Army ROTC, cooperative Air Force ROTC, off-campus living. *Payment Plan:* installment.

Contact Mr. John R. Sparks, Director of Admissions and Financial Aid, University of Pittsburgh at Greensburg, 1150 Mt. Pleasant Road, Greensburg, PA 15601-5860, 412-836-9880, fax: 412-836-7160.

UNIVERSITY OF PITTSBURGH AT JOHNSTOWN
Johnstown, Pennsylvania

About the Institution State-related, coed. Degrees awarded: A, B. Offers 40 undergraduate majors. Total enrollment: 3,143 (98% state residents). Freshmen: 769.

Undergraduate Expenses (1996–97) State resident tuition: $5416 (minimum). Nonresident tuition: $11,776 (minimum). Mandatory fees: $486. College room and board: $4770. College room only: $2670.

Applications 98% of all full-time undergraduates enrolled in fall 1996 applied for aid; of these, 91% were judged to have need according to Federal Methodology, of whom 92% were aided. *Financial aid deadline (priority):* 4/1. *Financial aid forms:* FAFSA, state form required. *Admission application deadline:* rolling.

Summary of Aid to Needy Students *From gift & self-help combined:* Average need met: 75%. Average amount awarded: $5055 (46% gift aid, 54% self-help). *Gift aid:* Total: $5,122,036 (10% from college's own funds, 5% from other college-administered sources, 85% from external sources). 116 Federal Work-Study jobs (averaging $1425); 161 part-time jobs.

Need-Based Scholarships & Grants Pell, FSEOG, state.

Loans Perkins, PLUS, Stafford, Unsubsidized Stafford, private, college/university short-term loans ($50 average), college/university long-term loans ($725 average).

Non-Need Awards In 1996, a total of 313 non-need awards were made. *Academic Interests/Achievement Awards:* 158 ($315,430 total): general academic. *Special Achievements/Activities Awards:* 22 ($44,000 total): leadership. *Special Characteristics Awards:* 104 ($461,352 total): children of faculty/staff. *Athletic:* Total: 29 ($185,170); Men: 14 ($119,307); Women: 15 ($65,863).

Other Money-Saving Options Accelerated degree, off-campus living. *Payment Plans:* installment, deferred payment. *Waivers:* full or partial for employees or children of employees.

Contact Ms. Julie A. Salem, Director, Student Financial Aid, University of Pittsburgh at Johnstown, 125 Biddle Hall, Johnstown, PA 15904-2990, 814-269-7045.

UNIVERSITY OF PORTLAND
Portland, Oregon

About the Institution Independent/religious, coed. Degrees awarded: B, M. Offers 43 undergraduate majors. Total enrollment: 2,639. Undergraduates: 2,078 (53% state residents). Freshmen: 538.

Undergraduate Expenses (1996–97) Comprehensive fee of $18,780 includes tuition ($14,300), mandatory fees ($100), and college room and board ($4380 minimum).

Applications Of all full-time undergraduates enrolled in fall 1996, 82% of those who applied for aid were judged to have need according to Federal Methodology, of whom 99% were aided. *Financial aid deadline*

(priority): 3/1. *Financial aid forms:* FAFSA, institutional form required. *Regular admission application deadline:* rolling. Early decision deadline: 11/15. Early action deadline: 11/15.

Summary of Aid to Needy Students *From gift & self-help combined:* Average need met: 90%. Average amount awarded: $13,196 (56% gift aid, 44% self-help). *Gift aid:* Total: $9,334,677 (78% from college's own funds, 4% from other college-administered sources, 18% from external sources). 275 Federal Work-Study jobs (averaging $1178); 600 part-time jobs.

Need-Based Scholarships & Grants Pell, FSEOG, state, private, college/university.

Loans Perkins, PLUS, Stafford, Unsubsidized Stafford, Federal Nursing, college/university short-term loans ($500 average).

Non-Need Awards In 1996, a total of 1,097 non-need awards were made. *Academic Interests/Achievement Awards:* 660 ($1,994,480 total): general academic, biological sciences, business, communication, computer science, education, engineering/technologies, English, foreign languages, health fields, humanities, mathematics, physical sciences, premedicine, religion/biblical studies, social sciences. *Creative Arts/Performance Awards:* 62 ($103,000 total): journalism/publications, music, performing arts, theater/drama. *Special Characteristics Awards:* 226 ($1,362,122 total): children of faculty/staff, relatives of clergy, ROTC participants. *Athletic:* Total: 149 ($1,457,488).

Other Money-Saving Options Accelerated degree, Army ROTC, Air Force ROTC, off-campus living. *Payment Plans:* installment, deferred payment. *Waivers:* full or partial for employees or children of employees.

Contact Ms. Rita Lambert, Director of Financial Aid, University of Portland, 5000 North Willamette Boulevard, Portland, OR 97203-5798, 503-283-7311, fax: 503-283-7508.

UNIVERSITY OF PUERTO RICO, AGUADILLA REGIONAL COLLEGE
Aguadilla, Puerto Rico

About the Institution Commonwealth-supported, coed. Degrees awarded: A, B. Offers 9 undergraduate majors. Total enrollment: 3,312 (100% commonwealth residents). Freshmen: 1,038.

Undergraduate Expenses (1996–97) Commonwealth resident tuition: $1020. Mandatory fees: $618.

Applications *Financial aid deadline (priority):* 6/30. *Financial aid forms:* FAFSA, institutional form required. State income tax form required for some. *Admission application deadline:* 3/29.

Summary of Aid to Needy Students Federal Work-Study jobs.

Loans College/university long-term loans.

Other Money-Saving Options Army ROTC. *Payment Plans:* installment, deferred payment. *Waivers:* full or partial for employees or children of employees.

Contact Office of Financial Aid, University of Puerto Rico, Aguadilla Regional College, Aguadilla, PR 00604-0160, 787-890-2681.

UNIVERSITY OF PUERTO RICO AT ARECIBO
Arecibo, Puerto Rico

About the Institution Commonwealth-supported, coed. Degrees awarded: A, B. Offers 15 undergraduate majors. Total enrollment: 4,715 (100% commonwealth residents). Freshmen: 1,233.

Applications Of all full-time undergraduates enrolled in fall 1996, 100% of those who applied for aid were judged to have need according to Federal Methodology, of whom 100% were aided. *Financial aid deadline:* Applications processed continuously. *Financial aid forms:* FAFSA, institutional form required. *Admission application deadline:* 11/17.

Summary of Aid to Needy Students *From gift & self-help combined:* Average need met: 53%. *Gift aid:* Total: $11,500,000 (24% from college-administered sources, 76% from external sources). 249 Federal Work-Study jobs (averaging $1500).

Need-Based Scholarships & Grants Pell, FSEOG.

Loans Perkins, Stafford, Unsubsidized Stafford.

Non-Need Awards *Academic Interests/Achievement Awards:* general academic. *Creative Arts/Performance Awards:* available. *Special Characteristics Awards:* general special characteristics, children of union members/company employees, local/state students. *Athletic:* Total: 182 ($86,450); Men: 95 ($45,125); Women: 87 ($41,325).

Other Money-Saving Options Army ROTC. *Payment Plan:* deferred payment. *Waivers:* full or partial for employees or children of employees.

Contact Mr. Luis Rodriguez, Director of Financial Aid, University of Puerto Rico at Arecibo, Arecibo, PR 00613, 787-878-2830 Ext. 2008.

UNIVERSITY OF PUERTO RICO AT BAYAMÓN
Bayamón, Puerto Rico

See Bayamón Technological University College

UNIVERSITY OF PUERTO RICO AT PONCE
Ponce, Puerto Rico

About the Institution Commonwealth-supported, coed. Degrees awarded: A, B. Offers 13 undergraduate majors. Total enrollment: 4,126. Freshmen: 1,230.

Applications 84% of all full-time undergraduates enrolled in fall 1996 applied for aid; of these, 93% were judged to have need according to Federal Methodology, of whom 100% were aided. *Financial aid deadline (priority):* 6/14. *Financial aid forms:* FAFSA, institutional form required. Commonwealth form required for some. *Regular admission application deadline:* 11/15. Early decision deadline: 1/15.

Summary of Aid to Needy Students *From gift & self-help combined:* Average need met: 40%. *Gift aid:* Total: $8,600,781 (13% from college-administered sources, 87% from external sources). Federal Work-Study jobs.

Need-Based Scholarships & Grants Pell, FSEOG, state, private, college/university.

Loans Stafford.

Non-Need Awards *Academic Interests/Achievement Awards:* available. *Creative Arts/Performance Awards:* available. *Special Achievements/Activities Awards:* available. *Special Characteristics Awards:* available. *Athletic:* available.

Other Money-Saving Options Accelerated degree, Army ROTC. *Payment Plan:* installment. *Waivers:* full or partial for employees or children of employees.

Contact Office of Financial Aid, University of Puerto Rico at Ponce, Box 7186, Ponce, PR 00732-7186, 787-844-8181.

UNIVERSITY OF PUERTO RICO, CAYEY UNIVERSITY COLLEGE
Cayey, Puerto Rico

About the Institution Commonwealth-supported, coed. Degrees awarded: A, B. Offers 24 undergraduate majors. Total enrollment: 3,758 (100% commonwealth residents).

Undergraduate Expenses (1996–97) Commonwealth resident tuition: $720. Mandatory fees: $276.

Applications 85% of all full-time undergraduates enrolled in fall 1996 applied for aid. *Financial aid deadline (priority):* 4/30. *Financial aid forms:* FAFSA, institutional form required. Commonwealth form required for some. *Admission application deadline:* 12/1.

Summary of Aid to Needy Students *Gift aid:* Total: $6,863,634 (4% from college's own funds, 11% from other college-administered sources, 85% from external sources). 264 Federal Work-Study jobs (averaging $1360); part-time jobs.

Need-Based Scholarships & Grants Pell, FSEOG, state, college/university.

Loans Stafford, Unsubsidized Stafford, college/university long-term loans.

Non-Need Awards In 1996, a total of 462 non-need awards were made. *Creative Arts/Performance Awards:* 141 ($63,730 total): music, theater/drama. *Special Achievements/Activities Awards:* 119 ($54,765 total): general special achievements/activities, cheerleading/drum major. *Special Characteristics Awards:* 140 ($61,356 total): children of faculty/staff, children of public servants, ROTC participants, veterans. *Athletic:* Total: 62 ($28,470); Men: 40 ($18,240); Women: 22 ($10,230).

Other Money-Saving Options Accelerated degree, Army ROTC. *Payment Plan:* deferred payment. *Waivers:* full or partial for employees or children of employees.

Contact Ms. Gloria Collazo, Director of Financial Aid, University of Puerto Rico, Cayey University College, Cayey, PR 00737, 787-738-2161.

UNIVERSITY OF PUERTO RICO, HUMACAO UNIVERSITY COLLEGE
Humacao, Puerto Rico

About the Institution Commonwealth-supported, coed. Degrees awarded: A, B. Offers 19 undergraduate majors. Total enrollment: 4,294 (100% commonwealth residents). Freshmen: 945.

Undergraduate Expenses (1996–97) Commonwealth resident tuition: $1020. Mandatory fees: $70 (minimum).

Applications Of all full-time undergraduates enrolled in fall 1996, 86% of those who applied for aid were judged to have need according to Federal Methodology, of whom 100% were aided. *Financial aid deadline:* Applications processed continuously. *Financial aid forms:* FAFSA, institutional form required. *Admission application deadline:* 11/15.

Summary of Aid to Needy Students *From gift & self-help combined:* Average need met: 47%. *Gift aid:* Total: $7,923,305 (6% from college's own funds, 14% from other college-administered sources, 80% from external sources). 816 Federal Work-Study jobs (averaging $1360).

Need-Based Scholarships & Grants Pell, FSEOG, state, college/university.

Loans Perkins, Stafford, Unsubsidized Stafford.

Non-Need Awards Not offered.

Other Money-Saving Options *Payment Plan:* deferred payment. *Waivers:* full or partial for employees or children of employees.

Contact Mr. Hector Maldonado, Director of Financial Aid, University of Puerto Rico, Humacao University College, CUH Station, Humacao, PR 00791, 787-850-9342, fax: 787-850-9371.

UNIVERSITY OF PUERTO RICO, MAYAGÜEZ CAMPUS
Mayagüez, Puerto Rico

About the Institution Commonwealth-supported, coed. Degrees awarded: A, B, M, D. Offers 51 undergraduate majors. Total enrollment: 12,594. Undergraduates: 11,703 (98% commonwealth residents). Freshmen: 2,626.

Applications Of all full-time undergraduates enrolled in fall 1996, 94% of those who applied for aid were judged to have need according to Federal Methodology, of whom 93% were aided. *Financial aid deadline (priority):* 5/1. *Financial aid forms:* FAFSA, institutional form required; CSS Financial Aid PROFILE acceptable. *Admission application deadline:* 12/15.

Summary of Aid to Needy Students *From gift & self-help combined:* Average need met: 45%. Average amount awarded: $3370 (76% gift aid, 24% self-help). *Gift aid:* Total: $17,357,746 (4% from college's own funds, 10% from other college-administered sources, 86% from external sources). 1,105 Federal Work-Study jobs (averaging $994); part-time jobs.

Need-Based Scholarships & Grants Pell, FSEOG, state, private, college/university.

Loans Perkins, Stafford, Unsubsidized Stafford, college/university short-term loans ($75 average), college/university long-term loans ($1000 average).

Non-Need Awards In 1996, a total of 2,104 non-need awards were made. *Academic Interests/Achievement Awards:* 811 ($378,525 total): general academic. *Creative Arts/Performance Awards:* 193 ($91,620 total): general creative, music. *Special Characteristics Awards:* 786 ($378,525 total): children of faculty/staff, ROTC participants. *Athletic:* Total: 314 ($150,675).

Other Money-Saving Options Co-op program, Army ROTC, Air Force ROTC. *Payment Plans:* installment, deferred payment. *Waivers:* full or partial for employees or children of employees.

Contact Ms. Ana T. Rodríguez, Assistant Director of Financial Aid, University of Puerto Rico, Mayagüez Campus, Box 5000, Mayagüez, PR 00681-5000, 787-265-3863, fax: 787-265-1920.

UNIVERSITY OF PUERTO RICO, MEDICAL SCIENCES CAMPUS
San Juan, Puerto Rico

About the Institution Commonwealth-supported, coed. Degrees awarded: A, B, M, D, P. Offers 14 undergraduate majors. Total enrollment: 2,712. Undergraduates: 1,128 (99% commonwealth residents).

Undergraduate Expenses (1996–97) Commonwealth resident tuition: $1050 (minimum). Mandatory fees: $400 (minimum).

Applications 77% of all full-time undergraduates enrolled in fall 1996 applied for aid; of these, 88% were judged to have need according to Federal Methodology, of whom 100% were aided. *Financial aid deadline:* continuous. *Financial aid forms:* FAFSA, institutional form required. *Admission application deadline:* 12/15.

Summary of Aid to Needy Students *From gift & self-help combined:* Average need met: 100%. *Gift aid:* Total: $2,674,186. Federal Work-Study jobs.

Need-Based Scholarships & Grants Pell, FSEOG, state, college/university.

Loans Perkins, Stafford, Unsubsidized Stafford, college/university short-term loans ($200 average).

Non-Need Awards *Academic Interests/Achievement Awards:* health fields. *Special Characteristics Awards:* children of faculty/staff.

Other Money-Saving Options *Payment Plan:* deferred payment. *Waivers:* full or partial for employees or children of employees.

Contact Lourdes Pont, Financial Aid Director, University of Puerto Rico, Medical Sciences Campus, Terreno Centro Médico-Edificio Decanato de Estudiante, Rio Piedras, PR 00936-5067, 787-763-7170, fax: 787-282-7117.

UNIVERSITY OF PUERTO RICO, RÍO PIEDRAS
San Juan, Puerto Rico

About the Institution Commonwealth-supported, coed. Degrees awarded: A, B, M, D, P. Offers 59 undergraduate majors. Total enrollment: 19,234. Undergraduates: 15,738 (99% commonwealth residents). Freshmen: 3,071.

Applications Of all full-time undergraduates enrolled in fall 1996, 38% of those who applied for aid were judged to have need according to Federal Methodology, of whom 50% were aided. *Financial aid deadline (priority):* 6/30. *Financial aid forms:* FAFSA, institutional form required. *Admission application deadline:* 11/15.

Summary of Aid to Needy Students *From gift & self-help combined:* Average need met: 100%. *Gift aid:* Total: $18,636,829. Federal Work-Study jobs; part-time jobs.

Need-Based Scholarships & Grants Pell, FSEOG, private.

Loans Perkins, PLUS, Stafford, Unsubsidized Stafford, college/university short-term loans ($85 average), law access loans.

Non-Need Awards Not offered.

Other Money-Saving Options Accelerated degree, co-op program, Army ROTC, Air Force ROTC, off-campus living. *Payment Plan:* installment. *Waivers:* full or partial for employees or children of employees.

Contact Mr. Efraim Williams, EDP Manager, University of Puerto Rico, Río Piedras, PO Box 23353, San Juan, PR 00931, 787-764-0000 Ext. 5573, fax: 787-764-0000.

UNIVERSITY OF PUGET SOUND
Tacoma, Washington

About the Institution Independent, coed. Degrees awarded: B, M. Offers 35 undergraduate majors. Total enrollment: 3,039. Undergraduates: 2,768 (27% state residents). Freshmen: 740.

Undergraduate Expenses (1997–98) Comprehensive fee of $23,860 includes tuition ($18,790), mandatory fees ($150), and college room and board ($4920). College room only: $2690.

Applications 75% of all full-time undergraduates enrolled in fall 1996 applied for aid; of these, 86% were judged to have need according to Federal Methodology, of whom 100% were aided. *Financial aid deadline (priority):* 2/1. *Financial aid forms:* FAFSA, CSS Financial Aid PROFILE required. Institutional form required for some. *Regular admission application deadline:* 2/1. Early decision deadline: 11/15.

Summary of Aid to Needy Students *From gift & self-help combined:* Average need met: 85%. Average amount awarded: $15,042 (57% gift aid, 43% self-help). *Gift aid:* Total: $14,581,000 (81% from college's own funds, 7% from other college-administered sources, 12% from external sources). 720 Federal Work-Study jobs (averaging $1833); 450 part-time jobs.

Need-Based Scholarships & Grants Pell, FSEOG, state, college/university.

Loans Perkins, PLUS, Stafford, Unsubsidized Stafford, private, college/university short-term loans ($100 average).

Non-Need Awards In 1996, a total of 414 non-need awards were made. *Academic Interests/Achievement Awards:* 349 ($1,845,000 total): general academic, biological sciences, business, computer science, humanities, mathematics, physical sciences. *Creative Arts/Performance Awards:* 33 ($174,000 total): art/fine arts, debating, music, theater/drama. *Special Achievements/Activities Awards:* 13 ($66,000 total): leadership, religious involvement. *Special Characteristics Awards:* 19 ($242,000 total): children of faculty/staff, members of minorities, religious affiliation, ROTC participants.

Other Money-Saving Options Co-op program, cooperative Army ROTC, off-campus living. *Payment Plans:* installment, deferred payment. *Waivers:* full or partial for employees or children of employees.

Contact Mr. Steven Thorndill, Director of Financial Aid, University of Puget Sound, 1500 North Warner Street, Tacoma, WA 98416-0005, 206-756-3214, fax: 206-756-3500.

UNIVERSITY OF REDLANDS
Redlands, California

About the Institution Independent, coed. Degrees awarded: B, M. Offers 52 undergraduate majors. Total enrollment: 3,584. Undergraduates: 2,636 (61% state residents). Freshmen: 383.

Undergraduate Expenses (1997–98) Comprehensive fee of $25,859 includes tuition ($18,300), mandatory fees ($245), and college room and board ($7314). College room only: $3954.

Applications 80% of all full-time undergraduates enrolled in fall 1996 applied for aid; of these, 94% were judged to have need according to Federal Methodology, of whom 100% were aided. *Financial aid deadline (priority):* 2/15. *Financial aid forms:* FAFSA required. *Admission application deadline:* 3/1.

Summary of Aid to Needy Students *From gift & self-help combined:* Average need met: 93%. Average amount awarded: $17,037 (60% gift aid, 40% self-help). *Gift aid:* Total: $9,886,300 (76% from college's own funds, 16% from other college-administered sources, 8% from external sources). 355 Federal Work-Study jobs (averaging $1833); 599 part-time jobs.

Need-Based Scholarships & Grants Pell, FSEOG, state, private, college/university.

Loans Perkins, Stafford, Unsubsidized Stafford, private, college/university short-term loans ($50 average), college/university long-term loans ($7500 average).

Non-Need Awards In 1996, a total of 600 non-need awards were made. *Academic Interests/Achievement Awards:* 195 ($961,175 total): general academic. *Creative Arts/Performance Awards:* 96 ($232,820 total): art/fine arts, creative writing, debating, music. *Special Achievements/Activities Awards:* 149 ($217,400 total): leadership. *Special Characteristics Awards:* 160 ($240,000 total): general special characteristics, ethnic background, out-of-state students.

Other Money-Saving Options Cooperative Army ROTC, cooperative Air Force ROTC. *Payment Plan:* installment. *Waivers:* full or partial for employees or children of employees.

Contact Office of Financial Aid, University of Redlands, PO Box 3080, Redlands, CA 92373-0999, 909-793-2121.

UNIVERSITY OF RHODE ISLAND
Kingston, Rhode Island

About the Institution State-supported, coed. Degrees awarded: B, M, D, P. Offers 101 undergraduate majors. Total enrollment: 13,261. Undergraduates: 10,136 (63% state residents). Freshmen: 1,968.

Undergraduate Expenses (1996–97) State resident tuition: $3154. Nonresident tuition: $10,846. Mandatory fees: $1306. College room and board: $5824 (minimum). College room only: $3276.

Applications Of all full-time undergraduates enrolled in fall 1996, 91% of those who applied for aid were judged to have need according to Federal Methodology, of whom 100% were aided. *Financial aid deadline (priority):* 3/1. *Financial aid forms:* FAFSA required. *Regular admission application deadline:* 3/1. Early action deadline: 12/15.

Summary of Aid to Needy Students *From gift & self-help combined:* Average need met: 72%. Average amount awarded: $7279 (23% gift aid, 77% self-help). *Gift aid:* Total: $12,692,491 (46% from college's

own funds, 26% from other college-administered sources, 28% from external sources). 1,600 Federal Work-Study jobs (averaging $800); 3,656 part-time jobs.

Need-Based Scholarships & Grants Pell, FSEOG, state, private, college/university.

Loans Perkins, PLUS, Stafford, Unsubsidized Stafford, Federal Nursing, college/university short-term loans ($200 average), college/university long-term loans ($1500 average).

Non-Need Awards In 1996, a total of 1,512 non-need awards were made. *Academic Interests/Achievement Awards:* 1,081 ($3,429,336 total): general academic. *Creative Arts/Performance Awards:* 41 ($44,481 total): music. *Athletic:* Total: 390 ($2,585,835).

Other Money-Saving Options Accelerated degree, co-op program, Army ROTC, off-campus living. *Payment Plan:* installment. *Waivers:* full or partial for minority students, employees or children of employees, senior citizens.

Contact Mr. Horace J. Aramal, Assistant Dean of Financial Aid, University of Rhode Island, Kingston, RI 02881, 401-874-2314.

UNIVERSITY OF RICHMOND
University of Richmond, Virginia

About the Institution Independent/religious, coed. Degrees awarded: A, B, M, P. Offers 59 undergraduate majors. Total enrollment: 4,366. Undergraduates: 3,586 (17% state residents). Freshmen: 809.

Undergraduate Expenses (1997–98) Comprehensive fee of $21,495 includes tuition ($17,570) and college room and board ($3925).

Applications 44% of all full-time undergraduates enrolled in fall 1996 applied for aid; of these, 77% were judged to have need according to Federal Methodology, of whom 94% were aided. *Financial aid deadline:* 2/25. *Financial aid forms:* FAFSA, institutional form required. State form required for some. *Regular admission application deadline:* 2/1. Early decision deadline: 11/15.

Summary of Aid to Needy Students *From gift & self-help combined:* Average need met: 94%. Average amount awarded: $12,017 (77% gift aid, 23% self-help). *Gift aid:* Total: $8,988,982 (85% from college's own funds, 2% from other college-administered sources, 13% from external sources). 300 Federal Work-Study jobs (averaging $1150); 500 part-time jobs.

Need-Based Scholarships & Grants Pell, FSEOG, state, college/university.

Loans Perkins, PLUS, Stafford, Unsubsidized Stafford, private, Charles B. Keesee Educational Loans (VA and NC residents).

Non-Need Awards In 1996, a total of 560 non-need awards were made. *Academic Interests/Achievement Awards:* 291 ($2,084,165 total): general academic. *Creative Arts/Performance Awards:* 12 ($32,500 total): music. *Special Characteristics Awards:* 49 ($401,820 total): members of minorities. *Athletic:* Total: 208 ($2,561,255).

Other Money-Saving Options Accelerated degree, Army ROTC, off-campus living. *Payment Plan:* installment. *Waivers:* full or partial for employees or children of employees.

Contact Office of Financial Aid, University of Richmond, Sarah Brunet Hall, University of Richmond, VA 23173, 804-289-8438.

UNIVERSITY OF RIO GRANDE
Rio Grande, Ohio

About the Institution Independent, coed. Degrees awarded: A, B, M. Offers 54 undergraduate majors. Total enrollment: 2,057. Undergraduates: 1,984 (80% state residents). Freshmen: 519.

Undergraduate Expenses (1996–97) Area resident tuition: $1764 (minimum). State resident tuition: $2058 (minimum). Nonresident tuition: $7362. Mandatory fees: $336. College room and board: $4263 (minimum).

Applications Of all full-time undergraduates enrolled in fall 1996, 74% of those who applied for aid were judged to have need according to Federal Methodology, of whom 100% were aided. *Financial aid deadline (priority):* 4/15. *Financial aid forms:* FAFSA, institutional form required. *Admission application deadline:* rolling.

Summary of Aid to Needy Students *From gift & self-help combined:* Average amount awarded: $4860 (56% gift aid, 44% self-help). *Gift aid:* Total: $4,241,956 (41% from college's own funds, 5% from other college-administered sources, 54% from external sources). 80 Federal Work-Study jobs (averaging $1200); part-time jobs.

Need-Based Scholarships & Grants Pell, FSEOG, state, private, college/university.

Loans Perkins, PLUS, Stafford, Unsubsidized Stafford.

Non-Need Awards In 1996, a total of 719 non-need awards were made. *Academic Interests/Achievement Awards:* 524 ($697,379 total): general academic. *Creative Arts/Performance Awards:* 37 ($89,640 total): music. *Special Characteristics Awards:* 40 ($76,699 total): children and siblings of alumni, children of faculty/staff, local/state students, out-of-state students. *Athletic:* Total: 118 ($365,860); Men: 62 ($209,547); Women: 56 ($156,313).

Other Money-Saving Options Accelerated degree, co-op program, cooperative Army ROTC. *Payment Plans:* tuition prepayment, installment. *Waivers:* full or partial for employees or children of employees.

Contact Dr. John Hill, Director of Financial Aid, University of Rio Grande, Rio Grande, OH 45674, 614-245-7218.

UNIVERSITY OF ROCHESTER
Rochester, New York

About the Institution Independent, coed. Degrees awarded: B, M, D. Offers 52 undergraduate majors. Total enrollment: 8,172. Undergraduates: 4,885 (40% state residents). Freshmen: 1,042.

Undergraduate Expenses (1996–97) Comprehensive fee of $27,010 includes tuition ($19,630), mandatory fees ($450), and college room and board ($6930 minimum). College room only: $4180.

Applications 86% of all full-time undergraduates enrolled in fall 1996 applied for aid; of these, 81% were judged to have need according to Federal Methodology, of whom 98% were aided. *Financial aid deadline (priority):* 2/1. *Financial aid forms:* FAFSA required. CSS Financial Aid PROFILE, state form, institutional form required for some. *Regular admission application deadline:* 1/31. Early decision deadline:

Summary of Aid to Needy Students *From gift & self-help combined:* Average need met: 86%. Average amount awarded: $19,227 (76% gift aid, 24% self-help). *Gift aid:* Total: $42,802,658 (80% from college's own funds, 11% from other college-administered sources, 9% from external sources). 1,319 Federal Work-Study jobs (averaging $1552); 886 part-time jobs.

Need-Based Scholarships & Grants Pell, FSEOG, state, private, college/university.

Loans Perkins, PLUS, Stafford, Unsubsidized Stafford, Federal Nursing, private, college/university long-term loans ($4943 average).

Non-Need Awards In 1996, a total of 639 non-need awards were made. *Academic Interests/Achievement Awards:* 286 ($1,820,388 total): general academic, biological sciences, humanities, mathematics, physical sciences, social sciences. *Special Achievements/Activities Awards:* 1 ($6000 total): leadership. *Special Characteristics Awards:* 352 ($1,762,500 total): children and siblings of alumni, ethnic background, local/state students, members of minorities, out-of-state students.

Other Money-Saving Options Naval ROTC, cooperative Army ROTC, cooperative Air Force ROTC, off-campus living (after sophomore year). *Payment Plans:* tuition prepayment, installment. *Waivers:* full or partial for employees or children of employees.

Contact Ms. Sherry Andersen, Acting Director of Financial Aid, University of Rochester, 318 Meliora Hall-River Campus, Rochester, NY 14627-0001, 716-275-3226, fax: 716-461-4595.

UNIVERSITY OF ST. THOMAS
St. Paul, Minnesota

About the Institution Independent/religious, coed. Degrees awarded: B, M, D, P. Offers 53 undergraduate majors. Total enrollment: 10,324. Undergraduates: 5,066 (84% state residents). Freshmen: 997.

Undergraduate Expenses (1997–98) Comprehensive fee of $19,429 includes tuition ($14,560), mandatory fees ($100), and college room and board ($4769). College room only: $2769.

Applications 73% of all full-time undergraduates enrolled in fall 1996 applied for aid; of these, 89% were judged to have need according to Federal Methodology, of whom 99% were aided. *Financial aid deadline (priority):* 4/1. *Financial aid forms:* FAFSA required; CSS Financial Aid PROFILE acceptable. *Admission application deadline:* rolling.

Summary of Aid to Needy Students *From gift & self-help combined:* Average need met: 86%. Average amount awarded: $11,893 (63% gift aid, 37% self-help). *Gift aid:* Total: $20,398,772 (66% from college's own funds, 3% from other college-administered sources, 31% from external sources). 1,021 Federal Work-Study jobs (averaging $1970); 1,212 part-time jobs.

Need-Based Scholarships & Grants Pell, FSEOG, state, private, college/university.

Loans Perkins, PLUS, Stafford, Unsubsidized Stafford, state, private.

Non-Need Awards In 1996, a total of 4,263 non-need awards were made. *Academic Interests/Achievement Awards:* 3,630 ($11,626,581 total): general academic, biological sciences, business, mathematics, physical sciences. *Creative Arts/Performance Awards:* 29 ($77,363 total): journalism/publications, music. *Special Achievements/Activities Awards:* 125 ($98,250 total): community service, leadership. *Special Characteristics Awards:* 479 ($2,014,549 total): children of educators, parents of current students, ROTC participants.

Other Money-Saving Options Air Force ROTC, cooperative Army ROTC, off-campus living. *Payment Plan:* installment. *Waivers:* full or partial for employees or children of employees and senior citizens.

Contact Ms. Lisa Moriarity, Assistant Director, New Student Financial Services, University of St. Thomas, 2115 Summit Avenue, AQU201, St. Paul, MN 55105-1096, 612-962-6550, fax: 612-962-6559.

UNIVERSITY OF ST. THOMAS
Houston, Texas

About the Institution Independent/religious, coed. Degrees awarded: B, M, D. Offers 34 undergraduate majors. Total enrollment: 2,504. Undergraduates: 1,497 (92% state residents). Freshmen: 226.

Undergraduate Expenses (1997–98) Comprehensive fee of $15,320 includes tuition ($10,962), mandatory fees ($108), and college room and board ($4250 minimum).

Applications *Financial aid deadline (priority):* 3/1. *Financial aid forms:* FAFSA, CSS Financial Aid PROFILE, institutional form required; state form acceptable. *Admission application deadline:* rolling.

Summary of Aid to Needy Students Federal Work-Study jobs; part-time jobs.

Non-Need Awards *Academic Interests/Achievement Awards:* general academic. *Creative Arts/Performance Awards:* debating, music, theater/drama. *Special Achievements/Activities Awards:* community service.

Special Characteristics Awards: general special characteristics, children of educators, members of minorities, religious affiliation.

Other Money-Saving Options Accelerated degree, co-op program, cooperative Army ROTC, cooperative Naval ROTC, off-campus living (after freshman year). *Payment Plans:* installment, deferred payment. *Waivers:* full or partial for employees or children of employees and senior citizens.

Contact Office of Financial Aid, University of St. Thomas, Houston, TX 77006-4694, 713-522-7911.

UNIVERSITY OF SAN DIEGO
San Diego, California

About the Institution Independent/religious, coed. Degrees awarded: B, M, D, P. Offers 39 undergraduate majors. Total enrollment: 6,603. Undergraduates: 4,299 (65% state residents). Freshmen: 1,048.

Undergraduate Expenses (1997–98 estimated) Comprehensive fee of $22,750 includes tuition ($15,680), mandatory fees ($100), and college room and board ($6970).

Applications 66% of all full-time undergraduates enrolled in fall 1996 applied for aid; of these, 76% were judged to have need according to Federal Methodology, of whom 100% were aided. *Financial aid deadline (priority):* 2/20. *Financial aid forms:* FAFSA required. State form, institutional form required for some. *Admission application deadline:* 1/15.

Summary of Aid to Needy Students *From gift & self-help combined:* Average amount awarded: $13,690 (65% gift aid, 35% self-help). *Gift aid:* Total: $18,726,652 (65% from college's own funds, 3% from other college-administered sources, 32% from external sources). 429 Federal Work-Study jobs (averaging $2218); 550 part-time jobs.

Need-Based Scholarships & Grants Pell, FSEOG, state, private, college/university.

Loans Perkins, PLUS, Stafford, Unsubsidized Stafford, college/university long-term loans ($2122 average).

Non-Need Awards In 1996, a total of 801 non-need awards were made. *Academic Interests/Achievement Awards:* 567 ($3,856,972 total): general academic. *Creative Arts/Performance Awards:* 12 ($84,000 total): music. *Special Characteristics Awards:* 98 ($620,603 total): children of faculty/staff, ROTC participants. *Athletic:* Total: 124 ($1,660,828); Men: 64 ($792,192); Women: 60 ($868,636).

Other Money-Saving Options Naval ROTC, cooperative Army ROTC, cooperative Air Force ROTC, off-campus living (after freshman year). *Payment Plan:* installment. *Waivers:* full or partial for employees or children of employees.

Contact Ms. Judith Lewis Logue, Director of Financial Aid, University of San Diego, 5998 Alcala Park, San Diego, CA 92110-2492, 619-260-4514.

UNIVERSITY OF SAN FRANCISCO
San Francisco, California

About the Institution Independent/religious, coed. Degrees awarded: B, M, D, P. Offers 64 undergraduate majors. Total enrollment: 7,888. Undergraduates: 3,622 (69% state residents). Freshmen: 622.

Undergraduate Expenses (1997–98) Comprehensive fee of $22,818 includes tuition ($15,850), mandatory fees ($100), and college room and board ($6868). College room only: $4396.

Applications 61% of all full-time undergraduates enrolled in fall 1996 applied for aid; of these, 94% were judged to have need according to Federal Methodology, of whom 97% were aided. *Financial aid deadline (priority):* 2/15. *Financial aid forms:* FAFSA required. *Regular admission application deadline:* 2/15. Early action deadline: 12/15.

Summary of Aid to Needy Students *From gift & self-help combined:* Average need met: 69%. Average amount awarded: $13,583 (62% gift aid, 38% self-help). *Gift aid:* Total: $16,072,442 (72% from college's own funds, 2% from other college-administered sources, 26% from external sources). 705 Federal Work-Study jobs (averaging $1799); 907 part-time jobs.

Need-Based Scholarships & Grants Pell, FSEOG, state, private, college/university.

Loans Perkins, PLUS, Stafford, Unsubsidized Stafford, Federal Nursing, private, college/university short-term loans ($150 average).

Non-Need Awards In 1996, a total of 578 non-need awards were made. *Academic Interests/Achievement Awards:* 153 ($1,367,218 total): general academic. *Special Achievements/Activities Awards:* 135 ($1,510,000 total): general special achievements/activities. *Special Characteristics Awards:* 147 ($1,228,342 total): general special characteristics, children of faculty/staff, ROTC participants. *Athletic:* Total: 143 ($1,367,639); Men: 72 ($636,313); Women: 71 ($731,326).

Other Money-Saving Options Accelerated degree, co-op program, Army ROTC, cooperative Air Force ROTC, off-campus living (after sophomore year). *Payment Plan:* installment. *Waivers:* full or partial for employees or children of employees.

Contact Office of Financial Aid, University of San Francisco, 2130 Fulton Street, San Francisco, CA 94117-1080, 415-422-6886.

UNIVERSITY OF SCIENCE AND ARTS OF OKLAHOMA
Chickasha, Oklahoma

About the Institution State-supported, coed. Degrees awarded: B. Offers 32 undergraduate majors. Total enrollment: 1,523 (97% state residents). Freshmen: 264.

Undergraduate Expenses (1996–97) State resident tuition: $1604 (minimum). Nonresident tuition: $3852 (minimum). College room and board: $2670 (minimum). College room only: $690.

Applications *Financial aid deadline (priority):* 8/15. *Financial aid forms:* FAFSA required; CSS Financial Aid PROFILE acceptable. *Admission application deadline:* rolling.

Summary of Aid to Needy Students *From gift & self-help combined:* Average need met: 95%. Average amount awarded: $2421 (58% gift aid, 42% self-help). *Gift aid:* Total: $1,367,407 (6% from college's own funds, 11% from other college-administered sources, 83% from external sources). 270 Federal Work-Study jobs (averaging $975); 25 part-time jobs.

Need-Based Scholarships & Grants Pell, FSEOG, state, private.

Loans Perkins, PLUS, Stafford, Unsubsidized Stafford, college/university short-term loans ($100 average).

Non-Need Awards In 1996, a total of 323 non-need awards were made. *Academic Interests/Achievement Awards:* 211 ($89,482 total): general academic. *Creative Arts/Performance Awards:* 20 ($8550 total): art/fine arts, music, theater/drama. *Special Achievements/Activities Awards:* 12 ($5400 total): cheerleading/drum major, leadership. *Special Characteristics Awards:* 38 ($26,765 total): international students, out-of-state students, previous college experience. *Athletic:* Total: 42 ($55,014); Men: 21 ($31,408); Women: 21 ($23,606).

Other Money-Saving Options Accelerated degree, co-op program, off-campus living. *Payment Plan:* installment. *Waivers:* full or partial for senior citizens.

Contact Ms. Laura Coponiti, Financial Aid Officer, University of Science and Arts of Oklahoma, PO Box 82345, Chickasha, OK 73018-0001, 405-224-3140, fax: 405-521-6244.

UNIVERSITY OF SCRANTON
Scranton, Pennsylvania

About the Institution Independent/religious, coed. Degrees awarded: A, B, M. Offers 65 undergraduate majors. Total enrollment: 4,906. Undergraduates: 4,173 (47% state residents). Freshmen: 948.

Undergraduate Expenses (1996–97) Comprehensive fee of $20,696 includes tuition ($13,176 minimum), mandatory fees ($920), and college room and board ($6600). College room only: $3938.

Applications Of all full-time undergraduates enrolled in fall 1996, 83% of those who applied for aid were judged to have need according to Federal Methodology, of whom 97% were aided. *Financial aid deadline (priority):* 2/1. *Financial aid forms:* FAFSA required; CSS Financial Aid PROFILE, institutional form acceptable. *Regular admission application deadline:* 3/1. Early action deadline: 11/1.

Summary of Aid to Needy Students *From gift & self-help combined:* Average need met: 78%. Average amount awarded: $10,850 (69% gift aid, 31% self-help). *Gift aid:* Total: $16,796,408 (80% from college's own funds, 1% from other college-administered sources, 19% from external sources). 540 Federal Work-Study jobs (averaging $1000); 182 part-time jobs.

Need-Based Scholarships & Grants Pell, FSEOG, state, private, college/university.

Loans Perkins, PLUS, Stafford, Unsubsidized Stafford, private.

Non-Need Awards In 1996, a total of 1,674 non-need awards were made. *Academic Interests/Achievement Awards:* 1,120 ($5,010,026 total): general academic. *Special Characteristics Awards:* 554 ($2,643,294 total): general special characteristics, children of faculty/staff, ethnic background, ROTC participants, siblings of current students.

Other Money-Saving Options Accelerated degree, Army ROTC, cooperative Air Force ROTC, off-campus living (after freshman year). *Payment Plan:* installment. *Waivers:* full or partial for employees or children of employees.

Contact Mr. William R. Burke, Director of Financial Aid, University of Scranton, Scranton, PA 18510-4622, 717-941-7701.

UNIVERSITY OF SIOUX FALLS
Sioux Falls, South Dakota

About the Institution Independent/religious, coed. Degrees awarded: A, B, M. Offers 57 undergraduate majors. Total enrollment: 947. Undergraduates: 829 (64% state residents). Freshmen: 140.

Undergraduate Expenses (1997–98) Comprehensive fee of $14,200 includes tuition ($10,750) and college room and board ($3450).

Applications 89% of all full-time undergraduates enrolled in fall 1996 applied for aid; of these, 89% were judged to have need according to Federal Methodology, of whom 100% were aided. *Financial aid deadline (priority):* 4/1. *Financial aid forms:* FAFSA, institutional form required; CSS Financial Aid PROFILE acceptable. State form required for some. *Admission application deadline:* rolling.

Summary of Aid to Needy Students *From gift & self-help combined:* Average need met: 75%. Average amount awarded: $8834 (43% gift aid, 57% self-help). *Gift aid:* Total: $1,716,144 (69% from college's own funds, 6% from other college-administered sources, 25% from external sources). 180 Federal Work-Study jobs (averaging $1200).

Need-Based Scholarships & Grants Pell, FSEOG, state, private, college/university.

Loans Perkins, PLUS, Stafford, Unsubsidized Stafford, private.

Non-Need Awards In 1996, a total of 602 non-need awards were made. *Academic Interests/Achievement Awards:* 234 ($405,281 total): general academic, biological sciences, business, communication, computer science, education, engineering/technologies, English, humanities, mathematics, physical sciences, premedicine, religion/biblical studies, social sciences. *Creative Arts/Performance Awards:* 77 ($46,525 total): music, theater/drama. *Special Achievements/Activities Awards:* 0: leadership, memberships. *Special Characteristics Awards:* 0: international students, out-of-state students, religious affiliation. *Athletic:* Total: 291 ($424,275); Men: 186 ($264,250); Women: 105 ($160,025).

Other Money-Saving Options Accelerated degree, co-op program, off-campus living (after sophomore year). *Payment Plan:* installment. *Waivers:* full or partial for employees or children of employees and senior citizens.

Contact Mr. David Vikander, Director of Financial Aid, University of Sioux Falls, 1101 West 22nd, Sioux Falls, SD 57105-1699, 605-331-6623.

UNIVERSITY OF SOUTH ALABAMA
Mobile, Alabama

About the Institution State-supported, coed. Degrees awarded: B, M, D, P. Offers 74 undergraduate majors. Total enrollment: 12,041. Undergraduates: 9,800 (71% state residents). Freshmen: 1,200.

Undergraduate Expenses (1996–97) State resident tuition: $2496. Nonresident tuition: $4992. Mandatory fees: $198. College room and board: $2835. College room only: $1485.

Applications Of all full-time undergraduates enrolled in fall 1996, 79% of those who applied for aid were judged to have need according to Federal Methodology, of whom 100% were aided. *Financial aid deadline (priority):* 5/1. *Financial aid forms:* FAFSA, institutional form required. *Admission application deadline:* 9/10.

Summary of Aid to Needy Students *From gift & self-help combined:* Average need met: 76%. Average amount awarded: $5716 (19% gift aid, 81% self-help). *Gift aid:* Total: $4,217,982 (9% from college-administered sources, 91% from external sources). 184 Federal Work-Study jobs (averaging $2103); 650 part-time jobs.

Need-Based Scholarships & Grants Pell, FSEOG, state, college/university.

Loans Perkins, PLUS, Stafford, Unsubsidized Stafford, state, college/university short-term loans ($150 average), college/university long-term loans.

Non-Need Awards In 1996, a total of 878 non-need awards were made. *Academic Interests/Achievement Awards:* 541 ($892,200 total). *Creative Arts/Performance Awards:* 77 ($56,306 total): music, theater/drama. *Special Achievements/Activities Awards:* 124 ($132,189 total): general special achievements/activities, hobbies/interest, Junior Miss, leadership. *Special Characteristics Awards:* 26 ($37,299 total): children and siblings of alumni, children of faculty/staff, members of minorities, ROTC participants. *Athletic:* Total: 110 ($622,788); Men: 52 ($287,451); Women: 58 ($335,337).

Other Money-Saving Options Accelerated degree, co-op program, Army ROTC, Air Force ROTC, off-campus living. *Waivers:* full or partial for employees or children of employees.

Contact Financial Aid Office, University of South Alabama, 260 Administration Building, Mobile, AL 36688-0002, 334-460-6231, fax: 334-460-7023.

UNIVERSITY OF SOUTH CAROLINA
Columbia, South Carolina

About the Institution State-supported, coed. Degrees awarded: B, M, D, P. Offers 89 undergraduate majors. Total enrollment: 25,489. Undergraduates: 15,747 (87% state residents). Freshmen: 2,703.

Undergraduate Expenses (1996–97) State resident tuition: $3362. Nonresident tuition: $8574. College room and board: $3692 (minimum). College room only: $1816 (minimum).

Applications 35% of all full-time undergraduates enrolled in fall 1996 applied for aid; of these, 82% were judged to have need according to

Federal Methodology, of whom 96% were aided. *Financial aid deadline (priority):* 4/15. *Financial aid forms:* FAFSA, institutional form required; CSS Financial Aid PROFILE acceptable. *Admission application deadline:* rolling.

Summary of Aid to Needy Students *From gift & self-help combined:* Average need met: 76%. Average amount awarded: $5926 (28% gift aid, 72% self-help). *Gift aid:* Total: $5,882,625 (21% from college's own funds, 27% from other college-administered sources, 52% from external sources). 1,082 Federal Work-Study jobs (averaging $2000); 1,437 part-time jobs.

Need-Based Scholarships & Grants Pell, FSEOG, state, private, college/university.

Loans Perkins, PLUS, Stafford, Unsubsidized Stafford, Federal Nursing, Primary Care.

Non-Need Awards In 1996, a total of 4,651 non-need awards were made. *Academic Interests/Achievement Awards:* 3,366 ($5,875,107 total): general academic. *Creative Arts/Performance Awards:* 473 ($473,939 total): art/fine arts, creative writing, debating, music, theater/drama. *Special Achievements/Activities Awards:* 56 ($42,525 total): cheerleading/drum major, community service. *Special Characteristics Awards:* 267 ($115,050 total): children and siblings of alumni, children of faculty/staff. *Athletic:* Total: 489 ($1,103,591); Men: 299 ($698,741); Women: 190 ($404,850).

Other Money-Saving Options Accelerated degree, co-op program, Army ROTC, Naval ROTC, Air Force ROTC, off-campus living (after freshman year). *Payment Plan:* deferred payment. *Waivers:* full or partial for senior citizens.

Contact Mr. Robert Patton, Financial Aid Officer, University of South Carolina, 1714 College Street, Columbia, SC 29208, 803-777-3205, fax: 803-777-0941.

UNIVERSITY OF SOUTH CAROLINA–AIKEN
Aiken, South Carolina

About the Institution State-supported, coed. Degrees awarded: A, B, M. Offers 25 undergraduate majors. Total enrollment: 3,027. Undergraduates: 2,981 (85% state residents). Freshmen: 445.

Undergraduate Expenses (1996–97) State resident tuition: $2708. Nonresident tuition: $6770. Mandatory fees: $140. College room and board: $2830 (minimum). College room only: $1990.

Applications *Financial aid deadline (priority):* 3/15. *Financial aid forms:* institutional form required; FAFSA, CSS Financial Aid PROFILE acceptable. *Admission application deadline:* 8/1.

Summary of Aid to Needy Students Federal Work-Study jobs; part-time jobs.

Loans College/university short-term loans, college/university long-term loans.

Non-Need Awards *Academic Interests/Achievement Awards:* general academic. *Creative Arts/Performance Awards:* art/fine arts, creative writing. *Athletic:* available.

Other Money-Saving Options Accelerated degree, co-op program, off-campus living. *Payment Plan:* deferred payment. *Waivers:* full or partial for employees or children of employees and senior citizens.

Contact Office of Financial Aid, University of South Carolina–Aiken, Aiken, SC 29801-6309, 803-648-6851.

UNIVERSITY OF SOUTH CAROLINA–SPARTANBURG
Spartanburg, South Carolina

About the Institution State-supported, coed. Degrees awarded: A, B, M. Offers 30 undergraduate majors. Total enrollment: 3,549. Undergraduates: 3,285 (94% state residents). Freshmen: 466.

Undergraduate Expenses (1996–97) State resident tuition: $2708. Nonresident tuition: $6570. Mandatory fees: $140.

Applications *Financial aid deadline (priority):* 5/1. *Financial aid forms:* FAFSA required. *Admission application deadline:* 8/15.

Summary of Aid to Needy Students *From gift & self-help combined:* Average amount awarded: $4438 (39% gift aid, 61% self-help). *Gift aid:* Total: $2,662,000 (21% from college's own funds, 19% from other college-administered sources, 60% from external sources). 200 Federal Work-Study jobs (averaging $1600); 150 part-time jobs.

Need-Based Scholarships & Grants Pell, FSEOG, state, private, college/university.

Loans Perkins, PLUS, Stafford, Unsubsidized Stafford.

Non-Need Awards In 1996, a total of 526 non-need awards were made. *Academic Interests/Achievement Awards:* 320 ($305,400 total): general academic. *Athletic:* Total: 206 ($253,700).

Other Money-Saving Options Accelerated degree, Army ROTC. *Payment Plan:* deferred payment. *Waivers:* full or partial for employees or children of employees and senior citizens.

Contact Office of Financial Aid, University of South Carolina–Spartanburg, Spartanburg, SC 29303-4932, 864-503-5340.

UNIVERSITY OF SOUTH DAKOTA
Vermillion, South Dakota

About the Institution State-supported, coed. Degrees awarded: A, B, M, D, P. Offers 81 undergraduate majors. Total enrollment: 7,028. Undergraduates: 5,215 (66% state residents). Freshmen: 899.

Undergraduate Expenses (1996–97) State resident tuition: $1696. Nonresident tuition: $5376. Mandatory fees: $1188. College room and board: $2647. College room only: $1283.

Applications Of all full-time undergraduates enrolled in fall 1996, 80% of those who applied for aid were judged to have need according to Federal Methodology, of whom 100% were aided. *Financial aid deadline (priority):* 3/1. *Financial aid forms:* FAFSA, state form required; CSS Financial Aid PROFILE acceptable. Institutional form required for some. *Admission application deadline:* rolling.

Summary of Aid to Needy Students *From gift & self-help combined:* Average need met: 68%. Average amount awarded: $5278 (32% gift aid, 68% self-help). *Gift aid:* Total: $5,606,323 (19% from college's own funds, 32% from other college-administered sources, 49% from external sources). 586 Federal Work-Study jobs (averaging $1086); 503 part-time jobs.

Need-Based Scholarships & Grants Pell, FSEOG, state, private, college/university, Bureau of Indian Affairs Grants.

Loans Perkins, PLUS, Stafford, Unsubsidized Stafford, Federal Nursing, Primary Care, private, college/university short-term loans ($99 average), college/university long-term loans ($1000 average).

Non-Need Awards In 1996, a total of 760 non-need awards were made. *Academic Interests/Achievement Awards:* 311 ($181,955 total): general academic, biological sciences, business, communication, computer science, education, English, foreign languages, mathematics, military science, premedicine, social sciences. *Creative Arts/Performance Awards:* 164 ($76,752 total): art/fine arts, creative writing, debating, journalism/publications, music, theater/drama. *Special Achievements/Activities Awards:* 27 ($6900 total): leadership. *Special Characteristics Awards:* 38 ($50,581 total): members of minorities, ROTC participants. *Athletic:* Total: 220 ($668,211); Men: 148 ($465,662); Women: 72 ($202,549).

Other Money-Saving Options Accelerated degree, Army ROTC, off-campus living (after sophomore year). *Payment Plan:* installment. *Waivers:* full or partial for employees or children of employees and senior citizens.

Contact Ms. Colleen Clifford, Associate Director Financial Aid, University of South Dakota, Slagle Hall 30, 414 East Clark, Vermillion, SD 57069-2390, 605-677-5005, fax: 605-677-6753.

UNIVERSITY OF SOUTHERN CALIFORNIA
Los Angeles, California

About the Institution Independent, coed. Degrees awarded: B, M, D, P. Offers 89 undergraduate majors. Total enrollment: 27,558. Undergraduates: 14,631 (69% state residents). Freshmen: 2,843.

Undergraduate Expenses (1996–97) Comprehensive fee of $26,228 includes tuition ($19,140), mandatory fees ($376), and college room and board ($6712). College room only: $3672.

Applications *Financial aid deadline:* Applications processed continuously. *Financial aid forms:* FAFSA, CSS Financial Aid PROFILE, state form, institutional form required. *Admission application deadline:* 2/1.

Summary of Aid to Needy Students Federal Work-Study jobs; part-time jobs.

Loans College/university short-term loans, college/university long-term loans.

Non-Need Awards *Academic Interests/Achievement Awards:* general academic, engineering/technologies. *Creative Arts/Performance Awards:* journalism/publications, music. *Special Characteristics Awards:* local/state students, ROTC participants. *Athletic:* available.

Other Money-Saving Options Accelerated degree, co-op program, Army ROTC, Naval ROTC, Air Force ROTC, off-campus living. *Payment Plans:* tuition prepayment, installment. *Waivers:* full or partial for employees or children of employees.

Contact Office of Financial Aid, University of Southern California, Los Angeles, CA 90089, 213-740-2311.

UNIVERSITY OF SOUTHERN COLORADO
Pueblo, Colorado

About the Institution State-supported, coed. Degrees awarded: B, M. Offers 70 undergraduate majors. Total enrollment: 4,109. Undergraduates: 3,806 (89% state residents). Freshmen: 608.

Undergraduate Expenses (1996–97) State resident tuition: $1682. Nonresident tuition: $7412. Mandatory fees: $410. College room and board: $4180. College room only: $1832.

Applications Of all full-time undergraduates enrolled in fall 1996, 82% of those who applied for aid were judged to have need according to Federal Methodology. *Financial aid deadline (priority):* 3/1. *Financial aid forms:* FAFSA, CSS Financial Aid PROFILE required. *Admission application deadline:* rolling.

Summary of Aid to Needy Students *From gift & self-help combined:* Average need met: 87%. Average amount awarded: $6325 (34% gift aid, 66% self-help). *Gift aid:* Total: $6,050,000 (35% from college's own funds, 20% from other college-administered sources, 45% from external sources). 160 Federal Work-Study jobs (averaging $1400); 145 part-time jobs.

Need-Based Scholarships & Grants Pell, FSEOG, state, college/university.

Loans Perkins, PLUS, Stafford, Unsubsidized Stafford, college/university short-term loans ($350 average).

Non-Need Awards *Academic Interests/Achievement Awards:* general academic. *Creative Arts/Performance Awards:* applied art and design, art/fine arts, journalism/publications, performing arts, theater/drama. *Special Achievements/Activities Awards:* general special achievements/activities, leadership. *Special Characteristics Awards:* general special characteristics. *Athletic:* available.

Other Money-Saving Options Accelerated degree, co-op program, off-campus living (after freshman year). *Payment Plans:* installment, deferred payment. *Waivers:* full or partial for employees or children of employees and senior citizens.

Contact Mr. Frederick L. Kidd, Director of Student Financial Aid, University of Southern Colorado, 2200 Bonforte Boulevard, Pueblo, CO 81001-4901, 719-549-2753, fax: 719-549-2419.

UNIVERSITY OF SOUTHERN INDIANA
Evansville, Indiana

About the Institution State-supported, coed. Degrees awarded: A, B, M. Offers 63 undergraduate majors. Total enrollment: 7,763. Undergraduates: 7,295 (92% state residents). Freshmen: 1,721.

Undergraduate Expenses (1996–97) State resident tuition: $2480. Nonresident tuition: $6053. Mandatory fees: $30. College room only: $1812.

Applications Of all full-time undergraduates enrolled in fall 1996, 77% of those who applied for aid were judged to have need according to Federal Methodology, of whom 92% were aided. *Financial aid deadline (priority):* 3/1. *Financial aid forms:* FAFSA, CSS Financial Aid PROFILE, institutional form required. *Admission application deadline:* 8/15.

Summary of Aid to Needy Students *From gift & self-help combined:* Average need met: 67%. Average amount awarded: $4313 (50% gift aid, 50% self-help). *Gift aid:* Total: $5,118,320 (16% from college's own funds, 3% from other college-administered sources, 81% from external sources). 74 Federal Work-Study jobs (averaging $1455); 400 part-time jobs.

Need-Based Scholarships & Grants Pell, FSEOG, state, private, college/university.

Loans Perkins, PLUS, Stafford, Unsubsidized Stafford, college/university short-term loans ($288 average).

Non-Need Awards In 1996, a total of 1,281 non-need awards were made. *Academic Interests/Achievement Awards:* 891 ($1,284,108 total): general academic, business, communication, education, engineering/technologies, foreign languages, health fields, humanities, physical sciences, premedicine, social sciences. *Creative Arts/Performance Awards:* 32 ($9150 total): art/fine arts, creative writing, music, theater/drama. *Special Achievements/Activities Awards:* 3 ($1800 total): leadership. *Special Characteristics Awards:* 130 ($183,371 total): adult students, children of faculty/staff, members of minorities, out-of-state students, spouses of current students, veterans' children. *Athletic:* Total: 225 ($306,077).

Other Money-Saving Options Co-op program, off-campus living. *Payment Plan:* installment. *Waivers:* full or partial for employees or children of employees and senior citizens.

Contact Ms. Rebecca Bryant, Financial Assistance Counselor, University of Southern Indiana, 8600 University Boulevard, Evansville, IN 47712-3590, 812-464-1767, fax: 812-465-7154.

UNIVERSITY OF SOUTHERN MAINE
Portland, Maine

About the Institution State-supported, coed. Degrees awarded: A, B, M, P. Offers 54 undergraduate majors. Total enrollment: 9,966. Undergraduates: 8,055 (94% state residents). Freshmen: 872.

Undergraduate Expenses (1996–97) State resident tuition: $3330. Nonresident tuition: $9420. Mandatory fees: $380. College room and board: $4554. College room only: $2358.

Applications 93% of all full-time undergraduates enrolled in fall 1996 applied for aid; of these, 79% were judged to have need according to Federal Methodology, of whom 94% were aided. *Financial aid deadline (priority):* 2/15. *Financial aid forms:* FAFSA required. *Admission application deadline:* rolling.

Summary of Aid to Needy Students *From gift & self-help combined:* Average need met: 71%. Average amount awarded: $5874 (33% gift aid, 67% self-help). *Gift aid:* Total: $4,667,016 (12% from college's own funds, 32% from other college-administered sources, 56% from external sources). 1,461 Federal Work-Study jobs (averaging $2100); 360 part-time jobs.

Need-Based Scholarships & Grants Pell, FSEOG, state, college/university.

Loans Perkins, PLUS, Stafford, Unsubsidized Stafford, Federal Nursing, private, college/university short-term loans ($100 average), college/university long-term loans ($1500 average).

Non-Need Awards In 1996, a total of 455 non-need awards were made. *Academic Interests/Achievement Awards:* general academic. *Creative Arts/Performance Awards:* music, theater/drama. *Special Achievements/Activities Awards:* community service. *Special Characteristics Awards:* general special characteristics, local/state students.

Other Money-Saving Options Co-op program, cooperative Air Force ROTC, off-campus living. *Payment Plan:* installment. *Waivers:* full or partial for minority students, employees or children of employees, senior citizens.

Contact Office of Financial Aid, University of Southern Maine, Portland, ME 04104-9300, 207-780-4141.

UNIVERSITY OF SOUTHERN MISSISSIPPI
Hattiesburg, Mississippi

About the Institution State-supported, coed. Degrees awarded: B, M, D. Offers 80 undergraduate majors. Total enrollment: 12,497. Undergraduates: 10,230 (83% state residents). Freshmen: 1,231.

Undergraduate Expenses (1996–97) State resident tuition: $2518. Nonresident tuition: $5338. College room and board: $2505. College room only: $1365 (minimum).

Applications Of all full-time undergraduates enrolled in fall 1996, 71% of those who applied for aid were judged to have need according to Federal Methodology, of whom 98% were aided. *Financial aid deadline (priority):* 3/15. *Financial aid forms:* FAFSA, institutional form required; CSS Financial Aid PROFILE acceptable. State form required for some. *Admission application deadline:* rolling.

Summary of Aid to Needy Students *From gift & self-help combined:* Average need met: 92%. Average amount awarded: $6599 (37% gift aid, 63% self-help). *Gift aid:* Total: $13,949,420 (35% from college's own funds, 15% from other college-administered sources, 50% from external sources). 662 Federal Work-Study jobs (averaging $1114); 600 part-time jobs.

Need-Based Scholarships & Grants Pell, FSEOG, state, private, college/university.

Loans Perkins, PLUS, Stafford, Unsubsidized Stafford, Federal Nursing, college/university short-term loans, college/university long-term loans.

Non-Need Awards In 1996, a total of 2,572 non-need awards were made. *Academic Interests/Achievement Awards:* 396 ($221,098 total): general academic. *Creative Arts/Performance Awards:* 354 ($366,121 total): art/fine arts, dance, music, theater/drama. *Special Achievements/Activities Awards:* 183 ($154,048 total): cheerleading/drum major, leadership. *Special Characteristics Awards:* 1,373 ($1,396,080 total): children and siblings of alumni, children of faculty/staff, ethnic background, out-of-state students, ROTC participants, veterans. *Athletic:* Total: 266 ($556,650); Men: 199 ($410,437); Women: 67 ($146,213).

Other Money-Saving Options Accelerated degree, co-op program, Army ROTC, Air Force ROTC, off-campus living. *Waivers:* full or partial for children of alumni and employees or children of employees.

Contact Mrs. Vernetta Fairley, Director of Financial Aid, University of Southern Mississippi, Box 5101, Hattiesburg, MS 39406-5167, 601-266-4774.

UNIVERSITY OF SOUTH FLORIDA
Tampa, Florida

About the Institution State-supported, coed. Degrees awarded: A, B, M, D, P. Offers 90 undergraduate majors. Total enrollment: 30,938. Undergraduates: 24,313 (94% state residents). Freshmen: 2,579.

Undergraduate Expenses (1997–98) State resident tuition: $2086. Nonresident tuition: $8003. College room and board: $4245. College room only: $2244.

Applications 57% of all full-time undergraduates enrolled in fall 1996 applied for aid; of these, 90% were judged to have need according to Federal Methodology, of whom 96% were aided. *Financial aid deadline (priority):* 3/1. *Financial aid forms:* FAFSA, CSS Financial Aid PROFILE acceptable. *Admission application deadline:* 5/1.

Summary of Aid to Needy Students *From gift & self-help combined:* Average need met: 63%. Average amount awarded: $5698 (38% gift aid, 62% self-help). *Gift aid:* Total: $16,749,000 (29% from college's own funds, 4% from other college-administered sources, 67% from external sources). 483 Federal Work-Study jobs (averaging $2500); 4,100 part-time jobs.

Need-Based Scholarships & Grants Pell, FSEOG, state, private, college/university.

Loans Perkins, PLUS, Stafford, Unsubsidized Stafford, Federal Nursing, private, college/university short-term loans ($880 average), college/university long-term loans ($5672 average).

Non-Need Awards *Academic Interests/Achievement Awards:* 1,853 ($2,900,000 total): general academic, architecture, biological sciences, business, communication, computer science, education, engineering/technologies, English, foreign languages, health fields, humanities, international studies, library science, mathematics, military science, physical sciences, premedicine, religion/biblical studies, social sciences. *Creative Arts/Performance Awards:* 206 ($163,000 total): applied art and design, art/fine arts, cinema/film/broadcasting, creative writing, dance, debating, journalism/publications, music, performing arts, theater/drama. *Special Achievements/Activities Awards:* general special achievements/activities. *Special Characteristics Awards:* general special characteristics. *Athletic:* Total: 192 ($587,138); Men: 101 ($245,138); Women: 91 ($342,000).

Other Money-Saving Options Accelerated degree, co-op program, Army ROTC, Air Force ROTC, off-campus living. *Payment Plan:* installment. *Waivers:* full or partial for senior citizens.

Contact Mr. Leonard Gude, Director of Financial Aid, University of South Florida, 4202 East Fowler Avenue, SVC 1102, Tampa, FL 33620-9951, 813-974-3039, fax: 813-974-5144.

UNIVERSITY OF SOUTH FLORIDA, NEW COLLEGE
Sarasota, Florida

See New College of the University of South Florida

UNIVERSITY OF SOUTHWESTERN LOUISIANA
Lafayette, Louisiana

About the Institution State-supported, coed. Degrees awarded: A, B, M, D. Offers 85 undergraduate majors. Total enrollment: 16,742. Undergraduates: 15,281 (97% state residents). Freshmen: 3,015.

Undergraduate Expenses (1996–97) State resident tuition: $1897. Nonresident tuition: $5633. College room and board: $2350 (minimum).

Applications Of all full-time undergraduates enrolled in fall 1996, 64% of those who applied for aid were judged to have need according to Federal Methodology, of whom 91% were aided. *Financial aid deadline (priority):* 3/1. *Financial aid forms:* FAFSA, institutional form required; CSS Financial Aid PROFILE, state form acceptable. *Admission application deadline:* rolling.

Summary of Aid to Needy Students *From gift & self-help combined:* Average need met: 90%. Average amount awarded: $4431. 674 Federal Work-Study jobs (averaging $1100); 938 part-time jobs.

Need-Based Scholarships & Grants Pell, FSEOG, state.

Loans Perkins, PLUS, Stafford, Unsubsidized Stafford, Federal Nursing, college/university short-term loans ($500 average).

Non-Need Awards *Academic Interests/Achievement Awards:* general academic, health fields. *Creative Arts/Performance Awards:* available. *Athletic:* available.

Other Money-Saving Options Accelerated degree, Army ROTC, off-campus living (after freshman year). *Payment Plan:* deferred payment. *Waivers:* full or partial for employees or children of employees and senior citizens.

Contact Office of Financial Aid, University of Southwestern Louisiana, USL Box 41206, Lafayette, LA 70504, 318-482-1000.

THE UNIVERSITY OF TAMPA
Tampa, Florida

About the Institution Independent, coed. Degrees awarded: A, B, M. Offers 44 undergraduate majors. Total enrollment: 2,712. Undergraduates: 2,190 (60% state residents). Freshmen: 427.

Undergraduate Expenses (1997–98) Comprehensive fee of $19,432 includes tuition ($13,890), mandatory fees ($762), and college room and board ($4780). College room only: $2280.

Applications 70% of all full-time undergraduates enrolled in fall 1996 applied for aid; of these, 91% were judged to have need according to Federal Methodology, of whom 100% were aided. *Financial aid deadline (priority):* 3/15. *Financial aid forms:* FAFSA required. State form required for some. *Admission application deadline:* rolling.

Summary of Aid to Needy Students *From gift & self-help combined:* Average need met: 70%. Average amount awarded: $13,930 (75% gift aid, 25% self-help). *Gift aid:* Total: $11,618,200 (63% from college's own funds, 22% from other college-administered sources, 15% from external sources). 161 Federal Work-Study jobs (averaging $1200); 200 part-time jobs.

Need-Based Scholarships & Grants Pell, FSEOG, state, private, college/university.

Loans Perkins, PLUS, Stafford, Unsubsidized Stafford, private, college/university short-term loans ($200 average), college/university long-term loans ($2100 average).

Non-Need Awards In 1996, a total of 1,479 non-need awards were made. *Academic Interests/Achievement Awards:* 1,007 ($3,871,000 total): general academic, biological sciences, business, communication, social sciences. *Creative Arts/Performance Awards:* 50 ($121,700 total): art/fine arts, creative writing, journalism/publications, music, performing arts. *Special Achievements/Activities Awards:* 200 ($492,000 total): general special achievements/activities, leadership. *Special Characteristics Awards:* 117 ($1,364,700 total): children of faculty/staff, international students, ROTC participants. *Athletic:* Total: 105 ($552,790); Men: 66 ($372,646); Women: 39 ($180,144).

Other Money-Saving Options Accelerated degree, co-op program, Army ROTC, cooperative Air Force ROTC, off-campus living (after sophomore year). *Payment Plan:* installment. *Waivers:* full or partial for employees or children of employees.

Contact Financial Aid Office, The University of Tampa, 401 West Kennedy Boulevard, Tampa, FL 33606-1490, 813-253-6219, fax: 813-258-7439.

UNIVERSITY OF TENNESSEE AT CHATTANOOGA
Chattanooga, Tennessee

About the Institution State-supported, coed. Degrees awarded: B, M. Offers 77 undergraduate majors. Total enrollment: 8,296. Undergraduates: 7,021 (89% state residents). Freshmen: 1,027.

Undergraduate Expenses (1996–97) State resident tuition: $2064. Nonresident tuition: $6400. College room only: $1430 (minimum).

Applications 91% of all full-time undergraduates enrolled in fall 1996 applied for aid; of these, 96% were judged to have need according to Federal Methodology, of whom 88% were aided. *Financial aid deadline (priority):* 3/1. *Financial aid forms:* FAFSA required; CSS Financial Aid PROFILE acceptable. State form required for some. *Admission application deadline:* rolling.

Summary of Aid to Needy Students *From gift & self-help combined:* Average need met: 78%. Average amount awarded: $6012 (28% gift aid, 72% self-help). *Gift aid:* Total: $1,550,809 (24% from college-administered sources, 76% from external sources). 212 Federal Work-Study jobs (averaging $1850); 1,000 part-time jobs.

Need-Based Scholarships & Grants Pell, FSEOG, state.

Loans Perkins, PLUS, Stafford, Unsubsidized Stafford, college/university short-term loans ($100 average), college/university long-term loans ($1405 average).

Non-Need Awards In 1996, a total of 1,390 non-need awards were made. *Academic Interests/Achievement Awards:* 709 ($898,163 total): general academic. *Creative Arts/Performance Awards:* 189 ($128,412 total): art/fine arts, music, theater/drama. *Special Characteristics Awards:* 242 ($315,404 total): members of minorities. *Athletic:* Total: 250 ($790,141); Men: 202 ($632,113); Women: 48 ($158,028).

Other Money-Saving Options Accelerated degree, co-op program, Army ROTC, off-campus living. *Payment Plan:* deferred payment. *Waivers:* full or partial for employees or children of employees and senior citizens.

Contact Mr. Joel Harrell, Director of Financial Aid, University of Tennessee at Chattanooga, 615 McCallie Avenue, Chattanooga, TN 37403-2598, 423-755-4677.

THE UNIVERSITY OF TENNESSEE AT MARTIN
Martin, Tennessee

About the Institution State-supported, coed. Degrees awarded: B, M. Offers 69 undergraduate majors. Total enrollment: 5,491. Undergraduates: 5,113 (90% state residents). Freshmen: 979.

Undergraduate Expenses (1996–97) State resident tuition: $2014. Nonresident tuition: $6350. College room and board: $2990 (minimum). College room only: $1560 (minimum).

Applications Of all full-time undergraduates enrolled in fall 1996, 94% of those who applied for aid were judged to have need according to Federal Methodology, of whom 95% were aided. *Financial aid deadline (priority):* 3/1. *Financial aid forms:* FAFSA or CSS Financial Aid PROFILE required. State form required for some. *Admission application deadline:* rolling.

Summary of Aid to Needy Students *From gift & self-help combined:* Average need met: 75%. Average amount awarded: $4455 (51% gift aid, 49% self-help). *Gift aid:* Total: $7,748,817 (48% from college's own funds, 21% from other college-administered sources, 31% from external sources). 300 Federal Work-Study jobs (averaging $850); 300 part-time jobs.

Need-Based Scholarships & Grants Pell, FSEOG, state, private, college/university.

Loans Perkins, PLUS, Stafford, Unsubsidized Stafford.

Non-Need Awards In 1996, a total of 1,029 non-need awards were made. *Academic Interests/Achievement Awards:* 527 ($969,647 total): general academic. *Creative Arts/Performance Awards:* 119 ($67,865 total): music. *Special Achievements/Activities Awards:* 89 ($85,610 total): cheerleading/drum major, rodeo. *Special Characteristics Awards:* 71 ($140,000 total): members of minorities. *Athletic:* Total: 223 ($1,217,186); Men: 144 ($820,088); Women: 79 ($397,098).

Other Money-Saving Options Accelerated degree, co-op program, Army ROTC, off-campus living (after sophomore year). *Payment Plan:* deferred payment. *Waivers:* full or partial for employees or children of employees and senior citizens.

Contact Mr. Randall Hall, Associate Dean of Financial Aid, The University of Tennessee at Martin, 205 Administration Building, Martin, TN 38238-1000, 901-587-7040.

UNIVERSITY OF TENNESSEE, KNOXVILLE
Knoxville, Tennessee

About the Institution State-supported, coed. Degrees awarded: B, M, D, P. Offers 164 undergraduate majors. Total enrollment: 25,517. Undergraduates: 18,825 (85% state residents). Freshmen: 3,692.

Undergraduate Expenses (1996–97) State resident tuition: $2060. Nonresident tuition: $6416. Mandatory fees: $140. College room and board: $3620. College room only: $1820.

Applications 63% of all full-time undergraduates enrolled in fall 1996 applied for aid; of these, 83% were judged to have need according to Federal Methodology, of whom 77% were aided. *Financial aid deadline (priority):* 2/15. *Financial aid forms:* FAFSA required; CSS Financial Aid PROFILE acceptable. *Admission application deadline:* 7/1.

Summary of Aid to Needy Students *From gift & self-help combined:* Average need met: 60%. Average amount awarded: $6484 (42% gift aid, 58% self-help). *Gift aid:* Total: $16,486,492 (21% from college's own funds, 35% from other college-administered sources, 44% from external sources). 296 Federal Work-Study jobs (averaging $2600); part-time jobs.

Need-Based Scholarships & Grants Pell, FSEOG, state, private, college/university.

Loans Perkins, PLUS, Stafford, Unsubsidized Stafford, Federal Nursing, state, private, college/university short-term loans ($50 average), college/university long-term loans ($1500 average).

Non-Need Awards *Academic Interests/Achievement Awards:* available. *Creative Arts/Performance Awards:* available. *Special Achievements/Activities Awards:* available. *Special Characteristics Awards:* members of minorities, ROTC participants. *Athletic:* Total: 359 ($2,327,384); Men: 214 ($1,377,564); Women: 145 ($949,820).

Other Money-Saving Options Accelerated degree, co-op program, Army ROTC, Air Force ROTC, off-campus living (after freshman year). *Payment Plans:* installment, deferred payment. *Waivers:* full or partial for employees or children of employees and senior citizens.

Contact Office of Financial Aid, University of Tennessee, Knoxville, 115 Student Services Building, Knoxville, TN 37996-0210, 423-974-1000.

THE UNIVERSITY OF TEXAS AT ARLINGTON
Arlington, Texas

About the Institution State-supported, coed. Degrees awarded: B, M, D. Offers 54 undergraduate majors. Total enrollment: 20,544. Undergraduates: 16,575 (95% state residents). Freshmen: 1,424.

Undergraduate Expenses (1996–97) State resident tuition: $960. Nonresident tuition: $7380. Mandatory fees: $1261. College room and board: $2900. College room only: $1500.

Applications Of all full-time undergraduates enrolled in fall 1996, 72% of those who applied for aid were judged to have need according to Federal Methodology, of whom 89% were aided. *Financial aid deadline (priority): 6/1. Financial aid forms: FAFSA, institutional form required. Admission application deadline: 8/1.*

Summary of Aid to Needy Students *From gift & self-help combined:* Average need met: 100%. Average amount awarded: $3286 (66% gift aid, 34% self-help). *Gift aid:* Total: $7,881,976 (24% from college's own funds, 22% from other college-administered sources, 54% from external sources). 1,033 Federal Work-Study jobs (averaging $2032); part-time jobs.

Need-Based Scholarships & Grants Pell, FSEOG, state, private, college/university.

Loans Perkins, PLUS, Stafford, Unsubsidized Stafford, state, private, college/university short-term loans ($270 average).

Non-Need Awards In 1996, a total of 1,082 non-need awards were made. *Academic Interests/Achievement Awards:* 578 ($727,454 total): general academic, biological sciences, business, communication, computer science, engineering/technologies, humanities, international studies, mathematics, physical sciences. *Creative Arts/Performance Awards:* 191 ($59,661 total): art/fine arts, debating, journalism/publications, music, theater/drama. *Special Achievements/Activities Awards:* 52 ($40,725 total): general special achievements/activities, cheerleading/drum major, Junior Miss, leadership. *Special Characteristics Awards:* 83 ($64,211 total): general special characteristics, first-generation college students, handicapped students, ROTC participants. *Athletic:* Total: 178 ($500,932); Men: 91 ($235,526); Women: 87 ($265,406).

Other Money-Saving Options Co-op program, Army ROTC, cooperative Air Force ROTC, off-campus living (after sophomore year). *Payment Plan:* installment.

Contact Ms. Judy Schneider, Director of Financial Aid, The University of Texas at Arlington, PO Box 19199, Arlington, TX 76019-0407, 817-272-3568, fax: 817-272-3555.

THE UNIVERSITY OF TEXAS AT AUSTIN
Austin, Texas

About the Institution State-supported, coed. Degrees awarded: B, M, D, P. Offers 110 undergraduate majors. Total enrollment: 48,008. Undergraduates: 35,789 (91% state residents). Freshmen: 6,430.

Undergraduate Expenses (1996–97) State resident tuition: $960. Nonresident tuition: $7380. Mandatory fees: $1652. College room and board: $4550.

Applications Of all full-time undergraduates enrolled in fall 1996, 78% of those who applied for aid were judged to have need according to Federal Methodology, of whom 95% were aided. *Financial aid deadline (priority): 4/1. Financial aid forms: FAFSA required. Admission application deadline: 2/1.*

Summary of Aid to Needy Students *From gift & self-help combined:* Average need met: 90%. Average amount awarded: $6690 (25% gift aid, 75% self-help). *Gift aid:* Total: $23,000,000 (40% from college's own funds, 8% from other college-administered sources, 52% from external sources). Federal Work-Study jobs; 4,800 part-time jobs.

Loans College/university short-term loans, college/university long-term loans.

Non-Need Awards *Academic Interests/Achievement Awards:* 7,091 ($17,630,000 total): general academic. *Athletic:* available.

Other Money-Saving Options Accelerated degree, co-op program, Army ROTC, Naval ROTC, Air Force ROTC, off-campus living. *Payment Plan:* installment.

Contact Office of Student Financial Services, The University of Texas at Austin, PO Box 7758, UT Station, Austin, TX 78713-7758, 512-475-6200.

THE UNIVERSITY OF TEXAS AT DALLAS
Richardson, Texas

About the Institution State-supported, coed. Degrees awarded: B, M, D. Offers 27 undergraduate majors. Total enrollment: 9,378. Undergraduates: 5,293 (90% state residents). Freshmen: 503.

Undergraduate Expenses (1996–97) State resident tuition: $960. Nonresident tuition: $7380. Mandatory fees: $1133. College room and board: $5102.

Applications *Financial aid deadline (priority): 4/1. Financial aid forms: FAFSA, institutional form, financial aid transcript (for transfers) required. Admission application deadline: 8/1.*

Summary of Aid to Needy Students *From gift & self-help combined:* Average amount awarded: $3382 (34% gift aid, 66% self-help). *Gift aid:* Total: $2,104,535. Federal Work-Study jobs; 21 part-time jobs.

Need-Based Scholarships & Grants Pell, FSEOG, state, college/university.

Loans Perkins, PLUS, Stafford, Unsubsidized Stafford, college/university short-term loans ($847 average).

Non-Need Awards *Academic Interests/Achievement Awards:* general academic, computer science, engineering/technologies. *Creative Arts/Performance Awards:* general creative.

Other Money-Saving Options Accelerated degree, co-op program, cooperative Army ROTC, cooperative Air Force ROTC, off-campus living. *Payment Plan:* installment. *Waivers:* full or partial for employees or children of employees and senior citizens.

Contact Office of Financial Aid, The University of Texas at Dallas, Richardson, TX 75083-0688, 972-883-2941.

THE UNIVERSITY OF TEXAS AT EL PASO
El Paso, Texas

About the Institution State-supported, coed. Degrees awarded: B, M, D. Offers 62 undergraduate majors. Total enrollment: 15,386. Undergraduates: 13,159 (88% state residents). Freshmen: 1,617.

Undergraduate Expenses (1996–97) State resident tuition: $960. Nonresident tuition: $7380. Mandatory fees: $1096. College room only: $1850 (minimum).

Applications 62% of all full-time undergraduates enrolled in fall 1996 applied for aid; of these, 84% were judged to have need according to Federal Methodology, of whom 80% were aided. *Financial aid deadline (priority): 3/15. Financial aid forms: FAFSA, institutional form required; CSS Financial Aid PROFILE acceptable. Admission application deadline: 7/1.*

Summary of Aid to Needy Students *From gift & self-help combined:* Average need met: 55%. Average amount awarded: $2193 (54% gift aid, 46% self-help). *Gift aid:* Total: $4,375,627 (2% from college's own funds, 28% from other college-administered sources, 70% from external sources). 696 Federal Work-Study jobs (averaging $2019).

Need-Based Scholarships & Grants Pell, FSEOG, state, college/university.

Loans Perkins, PLUS, Stafford, Unsubsidized Stafford, college/university short-term loans ($432 average).

Non-Need Awards *Academic Interests/Achievement Awards:* general academic, biological sciences, business, communication, computer science, education, engineering/technologies, English, health fields, humanities, international studies, mathematics, military science, physical sciences. *Creative Arts/Performance Awards:* applied art and design, art/fine arts, journalism/publications, music, performing arts, theater/drama. *Special Achievements/Activities Awards:* cheerleading/drum major, leadership. *Special Characteristics Awards:* ethnic background, international students, local/state students, members of minorities, out-of-state students, ROTC participants. *Athletic:* available.

Other Money-Saving Options Accelerated degree, co-op program, Army ROTC, Air Force ROTC, off-campus living. *Payment Plan:* installment.

Contact Ms. Linda Gonzales-Hensgen, Director of Financial Aid, The University of Texas at El Paso, El Paso, TX 79968-0001, 915-747-5204.

THE UNIVERSITY OF TEXAS AT SAN ANTONIO
San Antonio, Texas

About the Institution State-supported, coed. Degrees awarded: B, M, D. Offers 60 undergraduate majors. Total enrollment: 17,547.

Undergraduate Expenses (1996–97) State resident tuition: $960. Nonresident tuition: $7380. Mandatory fees: $1234. College room only: $2833.

Applications 62% of all full-time undergraduates enrolled in fall 1996 applied for aid; of these, 57% were judged to have need according to Federal Methodology, of whom 91% were aided. *Financial aid deadline (priority):* 3/31. *Financial aid forms:* FAFSA required; CSS Financial Aid PROFILE acceptable. *Admission application deadline:* 7/1.

Summary of Aid to Needy Students *From gift & self-help combined:* Average need met: 73%. Average amount awarded: $7499 (42% gift aid, 58% self-help). *Gift aid:* Total: $15,574,855 (20% from college's own funds, 34% from other college-administered sources, 46% from external sources). 288 Federal Work-Study jobs (averaging $2065).

Need-Based Scholarships & Grants Pell, FSEOG, state, private, college/university.

Loans Perkins, PLUS, Stafford, Unsubsidized Stafford, state, college/university short-term loans ($300 average), Tuition and Fees Emergency Loans.

Non-Need Awards In 1996, a total of 2,927 non-need awards were made. *Academic Interests/Achievement Awards:* 1,698 ($1,271,248 total): general academic, architecture, biological sciences, business, computer science, education, engineering/technologies, English, foreign languages, mathematics. *Creative Arts/Performance Awards:* 143 ($44,374 total): art/fine arts, music. *Special Achievements/Activities Awards:* 37 ($28,166 total): general special achievements/activities. *Special Characteristics Awards:* 880 ($627,263 total): general special characteristics, adult students, ethnic background, local/state students, out-of-state students. *Athletic:* Total: 169 ($783,189).

Other Money-Saving Options Accelerated degree, co-op program, Army ROTC, Air Force ROTC, off-campus living. *Payment Plan:* installment.

Contact Ms. Judy Curry, Assistant Director of Student Financial Aid, The University of Texas at San Antonio, 6900 North Loop 1604 West, San Antonio, TX 78249-0687, 210-458-4636, fax: 210-458-4638.

THE UNIVERSITY OF TEXAS OF THE PERMIAN BASIN
Odessa, Texas

About the Institution State-supported, coed. Degrees awarded: B, M. Offers 23 undergraduate majors. Total enrollment: 2,193. Undergraduates: 1,612 (97% state residents). Freshmen: 113.

Undergraduate Expenses (1996–97) State resident tuition: $960. Nonresident tuition: $7380. Mandatory fees: $960. College room only: $1350 (minimum).

Applications Of all full-time undergraduates enrolled in fall 1996, 81% of those who applied for aid were judged to have need according to Federal Methodology, of whom 97% were aided. *Financial aid deadline (priority):* 6/1. *Financial aid forms:* FAFSA, institutional form required; CSS Financial Aid PROFILE acceptable. *Admission application deadline:* 8/1.

Summary of Aid to Needy Students *From gift & self-help combined:* Average need met: 90%. Average amount awarded: $7970 (23% gift aid, 77% self-help). *Gift aid:* Total: $971,849 (17% from college's own funds, 6% from other college-administered sources, 77% from external sources). 20 Federal Work-Study jobs (averaging $2280); 150 part-time jobs.

Need-Based Scholarships & Grants Pell, FSEOG, state, college/university.

Loans PLUS, Stafford, Unsubsidized Stafford, state, college/university short-term loans ($500 average).

Non-Need Awards *Academic Interests/Achievement Awards:* general academic. *Creative Arts/Performance Awards:* general creative. *Special Characteristics Awards:* general special characteristics.

Other Money-Saving Options Off-campus living. *Payment Plan:* installment.

Contact Mr. Harold G. Whitis, Director of Financial Aid, The University of Texas of the Permian Basin, 4901 East University, Odessa, TX 79762-0001, 915-552-2620, fax: 915-552-2621.

THE UNIVERSITY OF TEXAS–PAN AMERICAN
Edinburg, Texas

About the Institution State-supported, coed. Degrees awarded: A, B, M, D. Offers 50 undergraduate majors. Total enrollment: 12,692. Undergraduates: 11,627 (95% state residents). Freshmen: 1,837.

Undergraduate Expenses (1996–97) State resident tuition: $900. Nonresident tuition: $7380. Mandatory fees: $693. College room and board: $2050.

Applications Of all full-time undergraduates enrolled in fall 1996, 93% of those who applied for aid were judged to have need according to Federal Methodology, of whom 99% were aided. *Financial aid deadline (priority):* 4/1. *Financial aid forms:* FAFSA, CSS Financial Aid PROFILE, institutional form required. State form required for some. *Admission application deadline:* 7/15.

Summary of Aid to Needy Students *From gift & self-help combined:* Average need met: 32%. Average amount awarded: $2189 (35% gift aid, 65% self-help). *Gift aid:* Total: $6,135,984 (10% from college's own funds, 14% from other college-administered sources, 76% from external sources). 800 Federal Work-Study jobs (averaging $900); 900 part-time jobs.

Need-Based Scholarships & Grants Pell, FSEOG, state, private, college/university.

Loans Perkins, PLUS, Stafford, Unsubsidized Stafford, college/university short-term loans ($148 average), college/university long-term loans ($1400 average).

Non-Need Awards In 1996, a total of 886 non-need awards were made. *Academic Interests/Achievement Awards:* 348 ($485,002 total): general academic, business, engineering/technologies. *Creative Arts/Performance Awards:* 89 ($38,942 total): art/fine arts, music, theater/drama. *Special Characteristics Awards:* 96 ($158,042 total): general special characteristics, members of minorities. *Athletic:* Total: 353 ($550,721); Men: 232 ($318,073); Women: 121 ($232,648).

Other Money-Saving Options Accelerated degree, co-op program, Army ROTC, off-campus living.

Contact Ms. Lucile Shabowich, Associate Director of Financial Aid, The University of Texas–Pan American, 1201 West University Drive, Edinburg, TX 78539-2999, 210-381-2507, fax: 210-381-2392.

UNIVERSITY OF THE ARTS
Philadelphia, Pennsylvania

About the Institution Independent, coed. Degrees awarded: B, M. Offers 30 undergraduate majors. Total enrollment: 1,399. Undergraduates: 1,268 (47% state residents). Freshmen: 330.

Undergraduate Expenses (1997–98) Tuition: $14,570. Mandatory fees: $500. College room only: $4100.

Applications *Financial aid deadline (priority):* 2/15. *Financial aid forms:* FAFSA required. *Admission application deadline:* rolling.

Summary of Aid to Needy Students *From gift & self-help combined:* Average need met: 65%. Average amount awarded: $9839 (55% gift aid, 45% self-help). *Gift aid:* Total: $6,000,000 (60% from college's own funds, 7% from other college-administered sources, 33% from external sources). Federal Work-Study jobs; 40 part-time jobs.

Need-Based Scholarships & Grants Pell, FSEOG, state, college/university.

Loans Perkins, PLUS, Stafford, Unsubsidized Stafford, private, college/university short-term loans.

Non-Need Awards *Academic Interests/Achievement Awards:* general academic. *Creative Arts/Performance Awards:* applied art and design, dance, music, performing arts, theater/drama.

Other Money-Saving Options Off-campus living. *Payment Plans:* installment, deferred payment. *Waivers:* full or partial for children of alumni and employees or children of employees.

Contact Office of Financial Aid, University of the Arts, 320 South Broad Street, Philadelphia, PA 19102-4944, 800-616-ARTS.

UNIVERSITY OF THE DISTRICT OF COLUMBIA
Washington, District of Columbia

About the Institution District-supported, coed. Degrees awarded: A, B, M. Offers 93 undergraduate majors. Total enrollment: 7,464. Undergraduates: 7,113 (87% district residents). Freshmen: 1,499.

Undergraduate Expenses (1997–98) District resident tuition: $2250. Nonresident tuition: $5550. Mandatory fees: $110.

Applications *Financial aid deadline (priority):* 4/15. *Financial aid forms:* FAFSA, institutional form required; CSS Financial Aid PROFILE, district form acceptable. *Admission application deadline:* 8/1.

Summary of Aid to Needy Students Federal Work-Study jobs; part-time jobs.

Loans College/university short-term loans.

Non-Need Awards *Academic Interests/Achievement Awards:* general academic. *Creative Arts/Performance Awards:* music. *Special Characteristics Awards:* children of faculty/staff. *Athletic:* available.

Other Money-Saving Options Accelerated degree, co-op program, cooperative Army ROTC, cooperative Air Force ROTC. *Payment Plans:* installment, deferred payment. *Waivers:* full or partial for employees or children of employees and senior citizens.

Contact Office of Financial Aid, University of the District of Columbia, Washington, DC 20008-1175, 202-274-5000.

UNIVERSITY OF THE OZARKS
Clarksville, Arkansas

About the Institution Independent/religious, coed. Degrees awarded: A, B. Offers 43 undergraduate majors. Total enrollment: 575 (65% state residents). Freshmen: 125.

Undergraduate Expenses (1997–98) Comprehensive fee of $10,990 includes tuition ($7250), mandatory fees ($140), and college room and board ($3600).

Applications 70% of all full-time undergraduates enrolled in fall 1996 applied for aid; of these, 94% were judged to have need according to Federal Methodology, of whom 100% were aided. *Financial aid deadline (priority):* 2/15. *Financial aid forms:* FAFSA required; CSS Financial Aid PROFILE acceptable. *Admission application deadline:* 8/15.

Summary of Aid to Needy Students *From gift & self-help combined:* Average need met: 57%. Average amount awarded: $7333 (60% gift aid, 40% self-help). *Gift aid:* Total: $1,374,001 (35% from college's own funds, 3% from other college-administered sources, 62% from external sources). 200 Federal Work-Study jobs (averaging $1275); 185 part-time jobs.

Need-Based Scholarships & Grants Pell, FSEOG, state, private, college/university.

Loans Perkins, PLUS, Stafford, Unsubsidized Stafford, college/university short-term loans ($100 average).

Non-Need Awards In 1996, a total of 311 non-need awards were made. *Academic Interests/Achievement Awards:* 215 ($901,121 total): general academic. *Creative Arts/Performance Awards:* 14 ($6117 total): art/fine arts. *Special Achievements/Activities Awards:* 35 ($55,500 total): leadership. *Special Characteristics Awards:* 47 ($184,394 total): children of faculty/staff, members of minorities, relatives of clergy.

Other Money-Saving Options *Payment Plan:* installment. *Waivers:* full or partial for employees or children of employees.

Contact Office of Financial Aid, University of the Ozarks, 415 North College Avenue, Clarksville, AR 72830-2880, 501-979-1000.

UNIVERSITY OF THE PACIFIC
Stockton, California

About the Institution Independent, coed. Degrees awarded: B, M, D, P. Offers 101 undergraduate majors. Total enrollment: 4,785. Undergraduates: 3,368 (80% state residents). Freshmen: 568.

Undergraduate Expenses (1997–98) Comprehensive fee of $24,436 includes tuition ($18,450 minimum), mandatory fees ($350), and college room and board ($5636).

Applications 75% of all full-time undergraduates enrolled in fall 1996 applied for aid; of these, 96% were judged to have need according to Federal Methodology, of whom 100% were aided. *Financial aid deadline (priority):* 3/2. *Financial aid forms:* FAFSA required. State form required for some. *Regular admission application deadline:* 3/1. Early action deadline: 12/15.

Summary of Aid to Needy Students *From gift & self-help combined:* Average need met: 86%. Average amount awarded: $18,475 (68% gift aid, 32% self-help). *Gift aid:* Total: $25,081,000 (73% from college's own funds, 19% from other college-administered sources, 8% from external sources). 1,600 Federal Work-Study jobs (averaging $1600); 150 part-time jobs.

Need-Based Scholarships & Grants Pell, FSEOG, state, private, college/university.

Loans Perkins, PLUS, Stafford, Unsubsidized Stafford, college/university short-term loans ($150 average), college/university long-term loans ($1500 average).

Non-Need Awards In 1996, a total of 541 non-need awards were made. *Academic Interests/Achievement Awards:* 240 ($2,100,000 total): general academic. *Creative Arts/Performance Awards:* 43 ($175,000 total): music. *Special Achievements/Activities Awards:* 60 ($150,000 total): religious involvement. *Athletic:* Total: 198 ($2,800,000); Men: 107 ($1,500,000); Women: 91 ($1,300,000).

Other Money-Saving Options Accelerated degree, co-op program, cooperative Air Force ROTC, off-campus living (after sophomore year). *Payment Plan:* installment. *Waivers:* full or partial for employees or children of employees.

Contact Office of Financial Aid, University of the Pacific, 3601 Pacific Avenue, Stockton, CA 95211-0197, 209-946-2011.

UNIVERSITY OF THE SACRED HEART
San Juan, Puerto Rico

About the Institution Independent/religious, coed. Degrees awarded: A, B, M. Offers 26 undergraduate majors. Total enrollment: 5,199. Undergraduates: 4,860 (99% commonwealth residents). Freshmen: 1,322.

Undergraduate Expenses (1996–97) Tuition: $3795. Mandatory fees: $240. College room only: $1400.

Applications Of all full-time undergraduates enrolled in fall 1996, 99% of those who applied for aid were judged to have need according to Federal Methodology, of whom 100% were aided. *Financial aid deadline (priority):* 6/30. *Financial aid forms:* FAFSA, institutional form, Territory of Puerto Rico income tax form required. *Admission application deadline:* 6/30.

Summary of Aid to Needy Students *From gift & self-help combined:* Average need met: 75%. *Gift aid:* Total: $3,382,325. 400 Federal Work-Study jobs (averaging $1000).

Need-Based Scholarships & Grants Pell, FSEOG, state, private, college/university.

Loans Perkins, PLUS, Stafford, Unsubsidized Stafford.

Non-Need Awards *Academic Interests/Achievement Awards:* 632 ($328,732 total): general academic. *Special Achievements/Activities Awards:* 9 ($605 total): memberships. *Special Characteristics Awards:* 50 ($112,720 total): children of faculty/staff. *Athletic:* available.

Other Money-Saving Options Accelerated degree, co-op program, off-campus living. *Payment Plan:* deferred payment. *Waivers:* full or partial for employees or children of employees.

Contact Ms. Maria Torres, Director of Financial Aid, University of the Sacred Heart, PO Box 12383 Loiza Station, San Juan, PR 00914-0383, 787-728-1515 Ext. 3608.

UNIVERSITY OF THE SOUTH
Sewanee, Tennessee

About the Institution Independent/religious, coed. Degrees awarded: B, M, D, P. Offers 41 undergraduate majors. Total enrollment: 1,346. Undergraduates: 1,266 (17% state residents). Freshmen: 366.

Undergraduate Expenses (1997–98) Comprehensive fee of $22,390 includes tuition ($17,555), mandatory fees ($175), and college room and board ($4660).

Applications 47% of all full-time undergraduates enrolled in fall 1996 applied for aid; of these, 85% were judged to have need according to Federal Methodology, of whom 99% were aided. *Financial aid deadline (priority):* 3/1. *Financial aid forms:* FAFSA, institutional form required; CSS Financial Aid PROFILE acceptable. State form required for some. *Regular admission application deadline:* 2/1. Early decision deadline: 11/15.

Summary of Aid to Needy Students *From gift & self-help combined:* Average need met: 100%. Average amount awarded: $14,422 (75% gift aid, 25% self-help). *Gift aid:* Total: $5,483,092 (89% from college's own funds, 3% from other college-administered sources, 8% from external sources). 415 Federal Work-Study jobs (averaging $955); 150 part-time jobs.

Need-Based Scholarships & Grants Pell, FSEOG, state, private, college/university.

Loans Perkins, PLUS, Stafford, Unsubsidized Stafford, private, college/university long-term loans ($1200 average).

Non-Need Awards In 1996, a total of 214 non-need awards were made. *Academic Interests/Achievement Awards:* 172 ($972,307 total): general academic. *Special Characteristics Awards:* 42 ($41,500 total): relatives of clergy, religious affiliation.

Other Money-Saving Options Accelerated degree. *Payment Plans:* installment, deferred payment. *Waivers:* full or partial for employees or children of employees.

Contact Mr. David R. Gelinas, Director of Financial Aid, University of the South, 735 University Avenue, Sewanee, TN 37383-1000, 615-598-1312, fax: 615-598-1667.

UNIVERSITY OF THE STATE OF NEW YORK, REGENTS COLLEGE
Albany, New York

About the Institution Independent, coed. Degrees awarded: A, B. Offers 35 undergraduate majors. Total enrollment: 18,432 (15% state residents).

Applications *Financial aid deadline (priority):* 7/1. *Financial aid forms:* institutional form required. FAFSA, state form required for some. *Admission application deadline:* rolling.

Need-Based Scholarships & Grants Pell, state, private, college/university.

Loans Private.

Non-Need Awards *Academic Interests/Achievement Awards:* general academic.

Other Money-Saving Options Accelerated degree. *Payment Plan:* installment. *Waivers:* full or partial for employees or children of employees.

Contact Ms. Cynthia L. Chalachan, Director of Financial Aid, University of the State of New York, Regents College, 7 Columbia Circle, Albany, NY 12203-5159, 518-464-8500, fax: 518-464-8777.

UNIVERSITY OF THE VIRGIN ISLANDS
Charlotte Amalie, St. Thomas, Virgin Islands

About the Institution Territory-supported, coed. Degrees awarded: A, B, M. Offers 25 undergraduate majors. Total enrollment: 2,898. Undergraduates: 2,666 (94% territory residents). Freshmen: 333.

Undergraduate Expenses (1996–97) Territory resident tuition: $2010. Nonresident tuition: $6030. Mandatory fees: $126. College room and board: $4810 (minimum).

Applications *Financial aid deadline:* 4/15. *Financial aid forms:* FAFSA, CSS Financial Aid PROFILE required. *Admission application deadline:* 4/15.

Summary of Aid to Needy Students *From gift & self-help combined:* Average need met: 75%. Average amount awarded: $5036 (71% gift aid, 29% self-help). *Gift aid:* Total: $2,172,103 (39% from college's own funds, 2% from other college-administered sources, 59% from external sources). 59 Federal Work-Study jobs (averaging $934); 50 part-time jobs.

Need-Based Scholarships & Grants Pell, FSEOG, state, college/university.

Loans PLUS, Stafford, Unsubsidized Stafford, college/university short-term loans ($200 average), college/university long-term loans ($400 average).

Non-Need Awards *Creative Arts/Performance Awards:* 1 ($9370 total): music. *Special Characteristics Awards:* children of faculty/staff. *Athletic:* Total: 15 ($21,638); Men: 14 ($19,638); Women: 1 ($2000).

Other Money-Saving Options Off-campus living. *Waivers:* full or partial for employees or children of employees and senior citizens.

Contact Ardrina Scott-Elliott, Financial Aid Supervisor, University of the Virgin Islands, No. 2 John Brewers Bay, Charlotte Amalie, St. Thomas, VI 00802-9990, 809-693-1090, fax: 809-693-1105.

UNIVERSITY OF TOLEDO
Toledo, Ohio

About the Institution State-supported, coed. Degrees awarded: A, B, M, D, P. Offers 140 undergraduate majors. Total enrollment: 21,692. Undergraduates: 18,187 (88% state residents). Freshmen: 2,442.

Undergraduate Expenses (1996–97) State resident tuition: $2997. Nonresident tuition: $8282. Mandatory fees: $781. College room and board: $4092. College room only: $2832.

Applications 58% of all full-time undergraduates enrolled in fall 1996 applied for aid; of these, 99% were judged to have need according to Federal Methodology, of whom 94% were aided. *Financial aid deadline (priority):* 3/1. *Financial aid forms:* FAFSA, institutional form required; CSS Financial Aid PROFILE acceptable. *Admission application deadline:* rolling.

Summary of Aid to Needy Students *From gift & self-help combined:* Average need met: 78%. Average amount awarded: $5689 (38% gift aid, 62% self-help). *Gift aid:* Total: $16,184,173 (25% from college's own funds, 12% from other college-administered sources, 63% from external sources). 589 Federal Work-Study jobs (averaging $1275); 1,200 part-time jobs.

Need-Based Scholarships & Grants Pell, FSEOG, state, private, college/university.

Loans Perkins, PLUS, Stafford, Unsubsidized Stafford, private, college/university short-term loans ($200 average).

Non-Need Awards In 1996, a total of 2,093 non-need awards were made. *Academic Interests/Achievement Awards:* 1,408 ($3,327,257 total): general academic, area/ethnic studies, business, communication, computer science, education, engineering/technologies, English, health fields, humanities, mathematics, military science, physical sciences, premedicine, social sciences. *Creative Arts/Performance Awards:* 68 ($36,196 total): art/fine arts, dance, journalism/publications, music, theater/drama. *Special Achievements/Activities Awards:* 181 ($195,479 total): general special achievements/activities, leadership, memberships. *Special Characteristics Awards:* 128 ($201,825 total): general special characteristics, adult students, children and siblings of alumni, children of educators, children of faculty/staff, ethnic background, handicapped students, local/state students, members of minorities, previous college experience, ROTC participants, siblings of current students, spouses of current students, veterans' children. *Athletic:* Total: 308 ($2,123,517); Men: 190 ($1,260,774); Women: 118 ($862,743).

Other Money-Saving Options Accelerated degree, co-op program, Army ROTC, cooperative Air Force ROTC, off-campus living (after freshman year). *Payment Plan:* installment. *Waivers:* full or partial for minority students, employees or children of employees, senior citizens.

Contact Ms. Carolyn G. Baumgartner, Assistant Director-Data Systems, University of Toledo, 2801 West Bancroft Street, Toledo, OH 43606-3398, 419-530-4181, fax: 419-530-7757.

UNIVERSITY OF TULSA
Tulsa, Oklahoma

About the Institution Independent/religious, coed. Degrees awarded: B, M, D, P. Offers 88 undergraduate majors. Total enrollment: 4,236. Undergraduates: 2,945 (64% state residents). Freshmen: 513.

Undergraduate Expenses (1996–97) Comprehensive fee of $17,520 includes tuition ($12,850), mandatory fees ($90), and college room and board ($4580). College room only: $2260.

Applications Of all full-time undergraduates enrolled in fall 1996, 98% of those who applied for aid were judged to have need according to Federal Methodology, of whom 100% were aided. *Financial aid deadline (priority):* 2/15. *Financial aid forms:* FAFSA, institutional form required. *Admission application deadline:* rolling.

Summary of Aid to Needy Students *From gift & self-help combined:* Average need met: 78%. Average amount awarded: $11,292 (67% gift aid, 33% self-help). *Gift aid:* Total: $14,163,719 (85% from college's own funds, 6% from other college-administered sources, 9% from external sources). 705 Federal Work-Study jobs (averaging $1750).

Need-Based Scholarships & Grants Pell, FSEOG, state, private, college/university.

Loans Perkins, PLUS, Stafford, Unsubsidized Stafford, private, college/university short-term loans ($200 average).

Non-Need Awards In 1996, a total of 1,631 non-need awards were made. *Academic Interests/Achievement Awards:* 926 ($2,738,773 total): general academic, biological sciences, business, communication, computer science, engineering/technologies, English, foreign languages, international studies, mathematics, premedicine, religion/biblical studies, social sciences. *Creative Arts/Performance Awards:* 202 ($856,110 total): art/fine arts, music, performing arts, theater/drama. *Special Achievements/Activities Awards:* 178 ($289,400 total): cheerleading/drum major, community service, leadership. *Special Characteristics Awards:* 113 ($113,000 total): general special characteristics, children and siblings of alumni. *Athletic:* Total: 212 ($3,113,789); Men: 133 ($2,080,299); Women: 79 ($1,033,490).

Other Money-Saving Options Off-campus living (after sophomore year). *Payment Plans:* tuition prepayment, installment. *Waivers:* full or partial for employees or children of employees.

Contact Mr. David L. Gruen, Director of Student Financial Services, University of Tulsa, 600 South College, Tulsa, OK 74104-3189, 918-631-2526, fax: 918-631-5105.

UNIVERSITY OF UTAH
Salt Lake City, Utah

About the Institution State-supported, coed. Degrees awarded: B, M, D, P. Offers 83 undergraduate majors. Total enrollment: 24,930. Undergraduates: 19,979 (90% state residents). Freshmen: 2,379.

Undergraduate Expenses (1997–98) State resident tuition: $2601. Nonresident tuition: $7998. College room and board: $4400. College room only: $1700.

Applications 47% of all full-time undergraduates enrolled in fall 1996 applied for aid; of these, 96% were judged to have need according to Federal Methodology, of whom 84% were aided. *Financial aid deadline (priority):* 3/1. *Financial aid forms:* FAFSA, institutional form required; state form acceptable. *Admission application deadline:* 7/1.

Summary of Aid to Needy Students *From gift & self-help combined:* Average need met: 54%. Average amount awarded: $5901 (54% gift aid, 46% self-help). *Gift aid:* Total: $23,602,644 (25% from college's own funds, 50% from other college-administered sources, 25% from external sources). 624 Federal Work-Study jobs (averaging $3819); 4,500 part-time jobs.

Need-Based Scholarships & Grants Pell, FSEOG, state, private, college/university.

Loans Perkins, PLUS, Stafford, Unsubsidized Stafford, Federal Nursing, Primary Care, state, private, college/university short-term loans ($650 average), college/university long-term loans ($1536 average).

Non-Need Awards In 1996, a total of 1,679 non-need awards were made. *Academic Interests/Achievement Awards:* 806 ($1,578,148 total): general academic, architecture, area/ethnic studies, biological sciences, business, communication, computer science, education, engineering/technologies, English, foreign languages, health fields, humanities, mathematics, physical sciences, social sciences. *Creative Arts/Performance Awards:* 60 ($77,672 total): dance, debating, journalism/publications, music, theater/drama. *Special Achievements/Activities Awards:* 147 ($185,646 total): general special achievements/activities, leadership. *Special Characteristics Awards:* 350 ($453,438 total): children of faculty/staff. *Athletic:* Total: 316 ($655,068); Men: 175 ($362,775); Women: 141 ($292,293).

Other Money-Saving Options Accelerated degree, co-op program, Army ROTC, Naval ROTC, Air Force ROTC, off-campus living. *Payment Plans:* installment, deferred payment. *Waivers:* full or partial for employees or children of employees and senior citizens.

Contact Mr. Doug Kenner, Senior Accountant, University of Utah, 105 Student Services Building, Salt Lake City, UT 84112, 801-581-8817, fax: 801-585-6350.

UNIVERSITY OF VERMONT
Burlington, Vermont

About the Institution State-supported, coed. Degrees awarded: A, B, M, D, P. Offers 118 undergraduate majors. Total enrollment: 8,929. Undergraduates: 7,375 (41% state residents). Freshmen: 1,799.

Undergraduate Expenses (1997–98) State resident tuition: $7032. Nonresident tuition: $17,580. Mandatory fees: $498. College room and board: $5272. College room only: $3432 (minimum).

Applications Of all full-time undergraduates enrolled in fall 1996, 97% of those who applied for aid were judged to have need according to Federal Methodology, of whom 100% were aided. *Financial aid deadline (priority):* 2/7. *Financial aid forms:* FAFSA required. State form, institutional form required for some. *Regular admission application deadline:* 2/1. Early decision deadline: 11/1. Early action deadline: 11/1.

Summary of Aid to Needy Students *From gift & self-help combined:* Average need met: 90%. Average amount awarded: $13,043 (40% gift aid, 60% self-help). *Gift aid:* Total: $16,394,547 (60% from college's own funds, 28% from other college-administered sources, 12% from external sources). 1,896 Federal Work-Study jobs (averaging $2000); part-time jobs.

Need-Based Scholarships & Grants Pell, FSEOG, state, private, college/university.

Loans Perkins, PLUS, Stafford, Unsubsidized Stafford, Federal Nursing, private, college/university long-term loans ($1850 average).

Non-Need Awards *Special Characteristics Awards:* adult students, ethnic background, first-generation college students, international students, members of minorities, ROTC participants. *Athletic:* Total: 145 ($1,796,121); Men: 61 ($939,900); Women: 84 ($856,221).

Other Money-Saving Options Co-op program, Army ROTC, cooperative Air Force ROTC, off-campus living (after sophomore year). *Payment Plans:* installment, deferred payment. *Waivers:* full or partial for employees or children of employees and senior citizens.

Contact Financial Aid Office, University of Vermont, 330 Waterman, South Prospect Street, Burlington, VT 05405-0160, 802-656-3156, fax: 802-656-4076.

UNIVERSITY OF VIRGINIA
Charlottesville, Virginia

About the Institution State-supported, coed. Degrees awarded: B, M, D, P. Offers 44 undergraduate majors. Total enrollment: 17,959. Undergraduates: 12,040 (66% state residents). Freshmen: 2,827.

Undergraduate Expenses (1997–98) State resident tuition: $4790. Nonresident tuition: $15,034. College room and board: $2700 (minimum). College room only: $1800 (minimum).

Applications Of all full-time undergraduates enrolled in fall 1996, 91% of those who applied for aid were judged to have need according to Federal Methodology, of whom 96% were aided. *Financial aid deadline (priority):* 3/1. *Financial aid forms:* FAFSA, institutional form required. *Regular admission application deadline:* 1/2. Early decision deadline: 11/1.

Summary of Aid to Needy Students *From gift & self-help combined:* Average need met: 90%. Average amount awarded: $8991 (51% gift aid, 49% self-help). *Gift aid:* Total: $18,465,000 (61% from college's own funds, 22% from other college-administered sources, 17% from external sources). 440 Federal Work-Study jobs (averaging $1608); 2,500 part-time jobs.

Need-Based Scholarships & Grants Pell, FSEOG, state, private, college/university.

Loans Perkins, PLUS, Stafford, Unsubsidized Stafford, Federal Nursing, college/university short-term loans ($500 average), college/university long-term loans ($1800 average).

Non-Need Awards In 1996, a total of 726 non-need awards were made. *Academic Interests/Achievement Awards:* 128 ($1,540,900 total): general academic. *Special Characteristics Awards:* 213 ($1,063,422 total): members of minorities. *Athletic:* Total: 385 ($4,252,146); Men: 230 ($2,572,718); Women: 155 ($1,679,428).

Other Money-Saving Options Accelerated degree, co-op program, Army ROTC, Naval ROTC, Air Force ROTC, off-campus living (after freshman year). *Payment Plan:* installment. *Waivers:* full or partial for employees or children of employees and senior citizens.

Contact Ms. Gail A. McDaniel, Assistant Director of Financial Aid, University of Virginia, PO 9021, Charlottesville, VA 22903, 804-982-5350, fax: 804-982-5222.

UNIVERSITY OF WASHINGTON
Seattle, Washington

About the Institution State-supported, coed. Degrees awarded: B, M, D, P. Offers 144 undergraduate majors. Total enrollment: 34,368. Undergraduates: 25,228 (90% state residents). Freshmen: 4,036.

Undergraduate Expenses (1996–97) State resident tuition: $3130. Nonresident tuition: $9713. Mandatory fees: $120. College room and board: $4455.

Applications Of all full-time undergraduates enrolled in fall 1996, 81% of those who applied for aid were judged to have need according to Federal Methodology, of whom 71% were aided. *Financial aid deadline (priority):* 2/28. *Financial aid forms:* FAFSA required. *Admission application deadline:* 2/1.

Summary of Aid to Needy Students *From gift & self-help combined:* Average need met: 84%. Average amount awarded: $7178 (35% gift aid, 65% self-help). *Gift aid:* Total: $27,078,250 (25% from college's own funds, 35% from other college-administered sources, 40% from external sources). Federal Work-Study jobs.

Need-Based Scholarships & Grants Pell, FSEOG, state, private, college/university.

Loans Perkins, PLUS, Stafford, Unsubsidized Stafford, Federal Nursing, Primary Care, private, college/university short-term loans ($800 average).

Non-Need Awards *Academic Interests/Achievement Awards:* general academic, architecture, biological sciences, business, communication, engineering/technologies, English, foreign languages, health fields, humanities, mathematics, physical sciences, social sciences. *Creative Arts/Performance Awards:* general creative, art/fine arts, creative writing, dance, journalism/publications, music, performing arts, theater/drama. *Special Achievements/Activities Awards:* general special achievements/activities, community service, leadership. *Special Characteristics Awards:* international students. *Athletic:* Total: ($3,513,523); Men: ($1,933,000); Women: ($1,580,523).

Other Money-Saving Options Accelerated degree, co-op program, Army ROTC, Naval ROTC, Air Force ROTC, off-campus living. *Payment Plan:* installment. *Waivers:* full or partial for employees or children of employees.

Contact Ms. Megan Davis, Assistant Director, University of Washington, Financial Aid Office, Box 355880, Seattle, WA 98195, 206-685-1698, fax: 206-685-1338.

THE UNIVERSITY OF WEST ALABAMA
Livingston, Alabama

About the Institution State-supported, coed. Degrees awarded: A, B, M. Offers 22 undergraduate majors. Total enrollment: 2,153. Undergraduates: 1,838 (77% state residents). Freshmen: 357.

Undergraduate Expenses (1996–97) Comprehensive fee of $5418 includes tuition ($2400), mandatory fees ($384), and college room and board ($2634 minimum). College room only: $1110 (minimum).

Applications 59% of all full-time undergraduates enrolled in fall 1996 applied for aid; of these, 93% were judged to have need according to Federal Methodology, of whom 100% were aided. *Financial aid deadline (priority):* 4/20. *Financial aid forms:* FAFSA acceptable. *Admission application deadline:* rolling.

Summary of Aid to Needy Students *Gift aid:* Total: $866,205 (35% from college's own funds, 15% from other college-administered sources, 50% from external sources). 150 Federal Work-Study jobs (averaging $1914); part-time jobs.

Need-Based Scholarships & Grants Pell, FSEOG, state, private, college/university.

Loans Perkins, PLUS, Stafford, Unsubsidized Stafford, college/university short-term loans, college/university long-term loans.

Non-Need Awards *Academic Interests/Achievement Awards:* ($117,378 total): computer science, English. *Creative Arts/Performance Awards:* ($7199 total): creative writing, journalism/publications, music. *Special Achievements/Activities Awards:* ($10,040 total): cheerleading/drum major, rodeo. *Special Characteristics Awards:* ($23,014 total): children of educators, children of faculty/staff. *Athletic:* Total: 137 ($122,003); Men: ($96,020); Women: ($25,983).

Other Money-Saving Options Accelerated degree, Army ROTC, Air Force ROTC, off-campus living (after sophomore year). *Payment Plan:* deferred payment. *Waivers:* full or partial for employees or children of employees.

Contact Mrs. Pat Reedy, Director of Financial Aid, The University of West Alabama, Station 3, Livingston, AL 35470, 205-652-3400.

UNIVERSITY OF WEST FLORIDA
Pensacola, Florida

About the Institution State-supported, coed. Degrees awarded: B, M, D. Offers 71 undergraduate majors. Total enrollment: 8,054. Undergraduates: 6,812 (92% state residents). Freshmen: 472.

Undergraduate Expenses (1996–97) State resident tuition: $1819. Nonresident tuition: $7064. College room and board: $4134. College room only: $1760.

Applications *Financial aid deadline (priority):* 3/1. *Financial aid forms:* FAFSA, state form, institutional form required. *Admission application deadline:* 6/30.

Summary of Aid to Needy Students *From gift & self-help combined:* Average need met: 100%. *Gift aid:* Total: $3,530,951 (17% from college's own funds, 19% from other college-administered sources, 64% from external sources). 89 Federal Work-Study jobs (averaging $2280); 839 part-time jobs.

Need-Based Scholarships & Grants Pell, FSEOG, state, college/university.

Loans Perkins, PLUS, Stafford, Unsubsidized Stafford, college/university short-term loans ($350 average).

Non-Need Awards In 1996, a total of 546 non-need awards were made. *Academic Interests/Achievement Awards:* 348 ($469,538 total):

general academic. *Creative Arts/Performance Awards:* 8 ($8000 total): applied art and design, art/fine arts, music, theater/drama. *Special Characteristics Awards:* 35 ($35,000 total): members of minorities. *Athletic:* Total: 155 ($470,622); Men: 88 ($256,314); Women: 67 ($214,308).

Other Money-Saving Options Co-op program, Army ROTC, Air Force ROTC, off-campus living.

Contact Ms. Georganne E. Major, Senior Financial Aid Officer, University of West Florida, 11000 University Parkway, Pensacola, FL 32514-5750, 904-474-2397.

UNIVERSITY OF WISCONSIN–EAU CLAIRE
Eau Claire, Wisconsin

About the Institution State-supported, coed. Degrees awarded: A, B, M. Offers 63 undergraduate majors. Total enrollment: 10,503. Undergraduates: 10,023 (80% state residents). Freshmen: 2,048.

Undergraduate Expenses (1996–97) State resident tuition: $2572. Nonresident tuition: $8036. Mandatory fees: $2. College room and board: $2904 (minimum). College room only: $1670.

Applications Of all full-time undergraduates enrolled in fall 1996, 78% of those who applied for aid were judged to have need according to Federal Methodology, of whom 98% were aided. *Financial aid deadline (priority):* 4/15. *Financial aid forms:* FAFSA, CSS Financial Aid PROFILE acceptable. *Admission application deadline:* 3/1.

Summary of Aid to Needy Students *From gift & self-help combined:* Average need met: 98%. Average amount awarded: $4455 (32% gift aid, 68% self-help). *Gift aid:* Total: $6,049,984 (6% from college's own funds, 35% from other college-administered sources, 59% from external sources). 878 Federal Work-Study jobs (averaging $1025); 925 part-time jobs.

Need-Based Scholarships & Grants Pell, FSEOG, state, private, college/university.

Loans Perkins, PLUS, Stafford, Unsubsidized Stafford, private, college/university short-term loans ($150 average), college/university long-term loans ($966 average).

Non-Need Awards In 1996, a total of 306 non-need awards were made. *Academic Interests/Achievement Awards:* 173 ($108,432 total). *Creative Arts/Performance Awards:* 95 ($34,945 total). *Special Achievements/Activities Awards:* 0. *Special Characteristics Awards:* 38 ($64,640 total).

Other Money-Saving Options Co-op program, off-campus living (after sophomore year). *Payment Plan:* installment. *Waivers:* full or partial for minority students and senior citizens.

Contact Financial Aid Office, University of Wisconsin–Eau Claire, 115 Schofield Hall, Eau Claire, WI 54701, 715-836-3373.

UNIVERSITY OF WISCONSIN–GREEN BAY
Green Bay, Wisconsin

About the Institution State-supported, coed. Degrees awarded: A, B, M. Offers 79 undergraduate majors. Total enrollment: 5,220. Undergraduates: 5,112 (95% state residents). Freshmen: 1,018.

Undergraduate Expenses (1996–97) State resident tuition: $2545. Nonresident tuition: $8009. College room and board: $2550 (minimum). College room only: $1650.

Applications 59% of all full-time undergraduates enrolled in fall 1996 applied for aid; of these, 98% were judged to have need according to Federal Methodology, of whom 93% were aided. *Financial aid deadline (priority):* 4/15. *Financial aid forms:* FAFSA required; CSS Financial Aid PROFILE acceptable. Institutional form required for some. *Admission application deadline:* 2/1.

Summary of Aid to Needy Students *From gift & self-help combined:* Average need met: 99%. Average amount awarded: $4738 (39% gift aid, 61% self-help). *Gift aid:* Total: $3,968,469 (9% from college's own funds, 35% from other college-administered sources, 56% from external sources). 253 Federal Work-Study jobs (averaging $1389); 600 part-time jobs.

Need-Based Scholarships & Grants Pell, FSEOG, state.

Loans Perkins, PLUS, Stafford, Unsubsidized Stafford, college/university short-term loans ($250 average).

Non-Need Awards In 1996, a total of 317 non-need awards were made. *Academic Interests/Achievement Awards:* 66 ($53,055 total): general academic, business, engineering/technologies. *Creative Arts/ Performance Awards:* 10 ($3425 total): art/fine arts, dance, music, theater/drama. *Special Characteristics Awards:* 34 ($119,500 total): adult students, international students. *Athletic:* Total: 207 ($475,146); Men: 93 ($194,076); Women: 114 ($281,070).

Other Money-Saving Options Accelerated degree, co-op program, off-campus living. *Payment Plan:* installment. *Waivers:* full or partial for senior citizens.

Contact Mr. Ron Ronnenberg, Director of Financial Aid, University of Wisconsin–Green Bay, 2420 Nicolet Drive, Green Bay, WI 54311-7001, 414-465-2075.

UNIVERSITY OF WISCONSIN–LA CROSSE
La Crosse, Wisconsin

About the Institution State-supported, coed. Degrees awarded: A, B, M. Offers 52 undergraduate majors. Total enrollment: 9,046. Undergraduates: 8,471 (82% state residents). Freshmen: 1,735.

Undergraduate Expenses (1996–97) State resident tuition: $2633. Nonresident tuition: $8097. Mandatory fees: $2. College room and board: $2800. College room only: $1400.

Applications Of all full-time undergraduates enrolled in fall 1996, 90% of those who applied for aid were judged to have need according to Federal Methodology, of whom 100% were aided. *Financial aid deadline (priority):* 3/15. *Financial aid forms:* FAFSA, institutional form, federal income tax form required. *Admission application deadline:* rolling.

Summary of Aid to Needy Students *From gift & self-help combined:* Average need met: 96%. Average amount awarded: $3355 (33% gift aid, 67% self-help). *Gift aid:* Total: $5,060,170 (5% from college's own funds, 48% from other college-administered sources, 47% from external sources). 450 Federal Work-Study jobs (averaging $1100); 1,800 part-time jobs.

Need-Based Scholarships & Grants Pell, FSEOG, state, private, college/university.

Loans Perkins, PLUS, Stafford, Unsubsidized Stafford, college/university short-term loans ($150 average).

Non-Need Awards In 1996, a total of 350 non-need awards were made. *Academic Interests/Achievement Awards:* 300 ($210,000 total): general academic, business, education, English, health fields, mathematics, physical sciences. *Creative Arts/Performance Awards:* 50 ($30,000 total): music, theater/drama.

Other Money-Saving Options Accelerated degree, co-op program, Army ROTC, off-campus living. *Payment Plan:* installment. *Waivers:* full or partial for minority students and senior citizens.

Contact Mr. A. C. Stadthaus, Director of Financial Aid, University of Wisconsin–La Crosse, 1725 State Street, La Crosse, WI 54601-3742, 608-785-8604, fax: 608-785-8843.

UNIVERSITY OF WISCONSIN–MADISON
Madison, Wisconsin

About the Institution State-supported, coed. Degrees awarded: B, M, D, P. Offers 138 undergraduate majors. Total enrollment: 39,826. Undergraduates: 26,910 (64% state residents). Freshmen: 5,455.

Undergraduate Expenses (1996–97) State resident tuition: $3040. Nonresident tuition: $10,210. College room and board: $4650.

Applications *Financial aid deadline (priority):* 3/1. *Financial aid forms:* FAFSA, institutional form required; CSS Financial Aid PROFILE acceptable. *Admission application deadline:* 2/1.

Summary of Aid to Needy Students *From gift & self-help combined:* Average amount awarded: $5765 (54% gift aid, 65% self-help). *Gift aid:* Total: $26,660,635 (31% from college's own funds, 11% from other college-administered sources, 58% from external sources). 2,110 Federal Work-Study jobs (averaging $1373); 6,500 part-time jobs.

Need-Based Scholarships & Grants Pell, FSEOG, state, private, college/university.

Loans Perkins, PLUS, Stafford, Unsubsidized Stafford, Federal Nursing, Primary Care, state, private, college/university short-term loans ($300 average), college/university long-term loans ($1260 average).

Non-Need Awards *Academic Interests/Achievement Awards:* available. *Creative Arts/Performance Awards:* available. *Special Achievements/ Activities Awards:* available. *Special Characteristics Awards:* available. *Athletic:* Total: 845 ($3,064,363); Men: 532 ($1,973,083); Women: 313 ($1,091,280).

Other Money-Saving Options Accelerated degree, co-op program, Army ROTC, Naval ROTC, Air Force ROTC, off-campus living.

Contact Office of Financial Aid, University of Wisconsin–Madison, 432 North Murray Street, Madison, WI 53706-1380, 608-262-1234.

UNIVERSITY OF WISCONSIN–MILWAUKEE
Milwaukee, Wisconsin

About the Institution State-supported, coed. Degrees awarded: B, M, D. Offers 111 undergraduate majors. Total enrollment: 21,877. Undergraduates: 15,272 (96% state residents). Freshmen: 2,253.

Undergraduate Expenses (1996–97) State resident tuition: $3102. Nonresident tuition: $9965. Mandatory fees: $2. College room and board: $2912 (minimum).

Applications Of all full-time undergraduates enrolled in fall 1996, 85% of those who applied for aid were judged to have need according to Federal Methodology, of whom 94% were aided. *Financial aid deadline (priority):* 3/1. *Financial aid forms:* FAFSA required. *Admission application deadline:* 6/30.

Summary of Aid to Needy Students *From gift & self-help combined:* Average need met: 77%. Average amount awarded: $7216 (26% gift aid, 74% self-help). *Gift aid:* Total: $10,856,990 (3% from college's own funds, 55% from other college-administered sources, 42% from external sources). 399 Federal Work-Study jobs (averaging $2184); part-time jobs.

Need-Based Scholarships & Grants Pell, FSEOG, state, Metropolitan Milwaukee Association of Commerce Awards, Lawton Grants.

Loans Perkins, PLUS, Stafford, Unsubsidized Stafford, Federal Nursing, college/university short-term loans ($150 average), college/university long-term loans ($1774 average).

Non-Need Awards In 1996, a total of 134 non-need awards were made. *Academic Interests/Achievement Awards:* general academic. *Creative Arts/Performance Awards:* music. *Athletic:* Total: 56 ($196,661); Men: 30 ($83,327); Women: 26 ($113,334).

Other Money-Saving Options Accelerated degree, co-op program, cooperative Army ROTC, cooperative Naval ROTC, off-campus living. *Payment Plan:* installment.

Contact Ms. Mary E. Roggeman, Director of Financial Aid, University of Wisconsin–Milwaukee, Milwaukee, WI 53201-0413, 414-29-4541.

Contact Office of Financial Aid, University of Wisconsin–Parkside, 900 Wood Road, Kenosha, WI 53141-2000, 414-595-2577.

UNIVERSITY OF WISCONSIN–OSHKOSH
Oshkosh, Wisconsin

About the Institution State-supported, coed. Degrees awarded: A, B, M. Offers 55 undergraduate majors. Total enrollment: 10,382. Undergraduates: 8,751 (96% state residents). Freshmen: 1,563.

Undergraduate Expenses (1996–97) State resident tuition: $2417. Nonresident tuition: $7881. Mandatory fees: $2. College room and board: $2511. College room only: $1551.

Applications Of all full-time undergraduates enrolled in fall 1996, 48% of those who applied for aid were judged to have need according to Federal Methodology, of whom 100% were aided. *Financial aid deadline (priority):* 3/15. *Financial aid forms:* FAFSA required. *Admission application deadline:* rolling.

Summary of Aid to Needy Students *From gift & self-help combined:* Average need met: 95%. Average amount awarded: $5200 (32% gift aid, 68% self-help). *Gift aid:* Total: $4,679,910 (1% from college's own funds, 17% from other college-administered sources, 82% from external sources). 475 Federal Work-Study jobs (averaging $1050); 1,600 part-time jobs.

Need-Based Scholarships & Grants Pell, FSEOG, state, private, college/university.

Loans Perkins, PLUS, Stafford, Unsubsidized Stafford, Federal Nursing, college/university short-term loans ($50 average).

Non-Need Awards In 1996, a total of 110 non-need awards were made. *Academic Interests/Achievement Awards:* 85 ($86,500 total): general academic, business, computer science, mathematics, physical sciences. *Creative Arts/Performance Awards:* 10 ($4500 total): art/fine arts, debating, music, theater/drama. *Special Characteristics Awards:* 15 ($14,000 total): children and siblings of alumni, local/state students, members of minorities.

Other Money-Saving Options Accelerated degree, Army ROTC, off-campus living (after sophomore year). *Payment Plan:* installment.

Contact Ms. Sheila Denney, Financial Aid Counselor, University of Wisconsin–Oshkosh, 800 Algoma Boulevard, Oshkosh, WI 54901-3551, 414-424-3377, fax: 414-424-0284.

UNIVERSITY OF WISCONSIN–PARKSIDE
Kenosha, Wisconsin

About the Institution State-supported, coed. Degrees awarded: B, M. Offers 48 undergraduate majors. Total enrollment: 4,254. Undergraduates: 4,124 (95% state residents). Freshmen: 744.

Undergraduate Expenses (1996–97) State resident tuition: $2523. Nonresident tuition: $7987. College room and board: $3166.

Applications *Financial aid deadline (priority):* 4/1. *Financial aid forms:* FAFSA, institutional form required. *Admission application deadline:* 8/1.

Summary of Aid to Needy Students *From gift & self-help combined:* Average need met: 80%. Average amount awarded: $4760 (48% gift aid, 52% self-help). *Gift aid:* Total: $4,800,000. Federal Work-Study jobs; 600 part-time jobs.

Need-Based Scholarships & Grants Pell, FSEOG, state, college/university.

Loans Perkins, PLUS, Stafford, Unsubsidized Stafford.

Non-Need Awards *Academic Interests/Achievement Awards:* general academic, premedicine. *Creative Arts/Performance Awards:* music. *Athletic:* available.

Other Money-Saving Options Accelerated degree, cooperative Army ROTC, off-campus living. *Payment Plan:* installment.

UNIVERSITY OF WISCONSIN–PLATTEVILLE
Platteville, Wisconsin

About the Institution State-supported, coed. Degrees awarded: A, B, M. Offers 48 undergraduate majors. Total enrollment: 4,998. Undergraduates: 4,665 (92% state residents). Freshmen: 935.

Undergraduate Expenses (1996–97) State resident tuition: $2143. Nonresident tuition: $7607. Mandatory fees: $448. College room and board: $2787 (minimum). College room only: $1376.

Applications Of all full-time undergraduates enrolled in fall 1996, 81% of those who applied for aid were judged to have need according to Federal Methodology, of whom 92% were aided. *Financial aid deadline (priority):* 3/15. *Financial aid forms:* FAFSA required. *Admission application deadline:* rolling.

Summary of Aid to Needy Students *From gift & self-help combined:* Average need met: 95%. Average amount awarded: $4381 (33% gift aid, 67% self-help). *Gift aid:* Total: $3,099,818 (3% from college's own funds, 10% from other college-administered sources, 87% from external sources). 656 Federal Work-Study jobs (averaging $1065); 700 part-time jobs.

Need-Based Scholarships & Grants Pell, FSEOG, state.

Loans Perkins, PLUS, Stafford, Unsubsidized Stafford, private, college/university short-term loans ($100 average).

Non-Need Awards *Academic Interests/Achievement Awards:* 374 ($340,272 total): general academic, agriculture, biological sciences, business, communication, education, engineering/technologies, health fields, mathematics. *Creative Arts/Performance Awards:* 39 ($7500 total): art/fine arts, music, theater/drama. *Special Achievements/Activities Awards:* leadership.

Other Money-Saving Options Accelerated degree, co-op program, off-campus living (after sophomore year). *Payment Plan:* installment.

Contact Office of Financial Aid, University of Wisconsin–Platteville, 1 University Plaza, Platteville, WI 53818-3099, 608-342-1491.

UNIVERSITY OF WISCONSIN–RIVER FALLS
River Falls, Wisconsin

About the Institution State-supported, coed. Degrees awarded: B, M. Offers 73 undergraduate majors. Total enrollment: 5,359. Undergraduates: 4,975 (55% state residents). Freshmen: 1,161.

Undergraduate Expenses (1996–97) State resident tuition: $2565. Nonresident tuition: $8029. College room and board: $2908. College room only: $1578.

Applications Of all full-time undergraduates enrolled in fall 1996, 88% of those who applied for aid were judged to have need according to Federal Methodology, of whom 100% were aided. *Financial aid deadline (priority):* 3/15. *Financial aid forms:* FAFSA, institutional form required; CSS Financial Aid PROFILE acceptable. *Admission application deadline:* rolling.

Summary of Aid to Needy Students *From gift & self-help combined:* Average need met: 80%. Average amount awarded: $5877 (48% gift aid, 52% self-help). *Gift aid:* Total: $9,045,471 (2% from college's own funds, 70% from other college-administered sources, 28% from external sources). 400 Federal Work-Study jobs (averaging $1050); 610 part-time jobs.

Need-Based Scholarships & Grants Pell, FSEOG, state, private, college/university.

Loans Perkins, PLUS, Stafford, Unsubsidized Stafford, state, college/university short-term loans ($100 average).

Non-Need Awards In 1996, a total of 460 non-need awards were made. *Academic Interests/Achievement Awards:* 450 ($216,000 total): general academic, agriculture, area/ethnic studies, biological sciences, business, communication, computer science, education, English, foreign languages, health fields, humanities, international studies, mathematics, physical sciences, premedicine, social sciences. *Creative Arts/ Performance Awards:* 10 ($4000 total): art/fine arts, music, theater/ drama.

Other Money-Saving Options Accelerated degree, co-op program, off-campus living (after sophomore year). *Payment Plan:* installment.

Contact Mr. David Woodward, Director of Financial Aid, University of Wisconsin–River Falls, 410 South Third Street, River Falls, WI 54022-5001, 715-425-3272, fax: 715-425-0708.

UNIVERSITY OF WISCONSIN–STEVENS POINT
Stevens Point, Wisconsin

About the Institution State-supported, coed. Degrees awarded: A, B, M. Offers 62 undergraduate majors. Total enrollment: 8,360. Undergraduates: 8,024 (92% state residents). Freshmen: 1,586.

Undergraduate Expenses (1996–97) State resident tuition: $2522. Nonresident tuition: $7986. College room and board: $3106. College room only: $1826.

Applications Of all full-time undergraduates enrolled in fall 1996, 65% of those who applied for aid were judged to have need according to Federal Methodology, of whom 94% were aided. *Financial aid deadline (priority):* 6/15. *Financial aid forms:* FAFSA required. Financial aid transcript (for transfers) required for some. *Admission application deadline:* rolling.

Summary of Aid to Needy Students *From gift & self-help combined:* Average need met: 91%. Average amount awarded: $5499 (28% gift aid, 72% self-help). *Gift aid:* Total: $5,409,902 (2% from college's own funds, 45% from other college-administered sources, 53% from external sources). 556 Federal Work-Study jobs (averaging $882); 958 part-time jobs.

Need-Based Scholarships & Grants Pell, FSEOG, state, college/ university.

Loans Perkins, PLUS, Stafford, Unsubsidized Stafford, college/university short-term loans ($75 average).

Non-Need Awards In 1996, a total of 644 non-need awards were made. *Academic Interests/Achievement Awards:* 344 ($171,991 total): general academic, architecture, biological sciences, business, communication, computer science, education, English, foreign languages, health fields, home economics, humanities, international studies, mathematics, military science, physical sciences, premedicine, social sciences. *Creative Arts/Performance Awards:* 100 ($39,200 total): applied art and design, creative writing, dance, music, performing arts, theater/ drama. *Special Achievements/Activities Awards:* 101 ($234,414 total): general special achievements/activities, leadership. *Special Characteristics Awards:* 99 ($371,657 total): general special characteristics, out-of-state students, ROTC participants.

Other Money-Saving Options Co-op program, Army ROTC, off-campus living (after sophomore year). *Payment Plan:* deferred payment.

Contact Mr. Philip George, Director, Financial Aid, University of Wisconsin–Stevens Point, 105 Student Services Center, Stevens Point, WI 54481-3897, 715-346-4771, fax: 715-346-3526.

UNIVERSITY OF WISCONSIN–STOUT
Menomonie, Wisconsin

About the Institution State-supported, coed. Degrees awarded: B, M. Offers 26 undergraduate majors. Total enrollment: 7,322. Undergraduates: 6,701 (73% state residents). Freshmen: 1,471.

Undergraduate Expenses (1996–97) State resident tuition: $2619. Nonresident tuition: $8083. College room and board: $2922. College room only: $1526.

Applications 65% of all full-time undergraduates enrolled in fall 1996 applied for aid; of these, 83% were judged to have need according to Federal Methodology, of whom 98% were aided. *Financial aid deadline (priority):* 4/1. *Financial aid forms:* FAFSA required. *Admission application deadline:* rolling.

Summary of Aid to Needy Students *From gift & self-help combined:* Average need met: 78%. Average amount awarded: $4838 (35% gift aid, 65% self-help). *Gift aid:* Total: $5,411,177 (33% from college-administered sources, 67% from external sources). 598 Federal Work-Study jobs (averaging $1231); 1,900 part-time jobs.

Need-Based Scholarships & Grants Pell, FSEOG, state, private, college/ university.

Loans Perkins, PLUS, Stafford, Unsubsidized Stafford, private, college/ university short-term loans ($100 average).

Non-Need Awards In 1996, a total of 238 non-need awards were made. *Academic Interests/Achievement Awards:* 238 ($185,975 total): general academic, business, education, engineering/technologies, home economics.

Other Money-Saving Options Accelerated degree, co-op program, off-campus living (after sophomore year). *Payment Plan:* installment.

Contact Ms. Suzanne Carlson, Director of Financial Aid, University of Wisconsin–Stout, 210 Bowman Hall, Menomonie, WI 54751, 715-232-1363.

UNIVERSITY OF WISCONSIN–SUPERIOR
Superior, Wisconsin

About the Institution State-supported, coed. Degrees awarded: A, B, M. Offers 67 undergraduate majors. Total enrollment: 2,647. Undergraduates: 2,117 (61% state residents). Freshmen: 321.

Undergraduate Expenses (1996–97) State resident tuition: $2463. Nonresident tuition: $7927. Mandatory fees: $2. College room and board: $3100. College room only: $1506.

Applications 100% of all full-time undergraduates enrolled in fall 1996 applied for aid; of these, 83% were judged to have need according to Federal Methodology, of whom 98% were aided. *Financial aid deadline (priority):* 4/15. *Financial aid forms:* FAFSA required. State form required for some. *Admission application deadline:* rolling.

Summary of Aid to Needy Students *From gift & self-help combined:* Average need met: 93%. Average amount awarded: $5398 (40% gift aid, 60% self-help). *Gift aid:* Total: $2,404,904 (8% from college's own funds, 28% from other college-administered sources, 64% from external sources). Federal Work-Study jobs; 283 part-time jobs.

Need-Based Scholarships & Grants Pell, FSEOG, state, private, college/ university.

Loans Perkins, PLUS, Stafford, Unsubsidized Stafford, state, college/ university short-term loans ($100 average), college/university long-term loans ($1100 average).

Non-Need Awards *Academic Interests/Achievement Awards:* 260 ($240,000 total): general academic, biological sciences, business, communication, computer science, education, English, health fields, humanities, mathematics, physical sciences, social sciences. *Creative Arts/

Performance Awards: general creative, art/fine arts, cinema/film/broadcasting, journalism/publications, music, performing arts, theater/drama.

Other Money-Saving Options Accelerated degree, co-op program, cooperative Air Force ROTC, off-campus living (after sophomore year). *Payment Plan:* installment. *Waivers:* full or partial for minority students, children of alumni, employees or children of employees, adult students.

Contact Ms. Anne E. Podgorak, Director of Financial Aid, University of Wisconsin–Superior, 1800 Grand Avenue, Superior, WI 54880-2873, 715-394-8203.

UNIVERSITY OF WISCONSIN–WHITEWATER
Whitewater, Wisconsin

About the Institution State-supported, coed. Degrees awarded: A, B, M. Offers 50 undergraduate majors. Total enrollment: 10,398. Undergraduates: 9,337 (94% state residents). Freshmen: 1,841.

Undergraduate Expenses (1996–97) State resident tuition: $2586. Nonresident tuition: $8050. College room and board: $2702. College room only: $1556.

Applications *Financial aid deadline (priority):* 4/15. *Financial aid forms:* FAFSA required; CSS Financial Aid PROFILE acceptable. *Admission application deadline:* rolling.

Summary of Aid to Needy Students Federal Work-Study jobs; part-time jobs.

Non-Need Awards *Academic Interests/Achievement Awards:* general academic. *Creative Arts/Performance Awards:* music, theater/drama. *Special Achievements/Activities Awards:* leadership. *Special Characteristics Awards:* local/state students.

Other Money-Saving Options Army ROTC, Air Force ROTC, off-campus living (after sophomore year). *Payment Plan:* installment.

Contact Office of Financial Aid, University of Wisconsin–Whitewater, Whitewater, WI 53190-1790, 414-472-1234.

UNIVERSITY OF WYOMING
Laramie, Wyoming

About the Institution State-supported, coed. Degrees awarded: B, M, D, P. Offers 84 undergraduate majors. Total enrollment: 11,251. Undergraduates: 8,820 (77% state residents). Freshmen: 1,239.

Undergraduate Expenses (1997–98) State resident tuition: $1944. Nonresident tuition: $7032. Mandatory fees: $382. College room and board: $4245. College room only: $1724.

Applications Of all full-time undergraduates enrolled in fall 1996, 79% of those who applied for aid were judged to have need according to Federal Methodology, of whom 98% were aided. *Financial aid deadline (priority):* 3/1. *Financial aid forms:* institutional form required. FAFSA required for some. *Admission application deadline:* 8/10.

Summary of Aid to Needy Students *From gift & self-help combined:* Average need met: 77%. Average amount awarded: $1643 (36% gift aid, 64% self-help). *Gift aid:* Total: $2,399,611 (61% from college's own funds, 6% from other college-administered sources, 33% from external sources). 324 Federal Work-Study jobs (averaging $1200); 2,600 part-time jobs.

Need-Based Scholarships & Grants Pell, FSEOG, private, college/university.

Loans Perkins, PLUS, Stafford, Unsubsidized Stafford, college/university short-term loans ($600 average), college/university long-term loans ($800 average).

Non-Need Awards In 1996, a total of 6,666 non-need awards were made. *Academic Interests/Achievement Awards:* 5,132 ($13,660,000 total): general academic. *Creative Arts/Performance Awards:* 311 ($394,208 total): dance, debating, music, theater/drama. *Special*

Achievements/Activities Awards: 127 ($153,300 total): leadership, rodeo. *Special Characteristics Awards:* 529 ($1,463,040 total): children and siblings of alumni, out-of-state students. *Athletic:* Total: 567 ($2,148,748); Men: 377 ($1,465,718); Women: 190 ($683,030).

Other Money-Saving Options Co-op program, Army ROTC, Air Force ROTC, off-campus living. *Payment Plans:* installment, deferred payment. *Waivers:* full or partial for children of alumni and senior citizens.

Contact Office of Financial Aid, University of Wyoming, Box 3335, University Station, Laramie, WY 82071-3335, 307-766-1121.

UPPER IOWA UNIVERSITY
Fayette, Iowa

About the Institution Independent, coed. Degrees awarded: A, B, M. Offers 39 undergraduate majors. Total enrollment: 695. Undergraduates: 630 (70% state residents). Freshmen: 127.

Undergraduate Expenses (1997–98) Comprehensive fee of $13,520 includes tuition ($9750) and college room and board ($3770).

Applications *Financial aid deadline (priority):* 7/1. *Financial aid forms:* FAFSA required. *Admission application deadline:* rolling.

Summary of Aid to Needy Students *From gift & self-help combined:* Average need met: 90%. Federal Work-Study jobs (averaging $846); 80 part-time jobs.

Need-Based Scholarships & Grants Pell, FSEOG, state.

Loans Perkins, PLUS, Stafford, Unsubsidized Stafford, private, TERI Loans.

Non-Need Awards *Academic Interests/Achievement Awards:* general academic. *Creative Arts/Performance Awards:* debating, music, theater/drama. *Special Characteristics Awards:* children and siblings of alumni, children of current students, parents of current students, religious affiliation, spouses of current students.

Other Money-Saving Options Accelerated degree. *Payment Plan:* installment. *Waivers:* full or partial for employees or children of employees.

Contact Office of Financial Aid, Upper Iowa University, Parker Fox Hall, Box 1859, Fayette, IA 52142-1859, 319-425-5274.

URBANA UNIVERSITY
Urbana, Ohio

About the Institution Independent/religious, coed. Degrees awarded: A, B. Offers 29 undergraduate majors. Total enrollment: 1,179 (96% state residents). Freshmen: 150.

Undergraduate Expenses (1997–98 estimated) Comprehensive fee of $14,880 includes tuition ($10,530) and college room and board ($4350 minimum). College room only: $1900.

Applications *Financial aid deadline (priority):* 6/1. *Financial aid forms:* FAFSA, institutional form required; state form acceptable. *Admission application deadline:* rolling.

Summary of Aid to Needy Students *From gift & self-help combined:* Average need met: 100%. Average amount awarded: $5101 (58% gift aid, 42% self-help). *Gift aid:* Total: $2,800,000. Federal Work-Study jobs.

Need-Based Scholarships & Grants Pell, FSEOG, state, college/university.

Loans Perkins, PLUS, Stafford, Unsubsidized Stafford.

Non-Need Awards *Academic Interests/Achievement Awards:* general academic. *Creative Arts/Performance Awards:* music, performing arts. *Special Achievements/Activities Awards:* community service, leadership, religious involvement. *Athletic:* available.

Other Money-Saving Options Accelerated degree, co-op program, off-campus living (after freshman year). *Payment Plans:* installment, deferred payment. *Waivers:* full or partial for children of alumni, employees or children of employees, senior citizens.

Contact Mrs. Jean Rabe, Director of Financial Aid, Urbana University, Urbana, OH 43078-2091, 513-484-1301.

URSINUS COLLEGE
Collegeville, Pennsylvania

About the Institution Independent/religious, coed. Degrees awarded: B. Offers 48 undergraduate majors. Total enrollment: 1,196 (66% state residents). Freshmen: 328.

Undergraduate Expenses (1996–97) Comprehensive fee of $22,090 includes tuition ($16,400), mandatory fees ($200), and college room and board ($5490).

Applications 94% of all full-time undergraduates enrolled in fall 1996 applied for aid; of these, 92% were judged to have need according to Federal Methodology, of whom 99% were aided. *Financial aid deadline (priority):* 2/15. *Financial aid forms:* FAFSA, CSS Financial Aid PROFILE, institutional form required. State form required for some. *Regular admission application deadline:* 2/15. Early decision deadline: 1/15.

Summary of Aid to Needy Students *From gift & self-help combined:* Average need met: 90%. Average amount awarded: $15,018 (65% gift aid, 35% self-help). *Gift aid:* Total: $10,304,723 (81% from college's own funds, 16% from other college-administered sources, 3% from external sources). 498 Federal Work-Study jobs (averaging $1400); 200 part-time jobs.

Need-Based Scholarships & Grants Pell, FSEOG, state, private, college/university, Office of Vocational Rehabilitation Awards.

Loans Perkins, PLUS, Stafford, Unsubsidized Stafford, private.

Non-Need Awards *Academic Interests/Achievement Awards:* general academic, health fields. *Special Achievements/Activities Awards:* leadership.

Other Money-Saving Options Accelerated degree, off-campus living. *Payment Plan:* installment. *Waivers:* full or partial for employees or children of employees and senior citizens.

Contact Ms. Suzanne B. Sparrow, Financial Aid Officer, Ursinus College, PO Box 1000, Collegeville, PA 19426-1000, 610-409-3600 Ext. 2242, fax: 610-409-3662.

URSULINE COLLEGE
Pepper Pike, Ohio

About the Institution Independent/religious, primarily women. Degrees awarded: B, M. Offers 32 undergraduate majors. Total enrollment: 1,312. Undergraduates: 1,153 (98% state residents). Freshmen: 80.

Undergraduate Expenses (1997–98) Comprehensive fee of $16,588 includes tuition ($11,424), mandatory fees ($704), and college room and board ($4460 minimum).

Applications 91% of all full-time undergraduates enrolled in fall 1996 applied for aid; of these, 96% were judged to have need according to Federal Methodology, of whom 100% were aided. *Financial aid deadline (priority):* 3/1. *Financial aid forms:* FAFSA, institutional form required. *Admission application deadline:* rolling.

Summary of Aid to Needy Students *From gift & self-help combined:* Average need met: 89%. Average amount awarded: $9870 (39% gift aid, 61% self-help). *Gift aid:* Total: $3,161,285. Federal Work-Study jobs; part-time jobs.

Need-Based Scholarships & Grants Pell, FSEOG, college/university.

Loans Perkins, PLUS, Stafford, Unsubsidized Stafford, private.

Non-Need Awards *Academic Interests/Achievement Awards:* general academic. *Creative Arts/Performance Awards:* general creative. *Special Achievements/Activities Awards:* community service, leadership. *Special Characteristics Awards:* children and siblings of alumni, children of faculty/staff, relatives of clergy, religious affiliation, ROTC participants, siblings of current students.

Other Money-Saving Options Co-op program, cooperative Army ROTC, off-campus living. *Payment Plan:* installment. *Waivers:* full or partial for employees or children of employees.

Contact Office of Financial Aid, Ursuline College, 2550 Lander Road, Pepper Pike, OH 44124-4398, 216-646-8329.

UTAH STATE UNIVERSITY
Logan, Utah

About the Institution State-supported, coed. Degrees awarded: A, B, M, D. Offers 93 undergraduate majors. Total enrollment: 20,808. Undergraduates: 16,703 (88% state residents). Freshmen: 2,442.

Undergraduate Expenses (1996–97) State resident tuition: $1584. Nonresident tuition: $5568. Mandatory fees: $387. College room and board: $3639. College room only: $1569.

Applications *Financial aid deadline:* continuous. *Financial aid forms:* FAFSA, institutional form, federal income tax form required; CSS Financial Aid PROFILE acceptable. *Admission application deadline:* 7/1.

Summary of Aid to Needy Students *From gift & self-help combined:* Average amount awarded: $2800 (28% gift aid, 72% self-help). *Gift aid:* Total: $9,000,000 (11% from college-administered sources, 89% from external sources). 500 Federal Work-Study jobs (averaging $3000); part-time jobs.

Need-Based Scholarships & Grants Pell, FSEOG, state, private, college/university.

Loans Perkins, PLUS, Stafford, Unsubsidized Stafford, college/university short-term loans ($350 average).

Non-Need Awards *Academic Interests/Achievement Awards:* general academic. *Creative Arts/Performance Awards:* available. *Special Achievements/Activities Awards:* available. *Special Characteristics Awards:* local/state students, members of minorities, out-of-state students. *Athletic:* available.

Other Money-Saving Options Accelerated degree, co-op program, Army ROTC, Air Force ROTC, off-campus living. *Payment Plan:* deferred payment. *Waivers:* full or partial for minority students, children of alumni, employees or children of employees, adult students, senior citizens.

Contact Information Specialists, Utah State University, Financial Aid Office, Logan, UT 84322-1800, 801-797-0173, fax: 801-797-0654.

UTICA COLLEGE OF SYRACUSE UNIVERSITY
Utica, New York

About the Institution Independent, coed. Degrees awarded: B. Offers 41 undergraduate majors. Total enrollment: 1,748 (87% state residents). Freshmen: 337.

Undergraduate Expenses (1997–98) Comprehensive fee of $20,562 includes tuition ($14,822), mandatory fees ($90), and college room and board ($5650). College room only: $2794.

Applications 94% of all full-time undergraduates enrolled in fall 1996 applied for aid; of these, 92% were judged to have need according to Federal Methodology, of whom 99% were aided. *Financial aid deadline (priority):* 2/15. *Financial aid forms:* FAFSA required. State form required for some. *Regular admission application deadline:* rolling. Early decision deadline: 12/1.

Summary of Aid to Needy Students *From gift & self-help combined:* Average amount awarded: $15,252 (52% gift aid, 48% self-help). *Gift aid:* Total: $10,038,499 (63% from college's own funds, 4% from other college-administered sources, 33% from external sources). 450 Federal Work-Study jobs (averaging $1194); 215 part-time jobs.

Need-Based Scholarships & Grants Pell, FSEOG, state, private, college/university.

Loans Perkins, PLUS, Stafford, Unsubsidized Stafford, private.

Non-Need Awards In 1996, a total of 204 non-need awards were made. *Academic Interests/Achievement Awards:* 204 ($774,863 total): general academic.

Other Money-Saving Options Accelerated degree, co-op program, Army ROTC, cooperative Air Force ROTC, off-campus living (after sophomore year). *Waivers:* full or partial for employees or children of employees.

Contact Office of Financial Aid, Utica College of Syracuse University, Burrstone Road, Utica, NY 13502-4892, 315-792-3111.

VALDOSTA STATE UNIVERSITY
Valdosta, Georgia

About the Institution State-supported, coed. Degrees awarded: A, B, M, D. Offers 64 undergraduate majors. Total enrollment: 9,810. Undergraduates: 8,338 (87% state residents). Freshmen: 2,520.

Undergraduate Expenses (1996–97) State resident tuition: $2043. Nonresident tuition: $5922. College room and board: $3300. College room only: $1515.

Applications *Financial aid deadline (priority):* 4/15. *Financial aid forms:* FAFSA, state form, institutional form required. CSS Financial Aid PROFILE required for some. *Admission application deadline:* rolling.

Summary of Aid to Needy Students *From gift & self-help combined:* Average need met: 80%. Average amount awarded: $4553 (34% gift aid, 66% self-help). *Gift aid:* Total: $10,450,150 (10% from college's own funds, 27% from other college-administered sources, 63% from external sources). 206 Federal Work-Study jobs (averaging $2900); 250 part-time jobs.

Need-Based Scholarships & Grants Pell, FSEOG, state, private, college/university.

Loans PLUS, Stafford, Unsubsidized Stafford, private, college/university short-term loans ($300 average).

Non-Need Awards In 1996, a total of 947 non-need awards were made. *Academic Interests/Achievement Awards:* 602 ($501,540 total): general academic, business, education, health fields, military science, social sciences. *Creative Arts/Performance Awards:* 35 ($41,350 total): art/fine arts, journalism/publications, music, theater/drama. *Special Achievements/Activities Awards:* 19 ($20,500 total): general special achievements/activities, community service, hobbies/interest. *Special Characteristics Awards:* 42 ($35,200 total): general special characteristics, children of public servants, international students, ROTC participants. *Athletic:* Total: 249 ($559,583); Men: 160 ($383,055); Women: 89 ($176,528).

Other Money-Saving Options Accelerated degree, co-op program, off-campus living (after freshman year). *Waivers:* full or partial for senior citizens.

Contact Mr. Douglas R. Tanner, Manager of Operations, Valdosta State University, 1500 North Patterson Street, Valdosta, GA 31698, 912-333-5935, fax: 912-333-5430.

VALLEY CITY STATE UNIVERSITY
Valley City, North Dakota

About the Institution State-supported, coed. Degrees awarded: B. Offers 27 undergraduate majors. Total enrollment: 1,121 (80% state residents). Freshmen: 183.

Undergraduate Expenses (1996–97) State resident tuition: $1680. Nonresident tuition: $4486. Mandatory fees: $213. College room and board: $2770 (minimum). College room only: $880.

Applications 75% of all full-time undergraduates enrolled in fall 1996 applied for aid; of these, 94% were judged to have need according to Federal Methodology, of whom 96% were aided. *Financial aid deadline*

(priority): 4/15. *Financial aid forms:* FAFSA required; CSS Financial Aid PROFILE, state form, institutional form acceptable. *Admission application deadline:* rolling.

Summary of Aid to Needy Students *From gift & self-help combined:* Average need met: 89%. Average amount awarded: $5413 (36% gift aid, 64% self-help). *Gift aid:* Total: $1,045,785 (34% from college's own funds, 11% from other college-administered sources, 55% from external sources). 56 Federal Work-Study jobs (averaging $1353); 130 part-time jobs.

Need-Based Scholarships & Grants Pell, FSEOG, state, private, college/university.

Loans Perkins, PLUS, Stafford, Unsubsidized Stafford, college/university short-term loans ($250 average).

Non-Need Awards In 1996, a total of 471 non-need awards were made. *Academic Interests/Achievement Awards:* 275 ($163,608 total): general academic, business, communication, education, engineering/technologies, library science, mathematics, physical sciences, social sciences. *Creative Arts/Performance Awards:* 43 ($12,600 total): art/fine arts, journalism/publications, music, theater/drama. *Special Characteristics Awards:* 36 ($25,000 total): children and siblings of alumni, local/state students. *Athletic:* Total: 117 ($83,595); Men: 81 ($56,195); Women: 36 ($27,400).

Other Money-Saving Options Accelerated degree, co-op program, off-campus living (after sophomore year). *Waivers:* full or partial for employees or children of employees.

Contact Mr. Ryan Graalum, Assistant Director, Financial Aid, Valley City State University, 101 College Street SW, Valley City, ND 58072, 701-845-7541, fax: 701-845-7245.

VALLEY FORGE CHRISTIAN COLLEGE
Phoenixville, Pennsylvania

About the Institution Independent/religious, coed. Degrees awarded: A, B. Offers 6 undergraduate majors. Total enrollment: 479 (98% state residents). Freshmen: 91.

Undergraduate Expenses (1997–98) Comprehensive fee of $10,040 includes tuition ($5360), mandatory fees ($1200), and college room and board ($3480). College room only: $1470.

Applications 92% of all full-time undergraduates enrolled in fall 1996 applied for aid; of these, 94% were judged to have need according to Federal Methodology, of whom 73% were aided. *Financial aid deadline (priority):* 5/1. *Financial aid forms:* FAFSA, institutional form required; CSS Financial Aid PROFILE, state form acceptable. *Admission application deadline:* 8/15.

Summary of Aid to Needy Students *From gift & self-help combined:* Average need met: 67%. Average amount awarded: $7508 (49% gift aid, 51% self-help). *Gift aid:* Total: $1,057,177 (22% from college's own funds, 37% from other college-administered sources, 41% from external sources). 35 Federal Work-Study jobs (averaging $1400); 38 part-time jobs.

Need-Based Scholarships & Grants Pell, FSEOG, state, private, college/university.

Loans Perkins, PLUS, Stafford, Unsubsidized Stafford, state, private.

Non-Need Awards In 1996, a total of 183 non-need awards were made. *Academic Interests/Achievement Awards:* 4 ($1250 total): general academic. *Creative Arts/Performance Awards:* 46 ($53,075 total): art/fine arts, music. *Special Achievements/Activities Awards:* 59 ($126,730 total): leadership. *Special Characteristics Awards:* 74 ($16,174 total): general special characteristics, children of current students, children of faculty/staff, members of minorities, siblings of current students, spouses of current students.

Contact Ms. Karen L. Fox, Director of Financial Aid, Valley Forge Christian College, 1401 Charlestown Road, Phoenixville, PA 19460-2399, 610-617-1416, fax: 610-935-9353.

VALPARAISO UNIVERSITY
Valparaiso, Indiana

About the Institution Independent/religious, coed. Degrees awarded: A, B, M, P. Offers 90 undergraduate majors. Total enrollment: 3,472. Undergraduates: 2,754 (38% state residents). Freshmen: 678.

Undergraduate Expenses (1997–98) Comprehensive fee of $18,990 includes tuition ($14,560 minimum), mandatory fees ($500), and college room and board ($3930). College room only: $2450.

Applications Of all full-time undergraduates enrolled in fall 1996, 91% of those who applied for aid were judged to have need according to Federal Methodology, of whom 99% were aided. *Financial aid deadline (priority):* 3/1. *Financial aid forms:* FAFSA required. Federal income tax form required for some. *Admission application deadline:* rolling.

Summary of Aid to Needy Students *From gift & self-help combined:* Average need met: 90%. Average amount awarded: $10,548 (67% gift aid, 33% self-help). *Gift aid:* Total: $12,534,809 (73% from college's own funds, 11% from other college-administered sources, 16% from external sources). 332 Federal Work-Study jobs (averaging $1200); 1,150 part-time jobs.

Need-Based Scholarships & Grants Pell, FSEOG, state, private, college/university.

Loans Perkins, PLUS, Stafford, Unsubsidized Stafford, private, college/university short-term loans ($500 average), college/university long-term loans ($2000 average).

Non-Need Awards In 1996, a total of 1,680 non-need awards were made. *Academic Interests/Achievement Awards:* 816 ($2,916,270 total): general academic, engineering/technologies, foreign languages, health fields, physical sciences. *Creative Arts/Performance Awards:* 88 ($71,850 total): music, performing arts, theater/drama. *Special Achievements/Activities Awards:* 22 ($32,500 total): leadership, religious involvement. *Special Characteristics Awards:* 589 ($1,907,751 total): children and siblings of alumni, children of faculty/staff, ethnic background, international students, members of minorities, relatives of clergy, religious affiliation, siblings of current students, twins. *Athletic:* Total: 165 ($1,353,742); Men: 83 ($610,852); Women: 82 ($742,890).

Other Money-Saving Options Accelerated degree, co-op program, off-campus living (after junior year). *Payment Plan:* installment. *Waivers:* full or partial for employees or children of employees.

Contact Mr. David Fevig, Director of Financial Aid, Valparaiso University, O. P. Kretzman Hall, Valparaiso, IN 46383-6493, 219-464-5015, fax: 219-464-5381.

VANDERBILT UNIVERSITY
Nashville, Tennessee

About the Institution Independent, coed. Degrees awarded: B, M, D, P. Offers 56 undergraduate majors. Total enrollment: 10,253. Undergraduates: 5,877 (12% state residents). Freshmen: 1,545.

Undergraduate Expenses (1997–98) Comprehensive fee of $27,198 includes tuition ($20,900), mandatory fees ($578), and college room and board ($5720 minimum). College room only: $4590 (minimum).

Applications Of all full-time undergraduates enrolled in fall 1996, 92% of those who applied for aid were judged to have need according to Federal Methodology, of whom 100% were aided. *Financial aid deadline (priority):* 2/15. *Financial aid forms:* FAFSA, CSS Financial Aid PROFILE, state form required. Institutional form required for some. *Regular admission application deadline:* 1/15. Early decision deadline: 11/1.

Summary of Aid to Needy Students *From gift & self-help combined:* Average need met: 95%. Average amount awarded: $19,168 (66% gift aid, 34% self-help). *Gift aid:* Total: $27,390,200 (84% from college's own funds, 2% from other college-administered sources, 14% from external sources). 845 Federal Work-Study jobs (averaging $1000); 1,000 part-time jobs.

Need-Based Scholarships & Grants Pell, FSEOG, state, private, college/university.

Loans Perkins, PLUS, Stafford, Unsubsidized Stafford, Federal Nursing, private, college/university short-term loans ($500 average), college/university long-term loans ($2120 average).

Non-Need Awards In 1996, a total of 1,303 non-need awards were made. *Academic Interests/Achievement Awards:* 720 ($6,000,000 total): general academic, education, engineering/technologies, humanities. *Creative Arts/Performance Awards:* 40 ($250,000 total): journalism/publications, music. *Special Characteristics Awards:* 320 ($2,200,000 total): local/state students, members of minorities, ROTC participants. *Athletic:* Total: 223 ($4,966,639); Men: 144 ($3,310,653); Women: 79 ($1,655,986).

Other Money-Saving Options Accelerated degree, Army ROTC, Naval ROTC, cooperative Air Force ROTC. *Payment Plans:* tuition prepayment, installment, deferred payment. *Waivers:* full or partial for employees or children of employees.

Contact Office of Student Financial Aid, Vanderbilt University, 2309 West End Avenue, Nashville, TN 37240-1001, 615-322-3591.

VANDERCOOK COLLEGE OF MUSIC
Chicago, Illinois

About the Institution Independent, coed. Degrees awarded: B, M. Offers 1 undergraduate major. Total enrollment: 175. Undergraduates: 65 (70% state residents). Freshmen: 25.

Undergraduate Expenses (1996–97) Comprehensive fee of $14,445 includes tuition ($9400), mandatory fees ($250), and college room and board ($4795).

Applications 93% of all full-time undergraduates enrolled in fall 1996 applied for aid; of these,100% were judged to have need according to Federal Methodology, of whom 100% were aided. *Financial aid deadline (priority):* 5/31. *Financial aid forms:* FAFSA required; CSS Financial Aid PROFILE acceptable. *Regular admission application deadline:* rolling. Early decision deadline: 12/1.

Summary of Aid to Needy Students *From gift & self-help combined:* Average need met: 58%. Average amount awarded: $6403 (67% gift aid, 33% self-help). *Gift aid:* Total: $262,374 (63% from college's own funds, 25% from other college-administered sources, 12% from external sources). 20 part-time jobs.

Need-Based Scholarships & Grants Pell, state, college/university.

Loans PLUS, Stafford, Unsubsidized Stafford.

Non-Need Awards *Academic Interests/Achievement Awards:* general academic. *Creative Arts/Performance Awards:* music.

Other Money-Saving Options Off-campus living. *Payment Plan:* installment.

Contact Ami Bartz, Admissions Counselor, VanderCook College of Music, 3140 South Federal Street, Chicago, IL 60616-3886, 312-225-6288, fax: 312-225-5211.

VASSAR COLLEGE
Poughkeepsie, New York

About the Institution Independent, coed. Degrees awarded: B, M. Offers 46 undergraduate majors. Total enrollment: 2,330. Undergraduates: 2,329 (32% state residents). Freshmen: 618.

Undergraduate Expenses (1997–98) Comprehensive fee of $28,560 includes tuition ($21,780), mandatory fees ($310), and college room and board ($6470).

Applications 63% of all full-time undergraduates enrolled in fall 1996 applied for aid; of these, 94% were judged to have need according to Federal Methodology, of whom 99% were aided. *Financial aid deadline:*

1/1. *Financial aid forms:* FAFSA, CSS Financial Aid PROFILE, state form, institutional form required. *Regular admission application deadline:* 1/1. Early decision deadline: 12/1.

Summary of Aid to Needy Students *From gift & self-help combined:* Average need met: 84%. Average amount awarded: $18,105 (73% gift aid, 27% self-help). *Gift aid:* Total: $17,695,603 (88% from college's own funds, 2% from other college-administered sources, 10% from external sources). 990 Federal Work-Study jobs (averaging $1300); 244 part-time jobs.

Need-Based Scholarships & Grants Pell, FSEOG, state, private, college/university.

Loans Perkins, PLUS, Stafford, Unsubsidized Stafford, private, college/university short-term loans ($100 average), college/university long-term loans ($2654 average).

Non-Need Awards Not offered.

Other Money-Saving Options Accelerated degree, off-campus living (after freshman year). *Waivers:* full or partial for employees or children of employees.

Contact Office of Financial Aid, Vassar College, Raymond Avenue, Poughkeepsie, NY 12604-0008, 914-437-7000.

VILLA JULIE COLLEGE
Stevenson, Maryland

About the Institution Independent, coed. Degrees awarded: A, B, M. Offers 53 undergraduate majors. Total enrollment: 1,866. Undergraduates: 1,844 (96% state residents). Freshmen: 287.

Undergraduate Expenses (1996–97) Tuition: $8510. Mandatory fees: $100. College room only: $3240.

Applications 87% of all full-time undergraduates enrolled in fall 1996 applied for aid; of these, 75% were judged to have need according to Federal Methodology, of whom 98% were aided. *Financial aid deadline (priority):* 3/1. *Financial aid forms:* FAFSA, institutional form required. *Admission application deadline:* 7/15.

Summary of Aid to Needy Students *From gift & self-help combined:* Average need met: 64%. Average amount awarded: $6912 (58% gift aid, 42% self-help). *Gift aid:* Total: $2,971,795 (42% from college's own funds, 42% from other college-administered sources, 16% from external sources). 46 Federal Work-Study jobs (averaging $1387); 10 part-time jobs.

Need-Based Scholarships & Grants Pell, FSEOG, state, private, college/university.

Loans Perkins, PLUS, Stafford, Unsubsidized Stafford.

Non-Need Awards In 1996, a total of 453 non-need awards were made. *Academic Interests/Achievement Awards:* 380 ($1,211,820 total): general academic. *Creative Arts/Performance Awards:* 2 ($8255 total): art/fine arts, creative writing. *Special Achievements/Activities Awards:* 55 ($116,250 total): general special achievements/activities, leadership. *Special Characteristics Awards:* 16 ($36,200 total): general special characteristics, ROTC participants.

Other Money-Saving Options Co-op program, cooperative Army ROTC, off-campus living. *Waivers:* full or partial for employees or children of employees.

Contact Office of Financial Aid, Villa Julie College, Greenspring Valley Road, Stevenson, MD 21153, 410-486-7000.

VILLANOVA UNIVERSITY
Villanova, Pennsylvania

About the Institution Independent/religious, coed. Degrees awarded: A, B, M, D, P. Offers 53 undergraduate majors. Total enrollment: 10,182. Undergraduates: 6,771 (31% state residents). Freshmen: 1,588.

Undergraduate Expenses (1997–98) Comprehensive fee of $26,430 includes tuition ($18,370 minimum), mandatory fees ($300), and college room and board ($7760). College room only: $4170.

Applications 59% of all full-time undergraduates enrolled in fall 1996 applied for aid; of these, 87% were judged to have need according to Federal Methodology, of whom 96% were aided. *Financial aid deadline (priority):* 2/15. *Financial aid forms:* FAFSA, institutional form, W-2 forms, federal income tax forms (student and parent) required. State form required for some. *Regular admission application deadline:* 1/15. Early action deadline: 12/1.

Summary of Aid to Needy Students *From gift & self-help combined:* Average need met: 73%. Average amount awarded: $12,285 (65% gift aid, 35% self-help). *Gift aid:* Total: $25,024,263 (79% from college's own funds, 2% from other college-administered sources, 19% from external sources). 700 Federal Work-Study jobs (averaging $2000).

Need-Based Scholarships & Grants Pell, FSEOG, state, private, college/university, endowed and restricted grants.

Loans Perkins, PLUS, Stafford, Unsubsidized Stafford, Federal Nursing, private.

Non-Need Awards In 1996, a total of 827 non-need awards were made. *Academic Interests/Achievement Awards:* 285 ($2,979,834 total): general academic. *Special Characteristics Awards:* 308 ($3,225,459 total): children of educators, members of minorities, religious affiliation, ROTC participants. *Athletic:* Total: 234 ($4,063,275); Men: 131 ($2,526,672); Women: 103 ($1,536,603).

Other Money-Saving Options Accelerated degree, Army ROTC, Naval ROTC, cooperative Air Force ROTC, off-campus living. *Waivers:* full or partial for employees or children of employees and senior citizens.

Contact Office of Financial Aid, Villanova University, 800 Lancaster Avenue, Villanova, PA 19085-1699, 610-519-4500.

VIRGINIA COMMONWEALTH UNIVERSITY
Richmond, Virginia

About the Institution State-supported, coed. Degrees awarded: B, M, D, P. Offers 104 undergraduate majors. Total enrollment: 21,681. Undergraduates: 12,527 (95% state residents). Freshmen: 1,928.

Undergraduate Expenses (1997–98) State resident tuition: $3125. Nonresident tuition: $11,293. Mandatory fees: $986. College room and board: $4352. College room only: $1690 (minimum).

Applications Of all full-time undergraduates enrolled in fall 1996, 91% of those who applied for aid were judged to have need according to Federal Methodology, of whom 96% were aided. *Financial aid deadline (priority):* 3/15. *Financial aid forms:* FAFSA required. *Regular admission application deadline:* 2/1. Early decision deadline: 11/1.

Summary of Aid to Needy Students *From gift & self-help combined:* Average need met: 64%. Average amount awarded: $6497 (38% gift aid, 62% self-help). *Gift aid:* Total: $14,765,620 (10% from college's own funds, 50% from other college-administered sources, 40% from external sources). 550 Federal Work-Study jobs (averaging $2000); 1,300 part-time jobs.

Need-Based Scholarships & Grants Pell, FSEOG, state, college/university.

Loans Perkins, PLUS, Stafford, Unsubsidized Stafford, Federal Nursing, Primary Care, private, college/university short-term loans ($200 average).

Non-Need Awards In 1996, a total of 1,727 non-need awards were made. *Academic Interests/Achievement Awards:* 753 ($2,259,869 total): general academic, health fields. *Creative Arts/Performance Awards:* 30 ($32,260 total): applied art and design, art/fine arts, music. *Special Characteristics Awards:* 795 ($1,408,737 total): general special characteristics, children of union members/company employees, first-generation college students, ROTC participants, veterans, veterans' children. *Athletic:* Total: 149 ($1,049,111); Men: 66 ($539,845); Women: 83 ($509,266).

Other Money-Saving Options Accelerated degree, co-op program, Army ROTC, off-campus living. *Payment Plan:* installment. *Waivers:* full or partial for senior citizens.

Contact Ms. Sherry Mikuta, Director of Support Services, Virginia Commonwealth University, PO Box 843537, Richmond, VA 23284-2527, 804-828-1280, fax: 804-828-6186.

VIRGINIA INTERMONT COLLEGE
Bristol, Virginia

About the Institution Independent/religious, coed. Degrees awarded: A, B. Offers 34 undergraduate majors. Total enrollment: 769 (72% state residents). Freshmen: 160.

Undergraduate Expenses (1997–98) Comprehensive fee of $15,550 includes tuition ($10,650), mandatory fees ($200), and college room and board ($4700). College room only: $2400.

Applications 96% of all full-time undergraduates enrolled in fall 1996 applied for aid; of these, 80% were judged to have need according to Federal Methodology, of whom 99% were aided. *Financial aid deadline (priority):* 4/15. *Financial aid forms:* FAFSA required. State form, institutional form required for some. *Admission application deadline:* rolling.

Summary of Aid to Needy Students *From gift & self-help combined:* Average need met: 80%. Average amount awarded: $7200 (61% gift aid, 39% self-help). *Gift aid:* Total: $1,259,180 (43% from college's own funds, 39% from other college-administered sources, 18% from external sources). 173 Federal Work-Study jobs (averaging $1500); 80 part-time jobs.

Need-Based Scholarships & Grants Pell, FSEOG.

Loans Perkins, PLUS, Stafford, Unsubsidized Stafford, Keesee Educational Funds.

Non-Need Awards In 1996, a total of 351 non-need awards were made. *Academic Interests/Achievement Awards:* 170 ($239,387 total): general academic. *Creative Arts/Performance Awards:* 87 ($47,725 total): general creative, applied art and design, art/fine arts, dance, performing arts. *Special Characteristics Awards:* 10 ($4025 total): religious affiliation. *Athletic:* Total: 84 ($163,518); Men: 48 ($98,449); Women: 36 ($65,069).

Other Money-Saving Options Off-campus living (after junior year). *Payment Plan:* installment. *Waivers:* full or partial for employees or children of employees.

Contact Mrs. Nancy Roberts, Director of Financial Aid, Virginia Intermont College, Bristol, VA 24201-4298, 540-669-6101 Ext. 209.

VIRGINIA MILITARY INSTITUTE
Lexington, Virginia

About the Institution State-supported, primarily men. Degrees awarded: B. Offers 14 undergraduate majors. Total enrollment: 1,218 (60% state residents). Freshmen: 390.

Undergraduate Expenses (1997–98) State resident tuition: $3655. Nonresident tuition: $10,680. Mandatory fees: $2725. College room and board: $3695. College room only: $1035.

Applications Of all full-time undergraduates enrolled in fall 1996, 85% of those who applied for aid were judged to have need according to Federal Methodology, of whom 98% were aided. *Financial aid deadline (priority):* 4/1. *Financial aid forms:* FAFSA, institutional form required. *Regular admission application deadline:* 4/1. Early decision deadline: 11/15.

Summary of Aid to Needy Students *From gift & self-help combined:* Average need met: 92%. Average amount awarded: $7189 (67% gift aid, 33% self-help). *Gift aid:* Total: $2,329,745 (47% from college's own funds, 25% from other college-administered sources, 28% from external sources). 57 Federal Work-Study jobs (averaging $1070); 160 part-time jobs.

Need-Based Scholarships & Grants Pell, FSEOG, state, private, college/university.

Loans Perkins, PLUS, Stafford, Unsubsidized Stafford, college/university short-term loans ($500 average).

Non-Need Awards In 1996, a total of 373 non-need awards were made. *Academic Interests/Achievement Awards:* 107 ($611,622 total): general academic, biological sciences, engineering/technologies, mathematics, premedicine. *Special Achievements/Activities Awards:* 3 ($4000 total): leadership. *Special Characteristics Awards:* 93 ($373,351 total): children and siblings of alumni, children of faculty/staff, local/state students, members of minorities, out-of-state students, ROTC participants. *Athletic:* Total: 170 ($1,043,051); Men: 170 ($1,043,051).

Other Money-Saving Options Accelerated degree, Army ROTC, Naval ROTC, Air Force ROTC. *Payment Plan:* installment.

Contact Office of Financial Aid, Virginia Military Institute, 306 Carroll Hall, Lexington, VA 24450, 540-464-7211.

VIRGINIA POLYTECHNIC INSTITUTE AND STATE UNIVERSITY
Blacksburg, Virginia

About the Institution State-supported, coed. Degrees awarded: A, B, M, D. Offers 112 undergraduate majors. Total enrollment: 24,812. Undergraduates: 20,525 (79% state residents). Freshmen: 4,976.

Undergraduate Expenses (1997–98) State resident tuition: $3500. Nonresident tuition: $10,464. Mandatory fees: $647. College room and board: $3420. College room only: $1568.

Applications Of all full-time undergraduates enrolled in fall 1996, 78% of those who applied for aid were judged to have need according to Federal Methodology, of whom 100% were aided. *Financial aid deadline (priority):* 3/1. *Financial aid forms:* FAFSA required. Institutional form required for some. *Regular admission application deadline:* 2/1. Early action deadline: 11/1.

Summary of Aid to Needy Students *From gift & self-help combined:* Average amount awarded: $5899 (50% gift aid, 50% self-help). *Gift aid:* Total: $27,963,888 (21% from college's own funds, 42% from other college-administered sources, 37% from external sources). 1,640 Federal Work-Study jobs (averaging $1171); 3,615 part-time jobs.

Need-Based Scholarships & Grants Pell, FSEOG, state, private, college/university, General Scholarship Program.

Loans Perkins, PLUS, Stafford, Unsubsidized Stafford, college/university short-term loans ($639 average), Health Professions Loans.

Non-Need Awards In 1996, a total of 2,182 non-need awards were made. *Academic Interests/Achievement Awards:* 927 ($1,248,167 total): general academic, agriculture, business, education, engineering/technologies, mathematics. *Creative Arts/Performance Awards:* 14 ($7200 total): journalism/publications, music, theater/drama. *Special Achievements/Activities Awards:* 288 ($623,719 total): community service, leadership, memberships. *Special Characteristics Awards:* 618 ($2,343,321 total): children of faculty/staff, members of minorities, out-of-state students, ROTC participants. *Athletic:* Total: 335 ($2,741,097); Men: 207 ($1,734,977); Women: 128 ($1,006,120).

Other Money-Saving Options Accelerated degree, co-op program, Army ROTC, Naval ROTC, Air Force ROTC, off-campus living (after freshman year). *Payment Plan:* installment. *Waivers:* full or partial for employees or children of employees.

Contact Mr. Gary Brewer, Assistant Director of Financial Aid, Virginia Polytechnic Institute and State University, 222 Burruss Hall, Blacksburg, VA 24061-0202, 540-231-9551, fax: 540-231-9139.

VIRGINIA STATE UNIVERSITY
Petersburg, Virginia

About the Institution State-supported, coed. Degrees awarded: B, M. Offers 26 undergraduate majors. Total enrollment: 4,014. Undergraduates: 3,053 (65% state residents). Freshmen: 790.

Undergraduate Expenses (1997–98) State resident tuition: $1951. Nonresident tuition: $6430. Mandatory fees: $1356. College room and board: $4910. College room only: $2800.

Applications 94% of all full-time undergraduates enrolled in fall 1996 applied for aid; of these, 89% were judged to have need according to Federal Methodology, of whom 97% were aided. *Financial aid deadline (priority):* 3/31. *Financial aid forms:* FAFSA, institutional form required. CSS Financial Aid PROFILE, state form, Stafford Student Loan form required for some. *Admission application deadline:* rolling.

Summary of Aid to Needy Students *From gift & self-help combined:* Average need met: 70%. Average amount awarded: $7590 (44% gift aid, 56% self-help). *Gift aid:* Total: $7,401,974 (11% from college's own funds, 43% from other college-administered sources, 46% from external sources). 309 Federal Work-Study jobs (averaging $2000); 51 part-time jobs.

Need-Based Scholarships & Grants Pell, FSEOG, state, private.

Loans Perkins, PLUS, Stafford, Unsubsidized Stafford, college/university short-term loans ($1000 average).

Non-Need Awards In 1996, a total of 404 non-need awards were made. *Academic Interests/Achievement Awards:* 200 ($400,000 total): general academic, agriculture, biological sciences, business, education, engineering/technologies, health fields, home economics, military science, premedicine, social sciences. *Creative Arts/Performance Awards:* 50 ($50,000 total): art/fine arts, music, performing arts. *Special Characteristics Awards:* 35 ($125,000 total): ROTC participants, veterans. *Athletic:* Total: 119 ($336,421); Men: 100 ($272,628); Women: 19 ($63,793).

Other Money-Saving Options Accelerated degree, co-op program, Army ROTC, off-campus living (after freshman year). *Payment Plan:* deferred payment. *Waivers:* full or partial for minority students and senior citizens.

Contact Ms. Angela Hamilton, Assistant Director, Student Services, Virginia State University, 101 Gandy Hall, PO Box 9031, Petersburg, VA 23806-2096, 804-524-5864, fax: 804-524-6818.

VIRGINIA UNION UNIVERSITY
Richmond, Virginia

About the Institution Independent/religious, coed. Degrees awarded: B, D, P. Offers 22 undergraduate majors. Total enrollment: 1,551. Undergraduates: 1,307 (49% state residents). Freshmen: 385.

Undergraduate Expenses (1996–97) Comprehensive fee of $12,849 includes tuition ($8579), mandatory fees ($490), and college room and board ($3780). College room only: $1790.

Applications 92% of all full-time undergraduates enrolled in fall 1996 applied for aid; of these, 95% were judged to have need according to Federal Methodology, of whom 100% were aided. *Financial aid deadline (priority):* 5/1. *Financial aid forms:* CSS Financial Aid PROFILE required; FAFSA acceptable. State form required for some. *Admission application deadline:* rolling.

Summary of Aid to Needy Students *From gift & self-help combined:* Average need met: 59%. Average amount awarded: $4555 (53% gift aid, 47% self-help). *Gift aid:* Total: $2,668,039 (44% from college's own funds, 24% from other college-administered sources, 32% from external sources). 304 Federal Work-Study jobs (averaging $884).

Need-Based Scholarships & Grants Pell, FSEOG, state, private.

Loans Perkins, PLUS, Stafford, Unsubsidized Stafford.

Non-Need Awards In 1996, a total of 272 non-need awards were made. *Academic Interests/Achievement Awards:* 96 ($376,830 total): general academic. *Creative Arts/Performance Awards:* 30 ($12,250 total): music. *Special Characteristics Awards:* 22 ($60,344 total): children of faculty/staff. *Athletic:* Total: 124 ($318,786); Men: 88 ($280,268); Women: 36 ($38,518).

Other Money-Saving Options Co-op program, cooperative Army ROTC, off-campus living. *Payment Plans:* installment, deferred payment. *Waivers:* full or partial for employees or children of employees.

Contact Mr. Nigel D. Edwards, Reports Coordinator, Virginia Union University, 1500 North Lombardy Street, Richmond, VA 23220-1170, 804-257-5763, fax: 804-257-5797.

VIRGINIA WESLEYAN COLLEGE
Norfolk, Virginia

About the Institution Independent/religious, coed. Degrees awarded: B. Offers 54 undergraduate majors. Total enrollment: 1,460 (71% state residents). Freshmen: 273.

Undergraduate Expenses (1997–98) Comprehensive fee of $18,950 includes tuition ($13,400) and college room and board ($5550).

Applications 86% of all full-time undergraduates enrolled in fall 1996 applied for aid; of these, 93% were judged to have need according to Federal Methodology, of whom 99% were aided. *Financial aid deadline (priority):* 3/1. *Financial aid forms:* FAFSA required. State form required for some. *Admission application deadline:* rolling.

Summary of Aid to Needy Students *From gift & self-help combined:* Average need met: 73%. Average amount awarded: $9510 (59% gift aid, 41% self-help). *Gift aid:* Total: $4,856,957 (66% from college's own funds, 21% from other college-administered sources, 13% from external sources). 226 Federal Work-Study jobs (averaging $1500).

Need-Based Scholarships & Grants Pell, FSEOG, state, private, college/university.

Loans Perkins, PLUS, Stafford, Unsubsidized Stafford.

Non-Need Awards In 1996, a total of 301 non-need awards were made. *Academic Interests/Achievement Awards:* 269 ($1,498,439 total): general academic. *Creative Arts/Performance Awards:* 13 ($27,165 total): music. *Special Characteristics Awards:* 19 ($1,309,800 total): children of educators, children of faculty/staff, local/state students, relatives of clergy.

Other Money-Saving Options Accelerated degree. *Waivers:* full or partial for employees or children of employees and senior citizens.

Contact Office of Financial Aid, Virginia Wesleyan College, 1584 Wesleyan Drive, Norfolk, VA 23502-5599, 757-455-3200.

VITERBO COLLEGE
La Crosse, Wisconsin

About the Institution Independent/religious, coed. Degrees awarded: B, M. Offers 45 undergraduate majors. Total enrollment: 1,914. Undergraduates: 1,637 (76% state residents). Freshmen: 292.

Undergraduate Expenses (1997–98) Comprehensive fee of $15,200 includes tuition ($10,880), mandatory fees ($270), and college room and board ($4050). College room only: $1770.

Applications 91% of all full-time undergraduates enrolled in fall 1996 applied for aid; of these, 94% were judged to have need according to Federal Methodology, of whom 100% were aided. *Financial aid deadline (priority):* 3/15. *Financial aid forms:* FAFSA, institutional form required. State form required for some. *Admission application deadline:* rolling.

Summary of Aid to Needy Students *From gift & self-help combined:* Average need met: 81%. Average amount awarded: $10,633 (60% gift aid, 40% self-help). *Gift aid:* Total: $6,904,130 (65% from college's own funds, 3% from other college-administered sources, 32% from external sources). 253 Federal Work-Study jobs (averaging $1400); 70 part-time jobs.

Need-Based Scholarships & Grants Pell, FSEOG, state, private, college/university.

Loans Perkins, PLUS, Stafford, Unsubsidized Stafford, Federal Nursing, college/university short-term loans ($200 average).

Non-Need Awards In 1996, a total of 1,341 non-need awards were made. *Academic Interests/Achievement Awards:* 1,107 ($3,863,818 total): general academic, health fields, international studies. *Creative Arts/Performance Awards:* 132 ($169,250 total): art/fine arts, music, performing arts, theater/drama. *Special Characteristics Awards:* 68 ($327,526 total): children and siblings of alumni, children of faculty/staff, ROTC participants. *Athletic:* Total: 34 ($33,250); Men: 16 ($18,500); Women: 18 ($14,750).

Other Money-Saving Options Accelerated degree, co-op program, cooperative Army ROTC, off-campus living (after sophomore year). *Payment Plan:* installment. *Waivers:* full or partial for minority students, employees or children of employees, senior citizens.

Contact Ms. Terry Norman, Director of Financial Aid, Viterbo College, 815 South Ninth Street, La Crosse, WI 54601-4797, 608-796-3900, fax: 608-796-3050.

VOORHEES COLLEGE
Denmark, South Carolina

About the Institution Independent/religious, coed. Degrees awarded: B. Offers 16 undergraduate majors. Total enrollment: 800 (73% state residents). Freshmen: 166.

Undergraduate Expenses (1996–97) Comprehensive fee of $7490 includes tuition ($4784) and college room and board ($2706).

Applications 98% of all full-time undergraduates enrolled in fall 1996 applied for aid; of these, 99% were judged to have need according to Federal Methodology, of whom 100% were aided. *Financial aid deadline (priority):* 4/1. *Financial aid forms:* FAFSA, institutional form required. *Admission application deadline:* rolling.

Summary of Aid to Needy Students *From gift & self-help combined:* Average need met: 61%. Average amount awarded: $6690 (51% gift aid, 49% self-help). *Gift aid:* Total: $2,653,286 (7% from college's own funds, 16% from other college-administered sources, 77% from external sources). 250 Federal Work-Study jobs (averaging $1428).

Need-Based Scholarships & Grants Pell, FSEOG, state, private, college/university, United Negro College Fund Scholarships.

Loans Perkins, PLUS, Stafford, Unsubsidized Stafford, state.

Non-Need Awards In 1996, a total of 119 non-need awards were made. *Academic Interests/Achievement Awards:* 28 ($55,873 total): general academic, business, computer science, education, premedicine. *Special Achievements/Activities Awards:* 50 ($25,000 total): community service. *Special Characteristics Awards:* 6 ($14,974 total): children of faculty/staff. *Athletic:* Total: 35 ($80,000); Men: 22 ($50,000); Women: 13 ($30,000).

Other Money-Saving Options Co-op program, cooperative Army ROTC, off-campus living (after sophomore year). *Payment Plans:* installment, deferred payment. *Waivers:* full or partial for employees or children of employees.

Contact Ms. Carolyn B. White, Director of Financial Aid, Voorhees College, Voorhees Road, Denmark, SC 29042, 803-793-3351, fax: 803-793-3068.

WABASH COLLEGE
Crawfordsville, Indiana

About the Institution Independent, men. Degrees awarded: B. Offers 24 undergraduate majors. Total enrollment: 824 (72% state residents). Freshmen: 248.

Undergraduate Expenses (1997–98) Comprehensive fee of $20,480 includes tuition ($15,400), mandatory fees ($300), and college room and board ($4780).

Applications 69% of all full-time undergraduates enrolled in fall 1996 applied for aid; of these, 95% were judged to have need according to Federal Methodology, of whom 100% were aided. *Financial aid deadline (priority):* 2/15. *Financial aid forms:* FAFSA, CSS Financial Aid PROFILE required. *Regular admission application deadline:* 3/1. Early decision deadline: 12/1. Early action deadline: 12/1.

Summary of Aid to Needy Students *From gift & self-help combined:* Average need met: 100%. Average amount awarded: $15,720 (77% gift aid, 23% self-help). *Gift aid:* Total: $6,596,011 (79% from college's own funds, 15% from other college-administered sources, 6% from external sources). 461 part-time jobs.

Need-Based Scholarships & Grants Pell, state, private, college/university.

Loans PLUS, Stafford, Unsubsidized Stafford, private, college/university short-term loans ($300 average), signature loans.

Non-Need Awards In 1996, a total of 653 non-need awards were made. *Academic Interests/Achievement Awards:* 534 ($2,527,079 total): general academic. *Creative Arts/Performance Awards:* 16 ($127,000 total): art/fine arts, creative writing, music, theater/drama. *Special Achievements/Activities Awards:* 103 ($1,022,953 total): community service, leadership.

Other Money-Saving Options Accelerated degree, off-campus living (after sophomore year). *Payment Plan:* installment. *Waivers:* full or partial for employees or children of employees.

Contact Mr. Clint Gasaway, Financial Aid Director, Wabash College, PO Box 352, Crawfordsville, IN 47933-0352, 800-718-9746, fax: 765-361-6166.

WADHAMS HALL SEMINARY-COLLEGE
Ogdensburg, New York

About the Institution Independent/religious, primarily men. Degrees awarded: B. Offers 2 undergraduate majors. Total enrollment: 28 (93% state residents). Freshmen: 9.

Undergraduate Expenses (1996–97) Comprehensive fee of $8900 includes tuition ($4490), mandatory fees ($210), and college room and board ($4200). College room only: $1990.

Applications 38% of all full-time undergraduates enrolled in fall 1996 applied for aid; of these, 60% were judged to have need according to Federal Methodology, of whom 100% were aided. *Financial aid deadline (priority):* 4/15. *Financial aid forms:* FAFSA, state form, institutional form required. *Admission application deadline:* rolling.

Summary of Aid to Needy Students Federal Work-Study jobs.

Non-Need Awards *Academic Interests/Achievement Awards:* general academic. *Special Characteristics Awards:* available.

Another Money-Saving Option *Payment Plan:* deferred payment.

Contact Office of Financial Aid, Wadhams Hall Seminary-College, Ogdensburg, NY 13669-9308, 315-393-4231.

WAGNER COLLEGE
Staten Island, New York

About the Institution Independent, coed. Degrees awarded: B, M. Offers 40 undergraduate majors. Total enrollment: 2,002. Undergraduates: 1,615 (73% state residents). Freshmen: 407.

Undergraduate Expenses (1997–98) Comprehensive fee of $22,000 includes tuition ($16,000) and college room and board ($6000).

Applications 70% of all full-time undergraduates enrolled in fall 1996 applied for aid; of these, 93% were judged to have need according to Federal Methodology, of whom 100% were aided. *Financial aid deadline (priority):* 4/1. *Financial aid forms:* FAFSA, institutional form required. State form required for some. *Regular admission application deadline:* rolling. Early decision deadline: 12/1.

Summary of Aid to Needy Students *From gift & self-help combined:* Average need met: 78%. Average amount awarded: $10,775 (66% gift aid, 34% self-help). *Gift aid:* Total: $7,003,235 (72% from college's own funds, 3% from other college-administered sources, 25% from external sources). 250 Federal Work-Study jobs (averaging $900); 100 part-time jobs.

Need-Based Scholarships & Grants Pell, FSEOG, state, private, college/university.

Loans Perkins, PLUS, Stafford, Unsubsidized Stafford, Federal Nursing, private.

Non-Need Awards In 1996, a total of 1,016 non-need awards were made. *Academic Interests/Achievement Awards:* 601 ($2,666,710 total): general academic. *Creative Arts/Performance Awards:* 179 ($980,710 total): music, theater/drama. *Special Achievements/Activities Awards:* 26 ($24,500 total): general special achievements/activities. *Athletic:* Total: 210 ($1,807,582); Men: 119 ($984,576); Women: 91 ($823,006).

Other Money-Saving Options Accelerated degree, cooperative Army ROTC, cooperative Air Force ROTC, off-campus living. *Payment Plan:* installment. *Waivers:* full or partial for employees or children of employees and senior citizens.

Contact Mr. Edward Keough, Director of Financial Aid, Wagner College, Staten Island, NY 10301, 718-390-3183, fax: 718-390-3203.

WAKE FOREST UNIVERSITY
Winston-Salem, North Carolina

About the Institution Independent, coed. Degrees awarded: B, M, D, P. Offers 37 undergraduate majors. Total enrollment: 5,910. Undergraduates: 3,771 (30% state residents). Freshmen: 940.

Undergraduate Expenses (1997–98) Comprehensive fee of $21,440 includes tuition ($16,300 minimum) and college room and board ($5140).

Applications Of all full-time undergraduates enrolled in fall 1996, 82% of those who applied for aid were judged to have need according to Federal Methodology, of whom 100% were aided. *Financial aid deadline (priority):* 3/1. *Financial aid forms:* FAFSA, CSS Financial Aid PROFILE, federal income tax forms and all schedules (student and parent) required. State form required for some. *Regular admission application deadline:* 1/15. Early decision deadline: 11/15.

Summary of Aid to Needy Students *From gift & self-help combined:* Average amount awarded: $11,667 (68% gift aid, 32% self-help). *Gift aid:* Total: $9,752,519 (74% from college's own funds, 10% from other college-administered sources, 16% from external sources). 200 Federal Work-Study jobs (averaging $1469); 11 part-time jobs.

Need-Based Scholarships & Grants Pell, FSEOG, state, college/university.

Loans Perkins, PLUS, Stafford, Unsubsidized Stafford, private, college/university long-term loans ($1978 average).

Non-Need Awards In 1996, a total of 826 non-need awards were made. *Academic Interests/Achievement Awards:* 227 ($1,756,594 total): general academic. *Creative Arts/Performance Awards:* 58 ($290,771 total): art/fine arts, cinema/film/broadcasting, creative writing, dance, debating, journalism/publications, music, performing arts, theater/drama. *Special Achievements/Activities Awards:* 78 ($440,178 total): leadership, religious involvement. *Special Characteristics Awards:* 200 ($1,474,758 total): children of faculty/staff, ROTC participants. *Athletic:* Total: 263 ($4,055,885); Men: 174 ($2,796,990); Women: 89 ($1,258,895).

Other Money-Saving Options Accelerated degree, Army ROTC, off-campus living (after freshman year). *Payment Plan:* installment. *Waivers:* full or partial for employees or children of employees.

Contact Office of Financial Aid, Wake Forest University, PO Box 7246, Winston-Salem, NC 27109, 910-759-5000.

WALLA WALLA COLLEGE
College Place, Washington

About the Institution Independent/religious, coed. Degrees awarded: A, B, M. Offers 63 undergraduate majors. Total enrollment: 1,763. Undergraduates: 1,606 (39% state residents). Freshmen: 300.

Undergraduate Expenses (1997–98) Comprehensive fee of $16,073 includes tuition ($12,570), mandatory fees ($123), and college room and board ($3380). College room only: $1836.

Applications Of all full-time undergraduates enrolled in fall 1996, 94% of those who applied for aid were judged to have need according to Federal Methodology, of whom 100% were aided. *Financial aid deadline (priority):* 4/1. *Financial aid forms:* FAFSA, institutional form required; CSS Financial Aid PROFILE acceptable. Verification worksheet required for some. *Admission application deadline:* rolling.

Summary of Aid to Needy Students *From gift & self-help combined:* Average need met: 87%. Average amount awarded: $14,074 (55% gift aid, 45% self-help). *Gift aid:* Total: $8,037,944 (48% from college's own funds, 9% from other college-administered sources, 43% from external sources). 560 Federal Work-Study jobs (averaging $1500); 500 part-time jobs.

Need-Based Scholarships & Grants Pell, FSEOG, state, private, college/university.

Loans Perkins, PLUS, Stafford, Unsubsidized Stafford, Federal Nursing, private, college/university short-term loans ($300 average), college/university long-term loans ($1100 average).

Non-Need Awards In 1996, a total of 1,168 non-need awards were made. *Academic Interests/Achievement Awards:* 683 ($870,533 total): general academic. *Creative Arts/Performance Awards:* 17 ($8400 total): general creative, music. *Special Achievements/Activities Awards:* 152 ($165,750 total): community service, leadership. *Special Characteristics Awards:* 316 ($2,577,247 total): children of faculty/staff.

Other Money-Saving Options Accelerated degree, co-op program, off-campus living (after junior year). *Payment Plan:* installment. *Waivers:* full or partial for employees or children of employees and senior citizens.

Contact Ms. Nancy Caldera, Associate Director of Financial Aid, Walla Walla College, 204 South College Avenue, College Place, WA 99324-1198, 509-527-2315, fax: 509-527-2253.

WALSH UNIVERSITY
North Canton, Ohio

About the Institution Independent/religious, coed. Degrees awarded: A, B, M. Offers 45 undergraduate majors. Total enrollment: 1,381. Undergraduates: 1,212 (95% state residents). Freshmen: 299.

Undergraduate Expenses (1996–97) Comprehensive fee of $14,960 includes tuition ($9900), mandatory fees ($300), and college room and board ($4760).

Applications 97% of all full-time undergraduates enrolled in fall 1996 applied for aid; of these, 89% were judged to have need according to Federal Methodology, of whom 100% were aided. *Financial aid deadline (priority):* 5/1. *Financial aid forms:* FAFSA, institutional form required; CSS Financial Aid PROFILE acceptable. *Admission application deadline:* rolling.

Summary of Aid to Needy Students *From gift & self-help combined:* Average need met: 90%. Average amount awarded: $5791 (38% gift aid, 62% self-help). *Gift aid:* Total: $1,761,990 (24% from college's own funds, 44% from other college-administered sources, 32% from external sources). 300 Federal Work-Study jobs (averaging $1500); part-time jobs.

Need-Based Scholarships & Grants Pell, FSEOG, state, private, college/university.

Loans Perkins, PLUS, Stafford, Unsubsidized Stafford, college/university long-term loans ($1000 average).

Non-Need Awards In 1996, a total of 609 non-need awards were made. *Academic Interests/Achievement Awards:* 276 ($597,633 total): general academic. *Special Characteristics Awards:* 131 ($124,125 total): children and siblings of alumni, local/state students, members of minorities, siblings of current students. *Athletic:* Total: 202 ($295,607); Men: 99 ($175,100); Women: 103 ($120,507).

Other Money-Saving Options Accelerated degree. *Payment Plans:* installment, deferred payment. *Waivers:* full or partial for children of alumni, employees or children of employees, senior citizens.

Contact Assistant Director of Financial Aid, Walsh University, North Canton, OH 44720-3396, 330-490-7146.

WARNER PACIFIC COLLEGE
Portland, Oregon

About the Institution Independent/religious, coed. Degrees awarded: A, B, M. Offers 38 undergraduate majors. Total enrollment: 601. Undergraduates: 595 (74% state residents). Freshmen: 55.

Undergraduate Expenses (1997–98) Comprehensive fee of $14,132 includes tuition ($10,240), mandatory fees ($142), and college room and board ($3750 minimum).

Applications *Financial aid deadline (priority):* 3/15. *Financial aid forms:* FAFSA required; CSS Financial Aid PROFILE, SINGLEFILE Form of United Student Aid Funds acceptable. Institutional form required for some. *Admission application deadline:* rolling.

Summary of Aid to Needy Students *From gift & self-help combined:* Average need met: 90%. Average amount awarded: $5782 (47% gift aid, 53% self-help). *Gift aid:* Total: $1,506,565 (59% from college's own funds, 25% from other college-administered sources, 16% from external sources). 99 Federal Work-Study jobs (averaging $2013); 12 part-time jobs.

Need-Based Scholarships & Grants Pell, FSEOG, state, private, college/university.

Loans Perkins, PLUS, Stafford, Unsubsidized Stafford, college/university.

Non-Need Awards In 1996, a total of 229 non-need awards were made. *Academic Interests/Achievement Awards:* 35 ($69,495 total): premedicine. *Creative Arts/Performance Awards:* 31 ($44,875 total): music. *Special Achievements/Activities Awards:* 22 ($25,000 total): leadership, religious involvement. *Special Characteristics Awards:* 141 ($294,117 total): children and siblings of alumni, members of minorities, religious affiliation.

Other Money-Saving Options Co-op program, cooperative Army ROTC, cooperative Air Force ROTC, off-campus living (after sophomore year). *Payment Plan:* installment. *Waivers:* full or partial for children of alumni and employees or children of employees.

Contact Mr. Rick Weems, Director of Financial Aid, Warner Pacific College, 2219 Southeast 68th Avenue, Portland, OR 97215-4099, 503-788-7422, fax: 503-788-7425.

WARNER SOUTHERN COLLEGE
Lake Wales, Florida

About the Institution Independent/religious, coed. Degrees awarded: A, B. Offers 23 undergraduate majors. Total enrollment: 601 (89% state residents). Freshmen: 71.

Undergraduate Expenses (1997–98) Comprehensive fee of $12,189 includes tuition ($7560), mandatory fees ($660), and college room and board ($3969). College room only: $1870.

Applications *Financial aid deadline (priority):* 5/1. *Financial aid forms:* FAFSA required; CSS Financial Aid PROFILE acceptable. State form required for some. *Admission application deadline:* rolling.

Summary of Aid to Needy Students *From gift & self-help combined:* Average need met: 92%. Average amount awarded: $7808 (34% gift aid, 66% self-help). *Gift aid:* Total: $2,106,827 (35% from college's own funds, 50% from other college-administered sources, 15% from external sources). 39 Federal Work-Study jobs (averaging $1368); 42 part-time jobs.

Need-Based Scholarships & Grants Pell, FSEOG, state, private, college/university.

Loans Perkins, PLUS, Stafford, Unsubsidized Stafford, private.

Non-Need Awards *Academic Interests/Achievement Awards:* general academic, business, communication, education, English, humanities. *Creative Arts/Performance Awards:* music. *Special Achievements/Activities Awards:* leadership. *Special Characteristics Awards:* children and siblings of alumni, children of educators, children of faculty/staff, international students, out-of-state students, relatives of clergy, spouses of current students, veterans, veterans' children. *Athletic:* Total: 63 ($163,855); Men: 42 ($109,575); Women: 21 ($54,280).

Other Money-Saving Options Accelerated degree, cooperative Army ROTC, off-campus living (after junior year). *Payment Plan:* installment. *Waivers:* full or partial for employees or children of employees.

Contact Mr. David Landen, Assistant Director of Financial Aid, Warner Southern College, 5301 US Highway 27 South, Lake Wales, FL 33853-8725, 941-638-7218, fax: 941-638-1472.

WARREN WILSON COLLEGE
Asheville, North Carolina

About the Institution Independent/religious, coed. Degrees awarded: B, M. Offers 23 undergraduate majors. Total enrollment: 655. Undergraduates: 620 (23% state residents). Freshmen: 173.

Undergraduate Expenses (1997–98) Comprehensive fee of $16,500 includes tuition ($12,250), mandatory fees ($250), and college room and board ($4000).

Applications 63% of all full-time undergraduates enrolled in fall 1996 applied for aid; of these, 86% were judged to have need according to Federal Methodology, of whom 100% were aided. *Financial aid deadline (priority):* 3/15. *Financial aid forms:* FAFSA, institutional form required. State form required for some. *Regular admission application deadline:* 3/15. Early decision deadline: 11/15.

Summary of Aid to Needy Students *From gift & self-help combined:* Average need met: 86%. Average amount awarded: $9211 (48% gift aid, 52% self-help). *Gift aid:* Total: $1,519,557 (65% from college's own funds, 8% from other college-administered sources, 27% from external sources). Federal Work-Study jobs (averaging $2040); part-time jobs.

Need-Based Scholarships & Grants Pell, FSEOG, state, college/university.

Loans Perkins, PLUS, Stafford, Unsubsidized Stafford, college/university short-term loans ($50 average), college/university long-term loans ($1900 average).

Non-Need Awards In 1996, a total of 72 non-need awards were made. *Academic Interests/Achievement Awards:* 51 ($53,500 total): general academic. *Special Achievements/Activities Awards:* 15 ($27,500 total): general special achievements/activities, leadership. *Special Characteristics Awards:* 6 ($4500 total): religious affiliation.

Other Money-Saving Options Accelerated degree, co-op program. *Payment Plan:* installment. *Waivers:* full or partial for employees or children of employees.

Contact Admissions Office, Warren Wilson College, Asheville, NC 28815-9000, 800-934-3536, fax: 704-298-1440.

WARTBURG COLLEGE
Waverly, Iowa

About the Institution Independent/religious, coed. Degrees awarded: B. Offers 47 undergraduate majors. Total enrollment: 1,467 (73% state residents). Freshmen: 406.

Undergraduate Expenses (1997–98) Comprehensive fee of $17,620 includes tuition ($13,470), mandatory fees ($140), and college room and board ($4010). College room only: $1860.

Applications 99% of all full-time undergraduates enrolled in fall 1996 applied for aid; of these, 73% were judged to have need according to Federal Methodology, of whom 100% were aided. *Financial aid deadline (priority):* 3/1. *Financial aid forms:* FAFSA required. Institutional form required for some. *Admission application deadline:* rolling.

Summary of Aid to Needy Students *From gift & self-help combined:* Average need met: 86%. Average amount awarded: $12,321 (66% gift aid, 34% self-help). *Gift aid:* Total: $7,936,824 (58% from college's own funds, 6% from other college-administered sources, 36% from external sources). 600 Federal Work-Study jobs (averaging $1141); 221 part-time jobs.

Need-Based Scholarships & Grants Pell, FSEOG, state, college/university.

Loans Perkins, PLUS, Stafford, Unsubsidized Stafford.

Non-Need Awards *Academic Interests/Achievement Awards:* general academic, biological sciences, English, mathematics, physical sciences. *Creative Arts/Performance Awards:* music. *Special Characteristics Awards:* children and siblings of alumni, religious affiliation, siblings of current students.

Other Money-Saving Options Accelerated degree. *Payment Plan:* installment. *Waivers:* full or partial for minority students, children of alumni, employees or children of employees, senior citizens.

Contact Mr. Dan Kielman, Assistant Director of Financial Aid, Wartburg College, 222 9th Street, NW, Waverly, IA 50677-1003, 319-352-8290, fax: 319-352-8247.

WASHBURN UNIVERSITY OF TOPEKA
Topeka, Kansas

About the Institution City-supported, coed. Degrees awarded: A, B, M, P. Offers 68 undergraduate majors. Total enrollment: 6,248. Undergraduates: 5,298 (94% state residents). Freshmen: 663.

Undergraduate Expenses (1997–98) State resident tuition: $3100. Nonresident tuition: $6758. Mandatory fees: $50. College room and board: $3300.

Applications *Financial aid deadline (priority):* 3/1. *Financial aid forms:* FAFSA, CSS Financial Aid PROFILE, institutional form acceptable. *Admission application deadline:* 8/6.

Summary of Aid to Needy Students Federal Work-Study jobs; 350 part-time jobs.

Need-Based Scholarships & Grants Pell, FSEOG.

Loans Perkins, PLUS, Stafford, Unsubsidized Stafford.

Non-Need Awards *Academic Interests/Achievement Awards:* general academic. *Creative Arts/Performance Awards:* art/fine arts, dance, music, theater/drama. *Athletic:* available.

Other Money-Saving Options Co-op program, Army ROTC, cooperative Air Force ROTC, off-campus living. *Payment Plan:* installment.

Contact Office of Financial Aid, Washburn University of Topeka, 1700 College, Topeka, KS 66621, 913-231-1010.

WASHINGTON AND JEFFERSON COLLEGE
Washington, Pennsylvania

About the Institution Independent, coed. Degrees awarded: B. Offers 25 undergraduate majors. Total enrollment: 1,128 (70% state residents). Freshmen: 321.

Undergraduate Expenses (1996–97) Comprehensive fee of $21,675 includes tuition ($17,190), mandatory fees ($280), and college room and board ($4205). College room only: $2035.

Applications 85% of all full-time undergraduates enrolled in fall 1996 applied for aid; of these, 94% were judged to have need according to Federal Methodology, of whom 99% were aided. *Financial aid deadline (priority):* 3/15. *Financial aid forms:* FAFSA, state form required. *Regular admission application deadline:* 2/1. Early decision deadline: 11/1.

Summary of Aid to Needy Students *From gift & self-help combined:* Average need met: 92%. Average amount awarded: $14,000 (86% gift aid, 14% self-help). *Gift aid:* Total: $10,251,283 (79% from college's own funds, 2% from other college-administered sources, 19% from external sources). 100 Federal Work-Study jobs (averaging $1000); 150 part-time jobs.

Need-Based Scholarships & Grants Pell, FSEOG, state, private, college/university.

Loans Perkins, PLUS, Stafford, Unsubsidized Stafford, college/university long-term loans ($1000 average).

Non-Need Awards In 1996, a total of 268 non-need awards were made. *Academic Interests/Achievement Awards:* 255 ($1,585,050 total): general academic, business. *Special Characteristics Awards:* 13 ($150,330 total): children and siblings of alumni, children of faculty/staff.

Other Money-Saving Options Accelerated degree, cooperative Army ROTC. *Payment Plans:* installment, deferred payment. *Waivers:* full or partial for employees or children of employees.

Contact Mr. Richard H. Soudan, Director of Financial Aid, Washington and Jefferson College, 60 South Lincoln Street, Washington, PA 15301-4801, 412-223-6019, fax: 412-223-5271.

WASHINGTON AND LEE UNIVERSITY
Lexington, Virginia

About the Institution Independent, coed. Degrees awarded: B, P. Offers 48 undergraduate majors. Total enrollment: 2,006. Undergraduates: 1,645 (12% state residents). Freshmen: 440.

Undergraduate Expenses (1997–98) Comprehensive fee of $21,815 includes tuition ($16,040), mandatory fees ($155), and college room and board ($5620).

Applications 37% of all full-time undergraduates enrolled in fall 1996 applied for aid; of these, 74% were judged to have need according to Federal Methodology, of whom 100% were aided. *Financial aid deadline (priority):* 2/1. *Financial aid forms:* FAFSA, CSS Financial Aid PROFILE, institutional form required. State form required for some. *Regular admission application deadline:* 1/15. Early decision deadline: 12/1.

Summary of Aid to Needy Students *From gift & self-help combined:* Average need met: 92%. Average amount awarded: $12,332 (63% gift aid, 37% self-help). *Gift aid:* Total: $3,569,495 (83% from college's

own funds, 3% from other college-administered sources, 14% from external sources). 275 Federal Work-Study jobs (averaging $1350); 50 part-time jobs.

Need-Based Scholarships & Grants Pell, FSEOG, state, private, college/university.

Loans Perkins, PLUS, Stafford, Unsubsidized Stafford, private, college/university short-term loans ($100 average), college/university long-term loans ($4000 average).

Non-Need Awards In 1996, a total of 96 non-need awards were made. *Academic Interests/Achievement Awards:* 95 ($775,000 total): general academic. *Special Characteristics Awards:* 1 ($7640 total): local/state students.

Other Money-Saving Options Accelerated degree, cooperative Army ROTC, off-campus living (after sophomore year). *Waivers:* full or partial for employees or children of employees.

Contact Ms. E. McClain Stradtner, Associate Director, Washington and Lee University, Gilliam House, Letcher Avenue, Lexington, VA 24450, 540-463-8729, fax: 540-463-8062.

WASHINGTON BIBLE COLLEGE
Lanham, Maryland

About the Institution Independent/religious, coed. Degrees awarded: A, B. Offers 8 undergraduate majors. Total enrollment: 319 (66% state residents). Freshmen: 84.

Undergraduate Expenses (1997–98) Comprehensive fee of $9210 includes tuition ($5040), mandatory fees ($180), and college room and board ($3990). College room only: $1690.

Applications 94% of all full-time undergraduates enrolled in fall 1996 applied for aid; of these, 92% were judged to have need according to Federal Methodology, of whom 78% were aided. *Financial aid deadline (priority):* 5/30. *Financial aid forms:* FAFSA, CSS Financial Aid PROFILE, institutional form required; state form acceptable. *Admission application deadline:* rolling.

Summary of Aid to Needy Students *From gift & self-help combined:* Average need met: 50%. Average amount awarded: $5376 (64% gift aid, 36% self-help). *Gift aid:* Total: $320,000 (46% from college's own funds, 23% from other college-administered sources, 31% from external sources). 20 Federal Work-Study jobs (averaging $2500); part-time jobs.

Need-Based Scholarships & Grants Pell, FSEOG, state, private, college/university.

Loans PLUS, Stafford, Unsubsidized Stafford.

Non-Need Awards In 1996, a total of 118 non-need awards were made. *Academic Interests/Achievement Awards:* 40 ($14,000 total): general academic. *Special Achievements/Activities Awards:* 35 ($20,000 total): leadership, religious involvement. *Special Characteristics Awards:* 43 ($46,000 total): relatives of clergy, religious affiliation.

Other Money-Saving Options Accelerated degree. *Payment Plans:* installment, deferred payment. *Waivers:* full or partial for employees or children of employees.

Contact Mr. Darrell DeHaven Jr., Financial Aid Administrator, Washington Bible College, 6511 Princess Garden Parkway, Lanham, MD 20706-3599, 301-552-1400 Ext. 222.

WASHINGTON COLLEGE
Chestertown, Maryland

About the Institution Independent, coed. Degrees awarded: B, M. Offers 27 undergraduate majors. Total enrollment: 1,009. Undergraduates: 952 (55% state residents). Freshmen: 312.

Undergraduate Expenses (1996–97) Comprehensive fee of $22,990 includes tuition ($16,800), mandatory fees ($450), and college room and board ($5740).

Applications 85% of all full-time undergraduates enrolled in fall 1996 applied for aid; of these,100% were judged to have need according to Federal Methodology, of whom 100% were aided. *Financial aid deadline (priority):* 2/15. *Financial aid forms:* FAFSA, CSS Financial Aid PROFILE, federal income tax form required. *Regular admission application deadline:* 2/15. Early decision deadline: 12/1.

Summary of Aid to Needy Students *From gift & self-help combined:* Average need met: 85%. Average amount awarded: $12,675 (75% gift aid, 25% self-help). *Gift aid:* Total: $7,927,208 (85% from college's own funds, 2% from other college-administered sources, 13% from external sources). Federal Work-Study jobs (averaging $1200).

Need-Based Scholarships & Grants Pell, FSEOG, state, private, college/university.

Loans Perkins, PLUS, Stafford, Unsubsidized Stafford, college/university long-term loans ($4000 average).

Non-Need Awards In 1996, a total of 638 non-need awards were made. *Academic Interests/Achievement Awards:* 401 ($2,491,617 total): general academic, biological sciences, foreign languages, physical sciences. *Creative Arts/Performance Awards:* 19 ($30,500 total): art/fine arts, creative writing, music, theater/drama. *Special Achievements/Activities Awards:* 161 ($161,000 total): memberships. *Special Characteristics Awards:* 57 ($670,975 total): children of educators, children of union members/company employees, members of minorities.

Other Money-Saving Options Off-campus living (after sophomore year). *Payment Plan:* installment. *Waivers:* full or partial for employees or children of employees and adult students.

Contact Ms. Jean M. Narcum, Director of Financial Aid, Washington College, 300 Washington Avenue, Chestertown, MD 21620-1197, 410-778-7214, fax: 410-778-7287.

WASHINGTON STATE UNIVERSITY
Pullman, Washington

About the Institution State-supported, coed. Degrees awarded: B, M, D, P. Offers 109 undergraduate majors. Total enrollment: 20,121. Undergraduates: 16,686 (85% state residents). Freshmen: 2,280.

Undergraduate Expenses (1996–97) State resident tuition: $3142. Nonresident tuition: $9758. Mandatory fees: $128. College room and board: $4150.

Applications Of all full-time undergraduates enrolled in fall 1996, 74% of those who applied for aid were judged to have need according to Federal Methodology, of whom 100% were aided. *Financial aid deadline (priority):* 3/1. *Financial aid forms:* FAFSA required; CSS Financial Aid PROFILE acceptable. State form, institutional form required for some. *Admission application deadline:* 5/1.

Summary of Aid to Needy Students *From gift & self-help combined:* Average need met: 98%. Average amount awarded: $8734 (25% gift aid, 75% self-help). *Gift aid:* Total: $14,610,002 (28% from college's own funds, 30% from other college-administered sources, 42% from external sources). 678 Federal Work-Study jobs (averaging $1400); 856 part-time jobs.

Need-Based Scholarships & Grants Pell, FSEOG, state, private, college/university.

Loans Perkins, PLUS, Stafford, Unsubsidized Stafford, Federal Nursing, private, college/university short-term loans ($2100 average).

Non-Need Awards In 1996, a total of 1,606 non-need awards were made. *Academic Interests/Achievement Awards:* 1,099 ($1,165,132 total): general academic, agriculture, architecture, business, education, engineering/technologies, English, health fields, home economics, humanities, mathematics, physical sciences. *Creative Arts/Performance*

Awards: 2 ($1700 total): art/fine arts, music, theater/drama. *Special Characteristics Awards:* 154 ($255,750 total): international students, members of minorities. *Athletic:* Total: 351 ($2,810,290); Men: 183 ($1,626,663); Women: 168 ($1,183,627).

Other Money-Saving Options Co-op program, Army ROTC, Air Force ROTC, cooperative Naval ROTC, off-campus living (after freshman year). *Waivers:* full or partial for employees or children of employees and senior citizens.

Contact Office of Student Financial Aid, Washington State University, PO Box 41068, Pullman, WA 99164-1068, 509-335-9711, fax: 509-335-1385.

WASHINGTON UNIVERSITY
St. Louis, Missouri

About the Institution Independent, coed. Degrees awarded: B, M, D, P. Offers 105 undergraduate majors. Total enrollment: 10,767. Undergraduates: 5,443 (14% state residents). Freshmen: 1,296.

Undergraduate Expenses (1997–98) Comprehensive fee of $27,803 includes tuition ($21,000), mandatory fees ($210), and college room and board ($6593). College room only: $3948.

Applications Of all full-time undergraduates enrolled in fall 1996, 89% of those who applied for aid were judged to have need according to Federal Methodology, of whom 98% were aided. *Financial aid deadline:* 2/15. *Financial aid forms:* FAFSA, Divorced/Separated Parents' Statement required. CSS Financial Aid PROFILE, institutional form required for some. *Regular admission application deadline:* 1/15. Early decision deadline: 1/1.

Summary of Aid to Needy Students *From gift & self-help combined:* Average need met: 94%. Average amount awarded: $18,568 (69% gift aid, 31% self-help). *Gift aid:* Total: $29,601,563 (83% from college's own funds, 4% from other college-administered sources, 13% from external sources). 1,277 Federal Work-Study jobs (averaging $1500); part-time jobs.

Need-Based Scholarships & Grants Pell, FSEOG, state, private, college/university.

Loans Perkins, PLUS, Stafford, Unsubsidized Stafford, college/university short-term loans ($200 average), college/university long-term loans ($3500 average).

Non-Need Awards In 1996, a total of 310 non-need awards were made. *Academic Interests/Achievement Awards:* 265 ($2,665,142 total): general academic, architecture, engineering/technologies, humanities, physical sciences, social sciences. *Creative Arts/Performance Awards:* 4 ($80,000 total): art/fine arts. *Special Characteristics Awards:* 41 ($919,122 total): members of minorities.

Other Money-Saving Options Accelerated degree, co-op program, Army ROTC, cooperative Air Force ROTC, off-campus living (after freshman year). *Payment Plans:* tuition prepayment, installment. *Waivers:* full or partial for employees or children of employees.

Contact Office of Financial Aid, Washington University, 1 Brookings Drive, Campus Box 1041, St. Louis, MO 63130-4899, 314-935-5000.

WAYNESBURG COLLEGE
Waynesburg, Pennsylvania

About the Institution Independent/religious, coed. Degrees awarded: A, B, M. Offers 38 undergraduate majors. Total enrollment: 1,288. Undergraduates: 1,229 (88% state residents). Freshmen: 310.

Undergraduate Expenses (1996–97) Comprehensive fee of $13,910 includes tuition ($9800), mandatory fees ($240), and college room and board ($3870 minimum). College room only: $2040 (minimum).

Applications Of all full-time undergraduates enrolled in fall 1996, 99% of those judged to have need according to Federal Methodology were aided. *Financial aid deadline (priority):* 3/15. *Financial aid forms:* FAFSA, institutional form required; CSS Financial Aid PROFILE acceptable. State form required for some. *Admission application deadline:* rolling.

Summary of Aid to Needy Students *From gift & self-help combined:* Average need met: 89%. Average amount awarded: $10,386 (60% gift aid, 40% self-help). *Gift aid:* Total: $7,101,817 (56% from college's own funds, 25% from other college-administered sources, 19% from external sources). 145 Federal Work-Study jobs (averaging $500); 108 part-time jobs.

Need-Based Scholarships & Grants Pell, FSEOG, state, private, college/university.

Loans Perkins, PLUS, Stafford, Unsubsidized Stafford, Federal Nursing, private, college/university short-term loans ($600 average).

Non-Need Awards In 1996, a total of 395 non-need awards were made. *Academic Interests/Achievement Awards:* 224 ($457,726 total): general academic. *Special Achievements/Activities Awards:* 120 ($230,465 total): community service, leadership. *Special Characteristics Awards:* 51 ($279,257 total): children of faculty/staff, ROTC participants.

Other Money-Saving Options Off-campus living (after junior year). *Payment Plan:* installment. *Waivers:* full or partial for employees or children of employees.

Contact Ms. Karen L. Pratz, Director of Financial Aid, Waynesburg College, 51 West College Street, Waynesburg, PA 15370-1222, 412-852-3227, fax: 412-627-6416.

WAYNE STATE COLLEGE
Wayne, Nebraska

About the Institution State-supported, coed. Degrees awarded: B, M. Offers 63 undergraduate majors. Total enrollment: 3,828. Undergraduates: 3,141 (82% state residents). Freshmen: 708.

Undergraduate Expenses (1996–97) State resident tuition: $1650. Nonresident tuition: $3300. Mandatory fees: $288. College room and board: $2870. College room only: $1350.

Applications 76% of all full-time undergraduates enrolled in fall 1996 applied for aid; of these, 86% were judged to have need according to Federal Methodology, of whom 97% were aided. *Financial aid deadline:* continuous. *Financial aid forms:* FAFSA, institutional form required. *Admission application deadline:* rolling.

Summary of Aid to Needy Students *From gift & self-help combined:* Average need met: 91%. Average amount awarded: $4715 (36% gift aid, 64% self-help). *Gift aid:* Total: $3,029,355 (20% from college's own funds, 5% from other college-administered sources, 75% from external sources). 170 Federal Work-Study jobs (averaging $981); 150 part-time jobs.

Need-Based Scholarships & Grants Pell, FSEOG, state, private, college/university.

Loans Perkins, PLUS, Stafford, Unsubsidized Stafford, private, college/university short-term loans ($250 average).

Non-Need Awards In 1996, a total of 943 non-need awards were made. *Academic Interests/Achievement Awards:* 297 ($492,415 total): general academic. *Creative Arts/Performance Awards:* 64 ($17,439 total): general creative, art/fine arts, cinema/film/broadcasting, creative writing, journalism/publications, music, theater/drama. *Special Achievements/Activities Awards:* 32 ($43,200 total): leadership. *Special Characteristics Awards:* 415 ($377,516 total): general special characteristics, children of faculty/staff, international students, members of minorities, out-of-state students, veterans' children. *Athletic:* Total: 135 ($197,585); Men: 88 ($144,624); Women: 47 ($52,961).

Other Money-Saving Options Co-op program, cooperative Army ROTC, off-campus living (after freshman year). *Waivers:* full or partial for employees or children of employees.

Contact Office of Financial Aid, Wayne State College, 1111 Main Street, Wayne, NE 68787, 402-375-7000.

WAYNE STATE UNIVERSITY
Detroit, Michigan

About the Institution State-supported, coed. Degrees awarded: B, M, D, P. Offers 119 undergraduate majors. Total enrollment: 31,185. Undergraduates: 18,200 (97% state residents). Freshmen: 1,970.

Undergraduate Expenses (1996–97) State resident tuition: $3255 (minimum). Nonresident tuition: $7254 (minimum). Mandatory fees: $144. College room only: $3880 (minimum).

Applications 66% of all full-time undergraduates enrolled in fall 1996 applied for aid; of these, 93% were judged to have need according to Federal Methodology, of whom 92% were aided. *Financial aid deadline:* Applications processed continuously. *Financial aid forms:* FAFSA required. *Admission application deadline:* 8/1.

Summary of Aid to Needy Students *From gift & self-help combined:* Average need met: 53%. *Gift aid:* Total: $11,816,070. 372 Federal Work-Study jobs (averaging $3297); 3,510 part-time jobs.

Loans College/university short-term loans ($400 average), college/university long-term loans ($2000 average).

Non-Need Awards *Academic Interests/Achievement Awards:* general academic. *Creative Arts/Performance Awards:* dance, debating, music. *Special Achievements/Activities Awards:* memberships. *Athletic:* Total: 211 ($298,418); Men: 140 ($176,510); Women: 71 ($121,908).

Other Money-Saving Options Accelerated degree, co-op program, Army ROTC, Air Force ROTC, off-campus living. *Payment Plan:* installment. *Waivers:* full or partial for employees or children of employees and senior citizens.

Contact Mr. Kevin J. Culler, Interim Director, Scholarships and Financial Aid, Wayne State University, HNJ Student Services Building, #3 West, Detroit, MI 48202, 313-577-4971, fax: 313-577-6648.

WEBBER COLLEGE
Babson Park, Florida

About the Institution Independent, coed. Degrees awarded: A, B. Offers 8 undergraduate majors. Total enrollment: 438 (58% state residents). Freshmen: 67.

Undergraduate Expenses (1997–98) Comprehensive fee of $10,690 includes tuition ($7390) and college room and board ($3300). College room only: $1650.

Applications 54% of all full-time undergraduates enrolled in fall 1996 applied for aid; of these, 87% were judged to have need according to Federal Methodology, of whom 100% were aided. *Financial aid deadline (priority):* 8/1. *Financial aid forms:* FAFSA, state form required; CSS Financial Aid PROFILE acceptable. *Admission application deadline:* rolling.

Summary of Aid to Needy Students *From gift & self-help combined:* Average amount awarded: $7392 (56% gift aid, 44% self-help). *Gift aid:* Total: $689,140 (33% from college's own funds, 33% from other college-administered sources, 34% from external sources). 25 Federal Work-Study jobs (averaging $637); 42 part-time jobs.

Need-Based Scholarships & Grants Pell, FSEOG, state, private, college/university.

Loans Perkins, PLUS, Stafford, Unsubsidized Stafford, private.

Non-Need Awards In 1996, a total of 271 non-need awards were made. *Academic Interests/Achievement Awards:* 58 ($29,100 total): general academic. *Special Achievements/Activities Awards:* 9 ($7850 total): general special achievements/activities, community service, leadership. *Special Characteristics Awards:* 61 ($150,500 total): general special characteristics, children and siblings of alumni, children of faculty/staff, local/state students. *Athletic:* Total: 143 ($225,873); Men: 84 ($135,150); Women: 59 ($90,723).

Other Money-Saving Options Accelerated degree, co-op program, off-campus living (after freshman year). *Payment Plan:* installment. *Waivers:* full or partial for children of alumni, employees or children of employees, adult students, senior citizens.

Contact Ms. Kathleen Wilson, Director of Financial Aid, Webber College, PO Box 96, Babson Park, FL 33827-0096, 941-638-2930, fax: 941-638-2919.

WEBB INSTITUTE
Glen Cove, New York

About the Institution Independent, primarily men. Degrees awarded: B, M. Offers 2 undergraduate majors. Total enrollment: 93. Undergraduates: 85 (23% state residents). Freshmen: 22.

Undergraduate Expenses (1997–98) Comprehensive fee of $6050 includes tuition ($0) and college room and board ($6050).

Applications *Financial aid deadline (priority):* 7/1. *Financial aid forms:* FAFSA required; CSS Financial Aid PROFILE acceptable. Institutional form required for some. *Regular admission application deadline:* 2/15. Early decision deadline: 10/15.

Non-Need Awards *Special Characteristics Awards:* general special characteristics.

Another Money-Saving Option Co-op program.

Contact Office of Financial Aid, Webb Institute, Glen Cove, NY 11542-1398, 516-671-2213.

WEBER STATE UNIVERSITY
Ogden, Utah

About the Institution State-supported, coed. Degrees awarded: A, B, M. Offers 106 undergraduate majors. Total enrollment: 13,906. Undergraduates: 13,728 (94% state residents). Freshmen: 2,199.

Undergraduate Expenses (1997–98) State resident tuition: $1935. Nonresident tuition: $5730. College room and board: $2955 (minimum). College room only: $1500 (minimum).

Applications Of all full-time undergraduates enrolled in fall 1996, 75% of those judged to have need according to Federal Methodology were aided. *Financial aid deadline (priority):* 4/1. *Financial aid forms:* FAFSA, institutional form required. *Admission application deadline:* rolling.

Summary of Aid to Needy Students *From gift & self-help combined:* Average need met: 82%. Average amount awarded: $3646 (32% gift aid, 68% self-help). *Gift aid:* Total: $7,306,083 (15% from college-administered sources, 85% from external sources). 822 Federal Work-Study jobs (averaging $1883); part-time jobs.

Need-Based Scholarships & Grants Pell, FSEOG, state, private.

Loans Perkins, PLUS, Stafford, Unsubsidized Stafford, college/university short-term loans ($1863 average).

Non-Need Awards *Academic Interests/Achievement Awards:* general academic. *Creative Arts/Performance Awards:* art/fine arts, debating, performing arts, theater/drama. *Special Achievements/Activities Awards:* leadership, rodeo. *Special Characteristics Awards:* adult students, members of minorities. *Athletic:* Total: 231 ($1,071,834); Men: 140 ($714,581); Women: 91 ($357,253).

Other Money-Saving Options Accelerated degree, co-op program, Army ROTC, cooperative Naval ROTC, cooperative Air Force ROTC, off-campus living. *Payment Plan:* deferred payment. *Waivers:* full or partial for employees or children of employees and senior citizens.

Contact Financial Aid Office, Weber State University, Ogden, UT 84408-1001, 801-626-7569.

WEBSTER UNIVERSITY
St. Louis, Missouri

About the Institution Independent, coed. Degrees awarded: B, M, D. Offers 71 undergraduate majors. Total enrollment: 12,319. Undergraduates: 3,784 (65% state residents). Freshmen: 277.

Undergraduate Expenses (1997–98) Comprehensive fee of $15,960 includes tuition ($10,860) and college room and board ($5100).

Applications 62% of all full-time undergraduates enrolled in fall 1996 applied for aid; of these, 93% were judged to have need according to Federal Methodology, of whom 100% were aided. *Financial aid deadline (priority):* 4/1. *Financial aid forms:* FAFSA, state form, institutional form required; CSS Financial Aid PROFILE acceptable. *Regular admission application deadline:* 8/1. Nonresident deadline: 4/1.

Summary of Aid to Needy Students *From gift & self-help combined:* Average amount awarded: $10,672 (52% gift aid, 48% self-help). *Gift aid:* Total: $6,196,048 (73% from college's own funds, 5% from other college-administered sources, 22% from external sources). 225 Federal Work-Study jobs (averaging $2172); 214 part-time jobs.

Need-Based Scholarships & Grants Pell, FSEOG, state, college/university.

Loans Perkins, PLUS, Stafford, Unsubsidized Stafford, college/university short-term loans ($100 average).

Non-Need Awards In 1996, a total of 723 non-need awards were made. *Academic Interests/Achievement Awards:* 653 ($2,050,381 total): general academic, biological sciences, business, communication, computer science, education, English, foreign languages, international studies, mathematics, social sciences. *Creative Arts/Performance Awards:* 70 ($174,798 total): art/fine arts, debating, journalism/publications, music, theater/drama.

Other Money-Saving Options Accelerated degree, co-op program, off-campus living (after freshman year). *Payment Plan:* installment. *Waivers:* full or partial for employees or children of employees.

Contact Office of Financial Aid, Webster University, 470 East Lockwood Avenue, St. Louis, MO 63119-3194, 314-968-6900.

WELLESLEY COLLEGE
Wellesley, Massachusetts

About the Institution Independent, women. Degrees awarded: B. Offers 48 undergraduate majors. Total enrollment: 2,319 (22% state residents). Freshmen: 597.

Undergraduate Expenses (1997–98) Comprehensive fee of $28,332 includes tuition ($21,256), mandatory fees ($406), and college room and board ($6670). College room only: $3400.

Applications Of all full-time undergraduates enrolled in fall 1996, 100% of those judged to have need according to Federal Methodology were aided. *Financial aid deadline:* 1/15. *Financial aid forms:* FAFSA, CSS Financial Aid PROFILE, institutional form, federal income tax forms required. *Regular admission application deadline:* 1/15. Early decision deadline: 11/1.

Summary of Aid to Needy Students *From gift & self-help combined:* Average need met: 100%. Average amount awarded: $16,946 (71% gift aid, 29% self-help). *Gift aid:* Total: $14,935,085 (93% from college's own funds, 3% from other college-administered sources, 4% from external sources). 801 Federal Work-Study jobs (averaging $1307); 30 part-time jobs.

Need-Based Scholarships & Grants Pell, FSEOG, state, private, college/university.

Loans Perkins, PLUS, Stafford, Unsubsidized Stafford, state, private, college/university short-term loans ($200 average), college/university long-term loans ($1127 average).

Non-Need Awards Not offered.

Other Money-Saving Options Accelerated degree, cooperative Army ROTC, cooperative Naval ROTC, cooperative Air Force ROTC, off-campus living. *Payment Plans:* tuition prepayment, installment. *Waivers:* full or partial for employees or children of employees.

Contact Ms. Kathryn Osmond, Director of Financial Aid, Wellesley College, 106 Central Street, Wellesley, MA 02181-8291, 617-283-2360.

WELLS COLLEGE
Aurora, New York

About the Institution Independent, women. Degrees awarded: B. Offers 41 undergraduate majors. Total enrollment: 425 (64% state residents). Freshmen: 100.

Undergraduate Expenses (1997–98) Comprehensive fee of $23,440 includes tuition ($17,100), mandatory fees ($440), and college room and board ($5900).

Applications 88% of all full-time undergraduates enrolled in fall 1996 applied for aid; of these, 96% were judged to have need according to Federal Methodology, of whom 100% were aided. *Financial aid deadline (priority):* 4/1. *Financial aid forms:* FAFSA required. CSS Financial Aid PROFILE, state form, institutional form required for some. *Regular admission application deadline:* 2/15. Early action deadline: 12/15.

Summary of Aid to Needy Students *From gift & self-help combined:* Average amount awarded: $17,497 (68% gift aid, 32% self-help). *Gift aid:* Total: $3,594,585 (75% from college's own funds, 17% from other college-administered sources, 8% from external sources). 109 Federal Work-Study jobs (averaging $1200); 198 part-time jobs.

Need-Based Scholarships & Grants Pell, FSEOG, state, college/university.

Loans Perkins, PLUS, Stafford, Unsubsidized Stafford, college/university short-term loans ($3000 average).

Non-Need Awards In 1996, a total of 168 non-need awards were made. *Academic Interests/Achievement Awards:* 50 ($300,418 total): general academic. *Special Achievements/Activities Awards:* 113 ($426,500 total): leadership. *Special Characteristics Awards:* 5 ($39,250 total): children and siblings of alumni, children of educators.

Other Money-Saving Options Accelerated degree, cooperative Army ROTC, cooperative Air Force ROTC. *Payment Plan:* installment. *Waivers:* full or partial for employees or children of employees and senior citizens.

Contact Ms. Cathleen A. Bellomo, Director of Financial Aid, Wells College, Route 90, Aurora, NY 13026, 315-364-3289, fax: 315-364-3227.

WESLEYAN COLLEGE
Macon, Georgia

About the Institution Independent/religious, women. Degrees awarded: B, M. Offers 26 undergraduate majors. Total enrollment: 476. Undergraduates: 469 (67% state residents). Freshmen: 151.

Undergraduate Expenses (1997–98) Comprehensive fee of $19,500 includes tuition ($14,000), mandatory fees ($200), and college room and board ($5300).

Applications 98% of all full-time undergraduates enrolled in fall 1996 applied for aid; of these, 93% were judged to have need according to Federal Methodology, of whom 100% were aided. *Financial aid deadline (priority):* 3/1. *Financial aid forms:* FAFSA, institutional form required. State form required for some. *Regular admission application deadline:* rolling. Early decision deadline: 11/1.

Summary of Aid to Needy Students *From gift & self-help combined:* Average need met: 90%. Average amount awarded: $12,744 (77% gift aid, 23% self-help). *Gift aid:* Total: $3,752,621 (72% from college's

own funds, 19% from other college-administered sources, 9% from external sources). 44 Federal Work-Study jobs (averaging $1000); 150 part-time jobs.

Need-Based Scholarships & Grants Pell, FSEOG, state, private, college/university.

Loans Perkins, PLUS, Stafford, Unsubsidized Stafford, state, private, college/university short-term loans ($2094 average), Presidents Foundation Student Loans, GATE Student Loan Program.

Non-Need Awards In 1996, a total of 291 non-need awards were made. *Academic Interests/Achievement Awards:* 152 ($1,023,926 total): general academic. *Creative Arts/Performance Awards:* 55 ($102,925 total): art/fine arts, music, theater/drama. *Special Achievements/Activities Awards:* 61 ($135,500 total): community service, leadership. *Special Characteristics Awards:* 23 ($82,142 total): general special characteristics, children and siblings of alumni, children of current students, children of faculty/staff, relatives of clergy.

Other Money-Saving Options Accelerated degree. *Payment Plans:* tuition prepayment, installment. *Waivers:* full or partial for children of alumni, employees or children of employees, senior citizens.

Contact Office of Financial Aid, Wesleyan College, 4760 Forsyth Road, Macon, GA 31210-4462, 912-477-1110.

WESLEYAN UNIVERSITY
Middletown, Connecticut

About the Institution Independent, coed. Degrees awarded: B, M, D. Offers 56 undergraduate majors. Total enrollment: 3,279. Undergraduates: 2,735 (9% state residents). Freshmen: 739.

Undergraduate Expenses (1997–98) Comprehensive fee of $29,200 includes tuition ($22,230), mandatory fees ($1110), and college room and board ($5860).

Applications Of all full-time undergraduates enrolled in fall 1996, 92% of those who applied for aid were judged to have need according to Federal Methodology, of whom 100% were aided. *Financial aid deadline:* 2/1. *Financial aid forms:* FAFSA, CSS Financial Aid PROFILE required. State form required for some. *Regular admission application deadline:* 1/1. Early decision deadline: 11/15.

Summary of Aid to Needy Students *From gift & self-help combined:* Average need met: 100%. Average amount awarded: $18,484 (61% gift aid, 39% self-help). *Gift aid:* Total: $15,743,447 (85% from college's own funds, 6% from other college-administered sources, 9% from external sources). 1,200 Federal Work-Study jobs (averaging $1450); 400 part-time jobs.

Need-Based Scholarships & Grants Pell, FSEOG, state, private, college/university.

Loans Perkins, PLUS, Stafford, Unsubsidized Stafford, private, college/university short-term loans ($250 average), college/university long-term loans ($3100 average).

Non-Need Awards Not offered.

Other Money-Saving Options Accelerated degree, co-op program, cooperative Army ROTC, cooperative Naval ROTC, cooperative Air Force ROTC. *Payment Plan:* installment. *Waivers:* full or partial for employees or children of employees.

Contact Office of Financial Aid, Wesleyan University, 237 High Street, Middletown, CT 06459-0260, 860-685-2000.

WESLEY COLLEGE
Dover, Delaware

About the Institution Independent/religious, coed. Degrees awarded: A, B. Offers 20 undergraduate majors. Total enrollment: 1,325 (66% state residents). Freshmen: 305.

Undergraduate Expenses (1997–98) Comprehensive fee of $16,684 includes tuition ($11,260), mandatory fees ($405), and college room and board ($5019). College room only: $2573.

Applications 92% of all full-time undergraduates enrolled in fall 1996 applied for aid; of these, 95% were judged to have need according to Federal Methodology, of whom 100% were aided. *Financial aid deadline (priority):* 4/15. *Financial aid forms:* FAFSA required. *Regular admission application deadline:* rolling. Early decision deadline: 11/15.

Summary of Aid to Needy Students *From gift & self-help combined:* Average need met: 87%. Average amount awarded: $6687 (48% gift aid, 52% self-help). *Gift aid:* Total: $2,051,323 (70% from college's own funds, 12% from other college-administered sources, 18% from external sources). 93 Federal Work-Study jobs (averaging $1000); 50 part-time jobs.

Need-Based Scholarships & Grants Pell, FSEOG, state, private, college/university.

Loans Perkins, PLUS, Stafford, Unsubsidized Stafford, state, private, college/university long-term loans ($500 average).

Non-Need Awards In 1996, a total of 104 non-need awards were made. *Academic Interests/Achievement Awards:* 57 ($189,800 total): general academic. *Special Achievements/Activities Awards:* 41 ($43,100 total): religious involvement. *Special Characteristics Awards:* 6 ($11,000 total): international students.

Other Money-Saving Options Accelerated degree. *Payment Plan:* installment. *Waivers:* full or partial for employees or children of employees and senior citizens.

Contact Ms. Marilyn M. Ambrose, Director of Financial Aid, Wesley College, 120 North State Street, Dover, DE 19901, 302-736-2338, fax: 302-736-2534.

WESLEY COLLEGE
Florence, Mississippi

About the Institution Independent/religious, coed. Degrees awarded: B. Offers 4 undergraduate majors. Total enrollment: 87 (25% state residents). Freshmen: 23.

Undergraduate Expenses (1996–97) Comprehensive fee of $4520 includes tuition ($1920), mandatory fees ($200), and college room and board ($2400). College room only: $1000.

Applications 59% of all full-time undergraduates enrolled in fall 1996 applied for aid; of these, 90% were judged to have need according to Federal Methodology, of whom 100% were aided. *Financial aid deadline (priority):* 7/1. *Financial aid forms:* FAFSA required. *Admission application deadline:* rolling.

Summary of Aid to Needy Students *From gift & self-help combined:* Average need met: 63%. Average amount awarded: $4200 (77% gift aid, 23% self-help). *Gift aid:* Total: $76,973 (10% from college's own funds, 3% from other college-administered sources, 87% from external sources). Federal Work-Study jobs.

Need-Based Scholarships & Grants Pell, FSEOG.

Loans PLUS, Stafford, Unsubsidized Stafford.

Non-Need Awards In 1996, a total of 16 non-need awards were made. *Academic Interests/Achievement Awards:* 4 ($4570 total): general academic. *Special Achievements/Activities Awards:* 3 ($1050 total): religious involvement. *Special Characteristics Awards:* 9 ($2500 total): international students.

Other Money-Saving Options *Payment Plan:* installment. *Waivers:* full or partial for employees or children of employees and senior citizens.

Contact Mr. William Devore Jr., Director of Financial Aid, Wesley College, PO Box 1070, Florence, MS 39073-1070, 601-845-2265.

WESTBROOK COLLEGE
Portland, Maine

See University of New England

WEST CHESTER UNIVERSITY OF PENNSYLVANIA
West Chester, Pennsylvania

About the Institution State-supported, coed. Degrees awarded: A, B, M. Offers 98 undergraduate majors. Total enrollment: 11,261. Undergraduates: 9,422 (89% state residents). Freshmen: 1,460.

Undergraduate Expenses (1996–97) State resident tuition: $3368. Nonresident tuition: $8566. Mandatory fees: $664. College room and board: $4312. College room only: $2738.

Applications 63% of all full-time undergraduates enrolled in fall 1996 applied for aid; of these, 96% were judged to have need according to Federal Methodology, of whom 87% were aided. *Financial aid deadline (priority):* 3/1. *Financial aid forms:* FAFSA required. State form required for some. *Admission application deadline:* rolling.

Summary of Aid to Needy Students *From gift & self-help combined:* Average amount awarded: $5944 (31% gift aid, 69% self-help). *Gift aid:* Total: $7,638,848 (6% from college's own funds, 53% from other college-administered sources, 41% from external sources). 397 Federal Work-Study jobs (averaging $940); 664 part-time jobs.

Need-Based Scholarships & Grants Pell, FSEOG, state, college/university.

Loans Perkins, PLUS, Stafford, Unsubsidized Stafford, Federal Nursing, college/university short-term loans ($125 average).

Non-Need Awards In 1996, a total of 248 non-need awards were made. *Academic Interests/Achievement Awards:* 41 ($100,000 total): general academic, business, social sciences. *Creative Arts/Performance Awards:* 25 ($15,682 total): music. *Athletic:* Total: 182 ($281,086); Men: 108 ($166,036); Women: 74 ($115,050).

Other Money-Saving Options Accelerated degree, cooperative Army ROTC, cooperative Air Force ROTC, off-campus living. *Payment Plans:* tuition prepayment, installment, deferred payment. *Waivers:* full or partial for employees or children of employees and senior citizens.

Contact Financial Aid Office, West Chester University of Pennsylvania, West Chester, PA 19383, 610-436-2627.

WESTERN BAPTIST COLLEGE
Salem, Oregon

About the Institution Independent/religious, coed. Degrees awarded: A, B. Offers 24 undergraduate majors. Total enrollment: 720 (71% state residents). Freshmen: 160.

Undergraduate Expenses (1997–98) Comprehensive fee of $17,170 includes tuition ($11,900), mandatory fees ($450), and college room and board ($4820).

Applications *Financial aid deadline (priority):* 2/15. *Financial aid forms:* FAFSA required; CSS Financial Aid PROFILE, state form acceptable. Institutional form required for some. *Admission application deadline:* rolling.

Summary of Aid to Needy Students *From gift & self-help combined:* Average need met: 60%. Average amount awarded: $10,306 (49% gift aid, 51% self-help). *Gift aid:* Total: $2,841,255 (72% from college's own funds, 15% from other college-administered sources, 13% from external sources). 356 Federal Work-Study jobs (averaging $933); part-time jobs.

Need-Based Scholarships & Grants Pell, FSEOG, state, private, college/university.

Loans Perkins, PLUS, Stafford, Unsubsidized Stafford, state, private, college/university long-term loans.

Non-Need Awards In 1996, a total of 434 non-need awards were made. *Academic Interests/Achievement Awards:* 222 ($348,000 total): general academic. *Creative Arts/Performance Awards:* 28 ($34,700 total): music, performing arts. *Special Achievements/Activities Awards:* 9 ($14,145 total): general special achievements/activities, cheerleading/drum major, hobbies/interest, leadership, memberships, religious involvement. *Special Characteristics Awards:* 71 ($233,864 total): general special characteristics, children of faculty/staff, relatives of clergy. *Athletic:* Total: 104 ($346,890); Men: 63 ($197,180); Women: 41 ($149,710).

Other Money-Saving Options Cooperative Army ROTC, cooperative Air Force ROTC. *Payment Plan:* installment. *Waivers:* full or partial for employees or children of employees.

Contact Office of Financial Aid, Western Baptist College, 5000 Deer Park Drive, SE, Salem, OR 97301-9392, 503-581-8600.

WESTERN CAROLINA UNIVERSITY
Cullowhee, North Carolina

About the Institution State-supported, coed. Degrees awarded: B, M, D. Offers 83 undergraduate majors. Total enrollment: 6,511. Undergraduates: 5,674 (93% state residents). Freshmen: 1,182.

Undergraduate Expenses (1996–97) State resident tuition: $874. Nonresident tuition: $8028. Mandatory fees: $931. College room and board: $2674. College room only: $1350.

Applications Of all full-time undergraduates enrolled in fall 1996, 75% of those who applied for aid were judged to have need according to Federal Methodology, of whom 95% were aided. *Financial aid deadline (priority):* 3/31. *Financial aid forms:* FAFSA, institutional form required. *Admission application deadline:* 8/1.

Summary of Aid to Needy Students *From gift & self-help combined:* Average need met: 95%. Average amount awarded: $4052 (42% gift aid, 58% self-help). *Gift aid:* Total: $3,664,604 (17% from college's own funds, 17% from other college-administered sources, 66% from external sources). 463 Federal Work-Study jobs (averaging $1475); 846 part-time jobs.

Need-Based Scholarships & Grants Pell, FSEOG, state, private, college/university.

Loans Perkins, PLUS, Stafford, Unsubsidized Stafford, college/university short-term loans ($100 average).

Non-Need Awards In 1996, a total of 877 non-need awards were made. *Academic Interests/Achievement Awards:* 570 ($478,786 total): general academic. *Creative Arts/Performance Awards:* 46 ($31,690 total): art/fine arts, music. *Special Characteristics Awards:* 40 ($60,650 total): ethnic background, local/state students, members of minorities. *Athletic:* Total: 221 ($763,598); Men: 157 ($553,116); Women: 64 ($210,482).

Other Money-Saving Options Accelerated degree, co-op program, Army ROTC, off-campus living (after freshman year). *Waivers:* full or partial for senior citizens.

Contact Ms. Nancy B. Dillard, Associate Director, Western Carolina University, 230 H. F. Robinson Administration Building, Cullowhee, NC 28723, 704-227-7290, fax: 704-227-7202.

WESTERN CONNECTICUT STATE UNIVERSITY
Danbury, Connecticut

About the Institution State-supported, coed. Degrees awarded: A, B, M. Offers 40 undergraduate majors. Total enrollment: 5,607. Undergraduates: 4,634 (87% state residents). Freshmen: 973.

Undergraduate Expenses (1997–98) State resident tuition: $2062. Nonresident tuition: $6674. Mandatory fees: $1564 (minimum). College room and board: $4718. College room only: $2600.

Applications *Financial aid deadline (priority):* 3/15. *Financial aid forms:* FAFSA, CSS Financial Aid PROFILE, institutional form required. *Regular admission application deadline:* 5/1. Early decision deadline: 12/1.

Summary of Aid to Needy Students Federal Work-Study jobs; part-time jobs.

Non-Need Awards *Academic Interests/Achievement Awards:* general academic.

Other Money-Saving Options Accelerated degree, co-op program, cooperative Army ROTC, cooperative Air Force ROTC, off-campus living. *Waivers:* full or partial for employees or children of employees and senior citizens.

Contact Office of Financial Aid, Western Connecticut State University, Danbury, CT 06810-6885, 203-837-8200.

WESTERN ILLINOIS UNIVERSITY
Macomb, Illinois

About the Institution State-supported, coed. Degrees awarded: B, M. Offers 51 undergraduate majors. Total enrollment: 12,184. Undergraduates: 9,644 (92% state residents). Freshmen: 1,506.

Undergraduate Expenses (1997–98) State resident tuition: $2119. Nonresident tuition: $6358. Mandatory fees: $766. College room and board: $3838.

Applications 86% of all full-time undergraduates enrolled in fall 1996 applied for aid; of these, 65% were judged to have need according to Federal Methodology, of whom 98% were aided. *Financial aid deadline (priority):* 3/1. *Financial aid forms:* FAFSA required. *Admission application deadline:* 8/10.

Summary of Aid to Needy Students *From gift & self-help combined:* Average need met: 84%. Average amount awarded: $7670 (38% gift aid, 62% self-help). *Gift aid:* Total: $13,082,742 (16% from college's own funds, 3% from other college-administered sources, 81% from external sources). 266 Federal Work-Study jobs (averaging $1005); 1,753 part-time jobs.

Need-Based Scholarships & Grants Pell, FSEOG, state, private, college/university.

Loans Perkins, PLUS, Stafford, Unsubsidized Stafford, private, college/university short-term loans ($250 average), college/university long-term loans ($2288 average).

Non-Need Awards In 1996, a total of 3,223 non-need awards were made. *Academic Interests/Achievement Awards:* 1,581 ($659,751 total): general academic, agriculture, biological sciences, business, education, foreign languages, home economics, mathematics, physical sciences, social sciences. *Creative Arts/Performance Awards:* 397 ($225,607 total): applied art and design, cinema/film/broadcasting, dance, debating, journalism/publications, music, performing arts, theater/drama. *Special Achievements/Activities Awards:* 168 ($58,926 total): community service, leadership. *Special Characteristics Awards:* 672 ($857,583 total): general special characteristics, children of faculty/staff, international students, members of minorities, veterans' children. *Athletic:* Total: 405 ($919,272); Men: 266 ($619,260); Women: 139 ($300,012).

Other Money-Saving Options Accelerated degree, co-op program, Army ROTC, off-campus living (after sophomore year). *Payment Plan:* installment. *Waivers:* full or partial for employees or children of employees.

Contact Financial Aid Office, Western Illinois University, 1 University Circle, 127 Sherman Hall, Macomb, IL 61455-1390, 309-298-2446, fax: 309-298-2353.

WESTERN KENTUCKY UNIVERSITY
Bowling Green, Kentucky

About the Institution State-supported, coed. Degrees awarded: A, B, M. Offers 119 undergraduate majors. Total enrollment: 14,613. Undergraduates: 12,475 (83% state residents). Freshmen: 2,338.

Undergraduate Expenses (1996–97) State resident tuition: $1740. Nonresident tuition: $5220. Mandatory fees: $290. College room and board: $2666. College room only: $1416 (minimum).

Applications 76% of all full-time undergraduates enrolled in fall 1996 applied for aid; of these, 65% were judged to have need according to Federal Methodology, of whom 94% were aided. *Financial aid deadline (priority):* 4/1. *Financial aid forms:* FAFSA required; CSS Financial Aid PROFILE acceptable. Proof of Selective Service registration (for men) required for some. *Regular admission application deadline:* 8/1. Nonresident deadline: 6/1.

Summary of Aid to Needy Students *From gift & self-help combined:* Average need met: 95%. Average amount awarded: $4806 (46% gift aid, 54% self-help). *Gift aid:* Total: $9,291,972 (3% from college-administered sources, 97% from external sources). 824 Federal Work-Study jobs (averaging $1612); 709 part-time jobs.

Need-Based Scholarships & Grants Pell, FSEOG, state.

Loans Perkins, PLUS, Stafford, Unsubsidized Stafford, state, private, college/university short-term loans ($200 average).

Non-Need Awards In 1996, a total of 3,619 non-need awards were made. *Academic Interests/Achievement Awards:* 2,566 ($3,668,912 total): general academic, agriculture, biological sciences, physical sciences. *Creative Arts/Performance Awards:* 55 ($37,850 total): music. *Special Characteristics Awards:* 193 ($220,946 total): children of faculty/staff, children of public servants, members of minorities, ROTC participants, veterans' children. *Athletic:* Total: 805 ($1,233,356); Men: 570 ($871,111); Women: 235 ($362,245).

Other Money-Saving Options Accelerated degree, co-op program, Army ROTC, cooperative Air Force ROTC, off-campus living (after sophomore year). *Payment Plans:* installment, deferred payment. *Waivers:* full or partial for children of alumni, employees or children of employees, senior citizens.

Contact Ms. Barbara M. Scheidt, Student Records Co-ordinator, Western Kentucky University, Potter Hall Room 317, 1 Big Red Way, Bowling Green, KY 42101-3576, 502-745-6385, fax: 502-745-6586.

WESTERN MARYLAND COLLEGE
Westminster, Maryland

About the Institution Independent, coed. Degrees awarded: B, M. Offers 35 undergraduate majors. Total enrollment: 2,592. Undergraduates: 1,382 (66% state residents). Freshmen: 385.

Undergraduate Expenses (1997–98) Comprehensive fee of $22,200 includes tuition ($16,850) and college room and board ($5350). College room only: $2540 (minimum).

Applications 73% of all full-time undergraduates enrolled in fall 1996 applied for aid; of these, 89% were judged to have need according to Federal Methodology, of whom 100% were aided. *Financial aid deadline (priority):* 3/1. *Financial aid forms:* FAFSA, institutional form required. *Regular admission application deadline:* 3/15. Early action deadline: 12/1.

Summary of Aid to Needy Students *From gift & self-help combined:* Average need met: 97%. Average amount awarded: $16,151 (70% gift aid, 30% self-help). *Gift aid:* Total: $9,307,050 (81% from college's own funds, 13% from other college-administered sources, 6% from external sources). 483 Federal Work-Study jobs (averaging $1190); 122 part-time jobs.

Need-Based Scholarships & Grants Pell, FSEOG, state, private, college/university.

Loans Perkins, PLUS, Stafford, Unsubsidized Stafford, private, college/university long-term loans ($1000 average).

Non-Need Awards In 1996, a total of 852 non-need awards were made. *Academic Interests/Achievement Awards:* 625 ($5,152,962 total): general academic. *Special Achievements/Activities Awards:* 13 ($26,000 total): leadership, memberships. *Special Characteristics Awards:* 214 ($294,488 total): local/state students, siblings of current students.

Other Money-Saving Options Army ROTC, cooperative Air Force ROTC, off-campus living (after junior year). *Payment Plans:* tuition prepayment, installment. *Waivers:* full or partial for employees or children of employees.

Contact Financial Aid Office, Western Maryland College, 2 College Hill, Westminster, MD 21157-4390, 410-857-2233.

WESTERN MICHIGAN UNIVERSITY
Kalamazoo, Michigan

About the Institution State-supported, coed. Degrees awarded: B, M, D. Offers 128 undergraduate majors. Total enrollment: 25,699. Undergraduates: 19,803 (92% state residents). Freshmen: 3,245.

Undergraduate Expenses (1996–97) State resident tuition: $2878 (minimum). Nonresident tuition: $7341 (minimum). Mandatory fees: $454. College room and board: $4257 (minimum). College room only: $1747.

Applications 56% of all full-time undergraduates enrolled in fall 1996 applied for aid; of these, 80% were judged to have need according to Federal Methodology, of whom 100% were aided. *Financial aid deadline (priority):* 3/1. *Financial aid forms:* FAFSA required. *Admission application deadline:* rolling.

Summary of Aid to Needy Students *From gift & self-help combined:* Average need met: 93%. Average amount awarded: $8981 (16% gift aid, 84% self-help). *Gift aid:* Total: $10,330,671 (36% from college's own funds, 6% from other college-administered sources, 58% from external sources). 1,189 Federal Work-Study jobs (averaging $2098); 5,025 part-time jobs.

Need-Based Scholarships & Grants Pell, FSEOG, state, private, college/university.

Loans Perkins, PLUS, Stafford, Unsubsidized Stafford, college/university short-term loans ($300 average).

Non-Need Awards *Academic Interests/Achievement Awards:* general academic, biological sciences, business, education, engineering/technologies, English, foreign languages, health fields, humanities, international studies, mathematics, military science, social sciences. *Creative Arts/Performance Awards:* applied art and design, art/fine arts, dance, music, performing arts, theater/drama. *Special Achievements/Activities Awards:* general special achievements/activities, community service. *Special Characteristics Awards:* general special characteristics, adult students, children and siblings of alumni, children of faculty/staff, children of union members/company employees, ethnic background, international students, members of minorities, out-of-state students, ROTC participants. *Athletic:* Total: 682 ($1,902,943); Men: 388 ($1,248,298); Women: 294 ($654,645).

Other Money-Saving Options Accelerated degree, co-op program, Army ROTC, cooperative Air Force ROTC, off-campus living. *Payment Plan:* installment. *Waivers:* full or partial for employees or children of employees and senior citizens.

Contact Mr. David Ladd, Business Manager, Western Michigan University, Kalamazoo, MI 49008, 616-387-6024, fax: 616-387-6989.

WESTERN MONTANA COLLEGE OF THE UNIVERSITY OF MONTANA
Dillon, Montana

About the Institution State-supported, coed. Degrees awarded: A, B. Offers 46 undergraduate majors. Total enrollment: 1,115 (91% state residents). Freshmen: 219.

Undergraduate Expenses (1996–97) State resident tuition: $2162. Nonresident tuition: $6154. College room and board: $3524. College room only: $1450.

Applications 90% of all full-time undergraduates enrolled in fall 1996 applied for aid; of these, 94% were judged to have need according to Federal Methodology, of whom 100% were aided. *Financial aid deadline (priority):* 3/1. *Financial aid forms:* FAFSA, CSS Financial Aid PROFILE required. *Admission application deadline:* rolling.

Summary of Aid to Needy Students *From gift & self-help combined:* Average need met: 64%. Average amount awarded: $5869 (31% gift aid, 69% self-help). *Gift aid:* Total: $1,101,029 (23% from college-administered sources, 77% from external sources). 110 Federal Work-Study jobs (averaging $1200); 28 part-time jobs.

Need-Based Scholarships & Grants Pell, FSEOG, state, private.

Loans Perkins, PLUS, Stafford, Unsubsidized Stafford, college/university short-term loans ($400 average).

Non-Need Awards In 1996, a total of 381 non-need awards were made. *Academic Interests/Achievement Awards:* 212 ($118,000 total): general academic, business, education, English. *Creative Arts/Performance Awards:* 26 ($26,000 total): art/fine arts. *Special Achievements/Activities Awards:* 35 ($29,700 total): rodeo. *Special Characteristics Awards:* 2 ($1000 total): members of minorities. *Athletic:* Total: 106 ($222,316); Men: 77 ($121,223); Women: 29 ($101,093).

Other Money-Saving Options Accelerated degree, co-op program, off-campus living (after freshman year). *Payment Plan:* deferred payment. *Waivers:* full or partial for minority students, employees or children of employees, senior citizens.

Contact Office of Financial Aid, Western Montana College of The University of Montana, 710 South Atlantic, Dillon, MT 59725-3598, 406-683-7011.

WESTERN NEW ENGLAND COLLEGE
Springfield, Massachusetts

About the Institution Independent, coed. Degrees awarded: A, B, M, P. Offers 32 undergraduate majors. Total enrollment: 4,574. Undergraduates: 2,902 (50% state residents). Freshmen: 479.

Undergraduate Expenses (1997–98) Comprehensive fee of $17,568 includes tuition ($10,580), mandatory fees ($868), and college room and board ($6120).

Applications 74% of all full-time undergraduates enrolled in fall 1996 applied for aid; of these, 76% were judged to have need according to Federal Methodology, of whom 98% were aided. *Financial aid deadline:* continuous. *Financial aid forms:* FAFSA, institutional form, federal income tax form required. *Admission application deadline:* rolling.

Summary of Aid to Needy Students *From gift & self-help combined:* Average need met: 70%. Average amount awarded: $10,052 (44% gift aid, 56% self-help). *Gift aid:* Total: $4,313,990 (68% from college's own funds, 5% from other college-administered sources, 27% from external sources). 622 Federal Work-Study jobs (averaging $1818); 235 part-time jobs.

Need-Based Scholarships & Grants Pell, FSEOG, state, private, college/university.

Loans Perkins, PLUS, Stafford, Unsubsidized Stafford, state, private.

Non-Need Awards Not offered.

Other Money-Saving Options Accelerated degree, Army ROTC, Air Force ROTC, off-campus living. *Payment Plans:* tuition prepayment, installment, deferred payment. *Waivers:* full or partial for employees or children of employees and senior citizens.

Contact Mrs. Kathy M. Chambers, Associate Director of Student Administrative Services, Western New England College, 1215 Wilbraham Road, Springfield, MA 01119-2654, 413-796-2080.

WESTERN NEW MEXICO UNIVERSITY
Silver City, New Mexico

About the Institution State-supported, coed. Degrees awarded: A, B, M. Offers 53 undergraduate majors. Total enrollment: 2,533. Undergraduates: 2,081 (86% state residents). Freshmen: 294.

Undergraduate Expenses (1996–97) State resident tuition: $1516. Nonresident tuition: $5604. Mandatory fees: $195. College room and board: $3014 (minimum). College room only: $1500 (minimum).

Applications Of all full-time undergraduates enrolled in fall 1996, 83% of those who applied for aid were judged to have need according to Federal Methodology, of whom 96% were aided. *Financial aid deadline (priority):* 4/1. *Financial aid forms:* FAFSA, institutional form required; CSS Financial Aid PROFILE acceptable. *Admission application deadline:* 8/15.

Summary of Aid to Needy Students *From gift & self-help combined:* Average need met: 70%. Average amount awarded: $2378 (68% gift aid, 32% self-help). *Gift aid:* Total: $1,591,390 (26% from college's own funds, 11% from other college-administered sources, 63% from external sources). 98 Federal Work-Study jobs (averaging $2040); 196 part-time jobs.

Need-Based Scholarships & Grants Pell, FSEOG, state, private, college/university.

Loans Perkins, PLUS, Stafford, Unsubsidized Stafford, state, college/university short-term loans ($100 average), college/university long-term loans ($1700 average).

Non-Need Awards In 1996, a total of 429 non-need awards were made. *Academic Interests/Achievement Awards:* 154 ($100,038 total). *Creative Arts/Performance Awards:* 24 ($10,977 total): performing arts. *Special Achievements/Activities Awards:* 59 ($9000 total). *Special Characteristics Awards:* 124 ($78,182 total): veterans. *Athletic:* Total: 68 ($84,583); Men: 52 ($63,838); Women: 16 ($20,745).

Other Money-Saving Options Accelerated degree, co-op program, off-campus living (after freshman year). *Payment Plan:* deferred payment. *Waivers:* full or partial for employees or children of employees and senior citizens.

Contact Office of Financial Aid, Western New Mexico University, PO Box 680, Silver City, NM 88062-0680, 505-538-6011.

WESTERN OREGON UNIVERSITY
Monmouth, Oregon

About the Institution State-supported, coed. Degrees awarded: A, B, M. Offers 47 undergraduate majors. Total enrollment: 4,030. Undergraduates: 3,798 (92% state residents). Freshmen: 742.

Undergraduate Expenses (1996–97) State resident tuition: $3096. Nonresident tuition: $9108. College room and board: $3839 (minimum).

Applications 70% of all full-time undergraduates enrolled in fall 1996 applied for aid; of these, 84% were judged to have need according to Federal Methodology, of whom 100% were aided. *Financial aid deadline (priority):* 3/1. *Financial aid forms:* FAFSA required. *Admission application deadline:* rolling.

Summary of Aid to Needy Students *From gift & self-help combined:* Average need met: 65%. Average amount awarded: $6550 (35% gift aid, 65% self-help). *Gift aid:* Total: $4,769,956 (24% from college's

own funds, 4% from other college-administered sources, 72% from external sources). 617 Federal Work-Study jobs (averaging $767); 172 part-time jobs.

Need-Based Scholarships & Grants Pell, FSEOG.

Loans Perkins, PLUS, Stafford, Unsubsidized Stafford, college/university short-term loans ($250 average), college/university long-term loans.

Non-Need Awards In 1996, a total of 595 non-need awards were made. *Academic Interests/Achievement Awards:* 454 ($410,812 total): general academic. *Creative Arts/Performance Awards:* 24 ($8990 total): art/fine arts, music, theater/drama. *Special Achievements/Activities Awards:* 10 ($15,156 total): general special achievements/activities. *Special Characteristics Awards:* 107 ($311,022 total): international students, members of minorities.

Other Money-Saving Options Accelerated degree, Army ROTC, cooperative Air Force ROTC, off-campus living (after freshman year). *Payment Plans:* installment, deferred payment. *Waivers:* full or partial for minority students.

Contact Ms. Sandra Mountain, Director of Financial Aid, Western Oregon University, 345 North Monmouth Avenue, Monmouth, OR 97361, 503-838-8684, fax: 503-838-8600.

WESTERN STATE COLLEGE OF COLORADO
Gunnison, Colorado

About the Institution State-supported, coed. Degrees awarded: B. Offers 51 undergraduate majors. Total enrollment: 2,534 (66% state residents). Freshmen: 637.

Undergraduate Expenses (1996–97) State resident tuition: $1440. Nonresident tuition: $6418. Mandatory fees: $636. College room and board: $4649. College room only: $2345.

Applications 75% of all full-time undergraduates enrolled in fall 1996 applied for aid; of these, 66% were judged to have need according to Federal Methodology, of whom 100% were aided. *Financial aid deadline (priority):* 4/1. *Financial aid forms:* FAFSA acceptable. *Admission application deadline:* rolling.

Summary of Aid to Needy Students *From gift & self-help combined:* Average need met: 100%. Average amount awarded: $2332 (30% gift aid, 70% self-help). *Gift aid:* Total: $842,000 (20% from college's own funds, 33% from other college-administered sources, 47% from external sources). 188 Federal Work-Study jobs (averaging $1263); 518 part-time jobs.

Need-Based Scholarships & Grants Pell, FSEOG, state, private, college/university.

Loans Perkins, PLUS, Stafford, Unsubsidized Stafford, private, college/university short-term loans ($713 average).

Non-Need Awards *Academic Interests/Achievement Awards:* general academic, biological sciences, business, communication, computer science, education, English, mathematics, social sciences. *Creative Arts/Performance Awards:* music, theater/drama. *Athletic:* Total: 192 ($300,000); Men: 116 ($180,000); Women: 76 ($120,000).

Other Money-Saving Options Accelerated degree, co-op program, off-campus living (after freshman year). *Payment Plans:* installment, deferred payment. *Waivers:* full or partial for employees or children of employees and senior citizens.

Contact Mr. Marty Somero, Director of Financial Aid, Western State College of Colorado, Gunnison, CO 81231, 970-943-3026, fax: 970-943-2277.

WESTERN WASHINGTON UNIVERSITY
Bellingham, Washington

About the Institution State-supported, coed. Degrees awarded: B, M. Offers 102 undergraduate majors. Total enrollment: 11,039. Undergraduates: 10,252 (92% state residents). Freshmen: 2,082.

Undergraduate Expenses (1996–97) State resident tuition: $2433. Nonresident tuition: $8616. Mandatory fees: $180. College room and board: $4478.

Applications Of all full-time undergraduates enrolled in fall 1996, 77% of those who applied for aid were judged to have need according to Federal Methodology, of whom 94% were aided. *Financial aid deadline (priority):* 2/15. *Financial aid forms:* FAFSA required. *Admission application deadline:* 3/1.

Summary of Aid to Needy Students *From gift & self-help combined:* Average need met: 81%. Average amount awarded: $5964 (33% gift aid, 67% self-help). *Gift aid:* Total: $8,971,769 (14% from college's own funds, 32% from other college-administered sources, 54% from external sources). 296 Federal Work-Study jobs (averaging $1430); 2,668 part-time jobs.

Need-Based Scholarships & Grants Pell, FSEOG, state, private, college/university.

Loans Perkins, PLUS, Stafford, Unsubsidized Stafford, private, college/university short-term loans ($600 average).

Non-Need Awards In 1996, a total of 646 non-need awards were made. *Academic Interests/Achievement Awards:* 300 ($291,391 total): general academic, biological sciences, business, communication, computer science, education, engineering/technologies, English, foreign languages, humanities, library science, mathematics, physical sciences, premedicine, social sciences. *Creative Arts/Performance Awards:* 52 ($32,932 total): art/fine arts, journalism/publications, music, theater/drama. *Special Achievements/Activities Awards:* 4 ($3871 total): leadership, memberships. *Special Characteristics Awards:* 164 ($277,819 total): international students, local/state students, members of minorities, veterans. *Athletic:* Total: 126 ($256,578); Men: 62 ($135,812); Women: 64 ($120,766).

Other Money-Saving Options Accelerated degree, co-op program, off-campus living. *Payment Plan:* installment. *Waivers:* full or partial for employees or children of employees and senior citizens.

Contact Ms. Jean Meyer, Systems Coordinator, Student Financial Resources, Western Washington University, OM 240 MS 9006, Bellingham, WA 98225-9006, 360-650-3470, fax: 360-650-7291.

WESTFIELD STATE COLLEGE
Westfield, Massachusetts

About the Institution State-supported, coed. Degrees awarded: B, M. Offers 52 undergraduate majors. Total enrollment: 4,878. Undergraduates: 4,137 (94% state residents). Freshmen: 729.

Undergraduate Expenses (1996–97) State resident tuition: $1338. Nonresident tuition: $5726. Mandatory fees: $1824. College room and board: $4146. College room only: $2680.

Applications 73% of all full-time undergraduates enrolled in fall 1996 applied for aid; of these, 81% were judged to have need according to Federal Methodology, of whom 100% were aided. *Financial aid deadline (priority):* 3/1. *Financial aid forms:* FAFSA required. *Admission application deadline:* rolling.

Summary of Aid to Needy Students *From gift & self-help combined:* Average need met: 75%. Average amount awarded: $6285 (19% gift aid, 81% self-help). *Gift aid:* Total: $2,241,796 (2% from college's own funds, 46% from other college-administered sources, 52% from external sources). 350 Federal Work-Study jobs (averaging $1000); 600 part-time jobs.

Need-Based Scholarships & Grants Pell, FSEOG, state, college/university.

Loans Perkins, PLUS, Stafford, Unsubsidized Stafford, state, private, college/university short-term loans ($300 average), college/university long-term loans ($995 average).

Non-Need Awards *Academic Interests/Achievement Awards:* general academic. *Special Achievements/Activities Awards:* community service.

Other Money-Saving Options Accelerated degree, cooperative Army ROTC, off-campus living. *Payment Plan:* installment. *Waivers:* full or partial for employees or children of employees and senior citizens.

Contact Ms. Michelle Mattie, Director of Financial Aid and Admissions, Westfield State College, Western Avenue, Westfield, MA 01086, 413-572-5407.

WEST LIBERTY STATE COLLEGE
West Liberty, West Virginia

About the Institution State-supported, coed. Degrees awarded: A, B. Offers 40 undergraduate majors. Total enrollment: 2,412 (70% state residents). Freshmen: 468.

Undergraduate Expenses (1997–98) State resident tuition: $2120. Nonresident tuition: $5560. College room and board: $3100.

Applications 65% of all full-time undergraduates enrolled in fall 1996 applied for aid; of these, 90% were judged to have need according to Federal Methodology, of whom 100% were aided. *Financial aid deadline (priority):* 3/1. *Financial aid forms:* FAFSA required. State form required for some. *Admission application deadline:* 8/1.

Summary of Aid to Needy Students *From gift & self-help combined:* Average need met: 85%. Average amount awarded: $5995 (41% gift aid, 59% self-help). *Gift aid:* Total: $2,447,924 (4% from college's own funds, 25% from other college-administered sources, 71% from external sources). 137 Federal Work-Study jobs (averaging $868); 128 part-time jobs.

Need-Based Scholarships & Grants Pell, FSEOG, state, private.

Loans Perkins, PLUS, Stafford, Unsubsidized Stafford, Federal Nursing.

Non-Need Awards In 1996, a total of 206 non-need awards were made. *Academic Interests/Achievement Awards:* 82 ($99,310 total): general academic, business, communication, education, English, mathematics, physical sciences. *Creative Arts/Performance Awards:* 20 ($38,910 total): art/fine arts, music, theater/drama. *Special Characteristics Awards:* 2 ($400 total): children of faculty/staff. *Athletic:* Total: 102 ($241,763); Men: 72 ($171,393); Women: 30 ($70,370).

Other Money-Saving Options Off-campus living. *Payment Plans:* installment, deferred payment.

Contact Mr. Frank J. Harrar, Dean of Students and Director of Financial Aid, West Liberty State College, West Liberty, WV 26074, 304-336-8016.

WESTMAR UNIVERSITY
Le Mars, Iowa

About the Institution Independent, coed. Degrees awarded: B. Offers 38 undergraduate majors. Total enrollment: 633 (40% state residents). Freshmen: 297.

Undergraduate Expenses (1997–98 estimated) Comprehensive fee of $14,026 includes tuition ($9980), mandatory fees ($296), and college room and board ($3750). College room only: $1680.

Applications 85% of all full-time undergraduates enrolled in fall 1996 applied for aid. *Financial aid deadline (priority):* 4/1. *Financial aid forms:* FAFSA, institutional form required. *Admission application deadline:* rolling.

Summary of Aid to Needy Students *From gift & self-help combined:* Average need met: 85%. 200 Federal Work-Study jobs (averaging $900); part-time jobs.

Need-Based Scholarships & Grants Pell, FSEOG, state, college/ university.

Loans Perkins, PLUS, Stafford, Unsubsidized Stafford, college/university short-term loans, college/university long-term loans.

Non-Need Awards *Academic Interests/Achievement Awards:* general academic. *Creative Arts/Performance Awards:* music. *Special Achievements/ Activities Awards:* Junior Miss. *Special Characteristics Awards:* children and siblings of alumni, children of faculty/staff, siblings of current students. *Athletic:* available.

Other Money-Saving Options Accelerated degree, co-op program, off-campus living (after junior year). *Payment Plan:* installment. *Waivers:* full or partial for employees or children of employees and senior citizens.

Contact Office of Financial Aid, Westmar University, 1002 3rd Avenue, SE, Le Mars, IA 51031-2697, 712-546-7081.

WESTMINSTER CHOIR COLLEGE OF RIDER UNIVERSITY
Princeton, New Jersey

About the Institution Independent, coed. Degrees awarded: B, M. Offers 6 undergraduate majors. Total enrollment: 398. Undergraduates: 280 (32% state residents). Freshmen: 55.

Undergraduate Expenses (1997–98) Comprehensive fee of $22,040 includes tuition ($15,120), mandatory fees ($310), and college room and board ($6610).

Applications 93% of all full-time undergraduates enrolled in fall 1996 applied for aid; of these, 95% were judged to have need according to Federal Methodology, of whom 100% were aided. *Financial aid deadline (priority):* 3/1. *Financial aid forms:* FAFSA required. *Regular admission application deadline:* rolling. Early decision deadline: 11/1.

Summary of Aid to Needy Students *From gift & self-help combined:* Average need met: 93%. Average amount awarded: $11,380 (64% gift aid, 36% self-help). *Gift aid:* Total: $1,766,692 (82% from college's own funds, 13% from other college-administered sources, 5% from external sources). Federal Work-Study jobs; part-time jobs.

Need-Based Scholarships & Grants Pell, FSEOG, state, private, college/ university.

Loans Perkins, PLUS, Stafford, Unsubsidized Stafford, state, college/ university long-term loans ($1000 average).

Non-Need Awards In 1996, a total of 208 non-need awards were made. *Academic Interests/Achievement Awards:* 90 ($389,620 total): general academic. *Creative Arts/Performance Awards:* 118 ($153,647 total): music.

Other Money-Saving Options Off-campus living (after junior year). *Payment Plan:* installment. *Waivers:* full or partial for employees or children of employees.

Contact Mr. John J. Williams, Director of Financial Aid, Westminster Choir College of Rider University, 2083 Lawrenceville Road, Lawrenceville, NJ 08648, 609-896-5360, fax: 609-895-6645.

WESTMINSTER COLLEGE
Fulton, Missouri

About the Institution Independent/religious, coed. Degrees awarded: B. Offers 46 undergraduate majors. Total enrollment: 653 (60% state residents). Freshmen: 216.

Undergraduate Expenses (1996–97) Comprehensive fee of $16,270 includes tuition ($11,700), mandatory fees ($240), and college room and board ($4330).

Applications Of all full-time undergraduates enrolled in fall 1996, 92% of those who applied for aid were judged to have need according to Federal Methodology, of whom 100% were aided. *Financial aid deadline*

(priority): 3/22. *Financial aid forms:* FAFSA required; CSS Financial Aid PROFILE acceptable. *Regular admission application deadline:* rolling. Early decision deadline: 11/1.

Summary of Aid to Needy Students *From gift & self-help combined:* Average need met: 94%. Average amount awarded: $12,367 (66% gift aid, 34% self-help). *Gift aid:* Total: $3,149,154 (78% from college's own funds, 15% from other college-administered sources, 7% from external sources). 263 Federal Work-Study jobs (averaging $900); 123 part-time jobs.

Need-Based Scholarships & Grants Pell, FSEOG, state, college/ university, Callaway Grants.

Loans Perkins, PLUS, Stafford, Unsubsidized Stafford.

Non-Need Awards In 1996, a total of 555 non-need awards were made. *Academic Interests/Achievement Awards:* 365 ($1,888,293 total): general academic. *Special Achievements/Activities Awards:* 173 ($205,800 total): leadership. *Special Characteristics Awards:* 17 ($154,837 total): children and siblings of alumni, ROTC participants.

Other Money-Saving Options Accelerated degree, cooperative Army ROTC, cooperative Air Force ROTC, off-campus living (after junior year). *Payment Plan:* installment. *Waivers:* full or partial for children of alumni and employees or children of employees.

Contact Ms. Karla Albert, Director of Admissions and Financial Aid, Westminster College, 501 Westminster Avenue, Fulton, MO 65251-1299, 800-475-3361, fax: 573-592-1255.

WESTMINSTER COLLEGE
New Wilmington, Pennsylvania

About the Institution Independent/religious, coed. Degrees awarded: B, M. Offers 52 undergraduate majors. Total enrollment: 1,584. Undergraduates: 1,469 (76% state residents). Freshmen: 301.

Undergraduate Expenses (1996–97) Comprehensive fee of $18,970 includes tuition ($14,085), mandatory fees ($765), and college room and board ($4120). College room only: $1980.

Applications Of all full-time undergraduates enrolled in fall 1996, 91% of those who applied for aid were judged to have need according to Federal Methodology, of whom 99% were aided. *Financial aid deadline (priority):* 5/1. *Financial aid forms:* FAFSA, institutional form, federal income tax forms required; CSS Financial Aid PROFILE, state form acceptable. *Admission application deadline:* rolling.

Summary of Aid to Needy Students *From gift & self-help combined:* Average need met: 95%. Average amount awarded: $12,758 (72% gift aid, 28% self-help). *Gift aid:* Total: $9,695,061 (71% from college's own funds, 6% from other college-administered sources, 23% from external sources). 202 Federal Work-Study jobs (averaging $1268); 35 part-time jobs.

Need-Based Scholarships & Grants Pell, FSEOG, state, private, college/ university.

Loans Perkins, PLUS, Stafford, Unsubsidized Stafford.

Non-Need Awards In 1996, a total of 729 non-need awards were made. *Academic Interests/Achievement Awards:* 336 ($1,693,864 total): general academic. *Creative Arts/Performance Awards:* 99 ($105,000 total): cinema/film/broadcasting, music, theater/drama. *Special Achievements/Activities Awards:* 16 ($54,526 total): leadership. *Special Characteristics Awards:* 133 ($304,429 total): general special characteristics, children and siblings of alumni. *Athletic:* Total: 145 ($398,334); Men: 90 ($314,459); Women: 55 ($83,875).

Other Money-Saving Options Accelerated degree, cooperative Army ROTC, off-campus living (after junior year). *Payment Plan:* installment. *Waivers:* full or partial for children of alumni, employees or children of employees, adult students.

Contact Mr. Robert A. Latta, Director of Financial Aid, Westminster College, South Market Street, New Wilmington, PA 16172-0001, 412-946-7102, fax: 412-946-7171.

WESTMINSTER COLLEGE OF SALT LAKE CITY
Salt Lake City, Utah

About the Institution Independent, coed. Degrees awarded: B, M. Offers 31 undergraduate majors. Total enrollment: 1,922. Undergraduates: 1,492 (92% state residents). Freshmen: 200.

Undergraduate Expenses (1997–98) Comprehensive fee of $15,604 includes tuition ($10,976), mandatory fees ($270), and college room and board ($4358 minimum). College room only: $1436 (minimum).

Applications 95% of all full-time undergraduates enrolled in fall 1996 applied for aid; of these, 70% were judged to have need according to Federal Methodology, of whom 99% were aided. *Financial aid deadline:* continuous. *Financial aid forms:* FAFSA required for some. *Admission application deadline:* rolling.

Summary of Aid to Needy Students *From gift & self-help combined:* Average need met: 98%. Average amount awarded: $12,479 (46% gift aid, 54% self-help). *Gift aid:* Total: $3,656,801 (68% from college's own funds, 6% from other college-administered sources, 26% from external sources). 163 Federal Work-Study jobs (averaging $2003).

Need-Based Scholarships & Grants Pell, FSEOG, state, private, college/university.

Loans Perkins, PLUS, Stafford, Unsubsidized Stafford, private, college/university short-term loans ($300 average).

Non-Need Awards In 1996, a total of 1,084 non-need awards were made. *Academic Interests/Achievement Awards:* 1,053 ($2,370,597 total): general academic, biological sciences, mathematics, physical sciences. *Creative Arts/Performance Awards:* 19 ($14,250 total): art/fine arts, journalism/publications, music, theater/drama. *Special Characteristics Awards:* 12 ($16,000 total): members of minorities, relatives of clergy, siblings of current students.

Other Money-Saving Options Cooperative Army ROTC, cooperative Naval ROTC, cooperative Air Force ROTC, off-campus living (after freshman year). *Payment Plans:* installment, deferred payment. *Waivers:* full or partial for employees or children of employees.

Contact Ms. Ruth Henneman, Director of Financial Aid, Westminster College of Salt Lake City, Salt Lake City, UT 84105-3697, 801-484-7651.

WESTMONT COLLEGE
Santa Barbara, California

About the Institution Independent/religious, coed. Degrees awarded: B. Offers 39 undergraduate majors. Total enrollment: 1,320 (75% state residents). Freshmen: 398.

Undergraduate Expenses (1997–98) Comprehensive fee of $24,046 includes tuition ($17,486), mandatory fees ($512), and college room and board ($6048). College room only: $3512.

Applications 88% of all full-time undergraduates enrolled in fall 1996 applied for aid; of these, 80% were judged to have need according to Federal Methodology, of whom 100% were aided. *Financial aid deadline (priority):* 3/1. *Financial aid forms:* FAFSA required; CSS Financial Aid PROFILE, institutional form acceptable. State form required for some. *Regular admission application deadline:* 3/1. Early action deadline: 12/1.

Summary of Aid to Needy Students *From gift & self-help combined:* Average need met: 85%. Average amount awarded: $15,000 (63% gift aid, 37% self-help). *Gift aid:* Total: $8,703,100 (73% from college's own funds, 18% from other college-administered sources, 9% from external sources). 225 Federal Work-Study jobs (averaging $625); 400 part-time jobs.

Need-Based Scholarships & Grants Pell, FSEOG, state, private, college/university.

Loans Perkins, PLUS, Stafford, Unsubsidized Stafford, private, college/university short-term loans ($100 average), college/university long-term loans ($2800 average).

Non-Need Awards In 1996, a total of 233 non-need awards were made. *Academic Interests/Achievement Awards:* 19 ($19,000 total): general academic. *Creative Arts/Performance Awards:* 48 ($48,000 total): art/fine arts, music, theater/drama. *Special Achievements/Activities Awards:* 36 ($36,000 total): leadership. *Special Characteristics Awards:* 38 ($200,184 total): ethnic background, international students. *Athletic:* Total: 92 ($397,500); Men: 55 ($229,300); Women: 37 ($168,200).

Other Money-Saving Options Accelerated degree, co-op program, cooperative Army ROTC, off-campus living. *Payment Plans:* installment, deferred payment. *Waivers:* full or partial for employees or children of employees.

Contact Financial Aid Office, Westmont College, Santa Barbara, CA 93108-1099, 888-963-4624.

WEST TEXAS A&M UNIVERSITY
Canyon, Texas

About the Institution State-supported, coed. Degrees awarded: B, M. Offers 98 undergraduate majors. Total enrollment: 6,482. Undergraduates: 5,330 (92% state residents). Freshmen: 883.

Undergraduate Expenses (1996–97) State resident tuition: $960. Nonresident tuition: $7380. Mandatory fees: $894. College room and board: $2846. College room only: $1308.

Applications 36% of all full-time undergraduates enrolled in fall 1996 applied for aid; of these, 86% were judged to have need according to Federal Methodology, of whom 91% were aided. *Financial aid deadline (priority):* 5/1. *Financial aid forms:* FAFSA required; CSS Financial Aid PROFILE, institutional form acceptable. Verification worksheet required for some. *Admission application deadline:* 8/16.

Summary of Aid to Needy Students *From gift & self-help combined:* Average need met: 75%. Average amount awarded: $6000 (39% gift aid, 61% self-help). *Gift aid:* Total: $2,963,389 (27% from college's own funds, 7% from other college-administered sources, 66% from external sources). 134 Federal Work-Study jobs (averaging $1200); 400 part-time jobs.

Need-Based Scholarships & Grants Pell, FSEOG, state, college/university.

Loans Perkins, PLUS, Stafford, Unsubsidized Stafford, state, college/university short-term loans ($831 average), college/university long-term loans ($1141 average).

Non-Need Awards In 1996, a total of 1,900 non-need awards were made. *Academic Interests/Achievement Awards:* 595 ($278,725 total): general academic, agriculture, business, computer science, education, English, health fields, humanities, mathematics, social sciences. *Creative Arts/Performance Awards:* 239 ($92,855 total): dance, journalism/publications, music, theater/drama. *Special Achievements/Activities Awards:* 155 ($79,157 total): cheerleading/drum major, leadership, memberships, rodeo. *Special Characteristics Awards:* 681 ($461,338 total): children of faculty/staff, first-generation college students, handicapped students. *Athletic:* Total: 230 ($326,948); Men: 166 ($246,698); Women: 64 ($80,250).

Other Money-Saving Options Accelerated degree, co-op program, off-campus living (after sophomore year). *Payment Plan:* installment.

Contact Mrs. Lynda R. Tinsley, Director of Financial Aid, West Texas A&M University, WTAMU Box 939, Canyon, TX 79016-0001, 806-656-2055, fax: 806-656-2924.

WEST VIRGINIA INSTITUTE OF TECHNOLOGY
Montgomery, West Virginia

See West Virginia University Institute of Technology

WEST VIRGINIA STATE COLLEGE
Institute, West Virginia

About the Institution State-supported, coed. Degrees awarded: A, B. Offers 48 undergraduate majors. Total enrollment: 4,545 (93% state residents). Freshmen: 729.

Undergraduate Expenses (1997–98) State resident tuition: $2184. Nonresident tuition: $5386. College room and board: $3450. College room only: $1650.

Applications Of all full-time undergraduates enrolled in fall 1996, 82% of those who applied for aid were judged to have need according to Federal Methodology, of whom 100% were aided. *Financial aid deadline:* Applications processed continuously. *Financial aid forms:* FAFSA, CSS Financial Aid PROFILE, institutional form required. Financial aid transcript (for transfers) required for some. *Admission application deadline:* 8/11.

Summary of Aid to Needy Students *From gift & self-help combined:* Average need met: 100%. Average amount awarded: $5156 (38% gift aid, 62% self-help). *Gift aid:* Total: $3,561,047 (10% from college's own funds, 33% from other college-administered sources, 57% from external sources). 162 Federal Work-Study jobs (averaging $3000); part-time jobs.

Need-Based Scholarships & Grants Pell, FSEOG, state, private, college/university.

Loans Perkins, PLUS, Stafford, Unsubsidized Stafford, college/university short-term loans ($1058 average).

Non-Need Awards *Academic Interests/Achievement Awards:* 249 ($359,247 total): general academic, biological sciences, business, communication, English, foreign languages, mathematics, military science. *Creative Arts/Performance Awards:* art/fine arts, music. *Special Achievements/Activities Awards:* general special achievements/activities, leadership. *Special Characteristics Awards:* general special characteristics, ethnic background, ROTC participants. *Athletic:* Total: 107 ($170,764).

Other Money-Saving Options Accelerated degree, co-op program, Army ROTC, off-campus living (after freshman year). *Payment Plan:* installment.

Contact Ms. Nancy Atkins, Student Loan Officer, West Virginia State College, Institute, WV 25112-1000, 304-766-3131.

WEST VIRGINIA UNIVERSITY
Morgantown, West Virginia

About the Institution State-supported, coed. Degrees awarded: B, M, D, P. Offers 74 undergraduate majors. Total enrollment: 21,743. Undergraduates: 14,897 (59% state residents). Freshmen: 3,151.

Undergraduate Expenses (1997–98) State resident tuition: $2336. Nonresident tuition: $7356. College room and board: $4832.

Applications Of all full-time undergraduates enrolled in fall 1996, 62% of those who applied for aid were judged to have need according to Federal Methodology, of whom 99% were aided. *Financial aid deadline:* Applications processed continuously. *Financial aid forms:* institutional form required. FAFSA, state form required for some. *Admission application deadline:* rolling.

Summary of Aid to Needy Students *From gift & self-help combined:* Average need met: 94%. Average amount awarded: $8521 (30% gift aid, 70% self-help). *Gift aid:* Total: $15,096,000 (9% from college's own funds, 29% from other college-administered sources, 62% from external sources). 1,500 Federal Work-Study jobs (averaging $1400); 1,488 part-time jobs.

Need-Based Scholarships & Grants Pell, FSEOG, state, private, college/university.

Loans Perkins, PLUS, Stafford, Unsubsidized Stafford, Federal Nursing, Primary Care, state, private, college/university short-term loans ($166 average), college/university long-term loans ($1211 average).

Non-Need Awards In 1996, a total of 2,523 non-need awards were made. *Academic Interests/Achievement Awards:* 924 ($1,975,600 total): general academic, agriculture, architecture, area/ethnic studies, biological sciences, business, communication, computer science, education, engineering/technologies, English, foreign languages, health fields, home economics, humanities, international studies, library science, mathematics, military science, physical sciences, premedicine, religion/biblical studies, social sciences. *Creative Arts/Performance Awards:* 101 ($499,600 total): art/fine arts, music, theater/drama. *Special Achievements/Activities Awards:* 789 ($555,700 total): general special achievements/activities, leadership. *Special Characteristics Awards:* 410 ($695,500 total): general special characteristics, children of faculty/staff, children of union members/company employees, children of workers in trades, ethnic background, international students, local/state students, members of minorities, ROTC participants. *Athletic:* Total: 299 ($2,772,900); Men: 205 ($1,754,400); Women: 94 ($1,018,500).

Other Money-Saving Options Accelerated degree, co-op program, Army ROTC, Air Force ROTC, off-campus living (after freshman year). *Payment Plans:* installment, deferred payment. *Waivers:* full or partial for employees or children of employees.

Contact Ms. Mary Ward, Scholars Program Coordinator, West Virginia University, PO Box 6004, Morgantown, WV 26506-6004, 304-293-4126, fax: 304-293-4890.

WEST VIRGINIA UNIVERSITY INSTITUTE OF TECHNOLOGY
Montgomery, West Virginia

About the Institution State-supported, coed. Degrees awarded: A, B, M. Offers 44 undergraduate majors. Total enrollment: 2,486. Undergraduates: 2,458 (92% state residents). Freshmen: 527.

Undergraduate Expenses (1997–98) State resident tuition: $2370. Nonresident tuition: $5946. College room and board: $3858. College room only: $1992.

Applications 67% of all full-time undergraduates enrolled in fall 1996 applied for aid; of these, 78% were judged to have need according to Federal Methodology, of whom 93% were aided. *Financial aid deadline (priority):* 4/1. *Financial aid forms:* FAFSA, institutional form required. *Admission application deadline:* rolling.

Summary of Aid to Needy Students *From gift & self-help combined:* Average need met: 91%. Average amount awarded: $4672 (44% gift aid, 56% self-help). *Gift aid:* Total: $1,927,394 (12% from college's own funds, 5% from other college-administered sources, 83% from external sources). 269 Federal Work-Study jobs (averaging $1082); 450 part-time jobs.

Need-Based Scholarships & Grants Pell, FSEOG, state, private, college/university.

Loans Perkins, PLUS, Stafford, Unsubsidized Stafford, college/university short-term loans ($100 average), college/university long-term loans ($500 average).

Non-Need Awards In 1996, a total of 111 non-need awards were made. *Academic Interests/Achievement Awards:* 25 ($26,017 total): general academic, engineering/technologies. *Creative Arts/Performance Awards:* 25 ($10,475 total): music. *Athletic:* Total: 61 ($91,965); Men: 47 ($73,917); Women: 14 ($18,048).

Other Money-Saving Options Accelerated degree, co-op program, Army ROTC, off-campus living (after sophomore year). *Payment Plan:* installment. *Waivers:* full or partial for employees or children of employees.

Contact Office of Financial Aid, West Virginia University Institute of Technology, Financial Aid Office-Box 51, Montgomery, WV 25136, 304-442-3071.

WEST VIRGINIA WESLEYAN COLLEGE
Buckhannon, West Virginia

About the Institution Independent/religious, coed. Degrees awarded: B, M. Offers 56 undergraduate majors. Total enrollment: 1,592. Undergraduates: 1,531 (45% state residents). Freshmen: 377.

Undergraduate Expenses (1996–97) Comprehensive fee of $19,150 includes tuition ($14,975), mandatory fees ($200), and college room and board ($3975). College room only: $1800.

Applications 95% of all full-time undergraduates enrolled in fall 1996 applied for aid. *Financial aid deadline (priority):* 2/15. *Financial aid forms:* FAFSA required. Institutional form required for some. *Admission application deadline:* rolling.

Summary of Aid to Needy Students 222 Federal Work-Study jobs (averaging $750); 519 part-time jobs.

Need-Based Scholarships & Grants Pell, FSEOG, state, private, college/university.

Loans Perkins, PLUS, Stafford, Unsubsidized Stafford, Federal Nursing, college/university short-term loans ($50 average), college/university long-term loans ($1200 average).

Non-Need Awards *Academic Interests/Achievement Awards:* 615 ($4,239,602 total): general academic. *Creative Arts/Performance Awards:* 218 ($613,455 total): art/fine arts, music, theater/drama. *Special Achievements/Activities Awards:* 66 ($24,235 total): community service. *Special Characteristics Awards:* general special characteristics, children of faculty/staff, international students, members of minorities, relatives of clergy. *Athletic:* Total: 197 ($1,622,811); Men: 113 ($922,275); Women: 84 ($700,536).

Other Money-Saving Options Accelerated degree. *Payment Plan:* installment. *Waivers:* full or partial for employees or children of employees.

Contact Ms. Lana Golden, Director of Financial Aid, West Virginia Wesleyan College, 59 College Avenue, Buckhannon, WV 26201, 304-473-8080.

WHEATON COLLEGE
Wheaton, Illinois

About the Institution Independent/religious, coed. Degrees awarded: B, M, D. Offers 42 undergraduate majors. Total enrollment: 2,697. Undergraduates: 2,315 (21% state residents). Freshmen: 558.

Undergraduate Expenses (1997–98) Comprehensive fee of $18,520 includes tuition ($13,780) and college room and board ($4740). College room only: $2730.

Applications 65% of all full-time undergraduates enrolled in fall 1996 applied for aid; of these, 87% were judged to have need according to Federal Methodology, of whom 96% were aided. *Financial aid deadline (priority):* 3/15. *Financial aid forms:* FAFSA, institutional form required. *Regular admission application deadline:* 2/1. Early action deadline: 11/15.

Summary of Aid to Needy Students *From gift & self-help combined:* Average need met: 78%. Average amount awarded: $10,913 (73% gift aid, 27% self-help). *Gift aid:* Total: $9,810,924 (64% from college's own funds, 12% from other college-administered sources, 24% from external sources). 284 Federal Work-Study jobs (averaging $826); 985 part-time jobs.

Need-Based Scholarships & Grants Pell, FSEOG, state, private, college/university.

Loans Perkins, PLUS, Stafford, Unsubsidized Stafford, state, private, college/university long-term loans ($1700 average).

Non-Need Awards *Academic Interests/Achievement Awards:* 471 ($355,250 total): general academic. *Creative Arts/Performance Awards:* 91 ($108,508 total): music. *Special Characteristics Awards:* children of faculty/staff, ROTC participants.

Other Money-Saving Options Army ROTC. *Payment Plan:* installment. *Waivers:* full or partial for employees or children of employees.

Contact Mrs. Donna Peltz, Director of Financial Aid, Wheaton College, 501 East College Avenue, Wheaton, IL 60187-5593, 630-752-5021, fax: 630-752-5245.

WHEATON COLLEGE
Norton, Massachusetts

About the Institution Independent, coed. Degrees awarded: B. Offers 35 undergraduate majors. Total enrollment: 1,350 (40% state residents). Freshmen: 449.

Undergraduate Expenses (1997–98) Comprehensive fee of $27,290 includes tuition ($20,620), mandatory fees ($200), and college room and board ($6470). College room only: $3410.

Applications 70% of all full-time undergraduates enrolled in fall 1996 applied for aid; of these, 94% were judged to have need according to Federal Methodology, of whom 100% were aided. *Financial aid deadline:* 2/1. *Financial aid forms:* FAFSA, CSS Financial Aid PROFILE required. *Regular admission application deadline:* 2/1. Early decision deadline: 11/15. Early action deadline: 12/15.

Summary of Aid to Needy Students *From gift & self-help combined:* Average need met: 95%. Average amount awarded: $16,895 (72% gift aid, 28% self-help). *Gift aid:* Total: $10,753,529 (89% from college's own funds, 4% from other college-administered sources, 7% from external sources). 796 Federal Work-Study jobs (averaging $1400); 162 part-time jobs.

Need-Based Scholarships & Grants Pell, FSEOG, state, private, college/university.

Loans Perkins, PLUS, Stafford, Unsubsidized Stafford, private, college/university short-term loans ($50 average).

Non-Need Awards In 1996, a total of 120 non-need awards were made. *Academic Interests/Achievement Awards:* 120 ($618,000 total): general academic.

Other Money-Saving Options Accelerated degree. *Payment Plans:* tuition prepayment, installment, deferred payment. *Waivers:* full or partial for employees or children of employees.

Contact Ms. Susan Beard, Associate Director of Student Aid, Wheaton College, East Main Street, Norton, MA 02766, 508-285-8232, fax: 508-285-8276.

WHEELING JESUIT UNIVERSITY
Wheeling, West Virginia

About the Institution Independent/religious, coed. Degrees awarded: B, M. Offers 40 undergraduate majors. Total enrollment: 1,527. Undergraduates: 1,313 (39% state residents). Freshmen: 283.

Undergraduate Expenses (1997–98) Comprehensive fee of $19,180 includes tuition ($14,200) and college room and board ($4980).

Applications 88% of all full-time undergraduates enrolled in fall 1996 applied for aid; of these, 87% were judged to have need according to Federal Methodology, of whom 100% were aided. *Financial aid deadline (priority):* 3/1. *Financial aid forms:* FAFSA required. State form required for some. *Admission application deadline:* rolling.

Summary of Aid to Needy Students *From gift & self-help combined:* Average need met: 88%. Average amount awarded: $11,064 (59% gift aid, 41% self-help). *Gift aid:* Total: $5,912,215 (80% from college's own funds, 3% from other college-administered sources, 17% from external sources). 250 Federal Work-Study jobs (averaging $1340); 250 part-time jobs.

Need-Based Scholarships & Grants Pell, FSEOG, state, private, college/university.

Loans Perkins, PLUS, Stafford, Unsubsidized Stafford, Federal Nursing.

Non-Need Awards In 1996, a total of 762 non-need awards were made. *Academic Interests/Achievement Awards:* 547 ($1,008,600 total): general academic, biological sciences, business, computer science, education, engineering/technologies, English, health fields, humanities, mathematics, physical sciences, premedicine, religion/biblical studies, social sciences. *Creative Arts/Performance Awards:* 31 ($64,000 total): creative writing, music. *Special Achievements/Activities Awards:* 29 ($42,750 total): community service, religious involvement. *Special Characteristics Awards:* 46 ($354,825 total): children and siblings of alumni, children of faculty/staff. *Athletic:* Total: 109 ($643,518); Men: 54 ($342,687); Women: 55 ($300,831).

Other Money-Saving Options Co-op program, off-campus living (after sophomore year). *Payment Plan:* guaranteed tuition. *Waivers:* full or partial for employees or children of employees and senior citizens.

Contact Ms. Su Saunders, Director of Student Financial Planning, Wheeling Jesuit University, 316 Washington Avenue, Wheeling, WV 26003-6295, 304-243-2304, fax: 304-243-2500.

WHEELOCK COLLEGE
Boston, Massachusetts

About the Institution Independent, primarily women. Degrees awarded: B, M. Offers 7 undergraduate majors. Total enrollment: 1,369. Undergraduates: 682 (54% state residents). Freshmen: 135.

Undergraduate Expenses (1997–98) Comprehensive fee of $21,520 includes tuition ($15,520) and college room and board ($6000).

Applications Of all full-time undergraduates enrolled in fall 1996, 100% of those who applied for aid were judged to have need according to Federal Methodology, of whom 100% were aided. *Financial aid deadline:* Applications processed continuously. *Financial aid forms:* FAFSA, CSS Financial Aid PROFILE, verification worksheet required. State form required for some. *Regular admission application deadline:* 2/15. Early decision deadline: 12/1.

Summary of Aid to Needy Students *From gift & self-help combined:* Average need met: 100%. Average amount awarded: $12,000 (60% gift aid, 40% self-help). *Gift aid:* Total: $3,859,000 (81% from college's own funds, 6% from other college-administered sources, 13% from external sources). 250 Federal Work-Study jobs (averaging $890); part-time jobs.

Need-Based Scholarships & Grants Pell, FSEOG, state, college/university.

Loans Perkins, PLUS, Stafford, Unsubsidized Stafford, state, college/university long-term loans ($2050 average).

Non-Need Awards Not offered.

Other Money-Saving Options Off-campus living (after sophomore year). *Payment Plan:* installment. *Waivers:* full or partial for employees or children of employees.

Contact Office of Financial Aid, Wheelock College, Boston, MA 02215, 617-734-5200 Ext. 191.

WHITMAN COLLEGE
Walla Walla, Washington

About the Institution Independent, coed. Degrees awarded: B. Offers 25 undergraduate majors. Total enrollment: 1,309 (45% state residents). Freshmen: 357.

Undergraduate Expenses (1997–98) Comprehensive fee of $25,396 includes tuition ($19,580), mandatory fees ($176), and college room and board ($5640). College room only: $2580.

Applications Of all full-time undergraduates enrolled in fall 1996, 92% of those who applied for aid were judged to have need according to Federal Methodology, of whom 91% were aided. *Financial aid deadline:* 2/1. *Financial aid forms:* FAFSA, CSS Financial Aid PROFILE required. Parent and student tax returns required for some. *Regular admission application deadline:* 2/1. Early decision deadline: 11/15.

Summary of Aid to Needy Students *From gift & self-help combined:* Average need met: 80%. Average amount awarded: $11,925 (70% gift aid, 30% self-help). *Gift aid:* Total: $10,500,000 (90% from college's own funds, 3% from other college-administered sources, 7% from external sources). 297 Federal Work-Study jobs (averaging $336); 737 part-time jobs.

Need-Based Scholarships & Grants Pell, FSEOG, state, college/university.

Loans Perkins, PLUS, Stafford, Unsubsidized Stafford, private, college/university short-term loans ($137 average).

Non-Need Awards In 1996, a total of 511 non-need awards were made. *Academic Interests/Achievement Awards:* 413 ($1,900,000 total): general academic. *Creative Arts/Performance Awards:* 10 ($96,400 total): art/fine arts, debating, music, theater/drama. *Special Achievements/Activities Awards:* 31 ($259,100 total): general special achievements/activities, leadership. *Special Characteristics Awards:* 57 ($768,230 total): ethnic background, international students.

Other Money-Saving Options Accelerated degree, off-campus living (after sophomore year). *Payment Plans:* installment, deferred payment. *Waivers:* full or partial for minority students and employees or children of employees.

Contact Ms. Varga Fox, Manager of Financial Aid Services, Whitman College, 515 Boyer, Walla Walla, WA 99362-2083, 509-527-5188, fax: 509-527-4967.

WHITTIER COLLEGE
Whittier, California

About the Institution Independent, coed. Degrees awarded: B, M, P. Offers 42 undergraduate majors. Total enrollment: 2,165. Undergraduates: 1,301 (66% state residents). Freshmen: 338.

Undergraduate Expenses (1997–98) Comprehensive fee of $24,780 includes tuition ($18,334), mandatory fees ($300), and college room and board ($6146).

Applications Of all full-time undergraduates enrolled in fall 1996, 96% of those who applied for aid were judged to have need according to Federal Methodology, of whom 100% were aided. *Financial aid deadline (priority):* 2/1. *Financial aid forms:* FAFSA, CSS Financial Aid PROFILE required. State form required for some. *Regular admission application deadline:* rolling. Early action deadline: 12/1.

Summary of Aid to Needy Students *From gift & self-help combined:* Average need met: 92%. Average amount awarded: $17,051 (65% gift aid, 35% self-help). *Gift aid:* Total: $11,272,697 (77% from college's own funds, 3% from other college-administered sources, 20% from external sources). 675 Federal Work-Study jobs (averaging $2215); 110 part-time jobs.

Need-Based Scholarships & Grants Pell, FSEOG, state, private, college/university.

Loans Perkins, PLUS, Stafford, Unsubsidized Stafford, college/university long-term loans ($1819 average).

Non-Need Awards In 1996, a total of 603 non-need awards were made. *Academic Interests/Achievement Awards:* 511 ($2,079,729 total): general academic. *Creative Arts/Performance Awards:* 44 ($292,500 total): art/fine arts, music, theater/drama. *Special Characteristics Awards:* 48 ($161,800 total): children and siblings of alumni, international students.

Other Money-Saving Options Accelerated degree, cooperative Army ROTC, cooperative Air Force ROTC, off-campus living (after junior year). *Payment Plan:* installment. *Waivers:* full or partial for children of alumni and employees or children of employees.

Contact Office of Financial Aid, Whittier College, 13406 East Philadelphia Street, Whittier, CA 90608-0634, 310-907-4200.

WHITWORTH COLLEGE
Spokane, Washington

About the Institution Independent/religious, coed. Degrees awarded: B, M. Offers 44 undergraduate majors. Total enrollment: 2,026. Undergraduates: 1,672 (52% state residents). Freshmen: 315.

Undergraduate Expenses (1996–97) Comprehensive fee of $19,524 includes tuition ($14,110), mandatory fees ($314), and college room and board ($5100).

Applications 89% of all full-time undergraduates enrolled in fall 1996 applied for aid; of these, 96% were judged to have need according to Federal Methodology, of whom 100% were aided. *Financial aid deadline (priority):* 3/1. *Financial aid forms:* CSS Financial Aid PROFILE required; FAFSA acceptable. *Regular admission application deadline:* 3/1. *Early action deadline:* 11/30.

Summary of Aid to Needy Students *From gift & self-help combined:* Average need met: 85%. Average amount awarded: $13,846 (56% gift aid, 44% self-help). *Gift aid:* Total: $10,000,000 (73% from college's own funds, 8% from other college-administered sources, 19% from external sources). 586 Federal Work-Study jobs (averaging $2066); 340 part-time jobs.

Need-Based Scholarships & Grants Pell, FSEOG, state, private, college/university.

Loans Perkins, PLUS, Stafford, Unsubsidized Stafford, private, college/university long-term loans ($1443 average).

Non-Need Awards In 1996, a total of 1,074 non-need awards were made. *Academic Interests/Achievement Awards:* 818 ($3,860,220 total): general academic. *Creative Arts/Performance Awards:* 92 ($202,370 total): art/fine arts, debating, music, theater/drama. *Special Characteristics Awards:* 164 ($211,300 total): children and siblings of alumni, relatives of clergy, ROTC participants.

Other Money-Saving Options Co-op program, cooperative Army ROTC, off-campus living (after sophomore year). *Payment Plans:* tuition prepayment, installment. *Waivers:* full or partial for children of alumni and employees or children of employees.

Contact Ms. Wendy Z. Olson, Director of Financial Aid, Whitworth College, 300 West Hawthorne Road, Spokane, WA 99251-0001, 509-466-3215.

WICHITA STATE UNIVERSITY
Wichita, Kansas

About the Institution State-supported, coed. Degrees awarded: A, B, M, D. Offers 64 undergraduate majors. Total enrollment: 14,264. Undergraduates: 11,280 (87% state residents). Freshmen: 1,061.

Undergraduate Expenses (1997–98 estimated) State resident tuition: $1845. Nonresident tuition: $7965. Mandatory fees: $644. College room and board: $3639 (minimum).

Applications Of all full-time undergraduates enrolled in fall 1996, 79% of those who applied for aid were judged to have need according to Federal Methodology, of whom 70% were aided. *Financial aid deadline (priority):* 3/15. *Financial aid forms:* FAFSA required. *Admission application deadline:* rolling.

Summary of Aid to Needy Students *From gift & self-help combined:* Average need met: 54%. Average amount awarded: $5725 (30% gift aid, 70% self-help). *Gift aid:* Total: $4,033,547 (26% from college's own funds, 12% from other college-administered sources, 62% from external sources). 224 Federal Work-Study jobs (averaging $1570); 770 part-time jobs.

Need-Based Scholarships & Grants Pell, FSEOG, state, college/university.

Loans Perkins, PLUS, Stafford, Unsubsidized Stafford, private, college/university short-term loans ($943 average).

Non-Need Awards In 1996, a total of 790 non-need awards were made. *Academic Interests/Achievement Awards:* 412 ($270,000 total): general academic, business, communication, computer science, education, engineering/technologies, English, health fields, mathematics, premedicine. *Creative Arts/Performance Awards:* 45 ($29,250 total): applied art and design, art/fine arts, dance, debating, journalism/publications, music, performing arts, theater/drama. *Special Characteristics Awards:* 168 ($36,000 total): adult students. *Athletic:* Total: 165 ($787,437); Men: 87 ($375,433); Women: 78 ($412,004).

Other Money-Saving Options Accelerated degree, co-op program, off-campus living (after freshman year). *Payment Plan:* deferred payment. *Waivers:* full or partial for senior citizens.

Contact Office of Financial Aid, Wichita State University, 1845 Fairmount, Wichita, KS 67260-0024, 316-978-3456.

WIDENER UNIVERSITY
Chester, Pennsylvania

About the Institution Independent, coed. Degrees awarded: A, B, M, D, P. Offers 44 undergraduate majors. Total enrollment: 8,150. Undergraduates: 3,850 (55% state residents). Freshmen: 527.

Undergraduate Expenses (1997–98) Comprehensive fee of $20,580 includes tuition ($14,380 minimum) and college room and board ($6200 minimum).

Applications 71% of all full-time undergraduates enrolled in fall 1996 applied for aid; of these, 91% were judged to have need according to Federal Methodology, of whom 97% were aided. *Financial aid deadline (priority):* 4/1. *Financial aid forms:* FAFSA, state form, institutional form required; CSS Financial Aid PROFILE acceptable. *Admission application deadline:* rolling.

Summary of Aid to Needy Students *From gift & self-help combined:* Average need met: 77%. Average amount awarded: $12,370 (58% gift aid, 42% self-help). *Gift aid:* Total: $10,341,581. 1,211 Federal Work-Study jobs (averaging $748); 209 part-time jobs.

Need-Based Scholarships & Grants Pell, FSEOG, state, private, college/university.

Loans Perkins, PLUS, Stafford, Unsubsidized Stafford, private.

Non-Need Awards In 1996, a total of 1,125 non-need awards were made. *Academic Interests/Achievement Awards:* 873 ($1,491,920 total): general academic, business, engineering/technologies, health fields. *Creative Arts/Performance Awards:* 18 ($35,000 total): music. *Special Achievements/Activities Awards:* 91 ($89,500 total): leadership. *Special Characteristics Awards:* 143 ($1,203,506 total): children of faculty/staff, ethnic background, ROTC participants.

Other Money-Saving Options Accelerated degree, co-op program, Army ROTC, cooperative Air Force ROTC. *Payment Plan:* installment. *Waivers:* full or partial for employees or children of employees.

Contact Ms. Ethel M. Desmarais, Director of Financial Aid, Widener University, One University Place, Chester, PA 19013-5792, 610-499-4194, fax: 610-499-4687.

WILBERFORCE UNIVERSITY
Wilberforce, Ohio

About the Institution Independent/religious, coed. Degrees awarded: B. Offers 22 undergraduate majors. Total enrollment: 897 (44% state residents). Freshmen: 194.

Undergraduate Expenses (1996–97) Comprehensive fee of $11,920 includes tuition ($7290), mandatory fees ($530), and college room and board ($4100).

Applications 94% of all full-time undergraduates enrolled in fall 1996 applied for aid; of these,100% were judged to have need according to Federal Methodology, of whom 100% were aided. *Financial aid deadline (priority):* 4/30. *Financial aid forms:* FAFSA, state form, institutional form required; CSS Financial Aid PROFILE acceptable. *Admission application deadline:* 6/1.

Summary of Aid to Needy Students *From gift & self-help combined:* Average need met: 80%. Average amount awarded: $9311 (41% gift aid, 59% self-help). *Gift aid:* Total: $3,250,000 (14% from college's own funds, 49% from other college-administered sources, 37% from external sources). Federal Work-Study jobs (averaging $1025).

Need-Based Scholarships & Grants Pell.

Loans Perkins, PLUS.

Non-Need Awards In 1996, a total of 106 non-need awards were made. *Academic Interests/Achievement Awards:* 106 ($170,000 total): general academic.

Other Money-Saving Options Co-op program, cooperative Army ROTC, cooperative Air Force ROTC, off-campus living (after junior year). *Payment Plans:* installment, deferred payment. *Waivers:* full or partial for employees or children of employees.

Contact Ms. Patricia A. Copely, Director of Financial Aid, Wilberforce University, 1055 North Bickett Road, Wilberforce, OH 45384, 937-376-2911 Ext. 724.

WILEY COLLEGE
Marshall, Texas

About the Institution Independent/religious, coed. Degrees awarded: A, B. Offers 27 undergraduate majors. Total enrollment: 508 (61% state residents). Freshmen: 135.

Undergraduate Expenses (1996–97) Comprehensive fee of $7694 includes tuition ($3960), mandatory fees ($596), and college room and board ($3138).

Applications *Financial aid deadline:* Applications processed continuously. *Financial aid forms:* FAFSA required. *Admission application deadline:* 8/1.

Summary of Aid to Needy Students Federal Work-Study jobs; part-time jobs.

Need-Based Scholarships & Grants Pell.

Loans Perkins, Stafford, Unsubsidized Stafford, private.

Non-Need Awards *Creative Arts/Performance Awards:* music. *Special Achievements/Activities Awards:* memberships. *Special Characteristics Awards:* children of faculty/staff, relatives of clergy, religious affiliation. *Athletic:* available.

Another Money-Saving Option Off-campus living.

Contact Financial Aid Office, Wiley College, Marshall, TX 75670-5199, 800-658-6889 Ext. 215.

WILKES UNIVERSITY
Wilkes-Barre, Pennsylvania

About the Institution Independent, coed. Degrees awarded: B, M. Offers 47 undergraduate majors. Total enrollment: 2,800. Undergraduates: 1,800 (82% state residents). Freshmen: 451.

Undergraduate Expenses (1997–98) Comprehensive fee of $21,655 includes tuition ($14,474), mandatory fees ($617), and college room and board ($6564).

Applications *Financial aid deadline (priority):* 5/1. *Financial aid forms:* FAFSA, state form, institutional form required; CSS Financial Aid PROFILE acceptable. *Admission application deadline:* rolling.

Summary of Aid to Needy Students *From gift & self-help combined:* Average need met: 78%. Average amount awarded: $11,589 (61% gift aid, 39% self-help). *Gift aid:* Total: $9,710,064 (64% from college's own funds, 3% from other college-administered sources, 33% from external sources). 418 Federal Work-Study jobs (averaging $562); 287 part-time jobs.

Need-Based Scholarships & Grants Pell, FSEOG, state, private, college/university.

Loans College/university short-term loans ($100 average), college/university long-term loans ($1550 average).

Non-Need Awards In 1996, a total of 1,016 non-need awards were made. *Academic Interests/Achievement Awards:* 784 ($2,910,354 total): general academic, engineering/technologies, health fields, physical sciences. *Creative Arts/Performance Awards:* 46 ($88,650 total): performing arts. *Special Achievements/Activities Awards:* 114 ($160,796 total): general special achievements/activities, leadership. *Special Characteristics Awards:* 72 ($109,446 total): children of current students, children of faculty/staff, ethnic background, members of minorities, siblings of current students, spouses of current students.

Other Money-Saving Options Accelerated degree, co-op program, Air Force ROTC, cooperative Army ROTC, off-campus living (after sophomore year). *Payment Plan:* installment. *Waivers:* full or partial for children of alumni, employees or children of employees, senior citizens.

Contact Mrs. Rachel L. Lohman, Director of Financial Aid, Wilkes University, PO Box 111, Wilkes-Barre, PA 18766-0002, 717-831-4346.

WILLAMETTE UNIVERSITY
Salem, Oregon

About the Institution Independent/religious, coed. Degrees awarded: B, M, P. Offers 42 undergraduate majors. Total enrollment: 2,501. Undergraduates: 1,727 (52% state residents). Freshmen: 431.

Undergraduate Expenses (1997–98) Comprehensive fee of $25,570 includes tuition ($20,200), mandatory fees ($90), and college room and board ($5280).

Applications Of all full-time undergraduates enrolled in fall 1996, 87% of those who applied for aid were judged to have need according to Federal Methodology, of whom 99% were aided. *Financial aid deadline (priority):* 2/1. *Financial aid forms:* FAFSA required. CSS Financial Aid PROFILE required for some. *Regular admission application deadline:* 2/1. Early decision deadline: 11/1.

Summary of Aid to Needy Students *From gift & self-help combined:* Average need met: 80%. Average amount awarded: $15,150 (64% gift aid, 36% self-help). *Gift aid:* Total: $10,798,110 (86% from college's own funds, 9% from other college-administered sources, 5% from external sources). 756 Federal Work-Study jobs (averaging $1500); 200 part-time jobs.

Need-Based Scholarships & Grants Pell, FSEOG, state, private, college/university.

Loans Perkins, PLUS, Stafford, Unsubsidized Stafford, private.

Non-Need Awards *Academic Interests/Achievement Awards:* general academic. *Creative Arts/Performance Awards:* debating, music, theater/drama. *Special Achievements/Activities Awards:* leadership. *Special Characteristics Awards:* international students, members of minorities.

Other Money-Saving Options Accelerated degree, cooperative Air Force ROTC, off-campus living (after sophomore year). *Payment Plans:* guaranteed tuition, installment, deferred payment. *Waivers:* full or partial for employees or children of employees.

Contact Ms. Leslie Limper, Director of Financial Aid, Willamette University, 900 State Street, Salem, OR 97301-3931, 503-370-6273, fax: 503-370-6588.

WILLIAM CAREY COLLEGE
Hattiesburg, Mississippi

About the Institution Independent/religious, coed. Degrees awarded: B, M. Offers 42 undergraduate majors. Total enrollment: 2,254. Undergraduates: 1,902 (68% state residents). Freshmen: 155.

Undergraduate Expenses (1997–98) Comprehensive fee of $8340 includes tuition ($6624) and college room and board ($1716 minimum).

Applications *Financial aid deadline (priority):* 4/1. *Financial aid forms:* FAFSA, institutional form required; CSS Financial Aid PROFILE acceptable. *Admission application deadline:* rolling.

Summary of Aid to Needy Students *From gift & self-help combined:* Average need met: 76%. Average amount awarded: $6412 (40% gift aid, 60% self-help). *Gift aid:* Total: $4,400,000 (57% from college's own funds, 9% from other college-administered sources, 34% from external sources). 300 Federal Work-Study jobs (averaging $1000).

Need-Based Scholarships & Grants Pell, FSEOG, state, private.

Loans Perkins, PLUS, Stafford, Unsubsidized Stafford, college/university short-term loans ($300 average).

Non-Need Awards *Academic Interests/Achievement Awards:* general academic. *Creative Arts/Performance Awards:* art/fine arts, debating, music, theater/drama. *Special Achievements/Activities Awards:* cheerleading/drum major, Junior Miss, leadership, religious involvement. *Special Characteristics Awards:* children and siblings of alumni, children of educators, children of faculty/staff, first-generation college students, international students, relatives of clergy, religious affiliation, ROTC participants, veterans. *Athletic:* Total: 125 ($350,000).

Other Money-Saving Options Accelerated degree, cooperative Army ROTC, cooperative Air Force ROTC.

Contact Ms. Brenda Pittman, Assistant Director of Financial Aid, William Carey College, Hattiesburg, MS 39401-5499, 601-582-6153.

WILLIAM JEWELL COLLEGE
Liberty, Missouri

About the Institution Independent/religious, coed. Degrees awarded: B. Offers 33 undergraduate majors. Total enrollment: 1,172 (74% state residents). Freshmen: 269.

Undergraduate Expenses (1997–98) Comprehensive fee of $15,410 includes tuition ($11,850) and college room and board ($3560). College room only: $1500.

Applications 96% of all full-time undergraduates enrolled in fall 1996 applied for aid; of these, 68% were judged to have need according to Federal Methodology, of whom 100% were aided. *Financial aid deadline (priority):* 3/1. *Financial aid forms:* FAFSA, institutional form required. *Regular admission application deadline:* rolling. Early action deadline: 11/15.

Summary of Aid to Needy Students *From gift & self-help combined:* Average need met: 95%. Average amount awarded: $9994 (58% gift aid, 42% self-help). *Gift aid:* Total: $4,332,262 (68% from college's

own funds, 16% from other college-administered sources, 16% from external sources). 650 Federal Work-Study jobs (averaging $1500); 100 part-time jobs.

Need-Based Scholarships & Grants Pell, FSEOG, state, college/university.

Loans Perkins, PLUS, Stafford, Unsubsidized Stafford, Federal Nursing, private.

Non-Need Awards In 1996, a total of 1,159 non-need awards were made. *Academic Interests/Achievement Awards:* 586 ($1,754,488 total): general academic, education. *Creative Arts/Performance Awards:* 172 ($238,825 total): art/fine arts, debating, journalism/publications, music, theater/drama. *Special Achievements/Activities Awards:* 60 ($84,270 total): cheerleading/drum major, religious involvement. *Special Characteristics Awards:* 148 ($486,614 total): children of faculty/staff, relatives of clergy. *Athletic:* Total: 193 ($493,142); Men: 130 ($340,412); Women: 63 ($152,730).

Other Money-Saving Options Accelerated degree, off-campus living (after junior year). *Payment Plans:* tuition prepayment, installment. *Waivers:* full or partial for employees or children of employees and senior citizens.

Contact Ms. Sue Armstrong, Director of Student Financial Planning, William Jewell College, 500 College Hill, Liberty, MO 64068-1843, 816-781-7700 Ext. 5146.

WILLIAM PATERSON UNIVERSITY OF NEW JERSEY
Wayne, New Jersey

About the Institution State-supported, coed. Degrees awarded: B, M. Offers 53 undergraduate majors. Total enrollment: 8,941. Undergraduates: 7,654 (98% state residents). Freshmen: 929.

Undergraduate Expenses (1996–97) State resident tuition: $3380. Nonresident tuition: $5360. College room and board: $4960 (minimum). College room only: $3100.

Applications 58% of all full-time undergraduates enrolled in fall 1996 applied for aid; of these, 84% were judged to have need according to Federal Methodology, of whom 93% were aided. *Financial aid deadline (priority):* 4/1. *Financial aid forms:* FAFSA required. *Admission application deadline:* 5/15.

Summary of Aid to Needy Students *From gift & self-help combined:* Average amount awarded: $5369 (55% gift aid, 45% self-help). *Gift aid:* Total: $7,602,719 (7% from college's own funds, 17% from other college-administered sources, 76% from external sources). 154 Federal Work-Study jobs (averaging $1300); 400 part-time jobs.

Need-Based Scholarships & Grants Pell, FSEOG, state.

Loans Perkins, PLUS, Stafford, Unsubsidized Stafford, state.

Non-Need Awards In 1996, a total of 378 non-need awards were made. *Academic Interests/Achievement Awards:* 297 ($648,643 total): general academic. *Creative Arts/Performance Awards:* 12 ($2875 total): music. *Special Characteristics Awards:* 69 ($65,000 total): members of minorities.

Other Money-Saving Options Accelerated degree, cooperative Air Force ROTC, off-campus living. *Payment Plan:* installment.

Contact Financial Aid Office, William Paterson College of New Jersey, Wayne, NJ 07470-8420, 973-595-2928.

WILLIAM PENN COLLEGE
Oskaloosa, Iowa

About the Institution Independent/religious, coed. Degrees awarded: B. Offers 39 undergraduate majors. Total enrollment: 472 (70% state residents). Freshmen: 102.

Undergraduate Expenses (1997–98) Comprehensive fee of $15,600 includes tuition ($11,000), mandatory fees ($490), and college room and board ($4110). College room only: $1410.

Applications *Financial aid deadline (priority):* 7/15. *Financial aid forms:* FAFSA required.

Summary of Aid to Needy Students *From gift & self-help combined:* Average need met: 90%. Average amount awarded: $11,922 (62% gift aid, 38% self-help). *Gift aid:* Total: $3,395,267 (59% from college's own funds, 28% from other college-administered sources, 13% from external sources). 304 Federal Work-Study jobs (averaging $1488); 10 part-time jobs.

Need-Based Scholarships & Grants Pell, FSEOG, state, private, college/university.

Loans Perkins, PLUS, Stafford, Unsubsidized Stafford.

Non-Need Awards *Academic Interests/Achievement Awards:* 108 ($534,517 total): general academic. *Creative Arts/Performance Awards:* art/fine arts, creative writing, journalism/publications, music, theater/drama. *Special Achievements/Activities Awards:* 25 ($78,015 total): Junior Miss, leadership, religious involvement. *Special Characteristics Awards:* 12 ($18,015 total): religious affiliation.

Other Money-Saving Options Accelerated degree, co-op program, off-campus living (after junior year).

Contact Ms. Nancy Ferguson, Director of Financial Aid, William Penn College, 201 Trueblood Avenue, Oskaloosa, IA 52577-1799, 515-673-1060, fax: 515-673-1396.

WILLIAMS BAPTIST COLLEGE
Walnut Ridge, Arkansas

About the Institution Independent/religious, coed. Degrees awarded: A, B. Offers 25 undergraduate majors. Total enrollment: 564 (71% state residents). Freshmen: 106.

Undergraduate Expenses (1997–98) Comprehensive fee of $8182 includes tuition ($5000), mandatory fees ($260), and college room and board ($2922).

Applications Of all full-time undergraduates enrolled in fall 1996, 100% of those judged to have need according to Federal Methodology were aided. *Financial aid deadline (priority):* 4/1. *Financial aid forms:* FAFSA, institutional form required. State form required for some. *Admission application deadline:* rolling.

Summary of Aid to Needy Students *From gift & self-help combined:* Average need met: 71%. Average amount awarded: $3500 (57% gift aid, 43% self-help). *Gift aid:* Total: $680,836 (53% from college's own funds, 17% from other college-administered sources, 30% from external sources). Federal Work-Study jobs; 28 part-time jobs.

Need-Based Scholarships & Grants Pell, FSEOG, state.

Loans PLUS, Stafford, Unsubsidized Stafford, private, college/university short-term loans ($200 average).

Non-Need Awards *Academic Interests/Achievement Awards:* general academic. *Creative Arts/Performance Awards:* 20 ($7000 total): music. *Special Characteristics Awards:* 10 ($2500 total): religious affiliation. *Athletic:* Total: 18 ($67,698); Men: 9 ($33,849); Women: 9 ($33,849).

Other Money-Saving Options Cooperative Army ROTC. *Payment Plan:* installment. *Waivers:* full or partial for employees or children of employees and senior citizens.

Contact Financial Aid Department, Williams Baptist College, Walnut Ridge, AR 72476, 501-886-6741 Ext. 121.

WILLIAMS COLLEGE
Williamstown, Massachusetts

About the Institution Independent, coed. Degrees awarded: B, M. Offers 29 undergraduate majors. Total enrollment: 2,138. Undergraduates: 2,084 (12% state residents). Freshmen: 554.

Undergraduate Expenses (1997–98) Comprehensive fee of $29,340 includes tuition ($22,889), mandatory fees ($101), and college room and board ($6350). College room only: $3180.

Applications Of all full-time undergraduates enrolled in fall 1996, 89% of those who applied for aid were judged to have need according to Federal Methodology, of whom 100% were aided. *Financial aid deadline:* 2/1. *Financial aid forms:* FAFSA, CSS Financial Aid PROFILE required. State form required for some. *Regular admission application deadline:* 1/1. Early decision deadline: 11/15.

Summary of Aid to Needy Students *From gift & self-help combined:* Average need met: 100%. Average amount awarded: $19,100 (74% gift aid, 26% self-help). *Gift aid:* Total: $11,677,000 (87% from college's own funds, 4% from other college-administered sources, 9% from external sources). 361 Federal Work-Study jobs (averaging $1559); 356 part-time jobs.

Need-Based Scholarships & Grants Pell, FSEOG, state, private, college/university.

Loans Perkins, PLUS, Stafford, Unsubsidized Stafford, college/university short-term loans ($100 average), college/university long-term loans ($4000 average).

Non-Need Awards Not offered.

Other Money-Saving Options Accelerated degree. *Payment Plan:* installment. *Waivers:* full or partial for employees or children of employees.

Contact Mr. Philip G. Wick, Director of Financial Aid, Williams College, PO Box 37, Williamstown, MA 01267, 413-597-4181, fax: 413-597-2999.

WILLIAM SMITH COLLEGE
Geneva, New York

See Hobart and William Smith Colleges

WILLIAM TYNDALE COLLEGE
Farmington Hills, Michigan

About the Institution Independent/religious, coed. Degrees awarded: A, B. Offers 16 undergraduate majors. Total enrollment: 512 (96% state residents). Freshmen: 37.

Undergraduate Expenses (1997–98) Tuition: $6000. College room only: $3600.

Applications Of all full-time undergraduates enrolled in fall 1996, 80% of those who applied for aid were judged to have need according to Federal Methodology, of whom 100% were aided. *Financial aid deadline:* continuous. *Financial aid forms:* FAFSA, CSS Financial Aid PROFILE, state form, institutional form required. *Admission application deadline:* rolling.

Summary of Aid to Needy Students *From gift & self-help combined:* Average need met: 27%. Average amount awarded: $5509 (74% gift aid, 26% self-help). *Gift aid:* Total: $747,000 (36% from college's own funds, 47% from other college-administered sources, 17% from external sources). 17 Federal Work-Study jobs (averaging $1500); 11 part-time jobs.

Need-Based Scholarships & Grants Pell, FSEOG, state, private, college/university.

Loans PLUS, Stafford, Unsubsidized Stafford, college/university short-term loans ($100 average).

Non-Need Awards *Academic Interests/Achievement Awards:* 200 ($500,000 total): general academic. *Creative Arts/Performance Awards:* 8 ($24,586 total): music. *Special Characteristics Awards:* children of faculty/staff.

Other Money-Saving Options Accelerated degree, off-campus living. *Payment Plan:* deferred payment. *Waivers:* full or partial for employees or children of employees and senior citizens.

Contact Ms. Bernitha Williams, Director of Financial Aid, William Tyndale College, 35700 West Twelve Mile Road, Farmington Hills, MI 48331, 810-533-7200, fax: 810-553-5963.

WILLIAM WOODS UNIVERSITY
Fulton, Missouri

About the Institution Independent/religious, coed. Degrees awarded: B, M. Offers 40 undergraduate majors. Total enrollment: 1,151. Undergraduates: 861. Freshmen: 104.

Undergraduate Expenses (1997–98) Comprehensive fee of $17,200 includes tuition ($12,200) and college room and board ($5000). College room only: $2550.

Applications 96% of all full-time undergraduates enrolled in fall 1996 applied for aid; of these, 90% were judged to have need according to Federal Methodology, of whom 98% were aided. *Financial aid deadline (priority):* 3/1. *Financial aid forms:* FAFSA, state form, institutional form required. *Admission application deadline:* rolling.

Summary of Aid to Needy Students *From gift & self-help combined:* Average need met: 88%. Average amount awarded: $12,386 (68% gift aid, 32% self-help). *Gift aid:* Total: $5,044,338 (40% from college's own funds, 15% from other college-administered sources, 45% from external sources). 143 Federal Work-Study jobs (averaging $1200); 98 part-time jobs.

Need-Based Scholarships & Grants Pell, FSEOG, state, private, college/university.

Loans Perkins, PLUS, Stafford, Unsubsidized Stafford, private, college/university long-term loans ($2500 average).

Non-Need Awards *Academic Interests/Achievement Awards:* ($619,774 total): general academic. *Creative Arts/Performance Awards:* ($32,600 total): applied art and design, art/fine arts, performing arts, theater/drama. *Special Achievements/Activities Awards:* ($172,000 total): general special achievements/activities, community service, leadership, memberships. *Special Characteristics Awards:* ($299,825 total): children and siblings of alumni, children of faculty/staff, ethnic background, local/state students, members of minorities, relatives of clergy, religious affiliation, siblings of current students. *Athletic:* Total: ($494,242); Men: 0; Women: ($494,242).

Other Money-Saving Options Accelerated degree, cooperative Air Force ROTC. *Payment Plan:* installment. *Waivers:* full or partial for employees or children of employees.

Contact Mrs. Laura L. Archuleta, Director for Student Financial Aid, William Woods University, 200 West Twelfth Street, Fulton, MO 65251-1098, 573-592-4232, fax: 573-592-1146.

WILMINGTON COLLEGE
New Castle, Delaware

About the Institution Independent, coed. Degrees awarded: A, B, M, D. Offers 18 undergraduate majors. Total enrollment: 5,500. Undergraduates: 2,500 (86% state residents). Freshmen: 900.

Undergraduate Expenses (1997–98) Tuition: $5700. Mandatory fees: $50.

Applications 49% of all full-time undergraduates enrolled in fall 1996 applied for aid; of these, 74% were judged to have need according to Federal Methodology, of whom 100% were aided. *Financial aid deadline*

(priority): 7/15. *Financial aid forms:* FAFSA required; CSS Financial Aid PROFILE acceptable. *Admission application deadline:* rolling.

Summary of Aid to Needy Students *From gift & self-help combined:* Average need met: 52%. Average amount awarded: $4256 (19% gift aid, 81% self-help). *Gift aid:* Total: $708,851 (31% from college's own funds, 18% from other college-administered sources, 51% from external sources). Federal Work-Study jobs; part-time jobs.

Need-Based Scholarships & Grants Pell, FSEOG, state, private, college/university.

Loans PLUS, Stafford, Unsubsidized Stafford.

Non-Need Awards In 1996, a total of 81 non-need awards were made. *Academic Interests/Achievement Awards:* 34 ($57,813 total): general academic. *Athletic:* Total: 47 ($75,430); Men: 21; Women: 26.

Other Money-Saving Options Accelerated degree, co-op program, cooperative Army ROTC, cooperative Air Force ROTC. *Payment Plan:* installment. *Waivers:* full or partial for employees or children of employees.

Contact Office of Financial Aid, Wilmington College, 320 DuPont Highway, New Castle, DE 19720-6491, 302-328-9401.

WILMINGTON COLLEGE
Wilmington, Ohio

About the Institution Independent/religious, coed. Degrees awarded: B. Offers 43 undergraduate majors. Total enrollment: 1,092 (93% state residents). Freshmen: 272.

Undergraduate Expenses (1997–98) Comprehensive fee of $17,090 includes tuition ($12,300), mandatory fees ($200), and college room and board ($4590).

Applications 85% of all full-time undergraduates enrolled in fall 1996 applied for aid; of these, 95% were judged to have need according to Federal Methodology, of whom 100% were aided. *Financial aid deadline (priority):* 3/1. *Financial aid forms:* FAFSA, institutional form required. *Admission application deadline:* rolling.

Summary of Aid to Needy Students *Gift aid:* Total: $4,700,000. Federal Work-Study jobs (averaging $1100); part-time jobs.

Need-Based Scholarships & Grants Pell, FSEOG.

Loans Perkins, PLUS, Stafford, Unsubsidized Stafford, college/university long-term loans ($1400 average).

Non-Need Awards *Academic Interests/Achievement Awards:* general academic, biological sciences, physical sciences. *Creative Arts/Performance Awards:* theater/drama. *Special Achievements/Activities Awards:* leadership. *Special Characteristics Awards:* children and siblings of alumni, members of minorities.

Other Money-Saving Options *Payment Plan:* installment. *Waivers:* full or partial for employees or children of employees.

Contact Office of Financial Aid, Wilmington College, Wilmington, OH 45177, 513-382-6661.

WILSON COLLEGE
Chambersburg, Pennsylvania

About the Institution Independent/religious, women. Degrees awarded: A, B. Offers 21 undergraduate majors. Total enrollment: 283 (63% state residents). Freshmen: 80.

Undergraduate Expenses (1997–98) Comprehensive fee of $18,555 includes tuition ($12,600), mandatory fees ($150), and college room and board ($5805). College room only: $2966.

Applications Of all full-time undergraduates enrolled in fall 1996, 96% of those who applied for aid were judged to have need according to Federal Methodology, of whom 100% were aided. *Financial aid deadline (priority):* 4/30. *Financial aid forms:* FAFSA, state form, institutional form required; CSS Financial Aid PROFILE acceptable. Financial statement for foreign students required for some. *Admission application deadline:* rolling.

Summary of Aid to Needy Students *From gift & self-help combined:* Average need met: 98%. Average amount awarded: $12,241 (62% gift aid, 38% self-help). *Gift aid:* Total: $1,793,457 (66% from college's own funds, 19% from other college-administered sources, 15% from external sources). 125 Federal Work-Study jobs (averaging $1094); 17 part-time jobs.

Need-Based Scholarships & Grants Pell, FSEOG, state, private, college/university.

Loans Perkins, PLUS, Stafford, Unsubsidized Stafford, private, college/university short-term loans ($100 average), college/university long-term loans ($2600 average).

Non-Need Awards In 1996, a total of 179 non-need awards were made. *Academic Interests/Achievement Awards:* 131 ($204,749 total): general academic. *Creative Arts/Performance Awards:* 1 ($1160 total): art/fine arts. *Special Achievements/Activities Awards:* 6 ($29,990 total): community service, religious involvement. *Special Characteristics Awards:* 41 ($117,000 total): children and siblings of alumni, local/state students, previous college experience, religious affiliation.

Other Money-Saving Options Cooperative Army ROTC, off-campus living (after junior year). *Payment Plans:* tuition prepayment, installment. *Waivers:* full or partial for children of alumni and employees or children of employees.

Contact Ms. Ruth K. Cramer, Director of Financial Aid, Wilson College, 1015 Philadelphia Avenue, Chambersburg, PA 17201-1285, 717-262-2016, fax: 717-264-1578.

WINGATE UNIVERSITY
Wingate, North Carolina

About the Institution Independent/religious, coed. Degrees awarded: B, M. Offers 52 undergraduate majors. Total enrollment: 1,275. Undergraduates: 1,185 (55% state residents). Freshmen: 331.

Undergraduate Expenses (1997–98) Comprehensive fee of $15,790 includes tuition ($11,250), mandatory fees ($440), and college room and board ($4100). College room only: $2000.

Applications Of all full-time undergraduates enrolled in fall 1996, 95% of those who applied for aid were judged to have need according to Federal Methodology, of whom 100% were aided. *Financial aid deadline (priority):* 3/1. *Financial aid forms:* FAFSA, institutional form required. State form required for some. *Regular admission application deadline:* 8/1. Early decision deadline: 12/1.

Summary of Aid to Needy Students *From gift & self-help combined:* Average need met: 78%. Average amount awarded: $9199 (68% gift aid, 32% self-help). *Gift aid:* Total: $4,563,006 (67% from college's own funds, 11% from other college-administered sources, 22% from external sources). 216 Federal Work-Study jobs (averaging $1200); 339 part-time jobs.

Need-Based Scholarships & Grants Pell, FSEOG, state, college/university.

Loans PLUS, Stafford, Unsubsidized Stafford.

Non-Need Awards In 1996, a total of 842 non-need awards were made. *Academic Interests/Achievement Awards:* 465 ($1,633,217 total): general academic. *Creative Arts/Performance Awards:* 57 ($68,219 total): music. *Special Achievements/Activities Awards:* 58 ($151,546 total): religious involvement. *Special Characteristics Awards:* 31 ($43,500 total): local/state students, relatives of clergy. *Athletic:* Total: 231 ($983,841); Men: 161 ($695,646); Women: 70 ($288,195).

Other Money-Saving Options Accelerated degree, cooperative Army ROTC, cooperative Air Force ROTC, off-campus living (after junior year). *Payment Plan:* installment. *Waivers:* full or partial for employees or children of employees.

Contact Ms. Betty C. Whalen, Director of Student Financial Planning, Wingate University, Box 3001, Wingate, NC 28174, 704-233-8209, fax: 704-233-9396.

WINONA STATE UNIVERSITY
Winona, Minnesota

About the Institution State-supported, coed. Degrees awarded: A, B, M. Offers 114 undergraduate majors. Total enrollment: 7,500. Undergraduates: 7,000 (65% state residents). Freshmen: 1,325.

Undergraduate Expenses (1997–98) State resident tuition: $2616. Nonresident tuition: $5760. Mandatory fees: $500. College room and board: $3200.

Applications 84% of all full-time undergraduates enrolled in fall 1996 applied for aid; of these, 74% were judged to have need according to Federal Methodology, of whom 100% were aided. *Financial aid deadline:* continuous. *Financial aid forms:* FAFSA required. *Admission application deadline:* rolling.

Summary of Aid to Needy Students *From gift & self-help combined:* Average need met: 90%. Average amount awarded: $3880 (31% gift aid, 69% self-help). *Gift aid:* Total: $4,165,000 (9% from college's own funds, 42% from other college-administered sources, 49% from external sources). Federal Work-Study jobs (averaging $1635); 900 part-time jobs.

Need-Based Scholarships & Grants Pell, FSEOG, state, private, college/university.

Loans Perkins, PLUS, Stafford, Unsubsidized Stafford, state, private, college/university short-term loans ($150 average).

Non-Need Awards In 1996, a total of 747 non-need awards were made. *Academic Interests/Achievement Awards:* 539 ($391,297 total): general academic. *Creative Arts/Performance Awards:* 15 ($7500 total): art/fine arts, music, theater/drama. *Special Characteristics Awards:* 43 ($30,749 total): members of minorities. *Athletic:* Total: 150 ($119,766).

Other Money-Saving Options Accelerated degree, cooperative Army ROTC, off-campus living. *Waivers:* full or partial for employees or children of employees and senior citizens.

Contact Office of Financial Aid, Winona State University, PO Box 5838, Winona, MN 55987-5838, 507-457-5000.

WINSTON-SALEM STATE UNIVERSITY
Winston-Salem, North Carolina

About the Institution State-supported, coed. Degrees awarded: B. Offers 35 undergraduate majors. Total enrollment: 2,781 (94% state residents). Freshmen: 493.

Undergraduate Expenses (1996–97) State resident tuition: $730. Nonresident tuition: $7046. Mandatory fees: $754. College room and board: $3265.

Applications Of all full-time undergraduates enrolled in fall 1996, 91% of those who applied for aid were judged to have need according to Federal Methodology, of whom 94% were aided. *Financial aid deadline (priority):* 5/1. *Financial aid forms:* FAFSA, institutional form required; CSS Financial Aid PROFILE acceptable. *Admission application deadline:* rolling.

Summary of Aid to Needy Students *From gift & self-help combined:* Average need met: 76%. Average amount awarded: $4458 (42% gift aid, 58% self-help). *Gift aid:* Total: $2,734,839 (14% from college's own funds, 14% from other college-administered sources, 72% from external sources). 388 Federal Work-Study jobs (averaging $1339); 13 part-time jobs.

Need-Based Scholarships & Grants Pell, FSEOG, state, private, college/university.

Loans Perkins, PLUS, Stafford, Unsubsidized Stafford, state, private, college/university short-term loans ($100 average), college/university long-term loans ($2050 average).

Non-Need Awards *Academic Interests/Achievement Awards:* 187 ($521,425 total): general academic, business, computer science, education, health fields, mathematics. *Creative Arts/Performance Awards:* 72 ($69,991 total): music. *Special Achievements/Activities Awards:* hobbies/interest. *Athletic:* Total: 79 ($294,627); Men: 62 ($258,485); Women: 17 ($36,142).

Other Money-Saving Options Accelerated degree, co-op program, Army ROTC, off-campus living. *Payment Plan:* installment. *Waivers:* full or partial for employees or children of employees and senior citizens.

Contact Mrs. Shirley P. Carter, Assistant Director of Financial Aid Office, Winston-Salem State University, 601 Martin Luther King, Jr. Drive, Winston-Salem, NC 27110-0003, 910-750-3280, fax: 910-750-3297.

WINTHROP UNIVERSITY
Rock Hill, South Carolina

About the Institution State-supported, coed. Degrees awarded: B, M. Offers 33 undergraduate majors. Total enrollment: 5,402. Undergraduates: 4,182 (85% state residents). Freshmen: 819.

Undergraduate Expenses (1997–98) State resident tuition: $3898. Nonresident tuition: $7026. Mandatory fees: $20. College room and board: $3680. College room only: $2260 (minimum).

Applications 63% of all full-time undergraduates enrolled in fall 1996 applied for aid; of these, 86% were judged to have need according to Federal Methodology, of whom 99% were aided. *Financial aid deadline (priority):* 5/1. *Financial aid forms:* FAFSA, institutional form required. *Admission application deadline:* 5/1.

Summary of Aid to Needy Students *From gift & self-help combined:* Average need met: 80%. Average amount awarded: $6707 (35% gift aid, 65% self-help). *Gift aid:* Total: $4,488,530 (27% from college's own funds, 21% from other college-administered sources, 52% from external sources). 536 Federal Work-Study jobs (averaging $800); 886 part-time jobs.

Need-Based Scholarships & Grants Pell, FSEOG, state, private, college/university.

Loans Perkins, PLUS, Stafford, Unsubsidized Stafford, state, private, college/university short-term loans ($200 average).

Non-Need Awards In 1996, a total of 1,161 non-need awards were made. *Academic Interests/Achievement Awards:* 497 ($1,652,039 total): general academic. *Creative Arts/Performance Awards:* 140 ($60,134 total): art/fine arts, dance, music, performing arts. *Special Characteristics Awards:* 419 ($1,100,336 total): adult students, out-of-state students. *Athletic:* Total: 105 ($348,799); Men: 54 ($173,808); Women: 51 ($174,991).

Other Money-Saving Options Co-op program, off-campus living. *Payment Plan:* installment. *Waivers:* full or partial for employees or children of employees and senior citizens.

Contact Ms. Geneva Drakeford, Financial Aid Counselor, Winthrop University, 119 Tillman Hall, Rock Hill, SC 29733, 803-323-2189, fax: 803-323-2557.

WISCONSIN LUTHERAN COLLEGE
Milwaukee, Wisconsin

About the Institution Independent/religious, coed. Degrees awarded: B. Offers 16 undergraduate majors. Total enrollment: 401 (76% state residents). Freshmen: 101.

Undergraduate Expenses (1996–97) Comprehensive fee of $15,160 includes tuition ($10,900), mandatory fees ($100), and college room and board ($4160). College room only: $2175.

Applications *Financial aid deadline (priority):* 3/1. *Financial aid forms:* institutional form required; CSS Financial Aid PROFILE acceptable. FAFSA required for some. *Admission application deadline:* 9/1.

Summary of Aid to Needy Students Federal Work-Study jobs; part-time jobs.

Non-Need Awards *Academic Interests/Achievement Awards:* general academic. *Special Achievements/Activities Awards:* general special achievements/activities.

Other Money-Saving Options *Payment Plan:* installment. *Waivers:* full or partial for employees or children of employees.

Contact Office of Financial Aid, Wisconsin Lutheran College, 8800 West Bluemound Road, Milwaukee, WI 53226-4699, 414-443-8800.

WITTENBERG UNIVERSITY
Springfield, Ohio

About the Institution Independent/religious, coed. Degrees awarded: B. Offers 81 undergraduate majors. Total enrollment: 2,000 (54% state residents). Freshmen: 505.

Undergraduate Expenses (1997–98) Comprehensive fee of $24,000 includes tuition ($18,228), mandatory fees ($912), and college room and board ($4860). College room only: $2416.

Applications 72% of all full-time undergraduates enrolled in fall 1996 applied for aid; of these, 94% were judged to have need according to Federal Methodology, of whom 100% were aided. *Financial aid deadline (priority):* 3/15. *Financial aid forms:* FAFSA, state form required; CSS Financial Aid PROFILE acceptable. *Regular admission application deadline:* 3/15. Early decision deadline: 11/15. Early action deadline: 12/1.

Summary of Aid to Needy Students *From gift & self-help combined:* Average need met: 96%. Average amount awarded: $17,408 (75% gift aid, 25% self-help). *Gift aid:* Total: $15,175,203 (85% from college's own funds, 2% from other college-administered sources, 13% from external sources). 226 Federal Work-Study jobs (averaging $1258); 1,000 part-time jobs.

Need-Based Scholarships & Grants Pell, FSEOG, state, private, college/university.

Loans Perkins, PLUS, Stafford, Unsubsidized Stafford, state, private, college/university long-term loans ($1000 average).

Non-Need Awards In 1996, a total of 1,302 non-need awards were made. *Academic Interests/Achievement Awards:* 686 ($3,708,744 total): general academic. *Creative Arts/Performance Awards:* 52 ($118,500 total): art/fine arts, dance, music, theater/drama. *Special Achievements/Activities Awards:* 127 ($358,830 total): general special achievements/activities, community service, leadership. *Special Characteristics Awards:* 437 ($1,924,966 total): children and siblings of alumni, children of faculty/staff, ethnic background, international students, local/state students, members of minorities, relatives of clergy, religious affiliation.

Other Money-Saving Options Accelerated degree, cooperative Army ROTC, cooperative Air Force ROTC, off-campus living (after sophomore year). *Payment Plans:* installment, deferred payment. *Waivers:* full or partial for children of alumni, employees or children of employees, adult students, senior citizens.

Contact Ms. Karen Hunt, Assistant Dean of Admission, Wittenberg University, PO Box 720, Springfield, OH 45501-0720, 937-327-6314, fax: 937-327-6340.

WOFFORD COLLEGE
Spartanburg, South Carolina

About the Institution Independent/religious, coed. Degrees awarded: B. Offers 26 undergraduate majors. Total enrollment: 1,115 (65% state residents). Freshmen: 291.

Undergraduate Expenses (1997–98) Comprehensive fee of $19,800 includes tuition ($15,085), mandatory fees ($305), and college room and board ($4410).

Applications 80% of all full-time undergraduates enrolled in fall 1996 applied for aid; of these, 73% were judged to have need according to Federal Methodology, of whom 99% were aided. *Financial aid deadline:* Applications processed continuously. *Financial aid forms:* FAFSA, CSS Financial Aid PROFILE, institutional form required. *Regular admission application deadline:* 2/1. Early action deadline: 12/1.

Summary of Aid to Needy Students *From gift & self-help combined:* Average need met: 93%. Average amount awarded: $12,480 (77% gift aid, 23% self-help). *Gift aid:* Total: $6,009,091. 180 Federal Work-Study jobs (averaging $1304); 235 part-time jobs.

Need-Based Scholarships & Grants Pell, FSEOG, state, private, college/university.

Loans Perkins, PLUS, Stafford, Unsubsidized Stafford, private.

Non-Need Awards In 1996, a total of 900 non-need awards were made. *Academic Interests/Achievement Awards:* 594 ($2,373,078 total). *Creative Arts/Performance Awards:* 25 ($25,000 total): music. *Special Achievements/Activities Awards:* 34 ($42,550 total): general special achievements/activities, cheerleading/drum major, community service, leadership, religious involvement. *Special Characteristics Awards:* 34 ($163,512 total): general special characteristics, children of faculty/staff, relatives of clergy. *Athletic:* Total: 213 ($1,581,474); Men: 147 ($1,178,764); Women: 66 ($402,710).

Other Money-Saving Options Accelerated degree, Army ROTC, off-campus living (after freshman year). *Waivers:* full or partial for employees or children of employees.

Contact Ms. Susan McCrackin, Director of Financial Aid, Wofford College, 429 North Church Street, Spartanburg, SC 29303-3663, 864-597-4160.

WOODBURY UNIVERSITY
Burbank, California

About the Institution Independent, coed. Degrees awarded: B, M. Offers 15 undergraduate majors. Total enrollment: 1,132. Undergraduates: 940 (88% state residents). Freshmen: 92.

Undergraduate Expenses (1997–98) Comprehensive fee of $20,855 includes tuition ($15,050 minimum), mandatory fees ($120), and college room and board ($5685). College room only: $3075.

Applications 69% of all full-time undergraduates enrolled in fall 1996 applied for aid; of these, 91% were judged to have need according to Federal Methodology, of whom 100% were aided. *Financial aid deadline (priority):* 3/1. *Financial aid forms:* FAFSA, institutional form required; CSS Financial Aid PROFILE acceptable. State form required for some. *Admission application deadline:* rolling.

Summary of Aid to Needy Students *From gift & self-help combined:* Average need met: 70%. Average amount awarded: $11,992 (59% gift aid, 41% self-help). *Gift aid:* Total: $3,279,360 (59% from college's own funds, 23% from other college-administered sources, 18% from external sources). 90 Federal Work-Study jobs (averaging $1100); 25 part-time jobs.

Need-Based Scholarships & Grants Pell, FSEOG, state, private, college/university.

Loans Perkins, PLUS, Stafford, Unsubsidized Stafford, private.

Non-Need Awards *Academic Interests/Achievement Awards:* general academic.

Other Money-Saving Options Accelerated degree, off-campus living. *Payment Plans:* installment, deferred payment. *Waivers:* full or partial for employees or children of employees.

Contact Financial Aid Office, Woodbury University, 7500 Glenoaks Boulevard, Burbank, CA 91510-7846, 818-767-0888 Ext. 273, fax: 818-767-4816.

WORCESTER POLYTECHNIC INSTITUTE
Worcester, Massachusetts

About the Institution Independent, coed. Degrees awarded: B, M, D. Offers 76 undergraduate majors. Total enrollment: 3,648. Undergraduates: 2,611 (47% state residents). Freshmen: 689.

Undergraduate Expenses (1997–98) Comprehensive fee of $25,148 includes tuition ($18,710), mandatory fees ($200), and college room and board ($6238). College room only: $3234.

Applications Of all full-time undergraduates enrolled in fall 1996, 93% of those who applied for aid were judged to have need according to Federal Methodology, of whom 99% were aided. *Financial aid deadline:* 3/1. *Financial aid forms:* FAFSA, CSS Financial Aid PROFILE, W-2 form, federal income tax form required; institutional form acceptable. *Regular admission application deadline:* 2/15. Early decision deadline: 12/1.

Summary of Aid to Needy Students *From gift & self-help combined:* Average need met: 90%. Average amount awarded: $15,337 (61% gift aid, 39% self-help). *Gift aid:* Total: $17,552,853 (76% from college's own funds, 17% from other college-administered sources, 7% from external sources). 650 Federal Work-Study jobs (averaging $900); 450 part-time jobs.

Need-Based Scholarships & Grants Pell, FSEOG, state, private, college/university.

Loans Perkins, PLUS, Stafford, Unsubsidized Stafford, college/university short-term loans ($50 average), college/university long-term loans ($2000 average), MassPlan Loans, TERI loans.

Non-Need Awards *Academic Interests/Achievement Awards:* 51 ($480,000 total): general academic. *Special Characteristics Awards:* children of workers in trades, ROTC participants.

Other Money-Saving Options Accelerated degree, co-op program, Army ROTC, Air Force ROTC, cooperative Naval ROTC, off-campus living. *Waivers:* full or partial for employees or children of employees.

Contact Office of Financial Aid, Worcester Polytechnic Institute, 100 Institute Road, Worcester, MA 01609-2280, 508-831-5000.

WORCESTER STATE COLLEGE
Worcester, Massachusetts

About the Institution State-supported, coed. Degrees awarded: B, M. Offers 25 undergraduate majors. Total enrollment: 5,369. Undergraduates: 4,782 (97% state residents). Freshmen: 447.

Undergraduate Expenses (1996–97) State resident tuition: $1338. Nonresident tuition: $5726. Mandatory fees: $1345. College room and board: $4120. College room only: $2830.

Applications 59% of all full-time undergraduates enrolled in fall 1996 applied for aid; of these, 94% were judged to have need according to Federal Methodology, of whom 100% were aided. *Financial aid deadline (priority):* 3/1. *Financial aid forms:* FAFSA, institutional form required. *Admission application deadline:* rolling.

Summary of Aid to Needy Students *From gift & self-help combined:* Average need met: 80%. Average amount awarded: $5881 (42% gift aid, 58% self-help). *Gift aid:* Total: $2,432,830 (3% from college's own funds, 36% from other college-administered sources, 61% from external sources). 166 Federal Work-Study jobs (averaging $1485); 25 part-time jobs.

Need-Based Scholarships & Grants Pell, FSEOG, state, college/university.

Loans Perkins, PLUS, Stafford, Unsubsidized Stafford, state.

Non-Need Awards In 1996, a total of 671 non-need awards were made. *Academic Interests/Achievement Awards:* 28 ($32,542 total): biological sciences, business, education, English, foreign languages, health fields. *Creative Arts/Performance Awards:* 1 ($300 total): art/fine arts. *Special Achievements/Activities Awards:* 95 ($38,765 total): general special achievements/activities. *Special Characteristics Awards:* 547 ($427,991 total): general special characteristics, children and siblings of alumni, children of faculty/staff, children with a deceased or disabled parent, handicapped students, local/state students, ROTC participants, veterans.

Other Money-Saving Options Cooperative Army ROTC, cooperative Naval ROTC, cooperative Air Force ROTC, off-campus living. *Payment Plan:* deferred payment. *Waivers:* full or partial for employees or children of employees and senior citizens.

Contact Ms. Carole Lapierre-Denning, Acting Director of Financial Aid, Worcester State College, 486 Chandler Street, Worcester, MA 01602-2597, 508-793-8056, fax: 508-793-8194.

WRIGHT STATE UNIVERSITY
Dayton, Ohio

About the Institution State-supported, coed. Degrees awarded: A, B, M, D, P. Offers 81 undergraduate majors. Total enrollment: 15,697. Undergraduates: 11,843 (97% state residents). Freshmen: 2,046.

Undergraduate Expenses (1996–97) State resident tuition: $3600. Nonresident tuition: $7200. College room and board: $4005 (minimum).

Applications *Financial aid deadline (priority):* 3/1. *Financial aid forms:* FAFSA, institutional form required. State form required for some. *Admission application deadline:* 9/1.

Summary of Aid to Needy Students *From gift & self-help combined:* Average amount awarded: $6908. *Gift aid:* Total: $10,514,000. Federal Work-Study jobs; part-time jobs.

Need-Based Scholarships & Grants Pell, FSEOG.

Loans Perkins, PLUS, Stafford, Unsubsidized Stafford, Federal Nursing, college/university short-term loans ($250 average), college/university long-term loans ($3234 average).

Non-Need Awards *Academic Interests/Achievement Awards:* general academic, biological sciences, physical sciences. *Creative Arts/Performance Awards:* creative writing, dance, debating, music, theater/drama. *Special Achievements/Activities Awards:* general special achievements/activities, leadership. *Special Characteristics Awards:* adult students, ethnic background. *Athletic:* available.

Other Money-Saving Options Co-op program, Army ROTC, Air Force ROTC, off-campus living. *Payment Plan:* installment. *Waivers:* full or partial for employees or children of employees and senior citizens.

Contact Mr. David R. Darr, Director of Financial Aid, Wright State University, Dayton, OH 45435, 937-873-5721.

XAVIER UNIVERSITY
Cincinnati, Ohio

About the Institution Independent/religious, coed. Degrees awarded: A, B, M, D. Offers 70 undergraduate majors. Total enrollment: 6,423. Undergraduates: 3,864 (68% state residents). Freshmen: 787.

Undergraduate Expenses (1997–98) Comprehensive fee of $19,090 includes tuition ($13,650) and college room and board ($5440 minimum). College room only: $3020.

Applications 67% of all full-time undergraduates enrolled in fall 1996 applied for aid; of these, 87% were judged to have need according to Federal Methodology, of whom 100% were aided. *Financial aid deadline (priority):* 2/15. *Financial aid forms:* FAFSA, financial aid transcript (for transfers) required. *Admission application deadline:* rolling.

Summary of Aid to Needy Students *From gift & self-help combined:* Average amount awarded: $12,114 (59% gift aid, 41% self-help). *Gift aid:* Total: $12,685,496 (76% from college's own funds, 14% from other college-administered sources, 10% from external sources). Federal Work-Study jobs; 100 part-time jobs.

Need-Based Scholarships & Grants Pell, FSEOG, state, private, college/university.

Loans Perkins, PLUS, Stafford, Unsubsidized Stafford, college/university long-term loans ($1400 average).

Non-Need Awards *Academic Interests/Achievement Awards:* general academic, business, education, foreign languages, mathematics, physical sciences, social sciences. *Creative Arts/Performance Awards:* art/fine arts, music, performing arts, theater/drama. *Special Achievements/Activities Awards:* community service, leadership. *Special Characteristics Awards:* general special characteristics, members of minorities, ROTC participants. *Athletic:* available.

Other Money-Saving Options Accelerated degree, Army ROTC, cooperative Air Force ROTC, off-campus living (after sophomore year). *Payment Plans:* installment, deferred payment. *Waivers:* full or partial for minority students, children of alumni, employees or children of employees.

Contact Ms. Marie Toon, Associate Director of Financial Aid, Xavier University, 3800 Victory Parkway, Cincinnati, OH 45207-5411, 513-745-3142, fax: 513-745-2806.

XAVIER UNIVERSITY OF LOUISIANA
New Orleans, Louisiana

About the Institution Independent/religious, coed. Degrees awarded: B, M, P. Offers 48 undergraduate majors. Total enrollment: 3,526. Undergraduates: 2,624 (57% state residents). Freshmen: 781.

Undergraduate Expenses (1997–98) Comprehensive fee of $12,215 includes tuition ($8100 minimum), mandatory fees ($115), and college room and board ($4000).

Applications Of all full-time undergraduates enrolled in fall 1996, 90% of those who applied for aid were judged to have need according to Federal Methodology, of whom 83% were aided. *Financial aid deadline (priority):* 6/30. *Financial aid forms:* FAFSA required; CSS Financial Aid PROFILE acceptable. *Admission application deadline:* 3/1.

Summary of Aid to Needy Students *From gift & self-help combined:* Average need met: 76%. Average amount awarded: $5419. *Gift aid:* Total: $10,154,670. 650 Federal Work-Study jobs (averaging $1000); part-time jobs.

Need-Based Scholarships & Grants Pell, FSEOG, state, private, college/university.

Loans Perkins, PLUS, Stafford, Unsubsidized Stafford, private.

Non-Need Awards In 1996, a total of 1,308 non-need awards were made. *Academic Interests/Achievement Awards:* general academic, biological sciences, business, computer science, education, engineering/technologies, foreign languages, humanities, mathematics, physical sciences, premedicine, social sciences. *Creative Arts/Performance Awards:* art/fine arts, music, performing arts. *Special Achievements/Activities Awards:* religious involvement. *Special Characteristics Awards:* children of faculty/staff. *Athletic:* Total: 55 ($423,127).

Other Money-Saving Options Co-op program, cooperative Army ROTC, cooperative Naval ROTC, cooperative Air Force ROTC, off-campus living. *Payment Plan:* installment. *Waivers:* full or partial for employees or children of employees and senior citizens.

Contact Mrs. Mildred Higgins, Director of Financial Aid, Xavier University of Louisiana, 7325 Palmetto Street, Box 40A, New Orleans, LA 70125-1098, 504-486-7411.

YALE UNIVERSITY
New Haven, Connecticut

About the Institution Independent, coed. Degrees awarded: B, M, D, P. Offers 64 undergraduate majors. Total enrollment: 11,047. Undergraduates: 5,401 (10% state residents). Freshmen: 1,409.

Undergraduate Expenses (1997–98) Comprehensive fee of $29,950 includes tuition ($23,100) and college room and board ($6850).

Applications *Financial aid deadline: 2/1. Financial aid forms:* FAFSA, CSS Financial Aid PROFILE required. State form, institutional form required for some. *Regular admission application deadline:* 12/31. Early decision deadline: 11/1.

Summary of Aid to Needy Students *From gift & self-help combined:* Average need met: 100%. Average amount awarded: $21,800 (73% gift aid, 27% self-help). *Gift aid:* Total: $33,092,000 (85% from college's own funds, 4% from other college-administered sources, 11% from external sources). Federal Work-Study jobs (averaging $2000); part-time jobs.

Need-Based Scholarships & Grants Pell, FSEOG, state, private, college/university, Alumni Club awards.

Loans Perkins, PLUS, Stafford, Unsubsidized Stafford, state, private, college/university short-term loans ($200 average), college/university long-term loans.

Non-Need Awards Not offered.

Other Money-Saving Options Accelerated degree, cooperative Army ROTC, cooperative Air Force ROTC, off-campus living (after sophomore year). *Payment Plans:* tuition prepayment, installment. *Waivers:* full or partial for employees or children of employees.

Contact Office of Financial Aid, Yale University, PO Box 208288, New Haven, CT 06520-8288, 203-432-4771.

YESHIVA BETH MOSHE
Scranton, Pennsylvania

About the Institution Independent/religious, men. Degrees awarded: B, M. Offers 1 undergraduate major.

Applications *Financial aid deadline:* continuous. *Financial aid forms:* FAFSA required.

Summary of Aid to Needy Students *Gift aid:* Total: $100,000. Federal Work-Study jobs.

Need-Based Scholarships & Grants Pell, FSEOG.

Loans Stafford, Unsubsidized Stafford.

Non-Need Awards Not offered.

Contact Financial Aid Office, Yeshiva Beth Moshe, 930 Hickory Street, Scranton, PA 18505-2124, 717-346-1747.

YESHIVA COLLEGE
New York, New York

See Yeshiva University

YESHIVA GEDDOLAH OF GREATER DETROIT RABBINICAL COLLEGE
Oak Park, Michigan

About the Institution Independent/religious, men. Degrees awarded: B.

Applications 74% of all full-time undergraduates enrolled in fall 1996 applied for aid; of these, 40% were judged to have need according to Federal Methodology, of whom 100% were aided. *Financial aid deadline (priority):* 9/1. *Financial aid forms:* FAFSA, institutional form required.

Summary of Aid to Needy Students *From gift & self-help combined:* Average need met: 57%. Average amount awarded: $3700 (94% gift aid, 6% self-help). *Gift aid:* Total: $75,220 (73% from college's own funds, 11% from other college-administered sources, 16% from external sources). 4 Federal Work-Study jobs (averaging $1000).

Need-Based Scholarships & Grants Pell, FSEOG, college/university.

Non-Need Awards In 1996, a total of 3 non-need awards were made. *Special Characteristics Awards:* 3 ($9100 total): children of faculty/staff, married students.

Contact Rabbi P. Rushnawitz, Executive Administrator, Yeshiva Geddolah of Greater Detroit Rabbinical College, 24600 Greenfield Road, Oak Park, MI 48237-1544, 810-968-3360, fax: 810-968-8613.

YESHIVA KARLIN STOLIN
Brooklyn, New York

About the Institution Independent/religious, men. Offers 3 undergraduate majors. Total enrollment: 53. Undergraduates: 36 (94% state residents). Freshmen: 10.

Undergraduate Expenses (1996–97) Comprehensive fee of $6800 includes tuition ($4200) and college room and board ($2600). College room only: $1300.

Applications *Financial aid deadline (priority):* 9/1. *Financial aid forms:* institutional form required. FAFSA required for some. *Admission application deadline:* rolling.

Summary of Aid to Needy Students Federal Work-Study jobs.

Need-Based Scholarships & Grants Pell, FSEOG.

Loans Perkins.

Other Money-Saving Options Off-campus living. *Payment Plan:* installment.

Contact Office of Financial Aid, Yeshiva Karlin Stolin, Brooklyn, NY 11204, 718-232-7800.

YESHIVA OF NITRA RABBINICAL COLLEGE
Mount Kisco, New York

About the Institution Independent/religious, men.

Applications 84% of all full-time undergraduates enrolled in fall 1996 applied for aid; of these,100% were judged to have need according to Federal Methodology, of whom 100% were aided. *Financial aid deadline:* continuous. *Financial aid forms:* FAFSA required.

Summary of Aid to Needy Students *From gift & self-help combined:* Average need met: 81%. Average amount awarded: $5723 (98% gift aid, 2% self-help). *Gift aid:* Total: $703,820 (30% from college's own funds, 4% from other college-administered sources, 66% from external sources). 8 Federal Work-Study jobs (averaging $1800).

Need-Based Scholarships & Grants Pell, FSEOG, private.

Non-Need Awards In 1996, a total of 115 non-need awards were made. *Academic Interests/Achievement Awards:* 115 ($210,820 total): general academic, education, religion/biblical studies.

Contact Mr. Yosef Rosen, Financial Aid Administrator, Yeshiva of Nitra Rabbinical College, 194 Division Avenue, Mount Kisco, NY 10549, 718-384-5460, fax: 718-387-9400.

YESHIVA OHR ELCHONON CHABAD/WEST COAST TALMUDICAL SEMINARY
Los Angeles, California

About the Institution Independent/religious, men. Degrees awarded: B. Offers 3 undergraduate majors. Total enrollment: 46 (50% state residents). Freshmen: 15.

Undergraduate Expenses (1996–97) Comprehensive fee of $7900 includes tuition ($4600) and college room and board ($3300).

Applications 75% of all full-time undergraduates enrolled in fall 1996 applied for aid; of these, 91% were judged to have need according to Federal Methodology, of whom 95% were aided. *Financial aid deadline (priority):* 8/15. *Financial aid forms:* FAFSA, CSS Financial Aid PROFILE required. State form, institutional form required for some. *Admission application deadline:* rolling.

Summary of Aid to Needy Students *From gift & self-help combined:* Average need met: 75%. Average amount awarded: $5000 (96% gift aid, 4% self-help). *Gift aid:* Total: $115,500 (53% from college's own funds, 5% from other college-administered sources, 42% from external sources). 5 Federal Work-Study jobs (averaging $1000); 2 part-time jobs.

Need-Based Scholarships & Grants Pell, FSEOG, state, college/university.

Non-Need Awards Not offered.

Other Money-Saving Options *Payment Plan:* installment. *Waivers:* full or partial for employees or children of employees.

Contact Ms. Hendy Tauber, Director of Financial Aid, Yeshiva Ohr Elchonon Chabad/West Coast Talmudical Seminary, 7215 Waring Avenue, Los Angeles, CA 90046-7660, 213-937-3763, fax: 213-937-9456.

YESHIVA SHAAR HATORAH TALMUDIC RESEARCH INSTITUTE
Kew Gardens, New York

About the Institution Independent/religious, men.

Applications 57% of all full-time undergraduates enrolled in fall 1996 applied for aid; of these, 92% were judged to have need according to Federal Methodology, of whom 100% were aided. *Financial aid deadline:* continuous. *Financial aid forms:* FAFSA required.

Need-Based Scholarships & Grants Pell, state, college/university.

Non-Need Awards *Academic Interests/Achievement Awards:* religion/biblical studies.

Contact Mr. Yocl Yankclcwitz, Executive Director, Financial Aid, Yeshiva Shaar Hatorah Talmudic Research Institute, Kew Gardens, NY 11418-1469, 718-846-1940.

YESHIVATH ZICHRON MOSHE
South Fallsburg, New York

About the Institution Independent/religious, men. Offers 1 undergraduate major.

Applications 91% of all full-time undergraduates enrolled in fall 1996 applied for aid; of these, 49% were judged to have need according to Federal Methodology, of whom 100% were aided. *Financial aid deadline (priority):* 8/30. *Financial aid forms:* FAFSA required; state form acceptable.

Summary of Aid to Needy Students *From gift & self-help combined:* Average need met: 66%. Average amount awarded: $3900 (96% gift aid, 4% self-help). *Gift aid:* Total: $279,080 (63% from college's own funds, 8% from other college-administered sources, 29% from external sources). 5 Federal Work-Study jobs (averaging $2900); 8 part-time jobs.

Need-Based Scholarships & Grants Pell, FSEOG, college/university.

Loans Perkins, PLUS, Stafford, Unsubsidized Stafford.

Non-Need Awards Not offered.

Contact Ms. Miryom R. Miller, Director of Financial Aid, Yeshivath Zichron Moshe, Laurel Park Road, South Fallsburg, NY 12779, 914-434-5240, fax: 914-434-1009.

YESHIVA TORAS CHAIM TALMUDICAL SEMINARY
Denver, Colorado

About the Institution Independent/religious, men. Degrees awarded: B, M. Offers 2 undergraduate majors.

Applications *Financial aid deadline (priority):* 8/15. *Financial aid forms:* FAFSA, institutional form required.

Summary of Aid to Needy Students Federal Work-Study jobs; part-time jobs.

Contact Office of Financial Aid, Yeshiva Toras Chaim Talmudical Seminary, Denver, CO 80204-1415, 303-629-8200.

YESHIVA UNIVERSITY
New York, New York

About the Institution Independent, coed. Degrees awarded: B, M, D, P. Offers 32 undergraduate majors. Total enrollment: 5,246. Undergraduates: 2,119 (57% state residents). Freshmen: 749.

Undergraduate Expenses (1996–97) Comprehensive fee of $20,530 includes tuition ($13,650), mandatory fees ($310), and college room and board ($6570). College room only: $3140.

Applications 70% of all full-time undergraduates enrolled in fall 1996 applied for aid; of these, 84% were judged to have need according to Federal Methodology, of whom 100% were aided. *Financial aid deadline (priority):* 4/15. *Financial aid forms:* FAFSA, state form, institutional form, federal income tax form required. *Admission application deadline:* 2/15.

Summary of Aid to Needy Students 324 Federal Work-Study jobs (averaging $1086).

Need-Based Scholarships & Grants Pell, FSEOG, state, private, college/university.

Loans Perkins, PLUS, Stafford, Unsubsidized Stafford, college/university long-term loans ($1500 average).

Non-Need Awards *Academic Interests/Achievement Awards:* general academic.

Other Money-Saving Options Off-campus living. *Payment Plan:* installment. *Waivers:* full or partial for employees or children of employees.

Contact Mr. Neal Harris, Acting Director of Student Finances, Yeshiva University, 500 West 185th Street, New York, NY 10033-3201, 212-960-5269, fax: 212-960-0037.

YORK COLLEGE
York, Nebraska

About the Institution Independent/religious, coed. Degrees awarded: A, B. Offers 38 undergraduate majors. Total enrollment: 452 (29% state residents). Freshmen: 126.

Undergraduate Expenses (1997–98) Comprehensive fee of $9865 includes tuition ($5785), mandatory fees ($780), and college room and board ($3300). College room only: $1095.

Applications 82% of all full-time undergraduates enrolled in fall 1996 applied for aid; of these, 92% were judged to have need according to Federal Methodology, of whom 100% were aided. *Financial aid deadline (priority):* 7/1. *Financial aid forms:* FAFSA, CSS Financial Aid PROFILE, state form acceptable. *Admission application deadline:* rolling.

Summary of Aid to Needy Students *From gift & self-help combined:* Average need met: 76%. Average amount awarded: $6819 (43% gift aid, 57% self-help). *Gift aid:* Total: $909,802 (57% from college's own funds, 12% from other college-administered sources, 31% from external sources). 200 Federal Work-Study jobs (averaging $700); part-time jobs.

Need-Based Scholarships & Grants Pell, FSEOG, state, college/university.

Loans Perkins, PLUS, Stafford, Unsubsidized Stafford, private, college/university short-term loans, college/university long-term loans ($500 average).

Non-Need Awards In 1996, a total of 434 non-need awards were made. *Academic Interests/Achievement Awards:* 226 ($197,167 total): general academic, business, communication, education, English, mathematics, religion/biblical studies. *Creative Arts/Performance Awards:* 72 ($51,000 total): art/fine arts, debating, music, performing arts, theater/drama. *Special Characteristics Awards:* 18 ($63,100 total): children of faculty/staff. *Athletic:* Total: 118 ($220,953); Men: 68 ($102,145); Women: 50 ($118,808).

Other Money-Saving Options Co-op program, cooperative Army ROTC, cooperative Naval ROTC, cooperative Air Force ROTC, off-campus living (after junior year). *Payment Plan:* installment. *Waivers:* full or partial for employees or children of employees.

Contact Ms. Debra Snider, Director of Financial Aid, York College, 912 Kiplinger Avenue, York, NE 68467-2699, 402-363-5624, fax: 402-363-5623.

YORK COLLEGE OF PENNSYLVANIA
York, Pennsylvania

About the Institution Independent, coed. Degrees awarded: A, B, M. Offers 62 undergraduate majors. Total enrollment: 5,046. Undergraduates: 4,858 (55% state residents). Freshmen: 812.

Undergraduate Expenses (1997–98) Comprehensive fee of $10,490 includes tuition ($5800), mandatory fees ($300), and college room and board ($4390). College room only: $2150.

Applications Of all full-time undergraduates enrolled in fall 1996, 72% of those who applied for aid were judged to have need according to Federal Methodology, of whom 87% were aided. *Financial aid deadline (priority):* 4/15. *Financial aid forms:* FAFSA, institutional form required; CSS Financial Aid PROFILE acceptable. State form required for some. *Admission application deadline:* rolling.

Summary of Aid to Needy Students *From gift & self-help combined:* Average need met: 90%. Average amount awarded: $4984 (39% gift aid, 61% self-help). *Gift aid:* Total: $2,919,232 (29% from college's own funds, 5% from other college-administered sources, 66% from external sources). 105 Federal Work-Study jobs (averaging $1500); 57 part-time jobs.

Need-Based Scholarships & Grants Pell, FSEOG, state, private, college/university.

Loans Perkins, PLUS, Stafford, Unsubsidized Stafford, Federal Nursing, college/university long-term loans ($500 average).

Non-Need Awards In 1996, a total of 458 non-need awards were made. *Academic Interests/Achievement Awards:* 458 ($831,839 total): general academic, health fields.

Other Money-Saving Options Accelerated degree, off-campus living (after freshman year). *Payment Plan:* installment. *Waivers:* full or partial for employees or children of employees.

Contact Office of Financial Aid, York College of Pennsylvania, Country Club Road, York, PA 17405-7199, 717-846-7788.

YORK COLLEGE OF THE CITY UNIVERSITY OF NEW YORK
Jamaica, New York

About the Institution State & locally supported, coed. Degrees awarded: B. Offers 46 undergraduate majors. Total enrollment: 6,335 (92% state residents). Freshmen: 578.

Undergraduate Expenses (1996–97) State resident tuition: $3200. Nonresident tuition: $6800. Mandatory fees: $92.

Applications *Financial aid deadline (priority):* 5/1. *Financial aid forms:* FAFSA, CSS Financial Aid PROFILE, state form, institutional form required. *Admission application deadline:* rolling.

Summary of Aid to Needy Students *From gift & self-help combined:* Average need met: 96%. Average amount awarded: $3910. 202 Federal Work-Study jobs (averaging $800).

Need-Based Scholarships & Grants Pell, FSEOG, state, college/university.

Loans Perkins, PLUS, Stafford, Unsubsidized Stafford.

Non-Need Awards Not offered.

Another Money-Saving Option Co-op program.

Contact Mr. Alan R. Rumberg, Director of Finance, York College of the City University of New York, 9420 Guy Brewer Boulevard, Jamaica, NY 11451-0001, 718-262-2230.

YOUNGSTOWN STATE UNIVERSITY
Youngstown, Ohio

About the Institution State-supported, coed. Degrees awarded: A, B, M, D. Offers 134 undergraduate majors. Total enrollment: 12,801. Undergraduates: 11,554 (93% state residents). Freshmen: 1,925.

Undergraduate Expenses (1997–98) State resident tuition: $2826. Nonresident tuition: $4512 (minimum). Mandatory fees: $732. College room and board: $4350.

Applications 80% of all full-time undergraduates enrolled in fall 1996 applied for aid; of these, 90% were judged to have need according to Federal Methodology, of whom 90% were aided. *Financial aid deadline (priority):* 3/1. *Financial aid forms:* FAFSA, institutional form required for some. *Admission application deadline:* 8/15.

Summary of Aid to Needy Students *From gift & self-help combined:* Average amount awarded: $1322 (35% gift aid, 65% self-help). *Gift aid:* Total: $2,449,964 (3% from college's own funds, 31% from other college-administered sources, 66% from external sources). 200 Federal Work-Study jobs (averaging $1500); part-time jobs.

Need-Based Scholarships & Grants Pell, FSEOG, state, private, college/university.

Loans Perkins, PLUS, Stafford, Unsubsidized Stafford, state, private, college/university short-term loans ($870 average).

Non-Need Awards In 1996, a total of 1,727 non-need awards were made. *Academic Interests/Achievement Awards:* 1,393 ($1,362,819 total): general academic. *Creative Arts/Performance Awards:* 64 ($16,768 total): music. *Special Characteristics Awards:* 179 ($141,955 total): children of faculty/staff. *Athletic:* Total: 91 ($280,513); Men: 67 ($209,842); Women: 24 ($70,671).

Other Money-Saving Options Accelerated degree, co-op program, Army ROTC, off-campus living. *Payment Plan:* installment. *Waivers:* full or partial for employees or children of employees and senior citizens.

Contact Ms. Beth Bartlett, Administrative Assistant II, Youngstown State University, One University Plaza, Youngstown, OH 44555-0002, 330-742-3504, fax: 330-742-1659.

SECTION 9

College

Financial Aid

Indexes

NON-NEED SCHOLARSHIPS FOR UNDERGRADUATES

This index lists the colleges that report that they offer scholarships to freshmen based on academic interests, abilities, achievements, or personal characteristics other than financial need. For any college listed in this index, the reader should refer to the *Non-Need Awards* section of that college's profile for specific information on the number and total dollar value of the scholarships offered.

Specific categories appear in alphabetical order under the following broad groups:

Academic Interests/Achievements

Agriculture, Architecture, Area/Ethnic Studies, Biological Sciences, Business, Communication, Computer Science, Education, Engineering/Technologies, English, Foreign Languages, Health Fields, Home Economics, Humanities, International Studies, Library Science, Mathematics, Military Science, Physical Sciences, Premedicine, Religion/Biblical Studies, Social Sciences

Creative Arts/Performance

Applied Art and Design, Art/Fine Arts, Cinema/Film/Broadcasting, Creative Writing, Dance, Debating, Journalism/Publications, Music, Performing Arts, Theater/Drama

Special Achievements/Activities

Cheerleading/Drum Major, Community Service, Hobbies/Interests, Junior Miss, Leadership, Memberships, Religious Involvement, Rodeo

Special Characteristics

Adult Students, Children/Siblings of Alumni, Children of Current Students, Children of Educators, Children of Faculty/Staff, Children of Public Servants, Children of Union Members/Company Employees, Children of Workers in Trades, Children of a Deceased or Disabled Parent, Ethnic Background, First-Generation College Students, Handicapped Students, International Students, Local/State Students, Married Students, Members of Minorities, Out-of-State Students, Parents of Current Students, Previous College Experience, Public Servants, Relatives of Clergy, Religious Affiliation, ROTC Participants, Siblings of Current Students, Spouses of Current Students, Spouses of Deceased or Disabled Public Servants, Twins, Veterans, Veterans' Children

---

ACADEMIC INTERESTS/ ACHIEVEMENTS

AGRICULTURE

Abilene Christian University, TX
Angelo State University, TX
Arkansas State University, AR
Arkansas Tech University, AR
Auburn University, AL
California Polytechnic State U, San Luis Obispo, CA
California State Polytechnic University, Pomona, CA
California State University, Chico, CA
California State University, Fresno, CA
Central Missouri State University, MO
Clemson University, SC
Clinch Valley College of the U of Virginia, VA
Delaware Valley College, PA
Dordt College, IA

Eastern Michigan University, MI
Eastern New Mexico University, NM
Eastern Oregon University, OR
Florida Agricultural and Mechanical University, FL
Florida Southern College, FL
Fort Hays State University, KS
Fort Valley State University, GA
Illinois State University, IL
Iowa State University of Science and Technology, IA
Louisiana State University and A&M College, LA
Louisiana Tech University, LA
McNeese State University, LA
Michigan State University, MI
MidAmerica Nazarene University, KS
Mississippi State University, MS
Montana State U–Bozeman, MT
Morehead State University, KY
Murray State University, KY

New Mexico State University, NM
Nicholls State University, LA
North Carolina State University, NC
North Dakota State University, ND
Northeast Louisiana University, LA
Northwestern Oklahoma State University, OK
Northwest Missouri State University, MO
The Ohio State University, OH
Oklahoma State U, OK
Prairie View A&M University, TX
Purdue University, West Lafayette, IN
Sam Houston State University, TX
South Dakota State University, SD
Southeastern Louisiana University, LA
Southeast Missouri State University, MO
Southern Arkansas University–Magnolia, AR
Southwest Missouri State University, MO
Southwest Texas State University, TX

State U of NY Coll of Environ Sci and
Forestry, NY
Stephen F. Austin State University, TX
Sul Ross State University, TX
Tennessee Technological University, TN
Texas A&M University, College Station,
TX
Texas A&M University–Commerce, TX
Texas A&M University–Kingsville, TX
Texas Tech University, TX
University of California, Davis, CA
University of California, Riverside, CA
University of Delaware, DE
University of Georgia, GA
University of Hawaii at Hilo, HI
University of Maryland Eastern Shore, MD
University of Massachusetts Amherst, MA
University of Minnesota, Crookston, MN
University of Minnesota, Twin Cities
Campus, MN
University of Nebraska–Lincoln, NE
University of Nevada, Reno, NV
University of Wisconsin–Platteville, WI
University of Wisconsin–River Falls, WI
Virginia Polytechnic Institute and State U,
VA
Virginia State University, VA
Washington State University, WA
Western Illinois University, IL
Western Kentucky University, KY
West Texas A&M University, TX
West Virginia University, WV

ARCHITECTURE
Auburn University, AL
Ball State University, IN
California Polytechnic State U, San Luis
Obispo, CA
California State Polytechnic University,
Pomona, CA
California State University, Fresno, CA
Clemson University, SC
Drury College, MO
Eastern Michigan University, MI
Eastern Washington University, WA
Endicott College, MA
Illinois Institute of Technology, IL
Iowa State University of Science and
Technology, IA
James Madison University, VA
Kent State University, OH
Lawrence Technological University, MI
Louisiana State University and A&M
College, LA
Michigan State University, MI
Mississippi State University, MS
Montana State U–Bozeman, MT
Newschool of Architecture, CA
North Dakota State University, ND
The Ohio State University, OH
Oklahoma State U, OK
Prairie View A&M University, TX
Pratt Institute, NY
Savannah College of Art and Design, GA
Syracuse University, NY
Texas A&M University, College Station,
TX

Texas Tech University, TX
University of Cincinnati, OH
University of Colorado at Boulder, CO
University of Kansas, KS
University of Massachusetts Amherst, MA
University of Michigan, Ann Arbor, MI
University of Minnesota, Twin Cities
Campus, MN
University of Nebraska–Lincoln, NE
University of Nevada, Las Vegas, NV
University of North Carolina at Charlotte,
NC
University of Oklahoma, OK
University of South Florida, FL
The University of Texas at San Antonio,
TX
University of Utah, UT
University of Washington, WA
University of Wisconsin–Stevens Point, WI
Washington State University, WA
Washington University, MO
West Virginia University, WV

AREA/ETHNIC STUDIES
American University, DC
Brigham Young University–Hawaii Campus,
HI
California State University, Chico, CA
California State University, Fresno, CA
Clear Creek Baptist Bible College, KY
College of New Rochelle, NY
Eastern Connecticut State University, CT
Indiana University of Pennsylvania, PA
Iowa State University of Science and
Technology, IA
Kent State University, OH
Mississippi State University, MS
Montana State U–Bozeman, MT
The Ohio State University, OH
Ohio University, OH
Oklahoma State U, OK
The Richard Stockton College of New
Jersey, NJ
Sonoma State University, CA
South Dakota State University, SD
State U of NY College at Geneseo, NY
Stetson University, FL
University of Cincinnati, OH
University of Colorado at Boulder, CO
University of Kansas, KS
University of Michigan, Ann Arbor, MI
University of Minnesota, Twin Cities
Campus, MN
University of Nevada, Reno, NV
University of Oklahoma, OK
University of Toledo, OH
University of Utah, UT
University of Wisconsin–River Falls, WI
West Virginia University, WV

BIOLOGICAL SCIENCES
Abilene Christian University, TX
Adams State College, CO
Agnes Scott College, GA
Alabama State University, AL
Albany State University, GA
Albertson College of Idaho, ID
Alfred University, NY

Allentown College of St. Francis de Sales,
PA
American University, DC
Anderson College, SC
Angelo State University, TX
Antioch College, OH
Arkansas State University, AR
Armstrong Atlantic State University, GA
Auburn University, AL
Augustana College, IL
Augustana College, SD
Austin College, TX
Baker University, KS
Ball State University, IN
Barat College, IL
Bard College, NY
Barry University, FL
Barton College, NC
Bellarmine College, KY
Bethel College, IN
Black Hills State University, SD
Bloomsburg University of Pennsylvania, PA
Boise State University, ID
Briar Cliff College, IA
Brigham Young University–Hawaii Campus,
HI
Buena Vista University, IA
Butler University, IN
California Lutheran University, CA
California Polytechnic State U, San Luis
Obispo, CA
California State Polytechnic University,
Pomona, CA
California State University, Bakersfield, CA
California State University, Chico, CA
California State University, Fresno, CA
California State University, Stanislaus, CA
Calvin College, MI
Carlow College, PA
Carthage College, WI
Cedar Crest College, PA
Centenary College of Louisiana, LA
Central College, IA
Central Missouri State University, MO
Chatham College, PA
Cheyney University of Pennsylvania, PA
The Citadel, The Military Coll of South
Carolina, SC
Clarion University of Pennsylvania, PA
Clarkson University, NY
Clemson University, SC
Clinch Valley College of the U of Virginia,
VA
Coe College, IA
College of New Rochelle, NY
College of St. Francis, IL
Coll of Staten Island of the City U of NY,
NY
The College of Wooster, OH
Columbia College, SC
Concordia College, NE
Cumberland College, KY
Davidson College, NC
Davis & Elkins College, WV
The Defiance College, OH
Delaware Valley College, PA
Denison University, OH

Biological Sciences (continued)

DePaul University, IL
DePauw University, IN
Eastern Mennonite University, VA
Eastern Michigan University, MI
Eastern New Mexico University, NM
Eastern Oregon University, OR
East Stroudsburg University of
  Pennsylvania, PA
East Texas Baptist University, TX
Edinboro University of Pennsylvania, PA
Elizabethtown College, PA
Elmhurst College, IL
Elon College, NC
Endicott College, MA
Felician College, NJ
Florida Institute of Technology, FL
Florida Southern College, FL
Fort Hays State University, KS
Fort Lewis College, CO
Framingham State College, MA
Francis Marion University, SC
Friends University, KS
Frostburg State University, MD
Gannon University, PA
George Fox University, OR
Georgian Court College, NJ
Georgia State University, GA
Goucher College, MD
Grambling State University, LA
Greenville College, IL
Grove City College, PA
Guilford College, NC
Gwynedd-Mercy College, PA
Hamline University, MN
Hardin-Simmons University, TX
Heritage College, WA
High Point University, NC
Hillsdale College, MI
Holy Names College, CA
Idaho State University, ID
Illinois Institute of Technology, IL
Illinois State University, IL
Indiana University of Pennsylvania, PA
Inter American U of PR, Aguadilla Campus,
  PR
Iowa State University of Science and
  Technology, IA
Iowa Wesleyan College, IA
Jacksonville State University, AL
James Madison University, VA
Jersey City State College, NJ
John Carroll University, OH
Juniata College, PA
Kalamazoo College, MI
Kennesaw State University, GA
Kent State University, OH
King's College, PA
Lander University, SC
Lebanon Valley College, PA
Limestone College, SC
Lincoln University, MO
Lincoln University, PA
Louisiana State University and A&M
  College, LA
Louisiana State University in Shreveport,
  LA

MacMurray College, IL
Maine Maritime Academy, ME
Malone College, OH
Manhattan College, NY
Mansfield University of Pennsylvania, PA
Marquette University, WI
Mass Coll of Pharmacy and Allied Health
  Sciences, MA
The Master's College and Seminary, CA
Mayville State University, ND
McKendree College, IL
McNeese State University, LA
Mesa State College, CO
Michigan State University, MI
Michigan Technological University, MI
Mills College, CA
Mississippi College, MS
Mississippi State University, MS
Missouri Western State College, MO
Montana State U–Bozeman, MT
Mount St. Clare College, IA
Murray State University, KY
New Mexico State University, NM
Norfolk State University, VA
North Carolina Agricultural and Technical
  State U, NC
North Carolina Central University, NC
North Carolina State University, NC
Northeastern State University, OK
Northeast Louisiana University, LA
Northwestern Oklahoma State University,
  OK
Northwest Missouri State University, MO
Oakland University, MI
The Ohio State University, OH
Ohio University, OH
Ohio Wesleyan University, OH
Oklahoma State U, OK
Old Dominion University, VA
Ottawa University, KS
Palmer College of Chiropractic, IA
Pepperdine University, Malibu, CA
Peru State College, NE
Piedmont College, GA
Pine Manor College, MA
Pittsburg State University, KS
Point Loma Nazarene College, CA
Purchase College, State U of NY, NY
Purdue University, West Lafayette, IN
Quincy University, IL
Reinhardt College, GA
The Richard Stockton College of New
  Jersey, NJ
Rochester Institute of Technology, NY
Rockford College, IL
Rowan University, NJ
Rutgers, State U of NJ, Cook College, NJ
Saginaw Valley State University, MI
St. Ambrose University, IA
St. Cloud State University, MN
St. Edward's University, TX
Saint Francis College, IN
St. John's University, NY
Saint Joseph's College, ME
Saint Paul's College, VA
Saint Vincent College, PA
Salisbury State University, MD

Sam Houston State University, TX
Savannah State University, GA
Seattle University, WA
Seton Hall University, NJ
Seton Hill College, PA
Shepherd College, WV
Slippery Rock University of Pennsylvania,
  PA
Sonoma State University, CA
South Dakota School of Mines and
  Technology, SD
South Dakota State University, SD
Southeastern Louisiana University, LA
Southeast Missouri State University, MO
Southern Methodist University, TX
Southern Oregon University, OR
Southwestern College, KS
Southwest Missouri State University, MO
Southwest State University, MN
Spelman College, GA
State U of NY at Oswego, NY
State U of NY College at Brockport, NY
State U of NY College at Fredonia, NY
State U of NY College at Geneseo, NY
State U of NY College at Old Westbury,
  NY
State U of NY College at Plattsburgh, NY
State U of NY Coll of Environ Sci and
  Forestry, NY
Stephen F. Austin State University, TX
Stetson University, FL
Sul Ross State University, TX
Tennessee Technological University, TN
Texas A&M University, College Station,
  TX
Texas A&M University–Kingsville, TX
Texas Tech University, TX
Texas Woman's University, TX
Truman State University, MO
Universidad Metropolitana, PR
The University of Akron, OH
U of Alaska Anchorage, AK
University of Arkansas at Little Rock, AR
University of California, San Diego, CA
University of Central Oklahoma, OK
University of Cincinnati, OH
University of Colorado at Boulder, CO
University of Delaware, DE
University of Denver, CO
University of Evansville, IN
University of Houston, TX
University of Kansas, KS
University of Mary Hardin-Baylor, TX
University of Massachusetts Amherst, MA
The University of Memphis, TN
University of Michigan, Ann Arbor, MI
University of Michigan–Dearborn, MI
University of Minnesota, Twin Cities
  Campus, MN
University of Missouri–St. Louis, MO
The University of Montana–Missoula, MT
University of Montevallo, AL
University of Nebraska at Omaha, NE
University of Nebraska–Lincoln, NE
University of Nevada, Las Vegas, NV
University of Nevada, Reno, NV
University of New England, ME

University of North Carolina at Greensboro, NC
University of North Carolina at Wilmington, NC
University of Northern Colorado, CO
University of Northern Iowa, IA
University of Oklahoma, OK
University of Pittsburgh at Bradford, PA
University of Portland, OR
University of Puget Sound, WA
University of Rochester, NY
University of St. Thomas, MN
University of Sioux Falls, SD
University of South Dakota, SD
University of South Florida, FL
The University of Tampa, FL
The University of Texas at Arlington, TX
The University of Texas at El Paso, TX
The University of Texas at San Antonio, TX
University of Tulsa, OK
University of Utah, UT
University of Washington, WA
University of Wisconsin–Platteville, WI
University of Wisconsin–River Falls, WI
University of Wisconsin–Stevens Point, WI
University of Wisconsin–Superior, WI
Virginia Military Institute, VA
Virginia State University, VA
Wartburg College, IA
Washington College, MD
Webster University, MO
Western Illinois University, IL
Western Kentucky University, KY
Western Michigan University, MI
Western State College of Colorado, CO
Western Washington University, WA
Westminster College of Salt Lake City, UT
West Virginia State College, WV
West Virginia University, WV
Wheeling Jesuit University, WV
Wilmington College, OH
Worcester State College, MA
Wright State University, OH
Xavier University of Louisiana, LA

BUSINESS

Abilene Christian University, TX
Adams State College, CO
Adrian College, MI
Albertson College of Idaho, ID
Albion College, MI
Alfred University, NY
Allentown College of St. Francis de Sales, PA
American University, DC
Anderson College, SC
Angelo State University, TX
Arkansas State University, AR
Auburn University, AL
Augustana College, SD
Augusta State University, GA
Austin College, TX
Baker University, KS
Ball State University, IN
Barry University, FL
Barton College, NC

Baylor University, TX
Bellarmine College, KY
Bellevue University, NE
Bethel College, IN
Birmingham-Southern College, AL
Bloomsburg University of Pennsylvania, PA
Boise State University, ID
Briar Cliff College, IA
Brigham Young University–Hawaii Campus, HI
Butler University, IN
California Lutheran University, CA
California Polytechnic State U, San Luis Obispo, CA
California State Polytechnic University, Pomona, CA
California State University, Bakersfield, CA
California State University, Chico, CA
California State University, Fresno, CA
California State University, Fullerton, CA
California State University, Northridge, CA
California State University, San Bernardino, CA
California State University, Stanislaus, CA
Calvin College, MI
Cameron University, OK
Carlow College, PA
Centenary College of Louisiana, LA
Central College, IA
Central Missouri State University, MO
Central State University, OH
Chapman University, CA
Clarion University of Pennsylvania, PA
Clarkson College, NE
Clarkson University, NY
Clearwater Christian College, FL
Clemson University, SC
Clinch Valley College of the U of Virginia, VA
College of New Rochelle, NY
College of Santa Fe, NM
The College of West Virginia, WV
Colorado Christian University, CO
Columbia College, SC
Concordia College, AL
Concordia College, NE
Cumberland College, KY
Dakota Wesleyan University, SD
Daniel Webster College, NH
David N. Myers College, OH
The Defiance College, OH
Delaware Valley College, PA
DePaul University, IL
DePauw University, IN
Detroit College of Business–Flint, MI
DeVry Institute of Technology, GA
Doane College, NE
Dordt College, IA
Drury College, MO
Eastern Mennonite University, VA
Eastern Michigan University, MI
Eastern New Mexico University, NM
Eastern Oregon University, OR
Eastern Washington University, WA
Edinboro University of Pennsylvania, PA
Elizabethtown College, PA
Elmhurst College, IL

Embry-Riddle Aeronautical University, FL
Endicott College, MA
Fairmont State College, WV
Five Towns College, NY
Flagler College, FL
Florida Agricultural and Mechanical University, FL
Florida Atlantic University, FL
Florida Metropolitan U-Tampa Coll, Lakeland, FL
Florida Southern College, FL
Fort Hays State University, KS
Fort Lewis College, CO
Fort Valley State University, GA
Francis Marion University, SC
Friends University, KS
Frostburg State University, MD
Gannon University, PA
Georgia College and State University, GA
Georgia State University, GA
Goldey-Beacom College, DE
Goucher College, MD
Grambling State University, LA
Grove City College, PA
Gwynedd-Mercy College, PA
Hardin-Simmons University, TX
Heritage College, WA
High Point University, NC
Hillsdale College, MI
Holy Names College, CA
Humphreys College, CA
Husson College, ME
Idaho State University, ID
Illinois State University, IL
Indiana University of Pennsylvania, PA
Indiana U–Purdue U Fort Wayne, IN
Inter American U of PR, Aguadilla Campus, PR
Iowa State University of Science and Technology, IA
Jacksonville State University, AL
Jacksonville University, FL
James Madison University, VA
Jersey City State College, NJ
Johnson & Wales University, RI
Johnson State College, VT
Jones College, FL
Juniata College, PA
Kean College of New Jersey, NJ
Kennesaw State University, GA
Kent State University, OH
Kentucky Christian College, KY
King's College, PA
Laboratory Institute of Merchandising, NY
Lakeland College, WI
Lander University, SC
Lawrence Technological University, MI
Limestone College, SC
Lincoln University, PA
Long Island U, Southampton College, NY
Longwood College, VA
Louisiana State University and A&M College, LA
Louisiana State University in Shreveport, LA
Louisiana Tech University, LA
Lyndon State College, VT

Business (continued)

Madonna University, MI
Malone College, OH
Manhattan College, NY
Mankato State University, MN
Marquette University, WI
Marygrove College, MI
Marymount University, VA
The Master's College and Seminary, CA
Mayville State University, ND
McKendree College, IL
McNeese State University, LA
Mesa State College, CO
Michigan State University, MI
Michigan Technological University, MI
Minot State University, ND
Mississippi State University, MS
Missouri Western State College, MO
Montana State U–Billings, MT
Montana State U–Bozeman, MT
Montana Tech of The University of
  Montana, MT
Morehead State University, KY
Morehouse College, GA
Morrison College, NV
Mount Mary College, WI
Mount St. Clare College, IA
Murray State University, KY
New Mexico State University, NM
New York University, NY
North Carolina Agricultural and Technical
  State U, NC
North Carolina State University, NC
North Dakota State University, ND
Northeastern State University, OK
Northeast Louisiana University, LA
Northern Michigan University, MI
Northwestern Oklahoma State University,
  OK
Northwest Missouri State University, MO
Northwood University, MI
Northwood University, Florida Campus, FL
The Ohio State University, OH
Ohio University, OH
Oklahoma Christian U of Science and Arts,
  OK
Oklahoma State U, OK
Old Dominion University, VA
Ottawa University, KS
Pepperdine University, Malibu, CA
Peru State College, NE
Pittsburg State University, KS
Point Loma Nazarene College, CA
Presentation College, SD
Providence College, RI
Purdue University, West Lafayette, IN
Quincy University, IL
Reinhardt College, GA
The Richard Stockton College of New
  Jersey, NJ
Robert Morris College, PA
Rochester Institute of Technology, NY
Rockford College, IL
Rowan University, NJ
Saginaw Valley State University, MI
St. Ambrose University, IA
St. Cloud State University, MN

St. Edward's University, TX
Saint Joseph's College, ME
Saint Vincent College, PA
Salisbury State University, MD
Sam Houston State University, TX
Seattle University, WA
Shenandoah University, VA
Shepherd College, WV
Siena Heights College, MI
Sierra Nevada College, NV
Sinte Gleska University, SD
Slippery Rock University of Pennsylvania,
  PA
Sonoma State University, CA
South Dakota State University, SD
Southeastern Louisiana University, LA
Southeastern Oklahoma State University,
  OK
Southeast Missouri State University, MO
Southern Adventist University, TN
Southern Methodist University, TX
Southern Oregon University, OR
Southern Utah University, UT
Southwestern College, KS
Southwest Missouri State University, MO
State U of NY College at Fredonia, NY
State U of NY College at Geneseo, NY
State U of NY College at Plattsburgh, NY
Stephen F. Austin State University, TX
Stetson University, FL
Strayer College, DC
Sul Ross State University, TX
Susquehanna University, PA
Teikyo Post University, CT
Tennessee Technological University, TN
Texas A&M University, College Station,
  TX
Texas A&M University–Kingsville, TX
Texas Tech University, TX
Texas Woman's University, TX
Tiffin University, OH
Trinity Christian College, IL
Truman State University, MO
United States International University, CA
The University of Akron, OH
The University of Alabama at Birmingham,
  AL
U of Alaska Anchorage, AK
University of Arkansas at Little Rock, AR
University of Central Oklahoma, OK
University of Cincinnati, OH
University of Colorado at Boulder, CO
University of Dayton, OH
University of Delaware, DE
University of Denver, CO
University of Evansville, IN
University of Georgia, GA
University of Great Falls, MT
University of Hawaii at Hilo, HI
University of Houston, TX
University of Idaho, ID
University of Kansas, KS
University of Maine at Fort Kent, ME
University of Mary Hardin-Baylor, TX
University of Maryland Eastern Shore, MD
University of Massachusetts Amherst, MA
The University of Memphis, TN

University of Michigan, Ann Arbor, MI
University of Michigan–Flint, MI
University of Minnesota, Crookston, MN
University of Minnesota, Twin Cities
  Campus, MN
University of Missouri–St. Louis, MO
The University of Montana–Missoula, MT
University of Nebraska at Kearney, NE
University of Nebraska at Omaha, NE
University of Nebraska–Lincoln, NE
University of Nevada, Las Vegas, NV
University of Nevada, Reno, NV
University of North Carolina at Charlotte,
  NC
University of North Carolina at Greensboro,
  NC
University of North Carolina at Pembroke,
  NC
University of North Carolina at
  Wilmington, NC
University of Northern Colorado, CO
University of Northern Iowa, IA
University of Oklahoma, OK
University of Portland, OR
University of Puget Sound, WA
University of St. Thomas, MN
University of Sioux Falls, SD
University of South Dakota, SD
University of Southern Indiana, IN
University of South Florida, FL
The University of Tampa, FL
The University of Texas at Arlington, TX
The University of Texas at El Paso, TX
The University of Texas at San Antonio,
  TX
The University of Texas–Pan American, TX
University of Toledo, OH
University of Tulsa, OK
University of Utah, UT
University of Washington, WA
University of Wisconsin–Green Bay, WI
University of Wisconsin–La Crosse, WI
University of Wisconsin–Oshkosh, WI
University of Wisconsin–Platteville, WI
University of Wisconsin–River Falls, WI
University of Wisconsin–Stevens Point, WI
University of Wisconsin–Stout, WI
University of Wisconsin–Superior, WI
Valdosta State University, GA
Valley City State University, ND
Virginia Polytechnic Institute and State U,
  VA
Virginia State University, VA
Voorhees College, SC
Warner Southern College, FL
Washington and Jefferson College, PA
Washington State University, WA
Webster University, MO
West Chester University of Pennsylvania,
  PA
Western Illinois University, IL
Western Michigan University, MI
Western Montana College of The U of
  Montana, MT
Western State College of Colorado, CO
Western Washington University, WA
West Liberty State College, WV

West Texas A&M University, TX
West Virginia State College, WV
West Virginia University, WV
Wheeling Jesuit University, WV
Wichita State University, KS
Widener University, PA
Winston-Salem State University, NC
Worcester State College, MA
Xavier University, OH
Xavier University of Louisiana, LA
York College, NE

COMMUNICATION

Abilene Christian University, TX
Adams State College, CO
Alfred University, NY
Allentown College of St. Francis de Sales, PA
American University, DC
Anderson College, SC
Angelo State University, TX
Arkansas State University, AR
Auburn University, AL
Augustana College, SD
Austin College, TX
Baker University, KS
Ball State University, IN
Barton College, NC
Baylor University, TX
Beaver College, PA
Bethel College, IN
Biola University, CA
Black Hills State University, SD
Bloomsburg University of Pennsylvania, PA
Boise State University, ID
Brenau University, GA
Briar Cliff College, IA
Brigham Young University–Hawaii Campus, HI
Butler University, IN
California Lutheran University, CA
California Polytechnic State U, San Luis Obispo, CA
California State University, Bakersfield, CA
California State University, Chico, CA
California State University, Fresno, CA
California State University, Fullerton, CA
California State University, Stanislaus, CA
Calvin College, MI
Cameron University, OK
Carlow College, PA
Central Christian College of the Bible, MO
Central College, IA
Central Missouri State University, MO
Clarion University of Pennsylvania, PA
Clemson University, SC
College of New Rochelle, NY
Columbia College, SC
Concordia College, NE
Cumberland College, KY
Dakota State University, SD
The Defiance College, OH
DePauw University, IN
Doane College, NE
Dordt College, IA
East Central University, OK
Eastern Michigan University, MI

Eastern New Mexico University, NM
East Stroudsburg University of Pennsylvania, PA
Edinboro University of Pennsylvania, PA
Elizabethtown College, PA
Elmhurst College, IL
Endicott College, MA
Flagler College, FL
Florida International University, FL
Florida Southern College, FL
Fordham University, NY
Fort Hays State University, KS
Fort Lewis College, CO
Frostburg State University, MD
Georgia State University, GA
Grove City College, PA
Gwynedd-Mercy College, PA
Heritage College, WA
Idaho State University, ID
Illinois State University, IL
Indiana University of Pennsylvania, PA
Iowa State University of Science and Technology, IA
Iowa Wesleyan College, IA
Jacksonville State University, AL
Jersey City State College, NJ
Kent State University, OH
King's College, PA
Limestone College, SC
Lincoln University, PA
Louisiana State University and A&M College, LA
Madonna University, MI
Malone College, OH
Mansfield University of Pennsylvania, PA
Marquette University, WI
McNeese State University, LA
Mesa State College, CO
Milligan College, TN
Minot State University, ND
Mississippi College, MS
Mississippi State University, MS
Missouri Western State College, MO
Montana State U–Bozeman, MT
Mount Mary College, WI
Mount St. Clare College, IA
Murray State University, KY
New Mexico Inst of Mining and Technology, NM
New Mexico State University, NM
Northeastern State University, OK
Northeast Louisiana University, LA
Northwestern Oklahoma State University, OK
The Ohio State University, OH
Ohio University, OH
Oklahoma Christian U of Science and Arts, OK
Oklahoma State U, OK
Ottawa University, KS
Pepperdine University, Malibu, CA
Pittsburg State University, KS
Point Loma Nazarene College, CA
Presentation College, SD
Roanoke Bible College, NC
Robert Morris College, PA
Rochester Institute of Technology, NY

Rowan University, NJ
St. Ambrose University, IA
St. Cloud State University, MN
Saint Joseph's College, ME
Salisbury State University, MD
Sam Houston State University, TX
Seattle University, WA
Shepherd College, WV
Sonoma State University, CA
South Dakota State University, SD
Southeastern College of the Assemblies of God, FL
Southeast Missouri State University, MO
Southern Methodist University, TX
Southern Utah University, UT
Southwest Baptist University, MO
Southwest Missouri State University, MO
Spring Arbor College, MI
State U of NY at Oswego, NY
State U of NY College at Fredonia, NY
State U of NY College at Geneseo, NY
State U of NY College at Plattsburgh, NY
Stephen F. Austin State University, TX
Stetson University, FL
Taylor University, Fort Wayne Campus, IN
Texas A&M University–Kingsville, TX
Texas Tech University, TX
Texas Woman's University, TX
Truman State University, MO
United States International University, CA
The University of Akron, OH
U of Alaska Anchorage, AK
University of Arkansas at Little Rock, AR
University of California, San Diego, CA
University of Cincinnati, OH
University of Colorado at Boulder, CO
University of Evansville, IN
University of Idaho, ID
University of Kansas, KS
University of Mary Hardin-Baylor, TX
University of Massachusetts Amherst, MA
The University of Memphis, TN
University of Minnesota, Twin Cities Campus, MN
University of Missouri–St. Louis, MO
University of Nebraska at Omaha, NE
University of Nevada, Las Vegas, NV
University of North Carolina at Greensboro, NC
University of North Carolina at Pembroke, NC
University of North Carolina at Wilmington, NC
University of Northern Colorado, CO
University of Oklahoma, OK
University of Portland, OR
University of Sioux Falls, SD
University of South Dakota, SD
University of Southern Indiana, IN
University of South Florida, FL
The University of Tampa, FL
The University of Texas at Arlington, TX
The University of Texas at El Paso, TX
University of Toledo, OH
University of Tulsa, OK
University of Utah, UT
University of Washington, WA

Communication (continued)

University of Wisconsin–Platteville, WI
University of Wisconsin–River Falls, WI
University of Wisconsin–Stevens Point, WI
University of Wisconsin–Superior, WI
Valley City State University, ND
Warner Southern College, FL
Webster University, MO
Western State College of Colorado, CO
Western Washington University, WA
West Liberty State College, WV
West Virginia State College, WV
West Virginia University, WV
Wichita State University, KS
York College, NE

COMPUTER SCIENCE

Adams State College, CO
Alfred University, NY
Allentown College of St. Francis de Sales, PA
American University, DC
Anderson College, SC
Angelo State University, TX
Arkansas State University, AR
Armstrong Atlantic State University, GA
Auburn University, AL
Baker University, KS
Barton College, NC
Baylor University, TX
Birmingham-Southern College, AL
Black Hills State University, SD
Bloomsburg University of Pennsylvania, PA
Boise State University, ID
Briar Cliff College, IA
Brigham Young University–Hawaii Campus, HI
Buena Vista University, IA
Butler University, IN
California Lutheran University, CA
California Polytechnic State U, San Luis Obispo, CA
California State Polytechnic University, Pomona, CA
California State University, Chico, CA
California State University, Fresno, CA
California State University, Northridge, CA
California State University, San Bernardino, CA
California State University, Stanislaus, CA
Carlow College, PA
Central Missouri State University, MO
Central State University, OH
Cheyney University of Pennsylvania, PA
Clarion University of Pennsylvania, PA
Clarke College, IA
Clarkson University, NY
Clemson University, SC
Clinch Valley College of the U of Virginia, VA
Cogswell Polytechnical College, CA
The College of West Virginia, WV
Concordia College, AL
Concordia College, NE
Cumberland College, KY
Dakota State University, SD
Daniel Webster College, NH

The Defiance College, OH
Delaware Valley College, PA
DePaul University, IL
DePauw University, IN
DeVry Institute of Technology, GA
Dordt College, IA
Eastern Michigan University, MI
Eastern New Mexico University, NM
East Stroudsburg University of Pennsylvania, PA
Edinboro University of Pennsylvania, PA
Elizabethtown College, PA
Elon College, NC
Embry-Riddle Aeronautical University, FL
Fontbonne College, MO
Fort Hays State University, KS
Fort Lewis College, CO
Georgia State University, GA
Grambling State University, LA
Gwynedd-Mercy College, PA
Heritage College, WA
Idaho State University, ID
Illinois Institute of Technology, IL
Illinois State University, IL
Indiana University of Pennsylvania, PA
Inter American U of PR, Aguadilla Campus, PR
Iowa State University of Science and Technology, IA
Jacksonville State University, AL
King's College, PA
Lander University, SC
Lawrence Technological University, MI
Limestone College, SC
Lincoln University, PA
Longwood College, VA
Louisiana State University and A&M College, LA
Louisiana State University in Shreveport, LA
Madonna University, MI
Malone College, OH
Mankato State University, MN
Marygrove College, MI
McNeese State University, LA
Mesa State College, CO
Michigan State University, MI
Michigan Technological University, MI
Minot State University, ND
Mississippi State University, MS
Missouri Western State College, MO
Montana State U–Bozeman, MT
Montana Tech of The University of Montana, MT
Mount St. Clare College, IA
Murray State University, KY
New Mexico State University, NM
Norfolk State University, VA
Northeastern State University, OK
Northeast Louisiana University, LA
Northwestern Oklahoma State University, OK
Northwest Missouri State University, MO
The Ohio State University, OH
Ohio University, OH
Ohio Wesleyan University, OH

Oklahoma Christian U of Science and Arts, OK
Oklahoma State U, OK
Old Dominion University, VA
Peru State College, NE
Pittsburg State University, KS
Polytechnic U, Brooklyn Campus, NY
Presentation College, SD
The Richard Stockton College of New Jersey, NJ
Rochester Institute of Technology, NY
Rollins College, FL
Rose-Hulman Institute of Technology, IN
Rowan University, NJ
Saginaw Valley State University, MI
St. Ambrose University, IA
St. Cloud State University, MN
St. John's University, NY
Saint Vincent College, PA
Sam Houston State University, TX
Seattle University, WA
Shepherd College, WV
Siena Heights College, MI
Slippery Rock University of Pennsylvania, PA
Sonoma State University, CA
South Dakota School of Mines and Technology, SD
South Dakota State University, SD
Southeast Missouri State University, MO
Southern Methodist University, TX
Spring Arbor College, MI
State U of NY at New Paltz, NY
State U of NY College at Geneseo, NY
State U of NY College at Plattsburgh, NY
Stephen F. Austin State University, TX
Stetson University, FL
Stevens Institute of Technology, NJ
Strayer College, DC
Texas A&M University, College Station, TX
Texas A&M University–Kingsville, TX
Texas Tech University, TX
Texas Woman's University, TX
Transylvania University, KY
University of Advancing Computer Technology, AZ
The University of Akron, OH
U of Alaska Anchorage, AK
University of Arkansas at Little Rock, AR
University of Central Oklahoma, OK
University of Cincinnati, OH
University of Colorado at Boulder, CO
University of Evansville, IN
University of Great Falls, MT
University of Hawaii at Hilo, HI
University of Houston, TX
University of Idaho, ID
University of Kansas, KS
University of Massachusetts Amherst, MA
University of Michigan, Ann Arbor, MI
University of Michigan–Dearborn, MI
University of Minnesota, Twin Cities Campus, MN
University of Missouri–St. Louis, MO
The University of Montana–Missoula, MT
University of Nebraska at Omaha, NE

University of Nebraska–Lincoln, NE
University of Nevada, Las Vegas, NV
University of Nevada, Reno, NV
University of North Carolina at Charlotte, NC
University of North Carolina at Wilmington, NC
University of Oklahoma, OK
University of Portland, OR
University of Puget Sound, WA
University of Sioux Falls, SD
University of South Dakota, SD
University of South Florida, FL
The University of Texas at Arlington, TX
The University of Texas at Dallas, TX
The University of Texas at El Paso, TX
The University of Texas at San Antonio, TX
University of Toledo, OH
University of Tulsa, OK
University of Utah, UT
The University of West Alabama, AL
University of Wisconsin–Oshkosh, WI
University of Wisconsin–River Falls, WI
University of Wisconsin–Stevens Point, WI
University of Wisconsin–Superior, WI
Voorhees College, SC
Webster University, MO
Western State College of Colorado, CO
Western Washington University, WA
West Texas A&M University, TX
West Virginia University, WV
Wheeling Jesuit University, WV
Wichita State University, KS
Winston-Salem State University, NC
Xavier University of Louisiana, LA

EDUCATION

Abilene Christian University, TX
Adams State College, CO
Alabama State University, AL
Albertson College of Idaho, ID
Alderson-Broaddus College, WV
Alfred University, NY
Allentown College of St. Francis de Sales, PA
American University, DC
Anderson College, SC
Angelo State University, TX
Antioch College, OH
Arizona Bible College, AZ
Arkansas State University, AR
Armstrong Atlantic State University, GA
Auburn University, AL
Augustana College, SD
Augusta State University, GA
Austin College, TX
Baker University, KS
Ball State University, IN
Baptist Bible College of Pennsylvania, PA
Barry University, FL
Barton College, NC
Baylor University, TX
Bethel College, IN
Birmingham-Southern College, AL
Black Hills State University, SD
Bloomsburg University of Pennsylvania, PA

Boise State University, ID
Briar Cliff College, IA
Brigham Young University–Hawaii Campus, HI
Buena Vista University, IA
Butler University, IN
California Lutheran University, CA
California Polytechnic State U, San Luis Obispo, CA
California State Polytechnic University, Pomona, CA
California State University, Bakersfield, CA
California State University, Chico, CA
California State University, Fresno, CA
California State University, Northridge, CA
California State University, San Bernardino, CA
California State University, Stanislaus, CA
Calvary Bible College and Theological Seminary, MO
Calvin College, MI
Carlow College, PA
Cedar Crest College, PA
Centenary College of Louisiana, LA
Central College, IA
Central Missouri State University, MO
Central State University, OH
Cheyney University of Pennsylvania, PA
Christopher Newport University, VA
Clarion University of Pennsylvania, PA
Clarke College, IA
Clearwater Christian College, FL
Clemson University, SC
Clinch Valley College of the U of Virginia, VA
College of New Rochelle, NY
College of Santa Fe, NM
Coll of Staten Island of the City U of NY, NY
Colorado Christian University, CO
Columbia College, SC
Concordia College, AL
Concordia College, NE
Concordia College, NY
Cumberland College, KY
Daemen College, NY
Davidson College, NC
The Defiance College, OH
Delaware Valley College, PA
DePaul University, IL
Doane College, NE
Dordt College, IA
Drury College, MO
Eastern Connecticut State University, CT
Eastern Mennonite University, VA
Eastern Michigan University, MI
Eastern New Mexico University, NM
Eastern Oregon University, OR
Eastern Washington University, WA
East Stroudsburg University of Pennsylvania, PA
Edinboro University of Pennsylvania, PA
Elizabethtown College, PA
Elon College, NC
Endicott College, MA
Fairmont State College, WV
Felician College, NJ

Five Towns College, NY
Flagler College, FL
Florida Institute of Technology, FL
Fort Hays State University, KS
Fort Lewis College, CO
Framingham State College, MA
Francis Marion University, SC
Friends University, KS
Frostburg State University, MD
Georgia State University, GA
Grambling State University, LA
Guilford College, NC
Gwynedd-Mercy College, PA
Hardin-Simmons University, TX
Hebrew College, MA
Heritage College, WA
High Point University, NC
Hillsdale College, MI
Holy Names College, CA
Huntington College, IN
Husson College, ME
Idaho State University, ID
Illinois State University, IL
Indiana University of Pennsylvania, PA
Indiana U–Purdue U Fort Wayne, IN
Inter American U of PR, Aguadilla Campus, PR
Iowa State University of Science and Technology, IA
Jacksonville State University, AL
James Madison University, VA
Jersey City State College, NJ
John Wesley College, NC
Juniata College, PA
Kean College of New Jersey, NJ
Kent State University, OH
King's College, PA
Lander University, SC
Lesley College, MA
Lewis-Clark State College, ID
Limestone College, SC
Lincoln University, MO
Lincoln University, PA
Livingstone College, NC
Long Island U, Southampton College, NY
Longwood College, VA
Louisiana State University and A&M College, LA
Louisiana State University in Shreveport, LA
Louisiana Tech University, LA
Lyndon State College, VT
Madonna University, MI
Malone College, OH
Mansfield University of Pennsylvania, PA
Marygrove College, MI
Maryville University of Saint Louis, MO
The Master's College and Seminary, CA
Mayville State University, ND
McNeese State University, LA
Meredith College, NC
Mesa State College, CO
Miami University, OH
Michigan State University, MI
Minot State University, ND
Mississippi College, MS
Mississippi State University, MS

Education (continued)

Missouri Western State College, MO
Montana State U–Bozeman, MT
Mount Mary College, WI
Mount St. Clare College, IA
Mount St. Mary's College, CA
Murray State University, KY
Nebraska Christian College, NE
New Mexico State University, NM
North Carolina State University, NC
North Central College, IL
North Dakota State University, ND
Northeastern State University, OK
Northeast Louisiana University, LA
Northwestern Oklahoma State University, OK
Northwest Missouri State University, MO
The Ohio State University, OH
Ohio University, OH
Oklahoma Christian U of Science and Arts, OK
Oklahoma State U, OK
Ottawa University, KS
Pepperdine University, Malibu, CA
Peru State College, NE
Piedmont College, GA
Pine Manor College, MA
Pittsburg State University, KS
Point Loma Nazarene College, CA
Purdue University, West Lafayette, IN
Quincy University, IL
Reinhardt College, GA
The Richard Stockton College of New Jersey, NJ
Rockford College, IL
Rowan University, NJ
Saginaw Valley State University, MI
St. Ambrose University, IA
St. Cloud State University, MN
St. Edward's University, TX
Saint Joseph's College, ME
Salisbury State University, MD
Sam Houston State University, TX
Seattle University, WA
Seton Hall University, NJ
Shaw University, NC
Shepherd College, WV
Sierra Nevada College, NV
Sinte Gleska University, SD
Slippery Rock University of Pennsylvania, PA
Sonoma State University, CA
South Dakota State University, SD
Southeastern Louisiana University, LA
Southeastern Oklahoma State University, OK
Southeast Missouri State University, MO
Southern Oregon University, OR
Southern Utah University, UT
Southern Wesleyan University, SC
Southwestern Adventist University, TX
Southwest Missouri State University, MO
Southwest Texas State University, TX
State U of NY at New Paltz, NY
State U of NY at Oswego, NY
State U of NY College at Brockport, NY
State U of NY College at Fredonia, NY

State U of NY College at Geneseo, NY
State U of NY College at Plattsburgh, NY
Stephen F. Austin State University, TX
Stetson University, FL
Stillman College, AL
Sul Ross State University, TX
Tennessee Technological University, TN
Texas A&M University, College Station, TX
Texas A&M University–Kingsville, TX
Texas Tech University, TX
Texas Woman's University, TX
Transylvania University, KY
Trinity Bible College, ND
Truman State University, MO
United States International University, CA
The University of Akron, OH
U of Alaska Anchorage, AK
University of Arkansas at Little Rock, AR
University of California, San Diego, CA
University of Central Oklahoma, OK
University of Cincinnati, OH
University of Colorado at Boulder, CO
University of Dayton, OH
University of Delaware, DE
University of Denver, CO
University of Evansville, IN
University of Georgia, GA
University of Great Falls, MT
University of Houston, TX
University of Idaho, ID
University of Kansas, KS
University of Maine at Fort Kent, ME
University of Mary Hardin-Baylor, TX
University of Maryland Eastern Shore, MD
University of Massachusetts Amherst, MA
The University of Memphis, TN
University of Michigan, Ann Arbor, MI
University of Michigan–Flint, MI
University of Minnesota, Twin Cities Campus, MN
University of Missouri–Rolla, MO
University of Missouri–St. Louis, MO
The University of Montana–Missoula, MT
University of Montevallo, AL
University of Nebraska at Omaha, NE
University of Nebraska–Lincoln, NE
University of Nevada, Las Vegas, NV
University of Nevada, Reno, NV
University of North Carolina at Greensboro, NC
University of North Carolina at Pembroke, NC
University of North Carolina at Wilmington, NC
University of Northern Colorado, CO
University of Northern Iowa, IA
University of Oklahoma, OK
University of Portland, OR
University of Sioux Falls, SD
University of South Dakota, SD
University of Southern Indiana, IN
University of South Florida, FL
The University of Texas at El Paso, TX
The University of Texas at San Antonio, TX
University of Toledo, OH

University of Utah, UT
University of Wisconsin–La Crosse, WI
University of Wisconsin–Platteville, WI
University of Wisconsin–River Falls, WI
University of Wisconsin–Stevens Point, WI
University of Wisconsin–Stout, WI
University of Wisconsin–Superior, WI
Valdosta State University, GA
Valley City State University, ND
Vanderbilt University, TN
Virginia Polytechnic Institute and State U, VA
Virginia State University, VA
Voorhees College, SC
Warner Southern College, FL
Washington State University, WA
Webster University, MO
Western Illinois University, IL
Western Michigan University, MI
Western Montana College of The U of Montana, MT
Western State College of Colorado, CO
Western Washington University, WA
West Liberty State College, WV
West Texas A&M University, TX
West Virginia University, WV
Wheeling Jesuit University, WV
Wichita State University, KS
William Jewell College, MO
Winston-Salem State University, NC
Worcester State College, MA
Xavier University, OH
Xavier University of Louisiana, LA
York College, NE

ENGINEERING/TECHNOLOGIES

Alfred University, NY
Arkansas State University, AR
Armstrong Atlantic State University, GA
Auburn University, AL
Austin College, TX
Baylor University, TX
Bluefield State College, WV
Boise State University, ID
California Polytechnic State U, San Luis Obispo, CA
California State Polytechnic University, Pomona, CA
California State University, Chico, CA
California State University, Fresno, CA
California State University, Fullerton, CA
California State University, Northridge, CA
Calvin College, MI
Centenary College of Louisiana, LA
Central State University, OH
The Citadel, The Military Coll of South Carolina, SC
Clarkson University, NY
Clemson University, SC
Cogswell Polytechnical College, CA
The College of New Jersey, NJ
Coll of Staten Island of the City U of NY, NY
Cumberland College, KY
Davis & Elkins College, WV
DeVry Institute of Technology, GA
Dordt College, IA

Eastern Michigan University, MI
Eastern New Mexico University, NM
Elizabethtown College, PA
Embry-Riddle Aeronautical University, FL
Fairmont State College, WV
Florida Agricultural and Mechanical University, FL
Florida Atlantic University, FL
Florida Institute of Technology, FL
Fort Hays State University, KS
Fort Lewis College, CO
Gannon University, PA
Geneva College, PA
The George Washington University, DC
Gonzaga University, WA
Greenville College, IL
Grove City College, PA
Idaho State University, ID
Illinois Institute of Technology, IL
Illinois State University, IL
Indiana University of Pennsylvania, PA
Indiana U–Purdue U Fort Wayne, IN
Iowa State University of Science and Technology, IA
Lakeland College, WI
Lawrence Technological University, MI
Louisiana State University and A&M College, LA
Louisiana Tech University, LA
Maine Maritime Academy, ME
Mankato State University, MN
Marquette University, WI
McNeese State University, LA
Mesa State College, CO
Miami University, OH
Michigan State University, MI
Michigan Technological University, MI
Mississippi State University, MS
Missouri Western State College, MO
Montana State U–Bozeman, MT
Montana Tech of The University of Montana, MT
New Mexico Inst of Mining and Technology, NM
New Mexico State University, NM
North Carolina Agricultural and Technical State U, NC
North Carolina State University, NC
North Dakota State University, ND
Northern Michigan University, MI
Oakland University, MI
The Ohio State University, OH
Ohio University, OH
Oklahoma Christian U of Science and Arts, OK
Oklahoma State U, OK
Old Dominion University, VA
Oral Roberts University, OK
Pittsburg State University, KS
Point Loma Nazarene College, CA
Polytechnic U, Brooklyn Campus, NY
Polytechnic U, Farmingdale Campus, NY
Purdue University, West Lafayette, IN
Rice University, TX
Rochester Institute of Technology, NY
Rollins College, FL
Rose-Hulman Institute of Technology, IN

Rowan University, NJ
Rutgers, State U of NJ, College of Engineering, NJ
St. Ambrose University, IA
St. Cloud State University, MN
Sam Houston State University, TX
Seattle University, WA
Shaw University, NC
Shepherd College, WV
South Dakota School of Mines and Technology, SD
South Dakota State University, SD
Southeastern Louisiana University, LA
Southeastern Oklahoma State University, OK
Southern Methodist University, TX
State U of NY at Binghamton, NY
State U of NY at New Paltz, NY
State U of NY Coll of Environ Sci and Forestry, NY
Stevens Institute of Technology, NJ
Tennessee Technological University, TN
Texas A&M University, College Station, TX
Texas Tech University, TX
The University of Akron, OH
The University of Alabama at Birmingham, AL
The University of Alabama in Huntsville, AL
U of Alaska Anchorage, AK
University of Arkansas at Little Rock, AR
University of California, Berkeley, CA
University of California, Riverside, CA
University of Cincinnati, OH
University of Colorado at Boulder, CO
University of Dayton, OH
University of Delaware, DE
University of Denver, CO
University of Evansville, IN
University of Houston, TX
University of Idaho, ID
University of Kansas, KS
University of Maine, Orono, ME
University of Maryland Eastern Shore, MD
University of Massachusetts Amherst, MA
The University of Memphis, TN
University of Michigan, Ann Arbor, MI
University of Michigan–Dearborn, MI
University of Minnesota, Twin Cities Campus, MN
University of Missouri–Rolla, MO
University of Missouri–St. Louis, MO
University of Nebraska at Omaha, NE
University of Nebraska–Lincoln, NE
University of Nevada, Las Vegas, NV
University of Nevada, Reno, NV
University of New Mexico, NM
University of North Carolina at Charlotte, NC
University of Oklahoma, OK
University of Portland, OR
University of Sioux Falls, SD
University of Southern California, CA
University of Southern Indiana, IN
University of South Florida, FL
The University of Texas at Arlington, TX

The University of Texas at Dallas, TX
The University of Texas at El Paso, TX
The University of Texas at San Antonio, TX
The University of Texas–Pan American, TX
University of Toledo, OH
University of Tulsa, OK
University of Utah, UT
University of Washington, WA
University of Wisconsin–Green Bay, WI
University of Wisconsin–Platteville, WI
University of Wisconsin–Stout, WI
Valley City State University, ND
Valparaiso University, IN
Vanderbilt University, TN
Virginia Military Institute, VA
Virginia Polytechnic Institute and State U, VA
Virginia State University, VA
Washington State University, WA
Washington University, MO
Western Michigan University, MI
Western Washington University, WA
West Virginia University, WV
West Virginia University Institute of Technology, WV
Wheeling Jesuit University, WV
Wichita State University, KS
Widener University, PA
Wilkes University, PA
Xavier University of Louisiana, LA

ENGLISH

Abilene Christian University, TX
Adams State College, CO
Agnes Scott College, GA
Alfred University, NY
Allentown College of St. Francis de Sales, PA
American University, DC
Anderson College, SC
Angelo State University, TX
Arkansas State University, AR
Auburn University, AL
Augustana College, SD
Augusta State University, GA
Austin College, TX
Baker University, KS
Ball State University, IN
Barton College, NC
Bassist College, OR
Baylor University, TX
Beaver College, PA
Berry College, GA
Bethel College, IN
Bloomsburg University of Pennsylvania, PA
Boise State University, ID
Briar Cliff College, IA
Brigham Young University–Hawaii Campus, HI
Butler University, IN
California Lutheran University, CA
California Polytechnic State U, San Luis Obispo, CA
California State University, Bakersfield, CA
California State University, Chico, CA
California State University, Fresno, CA

English *(continued)*

California State University, Stanislaus, CA
Calvin College, MI
Cameron University, OK
Carlow College, PA
Centenary College of Louisiana, LA
Central Missouri State University, MO
Clarion University of Pennsylvania, PA
Clemson University, SC
Clinch Valley College of the U of Virginia, VA
College of New Rochelle, NY
The College of Wooster, OH
Columbia College, SC
Concordia College, NE
Cumberland College, KY
Delaware Valley College, PA
Dordt College, IA
Drury College, MO
Eastern Mennonite University, VA
Eastern Michigan University, MI
Eastern New Mexico University, NM
East Stroudsburg University of Pennsylvania, PA
East Texas Baptist University, TX
Edinboro University of Pennsylvania, PA
Elizabethtown College, PA
Felician College, NJ
Fontbonne College, MO
Fort Hays State University, KS
Fort Lewis College, CO
Francis Marion University, SC
Frostburg State University, MD
Green Mountain College, VT
Gwynedd-Mercy College, PA
High Point University, NC
Hillsdale College, MI
Holy Names College, CA
Idaho State University, ID
Illinois State University, IL
Indiana University of Pennsylvania, PA
Iowa State University of Science and Technology, IA
Jacksonville State University, AL
James Madison University, VA
Kalamazoo College, MI
Kennesaw State University, GA
Kent State University, OH
King's College, PA
LaGrange College, GA
Limestone College, SC
Longwood College, VA
Louisiana State University in Shreveport, LA
MacMurray College, IL
Malone College, OH
Manchester College, IN
Mayville State University, ND
McNeese State University, LA
Meredith College, NC
Mesa State College, CO
Milligan College, TN
Minot State University, ND
Mississippi State University, MS
Missouri Western State College, MO
Montana State U–Billings, MT
Montana State U–Bozeman, MT

Mount Mary College, WI
Mount St. Clare College, IA
Murray State University, KY
New Mexico State University, NM
Northeastern State University, OK
Northeast Louisiana University, LA
Northwestern Oklahoma State University, OK
Northwest Missouri State University, MO
The Ohio State University, OH
Ohio University, OH
Ohio Wesleyan University, OH
Oklahoma State U, OK
Old Dominion University, VA
Ottawa University, KS
Peru State College, NE
Piedmont College, GA
Pittsburg State University, KS
Quincy University, IL
Reinhardt College, GA
Rockford College, IL
St. Ambrose University, IA
St. Cloud State University, MN
Saint Joseph's College, ME
Salisbury State University, MD
Sam Houston State University, TX
Seattle University, WA
Seton Hill College, PA
Shepherd College, WV
Slippery Rock University of Pennsylvania, PA
Sonoma State University, CA
South Dakota State University, SD
Southeastern Louisiana University, LA
Southeast Missouri State University, MO
Southern Wesleyan University, SC
Southwestern Adventist University, TX
State U of NY at New Paltz, NY
State U of NY at Oswego, NY
State U of NY College at Brockport, NY
State U of NY College at Fredonia, NY
State U of NY College at Geneseo, NY
State U of NY College at Plattsburgh, NY
Stetson University, FL
Sul Ross State University, TX
Teikyo Post University, CT
Tennessee Technological University, TN
Texas A&M University–Kingsville, TX
Texas Tech University, TX
Texas Woman's University, TX
Trinity Christian College, IL
Truman State University, MO
The University of Akron, OH
U of Alaska Anchorage, AK
University of Arkansas at Little Rock, AR
University of California, San Diego, CA
University of Cincinnati, OH
University of Colorado at Boulder, CO
University of Evansville, IN
University of Hawaii at Hilo, HI
University of Houston, TX
University of Idaho, ID
University of Kansas, KS
University of Mary Hardin-Baylor, TX
University of Maryland Eastern Shore, MD
University of Michigan, Ann Arbor, MI

University of Minnesota, Twin Cities Campus, MN
University of Missouri–St. Louis, MO
The University of Montana–Missoula, MT
University of Nebraska at Kearney, NE
University of Nebraska at Omaha, NE
University of Nebraska–Lincoln, NE
University of Nevada, Las Vegas, NV
University of Nevada, Reno, NV
University of North Carolina at Greensboro, NC
University of North Carolina at Pembroke, NC
University of North Carolina at Wilmington, NC
University of Northern Colorado, CO
University of Portland, OR
University of Sioux Falls, SD
University of South Dakota, SD
University of South Florida, FL
The University of Texas at El Paso, TX
The University of Texas at San Antonio, TX
University of Toledo, OH
University of Tulsa, OK
University of Utah, UT
University of Washington, WA
The University of West Alabama, AL
University of Wisconsin–La Crosse, WI
University of Wisconsin–River Falls, WI
University of Wisconsin–Stevens Point, WI
University of Wisconsin–Superior, WI
Warner Southern College, FL
Wartburg College, IA
Washington State University, WA
Webster University, MO
Western Michigan University, MI
Western Montana College of The U of Montana, MT
Western State College of Colorado, CO
Western Washington University, WA
West Liberty State College, WV
West Texas A&M University, TX
West Virginia State College, WV
West Virginia University, WV
Wheeling Jesuit University, WV
Wichita State University, KS
Worcester State College, MA
York College, NE

FOREIGN LANGUAGES

Abilene Christian University, TX
Adams State College, CO
Alfred University, NY
Allentown College of St. Francis de Sales, PA
American University, DC
Arkansas State University, AR
Auburn University, AL
Austin College, TX
Ball State University, IN
Barton College, NC
Baylor University, TX
Bloomsburg University of Pennsylvania, PA
Boise State University, ID
Briar Cliff College, IA

Brigham Young University–Hawaii Campus, HI
Butler University, IN
California Lutheran University, CA
California Polytechnic State U, San Luis Obispo, CA
California State University, Chico, CA
Castleton State College, VT
Centenary College of Louisiana, LA
Central College, IA
Central Missouri State University, MO
Clarion University of Pennsylvania, PA
Clemson University, SC
Coe College, IA
College of New Rochelle, NY
Columbia College, SC
Cumberland College, KY
Davidson College, NC
Dordt College, IA
Eastern Mennonite University, VA
Eastern Michigan University, MI
Eastern New Mexico University, NM
Eastern Washington University, WA
East Stroudsburg University of Pennsylvania, PA
Elizabethtown College, PA
Fairmont State College, WV
Fort Hays State University, KS
Fort Lewis College, CO
Franklin College of Indiana, IN
Friends University, KS
Frostburg State University, MD
Gannon University, PA
Georgian Court College, NJ
Grove City College, PA
High Point University, NC
Hillsdale College, MI
Holy Names College, CA
Idaho State University, ID
Illinois State University, IL
Indiana University of Pennsylvania, PA
Iowa State University of Science and Technology, IA
John Carroll University, OH
Kalamazoo College, MI
King's College, PA
Louisiana State University and A&M College, LA
Loyola University Chicago, IL
MacMurray College, IL
Malone College, OH
Manhattan College, NY
Marquette University, WI
McNeese State University, LA
Mississippi State University, MS
Montana State U–Bozeman, MT
Moravian College, PA
Mount St. Clare College, IA
Murray State University, KY
New Mexico State University, NM
Northeastern State University, OK
Northeast Louisiana University, LA
Northwestern Oklahoma State University, OK
Northwest Missouri State University, MO
The Ohio State University, OH
Ohio University, OH

Oklahoma State U, OK
Ottawa University, KS
Piedmont College, GA
Pittsburg State University, KS
St. Ambrose University, IA
Salisbury State University, MD
Sam Houston State University, TX
Seattle University, WA
Shepherd College, WV
Siena Heights College, MI
Sonoma State University, CA
South Dakota State University, SD
Southeast Missouri State University, MO
Southwestern Oklahoma State University, OK
Southwest Missouri State University, MO
State U of NY College at Brockport, NY
State U of NY College at Fredonia, NY
State U of NY College at Geneseo, NY
Stetson University, FL
Sul Ross State University, TX
Texas Tech University, TX
Texas Woman's University, TX
Truman State University, MO
United States International University, CA
The University of Akron, OH
University of Arkansas at Little Rock, AR
University of Central Oklahoma, OK
University of Cincinnati, OH
University of Colorado at Boulder, CO
University of Dallas, TX
University of Evansville, IN
The University of Findlay, OH
University of Idaho, ID
University of Kansas, KS
University of Maine at Fort Kent, ME
University of Mary Hardin-Baylor, TX
University of Michigan, Ann Arbor, MI
University of Minnesota, Twin Cities Campus, MN
University of Missouri–St. Louis, MO
The University of Montana–Missoula, MT
University of Nebraska at Kearney, NE
University of Nebraska at Omaha, NE
University of Nebraska–Lincoln, NE
University of Nevada, Reno, NV
University of North Carolina at Greensboro, NC
University of North Carolina at Wilmington, NC
University of Portland, OR
University of South Dakota, SD
University of Southern Indiana, IN
University of South Florida, FL
The University of Texas at San Antonio, TX
University of Tulsa, OK
University of Utah, UT
University of Washington, WA
University of Wisconsin–River Falls, WI
University of Wisconsin–Stevens Point, WI
Valparaiso University, IN
Washington College, MD
Webster University, MO
Western Illinois University, IL
Western Michigan University, MI
Western Washington University, WA

West Virginia State College, WV
West Virginia University, WV
Worcester State College, MA
Xavier University, OH
Xavier University of Louisiana, LA

HEALTH FIELDS

Adams State College, CO
Albany State University, GA
Alderson-Broaddus College, WV
Allentown College of St. Francis de Sales, PA
American University, DC
Arkansas State University, AR
Armstrong Atlantic State University, GA
Auburn University, AL
Augusta State University, GA
Austin College, TX
Averett College, VA
Azusa Pacific University, CA
Ball State University, IN
Barry University, FL
Barton College, NC
Baylor University, TX
Bethel College, IN
Biola University, CA
Birmingham-Southern College, AL
Bloomsburg University of Pennsylvania, PA
Boise State University, ID
Briar Cliff College, IA
California Polytechnic State U, San Luis Obispo, CA
California State University, Bakersfield, CA
California State University, Chico, CA
California State University, Fresno, CA
California State University, Los Angeles, CA
California State University, San Bernardino, CA
Calvin College, MI
Carthage College, WI
Cedar Crest College, PA
Central Missouri State University, MO
Chadron State College, NE
Clarkson College, NE
Clemson University, SC
Clinch Valley College of the U of Virginia, VA
College of New Rochelle, NY
Coll of Staten Island of the City U of NY, NY
The College of West Virginia, WV
Cumberland College, KY
Daemen College, NY
Davis & Elkins College, WV
Deaconess College of Nursing, MO
Eastern Michigan University, MI
Eastern New Mexico University, NM
Eastern Washington University, WA
East Stroudsburg University of Pennsylvania, PA
Edinboro University of Pennsylvania, PA
Elizabethtown College, PA
Elmhurst College, IL
Endicott College, MA
Fairmont State College, WV
Felician College, NJ

Health Fields (continued)

Florida Agricultural and Mechanical
University, FL
Fort Hays State University, KS
Francis Marion University, SC
Gardner-Webb University, NC
Georgia College and State University, GA
Georgia State University, GA
Gwynedd-Mercy College, PA
Hillsdale College, MI
Holy Names College, CA
Houston Baptist University, TX
Idaho State University, ID
Illinois State University, IL
Indiana University of Pennsylvania, PA
Iowa State University of Science and
Technology, IA
Jacksonville State University, AL
James Madison University, VA
Jones College, FL
Kean College of New Jersey, NJ
Kennesaw State University, GA
Kent State University, OH
King's College, PA
Lander University, SC
Lewis-Clark State College, ID
Long Island U, Brooklyn Campus, NY
Louisiana College, LA
Loyola University Chicago, IL
Lynchburg College, VA
Lynn University, FL
MacMurray College, IL
Malone College, OH
Mansfield University of Pennsylvania, PA
Marquette University, WI
Marygrove College, MI
Mass Coll of Pharmacy and Allied Health
Sciences, MA
McNeese State University, LA
Mesa State College, CO
MidAmerica Nazarene University, KS
Milligan College, TN
Minot State University, ND
Mississippi College, MS
Mississippi State University, MS
Missouri Western State College, MO
Montana State U–Bozeman, MT
Montana Tech of The University of
Montana, MT
Mount St. Clare College, IA
Murray State University, KY
New Mexico State University, NM
North Carolina Agricultural and Technical
State U, NC
Northeastern State University, OK
Northeast Louisiana University, LA
Northern Michigan University, MI
Northwest Missouri State University, MO
The Ohio State University, OH
Ohio University, OH
Old Dominion University, VA
Oral Roberts University, OK
Ottawa University, KS
Palmer College of Chiropractic, IA
Piedmont College, GA
Pittsburg State University, KS
Point Loma Nazarene College, CA

Presentation College, SD
Quincy University, IL
Reinhardt College, GA
Research College of Nursing–Rockhurst
College, MO
The Richard Stockton College of New
Jersey, NJ
Rochester Institute of Technology, NY
Rockhurst College, MO
Russell Sage College, NY
Saginaw Valley State University, MI
St. Ambrose University, IA
Saint Francis College, IN
St. John's University, NY
Saint Joseph's College, ME
Saint Louis University, MO
Seattle University, WA
Seton Hall University, NJ
Shepherd College, WV
Sonoma State University, CA
South Dakota State University, SD
Southeast Missouri State University, MO
State U of NY at New Paltz, NY
State U of NY College at Old Westbury,
NY
State U of NY College at Plattsburgh, NY
Stephen F. Austin State University, TX
Sul Ross State University, TX
Tennessee Technological University, TN
Texas A&M University, College Station,
TX
Texas A&M University–Kingsville, TX
Texas Woman's University, TX
Trinity Christian College, IL
The University of Akron, OH
The University of Alabama in Huntsville,
AL
U of Alaska Anchorage, AK
University of Arkansas at Little Rock, AR
University of Central Oklahoma, OK
University of Cincinnati, OH
University of Colorado at Boulder, CO
University of Evansville, IN
University of Hawaii at Hilo, HI
University of Houston, TX
University of Kansas, KS
University of Mary Hardin-Baylor, TX
University of Massachusetts Amherst, MA
The University of Memphis, TN
University of Michigan, Ann Arbor, MI
University of Minnesota, Twin Cities
Campus, MN
University of Missouri–St. Louis, MO
The University of Montana–Missoula, MT
University of Nebraska–Lincoln, NE
University of Nevada, Las Vegas, NV
University of Nevada, Reno, NV
University of North Carolina at Charlotte,
NC
University of North Carolina at Greensboro,
NC
University of North Carolina at Pembroke,
NC
University of North Carolina at
Wilmington, NC
University of Northern Colorado, CO
University of Portland, OR

U of Puerto Rico Medical Sciences
Campus, PR
University of Southern Indiana, IN
University of South Florida, FL
University of Southwestern Louisiana, LA
The University of Texas at El Paso, TX
University of Toledo, OH
University of Utah, UT
University of Washington, WA
University of Wisconsin–La Crosse, WI
University of Wisconsin–Platteville, WI
University of Wisconsin–River Falls, WI
University of Wisconsin–Stevens Point, WI
University of Wisconsin–Superior, WI
Ursinus College, PA
Valdosta State University, GA
Valparaiso University, IN
Virginia Commonwealth University, VA
Virginia State University, VA
Viterbo College, WI
Washington State University, WA
Western Michigan University, MI
West Texas A&M University, TX
West Virginia University, WV
Wheeling Jesuit University, WV
Wichita State University, KS
Widener University, PA
Wilkes University, PA
Winston-Salem State University, NC
Worcester State College, MA
York College of Pennsylvania, PA

HOME ECONOMICS

Abilene Christian University, TX
Baylor University, TX
California Polytechnic State U, San Luis
Obispo, CA
California State University, Fresno, CA
Central Missouri State University, MO
Eastern Michigan University, MI
Eastern New Mexico University, NM
Eastern Oregon University, OR
Fort Valley State University, GA
Framingham State College, MA
Idaho State University, ID
Illinois State University, IL
Indiana University of Pennsylvania, PA
Iowa State University of Science and
Technology, IA
Jacksonville State University, AL
Louisiana State University and A&M
College, LA
Louisiana Tech University, LA
McNeese State University, LA
Mississippi State University, MS
Montana State U–Bozeman, MT
Mount Mary College, WI
Murray State University, KY
New Mexico State University, NM
North Dakota State University, ND
Northeastern State University, OK
Northeast Louisiana University, LA
Northwest Missouri State University, MO
The Ohio State University, OH
Ohio University, OH
Oklahoma State U, OK
Pittsburg State University, KS

Point Loma Nazarene College, CA
Sam Houston State University, TX
Seton Hill College, PA
Shepherd College, WV
South Dakota State University, SD
Southeastern Louisiana University, LA
Southeast Missouri State University, MO
State U of NY College at Plattsburgh, NY
Stephen F. Austin State University, TX
Tennessee Technological University, TN
Texas A&M University–Kingsville, TX
Texas Tech University, TX
Texas Woman's University, TX
The University of Akron, OH
University of Central Oklahoma, OK
University of Delaware, DE
University of Idaho, ID
University of Maryland Eastern Shore, MD
University of Minnesota, Twin Cities
  Campus, MN
University of Nebraska at Omaha, NE
University of Nebraska–Lincoln, NE
University of North Carolina at Greensboro,
  NC
University of Northern Colorado, CO
University of Wisconsin–Stevens Point, WI
University of Wisconsin–Stout, WI
Virginia State University, VA
Washington State University, WA
Western Illinois University, IL
West Virginia University, WV

HUMANITIES

Adams State College, CO
Albertson College of Idaho, ID
Alderson-Broaddus College, WV
Alfred University, NY
Allentown College of St. Francis de Sales,
  PA
Alma College, MI
American University, DC
Antioch College, OH
Armstrong Atlantic State University, GA
Auburn University, AL
Austin College, TX
Baker University, KS
Barton College, NC
Baylor University, TX
Bellevue University, NE
Benedictine University, IL
Berry College, GA
Black Hills State University, SD
Bloomsburg University of Pennsylvania, PA
Brenau University, GA
Briar Cliff College, IA
Brigham Young University–Hawaii Campus,
  HI
Buena Vista University, IA
Butler University, IN
California Polytechnic State U, San Luis
  Obispo, CA
California State Polytechnic University,
  Pomona, CA
California State University, Bakersfield, CA
California State University, Chico, CA
California State University, Fresno, CA
California State University, Fullerton, CA

California State University, San Bernardino,
  CA
Calvin College, MI
Carlow College, PA
Centenary College of Louisiana, LA
Central College, IA
Central Missouri State University, MO
Chatham College, PA
Clarion University of Pennsylvania, PA
Clarkson University, NY
Clemson University, SC
Clinch Valley College of the U of Virginia,
  VA
College Misericordia, PA
College of New Rochelle, NY
College of Santa Fe, NM
Coll of Staten Island of the City U of NY,
  NY
College of the Holy Cross, MA
The College of West Virginia, WV
Colorado Christian University, CO
Concordia College, NE
The Defiance College, OH
Denison University, OH
DePauw University, IN
Doane College, NE
Dordt College, IA
Eastern Mennonite University, VA
Eastern Michigan University, MI
Eastern New Mexico University, NM
Edinboro University of Pennsylvania, PA
Elizabethtown College, PA
Elmhurst College, IL
Endicott College, MA
Fairmont State College, WV
Flagler College, FL
Fort Hays State University, KS
Fort Lewis College, CO
Francis Marion University, SC
Friends University, KS
Frostburg State University, MD
Gwynedd-Mercy College, PA
Hardin-Simmons University, TX
High Point University, NC
Hillsdale College, MI
Idaho State University, ID
Illinois State University, IL
Indiana University of Pennsylvania, PA
Iowa State University of Science and
  Technology, IA
Jacksonville State University, AL
James Madison University, VA
John Carroll University, OH
Juniata College, PA
Kean College of New Jersey, NJ
King's College, PA
Lander University, SC
Lawrence Technological University, MI
Limestone College, SC
Lincoln University, PA
Long Island U, Southampton College, NY
Longwood College, VA
Louisiana Tech University, LA
Lyndon State College, VT
Madonna University, MI
Malone College, OH
McNeese State University, LA

Mesa State College, CO
Minot State University, ND
Mississippi College, MS
Mississippi State University, MS
Missouri Western State College, MO
Montana State U–Billings, MT
Montana State U–Bozeman, MT
Mount Mary College, WI
Mount St. Clare College, IA
New Mexico State University, NM
North Carolina State University, NC
North Dakota State University, ND
Northeastern State University, OK
Northwestern Oklahoma State University,
  OK
The Ohio State University, OH
Ohio University, OH
Oklahoma State U, OK
Old Dominion University, VA
Ottawa University, KS
Pepperdine University, Malibu, CA
Peru State College, NE
Piedmont College, GA
Point Loma Nazarene College, CA
Reinhardt College, GA
The Richard Stockton College of New
  Jersey, NJ
Rowan University, NJ
St. Edward's University, TX
St. John Fisher College, NY
Saint Joseph's College, ME
Salisbury State University, MD
Sam Houston State University, TX
Seattle University, WA
Shepherd College, WV
Sierra Nevada College, NV
Sonoma State University, CA
South Dakota State University, SD
Southeastern Louisiana University, LA
Southeast Missouri State University, MO
Southern Methodist University, TX
Southwestern Adventist University, TX
Southwestern College, KS
State U of NY at New Paltz, NY
State U of NY at Oswego, NY
State U of NY College at Geneseo, NY
State U of NY College at Plattsburgh, NY
Stetson University, FL
Stevens Institute of Technology, NJ
Texas Woman's University, TX
The University of Akron, OH
U of Alaska Anchorage, AK
University of Arkansas at Little Rock, AR
University of California, San Diego, CA
University of Cincinnati, OH
University of Colorado at Boulder, CO
University of Dayton, OH
University of Delaware, DE
University of Denver, CO
University of Evansville, IN
University of Great Falls, MT
University of Houston, TX
University of Idaho, ID
University of Kansas, KS
University of Mary Hardin-Baylor, TX
University of Maryland Baltimore County,
  MD

Humanities (continued)

University of Massachusetts Amherst, MA
University of Michigan, Ann Arbor, MI
University of Minnesota, Twin Cities
  Campus, MN
University of Missouri–Rolla, MO
University of Missouri–St. Louis, MO
The University of Montana–Missoula, MT
University of Nebraska–Lincoln, NE
University of Nevada, Las Vegas, NV
University of Nevada, Reno, NV
University of North Carolina at Greensboro,
  NC
University of North Carolina at
  Wilmington, NC
University of Pittsburgh at Bradford, PA
University of Portland, OR
University of Puget Sound, WA
University of Rochester, NY
University of Sioux Falls, SD
University of Southern Indiana, IN
University of South Florida, FL
The University of Texas at Arlington, TX
The University of Texas at El Paso, TX
University of Toledo, OH
University of Utah, UT
University of Washington, WA
University of Wisconsin–River Falls, WI
University of Wisconsin–Stevens Point, WI
University of Wisconsin–Superior, WI
Vanderbilt University, TN
Warner Southern College, FL
Washington State University, WA
Washington University, MO
Western Michigan University, MI
Western Washington University, WA
West Texas A&M University, TX
West Virginia University, WV
Wheeling Jesuit University, WV
Xavier University of Louisiana, LA

INTERNATIONAL STUDIES

Alfred University, NY
American University, DC
Angelo State University, TX
Auburn University, AL
Austin College, TX
Baker University, KS
Barton College, NC
Baylor University, TX
Bloomsburg University of Pennsylvania, PA
Brigham Young University–Hawaii Campus,
  HI
Butler University, IN
California Polytechnic State U, San Luis
  Obispo, CA
California State University, Chico, CA
Central College, IA
Clarion University of Pennsylvania, PA
Clemson University, SC
Colorado Christian University, CO
Elizabethtown College, PA
Fort Hays State University, KS
Frostburg State University, MD
Georgia College and State University, GA
Guilford College, NC
Hampshire College, MA

High Point University, NC
Hillsdale College, MI
Idaho State University, ID
Illinois State University, IL
Indiana University of Pennsylvania, PA
Iowa State University of Science and
  Technology, IA
James Madison University, VA
Juniata College, PA
Kent State University, OH
Malone College, OH
Manchester College, IN
Mercer University, Macon, GA
Mississippi State University, MS
The Ohio State University, OH
Ohio University, OH
Oklahoma State U, OK
Ottawa University, KS
Pepperdine University, Malibu, CA
Pfeiffer University, NC
Quincy University, IL
Roanoke Bible College, NC
Robert Morris College, PA
Saginaw Valley State University, MI
St. Cloud State University, MN
Seattle University, WA
Sonoma State University, CA
South Dakota State University, SD
Southwest Texas State University, TX
State U of NY at Oswego, NY
State U of NY College at Plattsburgh, NY
Teikyo Post University, CT
Texas Tech University, TX
Thomas College, ME
United States International University, CA
The University of Akron, OH
University of Arkansas at Little Rock, AR
University of Colorado at Boulder, CO
University of Evansville, IN
University of Kansas, KS
University of Mary Hardin-Baylor, TX
The University of Memphis, TN
University of Michigan, Ann Arbor, MI
University of Michigan–Dearborn, MI
University of Minnesota, Twin Cities
  Campus, MN
University of Missouri–St. Louis, MO
The University of Montana–Missoula, MT
University of Nebraska–Lincoln, NE
University of Nevada, Las Vegas, NV
University of Nevada, Reno, NV
University of South Florida, FL
The University of Texas at Arlington, TX
The University of Texas at El Paso, TX
University of Tulsa, OK
University of Wisconsin–River Falls, WI
University of Wisconsin–Stevens Point, WI
Viterbo College, WI
Webster University, MO
Western Michigan University, MI
West Virginia University, WV

LIBRARY SCIENCE

Brigham Young University–Hawaii Campus,
  HI
California Polytechnic State U, San Luis
  Obispo, CA

Central Missouri State University, MO
Clarion University of Pennsylvania, PA
Fort Hays State University, KS
Illinois State University, IL
Iowa State University of Science and
  Technology, IA
Kent State University, OH
Mayville State University, ND
Mississippi State University, MS
Northeastern State University, OK
Northeast Louisiana University, LA
Northwestern Oklahoma State University,
  OK
Sam Houston State University, TX
University of Kansas, KS
University of Minnesota, Twin Cities
  Campus, MN
University of North Carolina at Greensboro,
  NC
University of Oklahoma, OK
University of South Florida, FL
Valley City State University, ND
Western Washington University, WA
West Virginia University, WV

MATHEMATICS

Abilene Christian University, TX
Adams State College, CO
Agnes Scott College, GA
Alabama State University, AL
Albertson College of Idaho, ID
Alfred University, NY
Allentown College of St. Francis de Sales,
  PA
American University, DC
Antioch College, OH
Arkansas State University, AR
Armstrong Atlantic State University, GA
Auburn University, AL
Augustana College, SD
Augusta State University, GA
Baker University, KS
Ball State University, IN
Barton College, NC
Baylor University, TX
Beaver College, PA
Bellevue University, NE
Bethel College, IN
Black Hills State University, SD
Bloomsburg University of Pennsylvania, PA
Boise State University, ID
Briar Cliff College, IA
Brigham Young University–Hawaii Campus,
  HI
Buena Vista University, IA
Butler University, IN
California Lutheran University, CA
California Polytechnic State U, San Luis
  Obispo, CA
California State Polytechnic University,
  Pomona, CA
California State University, Chico, CA
California State University, Fresno, CA
California State University, Fullerton, CA
California State University, San Bernardino,
  CA
California State University, Stanislaus, CA

Cameron University, OK
Carlow College, PA
Carthage College, WI
Centenary College of Louisiana, LA
Central College, IA
Central Missouri State University, MO
Cheyney University of Pennsylvania, PA
Clarion University of Pennsylvania, PA
Clarkson University, NY
Clearwater Christian College, FL
Clemson University, SC
Clinch Valley College of the U of Virginia, VA
College of New Rochelle, NY
The College of Wooster, OH
Columbia College, SC
Concordia College, NE
Cumberland College, KY
The Defiance College, OH
Delaware Valley College, PA
DePauw University, IN
Dordt College, IA
Drury College, MO
Duke University, NC
Eastern Mennonite University, VA
Eastern Michigan University, MI
Eastern New Mexico University, NM
Eastern Oregon University, OR
East Stroudsburg University of Pennsylvania, PA
Edinboro University of Pennsylvania, PA
Elizabethtown College, PA
Elmhurst College, IL
Elon College, NC
Fairmont State College, WV
Fort Hays State University, KS
Fort Lewis College, CO
Francis Marion University, SC
Franklin College of Indiana, IN
Friends University, KS
Frostburg State University, MD
Furman University, SC
Gannon University, PA
The George Washington University, DC
Georgian Court College, NJ
Georgia State University, GA
Greenville College, IL
Guilford College, NC
Gwynedd-Mercy College, PA
Hardin-Simmons University, TX
Heidelberg College, OH
High Point University, NC
Hillsdale College, MI
Humboldt State University, CA
Idaho State University, ID
Illinois Institute of Technology, IL
Illinois State University, IL
Indiana University of Pennsylvania, PA
Iowa State University of Science and Technology, IA
Jacksonville State University, AL
James Madison University, VA
Jersey City State College, NJ
Johnson State College, VT
Kalamazoo College, MI
Kennesaw State University, GA
Kent State University, OH

King's College, PA
Knox College, IL
LaGrange College, GA
Lander University, SC
Lawrence Technological University, MI
Limestone College, SC
Lincoln University, PA
Longwood College, VA
Louisiana State University and A&M College, LA
Malone College, OH
Manhattan College, NY
Mankato State University, MN
Mansfield University of Pennsylvania, PA
Marquette University, WI
Mayville State University, ND
McKendree College, IL
McNeese State University, LA
Meredith College, NC
Mesa State College, CO
Michigan Technological University, MI
Mills College, CA
Minot State University, ND
Mississippi College, MS
Mississippi State University, MS
Missouri Western State College, MO
Montana State U–Bozeman, MT
Montana Tech of The University of Montana, MT
Mount Mary College, WI
Mount St. Clare College, IA
Murray State University, KY
New Mexico State University, NM
Norfolk State University, VA
North Carolina State University, NC
Northeastern State University, OK
Northeast Louisiana University, LA
Northwestern Oklahoma State University, OK
Northwest Missouri State University, MO
The Ohio State University, OH
Ohio University, OH
Ohio Wesleyan University, OH
Oklahoma State U, OK
Old Dominion University, VA
Ottawa University, KS
Peru State College, NE
Piedmont College, GA
Pittsburg State University, KS
Point Loma Nazarene College, CA
Quincy University, IL
Reinhardt College, GA
The Richard Stockton College of New Jersey, NJ
Rochester Institute of Technology, NY
Rockford College, IL
Rollins College, FL
Rose-Hulman Institute of Technology, IN
Saginaw Valley State University, MI
St. Ambrose University, IA
St. Cloud State University, MN
St. John Fisher College, NY
St. John's University, NY
Saint Vincent College, PA
Salisbury State University, MD
Sam Houston State University, TX
Seattle University, WA

Seton Hill College, PA
Shaw University, NC
Shepherd College, WV
Siena Heights College, MI
Sonoma State University, CA
South Dakota School of Mines and Technology, SD
South Dakota State University, SD
Southeastern Louisiana University, LA
Southeast Missouri State University, MO
Southern Methodist University, TX
Southern Oregon University, OR
Southern Wesleyan University, SC
Southwest Missouri State University, MO
Southwest State University, MN
Spelman College, GA
State U of NY at New Paltz, NY
State U of NY at Oswego, NY
State U of NY College at Brockport, NY
State U of NY College at Geneseo, NY
State U of NY College at Plattsburgh, NY
Stephen F. Austin State University, TX
Stetson University, FL
Stevens Institute of Technology, NJ
Susquehanna University, PA
Teikyo Post University, CT
Tennessee Technological University, TN
Texas A&M University–Kingsville, TX
Texas Tech University, TX
Texas Woman's University, TX
Trinity Christian College, IL
Truman State University, MO
The University of Akron, OH
U of Alaska Anchorage, AK
University of Arkansas at Little Rock, AR
University of California, San Diego, CA
University of Central Oklahoma, OK
University of Cincinnati, OH
University of Colorado at Boulder, CO
University of Evansville, IN
University of Great Falls, MT
University of Idaho, ID
University of Kansas, KS
University of Mary Hardin-Baylor, TX
University of Massachusetts Amherst, MA
University of Michigan, Ann Arbor, MI
University of Minnesota, Twin Cities Campus, MN
University of Missouri–St. Louis, MO
The University of Montana–Missoula, MT
University of Nebraska at Omaha, NE
University of Nebraska–Lincoln, NE
University of Nevada, Las Vegas, NV
University of Nevada, Reno, NV
University of North Carolina at Charlotte, NC
University of North Carolina at Greensboro, NC
University of North Carolina at Wilmington, NC
University of Northern Colorado, CO
University of Northern Iowa, IA
University of Oklahoma, OK
University of Portland, OR
University of Puget Sound, WA
University of Rochester, NY
University of St. Thomas, MN

Mathematics (continued)

University of Sioux Falls, SD
University of South Dakota, SD
University of South Florida, FL
The University of Texas at Arlington, TX
The University of Texas at El Paso, TX
The University of Texas at San Antonio,
 TX
University of Toledo, OH
University of Tulsa, OK
University of Utah, UT
University of Washington, WA
University of Wisconsin–La Crosse, WI
University of Wisconsin–Oshkosh, WI
University of Wisconsin–Platteville, WI
University of Wisconsin–River Falls, WI
University of Wisconsin–Stevens Point, WI
University of Wisconsin–Superior, WI
Valley City State University, ND
Virginia Military Institute, VA
Virginia Polytechnic Institute and State U,
 VA
Wartburg College, IA
Washington State University, WA
Webster University, MO
Western Illinois University, IL
Western Michigan University, MI
Western State College of Colorado, CO
Western Washington University, WA
West Liberty State College, WV
Westminster College of Salt Lake City, UT
West Texas A&M University, TX
West Virginia State College, WV
West Virginia University, WV
Wheeling Jesuit University, WV
Wichita State University, KS
Winston-Salem State University, NC
Xavier University, OH
Xavier University of Louisiana, LA
York College, NE

MILITARY SCIENCE

Angelo State University, TX
Augusta State University, GA
Black Hills State University, SD
Boise State University, ID
California Polytechnic State U, San Luis
 Obispo, CA
California State University, San Bernardino,
 CA
Central Missouri State University, MO
Christopher Newport University, VA
The Citadel, The Military Coll of South
 Carolina, SC
Clarkson University, NY
Clemson University, SC
Cumberland College, KY
East Central University, OK
Eastern New Mexico University, NM
Edinboro University of Pennsylvania, PA
Fort Valley State University, GA
Illinois State University, IL
Jacksonville State University, AL
James Madison University, VA
Kent State University, OH
Louisiana State University and A&M
 College, LA

Mercer University, Macon, GA
Michigan State University, MI
Mississippi State University, MS
Missouri Western State College, MO
Montana State U–Bozeman, MT
Morehouse College, GA
New Mexico State University, NM
North Carolina Agricultural and Technical
 State U, NC
Northeast Louisiana University, LA
North Greenville College, SC
The Ohio State University, OH
Ohio University, OH
Oklahoma State U, OK
Pittsburg State University, KS
Providence College, RI
Radford University, VA
St. John's University, NY
Sam Houston State University, TX
Santa Clara University, CA
Seattle University, WA
Seton Hall University, NJ
South Dakota State University, SD
Southeast Missouri State University, MO
Stephen F. Austin State University, TX
Stetson University, FL
Tennessee Technological University, TN
Texas A&M University–Kingsville, TX
Truman State University, MO
The University of Akron, OH
University of Central Oklahoma, OK
University of Cincinnati, OH
University of Colorado at Boulder, CO
University of Houston, TX
University of Idaho, ID
University of Kansas, KS
University of Massachusetts Amherst, MA
The University of Memphis, TN
University of Michigan, Ann Arbor, MI
University of Minnesota, Twin Cities
 Campus, MN
University of Nevada, Reno, NV
University of Northern Colorado, CO
University of Oklahoma, OK
University of South Dakota, SD
University of South Florida, FL
The University of Texas at El Paso, TX
University of Toledo, OH
University of Wisconsin–Stevens Point, WI
Valdosta State University, GA
Virginia State University, VA
Western Michigan University, MI
West Virginia State College, WV
West Virginia University, WV

PHYSICAL SCIENCES

Abilene Christian University, TX
Agnes Scott College, GA
Albertson College of Idaho, ID
Alderson-Broaddus College, WV
Alfred University, NY
Allentown College of St. Francis de Sales,
 PA
Anderson College, SC
Angelo State University, TX
Antioch College, OH
Arkansas State University, AR

Auburn University, AL
Augustana College, SD
Augusta State University, GA
Austin College, TX
Baker University, KS
Barat College, IL
Bard College, NY
Barton College, NC
Baylor University, TX
Benedictine University, IL
Bethel College, IN
Black Hills State University, SD
Bloomsburg University of Pennsylvania, PA
Briar Cliff College, IA
Brigham Young University–Hawaii Campus,
 HI
Butler University, IN
California Lutheran University, CA
California Polytechnic State U, San Luis
 Obispo, CA
California State Polytechnic University,
 Pomona, CA
California State University, Bakersfield, CA
California State University, Chico, CA
California State University, Fresno, CA
California State University, Stanislaus, CA
Calvin College, MI
Carthage College, WI
Centenary College of Louisiana, LA
Central College, IA
Central Missouri State University, MO
Central State University, OH
Chatham College, PA
Chicago State University, IL
Clarion University of Pennsylvania, PA
Clarkson University, NY
Clemson University, SC
Clinch Valley College of the U of Virginia,
 VA
Coe College, IA
College of New Rochelle, NY
College of Santa Fe, NM
Coll of Staten Island of the City U of NY,
 NY
The College of Wooster, OH
The Colorado College, CO
Cumberland College, KY
Davidson College, NC
Davis & Elkins College, WV
The Defiance College, OH
Denison University, OH
DePauw University, IN
Doane College, NE
Dordt College, IA
Earlham College, IN
Eastern Connecticut State University, CT
Eastern Mennonite University, VA
Eastern Michigan University, MI
Eastern New Mexico University, NM
Eastern Oregon University, OR
Eastern Washington University, WA
East Texas Baptist University, TX
Edinboro University of Pennsylvania, PA
Elizabethtown College, PA
Elmhurst College, IL
Elon College, NC
Fairmont State College, WV

Florida Atlantic University, FL
Florida Institute of Technology, FL
Fort Hays State University, KS
Fort Lewis College, CO
Framingham State College, MA
Friends University, KS
Frostburg State University, MD
Georgia State University, GA
Goucher College, MD
Grove City College, PA
Heidelberg College, OH
Heritage College, WA
High Point University, NC
Hillsdale College, MI
Hiram College, OH
Hope College, MI
Idaho State University, ID
Illinois Institute of Technology, IL
Illinois State University, IL
Indiana University of Pennsylvania, PA
Iowa State University of Science and
   Technology, IA
Jacksonville State University, AL
Jacksonville University, FL
James Madison University, VA
John Carroll University, OH
Juniata College, PA
Kalamazoo College, MI
Kennesaw State University, GA
Kent State University, OH
King's College, PA
LaGrange College, GA
Lander University, SC
Lawrence Technological University, MI
Lincoln University, MO
Lincoln University, PA
Long Island U, Southampton College, NY
Louisiana State University and A&M
   College, LA
Loyola University Chicago, IL
MacMurray College, IL
Malone College, OH
Mankato State University, MN
Mansfield University of Pennsylvania, PA
Marygrove College, MI
The Master's College and Seminary, CA
Mayville State University, ND
McKendree College, IL
McNeese State University, LA
Mercer University, Macon, GA
Mesa State College, CO
Michigan Technological University, MI
Mills College, CA
Mississippi College, MS
Mississippi State University, MS
Missouri Western State College, MO
Montana State U–Bozeman, MT
Montana Tech of The University of
   Montana, MT
Moravian College, PA
Morehead State University, KY
Mount Mary College, WI
Mount St. Clare College, IA
Murray State University, KY
New Mexico Inst of Mining and
   Technology, NM
New Mexico State University, NM

North Carolina Central University, NC
North Carolina State University, NC
Northeastern State University, OK
Northeast Louisiana University, LA
Northwest Missouri State University, MO
The Ohio State University, OH
Ohio University, OH
Oklahoma State U, OK
Old Dominion University, VA
Ottawa University, KS
Peru State College, NE
Pittsburg State University, KS
Purdue University, West Lafayette, IN
Regis University, CO
The Richard Stockton College of New
   Jersey, NJ
Rochester Institute of Technology, NY
Rockford College, IL
Rollins College, FL
Rose-Hulman Institute of Technology, IN
Rowan University, NJ
St. Ambrose University, IA
St. Cloud State University, MN
St. Edward's University, TX
Saint Francis College, IN
St. John Fisher College, NY
Saint Vincent College, PA
Salisbury State University, MD
Sam Houston State University, TX
Savannah State University, GA
Seton Hall University, NJ
Seton Hill College, PA
Shepherd College, WV
Siena Heights College, MI
Sonoma State University, CA
South Dakota School of Mines and
   Technology, SD
South Dakota State University, SD
Southeastern Louisiana University, LA
Southeast Missouri State University, MO
Southern Methodist University, TX
Southern Oregon University, OR
Southwest State University, MN
Spelman College, GA
State U of NY at Binghamton, NY
State U of NY at New Paltz, NY
State U of NY at Oswego, NY
State U of NY College at Brockport, NY
State U of NY College at Fredonia, NY
State U of NY College at Geneseo, NY
State U of NY College at Old Westbury,
   NY
State U of NY College at Plattsburgh, NY
Stephen F. Austin State University, TX
Stetson University, FL
Stevens Institute of Technology, NJ
Texas A&M University, College Station,
   TX
Texas A&M University–Kingsville, TX
Texas Tech University, TX
Texas Woman's University, TX
Truman State University, MO
Universidad Metropolitana, PR
The University of Akron, OH
The University of Alabama in Huntsville,
   AL
University of Arkansas at Little Rock, AR

University of Central Oklahoma, OK
University of Cincinnati, OH
University of Colorado at Boulder, CO
University of Delaware, DE
University of Evansville, IN
The University of Findlay, OH
University of Houston, TX
University of Idaho, ID
University of Kansas, KS
University of Maine, Orono, ME
University of Mary Hardin-Baylor, TX
University of Massachusetts Amherst, MA
University of Michigan, Ann Arbor, MI
University of Michigan–Dearborn, MI
University of Minnesota, Twin Cities
   Campus, MN
The University of Montana–Missoula, MT
University of Montevallo, AL
University of Nebraska at Omaha, NE
University of Nebraska–Lincoln, NE
University of Nevada, Las Vegas, NV
University of Nevada, Reno, NV
University of North Carolina at Greensboro,
   NC
University of North Carolina at Pembroke,
   NC
University of North Carolina at
   Wilmington, NC
University of Northern Colorado, CO
University of Northern Iowa, IA
University of Oklahoma, OK
University of Portland, OR
University of Puget Sound, WA
University of Rochester, NY
University of St. Thomas, MN
University of Sioux Falls, SD
University of Southern Indiana, IN
University of South Florida, FL
The University of Texas at Arlington, TX
The University of Texas at El Paso, TX
University of Toledo, OH
University of Utah, UT
University of Washington, WA
University of Wisconsin–La Crosse, WI
University of Wisconsin–Oshkosh, WI
University of Wisconsin–River Falls, WI
University of Wisconsin–Stevens Point, WI
University of Wisconsin–Superior, WI
Valley City State University, ND
Valparaiso University, IN
Wartburg College, IA
Washington College, MD
Washington State University, WA
Washington University, MO
Western Illinois University, IL
Western Kentucky University, KY
Western Washington University, WA
West Liberty State College, WV
Westminster College of Salt Lake City, UT
West Virginia University, WV
Wheeling Jesuit University, WV
Wilkes University, PA
Wilmington College, OH
Wright State University, OH
Xavier University, OH
Xavier University of Louisiana, LA

Physical Sciences (continued)

PREMEDICINE
Adams State College, CO
Albertson College of Idaho, ID
Alfred University, NY
Allentown College of St. Francis de Sales, PA
Angelo State University, TX
Arkansas State University, AR
Auburn University, AL
Austin College, TX
Baylor University, TX
Birmingham-Southern College, AL
Boise State University, ID
Butler University, IN
California State University, Fresno, CA
Calvin College, MI
Carthage College, WI
Cedar Crest College, PA
Centenary College of Louisiana, LA
Central Missouri State University, MO
Clarion University of Pennsylvania, PA
Clearwater Christian College, FL
Clemson University, SC
Clinch Valley College of the U of Virginia, VA
Coe College, IA
Cumberland College, KY
The Defiance College, OH
Delaware Valley College, PA
Dordt College, IA
Drury College, MO
Eastern Mennonite University, VA
Eastern New Mexico University, NM
Edinboro University of Pennsylvania, PA
Elon College, NC
Fort Hays State University, KS
Fort Valley State University, GA
Francis Marion University, SC
Gwynedd-Mercy College, PA
High Point University, NC
Hillsdale College, MI
Idaho State University, ID
Illinois Institute of Technology, IL
Illinois State University, IL
Indiana University of Pennsylvania, PA
Iowa State University of Science and Technology, IA
James Madison University, VA
Kennesaw State University, GA
King's College, PA
Louisiana State University and A&M College, LA
Louisiana State University in Shreveport, LA
Louisiana Tech University, LA
Malone College, OH
McNeese State University, LA
Mississippi State University, MS
Mount St. Clare College, IA
Murray State University, KY
Northeastern State University, OK
Northern Michigan University, MI
Northwestern Oklahoma State University, OK
The Ohio State University, OH
Ohio University, OH

Oklahoma State U, OK
Ottawa University, KS
Peru State College, NE
Piedmont College, GA
Providence College, RI
Rochester Institute of Technology, NY
Rockford College, IL
St. Ambrose University, IA
Salisbury State University, MD
Seton Hall University, NJ
Shepherd College, WV
Siena College, NY
Sonoma State University, CA
South Dakota State University, SD
Southwestern Adventist University, TX
Southwest Missouri State University, MO
State U of NY at New Paltz, NY
State U of NY at Oswego, NY
State U of NY College at Geneseo, NY
State U of NY College at Plattsburgh, NY
Stephen F. Austin State University, TX
Stetson University, FL
Stevens Institute of Technology, NJ
Sweet Briar College, VA
Texas Tech University, TX
Texas Woman's University, TX
Truman State University, MO
The University of Akron, OH
University of California, Riverside, CA
University of California, San Diego, CA
University of Cincinnati, OH
University of Colorado at Boulder, CO
University of Denver, CO
University of Evansville, IN
University of Idaho, ID
University of Kansas, KS
University of Mary Hardin-Baylor, TX
University of Massachusetts Amherst, MA
The University of Memphis, TN
University of Michigan, Ann Arbor, MI
University of Minnesota, Twin Cities Campus, MN
The University of Montana–Missoula, MT
University of Nebraska at Omaha, NE
University of Nebraska–Lincoln, NE
University of Nevada, Las Vegas, NV
University of Nevada, Reno, NV
University of North Carolina at Greensboro, NC
University of Portland, OR
University of Sioux Falls, SD
University of South Dakota, SD
University of Southern Indiana, IN
University of South Florida, FL
University of Toledo, OH
University of Tulsa, OK
University of Wisconsin–Parkside, WI
University of Wisconsin–River Falls, WI
University of Wisconsin–Stevens Point, WI
Virginia Military Institute, VA
Virginia State University, VA
Voorhees College, SC
Warner Pacific College, OR
Western Washington University, WA
West Virginia University, WV
Wheeling Jesuit University, WV
Wichita State University, KS

Xavier University of Louisiana, LA

RELIGION/BIBLICAL STUDIES
Abilene Christian University, TX
Albertson College of Idaho, ID
Allentown College of St. Francis de Sales, PA
Anderson College, SC
Augustana College, SD
Austin College, TX
Azusa Pacific University, CA
Baker University, KS
Baptist Bible College of Pennsylvania, PA
Barton College, NC
Baylor University, TX
Belhaven College, MS
Berry College, GA
Bethel College, IN
Bethel College, TN
Bloomsburg University of Pennsylvania, PA
Boise Bible College, ID
Brewton-Parker College, GA
Briar Cliff College, IA
Brigham Young University–Hawaii Campus, HI
Butler University, IN
California Baptist College, CA
California Lutheran University, CA
Calvary Bible College and Theological Seminary, MO
Calvin College, MI
Centenary College of Louisiana, LA
Central Christian College of the Bible, MO
Central College, IA
Circleville Bible College, OH
Clear Creek Baptist Bible College, KY
Clearwater Christian College, FL
College of New Rochelle, NY
Columbia College, SC
Conception Seminary College, MO
Concordia College, AL
Concordia College, St. Paul, MN
Concordia College, NE
Concordia College, NY
Cumberland College, KY
Davis & Elkins College, WV
The Defiance College, OH
Dordt College, IA
Eastern Mennonite University, VA
Eastern Michigan University, MI
Eastern New Mexico University, NM
East Texas Baptist University, TX
Elizabethtown College, PA
Elmhurst College, IL
Eugene Bible College, OR
Eureka College, IL
Faulkner University, AL
Florida Southern College, FL
Friends University, KS
Gardner-Webb University, NC
George Fox University, OR
Great Lakes Christian College, MI
Greenville College, IL
Hampden-Sydney College, VA
Hardin-Simmons University, TX
High Point University, NC
Hillsdale College, MI

Hiram College, OH
Houston Baptist University, TX
Idaho State University, ID
James Madison University, VA
John Wesley College, NC
Kentucky Christian College, KY
King's College, PA
Limestone College, SC
Louisiana College, LA
MacMurray College, IL
Malone College, OH
Manchester College, IN
Manhattan Christian College, KS
Mars Hill College, NC
The Master's College and Seminary, CA
McKendree College, IL
McMurry University, TX
Mercer University, Macon, GA
Michigan Christian College, MI
Milligan College, TN
Minnesota Bible College, MN
Mississippi College, MS
Mississippi State University, MS
Missouri Baptist College, MO
Multnomah Bible College and Biblical
  Seminary, OR
Nazarene Indian Bible College, NM
Nebraska Christian College, NE
North Greenville College, SC
Northwest College of the Assemblies of
  God, WA
Oklahoma Baptist University, OK
Oklahoma Christian U of Science and Arts,
  OK
Oklahoma City University, OK
Ottawa University, KS
Ouachita Baptist University, AR
Ozark Christian College, MO
Pepperdine University, Malibu, CA
Piedmont College, GA
Point Loma Nazarene College, CA
Presentation College, SD
Puget Sound Christian College, WA
Quincy University, IL
Roanoke Bible College, NC
St. Ambrose University, IA
Seattle University, WA
Seton Hill College, PA
Southeastern Louisiana University, LA
Southern Wesleyan University, SC
Southwestern Adventist University, TX
Spring Arbor College, MI
Stetson University, FL
Tennessee Wesleyan College, TN
Texas Lutheran University, TX
University of Colorado at Boulder, CO
University of Evansville, IN
University of Great Falls, MT
University of Kansas, KS
University of Mary Hardin-Baylor, TX
University of Minnesota, Twin Cities
  Campus, MN
University of Mobile, AL
University of North Carolina at Greensboro,
  NC
University of Portland, OR
University of Sioux Falls, SD

University of South Florida, FL
University of Tulsa, OK
West Virginia University, WV
Wheeling Jesuit University, WV
York College, NE

SOCIAL SCIENCES

Abilene Christian University, TX
Adams State College, CO
Albany State University, GA
Alderson-Broaddus College, WV
Alfred University, NY
Allentown College of St. Francis de Sales,
  PA
American University, DC
Arkansas State University, AR
Auburn University, AL
Augustana College, SD
Austin College, TX
Baker University, KS
Ball State University, IN
Barton College, NC
Baylor University, TX
Bellevue University, NE
Bethel College, IN
Black Hills State University, SD
Bloomsburg University of Pennsylvania, PA
Boise State University, ID
Briar Cliff College, IA
Brigham Young University–Hawaii Campus,
  HI
Butler University, IN
California Lutheran University, CA
California Polytechnic State U, San Luis
  Obispo, CA
California State Polytechnic University,
  Pomona, CA
California State University, Bakersfield, CA
California State University, Chico, CA
California State University, Fresno, CA
California State University, Fullerton, CA
California State University, Northridge, CA
California State University, Stanislaus, CA
Calvin College, MI
Carlow College, PA
Centenary College of Louisiana, LA
Central Missouri State University, MO
Chapman University, CA
Chatham College, PA
Clarion University of Pennsylvania, PA
Clemson University, SC
Clinch Valley College of the U of Virginia,
  VA
College of New Rochelle, NY
College of Santa Fe, NM
Coll of Staten Island of the City U of NY,
  NY
The College of West Virginia, WV
The College of Wooster, OH
Concordia College, NE
Concordia College, NY
Cumberland College, KY
The Defiance College, OH
Delaware Valley College, PA
Doane College, NE
Dordt College, IA
Drury College, MO

Eastern Mennonite University, VA
Eastern Michigan University, MI
Eastern New Mexico University, NM
Eastern Washington University, WA
Edinboro University of Pennsylvania, PA
Elizabethtown College, PA
Elmhurst College, IL
Endicott College, MA
Fairmont State College, WV
Florida Atlantic University, FL
Florida Southern College, FL
Fort Hays State University, KS
Fort Lewis College, CO
Fort Valley State University, GA
Francis Marion University, SC
Friends University, KS
Frostburg State University, MD
Georgia State University, GA
Goucher College, MD
Grambling State University, LA
Gwynedd-Mercy College, PA
Hampshire College, MA
Heritage College, WA
Hiram College, OH
Idaho State University, ID
Illinois Institute of Technology, IL
Illinois State University, IL
Indiana University of Pennsylvania, PA
Iowa State University of Science and
  Technology, IA
Jacksonville State University, AL
James Madison University, VA
Juniata College, PA
Kalamazoo College, MI
Kennesaw State University, GA
Kent State University, OH
King's College, PA
LaGrange College, GA
Limestone College, SC
Long Island U, Southampton College, NY
MacMurray College, IL
Malone College, OH
Marygrove College, MI
McNeese State University, LA
Mesa State College, CO
Michigan State University, MI
Michigan Technological University, MI
Minot State University, ND
Mississippi State University, MS
Missouri Western State College, MO
Montana State U–Bozeman, MT
Mount Mary College, WI
Mount St. Clare College, IA
Murray State University, KY
New Mexico State University, NM
North Carolina Central University, NC
North Carolina State University, NC
North Dakota State University, ND
Northeastern State University, OK
Northeast Louisiana University, LA
Northwestern Oklahoma State University,
  OK
Northwest Missouri State University, MO
The Ohio State University, OH
Ohio University, OH
Oklahoma State U, OK
Ottawa University, KS

Social Sciences (continued)

Pepperdine University, Malibu, CA
Peru State College, NE
Pittsburg State University, KS
Point Loma Nazarene College, CA
Quincy University, IL
Reinhardt College, GA
The Richard Stockton College of New Jersey, NJ
Rochester Institute of Technology, NY
Rowan University, NJ
Saginaw Valley State University, MI
St. Ambrose University, IA
St. Cloud State University, MN
St. Edward's University, TX
Saint Joseph's College, ME
Saint Vincent College, PA
Salisbury State University, MD
Sam Houston State University, TX
Savannah State University, GA
Seattle University, WA
Shepherd College, WV
Siena Heights College, MI
Slippery Rock University of Pennsylvania, PA
Sonoma State University, CA
South Dakota State University, SD
Southeastern Louisiana University, LA
Southeast Missouri State University, MO
Southern Oregon University, OR
Southern Wesleyan University, SC
Southwest Missouri State University, MO
State U of NY at Oswego, NY
State U of NY College at Geneseo, NY
State U of NY College at Plattsburgh, NY
Stetson University, FL
Taylor University, Fort Wayne Campus, IN
Texas A&M University–Kingsville, TX
Texas Tech University, TX
Texas Woman's University, TX
Truman State University, MO
United States International University, CA
The University of Akron, OH
U of Alaska Anchorage, AK
University of Arkansas at Little Rock, AR
University of California, San Diego, CA
University of Central Oklahoma, OK
University of Cincinnati, OH
University of Colorado at Boulder, CO
University of Evansville, IN
University of Great Falls, MT
University of Hawaii at Hilo, HI
University of Houston, TX
University of Idaho, ID
University of Kansas, KS
University of Mary Hardin-Baylor, TX
University of Massachusetts Amherst, MA
The University of Memphis, TN
University of Michigan, Ann Arbor, MI
University of Minnesota, Twin Cities Campus, MN
The University of Montana–Missoula, MT
University of Nebraska at Omaha, NE
University of Nebraska–Lincoln, NE
University of Nevada, Las Vegas, NV
University of Nevada, Reno, NV

University of North Carolina at Greensboro, NC
University of North Carolina at Wilmington, NC
University of Northern Colorado, CO
University of Northern Iowa, IA
University of Oklahoma, OK
University of Pittsburgh at Bradford, PA
University of Portland, OR
University of Rochester, NY
University of Sioux Falls, SD
University of South Dakota, SD
University of Southern Indiana, IN
University of South Florida, FL
The University of Tampa, FL
University of Toledo, OH
University of Tulsa, OK
University of Utah, UT
University of Washington, WA
University of Wisconsin–River Falls, WI
University of Wisconsin–Stevens Point, WI
University of Wisconsin–Superior, WI
Valdosta State University, GA
Valley City State University, ND
Virginia State University, VA
Washington University, MO
Webster University, MO
West Chester University of Pennsylvania, PA
Western Illinois University, IL
Western Michigan University, MI
Western State College of Colorado, CO
Western Washington University, WA
West Texas A&M University, TX
West Virginia University, WV
Wheeling Jesuit University, WV
Xavier University, OH
Xavier University of Louisiana, LA

CREATIVE ARTS/ PERFORMANCE

APPLIED ART AND DESIGN

The American College, CA
Anderson College, SC
Art Academy of Cincinnati, OH
Art Institute of Boston, MA
Art Institute of Southern California, CA
Barry University, FL
Bowie State University, MD
Brenau University, GA
Brigham Young University, UT
California College of Arts and Crafts, CA
California Institute of the Arts, CA
California Polytechnic State U, San Luis Obispo, CA
California State University, Chico, CA
California State University, Long Beach, CA
Cazenovia College, NY
Ctr for Creative Studies—Coll of Art and Design, MI
Claflin College, SC
College of New Rochelle, NY
Columbia College, MO
Columbia College, SC

Dana College, NE
East Carolina University, NC
Eastern Michigan University, MI
Eastern New Mexico University, NM
The Evergreen State College, WA
Friends University, KS
Georgia State University, GA
Graceland College, IA
Huntingdon College, AL
Illinois State University, IL
Indiana University of Pennsylvania, PA
International Acad of Merchandising & Design, Inc, FL
Kendall College of Art and Design, MI
Kutztown University of Pennsylvania, PA
La Roche College, PA
Louisiana State University and A&M College, LA
Mankato State University, MN
Maryville University of Saint Louis, MO
Meredith College, NC
Milwaukee Institute of Art and Design, WI
Minneapolis College of Art and Design, MN
Mississippi College, MS
Mississippi State University, MS
Montserrat College of Art, MA
Mount Mary College, WI
Murray State University, KY
New Mexico State University, NM
Newschool of Architecture, CA
North Carolina School of the Arts, NC
Northeastern Illinois University, IL
Northeastern State University, OK
Northern Michigan University, MI
Northwest College of Art, WA
Ohio University, OH
Ohio University–Chillicothe, OH
Otis College of Art and Design, CA
Pratt Institute, NY
Radford University, VA
Rhode Island School of Design, RI
The Richard Stockton College of New Jersey, NJ
Ringling School of Art and Design, FL
Rochester Institute of Technology, NY
Rocky Mountain College of Art & Design, CO
St. Cloud State University, MN
School of Visual Arts, NY
Shepherd College, WV
Sonoma State University, CA
Southwest Texas State University, TX
Spalding University, KY
State U of NY College at Fredonia, NY
State U of NY College at Geneseo, NY
Stephen F. Austin State University, TX
Stetson University, FL
Texas Tech University, TX
Texas Woman's University, TX
The University of Akron, OH
University of Central Oklahoma, OK
University of Cincinnati, OH
University of Idaho, ID
University of Kansas, KS
University of Nebraska at Kearney, NE
University of Nevada, Las Vegas, NV

University of Nevada, Reno, NV
University of Northern Iowa, IA
University of Southern Colorado, CO
University of South Florida, FL
The University of Texas at El Paso, TX
University of the Arts, PA
University of West Florida, FL
University of Wisconsin–Stevens Point, WI
Virginia Commonwealth University, VA
Virginia Intermont College, VA
Western Illinois University, IL
Western Michigan University, MI
Wichita State University, KS
William Woods University, MO

ART/FINE ARTS

Abilene Christian University, TX
Academy of Art College, CA
Adams State College, CO
Adelphi University, NY
Adrian College, MI
Alabama State University, AL
Albertson College of Idaho, ID
Albion College, MI
Alderson-Broaddus College, WV
Alfred University, NY
Alma College, MI
Alverno College, WI
Anderson College, SC
Arkansas State University, AR
Armstrong Atlantic State University, GA
Art Academy of Cincinnati, OH
Art Institute of Boston, MA
Art Institute of Southern California, CA
Ashland University, OH
Atlanta College of Art, GA
Augustana College, IL
Augustana College, SD
Augusta State University, GA
Austin College, TX
Austin Peay State University, TN
Baker University, KS
Ball State University, IN
Barat College, IL
Barry University, FL
Barton College, NC
Baylor University, TX
Beaver College, PA
Belhaven College, MS
Bellarmine College, KY
Bellevue University, NE
Benedictine College, KS
Bethel College, IN
Bethel College, KS
Bethel College, MN
Biola University, CA
Birmingham-Southern College, AL
Bluefield College, VA
Bluffton College, OH
Boise State University, ID
Boston University, MA
Bowie State University, MD
Bowling Green State University, OH
Bradley University, IL
Brenau University, GA
Brescia College, KY
Briar Cliff College, IA

Brigham Young University, UT
Brigham Young University–Hawaii Campus, HI
Buena Vista University, IA
Butler University, IN
Caldwell College, NJ
California College of Arts and Crafts, CA
California Institute of the Arts, CA
California Lutheran University, CA
California Polytechnic State U, San Luis Obispo, CA
California State University, Bakersfield, CA
California State University, Chico, CA
California State University, Fullerton, CA
California State University, Stanislaus, CA
Calvin College, MI
Cameron University, OK
Campbell University, NC
Cardinal Stritch University, WI
Carson-Newman College, TN
Carthage College, WI
Case Western Reserve University, OH
Cazenovia College, NY
Cedar Crest College, PA
Centenary College of Louisiana, LA
Ctr for Creative Studies—Coll of Art and Design, MI
Central Bible College, MO
Central College, IA
Central Missouri State University, MO
Chadron State College, NE
Chapman University, CA
Charleston Southern University, SC
Chicago State University, IL
Christopher Newport University, VA
Claflin College, SC
Clarion University of Pennsylvania, PA
Clarke College, IA
Cleveland Institute of Art, OH
Cleveland State University, OH
Coastal Carolina University, SC
Coe College, IA
Coker College, SC
Colby-Sawyer College, NH
College of Charleston, SC
College of Mount St. Joseph, OH
College of New Rochelle, NY
College of Notre Dame of Maryland, MD
College of Saint Benedict, MN
College of Saint Elizabeth, NJ
College of Santa Fe, NM
Colorado Christian University, CO
Colorado State University, CO
Columbia College, SC
Columbus College of Art and Design, OH
Columbus State University, GA
Concord College, WV
Concordia College, MI
Concordia College, NE
The Corcoran School of Art, DC
Cornell College, IA
Cornish College of the Arts, WA
Culver-Stockton College, MO
Cumberland College, KY
Cumberland University, TN
Dakota Wesleyan University, SD
Dana College, NE

David Lipscomb University, TN
Davidson College, NC
Davis & Elkins College, WV
Delta State University, MS
DePaul University, IL
DePauw University, IN
Doane College, NE
Drake University, IA
Drury College, MO
East Carolina University, NC
Eastern Mennonite University, VA
Eastern Michigan University, MI
Eastern New Mexico University, NM
Eckerd College, FL
Edgewood College, WI
Edinboro University of Pennsylvania, PA
Elon College, NC
Emporia State University, KS
Escuela de Artes Plasticas de Puerto Rico, PR
Eureka College, IL
The Evergreen State College, WA
Fairmont State College, WV
Flagler College, FL
Florida Agricultural and Mechanical University, FL
Florida Southern College, FL
Fontbonne College, MO
Fort Lewis College, CO
Francis Marion University, SC
Freed-Hardeman University, TN
Friends University, KS
Frostburg State University, MD
Georgetown College, KY
Georgian Court College, NJ
Georgia Southwestern State University, GA
Georgia State University, GA
Goucher College, MD
Grace College, IN
Grand Valley State University, MI
Grand View College, IA
Green Mountain College, VT
Greensboro College, NC
Greenville College, IL
Guilford College, NC
Hannibal-LaGrange College, MO
Hardin-Simmons University, TX
Hastings College, NE
Hendrix College, AR
Hillsdale College, MI
Hobart and William Smith Colleges, NY
Hofstra University, NY
Holy Names College, CA
Houghton College, NY
Howard Payne University, TX
Howard University, DC
Huntington College, IN
Idaho State University, ID
Illinois College, IL
Illinois State University, IL
Illinois Wesleyan University, IL
Indiana State University, IN
Indiana University of Pennsylvania, PA
Indiana U–Purdue U Fort Wayne, IN
Indiana Wesleyan University, IN
Iowa Wesleyan College, IA
Jacksonville State University, AL

Art/Fine Arts (continued)

Jacksonville University, FL
James Madison University, VA
Jersey City State College, NJ
Johnson State College, VT
Judson College, IL
Kalamazoo College, MI
Kansas City Art Institute, MO
Kansas State University, KS
Keene State College, NH
Kendall College of Art and Design, MI
Kennesaw State University, GA
Kent State University, OH
Kentucky Wesleyan College, KY
Knox College, IL
LaGrange College, GA
Lake Erie College, OH
Lake Forest College, IL
Lander University, SC
Limestone College, SC
Lincoln University, MO
Lindsey Wilson College, KY
Long Island U, Brooklyn Campus, NY
Long Island U, C.W. Post Campus, NY
Long Island U, Southampton College, NY
Longwood College, VA
Louisiana State University and A&M College, LA
Lycoming College, PA
Lyme Academy of Fine Arts, CT
MacMurray College, IL
Maine College of Art, ME
Manchester College, IN
Mankato State University, MN
Mansfield University of Pennsylvania, PA
Marietta College, OH
Martin Methodist College, TN
Maryland Institute, College of Art, MD
Marymount College, NY
Marymount Manhattan College, NY
Maryville College, TN
Maryville University of Saint Louis, MO
Mary Washington College, VA
Marywood University, PA
McMurry University, TX
McNeese State University, LA
Memphis College of Art, TN
Mercyhurst College, PA
Meredith College, NC
Merrimack College, MA
Mesa State College, CO
Messiah College, PA
Miami University, OH
Midland Lutheran College, NE
Midway College, KY
Millersville University of Pennsylvania, PA
Milligan College, TN
Millikin University, IL
Millsaps College, MS
Milwaukee Institute of Art and Design, WI
Minnesota Bible College, MN
Mississippi College, MS
Mississippi State University, MS
Mississippi University for Women, MS
Mississippi Valley State University, MS
Missouri Southern State College, MO
Molloy College, NY

Monmouth College, IL
Montana State U–Bozeman, MT
Montana State U–Northern, MT
Montserrat College of Art, MA
Moore College of Art and Design, PA
Moorhead State University, MN
Morehead State University, KY
Morningside College, IA
Mount Mary College, WI
Mount Mercy College, IA
Mount Olive College, NC
Mount Union College, OH
Murray State University, KY
Muskingum College, OH
Nazareth College of Rochester, NY
Nebraska Wesleyan University, NE
New England College, NH
New Mexico Highlands University, NM
New Mexico State University, NM
North Central Bible College, MN
North Central College, IL
North Dakota State University, ND
Northeastern Illinois University, IL
Northeastern State University, OK
Northeast Louisiana University, LA
Northern Arizona University, AZ
Northern Illinois University, IL
Northern Kentucky University, KY
Northern State University, SD
North Greenville College, SC
North Park University, IL
Northwest College of Art, WA
Northwest College of the Assemblies of God, WA
Northwestern College, IA
Northwest Missouri State University, MO
Oakland City University, IN
Ohio Northern University, OH
Ohio University, OH
Ohio University–Chillicothe, OH
Ohio University–Lancaster, OH
Ohio Wesleyan University, OH
Oklahoma Baptist University, OK
Oklahoma Christian U of Science and Arts, OK
Old Dominion University, VA
Olivet Nazarene University, IL
Oral Roberts University, OK
Otis College of Art and Design, CA
Ottawa University, KS
Otterbein College, OH
Pacific Northwest College of Art, OR
Park College, MO
Parsons Sch of Design, New Sch for Social Research, NY
Pepperdine University, Malibu, CA
Peru State College, NE
Piedmont College, GA
Point Loma Nazarene College, CA
Portland State University, OR
Prairie View A&M University, TX
Purchase College, State U of NY, NY
Queens College, NC
Quincy University, IL
Radford University, VA
Reinhardt College, GA
Rhode Island College, RI

Rhode Island School of Design, RI
Rhodes College, TN
The Richard Stockton College of New Jersey, NJ
Rider University, NJ
Ringling School of Art and Design, FL
Roanoke College, VA
Roberts Wesleyan College, NY
Rochester Institute of Technology, NY
Rocky Mountain College, MT
Rocky Mountain College of Art & Design, CO
Rollins College, FL
Rosemont College, PA
Rowan University, NJ
St. Ambrose University, IA
St. Andrews Presbyterian College, NC
St. Cloud State University, MN
Saint Francis College, IN
Saint Francis College, PA
Saint John's University, MN
St. John's University, NY
Saint Louis University, MO
Saint Mary College, KS
Saint Mary-of-the-Woods College, IN
Saint Mary's College, IN
Saint Michael's College, VT
St. Norbert College, WI
Sam Houston State University, TX
San Francisco Art Institute, CA
Savannah College of Art and Design, GA
School of the Art Institute of Chicago, IL
School of Visual Arts, NY
Seattle Pacific University, WA
Seton Hall University, NJ
Seton Hill College, PA
Shepherd College, WV
Shimer College, IL
Shorter College, GA
Siena Heights College, MI
Sierra Nevada College, NV
Simpson College, IA
Sinte Gleska University, SD
Slippery Rock University of Pennsylvania, PA
Sonoma State University, CA
South Dakota State University, SD
Southeastern Oklahoma State University, OK
Southern Adventist University, TN
Southern Arkansas University–Magnolia, AR
Southern Illinois University at Edwardsville, IL
Southern Methodist University, TX
Southern Oregon University, OR
Southwestern Oklahoma State University, OK
Southwest Missouri State University, MO
Spalding University, KY
Spring Arbor College, MI
State U of NY at New Paltz, NY
State U of NY at Oswego, NY
State U of NY College at Brockport, NY
State U of NY College at Geneseo, NY
State U of NY College at Plattsburgh, NY
Stephen F. Austin State University, TX

Stetson University, FL
Sul Ross State University, TX
Syracuse University, NY
Texas A&M University–Commerce, TX
Texas Christian University, TX
Texas Tech University, TX
Texas Wesleyan University, TX
Texas Woman's University, TX
Thomas More College, KY
Towson University, MD
Transylvania University, KY
Trinity Bible College, ND
Truman State University, MO
The University of Akron, OH
The University of Alabama at Birmingham, AL
U of Alaska Anchorage, AK
University of Arkansas at Little Rock, AR
University of Arkansas at Pine Bluff, AR
University of California, Riverside, CA
University of Central Oklahoma, OK
University of Cincinnati, OH
University of Colorado at Boulder, CO
University of Connecticut, Storrs, CT
University of Dallas, TX
University of Dayton, OH
University of Delaware, DE
University of Denver, CO
University of Evansville, IN
University of Guam, GU
University of Hartford, CT
University of Hawaii at Hilo, HI
University of Houston, TX
University of Idaho, ID
University of Illinois at Chicago, IL
University of Indianapolis, IN
University of Kansas, KS
University of Maine, Orono, ME
University of Maine at Presque Isle, ME
University of Mary Hardin-Baylor, TX
University of Maryland Baltimore County, MD
University of Maryland College Park, MD
University of Maryland Eastern Shore, MD
University of Massachusetts Amherst, MA
The University of Memphis, TN
University of Minnesota, Duluth, MN
University of Mississippi, MS
University of Missouri–St. Louis, MO
University of Mobile, AL
The University of Montana–Missoula, MT
University of Montevallo, AL
University of Nebraska at Kearney, NE
University of Nebraska at Omaha, NE
University of Nebraska–Lincoln, NE
University of Nevada, Las Vegas, NV
University of Nevada, Reno, NV
University of New Mexico, NM
University of North Carolina at Asheville, NC
University of North Carolina at Wilmington, NC
University of North Dakota, ND
University of Northern Iowa, IA
University of Oklahoma, OK
University of Oregon, OR
University of Puget Sound, WA

University of Redlands, CA
University of Science and Arts of Oklahoma, OK
U of South Carolina, Columbia, SC
U of South Carolina–Aiken, SC
University of South Dakota, SD
University of Southern Colorado, CO
University of Southern Indiana, IN
University of Southern Mississippi, MS
University of South Florida, FL
The University of Tampa, FL
University of Tennessee at Chattanooga, TN
The University of Texas at Arlington, TX
The University of Texas at El Paso, TX
The University of Texas at San Antonio, TX
The University of Texas–Pan American, TX
University of the Ozarks, AR
University of Toledo, OH
University of Tulsa, OK
University of Washington, WA
University of West Florida, FL
University of Wisconsin–Green Bay, WI
University of Wisconsin–Oshkosh, WI
University of Wisconsin–Platteville, WI
University of Wisconsin–River Falls, WI
University of Wisconsin–Superior, WI
Valdosta State University, GA
Valley City State University, ND
Valley Forge Christian College, PA
Villa Julie College, MD
Virginia Commonwealth University, VA
Virginia Intermont College, VA
Virginia State University, VA
Viterbo College, WI
Wabash College, IN
Wake Forest University, NC
Washburn University of Topeka, KS
Washington College, MD
Washington State University, WA
Washington University, MO
Wayne State College, NE
Weber State University, UT
Webster University, MO
Wesleyan College, GA
Western Carolina University, NC
Western Michigan University, MI
Western Montana College of The U of Montana, MT
Western Oregon University, OR
Western Washington University, WA
West Liberty State College, WV
Westminster College of Salt Lake City, UT
Westmont College, CA
West Virginia State College, WV
West Virginia University, WV
West Virginia Wesleyan College, WV
Whitman College, WA
Whittier College, CA
Whitworth College, WA
Wichita State University, KS
William Carey College, MS
William Jewell College, MO
William Penn College, IA
William Woods University, MO
Wilson College, PA
Winona State University, MN

Winthrop University, SC
Wittenberg University, OH
Worcester State College, MA
Xavier University, OH
Xavier University of Louisiana, LA
York College, NE

CINEMA/FILM/BROADCASTING

Allentown College of St. Francis de Sales, PA
Baylor University, TX
Bowling Green State University, OH
Brigham Young University, UT
California Institute of the Arts, CA
California Polytechnic State U, San Luis Obispo, CA
California State University, Chico, CA
California State University, Long Beach, CA
Chapman University, CA
College of New Rochelle, NY
College of Santa Fe, NM
DePauw University, IN
Eastern New Mexico University, NM
Edinboro University of Pennsylvania, PA
Five Towns College, NY
Freed-Hardeman University, TN
Henderson State University, AR
Illinois State University, IL
Judson College, IL
Kalamazoo College, MI
Long Island U, Brooklyn Campus, NY
Long Island U, C.W. Post Campus, NY
Marygrove College, MI
Mississippi State University, MS
Montana State U–Bozeman, MT
Morningside College, IA
Mount Union College, OH
Muskingum College, OH
North Carolina School of the Arts, NC
North Central College, IL
Northern Arizona University, AZ
Ohio University, OH
Oklahoma Panhandle State University, OK
Oral Roberts University, OK
Purchase College, State U of NY, NY
Quincy University, IL
Radford University, VA
St. Cloud State University, MN
St. John's University, NY
Sam Houston State University, TX
Seton Hall University, NJ
Sonoma State University, CA
Southwestern College, KS
Sul Ross State University, TX
Texas Christian University, TX
University of Central Arkansas, AR
University of Colorado at Boulder, CO
University of Kansas, KS
The University of Memphis, TN
University of Nebraska at Kearney, NE
University of Nebraska–Lincoln, NE
University of Nevada, Las Vegas, NV
University of South Florida, FL
University of Wisconsin–Superior, WI
Wake Forest University, NC
Wayne State College, NE

Cinema/Film/Broadcasting (continued)

Western Illinois University, IL
Westminster College, PA

CREATIVE WRITING

Alderson-Broaddus College, WV
Arkansas Tech University, AR
Augustana College, IL
Brescia College, KY
Brigham Young University–Hawaii Campus, HI
California Lutheran University, CA
California Polytechnic State U, San Luis Obispo, CA
California State University, Bakersfield, CA
California State University, Chico, CA
Cameron University, OK
Campbell University, NC
Carlow College, PA
Case Western Reserve University, OH
Chapman University, CA
Clinch Valley College of the U of Virginia, VA
Coe College, IA
College of New Rochelle, NY
College of Santa Fe, NM
Colorado State University, CO
Davidson College, NC
Eastern New Mexico University, NM
Eckerd College, FL
Edgewood College, WI
The Evergreen State College, WA
Fontbonne College, MO
Free Will Baptist Bible College, TN
Graceland College, IA
Grove City College, PA
Hamline University, MN
Hobart and William Smith Colleges, NY
Hood College, MD
Illinois State University, IL
Knox College, IL
Long Island U, Southampton College, NY
Louisiana State University and A&M College, LA
Maharishi University of Management, IA
Mankato State University, MN
Mesa State College, CO
Michigan State University, MI
Mississippi State University, MS
Murray State University, KY
Northeast Louisiana University, LA
The Ohio State University, OH
Oklahoma Baptist University, OK
Plymouth State College of the U System of NH, NH
The Richard Stockton College of New Jersey, NJ
Rockhurst College, MO
St. Andrews Presbyterian College, NC
Saint Mary College, KS
Shimer College, IL
Sonoma State University, CA
State U of NY at Binghamton, NY
State U of NY at New Paltz, NY
State U of NY at Oswego, NY
State U of NY College at Geneseo, NY
The University of Akron, OH

U of Alaska Fairbanks, AK
University of California, Riverside, CA
University of Colorado at Boulder, CO
University of Houston, TX
University of Idaho, ID
University of Kansas, KS
University of Maryland Baltimore County, MD
University of Nebraska at Kearney, NE
University of Redlands, CA
U of South Carolina, Columbia, SC
U of South Carolina–Aiken, SC
University of South Dakota, SD
University of Southern Indiana, IN
University of South Florida, FL
The University of Tampa, FL
University of Washington, WA
The University of West Alabama, AL
University of Wisconsin–Stevens Point, WI
Villa Julie College, MD
Wabash College, IN
Wake Forest University, NC
Washington College, MD
Wayne State College, NE
Wheeling Jesuit University, WV
William Penn College, IA
Wright State University, OH

DANCE

Adelphi University, NY
Allentown College of St. Francis de Sales, PA
Alma College, MI
Ball State University, IN
Barat College, IL
Bay Path College, MA
Belhaven College, MS
Birmingham-Southern College, AL
Boston Conservatory, MA
Brenau University, GA
Brigham Young University, UT
Butler University, IN
California Institute of the Arts, CA
California Polytechnic State U, San Luis Obispo, CA
California State University, Chico, CA
California State University, Long Beach, CA
Case Western Reserve University, OH
Centenary College of Louisiana, LA
Chapman University, CA
Coker College, SC
College of New Rochelle, NY
The College of Wooster, OH
Colorado State University, CO
Columbia College, SC
Cornish College of the Arts, WA
Drexel University, PA
Duquesne University, PA
Eastern New Mexico University, NM
Florida International University, FL
Friends University, KS
Goucher College, MD
Grambling State University, LA
Hawaii Pacific University, HI
Hobart and William Smith Colleges, NY
Hofstra University, NY

Hope College, MI
Huntingdon College, AL
Indiana University of Pennsylvania, PA
Jacksonville University, FL
James Madison University, VA
Jersey City State College, NJ
Johnson State College, VT
Kansas Wesleyan University, KS
Lambuth University, TN
Lees-McRae College, NC
Lewis University, IL
Long Island U, Brooklyn Campus, NY
Long Island U, C.W. Post Campus, NY
Lyon College, AR
Mars Hill College, NC
Marygrove College, MI
Marymount Manhattan College, NY
Mary Washington College, VA
Mercyhurst College, PA
Mississippi State University, MS
Mississippi University for Women, MS
Missouri Western State College, MO
Montana State U–Bozeman, MT
Muhlenberg College, PA
Murray State University, KY
North Carolina School of the Arts, NC
Northeastern Illinois University, IL
Northeastern State University, OK
Northwestern State University of Louisiana, LA
The Ohio State University, OH
Ohio University, OH
Oklahoma City University, OK
Old Dominion University, VA
Point Park College, PA
Purchase College, State U of NY, NY
Radford University, VA
Rhode Island College, RI
The Richard Stockton College of New Jersey, NJ
Rockford College, IL
Sam Houston State University, TX
Shenandoah University, VA
Sonoma State University, CA
Southern Methodist University, TX
Southern Utah University, UT
Southwestern University, TX
Southwest Missouri State University, MO
State U of NY College at Geneseo, NY
Texas Christian University, TX
Texas Tech University, TX
Texas Woman's University, TX
Towson University, MD
The University of Akron, OH
University of California, Riverside, CA
University of Colorado at Boulder, CO
University of Hartford, CT
University of Idaho, ID
University of Kansas, KS
University of Maryland Baltimore County, MD
University of Massachusetts Amherst, MA
University of Nebraska at Kearney, NE
University of Nebraska–Lincoln, NE
University of Nevada, Las Vegas, NV
University of Nevada, Reno, NV
University of Northern Colorado, CO

University of Oklahoma, OK
University of Southern Mississippi, MS
University of South Florida, FL
University of the Arts, PA
University of Toledo, OH
University of Utah, UT
University of Washington, WA
University of Wisconsin–Green Bay, WI
University of Wisconsin–Stevens Point, WI
University of Wyoming, WY
Virginia Intermont College, VA
Wake Forest University, NC
Washburn University of Topeka, KS
Wayne State University, MI
Western Illinois University, IL
Western Michigan University, MI
West Texas A&M University, TX
Wichita State University, KS
Winthrop University, SC
Wittenberg University, OH
Wright State University, OH

DEBATING

Abilene Christian University, TX
Alderson-Broaddus College, WV
Allentown College of St. Francis de Sales, PA
Augustana College, IL
Augustana College, SD
Austin Peay State University, TN
Bartlesville Wesleyan College, OK
Baylor University, TX
Bethel College, MN
Biola University, CA
Bowling Green State University, OH
Bradley University, IL
California Polytechnic State U, San Luis Obispo, CA
California State University, Chico, CA
Cameron University, OK
Carroll College, MT
Carson-Newman College, TN
Cedarville College, OH
Central Missouri State University, MO
College of New Rochelle, NY
Colorado State University, CO
Concordia College, Moorhead, MN
Culver-Stockton College, MO
Dakota Wesleyan University, SD
Dana College, NE
David Lipscomb University, TN
The Defiance College, OH
DePaul University, IL
Eastern Michigan University, MI
Eastern New Mexico University, NM
Emory University, GA
Emporia State University, KS
Evangel College, MO
Ferris State University, MI
George Fox University, OR
The George Washington University, DC
Georgia College and State University, GA
Gonzaga University, WA
Graceland College, IA
Hastings College, NE
Henderson State University, AR
Illinois College, IL

Illinois State University, IL
Kansas Newman College, KS
Kansas State University, KS
Kentucky Christian College, KY
King's College, PA
Lewis & Clark College, OR
Louisiana Tech University, LA
Loyola Marymount University, CA
Loyola University Chicago, IL
Mankato State University, MN
Marist College, NY
Marshall University, WV
McNeese State University, LA
Mercer University, Macon, GA
Michigan State University, MI
Midland Lutheran College, NE
Mississippi State University, MS
Missouri Southern State College, MO
Mount Union College, OH
Murray State University, KY
Muskingum College, OH
North Central College, IL
Northeastern State University, OK
Northeast Louisiana University, LA
Northern Arizona University, AZ
Northwestern State University of Louisiana, LA
Northwest Missouri State University, MO
Oklahoma Panhandle State University, OK
Pacific University, OR
Palm Beach Atlantic College, FL
Point Loma Nazarene College, CA
Regis University, CO
Rhode Island College, RI
Ripon College, WI
Rocky Mountain College, MT
Saint Anselm College, NH
St. John's University, NY
Saint Joseph's University, PA
Saint Mary's University of Minnesota, MN
Santa Clara University, CA
Seton Hall University, NJ
South Dakota State University, SD
Southeastern Louisiana University, LA
Southern California College, CA
Southwestern College, KS
Southwest Missouri State University, MO
Sterling College, KS
Suffolk University, MA
Trinity International University, IL
Truman State University, MO
The University of Akron, OH
University of Arkansas at Monticello, AR
University of Georgia, GA
University of Kansas, KS
University of Kentucky, KY
University of La Verne, CA
University of Mary, ND
University of Missouri–Kansas City, MO
University of Nebraska at Kearney, NE
University of Nebraska at Omaha, NE
University of Nevada, Reno, NV
University of Puget Sound, WA
University of Redlands, CA
University of St. Thomas, TX
U of South Carolina, Columbia, SC
University of South Dakota, SD

University of South Florida, FL
The University of Texas at Arlington, TX
University of Utah, UT
University of Wisconsin–Oshkosh, WI
University of Wyoming, WY
Upper Iowa University, IA
Wake Forest University, NC
Wayne State University, MI
Weber State University, UT
Webster University, MO
Western Illinois University, IL
Whitman College, WA
Whitworth College, WA
Wichita State University, KS
Willamette University, OR
William Carey College, MS
William Jewell College, MO
Wright State University, OH
York College, NE

JOURNALISM/PUBLICATIONS

Abilene Christian University, TX
Anderson College, SC
Arkansas Tech University, AR
Austin College, TX
Baker University, KS
Ball State University, IN
Baylor University, TX
Benedictine College, KS
Berry College, GA
Boise State University, ID
Brigham Young University, UT
Brigham Young University–Hawaii Campus, HI
California Polytechnic State U, San Luis Obispo, CA
California State University, Bakersfield, CA
California State University, Chico, CA
California State University, Fresno, CA
California State University, Northridge, CA
Cameron University, OK
Campbell University, NC
Central Baptist College, AR
Chapman University, CA
Chicago State University, IL
The Citadel, The Military Coll of South Carolina, SC
Clinch Valley College of the U of Virginia, VA
College of New Rochelle, NY
David Lipscomb University, TN
DePauw University, IN
Dordt College, IA
Eastern New Mexico University, NM
Eastern Washington University, WA
Edinboro University of Pennsylvania, PA
Faulkner University, AL
Ferris State University, MI
Florida Agricultural and Mechanical University, FL
Freed-Hardeman University, TN
Georgia College and State University, GA
Hannibal-LaGrange College, MO
Henderson State University, AR
Huntington College, IN
Indiana University of Pennsylvania, PA
James Madison University, VA

Journalism/Publications *(continued)*

John Brown University, AR
Judson College, IL
Kent State University, OH
Lakeland College, WI
Lees-McRae College, NC
LeTourneau University, TX
Louisiana State University and A&M College, LA
Louisiana Tech University, LA
Marycrest International University, IA
Mary Washington College, VA
Mesa State College, CO
Michigan State University, MI
Midland Lutheran College, NE
Mississippi State University, MS
Mississippi Valley State University, MS
Missouri Southern State College, MO
Morehead State University, KY
Morningside College, IA
Mount Union College, OH
Murray State University, KY
New Mexico State University, NM
Northeastern State University, OK
Northeast Louisiana University, LA
Northern Arizona University, AZ
North Greenville College, SC
Northwestern College, IA
Northwest Missouri State University, MO
Nyack College, NY
Oglethorpe University, GA
The Ohio State University, OH
Ohio University, OH
Oklahoma Baptist University, OK
Oklahoma Christian U of Science and Arts, OK
Oral Roberts University, OK
Pepperdine University, Malibu, CA
Point Park College, PA
Rhode Island College, RI
The Richard Stockton College of New Jersey, NJ
St. Cloud State University, MN
St. John's University, NY
Saint Mary-of-the-Woods College, IN
Sam Houston State University, TX
Seton Hall University, NJ
Sonoma State University, CA
South Dakota State University, SD
Southeastern Louisiana University, LA
Southern Adventist University, TN
Southern Utah University, UT
Southwestern College, KS
Southwest Missouri State University, MO
State U of NY College at Geneseo, NY
Stephen F. Austin State University, TX
Sul Ross State University, TX
Texas A&M University, College Station, TX
Texas Christian University, TX
Texas Lutheran University, TX
Texas Tech University, TX
Texas Woman's University, TX
Trinity Christian College, IL
Trinity International University, IL
Troy State University, Troy, AL
The University of Akron, OH

University of Central Oklahoma, OK
University of Colorado at Boulder, CO
University of Georgia, GA
University of Guam, GU
University of Idaho, ID
University of Kansas, KS
University of La Verne, CA
University of Mary Hardin-Baylor, TX
The University of Memphis, TN
The University of Montana–Missoula, MT
University of Nebraska at Kearney, NE
University of Nebraska at Omaha, NE
University of Nebraska–Lincoln, NE
University of Nevada, Las Vegas, NV
University of Nevada, Reno, NV
University of North Alabama, AL
University of North Carolina at Pembroke, NC
University of Oklahoma, OK
University of Oregon, OR
University of Portland, OR
University of St. Thomas, MN
University of South Dakota, SD
University of Southern California, CA
University of Southern Colorado, CO
University of South Florida, FL
The University of Tampa, FL
The University of Texas at Arlington, TX
The University of Texas at El Paso, TX
University of Toledo, OH
University of Utah, UT
University of Washington, WA
The University of West Alabama, AL
University of Wisconsin–Superior, WI
Valdosta State University, GA
Valley City State University, ND
Vanderbilt University, TN
Virginia Polytechnic Institute and State U, VA
Wake Forest University, NC
Wayne State College, NE
Webster University, MO
Western Illinois University, IL
Western Washington University, WA
Westminster College of Salt Lake City, UT
West Texas A&M University, TX
Wichita State University, KS
William Jewell College, MO
William Penn College, IA

MUSIC

Abilene Christian University, TX
Adams State College, CO
Adelphi University, NY
Adrian College, MI
Agnes Scott College, GA
Alabama Agricultural and Mechanical University, AL
Alabama State University, AL
Alaska Bible College, AK
Albany State University, GA
Albertson College of Idaho, ID
Albion College, MI
Albright College, PA
Alcorn State University, MS
Alderson-Broaddus College, WV

Allentown College of St. Francis de Sales, PA
Allen University, SC
Alma College, MI
Alverno College, WI
American Conservatory of Music, IL
Anderson College, SC
Anderson University, IN
Angelo State University, TX
Anna Maria College, MA
Arizona Bible College, AZ
Arkansas State University, AR
Arkansas Tech University, AR
Armstrong Atlantic State University, GA
Asbury College, KY
Ashland University, OH
Atlanta Christian College, GA
Atlantic Union College, MA
Auburn University, AL
Augsburg College, MN
Augustana College, IL
Augustana College, SD
Augusta State University, GA
Austin College, TX
Austin Peay State University, TN
Azusa Pacific University, CA
Baker University, KS
Baldwin-Wallace College, OH
Ball State University, IN
Baptist Bible College of Pennsylvania, PA
Barber-Scotia College, NC
Bartlesville Wesleyan College, OK
Barton College, NC
Baylor University, TX
Belhaven College, MS
Bellarmine College, KY
Belmont University, TN
Beloit College, WI
Bemidji State University, MN
Benedict College, SC
Benedictine College, KS
Benedictine University, IL
Berklee College of Music, MA
Berry College, GA
Bethel College, KS
Bethel College, MN
Bethel College, TN
Bethune-Cookman College, FL
Biola University, CA
Birmingham-Southern College, AL
Black Hills State University, SD
Blue Mountain College, MS
Bluffton College, OH
Boise Bible College, ID
Boise State University, ID
Boston Conservatory, MA
Boston University, MA
Bowie State University, MD
Bowling Green State University, OH
Bradley University, IL
Brenau University, GA
Brescia College, KY
Brewton-Parker College, GA
Briar Cliff College, IA
Bridgewater College, VA
Brigham Young University, UT

Brigham Young University–Hawaii Campus, HI
Bryan College, TN
Buena Vista University, IA
Butler University, IN
Caldwell College, NJ
California Baptist College, CA
California Institute of the Arts, CA
California Lutheran University, CA
California Polytechnic State U, San Luis Obispo, CA
California State University, Bakersfield, CA
California State University, Chico, CA
California State University, Fresno, CA
California State University, Fullerton, CA
California State University, Hayward, CA
California State University, Long Beach, CA
California State University, Northridge, CA
California State University, San Bernardino, CA
California State University, Stanislaus, CA
Calvin College, MI
Cameron University, OK
Campbell University, NC
Capital University, OH
Carnegie Mellon University, PA
Carroll College, WI
Carson-Newman College, TN
Carthage College, WI
Cascade College, OR
Case Western Reserve University, OH
Castleton State College, VT
The Catholic University of America, DC
Cedarville College, OH
Centenary College of Louisiana, LA
Central Baptist College, AR
Central Bible College, MO
Central Christian College of the Bible, MO
Central College, IA
Central Methodist College, MO
Central Michigan University, MI
Central Missouri State University, MO
Central State University, OH
Central Washington University, WA
Chapman University, CA
Charleston Southern University, SC
Chatham College, PA
Chicago State University, IL
Christian Heritage College, CA
Christopher Newport University, VA
Cincinnati Bible College and Seminary, OH
Circleville Bible College, OH
The Citadel, The Military Coll of South Carolina, SC
Claflin College, SC
Clark Atlanta University, GA
Clarke College, IA
Clayton College & State University, GA
Clear Creek Baptist Bible College, KY
Clearwater Christian College, FL
Cleveland Institute of Music, OH
Cleveland State University, OH
Clinch Valley College of the U of Virginia, VA
Coastal Carolina University, SC
Coe College, IA

Coker College, SC
Colby-Sawyer College, NH
College of Charleston, SC
College of Mount St. Joseph, OH
The College of New Jersey, NJ
College of New Rochelle, NY
College of Notre Dame, CA
College of Saint Benedict, MN
College of St. Catherine, MN
College of St. Francis, IL
College of St. Scholastica, MN
College of Santa Fe, NM
Coll of Staten Island of the City U of NY, NY
College of the Holy Cross, MA
College of the Southwest, NM
The College of Wooster, OH
Colorado Christian University, CO
Colorado School of Mines, CO
Colorado State University, CO
Columbia College, MO
Columbia College, SC
Columbia International University, SC
Columbia Union College, MD
Columbus State University, GA
Concord College, WV
Concordia College, MI
Concordia College, Moorhead, MN
Concordia College, St. Paul, MN
Concordia College, NE
Concordia College, NY
Concordia University, CA
Concordia University, IL
Concordia University, OR
Concordia University at Austin, TX
Concordia University Wisconsin, WI
Converse College, SC
Cornell College, IA
Cornerstone College, MI
Cornish College of the Arts, WA
Covenant College, GA
Crichton College, TN
Culver-Stockton College, MO
Cumberland College, KY
The Curtis Institute of Music, PA
Dakota State University, SD
Dakota Wesleyan University, SD
Dallas Baptist University, TX
Dallas Christian College, TX
Dana College, NE
David Lipscomb University, TN
Davidson College, NC
Davis & Elkins College, WV
The Defiance College, OH
Delaware State University, DE
Delta State University, MS
Denison University, OH
DePaul University, IL
DePauw University, IN
Dickinson College, PA
Dickinson State University, ND
Doane College, NE
Dominican College of San Rafael, CA
Dordt College, IA
Drake University, IA
Drexel University, PA
Drury College, MO

Duquesne University, PA
East Carolina University, NC
East Central University, OK
East Coast Bible College, NC
Eastern College, PA
Eastern Connecticut State University, CT
Eastern Kentucky University, KY
Eastern Mennonite University, VA
Eastern Michigan University, MI
Eastern New Mexico University, NM
Eastern Oregon University, OR
Eastern Washington University, WA
East Tennessee State University, TN
East Texas Baptist University, TX
Eckerd College, FL
Edgewood College, WI
Edinboro University of Pennsylvania, PA
Elizabeth City State University, NC
Elizabethtown College, PA
Elmhurst College, IL
Elon College, NC
Emmaus Bible College, IA
Emory University, GA
Emporia State University, KS
Erskine College, SC
Eugene Bible College, OR
Evangel College, MO
Fairfield University, CT
Faith Baptist Bible Coll and Theological Seminary, IA
Faulkner University, AL
Fayetteville State University, NC
Ferris State University, MI
Ferrum College, VA
Fitchburg State College, MA
Five Towns College, NY
Florida Agricultural and Mechanical University, FL
Florida Christian College, FL
Florida International University, FL
Florida Southern College, FL
Florida State University, FL
Fordham University, NY
Fort Lewis College, CO
Fort Valley State University, GA
Francis Marion University, SC
Franklin College of Indiana, IN
Freed-Hardeman University, TN
Free Will Baptist Bible College, TN
Fresno Pacific University, CA
Friends University, KS
Frostburg State University, MD
Furman University, SC
Gardner-Webb University, NC
Geneva College, PA
George Fox University, OR
Georgetown College, KY
The George Washington University, DC
Georgia College and State University, GA
Georgian Court College, NJ
Georgia Southern University, GA
Georgia Southwestern State University, GA
Georgia State University, GA
Glenville State College, WV
God's Bible School and College, OH
Gonzaga University, WA
Gordon College, MA

Music (continued)

Goucher College, MD
Grace Bible College, MI
Grace College, IN
Graceland College, IA
Grace University, NE
Grambling State University, LA
Grand Valley State University, MI
Grand View College, IA
Great Lakes Christian College, MI
Green Mountain College, VT
Greensboro College, NC
Greenville College, IL
Grove City College, PA
Guilford College, NC
Gustavus Adolphus College, MN
Hannibal-LaGrange College, MO
Harding University, AR
Hardin-Simmons University, TX
Hartwick College, NY
Hastings College, NE
Hawaii Pacific University, HI
Heidelberg College, OH
Henderson State University, AR
Hendrix College, AR
Hillsdale College, MI
Hiram College, OH
Hobart and William Smith Colleges, NY
Hofstra University, NY
Hollins College, VA
Holy Names College, CA
Hope International University, CA
Houghton College, NY
Houston Baptist University, TX
Howard Payne University, TX
Howard University, DC
Huntingdon College, AL
Huntington College, IN
Huston-Tillotson College, TX
Idaho State University, ID
Illinois College, IL
Illinois State University, IL
Illinois Wesleyan University, IL
Immaculata College, PA
Indiana University of Pennsylvania, PA
Indiana U–Purdue U Fort Wayne, IN
Indiana Wesleyan University, IN
Inter American U of PR, Aguadilla Campus, PR
Iona College, New Rochelle, NY
Iowa State University of Science and Technology, IA
Iowa Wesleyan College, IA
Ithaca College, NY
Jackson State University, MS
Jacksonville State University, AL
Jacksonville University, FL
James Madison University, VA
Jersey City State College, NJ
John Brown University, AR
Johnson C. Smith University, NC
Johnson State College, VT
John Wesley College, NC
Kalamazoo College, MI
Kansas Newman College, KS
Kansas State University, KS
Kansas Wesleyan University, KS

Kean College of New Jersey, NJ
Keene State College, NH
Kennesaw State University, GA
Kent State University, OH
Kentucky Christian College, KY
Kentucky Mountain Bible College, KY
Kentucky State University, KY
Kentucky Wesleyan College, KY
King College, TN
Knox College, IL
Kutztown University of Pennsylvania, PA
LaGrange College, GA
Lake Forest College, IL
Lambuth University, TN
Lancaster Bible College, PA
Lander University, SC
Langston University, OK
La Sierra University, CA
Lawrence University, WI
Lebanon Valley College, PA
LeMoyne-Owen College, TN
Lenoir-Rhyne College, NC
LeTourneau University, TX
Lewis & Clark College, OR
Lewis-Clark State College, ID
Limestone College, SC
Lincoln Memorial University, TN
Lincoln University, MO
Lincoln University, PA
Lindsey Wilson College, KY
Linfield College, OR
Livingstone College, NC
Lock Haven University of Pennsylvania, PA
Long Island U, Brooklyn Campus, NY
Long Island U, C.W. Post Campus, NY
Longwood College, VA
Louisiana College, LA
Louisiana State University and A&M College, LA
Louisiana Tech University, LA
Loyola Marymount University, CA
Luther College, IA
Lycoming College, PA
Lynchburg College, VA
Lynn University, FL
MacMurray College, IL
Magnolia Bible College, MS
Maharishi University of Management, IA
Malone College, OH
Manchester College, IN
Manhattan Christian College, KS
Manhattan College, NY
Manhattan School of Music, NY
Mankato State University, MN
Mannes Coll of Music, New Sch for Social Research, NY
Mansfield University of Pennsylvania, PA
Marian College, IN
Marian College of Fond du Lac, WI
Marist College, NY
Marshall University, WV
Mars Hill College, NC
Martin Luther College, MN
Martin Methodist College, TN
Martin University, IN
Maryville College, TN
Mary Washington College, VA

Marywood University, PA
The Master's College and Seminary, CA
McKendree College, IL
McMurry University, TX
McNeese State University, LA
Mercer University, Macon, GA
Mercyhurst College, PA
Meredith College, NC
Mesa State College, CO
Messiah College, PA
Methodist College, NC
Metropolitan State College of Denver, CO
Miami University, OH
Michigan Christian College, MI
Michigan State University, MI
Mid-America Bible College, OK
MidAmerica Nazarene University, KS
Middle Tennessee State University, TN
Midland Lutheran College, NE
Midway College, KY
Miles College, AL
Milligan College, TN
Millikin University, IL
Millsaps College, MS
Mills College, CA
Minnesota Bible College, MN
Minot State University, ND
Mississippi College, MS
Mississippi State University, MS
Mississippi University for Women, MS
Mississippi Valley State University, MS
Missouri Baptist College, MO
Missouri Southern State College, MO
Missouri Western State College, MO
Molloy College, NY
Monmouth College, IL
Montana State U–Bozeman, MT
Montreat College, NC
Moorhead State University, MN
Morehead State University, KY
Morehouse College, GA
Morgan State University, MD
Morningside College, IA
Mount Marty College, SD
Mount Mary College, WI
Mount Mercy College, IA
Mount Olive College, NC
Mount St. Clare College, IA
Mount Union College, OH
Mount Vernon Nazarene College, OH
Muhlenberg College, PA
Murray State University, KY
Muskingum College, OH
Nazareth College of Rochester, NY
Nebraska Christian College, NE
Nebraska Wesleyan University, NE
Newberry College, SC
New Mexico Highlands University, NM
New Mexico State University, NM
Nicholls State University, LA
Norfolk State University, VA
North Carolina Agricultural and Technical State U, NC
North Carolina School of the Arts, NC
North Central Bible College, MN
North Central College, IL
North Dakota State University, ND

616

Northeastern Illinois University, IL
Northeastern State University, OK
Northeast Louisiana University, LA
Northern Arizona University, AZ
Northern Illinois University, IL
Northern Michigan University, MI
Northern State University, SD
North Greenville College, SC
Northland College, WI
North Park University, IL
Northwestern College, IA
Northwestern College, MN
Northwestern Oklahoma State University, OK
Northwestern State University of Louisiana, LA
Northwest Missouri State University, MO
Nyack College, NY
Oakland City University, IN
Oakland University, MI
Oberlin College, OH
Occidental College, CA
Oglethorpe University, GA
Ohio Northern University, OH
The Ohio State University, OH
Ohio University, OH
Ohio Wesleyan University, OH
Oklahoma Baptist University, OK
Oklahoma Christian U of Science and Arts, OK
Oklahoma City University, OK
Oklahoma Panhandle State University, OK
Oklahoma State U, OK
Old Dominion University, VA
Olivet College, MI
Olivet Nazarene University, IL
Oral Roberts University, OK
Oregon State University, OR
Ottawa University, KS
Otterbein College, OH
Ouachita Baptist University, AR
Our Lady of the Lake University of San Antonio, TX
Ozark Christian College, MO
Pacific University, OR
Paine College, GA
Palm Beach Atlantic College, FL
Peabody Conserv of Music of Johns Hopkins U, MD
Pepperdine University, Malibu, CA
Peru State College, NE
Philadelphia College of Bible, PA
Philander Smith College, AR
Phillips University, OK
Piedmont College, GA
Pittsburg State University, KS
Plymouth State College of the U System of NH, NH
Point Loma Nazarene College, CA
Portland State University, OR
Practical Bible College, NY
Prairie View A&M University, TX
Presbyterian College, SC
Purchase College, State U of NY, NY
Queens College, NC
Quincy University, IL
Radford University, VA

Reinhardt College, GA
Rhode Island College, RI
Rhodes College, TN
Rice University, TX
The Richard Stockton College of New Jersey, NJ
Ripon College, WI
Roanoke College, VA
Roberts Wesleyan College, NY
Rockford College, IL
Rocky Mountain College, MT
Rollins College, FL
Rowan University, NJ
Rust College, MS
Saginaw Valley State University, MI
St. Ambrose University, IA
St. Andrews Presbyterian College, NC
Saint Augustine's College, NC
St. Bonaventure University, NY
St. Cloud State University, MN
Saint Francis College, PA
Saint John's University, MN
St. John's University, NY
St. Louis Christian College, MO
Saint Louis University, MO
Saint Mary College, KS
Saint Mary-of-the-Woods College, IN
Saint Mary's College, IN
Saint Mary's University of Minnesota, MN
St. Mary's University of San Antonio, TX
St. Norbert College, WI
St. Olaf College, MN
Saint Vincent College, PA
Saint Xavier University, IL
Salem College, NC
Samford University, AL
Sam Houston State University, TX
Santa Clara University, CA
Scripps College, CA
Seattle University, WA
Seton Hall University, NJ
Seton Hill College, PA
Shaw University, NC
Sheldon Jackson College, AK
Shenandoah University, VA
Shepherd College, WV
Shorter College, GA
Siena Heights College, MI
Sierra Nevada College, NV
Silver Lake College, WI
Simpson College, CA
Simpson College, IA
Skidmore College, NY
Slippery Rock University of Pennsylvania, PA
Sonoma State University, CA
South Dakota State University, SD
Southeastern Baptist College, MS
Southeastern College of the Assemblies of God, FL
Southeastern Louisiana University, LA
Southeastern Oklahoma State University, OK
Southeast Missouri State University, MO
Southern Adventist University, TN
Southern Arkansas University–Magnolia, AR

Southern California College, CA
Southern Illinois University at Edwardsville, IL
Southern Methodist University, TX
Southern Nazarene University, OK
Southern Oregon University, OR
Southern Utah University, UT
Southern Wesleyan University, SC
Southwest Baptist University, MO
Southwestern Adventist University, TX
Southwestern Christian College, TX
Southwestern College, KS
Southwestern College of Christian Ministries, OK
Southwestern Oklahoma State University, OK
Southwestern University, TX
Southwest Missouri State University, MO
Southwest State University, MN
Southwest Texas State University, TX
Spring Arbor College, MI
State U of NY at Buffalo, NY
State U of NY at Oswego, NY
State U of NY College at Fredonia, NY
State U of NY College at Geneseo, NY
State U of NY College at Oneonta, NY
State U of NY College at Plattsburgh, NY
State U of NY College at Potsdam, NY
Stephen F. Austin State University, TX
Sterling College, KS
Stetson University, FL
Stillman College, AL
Sul Ross State University, TX
Susquehanna University, PA
Syracuse University, NY
Tabor College, KS
Tarleton State University, TX
Taylor University, IN
Temple University, Philadelphia, PA
Tennessee State University, TN
Tennessee Technological University, TN
Tennessee Temple University, TN
Tennessee Wesleyan College, TN
Texas A&M University–Commerce, TX
Texas A&M University–Kingsville, TX
Texas Christian University, TX
Texas Lutheran University, TX
Texas Tech University, TX
Texas Woman's University, TX
Thomas College, GA
Tiffin University, OH
Toccoa Falls College, GA
Tougaloo College, MS
Towson University, MD
Transylvania University, KY
Trevecca Nazarene University, TN
Trinity Christian College, IL
Trinity International University, IL
Trinity University, TX
Troy State University, Troy, AL
Truman State University, MO
Tuskegee University, AL
Union College, KY
Union College, NE
Union University, TN
The University of Akron, OH

Music (continued)

The University of Alabama at Birmingham, AL

The University of Alabama in Huntsville, AL

U of Alaska Anchorage, AK

U of Alaska Fairbanks, AK

University of Arkansas, Fayetteville, AR

University of Arkansas at Little Rock, AR

University of Arkansas at Monticello, AR

University of Arkansas at Pine Bluff, AR

University of Bridgeport, CT

University of California, Riverside, CA

University of Central Arkansas, AR

University of Central Florida, FL

University of Central Oklahoma, OK

The University of Charleston, WV

University of Cincinnati, OH

University of Colorado at Boulder, CO

University of Connecticut, Storrs, CT

University of Dayton, OH

University of Delaware, DE

University of Denver, CO

University of Dubuque, IA

University of Evansville, IN

The University of Findlay, OH

University of Hartford, CT

University of Hawaii at Hilo, HI

University of Hawaii at Manoa, HI

University of Houston, TX

University of Idaho, ID

University of Indianapolis, IN

The University of Iowa, IA

University of Kansas, KS

University of Kentucky, KY

University of Mary, ND

University of Mary Hardin-Baylor, TX

University of Maryland Baltimore County, MD

University of Maryland College Park, MD

University of Maryland Eastern Shore, MD

University of Massachusetts Amherst, MA

University of Massachusetts Lowell, MA

The University of Memphis, TN

University of Miami, FL

University of Michigan–Flint, MI

University of Mississippi, MS

University of Missouri–Kansas City, MO

University of Missouri–Rolla, MO

University of Missouri–St. Louis, MO

University of Mobile, AL

The University of Montana–Missoula, MT

University of Montevallo, AL

University of Nebraska at Kearney, NE

University of Nebraska at Omaha, NE

University of Nebraska–Lincoln, NE

University of Nevada, Las Vegas, NV

University of Nevada, Reno, NV

University of New Hampshire, Durham, NH

University of New Mexico, NM

University of North Alabama, AL

University of North Carolina at Asheville, NC

University of North Carolina at Greensboro, NC

University of North Carolina at Pembroke, NC

University of North Carolina at Wilmington, NC

University of North Dakota, ND

University of Northern Colorado, CO

University of Northern Iowa, IA

University of North Florida, FL

University of Oklahoma, OK

University of Portland, OR

U of Puerto Rico, Cayey University College, PR

U of Puerto Rico, Mayagüez Campus, PR

University of Puget Sound, WA

University of Redlands, CA

University of Rhode Island, RI

University of Richmond, VA

University of Rio Grande, OH

University of St. Thomas, MN

University of St. Thomas, TX

University of San Diego, CA

University of Science and Arts of Oklahoma, OK

University of Sioux Falls, SD

University of South Alabama, AL

U of South Carolina, Columbia, SC

University of South Dakota, SD

University of Southern California, CA

University of Southern Indiana, IN

University of Southern Maine, ME

University of Southern Mississippi, MS

University of South Florida, FL

The University of Tampa, FL

University of Tennessee at Chattanooga, TN

The University of Tennessee at Martin, TN

The University of Texas at Arlington, TX

The University of Texas at El Paso, TX

The University of Texas at San Antonio, TX

The University of Texas–Pan American, TX

University of the Arts, PA

University of the District of Columbia, DC

University of the Pacific, CA

University of the Virgin Islands, VI

University of Toledo, OH

University of Tulsa, OK

University of Utah, UT

University of Washington, WA

The University of West Alabama, AL

University of West Florida, FL

University of Wisconsin–Green Bay, WI

University of Wisconsin–La Crosse, WI

University of Wisconsin–Milwaukee, WI

University of Wisconsin–Oshkosh, WI

University of Wisconsin–Parkside, WI

University of Wisconsin–Platteville, WI

University of Wisconsin–River Falls, WI

University of Wisconsin–Stevens Point, WI

University of Wisconsin–Superior, WI

University of Wisconsin–Whitewater, WI

University of Wyoming, WY

Upper Iowa University, IA

Urbana University, OH

Valdosta State University, GA

Valley City State University, ND

Valley Forge Christian College, PA

Valparaiso University, IN

Vanderbilt University, TN

VanderCook College of Music, IL

Virginia Commonwealth University, VA

Virginia Polytechnic Institute and State U, VA

Virginia State University, VA

Virginia Union University, VA

Virginia Wesleyan College, VA

Viterbo College, WI

Wabash College, IN

Wagner College, NY

Wake Forest University, NC

Walla Walla College, WA

Warner Pacific College, OR

Warner Southern College, FL

Wartburg College, IA

Washburn University of Topeka, KS

Washington College, MD

Washington State University, WA

Wayne State College, NE

Wayne State University, MI

Webster University, MO

Wesleyan College, GA

West Chester University of Pennsylvania, PA

Western Baptist College, OR

Western Carolina University, NC

Western Illinois University, IL

Western Kentucky University, KY

Western Michigan University, MI

Western Oregon University, OR

Western State College of Colorado, CO

Western Washington University, WA

West Liberty State College, WV

Westmar University, IA

Westminster Choir Coll of Rider U, NJ

Westminster College, PA

Westminster College of Salt Lake City, UT

Westmont College, CA

West Texas A&M University, TX

West Virginia State College, WV

West Virginia University, WV

West Virginia University Institute of Technology, WV

West Virginia Wesleyan College, WV

Wheaton College, IL

Wheeling Jesuit University, WV

Whitman College, WA

Whittier College, CA

Whitworth College, WA

Wichita State University, KS

Widener University, PA

Wiley College, TX

Willamette University, OR

William Carey College, MS

William Jewell College, MO

William Paterson University of New Jersey, NJ

William Penn College, IA

Williams Baptist College, AR

William Tyndale College, MI

Wingate University, NC

Winona State University, MN

Winston-Salem State University, NC

Winthrop University, SC

Wittenberg University, OH

Wofford College, SC

Wright State University, OH

Xavier University, OH

Xavier University of Louisiana, LA
York College, NE
Youngstown State University, OH

PERFORMING ARTS

Adams State College, CO
Adelphi University, NY
Alabama State University, AL
Alderson-Broaddus College, WV
Alfred University, NY
Alma College, MI
Augsburg College, MN
Bartlesville Wesleyan College, OK
Bay Path College, MA
Biola University, CA
Birmingham-Southern College, AL
Boise State University, ID
California Polytechnic State U, San Luis
  Obispo, CA
California State University, Bakersfield, CA
California State University, Chico, CA
California State University, Long Beach,
  CA
California State University, San Bernardino,
  CA
Calvin College, MI
Catawba College, NC
Charleston Southern University, SC
Clarion University of Pennsylvania, PA
Clinch Valley College of the U of Virginia,
  VA
Coe College, IA
College of Charleston, SC
College of New Rochelle, NY
College of Santa Fe, NM
Coll of Staten Island of the City U of NY,
  NY
Concordia University Wisconsin, WI
Davis & Elkins College, WV
DePaul University, IL
East Central University, OK
East Coast Bible College, NC
Eastern New Mexico University, NM
Edgewood College, WI
Elizabeth City State University, NC
Elon College, NC
Emerson College, MA
Emory University, GA
Eureka College, IL
Ferrum College, VA
Florida International University, FL
Fort Lewis College, CO
Franklin College of Indiana, IN
Freed-Hardeman University, TN
Friends University, KS
Georgetown College, KY
The George Washington University, DC
Georgia State University, GA
Greenville College, IL
Hannibal-LaGrange College, MO
Hastings College, NE
Hobart and William Smith Colleges, NY
Hope College, MI
Idaho State University, ID
Illinois State University, IL
Indiana State University, IN
Indiana University of Pennsylvania, PA

Johnson State College, VT
Kennesaw State University, GA
Kentucky Christian College, KY
King College, TN
Lees-McRae College, NC
Limestone College, SC
Lindenwood College, MO
Louisiana College, LA
Louisiana State University and A&M
  College, LA
Louisiana Tech University, LA
Lyon College, AR
Manchester College, IN
Marian College, IN
Marycrest International University, IA
Marygrove College, MI
Michigan State University, MI
Millersville University of Pennsylvania, PA
Mississippi State University, MS
Mississippi University for Women, MS
Molloy College, NY
Muhlenberg College, PA
New Mexico State University, NM
Norfolk State University, VA
Northeastern State University, OK
Northeast Louisiana University, LA
Northern Illinois University, IL
Nyack College, NY
Oakland University, MI
Oglethorpe University, GA
The Ohio State University, OH
Ohio University, OH
Oklahoma Christian U of Science and Arts,
  OK
Oklahoma City University, OK
Old Dominion University, VA
Pepperdine University, Malibu, CA
Point Park College, PA
Prairie View A&M University, TX
Purchase College, State U of NY, NY
Reinhardt College, GA
The Richard Stockton College of New
  Jersey, NJ
Rockhurst College, MO
Rowan University, NJ
St. Cloud State University, MN
St. John's University, NY
Saint Louis University, MO
Sam Houston State University, TX
San Francisco Conservatory of Music, CA
Seattle Pacific University, WA
Shawnee State University, OH
Shenandoah University, VA
Shepherd College, WV
Sonoma State University, CA
South Dakota State University, SD
Southern Nazarene University, OK
Southern Utah University, UT
Southwest Missouri State University, MO
State U of NY College at Geneseo, NY
Tabor College, KS
Temple University, Philadelphia, PA
Texas A&M University, College Station,
  TX
Texas Tech University, TX
Troy State University, Troy, AL
Tusculum College, TN

The University of Akron, OH
The University of Alabama at Birmingham,
  AL
University of Arkansas at Pine Bluff, AR
University of Colorado at Boulder, CO
University of Dallas, TX
University of Hartford, CT
University of Hawaii at Hilo, HI
University of Idaho, ID
The University of Iowa, IA
University of Kansas, KS
University of Louisville, KY
University of Maine, Orono, ME
University of Maryland Eastern Shore, MD
University of Missouri–Kansas City, MO
The University of Montana–Missoula, MT
University of Nebraska–Lincoln, NE
University of Nevada, Las Vegas, NV
University of North Carolina at Greensboro,
  NC
University of Northern Colorado, CO
University of Oklahoma, OK
University of Oregon, OR
University of Portland, OR
University of Southern Colorado, CO
University of South Florida, FL
The University of Tampa, FL
The University of Texas at El Paso, TX
University of the Arts, PA
University of Tulsa, OK
University of Washington, WA
University of Wisconsin–Stevens Point, WI
University of Wisconsin–Superior, WI
Urbana University, OH
Valparaiso University, IN
Virginia Intermont College, VA
Virginia State University, VA
Viterbo College, WI
Wake Forest University, NC
Weber State University, UT
Western Baptist College, OR
Western Illinois University, IL
Western Michigan University, MI
Western New Mexico University, NM
Wichita State University, KS
Wilkes University, PA
William Woods University, MO
Winthrop University, SC
Xavier University, OH
Xavier University of Louisiana, LA
York College, NE

THEATER/DRAMA

Abilene Christian University, TX
Adams State College, CO
Adelphi University, NY
Adrian College, MI
Albertson College of Idaho, ID
Albion College, MI
Albright College, PA
Alderson-Broaddus College, WV
Allentown College of St. Francis de Sales,
  PA
Alma College, MI
Anderson College, SC
Angelo State University, TX
Arkansas State University, AR

Theater/Drama (continued)

Ashland University, OH
Augustana College, IL
Augustana College, SD
Augusta State University, GA
Austin College, TX
Azusa Pacific University, CA
Baker University, KS
Ball State University, IN
Barat College, IL
Barry University, FL
Bartlesville Wesleyan College, OK
Barton College, NC
Baylor University, TX
Bay Path College, MA
Bemidji State University, MN
Benedictine College, KS
Berry College, GA
Bethel College, IN
Bethel College, KS
Bethel College, MN
Birmingham-Southern College, AL
Boise State University, ID
Boston Conservatory, MA
Boston University, MA
Bowling Green State University, OH
Bradley University, IL
Brenau University, GA
Brewton-Parker College, GA
Briar Cliff College, IA
Brigham Young University, UT
Brigham Young University–Hawaii Campus, HI
Buena Vista University, IA
Butler University, IN
California Baptist College, CA
California Lutheran University, CA
California Polytechnic State U, San Luis Obispo, CA
California State University, Bakersfield, CA
California State University, Chico, CA
California State University, Fresno, CA
California State University, Long Beach, CA
Calvin College, MI
Cameron University, OK
Campbell University, NC
Carroll College, MT
Carroll College, WI
Carthage College, WI
Cascade College, OR
Case Western Reserve University, OH
Cedar Crest College, PA
Centenary College of Louisiana, LA
Central Bible College, MO
Central Christian College of the Bible, MO
Central College, IA
Central Methodist College, MO
Central Michigan University, MI
Central Missouri State University, MO
Chapman University, CA
Chatham College, PA
Clarke College, IA
Cleveland State University, OH
Clinch Valley College of the U of Virginia, VA
Coastal Carolina University, SC

Coe College, IA
Coker College, SC
College of Charleston, SC
College of New Rochelle, NY
College of Saint Benedict, MN
College of Santa Fe, NM
College of the Southwest, NM
The College of Wooster, OH
Colorado Christian University, CO
Concord College, WV
Concordia College, Moorhead, MN
Concordia College, NE
Concordia University, CA
Cornell College, IA
Cornish College of the Arts, WA
Crichton College, TN
Culver-Stockton College, MO
Dakota Wesleyan University, SD
Dana College, NE
David Lipscomb University, TN
Davis & Elkins College, WV
The Defiance College, OH
DePaul University, IL
DePauw University, IN
Doane College, NE
Dordt College, IA
Drake University, IA
Drexel University, PA
Drury College, MO
East Coast Bible College, NC
Eastern Connecticut State University, CT
Eastern Michigan University, MI
Eastern New Mexico University, NM
Eastern Oregon University, OR
Eastern Washington University, WA
Eckerd College, FL
Edgewood College, WI
Elmhurst College, IL
Elon College, NC
Emporia State University, KS
Erskine College, SC
Fairfield University, CT
Faulkner University, AL
Ferris State University, MI
Ferrum College, VA
Flagler College, FL
Florida International University, FL
Florida Southern College, FL
Fontbonne College, MO
Fort Lewis College, CO
Francis Marion University, SC
Franklin College of Indiana, IN
Freed-Hardeman University, TN
Fresno Pacific University, CA
Friends University, KS
Frostburg State University, MD
Gannon University, PA
George Fox University, OR
Georgetown College, KY
The George Washington University, DC
Georgia College and State University, GA
Georgia State University, GA
Goucher College, MD
Grace College, IN
Graceland College, IA
Grand Valley State University, MI
Grand View College, IA

Green Mountain College, VT
Greensboro College, NC
Gustavus Adolphus College, MN
Hannibal-LaGrange College, MO
Hardin-Simmons University, TX
Hastings College, NE
Henderson State University, AR
Hendrix College, AR
Hobart and William Smith Colleges, NY
Hofstra University, NY
Hope College, MI
Howard Payne University, TX
Howard University, DC
Huntingdon College, AL
Huntington College, IN
Idaho State University, ID
Illinois State University, IL
Illinois Wesleyan University, IL
Indiana University of Pennsylvania, PA
Indiana U–Purdue U Fort Wayne, IN
Ithaca College, NY
Jacksonville State University, AL
Jacksonville University, FL
James Madison University, VA
Johnson State College, VT
Kalamazoo College, MI
Kansas Newman College, KS
Kansas State University, KS
Kansas Wesleyan University, KS
Keene State College, NH
Kentucky Christian College, KY
Kentucky Wesleyan College, KY
King College, TN
Knox College, IL
LaGrange College, GA
Lake Forest College, IL
Lambuth University, TN
Lander University, SC
La Sierra University, CA
Lees-McRae College, NC
Lewis University, IL
Long Island U, C.W. Post Campus, NY
Longwood College, VA
Louisiana College, LA
Louisiana State University and A&M College, LA
Louisiana Tech University, LA
Loyola University Chicago, IL
Manchester College, IN
Mankato State University, MN
Marian College, IN
Marquette University, WI
Marshall University, WV
Mars Hill College, NC
Martin Methodist College, TN
Marymount Manhattan College, NY
Maryville College, TN
Mary Washington College, VA
Marywood University, PA
McMurry University, TX
McNeese State University, LA
Mercer University, Macon, GA
Merrimack College, MA
Mesa State College, CO
Methodist College, NC
Miami University, OH
Michigan Christian College, MI

Michigan State University, MI
Midland Lutheran College, NE
Milligan College, TN
Millikin University, IL
Millsaps College, MS
Minot State University, ND
Mississippi State University, MS
Mississippi University for Women, MS
Missouri Southern State College, MO
Monmouth College, IL
Montana State U–Bozeman, MT
Montreat College, NC
Moorhead State University, MN
Morehead State University, KY
Morningside College, IA
Mount Marty College, SD
Mount Mercy College, IA
Mount Union College, OH
Muhlenberg College, PA
Murray State University, KY
Muskingum College, OH
National-Louis University, IL
Nazareth College of Rochester, NY
Nebraska Wesleyan University, NE
Newberry College, SC
New Mexico Highlands University, NM
New Mexico State University, NM
Niagara University, NY
North Carolina Agricultural and Technical
   State U, NC
North Carolina Central University, NC
North Carolina School of the Arts, NC
North Central Bible College, MN
North Central College, IL
Northeastern Illinois University, IL
Northeastern State University, OK
Northeast Louisiana University, LA
Northern Arizona University, AZ
Northern Illinois University, IL
Northern Michigan University, MI
Northern State University, SD
North Greenville College, SC
North Park University, IL
Northwestern College, IA
Northwestern Oklahoma State University,
   OK
Northwestern State University of Louisiana,
   LA
Northwest Missouri State University, MO
Nyack College, NY
Oglethorpe University, GA
Ohio Northern University, OH
The Ohio State University, OH
Ohio University, OH
Ohio Wesleyan University, OH
Oklahoma Christian U of Science and Arts,
   OK
Oklahoma Panhandle State University, OK
Old Dominion University, VA
Ottawa University, KS
Otterbein College, OH
Palm Beach Atlantic College, FL
Park College, MO
Pepperdine University, Malibu, CA
Peru State College, NE
Piedmont College, GA

Plymouth State College of the U System of
   NH, NH
Point Loma Nazarene College, CA
Point Park College, PA
Portland State University, OR
Purchase College, State U of NY, NY
Radford University, VA
Rhode Island College, RI
Rhodes College, TN
The Richard Stockton College of New
   Jersey, NJ
Rider University, NJ
Ripon College, WI
Rockford College, IL
Rocky Mountain College, MT
Rollins College, FL
St. Ambrose University, IA
St. Cloud State University, MN
St. Edward's University, TX
Saint Francis College, PA
Saint John's University, MN
St. John's University, NY
Saint Joseph's University, PA
Saint Louis University, MO
Saint Mary College, KS
Saint Mary's University of Minnesota, MN
St. Norbert College, WI
Sam Houston State University, TX
Santa Clara University, CA
Seton Hill College, PA
Sheldon Jackson College, AK
Shenandoah University, VA
Shimer College, IL
Shorter College, GA
Siena Heights College, MI
Simpson College, IA
Sonoma State University, CA
South Dakota State University, SD
Southeastern Oklahoma State University,
   OK
Southeast Missouri State University, MO
Southern Adventist University, TN
Southern Arkansas University–Magnolia,
   AR
Southern Illinois University at
   Edwardsville, IL
Southern Methodist University, TX
Southern Oregon University, OR
Southern Utah University, UT
Southern Wesleyan University, SC
Southwest Baptist University, MO
Southwestern Adventist University, TX
Southwestern College, KS
Southwestern Oklahoma State University,
   OK
Southwestern University, TX
Southwest Missouri State University, MO
Southwest State University, MN
Southwest Texas State University, TX
State U of NY at Oswego, NY
State U of NY College at Fredonia, NY
State U of NY College at Geneseo, NY
State U of NY College at Plattsburgh, NY
Stephen F. Austin State University, TX
Stephens College, MO
Sterling College, KS
Stetson University, FL

Sul Ross State University, TX
Tabor College, KS
Tarleton State University, TX
Taylor University, IN
Texas A&M University, College Station,
   TX
Texas A&M University–Commerce, TX
Texas Christian University, TX
Texas Lutheran University, TX
Texas Tech University, TX
Texas Woman's University, TX
Thomas More College, KY
Towson University, MD
Trevecca Nazarene University, TN
Trinity Christian College, IL
Troy State University, Troy, AL
Truman State University, MO
The University of Akron, OH
The University of Alabama at Birmingham,
   AL
U of Alaska Fairbanks, AK
University of Arkansas at Little Rock, AR
University of California, Riverside, CA
University of Central Arkansas, AR
University of Central Oklahoma, OK
University of Colorado at Boulder, CO
University of Connecticut, Storrs, CT
University of Denver, CO
University of Evansville, IN
The University of Findlay, OH
University of Hartford, CT
University of Hawaii at Hilo, HI
University of Houston, TX
University of Idaho, ID
University of Indianapolis, IN
The University of Iowa, IA
University of Kansas, KS
University of La Verne, CA
University of Mary, ND
University of Maryland Baltimore County,
   MD
University of Maryland College Park, MD
University of Maryland Eastern Shore, MD
University of Massachusetts Amherst, MA
University of Michigan, Ann Arbor, MI
University of Michigan–Flint, MI
University of Minnesota, Duluth, MN
University of Mississippi, MS
University of Missouri–Rolla, MO
The University of Montana–Missoula, MT
University of Nebraska at Kearney, NE
University of Nebraska–Lincoln, NE
University of Nevada, Las Vegas, NV
University of Nevada, Reno, NV
University of New Mexico, NM
University of North Carolina at Asheville,
   NC
University of North Dakota, ND
University of Northern Colorado, CO
University of Northern Iowa, IA
University of Oklahoma, OK
University of Portland, OR
U of Puerto Rico, Cayey University
   College, PR
University of Puget Sound, WA
University of St. Thomas, TX

Theater/Drama (continued)

University of Science and Arts of
  Oklahoma, OK
University of Sioux Falls, SD
University of South Alabama, AL
U of South Carolina, Columbia, SC
University of South Dakota, SD
University of Southern Colorado, CO
University of Southern Indiana, IN
University of Southern Maine, ME
University of Southern Mississippi, MS
University of South Florida, FL
University of Tennessee at Chattanooga, TN
The University of Texas at Arlington, TX
The University of Texas at El Paso, TX
The University of Texas–Pan American, TX
University of the Arts, PA
University of Toledo, OH
University of Tulsa, OK
University of Utah, UT
University of Washington, WA
University of West Florida, FL
University of Wisconsin–Green Bay, WI
University of Wisconsin–La Crosse, WI
University of Wisconsin–Oshkosh, WI
University of Wisconsin–Platteville, WI
University of Wisconsin–River Falls, WI
University of Wisconsin–Stevens Point, WI
University of Wisconsin–Superior, WI
University of Wisconsin–Whitewater, WI
University of Wyoming, WY
Upper Iowa University, IA
Valdosta State University, GA
Valley City State University, ND
Valparaiso University, IN
Virginia Polytechnic Institute and State U,
  VA
Viterbo College, WI
Wabash College, IN
Wagner College, NY
Wake Forest University, NC
Washburn University of Topeka, KS
Washington College, MD
Washington State University, WA
Wayne State College, NE
Weber State University, UT
Webster University, MO
Wesleyan College, GA
Western Illinois University, IL
Western Michigan University, MI
Western Oregon University, OR
Western State College of Colorado, CO
Western Washington University, WA
West Liberty State College, WV
Westminster College, PA
Westminster College of Salt Lake City, UT
Westmont College, CA
West Texas A&M University, TX
West Virginia University, WV
West Virginia Wesleyan College, WV
Whitman College, WA
Whittier College, CA
Whitworth College, WA
Wichita State University, KS
Willamette University, OR
William Carey College, MS
William Jewell College, MO

William Penn College, IA
William Woods University, MO
Wilmington College, OH
Winona State University, MN
Wittenberg University, OH
Wright State University, OH
Xavier University, OH
York College, NE

SPECIAL ACHIEVEMENTS/ ACTIVITIES

CHEERLEADING/DRUM MAJOR

Abilene Christian University, TX
Alabama State University, AL
Angelo State University, TX
Anna Maria College, MA
Arkansas Tech University, AR
Auburn University, AL
Baker University, KS
Bellarmine College, KY
Benedictine College, KS
Bethel College, IN
Boise State University, ID
California Baptist College, CA
Campbell University, NC
Central Methodist College, MO
Central Missouri State University, MO
Charleston Southern University, SC
Claflin College, SC
College of St. Francis, IL
Cumberland College, KY
David Lipscomb University, TN
Drury College, MO
East Central University, OK
Emporia State University, KS
Faulkner University, AL
Francis Marion University, SC
Gardner-Webb University, NC
Georgia College and State University, GA
Grambling State University, LA
Harding University, AR
Hawaii Pacific University, HI
Huron University, SD
Iowa Wesleyan College, IA
Jacksonville State University, AL
James Madison University, VA
Kansas Wesleyan University, KS
Lambuth University, TN
Lees-McRae College, NC
Lincoln Memorial University, TN
Long Island U, Brooklyn Campus, NY
Louisiana Tech University, LA
McNeese State University, LA
MidAmerica Nazarene University, KS
Mississippi College, MS
Mississippi State University, MS
Missouri Baptist College, MO
Missouri Western State College, MO
Morehead State University, KY
Newberry College, SC
Northeastern State University, OK
Northeast Louisiana University, LA
North Greenville College, SC
Northwestern Oklahoma State University,
  OK

Northwestern State University of Louisiana,
  LA
Northwest Missouri State University, MO
The Ohio State University, OH
Oklahoma City University, OK
Oklahoma Panhandle State University, OK
Oral Roberts University, OK
Ottawa University, KS
Saint Francis College, PA
Saint Joseph's College, IN
St. Mary's University of San Antonio, TX
Sam Houston State University, TX
Southeastern Louisiana University, LA
Southeast Missouri State University, MO
Southern Arkansas University–Magnolia,
  AR
Southern Utah University, UT
Southwestern College, KS
Southwestern Oklahoma State University,
  OK
Stephen F. Austin State University, TX
Sterling College, KS
Stetson University, FL
Tabor College, KS
Tennessee Technological University, TN
Tennessee Wesleyan College, TN
Texas Wesleyan University, TX
Union College, KY
The University of Alabama at Birmingham,
  AL
University of Arkansas at Monticello, AR
University of Central Arkansas, AR
University of Mary Hardin-Baylor, TX
The University of Memphis, TN
University of Nebraska at Kearney, NE
University of Nebraska–Lincoln, NE
University of Nevada, Las Vegas, NV
University of Nevada, Reno, NV
University of North Alabama, AL
U of Puerto Rico, Cayey University
  College, PR
University of Science and Arts of
  Oklahoma, OK
U of South Carolina, Columbia, SC
University of Southern Mississippi, MS
The University of Tennessee at Martin, TN
The University of Texas at Arlington, TX
The University of Texas at El Paso, TX
University of Tulsa, OK
The University of West Alabama, AL
Western Baptist College, OR
West Texas A&M University, TX
William Carey College, MS
William Jewell College, MO
Wofford College, SC

COMMUNITY SERVICE

Adams State College, CO
Agnes Scott College, GA
Antioch College, OH
Aquinas College, MI
Augsburg College, MN
Barry University, FL
Baylor University, TX
Beaver College, PA
Bellarmine College, KY

Bentley College, MA
Berry College, GA
Bethel College, MN
Bluffton College, OH
Bradford College, MA
Brandeis University, MA
California Polytechnic State U, San Luis Obispo, CA
California State University, Chico, CA
Calvin College, MI
Canisius College, NY
Central Bible College, MO
Charleston Southern University, SC
Chatham College, PA
Cleary College, MI
Colby-Sawyer College, NH
College of Charleston, SC
College of New Rochelle, NY
College of St. Catherine, MN
College of St. Joseph, VT
Coll of Staten Island of the City U of NY, NY
The College of Wooster, OH
Concord College, WV
Crichton College, TN
The Defiance College, OH
DePaul University, IL
DePauw University, IN
Dominican College of San Rafael, CA
Dominican University, IL
Earlham College, IN
Eastern Nazarene College, MA
Eastern New Mexico University, NM
Eastern Oregon University, OR
Eckerd College, FL
Edgewood College, WI
Electronic Data Processing College of Puerto Rico, PR
The Evergreen State College, WA
Ferrum College, VA
Fresno Pacific University, CA
Georgia State University, GA
Grace College, IN
Green Mountain College, VT
Greensboro College, NC
Guilford College, NC
Gustavus Adolphus College, MN
Gwynedd-Mercy College, PA
Hampshire College, MA
Hillsdale College, MI
Howard Payne University, TX
Illinois Institute of Technology, IL
Illinois State University, IL
Immaculata College, PA
Indiana University of Pennsylvania, PA
Iowa State University of Science and Technology, IA
Johnson Bible College, TN
Johnson State College, VT
Juniata College, PA
Kean College of New Jersey, NJ
Kennesaw State University, GA
Kentucky Christian College, KY
Knox College, IL
La Salle University, PA
Lewis University, IL
Loras College, IA

Loyola Marymount University, CA
Lyndon State College, VT
Malone College, OH
Manhattan College, NY
Marymount College, NY
Maryville College, TN
Maryville University of Saint Louis, MO
McKendree College, IL
Mercyhurst College, PA
Michigan State University, MI
Mid-America Bible College, OK
Midland Lutheran College, NE
Miles College, AL
Millsaps College, MS
Missouri Western State College, MO
Montana State U–Northern, MT
Morehouse College, GA
Mount Angel Seminary, OR
Mount Carmel College of Nursing, OH
Mount St. Clare College, IA
Mount St. Mary's College, CA
New England College, NH
Northeast Louisiana University, LA
Nova Southeastern University, FL
Oglethorpe University, GA
Ohio Wesleyan University, OH
Old Dominion University, VA
Olivet College, MI
Oral Roberts University, OK
Otterbein College, OH
Ouachita Baptist University, AR
Portland State University, OR
Providence College, RI
Queens College, NC
Quincy University, IL
Regis College, MA
Robert Morris College, IL
Roberts Wesleyan College, NY
Rockhurst College, MO
St. John Fisher College, NY
St. John's University, NY
Saint Joseph's College, ME
St. Lawrence University, NY
St. Louis College of Pharmacy, MO
Saint Louis University, MO
Saint Mary College, KS
St. Olaf College, MN
St. Thomas Aquinas College, NY
San Diego State University, CA
Siena Heights College, MI
Sierra Nevada College, NV
Southern Adventist University, TN
Southern Wesleyan University, SC
Southwestern Adventist University, TX
Southwestern College, KS
Spalding University, KY
Spring Hill College, AL
State U of NY at New Paltz, NY
State U of NY College at Brockport, NY
State U of NY College at Geneseo, NY
Stetson University, FL
Texas Tech University, TX
Union College, NE
United States International University, CA
Unity College, ME
University of Arkansas at Little Rock, AR
University of California, San Diego, CA

University of Colorado at Colorado Springs, CO
University of Hawaii at Hilo, HI
University of Indianapolis, IN
University of Kansas, KS
University of La Verne, CA
University of Maryland Eastern Shore, MD
University of Michigan–Flint, MI
University of Nevada, Las Vegas, NV
University of New England, ME
University of St. Thomas, MN
University of St. Thomas, TX
U of South Carolina, Columbia, SC
University of Southern Maine, ME
University of Tulsa, OK
University of Washington, WA
Urbana University, OH
Ursuline College, OH
Valdosta State University, GA
Virginia Polytechnic Institute and State U, VA
Voorhees College, SC
Wabash College, IN
Walla Walla College, WA
Waynesburg College, PA
Webber College, FL
Wesleyan College, GA
Western Illinois University, IL
Western Michigan University, MI
Westfield State College, MA
West Virginia Wesleyan College, WV
Wheeling Jesuit University, WV
William Woods University, MO
Wilson College, PA
Wittenberg University, OH
Wofford College, SC
Xavier University, OH

HOBBIES/INTERESTS

Augusta State University, GA
California State Polytechnic University, Pomona, CA
California State University, Chico, CA
Capital University, OH
Central Washington University, WA
College of New Rochelle, NY
Eastern New Mexico University, NM
Edgewood College, WI
Emmaus Bible College, IA
Eugene Bible College, OR
Great Lakes Christian College, MI
Hardin-Simmons University, TX
Hawaii Pacific University, HI
Illinois State University, IL
Illinois Wesleyan University, IL
Indiana University of Pennsylvania, PA
Lake Erie College, OH
Lawrence Technological University, MI
Louisiana State University and A&M College, LA
Lycoming College, PA
Macalester College, MN
Mesa State College, CO
Michigan State University, MI
Montana State U–Northern, MT
Northeastern State University, OK
The Ohio State University, OH

Hobbies/Interests (continued)

Oklahoma Baptist University, OK
Rhode Island College, RI
Rhodes College, TN
Robert Morris College, PA
Sacred Heart University, CT
St. John's University, NY
Shimer College, IL
Stephen F. Austin State University, TX
University of Minnesota, Twin Cities Campus, MN
University of Nevada, Las Vegas, NV
University of New England, ME
University of South Alabama, AL
Valdosta State University, GA
Western Baptist College, OR
Winston-Salem State University, NC

JUNIOR MISS

Albertson College of Idaho, ID
Belhaven College, MS
Bethel College, MN
Birmingham-Southern College, AL
Brigham Young University–Hawaii Campus, HI
Caldwell College, NJ
Campbell University, NC
Charleston Southern University, SC
College of New Rochelle, NY
College of Saint Benedict, MN
College of Saint Elizabeth, NJ
Columbia College, MO
Elizabethtown College, PA
Hawaii Pacific University, HI
Huntingdon College, AL
Idaho State University, ID
Johnson & Wales University, FL
Johnson & Wales University, RI
Johnson & Wales University, SC
Lewis-Clark State College, ID
Lindsey Wilson College, KY
Malone College, OH
McMurry University, TX
Michigan State University, MI
Mississippi College, MS
Mississippi University for Women, MS
Mount Vernon Nazarene College, OH
Murray State University, KY
Northeastern State University, OK
North Greenville College, SC
Ohio Northern University, OH
Oklahoma City University, OK
Ottawa University, KS
Roberts Wesleyan College, NY
Saint Francis College, PA
South Dakota State University, SD
Tennessee Wesleyan College, TN
Thomas College, GA
University of Mobile, AL
University of Montevallo, AL
University of South Alabama, AL
The University of Texas at Arlington, TX
Westmar University, IA
William Carey College, MS
William Penn College, IA

LEADERSHIP

Abilene Christian University, TX
Adams State College, CO
Adrian College, MI
Alabama State University, AL
Alaska Pacific University, AK
Alderson-Broaddus College, WV
Alfred University, NY
Allentown College of St. Francis de Sales, PA
Anderson College, SC
Anna Maria College, MA
Aquinas College, MI
Ashland University, OH
Augsburg College, MN
Austin College, TX
Austin Peay State University, TN
Averett College, VA
Baldwin-Wallace College, OH
Ball State University, IN
Baptist Bible College of Pennsylvania, PA
Barclay College, KS
Barry University, FL
Barton College, NC
Baylor University, TX
Beaver College, PA
Becker College–Leicester Campus, MA
Becker College–Worcester Campus, MA
Belhaven College, MS
Bellarmine College, KY
Bellevue University, NE
Bethany College, WV
Bethel College, IN
Bethel College, MN
Bluffton College, OH
Boise Bible College, ID
Bowling Green State University, OH
Bradford College, MA
Brewton-Parker College, GA
Briar Cliff College, IA
Brigham Young University–Hawaii Campus, HI
Bryan College, TN
Bryant College, RI
Buena Vista University, IA
Butler University, IN
Caldwell College, NJ
California Lutheran University, CA
California Polytechnic State U, San Luis Obispo, CA
California State Polytechnic University, Pomona, CA
California State University, Chico, CA
California State University, Stanislaus, CA
Calumet College of Saint Joseph, IN
Cameron University, OK
Canisius College, NY
Capital University, OH
Cardinal Stritch University, WI
Carlow College, PA
Carroll College, MT
Carson-Newman College, TN
Carthage College, WI
Case Western Reserve University, OH
Catawba College, NC
Cedarville College, OH
Centenary College, NJ

Centenary College of Louisiana, LA
Central Christian College of the Bible, MO
Central Methodist College, MO
Central Missouri State University, MO
Central State University, OH
Chapman University, CA
Charleston Southern University, SC
Chatham College, PA
Chicago State University, IL
The Citadel, The Military Coll of South Carolina, SC
Clark Atlanta University, GA
Clarke College, IA
Clarkson University, NY
Colby-Sawyer College, NH
College of Charleston, SC
College of Mount St. Joseph, OH
College of Mount Saint Vincent, NY
College of New Rochelle, NY
College of Notre Dame of Maryland, MD
College of St. Joseph, VT
College of Saint Mary, NE
Coll of Staten Island of the City U of NY, NY
Colorado Christian University, CO
Columbia College, MO
Columbia College, SC
Columbia Union College, MD
Concordia University at Austin, TX
Concordia University Wisconsin, WI
Cornell College, IA
Cornerstone College, MI
Crichton College, TN
Crown College, MN
Cumberland University, TN
Dakota Wesleyan University, SD
Dallas Baptist University, TX
David Lipscomb University, TN
David N. Myers College, OH
Davidson College, NC
Deaconess College of Nursing, MO
The Defiance College, OH
Delaware State University, DE
Delta State University, MS
Denison University, OH
DePauw University, IN
Dickinson State University, ND
Dominican College of Blauvelt, NY
Dordt College, IA
Drury College, MO
East Carolina University, NC
East Coast Bible College, NC
Eastern College, PA
Eastern Michigan University, MI
Eastern Nazarene College, MA
Eastern New Mexico University, NM
Eastern Oregon University, OR
Eckerd College, FL
Edgewood College, WI
Elmira College, NY
Elon College, NC
Embry-Riddle Aeronautical University, AZ
Embry-Riddle Aeronautical University, FL
Embry-Riddle Aeronautical U, Extended Campus, FL
Emmaus Bible College, IA
Erskine College, SC

Eureka College, IL
Evangel College, MO
Fairleigh Dickinson U,
  Teaneck-Hackensack, NJ
Faith Baptist Bible Coll and Theological
  Seminary, IA
Faulkner University, AL
Flagler College, FL
Florida Institute of Technology, FL
Fontbonne College, MO
Franklin College of Indiana, IN
Franklin University, OH
Freed-Hardeman University, TN
Fresno Pacific University, CA
Friends University, KS
Gannon University, PA
George Fox University, OR
The George Washington University, DC
Georgia Institute of Technology, GA
Georgia Southwestern State University, GA
Georgia State University, GA
Golden Gate University, CA
Gordon College, MA
Grace College, IN
Graceland College, IA
Grambling State University, LA
Green Mountain College, VT
Greensboro College, NC
Greenville College, IL
Grove City College, PA
Gwynedd-Mercy College, PA
Hampshire College, MA
Hanover College, IN
Harding University, AR
Hardin-Simmons University, TX
Heidelberg College, OH
Hendrix College, AR
Hilbert College, NY
Hillsdale College, MI
Hiram College, OH
Hofstra University, NY
Hollins College, VA
Hood College, MD
Hope International University, CA
Howard Payne University, TX
Huntingdon College, AL
Huntington College, IN
Idaho State University, ID
Illinois Institute of Technology, IL
Illinois State University, IL
Immaculata College, PA
Indiana University of Pennsylvania, PA
Iowa State University of Science and
  Technology, IA
Jacksonville State University, AL
James Madison University, VA
Jamestown College, ND
John Brown University, AR
Johnson & Wales University, FL
Johnson & Wales University, RI
Johnson & Wales University, SC
Johnson Bible College, TN
Johnson State College, VT
Juniata College, PA
Kansas Newman College, KS
Kansas State University, KS
Kean College of New Jersey, NJ

Kendall College, IL
Kentucky Christian College, KY
Kentucky Wesleyan College, KY
Keuka College, NY
King's College, PA
Knoxville College, TN
Lake Forest College, IL
Lancaster Bible College, PA
Lander University, SC
La Sierra University, CA
Lees-McRae College, NC
Le Moyne College, NY
Lenoir-Rhyne College, NC
Lewis-Clark State College, ID
Lexington Baptist College, KY
Limestone College, SC
Lindsey Wilson College, KY
Long Island U, Brooklyn Campus, NY
Louisiana College, LA
Louisiana State University and A&M
  College, LA
Lynchburg College, VA
Lyndon State College, VT
Lyon College, AR
MacMurray College, IL
Malone College, OH
Manhattan Christian College, KS
Manhattan College, NY
Mankato State University, MN
Marquette University, WI
Marycrest International University, IA
Marygrove College, MI
Marymount College, NY
Marymount Manhattan College, NY
Marymount University, VA
Maryville University of Saint Louis, MO
McKendree College, IL
Menlo College, CA
Meredith College, NC
Merrimack College, MA
Messiah College, PA
Michigan Christian College, MI
Michigan State University, MI
Michigan Technological University, MI
Mid-America Bible College, OK
MidAmerica Nazarene University, KS
Middle Tennessee State University, TN
Midwestern State University, TX
Millsaps College, MS
Mills College, CA
Minnesota Bible College, MN
Mississippi College, MS
Mississippi State University, MS
Moody Bible Institute, IL
Morehead State University, KY
Mount Marty College, SD
Mount Mary College, WI
Mount Mercy College, IA
Mount Olive College, NC
Mount St. Mary's College, CA
Muhlenberg College, PA
Murray State University, KY
Muskingum College, OH
National University, CA
New England College, NH
New Mexico State University, NM
Nicholls State University, LA

Northeast Louisiana University, LA
Northern Michigan University, MI
Northern State University, SD
North Georgia College & State University,
  GA
Northland College, WI
Northwestern State University of Louisiana,
  LA
Northwest Missouri State University, MO
Nyack College, NY
Oakland University, MI
The Ohio State University, OH
Oklahoma Baptist University, OK
Oklahoma Christian U of Science and Arts,
  OK
Oklahoma City University, OK
Old Dominion University, VA
Olivet College, MI
Oral Roberts University, OK
Otterbein College, OH
Ouachita Baptist University, AR
Pace University, NY
Pacific Lutheran University, WA
Palm Beach Atlantic College, FL
Patten College, CA
Peru State College, NE
Philadelphia College of Bible, PA
Piedmont College, GA
Practical Bible College, NY
Presbyterian College, SC
Purdue University North Central, IN
Queens College, NC
Quincy University, IL
Quinnipiac College, CT
Radford University, VA
Reformed Bible College, MI
Regis College, MA
Reinhardt College, GA
The Richard Stockton College of New
  Jersey, NJ
Ripon College, WI
Robert Morris College, PA
Roberts Wesleyan College, NY
Rockhurst College, MO
Sacred Heart University, CT
St. Andrews Presbyterian College, NC
St. Edward's University, TX
Saint John's University, MN
St. John's University, NY
Saint Joseph's College, ME
St. Louis Christian College, MO
St. Louis College of Pharmacy, MO
Saint Louis University, MO
Saint Mary-of-the-Woods College, IN
Saint Mary's University of Minnesota, MN
Saint Peter's College, Jersey City, NJ
St. Thomas Aquinas College, NY
Saint Vincent College, PA
Saint Xavier University, IL
Salem College, NC
Samford University, AL
Sam Houston State University, TX
San Diego State University, CA
Seattle Pacific University, WA
Seattle University, WA
Seton Hall University, NJ
Shepherd College, WV

Leadership (continued)

Simpson College, CA
Slippery Rock University of Pennsylvania, PA
South Dakota State University, SD
Southeast Missouri State University, MO
Southern Adventist University, TN
Southern Arkansas University–Magnolia, AR
Southern Oregon University, OR
Southern Utah University, UT
Southern Wesleyan University, SC
Southwestern Adventist University, TX
Southwestern College, KS
Southwest State University, MN
Spalding University, KY
State U of NY at Oswego, NY
State U of NY College at Brockport, NY
State U of NY College at Fredonia, NY
State U of NY College at Geneseo, NY
State U of NY College at Plattsburgh, NY
Stephen F. Austin State University, TX
Sterling College, KS
Stetson University, FL
Stonehill College, MA
Sul Ross State University, TX
Sweet Briar College, VA
Taylor University, IN
Tennessee Temple University, TN
Tennessee Wesleyan College, TN
Texas A&M University, College Station, TX
Texas Christian University, TX
Texas Lutheran University, TX
Texas Wesleyan University, TX
Thiel College, PA
Thomas More College, KY
Trinity Baptist College, FL
Trinity Bible College, ND
Trinity Christian College, IL
Trinity College, DC
Trinity International University, IL
Trinity International U, South Florida Campus, FL
Truman State University, MO
Union College, NE
Union University, TN
United States International University, CA
Unity College, ME
The University of Alabama at Birmingham, AL
The University of Alabama in Huntsville, AL
University of Arkansas at Little Rock, AR
University of Arkansas at Monticello, AR
University of California, San Diego, CA
University of Central Arkansas, AR
University of Central Oklahoma, OK
The University of Charleston, WV
University of Colorado at Boulder, CO
University of Colorado at Colorado Springs, CO
University of Dallas, TX
University of Delaware, DE
University of Evansville, IN
University of Hawaii at Hilo, HI
University of Houston, TX

University of Idaho, ID
University of Kansas, KS
University of La Verne, CA
University of Mary Hardin-Baylor, TX
University of Maryland Eastern Shore, MD
The University of Memphis, TN
University of Michigan–Flint, MI
University of Minnesota, Crookston, MN
University of Mississippi, MS
University of Mobile, AL
The University of Montana–Missoula, MT
University of Nebraska at Kearney, NE
University of Nebraska at Omaha, NE
University of Nebraska–Lincoln, NE
University of Nevada, Las Vegas, NV
University of Nevada, Reno, NV
University of New England, ME
University of North Alabama, AL
University of Northern Iowa, IA
University of North Florida, FL
University of Oklahoma, OK
University of Pittsburgh at Johnstown, PA
University of Puget Sound, WA
University of Redlands, CA
University of Rochester, NY
University of St. Thomas, MN
University of Science and Arts of Oklahoma, OK
University of Sioux Falls, SD
University of South Alabama, AL
University of South Dakota, SD
University of Southern Colorado, CO
University of Southern Indiana, IN
University of Southern Mississippi, MS
The University of Tampa, FL
The University of Texas at Arlington, TX
The University of Texas at El Paso, TX
University of the Ozarks, AR
University of Toledo, OH
University of Tulsa, OK
University of Utah, UT
University of Washington, WA
University of Wisconsin–Platteville, WI
University of Wisconsin–Stevens Point, WI
University of Wisconsin–Whitewater, WI
University of Wyoming, WY
Urbana University, OH
Ursinus College, PA
Ursuline College, OH
Valley Forge Christian College, PA
Valparaiso University, IN
Villa Julie College, MD
Virginia Military Institute, VA
Virginia Polytechnic Institute and State U, VA
Wabash College, IN
Wake Forest University, NC
Walla Walla College, WA
Warner Pacific College, OR
Warner Southern College, FL
Warren Wilson College, NC
Washington Bible College, MD
Waynesburg College, PA
Wayne State College, NE
Webber College, FL
Weber State University, UT
Wells College, NY

Wesleyan College, GA
Western Baptist College, OR
Western Illinois University, IL
Western Maryland College, MD
Western Washington University, WA
Westminster College, MO
Westminster College, PA
Westmont College, CA
West Texas A&M University, TX
West Virginia State College, WV
West Virginia University, WV
Whitman College, WA
Widener University, PA
Wilkes University, PA
Willamette University, OR
William Carey College, MS
William Penn College, IA
William Woods University, MO
Wilmington College, OH
Wittenberg University, OH
Wofford College, SC
Wright State University, OH
Xavier University, OH

MEMBERSHIPS

Adams State College, CO
Alfred University, NY
Allentown College of St. Francis de Sales, PA
Aquinas College, MI
Art Institute of Boston, MA
Atlanta Christian College, GA
Auburn University, AL
Barry University, FL
Birmingham-Southern College, AL
Blue Mountain College, MS
California State University, Chico, CA
Cedar Crest College, PA
Central Washington University, WA
Charleston Southern University, SC
College of New Rochelle, NY
College of Saint Benedict, MN
College of St. Catherine, MN
Columbia College, MO
Columbia Union College, MD
Dallas Baptist University, TX
Eastern Connecticut State University, CT
Eastern New Mexico University, NM
Eastern Washington University, WA
Erskine College, SC
Georgia State University, GA
Hawaii Pacific University, HI
Hood College, MD
Idaho State University, ID
Illinois Institute of Technology, IL
Immaculata College, PA
Johnson & Wales University, FL
Johnson & Wales University, RI
Johnson & Wales University, SC
Johnson State College, VT
Kansas Newman College, KS
Lincoln University, MO
Lock Haven University of Pennsylvania, PA
Longwood College, VA
Loras College, IA
Loyola University Chicago, IL
Manchester College, IN

McNeese State University, LA
Michigan State University, MI
Mid-America Bible College, OK
Mississippi College, MS
Mississippi State University, MS
Montana State U–Northern, MT
Mount St. Clare College, IA
Muhlenberg College, PA
North Carolina Agricultural and Technical State U, NC
Northwestern Oklahoma State University, OK
Northwest Missouri State University, MO
Northwood University, Florida Campus, FL
The Ohio State University, OH
Old Dominion University, VA
Oral Roberts University, OK
Peru State College, NE
Portland State University, OR
Rhodes College, TN
Ripon College, WI
St. Andrews Presbyterian College, NC
Saint Joseph's College, ME
Saint Louis University, MO
Saint Mary's University of Minnesota, MN
Shawnee State University, OH
South Dakota State University, SD
Tennessee Technological University, TN
Tennessee Wesleyan College, TN
Texas A&M University, College Station, TX
Texas Tech University, TX
The University of Alabama at Birmingham, AL
University of Arkansas at Little Rock, AR
University of Missouri–St. Louis, MO
University of Nebraska at Kearney, NE
University of Nebraska at Omaha, NE
University of Nevada, Las Vegas, NV
University of Sioux Falls, SD
University of the Sacred Heart, PR
University of Toledo, OH
Virginia Polytechnic Institute and State U, VA
Washington College, MD
Wayne State University, MI
Western Baptist College, OR
Western Maryland College, MD
Western Washington University, WA
West Texas A&M University, TX
Wiley College, TX
William Woods University, MO

RELIGIOUS INVOLVEMENT

Alaska Bible College, AK
Allentown College of St. Francis de Sales, PA
Anderson College, SC
Anna Maria College, MA
Arizona Bible College, AZ
Atlanta Christian College, GA
Augsburg College, MN
Austin College, TX
Azusa Pacific University, CA
Baker University, KS
Baptist Bible College of Pennsylvania, PA
Barry University, FL

Bartlesville Wesleyan College, OK
Barton College, NC
Baylor University, TX
Bellarmine College, KY
Bethany College, WV
Bethune-Cookman College, FL
Bluefield College, VA
Blue Mountain College, MS
Boise Bible College, ID
Brewton-Parker College, GA
Briar Cliff College, IA
California Lutheran University, CA
Calvary Bible College and Theological Seminary, MO
Calvin College, MI
Campbell University, NC
Carlow College, PA
The Catholic University of America, DC
Centenary College of Louisiana, LA
Central Baptist College, AR
Central Bible College, MO
Central Christian College of the Bible, MO
Central College, IA
Central Methodist College, MO
Chapman University, CA
Charleston Southern University, SC
The Citadel, The Military Coll of South Carolina, SC
Clear Creek Baptist Bible College, KY
College of Charleston, SC
College of Notre Dame of Maryland, MD
College of Saint Mary, NE
The College of Wooster, OH
Colorado Christian University, CO
Columbia Union College, MD
Concordia University, CA
Concordia University, OR
Concordia University Wisconsin, WI
Cornerstone College, MI
Crichton College, TN
The Criswell College, TX
David Lipscomb University, TN
Davidson College, NC
The Defiance College, OH
Dominican University, IL
Drury College, MO
East Texas Baptist University, TX
Emmanuel College, GA
Emmaus Bible College, IA
Eugene Bible College, OR
Faulkner University, AL
Flagler College, FL
Florida Christian College, FL
Gardner-Webb University, NC
Georgetown College, KY
Grace College, IN
Graceland College, IA
Great Lakes Christian College, MI
Green Mountain College, VT
Hannibal-LaGrange College, MO
Harding University, AR
Hendrix College, AR
Hope International University, CA
Houghton College, NY
Howard Payne University, TX
Immaculata College, PA
Johnson Bible College, TN

John Wesley College, NC
Judson College, IL
Kansas Newman College, KS
Kentucky Christian College, KY
King College, TN
Lancaster Bible College, PA
Limestone College, SC
Lindsey Wilson College, KY
Loras College, IA
Loyola Marymount University, CA
Lynchburg College, VA
MacMurray College, IL
Malone College, OH
Manhattan Christian College, KS
Mars Hill College, NC
Mercyhurst College, PA
Michigan State University, MI
Mid-America Bible College, OK
Midland Lutheran College, NE
Minnesota Bible College, MN
Mississippi College, MS
Missouri Baptist College, MO
Moravian College, PA
Mount Marty College, SD
Mount St. Clare College, IA
Mount Vernon Nazarene College, OH
Muskingum College, OH
Neumann College, PA
North Carolina Agricultural and Technical State U, NC
North Central Bible College, MN
North Central College, IL
North Greenville College, SC
Nyack College, NY
Oakland City University, IN
Oglethorpe University, GA
Oklahoma Baptist University, OK
Oklahoma Christian U of Science and Arts, OK
Oklahoma City University, OK
Old Dominion University, VA
Olivet Nazarene University, IL
Oral Roberts University, OK
Ottawa University, KS
Ouachita Baptist University, AR
Ozark Christian College, MO
Palm Beach Atlantic College, FL
Patten College, CA
Paul Quinn College, TX
Philadelphia College of Bible, PA
Phillips University, OK
Reformed Bible College, MI
Roberts Wesleyan College, NY
St. Andrews Presbyterian College, NC
St. John's University, NY
Saint Leo College, FL
St. Louis Christian College, MO
St. Olaf College, MN
Shorter College, GA
Simpson College, CA
Southeastern Baptist College, MS
Southeastern College of the Assemblies of God, FL
Southern Adventist University, TN
Southern Wesleyan University, SC
Southwestern Adventist University, TX
Southwestern College, KS

Religious Involvement (continued)

Stetson University, FL
Tabor College, KS
Taylor University, IN
Tennessee Wesleyan College, TN
Texas Christian University, TX
Texas Lutheran University, TX
Texas Wesleyan University, TX
Thomas More College, KY
Transylvania University, KY
Trevecca Nazarene University, TN
Trinity Baptist College, FL
Trinity Bible College, ND
Trinity International University, IL
Union College, NE
University of Detroit Mercy, MI
University of Mary Hardin-Baylor, TX
University of Puget Sound, WA
University of the Pacific, CA
Urbana University, OH
Valparaiso University, IN
Wake Forest University, NC
Warner Pacific College, OR
Washington Bible College, MD
Wesley College, DE
Wesley College, MS
Western Baptist College, OR
Wheeling Jesuit University, WV
William Carey College, MS
William Jewell College, MO
William Penn College, IA
Wilson College, PA
Wingate University, NC
Wofford College, SC
Xavier University of Louisiana, LA

RODEO

Albertson College of Idaho, ID
Boise State University, ID
California Polytechnic State U, San Luis Obispo, CA
Chadron State College, NE
Dickinson State University, ND
Eastern New Mexico University, NM
Eastern Oregon University, OR
Idaho State University, ID
McNeese State University, LA
Montana State U–Northern, MT
Murray State University, KY
New Mexico State University, NM
Northwestern Oklahoma State University, OK
Oklahoma Panhandle State University, OK
Sam Houston State University, TX
Sinte Gleska University, SD
South Dakota State University, SD
Southern Arkansas University–Magnolia, AR
Southwestern Oklahoma State University, OK
Stephen F. Austin State University, TX
Tarleton State University, TX
Teikyo Post University, CT
Texas A&M University, College Station, TX
Texas A&M University–Kingsville, TX
Texas Tech University, TX

University of Idaho, ID
The University of Montana–Missoula, MT
University of Nevada, Las Vegas, NV
The University of Tennessee at Martin, TN
The University of West Alabama, AL
University of Wyoming, WY
Weber State University, UT
Western Montana College of The U of Montana, MT
West Texas A&M University, TX

SPECIAL CHARACTERISTICS

ADULT STUDENTS

Agnes Scott College, GA
Allentown College of St. Francis de Sales, PA
Anderson College, SC
Anderson University, IN
Arkansas State University, AR
Arkansas Tech University, AR
Barry University, FL
Bay Path College, MA
Bellarmine College, KY
Berry College, GA
Bethel College, IN
Biola University, CA
Boise Bible College, ID
California Lutheran University, CA
California State University, Chico, CA
Calumet College of Saint Joseph, IN
Central Baptist College, AR
Central Christian College of the Bible, MO
Central Michigan University, MI
Central Missouri State University, MO
Central Washington University, WA
Charleston Southern University, SC
Chatham College, PA
College of Charleston, SC
College of Mount St. Joseph, OH
College of Santa Fe, NM
Detroit College of Business, Dearborn, MI
Detroit College of Business–Flint, MI
East Carolina University, NC
Eastern Oregon University, OR
Eastern Washington University, WA
East Stroudsburg University of Pennsylvania, PA
Edinboro University of Pennsylvania, PA
Faulkner University, AL
Fort Hays State University, KS
Francis Marion University, SC
Franklin Pierce College, NH
Freed-Hardeman University, TN
Grace University, NE
Greensboro College, NC
Hastings College, NE
Indiana University of Pennsylvania, PA
Inter Amer U of PR, Barranquitas Campus, PR
Iowa State University of Science and Technology, IA
Juniata College, PA
Kentucky State University, KY
La Sierra University, CA
Long Island U, C.W. Post Campus, NY
Lyndon State College, VT

Manhattan Christian College, KS
Mars Hill College, NC
Marygrove College, MI
Mary Washington College, VA
Medaille College, NY
Michigan Christian College, MI
Millsaps College, MS
Mississippi State University, MS
Mississippi University for Women, MS
Montana State U–Northern, MT
Morehead State University, KY
Murray State University, KY
New Mexico State University, NM
North Central College, IL
Northwestern College, IA
Northwestern State University of Louisiana, LA
The Ohio State University, OH
Ohio University–Lancaster, OH
Oklahoma State U, OK
Old Dominion University, VA
Purdue University North Central, IN
Queens College, NC
Randolph-Macon Woman's College, VA
Reinhardt College, GA
The Richard Stockton College of New Jersey, NJ
St. Ambrose University, IA
St. Edward's University, TX
Saint Francis College, IN
Saint Francis College, PA
Saint Mary-of-the-Woods College, IN
Sonoma State University, CA
Southeastern Louisiana University, LA
Southern Arkansas University–Magnolia, AR
Southwest Missouri State University, MO
State U of NY at Oswego, NY
Stephen F. Austin State University, TX
Suffolk University, MA
Texas Christian University, TX
The University of Akron, OH
The University of Alabama at Birmingham, AL
University of Great Falls, MT
University of Kansas, KS
University of Maine at Fort Kent, ME
University of Maryland College Park, MD
The University of Memphis, TN
University of North Carolina at Charlotte, NC
University of Northern Colorado, CO
University of Pittsburgh, PA
University of Southern Indiana, IN
The University of Texas at San Antonio, TX
University of Toledo, OH
University of Vermont, VT
University of Wisconsin–Green Bay, WI
Weber State University, UT
Western Michigan University, MI
Wichita State University, KS
Winthrop University, SC
Wright State University, OH

CHILDREN AND SIBLINGS OF ALUMNI

Adelphi University, NY

Albany College of Pharmacy of Union
  University, NY
Albertson College of Idaho, ID
Albright College, PA
Alverno College, WI
Anderson College, SC
Anna Maria College, MA
Aquinas College, MI
Arizona Bible College, AZ
Arkansas State University, AR
Asbury College, KY
Ashland University, OH
Augustana College, IL
Augustana College, SD
Baptist Bible College of Pennsylvania, PA
Barclay College, KS
Barry University, FL
Bartlesville Wesleyan College, OK
Benedictine University, IL
Bloomfield College, NJ
Boston University, MA
Bradley University, IL
Brescia College, KY
Bryan College, TN
Cabrini College, PA
Caldwell College, NJ
California Lutheran University, CA
California State Polytechnic University,
  Pomona, CA
Capital University, OH
Carroll College, MT
Carroll College, WI
Carson-Newman College, TN
Carthage College, WI
Central Christian College of the Bible, MO
Central College, IA
Central Missouri State University, MO
Centre College, KY
Chaminade University of Honolulu, HI
Chapman University, CA
Chatham College, PA
Cincinnati Bible College and Seminary, OH
The Citadel, The Military Coll of South
  Carolina, SC
Clarke College, IA
Clarkson College, NE
Coe College, IA
Coker College, SC
Coleman College, CA
College of Charleston, SC
College of Mount St. Joseph, OH
College of Mount Saint Vincent, NY
College of St. Catherine, MN
College of Saint Elizabeth, NJ
College of St. Scholastica, MN
Colorado Christian University, CO
Colorado School of Mines, CO
Columbia College, MO
Columbia International University, SC
Concordia College, MI
Concordia College, NE
Crichton College, TN
Culver-Stockton College, MO
Cumberland College, KY
Daemen College, NY
Dallas Baptist University, TX
Dana College, NE

The Defiance College, OH
Delta State University, MS
DePauw University, IN
Detroit College of Business, Dearborn, MI
Detroit College of Business–Flint, MI
Dominican College of San Rafael, CA
Dominican University, IL
Dordt College, IA
Dowling College, NY
Drury College, MO
Eastern Mennonite University, VA
Eastern Michigan University, MI
Eastern Nazarene College, MA
Eastern New Mexico University, NM
Eastern Washington University, WA
Edinboro University of Pennsylvania, PA
Emmanuel College, MA
Emporia State University, KS
Erskine College, SC
Fairleigh Dickinson U,
  Teaneck-Hackensack, NJ
Fitchburg State College, MA
Florida Christian College, FL
Florida Southern College, FL
Fordham University, NY
Francis Marion University, SC
Franklin College of Indiana, IN
Friends University, KS
Frostburg State University, MD
George Fox University, OR
Gonzaga University, WA
Gordon College, MA
Grace University, NE
Grambling State University, LA
Greensboro College, NC
Greenville College, IL
Gustavus Adolphus College, MN
Hiram College, OH
Holy Names College, CA
Hope International University, CA
Howard Payne University, TX
Howard University, DC
Huron University, SD
Idaho State University, ID
Illinois Institute of Technology, IL
Indiana State University, IN
Indiana Wesleyan University, IN
James Madison University, VA
Kansas Newman College, KS
Kansas Wesleyan University, KS
Kent State University, OH
Kentucky Christian College, KY
Kentucky Wesleyan College, KY
Lake Forest College, IL
Lancaster Bible College, PA
Lenoir-Rhyne College, NC
Lewis University, IL
Long Island U, Brooklyn Campus, NY
Long Island U, Southampton College, NY
Longwood College, VA
Loras College, IA
Louisiana State University and A&M
  College, LA
Loyola Marymount University, CA
MacMurray College, IL
Maharishi University of Management, IA
Malone College, OH

Manchester College, IN
Maranatha Baptist Bible College, WI
Marymount Manhattan College, NY
Marymount University, VA
Mary Washington College, VA
McNeese State University, LA
Merrimack College, MA
Michigan Christian College, MI
Michigan State University, MI
Michigan Technological University, MI
Midway College, KY
Milwaukee School of Engineering, WI
Mississippi College, MS
Mississippi State University, MS
Mississippi University for Women, MS
Missouri Baptist College, MO
Montana State U–Billings, MT
Montana State U–Northern, MT
Moravian College, PA
Morehead State University, KY
Morningside College, IA
Mount St. Clare College, IA
Mount Senario College, WI
Mount Union College, OH
Murray State University, KY
Muskingum College, OH
Nazareth College of Rochester, NY
New Mexico State University, NM
Northern Arizona University, AZ
Northwestern College, IA
Northwestern State University of Louisiana,
  LA
Northwood University, MI
Northwood University, Florida Campus, FL
Northwood University, Texas Campus, TX
Notre Dame College, NH
Notre Dame College of Ohio, OH
Nyack College, NY
The Ohio State University, OH
Ohio University–Eastern, OH
Ohio Wesleyan University, OH
Oklahoma Baptist University, OK
Oklahoma Christian U of Science and Arts,
  OK
Oklahoma State U, OK
Oral Roberts University, OK
Ottawa University, KS
Otterbein College, OH
Pacific Lutheran University, WA
Philadelphia College of Bible, PA
Pine Manor College, MA
Practical Bible College, NY
Presentation College, SD
Principia College, IL
Quincy University, IL
Reinhardt College, GA
Ripon College, WI
Rockford College, IL
Rockhurst College, MO
Rocky Mountain College, MT
St. Ambrose University, IA
Saint Francis College, IN
St. John Fisher College, NY
St. John's University, NY
Saint Joseph's College, IN
St. Joseph's College, New York, NY
Saint Mary-of-the-Woods College, IN

Children and Siblings of Alumni
(continued)

Saint Mary's College of California, CA
Santa Clara University, CA
Seattle Pacific University, WA
Seattle University, WA
Seton Hill College, PA
Shimer College, IL
Siena Heights College, MI
Simpson College, IA
Sonoma State University, CA
Southwestern College, KS
Southwestern Oklahoma State University,
  OK
Southwestern University, TX
Southwest Missouri State University, MO
Spalding University, KY
State U of NY at Oswego, NY
State U of NY College at Fredonia, NY
Stevens Institute of Technology, NJ
Tabor College, KS
Taylor University, IN
Teikyo Post University, CT
Tennessee Temple University, TN
Trevecca Nazarene University, TN
Trinity Christian College, IL
Truman State University, MO
Union College, KY
The University of Alabama at Birmingham,
  AL
University of Arkansas at Pine Bluff, AR
University of Delaware, DE
University of Detroit Mercy, MI
University of Dubuque, IA
University of Evansville, IN
The University of Findlay, OH
University of Idaho, ID
University of La Verne, CA
University of Mary Hardin-Baylor, TX
University of Massachusetts Amherst, MA
University of Mississippi, MS
University of Missouri–Rolla, MO
The University of Montana–Missoula, MT
University of Nevada, Las Vegas, NV
University of Nevada, Reno, NV
University of North Carolina at Pembroke,
  NC
University of Northern Colorado, CO
University of Oklahoma, OK
University of Rio Grande, OH
University of Rochester, NY
University of South Alabama, AL
U of South Carolina, Columbia, SC
University of Southern Mississippi, MS
University of Toledo, OH
University of Tulsa, OK
University of Wisconsin–Oshkosh, WI
University of Wyoming, WY
Upper Iowa University, IA
Ursuline College, OH
Valley City State University, ND
Valparaiso University, IN
Virginia Military Institute, VA
Viterbo College, WI
Walsh University, OH
Warner Pacific College, OR
Warner Southern College, FL

Wartburg College, IA
Washington and Jefferson College, PA
Webber College, FL
Wells College, NY
Wesleyan College, GA
Western Michigan University, MI
Westmar University, IA
Westminster College, MO
Westminster College, PA
Wheeling Jesuit University, WV
Whittier College, CA
Whitworth College, WA
William Carey College, MS
William Woods University, MO
Wilmington College, OH
Wilson College, PA
Wittenberg University, OH
Worcester State College, MA

CHILDREN OF CURRENT STUDENTS

Anderson College, SC
Becker College–Worcester Campus, MA
Bloomfield College, NJ
California State Polytechnic University,
  Pomona, CA
Calvary Bible College and Theological
  Seminary, MO
Carlow College, PA
College of New Rochelle, NY
The Defiance College, OH
Huntington College, IN
Jacksonville University, FL
Johnson & Wales University, FL
Johnson & Wales University, RI
Johnson & Wales University, SC
Johnson Bible College, TN
Lasell College, MA
Maryville University of Saint Louis, MO
Mount St. Clare College, IA
North Central Bible College, MN
Nyack College, NY
Oklahoma Christian U of Science and Arts,
  OK
Olivet Nazarene University, IL
Palm Beach Atlantic College, FL
Presentation College, SD
Queens College, NC
Rockford College, IL
Southwestern College, KS
The University of Alabama at Birmingham,
  AL
University of Mary Hardin-Baylor, TX
Upper Iowa University, IA
Valley Forge Christian College, PA
Wesleyan College, GA
Wilkes University, PA

CHILDREN OF EDUCATORS

Agnes Scott College, GA
Allentown College of St. Francis de Sales,
  PA
Becker College–Leicester Campus, MA
Benedictine College, KS
Brigham Young University–Hawaii Campus,
  HI
Centenary College of Louisiana, LA
Clearwater Christian College, FL
Colby-Sawyer College, NH

College of St. Francis, IL
Crown College, MN
Emmanuel College, MA
Endicott College, MA
Ferrum College, VA
Franklin College of Indiana, IN
Gallaudet University, DC
Hannibal-LaGrange College, MO
Hastings College, NE
Hilbert College, NY
Illinois College, IL
James Madison University, VA
John Brown University, AR
Juniata College, PA
Lees-McRae College, NC
Lycoming College, PA
Mississippi State University, MS
New England College, NH
New York Institute of Technology, NY
Oklahoma Christian U of Science and Arts,
  OK
Pacific Lutheran University, WA
Practical Bible College, NY
Reinhardt College, GA
Rockford College, IL
Rosemont College, PA
St. Ambrose University, IA
Salem College, NC
Seattle University, WA
Shenandoah University, VA
Sonoma State University, CA
Tennessee Technological University, TN
The University of Alabama at Birmingham,
  AL
University of Central Arkansas, AR
The University of Charleston, WV
University of Dubuque, IA
The University of Memphis, TN
University of St. Thomas, MN
University of St. Thomas, TX
University of Toledo, OH
The University of West Alabama, AL
Villanova University, PA
Virginia Wesleyan College, VA
Warner Southern College, FL
Washington College, MD
Wells College, NY
William Carey College, MS

CHILDREN OF FACULTY/STAFF

Abilene Christian University, TX
Adrian College, MI
Agnes Scott College, GA
Alaska Bible College, AK
Albertson College of Idaho, ID
Albright College, PA
Alderson-Broaddus College, WV
Allentown College of St. Francis de Sales,
  PA
Alma College, MI
Alvernia College, PA
Anderson College, SC
Anderson University, IN
Anna Maria College, MA
Arizona Bible College, AZ
Arkansas Tech University, AR
Ashland University, OH

Atlanta Christian College, GA
Augustana College, IL
Austin College, TX
Azusa Pacific University, CA
Baker University, KS
Ball State University, IN
Barry University, FL
Bartlesville Wesleyan College, OK
Barton College, NC
Baylor University, TX
Bay Path College, MA
Becker College–Leicester Campus, MA
Becker College–Worcester Campus, MA
Belhaven College, MS
Bellarmine College, KY
Belmont University, TN
Benedictine College, KS
Bennett College, NC
Berry College, GA
Bethany College, WV
Bethel College, IN
Biola University, CA
Birmingham-Southern College, AL
Bloomsburg University of Pennsylvania, PA
Bluffton College, OH
Boise Bible College, ID
Boston College, MA
Brenau University, GA
Brescia College, KY
Brewton-Parker College, GA
Brigham Young University–Hawaii Campus, HI
Bryan College, TN
Cabrini College, PA
Caldwell College, NJ
California Baptist College, CA
California Lutheran University, CA
California State University, Chico, CA
California State University, Stanislaus, CA
Calumet College of Saint Joseph, IN
Calvin College, MI
Campbell University, NC
Capital University, OH
Cascade College, OR
Case Western Reserve University, OH
Catawba College, NC
The Catholic University of America, DC
Cedarville College, OH
Centenary College of Louisiana, LA
Central Bible College, MO
Central Christian College of the Bible, MO
Central College, IA
Central Methodist College, MO
Central Michigan University, MI
Central Missouri State University, MO
Central State University, OH
Centre College, KY
Chadron State College, NE
Chaminade University of Honolulu, HI
Chapman University, CA
Charleston Southern University, SC
Chatham College, PA
Cheyney University of Pennsylvania, PA
Chowan College, NC
Christian Heritage College, CA
Circleville Bible College, OH
Claflin College, SC

Clarke College, IA
Clarkson College, NE
Clarkson University, NY
Clear Creek Baptist Bible College, KY
Cleary College, MI
Clemson University, SC
Colby College, ME
Colby-Sawyer College, NH
College of Charleston, SC
College of Insurance, NY
College of Mount Saint Vincent, NY
College of New Rochelle, NY
College of St. Catherine, MN
College of St. Scholastica, MN
College of Santa Fe, NM
The College of West Virginia, WV
The College of Wooster, OH
Colorado Christian University, CO
Columbia College, SC
Columbia College of Nursing, WI
Concordia College, St. Paul, MN
Concordia College, NE
Concordia College, NY
Concordia University, CA
Cornell College, IA
Cornerstone College, MI
Covenant College, GA
Creighton University, NE
Crown College, MN
Cumberland College, KY
Dallas Baptist University, TX
Dana College, NE
David Lipscomb University, TN
David N. Myers College, OH
Davidson College, NC
The Defiance College, OH
Delta State University, MS
DePaul University, IL
DePauw University, IN
Dickinson College, PA
Dillard University, LA
Dordt College, IA
Dowling College, NY
Duquesne University, PA
East Carolina University, NC
East Coast Bible College, NC
Eastern Mennonite University, VA
Edinboro University of Pennsylvania, PA
Elizabethtown College, PA
Elmira College, NY
Elon College, NC
Emmanuel College, GA
Emmanuel College, MA
Emmaus Bible College, IA
Emory & Henry College, VA
Emory University, GA
Emporia State University, KS
Erskine College, SC
Evangel College, MO
Fairfield University, CT
Faith Baptist Bible Coll and Theological Seminary, IA
Faulkner University, AL
Ferrum College, VA
Fisk University, TN
Flagler College, FL
Florida Christian College, FL

Florida Metropolitan U-Orlando Coll, North, FL
Florida Southern College, FL
Fordham University, NY
Framingham State College, MA
Franciscan University of Steubenville, OH
Francis Marion University, SC
Franklin College of Indiana, IN
Franklin Pierce College, NH
Freed-Hardeman University, TN
Gallaudet University, DC
Geneva College, PA
Georgetown University, DC
The George Washington University, DC
Georgia College and State University, GA
Georgia Institute of Technology, GA
Grace College, IN
Graceland College, IA
Grace University, NE
Grambling State University, LA
Grand Valley State University, MI
Green Mountain College, VT
Greensboro College, NC
Greenville College, IL
Grove City College, PA
Guilford College, NC
Hamline University, MN
Hampden-Sydney College, VA
Hampshire College, MA
Hannibal-LaGrange College, MO
Hardin-Simmons University, TX
Hartwick College, NY
Hastings College, NE
Hawaii Pacific University, HI
Henderson State University, AR
Hendrix College, AR
Hillsdale College, MI
Holy Family College, PA
Hope International University, CA
Howard Payne University, TX
Huntington College, IN
Idaho State University, ID
Illinois College, IL
Illinois Institute of Technology, IL
Illinois State University, IL
Immaculata College, PA
Indiana State University, IN
Indiana U–Purdue U Fort Wayne, IN
Inter American U of PR, Aguadilla Campus, PR
Iowa Wesleyan College, IA
Jackson State University, MS
Jacksonville University, FL
James Madison University, VA
Jamestown College, ND
John Brown University, AR
John Carroll University, OH
Johns Hopkins University, MD
Johnson Bible College, TN
John Wesley College, NC
Judson College, IL
Juniata College, PA
Kalamazoo College, MI
Kansas Wesleyan University, KS
Kendall College, IL
Kentucky Christian College, KY
King College, TN

Children of Faculty/Staff (continued)

King's College, PA
Knoxville College, TN
Kutztown University of Pennsylvania, PA
Lake Erie College, OH
Lancaster Bible College, PA
La Salle University, PA
Lasell College, MA
La Sierra University, CA
Lawrence Technological University, MI
Lees-McRae College, NC
Lehigh University, PA
Lenoir-Rhyne College, NC
LeTourneau University, TX
Limestone College, SC
Lincoln Memorial University, TN
Lincoln University, MO
Lindenwood College, MO
Lindsey Wilson College, KY
Linfield College, OR
Long Island U, Brooklyn Campus, NY
Long Island U, C.W. Post Campus, NY
Long Island U, Southampton College, NY
Louisiana College, LA
Louisiana Tech University, LA
Loyola Marymount University, CA
Lycoming College, PA
Lynchburg College, VA
Lyndon State College, VT
Lynn University, FL
MacMurray College, IL
Maharishi University of Management, IA
Maine Maritime Academy, ME
Malone College, OH
Manhattan Christian College, KS
Manhattan College, NY
Marian College of Fond du Lac, WI
Mars Hill College, NC
Mary Baldwin College, VA
Maryland Institute, College of Art, MD
Marymount University, VA
Mary Washington College, VA
The Master's College and Seminary, CA
McKendree College, IL
McMurry University, TX
McNeese State University, LA
Mercer University, Macon, GA
Mercyhurst College, PA
Merrimack College, MA
Michigan Christian College, MI
Michigan State University, MI
Mid-America Bible College, OK
MidAmerica Nazarene University, KS
Midway College, KY
Milligan College, TN
Millsaps College, MS
Milwaukee Institute of Art and Design, WI
Milwaukee School of Engineering, WI
Minnesota Bible College, MN
Mississippi College, MS
Mississippi State University, MS
Mississippi University for Women, MS
Missouri Baptist College, MO
Missouri Southern State College, MO
Montreat College, NC
Morehouse College, GA
Morningside College, IA

Mount Marty College, SD
Mount St. Clare College, IA
Mount Saint Mary College, NY
Mount Senario College, WI
Mount Union College, OH
Mount Vernon Nazarene College, OH
Murray State University, KY
Nazareth College of Rochester, NY
Nebraska Christian College, NE
Neumann College, PA
Newberry College, SC
New England College, NH
New Hampshire College, NH
New Mexico State University, NM
New York Institute of Technology, NY
Niagara University, NY
Nichols College, MA
North Central Bible College, MN
North Central College, IL
Northeastern Illinois University, IL
Northeast Louisiana University, LA
Northern Illinois University, IL
North Greenville College, SC
Northwest College of the Assemblies of
   God, WA
Northwestern College, IA
Northwestern College, MN
Northwood University, MI
Northwood University, Florida Campus, FL
Northwood University, Texas Campus, TX
Notre Dame College of Ohio, OH
Nova Southeastern University, FL
Nyack College, NY
Oak Hills Bible College, MN
Oglethorpe University, GA
Ohio Northern University, OH
The Ohio State University, OH
Ohio University, OH
Ohio Wesleyan University, OH
Oklahoma Baptist University, OK
Oklahoma Christian U of Science and Arts,
   OK
Oklahoma City University, OK
Old Dominion University, VA
Olivet Nazarene University, IL
Oral Roberts University, OK
Ottawa University, KS
Otterbein College, OH
Ouachita Baptist University, AR
Our Lady of the Lake University of San
   Antonio, TX
Ozark Christian College, MO
Pacific Lutheran University, WA
Paine College, GA
Park College, MO
Pepperdine University, Malibu, CA
Philadelphia College of Bible, PA
Phillips University, OK
Piedmont Bible College, NC
Plymouth State College of the U System of
   NH, NH
Point Loma Nazarene College, CA
Practical Bible College, NY
Presentation College, SD
Puget Sound Christian College, WA
Purdue University, West Lafayette, IN
Purdue University North Central, IN

Quincy University, IL
Quinnipiac College, CT
Randolph-Macon Woman's College, VA
Reformed Bible College, MI
Regis University, CO
Reinhardt College, GA
Rhode Island School of Design, RI
Rhodes College, TN
Rice University, TX
The Richard Stockton College of New
   Jersey, NJ
Ripon College, WI
Roanoke Bible College, NC
Robert Morris College, IL
Robert Morris College, PA
Roberts Wesleyan College, NY
Rockford College, IL
Rockhurst College, MO
Rocky Mountain College, MT
Rust College, MS
Rutgers, State U of NJ, Camden Coll of
   Arts & Scis, NJ
Rutgers, State U of NJ, College of
   Engineering, NJ
Rutgers, State U of NJ, College of Nursing,
   NJ
Rutgers, State U of NJ, College of
   Pharmacy, NJ
Rutgers, State U of NJ, Cook College, NJ
Rutgers, State U of NJ, Douglass College,
   NJ
Rutgers, State U of NJ, Livingston College,
   NJ
Rutgers, State U of NJ, Mason Gross
   School of Arts, NJ
Rutgers, State U of NJ, Newark Coll of
   Arts & Scis, NJ
Rutgers, State U of NJ, Rutgers College, NJ
Rutgers, State U of NJ, U Coll–Camden,
   NJ
Rutgers, State U of NJ, U Coll–Newark, NJ
Rutgers, State U of NJ, U Coll–New
   Brunswick, NJ
St. Ambrose University, IA
Saint Anselm College, NH
Saint Augustine's College, NC
St. Bonaventure University, NY
St. Cloud State University, MN
St. Edward's University, TX
Saint Francis College, PA
St. John's College, NM
St. John's University, NY
Saint Joseph's College, IN
Saint Joseph's College, ME
St. Joseph's College, New York, NY
Saint Leo College, FL
St. Louis College of Pharmacy, MO
Saint Louis University, MO
Saint Mary College, KS
Saint Mary's College, IN
Saint Mary's College of California, CA
St. Mary's University of San Antonio, TX
St. Norbert College, WI
Saint Peter's College, Jersey City, NJ
Saint Xavier University, IL
Salem College, NC
Samford University, AL

Seattle University, WA
Seton Hall University, NJ
Seton Hill College, PA
Shaw University, NC
Sierra Nevada College, NV
Simpson College, IA
Slippery Rock University of Pennsylvania, PA
Sonoma State University, CA
Southeastern Baptist College, MS
Southeastern College of the Assemblies of God, FL
Southeastern Louisiana University, LA
Southern Arkansas University–Magnolia, AR
Southern California College, CA
Southern Connecticut State University, CT
Southern Methodist University, TX
Southern Oregon University, OR
Southern Wesleyan University, SC
Southwestern Adventist University, TX
Southwestern Christian College, TX
Southwestern College, KS
Southwestern University, TX
Southwest Missouri State University, MO
Spalding University, KY
Spring Arbor College, MI
Spring Hill College, AL
Stetson University, FL
Stevens Institute of Technology, NJ
Stillman College, AL
Stonehill College, MA
Syracuse University, NY
Tabor College, KS
Tarleton State University, TX
Taylor University, IN
Tennessee Technological University, TN
Tennessee Wesleyan College, TN
Texas A&M University, College Station, TX
Texas Christian University, TX
Texas Tech University, TX
Thiel College, PA
Thomas College, GA
Touro College, NY
Transylvania University, KY
Trinity Bible College, ND
Trinity Christian College, IL
Truman State University, MO
Tufts University, MA
Tulane University, LA
Tusculum College, TN
Tuskegee University, AL
United States International University, CA
The University of Alabama at Birmingham, AL
U of Alaska Anchorage, AK
University of Arizona, AZ
University of Arkansas at Monticello, AR
University of Bridgeport, CT
University of Central Arkansas, AR
The University of Charleston, WV
University of Cincinnati, OH
University of Dallas, TX
University of Detroit Mercy, MI
University of Dubuque, IA
The University of Findlay, OH

University of Guam, GU
University of Hartford, CT
University of Idaho, ID
University of Illinois at Chicago, IL
University of Indianapolis, IN
University of La Verne, CA
University of Maine at Presque Isle, ME
University of Mary, ND
University of Mary Hardin-Baylor, TX
University of Maryland College Park, MD
University of Maryland Eastern Shore, MD
University of Massachusetts Amherst, MA
The University of Memphis, TN
University of Nebraska at Kearney, NE
University of Nebraska at Omaha, NE
University of Nevada, Las Vegas, NV
University of Nevada, Reno, NV
University of New England, ME
University of New Hampshire at Manchester, NH
University of New Mexico, NM
University of North Alabama, AL
University of North Carolina at Asheville, NC
University of Northern Colorado, CO
University of Notre Dame, IN
University of Pittsburgh, PA
University of Pittsburgh at Johnstown, PA
University of Portland, OR
U of Puerto Rico, Cayey University College, PR
U of Puerto Rico, Mayagüez Campus, PR
U of Puerto Rico Medical Sciences Campus, PR
University of Puget Sound, WA
University of Rio Grande, OH
University of San Diego, CA
University of San Francisco, CA
University of Scranton, PA
University of South Alabama, AL
U of South Carolina, Columbia, SC
University of Southern Indiana, IN
University of Southern Mississippi, MS
The University of Tampa, FL
University of the District of Columbia, DC
University of the Ozarks, AR
University of the Sacred Heart, PR
University of the Virgin Islands, VI
University of Toledo, OH
University of Utah, UT
The University of West Alabama, AL
Ursuline College, OH
Valley Forge Christian College, PA
Valparaiso University, IN
Virginia Military Institute, VA
Virginia Polytechnic Institute and State U, VA
Virginia Union University, VA
Virginia Wesleyan College, VA
Viterbo College, WI
Voorhees College, SC
Wake Forest University, NC
Walla Walla College, WA
Warner Southern College, FL
Washington and Jefferson College, PA
Waynesburg College, PA
Wayne State College, NE

Webber College, FL
Wesleyan College, GA
Western Baptist College, OR
Western Illinois University, IL
Western Kentucky University, KY
Western Michigan University, MI
West Liberty State College, WV
Westmar University, IA
West Texas A&M University, TX
West Virginia University, WV
West Virginia Wesleyan College, WV
Wheaton College, IL
Wheeling Jesuit University, WV
Widener University, PA
Wiley College, TX
Wilkes University, PA
William Carey College, MS
William Jewell College, MO
William Tyndale College, MI
William Woods University, MO
Wittenberg University, OH
Wofford College, SC
Worcester State College, MA
Xavier University of Louisiana, LA
York College, NE
Youngstown State University, OH

CHILDREN OF PUBLIC SERVANTS

Bay Path College, MA
Carthage College, WI
Detroit College of Business, Dearborn, MI
Detroit College of Business, Warren Campus, MI
Framingham State College, MA
Graceland College, IA
Jackson State University, MS
Louisiana State University and A&M College, LA
Mississippi State University, MS
New York Institute of Technology, NY
Nicholls State University, LA
The Ohio State University, OH
Sonoma State University, CA
Tennessee Technological University, TN
The University of Alabama at Birmingham, AL
University of Delaware, DE
The University of Memphis, TN
University of Nevada, Las Vegas, NV
U of Puerto Rico, Cayey University College, PR
Valdosta State University, GA
Western Kentucky University, KY

CHILDREN OF UNION MEMBERS/COMPANY EMPLOYEES

Arkansas State University, AR
Barton College, NC
Chowan College, NC
Cornerstone College, MI
Dowling College, NY
Edinboro University of Pennsylvania, PA
Emporia State University, KS
Florida Agricultural and Mechanical University, FL
Fordham University, NY
Framingham State College, MA
Frostburg State University, MD

Children of Union Members/Company Employees (continued)

Grand Valley State University, MI
Illinois State University, IL
Mankato State University, MN
Mayville State University, ND
Michigan State University, MI
Northwood University, Florida Campus, FL
Oakland University, MI
The Ohio State University, OH
Philadelphia College of Pharmacy and Science, PA
Rhode Island College, RI
St. Cloud State University, MN
Slippery Rock University of Pennsylvania, PA
Sonoma State University, CA
Stephen F. Austin State University, TX
Texas Christian University, TX
The University of Alabama at Birmingham, AL
University of New Mexico, NM
University of Northern Colorado, CO
U of Puerto Rico at Arecibo, PR
Virginia Commonwealth University, VA
Washington College, MD
Western Michigan University, MI
West Virginia University, WV

CHILDREN OF WORKERS IN TRADES

Dowling College, NY
The Ohio State University, OH
Rockford College, IL
South Dakota State University, SD
State U of NY at Oswego, NY
The University of Alabama at Birmingham, AL
University of Nevada, Las Vegas, NV
West Virginia University, WV
Worcester Polytechnic Institute, MA

CHILDREN WITH A DECEASED OR DISABLED PARENT

Arkansas State University, AR
Bay Path College, MA
California State University, San Bernardino, CA
The Citadel, The Military Coll of South Carolina, SC
College of Charleston, SC
David Lipscomb University, TN
The Defiance College, OH
Edinboro University of Pennsylvania, PA
Erskine College, SC
Harding University, AR
Illinois State University, IL
Indiana State University, IN
Indiana U–Purdue U Fort Wayne, IN
Kentucky State University, KY
Lees-McRae College, NC
Louisiana State University and A&M College, LA
Marian College of Fond du Lac, WI
Nicholls State University, LA
Northeast Louisiana University, LA
The Ohio State University, OH
St. Norbert College, WI

The University of Alabama at Birmingham, AL
Worcester State College, MA

ETHNIC BACKGROUND

Adelphi University, NY
Alabama State University, AL
Alaska Pacific University, AK
Albertson College of Idaho, ID
Anna Maria College, MA
Arkansas State University, AR
Auburn University, AL
Austin College, TX
Azusa Pacific University, CA
Bellarmine College, KY
Benedictine College, KS
Bethany College, WV
Bethel College, MN
Biola University, CA
Boise State University, ID
Brigham Young University–Hawaii Campus, HI
California College of Arts and Crafts, CA
California State University, Bakersfield, CA
California State University, Chico, CA
California State University, Dominguez Hills, CA
California State University, Los Angeles, CA
California State University, San Bernardino, CA
Calvin College, MI
Capital University, OH
Central Bible College, MO
Cheyney University of Pennsylvania, PA
Clarkson College, NE
Clear Creek Baptist Bible College, KY
Clinch Valley College of the U of Virginia, VA
College of Charleston, SC
College of Saint Benedict, MN
College of St. Francis, IL
Dakota Wesleyan University, SD
Dana College, NE
The Defiance College, OH
DePauw University, IN
Detroit College of Business–Flint, MI
Dickinson State University, ND
Drake University, IA
Eastern Mennonite University, VA
Eastern New Mexico University, NM
Eastern Washington University, WA
Emporia State University, KS
Florida Agricultural and Mechanical University, FL
Fort Lewis College, CO
George Fox University, OR
Georgia Institute of Technology, GA
Guilford College, NC
Illinois Institute of Technology, IL
Indiana University of Pennsylvania, PA
Iowa State University of Science and Technology, IA
Iowa Wesleyan College, IA
Johnson Bible College, TN
Lenoir-Rhyne College, NC
Long Island U, Brooklyn Campus, NY

Long Island U, Southampton College, NY
Maharishi University of Management, IA
Michigan State University, MI
Milwaukee Institute of Art and Design, WI
Minot State University, ND
Mississippi University for Women, MS
Molloy College, NY
North Carolina Agricultural and Technical State U, NC
Northland College, WI
The Ohio State University, OH
Oregon Institute of Technology, OR
Pine Manor College, MA
Prairie View A&M University, TX
Regis University, CO
Rhodes College, TN
The Richard Stockton College of New Jersey, NJ
Robert Morris College, PA
Rust College, MS
St. John Fisher College, NY
Shepherd College, WV
Sierra Nevada College, NV
Slippery Rock University of Pennsylvania, PA
Sonoma State University, CA
Southern Utah University, UT
Southwestern College, KS
Southwest Missouri State University, MO
State U of NY at Oswego, NY
State U of NY College at Potsdam, NY
Taylor University, IN
Taylor University, Fort Wayne Campus, IN
Texas A&M University–Commerce, TX
Truman State University, MO
United States International University, CA
The University of Alabama at Birmingham, AL
U of Alaska Anchorage, AK
University of Arizona, AZ
University of California, San Diego, CA
University of Central Oklahoma, OK
University of Colorado at Boulder, CO
University of Dubuque, IA
University of Kansas, KS
University of Michigan–Dearborn, MI
University of Missouri–St. Louis, MO
University of Nebraska–Lincoln, NE
University of Nevada, Las Vegas, NV
University of Nevada, Reno, NV
University of New Hampshire at Manchester, NH
University of Northern Colorado, CO
University of Oklahoma, OK
University of Redlands, CA
University of Rochester, NY
University of Scranton, PA
University of Southern Mississippi, MS
The University of Texas at El Paso, TX
The University of Texas at San Antonio, TX
University of Toledo, OH
University of Vermont, VT
Valparaiso University, IN
Western Carolina University, NC
Western Michigan University, MI
Westmont College, CA

West Virginia State College, WV
West Virginia University, WV
Whitman College, WA
Widener University, PA
Wilkes University, PA
William Woods University, MO
Wittenberg University, OH
Wright State University, OH

FIRST-GENERATION COLLEGE STUDENTS

Austin College, TX
Boise State University, ID
California State University, Chico, CA
California State University, San Bernardino, CA
California State University, Stanislaus, CA
Colorado State University, CO
David N. Myers College, OH
Davidson College, NC
The Defiance College, OH
Dowling College, NY
Eastern New Mexico University, NM
Edinboro University of Pennsylvania, PA
Fort Lewis College, CO
Idaho State University, ID
Illinois State University, IL
Iowa State University of Science and Technology, IA
Long Island U, Brooklyn Campus, NY
Lyndon State College, VT
Michigan State University, MI
Mississippi State University, MS
Morningside College, IA
Saint Francis College, IN
Sonoma State University, CA
Southwest Missouri State University, MO
Stephen F. Austin State University, TX
Tennessee Technological University, TN
Texas Christian University, TX
Texas Lutheran University, TX
The University of Alabama at Birmingham, AL
University of Colorado at Boulder, CO
University of Kansas, KS
University of Maryland Eastern Shore, MD
University of Nevada, Las Vegas, NV
University of Nevada, Reno, NV
University of North Alabama, AL
The University of Texas at Arlington, TX
University of Vermont, VT
Virginia Commonwealth University, VA
West Texas A&M University, TX
William Carey College, MS

HANDICAPPED STUDENTS

Agnes Scott College, GA
Alabama State University, AL
Arkansas State University, AR
Austin College, TX
Barry University, FL
Barton College, NC
California State University, Chico, CA
California State University, Fresno, CA
Calvin College, MI
Clear Creek Baptist Bible College, KY
College of Charleston, SC
College of Saint Elizabeth, NJ

Coll of Staten Island of the City U of NY, NY
The College of Wooster, OH
East Carolina University, NC
Eastern Illinois University, IL
Eastern Washington University, WA
Edinboro University of Pennsylvania, PA
Elizabeth City State University, NC
Emporia State University, KS
Fordham University, NY
Francis Marion University, SC
Frostburg State University, MD
Gallaudet University, DC
Gardner-Webb University, NC
Grand Valley State University, MI
Idaho State University, ID
Illinois State University, IL
Indiana U–Purdue U Fort Wayne, IN
Kentucky State University, KY
Lebanon Valley College, PA
Marygrove College, MI
Midland Lutheran College, NE
Miles College, AL
Mississippi State University, MS
Murray State University, KY
North Carolina Agricultural and Technical State U, NC
Northern Arizona University, AZ
The Ohio State University, OH
Old Dominion University, VA
Rockford College, IL
Rowan University, NJ
Sam Houston State University, TX
San Diego State University, CA
Shenandoah University, VA
Sonoma State University, CA
South Dakota State University, SD
Southeastern Louisiana University, LA
Southwest Missouri State University, MO
Texas Tech University, TX
The University of Akron, OH
The University of Alabama at Birmingham, AL
University of California, San Diego, CA
University of Central Arkansas, AR
University of Idaho, ID
University of Mary Hardin-Baylor, TX
University of Maryland College Park, MD
University of Massachusetts Amherst, MA
The University of Memphis, TN
University of Nebraska–Lincoln, NE
University of Nevada, Las Vegas, NV
University of North Carolina at Asheville, NC
University of Northern Colorado, CO
The University of Texas at Arlington, TX
University of Toledo, OH
West Texas A&M University, TX
Worcester State College, MA

INTERNATIONAL STUDENTS

Adelphi University, NY
Alaska Pacific University, AK
Albright College, PA
Alderson-Broaddus College, WV
Alfred University, NY

Allentown College of St. Francis de Sales, PA
Alvernia College, PA
Anderson University, IN
Asbury College, KY
Augustana College, IL
Augustana College, SD
Augusta State University, GA
Austin College, TX
Azusa Pacific University, CA
Baker University, KS
Barclay College, KS
Barry University, FL
Barton College, NC
Bay Path College, MA
Belhaven College, MS
Bellarmine College, KY
Belmont Abbey College, NC
Bethel College, IN
Bethel College, MN
Bloomsburg University of Pennsylvania, PA
Bluffton College, OH
Boise Bible College, ID
Boise State University, ID
Brenau University, GA
Briar Cliff College, IA
Brigham Young University–Hawaii Campus, HI
Buena Vista University, IA
Caldwell College, NJ
California Lutheran University, CA
California State University, Chico, CA
Calvin College, MI
Capital University, OH
Centenary College of Louisiana, LA
Central College, IA
Central Methodist College, MO
Central Michigan University, MI
Central State University, OH
Chadron State College, NE
Chaminade University of Honolulu, HI
Chatham College, PA
Christian Heritage College, CA
Cincinnati Bible College and Seminary, OH
Circleville Bible College, OH
Clarkson College, NE
Clarkson University, NY
Coe College, IA
College of Charleston, SC
College of Notre Dame of Maryland, MD
College of Saint Benedict, MN
College of St. Catherine, MN
College of Saint Elizabeth, NJ
College of St. Scholastica, MN
The College of Wooster, OH
The Colorado College, CO
Columbia International University, SC
Covenant College, GA
Dana College, NE
DePauw University, IN
Dickinson State University, ND
Dominican University, IL
Dordt College, IA
Drake University, IA
Duquesne University, PA
Eastern Connecticut State University, CT
Eastern Kentucky University, KY

International Students (continued)

Eastern Mennonite University, VA
Eastern Michigan University, MI
Eastern New Mexico University, NM
Eastern Oregon University, OR
Eastern Washington University, WA
East Texas Baptist University, TX
Eckerd College, FL
Edinboro University of Pennsylvania, PA
Elizabethtown College, PA
Emmanuel College, MA
Emmaus Bible College, IA
Emporia State University, KS
Fairleigh Dickinson U,
  Teaneck-Hackensack, NJ
Faulkner University, AL
Fort Valley State University, GA
Franciscan University of Steubenville, OH
Francis Marion University, SC
Franklin Pierce College, NH
Fresno Pacific University, CA
Gallaudet University, DC
George Fox University, OR
The George Washington University, DC
Georgia College and State University, GA
God's Bible School and College, OH
Graceland College, IA
Grand Valley State University, MI
Greensboro College, NC
Hanover College, IN
Harding University, AR
Henderson State University, AR
Hendrix College, AR
Henry Cogswell College, WA
Hillsdale College, MI
Hope International University, CA
Huntington College, IN
Illinois Institute of Technology, IL
Iowa State University of Science and
  Technology, IA
Iowa Wesleyan College, IA
James Madison University, VA
John Brown University, AR
Johnson Bible College, TN
Judson College, IL
Kalamazoo College, MI
Kendall College, IL
Kentucky Christian College, KY
King's College, PA
Lancaster Bible College, PA
Lawrence University, WI
Lees-McRae College, NC
LeTourneau University, TX
Lindsey Wilson College, KY
Long Island U, Brooklyn Campus, NY
Long Island U, C.W. Post Campus, NY
Lutheran Bible Institute of Seattle, WA
Lynchburg College, VA
MacMurray College, IL
Maharishi University of Management, IA
Malone College, OH
Manchester College, IN
Maryland Institute, College of Art, MD
Marymount Manhattan College, NY
Marymount University, VA
Marywood University, PA
Mayville State University, ND

McMurry University, TX
McNeese State University, LA
Mercer University, Macon, GA
Merrimack College, MA
Michigan Technological University, MI
Mid-America Bible College, OK
Midland Lutheran College, NE
Millikin University, IL
Milwaukee School of Engineering, WI
Minnesota Bible College, MN
Minot State University, ND
Montana State U–Northern, MT
Montreat College, NC
Mount Marty College, SD
Mount Mary College, WI
Mount St. Clare College, IA
Mount Vernon College, DC
Mount Vernon Nazarene College, OH
Multnomah Bible College and Biblical
  Seminary, OR
Murray State University, KY
Nebraska Christian College, NE
North Central Bible College, MN
Northeast Louisiana University, LA
Northern Arizona University, AZ
Northern Illinois University, IL
Northwest College of the Assemblies of
  God, WA
Northwestern College, IA
Nyack College, NY
Oak Hills Bible College, MN
The Ohio State University, OH
Ohio Wesleyan University, OH
Oklahoma Christian U of Science and Arts,
  OK
Old Dominion University, VA
Olivet Nazarene University, IL
Oral Roberts University, OK
Otterbein College, OH
Ouachita Baptist University, AR
Pacific Lutheran University, WA
Pacific University, OR
Philadelphia College of Bible, PA
Pine Manor College, MA
Plymouth State College of the U System of
  NH, NH
Practical Bible College, NY
Purdue University, West Lafayette, IN
Queens College, NC
Ramapo College of New Jersey, NJ
Randolph-Macon Woman's College, VA
Reformed Bible College, MI
Rensselaer Polytechnic Institute, NY
The Richard Stockton College of New
  Jersey, NJ
Roanoke Bible College, NC
Roberts Wesleyan College, NY
Rochester Institute of Technology, NY
Rockford College, IL
Rowan University, NJ
Rust College, MS
Saginaw Valley State University, MI
St. Ambrose University, IA
Saint John's University, MN
Saint Joseph's College, ME
Saint Vincent College, PA
Saint Xavier University, IL

Seton Hill College, PA
Simpson College, IA
Sonoma State University, CA
South Dakota State University, SD
Southern Adventist University, TN
Southern Oregon University, OR
Southwestern College, KS
Spalding University, KY
Spring Arbor College, MI
Tabor College, KS
Taylor University, IN
Tennessee Wesleyan College, TN
Texas Christian University, TX
Texas Lutheran University, TX
Texas Tech University, TX
Tri-State University, IN
Truman State University, MO
Tusculum College, TN
United States International University, CA
U of Alaska Anchorage, AK
U of Alaska Southeast, AK
University of Arizona, AZ
University of California, Davis, CA
The University of Charleston, WV
University of Denver, CO
University of Evansville, IN
University of Hartford, CT
University of Idaho, ID
University of Indianapolis, IN
University of Kansas, KS
University of Maine at Fort Kent, ME
University of Maine at Presque Isle, ME
University of Mary Hardin-Baylor, TX
University of Montevallo, AL
University of Nebraska at Kearney, NE
University of Nebraska at Omaha, NE
University of Nebraska–Lincoln, NE
University of Nevada, Las Vegas, NV
University of Nevada, Reno, NV
University of Northern Colorado, CO
University of Science and Arts of
  Oklahoma, OK
University of Sioux Falls, SD
The University of Tampa, FL
The University of Texas at El Paso, TX
University of Vermont, VT
University of Washington, WA
University of Wisconsin–Green Bay, WI
Valdosta State University, GA
Valparaiso University, IN
Warner Southern College, FL
Washington State University, WA
Wayne State College, NE
Wesley College, DE
Wesley College, MS
Western Illinois University, IL
Western Michigan University, MI
Western Oregon University, OR
Western Washington University, WA
Westmont College, CA
West Virginia University, WV
West Virginia Wesleyan College, WV
Whitman College, WA
Whittier College, CA
Willamette University, OR
William Carey College, MS
Wittenberg University, OH

LOCAL/STATE STUDENTS

Abilene Christian University, TX
Alaska Bible College, AK
Alaska Pacific University, AK
Albertson College of Idaho, ID
Albright College, PA
Allegheny College, PA
Allentown College of St. Francis de Sales, PA
Arkansas State University, AR
Art Institute of Boston, MA
Austin College, TX
Averett College, VA
Barton College, NC
Bellarmine College, KY
Benedictine College, KS
Berry College, GA
Bethany College, WV
Bloomfield College, NJ
Bluefield College, VA
Boston University, MA
Brandeis University, MA
Bryan College, TN
California State University, Bakersfield, CA
California State University, Chico, CA
California State University, San Bernardino, CA
California State University, Stanislaus, CA
Calumet College of Saint Joseph, IN
Carroll College, MT
Carthage College, WI
Centenary College of Louisiana, LA
Central College, IA
Central Michigan University, MI
Centre College, KY
Chadron State College, NE
Chaminade University of Honolulu, HI
The Citadel, The Military Coll of South Carolina, SC
Clarion University of Pennsylvania, PA
Clarke College, IA
Clarkson University, NY
Clearwater Christian College, FL
Clinch Valley College of the U of Virginia, VA
College of Charleston, SC
The College of Wooster, OH
Columbia Union College, MD
Columbus College of Art and Design, OH
Concordia College, NE
Creighton University, NE
Culver-Stockton College, MO
Dana College, NE
Davis & Elkins College, WV
The Defiance College, OH
Detroit College of Business, Dearborn, MI
Detroit College of Business–Flint, MI
Dominican College of San Rafael, CA
Dordt College, IA
Dowling College, NY
East Carolina University, NC
Eastern Connecticut State University, CT
Eastern Mennonite University, VA
Eckerd College, FL
Edgewood College, WI
Edinboro University of Pennsylvania, PA
Elizabethtown College, PA

Elmira College, NY
Embry-Riddle Aeronautical University, AZ
Embry-Riddle Aeronautical University, FL
Emporia State University, KS
Fayetteville State University, NC
Ferrum College, VA
Flagler College, FL
Florida Southern College, FL
Florida State University, FL
Fort Lewis College, CO
Framingham State College, MA
Franciscan University of Steubenville, OH
Franklin and Marshall College, PA
Franklin College of Indiana, IN
Frostburg State University, MD
The George Washington University, DC
Georgia Southwestern State University, GA
GMI Engineering & Management Institute, MI
Goddard College, VT
Gonzaga University, WA
Graceland College, IA
Grand Valley State University, MI
Green Mountain College, VT
Hamline University, MN
Hardin-Simmons University, TX
Heidelberg College, OH
Hollins College, VA
Hope International University, CA
Idaho State University, ID
Illinois College, IL
Illinois Institute of Technology, IL
Illinois State University, IL
Indiana Institute of Technology, IN
Indiana U–Purdue U Fort Wayne, IN
Jarvis Christian College, TX
John Carroll University, OH
Johnson State College, VT
Judson College, IL
Kean College of New Jersey, NJ
Kennesaw State University, GA
Laboratory Institute of Merchandising, NY
Lake Erie College, OH
Lawrence University, WI
Lees-McRae College, NC
Lenoir-Rhyne College, NC
Lesley College, MA
LeTourneau University, TX
Limestone College, SC
Longwood College, VA
Lourdes College, OH
Loyola College, MD
Lynchburg College, VA
Maharishi University of Management, IA
Maine Maritime Academy, ME
Mankato State University, MN
Mansfield University of Pennsylvania, PA
Mars Hill College, NC
Martin Methodist College, TN
Marygrove College, MI
Maryland Institute, College of Art, MD
Maryville College, TN
Mary Washington College, VA
Marywood University, PA
Mayville State University, ND
McMurry University, TX
McNeese State University, LA

Mercer University, Macon, GA
Mercyhurst College, PA
Meredith College, NC
Mesa State College, CO
Miami University, OH
Milwaukee Institute of Art and Design, WI
Minot State University, ND
Mississippi State University, MS
Montana State U–Billings, MT
Montreat College, NC
Morehead State University, KY
Morningside College, IA
Mount Senario College, WI
Mount Vernon Nazarene College, OH
Murray State University, KY
Muskingum College, OH
National College, SD
Newberry College, SC
New England College, NH
New Hampshire College, NH
New Mexico Highlands University, NM
New Mexico State University, NM
New York Institute of Technology, NY
Northeastern University, MA
Northwood University, Florida Campus, FL
Northwood University, Texas Campus, TX
Nova Southeastern University, FL
Ohio University–Chillicothe, OH
Oklahoma Baptist University, OK
Old Dominion University, VA
Ottawa University, KS
Pacific University, OR
Philadelphia College of Pharmacy and Science, PA
Pine Manor College, MA
Point Loma Nazarene College, CA
Pontifical College Josephinum, OH
Principia College, IL
Queens College, NC
Quinnipiac College, CT
Randolph-Macon Woman's College, VA
Regis University, CO
Reinhardt College, GA
Rensselaer Polytechnic Institute, NY
The Richard Stockton College of New Jersey, NJ
Roanoke College, VA
Roger Williams University, RI
Rust College, MS
Sacred Heart Major Seminary, MI
St. Bonaventure University, NY
St. John Fisher College, NY
St. Louis Christian College, MO
St. Louis College of Pharmacy, MO
Saint Martin's College, WA
Saint Mary-of-the-Woods College, IN
Saint Michael's College, VT
Shawnee State University, OH
Shenandoah University, VA
Shorter College, GA
Sierra Nevada College, NV
Silver Lake College, WI
Simon's Rock College of Bard, MA
Southeastern University, DC
Southern Adventist University, TN
Southern Nazarene University, OK
Southwest Baptist University, MO

Local/State Students (continued)

Southwestern Christian College, TX
Southwestern College, KS
Southwestern Oklahoma State University, OK
Springfield College, MA
State U of NY at Buffalo, NY
State U of NY at Oswego, NY
State U of NY College at Brockport, NY
State U of NY College at Geneseo, NY
Stephen F. Austin State University, TX
Stephens College, MO
Stetson University, FL
Stevens Institute of Technology, NJ
Teikyo Post University, CT
Tennessee State University, TN
Tiffin University, OH
Trinity Christian College, IL
Tulane University, LA
Tusculum College, TN
Tuskegee University, AL
United States International University, CA
University of Advancing Computer Technology, AZ
The University of Akron, OH
The University of Alabama at Birmingham, AL
University of Arkansas at Little Rock, AR
The University of Charleston, WV
University of Colorado at Boulder, CO
University of Dayton, OH
University of Delaware, DE
University of Denver, CO
University of Georgia, GA
University of Hartford, CT
University of Hawaii at Hilo, HI
University of Idaho, ID
University of Kansas, KS
University of Michigan, Ann Arbor, MI
University of Mississippi, MS
University of Missouri–St. Louis, MO
University of Nevada, Las Vegas, NV
University of North Carolina at Asheville, NC
University of North Carolina at Wilmington, NC
University of Northern Colorado, CO
U of Puerto Rico at Arecibo, PR
University of Rio Grande, OH
University of Rochester, NY
University of Southern California, CA
University of Southern Maine, ME
The University of Texas at El Paso, TX
The University of Texas at San Antonio, TX
University of Toledo, OH
University of Wisconsin–Oshkosh, WI
University of Wisconsin–Whitewater, WI
Utah State University, UT
Valley City State University, ND
Vanderbilt University, TN
Virginia Military Institute, VA
Virginia Wesleyan College, VA
Walsh University, OH
Washington and Lee University, VA
Webber College, FL
Western Carolina University, NC

Western Maryland College, MD
Western Washington University, WA
West Virginia University, WV
William Woods University, MO
Wilson College, PA
Wingate University, NC
Wittenberg University, OH
Worcester State College, MA

MARRIED STUDENTS

Baptist Bible College of Pennsylvania, PA
California State University, Chico, CA
Central Christian College of the Bible, MO
Eugene Bible College, OR
John Wesley College, NC
New Mexico State University, NM
North Central Bible College, MN
Southwestern Adventist University, TX
The University of Alabama at Birmingham, AL
University of Kansas, KS

MEMBERS OF MINORITIES

Albertson College of Idaho, ID
Albright College, PA
Alice Lloyd College, KY
Allegheny College, PA
Allentown College of St. Francis de Sales, PA
Alvernia College, PA
Anna Maria College, MA
Arkansas State University, AR
Art Institute of Boston, MA
Auburn University, AL
Augustana College, IL
Baker University, KS
Baldwin-Wallace College, OH
Barry University, FL
Barton College, NC
Beloit College, WI
Benedictine College, KS
Berry College, GA
Bethel College, MN
Black Hills State University, SD
Bluefield College, VA
Bluffton College, OH
Bowling Green State University, OH
Bradley University, IL
Brenau University, GA
Brewton-Parker College, GA
Briar Cliff College, IA
California Maritime Academy, CA
California State Polytechnic University, Pomona, CA
California State University, Bakersfield, CA
California State University, Chico, CA
California State University, Dominguez Hills, CA
California State University, Los Angeles, CA
California State University, Stanislaus, CA
California University of Pennsylvania, PA
Calvin College, MI
Cameron University, OK
Capital University, OH
Centenary College of Louisiana, LA
Central College, IA
Central Connecticut State University, CT

Central Michigan University, MI
Centre College, KY
Chadron State College, NE
Clarion University of Pennsylvania, PA
Clarkson University, NY
Coastal Carolina University, SC
The College of New Jersey, NJ
College of Saint Benedict, MN
The College of Wooster, OH
Colorado School of Mines, CO
Columbia International University, SC
Concordia University, CA
Cornish College of the Arts, WA
Covenant College, GA
Creighton University, NE
Crichton College, TN
Dana College, NE
The Defiance College, OH
DePauw University, IN
Drake University, IA
Duquesne University, PA
East Central University, OK
Eastern Connecticut State University, CT
Eastern Illinois University, IL
Eastern New Mexico University, NM
Eastern Oregon University, OR
Eastern Washington University, WA
East Stroudsburg University of Pennsylvania, PA
East Tennessee State University, TN
Edgewood College, WI
Edinboro University of Pennsylvania, PA
Elizabeth City State University, NC
Elizabethtown College, PA
Elmhurst College, IL
Emporia State University, KS
The Evergreen State College, WA
Flagler College, FL
Florida Agricultural and Mechanical University, FL
Florida Atlantic University, FL
Florida International University, FL
Fort Lewis College, CO
Fort Valley State University, GA
Franklin University, OH
George Fox University, OR
Georgia College and State University, GA
Georgia Institute of Technology, GA
Golden Gate University, CA
Gonzaga University, WA
Graceland College, IA
Grand Valley State University, MI
Grove City College, PA
Guilford College, NC
Hanover College, IN
Hendrix College, AR
Hilbert College, NY
Huntington College, IN
Idaho State University, ID
Illinois College, IL
Illinois Institute of Technology, IL
Illinois State University, IL
Indiana State University, IN
Iowa State University of Science and Technology, IA
Iowa Wesleyan College, IA
James Madison University, VA

Johnson Bible College, TN
Johnson State College, VT
Kalamazoo College, MI
Kean College of New Jersey, NJ
Kendall College, IL
Kennesaw State University, GA
Kent State University, OH
Kentucky Christian College, KY
Lander University, SC
La Salle University, PA
Lawrence University, WI
Le Moyne College, NY
Lenoir-Rhyne College, NC
Lesley College, MA
Livingstone College, NC
Lock Haven University of Pennsylvania, PA
Lourdes College, OH
Loyola College, MD
Lynchburg College, VA
Mansfield University of Pennsylvania, PA
Marian College, IN
Mary Baldwin College, VA
Maryville University of Saint Louis, MO
Mary Washington College, VA
Mayo School of Health-Related Sciences, MN
Mayville State University, ND
McNeese State University, LA
Mercyhurst College, PA
Mesa State College, CO
Miami University, OH
Michigan State University, MI
Michigan Technological University, MI
Mid-America Bible College, OK
Middle Tennessee State University, TN
Midland Lutheran College, NE
Midway College, KY
Milwaukee Institute of Art and Design, WI
Minot State University, ND
Mississippi College, MS
Mississippi University for Women, MS
Missouri Western State College, MO
Montana State U–Northern, MT
Moorhead State University, MN
Morehead State University, KY
Mount Carmel College of Nursing, OH
Mount Saint Mary's College and Seminary, MD
Murray State University, KY
Muskingum College, OH
New Mexico Highlands University, NM
New Mexico State University, NM
North Carolina Agricultural and Technical State U, NC
Northeastern Illinois University, IL
Northern Arizona University, AZ
Northern Illinois University, IL
Northern Kentucky University, KY
Northern Michigan University, MI
Northwest Missouri State University, MO
The Ohio State University, OH
Ohio University–Chillicothe, OH
Ohio Wesleyan University, OH
Oklahoma State U, OK
Old Dominion University, VA
Oregon Institute of Technology, OR
Otterbein College, OH

Philadelphia College of Pharmacy and Science, PA
Piedmont College, GA
Pine Manor College, MA
Portland State University, OR
Queens College, NC
Radford University, VA
Regis University, CO
The Richard Stockton College of New Jersey, NJ
Rider University, NJ
Roanoke College, VA
Robert Morris College, PA
Rochester Institute of Technology, NY
Rose-Hulman Institute of Technology, IN
Rowan University, NJ
Rust College, MS
Saint Anselm College, NH
St. Bonaventure University, NY
St. Cloud State University, MN
St. John Fisher College, NY
Saint Joseph's College, IN
Saint Joseph's College, ME
St. Lawrence University, NY
Saint Leo College, FL
Saint Louis University, MO
Saint Martin's College, WA
Saint Michael's College, VT
St. Thomas University, FL
Saint Vincent College, PA
San Diego State University, CA
Seattle University, WA
Shawnee State University, OH
Shepherd College, WV
Siena Heights College, MI
Simpson College, IA
Slippery Rock University of Pennsylvania, PA
Sonoma State University, CA
South Dakota State University, SD
Southeastern Louisiana University, LA
Southern Adventist University, TN
Southern Oregon University, OR
Southwestern College, KS
Southwest Missouri State University, MO
Southwest State University, MN
Spring Arbor College, MI
Springfield College, MA
State U of NY at New Paltz, NY
State U of NY College at Brockport, NY
State U of NY College at Fredonia, NY
State U of NY College at Geneseo, NY
State U of NY College at Plattsburgh, NY
State U of NY Coll of Environ Sci and Forestry, NY
Stetson University, FL
Stevens Institute of Technology, NJ
Susquehanna University, PA
Taylor University, Fort Wayne Campus, IN
Teikyo Post University, CT
Tennessee State University, TN
Tennessee Technological University, TN
Tennessee Wesleyan College, TN
Texas A&M University–Commerce, TX
Transylvania University, KY
Trinity Christian College, IL
Tri-State University, IN

United States International University, CA
Unity College, ME
The University of Akron, OH
U of Alaska Anchorage, AK
University of Arkansas at Pine Bluff, AR
University of Central Florida, FL
University of Central Oklahoma, OK
University of Cincinnati, OH
University of Colorado at Boulder, CO
University of Dallas, TX
University of Denver, CO
University of Detroit Mercy, MI
University of Dubuque, IA
University of Georgia, GA
University of Houston–Downtown, TX
University of Idaho, ID
University of Illinois at Chicago, IL
University of Kansas, KS
University of Kentucky, KY
University of Maine, Orono, ME
University of Maine at Farmington, ME
University of Maine at Fort Kent, ME
The University of Memphis, TN
University of Michigan, Ann Arbor, MI
University of Minnesota, Crookston, MN
University of Minnesota, Morris, MN
University of Minnesota, Twin Cities Campus, MN
University of Missouri–Columbia, MO
University of Missouri–Kansas City, MO
University of Missouri–Rolla, MO
University of Missouri–St. Louis, MO
The University of Montana–Missoula, MT
University of Nebraska–Lincoln, NE
University of Nevada, Las Vegas, NV
University of Nevada, Reno, NV
University of New Hampshire at Manchester, NH
University of New Mexico, NM
University of North Carolina at Asheville, NC
University of North Carolina at Pembroke, NC
University of North Carolina at Wilmington, NC
University of North Dakota, ND
University of Northern Colorado, CO
University of Northern Iowa, IA
University of North Florida, FL
University of Oklahoma, OK
University of Pittsburgh, PA
University of Puget Sound, WA
University of Richmond, VA
University of Rochester, NY
University of St. Thomas, TX
University of South Alabama, AL
University of South Dakota, SD
University of Southern Indiana, IN
University of Tennessee at Chattanooga, TN
The University of Tennessee at Martin, TN
University of Tennessee, Knoxville, TN
The University of Texas at El Paso, TX
The University of Texas–Pan American, TX
University of the Ozarks, AR
University of Toledo, OH
University of Vermont, VT
University of Virginia, VA

Members of Minorities (continued)

University of West Florida, FL
University of Wisconsin–Oshkosh, WI
Utah State University, UT
Valley Forge Christian College, PA
Valparaiso University, IN
Vanderbilt University, TN
Villanova University, PA
Virginia Military Institute, VA
Virginia Polytechnic Institute and State U, VA
Walsh University, OH
Warner Pacific College, OR
Washington College, MD
Washington State University, WA
Washington University, MO
Wayne State College, NE
Weber State University, UT
Western Carolina University, NC
Western Illinois University, IL
Western Kentucky University, KY
Western Michigan University, MI
Western Montana College of The U of Montana, MT
Western Oregon University, OR
Western Washington University, WA
Westminster College of Salt Lake City, UT
West Virginia University, WV
West Virginia Wesleyan College, WV
Wilkes University, PA
Willamette University, OR
William Paterson University of New Jersey, NJ
William Woods University, MO
Wilmington College, OH
Winona State University, MN
Wittenberg University, OH
Xavier University, OH

OUT-OF-STATE STUDENTS

Abilene Christian University, TX
Adams State College, CO
Alaska Pacific University, AK
Anderson College, SC
Anderson University, IN
Arkansas State University, AR
Armstrong Atlantic State University, GA
Baker University, KS
Bay Path College, MA
Bellarmine College, KY
Bethel College, MN
Boise State University, ID
Bowie State University, MD
Buena Vista University, IA
Caldwell College, NJ
California State University, Chico, CA
Central College, IA
Central Missouri State University, MO
Chadron State College, NE
Chaminade University of Honolulu, HI
Charleston Southern University, SC
Christian Heritage College, CA
College of New Rochelle, NY
College of Saint Mary, NE
Dana College, NE
The Defiance College, OH
Delaware State University, DE

Delta State University, MS
Dordt College, IA
Eastern Kentucky University, KY
Eastern Michigan University, MI
Eastern New Mexico University, NM
Eastern Oregon University, OR
Eastern Washington University, WA
Edinboro University of Pennsylvania, PA
Emmaus Bible College, IA
Emporia State University, KS
Ferrum College, VA
Florida Southern College, FL
Fort Lewis College, CO
Francis Marion University, SC
Franklin Pierce College, NH
George Fox University, OR
Grand Valley State University, MI
Greenville College, IL
Hamline University, MN
Henderson State University, AR
Idaho State University, ID
Illinois Institute of Technology, IL
Indiana Institute of Technology, IN
Iowa State University of Science and Technology, IA
Judson College, IL
Juniata College, PA
Kansas Newman College, KS
Kent State University, OH
Kentucky Christian College, KY
Lander University, SC
Lewis-Clark State College, ID
Limestone College, SC
MacMurray College, IL
Maine Maritime Academy, ME
Mankato State University, MN
Marycrest International University, IA
Marygrove College, MI
McKendree College, IL
McNeese State University, LA
Mesa State College, CO
Miami University, OH
Michigan Christian College, MI
Michigan State University, MI
Michigan Technological University, MI
Mississippi State University, MS
Mississippi University for Women, MS
Missouri Western State College, MO
Montana State U–Northern, MT
Morehead State University, KY
New Mexico State University, NM
Northeast Louisiana University, LA
Northwestern College, MN
Nyack College, NY
Oakland University, MI
The Ohio State University, OH
Ohio Wesleyan University, OH
Oklahoma Baptist University, OK
Oklahoma State U, OK
Old Dominion University, VA
Pace University, NY
Purdue University, West Lafayette, IN
Ramapo College of New Jersey, NJ
Robert Morris College, IL
Robert Morris College, PA
Rockford College, IL
St. Cloud State University, MN

Saint Francis College, IN
Saint Mary College, KS
Saint Mary-of-the-Woods College, IN
St. Mary's University of San Antonio, TX
Shimer College, IL
Southern Adventist University, TN
Southern Arkansas University–Magnolia, AR
Southern Oregon University, OR
Southwestern Oklahoma State University, OK
Southwest Missouri State University, MO
Spring Arbor College, MI
Texas Tech University, TX
Thomas College, GA
Tiffin University, OH
Transylvania University, KY
Trinity Christian College, IL
University of Advancing Computer Technology, AZ
The University of Akron, OH
The University of Alabama at Birmingham, AL
University of Cincinnati, OH
University of Dubuque, IA
University of Florida, FL
University of Idaho, ID
University of Kansas, KS
University of Michigan, Ann Arbor, MI
University of Minnesota, Morris, MN
University of Mississippi, MS
University of Missouri–Columbia, MO
University of Missouri–Rolla, MO
University of Mobile, AL
University of Montevallo, AL
University of Nebraska at Kearney, NE
University of Nebraska at Omaha, NE
University of Nebraska–Lincoln, NE
University of Nevada, Las Vegas, NV
University of New Mexico, NM
University of North Alabama, AL
University of Northern Colorado, CO
University of Pittsburgh at Bradford, PA
University of Redlands, CA
University of Rio Grande, OH
University of Rochester, NY
University of Science and Arts of Oklahoma, OK
University of Sioux Falls, SD
University of Southern Indiana, IN
University of Southern Mississippi, MS
The University of Texas at El Paso, TX
The University of Texas at San Antonio, TX
University of Wisconsin–Stevens Point, WI
University of Wyoming, WY
Utah State University, UT
Virginia Military Institute, VA
Virginia Polytechnic Institute and State U, VA
Warner Southern College, FL
Wayne State College, NE
Western Michigan University, MI
Winthrop University, SC

PARENTS OF CURRENT STUDENTS

Anderson College, SC
Becker College–Worcester Campus, MA
Calvary Bible College and Theological
  Seminary, MO
College of New Rochelle, NY
College of Saint Mary, NE
The Defiance College, OH
Fairleigh Dickinson U,
  Teaneck-Hackensack, NJ
Great Lakes Christian College, MI
Houghton College, NY
Huntington College, IN
Johnson Bible College, TN
Malone College, OH
Maryville University of Saint Louis, MO
Minot State University, ND
Mount Mary College, WI
Mount St. Clare College, IA
Oklahoma Christian U of Science and Arts,
  OK
Olivet Nazarene University, IL
Presentation College, SD
Rockford College, IL
Seton Hill College, PA
The University of Alabama at Birmingham,
  AL
University of Bridgeport, CT
The University of Findlay, OH
University of St. Thomas, MN
Upper Iowa University, IA

PREVIOUS COLLEGE EXPERIENCE

Alma College, MI
Bellarmine College, KY
Benedictine College, KS
Benedictine University, IL
Calumet College of Saint Joseph, IN
Carthage College, WI
Cedar Crest College, PA
The Defiance College, OH
Eastern Connecticut State University, CT
Elmira College, NY
Hendrix College, AR
Illinois College, IL
Illinois Institute of Technology, IL
Illinois State University, IL
Johnson & Wales University, FL
Johnson & Wales University, RI
Kansas Newman College, KS
Lake Forest College, IL
Lees-McRae College, NC
MacMurray College, IL
Manchester College, IN
Marygrove College, MI
McMurry University, TX
Michigan Technological University, MI
Mississippi College, MS
Mississippi State University, MS
Mount Senario College, WI
New Mexico State University, NM
The Ohio State University, OH
Old Dominion University, VA
Otterbein College, OH
Pacific Lutheran University, WA
Queens College, NC

The Richard Stockton College of New
  Jersey, NJ
Sonoma State University, CA
State U of NY College at Fredonia, NY
Stephen F. Austin State University, TX
Texas Lutheran University, TX
The University of Alabama at Birmingham,
  AL
University of Minnesota, Crookston, MN
University of Oklahoma, OK
University of Science and Arts of
  Oklahoma, OK
University of Toledo, OH
Wilson College, PA

PUBLIC SERVANTS

David N. Myers College, OH
Hannibal-LaGrange College, MO
Michigan State University, MI
Missouri Baptist College, MO
New York Institute of Technology, NY
Park College, MO
The University of Alabama at Birmingham,
  AL
The University of Memphis, TN

RELATIVES OF CLERGY

Abilene Christian University, TX
Alderson-Broaddus College, WV
Allentown College of St. Francis de Sales,
  PA
Anderson College, SC
Anderson University, IN
Austin College, TX
Averett College, VA
Azusa Pacific University, CA
Baker University, KS
Baptist Bible College of Pennsylvania, PA
Bartlesville Wesleyan College, OK
Barton College, NC
Belhaven College, MS
Bennett College, NC
Bethany College, WV
Bethel College, IN
Bethel College, KS
Bethel College, MN
Biola University, CA
Birmingham-Southern College, AL
Bloomfield College, NJ
Bluefield College, VA
Bluffton College, OH
Boise Bible College, ID
Boston University, MA
Bryan College, TN
California Baptist College, CA
California Lutheran University, CA
Calvary Bible College and Theological
  Seminary, MO
Campbell University, NC
Capital University, OH
Carthage College, WI
Catawba College, NC
Cedar Crest College, PA
Centenary College of Louisiana, LA
Central Baptist College, AR
Central Bible College, MO
Central Christian College of the Bible, MO
Central College, IA

Central Methodist College, MO
Chapman University, CA
Charleston Southern University, SC
Chowan College, NC
Christian Heritage College, CA
Cincinnati Bible College and Seminary, OH
Circleville Bible College, OH
Claflin College, SC
Clarke College, IA
Colorado Christian University, CO
Columbia College, SC
Concordia College, MI
Concordia College, NY
Concordia University, CA
Concordia University, OR
Crichton College, TN
Crown College, MN
Cumberland College, KY
Dana College, NE
David Lipscomb University, TN
Davidson College, NC
The Defiance College, OH
DePauw University, IN
Dominican College of Blauvelt, NY
Drury College, MO
Eastern College, PA
Eastern Nazarene College, MA
Elon College, NC
Emory & Henry College, VA
Emory University, GA
Erskine College, SC
Eugene Bible College, OR
Faith Baptist Bible Coll and Theological
  Seminary, IA
Faulkner University, AL
Ferrum College, VA
Florida Christian College, FL
Florida Southern College, FL
Fresno Pacific University, CA
Friends University, KS
Furman University, SC
Gardner-Webb University, NC
Geneva College, PA
George Fox University, OR
Grace College, IN
Grace University, NE
Greensboro College, NC
Greenville College, IL
Hamline University, MN
Hannibal-LaGrange College, MO
Hardin-Simmons University, TX
Hastings College, NE
Hawaii Pacific University, HI
Hendrix College, AR
High Point University, NC
Hope International University, CA
Houghton College, NY
Howard Payne University, TX
Huntingdon College, AL
Illinois College, IL
Immaculata College, PA
Indiana Wesleyan University, IN
Iowa Wesleyan College, IA
John Brown University, AR
Johnson Bible College, TN
John Wesley College, NC
Judson College, AL

Relatives of Clergy (continued)

King College, TN
King's College, PA
Lancaster Bible College, PA
La Sierra University, CA
Lees-McRae College, NC
Lenoir-Rhyne College, NC
LeTourneau University, TX
Lindsey Wilson College, KY
Lutheran Bible Institute of Seattle, WA
Lycoming College, PA
Lynchburg College, VA
Malone College, OH
Maranatha Baptist Bible College, WI
Mars Hill College, NC
Mary Baldwin College, VA
Maryville College, TN
McMurry University, TX
Mercer University, Macon, GA
Merrimack College, MA
Messiah College, PA
MidAmerica Nazarene University, KS
Midway College, KY
Millikin University, IL
Mississippi College, MS
Missouri Baptist College, MO
Montreat College, NC
Moravian College, PA
Morningside College, IA
Mount Union College, OH
Mount Vernon Nazarene College, OH
Muhlenberg College, PA
Nebraska Christian College, NE
Nebraska Wesleyan University, NE
Newberry College, SC
Niagara University, NY
North Central Bible College, MN
North Central College, IL
Northwest Christian College, OR
Northwest College of the Assemblies of God, WA
Northwestern College, MN
Notre Dame College of Ohio, OH
Nyack College, NY
Oakwood College, AL
Ohio Northern University, OH
Ohio Wesleyan University, OH
Oklahoma Baptist University, OK
Oklahoma City University, OK
Olivet Nazarene University, IL
Oral Roberts University, OK
Otterbein College, OH
Ouachita Baptist University, AR
Pacific Lutheran University, WA
Palm Beach Atlantic College, FL
Philadelphia College of Bible, PA
Piedmont Bible College, NC
Point Loma Nazarene College, CA
Practical Bible College, NY
Presbyterian College, SC
Puget Sound Christian College, WA
Queens College, NC
Quincy University, IL
Randolph-Macon College, VA
Randolph-Macon Woman's College, VA
Reinhardt College, GA
Rhodes College, TN

Rockford College, IL
St. Ambrose University, IA
St. Bonaventure University, NY
St. John's University, NY
Saint Peter's College, Jersey City, NJ
Salem College, NC
Samford University, AL
Seattle Pacific University, WA
Seton Hall University, NJ
Shenandoah University, VA
Siena Heights College, MI
Simpson College, IA
Southeastern College of the Assemblies of God, FL
Southern California College, CA
Southern Methodist University, TX
Southern Wesleyan University, SC
Southwest Baptist University, MO
Southwestern College, KS
Southwestern College of Christian Ministries, OK
Southwestern University, TX
Spring Arbor College, MI
Stonehill College, MA
Tabor College, KS
Tennessee Temple University, TN
Tennessee Wesleyan College, TN
Texas Christian University, TX
Texas Wesleyan University, TX
Toccoa Falls College, GA
Transylvania University, KY
Trevecca Nazarene University, TN
Trinity Bible College, ND
Union University, TN
The University of Alabama at Birmingham, AL
University of Dubuque, IA
University of Indianapolis, IN
University of Portland, OR
University of the Ozarks, AR
University of the South, TN
Ursuline College, OH
Valparaiso University, IN
Virginia Wesleyan College, VA
Warner Southern College, FL
Washington Bible College, MD
Wesleyan College, GA
Western Baptist College, OR
Westminster College of Salt Lake City, UT
West Virginia Wesleyan College, WV
Whitworth College, WA
Wiley College, TX
William Carey College, MS
William Jewell College, MO
William Woods University, MO
Wingate University, NC
Wittenberg University, OH
Wofford College, SC

RELIGIOUS AFFILIATION

Abilene Christian University, TX
Alaska Bible College, AK
Alaska Pacific University, AK
Albertson College of Idaho, ID
Albright College, PA
Alderson-Broaddus College, WV

Allentown College of St. Francis de Sales, PA
American Baptist Coll of American Baptist Theol Sem, TN
Anderson College, SC
Arizona Bible College, AZ
Ashland University, OH
Augustana College, IL
Augustana College, SD
Averett College, VA
Barclay College, KS
Barry University, FL
Bartlesville Wesleyan College, OK
Barton College, NC
Belhaven College, MS
Belmont Abbey College, NC
Benedictine College, KS
Bennett College, NC
Bethany College, WV
Bethel College, IN
Bethel College, MN
Bethel College, TN
Birmingham-Southern College, AL
Bluffton College, OH
Boston University, MA
Bridgewater College, VA
Brigham Young University–Hawaii Campus, HI
Bryan College, TN
Buena Vista University, IA
Caldwell College, NJ
California Lutheran University, CA
Calumet College of Saint Joseph, IN
Calvin College, MI
Capital University, OH
Carlow College, PA
Carthage College, WI
Catawba College, NC
The Catholic University of America, DC
Cedar Crest College, PA
Cedarville College, OH
Centenary College, NJ
Centenary College of Louisiana, LA
Central Bible College, MO
Central College, IA
Central Methodist College, MO
Chaminade University of Honolulu, HI
Chapman University, CA
Circleville Bible College, OH
Claflin College, SC
Coe College, IA
College of Charleston, SC
College of St. Joseph, VT
Colorado Christian University, CO
Columbia College, MO
Conception Seminary College, MO
Concordia College, MI
Concordia College, NE
Concordia College, NY
Concordia University, CA
Concordia University, IL
Concordia University at Austin, TX
Concordia University Wisconsin, WI
Covenant College, GA
Creighton University, NE
Crichton College, TN
Culver-Stockton College, MO

Dakota Wesleyan University, SD
Dallas Christian College, TX
Dana College, NE
Davis & Elkins College, WV
Deaconess College of Nursing, MO
The Defiance College, OH
DePauw University, IN
Dillard University, LA
Doane College, NE
Dordt College, IA
Earlham College, IN
East Coast Bible College, NC
Eastern Mennonite University, VA
East Texas Baptist University, TX
Eckerd College, FL
Edgewood College, WI
Edinboro University of Pennsylvania, PA
Elmhurst College, IL
Emmanuel College, MA
Emory University, GA
Emporia State University, KS
Erskine College, SC
Eureka College, IL
Ferrum College, VA
Florida Baptist Theological College, FL
Florida Christian College, FL
Fontbonne College, MO
Franciscan University of Steubenville, OH
Franklin College of Indiana, IN
Fresno Pacific University, CA
Friends University, KS
Furman University, SC
Geneva College, PA
George Fox University, OR
Georgetown College, KY
Graceland College, IA
Grace University, NE
Greensboro College, NC
Greenville College, IL
Guilford College, NC
Hardin-Simmons University, TX
Hastings College, NE
Hawaii Pacific University, HI
Heidelberg College, OH
Hiram College, OH
Houghton College, NY
Howard Payne University, TX
Huntington College, IN
Indiana Wesleyan University, IN
Iowa Wesleyan College, IA
Jarvis Christian College, TX
Johnson Bible College, TN
John Wesley College, NC
Judson College, AL
Judson College, IL
Kansas Newman College, KS
Kentucky Christian College, KY
Kentucky Wesleyan College, KY
Lakeland College, WI
Lambuth University, TN
Lancaster Bible College, PA
La Sierra University, CA
Lees-McRae College, NC
Lenoir-Rhyne College, NC
Lexington Baptist College, KY
Lindsey Wilson College, KY
Loyola University Chicago, IL

Lutheran Bible Institute of Seattle, WA
Luther College, IA
Lynchburg College, VA
MacMurray College, IL
Malone College, OH
Manchester College, IN
Maranatha Baptist Bible College, WI
Marian College, IN
Mars Hill College, NC
Martin Methodist College, TN
Maryland Institute, College of Art, MD
Maryville College, TN
Maryville University of Saint Louis, MO
Marywood University, PA
McKendree College, IL
McMurry University, TX
Mercer University, Macon, GA
Messenger College, MO
Messiah College, PA
Michigan State University, MI
Mid-America Bible College, OK
MidAmerica Nazarene University, KS
Midland Lutheran College, NE
Midway College, KY
Millsaps College, MS
Minnesota Bible College, MN
Missouri Baptist College, MO
Morningside College, IA
Mount Marty College, SD
Mount Vernon Nazarene College, OH
Multnomah Bible College and Biblical
  Seminary, OR
Muskingum College, OH
Neumann College, PA
Newberry College, SC
North Central Bible College, MN
Northwest Christian College, OR
Northwest College of the Assemblies of
  God, WA
Northwestern College, IA
Nyack College, NY
Oakland City University, IN
Ohio Northern University, OH
Ohio Wesleyan University, OH
Oklahoma Baptist University, OK
Olivet Nazarene University, IL
Ottawa University, KS
Ouachita Baptist University, AR
Ozark Christian College, MO
Pacific University, OR
Paine College, GA
Park College, MO
Patten College, CA
Pepperdine University, Malibu, CA
Point Loma Nazarene College, CA
Reinhardt College, GA
Rhodes College, TN
Roanoke College, VA
Roberts Wesleyan College, NY
Rockhurst College, MO
Rocky Mountain College, MT
Rust College, MS
Sacred Heart Major Seminary, MI
St. Ambrose University, IA
St. Bonaventure University, NY
St. Edward's University, TX
St. John's Seminary College, CA

St. John's University, NY
Saint Joseph College, CT
St. Louis Christian College, MO
Saint Martin's College, WA
Saint Mary College, KS
Saint Mary-of-the-Woods College, IN
Saint Michael's College, VT
Saint Peter's College, Jersey City, NJ
Seattle Pacific University, WA
Shenandoah University, VA
Shorter College, GA
Siena Heights College, MI
Silver Lake College, WI
Simpson College, CA
Southeastern Louisiana University, LA
Southern California College, CA
Southern Nazarene University, OK
Southern Wesleyan University, SC
Southwestern College, KS
Southwestern College of Christian
  Ministries, OK
Southwestern University, TX
Spring Arbor College, MI
Stephen F. Austin State University, TX
Tabor College, KS
Taylor University, IN
Taylor University, Fort Wayne Campus, IN
Tennessee Wesleyan College, TN
Texas Christian University, TX
Texas Lutheran University, TX
Texas Wesleyan University, TX
Thiel College, PA
Thomas More College, KY
Transylvania University, KY
Trevecca Nazarene University, TN
Trinity International University, IL
Union College, KY
The University of Alabama at Birmingham,
  AL
University of Arkansas at Pine Bluff, AR
University of Dayton, OH
University of Dubuque, IA
University of Evansville, IN
The University of Findlay, OH
University of Indianapolis, IN
University of La Verne, CA
University of Mary Hardin-Baylor, TX
University of Mobile, AL
University of Puget Sound, WA
University of St. Thomas, TX
University of Sioux Falls, SD
University of the South, TN
Upper Iowa University, IA
Ursuline College, OH
Valparaiso University, IN
Villanova University, PA
Virginia Intermont College, VA
Warner Pacific College, OR
Warren Wilson College, NC
Wartburg College, IA
Washington Bible College, MD
Wiley College, TX
William Carey College, MS
William Penn College, IA
Williams Baptist College, AR
William Woods University, MO
Wilson College, PA

Religious Affiliation (continued)

Wittenberg University, OH

ROTC PARTICIPANTS

Alabama State University, AL
Alfred University, NY
Allentown College of St. Francis de Sales, PA
Arkansas State University, AR
Baylor University, TX
Bellarmine College, KY
Bethel College, MN
Boston College, MA
Boston University, MA
Brigham Young University, UT
California Polytechnic State U, San Luis Obispo, CA
Cameron University, OK
Capital University, OH
Carnegie Mellon University, PA
Case Western Reserve University, OH
Cedarville College, OH
Central Michigan University, MI
Central State University, OH
Centre College, KY
Chaminade University of Honolulu, HI
Charleston Southern University, SC
The Citadel, The Military Coll of South Carolina, SC
Clark Atlanta University, GA
Clarkson College, NE
Clarkson University, NY
Colby College, ME
College of St. Scholastica, MN
College of the Holy Cross, MA
College of the Ozarks, MO
Colorado School of Mines, CO
Columbia College, MO
Creighton University, NE
Davidson College, NC
Dickinson College, PA
Drake University, IA
Drexel University, PA
East Carolina University, NC
East Central University, OK
Eastern New Mexico University, NM
Eckerd College, FL
Edinboro University of Pennsylvania, PA
Electronic Data Processing College of Puerto Rico, PR
Elon College, NC
Embry-Riddle Aeronautical University, AZ
Embry-Riddle Aeronautical University, FL
Emporia State University, KS
Florida Agricultural and Mechanical University, FL
Florida Institute of Technology, FL
Florida Southern College, FL
Fordham University, NY
Fort Valley State University, GA
Free Will Baptist Bible College, TN
Georgetown University, DC
The George Washington University, DC
Georgia College and State University, GA
Georgia Institute of Technology, GA
Gonzaga University, WA
Gustavus Adolphus College, MN

Hampden-Sydney College, VA
Hawaii Pacific University, HI
Illinois Institute of Technology, IL
Illinois State University, IL
Iowa State University of Science and Technology, IA
Jacksonville University, FL
James Madison University, VA
John Carroll University, OH
King's College, PA
Lafayette College, PA
Lehigh University, PA
Limestone College, SC
Louisiana State University and A&M College, LA
Loyola College, MD
Loyola Marymount University, CA
Loyola University New Orleans, LA
Maine Maritime Academy, ME
Manhattan College, NY
Marian College of Fond du Lac, WI
Marquette University, WI
Marymount University, VA
Marywood University, PA
Mercer University, Macon, GA
Michigan State University, MI
Milwaukee School of Engineering, WI
Mississippi State University, MS
Missouri Western State College, MO
Morehouse College, GA
New Mexico State University, NM
North Carolina Agricultural and Technical State U, NC
Northeast Louisiana University, LA
Northern Arizona University, AZ
Northern Illinois University, IL
North Georgia College & State University, GA
Norwich University, VT
The Ohio State University, OH
Ohio University, OH
Oklahoma Christian U of Science and Arts, OK
Oklahoma State U, OK
Old Dominion University, VA
Olivet Nazarene University, IL
Pacific Lutheran University, WA
Pittsburg State University, KS
Plymouth State College of the U System of NH, NH
Point Loma Nazarene College, CA
Purdue University, West Lafayette, IN
Radford University, VA
Regis University, CO
Rensselaer Polytechnic Institute, NY
Rice University, TX
Rider University, NJ
Rochester Institute of Technology, NY
Rose-Hulman Institute of Technology, IN
Saint Augustine's College, NC
St. Bonaventure University, NY
St. Edward's University, TX
Saint John's University, MN
St. John's University, NY
Saint Joseph's College, ME
Saint Leo College, FL
Saint Mary's College, IN

St. Mary's University of San Antonio, TX
Saint Michael's College, VT
St. Norbert College, WI
Samford University, AL
Sam Houston State University, TX
San Jose State University, CA
Seattle Pacific University, WA
Seattle University, WA
Shaw University, NC
South Dakota State University, SD
Southeastern College of the Assemblies of God, FL
Southeastern Louisiana University, LA
Southern Connecticut State University, CT
Southwest Missouri State University, MO
State U of NY Coll of Environ Sci and Forestry, NY
Stephen F. Austin State University, TX
Stetson University, FL
Stevens Institute of Technology, NJ
Syracuse University, NY
Texas A&M University, College Station, TX
Texas A&M University–Kingsville, TX
Texas Christian University, TX
Texas Tech University, TX
Thomas College, GA
Transylvania University, KY
Truman State University, MO
Tulane University, LA
Tuskegee University, AL
The University of Akron, OH
The University of Alabama in Huntsville, AL
The University of Charleston, WV
University of Cincinnati, OH
University of Colorado at Boulder, CO
University of Idaho, ID
University of Illinois at Chicago, IL
University of Kansas, KS
University of Maryland Eastern Shore, MD
University of Massachusetts Amherst, MA
The University of Memphis, TN
University of Miami, FL
University of Michigan, Ann Arbor, MI
University of Minnesota, Duluth, MN
University of Missouri–Columbia, MO
University of Nebraska–Lincoln, NE
University of Nevada, Reno, NV
University of New Mexico, NM
University of North Alabama, AL
University of North Dakota, ND
University of Northern Colorado, CO
University of Pittsburgh at Bradford, PA
University of Portland, OR
U of Puerto Rico, Cayey University College, PR
U of Puerto Rico, Mayagüez Campus, PR
University of Puget Sound, WA
University of St. Thomas, MN
University of San Diego, CA
University of San Francisco, CA
University of Scranton, PA
University of South Alabama, AL
University of South Dakota, SD
University of Southern California, CA
University of Southern Mississippi, MS

The University of Tampa, FL
University of Tennessee, Knoxville, TN
The University of Texas at Arlington, TX
The University of Texas at El Paso, TX
University of Toledo, OH
University of Vermont, VT
University of Wisconsin–Stevens Point, WI
Ursuline College, OH
Valdosta State University, GA
Vanderbilt University, TN
Villa Julie College, MD
Villanova University, PA
Virginia Commonwealth University, VA
Virginia Military Institute, VA
Virginia Polytechnic Institute and State U, VA
Virginia State University, VA
Viterbo College, WI
Wake Forest University, NC
Waynesburg College, PA
Western Kentucky University, KY
Western Michigan University, MI
Westminster College, MO
West Virginia State College, WV
West Virginia University, WV
Wheaton College, IL
Whitworth College, WA
Widener University, PA
William Carey College, MS
Worcester Polytechnic Institute, MA
Worcester State College, MA
Xavier University, OH

SIBLINGS OF CURRENT STUDENTS

Albright College, PA
Allentown College of St. Francis de Sales, PA
Alverno College, WI
Anderson College, SC
Anna Maria College, MA
Arizona Bible College, AZ
Ashland University, OH
Augustana College, IL
Augustana College, SD
Azusa Pacific University, CA
Barry University, FL
Bartlesville Wesleyan College, OK
Bay Path College, MA
Becker College–Leicester Campus, MA
Becker College–Worcester Campus, MA
Beloit College, WI
Bethel College, IN
Bloomfield College, NJ
Bryant College, RI
Buena Vista University, IA
Cabrini College, PA
Caldwell College, NJ
Calvary Bible College and Theological Seminary, MO
Capital University, OH
Carlow College, PA
Carroll College, MT
Carson-Newman College, TN
Carthage College, WI
Cascade College, OR
Catawba College, NC
Central Bible College, MO

Central College, IA
Central Methodist College, MO
Chaminade University of Honolulu, HI
Clarke College, IA
College of Mount Saint Vincent, NY
College of New Rochelle, NY
College of St. Catherine, MN
College of St. Francis, IL
College of Saint Mary, NE
Colorado Christian University, CO
Columbia College of Nursing, WI
Creighton University, NE
Cumberland College, KY
Daemen College, NY
Dana College, NE
The Defiance College, OH
Doane College, NE
Dominican University, IL
East Coast Bible College, NC
Eastern Nazarene College, MA
Elizabethtown College, PA
Elmira College, NY
Embry-Riddle Aeronautical University, AZ
Embry-Riddle Aeronautical University, FL
Endicott College, MA
Erskine College, SC
Fairfield University, CT
Fairleigh Dickinson U, Teaneck-Hackensack, NJ
Faulkner University, AL
Florida Southern College, FL
Fontbonne College, MO
Franklin Pierce College, NH
The George Washington University, DC
Gonzaga University, WA
Grace University, NE
Great Lakes Christian College, MI
Green Mountain College, VT
Greensboro College, NC
Greenville College, IL
Harding University, AR
Hartwick College, NY
Hastings College, NE
Hope International University, CA
Houghton College, NY
Huntington College, IN
Illinois Institute of Technology, IL
Immaculata College, PA
Indiana Institute of Technology, IN
Indiana Wesleyan University, IN
Jacksonville University, FL
James Madison University, VA
Johnson & Wales University, FL
Johnson & Wales University, RI
Johnson & Wales University, SC
Johnson Bible College, TN
Judson College, IL
Kansas Newman College, KS
Kansas Wesleyan University, KS
King's College, PA
Knoxville College, TN
Lakeland College, WI
Lancaster Bible College, PA
Lasell College, MA
La Sierra University, CA
Lenoir-Rhyne College, NC
Limestone College, SC

Linfield College, OR
Long Island U, Southampton College, NY
Loras College, IA
Loyola College, MD
Lyndon State College, VT
Malone College, OH
Marian College of Fond du Lac, WI
Marquette University, WI
Mary Baldwin College, VA
Marymount University, VA
Maryville University of Saint Louis, MO
Mercer University, Macon, GA
Mercyhurst College, PA
Merrimack College, MA
Messiah College, PA
Michigan Christian College, MI
Midland Lutheran College, NE
Minnesota Bible College, MN
Missouri Baptist College, MO
Molloy College, NY
Mount Marty College, SD
Mount Mary College, WI
Mount St. Clare College, IA
Mount Saint Mary's College and Seminary, MD
Mount Union College, OH
Mount Vernon Nazarene College, OH
Multnomah Bible College and Biblical Seminary, OR
Muskingum College, OH
National College–Sioux Falls Branch, SD
Nazareth College of Rochester, NY
Nebraska Wesleyan University, NE
New England College, NH
North Central Bible College, MN
North Greenville College, SC
Northwest College of the Assemblies of God, WA
Northwestern College, IA
Northwestern College, MN
Northwood University, MI
Northwood University, Florida Campus, FL
Northwood University, Texas Campus, TX
Notre Dame College, NH
Oak Hills Bible College, MN
Oglethorpe University, GA
Ohio Northern University, OH
Oklahoma Christian U of Science and Arts, OK
Olivet Nazarene University, IL
Oral Roberts University, OK
Otterbein College, OH
Paine College, GA
Palm Beach Atlantic College, FL
Philadelphia College of Bible, PA
Pine Manor College, MA
Point Loma Nazarene College, CA
Presentation College, SD
Queens College, NC
Quincy University, IL
Randolph-Macon College, VA
Rockford College, IL
Rockhurst College, MO
Rosemont College, PA
St. Ambrose University, IA
Saint Anselm College, NH
St. Bonaventure University, NY

Siblings of Current Students (continued)

Saint Francis College, IN
Saint Francis College, PA
St. John's University, NY
Saint Joseph's College, IN
Saint Joseph's College, ME
Saint Louis University, MO
Saint Martin's College, WA
Saint Mary College, KS
Saint Mary's College, IN
Saint Michael's College, VT
Santa Clara University, CA
Seton Hall University, NJ
Seton Hill College, PA
Shorter College, GA
Sierra Nevada College, NV
Simpson College, IA
Southeastern College of the Assemblies of
 God, FL
Southern Wesleyan University, SC
Southwestern Adventist University, TX
Southwestern College, KS
Spalding University, KY
Spring Hill College, AL
Stephens College, MO
Stonehill College, MA
Suffolk University, MA
Tabor College, KS
Teikyo Post University, CT
Thiel College, PA
Trinity College, DC
The University of Alabama at Birmingham,
 AL
University of Bridgeport, CT
University of Dallas, TX
University of Dubuque, IA
University of Evansville, IN
The University of Findlay, OH
University of Hartford, CT
University of Mary Hardin-Baylor, TX
University of Scranton, PA
University of Toledo, OH
Ursuline College, OH
Valley Forge Christian College, PA
Valparaiso University, IN
Walsh University, OH
Wartburg College, IA
Western Maryland College, MD
Westmar University, IA
Westminster College of Salt Lake City, UT
Wilkes University, PA
William Woods University, MO

SPOUSES OF CURRENT STUDENTS

Alaska Bible College, AK
Anderson College, SC
Augustana College, SD
Becker College–Leicester Campus, MA
Becker College–Worcester Campus, MA
Bethel College, IN
Boise Bible College, ID
Bryan College, TN
Calvary Bible College and Theological
 Seminary, MO
Carlow College, PA
Central Christian College of the Bible, MO
Central Methodist College, MO

Chaminade University of Honolulu, HI
Cincinnati Bible College and Seminary, OH
College of New Rochelle, NY
College of Saint Mary, NE
Colorado Christian University, CO
Cornerstone College, MI
Dana College, NE
The Defiance College, OH
Dominican University, IL
East Coast Bible College, NC
Emmaus Bible College, IA
Fairleigh Dickinson U,
 Teaneck-Hackensack, NJ
Faith Baptist Bible Coll and Theological
 Seminary, IA
Florida Christian College, FL
Hope International University, CA
Illinois Institute of Technology, IL
Jacksonville University, FL
Johnson & Wales University, FL
Johnson & Wales University, RI
Johnson & Wales University, SC
Johnson Bible College, TN
John Wesley College, NC
Lancaster Bible College, PA
LeTourneau University, TX
Magnolia Bible College, MS
Malone College, OH
Maryville University of Saint Louis, MO
Mid-America Bible College, OK
Minnesota Bible College, MN
Mount St. Clare College, IA
Mount Vernon Nazarene College, OH
National College–Sioux Falls Branch, SD
New Mexico State University, NM
Northwest College of the Assemblies of
 God, WA
Oak Hills Bible College, MN
Oklahoma Christian U of Science and Arts,
 OK
Olivet Nazarene University, IL
Palm Beach Atlantic College, FL
Piedmont Bible College, NC
Pontifical Catholic University of Puerto
 Rico, PR
Practical Bible College, NY
Presentation College, SD
Puget Sound Christian College, WA
Reformed Bible College, MI
Roanoke Bible College, NC
St. Edward's University, TX
Saint Joseph's College, ME
Saint Martin's College, WA
St. Thomas Aquinas College, NY
Sierra Nevada College, NV
Spalding University, KY
Tabor College, KS
Trinity Baptist College, FL
Trinity Bible College, ND
The University of Alabama at Birmingham,
 AL
University of Bridgeport, CT
University of Southern Indiana, IN
University of Toledo, OH
Upper Iowa University, IA
Valley Forge Christian College, PA
Warner Southern College, FL

Wilkes University, PA

SPOUSES OF DECEASED OR DISABLED PUBLIC SERVANTS

College of Charleston, SC
Francis Marion University, SC
Michigan State University, MI
Mississippi State University, MS
New York Institute of Technology, NY
Southwest Missouri State University, MO
The University of Alabama at Birmingham,
 AL
U of Alaska Anchorage, AK

TWINS

Anderson College, SC
Bay Path College, MA
Becker College–Leicester Campus, MA
Becker College–Worcester Campus, MA
Cabrini College, PA
The Defiance College, OH
Dominican University, IL
Kansas Wesleyan University, KS
Lake Erie College, OH
Lasell College, MA
Maryville University of Saint Louis, MO
Mount St. Clare College, IA
Ohio Wesleyan University, OH
Sterling College, KS
The University of Alabama at Birmingham,
 AL
University of Hartford, CT
Valparaiso University, IN

VETERANS

Augustana College, SD
Barton College, NC
Belhaven College, MS
California State University, Fresno, CA
Cedarville College, OH
Central Michigan University, MI
Central State University, OH
Chadron State College, NE
Chaminade University of Honolulu, HI
Circleville Bible College, OH
Clarkson College, NE
David N. Myers College, OH
East Central University, OK
Eastern New Mexico University, NM
Eastern Washington University, WA
Edinboro University of Pennsylvania, PA
Electronic Data Processing College of
 Puerto Rico, PR
Emporia State University, KS
Ferrum College, VA
Framingham State College, MA
Francis Marion University, SC
Grambling State University, LA
Greensboro College, NC
Hope International University, CA
Illinois State University, IL
Inter American U of PR, Aguadilla Campus,
 PR
Inter Amer U of PR, Barranquitas Campus,
 PR
John Wesley College, NC
Lees-McRae College, NC
Maharishi University of Management, IA

Michigan State University, MI
Minot State University, ND
Montana State U–Northern, MT
Mount Vernon Nazarene College, OH
Northern Illinois University, IL
Piedmont Bible College, NC
Puget Sound Christian College, WA
Quinnipiac College, CT
Ramapo College of New Jersey, NJ
Robert Morris College, IL
Rust College, MS
St. John's Seminary College, CA
St. John's University, NY
Sonoma State University, CA
South Dakota State University, SD
Southern Connecticut State University, CT
Southwest Missouri State University, MO
Texas A&M University, College Station, TX
Texas Tech University, TX
Thomas College, GA
The University of Alabama at Birmingham, AL
University of Illinois at Chicago, IL
University of Massachusetts Amherst, MA
University of Montevallo, AL
University of Nebraska at Kearney, NE
University of New Mexico, NM
University of North Carolina at Asheville, NC
University of Northern Colorado, CO
U of Puerto Rico, Cayey University College, PR

University of Southern Mississippi, MS
Virginia Commonwealth University, VA
Virginia State University, VA
Warner Southern College, FL
Western New Mexico University, NM
Western Washington University, WA
William Carey College, MS
Worcester State College, MA

VETERANS' CHILDREN

Alabama State University, AL
California State University, Fresno, CA
Central Michigan University, MI
Central State University, OH
Chadron State College, NE
Circleville Bible College, OH
Coastal Carolina University, SC
David N. Myers College, OH
East Central University, OK
Edinboro University of Pennsylvania, PA
Electronic Data Processing College of Puerto Rico, PR
Emporia State University, KS
Florida Agricultural and Mechanical University, FL
Francis Marion University, SC
Hope International University, CA
Illinois State University, IL
Indiana State University, IN
Inter American U of PR, Aguadilla Campus, PR

John Wesley College, NC
Maharishi University of Management, IA
Marshall University, WV
Michigan State University, MI
Mount Vernon Nazarene College, OH
New Mexico State University, NM
Purdue University North Central, IN
Roanoke Bible College, NC
St. John's University, NY
South Dakota State University, SD
State U of NY College at Fredonia, NY
Texas A&M University, College Station, TX
Texas Tech University, TX
The University of Alabama at Birmingham, AL
University of California, San Diego, CA
University of Montevallo, AL
University of Nebraska at Kearney, NE
University of Nebraska at Omaha, NE
University of Nebraska–Lincoln, NE
University of North Carolina at Asheville, NC
University of Southern Indiana, IN
University of Toledo, OH
Virginia Commonwealth University, VA
Warner Southern College, FL
Wayne State College, NE
Western Illinois University, IL
Western Kentucky University, KY

ATHLETIC GRANTS FOR UNDERGRADUATES

This index lists the colleges that report offering scholarships for undergraduates on the basis of athletic achievements or abilities. For each college listed in this index, the reader should refer to the *Non-Need Awards* section of the college's profile for specific information on the number and value of the scholarships offered. Under each sport, each college is marked with an *M* (Men) to indicate scholarship programs awarded to men in that sport, a *W* (Women) to indicate women's scholarships, or *M,W* to show grants in the specified sport to students of both sexes.

These are the categories and the order in which they appear: Archery, Badminton, Baseball, Basketball, Bowling, Crew, Cross-Country Running, Equestrian Sports, Fencing, Field Hockey, Football, Golf, Gymnastics, Ice Hockey, Lacrosse, Racquetball, Riflery, Rugby, Sailing, Skiing—Cross Country, Skiing—Downhill, Soccer, Softball, Squash, Swimming and Diving, Table Tennis (Ping-Pong), Tennis, Track and Field, Volleyball, Water Polo, Weight Lifting, Wrestling.

BASEBALL

Abilene Christian University, TX	M
Adelphi University, NY	M
Alabama Agricultural and Mechanical University, AL	M
Albertson College of Idaho, ID	M
Alcorn State University, MS	M
Alderson-Broaddus College, WV	M
Alice Lloyd College, KY	M
American International College, MA	M
Anderson College, SC	M
Appalachian State University, NC	M
Aquinas College, MI	M
Arizona State University, AZ	M
Arkansas State University, AR	M
Armstrong Atlantic State University, GA	M
Ashland University, OH	M
Auburn University, AL	M
Auburn University at Montgomery, AL	M
Austin Peay State University, TN	M
Azusa Pacific University, CA	M
Baker University, KS	M
Ball State University, IN	M
Barry University, FL	M
Barton College, NC	M
Baylor University, TX	M
Becker College–Leicester Campus, MA	M
Becker College–Worcester Campus, MA	M
Belhaven College, MS	M
Bellarmine College, KY	M
Belmont Abbey College, NC	M
Belmont University, TN	M
Benedictine College, KS	M
Berry College, GA	M
Bethany College, KS	M
Bethel College, IN	M
Bethune-Cookman College, FL	M
Biola University, CA	M
Birmingham-Southern College, AL	M
Bloomfield College, NJ	M
Bluefield College, VA	M
Bluefield State College, WV	M
Bowie State University, MD	M
Bowling Green State University, OH	M
Bradley University, IL	M
Brewton-Parker College, GA	M
Briar Cliff College, IA	M
Butler University, IN	M
Caldwell College, NJ	M
California Baptist College, CA	M
California Polytechnic State U, San Luis Obispo, CA	M
California State Polytechnic University, Pomona, CA	M
California State University, Fresno, CA	M
California State University, Fullerton, CA	M
California State University, Northridge, CA	M
California State University, Sacramento, CA	M
California State University, San Bernardino, CA	M
Cameron University, OK	M
Campbell University, NC	M
Canisius College, NY	M
Carson-Newman College, TN	M
Catawba College, NC	M
Cedarville College, OH	M
Centenary College of Louisiana, LA	M
Central Connecticut State University, CT	M
Central Methodist College, MO	M
Central Michigan University, MI	M
Central Missouri State University, MO	M
Central State University, OH	M
Charleston Southern University, SC	M
Christian Brothers University, TN	M
The Citadel, The Military Coll of South Carolina, SC	M
Clarion University of Pennsylvania, PA	M
Cleveland State University, OH	M
Clinch Valley College of the U of Virginia, VA	M
Coastal Carolina University, SC	M
Coker College, SC	M
College of Charleston, SC	M
College of St. Francis, IL	M
College of the Ozarks, MO	M
College of William and Mary, VA	M
Colorado School of Mines, CO	M
Columbus State University, GA	M
Concord College, WV	M
Concordia College, MI	M
Concordia College, NE	M
Concordia College, NY	M
Concordia University, CA	M
Concordia University, OR	M
Concordia University at Austin, TX	M
Cornerstone College, MI	M
Creighton University, NE	M
Culver-Stockton College, MO	M
Cumberland College, KY	M
Cumberland University, TN	M
Dallas Baptist University, TX	M
Dana College, NE	M
David Lipscomb University, TN	M
Davis & Elkins College, WV	M
Delta State University, MS	M
Doane College, NE	M
Dominican College of Blauvelt, NY	M
Dowling College, NY	M
Drexel University, PA	M
Duke University, NC	M
Duquesne University, PA	M
East Carolina University, NC	M
Eastern Illinois University, IL	M
Eastern Kentucky University, KY	M
Eastern Michigan University, MI	M
Eastern New Mexico University, NM	M
East Texas Baptist University, TX	M
Eckerd College, FL	M
Edinboro University of Pennsylvania, PA	M
Elon College, NC	M

Embry-Riddle Aeronautical University, FL	M	Kansas Wesleyan University, KS	M	Mississippi Valley State University, MS	M
Emmanuel College, GA	M	Kennesaw State University, GA	M	Missouri Baptist College, MO	M
Emporia State University, KS	M	Kent State University, OH	M	Missouri Southern State College, MO	M
Erskine College, SC	M	Kentucky Wesleyan College, KY	M	Missouri Western State College, MO	M
Fairfield University, CT	M	King College, TN	M	Molloy College, NY	M
Fairleigh Dickinson U, Teaneck-Hackensack, NJ	M	Kutztown University of Pennsylvania, PA	M	Monmouth University, NJ	M
Faulkner University, AL	M	Lamar University, TX	M	Montreat College, NC	M
Flagler College, FL	M	Lambuth University, TN	M	Morehead State University, KY	M
Florida Atlantic University, FL	M	La Salle University, PA	M	Morningside College, IA	M
Florida Institute of Technology, FL	M	Lehigh University, PA	M	Morris College, SC	M
Florida International University, FL	M	Le Moyne College, NY	M	Mount Olive College, NC	M
Florida Southern College, FL	M	LeMoyne-Owen College, TN	M	Mount St. Clare College, IA	M
Florida State University, FL	M	Lenoir-Rhyne College, NC	M	Mount Saint Mary's College and Seminary, MD	M
Fordham University, NY	M	LeTourneau University, TX	M	Mount Vernon Nazarene College, OH	M
Fort Hays State University, KS	M	Lewis-Clark State College, ID	M	Murray State University, KY	M
Francis Marion University, SC	M	Lewis University, IL	M	Newberry College, SC	M
Franklin Pierce College, NH	M	Limestone College, SC	M	New Mexico Highlands University, NM	M
Freed-Hardeman University, TN	M	Lincoln Memorial University, TN	M	New Mexico State University, NM	M
Friends University, KS	M	Lincoln University, MO	M	New York Institute of Technology, NY	M
Furman University, SC	M	Lindenwood College, MO	M	Niagara University, NY	M
Gannon University, PA	M	Lindsey Wilson College, KY	M	Nicholls State University, LA	M
Geneva College, PA	M	Lock Haven University of Pennsylvania, PA	M	North Carolina Agricultural and Technical State U, NC	M
George Mason University, VA	M	Long Island U, Brooklyn Campus, NY	M	North Carolina State University, NC	M
Georgetown College, KY	M	Long Island U, C.W. Post Campus, NY	M	North Dakota State University, ND	M
Georgetown University, DC	M	Longwood College, VA	M	Northeastern Illinois University, IL	M
The George Washington University, DC	M	Louisiana College, LA	M	Northeastern State University, OK	M
Georgia College and State University, GA	M	Louisiana State University and A&M College, LA	M	Northeastern University, MA	M
Georgia Institute of Technology, GA	M	Louisiana State University in Shreveport, LA	M	Northeast Louisiana University, LA	M
Georgia Southern University, GA	M	Louisiana Tech University, LA	M	Northern Illinois University, IL	M
Georgia Southwestern State University, GA	M	Loyola Marymount University, CA	M	Northern Kentucky University, KY	M
Georgia State University, GA	M	Lubbock Christian University, TX	M	North Greenville College, SC	M
Gonzaga University, WA	M	Lynn University, FL	M	Northwestern College, IA	M
Grace College, IN	M	Lyon College, AR	M	Northwestern Oklahoma State University, OK	M
Graceland College, IA	M	Malone College, OH	M	Northwestern State University of Louisiana, LA	M
Grambling State University, LA	M	Manhattan College, NY	M	Northwestern University, IL	M
Grand View College, IA	M	Mankato State University, MN	M	Northwest Missouri State University, MO	M
Hannibal-LaGrange College, MO	M	Mansfield University of Pennsylvania, PA	M	Northwood University, MI	M
Hastings College, NE	M	Marian College, IN	M	Northwood University, Florida Campus, FL	M
Hawaii Pacific University, HI	M	Marist College, NY	M	Northwood University, Texas Campus, TX	M
Hillsdale College, MI	M	Marshall University, WV	M	Nova Southeastern University, FL	M
Hofstra University, NY	M	Martin Methodist College, TN	M	Oakland City University, IN	M
Huntington College, IN	M	Marycrest International University, IA	M	Oakland University, MI	M
Huron University, SD	M	The Master's College and Seminary, CA	M	Ohio Dominican College, OH	M
Illinois Institute of Technology, IL	M	McKendree College, IL	M	The Ohio State University, OH	M
Illinois State University, IL	M	McNeese State University, LA	M	Ohio University, OH	M
Indiana Institute of Technology, IN	M	Mercer University, Macon, GA	M	Oklahoma Baptist University, OK	M
Indiana State University, IN	M	Mercyhurst College, PA	M	Oklahoma Christian U of Science and Arts, OK	M
Indiana University Bloomington, IN	M	Merrimack College, MA	M	Oklahoma City University, OK	M
Indiana U–Purdue U Indianapolis, IN	M	Mesa State College, CO	M	Oklahoma State U, OK	M
Indiana Wesleyan University, IN	M	Metropolitan State College of Denver, CO	M	Old Dominion University, VA	M
Inter American U of PR, San Germán Campus, PR	M	Miami University, OH	M	Olivet Nazarene University, IL	M
Iowa State University of Science and Technology, IA	M	Michigan Christian College, MI	M	Oral Roberts University, OK	M
Iowa Wesleyan College, IA	M	MidAmerica Nazarene University, KS	M	Oregon State University, OR	M
Jackson State University, MS	M	Middle Tennessee State University, TN	M	Ottawa University, KS	M
Jacksonville State University, AL	M	Millersville University of Pennsylvania, PA	M	Pace University, NY	M
Jacksonville University, FL	M	Mississippi State University, MS	M	Paine College, GA	M
James Madison University, VA	M			Palm Beach Atlantic College, FL	M
Judson College, IL	M				
Kansas Newman College, KS	M				
Kansas State University, KS	M				

Baseball (continued)

Patten College, CA	M
Penn State U Univ Park Campus, PA	M
Pepperdine University, Malibu, CA	M
Peru State College, NE	M
Pfeiffer University, NC	M
Philadelphia College of Textiles and Science, PA	M
Phillips University, OK	M
Piedmont College, GA	M
Pikeville College, KY	M
Pittsburg State University, KS	M
Point Loma Nazarene College, CA	M
Point Park College, PA	M
Portland State University, OR	M
Providence College, RI	M
Purdue University, West Lafayette, IN	M
Queens Coll of the City U of NY, NY	M
Quincy University, IL	M
Quinnipiac College, CT	M
Radford University, VA	M
Regis University, CO	M
Research College of Nursing–Rockhurst College, MO	M
Rice University, TX	M
Rider University, NJ	M
Rockhurst College, MO	M
Rollins College, FL	M
Rutgers, State U of NJ, College of Engineering, NJ	M
Rutgers, State U of NJ, College of Pharmacy, NJ	M
Rutgers, State U of NJ, Cook College, NJ	M
Rutgers, State U of NJ, Livingston College, NJ	M
Rutgers, State U of NJ, Mason Gross School of Arts, NJ	M
Rutgers, State U of NJ, Rutgers College, NJ	M
Saginaw Valley State University, MI	M
St. Ambrose University, IA	M
St. Andrews Presbyterian College, NC	M
St. Bonaventure University, NY	M
St. Edward's University, TX	M
Saint Francis College, IN	M
St. Francis College, NY	M
St. John's University, NY	M
Saint Joseph's College, IN	M
Saint Joseph's University, PA	M
Saint Leo College, FL	M
Saint Louis University, MO	M
Saint Martin's College, WA	M
Saint Mary's College of California, CA	M
St. Mary's University of San Antonio, TX	M
Saint Paul's College, VA	M
Saint Peter's College, Jersey City, NJ	M
St. Thomas Aquinas College, NY	M
St. Thomas University, FL	M
Saint Vincent College, PA	M
Saint Xavier University, IL	M
Salem-Teikyo University, WV	M
Samford University, AL	M
Sam Houston State University, TX	M
San Diego State University, CA	M

San Jose State University, CA	M,W
Santa Clara University, CA	M
Seton Hall University, NJ	M
Shippensburg University of Pennsylvania, PA	M
Shorter College, GA	M
Siena College, NY	M
Siena Heights College, MI	M
Slippery Rock University of Pennsylvania, PA	M
South Dakota State University, SD	M
Southeastern Louisiana University, LA	M
Southeastern Oklahoma State University, OK	M
Southeast Missouri State University, MO	M
Southern California College, CA	M
Southern Illinois University at Carbondale, IL	M
Southern Illinois University at Edwardsville, IL	M
Southern Polytechnic State University, GA	M
Southern Utah University, UT	M
Southern Wesleyan University, SC	M
Southwest Baptist University, MO	M
Southwestern Oklahoma State University, OK	M
Southwest Missouri State University, MO	M
Southwest Texas State University, TX	M
Spring Arbor College, MI	M
Spring Hill College, AL	M
Stetson University, FL	M
Sue Bennett College, KY	M
Tabor College, KS	M
Tarleton State University, TX	M
Taylor University, IN	M
Teikyo Post University, CT	M
Temple University, Philadelphia, PA	M
Tennessee Technological University, TN	M
Tennessee Temple University, TN	M
Tennessee Wesleyan College, TN	M
Texas A&M University, College Station, TX	M
Texas Christian University, TX	M
Texas Lutheran University, TX	M
Texas Tech University, TX	M
Texas Wesleyan University, TX	M
Thomas College, GA	M
Tiffin University, OH	M
Towson University, MD	M
Transylvania University, KY	M
Trevecca Nazarene University, TN	M
Trinity Christian College, IL	M
Tri-State University, IN	M
Troy State University, Troy, AL	M
Truman State University, MO	M
Tulane University, LA	M
Tusculum College, TN	M
Tuskegee University, AL	M
Union College, KY	M
Union University, TN	M
U at Albany, State U of NY, NY	M
The University of Akron, OH	M

The University of Alabama at Birmingham, AL	M
The University of Alabama in Huntsville, AL	M
University of Arizona, AZ	M
University of Arkansas, Fayetteville, AR	M
University of Arkansas at Little Rock, AR	M
University of Bridgeport, CT	M
University of California, Los Angeles, CA	M
University of California, Riverside, CA	M
University of California, Santa Barbara, CA	M
University of Central Florida, FL	M
University of Central Oklahoma, OK	M
The University of Charleston, WV	M
University of Connecticut, Storrs, CT	M
University of Dayton, OH	M
University of Delaware, DE	M
University of Denver, CO	M
University of Detroit Mercy, MI	M
University of Evansville, IN	M
The University of Findlay, OH	M
University of Florida, FL	M
University of Georgia, GA	M
University of Hartford, CT	M
University of Hawaii at Hilo, HI	M
University of Hawaii at Manoa, HI	M
University of Illinois at Chicago, IL	M
University of Illinois at Urbana–Champaign, IL	M
University of Indianapolis, IN	M
The University of Iowa, IA	M
University of Kansas, KS	M
University of Louisville, KY	M
University of Maine, Orono, ME	M
University of Mary Hardin-Baylor, TX	M
University of Maryland Baltimore County, MD	M
University of Maryland Eastern Shore, MD	M
University of Massachusetts Amherst, MA	M
The University of Memphis, TN	M
University of Miami, FL	M
University of Michigan, Ann Arbor, MI	M
University of Minnesota, Crookston, MN	M
University of Minnesota, Duluth, MN	M
University of Minnesota, Twin Cities Campus, MN	M
University of Mississippi, MS	M
University of Missouri–Columbia, MO	M
University of Missouri–St. Louis, MO	M
University of Mobile, AL	M
University of Montevallo, AL	M
University of Nebraska at Kearney, NE	M
University of Nebraska at Omaha, NE	M
University of Nebraska–Lincoln, NE	M
University of Nevada, Las Vegas, NV	M
University of Nevada, Reno, NV	M

University of New Hampshire, Durham, NH	M
University of New Haven, CT	M
University of North Alabama, AL	M
University of North Carolina at Asheville, NC	M
University of North Carolina at Charlotte, NC	M
University of North Carolina at Greensboro, NC	M
University of North Carolina at Pembroke, NC	M
University of North Carolina at Wilmington, NC	M
University of North Dakota, ND	M
University of Northern Colorado, CO	M
University of Northern Iowa, IA	M
University of North Florida, FL	M
University of Notre Dame, IN	M
University of Oklahoma, OK	M
University of Pittsburgh, PA	M
University of Portland, OR	M
University of Rhode Island, RI	M
University of Richmond, VA	M
University of Rio Grande, OH	W
University of San Diego, CA	M
University of San Francisco, CA	M
University of South Alabama, AL	M
U of South Carolina, Columbia, SC	M
U of South Carolina–Aiken, SC	M
U of South Carolina–Spartanburg, SC	M
University of South Dakota, SD	M
University of Southern California, CA	M
University of Southern Indiana, IN	M
University of Southern Mississippi, MS	M
University of South Florida, FL	M
University of Southwestern Louisiana, LA	M
The University of Tampa, FL	M
The University of Tennessee at Martin, TN	M
The University of Texas at Arlington, TX	M
The University of Texas at Austin, TX	M
The University of Texas at San Antonio, TX	M
University of the Pacific, CA	M
University of Toledo, OH	M
University of Utah, UT	M
University of Virginia, VA	M
University of Washington, WA	M
The University of West Alabama, AL	M
University of West Florida, FL	M
University of Wisconsin–Parkside, WI	M
University of Wyoming, WY	M
Urbana University, OH	M
Valdosta State University, GA	M
Valley City State University, ND	M
Valparaiso University, IN	M
Vanderbilt University, TN	M
Villanova University, PA	M
Virginia Commonwealth University, VA	M
Virginia Intermont College, VA	M
Virginia Polytechnic Institute and State U, VA	M

Wagner College, NY	M
Wake Forest University, NC	M
Walsh University, OH	M
Warner Southern College, FL	M
Washburn University of Topeka, KS	M
Wayne State College, NE	M
Wayne State University, MI	M
Webber College, FL	M
West Chester University of Pennsylvania, PA	M
Western Carolina University, NC	M
Western Illinois University, IL	M
Western Kentucky University, KY	M
Western Michigan University, MI	M
West Liberty State College, WV	M
Westmar University, IA	M
Westmont College, CA	M
West Texas A&M University, TX	M
West Virginia University, WV	M
West Virginia University Institute of Technology, WV	M
Wichita State University, KS	M
William Carey College, MS	M
William Jewell College, MO	M
Williams Baptist College, AR	M
Wilmington College, DE	M
Wingate University, NC	M
Winona State University, MN	M
Winthrop University, SC	M
Wofford College, SC	M
Wright State University, OH	M
Xavier University, OH	M
York College, NE	M
Youngstown State University, OH	M

BASKETBALL

Abilene Christian University, TX	M,W
Adams State College, CO	M,W
Adelphi University, NY	M,W
Alabama Agricultural and Mechanical University, AL	M,W
Alabama State University, AL	M,W
Albany State University, GA	M,W
Albertson College of Idaho, ID	M,W
Alcorn State University, MS	M,W
Alderson-Broaddus College, WV	M,W
Alice Lloyd College, KY	M,W
Allen University, SC	M,W
American International College, MA	M,W
American University, DC	M,W
Anderson College, SC	M,W
Angelo State University, TX	M,W
Appalachian State University, NC	M,W
Aquinas College, MI	M,W
Arizona State University, AZ	M,W
Arkansas State University, AR	M,W
Arkansas Tech University, AR	M,W
Armstrong Atlantic State University, GA	M,W
Ashland University, OH	M,W
Assumption College, MA	M,W
Atlantic Union College, MA	M,W
Auburn University, AL	M,W
Auburn University at Montgomery, AL	M,W
Augustana College, SD	M,W
Augusta State University, GA	M,W

Austin Peay State University, TN	M,W
Azusa Pacific University, CA	M,W
Baker University, KS	M,W
Ball State University, IN	M,W
Barat College, IL	M
Barber-Scotia College, NC	M,W
Barry University, FL	M,W
Bartlesville Wesleyan College, OK	M,W
Barton College, NC	M,W
Bayamón Technological University College, PR	M,W
Baylor University, TX	M,W
Becker College–Leicester Campus, MA	W
Becker College–Worcester Campus, MA	M,W
Belhaven College, MS	M,W
Bellarmine College, KY	M,W
Bellevue University, NE	M
Belmont Abbey College, NC	M,W
Belmont University, TN	M,W
Bemidji State University, MN	M,W
Benedict College, SC	M,W
Benedictine College, KS	M,W
Bentley College, MA	M,W
Berry College, GA	M,W
Bethany College, KS	M,W
Bethel College, IN	M,W
Bethel College, KS	M,W
Bethel College, TN	M,W
Bethune-Cookman College, FL	M,W
Biola University, CA	M,W
Birmingham-Southern College, AL	M
Black Hills State University, SD	M,W
Bloomfield College, NJ	M,W
Bloomsburg University of Pennsylvania, PA	M,W
Bluefield College, VA	M,W
Bluefield State College, WV	M,W
Blue Mountain College, MS	W
Boise State University, ID	M,W
Boston College, MA	M,W
Boston University, MA	M,W
Bowie State University, MD	M,W
Bowling Green State University, OH	M,W
Bradley University, IL	M,W
Brescia College, KY	M,W
Brewton-Parker College, GA	M,W
Briar Cliff College, IA	M,W
Brigham Young University, UT	M,W
Brigham Young University–Hawaii Campus, HI	M
Bryan College, TN	M,W
Bryant College, RI	M,W
Butler University, IN	M,W
Caldwell College, NJ	M,W
California Baptist College, CA	M,W
California Polytechnic State U, San Luis Obispo, CA	M,W
California State Polytechnic University, Pomona, CA	M,W
California State University, Bakersfield, CA	M
California State University, Dominguez Hills, CA	M,W
California State University, Fresno, CA	M,W

Basketball (continued)

California State University, Fullerton, CA — M,W
California State University, Long Beach, CA — M,W
California State University, Los Angeles, CA — M,W
California State University, Northridge, CA — M,W
California State University, Sacramento, CA — M,W
California State University, San Bernardino, CA — M,W
California University of Pennsylvania, PA — M,W
Cameron University, OK — M,W
Campbell University, NC — M,W
Canisius College, NY — M,W
Carlow College, PA — W
Carroll College, MT — M,W
Carson-Newman College, TN — M,W
Catawba College, NC — M,W
Cedarville College, OH — M,W
Centenary College of Louisiana, LA — M
Central Connecticut State University, CT — M,W
Central Methodist College, MO — M,W
Central Michigan University, MI — M,W
Central Missouri State University, MO — M,W
Central State University, OH — M,W
Chadron State College, NE — M,W
Chaminade University of Honolulu, HI — M
Charleston Southern University, SC — M,W
Cheyney University of Pennsylvania, PA — M,W
Chicago State University, IL — M,W
Christian Brothers University, TN — M,W
Christian Heritage College, CA — M,W
The Citadel, The Military Coll of South Carolina, SC — M
Claflin College, SC — M,W
Clarion University of Pennsylvania, PA — M,W
Clark Atlanta University, GA — M,W
Clayton College & State University, GA — M
Clemson University, SC — M,W
Cleveland State University, OH — M,W
Clinch Valley College of the U of Virginia, VA — M,W
Coastal Carolina University, SC — M,W
Coker College, SC — M,W
Colegio Universitario del Este, PR — M
College of Charleston, SC — M,W
College of St. Francis, IL — M,W
College of St. Joseph, VT — M,W
College of the Ozarks, MO — M,W
The College of West Virginia, WV — M
College of William and Mary, VA — M,W
Colorado Christian University, CO — M,W
Colorado School of Mines, CO — M,W
Colorado State University, CO — M,W
Columbia College, MO — M
Columbia Union College, MD — M,W
Columbus State University, GA — M,W
Concord College, WV — M,W

Concordia College, AL — M
Concordia College, MI — M,W
Concordia College, NE — M,W
Concordia College, NY — M,W
Concordia University, CA — M,W
Concordia University, OR — M,W
Concordia University at Austin, TX — M,W
Cornerstone College, MI — M,W
Covenant College, GA — M,W
Creighton University, NE — M,W
Culver-Stockton College, MO — M,W
Cumberland College, KY — M,W
Cumberland University, TN — M,W
Daemen College, NY — M,W
Dakota State University, SD — M,W
Dakota Wesleyan University, SD — M,W
Dana College, NE — M,W
David Lipscomb University, TN — M,W
Davidson College, NC — M,W
Davis & Elkins College, WV — M,W
Delaware State University, DE — M,W
Delta State University, MS — M,W
DePaul University, IL — M,W
Dickinson State University, ND — M,W
Dillard University, LA — M,W
Doane College, NE — M,W
Dominican College of Blauvelt, NY — M,W
Dominican College of San Rafael, CA — M,W
Dowling College, NY — M,W
Drake University, IA — M,W
Drexel University, PA — M
Drury College, MO — M
Duke University, NC — M,W
Duquesne University, PA — M,W
D'Youville College, NY — M,W
East Carolina University, NC — M,W
East Central University, OK — M,W
Eastern Illinois University, IL — M,W
Eastern Kentucky University, KY — M,W
Eastern Michigan University, MI — M,W
Eastern New Mexico University, NM — M,W
Eastern Washington University, WA — M,W
East Stroudsburg University of Pennsylvania, PA — M,W
East Tennessee State University, TN — M,W
East Texas Baptist University, TX — M,W
Eckerd College, FL — M,W
Edinboro University of Pennsylvania, PA — M,W
Edward Waters College, FL — M,W
Electronic Data Processing College of Puerto Rico, PR — M,W
Elizabeth City State University, NC — M,W
Elon College, NC — M,W
Embry-Riddle Aeronautical University, FL — M
Emmanuel College, GA — M,W
Emporia State University, KS — M,W
Erskine College, SC — M,W
Evangel College, MO — M,W
Fairfield University, CT — M,W
Fairleigh Dickinson U, Teaneck-Hackensack, NJ — M,W
Fairmont State College, WV — M,W
Faulkner University, AL — M
Fayetteville State University, NC — M
Ferris State University, MI — M,W

Flagler College, FL — M,W
Florida Agricultural and Mechanical University, FL — M,W
Florida Atlantic University, FL — M,W
Florida Institute of Technology, FL — M,W
Florida International University, FL — M,W
Florida Memorial College, FL — M
Florida Southern College, FL — M,W
Florida State University, FL — M,W
Fordham University, NY — M,W
Fort Hays State University, KS — M,W
Fort Lewis College, CO — M,W
Fort Valley State University, GA — M,W
Francis Marion University, SC — M,W
Franklin Pierce College, NH — M,W
Freed-Hardeman University, TN — M,W
Fresno Pacific University, CA — M,W
Friends University, KS — M,W
Furman University, SC — M,W
Gannon University, PA — M,W
Gardner-Webb University, NC — M,W
Geneva College, PA — M,W
George Mason University, VA — M,W
Georgetown College, KY — M,W
Georgetown University, DC — M,W
The George Washington University, DC — M,W
Georgia College and State University, GA —
Georgia Institute of Technology, GA — M,W
Georgian Court College, NJ — W
Georgia Southern University, GA —
Georgia Southwestern State University, GA — M,W
Georgia State University, GA — M,W
Glenville State College, WV — M,W
Gonzaga University, WA — M,W
Goshen College, IN — M,W
Grace College, IN — M,W
Graceland College, IA — M,W
Grambling State University, LA — M,W
Grand Canyon University, AZ — M,W
Grand Valley State University, MI — M,W
Grand View College, IA — M,W
Green Mountain College, VT — M,W
Hannibal-LaGrange College, MO — M,W
Harding University, AR — M,W
Hastings College, NE — M,W
Hawaii Pacific University, HI — M
Henderson State University, AR — M,W
Hillsdale College, MI — M,W
Hofstra University, NY — M,W
Holy Family College, PA — M,W
Holy Names College, CA — M,W
Hope International University, CA — M,W
Houghton College, NY — M,W
Howard University, DC — M,W
Huntington College, IN — M,W
Huron University, SD — M,W
Idaho State University, ID — M,W
Illinois Institute of Technology, IL — M,W
Illinois State University, IL — M,W
Indiana Institute of Technology, IN — M,W
Indiana State University, IN — M,W
Indiana University Bloomington, IN — M,W
Indiana University of Pennsylvania, PA — M,W

Indiana U–Purdue U Fort Wayne, IN	M,W	Loyola Marymount University, CA	M,W	Mount Aloysius College, PA	M,W
Indiana U–Purdue U Indianapolis, IN	M,W	Loyola University Chicago, IL	M,W	Mount Marty College, SD	M,W
Indiana University South Bend, IN	M	Lubbock Christian University, TX	M,W	Mount Olive College, NC	M,W
Indiana University Southeast, IN	M,W	Lynn University, FL	M,W	Mount St. Clare College, IA	M,W
Indiana Wesleyan University, IN	M,W	Lyon College, AR	M,W	Mount Saint Mary's College and	
Inter American U of PR, Arecibo		Madonna University, MI	W	Seminary, MD	M,W
Campus, PR	M,W	Malone College, OH	M,W	Mount Vernon Nazarene College, OH	M,W
Inter American U of PR, Metropolitan		Manhattan College, NY	M,W	Murray State University, KY	M,W
Campus, PR	M	Mankato State University, MN	M,W	Newberry College, SC	M,W
Inter American U of PR, San Germán		Mansfield University of Pennsylvania,		New Hampshire College, NH	M,W
Campus, PR	M,W	PA	M,W	New Mexico Highlands University,	
Iona College, New Rochelle, NY	M,W	Marian College, IN	M,W	NM	M,W
Iowa State University of Science and		Marist College, NY	M,W	New Mexico State University, NM	M,W
Technology, IA	M,W	Marquette University, WI	M,W	New York Institute of Technology, NY	M
Iowa Wesleyan College, IA	M,W	Marshall University, WV	M,W	Niagara University, NY	M,W
Jackson State University, MS	M,W	Mars Hill College, NC	M,W	Nicholls State University, LA	M,W
Jacksonville State University, AL	M,W	Martin Methodist College, TN	M,W	Norfolk State University, VA	M,W
Jacksonville University, FL	M	Marycrest International University, IA	M,W	North Carolina Agricultural and	
James Madison University, VA	M,W	The Master's College and Seminary,		Technical State U, NC	M,W
John Brown University, AR	M,W	CA	M,W	North Carolina Central University, NC	M,W
Johnson C. Smith University, NC	M,W	Mayville State University, ND	M,W	North Carolina State University, NC	M,W
Judson College, IL	M,W	McKendree College, IL	M,W	North Dakota State University, ND	M,W
Kansas Newman College, KS	W	McNeese State University, LA	M,W	Northeastern Illinois University, IL	M,W
Kansas State University, KS	M,W	McPherson College, KS	M,W	Northeastern State University, OK	M
Kansas Wesleyan University, KS	M,W	Mercer University, Macon, GA	M,W	Northeastern University, MA	M,W
Kennesaw State University, GA	M,W	Mercyhurst College, PA	M,W	Northeast Louisiana University, LA	M,W
Kent State University, OH	M,W	Merrimack College, MA	M,W	Northern Arizona University, AZ	M,W
Kentucky State University, KY	M,W	Mesa State College, CO	M,W	Northern Illinois University, IL	M,W
Kentucky Wesleyan College, KY	M,W	Metropolitan State College of Denver,		Northern Kentucky University, KY	M,W
King College, TN	M,W	CO	M,W	Northern Michigan University, MI	M,W
Kutztown University of Pennsylvania,		Miami University, OH	M,W	Northern State University, SD	M,W
PA	M,W	Michigan Christian College, MI	M,W	North Georgia College & State	
Lamar University, TX	M,W	Michigan State University, MI	M,W	University, GA	M,W
Lambuth University, TN	M,W	Michigan Technological University,		North Greenville College, SC	M,W
Lander University, SC	M,W	MI	M,W	Northland College, WI	M,W
Langston University, OK	M,W	MidAmerica Nazarene University, KS	M,W	Northwest College of the Assemblies	
La Salle University, PA	M,W	Middle Tennessee State University,		of God, WA	M,W
Lees-McRae College, NC	M,W	TN	M,W	Northwestern College, IA	M,W
Lee University, TN	M,W	Midland Lutheran College, NE	M,W	Northwestern Oklahoma State	
Lehigh University, PA	M	Midway College, KY	W	University, OK	M,W
Le Moyne College, NY	M,W	Midwestern State University, TX	M,W	Northwestern State University of	
LeMoyne-Owen College, TN	M,W	Millersville University of		Louisiana, LA	M,W
Lenoir-Rhyne College, NC	M,W	Pennsylvania, PA	M,W	Northwestern University, IL	M,W
LeTourneau University, TX	M,W	Milligan College, TN	M,W	Northwest Missouri State University,	
Lewis-Clark State College, ID	M,W	Minot State University, ND	M,W	MO	M,W
Lewis University, IL	M,W	Mississippi State University, MS	M,W	Northwood University, MI	M,W
Limestone College, SC	M,W	Mississippi University for Women,		Notre Dame College, NH	M,W
Lincoln Memorial University, TN	M,W	MS	W	Nova Southeastern University, FL	M
Lincoln University, MO	M,W	Mississippi Valley State University,		Nyack College, NY	M,W
Lindenwood College, MO	M,W	MS	M,W	Oakland City University, IN	M,W
Lindsey Wilson College, KY	M,W	Missouri Baptist College, MO	M,W	Oakland University, MI	M,W
Livingstone College, NC	M,W	Missouri Southern State College, MO	M,W	Ohio Dominican College, OH	M,W
Lock Haven University of		Missouri Western State College, MO	M,W	The Ohio State University, OH	M,W
Pennsylvania, PA	M,W	Molloy College, NY	M,W	Ohio University, OH	M,W
Long Island U, Brooklyn Campus, NY	M,W	Monmouth University, NJ	M,W	Oklahoma Baptist University, OK	M,W
Long Island U, C.W. Post Campus,		Montana State U–Billings, MT	M,W	Oklahoma Christian U of Science and	
NY	M,W	Montana State U–Bozeman, MT	M,W	Arts, OK	M,W
Long Island U, Southampton College,		Montana State U–Northern, MT	M,W	Oklahoma City University, OK	M,W
NY	M,W	Montana Tech of The University of		Oklahoma Panhandle State University,	
Longwood College, VA	M,W	Montana, MT	M,W	OK	M,W
Louisiana College, LA	M,W	Montreat College, NC	M,W	Oklahoma State U, OK	M,W
Louisiana State University and A&M		Moorhead State University, MN	M,W	Old Dominion University, VA	M,W
College, LA	M,W	Morehead State University, KY	M,W	Olivet Nazarene University, IL	M,W
Louisiana State University in		Morehouse College, GA	M	Oral Roberts University, OK	M,W
Shreveport, LA	W	Morgan State University, MD	M,W	Oregon Institute of Technology, OR	M
Louisiana Tech University, LA	M,W	Morningside College, IA	M,W	Oregon State University, OR	M,W
Loyola College, MD	M,W	Morris College, SC	M,W	Ottawa University, KS	M,W

Basketball (continued)

Ouachita Baptist University, AR	M,W
Pace University, NY	M,W
Paine College, GA	M,W
Palm Beach Atlantic College, FL	M
Park College, MO	M,W
Patten College, CA	M,W
Penn State U Univ Park Campus, PA	M,W
Pepperdine University, Malibu, CA	M,W
Peru State College, NE	M,W
Pfeiffer University, NC	M,W
Philadelphia College of Textiles and Science, PA	M,W
Phillips University, OK	M,W
Piedmont College, GA	M,W
Pikeville College, KY	M,W
Pittsburg State University, KS	M,W
Point Loma Nazarene College, CA	M,W
Point Park College, PA	M,W
Portland State University, OR	W
Presbyterian College, SC	M,W
Providence College, RI	M,W
Purdue University, West Lafayette, IN	M,W
Purdue University Calumet, IN	M,W
Queens College, NC	M,W
Queens Coll of the City U of NY, NY	M,W
Quincy University, IL	M,W
Quinnipiac College, CT	M,W
Radford University, VA	M,W
Regis University, CO	M,W
Reinhardt College, GA	M,W
Research College of Nursing–Rockhurst College, MO	M,W
Rice University, TX	M,W
Rider University, NJ	M,W
Robert Morris College, PA	M,W
Roberts Wesleyan College, NY	M,W
Rockhurst College, MO	M,W
Rocky Mountain College, MT	M,W
Rollins College, FL	M,W
Rutgers, State U of NJ, College of Engineering, NJ	M,W
Rutgers, State U of NJ, College of Pharmacy, NJ	M,W
Rutgers, State U of NJ, Cook College, NJ	M,W
Rutgers, State U of NJ, Douglass College, NJ	W
Rutgers, State U of NJ, Livingston College, NJ	M,W
Rutgers, State U of NJ, Mason Gross School of Arts, NJ	M,W
Rutgers, State U of NJ, Rutgers College, NJ	M,W
Saginaw Valley State University, MI	M,W
St. Ambrose University, IA	M,W
St. Andrews Presbyterian College, NC	M,W
Saint Anselm College, NH	M,W
Saint Augustine's College, NC	M,W
St. Bonaventure University, NY	M,W
St. Cloud State University, MN	M,W
St. Edward's University, TX	M,W
Saint Francis College, IN	M,W
St. Francis College, NY	M,W
Saint Francis College, PA	M,W
St. John's University, NY	M,W
Saint Joseph's College, IN	M,W

Saint Joseph's University, PA	M,W
Saint Leo College, FL	M,W
Saint Louis University, MO	M,W
Saint Martin's College, WA	M,W
Saint Mary College, KS	M,W
Saint Mary-of-the-Woods College, IN	W
Saint Mary's College of California, CA	M,W
St. Mary's University of San Antonio, TX	M,W
Saint Michael's College, VT	M,W
Saint Paul's College, VA	M,W
Saint Peter's College, Jersey City, NJ	M,W
St. Thomas Aquinas College, NY	M,W
St. Thomas University, FL	M
Saint Vincent College, PA	M,W
Saint Xavier University, IL	M
Salem-Teikyo University, WV	M,W
Samford University, AL	M
Sam Houston State University, TX	M,W
San Diego State University, CA	M,W
San Jose State University, CA	M,W
Santa Clara University, CA	M,W
Savannah State University, GA	M,W
Seattle Pacific University, WA	M,W
Seton Hall University, NJ	M,W
Seton Hill College, PA	W
Shaw University, NC	M,W
Shepherd College, WV	M,W
Shippensburg University of Pennsylvania, PA	M,W
Shorter College, GA	M,W
Siena College, NY	M,W
Siena Heights College, MI	M,W
Slippery Rock University of Pennsylvania, PA	M,W
South Dakota School of Mines and Technology, SD	M,W
South Dakota State University, SD	M,W
Southeastern Louisiana University, LA	M,W
Southeastern Oklahoma State University, OK	M,W
Southeast Missouri State University, MO	M,W
Southern Arkansas University–Magnolia, AR	M,W
Southern California College, CA	M,W
Southern Illinois University at Carbondale, IL	M,W
Southern Illinois University at Edwardsville, IL	M,W
Southern Methodist University, TX	M,W
Southern Nazarene University, OK	M,W
Southern Oregon University, OR	M,W
Southern Polytechnic State University, GA	M
Southern University and A&M College, LA	M,W
Southern University at New Orleans, LA	M
Southern Utah University, UT	M,W
Southern Wesleyan University, SC	M,W
Southwest Baptist University, MO	M,W
Southwestern Christian College, TX	M,W
Southwestern College, KS	M,W
Southwestern Oklahoma State University, OK	M,W

Southwest Missouri State University, MO	M,W
Southwest State University, MN	M,W
Southwest Texas State University, TX	M,W
Spalding University, KY	M,W
Spring Arbor College, MI	M,W
Spring Hill College, AL	M,W
Stanford University, CA	M,W
State U of NY at Buffalo, NY	M,W
Stephen F. Austin State University, TX	M,W
Sterling College, KS	M,W
Stetson University, FL	M,W
Stonehill College, MA	M,W
Sue Bennett College, KY	M,W
Sullivan College, KY	M,W
Syracuse University, NY	M,W
Tabor College, KS	M,W
Talladega College, AL	M,W
Tarleton State University, TX	M,W
Taylor University, IN	M,W
Teikyo Post University, CT	M,W
Temple University, Philadelphia, PA	M,W
Tennessee State University, TN	M,W
Tennessee Technological University, TN	M,W
Tennessee Temple University, TN	M,W
Tennessee Wesleyan College, TN	M,W
Texas A&M University, College Station, TX	M,W
Texas A&M University–Commerce, TX	M,W
Texas A&M University–Kingsville, TX	M,W
Texas Christian University, TX	M,W
Texas Lutheran University, TX	M,W
Texas Southern University, TX	M,W
Texas Tech University, TX	M,W
Texas Wesleyan University, TX	M,W
Texas Woman's University, TX	W
Thomas College, GA	M
Tiffin University, OH	M,W
Tougaloo College, MS	M,W
Towson University, MD	M,W
Transylvania University, KY	M,W
Trevecca Nazarene University, TN	M,W
Trinity Christian College, IL	M,W
Trinity International University, IL	M,W
Tri-State University, IN	M,W
Troy State University, Troy, AL	M,W
Truman State University, MO	M,W
Tulane University, LA	M,W
Tusculum College, TN	M,W
Tuskegee University, AL	M,W
Union College, KY	M,W
Union University, TN	M,W
Unity College, ME	M
U at Albany, State U of NY, NY	M,W
The University of Akron, OH	M,W
The University of Alabama at Birmingham, AL	M,W
The University of Alabama in Huntsville, AL	M,W
U of Alaska Anchorage, AK	M,W
U of Alaska Fairbanks, AK	M,W
University of Arizona, AZ	M,W
University of Arkansas, Fayetteville, AR	M,W

University of Arkansas at Little Rock, AR	M
University of Arkansas at Monticello, AR	M,W
University of Arkansas at Pine Bluff, AR	M,W
University of Bridgeport, CT	M,W
University of California, Berkeley, CA	M,W
University of California, Irvine, CA	M,W
University of California, Los Angeles, CA	M,W
University of California, Riverside, CA	M,W
University of California, Santa Barbara, CA	M,W
University of Central Arkansas, AR	M,W
University of Central Florida, FL	M,W
University of Central Oklahoma, OK	M,W
The University of Charleston, WV	M,W
University of Cincinnati, OH	M,W
University of Colorado at Boulder, CO	M,W
University of Colorado at Colorado Springs, CO	M,W
University of Connecticut, Storrs, CT	M,W
University of Dayton, OH	M,W
University of Delaware, DE	M,W
University of Denver, CO	M,W
University of Detroit Mercy, MI	M,W
University of Evansville, IN	M,W
The University of Findlay, OH	M,W
University of Florida, FL	M,W
University of Georgia, GA	M,W
University of Guam, GU	M,W
University of Hartford, CT	M,W
University of Hawaii at Hilo, HI	M
University of Hawaii at Manoa, HI	M,W
University of Houston, TX	M,W
University of Idaho, ID	M,W
University of Illinois at Chicago, IL	M,W
University of Illinois at Urbana–Champaign, IL	M,W
University of Indianapolis, IN	M,W
The University of Iowa, IA	M,W
University of Kansas, KS	M,W
University of Kentucky, KY	M,W
University of Louisville, KY	M,W
University of Maine, Orono, ME	M,W
University of Mary, ND	M,W
University of Mary Hardin-Baylor, TX	M,W
University of Maryland Baltimore County, MD	M,W
University of Maryland College Park, MD	M,W
University of Maryland Eastern Shore, MD	M,W
University of Massachusetts Amherst, MA	M,W
University of Massachusetts Lowell, MA	M,W
The University of Memphis, TN	M,W
University of Miami, FL	M,W
University of Michigan, Ann Arbor, MI	M,W
University of Michigan–Dearborn, MI	M,W
University of Minnesota, Crookston, MN	M,W
University of Minnesota, Duluth, MN	M,W
University of Minnesota, Twin Cities Campus, MN	M,W
University of Mississippi, MS	M,W
University of Missouri–Columbia, MO	M,W
University of Missouri–Kansas City, MO	M,W
University of Missouri–Rolla, MO	M,W
University of Missouri–St. Louis, MO	M,W
University of Mobile, AL	M,W
The University of Montana–Missoula, MT	M,W
University of Montevallo, AL	M,W
University of Nebraska at Kearney, NE	M,W
University of Nebraska at Omaha, NE	M,W
University of Nebraska–Lincoln, NE	M,W
University of Nevada, Las Vegas, NV	M,W
University of Nevada, Reno, NV	M,W
University of New Hampshire, Durham, NH	M,W
University of New Haven, CT	M,W
University of New Mexico, NM	M,W
University of North Alabama, AL	M,W
University of North Carolina at Asheville, NC	M,W
University of North Carolina at Charlotte, NC	M,W
University of North Carolina at Greensboro, NC	M,W
University of North Carolina at Pembroke, NC	M,W
University of North Carolina at Wilmington, NC	M,W
University of North Dakota, ND	M,W
University of Northern Colorado, CO	M,W
University of Northern Iowa, IA	M,W
University of North Florida, FL	M,W
University of North Texas, TX	M,W
University of Notre Dame, IN	M,W
University of Oklahoma, OK	M,W
University of Oregon, OR	M,W
University of Pittsburgh, PA	M,W
University of Pittsburgh at Johnstown, PA	M,W
University of Portland, OR	M,W
U of Puerto Rico at Ponce, PR	M,W
U of Puerto Rico, Cayey University College, PR	M,W
U of Puerto Rico, Mayagüez Campus, PR	M,W
U of Puerto Rico, Río Piedras, PR	M,W
University of Rhode Island, RI	M,W
University of Richmond, VA	M,W
University of Rio Grande, OH	M,W
University of San Diego, CA	M,W
University of San Francisco, CA	M,W
University of Science and Arts of Oklahoma, OK	M,W
University of Sioux Falls, SD	M,W
University of South Alabama, AL	M,W
U of South Carolina, Columbia, SC	M,W
U of South Carolina–Aiken, SC	M,W
U of South Carolina–Spartanburg, SC	M,W
University of South Dakota, SD	M,W
University of Southern California, CA	M,W
University of Southern Colorado, CO	M,W
University of Southern Indiana, IN	M,W
University of Southern Mississippi, MS	M,W
University of South Florida, FL	M,W
University of Southwestern Louisiana, LA	M,W
The University of Tampa, FL	M,W
University of Tennessee at Chattanooga, TN	M,W
The University of Tennessee at Martin, TN	M,W
University of Tennessee, Knoxville, TN	M,W
The University of Texas at Arlington, TX	M,W
The University of Texas at Austin, TX	M,W
The University of Texas at El Paso, TX	M,W
The University of Texas at San Antonio, TX	M,W
The University of Texas–Pan American, TX	M,W
University of the District of Columbia, DC	M,W
University of the Pacific, CA	M,W
University of the Sacred Heart, PR	M
University of Toledo, OH	M,W
University of Tulsa, OK	M,W
University of Utah, UT	M,W
University of Vermont, VT	M,W
University of Virginia, VA	M,W
University of Washington, WA	M,W
The University of West Alabama, AL	M,W
University of West Florida, FL	W
University of Wisconsin–Green Bay, WI	M,W
University of Wisconsin–Madison, WI	M,W
University of Wisconsin–Milwaukee, WI	M,W
University of Wisconsin–Parkside, WI	M,W
University of Wyoming, WY	M,W
Urbana University, OH	M,W
Utah State University, UT	M
Valdosta State University, GA	M,W
Valley City State University, ND	M,W
Valparaiso University, IN	M,W
Vanderbilt University, TN	M,W
Villanova University, PA	M,W
Virginia Commonwealth University, VA	M,W
Virginia Intermont College, VA	M,W
Virginia Military Institute, VA	M
Virginia Polytechnic Institute and State U, VA	M,W
Virginia State University, VA	M,W
Virginia Union University, VA	M,W
Voorhees College, SC	M,W
Wagner College, NY	M,W
Wake Forest University, NC	M,W
Walsh University, OH	M,W
Warner Southern College, FL	M,W
Washburn University of Topeka, KS	M,W
Washington State University, WA	M,W
Wayne State College, NE	M,W
Wayne State University, MI	M,W
Webber College, FL	M,W
Weber State University, UT	M,W

Basketball (continued)

West Chester University of Pennsylvania, PA	M,W
Western Baptist College, OR	M,W
Western Carolina University, NC	M,W
Western Illinois University, IL	M,W
Western Kentucky University, KY	M,W
Western Michigan University, MI	M,W
Western Montana College of The U of Montana, MT	M,W
Western New Mexico University, NM	M,W
Western State College of Colorado, CO	M,W
Western Washington University, WA	M,W
West Liberty State College, WV	M
Westmar University, IA	M,W
Westminster College, PA	M,W
Westmont College, CA	M,W
West Texas A&M University, TX	M,W
West Virginia State College, WV	M,W
West Virginia University, WV	M,W
West Virginia University Institute of Technology, WV	M,W
West Virginia Wesleyan College, WV	M,W
Wheeling Jesuit University, WV	M,W
Wichita State University, KS	M,W
Wiley College, TX	M,W
William Carey College, MS	M,W
William Jewell College, MO	M,W
Williams Baptist College, AR	M,W
William Woods University, MO	W
Wilmington College, DE	M,W
Wingate University, NC	M,W
Winona State University, MN	M,W
Winston-Salem State University, NC	M,W
Winthrop University, SC	M,W
Wofford College, SC	M,W
Wright State University, OH	M,W
Xavier University, OH	M,W
Xavier University of Louisiana, LA	M,W
York College, NE	M,W
Youngstown State University, OH	M,W

BOWLING

Saginaw Valley State University, MI	M
Thomas College, GA	M

CREW

Barry University, FL	W
Boston University, MA	M,W
Brenau University, GA	W
California State University, Sacramento, CA	M,W
Creighton University, NE	W
Drexel University, PA	M
Florida Institute of Technology, FL	M,W
The George Washington University, DC	M,W
Jacksonville University, FL	M,W
La Salle University, PA	W
Mercyhurst College, PA	M,W
Northeastern University, MA	M,W
Rutgers, State U of NJ, College of Engineering, NJ	M,W
Rutgers, State U of NJ, College of Pharmacy, NJ	M,W

Rutgers, State U of NJ, Cook College, NJ	M,W
Rutgers, State U of NJ, Douglass College, NJ	W
Rutgers, State U of NJ, Livingston College, NJ	M,W
Rutgers, State U of NJ, Mason Gross School of Arts, NJ	M,W
Rutgers, State U of NJ, Rutgers College, NJ	M,W
Stetson University, FL	M,W
Syracuse University, NY	W
Temple University, Philadelphia, PA	M,W
The University of Charleston, WV	M,W
University of Kansas, KS	W
University of New Hampshire, Durham, NH	W
The University of Tampa, FL	W
University of Tennessee, Knoxville, TN	W
University of Virginia, VA	W
University of Washington, WA	M,W
University of Wisconsin–Madison, WI	M,W
Washington State University, WA	W

CROSS-COUNTRY RUNNING

Abilene Christian University, TX	M,W
Adams State College, CO	M,W
Adelphi University, NY	M,W
Alabama Agricultural and Mechanical University, AL	M,W
Albany State University, GA	M,W
Alcorn State University, MS	M,W
Alderson-Broaddus College, WV	M,W
Anderson College, SC	M,W
Angelo State University, TX	M,W
Appalachian State University, NC	M,W
Aquinas College, MI	M,W
Arizona State University, AZ	M,W
Arkansas State University, AR	M,W
Arkansas Tech University, AR	W
Armstrong Atlantic State University, GA	M
Ashland University, OH	M,W
Auburn University, AL	M,W
Augustana College, SD	M,W
Augusta State University, GA	M,W
Austin Peay State University, TN	M,W
Azusa Pacific University, CA	M,W
Baker University, KS	M,W
Ball State University, IN	M,W
Barber-Scotia College, NC	M,W
Bayamón Technological University College, PR	M,W
Baylor University, TX	M,W
Belhaven College, MS	M,W
Bellarmine College, KY	M,W
Belmont Abbey College, NC	M,W
Belmont University, TN	M,W
Berry College, GA	M,W
Bethany College, KS	M,W
Bethel College, IN	M,W
Bethune-Cookman College, FL	M,W
Biola University, CA	M,W
Black Hills State University, SD	M,W
Bloomsburg University of Pennsylvania, PA	W

Bluefield State College, WV	M,W
Boise State University, ID	M,W
Boston College, MA	W
Boston University, MA	M,W
Bowie State University, MD	M,W
Bowling Green State University, OH	M,W
Bradley University, IL	M,W
Brenau University, GA	W
Brigham Young University, UT	M,W
Brigham Young University–Hawaii Campus, HI	M,W
Butler University, IN	M,W
California Baptist College, CA	M,W
California Polytechnic State U, San Luis Obispo, CA	M,W
California State Polytechnic University, Pomona, CA	M,W
California State University, Fresno, CA	M
California State University, Fullerton, CA	M,W
California State University, Long Beach, CA	M,W
California State University, Los Angeles, CA	M,W
California State University, Northridge, CA	M,W
California State University, Sacramento, CA	M,W
California University of Pennsylvania, PA	M,W
Campbell University, NC	M,W
Canisius College, NY	M,W
Carlow College, PA	W
Carson-Newman College, TN	M,W
Catawba College, NC	M,W
Cedarville College, OH	M,W
Centenary College of Louisiana, LA	M,W
Central Connecticut State University, CT	M,W
Central Methodist College, MO	M,W
Central Michigan University, MI	M,W
Central Missouri State University, MO	M,W
Charleston Southern University, SC	M,W
Cheyney University of Pennsylvania, PA	M,W
Chicago State University, IL	M,W
Christian Brothers University, TN	M,W
The Citadel, The Military Coll of South Carolina, SC	M
Clarion University of Pennsylvania, PA	M,W
Clayton College & State University, GA	M,W
Clemson University, SC	M,W
Cleveland State University, OH	W
Coastal Carolina University, SC	M,W
College of Charleston, SC	M,W
College of St. Francis, IL	W
College of William and Mary, VA	M,W
Colorado School of Mines, CO	M
Colorado State University, CO	M,W
Columbia Union College, MD	M,W
Concordia College, MI	M,W
Concordia College, NE	M,W
Concordia University, CA	M,W
Cornerstone College, MI	M,W

Covenant College, GA	M,W
Creighton University, NE	M,W
Cumberland College, KY	M,W
Dakota State University, SD	M,W
Dakota Wesleyan University, SD	M,W
Dana College, NE	M,W
David Lipscomb University, TN	M,W
Davidson College, NC	W
Davis & Elkins College, WV	M,W
Delaware State University, DE	M,W
Delta State University, MS	W
DePaul University, IL	M,W
Dickinson State University, ND	M,W
Doane College, NE	M,W
Dominican College of San Rafael, CA	M,W
Drake University, IA	M,W
Drexel University, PA	M
Duquesne University, PA	M,W
D'Youville College, NY	M
East Carolina University, NC	M,W
Eastern Illinois University, IL	M,W
Eastern Kentucky University, KY	M,W
Eastern Michigan University, MI	M,W
Eastern Washington University, WA	M,W
East Stroudsburg University of Pennsylvania, PA	M
East Tennessee State University, TN	M,W
Eckerd College, FL	W
Edinboro University of Pennsylvania, PA	M,W
Electronic Data Processing College of Puerto Rico, PR	M
Elon College, NC	M,W
Emporia State University, KS	M,W
Erskine College, SC	M,W
Evangel College, MO	M,W
Fairleigh Dickinson U, Teaneck-Hackensack, NJ	M,W
Ferris State University, MI	W
Flagler College, FL	M,W
Florida Agricultural and Mechanical University, FL	M,W
Florida Atlantic University, FL	M,W
Florida International University, FL	M,W
Florida Southern College, FL	M,W
Florida State University, FL	M,W
Fordham University, NY	M,W
Fort Hays State University, KS	M,W
Francis Marion University, SC	M,W
Fresno Pacific University, CA	M,W
Furman University, SC	M,W
Gannon University, PA	M,W
Gardner-Webb University, NC	M
Geneva College, PA	M,W
George Mason University, VA	M,W
Georgetown College, KY	M,W
Georgetown University, DC	M,W
The George Washington University, DC	M,W
Georgia College and State University, GA	M,W
Georgia Institute of Technology, GA	M,W
Georgian Court College, NJ	W
Georgia Southern University, GA	M,W
Georgia Southwestern State University, GA	M,W
Georgia State University, GA	M,W
Gonzaga University, WA	M
Goshen College, IN	M,W
Graceland College, IA	M,W
Grand Canyon University, AZ	M,W
Grand Valley State University, MI	W
Harding University, AR	M,W
Hastings College, NE	M,W
Hawaii Pacific University, HI	M,W
Henderson State University, AR	W
Hillsdale College, MI	M,W
Hofstra University, NY	M,W
Holy Family College, PA	W
Holy Names College, CA	M,W
Houghton College, NY	M,W
Howard University, DC	M,W
Huntington College, IN	M,W
Huron University, SD	M,W
Idaho State University, ID	M,W
Illinois Institute of Technology, IL	M,W
Illinois State University, IL	M,W
Indiana State University, IN	M,W
Indiana University Bloomington, IN	M,W
Indiana University of Pennsylvania, PA	M,W
Indiana U–Purdue U Fort Wayne, IN	M,W
Indiana Wesleyan University, IN	M,W
Inter American U of PR, Metropolitan Campus, PR	M,W
Inter American U of PR, San Germán Campus, PR	M,W
Iowa State University of Science and Technology, IA	M,W
Iowa Wesleyan College, IA	M,W
Jacksonville University, FL	M,W
James Madison University, VA	M,W
Judson College, IL	M,W
Kansas State University, KS	M,W
Kansas Wesleyan University, KS	M
Kennesaw State University, GA	M,W
Kent State University, OH	M,W
Kentucky State University, KY	M,W
Kutztown University of Pennsylvania, PA	M,W
Lamar University, TX	M,W
Lambuth University, TN	M,W
Lander University, SC	M,W
La Salle University, PA	M,W
Lees-McRae College, NC	M,W
Lee University, TN	M,W
Lehigh University, PA	M,W
Le Moyne College, NY	M,W
LeMoyne-Owen College, TN	M
Lenoir-Rhyne College, NC	M,W
Lewis-Clark State College, ID	M,W
Lewis University, IL	M,W
Lincoln Memorial University, TN	M,W
Lindenwood College, MO	M,W
Lindsey Wilson College, KY	M,W
Long Island U, Brooklyn Campus, NY	W
Long Island U, C.W. Post Campus, NY	M,W
Louisiana College, LA	M,W
Louisiana State University and A&M College, LA	M,W
Louisiana Tech University, LA	M,W
Loyola University Chicago, IL	M,W
Lubbock Christian University, TX	M,W
Lyon College, AR	M,W
Malone College, OH	M,W
Manhattan College, NY	M,W
Mankato State University, MN	M,W
Marian College, IN	M,W
Marist College, NY	M,W
Marquette University, WI	M,W
Marshall University, WV	M,W
Mars Hill College, NC	M,W
The Master's College and Seminary, CA	M,W
Mayville State University, ND	M
McKendree College, IL	M,W
McNeese State University, LA	M,W
McPherson College, KS	M,W
Mercer University, Macon, GA	M,W
Mercyhurst College, PA	M,W
Merrimack College, MA	M,W
Mesa State College, CO	W
Miami University, OH	M,W
Michigan Christian College, MI	M,W
Michigan State University, MI	M,W
MidAmerica Nazarene University, KS	M,W
Middle Tennessee State University, TN	M,W
Midland Lutheran College, NE	M,W
Midway College, KY	W
Millersville University of Pennsylvania, PA	M,W
Minot State University, ND	M,W
Mississippi State University, MS	M,W
Mississippi Valley State University, MS	M,W
Missouri Southern State College, MO	M,W
Molloy College, NY	M,W
Monmouth University, NJ	M,W
Montana State U–Bozeman, MT	M,W
Morehead State University, KY	M,W
Morehouse College, GA	M
Morgan State University, MD	M,W
Morningside College, IA	M
Mount Olive College, NC	M,W
Mount St. Clare College, IA	M,W
Mount Saint Mary's College and Seminary, MD	M,W
Murray State University, KY	M,W
New Mexico Highlands University, NM	M,W
New Mexico State University, NM	M,W
New York Institute of Technology, NY	M,W
Niagara University, NY	M,W
Nicholls State University, LA	M,W
Norfolk State University, VA	M
North Carolina Agricultural and Technical State U, NC	M
North Carolina State University, NC	M,W
North Dakota State University, ND	M,W
Northeastern Illinois University, IL	M,W
Northeastern University, MA	M,W
Northeast Louisiana University, LA	M,W
Northern Arizona University, AZ	M,W
Northern Kentucky University, KY	M,W
Northern State University, SD	M,W
Northwest College of the Assemblies of God, WA	M,W
Northwestern College, IA	M,W

Cross-Country Running (continued)

Northwestern State University of Louisiana, LA	M,W
Northwest Missouri State University, MO	M,W
Northwood University, MI	M,W
Northwood University, Texas Campus, TX	M,W
Nova Southeastern University, FL	M,W
Oakland City University, IN	M,W
Oakland University, MI	M,W
The Ohio State University, OH	M,W
Ohio University, OH	M,W
Oklahoma Baptist University, OK	M,W
Oklahoma Christian U of Science and Arts, OK	M,W
Oklahoma State U, OK	M,W
Old Dominion University, VA	M,W
Olivet Nazarene University, IL	M,W
Oral Roberts University, OK	M,W
Oregon Institute of Technology, OR	M,W
Ottawa University, KS	M,W
Pace University, NY	M,W
Paine College, GA	M,W
Park College, MO	M,W
Penn State U Univ Park Campus, PA	M,W
Pfeiffer University, NC	M,W
Phillips University, OK	M,W
Pittsburg State University, KS	M
Point Loma Nazarene College, CA	M,W
Portland State University, OR	M,W
Providence College, RI	M,W
Purdue University, West Lafayette, IN	M,W
Quinnipiac College, CT	M,W
Radford University, VA	M,W
Rice University, TX	M,W
Rider University, NJ	M
Robert Morris College, PA	M,W
Roberts Wesleyan College, NY	M,W
Rutgers, State U of NJ, College of Engineering, NJ	M,W
Rutgers, State U of NJ, College of Pharmacy, NJ	M,W
Rutgers, State U of NJ, Cook College, NJ	M,W
Rutgers, State U of NJ, Douglass College, NJ	W
Rutgers, State U of NJ, Livingston College, NJ	M,W
Rutgers, State U of NJ, Mason Gross School of Arts, NJ	M,W
Rutgers, State U of NJ, Rutgers College, NJ	M,W
Saginaw Valley State University, MI	M,W
St. Ambrose University, IA	M,W
St. Andrews Presbyterian College, NC	M,W
Saint Augustine's College, NC	M,W
St. Bonaventure University, NY	M,W
St. Cloud State University, MN	M
Saint Francis College, IN	M,W
St. Francis College, NY	M,W
Saint Francis College, PA	M,W
St. John's University, NY	M,W
Saint Joseph's College, IN	M,W
Saint Joseph's University, PA	M,W
Saint Louis University, MO	M,W
Saint Martin's College, WA	M,W

Saint Mary's College of California, CA	M,W
Saint Peter's College, Jersey City, NJ	M,W
St. Thomas Aquinas College, NY	M,W
Saint Vincent College, PA	M,W
Saint Xavier University, IL	W
Samford University, AL	M,W
San Diego State University, CA	W
San Jose State University, CA	W
Santa Clara University, CA	M,W
Savannah State University, GA	M
Seattle Pacific University, WA	M,W
Seton Hall University, NJ	M,W
Seton Hill College, PA	W
Shippensburg University of Pennsylvania, PA	M,W
Shorter College, GA	M
Siena Heights College, MI	M,W
Slippery Rock University of Pennsylvania, PA	M,W
South Dakota School of Mines and Technology, SD	M,W
South Dakota State University, SD	M,W
Southeastern Louisiana University, LA	M,W
Southeast Missouri State University, MO	M,W
Southern California College, CA	M,W
Southern Illinois University at Carbondale, IL	M,W
Southern Illinois University at Edwardsville, IL	M,W
Southern Methodist University, TX	M,W
Southern Oregon University, OR	M,W
Southern University and A&M College, LA	M
Southern University at New Orleans, LA	M,W
Southern Wesleyan University, SC	M,W
Southwest Baptist University, MO	M,W
Southwestern College, KS	M,W
Southwestern Oklahoma State University, OK	W
Southwest Missouri State University, MO	M,W
Southwest Texas State University, TX	M,W
Spring Arbor College, MI	M,W
Spring Hill College, AL	W
Stanford University, CA	M,W
State U of NY at Buffalo, NY	M,W
Stephen F. Austin State University, TX	M,W
Sterling College, KS	M,W
Stetson University, FL	M,W
Syracuse University, NY	M,W
Tabor College, KS	M,W
Taylor University, IN	M,W
Teikyo Post University, CT	M,W
Tennessee State University, TN	M,W
Texas A&M University, College Station, TX	M,W
Texas A&M University–Commerce, TX	M,W
Texas A&M University–Kingsville, TX	M,W
Texas Christian University, TX	M,W
Texas Southern University, TX	M,W
Texas Tech University, TX	M,W
Tiffin University, OH	M,W

Tougaloo College, MS	M,W
Towson University, MD	M,W
Transylvania University, KY	M,W
Tri-State University, IN	M,W
Troy State University, Troy, AL	M
Truman State University, MO	M,W
Tulane University, LA	M,W
Tusculum College, TN	M,W
Unity College, ME	M,W
U at Albany, State U of NY, NY	M,W
The University of Akron, OH	M,W
The University of Alabama at Birmingham, AL	M,W
The University of Alabama in Huntsville, AL	M,W
U of Alaska Anchorage, AK	M
U of Alaska Fairbanks, AK	M,W
University of Arizona, AZ	M,W
University of Arkansas, Fayetteville, AR	M,W
University of Arkansas at Little Rock, AR	M,W
University of California, Berkeley, CA	M
University of California, Irvine, CA	W
University of California, Los Angeles, CA	M,W
University of California, Riverside, CA	M,W
University of California, Santa Barbara, CA	M,W
University of Central Florida, FL	M,W
University of Central Oklahoma, OK	M,W
University of Cincinnati, OH	M,W
University of Colorado at Boulder, CO	M,W
University of Colorado at Colorado Springs, CO	M,W
University of Connecticut, Storrs, CT	M,W
University of Dayton, OH	M,W
University of Detroit Mercy, MI	M,W
University of Evansville, IN	M,W
The University of Findlay, OH	M,W
University of Florida, FL	M,W
University of Georgia, GA	M,W
University of Hartford, CT	M,W
University of Hawaii at Hilo, HI	M,W
University of Hawaii at Manoa, HI	W
University of Houston, TX	M,W
University of Idaho, ID	M,W
University of Illinois at Chicago, IL	M,W
University of Illinois at Urbana–Champaign, IL	M,W
University of Indianapolis, IN	M,W
The University of Iowa, IA	M,W
University of Kansas, KS	M,W
University of Kentucky, KY	M,W
University of Louisville, KY	M,W
University of Maine, Orono, ME	M,W
University of Mary, ND	M,W
University of Maryland Baltimore County, MD	M,W
University of Maryland College Park, MD	M,W
University of Massachusetts Amherst, MA	M,W
University of Massachusetts Lowell, MA	M,W
The University of Memphis, TN	M

University of Miami, FL	M,W
University of Michigan, Ann Arbor, MI	M,W
University of Minnesota, Duluth, MN	M,W
University of Minnesota, Twin Cities Campus, MN	M,W
University of Mississippi, MS	M,W
University of Missouri–Columbia, MO	M,W
University of Missouri–Kansas City, MO	M,W
University of Missouri–Rolla, MO	M,W
University of Mobile, AL	M,W
The University of Montana–Missoula, MT	M,W
University of Nebraska at Kearney, NE	M,W
University of Nebraska at Omaha, NE	W
University of Nebraska–Lincoln, NE	M,W
University of Nevada, Las Vegas, NV	W
University of Nevada, Reno, NV	W
University of New Hampshire, Durham, NH	W
University of New Haven, CT	M
University of New Mexico, NM	M,W
University of North Alabama, AL	M,W
University of North Carolina at Asheville, NC	M,W
University of North Carolina at Charlotte, NC	M,W
University of North Carolina at Greensboro, NC	M,W
University of North Carolina at Pembroke, NC	M,W
University of North Carolina at Wilmington, NC	M,W
University of Northern Iowa, IA	M,W
University of North Florida, FL	M,W
University of North Texas, TX	M,W
University of Notre Dame, IN	M,W
University of Oregon, OR	M,W
University of Pittsburgh, PA	M,W
University of Portland, OR	M,W
U of Puerto Rico at Ponce, PR	M,W
U of Puerto Rico, Cayey University College, PR	M,W
U of Puerto Rico, Mayagüez Campus, PR	M,W
U of Puerto Rico, Río Piedras, PR	M,W
University of Rhode Island, RI	M,W
University of Rio Grande, OH	M,W
University of San Diego, CA	M,W
University of Sioux Falls, SD	M,W
University of South Alabama, AL	M,W
U of South Carolina, Columbia, SC	M,W
U of South Carolina–Aiken, SC	M,W
U of South Carolina–Spartanburg, SC	M
University of South Dakota, SD	M,W
University of Southern Colorado, CO	M,W
University of Southern Indiana, IN	M,W
University of Southern Mississippi, MS	M,W
University of South Florida, FL	M,W
University of Southwestern Louisiana, LA	M,W
The University of Tampa, FL	M,W
University of Tennessee at Chattanooga, TN	M,W

The University of Tennessee at Martin, TN	M
University of Tennessee, Knoxville, TN	M,W
The University of Texas at Arlington, TX	M,W
The University of Texas at Austin, TX	M,W
The University of Texas at El Paso, TX	M,W
The University of Texas at San Antonio, TX	M,W
The University of Texas–Pan American, TX	M,W
University of the Sacred Heart, PR	M,W
University of Toledo, OH	M,W
University of Tulsa, OK	M,W
University of Utah, UT	M,W
University of Virginia, VA	M,W
University of Washington, WA	M,W
University of West Florida, FL	M,W
University of Wisconsin–Green Bay, WI	M,W
University of Wisconsin–Madison, WI	M,W
University of Wisconsin–Milwaukee, WI	M,W
University of Wisconsin–Parkside, WI	M,W
University of Wyoming, WY	M,W
Utah State University, UT	M,W
Valdosta State University, GA	M,W
Valley City State University, ND	M,W
Valparaiso University, IN	M,W
Vanderbilt University, TN	M,W
Villanova University, PA	M,W
Virginia Commonwealth University, VA	M,W
Virginia Military Institute, VA	M,W
Virginia Polytechnic Institute and State U, VA	M,W
Virginia State University, VA	M,W
Virginia Union University, VA	M,W
Wagner College, NY	M,W
Wake Forest University, NC	M,W
Walsh University, OH	M,W
Warner Southern College, FL	M,W
Washington State University, WA	M,W
Wayne State College, NE	M,W
Wayne State University, MI	M,W
Webber College, FL	M
Weber State University, UT	M,W
Western Carolina University, NC	M,W
Western Illinois University, IL	M,W
Western Kentucky University, KY	M,W
Western Michigan University, MI	M,W
Western State College of Colorado, CO	M,W
Western Washington University, WA	M,W
Westmar University, IA	M,W
Westminster College, PA	W
Westmont College, CA	M,W
West Texas A&M University, TX	M,W
West Virginia University, WV	M,W
West Virginia Wesleyan College, WV	M,W
Wheeling Jesuit University, WV	M,W
Wichita State University, KS	M,W
William Jewell College, MO	M,W
Wingate University, NC	M
Winona State University, MN	W

Winston-Salem State University, NC	M,W
Winthrop University, SC	M,W
Wofford College, SC	M,W
Wright State University, OH	M,W
Xavier University, OH	M,W
York College, NE	M,W
Youngstown State University, OH	M,W

EQUESTRIAN SPORTS

Becker College–Leicester Campus, MA	M,W
Becker College–Worcester Campus, MA	M,W
Midway College, KY	W
Molloy College, NY	W
National College, SD	M,W
Oklahoma Panhandle State University, OK	M,W
St. Andrews Presbyterian College, NC	M,W
Southwestern Oklahoma State University, OK	M,W
University of Wyoming, WY	M,W
Virginia Intermont College, VA	M,W

FENCING

California State University, Fullerton, CA	M,W
Cleveland State University, OH	M,W
Fairleigh Dickinson U, Teaneck-Hackensack, NJ	W
The Ohio State University, OH	W
Penn State U Univ Park Campus, PA	M,W
Rutgers, State U of NJ, College of Engineering, NJ	M,W
Rutgers, State U of NJ, College of Pharmacy, NJ	M,W
Rutgers, State U of NJ, Cook College, NJ	M,W
Rutgers, State U of NJ, Douglass College, NJ	W
Rutgers, State U of NJ, Livingston College, NJ	M,W
Rutgers, State U of NJ, Mason Gross School of Arts, NJ	M,W
Rutgers, State U of NJ, Rutgers College, NJ	M,W
St. John's University, NY	M,W
Stanford University, CA	M,W
Temple University, Philadelphia, PA	W
Tri-State University, IN	M,W
University of Detroit Mercy, MI	M,W
University of Notre Dame, IN	M,W
U of Puerto Rico, Cayey University College, PR	M,W
Wayne State University, MI	M,W

FIELD HOCKEY

American International College, MA	W
American University, DC	W
Appalachian State University, NC	W
Ball State University, IN	W
Becker College–Leicester Campus, MA	W
Becker College–Worcester Campus, MA	W
Bellarmine College, KY	W
Bloomsburg University of Pennsylvania, PA	W

Field Hockey (continued)

Boston College, MA	W
Boston University, MA	W
Catawba College, NC	W
Central Michigan University, MI	W
College of William and Mary, VA	W
Davidson College, NC	W
Davis & Elkins College, WV	W
Drexel University, PA	W
Duke University, NC	W
Fairfield University, CT	W
Hofstra University, NY	W
Houghton College, NY	W
James Madison University, VA	W
Kent State University, OH	W
Kutztown University of Pennsylvania, PA	W
La Salle University, PA	W
Lehigh University, PA	W
Lock Haven University of Pennsylvania, PA	W
Long Island U, C.W. Post Campus, NY	W
Longwood College, VA	W
Mercyhurst College, PA	W
Merrimack College, MA	W
Miami University, OH	W
Michigan State University, MI	W
Millersville University of Pennsylvania, PA	W
Northeastern University, MA	W
Northwestern University, IL	W
The Ohio State University, OH	W
Ohio University, OH	W
Old Dominion University, VA	W
Penn State U Univ Park Campus, PA	W
Philadelphia College of Textiles and Science, PA	W
Providence College, RI	W
Radford University, VA	W
Rider University, NJ	W
Rutgers, State U of NJ, College of Engineering, NJ	W
Rutgers, State U of NJ, College of Pharmacy, NJ	W
Rutgers, State U of NJ, Cook College, NJ	W
Rutgers, State U of NJ, Douglass College, NJ	W
Rutgers, State U of NJ, Livingston College, NJ	W
Rutgers, State U of NJ, Mason Gross School of Arts, NJ	W
Rutgers, State U of NJ, Rutgers College, NJ	W
Saint Louis University, MO	W
Shippensburg University of Pennsylvania, PA	W
Slippery Rock University of Pennsylvania, PA	W
Southwest Missouri State University, MO	W
Stanford University, CA	W
Syracuse University, NY	W
Temple University, Philadelphia, PA	W
Towson University, MD	W
Transylvania University, KY	W

University of Connecticut, Storrs, CT	W
University of Delaware, DE	W
The University of Iowa, IA	W
University of Louisville, KY	W
University of Maine, Orono, ME	W
University of Maryland College Park, MD	W
University of Massachusetts Amherst, MA	W
University of Massachusetts Lowell, MA	W
University of Michigan, Ann Arbor, MI	W
University of New Hampshire, Durham, NH	W
University of Rhode Island, RI	W
University of Richmond, VA	W
University of the Pacific, CA	W
University of Virginia, VA	W
Villanova University, PA	W
Virginia Commonwealth University, VA	W
Wake Forest University, NC	W
West Chester University of Pennsylvania, PA	W

FOOTBALL

Abilene Christian University, TX	M
Adams State College, CO	M
Alabama Agricultural and Mechanical University, AL	M
Alabama State University, AL	M
Albany State University, GA	M
Alcorn State University, MS	M
American International College, MA	M
Angelo State University, TX	M
Appalachian State University, NC	M
Arizona State University, AZ	M
Arkansas State University, AR	M
Arkansas Tech University, AR	M
Ashland University, OH	M
Auburn University, AL	M
Augustana College, SD	M
Austin Peay State University, TN	M
Azusa Pacific University, CA	M
Baker University, KS	M
Ball State University, IN	M
Baylor University, TX	M
Bemidji State University, MN	M
Benedictine College, KS	M
Bethany College, KS	M
Bethel College, KS	M
Bethune-Cookman College, FL	M
Black Hills State University, SD	M
Bloomsburg University of Pennsylvania, PA	M
Boise State University, ID	M
Boston College, MA	M
Boston University, MA	M
Bowie State University, MD	M
Bowling Green State University, OH	M
Brigham Young University, UT	M
Butler University, IN	M
California Polytechnic State U, San Luis Obispo, CA	M
California State University, Fresno, CA	M

California State University, Northridge, CA	M
California State University, Sacramento, CA	M
California University of Pennsylvania, PA	M
Carroll College, MT	M
Carson-Newman College, TN	M
Catawba College, NC	M
Central Methodist College, MO	M
Central Michigan University, MI	M
Central Missouri State University, MO	M
Central State University, OH	M
Chadron State College, NE	M
Cheyney University of Pennsylvania, PA	M
The Citadel, The Military Coll of South Carolina, SC	M
Clarion University of Pennsylvania, PA	M
Clark Atlanta University, GA	M
Clemson University, SC	M
College of William and Mary, VA	M
Colorado School of Mines, CO	M
Colorado State University, CO	M
Concord College, WV	M
Concordia College, NE	M
Culver-Stockton College, MO	M
Cumberland College, KY	M
Dakota State University, SD	M
Dakota Wesleyan University, SD	M
Dana College, NE	M
Delaware State University, DE	M
Delta State University, MS	M
Dickinson State University, ND	M
Doane College, NE	M
Duke University, NC	M
East Carolina University, NC	M
East Central University, OK	M
Eastern Illinois University, IL	M
Eastern Kentucky University, KY	M
Eastern Michigan University, MI	M
Eastern New Mexico University, NM	M
Eastern Washington University, WA	M
East Stroudsburg University of Pennsylvania, PA	M
East Tennessee State University, TN	M
Edinboro University of Pennsylvania, PA	M
Elizabeth City State University, NC	M
Elon College, NC	M
Emporia State University, KS	M
Evangel College, MO	M
Fairfield University, CT	M
Fairmont State College, WV	M
Fayetteville State University, NC	M
Ferris State University, MI	M
Florida Agricultural and Mechanical University, FL	M
Florida State University, FL	M
Fordham University, NY	M
Fort Hays State University, KS	M
Fort Lewis College, CO	M
Fort Valley State University, GA	M
Friends University, KS	M
Furman University, SC	M
Gardner-Webb University, NC	M

Geneva College, PA	M
Georgetown College, KY	M
Georgia Institute of Technology, GA	M
Georgia Southern University, GA	M
Glenville State College, WV	M
Graceland College, IA	M
Grambling State University, LA	M
Grand Valley State University, MI	M
Harding University, AR	M
Hastings College, NE	M
Henderson State University, AR	M
Hillsdale College, MI	M
Hofstra University, NY	M
Howard University, DC	M
Huron University, SD	M
Idaho State University, ID	M
Illinois State University, IL	M
Indiana State University, IN	M
Indiana University Bloomington, IN	M
Indiana University of Pennsylvania, PA	M
Iowa State University of Science and Technology, IA	M
Iowa Wesleyan College, IA	M
Jackson State University, MS	M
Jacksonville State University, AL	M
James Madison University, VA	M
Johnson C. Smith University, NC	M
Kansas State University, KS	M
Kansas Wesleyan University, KS	M
Kent State University, OH	M
Kentucky State University, KY	M
Kutztown University of Pennsylvania, PA	M
Lamar University, TX	M
Langston University, OK	M
Lehigh University, PA	M
Lenoir-Rhyne College, NC	M
Lindenwood College, MO	M
Livingstone College, NC	M
Lock Haven University of Pennsylvania, PA	M
Louisiana State University and A&M College, LA	M
Louisiana Tech University, LA	M
Malone College, OH	M
Mankato State University, MN	M
Mansfield University of Pennsylvania, PA	M
Marshall University, WV	M
Mars Hill College, NC	M
Mayville State University, ND	M
McKendree College, IL	M
McNeese State University, LA	M
McPherson College, KS	M
Mesa State College, CO	M
Miami University, OH	M
Michigan State University, MI	M
Michigan Technological University, MI	M
MidAmerica Nazarene University, KS	M
Middle Tennessee State University, TN	M
Midland Lutheran College, NE	M
Midwestern State University, TX	M
Millersville University of Pennsylvania, PA	M
Minot State University, ND	M
Mississippi State University, MS	M
Mississippi Valley State University, MS	M
Missouri Southern State College, MO	M
Missouri Western State College, MO	M
Montana State U–Bozeman, MT	M
Montana Tech of The University of Montana, MT	M
Moorhead State University, MN	M
Morehouse College, GA	M
Morgan State University, MD	M
Morningside College, IA	M
Murray State University, KY	M
Newberry College, SC	M
New Mexico Highlands University, NM	M
New Mexico State University, NM	M
Nicholls State University, LA	M
Norfolk State University, VA	M
North Carolina Central University, NC	M
North Carolina State University, NC	M
North Dakota State University, ND	M
Northeastern State University, OK	M
Northeastern University, MA	M
Northeast Louisiana University, LA	M
Northern Arizona University, AZ	M
Northern Illinois University, IL	M
Northern Michigan University, MI	M
Northern State University, SD	M
North Greenville College, SC	M
Northwestern College, IA	M
Northwestern Oklahoma State University, OK	M
Northwestern State University of Louisiana, LA	M
Northwestern University, IL	M
Northwest Missouri State University, MO	M
Northwood University, MI	M
The Ohio State University, OH	M
Ohio University, OH	M
Oklahoma Panhandle State University, OK	M
Oklahoma State U, OK	M
Olivet Nazarene University, IL	M
Oregon State University, OR	M
Ottawa University, KS	M
Ouachita Baptist University, AR	M
Penn State U Univ Park Campus, PA	M
Peru State College, NE	M
Pittsburg State University, KS	M
Portland State University, OR	M
Presbyterian College, SC	M
Purdue University, West Lafayette, IN	M
Rice University, TX	M
Rocky Mountain College, MT	M
Rutgers, State U of NJ, College of Engineering, NJ	M
Rutgers, State U of NJ, College of Pharmacy, NJ	M
Rutgers, State U of NJ, Cook College, NJ	M
Rutgers, State U of NJ, Livingston College, NJ	M
Rutgers, State U of NJ, Mason Gross School of Arts, NJ	M
Rutgers, State U of NJ, Rutgers College, NJ	M
Saginaw Valley State University, MI	M
St. Ambrose University, IA	M
St. Cloud State University, MN	M
Saint Francis College, IN	M
Saint Joseph's College, IN	M
Saint Mary's College of California, CA	M
Saint Xavier University, IL	M
Samford University, AL	M
Sam Houston State University, TX	M
San Diego State University, CA	M
San Jose State University, CA	M
Savannah State University, GA	M
Shepherd College, WV	M
Shippensburg University of Pennsylvania, PA	M
Slippery Rock University of Pennsylvania, PA	M
South Dakota School of Mines and Technology, SD	M
South Dakota State University, SD	M
Southeastern Oklahoma State University, OK	M
Southeast Missouri State University, MO	M
Southern Arkansas University–Magnolia, AR	M
Southern Illinois University at Carbondale, IL	M
Southern Methodist University, TX	M
Southern Oregon University, OR	M
Southern University and A&M College, LA	M
Southern Utah University, UT	M
Southwest Baptist University, MO	M
Southwestern College, KS	M
Southwestern Oklahoma State University, OK	M
Southwest Missouri State University, MO	M
Southwest State University, MN	M
Southwest Texas State University, TX	M
Stanford University, CA	M
State U of NY at Buffalo, NY	M
Stephen F. Austin State University, TX	M
Sterling College, KS	M
Sue Bennett College, KY	M
Syracuse University, NY	M
Tabor College, KS	M
Tarleton State University, TX	M
Taylor University, IN	M
Temple University, Philadelphia, PA	M
Tennessee State University, TN	M
Tennessee Technological University, TN	M
Texas A&M University, College Station, TX	M
Texas A&M University–Commerce, TX	M
Texas A&M University–Kingsville, TX	M
Texas Christian University, TX	M
Texas Southern University, TX	M
Texas Tech University, TX	M
Tiffin University, OH	M

Football (continued)

Trinity International University, IL	M
Tri-State University, IN	M
Troy State University, Troy, AL	M
Truman State University, MO	M
Tulane University, LA	M
Tusculum College, TN	M
Tuskegee University, AL	M
The University of Akron, OH	M
University of Arizona, AZ	M
University of Arkansas, Fayetteville, AR	M
University of Arkansas at Monticello, AR	M
University of Arkansas at Pine Bluff, AR	M
University of California, Berkeley, CA	M
University of California, Los Angeles, CA	M
University of Central Arkansas, AR	M
University of Central Florida, FL	M
University of Central Oklahoma, OK	M
University of Cincinnati, OH	M
University of Colorado at Boulder, CO	M
University of Delaware, DE	M
The University of Findlay, OH	M
University of Florida, FL	M
University of Georgia, GA	M
University of Hawaii at Manoa, HI	M
University of Houston, TX	M
University of Idaho, ID	M
University of Illinois at Urbana–Champaign, IL	M
University of Indianapolis, IN	M
The University of Iowa, IA	M
University of Kansas, KS	M
University of Kentucky, KY	M
University of Louisville, KY	M
University of Maine, Orono, ME	M
University of Mary, ND	M
University of Maryland College Park, MD	M
University of Massachusetts Amherst, MA	M
The University of Memphis, TN	M
University of Miami, FL	M
University of Michigan, Ann Arbor, MI	M
University of Minnesota, Crookston, MN	M
University of Minnesota, Duluth, MN	M
University of Minnesota, Twin Cities Campus, MN	M
University of Mississippi, MS	M
University of Missouri–Columbia, MO	M
University of Missouri–Rolla, MO	M
The University of Montana–Missoula, MT	M
University of Nebraska at Kearney, NE	M
University of Nebraska at Omaha, NE	M
University of Nebraska–Lincoln, NE	M
University of Nevada, Las Vegas, NV	M
University of Nevada, Reno, NV	M
University of New Hampshire, Durham, NH	M
University of New Haven, CT	M

University of New Mexico, NM	M
University of North Alabama, AL	M
University of North Dakota, ND	M
University of Northern Colorado, CO	M
University of Northern Iowa, IA	M
University of North Texas, TX	M
University of Notre Dame, IN	M
University of Oklahoma, OK	M
University of Oregon, OR	M
University of Pittsburgh, PA	M
U of Puerto Rico, Cayey University College, PR	M
University of Rhode Island, RI	M
University of Richmond, VA	M
University of Sioux Falls, SD	M
U of South Carolina, Columbia, SC	M
University of South Dakota, SD	M
University of Southern California, CA	M
University of Southern Mississippi, MS	M
University of South Florida, FL	M
University of Southwestern Louisiana, LA	M
University of Tennessee at Chattanooga, TN	M
The University of Tennessee at Martin, TN	M
University of Tennessee, Knoxville, TN	M
The University of Texas at Austin, TX	M
The University of Texas at El Paso, TX	M
University of the District of Columbia, DC	M
University of Toledo, OH	M
University of Tulsa, OK	M
University of Utah, UT	M
University of Virginia, VA	M
University of Washington, WA	M
The University of West Alabama, AL	M
University of Wisconsin–Madison, WI	M
University of Wyoming, WY	M
Urbana University, OH	M
Utah State University, UT	M
Valdosta State University, GA	M
Valley City State University, ND	M
Vanderbilt University, TN	M
Villanova University, PA	M
Virginia Military Institute, VA	M
Virginia Polytechnic Institute and State U, VA	M
Virginia State University, VA	M
Virginia Union University, VA	M
Wake Forest University, NC	M
Walsh University, OH	M
Washburn University of Topeka, KS	M
Washington State University, WA	M
Wayne State College, NE	M
Wayne State University, MI	M
Weber State University, UT	M
West Chester University of Pennsylvania, PA	M
Western Carolina University, NC	M
Western Illinois University, IL	M
Western Kentucky University, KY	M
Western Michigan University, MI	M

Western Montana College of The U of Montana, MT	M
Western New Mexico University, NM	M
Western State College of Colorado, CO	M
Western Washington University, WA	M
West Liberty State College, WV	M
Westmar University, IA	M
Westminster College, PA	M
West Texas A&M University, TX	M
West Virginia State College, WV	M
West Virginia University, WV	M
West Virginia University Institute of Technology, WV	M
West Virginia Wesleyan College, WV	M
William Jewell College, MO	M
Wingate University, NC	M
Winona State University, MN	M
Winston-Salem State University, NC	M
Wofford College, SC	M
Youngstown State University, OH	M

GOLF

Abilene Christian University, TX	M
Adelphi University, NY	M
Albertson College of Idaho, ID	M,W
Alcorn State University, MS	M
Anderson College, SC	
Appalachian State University, NC	M,W
Aquinas College, MI	M,W
Arizona State University, AZ	M,W
Arkansas State University, AR	M,W
Arkansas Tech University, AR	M
Ashland University, OH	M
Auburn University, AL	M,W
Augusta State University, GA	M
Austin Peay State University, TN	M
Baker University, KS	M
Ball State University, IN	M
Barry University, FL	M
Barton College, NC	M
Baylor University, TX	M,W
Becker College–Leicester Campus, MA	M
Belhaven College, MS	M
Bellarmine College, KY	M,W
Belmont Abbey College, NC	M
Bemidji State University, MN	M
Benedictine College, KS	M,W
Berry College, GA	M
Bethany College, KS	M,W
Bethel College, IN	M
Bethel College, TN	M
Bethune-Cookman College, FL	M,W
Bluefield College, VA	M
Bluefield State College, WV	M
Boise State University, ID	M
Bowling Green State University, OH	M,W
Bradley University, IL	M,W
Brescia College, KY	M
Briar Cliff College, IA	M,W
Brigham Young University, UT	M,W
Butler University, IN	M
Caldwell College, NJ	M,W
California Baptist College, CA	M
California State University, Bakersfield, CA	M

California State University, Dominguez Hills, CA	M	Erskine College, SC	M	Lamar University, TX	M,W
		Fairfield University, CT	M,W	Lambuth University, TN	M
California State University, Fresno, CA	M	Fairleigh Dickinson U, Teaneck-Hackensack, NJ	M	La Salle University, PA	M,W
				Lees-McRae College, NC	M
California State University, Long Beach, CA	M,W	Fairmont State College, WV	M	Lee University, TN	M
		Ferris State University, MI	W	Lehigh University, PA	M
California State University, Northridge, CA	M	Flagler College, FL	M	Le Moyne College, NY	M
		Florida Agricultural and Mechanical University, FL	M,W	Lenoir-Rhyne College, NC	M
California State University, Sacramento, CA	M	Florida Atlantic University, FL	M,W	Lewis-Clark State College, ID	M,W
California State University, San Bernardino, CA	M	Florida International University, FL	M,W	Lewis University, IL	M,W
		Florida Southern College, FL	M,W	Limestone College, SC	M
Campbell University, NC	M,W	Florida State University, FL	M,W	Lincoln Memorial University, TN	M
Canisius College, NY	M	Fordham University, NY	M	Lincoln University, MO	M
Carson-Newman College, TN	M	Fort Hays State University, KS	M	Lindenwood College, MO	M,W
Catawba College, NC	M	Francis Marion University, SC	M	Lindsey Wilson College, KY	M
Cedarville College, OH	M	Franklin Pierce College, NH	M	Long Island U, Brooklyn Campus, NY	M
Centenary College of Louisiana, LA	M	Freed-Hardeman University, TN	M	Longwood College, VA	M,W
Central Connecticut State University, CT	M,W	Friends University, KS	M	Louisiana State University and A&M College, LA	M,W
Central Methodist College, MO	M,W	Furman University, SC	M,W	Louisiana Tech University, LA	M
Chadron State College, NE	W	Gannon University, PA	M	Loyola Marymount University, CA	M
Charleston Southern University, SC	M,W	Gardner-Webb University, NC	M	Loyola University Chicago, IL	M,W
Chicago State University, IL	M	George Mason University, VA	M	Lynn University, FL	M,W
Christian Brothers University, TN	M	Georgetown College, KY	M,W	Lyon College, AR	M
The Citadel, The Military Coll of South Carolina, SC	M	The George Washington University, DC	M	Malone College, OH	M
				Manhattan College, NY	M
Clarion University of Pennsylvania, PA	M	Georgia College and State University, GA	M	Mankato State University, MN	M,W
Clemson University, SC	M	Georgia Institute of Technology, GA	M	Marian College, IN	M,W
Cleveland State University, OH	M	Georgia Southern University, GA	M	Marquette University, WI	M
Coastal Carolina University, SC	M,W	Georgia Southwestern State University, GA	M	Marshall University, WV	M
Coker College, SC	M	Georgia State University, GA	M,W	Mars Hill College, NC	M
College of Charleston, SC	M,W	Glenville State College, WV	M	Martin Methodist College, TN	M,W
College of St. Francis, IL	M	Gonzaga University, WA	M,W	McKendree College, IL	M,W
College of Saint Mary, NE	W	Goshen College, IN	M	McNeese State University, LA	M
College of William and Mary, VA	M,W	Grace College, IN	M	McPherson College, KS	M,W
Colorado Christian University, CO	M	Grambling State University, LA	M	Mercer University, Macon, GA	M,W
Colorado School of Mines, CO	M,W	Grand Canyon University, AZ	M	Mercyhurst College, PA	M,W
Columbus State University, GA	M	Hastings College, NE	M,W	Mesa State College, CO	W
Concordia College, NE	M,W	Hillsdale College, MI	M	Miami University, OH	M
Concordia University at Austin, TX	M	Hofstra University, NY	M	Michigan State University, MI	M,W
Cornerstone College, MI	M	Holy Family College, PA	M	Middle Tennessee State University, TN	M
Creighton University, NE	M,W	Holy Names College, CA	M	Midland Lutheran College, NE	M,W
Culver-Stockton College, MO	M	Huntington College, IN	M,W	Millersville University of Pennsylvania, PA	M
Cumberland College, KY	M,W	Huron University, SD	M		
Dakota Wesleyan University, SD	M,W	Idaho State University, ID	M,W	Milligan College, TN	M
David Lipscomb University, TN	M	Illinois State University, IL	M,W	Mississippi State University, MS	M,W
Davis & Elkins College, WV	M	Indiana University Bloomington, IN	M,W	Mississippi Valley State University, MS	M
Delta State University, MS	M	Indiana U–Purdue U Fort Wayne, IN	M		
DePaul University, IL	M,W	Indiana Wesleyan University, IN	M	Missouri Baptist College, MO	M
Doane College, NE	M,W	Iowa State University of Science and Technology, IA	M,W	Missouri Southern State College, MO	M
Dominican College of Blauvelt, NY	M			Missouri Western State College, MO	M
Dowling College, NY	M	Iowa Wesleyan College, IA	M,W	Molloy College, NY	M
Drake University, IA	M	Jackson State University, MS	M	Montreat College, NC	M
Drury College, MO	M	Jacksonville State University, AL	M,W	Morehead State University, KY	M
Duke University, NC	M,W	Jacksonville University, FL	M,W	Mount Olive College, NC	M
Duquesne University, PA	M,W	James Madison University, VA	M,W	Mount St. Clare College, IA	M,W
East Carolina University, NC	M	Johnson C. Smith University, NC	M	Mount Vernon Nazarene College, OH	M
Eastern Kentucky University, KY	M	Kansas Newman College, KS	M	Murray State University, KY	M
Eastern Michigan University, MI	M	Kansas State University, KS	M,W	Newberry College, SC	M,W
Eckerd College, FL	M	Kansas Wesleyan University, KS	M,W	New Mexico State University, NM	M,W
Edinboro University of Pennsylvania, PA	M	Kennesaw State University, GA	M	Niagara University, NY	M
		Kent State University, OH	M	Nicholls State University, LA	M
Elon College, NC	M	Kentucky State University, KY	M,W	North Carolina State University, NC	M,W
Embry-Riddle Aeronautical University, FL	M	Kentucky Wesleyan College, KY	M,W	Northeastern Illinois University, IL	M,W
		King College, TN	M	Northeastern State University, OK	M
				Northeast Louisiana University, LA	M

Golf (continued)

Northern Arizona University, AZ	W
Northern Illinois University, IL	M,W
Northern Kentucky University, KY	M
Northern State University, SD	W
North Greenville College, SC	M
Northwestern College, IA	M,W
Northwestern State University of Louisiana, LA	M
Northwestern University, IL	M,W
Northwood University, MI	M
Northwood University, Florida Campus, FL	M,W
Northwood University, Texas Campus, TX	M,W
Nova Southeastern University, FL	M
Oakland City University, IN	M,W
Oakland University, MI	M,W
The Ohio State University, OH	M,W
Ohio University, OH	M
Oklahoma Christian U of Science and Arts, OK	M
Oklahoma City University, OK	M
Oklahoma State U, OK	M,W
Old Dominion University, VA	M
Oral Roberts University, OK	M,W
Oregon State University, OR	M,W
Penn State U Univ Park Campus, PA	M,W
Pepperdine University, Malibu, CA	M,W
Pfeiffer University, NC	M
Philadelphia College of Textiles and Science, PA	M
Phillips University, OK	M,W
Point Loma Nazarene College, CA	M
Portland State University, OR	M
Presbyterian College, SC	M,W
Providence College, RI	M
Purdue University, West Lafayette, IN	M,W
Queens College, NC	M
Quinnipiac College, CT	M
Radford University, VA	M,W
Regis University, CO	M
Rice University, TX	M
Rider University, NJ	M
Robert Morris College, PA	M
Rollins College, FL	M,W
Rutgers, State U of NJ, College of Engineering, NJ	M,W
Rutgers, State U of NJ, College of Pharmacy, NJ	M,W
Rutgers, State U of NJ, Cook College, NJ	M,W
Rutgers, State U of NJ, Douglass College, NJ	W
Rutgers, State U of NJ, Livingston College, NJ	M,W
Rutgers, State U of NJ, Mason Gross School of Arts, NJ	M,W
Rutgers, State U of NJ, Rutgers College, NJ	M,W
Saginaw Valley State University, MI	M
St. Ambrose University, IA	M,W
St. Andrews Presbyterian College, NC	M
Saint Augustine's College, NC	M
St. Bonaventure University, NY	M
St. Edward's University, TX	M
Saint Francis College, IN	M
Saint Francis College, PA	M,W
St. John's University, NY	M
Saint Joseph's College, IN	M,W
Saint Joseph's University, PA	M
Saint Louis University, MO	M
Saint Martin's College, WA	M,W
Saint Mary's College of California, CA	M
St. Mary's University of San Antonio, TX	M
St. Thomas Aquinas College, NY	M
St. Thomas University, FL	M,W
Samford University, AL	M,W
Sam Houston State University, TX	M
San Diego State University, CA	M,W
San Jose State University, CA	M,W
Santa Clara University, CA	M,W
Seton Hall University, NJ	M
Shaw University, NC	M
Shorter College, GA	M,W
Siena Heights College, MI	M
Slippery Rock University of Pennsylvania, PA	M,W
South Dakota State University, SD	M,W
Southeastern Louisiana University, LA	M
Southeast Missouri State University, MO	M
Southern Illinois University at Carbondale, IL	M,W
Southern Methodist University, TX	M,W
Southern Nazarene University, OK	M
Southern University and A&M College, LA	M
Southern Utah University, UT	M
Southern Wesleyan University, SC	M
Southwest Baptist University, MO	M
Southwestern College, KS	M
Southwestern Oklahoma State University, OK	M
Southwest Missouri State University, MO	M,W
Southwest Texas State University, TX	M
Spalding University, KY	M
Spring Arbor College, MI	M
Spring Hill College, AL	M,W
Stanford University, CA	M,W
Stephen F. Austin State University, TX	M
Stetson University, FL	M,W
Tabor College, KS	M
Taylor University, IN	M
Temple University, Philadelphia, PA	M
Tennessee State University, TN	M
Tennessee Technological University, TN	M
Tennessee Wesleyan College, TN	M
Texas A&M University, College Station, TX	M,W
Texas A&M University–Commerce, TX	M
Texas Christian University, TX	M,W
Texas Lutheran University, TX	M,W
Texas Southern University, TX	M
Texas Tech University, TX	M,W
Texas Wesleyan University, TX	M
Thomas College, GA	M
Tiffin University, OH	M,W
Towson University, MD	M
Transylvania University, KY	M
Trinity International University, IL	M
Tri-State University, IN	M,W
Troy State University, Troy, AL	M
Tulane University, LA	M,W
Tusculum College, TN	M,W
Union College, KY	M
Union University, TN	M
U at Albany, State U of NY, NY	W
The University of Akron, OH	M
The University of Alabama at Birmingham, AL	M,W
University of Arizona, AZ	M,W
University of Arkansas, Fayetteville, AR	M,W
University of Arkansas at Little Rock, AR	M,W
University of California, Berkeley, CA	M
University of California, Irvine, CA	M
University of California, Los Angeles, CA	M,W
University of California, Santa Barbara, CA	M
University of Central Florida, FL	M,W
University of Central Oklahoma, OK	M
The University of Charleston, WV	M
University of Cincinnati, OH	M
University of Colorado at Boulder, CO	M,W
University of Colorado at Colorado Springs, CO	M
University of Dayton, OH	M,W
University of Detroit Mercy, MI	M,W
University of Evansville, IN	M
The University of Findlay, OH	M,W
University of Florida, FL	M,W
University of Georgia, GA	M,W
University of Hartford, CT	M,W
University of Hawaii at Hilo, HI	M
University of Hawaii at Manoa, HI	M,W
University of Houston, TX	M
University of Idaho, ID	M,W
University of Illinois at Urbana–Champaign, IL	M,W
University of Indianapolis, IN	M,W
The University of Iowa, IA	M,W
University of Kansas, KS	M,W
University of Kentucky, KY	M,W
University of Louisville, KY	M
University of Mary Hardin-Baylor, TX	M
University of Maryland Baltimore County, MD	M
University of Maryland College Park, MD	M
The University of Memphis, TN	M,W
University of Miami, FL	W
University of Michigan, Ann Arbor, MI	M,W
University of Minnesota, Twin Cities Campus, MN	M,W
University of Mississippi, MS	M,W
University of Missouri–Columbia, MO	M,W
University of Missouri–Kansas City, MO	M,W
University of Missouri–Rolla, MO	M
University of Missouri–St. Louis, MO	M
University of Mobile, AL	M,W
University of Montevallo, AL	M,W

University of Nebraska at Kearney, NE	M,W
University of Nebraska–Lincoln, NE	M,W
University of Nevada, Las Vegas, NV	M
University of Nevada, Reno, NV	M
University of New Mexico, NM	M,W
University of North Alabama, AL	M
University of North Carolina at Charlotte, NC	M
University of North Carolina at Greensboro, NC	M,W
University of North Carolina at Pembroke, NC	M
University of North Carolina at Wilmington, NC	M,W
University of Northern Iowa, IA	W
University of North Florida, FL	M
University of North Texas, TX	M,W
University of Notre Dame, IN	M,W
University of Oklahoma, OK	M,W
University of Oregon, OR	M,W
University of Portland, OR	M
University of Rhode Island, RI	M
University of Richmond, VA	M
University of San Diego, CA	M
University of San Francisco, CA	M,W
University of South Alabama, AL	M,W
U of South Carolina, Columbia, SC	M,W
U of South Carolina–Aiken, SC	M
University of Southern California, CA	M,W
University of Southern Colorado, CO	M,W
University of Southern Indiana, IN	M,W
University of Southern Mississippi, MS	M,W
University of South Florida, FL	M,W
University of Southwestern Louisiana, LA	M
The University of Tampa, FL	M
University of Tennessee at Chattanooga, TN	M
The University of Tennessee at Martin, TN	M
University of Tennessee, Knoxville, TN	M,W
The University of Texas at Arlington, TX	M
The University of Texas at Austin, TX	M,W
The University of Texas at El Paso, TX	M
The University of Texas at San Antonio, TX	M
The University of Texas–Pan American, TX	M
University of the Pacific, CA	M
University of Toledo, OH	M,W
University of Tulsa, OK	M,W
University of Utah, UT	M
University of Virginia, VA	M
University of Washington, WA	M,W
University of West Florida, FL	M
University of Wisconsin–Green Bay, WI	M
University of Wisconsin–Madison, WI	M,W
University of Wisconsin–Parkside, WI	M
University of Wyoming, WY	M,W
Urbana University, OH	M
Utah State University, UT	M

Valdosta State University, GA	M
Vanderbilt University, TN	M,W
Virginia Commonwealth University, VA	M
Virginia Military Institute, VA	M
Virginia Polytechnic Institute and State U, VA	M
Virginia Union University, VA	M
Wagner College, NY	M,W
Wake Forest University, NC	M,W
Walsh University, OH	M
Washburn University of Topeka, KS	M
Washington State University, WA	M,W
Wayne State University, MI	M
Webber College, FL	M,W
Weber State University, UT	M,W
West Chester University of Pennsylvania, PA	M
Western Carolina University, NC	M,W
Western Illinois University, IL	M
Western Kentucky University, KY	M,W
Western Washington University, WA	M
Westmar University, IA	M,W
West Virginia University Institute of Technology, WV	M
West Virginia Wesleyan College, WV	M
Wheeling Jesuit University, WV	M
Wichita State University, KS	M,W
William Jewell College, MO	M
William Woods University, MO	W
Wingate University, NC	M
Winona State University, MN	M,W
Winston-Salem State University, NC	M
Winthrop University, SC	M,W
Wofford College, SC	M,W
Wright State University, OH	M
Xavier University, OH	M,W
Youngstown State University, OH	M

GYMNASTICS

Arizona State University, AZ	W
Auburn University, AL	W
Ball State University, IN	W
Boise State University, ID	W
Bowling Green State University, OH	W
Brigham Young University, UT	M,W
California Polytechnic State U, San Luis Obispo, CA	W
California State University, Fullerton, CA	W
California State University, Sacramento, CA	W
Centenary College of Louisiana, LA	W
Central Michigan University, MI	W
College of William and Mary, VA	M,W
Columbia Union College, MD	M,W
Eastern Michigan University, MI	W
The George Washington University, DC	W
Illinois State University, IL	W
Indiana University of Pennsylvania, PA	W
Inter American U of PR, Metropolitan Campus, PR	M,W
Iowa State University of Science and Technology, IA	W
James Madison University, VA	M,W

Kent State University, OH	W
Louisiana State University and A&M College, LA	W
Michigan State University, MI	M,W
North Carolina State University, NC	M,W
Northern Illinois University, IL	W
The Ohio State University, OH	M,W
Oregon State University, OR	W
Penn State U Univ Park Campus, PA	M,W
Radford University, VA	M,W
Rutgers, State U of NJ, College of Engineering, NJ	W
Rutgers, State U of NJ, College of Pharmacy, NJ	W
Rutgers, State U of NJ, Cook College, NJ	W
Rutgers, State U of NJ, Douglass College, NJ	W
Rutgers, State U of NJ, Livingston College, NJ	W
Rutgers, State U of NJ, Mason Gross School of Arts, NJ	W
Rutgers, State U of NJ, Rutgers College, NJ	W
San Jose State University, CA	M,W
Seattle Pacific University, WA	W
Southeast Missouri State University, MO	W
Southern Utah University, UT	W
Stanford University, CA	M,W
Syracuse University, NY	M
Temple University, Philadelphia, PA	M,W
Texas Woman's University, TX	W
Towson University, MD	W
U of Alaska Anchorage, AK	W
University of Arizona, AZ	W
University of Bridgeport, CT	W
University of California, Berkeley, CA	M
University of California, Los Angeles, CA	W
University of California, Santa Barbara, CA	M,W
University of Denver, CO	W
University of Florida, FL	W
University of Georgia, GA	W
University of Illinois at Chicago, IL	M,W
University of Illinois at Urbana–Champaign, IL	M,W
The University of Iowa, IA	M,W
University of Kentucky, KY	W
University of Maryland College Park, MD	W
University of Massachusetts Amherst, MA	M,W
University of Michigan, Ann Arbor, MI	M,W
University of Minnesota, Twin Cities Campus, MN	M,W
University of Missouri–Columbia, MO	W
University of Nebraska–Lincoln, NE	M,W
University of New Hampshire, Durham, NH	W
University of New Mexico, NM	M
University of Oklahoma, OK	M,W
University of Pittsburgh, PA	W
University of Rhode Island, RI	W
University of Utah, UT	W

Gymnastics (continued)

University of Washington, WA	W
Utah State University, UT	W
West Chester University of Pennsylvania, PA	W
Western Michigan University, MI	M,W
West Virginia University, WV	W
Winona State University, MN	W

ICE HOCKEY

American International College, MA	M
Bemidji State University, MN	M
Boston College, MA	M
Boston University, MA	M
Bowling Green State University, OH	M
Canisius College, NY	M
Clarkson University, NY	M
The Colorado College, CO	M
Fairfield University, CT	M
Ferris State University, MI	M
Mankato State University, MN	M
Merrimack College, MA	M
Miami University, OH	M
Michigan State University, MI	M
Michigan Technological University, MI	M
Northeastern University, MA	M,W
Northern Michigan University, MI	M
The Ohio State University, OH	M
Providence College, RI	M,W
Rensselaer Polytechnic Institute, NY	M
St. Cloud State University, MN	M
The University of Alabama in Huntsville, AL	M
U of Alaska Anchorage, AK	M
U of Alaska Fairbanks, AK	M
University of Connecticut, Storrs, CT	M
University of Denver, CO	M
The University of Findlay, OH	M
University of Illinois at Chicago, IL	M
University of Maine, Orono, ME	M
University of Massachusetts Lowell, MA	M
University of Michigan, Ann Arbor, MI	M
University of Minnesota, Crookston, MN	M
University of Minnesota, Duluth, MN	M
University of Minnesota, Twin Cities Campus, MN	M,W
University of New Hampshire, Durham, NH	M,W
University of North Dakota, ND	M
University of Notre Dame, IN	M
University of Vermont, VT	M
University of Wisconsin–Madison, WI	M
Western Michigan University, MI	M

LACROSSE

Adelphi University, NY	M
Bloomfield College, NJ	M
Boston College, MA	W
Boston University, MA	W
Butler University, IN	M
Canisius College, NY	M
College of William and Mary, VA	W
Drexel University, PA	M

Duke University, NC	M,W
Duquesne University, PA	W
Fairfield University, CT	M,W
Gannon University, PA	W
Georgetown University, DC	M
Hofstra University, NY	M,W
James Madison University, VA	W
Johns Hopkins University, MD	M
La Salle University, PA	M,W
Lees-McRae College, NC	M
Lehigh University, PA	M,W
Limestone College, SC	M,W
Long Island U, C.W. Post Campus, NY	M
Long Island U, Southampton College, NY	M
Loyola College, MD	M,W
Manhattan College, NY	M,W
Mercyhurst College, PA	M,W
Merrimack College, MA	M
Millersville University of Pennsylvania, PA	W
Monmouth University, NJ	W
Mount Saint Mary's College and Seminary, MD	M,W
New York Institute of Technology, NY	M
Northwood University, MI	M
The Ohio State University, OH	W
Old Dominion University, VA	W
Pace University, NY	M
Penn State U Univ Park Campus, PA	M,W
Pfeiffer University, NC	M
Philadelphia College of Textiles and Science, PA	W
Providence College, RI	M
Radford University, VA	M
Rutgers, State U of NJ, College of Engineering, NJ	M,W
Rutgers, State U of NJ, College of Pharmacy, NJ	M,W
Rutgers, State U of NJ, Cook College, NJ	M,W
Rutgers, State U of NJ, Douglass College, NJ	W
Rutgers, State U of NJ, Livingston College, NJ	M,W
Rutgers, State U of NJ, Mason Gross School of Arts, NJ	M,W
Rutgers, State U of NJ, Rutgers College, NJ	M,W
St. Andrews Presbyterian College, NC	M
Saint Joseph's University, PA	M,W
Saint Vincent College, PA	M
Shippensburg University of Pennsylvania, PA	W
Syracuse University, NY	M,W
Temple University, Philadelphia, PA	W
Towson University, MD	M,W
U at Albany, State U of NY, NY	M,W
University of Delaware, DE	M,W
University of Denver, CO	M
University of Hartford, CT	M
University of Maryland Baltimore County, MD	M,W
University of Maryland College Park, MD	M,W

University of Massachusetts Amherst, MA	M,W
University of New Hampshire, Durham, NH	W
University of Notre Dame, IN	W
University of Richmond, VA	W
University of Virginia, VA	M,W
University of Wisconsin–Madison, WI	W
Vanderbilt University, TN	W
Virginia Military Institute, VA	M
Virginia Polytechnic Institute and State U, VA	W
Wagner College, NY	W
West Chester University of Pennsylvania, PA	M,W
Wingate University, NC	M

RIFLERY

Austin Peay State University, TN	W
Canisius College, NY	M,W
Centenary College of Louisiana, LA	M,W
DePaul University, IL	M,W
Duquesne University, PA	M,W
Eastern New Mexico University, NM	M,W
Jacksonville State University, AL	M
Marquette University, WI	M,W
Mercer University, Macon, GA	M,W
Morehead State University, KY	M,W
Murray State University, KY	M,W
North Georgia College & State University, GA	M,W
St. John's University, NY	M,W
Saint Louis University, MO	M,W
Tennessee Technological University, TN	M,W
U of Alaska Fairbanks, AK	M,W
University of Missouri–Kansas City, MO	M,W
University of Nevada, Reno, NV	M,W
University of North Alabama, AL	M
The University of Tennessee at Martin, TN	M,W
Virginia Military Institute, VA	M
West Virginia University, WV	M,W
Xavier University, OH	M,W

SKIING—CROSS-COUNTRY

Northern Michigan University, MI	M,W
U of Alaska Anchorage, AK	M,W
U of Alaska Fairbanks, AK	M,W
University of Colorado at Boulder, CO	M,W
University of Denver, CO	M,W
University of Nevada, Reno, NV	M,W
University of New Hampshire, Durham, NH	M,W
University of New Mexico, NM	M,W
University of Utah, UT	M,W
University of Vermont, VT	M,W
University of Wisconsin–Green Bay, WI	M,W
Western State College of Colorado, CO	M,W

SKIING—DOWNHILL

Albertson College of Idaho, ID	M,W
Brigham Young University, UT	M,W
Green Mountain College, VT	M,W
Lees-McRae College, NC	M,W

Montana State U–Bozeman, MT	W	
Northern Michigan University, MI	W	
Rocky Mountain College, MT	M,W	
Sierra Nevada College, NV	M,W	
U of Alaska Anchorage, AK	M,W	
University of Colorado at Boulder, CO	M,W	
University of Denver, CO	M,W	
University of Massachusetts Amherst, MA	M	
University of Nevada, Reno, NV	M,W	
University of New Hampshire, Durham, NH	M,W	
University of New Mexico, NM	M,W	
University of Utah, UT	M,W	
University of Vermont, VT	M,W	

SOCCER

Adelphi University, NY	M,W
Alabama Agricultural and Mechanical University, AL	M
Albertson College of Idaho, ID	M,W
Alderson-Broaddus College, WV	M
American University, DC	M,W
Anderson College, SC	M,W
Angelo State University, TX	W
Appalachian State University, NC	M,W
Aquinas College, MI	M,W
Arizona State University, AZ	W
Ashland University, OH	M,W
Auburn University, AL	W
Auburn University at Montgomery, AL	M
Augusta State University, GA	M
Azusa Pacific University, CA	M,W
Baker University, KS	M,W
Barry University, FL	M,W
Bartlesville Wesleyan College, OK	M,W
Barton College, NC	M,W
Bayamón Technological University College, PR	M
Baylor University, TX	W
Becker College–Leicester Campus, MA	M,W
Becker College–Worcester Campus, MA	M,W
Belhaven College, MS	M,W
Bellarmine College, KY	M,W
Belmont Abbey College, NC	M,W
Belmont University, TN	M
Benedictine College, KS	M,W
Berry College, GA	M,W
Bethel College, IN	M,W
Bethel College, KS	M,W
Biola University, CA	M,W
Birmingham-Southern College, AL	M,W
Bloomfield College, NJ	M
Bloomsburg University of Pennsylvania, PA	W
Bluefield College, VA	M
Boston College, MA	M,W
Boston University, MA	M,W
Bowling Green State University, OH	M
Bradley University, IL	M
Brenau University, GA	W
Brescia College, KY	M
Brewton-Parker College, GA	M,W
Briar Cliff College, IA	M,W

Brigham Young University, UT	W
Bryan College, TN	M,W
Butler University, IN	M,W
Caldwell College, NJ	M
California Baptist College, CA	M,W
California State Polytechnic University, Pomona, CA	M,W
California State University, Bakersfield, CA	M
California State University, Dominguez Hills, CA	M,W
California State University, Fresno, CA	M,W
California State University, Fullerton, CA	M,W
California State University, Los Angeles, CA	M
California State University, Northridge, CA	M
California State University, Sacramento, CA	M,W
California State University, San Bernardino, CA	M,W
California University of Pennsylvania, PA	M
Campbell University, NC	M,W
Canisius College, NY	M,W
Carson-Newman College, TN	M,W
Catawba College, NC	M,W
Cedarville College, OH	M
Centenary College of Louisiana, LA	M,W
Central Connecticut State University, CT	M,W
Central Methodist College, MO	M,W
Charleston Southern University, SC	M,W
Christian Brothers University, TN	M,W
Christian Heritage College, CA	M
The Citadel, The Military Coll of South Carolina, SC	M
Clayton College & State University, GA	M,W
Clemson University, SC	M
Cleveland State University, OH	M
Coastal Carolina University, SC	M
Coker College, SC	M,W
College of Charleston, SC	M,W
College of St. Francis, IL	M,W
College of St. Joseph, VT	M,W
College of Saint Mary, NE	W
College of the Southwest, NM	W
College of William and Mary, VA	M,W
Colorado Christian University, CO	M,W
The Colorado College, CO	W
Colorado School of Mines, CO	M
Columbia College, MO	M
Columbia Union College, MD	M
Concordia College, MI	M,W
Concordia College, NE	M,W
Concordia College, NY	M,W
Concordia University, CA	M
Concordia University, OR	M,W
Cornerstone College, MI	M,W
Covenant College, GA	M,W
Creighton University, NE	M,W
Culver-Stockton College, MO	M
Cumberland College, KY	M,W
Cumberland University, TN	M

Dana College, NE	W
David Lipscomb University, TN	M
Davidson College, NC	W
Davis & Elkins College, WV	M
DePaul University, IL	M,W
Dominican College of Blauvelt, NY	M,W
Dominican College of San Rafael, CA	M,W
Dowling College, NY	M
Drake University, IA	M
Drexel University, PA	M
Duke University, NC	M,W
Duquesne University, PA	M,W
East Carolina University, NC	M,W
Eastern Illinois University, IL	M,W
Eastern Michigan University, MI	M,W
East Stroudsburg University of Pennsylvania, PA	M,W
Eckerd College, FL	M,W
Edinboro University of Pennsylvania, PA	W
Elon College, NC	M,W
Embry-Riddle Aeronautical University, FL	M
Erskine College, SC	M,W
Fairfield University, CT	M,W
Fairleigh Dickinson U, Teaneck-Hackensack, NJ	M
Flagler College, FL	M,W
Florida Atlantic University, FL	M,W
Florida Institute of Technology, FL	M
Florida International University, FL	M,W
Florida Southern College, FL	M
Florida State University, FL	W
Fordham University, NY	M,W
Fort Lewis College, CO	M,W
Francis Marion University, SC	M,W
Franklin Pierce College, NH	M,W
Fresno Pacific University, CA	M
Friends University, KS	M,W
Furman University, SC	M,W
Gannon University, PA	M,W
Gardner-Webb University, NC	M
Geneva College, PA	M,W
George Mason University, VA	M,W
Georgetown College, KY	M,W
The George Washington University, DC	M,W
Georgian Court College, NJ	W
Georgia Southern University, GA	M,W
Georgia State University, GA	M
Goldey-Beacom College, DE	M
Gonzaga University, WA	M,W
Goshen College, IN	M,W
Grace College, IN	M,W
Graceland College, IA	M,W
Grand Canyon University, AZ	M
Grand Valley State University, MI	W
Grand View College, IA	M
Green Mountain College, VT	M,W
Hartwick College, NY	M
Hastings College, NE	M,W
Hawaii Pacific University, HI	M,W
Hofstra University, NY	M,W
Holy Family College, PA	M,W
Hope International University, CA	M,W
Houghton College, NY	M,W
Howard University, DC	M

Soccer (continued)

Huntington College, IN	M
Illinois State University, IL	W
Indiana Institute of Technology, IN	M
Indiana University Bloomington, IN	M,W
Indiana U–Purdue U Fort Wayne, IN	M
Indiana U–Purdue U Indianapolis, IN	M
Indiana Wesleyan University, IN	M,W
Inter American U of PR, San Germán Campus, PR	M
Iowa State University of Science and Technology, IA	W
Iowa Wesleyan College, IA	M,W
Jacksonville University, FL	M,W
James Madison University, VA	M,W
John Brown University, AR	M
Judson College, IL	M,W
Kansas Newman College, KS	M,W
Kansas Wesleyan University, KS	M
Kentucky Wesleyan College, KY	M,W
King College, TN	M
Kutztown University of Pennsylvania, PA	M,W
Lambuth University, TN	M,W
Lander University, SC	M
La Salle University, PA	M,W
Lees-McRae College, NC	M,W
Lee University, TN	M,W
Lehigh University, PA	M,W
Le Moyne College, NY	M,W
Lenoir-Rhyne College, NC	M,W
LeTourneau University, TX	M
Lewis University, IL	M,W
Limestone College, SC	M,W
Lincoln Memorial University, TN	M,W
Lincoln University, MO	M
Lindenwood College, MO	M,W
Lindsey Wilson College, KY	M,W
Lock Haven University of Pennsylvania, PA	M,W
Long Island U, Brooklyn Campus, NY	M,W
Long Island U, C.W. Post Campus, NY	M,W
Long Island U, Southampton College, NY	M,W
Longwood College, VA	M
Louisiana State University and A&M College, LA	W
Loyola College, MD	M,W
Loyola Marymount University, CA	M,W
Loyola University Chicago, IL	M,W
Lynn University, FL	M,W
Malone College, OH	M
Manhattan College, NY	M,W
Mankato State University, MN	W
Marian College, IN	M
Marist College, NY	M,W
Marquette University, WI	M,W
Marshall University, WV	M,W
Mars Hill College, NC	M,W
Martin Methodist College, TN	M
Marycrest International University, IA	M,W
The Master's College and Seminary, CA	M,W
McKendree College, IL	M,W
McPherson College, KS	M,W
Mercer University, Macon, GA	M,W

Mercyhurst College, PA	M,W
Merrimack College, MA	M,W
Mesa State College, CO	W
Metropolitan State College of Denver, CO	M,W
Michigan Christian College, MI	M
Michigan State University, MI	M
Midland Lutheran College, NE	W
Midway College, KY	W
Midwestern State University, TX	M,W
Millersville University of Pennsylvania, PA	M,W
Milligan College, TN	M
Missouri Baptist College, MO	M,W
Missouri Southern State College, MO	M
Monmouth University, NJ	M,W
Montreat College, NC	M,W
Moorhead State University, MN	W
Mount Olive College, NC	M,W
Mount St. Clare College, IA	M,W
Mount Saint Mary's College and Seminary, MD	M,W
Mount Vernon Nazarene College, OH	M
National College, SD	M
Newberry College, SC	M,W
New Hampshire College, NH	M,W
New Mexico Highlands University, NM	W
New York Institute of Technology, NY	M,W
Niagara University, NY	M,W
North Carolina State University, NC	M,W
North Dakota State University, ND	W
Northeastern Illinois University, IL	M
Northeastern State University, OK	M
Northeastern University, MA	M,W
Northern Arizona University, AZ	W
Northern Illinois University, IL	M,W
Northern Kentucky University, KY	M,W
Northern Michigan University, MI	W
North Georgia College & State University, GA	M,W
North Greenville College, SC	M,W
Northland College, WI	M
Northwest College of the Assemblies of God, WA	M
Northwestern College, IA	M
Northwestern University, IL	W
Northwood University, MI	W
Northwood University, Florida Campus, FL	M
Notre Dame College, NH	M,W
Nova Southeastern University, FL	M,W
Nyack College, NY	M,W
Oakland University, MI	M,W
Ohio Dominican College, OH	M
The Ohio State University, OH	M,W
Oklahoma Christian U of Science and Arts, OK	M,W
Oklahoma City University, OK	M,W
Old Dominion University, VA	M,W
Oral Roberts University, OK	M,W
Oregon State University, OR	M,W
Ottawa University, KS	M,W
Palm Beach Atlantic College, FL	M
Park College, MO	M,W
Penn State U Univ Park Campus, PA	M,W
Pepperdine University, Malibu, CA	W

Pfeiffer University, NC	M,W
Philadelphia College of Textiles and Science, PA	M
Phillips University, OK	M,W
Piedmont College, GA	M,W
Point Loma Nazarene College, CA	M
Point Park College, PA	M
Portland State University, OR	M
Presbyterian College, SC	M,W
Providence College, RI	M,W
Purdue University Calumet, IN	M
Queens College, NC	M,W
Queens Coll of the City U of NY, NY	M
Quincy University, IL	M,W
Quinnipiac College, CT	M,W
Radford University, VA	M,W
Regis University, CO	W
Reinhardt College, GA	M
Research College of Nursing–Rockhurst College, MO	M,W
Rider University, NJ	M
Robert Morris College, PA	M,W
Roberts Wesleyan College, NY	M,W
Rockhurst College, MO	M,W
Rollins College, FL	M
Rutgers, State U of NJ, College of Engineering, NJ	M,W
Rutgers, State U of NJ, College of Pharmacy, NJ	M,W
Rutgers, State U of NJ, Cook College, NJ	M,W
Rutgers, State U of NJ, Douglass College, NJ	W
Rutgers, State U of NJ, Livingston College, NJ	M,W
Rutgers, State U of NJ, Mason Gross School of Arts, NJ	M,W
Rutgers, State U of NJ, Rutgers College, NJ	M,W
Saginaw Valley State University, MI	M,W
St. Ambrose University, IA	M,W
St. Andrews Presbyterian College, NC	M,W
Saint Augustine's College, NC	M
St. Bonaventure University, NY	M,W
St. Cloud State University, MN	W
St. Edward's University, TX	M,W
Saint Francis College, IN	M,W
St. Francis College, NY	M
Saint Francis College, PA	M,W
St. John's University, NY	M,W
Saint Joseph's College, IN	M,W
Saint Joseph's University, PA	M,W
Saint Leo College, FL	M
Saint Louis University, MO	M,W
Saint Mary College, KS	M,W
Saint Mary's College of California, CA	M,W
St. Mary's University of San Antonio, TX	M,W
Saint Peter's College, Jersey City, NJ	M
St. Thomas Aquinas College, NY	M,W
St. Thomas University, FL	M,W
Saint Vincent College, PA	M,W
Saint Xavier University, IL	M,W
Salem-Teikyo University, WV	M
San Diego State University, CA	M,W
San Jose State University, CA	M,W

Santa Clara University, CA	M,W	University of Bridgeport, CT	M,W	U of Puerto Rico, Río Piedras, PR	M
Seattle Pacific University, WA	M	University of California, Los Angeles, CA	M,W	University of Rhode Island, RI	M,W
Seton Hall University, NJ	M,W	University of California, Santa Barbara, CA	M,W	University of Richmond, VA	M,W
Seton Hill College, PA	W	University of Central Florida, FL	M,W	University of San Diego, CA	M,W
Shippensburg University of Pennsylvania, PA	M,W	The University of Charleston, WV	M,W	University of San Francisco, CA	M,W
Siena College, NY	M,W	University of Cincinnati, OH	M,W	University of South Alabama, AL	M,W
Siena Heights College, MI	M,W	University of Colorado at Boulder, CO	W	U of South Carolina, Columbia, SC	M
Slippery Rock University of Pennsylvania, PA	M,W	University of Colorado at Colorado Springs, CO	M	U of South Carolina–Aiken, SC	M
Southeastern Louisiana University, LA	W	University of Connecticut, Storrs, CT	M,W	U of South Carolina–Spartanburg, SC	M
Southern California College, CA	M,W	University of Dayton, OH	M,W	University of Southern California, CA	W
Southern Illinois University at Edwardsville, IL	M,W	University of Delaware, DE	M,W	University of Southern Indiana, IN	M
Southern Methodist University, TX	M,W	University of Denver, CO	M,W	University of South Florida, FL	M,W
Southern Nazarene University, OK	M,W	University of Detroit Mercy, MI	M,W	The University of Tampa, FL	M
Southern Wesleyan University, SC	M	University of Evansville, IN	M	University of Tennessee at Chattanooga, TN	M
Southwest Baptist University, MO	M,W	The University of Findlay, OH	M,W	University of Tennessee, Knoxville, TN	W
Southwestern College, KS	M,W	University of Guam, GU	M	
Southwest Missouri State University, MO	M	University of Hartford, CT	M,W	The University of Texas at Austin, TX	W
		University of Hawaii at Manoa, HI	W	University of the District of Columbia, DC	M
Spalding University, KY	M	University of Illinois at Chicago, IL	M	
Spring Arbor College, MI	M,W	University of Indianapolis, IN	M,W	University of the Pacific, CA	W
Spring Hill College, AL	M,W	University of Kansas, KS	W	University of Toledo, OH	W
Stanford University, CA	M	University of Louisville, KY	M,W	University of Tulsa, OK	M,W
State U of NY at Buffalo, NY	M,W	University of Maine, Orono, ME	M,W	University of Utah, UT	W
Stephen F. Austin State University, TX	W	University of Mary Hardin-Baylor, TX	M	University of Virginia, VA	M,W
Sterling College, KS	M	University of Maryland Baltimore County, MD	M,W	University of Washington, WA	M
Stetson University, FL	M,W			University of West Florida, FL	M,W
Sue Bennett College, KY	M	University of Maryland College Park, MD	M,W	University of Wisconsin–Green Bay, WI	M,W
Syracuse University, NY	M,W			
Tabor College, KS	M	University of Massachusetts Amherst, MA	M,W	University of Wisconsin–Madison, WI	M,W
Taylor University, IN	M	The University of Memphis, TN	M	University of Wisconsin–Milwaukee, WI	M,W
Teikyo Post University, CT	M,W	University of Minnesota, Duluth, MN	W	
Temple University, Philadelphia, PA	M,W	University of Mississippi, MS	W	University of Wisconsin–Parkside, WI	M
Tennessee Temple University, TN	M	University of Missouri–Columbia, MO	W	Urbana University, OH	M,W
Tennessee Wesleyan College, TN	M,W	University of Missouri–Kansas City, MO	M	Utah State University, UT	W
Texas A&M University, College Station, TX	W	University of Missouri–Rolla, MO	M,W	Valparaiso University, IN	M,W
		University of Missouri–St. Louis, MO	M,W	Vanderbilt University, TN	M,W
Texas Lutheran University, TX	M,W	University of Mobile, AL	M,W	Villanova University, PA	M,W
Texas Tech University, TX	W	University of Montevallo, AL	M,W	Virginia Commonwealth University, VA	M,W
Texas Wesleyan University, TX	M	University of Nebraska–Lincoln, NE	W	
Thomas College, GA	M	University of Nevada, Las Vegas, NV	M	Virginia Military Institute, VA	M
Tiffin University, OH	M,W	University of New Hampshire, Durham, NH	M,W	Virginia Polytechnic Institute and State U, VA	M,W
Towson University, MD	M,W			
Transylvania University, KY	M,W	University of New Haven, CT	M,W	Wagner College, NY	W
Trinity Christian College, IL	M,W	University of New Mexico, NM	M,W	Wake Forest University, NC	M,W
Trinity International University, IL	M,W	University of North Carolina at Asheville, NC	M,W	Walsh University, OH	M,W
Tri-State University, IN	M,W			Washington State University, WA	W
Truman State University, MO	M,W	University of North Carolina at Charlotte, NC	M,W	Webber College, FL	M,W
Tulane University, LA	W			West Chester University of Pennsylvania, PA	M,W
Tusculum College, TN	M,W	University of North Carolina at Greensboro, NC	M,W	
Union College, KY	M,W			Western Baptist College, OR	M
United States International University, CA	M,W	University of North Carolina at Pembroke, NC	M	Western Illinois University, IL	M
				Western Kentucky University, KY	M
Unity College, ME	M	University of North Carolina at Wilmington, NC	M,W	Western Michigan University, MI	M,W
U at Albany, State U of NY, NY	M,W			Western Washington University, WA	M,W
The University of Akron, OH	M	University of Northern Colorado, CO	W	Westmar University, IA	M,W
The University of Alabama at Birmingham, AL	M	University of North Florida, FL	M,W	Westmont College, CA	M,W
		University of Notre Dame, IN	M,W	West Texas A&M University, TX	M,W
The University of Alabama in Huntsville, AL	M,W	University of Oregon, OR	W	West Virginia University, WV	M,W
		University of Pittsburgh, PA	M,W	West Virginia Wesleyan College, WV	M,W
University of Arizona, AZ	W	University of Portland, OR	M,W	Wheeling Jesuit University, WV	M,W
University of Arkansas, Fayetteville, AR	W	U of Puerto Rico, Cayey University College, PR	M	William Carey College, MS	M,W
				William Jewell College, MO	M
University of Arkansas at Little Rock, AR	M,W			William Woods University, MO	M,W
				Wingate University, NC	M
				Winona State University, MN	W
				Winthrop University, SC	M

Soccer (continued)

Wofford College, SC	M,W
Wright State University, OH	M
Xavier University, OH	M,W
York College, NE	M,W

SOFTBALL

Abilene Christian University, TX	W
Adelphi University, NY	W
Alabama State University, AL	W
Alderson-Broaddus College, WV	W
American International College, MA	W
Anderson College, SC	W
Aquinas College, MI	W
Arizona State University, AZ	W
Ashland University, OH	W
Auburn University, AL	W
Augustana College, SD	W
Austin Peay State University, TN	W
Azusa Pacific University, CA	W
Baker University, KS	W
Barber-Scotia College, NC	W
Barry University, FL	W
Barton College, NC	W
Baylor University, TX	W
Becker College–Leicester Campus, MA	W
Becker College–Worcester Campus, MA	W
Belhaven College, MS	W
Bellarmine College, KY	W
Belmont Abbey College, NC	W
Belmont University, TN	W
Benedictine College, KS	W
Bethany College, KS	W
Bethel College, IN	W
Bethune-Cookman College, FL	W
Bloomfield College, NJ	W
Bloomsburg University of Pennsylvania, PA	W
Bluefield College, VA	W
Bluefield State College, WV	W
Boston College, MA	W
Boston University, MA	W
Bowie State University, MD	W
Bowling Green State University, OH	W
Bradley University, IL	W
Brescia College, KY	W
Brewton-Parker College, GA	W
Briar Cliff College, IA	W
Butler University, IN	W
Caldwell College, NJ	W
California Baptist College, CA	W
California Polytechnic State U, San Luis Obispo, CA	W
California State University, Bakersfield, CA	W
California State University, Fresno, CA	W
California State University, Fullerton, CA	W
California State University, Long Beach, CA	W
California State University, Northridge, CA	W
California State University, Sacramento, CA	W

California State University, San Bernardino, CA	W
Cameron University, OK	W
Campbell University, NC	W
Canisius College, NY	W
Carson-Newman College, TN	W
Catawba College, NC	W
Cedarville College, OH	W
Centenary College of Louisiana, LA	W
Central Connecticut State University, CT	W
Central Methodist College, MO	W
Central Missouri State University, MO	W
Charleston Southern University, SC	W
Christian Brothers University, TN	W
Clarion University of Pennsylvania, PA	W
Cleveland State University, OH	W
Coastal Carolina University, SC	W
Coker College, SC	W
College of Charleston, SC	W
College of St. Francis, IL	W
College of St. Joseph, VT	W
College of Saint Mary, NE	W
Colorado School of Mines, CO	W
Columbia College, MO	W
Columbus State University, GA	W
Concordia College, MI	W
Concordia College, NY	W
Concordia University, CA	W
Cornerstone College, MI	W
Creighton University, NE	W
Culver-Stockton College, MO	W
Cumberland College, KY	W
Cumberland University, TN	W
Dakota Wesleyan University, SD	W
Dana College, NE	W
Davis & Elkins College, WV	W
DePaul University, IL	W
Doane College, NE	W
Dominican College of Blauvelt, NY	W
Dowling College, NY	W
Drake University, IA	W
Drexel University, PA	W
East Carolina University, NC	W
Eastern Illinois University, IL	W
Eastern Kentucky University, KY	W
Eastern Michigan University, MI	W
Eckerd College, FL	W
Edinboro University of Pennsylvania, PA	W
Elon College, NC	W
Emmanuel College, GA	W
Emporia State University, KS	W
Erskine College, SC	W
Evangel College, MO	W
Fairfield University, CT	W
Faulkner University, AL	W
Florida Institute of Technology, FL	W
Florida Southern College, FL	W
Florida State University, FL	W
Fordham University, NY	W
Fort Lewis College, CO	W
Francis Marion University, SC	W
Franklin Pierce College, NH	W
Freed-Hardeman University, TN	M
Friends University, KS	W

Furman University, SC	W
Gannon University, PA	W
Gardner-Webb University, NC	W
Geneva College, PA	W
George Mason University, VA	W
Georgetown College, KY	W
Georgia College and State University, GA	W
Georgian Court College, NJ	W
Georgia Southern University, GA	W
Georgia Southwestern State University, GA	W
Georgia State University, GA	W
Goldey-Beacom College, DE	W
Goshen College, IN	W
Grace College, IN	W
Graceland College, IA	W
Grand Valley State University, MI	W
Grand View College, IA	W
Hannibal-LaGrange College, MO	W
Hastings College, NE	W
Hawaii Pacific University, HI	W
Hillsdale College, MI	W
Hofstra University, NY	W
Holy Family College, PA	W
Hope International University, CA	W
Huntington College, IN	W
Huron University, SD	W
Illinois State University, IL	W
Indiana Institute of Technology, IN	W
Indiana State University, IN	W
Indiana University Bloomington, IN	W
Indiana U–Purdue U Indianapolis, IN	W
Indiana Wesleyan University, IN	W
Iowa State University of Science and Technology, IA	W
Iowa Wesleyan College, IA	W
Jacksonville State University, AL	W
Judson College, IL	W
Kansas Newman College, KS	W
Kansas Wesleyan University, KS	W
Kennesaw State University, GA	W
Kent State University, OH	W
Kentucky Wesleyan College, KY	W
King College, TN	W
Kutztown University of Pennsylvania, PA	W
Lambuth University, TN	W
Lander University, SC	W
La Salle University, PA	W
Lees-McRae College, NC	W
Lee University, TN	W
Lehigh University, PA	W
Le Moyne College, NY	W
Lenoir-Rhyne College, NC	W
Lewis University, IL	W
Limestone College, SC	W
Lincoln Memorial University, TN	W
Lincoln University, MO	W
Lindenwood College, MO	W
Lindsey Wilson College, KY	W
Lock Haven University of Pennsylvania, PA	W
Long Island U, C.W. Post Campus, NY	W
Long Island U, Southampton College, NY	W

Louisiana Tech University, LA	W	Oklahoma Baptist University, OK	W	Samford University, AL	W
Loyola University Chicago, IL	W	Oklahoma Christian U of Science and Arts, OK	W	San Diego State University, CA	W
Malone College, OH	W			Santa Clara University, CA	W
Manhattan College, NY	W	Oklahoma City University, OK	W	Seton Hall University, NJ	W
Mankato State University, MN	W	Oklahoma State U, OK	W	Seton Hill College, PA	W
Marian College, IN	W	Olivet Nazarene University, IL	W	Shaw University, NC	W
Marist College, NY	W	Oregon Institute of Technology, OR	W	Shepherd College, WV	W
Marshall University, WV	W	Oregon State University, OR	W	Shippensburg University of Pennsylvania, PA	W
Mars Hill College, NC	W	Ottawa University, KS	W		
Martin Methodist College, TN	W	Pace University, NY	W	Shorter College, GA	W
Marycrest International University, IA	W	Penn State U Univ Park Campus, PA	W	Siena College, NY	W
McKendree College, IL	W	Peru State College, NE	W	Siena Heights College, MI	W
McNeese State University, LA	W	Pfeiffer University, NC	W	Slippery Rock University of Pennsylvania, PA	W
Mercer University, Macon, GA	W	Philadelphia College of Textiles and Science, PA	W	South Dakota State University, SD	W
Mercyhurst College, PA	W			Southeastern Louisiana University, LA	W
Merrimack College, MA	W	Phillips University, OK	W	Southeastern Oklahoma State University, OK	W
Mesa State College, CO	W	Piedmont College, GA	W		
Miami University, OH	W	Pikeville College, KY	W	Southeast Missouri State University, MO	W
Michigan Christian College, MI	W	Pittsburg State University, KS	W		
Middle Tennessee State University, TN	W	Point Park College, PA	W	Southern California College, CA	W
		Portland State University, OR	W	Southern Illinois University at Carbondale, IL	W
Midway College, KY	W	Providence College, RI	W		
Millersville University of Pennsylvania, PA	W	Purdue University, West Lafayette, IN	W	Southern Illinois University at Edwardsville, IL	W
Minot State University, ND	W	Queens College, NC	W	Southern Nazarene University, OK	W
Mississippi University for Women, MS	W	Queens Coll of the City U of NY, NY	M	Southern Utah University, UT	W
		Quincy University, IL	W	Southern Wesleyan University, SC	W
Missouri Baptist College, MO	W	Quinnipiac College, CT	W	Southwest Baptist University, MO	W
Missouri Southern State College, MO	W	Radford University, VA	W	Southwest Missouri State University, MO	W
Missouri Western State College, MO	W	Regis University, CO	W		
Molloy College, NY	W	Rider University, NJ	W	Southwest State University, MN	W
Monmouth University, NJ	W	Robert Morris College, PA	W	Southwest Texas State University, TX	W
Montreat College, NC	W	Rutgers, State U of NJ, College of Engineering, NJ	W	Spring Arbor College, MI	W
Moorhead State University, MN	W			Stephen F. Austin State University, TX	W
Morehead State University, KY	W	Rutgers, State U of NJ, College of Pharmacy, NJ	W	Stetson University, FL	W
Morris College, SC	W			Sue Bennett College, KY	W
Mount Olive College, NC	W	Rutgers, State U of NJ, Cook College, NJ	W	Tabor College, KS	W
Mount St. Clare College, IA	W			Tarleton State University, TX	W
Mount Vernon Nazarene College, OH	W	Rutgers, State U of NJ, Douglass College, NJ	W	Taylor University, IN	W
Newberry College, SC	W			Teikyo Post University, CT	W
New Mexico State University, NM	W	Rutgers, State U of NJ, Livingston College, NJ	W	Temple University, Philadelphia, PA	W
New York Institute of Technology, NY	W			Tennessee Technological University, TN	W
Niagara University, NY	W	Rutgers, State U of NJ, Mason Gross School of Arts, NJ	W		
Nicholls State University, LA	W			Tennessee Wesleyan College, TN	W
North Dakota State University, ND	W	Rutgers, State U of NJ, Rutgers College, NJ	W	Texas A&M University, College Station, TX	W
Northeastern Illinois University, IL	W				
Northeastern State University, OK	W	Saginaw Valley State University, MI	W	Texas Lutheran University, TX	W
Northeast Louisiana University, LA	W	St. Andrews Presbyterian College, NC	W	Texas Tech University, TX	W
Northern Illinois University, IL	W	St. Bonaventure University, NY	W	Texas Wesleyan University, TX	W
Northern Kentucky University, KY	W	St. Edward's University, TX	W	Texas Woman's University, TX	W
Northern State University, SD	W	Saint Francis College, IN	W	Thomas College, GA	W
North Greenville College, SC	W	St. Francis College, NY	W	Tiffin University, OH	W
Northwestern College, IA	W	Saint Francis College, PA	W	Towson University, MD	W
Northwestern State University of Louisiana, LA	W	St. John's University, NY	W	Transylvania University, KY	W
		Saint Joseph's College, IN	W	Trevecca Nazarene University, TN	W
Northwestern University, IL	W	Saint Joseph's University, PA	W	Trinity Christian College, IL	W
Northwest Missouri State University, MO	W	Saint Leo College, FL	W	Trinity International University, IL	W
		Saint Louis University, MO	W	Tri-State University, IN	W
Northwood University, MI	W	Saint Martin's College, WA	W	Truman State University, MO	W
Northwood University, Florida Campus, FL	W	Saint Mary College, KS	W	Tusculum College, TN	W
		Saint Mary-of-the-Woods College, IN	W	Union College, KY	W
Northwood University, Texas Campus, TX	W	Saint Mary's College of California, CA	W	Union University, TN	W
Nova Southeastern University, FL	W	St. Thomas Aquinas College, NY	W	U at Albany, State U of NY, NY	W
Oakland City University, IN	W	St. Thomas University, FL	W	The University of Akron, OH	W
Ohio Dominican College, OH	W	Saint Vincent College, PA	W	University of Arizona, AZ	W
The Ohio State University, OH	W	Saint Xavier University, IL	W		
		Salem-Teikyo University, WV	W		

Softball (continued)

University of Arkansas, Fayetteville, AR	W
University of Bridgeport, CT	W
University of California, Los Angeles, CA	W
University of California, Riverside, CA	W
University of California, Santa Barbara, CA	W
University of Central Oklahoma, OK	W
The University of Charleston, WV	W
University of Colorado at Colorado Springs, CO	W
University of Connecticut, Storrs, CT	W
University of Dayton, OH	W
University of Delaware, DE	W
University of Detroit Mercy, MI	W
The University of Findlay, OH	W
University of Florida, FL	W
University of Hartford, CT	W
University of Hawaii at Hilo, HI	W
University of Hawaii at Manoa, HI	W
University of Illinois at Chicago, IL	W
University of Indianapolis, IN	W
The University of Iowa, IA	W
University of Kansas, KS	W
University of Maine, Orono, ME	W
University of Mary, ND	W
University of Mary Hardin-Baylor, TX	W
University of Maryland Baltimore County, MD	W
University of Maryland College Park, MD	W
University of Massachusetts Amherst, MA	W
University of Michigan, Ann Arbor, MI	M
University of Minnesota, Crookston, MN	W
University of Minnesota, Duluth, MN	W
University of Mississippi, MS	W
University of Missouri–Columbia, MO	W
University of Missouri–Kansas City, MO	W
University of Missouri–Rolla, MO	W
University of Missouri–St. Louis, MO	W
University of Mobile, AL	W
University of Nebraska at Kearney, NE	W
University of Nebraska at Omaha, NE	W
University of Nebraska–Lincoln, NE	W
University of Nevada, Las Vegas, NV	W
University of New Haven, CT	W
University of New Mexico, NM	W
University of North Carolina at Asheville, NC	W
University of North Carolina at Charlotte, NC	W
University of North Carolina at Greensboro, NC	W
University of North Carolina at Pembroke, NC	W
University of North Carolina at Wilmington, NC	W
University of North Dakota, ND	W
University of Northern Iowa, IA	W

University of North Florida, FL	W
University of Notre Dame, IN	W
University of Oklahoma, OK	W
University of Oregon, OR	W
University of Rhode Island, RI	W
University of Rio Grande, OH	W
U of South Carolina, Columbia, SC	W
U of South Carolina–Aiken, SC	W
U of South Carolina–Spartanburg, SC	W
University of South Dakota, SD	W
University of Southern Colorado, CO	W
University of Southern Indiana, IN	W
University of South Florida, FL	W
University of Southwestern Louisiana, LA	W
The University of Tampa, FL	W
University of Tennessee, Knoxville, TN	W
The University of Texas at Arlington, TX	W
The University of Texas at Austin, TX	W
The University of Texas at San Antonio, TX	W
University of the Pacific, CA	W
University of Toledo, OH	W
University of Tulsa, OK	W
University of Virginia, VA	W
University of Washington, WA	W
The University of West Alabama, AL	W
University of West Florida, FL	W
University of Wisconsin–Green Bay, WI	W
University of Wisconsin–Madison, WI	W
University of Wisconsin–Parkside, WI	W
Urbana University, OH	W
Utah State University, UT	W
Valdosta State University, GA	W
Valley City State University, ND	W
Valparaiso University, IN	W
Villanova University, PA	W
Virginia Intermont College, VA	W
Virginia State University, VA	W
Virginia Union University, VA	W
Wagner College, NY	W
Walsh University, OH	W
Washburn University of Topeka, KS	W
Wayne State College, NE	W
Wayne State University, MI	W
Webber College, FL	W
West Chester University of Pennsylvania, PA	W
Western Illinois University, IL	W
Western Michigan University, MI	W
Western Washington University, WA	W
West Liberty State College, WV	W
Westmar University, IA	W
Westminster College, PA	W
West Virginia State College, WV	W
West Virginia University Institute of Technology, WV	W
West Virginia Wesleyan College, WV	W
Wichita State University, KS	W
William Jewell College, MO	W
William Woods University, MO	W
Wilmington College, DE	W
Wingate University, NC	W
Winona State University, MN	W

Winston-Salem State University, NC	W
Winthrop University, SC	W
Wright State University, OH	W
York College, NE	W
Youngstown State University, OH	W

SWIMMING AND DIVING

Adelphi University, NY	M,W
American University, DC	M,W
Arizona State University, AZ	M,W
Ashland University, OH	M,W
Auburn University, AL	M,W
Ball State University, IN	M,W
Bayamón Technological University College, PR	M,W
Bloomsburg University of Pennsylvania, PA	M,W
Boston College, MA	W
Boston University, MA	M,W
Bowling Green State University, OH	M,W
Bradley University, IL	M,W
Brigham Young University, UT	M,W
Butler University, IN	M,W
California State University, Bakersfield, CA	M,W
California State University, Fresno, CA	W
California State University, Long Beach, CA	M,W
California State University, Northridge, CA	M,W
California State University, San Bernardino, CA	M,W
Canisius College, NY	M,W
Catawba College, NC	W
Central Connecticut State University, CT	M,W
Chicago State University, IL	M,W
Clarion University of Pennsylvania, PA	M,W
Clemson University, SC	M,W
Cleveland State University, OH	M,W
College of Charleston, SC	M,W
College of William and Mary, VA	M,W
Colorado School of Mines, CO	M,W
Colorado State University, CO	W
Cumberland College, KY	M,W
Davidson College, NC	W
Delta State University, MS	M,W
Drexel University, PA	M,W
Drury College, MO	M,W
Duquesne University, PA	M,W
East Carolina University, NC	M,W
Eastern Michigan University, MI	M,W
Edinboro University of Pennsylvania, PA	M,W
Fairfield University, CT	M,W
Fairmont State College, WV	M,W
Florida Agricultural and Mechanical University, FL	M,W
Florida Atlantic University, FL	M,W
Florida State University, FL	M,W
Fordham University, NY	M,W
Gannon University, PA	M,W
The George Washington University, DC	M,W
Georgia Institute of Technology, GA	M

Georgia Southern University, GA	M,W	
Grand Valley State University, MI	W	
Henderson State University, AR	M,W	
Hillsdale College, MI	W	
Howard University, DC	M,W	
Illinois Institute of Technology, IL	M,W	
Illinois State University, IL	W	
Indiana University Bloomington, IN	M,W	
Inter American U of PR, Metropolitan Campus, PR	M,W	
Iowa State University of Science and Technology, IA	M,W	
James Madison University, VA	M,W	
John Brown University, AR	M,W	
Kutztown University of Pennsylvania, PA	M,W	
La Salle University, PA	M,W	
Lehigh University, PA	M,W	
Louisiana State University and A&M College, LA	M,W	
Mankato State University, MN	M,W	
Marist College, NY	M,W	
Metropolitan State College of Denver, CO	M,W	
Miami University, OH	M,W	
Michigan State University, MI	M,W	
Millersville University of Pennsylvania, PA	W	
Morehouse College, GA	M	
New Mexico State University, NM	M,W	
Niagara University, NY	M,W	
North Carolina State University, NC	M,W	
Northeastern Illinois University, IL	M,W	
Northeastern University, MA	W	
Northeast Louisiana University, LA	M	
Northern Arizona University, AZ	M,W	
Northern Illinois University, IL	M,W	
Northern Michigan University, MI	W	
Northwestern University, IL	M,W	
Oakland University, MI	M,W	
The Ohio State University, OH	M,W	
Ohio University, OH	M,W	
Old Dominion University, VA	M,W	
Oregon State University, OR	W	
Penn State U Univ Park Campus, PA	M,W	
Pepperdine University, Malibu, CA	W	
Pfeiffer University, NC	W	
Providence College, RI	W	
Purdue University, West Lafayette, IN	M,W	
Queens Coll of the City U of NY, NY	M,W	
Rice University, TX	M,W	
Rider University, NJ	M	
Rutgers, State U of NJ, College of Engineering, NJ	M,W	
Rutgers, State U of NJ, College of Pharmacy, NJ	M,W	
Rutgers, State U of NJ, Cook College, NJ	M,W	
Rutgers, State U of NJ, Douglass College, NJ	W	
Rutgers, State U of NJ, Livingston College, NJ	M,W	
Rutgers, State U of NJ, Mason Gross School of Arts, NJ	M,W	
Rutgers, State U of NJ, Rutgers College, NJ	M,W	
St. Bonaventure University, NY	M,W	
St. Cloud State University, MN	M,W	
St. Francis College, NY	M,W	
Saint Francis College, PA	W	
St. John's University, NY	M,W	
Saint Louis University, MO	M,W	
Saint Peter's College, Jersey City, NJ	M,W	
Salem-Teikyo University, WV	M,W	
San Diego State University, CA	W	
San Jose State University, CA	W	
Seton Hall University, NJ	M,W	
Shippensburg University of Pennsylvania, PA	M,W	
Slippery Rock University of Pennsylvania, PA	M,W	
South Dakota State University, SD	M,W	
Southern Illinois University at Carbondale, IL	M,W	
Southern Methodist University, TX	M,W	
Southwest Missouri State University, MO	M	
Stanford University, CA	M,W	
State U of NY at Buffalo, NY	M,W	
Syracuse University, NY	M,W	
Texas A&M University, College Station, TX	M,W	
Texas Christian University, TX	M,W	
Towson University, MD	M,W	
Transylvania University, KY	M,W	
Truman State University, MO	W	
Union College, KY	M,W	
U of Alaska Anchorage, AK	M	
University of Arizona, AZ	M,W	
University of Arkansas, Fayetteville, AR	M,W	
University of California, Berkeley, CA	M,W	
University of California, Irvine, CA	M,W	
University of California, Los Angeles, CA	W	
University of California, Santa Barbara, CA	M,W	
The University of Charleston, WV	M,W	
University of Cincinnati, OH	M,W	
University of Connecticut, Storrs, CT	M,W	
University of Denver, CO	M,W	
University of Evansville, IN	M,W	
The University of Findlay, OH	M,W	
University of Florida, FL	M,W	
University of Georgia, GA	M,W	
University of Hawaii at Manoa, HI	M,W	
University of Houston, TX	W	
University of Illinois at Chicago, IL	M,W	
University of Illinois at Urbana–Champaign, IL	W	
University of Indianapolis, IN	M,W	
The University of Iowa, IA	M,W	
University of Kansas, KS	M,W	
University of Kentucky, KY	M,W	
University of Louisville, KY	M,W	
University of Maine, Orono, ME	M,W	
University of Maryland Baltimore County, MD	M,W	
University of Maryland College Park, MD	M,W	
University of Massachusetts Amherst, MA	M,W	
University of Massachusetts Lowell, MA	M	
University of Miami, FL	M,W	
University of Michigan, Ann Arbor, MI	M,W	
University of Minnesota, Twin Cities Campus, MN	M,W	
University of Missouri–Columbia, MO	M,W	
University of Missouri–Rolla, MO	M	
University of Missouri–St. Louis, MO	M,W	
University of Nebraska at Kearney, NE	W	
University of Nebraska–Lincoln, NE	M,W	
University of Nevada, Las Vegas, NV	M,W	
University of Nevada, Reno, NV	W	
University of New Hampshire, Durham, NH	W	
University of New Mexico, NM	M,W	
University of North Carolina at Wilmington, NC	M,W	
University of North Dakota, ND	W	
University of Northern Colorado, CO	W	
University of Northern Iowa, IA	W	
University of Notre Dame, IN	M,W	
University of Pittsburgh, PA	M,W	
U of Puerto Rico, Cayey University College, PR	M	
U of Puerto Rico, Mayagüez Campus, PR	M,W	
U of Puerto Rico, Río Piedras, PR	M,W	
University of Rhode Island, RI	M,W	
University of Richmond, VA	W	
University of San Diego, CA	W	
U of South Carolina, Columbia, SC	M,W	
University of South Dakota, SD	M	
University of Southern California, CA	M,W	
The University of Tampa, FL	M,W	
University of Tennessee, Knoxville, TN	M,W	
The University of Texas at Austin, TX	M,W	
University of the Pacific, CA	M,W	
University of the Sacred Heart, PR	M,W	
University of Toledo, OH	M,W	
University of Utah, UT	M,W	
University of Virginia, VA	M,W	
University of Washington, WA	M,W	
University of Wisconsin–Green Bay, WI	M,W	
University of Wisconsin–Madison, WI	M,W	
University of Wisconsin–Milwaukee, WI	M,W	
University of Wyoming, WY	M,W	
Valparaiso University, IN	M,W	
Villanova University, PA	W	
Virginia Military Institute, VA	M	
Virginia Polytechnic Institute and State U, VA	M,W	
Walsh University, OH	W	
Washington State University, WA	W	
Wayne State University, MI	M,W	
West Chester University of Pennsylvania, PA	M,W	
Western Illinois University, IL	M,W	
Western Kentucky University, KY	M	
Westminster College, PA	W	
West Virginia University, WV	M,W	
West Virginia Wesleyan College, WV	M,W	
Wheeling Jesuit University, WV	M	
Wingate University, NC	W	

Swimming and Diving (continued)

Wright State University, OH	M,W
Xavier University, OH	M,W

TABLE TENNIS (PING-PONG)

Inter American U of PR, San Germán Campus, PR	M,W
U of Puerto Rico, Cayey University College, PR	M
U of Puerto Rico, Mayagüez Campus, PR	M,W
U of Puerto Rico, Río Piedras, PR	M,W

TENNIS

Abilene Christian University, TX	M,W
Adelphi University, NY	M,W
Albertson College of Idaho, ID	M,W
Alcorn State University, MS	M,W
American University, DC	W
Anderson College, SC	M,W
Appalachian State University, NC	M,W
Aquinas College, MI	M,W
Arizona State University, AZ	M,W
Arkansas State University, AR	W
Arkansas Tech University, AR	W
Armstrong Atlantic State University, GA	M,W
Auburn University, AL	M,W
Auburn University at Montgomery, AL	M,W
Augusta State University, GA	M,W
Austin Peay State University, TN	M,W
Azusa Pacific University, CA	M
Baker University, KS	M,W
Ball State University, IN	M,W
Barber-Scotia College, NC	M
Barry University, FL	M,W
Barton College, NC	M,W
Bayamón Technological University College, PR	M,W
Baylor University, TX	M,W
Becker College–Leicester Campus, MA	M,W
Becker College–Worcester Campus, MA	M,W
Belhaven College, MS	M,W
Bellarmine College, KY	M,W
Belmont Abbey College, NC	M,W
Belmont University, TN	M,W
Bemidji State University, MN	W
Berry College, GA	M,W
Bethany College, KS	M,W
Bethel College, IN	M,W
Bethel College, KS	M,W
Bethel College, TN	W
Bethune-Cookman College, FL	M,W
Biola University, CA	M,W
Birmingham-Southern College, AL	M,W
Bloomsburg University of Pennsylvania, PA	M,W
Bluefield College, VA	M,W
Bluefield State College, WV	M,W
Blue Mountain College, MS	W
Boise State University, ID	M,W
Boston College, MA	W
Boston University, MA	W
Bowling Green State University, OH	M,W

Bradley University, IL	M,W
Brenau University, GA	W
Brescia College, KY	M,W
Brewton-Parker College, GA	M,W
Brigham Young University, UT	M,W
Brigham Young University–Hawaii Campus, HI	M,W
Butler University, IN	M,W
Caldwell College, NJ	M,W
California Baptist College, CA	M,W
California State Polytechnic University, Pomona, CA	M,W
California State University, Bakersfield, CA	W
California State University, Fresno, CA	M,W
California State University, Fullerton, CA	W
California State University, Long Beach, CA	W
California State University, Los Angeles, CA	M,W
California State University, Northridge, CA	W
California State University, Sacramento, CA	M,W
California University of Pennsylvania, PA	W
Cameron University, OK	M,W
Campbell University, NC	M,W
Canisius College, NY	M,W
Carlow College, PA	W
Carson-Newman College, TN	M,W
Catawba College, NC	M,W
Cedarville College, OH	M,W
Centenary College of Louisiana, LA	M,W
Central Connecticut State University, CT	M,W
Central Methodist College, MO	M,W
Charleston Southern University, SC	M,W
Cheyney University of Pennsylvania, PA	M,W
Christian Brothers University, TN	M,W
The Citadel, The Military Coll of South Carolina, SC	M
Clarion University of Pennsylvania, PA	W
Clark Atlanta University, GA	M,W
Clayton College & State University, GA	W
Clemson University, SC	M,W
Cleveland State University, OH	W
Clinch Valley College of the U of Virginia, VA	M
Coastal Carolina University, SC	M,W
Coker College, SC	M,W
College of Charleston, SC	M,W
College of St. Francis, IL	M,W
College of Saint Mary, NE	W
College of William and Mary, VA	M,W
Colorado Christian University, CO	M,W
Colorado School of Mines, CO	M,W
Columbia College, SC	W
Columbus State University, GA	M,W
Concordia College, NE	M,W
Concordia College, NY	M,W
Concordia University at Austin, TX	M,W

Cornerstone College, MI	M
Creighton University, NE	M,W
Cumberland College, KY	M,W
Cumberland University, TN	M,W
David Lipscomb University, TN	M,W
Davidson College, NC	W
Davis & Elkins College, WV	M,W
Delta State University, MS	M,W
DePaul University, IL	M,W
Dominican College of San Rafael, CA	M,W
Dowling College, NY	M,W
Drake University, IA	M,W
Drexel University, PA	M
Drury College, MO	M,W
Duke University, NC	M,W
Duquesne University, PA	M,W
East Carolina University, NC	M,W
East Central University, OK	M,W
Eastern Illinois University, IL	W
Eastern Kentucky University, KY	M,W
Eastern Michigan University, MI	M,W
Eastern New Mexico University, NM	W
Eastern Washington University, WA	M,W
East Tennessee State University, TN	M,W
Eckerd College, FL	M,W
Edinboro University of Pennsylvania, PA	M,W
Edward Waters College, FL	M,W
Elon College, NC	M,W
Embry-Riddle Aeronautical University, FL	M
Emporia State University, KS	M,W
Erskine College, SC	M,W
Fairfield University, CT	M,W
Fairleigh Dickinson U, Teaneck-Hackensack, NJ	M,W
Fairmont State College, WV	M,W
Ferris State University, MI	M,W
Flagler College, FL	M,W
Florida Agricultural and Mechanical University, FL	M,W
Florida Atlantic University, FL	M,W
Florida Institute of Technology, FL	M
Florida International University, FL	M,W
Florida Southern College, FL	M,W
Florida State University, FL	M,W
Fordham University, NY	M,W
Fort Hays State University, KS	W
Fort Valley State University, GA	M,W
Francis Marion University, SC	M,W
Franklin Pierce College, NH	M,W
Freed-Hardeman University, TN	M,W
Friends University, KS	M,W
Furman University, SC	M,W
Gannon University, PA	M,W
Gardner-Webb University, NC	M,W
Geneva College, PA	M,W
George Mason University, VA	M,W
Georgetown College, KY	M,W
The George Washington University, DC	M,W
Georgia College and State University, GA	M,W
Georgia Institute of Technology, GA	M,W
Georgia Southern University, GA	M,W
Georgia Southwestern State University, GA	M,W

Georgia State University, GA	M,W	Lynn University, FL	M,W	Northwestern University, IL	M,W
Gonzaga University, WA	M,W	Lyon College, AR	M,W	Northwest Missouri State University, MO	M,W
Goshen College, IN	M,W	Malone College, OH	M,W	Northwood University, MI	M,W
Grace College, IN	M,W	Manhattan College, NY	M,W	Nova Southeastern University, FL	W
Graceland College, IA	M,W	Mankato State University, MN	M,W	Oakland University, MI	W
Grambling State University, LA	M	Marian College, IN	M,W	The Ohio State University, OH	M,W
Grand Canyon University, AZ	W	Marist College, NY	M,W	Oklahoma Baptist University, OK	M,W
Grand Valley State University, MI	W	Marquette University, WI	M,W	Oklahoma Christian U of Science and Arts, OK	M
Green Mountain College, VT	M,W	Marshall University, WV	W	Oklahoma City University, OK	M,W
Harding University, AR	M,W	Mars Hill College, NC	M,W	Oklahoma State U, OK	M,W
Hastings College, NE	M,W	McKendree College, IL	M,W	Old Dominion University, VA	M,W
Hawaii Pacific University, HI	M,W	McNeese State University, LA	W	Oral Roberts University, OK	M,W
Henderson State University, AR	M,W	McPherson College, KS	M,W	Pace University, NY	M,W
Hillsdale College, MI	M,W	Mercer University, Macon, GA	M,W	Penn State U Univ Park Campus, PA	M,W
Hofstra University, NY	M,W	Mercyhurst College, PA	M,W	Pepperdine University, Malibu, CA	M,W
Howard University, DC	M,W	Merrimack College, MA	M,W	Pfeiffer University, NC	M,W
Huntington College, IN	M,W	Mesa State College, CO	M,W	Philadelphia College of Textiles and Science, PA	M,W
Idaho State University, ID	M,W	Metropolitan State College of Denver, CO	M,W	Phillips University, OK	W
Illinois State University, IL	M,W	Miami University, OH	M,W	Pikeville College, KY	W
Indiana State University, IN	M,W	Michigan State University, MI	M,W	Point Loma Nazarene College, CA	M,W
Indiana University Bloomington, IN	M,W	Middle Tennessee State University, TN	M,W	Portland State University, OR	W
Indiana U–Purdue U Fort Wayne, IN	M,W	Midland Lutheran College, NE	M,W	Presbyterian College, SC	M,W
Indiana U–Purdue U Indianapolis, IN	M,W	Midway College, KY	W	Providence College, RI	M,W
Indiana Wesleyan University, IN	M,W	Millersville University of Pennsylvania, PA	M,W	Purdue University, West Lafayette, IN	M,W
Inter American U of PR, San Germán Campus, PR	M,W	Milligan College, TN	M,W	Queens College, NC	M,W
Iona College, New Rochelle, NY	M	Mississippi State University, MS	M,W	Queens Coll of the City U of NY, NY	M,W
Iowa State University of Science and Technology, IA	W	Mississippi University for Women, MS	W	Quincy University, IL	W
Jackson State University, MS	M	Mississippi Valley State University, MS	M	Quinnipiac College, CT	M,W
Jacksonville State University, AL	M,W	Missouri Southern State College, MO	W	Radford University, VA	M,W
Jacksonville University, FL	M,W	Missouri Western State College, MO	W	Regis University, CO	W
James Madison University, VA	M,W	Molloy College, NY	W	Rice University, TX	M,W
John Brown University, AR	M,W	Monmouth University, NJ	M,W	Rider University, NJ	M,W
Johnson C. Smith University, NC	M	Montana State U–Bozeman, MT	M,W	Robert Morris College, PA	M,W
Judson College, IL	M,W	Montreat College, NC	M,W	Rockhurst College, MO	M,W
Kansas State University, KS	W	Morehead State University, KY	M,W	Rollins College, FL	M,W
Kennesaw State University, GA	W	Morehouse College, GA	M	Rust College, MS	M,W
Kentucky State University, KY	M,W	Morgan State University, MD	M,W	Rutgers, State U of NJ, College of Engineering, NJ	M,W
Kentucky Wesleyan College, KY	M,W	Mount Olive College, NC	M,W	Rutgers, State U of NJ, College of Pharmacy, NJ	M,W
King College, TN	M,W	Mount St. Clare College, IA	M,W	Rutgers, State U of NJ, Cook College, NJ	M,W
Kutztown University of Pennsylvania, PA	M,W	Mount Saint Mary's College and Seminary, MD	M,W	Rutgers, State U of NJ, Douglass College, NJ	W
Lamar University, TX	M,W	Murray State University, KY	M,W	Rutgers, State U of NJ, Livingston College, NJ	M,W
Lambuth University, TN	M,W	Newberry College, SC	M,W	Rutgers, State U of NJ, Mason Gross School of Arts, NJ	M,W
Lander University, SC	M,W	New Mexico State University, NM	M,W	Rutgers, State U of NJ, Rutgers College, NJ	M,W
La Salle University, PA	M,W	Niagara University, NY	M,W	Saginaw Valley State University, MI	W
Lees-McRae College, NC	M,W	Nicholls State University, LA	W	St. Ambrose University, IA	M,W
Lee University, TN	M,W	North Carolina Agricultural and Technical State U, NC	M,W	St. Andrews Presbyterian College, NC	M,W
Lehigh University, PA	M,W	North Carolina State University, NC	M,W	Saint Augustine's College, NC	M
Le Moyne College, NY	M,W	Northeastern Illinois University, IL	M,W	St. Bonaventure University, NY	M,W
Lenoir-Rhyne College, NC	M,W	Northeastern State University, OK	M,W	St. Edward's University, TX	M,W
Lewis-Clark State College, ID	M,W	Northeast Louisiana University, LA	M,W	Saint Francis College, IN	W
Lewis University, IL	M,W	Northern Arizona University, AZ	M,W	St. Francis College, NY	M,W
Limestone College, SC	M,W	Northern Illinois University, IL	M,W	Saint Francis College, PA	M,W
Lincoln Memorial University, TN	M,W	Northern Kentucky University, KY	M,W	St. John's University, NY	M,W
Lincoln University, MO	W	Northern State University, SD	W	Saint Joseph's College, IN	M,W
Lindenwood College, MO	W	North Georgia College & State University, GA	M,W	Saint Joseph's University, PA	M,W
Lindsey Wilson College, KY	M,W	North Greenville College, SC	M,W	Saint Leo College, FL	M,W
Long Island U, C.W. Post Campus, NY	W	Northwestern College, IA	M,W	Saint Louis University, MO	M,W
Longwood College, VA	W	Northwestern State University of Louisiana, LA	W		
Louisiana College, LA	W				
Louisiana State University and A&M College, LA	M,W				
Louisiana Tech University, LA	W				
Loyola Marymount University, CA	W				

Tennis (continued)

Saint Mary's College of California, CA	M,W
St. Mary's University of San Antonio, TX	M,W
Saint Peter's College, Jersey City, NJ	M,W
St. Thomas University, FL	M,W
Saint Vincent College, PA	M
Samford University, AL	M,W
Sam Houston State University, TX	M,W
San Diego State University, CA	M,W
San Jose State University, CA	M,W
Santa Clara University, CA	M,W
Seton Hall University, NJ	M,W
Seton Hill College, PA	W
Shaw University, NC	M,W
Shippensburg University of Pennsylvania, PA	W
Shorter College, GA	M,W
Siena Heights College, MI	M,W
Slippery Rock University of Pennsylvania, PA	M,W
Southeastern Louisiana University, LA	M,W
Southeastern Oklahoma State University, OK	M,W
Southeast Missouri State University, MO	W
Southern California College, CA	M,W
Southern Illinois University at Carbondale, IL	M,W
Southern Illinois University at Edwardsville, IL	M,W
Southern Methodist University, TX	M,W
Southern Nazarene University, OK	M,W
Southern Polytechnic State University, GA	M
Southern University and A&M College, LA	M
Southern Utah University, UT	W
Southwest Baptist University, MO	M,W
Southwestern College, KS	M,W
Southwestern Oklahoma State University, OK	M,W
Southwest Missouri State University, MO	M,W
Southwest State University, MN	W
Southwest Texas State University, TX	M,W
Spring Arbor College, MI	M,W
Spring Hill College, AL	M,W
Stanford University, CA	M,W
State U of NY at Buffalo, NY	M,W
Stephen F. Austin State University, TX	W
Sterling College, KS	M,W
Stetson University, FL	M,W
Syracuse University, NY	W
Tabor College, KS	M,W
Taylor University, IN	M,W
Temple University, Philadelphia, PA	M
Tennessee State University, TN	M,W
Tennessee Technological University, TN	M,W
Tennessee Wesleyan College, TN	M,W
Texas A&M University, College Station, TX	M,W
Texas A&M University–Kingsville, TX	M,W
Texas Christian University, TX	M,W

Texas Lutheran University, TX	M,W
Texas Southern University, TX	M
Texas Tech University, TX	M,W
Texas Wesleyan University, TX	M,W
Texas Woman's University, TX	W
Tiffin University, OH	M,W
Towson University, MD	M,W
Transylvania University, KY	M,W
Trinity International University, IL	M,W
Tri-State University, IN	M,W
Troy State University, Troy, AL	M,W
Truman State University, MO	M,W
Tulane University, LA	M,W
Tusculum College, TN	M,W
Tuskegee University, AL	M,W
Union College, KY	M,W
Union University, TN	M,W
United States International University, CA	M,W
U at Albany, State U of NY, NY	W
The University of Akron, OH	M,W
The University of Alabama at Birmingham, AL	M,W
The University of Alabama in Huntsville, AL	M,W
University of Arizona, AZ	M,W
University of Arkansas, Fayetteville, AR	M,W
University of Arkansas at Little Rock, AR	M,W
University of California, Berkeley, CA	M
University of California, Irvine, CA	M,W
University of California, Los Angeles, CA	M,W
University of California, Riverside, CA	M,W
University of California, Santa Barbara, CA	M,W
University of Central Florida, FL	M,W
University of Central Oklahoma, OK	M,W
The University of Charleston, WV	M,W
University of Cincinnati, OH	M,W
University of Colorado at Boulder, CO	M,W
University of Colorado at Colorado Springs, CO	M,W
University of Dayton, OH	M,W
University of Denver, CO	M,W
University of Evansville, IN	M,W
The University of Findlay, OH	M,W
University of Florida, FL	M,W
University of Georgia, GA	M,W
University of Hartford, CT	M,W
University of Hawaii at Manoa, HI	M,W
University of Houston, TX	W
University of Idaho, ID	M,W
University of Illinois at Chicago, IL	M,W
University of Illinois at Urbana–Champaign, IL	M,W
University of Indianapolis, IN	M,W
The University of Iowa, IA	M,W
University of Kansas, KS	M,W
University of Kentucky, KY	M,W
University of Louisville, KY	M,W
University of Mary, ND	M,W
University of Mary Hardin-Baylor, TX	M,W
University of Maryland Baltimore County, MD	M,W

University of Maryland College Park, MD	M,W
University of Maryland Eastern Shore, MD	M
University of Massachusetts Amherst, MA	M,W
University of Massachusetts Lowell, MA	M,W
The University of Memphis, TN	M,W
University of Miami, FL	M,W
University of Michigan, Ann Arbor, MI	M,W
University of Minnesota, Duluth, MN	M,W
University of Minnesota, Twin Cities Campus, MN	M,W
University of Mississippi, MS	M,W
University of Missouri–Columbia, MO	M,W
University of Missouri–Kansas City, MO	M,W
University of Mobile, AL	M,W
The University of Montana–Missoula, MT	M,W
University of Montevallo, AL	W
University of Nebraska at Kearney, NE	M,W
University of Nebraska–Lincoln, NE	M,W
University of Nevada, Las Vegas, NV	M,W
University of Nevada, Reno, NV	M,W
University of New Hampshire, Durham, NH	W
University of New Haven, CT	W
University of New Mexico, NM	M,W
University of North Alabama, AL	M,W
University of North Carolina at Asheville, NC	M,W
University of North Carolina at Charlotte, NC	M,W
University of North Carolina at Greensboro, NC	M,W
University of North Carolina at Pembroke, NC	M,W
University of North Carolina at Wilmington, NC	M,W
University of Northern Colorado, CO	M,W
University of Northern Iowa, IA	W
University of North Florida, FL	M,W
University of North Texas, TX	W
University of Notre Dame, IN	M,W
University of Oklahoma, OK	M,W
University of Oregon, OR	M,W
University of Pittsburgh, PA	W
University of Portland, OR	M,W
U of Puerto Rico at Ponce, PR	M,W
U of Puerto Rico, Cayey University College, PR	M,W
U of Puerto Rico, Mayagüez Campus, PR	M,W
U of Puerto Rico, Río Piedras, PR	M,W
University of Rhode Island, RI	W
University of Richmond, VA	M,W
University of San Diego, CA	M,W
University of San Francisco, CA	M,W
University of Sioux Falls, SD	M,W
University of South Alabama, AL	M,W
U of South Carolina, Columbia, SC	M,W
U of South Carolina–Aiken, SC	M,W
U of South Carolina–Spartanburg, SC	M,W

University of South Dakota, SD — M,W
University of Southern California, CA — M,W
University of Southern Colorado, CO — M,W
University of Southern Indiana, IN — M,W
University of Southern Mississippi, MS — M,W
University of South Florida, FL — M,W
University of Southwestern Louisiana, LA — M,W
The University of Tampa, FL — M,W
University of Tennessee at Chattanooga, TN — M,W
The University of Tennessee at Martin, TN — M,W
University of Tennessee, Knoxville, TN — M,W
The University of Texas at Arlington, TX — M,W
The University of Texas at Austin, TX — M,W
The University of Texas at El Paso, TX — W
The University of Texas at San Antonio, TX — M,W
The University of Texas–Pan American, TX — M
University of the District of Columbia, DC — M,W
University of the Pacific, CA — M,W
University of the Sacred Heart, PR — M,W
University of Toledo, OH — M,W
University of Tulsa, OK — M,W
University of Utah, UT — M,W
University of Virginia, VA — M,W
University of Washington, WA — M,W
The University of West Alabama, AL — M,W
University of West Florida, FL — M,W
University of Wisconsin–Green Bay, WI — M,W
University of Wisconsin–Madison, WI — M,W
University of Wisconsin–Milwaukee, WI — M,W
University of Wisconsin–Parkside, WI — M,W
Utah State University, UT — M,W
Valdosta State University, GA — M,W
Valparaiso University, IN — M,W
Vanderbilt University, TN — M,W
Villanova University, PA — W
Virginia Commonwealth University, VA — M,W
Virginia Intermont College, VA — M,W
Virginia Military Institute, VA — M
Virginia Polytechnic Institute and State U, VA — M,W
Virginia State University, VA — M,W
Virginia Union University, VA — M
Wagner College, NY — M,W
Wake Forest University, NC — M,W
Walsh University, OH — M,W
Washburn University of Topeka, KS — M,W
Washington State University, WA — M,W
Wayne State University, MI — M,W
Webber College, FL — M,W
Weber State University, UT — M,W
West Chester University of Pennsylvania, PA — M,W
Western Carolina University, NC — W
Western Illinois University, IL — M,W

Western Kentucky University, KY — M,W
Western Michigan University, MI — M,W
West Liberty State College, WV — M,W
Westmar University, IA — M,W
Westminster College, PA — W
Westmont College, CA — M,W
West Texas A&M University, TX — M,W
West Virginia University, WV — M,W
West Virginia University Institute of Technology, WV — M,W
West Virginia Wesleyan College, WV — M,W
Wichita State University, KS — M,W
William Carey College, MS — M,W
William Jewell College, MO — M,W
William Woods University, MO — W
Wingate University, NC — M,W
Winona State University, MN — M,W
Winston-Salem State University, NC — M,W
Winthrop University, SC — M,W
Wofford College, SC — M,W
Wright State University, OH — M,W
Xavier University, OH — M,W
Xavier University of Louisiana, LA — M,W
York College, NE — M,W
Youngstown State University, OH — M,W

TRACK AND FIELD

Abilene Christian University, TX — M,W
Adams State College, CO — M,W
Alabama Agricultural and Mechanical University, AL — M,W
Albany State University, GA — M,W
Alcorn State University, MS — M,W
Allen University, SC — M,W
Anderson College, SC — M,W
Angelo State University, TX — M,W
Appalachian State University, NC — M,W
Aquinas College, MI — M,W
Arizona State University, AZ — M,W
Arkansas State University, AR — M,W
Ashland University, OH — M,W
Auburn University, AL — M,W
Augustana College, SD — M,W
Austin Peay State University, TN — W
Azusa Pacific University, CA — M,W
Baker University, KS — M,W
Ball State University, IN — M,W
Barber-Scotia College, NC — M,W
Bayamón Central University, PR — M,W
Bayamón Technological University College, PR — M,W
Baylor University, TX — M,W
Belmont University, TN — M,W
Benedict College, SC — M
Berry College, GA — M,W
Bethany College, KS — M,W
Bethel College, IN — M,W
Bethel College, KS — M,W
Bethune-Cookman College, FL — M,W
Biola University, CA — M,W
Black Hills State University, SD — M,W
Bloomsburg University of Pennsylvania, PA — M,W
Boise State University, ID — M,W
Boston College, MA — M,W
Boston University, MA — M,W
Bowie State University, MD — M,W

Bowling Green State University, OH — M,W
Brigham Young University, UT — M,W
Butler University, IN — M,W
California Baptist College, CA — M,W
California Polytechnic State U, San Luis Obispo, CA — M,W
California State Polytechnic University, Pomona, CA — M,W
California State University, Bakersfield, CA — M,W
California State University, Fresno, CA — M
California State University, Fullerton, CA — M,W
California State University, Long Beach, CA — M,W
California State University, Los Angeles, CA — M,W
California State University, Northridge, CA — M,W
California State University, Sacramento, CA — M,W
California University of Pennsylvania, PA — M,W
Campbell University, NC — M,W
Canisius College, NY — M,W
Carson-Newman College, TN — M,W
Cedarville College, OH — M,W
Central Connecticut State University, CT — M,W
Central Methodist College, MO — M,W
Central Michigan University, MI — M,W
Central Missouri State University, MO — M,W
Chadron State College, NE — M,W
Charleston Southern University, SC — M,W
Cheyney University of Pennsylvania, PA — M,W
Chicago State University, IL — M,W
The Citadel, The Military Coll of South Carolina, SC — M
Clarion University of Pennsylvania, PA — M,W
Clark Atlanta University, GA — M
Clemson University, SC — M,W
Cleveland State University, OH — W
Coastal Carolina University, SC — M,W
Colegio Universitario del Este, PR — M,W
College of William and Mary, VA — M,W
Colorado School of Mines, CO — M,W
Colorado State University, CO — M,W
Columbia Union College, MD — M,W
Concordia College, NE — M,W
Cumberland College, KY — M,W
Dakota State University, SD — M,W
Dakota Wesleyan University, SD — M,W
Dana College, NE — M,W
Davidson College, NC — W
Delaware State University, DE — M,W
DePaul University, IL — M,W
Dickinson State University, ND — M,W
Doane College, NE — M,W
Drake University, IA — M,W
Drexel University, PA — M
Duquesne University, PA — W
East Carolina University, NC — M,W
Eastern Illinois University, IL — M,W
Eastern Kentucky University, KY — M,W

Track and Field (continued)

Eastern Michigan University, MI	M,W
Eastern Washington University, WA	M,W
East Stroudsburg University of Pennsylvania, PA	M
East Tennessee State University, TN	M,W
Edinboro University of Pennsylvania, PA	M,W
Edward Waters College, FL	M,W
Electronic Data Processing College of Puerto Rico, PR	M,W
Emporia State University, KS	M,W
Evangel College, MO	M,W
Fairleigh Dickinson U, Teaneck-Hackensack, NJ	M,W
Ferris State University, MI	W
Florida Agricultural and Mechanical University, FL	M,W
Florida International University, FL	M,W
Florida State University, FL	M,W
Fordham University, NY	M,W
Fort Hays State University, KS	M,W
Fort Valley State University, GA	M,W
Francis Marion University, SC	M,W
Fresno Pacific University, CA	M,W
Furman University, SC	M,W
Geneva College, PA	M,W
George Mason University, VA	M,W
Georgetown University, DC	M,W
Georgia Institute of Technology, GA	M,W
Georgia State University, GA	M
Goshen College, IN	M,W
Grace College, IN	M,W
Graceland College, IA	M,W
Grambling State University, LA	M,W
Harding University, AR	M,W
Hastings College, NE	M,W
Hillsdale College, MI	M,W
Houghton College, NY	M,W
Howard University, DC	M,W
Huntington College, IN	M,W
Huron University, SD	M,W
Idaho State University, ID	M,W
Illinois State University, IL	M,W
Indiana State University, IN	M,W
Indiana University Bloomington, IN	M,W
Indiana Wesleyan University, IN	M,W
Inter American U of PR, Arecibo Campus, PR	M
Inter American U of PR, Metropolitan Campus, PR	M,W
Inter American U of PR, San Germán Campus, PR	M,W
Iona College, New Rochelle, NY	M
Iowa State University of Science and Technology, IA	M,W
Iowa Wesleyan College, IA	M,W
Jackson State University, MS	M,W
Jacksonville University, FL	W
James Madison University, VA	M,W
Johnson C. Smith University, NC	M,W
Kansas State University, KS	M,W
Kansas Wesleyan University, KS	M,W
Kent State University, OH	M,W
Kentucky State University, KY	M,W
Kutztown University of Pennsylvania, PA	M,W

Lamar University, TX	M,W
Langston University, OK	M,W
La Salle University, PA	M,W
Lehigh University, PA	M,W
LeMoyne-Owen College, TN	M,W
Lenoir-Rhyne College, NC	M
Lewis University, IL	M,W
Lincoln University, MO	M,W
Lindenwood College, MO	M,W
Livingstone College, NC	M,W
Lock Haven University of Pennsylvania, PA	M,W
Long Island U, Brooklyn Campus, NY	W
Long Island U, C.W. Post Campus, NY	M,W
Louisiana State University and A&M College, LA	M,W
Louisiana Tech University, LA	M,W
Loyola University Chicago, IL	M,W
Lubbock Christian University, TX	M,W
Malone College, OH	M,W
Manhattan College, NY	M,W
Mankato State University, MN	M,W
Marian College, IN	M,W
Marquette University, WI	M,W
Marshall University, WV	M
McKendree College, IL	M,W
McNeese State University, LA	M,W
McPherson College, KS	M,W
Miami University, OH	M,W
Michigan Christian College, MI	M,W
Michigan State University, MI	M,W
MidAmerica Nazarene University, KS	M,W
Middle Tennessee State University, TN	M,W
Midland Lutheran College, NE	M,W
Midway College, KY	W
Millersville University of Pennsylvania, PA	M,W
Minot State University, ND	M,W
Mississippi State University, MS	M,W
Mississippi Valley State University, MS	M,W
Missouri Southern State College, MO	M,W
Monmouth University, NJ	M,W
Montana State U–Bozeman, MT	M,W
Moorhead State University, MN	M,W
Morehead State University, KY	M,W
Morehouse College, GA	M
Morgan State University, MD	M,W
Morningside College, IA	M
Morris College, SC	M,W
Mount St. Clare College, IA	M,W
Mount Saint Mary's College and Seminary, MD	M,W
Murray State University, KY	M,W
New Mexico State University, NM	M,W
New York Institute of Technology, NY	M,W
Nicholls State University, LA	M,W
North Carolina Agricultural and Technical State U, NC	M,W
North Carolina State University, NC	M,W
North Dakota State University, ND	M,W
Northeastern State University, OK	M
Northeastern University, MA	M,W
Northeast Louisiana University, LA	M,W
Northern Arizona University, AZ	M,W

Northern State University, SD	M,W
Northwest College of the Assemblies of God, WA	M,W
Northwestern College, IA	M,W
Northwestern State University of Louisiana, LA	M,W
Northwest Missouri State University, MO	M,W
Northwood University, MI	M,W
Northwood University, Texas Campus, TX	M,W
The Ohio State University, OH	M,W
Ohio University, OH	M,W
Oklahoma Baptist University, OK	M,W
Oklahoma Christian U of Science and Arts, OK	M,W
Oklahoma State U, OK	M,W
Oral Roberts University, OK	M,W
Oregon Institute of Technology, OR	M,W
Ottawa University, KS	M,W
Pace University, NY	M,W
Paine College, GA	M,W
Park College, MO	M,W
Penn State U Univ Park Campus, PA	M,W
Pittsburg State University, KS	M,W
Point Loma Nazarene College, CA	M,W
Pontifical Catholic University of Puerto Rico, PR	M,W
Portland State University, OR	M,W
Providence College, RI	M,W
Purdue University, West Lafayette, IN	M,W
Queens Coll of the City U of NY, NY	M,W
Rice University, TX	M,W
Rider University, NJ	M,W
Robert Morris College, PA	M,W
Roberts Wesleyan College, NY	M,W
Rust College, MS	M,W
Rutgers, State U of NJ, College of Engineering, NJ	M,W
Rutgers, State U of NJ, College of Pharmacy, NJ	M,W
Rutgers, State U of NJ, Cook College, NJ	M,W
Rutgers, State U of NJ, Douglass College, NJ	W
Rutgers, State U of NJ, Livingston College, NJ	M,W
Rutgers, State U of NJ, Mason Gross School of Arts, NJ	M,W
Rutgers, State U of NJ, Rutgers College, NJ	M,W
Saginaw Valley State University, MI	M,W
St. Ambrose University, IA	M,W
Saint Augustine's College, NC	M,W
St. Cloud State University, MN	M,W
Saint Francis College, IN	M,W
St. Francis College, NY	M,W
Saint Francis College, PA	M,W
St. John's University, NY	M,W
Saint Joseph's College, IN	M,W
Saint Joseph's University, PA	M,W
Saint Peter's College, Jersey City, NJ	M,W
Samford University, AL	M,W
San Diego State University, CA	W
Savannah State University, GA	M,W
Seattle Pacific University, WA	M,W
Seton Hall University, NJ	M,W

Shaw University, NC	M,W	University of California, Irvine, CA	W	University of Northern Colorado, CO	M,W
Shippensburg University of Pennsylvania, PA	M,W	University of California, Los Angeles, CA	M,W	University of Northern Iowa, IA	M,W
Siena Heights College, MI	M,W	University of California, Riverside, CA	M,W	University of North Florida, FL	M,W
Slippery Rock University of Pennsylvania, PA	M,W	University of California, Santa Barbara, CA	M,W	University of North Texas, TX	M,W
South Dakota School of Mines and Technology, SD	M,W	University of Central Oklahoma, OK	M,W	University of Notre Dame, IN	M,W
South Dakota State University, SD	M,W	University of Cincinnati, OH	M	University of Oklahoma, OK	M,W
Southeastern Louisiana University, LA	M,W	University of Colorado at Boulder, CO	M,W	University of Oregon, OR	M,W
Southeastern Oklahoma State University, OK	W	University of Connecticut, Storrs, CT	M,W	University of Pittsburgh, PA	M,W
Southeast Missouri State University, MO	M,W	University of Detroit Mercy, MI	M,W	University of Portland, OR	M,W
Southern California College, CA	M,W	The University of Findlay, OH	M,W	U of Puerto Rico at Ponce, PR	M,W
Southern Illinois University at Carbondale, IL	M,W	University of Florida, FL	M,W	U of Puerto Rico, Cayey University College, PR	M,W
Southern Illinois University at Edwardsville, IL	M,W	University of Georgia, GA	M,W	U of Puerto Rico, Mayagüez Campus, PR	M,W
Southern Methodist University, TX	M,W	University of Houston, TX	M	U of Puerto Rico, Río Piedras, PR	M,W
Southern Oregon University, OR	M,W	University of Idaho, ID	M,W	University of Rhode Island, RI	M,W
Southern University and A&M College, LA	M,W	University of Illinois at Urbana–Champaign, IL	M,W	University of Rio Grande, OH	M,W
Southern University at New Orleans, LA	M,W	University of Indianapolis, IN	M,W	University of Sioux Falls, SD	M,W
Southern Utah University, UT	M,W	The University of Iowa, IA	M,W	University of South Alabama, AL	M,W
Southwestern Christian College, TX	M,W	University of Kansas, KS	M,W	U of South Carolina, Columbia, SC	M
Southwestern College, KS	M,W	University of Kentucky, KY	M,W	University of South Dakota, SD	M,W
Southwest Missouri State University, MO	M,W	University of Louisville, KY	M,W	University of Southern California, CA	M,W
Southwest Texas State University, TX	M,W	University of Maine, Orono, ME	M,W	University of Southern Mississippi, MS	M,W
Spring Arbor College, MI	M,W	University of Mary, ND	M,W	University of South Florida, FL	M,W
Stanford University, CA	M,W	University of Maryland Baltimore County, MD	M,W	University of Southwestern Louisiana, LA	M,W
State U of NY at Buffalo, NY	M,W	University of Maryland College Park, MD	M,W	The University of Tennessee at Martin, TN	W
Stephen F. Austin State University, TX	M,W	University of Massachusetts Amherst, MA	M,W	University of Tennessee, Knoxville, TN	M,W
Sterling College, KS	M,W	University of Massachusetts Lowell, MA	M,W	The University of Texas at Arlington, TX	M,W
Syracuse University, NY	M,W	The University of Memphis, TN	M	The University of Texas at Austin, TX	M,W
Tabor College, KS	M,W	University of Miami, FL	M,W	The University of Texas at El Paso, TX	M,W
Tarleton State University, TX	M,W	University of Michigan, Ann Arbor, MI	M,W	The University of Texas at San Antonio, TX	M,W
Taylor University, IN	M,W	University of Minnesota, Duluth, MN	M,W	The University of Texas–Pan American, TX	M,W
Temple University, Philadelphia, PA	M,W	University of Minnesota, Twin Cities Campus, MN	M,W	University of the District of Columbia, DC	M,W
Tennessee State University, TN	M,W	University of Mississippi, MS	M,W	University of the Sacred Heart, PR	M,W
Texas A&M University, College Station, TX	M,W	University of Missouri–Columbia, MO	M,W	University of Toledo, OH	M,W
Texas A&M University–Commerce, TX	M,W	University of Missouri–Kansas City, MO	M,W	University of Tulsa, OK	M,W
Texas A&M University–Kingsville, TX	M	University of Missouri–Rolla, MO	M,W	University of Utah, UT	M,W
Texas Christian University, TX	M,W	University of Mobile, AL	M,W	University of Vermont, VT	W
Texas Southern University, TX	M,W	The University of Montana–Missoula, MT	M,W	University of Virginia, VA	M,W
Texas Tech University, TX	M,W			University of Washington, WA	M,W
Towson University, MD	M,W	University of Nebraska at Kearney, NE	M,W	University of Wisconsin–Madison, WI	M,W
Tri-State University, IN	M,W	University of Nebraska–Lincoln, NE	M,W	University of Wisconsin–Milwaukee, WI	M,W
Troy State University, Troy, AL	M	University of Nevada, Las Vegas, NV	W	University of Wisconsin–Parkside, WI	M,W
Truman State University, MO	M,W	University of Nevada, Reno, NV	W	University of Wyoming, WY	M,W
Tulane University, LA	M,W	University of New Hampshire, Durham, NH	W	Utah State University, UT	M,W
Tuskegee University, AL	M,W	University of New Haven, CT	M	Valley City State University, ND	M,W
U at Albany, State U of NY, NY	M,W	University of New Mexico, NM	M,W	Vanderbilt University, TN	W
The University of Akron, OH	M,W	University of North Carolina at Asheville, NC	M,W	Villanova University, PA	M,W
The University of Alabama at Birmingham, AL	W	University of North Carolina at Charlotte, NC	M,W	Virginia Commonwealth University, VA	M,W
University of Arizona, AZ	M,W	University of North Carolina at Pembroke, NC	M	Virginia Military Institute, VA	M
University of Arkansas, Fayetteville, AR	M,W	University of North Carolina at Wilmington, NC	M	Virginia Polytechnic Institute and State U, VA	M,W
University of Arkansas at Little Rock, AR	W	University of North Dakota, ND	M,W	Virginia State University, VA	M,W
University of California, Berkeley, CA	M,W			Virginia Union University, VA	M,W
				Voorhees College, SC	M
				Wagner College, NY	M,W

Track and Field (continued)

Wake Forest University, NC	M,W
Walsh University, OH	M,W
Washington State University, WA	M,W
Wayne State College, NE	M,W
Weber State University, UT	M,W
West Chester University of Pennsylvania, PA	M,W
Western Carolina University, NC	M,W
Western Illinois University, IL	M,W
Western Kentucky University, KY	M,W
Western Michigan University, MI	M,W
Western State College of Colorado, CO	M,W
Western Washington University, WA	M,W
Westmar University, IA	M,W
Westmont College, CA	M,W
West Virginia University, WV	M,W
West Virginia Wesleyan College, WV	M,W
Wheeling Jesuit University, WV	M,W
Wichita State University, KS	M,W
Wiley College, TX	M,W
William Jewell College, MO	M,W
Winona State University, MN	W
Winston-Salem State University, NC	M,W
Winthrop University, SC	M,W
Wofford College, SC	W
York College, NE	M,W
Youngstown State University, OH	M,W

VOLLEYBALL

Abilene Christian University, TX	W
Adams State College, CO	W
Adelphi University, NY	W
Alabama Agricultural and Mechanical University, AL	W
Albany State University, GA	W
Albertson College of Idaho, ID	W
Alcorn State University, MS	W
Alderson-Broaddus College, WV	W
American International College, MA	W
American University, DC	W
Anderson College, SC	W
Angelo State University, TX	W
Appalachian State University, NC	W
Aquinas College, MI	W
Arizona State University, AZ	W
Arkansas State University, AR	W
Arkansas Tech University, AR	W
Armstrong Atlantic State University, GA	W
Ashland University, OH	W
Atlantic Union College, MA	W
Auburn University, AL	W
Augustana College, SD	W
Augusta State University, GA	W
Austin Peay State University, TN	W
Azusa Pacific University, CA	W
Baker University, KS	W
Ball State University, IN	M,W
Barat College, IL	W
Barber-Scotia College, NC	W
Barry University, FL	W
Bartlesville Wesleyan College, OK	W
Barton College, NC	W
Bayamón Central University, PR	M,W

Bayamón Technological University College, PR	M,W
Baylor University, TX	W
Becker College–Leicester Campus, MA	W
Becker College–Worcester Campus, MA	W
Belhaven College, MS	W
Bellarmine College, KY	W
Bellevue University, NE	W
Belmont Abbey College, NC	W
Belmont University, TN	W
Bemidji State University, MN	W
Benedictine College, KS	W
Bethany College, KS	W
Bethel College, IN	W
Bethel College, KS	W
Bethune-Cookman College, FL	W
Biola University, CA	W
Black Hills State University, SD	W
Bloomfield College, NJ	W
Bluefield College, VA	W
Boise State University, ID	W
Boston College, MA	W
Bowie State University, MD	W
Bowling Green State University, OH	W
Bradley University, IL	W
Brenau University, GA	W
Brescia College, KY	W
Briar Cliff College, IA	W
Brigham Young University, UT	W
Brigham Young University–Hawaii Campus, HI	W
Bryan College, TN	W
Butler University, IN	W
California Baptist College, CA	W
California Polytechnic State U, San Luis Obispo, CA	W
California State Polytechnic University, Pomona, CA	W
California State University, Bakersfield, CA	W
California State University, Dominguez Hills, CA	W
California State University, Fresno, CA	W
California State University, Fullerton, CA	W
California State University, Long Beach, CA	M,W
California State University, Northridge, CA	M,W
California State University, Sacramento, CA	W
California State University, San Bernardino, CA	W
California University of Pennsylvania, PA	W
Cameron University, OK	W
Campbell University, NC	W
Canisius College, NY	W
Carlow College, PA	W
Carroll College, MT	W
Carson-Newman College, TN	W
Catawba College, NC	W
Cedarville College, OH	W
Centenary College of Louisiana, LA	W

Central Connecticut State University, CT	W
Central Methodist College, MO	W
Central Michigan University, MI	W
Central Missouri State University, MO	W
Chadron State College, NE	W
Chaminade University of Honolulu, HI	W
Charleston Southern University, SC	W
Cheyney University of Pennsylvania, PA	W
Chicago State University, IL	W
Christian Brothers University, TN	W
Christian Heritage College, CA	W
Clarion University of Pennsylvania, PA	W
Clemson University, SC	W
Cleveland State University, OH	W
Coastal Carolina University, SC	W
Coker College, SC	W
Colegio Universitario del Este, PR	M,W
College of Charleston, SC	W
College of St. Francis, IL	W
College of Saint Mary, NE	W
College of the Ozarks, MO	W
College of the Southwest, NM	W
College of William and Mary, VA	W
Colorado Christian University, CO	W
Colorado School of Mines, CO	W
Colorado State University, CO	W
Columbia College, MO	M,W
Columbia College, SC	W
Columbia Union College, MD	W
Concord College, WV	W
Concordia College, MI	W
Concordia College, NE	W
Concordia College, NY	M,W
Concordia University, CA	W
Concordia University, OR	W
Concordia University at Austin, TX	W
Cornerstone College, MI	W
Covenant College, GA	W
Creighton University, NE	W
Culver-Stockton College, MO	W
Cumberland College, KY	W
Cumberland University, TN	W
Daemen College, NY	W
Dakota State University, SD	W
Dakota Wesleyan University, SD	W
Dallas Baptist University, TX	W
Dana College, NE	W
David Lipscomb University, TN	W
Davidson College, NC	W
DePaul University, IL	W
Dickinson State University, ND	W
Doane College, NE	W
Dominican College of Blauvelt, NY	W
Dominican College of San Rafael, CA	W
Dowling College, NY	W
Drake University, IA	W
Drury College, MO	W
Duke University, NC	W
Duquesne University, PA	W
D'Youville College, NY	W
East Carolina University, NC	W
Eastern Illinois University, IL	W
Eastern Kentucky University, KY	W

Eastern Michigan University, MI	W
Eastern New Mexico University, NM	W
Eastern Washington University, WA	W
East Tennessee State University, TN	W
Eckerd College, FL	W
Edinboro University of Pennsylvania, PA	W
Electronic Data Processing College of Puerto Rico, PR	M,W
Elon College, NC	W
Embry-Riddle Aeronautical University, AZ	W
Embry-Riddle Aeronautical University, FL	W
Emporia State University, KS	W
Erskine College, SC	W
Evangel College, MO	W
Fairfield University, CT	W
Fairleigh Dickinson U, Teaneck-Hackensack, NJ	W
Faulkner University, AL	W
Ferris State University, MI	W
Flagler College, FL	W
Florida Agricultural and Mechanical University, FL	W
Florida Atlantic University, FL	W
Florida Institute of Technology, FL	W
Florida International University, FL	W
Florida Southern College, FL	W
Florida State University, FL	W
Fordham University, NY	W
Fort Hays State University, KS	W
Fort Lewis College, CO	W
Fort Valley State University, GA	W
Francis Marion University, SC	W
Franklin Pierce College, NH	W
Freed-Hardeman University, TN	W
Fresno Pacific University, CA	W
Friends University, KS	W
Furman University, SC	W
Gannon University, PA	W
Gardner-Webb University, NC	W
Geneva College, PA	W
George Mason University, VA	M,W
Georgetown College, KY	W
Georgetown University, DC	W
The George Washington University, DC	W
Georgia Institute of Technology, GA	W
Georgia Southern University, GA	W
Georgia Southwestern State University, GA	W
Georgia State University, GA	W
Gonzaga University, WA	W
Goshen College, IN	W
Grace College, IN	W
Graceland College, IA	M,W
Grand Canyon University, AZ	W
Grand Valley State University, MI	W
Grand View College, IA	W
Green Mountain College, VT	W
Hannibal-LaGrange College, MO	W
Harding University, AR	W
Hastings College, NE	W
Hawaii Pacific University, HI	W
Henderson State University, AR	W
Hillsdale College, MI	W
Hofstra University, NY	W
Holy Names College, CA	W
Hope International University, CA	M,W
Houghton College, NY	W
Houston Baptist University, TX	W
Howard University, DC	W
Huntington College, IN	W
Huron University, SD	W
Idaho State University, ID	W
Illinois Institute of Technology, IL	W
Illinois State University, IL	W
Indiana State University, IN	W
Indiana University Bloomington, IN	W
Indiana U–Purdue U Fort Wayne, IN	M,W
Indiana U–Purdue U Indianapolis, IN	W
Indiana University Southeast, IN	W
Indiana Wesleyan University, IN	W
Inter American U of PR, San Germán Campus, PR	M,W
Iowa State University of Science and Technology, IA	W
Iowa Wesleyan College, IA	W
Jacksonville State University, AL	W
Jacksonville University, FL	W
James Madison University, VA	W
John Brown University, AR	W
Judson College, IL	W
Kansas Newman College, KS	W
Kansas State University, KS	W
Kansas Wesleyan University, KS	W
Kent State University, OH	W
Kentucky State University, KY	W
Kentucky Wesleyan College, KY	W
King College, TN	W
Kutztown University of Pennsylvania, PA	W
Lamar University, TX	W
Lambuth University, TN	W
La Salle University, PA	W
Lees-McRae College, NC	W
Lee University, TN	W
Lehigh University, PA	W
Le Moyne College, NY	W
LeMoyne-Owen College, TN	W
Lenoir-Rhyne College, NC	W
LeTourneau University, TX	W
Lewis-Clark State College, ID	W
Lewis University, IL	M,W
Limestone College, SC	W
Lincoln Memorial University, TN	W
Lindenwood College, MO	W
Lindsey Wilson College, KY	W
Lock Haven University of Pennsylvania, PA	W
Long Island U, Brooklyn Campus, NY	W
Long Island U, C.W. Post Campus, NY	W
Long Island U, Southampton College, NY	W
Louisiana State University and A&M College, LA	W
Louisiana Tech University, LA	W
Loyola College, MD	W
Loyola Marymount University, CA	M,W
Loyola University Chicago, IL	M,W
Lubbock Christian University, TX	W
Lyon College, AR	W
Madonna University, MI	W
Malone College, OH	W
Manhattan College, NY	W
Mankato State University, MN	W
Marian College, IN	W
Marist College, NY	W
Marquette University, WI	W
Marshall University, WV	W
Mars Hill College, NC	W
Martin Methodist College, TN	W
Marycrest International University, IA	M,W
The Master's College and Seminary, CA	W
Mayville State University, ND	W
McKendree College, IL	W
McNeese State University, LA	W
McPherson College, KS	W
Mercer University, Macon, GA	W
Mercyhurst College, PA	M,W
Mesa State College, CO	W
Metropolitan State College of Denver, CO	W
Miami University, OH	W
Michigan Christian College, MI	W
Michigan State University, MI	W
Michigan Technological University, MI	W
MidAmerica Nazarene University, KS	W
Middle Tennessee State University, TN	W
Midland Lutheran College, NE	W
Midway College, KY	W
Millersville University of Pennsylvania, PA	W
Milligan College, TN	W
Minot State University, ND	W
Mississippi State University, MS	W
Mississippi University for Women, MS	W
Missouri Baptist College, MO	W
Missouri Southern State College, MO	W
Missouri Western State College, MO	W
Molloy College, NY	W
Montana State U–Billings, MT	W
Montana State U–Bozeman, MT	W
Montana State U–Northern, MT	W
Montana Tech of The University of Montana, MT	W
Montreat College, NC	W
Moorhead State University, MN	W
Morehead State University, KY	W
Morningside College, IA	W
Mount Marty College, SD	W
Mount Olive College, NC	W
Mount St. Clare College, IA	W
Mount Vernon Nazarene College, OH	W
Murray State University, KY	W
National College, SD	W
Newberry College, SC	W
New Mexico Highlands University, NM	W
New Mexico State University, NM	W
New York Institute of Technology, NY	W
Niagara University, NY	W
Nicholls State University, LA	W
North Carolina Agricultural and Technical State U, NC	W

Volleyball (continued)

North Carolina State University, NC	W
North Dakota State University, ND	W
Northeastern Illinois University, IL	W
Northeastern University, MA	W
Northeast Louisiana University, LA	W
Northern Arizona University, AZ	W
Northern Illinois University, IL	W
Northern Kentucky University, KY	W
Northern Michigan University, MI	W
Northern State University, SD	W
North Greenville College, SC	W
Northland College, WI	W
Northwest College of the Assemblies of God, WA	W
Northwestern College, IA	W
Northwestern State University of Louisiana, LA	W
Northwestern University, IL	W
Northwest Missouri State University, MO	W
Northwood University, MI	W
Northwood University, Florida Campus, FL	W
Nova Southeastern University, FL	W
Nyack College, NY	W
Oakland City University, IN	W
Oakland University, MI	W
Ohio Dominican College, OH	W
The Ohio State University, OH	M,W
Ohio University, OH	W
Oral Roberts University, OK	W
Oregon State University, OR	W
Ottawa University, KS	W
Ouachita Baptist University, AR	W
Pace University, NY	W
Paine College, GA	W
Palm Beach Atlantic College, FL	W
Park College, MO	M,W
Penn State U Univ Park Campus, PA	M,W
Pepperdine University, Malibu, CA	M,W
Peru State College, NE	W
Pfeiffer University, NC	W
Philadelphia College of Textiles and Science, PA	W
Phillips University, OK	W
Piedmont College, GA	W
Pittsburg State University, KS	W
Point Loma Nazarene College, CA	W
Point Park College, PA	W
Portland State University, OR	W
Presbyterian College, SC	W
Providence College, RI	W
Purdue University, West Lafayette, IN	W
Purdue University Calumet, IN	W
Queens College, NC	W
Queens Coll of the City U of NY, NY	W
Quincy University, IL	W
Quinnipiac College, CT	W
Radford University, VA	W
Regis University, CO	W
Research College of Nursing–Rockhurst College, MO	W
Rice University, TX	W
Rider University, NJ	W
Robert Morris College, PA	W
Roberts Wesleyan College, NY	W

Rockhurst College, MO	W
Rocky Mountain College, MT	W
Rollins College, FL	W
Rutgers, State U of NJ, College of Engineering, NJ	W
Rutgers, State U of NJ, College of Nursing, NJ	M
Rutgers, State U of NJ, College of Pharmacy, NJ	W
Rutgers, State U of NJ, Cook College, NJ	W
Rutgers, State U of NJ, Douglass College, NJ	W
Rutgers, State U of NJ, Livingston College, NJ	W
Rutgers, State U of NJ, Mason Gross School of Arts, NJ	W
Rutgers, State U of NJ, Newark Coll of Arts & Scis, NJ	M
Rutgers, State U of NJ, Rutgers College, NJ	W
Saginaw Valley State University, MI	W
St. Ambrose University, IA	W
St. Andrews Presbyterian College, NC	W
Saint Augustine's College, NC	W
St. Bonaventure University, NY	W
St. Cloud State University, MN	W
St. Edward's University, TX	W
Saint Francis College, IN	W
St. Francis College, NY	W
Saint Francis College, PA	M,W
Saint Joseph's College, IN	W
Saint Leo College, FL	W
Saint Louis University, MO	W
Saint Martin's College, WA	W
Saint Mary College, KS	W
Saint Mary's College of California, CA	W
St. Mary's University of San Antonio, TX	W
Saint Peter's College, Jersey City, NJ	W
St. Thomas Aquinas College, NY	W
St. Thomas University, FL	W
Saint Vincent College, PA	W
Saint Xavier University, IL	W
Salem-Teikyo University, WV	W
Samford University, AL	W
Sam Houston State University, TX	W
San Diego State University, CA	M,W
San Jose State University, CA	W
Santa Clara University, CA	W
Seattle Pacific University, WA	W
Seton Hall University, NJ	W
Seton Hill College, PA	W
Shaw University, NC	M,W
Shepherd College, WV	W
Shippensburg University of Pennsylvania, PA	W
Siena Heights College, MI	W
Slippery Rock University of Pennsylvania, PA	W
South Dakota School of Mines and Technology, SD	W
South Dakota State University, SD	W
Southeastern Louisiana University, LA	W
Southeast Missouri State University, MO	W

Southern Arkansas University–Magnolia, AR	W
Southern California College, CA	W
Southern Illinois University at Carbondale, IL	W
Southern Methodist University, TX	W
Southern Nazarene University, OK	W
Southern Oregon University, OR	W
Southern University and A&M College, LA	W
Southern Wesleyan University, SC	W
Southwest Baptist University, MO	W
Southwestern College, KS	W
Southwest Missouri State University, MO	W
Southwest State University, MN	W
Southwest Texas State University, TX	W
Spalding University, KY	W
Spring Arbor College, MI	W
Stanford University, CA	M,W
State U of NY at Buffalo, NY	W
Stephen F. Austin State University, TX	W
Sterling College, KS	W
Stetson University, FL	W
Sue Bennett College, KY	W
Syracuse University, NY	W
Tabor College, KS	W
Tarleton State University, TX	W
Taylor University, IN	W
Temple University, Philadelphia, PA	W
Tennessee Technological University, TN	W
Tennessee Temple University, TN	W
Texas A&M University, College Station, TX	W
Texas A&M University–Commerce, TX	W
Texas A&M University–Kingsville, TX	W
Texas Lutheran University, TX	W
Texas Tech University, TX	W
Texas Wesleyan University, TX	W
Texas Woman's University, TX	W
Tiffin University, OH	W
Towson University, MD	M,W
Trevecca Nazarene University, TN	W
Trinity Christian College, IL	W
Trinity International University, IL	W
Tri-State University, IN	M,W
Troy State University, Troy, AL	W
Truman State University, MO	W
Tulane University, LA	W
Tusculum College, TN	W
Tuskegee University, AL	W
Union College, KY	W
Unity College, ME	W
U at Albany, State U of NY, NY	W
The University of Akron, OH	W
The University of Alabama at Birmingham, AL	W
The University of Alabama in Huntsville, AL	W
U of Alaska Anchorage, AK	W
U of Alaska Fairbanks, AK	W
University of Arizona, AZ	W
University of Arkansas, Fayetteville, AR	W

682

University of Arkansas at Little Rock, AR	W
University of Arkansas at Pine Bluff, AR	W
University of California, Irvine, CA	W
University of California, Los Angeles, CA	M,W
University of California, Riverside, CA	W
University of California, Santa Barbara, CA	M,W
University of Central Arkansas, AR	W
University of Central Florida, FL	W
University of Central Oklahoma, OK	W
The University of Charleston, WV	W
University of Cincinnati, OH	W
University of Colorado at Boulder, CO	W
University of Colorado at Colorado Springs, CO	W
University of Connecticut, Storrs, CT	W
University of Dayton, OH	W
University of Delaware, DE	W
University of Denver, CO	W
University of Evansville, IN	W
The University of Findlay, OH	W
University of Florida, FL	W
University of Georgia, GA	W
University of Guam, GU	M,W
University of Hartford, CT	W
University of Hawaii at Hilo, HI	W
University of Hawaii at Manoa, HI	M,W
University of Houston, TX	W
University of Idaho, ID	W
University of Illinois at Chicago, IL	W
University of Illinois at Urbana–Champaign, IL	W
University of Indianapolis, IN	W
The University of Iowa, IA	W
University of Kansas, KS	W
University of Kentucky, KY	W
University of Louisville, KY	W
University of Mary, ND	W
University of Mary Hardin-Baylor, TX	W
University of Maryland Baltimore County, MD	W
University of Maryland College Park, MD	W
University of Massachusetts Amherst, MA	W
University of Massachusetts Lowell, MA	W
The University of Memphis, TN	W
University of Michigan, Ann Arbor, MI	W
University of Michigan–Dearborn, MI	W
University of Minnesota, Crookston, MN	W
University of Minnesota, Duluth, MN	W
University of Minnesota, Twin Cities Campus, MN	W
University of Mississippi, MS	W
University of Missouri–Columbia, MO	W
University of Missouri–Kansas City, MO	W
University of Missouri–St. Louis, MO	W
The University of Montana–Missoula, MT	W

University of Montevallo, AL	W
University of Nebraska at Kearney, NE	W
University of Nebraska at Omaha, NE	W
University of Nebraska–Lincoln, NE	W
University of Nevada, Reno, NV	W
University of New Hampshire, Durham, NH	W
University of New Haven, CT	W
University of New Mexico, NM	W
University of North Alabama, AL	W
University of North Carolina at Asheville, NC	W
University of North Carolina at Charlotte, NC	W
University of North Carolina at Greensboro, NC	W
University of North Carolina at Pembroke, NC	W
University of North Carolina at Wilmington, NC	W
University of North Dakota, ND	W
University of Northern Colorado, CO	W
University of Northern Iowa, IA	W
University of North Florida, FL	W
University of North Texas, TX	W
University of Notre Dame, IN	W
University of Oklahoma, OK	W
University of Oregon, OR	W
University of Pittsburgh, PA	W
University of Portland, OR	W
U of Puerto Rico at Ponce, PR	M,W
U of Puerto Rico, Cayey University College, PR	M,W
U of Puerto Rico, Mayagüez Campus, PR	M,W
U of Puerto Rico, Río Piedras, PR	M,W
University of Rhode Island, RI	W
University of Rio Grande, OH	W
University of San Diego, CA	W
University of San Francisco, CA	W
University of Sioux Falls, SD	W
University of South Alabama, AL	W
U of South Carolina, Columbia, SC	W
U of South Carolina–Aiken, SC	W
U of South Carolina–Spartanburg, SC	W
University of South Dakota, SD	W
University of Southern California, CA	M,W
University of Southern Colorado, CO	W
University of Southern Indiana, IN	W
University of Southern Mississippi, MS	W
University of South Florida, FL	W
University of Southwestern Louisiana, LA	W
The University of Tampa, FL	W
University of Tennessee at Chattanooga, TN	W
The University of Tennessee at Martin, TN	W
University of Tennessee, Knoxville, TN	W
The University of Texas at Arlington, TX	W
The University of Texas at Austin, TX	W
The University of Texas at El Paso, TX	W

The University of Texas at San Antonio, TX	W
University of the District of Columbia, DC	W
University of the Pacific, CA	M,W
University of the Sacred Heart, PR	M,W
University of Toledo, OH	W
University of Tulsa, OK	W
University of Utah, UT	W
University of Virginia, VA	W
University of Washington, WA	W
The University of West Alabama, AL	W
University of Wisconsin–Green Bay, WI	W
University of Wisconsin–Madison, WI	M,W
University of Wisconsin–Milwaukee, WI	W
University of Wisconsin–Parkside, WI	W
University of Wyoming, WY	W
Urbana University, OH	W
Utah State University, UT	W
Valdosta State University, GA	W
Valley City State University, ND	W
Valparaiso University, IN	W
Villanova University, PA	W
Virginia Commonwealth University, VA	W
Virginia Polytechnic Institute and State U, VA	W
Virginia State University, VA	W
Virginia Union University, VA	W
Wagner College, NY	W
Wake Forest University, NC	W
Walsh University, OH	W
Warner Southern College, FL	W
Washburn University of Topeka, KS	W
Washington State University, WA	W
Wayne State College, NE	W
Wayne State University, MI	W
Webber College, FL	W
Weber State University, UT	W
West Chester University of Pennsylvania, PA	W
Western Baptist College, OR	W
Western Carolina University, NC	W
Western Illinois University, IL	W
Western Kentucky University, KY	W
Western Michigan University, MI	W
Western Montana College of The U of Montana, MT	W
Western New Mexico University, NM	W
Western State College of Colorado, CO	W
Western Washington University, WA	W
West Liberty State College, WV	W
Westmar University, IA	W
Westminster College, PA	W
Westmont College, CA	W
West Texas A&M University, TX	W
West Virginia University, WV	W
West Virginia University Institute of Technology, WV	W
West Virginia Wesleyan College, WV	W
Wheeling Jesuit University, WV	W
Wichita State University, KS	W
William Jewell College, MO	W
Williams Baptist College, AR	W

Volleyball (continued)

William Woods University, MO	M,W
Wilmington College, DE	W
Wingate University, NC	W
Winona State University, MN	W
Winston-Salem State University, NC	W
Winthrop University, SC	W
Wofford College, SC	W
Wright State University, OH	W
Xavier University, OH	W
York College, NE	W
Youngstown State University, OH	W

WATER POLO

Bayamón Technological University College, PR	M
California State University, Long Beach, CA	M
Fordham University, NY	M
The George Washington University, DC	M
Pepperdine University, Malibu, CA	M
Queens Coll of the City U of NY, NY	M
St. Francis College, NY	M
San Diego State University, CA	W
Santa Clara University, CA	M
Stanford University, CA	M
University of California, Berkeley, CA	M
University of California, Irvine, CA	M
University of California, Los Angeles, CA	M,W
University of California, Santa Barbara, CA	M
University of Massachusetts Amherst, MA	M,W
U of Puerto Rico, Mayagüez Campus, PR	M
U of Puerto Rico, Río Piedras, PR	M
University of Southern California, CA	M
University of the Pacific, CA	M,W

WEIGHT LIFTING

Bayamón Technological University College, PR	M
Electronic Data Processing College of Puerto Rico, PR	M
Inter American U of PR, San Germán Campus, PR	M
U of Puerto Rico at Ponce, PR	M,W
U of Puerto Rico, Mayagüez Campus, PR	M
U of Puerto Rico, Río Piedras, PR	M
University of the Sacred Heart, PR	M,W

WRESTLING

Adams State College, CO	M
American University, DC	M
Anderson College, SC	M
Appalachian State University, NC	M
Arizona State University, AZ	M
Ashland University, OH	M
Augustana College, SD	M
Bayamón Technological University College, PR	M
Bloomsburg University of Pennsylvania, PA	M
Boise State University, ID	M
Boston University, MA	M
Brigham Young University, UT	M
California Polytechnic State U, San Luis Obispo, CA	M
California State University, Bakersfield, CA	M
California State University, Fresno, CA	M
California State University, Fullerton, CA	M
California University of Pennsylvania, PA	M
Campbell University, NC	M
Carson-Newman College, TN	M
Central Michigan University, MI	M
Central Missouri State University, MO	M
Chadron State College, NE	M
Cheyney University of Pennsylvania, PA	M
Chicago State University, IL	M
The Citadel, The Military Coll of South Carolina, SC	M
Clarion University of Pennsylvania, PA	M
Clemson University, SC	M
Cleveland State University, OH	M
Colorado School of Mines, CO	M
Cumberland College, KY	M
Dakota Wesleyan University, SD	M
Dana College, NE	M
Delaware State University, DE	M
Dickinson State University, ND	M
Drexel University, PA	M
Duquesne University, PA	M
Eastern Illinois University, IL	M
Eastern Michigan University, MI	M
East Stroudsburg University of Pennsylvania, PA	M
Edinboro University of Pennsylvania, PA	M
Embry-Riddle Aeronautical University, AZ	M
Fort Hays State University, KS	M
Gannon University, PA	M
Gardner-Webb University, NC	M
George Mason University, VA	M
Georgia State University, GA	M
Hofstra University, NY	M
Howard University, DC	M
Indiana University Bloomington, IN	M
Inter American U of PR, San Germán Campus, PR	M
Iowa State University of Science and Technology, IA	M
James Madison University, VA	M
Kent State University, OH	M
Kutztown University of Pennsylvania, PA	M
La Salle University, PA	M
Lehigh University, PA	M
Lindenwood College, MO	M
Lock Haven University of Pennsylvania, PA	M
Longwood College, VA	M
Mankato State University, MN	M
Marquette University, WI	M
Mayville State University, ND	M
Miami University, OH	M
Michigan State University, MI	M
Millersville University of Pennsylvania, PA	M
Montana State U–Northern, MT	M
Moorhead State University, MN	M
North Carolina Agricultural and Technical State U, NC	M
North Carolina State University, NC	M
North Dakota State University, ND	M
Northern Illinois University, IL	M
Northern State University, SD	M
Northwestern College, IA	M
Northwestern University, IL	M
The Ohio State University, OH	M
Oklahoma State U, OK	M
Old Dominion University, VA	M
Oregon State University, OR	M
Penn State U Univ Park Campus, PA	M
Portland State University, OR	M
Purdue University, West Lafayette, IN	M
Rider University, NJ	M
Rutgers, State U of NJ, College of Engineering, NJ	M
Rutgers, State U of NJ, College of Pharmacy, NJ	M
Rutgers, State U of NJ, Cook College, NJ	M
Rutgers, State U of NJ, Livingston College, NJ	M
Rutgers, State U of NJ, Mason Gross School of Arts, NJ	M
Rutgers, State U of NJ, Rutgers College, NJ	M
St. Cloud State University, MN	M
Seton Hall University, NJ	M
Shippensburg University of Pennsylvania, PA	M
Slippery Rock University of Pennsylvania, PA	M
South Dakota State University, SD	M
Southern Illinois University at Edwardsville, IL	M
Southern Oregon University, OR	M
Southwest State University, MN	M
Stanford University, CA	M
State U of NY at Buffalo, NY	M
Syracuse University, NY	M
University of Central Oklahoma, OK	M
The University of Findlay, OH	M
University of Illinois at Urbana–Champaign, IL	M
University of Indianapolis, IN	M
The University of Iowa, IA	M
University of Mary, ND	M
University of Maryland College Park, MD	M
University of Massachusetts Lowell, MA	M
University of Michigan, Ann Arbor, MI	M
University of Minnesota, Twin Cities Campus, MN	M
University of Missouri–Columbia, MO	M
University of Nebraska at Kearney, NE	M
University of Nebraska at Omaha, NE	M
University of Nebraska–Lincoln, NE	M

University of New Mexico, NM	M	University of Pittsburgh at Johnstown, PA	M	Valley City State University, ND	M
University of North Carolina at Greensboro, NC	M	U of Puerto Rico, Mayagüez Campus, PR	M	Virginia Military Institute, VA	M
University of North Carolina at Pembroke, NC	M	University of Southern Colorado, CO	M	Virginia Polytechnic Institute and State U, VA	M
University of North Dakota, ND	M	University of Tennessee at Chattanooga, TN	M	Wagner College, NY	M
University of Northern Colorado, CO	M	University of Virginia, VA	M	Western State College of Colorado, CO	M
University of Northern Iowa, IA	M	University of Wisconsin–Madison, WI	M	Westmar University, IA	M
University of Oklahoma, OK	M	University of Wisconsin–Parkside, WI	M	West Virginia University, WV	M
University of Oregon, OR	M	University of Wyoming, WY	M	Wilkes University, PA	M
University of Pittsburgh, PA	M				

CO-OP PROGRAMS

This index lists the colleges that report offering cooperative education programs. These are formal arrangements with off-campus employers that are designed to allow students to combine study and work, often in a position related to the field of study. Salaries typically are set at a regular marketplace level, and sometimes academic credit is given for the work experience.

Abilene Christian University, TX
Alabama Agricultural and Mechanical University, AL
Alabama State University, AL
Albany State University, GA
Alcorn State University, MS
Alfred University, NY
Allegheny University of the Health Sciences, PA
Alverno College, WI
American Baptist Coll of American Baptist Theol Sem, TN
American University, DC
American University of Puerto Rico, PR
Anderson University, IN
Antioch College, OH
Aquinas College, MI
Arizona State University, AZ
Arkansas State University, AR
Armstrong Atlantic State University, GA
Atlanta College of Art, GA
Atlantic Union College, MA
Auburn University, AL
Auburn University at Montgomery, AL
Audrey Cohen College, NY
Augsburg College, MN
Augustana College, IL
Augustana College, SD
Augusta State University, GA
Austin Peay State University, TN
Azusa Pacific University, CA
Ball State University, IN
Barber-Scotia College, NC
Bayamón Technological University College, PR
Beaver College, PA
Becker College–Leicester Campus, MA
Becker College–Worcester Campus, MA
Belmont University, TN
Bemidji State University, MN
Benedictine College, KS
Bennett College, NC
Berry College, GA
Bethany College, KS
Bethune-Cookman College, FL
Beulah Heights Bible College, GA
Biola University, CA
Blackburn College, IL
Black Hills State University, SD
Bloomsburg University of Pennsylvania, PA
Boston Architectural Center, MA
Boston University, MA
Bowie State University, MD
Bowling Green State University, OH

Bradford College, MA
Bradley University, IL
Brescia College, KY
Brewton-Parker College, GA
Brigham Young University, UT
Brigham Young University–Hawaii Campus, HI
Bryn Athyn College of the New Church, PA
Burlington College, VT
Cabrini College, PA
Caldwell College, NJ
California Baptist College, CA
California College for Health Sciences, CA
California Institute of the Arts, CA
California Lutheran University, CA
California Polytechnic State U, San Luis Obispo, CA
California State Polytechnic University, Pomona, CA
California State University, Bakersfield, CA
California State University, Chico, CA
California State University, Dominguez Hills, CA
California State University, Fresno, CA
California State University, Fullerton, CA
California State University, Hayward, CA
California State University, Long Beach, CA
California State University, Los Angeles, CA
California State University, Sacramento, CA
California State University, San Bernardino, CA
California State University, Stanislaus, CA
California University of Pennsylvania, PA
Calumet College of Saint Joseph, IN
Calvin College, MI
Campbell University, NC
Capitol College, MD
Carnegie Mellon University, PA
Carroll College, MT
Case Western Reserve University, OH
Castleton State College, VT
Cazenovia College, NY
Central Connecticut State University, CT
Central Missouri State University, MO
Central State University, OH
Central Washington University, WA
Chadron State College, NE
Chapman University, CA
Chestnut Hill College, PA
Cheyney University of Pennsylvania, PA
Chicago State University, IL
Christopher Newport University, VA

City Coll of the City U of NY, NY
Clarion University of Pennsylvania, PA
Clark Atlanta University, GA
Clarke College, IA
Clarkson University, NY
Clayton College & State University, GA
Cleary College, MI
Clemson University, SC
Cleveland College of Jewish Studies, OH
Cleveland Institute of Art, OH
Cleveland State University, OH
Clinch Valley College of the U of Virginia, VA
Coker College, SC
College Misericordia, PA
College of Charleston, SC
College of Insurance, NY
College of Mount St. Joseph, OH
College of New Rochelle, NY
College of Notre Dame, CA
College of St. Francis, IL
College of Santa Fe, NM
College of the Atlantic, ME
College of the Ozarks, MO
The College of West Virginia, WV
Colorado Christian University, CO
Colorado School of Mines, CO
Colorado State University, CO
Colorado Technical University, CO
Columbia Union College, MD
Columbus State University, GA
Concordia College, Moorhead, MN
Concordia University, CA
Concordia University at Austin, TX
Cornell University, NY
Covenant College, GA
Cumberland University, TN
Daemen College, NY
Dakota State University, SD
Dakota Wesleyan University, SD
Daniel Webster College, NH
Davenport College of Business, Grand Rapids, MI
Davenport College of Business, Lansing Campus, MI
David N. Myers College, OH
Davis & Elkins College, WV
The Defiance College, OH
Delaware State University, DE
Delaware Valley College, PA
Denver Technical College, CO

Detroit College of Business, Dearborn, MI
Detroit College of Business–Flint, MI
Detroit College of Business, Warren
 Campus, MI
DeVry Institute of Technology, AZ
DeVry Institute of Technology, Pomona, CA
DeVry Institute of Technology, GA
DeVry Institute of Technology, Addison, IL
DeVry Institute of Technology, Chicago, IL
DeVry Institute of Technology, MO
DeVry Institute of Technology, OH
DeVry Institute of Technology, TX
Dickinson State University, ND
Doane College, NE
Dominican College of Blauvelt, NY
Dowling College, NY
Drake University, IA
Drexel University, PA
Duquesne University, PA
East Carolina University, NC
Eastern Connecticut State University, CT
Eastern Kentucky University, KY
Eastern Michigan University, MI
Eastern New Mexico University, NM
Eastern Oregon University, OR
Eastern Washington University, WA
East Tennessee State University, TN
Edward Waters College, FL
Elizabeth City State University, NC
Elmhurst College, IL
Elon College, NC
Embry-Riddle Aeronautical University, AZ
Embry-Riddle Aeronautical University, FL
Embry-Riddle Aeronautical U, Extended
 Campus, FL
Emporia State University, KS
Escuela de Artes Plasticas de Puerto Rico,
 PR
The Evergreen State College, WA
Fairleigh Dickinson U,
 Teaneck-Hackensack, NJ
Fashion Institute of Technology, NY
Fayetteville State University, NC
Ferris State University, MI
Fisk University, TN
Five Towns College, NY
Florida Agricultural and Mechanical
 University, FL
Florida Atlantic University, FL
Florida Institute of Technology, FL
Florida International University, FL
Florida Memorial College, FL
Florida Metropolitan U-Tampa Coll,
 Pinellas, FL
Florida Metropolitan U-Tampa Coll, FL
Florida State University, FL
Fontbonne College, MO
Fort Lewis College, CO
Fort Valley State University, GA
Franciscan University of Steubenville, OH
Francis Marion University, SC
Freed-Hardeman University, TN
Friends University, KS
Furman University, SC
Gallaudet University, DC
Gannon University, PA
Geneva College, PA

George Mason University, VA
Georgetown College, KY
The George Washington University, DC
Georgia College and State University, GA
Georgia Institute of Technology, GA
Georgia Southern University, GA
Georgia Southwestern State University, GA
Georgia State University, GA
GMI Engineering & Management Institute,
 MI
Goddard College, VT
Golden Gate University, CA
Goldey-Beacom College, DE
Gordon College, MA
Goshen College, IN
Grace University, NE
Grambling State University, LA
Grand Valley State University, MI
Grand View College, IA
Greenville College, IL
Gustavus Adolphus College, MN
Gwynedd-Mercy College, PA
Hamline University, MN
Hannibal-LaGrange College, MO
Harding University, AR
Hastings College, NE
Hawaii Pacific University, HI
Heritage College, WA
High Point University, NC
Hilbert College, NY
Holy Family College, PA
Hood College, MD
Howard University, DC
Humboldt State University, CA
Humphreys College, CA
Huntingdon College, AL
Huron University, SD
Husson College, ME
Huston-Tillotson College, TX
The Illinois Institute of Art, IL
Illinois Institute of Technology, IL
Illinois State University, IL
Indiana State University, IN
Indiana University Bloomington, IN
Indiana University Northwest, IN
Indiana University of Pennsylvania, PA
Indiana U–Purdue U Fort Wayne, IN
Indiana U–Purdue U Indianapolis, IN
Inter American U of PR, Arecibo Campus,
 PR
Inter American U of PR, Metropolitan
 Campus, PR
International Acad of Merchandising &
 Design, Inc, FL
International College, FL
Iowa State University of Science and
 Technology, IA
ITT Technical Institute, Maitland, FL
Jackson State University, MS
Jacksonville State University, AL
Jacksonville University, FL
Jamestown College, ND
Jarvis Christian College, TX
Jersey City State College, NJ
John Carroll University, OH
John Jay Coll of Criminal Justice, the City
 U of NY, NY

Johns Hopkins University, MD
Johnson & Wales University, FL
Johnson & Wales University, RI
Johnson & Wales University, SC
Johnson C. Smith University, NC
Kalamazoo College, MI
Kansas City Art Institute, MO
Kansas Newman College, KS
Kansas State University, KS
Kean College of New Jersey, NJ
Keene State College, NH
Kendall College, IL
Kendall College of Art and Design, MI
Kennesaw State University, GA
Kent State University, OH
Kentucky State University, KY
King's College, PA
Knoxville College, TN
Kol Yaakov Torah Center, NY
Laboratory Institute of Merchandising, NY
Lamar University, TX
Lander University, SC
Lane College, TN
Langston University, OK
La Roche College, PA
La Salle University, PA
Lawrence Technological University, MI
Lee University, TN
Lehigh University, PA
Lehman Coll of the City U of NY, NY
LeMoyne-Owen College, TN
LeTourneau University, TX
Lewis-Clark State College, ID
Lincoln University, MO
Lincoln University, PA
Lindenwood College, MO
Lindsey Wilson College, KY
Livingstone College, NC
Long Island U, Brooklyn Campus, NY
Long Island U, C.W. Post Campus, NY
Long Island U, Southampton College, NY
Louisiana State University and A&M
 College, LA
Louisiana State University in Shreveport,
 LA
Louisiana Tech University, LA
Lourdes College, OH
Lyndon State College, VT
Madonna University, MI
Maharishi University of Management, IA
Maine College of Art, ME
Maine Maritime Academy, ME
Malone College, OH
Manchester College, IN
Manhattan College, NY
Marian College, IN
Marian College of Fond du Lac, WI
Marist College, NY
Marquette University, WI
Marshall University, WV
Marycrest International University, IA
Marygrove College, MI
Maryville University of Saint Louis, MO
Mary Washington College, VA
Massachusetts College of Art, MA
Massachusetts Institute of Technology, MA
Massachusetts Maritime Academy, MA

Mayville State University, ND
McNeese State University, LA
Medgar Evers College of the City U of NY, NY
Mercer University, Macon, GA
Mercyhurst College, PA
Meredith College, NC
Merrimack College, MA
Metropolitan State College of Denver, CO
Miami University, OH
Michigan State University, MI
Michigan Technological University, MI
Middle Tennessee State University, TN
Miles College, AL
Millersville University of Pennsylvania, PA
Milligan College, TN
Mills College, CA
Minneapolis College of Art and Design, MN
Minot State University, ND
Mississippi College, MS
Mississippi State University, MS
Mississippi University for Women, MS
Mississippi Valley State University, MS
Missouri Baptist College, MO
Missouri Southern State College, MO
Missouri Valley College, MO
Molloy College, NY
Monmouth University, NJ
Montana State U–Billings, MT
Montana State U–Northern, MT
Montana Tech of The University of Montana, MT
Montclair State University, NJ
Montreat College, NC
Moore College of Art and Design, PA
Morehead State University, KY
Morehouse College, GA
Morgan State University, MD
Morris College, SC
Mount Marty College, SD
Mount Olive College, NC
Mount Saint Mary College, NY
Mount Saint Mary's College and Seminary, MD
Mount Senario College, WI
Mount Union College, OH
Mount Vernon College, DC
Murray State University, KY
National College, MO
National College, NM
National College, SD
National College–St. Paul Campus, MN
National College–Sioux Falls Branch, SD
The National Hispanic University, CA
Nazareth College of Rochester, NY
Neumann College, PA
New College of California, CA
New Hampshire College, NH
New Jersey Institute of Technology, NJ
New Mexico Highlands University, NM
New Mexico Inst of Mining and Technology, NM
New Mexico State University, NM
Newschool of Architecture, CA
New York Institute of Technology, NY
Niagara University, NY

Nicholls State University, LA
Norfolk State University, VA
North Carolina Agricultural and Technical State U, NC
North Carolina Central University, NC
North Carolina State University, NC
North Carolina Wesleyan College, NC
North Central Bible College, MN
North Central College, IL
North Dakota State University, ND
Northeastern Illinois University, IL
Northeastern University, MA
Northeast Louisiana University, LA
Northern Arizona University, AZ
Northern Illinois University, IL
Northern Kentucky University, KY
Northern State University, SD
North Georgia College & State University, GA
Northland College, WI
Northwest Christian College, OR
Northwestern College, IA
Northwestern State University of Louisiana, LA
Northwestern University, IL
Northwood University, Texas Campus, TX
Norwich University, VT
Notre Dame College of Ohio, OH
Nova Southeastern University, FL
Oakland University, MI
Oakwood College, AL
Oglala Lakota College, SD
Oglethorpe University, GA
Ohio Northern University, OH
The Ohio State University, OH
Ohio University, OH
Oklahoma Baptist University, OK
Oklahoma City University, OK
Oklahoma Panhandle State University, OK
Oklahoma State U, OK
Old Dominion University, VA
Olivet Nazarene University, IL
Oregon Institute of Technology, OR
Oregon State University, OR
Otis College of Art and Design, CA
Ouachita Baptist University, AR
Our Lady of Holy Cross College, LA
Our Lady of the Lake University of San Antonio, TX
Pace University, NY
Pacific Lutheran University, WA
Paine College, GA
Paul Quinn College, TX
Penn State U Univ Park Campus, PA
Peru State College, NE
Pfeiffer University, NC
Philadelphia College of Textiles and Science, PA
Philander Smith College, AR
Phillips University, OK
Pittsburg State University, KS
Pitzer College, CA
Point Park College, PA
Polytechnic U, Brooklyn Campus, NY
Polytechnic U, Farmingdale Campus, NY
Portland State University, OR
Prairie View A&M University, TX

Pratt Institute, NY
Presentation College, SD
Purdue University, West Lafayette, IN
Purdue University Calumet, IN
Purdue University North Central, IN
Queens Coll of the City U of NY, NY
Ramapo College of New Jersey, NJ
Reformed Bible College, MI
Regis University, CO
Rensselaer Polytechnic Institute, NY
Robert Morris College, IL
Robert Morris College, PA
Roberts Wesleyan College, NY
Rochester Institute of Technology, NY
Rockhurst College, MO
Rocky Mountain College, MT
Roger Williams University, RI
Rose-Hulman Institute of Technology, IN
Rowan University, NJ
Russell Sage College, NY
Rust College, MS
Rutgers, State U of NJ, Cook College, NJ
Sacred Heart University, CT
Saginaw Valley State University, MI
St. Ambrose University, IA
Saint Augustine's College, NC
St. Edward's University, TX
Saint Francis College, IN
Saint Joseph's College, IN
Saint Joseph's University, PA
Saint Martin's College, WA
Saint Mary's College, MI
St. Mary's University of San Antonio, TX
St. Norbert College, WI
Saint Paul's College, VA
Saint Peter's College, Jersey City, NJ
St. Thomas University, FL
Saint Vincent College, PA
Saint Xavier University, IL
Salisbury State University, MD
Samford University, AL
Sam Houston State University, TX
San Francisco State University, CA
San Jose State University, CA
Santa Clara University, CA
Savannah State University, GA
School of the Art Institute of Chicago, IL
Seattle Pacific University, WA
Seton Hall University, NJ
Seton Hill College, PA
Shepherd College, WV
Shimer College, IL
Sh'or Yoshuv Rabbinical College, NY
Siena Heights College, MI
Silver Lake College, WI
Simpson College, IA
South Dakota School of Mines and Technology, SD
South Dakota State University, SD
Southeastern University, DC
Southeast Missouri State University, MO
Southern California Institute of Architecture, CA
Southern Connecticut State University, CT
Southern Illinois University at Carbondale, IL

Southern Illinois University at
  Edwardsville, IL
Southern Methodist University, TX
Southern Oregon University, OR
Southern Polytechnic State University, GA
Southern University and A&M College, LA
Southern Utah University, UT
Southwest Baptist University, MO
Southwestern Adventist University, TX
Southwestern Oklahoma State University,
  OK
Southwest Missouri State University, MO
Springfield College, MA
Spring Hill College, AL
State U of NY at New Paltz, NY
State U of NY at Oswego, NY
State U of NY College at Brockport, NY
State U of NY College at Cortland, NY
State U of NY College at Plattsburgh, NY
State U of NY College at Potsdam, NY
Stevens Institute of Technology, NJ
Strayer College, DC
Suffolk University, MA
Syracuse University, NY
Talladega College, AL
Tarleton State University, TX
Taylor University, Fort Wayne Campus, IN
Teikyo Post University, CT
Temple University, Philadelphia, PA
Tennessee State University, TN
Tennessee Technological University, TN
Tennessee Temple University, TN
Texas A&M University, College Station,
  TX
Texas A&M University at Galveston, TX
Texas A&M University–Commerce, TX
Texas A&M University–Corpus Christi, TX
Texas A&M University–Kingsville, TX
Texas Southern University, TX
Texas Woman's University, TX
Thiel College, PA
Thomas College, GA
Thomas More College, KY
Tougaloo College, MS
Towson University, MD
Trevecca Nazarene University, TN
Trinity International University, IL
Tri-State University, IN
Tuskegee University, AL
Union College, KY
Union College, NE
Unity College, ME
Universidad Adventista de las Antillas, PR
Universidad Metropolitana, PR
The University of Akron, OH
The University of Alabama at Birmingham,
  AL
The University of Alabama in Huntsville,
  AL
U of Alaska Anchorage, AK
U of Alaska Southeast, AK
University of Arizona, AZ
University of Arkansas, Fayetteville, AR
University of Arkansas at Little Rock, AR
University of Arkansas at Pine Bluff, AR
University of Bridgeport, CT
University of California, Berkeley, CA

University of California, Riverside, CA
University of California, Santa Barbara, CA
University of Central Arkansas, AR
University of Central Florida, FL
University of Cincinnati, OH
University of Colorado at Boulder, CO
University of Colorado at Colorado Springs,
  CO
University of Colorado at Denver, CO
University of Connecticut, Storrs, CT
University of Dayton, OH
University of Delaware, DE
University of Denver, CO
University of Detroit Mercy, MI
University of Evansville, IN
The University of Findlay, OH
University of Florida, FL
University of Georgia, GA
University of Great Falls, MT
University of Hartford, CT
University of Hawaii at Manoa, HI
University of Houston, TX
University of Houston–Downtown, TX
University of Idaho, ID
University of Illinois at Chicago, IL
University of Illinois at Urbana–
  Champaign, IL
University of Indianapolis, IN
The University of Iowa, IA
University of Kansas, KS
University of Kentucky, KY
University of La Verne, CA
University of Louisville, KY
University of Maine, Orono, ME
University of Maine at Machias, ME
University of Mary, ND
University of Mary Hardin-Baylor, TX
University of Maryland Baltimore County,
  MD
University of Maryland College Park, MD
University of Maryland Eastern Shore, MD
University of Massachusetts Amherst, MA
University of Massachusetts Boston, MA
University of Massachusetts Dartmouth,
  MA
University of Massachusetts Lowell, MA
University of Michigan, Ann Arbor, MI
University of Michigan–Dearborn, MI
University of Michigan–Flint, MI
University of Minnesota, Twin Cities
  Campus, MN
University of Missouri–Columbia, MO
University of Missouri–Kansas City, MO
University of Missouri–Rolla, MO
University of Missouri–St. Louis, MO
The University of Montana–Missoula, MT
University of Nebraska at Kearney, NE
University of Nebraska at Omaha, NE
University of Nebraska–Lincoln, NE
University of Nevada, Las Vegas, NV
University of Nevada, Reno, NV
University of New England, ME
University of New Haven, CT
University of New Mexico, NM
University of North Alabama, AL
University of North Carolina at Charlotte,
  NC

University of North Carolina at Pembroke,
  NC
University of North Carolina at
  Wilmington, NC
University of North Dakota, ND
University of Northern Colorado, CO
University of Northern Iowa, IA
University of North Florida, FL
University of North Texas, TX
University of Oklahoma, OK
University of Pittsburgh, PA
U of Puerto Rico, Mayagüez Campus, PR
U of Puerto Rico, Río Piedras, PR
University of Puget Sound, WA
University of Rhode Island, RI
University of Rio Grande, OH
University of St. Thomas, TX
University of San Francisco, CA
University of Science and Arts of
  Oklahoma, OK
University of Sioux Falls, SD
University of South Alabama, AL
U of South Carolina, Columbia, SC
U of South Carolina–Aiken, SC
University of Southern California, CA
University of Southern Colorado, CO
University of Southern Indiana, IN
University of Southern Maine, ME
University of Southern Mississippi, MS
University of South Florida, FL
The University of Tampa, FL
University of Tennessee at Chattanooga, TN
The University of Tennessee at Martin, TN
University of Tennessee, Knoxville, TN
The University of Texas at Arlington, TX
The University of Texas at Austin, TX
The University of Texas at Dallas, TX
The University of Texas at El Paso, TX
The University of Texas at San Antonio,
  TX
The University of Texas–Pan American, TX
University of the District of Columbia, DC
University of the Pacific, CA
University of the Sacred Heart, PR
University of Toledo, OH
University of Utah, UT
University of Vermont, VT
University of Virginia, VA
University of Washington, WA
University of West Florida, FL
University of Wisconsin–Eau Claire, WI
University of Wisconsin–Green Bay, WI
University of Wisconsin–La Crosse, WI
University of Wisconsin–Madison, WI
University of Wisconsin–Milwaukee, WI
University of Wisconsin–Platteville, WI
University of Wisconsin–River Falls, WI
University of Wisconsin–Stevens Point, WI
University of Wisconsin–Stout, WI
University of Wisconsin–Superior, WI
University of Wyoming, WY
Urbana University, OH
Ursuline College, OH
Utah State University, UT
Utica College of Syracuse University, NY
Valdosta State University, GA
Valley City State University, ND

Valparaiso University, IN
Villa Julie College, MD
Virginia Commonwealth University, VA
Virginia Polytechnic Institute and State U,
 VA
Virginia State University, VA
Virginia Union University, VA
Viterbo College, WI
Voorhees College, SC
Walla Walla College, WA
Warner Pacific College, OR
Warren Wilson College, NC
Washburn University of Topeka, KS
Washington State University, WA
Washington University, MO
Wayne State College, NE
Wayne State University, MI
Webber College, FL
Webb Institute, NY

Weber State University, UT
Webster University, MO
Wesleyan University, CT
Western Carolina University, NC
Western Connecticut State University, CT
Western Illinois University, IL
Western Kentucky University, KY
Western Michigan University, MI
Western Montana College of The U of
 Montana, MT
Western New Mexico University, NM
Western State College of Colorado, CO
Western Washington University, WA
Westmar University, IA
Westmont College, CA
West Texas A&M University, TX
West Virginia State College, WV
West Virginia University, WV

West Virginia University Institute of
 Technology, WV
Wheeling Jesuit University, WV
Whitworth College, WA
Wichita State University, KS
Widener University, PA
Wilberforce University, OH
Wilkes University, PA
William Penn College, IA
Wilmington College, DE
Winston-Salem State University, NC
Winthrop University, SC
Worcester Polytechnic Institute, MA
Wright State University, OH
Xavier University of Louisiana, LA
York College, NE
York College of the City University of New
 York, NY
Youngstown State University, OH

ROTC PROGRAMS

This index lists the colleges that offer ROTC programs. This is arranged in three categories by branch of the service that sponsors the program, in this order: Army, Navy, Air Force.

An asterisk means that the program is offered at another college's campus site.

ARMY

Abilene Christian University, TX*
Adelphi University, NY*
Alabama Agricultural and Mechanical University, AL
Alabama State University, AL*
Albany State University, GA
Alcorn State University, MS
Alderson-Broaddus College, WV*
Alfred University, NY*
Allegheny College, PA*
Allen College of Nursing, IA*
Allentown College of St. Francis de Sales, PA*
Alma College, MI*
Alvernia College, PA*
American International College, MA*
American University, DC*
American University of Puerto Rico, PR*
Anderson College, SC*
Anna Maria College, MA*
Appalachian State University, NC
Arizona State University, AZ
Arkansas State University, AR
Arkansas Tech University, AR*
Armstrong Atlantic State University, GA
Art Academy of Cincinnati, OH*
Asbury College, KY*
Assumption College, MA*
Auburn University, AL
Auburn University at Montgomery, AL
Augusta State University, GA
Austin Peay State University, TN
Azusa Pacific University, CA*
Babson College, MA*
Baker University, KS*
Baldwin-Wallace College, OH*
Ball State University, IN
Baptist Bible College, MO*
Baptist Bible College of Pennsylvania, PA*
Barber-Scotia College, NC*
Bayamón Central University, PR*
Bayamón Technological University College, PR
Bay Path College, MA*
Beaver College, PA*
Becker College–Leicester Campus, MA*
Becker College–Worcester Campus, MA*
Bellarmine College, KY*
Bellevue University, NE*
Bellin College of Nursing, WI*
Belmont Abbey College, NC*
Belmont University, TN*
Benedict College, SC

Benedictine College, KS
Benedictine University, IL*
Bennett College, NC*
Bentley College, MA*
Bethel College, MN*
Beth-El College of Nursing and Health Sciences, CO*
Bethune-Cookman College, FL
Biola University, CA*
Birmingham-Southern College, AL*
Black Hills State University, SD
Bloomfield College, NJ*
Bloomsburg University of Pennsylvania, PA
Boise State University, ID
Boston College, MA*
Boston University, MA
Bowie State University, MD
Bowling Green State University, OH
Bradley University, IL
Brandeis University, MA*
Bridgewater State College, MA*
Brigham Young University, UT
Brigham Young University–Hawaii Campus, HI*
Brown University, RI*
Bryant College, RI
Bucknell University, PA
Butler University, IN*
Cabrini College, PA*
Caldwell College, NJ*
California Baptist College, CA*
California Institute of Technology, CA*
California Lutheran University, CA*
California Polytechnic State U, San Luis Obispo, CA
California State Polytechnic University, Pomona, CA
California State University, Dominguez Hills, CA*
California State University, Fresno, CA
California State University, Fullerton, CA
California State University, Long Beach, CA
California State University, Los Angeles, CA*
California State University, Northridge, CA*
California State University, Sacramento, CA*
California State University, San Bernardino, CA
California University of Pennsylvania, PA
Cameron University, OK
Campbell University, NC
Canisius College, NY

Capital University, OH
Capitol College, MD*
Caribbean University, PR*
Carlow College, PA*
Carnegie Mellon University, PA
Carson-Newman College, TN
Cascade College, OR*
Case Western Reserve University, OH*
Catawba College, NC
The Catholic University of America, DC*
Cazenovia College, NY*
Cedar Crest College, PA*
Cedarville College, OH*
Centenary College of Louisiana, LA*
Central Baptist College, AR*
Central Connecticut State University, CT*
Central Methodist College, MO*
Central Michigan University, MI
Central Missouri State University, MO
Central State University, OH
Central Washington University, WA
Centre College, KY*
Chaminade University of Honolulu, HI*
Chapman University, CA*
Chatham College, PA*
Chestnut Hill College, PA*
Cheyney University of Pennsylvania, PA
Chicago State University, IL
Christian Brothers University, TN*
Christian Heritage College, CA*
Christopher Newport University, VA
The Citadel, The Military Coll of South Carolina, SC
City Coll of the City U of NY, NY*
Claflin College, SC
Claremont McKenna College, CA
Clark Atlanta University, GA
Clarkson College, NE*
Clarkson University, NY
Clark University, MA*
Clayton College & State University, GA*
Clearwater Christian College, FL*
Clemson University, SC
Cleveland State University, OH
Coe College, IA*
Cogswell Polytechnical College, CA*
Colby College, ME*
Colby-Sawyer College, NH*
College Misericordia, PA*
College of Mount St. Joseph, OH*
College of Mount Saint Vincent, NY*
The College of New Jersey, NJ*
College of Notre Dame, CA*
College of Notre Dame of Maryland, MD*
College of Our Lady of the Elms, MA*

ARMY (continued)

College of Saint Benedict, MN*
College of Saint Mary, NE*
College of St. Scholastica, MN*
College of the Holy Cross, MA*
College of the Ozarks, MO
College of William and Mary, VA
Colorado Christian University, CO*
The Colorado College, CO*
Colorado School of Mines, CO
Colorado State University, CO
Colorado Technical University, CO*
Columbia College, MO*
Columbia College, SC*
Columbus State University, GA
Concordia College, MI*
Concordia College, Moorhead, MN*
Concordia College, St. Paul, MN*
Concordia College, NE
Concordia University at Austin, TX*
Conservatory of Music of Puerto Rico, PR*
Converse College, SC*
Cornell University, NY
Cornerstone College, MI*
Covenant College, GA*
Creighton University, NE
Cumberland College, KY
Curry College, MA*
Daemen College, NY*
Dallas Baptist University, TX*
Dana College, NE*
Daniel Webster College, NH*
Dartmouth College, NH
Davenport College of Business, Lansing
    Campus, MI*
David Lipscomb University, TN*
Davidson College, NC
Delaware State University, DE
Delta State University, MS
DePaul University, IL
DePauw University, IN*
DeVry Institute of Technology, Addison,
    IL*
DeVry Institute of Technology, OH*
Dickinson College, PA
Dillard University, LA
Doane College, NE*
Dominican College of Blauvelt, NY*
Dominican College of San Rafael, CA*
Dowling College, NY*
Drake University, IA
Drew University, NJ*
Drexel University, PA
Drury College, MO*
Duke University, NC
Duquesne University, PA
D'Youville College, NY*
East Carolina University, NC
East Central University, OK
Eastern College, PA*
Eastern Connecticut State University, CT*
Eastern Illinois University, IL
Eastern Kentucky University, KY
Eastern Michigan University, MI
Eastern New Mexico University, NM
Eastern Washington University, WA
East Tennessee State University, TN

East Texas Baptist University, TX*
Eckerd College, FL*
Edinboro University of Pennsylvania, PA
Edward Waters College, FL*
Electronic Data Processing College of
    Puerto Rico, PR*
Elizabeth City State University, NC
Elmhurst College, IL*
Elmira College, NY*
Elon College, NC*
Embry-Riddle Aeronautical University, AZ
Embry-Riddle Aeronautical University, FL
Emmanuel College, MA*
Emporia State University, KS
Evangel College, MO
Fairleigh Dickinson U,
    Teaneck-Hackensack, NJ*
Fairmont State College, WV
Ferris State University, MI*
Fisk University, TN*
Fitchburg State College, MA
Florida Agricultural and Mechanical
    University, FL
Florida Institute of Technology, FL
Florida International University, FL
Florida Memorial College, FL
Florida Southern College, FL
Florida State University, FL
Fontbonne College, MO*
Fordham University, NY
Fort Valley State University, GA
Framingham State College, MA*
Francis Marion University, SC
Franklin and Marshall College, PA*
Franklin College of Indiana, IN*
Franklin University, OH*
Free Will Baptist Bible College, TN*
Frostburg State University, MD
Furman University, SC
Gannon University, PA
George Mason University, VA
Georgetown College, KY
Georgetown University, DC
The George Washington University, DC*
Georgia College and State University, GA
Georgia Institute of Technology, GA
Georgia Southern University, GA
Georgia State University, GA
Golden Gate University, CA*
Gonzaga University, WA
Goucher College, MD*
Grambling State University, LA
Grand Canyon University, AZ
Grand View College, IA*
Green Mountain College, VT*
Greensboro College, NC*
Guilford College, NC*
Gustavus Adolphus College, MN*
Hamilton College, NY*
Hampden-Sydney College, VA*
Hampshire College, MA*
Harding University, AR*
Harvard University, MA*
Harvey Mudd College, CA*
Hawaii Pacific University, HI*
Hendrix College, AR*
High Point University, NC*
Hillsdale College, MI*

Hofstra University, NY
Holy Names College, CA*
Hood College, MD*
Houghton College, NY*
Houston Baptist University, TX*
Howard Payne University, TX*
Howard University, DC
Huntingdon College, AL*
Husson College, ME*
Idaho State University, ID*
Illinois Institute of Technology, IL
Illinois State University, IL
Illinois Wesleyan University, IL*
Indiana State University, IN
Indiana University Bloomington, IN
Indiana University Northwest, IN
Indiana University of Pennsylvania, PA
Indiana U–Purdue U Indianapolis, IN
Indiana University South Bend, IN*
Indiana University Southeast, IN*
Inter American U of PR, Arecibo Campus,
    PR*
Inter American U of PR, Guayama Campus,
    PR*
Inter American U of PR, Metropolitan
    Campus, PR*
Inter American U of PR, San Germán
    Campus, PR*
Iona College, New Rochelle, NY*
Iowa State University of Science and
    Technology, IA
Ithaca College, NY*
Jackson State University, MS
Jacksonville State University, AL
James Madison University, VA
Jersey City State College, NJ*
John Brown University, AR*
John Carroll University, OH
Johns Hopkins University, MD
Johnson & Wales University, RI*
Johnson C. Smith University, NC*
Judson College, AL*
Judson College, IL*
Kalamazoo College, MI*
Kansas State University, KS
Kean College of New Jersey, NJ*
Keene State College, NH*
Kennesaw State University, GA*
Kent State University, OH
Keuka College, NY*
King College, TN*
King's College, PA
Knoxville College, TN
Kutztown University of Pennsylvania, PA*
Lafayette College, PA*
Lander University, SC
Langston University, OK*
La Roche College, PA*
La Salle University, PA*
Lawrence Technological University, MI*
Lebanon Valley College, PA*
Lees-McRae College, NC*
Lehigh University, PA
Lehman Coll of the City U of NY, NY*
Le Moyne College, NY*
LeMoyne-Owen College, TN*
Lenoir-Rhyne College, NC*
Lewis-Clark State College, ID

*program is offered at another college's campus

Lewis University, IL
Limestone College, SC*
Lincoln University, MO
Lindenwood College, MO*
Lindsey Wilson College, KY*
Livingstone College, NC
Lock Haven University of Pennsylvania, PA
Long Island U, Brooklyn Campus, NY*
Long Island U, C.W. Post Campus, NY*
Long Island U, Southampton College, NY*
Longwood College, VA
Louisiana State University and A&M
  College, LA
Louisiana State University in Shreveport,
  LA
Lourdes College, OH*
Loyola College, MD
Loyola Marymount University, CA*
Loyola University Chicago, IL*
Loyola University New Orleans, LA
Lubbock Christian University, TX*
Lycoming College, PA*
Manhattan College, NY*
Mankato State University, MN
Marian College, IN*
Marian College of Fond du Lac, WI
Marietta College, OH*
Marquette University, WI
Marshall University, WV
Mary Baldwin College, VA*
Maryland Institute, College of Art, MD*
Marymount University, VA*
Maryville University of Saint Louis, MO*
Marywood University, PA*
Mass Coll of Pharmacy and Allied Health
  Sciences, MA*
Massachusetts Institute of Technology, MA
Massachusetts Maritime Academy, MA*
Mayville State University, ND*
McKendree College, IL*
McNeese State University, LA
Medaille College, NY*
Menlo College, CA*
Mercer University, Macon, GA*
Mercyhurst College, PA*
Meredith College, NC*
Methodist College, NC
Metropolitan State College of Denver, CO
Miami University, OH*
Michigan State University, MI
Michigan Technological University, MI
MidAmerica Nazarene University, KS*
Middle Tennessee State University, TN
Midway College, KY*
Miles College, AL*
Milligan College, TN*
Millsaps College, MS*
Milwaukee School of Engineering, WI*
Mississippi College, MS*
Mississippi State University, MS
Mississippi University for Women, MS*
Mississippi Valley State University, MS
Missouri Baptist College, MO*
Missouri Western State College, MO
Molloy College, NY*
Monmouth College, IL*
Montana State U–Billings, MT
Montana State U–Bozeman, MT

Moorhead State University, MN*
Moravian College, PA*
Morehead State University, KY
Morehouse College, GA
Morgan State University, MD
Morris College, SC
Mount Holyoke College, MA*
Mount Marty College, SD*
Mount Mary College, WI*
Mount Saint Mary College, NY*
Mount St. Mary's College, CA*
Mount Saint Mary's College and Seminary,
  MD
Mount Union College, OH*
Muhlenberg College, PA*
Murray State University, KY
National College, SD*
National University, CA*
Nebraska Methodist Coll of Nursing &
  Allied Health, NE*
Nebraska Wesleyan University, NE*
Neumann College, PA
Newberry College, SC
New College of the University of South
  Florida, FL*
New England College, NH*
New Hampshire College, NH*
New Mexico State University, NM
Niagara University, NY
Nichols College, MA
Norfolk State University, VA
North Carolina Agricultural and Technical
  State U, NC
North Carolina Central University, NC*
North Carolina State University, NC
North Central Bible College, MN*
North Central College, IL*
North Dakota State University, ND
Northeastern Illinois University, IL*
Northeastern University, MA
Northeast Louisiana University, LA
Northern Arizona University, AZ
Northern Illinois University, IL
Northern Kentucky University, KY*
Northern Michigan University, MI
North Georgia College & State University,
  GA
North Greenville College, SC
Northwest Christian College, OR*
Northwestern College, MN*
Northwestern State University of Louisiana,
  LA
Northwestern University, IL*
Norwich University, VT
Occidental College, CA*
Oglethorpe University, GA*
Ohio Dominican College, OH*
Ohio Northern University, OH*
The Ohio State University, OH
Ohio University, OH
Ohio University–Chillicothe, OH
Ohio University–Lancaster, OH*
Oklahoma Christian U of Science and Arts,
  OK*
Oklahoma City University, OK*
Oklahoma State U, OK
Old Dominion University, VA
Olivet Nazarene University, IL*

Oregon State University, OR
Otterbein College, OH*
Our Lady of Holy Cross College, LA*
Our Lady of the Lake University of San
  Antonio, TX*
Pacific Lutheran University, WA
Pacific University, OR*
Paine College, GA*
Park College, MO
Penn State U Abington College, PA
Penn State U Altoona College, PA
Penn State U Berks-Lehigh Valley Coll, PA
Penn State U Harrisburg Campus of the
  Capital Coll, PA*
Penn State U Schuylkill Campus of the
  Capital Coll, PA
Penn State U Univ Park Campus, PA
Pepperdine University, Malibu, CA*
Pfeiffer University, NC*
Philadelphia College of Pharmacy and
  Science, PA*
Philander Smith College, AR
Pittsburg State University, KS
Plymouth State College of the U System of
  NH, NH*
Point Loma Nazarene College, CA*
Point Park College, PA*
Polytechnic U, Brooklyn Campus, NY
Polytechnic U, Farmingdale Campus, NY
Polytechnic University of Puerto Rico, PR*
Pontifical Catholic University of Puerto
  Rico, PR*
Portland State University, OR
Prairie View A&M University, TX
Pratt Institute, NY*
Presbyterian College, SC
Presentation College, SD*
Princeton University, NJ
Providence College, RI
Purdue University, West Lafayette, IN
Purdue University Calumet, IN*
Queens College, NC*
Quinnipiac College, CT*
Radford University, VA
Ramapo College of New Jersey, NJ*
Randolph-Macon College, VA*
Reed College, OR*
Rensselaer Polytechnic Institute, NY
Research College of Nursing–Rockhurst
  College, MO*
Rhode Island College, RI*
Rhodes College, TN*
Rice University, TX*
The Richard Stockton College of New
  Jersey, NJ*
Rider University, NJ
Ripon College, WI
Robert Morris College, PA*
Roberts Wesleyan College, NY*
Rochester Institute of Technology, NY
Rockford College, IL*
Rockhurst College, MO*
Roger Williams University, RI*
Rose-Hulman Institute of Technology, IN
Rowan University, NJ
Russell Sage College, NY*
Rutgers, State U of NJ, Camden Coll of
  Arts & Scis, NJ

ARMY (continued)

Rutgers, State U of NJ, College of
Engineering, NJ

Rutgers, State U of NJ, College of Nursing,
NJ*

Rutgers, State U of NJ, College of
Pharmacy, NJ

Rutgers, State U of NJ, Cook College, NJ

Rutgers, State U of NJ, Douglass College,
NJ

Rutgers, State U of NJ, Livingston College,
NJ

Rutgers, State U of NJ, Mason Gross
School of Arts, NJ

Rutgers, State U of NJ, Newark Coll of
Arts & Scis, NJ*

Rutgers, State U of NJ, Rutgers College, NJ

Rutgers, State U of NJ, U Coll–Camden,
NJ*

Rutgers, State U of NJ, U Coll–Newark,
NJ*

Rutgers, State U of NJ, U Coll–New
Brunswick, NJ

Sacred Heart University, CT*

Saint Anselm College, NH*

Saint Augustine's College, NC

St. Bonaventure University, NY

St. Cloud State University, MN

St. Edward's University, TX*

St. Francis College, NY*

Saint Francis College, PA*

St. John Fisher College, NY*

Saint John's University, MN

St. John's University, NY

Saint Joseph's College, ME*

St. Joseph's College, Suffolk Campus, NY*

Saint Joseph's University, PA*

Saint Leo College, FL*

St. Louis College of Pharmacy, MO*

Saint Louis University, MO*

Saint Martin's College, WA*

Saint Mary College, KS

Saint Mary-of-the-Woods College, IN*

Saint Mary's College, IN*

Saint Mary's College of California, CA*

St. Mary's University of San Antonio, TX

Saint Michael's College, VT*

St. Norbert College, WI*

Saint Paul's College, VA

Saint Peter's College, Jersey City, NJ*

St. Thomas University, FL*

Salem College, NC*

Salem-Teikyo University, WV*

Salisbury State University, MD

Salve Regina University, RI

Samford University, AL*

Sam Houston State University, TX

Samuel Merritt College, CA*

San Diego State University, CA

San Francisco State University, CA*

San Jose State University, CA

Santa Clara University, CA

Savannah State University, GA

Scripps College, CA*

Seattle Pacific University, WA*

Seattle University, WA

Seton Hall University, NJ

Seton Hill College, PA*

Shaw University, NC

Shepherd College, WV*

Shippensburg University of Pennsylvania,
PA

Siena College, NY

Sierra Nevada College, NV*

Simmons College, MA*

Skidmore College, NY*

Slippery Rock University of Pennsylvania,
PA

Smith College, MA*

Sonoma State University, CA*

South Dakota School of Mines and
Technology, SD

South Dakota State University, SD

Southeastern College of the Assemblies of
God, FL*

Southeastern Louisiana University, LA*

Southeast Missouri State University, MO

Southern California College, CA*

Southern Connecticut State University, CT*

Southern Illinois University at Carbondale,
IL

Southern Illinois University at
Edwardsville, IL

Southern Methodist University, TX*

Southern Nazarene University, OK*

Southern Polytechnic State University, GA*

Southern University and A&M College, LA

Southern University at New Orleans, LA*

Southern Wesleyan University, SC*

Southwest Baptist University, MO*

Southwest Missouri State University, MO

Southwest Texas State University, TX

Spalding University, KY*

Spelman College, GA*

Springfield College, MA*

Spring Hill College, AL

Stanford University, CA*

State U of NY at Buffalo, NY*

State U of NY at Oswego, NY

State U of NY College at Brockport, NY

State U of NY College at Buffalo, NY*

State U of NY College at Cortland, NY*

State U of NY College at Fredonia, NY*

State U of NY College at Geneseo, NY*

State U of NY College at Old Westbury,
NY*

State U of NY College at Potsdam, NY*

State U of NY Coll of Environ Sci and
Forestry, NY*

Stephen F. Austin State University, TX

Stephens College, MO*

Stetson University, FL*

Stevens Institute of Technology, NJ*

Stillman College, AL*

Stonehill College, MA

Suffolk University, MA*

Susquehanna University, PA*

Swarthmore College, PA*

Sweet Briar College, VA*

Syracuse University, NY

Talladega College, AL*

Tarleton State University, TX

Teikyo Post University, CT*

Temple University, Philadelphia, PA

Tennessee State University, TN*

Tennessee Technological University, TN

Texas A&M University, College Station,
TX

Texas A&M University–Corpus Christi, TX

Texas A&M University–Kingsville, TX

Texas Christian University, TX

Texas Southern University, TX*

Texas Tech University, TX

Texas Wesleyan University, TX*

Thiel College, PA*

Thomas College, GA

Thomas College, ME*

Thomas More College, KY*

Tougaloo College, MS

Towson University, MD*

Transylvania University, KY*

Trevecca Nazarene University, TN*

Trinity College, CT*

Trinity College, DC*

Troy State University, Troy, AL

Troy State University Montgomery, AL*

Truman State University, MO

Tufts University, MA*

Tulane University, LA

Tuskegee University, AL

Union College, NY*

United States International University, CA*

Unity College, ME*

Universidad del Turabo, PR*

U at Albany, State U of NY, NY

The University of Akron, OH

The University of Alabama at Birmingham,
AL

The University of Alabama in Huntsville,
AL*

U of Alaska Fairbanks, AK

University of Arizona, AZ

University of Arkansas, Fayetteville, AR

University of Arkansas at Little Rock, AR

University of Arkansas at Pine Bluff, AR

University of Bridgeport, CT

University of California, Berkeley, CA

University of California, Davis, CA

University of California, Irvine, CA*

University of California, Los Angeles, CA

University of California, Riverside, CA*

University of California, Santa Barbara, CA

University of California, Santa Cruz, CA*

University of Central Arkansas, AR

University of Central Florida, FL

University of Central Oklahoma, OK

The University of Charleston, WV

University of Chicago, IL*

University of Cincinnati, OH

University of Colorado at Boulder, CO

University of Colorado at Colorado Springs,
CO

University of Colorado at Denver, CO

University of Connecticut, Storrs, CT

University of Dallas, TX*

University of Dayton, OH

University of Delaware, DE

University of Denver, CO*

University of Detroit Mercy, MI*

University of Florida, FL

University of Georgia, GA

University of Guam, GU

University of Hartford, CT*

*program is offered at another college's campus

University of Hawaii at Manoa, HI
University of Houston, TX
University of Houston–Downtown, TX*
University of Idaho, ID
University of Illinois at Chicago, IL
University of Illinois at Urbana–
  Champaign, IL
University of Indianapolis, IN*
The University of Iowa, IA
University of Kansas, KS
University of Kentucky, KY
University of La Verne, CA*
University of Louisville, KY
University of Maine, Orono, ME
University of Maryland Baltimore County,
  MD*
University of Maryland Eastern Shore,
  MD*
University of Massachusetts Amherst, MA
University of Massachusetts Dartmouth,
  MA
University of Massachusetts Lowell, MA
The University of Memphis, TN
University of Miami, FL*
University of Michigan, Ann Arbor, MI
University of Michigan–Dearborn, MI
University of Minnesota, Twin Cities
  Campus, MN
University of Mississippi, MS
University of Missouri–Columbia, MO
University of Missouri–Kansas City, MO
University of Missouri–Rolla, MO
University of Missouri–St. Louis, MO*
University of Mobile, AL*
The University of Montana–Missoula, MT
University of Montevallo, AL*
University of Nebraska at Omaha, NE*
University of Nebraska–Lincoln, NE
University of Nevada, Reno, NV
University of New England, ME*
University of New Hampshire, Durham, NH
University of New Hampshire at
  Manchester, NH*
University of New Mexico, NM
University of North Alabama, AL
The University of North Carolina at Chapel
  Hill, NC
University of North Carolina at Charlotte,
  NC
University of North Carolina at Greensboro,
  NC*
University of North Carolina at Pembroke,
  NC
University of North Dakota, ND
University of Northern Colorado, CO
University of Northern Iowa, IA
University of Notre Dame, IN
University of Oklahoma, OK
University of Oregon, OR
University of Pennsylvania, PA
University of Pittsburgh, PA
University of Pittsburgh at Bradford, PA
University of Pittsburgh at Greensburg, PA*
University of Portland, OR
U of Puerto Rico, Aguadilla Regional
  College, PR
U of Puerto Rico at Arecibo, PR
U of Puerto Rico at Ponce, PR

U of Puerto Rico, Cayey University
  College, PR
U of Puerto Rico, Mayagüez Campus, PR
U of Puerto Rico, Río Piedras, PR
University of Puget Sound, WA*
University of Redlands, CA*
University of Rhode Island, RI
University of Richmond, VA
University of Rio Grande, OH*
University of Rochester, NY*
University of St. Thomas, MN*
University of St. Thomas, TX*
University of San Diego, CA*
University of San Francisco, CA
University of Scranton, PA
University of South Alabama, AL
U of South Carolina, Columbia, SC
U of South Carolina–Spartanburg, SC
University of South Dakota, SD
University of Southern California, CA
University of Southern Mississippi, MS
University of South Florida, FL
University of Southwestern Louisiana, LA
The University of Tampa, FL
University of Tennessee at Chattanooga, TN
The University of Tennessee at Martin, TN
University of Tennessee, Knoxville, TN
The University of Texas at Arlington, TX
The University of Texas at Austin, TX
The University of Texas at Dallas, TX*
The University of Texas at El Paso, TX
The University of Texas at San Antonio,
  TX
The University of Texas–Pan American, TX
University of the District of Columbia, DC*
University of Toledo, OH
University of Utah, UT
University of Vermont, VT
University of Virginia, VA
University of Washington, WA
The University of West Alabama, AL
University of West Florida, FL
University of Wisconsin–La Crosse, WI
University of Wisconsin–Madison, WI
University of Wisconsin–Milwaukee, WI*
University of Wisconsin–Oshkosh, WI
University of Wisconsin–Parkside, WI*
University of Wisconsin–Stevens Point, WI
University of Wisconsin–Whitewater, WI
University of Wyoming, WY
Ursuline College, OH*
Utah State University, UT
Utica College of Syracuse University, NY
Vanderbilt University, TN
Villa Julie College, MD*
Villanova University, PA
Virginia Commonwealth University, VA
Virginia Military Institute, VA
Virginia Polytechnic Institute and State U,
  VA
Virginia State University, VA
Virginia Union University, VA*
Viterbo College, WI*
Voorhees College, SC*
Wagner College, NY*
Wake Forest University, NC
Warner Pacific College, OR*
Warner Southern College, FL*

Washburn University of Topeka, KS
Washington and Jefferson College, PA*
Washington and Lee University, VA*
Washington State University, WA
Washington University, MO
Wayne State College, NE*
Wayne State University, MI
Weber State University, UT
Wellesley College, MA*
Wells College, NY*
Wesleyan University, CT*
West Chester University of Pennsylvania,
  PA*
Western Baptist College, OR*
Western Carolina University, NC
Western Connecticut State University, CT*
Western Illinois University, IL
Western Kentucky University, KY
Western Maryland College, MD
Western Michigan University, MI
Western New England College, MA
Western Oregon University, OR
Westfield State College, MA*
Westminster College, MO*
Westminster College, PA*
Westminster College of Salt Lake City, UT*
Westmont College, CA*
West Virginia State College, WV
West Virginia University, WV
West Virginia University Institute of
  Technology, WV
Wheaton College, IL
Whittier College, CA*
Whitworth College, WA*
Widener University, PA
Wilberforce University, OH*
Wilkes University, PA*
William Carey College, MS*
Williams Baptist College, AR*
Wilmington College, DE*
Wilson College, PA*
Wingate University, NC*
Winona State University, MN*
Winston-Salem State University, NC
Wittenberg University, OH*
Wofford College, SC
Worcester Polytechnic Institute, MA
Worcester State College, MA*
Wright State University, OH
Xavier University, OH
Xavier University of Louisiana, LA*
Yale University, CT*
York College, NE*
Youngstown State University, OH

NAVY

Agnes Scott College, GA*
Armstrong Atlantic State University, GA
Art Academy of Cincinnati, OH*
Assumption College, MA*
Auburn University, AL
Augsburg College, MN*
Becker College–Leicester Campus, MA*
Becker College–Worcester Campus, MA*
Bethel College, IN*
Bethel College, MN*
Biola University, CA*
Boston College, MA*

NAVY (continued)

Boston University, MA
California Maritime Academy, CA*
California State University, Sacramento, CA*
Capitol College, MD*
Carlow College, PA*
Carnegie Mellon University, PA
The Catholic University of America, DC*
Chatham College, PA*
Chicago State University, IL*
Christian Brothers University, TN*
The Citadel, The Military Coll of South Carolina, SC
Claremont McKenna College, CA*
Clark Atlanta University, GA
College of Notre Dame, CA*
College of the Holy Cross, MA
Columbia College, MO*
Concordia College, St. Paul, MN*
Concordia College, NE*
Concordia University at Austin, TX*
Cornell University, NY
Dillard University, LA*
Dominican College of San Rafael, CA*
Drexel University, PA*
Duke University, NC
Eastern Michigan University, MI*
Florida Agricultural and Mechanical University, FL
Florida State University, FL*
Fordham University, NY*
Georgetown University, DC*
The George Washington University, DC
Georgia Institute of Technology, GA
Georgia State University, GA*
Golden Gate University, CA*
Green Mountain College, VT*
Harvard University, MA*
Hillsdale College, MI*
Houston Baptist University, TX*
Howard University, DC*
Husson College, ME*
Illinois Institute of Technology, IL
Indiana University South Bend, IN*
Inter American U of PR, Metropolitan Campus, PR*
Inter American U of PR, San Germán Campus, PR*
Iowa State University of Science and Technology, IA
Jacksonville University, FL
Jersey City State College, NJ*
John Jay Coll of Criminal Justice, the City U of NY, NY*
La Salle University, PA*
Lewis-Clark State College, ID*
Louisiana State University and A&M College, LA*
Loyola Marymount University, CA*
Loyola University Chicago, IL*
Loyola University New Orleans, LA*
Lubbock Christian University, TX*
Macalester College, MN*
Maine Maritime Academy, ME
Marquette University, WI
Mary Baldwin College, VA*

program is offered at another college's campus

Massachusetts Institute of Technology, MA
Miami University, OH
Morehouse College, GA
Mount St. Mary's College, CA*
Nebraska Methodist Coll of Nursing & Allied Health, NE*
Norfolk State University, VA
North Carolina Central University, NC*
North Carolina State University, NC
North Central College, IL*
Northeastern University, MA*
Northwestern University, IL
Norwich University, VT
Occidental College, CA*
The Ohio State University, OH
Old Dominion University, VA
Oregon State University, OR
Our Lady of Holy Cross College, LA*
Penn State U Univ Park Campus, PA
Pepperdine University, Malibu, CA*
Point Loma Nazarene College, CA*
Prairie View A&M University, TX
Purdue University, West Lafayette, IN
Rensselaer Polytechnic Institute, NY
Rice University, TX
Rochester Institute of Technology, NY*
Rutgers, State U of NJ, Camden Coll of Arts & Scis, NJ*
Rutgers, State U of NJ, U Coll–Camden, NJ*
St. Edward's University, TX*
Saint Joseph's University, PA*
Saint Mary's College, IN*
Saint Mary's College of California, CA*
Samuel Merritt College, CA*
San Diego State University, CA
San Francisco State University, CA*
San Jose State University, CA*
Santa Clara University, CA*
Savannah State University, GA
Seattle Pacific University, WA*
Seattle University, WA*
Sonoma State University, CA*
Southern California College, CA*
Southern Polytechnic State University, GA*
Southern University and A&M College, LA
Spelman College, GA*
Stanford University, CA*
State U of NY College at Brockport, NY*
State U of NY College at Cortland, NY*
State U of NY Maritime College, NY
Stephens College, MO*
Swarthmore College, PA*
Temple University, Philadelphia, PA*
Tennessee State University, TN*
Texas A&M University, College Station, TX
Texas A&M University at Galveston, TX
Texas Southern University, TX*
Trinity College, DC*
Tufts University, MA*
Tulane University, LA
Union College, NY*
U at Albany, State U of NY, NY*
University of Arizona, AZ
University of California, Berkeley, CA
University of California, Los Angeles, CA
University of Colorado at Boulder, CO

University of Colorado at Denver, CO*
University of Florida, FL
University of Houston, TX*
University of Houston–Downtown, TX*
University of Idaho, ID
University of Illinois at Chicago, IL*
University of Illinois at Urbana–Champaign, IL
University of Kansas, KS
University of Maine, Orono, ME
University of Maryland College Park, MD*
The University of Memphis, TN
University of Michigan, Ann Arbor, MI
University of Michigan–Dearborn, MI*
University of Minnesota, Twin Cities Campus, MN
University of Mississippi, MS
University of Missouri–Columbia, MO
University of Nebraska–Lincoln, NE
The University of North Carolina at Chapel Hill, NC
University of North Florida, FL
University of Notre Dame, IN
University of Oklahoma, OK
University of Pennsylvania, PA
University of Pittsburgh, PA*
University of Rochester, NY
University of St. Thomas, TX*
University of San Diego, CA
U of South Carolina, Columbia, SC
University of Southern California, CA
The University of Texas at Austin, TX
University of Utah, UT
University of Virginia, VA
University of Washington, WA
University of Wisconsin–Madison, WI
University of Wisconsin–Milwaukee, WI*
Vanderbilt University, TN
Villanova University, PA
Virginia Military Institute, VA
Virginia Polytechnic Institute and State U, VA
Washington State University, WA*
Weber State University, UT*
Wellesley College, MA*
Wesleyan University, CT*
Westminster College of Salt Lake City, UT*
Worcester Polytechnic Institute, MA*
Worcester State College, MA*
Xavier University of Louisiana, LA*
York College, NE*

AIR FORCE

Adelphi University, NY*
Agnes Scott College, GA*
Alabama State University, AL
Allentown College of St. Francis de Sales, PA*
Alverno College, WI*
American International College, MA*
American University, DC*
Anderson College, SC*
Angelo State University, TX
Arizona State University, AZ
Art Academy of Cincinnati, OH*
Ashland University, OH*
Assumption College, MA*
Auburn University, AL

Auburn University at Montgomery, AL*
Augsburg College, MN*
Baldwin-Wallace College, OH*
Barry University, FL*
Bayamón Central University, PR*
Bayamón Technological University College, PR*
Baylor University, TX
Becker College–Leicester Campus, MA*
Becker College–Worcester Campus, MA*
Bellarmine College, KY*
Bellevue University, NE*
Belmont Abbey College, NC*
Benedict College, SC*
Bennett College, NC*
Bentley College, MA*
Bethel College, IN*
Bethel College, MN*
Bethune-Cookman College, FL*
Biola University, CA*
Birmingham-Southern College, AL*
Bloomsburg University of Pennsylvania, PA*
Boston College, MA*
Boston University, MA
Bowie State University, MD*
Bowling Green State University, OH
Brandeis University, MA*
Bridgewater State College, MA
Brigham Young University, UT
Brigham Young University–Hawaii Campus, HI*
Bryn Mawr College, PA*
Butler University, IN*
California Baptist College, CA*
California Institute of Technology, CA*
California Lutheran University, CA*
California State University, Dominguez Hills, CA*
California State University, Fresno, CA
California State University, Long Beach, CA
California State University, Los Angeles, CA*
California State University, Northridge, CA*
California State University, Sacramento, CA*
California State University, San Bernardino, CA
California State University, San Marcos, CA*
Capitol College, MD*
Carlow College, PA*
Carnegie Mellon University, PA
Carson-Newman College, TN*
Carthage College, WI*
Cascade College, OR*
Case Western Reserve University, OH*
The Catholic University of America, DC*
Cazenovia College, NY*
Cedarville College, OH*
Central Connecticut State University, CT*
Central Washington University, WA
Centre College, KY*
Chaminade University of Honolulu, HI*
Chapman University, CA*
Charleston Southern University, SC

Chatham College, PA*
Cheyney University of Pennsylvania, PA*
Chicago State University, IL*
Christian Brothers University, TN*
Christian Heritage College, CA*
The Citadel, The Military Coll of South Carolina, SC
City Coll of the City U of NY, NY*
Claremont McKenna College, CA*
Clarkson University, NY
Clark University, MA*
Clearwater Christian College, FL*
Cleary College, MI*
Clemson University, SC
Cleveland State University, OH*
Coe College, IA*
Cogswell Polytechnical College, CA*
Colby-Sawyer College, NH*
College Misericordia, PA*
College of Aeronautics, NY
College of Charleston, SC*
College of Mount St. Joseph, OH*
College of Mount Saint Vincent, NY*
The College of New Jersey, NJ*
College of Notre Dame, CA*
College of Our Lady of the Elms, MA*
College of St. Catherine, MN*
College of Saint Mary, NE*
College of St. Scholastica, MN*
College of the Holy Cross, MA*
Colorado Christian University, CO*
Colorado School of Mines, CO*
Colorado State University, CO
Columbia College, MO*
Concordia College, MI*
Concordia College, Moorhead, MN*
Concordia College, St. Paul, MN*
Concordia College, NE
Concordia University at Austin, TX*
Cornell University, NY
Creighton University, NE*
Dakota State University, SD*
Dallas Baptist University, TX*
Dana College, NE*
Daniel Webster College, NH
David Lipscomb University, TN*
Davidson College, NC*
Delaware State University, DE
Delta State University, MS
DePauw University, IN*
Dillard University, LA*
Doane College, NE*
Dominican College of San Rafael, CA*
Dowling College, NY
Drake University, IA*
Drexel University, PA*
Duke University, NC
Duquesne University, PA*
East Carolina University, NC
Eastern College, PA*
Eastern Connecticut State University, CT*
Eastern Kentucky University, KY*
Eastern Michigan University, MI*
East Stroudsburg University of Pennsylvania, PA*
Eckerd College, FL*
Electronic Data Processing College of Puerto Rico, PR*

Elmhurst College, IL*
Elmira College, NY*
Embry-Riddle Aeronautical University, AZ
Embry-Riddle Aeronautical University, FL
Emory University, GA*
Fairmont State College, WV*
Fayetteville State University, NC
Fisk University, TN*
Florida Agricultural and Mechanical University, FL*
Florida International University, FL
Florida Memorial College, FL*
Florida State University, FL
Fordham University, NY*
Franklin Pierce College, NH*
Franklin University, OH*
Free Will Baptist Bible College, TN*
George Fox University, OR*
George Mason University, VA*
Georgetown College, KY*
Georgetown University, DC*
The George Washington University, DC*
Georgia Institute of Technology, GA
Georgia State University, GA*
Golden Gate University, CA*
Gordon College, MA*
Grambling State University, LA
Grand Canyon University, AZ*
Grand View College, IA*
Green Mountain College, VT*
Greensboro College, NC*
Guilford College, NC*
Hamilton College, NY*
Hamline University, MN*
Harvard University, MA*
Harvey Mudd College, CA
Hawaii Pacific University, HI*
High Point University, NC*
Hillsdale College, MI*
Holy Names College, CA*
Howard University, DC
Huntingdon College, AL*
Illinois Institute of Technology, IL
Indiana State University, IN
Indiana University Bloomington, IN
Indiana U–Purdue U Indianapolis, IN*
Indiana University South Bend, IN*
Indiana University Southeast, IN*
Inter American U of PR, Metropolitan Campus, PR*
Inter American U of PR, San Germán Campus, PR*
Iowa State University of Science and Technology, IA
Ithaca College, NY*
Jersey City State College, NJ*
John Brown University, AR*
John Jay Coll of Criminal Justice, the City U of NY, NY*
Johns Hopkins University, MD*
Johnson C. Smith University, NC*
Kansas State University, KS
Kean College of New Jersey, NJ*
Keene State College, NH*
Kent State University, OH
Kentucky State University, KY*
King's College, PA*
Knoxville College, TN

AIR FORCE (continued)

La Roche College, PA*
La Salle University, PA*
Lawrence Technological University, MI*
Le Moyne College, NY*
LeMoyne-Owen College, TN*
Lenoir-Rhyne College, NC*
Lewis-Clark State College, ID*
Lewis University, IL*
Lincoln University, PA*
Linfield College, OR*
Long Island U, C.W. Post Campus, NY*
Louisiana State University and A&M
  College, LA
Louisiana Tech University, LA
Loyola College, MD*
Loyola Marymount University, CA
Loyola University Chicago, IL*
Loyola University New Orleans, LA*
Lubbock Christian University, TX*
Lyndon State College, VT
Macalester College, MN*
Manhattan College, NY
Marian College, IN*
Marquette University, WI
Mary Baldwin College, VA*
Marywood University, PA*
Massachusetts Institute of Technology, MA
McKendree College, IL*
Meredith College, NC*
Merrimack College, MA*
Methodist College, NC*
Metropolitan State College of Denver, CO*
Miami University, OH
Michigan State University, MI
Michigan Technological University, MI
MidAmerica Nazarene University, KS*
Middle Tennessee State University, TN*
Miles College, AL*
Milwaukee School of Engineering, WI*
Mississippi State University, MS
Mississippi University for Women, MS*
Mississippi Valley State University, MS
Molloy College, NY*
Montana State U–Bozeman, MT
Moorhead State University, MN*
Morehouse College, GA*
Mount Holyoke College, MA*
Mount St. Mary's College, CA*
Mount Union College, OH*
National University, CA*
Nazareth College of Rochester, NY*
Nebraska Methodist Coll of Nursing &
  Allied Health, NE*
Nebraska Wesleyan University, NE*
New College of the University of South
  Florida, FL*
New England College, NH*
New Hampshire College, NH*
New Jersey Institute of Technology, NJ
New Mexico State University, NM
New York Institute of Technology, NY
New York University, NY*
North Carolina Agricultural and Technical
  State U, NC
North Carolina Central University, NC*
North Carolina State University, NC

North Central Bible College, MN*
North Central College, IL*
North Dakota State University, ND
Northeastern Illinois University, IL*
Northeastern University, MA*
Northern Arizona University, AZ
Northern Illinois University, IL*
Northern Kentucky University, KY*
Northwestern College, MN*
Northwestern University, IL*
Norwich University, VT
Notre Dame College, NH*
Occidental College, CA*
Oglethorpe University, GA*
Ohio Dominican College, OH*
Ohio Northern University, OH*
The Ohio State University, OH
Ohio University, OH
Ohio University–Chillicothe, OH*
Ohio University–Lancaster, OH*
Oklahoma Baptist University, OK*
Oklahoma Christian U of Science and Arts,
  OK*
Oklahoma City University, OK*
Oklahoma State U, OK
Oregon State University, OR
Otterbein College, OH*
Our Lady of Holy Cross College, LA*
Our Lady of the Lake University of San
  Antonio, TX*
Pace University, NY*
Penn State U Abington College, PA*
Penn State U Univ Park Campus, PA
Pepperdine University, Malibu, CA*
Plymouth State College of the U System of
  NH, NH*
Point Loma Nazarene College, CA*
Point Park College, PA*
Polytechnic U, Brooklyn Campus, NY*
Polytechnic U, Farmingdale Campus, NY*
Pontifical Catholic University of Puerto
  Rico, PR*
Portland State University, OR*
Princeton University, NJ*
Purdue University, West Lafayette, IN
Queens College, NC*
Quinnipiac College, CT*
Regis University, CO*
Rensselaer Polytechnic Institute, NY
Rhodes College, TN*
Rider University, NJ*
Rivier College, NH*
Robert Morris College, PA*
Roberts Wesleyan College, NY*
Rochester Institute of Technology, NY
Rose-Hulman Institute of Technology, IN
Russell Sage College, NY*
Rutgers, State U of NJ, Camden Coll of
  Arts & Scis, NJ*
Rutgers, State U of NJ, College of
  Engineering, NJ
Rutgers, State U of NJ, College of Nursing,
  NJ*
Rutgers, State U of NJ, College of
  Pharmacy, NJ
Rutgers, State U of NJ, Cook College, NJ
Rutgers, State U of NJ, Douglass College,
  NJ

Rutgers, State U of NJ, Livingston College,
  NJ
Rutgers, State U of NJ, Mason Gross
  School of Arts, NJ
Rutgers, State U of NJ, Newark Coll of
  Arts & Scis, NJ*
Rutgers, State U of NJ, Rutgers College, NJ
Rutgers, State U of NJ, U Coll–Camden,
  NJ*
Rutgers, State U of NJ, U Coll–Newark,
  NJ*
Rutgers, State U of NJ, U Coll–New
  Brunswick, NJ
Saint Anselm College, NH*
Saint Augustine's College, NC
St. Edward's University, TX*
St. Francis College, NY*
St. John Fisher College, NY*
St. Joseph's College, Suffolk Campus, NY*
Saint Joseph's University, PA
St. Lawrence University, NY*
Saint Leo College, FL*
St. Louis College of Pharmacy, MO*
Saint Louis University, MO
Saint Mary-of-the-Woods College, IN*
Saint Mary's College, IN*
Saint Mary's College of California, CA*
Saint Michael's College, VT*
Saint Peter's College, Jersey City, NJ*
St. Thomas Aquinas College, NY*
St. Thomas University, FL*
Saint Vincent College, PA*
Saint Xavier University, IL*
Salem-Teikyo University, WV*
Samford University, AL
Samuel Merritt College, CA*
San Diego State University, CA
San Francisco State University, CA*
San Jose State University, CA
Santa Clara University, CA*
Scripps College, CA*
Seattle Pacific University, WA*
Seattle University, WA*
Seton Hall University, NJ*
Shaw University, NC*
Shepherd College, WV*
Siena College, NY*
Skidmore College, NY*
Smith College, MA*
Sonoma State University, CA*
South Dakota State University, SD
Southeast Missouri State University, MO
Southern California College, CA*
Southern Connecticut State University, CT*
Southern Illinois University at Carbondale,
  IL
Southern Illinois University at
  Edwardsville, IL
Southern Methodist University, TX*
Southern Polytechnic State University, GA*
Southern University and A&M College,
  LA*
Southern University at New Orleans, LA*
Southern Wesleyan University, SC*
Southwest Texas State University, TX
Spalding University, KY*
Spelman College, GA*
Springfield College, MA*

*program is offered at another college's campus

Spring Hill College, AL
Stanford University, CA*
State U of NY at Binghamton, NY*
State U of NY College at Brockport, NY*
State U of NY College at Cortland, NY*
State U of NY College at Geneseo, NY*
State U of NY College at Old Westbury, NY*
State U of NY College at Potsdam, NY*
State U of NY Coll of Environ Sci and Forestry, NY*
State U of NY Maritime College, NY*
Stephens College, MO*
Stevens Institute of Technology, NJ*
Swarthmore College, PA*
Syracuse University, NY
Temple University, Philadelphia, PA*
Tennessee State University, TN
Tennessee Technological University, TN*
Texas A&M University, College Station, TX
Texas Christian University, TX
Texas Lutheran University, TX*
Texas Tech University, TX
Texas Wesleyan University, TX*
Thomas More College, KY*
Towson University, MD*
Transylvania University, KY*
Trinity College, DC*
Trinity College of Vermont, VT*
Trinity University, TX*
Troy State University, Troy, AL
Troy State University Montgomery, AL*
Tufts University, MA*
Tulane University, LA
Tuskegee University, AL
Union College, NY*
Universidad del Turabo, PR*
U at Albany, State U of NY, NY*
The University of Akron, OH
The University of Alabama at Birmingham, AL*
The University of Alabama in Huntsville, AL*
University of Arizona, AZ
University of Arkansas, Fayetteville, AR
University of California, Berkeley, CA
University of California, Davis, CA*
University of California, Irvine, CA*
University of California, Los Angeles, CA
University of California, Riverside, CA*
University of California, Santa Cruz, CA*
University of Central Florida, FL
University of Central Oklahoma, OK*
University of Chicago, IL*
University of Cincinnati, OH
University of Colorado at Boulder, CO
University of Colorado at Denver, CO*
University of Connecticut, Storrs, CT
University of Dallas, TX*
University of Dayton, OH*
University of Delaware, DE
University of Denver, CO*
The University of Findlay, OH*
University of Florida, FL
University of Georgia, GA
University of Hartford, CT*
University of Hawaii at Manoa, HI

University of Idaho, ID*
University of Illinois at Chicago, IL*
University of Illinois at Urbana–Champaign, IL
The University of Iowa, IA
University of Kansas, KS
University of Kentucky, KY
University of Louisville, KY
University of Maine, Orono, ME
University of Mary Hardin-Baylor, TX*
University of Maryland Baltimore County, MD*
University of Maryland College Park, MD
University of Massachusetts Amherst, MA
University of Massachusetts Lowell, MA
The University of Memphis, TN
University of Miami, FL
University of Michigan, Ann Arbor, MI
University of Michigan–Dearborn, MI*
University of Minnesota, Duluth, MN
University of Minnesota, Twin Cities Campus, MN
University of Mississippi, MS
University of Missouri–Columbia, MO
University of Missouri–Rolla, MO
University of Missouri–St. Louis, MO*
University of Mobile, AL*
University of Montevallo, AL*
University of Nebraska at Omaha, NE
University of Nebraska–Lincoln, NE
University of New Hampshire, Durham, NH
University of New Hampshire at Manchester, NH*
University of New Haven, CT*
University of New Mexico, NM
The University of North Carolina at Chapel Hill, NC
University of North Carolina at Charlotte, NC
University of North Carolina at Greensboro, NC*
University of North Carolina at Pembroke, NC
University of Northern Colorado, CO
University of North Texas, TX
University of Notre Dame, IN
University of Oklahoma, OK
University of Oregon, OR*
University of Pennsylvania, PA*
University of Pittsburgh, PA
University of Pittsburgh at Bradford, PA*
University of Pittsburgh at Greensburg, PA*
University of Portland, OR
U of Puerto Rico, Mayagüez Campus, PR
U of Puerto Rico, Río Piedras, PR
University of Redlands, CA*
University of Rochester, NY*
University of St. Thomas, MN
University of San Diego, CA*
University of San Francisco, CA*
University of Scranton, PA*
University of South Alabama, AL
U of South Carolina, Columbia, SC
University of Southern California, CA
University of Southern Maine, ME*
University of Southern Mississippi, MS
University of South Florida, FL
The University of Tampa, FL*

University of Tennessee, Knoxville, TN
The University of Texas at Arlington, TX*
The University of Texas at Austin, TX
The University of Texas at Dallas, TX*
The University of Texas at El Paso, TX
The University of Texas at San Antonio, TX
University of the District of Columbia, DC*
University of the Pacific, CA*
University of Toledo, OH*
University of Utah, UT
University of Vermont, VT*
University of Virginia, VA
University of Washington, WA
The University of West Alabama, AL
University of West Florida, FL
University of Wisconsin–Madison, WI
University of Wisconsin–Superior, WI*
University of Wisconsin–Whitewater, WI
University of Wyoming, WY
Utah State University, UT
Utica College of Syracuse University, NY*
Vanderbilt University, TN*
Villanova University, PA*
Virginia Military Institute, VA
Virginia Polytechnic Institute and State U, VA
Wagner College, NY*
Warner Pacific College, OR*
Washburn University of Topeka, KS*
Washington State University, WA
Washington University, MO*
Wayne State University, MI
Weber State University, UT*
Wellesley College, MA*
Wells College, NY*
Wesleyan University, CT*
West Chester University of Pennsylvania, PA*
Western Baptist College, OR*
Western Connecticut State University, CT*
Western Kentucky University, KY*
Western Maryland College, MD*
Western Michigan University, MI*
Western New England College, MA
Western Oregon University, OR*
Westminster College, MO*
Westminster College of Salt Lake City, UT*
West Virginia University, WV
Whittier College, CA*
Widener University, PA*
Wilberforce University, OH*
Wilkes University, PA
Willamette University, OR*
William Carey College, MS*
William University College of New Jersey, NJ*
William Woods University, MO*
Wilmington College, DE*
Wingate University, NC*
Wittenberg University, OH*
Worcester Polytechnic Institute, MA
Worcester State College, MA*
Wright State University, OH
Xavier University, OH*
Xavier University of Louisiana, LA*
Yale University, CT*
York College, NE*

This index lists the colleges that report offering tuition waivers for certain categories of students. For each college listed in this index, the reader should refer to the *Other Money-Saving Options* section of the college's profile for specific information on whether a full or partial tuition waiver is offered. A majority of colleges offer tuition waivers to employees or children of employees. Because this benefit is so common and the affected employees usually are aware of it, no separate index of schools offering this option is provided. However, this information is included in the individual college profiles.

Within each category, the colleges are arranged alphabetically by school name. These are the categories and their order: Minority Students, Children of Alumni, Adult Students, Senior Citizens.

MINORITY STUDENTS

Abilene Christian University, TX
Assumption College, MA
Bloomsburg University of Pennsylvania, PA
California State University, Fullerton, CA
Clarkson College, NE
The College of Wooster, OH
Columbia U, School of Engineering & Applied Sci, NY
Crichton College, TN
Dana College, NE
David Lipscomb University, TN
Dickinson State University, ND
Dowling College, NY
D'Youville College, NY
Fontbonne College, MO
George Fox University, OR
Huntington College, IN
Indiana University of Pennsylvania, PA
Inter Amer U of PR, Barranquitas Campus, PR
Johnson & Wales University, RI
Kansas Newman College, KS
Kentucky Christian College, KY
La Salle University, PA
Lock Haven University of Pennsylvania, PA
Mary Washington College, VA
Merrimack College, MA
Middlebury College, VT
Minot State University, ND
Mississippi University for Women, MS
Molloy College, NY
Montana State U–Bozeman, MT
Montana State U–Northern, MT
Montana Tech of The University of Montana, MT
Northern Illinois University, IL
Oakland City University, IN
Oklahoma State U, OK
Plymouth State College of the U System of NH, NH
Polytechnic U, Brooklyn Campus, NY
Polytechnic U, Farmingdale Campus, NY
Portland State University, OR
Prairie View A&M University, TX
Rockhurst College, MO
Sacred Heart Major Seminary, MI
Saint Joseph's College, IN
Saint Mary College, KS

Saint Mary-of-the-Woods College, IN
St. Thomas University, FL
Salem State College, MA
Shepherd College, WV
Shimer College, IL
Slippery Rock University of Pennsylvania, PA
Southern Oregon University, OR
State U of NY at Stony Brook, NY
Stonehill College, MA
Teikyo Post University, CT
Tennessee State University, TN
Tennessee Wesleyan College, TN
Texas Southern University, TX
Union College, NE
U of Alaska Anchorage, AK
University of Arizona, AZ
University of Hawaii at Manoa, HI
University of Illinois at Urbana–Champaign, IL
University of Maine at Farmington, ME
University of Maine at Presque Isle, ME
University of Maryland Eastern Shore, MD
University of Michigan–Flint, MI
University of Minnesota, Morris, MN
The University of Montana–Missoula, MT
University of New Hampshire, Durham, NH
University of Oregon, OR
University of Rhode Island, RI
University of Southern Maine, ME
University of Toledo, OH
University of Wisconsin–Eau Claire, WI
University of Wisconsin–La Crosse, WI
University of Wisconsin–Superior, WI
Utah State University, UT
Virginia State University, VA
Viterbo College, WI
Wartburg College, IA
Western Montana College of The U of Montana, MT
Western Oregon University, OR
Whitman College, WA
Xavier University, OH

CHILDREN OF ALUMNI

Albertson College of Idaho, ID
Alcorn State University, MS
Anna Maria College, MA
Aquinas College, MI

Arkansas State University, AR
Benedictine University, IL
Birmingham-Southern College, AL
Bloomfield College, NJ
Brescia College, KY
Cabrini College, PA
Calvary Bible College and Theological Seminary, MO
Carthage College, WI
Central Christian College of the Bible, MO
Chapman University, CA
Christian Brothers University, TN
Cincinnati Bible College and Seminary, OH
Clarke College, IA
College of St. Francis, IL
Colorado Christian University, CO
Columbia College, MO
Crichton College, TN
Culver-Stockton College, MO
Curry College, MA
Daemen College, NY
Dana College, NE
Delta State University, MS
Detroit College of Business, Dearborn, MI
Detroit College of Business–Flint, MI
Detroit College of Business, Warren Campus, MI
Dordt College, IA
Dowling College, NY
D'Youville College, NY
Erskine College, SC
Eureka College, IL
Florida Bible College, FL
Georgia Baptist College of Nursing, GA
Grace University, NE
Hellenic College, MA
Huntington College, IN
Illinois Institute of Technology, IL
Kansas Newman College, KS
Kansas Wesleyan University, KS
Kentucky Wesleyan College, KY
Lancaster Bible College, PA
La Salle University, PA
Lewis University, IL
LIFE Bible College, CA
Loras College, IA
Louisiana State University and A&M College, LA
Louisiana Tech University, LA

MacMurray College, IL
Maranatha Baptist Bible College, WI
Marian College, IN
Marymount University, VA
Michigan Christian College, MI
Middlebury College, VT
Mississippi University for Women, MS
Mississippi Valley State University, MS
Missouri Baptist College, MO
Missouri Valley College, MO
Molloy College, NY
Morningside College, IA
Mount Union College, OH
Murray State University, KY
Northern Michigan University, MI
Northern State University, SD
Northwestern State University of Louisiana, LA
Notre Dame College, NH
Oklahoma State U, OK
Paine College, GA
Philadelphia College of Bible, PA
Piedmont Bible College, NC
Pine Manor College, MA
Practical Bible College, NY
Reinhardt College, GA
Ripon College, WI
Rockhurst College, MO
Saint Francis College, IN
Saint Francis College, PA
Saint Joseph's College, IN
Saint Mary-of-the-Woods College, IN
St. Thomas University, FL
Shimer College, IL
South Dakota School of Mines and Technology, SD
Southeastern Bible College, AL
Southern Arkansas University–Magnolia, AR
Spalding University, KY
Tabor College, KS
Teikyo Post University, CT
Thomas More College, KY
Union College, KY
U of Alaska Anchorage, AK
U of Alaska Fairbanks, AK
University of Detroit Mercy, MI
University of Dubuque, IA
University of Maine at Presque Isle, ME
University of Mississippi, MS
University of Nevada, Las Vegas, NV
University of Nevada, Reno, NV
University of Oklahoma, OK
University of Southern Mississippi, MS
University of the Arts, PA
University of Wisconsin–Superior, WI
University of Wyoming, WY
Urbana University, OH
Utah State University, UT
Walsh University, OH
Warner Pacific College, OR
Wartburg College, IA
Webber College, FL
Wesleyan College, GA
Western Kentucky University, KY
Westminster College, MO
Westminster College, PA
Whittier College, CA

Whitworth College, WA
Wilkes University, PA
Wilson College, PA
Wittenberg University, OH
Xavier University, OH

ADULT STUDENTS
Albertson College of Idaho, ID
Anderson College, SC
Anderson University, IN
Art Institute of Boston, MA
Augustana College, SD
Barton College, NC
Berry College, GA
Bethel College, IN
Bloomfield College, NJ
Bluefield College, VA
Briar Cliff College, IA
Carlow College, PA
Clarke College, IA
Coe College, IA
Coker College, SC
College of the Atlantic, ME
Columbia Union College, MD
Converse College, SC
Cornell College, IA
Creighton University, NE
Crichton College, TN
Culver-Stockton College, MO
Dowling College, NY
Drury College, MO
D'Youville College, NY
Emmanuel College, GA
Faulkner University, AL
Hamilton College, NY
Hastings College, NE
Huntington College, IN
John Brown University, AR
Juniata College, PA
Lambuth University, TN
Lancaster Bible College, PA
Lynchburg College, VA
Medaille College, NY
Middlebury College, VT
Mississippi University for Women, MS
Muhlenberg College, PA
Nebraska Wesleyan University, NE
North Park University, IL
Piedmont Bible College, NC
Pine Manor College, MA
Randolph-Macon Woman's College, VA
Regis University, CO
Rockhurst College, MO
Saint Mary College, KS
Saint Mary's College, IN
Simmons College, MA
Southern Adventist University, TN
Sweet Briar College, VA
Tabor College, KS
Teikyo Post University, CT
U of Alaska Anchorage, AK
University of Hawaii at Manoa, HI
University of La Verne, CA
University of Maine at Presque Isle, ME
University of Wisconsin–Superior, WI
Utah State University, UT
Washington College, MD
Webber College, FL

Westminster College, PA
Wittenberg University, OH

SENIOR CITIZENS
Alaska Pacific University, AK
Albany State University, GA
Albertson College of Idaho, ID
Albertus Magnus College, CT
Albright College, PA
Alvernia College, PA
American International College, MA
American University, DC
Anderson College, SC
Andrews University, MI
Anna Maria College, MA
Appalachian State University, NC
Arkansas State University, AR
Arkansas Tech University, AR
Armstrong Atlantic State University, GA
Art Institute of Boston, MA
Asbury College, KY
Atlanta Christian College, GA
Atlantic Union College, MA
Augsburg College, MN
Augustana College, SD
Augusta State University, GA
Averett College, VA
Baker University, KS
Ball State University, IN
Baltimore Hebrew University, MD
Bartlesville Wesleyan College, OK
Baruch Coll of the City U of NY, NY
Bay Path College, MA
Becker College–Leicester Campus, MA
Becker College–Worcester Campus, MA
Belhaven College, MS
Bellarmine College, KY
Belmont Abbey College, NC
Belmont University, TN
Bemidji State University, MN
Benedict College, SC
Benedictine College, KS
Berry College, GA
Bethel College, MN
Black Hills State University, SD
Bloomfield College, NJ
Bluefield College, VA
Boise Bible College, ID
Boise State University, ID
Boston University, MA
Bowie State University, MD
Bowling Green State University, OH
Bradley University, IL
Brescia College, KY
Briar Cliff College, IA
Brooklyn Coll of the City U of NY, NY
Bryant College, RI
Bryn Athyn College of the New Church, PA
Bryn Mawr College, PA
Burlington College, VT
Cabrini College, PA
Caldwell College, NJ
California Polytechnic State U, San Luis Obispo, CA
California State Polytechnic University, Pomona, CA
California State University, Bakersfield, CA
California State University, Chico, CA

Senior Citizens (continued)

California State University, Fresno, CA
California State University, Hayward, CA
California State University, Northridge, CA
California State University, Sacramento, CA
California State University, San Marcos, CA
California State University, Stanislaus, CA
Calumet College of Saint Joseph, IN
Calvary Bible College and Theological
  Seminary, MO
Capital University, OH
Carroll College, MT
Carson-Newman College, TN
Cedarville College, OH
Centenary College, NJ
Central Bible College, MO
Central Connecticut State University, CT
Central Methodist College, MO
Central Washington University, WA
Chadron State College, NE
Chestnut Hill College, PA
Chicago State University, IL
Chowan College, NC
Christopher Newport University, VA
Cincinnati Bible College and Seminary, OH
Circleville Bible College, OH
City Coll of the City U of NY, NY
Clarke College, IA
Clayton College & State University, GA
Clemson University, SC
Cleveland College of Jewish Studies, OH
Cleveland State University, OH
Clinch Valley College of the U of Virginia,
  VA
Coastal Carolina University, SC
Colby College, ME
College of Charleston, SC
College of Mount St. Joseph, OH
College of Mount Saint Vincent, NY
The College of New Jersey, NJ
College of New Rochelle, NY
College of St. Catherine, MN
College of Saint Elizabeth, NJ
College of St. Joseph, VT
College of Saint Mary, NE
College of St. Scholastica, MN
College of Santa Fe, NM
Coll of Staten Island of the City U of NY,
  NY
College of William and Mary, VA
Columbia College, MO
Columbia Union College, MD
Columbus College of Art and Design, OH
Columbus State University, GA
Concordia College, St. Paul, MN
Concordia College, NY
Concordia University, OR
Converse College, SC
Cornell College, IA
Covenant College, GA
Crichton College, TN
Culver-Stockton College, MO
Cumberland University, TN
Curry College, MA
Daemen College, NY
Dakota State University, SD
Daniel Webster College, NH

The Defiance College, OH
Delaware State University, DE
Delta State University, MS
Dickinson State University, ND
Doane College, NE
Dominican College of Blauvelt, NY
Dordt College, IA
Dowling College, NY
Drake University, IA
Drew University, NJ
Drexel University, PA
Drury College, MO
Duquesne University, PA
D'Youville College, NY
East Carolina University, NC
East Central University, OK
Eastern Connecticut State University, CT
East Stroudsburg University of
  Pennsylvania, PA
East Tennessee State University, TN
Edinboro University of Pennsylvania, PA
Elizabeth City State University, NC
Elmhurst College, IL
Emmanuel College, GA
Emmaus Bible College, IA
Emporia State University, KS
Eugene Bible College, OR
Fairleigh Dickinson U,
  Teaneck-Hackensack, NJ
Fayetteville State University, NC
Felician College, NJ
Ferrum College, VA
Fitchburg State College, MA
Five Towns College, NY
Florida Agricultural and Mechanical
  University, FL
Florida Institute of Technology, FL
Florida International University, FL
Florida State University, FL
Fontbonne College, MO
Framingham State College, MA
Francis Marion University, SC
Franklin College of Indiana, IN
Franklin Pierce College, NH
Freed-Hardeman University, TN
Fresno Pacific University, CA
Frostburg State University, MD
Gannon University, PA
George Fox University, OR
Georgia College and State University, GA
Georgian Court College, NJ
Georgia Southern University, GA
Georgia Southwestern State University, GA
Georgia State University, GA
Gonzaga University, WA
Grace Bible College, MI
Graceland College, IA
Grace University, NE
Grambling State University, LA
Grand View College, IA
Greenville College, IL
Gustavus Adolphus College, MN
Hannibal-LaGrange College, MO
Harding University, AR
Henderson State University, AR
Heritage College, WA
Hilbert College, NY
Hofstra University, NY

Hood College, MD
Hope International University, CA
Houston Baptist University, TX
Howard Payne University, TX
Humboldt State University, CA
Hunter Coll of the City U of NY, NY
Huntington College, IN
Husson College, ME
Idaho State University, ID
Illinois State University, IL
Immaculata College, PA
Indiana University Northwest, IN
Iona College, New Rochelle, NY
Jacksonville State University, AL
James Madison University, VA
Jersey City State College, NJ
Jewish Theological Seminary of America,
  NY
John Brown University, AR
Johnson State College, VT
Kansas Newman College, KS
Kansas Wesleyan University, KS
Kean College of New Jersey, NJ
Keene State College, NH
Kennesaw State University, GA
Kentucky State University, KY
Kentucky Wesleyan College, KY
King's College, PA
Lake Erie College, OH
Lakeland College, WI
Lamar University, TX
Lambuth University, TN
Lancaster Bible College, PA
Lander University, SC
Lee University, TN
Lewis-Clark State College, ID
Lincoln Memorial University, TN
Lincoln University, MO
Lindenwood College, MO
Long Island U, Brooklyn Campus, NY
Long Island U, C.W. Post Campus, NY
Long Island U, Southampton College, NY
Longwood College, VA
Loras College, IA
Louisiana State University and A&M
  College, LA
Louisiana State University in Shreveport,
  LA
Louisiana Tech University, LA
Lourdes College, OH
Lynchburg College, VA
Lyndon State College, VT
MacMurray College, IL
Malone College, OH
Manhattan Christian College, KS
Mankato State University, MN
Marian College, IN
Marian College of Fond du Lac, WI
Marquette University, WI
Marygrove College, MI
Marymount University, VA
Maryville University of Saint Louis, MO
Marywood University, PA
Massachusetts College of Art, MA
McNeese State University, LA
Medaille College, NY
Medical College of Georgia, GA
Merrimack College, MA

Mesa State College, CO
Messiah College, PA
Methodist College, NC
Metropolitan State College of Denver, CO
Metropolitan State University, MN
Michigan Christian College, MI
Michigan Technological University, MI
MidAmerica Nazarene University, KS
Mid-Continent Baptist Bible College, KY
Middlebury College, VT
Middle Tennessee State University, TN
Midland Lutheran College, NE
Minnesota Bible College, MN
Mississippi State University, MS
Missouri Baptist College, MO
Missouri Southern State College, MO
Missouri Western State College, MO
Molloy College, NY
Monmouth University, NJ
Montana State U–Billings, MT
Montana State U–Bozeman, MT
Montana State U–Northern, MT
Montana Tech of The University of
  Montana, MT
Montclair State University, NJ
Montreat College, NC
Moorhead State University, MN
Morehead State University, KY
Morgan State University, MD
Morningside College, IA
Mount Olive College, NC
Mount St. Clare College, IA
Murray State University, KY
Muskingum College, OH
National American University, Denver, CO
National College–St. Paul Campus, MN
Nebraska Wesleyan University, NE
New Hampshire College, NH
New Mexico Highlands University, NM
New Mexico State University, NM
New York Institute of Technology, NY
Nicholls State University, LA
Nichols College, MA
North Carolina State University, NC
North Carolina Wesleyan College, NC
North Central Bible College, MN
North Central College, IL
Northeastern Illinois University, IL
Northeastern University, MA
Northeast Louisiana University, LA
Northern Kentucky University, KY
Northern Michigan University, MI
North Georgia College & State University,
  GA
Northwest College of the Assemblies of
  God, WA
Northwestern College, MN
Northwestern Oklahoma State University,
  OK
Northwest Missouri State University, MO
Notre Dame College, NH
The Ohio State University, OH
Ohio University–Chillicothe, OH
Ohio University–Zanesville, OH
Oklahoma Baptist University, OK
Old Dominion University, VA
Ozark Christian College, MO
Pacific Lutheran University, WA

Paier College of Art, Inc., CT
Palm Beach Atlantic College, FL
Park College, MO
Penn State U Abington College, PA
Penn State U Altoona College, PA
Penn State U at Erie, The Behrend College,
  PA
Penn State U Berks-Lehigh Valley Coll, PA
Penn State U Harrisburg Campus of the
  Capital Coll, PA
Penn State U Schuylkill Campus of the
  Capital Coll, PA
Penn State U Univ Park Campus, PA
Phillips University, OK
Piedmont College, GA
Point Loma Nazarene College, CA
Point Park College, PA
Portland State University, OR
Presbyterian College, SC
Presentation College, SD
Puget Sound Christian College, WA
Purchase College, State U of NY, NY
Purdue University Calumet, IN
Purdue University North Central, IN
Quincy University, IL
Quinnipiac College, CT
Ramapo College of New Jersey, NJ
Regis University, CO
Reinhardt College, GA
Research College of Nursing–Rockhurst
  College, MO
Rhode Island College, RI
The Richard Stockton College of New
  Jersey, NJ
Rivier College, NH
Roanoke Bible College, NC
Roanoke College, VA
Robert Morris College, PA
Rockhurst College, MO
Rosemont College, PA
Sacred Heart University, CT
Saginaw Valley State University, MI
Saint Anselm College, NH
St. Bonaventure University, NY
St. Cloud State University, MN
Saint Francis College, IN
St. John Fisher College, NY
Saint Joseph College, CT
Saint Joseph's College, ME
St. Joseph's College, Suffolk Campus, NY
Saint Joseph Seminary College, LA
Saint Mary's College, IN
St. Mary's College of Maryland, MD
St. Thomas Aquinas College, NY
Saint Xavier University, IL
Salem State College, MA
Salem-Teikyo University, WV
Salisbury State University, MD
San Diego State University, CA
San Jose State University, CA
School of the Art Institute of Chicago, IL
Seattle Pacific University, WA
Seton Hall University, NJ
Shawnee State University, OH
Shimer College, IL
Shippensburg University of Pennsylvania,
  PA
Shorter College, GA

Siena College, NY
Silver Lake College, WI
Simmons College, MA
Slippery Rock University of Pennsylvania,
  PA
South Dakota School of Mines and
  Technology, SD
South Dakota State University, SD
Southeastern Louisiana University, LA
Southeast Missouri State University, MO
Southern Adventist University, TN
Southern Arkansas University–Magnolia,
  AR
Southern Connecticut State University, CT
Southern Illinois University at Carbondale,
  IL
Southern Nazarene University, OK
Southern Polytechnic State University, GA
Southern Wesleyan University, SC
Southwest Baptist University, MO
Southwestern College, KS
Southwestern Oklahoma State University,
  OK
Southwest Missouri State University, MO
Southwest State University, MN
Spalding University, KY
Spring Arbor College, MI
State U of NY College at Brockport, NY
State U of NY College at Old Westbury,
  NY
Stonehill College, MA
Sue Bennett College, KY
Suffolk University, MA
Sweet Briar College, VA
Tabor College, KS
Tarleton State University, TX
Taylor University, Fort Wayne Campus, IN
Teikyo Post University, CT
Texas A&M University–Commerce, TX
Texas Woman's University, TX
Thomas College, GA
Toccoa Falls College, GA
Towson University, MD
Trevecca Nazarene University, TN
Trinity Christian College, IL
Trinity College of Florida, FL
Trinity College of Vermont, VT
Tri-State University, IN
Truman State University, MO
Union College, KY
Union College, NY
U at Albany, State U of NY, NY
The University of Akron, OH
U of Alaska Anchorage, AK
U of Alaska Fairbanks, AK
U of Alaska Southeast, AK
University of Arkansas, Fayetteville, AR
University of Arkansas at Little Rock, AR
University of Arkansas at Monticello, AR
University of Bridgeport, CT
University of California, Santa Cruz, CA
University of Central Arkansas, AR
University of Central Florida, FL
The University of Charleston, WV
University of Colorado at Boulder, CO
University of Connecticut, Storrs, CT
University of Delaware, DE
University of Detroit Mercy, MI

Senior Citizens (continued)

University of Dubuque, IA
The University of Findlay, OH
University of Florida, FL
University of Georgia, GA
University of Great Falls, MT
University of Guam, GU
University of Hartford, CT
University of Hawaii at Hilo, HI
University of Hawaii at Manoa, HI
University of Illinois at Chicago, IL
University of Illinois at Urbana–
  Champaign, IL
University of Indianapolis, IN
University of Kansas, KS
University of Kentucky, KY
University of Louisville, KY
University of Maine, Orono, ME
University of Maine at Fort Kent, ME
University of Maine at Machias, ME
University of Maine at Presque Isle, ME
University of Maryland Baltimore County,
  MD
University of Maryland College Park, MD
University of Maryland Eastern Shore, MD
University of Massachusetts Amherst, MA
University of Massachusetts Boston, MA
University of Massachusetts Dartmouth,
  MA
The University of Memphis, TN
University of Michigan, Ann Arbor, MI
University of Michigan–Dearborn, MI
University of Michigan–Flint, MI
University of Minnesota, Crookston, MN
University of Minnesota, Duluth, MN
University of Minnesota, Morris, MN
University of Minnesota, Twin Cities
  Campus, MN
University of Mississippi, MS
The University of Montana–Missoula, MT
University of Montevallo, AL
University of Nevada, Las Vegas, NV
University of Nevada, Reno, NV
University of New Hampshire, Durham, NH
University of New Hampshire at
  Manchester, NH
University of New Haven, CT

University of New Mexico, NM
University of North Carolina at Asheville,
  NC
University of North Carolina at Charlotte,
  NC
University of North Carolina at Greensboro,
  NC
University of North Carolina at Pembroke,
  NC
University of North Carolina at
  Wilmington, NC
University of North Dakota, ND
University of North Florida, FL
University of North Texas, TX
University of Oklahoma, OK
University of Pittsburgh, PA
University of Rhode Island, RI
University of St. Thomas, MN
University of St. Thomas, TX
University of Science and Arts of
  Oklahoma, OK
University of Sioux Falls, SD
U of South Carolina, Columbia, SC
U of South Carolina–Aiken, SC
U of South Carolina–Spartanburg, SC
University of South Dakota, SD
University of Southern Colorado, CO
University of Southern Indiana, IN
University of Southern Maine, ME
University of South Florida, FL
University of Southwestern Louisiana, LA
University of Tennessee at Chattanooga, TN
The University of Tennessee at Martin, TN
University of Tennessee, Knoxville, TN
The University of Texas at Dallas, TX
University of the District of Columbia, DC
University of the Virgin Islands, VI
University of Toledo, OH
University of Utah, UT
University of Vermont, VT
University of Virginia, VA
University of Wisconsin–Eau Claire, WI
University of Wisconsin–Green Bay, WI
University of Wisconsin–La Crosse, WI
University of Wyoming, WY
Urbana University, OH
Ursinus College, PA

Utah State University, UT
Valdosta State University, GA
Villanova University, PA
Virginia Commonwealth University, VA
Virginia State University, VA
Virginia Wesleyan College, VA
Viterbo College, WI
Wagner College, NY
Walla Walla College, WA
Walsh University, OH
Wartburg College, IA
Washington State University, WA
Wayne State University, MI
Webber College, FL
Weber State University, UT
Wells College, NY
Wesleyan College, GA
Wesley College, DE
Wesley College, MS
West Chester University of Pennsylvania,
  PA
Western Carolina University, NC
Western Connecticut State University, CT
Western Kentucky University, KY
Western Michigan University, MI
Western Montana College of The U of
  Montana, MT
Western New England College, MA
Western New Mexico University, NM
Western State College of Colorado, CO
Western Washington University, WA
Westfield State College, MA
Westmar University, IA
Wheeling Jesuit University, WV
Wichita State University, KS
Wilkes University, PA
William Jewell College, MO
Williams Baptist College, AR
William Tyndale College, MI
Winona State University, MN
Winston-Salem State University, NC
Winthrop University, SC
Wittenberg University, OH
Worcester State College, MA
Wright State University, OH
Xavier University of Louisiana, LA
Youngstown State University, OH

TUITION PAYMENT ALTERNATIVES

This index lists the colleges that report offering alternative tuition payment plans. *D* (deferred) indicates that a system of deferred payments is a possible option. *G* (guaranteed) indicates that the college offers a plan that guarantees that the tuition rate of an entering student will not increase during the student's entire term of enrollment, from entrance to graduation. *I* (installment) indicates that the school has a plan to permit payment of the tuition in planned installments. *P* (prepayment) means that an entering student may lock in the current tuition rate for the entire term of enrollment by paying the full amount in advance rather than year-by-year.

Abilene Christian University, TX	I,P	Art Institute of Boston, MA	I	Benedictine College, KS	I
Academy of Art College, CA	I	Art Institute of Southern California,		Benedictine University, IL	D,I
Adams State College, CO	I	CA	G,I	Bennett College, NC	D
Adelphi University, NY	D,I,P	Asbury College, KY	D,I	Bennington College, VT	I
Adrian College, MI	D,I	Ashland University, OH	I	Bentley College, MA	I,P
The Advertising Arts College, CA	I,P	Assumption College, MA	I	Berea College, KY	D
Agnes Scott College, GA	I	Atlanta Christian College, GA	I	Berklee College of Music, MA	I
Alabama Agricultural and Mechanical		Atlanta College of Art, GA	D,I	Berry College, GA	I
University, AL	D	Atlantic Union College, MA	I	Bethany College, KS	I
Alaska Bible College, AK	I	Auburn University at Montgomery,		Bethany College, WV	I
Alaska Pacific University, AK	D	AL	D	Bethel College, IN	I
Albany College of Pharmacy of Union		Audrey Cohen College, NY	G,I	Bethel College, KS	D,I
University, NY	I	Augsburg College, MN	D,I	Bethel College, MN	I
Albertson College of Idaho, ID	I	Augustana College, IL	I,P	Bethel College, TN	I
Albertus Magnus College, CT	I	Augustana College, SD	G,I	Beth-El College of Nursing and	
Albion College, MI	D	Austin College, TX	I	Health Sciences, CO	D,I
Albright College, PA	I	Averett College, VA	I	Beulah Heights Bible College, GA	D,I
Alderson-Broaddus College, WV	D,I	Azusa Pacific University, CA	I	Biola University, CA	I
Alfred University, NY	D,I,P	Babson College, MA	I	Birmingham-Southern College, AL	I
Alice Lloyd College, KY	I	Baker University, KS	I	Blackburn College, IL	I
Allegheny College, PA	I,P	Baldwin-Wallace College, OH	D,I	Black Hills State University, SD	I
Allegheny University of the Health		Ball State University, IN	I	Bloomfield College, NJ	D,I
Sciences, PA	I	Baltimore Hebrew University, MD	I	Bluefield College, VA	I
Allen College of Nursing, IA	I	Baptist Bible College of Pennsylvania,		Blue Mountain College, MS	I
Allentown College of St. Francis de		PA	I	Bluffton College, OH	I
Sales, PA	D,I	Baptist Missionary Assoc Theol Sem,		Boise Bible College, ID	I
Alma College, MI	I,P	TX	I	Boise State University, ID	D
Alvernia College, PA	I	Barat College, IL	D	Boricua College, NY	D
Alverno College, WI	D,I	Barber-Scotia College, NC	I	Boston Architectural Center, MA	D
The American College, CA	D,I	Bard College, NY	I	Boston College, MA	I,P
American Conservatory of Music, IL	I	Barnard College, NY	D,I,P	Boston University, MA	I,P
American International College, MA	D,I,P	Barry University, FL	I	Bowdoin College, ME	I
American University, DC	D,I,P	Bartlesville Wesleyan College, OK	D,I	Bowie State University, MD	D
American University of Puerto Rico,		Barton College, NC	I	Bowling Green State University, OH	I
PR	G	Bassist College, OR	D,G,I	Bradford College, MA	D,I
Amherst College, MA	D,I	Bates College, ME	I	Bradley University, IL	D,I
Anderson College, SC	I	Baylor University, TX	G	Brandeis University, MA	I,P
Anderson University, IN	I	Bay Path College, MA	D,I	Brescia College, KY	D
Andrews University, MI	I	Beaver College, PA	D,I	Brewton-Parker College, GA	I
Angelo State University, TX	I	Becker College–Leicester Campus,		Briar Cliff College, IA	D
Anna Maria College, MA	I,P	MA	I	Bridgewater College, VA	I
Antioch College, OH	I	Becker College–Worcester Campus,		Bridgewater State College, MA	I
Appalachian Bible College, WV	I	MA	I	Brooks Institute of Photography, CA	D,I
Aquinas College, MI	D,I	Belhaven College, MS	I	Brown University, RI	D,I,P
Arizona Bible College, AZ	I	Bellarmine College, KY	D,I	Bryan College, TN	I
Arkansas State University, AR	I	Bellevue University, NE	D,I	Bryant and Stratton Coll, Cleveland,	
Arkansas Tech University, AR	D	Bellin College of Nursing, WI	I	OH	G
Arlington Baptist College, TX	D,I	Belmont Abbey College, NC	I	Bryant College, RI	I
Art Academy of Cincinnati, OH	I	Belmont University, TN	D,I	Bryn Athyn College of the New	
Art Center College of Design, CA	I	Beloit College, WI	I	Church, PA	I

Bryn Mawr College, PA	D,I,P	Chaminade University of Honolulu,		College of William and Mary, VA	I
Bucknell University, PA	I,P	HI	D	The College of Wooster, OH	I
Buena Vista University, IA	I	Chapman University, CA	D,I	Colorado Christian University, CO	I
Burlington College, VT	I	Chatham College, PA	I	The Colorado College, CO	I
Butler University, IN	I,P	Chestnut Hill College, PA	D,I	Colorado School of Mines, CO	I
Cabrini College, PA	I	Cheyney University of Pennsylvania,		Colorado State University, CO	I
Caldwell College, NJ	D,I	PA	D	Colorado Technical University, CO	I
California Baptist College, CA	D,I	Chicago State University, IL	D	Columbia College, IL	D
California College for Health		Chowan College, NC	I	Columbia College, MO	D
Sciences, CA	I	Christendom College, VA	I	Columbia College, NY	I,P
California College of Arts and Crafts,		Christian Brothers University, TN	D,I	Columbia College, PR	G
CA	D,I	Christian Heritage College, CA	I	Columbia College, SC	I
California Institute of Technology, CA	D,I	Christopher Newport University, VA	I	Columbia College–Hollywood,	
California Lutheran University, CA	I	Cincinnati Bible College and		Hollywood, CA	I
California Polytechnic State U, San		Seminary, OH	D	Columbia International University, SC	I
Luis Obispo, CA	I	Circleville Bible College, OH	I	Columbia Union College, MD	D,I
California State Polytechnic		City Coll of the City U of NY, NY	D	Columbia U, School of Engineering &	
University, Pomona, CA	I	Claremont McKenna College, CA	I	Applied Sci, NY	D,I,P
California State University,		Clarion University of Pennsylvania,		Columbus College of Art and Design,	
Bakersfield, CA	I	PA	I	OH	I
California State University, Chico, CA	I	Clark Atlanta University, GA	D	Concord College, WV	D,I
California State University, Hayward,		Clarke College, IA	D,I	Concordia College, AL	I
CA	I	Clarkson College, NE	D,I	Concordia College, MI	I
California State University, Long		Clarkson University, NY	I	Concordia College, Moorhead, MN	I
Beach, CA	I	Clark University, MA	I,P	Concordia College, St. Paul, MN	I
California State University,		Clear Creek Baptist Bible College,		Concordia College, NE	D,I
Sacramento, CA	I	KY	I	Concordia College, NY	I
California University of Pennsylvania,		Clearwater Christian College, FL	I	Concordia University, OR	I
PA	I	Cleary College, MI	D,I	Concordia University at Austin, TX	I
Calumet College of Saint Joseph, IN	I	Clemson University, SC	D	Concordia University Wisconsin, WI	D,I
Calvary Bible College and Theological		Cleveland College of Jewish Studies,		Connecticut College, CT	I
Seminary, MO	D,I	OH	I	Converse College, SC	I
Calvin College, MI	I,P	Cleveland Institute of Art, OH	I	The Corcoran School of Art, DC	I
Campbell University, NC	I	Cleveland Institute of Music, OH	I	Cornell College, IA	I
Canisius College, NY	D,I,P	Cleveland State University, OH	I	Cornell University, NY	I,P
Capital University, OH	I	Coastal Carolina University, SC	D,I	Cornerstone College, MI	I
Capitol College, MD	D,I	Coe College, IA	I,P	Cornish College of the Arts, WA	I
Cardinal Stritch University, WI	I	Cogswell Polytechnical College, CA	D	Creighton University, NE	I
Carleton College, MN	I,P	Coker College, SC	G,I	The Criswell College, TX	I
Carlow College, PA	D,I	Colby College, ME	I	Crown College, MN	I
Carnegie Mellon University, PA	I	Coleman College, CA	G,I	Culver-Stockton College, MO	I
Carroll College, MT	I	Colgate University, NY	D,I,P	Cumberland College, KY	I
Carroll College, WI	D,I	College Misericordia, PA	D,I	Cumberland University, TN	I
Carson-Newman College, TN	I	College of Aeronautics, NY	I	Curry College, MA	I
Carthage College, WI	I	College of Charleston, SC	I	Daemen College, NY	D,I
Case Western Reserve University, OH	I,P	College of Insurance, NY	I	Dakota State University, SD	D
Castleton State College, VT	I	College of Mount St. Joseph, OH	I	Dakota Wesleyan University, SD	I
Catawba College, NC	I	College of Mount Saint Vincent, NY	I	Dallas Baptist University, TX	I
The Catholic University of America,		The College of New Jersey, NJ	D,I	Dallas Christian College, TX	I
DC	D	College of New Rochelle, NY	P	Dana College, NE	I
Cazenovia College, NY	I	College of Notre Dame, CA	I	Daniel Webster College, NH	I
Cedar Crest College, PA	I	College of Notre Dame of Maryland,		Dartmouth College, NH	I,P
Cedarville College, OH	I	MD	I	Davenport College of Business,	
Centenary College, NJ	I	College of Our Lady of the Elms, MA	I,P	Kalamazoo Campus, MI	D,I
Centenary College of Louisiana, LA	D,I,P	College of Saint Benedict, MN	D,I,P	Davenport College of Business,	
Ctr for Creative Studies—Coll of Art		College of St. Catherine, MN	I	Lansing Campus, MI	I
and Design, MI	D,I	College of Saint Elizabeth, NJ	I	David Lipscomb University, TN	I
Central Baptist College, AR	D,I	College of St. Francis, IL	I	David N. Myers College, OH	D,I
Central Bible College, MO	I	College of St. Joseph, VT	I	Davidson College, NC	I
Central Christian College of the Bible,		College of Saint Mary, NE	D,I	Davis & Elkins College, WV	I
MO	D	College of St. Scholastica, MN	I	Deaconess College of Nursing, MO	D,I
Central College, IA	I	College of Santa Fe, NM	I	Delaware State University, DE	D,I
Central Connecticut State University,		Coll of Staten Island of the City U of		Delaware Valley College, PA	I
CT	D,I	NY, NY	D	Delta State University, MS	I
Central Methodist College, MO	I	College of the Atlantic, ME	I	Denison University, OH	I
Central Missouri State University, MO	I	College of the Holy Cross, MA	I,P	Denver Institute of Technology, CO	D,G,I
Centre College, KY	I	College of the Southwest, NM	D	Denver Technical College, CO	G
Chadron State College, NE	I	The College of West Virginia, WV	I	DePaul University, IL	D,I

DePauw University, IN	D,I,P	Erskine College, SC	I	Georgian Court College, NJ	D,I
Design Institute of San Diego, CA	I	Escuela de Artes Plasticas de Puerto Rico, PR	D	Gettysburg College, PA	I
Detroit College of Business, Dearborn, MI	D,I	Eugene Bible College, OR	I,P	Glenville State College, WV	I
Detroit College of Business–Flint, MI	D,I	Eugene Lang College, New Sch for Social Research, NY	I	GMI Engineering & Management Institute, MI	I
Detroit College of Business, Warren Campus, MI	D,I	Eureka College, IL	I	Goddard College, VT	I
DeVry Institute of Technology, AZ	D,I	Evangel College, MO	I	Golden Gate University, CA	I
DeVry Institute of Technology, Long Beach, CA	I	Fairfield University, CT	I	Goldey-Beacom College, DE	D,I
DeVry Institute of Technology, Pomona, CA	D,I	Fairleigh Dickinson U, Teaneck-Hackensack, NJ	D,I	Gonzaga University, WA	I
DeVry Institute of Technology, GA	D,I	Fairmont State College, WV	D	Gordon College, MA	I,P
DeVry Institute of Technology, Addison, IL	D,I	Faith Baptist Bible Coll and Theological Seminary, IA	I	Grace Bible College, MI	I
DeVry Institute of Technology, Chicago, IL	D,I	Fashion Institute of Technology, NY	I	Grace College, IN	I
DeVry Institute of Technology, MO	D,I	Faulkner University, AL	D,I	Graceland College, IA	I
DeVry Institute of Technology, OH	D,I	Fayetteville State University, NC	I	Grace University, NE	D
DeVry Institute of Technology, TX	D,I	Felician College, NJ	I	Grambling State University, LA	I
Dickinson College, PA	I	Ferris State University, MI	D,I	Grand Canyon University, AZ	I
Dillard University, LA	I	Ferrum College, VA	I	Grand Valley State University, MI	D,I
Doane College, NE	I	Fitchburg State College, MA	I	Grand View College, IA	D,I
Dominican College of Blauvelt, NY	G,I	Five Towns College, NY	D,I	Green Mountain College, VT	I
Dominican College of San Rafael, CA	D,G,I	Florida Agricultural and Mechanical University, FL	D,P	Greensboro College, NC	I
Dominican University, IL	I	Florida Atlantic University, FL	D,I	Greenville College, IL	I
Dordt College, IA	I	Florida Baptist Theological College, FL	D	Grinnell College, IA	I,P
Dowling College, NY	D,G,I	Florida Bible College, FL	D	Guilford College, NC	I
Drake University, IA	I	Florida Christian College, FL	I	Gustavus Adolphus College, MN	I,P
Drew University, NJ	D,I,P	Florida Institute of Technology, FL	I	Gwynedd-Mercy College, PA	I
Drexel University, PA	D,I	Florida International University, FL	P	Hamilton College, NY	D,I
Drury College, MO	D,I,P	Florida Metropolitan U-Fort Lauderdale Coll, FL	I	Hamilton Technical College, IA	G
Duke University, NC	D,I,P	Florida Metropolitan U-Orlando Coll, FL	D,G,I,P	Hamline University, MN	I
Duquesne University, PA	D,I	Florida Metropolitan U-Tampa Coll, Pinellas, FL	G,I	Hampden-Sydney College, VA	I
D'Youville College, NY	D,I	Florida Metropolitan U-Tampa Coll, Lakeland, FL	I	Hampshire College, MA	D,I
Earlham College, IN	D,I	Florida Metropolitan U-Tampa Coll, FL	G,I	Hannibal-LaGrange College, MO	D
East Carolina University, NC	D	Florida Metropolitan U-Tampa Coll, Brandon, FL	I	Hanover College, IN	I
East Coast Bible College, NC	D	Florida State University, FL	I,P	Harding University, AR	I,P
Eastern College, PA	I	Fontbonne College, MO	D,I	Hardin-Simmons University, TX	D,G,I
Eastern Connecticut State University, CT	D,I	Fordham University, NY	I,P	Harrington Institute of Interior Design, IL	I
Eastern Illinois University, IL	I	Framingham State College, MA	I	Hartwick College, NY	I
Eastern Mennonite University, VA	I	Franciscan University of Steubenville, OH	I	Harvard University, MA	I,P
Eastern Michigan University, MI	I	Franklin and Marshall College, PA	I	Harvey Mudd College, CA	I
Eastern New Mexico University, NM	I	Franklin College of Indiana, IN	I	Hastings College, NE	D,I
Eastern Oregon University, OR	D	Franklin Pierce College, NH	I	Haverford College, PA	I
East Stroudsburg University of Pennsylvania, PA	I	Franklin University, OH	D,I	Hawaii Pacific University, HI	I
East Texas Baptist University, TX	I	Freed-Hardeman University, TN	I	Hebrew College, MA	I
East-West University, IL	D,I	Free Will Baptist Bible College, TN	D,I	Hebrew Theological College, IL	I
Eckerd College, FL	I	Fresno Pacific University, CA	I	Heidelberg College, OH	D,I
Edgewood College, WI	D	Friends University, KS	I	Hendrix College, AR	I
Edinboro University of Pennsylvania, PA	I	Frostburg State University, MD	D,I	Henry Cogswell College, WA	D,I
Elizabethtown College, PA	I	Furman University, SC	I	Heritage Bible College, NC	D,I
Elmhurst College, IL	D,I	Gallaudet University, DC	I	Heritage College, WA	D,I
Elmira College, NY	I,P	Gannon University, PA	I	Hilbert College, NY	D,I
Elon College, NC	I	Geneva College, PA	I	Hiram College, OH	I
Embry-Riddle Aeronautical University, FL	D,I	George Fox University, OR	I	Hobart and William Smith Colleges, NY	D,I,P
Emerson College, MA	D,P	George Mason University, VA	D,I	Hobe Sound Bible College, FL	I
Emmanuel College, GA	I	Georgetown College, KY	D	Hofstra University, NY	D,I
Emmanuel College, MA	D,I	Georgetown University, DC	I	Hollins College, VA	D,I,P
Emmaus Bible College, IA	I	The George Washington University, DC	D,I	Holy Apostles College and Seminary, CT	I
Emory & Henry College, VA	I			Holy Family College, PA	I
Emory University, GA	I,P			Holy Names College, CA	D,I
Emporia State University, KS	D,I			Hood College, MD	D,I,P
Endicott College, MA	I			Hope College, MI	I
				Hope International University, CA	I
				Houghton College, NY	I
				Houston Baptist University, TX	D,I
				Humboldt State University, CA	I
				Humphreys College, CA	I,P
				Hunter Coll of the City U of NY, NY	D

Huntingdon College, AL	D	Kansas Wesleyan University, KS	I	Loyola University Chicago, IL	I
Huntington College, IN	G,I	Keene State College, NH	I	Loyola University New Orleans, LA	I
Husson College, ME	I,P	Kendall College, IL	I	Lubbock Christian University, TX	I
Huston-Tillotson College, TX	I	Kendall College of Art and Design,		Lutheran Bible Institute of Seattle,	
Idaho State University, ID	D	MI	D,I,P	WA	I
Illinois College, IL	D,I	Kennesaw State University, GA	D	Luther College, IA	G,I
The Illinois Institute of Art, IL	I	Kent State University, OH	I	Luther Rice Bible College and	
Illinois Institute of Technology, IL	I	Kentucky Christian College, KY	I,P	Seminary, GA	I
Illinois State University, IL	I	Kentucky State University, KY	D,I	Lycoming College, PA	I
Illinois Wesleyan University, IL	I	Kentucky Wesleyan College, KY	D,I	Lyme Academy of Fine Arts, CT	I
Immaculata College, PA	I	Kenyon College, OH	I	Lynchburg College, VA	I
Indiana State University, IN	D,I	Keuka College, NY	I	Lynn University, FL	D,I
Indiana University Bloomington, IN	D	King College, TN	I	Lyon College, AR	I
Indiana University East, IN	D	King's College, PA	D,I	Macalester College, MN	I
Indiana University Northwest, IN	D,P	Knox College, IL	D,P	Machzikei Hadath Rabbinical College,	
Indiana University of Pennsylvania,		Kutztown University of Pennsylvania,		NY	D,I
PA	D,I	PA	D,I	MacMurray College, IL	I
Indiana U–Purdue U Indianapolis, IN	D,I	Laboratory Institute of Merchandising,		Madonna University, MI	D
Indiana University South Bend, IN	D,I	NY	I	Magnolia Bible College, MS	D
Indiana Wesleyan University, IN	I	Lafayette College, PA	D,P	Maharishi University of Management,	
Inter American U of PR, Arecibo		LaGrange College, GA	I	IA	I
Campus, PR	G	Lake Erie College, OH	I	Maine College of Art, ME	D,I
Inter Amer U of PR, Barranquitas		Lake Forest College, IL	I	Malone College, OH	I
Campus, PR	D,G	Lakeland College, WI	I	Manchester College, IN	D,I
Inter American U of PR, Fajardo		Lamar University, TX	I	Manhattan Christian College, KS	I
Campus, PR	D	Lambuth University, TN	D,I	Manhattan College, NY	I
Inter American U of PR, Guayama		Lancaster Bible College, PA	I	Manhattan School of Music, NY	I
Campus, PR	D	Lander University, SC	I	Manhattanville College, NY	I
Inter American U of PR, San Germán		Lane College, TN	D,I	Mannes Coll of Music, New Sch for	
Campus, PR	D	La Roche College, PA	I	Social Research, NY	I
International Acad of Merchandising		La Salle University, PA	D,I	Mansfield University of Pennsylvania,	
& Design, Inc, FL	D,I	Lasell College, MA	I	PA	D,I
International Acad of Merchandising		La Sierra University, CA	I	Maranatha Baptist Bible College, WI	I
& Design, Ltd, IL	D,I	Lawrence University, WI	I	Marian College, IN	D,I
International Bible College, AL	D,I	Lees-McRae College, NC	I	Marian College of Fond du Lac, WI	I
International College, FL	I	Lee University, TN	I	Marietta College, OH	I
Iona College, New Rochelle, NY	D,I	Lehigh University, PA	D,I,P	Marist College, NY	I
Iowa State University of Science and		Le Moyne College, NY	I	Marlboro College, VT	I
Technology, IA	I	LeMoyne-Owen College, TN	D,I,P	Marquette University, WI	I,P
Iowa Wesleyan College, IA	D,I	Lenoir-Rhyne College, NC	D,I	Marshall University, WV	D,I
Ithaca College, NY	I	Lesley College, MA	I	Mars Hill College, NC	I
ITT Technical Institute, Maitland, FL	G	LeTourneau University, TX	I	Martin Luther College, MN	I
Jackson State University, MS	D,I	Lewis & Clark College, OR	I	Martin Methodist College, TN	I
Jacksonville University, FL	I	Lewis-Clark State College, ID	D	Martin University, IN	D,I
James Madison University, VA	I	Lewis University, IL	I	Mary Baldwin College, VA	I
Jamestown College, ND	I	LIFE Bible College, CA	I	Marycrest International University, IA	D
Jarvis Christian College, TX	D,P	Limestone College, SC	I	Marygrove College, MI	I
Jersey City State College, NJ	D	Lincoln Christian College, IL	D,I	Maryland Institute, College of Art,	
Jewish Hospital Coll of Nursing and		Lincoln Memorial University, TN	I	MD	I
Allied Health, MO	D,I	Lincoln University, MO	D	Marymount College, NY	D,I
Jewish Theological Seminary of		Lindenwood College, MO	D,I	Marymount Manhattan College, NY	D
America, NY	I	Lindsey Wilson College, KY	I	Marymount University, VA	D,I
John Brown University, AR	I	Linfield College, OR	I	Maryville College, TN	D,I
John Carroll University, OH	I	Livingstone College, NC	I	Maryville University of Saint Louis,	
Johns Hopkins University, MD	I,P	Long Island U, C.W. Post Campus,		MO	D,I
Johnson & Wales University, FL	I	NY	D,I	Mary Washington College, VA	I
Johnson & Wales University, RI	I	Long Island U, Southampton College,		Marywood University, PA	D,I
Johnson & Wales University, SC	I,P	NY	I	Massachusetts College of Art, MA	I
Johnson Bible College, TN	I	Longwood College, VA	I	Massachusetts Institute of Technology,	
Johnson State College, VT	D	Loras College, IA	I	MA	D
John Wesley College, NC	I	Louise Salinger Academy of Fashion,		The Master's College and Seminary,	
Judson College, AL	I	CA	I	CA	D,I
Judson College, IL	I	Louisiana State University and A&M		McKendree College, IL	D,I
The Juilliard School, NY	I	College, LA	D	McMurry University, TX	G,I
Juniata College, PA	I	Louisiana State University in		McNeese State University, LA	I
Kalamazoo College, MI	D,I	Shreveport, LA	D	Medaille College, NY	I
Kansas Newman College, KS	D,I	Lourdes College, OH	D,I	Memphis College of Art, TN	D,I,P
Kansas State University, KS	D,I	Loyola Marymount University, CA	I	Menlo College, CA	I

Mercer University, Macon, GA	I	Mount Saint Mary College, NY	I	Northwestern State University of	
Mercyhurst College, PA	I	Mount St. Mary's College, CA	D	Louisiana, LA	I
Meredith College, NC	I	Mount Saint Mary's College and		Northwestern University, IL	I
Merrimack College, MA	D,I	Seminary, MD	I,P	Northwest Missouri State University,	
Messiah College, PA	I	Mount Senario College, WI	I	MO	I
Methodist College, NC	D,I	Mount Union College, OH	I,P	Northwood University, Florida	
Metropolitan State College of Denver,		Mount Vernon College, DC	I	Campus, FL	I
CO	D	Muhlenberg College, PA	I	Northwood University, Texas Campus,	
Miami University, OH	I	Multnomah Bible College and Biblical		TX	I
Michigan Christian College, MI	I	Seminary, OR	I	Notre Dame College, NH	I
Michigan State University, MI	D	Murray State University, KY	D,I	Notre Dame College of Ohio, OH	I
Michigan Technological University,		Muskingum College, OH	I	Nova Southeastern University, FL	I
MI	I	NAES College, IL	P	Nyack College, NY	I
Mid-America Bible College, OK	I	National American University, Denver,		Oak Hills Bible College, MN	I
MidAmerica Nazarene University, KS	I	CO	I	Oakland City University, IN	D,I
Mid-Continent Baptist Bible College,		National College, MO	I	Oakland University, MI	I
KY	I	National College, SD	I	Oberlin College, OH	I
Middlebury College, VT	D,I,P	National College–St. Paul Campus,		Occidental College, CA	I,P
Midland Lutheran College, NE	I	MN	D,I	Oglala Lakota College, SD	I
Midwestern State University, TX	I	National College–Sioux Falls Branch,		Oglethorpe University, GA	I,P
Millersville University of		SD	G	Ohio Dominican College, OH	I
Pennsylvania, PA	I	National-Louis University, IL	I	Ohio Northern University, OH	I
Milligan College, TN	I	National University, CA	P	The Ohio State University, OH	I
Millikin University, IL	I	Nazareth College of Rochester, NY	I	Ohio University, OH	I
Millsaps College, MS	I	Nebraska Wesleyan University, NE	I	Ohio Wesleyan University, OH	I
Mills College, CA	I	Neumann College, PA	D,I	Oklahoma Baptist University, OK	I
Milwaukee Institute of Art and		New College of the University of		Oklahoma Christian U of Science and	
Design, WI	D	South Florida, FL	I,P	Arts, OK	P
Milwaukee School of Engineering, WI	I	New England College, NH	I	Oklahoma City University, OK	D,I
Minneapolis College of Art and		New Hampshire College, NH	I	Oklahoma State U, OK	D,I
Design, MN	I	New Jersey Institute of Technology,		Old Dominion University, VA	D,I
Minnesota Bible College, MN	I	NJ	D,I	Olivet College, MI	I
Mississippi College, MS	D,I	New Mexico Highlands University,		Olivet Nazarene University, IL	I
Mississippi State University, MS	D	NM	D	Oral Roberts University, OK	I
Mississippi University for Women,		New Mexico Inst of Mining and		Oregon College of Art and Craft, OR	I
MS	D,I	Technology, NM	D	Oregon Institute of Technology, OR	D,I
Mississippi Valley State University,		New Mexico State University, NM	D	Oregon State University, OR	D
MS	I	New Orleans Baptist Theological		Ottawa University, KS	D,I
Missouri Baptist College, MO	I	Seminary, LA	D	Otterbein College, OH	I
Missouri Southern State College, MO	D	Newschool of Architecture, CA	D,I,P	Ouachita Baptist University, AR	I
Missouri Valley College, MO	I	New York Institute of Technology, NY	I	Our Lady of the Lake University of	
Missouri Western State College, MO	D,I	New York School of Interior Design,		San Antonio, TX	I
Molloy College, NY	I	NY	D,I	Ozark Christian College, MO	D,I
Monmouth College, IL	I	New York University, NY	D,I,P	Pace University, NY	I
Monmouth University, NJ	I	Niagara University, NY	D,I	Pacific Lutheran University, WA	I
Montana State U–Bozeman, MT	D,I	Nichols College, MA	I	Pacific Northwest College of Art, OR	I
Montana State U–Northern, MT	D	North Adams State College, MA	I	Pacific University, OR	D,I
Montana Tech of The University of		North Carolina Agricultural and		Paier College of Art, Inc., CT	I
Montana, MT	D	Technical State U, NC	D	Paine College, GA	I
Montclair State University, NJ	I	North Carolina School of the Arts, NC	I	Palm Beach Atlantic College, FL	I
Montreat College, NC	I	North Carolina Wesleyan College, NC	I	Palmer College of Chiropractic, IA	D
Montserrat College of Art, MA	I	North Central Bible College, MN	I	Park College, MO	I
Moody Bible Institute, IL	I	North Central College, IL	I	Parsons Sch of Design, New Sch for	
Moore College of Art and Design, PA	I	North Dakota State University, ND	I	Social Research, NY	I
Moorhead State University, MN	D	Northeastern Illinois University, IL	D	Patten College, CA	I
Moravian College, PA	I	Northeastern University, MA	D,I	Paul Quinn College, TX	I
Morehead State University, KY	D,I	Northern Illinois University, IL	I	Penn State U Abington College, PA	D
Morehouse College, GA	I	Northern Kentucky University, KY	I	Penn State U Altoona College, PA	D
Morgan State University, MD	D,I	Northern Michigan University, MI	I	Penn State U at Erie, The Behrend	
Morningside College, IA	I	Northern State University, SD	I	College, PA	D
Morris College, SC	I	North Greenville College, SC	I	Penn State U Berks-Lehigh Valley	
Morrison College, NV	G,I	Northland College, WI	I,P	Coll, PA	D
Mount Holyoke College, MA	I,P	North Park University, IL	I	Penn State U Harrisburg Campus of	
Mount Marty College, SD	I	Northwest Christian College, OR	D,I	the Capital Coll, PA	D
Mount Mary College, WI	I	Northwest College of Art, WA	I	Penn State U Schuylkill Campus of	
Mount Mercy College, IA	I	Northwest College of the Assemblies		the Capital Coll, PA	D
Mount Olive College, NC	I	of God, WA	D,I,P	Penn State U Univ Park Campus, PA	D
Mount St. Clare College, IA	I	Northwestern College, IA	I	Pepperdine University, Malibu, CA	D,I,P

Pfeiffer University, NC	D,I	Robert Morris College, PA	D,I	St. Lawrence University, NY	D,I
Philadelphia College of Bible, PA	I	Roberts Wesleyan College, NY	I	Saint Leo College, FL	I
Philadelphia College of Pharmacy and Science, PA	D,I	Rochester Institute of Technology, NY	D,I,P	St. Louis Christian College, MO	I
		Rockford College, IL	D,I	St. Louis College of Pharmacy, MO	D
Philadelphia College of Textiles and Science, PA	D,I	Rockhurst College, MO	D,I	Saint Louis University, MO	I
		Rocky Mountain College, MT	I	Saint Martin's College, WA	I
Phillips University, OK	D,I	Rocky Mountain College of Art & Design, CO	I	Saint Mary College, KS	I
Piedmont Bible College, NC	I			Saint Mary-of-the-Woods College, IN	I
Piedmont College, GA	I	Roger Williams University, RI	D,I	Saint Mary's College, IN	D,I
Pikeville College, KY	I	Rollins College, FL	I,P	Saint Mary's College, MI	I
Pillsbury Baptist Bible College, MN	I	Rose-Hulman Institute of Technology, IN	I,P	Saint Mary's College of California, CA	I,P
Pine Manor College, MA	I,P			
Pittsburg State University, KS	D	Rosemont College, PA	I	Saint Mary's University of Minnesota, MN	I
Pitzer College, CA	D,I	Rowan University, NJ	D	
Point Loma Nazarene College, CA	I	Rust College, MS	I	St. Mary's University of San Antonio, TX	D,I,P
Point Park College, PA	D,I	Rutgers, State U of NJ, Camden Coll of Arts & Scis, NJ	I	
Polytechnic U, Brooklyn Campus, NY	D,P			Saint Meinrad College, IN	D,I
Polytechnic U, Farmingdale Campus, NY	D,P	Rutgers, State U of NJ, College of Engineering, NJ	I	Saint Michael's College, VT	I
				St. Norbert College, WI	D,G,I
Polytechnic University of Puerto Rico, PR	D	Rutgers, State U of NJ, College of Nursing, NJ	I	St. Olaf College, MN	I,P
				Saint Peter's College, Jersey City, NJ	D,I
Pomona College, CA	I	Rutgers, State U of NJ, College of Pharmacy, NJ	I	St. Thomas Aquinas College, NY	D,I
Pontifical College Josephinum, OH	D,I			St. Thomas University, FL	I
Portland State University, OR	D,I	Rutgers, State U of NJ, Cook College, NJ	I	Saint Vincent College, PA	D,I
Practical Bible College, NY	I			Saint Xavier University, IL	I
Prairie View A&M University, TX	I	Rutgers, State U of NJ, Douglass College, NJ	I	Salem College, NC	I
Pratt Institute, NY	D,I			Salem State College, MA	D
Presbyterian College, SC	I,P	Rutgers, State U of NJ, Livingston College, NJ	I	Salem-Teikyo University, WV	I
Prescott College, Resident Degree Program, AZ	I			Sam Houston State University, TX	I
		Rutgers, State U of NJ, Mason Gross School of Arts, NJ	I	Samuel Merritt College, CA	D,I
Princeton University, NJ	D,I			San Diego State University, CA	I
Principia College, IL	I	Rutgers, State U of NJ, Newark Coll of Arts & Scis, NJ	I	San Francisco Art Institute, CA	I
Providence College, RI	I			San Francisco Conservatory of Music, CA	I
Puget Sound Christian College, WA	I,P	Rutgers, State U of NJ, Rutgers College, NJ	I	
Purchase College, State U of NY, NY	I			San Jose Christian College, CA	D
Purdue University, West Lafayette, IN	I	Rutgers, State U of NJ, U Coll– Camden, NJ	I	Santa Clara University, CA	D,I,P
Purdue University Calumet, IN	D			Sarah Lawrence College, NY	D,I
Queens College, NC	D,I	Rutgers, State U of NJ, U Coll– Newark, NJ	I	Savannah College of Art and Design, GA	I
Queens Coll of the City U of NY, NY	I			
Quincy University, IL	G,I	Rutgers, State U of NJ, U Coll–New Brunswick, NJ	I	School of the Art Institute of Chicago, IL	I
Quinnipiac College, CT	I			
Rabbinical College of America, NJ	I	Sacred Heart Major Seminary, MI	D,I	School of the Museum of Fine Arts, MA	I
Rabbinical Seminary of America, NY	I	Sacred Heart University, CT	D,I	
Radford University, VA	I	St. Ambrose University, IA	I	School of Visual Arts, NY	I
Ramapo College of New Jersey, NJ	I	St. Andrews Presbyterian College, NC	I	Scripps College, CA	I
Randolph-Macon College, VA	I	St. Bonaventure University, NY	D,I	Seattle Pacific University, WA	I
Randolph-Macon Woman's College, VA	I	St. Charles Borromeo Seminary, Overbrook, PA	I	Seattle University, WA	I
				Seton Hall University, NJ	D,I
Reed College, OR	I	St. Edward's University, TX	I	Seton Hill College, PA	I
Reformed Bible College, MI	D	Saint Francis College, IN	I	Shaw University, NC	I
Regis College, MA	D,I,P	St. Francis College, NY	I	Sheldon Jackson College, AK	I
Regis University, CO	D	Saint Francis College, PA	D,I	Shenandoah University, VA	D
Reinhardt College, GA	I	St. John Fisher College, NY	D,I	Shepherd College, WV	I
Rensselaer Polytechnic Institute, NY	I	St. John's College, MD	I,P	Shimer College, IL	I
Research College of Nursing– Rockhurst College, MO	D,G,I	St. John's College, NM	I,P	Shorter College, GA	I
		St. John's Seminary College, CA	D,I	Siena College, NY	I
Rhode Island College, RI	I	Saint John's University, MN	D,I,P	Siena Heights College, MI	D
Rhode Island School of Design, RI	I	St. John's University, NY	I	Sierra Nevada College, NV	G,I
Rhodes College, TN	I	St. John Vianney College Seminary, FL	I	Silver Lake College, WI	I
Rice University, TX	I			Simmons College, MA	I
The Richard Stockton College of New Jersey, NJ	I	Saint Joseph College, CT	I	Simon's Rock College of Bard, MA	I
		Saint Joseph's College, IN	I	Simpson College, CA	I
Ringling School of Art and Design, FL	I	Saint Joseph's College, ME	I	Simpson College, IA	I
		St. Joseph's College, New York, NY	D,I	Sinte Gleska University, SD	I
Ripon College, WI	I	St. Joseph's College, Suffolk Campus, NY	I	Skidmore College, NY	I,P
Rivier College, NH	D,I			Slippery Rock University of Pennsylvania, PA	I
Roanoke Bible College, NC	D,I	Saint Joseph Seminary College, LA	I	
Robert Morris College, IL	I	Saint Joseph's University, PA	D,I	Smith College, MA	I,P

Sojourner-Douglass College, MD	D,I	Stephens College, MO	I	Trinity International U, South Florida	
South Dakota School of Mines and		Sterling College, KS	I	Campus, FL	I
Technology, SD	I	Stetson University, FL	I	Trinity University, TX	I,P
South Dakota State University, SD	D,I	Stevens Institute of Technology, NJ	I	Tri-State University, IN	I
Southeastern Baptist College, MS	I	Stillman College, AL	I	Troy State University, Troy, AL	I
Southeastern Bible College, AL	I	Stonehill College, MA	I,P	Troy State University Montgomery,	
Southeastern College of the		Strayer College, DC	I	AL	D
Assemblies of God, FL	I	Sue Bennett College, KY	I	Truman State University, MO	I
Southeastern University, DC	I	Suffolk University, MA	D,I	Tufts University, MA	I,P
Southeast Missouri State University,		Sullivan College, KY	D,I	Tulane University, LA	I
MO	D,I	Sul Ross State University, TX	I	Tusculum College, TN	I
Southern Adventist University, TN	I,P	Susquehanna University, PA	D,I,P	Tuskegee University, AL	I
Southern Arkansas University–		Swarthmore College, PA	I	Union College, KY	I
Magnolia, AR	D,I	Sweet Briar College, VA	I	Union College, NE	I,P
Southern California College, CA	I	Syracuse University, NY	I,P	Union College, NY	I
Southern Connecticut State University,		Tabor College, KS	I	The Union Institute, OH	I
CT	I	Talladega College, AL	I	Union University, TN	D,I
Southern Illinois University at		Talmudical Institute of Upstate New		United States International University,	
Carbondale, IL	I	York, NY	I	CA	D
Southern Illinois University at		Talmudical Seminary Oholei Torah,		Unity College, ME	I
Edwardsville, IL	D,I	NY	I	Universidad Adventista de las Antillas,	
Southern Methodist University, TX	I,P	Tarleton State University, TX	I	PR	D,I
Southern Nazarene University, OK	I,P	Taylor University, IN	I	U at Albany, State U of NY, NY	I
Southern Oregon University, OR	D	Taylor University, Fort Wayne		The University of Akron, OH	I
Southern Vermont College, VT	D,I	Campus, IN	I	U of Alaska Anchorage, AK	D
Southern Wesleyan University, SC	I	Teikyo Post University, CT	D,I	U of Alaska Fairbanks, AK	D
Southwest Baptist University, MO	I	Temple University, Philadelphia, PA	I	U of Alaska Southeast, AK	D,I
Southwestern Adventist University, TX	I	Tennessee State University, TN	D	University of Arkansas, Fayetteville,	
Southwestern Assemblies of God		Tennessee Temple University, TN	I	AR	I
University, TX	G,I	Tennessee Wesleyan College, TN	D	University of Arkansas at Little Rock,	
Southwestern College, KS	I	Texas A&M International University,		AR	D
Southwestern College of Christian		TX	I	University of Bridgeport, CT	D,I
Ministries, OK	I	Texas A&M University, College		University of California, Berkeley, CA	I
Southwestern Oklahoma State		Station, TX	I	University of California, Riverside,	
University, OK	I	Texas A&M University at Galveston,		CA	D,I
Southwestern University, TX	D,I,P	TX	I	University of California, San Diego,	
Southwest Missouri State University,		Texas A&M University–Commerce,		CA	D
MO	D	TX	I	University of California, Santa Cruz,	
Southwest State University, MN	D,I	Texas A&M University–Corpus		CA	D
Southwest Texas State University, TX	I	Christi, TX	D,I	University of Central Arkansas, AR	I
Spalding University, KY	I	Texas A&M University–Kingsville,		University of Central Florida, FL	D
Spelman College, GA	I	TX	I	The University of Charleston, WV	I
Spring Arbor College, MI	D,I	Texas Christian University, TX	I	University of Chicago, IL	I,P
Spring Hill College, AL	D	Texas Lutheran University, TX	I	University of Cincinnati, OH	I
Stanford University, CA	D,I	Texas Southern University, TX	I	University of Colorado at Boulder, CO	D
State U of NY at Binghamton, NY	I	Texas Tech University, TX	I	University of Colorado at Colorado	
State U of NY at Buffalo, NY	I	Texas Wesleyan University, TX	D,I	Springs, CO	D
State U of NY at New Paltz, NY	I	Texas Woman's University, TX	I	University of Colorado at Denver, CO	D,I
State U of NY at Oswego, NY	D,I	Thiel College, PA	I	University of Connecticut, Storrs, CT	D,I
State U of NY at Stony Brook, NY	D,I	Thomas Aquinas College, CA	I	University of Dallas, TX	D,I
State U of NY College at Brockport,		Thomas College, GA	I	University of Dayton, OH	D,I
NY	I	Thomas College, ME	I	University of Delaware, DE	I,P
State U of NY College at Buffalo, NY	I	Thomas More College, KY	I	University of Denver, CO	D
State U of NY College at Fredonia,		Thomas More College of Liberal Arts,		University of Detroit Mercy, MI	D,I
NY	I	NH	D,I	University of Dubuque, IA	D,I
State U of NY College at Geneseo,		Tiffin University, OH	I	University of Evansville, IN	I
NY	D,I	Toccoa Falls College, GA	I	The University of Findlay, OH	I
State U of NY College at Old		Transylvania University, KY	D,I	University of Florida, FL	P
Westbury, NY	I	Trevecca Nazarene University, TN	I	University of Great Falls, MT	D
State U of NY College at Plattsburgh,		Trinity Baptist College, FL	G,I	University of Guam, GU	D,I
NY	I	Trinity Bible College, ND	D,I	University of Hartford, CT	I,P
State U of NY College at Potsdam,		Trinity Christian College, IL	I	University of Houston, TX	I
NY	I	Trinity College, CT	I	University of Houston–Downtown, TX	I
State U of NY Coll of Environ Sci		Trinity College, DC	D,I	University of Idaho, ID	D
and Forestry, NY	D	Trinity College of Florida, FL	D	University of Illinois at Urbana–	
State U of NY Health Science Center		Trinity College of Vermont, VT	D,I	Champaign, IL	I
at Syracuse, NY	I	Trinity International University, IL	I	University of Indianapolis, IN	D,I
Stephen F. Austin State University, TX	I			The University of Iowa, IA	I

University of La Verne, CA	D,I,P
University of Louisville, KY	I
University of Maine, Orono, ME	I
University of Maine at Farmington, ME	I
University of Maine at Fort Kent, ME	I
University of Maine at Machias, ME	D,I
University of Maine at Presque Isle, ME	D,I
University of Mary, ND	I
University of Mary Hardin-Baylor, TX	I
University of Maryland Baltimore County, MD	I
University of Maryland College Park, MD	D
University of Maryland Eastern Shore, MD	D,I
University of Massachusetts Amherst, MA	I
University of Massachusetts Boston, MA	I
University of Massachusetts Dartmouth, MA	I
University of Massachusetts Lowell, MA	I
The University of Memphis, TN	I
University of Miami, FL	I,P
University of Michigan, Ann Arbor, MI	I
University of Michigan–Dearborn, MI	I
University of Michigan–Flint, MI	D
University of Minnesota, Crookston, MN	G,I
University of Minnesota, Duluth, MN	I
University of Minnesota, Morris, MN	D,I
University of Minnesota, Twin Cities Campus, MN	G,I
University of Mississippi, MS	D
University of Missouri–Columbia, MO	I
University of Missouri–Rolla, MO	I
University of Missouri–St. Louis, MO	I
The University of Montana–Missoula, MT	I
University of Nebraska at Kearney, NE	I
University of Nebraska at Omaha, NE	D
University of Nevada, Las Vegas, NV	D
University of Nevada, Reno, NV	D
University of New England, ME	D,I
University of New Hampshire at Manchester, NH	I
University of New Haven, CT	I
University of New Mexico, NM	I
University of North Carolina at Asheville, NC	I
University of North Carolina at Pembroke, NC	I
University of North Carolina at Wilmington, NC	I
University of Northern Colorado, CO	D
University of Northern Iowa, IA	I
University of North Florida, FL	D
University of North Texas, TX	I
University of Notre Dame, IN	I
University of Oklahoma, OK	I
University of Oregon, OR	D
University of Pennsylvania, PA	I,P
University of Pittsburgh, PA	D,I

University of Pittsburgh at Bradford, PA	D,I
University of Pittsburgh at Greensburg, PA	I
University of Pittsburgh at Johnstown, PA	D,I
University of Portland, OR	D,I
U of Puerto Rico, Aguadilla Regional College, PR	D,I
U of Puerto Rico at Arecibo, PR	D
U of Puerto Rico at Ponce, PR	I
U of Puerto Rico, Cayey University College, PR	D
U of Puerto Rico, Humacao University College, PR	D
U of Puerto Rico, Mayagüez Campus, PR	D,I
U of Puerto Rico Medical Sciences Campus, PR	D
U of Puerto Rico, Río Piedras, PR	I
University of Puget Sound, WA	D,I
University of Redlands, CA	I
University of Rhode Island, RI	I
University of Richmond, VA	I
University of Rio Grande, OH	I,P
University of Rochester, NY	I,P
University of St. Thomas, MN	I
University of St. Thomas, TX	D,I
University of San Diego, CA	I
University of San Francisco, CA	I
University of Science and Arts of Oklahoma, OK	I
University of Scranton, PA	I
University of Sioux Falls, SD	I
U of South Carolina, Columbia, SC	D
U of South Carolina–Aiken, SC	D
U of South Carolina–Spartanburg, SC	D
University of South Dakota, SD	I
University of Southern California, CA	I,P
University of Southern Colorado, CO	D,I
University of Southern Indiana, IN	I
University of Southern Maine, ME	I
University of South Florida, FL	I
University of Southwestern Louisiana, LA	D
The University of Tampa, FL	I
University of Tennessee at Chattanooga, TN	D
The University of Tennessee at Martin, TN	D
University of Tennessee, Knoxville, TN	D,I
The University of Texas at Arlington, TX	I
The University of Texas at Austin, TX	I
The University of Texas at Dallas, TX	I
The University of Texas at El Paso, TX	I
The University of Texas at San Antonio, TX	I
The University of Texas of the Permian Basin, TX	I
University of the Arts, PA	D,I
University of the District of Columbia, DC	D,I
University of the Ozarks, AR	I
University of the Pacific, CA	I
University of the Sacred Heart, PR	D

University of the South, TN	D,I
U of the State of NY, Regents College, NY	I
University of Toledo, OH	I
University of Tulsa, OK	I,P
University of Utah, UT	D,I
University of Vermont, VT	D,I
University of Virginia, VA	I
University of Washington, WA	I
The University of West Alabama, AL	D
University of Wisconsin–Eau Claire, WI	I
University of Wisconsin–Green Bay, WI	I
University of Wisconsin–La Crosse, WI	I
University of Wisconsin–Milwaukee, WI	I
University of Wisconsin–Oshkosh, WI	I
University of Wisconsin–Parkside, WI	I
University of Wisconsin–Platteville, WI	I
University of Wisconsin–River Falls, WI	I
University of Wisconsin–Stevens Point, WI	D
University of Wisconsin–Stout, WI	I
University of Wisconsin–Superior, WI	I
University of Wisconsin–Whitewater, WI	I
University of Wyoming, WY	D,I
Upper Iowa University, IA	I
Urbana University, OH	D,I
Ursinus College, PA	I
Ursuline College, OH	I
Utah State University, UT	D
Valparaiso University, IN	I
Vanderbilt University, TN	D,I,P
VanderCook College of Music, IL	I
Virginia Commonwealth University, VA	I
Virginia Intermont College, VA	I
Virginia Military Institute, VA	I
Virginia Polytechnic Institute and State U, VA	I
Virginia State University, VA	D
Virginia Union University, VA	D,I
Viterbo College, WI	I
Voorhees College, SC	D,I
Wabash College, IN	I
Wadhams Hall Seminary-College, NY	D
Wagner College, NY	I
Wake Forest University, NC	I
Walla Walla College, WA	I
Walsh University, OH	D,I
Warner Pacific College, OR	I
Warner Southern College, FL	I
Warren Wilson College, NC	I
Wartburg College, IA	I
Washburn University of Topeka, KS	I
Washington and Jefferson College, PA	D,I
Washington Bible College, MD	D,I
Washington College, MD	I
Washington University, MO	I,P
Waynesburg College, PA	I
Wayne State University, MI	I
Webber College, FL	I
Weber State University, UT	D

Webster University, MO	I	Westminster College, MO	I	Williams College, MA	I
Wellesley College, MA	I,P	Westminster College, PA	I	William Tyndale College, MI	D
Wells College, NY	I	Westminster College of Salt Lake		William Woods University, MO	I
Wesleyan College, GA	I,P	City, UT	D,I	Wilmington College, DE	I
Wesleyan University, CT	I	Westmont College, CA	D,I	Wilmington College, OH	I
Wesley College, DE	I	West Texas A&M University, TX	I	Wilson College, PA	I,P
Wesley College, MS	I	West Virginia State College, WV	I	Wingate University, NC	I
West Chester University of		West Virginia University, WV	D,I	Winston-Salem State University, NC	I
Pennsylvania, PA	D,I,P	West Virginia University Institute of		Winthrop University, SC	I
Western Baptist College, OR	I	Technology, WV	I	Wisconsin Lutheran College, WI	I
Western Illinois University, IL	I	West Virginia Wesleyan College, WV	I	Wittenberg University, OH	D,I
Western Kentucky University, KY	D,I	Wheaton College, IL	I	Woodbury University, CA	D,I
Western Maryland College, MD	I,P	Wheaton College, MA	D,I,P	Worcester State College, MA	D
Western Michigan University, MI	I	Wheeling Jesuit University, WV	G	Wright State University, OH	I
Western Montana College of The U of		Wheelock College, MA	I	Xavier University, OH	D,I
Montana, MT	D	Whitman College, WA	D,I	Xavier University of Louisiana, LA	I
Western New England College, MA	D,I,P	Whittier College, CA	I	Yale University, CT	I,P
Western New Mexico University, NM	D	Whitworth College, WA	I,P	Yeshiva Karlin Stolin, NY	I
Western Oregon University, OR	D,I	Wichita State University, KS	D	Yeshiva Ohr Elchonon Chabad/W	
Western State College of Colorado,		Widener University, PA	I	Coast Talmudical Sem, CA	I
CO	D,I	Wilberforce University, OH	D,I	Yeshiva University, NY	I
Western Washington University, WA	I	Wilkes University, PA	I	York College, NE	I
Westfield State College, MA	I	Willamette University, OR	D,G,I	York College of Pennsylvania, PA	I
West Liberty State College, WV	D,I	William Jewell College, MO	I,P	Youngstown State University, OH	I
Westmar University, IA	I	William Paterson University of New			
Westminster Choir Coll of Rider U,		Jersey, NJ	I		
NJ	I	Williams Baptist College, AR	I		

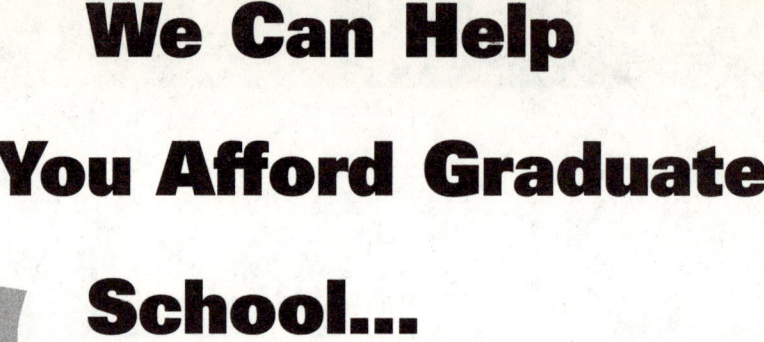